D0065120

The
Oxford Companion
to the
English Language

The
Oxford Companion
to the
English Language

Editor
TOM McARTHUR

Managing Editor
FERI McARTHUR

Oxford   New York
OXFORD UNIVERSITY PRESS
1992

Oxford University Press, Walton Street, Oxford OX2 6DP

Oxford New York Toronto
Delhi Bombay Calcutta Madras Karachi
Kuala Lumpur Singapore Hong Kong Tokyo
Nairobi Dar es Salaam Cape Town
Melbourne Auckland Madrid
and associated companies in
Berlin Ibadan

Oxford is a trade mark of Oxford University Press

Published in the United States
by Oxford University Press, New York

© *Tom McArthur 1992*

All rights reserved. No part of this publication may be reproduced,
stored in a retrieval system, or transmitted, in any form or by any means,
electronic, mechanical, photocopying, recording, or otherwise, without
the prior permission of Oxford University Press

This book is sold subject to the condition that it shall not, by way
of trade or otherwise, be lent, re-sold, hired out or otherwise circulated
without the publisher's prior consent in any form of binding or cover
other than that in which it is published and without a similar condition
including this condition being imposed on the subsequent purchaser

British Library Cataloguing in Publication Data
Data available

Library of Congress Cataloging in Publication Data
Data available
ISBN 0-19-214183-X

Typeset by Latimer Trend Ltd., Plymouth
Printed in the United States of America
on acid free paper

Contents

To the staff of Addenbrookes Hospital, Cambridge

Preface

TOWARDS the end of lunch one day in Oxford, in the summer of 1986, David Attwooll asked me if I would consider editing a *Companion to the English Language*. The idea took some moments to sink in, and when it did was both appealing and appalling. It appealed because the time was right for such a book: English had become so internationally significant and was the object of so much research that an overview was badly needed. It appalled because trying to produce an A to Z survey of the language over all its centuries, as used by all manner of folk, in all kinds of places, for all sorts of purposes, made going to sea in a sieve look quite safe.

I thought: one editor, many contributors—there would be chaos in the making of this book. Everybody would have an opinion on everything, endlessly, yet I would have to close the circle somewhere and let the results be printed. Purists would want one thing, permissivists another, and neither would compromise. Pedants would want every *i* dotted and *t* crossed, with quibbles till Kingdom come, while Plain English campaigners would want a prose style with only active sentences each fifteen words long. Liberals would want to be fair to everyone, balancing every viewpoint and counter-viewpoint, until from the point of view of conservatives everything cancelled out everything else. Some writers would want maximum concision, using plenty of abbreviations and symbols; others would want optimum flow and as few abbreviations and symbols as possible. And all the while I would have to step with care among land-mines labelled 'class' and 'colonialism', 'colour' and 'creed', 'ethnicity' and 'foreignness', 'feminism' and 'gender', 'nationality' and 'nativeness', 'prejudice', 'special pleading', and 'taste'.

Finally, the day after publication, sins of omission and commission would be mercilessly listed by reviewers and readers: 'There is no entry on antimetabole!'; 'They've put in Boontling but left out Bungo Talk!'; 'There is, I am sorry to report, a dangling participle in the entry on illiteracy.'

After I agreed to put my head in the lion's mouth, it took a year to think about the issues and talk to people whose help and support I would need. At one point, a friend observed: 'It's like being asked to write the Bible.' There was truth in that. Sacred threads run through the world of reference books, and one of them bears the colours of Oxford. There were strong views (both inside and outside the Press) about what a companion to English should be and what an *Oxford* companion should *not* be: not a gazetteer of the international language (warts and all), not a guide to style and usage (there were enough of those), not a grammar book in disguise or a hidden history or a companion to literature by other means, not a compendium on linguistics or a coffee-table book full of pictures and maps, and certainly not a dictionary of allusions, quotations, origins, phrases, and fables. When the negatives were all added up, the project became impossible—unless one could somehow co-opt features from all such books into a pattern that served new ends and was in the end much more than the sum of its parts.

Six years have passed. In that time, there have been a first and second plan, a first, second, and third master list of entries, a set of guidelines, a growing list of writers and advisers, and a build-up of entries written, edited, amended, reviewed, often rewritten and re-edited, sometimes re-reviewed, sometimes re-rewritten and then re-re-rewritten, and finally all dropped into place by means of a versatile and fascinating technology. Without its IBM hardware and Nota Bene software, the project would, I suspect, have taken twice as long and may well never have been finished at all. Throughout the work, I have adhered to the original Oxford plan, which was that some 60 per cent of the entries should be the work of contributors, and the rest my own.

Sometimes it was easy; sometimes it was hard. Alongside the triumphs and trials of the work there have been tribulations of illness and death. Martyn Wakelin died in 1988, just as he was about to start on the dialects of England; Peter Strevens died in 1989, half-way through his entries on language teaching; and John Platt died in 1990 while his contributions on English in East and South-East Asia were being edited. These were heartfelt losses.

At home, Feri McArthur, Managing Editor, and my wife of nearly 30 years, fell victim in 1989 to acute myeloid leukaemia, but, despite spells in hospital and the ongoing threat, she built up and sustained our worldwide network of contributors and consultants. Then, as the work entered its closing phase, our 20-year-old son (in defiance of all the laws of medical probability) fell ill with acute lymphoblastic leukaemia. The same hospital and the same unit in that hospital cared for him as had cared for Feri, and coaxed him safely out of danger during the long slow months when the *Companion* was being copy-edited and prepared for press.

I am indebted, beyond words in any language, to the staff of the Haematological Unit and Ward C10 of Addenbrookes Hospital, Cambridge: especially to Consultants Robert Marcus and Trevor Baglin, Sister Alison Wetherall, Staff Nurse Nicki de Zeeuw, and Housekeeper Pat McVeigh. I am also deeply appreciative of the efficient and sympathetic help that I myself received at Addenbrookes when, in mid-1991, half-way through the copy-editing, I had an experience of angina pectoris. Because this remarkable hospital became for a time home from home for the McArthur clan, we decided to dedicate the *Companion* to the entire staff.

We are grateful to all our companions and helpers on the way, for the work they have done, the patience they have shown, and especially the heart-warming personal support of so many. We would like, in particular, to thank our ten Associate Editors for involvement well beyond the call of academic duty. I would also like to record my admiration for and special thanks to George Tulloch, copy-editor extraordinary.

The *Companion* has been a great affair, with a scale and momentum that still excite and surprise me. Yet, in the course of the work, I have from time to time felt a twinge of sympathy for Samuel Johnson, when he finished what he had set out to do, and wrote in the preface to his *Dictionary* in 1755: 'It may repress the triumph of malignant criticism to observe, that if our language is not here fully displayed, I have only failed in an attempt which no human powers have hitherto completed.'

I know just how he felt.

Tom McArthur

Cambridge, 1992

THE OXFORD COMPANION TO THE ENGLISH LANGUAGE

EDITOR
TOM McARTHUR

MANAGING EDITOR
FERI McARTHUR

Associate Editors

John Algeo
Robert E. Allen
Richard W. Bailey
W. F. Bolton
Raymond Chapman

Sidney Greenbaum
Braj B. Kachru
Suzanne Romaine
Loreto Todd
Christopher Upward

Copy-Editor
George S. Tulloch

Contributors

In the following list, the contributors are arranged alphabetically by surname. The topics on which each has contributed are shown in square brackets.

J.M.A.
JEAN AITCHISON, Senior Lecturer in Linguistics, London School of Economics; author, *The Articulate Mammal* and *Words in the Mind*. [*linguistics*]

A.J.A.
A. J. AITKEN, Honorary Professor, University of Edinburgh; (formerly) editor, *A Dictionary of the Older Scottish Tongue.* [*Scottish English, lexicography*]

J.A.
JOHN ALGEO, Professor of English, University of Georgia; (formerly) editor, *American Speech.* [*American English, lexicology, names (onomastics)*]

R.E.A.
ROBERT E. ALLEN, editor, *The Concise Oxford Dictionary* (8th edition). [*Oxford University Press, punctuation, usage*]

J.AM.
JON AMASTAE, Associate Professor of Linguistics, University of Texas at El Paso; author, *Official English and the Learning of English.* [*Spanish and English, Hispanic America*]

T.A.
TONY AUGARDE, (formerly) Departmental Manager, Oxford English Dictionaries;
author, *The Oxford Guide to Word Games.* [*word games*]

R.W.B.
RICHARD W. BAILEY, Professor of English Language and Literature, University of Michigan; co-editor, *English as a World Language.* [*lexicography, literacy, North American English*]

W.W.B.
WILLIAM W. BARKER, Assistant Professor of English, Memorial University of Newfoundland; research editor, *The Spenser Encyclopedia.* [*typography, writing*]

D.E.B.
Dennis E. Baron, Professor of English and Linguistics, University of Illinois; author, *Grammar and Good Taste: Reforming the American Language.* [*grammar, usage*]

L.J.B.
LAURIE J. BAUER, Reader in Linguistics, Victoria University, Wellington; author, *English Word-Formation.* [*New Zealand English*]

J.BA.
JOHN BAUGH, Professor of Education and Linguistics, Stanford University, California; author, *Black Street Speech.* [*Black English Vernacular*]

P.B.
PAUL BEALE, Assistant Librarian, Loughborough College; editor, Partridge's *Dictionary of Slang and Unconventional English* (8th edition). [*Partridge, slang*]

F.M.B.
FRANK M. BIRBALSINGH, Associate Professor, York University, Toronto; author, *Passion and Exile*. [*Caribbean literature*]

D.B.
DAVID BLAIR, Senior Lecturer in Linguistics, Macquarie University, Sydney; editor, *Australian English: The Language of a New Society*. [*Australasian English*]

E.G.B.
EYAMBA G. BOKAMBA, Associate Professor of Linguistics and African Languages, University of Illinois. [*African English*]

W.F.B.
WHITNEY F. BOLTON, Professor of English, Rutgers University; author, *The Living Language: The History and Structure of English* and *The Language of 1984: Orwell's English and Ours*. [*history, Chaucer, Shakespeare, Orwell*]

J.B.
JEAN BRANFORD, (formerly) Honorary Research Associate of Rhodes University, Grahamstown; editor, *A Dictionary of South African English*. [*South African English*]

W.B.
WILLIAM BRANFORD, (formerly) Professor of Linguistics and English Language, Rhodes University, Grahamstown. [*South African English*]

L.B.B.
LAWRENCE B. BREITBORDE, Professor of Anthropology, Beloit College, Wisconsin. [*Liberian English*]

C.J.B.
CHRISTOPHER J. BRUMFIT, Professor of Education, University of Southampton; editor, ELT Documents Series. [*education, language teaching*]

RO.W.B.
ROBERT W. BURCHFIELD, (formerly) Chief Editor, Oxford English Dictionaries; editor, *The New Zealand Pocket Oxford Dictionary*. [*Fowler, New Zealand English, Oxford University Press*]

G.C.
GARLAND CANNON, Professor of Linguistics, Texas A & M University; author, *Historical Change and English Word-Formation*. [*word borrowing, China*]

L.D.C.
LAWRENCE D. CARRINGTON, Senior Research

Fellow, Faculty of Education, University of the West Indies, Trinidad and Tobago; President, Society for Caribbean Linguistics. [*Caribbean English*]

F.G.C.
FREDERIC G. CASSIDY, Professor Emeritus, University of Wisconsin-Madison; chief editor, *Dictionary of American Regional English*. [*Caribbean, dialect, lexicography*]

S.C.
SYLVIA CHALKER, staff member, Survey of English Usage, University College London; author, *Current English Grammar*. [*grammar*]

R.C.
RAYMOND CHAPMAN, Professor Emeritus of English Studies, University of London; author, *The Treatment of Sounds in Language and Literature*. [*Bible, language and literature, usage in England*]

P.C.
PAUL CHRISTOPHERSEN, Professor Emeritus of English, University of Ulster; co-author (with Otto Jespersen), *A Modern English Grammar*, vol. 6. [*language teaching, Scandinavian languages, history*]

I.R.C.
ISAGANI R. CRUZ, Professor of Literature, De La Salle University, Manila; author, *Beyond Futility: The Filipino as Critic*. [*imperialism, Philippines*]

D.C.
DAVID CRYSTAL, Honorary Professor of Linguistics, University College of North Wales, Bangor; author, *The Cambridge Encyclopedia of Language*. [*communication, child language, language pathology*]

W.D.
WIMAL DISSANAYAKE, Associate Director, Institute of Culture and Communication, East–West Center, Honolulu. [*English in Sri Lanka*]

A. DU P.
ADRIAN DU PLESSIS, Editorial Director (Reference), Cambridge University Press. [*publishing*]

C.C.E.
CONNIE C. EBLE, Associate Professor of English, University of North Carolina, Chapel Hill; editorial adviser, *American Speech*. [*education, slang, Southern English (USA)*]

J.E.
JOHN EDWARDS, Professor of Psychology, St Francis Xavier University, Nova Scotia; author, *Language, Society and Identity* and *The Irish Language*. [*ethnicity, Ireland*]

S.E.

STANLEY ELLIS, Honorary Lecturer, University of Leeds; principal fieldworker, The Survey of English Dialects. [*dialects of England*]

M.F.

MARGERY FEE, Director, Strathy Language Unit, Queen's University, Kingston, Ontario; author, *Canadian Fiction: An Annotated Bibliography*. [*Canadian English*]

J.M.G.

JEAN-MARC GACHELIN, Professor of English, University of Rouen; author, *William Barnes and the Dorset Dialect*. [*French and English, history*]

C.G.

CHARLES GILMAN, English Language Consultant, Africa Consultants International, Dakar, Senegal. [*Cameroon*]

A.G.

ANDREW GONZALES, President, De La Salle University, Manila; editor, *Philippine Journal of Linguistics*. [*Philippine English*]

K.L.G.

KEN L. GOODWIN, Professor of English, University of Queensland; author, *A History of Australian Literature*. [*Australian literature*]

S.G.

SIDNEY GREENBAUM, Director, Survey of English Usage; co-author, *A Comprehensive Grammar of the English Language*. [*grammar*]

M.D.G.

MARK D. GRIFFITHS, Fellow of the Linnean Society; editor, *Royal Horticultural Society Dictionary of Gardening*. [*binomial nomenclature*]

A.R.H.

ANJUM R. HAQUE, Director, National Academy for Higher Education, Islamabad. [*English in Pakistan*]

R.H.

REINHARD HARTMANN, Reader in Applied Linguistics, and Director, Dictionary Research Centre, University of Exeter; author, *Contrastive Textology*. [*translation, lexicography*]

M.H.

MOHAMED HELIEL, Professor of Phonetics and Linguistics, Alexandria University, Egypt; author, *Terminological Lexicography: Bilingual Dictionaries of Linguistic Terms (English–Arabic)*. [*Arabic, English in the Arab world*]

G.H.

GEOFFREY HUGHES, Professor of the History of the English Language, University of the Witwatersrand, Johannesburg; author, *Words*

in Time: A Social History of the English Vocabulary. [*media*]

R.F.I.

ROBERT F. ILSON, Associate Director, Survey of English Usage, University College London; editor, *International Journal of Lexicography*. [*American and British English, lexicography, swearing*]

B.B.K.

BRAJ B. KACHRU, Professor of Linguistics, and Director, Division of English as an International Language, University of Illinois, Urbana; author, *The Indianization of English*; co-editor, *World Englishes*. [*linguistics, New Englishes, South Asian English*]

Y.K.

YAMUNA KACHRU, Professor of Linguistics and English, University of Illinois, Urbana; author, *An Introduction to Hindi Syntax*. [*Indian languages*]

G.S.K.

GILLIAN S. KAY, Lecturer in English, Toyama Medical and Pharmaceutical University, Toyama. [*Japan and English*]

G.D.K.

G. DOUGLAS KILLAM, Professor of Language and Literature, University of Guelph, Ontario; author, *Africa in English Fiction*. [*African literature in English*]

F.E.K.

FRANCIS E. KNOWLES, Professor of Language, Department of Modern Languages, Aston University, Birmingham. [*Russian, Slavonic languages*]

G.K.

GERALD KNOWLES, Lecturer in Linguistics, University of Lancaster; author, *Patterns of Spoken English*. [*phonetics*]

M.LA.

MARGOT LAWRENCE, Honorary Secretary, Prayer Book Society of England; author, *Poetry of the Book of Common Prayer*. [*Bible, Biblical English, house style*]

B.L.

BENJAMIN LEASE, Professor Emeritus of English, Northeastern Illinois University; author, *Anglo-American Encounters: England and the Rise of American Literature*. [*American literature*]

S.L.

SANGSUP LEE, Professor of English and Director, the Lexicographical Center, Yonsei University, Seoul. [*Korea*]

M.L.

MICHAEL LESK, Executive Director, Computer Sciences Research, Bell

Communications Research, New Jersey. [*computing, information technology*]

M.LE.

MARCIA LEVESON, Senior Lecturer, University of the Witwatersrand, Johannesburg; editor, *Vita Anthology of New South African Short Fiction*. [*South African literature in English*]

P.H.L.

PETER H. LOWENBERG, Associate Professor of Linguistics, San Jose State University; editor, *Language Spread and Language Policy*. [*Malaysian English*]

W.D.L.

WILLIAM D. LUTZ, Professor of English, Rutgers University, New Jersey; editor, *Quarterly Review of Doublespeak*. [*doublespeak, jargon*]

T.MCA.

TOM MCARTHUR, Editor, *English Today: The International Review of the English Language*; author, *Worlds of Reference*. [*lexicography, media, reference, varieties of English, words and word-formation*]

M.MCC.

MICHAEL MCCARTHY, Lecturer in Modern English Language, University of Nottingham; author, *Discourse Analysis for Language Teachers*. [*discourse analysis*]

J.D.M.

J. DERRICK MCCLURE, Senior Lecturer in English, University of Aberdeen; editor, *Scottish Language*. [*Scottish literature*]

I.C.M.

ISEABAIL C. MACLEOD, Editorial Director, Scottish National Dictionary Association; editor, *The Scots Thesaurus*. [*Scottish languages*]

R.M.

RAJEND MESTHRIE, Lecturer in Linguistics, University of Cape Town; author, *English in Language Shift: The History, Structure and Sociolinguistics of South African Indian English*. [*South African English*]

L.M.

LESLIE MONKMAN, Professor of English, Queen's University, Kingston, Ontario; author, *A Native Heritage: Images of the Indian in English-Canadian Literature*. [*Canadian literature in English*]

S.S.M.

SALIKOKO S. MUFWENE, Professor of Linguistics, University of Chicago; review editor, *Journal of Pidgin and Creole Languages*. [*Gullah, West African English*]

W.N.

WALTER NASH, Emeritus Professor of Modern English Language, University of Nottingham; author, *The Language of Humour* and *Rhetoric: The Wit of Persuasion*. [*humour*]

C.L.N.

CECIL L. NELSON, Associate Professor of Linguistics, Department of English, Indiana State University. [*African English*]

N.E.O.

NOEL E. OSSELTON, Professor of English Language, University of Newcastle upon Tyne; author, *Engels Woordenboek*; general editor, Oxford Monographs in Lexicography and Lexicology. [*Dutch, lexicography*]

F.R.P.

FRANK R. PALMER, Professor Emeritus, University of Reading; author, *The English Verb* and *Modality and the English Modals*. [*grammar, linguistics, semantics*]

R.P.

RAJESHWARI PANDHARIPANDE, Assistant Professor of Linguistics and Religious Studies, University of Illinois, Urbana; author, *Saṃsāra: Introduction to Asian Mythology and Religion*. [*Indian languages*]

J.P.

JOHN PLATT, (formerly) Professor of Linguistics, Monash University, Victoria; co-author, *The New Englishes* and *English in Singapore and Malaysia*. [*East and South-East Asian English*]

R.J.Q.

RENÉ JAMES QUINAULT, Honorary Research Fellow, Department of English, University College London; (formerly) editor, English by Radio and Television, BBC World Service. [*British broadcasting*]

W.S.R.

WILLIAM S. RAMSON, Australian National University, Canberra; editor, *Australian National Dictionary*. [*Australian English*]

R.R.

ROGER ROBINSON, Professor of English, Victoria University of Wellington. [*New Zealand literature*]

S.R.

SUZANNE ROMAINE, Merton Professor of English Language, University of Oxford; author, *Pidgin and Creole Languages* and *Bilingualism*. [*linguistics, pidgins and creoles*]

A.R.

ADRIAN ROOM, author, *Dictionary of Place-Names in the British Isles* and *Place-Names of the World*. [*place-names*]

P.SH.

PAUL SHARRAD, Lecturer in English, University of Wollongong, New South

Wales; co-editor, *New Literature Review.* [*Philippine literature in English*]

W.S.
WILLIAM SHEPHARD, (formerly) Secretary, Examinations in English, University of Cambridge Local Examination Syndicate; author, *Students' Handbook to the Cambridge EFL Examinations.* [*examining in English*]

L.E.S.
LARRY E. SMITH, Research Associate, East–West Center, Honolulu; author, *Discourse across Cultures*; co-editor, *World Englishes.* [*communication, English as an International Language*]

S.N.S.
S. N. SRIDHAR, Associate Professor of Linguistics, State University of New York, Stonybrook; associate editor, *World Englishes.* [*English in South India*]

J.S.
JAMES STANLAW, Assistant Professor of Asian Studies, St John's University, Jamaica, New York. [*Japan and English*]

S.S.
SOL STEINMETZ, Executive Editor, Random House Dictionaries; author, *Yiddish and English.* [*Jewish English*]

P.S.
PETER STREVENS, (formerly) Director-General, Bell Educational Trust; Fellow of Wolfson College, Cambridge; author, *Teaching English as an International Language.* [*education, language teaching*]

M.T.
MARY TAY, Professor of English, National University of Singapore. [*English in Singapore*]

L.T.
LORETO TODD, Senior Lecturer in English, University of Leeds; co-author, *International English Usage*; author, *Pidgins and Creoles* and *The Language of Irish Literature.* [*African English, dialects of England, Irish English, pidgins and creoles*]

B.T.
BARRY TOMALIN, Head of Marketing, BBC English; author, *Video, TV and Radio in the English Class.* [*British broadcasting*]

P.T.
PETER TRUDGILL, Professor of Sociolinguistics, University of Essex; editor, *Language in the British Isles*; author, *The Dialects of England.* [*sociolinguistics*]

C.U.
CHRISTOPHER UPWARD, Senior Lecturer in German, Department of Modern Languages, Aston University, Birmingham; editor, *Journal of the Simplified Spelling Society.* [*orthography*]

L.U.
LAURENCE URDANG, managing editor, *Random House Dictionary of English* (1st edition); editorial director, *Collins English Dictionary*; editor, *Verbatim: The Language Quarterly.* [*lexicography, semantics*]

K.W.
KATIE WALES, Senior Lecturer in English, University of London (Royal Holloway and Bedford New College); author, *A Dictionary of Stylistics.* [*style and stylistics*]

H.W.
HEIDI WEBER, co-author, *The New Englishes* and *English in Singapore and Malaysia.* [*East and South-East Asian English*]

E.W.
EDMUND WEINER, co-editor, *The Oxford English Dictionary* (2nd edition); editor, *The Oxford Guide to English Usage.* [*orthography*]

L.S.W.
LISE S. WINER, Assistant Professor of Linguistics, Southern Illinois University at Carbondale. [*sexism and language, TESD*]

M.E.W.
MARGARET E. WINTERS, Associate Professor of Linguistics and French, Southern Illinois University at Carbondale. [*sexism and language*]

Consultants

Richard Allwright (TESOL), Reinhold Aman (*Maledicta*), Jacqueline Anderson (United States), Peter M. Bassett (Queen's English Society), Lourdes B. Bautista (Philippines), Yolanda Beh (RELC), Ben Benedikz (Scandinavia), John Bodley (Faber), Roger Bowers (British Council), Melanie Butler (*EFL Gazette*), J. K. Chambers (Canada), Sandra Clarke (Canada), John Clement (W. & R. Chambers), Rachel Davis (Lancashire, Scouse), Agnes Drever (classical languages), Peter Ducker (typography), Robert A.

Dunbar (Ireland), Anna Dunlop (Italian), Thomas M. Farmiloe (Macmillan), Helen Fraser (Heinemann), Barbara Goldsmid (BBC English), Alan Goodworth (Facts on File), Manfred Görlach (*English World-Wide*, Varieties of English around the World), David Gough (South Africa), Barbara Harris (Canada), Tom Hecht (Tristan da Cunha), David Hicks (English-Speaking Union), Robin Hosie (*Reader's Digest*), Joan Hughes (Australia), Sally Hunt (South Africa), Michal Jankowski (Polish), Fadilah Jasmani (Malaysia), S. Johansson (Scandinavia), Geoffrey Kaye (information technology), Damian J. Kelly (Birmingham), Virginia LaCastro (Japan), James Lake (Penguin), Joseph Lease (American literature), Leonhard Lipka (lexicology), Robert McHenry (*Encyclopaedia Britannica*), Louise McIvor (Ireland), Kevin McNamee (Pitman), David I. Masson (master list), Dhun Mehta (India), Godfrey Meintjes (South Africa), Tatsuo Miyajima (Japan),

Anne C. Newton (*English Language Forum*), Diarmaid Ó hAirt (Ireland), Brian O'Kill (Longman), Maria-Grazia Pederzani (Italian), Mary Penrith (Wales, Daniel Jones), Frederick H. G. Percy (master list), Peter Pitman (Pitman), Arnold D. N. Pitt (Esperanto), Graham Pointon (BBC English), Velma Pollard (Caribbean), Camilla Raab (Eric Partridge), F. Gordon Rohlehr (Caribbean), A. O. Sanved (Scandinavia), Sybil Sarel (master list), Zakia Sarwar (SPELT), Donald Scragg (spelling), John Singler (Liberia), Brian Smith (Indonesia), K. Sørenson (Scandinavia), Mats-Peter Sundström (Scandinavia, Finland), Paul Thompson (master list), Ronald Threadgall (initial teaching alphabet), Hamish Todd (Japan), Henry Warkentyne (Canada), Junko Uozu (Japan), Henry Widdowson (education, language teaching), David Williamson (Debretts: titles and forms of address), Carol Winkelmann (United States).

The Organization of the *Companion*

IN the closing years of the twentieth century, the English language has become a global resource. As such, it does not owe its existence or the protection of its essence to any one nation or group. Inasmuch as a particular language belongs to any individual or community, English is the possession of every individual and every community that in any way uses it, regardless of what any other individual or community may think or feel about the matter.

During the 1980s, there was considerable discussion about the nature and use of English, especially what Robert W. Burchfield called 'its innumerable clearly distinguishable varieties' (*A Supplement to the Oxford English Dictionary*, vol. 4, 1986, Introduction). Scholars discussed both usage (local, regional, and international) and varieties (standard and non-standard), while in a broader public debate many people wondered whether the language was in decline and might even break up into various mutually unintelligible forms: in effect, into 'the English languages'.

The aim of the contributors to *The Oxford Companion to the English Language* has been to survey all such matters, distilling from past and present scholarship an interim report that can serve specialists, students, and general readers alike. At the same time, the editorial aim has been to present both fact and opinion in an impartial manner that is neither bland nor evasive, and in an accessible style that is neither overly popular nor too academic and technical.

Although the entries are alphabetical, they have been written in sets and subsets within a group of themes. As a result, readers can consult an individual entry like *accent* in its own right, without regard to the rest of the book, or move from such an entry by means of cross-references to others that are related to it: in this instance, to *brogue, burr, drawl,* and *twang,* among other entries (all of which are members of the Speech theme). Cross-references, printed in small capitals, sometimes appear in the body of the text, but are generally listed at the ends of entries, those that identify themes being placed last of all, in square brackets. Readers who wish to see all the entries in a theme, perhaps to help them formulate a reading plan or draw up their own list of terms within a field of study, can consult the thesaurus-like list which follows the overview entry for that theme (see below).

THE CIRCLES OF ENGLISH

The model for the *Companion* consists of three concentric circles, and is a development of 'the circle of the English language' displayed by Sir James

FIG. I

Murray in the General Explanations of *The Oxford English Dictionary* (vol. i, p. xxiv: see Fig. 1). The innermost circle in the *Companion* (see Fig. 2) represents 'core' entries covering such immediately obvious aspects of the language as its grammar, history, pronunciation, punctuation, usage, and word-formation. The leading core entries are *English* and *standard English*; shorter core entries include, for example, *acronym, adjective, apostrophe, comma, L, Middle English, Orwell, participle*, and *R-sounds*. Most such entries refer outward to a second circle that represents major language issues and contains such entries as *bilingualism, child language acquisition, education, etymology, literature, metaphor*, and *phonetics*.

In turn, entries in the first and second circles reach out further still, to subjects such as art, communication, culture, geography, mathematics, philosophy, and politics: to varying degrees, all of these impinge on English and English impinges on them. Deciding where to draw the outer line of the outermost circle has been a thorny task. Some of these 'general' outer entries may make immediate sense to the reader (such as *culture, logic, medium, norm, number*[2], *sign*, and *symbol*), but others may at first sight seem unlikely candidates (such as *book, chapter, form, line, mark, model, modern, network, note, space*, and *system*). They have been included, however, because they have cropped up constantly in describing and discussing the central subjects; they represent objects, concepts, activities, and techniques so basic to any discussion of language that they are often overlooked or even considered trivial. Paradoxically, in preparing the *Companion*, they have proved to be in their own right a second set of 'core' entries.

Inevitably, many entries and groups of entries range through all three circles. For example, the entry *dialect* discusses a key concept in general terms, while follow-on entries such as *dialect in America* and *dialect in England* focus on specific regions, and direct readers to further topics that are even more specific, such as *Cajun* and *Ottawa Valley* in North America and *Gutter Scots* and *Scouse* in Britain. Lastly, although the circle model is fundamental to the structure of the book, it does not figure explicitly in any theme or entry that appears in the book; it is an organizational aid, not a theory of language.

Because of the great range of terms and topics covered, it proved impossible to develop one entry format that would serve all entries equally well.

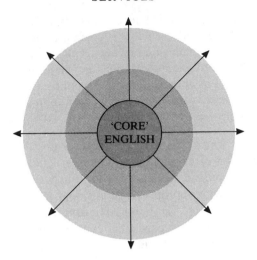

'CORE'
ENGLISH

Fig. 2

Rather, in the process of compiling the *Companion*, three distinct types of format emerged: (1) The essay-like entry, either concise, as with *indefinite article*, *obelisk*, *stage*, and *Websters*, or extensive and with subsections, as with *abbreviation*, *modal verb*, *name*, and *poetry*. (2) The dictionary-style entry, enumerating the senses of a term and usually concise, as in *Cajun*, *Gothic*, *medium*, and *message*. (3) The biographical entry, much like those in standard biographical dictionaries and of varying lengths, as with *Craigie*, *Gordimer*, *Murray*, and *Nehru*. Quite often, hybridization has taken place among the three types, as with *Carroll* and *Shakespeare* (which blend biography and essay) and *Lancashire* and *semantics* (in which a dictionary-like opening leads on to a subheaded essay).

SERVICES

As part of or in addition to its main text, the *Companion* provides: a chronology of English; etymologies; sources, quotations, and bibliographies; the initials, names, and some personal information about its contributors; and an index of most of the people mentioned in the text.

Chronology. Following the entry *history of English* is a detailed list of dates and events relating to the language, from Roman times to the present day. Some of this information can also be found in various entries, but the distribution of these entries through the book does not lend itself to the easy comparisons and overviews that the chronological list makes possible.

Etymologies. Many entries open with information in square brackets about the history of their headword(s). The etymologies are usually brief, as with those for *antecedent* and *Gothic*, but are sometimes long and detailed, as with those for *aesthetics/esthetics* and *grammar*. Most of them open with the date in which a term was, as far as is known, first used in English. For recent coinages, a year date is given if known, such as *1982*; for nineteenth- and twentieth-century terms, a decade date is given if known, such as *1880s*; and for earlier or less well-documented recent terms, a century or part-century date is given, such as *14c* or *mid-19c*. Languages mentioned in the etymologies appear in full and not as abbreviations (for example, *Latin* and not *L.*), and no specialist symbols are used. The aim has been to make the information as accessible as possible.

Sources, quotations, and bibliographies. Wherever possible, information provided in the entries is strengthened with source details for quotations and cited authorities. Published works providing further information are often cited within entries, with appropriate details, and select bibliographies generally follow major entries. The hundreds of quotations and excerpts were chosen for their relevance in particular contexts and their representative value as a historical and geographical cross-section of specimens of how the language has been used.

Contributors' initials and index of persons. All entries, however brief, are followed by the initials of those who wrote them, including the Editor where appropriate. Most entries are primarily the work of individuals, but many are joint efforts or composites created from several original texts. In all cases, initials can be checked in the list of contributors on pp. xi–xv. In addition, there is an index of the names of a majority of persons mentioned in entries. The names are followed, not by page references, but by the headwords of the entries in which they appear, so that readers can see at a glance the context(s) in which a person is mentioned. In those cases where someone has both a biographical entry and an index entry, the index entry provides the set of cross-references for the biography.

THEMES

There are 22 themes or topic areas in the *Companion*. They often overlap and many entries belong to more than one theme. The themes, arranged in pairs, are shown in Fig. 3 as aspects of the circle model described above. The themes are not absolute or watertight entities, and it is probably impossible to specify their natures, limits, and relationships precisely. They are:

Geography. Entries associated with places, and with the geopolitics of English. Specific gazetteer entries range from scene-setting articles such as *Australia* and *Canada* to capsule entries such as *Gibraltar* (a territory where English and Spanish meet) and *Vanuatu* (a Pacific nation of some 150,000 people who use at least four languages: ni-Vanuatu, Bislama, English, and French). Theme list p. 436. The Geography theme is so large, however, that for convenience it has been divided into five regional sub-themes, treated in effect as themes in their own right. They are:

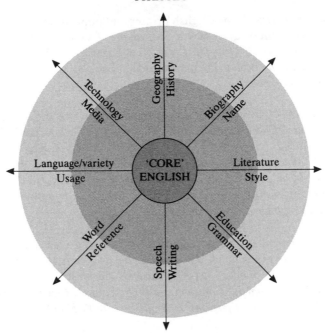

FIG. 3

- *Africa*, with entries such as *African English, Bantu, Flytaal, Krio, Ngugi wa Thiong'o, South African broadcasting*, and *Zambia*. Theme list p. 19.
- *Americas*, with entries such as *American English, Black English Vernacular, Dictionary of Bahamian English, New Orleans, Quebec*, and *Rasta Talk*. Theme list p. 34.
- *Asia*, with entries such as *Babu English, Filipino literature in English, Gairaigo, Hobson-Jobson, Indianism, Pacific Rim*, and *Taglish*. Theme list p. 85.
- *Europe*, with entries such as *Black Irish, English in England, European Community, Germanic languages, Latin*[1], *Jespersen, Malta, Norn*, and *Shakespeare*. Theme list p. 389.
- *Oceania* (treated here as including Australasia), with entries such as *Australian English, Godzone, Hawaii Pidgin English, Kriol, Maori English, New Zealand literature*, and *Tok Pisin*. Theme list p. 721.

History. Entries for events, conditions, concepts, institutions, persons, and works considered significant in the development of the language, such as *Anglo-Saxon Chronicle, Bible, Defoe (Daniel), etymology, Great Vowel Shift, Indo-European roots, Library of Congress, Renaissance*, and *Royal Society*. Theme list p. 475.

Biography. Capsule reviews of the careers, activities, and views (often with quotations) of individuals influential in the use and study of the language, such as the American lexicographer *Barnhart (Clarence L.)*, the Scottish rhetorician *Blair* (*Hugh*), the English printer and publisher *Caxton* (*William*), the Canadian communications critic *McLuhan* (*Marshall*), the English experimental novelist *Woolf* (*Virginia*), and the Nigerian Nobel Prize winning playwright *Soyinka* (*Wole*). Theme list p. 130. See also the description of the index of persons (above).

Name. (1) Entries that are part of the naming system of the language, such as *Botswana* and *Cumbria* (place-names), *Brontë* (*Charlotte* and *Emily*) and *Gandhi* (*Mohandas K.*) (personal names), and *Kiwi* and *Yankee* (ethnic nicknames). (2) General entries such as *binomial nomenclature, eponym, forms of address, Irish place-names, onomastics, terminology,* and *trademark.* (3) Entries for words ending in *-onym,* such as *homonym, retronym, synonym,* and *toponym.* Theme list p. 679.

Literature. Entries relating especially to: (1) Linguistic aspects of literary and related topics, as in the entries *alexandrine, diary, intertextuality, macaronic, poetic diction,* and *spondee.* (2) The various literatures of English, as in the entries *Behn* (*Aphra*), *Commonwealth literature, Joyce* (*James*), *Scots literature, South African literature in English,* and *Twain* (*Mark*). Theme list p. 622.

Style. Entries relating to ways in which language is used, including register (such as *Biblical English, Caribbeanism, legal usage,* and *psychobabble*), humour (such as *Aberdeen joke, Irish bull, repartee,* and *wit*), swearing (such as *blasphemy, four-letter word, great Australian adjective,* and *taboo*), styles, genres, and usages (such as *archaism, blarney, caricature, plain English, Saxonism,* and *sexism*), and rhetoric (such as *anachronism, metaphor, polemic, synecdoche,* and *trope*). Theme list p. 994.

Education. Entries relating to educational theory and practice as they relate to English, as both a mother tongue and a foreign, second, or international language, such as *applied linguistics, ARELS, Bullock Report, EFL Gazette, feedback, interference, NCTE, reading, Strevens* (*Peter*), *TEFL, TESOL, UCLES,* and *West* (*Michael*). Theme list p. 340.

Grammar. Entries that cover concepts and features of grammar both in general terms and in relation to English, grammar projects associated with the language, and grammarians, such as *apposition, case grammar, determiner, existential sentence, Jonson* (*Ben*), *modal verb, part of speech, Quirk* (*Sir Randolph*), *relative clause, Survey of English Usage, tag, voice,* and *word class.* Theme list p. 450.

Writing. Entries relating to the nature and history of writing in its various aspects, including *alphabet, calligraphy, creative writing, dialog(ue), dysgraphia, euphuism, paragraph, Pitman* (*Isaac*), *prose, semicolon, shorthand, spelling reform, theme,* and *uncial.* Theme list p. 1134.

Speech. Entries relating to both technical and popular discussions of accents, pronunciations, and the like, including *affricate, broad, clipped, drawl, International Phonetic Alphabet, Jones (Daniel), minimal pair, monophthong, phoneme, Received Pronunciation, Pygmalion,* and *voice*. In many instances, phonetic symbols have been used to indicate pronunciations; they have, however, been replaced by or supplemented with quasi-phonetic spellings (such as 'yeller' for one pronunciation of *yellow*) when these were considered to be a sufficiently clear means of indicating a pronunciation. Theme list p. 967.

Reference. Entries dealing with the concept of referring, with works of reference, and with aspects of lexicography and associated topics, such as *allusion, concordance, Dictionary of Jamaican English, Gowers (Sir Ernest), index, Linguistic Atlas of the United States and Canada, New Zealand dictionaries, quotation, semantic field,* and *thesaurus*. Theme list p. 855.

Word. Entries relating to vocabulary and word-formation, including *abbreviation, antonym, buzz word, calque, confusible, derivation, homophone, initialese, nonce word, reversal, root-creation, Scotticism, suffix, word*. Theme list p. 1122.

Usage. Entries relating to language use and judgements made about it, such as *authority, bad English, barbarism, Doublespeak Award, Fowler (Henry W.), usage guidance and criticism, Webster's Dictionary of English Usage,* and usage in the sense of register (*legal usage, plain language*). Theme list p. 1075.

Language. Entries relating to linguistics, language in general, specific languages, and prominent linguists, such as *Afrikaans, agglutinating, American Dialect Society, Australian languages, Bloomfield (Leonard), Chomsky (Noam), computational linguistics, echolalia, foreigner talk, Germanic languages, language pathology, Norman French, Polari, Scots,* and *sociolinguistics*. Theme list p. 573.

Variety. Entries relating to the many varieties (dialects, registers, and related forms) of English, and the places in which they occur, such as *academic English, Appalachian English, Briticism, Chancery Standard, educated English, Gambia, Miskito Coast Creole, Mummerset, Seaspeak, Singapore English, strine,* and *Zimbabwe*. Theme list p. 1081.

Media. Entries relating to the term 'media' understood in its widest sense, including publishing and language-related organizations as well as broadcasting, journalism, motion pictures, and the like, such as *American broadcasting, BBC English*[1], *ELT publishing, headline, Indian publishing, journalese, motion picture, Random House, South African press, telephone*. Theme list p. 647.

Technology. Entries relating to the technical concepts, physical systems, and kinds of apparatus associated with language, especially in its written and printed forms, such as *algorithm, boilerplate, codex, computing, keyboard, line, mark, mouse, pica, quarto, QWERTY, script, serif, typography,* and *white space.* Theme list p. 1026.

PROSPECTS

Although the *Companion* is complex and detailed, it is nonetheless, as stated above, 'an interim report'. No work describing a living language can ever be complete, and no printed product can directly exhibit the diversity of spoken language, nor hope to cover every feature and nuance of written, printed, and electronic expression. In addition, in the last year of preparation, after all the entries were technically complete, various changes had to be made so as to ensure that everything was as up-to-date as possible. In due course, there will be a second edition of the *Companion*, in which further developments in usage and in scholarly opinion will be suitably reflected. For this ongoing work, constructive comment and suggestions are welcomed by: The Editor, *The Oxford Companion to the English Language*, Oxford University Press, Walton Street, Oxford OX2 6DP, England.

Abbreviations

Only those abbreviations are listed that are not explained in the entries in which they occur.

AfrE	African English	NZE	New Zealand English
AmE	American English	*OED*	*Oxford English Dictionary*
AusE	Australian English	PakE	Pakistani English
AV	Authorized Version of the	RP	Received Pronunciation
	Bible	ScoE	Scottish English
BrE	British English	TEFL/EFL	(Teaching) English as a
c	century/centuries		Foreign Language
CanE	Canadian English	TEIL/EIL	(Teaching) English as an
CarE	Caribbean English		International Language
ELT	English Language Teaching	TESL/ESL	(Teaching) English as a
EngE	English in England		Second Language
ESP	English for Special/Specific	TESOL	Teaching of English to
	Purposes		Speakers of Other
IE	Indo-European		Languages
IndE	Indian English	U.	University
IPA	International Phonetic	UCLES	University of Cambridge
	Alphabet/Association		Local Examination
IrE	Irish English		Syndicate
MLA	Modern Language	WAE	West African English
	Association	WelshE	Welsh English

The asterisk symbol (*) has two uses in the body of the *Companion*: it marks either a grammatically unacceptable form (as in *has went*) or an unattested or hypothetical form (as in *ultraticum*). For its use in the Index, see p. 1149.

Values of phonetic symbols used in the *Companion*

a	*a* as in ScoE *pat* and Parisian French *patte*
aɪ	*y* and *i-e* as in RP and AmE *try, write*
aʊ	*ou* and *ow* as in RP and AmE *noun, now*
ɑ	*a* as in RP *father*; *a* and *o* as in AmE *father, bother*
ɒ	*a* and *o* as in RP *wash, odd*
æ	*a* as in traditional RP and in AmE *cat, trap*
b	*b* as in *back*; *bb* as in *rubber*
ç	*ch* as in German *ich*; h as in Japanese *hito*; occasionally, *h* as in *hue*
d	*d* as in *day*; *dd* as in *rudder*
dʒ	*j* and *dge* as in *judge*, and *ge* as in *George*; *j* as in Hindi *raj*
ð	*th* as in *this, other*; *d* as in Spanish *nada*
e	*ay* as in ScoE *day*; *é* as in French *thé*; *e* as in Italian *pesca* (fishing)
eɪ	*ay*, *a-e*, and *ea* as in RP and AmE *day, face, steak*
ə	[the schwa or neutral vowel] *a* as in *about, sofa*, *e* as in *hyphen*, *o* as in *reckon* (etc.)
əʊ	*o* and *oa* as in RP *go, goat*
ε	*e* as in *get*, German *Bett*, and Italian *pesca* (peach)
εə	*ai* and *a-e* as in RP *fair, square*
ɜ	*e, i, o, u* as in RP and AmE *her, stir, word, nurse*
f	*f* as in *few*; *ff* as in *puff*
g	*g* as in *got*; *gg* as in *bigger*
h	*h* as in *hot*
i	*e* as in *he*, *ee* as in *see*; *i* as in Spanish and French *si*; *ie* as in German *sie*
ɪ	*i* as in *ship* and in German *Schiff*
ɪə	*ea* and *e-e* as in RP *hear, here*
j	*y* as in *yet*; *j* as in German *ja*
k	*c* as in *car*; *k* as in *key*; *ck* as in *clock*; *kk* as in *trekked*; *qu* as in *quay*
l	[clear l] *l* as in RP *lip*
ł	[dark l] *l* as in RP *all*; as commonly in ScoE *all, lip, hilly*
ɬ	*ll* as in Welsh *Llanelli*
m	*m* as in *much*; *mm* as in *hammer*
n	*n* as in *now*; *nn* as in *runner*
ŋ	*ng* as in RP and AmE *sing*; *n* as in Spanish *cinco*
o	*o* as in ScoE *no*, in advanced RP *force*, and in Italian *dove*; *eau* as in French *beau*; *oh* as in German *wohl*
oʊ	*o* and *oa* as in AmE *go, goat*
ø	*eu* as in French *peu*; *ö* as in German *schön*

œ	*eu* as in French *veuve*; *ö* as in German *zwölf*
ɔ	*o* as in *north* and in German *Sonne*; *a* as in *war*
ɔɪ	*oi* and *oy* as in *noise*, *toy*
p	*p* as in *pen*; *pp* as in *pepper*
r	generally, *r* as in *round* and *rr* as in *sorry* (however pronounced); strictly, the rolled *r* of traditional ScoE, and of Spanish and Italian
ʀ	uvular *r* as in Parisian French *rue* and the Northumbrian burr
s	*s* as in *see*; *ss* as in *missed*
ʃ	*sh* as in *ship*; *ssi* as in *mission*; *ti* as in *motion*; *ch* as in French *chose*; *sch* as in German *Schiff*
t	*t* as in *ten*; *tt* as in RP *written*
tʃ	*ch* as in *church*; *tch* as in *latch*; *c* as in Italian *cello*, *ciao*; *tsch* as in German *Deutsch*
θ	*th* as in *three*, *heath*, and Greek *thésis*; *c* and *z* as in Castilian Spanish *cerveza*
u	*u* as in *lunar* and *oo* as in RP *pool*; *u* as in Italian *subito* and German *gut*; *ou* as in French *tout*
ʉ	*ui*, *ou* (etc.) in Scots *puir* (poor) and *doun/doon* (down), and as in Norwegian *hus*
ʊ	*oo* and *u* as in RP and AmE *foot* and *put*
ʊə	*u* and *u-e* as in RP *pure*
v	*v* as in *very* and in French *vrai*; *w* as in German *wohl*
ʌ	*u*, *oo*, and *o-e* as in RP and ScoE *bud*, *blood*, *love*
w	*w* as in *will*; *ou* as in French *oui*
hw	*wh* as in ScoE and IrE *when*, *white*
x	*ch* as in ScoE and German *ach*; *j* and *g* as in Spanish *jabón* and *gente*
y	*u-e* as in French *lune*; *ü* as in German *über*
ɣ	*g* as in Spanish *luego*
z	*z* as in *zeal* and French *zèle*; *s* as in *position*; *ss* as in *scissors*
ʒ	*s* as in *decision* and *measure*; *j* and *g* as in French *Jacques* and *rouge*
ʔ	[glottal stop] *tt* as in Cockney and Glasgow pronunciations of *better butter*, and as a phoneme in Arabic and Hawaiian
ː	[the length mark] used to indicate a long vowel, as in /uː/, in RP *loose*, *truce*
~	[the tilde] set over a symbol to indicate nasality

English throughout the world

A numbered list and map of territories for
which English is a significant language

1 Anguilla
2 Antigua and Barbuda
3 Argentina
4 Ascension
5 Australia
6 Bahamas
7 Bahrain
8 Bangladesh
9 Barbados
10 Belize
11 Bermuda
12 Botswana
13 British Indian
   Ocean Territory
14 Brunei
15 Cameroon
16 Canada
17 Cayman Islands
18 Channel Islands
19 China
20 Cook Islands
21 Dominica
22 Egypt
23 England
24 Falkland Islands
25 Fiji
26 Gambia
27 Ghana
28 Gibraltar
29 Grenada
30 Guyana
31 Hawaii
32 Honduras
33 Hong Kong
34 India
35 Indonesia
36 Iraq
37 Irish Republic
38 Isle of Man
39 Israel
40 Jamaica
41 Japan
42 Jordan
43 Kenya
44 Kiribati
45 Korea

46 Kuwait
47 Lesotho
48 Liberia
49 Malawi
50 Malaysia
51 Maldives
52 Malta
53 Maritime Provinces
54 Mauritius
55 Montserrat
56 Namibia
57 Nauru
58 Nepal

59 New England
60 Newfoundland
61 New Zealand
62 Nicaragua
63 Nigeria
64 Northern Ireland
65 Oman
66 Orkney
67 Pakistan
68 Panama
69 Papua New Guinea
70 Philippines
71 Puerto Rico

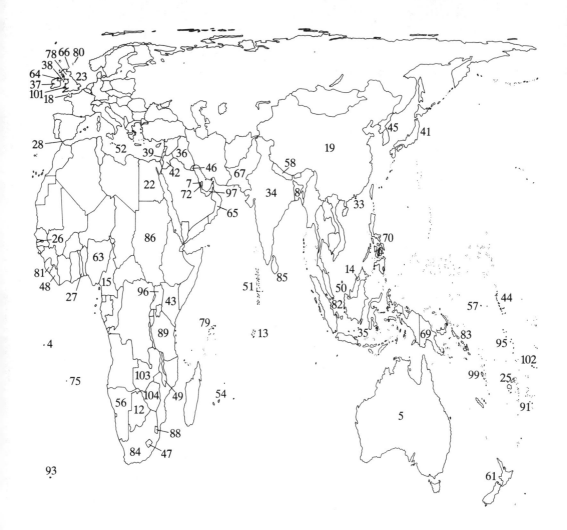

A

A, a [Called *ay*, rhyming with *say*]. The 1st letter of the Roman alphabet as used for English. It descends from the Phoenician symbol for a glottal stop, the sound at the beginning of its name, *'aleph* ('ox'). This letter, a consonant in Phoenician, was adopted by the Greeks as a vowel, A, to which they gave the name *alpha*. It was later adopted as *A* first by the Etruscans, then the Romans.

Sound values. (1) Short, as in *hat, lack, apple*. (2) Long, as in *hate, lake, maple, chaos*. In many accents of English, this sound is a diphthong, /eɪ/, often in RP with a special value before *r*, /eə/, as in *vary, scarce*. (3) In RP and related accents, phonetically long and open, /ɑː/, in such words as *calm, dance, far, father*. (4) Schwa in weak syllables, as in *avoid, prevalent, viable, vital, relevant, vicar, villa*. In RP, the weak form sometimes has the value of short *i*, /ɪ/, as in *private, village*. (5) After /w/ and before /l/, a phonetically long, open value of *o*, /ɔː/, as in *wall, war, water, quarter, tall*; in RP, after *w*, a short *o*-sound, /ɒ/, as in *swamp, swastika*; likewise in *yacht*. (6) In *any, many*, the short *e*-sound in *hen*.

Digraphs and other combinations. With the value of long *a* in cases 1–3. (1) *a–e*, where one or more consonants separate *a* and *e*: *hate, pale, waste*. (2) *ai*, initially and medially: *aid, pail, maintain*. The value of short *e* is often heard in *again, against, said*. (3) *ay*, in final positions: *day, dismay, relay*. The value of short *e* is often heard in *says*. (4) *au*, initially and medially: *sauce, author, because, laurel*. These have values of *o* that tend to be accent-dependent: for example, /ɔ/ in RP, and /ɒ/ in AmE, sometimes with length variation. (5) *aw*, in all positions, but especially finally: *awful, drawl, saw* (with various values, many comparable to those of *au*). (6) *aa*, only in loans, such as: names from Hebrew, with the long-*a* value in *Aaron, Canaan*, and schwa in *Isaac*; from Afrikaans, with the value of phonetically long, open *a* (*aardvark, kraal*). (7) *ae*, in diverse loans, usually with the value of long *a*: *maelstrom*, from Dutch; *Gael*, from Celtic; *Ishmael, Israel*, from Hebrew. (8) As second element in a digraph (*ea, oa*), *a* usually indicates a special value for the first vowel, but is not itself pronounced: long *e* in *east, beat, cheated*, long *o* in *oats, boat, soaked*, with a glide effect before *r* in non-rhotic accents, as in *fear, boar*. (9) In four words, *ea* has the value of long *a*: *break, great, steak, yea*. (10) In many common words, the digraph *ea* is pronounced as short *e*: *bread, meadow, ready, sweat, zealous*. (11) The letter *a* combines in unusual, sometimes unique ways with other vowel letters in: *aisle, aunt, beauty, broad, guinea, laugh, quay*. (12) Distinctive values in loanwords are usually preserved: *bureau, gauche, gaucho, naive/naïve*. For the symbol *æ*, see DIGRAPH.

Variations. (1) In some pairs of derivationally associated words, *a* has been replaced or has disappeared in unstressed syllables (*abstain/abstinence, maintain/maintenance, float/flotation*); in others, it alternates with other letters (*appearance/apparent, comparative/comparison, message/messenger*). (2) There is variation in the endings *-ant/ent, -ance/ence, -ancy/ency*, producing such forms as *assistant, concomitant, consistent, insistent, persistent, resistant*. These differences relate to the historical derivation of the words in question: whether they were acquired directly from Latin or through French. If taken straight from Latin, the words derive from the participles of verbs that have either an *a*-stem (as with *concomitant*, from *concomitans* accompanying) or an *e*-stem (as with *consistent, insistent*, and *persistent*, from variations on the base form *-sistens* standing, setting). If, however, they are taken from French, they derive from participles all of which end in *-ant*, regardless

THE CAPITAL LETTER

EARLY FORMS				CURRENT FORMS	
Phoenician	Greek	Etruscan	Roman (Latin)	roman	italic
Ƙ	ΔΛ	Ꙓ	A	A	*A*

THE SMALL LETTER

EARLY FORMS			CURRENT FORMS	
Roman cursive	Roman uncial	Carolingian minuscule	roman	italic
λ	ᴀ	ᴀ	a	*a*

of verb class (as with *assistant* and *resistant*). Sometimes, a distinction in meaning and use arises, as in *dependant/dependent*, but in *ambiance/ambience* there is no such distinction. See ALPHABET, GLOTTAL STOP, LETTER[1], LONG AND SHORT, S(C)HWA, SPELLING. [WRITING].

C.U., T.MCA., E.W.

ABBREVIATION [15c: through French *abré-viation* from Latin *abbreviatio/abbreviationis* shortening, from *brevis* short. Compare ABRIDG(E)MENT]. The shortening of words and phrases (*kilogram* to *kg*, *Imperial Chemical Industries* to *ICI*) and a result of such shortening (*MA* for *Master of Arts*, *sitcom* for *situation comedy*).

History. In ancient Egypt, although hieroglyphic signs were primarily pictorial and ideographic, some also served as *acrophones*, signs that represent not whole words but only their initial sounds: for example, the sign for *mulotch* (a horned owl) also represented an /m/ in personal names. If such a system were used in English, the picture of an owl might stand for the *o* in *Oliver*, a lion for the *l*, an ibis for the *i*, and so on. The whole name would be represented by word-signs interpreted as speech sounds. In a system of acrophonic abbreviation, there is no visible shortening; the reader decides from the context how to interpret a sign. Alphabetic abbreviation became possible around 1000 BC and was common in the classical world: the Greek letters *ΙΧΘΥΣ* (making up the word for 'fish') stood for Ἰησοῦς Χριστὸς Θεοῦ Ὑιὸς Σωτήρ (Jesus Christ Son of God Saviour), and as a result of their use the fish became a Christian symbol; the Latin letters *SPQR* stood for *Senatus Populusque Romanus* (the Senate and the Roman people), and *INRI* for *Iesus Nazaraeus Rex Iudaeorum* (Jesus of Nazareth King of the Jews). In addition, short forms such as *IMP CAES* (*Imperator Caesar* Emperor Caesar) were common on inscriptions and coins.

Although present-day abbreviation in English descends from such forms, its more immediate origin was in the practices of medieval scribes, among whom short forms were mnemonic and a means of economizing on parchment, effort, and time. As writing extended from Latin into the European vernacular languages, short forms went with it, first as loans (such as *AD* for *Anno Domini*: from the year of the Lord), then as native creations (such as *BC* for *Before Christ*). All such devices combine economy (of effort, space, and reference) with repetition (of the familiar and formulaic); although some are casual or temporary creations, others have become over the centuries so institutionalized that their origins and natures are seldom considered: as for

example *AD* and *BC*, when used for everyday secular purposes.

Nature. Although abbreviations usually need to be concise, convenient, and easy to remember, they do not need to be fully understood to serve their purpose. People literate in English can work successfully with such formulas as *e.g.* and *q.v.* whether or not they know their full Latin forms *exempli gratia* (for the sake of example) and *quod vide* (which see). Similarly, people can talk about *IBM* and *Amoco* without knowing (or needing to know) that these shortened names stand for *International Business Machines* and *American Oil Company*. This is especially true of foreign abbreviations such as *BMW*, the common name for a company that makes cars; few users of English know that the full German form is *Bayerische Motoren Werke*. The more familiar and successful the short form, the less need for the full form, which may in course of time be forgotten. The full forms of *mob* (Latin *mobile vulgus* the fickle crowd) and *radar* (radio detection and ranging) have no functional value in the 1990s, and many are entirely unaware that these words are (or were) abbreviations. The members of organizations usually have little difficulty with the abbreviations they use, because of sheer familiarity, but people who are not part of the in-group may regard their use as (sometimes frustrating and provocative) jargon. They may be irritated by the number, opacity, and ambiguity of forms that they meet in new contexts: for example, the letters *AAA* have many meanings (such as *Amateur Athletic Association*, *American Automobile Association*, *Australian Automobile Association*, and *Art Against Apartheid*), and the syllable *con* represents various full words (such as *convict*, *confidence trick*, *concentration*, *consols*, *consul*), but an awareness of such established uses may be no help at all on meeting the abbreviated phrase *an AAA con* in a new situation.

Orthography. There are six conventions for writing and printing abbreviations: (1) Capital letters and points: *I.N.S.E.A.* for 'International Society for Education through Art'. (2) Capital letters without points: *BBC* for 'British Broadcasting Corporation'; *NATO* for 'North Atlantic Treaty Organization'. (3) Lower-case letters with points for formulas such as *e.g.* and *q.v.*, and without points for items that have become everyday words, such as *laser*, *radar*. (4) Mixed capitals and lower case, without points, capitals usually for lexical words, lower case for grammatical words: *DoWLT* for 'Dictionary of World Literary Terms'; *MoMA* for 'Museum of Modern Art'; *mRNA* for 'messenger ribonucleic acid'; *WiB* the organization 'Women in Business'. (5) Internal capitals, as in *CompuSex* for 'Computer

Sex', and *DigiPulse* for 'Digital Pulse'. (6) Hybrid forms: *B.Com.* for 'Bachelor of Commerce'.

Typology. There are three types of abbreviation: (1) Letter-based, such as *AAA*. (2) Syllable-based, such as *con.* (3) Hybrid, such as *B.Com.* All may have a symbolic or a lexical function: symbolic abbreviations serve as formulas, as with *c.c.* or *cc* (cubic centimetres/meters), *Fe* (iron, from Latin *ferrum*); lexical abbreviations are generally word-like, some less so because they are spoken as letter sequences, as with *BBC*, some more so because they are spoken as words and often cannot be usefully distinguished from them, as with *NATO, radar.*

Symbolic abbreviations. Abbreviations that serve as symbols are usually pronounced as letter sequences or as their full originating words, as with *c.c.* ('cee-cee', 'cubic centimetres'). Some are spoken very differently from anything suggested by etymology or appearance: for example, the former British symbol *£.s.d.* is pronounced either 'ell-ess-dee' or 'pounds, shillings, and pence', not **Librae, solidi, et denarii* (the Latin for which the signs stand). Abbreviated titles such as *M.A.* for *Magister Artium* and *Ph.D.* for *Philosophiae Doctor* are comparable: 'em-ay', 'Master of Arts'; 'pee-aitch-dee', 'Doctor of Philosophy'. In some instances, where abbreviations start with a vowel, the use of *a* or *an* indicates whether a writer is thinking of them as letters or words: *a MP* 'a Member of Parliament'; *an MP* 'an em-pee'.

Lexical abbreviations. Abbreviations that serve as words fall into three types that shade into a fourth less clear-cut type: (1) *Initialism*. A letter group that cannot be pronounced as a word, and must therefore be spoken as letters: *BBC* spoken as 'bee-bee-cee'. (2) *Acronym*. A letter group that can be, and is, pronounced as a word: *NATO* spoken as 'Nay-toe'. (3) *Clipping*. A part of a word standing for the whole: *pro* for *professional* and *phone* for *telephone*. (4) *Blend*, also *portmanteau word*. A word made from two or more other words, by fusion (*brunch* from *breakfast* and *lunch*) or by putting together syllabic elements from other words (*Oxbridge* from *Oxford* and *Cambridge*). There are variations and hybrids of these basic types: (1) Both initialisms and acronyms: *VAT* (Value Added Tax) is referred to as both 'vat' and 'vee-ay-tee'. (2) Forms that look like one type but behave like another: *WHO* (World Health Organization) is 'double-you-aitch-oh', not 'hoo'; *POW* (prisoner of war) is 'pee-oh-double-you', not 'pow'. (3) Part-initialism, part-acronym: *VTOL* (vertical take-off and landing) is pronounced 'vee-tall'; *CD-ROM* (compact disc read-only memory) is 'cee-dee-rom'. (4) Combinations of letter groups and clippings: *ARPAnet* (Advanced Research Projects Agency computer network). (5) Initialisms adapted as acronyms: 'GLCMs (ground-launched cruise missiles) and SLCMs (sea-launched cruise missiles) are called Glickems and Slickems by those in the know' (from *Time*, 18 Feb. 1985).

Occurrence in texts. When abbreviations are familiar, they are used without explanation but, because they cannot always be presented without a gloss, there are at least six ways of bringing them into a text:

Indirect association. 'The Art Gallery of Nova Scotia is now touring three other national exhibitions . . . In the last fiscal year AGNS sent 23 exhibitions to 63 centres' (Halifax *Chronicle Herald*, 11 Nov. 1982); 'London & Scottish Marine Oil are going to drill onshore in Scotland again. . . . The spot where LASMO want to put down their drill is near Loanhead, Midlothian' (*Scotsman*, 24 Aug. 1983).

Full form, bracketed abbreviation. 'Britain may ban imports [of blood] that could be spreading the killer disease Acquired Immune Deficiency Syndrome (AIDS)' (Montreal *Gazette*, 3 May 1983); 'The strike is in response to a call by the All-India Federation of University and College Teachers Organisations (AIFUCTO)' (*Times of India*, 5 Aug. 1987).

Abbreviation, bracketed full form. 'The uncertainty surrounding SERPS (State earnings related pension scheme) deepens' (*Times*, 11 May 1985); 'They are the acknowledged codiscoverers of the virus that causes AIDS (Acquired Immune Deficiency Syndrome)' (*Observer*, 6 Oct. 1985).

Using '(stands) for'. 'Here's an acronym you should know: MEGO. It stands for "My Eyes Glaze Over" ' (William Safire, *New York Times*, Jan. 1988); 'AIDS—an acronym for acquired immune deficiency syndrome' (Montreal *Gazette*, 7 May 1983).

Using 'or'. 'Ethylene dibromide, or EDB, has been described as the most powerful cancer-causing agent the Environmental Protection Agency has tested' (*International Herald Tribune*, 4/5 Feb. 1984); 'That capital base appeared to give Arab Insurance Group, or ARIG, the power to take on the likes of Munich Reinsurance and Lloyd's of London' (*IHT*, 29 Sept. 1983).

Using 'as it is known'. 'The failure may explain the absence so far of any announcement about "Initial Operating Capability," due to have been achieved at Greenham Common on Thursday. IOC, as it is known, means that one flight of missiles is declared officially capable of being launched on a "mission"' (*Observer*, 18 Dec. 1983).

Occasionally, an abbreviation is glossed not by the word or words it shortens but by others with which it has semantic links: 'Paris imposed the ban [on British beef] . . . because of concern over BSE, or "mad cow" disease' (*The European*, 1–3 June 1990). *BSE* in fact stands for *bovine spongiform encephalopathy*.

Word-formation. Because they are word-like, abbreviations play a part in word-formation:

Conversion. The word *overdose* is used as a noun and a verb. So also is its medical abbreviation *OD*: '*OD*ing on aspirin' (overdosing on aspirin). In the British Army, *RTU*ed personnel have been 'returned to unit'.

Derivation. (1) With prefixes: an *ex-PoC* is someone no longer a prisoner of conscience (Amnesty International); *pro-JLP* means in favour of the Jamaican Labour Party. (2) With suffixes: *Rabisms* are noteworthy sayings of the British politician R. A. Butler; *WASPy* means like a White Anglo-Saxon Protestant. See WASP. (3) With both: an *ex-CFL-er* is a former member of the Canadian Football League.

Attribution. Like *steel* in *steel bridge*: an *AI gambit* is a gambit relating to artificial intelligence; an *IRA gunman* is a gunman belonging to the Irish Republican Army; an *RCMP superintendent* is a superintendent in the Royal Canadian Mounted Police. Abbreviations occur attributively before other abbreviations: a *BBC micro* is a British Broadcasting Corporation microcomputer; an *IBM PC* is an International Business Machines personal computer; *Mr TV Exec* means Mister Television Executive. Abbreviations may occur in a string in which precise attribution is not easily determined: *NYS ESOL BEA* refers to the composite New York State English to Speakers of Other Languages Bilingual Educators Association.

Compounding. With the same stress patterns as *teapot* and *blackbird*: *A-bomb*, *AIDS cure*, *B-movie*, *CCAT* ('See-cat': Cambridge College of Arts and Technology), *kiddie porn*. Composites containing abbreviations are common and often intricate, mixing compounding and attribution: *NY kiddie porn*, an *AIDS-Africa link*, *Metro-Montreal QPF contingent patrols* (Metropolitan Montreal Quebec Police Force contingent patrols). Combining forms may precede or follow abbreviations: *pseudo-* in a *pseudo-BBC accent*; *-logy* in *UFOlogy*, the study of Unidentified Flying Objects. In some classical compounds, a syllable is dropped for ease of expression: *fathometer*, formed from *fathom* and *meter*; *symbology* from *symbol* and *-ology*.

Blending. Because blending is associated with abbreviation, the analysis of formations is particularly complex. A blend may be created for stunt purposes or convenience and bring together an abbreviation and part of a word: for example, *IBMulation* is the emulation of International Business Machines, and the *EYE-catcher Award* was a particularly eye-catching award because it was given in 1987 (which was the EYE or European Year of the Environment).

Ad-hoc usage. The use of abbreviations has long been part of note-taking, file-making, cataloguing, and the making of inventories. In such activities, short forms are often created for ad-hoc purposes, used for a time, then dispensed with and forgotten. In such restricted systems, *LA* may mean not *Los Angeles* but *late arrivals*, and *BBC* may mean *best before Christmas*. Ad-hoc abbreviation is a major feature of computer use, especially in the creation of commands and file names: for example, in the making of this volume, two commands have been *ca* (for calling up a file) and *ne* (for making a new file), while *oc/hist/shak* was the shorthand filename meaning 'Oxford Companion/History theme/Shakespeare file'. In the checklists inserted in their catalogues by the University of California Press, books have acronymic names for ordering, formed from the first three letters of the author's name followed by the first three letters of the title: for example, *ABBANA* from *Abbate* and *Analyzing Opera*, *DAMTHE* from *D'Amico* and *Theory and Practice*, and *PELSHA* from *Peletz* and *Share of the Harvest*.

Special effects. Abbreviations may be ironic, humorous, or whimsical: for example, the rail link between the town of *Bed*ford and the London station of St *Pan*cras is locally known as *the Bedpan Line*; a comparable link for *Bos*ton, New York, and *Wash*ington is *the Bosnywash circuit*. Comments on life may be telescoped into such sardonic packages as: *BOGSAT* a Bunch Of Guys Sitting Around a Table (making decisions about other people); *GOMER* Get Out of My Emergency Room (said by physicians to hypochondriacs); *MMBA* Miles and Miles of Bloody Africa (an in-group term among people who have to travel those miles); *TGIF* Thank God It's Friday (after a particularly hard working week). In addition, some institutionalized abbreviations have more than one interpretation. This double meaning may be intentional, as with *ATI*, whose primary meaning is *American Tours International* and secondary sense, as a kind of business motto, is *Attitude, Teamwork, Initiative*. More commonly, however, secondary meanings are ironic: for example, in the British honours system, the forms *CMG* (Commander of St Michael and St George), *KCMG* (Knight C. of

St Michael and St George), and *GCMG* (Grand C. of St Michael and St George) are often glossed as *Call Me God, Kindly Call Me God,* and *God Calls Me God.*

See ABRIDG(E)MENT, ACRONYM/PROTOGRAM, AGGLOMERESE, AMPERSAND, AUSTRALIAN ENGLISH, BINOMIAL NOMENCLATURE, BLEND, CLIPPING, COMPUTERESE, CONTRACTION, DIACRITIC, GAIRAIGO, HOUSE STYLE, INITIAL, INITIALISM, LATIN, LATIN TAG, LETTER[1], LETTER WORD, NOTES AND REFERENCES, NUMBER[1], POINT, PUNCTUATION, REDUNDANCY, SHORTHAND, SYLLABLE WORD, TECHNOSPEAK, TELEGRAPHESE, TELESCOPING, WORD-FORMATION. [USAGE, WORD, WRITING].

T.MCA.

Bauer, Laurie. 1983. *English Word-Formation.* Cambridge: University Press.
Marchand, H. 1969. *Categories and Types of Present-Day English Word-Formation,* 2nd edition. Munich: C. H. Beck.
Paxton, J. 1986. *Everyman Dictionary of Abbreviations.* London: Dent.
Sola, R. de. 1985. *Abbreviations Dictionary.* Amsterdam: Elsevier.
Towell, J. E., & Sheppard, H. E. 1986. *International Acronyms, Initialisms & Abbreviations Dictionary,* 2nd edition. Detroit: Gale.
—— 1989. *Acronyms, Initialisms & Abbreviations Dictionary,* 13th edition. Three volumes. Detroit: Gale.

ABC. See AMERICAN BROADCASTING.

ABERCROMBIE, David [b.1909]. British phonetician and language teacher, born in Birkenhead, son of the poet Lascelles Abercrombie, and educated at Leeds Grammar School, the U. of Leeds, U. College London, and the Sorbonne in Paris. A student of Daniel Jones at UCL, he taught in Jones's department, then at the London School of Economics (1934-8), the Institute of English Studies, Athens (1938-40), and Cairo U. (1940-5). After teaching EFL at the London School of Economics and then phonetics at Leeds, he established the Department of Phonetics at the U. of Edinburgh, where he became Professor in 1964 and remained until his retirement in 1980. His publications include: *Problems and Principles: Studies in the Teaching of English as a Second Language* (1956, 2nd edition in 1963 retitled *Problems and Principles in Language Study*); *Studies in Phonetics and Linguistics* (1965); and *Elements of General Phonetics* (1967). His special interests include the history of phonetics, speech therapy, rhythm and stress in teaching English, a phonetic approach to English prosody, writing systems, spoken prose, and the social impact of Received Pronunciation. See index. [BIOGRAPHY, EDUCATION, EUROPE, LANGUAGE, SPEECH].

P.S., T.MCA.

ABERDEEN JOKE, also **Aberdonian joke.** A joke characterizing the supposedly mean habits and parochial mentality of the people of Aberdeen in Scotland: 'Two taxis collided this morning in Aberdeen, and 24 passengers were taken to hospital'; 'local headline *Titanic sunk; Aberdeen woman missing*'. See JOKE, SCOTTISH JOKE. [STYLE].

W.N.

ABERDEENSHIRE DIALECT. See DIALECT IN SCOTLAND.

ABLATIVE ABSOLUTE. See ABSOLUTE CLAUSE.

ABLATIVE CASE [15c: from Latin *casus ablativus* the case directing away (from a position)]. A term in the case system of Latin. The ablative is the form of a noun, adjective, or pronoun when it expresses meanings usually shown in English through *by, with,* and *from*: agency, instrumentality, source, association, removal, distance. The noun and adjective in the phrase *magna cum laude* ('great with praise', with great praise) are in the ablative. See ABSOLUTE CLAUSE, CASE[1]. [GRAMMAR].

S.C.

ABLAUT [1840s: from German *Ablaut,* from *ab* off, *Laut* sound. Coined in 1819 by Jakob Grimm]. Terms used in philology for both the diachronic shifting of vowels (also known as *vowel shift*) and the synchronic grading of vowels (also known as *vowel gradation*), especially in the Indo-European languages. Vowel gradation occurs in English in the formation of some irregular noun plurals (*man, men; goose, geese*) and some irregular verbs (*sing, sang, sung; swim, swam, swum*). See GREAT VOWEL SHIFT, STRONG VERB, VOWEL SHIFT. [GRAMMAR, SPEECH]. T.MCA.

ABORIGINAL ENGLISH. The technical name given to a continuum of varieties of English, ranging between standard AusE and creoles, acquired and used by Aboriginal Australians and often referred to by their speakers as *blackfella English* or *blackfella talk.* In some parts of Australia, the transition from a traditional language to Aboriginal English has occurred within four generations in the 20c. It is used by Aborigines both among themselves and with non-Aborigines. Most varieties are intelligible to speakers of standard AusE, though certain norms for the use of language are very different (for example, direct questions are not typically used to elicit information), and there are considerable differences in grammar and phonology. Some of the features of Aboriginal English are shared by non-standard varieties around the world, such as the use of past and participial forms of certain verbs (*brang,* not *brought*), and double negatives (*He hasn't got no toys*). Others are more characteristic of creoles, such as the non-occurrence of the copula (*His name John*, not *His name is John*) and lack of plural marking with *-s* (*two bird*, not *two birds*). In areas where speakers still use traditional languages such as Warlpiri and Pitjantjatjara, their English often displays features borrowed from them: for example, in phonology, affricates and fricatives alternate with palatals, as in *tjicken* (chicken). There are also lexical differences, including words borrowed from such languages, and distinctive uses of English words: *granny* can be used in the South-West to refer to any male or female relative of a person's grandparents' generation. Some words can be used with a different grammatical function: *grow up* and *growl* may be used transitively, as in *My mother grew me up* and *She growled him*. Although the variety is generally stigmatized by white Australian society, it often functions as a symbol of Aboriginal identity. See ABORIGINES, AUSTRALIAN PIDGIN, KRIOL, PIDGIN. [OCEANIA, VARIETY]. S.R.

ABORIGINES [16c: a plural given to the Latin phrase *ab origine* from the beginning]. A plural word for the indigenous people of a country, applied especially to the original inhabitants of Australia and for a time New Zealand. Two singulars coexist: *Aborigine*, *Aboriginal*. In Australia, *Aborigine* and *Aborigines* are currently the singular and plural preferred by standardizing agencies, though there is good citation evidence for *Aboriginal*, *Aboriginals*. European settlers have also called the indigenous inhabitants *Australians*, *Blacks*, *Blackfellows*, *Indians*, and *Natives*. *Aborigines* seems to have been established as the preferred term by the 1820s (when both singulars came into use), because of its degree of neutrality, because native-born whites had begun to call themselves *Australians* and *natives*, and because the inappropriateness of *Indians* was recognized. *Blackfellow* was frequently used, especially in pidgin, but is now offensive in white use, as is the abbreviation *Abo*. *Black* has been in use throughout, more recently developing new strength, as elsewhere, in the context of black activism. Associated in Australia with a land rights movement, which began in the 1960s, this political activism has led to a manifestation of *Aboriginality*, a facet of which is the use of indigenous generics meaning 'being' or 'man': *koori* from Awabakal, *murri* from Kamilaroi, *nyoongah* from Nyungar, and others, as alternatives to the term *Aborigine*. See ABORIGINAL ENGLISH, AUSTRALIAN LANGUAGES, AUSTRALIAN PLACE-NAMES. [NAME, OCEANIA]. W.S.R.

ABRIDGEMENT, also **abridgment** [15c: from Old French *abregement*, from *abreger*, from Latin *abbreviare/abbreviatum* to shorten. Compare ABBREVIATION]. (1) The act, process, or result of shortening or condensing a text, usually to a given length such as half or one-third, or to a required number of words. (2) A work produced in this way: an abridgement of Thomas Hardy's novel *Far from the Madding Crowd*. The process might include removing matter that the abridger considers less important or central (such as repetition), less relevant for the purposes in mind (such as certain kinds of detail and description), or more difficult to understand (such as technical or archaic usage). It may include a simplification of such structural elements as paragraph length and sentence complexity, and in some cases (usually political, religious, or aesthetic) may include censorship. In most abridgements, the intention is to keep the main sense and substance of a work, such as the main plot and characters in a novel. Abridgements are undertaken because: (1) A text may be longer than a given group (such as younger readers) is willing to attempt, but nonetheless of intrinsic interest to them: for example, by current standards, 19c novels like those of Hardy are too long and leisurely in their development, but nevertheless have plots and motifs of wide appeal. (2) Foreign learners of a language like English might benefit from a simplified abridgement of a novel that retains the human interest but replaces more difficult and longer passages with easier vocabulary and syntax and less bulk. See ABSTRACT, BOWDLERIZE, CENSORSHIP, CONDENSED BOOK, DIGEST, PRÉCIS, READER, SUMMARY, SYNOPSIS, UNABRIDGED. [MEDIA, WRITING]. T.MCA.

ABSOLUTE [14c: from Latin *absolutus* free from restriction, translating Greek *apoleluménos*]. A term indicating that a word, phrase, or clause stands apart from the usual relations with other elements in a sentence: *This being so* is absolute in *This being so, we'll have to make new plans*. Traditionally, such a combination is an *absolute phrase*, but it is now widely referred to as an *absolute clause*. See ABSOLUTE CLAUSE. [GRAMMAR]. T.MCA.

ABSOLUTE CLAUSE. An adverbial clause that has its own subject, and has a participle as its verb or no verb at all: '*The dinner having been prepared*, I had time to take a nap before the guests arrived'. Here, the verb is the participle phrase *having been prepared* and the subject is *the dinner*. Contrast the adverbial participle clause in '*Having prepared the dinner*, I had time to take a nap', where the subject of *having prepared the dinner* is understood to be identical with the main subject *I*. An absolute clause is not introduced by a *subordinating conjunction*:

after having prepared the dinner and *while preparing the dinner* are not absolute clauses. The participle may end in *-ing* (*trembling* in '*His voice trembling*, he described what had happened') or *-ed* (*wasted* in '*Their money wasted on imprudent schemes*, they could not expect any further help'). With some irregular verbs, the participle may not end in *-ed*: *spent* in '*Their money spent on imprudent schemes*, they could expect no further help.' Absolute clauses may be without a verb, as in 'The soldiers emerged from their hiding places, *their hands high above their heads*', a corresponding participle clause being *their hands held high above their heads*. (The end of the previous sentence itself contains an absolute clause with the participle *being* as its verb.) Outside a few set phrases such as *all being/going well, weather permitting, present company excluded/excepted*, absolute clauses are infrequent and usually confined to formal written English. Absolute clauses in Latin are in the ablative case, and are therefore said to be *ablative absolutes*: for example, *Gallis victis* (literally 'with the Gauls having been conquered') means 'when the Gauls had been conquered'. There is no ablative case in English. Pronouns in absolute constructions are in the subjective case: *he* (not objective *him*) in 'The police located the terrorist by tapping his parents' telephone line, *he having mentioned his hideout when talking to his father.*' Since the corresponding case in Latin is the nominative, English absolute constructions are sometimes called *nominative absolutes*. See ABSOLUTE, CLAUSE. [GRAMMAR]. S.G.

ABSOLUTE DEGREE. See POSITIVE DEGREE.

ABSTRACT [16c in this sense: from Latin *abstractus* drawn away]. A summary of a statement, thesis, paper, or other document, usually providing its *gist* (essential elements and argument). After reading the abstract, someone may decide to read the whole document or (in the case of a public presentation) attend the meeting at which the document will be read out and/or discussed. Abstracts are routinely printed in the programmes of academic and scientific conferences, at the beginnings of papers published in the proceedings of such conferences, and in issues of learned journals at the start of most papers or articles. Some publications consist almost entirely of abstracts of papers that have appeared in other journals: for example, *Language Teaching: The International Abstracting Journal for Language Teachers and Applied Linguists* (Cambridge University Press). See ABRIDG(E)MENT. [EDUCATION, MEDIA, WRITING]. T.MCA.

ABSTRACT AND CONCRETE [*abstract* 15c, from Latin *abstractus* drawn away; *concrete* 14c, from Latin *concretus* grown together]. Contrasting terms in traditional philosophy and grammar, *concrete* referring to the material and specific, *abstract* to the ideal and general. Abstraction as a mental process starts with many particular things or events and moves to a single generality within or behind them, such as the concept *time* abstracted from such changes as day and night, the seasons, and ageing. Although the use of language depends on abstract thought and everyone therefore engages in it, such thought is widely regarded as difficult, the domain of intellectuals and scholars. In grammar, an *abstract noun* refers to an action, concept, event, quality, or state (*love, conversation*), whereas a *concrete noun* refers to a touchable, observable person or thing (*child, tree*). This semantic classification cuts across the syntactic division countable/uncountable noun. Although abstract nouns tend to be uncountable (*courage, happiness, news, tennis, training*), many are countable (*an hour, a joke, a quantity*). Others can be both, often with shifts of meaning from general to particular (*great kindness/many kindnesses; not much industry/a major industry; some success/a remarkable success*). See NOUN. [GRAMMAR, LANGUAGE]. T.MCA., S.C.

ABUSAGE [16c]. An archaic term for misuse and defilement, revived in 1942 by Eric Partridge in the title *Usage and Abusage: A Guide to Good English* (1942). It is currently used only in his sense of improper, unidiomatic, and ungrammatical language. Compare CONFUSAGE. [USAGE]. T.MCA.

ABUSE [15c: from Old French *abus*, Latin *abusus* misuse, waste]. (1) Wrong or improper use of anyone or anything. The term is often (usually emotively) applied to language:

Some native speakers claim that the *use* of the language is deteriorating. One charge is ethical: people are said to be abusing the language, more so than in the past, with intent to conceal, mislead, or deceive, generally through euphemism or obscure language. Usually, the accusation is directed principally against politicians, bureaucrats, and advertisers, but the abuse is felt to have an adverse effect on the language as such. Certainly, the contemporary mass media facilitate the rapid and widespread dissemination of such language abuses. The other charge is aesthetic or functional: people are said to be using the language less elegantly or less efficiently than in the recent past, a charge that is commonly directed against young people. The charge may or may not have some justification, but in any case is impossible to substantiate. Many variables inhibit the feasibility of making valid and reliable comparisons with earlier periods: for example, the phenomenal growth of the literate population and of the use of the written language ('Standards of English', section 1.11 in Quirk *et al.*, *A Comprehensive Grammar of the English Language*, 1985).

(2) Harsh or coarsely insulting language: *to hurl abuse at people*. See SWEARING. [MEDIA, STYLE, USAGE].   T.MCA.

ACADEMESE. See ACADEMIC USAGE, -ESE, PEDANT.

ACADEMIC USAGE, also **academic English**. The register of English used by scholars and scientists: an elevated and often complex style associated with concern for accuracy, objectivity, and dispassionate comment, and characterized by: (1) Qualifying expressions such as *at least, may, probably, under such conditions, usually*. (2) Parenthetical asides, intended to modify, support, or otherwise affect statements: *according to the data, apparently, as far as we can tell at this stage*. (3) Passive constructions serving to minimize or remove personality: *It was found that . . ., The data were analysed, When completed, the experiment was discussed*. (4) Impersonal and non-dramatic ('dry') speech that may consist of reading a prepared paper (with or without extempore comments) or making extempore remarks supported by notes. Replies to comments and questions are often marked by pauses to rephrase a statement for the sake of precision and self-defence. Speakers may announce such rephrasing as they engage in it, using such formulas as *that is (to say), . . ., or, more precisely . . ., Let me rephrase that so as to . . .* Concern for precision sometimes leads to statements framed so as to cover every possible aspect of a topic, with detailed annotation full of supporting documentation in written work.

Academic writing generally makes use of such *scholarly apparatus* as introductions, provisos, disclaimers, acknowledgements, notes, references, bibliographies, and indexes. Such apparatus descends from the Middle Ages and the Renaissance and became more easily organized with the printing of books and papers. For many lay people, academic usage is often rarefied and pedantic. It can intimidate and appear to be at odds with plain English. As a result, many regard it as acceptable in the ivory tower but impractical elsewhere. Many academics, however, see such a style as the proper and perhaps sole medium of rational expression, and dislike the implication that it can be used as a shield against the world. Extreme styles are pejoratively referred to as *academese*, such as: 'Chieftaincy as a sanctional source, a symbolic referent, an integrational integer, and for ethnic and sub-ethnic definition, represents an orientational base for the charismatic persona' (from a 1960s sociology paper).

Not all academics accept the prevailing styles in research papers and other documents. For example, the US physicist N. David Mermin has observed:

Over the past fifty years or so, scientists have allowed the conventions of expression available to them to become entirely too confining. The insistence on bland impersonality and the widespread indifference to anything like the display of a unique human author in scientific exposition, have not only transformed the reading of most scientific papers into an act of tedious drudgery, but have also deprived scientists of some powerful tools for enhancing their clarity in communicating matters of great complexity. Scientists wrote beautifully through the 19th century and on into the early 20th. But somewhere after that, coincident with the explosive growth of research, the art of writing science suffered a grave setback, and the stultifying convention descended that the best scientific prose should sound like a non-human author addressing a mechanical reader (Preface, *Boojums All The Way Through: Communicating Science In a Prosaic Age*, Cambridge University Press, 1990).

See EAP, NOTES AND REFERENCES, REGISTER, SOCIOLOGESE. [STYLE, USAGE].   T.MCA.

ACADEMY [16c: from French *académie*, Latin *academia*, Greek *Akadḗmeia* a grove in Athens where Plato established a school]. (1) A school, college, or other educational institution. (2) A cultural institution for the maintenance or raising of standards in art, science, or language, such as the *Académie française*, founded in 1634. The members of this academy ('the forty immortals') meet in the Institut de France in Paris, where they have a dual mandate: to maintain a dictionary of French and to adjudicate on grammar, vocabulary, and usage. The Académie made such a profound impression in 17c England that the issue of whether English should also have such an institution was discussed for many years. Daniel Defoe argued:

The *English* Tongue is a Subject not at all less worthy the Labour of such a Society than the *French*, and capable of a much greater Perfection. . . . The Work of this Society shou'd be to encourage Polite Learning, to polish and refine the *English* Tongue, and advance the so much neglected Faculty of Correct Language, to establish Purity and Propriety of Stile, and to purge it from all the Irregular Additions that Ignorance and Affectation have introduc'd (*An Essay upon Projects*, 1697).

Nothing came of the plan. When from time to time the question of the 'missing' English Academy is raised, authoritarians deplore and libertarians applaud its absence. See ADDISON, AUGUSTAN, DEFOE, EDUCATION, ENGLISH IN ENGLAND, ENGLISH LITERATURE, FRENCH, FRISIAN, HOUSE STYLE, LONDON, ROYAL SOCIETY, SOUTH AFRICAN LANGUAGE ORGANIZATIONS, SPELLING, SPELLING REFORM, STANDARD, [HISTORY, STYLE, USAGE].   T.MCA.

ACCENT [16c: through French from Latin *accentus* signal, stress, from *ad-* to, *cantus* song: translating Greek *prosōidía*: compare PROSODY]. (1) A way of speaking that indicates a person's place of origin and/or social class: *a working-class accent, a London accent, a working-class London accent; a regional accent; an American accent; an American regional accent*. In phonetic terms, an accent is a set of habits that make up someone's pronunciation of a language or language variety. (2) In poetics and phonetics, the prominence of a syllable: in *dogmatic*, the accent (or stress) is on the second syllable, *dogMAtic*. (3) A diacritical mark, as over the first *e* in *élite* (an acute accent). Acute accents are often used over vowels to mark prominent syllables, as in *This is the wáy it's dóne*. When so used, they are called *accent marks*. *Accent* in this sense is also used figuratively for emphasis (*The accent is on entertainment*) or special detail (*a dress with vivid blue accents*).

Accent as pitch. In classical Greek, the technical term *prosōdia* referred to pitch, tone, and melody. It was loan-translated into Latin as *accentus* and directly borrowed as *prosodia*, but despite this background *accent* and *prosody* have never been synonyms. Each covers different aspects of vocal sound. In Greek, but not Latin, variation in the pitch of a syllable was marked in writing: (1) A syllable with a *prosōidía bareîa* or heavy tone was spoken with a low pitch, and above its written vowel was placed a mark sloping down from left to right. The Romans called this an *accentus gravis* (grave accent). (2) A syllable with a *prosōidía oxeîa* or sharp tone was higher, and above its written vowel was placed a mark that sloped up from left to right. The Romans called this an *accentus acutus* (acute accent). (3) A syllable with a *prosōidía perispōménē* or a rising-then-falling pitch had a mark that also rose then fell. The Romans called this an *accentus circumflexus* (a circumflex or 'bent round' accent). The precise details of how these marks were used are not known, but it was in this way that three of the best-known diacritical marks in modern use came into existence.

Accent as stress. In phonetics and linguistics, *accent* may mean the stress or pitch prominence of a syllable, or both. In English, *word stress* is often marked with an acute on the vowel of a stressed syllable (*atómic, diréction*). In *sentence stress*, acutes may mark stressed syllables while such a device as capital letters marks a tonic syllable (that on which change of pitch occurs), as in *Whát a reMARkable idéa!*, in which the tonic is *MAR* (emphasizing *remarkable*), as opposed to *Whát a remárkable iDEa*, in which the tonic is *DE* (emphasizing *idea*). Many con-

ventions have been used to exhibit degrees of prominence, including circles and boxes of various sizes above the words, but none is standard, and no graphic formulas ever catch all the subtleties of speech. In some theories, *accent* is the tonicity of syllables (such as the *MAR* and *DE* of the above examples) and does not refer to non-tonic stress (for which, however, acute 'accents' may be used). Acutes are also used idiosyncratically; for example, the poet Gerard Manley Hopkins used them to indicate how he wanted certain words stressed, as in 'And áll trádes, their gear and tackle and trim'. See SPRUNG RHYTHM.

Accent as diacritic. The marks known as 'accents' have a wider range of uses today than in classical times. French for example uses them in three ways, none of which relates to pitch or stress: (1) For particular values of letters, unmarked *e* contrasting with *é* (e-acute) and *è* (e-grave). The word *élève* has three values of *e*. (2) To prevent certain homophones from also being homographs: *la* and *là*, *vit* and *vît*. (3) To mark a historical change, the circumflex in *être* for example marking the *s* lost from earlier *estre*. English may or may not keep the accentuation in such words as *élite, café, pâté, fête, gîte, rôle, pied à terre, pièce de résistance*. They are often dropped for typographic convenience, especially in AmE, even when they offer strong visual contrast: *pâté* may be shown as *paté* or even *pate*, despite possible confusion with *pate* (head).

Accent as way of speaking. In everyday usage, *accent* means 'way of speaking', a sense that may have developed in the Middle Ages in reference to the distinctive 'tunes' of speech. Since the 16c, the term has been used in English for styles of speech that mark people off from each other, principally by region: 'We fynd the south and north to differ more in accent than symbol' (Alexander Hume, *Of the orthographie and congruitie of the British tongue*, c.1620). Most people can identify the main accent types in their language and those of some groups of foreigners speaking that language, and may have feelings and opinions about them. Even so, however, it is not easy to say just what an accent is. Phoneticians and linguists do not know why particular features come together to form accents, although they can list such features and show how they cluster as aspects of particular accents.

Accent and dialect. It is also not easy to separate *accent* from *dialect*. The terms have long been used together and certain accents are considered to belong 'naturally' to certain dialects: in the North of England, the Geordie accent of Tyneside is part of Geordie dialect; in New York, a Brooklyn accent is part of Brooklyn dialect.

Most individuals, however, have personal ways of speaking (their *idiolects*), and may conform more or less to particular kinds of accent and dialect. Britons who live for a time in the US may incorporate accentual Americanisms into their speech; Americans may take on local linguistic colour in Britain. For many people, especially if they belong to a privileged group or to a community that has little contact with outsiders, an accent is someone else's way of speaking. In such cases, the group's speech is often thought of as *accentless*: only outsiders 'speak with an accent'. Certain words, some dismissive and pejorative, are used to describe speech, including *adenoidal, barbarous, broad, cute, distinct, educated, flat, foreign, funny, guttural, harsh, heavy, lilting, nasal, posh, provincial, quaint, rough, rustic, sing-song, strong, uneducated.* By means of such words, people can be marked out as having, for example, *a distinct New England accent, a strong Scottish accent, a broad Yorkshire accent, a posh public-school accent,* and so forth. All such informal accentual labels have social implications, some of which are strong and long-lasting, both in social and personal terms.

Some phoneticians and linguists treat accent as part of dialect; others treat it as separate or separable from dialect, especially with regard to use of the standard variety of a language. Many argue that standard English can be spoken with a range of more or less 'educated' accents. Others consider that it can only be spoken with one accent (such as RP in England) or a small group of accents (such as those which have social and educational prestige in the major English-speaking countries). Others again consider that there is a continuum of possibilities, some accents being 'modified' more, some less, towards a perceived regional or other standard, with the result that people may be speaking more or less 'standardly', or may come closer to a standard in some contexts and move farther from it in others. The matter is controversial, especially when applied linguists and others seek to use the theories and findings of phonetics and linguistics to influence policies for the teaching of English either as a mother tongue or a second or foreign language. However, all phoneticians and linguists agree that the widely held view that many accents are corruptions of a pure pronunciation has no scientific basis whatsoever.

Defining an accent. Two features commonly characterize accents: (1) Their 'tunes' (melodies and tones), usually described in evaluative terms, such as *flat*, used of such urban accents as Scouse (Liverpool), *lilting*, used of Irish and Scottish accents associated with Gaelic, and of Caribbean accents associated with Creole, and *sing-song*,

used of Welsh, Anglo-Indian, and Filipino accents. (2) Kinds of articulation and voice quality, often identified with anatomical features, such as *adenoidal*, used of Scouse, and *nasal*, used of many North American accents. More or less precise non-technical names are often given to voice qualities, such as *drawl, brogue, burr, twang.* Some names figure frequently in the informal description of particular accents: for example, *a distinct Dublin brogue, a soft Highland lilt, a guttural Northumberland burr, a laid-back Southern drawl, a sharp Yankee twang.* Although voice quality is often a part of accent, people with the same accents may have different voice qualities, so that not all Highland voices softly lilt, and not all Liverpool voices are flatly adenoidal. Even where accents are thought to be well delineated, features that contribute to them are unevenly distributed, so that there are more or less American, Brooklyn, British, Cockney, and other accents. In addition, the accents of people who have lived for long periods in various places lay down a kind of 'vocal geology', with strata from the different times and places in their lives.

See ACCENT BAR, ACUTE ACCENT, ADVANCED, ARTICULATORY SET(TING), BROAD, BROGUE, BURR, CIRCUMFLEX, CLIPPED, DIACRITIC, DIALECT, DRAWL, EDUCATED AND UNEDUCATED, ELOCUTION, ENGLISH IN ENGLAND, FLAT, GLOTTAL STOP, GRAVE ACCENT, GUTTURAL, HARD AND SOFT, HARSH, HEAVY, INTONATION, L-SOUNDS, METRE/METER, NASAL, ORTHOEPY, PHONETICS, POSH, PRONUNCIATION, PROPER, PROVINCE (PROVINCIAL), PUBLIC SCHOOL ACCENT, PYGMALION, RECEIVED PRONUNCIATION, RECEIVED STANDARD AND MODIFIED STANDARD, RHOTIC AND NON-RHOTIC, RHYTHM, ROUGH, R-SOUNDS, SINGSONG, SOCIOLINGUISTICS, SOFT, STAGE, STRESS, STRONG LANGUAGE, THESIS, TONE, TWANG, VOICE, WELL-SPOKEN, VOICE. [LANGUAGE, SPEECH, USAGE, WRITING].   T.MCA., G.K.

Honey, John. 1989. *Does Accent Matter?—The Pygmalion Factor.* London: Faber.
Trudgill, Peter (ed.). 1984. *Language in the British Isles.* Cambridge: University Press.
Wells, John C. 1982. *Accents of English.* Three volumes: (1) *An Introduction,* (2) *The British Isles,* (3) *Beyond the British Isles.* With cassette. Cambridge: University Press.

ACCENT BAR [1951: coined by David Abercrombie]. A name for a perceived social barrier in Britain that favours or favoured *Received Pronunciation.* Abercrombie notes:

And very often the first judgement made on a stranger's speech is the answer to the question: which side of the accent-bar is he? Though, needless to say, the question is never formulated explicitly. . . . Many people, I know, feel a vague disquiet at this situation, but it is all very well just to ask for tolerance. The accent-bar is a little like a colour-bar—to many people, on the right side of the bar, it appears eminently reasonable. It is very difficult to believe, if you talk R.P. yourself, that it is not intrinsically superior to other accents (*Studies in Linguistics and Phonetics*, 1965).

Since Abercrombie first discussed the matter, there has been some measure of erosion in the barrier described, especially in the media. See ABERCROMBIE, ACCENT, BBC ENGLISH¹, LEXICAL BAR, RECEIVED PRONUNCIATION. [EUROPE, SPEECH, USAGE].   T.MCA.

ACCENT SHIFT. See STRESS.

ACCENTUAL METRE/METER. See METRE/METER.

ACCEPTABILITY [20c in this sense]. A term in linguistics relating to whether a phrase or sentence is grammatically or semantically acceptable to a native speaker. Chomsky's sentence *Colourless green ideas sleep furiously* (in *Aspects of the Theory of Syntax*, 1965) is said to be grammatically acceptable because of its syntactic structure but semantically unacceptable because it cannot be interpreted or too much effort and ingenuity are needed to interpret it. Compare CORRECT, GRAMMATICALITY. [GRAMMAR, LANGUAGE, USAGE].   T.MCA.

ACCIDENCE [16c: from Latin *accidentia* things that befall, from *cadere/casum* to fall, translating Greek *parepómena* accompaniments]. The part of traditional grammar dealing with inflections (changes in the forms of words to express such grammatical meanings as case, number, and tense). In English, the differences between *work, works, worked, working*, and between *worker, workers, worker's, workers'* would be described and explained under accidence. Nowadays, these differences are usually handled in *inflectional morphology*, a division of *morphology* (the study of word form) that deals with the formation and uses of inflections. See INFLECTION/INFLEXION, MORPHOLOGY. [GRAMMAR].   S.G.

ACCUSATIVE CASE [15c: from Latin *casus accusativus* the objectifying case]. A term in the case system of Latin. The accusative is the form of a noun marking the direct object of the verb. The noun *mensa* (table) is accusative in the sentence *Mensam vidi* (I saw the table). The term has sometimes been used to label words functioning as objects of verbs in English sentences. Although nouns in English do not have accusative forms, seven pronouns inflect in this way: *I/me, thou/thee, he/him, she/her, we/us, they/them, who/whom. Me* can therefore be described as the accusative of *I*. See CASE¹, DOUBLE ACCUSATIVE, OBJECT. [GRAMMAR].   S.C.

ACHEBE, Chinua [b.1930]. Nigerian writer, born at Ogidi in Eastern Nigeria, and educated at Umuahia Government College and the U. of Ibadan. Director of External Broadcasting for the Nigerian Broadcasting Corporation (1956-66). His first novel, *Things Fall Apart* (1958), re-creates life in Igboland before and during the early period of British imperialism. It was followed by *No Longer at Ease* (1960), *Arrow of God* (1963), *A Man of the People* (1966), *Anthills of the Savannah* (1986), as well as stories for children and collections of poems, essays, and short stories. Awards include the *New Statesman* award for fiction and the Nigerian National Merit Award (twice). Achebe has defended his choice of English as not only a medium of international exchange but more importantly the only medium of national linguistic exchange in Nigeria and the only medium for forging national unity. He has modified European traditions of fiction and provided connections between traditional and experimental. His art is transitional in a society where the public act of telling a story is giving way to the private forms of the printed word. See index. [AFRICA, BIOGRAPHY, LITERATURE].   G.D.K.

ACROLECT [1960s: from Greek *ákros* top, tip, and *-lect* as in *dialect*]. (1) The variety of language in a post-creole continuum closest to the standard or superstrate language: for example, in Jamaica a local variety of standard English. (2) The most prestigious variety of a language, such as standard BrE with an RP accent in England. See LECT. [LANGUAGE].   S.R.

ACRONYM [1940s: from Greek *ákros* point, ónuma name]. Also **protogram** [from Greek *prôtos* first, *grámma* letter]. An abbreviation formed from the first letters of a series of words and pronounced as one word: *NATO* from *North Atlantic Treaty Organization*, pronounced 'Nay-toe'; *radar* from *radio detection and ranging*, pronounced 'ray-dar'. Some lexicologists regard the acronym as a kind of initialism; others see it as contrasting with the initialism, in which case that term is restricted to abbreviations that are pronounced only as sequences of letters: for example, *BBC* as 'bee-bee-cee'. In this entry, acronyms and initialisms are treated as distinct. Informally, it is not unusual for both kinds of abbreviation to be lumped together as *letter words*, and there are many grey areas between them. In structural terms, there are three kinds of acronym: (1) Letter acronyms, such as *NATO, radar.* (2) Syllabic acronyms, such as *Asda* (Associated Dairies) and *sitcom* (situation comedy). (3) Hybrids of these, such as *CoSIRA* (Council for Small Industries in Rural Areas) and *MATCON* (microwave aerospace terminal control).

Pronunciation and orthography. The pronunciation of letter acronyms has encouraged two tendencies in abbreviation: to omit points (*NATO* rather than *N.A.T.O.*); to use lower-case letters (*radar* rather than *RADAR*). As a result, an acronym may become so fully a word that its letter-based origin ceases to signify or be remembered, as with *radar*. Occasionally, contrasts occur, such as lower-case *radar* and upper-case *RADAR* (Royal Association for Disability and Rehabilitation). There are variations, inconsistencies, and idiosyncratic practices in the presentation of letter acronyms: the United Nations Educational, Scientific, and Cultural Organization is conservatively contracted to *U.N.E.S.C.O.*, but commonly contracted to *UNESCO* and sometimes *Unesco*. In the house styles of some publications, common acronyms are presented as if they were proper nouns: 'When the Vice-President explicitly links European concessions on Gatt [General Agreement on Tariffs and Trade] to the continuance of Nato, he bangs a crude drum' (editorial, *Guardian*, 11 Feb. 1992). Syllabic and hybrid acronyms do not have points (*Asda*, *sitcom*), may be lower-case, upper-case, or mixed, and sometimes have internal capitals: for example, *HoJo*, short for the US hotel-and-restaurant group *Howard Johnson*.

The effects of pronounceability. Because acronyms are pronounceable and easy to create, they make convenient shorthand labels, mnemonic aids, and activist slogans. A typical *shorthand acronym* is Disney's *EPCOT* or *Epcot*: Experimental Prototype Community of Tomorrow (in Florida). *Mnemonic acronyms* are often homonyms of existing words that help fix events and ideas in people's minds: *SALT*, which is not connected with sodium chloride and means 'Strategic Arms Limitation Talks'; *SQUID*, which has nothing to do with the sea and means 'superconducting quantum interference device'. *Slogan acronyms* are parasitic on existing words, coined to label a cause and send a message at the same time: *ASH* for 'Action on Smoking and Health'; *DUMP* for 'Disposal of Unused Medicines and Pills'; *NOW* for 'National Organization of Women'. Mnemonic and slogan acronyms are particularly subject to word-play, especially in headlines: *Can START be stopped?* refers to Strategic Arms Reduction Talks; *A ConCERNed Pope* refers to the Vatican's interest in radiation and in CERN, the Centre européen pour la recherche nucléaire.

A spectrum of acronyms. There is no sharp dividing line between initialisms and acronyms, and among acronyms the dividing line is not sharp between the pronounceable but meaningless and forms that have been chosen because they give 'added value'. The five stages below represent the continuum from initialisms to slogan acronyms.

Unpronounceable initialisms

Amateur Athletic Association	AAA
Graduate of the Royal School of Music	G.R.S.M.

Semi-acronyms

British Broadcasting Corporation (informal usage, omitting the C)	BBC (Beeb)
Cambridge College of Arts and Technology	CCAT (See-cat)

Shorthand acronyms

Experimental Prototype Community of Tomorrow	EPCOT/Epcot
Roll-on, roll-off (ferries)	RO-RO/ro-ro

Mnemonic acronyms

Strategic Arms Limitation Talks	SALT
Superconducting quantum interference device	SQUID

Slogan acronyms

Aboriginal Lands of Hawaiian Ancestry	ALOHA
National Organization of Women	NOW

In addition, because acronyms are so much like words, they can become part of further acronyms, as when *AIDS* (Acquired Immune Deficiency Syndrome) contributes the *A* in both *ARC* (AIDS-related complex) and *DIFA* (Design Industries Foundations for AIDS).

Syllabic and hybrid acronyms. Syllabic acronyms, currently fashionable in many languages, are related to word blends such as *brunch* and *electrocute*. Some two-syllable and three-syllable forms are: *Amoco* American Oil Company; *Asda* Associated Dairies; *Con Ed* Consolidated Edison; *Fedeco* Federal Electoral Commission (Nigeria); *HoJo* Howard Johnson [Motor Lodges] (US); *op-ed* opposite the editorial page (journalese); *sitcom* situation comedy (television drama). The factors that have encouraged their spread include computer usage, telex addresses, the naming of scientific and technical devices and activities, the often flamboyant labelling of commercial products, and the influence of Japanese, whose speech and writing systems favour the usage. International acronyms like *Amoco* and *Texaco* have the same syllabic structure as Japanese names like *Toshiba* and *Tokyo*. As a result, such acronyms fit easily into Japanese. Syllabic acronyms of Japanese provenance that relate to English include *wapuro* from 'word processor' and *Mavica*, a trade name formed from 'magnetic video camera'.

Creativity. Acronyms are numerous and more are constantly being coined. As a result, they are often gathered, with other abbreviations, in such collections as *Elsevier's Foreign-Language Teacher's Dictionary of Acronyms and Abbreviations* (Udo O. H. Jung, 1985), which contains more than 3,500 items like *Flint* (Foreign Language Instructional Technology) and *Team* (Teachers of English Arabic Monthly). Although many acronyms are soberly functional, others have a touch of whimsy about them, such as *BOMFOG* (Brotherhood of Man, Fatherhood of God), a term used by US journalists for pious and platitudinous speeches, evidently an abbreviation of phrases with which Nelson Rockefeller liked to end his speeches. The informal BrE term *bumf* (unnecessary papers and paperwork) is comparable; it derives from public-school and Armed Forces slang for toilet paper, which in turn descends from *bum fodder*, a 17c expression for trashy printed matter. Length can be part of the humour, as with *ABRACADABRA*, a facetious mnemonic acronym used as the title of a US list of abbreviations published by the Raytheon Company in the 1960s; it stands for 'Abbreviations and Related Acronyms Associated with Defense, Astronautics, Business and Radio-electronics'. In 1987, during the compiling of the second edition of the *OED*, a system was created for examining and correcting text on computer screen. It was called the *Oxford English Dictionary Integration, Proofing, and Updating System*, partly so that it could be shortened to *OEDIPUS*. However, to avoid the kind of retribution inflicted on the original Oedipus, the editors called it *OEDIPUS LEX*. See ABBREVIATION, GAIRAIGO, -ONYM. [USAGE, WORD].   T.MCA.

ACROSTIC [16c: from French *acrostiche*, Greek *akrostikhís* point or end of line]. A poem or a puzzle in which the first letters of each line spell out a word or phrase:

Sleep hath treasures worth retracing:
Are you not in slumbers pacing
Round your native spot at times,
And seem to hear Beguildy's chimes?
Hold the airy vision fast.
(Charles Lamb, 'To Sarah James of Beguildy')

When the last letters of each line also spell something, the puzzle is a *double acrostic*, while *triple acrostics* also use a series of letters in the middle of the lines. In 1599, Sir John Davies praised Queen Elizabeth in a sequence of 26 acrostic poems spelling out the name *Elisabetha Regina*. In the 19c, Lewis Carroll published acrostic poems at the beginning of *Sylvie and Bruno* and at the end of *Through the Looking-Glass*. Acrostic puzzles, in which one has to form words from clues, were popular in Victorian times, but have been replaced in popularity by crosswords,

which evolved from them. See WORD GAME. [WORD].   T.A.

ACTIVE VOCABULARY. See VOCABULARY.

ACTIVE (VOICE). See PASSIVE (VOICE), VERB, VOICE.

ACUTE ACCENT [17c: from Latin *accentus acutus* sharp tune or accent]. A right-inclined oblique stroke over a letter, as in French *é* (*café, élite, née*), transliterated Sanskrit *ś* (*śastra, Śiva*), Spanish (to mark the vowels of stressed syllables, as in *nación*), and the rising tonal accent of classical Greek (*logikós, prótasis*). In English, the acute accents present in loans from other languages are often dropped (*cafe, elite, nee*) or replaced by some other device (such as *h* in *shastra, Shiva*), except when the use of foreign conventions is necessary for accuracy or effect, or occasionally to preserve a pronunciation, as for example in *café*, a word sometimes informally and jocularly pronounced 'kaff' or 'kayf' in BrE, especially if the establishment in question is considered seedy. See ACCENT, DIACRITIC, TRANSLITERATION. [WRITING].   T.MCA.

ADAGE [16c: through French from Latin *adagium* saying]. A usually traditional saying that sums up an aspect of common experience or observation as a capsule-like piece of advice or admonition, such as *The more hurry the less speed*. See PROVERB, SAYING. [STYLE, WORD].   T.MCA.

ADDISON, Joseph [1672–1719]. English essayist. Born in Lichfield and educated at Charterhouse and Oxford, he became under-secretary of state in 1706, a Whig Member of Parliament in 1708, and later chief secretary for Ireland. He was a leading member of the Kit-Kat Club of Whig writers. Although he was known as a poet and playwright, his principal achievement was as an essayist. He wrote papers for *The Tatler*, edited by Richard Steele, and in 1711 they collaborated to produce *The Spectator*. This daily periodical commented on contemporary manners, fashions, and writing, with the declared object 'to enliven morality with wit and to temper wit with morality'. It was widely read, notably by the emerging London middle class. Later, his friendship with Steele cooled and he aroused the hostility of Pope, who satirized him as 'Atticus'. Addison used the plain but elegant prose style of the late 17c and early 18c, was critical of Restoration bawdiness, and anxious to establish standards of middle-class good taste. With Steele, he created the squire Sir Roger de Coverley and other characters, moving from the early 17c 'character books' towards the novel. Addison supported the idea of an English Academy, writing that questions of usage could not be settled without 'something like an Academy, that by the best authorities and rules drawn from the analogy of languages shall settle all controversies between grammar and idiom' (*Spectator* 135). See index. [BIOGRAPHY, EUROPE, LITERATURE, MEDIA].   R.C.

ADJECTIVE [14c: from Latin *adiectivus* added, as in *nomen adiectivum* added noun, translating Greek *ónoma epítheton*; the term reflected the classical view that an adjective is a kind of noun]. A part of speech or word class chiefly used to premodify nouns (*romantic* in *romantic story*) and as a complement to copular verbs such as *be* and *seem* (*happy* and *healthy* in *Jeremy is happy, Mervyn seems healthy*).

Form. (1) Simple adjectives such as *good, sad, old, yellow, bitter*. (2) Derived adjectives, formed through adding suffixes to nouns and verbs, such as *-able* adorable, *-ful* careful, *-ic* heroic, *-ish* foolish, *-ive* attractive, *-ous* (famous), *-y* (tasty).

Function. Adjectives function attributively as pre-modifiers (*my forgetful parents*) and predicatively as complements to the subject (*My parents are forgetful*) and the object (*They found my parents forgetful*). Many adjectives have only one of these functions, at least as used in a particular sense. In the following phrases, *utter, certain*, and *former* are attributive only: *an utter lie, a certain person, our former friends*. Some adjectives are predicative only, as with *afraid, loath*, and *aware* in: *Your brother is afraid of them, My friends seem loath to interfere, The manager became aware of her attitude*. Adjectives that occur predicatively can also post-modify certain pronouns, usually when the adjectives are part of a larger adjective phrase: (*those*) *forgetful* (*of their duties*), (*somebody*) *afraid* (*of me*). Adjectives ending in *-able* or *-ible* can function as post-modifiers in certain circumstances: *the best treatment available, the only teacher suitable*. There are also some fixed phrases (mostly legal terms derived from French) that have an adjective following the noun: *heir apparent, court martial, attorney general*, with the formal plurals *heirs apparent, courts martial, attorneys general*.

Adjectives that refer to people are sometimes introduced by the definite article *the* or by a possessive pronoun. They can function in the same way as nouns, namely as subject, object, etc.: *The poor require our help, We should look after our young, The British are coming*. The adjective phrases *the poor, our young* and *the British* are plural and refer to a group of people. A few adjectives are used in the same way as singular abstract nouns, mainly in set phrases: *for good, in private, in common*. The semantic distinction between *restrictive* and *non-restrictive modification* applies to adjectives that modify nouns as well as to *relative clauses*. The adjective *clever* in *my clever daughter* is restrictive if its function is to distinguish one daughter from the others; it is non-restrictive if there is only one daughter in question and the adjective is conveying a characteristic of that daughter rather than defining which daughter is being referred to.

Comparison. The comparative and superlative degrees in adjectives are shown in two ways: (1) For shorter, usually monosyllabic, words, through a comparative inflection *-er* as in *older* and a superlative inflection *-est* as in *oldest*. (2) For longer words, through the addition of premodifiers, the comparative *more* in *more hostile* and superlative *most* in *most hostile*. Some adjectives may take both constructions: *common* with *commoner/more common* and *commonest/most common, friendly* with *friendlier/more friendly* and *friendliest/most friendly*. Sometimes, for emphasis, shorter adjectives may take *more* and *most*: *Could you be more clear so that we all understand?* There are also some irregular forms: *good, well* (that is, healthy) with *better/best, bad* with *worse/worst*, and *far* with *farther/farthest* or *further/furthest*. Comparison applies only to adjectives that are *gradable*, that is, that can be viewed as on a scale of intensity, such as those illustrated above. Adjectives that are not gradable, such as *utter* and *atomic*, cannot be compared or modified by an *intensifier* such as *very*. There are differences in usage with a few adjectives, such as *perfect, complete, unique*, since some people but not others will use *more perfect, very complete, really unique*, etc. See DEGREE, INTENSIFIER.

Modification. Gradable adjectives are premodified by intensifying adverbs such as *very, extremely*, and *completely*: *very young, extremely cold, completely unfriendly*. Examples of phrases where the adjective is postmodified are: *trustworthy indeed, clever enough to help, fond of you, glad that you could make it*. See PART OF SPEECH. [GRAMMAR].   S.G.

ADJECTIVE CLAUSE, also **adjectival clause**. The traditional name for a relative clause, because such clauses modify nouns. The term is also used for constructions in which an adjective phrase is felt to function as a clause: *Aware of his difficulties* (Since she was aware of his difficulties), *she did not press for an immediate answer*. See ADJECTIVE, CLAUSE, RELATIVE CLAUSE. [GRAMMAR].   S.G.

ADJUNCT. See ADVERBIAL.

ADNOMINAL [19c: from *ad-* and *nominal*, on the analogy of *adverbial*]. In contemporary grammar, a word or phrase that modifies a noun and forms part of a noun phrase. Adnominals may precede or follow their nouns: '*her new house*', '*the little red* book', '*a library* book', '*the manager's* book', '*a book about* dinosaurs', 'a book *to read*', 'a book (*that*) *I've been meaning to read*'. See RELATIVE CLAUSE. [GRAMMAR]. S.C.

ADVANCED. (1) In phonetics, said of a sound articulated with a tongue position closer to the front of the mouth. (2) In phonetics and linguistics, said of an accent or elements of an accent that are further along certain lines of change than others, to which the term *conservative* is given. Some linguists dislike the term because it may be taken to mean that the form in question reflects social progress or importance, as for example in the phrase *advanced RP*, a term used for the RP of some members of the upper class and royal family in Britain. (3) In language teaching and applied linguistics, said of a student whose competence in a foreign language has passed beyond the intermediate stage. See LANGUAGE LEARNING, LEARNER'S DICTIONARY, RECEIVED PRONUNCIATION. [EDUCATION, LANGUAGE, SPEECH]. T.MCA.

ADVANCED LEARNER'S DICTIONARY.
See LEARNER'S DICTIONARY.

ADVERB [16c: from Latin *adverbium* (a word) added to a word or verb: a loan translation of Greek *epírrhēma*]. A part of speech or word class chiefly used to modify verbs, adjectives, or other adverbs.

Form. (1) Most adverbs are formed from adjectives by the addition of the ending *-ly* as in *suddenly, playfully, interestingly*, or *-ally* after *-ic* as in *automatically, spasmodically* (with the exception *publicly*). (2) Some are formed from nouns in combination with other suffixes: *-wise* as in *clockwise, lengthwise*, and *-ward(s)* as in *northwards, skyward*. (3) A set of common adverbs have no suffixes (*here, there, now, just, well*), though some are compounds (*therefore, nevertheless*). (4) A set of common adverbs, also known as *adverbial particles*, are used along with verbs: *in, out, on, off, up, down*, etc. See PHRASAL VERB.

Function. The class is heterogeneous, and some grammarians have attempted to establish separate classes for some sets of words that are traditionally regarded as adverbs, such as intensifiers. Within the traditional adverb class, a distinction is made between adverbs that modify adjectives or other adverbs (the most frequent being *very* as in *very quick*), and adverbs that modify verbs or verbs together with some other part of the sentence (such as *competently* in *She* handled the matter competently). Adverbs in the second group are sometimes said to have an adverbial function, a function also performed by such constructions as prepositional phrases and clauses. The adverb *competently* is an adverbial in *She handled the matter competently*, as are the prepositional phrase *in a competent manner* in *She handled the matter in a competent manner* and the clause *as everybody expected her to do* in *She handled the matter as everybody expected her to do*.

Sentence adverbs. Adverbials that modify the sentence as a whole are *sentence adverbials*, and adverbs that function as sentence adverbials are *sentence adverbs*. In the following examples, *fortunately* and *however* are both sentence adverbs: *Fortunately, she handled the matter competently; The task was formidable; however* (that is, despite the task being formidable), *she handled the matter competently*.

Wh-adverbs. There is a subclass of so-called *wh*-adverbs: *how, when, where, why*, and combinations such as *whenever* and *wherever*. The four simple adverbs introduce *wh*-questions (*When did they come?*), and they and the others introduce certain types of subordinate clauses (*He told us when they had come*).

Comparison and modification. (1) Apart from modifying adjectives and adverbs, some adverbs may modify prepositions (*well* in *He kicked the ball well past the line*), certain pronouns and determiners (*virtually* in *They admitted virtually everybody*), noun phrases (*quite* in *It was quite a quarrel*), and nouns of time and place (*afterwards* in *the week afterwards*). (2) Some adverbs may also function as the complement of certain prepositions (*now* in the phrase *by now*). (3) Like gradable adjectives, *gradable adverbs* allow comparison and modification by intensifying adverbs: *more humbly, very humbly*. Only a small number of gradable adverbs take comparative and superlative inflections, many of them having the same forms as the corresponding ad-jective: *work hard/harder/hardest; drive fast/faster/fastest*. There are also some irregular forms: *plays well/better/best* (compare *good/better/best* plays), *sings badly/worse/worst* (compare *bad/worse/worst* songs). See ADVERBIAL, ADVERBIAL CLAUSE, ADVERBIAL PARTICLE, PART OF SPEECH, DEGREE, INTENSIFIER, PERIPHRASIS. [GRAMMAR]. S.G.

ADVERBIAL [17c]. (1) Relating to an adverb: *an adverbial clause*. (2) A word, phrase, or clause that modifies a verb or a verb plus other words: *usually* and *on the terrace* in 'Breakfast is *usually* served *on the terrace*'; *more quietly* in 'You must close the door *more quietly*'. Unlike subjects, verbs, and objects, most adverbials are optional and may be omitted without making a sentence ungrammatical: '*At this time of the year* they *usually* serve cider *with the meal, if the guests don't object*'. Some verbs, however, require an adverbial: *put* needs a place adverbial ('Put the dog *outside*'), *last* an adverbial of duration ('The meeting lasted *nearly two hours*'). Grammarians usually distinguish between *sentence adverbials* (adverbials that modify the sentence as a whole) and *adjuncts* (all other adverbials).

Sentence adverbials. There is no agreement on the adverbials to be counted as *sentence adverbials* (sometimes also called *sentence adverbs*). Such an item, however, modifies either a sentence as a whole (*unfortunately* in *Unfortunately, the bank will not give me a large enough mortgage*) or a clause within a sentence (*unfortunately* in *I wanted to buy the house, but unfortunately the bank will not give me a large enough mortgage*). The two major classes of sentence adverbs are *conjuncts* and *disjuncts*. Conjuncts indicate a connection between the unit in which they appear and another usually preceding unit: *for example, accordingly*. Disjuncts are a comment on the content or manner of what is being said or written: *frankly, surprisingly*. Most adverbs that function as conjuncts or disjuncts may have other functions.

Conjuncts. Most conjuncts are adverbs (also known as *conjunctive adverbs*) and prepositional phrases. Their role can be demonstrated through paraphrases. In the sentence *The shop ran out of liver before my turn came, so I raced to another shop, so* can be paraphrased as 'because the shop ran out of liver before my turn came', giving the reason for what is said in the sentence or clause that it introduces. Conjuncts are grammatically distinct from *coordinating conjunctions* such as *and*, because the two types can occur together: in *. . . and so I raced to another shop*. Furthermore, unlike such conjunctions, most conjuncts are not restricted to initial position, as when *so* is replaced by *therefore*. The units linked by conjuncts vary in size, though typically they are sentences or clauses. The example with *so* demonstrates a link between two possibly independent sentences, but the connection may be between smaller units: *yet* in *She was over ninety and yet in full possession of her mental faculties*. Conjuncts can also link paragraphs or sequences of paragraphs. They signal a variety of connective meanings, such as: listing (*first, firstly, first of all, second, secondly, next, finally, also, furthermore*); summarizing (*overall*); apposition (*for example, for instance, namely, in other words*); result (*so, therefore, consequently*); inference (*then*); contrast (*on the one hand/on the other hand, rather, however, nevertheless*); transition (*incidentally*). On the whole, conjuncts are

a closed class of items that can be listed, with the exception of enumerative adverbs (*first, second*, etc.) which make up a potentially infinite list.

Disjuncts. There are two kinds of disjuncts: *style disjuncts* and *content disjuncts*. Style disjuncts express comments by speakers on the style or manner in which they are speaking: *frankly*, as in *Frankly, you have nothing to do with them*; *with respect* in *With respect, it is not up to you to decide*; *if I may say so* in *They are rather rude, if I may say so*; *because she told me so* in *She won't be there, because she told me so* (= I know that because she told me so). Content disjuncts comment on the content of what is being said. The most common express degrees of certainty and doubt as to what is being said: *perhaps* in *Perhaps you can help me*; *undoubtedly* in *Undoubtedly, she is the winner*; *obviously* in *Obviously, she had no wish to help us*. Others evaluate the content of the utterance, conveying some attitude towards it: that it is surprising (*Unexpectedly, he arrived home and found them*; *To my surprise, nobody came*) or not surprising (*Naturally, I wanted to help*; *Understandably, she was annoyed*); that it is fortunate (*Happily, they came to me first*; *Luckily, we already knew about it*) or unfortunate (*Sadly, he died in an air crash*; *Tragically, we heard about it too late*). Some pass judgement on the topic raised or indicate an emotional position: *Rightly, she objected to what they were doing*; *Foolishly, he asked for more money*; *To my annoyance, nobody came*.

Adverbs that typically have other functions also serve as disjuncts. Such a use occasionally arouses objections, as when *hopefully*, usually a manner adverb as in *He waited hopefully for his results*, is used as a content disjunct, as in *Hopefully, we won't have to wait much longer*. The use of an adverb as a disjunct can be unusual, as in: '*Awkwardly*, President Reagan's most forceful and innovative cabinet officer is in charge of a department that has marginal responsibility . . .' (*The Economist*, 23 Nov. 1985); 'Borges signed manifestos against the dictator and the dictator *famously* took his job away . . .' (*London Review of Books*, 7 Aug. 1986). The functions of conjuncts and disjuncts are found in units other than adverbs: like *finally* are *in conclusion* and *to sum up*; like *frankly* are *frankly speaking* and *if I may be frank*; like *probably* are *in all probability*.

Adjuncts. Adverbials integrated within the structure of the sentence are *adjuncts*. Among the features indicating that an adverbial is an adjunct is the ability to be questioned and negated. The *because*-clause in *She took off her jacket because she felt hot* can be questioned (Why did she take off her jacket?—Because she felt hot) and negated (She didn't take off her jacket because she felt hot, but for some other reason). Another common feature is that the *because*-clause can become the focus of a cleft sentence: *It was because she felt hot that she took off her jacket.* See ADVERB, PART OF SPEECH, VERB. [GRAMMAR, USAGE].   S.G.

ADVERBIAL CLAUSE. A subordinate clause with an adverbial function: the *when*-clause in 'He got angry *when I started to beat him at table-tennis.*' Adverbial clauses express such meanings as time, place, condition, concession, reason, purpose, and result. See ADVERB, CLAUSE, SUB-ORDINATION. [GRAMMAR].   S.G.

ADVERBIAL PARTICLE. A particle with an adverbial function, as in phrasal verbs: for example, *out* in *I've turned out the light,* and *up* in *We gave up.* See ADVERB, PARTICLE, PHRASAL VERB. [GRAMMAR].   S.G.

AELFRIC OF EYNSHAM [*c.*955–*c.*1020]. Also **Ælfric.** West Saxon monk, teacher, and writer, Abbot of Eynsham from 1005. He wrote homilies, saints' lives, translations from the Old Testament, treatises, and letters, and for learners of Latin a grammar, glossary, and teaching dialogue. He used Latin literary devices in his English works, alliteration and verse rhythm from poetry in his prose, and was influential until long after the Norman Conquest of 1066. See index. [BIOGRAPHY, EUROPE, GRAMMAR, HISTORY, LITERATURE, WRITING].   W.F.B.

AESTHETICS, AmE also **esthetics** [1810s: under the influence of German *ästhetik* and French *esthétique,* from Latin *aestheticus,* Greek *aisthētikós* of perception, perceptive, from *aisthētá* things the senses perceive. The term was first used in German by the philosopher Alexander Baumgarten, in *Æsthetica* (1750), to denote poetic feeling, a use that became popular throughout Europe despite objections by the philosopher Immanuel Kant, who used the term to mean the science of physical perception. The contemporary sense derives largely from Baumgarten]. A branch of philosophy concerned with the understanding of beauty and taste and the appreciation of art, literature, and style. It seeks to answer the question: is beauty or ugliness inherent in the object in question, or is it 'in the eye of the beholder'? Among other things, aesthetics has sought to analyse the concepts and arguments used in discussing such matters, to examine aesthetic states of mind, and to assess the objects themselves about which aesthetic statements are made. Out of aesthetics developed *aestheticism,* a literary and artistic movement of the late 19c and early 20c associated with the poets Wilde, Yeats, and Swinburne, whose slogan was *art for art's sake.* Such critics as the Russian Formalists and in particular Roman Jakobson regard poetic expression as especially manifesting 'the aesthetic', as 'language used autonomously for the sake of the work of art itself, with textual and thematic reference, rather than for an extra-textual communicative or informational purpose' (Katie Wales, *A Dictionary of Stylistics,* 1989). At the same time, however, many literary forms have clear-cut non-artistic functions (as with love poems and didactic drama) and word-play is often used for such rhetorical ends as advertising and propaganda.

The term *aesthetic* often refers to responses, judgements, and statements that are subjective and emotive rather than objective, clinical, and detached. These have social power, and serve a variety of rhetorical ends, such as asserting a point of view (*What thrilling words!*; *That accent is ugly*), presenting opinion as fact (*Shakespeare is the greatest writer in the world*), seeking to persuade (*Don't you think he speaks very coarsely? Doesn't she have a delightful voice!*), seeking to coerce (*You really must learn to appreciate the classics—Nobody in their right mind reads rubbish like that!*), dismissing the unacceptable (*Can't they write better than that? Even a monkey could write better than that!*), and asserting or maintaining stock responses, especially of a social, ethnic, or linguistic kind (*BBC English is the best English*; *Wogs begin at Calais*; *I really like her soft Irish lilt*; *I don't like her Irish brogue*).

The ability to appreciate and produce language that is considered aesthetically pleasing (or at least adequate) has been associated with such concepts as 'refinement', 'culture', and 'cultivation'. A refined or cultured person is widely taken to be able to distinguish the good from the bad, the beautiful from the ugly, and to know when it is not right to make such judgements at all; it is also often considered that the less cultured or the uncultured should learn, gladly or grudgingly, from such a person. Ability with language has been ascribed to divine inspiration or grace, to good breeding or the right social background, to the right kind of teacher, to proper observance of the rulings of a group with privilege and authority, or to a mix of these. By and large, good taste has traditionally been considered to have an absolute form: some people have it or approximate to it; others do not have it or are deficient in it. Sometimes, creative speakers and writers may be seen as having great skill but deplorable taste in how they use that skill.

Sociologists of language generally consider that a sense of the correctness, goodness, or beauty of something results from exposure to the norms and expectations of a community: the individual learns or fails to learn how to respond in terms of the values of the group. Aesthetics, from this point of view, is relative, and good taste varies from community to community. A sense of the acceptable may be more fully reinforced in the centre or heartland of a society than at its periphery, where other societies may exert an influence. When distinct groups (tribes, nations, classes, religions, and speakers of certain languages or varieties of a language) are neighbours, become mixed, or are in competition, uncertainties about aesthetic and other values arise, along with problems of choice. These may lead to a search for security in terms of fundamentals (good religion, good grammar), may prompt an eclectic pragmatism (a certain thing is good in one place but not in another; is sometimes good and sometimes not), or may offer greater or less confusion (with no clear conception of what is good or bad, or with uneasily shifting conceptions). Whatever the case, however, people constantly make aesthetic judgements and often institutionalize them in terms of praise or abuse, compliments or insults, affectionate or dismissive names, and a wide range of judgemental expressions such as (for language) the adjectives *bad, good, harsh, lovely, plain,* and *pure.*

See ABUSAGE, ABUSE, ACCENT, BAD ENGLISH, BAD LANGUAGE, BROGUE, BURR, CRITICISM, CULTURE, DEROGATORY, DESCRIPTIVISM AND PRESCRIPTIVISM, DETERIORATION AND DECAY IN LANGUAGE, DIACRITIC, DIALECT, DISEASED ENGLISH, DRAWL, EDUCATED AND UNEDUCATED, EDUCATED ENGLISH, EUPHONY, FLAT, FRUITY, GOOD ENGLISH, GUTTURAL, HARD AND SOFT, HARSH, HEAVY, ILLITERACY, LONG AND SHORT, NON-STANDARD, NORMATIVE, PEJORATIVE, PLAIN, PLUMMY, POLITE, PROGRESS AND DECAY IN LANGUAGE, PROPER, PURE, QUEEN'S ENGLISH SOCIETY, REFINED, RHYME, ROUGH, SEMI-LITERATE, SINGSONG, SOCIETY FOR PURE ENGLISH, STANDARD, SUBSTANDARD, TWANG, WILDE. [STYLE, USAGE].
                                                    T.MCA.

AFFECTATION [16c: from Latin *affectatio/ affectationis* a striving towards]. Behaviour that does not come easily or naturally and therefore seems stilted, false, and often exaggerated. People 'affecting' the style or accent of an élite may be dismissed or condemned as *putting on airs* or *getting above themselves.* Élites affecting particular usages, however, may be regarded as leaders of fashion. In the 18c, 'polite' society in England affected fashionable French expressions, while in Scotland it affected both fashionable French and English expressions. In some parts of the world in the late 20c, affectation may include adding words and phrases of English to a local language or using English instead of that language. See GENTEELISM, HYPERCORRECTION, KENSINGTON, LITERARY, MORNINGSIDE AND KELVINSIDE, NICE-NELLYISM, OXFORD ENGLISH. Compare STILTED. [STYLE, USAGE].   T.MCA.

AFFIRMATIVE. See POSITIVE.

AFFIX [16c: from French *affixe,* Latin *affixus* attached to]. An element added to a word, base, or root to produce an inflected or derived form, such as *-s* added to *house* to form *houses* and *re-* added to *write* to form *re-write.* Affixed elements include the prefix (*anti-* in *anti-war*), the suffix (*-ity* in *formality*), the infix (*-m-* in *recumbent* but not *cubicle,* a relic from Latin), and the interfix (reduced *and* in *sun 'n' sand*). See DERIVATION, ENDING, INFIX, INTERFIX, PREFIX, SUFFIX, WORD-FORMATION. [WORD].   T.MCA.

AFFRICATE [19c: from Latin *affricatus* rubbed against]. In phonetics, a stop consonant that is released slowly into a period of fricative noise: for example, the *ch*-sounds in *church* and *j*-sounds in *judge.* See CONSONANT, FRICATIVE. [SPEECH].   G.K.

AFRICA [Before 10c: from Latin *Africa (terra),* land of the Afers, from *Afer,* singular of *Afri,* a people perhaps linked with the present-day Afars of the Red Sea coast]. Sometimes in poetry *Afric.* Originally, the name of a land mass immediately south of the Mediterranean Sea and a Roman province between *Mauretania* [Greek: Blackland] and *Aegyptus* (Egypt). The province covered much of present-day Algeria, Tunisia, and Libya. To its south lay an indeterminate region called *Aethiopia* [Greek: Land of Burnt Faces], with which the name of the Greek slave and fabulist *Aesop* has been associated. On 16–19c maps, the name *Africa* was given to the entire continent, its largely uncharted interior being called *Aethiopia* and/or *Nigritia* [Latin: Blackland]. Occasionally, *Kaffraria* [Latin from Arabic: Land of the Kaffirs/Infidels] was also used, and for a time in the 19c was a name for part of Cape Colony. In the West, geographical ignorance together with an awareness of dark-skinned peoples south of the Sahara encouraged the phrases *the Dark Continent* for Africa at large and *Darkest Africa* for its most poorly known areas: compare the title of Joseph Conrad's novella about Central Africa, *Heart of Darkness* (1902).

By the late 19c, travellers had largely dispelled Western ignorance and the European powers were engaged in 'the scramble for Africa', especially after the Berlin Conference of 1885. Until then, European languages had been generally confined to the coasts, but the acquisition of colonies took them inland. In the late 19c and early 20c, there was in Britain and North America a romantic view of Africa as a haven of 'lost' kingdoms like Great Zimbabwe and the homeland of Prester John. Missionaries, explorers, gold- and diamond-miners, colonial officers, and white hunters performed on this vast stage against a backdrop of jungle, desert, wild animals, and 'savage' tribes. Public interest was fed by, and guaranteed the success of, such novels as Henry Rider Haggard's *King Solomon's Mines* and *She* (1886, 1887), Edgar Wallace's *Sanders of the River* (1911), and Edgar Rice Burroughs's *Tarzan of the Apes* (1914). Novels of this kind and later motion pictures on the same themes helped form Western opinions of what Africa and Africans were like.

Regions and names. A variety of cultural, political, and racial factors have affected the way in which Africa is discussed in English, including names for the regions of the continent:

North Africa. The Mediterranean littoral and the Sahara Desert, from the Red Sea to the Atlantic: Egypt, northern Sudan, Eritrea, Libya, Tunisia, Algeria, Chad, Mauritania, Morocco. The region has for centuries been part of the Arab and Islamic world, its inhabitants generally described as *North African* but not necessarily usually *African*.

West Africa. Not the whole west coast, but the lands along the Gulf of Guinea: Senegal, Gambia, Guinea-Bissau, Guinea, Mali, Sierra Leone, Liberia, Ivory Coast, Burkina Faso, Ghana, Togo, Benin, Nigeria, and Cameroon and Rio Muni (also classed as Central African). The inhabitants of this region have been traditionally known as *Negro* (Spanish: black), as opposed to *Hamites* (the Biblical 'sons of Ham') in parts of Egypt, Sudan, and Ethiopia. The terms have, however, often been used as synonyms.

Central Africa. The equatorial lands around the River Zaïre, including the central west coast but usually none of the east coast: Cameroon, Central African Republic, Congo, Equatorial Guinea, Gabon, Zaïre, Rwanda, Burundi, perhaps southern Sudan, perhaps Uganda, and shading south into Zambia and Malawi. The term *Equatorial Africa* covers much of this area and the relevant parts of East Africa.

East Africa. The coastal lands and neighbouring islands of the Indian Ocean from the Horn of Africa south: Ethiopia, Somalia, Uganda, Kenya, Seychelles, Tanzania, and sometimes the southern Sudan.

South Africa. This term once referred to the south of the continent generally, but is currently restricted to the Republic of South Africa. The term *Southern/southern Africa*, however, generally includes Angola, Botswana, Lesotho, Malawi, Mozambique, Namibia, South Africa, Swaziland, Zambia, and Zimbabwe. It is sometimes used to include the island states of Madagascar (the Malagasy Republic), Mauritius, and the Comoros Islands, in the Indian Ocean.

Black Africa. Countries inhabited and controlled by non-Europeans and non-Arabs, whose inhabitants are often regarded and generally regard themselves as Africans properly so called. The term *Sub-Saharan Africa* technically refers to all of Africa south of the Sahara, but is often used to mean Black Africa.

Nations and names. For almost 200 years, the regional, national, and other names of the continent have been unstable, largely because of colonialism: the state derived from an empire in the Horn of Africa has been known as both *Abyssinia* and *Ethiopia*; the British colony of *the Gold Coast* is now the republic of *Ghana*, reviving the name of a medieval empire; the Congo River is now called the Zaïre and the former *Belgian Congo* is Zaïre; the ex-British colonies of *Northern Rhodesia* and *Southern Rhodesia* are *Zambia* and *Zimbabwe*, and *Nyasaland* is now *Malawi*; *Portuguese Guinea* is *Guinea-Bissau*; *Dahomey* is *Benin*; *Upper Volta* is *Burkina Faso*; *Bechuanaland* is *Botswana*; *South West Africa* is *Namibia*; and *Tanganyika* and *Zanzibar* have combined as *Tanzania*. Radical anti-apartheid activists refer to the *Republic of South Africa* as *Azania* (from Arabic *zanj* black, as in *Zanzibar* and *Tanzania*). In the unification of British and Italian *Somaliland* into *Somalia*, vernacular *-land* has given way to Latinate *-ia*. Elsewhere, old and new coexist: *Ovamboland* is part of *Namibia*; *Mashonaland* and *Matabeleland* are parts of *Zimbabwe*; the former British protectorate of *Basutoland* is *Lesotho*, but another ex-protectorate continues to be known as *Swaziland*. [AFRICA, GEOGRAPHY, HISTORY, NAME].

T.MCA.

The Africa theme.
ACHEBE, AFRICA, AFRICAN, AFRICAN-AMERICAN, AFRICAN ENGLISH, AFRICANISM, AFRICAN LANGUAGES, AFRICAN LITERATURE IN ENGLISH, AFRIKAANS, AFRIKAANS ENGLISH, AFRO-, AFRO-SEMINOLE, AKU, ANGLIKAANS, ANGLO, ANGLOPHONE, ARABIC, ATLANTIC CREOLES, BANTU, BLACK, BLACK AFRICA, BLACK ENGLISH, BOTSWANA, BRITISH COUNCIL, BRITISH EMPIRE, BRITISH INDIAN OCEAN TERRITORY, BUSH, CAMEROON, CAMEROONIAN ENGLISH, CAMEROON(IAN) PIDGIN, CAMFRANGLAIS, CAPE DUTCH, CLICK, COMMONWEALTH, COMMONWEALTH LITERATURE, CONRAD, CONTINENT, COUNTRY TALK, DIALECT IN SOUTH AFRICA, DUTCH, EAST AFRICAN ENGLISH, ENGLISH, ENGLISH LITERATURE, ETHNIC NAME, FANAKALO/FANAGALO, FLYTAAL, FRENCH,

GAMBIA, GHANA, GORDIMER, GULLAH, KAMTOK, KENYA, KISETTLA/KISETTLER, KITCHEN, KRIO, KRU PIDGIN ENGLISH, LESOTHO, LIBERIA, MALAWI, MAURITIUS, MERICO, NAMIBIA, NGUGI, NIGERIA, NOVEL, PORTUGUESE, RACISM, RASTA TALK, REGGAE, RHODESIA, ROTTEN ENGLISH, SAINT HELENA, SETTLER ENGLISH, SEYCHELLES, SIERRA LEONE, SOLDIER ENGLISH, SOUTH AFRICA, SOUTH AFRICAN BROADCASTING, SOUTH AFRICAN ENGLISH, SOUTH AFRICAN ENGLISH DICTIONARIES, SOUTH AFRICAN INDIAN ENGLISH, SOUTH AFRICANISM, SOUTH AFRICAN LANGUAGE ORGANIZATIONS, SOUTH AFRICAN LANGUAGES, SOUTH AFRICAN LITERATURE IN ENGLISH, SOUTH AFRICAN PLACE-NAMES, SOUTH AFRICAN PRESS, SOUTH AFRICAN PUBLISHING, SOYINKA, SPANISH, SUDAN, SWAHILI, SWAZILAND, TANZANIA, TEFL, TEIL, TESL, TRISTAN DA CUNHA, TSOTSI-TAAL, TURNER (L.), UGANDA, VELARIC, WEST AFRICAN ENGLISH, WEST AFRICAN EXAMINATIONS COUNCIL, WEST AFRICAN PIDGIN ENGLISH, ZAMBIA, ZIMBABWE.

AFRICAN [From Old English *Africanas* people of Africa, from Latin *Africanus* relating to Africa]. (1) Of Africa: *The Organization of African Unity (OAU)*, *Pan-Africanism*. (2) Of Black Africa: 'Turks and Egyptians controlled the north and raided the African tribes of the south for human plunder' (*Newsweek*, 12 Feb. 1990). The demographic results of the Atlantic slave trade are sometimes referred to as the *African* or *Black diaspora*: 'The neighbourhood's sense of being part of the African diaspora is reflected in the street-name plaques. A local artist has painted them red, gold and green. With the original black of the letterings, these colours can be a re-assuring sign to a stranger who is familiar with the notion of a Black diaspora' ('Britain's black cities', *The Listener*, 30 Apr. 1987). See AFRICANISM, BLACK, DIASPORA. [AFRICA, NAME].   T.MCA.

AFRICAN-AMERICAN, also **African American** [1980s]. A term (noun and adjective) for Americans of black African origin: 'I've lived through all the changes—from nigger to negro to black to Afro-American to African-American' (John H. Johnson, quoted in 'Success Story: Color it Black, and Angry', *International Herald Tribune*, 21 Nov. 1990). See AFRICAN, AFRO-, AMERICAN[1], AMERICAN ENGLISH, BLACK, ETHNIC NAME, TESD, [AFRICA, AMERICAS, NAME].   T.MCA.

AFRICAN ENGLISH, short form *AfrE*. The English language as used in Africa. In principle, the term can refer to English used anywhere from the Mediterranean to the Cape of Good Hope, including English as used in Egypt by speakers of Arabic, in Nigeria by speakers of Hausa, Igbo, and Yoruba, and in the Republic of South Africa by speakers of Afrikaans, Xhosa, Zulu, and other regional languages, as well as by settlers of British origin. In practice, however, the term is usually restricted to Black

Africa, especially to ex-British colonies, with three subcategories: *West African English* (Cameroon, Gambia, Ghana, Nigeria, Sierra Leone, with Liberia as a special case because of its American associations), *East African English* (Kenya, Tanzania, Uganda, and perhaps Sudan), and *Southern African English* (Botswana, Lesotho, Malawi, Namibia, Swaziland, Zambia, Zimbabwe, with South Africa as a special case because of its history and ethnic diversity).

In the second sense, the term is open to two further interpretations: as either all forms of English since the establishment of trading posts in the 17c, including pidgins and creoles, or only the forms spoken and written by educated Black Africans after some territories were administered by the British (such as Ghana and Nigeria) and/or settled by the British (such as Kenya and Zimbabwe). If the first sense is adopted, English has been in Africa for nearly 400 years. If the second sense is adopted, English in Africa dates from the mid-19c. However the term is interpreted, the reality and worth of an indigenized *African English* (with subvarieties such as *Kenyan English* and *Nigerian English*) are controversial matters, asserted by some, denied by others, advocated by some and denounced by others. English is in daily use for many purposes in 18 sub-Saharan countries (including as a lingua franca between speakers of different indigenous languages), and reflects all manner of local and regional influences. It is also taught as a second language in francophone countries. To discuss such matters, the term *African English* seems inescapable.

History. The English pidgins and creoles of West Africa have been the product of contacts between Africans and Europeans who were concerned at first with trade and later with colonialism. These varieties were significant not only in West Africa but also in the development of creoles elsewhere, particularly in the New World. Educated AfrE, however, evolved out of the formal teaching of English as a second language during the colonial era, when the grammar-translation method was the dominant approach to language learning and the teaching of English literature was central to all advanced work. Most teachers were British, with little or no knowledge of indigenous languages. During this period, the language was taught to multilingual Africans by multidialectal Britons, so that two kinds of variation were present from the start. Multilingualism and the difficulty of establishing a single national African language in each of the countries concerned made it easy to impose and then continue the use of English as the language for education, administration, and pan-regional communication.

Like French, Portuguese, and Spanish in other colonies, English became the medium of communication between the administration and its educated subjects as well as the prized vehicle of upward mobility. Formal education was a primary agent in its spread to the relatively few Africans admitted to the school system. As a result, English became the shared language of the colonial establishment and a Western-educated élite, while such African lingua francas as Hausa and Swahili continued to serve the everyday needs of the masses. Contact between standard English and these lingua francas (including the pidgin and creole Englishes of West Africa) has added to the complexity of AfrE and provided it with a range of situations in which diglossia, code-switching, and borrowing have been common.

Creative writing. As in other former colonial societies, creative writing has contributed to the emergence and recognition of AfrE as a distinct variety or group of varieties. In attempting to transcreate African cultures through their literary works in English, African writers have found it necessary to adapt and indigenize certain aspects of the language, including both lexicon and narrative style. The work of the Nigerian novelist Chinua Achebe is an example of such creative indigenization. He has observed:

My answer to the question, can an African ever learn English well enough to be able to use it effectively in creative writing? is certainly yes. If on the other hand you ask: Can he ever learn to use it like a native speaker? I should say: I hope not. It is neither necessary nor desirable for him to be able to do so. The price a world language must be prepared to pay is submission to many different kinds of use. The African writer should aim to use English in a way that brings out his message best without altering the language to the extent that its value as a medium of international exchange will be lost (*Transition* 18, 1965).

This adaptation of the language to accommodate the African cultural experience, combined with the unconscious structural adjustments attendant on language contact and foreign-language learning, accounts for the development of an English that is distinctively African.

The contemporary situation. English is an official language of 16 countries: in *West Africa* Cameroon (with French), Gambia, Ghana, Liberia, Nigeria, and Sierra Leone; in *East Africa* Sudan (with Arabic), Uganda; in *Southern Africa* Botswana, Lesotho (with Sesotho), Malawi (with Chichewa), Namibia, South Africa (with Afrikaans), Swaziland, Zambia, and Zimbabwe. In Kenya and Tanzania, Swahili is the official language, English the second language and medium of higher education. Because of its official role and use by the media, standard English occupies a privileged place in the stratification of languages in these regions, but is by and large a minority language learned mainly through formal education. Depending on situation, the choice of code to be used in a conversation is generally a local language, a national language or lingua franca, or English. Other elements in such a range of choices are the pidgins and creoles of English in West Africa and of Afrikaans in South Africa and Namibia. Because of the large number of countries and the vast distances and considerable cultural differences involved, it is not easy to list examples of usages that are true for AfrE as a whole, but some generalizations are possible.

Pronunciation. (1) Non-rhotic and generally syllable-timed. (2) West African speakers tend to have antepenultimate word stress as in 'condition, East and Southern African speakers to have penultimate word stress as in main'tenance, reflecting that of the Bantu languages. (3) By and large, there is a reduced system of five to seven vowels /i, e, a, o, u/ and perhaps /ɔ, ɛ/, with such homophones as *bit/beat* (sometimes distinguished by length), *had/hard* as /had/, *full/fool* as /ful/, and *cut/court/caught* as /kɔt/. Individual items may be variously realized: *bed* as /bed/ or /bɛd/, *bird* as /bed/ or /bɔd/. (4) The consonants /θ, ð/, are usually realized in West Africa as /t/ and /d/ ('tree of dem' for *three of them*), in East and Southern Africa as /s/ and /z/ ('sree of zem' for *three of them*). *Useful/youthful* and *breeze/breathe* may be homophones, having the first pronunciation for both members of each pair. (5) The nasal /ŋ/ is often pronounced as /n/ or /ŋg/ ('singin' for *singing*). (6) The consonants /l/ and /r/ are often exchanged ('load' for *road*, 'rolly' for *lorry*, 'fright' for *flight*), but this is becoming rare in West Africa. In parts of Nigeria, there is an exchange of /l/ and /n/, as in *lomba wan* for *number one*. (7) Word-final consonant clusters are often simplified: 'nest' for *next*, 'nees' for *needs*.

Grammar. The discussion of syntax tends to centre on deviation from standard English rather than a consideration of distinctively AfrE forms. Features include: (1) Sporadic countable use of usually uncountable nouns: *firewoods* for bits of firewood, *furnitures* for pieces of furniture, *correspondences* for letters. (2) The inconsistent omission of the plural in some contexts: *Madam X gave birth to triplet.* (3) A tendency to repeat words for emphasis and rhetorical purposes: *Do it small small* Do it slowly, bit by bit; *What you* *say, you say; My boy, I see what I see; They blamed them, they blamed them for all the troubles that have befallen our land.* (4) A common use of resumptive pronoun subjects: *My daughter she is attending that school, My father he is very tall.* (5) *Yes-no* questions typically answered to accord with form rather than meaning: *Hasn't he left yet?—Yes, he hasn't; Didn't you break that?—Yes, I didn't.* (6) Simple verbs often used instead of their phrasal-verb derivatives: *crop* crop up, *pick* pick up, *leave* leave out, leave in.

Vocabulary. (1) Words and phrases borrowed from local languages: West African *oga* master, boss (Yoruba); South African *madumbi* tubers (Zulu), East African *pombe* local traditional beer (Swahili). (2) Hybrids from English and local languages: Southern African *lobola-beast*, from Nguni *ukolobola* (to give dowry), an enemy who uses a bride price as a means of exploitation while feigning friendship, *kwela music*, from Xhosa *kwela* (to get moving), penny-whistle music; East African *mabenzi people* and *wabenzi*, from Swahili, people who own Mercedes-Benz cars, the rich. (3) Loan translations from local languages: West African *chewing stick* a piece of wood used as a toothbrush, *cornstick* a corncob, *tight friend* a close friend, intimate, *mami water* a female water spirit, *enstool* to enthrone, *destool* to overthrow (a chief), with derivatives *enstoolment, destoolment.* (4) Semantic shift in the use of everyday words: Nigerian and Cameroonian *in state* pregnant, Nigerian *to have long legs* to wield power and influence, West African *high life* local music similar to jazz, Kenyan *thank you* reply to 'goodbye', East African *beat me a picture* take my photograph, and *It's/that's porridge* It's/that's a piece of cake.

Style. (1) AfrE, especially in works of fiction and the media, is marked by the use of African proverbs and figurative usage, and by a narrative style characteristic of African rhetoric, using titles, praise words, and special epithets: *My brother, son of my fathers, you have failed; You are mighty, my brother, mighty and dangerous; Do you blame a vulture for perching over a carcass?; Father, isn't it true that a wise man becomes wiser by borrowing from other people's heads? Isn't it true that a rich man becomes richer through the toils of his exploits?* (2) It is frequently marked by code-mixing involving various lingua francas: 'He paraded me to the world, l'ogolonto' (Igbo 'stark-naked', in Wole Soyinka's *Kongi's Harvest*, 1967); 'Each feared onwana wa rikutene—a bastard child' (in Abel Mwanga's *Nyangeta: The Name from the Calabash*, 1976). This mixing may also include the use of pidgin: ' "He no be like dat," said

Joseph. "Him no gentleman. Not fit take bribe" ' (Chinua Achebe, *No Longer at Ease*, 1960).

Conclusion. As English continues to spread, through education, the media, and administrative institutions, with Africans serving as models for Africans, the distinctness of the varieties subsumed under the term *African English* is likely to become more evident and the varieties are more likely to be recognized as legitimate by both their own users and the rest of the English-speaking world. See EAST AFRICAN ENGLISH, SOUTH AFRICAN ENGLISH, WEST AFRICAN ENGLISH. [AFRICA, HISTORY, VARIETY].   E.G.B., L.T.

Angogo, R., & Hancock, I. 1980. 'English in Africa: Emerging Standards or Diverging Regionalisms?', in *English World-Wide* 1: 1.

Blakemore, K., & Cooksey, B. 1981. *A Sociology of Education for Africa.* London: Allen & Unwin.

Bokamba, Eyamba G. 1982. 'The Africanization of English', in Braj B. Kachru (ed.), *The Other Tongue: English across Cultures.* Champaign, Ill.: University of Illinois Press. Oxford: Pergamon.

Dalgish, G. M. 1982. *A Dictionary of Africanisms: Contributions of Sub-Saharan Africa to the English Language.* Westport, Conn., & London: Greenwood Press.

Dathorne, O. R., & Feuser, Willfried (eds.). 1969. *Africa in Prose.* Harmondsworth: Penguin.

Garcia O., & Otheguy, R. (eds.). 1989. *English across Cultures, Cultures across English.* Berlin & New York: Mouton de Gruyter.

Görlach, Manfred. 1984. 'English in Africa—African English?', in *Revista Canaria de Estudios Ingleses* 8, reprinted in Görlach, *Englishes: Studies in Varieties of English 1984-1988,* 1991. Amsterdam & Philadelphia: John Benjamins.

Pride, J. 1982. *New Englishes.* Rowley, Mass.: Newbury House.

Todd, L., & Hancock, I. F. 1986. *International English Usage.* London: Croom Helm.

AFRICANISM [17c]. (1) An African usage, style, or way of thought; a word or phrase from an African language, such as *juju* a charm or fetish (probably from Hausa *djudju* evil spirit, fetish): 'These Englishes share certain properties that can be identified as *Africanisms*, in that they reflect structural characteristics of African languages' (Eyamba K. Bokamba, 'Africanization of English', in *The Other Tongue*, 1982). The term is sometimes modified to refer to parts of the continent: *South Africanism, West Africanism.* (2) A policy or attitude promoting the primacy of Africans; African culture and ideals: *pan-Africanism.* See AFRICAN, AFRICAN ENGLISH, TURNER (L.). [AFRICA, VARIETY, WORD].   T.MCA.

AFRICAN LANGUAGES. Traditionally, a term referring to the indigenous languages of sub-Saharan or Black Africa. More pragmatically, all languages used in Africa, including the sub-Saharan languages, the North African languages, especially Arabic, and immigrating languages such as English, Dutch, French, German, Gujarati, Hindi, Italian, Portuguese, Spanish, and Urdu.

Indigenous languages. Scholars do not agree in describing the indigenous languages of Africa, either in terms of some 1,000 distinct forms or the families into which they may be grouped. The people of many parts of Africa use several languages: a mother tongue, one or more lingua francas, and a language or languages of religion, education, and administration. Hausa, spoken by some 30m people, is both the language of the Hausa people and a lingua franca of the western Sahel, the semi-arid regions below the Sahara Desert. The *Hamitic* language family includes Berber in the Maghreb, Coptic in Egypt, Gallinya in Ethiopia, and Somali in the Horn of Africa. The *Semitic* family includes Amharic and Tigrinya in Ethiopia. These two families are sometimes grouped together as the *Hamito-Semitic* or *Afro-Asiatic languages*. The *Niger-Congo* family of languages is spoken from Mauritania to South Africa, and includes the *Bantu* subfamily. The *Nilo-Saharan* languages are spoken from Sudan and Nigeria to Tanzania, and include Dinka in Sudan, Lango in Uganda, and Luo in Kenya. The *Khoisan* languages (Bushman and Hottentot) are spoken in southern Africa.

Immigrating languages. Non-African languages have been introduced into the continent since the earliest recorded times: Phoenician in Carthage, Greek in Egypt and Libya, Latin as the language of the Roman Empire and then of the Roman Catholic Church. Arabic, an imperial language of the early Middle Ages, has for centuries been indigenous in the north, important in the Sahel, and influential among Muslims elsewhere. Turkish, an imperial language in North Africa until the 19c, is no longer used. The languages of European colonialism were introduced from the 16c onward, and have led to a variety of pidgins and creoles. In addition, such Asian languages as Gujarati, Hindi, and Urdu were introduced into British territories in the 19-20c by immigrants from the Indian subcontinent.

The earliest of the European languages have been used as long in Africa as in the Americas, but continue by and large to be considered non-African, especially by writers and scholars who seek to resist their influence and strengthen the roles of various Black African languages. The European languages currently serve three roles: (1) As native languages among white communities long established in southern Africa (principally Dutch from the 17c, becoming Afrikaans, and English from the 18c) and as native and near-native languages among non-white groups (such as Portuguese in West Africa from the 16c, especially in the Cape Verde Islands, the English of Liberia, and South African Indian English, both from the 19c). (2) As national, international, official, and administrative languages, such as English in Nigeria, French in Senegal, and Portuguese in Angola. (3) As cultural languages, such as English and French in schools and colleges in many Black African countries, and Arabic for religious purposes.

Africanization. The governments of many Black African states have found it difficult to decide which indigenous languages to adapt and standardize for official and/or educational purposes. They have therefore tended to retain an ex-colonial language because it has already been established, poses fewer problems of loyalty and rivalry, may serve as a unifying factor in areas of social diversity, and is often already a lingua franca among disparate communities. Some argue that the use of a European language for such purposes de-Africanizes the educated élite in such states, others that the ex-colonial language itself becomes Africanized.

English influence. The influence of English on African languages varies considerably, depending on the extent of contact in an area. In some languages, such as those in the francophone zones, English has supplied very few words: for example, forms of *kitchen*, *matches*, and *school*. In others, such as Hausa, Shona, and Swahili, because of bilingualism and code-mixing, the influence may have affected not only vocabulary but also structure. Anglicisms typically occur in such registers as administration, education, finance, and technology, such as: Hausa *cifjoji* chief judge, *satifiket* certificate, *dala* dollar, *injin* engine; Shona *inispekita* inspector, *chikoro* school, *cheki* cheque, *rori* lorry; and Swahili *meneja* manager, *jiografia* geography, *pensheni* pension, *beteri* battery. See AFRICAN ENGLISH, BANTU, BORROWING, SOUTH AFRICAN LANGUAGES. [AFRICA, LANGUAGE].   T.MCA., L.T.

AFRICAN LITERATURE IN ENGLISH.

Literature has been produced in English in all sub-Saharan countries which were at any time part of the British Empire. Much of the early writing is perhaps more interesting from a linguistic than a literary point of view, but *The Interesting Narrative of the Life of Olaudah Equiano or Gustavus Vassa the African* (1789, edited by P. Edwards as *Equiano's Travels*, Heinemann, 1967) may be read as biography. The first texts written by Africans and read widely in the English-speaking world include Amos Tutuola's novel *Palm Wine Drinkard* (Faber, 1953), Cyprian Ekwensi's *People of the City* (Hutchinson, 1956), Chinua Achebe's *Things Fall Apart* (Heinemann, 1958), all Nigerian, and Ngugi wa Thiong'o's *Weep Not, Child* (Heinemann, 1964), Kenyan. The third of these has become a world classic, setting the standard by which all subsequent writing has been measured. Since 1960, there has been a steady flow of novels, plays, poetry, and short stories, many of these re-creating oral traditions. Drama, myth, story, song and dance, and poetry often of epic proportions have always been part of Black African culture, many elements of which were tenaciously maintained by slaves carried to the New World.

The fact that English was an alien language caused heated debate both before and after independence. Africans such as the Nigerian Obiajunwa Wali and the Kenyan Ngugi wa Thiong'o have argued that the use of English as a literary medium is élitist, a colonial remnant, an imposer of Western culture and ideology, and the cause of the impoverishment or even death of mother tongues. Such writers and their followers have proposed the use of African languages, including Ewe, Kikuyu, Igbo, Yoruba, and Swahili, the last being recommended as a pan-African lingua franca. Many writers, including Achebe, have supported the use of English, emphasizing its international status and readership, its ability to be moulded to reflect African culture and traditions, and the role it has played in Africa's liberation movements. They often quote Caliban's claim to Prospero:

> You taught me language; and my profit on't
> Is, I know how to curse: the red plague rid you
> For learning me your language!
> (William Shakespeare, *The Tempest*, I. 2),

and argue that English must be considered part of the African's linguistic repertoire. Echoing Caliban, Achebe has insisted, 'I have been given this language, and I intend to use it.'

Most African writers look for ways in which to put their writing at the disposal of their people. They use English but are aware of their limited readership in countries where universal education is not always the norm. In trying to reach their audience, they have developed a unique English that incorporates the legacy of a communal oral past. Many West African writers make use of Pidgin English as part of the spectrum of Englishes available to them. In Nigeria, Achebe has used it in prose, Aik-Imoukhuede in poetry, and Ola Rotimi in drama. Literature is also being provided for an African audience through the medium of radio and television, which broadcast poetry, plays, stories, and serials by local writers who often write both in English and in their mother tongue. The English may show influences from Swahili or Akan or Lamso or Afrikaans, but it is still 'in communion' with world English and still capable of reaching the widest audience in Africa on a national and transnational basis. See ACHEBE, CALIBAN, COMMONWEALTH LITERATURE, ENGLISH LITERATURE, GORDIMER, HEINEMANN, NGUGI, ROTTEN ENGLISH, SOUTH AFRICAN LITERATURE IN ENGLISH, SOYINKA, WEST AFRICAN PIDGIN ENGLISH. [AFRICA, LITERATURE, VARIETY]. G.D.K., L.T.

Achebe, C. 1975. *Morning Yet on Creation Day.* London: Heinemann.
—— 1986. *Hopes and Impediments.* London: Heinemann.
Brown, Lalage (ed.). 1973. *Two Centuries of African English: A Survey and Anthology of Non-Fictional Prose by African Writers since 1769.* London: Heinemann.
Chinweizu, O. J., & Ihechukwu, M. 1980. *Towards the Decolonization of African Literature.* Enugu: Fourth Dimension.
Gikandi, Simon. 1986. *Readings in the African Novel.* London: James Currey.
Killam, G. D. (ed.). 1973. *African Writers on African Writing.* London: Heinemann.
—— (ed.). 1984. *The Writings of East and Central Africa.* London: Heinemann.
wa Thiong'o, Ngugi. 1981. *Decolonising the Mind: The Politics of Language in African Literature.* London: James Currey.
Wright, E. (ed.). 1973. *The Critical Evaluation of African Literature.* London: Cox & Wyman.

AFRIKAANS. A language related to Dutch, the mother tongue of about 6m people in Southern Africa and a second language for millions of South Africans and Namibians. It is the source of many hundreds of loanwords in the English of South Africans, including such internationally known words as *apartheid, boer, laager, trek, veld,* and has in turn borrowed extensively from English.

The Dutch spoken by the first colonists sent to the Cape by the Dutch East India Company in the 17c gradually evolved, with the loss of inflections, into a language known as *Cape Dutch, Colonial Dutch,* or *the Taal* (the language). It was considerably influenced by *Vreemdelinge-Nederlands* ('Foreigners Dutch'), a form of Dutch spoken by German and French colonists as well as by the local population and slaves. Discrimination against Dutch by British colonial authorities fuelled a strong language movement, *Die Eerste Afrikaanse Taalbeweging* (First Afrikaans Language Movement) from the mid-1870s, in which the word *Afrikaans* is first recorded. To the Afrikaner community, English is a foreign or partially foreign language that some have called *die vyand se taal* (the enemy's language). The survival and recognition of 'the Taal' has been a matter of great emotional and political significance to the Afrikaner people.

In 1910, Dutch and English became the two official languages of the Union of South Africa. In 1925, Dutch was replaced by Afrikaans.

Large sums and great effort have been expended on its promotion, including a National Dictionary project at the U. of Stellenbosch. Among its early texts were those produced for religious instruction in Islamic schools (the Moslem Theological School in Cape Town was founded in 1862). Translation of the Bible was promoted by Arnoldus Pennevis from 1872 onwards, and the first complete Afrikaans Bible was published in 1933. Since 1919, Afrikaans has replaced Dutch as the language of the Dutch Reformed Churches in Southern Africa.

In 1914, years of emotional and sometimes bitter struggle culminated in the acceptance of Afrikaans as medium of instruction in schools. The association of Afrikaans with the Nationalist party, which came into power in 1948, caused the language to be identified with apartheid, and its compulsory use as a medium in many black schools was one cause of the uprising in Soweto in 1976. Even so, however, a black *resistance Afrikaans* developed and current work on *People's Afrikaans* is adapting the language for a South Africa without apartheid. There is a vigorous literature, including fiction, poetry, and drama; much of it, such as the novels of Andre P. Brink, is available in English translation. See AFRICAN LANGUAGES, AFRIKAANS ENGLISH, ANGLIKAANS, DUTCH, FANAKALO/ FANAGALO, FLYTAAL, GERMANIC LANGUAGES, NAMIBIA, SOUTH AFRICA, SOUTH AFRICAN ENGLISH, SOUTH AFRICAN LANGUAGE ORGANIZATIONS, SOUTH AFRICAN LANGUAGES, SOUTH AFRICAN PLACE-NAMES, [AFRICA, LANGUAGE].

J.B., W.B.

AFRIKAANS ENGLISH. English used as a second language in South Africa and Namibia by speakers of Afrikaans. It is generally rhotic, characterized by a trilled or rolled *r*. It also has schwa where RP has the vowel /ɪ/ in such words as *pin* and *sit* (/pən/ and /sət/), a sound regarded as the characteristic South African vowel, with a varying influence on South African English. Initial and medial /h/ is often voiced, and gives the impression of being dropped, so that *red hair* may be heard as 'red air'. Conversely, there is often an intrusive aspirate between vowels, as in 'cre-haytion' for *creation* and 'hi-haytus' for *hiatus*. Before /ju/, as in *you*, the intrusive /h/ is palatalized as in English *huge*, whilw *huge* is often rendered as 'yoodge'. Final voiced consonants tend to be devoiced: 'dok' for *dog*, 'piecess' for *pieces*. Because Afrikaans verbs are not marked for third-person singular, confusion of concord is common, including in the media, particularly with *is/are*, *has/have*, *does/do*. Use of prepositions is also influenced by Afrikaans: *He's by the house* (at the house), *She's not here on the moment* (at the

moment), *They're waiting on their results* (for their results). Many expressions are carried over from Afrikaans: 'I *rode* (drove) all over town looking for my shoes but didn't find it (compare *dit*, the Afrikaans inanimate pronoun for 'them'). Most frequently heard is the phrase *Is it?*, from Afrikaans *Is dit?* (Really? Is that so? Are they?, etc.). Some Afrikaans-derived expressions have been assimilated into South African English, such as *He's lazy to get up* He's too lazy to get up, *The tree is capable to withstand frost* The tree is capable of withstanding frost, *He farms with wine grapes* He grows grapes for wine, and *The village boasts with beautiful vineyards* The village boasts beautiful vineyards. See AFRIKAANS, ANGLIKAANS, SOUTH AFRICAN ENGLISH. [AFRICA, VARIETY].

J.B.

AFRO- [19c: from Latin *Afer* African]. A combining form meaning (*Black*) *Africa(n)*: 'Among the enduring legacies of 1884, the most far-reaching are the transformation, through colonisation, of African life and culture from endogenous and Afrocentric to exogenous and Eurocentric' (*South*, Dec. 1984). Combinations include: *Afro-American*, *Afro-British*, *Afro-Canadian*, *Afro-Caribbean*, *Afrobeat*, *Afro-style*. The form is sometimes used as a word, as in *an Afro hairdo* or *an Afro*. See AFRICAN, AFRICAN-AMERICAN, ANGLO-SAXON. [AFRICA, NAME]. T.MCA.

AFRO-ASIATIC LANGUAGES. See AFRICAN LANGUAGES, HAMITO-SEMITIC LANGUAGES, LANGUAGE.

AFRO-SEMINOLE [Date uncertain: from *Afro-* and *Seminole*, from Creek *simanóli* wild, runaway, from earlier *simalóni*, from American Spanish *cimarrón* wild: compare *maroon*]. An English-based creole descended from Gullah, formed when slaves escaped to Florida in the 18c, and traded and intermingled with the Seminole Indians, who were themselves runaways from the Creek Federation. In the First Seminole War (1817-18), US forces led by Andrew Jackson forced the mixed population farther into the Florida swampland. When Spain sold the territory to the US in 1819, the Seminoles resisted attempts at settlement by whites, and the government's decision to relocate them to Indian territory provoked the Second Seminole War (1835-42). Some Seminoles chose to hide and others were dispersed to Oklahoma, Texas, Mexico, and the Bahamas. Afro-Seminole is spoken today by several hundred people in Bracketville, Texas, near the border with Mexico, and in Nacimiento de los Negros, 200 miles south of the border; it is not certain whether it is still spoken in the Bahamas and Florida. In Bracketville, it is used mainly by older people, who also speak

Spanish or English; in Nacimiento, they also speak Spanish. See GULLAH. [AFRICA, AMERICAS, VARIETY].   S.R.

AGENT [16c: from Latin *agens/agentis* a person or thing that acts]. In grammar, the person or other being that instigates the happening denoted by the verb: *Jenny* in the sentences *Jenny has written me a letter* and *Jenny made Henry angry* refers to the doer of the action or the causer of the event. In English, the semantic role of the subject in active constructions is typically agentive, but not exclusively so: *books* in *These books sell well* is not the agent but the affected. In a passive construction, the agent may be represented in an optional *by*-phrase: *Anita and Michael were mugged (by some louts) on their way home last night.* The term *agent* or *agentive* is used in case grammar for one of the semantic cases. AGENTLESS PASSIVE, see CASE GRAMMAR. [GRAMMAR].   S.G.

AGENTLESS PASSIVE. A common type of passive construction in English, in which the role of the agent is not represented, as in *Michael was mugged on his way home.* Here, such a *by*-phrase as *by some louts*, the agents of the mugging, has been omitted. The agentless passive is common in formal reports: *Although insufficient funds had been allocated, the decision was taken to continue for another six months in the hope that more money would be made available.* See AGENT, PASSIVE (VOICE), VOICE. [GRAMMAR].   S.G.

AGGLOMERESE [1959: coined from *agglomer(ate)* and *-ese* by Robert C. Doty, *New York Times*]. An informal, usually pejorative term for speech or writing packed with numbers and abbreviations: 'The D200 has a dual Centronics parallel/RS232C serial interface plus IBM PC compatibility and Epson emulation' (Smith Corona ad, 1980s). See -ESE. Compare TECHNOSPEAK. [STYLE, VARIETY].   T.McA.

AGGLUTINATING, also **agglutinative** [16c: from Latin *agglutinare/agglutinatum* to fix with glue]. A term in linguistics for a language whose words are mostly made up of units (morphemes) that are easily distinguishable, as in: Turkish *evlerde* (*ev-ler-de*, house-*plural*-in, 'in the houses'); Swahili *ninakupenda* (*ni-na-ku-penda*, I-*present*-you-love, 'I love you'). Most languages have some agglutination, as in English *cows* (cow-s), *goodness* (good-ness), *distasteful* (distaste-ful), but in some languages such as Turkish or Swahili, it predominates. See LINGUISTIC TYPOLOGY, SWAHILI. [LANGUAGE].   J.M.A.

AGNOSIA. See LANGUAGE PATHOLOGY.

AGRAMMATISM [1880s: from Greek *agrámmatos* unlettered, and *-ism* as in *autism*]. A characteristic of certain kinds of language disorder, in which grammatical structure has become elliptical or telegrammatic; an important symptom of *Broca's aphasia*. Its features are: reduced processes of sentence construction, omission of grammatical words, disturbed intonation and rhythm, and laboured articulation, as in this 65-year-old man's attempt to describe a picture of someone pouring a drink (with a speech therapist's prompts in parentheses): *girl—(the girl's)—pour—pouring—orange—(in the)—(in the) glass—it drink—(say the whole thing, the)—girl—(is)— taking top off—(is pouring)—pouring—(a)—a drink.* See APHASIA. [GRAMMAR, LANGUAGE].   D.C.

AGRAPHIA. See DYSGRAPHIA.

AGREEMENT. See CONCORD.

AILA. See BAAL.

AIRSPEAK [c.1970s]. Also **air traffic control English, Aviation English**. The English of international civil aviation, a restricted language established after the Second World War by the *International Civil Aviation Organization* (*ICAO*). Although in some conditions aircraft may use a local language, commercial flying is universally conducted in English. When speech is necessary, it is as concise and unambiguous as possible, uses only accepted conventions for procedures and message types, is not too dense (that is, does not contain too many propositions before allowing the interlocutor to speak), and has checkbacks so that speakers can be sure that what was said is what was heard. Everything used for these purposes is English in grammar, vocabulary, or pronunciation, but some of the vocabulary is technical and specialized. Radio conversation not relevant to a flight is forbidden. International agreements ensure that all pilots are trained in this English, and cockpit conversations are monitored to ensure that rules are adhered to. The following extract, for an aircraft descending from cruise height towards its destination airport, is typical:

Control. BA six zero six Alfa: squawk ident.
Pilot. Identing, BA six zero six Alfa.
Control. BA six zero six Alfa, radar contact. Descend to flight level three one zero.
Pilot. Leaving flight level three nine zero. Descending to level three one zero. BA six zero six Alfa.

[Glossary: *ident* identity, *identing* identifying, *squawk* reveal, make known.] See ENGLISH FOR SPECIFIC PURPOSES, RESTRICTED LANGUAGE, SEASPEAK, -SPEAK. [EDUCATION, VARIETY].   P.S.

AIR-STREAM MECHANISM. In phonetics, the mechanism that uses a stream of air to produce speech. It is created by the action of the lungs (*pulmonic action*), and may be blown out (*egressive*) or sucked in (*ingressive*). Normal speech is produced with an *egressive pulmonic air-stream mechanism.* See GLOTTALIC, VELARIC. [SPEECH].   G.K.

AIR TRAFFIC CONTROL ENGLISH. See AIRSPEAK.

AITCH [from Old French *ache*, Latin **hacca* or *accha*]. The name for the letter *h*, often used disparagingly in such expressions as *an aitch-dropper, aitch-free,* and *aitchless*. In phonetics, the term *aitch-dropping* refers to the absence of initial /h/ in such words as *harm* and *here* (usually shown in writing as *'arm* and *'ere*), common in working-class and lower middle-class speech in much of England; the use of the term, however, is controversial because one cannot 'drop' a sound that one has not first 'held'. Absence of initial /h/, though widespread, is non-standard in BrE. On its absence from Cockney speech, Robert Barltrop and Jim Wolveridge make the following comment in *The Muvver Tongue* (1980, pp. 6 and 101):

Cockneys drop h's. So do the French. . . . The teacher's case is that 'h' should be sounded on English words because this is the established practice. So it is—but not among Cockneys. They know that h's are there and put them in in writing; but to use them in speech is 'talking posh'. Their omission does not lead to misunderstandings, except by non-Cockneys. . . . One Sunday morning some years ago I sat in a bus behind a man who had his little boy of about four on his lap. The child had a picture-alphabet book, and the father was explaining it carefully; when they came to h, the picture was of a hedgehog. The man said: 'that's an edgeog. It's really two words, edge and og. They both start with h.'

Many upwardly mobile non-aitch-using people in England have sought to 'restore' (that is, acquire) initial /h/, with varying success. Some socialists, however, have made a political point of its absence from their speech or, if brought up 'aitch-fully', have sought to drop their aitches as a token of working-class solidarity. In 1903, Shaw observed in *Man and Superman*: 'This man takes more trouble to drop his aitches than ever his father did to pick them up.' See ARTICLE[1], ASPIRATE, COCKNEY, DIALECT IN ENGLAND, GEORDIE, H, ORWELL, STRESS. [SPEECH].   T.MCA.

AITKEN'S LAW [1950s: coined by David Murison]. A name for the *Scottish vowel-length rule* that recognizes A. J. Aitken's insistence on its importance as a diagnostic principle of Scottish speech. See SCOTTISH VOWEL-LENGTH RULE. [EUROPE, SPEECH].   T.MCA.

AITKEN'S VOWEL [1949: so named because first noted by A. J. Aitken]. In phonetics, a stressed vowel in the speech of many Scots, the centralized mid vowel /ɛ̈/. It occurs in such words as *never* (Scots *nivver*), *next* (Scots *nixt*). In ScoE, *never* with /ɛ̈/ contrasts with *sever* with /ɛ/ and *river* with /ɪ/; similarly, *next* contrasts with *vexed* and *mixed*. Speakers of ScoE vary in their selection of this vowel, some using it in only a few, others in most, of the words in which it can occur. See SCOTTISH ENGLISH. [EUROPE, SPEECH].   T.MCA.

AKU, also **Aku Talk, Gambian Krio**. An English-based creole spoken in Gambia and closely related to Krio in Sierra Leone. See GAMBIA, KRIO, WEST AFRICAN PIDGIN ENGLISH. [AFRICA, VARIETY]. T.MCA.

ALBA [10c: an adaptation of Latin *Albania* Scotland]. The Gaelic name for Scotland, adopted *c.*10c for the kingdom of the Scots north of the Forth. In Gaelic, the Scots are the *Albannaich*. See CALEDONIA, SCOTLAND. Compare ALBION. [EUROPE, NAME].   T.MCA.

ALBION [From Old English, from Latin *Albio/Albionis* (Pliny) and Greek *Alouiōn* (Ptolemy), probably from a shared Celtic and Latin root meaning 'white' (compare Latin *albus*), and meaning 'the white land' (evidently referring to the White Cliffs of Dover), perhaps from Celtic *alp*]. Also *Albany*. An ancient, poetic name for Britain, said to derive variously from a giant of that name (a son of the sea god Neptune), a Christian martyr of that name (the first in Britain), and the princess Albia, oldest of 50 daughters of the king of Syria who, forced to migrate west, settled in Britain. The phrase *perfidious Albion* (in French *la perfide Albion*) is from a poem written in 1793 by the Marquis de Ximenès. It appeared again in a poem by Henri Simon in 1809 and was a slogan in the Napoleonic recruiting drive of 1813. It is often mistakenly attributed to Jacques Bossuet in 1653, who wrote *la perfide Angleterre.* Sir Francis Drake called California *New Albion* in 1579, when he tried without success to annex it. Compare ALBA. [AMERICAS, EUROPE, NAME].   T.MCA.

ALEXANDER, Henry [1890-1975]. Canadian dialectologist and writer, born in Liverpool, and educated at the School of English at the U. of Liverpool, where Henry Cecil Wyld supervised a dissertation that later became *The Place Names of Oxfordshire* (1912). He taught at Queen's U., Kingston, Ontario (1922-57), becoming head of the Department of English in 1949. He was first president of the Canadian Linguistic Association (1954-65), author of *The Story of Our Language* (1940), trained fieldworkers for the *Linguistic Atlas of Canada and the United States,* and did fieldwork for the atlas, mostly in Nova Scotia (1939-40). [AMERICAS, BIOGRAPHY, HISTORY].   M.F.

ALEXANDER, L(ouis) G(eorge) [b.1932]. British author of EFL course books. Born in London and educated at Godalming Grammar School and London U., he taught English in Germany (1954-6) and Greece (1956-65), where he was head of English at the Protypon Lykeion, Athens (now the Scholi Moraïti). He was a member of the Council of Europe Committee on Modern Language Teaching (1973-8), and one of the authors of *The Threshold Level* (1975) and *Waystage* (1977), works developed for the Council of Europe that have been the bases of many communicative language courses. He has served on the Committee of Management of the Society of Authors (1980-3). In 1986-8, he was adviser to UCLES for the *Cambridge Certificate in English for International Communication*. He has been a writer of EFL course materials since the 1960s. His publications include: *A First Book in Comprehension* (1964), *New Concept English* (1967), *Look, Listen and Learn!* (1968-71), *Target* (1972-4), *Mainline* (1973-81), *Follow Me* (1979-80), *Plain English* (1987-8), *Longman English Grammar* (1988), and *Longman English Grammar Practice* (1990). He was consultant for *Junior English for China* (1988-) on behalf of UNESCO. He has created the blueprint for the *Survive* self-study series (1980-3, reissued 1989) for modern languages and has published courses in the field of computer-assisted language learning. Alexander has consistently supported the cause of the relatively untrained non-native-speaking teacher of English. See index. [BIOGRAPHY, EDUCATION, EUROPE, MEDIA].   T.MCA., C.J.B.

ALEXANDRINE [16c: from French *alexandrin*, after *Alexandre* the title of a 15c poem about Alexander the Great]. A line of iambic hexameter verse, standard in classical French drama but rare in English, where it may seem long and heavy, with a tendency to break in the middle (creating the effect of two trimeters written as one line). Pope showed its effect in *Essay on Criticism* (1711), by comment and example, in the second line of the couplet: 'A needless Alexandrine ends the song, / That, like a wounded snake, drags its slow length along.' See BRIDGES, SPENSERIAN STANZA. [LITERATURE].   R.C.

ALEXIA. See DYSLEXIA.

ALFRED [849-99]. Old English *Ælfred*. Scholar king of the West Saxons (871-99), often called *Alfred the Great*, who prevented the Danes from conquering all of England, and promoted learning and literacy in English and Latin. In the preface to his translation of Gregory the Great's *Pastoral Care*, he reasoned that Greek and Latin translations of Old Testament were a precedent for translating some Latin classics into English for the children of free men to read. Although he lacked a profound knowledge of Latin, his translations initiated Old English prose writing. Alfred was assisted by the Welsh priest Asser (who wrote his biography, 893), Plegmund, a Mercian, and Grimbald, a Frank. The Anglo-Saxon Chronicle probably began during his reign (c.890) and may reflect his influence. At the time when the Vikings were destroying the celebrated Latin culture of Northumbria, Alfred's programme of translations gave English an important place in early medieval culture, an unparalleled development among European vernaculars of the time. His books continued to be copied in Norman England. See index. [BIOGRAPHY, EUROPE, HISTORY].   W.F.B.

ALGORITHM [Late 19c: a variant (by association with Greek *arithmós* a number) of *algorism*, which entered English in the 13c, denotes Arabic numbers and their use, and derives from Arabic *Al Khwarizmi* (The Man from Khwarizm), the surname of a 9c Persian mathematician]. In mathematics and computing, a set of rules for solving a problem by means of a finite series of steps: for example, a simple algorithm for putting a set of items into alphabetical order goes through them repeatedly from first to last, exchanging any adjoining pair which is out of order. To sort 100 items in this way takes about 10,000 operations. [TECHNOLOGY].   M.L.

ALLEGORY [14c: from French *allégorie*, Latin *allegoria*, from Greek *allēgoría* speaking in another way]. A story, such as George Orwell's *Animal Farm* (1945), that can be read on two levels: as a surface narrative that may or may not be realistic and at a deeper level that is often didactic and moralistic, and sometimes satirical. Characters and episodes are intended to represent some elements in human life: Orwell's farm is a national state and his pigs are Marxist revolutionaries. Allegory may occur in any genre, does not constitute a literary form, and is in effect an extended metaphor. Greek and Roman stories of the gods were often interpreted allegorically, and *Aesop's Fables* (6c BC) commented on human behaviour through tales about animals. Early examples in English are Langland's poem *Piers Plowman* (14c) and the morality play *Everyman* (16c). Langland writes of a dream in which he sees a tower where Truth lives and the Seven Deadly Sins are people, while Everyman is summoned by Death, abstractions like Kindred and Goods appear and are not allowed to go with him, but Knowledge says, 'I will go with thee and be thy guide.' Spenser's *Faerie Queene* (1590-6) is an allegory of the virtues of chivalry, and the most famous religious allegory in

English is Bunyan's *Pilgrim's Progress* (1678), in which Christian passes such obstacles as the Slough of Despond and Vanity Fair to reach the Celestial City. Allegory may figure in other works, as in the episode of Sin and Death in John Milton's *Paradise Lost*, Book 2 (1667). Typically, common nouns are capitalized to serve as characters' names (*Knowledge*, *Sin*) and incorporated into features of the landscape (*the Slough of Despond*). Although allegory in England flourished chiefly from the Middle Ages to the 17c, allegorical elements appear in more recent works, such as Thomas Hardy's *The Dynasts* (1904-8) and Virginia Woolf's *Between the Acts* (1941). See ANALOGY, APTRONYM, BUNYAN, FANTASY, JOHN BULL, METAPHOR, ONOMASTICS (CHARACTERNYMS), ORWELL, PARABLE. [LITERATURE].   R.C.

ALLIANCE QUEBEC. A pressure group in the Canadian province of Quebec, formed in 1982 to protect the rights of English-speaking Quebecers (*anglophone/anglo rights*), as a response to the passing into law in 1977 of Bill 101 (the Charter of the French Language) by the Parti Québécois government. It was formed from several organizations that arose to defend minority language rights, and is funded by the Canadian Secretary of State through the Official Languages Minority Community Program. It has 40,000 members and a staff of 25. See QUEBEC. [AMERICAS, MEDIA].   M.F.

ALL INDIA RADIO (AIR). See SOUTH ASIAN BROADCASTING.

ALLITERATION [17c: from Latin *alliteratio/ alliterationis* putting (the same) letters together]. Also **head rhyme, initial rhyme.** Terms in rhetoric, poetics, and general usage for the repetition of the same sound, usually an initial consonant such as the *f* in 'Fixed fate, free will, foreknowledge absolute' (Milton). Alliteration can serve both a mnemonic and an ornamental purpose, and is common in: *verse* O Wild West Wind, thou breath of autumn's being (Shelley); *story-telling prose* the great grey-green, greasy Limpopo River (Kipling), Tune the pipes to the tragedy of tallow, the bane of bulk, the calamity of corpulence (O. Henry); *speech-making* Do not let us speak of darker days; let us rather speak of sterner days (Churchill); *advertising* Guinness is good for you, You can be sure of Shell; *tongue-twisters* Peter Piper picked a peck of pickled peppers, She sells sea-shells on the seashore; *similes* cool as a cucumber, dead as a doornail; *reduplicative words* flimflam, tittle-tattle; *collocations, idiomatic phrases, proverbs* bed and breakfast, footloose and fancy-free, Look before you leap; *nicknames and epithets* Battling Bill, Tiny Tim, the Broadway Butcher; *tabloid newspaper headlines* Saucy Sue brings home the bacon. Alliteration is often used as a means of emphasizing

the reach or range of a subject, by listing pairs of place-names that begin with the same sound: 'But Pooh is loved in Consett and Calgary, in Kalamazoo and Kalgoorlie, as tenderly as in Camberley and Carshalton' (Godfrey Hodgson, *Independent*, 2 June 1990). See AELFRIC, ALLITERATIVE VERSE, ASSONANCE, CONSONANT, ENGLISH LITERATURE, HOMEOTELEUTON, JINGLE, METRE/ METER, PROVERB, REDUPLICATION, REPETITION, TONGUE-TWISTER. [SPEECH, STYLE].   T.MCA.

ALLITERATIVE VERSE. Verse that depends for its effect on alliteration. Such verse was unknown in classical Greek but common in Latin and the Celtic and Germanic languages. Old English verse was alliterative, as in the opening lines of the epic poem *Beowulf*: 'Hwæt, we gardena in geardagum, / þeodcyninga þrym gefrunon, / hu ða æþelingas ellen fremedon'. These lines have been translated into modern alliterative verse in 1973 by Michael Alexander as: 'Attend! We have heard of the thriving of the throne of Denmark, / how the folk-kings flourished in former days'. Such verse died out with the coming of the Normans and consequent French influence, but was revived in the 13c. The best-known poems are Langland's *Piers Plowman* and the anonymous *Sir Gawain and the Green Knight* (both 14c). Two lines from Langland run: 'In a somer seson whan soft was the sonne, / I shope me in shroudes, as I a shepe were' (*shope* dressed, *shepe* ship). Alliterative verse continued until the 16c, surviving longer in Scotland than England. Although the tradition died out, alliterative phrasing continues, as in: 'Down dropt the breeze, the sails dropt down, / 'Twas sad as sad could be; / And we did speak only to break / The silence of the sea!' (Coleridge, *The Rime of the Ancient Mariner*, 1797-8); 'Eyes I dare not meet in dreams / In death's dream kingdom / These do not appear' (Eliot, 'The Hollow Men', 1925). See ALLITERATION, LITERARY CRITICISM, VERSE. [LITERATURE].   T.MCA.

ALLOPHONE. See (1) ANGLOPHONE, (2) PHONEME.

ALLUSION [16c: from Latin *allusio/allusionis* a playful reference, from *ad-* towards, and *ludere/ lusum* to play]. An indirect reference. The term formerly included metaphors, parables, and puns, but now generally means implicit use of someone else's words. Whereas quotations usually come with acknowledged sources, allusions are indirect, even cryptic, sometimes dropped in passing, with little thought, sometimes used with care, so that a speaker or writer can share an understanding with certain listeners or readers. Allusions often adapt their originals to new ends, the audience making or failing to make the connections, as when the

US journalist William Safire cries out in his column: 'Ah, Fowler! Thou shouldst be living at this hour; usage hath need of thee' (*New York Times*, July 1989). Here, Safire addresses the master of his craft much as Wordsworth once opened a sonnet: 'Milton! Thou shouldst be living at this hour, / England hath need of thee.' Similarly, Wordsworth's paradoxical statement 'The Child is father of the Man' is embroidered by the British television critic John Naughton when saying of Richard Burton, 'the abandoned, motherless child was father to the volatile, generous, self-hating man' (*Observer*, Sept. 1988). Newspaper headlines are often allusive: *Amid the Alien Porn*; *Brontë village fears wuthering blight*; *A Chase That Stopped a Thousand Trips*; *The Laser's Edge*; *Comedy of Terrors*. See ANALOGY, BIBLE, ECHOISM, FACTS ON FILE, QUOTATION, SHAKESPEARE. [REFERENCE, STYLE].   T.MCA.

ALPHABET [14c: from Latin *alphabetum*, Greek *alphábētos*, an adjective and noun that, combining the names of the first two letters of the Greek alphabet, *alpha* and *beta*, was used to refer to the whole set of letters, which were however commonly known as *tá grámmata* ('the written things') the letters: compare GRAMMAR]. A system of written and printed language in which each symbol generally represents one sound, as with *b* for the voiced bilabial stop at the beginning of the word *boat* in the Roman alphabet as used for English.

Nature. In most alphabetic systems, such as the Roman alphabet as used for Spanish, the correlation of symbol to sound is close, representing with considerable success a language's inventory of *phonemes* (smallest identifiable units of speech). The system used for English, however, falls well short of ideal *phonographic* (sound/spelling) equivalence: for example, the letter *f* conventionally represents the voiceless labio-dental fricative sound /f/, as in *fast*, but in some words this sound is represented by *gh* as in *tough*, and in others by *ph* as in *phone*. Again, in French, the letter *d* generally represents the voiced alveolar plosive sound /d/ in *dans*, but has no phonetic value in, for example, *canard* (where the *d* is said to be 'silent').

Alphabets and syllabaries. A clear-cut distinction cannot always be made between alphabets proper and *syllabaries*, sets of syllabic symbols as in the Japanese *kana* systems: see JAPAN. Syllabic signs, like letters, represent small units of pronunciation, typically a spoken consonant followed by a spoken vowel, as in the four signs for the syllables *yo*, *ko*, *ha*, *ma* in the place-name *Yokohama*. Single alphabetic letters may represent a double sound, as with the letter *x*, which in Roman-derived alphabets generally stands for the two sounds /ks/, and sometimes a representation is syllabic, as with the letter *m* in the English word *spasm*, which consists of the 'ordinary' syllable *spas* and

the syllabic consonant *m*. In addition, alphabets are commonly part of a graphic inventory that includes non-alphabetic signs, such as *punctuation marks* (?, !, " ", etc.), *diacritics* (ˆ, ΄, ˜, etc.), *ideograms* (representing such concepts as the numbers 1, 2, 3), and *logograms* (standing for specific words, as with &, $, £).

Phonography and ideography. Probably the most fundamental distinction among writing systems, however, is between the *phonographic principle* (in which writing is done by means of sound symbols organized in alphabets and syllabaries) and the *ideographic* or *logographic principle* (in which writing is done by means of symbols that directly represent ideas or words). Traditional Chinese writing is typically ideographic, its thousands of characters generally representing meanings and not sounds, whereas the symbols of phonographic systems represent sounds and not meanings: see CHINA. There are, however, few if any pure phonographic or ideographic systems: the English writing system, for example, employs such ideograms as numeral signs and such logograms as the ampersand and dollar sign (as indicated above), and is part of a general system that adds iconic forms such as a pointing hand indicating a direction to take or male and female figures for toilet facilities, often part of an international system reminiscent of the hieroglyphs of ancient Egypt.

Origin. Scholars who study the world's writing systems generally agree that the alphabetic principle was invented only once, in West Asia. The original set of some 30 signs, known as the *North Semitic alphabet*, was used in and around Canaan and Phoenicia from *c*.1700-1500 BC onwards. It was the ultimate ancestor (by evolution or through analogy) of all later alphabets, such as those used for Phoenician, Hebrew, Greek, Arabic, Latin, English, French, Russian, the languages of the Indian subcontinent, and those of Ethiopia. Some Indian scholars argue that their scripts were entirely indigenous achievements, and a separate origin has been claimed for the *han-gul* alphabet created for Korean in the 15c: see KOREA. It seems likely, however, that the older Indian alphabets were innovatively adapted from West Asian predecessors, and that the idea for the Korean script emerged from an appreciation of how pre-existing alphabetic systems worked elsewhere in the world.

From the 11c BC, Phoenicians using a 22-sign variant of the North Semitic alphabet traded throughout the Mediterranean littoral, sometimes setting up colonies. In Carthage, a colony established in present-day Tunisia, the Punic version of their alphabet continued in use until the 3c AD. Like all early Semitic systems, the Phoenician scripts were written from right to left and consisted only of signs for consonants, because of the preeminence of consonants in the formation of Semitic word forms. The Greeks, *c*.1000-900 BC, developed a script heavily influenced by this alphabet, in which, however, they reassigned certain symbols that had no spoken equivalents in their own language to represent vowel sounds, which were central to their system of word-formation and word use. In the Greek alphabet, the letter *aleph*, which in Phoenician stood for a consonantal glottal stop (compare ARABIC), was adopted and adapted as the sign for a sound like 'ah', to which the Greeks gave the name *alpha*.

Initially, Greek was written from right to left like Phoenician, but later changed from left to right. The reason for this development is unknown. There was, however, for a time a technique in which letters were inscribed on stone with one line running from right to left (the letters facing one way), then the next line from left to right (the letters facing the opposite way). This convention was known as *boustrophedon* ('ox-turning'), because it worked on the same principle as an ox ploughing a field. It appears to have been dictated by convenience when cutting and then reading a text with long lines: readers did not need to track back across a wide surface to find the beginning of the next line, but could carry on like the ox 'on the turn' of the furrow-like line. The system was short-lived, and may have served as an intermediate stage between moving to a permanent left-to-right sequence first for Greek and ultimately for all Western alphabets.

The Greek, Etruscan, and Roman alphabets. The pre-classical Greek alphabet contained several symbols that did not survive into classical times but nonetheless had an influence beyond Greek. They included the letters *digamma* and *koppa*, the ancestors of Roman *F* and *Q* (see F, Q) and a modification of P written with a tail, which served as an early model for Roman *R* (see P, R). These forms gradually disappeared from the writing of the classical language, but were adopted by other Mediterranean peoples into their own Greek-derived alphabets. The mature Greek alphabet of *c*.400 BC contained several new letters, such as *phi* (Φ), *chi* (X), *psi* (Ψ), *omega* (Ω), all added at the end of the traditional alphabetic list. *Phi* and *chi* were later taken over with the same values (along with many other Greek letters) into the Cyrillic alphabet in which Russian and some other Slavonic languages are written. *Psi* and *omega*, however, have remained special to Greek.

Among the Mediterranean peoples who developed their own versions of the Greek alphabet were the Etruscans in Italy *c*.800 BC. Their alphabet was in turn adopted and adapted by their neighbours the Romans, and the Roman alphabet as used for classical Latin can be related as follows to that of classical Greek: (1) The capital forms (but often not the later small forms) of the letters *A*, *B*, *E*, *I*, *K*, *M*, *N*, *O*, *T*, *Y*, *Z*, and their sound values, remained broadly the same as in Greek. (2) Earlier Greek letters, abandoned in the classical alphabet, were retained in Roman *F*, *Q*. (3) Earlier Greek sound values were retained for Roman *H*, *X*. (4) Changes in form occurred in *D*, *L*, *P*, *R*, *S*, *V*. (5) A change of form and sound value occurred in *C*, and the letter *G* was invented for Latin. (6) The original Roman alphabet comprised 23 letters, but the germs of the future *J* and *U* were contained in the letters *I* and *V*, although the graphic distinction between the vowel and consonant letters in the pairs *I*, *J* and *U*, *V* was not universally accepted until the 17-19c. The letter *W* emerged in the Middle Ages from the doubling of *U/V*.

Many languages that use variants of the Roman alphabet employ *diacritics* to enable a given letter to represent more than one sound unambiguously, as when German writes *ö* to indicate a different value from *o*. Scandinavian languages in particular have created extra letters: Danish and Norwegian have extended the alphabet by adding the letters *æ* and *ø* while Icelandic includes *ð* and *þ* to represent voiced and voiceless *th* respectively. Sometimes a letter with a diacritic may be listed separately from its plain form, as with *å* in Danish, Norwegian, and Swedish, which is added at the end of the alphabet list, and *ñ* in Spanish, which follows plain *n*. Sometimes a language that uses a digraph (double-letter combination) to represent a distinct phoneme will list the digraph separately in the alphabet too: in Spanish, the digraphs *ch*, *ll*, *rr* follow *c*, *l*, *r* respectively, and in Welsh *ch*, *dd*, *ff*, *ll*, *ph*, *rh* are listed after their first letter, while *ng* occurs between *g* and *h*. Conversely, a language that does not use certain of the conventional 26 letters to spell its native vocabulary may not include them in its alphabet: in Welsh, *j*, *k*, *q*, *v*, *x*, *z* are not used, and *w* generally represents a vowel. Variants of the Roman alphabet are used throughout Europe and the Americas, in most of sub-Saharan Africa, in Australasia, in parts of South-East Asia, and as a secondary system in most of the rest of the world.

The English alphabet. Old English was first written in the runic alphabet known as *futhork*, and isolated runic inscriptions continued to be made in Britain until the 12c: see RUNE. With the advent of Christianity, the Roman alphabet was applied to the language with fairly regular sound-symbol correspondence but sometimes with different spoken realizations in different dialects: see OLD ENGLISH[1]. Because Old English had phonemes not present in Latin, however, a number of new symbols were introduced: *æ* (ash), *þ* (thorn), *ð* (eth), and *p* (wynn), thorn and wynn being taken from futhork. The letter *g* was modified as *ȝ* (yogh), which existed alongside continental *g* for some centuries after the Norman Conquest in 1066. The use of these symbols was discontinued after the introduction of printing in the 15c, partly because printers' sets of continental typefaces lacked them. By that time, the sound of *æ* had merged with that of short *a*, the sound of thorn and eth was already spelt *th* in words transliterated from Greek into Latin, and wynn had been largely superseded by *w*. The loss of these letters left an alphabet of 24 letters, in which *i/j* and *u/v* were not clearly distinguished. From about 1600, however, they were gradually separated over a period of more than two centuries into the vowel letters *i*, *u* and the consonant letters *j*, *v*. Graphic variation was long preserved with the two forms of lower-case *s*, written either as *s* or *ſ* (long *s*), the latter normally in medial position, as in *poſſeſs* (roman: poſſefs) possess. The greater typographical simplicity of using only one form of *s* led to the rapid abandonment of the long form by printers after 1800, and by the general public soon after. The Roman alphabet as currently used for English consists of the 26 large and small letters *Aa*, *Bb*, *Cc*, *Dd*, *Ee*, *Ff*, *Gg*, *Hh*, *Ii*, *Jj*, *Kk*, *Ll*, *Mm*, *Nn*, *Oo*, *Pp*, *Qq*, *Rr*, *Ss*, *Tt*, *Uu*, *Vv*, *Ww*, *Xx*, *Yy*, *Zz*. No diacritic marks are normally used for native English words, unless the apostrophe and the diaeresis sign (see entries) are counted as such.

See ACCENT, ALGORITHM, ASH, CIPHER (ALPHABET), CODE, COMMUNICATIVE SHIFT, DIACRITIC, ENG, ESH, ETH, INITIAL, INTERNATIONAL PHONETIC ALPHABET, KEYBOARD, LETTER[1], LONG S, OLD ENGLISH[1], PHONEME, QWERTY, ROMAN, RUNE, SCRIPT, SPELLING, SPELLING REFORM, THORN, TRANSCRIPTION, TRANSLITERATION, WRITING (WRITING SYSTEM), WYN(N), YOGH, and the letter entries A to Z. [HISTORY, TECHNOLOGY, WRITING]. C.U., T.MCA.

ALPHABETICAL ORDER, also **alphabetic order, ABC order, alphabetic(al) arrangement**. The order used for presenting, teaching, memorizing, or otherwise using the letters of an alphabet. It is particularly favoured as an invariant series by which information can be organized in catalogues, concordances, dictionaries, directories, encyclopedias, indexes, and the like. In the Middle Ages, such ordering was rare and often haphazard, seldom going beyond grouping words according to first letters only (all the *a*-words, then all the *b*-words, etc.), or at most second-order arrangement (*ab-*, *ac-*, *ad-*, etc.). Thoroughgoing alphabetization did not establish itself fully until printing had become widespread and printers had become used to manipulating letters first physically (as bits of metal in alphabetized trays), then conceptually.

Conventionally, alphabetical ordering must be consistent through words, word groups, names, name groups, etc., so that, for example, *access* precedes *accessibility* which precedes *accessible* which precedes *accessibly*. Word groups may be ordered strictly by letter throughout the group, ignoring spaces (as are the headwords in this book); alternatively, they may be ordered word by word, a shorter word then preceding all longer words that begin with the same sequence of letters. Compare the following:

Letter-by-letter order	Word-by-word order
American	American
American English	American English
Americanese	American language
Americanism	Americanese
American language	Americanism

Difficulties may arise in English over certain placings, such as *Mac* and *Mc* names and the names of saints. In the first case, the names may be taken to be in effect the same and presented in a single series as *McArthur*, *MacLean*, *Macmahon*, *McMillan*, or they may be regarded as two series, first *Mac*, then *Mc*. The names of saints, even when abbreviated (as with *St Mark*), are usually placed in the *sai* series with such words as *sail*, either as *Saint Mark* or as if *St* were *Saint*, rather than in the *st* series with such words as *stand*. Further complications include ordering according to personal names that follow surnames in a directory, as with *Macleod*, *John*; *McLeod*, *Margaret*; *MacLeod*, *Morag*; *McLeod*, *Murdo*, etc. See ALPHABET, CONCORDANCE, INDEX. Compare THEMATIC ORDER. [REFERENCE]. T.MCA.

ALPHANUMERIC [1950s: a blend of *alpha(bet)* and *numeric*]. A term in computing and related subjects that refers to any circumstance in which letters and numbers occur together, often also along with such other characters as punctuation marks: *an alphanumeric code*. See ALPHABET, NUMERAL. [TECHNOLOGY]. T.MCA.

ALPHA PRIVATIVE. See PRIVATIVE.

ALVEOLAR [1790s: from Latin *alveolus* a hollow, a socket of a tooth, and *-ar* as in *similar*. Stress: 'al-VEE-o-lar']. (1) Relating to either of the bony ridges in the mouth that contain the teeth, but especially in phonetics to the ridge behind the upper teeth (*the alveolar ridge*), and to any sounds made when the tongue touches or comes close to it: for example, the consonants /t, d/ are alveolar stops, while /s, z/ are alveolar fricatives. (2) A sound made in this way: /d/ is a voiced alveolar. See CONSONANT, L-SOUNDS, PALATE, R-SOUNDS, TONGUE. [SPEECH]. T.MCA.

AM- [20c]. A combining form for *America(n)*, used especially in trade-names: *Amexco* American Express Company, *Aramco* Arabian-American Oil Company, *Pan Am* Pan-American Airways. Compare AMER-. [AMERICAS, NAME]. T.MCA.

AMBIGUITY [14c: from Latin *ambiguitas* acting both ways, shifting, from *ambi-* both ways, *agere/ actum* to drive, act]. Actual or potential uncertainty of meaning, especially if a word, phrase, or sentence can be understood in two ways: for example, the written statement *They can fish*, which could mean *They may or are able to fish* and *They put fish in cans*. Many statements are ambiguous in isolation but clear in context or are amenable to logical analysis: although there are scores of meanings of *run*, someone who speaks of *running the marathon* is not likely to be using the word in the sense of *running a company*, although that is possible and may in some circumstances be so. In conversation, ambiguity can usually be resolved by asking, 'What do you mean, X or Y?', but in reading there is no one to ask and, unless the term is marked so as to designate the meaning intended, it may be impossible to distinguish one meaning from another.

Lexical ambiguity. Most words are polysemous: a dictionary may list some 80 definitions for *take*, including 'acquire', 'steal', 'deceive', 'accept', 'regard', 'require', and 'occupy', yet when a native user of English encounters *take* there is rarely any ambiguity, because the context is usually clear. Words that are spelled identically but have different origins are *homographs*, whether pronounced identically, like *bear* (animal), *bear* (carry), or differently, like *lead* (metal), *lead* (conduct). A reader might regard *lead* as a visual ambiguity, but would probably not be confused by listening to a passage containing either or both words. *Bear* is ambiguous phonetically as well as visually. A word like *scan*, meaning either 'read rapidly and superficially' or 'read with great care, scrutinize', presents a problem of ambiguity not readily soluble by context because both its meanings have to do with reading. *Cleave* can mean either 'split asunder' or 'cling', which are virtual opposites. Although context resolves ambiguities most of the time, it does not always do so, and the amount of context required for resolution varies.

Grammatical ambiguity. In a written sentence like *They are cooking apples*, the syntax is inherently ambiguous, allowing two incompatible readings: *There are some people and some apples, and the people are cooking the apples* and *There are some apples, of the kind that are better cooked than eaten fresh*. In isolation, the meaning of such a sentence cannot be resolved, but in such sentences as *They are cooking apples* and *They can fish* some distinction can be made in speech through stress and intonation. Because of their compactness, newspaper headlines are particularly prone to peculiar elliptical effects, as in *MACARTHUR FLIES BACK TO FRONT*, referring to US general Douglas MacArthur during the Korean War.

Literary ambiguity. In *Seven Types of Ambiguity* (1930), the English critic William Empson considered ambiguity as a literary device and classified it into categories 'intended as stages of advancing logical disorder'. He allows for both deliberate or unintentional ambiguities created by the author and confusion in the mind of a reader, whether literal, logical, or psychological. Empson's types are: *ambiguity of reference*, the result of metaphoric manipulation; *ambiguity of referent*, the grammatical running of alternative meanings into one; *ambiguity of sense*, including puns, allusions, and allegories; *ambiguity of intent*, in which the author's purpose is unclear; *ambiguity of transition*, marked by a change in the author's perspective of his or her subject; *ambiguity of contradiction*, in which the author confuses an image owing to tautology, contradiction, or irrelevancy; and *ambiguity of meaning*, as in words like *let* ('allow' or 'hinder') and *cleave* ('split asunder' or 'embrace').

See AMPHIBOLY, COMPUTATIONAL LINGUISTICS, DISAMBIGUATE, DOUBLE MEANING, DOUBLE TALK, ENGLISH, EQUIVOCATION, HEADLINE, HOMOGRAPH, JANUS WORD, MACHINE TRANSLATION, PUN, PUNCTUATION. [LANGUAGE, STYLE]. L.U.

AMELIORATION. See MELIORATION.

AMER-, also **Ameri-** [1900s]. Combining forms for *America(n)*, as in: *Amerasian*, of American and Asian parentage (compare *Eurasian*); *Amerind*, *Amerindian*, American Indian; commercial terms such as *Americash*, *Americar*, *Ameritech*, and the facetious *Ameri-think*, American thinking (Jane Walmsley, 'A Native's Guide to Ameri-think', *Company*, Mar. 1984) and *Amerispeak*, American buzz-words and jargon (*She*, May 1987). Compare AM-, AMERICO-. See AMERENGLISH. [AMERICAS, NAME]. T.MCA.

AMERENGLISH [Later 20c: both with and without a capital *E*]. An occasional, mainly British, and usually facetious or pejorative term for American English: 'He lives in a duplex in one of the citadels of Amerenglish, downtown Manhattan' (*Encounter*, Oct. 1974); 'The English of America is Amer-English' (*Siwanee Review*, 1978). See AMER-. Compare AMERICAN[2], AMERICANESE, AMERICAN LANGUAGE. [AMERICAS, VARIETY]. T.MCA., J.A.

AMERICA [16c: from the feminine of *Americus*, the Latinized first name of the Italian explorer Amerigo Vespucci (1454-1512). A claim is also made for the name of Richard Ameryk, sheriff of Bristol and patron of John Cabot (Giovanni Caboto), the 16c Anglo-Italian explorer of North America. The name *America* first appeared on a map in 1507 by the German cartographer Martin Waldseemüller, referring to the area now called Brazil]. Since the 16c, a name of the western hemisphere, often in the plural *Americas* and more or less synonymous with *the New World*. Since the 18c, a name of the United States of America. The second sense is now primary in English: 'The American president of the American University of

Beirut was murdered because he was the symbol of America' (*International Herald Tribune*, 9 May 1984). However, the term is open to uncertainties: the name *The American Heritage Publishing Company* (New York) refers to the US alone; in the company's publication *The Golden Book of America* (1974), a children's book about the US, the first chapter asks 'Did Columbus Discover America?', without making it clear that a different sense of the word is needed when discussing Columbus. [AMERICAS, GEOGRAPHY, HISTORY, NAME].   T.MCA.

The Americas theme

A. AFRICAN-AMERICAN, AFRO-SEMINOLE, ALBION, ALEXANDER (H.), ALLIANCE QUEBEC, AM-, AMER, AMERENGLISH, AMERICA, AMERICAN[1], AMERICAN[2], AMERICAN BLACK ENGLISH, AMERICAN BROADCASTING, AMERICAN DIALECT SOCIETY, AMERICAN ENGLISH, AMERICAN ENGLISH AND BRITISH ENGLISH, AMERICANESE, AMERICAN HERITAGE DICTIONARY, AMERICANISM, AMERICANISTICS, AMERICAN LANGUAGE, AMERICAN LANGUAGE (THE), AMERICAN LANGUAGES, AMERICAN LITERATURE, AMERICAN NAME SOCIETY, AMERICAN PLACE-NAMES, AMERICAN PRESS, AMERICAN PUBLISHING, AMERICAN SIGN LANGUAGE, AMERICAN SPEECH, AMERICO-, AMESLAN, ANGLO, ANGLO-AMERICAN, ANGLO-CANADIAN, ANGLO ENGLISH, ANGLO-IRISH, ANGLOPHONE, ANGUILLA, ANTIGUA AND BARBUDA, ANTILLES, APPALACHIAN ENGLISH, ARGENTINA, ASSIMILATION, ATLANTIC, ATLANTIC CREOLES, AVIS.

B–C. BADIAN, BAHAMAS, BAILEY (B.), BAJAN, BARBADOS, BARNHART, BAY ISLANDS, BELIZE, BERLITZ, BERMUDA, BIERCE, BLACK, BLACK ENGLISH, BLACK ENGLISH VERNACULAR, BLACK IRISH, BLOOMFIELD, BOLINGER, BONEHEAD ENGLISH, BOSTON, BRATHWAITE, BROOKLYNESE, BURGESSISM, BUSH, CAJUN, CAN-, CANADA, CANADIAN, CANADIAN BROADCASTING, CANADIAN DICTIONARIES IN ENGLISH, CANADIAN ENGLISH, CANADIANISM, CANADIAN LANGUAGE ORGANIZATIONS, CANADIAN LANGUAGES, CANADIAN LITERATURE IN ENGLISH, CANADIAN PLACE-NAMES, CANADIAN PRESS, CANADIAN PUBLISHING, CANADIAN STYLE GUIDES, CARIBBEAN, CARIBBEAN ENGLISH, CARIBBEAN ENGLISH CREOLE, CARIBBEAN EXAMINATIONS COUNCIL, CARIBBEAN LANGUAGES, CARIBBEAN LITERATURE IN ENGLISH, CASSIDY, CAYMAN ISLANDS, CENTRAL AMERICA, CHICANO, CHICANO ENGLISH, CHINOOK JARGON, CHOMSKY, CLASSICAL LANGUAGE, COLLEGE ENGLISH ASSOCIATION, COLONIAL, COMMONWEALTH, COMMONWEALTH CARIBBEAN, COMMONWEALTH LITERATURE, CONTINENT, CRAIGIE, CULTURA, CURME.

D–H. DIALECT IN AMERICA, DIALECT IN CANADA, DICKINSON, DICTIONARY OF AMERICANISMS, DICTIONARY OF AMERICAN REGIONAL ENGLISH, DICTIONARY OF BAHAMIAN ENGLISH, DICTIONARY OF CANADIANISMS, DICTIONARY OF JAMAICAN ENGLISH, DICTIONARY OF NEWFOUNDLAND ENGLISH, DICTIONARY OF PRINCE EDWARD ISLAND ENGLISH, DICTIONARY SOCIETY OF NORTH AMERICA, DIXIE, DOMINICA, DUB, DUTCH, EDUCATIONAL TESTING SERVICE, ELEMENTS OF STYLE (THE), ELIOT, ENGLISH, ENGLISH CANADA, ENGLISH CANADIAN, ENGLISH LANGUAGE AMENDMENT, ENGLISH LITERATURE, ENGLISH-SPEAKING UNION, ENGLISH TEACHING FORUM, ETHNIC NAME, EXAMINING IN ENGLISH, FALKLAND ISLANDS, FRANCIZATION, FRANGLAIS, FRENCH, FRIES, FUNK, FUNK & WAGNALLS, GEECHEE, GEISEL, GENERAL AMERICAN, GENERAL AMERICAN ENGLISH, GRENADA, GRINGO, GULLAH,

GUYANA, HALLIDAY, HANLEY, HAWAII, HAWAIIAN, HAWAIIAN ENGLISH, HAWAII CREOLE ENGLISH, HAWAII PIDGIN ENGLISH, HEMPL, HERITAGE LANGUAGE, HILLBILLY, HILL SOUTHERN, HISPANIC, HONDURAS, HOUSE STYLE.

I–M. INDIA, INDIAN, INDIAN ENGLISH[2], INDIES, INNIS, INTERNATIONAL LINGUISTIC ASSOCIATION, INUIT, JAMAICA, JAMAICAN CREOLE, JAMAICAN ENGLISH, JIVE (TALK), KRAPP, KUHN, KURATH, KWEYOL, LANGUAGE, LANGUAGE POLICE, LATIN[2], LATINO, LEACOCK, LEEWARD ISLANDS, LIBRARY OF CONGRESS, LIEBER, LINGUISTIC ASSOCIATION OF CANADA AND THE UNITED STATES, LINGUISTIC ATLAS, LINGUISTIC ATLAS OF THE UNITED STATES AND CANADA, LINGUISTIC SOCIETY OF AMERICA, MCDAVID, MCLUHAN, MCWORD, MAGAZINE, MALEDICTA, MARCH, MARITIME PROVINCES/MARITIMES, MARSH, MATHEWS, MELVILLE, MENCKEN, MERRIAM-WEBSTER, MESTIZO, MÉTIS, MID-ATLANTIC, MISKITO COAST CREOLE, MODERN LANGUAGE ASSOCIATION, MONTSERRAT, MOTION PICTURE, MOVIE, MULATTO, MULTICULTURALISM.

N–S. NAIPAUL, NATIONAL COUNCIL OF TEACHERS OF ENGLISH, NATION LANGUAGE, NATIVISM, NCTE, NETWORK STANDARD, NEW ENGLAND, NEWFIE JOKE, NEWFOUNDLAND, NEWFOUNDLAND ENGLISH, NEW ORLEANS, NEW YORK, NEW YORKER (THE), NEW YORKESE, NEW YORRICAN, NICARAGUAN ENGLISH, NORTH AMERICAN, NOVEL, OFFICIAL ENGLISH (MOVEMENT), OTTAWA VALLEY, OXFORD ENGLISH DICTIONARY, PACIFIC RIM, PANAMA, PATOIS, PENNSYLVANIA DUTCH, PLAIN ENGLISH, PLANTATION SOUTHERN, POLITICALLY CORRECT, PORTUGUESE, POUND (L.), PUERTO RICO, QUEBEC, RACISM, RANDOM HOUSE, RANDOM HOUSE DICTIONARY, RAP, RASTA TALK, READ, REGGAE, RICKERT, SAINT CHRISTOPHER AND NEVIS, SAINT LUCIA, SAINT VINCENT AND THE GRENADINES, SAMANA, SAPIR, SARAMACCAN, SCOTCH-IRISH, SOUTH, SOUTHERN ENGLISH, SOUTHRON, SPANGLISH, SPANISH, SRANAN, STANDARD AMERICAN, STANDARD AMERICAN ENGLISH, STANDARD BLACK ENGLISH, STANDARD CANADIAN ENGLISH, STRATHY LANGUAGE UNIT, SURINAM(E), SYNECDOCHE.

T–Z. TEFL, TEIL, TESD, TESL, TESL CANADA, TESOL, TEXAS, TEXIAN, TEX-MEX, THORNDIKE, TIME MAGAZINE, TIMESPEAK, TRIN(I)BAGONIAN, TRINIBAGIANESE, TRINIDAD AND TOBAGO, TURKS AND CAICOS ISLANDS, TURNER (L.), TWAIN, UNCLE SAM, UNITED STATES, UNITED STATES ENGLISH, URDANG, US, USA, US ENGLISH, USIA, USIS, VERBATIM, VIRGIN ISLANDS, VOICE OF AMERICA, WASP, WEBSTER, WEBSTERS, WEBSTER'S COLLEGIATE DICTIONARIES, WEBSTER'S DICTIONARY OF ENGLISH USAGE, WEBSTER'S NEW INTERNATIONAL DICTIONARY, WEBSTER'S NEW WORLD DICTIONARY, WEST INDIAN, WEST INDIES, WHITE, WHITE ENGLISH, WHITNEY, WHORF, WINDWARD ISLANDS, WORCESTER, YANK(EE), YIDDISH, YIDDISHISM, YINGLISH, Z.

AMERICAN[1] [16c]. A term that first referred to the entire western hemisphere, its peoples, animals, and plants, then to the British colonies which became the United States of America. In 1697, the Boston clergyman Cotton Mather applied the term as a noun to settlers from England, but the use was slow in spreading; when Joseph Addison noted (1711, *Spectator* 56) that 'the Americans believe that all things have souls', he was referring not to the colonists but to the indigenous peoples. As late as 1809, a traveller writing about the people of the ex-colonies as *the Americans* added: 'that is, the subjects of the United States' (Edward A. Kendall, *Travels through the Northern Parts of the United States*).

A Brazilian is *South American* and *Latin American*, but not, in English, *American*; a Canadian is a *North American*, but not an American. Costa Ricans and Nicaraguans are *Central Americans* or *Meso-Americans*, but not *Middle Americans*, who are typical US citizens (whether they live in Kansas or Hawaii). The term *Pan-American* refers to the hemisphere, while *All-American* is used only of the US (for whatever is characteristic of the whole country and excludes foreign elements); to be *un-American*, however, is to fail to represent the assumed values of the US. *Irish-American*, *Italian-American* (sometimes *Italo-American*), and other hyphenated usages also relate only to the US: a *Cuban-American* is a US citizen of Cuban background, even though Cubans are American in the hemispheric sense. The use in the late 20c of such hyphenless variants as *Irish American* and *Italian American* may express greater confidence in a dual heritage. There continues, however, to be uncertainty as to the best name for Americans of African provenance: *Black American*, *Afro-American*, and *African-American* are all used. Such naming of the people of the US in terms of their non-American ancestors occasionally provokes wry comment:

As yet we have no 'African-American' parade, but its time is probably coming. And can the Scottish-American Tattoo be far behind? There will have to be an Indian-American celebration, of course. But here we begin to run into labeling problems, Indian-Americans of Indian descent (as opposed to Pakistani-Americans) will not want to march alongside of—you know, American-Indians. Perhaps the last-named, being firstcomers, should be allowed to call themselves American-Americans (Edmund Morris, *The Washington Post*, Jan. 1989).

In Spanish, *América* refers to the hemisphere, to Latin America, and to the US. *América del Norte* is North America at large, but *un norteamericano* is usually a US citizen and *El Norte* is the US. There are other *Estados Unidos* (United States), such as of Mexico and of Venezuela, and so the US is often called *Los Estados Unidos del Norte* and its citizens *estadounidenses*, a word for which there is no strict equivalent in English. See AMERICA, NATIVE AMERICAN. [AMERICAS, NAME].   T.MCA.

AMERICAN[2] [19c in this sense: by ellipsis from *American English/language*]. An occasional term for English as used in the US, often in contrast with *English* (sometimes *British*), and seriously or facetiously implying a distinct language: 'The American I have heard up to the present, is a tongue as distinct from English as Patagonian' (Kipling, *From Sea to Sea*, 1889); 'Too often are spoken English and spoken American criticized as though it were impossible for them to have any

laws of their own' (Partridge, *Usage and Abusage*, 1947/57); 'Brandon has a beaut: the transmission from American to English of *cost-effective*' (Safire, *New York Times*, Oct. 1988). Compare AMER-ENGLISH, AMERICANESE, AMERICAN ENGLISH, AMERICAN LANGUAGE. [AMERICAS, VARIETY].   T.MCA.

AMERICAN BLACK ENGLISH. See BLACK ENGLISH VERNACULAR.

AMERICAN BROADCASTING. In the United States there are more than 10,000 radio stations, 1,342 television stations, and over 90m homes (98%) with one or more television sets. The three main TV networks account for more advertising dollars than any other medium and in 1985 their pre-tax profits were over $1,000m.

Radio. There was sporadic broadcasting as early as 1906, but scheduled broadcasting began in Pittsburgh in 1920 and the first advertising was sold in 1922. A coast-to-coast hook-up was made in 1924, and the principal networks were formed shortly afterwards: the *National Broadcasting Corporation* (*NBC*) in 1926, the *Columbia Broadcasting Corporation* (*CBS*) in 1927. The NBC had two networks under its control, Red and Blue, but the *Federal Communications Commission* (*FCC*), a regulatory agency created in 1934, eventually forced their separation. The Blue network was sold in 1945 and renamed the *American Broadcasting Company* (*ABC*). The *Mutual Broadcasting System* (1934) was the only network not to move eventually into television. Radio has been mainly private and commercial, regulated by government agencies that license and supervise stations but have no control over content. In addition to reportage, this has mainly been music and dramatization: an early success was *Amos 'n' Andy* (1929), a blackface vaudeville act, and a famous drama was Orson Welles's version of H. G. Wells's *War of the Worlds* (1938), which created widespread panic when many listeners mistook its reports of a Martian invasion for real news. Radio also became an important political tool. During the 1930s, President Franklin D. Roosevelt used it in his 'fireside chats' to allay anxiety over the Depression and gain support for his policies. Public perceptions of national policy were influenced by such commentators as Father Charles Coughlin, Hans von Kaltenborn, Fulton Lewis Jr., Edward R. Murrow, and Dorothy Thompson, spanning the political spectrum from liberal internationalist to conservative isolationist.

Television. Although experimental TV had been available from the 1920s, the US lagged behind Britain in developing it: many Americans did not see a broadcast until the New York World's Fair of 1939. Licensing of commercial stations followed, but development was inhibited by World

War II. After the war TV began to expand, and by the 1952 presidential election campaign between Dwight D. Eisenhower and Adlai E. Stevenson it was a significant political tool. In that year, a third of all homes had a set, and the distinction was established between VHF (very high frequency) channels 2 to 13 and UHF (ultra high frequency) up to 83, allowing in due course a proliferation of channels and programming. By 1960, more than four-fifths of US homes had a set, and viewing had become an established and influential part of life. In 1953, viewers in more than 15m homes watched Lucille Ball, who was pregnant at the time, enact a birth scene on the *I Love Lucy* show. The following year, a broadcast of the Senate investigation into alleged pro-Communist activities in the military helped to arouse public sentiment against the browbeating tactics to which Senator Joseph R. McCarthy of Wisconsin gave his name. The increasing popularity of TV over radio and the proliferation of channels had effects on both media, radio being increasingly devoted to music, sports, news, and call-in programmes. In the early days of TV, programmes were live; later they were usually taped and the increasing number of time slots made it difficult to satisfy demand. Television consequently turned to motion pictures to fill its needs, at a time when Hollywood was becoming concerned about people staying at home rather than going to the movies.

Impacts and attitudes. Television has been a force in American life, especially in politics: John F. Kennedy's close victory over Richard M. Nixon in the presidential election of 1960 was probably due to his better showing in televised debates. Popular disenchantment with government policy during the Vietnam conflict was fuelled by the graphic reportage of the events of that war on television; President Lyndon B. Johnson's decision not to stand for a second term in office was a direct result of the unpopularity of the war, as seen on the nation's screens. American television is often criticized in other English-speaking countries for vacuousness of content, despite the fact that US programmes are often a mainstay of broadcasting in those countries. Canada and Ireland take steps to counteract the threat they see from American TV, especially by legislating for the showing of a percentage of home-produced material.

Television's ability to bring the distant into focus and make it immediate reached an apogee in July 1969 when it brought the moon landing into the living-rooms of millions worldwide. The normally articulate Walter Cronkite, a leading newscaster of the period, embodied the general response when he was reduced to 'My golly!' The Watergate crisis (1972-4) was another example of the ability of TV to create a sense of immediacy and urgency around events far from the everyday lives of its viewers.

Although the reporting that contributed to exposing the attempted cover-up by the administration was chiefly the work of print journalists, broadcasts of the Senate Select Committee hearings, under the chairmanship of Sam Ervin of North Carolina, gripped the nation's attention. Ervin's Southern accent, suggesting unpretentiousness and trustworthiness, avuncular concern for running his committee fairly and effectively, and old-home-boy plainness contrasted with the style of many whom his committee questioned and helped shift sympathy away from Nixon.

Public broadcasting. Only relatively recently has an effort been made to create an agency of public broadcasting. In the late 1960s, the *Corporation for Public Broadcasting* was chartered to create a network of local and national programmes, the *Public Broadcasting Service* (*PBS*), which aspired to be a fourth, non-commercial network. It depended on already existing *National Educational Television* (*NET*) for much of its early programming. *National Public Radio* (*NPR*) is a comparable network for radio. Initially, public broadcasting was funded by private foundations (especially the Ford Foundation) and government subsidy through laws enacted during the administrations of Presidents Gerald Ford and Jimmy Carter. Under the Reagan administration, however, funds were severely cut, and local stations were forced to engage in fund-raising campaigns and broadcast advertisements of a restrained kind. Without government financial support from a licensing fee, common in Britain and other English-speaking countries, public broadcasting has little prospect of fulfilling its ambition to match the three commercial networks or public channels in other nations.

Satellite and cable. A significant development of the 1970s-80s was the proliferation of *satellite transmission* and *cable television*. Originally intended for houses in areas of poor reception or limited options, cable TV (also known as *cablevision* or *CATV* for *community antenna television*) expanded so much that the companies offering it began to originate their own programmes. By the end of the 1980s, about half of national TV reception was via cable. Many networks developed, of which perhaps the most notable is Ted Turner's *Cable News Network* (*CNN*), based in Atlanta, Georgia, which is respected for both the timeliness and depth of its news reporting. It is an international enterprise, with many foreign bureaus and reception in more than 50 nations.

Broadcasting and language. A popular belief holds that radio and television have homogenized the language of Americans, but there is little evidence that people change their speechways as a result of passive exposure. Change is more often the result of interaction, as speakers feel the need to adapt what they say to the understanding or style of those they address. Scholars disagree about the basic question of whether AmE is becoming homogeneous or more diverse; there are no generally accepted scales to measure sameness or difference between varieties. Another popular belief is that radio and TV announcers use a variety called *Network Standard* or *General American*. However, the former implies an institutionalization that does not exist and the latter has been misunderstood, especially in Europe, as denoting a well-defined dialect. The efforts of some networks, such as NBC, to provide their announcers with authoritative guidance on pronunciation have not been widely influential or successful.

On the other hand, broadcasters hoping to work on large metropolitan stations or national networks tend to modify their speechways by eliminating pronunciations or other usages likely to be associated by listeners with a particular area or social group. Certain broadcasters, however, such as sports reporters, folksy humorists, and meteorologists, are less likely to feel the need to change the way they talk, because they may be expected to sound local; anchors and serious news reporters or commentators are supposed to be more cosmopolitan. The outcome of efforts to weed out regional features is not an accent as unified or well-defined as traditional BBC English, but rather one whose core is shared by most Americans and which includes diverse regional or social features that most people are not aware of or do not respond to as 'dialect'. Such a variable, artificial, and negatively defined speechway might be called *General American* and be useful as a model for foreign learners, as well as ambitious broadcasters. On the whole, however, it is not clear that broadcasting has effected any changes in the way most Americans talk. See BROADCASTING, CABLE NEWS NETWORK, VOICE OF AMERICA, RAP, SOAP OPERA. [AMERICAS, MEDIA].   J.A.

Emery, Michael & Edwin. 1988. *The Press and America: An Interpretive History of the Mass Media*, 6th edition. Englewood Cliffs, NJ: Prentice Hall.

AMERICAN COLLEGE DICTIONARY. See
BARNHART.

AMERICAN DIALECT SOCIETY, short form
ADS. One of the oldest learned societies in the US, founded 1889 in Cambridge, Massachusetts, to study the English language in the western hemisphere, together with other languages influencing it or influenced by it. The first president was the folklorist Francis James Child; other founding members included George L. Kitteredge, Charles H. Grandgent, James R. Lowell, John M. Manly, and Henry Sweet. The original individual and institutional membership was 140; a century later, after periods of inactivity and near-bankruptcy,

ADS has some 550 individual and 300 institutional members. The Society's primary objective has been to publish a dictionary on the model of Wright's *English Dialect Dictionary*. Collected materials, housed for many years at Harvard in anticipation of this project, were found in 1941 to be missing. More recent archives are at the U. of Wisconsin, where Frederic G. Cassidy is editing the *Dictionary of American Regional English*. From 1890 to 1942, ADS published only six volumes of its journal *Dialect Notes*. After reorganization in 1943, it began to issue an annual monograph series called *Publication of the American Dialect Society* (*PADS*). In 1972, the Society assumed sponsorship of *American Speech*. It also publishes a newsletter (*NADS*) three times a year. The annual meeting is held in conjunction with the conference of the *Modern Language Association*, with other meetings at the conferences of the *Linguistic Society of America*, the *National Council of Teachers of English*, the *Conference on Methods of Dialectology*, the *Linguistic Institute of the LSA*, the *Dictionary Society of North America*, and the regional sections of the MLA. See AMERICAN SPEECH, DICTIONARY OF AMERICAN REGIONAL ENGLISH. [AMERICAS, LANGUAGE, MEDIA].   D.E.B.

AMERICAN ENGLISH, short forms *AmE*, *AE*. Also **United States English**, short form *USE*. The English language as used in the United States of America. The speakers of AmE outnumber all native speakers of English outside the US by about two to one and those of BrE by nearly four to one. This advantage, strengthened by US involvement with world affairs, has given AmE a global importance in the late 20c comparable to that of BrE in the late 19c. The history of the variety falls into three periods, whose dates correspond to political and social events with important consequences for the language: (1) *The Colonial Period*, during which a distinctive AmE was gestating. (2) *The National Period*, which saw its birth, establishment, and consolidation. (3) *The International Period*, during which it has come increasingly under foreign influence and has exerted influence on other varieties of English and on other languages.

The Colonial Period (1607-1776). English colonization of the Americas came relatively late, as compared for example with Spanish settlement in Central and South America. In 1497, John Cabot explored the coast of what became the Canadian province of Nova Scotia, but no effort was made to establish a colony for nearly another century, when Humphrey Gilbert claimed the island of Newfoundland (1583) and Walter Raleigh attempted his ill-fated settlement at Roanoke, Virginia (1584). Raleigh's 'lost colony' did not survive, so the first permanent English settlement on the mainland was at Jamestown in 1607. Both religious and commercial motives prompted the founding of the Plymouth colony of 1620 and the Maryland colony of 1634. Colonization of the Carolinas began in 1663. The Dutch settled Manhattan Island in 1624, but were brought under English rule in 1664. European settlement of Pennsylvania, partly by the Dutch and Swedes, preceded the English chartering of a Quaker colony there in 1681 under William Penn. From the beginning, the colonies were of mixed origin. Because settlers came from a variety of locations, there was no simple transplanting of British dialects, but rather a combination of features in a single colony, resulting in the levelling of divergent features and the apparently random survival of features from disparate sources. The result was more uniform speech in the colonies than in the motherland. The barrier of the Atlantic began the process of divergence of American from British usage almost immediately. Changes in the motherland were slow to reach the colonies, the colonists adapted old uses to new purposes, and borrowed from other groups, especially the Amerindians, Dutch, and French. Although still depending on England for authority and a standard, the colonies were forced to develop their own resources.

The National Period (1776–1898). The War of Independence (1776-83) brought the Colonial Period to a close. Several of the Founding Fathers of the new republic recognized that political independence would require cultural independence as well. Linguistically, this period faced two related challenges: the evolution and recognition of a separate standard English for the US and the extension of that standard over the whole nation as it expanded westward. Noah Webster is most closely associated with linguistic nationalism in promoting what he called Federal English, but others contributed to it. The Civil War (1861-5) disrupted the fabric of the Union in politics, culture, and language. By the time it began, US sovereignty extended to the Pacific, fulfilling a sense of a mission (the 'Manifest Destiny' of the US) which motivated national policy during this period. The assimilation of foreign influences continued, including large numbers of immigrants from Europe and contacts with speakers of Spanish in Florida and the West. Developments which moulded the language of Americans during the 19c included the settlement of the West, the extension of the railroads, the growth of industry, the labour movement, the invention of the telegraph and telephone, the burgeoning of journalism, the expansion of education at all levels, and the publication of textbooks and dictionaries. The establishment of a national identity and its domestic elaboration were the preoccupation of this period, but by the end of the century new directions in national policy began to affect the language. By the 1890s, the

domestic frontier was exhausted, and expansionism took Americans into territories overseas. The Spanish-American War (1898) lasted barely four months, but was a turning-point in foreign policy. During the 120 years since the founding of the nation, the US had generally observed George Washington's counsel to avoid foreign alliances and followed an isolationist policy concentrating on domestic matters. With this war, however, the US and its English became internationally significant.

The International Period (from 1898). The Hawaiian Islands were annexed during the course of the Spanish-American War, the island of Puerto Rico was ceded to the US, and the Philippines were bought for $20m. In the following years, the US extended its overseas interests: an Open Door policy was affirmed for China; the US mediated the Russo-Japanese war of 1905; the Panamanian revolution against Colombia was supported (if not actually fomented), so that the US could build a canal across the isthmus of Panama; intervention in Latin American affairs became frequent, to prevent European involvement and secure American interests; the Virgin Islands in the Caribbean were purchased from Denmark; and in 1917 the US entered World War I. Thereafter, Americans played an increasing role in world politics and economics with a consequent effect on AmE usage. In turn, such US institutions as the movie industry in Hollywood, jazz and popular music from the South, participation in World War II, post-war technological developments such as the computer, and the activities and products of major US corporations and publications, from Coca-Cola to *Time* magazine, have helped disseminate Americanisms throughout the world.

Variation. Variation within AmE is far less than within many other national languages. Although Americans are conscious of the odd way their fellow citizens in other communities talk, considering the size and population of the US, its language is relatively homogeneous. Yet there are distinctive speechways in particular communities: the Boston Brahmins, the old families of New England who pride themselves on their culture and conservative attitudes and are noted for their haughtiness; the Gullah, who live on the islands off the shore of South Carolina and Georgia and talk with heavy West African influence; the Cajuns of Louisiana, descended from Acadian French immigrants, with folkways, cuisine, and speechways that blend influences from several traditions; the Appalachian mountain people; the Tex-Mex bronco-busters; the laid-back life-stylers of Marin County, California; the Charlestonian Old South aristocracy; the inner-city African Americans; the Minnesota Swedes; the Chicanos of the Southwest; and many others. Beneath the relative uniformity of its stand-ard, edited variety, American English is a rich gal-limaufry of exotic and native stuffs.

Pronunciation. Underlying the regional accents of the US are some widespread features that are typ-ical of AmE: (1) With the exception of the South-ern states, eastern New England, and New York City, pronunciation is rhotic, postvocalic /r/ being pronounced in such words as *part, four, motor*. (2) The AmE /r/ is retroflex, and is often lost after an unstressed vowel if another /r/ follows: the *r* in *govern* is pronounced but is dropped in *governor*. (3) The vowels of words like *hoarse* and *horse* are increasingly merged in favour of a vowel of the quality in *haw* or *hoe*. (4) In words like *path, can't, dance*, AmE generally has the vowel of *pat* and *cant*. (5) The vowels of the stressed syllables in such words as *father* and *fodder* are generally ident-ical. (6) The *o*-sound of *go, note, soap* begins with a rounded vowel, while the *o*-sound in *not* is unrounded. (7) Generally there is no /j/ glide before a stressed *u*-vowel in words like *tune, duke, new, sue, thews, lute* ('toon', 'dook', 'noo', etc.), in which a dental consonant precedes, but the glide is retained in unstressed syllables (the second syl-lables of *menu, value*), when the vowel is initial (*ewe*), and when it is preceded by a labial or velar sound (*pew, cute*). (8) Among changes already under way and likely to become general is a merger of the vowel sounds in words like *caught, cot*. The resulting vowel is sometimes lightly rounded but more often unrounded, like the stressed vowel of *father*. (9) A /d/ typically occurs where the spelling has *t* or *tt* in words like *latter, atom, metal, bitty*, which are homophonous with *ladder, Adam, medal, biddy*. (10) Similarly, /t/ is often lost from /nt/ in *winter* ('winner'), *anti* ('annie', though retained when the second vowel has full value and some stress, 'an-tie'), *international* ('inner-national'). The *t* of words like *eaten* is usually glot-talized and is followed by a syllabic *n*. (11) The *l* at the end of words and between vowels (*bill, pil-low*) is typically dark: pronounced with the back of the tongue lifted toward the soft roof of the mouth. (12) Secondary stress is normal on the pen-ultimate syllables of words like *laboratory* and *sec-retary*, so that these words end like *Tory* and *Terry*. At the same time, syncope is common in words like *fam'ly, fed'ral, happ'ning*.

Grammar. (1) For the verb *get*, the old past par-ticiple *gotten* occurs alongside the newer *got*. Americans use both, but differently. *Gotten* gen-erally occurs when a process rather than a state or condition is intended: *I've gotten it* means 'acquired', whereas *I've got it* means 'possess'. Sim-ilarly, *I've gotten to go* means 'received permission or opportunity', whereas *I've got to go* means 'am obliged'. (2) *I will, you will, he will*, etc., are usual. *Shall* is rare in AmE, being largely restricted to

formal invitation (*Shall we dance?*) and emphasis (*I shall return*). (3) A simple preterite rather than a perfect form is sometimes used for action leading up to the present time, even with adverbs: *Did you ever hear that?*; *I already did it*. (4) In formal mandative constructions, with clauses following verbs, adjectives, and nouns of requiring and urging, AmE prefers the present subjunctive form: *They insisted that he go with them, It is imperative that you be here on time*. (5) When the subject of a clause is a collective noun, there is generally a singular verb, in concord with the form rather than the sense of the subject: *The airline insists . . .*; *The government is . . .* (6) The use of pre-positions is often distinctive: Americans live *on* a street (BrE *in*), cater *to* people (BrE *for*), do things *on* the weekend (BrE *at*), are *of* two minds about something (BrE *in*), have a new lease *on* life (BrE *of*), and when mentioning dates when things happen, may use or omit *on* (*Jack went home on Monday and came back Thursday*).

Vocabulary. A distinctive vocabulary developed from the Colonial Period until the present, includ-ing: (1) Old words put to new uses: *creek* for a small stream (compare AusE) rather than an estu-ary (as in BrE). This use probably arose because the term was first applied to the mouths of streams along coasts settled by the colonists then extended to the whole watercourse. (2) New words made up from old resources: *lengthy* from *length* and *-y* for the marked sense of *long* (of greater length than usual) as distinct from the unmarked sense (How long is it?), which does not imply great length; *Briticism* an expression peculiar to Britain; *com-plected* in combinations like *dark-complected* (hav-ing a dark complexion). (3) Borrowing from Amerindian languages: *chipmunk, hickory, moc-casin, pecan, skunk, squash, totem, wigwam*. Some-times such words came through French: *caribou, toboggan*. (4) Borrowing from other colonial lan-guages: French *chowder, prairie*; Dutch *boss, cole-slaw, cookie, Santa Claus, sleigh, snoop, waffle*, and probably *Yankee*; Spanish *corral, lasso, ranch*. (5) Borrowing from later immigrant languages: African *goober, gumbo, juke, voodoo, zombie*; Ger-man (especially through Pennsylvania Dutch) *dumb* stupid, *noodle, sauerkraut, snorkel*, and the *-fest* and *-burger* endings in *bookfest, cheeseburger*, etc. Among food terms are Mexican Spanish *chili* (*con carne*), Chinese *chop suey*, Czech *kolach* a kind of sweet bun, Italian *pizza*, Swedish *smorgasbord*, Japanese *sukiyaki*, Nahuatl-Spanish *tamale*, Ger-man *wiener*. (6) Some typically AmE words with complex histories: *lagniappe*, a term for a small present given by merchants to their customers, extended to any little extra benefit. Associated with the South, it is from Louisiana French, borrowed from Spanish *la ñapa* the gift, from Quechua *yapa*.

A selection of words of American origin indicates the variety and significance of the AmE contribution to English at large: *airline, boondoggle, checklist, disco, expense account, flowchart, geewhiz, halfbreed, inner city, junk food, kangaroo court, laser, mass meeting, nifty, ouch, pants, quasar, radio, soap opera, teddy bear, UFO, vigilante, wholehearted, xerox, yuppie, zipper.*

The story of OK. The best-known and most exported item in AmE, *OK* or *okay*, has a particularly complex history tracked down by Allen Walker Read to two fads of the 1830s in the city of Boston. In the first, the initials of the words in a phrase were used instead of the phrase itself: *OFM* for *our first men*; *ng* for *no go/no good*. In the second, comic misspellings of words were favoured: *oll wright* for all right. The two came together to produce initialisms like *OW* ('oll wright'), *KY* ('know yuse': no use), and *OK* ('oll korrect': all correct). *OK* would probably have gone the way of *OFM* and *OW* into the graveyard of forgotten usage, except that it was taken up as a pun on the nickname of the politician Martin Van Buren: *Old Kinderhook* (after the town in New York state in which he was born). A political organization, the OK Club, was formed to support his political fortunes, and its use of the term in the election campaign of 1840 spread knowledge of the word. Van Buren lost the election, but his catchword endured. (Other etymologies for *OK* have been proposed, tracing it to French, Finnish, Norwegian, Greek, German, Scots, Cockney, Choctaw, and several African languages, as well as to a number of personal names. All are imaginative, but lack documentary support.)

Social issues. Through the closing years of the 19c and throughout the 20c, the American concern over correct usage seems to have been more intense than the British. Questions of language engineering have generally been more vigorously considered in the US than in other English-speaking countries. Three issues in particular have powerful and volatile social repercussions: feminist concern for sexist language; the relationship between Black English and the standard language; and the relationship between English and other languages in the US, particularly Spanish:

Sexism. The question of sexism in language arouses violent partisanship. One of its simpler manifestations is the use of words with masculine implications (*man, he*) when both sexes are intended or appropriate. Occupational terms like *chairman, foreman, policeman, mail man,* and *airline stewardess,* with real or perceived sexual reference, are now being replaced by sexually neutral terms like *chair, supervisor, police officer, letter carrier,* and *flight attendant.* A brief fad for the use of *person* instead of *man* in such forms seems to have run its course, leaving some words, such as *chairperson,* in widespread use and others, such as *foreperson,* as curiosities. Another sore point is the requirement that a woman's social title (*Mrs.* or *Miss*) specify her marital status, whereas a man's (*Mr.*) does not; as a consequence, the female title *Ms* has become very widely used, partly because it is handy when the marital status of a woman is unknown even for those who are otherwise indifferent to the problem. A subtler form of sexism in language is the use of *girls* and *ladies* with reference to mature women; both are thought to be condescending, the first because it labels women as immature and the second because it isolates them socially. In this, as in other matters, however, much depends on one's age and social status. Among many middle-aged clubby women, *the girls* is the normal way of referring to one's intimates (just as *the boys* is among men), and *ladies* is the preferred general term, *women* sounding abrupt and rude. In general, consciousness of sexism in language is a younger-generation, urban, and politically liberal concern. See SEXISM.

Black English. The terms used for Americans descended from African slaves continue to fluctuate as members of the group change the name by which they prefer to be known. At one time, *colored person* was the preferred term, enshrined in the National Association for the Advancement of Colored People (NAACP). It was replaced by *Negro* (with a first vowel like *league,* as opposed to the sound in the variant *nigra*), then by *Black,* and more recently *African American* has been favoured. Considerable controversy has existed about *Black English (Vernacular)* or *BEV,* the language associated with African Americans. There has been argument about whether such usage should be a medium of instruction as an alternative to standard English. Among the strongest opponents of such a development have been older members of the group. The origin and history of Black English has also been a subject of controversy among scholars, and the very existence of such a discrete dialect has been questioned.

English and Spanish. There is a similar controversy about the official use of any non-English languages, but particularly of Spanish, as a medium of instruction in public schools, for voting in elections, and for other governmental and official functions. Pressure for such use of other languages comes from immigrant communities desirous of maintaining their identity within US society and has generated a counter-pressure to declare English the official language of the US. Several communities and states have passed laws or resolutions to that effect. The *English for US, English First,* or *Official English* movement has been called xenophobic, but can be seen as an extension of the 'Federal English' campaign of the early Republic, whose aim was the establishment of a uniform national language.

Conclusion. Regardless of the constitutional or other status of English in the US, the future of AmE is hardly in doubt. The international use of English seems assured for the foreseeable future. The extent to which international English reflects the standards of BrE or AmE, or a mid-Atlantic compromise, is open to speculation, but the question is of no great practical consequence: all national standards of English are close to one another. The growth of 'New Englishes' in the nations that have emerged since World War II may diversify the total range of the language, but international use is closely tied to the relatively uniform American–British complex.

See AFRO-SEMINOLE, AMERENGLISH, AMERICAN[2], AMERICAN BROADCASTING, AMERICAN DIALECT SOCIETY, AMERICAN ENGLISH, AMERICAN ENGLISH AND BRITISH ENGLISH, AMERICANESE, AMERINDIAN PIDGIN, AMERICANISM, AMERICAN LANGUAGE, AMERICAN LANGUAGE (THE), AMERICAN LANGUAGES, AMERICAN PRESS, AMERICAN PUBLISHING, AMERICAN SPEECH, ANGLO, ANGLO-AMERICAN, ANGLO-ENGLISH, BLACK ENGLISH, BLACK ENGLISH VERNACULAR, BOSTON, BROOKLYNESE, CANADIAN ENGLISH, CHICANO ENGLISH, CHINOOK JARGON, DIALECT IN AMERICA, ENGLISH LANGUAGE AMENDMENT, GEECHEE, GENERAL AMERICAN, GULLAH, INDIAN ENGLISH[2], JEWISH ENGLISH, LIEBER, MENCKEN, NASAL, NETWORK STANDARD, NEW ENGLAND, NEW ORLEANS, NEW YORK, NEW YORKESE, POUND (L.), RED ENGLISH, SEXISM, SOUTHERN ENGLISH, SPANISH, TEXAS, TEX-MEX, YIDDISHISM. [AMERICAS, HISTORY, VARIETY].   J.A.

Algeo, John. 1988. 'British and American Grammatical Differences', in *International Journal of Lexicography* 1. Oxford: University Press.

Baron, Dennis. 1982. *Grammar and Good Taste: Reforming the American Language*. New Haven: Yale University Press.

—— 1986. *Grammar and Gender*. New Haven: Yale University Press.

Mencken, H. L. 1963. *The American Language*. Revised by Raven I. McDavid Jr. New York: Knopf.

Neufeldt, Victoria, & Guralnik, David (eds.). 1988. *Webster's New World Dictionary of American English*, 3rd college edition. New York.

Pyles, Thomas. 1952. *Words and Ways of American English*. New York: Random House.

Read, Allen Walker. 1963. 'The First Stage in the History of O.K.' and 'The Second Stage in the History of O.K.', in *American Speech* 38.

Simpson, David. 1986. *The Politics of American English, 1776-1850*. New York: Oxford University Press

AMERICAN ENGLISH AND BRITISH ENGLISH.

Because BrE and AmE are the foremost varieties of the English language and serve as reference norms for other varieties, they have often been compared and contrasted. Such comparison and contrast are complex matters, made even more complex by the ambiguity and vagueness of the terms themselves. They are ambiguous in that each has more than one meaning; they are vague in that the boundaries between them are often fuzzy. For example, to say that the spelling *colour* is BrE means that it is used widely in the UK, is not used, or not widely used, or no longer used, in the US, may or may not be used in Canada, and may also be widely used in other parts of the English-speaking world. To say that the spelling *color* is AmE means that it is used widely in the US, is not used, or not widely used, or no longer used, in Britain, is probably used widely in Canada, and may or may not be used in other parts of the English-speaking world.

General ambiguity and vagueness. The terms *British English* and *American English* are used in different ways by different people for different purposes. They may refer to: (1) Two national varieties, each subsuming regional and other subvarieties, standard and non-standard. They do not extend beyond the frontiers of their states, but within those frontiers everything is included. (2) Two national standard varieties, each excluding the national non-standard varieties, but to some extent merging with at least some of these. Each is only part of the range of English within its own state, but the most prestigious part. (3) Two international varieties, focused on particular nations, but each subsuming other varieties in a more or less ill-defined way. Each is more than a national variety of English. (4) Two international standard varieties that may or may not each subsume other standard varieties. Each serves in a more or less ill-defined way as a reference norm for users of the language elsewhere. Furthermore, whether BrE and AmE are understood as national or international varieties, there is so much communication between them that items of language pass easily and quickly from one to the other, often without clear identification as primarily belonging to one or the other, or to some other variety.

Lexicographical ambiguity and vagueness. The ambiguity of the terms is reflected in dictionaries. When a dictionary labels something *BrE*, users can safely assume that it has more currency in Britain than in the US, but cannot be sure whether it is restricted to Britain or is used elsewhere, as for example in Australia or New Zealand. Often enough, the lexicographer using the label does not know either. The vagueness due to the easy passage between the two varieties is also reflected in dictionaries, by the tendency to qualify the labels with some such word as *chiefly* or *especially*, a tendency that appears to be increasing as communication between AmE and BrE increases: the 1st edition of the *American Heritage Dictionary* (1969) used both *British* and *Chiefly British* as labels, but the 2nd (1982) uses *Chiefly British* only. The use of qualifiers with BrE and AmE is in sharp contrast to their non-use with labels of certain other types: an item may be labelled *Slang* or *Archaic*, but not **Chiefly slang* or **esp archaic*. An item labelled *Chiefly BrE* or *esp BrE* is not more likely to be used in, say, Australia: it is more likely to be used in the US. Similarly, an item labelled *Chiefly AmE* or *esp AmE* is not more likely to be used in, say, Canada: it is more likely to be used in Britain. In this respect, qualifiers like *Chiefly* and *esp* loosen the national restrictions on BrE and AmE, but do not affect their international range, which is already rather ill defined.

National standards. In the following discussion, the emphasis is first on AmE and BrE as two national standard varieties and then on their differences rather than their similarities. Paradoxically, the desire for a discussion of British/American differences reflects an underlying confidence that the similarities between them are greater: even if Americans and Britons are said to be 'divided by a common language', the language remains essentially common, especially in terms of standard usage. The two standard varieties are contrasted below in terms of spelling, pronunciation, grammar, vocabulary, and idioms.

Spelling. Most spelling differences between BrE and AmE do not signal differences in pronunciation. Rather, they serve as emblems or shibboleths of linguistic nationalism. It is primarily spelling that indicates whether a text is British or American in origin. By and large, the adoption of certain spellings in AmE has impeded their use in BrE or hastened their decline if they were used in that variety: such AmE *-or* spellings as *color* were once freely available alternatives to *-our* in BrE. However, when spelling is 'normalized' to one or other print standard, it may no longer be possible to identify the source of a text. It was once common to change the spelling of American books published in Britain, but in recent years the practice has been less common. This may mean that British linguistic nationalism is waning, or simply that the practice costs less, but since it also makes American texts easier to identify in British editions, it may slow down the adoption of expressions and constructions identified as AmE in those texts. There are two ways in which the orthographic differences can be classified: systemic or non-systemic; exclusive or non-exclusive.

(1) *Systemic or non-systemic differences*. If a difference is systemic, it affects large classes of words; if non-systemic, it affects only one word or a small group of words. By and large, the difference between BrE *colour*, AmE *color* is systemic, affecting such words as *hono(u)r*, *favo(u)r*, *neighbo(u)r*, *vigo(u)r* (but note *languor*, *stupor*, *torpor*, etc., in both varieties). The BrE variant *gaol* (by contrast with the common *jail*) is non-systemic, affecting

only one word and its inflections (*gaols*), derivatives (*gaoler*), and compounds (*gaolbird*). Occasionally, variants exist in both varieties: the optional *e* in *abridg(e)ment*, *acknowledg(e)ment*, *judg(e)ment* can be found in both AmE and BrE.

(2) *Exclusive or non-exclusive differences*. When writing *colo(u)r*, either a BrE or an AmE spelling must be chosen; there is no international alternative. In the case of *gaol/jail*, however, there is a choice between local *gaol* and international *jail*. In the case of *ax(e)*, an international variant *axe* coexists with an *ax* that is now AmE, though it was once used in BrE: in 1884, the *Oxford English Dictionary* favoured this spelling, but in 1989 2nd edition has changed to *axe*. There seem to be no cases of an international spelling variant coexisting with a marked BrE variant on one side and a marked AmE variant on the other.

All permutations and combinations of the two categories are possible: *colour/color*, systemic exclusive variants; the suffixes *-ise/-ize*, systemic non-exclusive variants in BrE; *gaol/jail*, *axe/ax*, non-systemic, non-exclusive variants in BrE and AmE respectively; in banking, *cheque/check*, non-systemic exclusive variants. Among the principal systemic variants are:

(1) *The colo(u)r group*. Most words of the type *color/colour* are from Latin or French: *arbo(u)r*, *armo(u)r*, *endeavo(u)r*, *favo(u)r*, *flavo(u)r*, *hono(u)r*, *humo(u)r*, *labo(u)r*, *odo(u)r*, *rigo(u)r*, *savo(u)r*, *tumo(u)r*, *valo(u)r*, *vigo(u)r*. In Latin, their forms are uniformly *-or* (*arbor*, *odor*) and in Modern French their cognates may have *-eur* (*couleur*, *honneur*). Some, however, are Germanic in origin (*harbo(u)r*, *neighbo(u)r*) and seem to have picked up their *u* by analogy. The BrE *u* is not used in words, other than *neighbo(u)r*, that readily refer to people: *actor*, *author*, *emperor*, *governor*, *survivor*, *tenor* are the same in both varieties, though especially during the 16–17c such spellings as *emperour*, *governour* occurred. In such cases, the *-or* is generally interpreted as an agent suffix like the vernacular *-er*: *author* is as invariable in its spelling as *writer*. There are, however, a number of anomalies: such words as *error*, *mirror*, *pallor*, *terror*, *tremor* have no *u* in BrE, and in AmE the spellings *glamor*, *savior*, *savor* are non-exclusive variants, coexisting with the international *glamour*, *saviour*, *savour*. *Saviour* appears to be the last surviving *-our* agent suffix referring to a person. In AmE, the *colo(u)r* group has *-or-* in its inflections (*coloring*), derivatives (*colorful*, *coloration*), and compounds (*color-blind*). BrE derivatives are more complex. Before vernacular suffixes, the *u* is retained: *armourer*, *colourful*, *flavoursome*, *savoury*. It is also kept before the French suffix *-able*: *honourable*. Before Latinate suffixes, however, it is dropped: *honorary*, *honorific*, *humorous*, *humorist*, *coloration*, *deodorize*, *invigorate*. In such cases, AmE and BrE

spellings are the same. Even so, there are some residual anomalies: BrE keeps the *u* in *colourist* and AmE can have the *u* in *savoury* and appears to be more likely than BrE to have a *u* in *glamo(u)rize* and *glamo(u)rous*.

(2) *The centre/center group*. In words of this type, BrE has -*re* and AmE -*er*, and the difference is exclusive. The chief members are of non-Germanic origin and are: *centre/center*, *fibre/fiber*, *goitre/goiter*, *litre/liter*, *meagre/meager*, *mitre/miter*, *sabre/saber*, *sombre/somber*, *spectre/specter*, *theatre/theater*. The agent suffix -*er* (as in *writer*) and comparative ending -*er* (as in *colder*) are unaffected. Many words in both varieties have -*er* (*banter, canter*) and -*re* (*acre, lucre, massacre, mediocre, ogre*). In the case of the second group, an -*er* spelling would suggest a misleading pronunciation (therefore no **acer, *lucer*, etc.). BrE distinguishes *metre* (unit of measurement) from *meter* (instrument for measuring; prosody), but AmE uses *meter* for both. Though *theater* is the preferred AmE spelling, *theatre* is common as a part of a name. Generally, the differences are preserved in inflections (*centred/centered*) and compounds (*centrefold/centerfold*), but usually vanish in derivatives through the loss of the *e*, which is no longer pronounced (*central, fibrous, metric/metrical, theatrical*).

(3) *The (o)estrogen group*. In words of Greek origin (in which an original *oi* became a Latin ligature *æ*), BrE has *oe* in exclusive variants, AmE *e* or less commonly *oe*, typically in non-exclusive variants: *am(o)eba, diarrh(o)ea, hom(o)eopathy, (o)esophagus, (o)estrogen, (o)estrous*. The differences are maintained in all inflections, derivatives, and compounds. Two words of Latin origin have been assimilated into this class, *f(o)etus* and *f(o)etid*. In both varieties, all trace of the earlier *oeconomy, oeconomical, oecumenical* has gone (in *economy, economic/economical, ecumenical*, etc.). Within a word, (*o*)*e* is pronounced /iː/ in both varieties; at the beginning it is pronounced /iː/ in BrE and may be so pronounced in AmE, though *e* tends to be pronounced /ɛ/. The pronunciation of BrE *oestrogen* is therefore 'ees-', of AmE *estrogen* is generally 'ess-'.

(4) *The (a)esthete group*. In words of classical (ultimately Greek) origin in which a Neo-Latin *æ* passed into English as *æ* then *ae*, BrE has tended to keep *ae* as an exclusive variant and AmE has had *e* and *ae* as non-exclusive variants: (*a*)*eon*, *arch(a)eology, gyn(a)ecology, (a)esthetics, an(a)emia, encyclop(a)edia, h(a)emophilia, h(a)emorrhage, medi(a)eval, pal(a)eontology*. The spelling differences are maintained in inflections, derivatives, and compounds. In the case of (*a*)*esthete* and its derivatives, the spelling can signal a difference in pronunciation: beginning in BrE with /iː/, /i/, or /ɛ/

and in AmE with /ɛ/. Elsewhere in this class, however, (*a*)*e* is pronounced /iː/ in both varieties. One classical form keeps *ae* in both varieties: *aer-* as in *aerate, aerobics, aerodynamics, aerosol*. In both varieties, *encyclopedia* and *medieval* are commoner than *encyclopaedia* and *mediaeval*, but where BrE pronunciation typically begins 'meddy', AmE pronunciation often begins 'meedy'. There is now a tendency for *e* and *ae* to become non-exclusive variants in BrE in such words as *co-eval, primeval* and *archeology, gynecology*.

(5) *The instil(l) group*. In such words, BrE has a single written vowel plus -*l* and AmE has a single written vowel plus -*ll*, and the exclusive variants are all disyllabic verbs stressed on the second syllable: *distil(l), enrol(l), fulfil(l), instil(l)*. Exceptionally, *extol* prevails in AmE over *extoll*. Verbs like this but with *a* in the second syllable belong to this class in AmE: *appall, enthrall, install*. In BrE, however, the preferences vary: *appal, befall, enthral, install*. The verb *annul* has -*l* in both varieties.

(6) *The final -l(l) group*. In BrE, verbs that end in a single written vowel plus -*l* or -*ll* keep them before -*s* (*travels, fulfills*), have -*l* before -*ment* (*instalment, fulfilment*), and have -*ll* before a suffix beginning with a vowel (*travelling, fulfilling*). In AmE, verbs that end with a single written vowel plus -*l* or -*ll* keep them before -*s* and -*ment* (*fulfillment, installment*); before a suffix beginning with a vowel, the verbs ending with -*ll* keep both letters (*fulfilling*), but the verbs ending with -*l* either have -*ll* as in BrE (*compelling, cavilling*) or more usually follow the general rules for doubling final consonants (*compelling, caviling*). Sometimes the result is the same for both varieties: *compel, compels, compelled*. Sometimes it is different: *travel, travels, travelled, traveller* shared by both, but AmE generally *travels, traveled, traveler*. *Parallel* does not usually double its final -*l* in either variety.

(7) *The -ize and -ise group*. Some verbs can only have -*ize*: *capsize, seize*. In some, only -*ise* is possible: *advise, surprise*. In many, both -*ise* and -*ize* are possible, as in *civilise/civilize, organise/organize*, and the -*s*- or -*z*- is preserved in derivatives: *civilisation/civilization*. For such verbs, AmE has systemic, exclusive -*ize*, and BrE has both -*ise* and -*ize*. In AusE, -*ise* is preferred. British publishers generally have their own house styles: among dictionary publishers, -*ize* is preferred by Cassell, Collins, Longman, Oxford, -*ise* by the Reader's Digest (UK). Chambers has -*ise* for its native-speaker dictionaries, -*ize* for its EFL learners' dictionary, intended for an international public. There is no infallible rule identifying the verbs that take both, but they generally form nouns in -*tion*. With the exception of *improvise/improvisation*, verbs that take only -*ise* do not generally have a noun in -*tion*: *revise/revision, advise/advice*. However, some verbs that allow

both forms do not form nouns in *-tion*: *apologise/ize*, *apology*; *aggrandise/ize*, *aggrandisement*, *aggrandizement*.

(8) *The -lyse and -lyze group*. In such verbs as *analyse/analyze* and *paralyse/paralyze*, BrE prefers *-lyse* and AmE *-lyze*. The variants are systemic and have been mutually exclusive, but recently *analyze* has begun to appear in BrE. The difference disappears in corresponding nouns: *analysis*, *paralysis* are international, as the /z/ of the verbs becomes /s/ in the nouns.

(9) *The -og(ue) group*. Although in words like *catalog(ue)*, *dialog(ue)*, *monolog(ue)*, *pedagog(ue)*, *prolog(ue)*, AmE sometimes drops *-ue*, only *catalog* is a widely used AmE variant. Thus, such spellings are systemic, non-exclusive variants in AmE. *Analog(ue)* is a special case: the spelling *analog* prevails in contrast with *digital* when referring to such things as computers, but that is true not only in AmE but also in BrE, where AmE spellings are generally used in the register of computing.

Conclusion. (1) Where differences exist, AmE spellings tend to be shorter than BrE spellings: *catalog*, *color*; AmE *jewelry*, *jeweler*, BrE *jewellery*, *jeweller*; AmE *councilor*, *counselor*, BrE *councillor*, *counsellor*. Exceptions include: AmE *instill* and *installment*, BrE *instil* and *instalment*; AmE *skillful* and *thralldom*, BrE *skilful* and *thraldom*. (2) In general terms, a spelling used in Britain is more likely to be acceptable in America than is an American spelling in Britain. BrE seems sometimes to use spelling to distinguish items with the same pronunciation: *tyre* and *tire*, *cheque* and *check*, *kerb* in a street and *curb* restrain/restraint. AmE seems to do this rarely: moral *vice* and *vise* the tool.

Pronunciation. Because BrE and AmE spelling can be seen in printed and edited texts, comparing and contrasting them is more or less straightforward, but because of the diversity of speech forms within AmE and BrE, there is no analogous basis for comparing BrE and AmE pronunciation. What follows is a comparison of two major features in the pronunciations shown in British dictionaries, typically based on the accent called *Received Pronunciation* or *RP*, with those in American dictionaries, typically clustering round a set of pronunciations often called *General American* or *GA*: see GENERAL AMERICAN, RECEIVED PRONUNCIATION.

(1) *The treatment of R*. GA is rhotic and RP non-rhotic: that is, in GA, /r/ is pronounced in all positions in words like *rare*, *rarer*, but in RP it is not pronounced unless a vowel follows. In RP, therefore, /r/ does not occur finally in *rare* and *rarer* unless followed by a word beginning with a vowel: *a rare article*, *a rarer article*. Generally, /r/ is a retroflex consonant in GA and

an alveolar consonant in RP: see RHOTIC AND NON-RHOTIC, R-SOUNDS.

(2) *The treatment of A*. In about 150 words where the sound represented by the letter *a* precedes a fricative (such as /s, f, θ/) or a nasal (such as /n, m/) followed by another consonant, GA has /a/ and RP /ɑ/, as in: *after*, *can't*, *dance*, *fast*, *half*, *pass*, *past*. Other cases of /a/ versus /ɑ/ include *aunt*, *example*, *laugh*, *draught*, *sample*, and the second *a* of *banana*. The RP pronunciation is widely known as the 'broad *a*', and is considered 'posh' in Britain and 'tony' or affected in America. It is in fact a phonological bone of contention throughout the English-speaking world. In RP, in the pronunciation of the broad *a*, there are many traps for the unwary: *grant*, *slant* have the broad *a*, but *cant*, *grand*, *hand*, *pant* do not. Words such as *translate* and *telegraph* may or may not have it, and *telegraphic* does not.

Grammar. A discussion of grammatical differences is closer to a discussion of spelling than of pronunciation, because it can be based on textual evidence. The following are significant contrasts:

(1) *Shall/will*. Though *shall* is even less common in AmE than in BrE, the only significant differences concern two of the least common BrE uses: second-person questions and the contraction *shan't*, as in *Shall you be at the embassy reception?—No, I'm afraid I shan't*. Both are virtually unknown in AmE. As for *will*, two of its BrE uses are much less likely in AmE: inference *will*, roughly equivalent to *must* (*That will be the postman at the door*); stressed *will* indicating a disagreeable habit or practice (*He WILL keep telling us about his operation!*).

(2) *Should/would*. In polite first-person statements (*We should be happy to comply with your request*), *should* is rarer in AmE than in BrE, particularly in advice-giving formulas (*I should dress warmly if I were you*). *Should* is also rarer in AmE in its putative use: *I demand that they should leave*; *It is astonishing that they should have left without telling me*. *Would* is primarily BrE in uses that parallel *will* above: *That would have been the postman at the door*; *He WOULD keep telling us about his operation!* However, it seems to be primarily AmE as an initial equivalent of *used to*: *When I was young, I would get up early*, though as a subsequent substitute for *used to* it is shared: *I used to get up early and before breakfast I would go jogging*.

(3) *Can/may*. Both varieties use *can* freely for permission as well as ability, a usage formerly discouraged on both sides of the Atlantic: *You can see him now* (*You are permitted to see him*). In a negative inferential sentence like *If you got wet you can't have taken your umbrella*, *can't*

is more likely in BrE than AmE, which allows *mustn't* (see following).

(4) *Must/have (got) to.* An affirmative inferential sentence like *This has to be/This has got to be the best novel this year* is more likely to be AmE than BrE, though it is becoming an alternative in BrE to the shared *This must be the best novel this year.* A negative inferential sentence like *If you got wet you mustn't have taken your umbrella* is AmE rather than standard BrE, which uses *can't* (see preceding).

(5) *Have (got).* There have been differences between BrE and AmE in the use of *have,* but in the last decade they have become largely of historical interest only. The major surviving difference is the past form *had got: She left because she'd got a lot to do/she'd got to do a lot* is a largely BrE alternative to the shared *She left because she had a lot to do/she had to do a lot.*

(6) *Let's.* The negative form *let's not (argue)* is shared, coexisting with the chiefly BrE variant *don't let's (argue)* and the AmE variant *let's don't (argue),* often reproved as non-standard.

(7) *Subjunctive forms.* After words like *demand,* several constructions are possible: *I demanded that he should (not) leave* (more BrE than AmE), *I demanded that he (not) leave* (somewhat more AmE than BrE, especially with *not*), *I demanded that he left/didn't leave* (far more BrE than AmE).

(8) *Perfective forms.* With *yet* and *already,* such perfective sentences as *Have you eaten yet?* and *They've already left* are shared usages. Such alternatives as *Did you eat yet?* and *They left already* are virtually exclusive to AmE, but may be regarded as non-standard.

(9) *Tag forms.* Such sentences as *They're here, aren't they?* combine positive and negative verb forms and are shared. Such sentences as *So they're/They're here, are they?* combine positive with positive and are somewhat more BrE than AmE. Such sentences as *So they/They didn't do it, didn't they?* combine negative with negative, are virtually exclusive to BrE, and are not used freely even by all BrE speakers. Tags used otherwise than to elicit or confirm information tend to be more BrE than AmE, in particular peremptory and aggressive tags such as *You'll just have to wait and see, won't you?* and *I don't know the answer, do I?*

(10) *Give.* The form *Give me it* is shared, while *Give it me* is BrE.

(11) *Provide.* The form *That provided us with an excuse* is shared, while *That provided us an excuse* is AmE.

(12) *Enough.* The form *They're rich enough to retire* is shared, while *They're rich enough that they can retire* is chiefly AmE.

(13) *Agree, approximate, protest.* The forms *They agreed to the plan* and *They agreed on the plan* are shared, while *They agreed the plan* is BrE. *That approximates to the truth* is chiefly BrE, while *That approximates the truth* is AmE. *They protested their innocence* and *They protested against/at the verdict* are shared; *They protested the verdict* is AmE.

(14) *Time expressions.* The form *Monday to Friday inclusive* is shared, while the synonymous *Monday through Friday* is AmE. *Monday through to Friday* is BrE, and may be ambiguous as to whether Friday itself is included. The forms *a week from today* and *a week from Friday* are shared, while *a week today, a week on Friday, Friday week* are BrE. The form *half past six* is shared, and coexists with the informal BrE *half six.* The use of *past* in time expressions (*10 past 6,* (*a*) *quarter past 6*) is shared; the corresponding use of *after* (*10 after 6,* (*a*) *quarter after 6*) is chiefly AmE. The form *ten (minutes) to six* is shared, while *ten (minutes) of six* is AmE.

(15) *Go, come.* The forms *Go and see/Come and see what you have done* are shared, while *Go see/Come see what you have done* are AmE.

(16) *One.* The form *If one does one's best, one will succeed* is shared and tends to be formal in both varieties, while *If one does his best, he will succeed* is AmE (and under attack by feminists and others as sexist usage).

(17) *Group nouns.* Such a collective usage as *The government is divided* is shared, while *The government are divided,* emphasizing the members of the group, is chiefly BrE.

(18) *Collocations.* There are many differences of idiom. The collocations *go to church/school/college* and *be at church/school/college* are shared, but *go to university/be at university* and *go to hospital/be in hospital* are BrE, AmE requiring *the* as in *go to the university.* Forms like *in a jubilant mood* are shared, but *in jubilant mood* is BrE. The expressions *on offer* and *in future* are BrE, the former the equivalent of the shared *being offered,* the latter of the shared *from now on/from then on.* The form *in the future* is shared. The form *do a deal* is BrE and *make a deal* is AmE. *Take a decision* is chiefly BrE, though *make a decision* is shared. *Seems/Looks like a good deal* is shared, but *Seems/Looks a good deal* is chiefly BrE. *Members of* is shared; *membership of* is BrE; *membership in* is AmE.

Vocabulary and idioms. As with differences in spelling, lexical differences can be divided into the exclusive (such as BrE *windscreen,* AmE *windshield*), and the non-exclusive. The non-exclusive differences subdivide into those in which the shared variant coexists with an exclusive usage (such as shared *editorial,* BrE *leader;*

shared *autumn*, AmE *fall*), and those in which a shared variant coexists with both a BrE variant and an AmE variant (shared *socket*, BrE *power point*, AmE *outlet*). Systemic differences in vocabulary are due to two factors: source and subject. AmE and BrE draw on different sources for certain words, especially in informal styles, AmE drawing for example on Spanish because of its associations with Latin America (see AMERICAN ENGLISH, DIALECT IN AMERICA), BrE drawing for example on Hindustani because of its long connection with India (see COCKNEY). They have also developed differences in some subjects more than others. In areas of technology that developed before the European settlement of America, such as sailing, differences are small; in those developed in the 19c, such as rail and automotive transport, they are much greater, but in 20c technology, such as aviation, they are few. In the vocabulary of computing, AmE spellings are used in BrE, such as *program*, *disk*, while BrE *programming* is used in AmE. For further discussion and examples of differences, see AMERICANISM, BRITICISM.

AmE and BrE sometimes have slightly different idioms, such as: BrE *a home from home, leave well alone, a storm in a teacup, blow one's own trumpet, sweep under the carpet*, AmE *a home away from home, leave well enough alone, a tempest in a teacup/teapot, blow one's own horn, sweep under the rug*. The use of prepositions is often different: for example, Americans live *on* a street while Britons live *in* a street; they cater *to* people where Britons cater *for* them; they do something *on* the weekend where Britons do it *at* the weekend; are *of* two minds about something while Britons are *in* two minds; have a new lease *on* life where Britons have a new lease *of* life. American students are *in* a course and British students are *on* a course. Americans can leave Monday while Britons must leave *on* Monday. See AMERICAN ENGLISH, BRITISH ENGLISH, DATE, ENGLISH, STANDARD, VARIETY, and the letter entries E, L, O, R, Z. [AMERICAS, EUROPE, VARIETY]. R.F.I.

Algeo, John. 1989. 'British–American Lexical Differences: A Typology of Interdialectal Variation', in O. Garcia & R. Otheguy (eds.), *English across Cultures, Cultures across English*. Berlin & New York: Mouton de Gruyter.
Benson, Morton, Benson, Evelyn, & Ilson, Robert. 1986. *Lexicographic Description of English*. Amsterdam & Philadelphia: John Benjamins. Especially ch. 2, 'Modern Varieties of English: British and American'.
Ilson, Robert. 1985. 'Diversity in Unity: American and British English', in *English Today*, no. 4.
Schur, Norman W. 1973. *British Self-Taught: With Comments on American*. New York: Macmillan. 1974: a slightly revised edition, London & Edinburgh: Johnston & Bacon. 1980: reissued as *English*, Essex, Connecticut: Verbatim Books. 1987: revised and reissued as *British English, A to Zed*, New York & Oxford: Facts on File.

AMERICANESE [Late 20c]. An occasional disparaging or facetious term for American English: 'People in this country do not speak the Queen's English—they speak Americanese, which at times bears only a passing resemblance to my native tongue' (Angela Rippon, 'Boston Diary', *Sunday Times*, 15 July 1984). Compare AMERENGLISH, AMERICAN[2], AMERICAN ENGLISH, AMERICAN LANGUAGE, AUSTRALIANESE. See -ESE. [AMERICAS, VARIETY]. T.MCA.

AMERICAN HERITAGE DICTIONARY, full form *American Heritage Dictionary of the English Language*. Short form *AHD*. A major contemporary American dictionary. Following the adversely critical reception of the 3rd edition of *Webster's New International Dictionary* (Merriam, 1961), James Parton, founder of *American Heritage* (a publisher of history and culture magazines), announced his intention to purchase Merriam and revise *Webster's Third* to reflect the taste of most of its reviewers. Failing in this aim, in 1964 he entered into an agreement with Houghton Mifflin to bring out a new dictionary edited by William Morris. *The American Heritage Dictionary of the English Language* was published in 1969, larger than the desk dictionaries of the day but much smaller than *Webster's Third* and *The Random House Dictionary of the English Language*. Innovations included illustrations in the outside margins of every page, an appendix of Indo-European roots (later dropped for lack of popular interest, but published as a separate title in 1985), and a usage panel (whose average age was 64, with 11 women members out of 105). While the panel's comments are reported for only 318 items, sales promotion presented the *AHD* as an alternative to dictionaries that reflect 'these permissive times' and as 'the single source for people who need to be right'. In 1969, American Heritage was sold to McGraw-Hill, which gave control of its dictionary department to Houghton Mifflin. A college version appeared in 1970, a photo-reduction of the original intended to match competitors in page size. A second college edition (1985), with Margery S. Berube as editorial director, had a reconstituted usage panel and 'over 400 new usage notes', including minor rewriting of the original notes. In other respects, the *AHD* resembled its competition in coverage, pronunciation, and sense analysis. See READER'S DIGEST, USAGE GUIDANCE AND CRITICISM, WEBSTER'S NEW INTERNATIONAL DICTIONARY. [AMERICAS, REFERENCE, USAGE]. R.W.B.

AMERICANISM [18c: on the analogy of *Scotticism*, first used in a publication in Philadelphia in 1781 by the Revd John Witherspoon, a Scot and a signer of the Declaration of Independence]. A usage or custom peculiar to, or common in, the US. The term refers primarily to English words and phrases that acquired a new sense (*bluff, corn, lumber*) or entered the language (*OK, raccoon, squash*) in what is now the US, but also to features of pronunciation, grammar, and sentence structure. A discussion of the problem of defining the term, with many examples, appears in H. L. Mencken's *The American Language* (4th edition, 1936). *A Dictionary of Americanisms* (1951), by Mitford Mathews, lists words and senses that originated in what is now the US but it is out of date; it is supplemented by *Webster's New World Dictionary* (3rd college edition, 1988), which marks US forms and senses with stars. *A Dictionary of American English* (1938–44), ed. William A. Craigie and James R. Hulbert, lists two kinds of Americanism: forms that originated in the US and those that are characteristic of US life, even though originally British. The term has often been used contrastively, especially in the US with *Briticism*. 'Bilingual' lists, drawn up for both academic and popular purposes, commonly contrast items in pairs, one being identified as the American usage, the other as the British equivalent (or vice versa). The following list contains a number of pairs of words and phrases (Briticisms first, Americanisms second) widely regarded as distinguishing AmE from BrE: *accommodation* (uncountable), *accommodations* (countable plural), with regard to rooms in hotels, etc.; *aluminium, aluminum; anticlockwise, counterclockwise; biscuit, cookie; bonnet, hood* (of a car); *boot, trunk* (of a car); *candy floss, cotton candy; caravan, trailer* (pulled by a car); *cornflour, cornstarch; cot, crib; drawing pin, thumbtack; fanlight, transom; founder member, charter member; goods train, freight train; high street, main street* (of a town); *hoarding, billboard; jumble sale, rummage sale; lift, elevator;* the abbreviations *maths* and *math; nappy, diaper; noticeboard, bulletin board; noughts and crosses, tick-tack-toe; number plate, licence plate* (for a road vehicle); *pavement, sidewalk; pelmet, valence; petrol, gas(oline); post code, zip code; return ticket, round trip ticket; right-angled triangle, right triangle;* a *rise, raise* (in salary); *rowing-boat, rowboat; sailing boat, sailboat; silencer, muffler* (on a car); *single ticket, one way ticket; skirting board, baseboard; sledge, sled; sweets, (hard) candy; torch, flashlight* (powered by batteries); *windscreen, windshield* (on a vehicle); *zip, zipper*. See AMERICAN ENGLISH AND BRITISH ENGLISH, AMERICAN LANGUAGE (THE), BRITICISM, DICTIONARY OF AMERICAN ENGLISH, DICTIONARY OF AMERICANISMS, -ISM, MATHEWS, MENCKEN. [AMERICAS, STYLE, VARIETY, REFERENCE, WORD].
C.C.E., J.A., T.MCA.

AMERICANISTICS. See ANGLICIST.

AMERICAN LANGUAGE [19c]. A term that presents American English as a national language, sometimes as an aggressive assertion of independence from the standard language of England: 'This occasional tolerance for things American was never extended to the American language' (H. L. Mencken, *The American Language*, 4th edition, 1936); 'The official language of the State of Illinois shall be known hereafter as the American language, and not as the English language' (Act of the Legislature of Illinois, ch. 127, sect. 178, 1923); 'George Bush is hardly known for his rhetorical gifts. But his speech at last summer's Republican Convention has already left its mark on the American language' (Laurence Zuckerman, 'Read My Cliché', *Time*, 16 Jan. 1989). Compare AMERICAN[2], AMERICANESE. See AMERICAN ENGLISH, AMERICAN LITERATURE. [AMERICAS, VARIETY].
T.MCA.

AMERICAN LANGUAGE, The, short form *AL*. An encyclopedic study of English in the US by Henry Louis Mencken (New York: Alfred A. Knopf, 1919), which demonstrates the distinctness of AmE, chronicles the contributions of each of the nation's major ethnic groups to the language, and stresses American linguistic creativity and independence. With *AL*, Mencken sought to remedy the lack of information available on AmE varieties and its neglect by the academic community. His work stimulated so much interest in the subject that his goal has been fulfilled. The first edition appeared at the end of World War I, at a time of isolationism and anti-British feeling over Ireland and Palestine. Between 1917 and 1923, many US states and cities were passing laws of various kinds relating to English and other languages: making English, or, in some cases, American, their official language; curtailing the teaching of foreign languages in schools; or even prohibiting the use of foreign languages in public.

The timeliness of Mencken's book and his criticism of the English of England as stuffy and artificial made the initial edition immensely popular. Mencken, however, was not entirely an anglophobe. He insisted that he was 'bilingual', adding, 'I can write English, as in this clause, quite as readily as American, as in this here one.' As this example shows, Mencken's book is based on a joke, by which he compares formal standard BrE with informal non-standard AmE. He preferred AmE spelling but BrE intonation, seeking 'a compromise dialect which embodies the common materials of both', though he acknowledged that such a dialect 'is the living speech of neither' (1919). In *AL*, he explores many aspects of AmE use, such as slang (for example the derivation of *OK*), the process of word coinage (his own inventiveness produced *ecdysiast* for *stripper*), and lists of non-standard American pronouns (*this-here, hisn, thesen*). Although his judgements are often more chauvinistic than scientific, his lists and citations provide valuable data. In 1919, he assured his readers of the inevitable divergence of the two major streams of English, an 18c theme on both sides of the Atlantic revived in the 1970s by Robert Burchfield, editor of the *OED* Supplements.

By the 4th edition, however, Mencken had come to believe that the gap was narrowing. Insisting 'that the American of today is much more honestly English . . . than the so-called Standard English of England' (1936), he predicted that instead of diverging, English in England would one day become a dialect of American. Revised and enlarged editions of the *AL* appeared in 1921, 1923, and 1936, and two large supplements to the 4th edition in 1945 and 1948. The later editions used anecdotal contributions from readers as well as contemporary AmE scholarship. Mencken ignored 20c developments in linguistics. A 1963 abridgement and conflation of the 4th edition and its supplements (which remain in print as a three-volume set) was edited with additions by Raven I. McDavid Jr. Compare AUSTRALIAN LANGUAGE (THE), KING'S ENGLISH (THE). See AMERICAN SPEECH, MENCKEN. [AMERICAS, MEDIA, USAGE].   D.E.B.

AMERICAN LANGUAGES. A term that covers both the languages of the western hemisphere and the languages of the US (indigenous and immigrant). In the hemispheric sense, the indigenous languages (often referred to as *Native American languages*) range from Alaska to Tierra del Fuego, and include the Amerindian languages and those of the Aleut and Inuit (Eskimo). Indigenous mainland communities in Central and South America have had close contact with Spanish (and with Portuguese in Brazil), but little contact with English, with the exception of Belize, Guyana, Honduras, Nicaragua, and Panama. In the national sense, the indigenous languages constitute a diverse group from the Atlantic to the Pacific (*Algonquian, Iroquoian, Siouan, Hopi, Navajo, Chinook*, etc.), as well as the languages of Alaska and Hawaii. Contacts with European languages have prim-

arily been with Dutch, English, French, Russian, and Spanish. Before the arrival of Europeans, lingua francas were used among various peoples; afterwards, pidgins based on European languages also developed.

The number of languages used in the United States is large. It has been estimated that 'about twenty-eight millions, or about 1 in 8, of the inhabitants of the USA have a language other than English as their mother tongue or live in a household where such a language is spoken' (Ferguson & Heath, introduction; below). In addition, there are scores of minority-language newspapers and radio stations. The US situation is marked by the dominance of English, the spread of Spanish, the survival of French in enclaves, the concentration of immigrant languages in certain areas, and the weakness of the Native American languages. In descending order for numbers of speakers, the main languages of the US are: English, Spanish, Italian, German, French, Polish, Chinese, Filipino, Japanese, Korean, and Vietnamese. Works on language in the US include *A Pluralistic Nation: The Language Issue in the United States*, ed. Margaret A. Lourie & Nancy F. Conklin (Newbury House, 1978) and *Language in the USA*, ed. Charles A. Ferguson & Shirley B. Heath (Cambridge University Press, 1981).

See AFRO-SEMINOLE, AMERICAN ENGLISH, AMERICAN PLACE-NAMES, AMERINDIAN PIDGIN ENGLISH, BAY ISLANDS, BELIZE, BLACK ENGLISH VERNACULAR, BORROWING, CANADIAN LANGUAGES, CARIBBEAN LANGUAGES, CHINOOK JARGON, DUTCH, FRENCH, GULLAH, GUYANA, INDIAN ENGLISH[2], PANAMA, PENNSYLVANIA DUTCH, PORTUGUESE, RED ENGLISH, SPANISH. [AMERICAS, LANGUAGE].

T.MCA.

AMERICAN LITERATURE. In the 18c, as the ties between the American colonies and Great Britain were weakening, the expression of sentiments urging writers to turn away from British literary models and celebrate the grandeur of the New World became increasingly strong. At the end of the Revolutionary War (1775–83), literary independence seemed to many as important as political independence. A bit of verse in 1786 conveys the mood: 'Shall we ever be thought to have learning or grace, / Unless it be brought from that damnable place?' (in Leary, below). In the wake of a second war in 1812, Sydney Smith asked in the *Edinburgh Review* (Jan. 1820) the infuriating question: 'In the four quarters of the globe, who reads an American book?' Still smouldering thirty years later, Herman Melville, while reviewing Nathaniel Hawthorne's *Mosses from an Old Manse* (1846), responded to Smith's taunt: 'And the day will come when you shall say who reads an English book that is a modern?'

The books that Hawthorne, Melville, Harriet Beecher Stowe, Henry David Thoreau, Frederick Douglass, and Walt Whitman produced between 1850 and 1855 were powerful answers to Smith's question. To these books, the crowning achievement of what has come to be known as the *American Renaissance*, should be added Emily Dickinson's poetry, begun about 1858 and unpublished during her lifetime. These writings incorporate, in different ways and degrees, what Perry Miller has called 'the majesty of the truly plain style' (below).

Puritan plain style. In the beginning was the Word and it was to the Word that the English Puritans of the 17c entrusted their lives and salvation. Miller has described how, during the years in which John Cotton became famous for his pulpit oratory at the University of Cambridge, 'crowds came to revel in his erudition and fancy, much as other crowds came to admire the spectacle of John Donne at St. Paul's in London'. Cotton's conversion to Puritanism was made instantly obvious not by doctrinal exposition but when, abruptly on a memorable Sunday, he began speaking in the plain style. A few years after his emigration to New England, Cotton wrote in the preface of *The Bay Psalm Book* (1639): 'If therefore the verses are not always so smooth and elegant as some may desire or expect; let them consider that Gods Altar needs not our pollishings.' The Altar of God for the American Puritans included not only verses in the Bible but also the ways in which divine providence was revealed among people and in nature, including the wilderness, in which the plain style was an essential tool for spiritual survival. Even after intellectual upheavals undermined the promises of the Puritan migration, these citizens of the wilderness (now spokesmen of the Revolution) made use of a forceful homely discourse that permeated 'the very language of the Declaration of Independence'. The American Literary Revolution, as it has been called, was in the making.

Colloquialism and dialect. A significant feature of that literary revolution was an extension of the plain style to include colloquial language and dialect. Long before the publication of Mark Twain's *Adventures of Huckleberry Finn* in 1884, in which dialect predominates, American writers such as Fenimore Cooper, Melville, Whitman, and Dickinson deployed a flexible and authentic colloquialism as an important tool in their powerful evocations of dark and bright truths about America and Americans. Though his language was occasionally high-flown and ornate, Cooper was a master of the colloquial style, and *The Pioneers* (1823) represents a significant turning-point in the rise of the American novel.

Offended by its coarse realism, the critic James G. Percival suggested that the novel was fit only 'to amuse the select society of a barber's shop or a porter-house'. Cooper was, however, aware of the sensibilities he was offending and has his narrator incorporate such a genteel critic into a passage giving an account of Ben Pump's not-so-genteel epithets. In addition, the frontiersman Natty Bumppo, unlike the dialect speakers in other novels of the period (who are usually treated in a comic way), powerfully expresses some of the writer's own views. In *The Pioneers* and other novels, Cooper creates a gallery of characters whose simple-shrewd attitudes are conveyed in a colourful idiom that points toward Mark Twain.

In *Moby-Dick*, Ishmael proclaims that a whaling vessel was his Yale College and his Harvard, as was also true for his creator, who gave up the sea to become a writer. At the heart of *Moby-Dick* is Father Mapple's sermon; the homely eloquence of a minister who was an ex-seaman and harpooneer speaks directly to the sailors of New Bedford. Ahab's speech in the novel veers from the nautical and homespun ('What say ye, men, will ye splice hands on it, now? I think ye do look brave') to the Shakespearian. In a lengthy footnote aimed at readers of *The Whale* (the British edition of *Moby-Dick*), Melville defended his use of nautical words as 'some of the best and furthest-descended English words—the etymological Howards and Percys—now democratised, nay, plebeianised—so to speak—in the New World'. His assertion that these 'sinewy Saxonisms' are neither corruptions nor inventions echoes a view widely held in America at the time. His defence, however, did not protect him from editorial interventions: 'Who aint a slave?' asks Ishmael in the opening chapter, a question decorously transformed by the British editor to 'Who is not a slave?'

An American language. In his old age, the poet Walt Whitman spoke of his lifelong preoccupation with a distinctively American language. Of *Leaves of Grass* (1855), the book he kept writing and rewriting all his life, he said: 'I sometimes think the Leaves is only a language experiment—that it is an attempt to give the spirit, the body, the man, new words, new potentialities of speech—an American, a cosmopolitan range of self-expression.' In the 1850s, he amassed notes for a lecture on the subject, published posthumously as *An American Primer* (1904). In them, he focused on the power and growth of an American English 'enjoying a distinct identity'. In the opening poem of *Leaves of Grass*, the speaker announces, 'I sound my barbaric yawp over the roofs of the world.' The phrase *barbaric yawp* pre-empts the criticism of the genteel reader while making an ally of the reader eager to turn away from gentility to confront a living voice. The book's format reinforced its message as a new American Bible: a slim quarto whose frontispiece portrait is of a bearded young man looking more like a working man than a poet.

Ralph Waldo Emerson responded enthusiastically to the copy that Whitman sent him. He had invoked just such a poet, one who would leave behind the dead language of libraries and lecture halls and respond to 'the voice of orators' and the 'Rude voices of the tavern hearth'. For 'the wonderful gift' of *Leaves of Grass*, Emerson conveyed his gratitude, and announced to the poet and the world: 'I greet you at the beginning of a great career, which yet must have had a long foreground, for such a start.' That career had its beginnings, in a real sense, in the shaping of a distinctively American language and literature, a shaping that began with the Puritan migration and continues today, many migrations later.

Genteel editing. Though Emily Dickinson's compression and hymn metres were far removed from Whitman's expansiveness and Biblical cadences, both were experimenters with the language. At the beginning of her correspondence with Thomas Wentworth Higginson, Dickinson told of her lexicon's great importance to her, referring to the family copy of the 1844 printing of Webster's *American Dictionary of the English Language*. Her lifelong search for the elusive words that 'Tell all the Truth but tell it slant' involved a syntactical and colloquial adventurousness that her New England editors tamed when a selection of her poems was posthumously printed in the 1890s, versions still reprinted in anthologies. A well-known poem about a certain slant of light that oppressed like the *heft of cathedral tunes* was changed to the more genteel *weight of cathedral tunes*; the last line of 'I never saw a Moor' was altered so that the colloquial term *checks* (stubs marked by a train conductor to validate a traveller's journey) was changed to a *chart* showing the way to heaven. Hundreds of such interventions were not corrected until 1955, when Thomas H. Johnson's monumental edition made Dickinson's 'letter to the world' (almost 1,800 poems) available as she had written it.

Mark Twain's South. 'In my opinion,' said William Faulkner late in his career, 'Mark Twain was the first truly American writer, and all of us since are his heirs' (*Faulkner at Nagano*, ed. Robert A. Jelliffe, 1956). Twain's revolutionary advance was to put an entire book, *Adventures of Huckleberry Finn* (1884), in the mouth of an illiterate country boy, whose story would artfully be told in an extreme form of the backwoods Southwestern dialect. At the outset, the author offers an explanatory note about these linguistic features, so that readers will not mistakenly 'suppose that all these characters were trying to talk alike and not succeeding'. Twain's linguistic virtuosity served the larger purpose of bringing to life, through numerous characters and shifting scenes, the antebellum world of the Mississippi and its villages. At one point, Huck makes up a story to explain his late appearance at the Phelps farm to kindly Aunt Sally:

'We been expecting you a couple of days and more. What kep' you?—boat get aground?'
    'Yes'm—she—'
    'Don't say yes'm—say Aunt Sally. Where'd she get aground?'
I didn't rightly know what to say, because I didn't know whether the boat would be coming up the river or down. . . . Now I struck an idea and fetched it out:
    'It warn't the grounding—that didn't keep us back just a little. We blowed out a cylinder-head.'
    'Good gracious! anybody hurt?'
    'No'm. Killed a nigger.'
    'Well, it's lucky; because sometimes people do get hurt.'

This grim joke was anticipated 23 years earlier by Melville in *Moby-Dick*: when gloomy Ahab asks the jovial captain of the whaler the *Bachelor*, 'Hast lost any men?' the answer comes back: 'Not enough to speak of—two [Polynesian] islanders, that's all . . .'. Alongside the frailties, fakeries, and cruelties wittily and savagely laid bare by Twain's experiment in language are passages (such as Huck telling of the coming of a dawn on the Mississippi) that stand alongside the haunting pictures of nature in *Moby-Dick* and *Walden*, pictures enlarged and vivified by a colloquial and distinctively American prose-poetry. 'The fantastic requirement of the plain style,' suggests Perry Miller (below), 'whether in the Puritan sermon or in *Huckleberry Finn*, is simply that language as printed on the page must convey the emphasis, the hesitancies, the searchings of language as it is spoken.' In a world of genteel literary language, 'it takes the ruse of speaking through the tongue of Huck Finn for a master stylist to put into print a prose that conforms to the irreducible plainness of the word spoken'. Such a prose tells 'more than he ever would attempt to say openly'.

William Faulkner's South. Although William Faulkner valued Twain as 'all of our grandfather', he rated *Moby-Dick* over *Huckleberry Finn* because 'it was bigger than one human being could do'. He found in Melville's style a fusion of grandeur and colloquialism that pointed the way to his own sagas of Yoknapatawpha county. Stephen M. Ross (below) sums up Faulkner's style as follows: 'Recordings of regional dialect ('Likely hit ain fittin for hawgs') harmonize, amazingly, with renderings of rhetorical floridity "constant and inflectioned and ceaseless".' From childhood, Faulkner listened to the voices around him in order to find his own: 'The South's the place for a novelist to grow up because the folks there talk so much about the past. Why, when I was a little boy there'd be sometimes twenty or thirty people in the house, mostly relatives . . . swapping stories about the family and about the past, while I sat in a corner and listened. That's where I got my books.' Faulkner was haunted by these voices and once told Malcolm Cowley that 'Sometimes I don't like what [the voices] say, but I don't change it.' Public oratory also helped to shape Faulkner's style, echoed in the prose of Thomas Wolfe, Robert Penn Warren, William Styron, and James Baldwin.

Black writing. 'Who aint a slave?' asks Ishmael in *Moby-Dick*; it was a question that haunted Melville, Twain, and Faulkner, and continues to haunt American writers. 'In the beginning was not only the word but the contradiction of the word', wrote Ralph Ellison about America's unresolved historical and moral predicament (*Going to the Territory*, 1986). The black writer Frederick Douglass, who was born in slavery in Maryland, drew on the call-and-response mode of discourse, the African and African-American form of song, speech, and sermons that he grew up with, to create enduring works of the American Renaissance: *Narrative of the Life of Frederick Douglass* (1845) and *My Bondage and My Freedom* (1855). An example of his deployment of call-and-response may be cited from this passage in Douglass's 1852 address to his fellow citizens in Rochester on the occasion of the great national holiday commemorating the adoption of the Declaration of Independence:

Would you have me argue that man is entitled to liberty? that he is the rightful owner of his own body? You have already declared it. Must I argue the wrongfulness of slavery? Is that a question for republicans? Is it to be settled by the rules of logic and argumentation, as a matter beset with great difficulty, involving a doubtful application of the principle of justice, hard to be understood? How should I look to-day in the presence of Americans, dividing and subdividing a discourse, to show that men have a natural right to freedom, speaking of it relatively and positively, negatively and affirmatively? To do so, would be to make myself ridiculous, and to offer an insult to your understanding. There is not a man beneath the canopy of heaven that does not know that slavery is wrong *for him* ('What to the Slave is the Fourth of July?', in *My Bondage and My Freedom*, ed. William L. Anderson, 1987).

John F. Callahan sees Douglass's art as linked to 'that organic American vernacular expression urged and practiced by Ralph Waldo Emerson in his lectures and essays' (below). Callahan

explores the ways in which Zora Neale Hurston, Ralph Ellison, Alice Walker, Ernest Gaines, and others 'use elements of call-and-response to overcome distrust and build a readership based on the trust that, however guardedly and complexly, informs the relationship between storyteller and audience in oral storytelling'.

Ethnic idiom. In 1904, when the novelist Henry James returned to America for a temporary visit after decades abroad, he was appalled to hear what had happened to the language. He referred to the cafés of New York as 'torture-rooms of the living idiom' and reflected gloomily on the ethnic synthesis of the future language. Whatever that will be, he observes, 'we shall not know it for English—in any sense for which there is an existing literary measure'. However, F. O. Matthiessen has noted that the prose of Sherwood Anderson, Ring Lardner, and Ernest Hemingway 'found its sources of life in James' "torture-rooms"; and poets as distant from one another as Robert Frost and e.e. cummings have demonstrated their return to Emerson's prime belief that the language of poetry takes its impulse from the speech of the common man' (*Henry James: The Major Phase*, 1944).

Saul Bellow tells how inconceivable daily life would have been for East European Jews without storytelling, how his father would respond with a story to any request for an explanation from his son. Growing up as a first-generation American on the streets of Montreal and Chicago, Bellow found the sources of life for his own stories. Harold Bloom has described Saul Bellow as 'a humane comic novelist of superb gifts, almost unique in American fiction since Mark Twain' (*Modern Critical Views: Saul Bellow*, 1988). What seems to set Bellow apart from many other writers since World War II, such as Norman Mailer, John Updike, Walker Percy, and Thomas Pynchon, is his exuberant and wide-ranging rhetorical virtuosity. According to Irving Howe, 'Bellow has brought to completion the first major new style in American fiction since those of Hemingway and Faulkner: a mingling of high-flown intellectual bravado with racy-tough street Jewishness, all in a comic rhetoric that keeps turning its head back toward Yiddish even as it keeps racing away from it' (*World of Our Fathers*, 1976). Bellow's idiom both invites and defies explanations of its special force and rhythm. Philip Stevick calls attention to a passage from 'A Silver Dish': 'How, against a contemporary background, do you mourn an octogenarian father, nearly blind, his heart enlarged, his lungs filling with fluid, who creeps, stumbles, gives off the odors, the moldiness or gassiness of old men. I *mean!* As Woody put it, be realistic.' Such a passage, Stevick suggests, illustrates Bellow's gift for conveying, through slight variations from standard speech patterns, 'a rhythmic sense of who the speakers are'.

Twentieth-century poetry. The poet William Carlos Williams brought Walt Whitman's 'language experiment' into the 20c. In *Spring and All* (1923), Williams sets side by side ranting paragraphs comparable to the manifestos of the European movements Cubism and Futurism with lyrics that describe moments of American daily life. Poems such as 'The Red Wheelbarrow', 'At the Ball Game', 'Spring and All', and 'To Elsie' are celebrated for their immediacy and directness, but in the context Williams originally intended for them they are part of a weave of prose and free verse, aesthetic meditation and pragmatic experience. His language seeks to construct an unmediated experience of 'the thing itself'. His faith in the efficacy of language, inherited from Emerson and Whitman, sets the tone for many experiments with poetic diction and lyric structure by later 20c American poets. So great was the influence of the Anglo-American poet and critic T. S. Eliot during the 1920s and 1930s that Williams conceived of his own experimental poetics in opposition to Eliot's academic cosmopolitanism. At the same time, Hart Crane tried to assimilate Eliot's epic scope and ambitious use of myth into Whitman's vision of American potential, developing an idiom both distinctly American and far more traditional than that of Williams. He uses metres, diction, syntax, and rhetorical figures from Elizabethan and Romantic poetry, but uses them in so distinctive a way that his verse is unmistakably modern and American, as in:

> Macadam, gun-grey as the tunny's belt,
> Leaps from Far Rockaway to Golden Gate. . . .
> Keep hold of that nickel for car-change, Rip,—
> Have you got your '*Times*'—?
> And hurry along, Van Winkle—it's getting late!
> (from 'Van Winkle', *The Bridge*, 1930)

The tone or illusion of an ordinary voice characterizes 20c American poetry, especially in the work of Robert Frost and Elizabeth Bishop:

> But no, I was out for stars:
> I would not come in.
> I meant not even if asked,
> And I hadn't been.
> (Frost, from 'Come In', 1941)

> . . . one seal particularly
> I have seen here evening after evening.
> He was curious about me. He was interested in music,
> like me a believer in total immersion,
> so I used to sing him Baptist hymns
> (Bishop, from 'At the Fishhouses', 1947)

Conclusion. This survey has dealt with a limited number of writers whose voices and characters have entered the national consciousness: *Rip*

Van Winkle and *Moby-Dick* are familiar names even to those who do not link them to Washington Irving and Herman Melville. Classic American writers, now world-renowned, were largely misunderstood or ignored when they made their first appearance. Melville, Whitman, and Dickinson achieved critical acceptance and a wide audience only posthumously. But misunderstanding and neglect are not invariable prerequisites for eventual fame. Fenimore Cooper's *The Pioneers* (1823) and Harriet Beecher Stowe's *Uncle Tom's Cabin* (1852) were instantaneous best-sellers, and acceptance by scholars and critics has lagged behind that of the general public. Whether fame came early or late, all these writers were responsive not only to great literary models of earlier times but also to the popular culture, now largely forgotten, of their own time, such as magic-lantern shows (Hawthorne), interest in mythic sea monsters (Melville), religious prophecies (Whitman), and spiritualism (Dickinson). In the 20c, popular expression in various forms (comic strips, jazz and rock music, movies, and television) has equally influenced writers, and writers have often been involved not only in extending a literary canon but also reaching new audiences by the writing of scripts for movies and television. The 21c will have a clearer understanding of the relationship between traditional literature and more recent media and of what passes away and what remains.

See AMERICAN ENGLISH, BIERCE, CANON, CLASSICAL LANGUAGE, DICKINSON, ELIOT, ENGLISH LITERATURE, LITERATURE, MELVILLE, TWAIN. [AMERICAS, LITERATURE]. B.L.

Blair, Walter. 1960. *Native American Humor*. San Francisco: Chandler.

Bridgman, Richard. 1966. *The Colloquial Style in America*. New York: Oxford University Press.

Callahan, John F. 1988. *In the African-American Grain: The Pursuit of Voice in Twentieth-Century Black Fiction*. Urbana: University of Illinois Press.

Gohdes, Clarence, & Marovitz, Sanford E. 1984. *Bibliographical Guide to the Study of the Literature of the U.S.A*. Durham, NC: Duke University Press.

Hart, James D. 1985. *The Oxford Companion to American Literature*. Oxford: University Press.

Inge, M. Thomas (ed.). 1989. *Handbook of American Popular Culture*. New York: Greenwood Press.

Koster, Donald N. 1982. *American Literature and Language: A Guide to Information Sources*. Detroit: Gale Research Co.

Leary, Lewis. 1976. *American Literature: A Study and Research Guide*. New York: St Martin's Press.

Lease, Benjamin. 1981. *Anglo-American Encounters: England and the Rise of American Literature*. Cambridge: University Press.

Matthiessen, F. O. 1941. *American Renaissance: Art and Expression in the Age of Emerson and Whitman*. Oxford: University Press.

Miller, Perry. 1967. *Nature's Nation.* Cambridge, Mass.: Harvard University Press.
Sewell, David R. 1988. *Mark Twain's Languages: Discourse, Dialogue, and Linguistic Variety.* Berkeley: University of California Press.
Tallack, Douglas. 1991. *Twentieth-Century America: The Intellectual and Cultural Context.* London & New York: Longman.

AMERICAN NAME SOCIETY. An organization devoted to the study of names, especially place and personal names, but also proper names and terminologies of all kinds, including names in literature. Founded in 1951, the Society's membership encompasses not only academics and other professionals concerned with various aspects of onomastics (literary scholars, philologists, geographers, historians, and psychologists), but also genealogists and lay-persons with an interest in names. Its quarterly journal, *Names*, began publication in 1953. The Society also publishes an informal newsletter entitled *Bulletin of the American Name Society* and an annual report of work completed and in progress. [AMERICAS, NAME].　　J.A.

AMERICAN PLACE-NAMES. The place-names of the US derive from many sources, but primarily are adoptions from indigenous languages, inventions by the early British settlers, and borrowings from other European explorers and settlers, especially the Spanish and French. The range is suggested by the origins of the names of the 50 states of the Union: 25 of Amerindian origin, 16 English-language inventions, 9 of Spanish, French, or other origins.

Amerindian. Many present-day names of Amerindian origin do not correspond to native designations for the places that bear those names. The original inhabitants belonged to a large number of cultures and languages with diverse naming customs. Relatively little is known about what names the various groups gave to the landscape or what sort of systems they used. Like the early Anglo-Saxons, they were doubtless more used to names for people than places. Just as the early English place-names *Sussex* and *Wessex* were primarily names for groups and only secondarily for territories, so Amerindians probably used tribal names for territories. Typically, European settlers would learn the name of a tribe and apply it to some geographical feature prominent in the area where they found the tribe, often a stream. The name would then be applied to watercourses further downstream from the original site, then extended to the region of land about the site, sometimes transferred to other regions, and finally adopted as the official name of a political unit: a territory and eventually a state. Thus, the name *Mississippi* was first

applied by the French (early form *Messipi*) to part of the northern reaches of the great river. It extended southward, eventually becoming the name of the main river. When a territory on the southern banks of the river was organized, the name was given to it, having been displaced by nearly the full north–south length of the country.

Like *Mississippi*, Amerindian names often entered English indirectly through French or Spanish: *Arkansas*, originally a tribal name, was borrowed through French, the silent final -*s* a sign of the plural. The original spelling *Arkansaw* reflects the word's pronunciation, with first- and third-syllable stress). Similarly, *Illinois* has an originally plural -*s*, usually not pronounced today; the name originally meant 'men'. Other French-mediated native names are *Iowa* and *Wisconsin*. Spanish-mediated names include *Alabama*, *Arizona* (originally 'place of the small spring', a local name that spread), *Tennessee*, and *Texas* (meaning 'friends/allies', but mistaken as a tribal name and extended to a region). *Kansas* is a tribal name that was filtered through both Spanish (*Escansaque*) and French before reaching English.

The Algonquian group of languages have had a considerable influence on US place-names: the state names *Connecticut* 'at the long river' (the unpronounced second *c* perhaps added to the spelling by association with the word *connect*), *Massachusetts* 'at the big hills', *Michigan* 'big lake', *Missouri* 'people of the big canoes', and *Wyoming*, a notable example of displacement. Originally something like *meche-weami-ing* 'at the big flats', the name was applied to a valley in Pennsylvania. Thomas Campbell's poem 'Gertrude of Wyoming' (1809) popularized and romanticized the name, which was applied to a new territory (later state) with which it had no connection. The name has moved from east to west through the influence of literature.

Other Amerindian state names are *Idaho*, an Apache name for the Comanches, unsuccessfully proposed for the Colorado territory and later shifted to the state that now bears it, *Kentucky* (Iroquoian) 'meadowlands', *Minnesota* (Siouan) 'cloudy water', an allusion to a turbid stream, *Nebraska* (Siouan) 'flat water', that is, a river on a plain, originally applied to what is now called *Platte River*, *North Dakota* and *South Dakota* (Siouan) from a tribal name, *Ohio* (Iroquoian) 'fine river', interpreted by the French as *Belle Rivière*, *Utah* from the Ute tribe (adopted by the US Congress as a name for the territory in preference to *Deseret*, the choice of the Mormon settlers, drawn from the *Book of Mormon*, in which it means 'honey bee', with implications of industry and productivity). One of the few Amerindian names traceable to a specific source is *Oklahoma*, a Muskogean term meaning 'red people', coined by a Choctaw chief for the western land known for a time as *Indian Territory*, to which tribes from the south-east were forcibly removed. When the territory became a state, the name was adopted for it. The name *Oregon* appears to be a mistake name, with the following possible history. An early French designation for the Wisconsin River was *Ouisconsink*; a French map of 1715 misspelled the name and printed it on two lines as *Ouaricon* with *sint* below. In various forms (*Ouragon, Ourgan, Ourigan, Oregon*), the first part of the name was used for a legendary great river flowing into the Pacific Ocean. When the Columbia River was discovered, it was associated with the legend, and the territory around it called *Oregon*.

The notion that European explorers moved into the new world, learned native names for places, and adopted them from the tribes does not correspond with the facts. The many Amerindian names in the present US are frequently displaced geographically and referentially. The adoption of such names was largely a consequence of romanticism and of the picturesque value they had for settlers with little knowledge of or concern about their original application. *Pasadena*, California, is an extreme example, a pseudo-Amerindian name concocted by English-speakers according to their idea of what a nice native name should be like.

Two states bear names that are neither Amerindian nor European. *Alaska* is from an Aleut word, meaning 'mainland' (from the perspective of the islands). Before the US purchase of the region in 1867, it was known as *Russian America*; a more suitably indigenous name was thought proper when it became an American territory. *Hawaii* is a Polynesian name brought by the island people when they settled the place. Its meaning is unknown. Apart from the state names, Amerindian and other native names are abundant for counties, cities, rivers, lakes, mountains, valleys, and other features of the landscape. *Manhattan* is said to mean etymologically 'island mountain', prophetic in view of later architecture. *Tallahassee*, capital of Florida, is from a Muskogean word meaning 'old town'. *Chesapeake* looks as though it might be an English place-name, except that its earliest spelling was *Chesepiooc* 'place on a big river'. *Chicago* is from an Algonquian word meaning 'onion field', by way of French. The *Appalachian Mountains* were named via Spanish *Apalachan*, a term used vaguely for an interior mountainous region. The *Allegheny Mountains* were named for the river, the term being from Algonquian with the sense 'beautiful stream', thus being synonymous with the *Ohio River*, of which it is a tributary.

Spanish. Spanish explorers and settlers were prominent across much of what is now the southern and western US. *Florida* 'flowery', the first European name to be given in North America, was bestowed by Ponce de León in 1513. It both described the locality and commemorated the Easter season when the Spanish went there. *California*, on the other side of the continent, was a literary name, from the poem 'Las Sergas de Esplandián', which described an island rich in gold and jewels and inhabited by a group of Amazon-like women. The Spanish explorer Cortés gave the name to the peninsula of Baja (Lower) California, which was mistaken for an island, and the name was extended northward to the present state. *Colorado* ('coloured, red') was applied to the Colorado River because of the sediment in it and officially extended to the bordering territory in 1861. *Nevada* ('snowy') was first used for a mountain range. When the Washoe Territory (named for a native tribe) was admitted to the Union, a more euphonious name was thought desirable, and *Nevada* was adopted for the state. *Washoe* remains as a name for a county within the state, from which the name was taken for the first chimpanzee successfully taught sign language. *New Mexico* is ultimately of Central American origin, and was applied in 1562 in the form *Nuevo Mexico* to the lands north of Mexico proper.

Many early Spanish names were religious. Settlements were often missions, named after saints and feast days. On the east coast, the now Anglicized *St Augustine* was the capital of Spanish Florida. In Texas, *San Antonio* retains its Spanish form, sometimes colloquially shortened to *San Anton*; *Corpus Christi* is of Latin form but Hispanic provenance, commemorating a Catholic feast day. The far West is particularly rich in mission names: *San Diego, San Francisco, San Luis Obispo, Santa Ana, Santa Barbara, Santa Cruz*. Such names extend to the far northwestern reaches of the US, with the *San Juan* islands off the coast of Washington State. Some such names are partially disguised, for example, *Ventura*, a shortening of *San Buenaventura* (St Bonaventure) and *Los Angeles*, originally the mission of *Nuestra Señora de los Angeles de la Porciúncula* Our Lady of the Angels of the Little Portion (the last term referring to a Franciscan shrine near Assisi). Non-religious Spanish names include: the *Alamo* (cottonwood), a celebrated fort in Texas; the related *Los Alamos*, New Mexico; *Boca Raton* (rodent mouth) in Florida, perhaps describing the shape of the shoreline; and the *Rio Grande* (great river), sometimes pleonastically called the *Rio Grande River*, the Spanish sense overlooked.

French. Although many Amerindian state names were filtered into English through French, only two state names come directly from French, in adapted forms, while a third is controversial. In 1682, the Mississippi valley was named *Louisiane* for King Louis XIV by the explorer La Salle. When the Spanish acquired the area in 1762, they Hispanicized the name to *Luisiana*. When the territory was purchased by the US in 1803, the two forms of the name were blended as *Louisiana*, the name given to the state in 1812. *Vermont* appears in 1777, probably invented in English from French roots; the French arrangement of those roots would be *le mont vert* 'green mountain'. *Maine* appears to be a simple transfer of name from Maine in western France, but has been accounted for as a variant of *main* (mainland), used from the 17c and adopted for the state when it was admitted to the Union in 1820. French names for other geographical and political features are more numerous: *St Croix River* named by the explorer Jacques Cartier on the feast of the Holy Cross, *St Joseph* Missouri, named by Joseph Robidoux for his patron saint, *St Louis* Missouri, named for Louis IX, the saint-king, and pronounced by native citizens as 'Saint Lewis'. A number of French names were given early in the history of the US out of gratitude for French aid during the Revolution: for example, *Paris* and *Versailles*, Kentucky, but gratitude did not extend to pronunciation, as this *Versailles* rhymes with 'her sails'. The name of the *Teton* mountains is from French ('teat'), a metaphor usually left untranslated, especially in the name of the highest of the mountains, *Grand Teton*.

Dutch. There are no state names from Dutch, but *New York* may show Dutch influence. The city was called by the original Dutch settlers *Nieuw Amsterdam*. When the English acquired it in 1644, they wanted to name it after the city of York in honour of their patron, the Duke of York. The resulting name follows the Dutch model. Adapted Dutch names are characteristic of the area around New York where the Dutch settled. *Flatbush* is a calque on *Vlak-bosch* (level forest), *Flushing* is the English form of the Dutch town *Vlissingen* (for which the settlement on Long Island was named), *Brooklyn* is Anglicized *Breukelyn*, another transferred name from Holland, and *The Bronx*, a borough of New York, is said to come from a farm belonging to Jonas Bronck, referred to as 'the Bronck's (farm)' (hence the definite article). The *Catskill* mountains derive their name from Dutch *Kats Kill* (cat stream). *Kill* is used in the area as a generic term for creeks.

English. Many US state names are made from English words, sometimes disguised. *Delaware* is from the title of the first colonial governor of neighbouring Virginia, Thomas West, Lord de la Warr. It was applied first to a cape, then a bay, a river, and a valley, and thence to the colony that eventually became the state. By a reversal of the usual pattern, it was also extended to the Delaware Indians, who lived in the area. Some names appear in a Latinized form. *Georgia* was named for King George II, in whose reign the colony was established. *Indiana* was derived from the name of land developers, the Indiana Company, as a picturesque term for uncivilized areas to be settled. *Montana* is a Latinized or Hispanicized English invention, originally used for a town near Pike's Peak. The name was proposed for the territory finally called *Idaho*, then given to the state that now bears it, which is not conspicuously mountainous. *North Carolina* and *South Carolina* were named in 1629 for King Charles I as *Carolina* and rechartered in 1663 by Charles II in the present form. *Pennsylvania* was settled by the Quaker William Penn, who wanted to call the colony *New Wales*; Charles II, however, chartered it under the name it now bears, combining Penn's name with the Latin *silva* (Penn's Forest Land: compare *sylvan*). *Virginia* was named for and perhaps by Queen Elizabeth I, the Virgin Queen. *West Virginia* was a later break-off from the extensive lands of the original colony.

Other state names from English have various origins. *Maryland* was ostensibly named for Henrietta Maria, the Queen of Charles I, but its Roman Catholic settlers must early have associated it with St Mary. *New Hampshire* was named by John Mason after the English county from which he came. *New Jersey* was named after the island of Jersey, the home of one of the proprietors of the colony, Georges Carteret. *Rhode Island* has been traced to a comment by the explorer Giovanni di Verrazano, who in 1524 mentioned an island about the size of the Aegean island of Rhodes. The Dutch called the place *Roodt Eylandt* ('red island'), so both Greek *Rhodos* (compare Greek *rhódon* a usually red rose) and Dutch *roodt* may have entered into the name of the state, making it a name invented in English, but with roots in several other languages. The only 'pure' American name is *Washington*, so called in honour of the first president of the US, whose surname originates in the town of Washington in England.

Commemorative names. Settlers frequently remembered their mother country by transferring place-names from their homeland to the new locale or honouring important persons by naming places after them. Transferred names might be the original homes of the settlers, such as *Birmingham*, *Boston*, *Burlington*, *Montgomery*, *Swansea*, sometimes with 'new', as in *New*

England, New London, New Orleans. Name-givers also commemorated famous locales with which they had no direct connection, such as the classical names *Rome, Syracuse, Olympia, Parnassus.* The same name may be found in various states, such as *Athens* in Georgia and Ohio and *Burlington* in Vermont and New Jersey. An area along the Mississippi is known as 'Little Egypt' because of the number of Egyptian places commemorated there, such as *Memphis*, Tennessee, and *Cairo*, Illinois. *Berlin* (often rhyming with 'Merlin') was a popular name before World War I. As the pioneers moved westward, they often transferred names from the east: for example, *Salem*, Massachusetts, was a Biblical name, from Hebrew, but *Salem*, Oregon, was named after the town in Massachusetts.

Place-names honouring persons began at least as early as *Jamestown*, Virginia, named for the new king of the newly united kingdoms of England and Scotland. American patriots were early so honoured, the most widely remembered being George *Washington*, for whom were named the capital of the nation, one of its states, and many towns, lakes, mountains, and other places and institutions. Other presidents and founding fathers, such as *Jefferson, Madison, Monroe,* and *Franklin* have been similarly honoured. So have Casimir *Pulaski*, a Polish military officer, and the Marquis de *Lafayette*, a French general who fought for the colonists in the Revolutionary War. Famous persons in history without American connections were also recalled, as in *Cicero*, New York, named for the Roman statesman during the 18–19c vogue for classical names. Settlers and entrepreneurs are the namesakes of other places, such as *Flagler*, a county in Florida named for the founder of the Florida East Coast Railway. *Pikes Peak* was named for Zebulon Pike, the explorer who described it. Some names are for persons of modest fame or no fame at all: *Martha's Vineyard* is an island in Massachusetts once notable for its wines, but Martha is unknown. *Atlanta*, Georgia, is said to have been named after the Western Atlantic Railroad, of which it was the terminus in the mid-19c. Another postulated origin, however, is the second given name of *Martha Atalanta Lumpkin*, daughter of a Georgia governor, and an earlier settlement was called *Marthasville*.

A specific event is the basis for some place-names. For example, *Flagstaff*, Maine, is said to have been so called because a flag was raised on a pole there at the time of General Benedict Arnold's campaign against Quebec in 1775. Many areas have a high overlook named *Lovers Leap*, usually accompanied by a popular legend of the death of frustrated lovers, often Amerindians. In fact, the name is common for a precipice regardless of its romantic history.

Descriptive names. Many names describe the natural characteristics of a locality or feature: *the Black Hills* of Dakota, *the Blue Ridge Mountains* of the Appalachians, *Long Island*, New York, *the Great Salt Lake*, Utah, *the Great Smoky Mountains*, North Carolina, *Green Bay*, Wisconsin, *the Red River* and *Red Lake*, in several states. *Lake Superior* (a translation from French) was so called because it was the uppermost of the *Great Lakes. Roaring Gap*, North Carolina, was named from the sound of the wind passing through the mountains, although *roaring* is also used in many names of watercourses. *Rock* and *Rocky* are similarly widespread name elements, most notably used in *the Rocky Mountains* (often shortened to *the Rockies*), which may also be called from their craggy appearance (in contrast with the older, rounded, and vegetation-covered eastern mountains, like the Appalachians) or which may be after a group of Amerindians nicknamed 'the Rocks' from a translation of their tribal name.

Other names associate their places with flora, fauna, minerals, activities, or some mix of these: *Cedar Rapids*, Iowa, *Hog Island*, Michigan, *Mica Mountains*, Arizona, *Milltown*, New Jersey, *Paper Mill Creek*, California. *Newspaper Rock*, Arizona, is so called because of the petroglyphs that were imaginatively thought to have been the journalism of their day. *Enterprise* and *Commerce* are found in various states as names of towns that were (hoped to be) commercial centres. *Intercourse*, Pennsylvania, probably had a similar origin, but is currently known chiefly as a joke town. *Philadelphia* (the City of Brotherly Love, as it is etymologically nicknamed) expressed the humanitarian sentiment of its Quaker founders.

Blended, concocted, and other names. Many names arise from blends of pre-existing names or other sources. *Texarkana* blends the names of three states, Texas, Arkansas, and Louisiana, being located close to their meeting points. Another such border name is *Mexhoma*, combining the names of New Mexico and Oklahoma. *Neyami*, Georgia, is a syllabic acronym from the names of three 1920s developers: *Newton, Yancy,* and *Miller. Tesnus* in Texas is said to be a reverse spelling of *sunset*, and *Tarzana* in California was named by the writer Edgar Rice Burroughs after his hero Tarzan, Lord of the Jungle. It is said that *Nome* in Alaska rose from the notation of an early map-maker, who wrote '? name' on a chart for a cape in Alaska. Others misinterpreted the notation as *Cape Nome*, which became the designation of the place. This etymology has been widely cited as an example of a mistake name, but such stories are often told as folk etymologies of place-names. See PLACE-NAME. [AMERICAS, NAME]. J.A.

AMERICAN PRESS. The first regular newspaper in the US was the *Boston News-Letter*, begun in 1704 by a postmaster, John Campbell. An earlier effort, *Publick Occurrences, Both Foreign and Domestick* (1690), had been suppressed by the colonial government of Massachusetts. From that unpromising beginning sprang the vast American Fourth Estate: by the late 1980s, there were over 1,600 US daily newspapers, with a circulation approaching 63m copies.

Crusading editors. Benjamin Franklin, one of the Founding Fathers of the Republic, included journalism among his many activities. In 1729, he became publisher of the *Pennsylvania Gazette*, whose front page might be devoted to announcements of missing persons, notices of ship sailings, financial statements, rewards for runaway indentured servants from England, and advertisements for the sale of broadcloth or other stuffs, loaf sugar, *Poor Richard's Almanack*, and Negro slaves newly imported from Barbados. The colonial press was influential in furthering the Revolution by spreading sentiments that the British regarded as seditious. Newspapers, ever since, have been politically active. In the 19c, Horace Greeley, editor of the *New York Tribune*, espoused the causes of equal rights for women, temperance, universal education, the organization of labour, the prudent control of capitalism, the abolition of slavery, penal reform, and social justice; Frederick Douglass, born a slave, became a crusading journalist in the cause of abolition; and Henry W. Grady, owner-editor of the *Atlanta Constitution*, articulated the spirit of 'The New South', which involved the modernization, industrialization, and reintegration of the region into the Union following the Civil War.

Competitive press barons. Joseph Pulitzer (1847–1911), of Hungarian-Jewish ancestry, is probably the best-known name in American journalism. An immigrant at the time of the Civil War, he became owner-editor of the *Saint Louis Post-Dispatch* and later of the *New York World*. A political supporter of Greeley, he endowed the Columbia University School of Journalism and founded the Pulitzer prizes, awarded since 1917 for excellence in various categories of literature, the arts, and journalism. The Californian William Randolph Hearst (1863–1951) was a competitor of Pulitzer's, associated with the *San Francisco Examiner* and the *New York Journal-American*, and an anti-British isolationist during World War I. Pulitzer's *New York World* had pioneered a comic section in colour, one of whose most popular drawings, 'Hogan's Alley', dealt with life in the New York tenements and included a bald-headed, toothless, grinning figure in a yellow night dress: the Yellow Kid. Hearst hired its cartoonist away from Pulitzer's paper and featured the Kid in posters intended to boost his paper's circulation. The character became symbolic of fiercely competitive and irresponsible newspaper practices and is the source of the term *yellow journalism*. Today, Hearst may be best remembered as the model for the title character of Orson Welles's film *Citizen Kane* (1941).

Pulitzer prize-winners. Other journalists have been less flamboyant. William Allen White (1868-1944), editor of the *Emporia Gazette*, Kansas, was the archetype of the small-town editor as a figure of simple wisdom, tolerance, good nature, optimism, and liberal conservatism: a combination of political qualities not thought impossible in the US. A supporter of William McKinley and Theodore Roosevelt, he won the Pulitzer Prize in 1923 for his editorials. In more recent years, journalists have become less well known. The press played a major role during the Watergate crisis in bringing the investigation of crimes and cover-ups to a head, with the resulting resignation of Richard M. Nixon. The *Washington Post* was awarded a Pulitzer for its *investigative reporting* (a collocation popularized at the time). The *Post* reporters most active in tracking the story were Bob Woodward and Carl Bernstein, but even at the time they were indistinct figures in the public mind, sometimes blended into a Siamese-twin figure 'Woodstein.'

Leading contemporary newspapers. Today, the two most widely circulated daily newspapers are aiming at a national circulation: *The Wall Street Journal*, which specializes in financial news but also provides general news reportage, and *USA Today*, which has regional editions and consists of pictures and headlines accompanied by short articles sometimes dismissed as *News McNuggets*. Daily papers with the next five largest circulations are the *New York Daily News*, *Los Angeles Times*, *New York Times*, *Chicago Tribune*, and *Washington Post*. Although they are all local papers, most enjoy some national circulation, particularly the *New York Times*.

Leading contemporary magazines. The five magazines with the largest paid circulations are *TV Guide* (a weekly listing of television programmes on major channels, with articles relating to them), *Modern Maturity* (a publication of the American Association of Retired Persons, specializing in articles of interest to older people), *Reader's Digest* (which began by publishing condensations of articles from other sources, but whose success soon led it to commission original articles), *NRTA/AARP News Bulletin* (a newsletter of the National Retired Teachers Association and American Association of Retired Persons, concerned with matters of political or other interest to them), and *National Geographic* (specializing in illustrated articles about places and peoples around the world). The next six are aimed at a female or domestic readership: *Better Homes and Gardens, Woman's Day, Family Circle, McCall's, Good Housekeeping*, and *Ladies' Home Journal*. Others are newsmagazines such as *Time, Newsweek, U.S. News & World Report*, tabloids such as *National Enquirer, Star*, religious magazines such as *Guideposts*, men's magazines such as *Playboy, Sports Illustrated, American Legion, Penthouse, Field & Stream, Popular Science*, and gossipy publications such as *People* (a compromise between a tabloid and a newsmagazine). Some high-circulation magazines are aimed at fairly specific readership, such as *Ebony* (African Americans), *The American Rifleman* (hunters), and *Bon Appetit* (gourmets). See JOURNALISM, MAGAZINE, NEWSPAPER, PRESS. [AMERICAS, MEDIA].

J.A.

AMERICAN PUBLISHING.

AMERICAN PUBLISHING. The first American printing press was established at Cambridge, Massachusetts, in 1639, and the first book to be printed on it was the Bay Psalm Book of 1640. Although printing in the English colonies began in New England, it soon spread to other regions: presses were set up in Jamestown, Virginia, in 1682, and in St Mary's City, Maryland, and Philadelphia, both in 1685. The most frequent subjects for colonial American books were theology, law, and literature, but the kinds of books printed varied from one region to another: in New England, nearly half the total output was in theology; in the Southern colonies, over half was in law; in the Middle colonies, the three subjects of literature, theology, and law were more nearly equal, with literature the most numerous and the law the least (Lehmann-Haupt, p. 33; below). That distribution reflects the interests of the regions.

Literary property. The concept of literary property was not strong during the colonial period, and copyright laws were lacking. This lack was recognized by the framers of the Constitution, who included the following in Section 8 (Powers of Congress) of Article 1: 'To promote the progress of science and useful arts, by securing for limited times to authors and inventors the exclusive right to their respective writings and discoveries.' Before the Constitution was adopted, authors had to depend on separate copyright laws in the various states. That such laws existed at all was largely due to the exertions of Noah Webster, who travelled over the states urging their adoption of copyright legislation, because of which he is known as 'The Father of American Copyright'. Webster's motives were by no means disinterested, because he was concerned with protecting his own literary property, especially his schoolbooks: a speller and a grammar.

During Colonial times, printers had a continuing struggle with governments over the censorship of printed works and prior restraint by licensing. King James II had directed the royal governor of the colony of New York as follows: 'And for as much a great inconvenience may arise by the liberty of printing within our province of New York, you are to provide by all necessary orders that noe person keep any press for printing, nor that any book, pamphlet or other matters whatsoever bee printed without your special leave & license first obtained' (cited by Tebbel, p. 4; below). As a result of such efforts at control and restraint, the first amendment to the Constitution in the Bill of Rights provides that 'Congress shall make no law . . . abridging the freedom of speech, or of the press.' These two principles, that authors have a right to their intellectual property and that government should not control ideas or their expression, are fundamental to publishing in the US.

Publishing for a new nation. The establishment of the new nation was a powerful stimulus to book publishing. In the twenty years following the Revolution, total book production increased fourfold, and the publishing of works of literature and political science increased twelvefold. The existence of a new nation called for new books on its government and for its culture. On the other hand, subjects such as medicine, music, and theology, to which the existence of a new social order was not directly relevant, saw more modest increases. Noah Webster, who has been called 'School Master to America', wrote distinctively American textbooks for language instruction after experience as a teacher left him dissatisfied with books that ignored American life and culture. His major textbook was *A Grammatical Institute of the English Language*, which included what came to be known familiarly as the 'Blue-Backed Speller' as its first part; the second and third parts were a grammar and a reader. His work in lexicography resulted in *An American Dictionary of the English Language* (1828) and its line of successors in the longest unbroken lexicographical tradition in the English-speaking world: the Merriam-Webster dictionaries. Webster was a spelling reform enthusiast, but his reforms were unenthusiastically received by Benjamin Franklin (who had toyed with spelling reform himself) and others to whom he presented them. However, through his spelling book and dictionaries, Webster was influential in establishing the pattern of American spelling, although that spelling was not a reform as such and Webster did not invent it. See SPELLING.

Commercial publishers. Several existing publishing houses trace their history to the early years of the Republic, beginning and often continuing to the 20c as family businesses. Today such family control is generally a thing of the past, as publishing houses have been the objects of corporate mergers. A widely lamented result of such change is that personal control over and concern for the quality of books has been replaced by impersonal marketing decisions that treat books simply as products. Some long-established companies are:

John Wiley & Sons. Charles Wiley, son of an officer in the Revolutionary army, ran a book-shop and operated a printing press. His establishment was known as a gathering place for intellectuals: Samuel F. B. Morse, William Cullen Bryan, Richard Dana, and James Fenimore Cooper, whom Wiley began to publish in 1821. The present firm, John Wiley & Sons, traces its foundation to 1807, though its significant activity as a publisher was somewhat later.

Harper & Row. In 1817, two brothers of the Harper family began to publish a general line of books in New York City, and can lay claim to being the oldest American publishing house in the contemporary sense. They declined to publish Melville's *Typee* when it was offered to them, in one of those errors of judgement that plague publishers. However, when Melville offered them *Omoo* (1847) and *Moby-Dick* (1851), they snatched them up.

G. P. Putnam Sons. George Palmer Putnam had formed an association with the Wiley firm in 1833, and together they published such works as Poe's *Tales* (1845) and Melville's *Typee* (1846). After the partnership dissolved in 1848, Wiley became primarily a publisher in science and technology, whereas Putnam continued the literary titles.

Appleton-Century-Crofts. Daniel Appleton was a dry-goods merchant who ran a chain of stores in New England and New York. His stores included a book department, which became so successful that it crowded out the rest of the merchandise, so that Appleton became a book-seller and by natural progression in 1831 a publisher. The house specialized in religious, medical, scientific, and other works of an earnest nature. As the result of the mergers, the firm became Appleton-Century in 1933 and Appleton-Century-Crofts in 1948.

A. S. Barnes. Beginning his career as a clerk in a book-dealer's office in Hartford, Connecticut, A. S. Barnes launched his own publishing business in 1838, specializing in textbooks. As a result of aggressive marketing directly to teachers and a prudent choice of books, Barnes prospered, eventually relocating in New York City. Among his most successful books was S. W. Clark's *Practical Grammar*, which helped to popularize the diagramming of sentences. Clark's system did not become the most widely practised (that was the Reed and Kellogg system), but used cartouche-shaped enclosures to identify syntactic functions in a sentence, from which it was sometimes satirized as 'sausage-link' grammar.

Other early names in publishing that continue to be part of American life (with the founding dates of their firms) are: G. & C. Merriam (1831: see MERRIAM WEBSTER), J. B. Lippincott (1836), Charles C. Little and James Brown (1837), Charles Scribner (1846), David Van Nostrand (1848), E. P. Dutton (1852), Henry O. Houghton (1864), and Frank N. Doubleday (1897). The extent of publishing in the US can be inferred from the following list of other imprints (in their present form, but with the firm's claimed date of founding): Thomas Y. Crowell (1834), Bobbs-Merrill (1838), Henry Holt (1866), Silver Burdett & Ginn (1867), Allyn and Bacon (1868), Macmillan (UK 1843, US 1869), R. R. Bowker (1872), Funk & Wagnalls (1876: see entry), David McKay (1882), D. C. Heath (1885), Longman (UK 1724, US 1887), AMS (1889), Scott, Foresman (1896), Grosset & Dunlap (1898), McGraw-Hill (1909), Prentice-Hall (1913), Liveright (1917), Harcourt Brace Jovanovich (1919), W. W. Norton (1924), Simon & Schuster (1924), Random House (1925: see entry), Viking Penguin (1925: see PENGUIN), Peter Lang (1926), William Morrow (1926), New Directions (1936), Scholars' Facsimiles & Reprints (1936), Pantheon (1942), Farrar, Strauss & Giroux (1945), Johnson Reprint (1945), Hafner (1946), Humanities (1950), Scarecrow (1950), Grove (1952), St Martin's (1952), Gale Research Company (1954), Hill & Wang (1956), Atheneum (1959), G. K. Hall (1959), Twayne (1959), Newbury House (1970), and Peachtree (1977).

Academic publishers. American university presses were late in developing, and when they did it was largely as a result of the growth of graduate schools, which exerted pressure for channels of scholarly publication that commercial presses could not satisfy. The first such press was Cornell University Press (1869), the second Johns Hopkins (1878), followed by Chicago (1891), California (1893), and Columbia (1893). Most American university presses are

20c: Teachers College (1904), Yale (1908), Washington (1909), Loyola in Chicago (1912), Harvard (1913), New York (1916), Illinois (1918), Duke (1921), Delaware (1922), North Carolina (1922), Iowa State (1924), Stanford (1925), Duquesne (1927), Minnesota (1927), Oklahoma (1928), New Mexico (1929), Michigan (1930), Brown (1932), Louisiana State (1935), Northwestern (1936), Pittsburgh (1936), Rutgers (1936), Southern Methodist (1937), Wisconsin (1937), Georgia (1938), and Iowa (1938). A good many others came into existence during the expansionist period in higher education after World War II and later conflicts, when veterans were returning to school.

Paperback publishing. It is often assumed that paperback publishing is a recent phenomenon. In fact, most colonial books were paper bound, and even after cloth- or leather-bound volumes became the norm, there were explosive periods when paperbacks enjoyed great popularity: (1) From 1830 to the Civil War, when an effort to appeal to a mass market resulted in reprinting books cheaply and produced the *dime novel* of the 1860s. (2) After the Civil War, when series and sets of books called *libraries* became common: for example, the works of Horatio Alger, the most popular US author of the late 19c, whose stories typically concerned the rise from rags to riches of an honest, industrious young man. (3) During and after World War II, when imprints such as Pocket Books (1939), Avon (1941), Dell (1942), Bantam Books (1945), Signet & Mentor (1948) changed public reading and buying habits.

Book clubs. An innovation with a considerable effect on purchasing and availability was the book club. Beginning in the 1920s, such clubs were merchandising organizations that distributed selected books by mail to subscribers, usually at reduced prices and sometimes in special editions. The first and most famous were the *Book-of-the-Month Club* (1926) and the *Literary Guild* (1927). Specialized book clubs developed for fans of detective stories, science fiction, children's books, literary classics, fine binding, and many other categories. Some book clubs were independent operations, such as the Book-of-the-Month Club; others were run by magazines, such as the *Reader's Digest Book Club* of condensed books; and others were subsidiaries of publishing houses, such as the Literary Guild (of Doubleday).

Distributing and selling. Although the large book clubs function as publishers, they are primarily distributors, whose function is a significant part of book production in the US. Although independent bookshops still exist, much selling is now done by firms that depend on volume sales.

Chain bookstores such as *Bookland, Crown*, and *Waldenbooks* are found in shopping centres and malls across the land. Mail-order houses typically offer remaindered or sharply discounted titles; companies such as the *Publishers Clearing House* and *Barnes & Noble* send catalogues to prospective purchasers and conduct most of their business by mail, although some also maintain retail stores.

Books and language. Publishing and distribution on such a vast scale has made the written word more available in the US than ever before, and a consequence of that availability is an increased influence of written on spoken English. The custom in AmE of preserving secondary stresses and giving full value to sounds that would otherwise be reduced or lost has been traced partly to the influence of the *spelling bee* and partly to a general regard for writing as more important than speech. Examples are the full-vowel pronunciation of the last syllable of words like *governor* and *educator* to rhyme with *war*, the analytical pronunciation of old compounds like *forehead* ('fore-head' rather than 'forrid'), and the repronunciation of the silent *l* in words like *palm* and *calm* or even occasionally *walk* and *talk*: see SPELLING BEE, SPELLING PRONUNCIATION. In addition to such specific influences, the abundance of published matter, in the US as in the rest of the English-speaking world, has had the effect of supporting and extending the institutionalized form of the language, standard English. Standardization has been a major consequence of the printing press. A time may dawn when the electronic storage and transmission of language will have new and as yet unimaginable effects on language and on the people who use it, but there is no reason to suppose that the electronic media will undo or seriously modify the importance of the printed word. See BOOK, PUBLISHING. [AMERICAS, MEDIA].   J.A.

Emery, Michael & Edwin. 1988. *The Press and America: An Interpretive History of the Mass Media*, 6th edition. Englewood Cliffs, NJ: Prentice Hall.

Lehmann-Haupt, Hellmut. 1951. *The Book in America: A History of the Making and Selling of Books in the United States*, 2nd edition. New York: Bowker.

Tebbel, John. 1987. *Between Covers: The Rise and Transformation of Book Publishing in America*. New York: Oxford University Press.

AMERICAN SIGN LANGUAGE. See SIGN LANGUAGE.

AMERICAN SPEECH, full form *American Speech: A Quarterly of Linguistic Usage*. Short form *AS*. A journal devoted to the study of English in America, founded in 1925 by H. L. Mencken. In the third edition of *American Language* (1923) he wrote: 'No attempt to deduce the principles of vulgar American grammar from the everyday speech of the people has ever been made by an American philologist. There is no scientific study, general and comprehensive in scope, of the American vocabulary, of the influences lying at the root of American word-formation. No professor, so far as I know, has ever deigned to give the same sober attention to the *sermo plebeius* of his country that his colleagues habitually give to the pronunciation of Latin, or to the irregular verbs in French.' To correct such neglect, he envisioned a magazine that would be scholarly but popular. To edit it, he recruited Louise Pound, a professor of English, the philologist Kemp Malone, and the bibliographer Arthur G. Kennedy. He arranged for its publication in Baltimore as a monthly. The magazine became bimonthly two years later in 1927 and after seven years was clearly not going to be a commercial success. Beginning with volume 8 it was published quarterly by Columbia University Press in New York, becoming more academic but without completely losing the popular slant. The new editor was William Cabell Greet, assisted by, among others, Clarence L. Barnhart and Allen Walker Read. In 1952, control was passed to an editorial board, of which Allan F. Hubbell was managing editor, succeeded in 1961 by James Macris. By 1971, *AS* was several years behind schedule and seemed likely to expire. Some members of the American Dialect Society proposed to Columbia that the Society assume sponsorship and editorial control. John Algeo of the U. of Georgia became the Society's first editor in 1972, with James W. Hartman and A. Murray Kinloch as associate editors. Columbia gave up publication in 1977 and the journal moved in 1978 to the U. of Alabama Press. By 1982, when Ronald R. Butters of Duke U. assumed the editorship, *AS* was again on schedule. The associate editors continued, Kinloch being replaced in 1984 by Charles Clay Doyle. The goal of serving as a dispassionate, if sometimes amused, observer of AmE has been fulfilled. See AMERICAN DIALECT SOCIETY, BARNHART, MENCKEN, POUND, READ. [AMERICAS, MEDIA, REFERENCE].　　　J.A.

AMERICO- [18c]. A rare combining form for *America* and *American*: *Americomania*, a great enthusiasm for America; *Americo-Liberian* (informal *Merico*), a Liberian whose ancestors were freed American slaves. Compare AMER-. See LIBERIA. [AMERICAS, NAME].　　　T.MCA.

AMERINDIAN [1900: a blend of *Amer(ican)* and *Indian*]. (1) Relating to the indigenous peoples of the Americas, more commonly known as *American Indians* or (*Red*) *Indians*, and often referred to in recent years as *Native Americans*:

Amerindian mythology. (2) Also *Amerind*. A Native American. See AMER-, AMERICAN[1], AMERICAN LANGUAGES, AMERICAN PLACE-NAMES, AMERINDIAN PIDGIN ENGLISH, BORROWING, CANADIAN PLACE-NAMES, CARIBBEAN LANGUAGES, CHINOOK JARGON, DIALECT IN AMERICA, HOBSON-JOBSONISM, INDIAN, INDIAN ENGLISH[2], MESTIZO, MÉTIS, NEWFOUNDLAND, RED ENGLISH, REVERSAL, SAPIR, SAPIR-WHORF HYPOTHESIS, WHORF. [AMERICAS, NAME].　　　T.MCA.

AMERINDIAN PIDGIN ENGLISH. In linguistics, a general term for: (1) Pidgin languages based on the indigenous languages of the Americas, such as *Chinook Jargon*, *Delaware Jargon*, *Mobilian Jargon*, *Trader Navajo/Navaho*. The term sometimes includes pidgins based on non-Amerindian languages, such as *Eskimo trade jargon*, and South American languages, such as *língua geral* (Portuguese: general language) in Brazil. Many developed before contact with Europeans. (2) Amerindian varieties of English descended from a makeshift language used between Indians and white settlers, especially in the US. Each variety retains features of its ancestral languages, but a striking shared feature is the transitivizing suffix *-um* after verbs (*Squaw makum bed*), also found in Melanesian Pidgin English and Kriol in Australia. Both loanwords (*chipmunk, moose, squash*) and loan translations (*firewater, peacepipe, warpath*) from this pidgin can be found in AmE. See AFRO-SEMINOLE, AMERICAN LANGUAGES, CHINOOK JARGON, INDIAN ENGLISH[2], HOBSON-JOBSONISM, PIDGIN. [AMERICAS, VARIETY].　　　S.R.

AMESLAN. See SIGN LANGUAGE.

AMPERSAND [17c: a contraction of *and per se and* and by itself (means) and]. A printer's term for the characters & and &, originally forms of Latin *et* (and), as in *Gilbert & Sullivan*, *Brown & Co.* Both & and £ (short for *libra* pound) survive from the system of abbreviation used by medieval scribes. Once a common replacement for *and*, it is now largely a flourish on business cards and letterheads. It also occurs in *&c*, a variant of *etc*. See ABBREVIATION. [TECHNOLOGY, WRITING].　　　W.W.B.

AMPHIBOLY [16c: from French *amphibolie*, Latin *amphibolia*, Greek *amphibolia* throwing in two directions. Stress: 'am-FI-bo-ly']. Also *amphibology*. Ambiguity caused by lack of grammatical clarity, in which, especially out of context, a phrase or sentence can be understood in two ways: *the shooting of the hunters* meaning either 'the hunters shot (someone/thing)' or 'the hunters were shot (by someone)'. See AMBIGUITY, EQUIVOCATION. [GRAMMAR, LANGUAGE].　　　T.MCA.

AMPHIBRACH [16c: from Greek *amphibrakhus* both short]. A metrical foot of three syllables, ∪–∪, short/long/short in quantitative measure, as in Latin, weak/strong/weak in accentual metre, as in the English words *replacement* and *vacation*. Not common in English, it sometimes occurs in blank verse when an extra weak stress is added at the end of a line, to give a feminine ending: 'A thing of beauty is a joy *for ever*' (Keats). See FOOT, METRE/METER, SCANSION. [LITERATURE].   R.C.

ANACHORISM [19c: from Greek *anakhōrismós* 'out-of-place-ness'. Stress: 'a-NA-ko-rizm']. (1) In rhetoric, literature, and drama, a rare term for the occurrence or use of something in an inappropriate place: tigers in Africa in Edgar Rice Burroughs's *Tarzan of the Apes* (1912); calling *Loch Lomond* in Scotland 'Lake Lomond'. (2) A foreign or exotic word or expression, such as South Asian English *godown* (warehouse), occurring in BrE. Compare FOREIGNISM. [STYLE, WORD].   T.MCA.

ANACHRONISM [17c: from Greek *anakhronismós* 'out-of-time-ness'. Stress: 'a-NA-kronizm']. In rhetoric, the appearance of a person or thing in the wrong epoch, such as the clock in Shakespeare's *Julius Caesar*. Playwrights in the 16c were not greatly interested in historical accuracy, but a later concern for realism has made such casual anachronism unacceptable, as when an attendant on Pharaoh wears tennis shoes in Cecil B. deMille's film *The Ten Commandments* (1956). Anachronism as a deliberate device, however, brings people and perspectives together from different times, as in Mark Twain's *A Connecticut Yankee in King Arthur's Court* (1889). It is common in science fiction: in 'The Last Gunfight', an episode of the 1960s TV series *Star Trek*, the officers of the Starship *Enterprise* meet 19c Western gunslingers on a remote planet. In due course, these prove to have been spun from Captain Kirk's mind by local telepaths. Social anachronisms include people as well as practices: 'Some [people] also ask me: do I know that being a Duke is an anachronism? Yes, I know that too. There is no contradiction in that: one may enjoy an anachronism' (Duke of Bedford, *How to Run a Stately Home*, 1971). Linguistic anachronisms are generally a matter of awareness, context, and expectation: for example, the archaism *wight* (person, man) may be appropriate at a seminar on the Elizabethan poet Spenser, but is incongruous and probably unintelligible elsewhere. Similarly, a character in a period novel who says *OK* long before the phrase was current rings false for anyone who knows (or senses) that its time is out of joint. Compare ARCHAISM. [STYLE, WORD].   T.MCA.

ANACHRONY [1980: from French *anachronie*: see ANACHRONISM. Stress: 'a-NA-kro-ny']. A change in the sequence of time in a narrative, including *analepsis* (switching to an earlier time, as in a *flashback*) and *prolepsis* (switching to a later time, by *anticipation* or a *flashforward*). provides information necessary to a plot, helps create suspense, and often occurs in stream-of-consciousness prose, contributing to the non-linear effect. See PLOT, STREAM OF CONSCIOUSNESS. [LITERATURE, WRITING].   T.MCA.

ANACOLUTHON [18c: from Greek *anakólouthon* not in proper sequence. Stress: 'a-na-ko-L(Y)OO-thon']. Also **anacoluthia**. In rhetoric, a break or change of direction in a speech: 'I will have such revenges on you both, / That all the world shall—I will do such things, / What they are, yet I know not' (Shakespeare, *King Lear*, 2. 4). In texts, the break is often signalled by a dash: 'I was listening to the news—this man, he's a company director in London—the police arrested him.' See APOSIOPESIS, DASH. [SPEECH, STYLE, WRITING].   T.MCA.

ANADIPLOSIS [16c: from Greek *anadiplōsis* doubling up. Stress: 'a-na-di-PLO-sis']. In rhetoric, a word repeated for effect: 'Victory at all costs, victory in spite of all terror, victory however long and hard the road may be' (Winston Churchill, House of Commons, 4 June 1940). Compare ANAPHORA, EPANALEPSIS, REDUNDANCY, REPETITION. [STYLE].   T.MCA.

ANAGNORISIS [18c: through Latin from Greek *anagnōrisis* recognition, revelation. Stress: 'an-ag-nor-EYE-sis']. In drama, the point of discovery that leads to a reversal of fortune, catastrophic in tragedy, happily resolved in comedy. The protagonist comes to know what has previously been hidden: in Shakespeare, Othello understands Iago's treachery, and Leontes learns that Hermione is not dead (*The Winter's Tale*). The device has been used in novels since the 18c: in Dickens, when Oliver Twist learns his true identity; in Hardy's *Tess of the D'Urbervilles*, when Angel Clare receives Tess's confession too late. In plays and novels, anagnorisis is often the climax of the plot. See DENOUEMENT, DETECTIVE STORY, IRONY, PLOT. [LITERATURE].   R.C.

ANAGRAM [16c: from French *anagramme*, Latin *anagramma*, from Greek *aná* back, *grámma* a letter]. A word or phrase made by rearranging the letters of another word or phrase: *mad policy* from *diplomacy*. The most satisfying anagrams are generally considered to reflect the meaning of the original word (such as *angered* from *enraged*) or describe a person's character (Lewis Carroll turned the name of the British politician *William Ewart Gladstone* into *Wild agitator! Means well*). *Antigrams* have the opposite meaning to the original word or phrase: *violence* changed to *nice love*. Anagrams are used mainly in games and puzzles, especially crosswords, where a clue like 'a confused tailor in Venice' leads to *Rialto*, an anagram of *tailor*. See CROSSWORD, WORD GAME. [WORD].   T.A.

ANALOGY [16c: from French *analogie*, Greek *analogía* double relation]. A comparison or correspondence between two things because of a third element that they are considered to share. An analogy is usually framed in order to describe or explain the nature of something: for example, *time* in 'Let me give you an analogy. Time is like a river. Just as the river flows from higher to lower ground, so time flows from the past into the future.' Once the time/river analogy has been drawn, people can talk about *the flow of time* and *the currents of history*. When such usages are established, their users may forget the analogy and come to think of them as statements of fact: what else can time do but flow? Because analogies depend on the concept *as if*, they often take the form of metaphors and similes.

Mathematics and logic. Among the ancient Greeks, *analogía* referred to a similarity between two proportions, such as $1:2::6:12$. The resemblance in this instance is *the second item in each pair is twice the first item*. All subsequent uses of the word and idea stem from this use. In mathematics, a statement in the form $a \times b = c \times d$ can provide the value of d if the values of a, b, and c are known: if $a = 2$, $b = 15$, $c = 3$, then $d = 10$, because both 2×15 and $3 \times 10 = 30$. Analogy is a form of inference: that if two things agree in at least one respect, they may agree in other respects. If a sheep has four legs, a head, and a tail, and a cow has the same, then the cow may also have eyes, ears, and skin, just like the sheep. Such analogies often hold true, but may break down at any point: it is wrong to suppose that if a cow is like a sheep in these ways it also has a fleece.

Grammar. In traditional language teaching, such paradigms as the conjugations of Latin and French display inflections in a fixed order, using a regular form of the verb for each class of inflections. In French, *j'aime* (I love) is to *tu aimes* (thou lovest) as *j'adore* (I adore) is to *tu adores* (thou adorest). Students learn to apply the basic example to all words of the same type and in this way can form *nous adorons* (we adore) from *nous aimons* (we love). In learning a language, children and students constantly make such analogies, both on their own and under

guidance. Sometimes, however, they engage in *false analogy*. Here, the child or student uses such known relationships as *cat : cats* and *dog : dogs* to produce *sheep : *sheeps*. The analogy has been correctly applied but is false because languages are not completely logical or analogical.

Word-formation. In lexicology, many words are described as created by analogy with other words: that is, new forms are modelled on older forms, as when *cavalcade* (a procession of horses and riders) prompted the formation of *camelcade* (a procession of camels) and *motorcade* (a procession of cars). In addition to the semantics of processions, important factors here appear to be a pattern of three syllables in which sole or primary stress falls on the first. The phonologically suitable **beavercade* is semantically unlikely, however, while the semantically suitable **elephantcade* is phonologically unlikely. Through such analogizing, the suffix *-cade* (meaning 'procession of') is added to the language, its use subject to certain constraints. This kind of analogy is fundamental to the formation of compound and derived words.

Rhetoric. Analogies are commonly employed for rhetorical, stylistic, or dramatic effect, often in the service of a social or political position:

Planet Earth is 4,600 million years old. If we condense this inconceivable time-span into an understandable concept, we can liken Earth to a person of 46 years of age. Nothing is known about the first 7 years of this person's life, and whilst only scattered information exists about the middle span, we know that only at the age 42 did the Earth begin to flower. Dinosaurs and great reptiles did not appear until one year ago, when the planet was 45. Mammals arrived only 8 months ago; in the middle of last week man-like apes evolved into ape-like men, and at the weekend the last ice age enveloped the Earth. Modern man has been around for four hours. During the last hour, Man discovered agriculture. The industrial revolution began a minute ago. During those sixty seconds of biological time, Modern Man has made a rubbish tip of Paradise (from a Greenpeace recruiting and fund-raising pamphlet, 1989).

See ALLUSION, DERIVATIONAL PARADIGM, FANTASY, FIGURATIVE LANGUAGE, LOGIC, METAPHOR, MODEL, PARABLE, PARADIGM, REGULAR AND IRREGULAR, SIMILE, USAGE, WORD-FORMATION. [GRAMMAR, LANGUAGE, STYLE].   T.MCA.

ANALOGY AND ANOMALY [16c: from Greek *analogía* ratio, and *anōmalía* lawlessness]. In philosophy and grammar, terms lying behind the concepts of *rule* and *regularity*. In Greece there were two controversies concerning language: *phúsis* (nature) versus *nómos* (convention), and *analogía* (order) versus *anomalía* (disorder). In the first, the naturalists claimed that language reflects reality, while the conventionalists argued that it is a social contract whose elements have an indirect and arbitrary relationship with matters outside themselves. The conventionalists by and large won this debate, which evolved into whether language is essentially an orderly (analogical) or disorderly (anomalous) phenomenon. Analogy meant ratio and proportion, as in *cat : cats : : dog : dogs*, a relationship that can be re-expressed as the rule 'Add -*s* to such regular nouns as *cat* and *dog* to form the plural', but because the analogy is implicit in such a rule it risks being overlooked. The analogists argued that such ratios could be formulated so easily because they were simply there to be discovered, but the anomalists considered that the analogists were overgeneralizing. The manifestations of plurality were closer to *cat : cats : : man : : men : : goose : geese : : sheep : sheep*. When the empire of Alexander the Great broke up (4c BC), pride of place as centres of learning in the Greek world was disputed by Pergamon in Asia Minor and Alexandria in Egypt. As explanations of language, anomalism was favoured in the first, analogism in the second. The Alexandrians won out, and when Dionysius Thrax wrote in Alexandria the first grammar of Greek he stressed regularity. From time to time, enthusiastic analogists have taken the view that regularities can be strengthened by judiciously straightening out the irregular. However, such items as *children* and *mice* are not easily analogized out of existence. See ANALOGY, REGULAR, RULE. [GRAMMAR, LANGUAGE].   T.MCA.

ANALYTIC [16c: from Latin *analyticus*, Greek *analutikós* separated into component parts]. Also **isolating**. A term in linguistics for a language in which each basic grammatical unit (morpheme) tends to form a separate word, as in Vietnamese, which has been estimated to have 1.06 morphemes per word: *tôi sé làm cho ông* (I *future* do benefit man, 'I'll do it for you'). English is a mildly analytic language, with an estimated 1.68 morphemes per word, though this is seen mainly in vocabulary from sources other than Latin and Greek: *Pick it up and put it in the bag*; *The dog can sleep on the floor*. Analytic languages are sometimes assumed to be monosyllabic, but morphemes can be of any size: the words *tulip* and *asparagus* each contain a single morpheme. See LINGUISTIC TYPOLOGY. [LANGUAGE].   J.M.A.

ANAPAEST BrE, **anapest** AmE [16c: from Latin *anapaestus*, Greek *anápaistos* reversed]. A metrical foot of three syllables, ∪∪–, short/short/long in quantitative metre, as in Latin, weak/weak/strong in accentual metre, as in the English phrase *in the room*. Byron's use of anapaests produces an effect of swift action in:

∪ ∪ – ∪ ∪ – ∪ ∪ –
The Assyr/ian came down / like the wolf /
∪ ∪ –
on the fold

The anapaest, the reverse of a dactyl, is the most common trisyllabic foot in English. See FOOT, METRE/METER, SCANSION. [LITERATURE].   R.C.

ANAPHORA [16c: from Greek *anaphorá* a carrying back. Stress 'a-NA-fo-ra']. (1) Also *anaphoric reference*. A term in grammar and linguistics for referring back in a stretch of language, as with *it* in: 'Although *the aircraft* had been damaged, *it* could still fly.' Here, the pronoun *it* substitutes for its antecedent *the aircraft*. In the next example, the definite article *the* in *the conference* is anaphoric, referring back to *a conference*: 'The EC leaders agreed to hold *a conference* on economic and monetary union, and have now fixed a date for *the conference*.' Anaphoric reference may be achieved through ellipsis, as in 'We asked them to join us, but they wouldn't', where *they wouldn't* means *they wouldn't join us*. The term is sometimes extended to include *cataphora* (forward reference to a following part of the text). (2) Also *epanaphora*. A term in rhetoric for the repetition of the same word or phrase at the beginning of successive phrases, clauses, sentences, and stanzas: 'He shows us a country where a man can be denied the right to know of what and by whom he is accused. A country where some police shoot first and ask questions later. A country where secrecy and short-term political goals may be put before freedom of speech and due process. If what Stalker says is true, Britain has paid for the Anglo-Irish accord by selling out its most cherished ideals' (*Christian Science Monitor*, international weekly edition, 11 Apr. 1988). Compare ANADIPLOSIS, CATAPHORA. [GRAMMAR, STYLE].   S.G., T.MCA.

ANASTROPHE. See INVERSION.

ANECDOTE [17c: through French from Latin *anecdota*, Greek *anékdota* ('not given out') unpublished stories]. A short account of an event or incident, often biographical, gossipy, and intended to entertain. Scientists often use the term *anecdotal* dismissively, especially in the phrase *anecdotal evidence*, to describe data drawn from casual reports rather than systematic study. See FACTS ON FILE, JOKE, SHAGGY DOG STORY, STORY. [STYLE].   T.MCA.

ANGELCYNN. See DIALECT IN ENGLAND, ENGLISH.

ANGLE [14c: through French from Latin *angulus* corner]. In journalism, advertising, etc., a viewpoint or perspective from which an article or feature is written or edited: *Do Florence from the up-market art-lover's angle.* Compare SLANT. [STYLE, WRITING].   T.MCA.

ANGLES [From Old English *Engle, Angle*, associated with *Angul*, the district now called Angeln, in Schleswig]. Germanic settlers in Britain some 1,500 years ago. According to Bede, the fair skin and blue eyes of Angle children in a slave market evoked from Pope Gregory the Great (6–7c) the comment that they were not Angles, but angels. The Angles, who settled to the north of the Saxons, along the east coast and in the Midlands, gave their name to *England, the English*, and *English*. See ANGLIA, ANGLIAN, ANGLIC, ANGLO-, ANGLO-SAXON, DIALECT IN ENGLAND, ENGLAND, ENGLISH, MERCIA, NORTHUMBRIA, OLD ENGLISH[1], SAXON. [EUROPE, HISTORY, NAME].   T.MCA.

ANGLIA [Latin: Land of the Angles, England]. (1) A name for England used mainly for commercial purposes: the *Ford Anglia* car, *the Anglia Building Society.* (2) A short form of *East Anglia*, the region between Essex and the Wash: *Anglia Television, the Royal Anglian Regiment.* See EAST ANGLIA. [EUROPE, NAME].   T.MCA.

ANGLIAN [18c]. (1) Relating to Anglia and the Angles. (2) Also *Anglic*. The language or dialect(s) of the Angles. (3) A variety of runic script. See ANGLES, NORTHUMBRIA, OLD ENGLISH[1], RUNE, SCOTTISH PLACE-NAMES. [EUROPE, HISTORY, NAME, VARIETY].   T.MCA.

ANGLIC [1860s: from Latin *Anglicus* English]. (1) A simplifed form of spelling invented in 1930 by the Swedish philologist R. E. Zachrisson to make English easier as an international language. About 40 frequent words keep their traditional spelling, the rest becoming phonetic. In 1937, the linguist J. R. Firth wrote: 'Anglic simplifies the spelling, Basic English the vocabulary' (*The Tongues of Men*). (2) Anglian (sense 2). See SPELLING REFORM. [EUROPE, HISTORY, VARIETY].   T.MCA.

ANGLICE [16c: from Latin *Anglice* in English. With or without an initial capital. Pronounced: 'ANG-li-sy, AN-gli-see']. Also **Anglicè**. A term marking: (1) A translation into English: 'the Latin "non sequitur" (*Anglice*, it does not follow)'. (2) The conversion of difficult usage, jargon, slang, etc., into plain language: 'Here we lay at the Sign of the Moon and seven Stars (*anglicè* in the open Air)' (J. Ozell, 1718). (3) A gloss of an AmE usage in BrE: 'A Manhattan store (*Anglice* shop) says that all the debutantes are describing one of its new "creations" in winter headgear as "definitely divine" ' (Wilson Follett, 'Words across the Sea', *Atlantic Monthly*, Mar. 1938). [LANGUAGE].   T.MCA.

ANGLICISM [17c: with or without an initial capital]. (1) An expression from English used in another language, such as *le fairplay* in French. (2) A characteristic, quality, fashion, or fad deriving from England, such as cricket or afternoon tea in Pakistan. (3) A feature of the English language that is peculiar to England, such as the working-class phrase *feelin' proper poorly* feeling really ill. See BRITICISM/BRITISHISM, -ISM. [EUROPE, VARIETY, WORD].   T.MCA.

ANGLICIST [1860s]. (1) Someone who favours the use of English. See INDIAN ENGLISH[1]. (2) Also *Anglist*. A scholar who specializes in English, especially in continental Europe (compare French *Angliciste*, German *Anglist*). In German and some other languages, *Anglistik* is English Studies at the university level, sometimes restricted to England or Britain in contrast with *Amerikanistik* American Studies. The translations *Anglistics* and *Americanistics* are sometimes used. See ENGLISH STUDIES. [EDUCATION, EUROPE].   T.MCA.

ANGLICITY [19c]. A quality that characterizes English; the essential nature of the English language: 'So the English vocabulary contains a nucleus or central mass of many thousand words whose "Anglicity" is unquestioned' (James A. H. Murray, General Explanations, *OED*). Compare LATINITY. [LANGUAGE, STYLE].   T.MCA.

ANGLICIZE AmE & BrE, **Anglicise** AusE & BrE [Early 18c: with and without an initial capital]. (1) To make (someone or something) English in nationality, culture, or language: 'What a strange character is Tennyson's Arthur in *Idylls of the King* . . . the most rigorously de-Celticised and Anglicised figure since Layamon's' (Tom Shippey, *London Review of Books*, 26 July 1990). (2) To adopt the English language: 'Are they allowed to *Anglicise* if they like, as the Scottish Highlanders were?' (P. Thompson, 1857, cited in *OED*). (3) To turn into an English form: 'Fort Ross—an anglicized abbreviation of *Fuerte de los Rusos*' (*Harper's Magazine*, Jan. 1883). Compare ANGLIFY, ENGLISHIZE, HOBSON-JOBSONISM. See SCOTS. [EUROPE, VARIETY].   T.MCA.

ANGLIFY [18c: with or without an initial capital]. A usually informal and sometimes pejorative alternative to *Anglicize*: 'the dark dialect of the Anglified Erse' (*Quarterly Review* 15, 1816); 'The greatest American linguistic investment by far has been the Anglification of the millions of immigrant and indigenous speakers of other languages' (Joshua A. Fishman, in Ferguson & Heath (eds.), *Language in the USA*, 1981). Compare the relationship between *Frenchify* and *Gallicize*. See ANGLICIZE. [EUROPE, VARIETY].

T.MCA.

ANGLIKAANS [Mid-20c: a blend of *Anglo* and *Afrikaans*]. An occasional informal term for a colloquial mixture of English and Afrikaans: 'In the popular press, the speech style combining English and Afrikaans elements is sometimes called *Anglikaans* in imitation of *franglais*. . . . Many literal translations from Afrikaans give this variety its typical flavor: *bell* "to telephone" (e.g. *I'll bell some of the chicks*)' (L. W. Lanham, 'English in South Africa', in Bailey & Görlach (eds.), *English as a World Language*, 1982). See AFRIKAANS ENGLISH, CODE-MIXING AND CODE-SWITCHING, SOUTH AFRICAN ENGLISH. [AFRICA, VARIETY].

T.MCA.

ANGLO [1830s: a free form of *Anglo*-]. (1) In and around the US Southwest, a clipping of Spanish *anglo-americano* and English *Anglo-American* standing, sometimes pejoratively, for a (white) speaker of English: 'Chicano norms always seem to be somewhat less formal than Anglo norms' (Fernando Peñalosa, *Chicano Sociolinguistics*, 1980). (2) In Canada and especially Quebec, a clipping of *anglophone*, standing for a speaker of English: *anglo rights*. It does not usually have a capital and may contrast with *franco*: see ALLIANCE QUEBEC, ANGLOPHONE. (3) In Scotland, a clipping of *Anglo-Scot*, standing for someone who is half-English, half-Scottish, a Scot who has been influenced by English ideas, mannerisms, etc., and a Scot who plays for an English soccer team. (4) In South Africa, a clipping of the company name *Anglo American Corporation*: 'He joined Anglo as a consultant.' [AFRICA, AMERICAS, EUROPE, NAME].

T.MCA.

ANGLO- [16c: from Latin *Anglus* English]. A combining form relating to: the Angles (*Anglo-Saxon culture*), England and the English (*Anglo-Welsh relations*) or Britain and the British (*the Anglo-Irish agreement*), location in England (*Anglo-Jewry* the Jews of England), and the English language (*Anglo-Danish pidgin*). In Northern Ireland, Scotland, and Wales, the use of the term to mean *Britain/British* is widely disliked. In Scotland, newspapers tend to avoid this sense of *Anglo*-, using instead such phrases as *the British–Irish agreement*. See ANGLO, ANGLO-SAXON, BRITISH-. [EUROPE, NAME].

T.MCA.

ANGLO-AMERICAN [Early 18c]. (1) Relating to England or Britain and the US: *Anglo-American trade talks*. (2) A citizen of the US

born in England or of English origin. (3) An American who speaks English: compare ANGLO. (4) A term for the English language proposed by the British zoologist and amateur linguist Lancelot Hogben in *The Mother Tongue* (1964). (5) American English: 'Since the Second World War, the Nordic languages have taken over not only direct loans, but also calques and grammatical constructions from Anglo-American' (*Language International* 2: 2, 1990). [AMERICAS, EUROPE, NAME].

T.MCA.

ANGLO-ARGENTINE. See Argentina.

ANGLO-AUSTRALIAN. See ANGLO-CELTIC.

ANGLO-CANADIAN [19c]. (1) Relating to England or Britain and Canada: *Anglo-Canadian ties*. (2) Formerly, a citizen or resident of Canada born in England or of English origin. (3) Currently and especially in Quebec, an English-speaking or anglophone Canadian, usually without regard to ethnic background. See ANGLO, ANGLOPHONE. [AMERICAS, EUROPE, NAME].

T.MCA.

ANGLO-CELTIC [19c]. (1) Relating to the Angles, England, the English, or the English language on the one hand and the Celts (in Ireland, Scotland, Wales, the Isle of Man, or elsewhere) on the other: 'The relative importance of the formal rules of communication in Anglo-Celtic cultures as opposed to those of the German-speaking countries can be seen in the conduct of formal meetings' (Larry E. Smith, *Discourse Across Cultures: Strategies in World Englishes*, 1987). (2) By nature or in origin both English or British and Celtic, as used by the English physician and anthropologist John Beddoe (1823-1911) in an article comparing mortality rates in Britain and Australia. From the 1880s, the term acquired a special significance in Australia; unlike *Anglo-Australian* and *Anglo-colonial*, it recognized the Irish-Catholic section of the population. As Australia has become multicultural, *Anglo-Celtic* has been used to distinguish people of British and Irish descent from immigrants of European or Asian descent, and from the Aborigines. See ANGLO-, CELTIC. [EUROPE, NAME, OCEANIA].

T.MCA., W.S.R.

ANGLOCENTRIC [1880s]. Centred on England and the English (or Britain and the British), or on the English language: 'The Commonwealth has moved further and further away from being Anglocentric' (*The Economist*, 26 May 1962). See BRITOCENTRIC, CENTRICITY. [EUROPE, LANGUAGE, NAME].

T.MCA.

ANGLO-CHINESE SCHOOLS. See HONG KONG.

ANGLO-DANISH. Old Danish as spoken in England (9–11c). Some scholars used the term *Anglo-Danish pidgin* for a contact language between speakers of Old English and Old Danish (*c.*10–11c), to account for simplifications that developed in English and the influence of Danish on English grammar and vocabulary. Because the two groups could not fully understand each other, a trade pidgin may have arisen: 'As the bilingual situation receded, the varieties that remained must have been effectively Anglo-Norse creoles' (James Milroy, 'The History of English in the British Isles', in *Language in the British Isles*, ed. P. Trudgill, 1984). See DANELAW, NORSE, PIDGIN. [EUROPE, HISTORY, LANGUAGES, VARIETY].   T.MCA.

ANGLO ENGLISH [1980s]. An occasional term in especially the Southwest of the US for English as used by Anglos: 'It is not known whether Chicanos who wish to replace their Chicano English with Anglo English turn primarily to regional or to national standards of English' (Fernando Peñalosa, *Chicano Sociolinguistics*, 1980). See ANGLO, CHICANO ENGLISH. [AMERICAS, VARIETY].   T.MCA.

ANGLO-ENGLISH [1970s]. An occasional term for the (standard) English language as used in England: 'I have chosen one accent for Scottish Standard English and one for "Anglo-English" (a convenient term for English Standard English recently introduced in the correspondence columns of *The Scotsman*)' (David Abercrombie, in *Languages of Scotland*, 1979). See ENGLISH ENGLISH, ENGLISH IN ENGLAND. [EUROPE, VARIETY].   T.MCA.

ANGLO-FRISIAN [1877: coined by Henry Sweet]. A term in philology linking the Old English and Old Frisian languages and the Angle and Frisian peoples who settled in Britain (5–7c), and naming a hypothetical subdivision of the West Germanic branch of the Indo-European language family, the parent of Old English and Old Frisian. See INGVAEONIC. [EUROPE, LANGUAGE].   T.MCA.

ANGLO-GAELIC [1980s]. An occasional informal term for elements of English and Gaelic used together: 'calling from an upstairs landing for "a cuppa tea, *le do thoil* (please)," an Anglo-Gaelic mix favoured by Falls Road revolutionaries' (Cal McCrystal, *Independent on Sunday*, 25 Feb. 1990). See ANGLO-GAELIC. [EUROPE, LANGUAGE, VARIETY].   T.MCA.

ANGLO-INDIAN [1800s]. (1) Now rare: relating to England or Britain, and India: *Anglo-Indian ties*. (2) Of English or British people and their activities in India during the Raj: *Anglo-Indian words and phrases*; *an Anglo-Indian colonel*. (3) Of the community of Eurasians in India descended from European fathers and Indian mothers, often disdained by both British and Indians and referred to in the 19c and earlier 20c as 'European half-castes'. The Indian Constitution defines an *Anglo-Indian* as 'a person whose father or any of whose other male progenitors in the male line is or was of European descent but who is domiciled within the territory of India and is or was born within such territory of parents habitually resident therein and not established there for temporary purposes only.' The mother tongue of the Anglo-Indian community is English. In present-day India, an *Anglo-Indian school* is an English-medium private school associated with the community and a Christian denomination, but open to students of all backgrounds. *Anglo-Indian English* is a subvariety of IndE. See Frank Anthony, *Britain's Betrayal in India: The Story of the Anglo-Indian Community* (Allied Publishers, Bombay, 1969), and R. A. Schermerhorn, 'Anglo-Indians: An Uneasy Minority', in *Ethnic Plurality in India* (University of Arizona Press, 1978). (4) Relating to the body of writing in English centred on the Indian subcontinent and written by such non-Indians as Rudyard Kipling, E. M. Forster, and John Masters, making use of forms of language appropriate to the cultural, sociolinguistic, and political contexts of the region: *Anglo-Indian literature*. See Ivor Lewis, *Sahibs, Nabobs and Boxwallahs: A Dictionary of the words of Anglo-India* (Oxford University Press, Bombay, 1991). See BURGHER ENGLISH, CHEE-CHEE ENGLISH, CONVENT ENGLISH, ENGLISH-MEDIUM SCHOOL, HOBSON-JOBSON, INDIAN ENGLISH[1], INDIAN ENGLISH LITERATURE, INDO-ANGLIAN, KIPLING. [ASIA, EUROPE, LITERATURE, NAME, VARIETY].   T.MCA., B.B.K.

ANGLO-IRISH [1830s]. (1) Relating to England or Britain and Ireland: *the Anglo-Irish agreement*, *Anglo-Irish tensions*. See ANGLO-. (2) Relating to the English in Ireland and the Protestant Ascendancy: 'PAT. He was an Anglo-Irishman. / MEG. In the blessed name of God, what's that? / PAT. A Protestant with a horse' (Brendan Behan, *The Hostage*, 1958, Act I). The term is disliked by many Irish nationalists when used to refer to Irish literature in English or when it obtrusively recalls the centuries of English/British rule over Ireland. (3) A term, especially in linguistics, for a variety of English spoken over most of Ireland. It derives mainly from the English brought to Ireland by 17c *Planters* (settlers) from England, modified by contacts with Irish Gaelic, Ulster Scots, and Hiberno-English. It is a continuum of usage influenced by the level of education of its speakers, their regional origin, and the area of original settlement. The usage of more educated speakers approximates to Irish broadcasting norms, whereas less educated speakers have more distinctive accents and non-standard usages.

Pronunciation. The middle-class Anglo-Irish accent has been influenced by and continues to be close to RP. However, it is rhotic (with a retroflex *r*) and the /t, d/ in words like *true* and *drew* tend to be dental rather than alveolar, suggesting 'thrue' and 'dhrew'. In working-class speech, the following features are common: (1) Words such as *leave* and *tea* sound like 'lave' and 'tay', *cold* and *old* sound like 'cowl' and 'owl', *bull* and *could* can rhyme with 'cull' and 'bud', and *which* and *whether* are distinguished from *witch* and *weather* (beginning with /hw/, not /w/). (2) In such words as *arm* and *film*, a vowel often opens up the consonant clusters: 'aram' and 'fillim'. (3) In the South, words such as *pence* are often pronounced 'pensh' (an /ʃ/ in word-final position) and *story* and *small* are often pronounced 'shtory' and 'shmall' (an /ʃ/ in consonant clusters). Less often, such words as *fizzed* and *puzzle* sound like 'fizhd' and 'puzhl' (a /ʒ/ in consonant clusters). Also in Southern Anglo-Irish, words such as *thin* and *then* sound like 'tin' and 'den' (/ð, θ/ replaced by /t, d/). Words such as *try, dry, butter*, and *under* sound like *thry, dhry, butther* and *undher* (with interdental rather than alveolar plosives).

Grammar. Standard Anglo-Irish is close to the standard BrE varieties. Non-standard Anglo-Irish syntax has six features also found outside Ireland: (1) *Done* and *seen* in the past tense: *She done it because she seen me do it.* (2) Special past participles: *He has div* He has dived; *They have went* They have gone. (3) Auxiliary *have* reduced to *a*: *You should a knew* You should have known; *They would a helped you.* (4) *Them* as a demonstrative plural adjective and pronoun: *Them shoes is lovely yet. Them's the ones I wanted.* (5) A plural form of *you*. In the South, it tends to be *ye* (rhyming with *he*: *Ye'll all get what's comin to ye*) or *youse* (rhyming with *whose*: *Youse childher will get a good beatin' when your father gets in!*). In the North, it is *yiz* (rhyming with *his*: *Yiz'll all get what's comin to yiz, Yiz childher will get . . .*). (6) Singular *be* with plural subjects: *Me and Mick's fed up, Mary and the daughter's out shopping, Yiz is late, Themins* (those ones) *is no use.* Such features are probably tolerated higher up the social ladder than in Britain.

Vocabulary. (1) Distinctive words never current in the standard language: *atomy* a small, insignificant person, as in *Did you ever see such a wee atomy of a man?*; *cog* to cheat, for example by copying, as in *I wouldn't let just anybody cog my*

exercise; *thole* to endure, as in *There was nothin for it but to thole* (shared with ScoE). (2) General words with distinctive senses: *backward* shy, *bold* naughty, *doubt* strongly believe, as in *I doubt he's coming* (shared with ScoE). Most regionally marked words occur in the speech of older, often rural people; it is unlikely that *biddable* obedient, *feasant* affable, *pishmire/pismire* ant, occur in the natural usage of people under 40. See BELFAST, DUBLIN, IRISH ENGLISH, NEWFOUNDLAND ENGLISH, NORTHERN IRISH ENGLISH, SHERIDAN (R.), SHERIDAN (T.), STEELE, STERNE, SWIFT. [AMERICAS, EUROPE, NAME, VARIETY].   L.T.

ANGLO-IRISH LITERATURE. Literature written by Irish authors in English. Many Irish people dislike the term, preferring to use *Irish literature* to comprehend all the literature written in Ireland, whether in Irish (Gaelic), English, French, or Latin. Literature in Irish dates from the 7c and in English from the 14c, when the so-called 'Kildare Poems' were written in a dialect that has strong links with early southwestern dialects in England. These poems seem to have been a product of the first quarter of the 14c and may have been composed in the monastic settlements of the town of Kildare. The subject matter is varied and includes verse on the transitory nature of earthly love and life ('This world is love is gone awai, / So dew on grasse in somer is dai'), on God's love, on religious themes, on battles, and on the punishment due to lawless men: 'Men ne schold ham biri in non church, / Bot cast ham ute as a hund' (quotations from J. J. Hogan, *The English Language in Ireland*, 1927). Similar poetry continued to be written in the 15c and early 16c and was augmented by prose that was often of a didactic nature. The second wave of colonization dates from the end of the 16c, with settlers from both England and Scotland. They differed from the native Irish and the first English colonists in being Protestant and in having closer links with Britain. The writing of the new Protestant, Anglo-Irish élite covers all the genres and becomes particularly noteworthy from the 17c. Among the early dramatists with strong Irish connections were William Congreve, George Farquhar, Oliver Goldsmith, and Richard Brinsley Sheridan. Prose writers include Jonathan Swift, George Berkeley, Laurence Sterne, and Edmund Burke. Poetry was written by many of these writers and by Charlotte Brooke, who also translated poems from Irish.

In the 19c, three trends in particular were significant: (1) Anglo-Irish novelists such as Maria Edgeworth and Lady Morgan wrote about Irish subjects with sensitivity and generosity. (2) Native Irish writers began to use the English language with skill and flexibility. They include the poet and musician Thomas Moore, the novelist William Carleton, and the poet James Clarence Mangan. (3) Towards the end of the century, Anglo-Irish authors such as Oscar Wilde, William Allingham, and George Bernard Shaw were among the most internationally renowned writers in the English language. From the middle of the 19c onward, it is difficult to draw distinctions between the works of writers of Anglo-Irish and of Gaelic origin, in that both groups used English for themes that included and excluded Ireland and Irish preoccupations. However, many, from Farquhar to Samuel Beckett, found fame as expatriate writers, and many more, including William Butler Yeats, James Joyce, Louis MacNeice, and Sean O'Casey, found fame on an international stage. Literature in Irish Gaelic continues to be written but is increasingly aimed at a specialist audience. Its influence on writers in English is apparent in Seamus Heaney, who brought the medieval poem 'Buille Suibhne' up to date in *Sweeney Astray* (1983), or Paul Muldoon, who continues to find inspiration in the Immrama ('Rowings') or journeys into the unknown. There does not seem to be any set of linguistic signals that mark off the work of major writers born in Ireland from their peers elsewhere, with the possible exception (as has from time to time been asserted) of their awareness of language and their ability to manipulate it with wit and skill. See ENGLISH LITERATURE, JOYCE, SHAW, SPENSER, SWIFT. [EUROPE, LITERATURE, VARIETY].   L.T.

ANGLO-LATIN. Medieval, Renaissance, and later Latin as used in England. See FRENCH, LATIN[1]. [EUROPE, LANGUAGE].   T.MCA.

ANGLO-MALAY. See MALAYSIAN ENGLISH.

ANGLOMANIA [18c: through French *anglomanie* from Latin *Anglus* English, Greek *mania* madness]. Excessive respect, love, and enthusiasm for England and the English, and/or the English language. The term may include Britain at large, but non-English Britons may also feel Anglomania. Parallel usages exist for other nations and languages, such as *Francomania* or *Gallomania*, an obsession with France, the French, and French. See FRENCH. [EUROPE, NAME].   T.MCA.

ANGLO-NORMAN [18c]. (1) Of the Normans in England or both the Normans and the indigenous English: *Anglo-Norman culture*. (2) of Norman French as used in England or a contact language mixing French and English, used between the Normans and their subjects: 'The Anglo-Norman jargon was only employed in the commercial intercourse between the conquerors and the conquered' (George Ellis, *Specimens of*

the Early English Poets, 1801). See CRAIGIE, IRELAND, IRISH ENGLISH, IRISH PLACE-NAMES, NORMAN, NORMAN FRENCH, SCOTS. [EUROPE, HISTORY, LANGUAGE].   T.MCA.

ANGLO-NORSE. See ANGLO-DANISH.

ANGLOPHILE [1860s: from French *anglophile*, from Latin *Anglus* English, Greek *philos* loving]. (1) Admiring or loving England and the English and/or the English language: *the Anglophile party in Scotland*. (2) Someone with such an attitude: *unrepentant Anglophiles*. The term may or may not include Britain as a whole, and non-English Britons may experience *Anglophilia*. [EUROPE, NAME].   T.MCA.

ANGLOPHOBE [1860s: from French *anglophobe*, from Latin *Anglus* English, Greek *phóbos* fear]. (1) Also *Anglophobic*. Fearing or hating England and the English and/or the English language: *Anglophobe reaction*. (2) Someone with such an attitude: *an inveterate Anglophobe*. The term may or may not include Britain as a whole, and non-English Britons may experience *Anglophobia*. [EUROPE, NAME].   T.MCA.

ANGLOPHONE [1960s: from French *anglophone*, from Latin *Anglus* English, Greek *phōnē* voice: often used in the French style without an initial capital]. (1) A speaker of English: (Africa) *locally born anglophone whites*; (Quebec) *certified anglophones*, permitted by law to send their children to English-medium schools. (2) Of speakers of English: *an anglophone school*. The term occurs mainly where French is also used. It contrasts with *francophone* (French-speaking), *allophone* (speaking a language other than French or English), *arabophone* (speaking Arabic), *hispanophone* (speaking Spanish), and *lusophone* (speaking Portuguese), etc. [AFRICA, AMERICAS, NAME].   T.MCA.

ANGLO-ROMANI. See ROMANI/ROMANY.

ANGLO-SAXON [16c: from Latin plural *Anglo-Saxones*. Compare Old English *Angulseaxan*]. Originally a name for the Saxons who with the Angles invaded and settled in Britain (5–7c), to contrast them with the *Old Saxons* of Germany. The name was later given both to the Angles and Saxons, also known as *the old English* (*Anglo-Saxon law*) and to their language, also known as *old English* (*Anglo-Saxon grammar*). More broadly and recently, it has served to identify a culture, spirit, style, heritage, or ethnic type associated with England, Britain, the British Empire, and/or the US: *Anglo-Saxon civilization*. It is also used to label vernacular English, especially when considered plain, monosyllabic, crude, and vulgar: *Anglo-Saxon words*.

History. For many centuries there was no agreed collective name for the Germanic peoples who settled in Britain. By the time of the Norman Conquest (1066), *English* had emerged for the peoples and their language, but when the Normans began to call themselves English the older sense of the word was obscured and the identification of *English* with post-Conquest England was strengthened. The mass of the people were classed by their overlords as *Saxon*. Medieval Latin chroniclers used *Anglo-Saxones* and *Angli Saxones* to refer to both Angles and Saxons, a practice that became universal after 1600 for anything before the Conquest. In 1884, James Murray noted in the *OED* entry *Anglo-Saxon* that this practice had led 'to an erroneous analysis of the word, which has been taken as = *Angle* + *Saxon*, a union of Angle and Saxon; and in accordance with this mistaken view, modern combinations have been profusely formed in which *Anglo-* is meant to express "English and . . .", "English in connexion with . . .", as "the Anglo-Russian war"; whence, on the same analogy, Franco-German, Turko-Russian, etc.'

Culture. An extension of the term to mean the people of England and (loosely) Britain developed in the 19c, for example when the journalist Walter Bagehot referred in a speech to wealth as 'the obvious and national idol of the Anglo-Saxon'. In 1956, the novelist Angus Wilson revived a phrase of Lewis Carroll's as the title of his satirical novel *Anglo-Saxon Attitudes*. The term *Anglo-Saxon* now refers to anyone in any way linked with England, the English language, and their traditions: in France, *anglosaxon* has been used, often negatively, for shared 'Anglo-American' attitudes and culture, while in 1975 the Tanzanian writer Ali Mazrui coined *Afro-Saxon* to describe Black Africans who adopt English as the language of the home and with it cultural attitudes and values which in effect make them Black Englishmen.

Plain usage. In Victorian times, the term was associated with the Germanic element in English vocabulary, especially by such purists as William Barnes. Its use as a label for direct and often coarse language marks a perception of Old English as a medium that called a spade a spade. This view contrasts a simple, vigorous vernacular with an effete Latinate style little understood and seldom used by the people at large. For those who hold this view, *smell* and *sweat* are plainer, briefer, and better than *odour* and *perspiration*. More pointedly still, the term is used for vulgar expressions. Webster's *Third New International Dictionary* (1966) gives *Anglo-Saxon word* as a synonym of *four-letter*

word, and Charles Berlitz has observed: 'In general, almost all the polysyllabic words in English are of French-Latin origin while the one-syllable words come from Anglo-Saxon' (*Native Tongues*, 1982). There are, however, many Anglo-Saxon polysyllables, such as *bloodthirstily* and *righthandedness*. See ANGLES, BIG WORD, OLD ENGLISH[1], PLAIN, RUNE, SAXON. [EUROPE, HISTORY, LANGUAGE, NAME].   T.MCA.

ANGLO-SAXON CHRONICLE [*c*.891–1154]. Also *Old English Annals*, *Old English Chronicle*. A set of annals, the first extended original composition in English, probably begun in the court of King Alfred and continued in monasteries, in which the seven surviving manuscripts were written. The last, for 1154, is also the last known document in Old English. The Chronicle includes six poems amidst the prose entries, starting with the 937 annal on the battle of Brunanburh. Anne Savage's modern rendering (*The Anglo-Saxon Chronicles*, 1983) conveys in prose a sense of the original poetry:

Aethelstan, king, lord of eorls, ring-giver to men, and his brother also, the atheling Edmund, lifelong glory struck in battle with sword's edge at Brunnanburh, broke the shield-wall, hewed linden-wood with hammer's leaving. Edward's sons, as they were noble-born, accustomed to battle, often on campaign had defended their land from each foe, hoard and home; the hated ones were crushed, people of the Scots, men of the ships, fated fell.

The chroniclers used many sources, including Bede's history, other annals and records, and popular stories. The use of the vernacular rather than Latin for chronicles was rare at that time. See ALFRED, BEDE, OLD ENGLISH[1]. [EUROPE, HISTORY, MEDIA].   W.F.B.

ANGLO-SAXONISM. See SAXONISM.

ANGLO-SCOT. See ANGLO.

ANGLO-WELSH LITERATURE. The term *Anglo-Welsh* was first used with a literary connotation by H. Idris Bell in 1922, and has subsequently been applied to Welsh writers of English, their work, Welsh literature in English generally, and Welsh writers who use English but are concerned to see their work as part of an indigenous cultural tradition. Many Welsh writers dislike the term, preferring to use *Welsh literature* to encompass all the literature of Wales: Welsh, Latin, or English. There has been an unbroken tradition of Welsh literature in English since the 15c. The first poem in English is reputed to have been written in 1470 by an Oxford-educated man from Powys, called Ieuan ap Hywel Swrdwal. His intricate poem to the Virgin Mary includes the following short stanza:

Kwin od off owr God, owr geiding
mwdyr, maedyn notwythstanding,
hwo wed syts wyth a ryts ring,
as God wod ddys gyd weding.
[Sole queen of our God, our guiding
mother, maiden notwithstanding,
who wed such with a rich ring,
since God desired this good wedding.]

The earliest prose was probably an *Abridgement of the Common Law* by William Owen of Henllys in 1499. Throughout the 15c and early 16c, Welsh writers produced poetry and prose, often of a religious nature, in English. The first Welsh writer of international status was the metaphysical poet Henry Vaughan (1622–95), who knew Welsh but does not seem to have been overtly influenced by the language or the intricacies of Welsh versification. Wales also produced a number of female writers although, until the 19c, it was not easy for women to get their works published. Jane Brereton (née Hughes in 1685) had her *Poems on Several Occasions* published posthumously in 1744. Anne Penny's *Poems with a Dramatic Entertainment* were published in 1771 and Anna Williams had the assistance of Samuel Johnson in publishing *Miscellanies in Prose and Verse* in 1766.

Most Anglo-Welsh writings appear to have been similar in form and theme to their English counterparts until the end of the 18c. At this time, a Romantic interest in Celtic culture developed and Welsh writers could again take an overt pride in their own literature and literary conventions. The novel was the main Anglo-Welsh medium in the 19c. Thomas Love Peacock (1785–1866) was not Welsh (although he married a Welshwoman), but the Welsh backgrounds of *Headlong Hall* (1816) and *Crotchet Castle* (1831) helped to foster an interest in Welsh novels, including *Cometh up as a Flower* (1867) and *Red as a Rose is She* (1870) by Rhoda Broughton (1840–1920). Gerard Manley Hopkins (1844–89) was not Welsh, but his recharging of poetic language owes much to his time in Wales and to his study of Welsh patterns of verse.

The 20c has seen the publication of works by Welsh writers widely read in the English-speaking world. The best-known novelists are Howard Spring (*O Absalom*, 1938, and *Fame is the Spur*, 1940) and Richard Llewellyn (*How Green Was My Valley*, 1939). The short story was adapted for expressing a Welsh point of view by writers such as Geraint Goodwin and Rhys Davies. There have also been many plays, including the work of Caradoc Evans, Saunders Lewis, and Gwyn Thomas, and television plays with a Welsh theme have increased the audience for Anglo-Welsh writing. Best known of all Anglo-Welsh writers is Dylan Thomas (1914–53), who wrote short stories, plays (including *Under Milk Wood*, 1954), and poetry that was elegant and eloquent, passionate, and complexly patterned. Anglo-Welsh literature continues to draw from and influence literature in Welsh; increasingly, writers are using both languages to deal with themes of national and international significance. In the principality, the literature in English has a wider audience but not necessarily greater prestige. See THOMAS, WALES, WELSH ENGLISH, WELSH LITERATURE. [EUROPE, LITERATURE]. L.T.

Garlick, Raymond. 1970. *An Introduction to Anglo-Welsh Literature*. University of Wales Press.
—— & Mathias, Roland (eds.). 1984. *Anglo-Welsh Poetry 1480–1980*. Bridgend: Poetry Wales Press.
Hughes, W. J. 1924. *Wales and the Welsh in English Literature*. Wrexham: Hughes and Son.
Jones, Gwyn (ed.). 1977. *The Oxford Book of Welsh Verse in English*. Oxford: University Press.
Mathias, Roland. 1987. *Anglo-Welsh Literature: An Illustrated History*. Bridgend: Poetry Wales Press.

ANGUILLA. A British dependency, the most northerly of the Leeward Islands. Capital: The Valley. Currency: the East Caribbean dollar. Economy: tourism and fishing. Population: 6,500 (1974), mainly African. Languages: English, Creole. English settlers from St Kitts colonized the island in 1650. See CARIBBEAN, ENGLISH, SAINT CHRISTOPHER AND NEVIS. [AMERICAS, NAME, VARIETY]. T.MCA., L.D.C.

ANGUISH. See BONEHEAD ENGLISH.

ANIMATE NOUN. A semantic category of noun, referring to a person, animal, or other creature (*boy*, *sheep*, *worm*), in contrast to an *inanimate noun*, which refers to a thing or concept (*corn*, *boyhood*, *sleep*). In general, animate nouns correlate with the pronouns *he*, *she*, *who* and inanimate nouns with *it*, *which*. See NOUN. [GRAMMAR]. S.C.

ANNOTATION. See NOTES AND REFERENCES.

ANOMIA [Date uncertain: from Greek *a-* not, Latin *nomen* name, and *-ia* as in *dyslexia*]. A characteristic of certain types of aphasia, where the speaker is unable to find the words for everyday concepts. See APHASIA. [LANGUAGE]. D.C.

ANTECEDENT [14c: from French *antécédent*, from Latin *antecedere* to go before]. (1) The words in a text, usually a noun phrase, to which a pronoun or other grammatical unit refers back. *Cook* is the antecedent of *him* in: 'In 1772, *Cook* began his second voyage, which took *him* further south than he had ever been.' Similarly, *his second voyage* is the antecedent of *which*. With impersonal *it, this, that, which*, the antecedent may be a whole clause or paragraph, as in: '*Might not the coast of New South Wales provide an armed haven*? To some people *this* looked good on paper, but there is no hard evidence that *it* did so to William Pitt or his ministers.' Despite the implications of the name, an antecedent can follow rather than precede: 'For *his* first Pacific voyage, *Cook* had no chronometer.' (2) In logic, the conditional element in a proposition. In *If they did that, they deserve our respect, they did that* is the antecedent. [GRAMMAR].   S.C., T.MCA.

ANTHROPONYMY [1930s: from Greek *ánthrōpos* human being, *ónuma* name]. The study of personal names. See ONOMASTICS, -ONYM, PERSONAL NAME. [NAME].   J.A.

ANTICIPATORY IT. A term for the pronoun *it* used in advance of the word, phrase, or clause to which it relates: '*It*'s clear to me (*that*) you never meant to do that'; 'I take *it that you are annoyed*.' This use is usually distinguished from another known as prop, empty, dummy, and introductory *it*, where the pronoun does not refer to anything: '*It*'s seven o'clock, and *it*'s still raining.' The pronoun may serve as either subject or object: (1) Also *anticipatory subject, introductory subject, preparatory subject*. The use of *it* as grammatical subject, the semantic subject coming later, often in the form of a clause or phrase: '*It is a waste of time telling you anything*'; '*It is extraordinary the lengths some people will go to*'; '*It seems that he didn't take the job after all*.' (2) Also *anticipatory object*. The use of *it* as the grammatical object, with the semantic object coming later, often as a clause or phrase: 'I take *it that you are annoyed*'; 'I find *it* difficult *to understand how anyone could think that*.' See CLEFT SENTENCE, DUMMY. [GRAMMAR].   S.C.

ANTICLIMAX [18c: through Latin from Greek *antiklimax* down a ladder]. (1) In rhetoric, a descent from the elevated and important to the low and trivial: 'Here thou, Great Anna! whom three realms obey, / Dost sometimes counsel take— and sometimes Tea' (Pope, *The Rape of the Lock*, 1712). (2) In drama, the lowered state after a climax; in life, an outcome that fails to live up to expectation. See BATHOS, CLIMAX, FIGURE OF SPEECH. [LITERATURE, STYLE].   T.MCA.

ANTIGRAM. See ANAGRAM.

ANTIGUA AND BARBUDA. A Caribbean country and member of the Commonwealth. Capital: Saint John's, Antigua. Currency: the East Caribbean dollar. Economy: tourism,

sugar. Population: 83,000 (1988), 97,000 (projection for 2000). Ethnicity: 92% African, 4% mixed, 4% Caucasian. Languages: English, Creole. Education: primary/secondary 63%, tertiary 11%, literacy 98%. In 1493, Columbus named the major island after the church of Santa Maria de la Antigua in Seville. English colonists settled Antigua in 1632, and Spain ceded it to Britain in 1667. Barbuda was colonized from Antigua in 1661. The islands, part of the Leeward Island Federation from 1871 to 1956, became independent in 1981. See CARIBBEAN, ENGLISH. [AMERICAS, NAME, VARIETY].   T.MCA.

ANTILLES [From *Antilia*, the name of a hypothetical island shown on charts in the early 15c and applied to the West Indies in 1493]. The islands of the Caribbean excluding the Bahamas. The *Greater Antilles* are Cuba, Jamaica, Hispaniola (Haiti, the Dominican Republic), and Puerto Rico. The *Lesser Antilles* are the Windward Islands, the Leeward Islands, and the *Netherlands Antilles*. See CARIBBEAN, WEST INDIES. [AMERICAS, NAME].   T.MCA.

ANTIPHRASIS. See IRONY.

ANTIPODEAN ENGLISH. See AUSTRALASIAN ENGLISH.

ANTIPODES [14c: through Latin from Greek *antipodes*, plural of *antipous/antipodos* having the foot opposite. Stress: 'an-TI-po-deez'. Former stress: 'AN-ti-poads'. Both with or without an initial capital]. A term first applied in English to the people of Ethiopia, once believed to live on the opposite side of the globe; by the 16c, applied to places directly opposite one other on the surface of the earth and to that place directly 'under' one's own location. A group of islands opposite Greenwich in England and south-east of New Zealand was named *the Antipodes* in 1800. From the 1830s, British travellers to Australia and New Zealand (but especially Australia) were encouraged by the reversal of the seasons and the unusualness of much of the flora and fauna to see an antipodean 'world turned upside down', in which 'everything goes by contraries'. Compare DOWN UNDER. [HISTORY, NAME, OCEANIA].   W.S.R.

ANTITHESIS [15c: through Latin from Greek *antithesis* setting against, opposition. Stress: 'an-TI-the-sis']. (1) In rhetoric, a construction in which words are opposed but balanced: 'For many are called, but few are chosen' (Matthew 22: 14); 'To err is human, to forgive, divine' (Pope, 1711). Technically, the first part of such constructions is the *thesis* ('for many are called'), the second the antithesis ('but few are chosen').

(2) In general usage, opposite: *This policy is the antithesis of everything we believe in.* See CHIASMUS, THESIS. [STYLE].   T.MCA.

ANTONOMASIA [16c: through Latin from Greek *antonomasia* 'a naming instead': that is, replacing one name with another. Stress: 'an-to-no-MAY-zy-a']. (1) In rhetoric, the use of an epithet to acknowledge a quality in one person or place by using the name of another person or place already known for that quality: *Henry is the local Casanova*; *Cambridge is England's Silicon Valley.* In 'An Elegy written in a Country Church-Yard' (1751), Thomas Gray used antonomasia to help identify people whose names he did not know: 'Some village Hampden that with dauntless breast / The little tyrant of his fields withstood, / Some mute inglorious Milton, here may rest, / Some Cromwell guiltless of his country's blood.' (2) The use of an epithet instead of the name of a person or thing: *the Swan of Avon* William Shakespeare; *the Athens of the North* Edinburgh. See FIGURE OF SPEECH. [NAME, STYLE].   T.MCA.

ANTONYM [1860s: on the analogy of *synonym*, using the Greek-derived prefix *anti-* against]. One of two words or other expressions that have opposite meanings: *fast* and *slow*, *hot* and *cold*. Some words are antonymous in some contexts but not others: *straight* is generally the opposite of *bent/curved*, but is the antonym of *gay* in the context of homosexuality. Linguists identify three types of antonymy: (1) *Gradable antonyms*, which operate on a continuum: *(very) big*, *(very) small*. Such pairs often occur in binomial phrases with *and*: *(blow) hot and cold*, *(search) high and low*. (2) *Complementary antonyms*, which express an either/or relationship: *dead* or *alive*, *male* or *female*. (3) *Converse* or *relational antonyms*, expressing reciprocity: *borrow* or *lend*, *buy* or *sell*, *wife* or *husband*. See SEMANTICS, SYNONYM. [LANGUAGE, STYLE, WORD].   T.MCA.

AORIST [16c: from Greek *aóristos* indefinite. Pronounced: 'AY-o-rist']. A tense expressing past action without any implication of completion or progression. Because the classical Greek aorist is generally translated into English as the simple past, this tense has sometimes been given the same name. [GRAMMAR].   T.MCA.

AOTEAROA [19c: Maori, long white cloud]. The Maori name for New Zealand, often also used in English. The Maori-language broadcasting system is called *Te reo o Aotearoa*. See NEW ZEALAND. [NAME, OCEANIA].   T.MCA.

APHAERESIS BrE, **apheresis** AmE [17c: from Latin *aphaeresis*, Greek *aphaíresis* a taking away. Stress: 'a-FER-e-sis']. The removal of an element from the beginning of a word, usually for informal economy of expression: *copter* and *gator* from *helicopter* and *alligator*. Sometimes aphaeresis and apocope occur together: *tec* from *detective*, *flu* from *influenza*. The use of an apostrophe to mark aphaeresis ('*gator*, '*phone*, '*plane*) is now rare, except when used to mark novel or unusual forms, as in '*kyou* for 'thank you'. See APHESIS, APOCOPE, APOSTROPHE[1], CLIPPING, ELISION. [SPEECH, STYLE].   T.MCA.

APHASIA [1860s: from Greek *áphatos* speechless, and -*ia* as in *dyslexia*]. Also, especially BrE, *dysphasia*. A language disorder that arises when an area of the brain specifically involved with language processing is damaged. About 85% of all cases are caused by strokes, in which the blood supply to an area is interrupted by blockage or haemorrhage. Other causes include kinds of brain disease and head injuries, traffic accidents, and other traumatic events. Many types of aphasia have been recognized, and classifications vary, but two broad types are generally distinguished:

(1) *Expressive* or *motor aphasia* primarily affects ability to speak. Speech is effortful and hesitant, grammar is reduced, and there is difficulty in finding words, but comprehension is still good. This kind of aphasia is classically related to damage to the anterior part of the brain in the frontal region known as *Broca's area*, after the French neurologist Paul Broca (1824-80). It is therefore also known as *Broca's aphasia*. Recent research, however, suggests that the area involved is not as clear-cut as was once hoped.

(2) *Receptive* or *sensory aphasia* primarily affects ability to understand. Speech is fluent, with little or no articulatory difficulty and normal intonation, but comprehension is disturbed. Speech contains stereotyped phrases, circumlocutions, unintelligible sequences (known technically as *jargon*), errors in choosing words and phonemes, and problems in retrieving words from memory. This kind of aphasia is classically related to damage to the posterior part of the brain in the temporal region known as *Wernicke's area*, after the German neurologist Carl Wernicke (1848-1905). It is therefore also called *Wernicke's aphasia*.

The study of aphasia is known as *aphasiology*. See AGRAMMATISM, ANOMIA, LANGUAGE PATHOLOGY. [LANGUAGE, SPEECH].   D.C.

APHESIS [1880: as if through Latin from Greek *áphesis* letting go. Coined by James A. H. Murray. Stress: 'AH-fe-sis']. The loss of an unstressed vowel at the beginning of a word, as in *prentice* from *apprentice*, sometimes leading to a word with a new meaning and use: *lone* from *alone*, *slant* from *aslant*, *squire* from *esquire*. Younger children often speak aphetically, a style that Rudyard Kipling imitates in *Just So Stories* (1902), marking the loss with an apostrophe: *'Stute Fish*, *'scruciating idle*, *'sclusively bare*, *'satiable curtiosity*. See APH(A)ERESIS, ELISION. [SPEECH, STYLE].   T.MCA.

APHORISM [16c: from French *aphorisme*, Latin *aphorismus*, Greek *aphorismós* a definition]. A compact saying, often one of a series, that states a principle, offers an insight, or teaches a point: 'Ignorance thinks of the perishable as imperishable, of the pure as impure, of the painful as pleasurable, of the non-Self as Self' (*Bhagwan Shree Patanjali: Aphorisms of Yoga*, Shree Purohit Swami, 1938). Compare ADAGE, MAXIM, SAYING. [STYLE].   T.MCA.

APICAL [19c: from Latin *apex/apicis* a point]. An anatomical term relating to the tip of the tongue. See LINGUAL, TONGUE. [SPEECH].   G.K.

APOCOPE [16c: through Latin from Greek *apokopé* cutting off. Stress: 'a-POK-o-py']. (1) The removal of an element at the end of a word, usually for informal economy of expression, as in: *kit* and *marge*, formed from *kitten* and *margarine*. Sometimes a suffix is added to the apocopated form, as in *kitty* from *kitten* and AusE *journo* from *journalist*. Apocope is common in especially affectionate nicknames: *Margery* becomes *Marge*, *William* becomes *Will*. Sometimes aphaeresis and apocope occur together: *Elizabeth* cut to *Liz*, *detective* to *tec*. (2) The loss of the inflectional endings of Old English, as when *singan* became *sing*. See APH(A)ERESIS, CLIPPING, ELISION. [SPEECH, STYLE].   T.MCA.

APODOSIS. See PROTASIS AND APODOSIS.

APOPHTHEGM, also **apothegm** [16c: from French *apophthegme*, Latin *apophthegma*, Greek *apóphthegma* an opinion. Stress: 'AH-po-them' (*th* as in *theme*)]. A short, often cryptic saying: 'Many a mickle maks a muckle' (Scots and Northern English: Every little helps). See SAYING. [STYLE].   T.MCA.

APORIA [16c: through Latin from Greek *aporia* difficulty in passing, impasse, puzzle. Pronounced 'ay-PAW-ri-a']. (1) In rhetoric, the expression of a real or simulated doubt or perplexity: *I hardly know where to start, it's really all so confusing*. (2) In logic, difficulty in establishing the truth of a proposition, caused by the presence of both favourable and unfavourable evidence. [STYLE].   T.MCA.

APOSIOPESIS [16c: through Latin from Greek *aposiópēsis* becoming silent. Stress: 'a-po-si-o-PEE-sis']. In rhetoric, breaking off in mid-sentence, an occurrence common in both real life and fiction. Both elliptical points (. . .) and a dash (—) may mark it in print, but occasionally the prose simply stops: 'How the devil did Rick L. Tucker manage to get hold of a gu' (the last words of *The Paper Men*, by William Golding, 1984). See ANACOLUTHON, DASH, ELLIPSIS. [STYLE, WRITING].   T.MCA.

APOSTROPHE[1] [16c: through French *apostrophe* and Late Latin *apostrophus* from Greek *apóstrophos*, short for *apóstrophos prosōidía* ('the turning-away accent') a mark indicating elision, from *apó* away, *stréphein* to turn. Pronunciation and stress: 'a-POS-tro-fy'. The French-based pronunciation 'AP-o-stroff' gave way in the 19c to that of a rhetorical term with the same spelling but a slightly different derivation: see APOSTROPHE[2]. Scholarly dislike for the change is exemplified by James Murray, Editor of the *OED*, in his entry on the subject (written in the 1880s), where he states that the two words were 'ignorantly confused']. The sign ('), sometimes regarded as a punctuation mark, sometimes as a diacritic. The apostrophe has three uses: (1) To mark the omission or elision of letters and sounds, as in *didn't* for *did not* and *fo'c'sle* or *fo'c's'le* for *forecastle*. (2) To indicate a plural form, especially in abbreviations, as in *V.I.P.'s* (short for *very important persons*). (3) To mark possession in nouns, as in *Jack's house* (the house belonging to Jack), but not in possessive pronouns (*hers, ours*, etc., not **her's, *ours*'), with the exception of *ones*. Each of the functions is discussed in detail below.

Omission and elision. The apostrophe was introduced into English in the 16c from Latin and Greek, in which it served to mark the loss of letters, as in the systematic dropping of *er* in Latin writing: for example, the word *tercius* ('third': classical form *tertius*) was commonly reduced in manuscripts to *t'cius*. Printers used the mark in the same way in English: for example, in *o'er*, a short form of *over*, and *'tis*, a short form of *it is*. By the end of the 16c, the sign was commonly used in this role: 'Nay sure, hee's not in Hell: hee's in *Arthurs* Bosome' (Shakespeare, *Henry V*, 2. 3). Since the 19c, the convention has stabilized in four related areas: (1) The representation of colloquial or informal elisions, such as the reduced *not* in *couldn't, hadn't, wasn't* and the reduced *-ing* in *huntin'*, *shootin'*, and *fishin'*. (2) The marking of initial word clippings, as in *'fraid so* for *afraid so* and *'gator* for *alligator*. (3) the omission of prefixed numbers, as with *the '80s* for *the 1980s*. (4) The representation of non-standard speech and dialect, as in *reg'lar, fr'en's o' mine*, and *fa' doun* (Scots: fall down). Increasingly, however, 20c writers of dialect have regarded this use of the apostrophe as a patronizing convention marking dialect as deviant from, and subordinate to, standard usage. Many have therefore dispensed with it in their work. Bernard Shaw disliked the use of the apostrophe of omission in such forms as *didn't*, which he changed to *didnt*, a convention that continues to be followed when his works are printed.

Plurality. There was formerly a respectable tradition (17–19c) of using the apostrophe for noun plurals, especially in loanwords ending in a vowel (as in *We doe confess Errata's*, Leonard Lichfield, 1641, and *Comma's are used*, Phillip Luckcombe, 1771) and in the consonants *s, z, ch, sh* (as in *waltz's and cotillions*, Washington Irving, 1804). Although this practice is rare in 20c standard usage, the apostrophe of plurality continues in at least five areas: (1) With abbreviations such as *V.I.P.'s* or *VIP's*, although forms such as *VIPs* are now widespread. (2) With letters of the alphabet, as in *His i's are just like his a's* and *Dot your i's and cross your t's*. In the phrase *do's and don'ts*, the apostrophe of plurality occurs in the first word but not the second, which has the apostrophe of omission: by and large, the use of two apostrophes close together (as in *don't's*) is avoided. (3) In decade dates, such as *the 1980's*, although such apostrophe-free forms as *the 1980s* are widespread, as are such truncations as *the '80s*, the form *the '80's* being unlikely. (4) In family names, especially if they end in *-s*, as in *keeping up with the Jones's*, as opposed to *the Joneses*, a form that is also common. (5) In the non-standard ('illiterate') use often called in BrE the *greengrocer's apostrophe*, as in *apple's 55p per lb* and *We sell the original shepherds pie's* (notice in a shop window, Canterbury, England).

Possession. Although apostrophes began to be used to mark possession in the late 16c, only 4% of the possessives in the First Folio edition of Shakespeare (1623) had them. Most of the nouns using such apostrophes were loanwords ending in *-o*, such as *Romeo's*. The device proved useful, however, as a means of visibly distinguishing the possessive case, so that the Fourth Folio of Shakespeare (1685) made fairly consistent use of it in the singular. Scholars have generally regarded this use of the apostrophe as arising from the omission of the letter *e* in Old and Middle English *-es* genitive singular endings (such as *mannes* man's, *scipes* ship's), spreading in due course to all genitives, with or without an *e* and plural as well as singular. Others have cited a

noun-and-pronoun pattern of possession common in the 16–17c, as in *Charles his name*, where noun and pronoun came together as *Charles's name* and then spread to all possessives, male or female, singular or plural. However, it is the Old English inflection that more directly accounts for the use of the apostrophe in Modern English.

Variations in the use of the possessive marker continued for a long time, however: 'As late as 1794 Washington Irving used apostrophes in only 38% of the possessives in his personal correspondence' (Greta D. Little, 'The Ambivalent Apostrophe', *English Today*, 8 Oct. 1986). By the mid-18c, however, the convention had extended to the possessive use of irregular noun plurals (*children's, men's, and women's clothing*), but the treatment of regular *s*-plurals posed problems. Some grammarians of the period, for example, saw no need for the mark in such phrases as *the soldiers hats*, because nothing was omitted; indeed, there was debate as to whether a distinct plural genitive existed in Modern English. By the middle of the 19c, however, such forms as *the soldiers' hats* were more or less established, but even so it appears from the evidence that there was never a golden age in which the rules for the use of the possessive apostrophe in English were clear-cut and known, understood, and followed by most educated people.

The conventions for the use of the possessive apostrophe in late 20c standard English are: singular nouns add *'s* (known as *apostrophe s*), as in *John's new suit* and *Your mother's job*. Plural nouns have *s'* (known as *s apostrophe*), as in *the Smiths' cat* and *my parents' house* (the house belonging to my parents). If a plural does not end in *s*, an apostrophe *s* is added: *the children's food*. Such a phrase as *the sheep's behaviour* is ambiguous out of context: it can be singular or plural. Beyond this point difficulties and inconsistencies are as common in the 1990s as in earlier times, especially with proper nouns. Singular use varies with place-names (*St John's, Newfoundland*, but *St Albans, England* and *St Andrews, Scotland*). There has been an accelerating tendency since the turn of the century to drop the apostrophe in the names of organizations and publications as well as place-names, as in: *Barclays Bank, Collins English Dictionary, Crows Nest, Debenhams, Harrods, Marks and Spencers, McMahons Point, Pikes Peak*. There is also widespread difficulty with *its* and *it's*. *Its* is the genitive or possessive of the personal pronoun *it*, as in *The cat licked its paws*, where it is possessive but does not have an apostrophe. *It's* is a contraction of *it is*, as in *It's too late* (It is too late), or *it has*, as in *It's made a mess* (It has made a mess); it is not possessive, but does have an apostrophe, because letters have been omitted.

There is widespread inconsistency and uncertainty in the use of the apostrophe when a singular noun already ends in -*s*. Traditional usage adds the apostrophe *s* if it is pronounced: *the boss's explanation*. With names of classical origin, a second *s* is not usually added, especially when the end sound of a word is /z/ rather than /s/: *Xerxes' battle, Socrates' pupils*. In speaking, a further syllable is less likely with such names as *Xerxes'*, where the last syllable already has two sibilant sounds, but might or might not be pronounced with *Socrates'*. With non-classical names ending in -*s*, again spoken and written forms may or may not have the same number of syllables. With short names, an extra syllable is generally pronounced, although the possessive can be written either way: *Mr Harris' job, Mr Harris's job*; *Keats' poetry, Keats's poetry*. The extra syllable for *Jesus* is optional in both writing and speech: *in Jesus' name, in Jesus's name*. The possessive plural of a singular name ending in -*s* (*Jones*) may be written either *'s* or *s'*: *the Jones's house*; *the Jones' house*. The tendency seems to be towards simplification and omitting the apostrophe: a century ago, *Chambers English Dictionary* was *Chambers's English Dictionary*.

Instability. Some observers consider that the general use of the apostrophe, especially for possession and plurality, is in decline, because it bears little relation to the spoken word and is a source of confusion in writing and print. Others urge that it be abandoned in some or all of its roles, a position that, if carried to the extreme, would make homographs of *he'll* and *hell*. Still others prefer a middle option that keeps the apostrophe for omission and elision but drops it for plurality and possession. Greta Little (above) sees the following forms (all authentic) as typifying many present-day public signs: *Dads Favorite Shop, Chelsea Mans Shop, Men's and Ladies Wear, Ladies and Mens Hair Styling, Childrens section, First 200 Mom's Get a Free Rose, Knoxville Welcome's Big John Tate, Violators will be towed at owners expense, Joe's Joke Book, Poes Kiddie Komics*. Because such conflicting forms occur close to each other in prominent places such as shopping malls in the US, she notes:

In and of itself the diversity can be confusing to youngsters on their way to achieving literacy. But what are these learners to make of direct contradictions like *Vella's Deli* and *Vellas Deli* or *Richie's Lounge* and *Richies Lounge*? They are very likely to conclude that the apostrophe means nothing, that it plays some non-significant, decorative role. And there is often evidence which would support that hypothesis: Kelly's with a shamrock 'apostrophe', Moma's Restaurant with a heart, and Patricia's Toy Closet where the apostrophe is a claw on the paw of a tiger that is stretched out atop the sign.

It is likely, however, that the many and varied uses of the apostrophe will remain part of the language for a long time to come, despite some reduction in range, and accompanied by a great deal of inconsistency and error in practice.

See AITCH, APH(A)ERESIS, APHESIS, CLIPPING, ELISION, DIACRITIC, GENITIVE CASE, H, POSSESSION, POSSESSIVE CASE, PUNCTUATION, S, SAXON GENITIVE, SHAW. [GRAMMAR, STYLE, USAGE].

T.MCA., S.C., R.E.A.

APOSTROPHE[2] [16c: through Latin from Greek *apostrophḗ* a turning away. Stress: 'a-POS-tro-fy']. (1) Rhetorically addressing someone or something that cannot respond, such as: a dead person ('Milton! thou shouldst be living at this hour': Wordsworth), a place ('Sweet Auburn! loveliest village of the plain': Goldsmith), or an idea ('O liberty! O liberty! what crimes are committed in thy name!': translating Mme Roland). Originally, the term referred to the invocation opening such epics as Homer's *Iliad*: 'Sing, Goddess, of the deadly wrath of Achilles, son of Peleus.' (2) A deliberate interruption, as when a lawyer breaks off from an argument to address a judge or turn on an opponent, usually for rhetorical effect or to divert attention from a tricky issue or a weak argument. [STYLE].   T.MCA.

APOTHEGM. See APOPHTHEGM.

APPALACHIAN ENGLISH. The English of the mountain region of Appalachia in the southeastern US: in parts of Kentucky, North Carolina, Tennessee, Virginia, and all of West Virginia. The most influential settlers in these areas were the Scots-Irish, who began arriving in the British American colonies *c*.1640 and moved to the south and west. Because of the relative isolation in which it has developed and the continuance of forms regarded elsewhere as archaisms, Appalachian English has been regarded (popularly but incorrectly) as a kind of Elizabethan or Shakespearian English. However, it shares features with other kinds of non-standard English, particularly in the South: absence of the copula (*That alright*); the use of *right* and *plumb* as intensifying adverbs (*I hollered right loud, The house burnt plumb down*). Phonological features include: initial /h/ in such words as *hit* for *it*, *hain't* for *ain't*; -*er* for -*ow* as in *feller/tobaccer/yeller* (fellow/tobacco/yellow). Grammatical features include: *a*-prefixing with -*ing* participial forms (*He just kept a-beggin' an' a-cryin'*) and the use of *done* as a perfective marker (*He done sold his house*: He has sold his house). *A*-prefixing is a relic of a construction containing the Old English preposition *on* in unstressed positions before certain participles: *He was on hunting* (He was engaged in hunting). Currently, Appalachian English is often socially stigmatized because it is spoken in its most distinctive form by poor, often uneducated, mountain people. See DIALECT IN AMERICA, HILLBILLY, SOUTH (THE), SOUTHERN ENGLISH. [AMERICAS, VARIETY]. S.R.

APPENDIX [16c: from Latin *appendix/ appendicis* something added on, from *appendere* to hang (something) on. Plural: traditionally *appendices*, less formally *appendixes*]. Short written forms *app.* and *appx.* Supplementary or appended material at the end of a book, document, article, or other text, such as a bibliography or notes, often numbered: *Appendix 1, Appx 2*, etc. See BACK MATTER, FORMAT, NOTES AND REFERENCES. Compare EPILOG(UE), POST-SCRIPT. [MEDIA, WRITING]. T.MCA.

APPLIED LINGUISTICS [1940s]. The application of linguistics to the study and improvement of language teaching and learning, language planning, communication between groups, speech therapy and the management of language handicap, systems of communications, translating and interpreting, and lexicography. The bulk of the work of applied linguists to date has related to language teaching and language learning and especially English as a foreign or second language. The term owes its origin to US language-teaching programmes during and after the Second World War, largely based on Leonard Bloomfield's *Outline Guide for the Practical Study of Foreign Languages* (1942), which was influenced by the early, mainly European, advocates of the Direct Method, in particular Henry Sweet. In 1948, *Language Learning: A Quarterly Journal of Applied Linguistics* was started at the U. of Michigan by Charles C. Fries, supported among others by Kenneth L. Pike and W. Freeman Twaddell, to disseminate information about work at Fries's English Language Institute (founded 1941). In Britain, a *School of Applied Linguistics* was established by J. C. Catford at the U. of Edinburgh in 1956, and the *Center for Applied Linguistics* was set up in Washington, DC, under Charles Ferguson in 1959. Similar institutes have since been set up in various parts of the world. National associations of applied linguists came together in 1964 to form the *Association internationale de la linguistique appliquée* (*AILA*), which holds a four-yearly international congress with published proceedings. Journals include: *International Review of Applied Linguistics* (since 1963: Julius Groos Verlag, Heidelberg), *Applied Linguistics* (since 1980: Oxford University Press), and *Annual Review of Applied Linguistics* (since 1980:

Cambridge University Press). Relevant publications include: Henry G. Widdowson, *Explorations in Applied Linguistics* (Oxford University Press, 1979/84, two volumes), and Jack Richards, John Platt, and Heidi Weber, *Longman Dictionary of Applied Linguistics* (1985). See BAAL, HALLIDAY, LANGUAGE LEARNING, LANGUAGE TEACHING, STREVENS. [EDUCATION, LANGUAGE, MEDIA]. P.S., T.MCA.

APPOSITION [15c: through French from Latin *appositio/appositionis* placing close]. Two consecutive, juxtaposed nouns or noun phrases are in apposition when they refer to the same person or thing, and when either can be omitted without seriously changing the meaning or the grammar of a sentence. *Mrs Thatcher* and *the British Prime Minister* are in apposition in *Mrs Thatcher, the British Prime Minister, became leader of the Tory party in 1975*. Here, both *Mrs Thatcher became leader . . .* and *The British Prime Minister became leader . . .* could serve equally well alone. The term is often used when these criteria only partly apply, some grammarians using terms like *partial* or *weak apposition* to distinguish various types of lesser acceptability: '*The heir to the throne* arrived, *Prince Charles*' (where only the second noun phrase can be omitted); '*Todor Zhivkov, until recently the Communist party leader in Bulgaria*, has been placed under house arrest' (where the second phrase as a whole cannot serve, unless slightly modified, as the subject in this sentence). Some grammarians argue that apposition includes the relationship between the two parts in such forms as: *Queen Elizabeth the Second*; *presidential candidate Jesse Jackson*; *the continent of Asia*; *some Canadian cities, for example Winnipeg*; *an unforgettable sight on television, the breaching of the Berlin Wall*; *the word 'architecture'*. [GRAMMAR]. S.C.

APPOSITIVE CLAUSE. See RELATIVE CLAUSE.

APPROACH. In language teaching and applied linguistics, a term for an attitude towards how languages can or should be taught. In EFL and ESL, recent developments in methodology have tended to be called *approaches* (*the situational approach, the communicative approach*), whereas earlier developments were often called *methods* and capitalized (*the Direct Method, the Natural Method*). In practical terms, it is not easy to distinguish the two, and in recent years there has been a tendency to use *approach* as a generic term containing *method*. See LANGUAGE TEACHING, METHOD. [EDUCATION]. P.S.

APPROPRIATENESS, also **appropriacy**. A term in linguistics for the intuitive expectation that styles of language vary between situations.

It provides a theoretical alternative to the traditional notion of *correctness*, which is an absolute standard against which all usage must be judged, and which invariably reflects the formal and written norms of language, especially as institutionalized in grammars, dictionaries, and manuals of style. The difference in approach can be illustrated by such sentences as *There's the man Mary spoke to*. Traditionally, this sentence would be considered incorrect, as it breaks the prescriptive rule that sentences in English should not end with a preposition; the recommended alternative would be *There is the man to whom Mary spoke*. In terms of appropriateness, each sentence has its own validity: the former in informal settings, the latter in formal settings. See CORRECT, DECORUM, REGISTER. [LANGUAGE, STYLE, USAGE]. D.C.

APPROXIMANT [20c: from Latin *approximare* to draw near]. Also **continuant**. In phonetics, a sound, usually a consonant, with a manner of articulation more open than a stop or fricative, as in the /r/ of *rink* compared with the /z/ of *zinc*. Approximants are normally voiced (/r/ after /d/ as in *drink*), but are often devoiced after a voiceless stop or a fricative (/r/ after /t/ as in *trinket*). The increased flow of air that results from the devoicing produces noise similar to that of a fricative. The set of approximants includes liquids, nasals, and glides. See CONSONANT, GLIDE, LIQUID, NASAL. [SPEECH]. G.K.

APRAXIA. See LANGUAGE PATHOLOGY.

APTRONYM [20c AmE: from *apt* and *-onym*, with epenthetic *r*. Coined by Franklin P. Adams]. A name that matches its owner's occupation or character, often in a humorous or ironic way, such as *William Rumhole*, a London taverner. Many surnames have been conferred on people because of what they do for a living (the original *Baker* being a baker), but the aptronym is not so straightforward as this. It has two applications: (1) *Factual aptronyms* belong to real people and their effect is usually fortuitous: 'When Pentagon reporters ventured north for the cold facts in Alaska last month, the Northern Warfare Training Center assigned Lieutenant Colonel Will B. Snow to issue their Arctic gear' (Lewis H. Diuguid, 'What's In a Name? Maybe a Destiny', *Washington Post*, Jan. 1989). (2) *Fictional aptronyms*, also known as *label names*, are generally used for allegorical and satirical purposes: 'Does Sir Midas Mammon need someone to negotiate a shady deal in the Third World? Who more suitable than old Sir Elegant Smoothways, who looks so fastidious' (Anthony Sampson, *Independent Magazine*, 2 June 1990). See ALLEGORY, DICKENS,

JONSON, ONOMASTICS (CHARACTERNYMS), -ONYM, SHERIDAN (R.). [NAME, STYLE, WORD]. T.MCA.

ARABIC [14c: through French from Latin *Arabicus* Arabian: known to its speakers as *al-'Arabiyya*]. A Semitic language of West Asia and North Africa that originated in the Arabian peninsula in the early first millennium AD. It is the mother tongue of c.150m people in Algeria, Bahrain, Chad, Egypt, Iraq, Jordan, Kuwait, Lebanon, Libya, Mali, Mauritania, Morocco, Oman, Qatar, Saudi Arabia, Sudan, Syria, Tunisia, the United Arab Emirates, and Yemen, as well as communities elsewhere in Asia and Africa, and immigrant communities in Europe (especially France). Because of its role as the scriptural language of Islam, it has cultural significance and linguistic influence in Bangladesh, India, Indonesia, Iran, Malaysia, Nigeria, Pakistan, the Philippines, Somalia, Turkey, various republics of the Soviet Union, and other countries where there are Muslim communities. Arabic has influenced such languages of southern Europe as Italian, Portuguese, and Spanish. It was formerly a major language of Europe, being spoken for some 400 years in the Iberian peninsula, and is still represented there by its offshoot *Maltese*, which has been strongly influenced by both Italian and English.

Classical and colloquial Arabic. The Arabic language is generally described as having two forms: *classical Arabic* and *colloquial Arabic*. The classical or literary language includes and is based on the Arabic of the *Qur'ān* (Recitation), the text of the teachings of the Prophet Muhammad in the 7c. The colloquial form consists of many dialects that are in the main mutually intelligible and fall into several groups: those of Arabia, Egypt, the Maghreb (North Africa west of Egypt), Iraq, and Syria. Classical usage is uniform throughout the Arab world, and all colloquial varieties have been influenced by it. Classical Arabic has immense prestige and liturgical significance wherever Muslims live, but, just as there are Muslims who do not speak Arabic, so there are speakers of Arabic who are not Muslim.

Speech and script. (1) Arabic has a series of velarized consonants, pronounced with constriction of the pharynx and raising of the tongue, and a group of uvular and pharyngeal fricatives that give the language a characteristic throaty sound. (2) The glottal stop is a consonantal phoneme, represented in Arabic script by the letter *alif* and in Roman transliteration by the lenis symbol ' (or the apostrophe '): *'ana* I, *sa'al* he asked. The sign *hamza* also represents a glottal stop and is transliterated in the same way. In the transliteration of the letter *ain*, a voiced pharyngeal fricative, the asper symbol ' (or the turned comma ') is used, as in *'āmiyya* colloquial, *sharī'a* Islamic law. (3) There are three short and three long vowels, transliterated as *a, i, u, ā, ī, ū*. (4) Words start with a consonant followed by a vowel. Clusters of more than two consonants do not occur. (5) Arabic script, which probably developed in the 4c, is the next most widely used writing system after the Roman alphabet. It has been adapted as a medium for such non-Semitic languages as Malay, Persian, Spanish, Swahili, Turkish, and Urdu. It has 28 letters, all representing consonants, and runs from right to left. (6) A set of diacritics, developed in the 8c, can be used for short vowels and some otherwise unmarked grammatical endings.

Grammar and word-formation. Arabic syntax and word-formation centre on a system of *triconsonantal roots* that provide the basic lexical content of words: for example, the root *k–t–b* underlies words relating to writing and books, and *s–l–m* underlies words relating to submission, resignation, peace, and religion. Such roots are developed in patterns of vowels and affixes: words formed from *k–t–b* include the nouns *kitāb* (book) and *kātib* (one who writes, a clerk or scribe); words formed from *s–l–m* include *'aslama* (he submitted), *islām* (submission to the will of God), *muslim* (one who so submits), and *salām* (peace, safety, security).

Arabic in English. Contacts between Arabic and English date from the Crusades (11–13c). Borrowings, though often individually significant, have never been numerous: for example, in the 14c *admiral, alchemy, alkali, bedouin, nadir, syrup*; 16c *alcohol, algebra, magazine, monsoon, sheikh, sultan*; 17c *albatross, alcove, assassin, ghoul, harem, jinn, mullah, sofa, zenith*; 19c *alfalfa, jihad/jehad, majlis, safari, yashmak*; 20c *ayatollah, intifada, mujahedin*. Arabic words in English tend to relate to Islam (*ayatollah, mullah*), Arab society and culture past or present (*alcove, bedouin, sultan*), and learning (*alchemy, alkali*), including mathematics and astronomy (*algebra, nadir, zenith*). Many have come into English through a third language: *admiral* through French, *albatross* through Portuguese and Spanish, *safari* through Swahili, *ayatollah* through Persian. One set of loanwords incorporates the Arabic definite article *al*, and includes *albatross, alchemy, alcohol, alcove, alembic, alfalfa, algebra, alhambra, alkali, almanac*.

Variations in spelling. Some Arabic words have more than one spelling in English. Of these, the more traditional forms, usually because of rivalry and animosity between Christians and Muslims, have taken little account of Muslim sensibilities. Vernacular and academic orthography are therefore often sharply contrasted,

the latter having strict conventions for transliterating Arabic into Roman script. Forms of the name of the Prophet include the obsolete and highly pejorative *Mahound* (equating him with a devil, false god, or idol), the archaic *Mahomet* (disliked by Muslims because *ma-* is a negative Arabic prefix), *Mohammed* and *Mohamed* (currently common among Muslims and others), and *Muhammad* (used principally by scholars). Similarly, a believer in Islam has been a *Mahometan* or *Mohammedan* (on the analogy of *Christian*, terms disliked by Muslims because they emphasize the Prophet and not God), *Moslem* (widely used), and *Muslim* (used especially by scholars, but increasingly in general writing). Names for Islam have included the obsolete and offensive *Mahometry* and *Maumetry* (meaning 'false religion') and the more recent *Mahometanism* and *Mohammedanism*, neither of which is acceptable to Muslims. The name for the Islamic scriptures has been *the Alcoran* (archaic: redundantly incorporating the definite article), *the Koran* (in general use), and *the Qur'ān* (especially among scholars). In the following excerpt, the Arabic words are transliterated using current scholarly conventions:

The Shāfi'ī school traces its founding to Abū 'Abdallah Muḥammad ibn Idrīs al-Shāfi'ī, a Meccan of the Quraysh, who taught in Egypt in Fusṭāṭ (now part of Cairo). He died there A.H. 204/AD 920

(J. E. Williams, *Islam*, 1962).

English in Arabic. Because of increasing contacts between the Arab world and English, many words have been borrowed into both spoken and written Arabic: for example, in Egypt, where the British had a colonial presence for 72 years (1882–1954), loans span many spheres and include the colloquial, such as: general *aftershave, ceramic, shampoo, spray*; architectural *motel, roof garden, shopping centre, supermarket*; clothing *cap, overall, shorts*; foodstuffs *grapefruit, ice cream*; sport *football, half-time, match, tennis*. The question of how to transfer foreign terms into the written language, especially scientific and technical terms, has long been hotly debated; innovators advocate borrowing terms where there are gaps, while purists urge the use of equivalents coined for the purpose. By and large, the Arabization of such words takes three forms: loan concepts that use the language's own system of roots and derivatives (*adā'a* to broadcast, *idā'a* broadcasting, *mūdī'* broadcaster); loan translations that create new Arabic forms (*semiotics* becoming *'ilm al-rumūz*); loan adaptations that give an Arabic look to foreign borrowings (*philosophy* becoming *al-falsafa*, *morpheme* becoming *al-murfīm*).

English in the Arab world. In the late 20c, English is a significant additional language in most Arab countries. Four European languages of empire have affected the Arab world, especially in the 19-20c: English especially in Bahrain, Egypt, Iraq, Jordan, Kuwait, Oman, Qatar, Saudi Arabia, Sudan, the United Arab Emirates, and Yemen; French especially in Algeria, Egypt, Lebanon, Morocco, Syria, and Tunisia; Spanish in Morocco; and Italian in Libya. Although the age of European colonial power passed in the 1950s/1960s, the English and French spheres of linguistic influence in particular are still detectable. Currently, English is extensively used for business, technical, and other purposes, especially in and around the Arabian peninsula and the Gulf, and is an increasingly important technical and educational resource in countries formerly closely associated with French.

See AFRICAN LANGUAGES, ARAMAIC, ASIAN LANGUAGES, AUSTRALIAN LANGUAGES, BISOCIATION, BORROWING, DIGLOSSIA, ETHNIC NAME, EUROPEAN LANGUAGES, GAMBIA, -GLISH AND -LISH, GLOTTAL STOP, GUTTURAL, HAMITO-SEMITIC LANGUAGES, HEBREW, HINDI-URDU, ISRAEL, LINGUISTIC TYPOLOGY, MALAY, MALTA, PHARYNX, Q, ROMAN, SPANISH, SUDAN, SWAHILI, TRANSLITERATION, URDU, WORLD LANGUAGE. Compare SANSKRIT. [AFRICA, ASIA, LANGUAGE]. T.MCA., M.H.

ARAMAIC [1880s: from Greek *Aramaîos* of Aram, from Hebrew *'Arām* Syria]. A Semitic language related to Hebrew, documented since *c.*7c BC, and the most widely spoken vernacular of West Asia until replaced by Arabic in the 7c. Jesus is considered to have spoken the Galilean dialect of Aramaic. Parts of the Old Testament (Ezra, Daniel), most of the Talmud, portions of Jewish liturgy, and major works of Jewish mysticism are written in dialects of Aramaic, which figured prominently in the formation of Jewish languages. Many Yiddish words and expressions are of Aramaic origin. Literary English includes some Aramaic words and phrases, such as *mene, mene, tekel, upharsin* (the handwriting on the wall in Daniel 5: 25-31) and *maranatha* (1 Corinthians 16: 22). There are small communities of Aramaic speakers in West Asia. See BIBLE, BORROWING, HAMITO-SEMITIC LANGUAGES, JEWISH LANGUAGES, PUN. [ASIA, LANGUAGE]. S.S.

ARCHAISM [17c: from Latin *archaismus*, Greek *arkhaismós* something old]. In rhetoric, literary criticism, and philology, a style that reflects the usage of an earlier period (*literary archaism*) and an out-of-date or old-fashioned word or phrase (*a lexical archaism*). *Literary archaism* occurs when a style is modelled on older works, so as to revive earlier practices or achieve a desired effect. *Lexical archaisms* are a

common feature of such a style and of such registers as religion and law. Archaism is often a consequence of purism and may rest on the belief that language and life in days of yore were plainer, more democratic, and more natural. In English, an archaizing social movement has appeared at least twice: (1) In the 16c, as a reaction to Latinate *inkhorn terms* and part of a renewed interest in medieval texts. In the 'Epistle Dedicatory' to Edmund Spenser's *Shepherds Calendar* (1579), 'E.K.' defends the poet's use of archaic language as appropriate for shepherds, and Richard Verstegen (*A Restitution of Decayed Intelligence*, 1605) lists a number of words he would like to see revived, including: *bead* prayer; *dugud* honour; *thorp* village; *wod* mad. (2) As an aspect of the 19c revival of antiquarianism that produced the old-fashioned style of Walter Scott and of Coleridge's poem *The Ancient Mariner*, the Middle English editions of the Early English Text Society, and the work of the Philological Society that became *The Oxford English Dictionary*.

Such archaisms as *ere* before, *prithee* I pray you, are often used for effect, especially in the dialogue of historical novels: 'Dear father, prithee add thyself to that venerable company ere the soup cools' (Margaret in Charles Reade's *The Cloister and the Hearth*, 1861). Sometimes, contemporary and ancient can be mixed for archaic effect, as when Middle English is paraphrased into Modern to open a contemporary campus novel: 'When April with its sweet showers has pierced the drought of March to the root, and bathed every vine of earth with that liquid by whose power the flowers are engendered' (David Lodge, *Small World*, 1984, adapting the opening lines of Chaucer's *Canterbury Tales*). The paraphrase is meant to draw a parallel between modern academics at conferences and medieval pilgrims going to Canterbury. Larger dictionaries of English generally make an attempt to label archaisms, but there is seldom a consensus: out of four dictionaries, only *Collins English Dictionary* marks *bantling* and *verily* archaic, only *Collins* and *Chambers English Dictionary* mark *wight* archaic, and *Collins, Random House,* and *Webster's Ninth Collegiate* mark *prithee* archaic, while *Chambers* does not. See ANACHRONISM, BARNES, CARLYLE, JOURNALESE, SAXONISM, SPENSER, TENNYSON, TIMESPEAK. [HISTORY, STYLE]. D.E.B., T.MCA.

ARCHETYPE [16c: from Latin *archetypum*, Greek *archétupon* impression, pattern, from *archétupos* of the mould: compare TYPE]. (1) A pattern, mould, or prototype, from which copies are made. (2) A concept or representation like a Platonic Idea: one of a number of ideal forms or patterns considered to lie 'behind' the fluctuations of existence, accessible only through intellectual analysis and/or aesthetic awareness. (3) A recurring image, symbol, or motif in art, literature, culture, and religion that appeals to instinct, emotion, and creative inspiration. (4) In the theories of the Swiss analytical psychologist Carl Gustav Jung (1875-1961), a primordial mental form, common to all humanity, one of a number in the Collective Unconscious. Such archetypes are not directly accessible, but show themselves through *archetypal images/symbols* (also commonly referred to as archetypes), in dreams, visions, myths, arts, languages, and literatures: God the Father, Mother Nature, Madonna and Child, Sage, Warrior, Mountain/Breast, Cave/Womb, Sword/ Phallus. Commonly, as above, archetypes are identified in print by an initial capital. In literary criticism, archetypes have been widely discussed and developed, for example in the theories of the Canadian critic Northrop Frye:

I mean by an archetype a symbol which connects one poem with another and thereby helps to unify and integrate our literary experience. And as the archetype is the communicable symbol, archetypal criticism is primarily concerned with literature as a social fact and as a mode of communication. By the study of conventions and genres, it attempts to fit poems into the body of poetry as a whole. The repetition of certain common images of physical nature like the sea or the forest in a large number of poems . . . does indicate a certain unity in the nature that poetry imitates, and in the communicating activity of which poetry forms part (*Anatomy of Criticism*, 1957, p. 99).

In title and content, Nicholas Monsarrat's novel *The Cruel Sea* (1951) focuses on one quality (Cruelty) of one force (the Sea). Similarly, Ernest Hemingway's *The Old Man and the Sea* (1952) brings two archetypes together in one setting. Idioms such as *all at sea, between the devil and the deep blue sea, plenty more fish in the sea*, and *worse things happen at sea* express archetypal assumptions about Sea and by analogy Life as vast, risky, fertile, fascinating expanses. No one can prove or disprove the existence of archetypes as features of neurology and psychology, but the associated symbols (however accounted for) have long been part of language and culture. See BIBLE, FRYE, ICON, IDEA, IMAGE, MYTH, NOVEL, SYMBOL. [LITERATURE].   T.MCA.

ARELS, short for *Association of Recognized English Language Schools*. An association of British private language schools, some commercial, some charitable, whose standards are periodically assessed and confirmed on behalf of the government. ARELS was founded in 1960 to establish a guaranteed minimum level of service in English-language schools, and negotiated inspection by the Department of Education of all schools willing to be so assessed. Those meeting certain levels in teaching, staffing, welfare, premises, and administration were then 'recognized as efficient' and could become members. ARELS has organized in-service training courses, and such members as the Bell Schools, Eurocentres, and International House have engaged in course design and methodology. The Association sponsored the *ARELS Oral Examinations*, a statistically validated test of spoken English available internationally. In 1985, this test was linked with an Oxford University written EFL examination, to produce a joint certificate, and the system of inspection and recognition was transferred from the Department of Education to the British Council. In the same year, ARELS merged with the *Federation of English Language Course Organisers*, whose members offer mainly holiday courses. The joint organization is known as *ARELS-FELCO*. In 1960, ARELS had 20 members; in 1989, ARELS-FELCO had 200. In 1990, however, because of disagreements about rates of subscription and quality control, 17 schools withdrew from the organization, including the three major institutions listed above. See BRITISH COUNCIL, ENGLISH LANGUAGE SCHOOL, TEFL. [EDUCATION].   P.S.

ARGENTINA. Official titles: Spanish *República Argentina*, English *Argentine Republic*. A state of South America. Capital: Buenos Aires. Currency: the austral. Economy: mixed. Population: 31.8m (1988), 36.2m (projection for 2000). Ethnicity: 90% Caucasian, 10% Amerindian and mestizo. Languages: Spanish (official); English, French, German, and Italian widely spoken. Education: primary/secondary 94%, tertiary 36%, literacy 96%. Colonized in the 16c by Spain, Argentina gained its independence in 1816. Immigration from Britain dates from the 18c: for example, Hispanicized Scottish surnames can be traced to refugees from the Jacobite Rebellion in 1745. An English-medium newspaper, the *Buenos Aires Herald*, dates from the late 19c. Among the Anglo-Argentine community (numbering over 100,000), it is a shibboleth to pronounce *Buenos Aires* 'Bonos Airs'. Long-established private bilingual schools (Spanish and English) have used the Cambridge overseas examinations since the 1940s, a practice scarcely interrupted by the Falklands War in 1982. See CULTURA, ENGLISH, FALKLAND ISLANDS, MESTIZO. [AMERICAS, NAME, VARIETY].

W.S., T.MCA.

ARGOT [19c: from French *argot* a beggars' guild, criminal cant, slang]. The slang of a restricted, often suspect, social group: 'They have their own argot: they bimble, yomp, or tab across the peat and couth a shirt in readiness for a Saturday night bop with the Bennies (locals)' (Colin Smith, *Observer*, 26 May 1985, writing about British soldiers in the Falkland Islands); 'I was obsessed by public lavatories—"cottages" or "tea-rooms" in the gay argot that was so very far from gay' (James Kirkup, quoted in the book review 'Erotica and Exotica', *Sunday Times*, 30 June 1991). See BURGESS, CANT, JARGON, POLARI, ROMANI/ROMANY, SLANG. [STYLE]. T.MCA.

ARGUMENT [14c: through Old French from Latin *argumentum*, assertion, proof]. (1) In general usage, a disagreement or dispute; more formally, the case for or against something. (2) In logic, such a case formulated so that a particular conclusion can be drawn from certain premisses. Such arguments are procedures to be followed in developing a rational theme, either for its own sake (as in mathematics and science) or in order to win a debate or point (as in theological disputation and courts of law). When used in debate, arguments are as much a matter of rhetoric as logic, bringing in partisanship, special pleading, emotive language, and overt and covert tactical manœuvring. See DIALECTIC, DIATRIBE, FALLACY, LOGIC, POLEMIC, PROPOSITION, RATIONALIZATION, RHETORIC. (3) In linguistics an especially case grammar, a term used to refer to the complements of a verb: for example, *John gave a book to Mary* has three arguments, *John*, *Mary*, and *book*, because the verb *give* requires three noun phrases to complete its meaning. Arguments have various semantic roles such as *agent*, *patient*, and *instrumental*. See CASE GRAMMAR. [LANGUAGE, STYLE]. T.MCA., S.R.

ARNOLD, Matthew [1822-88]. English poet, academic, and critic. Born at Laleham, Middlesex, son of Thomas Arnold, and educated at Rugby and Oxford, he became secretary to Lord Lansdowne, then an inspector of schools when elementary education for all was being developed. At first he disliked the work, but became committed to trying to improve the national system. He favoured setting up infant schools and opposed the method of payment by results. Arnold published a volume of poems in 1849 and further collections followed. He attempted unrhymed classical metres, notably in the verse tragedy *Merope* (1858); he was appointed Professor of Poetry at Oxford in 1857. His later prose shows a sense of mission not only in education but in the improvement of society at large (*Culture and Anarchy*, 1867-9). Although his literary criticism was not systematic, he was a leading critic of the period (*Essays in Criticism*, 1865/1887), trying to improve contemporary standards by studying what he saw as past excellence and looking to literature for values in life. His coinages include such phrases as *sweetness*

and light, *high seriousness*, and *the higher journalism*. See index. [BIOGRAPHY, EDUCATION, EUROPE, LITERATURE]. R.C.

ARNOLD, Thomas [1795-1842]. English clergyman and schoolmaster. Born at Cowes, Isle of Wight, and educated at Winchester and Oxford, he was appointed Headmaster of Rugby in 1828 and worked to raise its standard of learning and behaviour. He took care to know the boys individually, entrusted the older ones with responsibility, and sought to inculcate a sense of duty and religion. He introduced the study of modern languages, mathematics, and modern history. In 1841, he became Professor of Modern History at Oxford. He did not regard English as a separate academic subject, believing that it could be learned through the study of Greek and Latin. He chose passages of English for composition into those languages and required translation from them to be idiomatic and in an appropriate style. His influence on the public (that is, private) schools was considerable; he attracted the rising middle class and the effect of his work continued well into the 20c. See index. [BIOGRAPHY, EDUCATION, EUROPE]. R.C.

ARSIS. See THESIS.

ARTICLE[1] [13c: from Old French *article*, Latin *articulus* a little joint, translating Greek *árthron* a joint]. A traditional part of speech, in contemporary grammar often included in the word class *determiner*. Some languages, such as classical Greek, have complex systems of articles varying according to person, gender, number, and case, but in English there are only two: *the*, the *definite article*, and *a/an*, the *indefinite article*.

Functions. The definite article marks a phrase as uniquely identifiable and can be used with any common noun: singular (*the house*), plural (*the houses*), uncountable (*the bread*). It also forms an essential part of some proper names: *The Hague*, *the Pennines*, *the Vatican*. *A/an* is used with singular countable nouns: *Give me a bag*, not *Give me bag. The form *a* is used before consonant sounds (*a book*, *a house*) and the semi-vowel /j/ (*a European*, *a UN official*, *a year*). The form *an* is used before vowel sounds, however spelled: *an American*, *an honour*, *an MP*, *an uncle*. There is some uncertainty about words beginning with a pronounced *h* and an unstressed first syllable, and practices vary: *a/an hotel*, *a/an historical event*. For more detail see the entry for H. Exceptionally and for emphasis, *a/an* is used before an uncountable noun with the meaning 'an example of', as in: *They displayed a breathtaking indifference to my problems.*

Zero article and ellipsis. Some grammarians use the term *zero* for the absence of an article before uncountable and plural nouns, such as *wine* and *bottles* in *He puts wine in bottles*. They argue that a zero article has the same sort of indefinite meaning as *a/an* before singular nouns. This convention and the usage it describes is distinct from the suppression of articles in certain kinds of writing and speaking, such as note-taking (*have suitcase, will travel*: I have a suitcase and I am willing to travel) and elliptical instructions (as in dramatic scripts, *leaves room*: the actor leaves the room).

Specific versus generic. The distinction of specific and generic cuts across the distinction between definite and indefinite. Specific reference is to particular people or things: *The Browns live next door to me*; *Shut the door*; *I went to a marvellous party last night*; *Help yourself to coffee*; *Biscuits are on the table*. In the last two examples, with the zero article, *some* could be added to the uncountable noun *coffee* and the plural noun *biscuits* without an appreciable change of meaning. Generic reference is to people or things as examples of a class in general: *The kangaroo is an Australian animal*, *A kangaroo is an Australian animal*, *Kangaroos are Australian animals*. As these examples illustrate, if the nouns are countable generic reference can be shown by the singular with the definite or indefinite article and the plural with the zero article. However, *the* with the plural has generic reference in two cases: nationality nouns (*The Afghans are engaged in a civil war*) and adjectives denoting a class of people (*The poor are always with us*).

A further distinction is sometimes made between specific reference (where particular people or things are intended) and non-specific reference (where instances of the kind of people or things are intended): for example, *I want to buy a secondhand car* or *Sue is looking for a partner*, where *a secondhand car* and *a partner* do not have reference to a specific car or partner. For non-specific relations, the indefinite article is used with singular countable nouns (as in the two examples above) and the zero article or *some* is used with plural and uncountable nouns: *I want to buy (some) secondhand cars*; *She is looking for (some) partners.* [GRAMMAR].   S.C., S.G.

ARTICLE² [13c: from Old French *article*, Latin *articulus* a little joint. In origin, written articles as sections in a text were likened to jointed bones. Compare CONJUNCTION, DACTYL]. (1) An element of the Apostles' Creed or any similar summary of religious belief: *the Articles of Faith*; *an article of faith in Islam*. (2) A distinct, usually numbered clause in an official or legal document:

the Articles of War (regulations relating to military forces); *articles of association* (rules and conditions on which a commercial agreement is based). (3) A piece of writing especially by a journalist or writer of reference material, usually on one topic: 'They read the Advertisements with the same curiosity as the Articles of publick News' (Joseph Addison, *Spectator* 452, 1712); 'The book . . . became the subject—not merely of reviews, but also—of what they call "articles" ' (Alexander W. Kinglake, *The Invasion of the Crimea*, 1870). Articles generally do not exceed a specified number of words and usually adopt, or are edited to fit, the prevailing style in the publication in which they appear. In a newspaper or magazine, a *feature article* or *feature story* deals with something important and is given a prominent position. The article is an adaptation of the essay and in journalism is often referred to as a *piece*. See ESSAY, FEATURE, STORY. [MEDIA, WRITING].   T.MCA.

ARTICULATION [15c: from Latin *articulatio/articulationis* division into joints or sections, from *articulus* a little joint, from *artus* a joint. Compare ARTICLE²]. (1) In general usage, the act or process of speaking, especially so that every element can be clearly heard. See DICTION, ELOCUTION, ORTHOEPY. (2) In phonetics, the production of speech sounds, especially that part of the process taking place above the larynx. See ARTICULATORY SET(TING), DOUBLE ARTICULATION, LARYNX, VOICE. [SPEECH].   T.MCA.

ARTICULATORY SETTING, sometimes **articulatory set**. A term in phonetics for the preferred positions of the organs of the vocal tract, such as for French (compared with other languages) or the English of Dublin or New York (compared with other accents). Such settings do not make linguistic contrasts, but are characteristic of communities and individuals: for example, the complaint that people in England do not open their mouths when they speak refers to the setting of lips and jaw (producing either a tight, clipped effect or a slurred effect that elides syllables). So-called *nasal twangs* and *adenoidal voices* are produced by different settings of the velum, while the settings of the pharynx and larynx produce the typical quality of a person's voice. See ACCENT, PRONUNCIATION, VOICE QUALITY. [SPEECH].   G.K., T.MCA.

ARTIFICIAL INTELLIGENCE, short form *AI*. The capacity of a computer or other device to imitate aspects of human intelligence; theory and practice aimed at creating this capacity. When applied to processing language in a computer, AI attempts to enable programs that model or learn about the world to understand spoken or written language. English is the language most frequently studied by researchers. The main branches of AI are: (1) *Expert systems*, which attempt to reason, using rules analogous to those a knowledgeable person would use, such as, in medicine, 'a high white blood cell count implies bacterial infection'. (2) *Natural language processing systems*, which accept a human rather than an artificial language as input, such as systems which attempt machine translation. (3) *Speech understanding systems*, which attempt to transcribe spoken language into written, such as the HEARSAY program at Carnegie-Mellon University, which recognizes spoken chess moves. (4) *AI computers*, designed to process AI programs, such as the Symbolics workstations or the Fifth Generation Computer project in Japan. (5) *Robotics*, the construction and operation of machines that manipulate objects rather than information, now common in factories for tasks they can do faster or more safely than people. See AMBIGUITY, COMPUTING. [LANGUAGE, TECHNOLOGY].   M.L.

ARTIFICIAL LANGUAGE [1860s]. (1) An invented language, such as Zamenhof's *Esperanto*, formed by blending elements of various Indo-European languages, or an adapted language, such as Ogden's *Basic English*, formed by radically reducing standard English. Hundreds of artefacts of this type have been created and many promoted over the last 150 years, mostly without success. Esperanto is, however, well known and its name serves virtually as a generic term for all kinds of artificial communication. Such languages are discussed in detail by Andrew Large in *The Artificial Language Movement* (Blackwell, 1985). (2) A system of symbols constructed for a particular purpose, such as a computer language or a system of symbolic logic. Such systems originated in the 17c, as part of a search for a universal logical system that would transcend all natural language. An early form was *Real Character*, a code-like writing system invented by Bishop John Wilkins, a member of the Royal Society. Since then, philosophers have developed a variety of systems, such as symbolic logic and Boolean algebra, which can be regarded as language-like. The practical side of systems of this kind includes such computer languages as *BASIC* and *COBOL*, procedures by which programs can be written for machines to follow. See AIRSPEAK, BASIC ENGLISH[1], COMPUTING, CORNISH, ESPERANTO, INTERLANGUAGE, LOGIC, NEWSPEAK, RESTRICTED LANGUAGE, SEASPEAK. [LANGUAGE, TECHNOLOGY].   T.MCA.

ARYAN [Late 18c: from Sanskrit *ārya* noble. Pronounced both 'AY-rian' and 'AH-rian']. A term used by 19c philologists for the common ancestor of many Indian and European languages. When the terms *Indo-Germanic* and *Indo-European* were adopted as more accurate, *Aryan* was restricted to the Indo-Iranian branch of the Indo-European language family. In Nazi terminology, the word was used to mean white and especially Nordic by race: *the Aryan Master Race*. Because of the disrepute of this third sense and confusion about the earlier senses, the term is now used in linguistics and ethnology only in the combination *Indo-Aryan*, referring to the Indo-European languages of India. See INDIAN LANGUAGES, INDO-EUROPEAN LANGUAGES, RACISM. [ASIA, EUROPE, HISTORY, LANGUAGE].
                                              W.F.B., T.MCA.

ASCENDER AND DESCENDER [17c]. Contrasting terms in printing and calligraphy. An *ascender* is the part of a minuscule or lower-case letter such as *b*, *d*, *f*, *h* that rises above *x-height* (the median height for Roman letters). A *descender* is the part of a minuscule, such as *g*, *j*, *p*, *y*, that falls below x-height. The terms are also used for the letters themselves. See LETTER[1]. [TECHNOLOGY, WRITING].   T.MCA.

ASCENSION, also **Ascension Island**. A British dependency in the South Atlantic. Population: *c*.1,400. Language: English. The island was discovered by the Portuguese on Ascension Day, 1501. A cable station links it with St Helena, from which it is administered. See ENGLISH, SAINT HELENA. [NAME, VARIETY].   T.MCA.

ASCII. See CHARACTER SET.

ASH, also **æsc, aesc** [From Old English *æsc* ash (tree), a mnemonic name for the rune to which the character corresponds]. The scholarly name for the ligature (upper case *Æ*, lower case *æ* or *æ*) of *a* and *e*, used in Old English orthography for a sound related to but distinct from the sound represented by each letter separately. The form *æ* is used in IPA for a not quite open, front unrounded vowel, higher than Cardinal 4 and lower than Cardinal 3, as in many pronunciations of *cat* /kæt/. This was probably the sound represented by the Old English symbol. See ALPHABET, DIGRAPH, LETTER[1], LIGATURE, RUNE. [SPEECH, WRITING].   T.MCA., E.W.

ASIA [From Greek *Asía*, mother of Atlas and Prometheus]. The largest continent. Originally, *Asia* was the imprecise term for an area east of the Aegean. Beyond lay *Anatolia* (Land of the Rising Sun), which by the time of the Romans was included in *Asia Minor* (roughly present-day Turkey), in contrast to *Asia* proper, the entire eastern land mass. For the Romans, this area was *Oriens* (Rising: Land of the Sunrise) while

Europe was *Occidens* (Falling: Land of the Sunset), terms that have passed into English as *the Orient* and *the Occident*. *Orient* and *Oriental* have tended to refer to East Asia and *Oriental* as a noun has often been pejorative: *wily Oriental, inscrutable Orientals*. *The East* and *the Orient* are broadly synonymous, suggesting the exotic: *the Mystic East, the mysterious Orient*. The traditional adjective *Asiatic*, as in the *Royal Asiatic Society*, has been so generally used pejoratively that it has been replaced in everyday use by *Asian*. Some phrases containing *East* are Eurocentric: (1) *The Near East* and *the Levant* (from French *lever*, to rise) are both now little used. They imprecisely cover Turkey, Cyprus, Lebanon, Syria, and sometimes Greece, Egypt, Iraq, Iran, Arabia, the Gulf. (2) *The Middle East*, both *Middle-East*, and *Mid-East* meant in the 19c and early 20c India and its environs but now covers the general area from Lebanon to Iran and the Gulf. (3) *The Far East* refers to regions beyond India. Neutral alternatives for divisions of the continent are *West Asia*, *South Asia*, *Central Asia*, *East Asia*, and *South-East Asia*. Compare EUROPE, NORTH, SOUTH, WEST. [GEOGRAPHY, HISTORY, NAME].   T.MCA.

The Asia theme.
ANGLO-CHINESE SCHOOLS, ANGLO-INDIAN, ARABIC, ARAMAIC, ARYAN, ASIA, ASIAN ENGLISH, ASIAN LANGUAGES, ASIATIC, AUSTRALASIA, BABU ENGLISH, BAHASA INDONESIA, BANGLADESH, BEARER ENGLISH, BENGALI, BORROWING, BOXWALLAH ENGLISH, BRITISH COUNCIL, BRITISH EMPIRE, BRUNEI, BURGHER ENGLISH, BURMA, BUTLER ENGLISH, CENTRAL INSTITUTE OF ENGLISH AND FOREIGN LANGUAGES, CHEE-CHEE ENGLISH, CHINA, CLASSICAL LANGUAGE, CONTINENT, DECORATIVE ENGLISH, DIASPORA, DUTCH, EAST ASIAN ENGLISH, EAST INDIAN, EAST INDIES, ENGLISH, ENGLISH LITERATURE, ETHNIC NAME, EURASIAN, EXAMINING IN ENGLISH, FILIPINISM, FILIPINO/PILIPINO, FILIPINO LITERATURE IN ENGLISH, FRENCH, GAIRAIGO, GUJARATI/GUJERATI, HALLIDAY, HAMITO-SEMITIC LANGUAGES, HEBRAISM, HEBREW, HINDLISH/HINGLISH, HINDI, HINDI-URDU, HINDUSTANI, HOBSON-JOBSON, HOBSON- JOBSONISM, HOME, HONG KONG, HORNBY, INDIA, INDIAN, INDIAN ENGLISH¹, INDIAN ENGLISH LITERATURE, INDIANISM, INDIAN LANGUAGES, INDIAN PRESS, INDIAN PUBLISHING, INDIAN RECOMMENDED PRONUNCIATION, INDIES, INDO-, INDO-ANGLIAN, INDO-ARYAN, INDO-BRITISH, INDO-EUROPEAN LANGUAGES, INDO-EUROPEAN ROOTS, INDO-GERMANIC, INDONESIA, JANGLISH, JAPAN, JAPANESE PIDGIN ENGLISH, JAPLISH, JEWISH LANGUAGES, JONES (W.), KANNADA/KANNARESE, KIPLING, KITCHEN, KOREA, KOREAN BAMBOO ENGLISH, MACAO, MACAULAY, MALAY, MALAYALAM, MALAYO-POLYNESIAN LANGUAGES, MALAYSIA, MALAYSIAN ENGLISH, MALDIVES, MARATHI, MESTIZO, NEPAL, NOVEL, PACIFIC RIM, PAKISTAN, PAKISTANI ENGLISH, PALMER, PANJABI/PUNJABI, PERSIAN, PHILIPPINE, PHILIPPINE ENGLISH, PHILIPPINES (THE), PORTUGUESE, RACISM, RELC, ROMANY/ROMANI, RUSSIAN, SINGAPORE, SINGAPORE ENGLISH, SINGLISH, SINHALA/SINHALESE, SINO-TIBETAN LANGUAGES, SOCIETY OF PAKISTANI ENGLISH LANGUAGE TEACHERS, SOUTH AFRICAN INDIAN ENGLISH, SOUTH ASIAN BROADCASTING, SOUTH ASIAN ENGLISH, SOUTH-EAST ASIAN ENGLISH, SPANISH, SPELT, SRI LANKA, TAGALOG, TAGLISH, TAIWAN, TAMIL, TELUGU/TELEGU, TESL, TURKISH, URDU, URO-ALTAIC LANGUAGES, WHITNEY.

ASIAN ENGLISH. See ASIAN LANGUAGES, EAST ASIAN ENGLISH, SOUTH ASIAN ENGLISH, SOUTH-EAST ASIAN ENGLISH.

ASIAN LANGUAGES. The languages of Asia, mainly grouped in such distinctive families as the Dravidian, Sino-Tibetan, and Malayo-Polynesian languages, as well as the Indo-European and Uro-Altaic families (also found in Europe) and the Hamito-Semitic languages (also found in Africa). The term currently excludes any originally European language currently used in Asia, however extensively. In pragmatic terms, however, a case can be made for Russian as an Asian language because of its widespread use across North and Central Asia, and for English as an Asian language because of its official use in India, Hong Kong, Pakistan, the Philippines, and Singapore, and significant status and use elsewhere.

See ARABIC, ARAMAIC, BANGLADESH, BORROWING, BURMA/MYANMAR, CHINA/CHINESE, EAST ASIAN ENGLISH, ENGLISH, FILIPINO/PILIPINO, HAMITO-SEMITIC LANGUAGES, HEBREW, INDIA, INDIAN LANGUAGES, INDO-EUROPEAN LANGUAGES, JAPAN, JEWISH LANGUAGES, KOREA, MALAYO-POLYNESIAN LANGUAGES, MALAYSIA, NEPAL, PAKISTAN, PERSIAN, PHILIPPINES, RUSSIAN, SINGAPORE, SINO-TIBETAN LANGUAGES, SOUTH ASIAN ENGLISH, SOUTH-EAST ASIAN ENGLISH, SRI LANKA, TAGALOG, URO-ALTAIC LANGUAGES. [LANGUAGE].   T.MCA.

ASIATIC. See ASIA.

ASIDE [18c in this sense]. (1) A remark spoken in an undertone so as not to be heard by everyone present, often behind a hand raised to the mouth. (2) A comment inserted into a speech or other presentation, for dramatic effect or to add humour, topicality, or additional information. Casual asides are often marked in print by parenthetical dashes: 'I was out shopping—looking for a pair of shoes actually—when . . .'. (3) In drama, a statement assumed to be unheard by other characters on the stage, used to express reactions to a situation, reveal intentions, or give information to the audience: 'A little more than kin and less than kind' (Shakespeare, *Hamlet*, 1. 2). The aside was popular in 16–17c drama and 19c melodrama. It is distinguished from the *soliloquy* by the presence of other characters, but there is some overlap, as in *Richard II*, where some of Richard's speeches reveal his thoughts but are not spoken when he is alone: 'Oh God, O God! that e'er this tongue of mine / That laid the sentence of dread banishment / On yon proud man should take it off again / With words of sooth!' (3. 3). See DASH, EXCLAMATION MARK/ POINT, PARENTHESIS, SOLILOQUY. [LITERATURE, SPEECH]. R.C.

ASPECT [14c: from Latin *aspectus* how something looks, from *ad-* towards, *specere/spectum* to look]. The grammatical category (expressed in verb forms) that refers to a way of looking at the time of a situation: for example, its duration, repetition, completion. Aspect contrasts with *tense*, the category that refers to the time of the situation with respect to some other time: for example, the moment of speaking or writing. There are two aspects in English: the *progressive aspect* ('We *are eating* lunch') and the *perfect aspect* ('We *have eaten* lunch'). See TENSE[1]. [GRAMMAR]. S.G.

ASPER. See ARABIC, DIACRITIC.

ASPIRATE [17c: from Latin *aspirare/aspiratum* to breathe out]. A term in phonetics for the *h*-sound, as in *hope*. *Aspiration* is a delay in voicing: for example, the release of the voiceless stops /p, t, k/ is often followed by further voicelessness like a brief *h*-sound, as in *tick* /tʰɪk/. Such stops are not aspirated after an *s*-sound, as in *stick* /stɪk/. See AITCH, ARTICLE[1], H, HIBERNO-ENGLISH. [SPEECH, STYLE]. G.K.

ASSIMILATION [16c: from Latin *assimilatio/ assimilationis* making one thing like another, from *similis* like]. (1) In phonetics, a process of connected speech in which one sound becomes similar to another, neighbouring sound. In the commonest type of assimilation in English, an alveolar consonant anticipates the place of articulation of a following sound: for example, in *good boy* the /d/ anticipates the labial articulation of /b/. When the process is complete, and the /d/ can be said to have changed into /b/. (2) The same process exhibited orthographically: for example, in the Latin-derived word *aggression* (originally *adgressio*), the *d* of the prefix *ad-* has been assimilated to the *g* of the base *-gress-*; in the informal English word *wanna* ('want to'), the *t* of both *want* and *to* have been assimilated to the preceding *n*. (3) In lexicology, the adaptation of items into one language from another, such as into English from French. The degree of assimilation of loanwords generally depends on the length of time since the borrowing took place and on the frequency of use. Compare the degree of spoken and written assimilation of *honour* (c.1400), *salon* (c.1700), *sabotage* (c.1900): see

BORROWING, LOAN. Assimilation of this type is often to elements that are already familiar in the receiving language, as with Spanish *cucuracha* becoming English *cockroach*, and Hindi *banglā* becoming English *bungalow*: compare HOBSON-JOBSONISM. (4) In sociolinguistics, the absorption of speakers of one language or dialect into another, such as Albanian immigrants in Greece and Italy. The degree of assimilation depends on such factors as receptiveness, the possibility of acceptance, and the degree of similarity. Albanians in Greece have more readily given up their language than in Italy, where attitudes towards diversity are more favourable. Immigrants into the English-speaking world experience pressure to adapt and different metaphors are sometimes used to discuss and even euphemize the processes involved: immigrants to the US are said to enter a *melting pot*, while immigrants to Canada become part of a *mosaic*. In Australia, the term has been applied to the policy of integrating all minorities into the dominant Anglo-Celtic society. This policy, now discredited, was until the early 1970s a contributory factor in the decline of Aboriginal languages and the languages of European immigrants. *Reverse assimilation* has been true in New Zealand, where the indigenous Maori became a minority assimilated towards the immigrant European majority. [AMERICAS, LANGUAGE, MEDIA, OCEANIA, SPEECH]. G.K., S.R., W.S.R., T.MCA.

ASSOCIATED EXAMINING BOARD, short form *AEB*. An examining board in England and Wales, founded in 1953. It operates the *General Certificate of Secondary Education* (*GCSE*) as part of the Southern Examining Group, and has examined at the level of Further Education in the UK and overseas, especially Africa. It has close links with commerce, industry, and the professions, and administers a *Test of English for Academic Purposes* (*TEAP*), used to screen overseas applicants for higher education in the UK. See EAP, EXAMINING IN ENGLISH. [EDUCATION]. W.S.

ASSOCIATION OF RECOGNIZED ENGLISH LANGUAGE SCHOOLS. See ARELS.

ASSONANCE [18c: through French from Latin *assonare* ('to sound towards') to answer something, in the manner of an echo. Stress: 'ASS-o-nanss']. In rhetoric and poetics, a resemblance or correspondence of sound between syllables or words, such as the repeated vowel in *easy to please* and the repeated consonant pattern *b-t-d* in *bright-eyed* and *bushy-tailed*. Traditionally, the term has been reserved for vowel repetition alone and *consonance* has been reserved for consonants, but this distinction is now rare. Assonance has been described as both a kind of rhyme and an alternative to rhyme. Sounds that echo each other occur in a wide range of English verse, such as the complex *s–th–b–y* pattern in this excerpt from Emily Dickinson (1890):

Some things that fly there be—
Birds—Hours—the Bumblebee—
Some things that stay there be—
Grief—Hills—Eternity.
Of these no Elegy.

The terms *alliteration, assonance,* and *rhyme* identify kinds of recurring sound that in practice are often freely mixed together. In considering a poem, it may not be easy or useful to decide where one stops and another starts. Poets and others are concerned with such matters, but are not necessarily interested in making fine distinctions. See ALLITERATION, ECHOISM, JINGLE, REPETITION, RHYME. [SPEECH, STYLE].   T.MCA.

ASTERISK [14c: from Latin *asteriscus*, Greek *asteriskos* a small star]. A star-shaped mark (*), used in writing and printing: (1) To indicate a reference or annotation, especially a first footnote, in which case it follows the word, phrase, or sentence being marked in a text, and precedes the footnote or reference: compare OBELISK. (2) To mark a cross-reference in an encyclopedia or similar work: *Darwin or Darwin*, meaning 'Darwin (see entry under that name)'. (3) To mark the omission of a letter, especially in four-letter words: *f**k* for *fuck*. (4) In philology, to mark a reconstructed form not (yet) attested in a text or inscription: for example, the hypothetical Latin word *ultraticum proposed as the source of English *outrage* and Italian *ultraggio*. (5) In linguistics, to mark a word, phrase, sentence, or utterance as unacceptable for grammatical, semantic, or other reasons: for example, **I went for to do it* discounted as a sentence of standard English. See ELLIPSIS, PROVERB. [REFERENCE, WRITING].   T.MCA.

ATLANTIC [14c: from Latin *Atlanticum (Mare)* Atlantic Sea, from Greek *Atlantikós* of (Mount) Atlas, from *Atlas* the titan who held the heavens or the world on his shoulders]. The ocean between Europe and Africa in the east and the Americas in the west, a barrier to travel until the 15c, when the Portuguese began to sail to Asia round southern Africa and the Spanish began to explore the New World. From *Atlantic* derive several words with linguistic and other associations, such as *transatlantic* (referring in Europe to North America and in North America to Europe), *Atlanticism* (a policy of close ties between the US and Europe, in such forms as the *North Atlantic Treaty Organization*), *mid-Atlantic* (accent), *Atlantic creoles*, and *Atlantic Englishes* (the varieties of English used on the shores of the Atlantic, as in John Harris,

'Expanding the Superstrate: Habitual Aspect Markers in Atlantic Englishes', *English World-Wide* 7: 2, 1986). See AFRICA, AMERICAS, ASCENSION (ISLAND), ATLANTIC CREOLES, BERMUDA, CARIBBEAN, EUROPE, FALKLAND ISLANDS, MID-ATLANTIC, SAINT HELENA, TRISTAN DA CUNHA. [GEOGRAPHY, NAME].   T.MCA.

ATLANTIC CREOLES. A group of related creole languages on both sides of the Atlantic, such as West African Pidgin English, Caribbean Creole, and Gullah. See ATLANTIC, CREOLE. [AFRICA, AMERICAS, VARIETY].   T.MCA.

ATMOSPHERE ENGLISH. See DECORATIVE ENGLISH.

ATTIC AND DORIC [16c: from Latin *Atticus, Doricus,* from Greek *Attikós, Dōrikós* Athenian, Dorian]. A classical contrast between the refined and the rustic, popular in the 18c, when Edinburgh came to be called 'the Athens of the North'. Just as the 'refined' Athenians were contrasted with their 'rougher' Dorian cousins in the Peloponnese, so Attic urban refinement was contrasted with Doric rusticity. See ATTICISM, DORIC. [HISTORY, NAME, STYLE].   T.MCA.

ATTICISM [17c: from Latin *Atticismus*, Greek *Attikismós* the style of Attica]. A now little-used term for witty refinement and a well-turned phrase. In classical times, the Athenian state (Attica) was a centre of social and cultural interest and Atticism was a predilection for anything Athenian; its dialect was extolled as the best Greek. In Rome, the rival schools of oratory were the *Atticists* (including Cicero and Caesar), who favoured a sharp, direct, witty style, and the *Asians*, who favoured the indirect and ornate. In the 2c, compilers of lexicons of the 'best' Greek were known as Atticists, because Attic was their reference norm. In 17–18c English, the term referred to such witty comments as those of Samuel Johnson's: 'A man is generally better pleased when he has a good dinner upon his table, than when his wife talks Greek.' See ATTIC AND DORIC, ATTIC SALT, BARBARISM, CLASSICISM, -ISM, KOINÉ, SOLECISM, VERNACULARISM. [HISTORY, STYLE, WORD].   T.MCA.

ATTIC SALT [18c: a translation of Latin *sal Atticum* 'salty' Athenian wit]. A traditional metaphor for wit: 'Triumph swam in my father's eyes, at the repartee; the Attic salt brought water to them' (Laurence Sterne, *Tristram Shandy,* 1760). See ATTICISM, WIT. [STYLE].   T.MCA.

ATTRIBUTIVE [17c: through French from Latin *attributivus* for the purpose of ascribing or associating]. A grammatical term contrasting with *predicative*. The attributive position is in front of a noun: the position of *new* in *a new house* and *steel* in *steel bridge*. It may imply a permanent attribute, as a result of which some adjectives and most nouns can only be attributive: *an atomic scientist* but not **the scientist was atomic*; *the greenhouse effect* but not **the effect is greenhouse*. Some attributive-only adjectives refer to relationships (a *former* chairman), intensify a noun (It's a *downright* swindle), or limit it (the *only* time, the *main* idea). Some adjectives that are both attributive and predicative can have a special meaning when attributive (my *late* uncle, a *certain* person, a *perfect* nuisance, a *good* listener, *poor old* you). Some phrases that are otherwise not hyphenated are hyphenated when attributive: *well known* in *a well-known politician*, *round the clock* in *a round-the-clock vigil*, *right to life* in *the right-to-life movement*, but hyphens are not usual after an adverb ending in *-ly* (contrast *a carefully written report* with *a well-written report*). See ABBREVIATION, ATTRIBUTIVE NOUN, PARTICIPLE, PHRASE WORD, PREDICATIVE ADJECTIVE, SENTENCE WORD. [GRAMMAR].   S.C.

ATTRIBUTIVE NOUN. A noun that modifies another noun: *steel* in *steel bridge*; *London* in *London house*. Nouns used in this way are sometimes said to be adjectives or to behave like adjectives. They are generally not used predicatively: *the bridge is steel* is possible, **the house is London* impossible. Phrases with attributive nouns are common, and are similar to noun compounds like *teapot* and *coffee jug*. However, such phrases have the same stress patterns as adjectival phrases (equal stress: *a bíg hóuse, a Lóndon hóuse*), but compounds take contrastive stress, emphasizing the first element in a pair: *the WHITE Hóuse in Wáshington*, rather than *the white hóuse next dóor*; *COFfee pót* as opposed to *stéel brídge*. In answer to questions or for emphasis, however, phrases with attributive nouns are contrastively stressed and sound like compounds: *What kind of bridge is it?—A STEEL bridge*. Noun compounds and phrases with attributive nouns can usually be paraphrased in the same way: *A steel bridge* a bridge made of steel; *a coffee pot* a pot for (making) coffee (in). An attributive noun can modify a compound (*china* in *a china téapot*) and one compound can modify another attributively (*STRIKE committee* modifying *POLicy decision* in *a STRIKE commíttee POLicy decision*). Such phrases are numerous and unpredictably creative, especially when they incorporate one or more loanword: *alfresco staircase, glissando laugh, goy Zionist, Uzbek mafia*. See ATTRIBUTIVE, EPONYM. [GRAMMAR, WORD].   T.MCA.

AUDIOBOOK [1980s]. A name for one or more audio cassettes that contain the taped version of a printed book, sometimes abridged, sometimes in full, and often read by an actor or author. Such books have rapidly found a market among the visually impaired, drivers, and people who prefer to listen rather than read. See BIBLE, BOOK, TALKING BOOK. [MEDIA, TECHNOLOGY].   T.MCA.

AUDIO-LINGUAL METHOD. See LANGUAGE TEACHING.

AUDIO-VISUAL METHOD. See LANGUAGE TEACHING.

AUGUSTAN [17c: from Latin *Augustanus* referring to Augustus Caesar, the first Roman emperor]. A term referring to two eras, both known as *the Augustan Age*: (1) In ancient Rome, the reign of Augustus, 27 BC to AD 14, traditionally considered the golden age of Latin literature. The period is sometimes widened to 43 BC to AD 18, to include more of the leading writers. In the decade 29 to 19 BC, Virgil produced the *Georgics* and the *Aeneid*, Horace his *Odes* 1–3, and *Epistles* 1, and Livy began his history of Rome. (2) By analogy, a neo-classical period widely considered a golden age of English letters. Some limit it to the reign of Queen Anne (1702–14), during which Addison, Defoe, Pope, Steele, and Swift had their heyday; others extend it back to Dryden and forward to Johnson. See ATTICISM, CLASSICAL LANGUAGE, CLASSICISM, EARLY MODERN ENGLISH, ENGLISH IN ENGLAND, ENGLISH LITERATURE, HUMO(U)R, RESTORATION, ROMANTICISM. [EUROPE, HISTORY, NAME, STYLE].   T.MCA.

AUNTIE. Also **Auntie/Aunty Beeb.** An informal, sometimes affectionate, sometimes dismissive, name for the British Broadcasting Corporation: 'Aunty Beeb's power to pervert our language is indeed impressive' (Dr Herbert Sandford, quoted in 'Three cheers for plain old English', *The Times*, 31 August 1991). See BRITISH BROADCASTING. [EUROPE, MEDIA, NAME].   T.MCA.

AUREATE DICTION [15c: from Latin *aureatus* gilded, *dictio* speech]. Also **aureate language, aureation.** An ornate style fashionable among such 15c poets as John Lydgate in England and William Dunbar in Scotland, whose aim was to gild or 'illumine' the vernacular with classicisms, such as *superne* and *eterne* in 'Hale, Sterne Superne! Hale, in eterne, In Godis Sicht to schyne!' (Dunbar, *Ballad of Our Lady*). Later critics have generally regarded the results as florid and overdone. See DICTION, EUPHUISM, HOLOFERNES, INKHORN TERM. [HISTORY, STYLE, WRITING].   T.MCA.

AUSSIE [1910: an abbreviation of *Australia(n)*. Usually pronounced with /z/, sometimes /s/]. Also *Ozzie, Ossie*. An informal term for Australia, an Australian, or anything Australian. First recorded in New Zealand, *Aussie* became popular among service personnel during the First World War, and is now international. The game *Australian Rules*, not unlike Gaelic football in Ireland, is familiarly known as *Aussie Rules*. *Aussieland* is sometimes used for Australia and *Aussielander* for an Australian. Compare oz. [NAME, OCEANIA].   W.S.R.

AUSTEN, Jane [1775-1817]. English novelist, born at Steventon, Hampshire, where her father was the rector. She lived, unmarried, with her family, in Bath, Southampton, and Chawton. She published six novels, including *Sense and Sensibility* (the first: 1811), *Pride and Prejudice* (1813), and *Emma* (1816), all gently ironic accounts of middle-class life. She tried to achieve what she called in a letter to her sister 'the playfulness and epigrammatism of the general style'. Austen had an acute ear for dialogue and the social nuances of speech. See index. [BIOGRAPHY, EUROPE, LITERATURE, STYLE].   R.C.

AUSTRAL [14c: from Latin *Auster* the south wind]. A poetic synonym for *southern*, often applied to Australasia: 'Grant that yet an Austral Milton's song . . . flow deep and rich along . . . An Austral Shakespeare rise' (W. C. Wentworth, *Australasia*, 1823). See ARGENTINA, AUSTRALASIAN ENGLISH. [NAME, OCEANIA]. T.MCA.

AUSTRALASIA [18c: from French *Australasie*, from Latin *australis* southern, and *Asia*: a name for part of the hypothetical continent *Terra Australis*]. Formerly, Australia and neighbouring islands; currently, Australia, New Zealand, and adjacent islands. [NAME, OCEANIA].   T.MCA.

AUSTRALASIAN ENGLISH, sometimes **Antipodean English, Austral English**. Australian English and New Zealand English taken together; all three terms have been popular in the past as a reflection of the similarities between the two varieties, but have fallen into disuse. Similar histories led to near-identity of the varieties: both are non-rhotic and based on late 18c southern BrE, and the lexicon of each has been heavily influenced by immigration from rural Britain. It is arguable that elements of ScoE are evident in New Zealand, as are elements of IrE in Australia, but the differences between the two countries were never substantial enough to distinguish speakers with any certainty. As late as 1970, Australians could only volunteer that the speech of New Zealanders was more 'English', while some New Zealanders saw AusE as more

'broad'. Speakers of BrE and AmE could normally do no more than distinguish the two from the English of South Africa. Linguists commonly treated the varieties together in the same publications, under such headings as 'Australia and New Zealand'.

Since *c*.1970, however, AusE and NZE have begun to show a publicly noted divergence in phonology almost entirely due to a shift in the NZ short front vowels, which have been raised and retracted. One effect of this shift has been the merging of /ɪ/ with /ə/. Australians now characterize New Zealanders as eating 'fush and chups', while New Zealanders return the compliment by hearing Australian 'feesh and cheeps'. Phonologically inspired graffiti near Bondi Beach in Sydney run: NEW ZEALAND SUCKS, AUSTRALIA SEVEN. The merging of /ɪ + ə/ with /ɛ + ə/ in most speakers, so that *ear* and *air* become homophones, further reduces the phonemic inventory of NZE. The rapidity of these changes has produced a distinctive age-grading in NZE phonology. Speakers over 50 cannot often be identified as New Zealanders or Australians, except by a degree of /ɪ/ retraction. Those under 30, however, show that the notion of a uniform spoken 'Australasian English' is out of date. Observations suggest that some Australians may be following the NZ lead in the vowel shift, but the pattern appears to be increasing divergence from the old near-identity. Younger speakers of AusE and NZE appear on the whole to respond readily to the opposing linguistic stereotypes. See AUSTRAL. [OCEANIA, VARIETY].   D.B.

AUSTRAL ENGLISH. See AUSTRALASIAN ENGLISH.

AUSTRALIA [18c: an Anglicization of Latin *Terra Australis* the southern land]. Official title *Commonwealth of Australia*. A country in Oceania and a member of the Commonwealth. Federal capital: Canberra. Population: 16.39m (1988), 18.4m (projection for 2000). Currency: the dollar (100 cents). Economy: agriculture, livestock, minerals, mixed. Ethnicity: 75% Anglo-Celtic, 19% other European (especially German, Italian, Greek), 5% Asian (Chinese, Jewish, Lebanese), 1% Aboriginal. Languages: English (official), Aboriginal languages and English-based creoles, and immigrant languages. Education: primary 98%, secondary 95%, tertiary 28%, literacy 98%. The state includes the Australian land mass, Tasmania, and a number of smaller islands.

Terra australis. Australia has sometimes been called *the Last of Lands* because it was the last large, habitable territory to be explored and settled by Europeans. Geographers and travellers had long speculated about a *terra australis incognita* [Latin: unknown southern land] to the south of Asia and Africa. Exploration established that this was in fact two continents: Antarctica and another beyond the East Indies. In the mid-17c, the Dutch charted the western coastline of a continent they named *New Holland*. In 1770, James Cook took possession of the eastern coast for Britain, later naming it *New South Wales*. *Australia* was preferred as a name for the continent by the explorer Matthew Flinders, for reasons of 'geographical propriety', and, promoted by Lachlan Macquarie, was in general use in the colonies in the 1820s. The wider term *Australasia* [Latin: southern Asia] was sometimes also used of the continent only.

Aborigines and settlers. At the time of the first white settlement in 1788, Australia was inhabited by upwards of 300,000 Aborigines speaking some 200 languages, whose occupation of the continent began 40,000 years earlier. Settlement and land use dispossessed and dispersed the Aborigines, their numbers reducing (largely through introduced diseases like smallpox) to about 50,000 within a century. The word *disperse* was sometimes used as a euphemism for 'kill'. Initial white settlement spread from New South Wales during the 19c, both south to Tasmania (then called *Van Diemen's Land*) and Victoria, and north to Queensland. Convicts transported to all the colonies except South Australia (1788–1868) were important as a labour force in both public and private employment. Separate settlements were effected in South Australia and Western Australia. The colonies federated as states in 1901, with state and federal governments.

The cities and the bush. The present-day population of Australia is largely urban, on or near the coast, in such cities as Sydney, Melbourne, Adelaide, Brisbane, and Perth, but the *bush*, the intractable natural environment, and beyond that the *outback*, and in particular the *dead* or *red centre*, have a place in the Australian consciousness akin to that of 'the great white north' in the Canadian. Until after the Second World War, immigrants were mainly from Britain and Ireland. All colonies attempted to restrict Asian immigration and after federation the Commonwealth Parliament introduced a *White Australian Policy* that remained effective into the 1950s. European immigration, much of it financially assisted, began on a large scale after the war, and the policy was one of assimilation into Anglo-Celtic society until the mid-1970s. Progressive relaxation of restrictions and a shift in internal policy have, however, moved a society

of whom one in four is born abroad towards multiculturalism, if not multilingualism.

See ABORIGINAL ENGLISH, ABORIGINES, ANGLO-CELTIC, ANTIPODEAN ENGLISH, ANTIPODES, ASSIMILATION, AUSSIE, AUSTRAL, AUSTRALASIA, AUSTRALASIAN ENGLISH, AUSTRALIAN, AUSTRALIAN BROADCASTING, AUSTRALIAN DICTIONARIES, AUSTRALIAN ENGLISH, AUSTRALIANESE, AUSTRALIANISM, AUSTRALIAN LANGUAGE, AUSTRALIAN LANGUAGE RESEARCH CENTRE, AUSTRALIAN LANGUAGES, AUSTRALIAN LITERATURE, AUSTRALIAN NATIONAL DICTIONARY CENTRE, AUSTRALIAN PIDGIN, AUSTRALIAN PLACE-NAMES, AUSTRALIAN PRESS, AUSTRALIAN PUBLISHING, BROAD AUSTRALIAN, BULLETIN (THE), BUSH, CLIPPING, COLONIAL, COMMUNITY LANGUAGE, CULTIVATED, CULTURAL CRINGE, DIALECT IN AUSTRALIA, DOWN UNDER, ELICOS, ENGLISH, GENERAL AUSTRALIAN, GREAT AUSTRALIAN ADJECTIVE, GREAT AUSTRALIAN SLANGUAGE, KRIOL, MOTHER COUNTRY, NAURU, OCEANIA, OLD COUNTRY, OZ, PACIFIC RIM, PITCAIRNESE/PITCAIRN–NORFOLK CREOLE, POM, SCOSE, STRINE. [HISTORY, NAME, OCEANIA].

W.S.R., T.MCA.

AUSTRALIAN [17c: from French *australien*, relating to *Terra Australis*: see AUSTRALIA]. (1) A native of the continent of Terra Australis and its islands: 'It is easie to judge of the incomparability of the Australians with the people of Europe' (*New Discoveries: Terra Australis Incognita*, 1693). (2) An original inhabitant of Australia, later referred to as *an Australian Aborigine*: see ABORIGINES. (3) A native or citizen of Australia, regardless of origin. (4) Relating to Australia and Australians: *an Australian accent*. (5) Australian English: 'English and French spoken; Australian understood' (O. Hogue, *Trooper Bluegum at the Dardanelles*, 1916). (6) Australian bad language: 'Then he began to speak some pure Australian, and the language that came out of the hole in that driver's face heated the air for yards around' (*Honk*, France, 1915). Compare AMERICAN, AUSTRALIAN LANGUAGE, CANADIAN, GREAT AUSTRALIAN SLANGUAGE. [NAME, OCEANIA, VARIETY].

T.MCA., W.S.R.

AUSTRALIAN ADJECTIVE. See GREAT AUSTRALIAN ADJECTIVE.

AUSTRALIAN BROADCASTING. Radio and television services in Australia fall into three categories: national, commercial, and public. The *Australian Broadcasting Corporation* (*ABC*) provides a radio and TV service within Australia and an overseas shortwave service, *Radio Australia*, directed primarily at the Asia–Pacific region. Established as the *Australian Broadcasting Commission* in 1932 and incorporated in

1983, the ABC is modelled on the British Broadcasting Corporation, and is similarly known as 'Auntie'. It has been a powerful, generally conservative force in Australian life, devoting time mainly to music, news, drama, education, sport, and rural concerns. From 1943 to 1951, a *Pronunciation Advisory Committee* sought to maintain pronunciations comparable to those of the BBC, but from 1952 a committee known from 1954 as the *Standing Committee on Spoken English* (*SCOSE*) has recognized the distinctiveness of AusE, given advice on acceptable styles of educated speech, and encouraged such speech in broadcasting. Its recommendations tend to be followed by other broadcasters and the community at large. SCOSE has published *A Guide to the Pronunciation of Australian Place Names* (1957) and *Watch Your Language* (1982), a collection of notes on usage.

There are special roles for two-way radio in two provisions made for remote communities: the *Flying Doctor Service*, established in 1928 as the *Aerial Medical Service* (under the auspices of the Presbyterian Church's Australian Inland Mission), and the *School of the Air*, established in 1951 to add 'classroom contact' to correspondence courses. Australian commercial and public services are operated under licence from the statutory *Australian Broadcasting Tribunal*. Commercial services, especially in television, are linked to major media groups. There are regulations governing Australian content. The *Special Broadcasting Service* (*SBS*) is federally funded and was introduced in the 1970s to provide programmes in ethnic languages. Audiences are small, but the television service is valued for its coverage of international news and readiness to programme films with limited appeal. Satellite services broadcast to all corners of the continent. [MEDIA, OCEANIA].　　W.S.R.

AUSTRALIAN DICTIONARIES. Dictionaries in Australia fall into two types: historical dictionaries and general reference dictionaries that recognize AusE as a national variety and are produced primarily for the local market.

Historical dictionaries. There are three such works: (1) *A Dictionary of Austral English* (Macmillan, London, 1898), ed. Edward Ellis Morris (1843-1902), professor of English, French, and German at Melbourne. His interest in Australasian English was aroused by James Murray, editor of the *OED*, and he followed Murray's principles and practices. His work is biased towards scientific terms and away from the colloquial, and many entries concern flora and fauna. The work records both Australianisms and New Zealandisms and is of historical interest. (2) *A Dictionary of Australian Colloquialisms*

(1978), compiled by G. A. Wilkes, Challis Professor of English Literature at Sydney. It provides the first documented record of many of the colloquialisms identified by S. J. Baker in *The Australian Language*. The revised edition of 1985 has *c*.3,000 entries. (3) *The Australian National Dictionary*, a dictionary of Australianisms on historical principles, ed. W. S. Ramson and published in Melbourne by Oxford University Press Australia (1988). The *AND* contains *c*.6,000 headwords and 4,000 combinations and collocations. The use and development of the words are documented with *c*.60,000 dated and referenced quotations drawn from over 9,000 printed sources. The dictionary was compiled at the Australian National U., Canberra, its sponsors including the University, the Australian Research Grants Scheme, and OUP Australia. The collection of data began in 1978 and publication took place as planned in 1988, Australia's bicentennial year.

General dictionaries. (1) *The Australian Pocket Oxford Dictionary* (1976), a revision and adaptation by Grahame Johnston of the *POD*. This was the first significant attempt to produce a general dictionary for the Australian market. Existing *POD* entries were revised where necessary to take account of their Australian application, and many new and peculiarly Australian words were added. The pronunciations remained British RP, but a prefatory note described the main divergences from this accent. George W. Turner's 2nd edition (1984) took the Australianization further, providing Cultivated Australian pronunciations. (2) *The Macquarie Dictionary*, ed. A. Delbridge, J. R. L. Bernard, D. Blair, and W. S. Ramson, was published by Macquarie Library, Sydney, in 1981 (revised 1985, 1987). It was the first to attempt a comprehensive coverage of regional vocabulary and record pronunciations. It takes its name from the Macquarie U., Sydney: three of the four editors were on the staff of the university, which holds copyright, and has made a substantial contribution to the development and maintenance of the dictionary. With the publication of derivative dictionaries and other popular reference works, the name has become a household word. The *MD* is an Australianization of Patrick Hanks's *Hamlyn Encyclopedic World Dictionary* (1971), itself a Briticization of *The American College Dictionary*. Nationalistic in its stance, as is *The Macquarie Thesaurus* (ed. J. R. L. Bernard, 1984), it has influenced consumer preference for dictionaries of Australian provenance. (3) Other works include *The Australian Concise Oxford Dictionary* (1987), ed. George W. Turner, and the Australian edition of the *Collins Dictionary* *of the English Language* (1986), ed. G. A. Wilkes. See DICTIONARY. [OCEANIA, REFERENCE].   W.S.R.

AUSTRALIAN ENGLISH, short form *AusE.* The English language as used in Australia. It has a short history, reflecting some 200 years of European settlement, and an even shorter period of recognition as a national variety, the term being first recorded in 1940. It is only since then that features of AusE have been regarded as distinctively and respectably Australian, instead of as evidence of colonial decline from the norms of the standard English of England.

Background. Initially, and uniquely, a majority of the British colonies in Australia were penal. As they expanded and as free colonies were developed, immigrants using languages other than English were insignificant. Relations with the Aborigines were generally poor and after an initial intake of words from their languages (such as *boomerang, dingo, kangaroo, koala, kookaburra, wombat*) were not conducive to extensive borrowing. The settlers were almost all Anglo-Celtic and geographical isolation was of great importance. The preoccupations of the colonists were the discovery and exploration of a new land, rich in exotic flora and fauna, and pastoral occupations such as raising sheep and cattle under circumstances vastly different from 'the Old Country'. In the late 20c, however, Australians are predominantly urban and increasingly multicultural. The major areas of lexical growth are international, as in computing and surfing. In the 19c, the situation was the reverse.

Pronunciation. The most marked feature of the Australian accent is its homogeneity, with no regional differences as marked as those in BrE and AmE, though recent studies have associated particular phonological characteristics with state capitals. There is, however, a social continuum in which three varieties are generally recognized: *Broad Australian, General Australian,* and *Cultivated Australian.* Of these, Cultivated Australian most closely approaches British RP and Broad Australian most vigorously exhibits distinctive regional features. It is generally assumed that the Australian accent derives from the mixing of British and Irish accents in the early years of settlement. However, although most convicts and other settlers came from London, the Midlands, and Ireland, the influence of the original accents cannot be conclusively quantified. The present spectrum was probably established by the early 19c. The major features of AusE pronunciation are:

(1) It is non-rhotic. (2) Its intonation is flatter than that of RP. (3) Speech rhythms are slow, stress being more evenly spaced than in RP. (4) Consonants do not differ significantly from those in RP. (5) Vowels are in general closer and more frontal than in RP, with /i/ and /u/ as in *tea, two* diphthongized to /əɪ/ and /əʊ/ respectively. (6) The vowel in *can't dance* may be /æ/ or /a/. (7) The schwa is busier than in RP, frequently replacing /ɪ/ in unaccented positions, as in *boxes, dances, darkest, velvet, acid.* (8) Some diphthongs shift, RP /eɪ/ towards /ʌɪ/, as in *Australia, day, mate,* and /aɪ/ towards /ɒɪ/, as in *high, wide.* (9) Speakers whose first language is not English or who have a bilingual background (Aboriginal, immigrant) often use sounds and a delivery influenced by the patterns of the first or other language. (10) The name of the letter *h* is often pronounced 'haitch' by speakers wholly or partly of Irish-Catholic background.

Grammar and vocabulary. There are no syntactic features that distinguish standard AusE from standard BrE, or indeed any major non-standard features not also found in Britain, but there are many distinctive words and phrases. However, although AusE has added some 10,000 items to the language, few have become internationally active. The largest demand for new words has concerned flora and fauna, and predominant occupations like stock-raising have also required new terms. Because of this, Australianisms are predominantly naming words: single nouns (*mulga* an acacia, *mullock* mining refuse, *muster* a round-up of livestock), compounds (*black camp* an Aboriginal settlement, *black tracker* an Aboriginal employed by the police to track down missing persons, *black velvet* Aboriginal women as sexual objects, *red-back* a spider, *redfin* a fish, *red gum* a eucalypt), nouns used attributively (*convict colony* a penal colony, *convict servant* or *convict slave* a convict assigned as a servant).

The penal settlements. The first settlements were penal colonies and until 1868, when transportation ceased, a vocabulary similar to that in a slave society described the life of the convicts. A major distinction was maintained between *bond* and *free*, as in *free emigrant, free native, free labourer, free servant*, and the distinction between *free* and *freed*. The settlements were populated in part by convicts and the attendant military forces, in part by free settlers. Though convicts who had served their sentences or obtained pardons (known from 1822 as *emancipists*) became *free* in their own eyes and those of the law, they often had difficulty escaping the stigma of servitude and obtained only a measure of freedom, being known by the *exclusives* or *exclusionists* as *free convicts* or *freed men.*

Stock-raising. Concomitantly, the land was explored and opened up for settlement and the stock-raising industry was developing. *Squatters* (stock-raisers or *graziers* occupying large tracts of Crown land under lease or licence) moved inland from the *limits of location* (the frontier of settlement) into the *back country* or *back of beyond* in search of land suitable for *runs* (tracts of grazing land) or *stations* (ranches). They looked for *open* land (free from forest or undergrowth), seeking *open forest* or *open plains*, and using words like *brush* (dense natural vegetation), *bush* (the distinctive Australian natural vegetation), *mallee* or *mulga* (forms of natural vegetation giving their name to their habitat), and *scrub* (generally, poor vegetation) to describe features of an unfamiliar environment. The stock industry employed *overseers* or *superintendents* (both convict terms), *stockmen*, and *rouseabouts* (general hands). *Drovers* travelled stock long distances *overland*, the original *overlanders* driving stock from New South Wales to South Australia. The importance of sheep in opening up the country and establishing a frontier society was such that the occupational vocabularies of droving and shearing figure largely in Australian literature.

The goldfields. Gold was discovered in the 1850s, leading to movement between the Californian, Australian, and New Zealand goldfields. *Rushes* (first used of the sudden escape of a number of convicts and then of the sudden movement of a number of miners to a particular place or *goldfield*) followed when a *prospector* (*goldfinder, gold-hunter, gold-seeker*) made a *find* and established a *claim*. A number of mining terms originated in Australia, but many are shared with other varieties of English, and the importance of the discovery of gold, and of the rushes that followed, lies in the mobility it encouraged and the effect of this on the homogeneity of the accent.

Colloquialisms. A growing sense of national identity was fostered by involvement in the First World War. The line between formal and informal usage is perhaps less rigidly drawn in Australia than elsewhere, colloquialisms being more generally admissible than in Britain. In informal usage, the suffixes *-ie* or *-y* and *-o* or *-oh* are freely attached to short base words (*roughie* a trick, *tinnie* a can of beer, *bottle-oh* a bottle merchant, *plonko* an addict of *plonk* or cheap wine, *smoko* a work break) and clippings (*Aussie* an Australian, *arvo* an afternoon, *barbie* a barbecue, *Chrissy* Christmas, *compo* workers' compensation, *derro* a derelict or down-and-out, *reffo* a refugee).

Kinds of Australianism. In terms of origin and structure, Australianisms fall into six categories: (1) Words from Aboriginal languages: *boomerang* a throwing weapon, *corroboree* a ceremonial dance, *jackeroo* a trainee farm manager, *kangaroo* a large hopping marsupial, *kookaburra* a kind of bird, *wombat* a burrowing marsupial. (2) Extensions of pre-existing senses: *bush* natural vegetation, or rural as opposed to urban life, *station* a garrison, colonial outpost, tract of grazing land, ranch. (3) Novel compounds: *bushman* someone skilled in traversing the bush, *bushranger* an armed bandit; *convict overseer* a convict appointed to supervise other convicts, *convict police* convicts appointed as police; *cattle/sheep station* station for raising cattle or sheep, *station black* an Aboriginal employed on a station; *stock agent* someone buying and selling livestock, *stockman* someone employed to tend livestock. (4) Novel fixed phrases: *black bream, black swan; colonial ale, colonial tobacco; native plum, native potato; red ash, red cedar; white box, white cockatoo; wild banana, wild spinach*. (5) Coinage: *emancipist* a freed convict, *go slow* a form of industrial protest in which employees work to rule (now international), *woop-woops* remote country. (6) Words with greater currency in Australia than elsewhere include new applications of words from British regional dialects: *dinkum* reliable, genuine, *dunny* a privy, *larrikin* a hooligan, *wowser* a killjoy.

Style and usage. By and large, printed English is much the same as elsewhere. The authoritative style guide is the Australian Government Printing Service's *Style Manual for Authors, Editors and Printers*, first published in 1966 and in its 4th edition. The manual was intended to set standards for government publications, but is widely used and has received input from the community at large through the Macquarie *Style Councils*. An informal guide is Stephen Murray-Smith's *Right Words: A Guide to Usage in Australia* (Viking, 1987, revised edition 1989). Where BrE and AmE spelling norms differ, BrE is preferred: *honour*, but *Labor* the name of the political party, *centre, licence*. The *-ise* spelling, as in *realise*, is generally preferred to *-ize*.

Strine and stereotyping. Australian usage has attracted comic stereotyping. The term *strine* refers to a kind of stage Australian in which vowels are distorted and syllables reduced (as in *strine* itself, collapsing the four syllables of *Australian* to one, and in *Emma Chisit*, a joke name derived from *How much is it?* The usage of the comedian Barry Humphries (b.1934), created by exaggerating certain features of pronunciation, delivery, or vocabulary, reflects a longstanding deference to BrE models combined with a new-found and exuberant recognition of national identity. Humphries' use of English has contributed both to colloquial idiom and a widespread perception of AusE as casual and vulgar. His characters include Dame Edna Everage (Average), a suburban Melbourne housewife turned megastar, Sir Les Patterson, an Australian 'cultural ambassador', and Barry McKenzie, an *ocker* (uncultured Australian male) in a comic strip in the British satirical magazine *Private Eye*.

Social issues. Until recently, Australia was determinedly assimilationist. Although immigrant languages such as Greek and Italian are now accorded the status of *community languages*, and bilingualism is actively encouraged by the government, the impact of these languages on AusE has been negligible. Two issues currently dominate the linguistic scene:

Multiculturalism. The arrival of immigrants (locally known as *migrants*) is slowly converting a homogeneous Anglo-Celtic society into a multilingual, multicultural society that is more or less tolerant of difference. A recent development has been the publication of a *National Policy on Languages* (J. Lo Bianco, 1987), a report commissioned by the Commonwealth Department of Education in 1986, a key document for federal and state initiatives to improve the teaching of English as a first and a second language, promote bilingualism, especially in those whose only language is English, and preserve and foster the teaching of community languages, including Aboriginal languages. Important also has been the increased prominence of Aboriginal English within the spectrum accessible to the average Australian.

American, British, and New Zealand influence. Despite a new-found sense of independence (including the export of Australian films and television series), AusE is subject to the media-borne influences of BrE and AmE. By and large, because of traditional ties, there is less resistance to BrE than to AmE, particularly in pronunciation and spelling. Although it is 1,200 miles away, New Zealand is considered to be a close geographical, cultural, and linguistic neighbour. The constant movement of labour between the two countries ensures continuing exchange and sharing of features with NZE.

See ABORIGINAL ENGLISH, AUSTRALASIAN ENGLISH, AUSTRALIAN, AUSTRALIAN DICTIONARIES, AUSTRALIANESE, AUSTRALIANISM, AUSTRALIAN LANGUAGE, AUSTRALIAN LANGUAGE (THE), AUSTRALIAN LANGUAGES, AUSTRALIAN LITERATURE, AUSTRALIAN PIDGIN, CULTURAL CRINGE, DIALECT IN AUSTRALIA, GREAT AUSTRALIAN ADJECTIVE, GREAT AUSTRALIAN SLANGUAGE, L-SOUNDS, NEW ZEALAND ENGLISH, STRINE. [OCEANIA, HISTORY, VARIETY].   W.S.R.

Baker, S. J. 1945. Revised edition 1966. *The Australian Language*. Sydney: Currawong Press.
Baldauf, Richard, & Luke, Allan (eds.). 1990. *Language Planning and Education in Australasia and the South Pacific*. Clevedon & Philadelphia: Multilingual Matters.
Collins, P., & Blair, D. (eds.). 1989. *Australian English: The Language of a New Society*. Brisbane: University of Queensland Press.
Görlach, Manfred. 1991. 'Australian English: Standards, Stigmata, Stereotypes and Statistics', in Görlach, *Englishes: Studies in Varieties of English 1984–1988*. Amsterdam & Philadelphia: John Benjamins.
Hughes, J. M. 1989. *Australian Words and their Origins*. Melbourne: Oxford University Press Australia.
Mitchell, A. G., & Delbridge, A. 1965. *The Pronunciation of English in Australia*. Sydney: Angus & Robertson.
Murray-Smith, S. 1989. *Right Words: A Guide to English Usage in Australia*, revised edition. Ringwood, Victoria: Viking.
Purchase, S. (ed.). 1990. *Australian Writers' and Editors' Guide*. Melbourne: Oxford University Press Australia.
Ramson, W. S. 1966. *Australian English: An Historical Study of the Vocabulary 1788–1898*. Canberra: Australian National University Press.
——, (ed.). 1970. *English Transported: Essays on Australasian English*. Canberra: Australian National University Press.
Style Manual for Authors, Editors and Printers 1988. 4th edition. Canberra: Australian Government Publishing Service.
Turner, G. W. 1966. *The English Language in Australia and New Zealand*. London: Longman.

AUSTRALIANESE [1910s]. An informal term for Australian English: 'The Australianese that the "Gyppos" picked up is not commonly used in polite society' (1918). Compare AMERICANESE, AUSTRALIAN, AUSTRALIAN LANGUAGE. See -ESE. [OCEANIA, VARIETY].   T.MCA.

AUSTRALIANISM [1890s: from *Australian* and *-ism* as in *Scotticism*]. A word, phrase, pronunciation, idiom, or other usage peculiar to, or particularly common in, Australia. Australianisms include loans from Aboriginal languages, such as *kangaroo*, *wombat* names of kinds of marsupial, and 'national treasures' such as *cobber* a companion, friend, *ocker* a rough and uncultivated Australian male. See AUSTRALIAN DICTIONARIES, AUSTRALIAN ENGLISH, -ISM. [OCEANIA, STYLE, VARIETY, WORD].   W.S.R.

AUSTRALIAN LANGUAGE [Later 19c]. (1) An Australian aboriginal language: 'In no Australian language is there any word for "five" ' (J. Fraser, *The Aborigines of Australia*, 1888). (2) Australian English 'The Australian language developed during the 19th century, first mainly in the penal settlements' (Richard D. Lewis, 'Let's Talk Strine', in *The Linguist*, Vol. 30 No. 2, 1991). See AUSTRALIAN LANGUAGE (THE). (3) Especially formerly, bad language used by Australians: 'I tried to back the bullocks, but they scorned me utterly, in spite of the Australian language I used' (M. Roberts, *Land Travel and Sea-Faring*, 1891); 'All barracking to be screamed, yelled, or bellowed in French. Australian language barred' (*Honk*, France, 1915). Compare AUSTRALIAN, GREAT AUSTRALIAN SLANGUAGE. See AUSTRALIAN LANGUAGES. [LANGUAGE, OCEANIA, STYLE, VARIETY].   T.MCA.

AUSTRALIAN LANGUAGE, The. The title of a book on Australian English by Sidney James Baker (1912-76), a New-Zealand-born journalist working in Sydney (1945, Angus & Robertson; 1966, revised, Currawong). Baker attempted to do what H. L. Mencken had done for AmE: establish the independence of the variety and find in it the fullness of an Australian cultural identity. Always tendentious, often idiosyncratic, frequently exasperating because assertive and undocumented, the work has none the less been popular and influential. Baker was interested primarily in the colloquial and in slang. Drawing on written and oral sources, he compiled lists of words from all walks of life, many subsequently shown not to be exclusively Australian. However, his division of local vocabulary into such subject areas as the bush, the road, and the city was influential in shaping the perception of AusE. Compare AMERICAN LANGUAGE (THE). [MEDIA, OCEANIA, VARIETY].   W.S.R.

AUSTRALIAN LANGUAGE RESEARCH CENTRE. A centre established in the English department of the U. of Sydney in 1962, to foster research into AusE. It has a citation archive and publishes a series of occasional papers, most of which present evidence for specific subject areas of vocabulary. [MEDIA, OCEANIA].   W.S.R.

AUSTRALIAN LANGUAGES. Some 200 Aboriginal languages were spoken in Australia when British settlers arrived in the later 18c. About 50 are now extinct, 100 are dying, and some 50 are in active first-language use, especially along the north coast of western and central Australia, on Cape York, and in the western and central interior: that is, in places remote from major population centres. There are several thousand speakers of dialects of the *Western Desert language* (the best-known of which is Pitjantjatjara) and of Aranda, around Alice Springs. There are many more speakers of Kriol and Torres Strait Creole. English is the first and only language of some 83 per cent of Australia's 16m people. Minority languages during the 19c included Chinese in goldfield communities, German in a Lutheran settlement in South Australia, and Gaelic and Welsh in rural families. Non-British immigration increased greatly after the Second World War and multilingualism has been encouraged since the 1970s. Immigrant

languages spoken by more than 100,000 people are (in decreasing order) Italian, Greek, Chinese, Arabic, and German. See ABORIGINES, AUSTRALIAN ENGLISH, AUSTRALIAN PLACE-NAMES, BORROWING. [LANGUAGE, OCEANIA].   W.S.R.

AUSTRALIAN LITERATURE. The literature of Australia can be read in several ways: (1) As a discourse about political, economic, and spiritual colonialism and post-colonialism, with emphasis on such themes as convictism, exile, the hope of return, the imperial cultural centre and the colonial periphery, the imposition of a colonizing language on a resistant land, or the conflict between urban culture and the terror of 'the bush'. In these terms, features such as brutality and the desire for metamorphosis constantly occur. (2) As a struggle to assert a unique nationality while assimilating international literary concerns and modes. (3) As a site for conflict between a fiction of male supremacy (the heroic male struggle against the bush, survival against the odds, woman as a necessary impediment partaking of the intractability of the land) and one of female assertiveness and re-assertiveness (emphasizing the essential female contribution to the development of the sheep industry and of small land-holdings, the history of neglect of and brutality to women, and female understanding of the land and its demands, as well as of its inhabitants).

Specifically Australian usage occurs in writing almost from the beginnings of white settlement in 1788. James Hardy Vaux, a transported convict, included a dictionary of convict canting terms, mostly from London, in *Memoirs of James Hardy Vaux* (1819). Alexander Harris's *Settlers and Convicts: Or, Recollections of Sixteen Years' Labour in the Australian Backwoods* (1847), and *The Emigrant Family: Or, The Story of an Australian Settler* (1849) were handbooks for intending migrants, providing details of colonial society, including the flash neighbourhood of the Rocks district in Sydney, convicts and ticket-of-leave men, squatters and selectors, the eating of steak and damper, boiling the billy, bullock driving, the stealing of cattle, bushrangers, and the Aborigines. C. J. Dennis's narrative poem, *The Songs of a Sentimental Bloke* (1915), once a popular recitation piece, represents the language of a Melbourne larrikin push (a street gang), though with substantial intrusions of stage Cockney. A similar combination of empirical authenticity and stage convention in language can be found in *They're a Weird Mob* (1957) by 'Nino Culotta' (John O'Grady), supposedly written by an Italian migrant working as a builder's labourer in Sydney. A more authentic impression of non-

English-speaking migrants is available in Rosa Cappiello's *Oh Lucky Country* (1984), published originally in Italian in 1981.

The works of Barry Humphries, who performs his own one-man scripts, contain much contemporary and slightly obsolescent Australian slang, such as *A Nice Night's Entertainment: Sketches and Monologues 1956-1981* (1981). Humphries, as a satirist, improves on and extends the expressions he has collected. A less farcical example of slang transmogrified into theatre occurs in Jack Hibberd's *A Stretch of the Imagination* (1973), which in published form contains a useful glossary. Several varieties of Aboriginal English (varied according to period, education, location, and purpose of speech) can be found in works by Aboriginal writers, such as Jack Davis's plays, especially *Kullark* (1979) and *The Dreamers* (1982), Colin Johnson's novels, especially *Doctor Wooreddy's Prescription for Enduring the Ending of the World* (1983) and *Doin Wildcat* (1988), and Archie Weller's novel, *The Day of the Dog* (1981). [LITERATURE, OCEANIA, VARIETY].   K.L.G.

Goodwin, Ken. 1986. *A History of Australian Literature*. London: Macmillan.

Green, H. M. 1961. Revised by Dorothy Green, 1985. *A History of Australian Literature*. Sydney: Angus & Robertson.

Hergenhan, Laurie (ed.). 1988. *The Penguin New Literary History of Australia*. Ringwood: Penguin.

Kramer, Leonie (ed.). 1981. *The Oxford History of Australian Literature*. Melbourne: Oxford University Press Australia.

MacLaren, John. 1989. *Australian Literature: An Historical Introduction*. Melbourne: Longman Cheshire.

Wilde, William H., Hooton, Joy, & Andrews, Barry. 1981. *The Oxford Companion to Australian Literature*. Melbourne: Oxford University Press Australia.

AUSTRALIAN NATIONAL DICTIONARY. See AUSTRALIAN DICTIONARIES and AUSTRALIAN NATIONAL DICTIONARY CENTRE.

AUSTRALIAN NATIONAL DICTIONARY CENTRE. A centre at the Australian National U., Canberra, for research into AusE. Its major resource is the continuously evolving archive of the *Australian National Dictionary*. The centre is jointly funded by the University and Oxford University Press Australia, undertakes research, and has editorial responsibility for the Australian range of Oxford dictionaries. See AUSTRALIAN DICTIONARIES, OXFORD UNIVERSITY PRESS. [MEDIA, OCEANIA].   W.S.R.

AUSTRALIAN PIDGIN. A general name for contact varieties of English, used especially between Aborigines and European settlers from the late 18c, which spread from Sydney to other settlements. One of the most important, pidgin English in Queensland (also known as *Queensland Canefields English* and *Queensland Kanaka English*) was used on the sugar plantations *c*.1860-1910. It appears to be descended from *New South Wales pidgin*, an early contact language taken north by explorers, convicts, and settlers, and spoken mainly by Melanesian indentured labourers rather than by Aborigines. Most returned to their home islands by 1910 and the pidgin currently exists only in fragmentary form among the elderly. However, it had a great influence on the subsequent development of *Melanesian Pidgin English* (see Tom Dutton & Peter Mühlhäusler, 'Queensland Kanaka English', *English World-Wide* 4: 2, 1984). Other varieties include *Kriol*, in the Northern Territory and parts of Western Australia, and *Torres Strait Broken*, in the Torres Strait Islands. See ABORIGINAL ENGLISH, BROKEN, KRIOL, MELANESIAN PIDGIN ENGLISH, PACIFIC JARGON ENGLISH. [OCEANIA, VARIETY].   S.R., T.MCA.

AUSTRALIAN PLACE-NAMES. There are some 4m place-names in Australia. They reflect the peopling of the country and are in the main Aboriginal or English in origin. There are three main types: borrowings, transferred uses of existing British names, and descriptive compounds.

Aboriginal. The greater number of place-names are Aboriginal in origin: recorded by explorers, especially from the 1820s onward, but the majority borrowed by settlers. Most underwent change because the sounds were heard imprecisely and were Anglicized in transcription. Words which were not place-names have also been given as such (*Bunyip* a mythical animal, *Wallaroo* a kind of marsupial), and names of animals like *dingo* (a dog domesticated by the Aborigines) and *warrigal* (a wild dog) are used in numerous compounds. Aboriginal place-names are mostly polysyllabic: *Indooroopilly, Murrumbidgee, Wollongong, Wooloongabba*. Many end in vowels (*Boggabri, Gunnedah, Merimbula, Tantanoola*), and a number are reduplicative (*Goonoo Goonoo, Tilba Tilba, Wagga Wagga, Woy Woy*). Their meanings are often uncertain: *Canberra*, the name of the capital, is anecdotally said to mean Woman's Breasts (after a pair of hills) or Meeting Place.

Dutch and French. A few names survive as a record of Dutch and French exploration, given by the explorers themselves or later in their honour. The original name of the continent, *New Holland*, remained in use in the early 19c and survives in its Latin form *Nova Hollandia* in scientific nomenclature and such popular names as *New Holland honeyeater*. Other names given by the Dutch include *Van Diemen's Land* (later named *Tasmania* after Abel Tasman), *Groote Eylandt* (in the Gulf of Carpentaria), and *Rottnest Island* (off the west coast). Names commemorating the Dutch visits include *Arnhem Land* (after one of Carstensz's vessels) and *Dirk Hartog Island* (after the seaman). Names given by French explorers include *Huon River* (after Huon de Kermadec), *D'Entrecasteaux Channel* (after the explorer), and *Freycinet Peninsula* (after the explorer), all in Tasmania. Other names like *La Perouse* (a Sydney suburb) commemorate explorers.

English. Existing British names for people and places were freely applied in the new context. Names were given: (1) In honour of people prominent in Britain: *Adelaide* after William IV's queen, *Melbourne* after the Prime Minister at the time of its foundation, *Hobart* after the Secretary of State for War and the Colonies, *Wellington* after the Duke of Wellington, *Moreton Bay* after the Earl of Morton, President of the Royal Society. (2) To commemorate people prominent in Australia: *Brisbane* after the governor, *Campbelltown* after the family name of the wife of Governor Macquarie, *Lake Eyre* after the explorer, *Ayers Rock* after a premier of South Australia, *Lake Pedder* after a Chief Justice of Tasmania, *Reynella* after John Reynell, who had established a vineyard nearby. (3) Because of some association, real or fancied, with a place in England (*Morpeth, Newcastle, Windsor*), Scotland (*Armidale* [sic], *Eildon Weir, Perth*), or, less frequently, Ireland and Wales. (4) With reference to people and places elsewhere: Australia's highest mountain, *Mount Kosciusko*, named by the explorer Strzelecki after the Polish patriot. The significance of many names is uncertain. (5) Descriptive names proliferated as the country was settled. They are either figurative (*Glass House Mountains, Mount Dromedary, Pigeon House Mountain*: all given by the explorer James Cook in 1770), indicate a dominant characteristic (*Bald Hill, Four Mile Bore, Kangaroo Flat, One Tree Hill, Sandy Creek*), or record an event (*Dinner Creek, Mistake Creek, Mount Misery*). Many such names were given locally, leading to duplication: *Sandy Creek* occurs some 400 times.

Toponymy. Little attention has been given to Australian toponymy. The states operate independently, but a National Mapping Council (established 1945) effects coordination for cartographical purposes. A pilot survey under the auspices of the Australian Academy of the Humanities (1971-4) established guidelines for a long-term research project, but no programme has been implemented. [NAME, OCEANIA]. W.S.R.

AUSTRALIAN PRESS. The older-established daily newspapers of Australia are associated with the capital cities of the states (formerly colonies) of the Commonwealth of Australia. These are *The Sydney Morning Herald* (1831), *The Age* (Melbourne, 1854), *The Advertiser* (Adelaide, 1858), *The West Australian* (1879), *The Courier-Mail* (Brisbane, 1846), and *The Mercury* (Hobart, 1854). All of the above are broadsheets except for the tabloid *West Australian*. A national daily, *The Australian*, began publication in 1964. A national weekly is *The Bulletin*. There are numerous, small-circulation country newspapers. Saturday editions tend to carry feature articles and book reviews and there is no tradition of 'quality Sundays'. Newspapers are politically vocal but have varied their alignment. Ownership tends to rest in the hands of major media groups. There is some movement towards AmE spelling norms (*honor*, but not *center*), notably in *The Advertiser* and *The Age*. See BULLETIN (THE), NEWSPAPER, PRESS. [MEDIA, OCEANIA]. W.S.R.

AUSTRALIAN PUBLISHING. The first book published in Australia, *New South Wales General Standing Orders*, appeared in 1802 at the hands of George Howe, a convict appointed Government Printer, but it was not until the end of the 19c, with the partnership of two Scots, G. M. Angus and George Robertson, that publishing became established. Angus and Robertson played a key role in the collecting, sale, and from 1888 publishing of Australiana, Robertson being instrumental in the development of public and private collections and a publishing programme that responded to and cultivated a growing interest in Australian writing. The firm is now a division of Nationwide News Pty Ltd. A. C. Rowlandson, through the NSW Bookstall Co., and the Lothian Publishing Co. (1905-) were part of the same boom. A second expansion came after the Second World War. Several university presses joined Melbourne University Press (1922 and still pre-eminent) and the University of Queensland Press with an Australian literature programme. British publishers established in Australia include William Collins Australia, Penguin Australia, and Oxford University Press Australia. The market is vigorous and volatile, and includes many small semi-specialist firms. See PUBLISHING. [MEDIA, OCEANIA]. W.S.R.

AUSTRALIAN SLANGUAGE. See GREAT AUSTRALIAN SLANGUAGE.

AUSTRONESIAN LANGUAGES. See LANGUAGE, MALAYO-POLYNESIAN LANGUAGES.

AUTHOR [13c: from Latin *auctor/auctoris* one who increases, creates, fathers, founds, or writes, from *augere/auctum* to increase; cognate with *augment, authority*]. (1) A person who writes a work of some significance, especially if published, such as a book of any kind, and more particularly a narrative work such as a novel, whether literary or popular. The term is often used to contrast with a range of associated terms, such as *compiler* (of works of reference), *copyist* (of manuscripts, etc.), *editor* (of a periodical or work of reference, etc.), and *writer* (in the professional and general senses of the word). It also often contrasts with such specific terms as *journalist, critic, essayist, poet, publisher, printer*, etc. Under certain conditions, however, all such persons can be an author, in the sense of 'one who has created a document'. One author who cooperates with another is a *co-author* or *coauthor*. In AmE, the verbal use (*to author a book*) is increasingly common. (2) The creator of something: *the author of a plan*. Compare POET, WRITER. See BRITISH PUBLISHING. [LITERATURE, WRITING]. T.MCA.

AUTHORITY [13c: from Latin *auctoritas/ auctoritatis* the capacity to produce, invent, counsel, decree, judge, etc.: compare AUTHOR]. (1) The power to establish rules and precedents and/or determine, judge, or settle issues or disputes: *Johnson and Webster have been widely regarded as having authority in matters of language.* (2) A person with such power or to whom such power is entrusted; someone known to be extremely well versed in a subject; an expert: *Jespersen was an authority on English grammar.* (3) Persuasive or convincing ability or knowledge: *She spoke with the authority of 40 years' experience.* (4) The justification for making a statement or doing a thing: *On what authority do you decide whether 'colour' or 'color' is the right spelling?* (5) An accepted source of information, advice, reassurance, etc., whether a person, a book, or an institution: *For many, the Oxford English Dictionary is the ultimate authority on words and their use; The Académie française is the major authority for formal French usage.* See: James & Leslie Milroy, *Authority in Language: Investigating Language Prescription and Standardisation* (London: Routledge, 1985). See ACADEMY, BOOK, DESCRIPTIVISM AND PRESCRIPTIVISM, HOUSE STYLE, STANDARD, USAGE GUIDANCE AND CRITICISM. [STYLE, USAGE]. T.MCA.

AUTHORIZED VERSION. See BIBLE.

AUTHORS' AND PRINTERS' DICTIONARY. See HOUSE STYLE.

AUTOBIOGRAPHY [19c: from *auto-* self, and *biography*]. A biography written by its subject, often to explain and justify as well as to inform: John Henry Newman's *Apologia pro Vita Sua* (Defence of his life: 1864) is a 'confessional' autobiography in the tradition begun by St Augustine's *Confessions* (4–5c AD) and responds to an attack. Some autobiographies come near to being works of fiction and many works of fiction have autobiographical aspects. Novels and other works are often written in the first person to suggest that they are autobiographical, as with Daniel Defoe's *Robinson Crusoe* (1719) and Jonathan Swift's *Gulliver's Travels* (1726). See BIOGRAPHY, NOVEL. [LITERATURE]. R.C.

AUXILIARY VERB [18c: from Latin *auxiliarius* helping, and *verb*]. Also **helping verb**. A category of verbs that regularly accompany full verbs such as *write, run, shoot*: *is* in *is writing*, *has* in *has run*, *may be* in *may be shooting*. In English, auxiliary verbs are customarily divided into: (1) The primary auxiliaries *be, have, do*. (2) The modal auxiliaries or modal verbs *can, could, may, might, shall, should, will, would, must*. The marginal modal auxiliaries, also called *semi-modals*, are *dare, need, ought to, used to*. They are marginal because they do not share all the properties of the others or do not do so regularly. Auxiliaries have four properties: (1) They are used with the negative *not* to make a sentence negative: *Frank may buy me a sweater/may not buy me a sweater.* Most have reduced negative forms: *isn't, hasn't, doesn't, can't, won't*, but not usually **mayn't*. (2) They form questions by changing positions with the subject: *Wendy has invited me/Has Wendy invited me?* (3) To avoid repetition, they can occur without a full verb: *Has Jonathan written to you yet?—Yes, he has.* (4) They can emphasize the positive, in which case they carry the accent: *David may not be there.—His mother told me he WILL be there.* The same properties apply to *be* as a full verb (*Jonathan isn't tired*) and particularly in BrE as an alternative to *have* as a full verb (*I haven't a headache*). In the absence of any other auxiliary, *do* is introduced for these functions: *Leslie didn't tell Doreen; Did Leslie tell Doreen?; Yes, he did; He DID tell her.*

The auxiliary *be* is used to form, with a following -*ing* participle, the progressive (*is employing, may have been proving*) and with a following -*ed* participle the passive (*is employed, may have been proved*). The auxiliary *have* is used with a following -*ed* participle to form the perfect (*has employed, may have proved*). The modal auxiliaries convey notions such as possibility, obligation, and permission. They are the only verbs not to have a distinctive third-person form in the present: *He can/They can* contrasts with *He is/They are, He has/They have, He sees/They see*. Like auxiliary *do*, they are always the first verb in the verb phrase (*should have apologized, could be making, did tell*) and are followed by the bare infinitive. In standard English, two modal auxiliaries cannot co-occur, but they can in some non-standard varieties, such as Appalachian English *They might could come*. See MODALITY, MODAL VERB, VERB. [GRAMMAR].   S.G.

AVIATION ENGLISH. See AIRSPEAK.

AVIS, Walter S. [1919-79]. Canadian lexicographer and dialectologist, born in Toronto, educated at Queen's U., Kingston, Ontario, and the U. of Michigan (Ph.D. 1965). From 1952 until his death, he taught at the Royal Military College of Canada, Kingston. He was a founding member of the Canadian Linguistic Association (1954) and its president (1968-70). Avis was editor-in-chief of the Gage Dictionary of Canadian English series, including *A Dictionary of Canadianisms on Historical Principles* (1967), *Dictionary of Canadian English: The Senior Dictionary* (1967, 1973) and its revision as *Canadian Senior Dictionary* (1979). Its further revision as *Gage Canadian Dictionary* (1983) was posthumously dedicated to him. See index. [AMERICAS, BIOGRAPHY, REFERENCE].   M.F.

AXIOM [15c: from Latin *axioma*, Greek *axiōma* something worthy or appropriate]. (1) A generally accepted principle or rule, especially when framed as a brief statement; a self-evident truth considered to require no proof: *What goes up must come down*. Compare TRUISM. (2) In logic, mathematics, and sometimes linguistics, a proposition assumed without the provision of proof, for the sake of studying the consequences that follow from it. In the linguistic theory of Noam Chomsky, it is axiomatic that a language consists of an indefinite number of grammatically well-formed sentences. Compare PREMISS/PREMISE. See LOGIC, SAYING. [LANGUAGE].

B

B, b [Called 'bee']. The 2nd letter of the modern Roman alphabet as used for English. It descends from the Phoenician symbol *bēth* ('house'), which was adopted by the Greeks as *beta*, B, then by the Romans as *B*.

Sound values. In English, *b* normally represents the voiced bilabial stop, with *p* as its voiceless equivalent: *bad/pad*. Word-final *b* is rare, occurring mainly in monosyllables (*hub, rib, scab*), but occasionally in longer words (*superb, disturb, cherub*).

Double B. (1) The doubling of *b* occurs when monosyllables with a short vowel are followed by *-er*, *-ed*, and *-ing*: *rob/robber/robbed/robbing* (contrast the phonetically long vowel in *daub/dauber/daubed/daubing*). (2) Many disyllables contain double *b* after a stressed short vowel (*abbey, rabbit, ribbon, rubber, rubble*), but many others do not (*cabin, debit, double, habit, robin*).

Silent B. *B* is silent after syllable-final *m* (*dumb, numb, tomb*), including in some words of Germanic origin in which it was formerly pronounced (*climb, comb, dumb, lamb, womb*) and in French-derived words with final *mb* (*aplomb, bomb, jamb, plumb, succumb, tomb*). In a number of words, a silent *b* has been added by analogy: *crumb, limb, numb, thumb*. In some of these, it was created by back-formation from words of the type *crumble, thimble* (formerly without *b*). *Crum* began to be written with *b* in the 16c, but occurs without it in Johnson's dictionary (1755) and in some 19c dictionaries. Derivatives from *mb*-words mostly keep the silent *b*, as in *climber, lambing, thumbing*, but *b* is pronounced in such non-derivative polysyllables as *cucumber, encumber, Humber, slumber*. There is no *b* in *dummy*, derived from *dumb*, or *crummy*, derived from *crumb*, and although *b* is not pronounced finally in *bomb*, medial *b* is pronounced in *bombard*.

Epenthetic B. *B* is epenthetic in *debt, doubt*, and *subtle*, which entered English from French as *dette, doute*, and *soutil*. As in French, these words were given a *b* in deference to their Latin etymons *debitum, dubitum,* and *subtilis*. However, while French shed *b* in *dette* and *doute* in the 18c and came to pronounce the *b* in *subtil*, English has kept a silent *b* in all three. Epenthesis also occurs after medial *m* in some words: for example, Latin *camera* and *numerus* became French *chambre* and *nombre*, English *chamber* and *number*. Compare German *fummeln* and *rummeln* with English *fumble* and *rumble*. See ALPHABET, EPENTHESIS, LETTER[1], SPELLING. [WRITING].   C.U., T.MCA.

BAAL, full form *British Association for Applied Linguistics*. An association founded in 1967 to foster and promote the study of language use, learning, and teaching, and interdisciplinary cooperation in these areas. Affiliated to the *Association Internationale de Linguistique Appliquée* (*AILA*), it has provided a forum for discussion and research in the teaching of English internationally. It publishes a newsletter, sponsors the journal *Applied Linguistics*, and with the Linguistics Association of Great Britain supports the *Committee for Linguistics in Education* (*CLIE*), founded in 1978 to 'foster an active interest in linguistics in schools, both as a subject in its own right, and as a resource for teachers in other subject areas'. See APPLIED LINGUISTICS. [EDUCATION, EUROPE, LANGUAGE, MEDIA].   C.J.B.

BABBLE [13c: from *bab*, probably echoing an infant's *ba-ba-ba*, and the iterative suffix *-le* again and again]. (1) To speak meaninglessly, foolishly, or so quickly that no one can follow. (2) The act, process, or result of speaking like this: *a babble of voices*; *Eurobabble*, a pejorative

THE CAPITAL LETTER						THE SMALL LETTER				
EARLY FORMS				CURRENT FORMS		EARLY FORMS			CURRENT FORMS	
Phoenician	Greek	Etruscan	Roman (Latin)	roman	italic	Roman cursive	Roman uncial	Carolingian minuscule	roman	italic
𐤁	𐌁Β	𐌁	B	B	*B*	⅃	B	ƅ	b	*b*

term for the many languages and distinctive jargon used in the European Community. See BARBARISM, EURO-, PSYCHOBABBLE, TECHNOBABBLE. Compare -ESE, -SPEAK. [SPEECH, STYLE].   T.MCA.

BABBLING. A stage in the development of speech that usually appears when an infant is between six and twelve months old. It is less varied than the preceding stage of *vocal play*, which displays great range and variability. A smaller range of sounds is used with greater frequency and stability, to produce sequences known as *reduplicated babbling*. About half-way through the stage, there emerges *variegated babbling*, in which vowels and consonants may change between syllables, as in [aguː]. Syllable length and utterance rhythm are much closer to adult speech and some utterances resemble words. When speech begins, babbling may continue, often until around 18 months. There has been debate over the function of this stage. The sounds are not random, but a small set similar to those used in the early words that the child eventually speaks. The increasing approximation of babbling to the sounds of the target language is known as *babbling drift*. See BABBLE, CHILD LANGUAGE ACQUISITION. [LANGUAGE, SPEECH].   D.C.

BABEL [14c: from Hebrew *bābel* Babylon, Assyrian *bāb-ilu* gate of God or *bāb-ili* gate of the gods. Pronounced 'bayble']. (1) Also *Tower of Babel*. The Biblical tower whose builders intended it to reach heaven. According to the Book of Genesis, all people once spoke the same language, but to prevent the completion of the tower God confounded their tongues. (2) A scene of confusion; a confused gathering; a turbulent medley of sounds, especially arising from the use of many languages. *Babelize* and *Babelization* are sometimes used disparagingly of the growth of multiethnic, multicultural, and multilingual societies. [SPEECH, STYLE].   T.MCA.

BABU ENGLISH, also **Baboo** [Late 19c: from *bābū*, a mode of address and reference in several Indo-Aryan languages, including Hindi, for officials working for rajahs, landlords, etc. It became a generic term during the British Raj for Hindu and especially Bengali officials and clerks working in English, and was often disparaging]. A variety of South Asian English used by middle-level bureaucrats and associated with a flowery, extremely deferential, and indirect style of writing and speaking. It has attracted the attention of scholars for over a century (see *Hobson-Jobson*, 1886, p. 44) and provided entertainment in such works as *Babu Jabberjee, BA,* by Thomas Anstey Guthrie (Dent, 1898), *Honoured Sir—from Babujee* by Cecil Hunt (Allan,

1931), and *Babuji Writes Home: Being a New Edition of 'Honoured Sir' with Many Additional Letters* (Allan, 1935). The following excerpt is representative:

Sir, Being in much need and suffering many privations I have after long time come to the determination to trouble your bounteous goodness. To my sorrow I have not the good friendships with many people hence my slow rate of progression and destitute state. Here on earth who have I but thee, and there is Our Father in heaven, needless to say that unless your milk of human kindness is showered on my sad state no other hope is left in this world (from *Baboo English; or Our Mother-tongue as our Aryan brethren understand it; Amusing specimens of Composition and Style, or English as written by Her Majesty's Indian subjects,* collected and edited by T.W.J.: Calcutta: H. P. Kent & Co., no date: late 19c).

Kipling, in his novel *Kim* (1901), has a Bengali character named Hurree Babu, who on one occasion observes: 'I am of opeenion it is not your old gentleman's precise releegion, but rather sub-variant of same. I have contributed rejected notes to *Asiatic Quarterly Review* on these subjects.' The classic parody of Babu English is to be found in G.V. Desani's *All About H. Hatterr* (1948). See HOBSON-JOBSON, INDIAN ENGLISH[1], INDO-ENGLISH. [ASIA, VARIETY].   B.B.K., T.MCA.

BABY TALK [1830s]. Kinds of speech used by small children. When used by adults, it is sometimes known technically as *motherese, caretaker language, caregiver language*. In the utterances of young children there is little grammar, vocabulary is idiosyncratic, and pronunciation immature, such as *Dada gone car* (Daddy has gone in the car). Adults speaking to small children adopt simplified grammar, special vocabulary, and exaggerated intonations: *All gone, doggie* The dog has gone. The appropriateness of 'adult baby talk' is sometimes questioned on the grounds that to provide a child with such a distortion of normal speech hinders the process of language learning. However, many researchers consider that the simplified grammar and marked stress patterns have an important role in making the structure of speech more accessible to the child. Forms of baby talk are also used in jocular, intimate conversation (*Aw, diddums hurt his finger, then?*, wife to husband complaining about minor injury) and with pets (*Oh, pretty boy, kootchee, kootchee, kootchee,* addressed to a budgerigar). See CHILD LANGUAGE ACQUISITION, MOTHERESE. [LANGUAGE].   D.C.

BACK-FORMATION [1880s]. Also **back-derivation** [1960s]. The creation of one word from another by removing rather than adding an element: *laze* from *lazy*; *gruntled* from *disgruntled*. Such words are usually coined for effect or because people think they exist or ought to exist. Some offend for aesthetic or conservative reasons, such as *enthuse* from *enthusiasm* (1820s AmE), *intuit* from *intuition* (1770s BrE), *liaise* from *liaison* (1920s BrE). Some usages may be denounced as back-formations when they are in fact long-established words: for example, the verbs *aggress* and *resile* are attested from the 16c, but are often taken to be back-formed from *aggression* and *resilient*. To *back-form* is itself a back-formation. Back-formations may fill structural as well as semantic gaps: aircraft *formate* when flying in formation, commentators *commentate* when reporting on games. Stunt and nonce forms are common: 'Do your leching away from the office!' (Maurice West, *Backlash*, 1958), 'illicit rendezvous between well-knowns who should well-know better' (James Herbert, *Shrine*, 1984), 'Mr. Gorbachev charges Mr. Shcherbitsky with failure to perestroik' (William Safire, *New York Times*, Apr. 1989). See NOUN-INCORPORATION, WORD-FORMATION. [WORD].

T.MCA.

BACK MATTER [1940s]. A collective term for parts of a book or other publication that appear after the main text, such as appendices, notes and references, bibliography, and indexes. Compare FRONT MATTER. See APPENDIX, FORMAT. [MEDIA, TECHNOLOGY].

T.MCA.

BACK SLANG [mid-19c]. A form of slang used especially in Britain, in which words are spoken or spelt backwards: *yob* boy (originally to disguise the word, now used to mean a 'backward' boy or lout); *ecilop* police, often modified to *slop* (*The slops are after you*). Market vendors and shop assistants have used back slang so that customers will not understand them: for example, a butcher saying *Evig reh emos delo garcs dene* Give her some old scrag end. Here, an inserted *e*-sound breaks up the difficult consonant clusters in *dlo* for 'old' and *dne* for 'end'. See COCKNEY, PIG LATIN, PRIVATE LANGUAGE, REVERSAL. [STYLE].

T.MCA.

BACK-SLASH. See OBLIQUE.

BAD ENGLISH. An informal term for English that does not measure up to approved norms, because it is ungrammatical, poorly spelt, or uses expletives: 'What is called "bad English" in the usual sense may be highly effective in the appropriate context' (W. Nelson Francis, *The English Language*, 1967). See (A)ESTHETICS, BAD LANGUAGE, GOOD ENGLISH, STANDARD ENGLISH. [USAGE, VARIETY].

T.MCA.

BADIAN. See BAJAN.

BADINAGE [17c: from French *badiner* to joke, tease, bandy witty remarks]. Clever, teasing

humour that involves people in good-natured remark and counter-remark. 'We shall not all sleep,' grumbles the hospital patient wakened for the morning routine of washing and bed-making. 'But we shall all be changed,' says the staff nurse, who has brought clean sheets and knows her Bible: 'Behold, I shew you a mystery: we shall not all sleep, but we shall all be changed' (St Paul, 1 Corinthians 15: 51). See BANTER, HUMO(U)R, PATTER, REPARTEE. [STYLE].

W.N.

BAD LANGUAGE. An informal term for expressions that offend against taste. Although often a weaker synonym of *foul language*, it is more likely to include obscene expressions and those that are blasphemous or abusive. The term does not usually include language considered stylistically bad, situationally inappropriate, or difficult to understand. In Britain, complaints about the bad language allegedly permitted on radio and television continue to rank high among criticisms levelled at such institutions as the BBC. Lars Andersson and Peter Trudgill, in *Bad Language* (Oxford: Blackwell, 1990), discuss the nature and consequences of negative judgements of language in general and English in particular. See (A)ESTHETICS, BAD ENGLISH, SWEARING. [STYLE, USAGE].

R.F.I.

BAFFLEGAB [1950s: AmE, from *baffle* and *gab* mouth. See GIFT OF THE GAB]. An informal pejorative term for fluent language that sounds impressive but confuses and confounds, and is often associated with politicians. In 1988, Senator J. Danforth Quayle, then a candidate for US Vice-President, explained his position on the need for a strategic defence initiative by saying, 'Why wouldn't an enhanced deterrent, a more stable peace, a better prospect to denying the ones who enter conflict in the first place to have a reduction of offensive systems and an introduction to defensive capability?' See JARGON. [STYLE, USAGE].

W.D.L.

BAHAMAS, The. Official title *Commonwealth of the Bahamas*. A Caribbean country and member of the Commonwealth, consisting of 700 islands and 2,000 cays. The islands have a mixture of English, Amerindian, Spanish, and Greek names, as in *Grand Bahama, Great Abaco, Bimini, Andros, Eleuthera, Cat Island, San Salvador, Great Exuma, Long Island, Acklins Island, Mayaguana, Great Inagua*. Capital: Nassau, on New Providence Island. Currency: the dollar. Economy: tourism, finance, fishing, rum. Head of state: the British monarch, represented by a governor-general. Population: 150,000 (1988), 300,000 (projection for 2000). Ethnicity: 85% African and mixed, 15% Caucasian (American, British, Canadian, others). Languages: English,

Creole. Education: primary/secondary 74%, tertiary 5%, literacy 93%. Columbus visited the islands 1492. First European settlement 1647, by religious refugees from Bermuda. British colony 1717. Independence 1973. The term *Bahamian English* refers to a continuum of usage from creole to standard. It has been influenced by migration between the Bahamas and the US and by a tourist industry that caters mainly for Americans. Of all CarE varieties, Bahamian English most closely follows AmE. See CARIBBEAN, CARIBBEAN BROADCASTING, CARIBBEAN ENGLISH, CARIBBEAN ENGLISH CREOLE, CARIBBEAN PRESS, DICTIONARY OF BAHAMIAN ENGLISH, ENGLISH. [AMERICAS, NAME, VARIETY]. L.D.C., T.MCA.

BAHASA INDONESIA, BAHASA MALAYSIA. See MALAY.

BAHRAIN. See ARABIC, ENGLISH.

BAILEY, Beryl Loftman [1920-77]. American linguist, born in Jamaica and a native speaker of Jamaican Creole, educated at undergraduate and graduate level at Columbia U., New York. Her doctoral dissertation was published as *Jamaican Creole Syntax: A Transformational Approach* (1966), as an extension of her *Language Guide to Jamaica* (1962). A faculty member at Yeshiva U. and Hunter College (both in New York City), she pioneered the study of American Black English as a systematic language variety rather than a dialect typified by error or randomness. In 1965, she established an agenda for future research when she wrote: 'I would like to suggest that the Southern Negro "dialect" differs from other Southern speech because its deep structure is different, having its origins . . . in some Proto-Creole grammatical structures. Hence, regardless of the surface resemblances to other dialects . . . we must look into the system itself for an explanation of seeming confusion of persons and tenses' (*American Speech*, 1965, p. 172). She was influential as an author and consultant on the teaching of African-American schoolchildren. [AMERICAS, BIOGRAPHY, LANGUAGE]. R.W.B.

BAILEY, Nathan(iel). English lexicographer, compiler of the *Universal Etymological English Dictionary* (1721) and the *Dictionarium Britannicum* (1730). The *UEED* was one of the most successful 18c dictionaries of English, with 27 editions before 1800. Its 28,000 entries include technical, dialect, and obsolete words. The *DB* is notable for its encyclopedic information and use of illustration; it has more entries than the later dictionary of Samuel Johnson, who drew on the 2nd edition (1736) for his word list. See index. [MEDIA, REFERENCE]. N.E.O.

BAJAN [1900s: a contraction of *Barbadian*. Compare CAJAN, INJUN]. Also **Badian, Bajun**. An abbreviation of *Barbadian* and the informal name for Barbadian Creole. Because British colonization started in 1627, Bajan is one of the earliest English-based creoles. The function of Barbados as a slavers' entrepôt for the Caribbean and North America made Bajan a contributor to the characteristics of such other creoles as Gullah, Jamaican, and Sranan. It has been so eroded by the spread of English that some scholars consider it better classified as a dialect than a creole. However, the presence of features similar to those of such conservative creoles as Jamaican allows its continued classification as a creole. See BARBADOS, CARIBBEAN ENGLISH CREOLE. [AMERICAS, VARIETY]. L.D.C.

BALLAD [14c: through Old French *balade* (Modern *ballade*), from Provençal *balada* a dance, dancing song, from *balar*, to dance]. The name of several kinds of poem and song. Traditionally and primarily, a ballad is an oral narrative poem, often sung to a simple instrumental accompaniment and without an acknowledged author. Such works may have passed through several generations and been adapted by many presenters. They tell the stories of a community and often have a supernatural element. The great period of such ballads in English was the late Middle Ages, especially in Lowland Scotland and the Border counties of England. For this reason, such poems are often called *Border ballads*. Many were collected by Thomas Percy (*Reliques of Ancient English Poetry*, 1765) and Francis J. Child (*English and Scottish Popular Ballads*, 1882-98). The following are the last three stanzas of 'Sir Patrick Spens':

> O lang, lang may their ladies sit,
> Wi' their fans into their hand,
> Or ere they see Sir Patrick Spens
> Come sailing to the land.

> O lang, lang may the ladies stand
> Wi' their gold kems in their hair,
> Waiting for their ain dear lords,
> For they'll see them na mair.

> Half o'er, half o'er to Aberdour
> It's fifty fadom deep,
> And there lies guid Sir Patrick Spens
> Wi' the Scots lords at his feet.

[*lang* long, *or ere* before, *kems* combs, *ain* own, *na mair* no more, *fadom* fathom, *guid* good]

Printed poems known as *broadside ballads* became popular in the 16c and endured into the 20c. They were printed on one side of a broadside sheet and were usually concerned with recent sensational events. In Shakespeare's *A Winter's Tale* (4. 4), the roguish pedlar

Autolycus hawks such ballads to the Clown and Mopsa:

CLOWNE. What hast heere? Ballads?

MOPSA. Pray now buy some: I loue a ballet in print, a life, for then we are sure they are true.

AUTOLICUS. Here's one, to a very dolefull tune, how a Vsurers wife was brought to bed of twenty money baggs at a burthen, and how she long'd to eate Adders heads, and Toads carbonado'd.

During the 18c and 19c, the *literary ballad* told a simple story with a strong climax, as in Coleridge's 'The Ancient Mariner' (in *Lyrical Ballads*, 1798) and Keats's 'La Belle Dame sans Merci'. The usual *ballad stanza* has four iambic lines, alternately tetrameter and trimeter running *abcb*, but there is no set form. At about the same time, the *popular ballad* developed mainly in the US and Australia, where traditional stories were retold to fit new conditions, and where the deeds of cowboys, railwaymen, miners, outlaws, and others were versified. In popular culture, the term is also used for slow, romantic and usually sentimental songs that tell a story of love and loss. See BALLADE, BROADSIDE, BUSH BALLAD, POUND, SINGSONG. [MEDIA, LITERATURE].   R.C.

BALLADE [15c: from Old French *balade*. See BALLAD]. A poem, usually three stanzas with the same rhyme scheme, followed by an envoi, the same last line being shared by stanzas and envoi. [LITERATURE].   T.MCA.

BALLOON. See CARTOON.

BAMBOO ENGLISH. See EAST ASIAN ENGLISH, JAPANESE PIDGIN ENGLISH.

BANGLADESH. Official title: Bengali *Gana Prajatantri Bangladesh*, English *People's Republic of Bangladesh*. A country of South Asia. Capital: Dhaka (formerly Dacca). Currency: the taka (100 poisha). Economy: agriculture, cotton fabrics, fishing. Population: 108.6m (1988), 145.8m (projection for 2000). Ethnicity: 98% Bengali, 2% Bihari and tribal. Religion: 83% Muslim, 16% Hindu, 1% Buddhist. Languages: Bengali (official), English for higher education, indigenous languages. Education: primary 55%, secondary 18%; tertiary 5%, literacy 35%. Local links with English date from the 17c; from the 18c till 1947, Bengal was part of British India. In 1947, East Bengal became *East Pakistan*. In 1971, the territory seceded from Pakistan during a short war and became independent. During the Pakistani period, Urdu was the national language, and English was the official second language (used for administration, higher education, and as a link language between educated speakers of Bengali and Urdu). Bengali came third. Resentment of Urdu led to a prolonged and violent language movement. When in 1987 the *Bangla Procolon Ain/Bengali Implementation Act* was passed, Bengali became the main language of education and English ceased to be the official second language. It continues, however, to be used as the language of the higher law courts and of South Asian communication, and has a place in radio and television. A number of newspapers and magazines are published in English. In 1989, English was made a compulsory language for primary and secondary education: a pass in Bengali and English is mandatory for the Secondary Certificate. At university level, English is a popular optional subject. English as used in Bangladesh is similar to that in West Bengal in India. Currently, Bangladesh is neither an ESL nor an EFL country. See BENGALI, ENGLISH, SOUTH ASIAN ENGLISH, TESL. [ASIA, NAME, VARIETY].   B.B.K., T.MCA.

BANTER [17c: origin uncertain. Swift regarded it as vulgar slang]. A kind of badinage, often with a butt who cannot easily answer back. When young Smith, normally a sloven, comes to work one day all brushed and groomed and wearing a suit, his colleagues enjoy shouting such comments as 'Lock up your daughters!' and 'A vision of loveliness!' See BADINAGE, HUMO(U)R. [STYLE].   W.N.

BANTU [1862, as proposed for philological use by W. H. I. Bleek: from Bantu *ntu* a person, the base of: singular *umuntu* a person, a human being; plural *abantu* people, humanity; the abstract nouns *ubuntu* humanity and compassion (especially if African), and *isintu* characteristically African language, behaviour, customs, and other positive qualities]. A term with a neutral, scholarly use throughout the world and a sociopolitical use in South Africa that, in the context of apartheid, has been largely pejorative and therefore greatly resented by black Africans.

The scholarly sense. The international sense relates to a group of over 300 widely distributed and closely related languages of Black Africa south of a line from Cameroon to Kenya, and by extension to c.60m people of various ethnic backgrounds who speak these languages. The *Bantu languages* belong to the Niger-Congo family and include: Douala in Cameroon, Ganda in Uganda, Kongo in Zaïre, Nyanja in Malawi, Shona and Ndebele in Zimbabwe, Sotho in Lesotho and South Africa, Tsonga in Mozambique and South Africa, Tswana in Botswana and South Africa, Siswati in Swaziland, and Xhosa and Zulu in South Africa. The most widely used Bantu language is Swahili, a lingua franca of East and Central Africa that has been strongly influenced by Arabic. The original

Bantu-speaking peoples appear to have originated in the region of Cameroon. In the structure of their languages, bases and affixes play a pre-eminent role: for example, from the base *Tswana* are formed *Batswana* the Tswana people (formerly rendered in English as *Bechuana*), *Motswana* an individual Tswana, *Botswana* land of the Tswana, and *Setswana* the Tswana language. Bantu loanwords in English are relatively few. Among them are: the animal names *impala*, *zebra*; *boma* a thorn-bush enclosure; (Zulu) *impi* regiment, *indaba* gathering, conference; (Swahili) *uhuru* freedom. English words associated with the Bantu-speaking peoples can be etymologically deceptive: Swahili *bwana* (master, boss) is from Arabic *abuna* (our father); *assegai* (spear, lance) has passed from Berber into Arabic and thence to Southern Africa; *kraal* is from Portuguese through Afrikaans, and is a doublet of *corral*. Bantu languages have borrowed extensively from English, especially in South Africa: for example, Zulu *ikhalenda* calendar, *ukheroti* carrot, *ukholiflawa* cauliflower; Xhosa *ibhentshi* bench, *ikati* cat, *ukubhaptiza* to baptise.

The sociopolitical sense. In 1964-78, the black population of the Republic of South Africa was officially referred to as *Bantu*, as in the terms *Bantu Affairs* and *Bantu Education*. Before this period, the term *Native* was used, and after it the term has been *Black*. Individuals were commonly referred to in the singular as *a Bantu* and in the plural as *Bantus*, terms generally detested by black South Africans as violations of the conventions of the Bantu languages (see etymology, above). Because the term was an imposed catchall for black people (Bantu-speaking or otherwise), it has been fiercely resented by them: 'In South Africa today, the word Bantu has become a swear word . . . part and parcel of the apartheid structures. . . . There is no such thing as "a Bantu" ' (*Voice*, 9 May 1982). A key element in the official policy of 'separate development' (apartheid) was the creation of ten (*Bantu*) homelands, territories set aside for specific groups. The term *bantustan* (combining Zulu *bantu* and Hindi/Persian *-stan*, as in *Afghanistan*) was used facetiously in the Republic of South Africa for these homelands, especially by the English-language press, and was assumed internationally to be a standard local term. Its current use is derisive, in the black South African press. The designated homelands are: *Bophuthatswana*, *Ciskei*, *Gazankulu*, *KaNgwane*, *KwaNdebele*, *KwaZulu*, *Lebowa*, *QwaQwa*, *Transkei*, *Venda*. Some have been granted quasi-autonomous status by the South African government but none have been recognized outside the country. See AFRICAN LANGUAGES, BORROWING, LANGUAGE FAMILY, SOUTH AFRICAN ENGLISH, SWAHILI. [AFRICA, LANGUAGE].   T.MCA.

BAR [12c: from Old French *barre* rod, of uncertain origin]. (1) In typography, a horizontal stroke, especially used as part of a character, as in 'H' and 'e'. See MACRON. (2) In compounds: a social barrier, as in *colour bar* a barrier based on the colour of one's skin. See ACCENT BAR, LEXICAL BAR. [STYLE, TECHNOLOGY].   T.MCA.

BARBADOS, informal **B'bados**. A Caribbean country and member of the Commonwealth. Capital: Bridgetown. Currency: the dollar. Economy: sugar, rum, tourism. Head of state: the British monarch, represented by a governor-general. Population: 254,000 (1988), 300,000 (projection for 2000). Ethnicity: 80% African, 16% mixed, 4% Caucasian. Languages: English, Bajan Creole. Education: primary 100%, secondary 89%, tertiary 8%, literacy 99%. British colony 1627. Independence 1961. The Barbadian variety of English is rhotic with stronger nasalization than in other CarE varieties. Word-final /t/ as in *about*, *but* is glottalized and /ai/ as in *mine*, *try* is narrowed to /ɘɪ/. See BAJAN, BLACK IRISH, BRATHWAITE, CARIBBEAN, CARIBBEAN ENGLISH, CARIBBEAN ENGLISH CREOLE, ENGLISH, LAMMING. [AMERICAS, NAME, VARIETY]. L.D.C., T.MCA.

BARBARISM [16c: from French *barbarisme*, Latin *barbarismus*, Greek *barbarismós* foreign speech. The classical Greek word *bárbaros* foreign, cognate with Sanskrit *balbala/barbara* stammering, Latin *balbutire* to stammer, and English *babble*, implied that foreigners spoke gibberish. *Barbarismós* was the babble of the non-Greek world. The Romans, refusing to be barbarians, borrowed the terms and the concept]. A word considered to offend against good taste by combining elements from different languages, especially classical with vernacular, or being used in an unsatisfactory way. The following words were considered to be barbarisms when first used: *escalate*, back-formed from *escalator*; *finalize*, Greek *-ize* added to Latin *final*; *mob* a clipping of Latin *mobile vulgus*; *television* a hybrid of Greek *tele-* and Latin *vision*.

In medieval Europe, educated descendants of the northern 'barbarians' were often insecure under the pressure of their classical inheritance and regarded their own speech as 'barbarous'. Most held that the vernaculars should therefore be kept from contaminating and debasing Latin. Mixing took place freely, however, and during the Renaissance purists and innovators debated the wisdom of transferring classical expressions *en masse* into the vernaculars. The purists feared that 'barbarous' abuses would result. The debate was largely over by the beginning of the 19c, settled in practical terms in favour of hybridization, but unease has survived into the 20c. In *Modern English Usage*, Fowler pointed to two problems: one might lack the information to decide whether an item is a barbarism or not ('life is not long enough to consult a competent philologist every time one of the hundreds of dubious words confronts us'); even if a philologist were consulted and a barbarism identified, people would not necessarily stop using it ('A barbarism is like a lie; it has got the start of us before we have found it out. That barbarisms should exist is a pity. To expend much energy on those that do exist is a waste. To create them is a grave misdemeanour; and the greater the need of the word that is made, the greater the maker's guilt if he miscreates it': 1965, ed. Ernest Gowers). In present-day usage, despite Fowler's strictures, concern for classical and linguistic purity is minimal and the coining of hybrids is casual and massive. See ATTICISM, CLASSICAL COMPOUND, CORRECT, GREEK, HYBRID, -ISM, SOLECISM, THEMATIC VOWEL. [STYLE, USAGE].   T.MCA.

BARDOLATRY [1901: a blend of Gaelic *bard* poet and singer, and Greek-derived *-latry* worship. Coined by Bernard Shaw]. Reverence for William Shakespeare (the 'Bard of Avon') as the greatest figure in English literature. The notion that Shakespeare 'doth not wrong' is recent, especially in terms of uncritical acceptance of his language. Some early defenders of his 'lapses' of decorum venerated him as an untutored genius ('fancies childe': Milton), but Jonson faulted him for lack of linguistic erudition and stylistic care (*c.*1618). Dryden discovered 'in every page either some *Solecism* of Speech, or some notorious flaw in Sence' (1672), and Shakespeare's editor Warburton found him guilty of 'licentious Use of Words' (1747). Even his admirer Johnson deplored a weakness for word-play. Johnson's contemporary Arthur Murphy, however, described Shakespeare as 'a kind of established religion in poetry', heralding the veneration dominating 19c and much of 20c commentary. Philological research corrected some strictures on Shakespeare's language, and 'practical criticism' (sympathetic study of a text as well-wrought and self-contained) displaced the arbitrary standards of correctness established in earlier centuries. Hence, the 20c English critic I. A. Richards extolled Shakespeare's 'really masterly use of a language' (1936), an endorsement as far from Milton's defence as it is from Warburton's attack. [HISTORY, LITERATURE].   W.F.B.

BARE INFINITIVE. An infinitive without *to* (*win* rather than *to win*), used: (1) After modal verbs: *I must go.* (2) In the pattern verb of perception plus object plus infinitive: *I saw Fonteyn*

dance; *We heard the door bang.* (3) With some verbs: *Let go*; *Help me do this*; *Make them pay*; *I've known this happen before.* (4) After *rather than* and *sooner than*: *I'll go without rather than pay so much.* (5) In cleft sentences: *All I did was ask.* See INFINITIVE. [GRAMMAR].   S.C.

BARNES, William [1801–86]. English dialectologist and poet. Born in Dorset of a farming family, he became a schoolmaster in 1823 and after studying at Cambridge a clergyman in 1848. In addition to textbooks, grammars, and articles on etymology, philology, archaeology, and local history, he produced a primer of Old English (*Se Gefylsta*, 1849) and collected dialect material. Most of his poetry was in dialect (*Poems of Rural Life in the Dorset Dialect*, 1844, and *Hwomely Rhymes*, 1859), with a volume in standard English (*Poems of Rural Life*, 1868). He wrote two grammars and glossaries of the Dorset dialect, which, together with *Philological Grammar* (1854), compared features of standard English and the Dorset dialect with those of other languages. As a teacher and clergyman, he was distressed by the intricacies of English vocabulary, blaming its shortcomings, as he saw them, on its hybrid nature. He set out therefore to counteract the classical influence. He revived Old English usages, such as *hearsomeness* and *forewit* to replace *obedience* and *caution*, drew on dialect, using *fore-elders* and *outstep* to replace *ancestors* and *remote*, made loan translations from other Germanic languages, such as *birdlore* and *speechlore* to replace *ornithology* and *grammar*, and coined new words on vernacular principles, such as *birdstow* and *beestow* to replace *aviary* and *apiary*. Although his purism had little impact, it was comparable to that in other parts of 19c Europe. See index. [BIOGRAPHY, EDUCATION, EUROPE, HISTORY].   J.M.G.

BARNHART, Clarence L(ewis) [b. 1900]. American editor and lexicographer, born near Plattsburg, Missouri, and educated at the U. of Chicago. He began his career by editing school dictionaries (1929–45) for Scott, Foresman & Co. Work on the dictionaries while studying with Leonard Bloomfield (1934–7) convinced him that lexicographers depend too heavily on written sources for their information. He therefore decided to make his publications descriptive of spoken AmE and refused to pass judgement on correctness or usage: 'Every person has his own style of English; there is no English language. There's your English language, XYZ's English language, and they overlap, and it is the overlapping that I try to get at' (in *Wilson Library Bulletin*, 1985). Barnhart edited the *Thorndike Century Junior Dictionary* (1935) and *Thorndike Century Senior Dictionary* (1941), and during World War II was invited by the War Department to oversee the *Dictionary of United States Army Terms* (1943), intended to acquaint allies with US technical terminology. After the war, he became an associate at the Institute of Psychological Research at Columbia U. (New York, 1945-6), where, encouraged by Edward Thorndike and Irving Lorge, he sought to apply a scientific approach to language problems.

Seeking ways to establish the dictionary as a regular classroom tool rather than an occasional resource, he designed the Random House *American College Dictionary* (1947), which set the pattern for subsequent AmE reference books. It reversed the practice of placing original, often obsolete, meanings before current definitions, included foreign words, neologisms, geographical names, and proper names in the main alphabet, employed spot maps to locate places, and used several characters from the IPA. Later, Barnhart used the semantic counts from the Thorndike-Lorge word-frequency lists to produce *The Thorndike-Barnhart Comprehensive Desk Dictionary* (1951), in which he included many Americanisms. He later published the series *The Barnhart Dictionary of New English since 1963* (1973), *The Second Barnhart Dictionary of New English* (1980), and *The Third Barnhart Dictionary of New English* (1990, combining and supplementing the preceding volumes). *The Barnhart Dictionary Companion* is a quarterly update published by Lexik House, whose editors scan American, Australian, British, Canadian, and South African newspapers, monitor television shows for new or unfamiliar words, and provide citations with enough surrounding context to show how they are used. In 1947, Barnhart founded *C. L. Barnhart Inc.* to produce reference books for publishers, chief among which has been the yearly edition of *The World Book Dictionary* (two volumes). Past president of the American Name Society, Barnhart co-edited *The New Century Cyclopedia of Names* (three volumes, 1954). He has been an associate editor of *American Speech*, has edited and co-written with Leonard Bloomfield a series of readers *Let's Read: A Linguistic Approach* (1961-6), and has edited and published many school and trade dictionaries. See index. [AMERICAS, EDUCATION, REFERENCE].
R.W.B.

BASCELT, full form *British Association of State Colleges in English Language Teaching*. An organization founded in 1982 to promote the work of the departments in technical colleges and colleges of technology which provide courses for foreign learners of English. It operates a formal validation scheme for inspected colleges in collaboration with the British Council, and guarantees standards in respect of such matters as course organization and student welfare. [EDUCATION, EUROPE, MEDIA]. W.S.

BASE [13c: through French from Latin *basis*, Greek *básis* a step, stance, pedestal]. Also **base form**. A word or lexeme from which another is derived: the base of *sharpen* is *sharp*, of *dorsal* is *dors-*. Within a series, successive forms are bases: *sharp* for *sharpen*, *sharpen* for *sharpener*. Here, *sharp* is a primary base and *sharpen* a secondary base. A word that serves as a base is a *base word*; part of a word that serves as a base is a *bound base*. See BOUND AND FREE, MORPHOLOGY, ROOT, STEM. [LANGUAGE, WORD]. T.MCA.

BASIC. See (1) BASIC ENGLISH[1], (2) COMPUTING.

BASIC ENGLISH[1], also **Ogden's Basic English, Basic** [1928: an acronym for *British, American, Scientific, International, Commercial*]. A reduced form of English devised in the 1920s by the writer and linguist C. K. Ogden, in cooperation with the critic I. A. Richards. It was favoured by the British Prime Minister Winston S. Churchill, with some support from the US President Franklin D. Roosevelt. Basic was an exercise in language planning, intended to extract from standard English the minimum grammar and vocabulary needed for everyday communication. Ogden saw it as serving three ends at the same time: an international medium in its own right, an introduction to 'full' English, and a kind of plain English. The name of the organization created to further Basic, the Orthological Institute, echoes such terms as *orthodoxy, orthography,* and *orthoepy.*

Nature. Ogden and Richards' *The Meaning of Meaning* (1923) contains in its chapter on definition the germ of Basic, which took final shape in 1928. Its minimal syntax has a fixed analytic word order (as in *I will put the record on the machine now*) and six affixes (*-s* for plurals and verbs, *un-* to negate adjectives, *-ed* and *-ing* to form participles, *-ly* for adverbs, and *-er* as an agent suffix). Ogden encouraged compounding such as *farmhouse* and *teapot, madman* and *blackbird,* and *get up, go out, put on*. The syntax was accompanied by a reduced vocabulary of 850 words in sets: 400 general words and 200 picturable words (600 nouns), 150 adjectives, 82 grammatical words, such as *across, all, can,* and 18 operators (such verbs as *get* and *put*). Operators had three roles: to replace more difficult words (*get* replacing *receive, obtain, become*), to form phrases that would obviate other verbs (*give money for* replacing *buy, give him a push* instead of *push him*), and to be part of a phrasal verb (*put together* replacing *assemble*). By such means, he considered that his operators could stand in for some 4,000 verbs. He accepted figurative extensions of meaning and supplemented the basic words with numbers, names, and lists of technical terminology according to need.

Ogden described the system in *Basic English* (1930) and *The System of Basic English* (1934). In 1940 he published *The General Basic English Dictionary*, which gave 'more than 40,000 senses of over 20,000 words, in basic English'. This work went into over 20 impressions until discontinued in the late 1980s, one of the first dictionaries for learners to use a defining vocabulary. In the introduction, Ogden stated:

With its help, anyone who has had some training in the structure of English, through Basic or any other system, will be able to make headway by himself with the English of Library, Radio, and Newspaper. . . . Words which are now come across only in the works of early writers and words which are the stamp of the old learning based on Greek and Latin are looked on as no less the apparatus of the expert than the words of some branch of science, and have been given no more space. As far as possible a balance has been kept between the interests of the old education and the new, without overlooking the fact that, for the learner, what is current is more important than what is past.

This extract is composed entirely in Basic, which includes the word *apparatus*. The following passages compare Basic and standard English. The first is from 'Time in Philosophy and Physics' (Herbert Dingle, *Philosophy* 54, 1979), the second its restatement in Basic:

Original. Let us look first at the question 'What is time?' Time is an inescapable—perhaps the most inescapable—fact of experience, but we cannot define it. The final word on this was said by St Augustine. 'What is time?' he asked, and replied 'If no one asks me I know; if I want to explain it to a questioner, I do not know.'

Basic. Let us give a look first at the question 'What is time?' Time is a fact of experience from which there is no getting away—possibly the only such fact of which this is completely true—, but we are unable to give any clear account of it. The statement which says the most it is possible to say about it was made by St. Augustine. His answer to the question 'what is time?' was: 'If no-one puts the question to me, I am certain about it; if I have a mind to give a questioner an account of it, I am uncertain.'

Critical responses. Most commentators have agreed that Basic is ingenious. Some have expressed sympathy for one or more of its aims, and enthusiasm for some or all of Ogden's principles and practices, but others have regarded it as pernicious. Basic was the subject of an acrimonious debate in the 1930s between Ogden and Michael West (see West *et al.*, *A Critical Examination of Basic English*, University of Toronto Press, 1934; Ogden, *Counteroffensive: An Exposure of Certain Misrepresentations of Basic English*, Cambridge, the Orthological Institute,

1935). West argued that Basic was a sort of pidgin English, and feared alike its success or failure: if successful, it would endanger such other forms of simplified English as his own, and lead to a deterioration in usage; if a failure, it would cast doubt on the approach he endorsed. It was, he claimed, 'an incalculably grave disservice' to humanity. Ogden in turn accused West of 'grave errors' and 'ludicrous' views.

Both adverse and favourably disposed critics generally agree that Basic has three weaknesses: (1) It cannot be a world auxiliary language, an avenue into standard English, and a reminder of the virtues of plain usage at one and the same time. (2) Its dependence on operators and combinations produces circumlocutions at times unacceptable in standard English (as above, where Dingle's 'If no one asks me I know' becomes 'If no-one puts the question to me, I am certain about it'). (3) The Basic words, mainly common, short words like *get*, *make*, *do*, have some of the widest ranges of meaning in the language and may be among the most difficult to learn adequately. Charles C. Fries and A. Aileen Traver reported that for the 850 words the *OED* lists no fewer than 18,416 senses (*English Word Lists*, Ann Arbor, 1950).

Vernacular English. Apart from a few items like *account*, *experience*, *machine*, *question*, and *apparatus*, Ogden's words are drawn from the vernacular stratum of English vocabulary. Like the 19c purist William Barnes, he appears to impute special merit to a core of words that were there before the majority of Latin and Greek 'big words' arrived. The syntax and word structures singled out for inclusion are Germanic, and the active-voice model for sentences rejects the passives common in academic and technical language, and originally based on Latin models. Like the early 17c lexicographer Robert Cawdrey, Ogden explains and replaces Latin-derived verbs like *impose* with vernacular verbs like *lay on*. However, as critics and many foreign learners have often pointed out, such vernacular forms as *lay on* can be harder to use than their Latinate partners.

Conclusion. In 1943, Churchill asked Harold Palmer to consider changes that would make Basic more flexible and useful as an international medium. Palmer suggested the addition of 'an adequate number of verbs' (so that, for example, *give him a push* could once again if necessary be *push him*), more grammatical words, and the replacement of non-standard compounds with their everyday equivalents. These recommendations were not adopted, but many word lists used in writing simplified readers and in introductory language courses, as well as defining vocabularies in learner's dictionaries, owe much to Ogden's pioneering efforts. Although the logical minimalism of Basic has few advocates and the system is now little used, its indirect influence has been considerable.

See ANGLIC, ARTIFICIAL LANGUAGE, DEFINING VOCABULARY, NEWSPEAK, PLAIN ENGLISH, RESTRICTED LANGUAGE, VOCABULARY CONTROL. [EDUCATION, VARIETY].   T.MCA.

BASIC ENGLISH². See BONEHEAD ENGLISH.

BASILECT [1960s: from Greek *básis* (lowest) step, and *-lect* as in *dialect*]. (1) The variety of language in a post-creole continuum most different from the standard or superstrate language: for example, Jamaican Creole as opposed to standard English. (2) The least prestigious variety of a language, such as *Gutter Glasgow* in Scotland and *Brooklyn* in New York City. See DIALECT, LECT. [LANGUAGE].   S.R.

BASIONYM. See BINOMIAL NOMENCLATURE.

BATHOS [18c: from Greek *báthos* depth]. A term in rhetoric for a ludicrous anticlimax: 'For God, for country, and for Acme Gasworks' (*Random House Dictionary*, 1987). Satire is often deliberately bathetic; in Swift's *Gulliver's Travels* (1726), the real-life disputes of Protestants and Catholics are presented as a Lilliputian war in which Big-Endians and Little-Endians fight over where to open a boiled egg. See ANTICLIMAX. [STYLE].   T.MCA.

BAY ISLANDS, Spanish *Islas de la Bahía*. A group of coastal islands in the western Caribbean, constituting a department of Honduras. Chief town: Roatán, on Roatán Island. Population: 18,744 (1983). The Bay Islanders speak a Creole descended from the English of British settlers, and of African and Carib slaves brought by them from the West Indies. The area was held by Britain between 1850 and 1858, then ceded to Honduras. See CARIBBEAN, CENTRAL AMERICA. [AMERICAS, NAME, VARIETY].   L.D.C., T.MCA.

BAYMEN. See BELIZE, NEWFOUNDLAND ENGLISH.

BBC, short form of *British Broadcasting Corporation*. A broadcasting organization, perhaps the best-known in the world: a non-commercial public service centred on London, with stations throughout the UK, providing radio and television services financed through licence fees paid annually by owners of TV receivers, as well as radio and television services throughout the world (the *BBC World Service*), financed by the Foreign and Commonwealth Office. The BBC

broadcasts primarily in English, but its local services include Welsh and Gaelic and its world services are transmitted in 36 different languages. See BBC ENGLISH¹, BBC ENGLISH², *BBC ENGLISH³*, BBC PRONUNCIATION UNIT, BBC PUBLICATIONS, BRITISH BROADCASTING, BROADCASTING, RECEIVED PRONUNCIATION, WELSH LANGUAGE SERVICE. [EUROPE, MEDIA]. B.T., T.MCA.

BBC ACCENT. See BBC ENGLISH¹, RECEIVED PRONUNCIATION.

BBC ADVISORY COMMITTEE ON SPOKEN ENGLISH. See BBC ENGLISH¹.

BBC ENGLISH¹ [1920s: evidently at first a disparaging term among regional BBC staff resentful of the better prospects of speakers with public-school accents]. A non-technical term for the speech of newsreaders and presenters of the national and international English-language programmes of the British Broadcasting Corporation. The phrase refers to the accent known to phoneticians as *Received Pronunciation* (*RP*) and sometimes informally referred to as *a BBC accent*. The term is used in at least three ways: neutrally, in the sense of English as heard on BBC news; positively, as the exemplary English of BBC announcers; negatively, as the accent of privilege imposed on the nation by a monopolistic and allegedly patronizing state institution. In recent years, while RP and near-RP accents continue to dominate BBC newsreading and presentation, they are no longer exclusive for announcements and continuity on radio and television. Reasons include the limited numbers of RP speakers available for training as broadcasters, the rise of local radio and TV stations with a demotic style in which RP might be a handicap, a gradually increasing national use of speakers with other accents in tandem with a degree of social levelling, and changes in the nature of RP itself, including forms blending with some southern accents. The use of RP remains strong in the World Service, and for many overseas listeners the traditional BBC voice is equated with good English.

The BBC and spoken English. The BBC was founded in 1922 and in 1924 its managing director, John C. W. Reith, a Scottish engineer, published the book *Broadcast over Britain*. In a chapter devoted to 'The King's English', he observed:

I have heard it said that one can place a man socially and educationally from the first few dozen words he utters. There is a measure of truth in the statement. It is certainly true that even the commonest and simplest words are subjected to horrible and grotesque abuse. One hears the most appalling travesties of vowel pronunciation. This is a matter in which broadcasting may be of immense assistance. Pride in a local or national intonation is perhaps quite natural; this is not necessarily mutilation. I do not suppose that any man wishes to go through life handicapped by the mistakes or carelessness of his own pronunciation, and yet this is what happens. We have made a special effort to secure in our stations men who, in the presentation of programme items, the reading of news bulletins and so on, can be relied upon to employ the correct pronunciation of the English tongue. . . . I have frequently heard that disputes as to the right pronunciation of words have been settled by reference to the manner in which they have been spoken on the wireless. No one would deny the great advantage of a standard pronunciation of the language, not only in theory but in practice. Our responsibilities in this matter are obvious, since in talking to so vast a multitude, mistakes are likely to be promulgated to a much greater extent than was ever possible before.

The Advisory Committee. To implement and supplement his language policy, Reith established in 1926 an *Advisory Committee on Spoken English*. Its chairman was Robert Bridges, the Poet Laureate and a founder of the Society for Pure English, and its honorary secretary Arthur Lloyd James, a Welsh phonetician at the School of Oriental and African Studies, U. of London. Its other original members were Daniel Jones, Professor of Phonetics at U. College London and compiler of the *English Pronouncing Dictionary* (1917), the actor Sir Johnston Forbes-Robertson, the naturalized American scholar Logan Pearsall Smith, and the Irish playwright and critic George Bernard Shaw. The committee's task was to make recommendations on policy and on the pronunciation of contentious words, both native and foreign, decisions being reached by majority vote. Reith sought 'a style or quality of English that would not be laughed at in any part of the country'. It was generally agreed that the most appropriate medium was the accent which Jones at that time referred to as *Public School Pronunciation* and shortly afterwards began to call *Received Pronunciation*. The committee considered that PSP would convey a suitable sense of sobriety, impartiality, and impersonality. A necessary implication of the decision, however, was that posts as announcers would only be filled by men of a certain class and type.

The committee's recommendations on the pronunciation of individual words were mandatory for announcers and newsreaders. To some extent, the presence of phoneticians on the committee ensured that the strict prescriptivism expressed by Reith in 1924 was to some extent mitigated. In the foreword to *Broadcast English I* (1928), the first booklet of recommendations (covering 332 words), Reith wrote: 'There has been no attempt to establish a uniform spoken language. . . . The policy might be described

as that of seeking a common denominator of educated speech.' Lloyd James noted in the *BBC Handbook* (1929) that recommending certain pronunciations to announcers 'is *not* to be regarded as implying that all other pronunciations are wrong: the recommendations are made in order to ensure uniformity of practice, and to protect the Announcers from the criticism to which the very peculiar nature of their work renders them liable'. There was from the earliest years an element of tension and disagreement among those responsible for shaping language policy as well as among the listeners, some of whom took BBC usage to be authoritative while others did not.

Recommended pronunciations were not written in IPA symbols but in a respelling system (with an acute accent marking stress) that would be more readily intelligible to the BBC's staff. Early recommendations that had no long-term effect include *allies* and *mishap* stressed on the second syllable, *immanent* as 'immáynent', to avoid confusion with *imminent*, *pejorative* as 'péejorativ', and *quandary* as 'kwondáiry'. The membership of the committee grew over the years, until it was over 20 strong. Bridges died in 1930 and Shaw became chairman; new members included Alistair Cooke because of his work with the American Dialect Society, the *OED* editor C. T. Onions, the dialectologist Harold Orton, and the lexicographer Henry Cecil Wyld. It was not easy to agree on the pronunciations of many words: in 1928 the committee recommended the pronunciation 'gárrazh' for *garage*, in 1931 changed to 'gárredge', then in 1935 returned to 'gárrazh'. In the same year, under the leadership of Lloyd James, it published its recommendations for place-names and family names in six volumes that served as an internal BBC standard for many years. Words whose recommended pronunciation has stood the test of time include *Auld Lang Syne* ('sign', not 'zine'), *centenary* ('sentéenàri', not '-tenn-'), *controversy* (stress on the first syllable), and *machination* ('mack-').

In 1939, at the beginning of the Second World War, the committee was suspended. Lloyd James and Jones remained as advisers for the rest of their lives and day-to-day work was taken over by Miss G. M. Miller, assistant secretary to the committee, with the title of Pronunciation Assistant, and Miss E. D. Anderson, both Scots and graduates of London U. trained in phonetics. After the war, the committee was not reactivated and at an uncertain date in the 1940s the group became known as the *BBC Pronunciation Unit*, whose brief was to give guidance to newsreaders and announcers on the pronunciation of place and personal names: see entry.

Reithian broadcasting. From 1926, newsreaders and programme announcers were required to wear dinner-jackets when on duty in the evenings. In his memoirs, Stuart Hibberd observed: 'Personally, I have always thought it only right and proper that announcers should wear evening dress on duty. After all, announcing is a serious, if new, profession, and the wearing of evening dress is an act of courtesy to the artists, many of whom will almost certainly be similarly dressed if they are taking part in a programme from 8 p.m. onwards. There are, of course, certain disadvantages. It is not ideal kit in which to read the News—I myself hate having anything tight round my neck when broadcasting—and I remember that more than once the engineers said that my shirt-front creaked during the reading of the bulletin' (*This—is London*, 1950). Informality was forbidden, as were impromptu additions and statements of personal opinion. However, when the newsreader Frank Philips, after the late-night shipping forecast, said to sea captains, 'Good night, gentlemen, and good sailing', listeners approved of it as a pleasant and worthy departure from the norm. The stiff upper lip also relaxed when Alvar Lidell announced the British victory at the Battle of El Alamein (1943): 'I'm going to read you the news and there's some cracking good news coming.'

Before the Second World War, announcers and newsreaders were anonymous, though outside-broadcast commentators were not. In 1940, John Snagge, as head of presentation, removed the anonymity and the new formula was: 'Here is the news and this is Alvar Lidell reading it.' The justification for this change was that German intelligence had trained their own announcers to imitate BBC newsreaders, so as to mislead the public during and after a German invasion. The best-known newsreaders of the period were Stuart Hibberd, Frank Philips, and Alvar Lidell. During the war, the Ministry of Information selected a BBC entertainer from the North of England, Wilfred Pickles, as a newsreader, to redress to some extent the dominance of RP and because it was thought that the Germans would find it harder to copy his accent. The experiment failed. Pickles felt that the bulletins were written by southerners for southerners and that this made a difference to the choice and order of the words. Many listeners complained about his voice, claiming that such an accent compromised the integrity of the news. Door-to-door research is said to have revealed that the use of a northern accent was more popular in the south of England than in the north.

Changes in policy. Although the official voice of the BBC continued to be that of the public school and Oxbridge, in some kinds of broadcasting non-RP speakers were used, such as weather forecasting, sports commentating, discussions of gardening, and drama and entertainment. In the 1950s, the BBC's approach was challenged by the more demotic style of new Independent Television. The BBC began to use some announcers and commentators from regional stations on network current affairs, especially for sport. The new radio networks in the 1960s led to a further relaxation, and in 1979 the retired newsreader Alvar Lidell complained about declining standards in an article in *The Listener*. A committee was set up to monitor the situation, one of whose members was Robert Burchfield, editor of the *OED Supplement*. In a booklet called *The Spoken Word* (1981), he stated that although standards had in some respects become more relaxed, there had been no decline. Radio 3 and the BBC World Service continued the RP tradition, but in 1989 the World Service announced a new policy of using announcers and newsreaders with a more representative range of accents. See ACCENT BAR, BBC, JONES (D.), RECEIVED PRONUNCIATION. [EUROPE, MEDIA, VARIETY].   B.T., P.S., T.MCA.

BBC ENGLISH[2], formerly *BBC English by Radio* and *BBC English by Radio and Television*. The department of the BBC World Service responsible for producing English language teaching programmes, so named since 1988. It is the largest radio and TV organization in existence for the teaching of English, sometimes called 'the largest classroom in the world'. It provides 30 hours a week of radio lessons from London and 30 hours a week of lessons and commentary in the learner's mother tongue, broadcast through the 36 language sections of the World Service. Programmes are re-broadcast for a nominal fee in over 50 countries. The series are made for use worldwide and are supported by the *BBC English* magazine.

As part of the World Service, BBC English is financed by a grant-in-aid from the British Foreign and Commonwealth Office, which decides to which regions broadcasts should be directed but has no influence over content. The estimate of an audience of 25m worldwide for the BBC World Service is based on extrapolation from audience research, listeners' letters, reports from overseas stations and correspondents, and the BBC's listening panels in different countries. Related publications are used in over 100 countries and are self-financing, the profits being used in new productions and a more extensive operation. The service has evolved from teaching only standard BrE to exposing the learner to many varieties in its audio and video material. It makes a distinction, however, between what learners hear and see and what they are taught to produce: standard BrE with RP as the pronunciation model.

History. The first BBC section to have lessons in English was the Arabic Service of the BBC World Service in 1939. Early programmes were called *The Radio Teaches You English* and were broadcasts of two or three minutes of selected utterances followed by translations. When such programmes were revised in 1941 they used Ogden's Basic English, although this was never publicly stated. In 1943, under the title *English by Radio*, a daily five-minute lesson in English for those with the rudiments of the language was introduced in the European Service, transmitting such programmes as *How good is your English?* and *What's the news?* The series *Ann and her Grandfather* began, with actors Alan Wheatley and Brenda Cleather, and lasted until 1970. Towards the end of the war, lessons with explanations in the learners' own languages began to be introduced in a number of the BBC's foreign-language services. German troops in Norway heard of the order to lay down their arms while listening to an English by Radio lesson in the German Service. Publication of some of the texts, with backup notes, followed later in the European programme bulletins *London Calling Europe, Ici Londres,* and *Hier Spricht London.*

Vernon Duckworth Barker, the first editor of *English by Radio*, was succeeded in 1945 by René Quinault, who enlisted the help of experienced teachers from the British Council and elsewhere, including C. E. Eckersley, A. S. Hornby, J. D. O'Connor, Michael West, and Stannard Allen, to ensure the professional standards of the department, and this tradition continues. In 1949, Sydney (S. F.) Stevens was appointed Manager and commissioned new programmes and backup books. He appointed publishers abroad to sell local editions and records, such as Editorial Alhambra in Spain, which first issued BBC English materials in 1947, Valmartina in Italy, and Disques BBC in France. Currently, *BBC English* courses are sold through over 80 agents worldwide, many of them publishers in their own right who have produced bilingual versions of courses.

In the 1950s, after a major beginners' course devised by Valentine Elliott and James Noonan of the London U. Institute of Education, *Listen and Speak*, a further coordinated scheme to teach listeners from beginner to advanced level was started with a bilingual radio series and book by David Hicks. The course, which continues to be used, was called *Calling all Beginners* and was followed by *Getting on in English* and *Choosing your English*, both by John Haycraft. Another development was the *BBC English Language Summer School* (1952), with students drawn originally from leaders of listening groups in Europe, established to provide feedback on programmes broadcast on direct transmission. The school continues, with some 160 students each year from all over the world and courses ranging from general English to the training of broadcasters.

TV and multimedia. Stevens retired in 1959 and his successor Christopher Dilke began an expansion into TV in 1962, with the first series of *Walter and Connie*, produced in collaboration with the British Council. This black-and-white series is still on air in some countries. The first material in colour was a business course, *The Belcrest Story*, which showed that TV could have an impact in the ELT classroom. On Dilke's retirement in 1973, Hugh Howse, former head of the BBC Far Eastern Service, took over and developed the service as a multimedia broadcasting and publishing organization. His greatest achievement was *Follow Me*, the world's most successful TV-based English course: shown in over 80 countries, including some 100m viewers in China. It was the biggest of a series of co-productions that the BBC has undertaken with government, broadcasting, publishing, and educational partners in the last 20 years. Hugh Howse was succeeded by Barbara Goldsmid in 1982, and Julian Amey was appointed first Executive Director in 1989. [EDUCATION, EUROPE, MEDIA].   B.T., R.J.Q.

BBC ENGLISH[3]. A bimonthly magazine with backup articles for listeners to BBC English and the BBC World Service. Intended primarily for foreign learners, its articles are often accompanied by keyed glossaries and it has exercises based on its own content, aimed at all levels of learner. Initially, the BBC published language notes in its European programme bulletins, then in 1976 published programme notes in *Modern English*, a magazine co-published with International House, a private EFL school. In 1982, BBC English took over the magazine, called it *BBC English*, and co-published it with *Middle Eastern Economic Digest*. In 1986, a new co-publisher *World of Information* took over its printing and distribution. See BBC ENGLISH[2]. [EUROPE, MEDIA].   B.T.

BBC PRONUNCIATION UNIT, The. A body of 'assessors and interpreters of educated usage' (*BBC Pronunciation Policy and Practice*, leaflet, 1974/9), set up in the 1940s as part of the BBC Presentation Department to replace the Advisory Committee on Spoken English, and now part of the BBC's Corporate Library Services: see BBC ENGLISH[1] for preceding events. The Unit does not promote a standard BBC accent, but decides on the pronunciation of individual words and names. Its decisions are mandatory only for announcers and newsreaders, not for other BBC broadcasters, professional or casual. Any influence it may have on BrE is therefore indirect and limited. Where names are concerned, the Unit's policy covers two areas: those used in English-speaking countries and those from other languages.

Names in English-speaking countries. (1) *The United Kingdom.* For personal names and titles, the BBC uses the pronunciation preferred by the person(s) concerned. To check such usage, the Unit consults them or near relations or colleagues. Some names are perennial problems, because of different preferences in vowel quality and stress: *Burnett, Izard, Jervis, Laing, Powell, Symon(d)s.* For place-names, local educated usage is followed, established when necessary by consulting local clergy, councillors, or police. Special policies have been developed for such bilingual regions as Wales, the treatment of place-names generally requiring English pronunciations for English-based names (*Bridgend, Newport*) and Welsh pronunciations for Welsh-based names (*Ystrad Mynach, Llanfair*). Because Wales is only partly bilingual, Welsh-language names in English-dominant areas are given local Anglicized pronunciations. (2) *Elsewhere.* For such countries as Australia, Canada, New Zealand, and the US, the Unit seeks to follow personal and local usage, consulting appropriate government offices, the works of reference of local broadcasting organizations, established gazetteers, and resident BBC colleagues.

Foreign names. (1) Where a well-established pronunciation and perhaps written form already exist, such as *Florence* for *Firenze* and *Munich* for *München*, they are used. Some pronunciations, however, change over time: where once *Calais* and *Cadiz* were 'káliss' (like *chalice*) and 'káydiz' (like *sadist*), they are now pronounced more or less as in French and Spanish. *Seville* no longer rhymes with *Greville*, but is stressed on the second syllable. In difficult cases, the Unit assesses the situation and makes its decision: for example, that *Majorca* remains Anglicized with a *y*-sound ('mi-yórkǎ'), while *Marbella* has a Castilian-like pronunciation ('maarbélyǎ'). (2) When there is no established usage, an Anglicization is recommended, based on the native pronunciation or the usage of long-term English-speaking residents. Thus, *Chernobyl* in the Ukraine becomes 'chěrnóbbil'. From time to time, adjustments are necessary: *Kenya*, once 'kéen-yǎ', is now 'kén-yǎ', after a request from the Kenyan government.

English-language usage. The BBC policy leaflet notes that the Unit 'normally does not step outside its advisory role to lay down the law on the pronunciation of individual words from the general vocabulary stock; but occasionally after pressure from outside, it issues reminders about this or that "desirable" pronunciation. Some modern phoneticians might be inclined to consider even this misguided.' The aim is not to lead the way in language change, but to keep 'an ear to the ground for the moment when a new pronunciation begins to displace an old one'. The leaflet notes: 'The Pronunciation Unit is equipped to advise good speakers, indeed any speaker, on the finer or more controversial points of educated usage. It cannot eradicate overnight the habits of a lifetime from the speech of a bad speaker.'

In recent years, the Unit has found it 'less useful to make rulings on English vocabulary words, as educated usage now accommodates far more variation than formerly, but certain words of more than one pronunciation have one which causes less annoyance than the others, and in these cases we do make recommendations which we like broadcasters to follow: *controversy* (first syllable stress), *dispute* (second syllable stress for both noun and verb), *kilometre* (first syllable stress), *soviet* (*-o* as in *no* rather than in *not*), *cervical* (first syllable stress, *-i* as in *pin*, not as in *nine*)' (Graham Pointon, Director of the BBC Pronunciation Unit, in *English Today* 15, July 1988). The seven published pre-war *Broadcast English* booklets have long been out of print, but in 1971 Oxford University Press published the *BBC Pronouncing Dictionary of British Names*, ed. G. M. Miller (2nd edition, enlarged, 1983). This work incorporates information from most of the booklets. The Unit publishes a series of Pronunciation Guides which it has compiled: lists of names of musicians, British politicians, and others, as well as Chinese syllables in their Pinyin and Wade–Giles transliterations, with BBC recommendations. It also publishes update bulletins for subscribers. The Unit is not perceived by the BBC as a guardian of the language but as a reflection of the preferred usage of the British public. See BBC, PRONUNCIATION. [EUROPE, MEDIA, NAME, SPEECH].   T.McA.

BBC PUBLICATIONS. The publishing arm of the British Broadcasting Corporation, founded in 1926 as the *Publications Management Department*. The name covers two organizations publishing books, video cassettes, and magazines based on BBC broadcasts. The periodicals are: (1) *Radio Times*, the domestic weekly programmes bulletin. It began in 1923, published by George Newnes on a profit-sharing basis. The BBC provided programme details while Newnes provided editorial content under the editor, Leonard Crocombe. In 1926, the BBC assumed full editorial control and the editor became a member of staff. Currently, it also includes non-BBC programming information. The name echoes that of *The Times* newspaper. (2) *The Listener*, a weekly magazine first published in 1929, mainly to print significant broadcast talks. It was discontinued in 1990. (3) *London Calling*, the monthly programme bulletin of the BBC World Service, first published in 1932 as the *Empire Programme Pamphlet* but changed to its present title in 1939. It gives details of and background information about forthcoming programmes, together with radio broadcast frequencies, and is available only on subscription. BBC publications obtained a boost from the introduction in 1963 of adult educational broadcasting, which led to increased demand for booklets on a variety of broadcast topics. It also benefits from the publication, often jointly with other publishers, of books relating to TV documentary series. See BBC, FABER. [EUROPE, MEDIA].   B.T.

BBC WORLD SERVICE. See BBC, BBC ENGLISH[1], BBC ENGLISH[2], BBC ENGLISH[3], BBC PRONUNCIATION UNIT, BBC PUBLICATIONS, CHINA.

BEACH LA MAR [19c: from French *bêche-de-mer*, Portuguese *bicho do mar* ('small sea creature') the sea slug]. Also *Sandalwood English*. An English-based contact language used from the 1840s in parts of the New Hebrides (now Vanuatu), New Caledonia, and the Loyalty Islands, and the ancestor of *Bislama*. The names derive from trade in sea slugs and sandalwood, the main products of the islands. Some writers associate *Beach La Mar* with the entire pidgin-speaking area from Papua New Guinea to New Caledonia for the whole of the 19c. See BISLAMA, MELANESIAN PIDGIN, VANUATU. [OCEANIA, VARIETY].   S.R.

BEARER ENGLISH [Date uncertain: from *bearer*, applied in the 18c to a palanquin carrier in India, then to a domestic servant who has charge of his master's clothes, household goods, etc., perhaps from, or influenced by, Bengali *behārā*, from Sanskrit *vyavhārī*. The use has extended to a servant in the kitchen]. A term for the English used by (and sometimes with) servants, shopkeepers, etc., in South Asia. It is marked by the omission of auxiliaries, pronouns, conjunctions, and plural endings, and articles are not generally used. There is extensive code-mixing with Hindustani or the individual's native language. See BUTLER ENGLISH, CODE-MIXING AND CODE SWITCHING, INDIAN ENGLISH[1], PIDGIN. [ASIA, VARIETY].   B.B.K.

BEDE [672?-735]. Old English *Bæda*. Also *the Venerable Bede*. Northumbrian monk and historian, wrote some 35 prose and some verse works in Latin, including Bible commentary and saints' lives, the most famous of which is *Historia Ecclesiastica Gentis Anglorum* (An Ecclesiastical History of the English People, 731), a review of British history from Caesar's invasion in 55 BC to his own day. The history was anonymously translated before 900 and by Thomas Stapleton in 1565. Bede's Bible commentaries influenced later authors, including writers of Middle English sermons and Milton in *Paradise Regained*. See index. [BIOGRAPHY, EUROPE, HISTORY]. W.F.B.

BEEB. See ACRONYM, AUNTIE, BRITISH BROADCASTING.

BEGGING THE QUESTION. (1) Assuming the truth of a point raised in a question or discussion, so that it illogically serves as its own proof: *Good English is the English used by well-spoken people; what well-spoken person doesn't use good English?* Arguing in this way is traditionally referred to as the fallacy of circular reasoning, known in Latin as *petitio principii* (seeking the start) and *circulus in probando* (arguing in a circle). (2) Avoiding giving an answer or facing an issue. Henry Fowler, in *Modern English Usage* (ed. Ernest Gowers, 1965), calls the second sense a misapprehension 'of which many writers need to disabuse themselves'. Contemporary dictionaries differ in discussing the two senses: *Collins English Dictionary* (1986) lists both, putting the fallacy second; *The American Heritage Dictionary* (1985) lists both, the fallacy first; *Webster's Ninth New Collegiate Dictionary* (1984) and *Longman Dictionary of the English Language* (1984) give *evade* as a sense of *beg* but *beg the question* for the fallacy only; *Chambers English Dictionary* (1988) has the fallacy only. [LANGUAGE, STYLE].   T.MCA.

BEHAVIOURISM BrE, **behaviorism** AmE, also **behavio(u)ral psychology** [1910s]. In psychology, a theory that presents behaviour as the product of heredity and environment, and in particular of a process of *conditioning* in which certain stimuli promote certain responses. Ivan Pavlov (1849-1936) was a forerunner, John Watson (1878-1958), was founder, and Burrhus Frederic Skinner (1904-90) was a major proponent of the theory. It influenced ESL teaching from the mid-1950s to the late 1980s, especially in the US, part of an association of structural linguistics, behavioural psychology, and language teaching promoted by Leonard Bloomfield. This led in the 1950s to the *audio-lingual method*, in which human learning was compared to that of rats in laboratory mazes and pigeons taught to play table-tennis. Language learning was seen as a process of habit formation. In 1959, Noam Chomsky challenged both behaviourism and structuralism in a critique of Skinner's work, as a result of which the use of teaching techniques and materials based on behaviourism had by 1980 greatly declined. See BLOOMFIELD, LANGUAGE TEACHING, PSYCHOLINGUISTICS. [EDUCATION]. P.S.

BEHEADMENT AND CURTAILMENT. Word games in which letters are removed from a word to form a shorter word. In *beheadment*, an initial letter is removed: *about* becoming *bout* then *out*. In *curtailment*, a final letter is removed: *codex* becoming *code* then *cod*. The two processes can be used together, sometimes until only a single-letter word is left: *sheathed—sheathe— sheath—heath—heat—eat—at—a*. In a further variant, a letter may be removed from within a word: *startling* becoming *starting* then *staring*. See WORD GAME. [WORD]. T.MCA.

BEHN, Aphra or Afra [1640–89]. English writer, born at Wye in Kent, her surname probably Johnson. She lived for a time in Surinam, and on her return she married a merchant named Behn. She was a secret agent at Antwerp in 1666. *Forced Marriage* (1670) was the first of her fifteen plays, mainly comedies of intrigue, the most successful of which were *The Rover* (1677) and *The City Heiress* (1682). Behn's fiction includes *Oronooko, or the History of the Royal Slave* (*c.*1688), the story of an African prince shipped to the New World, where he rebels and is executed (based loosely on Oroono, the leader of an uprising that took place while she was in South America). The book attacked both slavery and Christian hypocrisy. Woolf described Behn as the first woman to earn her living by writing; she is also widely regarded as the first woman novelist in English. See NOVEL, SURINAME. [BIOGRAPHY, LITERATURE]. R.C.

BELFAST [From Gaelic *Béal Feirste* mouth of (the river) Feirste]. The capital of Northern Ireland, settled in the early 17c with *planters* (settlers) mainly from England. The numbers of Scottish Protestants increased in the 18c and of Irish Catholics in the 19c, the often mutually hostile communities tending to live in different parts of the city. There is a range of usage varying according to level of education, with some homogeneity in working-class speech. Such words as *true* and *drew* sound like 'thrue' and 'dhrew' (an interdental pronunciation), *good* and *cap* sound like 'gyood' and 'kyap' (addition of the semi-vowel /j/), *cheap* and *speak* sound like 'chape' and 'spake' (with the vowel sound /e/), *push* and *took* rhyme with 'rush' and 'luck', *ever* and *yet* sound like 'ivver' and 'yit', *deck* and

penny sound a little like 'dack' and 'panny' (having a close /a/ vowel), *board* and *course* sound like 'boored' and 'koors' (the /ou/ diphthong), *cold* and *hold* sound like 'cowl' and 'howl', *berry/bury* and *cherry* sound like 'barry' and 'charry', *bag* and *can* sounding like 'beg' and 'ken', *off* and *shop* sound like 'aff' and 'shap'. *Y'are not* is commoner than *you're not*. None of the above features are exclusive to Belfast, but their co-occurrence and the rapidity of informal speech distinguish Belfast speakers from other speakers of IrE. These features of pronunciation are associated with the vocabulary and the grammatical patterns described for non-standard Anglo-Irish, but lexical influence from Ulster Scots also occurs, especially in the north and east. See ANGLO IRISH, NORTHERN IRISH ENGLISH, ULSTER SCOTS. [EUROPE, NAME, VARIETY]. L.T.

BELIZE [Pronounced 'Be-LEEZ']. A country of the Central American Caribbean and member of the Commonwealth. Its districts have names deriving from English, Spanish, and Amerindian languages: *Corozal, Orange Walk, Belize, Cayo, Stann Creek, Toledo*. Capital: Belmopan. Currency: the dollar. Economy: timber, agriculture. Population: 180,000 (1988), 200,000 (projection for 2000). Ethnicity: 51% African and mixed, 22% Spanish-Mayan, 13% Amerindian, 3% Chinese, 2% East Indian, 2% Caucasian. Languages: English (official), Creole, Spanish, Mayan, Carib. Education: primary/secondary 84%, tertiary 3%, literacy 80%. Colonized in the 17c by shipwrecked British sailors and disbanded soldiers known as *baymen*. After the Treaty of Paris in 1763, they became loggers. Supported by the Royal Navy, they defeated the Spanish in 1798. The colony of *British Honduras* was established in 1862, changed its name to Belize in 1973, and became independent in 1981. Loan in Belizean English from Central American Spanish include *karbown* charcoal, *kwartel* jailhouse, *potrero* pasture, and from Miskito Indian include *pitpan* canoe, *rahti* a kind of crab, *wawla* boa constrictor. See CARIBBEAN, CENTRAL AMERICA, ENGLISH. [AMERICAS, NAME, VARIETY]. L.D.C., T.MCA.

BELLES LETTRES, also **belles-lettres** [18c: from French, fine letters]. An obsolescent term for literature valued for its formal beauty, refinement, and moral tone, usually applied to short texts such as poems and essays. It was used for literature taught as a necessary acquisition for a person of breeding. At the U. of Edinburgh from 1762 there was a Chair of Rhetoric and Belles Lettres whose named changed in 1865 to Rhetoric and English Literature. Hugh Blair, its first holder, dealt mostly with grammatical propriety. The term *belletrist* is used for both a literary stylist and a literary dilettante. Adjective: *belletristic*. See BLAIR. [LITERATURE].   R.C.

BENGALI. A language of South Asia, the official language of Bangladesh and the state language of West Bengal in India, as well as one of the 15 major languages of India. It has 160m speakers, is written in modified Devanagari script, and its literary tradition dates from the 10c. It is diglossic between literary and colloquial varieties. Its most famous exponent is the poet and Nobel Prize winner Rabindranath Tagore, the first to use colloquial Bengali for literary purposes. Bengali and English have been associated since 1690, when the East India Company founded Calcutta. See BABU ENGLISH, BANGLADESH, INDIAN ENGLISH[1], INDIAN LANGUAGES. [ASIA, LANGUAGE].   Y.K.

BEOWULF. The longest of the known poems in Old English and the first major recorded poem in a European vernacular language. Its 3,182 lines survive in one manuscript (BL Cotton Vitellius A.15) of *c.*1000, which was damaged in a fire in 1731, first transcribed in 1787, and first published in 1815. The poem tells the story of its Geatish hero Beowulf in two parts: ridding the Danes of the monster Grendel and his mother, and a fatal struggle against a fire dragon after he became king of the Geats. Retrospects, anticipations, and digressions mark the course of the narrative, whose style is characterized by parallel constructions, periphrastic figures of speech, and a large vocabulary. Modern interpretations vary, some taking folkloric approaches in the poem, some stressing the pagan setting (associated with the mid-6c), some emphasizing the Christian literary background. See ALLITERATIVE VERSE, ENGLISH, ENGLISH LITERATURE, OLD ENGLISH[1]. [EUROPE, HISTORY, LITERATURE].   W.F.B.

BERLITZ, Maximilian Delphinus (later **David**) [1852–1921]. German-American language teacher and organizer of the Berlitz Method. Born in Württemberg, Germany, he emigrated to the US in the 1870s and opened a language school in Providence, Rhode Island (1878), the first of many in the US and elsewhere. Among the languages taught by conversational means was English as a foreign language. From the first lesson, only the target language was used in class, and no translation was allowed. The teachers were native speakers of the language, and the materials used were so systematized and the directions so precise that it was possible to employ quite young and relatively untried people as teachers. The Berlitz Method has often been referred to as the *Direct Method*, with the

result that it has become associated with the method of the Reform Movement initiated by Wilhelm Viëtor and other scholars from the 1880s onwards. This, however, differed in using phonetic texts and phonetically trained teachers who were usually the same nationality as the learners, in using translation sparingly, and in having broader educational aims. See LANGUAGE TEACHING. [AMERICAS, BIOGRAPHY, EDUCATION, EUROPE].   P.C.

BERMUDA, formerly *Somers Islands.* A self-governing British dependency in the Western Atlantic, comprising 138 islands of which 20 are inhabited and seven linked by causeways and bridges. The main islands are *Main Island* (*Great Bermuda*), *Somerset Island, Ireland Island, St George's Island, St David's Island.* Capital: Hamilton. Currency: the Bermuda dollar. Economy: mixed, finance, tourism. Population: 54,670 (1980). Ethnicity: 66% African, mixed, 34% British, Portuguese. Language: English. The islands were named after Juan Bermudez, the Spanish mariner who discovered them in the early 16c. They were settled in 1612 by the Virginia Company, became a colony in 1684, and gained internal self-government in 1968. Bermudian English mixes BrE and AmE influences. See ENGLISH. [AMERICAS, NAME, VARIETY].   T.MCA.

BERWICKSHIRE BURR. See BURR, R-SOUNDS.

BIBLE [14c: from French *Bible,* Latin *Biblia,* a feminine singular adaptation of Greek neuter plural *Biblia* little papyrus rolls, a description of the Hebrew scriptures]. A collection of sacred texts usually regarded as a unified whole and published as a book consisting of a number of books. For Christians these are in two groups, an Old Testament (OT), whose original texts are Hebrew (and some Aramaic), and a New Testament (NT), whose original texts are Greek. The first five OT books are known in Hebrew as the *Torah* (instruction, law) and in Greek as the *Pentateuch* (five scrolls). Tradition ascribes them to Moses. The first seven make up the *Heptateuch* (seven scrolls). The translation of all OT writings into Greek, including the Apocrypha or non-canonical texts, is known by the Latinate name *Septuagint* (seventy), after the number of scholars believed to have engaged in their translation in Alexandria (3–2c BC). The term *testament* (from Latin *testamentum* a witnessed contract) reflects the Christian belief that God made two covenants with humanity, the first with the Hebrews as a chosen people, the second with the followers of Jesus Christ. When, in the 4–5c, St Jerome translated OT Hebrew and NT Greek into one language, Latin, the Christian scriptures in the West acquired a linguistic homogeneity that strengthened perceptions of the Bible as a single text providing an unbroken account of events and prophecies. Although generally aware of the heterogeneous origins of the Bible, Christians in recent centuries have tended not to dwell on them.

The Bible as scripture. The books of the Bible were accumulated over some 1,300 years and are not set out in the order in which they appear to have been written. Although there are names attached to most of them (such as the OT *Book of Job*, the NT *Gospel according to Mark*), there is no firm evidence of authorship for most of them and little indication of how they were edited into their present forms. Since the 18c, however, there has been close scholarly scrutiny of the texts and their sources. The Bible is a miscellany of genres: story, history, law, prophecy, song, poetry, and letters, making up a sacred 'encyclopedia' which has for centuries been a prime source of reading throughout the world. For Christians, it is the foundation document of their faith; some admit no other authority, while others respect or insist on certain pastoral traditions and later documents. The books of the OT and NT have reached their present number and arrangement by a process of adjustment and elimination over centuries. As a selection from a larger number of texts, they constitute the Christian canon and stand in contrast with the deutero-canonical (secondary) or non-canonical works known as the *Apocrypha* (Greek: hidden), which may or may not appear as an appendix to the OT in Protestant Bibles. Following a long-standing tradition, *The New English Bible* (1970, Oxford and Cambridge University Presses) appends the 15 traditional apocryphal works to the 39 canonical books of the OT, but excludes the various apocryphal gospels from the NT, which are regarded as non-canonical by all mainstream Christian groups. Its successor, *The Revised English Bible* of 1989, excludes both.

The Bible as social archetype. For cultures with their roots in medieval Western Christendom, the word *bible* is both symbolic and archetypal. The symbolism is explicit when the *Longman Dictionary of Geography* is reviewed as 'the geographer's bible' and Plain English campaigners describe Ernest Gowers's *Complete Plain Words* as 'the bible of techniques for clear writing'. It is implicit in the use of the definite article in such expressions as *the Dictionary* and *the telephone directory*, as if such works were as fundamental as *the Bible*. Both name and object are associated in many places with the Christian missions that often paralleled European colonial and commercial expansion. The ties between missionaries and colonialism were lightly touched on by Archbishop Desmond Tutu of South Africa on a visit to the US in 1984: 'When the missionaries first came to Africa they had the Bible and we had the land. They said, "Let us pray." We closed our eyes. When we opened them again we had the Bible and they had the land.'

The Bible as literature. The Bible, whether in the original or in translation, both in itself and because of its influence, is among the great literary achievements of the world. As such, it can be considered in terms of both its genres (poetry, prose, prophecy, gospels, and epistles) and its many translations. In recent decades, a sense of the uniqueness and inviolability of the Bible has given way to scholarly inquiry and an interest in content for its own sake, and the study of the Bible as a text, apart from and/or in addition to its significance as a religious document, has increased. In addition, interest in its language and rhetoric has been stimulated by scholarly study of how this work relates to and has influenced the culture of the peoples who were once part of Western Christendom. As the Canadian critic Northrop Frye has put it:

My interest in the subject began when I found myself teaching Milton and writing about Blake, two authors who were exceptionally Biblical even by the standards of English literature. I soon realized that a student of English literature who does not know the Bible does not understand a great deal of what is going on in what he reads: the most conscientious student will be continually misconstruing the implications, even the meaning (1981, below).

Biblical poetry. The Bible's poetic aspect is most obvious in the Psalms, an anthology of pieces which have for centuries formed part of Jewish and Christian liturgies. There is also poetry in the prophetic books, the *Book of Job*, and elsewhere, but it has often been concealed by the prose form of the older English translations. The *Song of Solomon* is a cycle of love poems to which allegorical meaning was given by the early Church, and in the Authorized Version (AV) has the intensity of medieval and Tudor love lyrics (original spelling):

13 A bundle of myrrhe is my welbeloued vnto me; he shall lie all night betwixt my breasts.
14 My beloued is vnto me, as a cluster of Camphire in the vineyards of Engedi.
15 behold, thou art faire, my loue: behold, thou art faire, thou hast doues eyes.
16 Behold, thou art faire, my beloued; yea pleasant: also our bedde is greene.
17 The beames of our house are Cedar, and our rafters of firre.

Classical Hebrew poetry depends not on rhyme and metre but on parallelism. The phonetic pattern is almost impossible to reproduce in English, but the parallelisms of thought can be seen in familiar versions (modern spelling):

Synonymous. The second half-line emphasizes the first: 'The heavens declare the glory of God: and the firmament showeth his handywork' (Psalms 19: 1).

Antithetical. The second half-line contrasts with the first: 'I see that all things come to an end: but thy commandment is exceeding broad' (Psalms 119: 96).

Synthetic. The second half-line supplements the first with a consequence or example: 'I did call upon the Lord with my voice: and he heard me out of his holy hill' (Psalms 3: 4).

Progressive. Building to a climax by repetition: 'Hear the right, O Lord, consider my complaint: and hearken unto my prayer, that goeth not out of feigned lips' (Psalms 17: 1).

Stepped. Each statement reinforced by a refrain, similar to many Border ballads: 'O give thanks unto the God of all gods: for his mercy endureth for ever. / O thank the Lord of all lords: for his mercy endureth for ever' (Psalms 136: 2–3).

The poetry of the Bible is expressed not only in formal structure. There is much use of imagery, usually direct and simple in keeping with the concrete thought and limited lexical range of OT Hebrew. It reflects the life of a people close to the wilderness, exposed to extremes of climate, and the constant threat of enemies. NT Greek imagery, however, shows a more settled life of agriculture. Much of the linguistic power of the Bible lies in the archetypal nature of its imagery: fire and water, night and day, wind and sun. Similes and metaphors are common and animals and birds are frequent sources of analogy: 'He is like a refiner's fire, and like fullers' soap' (Malachi 3: 2); 'His truth shall be thy shield and buckler' (Psalms 91: 4); 'They were swifter than eagles, they were stronger than lions' (2 Samuel 1: 23).

Biblical prose. Much of the Bible is narrative and its style immediate, like unadorned speech:

OT. And Cain talked with Abel his brother: and it came to pass, when they were in the field, that Cain rose up against Abel his brother, and slew him. And the Lord said unto Cain, Where is Abel thy brother? And he said, I know not (Genesis 4).

NT. And all the city was gathered together at the door. And he healed many that were sick of divers diseases, and cast out many devils; and suffered not the devils to speak, because they knew him (Mark 1).

The force of the stories lies not in embellishment or subtle plotting but in sequential events moving to a climax. They can be exciting and dynamic, often moving to a violent or tragic end like the sacrifice of Jephthah's daughter or the death of Absalom, or to rescue by divine intervention like the story of Abraham and Isaac. There is little detail of characterization; people are described mainly in brief physical terms. The

good and the bad, Moses, David, Jezebel, Elijah, Jonah, and the rest come to life as they are seen acting and responding to the consequences of action.

There are some more sophisticated compositions: the *Book of Ruth* is a compelling and well-knit novella, with a few interacting characters and the finale of a fruitful marriage after tribulation. The *Book of Job* has the qualities of epic drama as Job (with a background chorus of friends) wrestles with disaster and his changing attitude to God, who at the end intervenes like a classical *deus ex machina.* Even the historical books have tragic attributes: David is punished for his hubris in numbering the people; Samson wins great victories but a fatal weakness exposes him to the wiles of a false woman and the catastrophe of blindness and captivity, followed by triumph in death. The constant wars and feuds of the ancient world have the grim vigour of the heroic sagas.

Prophecy. This distinctive genre is less concerned with foretelling events than with warnings of consequences if wrong behaviour persists; its denunciations are akin to the 20c dystopias of Aldous Huxley and George Orwell, though the impetus is theological, not sociopolitical. There is imagination and poetry in both the positive and negative visions of the prophets, as in the *Book of Isaiah* (from ch. 40):

1 Comfort ye, comfort ye my people, saith your God.

2 Speak ye comfortably to Jerusalem, and cry unto her, that her warfare is accomplished, that her iniquity is pardoned: for she hath received of the Lord's hand double for all her sins.

3 The voice of him that crieth in the wilderness, Prepare ye the way of the Lord, make straight in the desert a highway for our God.

4 Every valley shall be exalted, and every mountain and hill shall be made low: and the crooked shall be made straight, and the rough places plain.

The Gospels and Epistles. The books of the NT were written with urgency and immediacy, to spread the good news (gospel) of recent events and in expectation of the end of the world. The parables of Jesus, based on a tradition of moral tales, contain many vignettes of contemporary life: the sower, the shepherd and his flock, the woman seeking a lost coin, the farmer hiring labourers. The Gospels (Matthew, Mark, Luke, John) are a genre without counterparts in the ancient world, written not so much as biography but to awake belief. Much of the NT is in the form of pastoral letters (the Epistles), written with conviction rather than in the forms of strict classical rhetoric. There are, however, many indications of literary skill. Thus, Luke's report of Paul's speech at Athens (Acts 17: 22–31) has the established oratorical pattern of *exordium, narratio, divisio,* and *conclusio.*

Influence. In addition to its literary quality, the Bible has been an influence on English literature and culture. Stories and characters from the Bible have been treated imaginatively by writers ranging from John Milton (*Paradise Lost* 1667, *Paradise Regained* 1671, *Samson Agonistes* 1671), to Christopher Smart (*A Song to David* 1763), Lord Byron (*Cain* 1821), and in the 20c James Bridie (*Jonah and the Whale* 1932) and Christopher Fry (*A Sleep of Prisoners* 1951). The style of the AV has influenced many, most noticeably John Bunyan's use of a Biblical style of narrative in *The Pilgrim's Progress* (1678–84). Swift praised the simplicity of Biblical English in *A Proposal for Correcting the English Tongue* (1712). The complex and eclectic style of Thomas Carlyle has the Bible as one of its strands. John Ruskin acknowledged the effect of frequent Bible reading in his early life and his prose sometimes echoes its more sonorous and stately passages.

The language of hymnology has often been strongly Biblical, especially in the compositions of John and Charles Wesley and Isaac Watts. Because the Bible was for so long a part of the common cultural heritage of English-speaking people, allusions and direct quotations are frequent in all literary genres. The speech of fictional characters includes many such references, often incidentally and naturally, but sometimes satirically exaggerated, as in Dickens's *Bleak House* (1853) and the Evangelical Cambridge group in Samuel Butler's *The Way of All Flesh* (1903).

Popular usage continues to incorporate Biblical allusions such as *coals of fire, a soft answer, a broken reed, the root of all evil, a word in season, the eleventh hour, a thorn in the flesh, cover a multitude of sins, the old Adam, riotous living.* Page headings in the AV have contributed *the Prodigal Son* and *the Good Samaritan,* the latter adopted in part by the helping organization, the Samaritans. Many English forenames are derived from the Bible: the continuingly popular *John, Mary, Peter, James, Elizabeth, Thomas, David,* and the less frequent or once fashionable *Abraham, Isaac, Daniel, Rebecca, Enoch, Nathaniel, Martha.* The less virtuous characters of the Bible, like Jezebel, Herod, and Judas, have not been adopted, but Thomas Hardy introduces a character christened *Cain* in *Far from the Madding Crowd* (1874), because his mother got confused and thought that it was Abel who killed Cain.

Translation. Much of the literary quality of the Bible is lost in translation, even in the 'Biblical' prose of the King James Version. English cannot reproduce the cadence of Hebrew poetry, such puns as the comparison of Peter to a rock (Greek *Pétros/pétra*), or the acrostic in the closing verses of *Proverbs.* However, in the 1611 version and other translations, writers have created a Bible tradition native to English, in which such themes as conflict and triumph, suffering and joy, can seize the imagination of readers with no knowledge of Hebrew or Greek, just as translation has served, in secular terms, to pass on through English the epics of Homer. The vigour and simplicity of OT Hebrew and NT Greek have to a great extent been successfully conveyed in Biblical English, especially in narrative. Both often had a direct paratactic style, with strong, concrete images and vivid, physical metaphors. There is often repetitive and incremental emphasis, as in: 'Hast thou not knowen? hast thou not heard, that the euerlasting God, the Lord, the Creatour of the ends of the earth, fainteth not, neither is wearie?' (Isaiah 40: 28), and balanced antithesis, as in: 'The Lord will not suffer the soule of the righteous to famish: but he casteth away the substance of the wicked. Hee becommeth poore that dealeth with a slack hand: but the hand of the diligent maketh rich' (Proverbs 10: 3–4).

Translators. The early translations were made at a time of change, as the language moved from its 'Middle' to its 'Modern' phases, when printing and standardizing were becoming central elements in the spread of literacy, and when religious protest then reformation inspired the translators. They preferred the vernacular to a high Latinate style, because they wished their work to reach, and be understood by, the mass of the people. In the view of the martyred 16c translator William Tyndale, ordinary English was better suited to translate both Hebrew and Greek than Latin and German, because: 'In a thousand places thou needest but to translate it into English word for word' (in 'Obedience of a Christian Man', 1528). Like the originals, Tyndale's style was paratactic and immediate. His frequent use of 'and' (following the Hebrew) may have influenced later generations of writers of English prose (compare the AV rendering of Mark, on p. 118). The early translators also influenced general vocabulary: the common word *nowadays* goes back to Wycliffe, and Tyndale's use of *beautiful* rather than the earlier and commoner *belle* and *fair* helped establish the word. *Peacemaker, long-suffering,* and *scapegoat* are other examples of his inventiveness. The vocabulary of the AV is relatively small, some 6,000 words of which a high proportion are vernacular.

Quotation and allusion. For centuries, the Bible was read both aloud and silently, and people were used to hearing long excerpts from it in sermons and speeches. After the establishment of lectern Bibles in all churches in 1538 and then the publication of the AV in 1611, the Bible was so well known that even unattributed quotations and allusions were instantly recognized. When Sir Richard Grenville said, 'Let me fall into the hand of God not the hand of Spain' (1591), he was adapting David's words in 2 Samuel (24: 14). The style of the AV directly influenced many writers, most prominently John Bunyan in *The Pilgrim's Progress* (1678), which opens:

As I walked through the wilderness of this world I lighted on a certain place where was a den, and laid me down in that place to sleep; and, as I slept, I dreamed a dream. I dreamed, and behold I saw a man clothed with rags standing in a certain place, with his face from his own house, a book in his hand, and a great burden upon his back.

The early translations. The translations of the Bible in the 15–17c have been a powerful influence on the development of English. The entire corpus of Modern English prose has grown up since, and been influenced by, the works of Tyndale and Coverdale, and during the formative period of the early translations there was little other widely available reading matter. Through private and public reading, the successive early translations introduced the general population to a range of genres, styles, and subjects distinct from song, folk-tale, and popular romance. The 16c Bible in particular provided a model of expression which was the chief written source of formal English for many people well into the 19c. There were translations of parts of the Bible in Anglo-Saxon times, associated with Alfred and Aelfric. Between the 11c and 13c, when Norman French was the dominant language and Latin the language of religious authority, translation into English lapsed, and though copies of earlier translations appear to have circulated, they have not survived. The translation into the 14c dialect of the East Midlands and London by John Wycliffe and such helpers as Nicholas Hereford and John Purvey was the first attempt to produce the complete Bible in English. It was hugely popular and widely circulated by itinerant *bible-men*, with manuscript copies of the NT selling for six months' wages; one copy of a few chapters sold for a load of hay. This translation was also important in helping to fix the dialect used as standard and spread it through England. Wycliffe's Bible was more often heard and listened to than read privately, and so influenced both those who could and those who could not read. Despite its being proscribed with severe penalties, some 170 manuscripts have survived.

Sixteenth-century Bibles. Wycliffe's translation was from the Vulgate and was not printed until after it had been superseded by the translations of Tyndale and Coverdale. These were made under the influence of the 'new learning' from Greek and Hebrew; Coverdale's was the first published translation into English and both translations had to be printed abroad, being at first smuggled into England as 'waste paper'. The first translation printed in England, in 1536, was a reprint of Tyndale's NT of 1534. Once Bible printing in England was legalized in 1537, publishing enterprise resulted in fresh editions such as *Matthew's Bible* (a synthesis of Tyndale and Coverdale with a commentary) and *Taverner's Bible*, a revised printed version of Matthew's.

The *Great Bible* of 1539 was the first officially authorized version, produced by a group headed by Coverdale and based on Matthew's. Largely printed abroad, where the technology was more advanced, this work went into seven editions in two years, because it was required in all churches and other versions were proscribed by law. The division of the Bible into chapters dates from the 13c, attributed both to Stephen Langton, Archbishop of Canterbury (d. 1228), and Hugo de Sancto Caro, who produced a concordance of the Vulgate in 1244. OT verses were numbered in the early 16c in Hebrew and in Latin, and Robert Estienne numbered the verses in his French NT in 1551. The numbering of verses was adopted in the English NT of 1557, the work of refugees in Geneva who undertook the revision of the entire English Bible, culminating in the *Geneva Bible* of 1560, which had both chapter and verse numbered. This work was also known as the *Breeches Bible*, because it described Adam and Eve as sewing themselves breeches. It included marginal notes which commended it to the Puritans, who wished to study it without need of priestly interpretation.

The King James Bible (also *The Authorized Version*; short forms *KJB, AV*). The popularity of the Geneva Bible prompted Archbishop Parker to revive a long-discussed project for an authorized revision approved by the English bishops. The Bishops' Bible was first published in 1568, a revision of Coverdale's Great Bible of 1539. One of the first acts of James VI King of Scots, on accession to the throne of England in 1603 as James I, was to approve a suggestion for a new translation, 'as consonant as can be to the original Hebrew and Greek . . . and only to be used in all churches of England'. He apparently appointed 54 'learned men' to work on the project, 50 of whom have been identified. They included scholars from Oxford, Cambridge, and Westminster (prominent among them Lancelot

Andrewes, John Hardinge, John Harmer, John Reynolds, Henry Saville, Miles Smith, and Robert Spalding), working in five committees which invited comment and observations from the clergy in general as the work progressed. The rules for the project included: (1) Following the 1572 edition of the Bishops' Bible so far as fidelity to the original sources would allow. (2) The division into chapters to be altered only where strictly necessary. (3) Where specially difficult passages occurred, consultation to follow with 'any Learned Man in the Land, for his Judgement of such a place' (*Rules to be Observed in the Translation of the Bible*). (4) Where a Hebrew or Greek word admitted of more than one possible meaning, one to be in the text, the other in the margin. (5) Any words that had to be inserted for colloquial reasons to be printed in italics. The new work appeared in 1611.

The KJB has been acclaimed as a landmark in both religious literature and the evolution of the English language, an achievement that comprises all earlier Bible translation and that has served for many as a standard against which all subsequent Bible translation must be judged. Many also consider that its verbal beauty is unsurpassed in the whole of English literature. It has provided many quotations and allusions which have become proverbial, and has been quoted, knowingly and unknowingly, in literature and in conversation at every level for centuries, from pubs to Parliament. Well-known quotations include:

Genesis. And the evening and the morning were the first day; Be fruitful, and multiply, and replenish the earth; bone of my bones and flesh of my flesh. *Exodus*. Let my people go; the burning bush; the golden calf; Eye for eye, tooth for tooth. *Ruth*. For whither thou goest I will go. *Job*. Man is born unto trouble, as the sparks fly upward. *Proverbs*. Go to the ant thou sluggard; consider her ways, and be wise. *Ecclesiastes*. Vanity of vanities; all is vanity. *Isaiah*. For unto us a child is born, unto us a son is given. *Jeremiah*. Is there no balm in Gilead? *Matthew*. Repent ye: for the kingdom of heaven is at hand; The voice of one crying in the wilderness, Prepare ye the way of the Lord (quoting Isaiah). *Mark*. My name is Legion; Suffer the little children to come unto me. *Luke*. Judge not, and ye shall not be judged; For the labourer is worthy of his hire. *John*. In the beginning was the Word; I am the way, the truth, and the life. *Paul* (*1 Corinthians*). Though I speak with the tongues of men and of angels; For now we see through a glass darkly. *Revelation*. And I saw a new heaven and a new earth: for the first heaven and the first earth were passed away.

Bible publication. In England, the publishing rights of the AV are vested in the Crown and in practice limited to the printing house holding the royal appointment, together with the universities of Oxford and Cambridge, whose privilege under their 16c charters allowed them to publish bibles. This exclusive right of printing the Bible had earlier come into being in the reign of Elizabeth I. Since 1769, the Royal Printers have been Eyre and Spottiswoode, in London. In Scotland, the Lord Advocate, representing the Crown, holds the patent and approves the choice of publishers, in practice the Glasgow publisher William Collins. In the US, no such restrictions have been placed on the publishing of the Bible; many publishers have brought out editions of the AV, amending it on their own initiative and responsibility. On many occasions, editions of the AV have contained misprints which have led to their receiving special names, such as the *Wicked Bible* (1632), so called because the word 'not' was omitted in the Seventh Commandment, making it read *Thou shalt commit adultery*; the *Vinegar Bible* (1717), so called because the Parable of the Vineyard became *The Parable of the Vinegar*; and the *Printer's Bible*, where a misprint makes the Psalmist complain that *printers have persecuted me without cause*, as opposed to *princes*.

Later translations. The publication of the AV, though intended to be definitive, did not put an end to Bible translation, especially by Protestant nonconformists and would-be popularizers: for example, John Wesley, founder of Methodism, who in 1755 published his own NT for 'unlettered men who understand only their mother tongue'. Subsequent translations, from the *Revised Version* (1884) through to late 20c versions, have not had the aim of producing work in an improved literary style, but of claiming greater fidelity to the original Hebrew or Greek as understood by the most recent scholarship. Some of these claims have been contested and the translations have made no special impact on the language. The *Revised Version* was the result of over ten years' work by Protestant scholars in the UK and US, following a decision in the Church of England in 1870 to set up a group of its members to work with others, irrespective of nation or religious affiliation. The revised OT was based on virtually the same Hebrew text as the AV, but the NT translators worked on a considerably reconstructed Greek text (itself the subject of controversy) and adopted the plan (rejected by the 1611 translators) of always translating the same Greek word by the same English word, which it was claimed preserved the meaning more faithfully. This version was less well received than had been hoped.

The Presbyterian scholar James Moffat brought out a colloquial translation in 1913 and the Anglican priest J. B. Phillips produced a NT in contemporary English in 1958. By contrast, *The New English Bible* (1961), *The Good News Bible* (1976), and the *New International Version* (1978) were produced by panels of scholars, each with the aim of a Bible in the language of the present day. NEB resulted from an inter-denominational conference initiated by the Church of Scotland and had the aim of aiding private study and scholarship rather than reading aloud. GNB was produced by William Collins and the United Bible Societies, based on the latter's simplified and colloquial versions originally aimed at the mission field, where users were mostly not speakers of English as a first language. NIV was intended to attract readers without prior religious commitment. All three followed the precedent of the RV in relying to an increasing extent on reconstructed or redis-covered texts unavailable to, or rejected by, the translators of the KJB.

Anglo-Jewish versions of the OT began to appear in the 19c. A translation by Isaac Leeser, a US rabbi and educator, was completed in 1853 and became the standard American Jewish Bible for over 50 years. By the turn of the century, progress in Bible scholarship made a new trans-lation imperative, and a committee of scholars representing both traditional and Reform Juda-ism was organized in 1903 by the Jewish Pub-lication Society of America to undertake a new translation. This version, based on the Masoretic text, but taking into account rabbinical com-mentary as well as modern scholarship, was deeply influenced in language and style by the AV and RV. It was published in 1917 and remains the most popular and authoritative Eng-lish translation of the OT among Jews.

Inclusive language. In the last two decades, efforts have been made to produce 'non-sexist' versions of the Bible in English, to meet the theo-logical and social contention of feminists and others that male terms for the Deity are inad-equate and inappropriate, for example *Give thanks unto the Lord; call upon his name: make known his deeds* (Psalm 105: 1), because they attribute maleness to a being believed to be above considerations of gender. The problems of reconciling fidelity to the original Hebrew and Greek with inclusive late 20c usage have proved considerable and controversial, relating not only to specific Biblical texts but also to general assumptions in Christianity and other religions about the nature and naming of Divinity.

The strata of translation. The following trans-lations of the Gospel of Matthew (25: 14-15) show how language, style, and interpretation have changed over six centuries of translation into English.

Ὥσπερ γὰρ ἄνθρωπος ἀποδημῶν ἐκάλεσε τοὺς ἰδίους δούλους, καὶ παρέδωκεν αὐτοῖς τὰ ὑπάρχοντα αὐτοῦ· καὶ ᾧ μὲν ἔδωκε πέντε τάλαντα, ᾧ δὲ δύο, ᾧ δὲ ἕν, ἑκάστῳ κατὰ τὴν ἰδίαν δύναμιν· καὶ ἀπεδήμησεν εὐθέως.

1380. Sothely as a man goynge fer in pilgrimage, clepide his seruauntis, and bitoke to hem his goodis; And to oon he ʒaue fyue talentis, for-sothe to an other two, but to an other oon, to eche after his owne vertu; and went forth anoon. (Wycliffe)

1526. Lykewise as a certeyne man redy to take his iorney to a straunge countre, called hys seruantes to hym, and delyvered to them hys gooddes; And vnto won he gave v. talentes, to another ij, and to another one, to every man after his abilite; and streyght waye departed. (Tyndale)

1611. 14 For *the kingdome of heauen is* as a man trauailing into a farre countrey, who called his owne seruants, and deliuered vnto them his goods. 15 And vnto one he gaue fiue talents, to another two, and to another one, to euery man according to his seuerall ability, & straightway tooke his iourney. (King James)

1913. For the case is that of a man going abroad, who summoned his servants and handed over his property to them; to one he gave twelve hundred pounds, to another five hundred, and to another two hundred and fifty; each got according to his capacity. Then the man went abroad. (Moffat)

1941. 14. For it is as when a man, about to take a journey, got his servants together, and gave them his property. 15. And to one he gave five pounds, to another two, to another one; to everyone as he was able; and he went on his journey. (Basic English)

1958. It is just like a man going abroad who called his household servants together before he went and handed his property over to them to manage. He gave one five thousand pounds, another two thousand and another one thou-sand—according to their respective abilities. Then he went away. (Phillips)

1970. "It is like a man going abroad, who called his servants and put his capital in their hands; to one he gave five bags of gold, to another two, to another one, each according to his capacity. Then he left the country." (New English Bible)

1976. 14 "At that time the Kingdom of heaven will be like this. Once there was a man who was about to go on a journey; he called his servants and put them in charge of his property. 15He gave to each one according to his ability: to one he gave five thousand gold coins, to another he gave two thousand, and to another he gave one thousand. Then he left on his journey." (The Good News Bible: BrE)

1982. "For it will be as when a man going on a journey called his servants and entrusted to them his property; to one he gave five talents, to another two, to another one, to each according to his ability. Then he went away." (Reader's Digest Bible)

1983. Or again, it is like this. A man at wis gaein out o the kintra ca's up his servans an haundit his haudin owre tae them tae gyde. He lippent ane wi five talents, anither wi twa, an a third wi ane—ilkane wi the soum confeirin til his capacitie. Syne he gaed his waas out o the kintra. (William L. Lorimer, *The New Testament in Scots*)

1989. [14]"It is like a man going abroad, who called his servants and entrusted his capital to them; [15]to one he gave five bags of gold, to another two, to another one, each according to his ability. Then he left the country.' (The Revised English Bible)

Conclusion. The existence of vernacular Bibles was important for the growth, enrichment, and even preservation of many of the languages of Europe, and the early translations into English were profoundly important for the development of the language. In English, both the established churches and nonconformists in 17–18c Britain, Ireland, and North America emphasized Bible study and reading aloud, and so encouraged a culture focused on the printed word. Bible translation in its most active stage coincided with both the development of printing and the need for standard languages in the nation-states of late medieval and Renaissance Europe. Because the Protestant nonconformists took the Bible (Geneva or AV) as their standard, it strongly influenced such writers as John Milton, George Fox, John Bunyan, and Richard Baxter, and through them later polemical and political writers in the UK, USA, and elsewhere. Its influence is also evident in the works of 19–20c writers as diverse as John Betjeman, George Eliot, T. S. Eliot, Thomas Hardy, Rudyard Kipling, Sean O'Casey, Dylan Thomas, Mark Twain, Evelyn Waugh, and P. G. Wodehouse. At least three factors contributed to the survival influence of the Bible on English from the 16c to the 20c century: the 16–17c legal requirement that all should attend the parish church, later transmuted into a widely respected social custom; the use of the Bible in legally required school assemblies till well after the Second World War; and compulsory church parades in the armed services of the British Empire until the 1950s. These ensured that vast numbers of people for generation after generation were exposed to the English of the King James Bible

as a living variety. It is to these factors, as much as to studies and use by scholars and writers, that the widespread survival of Biblical usage and allusion can be attributed.

See ALLUSION, AMERICAN ENGLISH, ARAMAIC, ARCHAISM, BABEL, BEDE, BIBLICAL ENGLISH, BOOK, BOOK OF COMMON PRAYER, BUNYAN, CAMBRIDGE UNIVERSITY PRESS, CANON, CENSORSHIP, CHAUCER, COLLINS, CONCORDANCE, COVERDALE, CRANMER, DRAMA, ENGLISH LITERATURE, EPITAPH, EUPHUISM, FANTASY, FREE VERSE, FRYE, GLOSSOLALIA, GREEK, HEBREW, HISTORY, HOMILY, HYMN, HYPERBATON, INCLUSIVE LANGUAGE, JEWISH LANGUAGES, LETTER[2], LORIMER, MILTON, OXFORD UNIVERSITY PRESS, POLYGLOT, PROSE, PROVERB, PSALM, PUN, RASTA TALK, SAXONISM, SCRIPTURE, SERMON, SHIBBOLETH, STANDARD, TRANSLATION, TYNDALE, WYCLIFFE. [HISTORY, LITERATURE, MEDIA].   R.C., M.LA, T.MCA.

Alter, Robert, & Kermode, Frank (eds.). 1987. *The Literary Guide to the Bible*. London & Glasgow: Collins.

Barker, William P. 1966. *Everyone in the Bible*. New Jersey: Fleming H. Revell.

Bruce, F. 1979. *History of the Bible in English*. London: Lutterworth Press.

Fox, Roland L. 1991. *The Unauthorized Version: Truth and Fiction in the Bible*. London & New York: Viking Penguin.

Frye, Northrop. 1981. *The Great Code: The Bible and Literature*. Toronto: Academic Press. London: Routledge & Kegan Paul.

Hammond, G. 1982. *The Making of the English Bible*. Manchester: Carcanet New Press.

Josipovici, Gabriel. 1988. *The Book of God: A Response to the Bible*. New Haven, Conn.: Yale University Press.

Levine, Mark L., & Rachlis, Eugene. 1986. *The Complete Book of Bible Quotations*. London: Robert Hale.

Mombert, J. I. 1906. *English Versions of the Bible*. London: Bagster & Sons.

Moulton, W. F. 1911. *The History of the English Bible*. London: Charles H. Kelly.

Pollard, A. W. 1911. *Records of the English Bible*. Oxford: Henry Frowde.

Robinson, H. Wheeler (ed.). 1940. *The Bible in its Ancient and English Versions*. Oxford: Clarendon Press.

Storr, V. F. (ed.). 1938. *The English Bible*. London: Methuen.

BIBLICAL ENGLISH. The register of English based on the Authorized Version (AV) of the Bible (1611), as in: 'And Jesus entered and passed through Jericho. And, behold, there was a man named Zacchaeus, which was the chief among the publicans, and he was rich. And he sought to see Jesus who he was; and could not for the press, because he was little of stature' (Luke 19: 1–3, modern spelling). Since the AV, translations have to a greater or less degree departed from this style, and so, paradoxically, many English-language Bibles are not in Biblical English. The New English Bible (1961) translates the same passage of Luke as: 'Entering Jericho he made his way through the city. There was a man there named Zacchaeus; he was superintendent of taxes and very rich. He was eager to see what Jesus looked like; but, being a little man, he could not see him for the crowd.'

Elevated Jacobean English. By and large, Biblical English is elevated Jacobean English, comparable to the style of Shakespeare and Thomas Browne. The AV, however, had a tradition of its own, evolving from or related to earlier works whose style is also recognizably Biblical: for example, the *Great Bible* of 1539 and the *First Prayer Book* of 1549 (later the *Book of Common Prayer* of the Anglican communion). Biblical English, therefore, is not a variety which appeared suddenly in the early 17c, but evolved from the Wycliffite translations of the 14c, and in various forms has continued into the 20c. Two main factors have shaped it: the style of the original texts and the ideology and situation of the early translators. In addition, English literature is full of quotations in which Bible sentences or phrases are worked into an author's own language: Shakespeare, 'come *the four corners of the world* in arms' (*King John*, c.1595); Trollope, 'Vavasour's friends knew that *his goings-out and his comings-in* were seldom accounted for openly' (*Can You Forgive Her?* 1864); Kipling, a book title, *Thy Servant a Dog* (1930); Wodehouse: 'I was one of the idle rich. I *toiled not, neither did I*—except for a bump supper at Cambridge—*spin*' (*Leave it to Psmith*, 1923).

The AV had a lasting effect on people's passive vocabulary, and more than any other text (apart from the Book of Common Prayer) has been responsible for the ongoing capacity to recognize and interpret *thou* and *-est* (*whither thou goest I will go*), *-eth* (*I say to this man, Go, and he goeth; and to another, Come, and he cometh*), and inverted negation and interrogation (*I think not; What say you?*). In addition, preachers, writers, and others grew accustomed to inserting elements from the AV into everyday language: (1) Words: *beget, apostle, parable, talent*. (2) Names: personal like *Ruth, Rebecca, Samuel, Simon*, such names serving as the baptismal names of millions; place-names like *Bethesda, Bethlehem, Eden, Salem*, such names often being given to settlements established by Bible-reading colonists. (3) Noun phrases: *broken reed, burnt offering, fatted calf, stony ground*. (4) Linking statements: *and it came to pass; I looked, and behold; then he answered and said*. (5) Proverb-like phrases: *a word in season, don't hide your light under a bushel, gird up your loins, not my brother's keeper, a multitude of sins*.

A whole European culture of Bible-influenced languages spread to every continent in the world, its members sharing an appreciation of allusions to an enormous range of topics such as *Noah's Ark, the Tower of Babel, the waters of Babylon, the writing on the wall*, and *the money-changers in the Temple*. A symbol system from the Bible in the language of the AV has tended, at least as much as that of classical Greek and Latin, to dominate writers' minds; as C. S. Lewis has pointed out, English authors in elevated contexts have tended to use the symbols *corn and wine* rather than 'beef and beer', *sword* rather than 'gun' or 'pike', *bread* rather than 'potatoes', *trumpet* rather than 'bugle', and *stone* rather than 'brick' (Ethel M. Wood Lecture, 1950). Samuel Taylor Coleridge contended that intense study of the Bible would elevate the style of any writer (*Table Talk*, 1830).

Modern developments. Biblical English is, however, most immediately recognized as extended discourse rather than as words, phrases, and styles. Many late 20c users of English recognize the vocabulary, the grammar, and the cadences of Biblical English without supposing that it has a living presence beyond church services, or that it is a resource on which various groups draw. In the 19c and 20c, however, at least three movements have adopted Biblical styles:

1. The US civil rights movement, as exemplified in the language of preachers such as Martin Luther King Jr. The following is from a speech by Martin Luther King Sr., when his son received the Nobel Prize: 'I always wanted to make a contribution. And all you got to do if you want to contribute, you got to ask the Lord, and let Him know, and the Lord heard me and in some kind of way I don't even know he laid His hand on me and my wife and He gave us Martin Luther King and our prayers were answered.'

2. The Church of Latter-Day Saints, especially in *The Book of Mormon: Another Testament of Jesus Christ* (as published by Joseph Smith in 1830): 'For behold, it came to pass that the Lord spake unto my father, yea, even in a dream, and said unto him: Blessed art thou Lehi, because of the things which thou hast done; and because thou hast been faithful and declared unto this people the things which I commanded thee, behold, they seek to take away thy life' (First Book of Nephi, 2: 1).

3. The Baha'i World Faith, in a policy adopted in the early 20c of translating the writings of the founder Bahá'u'lláh and his son 'Abdu'l-Bahá, as in: 'Ye are but vassals, O Kings of the earth! He Who is the King of Kings hath appeared, arrayed in His most wondrous glory, and is summoning you unto Himself, the Help

in Peril, the Self-Subsisting' (Bahá'u'lláh, 'Proclamation to the Kings and Leaders of Religion', c.1860).

Compare BUNYAN. See BIBLE. [HISTORY, STYLE, VARIETY].   T.MCA., M.LA., R.C.

BIBLIOGRAPHY [17c: from Greek *bibliographia* ('book-writing') a written list of books]. (1) A branch of library science dealing with the description, history, comparison, and classification of documents. (2) A list, sometimes as comprehensive as possible, but usually selective (a *select bibliography*), of documents compiled according to a particular need and/or principle of classification, such as 20c books on gardening published in Britain or the printed sources used in a piece of research or a published work. Most bibliographies are relatively straightforward lists, but some, such as *The Year's Work in English Studies* (published by the English Association), embody general surveys and critical reviews. All such lists are organized alphabetically, but may otherwise vary greatly. Usually keyed to authors' names, they may also be organized according to subject, place of publication, publisher, or some other criterion; in an electronic database, a bibliography may be variously tagged, to make its information accessible according to authors, topics in titles, publishers, etc. Bibliographies ordered according to surname take many forms, according to rules laid down by academic and other institutions, practices favoured in publishers' house styles, or authors' preferences. Such lists may be long enough to be documents in their own right or published as works of reference, but most are appendices to books, articles, and dissertations. In this volume, many of the longer entries (such as *Bible*) have bibliographies that provide authors' names in full (if known), dates of first publication (if known), titles, places of publication, and publishers. Below are four possible formats for the same title:

Watson, James, & Hill, Anne (eds.). 1984. *A Dictionary of Communication and Media Studies*. London: Edward Arnold.
Watson, J., and Hill, A. (eds.). *A Dictionary of Communication and Media Studies* (London: Edward Arnold, 1984).
Watson, J., and Hill, A., *A Dictionary of Communication and Media Studies*, London, 1984.
Watson, James, and Hill, Anne. *A Dictionary of Communication and Media Studies* (London, 1984).

Most print formats agree in italicizing titles (underlined or italicized in typescript). The cardinal requirement of a bibliography, whatever the nature or purpose of the list, is the consistent use of one style. See APPENDIX, BACK MATTER, BRITISH LIBRARY, CATALOG(UE), INDEX, LIBRARY, NOTES AND REFERENCES, REFERENCE GUIDE FOR ENGLISH STUDIES, YEAR'S WORK IN ENGLISH STUDIES, [REFERENCE, STYLE, WRITING].   T.MCA.

BICULTURALISM [1950s: on the analogy of *bilingualism*]. (1) Two cultures in one area, such as those of French and English in Montreal, Quebec. In such situations, mixing may result in a third, hybrid culture. (2) Familiarity with and membership of two cultures, often including a knowledge of two languages or varieties of the same language. In situations of hostility between communities, bicultural individuals, marriages, groups, and institutions may be insecure and perceived as insufficiently loyal to one side or the other. See BILINGUALISM, CULTURE, MULTICULTURALISM. [LANGUAGE].   L.E.S., T.MCA.

BIERCE, Ambrose (Gwinnett) [1842–1914]. American journalist and satirist, born in Meigs County, Ohio, and raised in Kosciusko County, Indiana. After a year in high school, he became a printer's devil on a local newspaper. In the Civil War, he served with the Indiana Volunteers, becoming a major in 1867. He worked as a journalist and editor mainly in San Francisco, with three years in London (1872–5) and some time as an unsuccessful gold miner in the Black Hills of Dakota. From 1887 to 1896 he wrote the 'Prattler' column in William Randolph Hearst's *San Francisco Examiner*, after which he moved to Washington, DC. In 1913, claiming to have tired of life in the US, he went to Mexico at the height of the revolution led by Pancho Villa, and vanished, probably killed at the siege of Ojinaga. Bierce is renowned for an acid and misanthropic style. His many publications include *In the Midst of Life* (1891), a collection of short stories, and *The Devil's Dictionary* (1906), a volume of mordant comment on humanity that evolved from his newspaper writings. It has often been reprinted. The *Enlarged Devil's Dictionary*, edited by E. J. Hopkins, appeared in 1967. It contains 1,851 words and definitions addressed to 'enlightened souls who prefer dry wines to sweet, sense to sentiment, wit to humour'. Typical entries: '*Conservative* A statesman who is enamored of existing evils, as distinguished from the Liberal, who wishes to replace them with others'; '*Fable* A brief lie intended to illustrate some important truth'; '*Tedium* Ennui, the state or condition of one that is bored. Many fanciful derivations of the word have been affirmed, but so high an authority as Father Jape says that it comes from a very obvious source—the first words of the ancient Latin *Te Deum Laudamus*. In this apparently natural derivation there is something that saddens.' See index. [AMERICAS, BIOGRAPHY, REFERENCE, STYLE].   T.MCA.

BIG WORD. See LONG WORD.

BILABIAL [19c: from Latin *bilabialis* two-lipped]. A term in phonetics for a sound made with both lips: for example, /m/ as in *move*. See LABIAL. [SPEECH].   G.K.

BILDUNGSROMAN [20c: from German *Bildung* growth, *Roman* novel]. Also **Erziehungsroman** [education novel]. A novel showing the development of its central character, usually from childhood to maturity, as in Goethe's *Wilhelm Meister* (1795–6). It differs from earlier personal narratives like Defoe's *Moll Flanders* (1722) in its psychological approach and its movement towards a goal. The term covers some 19c novels with different narrative points of view: Dickens wrote *Great Expectations* (1861) in the first person, George Eliot *The Mill on the Floss* (1860) in the third person, and Samuel Butler used a mature first person to describe his younger self in *The Way of All Flesh* (1903). James Joyce's *Portrait of the Artist as a Young Man* (1916) is a type of *Kunstlerroman* (artist novel), in which the protagonist is an aspiring writer. See AUTOBIOGRAPHY, BIOGRAPHY, MEMOIR, NOVEL. [LITERATURE].   R.C.

BILINGUAL DICTIONARY, sometimes **translation dictionary**. A dictionary that defines a selection of the vocabulary of two languages, usually each through the other, as in the *Collins Robert French Dictionary* (1978). In English as in many other languages, one-way bilingual dictionaries preceded monolingual dictionaries, as with the *Ortus vocabulorum* (Garden of Words) before 1450 and the *Catholicon anglicum* (English Universal) for Latin in 1483, then dictionaries for Welsh (1547), French (1570, 1580, 1593), Spanish (1591, 1599), and Italian (1598), all before the first English-only dictionary in 1604. Bidirectional or two-way works developed later. Bilingual dictionaries have been compiled for English and many European, Asian, African, and Amerindian languages, some developing distinct traditions due particularly to special scripts and conventions, as for Chinese and Japanese, in which non-English entries are arranged not in alphabetical sequence, but on the basis of the structure of the written characters. The difficulty of finding direct equivalents between the words of two languages is constant. Lexical equivalents are rarely one-to-one, and a high level of competence is needed to match words and expressions. Where close equivalents do not exist, as with idioms, dictionary makers resort to near-synonymous words, paraphrases, and explanations. Design depends on purpose. A distinction is made, for example, between the *passive* comprehension dictionary and the *active* dictionary for translating into or writing in the

foreign language. Electronic bilingual dictionaries, benefiting from large storage and fast access, are likely to produce flexible new forms. Works on the subject include: Robert Collison, *A History of Foreign-Language Dictionaries* (Blackwell, 1982); Ladislav Zgusta, *Problems of the Bilingual Dictionary* (Niemeyer, 1986). See BILINGUALISM, CANADIAN DICTIONARIES IN ENGLISH, COLLINS, DICTIONARY, EURODICAUTOM, TERMINOLOGY, TRANSLATION, TRANSLITERATION. [LANGUAGE, REFERENCE].   R.H.

BILINGUALISM [1870s: from Latin *bi-* two, *lingua* tongue, and *-alism* as in *nationalism*]. The capacity to make alternate (and sometimes mixed) use of two languages, in contrast to *monolingualism* or *unilingualism* and *multilingualism*. In the social context of languages like English, especially in England and the US, the traditional tendency has been to consider the possession and use of one language the norm. Bilingualism, however, is at least as common as monolingualism; about half the world's population (some 2.5bn people) is bilingual and kinds of bilingualism are probably present in every country in the world. The capacity to function in two (or more) languages has been closely researched in recent years and is often discussed in terms of such categories, scales, and dichotomies as:

Individual and societal bilingualism. Some countries are officially and institutionally bilingual, such as Canada (with English and French), but many Canadians are not bilingual or are not bilingual in these languages. In proportion to population size, probably more French Canadians learn and use English than English Canadians learn and use French, but large numbers of both communities function only in their mother tongue. In other countries, such as India, there is a high degree of individual bilingualism, the average person knowing and using two or more languages. The bulk of the population lives in *linguistic states*, in which one language dominates (such as Gujarati in Gujarat, Marathi in Maharashtra) but many other languages are in daily use.

Balanced bilingualism. Ability with more than one language can be thought of as a continuum. At one end, there are the so-called *balanced bilinguals*, who have a native-like control of two or more languages, while at the other are people with minimal competence in a second language and/or limitations in the use of both languages. Individuals may be bilingual to various degrees depending on such factors as circumstances of acquisition, opportunities for use of the other language, aptitude, and motivation. A *passive* *bilingual* may be able to understand another language without being able to speak it well or even at all. Degree of proficiency is also related to the functions a language is used for. Individuals who do not have the opportunity to use a language for particular purposes may not develop full proficiency in it. In some societies, *diglossia* occurs, a situation in which more than one language or varieties of the same language are used in different functions: among many North Indian and Pakistani immigrants to the UK, Panjabi functions mainly as a home language and perhaps as a religious language, while English is the language of society at large. Children of Panjabi-speaking parents are often English-dominant and do not become fully proficient in Panjabi, because they are educated in English and Panjabi receives little reinforcement outside the home.

Bilinguals are rarely equally fluent about all topics in all contexts. In each situation, there may be pressures of various kinds (administrative, cultural, economic, political, and religious) which influence the individual towards one language rather than the other. The extent to which bilinguals are able or need to keep their languages separate depends on many factors. In many cases, they may more or less freely mix elements of both and frequently switch between them: see CODE-MIXING AND CODE-SWITCHING.

Compound and coordinate bilingualism. Two kinds of bilingualism are associated with how languages are learned. In *compound bilingualism*, they are learned in the same context and are more or less interdependent. Thus, some researchers maintain that a child who acquired both French and English in the home would know both French *livre* and English *book*, but would probably have one mental representation and one meaning for both. In *coordinate bilingualism*, the languages are learned separately and are more or less independent. In such cases, they are believed to be independently stored and represented in the brain, so that *livre* and *book* in such circumstances would not be so readily associated. The compound bilingual is therefore thought to have one set of meanings with two linguistic systems tied to them, and the coordinate bilingual two sets of meanings and linguistic systems.

Many early studies of bilingualism in the 1920s and 1930s claimed that bilingualism had negative effects on children's development. Most of these studies were based on immigrant and/or ethnic minority populations, especially in the US, where other factors (such as low social status and lack of familiarity with testing procedures and the language of tests) may have affected the investigators' perceptions of the abilities of the children tested. Many of the groups tested were in the process of shifting from their own to a more dominant language, which posed a threat to their bilingualism. More recent research, particularly in Canada from the late 1950s onwards, has claimed that bilingualism is an advantage which fosters cognitive flexibility and creative thinking.

Additive and subtractive bilingualism. The Canadian studies have generally been conducted in circumstances where a second language has been acquired without posing a threat to the development and maintenance of the first: it is additive rather than subtractive. *Additive bilingualism* refers to cases in which bilinguals learn a second language without adverse effects on any language already known, and bilingualism acquired under these circumstances is believed to have positive effects on mental development. *Subtractive bilingualism* refers to cases in which the acquisition of a second language interferes with the development of a first language. This kind of bilingualism often obtains when children from minority groups attend school in the second language and are not given the opportunity to develop their native-language skills. It is believed to have negative effects on mental development and has been common in the Highlands of Scotland, among the Maori of New Zealand, and among Hispanics in the US. It is likely that the nature of the relationship between bilingualism and intelligence is variable, depending on circumstances such as context of acquisition and use.

See BICULTURALISM, CANADA, CANADIAN LANGUAGES, CODE-MIXING AND CODE-SWITCHING, -GLISH AND -LISH, HIGHLAND ENGLISH, IRELAND, IRISH ENGLISH, LINGUAL, MAORI ENGLISH, MULTILINGUALISM, NEW ZEALAND, QUEBEC, WALES, WELSH ENGLISH. [LANGUAGE]. S.R.

Cummins, Jim, & Swain, Merill. 1986. *Bilingualism in Education*. London & New York: Longman.
De Jong, Eveline. 1986. *The Bilingual Experience: A Book for Parents*. Cambridge: University Press.
Romaine, Suzanne. 1989. *Bilingualism*. Oxford: Blackwell.
Saunders, George. 1988. *Bilingual Children: From Birth to Teens*. Clevedon & Philadelphia: Multilingual Matters.

BINOMIAL [16c: from Latin *binomius* having two names, and *-al*]. (1) A two-part Latin name of a plant or an animal, such as *Rana vulgaris* (the common frog). Although the term is generally reserved for biological labels, several other groups of Latinate terms are structurally binomial: such phrases as *miles gloriosus, pax Britannica, terra incognita*; the names of stars in constellations, such as *Alpha Centauri* and *Eta Carinae*, the first element a letter of the Greek alphabet, the second the genitive of the name for the constellation; and anatomical names such as *gluteus maximus* and *latissimus dorsi* (kinds of muscle). The orthography differs for each group: in zoology, italics, and capital and lower-case; in the general phrases, either italic or roman, and capitals as needed; for stars, roman and a capital in both cases; in anatomy, usually roman and no capitals. (2) Two-part phrases such as *snow and ice*, *neat but nasty*. The US linguist Yakov Malkiel in 1959 coined the term *irreversible binomial* for such fixed-order idioms as *odds and ends* and *raining cats and dogs* (never *ends and odds and *raining dogs and cats). See BINOMIAL NOMENCLATURE, LATIN TAG. [NAME, WORD].   T.MCA.

BINOMIAL NOMENCLATURE, sometimes **binominal nomenclature**. The international system of scientific naming in a modern form of Latin of types of animals and plants. The basic unit, the *binomial*, names genus and species: the capitalized first word (the *generic term*) identifies the genus, the lower-case second word (the *specific term* or *epithet*) names the species: *Homo sapiens* ('Man wise') the human race, *Rana vulgaris* ('Frog common') the common frog. In running text, binomials are usually italicized or underlined, the generic term often reduced to its initial: *H. sapiens*, *R. vulgaris*. The forms usually follow Latin gender (masculine *Dianthus alpinus*, feminine *Echeveria alpina*, neuter *Chrysanthemum alpinum*), but a specific attributive noun has its own gender (*Achillea millefolium* Achilles plant, thousand-leaf). Trees named in classical times are feminine despite appearances, as with *Ficus carica*, *Fagus sylvatica*. A possessive epithet has a genitive ending: *Magnolia delavayi* Delavay's Magnolia. Commemorative names are also important; they have adjectival rather than genitive endings: compare *Crinodendron hookeranum* with *Berberis hookeri*. Popular names for plants tend to be binomial in many languages, a single epithet locating a member of a class, as with the English *Common Speedwell*, *Germander Speedwell*, *Marsh Speedwell*, *Thyme-leaved Speedwell*. The Latin system parallels these, with *Veronica officinalis*, *V. chamaedrys*, *V. scutellata*, and *V. serpyllifolia*.

History. The current system is based on the work of the 18c Swedish biologist Linnaeus (Carl von Linné), who called his pairs *biverbal names*. He saw the challenge of naming the diversity of living forms as a problem of language, and to separate the processes of naming and describing he created a shorthand, arbitrary system. Before Linnaeus, units of nomenclature (*taxa*, singular *taxon*) were unregulated, descriptive, and sometimes rambling, such as the name of a grass from an early work of Linnaeus himself, *Lolium spicis muticis radice perenni* ('darnel with docked spikes and a perennial root'), which he reduced in his landmark work *Species Plantarum* (1753) to *Lolium perenne* ('perennial darnel'). It has become standard practice to attach to every binomial the abbreviated name of its creator in roman letters, in this case *Lolium perenne* L.; a binomial is taxonomically meaningless without its author abbreviation. A generally agreed rule of priority states that the first name validly published for a species has precedence over any later name: thus, *Helleborus olympicus*, named in 1841 by Lindley, is properly *Helleborus orientalis*, coined by Lamarck in 1789. Such invalid later names are known technically as 'synonyms'. By this means, the system seeks to ensure that a rose cannot be a rose by any other name.

An international vocabulary. Linnaeus intended to provide points of reference within an integrated system that would be comprehensible to all naturalists and other interested persons, regardless of mother tongue. That it has succeeded in difficult situations is shown in a report by the English broadcaster and traveller Sir David Attenborough:

The first time I travelled in the forests of Borneo, I knew no Malay. My guide, a Dyak hunter who, with his blowpipe, regularly collected birds for the local museum, knew no English. So, to begin with, we had some difficulty—to put it mildly—in sorting out where we should go and what we should do. On our first day out together, we were paddling up a river in a canoe, when I heard a sonorous *tok-tok-tok-tok* call echoing through the trees . . . I cupped my hand round my ear and raised my eyebrows towards my guide. He then, for the very first time in our acquaintance, spoke words that I precisely understood. '*Caprimulgus macrurus*', he said and I knew immediately that I was listening to the voice of the long-tailed night-jar. It was a nice demonstration that those cumbersome Latin names, sometimes mocked by the ignorant as pretentious obfuscations invented by scientists to prevent others understanding what they are talking about, do indeed constitute a truly international lingua franca (Foreword, *Oxford Dictionary of Natural History*, 1985).

Structures and usages. (1) Epithets may describe key features (*alba* white, *pubescens* hairy, *pendula* weeping, *arborescens* tree-like), geographical distribution (*amboinensis*, *californica*, *indica*), or type of habitat (*alpinum*, *aquaticum*, *littoralis*, *montanum*). (2) The use of classical derivation and compounding is common: the Dawn Redwood is *Metasequoia glyptostroboides*, whose generic term combines the Greek prefix *meta*- (across or beside) and *Sequoia*, the name of a genus of conifers in turn named for the Cherokee chief Sequoyah, while its specific epithet combines *glypto*- carved, *strobo*- twisted, -*oides* of that kind, the whole meaning 'something close in appearance to the genus *Sequoia*, but of a kind with twisted, riven bark'. Such a name, however, has significance not because of its highly descriptive character, but because it is an arbitrary and neat tag clearly assigned a place within a system of labels. (3) Latinized borrowings occur: *Tamarindus*, from Arabic *tamar hindi*, the Indian date; *Ananassa*, from Guarani *anana*, pineapple. (4) Sometimes anagrams of existing names are used for new (segregate) genera split from them: *Muilla* from *Allium*, *Tellima* from *Mitella*. (5) There are many eponyms, usually intended to honour the person who discovered a genus or species: *Macadamia ternifolia*, after John Macadam. (6) Some names are formed through complex analogies and associations: *Cycas*, based purposefully vaguely on Greek *koikas*, Pliny's name for a plant it only remotely resembles; *Andromeda*, a plant genus whose *type* (first specimen) was found attached to a rock like the mythic heroine. (7) Names of intergeneric hybrids may blend parents' names: for example, X *Brassocattleya*, signifying crosses between the orchids *Brassavola* and *Cattleya* (where X indicates hybrid status).

Accuracy of naming. The nomenclature of biology involves more than the formation of binomials. A name is acceptable only if it conforms to one of the codes that regulate the naming of animals, micro-organisms, and plants and confer legitimacy through valid publication. A taxon is validly published when it is named correctly and (unless it is subject to a taxonomic revision) for the first time, its author and type designated, and the type described in Latin, deposited in a collection, and preferably illustrated. A binomial without a type or description is a *nomen nudum* or *nom. nud.* (naked name); one lacking conceptual clarity is a *nomen confusum* or *nom. confus.* (confused name). Naming is further confused by the use of the same name for different plants, usually through ignorance or misunderstanding. Although only one name is correct, differences of usage must be stated. The author abbreviations of faulty names are modified by the formula *sensu x non y* (in the sense of x not y). *Hypericum hookeranum* Wight & Arn. is the accepted and valid name for a plant, given by Wight and Arnott. It was first described by Hooker, however, as *Hypericum oblongifolium*, but this name had to be rejected because it had already been applied by Choisy to a different plant. The misleading synonym is therefore described as *Hypericum oblongifolium* sensu Hook. non Chois. (a taxonomic warning like an editor's *sic*).

Taxonomy. The science of classification or *taxonomy* has a bearing on nomenclatural procedure. When taxonomists group taxa, they may transfer species from one genus to another and relegate or promote them within the taxonomic hierarchy. These activities are reflected in the accumulation of synonyms and author abbreviations. Thus, the Bluebell is currently labelled *Hyacinthoides non-scripta* (L.) Chouard ex Rothmaler (where *ex* means that Rothmaler validly published a name proposed by Chouard). It was published as such in 1944, but the bracketed 'L.' shows that it is a recombination of an earlier Linnaean name, *Hyacinthus non-scriptus* (the first name or *basionym* published in 1753). By means of this bracketing convention, the stages of the naming process are indicated. The stability of botanical nomenclature is also sought through clear naming of ranks below the species level. The taxonomic hierarchy of botany is *Family*, *Genus*, *species* (abbreviated *sp*, plural *spp*), *subspecies* (*ssp*, *sspp*), *varietas* (*var*, *vars*), *forma* (*f* or *fa*, plural *ff*). Hybrids and cultivars (abbreviation *cv*), that is, plants originating or maintained in cultivation, can be coextensive with or attached to any rank below genus. The binomial is therefore only part of a fuller name, such as *Rosa sericea* var *omeiensis* (Rolfe) Rowley, which states that the Omei rose is a variant of *R. sericea* that was named by Rowley, who adapted a basionym created by Rolfe. Some names occupy all ranks, as with *Macrozamia tridentata* ssp *cylindrica* var *corallipes* f *vavilovii* Schuster. The special names of cultivars (garden 'varieties') are added in roman, as in *Buddleia davidii* cv Black Knight or *Buddleia davidii* 'Black Knight'. Since cultivar names may be coextensive with species names, this plant can also be accurately described as *Buddleia* cv Black Knight or *Buddleia* 'Black Knight'.

Trinomials. Trinomials or three-term labels do not occur in botany but are used in zoology to name subspecies: *Homo sapiens neanderthalensis* ('Man wise, from the Neanderthal valley in Germany') the Neanderthal branch of the human race. Repetition of the epithet sometimes occurs, as in *Homo sapiens sapiens* ('wise wise man'), a label that distinguishes the contemporary human subspecies from such extinct subspecies as Neanderthal. In at least one instance the same name is repeated three times: *Troglodytes troglodytes troglodytes* ('cave-dweller' × 3), the common wren.

Informal uses. The technical terms of biology are sometimes used informally for purposes of explanation and identification: 'the Crown Imperial fritillary, *Fritillaria imperialis*' and 'Pellaea rotundifolia (button fern)'. Occasionally, quasi-scientific binomials are coined for rhetorical purposes: a book on language entitled *Homo Loquens* speaking human; intelligent computers labelled *Machina sapiens* wise engine. See BINOMIAL, LATIN, NOMENCLATURE, VERNACULAR. [NAME, WORD].   M.D.G., T.MCA.

BIOGRAPHY [17c: from French *biographie*, Latin *biographia*, Greek *biographia* life-writing]. A written account of a human life, often referred to in title or subtitle as a *life*, as in *The Vicar of Morwenstow: Being a Life of Robert Stephen Hawker* (S. Baring-Gould, 1899). The lives of famous people have been recorded from antiquity, in such works as Plutarch's *Parallel Lives of Illustrious Greeks and Romans* (1–2c), and continued in the Middle Ages in the lives of saints. The modern biography appeared after the Renaissance and began in English with the short lives by John Aubrey and Isaac Walton (17c), extended by Johnson's *Lives of the Poets* (1779–81) and Boswell's *Life of Samuel Johnson* (1791). Because 19c biographers tended to write reverently, the frankness of Elizabeth Gaskell's *Life of Charlotte Brontë* (1857) and J. A. Froude's *Reminiscences* and biography of Carlyle (1881–4) caused controversy. In the early 20c, Lytton Strachey set the fashion for a more ironic and debunking treatment: 'There was humour in her face; but the curious watcher might wonder whether it was humour of a very pleasant kind' (on Florence Nightingale, *Eminent Victorians*, 1918). Late 20c biographers usually seek or claim detachment and generally engage in detailed research. Short biographies are commonly collected for reference, as in *The Dictionary of National Biography*, which was begun in Britain in 1882 under the editorship of Leslie Stephen and has been kept up to date by supplements. Biographies are common in general encyclopedias and appear in some dictionaries. Living subjects compile their own entries for such social registers as *Who's Who* (published annually in Britain since 1897) and its equivalents in other English-speaking countries. The *capsule biography* is usually formulaic: name, life dates, place of birth, family situation, education, general career, main achievements, aspects of personal life, and perhaps a brief critical assessment. Variations include *potted biographies* or *biodata* placed alongside articles in periodicals and *obituary* notices and articles in the print and sound media. See AUTOBIOGRAPHY, BILDUNGSROMAN, LEGEND, MEMOIR, NOVEL. [LITERATURE, MEDIA].

R.C.

The biography theme.
ABERCROMBIE, ACHEBE, ADDISON, AELFRIC, ALEXANDER (H.), ALFRED, ARNOLD (M.), ARNOLD (T.), AUSTEN, AVIS, BAILEY (N.), BARNES, BARNHART, BEDE, BEHN, BERLITZ, BIERCE, BLAIR, BLOOMFIELD, BOLINGER, BOSWELL, BRADLEY, BRATHWAITE, BRIDGES, BRITTON, BRONTË SISTERS, BUNYAN, BURCHFIELD, BURGESS, BURNS, BUTLER, CAMDEN, CARLYLE, CARROLL, CASSIDY, CAWDREY, CAXTON, CHAUCER, CHOMSKY, CHURCHILL, COBBETT, COLERIDGE (H.), COLERIDGE (S.), CONRAD, COOPER, COVERDALE, CRAIGIE, CRANMER, CURME, DEFOE,

DICKENS, DICKINSON, DRYDEN, ELIOT, ELLIS, ELYOT, FIELDING, FOWLER, FRIES, FUNK, FURNIVALL, GANDHI, GORDIMER, GOWERS, HALLIDAY, HANLEY, HARDY, HAZLITT, HEMPL, HORNBY, INNIS, JENNINGS, JESPERSEN, JOHNSON, JONES (D.), JONES (W.), JONSON, JOYCE, KERSEY, KIPLING, KRAPP, KUHN, KURATH, LAMB, LAWRENCE, LEACOCK, LEAVIS, LIEBER, LORIMER, LOWTH, LYLY, MACAULAY, MCDAVID, MACDIARMID, MCLUHAN, MARCH, MARSH, MATHEWS, MELVILLE, MENCKEN, MILTON, MORRIS, MULCASTER, MURISON, MURRAY, NAIPAUL, NEHRU, NGUGI, ONIONS, ORTON, ORWELL, PALMER, PARTRIDGE, PASSY, PIOZZI (THRALE), PITMAN (I.), PITMAN (J.), POPE, POUND (L.), PUTTENHAM, QUIRK, READ, RICHARDS, RICHARDSON, ROGET, SAPIR, SCOTT, SHAKESPEARE, SHAW, SHERIDAN (R.), SHERIDAN (T.), SIDNEY, SKEAT, SMOLLETT, SOYINKA, SPENSER, STEELE, STERNE, STEVENSON, STRANG, STREVENS, SWEET, SWIFT, TENNYSON, THOMAS, THORNDIKE, TRENCH, TURNER (G.), TURNER (L.), TWAIN, TYNDALE, URDANG, VIËTOR, WATSON, WEBSTER, WEEKLEY, WELLS, WEST, WHITNEY, WHORF, WILDE, WILSON, WOLLSTONECRAFT, WOOLF, WORCESTER, WORDSWORTH, WREN, WRIGHT, WYCLIF(FE), WYLD.

BIRMINGHAM. A large industrial city in the West Midlands of England, often referred to as *Brum*, an abbreviation of the metathesis *Brummagem*. The city's inhabitants are *Brummies*, and their speech is known as *Brummie*, *Birmingham*, and *Brummagem*. Accents vary according to such factors as age, education, locality, region of origin, and social aspirations.

Pronunciation. Middle-class speech in the city is either RP or near-RP. The following points apply mainly to working-class speech: (1) It is non-rhotic and generally aitchless. (2) The vowel /a/ tends to be used in both *bat* and *bath*. The pronunciation of *Edgbaston* (the name of a better-off part of the city) is a class shibboleth: the *a* is short among the working class, who stress the first syllable ('EDGE-biston'), and long in 'posh' usage, with stress on the second syllable ('Edge-BAHston'). (3) There is a tendency towards /ʊ/ in both *but* and *boot*, although the /ʌ/ pronunciation in words such as *but*, *cut*, and *shut* is spreading. (4) Words such as *course* and *force* are sometimes realized with a triphthong /ʌʊə/, especially among older speakers. (5) The monophthong /ɪ/ is close, so that *it* often sounds like *eat* and *did* like *deed*. (6) The *-y* ending of words such as *happy* is often pronounced /əi/ or /ʌi/. (7) The diphthongs in *gate* and *goat* tend to vary as between /aɪ ~ ʌɪ/ and /aʊ ~ ʌʊ/ rather than the /eɪ/ and /əʊ/ of RP. (8) The diphthong of *house* and *mouth* is /æʊ/. (9) The diphthongs in *tie* and *toy* have merged in /ɒɪ/, producing homophones and uncertainty in such sentences as *Where's your tie/toy?* (10) Words and syllables ending in *-ng* tend to close with a voiced velar plosive: for example, /sɪŋgɪŋg/ for *singing* and /kɪŋglʊɪ/ for *kingly*. This feature has been criticized so often that many Birmingham speakers tend to overcompensate in the attempt to avoid it, using /ŋ/ where /ŋg/ is standard, as in /fɪŋə/ for *finger*. (11) To the north of the city, some speakers use /au/ for /u/, so that *you* rhymes with *how*: 'Yow coom from Staffid' for *You come from Stafford*.

Grammar and vocabulary. (1) Like people in most large cities, Birmingham speakers fall into many categories, from those who use standard grammar, with or without a local accent, through those whose English is influenced by a mother tongue such as a Caribbean creole, Punjabi, or Urdu, to working-class speakers who tend to use non-standard forms that also occur elsewhere in Britain. These include the use of *them* as a demonstrative adjective (*them things*), non-standard verb forms (*I seen it, I done it; It's broke; She give it in yesterday; We come here last year*), and *was* for *were* (*They didn't know where they was*). (2) Especially among older speakers, the following features also occur: *up* instead of *to*, as in *He went up the pub half an hour ago* and *We'll go up town tomorrow*; use of *her* instead of *she*, as in *What's 'er doing then?*; use of *as* as a relative pronoun, as in *It wasn't 'im as went*; use of /dai/ for *did not*, especially with *know*, as in *They dai know where they was*. (3) Most people use the standard vocabulary. Older speakers, however, may continue to use such words as *brewins* an outhouse, *closet* a toilet, *miskin* BrE dustbin, AmE trashcan, and *suff* a drain. See MIDLANDS. [EUROPE, VARIETY].   L.T., S.E.

BISLAMA [From French *bichelamar*, variant of *bêche-de-mer*: see BEACH LA MAR]. A variety of Melanesian pidgin and the national language of Vanuatu, sharing official status with English and French, which are the principal languages of education. Bislama, which is descended from *Beach La Mar*, is a lingua franca for a population speaking some 100 distinct local languages, and is more or less evenly distributed throughout the country. It used to be learned mainly in adulthood by men, usually through work on plantations, in town, or on ships. Most adult males probably speak it, except in isolated parts of the islands. In towns today, most children speak their vernacular and Bislama. It is the only one of the three Melanesian pidgins to develop and be spoken *in situ* over its entire history, unlike *Tok Pisin* and *Pijin*, which were introduced after a period of initial development outside Papua New Guinea and the Solomon Islands respectively. In the southern islands there has been an unbroken tradition of Bislama for almost 150 years. The constitution of Vanuatu states: *Lanwis blong Ripablik blong Vanuatu, hemia Bislama. Trifala lanwis blong mekem ol wok blong kantri ya, i gat Bislama mo Inglis mo Franis* The language of the Republic of Vanuatu is Bislama. There are three languages for conducting the business of the country, Bislama, English, and French. See MELANESIAN PIDGIN ENGLISH, VANUATU. [OCEANIA, VARIETY].   S.R.

BISOCIATION [1990: a blend of *bi*- two, and *association*. Coined by Tom McArthur: 'English in Tiers', *English Today* 23]. The occurrence in a language of pairs of words with similar meanings, one member of each pair being native to that language (such as everyday English *sight*), the other being a loanword from an influential foreign source (such as *vision*, a loanword from Latin). In English, the vernacular members of such pairs are mainly Germanic (usually from Old English or Old Norse), while the loanwords are mainly classical (usually from Latin, often mediated by French), as in: *freedom/liberty, hearty/cordial, go up/ascend, go down/descend*. Occasionally, such lexical parallelism is put to humorous ends, as when a *wisecrack* becomes a *sagacious crevice*. Bisociation in English has often been remarked on. Simeon Potter, for example, observes that 'English and French expressions may have similar denotations but slightly different connotations and associations. Generally the English words are stronger, more physical, and more human. We feel more at ease after getting a *hearty welcome* than after being granted a *cordial reception*' (*Our Language*, 1950/66). Similarly, Thomas Finkenstaedt has noted: 'Apparently the Elizabethans discovered the possibilities of etymological dissociation in language: *amatory* and *love*, *audition* and *hearing*, *hearty welcome* and *cordial reception*: these quasisynonyms offer new opportunites for semantic differentiation' (in *Ordered Profusion*, 1973).

This kind of semantic parallelism usually arises when one language borrows so freely from another that it gains an entire extra stratum of words and word elements, as Persian has done from Arabic, and Kannada and Malayalam in southern India from Sanskrit. It has also occurred in Latin, which has absorbed many words from Greek, creating such pairs as Latin *circumlocutio* and Greek-derived *periphrasis*, *compassio* and *sympathia*, *compositio* and *synthesis*, *conspectus* and *synopsis*, *suppositio* and *hypothesis*, *transformatio* and *metamorphosis*. In many instances, bisociate Latin pairs have passed into English, leading to a threefold condition, or *trisociation*, as with Germanic *fellow feeling*, Latinate *compassion*, and Greek-derived *sympathy*. In addition to words and phrases, trisociate sets or 'triples' include the three main morphological elements: prefixes (as in the case of *over*sensitive, *super*sensitive, and *hyper*sensitive, each word having its distinctive nuances); suffixes (as in hard*en*, magn*ify*, harmon*ize*, each suffix being inceptive and causative, but attaching to different kinds of base); and both free and bound bases (as in *heart*y, *cord*ial, and *cardi*ac, and *ant*-hill, *formic*ary, and *myrmec*ology). There are scores of such correspondences in English, the Germanic material tending to be part of everyday usage (as with *new*ness), the Latinate tending to be more formal and 'educated' (as with in*nova*te), and the Greek tending to be highly technical and even arcane (as with *neo*phyte). However, not all such triples are from these three sharply differing sources: for example, *kingly* is Germanic, *royal* is from Old French and ultimately Latin, and *regal* is from Latin, but perhaps through Old French. Compare CALQUE, DOUBLET. See BOOK OF COMMON PRAYER, CLASSICAL LANGUAGE, ELYOT, FRENCH, LEXICAL BAR. [HISTORY, LANGUAGE, STYLE, WORD].   T.MCA.

BIT. See COMPUTING, INFORMATION.

BLACK [From Old English *blæc*, *blac*, sometimes confused in the reading of ancient texts with the similar *blāc*, which however meant 'shining']. A word associated with absence of light, dead of night, soot, coal, etc., and with various shades of brown, especially in skin, eyes, and hair, as in *the black Irish* (Irish people with very dark hair). The term has also long been associated with death, evil, ill luck, and rage ('Many a black curse haue they of the poore commons', Philip Stubbes, *The Anatomie of Abuses*, 1583), and has pointed up differences in appearance ('the Fair, the Black, the Learned, the Unlearned, do all pass away', Robert Nelson, *A Kempis' Christian Exercises*, 1715). Black animals have been associated with practitioners of *the Black Arts* and *the Black Mass*, villains are *black-hearted* and *blackguards*, people are *black-balled* from clubs, and subjected to *blackmail* or *black propaganda*. Dark people have often been considered further from God's grace than the fair-haired and blue-eyed. There are in Spenser's *Faerie Queene* (1590-6) two symbolic women: Una (fair, honest, virginal) and Duessa (darkly deceiving and seductive).

After the European diaspora, which began in the 16c, these ancient associations tended to merge with perceptions of dark-skinned peoples encountered in Africa, South Asia, Australasia, Melanesia, and Polynesia, especially in colonial situations. Although slavery had previously been a condition into which members of any race might fall, from the 17c onward it became in European eyes a condition of 'black' people, also widely regarded as 'benighted' heathen in need of conversion. William Blake's poem 'The Little Black Boy' (1789) opens:

> My mother bore me in the southern wild,
> And I am black, but O! my soul is white;
> White as an angel is the English child,
> But I am black, as if bereav'd of light.

In the next stanzas, the boy recalls his mother pointing to the sun, from which God gives light and life to the world in which they live briefly in 'these black bodies'. The boy adds:

> Thus did my mother say, and kissed me;
> And thus I say to little English boy.
> When I from black and he from white cloud free,
> And round the tent of God like lambs we joy,
>
> I'll shade him from the heat, till he can bear
> To lean in joy upon our father's knee;
> And then I'll stand and stroke his silver hair,
> And be like him, and he will then love me.

In recent years, people of African descent in the US and UK have drawn attention to the symbolic and racist connotations of *black*, and have sought to create new, more positive associations through such slogans as *Black is beautiful*. A viewpoint far from that of Blake's little boy occurs in Mikey Smith's poem 'Nigger Talk' (1984):

> Funky talk
> Nitty gritty grass-root talk
> Dat's what I da talk
> Cause de talk is togedder talk.
> Like right on, out-a-sight, kind-a-too-much.
> Ya hip to it yet?
> Ya dig de funky way to talk
> Talk talk?
> Dis na white talk
> Na white talk dis.
> It is coon, nignog sambo wog talk.

In the UK in the 1980s, social and political activists of African, South Asian, and other backgrounds began to adopt *black* as a term that marks their shared status and problems in a predominantly white country:

The definition of 'black' as a cultural and political term has generated a wide debate in Britain recently. 'Black' has now come to denote people descended from Africa, Asia, Latin America, the Pacific (so-called Third World Peoples) . . . . This debate is not just a matter of semantics but to do with an analysis of racism. It aims to make 'black' a political term rather than one which refers solely to skin colour and covers different groups to stress common interests and experiences (from the 'Black Students' section of the students' handbook of the U. of East Anglia, England, 1989/90).

A friend of mine, a professional writer with lofty degrees from British universities and teaching experience in the US—in fact, much more of a native speaker than the husband of the Queen—was offered a job in Southern Germany. However, when the director of the school learnt that my friend was black, he was told not to bother to come as 'the people here don't consider black people to be teachers'. By black, I mean people of Asian/Afro-Caribbean origin (Rakesh Bhanot, 'The Native Speaker and the Enemy Within', *EFL Gazette*, Mar. 1990).

Many Asians in the UK, however, from the subcontinent of India, Chinese backgrounds, and elsewhere, resist (and may resent) this conflation, preferring the three-term contrast *white*, *black*, and *Asian*. See ABORIGINES, AFRICAN LITERATURE IN ENGLISH, AMERICAN ENGLISH, BANTU, BLACK ENGLISH, BLACK ENGLISH VERNACULAR, BLACK IRISH, BRITISH BLACK ENGLISH, CALIBAN, CELT, DIALOG(UE) (NAIPAUL), ETHNIC NAME, MELANESIA, RACISM, RAP, WHITE. [AFRICA, AMERICAS, EUROPE, LANGUAGE].   T.MCA.

BLACK AFRICA, BLACK AFRICAN. See AFRICA, AFRICAN.

BLACK AFRICAN LITERATURE. See AFRICAN LITERATURE IN ENGLISH, SOUTH AFRICAN LITERATURE IN ENGLISH.

BLACK CELT. See CELT.

BLACK ENGLISH [Late 20c]. A controversial term for the English of people of African origin or for English in Black Africa. In the US, the term generally refers to the vernaculars of descendants of slaves, some called dialects, some creoles. In the UK, the term generally refers to the usage of West Indian immigrant communities. The term *white English* has occasionally been used in contrast: 'local "white" English, BBC English' (David Sutcliffe, 'British Black English and West Indian Creoles', in P. Trudgill (ed.), *Language in the British Isles*, 1984). Compare BLUE-EYED ENGLISH, RED ENGLISH, WHITE ENGLISH. See AMERICAN ENGLISH, AMERICAN LITERATURE, BLACK ENGLISH VERNACULAR, BRITISH BLACK ENGLISH. [AFRICA, AMERICAS, EUROPE, VARIETY].   T.MCA.

BLACK ENGLISH VERNACULAR [1972: coined by William Labov]. Short form *BEV*. Also **African-American English, Afro-American English, Afro-American, (American) Black English, black English**. Terms in sociolinguistics for English as used by a majority of US citizens of Black African background, consisting of a range of socially stratified urban and rural dialects. The most non-standard varieties are used by poor blacks with limited education, who have restricted social contact beyond their native communities. Standard varieties are influenced by regional norms: black standard English in the South is different from the African-American standard in the North, and each in turn reflects colloquial usage among educated whites in the

same areas. Considerable style-shifting occurs between blacks talking to non-blacks and especially on less formal occasions when blacks prefer to use vernacular speech among themselves. The corresponding variation is pervasive, occurring with phonology, intonation, morphology, syntax, African-American slang, idioms, and ritualized verbal confrontations.

Origins. American Black English was born of slavery between the late 16c and mid-19c, and followed black migration from the southern states to racially isolated ghettos throughout the US. According to J. L. Dillard (1972, below), some 80% of black Americans speak the vernacular, and he and several other commentators stress its African origins. The pidginization and creolization that resulted from slavery linger on the tongues of Americans of African descent. Slave labour in the South gave birth to diverse linguistic norms; former indentured servants from all parts of the British Isles, who often became overseers on plantations, variously influenced the foundations of BEV. See GULLAH. First the industrial revolution then the Civil War disrupted slavery and promoted African-American migration within the US, as a result of which slave dialects were transplanted from Southern plantations to the factories of the North and Midwest. When 'smokestack' industries grew, so too did urban employment for blacks, but racial segregation, rigorous in the South, was maintained in various forms throughout the entire US, and has not yet come to an end.

Pronunciation. (1) Like the English of the Southern states in general, BEV is non-rhotic: 'ca' for *car*, 'pahty' for *party*. Comparably, /l/ is absent in word-final consonant clusters with labials ('hep' for *help*, 'sef' for *self*), and both /r/ and /l/ are absent in such usages as 'We comin' for *We're coming* and 'We be here' for *We'll be here*. (2) A syllabic /n/ commonly replaces /ŋ/ in *-ing* forms: 'comin' and 'runnin' for *coming* and *running*. (3) Word-final consonant clusters are reduced: 'des' for *desk*, 'tes' for *test*, 'col' for *cold*. (4) Past-tense endings are also absent in such clusters: 'look' for *looked*, 'talk' for *talked*. (5) Word-initial /d/ often takes the place of /ð/, as in 'dat day' for *that day* and 'dis house' for *this house*. (6) Word-final /f/ often replaces /θ/, as in 'boof' for *booth* and 'souf' for *south*. (7) There is often heavy initial stress in disyllabic words: *pólice* for *police*, *défine* for *define*.

Grammar. (1) Multiple negation is common, as with many non-standard English dialects: *No way no girl can't wear no platform shoes to no amusement park* There is no way that any girl can wear platform shoes to an amusement park.

(2) Existential *it* replaces *there*: *It ain't no food here* There is no food here. (3) Inflected forms such as plural, possessive, and singular *-s* and past *-ed* are variably omitted (as illustrated for pronunciation, points 3 and 4, above): *He got three cent*; *That's my brother book*; *She like new clothes*; *They talk* (= talked) *all night*. (4) Some inversion occurs with questions: *What it is?*, *How you are?* (5) Auxiliary *do* can replace *be* in a negative statement: *It don't all be her fault* It isn't always her fault. (6) Auxiliary *be* is often used to indicate habitual occurrence: *They be fightin* They are always fighting, *He be laughin* He laughs all the time. (7) Stressed *been* conveys long-standing events with remote pasts: *I béen see dat movie* I saw that movie long ago; *She béen had dat hat* She has had that hat for some time. (8) Intention is sometimes expressed by the particle *a*: *I'm a shoot you* I'm going to shoot you: compare Appalachian English *I'm a gonna* for 'I am going to'. (9) Aspectual usage with *steady* occurs before progressive verbs or with heavy stress in sentence-final position; greater emphasis occurs when sentences conclude with *steady*: *We be steady rappin*, *We steady be rappin*, *We be rappin stéady* We are always talking; *They steady be high*, *They be steady high*, *They be high stéady* They are always intoxicated (from drugs or alcohol). In such cases, *steady* indicates that the activity is persistent, consistent, and intense. (10) *Come* sometimes functions as a semi-auxiliary: *He come tellin me some story* He told me a lie; *They come comin in here like they own de place* They came in here like they owned the place. (11) Adverbial use of *like to* meaning 'almost': *I like to die(d)* I almost died; *He like to hit his head on that branch* He almost hit his head on that branch.

Vocabulary. (1) Such terms as *goober* (peanut), *yam* (sweet potato), *tote* (to carry), and *buckra* (white man) trace their history to West Africa, as do the grammatical functions of habitual *be* and aspectual *steady* (above). (2) Several in-group terms are used to refer to intimates or to other African Americans in general. For example, *homeboy* was coined by convicts who served prison terms with other 'boys from home': that is, other convicts from the same neighbourhood. The bond between *homeboys* is stronger than that between other *brothers* or *bloods* (other blacks) who have had no relationship prior to imprisonment. This term moved from prisons to the black communities where most (ex)convicts live(d). *Homies* is the plural form and *homegirl* the feminine equivalent of *homeboy*. (3) Pejorative ethnic terms for whites include *honkie* and *whitey* for all whites, and *redneck* and *peckerwood* for poor and/or rural and/or Southern whites, especially such overt racists as members of the Ku Klux Klan.

Slang. (1) Established slang includes significant changes in the senses and applications of words: *bad* is used to mean 'good' (*Hey, that's a bad car, man!*); *cool* and *hot* are used with equal intensity to mean 'very good' (*That car is real cool/hot*); *crib*, usually associated with infants, can mean any home, apartment, or place where one lives, including a federal housing project; *short* and *ride* can refer to an automobile: *Homeboy be steady driving that short/ride*. (2) Everyday idioms include: *stepped-to* (subject to a physical advance by an opponent before a possible exchange of blows), as in *So I said, 'What's up?' and I got stepped-to*; *upside the head* (against the head), as in *He got hit upside the head*; *ashy*, in reference to a dry skin condition that appears as a slight discoloration: *His skin always be so ashy*. (3) Many expressions used in BEV have 'crossed over' into mainstream colloquial AmE: *hip* or *hep*, referring to someone who is very knowledgeable about popular (especially inner-city African-American) culture; *dude* as a generic reference for any male: *That dude be crazy*.

Usage. Many kinds of African-American speech acts go back to African oral traditions: *the dozens* verbal insults towards an opponent's mother; *rapping* a voluble, rhythmic eloquence that includes both the language of seduction and the lyrics of popular music; *shucking*, *jiving* deceiving whites through verbal trickery without their knowledge; *sounding* engaging in verbal duels. The 'men and women of words' who embody these traditions are common in most black communities; preachers, poets, musicians, and political radicals tend to be consummate practitioners of a rhetoric derived from Africa and often influenced by the Bible. Although men are perceived as dominating these traditions, women have played a significant role in the oral traditions of African America. Such music as Negro spirituals and jazz, as well as dance, poetry, rap, and even elaborate handshakes have substantially 'crossed over' and become part of popular culture in the US and elsewhere.

Literary BEV. The implementation of BEV in AmE literature is comparable to that of literary Cockney in England. J. L. Dillard (below) observed that the earliest literary renditions appeared before 1790: 'Attestation (recorded literary examples) from Crèvecoeur, Cotton Mather, Benjamin Franklin, the court records of Salem, Massachusetts, and several other sources may be found before the 1790's—and all without any recourse to fictional sources. The wealth of material after that date is simply astonishing. There is, in fact, a very great deal of pre-Civil War literary Negro dialect' (1972). Dillard was reacting to such statements by H. L. Mencken as: 'The Negro dialect, as we know it today, seems to have been formulated by the song-writers for the minstrel shows; it did not appear in literature until the time of the Civil War; before that . . . it was a vague and artificial lingo which had little relation to the actual speech of Southern blacks' (*The American Language*, 4th edition, 1936). Minstrel shows, usually scripted and performed by whites, did not reflect the true voices of slavery; rather, they employed exaggerated stereotypes that have, often inadvertently, served to perpetuate linguistic myths across racial, regional, and class boundaries. Contemporary African-American writers, including Maya Angelou, Langston Hughes, Toni Morrison, Alice Walker, and Richard Wright, have provided insights, vitality, and authenticity to literary versions of Black English in the US that continue to have an impact on broader interpretations of English usage and American literature.

Social issues. Although this cross-over provides some evidence of cultural progress and racial tolerance, many misconceptions about BEV prevail, especially that it is simply 'bad English' and that it holds African Americans back in education and employment opportunities because of this. The dominant issue for BEV is a stereotype that equates non-standard usage with stupidity. Its negative consequences continue to affect the prospects of black American children. Because BEV is devalued and misunderstood, uninformed citizens (including many teachers with excellent intentions) continue to denigrate it in favour of standard AmE. Few such educators, whether or not they have a training in linguistics, have learned about the history and nature of African-American English, and fail therefore to appreciate its diversity and logical integrity as a long-established variety of the language.

Conclusion. African-American varieties of English vary considerably, tending to reflect the social background and personal aspirations of individual speakers as well as the social circumstances in which different dialects thrive. The historical evidence confirms a combination of African, English, Scots, and Irish influences that have evolved through complex processes of pidginization and creolization. Ever-changing racial attitudes and capricious social opportunities for blacks in the US have exacerbated linguistic diversity among the descendants of American slaves.

See AFRICA, AFRICAN, AFRICAN-AMERICAN, AFRICAN ENGLISH, AFRO-, AFRO-SEMINOLE, AMERICAN[1], AMERICAN ENGLISH, AMERICAN LITERATURE, ATLANTIC CREOLES, BLACK, BLACK ENGLISH, BRITISH BLACK ENGLISH, CARIBBEAN ENGLISH, CARIBBEAN ENGLISH CREOLE, CREOLE, DIALECT IN AMERICA, GEECHEE, GULLAH, JIVE (TALK), NEW ORLEANS, PIDGIN, SAMANA, SOUTHERN ENGLISH, TESD. [AMERICAS, VARIETY]. J.Ba.

Baratz, Joan C., & Shuy, Robert W. (eds.). 1969. *Teaching Black Children to Read*. Washington, DC: Center for Applied Linguistics.
Baugh, John. 1983. *Black Street Speech: Its History, Structure, and Survival*. Austin: University of Texas Press.
Brooks, Charlotte K. (ed.). 1985. *Tapping Potential: English and Language Arts for the Black Learner*: Urbana, Ill.: National Council of Teachers of English.
Burling, Robbins. 1973. *English in Black and White*. New York: Holt, Rinehart & Winston.
Dillard, J. L. 1972. *Black English*. New York: Random House.
Kochman, Thomas. 1981. *Black and White Styles in Conflict*. Chicago: University Press.
Labov, William. 1972. *Language in the Inner-City: Studies in the Black English Vernacular*. Philadelphia: University of Pennsylvania Press.
Smitherman, Geneva. 1978. *Talkin' and Testifyin'*. Boston: Houghton Mifflin.
—— (ed.). 1981. *Black English and the Education of Black Children and Youth*. Detroit: Wayne State University Press.
Whiteman, Marcia Farr (ed.). 1980. *Reactions to Ann Arbor: Vernacular Black English and Education*. Arlington, Va.: Center for Applied Linguistics.
Wolfram, Walt. 1969. *A Sociolinguistic Description of Detroit Negro Speech*. Washington, DC: Center for Applied Linguistics.

BLACKFELLA ENGLISH, BLACKFELLA TALK. See ABORIGINAL ENGLISH.

BLACK IRISH. (1) Irish people with dark hair: 'Those are the Black Oirish an' 'tis they that bring dishgrace upon the name av Oireland' (Kipling, *Soldiers Three*, 1890); 'a black Irish type, with centuries of rebelliousness behind him' (J. B. Priestley, *Saturn over Water*, 1961). In IrE, *black* translates Irish *dubh* and can mean both 'dark' and 'black': 'Some say he's black / But I say he's bonny / And the finest of them all / Is my handsome, winsome Johnny' (folksong). In Northern Ireland, *black* can mean Protestant (also called 'Orange', after William of Orange'): *Was he Orange?—Orange? He was as black as your boot*. (2) In the 17c, during Cromwell's Irish campaigns, thousands were transported to Barbados, where they were called *Redlegs* and *Black Irish*. Irish men on Montserrat married African women, the resulting Afro-Irish community being known there as *Black Irish*. See BLACK, CELT, IRISH, MONTSERRAT, WILD IRISH. [AMERICAS, EUROPE, NAME].

T.MCA., L.T.

BLACK LETTER. See GOTHIC.

BLADE. The part of the tongue between tip and front. See TONGUE. [SPEECH].   G.K.

BLAIR, Hugh [1718–1800]. Clergyman and teacher, the most widely known of the Scottish rhetoricians who laid the foundations of a modern rhetorical theory for English by extending classical rhetoric and poetics into a system for promoting effective writing, speaking, and criticism in literature, philosophy, theology, history, psychology, and natural science. He was named the first Regius Professor of Rhetoric in 1762 by George III, in recognition of the series of lectures he regularly delivered to students at the U. of Edinburgh. He also enjoyed influence as the minister of the High Church at St Giles, Edinburgh, siding with the moderates on theological and intellectual issues. Blair's *Lectures on Rhetoric and Belles-Lettres* (1783) were based on ideas brought from the Continent by Adam Smith and influenced by Henry Home, Lord Kames. They include lectures on the origin and nature of figurative language, the structure of sentences, and different kinds of public speaking. Like others at the time, Blair asserted a connection between training in the correct and refined use of language and the development of virtue. His *Lectures* attracted a wide readership, particularly in the US, where it became the standard text for several generations. For a century this work was reprinted, abridged, or translated in some 130 editions. See RHETORIC. [BIOGRAPHY, EUROPE, HISTORY, STYLE].   C.C.E.

BLANK VERSE [16c]. Unrhymed verse, almost always in iambic pentameters. It was introduced into English *c*.1540 by Henry Howard, Earl of Surrey, in his translation of Virgil's *Aeneid*, and adopted by the Elizabethan dramatists as their principal verse form. Milton, by using it in *Paradise Lost*, established it as a medium for narrative verse, although Pope favoured the heroic couplet. In the 19c, Thomson, Wordsworth, Coleridge, Tennyson, and Browning all used it for long poems. In the 20c, it has been superseded by *free verse* and the fashion for shorter poems, but was revived by the American poets Robert Frost and Wallace Stevens. T. S. Eliot used a loose type of blank verse in his later plays. Poets who have used it for epic or narrative purposes have generally divided their work into blocks of lines (verse paragraphs). Extended blank verse seldom keeps the iambic pentameter throughout, and poets have varied the line with additional syllables and occasional irregular feet. See VERSE. [LITERATURE].   R.C.

BLARNEY [*c*.1600]. Extravagant eloquence that beguiles and flatters, impresses and deceives, often taken to be typically Irish. In 1602, Cor-

mac Teige Macarthy unwillingly agreed to surrender Blarney Castle in County Cork, so as to have it returned to him as a loyal retainer of Elizabeth I. Afterwards he stalled and, tired of his glib equivocation, the queen is said to have shouted, 'This is all Blarney—he never means what he says, he never does what he promises.' In the wall of Blarney Castle is the *Blarney Stone*, said to bestow Macarthy's gift of eloquence on whoever kisses it. The ritual of kissing the stone by hanging head-down from the battlements appears to date from the 18c. Tourists can now reach its inner face awkwardly but with less risk through a specially made hole. Sir Walter Scott kissed the stone during a visit to Cork in 1825, but after most of his works had been written. Compare GIFT OF THE GAB, PATTER. [EUROPE, HISTORY, STYLE].   T.MCA.

BLASPHEMY [12c: through French from Latin *blasphemia* profanity, from Greek *blasphēmeîn* to speak evil]. A general and legal term for impious or irreverent usage; any form of strong language that uses religious expressions in a disrespectful and obscene way. Blasphemy is a common-law offence in Britain: 'Every publication is said to be blasphemous which contains any contemptuous, reviling, scurrilous or ludicrous matter relating to God, Jesus Christ, or the Bible, or the formularies of the Church of England as by law established. It is not blasphemous to speak or publish opinions hostile to the Christian religion, or to deny the existence of God, if the publication is couched in decent and temperate language. The test to be applied is as to the manner in which the doctrines are advocated and not as to the substance of the doctrines themselves' (*Stephen's Digest of the Criminal Law*, 9th edition, 1950). In the 1970s, the publication *Gay News* was found guilty of blasphemous libel for having published a poem depicting Jesus as a homosexual. It has since been proposed that the blasphemy law in England, traditionally referring only to attacks on Christianity, should be widened to include attacks on other religions. In 1989, Muslims scandalized by the portrayal of Islam in Salman Rushdie's *Satanic Verses* found that the existing law could not give them redress against author and publisher. Because the scandalized response to blasphemy is comparable to the shocked response to obscenity, the term has come to be applied to obscene language and strong language. See SWEARING. [STYLE, USAGE].   R.F.I.

BLEND [Early 20c]. Also **blend word, word blend, amalgam, fusion**. A word formed by fusing elements of two other words, such as Lewis Carroll's *slithy* from *slimy* and *lithe*. He called such forms *portmanteau words*, because they were like a two-part portmanteau bag. Blending is related to abbreviation, derivation, and compounding, but distinct from them all. In the making of *slithy* it is hard to identify the precise contributions of the source words, but some blends follow clearcut boundaries, as in *Oxbridge*, formed from *Oxford* and *Cambridge*. Many begin and end as nonce words, like *chimpanutang* and *orangorilla*. Others serve as slogans: *Cocacolonization* asserting that a country has been taken over by American values, *Don't Californicate Oregon* warning one US state against influences from another. Although blending is distinct from derivation, it may affect it. Forms like *electrocute* (1880s) bring *electro-* and *execute* together so as to suggest a suffix *-cute* that means 'kill by means of'. This element has not been exploited, but *motorcade* (*c*.1913) blends *motor* and *cavalcade* and has prompted *aerocade*, *aquacade*, and *camelcade*. As a result, the *OED* lists *-cade* as a suffix 'taken by a false division of CAVAL)CADE'. Several recent combining forms have emerged from such blending: *econo-* in *econometrics*, *-nomics* in *Reaganomics*, *-gate* in *Irangate*, *maxi-* in *maxiskirt*, *mini-* in *miniboom*, and *-thon* in *telethon*.

Blending has been used to create combination place-names: *Calexico* and *Mexicali* combine *California* and *Mexico* in forms appropriate to the side of the border on which each is found. Business names are created in the same way: *Amoco* from *American Oil Company* and a guest-house called *Kenricia* that is owned and run by a Kenneth and a Patricia. The elements of blends are sometimes presented separately in print: for example, contractions of *high technology* are commonly hyphenated as *hi-tech*, *high-tech*, *high-tec*, and have such variants and extensions as *High Tech*, *Low Tech*, *No Tech*, *Lie Tech*, *high tack*, *My Tec* (all rhyme blends or assonance blends). The variants *Hi-Tech*, *HiTech*, *HiTec*, *HyTek* employ orthographic variation for effect, as do such commercial names as *DigiPulse*, *VisiTel*, *CompuSex*. See CAPITAL. Such blending is increasing because of the need for compact scientific and technical names such as *amatol* from *ammonium nitrate* and *trinitrotoluene*, and for associated commercial names, often quasi-blends such as *Mentadent*, a toothpaste flavoured with menthol, and *Trexan*, trade name for a drug called *naltrexone*. *Atomergic Chemetals* is the portmanteau name for a company with varied interests. See ABBREVIATION, CARROLL, EPONYM, WORD-FORMATION. [WORD].   T.MCA.

BLOCK CAPITALS/LETTERS. See CAPITAL.

BLOOMFIELD, Leonard [1887-1949]. American philologist and linguist, born in Chicago, Illinois, and educated at Harvard, Wisconsin, and Chicago. He taught at several universities (1909-27) before becoming Professor of Germanic Philology at Chicago (1927-40) and Professor of Linguistics at Yale (1940-9). Initially, he was interested in Indo-European, and particularly Germanic, speech sounds and word-formation. Later, he undertook pioneering studies in the Malayo-Polynesian languages, including Tagalog in the Philippines, and made a detailed study of the North American Indian languages, in particular the Algonquian family. His publications include: *An Introduction to the Study of Language* (1914), *Language* (1933), and *Outline Guide for the Practical Study of Foreign Languages* (1942). *A Leonard Bloomfield Anthology*, edited by Charles F. Hockett, appeared in 1970. Influenced by European structuralism, Bloomfield is generally regarded as the founder of American structural linguistics. He wished to introduce greater scientific rigour into the study of language, and believed that the only useful generalizations about it are based on induction. He argued for a mechanistic and experimental rather than an introspective and mentalist approach to its study, considering ideas, feelings, and volitions to be 'merely popular terms for various bodily movements' (*Language*, 1933, p. 142).

Bloomfield's mechanistic approach is particularly evident in a treatment of meaning which derives from behavioural psychology. He interpreted a situation in which Jack gets Jill an apple (at her request) in terms of stimulus and response: a practical stimulus S (Jill sees the apple), a linguistic response r (Jill speaks), a linguistic stimulus s (Jack hears Jill's request), and a practical response R (Jack picks the apple and gives it to Jill). He argued that the meaning of Jill's utterance, or any other linguistic form, can be defined as 'the situation in which a speaker utters it and the response which it calls forth in the hearer' (p. 139). He noted that no one has a 'scientifically accurate knowledge of everything in the speaker's world' and that therefore 'the study of meaning is . . . the weak point in language study'. He largely excluded it from his own studies and for several decades his successors more or less ignored semantics.

Bloomfield's definitions of the basic units of language were influential. He defined the phoneme as 'a minimum same of vocal feature' (that is, as a physical piece of speech rather than as an abstract construct of the linguist) and believed (mistakenly, as it proved) that within a few decades it would be possible to establish the phonemes of a language in the laboratory. He defined the morpheme as the basic unit of grammatical arrangement, a 'minimal form which bears no partial phonetic-semantic resemblance to any other form' (p. 161). The word was a 'mininum free form', the smallest unit that can occur in isolation, and might consist of one morpheme (*boy*, *but*) or more than one (*boyish*, *carelessness*). However, in order to handle special morphological cases, Bloomfield crucially revised his definition of the morpheme by introducing the concept of morpheme *alternants*. These involved phonetic modification (*feel* becoming *felt*, not **feeled*), zero features (*sheep* both singular and plural), minus features (minus final /t/ where the French *petite* becomes *petit*), and suppletion (*-s* changed to *-en* in *oxen*). This change from a definition based on physical arrangement to one that incorporates process led his successors in due course to modify the definitions of both phoneme and morpheme, making them more abstract and removing the semantic element from the definition of the morpheme. See index. [AMERICAS, BIOGRAPHY, GRAMMAR, LANGUAGE].

F.R.P., T.MCA.

BLUE-EYED ENGLISH [Early 20c]. A name given by the Australian composer Percy Grainger (1882–1961) to English without its Latinate element. He worked on an unpublished 'Blueeyed dictionary' and sought to rid his own usage as far as possible of non-Germanic elements: 'Nothing should be done for take-it-easy, knownothing & care-less keyed-hammer-string players. We tone-wrights should be-shame them all we can' (quoted in John Bird, *Percy Grainger*, Melbourne, 1977) [*take-it-easy* relaxed, *knownothing* ignorant, *keyed-hammer-string* piano, *tone-wright* musician, *be-shame* to humiliate]. See BARNES, SAXONISM. [HISTORY, OCEANIA, STYLE].   T.MCA.

BLURB [1907: coined by Frank Gelett Burgess to describe a comic-book jacket that he created, embellished by a sexy young woman whom he called Miss Blinda Blurb]. (1) A usually brief and excited promotional description on the jacket, cover, or wrapper of a newly published book or similar item: 'A flamboyant advertisement; an inspired testimonial. . . . On the "jacket" of the "latest" fiction, we find the blurb, abounding in agile adjectives and adverbs, attesting that this book is the "sensation of the year" ' (F. G. Burgess, *Burgess Unabridged*, 1914); 'For why must publishers prefix to novels of this school a blurb in which much of the substance of the thriller is already revealed?' (*The Times*, 4 Aug. 1955). (2) A similarly brief promotional statement of any kind. (3) To advertise or praise (a new book, etc.) in the style of a blurb. See BURGESSISM, EDITING. [MEDIA].   T.MCA.

BODY LANGUAGE [1920s]. An informal, non-technical term for physical movement that expresses meaning, usually distinguished from *verbal communication* and often referred to technically as *non-verbal communication*. There are two aspects: facial expressions and bodily gestures, the study of which is *kinesics*, and the use of touch and body position with reference to other people, the study of which is *proxemics*. See COMMUNICATION, GESTURE, KINESICS, PROXEMICS, SEMIOTICS. [LANGUAGE].   D.C.

BOG LATIN. See SHELTA.

BOILERPLATE [1890s: by analogy with the production of steel plates for boilers. Compare CLICHÉ, STEREOTYPE]. A term in journalism, publishing, advertising, computing, etc., for: (1) Ready-to-print, syndicated copy turned out according to formula and used by small-town weekly newspapers. (2) Trite and hackneyed writing. (3) The standard wording of contracts, warranties, and similar documents. (4) Phrases, sentences, and paragraphs stored in a computer for repeated insertion in letters and other documents. See FORMULA. [STYLE, TECHNOLOGY, WRITING].   T.MCA.

BOLINGER, Dwight L(emerton) [b. 1907]. American linguist, born in Topeka, Kansas, and educated at Washburn U., the U. of Kansas, and the U. of Wisconsin. A specialist in English and Spanish, he has taught at the U. of Southern California, Harvard, and Stanford, where he has been Visiting Professor Emeritus since 1978. He founded the section on neologisms, 'Among the New Words', in the journal *American Speech* in 1941. His publications include a general introduction to linguistics, *Aspects of Language* (1968; 3rd edition, 1981), *Intonation and its Parts: Melody in Spoken English* (1985), and, aimed at a non-specialist audience, *Language, the Loaded Weapon: The Use and Abuse of Language Today* (1980), which discusses 'the influences of language on thinking and behavior' and won the Orwell Award of the National Council of Teachers of English. See index. [AMERICAS, BIOGRAPHY, LANGUAGE].   D.E.B.

BOMBAST [16c: from Old French *bombace*, Latin *bombax* silk, cotton, padding, from Greek *bómbux* a silkworm, silk]. A pejorative term for language considered padded and pompous. See JARGON. [STYLE].   T.MCA.

BOMFOG. See ACRONYM.

BONEHEAD ENGLISH, also **boneheaded English, Anguish.** College slang terms in the US since the 1920s for remedial courses intended for students who are insufficiently prepared for college-level writing. Officially, such courses have such names as *Basic English* and *English*

BOOK 139

100, and traditionally they include doses of grammar, punctuation, and usage. Unlike other watered-down (*gut* or *snap*) courses, with slang titles such as *Rocks for Jocks* (geology for athletes) and *Bolts for Dolts* (basic engineering), bonehead English is usually regarded as difficult by instructors and students alike. [AMERICAS, EDUCATION, VARIETY].   D.E.B.

BON MOT [18c: French, good word]. A well-chosen and well-used word or expression; a clever saying; a witty remark. Compare JOKE, SAYING, WITTICISM. [STYLE].   T.MCA.

BOOK [Before 10c: from Old English *bōc*, plural *bēc*, cognate with *beech*. Runic tablets were made from beechwood]. A collection of leaves of paper or other material, defined by UNESCO as a printed and bound document with more than 48 pages. In a broader sense, however, a book can have many forms: a printed and bound document, a series of clay tablets, a set of wall panels, numbered but unbound sheets, microfilm or microfiche reproduction, a machine-readable disc, etc. The primary shape, however, derives from the *codex*, a collection of leaves bound along one side, which began to prevail over papyrus and parchment rolls in the 4c. Although such rolls were expandable by gluing on further lengths, and continued in use throughout the Middle Ages, the codex was the principal medium for learned texts. Its shape remains standard, despite competition from electronic and photographic storage media.

Authority. The book is the most authoritative medium of print, but not the most pervasive. According to figures for the US in *Communication Flows* (I. De Sola Pool and others, Tokyo, 1984), 80% of published material is in newspapers, 10% in magazines, 8% in brochures and pamphlets by direct mail, and 2% in books. *CF* estimates that Americans spend an average of 9 minutes per day reading a book (with similar reading patterns for comparable nations). This is far less time than people spend on other media. When compared with these, the book is a lesser medium, but despite the limited time spent on them, books have an authority drawn in part from a complex relationship with religion. In classical and medieval times, the book was the principal form of scribal culture, its authority apparent in the Bible, often referred to simply as *the (Good) Book*. The book as word of God was, during and after the Reformation, a central authoritative document, and the idea of the Book as a source of truth was extended to other works. Hence, in many societies, censorship, undue taxation, import restriction, or limitation in the production or movement of books is seen as an attack on the freedom to share ideas. To

those brought up in such societies, whether they read or not, the book is virtually sacred. In addition, the special status of the book is reinforced by its central position in most systems of education.

Decline? Books require a long lead time for writing, manufacture, and distribution; other media can move data more rapidly. Although several books together can provide a rich spread of information, they cannot be combined, sorted, and recombined as rapidly as in electronic systems. Books are, however, superb media for sustained thought: the text is stable and can be read again and again. Although it has been said that print culture is in decline, the book industry has been growing during the later 20c. Annual production in the English-speaking world is enormous: over 2bn copies of new books annually in the US alone. The UK and the US each report over 40,000 new editions every year, with an estimated growth of over 2% every year in the US since 1970. Much of this production is educational and informational, but works of literature, philosophy, and poetry also abound. People appear in fact to be reading and consulting more books than ever before.

Formats. Though books may be seen as quasi-spiritual, they remain material objects. Special technical terms, commonly known and used in the high era of the book (late 15c to mid-20c), describe their shapes and sizes. In the era of hand-printing, size was determined by the size of sheets used and the way in which they were printed, folded, sewn, and cut to produce leaves that could be turned and read. An average-sized sheet might measure from around 12 × 16 inches (30 × 40 cm), the size known as *pot* or *pott*, to around 18 × 24 inches (45 × 60 cm), the size known as *royal*. Other sizes were *foolscap*, *crown*, *demy*, *elephant*, and *imperial*. If a printer covers one side of a sheet with one block of type, the result is a *broadsheet* or *broadside*. If two blocks of type are printed on each side and the sheet is folded to produce two leaves or four pages of print, the result is a *folio*. It is impractical to sew single folios together to make a whole book; the stitching in the binding would be thicker than the pages. Three or four folios are therefore gathered together into a *gathering* or *quire* which is then stitched in a binding. These are called *folios in sixes/eights*, depending on the number of leaves the gathering presents. As every leaf is in two *pages*, a folio in eights has 16 pages in each gathering.

Folios are large books; smaller formats are obtained by printing more pages on the single sheet and folding the sheet to present more pages. A *quarto* is the sheet folded twice to present four leaves, an *octavo* the sheet folded three times to present eight leaves. *Duodecimo* (or *twelvemo*) is the folding needed to produce a 12-leaf gathering; others are *sixteenmo* and *thirty-two-mo* (in Latin *sextodecimo, tricesimosecundo*). The range of size of the books is only partly indicated by the format name: a quarto could be impressive or insignificant, in the latter instance, even a *pamphlet*, as were first editions of some of Shakespeare's plays. There is a limit to how many times even a thin piece of paper can be folded, so that a tiny format like *sixty-four-mo* is unusual.

Hierarchies. In the era of the hand-press, certain books were associated with certain formats. Folios were often seen as books of great learning; standard editions of the great philosophers would appear in this format. When Ben Jonson prepared a folio edition of his works in 1616, he was indulging in extraordinary self-aggrandizement for a writer of plays. The 1623 First Folio of Shakespeare showed a similar extravagance on the part of his editors. There was a pecking order in the formats. Joseph Addison comments in 1712 that 'The Author of a *Folio* . . . sets himself above the Author of a *Quarto*; the Author of a *Quarto* above the Author of an *Octavo*; and so on, by a gradual Descent and Subordination, to an Author in *Twenty-Fours*' (*Spectator* 529).

Writing to fit. In the 17–18c, books were not always well finished, and they were often accompanied by errata lists. Because a book was not sold bound, but in folded sheets, the buyer could rearrange material: books printed in parts are bound whole, in parts, or in mixed sets, where owners would complete a set by mixing in later editions of other works or works by other authors on the same topic, all in the same binding. Sometimes books would be published in one form with the intention of rebinding or reuse in another. Dickens wrote many of his novels for magazines printed in octavo gatherings. The publisher or the reader could gather up the sheets and rebind them as a book. Indeed, Dickens, Scott, and others wrote their chapters to fit these gatherings. The fifth monthly instalment of Dickens's *Nicholas Nickleby* runs from ch. 15 through 18 and fills two octavo gatherings. A knowledge of printer's gatherings and how 19c part-publication was organized helps one understand the way in which Dickens structured his narrative.

New shapes. Many books continue to be printed from sheets, and editors and printers know that a work is to be printed *sixteen-up* or *thirty-two-up* (the number of pages printed on one side of the sheet), but the sheets are much larger, so that a book with sections of 16 leaves could be the size of an old quarto or even a folio. With web-fed presses, the number of pages on a single side of a sheet before cutting becomes complex: there are large machines that print entire editions of paperback books, the finished product not just printed and folded but also bound and ready for packing. Although such books have no precise name, standard sizes exist, even though with contemporary technology the possibilities of size and shape are limitless. The typical paperback is about 7×5 inches (18×13 cm) and half an inch thick. The typical hardcover or trade paperback is about 10×7 inches (25×18 cm). These sizes are in large part conventional. In physical terms, the book is simply a commodity in a system of presses, shipping and packing machines, warehouse and bookstore shelving, and the needs of librarians and others for storage space. Yet even the most ordinary and ephemeral mass-market paperback is part of a cultural history that stretches back in the West for some two and a half millennia, in which the book served as the privileged medium for both faith and learning.

See AUDIOBOOK, BACK MATTER, BIBLE, BIBLIOGRAPHY, BOOKLET, BOOK OF COMMON PRAYER, BRITISH LIBRARY, BROADSHEET, BROCHURE, CANON, CASE[2], CATALOG(UE), CHAPTER, CODEX, COMMUNICATIVE, COMMUNICATION SHIFT, CROWN, DEMY, DIARY, EDITING, EDUCATION, FICTION, FOLIO, FOOLSCAP, FRONT MATTER, IMPERIAL, JOURNAL, LEAF, LEAFLET, LIBRARY, LIBRARY OF CONGRESS, LITERATURE, MAGAZINE, -MO, OCTAVO, PAGE, PAGINATION, PAMPHLET, PAPER, PAPERBACK, PARCHMENT, PERIODICAL, PREFACE, PRELIM(INARIE)S, PRINTING, PUBLISHING, QUARTO, READING, REFERENCE, SCRIPTURE, SIGNATURE, SIXTEENMO, TALKING BOOK, TEXT, TEXTBOOK, TITLE, VOLUME, WRITING. [HISTORY, MEDIA, TECHNOLOGY].   W.W.B.

BOOKLET [19c]. A thin or small book, especially one with paper covers. In the 19c, forerunners of the paperback, capable of being put conveniently in the pocket, were referred to as *booklets*. Compare BROADSIDE, PAMPHLET. [MEDIA, TECHNOLOGY].   T.MCA.

BOOK OF COMMON PRAYER, short form *BCP*. The book used for public worship by Anglican Christians for over 400 years, and regarded as authoritative for doctrine. It originated with the First and Second Prayer Books of King Edward VI (1549, 1552), was mainly compiled by Thomas Cranmer, and drew on Latin, Orthodox, German, and Spanish liturgies. It underwent revisions, notably in 1662 when restored to use after being banned during the Commonwealth, but is recognizably Cranmer's original. A further revision in 1928, though not officially authorized, is in use in some places. *BCP* is the earliest source for many common words and phrases, such as *all one's worldly goods, at death's door, to have and to hold, in sickness and in health, land of the living, like lost sheep, tender mercy, to lead a new life*. Complex sentence structure with long subordinate clauses is a feature widely assimilated into the language: 'Almighty God, unto whom all hearts be open, all desires known, and from whom no secrets are hid; Cleanse the thoughts of our hearts by the inspiration of thy Holy Spirit, that we may perfectly love thee, and worthily magnify thy holy Name' (Collect at commencement of Holy Communion). *BCP* contains many pairs of synonyms, such as *praise and magnify, erred and strayed, prisoners and captives, prepare and make ready*, usually one word from Latin, the other Anglo-Saxon, the aim of which was comprehensibility among all levels of society. Because for 400 years a high degree of uniformity in worship was imposed by law, *BCP* has influenced vocabulary and syntax to an extent comparable to the Bible and Shakespeare. See BIBLE, BIBLICAL ENGLISH, BISOCIATION, CRANMER. [HISTORY, LITERATURE].   M.LA.

BOONTLING, BOONVILLE LINGO. See DIALECT IN AMERICA, PRIVATE LANGUAGE.

BORDER LINGO. See LINGO, TEX-MEX.

BORROWING [Before 10c: from Old English *borgian* to borrow, lend, from *borg* a pledge]. (1) Taking a word or phrase from one language into another, or from one variety of a language into another. (2) The item so taken, such as *arpeggio* from Italian into English, and *schlock* from Yiddish into AmE, then into BrE. Borrowing is a major aspect of language change, but the term itself is a misnomer: it presumes repayment, whereas there is no *quid pro quo* between languages. The item borrowed is not returned, because it never left the source language and in any case changes in the transfer. Compare LOAN, LOANWORD.

Patterns of borrowing. Any language, under appropriate circumstances, borrows lexical material from other languages, usually absorbing the exotic items or translating them into native equivalents. Some languages borrow more than others, and borrow more from some sources than others. English has borrowed massively from French, Latin, and Greek, significantly from Italian, Spanish, German, Danish, and Dutch, and to varying degrees from every other language with which it has come in contact. The Cannon corpus of 13,683 new English words shows that this process continues unabated; the 1,029 transfers listed in the corpus entered English from 84 languages (1987-9) as follows: French 25%, Spanish and Japanese both

8%, Italian 6.3%, Latin 6.1%, Greek 6%, German 5.5%, and 77 languages contributed 1-39 items each. Here, only the Japanese element breaks the traditional pattern, in which European languages predominate.

Reasons for borrowing. The preconditions for borrowing are: (1) Close contact in especially multilingual situations, making the mixing of elements from different languages more or less commonplace. (2) The domination of some languages by others (for cultural, economic, political, religious, or other reasons), so that material flows 'down' from those 'high' languages into 'lower' vernaculars. (3) A sense of need, users of one language drawing material from another for such purposes as education and technology. (4) Prestige associated with using words from another language. (5) A mix of some or all of these. Individuals may use an exotic expression because it seems to them to be the most suitable term available, the only possible term (with no equivalent in any other language), or the most impressive term. Much of the vocabulary of French entered English in the Middle Ages because French was the language of political and social power and the channel through which mainland European culture reached Britain. Much of the vocabulary of Latin entered English during the Renaissance (directly or via French) because Latin was the European language of religion, education, and learning. While so prestigious a language could provide time-hallowed resources, there was little encouragement to develop the resources of relatively insignificant vernaculars like English. In the late 20c, English sometimes serves in its turn as a kind of Latin in the main because both have been languages of empire. Thus, as part of the Malaysian Government's educational programme based on Malay (intended to unify the nation's ethnic groups), the already polyglot scientific and technical vocabulary of English has been massively adopted into Malay: see MALAY.

Reasons for resisting borrowing. Listeners and readers have their own responses to the use of an exotic term, and these responses affect their inclination to repeat it. Although such reactions are not properties of the item itself, the associations formed may affect its new use, so that it may remain in a limited field, such as French *œuvre* and *auteur* in English literary criticism. Such a term may not be understood outside its field or may be considered pretentious. However, some items are so universally apt that they swiftly occupy a niche in the language at large, such as French *garage* and *cliché*. In addition, there may be personal and communal reasons for resisting the influx of foreignisms: for example, a protectionist language policy (as in

Iceland), on the grounds that the community is small and linguistically fragile; a sense of past oppression (as in such ex-colonial countries as Tanzania), where Swahili is promoted as a national medium rather than English; and pride in the home language and culture (as in Iran). All three factors were present in the Canadian province of Quebec in the 1970s, when official legislation militated against English influence on French.

Diffusion and adaptation. Borrowing is sometimes simple and limited (a few words taken from Language A into Language B), sometimes complex and extensive (much of the vocabulary of A becoming available for use in B, and perhaps C and D as well as with Sanskrit in India, Arabic in West Asia, and Latin in Europe). What appears to be a single process affecting two languages may be multiple, in that an item may be diffused as a *pilgrim word* into a range of languages, usually adapting as it goes: (1) Greek *phantasía* has become French *fantaisie*, German *Fantasie*, Italian *fantasia*, Portuguese *fantazia*, Spanish *fantasía*, and English *fancy*, along with *fantasy*, *fantasia*, and archaic *phantasy*. (2) Latin *planta* (sprout, offspring) passed into Italian as *pianta*, Old English and Old French as *plante*, Spanish *llanta*, Portuguese *chanta*, German *Pflanze*, Welsh *plant*, and Old Irish as *cland*, whence it became Gaelic *clann* (offspring, family, stock, race). Both *plant* and *clan* are now English words. (3) Sanskrit *dhyāna* (meditation) passed into Pali as *jhāna*, into Chinese as *ch'an*, then into Japanese as *zen*. Both *dhyana* and *Zen* are now English words.

There is a continuum in borrowing, from words that remain relatively alien and unassimilated in pronunciation and spelling (as with *blasé* and *soirée* from French), through those that become more or less acclimatized (as with *elite* rather than *élite*, while retaining a French-like pronunciation, and *garage* with its various pronunciations) to forms that have been assimilated so fully that their exotic origin is entirely obscured (as with *cockroach*, from Spanish *cucaracha*, and *chocolate* through Spanish from Nahuatl *chocolatl*).

A word taken from a typologically or genetically related language would appear to be more easily assimilated than one taken from a very different kind of language. Like English, Spanish is an Indo-European language written in the Roman alphabet, and so the absorption of items like *armada* and *guerrilla* into English offers few problems. However, some elements may be too alien for convenient absorption: for example, although Mexican Spanish *chili* and *taco* have been easily absorbed, the phrase *frijoles refritos* has posed a problem, because the order of noun and adjective and the double plural are not native to English. As a result, the loan translation *refried beans* has become the choice for non-bilinguals. On the other hand, Chinese is a tone language usually written ideographically; in theory, this should deter transfer, but large-scale English–Chinese and Chinese–English borrowing has gone ahead without much difficulty, English for example acquiring *chow mein*, *ginseng*, *kaolin*, *taipan*, and *tea/char*.

Linguistic effects of borrowing. Transfers may have an influence on such basic aspects of a language as its pronunciation, spelling, syntax, and semantics. The local system usually overwhelms the acquisition; thus, when numbers of items with aspirated voiced stops came into English, spelled with *h*, the consonantal system remained unchanged, *bhang* being pronounced like *bang*, *dhow* like *dow*, *ghat* like *gat*. However, transfers into English from French may be pronounced as closely as possible to the French (as with *raison d'être*, *sabotage*), or with concessions to French and adaptations into English (the various pronunciations of *garage*). Morphological impact may introduce different plural forms: for example, such sets as Greek *criterion/criteria*, *thesis/theses*, Latin *appendix/appendices*, *stimulus/stimuli*, Italian *graffito/graffiti*, and Hebrew *cherub/cherubim*, *kibbutz/kibbutzim*. However, such adoptions are not always stable, and conflict may occur between foreign and nativized forms, as with *cactus/cacti ~ cactuses*. See CLASSICAL ENDING. Perhaps the largest morphological impact on English has been the addition of French, Latin, and Greek affixes such as *dis-*, *pro-*, *anti-*, *-ity*, *-ism*, and such combining forms as *bio-*, *micro-*, *-metry*, *-logy*, which replaced many of the original Germanic affixes in English. Only rarely do affixes from other sources establish themselves to any degree in English: for example, the suffix *-nik*, from Russian, as in *kolkhoznik*, and Yiddish, as in *kibbutznik*, and nativized, as in *beatnik* and *peacenik*.

Kinds of words borrowed. Nouns make up the highest proportion of transfers, followed by adjectives. Verbs are usually few, with even fewer adverbs and grammatical words like pronouns. However, the replacement of the Old English third-person plural *hīe* by Old Danish *they* shows that such transfers sometimes occur. The 1,029 recent transfers in the Cannon corpus break down into 916 nouns (such as *art trouvé*, *honcho*, *pita*), 86 adjectives (such as *gauchesco*, *kitschy*, *Namibian*), 12 verbs (such as *francicize*, *nosh*, *vinify*), 3 interjections (*arigato* from Japanese, *ciao* from Italian, *inshallah* from Arabic), and 12 bound forms (including *atto-* from Danish/Norwegian, *-nik* from Russian, and *ur-* from

German). This does not, however, mean that nouns are most and interjections least easily transferred; nouns in any case predominate in a language. In terms of such proportions, interjections are at least as easily borrowed, when the conditions are appropriate, as the worldwide spread of AmE *OK* testifies. Phrases are also commonly transferred, as with *drame à clef* and *roman à clef* from French into English. Sentences are less common, although English has a tradition of using short Latin and French sentences like *Tempus fugit* and *C'est la vie.*

Borrowings into English. In the following sections, arranged according to the world's major regions, is a wide selection of languages from which at various times and in various ways English has borrowed. The samples are organized so as to suggest the proportions in which material from other languages is present in English, but no section seeks to be exhaustive and the historical dimension (for example, the periods when particular words entered English) is not explored. In some cases, the intermediary languages through which material has passed are indicated.

The Americas. (1) Algonquian, including Abnaki, Cree, Micmac, Ojibway, Narragansett, Shawnee: *caucus, chipmunk, hickory, manitou, moccasin, moose, muskrat, opossum, papoose, pecan, pemmican, persimmon, pow-wow, rac-(c)oon, skunk, squash, squaw, succotash, toboggan, tomahawk, wampum, wapiti, wigwam, woodchuck.* (2) Aleut and Inuit: *anorak, igloo, kayak, parka.* (3) Araucanian through Spanish: *coypu, poncho.* (4) Arawakan, especially through Spanish: *barbecue, cacique, hammock, iguana, potato, tobacco, savanna(h).* (5) Carib, especially through Spanish: *cannibal, canoe, hurricane, macaw, maize, manatee, papaya/pa(w)paw, peccary, tomalley, yucca.* (6) Creek: *catalpa, tupelo.* (7) Nahuatl through Spanish: *avocado, axolotl, cacao/cocoa, chili/chilli, chocolate, coyote, mescal, ocelot, peyote, teocalli, tomato.* (8) Quechua through Spanish: *alpaca, charqui/jerky, coca(ine), condor, guanaco, guano, llama, pampas, puma, quinine, vicuna.* (9) Tupi-Guaraní through French, Portuguese, Spanish: *buccaneer, cashew, cayenne, cougar, ipecac(uanha), jaguar, manioc, petunia, tapioca, tapir, toucan.*

Africa. (1) Afrikaans: *aardvaark, aardwolf, apartheid, Boer, commando, dorp, kop, kopje/koppie, outspan, spoor, springbok, trek.* (2) Bantu languages, including Kongo, Swahili, Tswana, Xhosa, Zulu: *boma, bwana, chimpanzee, impala, impi, indaba, mamba, marimba, tsetse, zombie.* (3) West African languages, including Ewe, Fanti, Hausa, Mandingo, mainly through the Atlantic creoles: *anansi, gumbo, harmattan, juju, juke(box), mumbo-jumbo, okra, voodoo, yam;*

perhaps *banjo, jazz.* (4) Malagasy: *raffia.* (5) Khoisan languages: *gnu, quagga.*

Asia: Western. (1) Arabic, through European languages: *admiral, albatross, alchemy, alcohol, alcove, alembic, algebra, alkali, almanac, apricot, arsenal, assassin, assegai, attar, aubergine, azimuth, bedouin, caliph, cipher/cypher, emir, gazelle, genie/jinn, ghoul, giraffe, hazard, jasmine, kismet, Koran, lemon, magazine, minaret, mohair, monsoon, Moslem, nadir, saffron, sash, scarlet, sequin, sheik(h), sherbet, simoom/simoon, sirocco, sofa, syrup, talisman, tariff, zero*; direct or through Afro-Asian languages: *ayatollah, harem, hashish, henna, hooka(h), imam, Islam, jihad, kaffir, muezzin, mufti, mujahedin, mullah, Muslim, nadir, Qur'ān, safari, sahib, salaam, Sharia, shaykh, zenith.* (2) Aramaic: *abbot, kaddish, pharisee.* (3) Hebrew, especially through Greek, Latin, and Yiddish: *alphabet, amen, bedlam, camel, cherub, cinnamon, hosanna, Jehovah, manna, maudlin, nard, nitre, rabbi, seraph, shemozzle, simony, sodomy*; more or less direct: *behemoth, cabal, Cabala, chazan/haz(z)an, golem, hallelujah, leviathan, messiah, sabbath, shalom, shibboleth, Talmud, Torah, Yahweh.* (4) Persian through European languages: *arsenic, azure, check, checkmate, magus/magic, paradise, peach, pilaf, pistachio, spinach, talc*; direct or through Asian languages: *bazaar, caravan/caravanserai, dervish, durbar, jackal, khaki, kiosk, lilac, maidan, mogul, pilau/pulao, pyjamas/pajamas, shah, shawl, sherbet, tiara, tulip, turban.* (5) Turkish/Tatar: *bosh, caftan/kaftan, caique, coffee, cossack, divan, horde, kavass, khan, kumiss, mammoth, pasha, Tartar, turkey, turquoise, yoghurt/yogurt/(CanE) yoghourt.*

Asia: Southern and South-Eastern. (1) Hindi/Urdu: *bungalow, crore, dacoit, deodar, dinghy, dungaree, ghee, gymkhana, lakh/lac, loot, paisa, pakora, Raj, samo(o)sa, shampoo, tandoori, tom-tom, wallah.* (2) Javanese: *bantam, batik, gamelan, junk.* (3) Malay: *amok/amuck, bamboo, caddy, camphor, cassowary, cockatoo, dugong, durian, gecko, gingham, gong, kampong/compound, kapok, kris, lory, mangosteen, orang-utan/orang-outang, paddy, pangolin, rattan, sago, sarong.* (4) Malayalam: *betel, coir, copra, ginger, teak.* (5) Marathi: *mongoose.* (6) Sanskrit through various languages: *ashram, avatar, banya, banyan, beryl, brahmin, carmine, cheetah, chintz, chutney, crimson, juggernaut, jungle, jute, lacquer, mandarin, palanquin, pundit, sapphire, sugar, suttee*; more or less direct: *ahimsa, asana, ashrama, atman, avatara, bodhisattva, brahmana, Buddha, chakra, guru, hatha yoga, karma, lingam, maharaja(h), mahatma, mantra, Maya, nirvana, raja(h), rani/ranee, satyagraha, sutra, swastika, yantra, yoga, yogasana.* (7) Sinhala:

anaconda, tourmaline. (8) Tagalog: *boondock, ylang-ylang.* (9) Tamil: *catamaran, cheroot, curry, mango, mulligatawny, pariah.* (10) Telugu: *bandicoot.*

Asia: Central and Eastern. (1) Chinese languages: *china, chin-chin, chopsticks, chopsuey, chow chow, chow mein, fan-tan, ginseng, gung-ho, kaolin, ketchup/catsup, kowtow, kung fu, litchi/ lichee/lychee, loquat, mahjong, pekoe, sampan, tai chi, taipan, Tao, tea, yang, yen, yin.* (2) Japanese: *aikido, banzai, bonsai, bushido, futon, geisha, haiku, hara-kiri, judo, jujitsu, Kabuki, kamikaze, kimono, koan, mikado, sake, samisen, samurai, sayonara, Shinto, shogun, soy(a), sushi, teriyaki, tofu, tycoon, yen, Zen.* (3) Tibetan: *lama, yak, yeti.* (4) Tungus: *shaman.*

Europe: the Celtic languages. (1) Breton through French: *bijou, dolmen, menhir.* (2) Celtic before Gaelic, Welsh, Breton, and Cornish, and through Latin, French, and Old English: *ambassador/embassy, bannock, bard, bracket, breeches, car/carry/career/ carriage/ cargo/carpenter/charge, crag, druid, minion, peat, piece, vassal/valet/varlet.* (3) Cornish: *porbeagle, wrasse.* (4) Gaelic, general: *bog, cairn, clarsach, coronach, crag, crannog, gab/gob, galore, skene, usquebaugh/whisk(e)y;* Irish: *banshee, blarney, brogue, colleen, hooligan, leprechaun, lough, macushla, mavourneen, poteen, shamrock, shebeen, shillelagh, smithereens, spalpeen, Tory;* Scottish: *caber, cailleach, cairngorm, clachan, clan, claymore, corrie, glen, loch, lochan, pibroch, plaid, ptarmigan, slogan, sporran, strath, trews, trousers.* (5) Welsh: *bug, coracle, corgi, cromlech, cwm, eisteddfod, flannel, flummery.*

Europe: the Germanic languages. (1) Danish: *smørrebrød/smorrebrod.* (2) Dutch, including Flemish and Low German (but not Afrikaans: see Africa): *bluff, boor, boss, brandy, bully, bumpkin, clamp, clipper, coleslaw, cookie, cruise, dapper, derrick, dope, drill, drum, easel, frolic, golf, grime, hunk, kink, landscape, loiter, poppycock, rant, runt, scow, skipper, sled, sledge, sleigh, slim, smack, smuggle, snap, snoop, splint, spook, stoop, yacht, yawl.* (3) German: *blitz- (krieg), dachshund, fahrenheit, flak, frankfurter, glockenspiel, gneiss, hamburger, hamster, kaffeeklatsch, kindergarten, kitsch, leberwurst, leitmotiv, nix, pretzel, quartz, realpolitik, sauerkraut, schadenfreude, schmaltz, schnitzel, schwa, strafe, waltz, weltanschauung, weltgeist, yodel, zeitgeist.* (4) Icelandic: *auk, eider, geyser, saga.* (5) Norse: *anger, balderdash, bing, bleak, blether, blink, bloom, blunder, blur, call, clamber, creek, crook, die, dirt, dowdy, doze, dregs, egg, fellow, flat, flaunt, flaw, fleck, flimsy, gasp, gaunt, gaze, girth, glint, glitter, gloat, happen, harsh, inkling, kick, kilt, law, leg, loan, meek, midden, muck, muggy, nasty, nudge, oaf, odd, raise, root, scalp,*

scant, scowl, seat, skerry, skewer, skid, skill, skin, skull, sky, sniff, snub, squall, squeal, take, they, thrall, thrift, thrust, ugly, vole, want, weak, window. (6) Norwegian: *fjord/fiord, floe, kraken, krill, lemming, ski, slalom.* (7) Scots, in English at large: *balmoral, burn, canny, carfuffle, collie, cosy, eerie, eldritch, forebear, glamour, glengarry, gloaming, glower, gumption, guddle, lilt, pony, raid, rampage, uncanny, wee, weird, wizened, wraith;* mainly in Scotland: *ashet, bogle, bonnie, burn, cleg, dreich, dwam, fornent, furth of, glaikit, glaur, hochmagandy, howf, leal, lowp, outwith, scunner, speir, stot, thole, trauchle.* (8) Swedish: *glogg, ombudsman, smörgåsbord/smorgasbord, tungsten.* (9) Yiddish: *chutzpah, shlemiel, shlep, shlock, schmaltzy.*

Europe: Greek. (1) Inflectional endings retained but spelt in the Latin style: *abiogenesis, aegis, analysis, anemone, antithesis, automaton, charisma, cinema, crisis, criterion, cytokinesis, diagnosis, dogma, drama, electron, enigma, genesis, gnosis, hoi polloi, kerygma, lalophobia, magma, osteoporosis, phenomenon, photon, rhinoceros, rhododendron, stigma, synthesis, thesis.* (2) With Latin endings: *brontosaurus, chrysanthemum, diplodocus, hippopotamus, Pliohippus.* (3) Endings dropped or adapted: *agnostic, agnosticism, alphabet, alphabetic, analyst, analytic, anthocyanin, astrobleme, atheism, automatic, biologist, biology, blasphemy, charismatic, chemotherapy, chronobiology, cinematography, critic, criticism, dinosaur, dogmatic, dogmatism, dramatic, dramatist, electric, electronic, enigmatic, epistemic, epistemology, gene, genetic, herpetology, narcolepsy, odyssey, oligarchy, patriarch, phenomenology, photograph, pterodactyl, sympathomimetic.* (4) Modern: *bouzouki, moussaka, ouzo, rebetika, sirtaki, souvlaki.*

Europe: Latin. (1) Inflectional endings retained: *addendum, albumen, apex, area, bacterium/ bacteria, cactus, calix, camera, cancer, circus, colossus, complex, datum/data, discus, equilibrium, fauna, flora, formula, fungus, genius, genus, homunculus, honorarium, inertia, interim, latex, locus, medium/media, memorandum, momentum, onus, opera, ovum, pauper, pendulum, peninsula, propaganda, radium, referendum, series, simile, simplex, status, stimulus, terminus, vertigo, victor.* (2) Actual inflected Latin verbs used as nouns: *audio, audit, caveat, exeunt, fiat, floruit, imprimatur, mandamus, video.* (3) Fixed phrases: *ad hoc, a posteriori, de facto, de jure, extempore, (ex) post facto, post mortem, quid pro quo, sine die.* (4) Binomials: *Homo sapiens, Pax Britannica, miles gloriosus, gluteus maximus.* (5) Endings dropped or adapted, often through French: *add, addition, additive, agent, agentive, aqueduct, candle, colo(u)r, colossal, consider, contemplate, decide,* *decision, erupt, eruption, general, generic, hono(u)r, hono(u)rable, honorary, igneous, ignite, ignition, ignoble, illiteracy, illiterate, immoral, immorality, ingenious, ingenuity, literacy, literate, literature, meditate, meditation, meditative, memorable, memory, moment, momentary, momentous, moral, morality, nobility, noble, pendulous, peninsular, revise, revision, sex, similar, similarity, temple.*

Europe: the Romance languages. (1) French, Old: *allow, bastard, beauty, beef, brush, castle, chivalry, choice, cloister, conquest, constraint, court, defeat, destroy, dinner, forest, frail, garden, govern, honest, hostel, interest, judge, loyal, marvel, mutton, paste, place, poison, pork, priest, push, quarter, quest, royal, stuff, sure, tempest, ticket, trick*; Modern: *aperitif/apéritif, apres-ski/après-ski, avant-garde, bidet, bourgeois(ie), brasserie, brassiere/brassière, cafe/café, camouflage, canard, chateau/château, chef, chevalier, coup de grace/grâce, coup d'etat/état, croissant, cuisine, debacle/débacle/débâcle, debut/début, dessert, elite/élite, esprit de corps, etiquette, fiance(e)/fiancé(e), fricassee/fricassée, frisson, garage, gourmand, gourmet, hors d'oeuvre, hotel, joie de vivre, liaison, limousine, lingerie, marionette, morale, nee/née, objet d'art, parole, pastiche, patisserie/pâtisserie, petite, pirouette, prestige, regime/régime, risque/risqué, silhouette, souvenir, toilette, vignette, voyeur.* (2) Italian, through French: *balcony, battalion, brigade, charlatan, design, frigate, granite, squadron*; direct: *alto, arpeggio, bordello, broccoli, cameo, canto, confetti, contralto, cupola, ghetto, graffiti, grotto, imbroglio, lasagne, libretto, mozzarella, pasta, piano(forte), piazza, piccolo, pizza, pizzeria, pizzicato, ravioli, risotto, sonata, seraglio, soprano, spaghetti, staccato, stanza, studio, tagliatelle, vermicelli.* (3) Occitan/Provençal, usually through French: *ballad, beret, cocoon, funnel, nutmeg, troubadour.* (4) Portuguese: *albino, caste, marmalade, molasses, palaver.* (5) Spanish, adapted: *alligator, anchovy, barricade, cask, cedilla, galleon, grenade, hoosegow, lariat, ranch, renegade, sherry, stampede, stevedore, vamoose*; direct: *adobe, armada, armadillo, borracho, bravado, chili, chinchilla, embargo, guerrilla, hacienda, mosquito, mulatto, negro, peccadillo, pinto, pronto, sarsaparilla, silo, sombrero, vigilante.*

Europe: the Slavonic languages. (1) Czech: *howitzer, pistol, robot.* (2) Polish: *mazurka, polka.* (3) Russian: *agitprop, borsch, cosmonaut, czar/tsar, dros(h)ky, glasnost, gulag, perestroika, pogrom, samizdat, samovar, steppe, troika, vodka.*

Europe: the unique languages. (1) Basque through Spanish: *chaparral, jai alai.* (2) Finnish: *sauna.* (3) Hungarian: *coach, czardas/csárdás, goulash, hussar, paprika, tokay.* (4) Romany: *nark, pal.*

Oceania. (1) Australian Aboriginal: *billabong, boomerang, corroboree, kangaroo, koala, kookaburra, murree, wallaby, wombat, yabber, yakka/yacker.* (2) Polynesian, including: Hawaiian *aloha, heiau, hula, kapu, lanai, lei, muumuu, ukulele/ukelele, wahine*; Maori *aroha, iwi, kauri, kiwi, Maoritanga, marae, moa, ngati, pakeha, pohutukawa, tangata whenua, tangi, toheroa, tuatara, whakapapa, whare*; Tahitian *tattoo*; Tongan *kava, taboo/tabu.*

See AFRICAN LANGUAGES, AFRIKAANS, AMERICAN LANGUAGES, ARABIC, ASSIMILATION, AUSTRALIAN LANGUAGES, BANTU, BISOCIATION, BRETON, CALQUE, CHINA, CLASSICAL COMPOUND, CLASSICAL ENDING, CODE-MIXING AND CODE-SWITCHING, COMBINING FORM, DANISH, DOUBLET, DUTCH, ENGLISHIZE, ETYMOLOGY, EUROPEAN LANGUAGES, FOREIGNISM, FRENCH, GAELIC, GERMAN, GREEK, HAMITO-SEMITIC LANGUAGES, HISTORY, INDIAN LANGUAGES, INDO-EUROPEAN LANGUAGES, INTERNATIONAL SCIENTIFIC VOCABULARY, ITALIAN, JAPAN, LANGUAGE CHANGE, LATIN, LEXICAL BAR, LOAN, LOANWORD, MALAY, MALAYALAM, MAORI, MARATHI, NEOLOGISM, NONCE WORD, NORSE, NORWEGIAN, PERSIAN, PHILOLOGY, PORTUGUESE, ROMANI/ROMANY, SANSKRIT, SOUTH AFRICAN LANGUAGES, SPANISH, SWEDISH, TAGALOG, TAMIL, WELSH, YIDDISH. [AFRICA, AMERICAS, ASIA, EUROPE, HISTORY, LANGUAGE, OCEANIA, WORD].   G.C., T.MCA., J.M.G.

BOSTON. The capital of the state of Massachusetts and cultural centre of New England, one of the earliest areas of English settlement in what is now the US and a focal point from which English spread. Its social leaders are called *Boston Brahmins*, a wry allusion to the priestly caste of India. In the 19c, they included such literary figures as Oliver Wendell Holmes Sr., Henry Wadsworth Longfellow, and James Russell Lowell, whose tastes were European and unsympathetic to the major 19c US writers, such as Ralph Waldo Emerson, Edgar Allan Poe, Mark Twain, and Walt Whitman. Boston represented a 'genteel' tradition in literature and language that has not survived. Currently, Bostonian speech is most widely known from the usage of President John F. Kennedy and his brothers, as stereotyped for example by the long 'flat' vowel and r-lessness of expressions like *paak the caa* (park the car) and the intrusive r of *Cuba/r is a problem*. Bostonian speech ranges from low-prestige to Boston Brahmin, which, although educated and cultured, is not widely admired outside the city. Compare NEW YORK. See DIALECT IN AMERICA (THE NORTH), NEW ENGLAND. [AMERICAS, VARIETY].   J.A.

BOSWELL, James [1740-95]. Scottish writer, born in Ayrshire, and educated at Edinburgh,

Glasgow, and Utrecht. He took up radical politics, met Rousseau and Voltaire, and supported the cause of liberty for Corsica; his *Account of Corsica* appeared in 1768. In 1760 he met Samuel Johnson. Their visit to Scotland in 1773 was recorded in *Journal of a Tour of the Hebrides* (1785) and their friendship led to his *Life of Samuel Johnson* (1791), one of the most famous biographies in English. It was mainly through this work that Johnson came to be so well known to posterity. Boswell preserves both Johnson's views on many subjects and his witty, often acerbic, replies to interlocutors. He created not only a pen portrait of Johnson but also a record of 18c conversation valuable to historians of the language and students of dialogue in the early novels. He also left letters and diaries. An abridged and annotated edition by John Canning was published by Methuen (London) in 1991. See index. [BIOGRAPHY, EUROPE, HISTORY, LITERATURE].   R.C.

BOTSWANA. Official title *Republic of Botswana*. A country in southern Africa and member of the Commonwealth. Capital: Gaborone. Currency: pula (100 thebe). Population: 1.19m (1988), 1.2m (projection for 2000). Ethnicity: Batswana 94%, Bushman 5%, European 1%. Religion: 50% Christian, 50% traditional. Languages: Setswana (national), English (official). Education: primary 76%, secondary 18%, tertiary 1%; literacy 71%. During the early 19c, the missionaries Robert Moffat and David Livingstone visited the Batswana. In 1885, under threat of settlement by Boer farmers from the Transvaal, their lands came under British influence and were divided into a southern colony, now part of the Cape province, South Africa, and the northern protectorate of *Bechuanaland*, which became independent as Botswana in 1966. See AFRICAN ENGLISH, AFRICAN LANGUAGES, BANTU, ENGLISH, JONES (D.). [AFRICA, NAME, VARIETY].   T.MCA.

BOUND AND FREE [1930s]. Contrasting terms in linguistics, used to describe elements in words. A *bound form* is part of a word and cannot stand alone: *un-* and *-ly* in *unhappily*, *bash-* in *bashful*, *tang-* in *tangible*. Affixes are bound, but sometimes break free as words: *ex*, *ism*. A base that cannot stand alone is a *bound base*: *vis-* in *visible*. A *free form* or *free word* can stand alone: *happy*. All such forms are known in linguistics as *bound* and *free morphemes*. See BASE, MORPHEME. [LANGUAGE, WORD].   T.MCA.

BOUTS-RIMÉS [18c: from French *bouts rimés* rhymed ends]. Words or word endings that form a set of rhymes that can be used (in a given order) in a piece of verse, such as *hail* and *sail*, *run* and *gun*, *boot* and *suit*. Such sets were used in an 18c pastime of the same name, in which one person gave a set of words to another, who was required to write a poem using the rhymes, and send it back with another set as a challenge to the challenger. See VERSE, WORD GAME. [LITERATURE, WORD].   T.MCA.

BOWDLERIZE, also BrE & AusE **bowdlerise** [1830s: after Thomas Bowdler (1754-1825), editor of an edition of Shakespeare's plays from which explicit sexual references and avowedly vulgar elements were removed]. To censor or expurgate a text by removing or modifying elements considered for any reason objectionable: 'When *The Taming of the Shrew* was staged in New York's Shakespeare festival this summer, it was bowdlerised to dilute the bard's misogynist sentiments' ('Male, modern, macho', *The Times Saturday Review*, 10 Nov. 1990). See CENSORSHIP, EDITING. [STYLE].   T.MCA.

BOXWALLAH ENGLISH [From English *box* and *wallah*, someone involved with or in charge of something, from Hindi/Urdu *wālā*, an owner, Sanskrit *pāla*, a protector]. Also **boxwalla, boxwala**. A South Asian pidgin English used primarily by *boxwallahs*, pedlars who carry a box or bundle containing such wares as shawls and jewellery. Their English is mixed with other languages and has a simplified syntax. Compare BUTLER ENGLISH. See INDO-ENGLISH, SOUTH ASIAN ENGLISH. [ASIA, VARIETY].   B.B.K.

BRACKETS [16c: from the singular *bragget* and *braget*, from French *braguette* a codpiece, diminutive of *brague* mortice (in plural, breeches), from Latin *bracae* breeches, from Gaulish. The bracket in architecture and shipbuilding may have been so called because it resembled a codpiece or a pair of breeches]. The name for punctuation marks of various kinds that mark off (more strongly than pairs of commas) certain matter as distinct, parenthetical, or interpolated. Material set between brackets is not grammatically essential to a sentence, which would be complete without it. Kinds of brackets include: *round brackets* BrE, *parentheses* AmE ( ); *square brackets* BrE, *brackets* AmE [ ]; *brace brackets* or less formally *curly brackets* { }; and *angle brackets* ⟨ ⟩.

Round brackets/parentheses. Extra statements that provide an explanation, a comment, an aside, an afterthought, a reference, or more information may be placed between commas, but are often more clearly set apart from the main text by means of round brackets: *Bristol (and some other cities) were mentioned*; *Zimbabwe (formerly Rhodesia)*; *We shall now discuss* the ode (*or lyric poem*); *They then decided (to everyone's dismay) to withdraw; their new house (an extremely smart one) is in London; there are many (apparent) difficulties; His next book (Fire Down Below) was well received; see the next chapter (pages 32–4); He is (as he always was) a rebel.* If overused, such parentheses can break up the flow of writing and become a distraction. The decision whether matter should be between commas, round brackets, or dashes is decided by author or editor, and may be a matter of personal, editorial, or house style.

Square brackets/brackets. Extra information attributable to someone other than the writer of the text is usually placed between square brackets: *Carol walked in, and her sister [Sarah] greeted her.* Such interpolations are usually made by an editor who wishes to add a comment (often information unknown to the original writer) to part of a text. The added item may replace a word or phrase in the original sentence: such a statement as *It is one of Shakespeare's less well-known plays* may become when cited *[Timon of Athens] is one of Shakespeare's less well-known plays.* In dictionaries, square brackets are often used to enclose etymological and other information at the beginning or end of entries (as at the beginning of this article). They are also often used in the texts of plays, to enclose stage directions (usually printed in italics), and in reports of meetings or proceedings, where they may be used to make asides, such as '*[shouts from audience]*', to indicate an occurrence or circumstance that is not an essential part of the reported information.

Brace brackets. Seldom used in ordinary writing, brace or curly brackets are common in mathematics and other formulaic usage, where they serve to enclose complex sets of symbols. A single brace is used to indicate displayed groupings and sets:

man
cats } carnivores
dogs

cattle
elephants } herbivores
giraffes

Angle brackets. Special words, phrases, and symbols may be highlighted by means of angle brackets when other parenthetical devices have already been assigned a use. In linguistics, *graphemes* or minimal elements in writing are often exhibited between angle brackets, as with the digraph ⟨ou⟩ in *shout*. Angle brackets are, however, rare in English and are generally used to enclose material that is not part of the text: for example, instructions to a printer typesetting a text.

Nesting. The nesting or embedding of brackets within brackets is not common in everyday print, but is not unusual in casual writing (especially handwritten letters), and is standard practice in some kinds of technical writing, such as grammatical analysis and computer programming. When complex nesting occurs, the number of opening and closing brackets has to be the same, as in the analytical version of *Coventry car factory strike committee policy decision*: ((((Coventry) (car factory)) (strike committee)) (policy decision)). See COMMA, DASH, PARENTHESIS, PUNCTUATION. [WRITING].   R.E.A., T.MCA.

BRADLEY, Henry [1845–1923]. English lexicographer, an editor of *The Oxford English Dictionary*. Born in Manchester and educated at Chesterfield Grammar School, he worked for 20 years (1863–83) as a clerk and correspondent with a Sheffield cutlery firm, during which time he acquired a knowledge of Greek, Latin, Hebrew, and a number of modern European languages. In London, from 1884 onward, he maintained himself by literary reviewing and philological work; his review of the first fascicle (A–ANT, 1884) of the *OED* in *The Academy* (1884) led to his appointment to its staff later the same year. He became second Editor in 1889 and moved to Oxford in 1896, where he remained until his death. Bradley edited some 4,590 pages of the *OED* out of a total of 15,487, including E, F, G, L, M, and parts of S and W. His publications include: *A Middle-English Dictionary* (1891), based on the 3rd edition of the work by Franz Heinrich Stratmann (1878); *The Making of English* (1904), a monograph on the history of the language; and an edition of Caxton's *Dialogues, English and French* (Early English Text Society, 1900), as well as articles on runes and place-names. See index. [BIOGRAPHY, EUROPE, REFERENCE].   RO.W.B.

BRAID SCOTS. See BROAD SCOTS.

BRAILLE [1850s: used with or without an initial capital]. A universally accepted system for writing and printing texts for the blind, devised by and named after the French teacher Louis Braille, who was himself blind from the age of three. He invented the system in Paris in 1824, when he was 16. Braille uses combinations of raised dots arranged in grids or cells of six paired spaces, numbered 1–2–3 down left, and 4–5–6 down right. Groups of from one to six dots within each grid represent letters and other symbols: for example, the equivalent of *a* is a dot in space 1 (top left-hand), of *b* is dots in spaces 1–2, and of *c* dots 1–4. For English, some groups of dots represent whole words, such as *and* (1–2–3, 4–6) and *for* (all six spaces). The idea of such combinations developed from two earlier French experiments, one with the embossing on paper of alphabetic letters, the other with raised dots in *night writing*, a system intended to be read by touch on the battlefield at night. The technique of embossed letters survives in limited use in *Moon type*, invented in 1845 by William Moon in Brighton, England; it uses roman outlines and is easier to learn by people who go blind later in life. The Braille system adapted night writing by simplifying its 12-dot grid to six. A universal Braille code for the English-speaking world was adopted in 1932, when UK and US representatives met in London and agreed the system known as *Standard English Braille* (further improved in 1957). A machine similar to a typewriter and known as a *Braillewriter* or *Brailler* (with or without an initial capital), first developed in 1892, is used to type texts. [TECHNOLOGY, WRITING].   T.MCA.

BRATHWAITE, Edward Kamau [b.1930]. Caribbean poet, essayist, critic, and social historian, born in Bridgetown, Barbados, and educated at Harrison College, Barbados, the U. of Cambridge, and the U. of Sussex (Ph.D. 1969). He has been a United Nations plebiscite officer (Ghana, 1953-4), an education officer (Ghana, 1955-62), a resident tutor at the Department of Extra-Mural Studies, U. of the West Indies (in St Lucia, 1962-3), a lecturer in history at the UWE (Mona, Jamaica, since 1963), where he is currently Professor of Social History. Brathwaite co-founded the Caribbean Artists' Movement in London (1966) and is with his wife Doris Monica Brathwaite co-editor of *Savacou*, a literary journal. His publications include: *Four Plays for Primary Schools* (1964); *Odale's Choice* (1967); the trilogy of long poems *Rights of Passage* (1967), *Masks* (1968), and *Islands* (1969), published together as *The Arrivants* (1974); *Other Exiles* (1975); *Black and Blues* (1976); *Mother Poem* (1977); *Third World Poems* (1982); *Sun Poem* (1982); and *X/Self* (1987). Among his historical works are *The Development of Creole Society in Jamaica* (Oxford University Press, 1971) and *Nanny, Sam Sharpe and the Struggle for People's Liberation* (Kingston: API, 1977). His works are listed in Doris M. Brathwaite, *A Descriptive and Chronological Bibliography 1950-1982 of the Work of Edward Kamau Brathwaite* (London: New Beacon, 1988). Honours include the Guggenheim Award (1972), the Casa de las Americas 1st Prize (1976, 1986), and a Barbados National Award. His poetry, history, and essays concern the coming into being of the New World person through the processes of enslavement, resistance, submergence, and revolution. See index. [AMERICAS, BIOGRAPHY, LITERATURE].   L.D.C.

BREAK HYPHEN. See HYPHEN.

BREATH. See AIR-STREAM MECHANISM, SPEECH, TONE (GROUP).

BREATH GROUP. See TONE (GROUP).

BRETON [14c: from French *Breton*, Latin *Brito/Britonis* a native of Britain. In Middle English, *Breton* and *Briton* were variants of the same word]. (1) A native of Brittany. (2) The Celtic language of Brittany. (3) Relating to Brittany, the Bretons, and Breton. French-speaking Breton minstrels and clerics greatly influenced Anglo-Norman culture from the 11c: 'Thise olde gentil Britons . . . Of diuerse auentures maden layes' (Chaucer, Prologue to *The Franklin's Tale*, c.1386). See ANGLO-NORMAN, BORROWING, BRITON, BRITTANY, CELTIC LANGUAGES, CORNISH, EUROPEAN COMMUNITY, FRENCH. [EUROPE, LANGUAGE, NAME].   T.MCA.

BREVE [13c: from Latin *breve*, neuter of *brevis* short. A doublet of *brief*]. A cup-like diacritic (˘) placed over a vowel letter to show that it is short. From its use in classical scansion to indicate a short syllable, it has come to indicate in English scansion that the syllable to which it belongs is not stressed. See DIACRITIC, LONG AND SHORT, MACRON, SCANSION. [LITERATURE, SPEECH, WRITING].   T.MCA., E.W.

BREWER'S DICTIONARY OF PHRASE AND FABLE. A 'Treasury of Literary bric-à-brac' originally compiled by the Victorian polymath clergyman, schoolmaster, and editor Dr Ebenezer Cobham Brewer. It has been published continuously by Cassell since 1870; revised editions include a Centenary Edition in 1970, revised by Ivor H. Evans, and an updated edition in 1989. It is the only work among some 40 publications by Brewer that continues in print, and has become one of the few works of reference (like the *Webster* dictionaries in the US and *Roget's Thesaurus* worldwide) that are close to household words: *Look it up in Brewer*. From the classical, Germanic, and other mythologies, the Bible, Chaucer, Shakespeare, Milton, and a kaleidoscope of other sources, Brewer and his successors have mined nuggets of information on matters of etymological, historical, literary, and idiomatic interest. Beyond such staples as the gods of Greece and Rome, the entries are unpredictable, archaic, and arcane. They include, for example, *Agapemone*, the name of a 19c Anglican sect, *Beefeaters*, a nickname for the Yeomen of the Guard of the Tower of London, *caul* 'a net in which women enclosed their hair, now called a snood', *dinkum*, an Australian term for 'genuine, sincere, honest', idioms associated with *eye* (including *In the wind's eye*, *Mind your eye*, *To pipe your eye*), *gong* 'A Service nickname for a medal', *Knockers* 'goblins or cobolds who dwell in mines', and *pam* 'the knave of clubs in certain card-games'. [REFERENCE].   T.MCA.

BRIDGES, Robert Seymour [1844-1930]. English poet and language reformer, born at Walmer in Kent. After education at Eton and Oxford, he studied medicine in London. In 1881, he gave up medicine and turned to literature. His first volume of poems was published in 1873. Bridges was probably the first English-language poet to understand phonetics. An interest in music led him to hymnology and he edited several editions of the *Yattendon Hymnal*. He experimented in prosody, influenced by Gerard Manley Hopkins, whose poems he edited and published in 1918. Bridges tried to escape from syllabic verse and attempted to reproduce classical quantitative metre in English, developing a flexible alexandrine line which he used in his long poem 'The Testament of Beauty' (1929). He founded the *Society for Pure English* (see entry) and wrote some of its tracts, and was chairman of the BBC's *Advisory Committee on Spoken English* in the 1920s/30s. He was also interested in spelling reform and devised a phonetic system which he used in some of his essays. He became poet laureate in 1913. See index. [BIOGRAPHY, EUROPE, LANGUAGE, LITERATURE].   R.C.

BRISTOL, BRISTOL L. See SOMERSET.

BRIT. (1) [From Old English *Bret* (plural *Brettas*) a Briton, probably from Celtic **Brittos*]. A Briton: the common term in the Anglo-Saxon Chronicle and until *c.*1300 for the Britons of Strathclyde, as in 'the Laws between the Scots and the Bretts'. The term is currently little used, except in such informal phrases as *the Ancient Brits*. (2) [1900s: probably from *Brit.*, an abbreviation in works of reference for *Britain* and *British*, its use perhaps strengthened by such patterns as *Scot/Scottish*, *Dane/Danish*]. An informal, often equivocal, name for a citizen of the UK: 'The best way to deal with a foreigner, any old-school Brit will tell you, is to shout at the blighter in English until he catches on' (Pico Iyer, *Time*, 9 July 1990). The term is used neutrally (*The Brits are coming*), affectionately (*It's nice to see some Brits here!*), and disparagingly (*Brits out!*, an anti-British slogan in Ireland). Because of its compactness, it is often used in headlines, such as (UK) *GLITZ BRITS BLITZ NEW YORK*, (US) *How the Brits Shaped the West*. Its various uses have greatly increased in the late 20c. See BRITISH, ETHNIC NAME. Compare BRETON, BRIT-, BRITISHER, BRITON. [EUROPE, HISTORY, NAME].
                T.MCA.

BRIT- [Late 20c]. A combining form of *British* in such names as *Britgas* and *Britoil*. Compare AMER-, BRITISH-, CAN-. [EUROPE, NAME].   T.MCA.

BRITAIN [*c.*13c: from Old French *Bretaigne*, Latin *Brittania* (later *Britannia*). The Old English forms *Breten*, *Bryten* may be directly from West Germanic **Brituna*. All mean 'land of the Britons'. Old Celtic appears to have had no name for the island as distinct from the people]. The name for the largest offshore island of Western Europe and semi-formally of the state whose official title is *the United Kingdom of Great Britain and Northern Ireland*. The earliest known reference to the people of the island, Greek *Pretanoi* (4c BC), was rendered in Latin as *Brittani* and *Britanni*. The names appear to have referred to a practice of painting or tattooing associated with the bluish dye known as woad. When the Angles and Saxons invaded Roman Britannia in the 5c, they called it, among other names, *Bretenland* and some of their kings were given the title *Bretwalda*, echoing the Latin *Dux Britanniarum* Leader of the Britains. However, when England, Scotland, and Wales became distinct entities in the Middle Ages, the term ceased to be political or ethnic and had little significance apart from the Arthurian romances, which were known as *the Matter of Britain*.

When in 1485 the part-Welsh Tudors gained the English throne and united Wales with England in 1536, many Welsh people favoured *Britain* as a name for the union. The name was further extended at the Union of the Crowns of England and Scotland in 1603. In 1604, when James VI King of Scots became James I of England he was also proclaimed King of Great Britain, but the title had little general appeal or value. In 1707, however, with the Union of the Parliaments, more serious official efforts were made to replace or complement the old names. In acts of Parliament, England and Scotland were often referred to as *South Britain* and *North Britain* within the framework of *Great Britain*, a term that had originally served to distinguish the island from *Less Britain* (Brittany in France). Later, when Ireland was brought into the Union in 1803, it was referred to as *West Britain*. In the later 19c, the phrase *Greater Britain* was sometimes used for the British Empire. Apart from *Great Britain*, all such usages failed. For the Scots, Welsh, and Northern Irish, however, the term *Britain* has been an essential psychological aid, making it possible to coexist with the English in a single state ruled from London.

Since the 18c, however, the terms *Britain* and *England* have been widely used as synonyms, especially in England: 'By the late nineteenth century such a thing was regarded as intolerable in Britain. It was not only that many Englishmen now regarded England's prosperity as being bound up with that of India; England's prestige too was now heavily committed' (M. E. Chamberlain, *Britain and India*, 1974); 'For four decades, since he had joined the Commons, [Churchill's] voice had given utterance in that hall to Britain's imperial dream, just as, for the past decade, it had been the goad of England's conscience' (Collins & Lapierre, *Freedom at Midnight*, 1975).

See ALBA, ALBION, BRETON, BRIT, BRIT-, BRITAIN, BRITANNIA, BRITISH, BRITISH EMPIRE, BRITISH ENGLISH, BRITISHER, BRITISH ISLES, BRITISH LANGUAGES, BRITO-, BRITON, BRITTANY, BRYTHONIC, CALEDONIA, CELT, CELTIC, CELTIC LANGUAGES, CHANNEL ISLANDS, COMMONWEALTH, CONTINENT, CORNWALL, CUMBRIA, ENGLAND, ENGLISH, EUROPE, EUROPEAN LANGUAGES, FRENCH, HISTORY OF ENGLISH, ISLE OF MAN, LONDON, MANX, NORMAN, NORMAN FRENCH, NORN, NORTHERN IRELAND, PICT, PICTISH, SCOTCH, SCOTLAND, SCOTS, SCOTTISH, ULSTER, WALES, WELSH. [EUROPE, HISTORY, NAME]. T.MCA.

BRITANNIA [See BRITAIN]. (1) The Roman name for Britain as a whole and for that part of Britain which the Romans controlled. The Emperor Claudius established a province in AD 43 which expanded in stages until it reached the Solway and Tyne. To keep the province of *Britannia Romana* (Roman Britain) safe, a wall was built between these rivers, completed in 128 by the Emperor Hadrian and known thereafter as Hadrian's Wall. The Emperor Severus (d.211) divided the territory south of the wall into two provinces: *Britannia superior* Upper Britain, closer to Rome, its capital Londinium (London), and *Britannia inferior* Lower Britain, its capital Eboracum (York). Beyond the wall lay *Britannia barbara* Barbarian Britain, made up of a neutral border area and unconquered Caledonia. (2) A female figure with a helmet and a shield. She dates from Roman times, but was more or less forgotten until her revival in 1665 by Charles II, who put her on a coin to symbolize the unity of England and Scotland. Both word and symbol have social, historical, and imperial connotations, linked with the vision of a God-favoured island identified by Shakespeare in *Richard II* (1595) as a 'sceptr'd isle . . . the envy of less happier lands'. In 1735, William Somerville addressed the same thought with: 'Hail, happy Britain! highly favoured isle, and Heaven's peculiar care!' The supreme panegyric was the poem and song 'Rule Britannia' by the Scottish poet James Thomson (1740), whose first stanza runs:

When Britain first, at heaven's command,
Arose from out the azure main,
This was the charter of the land,
And guardian angels sung the strain:
'Rule Britannia, rule the waves;
Britons never shall be slaves'.

The image of Britannia has to some extent blended with that of Boadicea/Boudic(c)a, an ancient British queen who fought the Romans, but has not been used in relation to such later queens as Elizabeth I and II or Victoria. In the 1980s, however, especially in cartoons and satire, the Boadicea and Britannia images were often applied to Margaret Thatcher, first British woman prime minister. The name *Britannia* often occurs in commercial names, such as *the Britannia Building Society*; the adjective *Britannic* is less likely to do so, having retained its regal and imperial connotations, especially in the phrase *her Britannic Majesty*. Currently, both words are sometimes used with a tinge of irony, contrasting the reduced present-day status of Britain with its imperial heyday. See CAMDEN. [EUROPE, HISTORY, NAME]. T.MCA.

BRITICISM [1868 AmE: coined by Richard Grant White: from *British* adapted to *Britic-* and *-ism* as in *Scotticism*]. Also **Britishism** [1890s]. A word or other expression typical of English as used in Britain, particularly after the late 18c, when varieties of the language were established beyond the British Isles and, especially in the case of AmE, began to develop their own standard and critical traditions. The term may or may not subsume *Anglicism* and *Scotticism*, and contrasts with *Americanism* in particular and also with *Australianism*, *Canadianism*, *Indianism*, *Irishism*, *New Zealandism*, etc. Because BrE and AmE are the major forms of the language, are used by the largest number of native speakers, and are the most widely known of all national varieties, they tend to be defined in terms of each other. Scholars of English in the US are as inclined to point out Briticisms as their colleagues in the UK are to point out Americanisms. The term applies to all aspects of usage, but is most often applied to vocabulary: where *government* is often used in the UK in the sense of Prime Minister and Cabinet, the nearest US equivalent is *administration*; while in BrE *school* is generally restricted to pre-university education, in AmE it applies to any educational level. Technological fields that developed independently in the two nations have often had different terminologies, as in the automotive industry (BrE first in each pair): *bonnet/hood*, *boot/trunk*, *bumper/fender*, *dip switch/dimmer*, *dynamo/generator*, *fascia/dashboard*, *indicator/blinker*, *quarterlight/vent*, *silencer/muffler*, *windscreen/windshield*, *wing/fender*. See AMERICAN ENGLISH AND BRITISH ENGLISH, AMERICANISM, -ISM. [EUROPE, VARIETY]. J.A., T.MCA.

BRITISH [From Old English *Brettisc*: see BRIT]. (1) A term for the mainly Celtic peoples of Britain before the arrival of the English and during the period in which the English were establishing themselves. (2) Also *Brythonic*. The Celtic language of the ancient Britons. (3) From the 16c, a collective term for the peoples of England, Scotland, and Wales, extended at various times and in various ways to all or some of the people of Ireland. The people of present-day Northern Ireland are British, but while the Protestant majority are known as 'loyalists', many Roman Catholics do not consider themselves British, despite their British nationality. The once common monarchic phrase *British subject* has been largely replaced by *British citizen* or *national*. (4) At the height of the Empire, a term that covered both 'mother country' and overseas 'possessions': *British India, British North America, British Honduras*, etc. The phrase *the British Commonwealth* has been used for the association of independent post-imperial nations now known as *the Commonwealth*. (5) The phrase *the British way of life* (compare *the American dream* and *the Canadian mosaic*) suggests a traditional aspiration towards decency and fair play accompanied by a paradoxical mixture of reserve, muddle, and arrogance. There is irony in the recent amused use of such expressions as *I say, that just isn't British/cricket* (it isn't right and proper) and the facetious *No sex, please, we're British*. (6) An occasional term for BrE, as in the American question and British answer while frying eggs: *What's the British for 'easy over'?— Turned*. See BRITISH-, BRITISH ENGLISH, BRYTHONIC, COMMONWEALTH, INDO-BRITISH. [EUROPE, HISTORY, NAME, VARIETY].   T.MCA.

BRITISH- [Apparently 20c]. *British* used as a combining form, especially when the less accurate *Anglo-* cannot be used: 'the present spate of British-Indian fictions' (Salman Rushdie, *The Observer*, 1 Apr. 1984). Here, *Anglo-Indian* would be ambiguous. The usage appears to be increasing: *British-Iranian, British-Nigerian, British-Soviet*. Compare BRIT-. See ANGLO-, BRITISH. [EUROPE, NAME].   T.MCA.

BRITISH ASSOCIATION FOR APPLIED LINGUISTICS. See BAAL.

BRITISH ASSOCIATION OF STATE COLLEGES IN ENGLISH LANGUAGE TEACHING. See BASCELT.

BRITISH BLACK ENGLISH, also known as **patois**. Any of several varieties of creole English used in the UK by the children of immigrants from the Commonwealth Caribbean since the 1950s. While the older generation often retain their creoles, younger speakers have acquired local varieties of BrE and in some cases a modified variety of their parents' creole which may emerge during adolescence as an assertion of black identity. Its use is often associated with black youth culture, Rastafarianism, and reggae. Although speakers sometimes call it *Jamaican*, it is in many respects different from Jamaican Creole, which has no gender distinction, so that both male and female are referred to as *im*. In *London Jamaican, shi* is also used, probably under the influence of mainstream English. Linguists are not agreed whether there is a continuum of varieties linking English and the creole, as in Jamaica, or whether there are discrete, diglossic systems. Many speakers code-switch between English and patois and there are few intermediate forms. Most speakers live in the London area, with other concentrations in Birmingham and Leeds, where there is some influence from local speech. Patois is also used by some white children in black peer groups. There has been in recent years an increasing range of literature, especially poetry, in British Black English. See BLACK, BLACK ENGLISH, CREOLE, DIGLOSSIA, JAMAICAN CREOLE, PATOIS. [AMERICAS, EUROPE, VARIETY].   S.R.

BRITISH BROADCASTING. Broadcasting as a significant non-commercial public service began in the UK in 1922, with the formation of a consortium of radio manufacturers administered by the Post Office. The organization was called the *British Broadcasting Company* with the Scottish engineer John C. W. Reith (later Lord Reith) as general manager. The aim was to establish a national network with transmitters in all major cities, financed first in part, later entirely, by licences to operate 'wireless' receiving equipment. The first transmissions on Station 2LO took place on 22 May 1922 at Marconi House in Aldwych, London. Soon after, headquarters moved to Savoy Hill, and the company developed separate transmissions from Manchester and Birmingham. In 1927, a royal charter changed this company into the *British Broadcasting Corporation* (motto: 'Nation shall speak peace unto nation'), which moved in 1932 into Broadcasting House, Portland Place, London. It was enjoined by the charter to 'inform, educate and entertain' its listeners. The audience in the 1930s was some 40–50% of the adult population and to address this enormous listenership a more informal style in talks and continuity developed than in the 1920s. The Corporation was, however, often criticized by the press as arrogant, snobbish, smug, and overly eager to educate the public, whence in the early 1960s its equivocal nickname *Auntie*. The informal and usually affectionate acronym *the Beeb* (from the beginning of 'bee-bee-cee') emerged somewhat later. The two are sometimes combined as *Auntie Beeb*, while for the BBC in Scotland *MacBeeb* is sometimes used.

The BBC in the 1930s. Four major developments took place in the 1930s: (1) The nation became accustomed to hearing predominantly male middle- and upper-class voices providing news and other information on a daily basis. Their style, which came to be known as *BBC English*, acquired great prestige at home and abroad, although it was also often resented as arrogant and snobbish. See BBC ENGLISH[1]. (2) Remote individuals, such as members of the royal family, became familiar to the nation as voices broadcasting at ritualized or otherwise significant times: George V made the first royal *Christmas Day broadcast* in 1932, and Edward VIII broadcast his abdication speech in 1936. They shared the linguistic manner of the announcers, a speech form referred to as the *King's English*. (3) In 1932, the *BBC Empire Service* was developed, initially at Broadcasting House, and grew by stages first into the BBC's Overseas Services, then the BBC World Service. (4) A television broadcasting service was launched in 1936 at the Radio Olympia exhibition in London, followed by regular broadcasts from Alexandra Palace that reached some 25,000 homes before it was suspended in 1939 on the outbreak of the Second World War. The suspension was necessary because BBC TV, broadcasting on 45 megahertz, would have been an ideal homing beacon for German bombers.

In the late 1930s, the Continental commercial station *Radio Luxembourg* became a major competitor, some 70% of the listening audience tuning to it at weekends. In addition, the outbreak of war raised considerable criticism of the BBC for not providing enough entertainment for the armed forces, especially in France, where most of the expeditionary force were listening to *Radio Normandie* or Radio Luxembourg. The result in 1940 was the *Allied Expeditionary Forces Programme (AEFP)*, later the *Forces Programme*, broadcasting mainly light entertainment at home and in Europe. To combat German propaganda broadcasts to Africa and the Middle East, broadcasts in Arabic began in 1938, becoming the first of the BBC's foreign-language sections. In 1939, on the outbreak of war, the European Service was started, and the BBC regional services merged into one Home Service.

Lord Haw Haw. An additional wartime stimulus was the foreign broadcasting activities of the Germans, especially the transmissions of an Anglo-Irish pro-German broadcaster known as 'Lord Haw Haw'. He was given this nickname by Jonah Barrington of the *Daily Express* because of his supercilious manner and pseudo-upper-class tones ('Jairmany calling, Jairmany calling . . .') and was eventually identified as William Joyce, a breakaway member of the British Union of Fascists. It is likely, however, that for the most influential period of broadcasting the voice belonged to someone as yet unidentified. To combat these broadcasts, which were avidly listened to, the Ministry of Information set up outside the BBC an 'anti-lie bureau' through the *Joint Broadcasting Committee*, directed by Hilda Matheson. The details of these activities are still secret.

Post-war prestige. At the end of the war, the BBC was widely considered the most influential and prestigious broadcasting organization in the world. Its wartime broadcasts to enemy-occupied Europe were a 'voice of freedom' to which millions secretly listened, often despite great personal risk. In Britain, the BBC was the main channel of communication between government and people. Listening to the news was a daily ritual, and Winston Churchill made some of his most memorable speeches as Prime Minister on the radio. During the war, the UK audience was served by the *Home Service* and the *Forces Programme*, audiences in Europe by the *European Service*, and British forces abroad and world audiences by the *Overseas Service* in 43 languages. In 1945, the BBC stabilized its domestic format as a *Home Service*, a *Light Programme*, and in 1946 a cultural *Third Programme*. Also in 1946, experimental TV transmissions began again from Alexandra Palace, but most of the UK did not receive regular TV transmissions until 1952. By the end of the 1950s, however, a massive shift from listening to radio to watching television was well under way.

ITA, IBA, and ITC. In the 1950s, the BBC monopoly on broadcasting in Britain came to an end. The Television Act of 1954 promoted a commercial television service under the control of the *Independent Television Authority (ITA)*. Franchises were awarded to regional groups to provide programmes for regional networks. Commercial television began in 1955, the programmes funded, as in the US, through advertising. In 1972, the ITA became the *Independent Broadcasting Authority (IBA)*, commercial radio stations being added to its range. Its primary responsibility was to license and periodically reallocate television franchises, as well as allocating programme transmission times and prohibiting transmissions. It also required that one-third of all materials broadcast on ITV should be 'serious non-fiction, sensibly distributed throughout the week as a whole in appropriate times'. The IBA also had an important role in determining the quality of entertainment on ITV by determining how much should be home-produced and how much and what quality of imported material should be shown. In 1990, the IBA was replaced by the *Independent Television Commission (ITC)*, which initiated a policy of periodically auctioning franchises to the highest bidder regarded as able to sustain quality programming. The first auction took place in 1991.

Educational broadcasting. Schools radio and TV have had a strong tradition in the BBC, complemented in the 1960s by educational TV for adults. *BBC Continuing Education* began in 1963, as did two of the larger independent franchises: *Associated Broadcasting Company (ABC)* and *Associated Television (ATV)*. The ITA appointed an *Adult Education Advisory Committee* in 1962. Many educational programmes were broadcast on the second BBC TV channel opened in 1964. Although initially conceived as a minority cultural channel, *BBC2* has become a broadly based channel allowing larger-scale coverage of cultural events, drama, opera productions, and outside broadcasts. A major educational development in 1969 was the *Open University* (originally known as 'The University of the Air'), based at Milton Keynes, Buckinghamshire: a degree-granting, distance-learning institution that uses broadcasts on BBC channels as part of its teaching material. The aim of the partnership is to provide a multimedia learning system of correspondence courses, radio and TV broadcasts, tutorial support and assessment, summer schools, and software. The first intake of students was in 1972 and courses are offered in arts, social sciences, mathematics, science, technology, education, and management.

Greater diversity. In the late 1960s, plans for local BBC radio stations were developed. Leicester, Sheffield and Merseyside (Liverpool) opened in 1967 and by 1971 twenty stations were in operation. Independent radio stations followed. The aim of local radio has been to provide community support with news, weather, publicity for local events, reporting on local issues, and entertainment. These stations have served to make local language a matter of course in British broadcasting, and have contributed to the breakdown of a monolithic 'BBC English'. The activities of pirate radio stations broadcasting mainly pop music from studios on ships anchored just beyond territorial waters spurred a reorganization of BBC radio in the 1970s. Following the document *Broadcasting in the Seventies* (1969), *generic programming* was introduced with a pop network *Radio 1* and a renaming of the older networks as *Radio 2* (the Light Programme), *Radio 3* (the Third Programme), and *Radio 4* (the Home Service). This change broke with the Reithian tradition of mixed programming on all networks. In the 1980s, there was increased regional output and community radio stations were introduced.

Prospects. Following the Conservative government White Paper on Broadcasting in 1989, further adjustments to British broadcasting were proposed, including a fifth TV channel, a fifth BBC radio network (introduced in 1990 as *Radio 5*), and the possibility of pay TV as a partial alternative to funding by licence fee. In 1989, commercial satellite broadcasting was introduced: *Sky Television* started up in that year and *British Satellite Broadcasting (BSB)* in 1990, the two operations merging late the same year, as *British Sky Broadcasting (BSkyB)*. The impact of such broadcasting was slowed by the need for specially installed equipment to receive the satellite signals, as well as by the success of video recording technology, which became immensely popular in the late 1980s and led to the opening of video shops serving as lending libraries. By 1990, millions were watching both rented videos and programmes recorded off-air at times of their own choosing.

See BBC, BBC ENGLISH[1], BBC ENGLISH[2], BBC ENGLISH[3], BROADCASTING, CALL MY BLUFF, EUROPEAN COMMUNITY, WELSH LANGUAGE SERVICE. [EUROPE, HISTORY, MEDIA]. B.T., R.J.Q.

BRITISH COUNCIL, The, short forms *the Council, the BC.* An autonomous, non-political organization set up in the UK in 1934 to counter Fascist propaganda in Europe by promoting a wider knowledge of Britain and the English language, and developing cultural relations with other countries. It was incorporated by Royal Charter in 1940 and is run from London by a director general and a board with 17 advisory committees. Its first overseas offices were in Europe, Latin America, and West Asia; since the 1950s it has been involved with educational work in Commonwealth and other countries as the agent of what is now the *British Overseas Development Administration*. In the 1980s, the Council merged with the *Inter-University Council*, a body that set up links between British and overseas universities. In matters of language scholarship and teaching, it is advised by an *English Teaching Advisory Committee*. In 1990, it had offices in 84 countries with 54 teaching centres in 35 countries. It organizes a wide range of educational, technical, and cultural activities, and

Council Directors work closely with but separately from British embassies and high commissions.

Funding and services. In 1990/1, the Council's budget was £348m, derived from three sources: a direct government grant (£121.8m); fees and agency funds from the Overseas Development Administration (£125.3m), the Foreign and Commonwealth Office (£20.9m), and other agencies (£24.4m); and earnings (£55.7m), including library fees, agency fees, the administration of examinations, commercial sponsorship, and English teaching services. Of this income, 60% was spent on the interchange of people, 12% on libraries and information, 12% on English language and literature, 11% on science and education, and 5% on the arts; 30% was spent in Africa, 18% in Western Europe, 17% in East Asia, 15% in South Asia, 9% in West Asia and North Africa, 7% in the Americas, and 4% in Eastern Europe. In 1988/9, the Council brought 35,000 people to Britain and sent 3,500 British specialists overseas on short-term advisory visits. Its network of teaching centres, managed from London, employed some 1,200 British teachers and other staff and had a turnover of £25.3m. Enrolment in these centres went from 51,300 in 1984/5 to 65,910 in 1988/9. The largest centres were Hong Kong and Madrid, with 80 teachers each. The BC network of 116 libraries and 428,000 library members made loans of close to 8m. The 13 libraries run jointly with the *Indian Council for Cultural Relations* had over 90,000 members and lent 2.25m books, periodicals, and videos.

The BC and ELT. During the 1960s, the Council through its advisory committee was instrumental in setting up the first departments of applied linguistics in British universities, to train, among others, those working overseas on Council and government contracts. Council-supported scholars remain a major source of students of applied linguistics and TEFL. The BC was the original publisher of *English Language Teaching* (now *English Language Teaching Journal*: see IATEFL), *Language Teaching Abstracts* (now *Language Teaching*: see ABSTRACT), and *ELT Documents* (see entry). Its management of the government-funded *Aid to Commonwealth English* (*ACE*) (1962–76) and *Key English Language Teaching* (*KELT*) (1977–89) schemes, now superseded, led to involvement in teacher education, curriculum development, and particularly *English for Special Purposes*. More recently, attention has turned to the promotion of British public- and private-sector services, and a Promotion Unit with its own representative steering group was set up in 1989.

The BC and British English. In 1985, the then director general Sir John Burgh noted in an interview that the Council does not 'actively propagate *British* English as a commodity or as the proper model for foreign users. It so happens that for all sorts of reasons—including, of course, that the very name *English* suggests to many foreign learners that we in this country speak the "purest", and, therefore, the best form of the language—British English is often the preferred model . . . The Council has no tradition or policy of preferring or propagating any one *accent* over another, and communicates with its many clients in standard written English. It occasionally happens that when recruiting staff for service with an overseas employer the Council will be asked for a speaker of Received Pronunciation or of BBC English' (*English Today* 3, July 1985). In 1989, the current director general, Sir Richard Francis, said in an interview: 'Britain's real black gold is not oil, but the English language' (to William Greaves, *The Times*, 24 Oct. 1989). He referred to the Council as *brokers* who assisted the British ELT *industry* to promote a *product* around the world, adding that 'it's difficult to quantify [English] as a national resource. The value, in the post-industrial age, of having people use the language of one's own culture is virtually inestimable. . . . I often refer to English as a linguistic continent, which isn't confined to the bounds of Africa or America or whatever.' See ARELS, BASCELT, BBC ENGLISH[1], CULTURA, ELT, ELT DOCUMENTS, IELTS, PROPAGANDA, TEFL. [AFRICA, ASIA, EDUCATION, EUROPE]. T.MCA.

BRITISH EMPIRE, The. A term for Britain and its colonies and for the colonies collectively. Although the Empire is now largely a matter of history, Britain continues to administer a number of dependencies in various parts of the world, among which the Falkland Islands and Gibraltar remain bones of contention with other states. The British monarch is head of state in many ex-imperial countries, including Australia, Canada, New Zealand, and several Caribbean nations, and holds the symbolic role of head of the Commonwealth. In the UK, honours continue to be bestowed with such titles as *Order of the British Empire* (*OBE*) and *British Empire Medal* (*BEM*). Irish nationalists argue that the province of Northern Ireland is a continuing manifestation of empire; Scottish and Welsh nationalists hold that the British state has served and continues to serve the imperial ends of England within the British Isles.

Duration. There are at least three views on the duration and nature of the Empire: (1) If the empire is English, it started with the invasion of

Ireland in 1171 and lasted in various forms for over 800 years. (2) If the empire is British, three dates mark the beginnings of 'Britishness': the incorporation of Wales into England in the 1530s-40s, the Union of the Crowns of England and Scotland in 1603, and the Union of the Parliaments of England and Scotland in 1707. (3) If the empire combines the expansion of England and some sharing of power with the Scots and Welsh, empire began in the 16c with the annexation of Wales and the conquest of Ireland, followed by the union of Scotland and England, and the colonizing of North America. Historians tend to favour the third view, often talking about a first empire based on commerce and profit in the 16-17c, and a second empire beginning in the 18c, when large overseas territories were acquired. Together, these empires span 400 years. Whenever the Empire began, however, its dissolution was swift after the Second World War, with a mass shedding of possessions between 1947 and the 1960s. For dates and events, see HISTORY OF ENGLISH (CHRONOLOGY).

Nature. The heyday of empire was 1890 to 1920, when one-fifth of the world's land mass was under the Union Flag and it was asserted that 'the sun never sets on the British Empire'. Although much was made of a duty to educate non-white subjects (characterized by Kipling as 'new-caught, sullen peoples, / Half-devil and half-child', *The White Man's Burden*), the primary motivations were commercial, industrial, and political, often haphazard and at times touched by humanitarianism, as with the abolition of slavery in 1833. Colonialism brought together venture capital, the pioneering spirit, and government expediency, as for example in shipping convicts to distant lands. In maintaining the Empire, the British sustained a high level of class and regional distinction among themselves and race distinction in dealing with others. Traders and plantation managers dealt profitably in such commodities as tobacco, sugar, minerals, and human beings, much as their equivalents did in the empires of France, Spain, Portugal, and the Netherlands. Influence spread beyond the Empire into such regions as China during the 19c Opium Wars and Iran in the 20c search for petroleum. Especially during the reign of Victoria, the British were buoyed by the Protestant ethic, social Darwinism, and a sense that 'God is an Englishman'. Pride in empire often dulled tensions at home, releasing them elsewhere in building 'the colonies'.

Imperial English. In the British Isles, English had by the beginning of the 19c largely supplanted the Celtic languages. Elsewhere, linguistic success from time to time mirrored this relationship. As in Wales, there was uneasy coexistence between English and one other language, such as English and Dutch (later Afrikaans) in South Africa, English and French in Canada, English and Maori in New Zealand. As with Cornish in England and Gaelic in Scotland and Ireland, English often swamped indigenous languages, as in North America and Australia. The casual and widespread mixing of English with other languages produced pidgins from which have arisen the English-based creoles of Africa, the Caribbean, and Oceania. English also served as a challenge to such languages as Bengali, Hindi, and Tamil in India, and Swahili, Yoruba, and Zulu in Africa, moving them towards a Westernized modernity involving print technology and such media as newspapers, radio, and television.

Circles of English. Within the Empire there grew up 'circles' of English: a prestigious core among the upper classes of London, Oxford, Cambridge, the Home Counties, and later in the BBC; an inner circle of non-Home Counties England, Scotland, Ireland, and Wales; an outer circle of the white dominions (Australia, Canada, New Zealand, and to some extent South Africa); and a further circle of non-white territories such as India and Nigeria. Because the US removed itself through revolution in 1776, AmE is not within the circles, but in Britain it has nonetheless often been characterized as 'colonial', sometimes humorously, sometimes seriously. The linguistic outcome of empire is not simple, yet it was curiously 'predicted' by the Elizabethan poet Samuel Daniel:

And who in time knowes whither we may vent
The treasure of our tongue, to what strange shores
This gaine of our best glorie shal be sent.
T'inrich vnknowing Nations with our stores?
What worlds in th'yet vnformed Occident
May come refin'd with th'accents that are ours?
(*Musophilus, or a generall defence of learning*, 1599)

Daniel's question was inspired by thoughts of the New World. The empire-builders there and elsewhere did 'vent' his tongue to every continent of the world, apparently as both a treasure and a tribulation.

See ACHEBE, AFRICA, AMERICA, ARABIC, ASCENSION (ISLAND), AUSTRALIA, BANGLADESH, BARBADOS, BELIZE, BOTSWANA, BRITAIN, BRITANNIA, BURMA/MYANMAR, CALIBAN, CAMEROON, CANADA, CARIBBEAN, CAYMAN ISLANDS, CLASSICAL LANGUAGE, COLONIAL, COMMONWEALTH, CYPRUS, DIASPORA, ENGLISH AS A SECOND LANGUAGE, ENGLISH LANGUAGES, ENGLISH LITERATURE, ENGLISH-MEDIUM SCHOOL, EUROPE, FALKLAND ISLANDS, FIJI, GAMBIA, GHANA, GIBRALTAR, HISTORY OF ENGLISH, HOME, HONG KONG, IMPERIALISM, INDIA, JAMAICA, KENYA, KIRIBATI, LESOTHO, MALAWI, MALAYSIA, MALTA, MAURITIUS, MONTSERRAT, MOTHER COUNTRY, NAMIBIA, NEW ZEALAND,

NGUGI, NIGERIA, OLD COUNTRY, PAKISTAN, PAPUA
NEW GUINEA, RACISM, SAINT CHRISTOPHER AND
NEVIS, SAINT HELENA, SAINT VINCENT AND THE
GRENADINES, SIERRA LEONE, SINGAPORE, SOLOMON
ISLANDS, SOUTH AFRICA, SRI LANKA, STANDARD
ENGLISH, SUDAN, SWAZILAND, TANZANIA, TRIN-
IDAD AND TOBAGO, TRISTAN DA CUNHA, TURKS
AND CAICOS ISLANDS, UGANDA, VANUATU, VIC-
TORIAN, VIRGIN ISLANDS, WESTERN SAMOA, WEST
INDIES, WORLD ENGLISH, ZAMBIA, ZIMBABWE.
[GEOGRAPHY, HISTORY].   T.MCA.

BRITISH ENGLISH, short form *BrE*. The English language as used in Britain. The phrase contrasts with kinds of English used elsewhere, and
especially with AmE. For many people,
however, especially in England, the usage is tautologous. For example, the language-teaching
organization Linguaphone makes a distinction
in advertising its courses between simply
'English' and 'American English'. In addition,
the phrase *British English* has a monolithic quality, as if it were a homogeneous variety and a
straightforward fact of life. The term, however,
shares in the ambiguities and tensions associated
with the term *British*, and can be used and interpreted in two ways, with some blurring between
them:

A broader interpretation. Broadly understood,
BrE is the English language as used in Great
Britain (England, Scotland, and Wales) or the
United Kingdom of Great Britain and Northern
Ireland, depending on the use of *British*
employed. In this sense, the term covers all varieties, standard and non-standard, at all times, in
all regions, and at all social levels. It is unlikely,
however, to include the variety known as *Scots*,
which in this context is usually treated, explicitly
or implicitly, as a separate entity. In this interpretation, BrE is a heterogeneous range of
accents and dialects, including standard varieties
used in several systems of education.

A narrower interpretation. Narrowly understood,
BrE is the form of standard English used in Britain at large or more specifically in England, and
more specifically still in south-eastern England.
It is essentially the medium of the middle and
upper classes. Although not confined to one
accent, especially in recent decades, it has been
associated since at least the late 19c with the
accent known since the 1920s as *Received Pronunciation* (*RP*), and with the phrases *the
Queen's English*, *Oxford English*, and *BBC
English*. When BrE refers to a model of English
taught to foreigners, it is an idealization of the
south-eastern middle-class standard, as presented in dictionaries and other materials prepared for learners.

Tensions and controversies. The precise naming
of the kind or kinds of English used in the UK,
and in those parts of the English-speaking world
which have been closely influenced by it (mainly
in the Commonwealth), is affected by tensions
and controversies that fall into three groups:

Regional antagonism. There are different perspectives and preferences in different parts of
Britain. These include objections among the
non-English to being categorized as English.
While they object to this on grounds of ethnic
reality, they also object to occasions when especially the southern English treat their use of English as quaint or inferior. Scots often argue that
they exist in the worst of both worlds: they are
called English when they are not English at the
same time as their use of English is dismissed as
not English. To a lesser degree, there are also
within England tensions between in particular
the North and the South, in which Northern
English is often seen as secondary to Southern
English, principally because it has no educated
spoken standard to weigh against RP.

Class antagonism. Issues of class remain significant in Britain, often mixed with regional,
ethnic, and linguistic issues. Many working-class
people regard the standard language and RP as
beyond their reach, as middle-class impositions,
or both. Standard usage containing 'big words'
is sometimes seen as a kind of social and educational conspiracy, while RP and near-RP
accents, despite their general prestige, or perhaps
because of it, are perceived as *posh, hoity-toity,
put on*, or *toffee-nosed* (snobbish and affected).

Precision of reference. The issues relating to
region and class become linguistic when their
clarification depends on the preciseness or loose-
ness of the terms used to discuss them. The scholarly debate includes both defences of and
objections to the presentation of the traditional,
standard, RP-linked variety as a single, prestige
form when it is used by a small minority. The
English sociolinguist Peter Trudgill has
observed: 'My own preferred label for varieties
of English from England is "English English",
by analogy with "American English", "Australian English" etc. . . . Note that, whatever
label is used, we have been careful in this book to
distinguish between the terms "English English"
and "British English". The latter is often used
in literature, particularly, it seems, by Americans
and writers on English as a foreign language,
where it is really the former that is intended'
(Introduction, *Language in the British Isles*,
1984).

Kinds of British English. It is not, however, surprising that the term *English English* is not
widely used. To the English it seems as tautologous or as silly and inelegant as 'German

German' and 'French French', whether or not there may be grounds for using those names, as for example to distinguish German in Germany from Austrian German and French in France from Quebec French. However, to many Scots, Irish, and Welsh people, and to others with comparable perspectives, some such term is essential to allow an explicit and productive contrast among the British varieties of English. Equally, however, the term *Scottish English* can seem odd to English and Scots alike, because of the ethnic sense of the word 'English': *Scottish English* seems a contradiction in terms. Similarly, the term *Irish English* may seem bizarre, both because of centuries-old connotations of illogic and whimsy acquired by the word *Irish* and because of the hostility of many in Ireland towards anything that links them too closely with England.

Because they belong to groups with strong positions in the 'pecking order' of the language, English and American scholars have tended to find 'British English' and 'American English' convenient labels for their respective varieties and standards, without further qualification. However, in recent years interest in and action on behalf of other varieties has made it difficult for these labels to be used as sweepingly and uncritically as in the past. It has also become increasingly difficult to resist the use of such terms as *English English, Scottish English, Welsh English, Hawaiian English, Indian English, Singapore English* on the grounds that they are tautologous, paradoxical, bizarre, or dubious.

See AMERICAN ENGLISH AND BRITISH ENGLISH, BRITICISM/BRITISHISM, BRITISH, BRITISH COUNCIL, BRITISH LANGUAGE, ENGLISH, ENGLISH IN ENGLAND, NORTHERN IRISH ENGLISH, RECEIVED PRONUNCIATION, SCOTTISH ENGLISH, STANDARD ENGLISH, WELSH ENGLISH. [EUROPE, HISTORY, VARIETY]. T.MCA.

BRITISHER [1820s: perhaps originating during or just after the American War of Independence (1776–83), to name a willing subject of the British king]. A person born in Britain. The term is both widely used and widely disowned. It was the first of the inclusive terms for people from Britain who may or may not be English: compare BRIT, BRITON. Typical of the unease surrounding such terms is a comment by Jawaharlal Nehru: 'Individual Englishmen, educationists, orientalists, journalists, missionaries, and others played an important part in bringing western culture to India, and in their attempts to do so often came into conflict with their own Government. . . . When I say Englishmen, I include, of course, people from the whole of Great Britain and Ireland, though I know this is improper and incorrect. But I dislike the word Britisher,

and even that probably does not include the Irish. My apologies to the Irish, the Scots, and the Welsh' (*The Discovery of India*, 1946). [EUROPE, NAME]. T.MCA.

BRITISH INDIAN OCEAN TERRITORY. A British dependency in the Indian Ocean, comprising the Chagos Archipelago, annexed from France in 1814 and administered from Mauritius until 1965, when the Territory was established as a UK/US naval base. The 1,500 Ilois (Islanders), descendants of African slaves on the islands' copra plantations, are speakers of a French-based creole, and were resettled under pressure on Mauritius. See ENGLISH. [AFRICA, NAME, VARIETY]. T.MCA.

BRITISH ISLES, The. The archipelago off the west coast of Europe, which includes Britain, Ireland, the Northern Isles (Orkney and Shetland), the (Inner and Outer) Hebrides (also known as the Western Isles), Man, Wight, and Anglesey, but not usually the Channel Islands which, though British, are geographically closer to France. In Ireland, many people object to including that island in anything British, but the usage is ancient and no alternative has been proposed. [EUROPE, NAME]. T.MCA.

BRITISH LANGUAGE. An occasional term for British English: 'Sir Richard Francis, director general of the British Council, strides around his office high above Trafalgar Square with all the irrepressible good humour of a man who has just struck oil. . . . His job, among others, is to sell the British language to the rest of the world' ('Selling English by the Pound', *The Times*, 24 Oct. 1989). Compare BRITISH, BRITISH ENGLISH. [EUROPE, VARIETY]. T.MCA.

BRITISH LANGUAGES. Many languages have been and are used in Britain. The indigenous living languages are *English, French* in the Channel Islands, *Scottish Gaelic, Welsh*, and (depending on definition) *Scots*. Languages now extinct are *Anglo-Danish, Anglo-Saxon (Old English), Brythonic* or *British* (a language of pre-Roman and Roman times), *Cornish, Anglo-Latin, Manx Gaelic, Norman French (Anglo-Norman), Norn* (the Norse of Caithness, Orkney, and Shetland), and *Pictish* (in ancient Caledonia). The dominant language since the 16c has been English. Welsh is spoken by a minority in Wales and Gaelic by a minority in Scotland. Various immigrant languages, especially *Hindi, Urdu, Gujarati,* and *Punjabi* from the Indian subcontinent and *Cantonese* from Hong Kong, are spoken in such cities as London, Birmingham, Glasgow, and Cardiff.

Caribbean English Creole and *British Black English* are used among West Indian communities especially in such cities as London, Birmingham, and Leeds. Currently, all the world's major languages can be heard in London. See Glanville Price, *The Languages of Britain* (Edward Arnold, 1984) and Peter Trudgill (ed.), *Language in the British Isles* (Cambridge University Press, 1984).

See ANGLO-DANISH, ANGLO-SAXON, BRITISH, BRITISH BLACK ENGLISH, CARIBBEAN ENGLISH, CELTIC LANGUAGES, CORNISH, CREOLE, CUMBRIC, ENGLISH, ENGLISH IN ENGLAND, FRENCH, INDIAN LANGUAGES, ISLE OF MAN, LATIN¹, NORMAN FRENCH, NORN, NORSE, PICTISH, POLARI, ROMANI/ ROMANY, SCOTS, SCOTTISH ENGLISH, SCOTTISH GAELIC, SCOTTISH LANGUAGES, WELSH, WELSH ENGLISH. [EUROPE, HISTORY, LANGUAGE].   T.MCA.

BRITISH LIBRARY. The national library of the UK, created by the British Library Act of 1972. Its main reading-room has traditionally been in the British Museum in London, but a large new independent building is due to open nearby in 1992 and includes among its services a *Centre for the Book* (established in 1990). There are three divisions of the British Library: *reference* (over 10m books, 120,000 manuscripts, 100,000 seals, 3,000 papyri, etc.); *lending*, at the *Document Supply Centre* at Boston Spa in Yorkshire (some 4.5m volumes, 55,000 current periodicals, and 3.5m documents on microfilm, for loan to other libraries); and the *bibliographic service*, which publishes the *British National Bibliography*, which catalogues British publishing. It is the largest library in Europe and the second largest in the world after the US *Library of Congress*. Its more than 1,000 miles of shelves stores some 23m books, periodicals, theses, maps, patents, and other documents, and increases at some six shelf-miles a year. In 1983 the library acquired the *National Sound Archive*.

History. The Library was created from four institutions: the *British Museum Library*, the *National Central Library*, the *National Lending Library for Science and Technology*, and the *British National Bibliography*. The British Museum and its Library were founded in 1753, when the government acquired collections made by Sir Hans Sloane, Anglo-Saxon manuscripts and Latin codices collected by Edward and Robert Harlet, earls of Oxford, and collections made by Sir Robert Cotton. They were established by an act of Parliament in 1759 and kept in Montagu House in London (erected 1823-52). In 1757, George II added the *Royal Library*, which brought with it the right of a copy of all books published in Britain. An additional royal collection was purchased in 1823. The National Central Library was founded in 1916 as the *Central Library for Students* and was the centre for interlibrary lending. The National Lending Library for Science and Technology was founded in 1961, administered by the Department of Science and Education and open only to organizations and libraries in the UK. The National Bibliography was founded in 1950.

On-line services. In addition to traditional services, the British Library has in recent years developed *BLAISE-LINE* (*British Library's Automated Information Service Line*), a worldwide on-line service for academics, researchers, librarians, and businesspeople. It is made up of 18 databases with some 8.5m records, such as catalogues of government publications, publications in libraries worldwide, antiquarian material, and the Library's own resources, including the catalogue of the *Science Reference Information Service*, the world's largest collection of document titles for science and industry. BLAISE-LINE greatly economizes on visits and correspondence. It supplied during 1988 over 25,000 records, and its service appears to be doubling every one or two years. Items may be traced through ISBN, Library of Congress number, Dewey decimal heading, or Boolean logic combinations relating to author, date, and title. Work is proceeding in tandem with British Telecom on worldwide fax transmission of documents, including where possible those located by BLAISE-LINE. See BOOK, BRITISH NATIONAL CORPUS, BRITISH PUBLISHING, LIBRARY. Compare LIBRARY OF CONGRESS. [EUROPE, HISTORY, MEDIA, TECHNOLOGY].   T.MCA.

BRITISH NATIONAL CORPUS, The. A cooperative venture, begun in 1991, with the aim of creating a computer-based corpus of 100m running words of BrE. There are six partners: Oxford University Press, Longman, W. & R. Chambers, Oxford U. Computing Services, the Unit for Computer Research on the English Language at Lancaster U., and the Research and Development Department of the British Library. The project is supported by the Department of Trade and Industry and the Science and Engineering Research Council. The sources for the corpus will include 90m words of text from books, newspapers, magazines, letters, memos, and advertisements, and 10m words of transcribed speech from radio and TV broadcasts, meetings, and the conversation of volunteers. The database is intended not only for the use of the collaborators but also, at cost price (as a national resource), for industry and researchers. Anticipated applications include: improved information in dictionaries; better grammar- and style-checking software for word-processing and desktop publishing; and linguistic analyses of value in information technology and machine translation. See CORPUS. Compare SURVEY OF ENGLISH USAGE (INTERNATIONAL CORPUS OF ENGLISH). [EUROPE, LANGUAGE]. T.MCA.

BRITISH PRESS. See JOURNALISM, NEWSPAPER, PRESS, TIMES (THE).

BRITISH PUBLISHING. Publishing in Britain began in England in 1476, when William Caxton introduced the first printing press. For several centuries after he produced and sold the first printed publications in English, there was no distinction between printer and publisher. Caxton and his successors followed their trade at a time when the language was in flux: see EARLY MODERN ENGLISH. They had a significant impact not only on the promotion and circulation of reading matter but also on the standardization of the written language. The introduction of the hand press and movable type revolutionized the process by which texts were prepared, bypassing the laborious hand-copying of manuscripts and the monopolies on knowledge of the Church and the rich. The process continues today, new technology making books and other publications cheaper and encouraging more purchasers and readers, who in turn prompt further innovations by authors, printers, publishers, and booksellers.

The Crown and the Stationers' Company. At first, printing and publishing grew slowly. By 1500, there were only five printers in England, all foreign apart from Caxton: to encourage the fledgeling trade, Richard III had exempted printers from the Act of 1484 that prevented foreigners from engaging in any trade. Henry VIII brought this period of relative freedom to an end, with a series of Acts between 1523 and 1534 that sought to impose restraints on what could be printed. Throughout the 16c, a series of proclamations aimed at controlling what seemed to the authorities, both secular and religious, to be a dangerous new undertaking. In 1538, a government proclamation inveighed against 'naughty printed books' and made it necessary to acquire a licence from the Privy Council or another royal nominee before any book could be printed. In 1557, Mary Tudor granted to the Stationers' Company a charter that gave it a near-monopoly on printing, in that only its members, or others with special patents, such as the University of Cambridge, had permission to engage in it. All books had to be registered with the Company, the first person registering a title acquiring all rights to it. This was, in effect, the beginning of *copyright*, and imposed a degree of regulation on what had until then often been a free-for-all in which many printers pirated works with impunity.

The first publishers. In 1586, Elizabeth I granted the Stationers powers to seize and destroy offending material and presses; at the same time, the Crown monopoly was extended to law books and catechisms, which could only be printed after payment of a fee. The Stationers' Company began to buy up existing patents and became a publisher in its own right, leasing patents to members and extending its control over most of the printers in London. Some book-seller members of the Company began to seek out authors, persuading them to write and funding the printing of their books. These book-sellers were among the first publishers, but the term *publisher* was not widely used for the commissioning, sale, and distribution of printed material until the 18c. Whatever arrangements were made between the Crown and the Stationers' Company, or between individual members of the Company and printers, binders, and paper-makers, authors were rarely beneficiaries. Some significant works were, however, published in the late 16c and early 17c, such as North's translation of *Plutarch's Lives* (1579), Spenser's *The Faerie Queene* (1589-96), and the King James Authorized Version of the Bible (1611). The publishing of drama and popular literature was at the time an exception to the general rule: not controlled by patent and left to non-members of the Company. These included some unscrupulous printer-publishers, such as Thomas Thorpe, who published an unauthorized copy of Shakespeare's sonnets in 1609. John Danter, a well-known pirate publisher, brought out the first of Shakespeare's plays to be published, *Titus Andronicus*, in 1594, and a corrupt version of *Romeo and Juliet* in 1597 that apparently derived largely from notes taken during a performance of the play.

Authors' rights. Throughout the 17c, the Crown repeatedly sought to exercise more control over printing. One attempt prompted Milton to produce *Areopagitica* (1643), a polemic against censorship and in favour of the freedom of the press. In 1694, Parliament refused to renew a licensing system that had been introduced by James II in 1685; from that point, state influence on what could or could not be published was exerted indirectly, through the laws of libel. The Copyright Act of 1709 introduced two radical principles: recognition of the rights of the author and protection of those rights for a fixed period of time. This Act, probably the most significant event in the early history of copyright, sought a balance between the interests of those who live by buying and selling printed works (printers, publishers, and authors); subsequent legislation has generally continued in the same vein.

Publishing technology. Developments in technology influence publishing: for example, in

1795 the Stanhope iron press was introduced, producing works of much better quality than the wooden press, because it exerted greater and more even pressure in the application of ink to paper. In 1803, an improved method of stereotyping was invented that reduced costs substantially: by taking a cast from the surface of a whole page of type, a mould could be obtained and then used to cast new printing plates for any reprint. Before this development, to be ready for reprints, printers needed either to keep expensive movable type standing indefinitely or to reset a book entirely. In the same year, a successful paper-making machine was invented and within ten years machine-made paper had become plentiful and cheap. In the 1830s, improved presses harnessed to steam power greatly accelerated output and, towards the end of the 19c, typesetting and binding were mechanized, with further increases in productivity and reductions in costs.

The book trade. In the later 19c, there were important developments in the structure and politics of the book trade. Authors, who tended to be the least powerful voice in the trade, were the first to organize. The *Society of Authors* was formed in 1884 and, with the rise of literary agents, there began a shift of power that in the 20c has led to further protection of authors' rights in copyright legislation. Intense competition between book-sellers in the late 19c produced price-cutting wars in Britain and elsewhere; for years, there had been attempts to introduce a net price principle under which publishers would sell to book-sellers at agreed discounts on condition that the book-seller would not sell books at less than the prices fixed by the publishers. However, a mutually satisfactory arrangement was not worked out until after the founding of the *Association of Booksellers of Great Britain and Ireland* (1895) and the *Publishers' Association* (1896). This agreement is incorporated in the *Net Book Agreement* (1901), which continues to operate in Britain, and is widely held to be crucial to the health of the book trade. Its supporters argue that without it bookshops could not afford a wide stock-holding as they would be forced to concentrate on a limited number of best-selling titles at substantially discounted prices. Its opponents argue that such resale price maintenance benefits publisher and book-seller (and perhaps author) at the cost of the consumer, and there have been recent attempts to circumvent it.

The paperback revolution. In the 20c, British publishing has grown into a substantial industry. Demand for books has continued to rise, fed by greater affluence and the spread of state education, which have created an ever-widening reading public and a need for educational books. The First World War disrupted but did not destroy the industry: paper was rationed, but demand remained high and publishers sold all that they produced. However, the post-war years were lean and caused a number of bankruptcies. Some publishers turned to educational publishing in the UK and colonies to help them through this period. The Great Depression, which began in 1929, produced further bankruptcies, but even so publishers continued their search for bigger markets. One of the most imaginative was Allen Lane, who in 1935 launched with *Penguin Books* (at sixpence a copy) a major sector of contemporary British book publishing: inexpensive paperbacks. The Second World War proved less destructive of the industry than had been expected: demand for reading material went up and publishers who could get enough paper achieved record sales. Again, the immediate post-war period was lean, but by the 1950s the paperback revolution was well under way; once again, cheaper books created new markets, not just in bookshops but in newsagents, corner shops, supermarkets, hotel lounges, and airport waiting-rooms. Books were everywhere, often impulse purchases designed for a single read before being discarded.

A representative list of publishers. The development of British publishing since the 16c can be inferred from the following list of major publishers with each firm's claimed date of founding: Cambridge University Press (1534: see entry), Oxford University Press (1584: see entry), Longman (1724: see entry), John Murray (1768), Thomas Nelson & Sons (1798), Blackie & Son (1809), Butterworths (1818), William Collins & Sons (1819: see entry), W. & R. Chambers (1820: see entry), John Bartholomew (1826), Macmillan (1843: see entry), Pitman Publishing (1845: see entry), Cassell (1848), Chatto & Windus (1855), Ginn & Co. (1867), British Museum (Natural History) (1881), J. M. Dent & Sons (1888), Heinemann (1890: see entry), Edward Arnold (1890), Gerald Duckworth & Co. (1898), Mills & Boon (1908), Sidgwick & Jackson (1908), Secker & Warburg (1910), Geographia (1921), Jonathan Cape (1921), Basil Blackwell (1922), Victor Gollancz (1927), Faber & Faber (1929: see entry), Hamish Hamilton (1931), Penguin Books (1935: see entry), Pan Books (1944), Hamlyn (1947), Pergamon Press (1948), Weidenfeld & Nicolson (1949), André Deutsch (1950), Ward Lock (1952), Mary Glasgow Publications (1956), David & Charles (1960), Sphere Books (1966), Mitchell Beazley (1969), Octopus (1971), British Museum Publications (1973),

British Library (1973: see entry), Virago (1974), Open University Press (1977), Women's Press (1978), Bloomsbury (1986), Paul Chapman (1987).

Revolutions in technology. In the 1950s–60s, there was a move away from metal typesetting and letterpress printing to the technology of photo-typesetting and lithographic printing, which required less skilled manual work. Costs were lower and new large presses achieved enormous economies of scale over long runs that were in turn made possible by improved marketing and distribution. Computer-aided composition in the 1960s–70s led to further economies and, in the 1980s, as computers became smaller and more sophisticated, a cottage industry came into being: people with a minimum of training could do their own typesetting and provide printers with electronic disks that could drive their photo-typesetting equipment. As microcomputers spread, authors began to be involved more directly in the publishing process, as the disks on which they created their texts could be used to avoid the re-keying of typescripts.

Communications and corporations. Other developments have in recent years changed the nature of publishing in the UK and elsewhere. The spread of radio, films, television, audio and video recording, and of such newer media as *compact disks* (CD-ROM and CD Interactive) all affect the nature of the industry, which can no longer be defined as dealing only with printed matter. For this reason, a new kind of publishing house has appeared in the late 20c: the international communications corporation that defines its interests not as books or magazines or films or television, but as 'information' and 'entertainment'. Traditional publishers are being acquired by such corporations, which see books as one package (by no means the most profitable) whose content can be marketed and sold alongside videos, films, TV (terrestrial and satellite), compact disks, databases, computer games, and the like. The long-established tendency for larger publishers to absorb smaller ones has become part of the process by which media empires have developed in recent years. For example, at the beginning of the 1990s:

(1) *News Corporation*, built by the Australian-born tycoon Rupert Murdoch, in addition to its newspaper and television interests, controlled: Collins, including Angus & Robertson, Collins Cartographic, Collins Educational, Collins Harvill, Bartholomew, Geographia, Robert Nicolson, Thorsons (including Aquarian and Crucible), Times Books, and Willow; Grafton (formerly Granada), including Adlard Coles and Paladin; and Marshal Pickering (as well as the US company Harper & Row).

(2) *Random House*, a US publishing corporation belonging to the Newhouse family, controlled the British *Random Century*, which in turn controlled: *Century Hutchinson*, including Century (including Rider), Hutchinson (including Muller and Radius), Ebury Press (including Benham), Barrie & Jenkins, and Stanley Paul; *Random House Division*, including Bodley Head, Chatto & Windus, Jonathan Cape, and Fodor; and the *Paperback Division*, including Arena, Arrow, Bearer, Legend, and Mysterious Press.

(3) *Reed International* controlled the *Octopus Group*, which included Bounty, Hamlyn, Heinemann, Mammoth, Mandarin, Methuen, Mitchell Beazley, Secker & Warburg, and Spring; and Butterworths (as well as the US company R. R. Bowker).

Pressures at the end of the 20c seem to be different in kind from those that existed before: vast sums of money are involved and there is a concentration of power in fewer hands. The traditional process by which small houses have arisen, replacing those absorbed by large corporations, faces great difficulties in competing with the buying power of the corporations (when negotiating with authors and particularly their agents) or with demands for bigger discounts made by an increasingly aggressive retail trade (that is also changing rapidly as large chains buy up independent bookshops).

Copyright, rights, and markets. Copyright remains the heart of the publishing industry. It is now recognized to be divisible into different *rights*, so that the contemporary author or agent may sell *hardback rights* to one publisher, *paperback rights* to another, *bookclub rights* separately, and *translation rights* to a variety of foreign publishers. The *non-print rights* in a work can be sold, for stage, film, television, audio or video recording, and for use in a database or as computer software. While new technologies have created new markets for rights, they are also often thought to create threats to markets for print publications. Radio, film, television, and computers have all in their time been seen as sounding the death-knell of traditional book publishing, but to date they have largely had the opposite effect: they have created new markets and introduced more people to reading for leisure and informational purposes. As a result, there are often *tie-ins* between one medium and another, such as the book of the TV series, or the novelization of a film script.

Conclusion. Currently, British publishing is a large and sophisticated industry that annually produces over £1bn turnover and publishes more than 70,000 new titles and new editions on every imaginable subject. A large percentage of these books are exported to countries where English is a first, second, or foreign language, and a smaller but significant proportion is translated into a large number of other languages. A striking feature has been a series of take-overs that has led to the assimilation of many well-known imprints into large multinational conglomerates: communications empires that recognize in book publishing raw material to feed other parts of the empire (usually film or television but increasingly computer databases). Though the process is not new, the scale at which it took place in the 1980s was unparalleled, as was its internationalization. See BIBLE, BOOK, BRITISH LIBRARY, CAXTON, ELT PUBLISHING, PUBLISHING. [MEDIA]. A. DU P., T.MCA.

BRITISH RAJ. See INDIA.

BRITISH SIGN LANGUAGE. See SIGN LANGUAGE.

BRITISH VIRGIN ISLANDS. See VIRGIN ISLANDS.

BRITO- [17c]. A relatively rare combining form of *Britain/British*, as in *Brito-Roman* relating to the ancient Britons and the Romans, and *Brito-Japanese* relating to Britain and Japan. See BRITOCENTRIC. Compare BRIT-, BRITISH-. [EUROPE, NAME]. T.MCA.

BRITOCENTRIC [1920s]. Centred in or on Britain and the British: 'Murray's model [in the *OED*] is unblushingly Britocentric. Words and senses not used in Britain are labelled "U.S.," "Austral.," and so on. Words used in Britain but not used in other regions are almost never labeled "U.K." ' (E. S. C. Weiner, in Ricks & Michaels, *The State of the Language*, 1990). See BRITO-, CENTRICITY. [EUROPE, STYLE]. T.MCA.

BRITON [13c: from Middle English *Breton*, French *breton*, from Latin *Britto* (plural *Brittones*), from Old Celtic, whence the Welsh plural *Brython*. The present form follows medieval Latin *Brito* (plural *Britones*)]. (1) Also *Brython*. A British Celt before the coming of the Anglo-Saxons and during the period when England, Scotland, and Wales were in the process of development. Often *ancient Briton*. (2) A native of Britain or a UK citizen, a term widely used in the media: *Briton jailed for life*; *35% of Britons Polled Admit to Racial Bias*. Although few British people refer to themselves as Britons, they are accustomed to seeing the term in print. See BRIT, BRITISHER. [EUROPE, HISTORY, NAME]. T.MCA.

BRITTANY [Before 10c: from Latin *Brittania* Britain: French *Bretagne* contrasts with *Grande Bretagne* Great Britain]. Also **Armorica**. A region of France between the English Channel and the Bay of Biscay, so named after the many Britons who fled there in the 5-6c. It was formerly known as *Less Britain* in contrast to the island of *Great Britain*. Its toponymy has much in common with that of Cornwall, especially in the use of saints' names: *Saint-Malo, Saint-Tugdual, Mont-Saint-Michel*. The Bretons resisted the Norse in the 9c, but in 1066 helped William of Normandy conquer England. In the late Middle Ages, they were often allies of England, but became French in 1532. There is a separatist movement comparable to that in Wales. See BRETON, BRITAIN, CORNWALL. [EUROPE, NAME]. T.MCA.

BRITTON, James N. [b.1908]. British theorist of teaching English as a mother tongue. Born in Scarborough, Yorkshire, and educated at the U. of London, he taught in various schools and in the London U. Institute of Education before becoming Professor of Education in 1970. Influential in the drafting of the Bullock Report, he has emphasized the role of talk as an important area for formal language teaching, and sought to classify modes of writing for school purposes. During his period of influence (1970s–80s), English teaching in England and Wales acquired something of the prestige previously held by Classics, and such movements as 'Language across the curriculum' extended the role of English teachers beyond their traditional boundaries. He is the author of *Language and Learning* (Allen Lane, 1970). See BULLOCK REPORT. [BIOGRAPHY, EDUCATION, EUROPE]. C.J.B.

BROAD. (1) An often dismissive term for a dialect, accent, or usage considered coarse, rustic, uneducated, and difficult to understand: 'I toke an olde boke, and the englysshe was so rude and brood that I coude not wele vnderstande it' (Caxton, *Eneydos*, 1490); 'Broad Yorkshire talked all over the ship' (*Blackwood's Magazine*, 1859). In linguistics, the concept *breadth of accent* is used to discuss distance from a norm, entailing greater risk of social disapproval the further an accent is from that norm: 'The most educated Scottish, Northern Irish, and Welsh accents are highly acceptable in Britain generally, though when any significant degree of breadth is used outside the region concerned there is a danger of unintelligibility, or at least of distraction from the speaker's message, *and even of actual hostility*' (John Honey, *Does Accent Matter?*, 1989). See ACCENT, AUSTRALASIAN ENGLISH, BROAD AUSTRALIAN, BROAD NEW ZEALAND, BROAD SCOTS. (2) In phonetics, a term referring to a transcription in which only significantly different sounds are marked, as opposed to a *narrow* transcription. See PHONETIC TRANSCRIPTION. [SPEECH].   T.MCA.

BROAD AUSTRALIAN. The pronunciation of AusE in which local features are most marked. See AUSTRALIAN ENGLISH, BROAD, STRINE. [OCEANIA, SPEECH, VARIETY].   W.S.R.

BROADCASTING [1920s: from 18c *broadcast* scattered around (said of seeds and by extension ideas, statements, etc.). Compare *dissemination*, from Latin *semen/seminis* seed]. The electronic transmission of speech, music, and images for public consumption and the activities and professions that support it, including *broadcast journalism*. Broadcasting organizations, whose administration, nature, and status vary from country to country, generally provide scheduled services of programmes that are analogues and extensions of magazines and other periodicals. As a result, many of the terms of journalism, publishing, and printing have been adapted for radio and television, such as *bulletin, correspondent, documentary, feature, format, journalism, news, newsdesk, newsroom, reporter, story* alongside such new terms as *anchor, continuity, docudrama, fade, network, station, voiceover*. Like print, the aim of broadcasting is usually to inform, entertain, and educate, but may include advertising, political indoctrination and manipulation, and propaganda. Like all media, it is often subject to degrees of state control and political and other kinds of intervention, including censorship. Broadcasting often implicitly or explicitly serves to standardize forms of spoken language, much as printed matter promotes a standard written language.

Radio. Broadcasting was implicit in the invention by the Italian physicist Guglielmo Marconi of a system of radio telegraphy patented in England in 1896. Despite initial scepticism and indifference, it became explicit in 1901 with his 'wireless' transmission of Morse code from Poldhu in Cornwall to St John's in Newfoundland. In the US, radio broadcasts were pioneered by amateurs, one of whom, R. A. Fessenden, first transmitted speech and music in 1906. In 1916, the *American Radio and Research Company* broadcast concerts twice a week. The military value of radio was recognized before and during the First World War, and contributed to its later civilian success. In 1920, the commercial station *KDKA Pittsburgh* went 'on air' in the US and the *Marconi Company* in the UK began broadcasting first from Chelmsford and Writtle in Essex, then as *Station 2LO* from London. By 1922, the US and the UK had developed very different responses to public radio: there were 564 licensed broadcasters in the US as against

one consortium in the UK, the *British Broadcasting Company*, established as a consequence of almost 100 applications for licences to broadcast. In 1927, the multiplicity of US stations maintained by commercial advertising was regulated by the Radio Act, and the single service in the UK became by royal charter the *British Broadcasting Corporation* (*BBC*), a public service monopoly financed by licences paid by owners of receiving sets.

The heyday of radio was the 1930s and 1940s, leading on both sides of the Atlantic to communicative forms that extended literature and drama. Novel conventions used by announcers and continuity voices served to separate programmes; news bulletins and current-affairs programmes were given formats modelled on the reports, features, editorials, and columns of journalism; plays were often serialized; entertainment was magazine-like (with interviews, storytelling, talks, variety performances, games, and competitions); and the performance of music became a staple both as programmes and as accompaniment to other programmes. National leaders and politicians also used the medium to communicate messages to the people and canvass for support. As a result, in addition to literacy acquired in school, millions in the mid-20c acquired oral/aural skills and expectations that included exposure to a variety of accents, styles, and usages. However, until the development of such programmes as the *phone-in* or *call-in*, radio allowed little more two-way communication than a printed page.

Television. The transmission of black-and-white visual images became technically feasible in the UK at the end of the 1920s, as a consequence of competition between the Scottish inventor John Logie Baird and the Russian-born engineer Isaac Shoenberg. Where Baird favoured a technique of mechanical scanning demonstrated in 1926, Shoenberg opted for electronic scanning, a more successful system adopted by the BBC for the world's first high-definition TV service in 1936. In the US, the first public transmission was made in 1939 by the *National Broadcasting Company* at the New York World's Fair. Further development was, however, delayed by the Second World War, in which radio served as a powerful instrument of social solidarity and wartime propaganda. Television developed rapidly after the war, especially in the US, and since the late 1950s television has been the dominant medium. Colour became available in 1954 and widespread in the 1960s, by which time a TV set in every home was becoming the norm for Western countries. The use of motion pictures, the creation of made-for-television films, the development of video recorders, and the universality of satellite transmission have greatly extended the range of services. Millions of viewers currently depend on their sets for the bulk of their news and entertainment. In tandem, the adaptation of literary genres has continued, turning living-rooms into miniature theatres at the press of a button.

As a consequence of this dual revolution, a major part of the world's use of language is in broadcasting and much of that broadcasting is in English. This is accounted for by the strong initial position of the UK and the US in the development of radio and television, the overwhelming predominance of the US in the making and marketing of motion pictures subsequently shown on television or specifically made for television, the distribution of English-language broadcasting throughout the world, so that its transmissions can be picked up everywhere, and the widespread association of English-language broadcasting with a modernity that includes print media, publishing, the telephone, and computer technology.

See AMERICAN BROADCASTING, AUSTRALIAN BROADCASTING, BBC, BBC ENGLISH[1], BBC ENGLISH[2], BBC ENGLISH[3], BRITISH BROADCASTING, CABLE NEWS NETWORK, CANADIAN BROADCASTING, COMMUNICATIVE SHIFT, IRISH BROADCASTING, MAGAZINE, NETWORK, NEW ZEALAND BROADCASTING, RECEIVED PRONUNCIATION, SCOSE, SERIAL, SERIES, SHORT STORY, SOAP OPERA, SOUTH AFRICAN BROADCASTING, WELSH LANGUAGE SERVICE. [MEDIA, TECHNOLOGY].   T.MCA.

BROAD NEW ZEALAND. The pronunciation of NZE in which local features are most marked. See BROAD, NEW ZEALAND ENGLISH. [OCEANIA, SPEECH, VARIETY].   T.MCA.

BROAD SCOTS, also **Broad Scotch, Braid Scots.** Traditional terms for Scots or for its more distinctive dialects. Unlike many other expressions involving *broad*, the terms are generally neutral or positive: 'In plain braid Scots hold forth a plain braid story' (Robert Burns, *Brigs of Ayr*, 1787). See BROAD, SCOTS. [EUROPE, SPEECH, VARIETY].   T.MCA.

BROADSHEET [18c: perhaps influenced by *broadside*]. (1) A large sheet of paper, usually a quarto page, printed on one side, originally containing royal proclamations, papal indulgences, and similar institutional statements. (2) Also *broadside*. A topical song or poem printed on a broadsheet, containing controversial, sometimes scurrilous comment, and used as a vehicle of political agitation. The format allowed swift production and easy distribution. Some 17c poems, by such writers as Butler and Dryden, first appeared as broadsheets. (3) A large-format newspaper with pages approximately 15×24

inches (38×61 cm): *The Times* of London as opposed to the tabloid *Daily Mirror*. Compare BROADSIDE. [MEDIA, TECHNOLOGY].   G.H., T.MCA.

BROADSIDE [16c: extending the term for a cannonade from one side of a warship]. (1) Also *broadsheet*. A sheet of paper usually printed on one side only. (2) Verse printed on such a sheet, and hawked and sung on the streets from the 16c. The verse might be doggerel or a *broadside ballad* sung to a popular tune: see BALLAD. (3) A standard size of paper before cutting or folding. (4) A printed circular for advertising. Compare BROADSHEET. [MEDIA, TECHNOLOGY].   T.MCA.

BROCHURE [18c: French, from *brocher* to stitch]. A leaflet or a magazine, originally a number of leaves stitched together, now often thick and providing information of a promotional nature: *travel brochures*. The style of language used is sometimes referred to, often pejoratively, as *brochurese*. See -ESE. [MEDIA, STYLE, TECHNOLOGY].   T.MCA.

BROGUE [17c: probably from Gaelic *bróg* a shoe, originally a leg-covering, cognate with *breeches*. The term referred especially to the footwear of the Irish peasantry and has been used in *sean-bhróg* old shoe, to refer to a story often repeated. The linguistic sense is sometimes said to derive from *barróg teangan* tongue hold, a lisp or speech defect]. An informal, nontechnical term for an Irish and sometimes a Scottish or West Country accent. In the 18c, the expression *to have the brogue on one's tongue* was common for an Irish accent and the word has been used at least since the 17c: '[They] had both their Education at the English Court, which something refin'd their Gibberish, yet not so much, but that there is still a Brogue' (James Farewell, *The Irish Hudibras*, London, 1689). The term is used humorously and facetiously in Ireland. See ACCENT. Compare LILT. [EUROPE, SPEECH].   T.MCA., L.T.

BROKEN [16c in this sense]. (1) An informal, non-technical term for a foreigner's limited and ungrammatical use of a language: 'The skipper asked in broken English for his help' (*Observer*, 2 Sept. 1990). (2) Also *Torres Strait Broken*. The name given by its speakers to the English-based creole of the Torres Strait islands between Cape York in Australia and Papua New Guinea, known technically as *Torres Strait Creole*. See BROKEN ENGLISH. [OCEANIA, SPEECH, STYLE, VARIETY].   T.MCA., S.R.

BROKEN ENGLISH [16c]. An informal and usually dismissive term for English when considered badly spoken or imperfectly learned:

'Breake thy mind to me in broken English' (Shakespeare, *Henry V*, 5. 2); 'English is the international language. Or, I should say, broken English is the international language' (Akira Nambara, quoted in the *International Herald Tribune*, 28 Sept. 1987). The term has often been used to describe the English used by aboriginal peoples, refugees, street traders, servants, and slaves, and has often been portrayed in literature: ' "Yes, yes," says I [to Man Friday], "God is above the devil, and therefore we pray to God to enable us to resist his temptations and quench his fiery darts." "But," says he again, "if God much strong, much might as devil, why God no kill the devil, so make him no more wicked?" ' (Defoe, *Robinson Crusoe*, 1719). See BROKEN, FOREIGNER TALK, FRACTURED ENGLISH, JARGON, PATOIS, PIDGIN. [LITERATURE, SPEECH, STYLE, VARIETY].   T.MCA.

BRONTË SISTERS, The. *Charlotte* [1816–55], *Emily* [1818–48]. Also **Bronte**. English writers, born near Bradford in Yorkshire and moved in infancy to Haworth, where their father was vicar. After unhappy early schooling, they studied in Brussels, where Charlotte briefly taught English, then taught in schools and as governesses. In 1846, with their sister Anne, they published a volume of poems under the pseudonyms Currer, Ellis, and Acton Bell. It had little success and only Emily won a reputation as a poet. They remained at home, contending with poor health, the ailments of an ageing father, and the alcoholism of their brother Branwell. Their fiction includes Emily's one novel *Wuthering Heights* (1842) and Charlotte's four, of which *Jane Eyre* (1847) is the best-known. After the deaths of her brother and sisters, Charlotte lived on with her father, married his curate in 1854, and died within a year. In their writing, Romantic and Gothic elements mingle with realism. Charlotte reproduces the style of Evangelical speakers and both portrayed Yorkshire dialect. Their skill in expressing thoughts and memories foreshadowed the development of interior monologue. While accepting male domination, both show the strains and disabilities of women in 19c English society. See index. [BIOGRAPHY, EUROPE, LITERATURE].   R.C.

BROOKLYNESE [1940s]. The dialect of the people of Brooklyn, one of the five boroughs of New York City. Originally a Dutch settlement, Brooklyn is currently both residential and industrial, as well as a centre of transport. The dialect has been stereotyped as an artificial dialect, especially in films. A typical feature is the vowel of *earl*, pronounced /ɔɪl/, a pronunciation found also in New Orleans and other parts of the South. In some varieties, *oil* has the same vowel,

a pronunciation once common in other forms of English, so that the two words are identical in sound. In stereotypical Brooklynese, the pronunciation of the words is reversed, so that *earl* is 'oil' and *oil* is 'earl'. This stage dialect is perceived as ignorant, comic, and crude, but the characteristic features of Brooklynese are survivals of older well-respected forms. See -ESE, NEW YORK CITY, NEW YORKESE. [AMERICAS, SPEECH, VARIETY].   J.A.

BROWN CORPUS, The. A pioneering computer-based corpus of 1m running words of English developed in the US in 1963–4 by Henry Kucera and W. Nelson Francis at Brown University, Providence, Rhode Island, for the statistical analysis of words in texts. Representative extracts of 2,000 words each were taken from a selection of texts that sought to balance registers, styles, and genres, and included material from newspapers, scientific writing, romantic novels, and westerns. See CORPUS, FREQUENCY COUNT. [LANGUAGE, WORD].   T.MCA.

BRUMMAGEM, BRUMMIE. See BIRMINGHAM.

BRUNEI. Official titles: Malay *Negara Brunei Darussalam*, English *State of Brunei Darussalam*. A country in South-East Asia, in the island of Borneo (a variant of the same name). Capital: Bandar Seri Begawan. Currency: the dollar (100 sen or cents). Economy: mainly oil, natural gas. Population: 250,000 (1988), 380,000 (projection for 2000). Ethnicity: 64% Malay, 20% Chinese, 16% others. Religions: 60% Muslim, 16% traditional, 14% Buddhist, 10% Christian. Languages: Malay, English (both official), Chinese. Education: primary and secondary 100%, tertiary 8%, literacy 78%. Brunei was a British protectorate from 1888 and gained its independence in 1984. See ENGLISH, MALAY, MALAYSIA. [ASIA, NAME, VARIETY].   T.MCA.

BRYTHONIC [1880s: from Welsh *Brython* a Briton. Stress: 'bri-THON-ik']. (1) An academic adjective, introduced by Sir John Rhys (1884), used to refer to the Brythons/Britons, the people of ancient Britain, and their descendants who, after the Anglo-Saxon settlement, lived mainly in Wales, Cornwall, and Strathclyde. (2) Also *British*. The language of the ancient Britons. See BRITISH, BRITON, CELTIC LANGUAGES, CUMBRIC. [EUROPE, LANGUAGE].   T.MCA.

BULL [17c: from Latin *bulla* bubble, game, joke, influenced by the name of the animal: compare BULLETIN]. A slang term for nonsense and foolish exaggeration: *What a lot/load of (old) bull!* The more emphatic form *bullshit* also refers to excessive zeal and pretentious usage, as in the British

Army adage *Bullshit baffles brains.* The AmE expression *to shoot the bull* means to talk aimlessly. See IRISH BULL, JARGON. [STYLE, USAGE].

T.MCA.

BULLETIN [17c: through French from Italian *bullettino*, a little document, from *bulla* a bubble, seal, document with a seal, and the origin of *papal bull*: compare BULL]. (1) A brief statement issued to the public, often by radio or television. In an institution or club, especially in the US, notices may appear ('be posted') on a *bulletin board*. (2) A brief, up-to-the-minute account in the media of news or events of public interest. (3) A summary cataloguing the activities of an agency, association, company, educational institution, etc. (4) An official or scholarly periodical. (5) The name of a periodical. (6) Although messages sent electronically are not usually called bulletins, the term (*electronic*) *bulletin board* is widely used, especially in North America, for a list of regularly updated messages maintained by a computer and 'posted' (made available) to other terminals in a network. See BULLETIN (THE), ELECTRONIC PUBLISHING, NEWS. [MEDIA].

T.MCA.

BULLETIN, The. A weekly Australian newsmagazine that incorporates the Pacific edition of *Newsweek.* Founded in 1880, it was for many years Australia's most significant literary magazine, its most vital period coinciding with the rise of nationalism in the 1890s. It encouraged items from 'the man in the bush' and became known as 'the Bushman's Bible'. It gave currency to the vocabularies of shearing and droving as part of outback life and its use of rural colloquialisms helped enshrine terms like *battler* someone who struggles to make a living, *bonzer* good, a good thing, *dinkum* true, genuine, honest, and *mate* a sworn friend, as part of an Australian stereotype. See AUSTRALIAN PRESS, NEWSMAGAZINE. [MEDIA, OCEANIA].

W.S.R.

BULLOCK REPORT. A British report on the teaching of English as a mother tongue, presented by the Committee of Inquiry set up by the Secretary of State for Education and Science, Margaret Thatcher, in 1972. The Committee was chaired by the historian Sir Alan Bullock, and reported in 1975. Its remit was 'to consider in relation to schools: (a) all aspects of teaching the use of English, including reading, writing, and speech; (b) how present practice might be improved and the role that initial and in-service training might play; (c) to what extent arrangements for monitoring the general level of attainment in these skills can be introduced or improved; and to make recommendations'. In a report of over 600 pages, with 333 recommendations, the Committee summarized much of the consensus of the 1970s on the nature of English teaching, particularly reflecting attitudes associated with the work of James N. Britton. Although sceptical about claims that literacy rates had fallen substantially, the Committee called for a major investment in training and development to improve linguistic skills and linguistic awareness among both teachers and learners, and drew attention to the number of English teachers whose training was not specifically for teaching in this area. The report has been criticized for its optimism, but reflects clearly the views on language which underlay the moves to a mass, comprehensive system of schooling through the 1960s–70s. See BRITTON, KINGMAN REPORT, LANGUAGE AWARENESS, NEWBOLT REPORT, TEACHING ENGLISH. [EDUCATION, EUROPE].

C.J.B.

BUNGEE. See MÉTIS.

BUNYAN, John [1628–88]. English religious writer and nonconformist preacher. The son of a Bedfordshire tinker, he learned the rudiments of reading and writing at a village school, was highly strung and prone to depression, and had an acute sense of sin and punishment. After serving in the Parliamentary forces in the Civil War, in which his life seemed to him to have been preserved by the grace of God, a long religious struggle led him to become a Baptist. He told the story of his conversion in *Grace Abounding* (1666), written when imprisoned as a dissenter after the Restoration in 1660. He spent most of 12 years in prison, but with a certain amount of freedom of action that he used to write tracts and to work on *The Pilgrim's Progress: From this world to that which is to come.* This allegory of the human spiritual predicament was written in the style and language of the King James Bible and told, through the device of a dream, how its hero Christian, after abandoning the City of Destruction and many subsequent trials, reached the Celestial City. It was published in 1678, went into ten editions in his lifetime, became the most widely read book in English after the Bible, and was highly popular in the American colonies. It was not, however, accepted in literary circles until the early 19c. After his release from prison, Bunyan became a leading dissenting minister, preached to huge congregations throughout England, administered the affairs of his sect, and wrote various other works. *The Pilgrim's Progress*, however, remains his monument. It contributed to the evolution of the novel through directness of style, narrative power, and use of dialogue. Such characters as Faithful, Mr Worldly Wiseman, Mr Standfast, Mr Facing-Both-Ways, and Giant Despair, and such places as the Slough of Despond, Doubting Castle, and Vanity Fair have become part of the language. See index. [EUROPE, LITERATURE].   M.LA.

BURCHFIELD, Robert W(illiam) [b.1923]. Lexicographer and linguist, born in Wanganui, New Zealand, and educated at Victoria U. College, Wellington, and Magdalen College, Oxford. After service in the Royal New Zealand Artillery during the Second World War (1941-6), he became a Rhodes scholar in 1949, a lecturer in English at Oxford at Magdalen College (1952-63), Tutorial Fellow of St Peter's College (1963-79), and Senior Research Fellow of St Peter's (from 1979). He was Editor of *A Supplement to the Oxford English Dictionary* (1957-86), Chief Editor, the Oxford Dictionaries (1971-84), Honorary Secretary of the Early English Text Society (1955-68), and President of the English Association (1978-9). His publications include: with C. T. Onions & G. W. S. Friedrichsen, *The Oxford Dictionary of English Etymology* (1966); the *OED Supplement* (vol. i 1972, vol. ii 1976, vol. iii 1982, vol. iv 1986); with D. Donoghue & A. Timothy, *The Quality of Spoken English on BBC Radio* (1979); *The Spoken Language as an Art Form* (1981); *The Spoken Word* (1981); *The English Language* (1985); *The New Zealand Pocket Oxford Dictionary* (1986). See index. [BIOGRAPHY, EUROPE, REFERENCE].   T.MCA.

BUREAUCRATESE [Late 20c: from *bureaucrat* and *-ese*]. A pejorative non-technical term for the language of bureaucrats. In Canada, for example, the duties of the government position of Senior Projects Officer were described as: '[Such an officer] leads project teams to implement Branch plans; coordinates select horizontal administrative activities and acts as a functional co-ordinator for cross-sectoral development initiatives; assists in Branch policy formulation in response to horizontal strategic issues impacting on the sector development process and then formulates and recommends strategies and initiatives to address these issues; develops, delivers, administers and monitors projects under Branch programs to foster development of the sector.' See ABUSE, -ESE, JARGON, OFFICIALESE. [STYLE, USAGE].   W.D.L.

BURGESS, Anthony, pen name of *John Anthony Burgess Wilson* [b.1917]. British novelist, critic, scriptwriter, teacher, and composer, born in Manchester and educated at the U. of Manchester. After service in the Second World War, he worked as a teacher, lectured at the U. of Birmingham (1946-8), and was an education officer in Malaya and Brunei (1954-9). Experience there provided material for his first novels, *Time for a Tiger* (1956), *The Enemy in the Blanket* (1958),

and *Beds in the East* (1959), published together as *The Malayan Trilogy* (1972). He has written educational texts, such as *English Literature: A Survey for Students* (1958), critical works, such as *Here Comes Everybody* (1956), on James Joyce, and the comic *Enderby* novels (as 'Joseph Kell'), has composed orchestral music, and written for cinema and television. Burgess's linguistic training is shown in dialogue enriched by distinctive pronunciations and the niceties of register; in *The Doctor is Sick* (1960) the protagonist is a linguist who suffers misadventures in London. His dystopian novel *A Clockwork Orange* (1962) is a violent tale told in the first person by an adolescent who uses *nadsat* (from Russian *nadtsat'* teen), a Russianized English argot used by teenagers. It opens:

There was me, that is Alex, and my three droogs, that is Pete, Georgie, and Dim, Dim being really dim, and we sat in the Korova Milkbar making up our rassoodocks what to do with the evening, a flip dark chill winter bastard though dry. The Korova Milkbar was a milk-plus mesto, and you may, O my brothers, have forgotten what these mestos were like.

[*droog* friend, *rassoodock* mind, *mesto* place].

Both the book and its film version by Stanley Kubrick (1972) achieved for a time virtual cult status. See index. [BIOGRAPHY, EUROPE, LANGUAGE, LITERATURE].   R.C., T.MCA.

BURGESSISM [20c]. A word or sense of a word coined by the US humorist Frank Gelett Burgess (1866-1951), who created many words that he felt the language lacked. The most successful were the word *blurb* (a highly favourable description of a book, usually on its cover) and the sense *bromide* (a boring person). In *Burgess Unabridged: A New Dictionary of Words You Have Always Needed* (1914), he created and defined such items as: *bleesh* obscene art, *fidgeltick* food that is a bore to eat, and *gloogo* a devoted adherent. The term is sometimes extended to any word coined to fill a lexical gap, such as *malefit* to balance *benefit*. See BLURB, -ISM, ROOT-CREATION. [STYLE, WORD].   T.MCA.

BURGHER ENGLISH [From *burgher* an Anglicized spelling of Dutch *burger* townsperson, citizen. The term has been used in Sri Lanka, formerly Ceylon, first for the descendants of European settlers, then for people of mixed European and local blood]. The English of Eurasians in Sri Lanka, whose pronunciation and usage distinguish it from the general English of Sri Lanka: 'The Burghers were indisputably superior to every other indigenous community in Ceylon in their command of the English language. . . . It was easy for Burghers to take to English education because from the early days they had adopted English as their home language' (Tissa Fernando, 'The Burghers of Ceylon', in Noel P. Gist & A. G. Dworkin (eds.), *The Blending of Races: Marginality and Identity in World Perspectives*, John Wiley, 1972). See ANGLO-INDIAN, EURASIAN, SRI LANKA. [ASIA, VARIETY].   B.B.K.

BURLESQUE [17c: from French *burlesque*, Italian *burlesco*, from *burla* a joke, ridicule]. (1) A comic work that satirizes in an exaggerated way, especially a play parodying social events or prevailing dramatic fashion, such as Richard Sheridan's *The Critic* (1779). (2) Also *burleycue*. In North America in the 19c and early 20c, a bawdy comedy show made up of short turns and sketches, in which striptease often featured latterly. See CARICATURE, COMEDY, MACARONIC, SATIRE. [LITERATURE].   T.MCA.

BURMA. Official title: Burmese *Pyidaungsu Socialist Thammada Myanma Naingngadaw*, English *Socialist Republic of the Union of Burma*. Although the country was officially renamed *Myanmar* in 1989, the new name has not to date been widely adopted. A country of South Asia. Capital: Rangoon/Yangon. Currency: the kyat (100 pyas). Economy: mainly agriculture. Population: 39.2m (1988), 51.8m (projection for 2000). Ethnicity: 68% Burman, 9% Shan, 7% Karen, 2% Chin, 2% Chinese. Religions: 85% Buddhist, 8% traditional, 3% Muslim, 2% Hindu, 2% Christian. Languages: Burmese (official), and indigenous, such as Shan and Karen. Burma was annexed to India during three wars with the British between 1824 and 1886. It gained internal self-government in 1937, and became independent in 1948. Burma did not join the Commonwealth, and discontinued the use of English as a language of administration and education. [ASIA, NAME].   T.MCA.

BURNS, Robert [1759–96]. Scottish national poet, born in Alloway, Ayrshire, and educated by a tutor, by his father at home, and by his own wide reading. His childhood and youth were spent helping his father in unsuccessful farming ventures. His first volume of poems, the Kilmarnock Edition of 1786, aroused great enthusiasm and he was fêted in Edinburgh social circles. He had friends and patrons of high rank, despite his radical views, but it was not until 1789 that he obtained in Dumfries the excise appointment he sought, and not until 1791 that he gave up farming to become a full-time exciseman. In his earliest poems, Burns hesitates between Scots and English, but the influence of Robert Fergusson confirmed his preference for Scots. Widely considered the supreme poet in that tongue, Burns draws on the registers of folk-song, storytelling, preaching, social banter,

and daily work, as well as the Bible and Augustan English poetry, and is noted for his ability to modulate between English and Scots for subtle effects:

> But pleasures are like poppies spread;
> You seize the flow'r, its bloom is shed;
> Or like the snow falls in the river,
> A moment white—then melts for ever;
> Or like the Borealis race,
> That flit ere you can point their place;
> Or like the rainbow's lovely form
> Evanishing amid the storm.
> Nae man can tether time or tide;
> The hour approaches Tam maun ride;
> That hour, o' night's black arch the key-stane,
> And sic a night he taks the road in,
> As ne'er poor sinner was abroad in.
>   (from *Tam o' Shanter*, 1791)

A central theme in his poetry is the injustice of society, expressed by celebrating the peasantry and the conviviality which lightened their lives, and by unrestrained, sometimes venomous satire on the pretentiousness and oppression of landowners. Religious hypocrisy was another target. The main achievement of his later years was a body of Scots songs, some 250 of them partly or wholly his own, contributed to the collections of James Johnson (six volumes, 1787–1803) and George Thomson (five volumes, 1793–1818). The work of matching verses to existing tunes and adapting unsophisticated original lyrics demonstrates an intense feeling for traditional Scottish folk music. See index. [BIOGRAPHY, EUROPE, LITERATURE].   J.D.M.

BURR [18c: imitative, from *bur, burr* a rough seed-container or flower head with a tendency to stick to clothes. Compare *a bur in the throat*, referring to huskiness]. An informal term for a pronunciation of *r* that is perceived as 'rough', especially the uvular trill once widespread in north-east England (the *Durham/Northumbrian/Northumberland burr*) and south-east Scotland (the *Berwick/Berwickshire burr*). This 'Parisian' *r* is prestigious in French (*r grasseyé*: guttural *r*) but often stigmatized in English; speech therapists traditionally treating it as a defect. Commentators on strong *r*-pronunciation do not, however, always distinguish uvular from alveolar; defining *burr* in the *OED* (1880s), James A. H. Murray noted: 'Writers ignorant of phonology often confuse the Northumberland *burr* with the entirely different Scotch *r*, which is a lingual trill.' The term is also used for an accent in which a burr is prominent: 'Miss Keith spoke with a Scotch burr' (Somerset Maugham, *The Razor's Edge*, 1967). See ACCENT, GEORDIE, GUTTURAL, RHOTACISM, R-SOUNDS. [SPEECH].   T.MCA.

BUSH [18c: from Dutch *bosch* woodland, first used in South Africa and the US]. Open country in a British colony or ex-colony: 'His house was well enough for the bush, as the country is generally termed in the colony' (J. Lang, *New South Wales*, 1837). It is evocative in AusE, meaning natural vegetation, land covered in such vegetation, country in its natural, unsettled state: the outback as opposed to town and city. The many AusE compounds include *bush fence*, *bush hospitality*, *bush lore*, and *bush poet*. It has a peculiar potency because of the associations formed by writers between the national character and the bush as an environment in which it was formed. In NZE, *bush* refers to country covered in native forest. In Canada, it refers to remote unsettled areas, including the treeless Arctic, and also occurs in compounds: *bush pilot*. *To be bushed*, in addition to meaning 'to be tired', can in CanE mean 'to be acting oddly because of long isolation'. See BULLETIN (THE), BUSH BALLAD, NDJUKA, SARAMACCAN. [AFRICA, AMERICAS, NAME, OCEANIA].   W.S.R., L.B., M.F.

BUSH BALLAD [19c]. A song associated with the Australian bush, as collected in *Australian Bush Ballads* (1955) and *Old Bush Songs* (1957), edited by D. A. Stewart and N. Keesing. A composer of such songs is a *bush balladist*. See BALLAD, BUSH. [LITERATURE, OCEANIA].   T.MCA.

BUSINESS ENGLISH. The register of English appropriate to commerce and industry, and the name for training courses in business usage, especially if offered to foreign learners: '*BBC Business English*: A self-study course in business English for intermediate level business people wanting to use English at work' (*BBC English* catalogue, 1991); 'Much business English teaching concentrates on communication skills: meetings; presentation; telephoning, and social skills in a business context etc.' (*EFL Gazette*, Nov. 1990). Some observers regard international business English as a neutral, pragmatic means of communication among non-native users of the language. Andrew Fenner has labelled it *IBL* (*international business language*): 'In a European context, IBL is the sort of English a Norwegian would use when trying to communicate with an Italian in Belgium. In other words, it is a *lingua franca* used between those for whom English is not their native language, but the only common language in which any sort of communication is possible. Its grammar and syntax vary, being modelled on those of the language of the person speaking in each case' ('Lingua Anglica: The Emergence of International Business English', *Language International* 2: 1, 1990). See COMMERCIALESE, ESP, GENERAL ENGLISH, INSTITUTE OF LINGUISTS, PITMAN PUBLISHING, REGISTER, SHORTHAND, TEIL. [EDUCATION, VARIETY].   T.MCA.

BUTLER ENGLISH, also **Kitchen English, Bearer English**. A reduced form of English used in South Asia. It probably arose in the 19c in the Madras Presidency of British India (now the state of Tamil Nadu), as a means of communication between the British and their *bearers* (valets, butlers). It is a minimal pidgin that takes on characteristics from the language of the area in which it is used. The present participle is used for the future (*I telling* I'll tell) and the perfect is formed by *done* (*I done tell* I have told). Auxiliaries and verb inflections are omitted, and words often have adapted meanings, such as *family* used to mean *wife*. Compare BEARER ENGLISH. See INDO-ENGLISH, KITCHEN, PIDGIN, SOUTH ASIAN ENGLISH. [ASIA, VARIETY].   B.B.K.

BUTLER, Samuel [1835-1902]. English novelist and painter, born at Langar, Nottinghamshire, and educated at Shrewsbury School and Cambridge. He was expected to follow his father and grandfather into holy orders but developed doubts and went to New Zealand, where he prospered as a sheep-farmer. He returned in 1864 and published anonymously his fantasies *Erewhon* (1872) and *Erewhon Revisited* (1901), in which an imaginary utopian community in New Zealand serves to satirize the follies of contemporary England as he saw them. The satire is partly achieved by reversed names: *Yram*, *Nosnibor*, and *Erewhon* itself. See index. [BIOGRAPHY, EUROPE, LITERATURE].   R.C.

BUZZ WORD [1960s: from *buzz* in the sense of excitement and gossip]. An informal term for a word that is fashionable and used more to impress than inform: for example, *power* with the sense 'pertaining to powerful persons, indicating political or economic power', which appeared in the US in the 1980s in such phrases as *power breakfast*, *power colour*, *power necktie*, *power suit*, *power writing*. Buzz words are particularly associated with the terminology and jargon of corporate business, government, and the sciences. Compare KEYWORD, VOGUE. See TIMESPEAK. [STYLE, WORD].   J.A.

BY-LINE, also **byline** [1920s]. A term in journalism for a line that provides a writer's name, set at the beginning or end of a story or feature: 'In the media club we tend to become very byline-conscious, whereas I suspect the public are almost byline-blind' (Mark Jones, in *Journalist's Week*, 21 Nov. 1990). A story accompanied by a by-line is *by-lined*; a journalist prominent enough to have a by-line is a *by-liner*. [MEDIA, NAME].   T.MCA.

BY-NAME, also **byname** [14c]. A nickname, surname, or secondary name. See NICKNAME. [NAME].   T.MCA.

BYTE. See COMPUTING, INFORMATION.

C

C, c [Called 'cee']. The 3rd letter of the Roman alphabet as used for English. It descends from the hook-shaped Phoenician symbol *gimel* (a name probably related to *camel*), which represented the voiced velar stop /g/. This letter was altered by the Greeks to Γ (*gamma*), with the same sound value. Gamma was then adapted by the Etruscans to represent the voiceless velar stop /k/, a use taken over by the Romans. In Old English, *c* represented both the sound /k/ as in *cynn* ('kin') and the sound *ch* /tʃ/ as in *cinn* ('chin'). In the Romance languages, and in English under the influence of Norman French, *c* acquired a second palatalized pronunciation /s/ before *e* and *i*: a 'soft' pronunciation, as in *cell* and *cite*, contrasting with the 'hard' *c* in *crown*. This development occurred after 1066 and resulted in a shift of spelling patterns and sound–symbol correspondences, Old English forms such as *cild, cyng, cwic, is* becoming *child, king, quick, ice*. In addition, such *c/k* pairs arose as *cat* and *kitten, cow* and *kine*.

Sound values. *C* has the greatest sound range of all English consonants, overlapping with the values of *k, q, s, t, x*: (1) It has the hard velar value /k/ before the vowels *a, o, u* (*cat, cot, cut*) and before consonants (*clip, creep, act, tics*). (2) It has the soft, palatalized value /s/ before *e, i, y*: *cell, city, cite, cycle, fancy*. (3) When *ce, ci* are followed by another vowel or vowels, usually pronounced as a schwa, soft *c* is often modified to a *sh*- sound: *ocean, herbaceous, special, efficient, suspicion*. (4) In some sets of derivationally associated words, *c* alternates between the above values: /k/ and /s/ in *electric/electricity*, /k/ and /ʃ/ in *logic/logician*. (5) Elsewhere, especially in some loans, *c* is soft before *ae, oe* in Latin *caesura* and Greek *coelacanth*, soft in French *façade* (often written without the cedilla, as *facade*), and generally hard in *Celt/Celtic*. It has a *ch*-sound as in *cheese*, in such loans from Italian as *cello, Medici*. (6) The *c* is silent in *indict, muscle* (but note *muscular*), and *victuals* ('vittles'), and may be regarded as silent before *q* in *acquaint, acquire*, etc., and after *x* in *excel, except*, etc. (7) The values of *cz* in *Czech* (/tʃ/) and *czar* (/z/), also spelt *tsar*, are unique.

Double C. The following patterns for the pronunciation of double *c* are consistent with the basic hard and soft values of *c*: (1) Hard before *a, o, u: saccade, account, occult*. (2) Hard then soft before *e, i* (with the same value as *x*): *accept, accident* (but note the hard value in *soccer*).

CH. (1) *Vernacular*. Affricate /tʃ/ in word-initial position (*chase, cheese, choose*) and word-finally in *each, teach*. After single short vowels, *t* usually precedes *ch*: *match, fetch, kitchen, botch, hutch* (but note *t* after a long vowel in *aitch* and no *t* after short *ou* in *touch*). However, no *t* occurs in several grammatical words (*much, such, which*), in *rich*, after another consonant (*belch, lunch*), and in some longer words (*duchess*). (2) *Greek and Italian*. The value of /k/ in words derived from Greek (*chaos, technique, monarch*) and in loans from Italian before *e, i* (*scherzo, Chianti*). (3) *French*. Commonly, a *sh*-sound in loans from French: *Charlotte, chef, machine*. (4) *German*. The *ch* in *Bach, Aachen* is generally pronounced with /k/, but may have the German value /x/, especially in ScoE. (5) *Scottish*. A voiced velar fricative in many ScoE words (*loch, pibroch*) and in traditional Scots (*bricht, micht, nicht* = *bright, might, night*). Outside Scotland, such words as *loch, clarsach* are usually pronounced with /k/. (6) *Other values*. In *spinach, sandwich*, and a common local pronunciation for the English city of Norwich, the *ch* is often voiced ('spinnidge', 'san(g)widge', 'Norridge'). In *yacht* (from Dutch), and *fuchsia* (from German), the *ch* has probably never been sounded in English.

THE CAPITAL LETTER						THE SMALL LETTER				
EARLY FORMS				CURRENT FORMS		EARLY FORMS			CURRENT FORMS	
Phoenician	Greek	Etruscan	Roman (Latin)	roman	italic	Roman cursive	Roman uncial	Carolingian minuscule	roman	italic
↑	↑Γ	↑	C	C	C	C	C	C	c	c

CK. (1) *Ck* with the value /k/ is common after short vowels in short words: *cackle, peck, flicker, lock, suck*. The ending *-ic* was formerly spelt *-ick* in such words as *logic* (*logick*) and *magic* (*magick*), the shorter form becoming general first in AmE, then spreading to BrE in the 19c. Recent French loans like *bloc, chic, tic* have only *c*. (2) When suffixes are added to words ending in *c*, the hard value can be preserved by adding *k*: *panic/panicking, picnic/picnicker* (but note *arc/arced, arcing*). An inhabitant of *Quebec* may be a *Quebecker* or a *Quebecer*, both pronounced with /k/.

SC. Before *e, i*, the value of *sc* is generally that of *s* alone: *scene, science, ascetic, descend, disciple, coalesce*. Some words containing *sc* acquired the *c* fairly late, sometimes by mistaken etymology: *scent, scissors*, and *scythe* were written *sent, sizars*, and *sithe* until the 17c. When followed by schwa, *sc* before *e* or *i* has the *sh*-sound of *c* alone in such a position: *conscience, conscious, luscious*. Loans from Italian also give *sc* the *sh*-sound before *e, i*: *crescendo, fascist*.

SCH. (1) Pronounced as /sk/ when it contains Greek *ch*: *scheme, schizoid, school*. (2) Pronounced as if *sh* in loans from German: *schadenfreude, Schubert*. *Schist* is usually pronounced as in German ('shist'), despite its ultimate Greek origin and its arrival in English through French. Greek-derived *schism* (spelt *scism* until the 15c) is either 'skism' or 'sism'.

Variation. (1) The use of *c* may depend on orthographic context. Word-finally, especially after long vowels, the hard value is normally represented by *k* (*take, speak, like, oak, rook, lurk*), but when such forms as *bicycle* and *Michael* are abbreviated, *c* becomes *k* (*bike* and *Mike*). If *l* or *r* follows, *c* may be found: *treacle, acre*. (2) A soft value in word-final position may be spelt *-ce* or *-se*: compare *mortice/mortise, fence/tense, fleece/geese* and BrE *licence/license*. (3) Sometimes, although there is no *c* in a base word, a secondary form has the letter: *louse/lice, mouse/mice, die/dice, penny/pence, despise/despicable, opaque/opacity*. (4) There is variation between *c* and *t* among some adjectives derived from nouns in *c*: *face/facial, palace/palatial, race/racial, space/spatial, finance/financial, substance/substantial*. (5) There has long been uncertainty about when to write *ct* and when to write *x* in such pairs as *connection/connexion* and *inflection/inflexion*, but not now in *complexion* (formerly also *complection*). (6) There is more or less free variation in the pairs *czar/tsar* and *disc/disk*, and a mild tendency for *cs* and *cks* to be replaced by *x*, as in *facsimile* shortened to *fax* and *Dickson* also spelt *Dixon*. (7) Common spelling errors include *supersede* spelt

*supercede on the analogy of *precede*, and *consensus* spelt **concensus* through the influence of *census*.

American and British differences. (1) AmE *defense, offense* (and optionally *pretense*) contrast with BrE *defence, offence, pretence*. (2) In BrE, there is a distinction between *practice* (noun) and *practise* (verb), but not in AmE, which has *practice* for both. (3) Only *vice* occurs in BrE, but AmE distinguishes *vice* (moral depravity) from *vise* (tool). (4) BrE has an anomalous hard *c* before *e* in *sceptic* (contrast *sceptre* and *septic*), but AmE has an unambiguous *k* in *skeptic*. (5) AmE prefers *mollusk* to *mollusc*, the only possible spelling in BrE. (6) AmE prefers *ck* in *check* to *que* in *cheque*, the only possible spelling in BrE. (7) *Sch* in *schedule* has the value *sh* in BrE, *sk* in AmE. Compare G, K, Q, X. See ALPHABET, HARD AND SOFT, LETTER[1], SPELLING. [WRITING].   C.U., T.MCA., E.W.

CABLE NEWS NETWORK, short form *CNN*. A 24-hour US TV news service, based in Atlanta, Georgia, whose live worldwide coverage has been made possible by satellite technology, which has also enabled CNN to be received throughout the world. The network's output is almost entirely in English, with the exception of a limited service in Spanish. CNN was founded in 1980 by the advertising and media entrepreneur Ted Turner [b. 1938]; once ridiculed because of its size, amateurism, and low wages as the 'Chicken Noodle Network', it has, since the late 1980s, become noted as a global medium for the reporting of 'raw' events as they occur: for example, in 1991 CNN enabled millions around the world to follow aspects of first the Gulf War then the breakup of the Soviet Union. For many TV services and newspapers, as well as governments, business groups, and populations at large, CNN currently serves as a primary source of news and comment:

For some social theorists, CNN has become far more than a news medium. It is considered prime evidence for the evolution of McLuhan's borderless world. As corporations become multinational and free trade transcends tariffs, as Europe develops a single currency and other regions build spheres of economic cooperation, as pop culture and air travel and migration and, yes, television make the world psychologically smaller, these theorists contend that the concept of nationalism recedes. Says Joshua Meyrowitz, professor of communication at the University of New Hampshire: 'Many of the things that define national sovereignty are fading. National sovereignty wasn't based only on power and barbed wire, it was based also on information control. Nations are losing control over informational borders because of CNN' (William A. Henry, 'History as It Happens', *Time*, 6 Jan. 1992).

In the same issue, *Time* featured Ted Turner as Man of the Year, giving him the title 'Prince of the Global Village'. It also described CNN as 'now the world's most widely heeded news organization'. See AMERICAN BROADCASTING, MCLUHAN. [AMERICAS, MEDIA, TECHNOLOGY].

T.MCA.

CABLESE [1890s]. Also **cablegramese**. The condensed style of messages sent by cable/telegram, especially formerly by journalists sending maximum information at minimum cost. Special affixes were once common: -*warding*, as in *Nairobiwarding soonest* going to Nairobi as soon as possible; Latin *inter-* among, -*que* and, as in *trouble interhindus muslimsque* trouble between Hindus and Muslims. See -ESE, TELEGRAPHESE. [MEDIA, STYLE].

T.MCA.

CACOPHEMISM. See DYSPHEMISM.

CAESURA, AmE also **cesura** [16c: from Latin *caesura* a cutting]. In Greek and Latin verse, a break caused by ending a word within a metrical foot. In English verse, a pause or break within a line, demanded by rhythm, syntax, and sense, and usually marked in scansion by //. It is a regular feature of Old English poetry and of such medieval poems as William Langland's *Piers Plowman*:

I loked on my left half // as the lady me taughte,
And was war of a womman // wortheli yclothed.

The caesura works with enjambement to give variety in long lines, particularly in blank verse and heroic couplets. It can appear at any point in the line: initial, medial, or terminal:

Uncrowded // yet safe-sheltered from the storm
(Cowper, 'Yardley Oak')

Who think too little // and who talk too much
(Dryden, *Absalom and Achitophel*)

Bore him slope downward to the sun // now fall'n
(Milton, *Paradise Lost*)

The usual position is medial, but a caesura early or late in the line can be effective in drawing attention to a word or phrase. A *masculine caesura* follows a stressed syllable, a *feminine caesura* an unstressed syllable. The medial caesura can emphasize antithesis: 'To err is human, // to forgive, divine' (Pope). The term can be used to describe the pause after an end-stopped line, but generally refers to an internal break. See SCANSION. [LITERATURE].

R.C.

CAJUN, sometimes **Cajan** [19c: an aphetic adaptation of *Acadian*. Compare *Bajan* from *Barbadian*, *Injun* from *Indian*]. (1) Also *Cajun French*. A dialect of French in southern Louisiana, developed from the regional French carried there in the 18c by immigrants expelled from Acadia (part of the colony of Nova Scotia

in Canada). Cajun is one of three kinds of local French: Louisiana Standard French, Cajun, and Creole. All three are spoken varieties, although the now rare standard form is written for ceremonial occasions. *Creole*, also called *gumbo* or *francais neg*, developed from the French-based creole brought by black slaves from the Caribbean. Cajun and Creole are spoken side by side and have been influenced by each other and by English. (2) Also *Cajun English*. The English that has arisen in the 23 parishes of Louisiana called Acadiana, where about 16% of the population still speaks Cajun French. Several characteristics are borrowings or translations from French, such as *cher* as a term of endearment, *make* (compare French *faire*) as an auxiliary verb (*He made closed the door*), *hair* as a count noun (*I have to wash my hairs*: compare French *cheveux*), and the object pronoun used for emphasis at the beginning or end of a sentence (*Me, I'm going to the store*; *I was late, me*: compare *moi*). (3) Someone descended from the original immigrants, especially if living in Acadiana and speaking Cajun French and English. Cajuns are known for devotion to family life, Roman Catholicism, hunting and fishing, and 'passing' a good time. Their cuisine and music enjoy widespread popularity in the US, as manifestations of the Cajun motto: *Laissez les bons temps rouler!* Let the good times roll! See AMERICAN ENGLISH, CREOLE. [AMERICAS, NAME, VARIETY].

C.C.E.

CALEDONIA [From Latin *Caledonii*, a tribal name]. (1) A name for Scotland north of the Forth and Clyde, recorded in 1–2c classical writers such as Tacitus and Ptolemy. (2) This name revived in the 17c, with a derivative *Caledonian*, usually referring to the whole of Scotland, as in *Mercurius Caledonius* (founded 1667) and *The Caledonian Mercury* (founded 1720), Edinburgh newspapers. It is used rhetorically, humorously, and commercially: 'Caledonia, and Caledonia's Bard, brother Burns' (Masonic toast to Robert Burns, 1787), *The Unfortunate Caledonian in England* (book title, 1781), the airline *British Caledonian*. It also appears in poems and songs: 'O Caledonia, stern and wild' (Sir Walter Scott), 'Hail, Caledonia, land of my childhood' (Hugh Ogilvie, 1912). Compare ALBA, SCOTLAND. [EUROPE, NAME].

A.J.A.

CALIBAN [16c: an anagram of *can(n)ibal*, a word evidently derived by scribal mistake from *Caribal* a Carib Indian: cognate with *Caribbean*]. A character in Shakespeare's romantic drama *The Tempest* (c.1611), a misshapen monster, half-human, half-beast, and son of the witch Sycorax. He is contrasted with the sprite Ariel, perhaps to suggest the gulf between body and spirit. Originally, Caliban was the only inhabitant of an island that might be anywhere in the Mediterranean or the Atlantic. When Prospero, a magician and the erstwhile Duke of Milan, is shipwrecked there, Caliban and Ariel become his slaves. Both want their freedom, but whereas Ariel is patient, Caliban is filled with rage. He asserts that Prospero treated him well at first ('Thou stroakst me, & made much of me'), then took the island from him and penned him up on a rock. Prospero answers that at first he had been kind to Caliban, but imprisoned him because he tried to rape Prospero's daughter Miranda:

CALIBAN. Oh ho, oh ho, would't had bene done:
    Thou didst preuent me, I had peopel'd else
    This Isle with *Calibans.*
MIRANDA.   Abhorred slaue,
    Which any print of goodnesse wilt not take,
    Being capable of all ill: I pittied thee,
    Took pains to make thee speak, taught thee each
    houre
    One thing or other: when thou didst not (Sauage)
    Know thine owne meaning; but wouldst gabble, like
    A thing most brutish, I endow'd thy purposes
    With words that made them knowne: But thy vild
    race
    (Tho thou didst learn) had that in't, which good
    natures
    Could not abide to be with; therefore wast thou
    Deseruedly confin'd into this Rocke,
    Who hadst deseru'd more then a prison.
CALIBAN. You taught me Language, and my profit
    on't
    Is, I know how to curse: the red-plague rid you
    For learning me your language.
                                        (Act 1, Scene 2)

Caliban seeks to rebel against his master, in the company of some men from a ship more recently wrecked on the island. The rebellion fails, but when the play ends the strangers depart, leaving Caliban once again alone. In the poem *Caliban Upon Setebos, or, Natural Theology in the Island* (1864), Robert Browning uses the character to speculate on the nature of his god, Setebos, and by this means obliquely discusses such topics as the Bible and evolution. In the late 20c, Caliban has been seen by black writers in English as linked with Africa and the Caribbean, in effect a symbol of slavery. In discussing the situation of the black Commonwealth writer, David Dabydeen observes: 'the pressure is to become a mulatto and house-nigger (Ariel) rather than stay a field-nigger (Caliban)', but even so, 'Caliban is tearing up the pages of Prospero's magic book and repasting it in his own order, by his own method, and for his own purpose' ('Nigger Talk in England Today', in Ricks & Michaels (eds.), *The State of the Language*, 1990). See AFRICAN LITERATURE IN ENGLISH, RACISM. [AFRICA, AMERICAS, LITERATURE, NAME]. T.MCA.

CALLIGRAPHY [17c: from Greek *kalligraphia* beautiful writing]. The art of handwriting (tra-

ditionally also known as *penmanship*), especially if stylized in some way, such as a cursive or angular script or a decorative style with many flourishes. Formerly, the term *calligraph* was used for both a person with a beautiful or ornamental 'hand' and a specimen of writing considered beautiful; currently, *calligrapher* (common) and *calligraphist* (rare) are terms used for someone who engages in calligraphy. Calligraphers who write in English may learn such 'hands' as *Roman, Italic, Italian Humanist, Gothic* or *Black Letter* (including *Rotunda* or *Round Gothic*), *Uncial, Copperplate,* the *Johnston Foundational Hand,* and *Basic Modern* or *Modern Round,* as well as various kinds of calligraphic drawing. Published works that describe calligraphy are sometimes entirely manuscript (without a single typographic letter), such as Tom Gourdie's *Calligraphic Styles* (New York: Tapfinger Publishing Company, 1979). The skills and styles of the calligrapher can be used in preparing 'Announcements, Banners, Business Cards, Bookplates, Brochures, Catalogues, Certificates, Condolences, Commendations, Christmas Cards, Congratulations, Diplomas, Family Trees, Envelopes, Guest Places, Menus, Inscriptions, Invitations, Letterheads, Memorials, Mottos, Logos, Name tags, Poems, Posters, Scrolls, Testimonials, Signs, Speeches, Show Cards, Title Pages, etc.' (Christopher Jarman, *The Osmiroid Book of Calligraphy,* Gosport, England: Osmiroid Pens, 1983). See COPPERPLATE, GOTHIC, HAND, ITALIC(S), LETTER[1], UNCIAL. [STYLE, WRITING].   T.MCA.

CALL MY BLUFF. A word game devised by the Americans Mark Goodson and Bill Todman and broadcast in an annual series since 1965 by BBC television. In it, two teams of three (consisting of 'resident' leaders, such as the humorist Frank Muir, and celebrity guests) compete in presenting and guessing definitions of rare words from *The Oxford English Dictionary.* The teams take turns in presenting sets of three definitions, one true, the others bluffs. Each person in turn has to decide which is true, gaining a point if correct, losing a point if wrong. In the process of guessing, participants are expected to explain their decisions. The words are so obscure and the definitions so urbane and yet so improbable that a confident choice is difficult to make. Other names for this game are the *Dictionary Game, Dictionary,* and *Fictionary Dictionary.* See ETYMORPHS, WORD GAME. [MEDIA, WORD]. T.MCA.

CALQUE [17c: from French, from *calquer* to trace or copy, from Italian *calcare* to trace, tread, from Latin *calx* heel]. Also **loan translation.** A word or other expression formed by translating from another language, such as Shaw's *superman* (1903), from German *Übermensch* (coined by Nietzsche in 1883). The Romans calqued freely from Greek; from *poiótēs* (suchness), *posótēs* (muchness), they formed *qualitas* and *quantitas*. Calques are often used for ad-hoc glossing, as with 'suchness' and 'muchness' above. Sometimes, a Greek original and its Latin calque have both entered English: *apátheia* and its calque *indolentia* provide English with both *apathy* and *indolence*. Calques are often formed from compounds in a source language: for example, German *Weltanschauung* becoming English 'world view'. They may also consist of entire translated phrases, such as 'Time flies' from Latin *Tempus fugit* and 'that goes without saying' from French *cela va sans dire*. See BORROWING, FOREIGNISM, FRENCH, LOAN, LOAN TRANSLATION. [WORD].   T.MCA.

CAMBRIDGE CERTIFICATE OF PROFICIENCY IN ENGLISH, short form *CPE*. Also referred to as *Cambridge Proficiency in English, Cambridge Proficiency, Proficiency*. A prestigious EFL examination introduced by UCLES in 1913 for foreign teachers of English, and taken throughout the world by advanced learners of English. It has no teacher-training content, but has an academic orientation and its standard is equivalent to GCE A Level (UK: General Certificate of Education Advanced Level). See EXAMINING IN ENGLISH, UCLES. [EDUCATION].   W.S.

CAMBRIDGE ENGLISH [20c]. A name for English literature as taught at the U. of Cambridge since the establishment in 1912 of the Edward VII Chair of English Literature, whose first incumbent was Arthur Quiller-Couch: 'Eventually an English Tripos [final honours degree examination] was proposed and agreed to in 1917, when, it was remarked, many of the dons who might have opposed it were away at the war. The ensuing Golden Age of Cambridge English has been widely commemorated in myth and memoir' (Bernard Bergonzi, *Exploding English*, 1990). Major figures of the 'golden age' (1920s-30s) included I. A. Richards, William Empson, and F. R. Leavis. See AMBIGUITY, LEAVIS, OXFORD ENGLISH, QUILLER-COUCH, RICHARDS. [LITERATURE, VARIETY].   T.MCA.

CAMBRIDGE FIRST CERTIFICATE. See FIRST CERTIFICATE IN ENGLISH.

CAMBRIDGE SYNDICATE. See UCLES.

CAMBRIDGE UNIVERSITY PRESS, short form *CUP*. The publishing and printing department of the U. of Cambridge, the oldest press in the world and consequently the oldest printer and publisher in English. In 1534, the University received from Henry VIII Royal Letters Patent licensing the printing and sale of *omnimodos libros* ('all manner of books') both in the university and 'elsewhere in our realm, wherever they please'. The University appointed a printer, but the first book was not produced until 50 years later, in 1584. The first Cambridge Bible, the Geneva, was published in 1591, making the Press the oldest extant Bible printer and publisher. It is one of the three English publishers authorized by the Crown to print the King James Bible, which it has done since 1629. The Press's authors in the humanities include John Milton, John Donne, Sir Thomas Browne, George Herbert, Samuel Butler, G. E. Moore, A. E. Housman, Alfred North Whitehead, Bertrand Russell, Sir Arthur Quiller-Couch, Dover Wilson, Steven Runciman, and F. R. Leavis, and in the sciences include William Harvey, Sir Isaac Newton, Ernest Rutherford, Sir Arthur Eddington, Albert Einstein, Joseph Needham, Stephen Hawking, and S. Chandrasekhar. The Press is a self-financing educational charity whose income finances further publishing, currently over 1,000 titles a year, from primary and secondary school to advanced research monographs and professional journals. Every publication requires the approval in advance of a committee of senior academics, the Syndicate, appointed by the University. Areas of expansion are reference, journals, and ELT publications, which include: *The Cambridge English Course* and the *New Cambridge English Course*, by Michael Swan and Catherine Walter; *English Grammar in Use* and *Essential Grammar in Use*, by Raymond Murphy; *Meanings into Words*, by Adrian Doff, Christopher Jones, and Keith Mitchell; *International Business English*, by Leo Jones and Richard Alexander; *Functions of American English*, by Leo Jones and C. von Baeyer; *Literature in the Language Classroom*, by Joanne Collie and Stephen Slater. See BIBLE, BRITISH PUBLISHING, ELT PUBLISHING, ENGLISH TODAY. [EDUCATION, EUROPE, MEDIA].   A. DU P.

CAMDEN, William [1551-1623]. English historian and antiquary, headmaster of Westminster School in 1592, royal Herald in 1597, and later a King-of-Arms. He wrote in Latin, in the belief common among scholars at the time that English was not suitable for work of lasting importance. He learned Welsh and Old English in order to study early chroniclers and showed no interest in the literature and theatre of his time. In 1580, he published *Britannia*, a survey based on observations during journeys around Britain. His major historical work was his

Annales of the reign of Elizabeth I, in two volumes (1615, 1629). Both were later translated into English. See LATIN[1]. [BIOGRAPHY, EUROPE, HISTORY, LANGUAGE].   R.C.

CAMEROON. Official titles: French *République Unie du Cameroun*, English *United Republic of Cameroon*. A country of West Africa. Capital Yaoundé. Currency: the franc. Population: 11.3m (1988), 16.6m (projection for 2000). Ethnicity: Bamileke, Douala, Fang, Fulani, Hausa, etc. Religion: 51% traditional, 33% Christian, 16% Muslim. Languages: English, French (both official, but to be legally binding a document must be in French), Kamtok or Cameroonian Pidgin, and indigenous languages. Education: primary/secondary 67%, tertiary 2%, estimated literacy 57%. The first Europeans in the area were the Portuguese in the 15c, who established a trade in slaves that in the early 17c passed to the Dutch. The British declared this trade illegal in 1807 and policed the waters until it ended in the 1840s. Although the British established settlements, the territory became the German protectorate of *Kamerun* in 1884, which ceased to exist during the First World War. In 1919, the region was divided into French and British zones, which became League of Nations mandates in 1922 and United Nations trusteeships in 1946. French Cameroon became an independent republic in 1960. The southern part of British Cameroon voted to join it in 1961, while the remainder joined Nigeria.

The English of Cameroon is distinguished by its coexistence with French (for administration, commerce, and education) and with *Cameroonian Pidgin* or *Kamtok*, an English-based pidgin of relatively high prestige in many communities, but no official recognition. In anglophone Cameroon (former West Cameroon, under British administration 1919–60), English is the first language of local government and education. All Cameroonian post-primary students receive a bilingual education in French and English. The speech of educated Cameroonians is distinguished by local vocabulary for foods and cultural items and by phonological peculiarities shared with Kamtok. In the metropolitan varieties of English, BrE and AmE usages and informal local usages are melded into a variety that becomes more and more affected by Pidgin as situations become less formal and speakers are further from the highest social levels. Cameroonian English is part of a national network of linguistic repertoires, including at its maximum several indigenous languages, possibly pidginized varieties of such languages, Pidgin English, and a Cameroonian French that has the same relation to French elsewhere as Cameroonian English has to English elsewhere.

See CAMFRANGLAIS, ENGLISH, KAMTOK, WEST AFRICAN ENGLISH, WEST AFRICAN PIDGIN ENGLISH. [AFRICA, NAME, VARIETY].   T.MCA., C.G.

CAMEROONIAN ENGLISH. See CAMEROON.

CAMEROON(IAN) PIDGIN. See KAMTOK.

CAMFRANGLAIS [Later 20c: from *Cam-(eroon)* and *franglais*]. An informal term for the use of words from French, Kamtok, and local languages in the English of Cameroon: *I am come to follow my dossier* I have come to find out what has happened to my file, *Garçon, dash me one bottle Trente trois* Waiter, give me a bottle of Trente Trois (a local beer). It is common among young people in the towns, is spreading in rural areas, and is volatile. The opening of a facetious editorial in *Cameroon Life* (Aug. 1990) runs: 'Nous are well dans our third meeting and je must say it is difficile to determine where to commencer. . . . Le multitude of journaux make les choses even more complicated.' See CAMEROON, FRANGLAIS, KAMTOK. [AFRICA, VARIETY].   T.MCA.

CAN- [20c: a clipping of *Canada* or *Canadian*]. A combining form: *Can Lit* Canadian Literature; *Statscan* Statistics Canada. Compare AM-. [AMERICAS, NAME].   T.MCA.

CANADA [16c: probably from Iroquois *kanata* village. First used by the Breton explorer Jacques Cartier in 1535 to designate the Gaspé and Saguenay regions of North America. Cartier is said to have asked for the name of the land in which he found himself. An Iroquois, assuming that he was asking about a local settlement, pointed to it and said 'village']. A country of North America and member of the Commonwealth: a constitutional monarchy and confederation of ten provinces and two territories. Head of state: the British monarch, represented by a governor-general. Capital: Ottawa. Currency: the dollar (100 cents). Economy: mixed. Languages: English, French (both official), various European, Asian, and other ethnic languages, and Amerindian languages. Population: 26.1m (1988), 28.2m (projection for 2000). Ethnicity: 45% British/Irish, 29% French, 24.5% other immigrant groups, 1.5% Native Peoples. Religion: 89% Christian (47% Roman Catholic, 41% Protestant, 1% Orthodox), 10% non-professing, 1% Jewish. Education: primary 97%, secondary 87%, higher 55%, estimated functional literacy 83%.

The term *Canada* did not designate the nation until Confederation in 1867, before which it was officially *British North America*. *Canada* at first referred to French settlements which, after the

American War of Independence (1776-83), became *Lower Canada* (Quebec) while the newer British settlements to the west became *Upper Canada* (now Ontario). The British maritime colonies of Nova Scotia, New Brunswick, and Prince Edward Island were distinct until Confederation and for many years after 1867 saw 'Canada' as another place. The feminist writer Gail Scott, a Quebecer, uses the term this way in her account of a visit outside Quebec: 'A Visit to Canada' (in *Spaces like Stairs*, 1989). The British colony of Newfoundland joined the confederation in 1949. Although enormous in area, Canada is thinly populated, with most of its people concentrated along the US border, particularly in the corridor from Quebec City to Windsor, Ontario, and on the Pacific coast around Vancouver.

Three social, historical, and linguistic factors have shaped the nation: (1) The tug of war between Britain and France, including religious differences, British settlers being mainly Protestant, French and Irish mainly Roman Catholic. In Quebec a strong nationalist minority has insisted on the special nature of the province in its own right and as the heartland of French Canada, and frequently raises calls for Quebec independence. (2) Even in the cities, Canadians are aware of the emptiness of the Arctic and sub-Arctic north, whose images and descriptions are a constant in much of Canadian literature. (3) Relations with Canada's powerful and populous southern neighbour are peaceful, usually friendly, and always ambivalent. Canadians often complain of an American tendency to take them for granted or pay little or no attention to what goes on in Canada. They often find it necessary to engage in negative self-definition, as 'not-American'. The sense of domination is powerful and pervasive: 'The United States makes a rule today and we follow it tomorrow; or, to put it differently, they take the snuff and we do the sneezing' (Samuel Jacobs, Canadian House of Commons, *Debates*, 30 Mar. 1921); 'Ours is a sovereign nation / Bows to no foreign will / But whenever they cough in Washington / They spit on Parliament Hill' (Joe Wallace, in *The Maple haugh Forever*, 1981).

See ALEXANDER, ALLIANCE QUEBEC, ANGLO, ANGLO-CANADIAN, ANGLOPHONE, AVIS, BILINGUALISM, CAN-, CANADIAN, CANADIAN BROADCASTING, CANADIAN DICTIONARIES IN ENGLISH, CANADIAN ENGLISH, CANADIANISM, CANADIAN LANGUAGE ORGANIZATIONS, CANADIAN LANGUAGES, CANADIAN LITERATURE IN ENGLISH, CANADIAN PLACE-NAMES, CANADIAN PRESS, CANADIAN PUBLISHING, CANADIAN RAISING, CANADIAN STYLE GUIDES, CHINOOK JARGON, DIALECT IN CANADA, ENGLISH, ENGLISH CANADA, ENGLISH CANADIAN, ETHNIC NAME, FRANCIZATION, FRANGLAIS, GENERAL CANADIAN, INNIS, INUIT, LANGUAGE POLICE, LEACOCK, MARITIME PROVINCES/MARITIMES, MCLUHAN, MÉTIS, NEWFIE JOKE, NEWFOUNDLAND, NEWFOUNDLAND ENGLISH, NORTH AMERICAN, OTTAWA VALLEY, QUEBEC, STRATHY LANGUAGE UNIT, TELEPHONE, TESD, TESL, TESL CANADA. [AMERICAS, HISTORY, NAME]. T.MCA., M.F.

CANADIAN [16c: from French *canadien*]. (1) Initially and into the 19c, the name for the indigenous peoples of north-eastern North America: 'John was not a pure blooded micmac. His father was a Canadian belonging to some of the tribes along the St Lawrence' (1872, cited in *Dictionary of Newfoundland English*, 1982). (2) From the 17c, the name of the French settlers along the St Lawrence. (3) From the later 18c, the name for the people of the British colonies Lower Canada (Quebec) and Upper Canada (Ontario), often referred to in linguistic and cultural terms as *English Canadians* and more commonly as *French Canadians*. The terms *French* and *English* on their own refer in a Canadian context to the language used or preferred rather than to ethnic origin. Someone 'English' may be of Scottish, Ukrainian, Italian, or other background; someone 'French' may be of Haitian or Belgian background. (4) An informal term for the English language in Canada: 'What language is spoken in the Dominion of Canada? Canadian' (James D. Gillis, *Canadian Grammar*, 1925, p. 3). [AMERICAS, NAME, VARIETY]. T.MCA.

CANADIAN BROADCASTING. In bringing together its far-flung communities, Canada has developed one of the most advanced broadcasting systems in the world. Radio and television in both official languages reach almost every part of Canada. While the *Canadian Broadcasting Corporation* (*CBC*) operates national radio and TV networks in English and French, the privately owned *Canadian Television Network* (*CTV*) operates nationally in English only. In the province of Quebec, in addition to CBC (there known as *Radio-Canada*), private French TV networks are operated by *TVA/Télémetropole, Telemedia Communications*, and *Quatre Saisons*. The Quebec government operates *Radio Québec*, a French educational TV network. Private French-language radio stations and English-language TV and radio stations also operate in the province. There are CBC French-language TV production centres and radio stations in British Columbia, Alberta, Saskatchewan, Manitoba, Ontario, and New Brunswick. In addition, in Toronto, the private company Multilingual Television broadcasts to local ethnic communities.

The CRTC. Both public and private broadcasting are regulated by the *Canadian Radio-Television and Telecommunications Commission* (*CRTC*). This government agency has the role of ensuring that the system 'should be effectively owned and controlled by Canadians so as to safeguard, enrich and strengthen the cultural, political, social and economic fabric of Canada' and that programming be 'of high standard, using predominantly Canadian creative and other resources' (Act, 1968). However, most Canadians live within receiving distance of US television and radio signals, and the CBC and independent stations have always had to compete for their audience share with US networks.

Canadian content. The CRTC has found it difficult to insist on Canadian-content rules that run counter to demand and might drive private stations out of business. Nonetheless, it requires that the broadcasts of private stations provide 60% Canadian content, 50% between 6 and 12 p.m. The major source of programming has traditionally been the CBC. In 1985-6, Canadian content reached 77% on the English and 79% on the French television network. However, of the 24.2 hours per week that Canadians spent watching television in 1986, 64% was devoted to foreign programming. CBC Radio attracts 10% of the potential audience. Now that 80% of Canadian homes have access to radio and to television signals on cable, which delivers many American and Canadian educational, public, and commercial channels, the CBC has to work harder than ever to create a distinctive profile.

CBC English. The CBC takes pride in the pronunciation and usage of its announcers and newsreaders, and its English is more conservative than that of most Canadians. From 1940 to 1989, it maintained an *Office of Broadcast Language* which from 1975 to 1983 produced 100 issues of an advice sheet called *You Don't Say*, promoting pronunciations such as *schedule* with 'sh' and not 'sk' and favouring many BrE over AmE pronunciations. However, the relative ease with which Canadian announcers can move to US networks demonstrates that there is little difference between network accents in the two countries. See BROADCASTING, NETWORK STANDARD. [AMERICAS, MEDIA].   M.F.

CANADIAN DICTIONARIES IN ENGLISH.

Because dictionaries are expensive to produce, English Canadians have traditionally relied on British or American dictionaries and French Canadians on dictionaries from France. Canadian editions of foreign dictionaries have often been produced, usually with the help of Canadian lexicographers: Walter S. Avis provided the local material for the Canadian edition of *Funk and Wagnalls Standard College Dictionary* (1982 edition). Other 'Canadian' editions, such as the *Dictionnaire Beauchemin canadien* (1968), have been minimally adapted. In the late 1950s, several projects led to the production of indigenous dictionaries and this initiative was strengthened by the rise of nationalism in the 1960s. Several such projects are associated with the *Canadian Linguistic Association* (founded in 1954). In 1957, the CLA established a Lexicographical Committee, chaired by M. H. Scargill, and this group initiated a bilingual French-English dictionary, a dictionary of Canadian French, and a dictionary of Canadian English.

Historical dictionaries. In 1967, Gage in Toronto brought out *A Dictionary of Canadianisms on Historical Principles*, edited by Walter S. Avis, Charles Crate, Patrick D. Drysdale, Douglas Leechman, and M. H. Scargill, with an abridged paperback edition, *A Concise Dictionary of Canadianisms* in 1973. The editors define *Canadianism* as 'a word, expression, or meaning which is native to Canada or which is distinctively characteristic of Canadian usage though not necessarily exclusive to Canada: *Winnipeg couch* falls into the first category, *chesterfield* ("sofa") into the second'. The *c*.10,000 entries are supported by quotations from published material.

The *Dictionary of Newfoundland English*, ed. G. M. Story, W. J. Kirwin, and J. D. Widdowson (University of Toronto Press, 1982), is an account of 'words which appear to have entered the language in Newfoundland or to have been recorded first, or solely, in books about Newfoundland; words which are characteristically Newfoundland by having continued in use here after they died out or declined elsewhere, or by having acquired a different form or developed a different meaning, or by having a distinctly higher or more general degree of use'. For its citations, the *DNE* has used printed, written, and oral records, and in the introduction there is a description of the features of local speech. Many local words relate to fishing, with over 30 items relating to *cod*, including *cod blubber*, *cod-fish weather*, *cod jigger*; sealing, with many terms for seals at particular stages of development, including *bedlamer*, *dotard*, *gun seal*, *jar*, *nog-head*, *ragged-jacket*, *turner*, *white-coat*; and seafaring and weather conditions, with such special kinds of ice as *ballacatter*, *clumper*, *quarr*, *sish*, *slob*. Other words and senses come from IrE (such as *after*: 'Some poor fellers are after courting for 6 or 7 years, just trying to get a little money to buy a house') and the English West Country (*planchion* for *floor*, *plim* for *to swell*).

The *Dictionary of Prince Edward Island English*, ed. T. K. Pratt (University of Toronto

Press, 1988) is a 'record of non-standard words as used, or once used, on Prince Edward Island'. It excludes words found without a qualifying label in any two of the *OED* (to the 1982 Supplement), *Webster's New World Dictionary* (1970), and *Funk and Wagnalls Standard College Dictionary* (Canadian edition, 1976) and any word found in the *Gage Canadian Dictionary* (1983) without such a label. Words unique to PEI are included, as are dialect words in use on the island from other parts of Canada, the US, and the UK. The 873 main entries are based on printed and written sources, local observers' reports, postal questionnaires, and fieldwork with informants selected by gender, age, socioeconomic status, and domicile. Detailed attention was paid to the usage of such occupations as potato farming, lobster and oyster fishing, fox ranching, and Irish moss harvesting. Localisms include *black moss* (unbleached Irish moss), *mussel mud* (mud rich in shells, formerly a fertilizer), *sheep storm* (a storm of wind and rain, usually in early June), *trap smasher* (in lobster fishing, a severe storm), and *windrower* (a machine that digs potatoes).

General dictionaries. In 1983, Gage in Toronto brought out the *Gage Canadian Dictionary*, edited by Walter S. Avis, Patrick D. Drysdale, Robert J. Gregg, Victoria E. Neufeldt, and Matthew H. Scargill, a major revision of the *Gage Senior Dictionary* (1979). It has 400 line drawings, entries for important people and places, and includes more examples and idioms than most desk dictionaries, making it suitable for ESL students. Most sales are to schools and the dictionary is more a learner's dictionary than a collegiate. Thomas M. Paikeday's *Compact Dictionary of Canadian English* (Toronto: Holt, Rinehart & Winston, 1970) has *c*.65,000 entries and serves senior high school students. His *Penguin Canadian Dictionary* (1990: 75,000 entries) is intended for senior elementary and high school students. Collier Macmillan, Gage, Winston, and Houghton Mifflin all produce Canadian elementary and intermediate-level school dictionaries.

Bilingual dictionaries. In 1962, McClelland & Stewart published the concise *Dictionnaire canadien/Canadian Dictionary*, compiled by Jean-Paul Vinay, Pierre Daviault, and Henry Alexander, a general bilingual dictionary that gives 'direct guidance on the terminology and style which are peculiar to the English and French of Canada'. The project has lately been revived as *The Bilingual Canadian Dictionary*, with the intention of producing a larger edition edited by André Clas of the Université de Montréal and Roda Roberts of the University of Ottawa. The Secretary of State's *Translation Bureau* issues many publications designed to assist translators with specialized terminology in both official languages and maintains *Termium*, a database of over 700,000 terms in English and French. In Quebec, a similar function is performed by the *Office de la langue française* (founded 1977), which sponsors research into linguistics and terminology and administers the *Banque de terminologie du Québec*, a lexicographical database of French and English holding over 3.5m words. Léandre Bergeron's French *Dictionnaire de la langue québécoise* (1980) has an English version, *The Québécois Dictionary* (Toronto: James Lorimer, 1982), that contains over 6,000 usages of Quebec French. See CANADA, DICTIONARY. [AMERICAS, REFERENCE, VARIETY]. M.F.

CANADIAN ENGLISH, short form *CanE*. The English language as used in Canada. This national variety has coexisted for some 230 years with Canadian French, which is almost a century older, as well as with a range of indigenous languages such as Cree, Iroquois, and Inuktitut and a number of immigrant languages such as Italian and Ukrainian. It has been marked by the now less significant influence of BrE and the enormous ongoing impact of AmE. Because of the similarity of American and Canadian accents, English Canadians travelling abroad are virtually resigned to being taken for Americans. However, as Gerald Clark has noted, although Canadians seem 'indistinguishable from the Americans the surest way of telling the two apart is to make the observation to a Canadian' (*Canada: The Uneasy Neighbour*, 1965). Because CanE and AmE are so alike, some scholars have argued that in linguistic terms Canadian English is no more or less than a variety of (*Northern*) *American English*. In response to the dominance of AmE, some Canadians have tended to stress the indigenous or even British features in their variety while others have felt that to do so is pretentious. Studies of CanE of necessity compare it to BrE or AmE or both, and many do nothing else. Recently, however, the view that only highly distinctive varieties are 'true' national languages is changing. The US linguist Richard W. Bailey notes: 'What is distinctly Canadian about Canadian English is not its unique linguistic features (of which there are a handful) but its combination of tendencies that are uniquely distributed' (1982, p. 161; below). In addition, the environment of CanE differs significantly from that of other varieties in two ways:

(1) *The presence of French as co-official language.* Spoken French is concentrated in Quebec, New Brunswick, and eastern Ontario, while written

French is ubiquitous. It appears with English on everything from signs in post offices to boxes of cornflakes, which have long been the stereotypical example of how French was being 'rammed down' unwilling English throats. In English broadcasts, a simultaneous translation formerly drowned spoken French, but lately CBC news broadcasts allow the French speaker to be heard and rely on the commentator to make the message comprehensible to anglophones without a knowledge of French. The first *Official Languages Act* (1969) confirmed the bilingual nature of Canada at the federal level and set up the *Office of the Commissioner of Official Languages*. The Commissioner deals with complaints concerning the infringement of language rights and oversees the implementation of the Act. The Office publishes a bilingual quarterly, *Language and Society/Langue et société*.

(2) *A preoccupation with the wilderness*. An awareness of the great empty northern spaces exists even among urban Canadians. Much as Australians are preoccupied with their myth of 'mates in the Outback', contending against nature, many Canadians are conscious of the vast extent of Canada.

The Canadian population is highly urbanized and mobile, 80% living in urban areas within 200 km of the US border. *Canadian Standard English (CSE)*, the English spoken in cities from Ontario to British Columbia by the middle and upper classes, is remarkably homogeneous, but the non-standard language varies, depending on which groups originally settled an area. The differences between the main regional varieties (such as in Newfoundland, the Maritimes, Quebec, and from Ontario westwards) can be accounted for primarily by settlement history. The history of Ontario, the province which currently has the largest number of English-speakers and dominates the country politically, economically, and linguistically, explains why CanE sounds very much more like AmE than like BrE.

History. English-speaking settlers began to enter mainland Canada in significant numbers after the Treaty of Paris ceded New France to Great Britain in 1762. Most were from the New England colonies and went to what are now the provinces of Nova Scotia and New Brunswick. During and immediately after the American Revolution (1776-83), a wave of some 50,000 settlers arrived from the US, usually called *Loyalists* or *United Empire Loyalists* (*UELs*). Some 10,000 went to Quebec, 2,500 settling in the Eastern Townships south-east of Montreal and 7,500 in western Quebec, which was named Upper Canada in 1791, Canada West in 1840, and

Ontario in 1867. Government promotion of settlement resulted in the arrival from the US of at least 80,000 'late loyalists' after 1791. By 1812, Upper Canada's population of around 100,000 was 80% of American background. This population consolidated its values by fighting against American attack during the War of 1812. By 1871, the population of Ontario had risen to 1.6m.

Canadian linguists disagree about the reasons for the similarity between CanE and Northern AmE. Partly in reaction to American linguists' suggestions that CanE is simply derivative from AmE, M. H. Scargill (1988, below) has argued that the flood of immigrants that arrived after 1814 overwhelmed the dialect they found in Canada. In his view, CanE is the result of a mixture of northern British dialects. Its similarity to Northern AmE thus would be accounted for by common origins in the mix of British dialects. Walter S. Avis, however, has argued that by the time the first major wave of British immigrants arrived 'the course of Ontario speech had been set, American speech habits of the Northern variety having been entrenched from the beginning' (1973, below). Current opinion rests with Avis, although to call the UEL dialect 'American' invites debate. The Loyalists who arrived in Canada were far from homogeneous linguistically: some had been in the US for generations, others were recently arrived British soldiers, some were Gaelic- and others German-speaking. However, once the Loyalists did arrive, the process of dialect mix would have begun.

Although their descendants' tendency to overstate the loyalty and status of these settlers has been called 'the myth of the UEL', they had over a generation to establish themselves and their dialect before the first influx of British settlers. Since children generally adopt the usage of their peers rather than their parents, later British settlers had to accept the assimilation of their children's speech to an 'American' dialect:

Listening to the children at any school, composed of the children of Englishmen, Scotchmen, Americans, and even of Germans, it is impossible to detect any marked difference in their accent, or way of expressing themselves (William Canniff, *The Settlement of Upper Canada*, 1869).

Indeed, the Irish and Scottish immigrants may well have embraced a patently non-English dialect as a sign of their rejection of England and its values. As Catharine Parr Traill observed:

Persons who come to this country are very apt to confound the old settlers from Britain with the native Americans; and when they meet with people of rude, offensive manners, using certain Yankee words in their conversations, and making a display of independence not exactly suitable to their own aristocratic notions, they immediately suppose they must be genuine Yankees, while they are, in fact, only imitators. . . . You would be surprised to see how soon the newcomers fall into this disagreeable manner and affectation of quality, especially the inferior class of Irish and Scotch; the English less so (in *The Backwoods of Canada: Being Letters from the Wife of an Emigrant Officer*, 1836).

The English spoken in Ontario is the dominant urban form westwards because settlement west of Ontario was led by Ontario anglophones, who formed the middle and professional classes. It was deliberate government policy to ensure that non-English-speaking immigrants conformed culturally, not to their American immigrant neighbours, but to the values of the Ontario heartland, a policy accomplished primarily through the education systems.

Pronunciation. Generally, the standard forms of CanE and Northern AmE are alike, whereas such regional varieties as the Maritimes and Newfoundland are more distinctive. The main features of standard CanE are: (1) *Canadian Raising*. There is a shibboleth that Canadians say such words as *house* and *out* differently from Americans, and by and large they do. *Canadian raising* (a term coined by J. K. Chambers in 1973) is a convenient term for what is in fact a non-lowering of certain diphthongs that are lowered in most other dialects. The tongue is raised higher to produce the diphthong in *knife*, *house* than in *knives*, *houses*. In general terms, these diphthongs have a raised onset before voiceless consonants: /ai/ becomes /ʌi/ and /au/ becomes /ʌu/. In the following pairs, only the first word has the raised onset: *tripe/tribe*, *bite/bide*, *tyke/tiger*, *knife/knives*, *price/prizes*, *lout/loud*, *mouth* (*n*)/*mouth* (*v*). Many Americans from western New England across the Great Lakes have the raised onset for /ai/, but far fewer have it for /au/. These raised diphthongs appear to be an innovation resulting from dialect mix. Studies of the speech of Montreal, Ottawa, Toronto, Vancouver, and Victoria show that Canadian Raising is a majority usage (over 90% in Vancouver, over 60% in Ottawa), but that there is a trend away from raising toward standard AmE values, led by women under 40. (2) *The cot/caught distinction.* Many phonological features shared with Northern AmE are distributed distinctively in standard CanE: for example, the low back vowels have merged, so that Canadians pronounce *cot/caught*, *Don/ Dawn*, *awful/offal*, *caller/collar* with the same vowel sound, although the quality of this sound varies. This merger is widespread in the US (in eastern New England and western Pennsylvania) and is spreading in the Midwest and West, but a distinction between *cot/caught*, etc. is maintained in all US areas bordering on Canada. (3) *T-flapping and T-deletion.* Especially in casual speech, many Canadians, like many Americans, pronounce /t/ as /d/ between vowels and after /r/, a feature known as *t-flapping*. Such pairs as *waiting/wading*, *metal/medal*, *latter/ladder*, *hearty/hardy* are therefore often homophones and the city of Ottawa is called 'Oddawa'. In addition, the /t/ is usually deleted after *n*, so that *Toronto* is pronounced 'Toronna' or 'Trawna' by most of the city's inhabitants. (4) *Use of WH.* Speakers of standard CanE tend more than speakers of standard Northern AmE to drop the distinction between initial /hw/ and /w/, making homophones out of *which/witch*. (5) Different regional and social groups vary the pronunciation of some words, such as *lever*, *schedule*, *aunt*, *route*, *hostile*. As with the lexical variants like *tap/faucet*, *pail/bucket*, *porch/ verandah*, the differences are generally ascribed to the degree of influence from AmE.

Grammar. Where CanE differs grammatically from BrE it tends to agree with AmE. However, where such differences exist, Canadians are often more aware of both usages than Americans, either because they use both or have been exposed to both. Middle-class Canadians over 40 prefer *have you got* as in *Have you got a match?* to either the AmE *Do you have a match?* or the conservative BrE *Have you a match?*, but the younger generation and those with some post-secondary education are moving to the American form.

Canadian EH. The belief, especially among Americans, that Canadians frequently use *eh* (*It's nice, eh?*) is borne out by research, but until more comparative work can be done, the assertion of Walter Avis (1972, below) that it is not uniquely a Canadianism must stand. As elsewhere, this interjection is used in Canada to mean *could you please repeat what you said*, but more commonly it is a tag question (*You do want to go, eh? = don't you?*) or serves to elicit agreement or confirmation (*It's nice, eh?*) and to intensify commands, questions, and exclamations (*Do it, eh?*). It is also common in anecdotes: *He's holding on to a firehose, eh? The thing is jumping all over the place, eh, and he can hardly hold on to it, eh? Well, he finally loses control of it, eh, and the water knocks down half a dozen bystanders.* This last use, the anecdotal *eh*, is the most stigmatized.

Vocabulary. English Canadians have developed the vocabulary they have needed in their special environment by borrowing from indigenous languages and from French, by extending and adapting traditional English words, and by coining new words, in addition to which, CanE vocabulary has been affected by institutional bilingualism:

(1) *Borrowing from indigenous languages.* There are two sources of native borrowing: the Canadian Indian languages such as Cree, Dene, and Ojibwa, and Inuktitut, the language of the Inuit or Eskimo. Such words tend to relate to flora and fauna, early economic and social activities, travel, and survival. From the Indian languages come *chipmunk*, *mackinaw* (a bush jacket), *moose*, *muskeg* (boggy, mossy land), *muskrat*. From Inuktitut come *kayak*, *mukluk*, *anorak*, *parka*, *malemute*, *husky*. A productive borrowing from Micmac through French is *toboggan*, a runnerless wooden sled still used by children. The word produced the logging terms *bogan* and *logboggan*. A motorized sled was first called a *motor toboggan* and *autoboggan*, then *bombardier* (after the trade name of one such vehicle). Now a vehicle of this kind, widely used in the North instead of a dog team and in the South for sport, is a *skimobile*, *skidoo*, or *snowmobile*.

(2) *Borrowing from French.* In addition to the ancient legacy of French expressions in English, CanE has a range of usages which are distinctively North American: *caboteur* (a ship engaged in coastal trade), *cache* (a place for storing supplies; a supply of goods kept for future use), *coureur du bois* (a French or Métis trader or woodsman), *Métis* (a person or people of 'mixed' blood), *portage* (the carrying of canoes past rapids), *voyageur* (a French-Canadian canoeman in the service of the fur companies; someone travelling the northern wilderness), *mush* (from French *marcher*, used to order sled dogs to run), and *tuque* (a knitted cap). In addition, there are such technical terms as *anglophone* and *francophone* (without an initial capital, in the French style), *caisse populaire* (a credit union, a bank-like institution, especially in Quebec): see QUEBEC (ENGLISH). The existence of two official languages has led to various usages, including the attributive use of *Canada* in the names of government departments, crown corporations, and national organizations, often with French word order, the attributive after the noun: *Canada Post*, *Revenue Canada*, *Air Canada*, *Loto Canada*. French and English often mix, as in names like the *Jeunesses Musicales of Canada* and on hybrid signs, especially those used for official purposes: *Postes Canada Post*. During the recent Canada games, some anglophone announcers referred to them as *the Jeux Canada Games* as if *Jeux* were an English word. In addition, the delicate relationship between English and French allows for originality: for example, the visual form of the name of the airline called *Canadian* in English and *Canadien* in French, in which the variable vowel is replaced by the company logo, a red arrow.

(3) *Extension and adaptation of traditional words.* Many BrE words have had their meanings extended and adapted to conditions in North America. CanE shares with AmE many usages relating to landscape and social life, etc., but has a range of distinctive additional usages, such as: *Native* officially referring to the indigenous peoples of Canada (*the Native Peoples*); the distinction between *prime minister* (federal chief minister) and *premier* (provincial chief minister); *province*, *provincial* (referring to the major political divisions of the country, most of which were once distinct British colonies); *riding* (a political constituency); *status Indian* (someone officially registered as a Canadian Indian); CanE *reserve* as opposed to AmE *reservation* as a term describing land set aside for Native peoples.

British influence. The social institutions of Canada have been profoundly influenced by the British imperial connection: for example, Parliament in Ottawa, in which usage is comparable to that of the British Parliament in Westminster. The ties of blood are still strong in many places, but have been considerably weakened by the influx into Canada of immigrants from parts of the world where the British connection has been either minimal (as with China and Vietnam) or equivocal (as with India and the West Indies). In addition, the generation that fought alongside the British in the Second World War is growing old, the Queen's representative in Canada (the Governor-General) is no longer a British aristocrat but a Canadian, and where Britain's economic and military interests now lie with Europe, Canada's lie with the US. Nonetheless, some BrE forms are either holding their own or gaining. Younger Canadians of both sexes pronounce *been* to rhyme with *queen* and not *bin*; *anti-*, *semi-*, and *multi-* to rhyme with *me*, not with *my*; words ending in *-ile* to rhyme with *Nile* and not *ill*. These all run against the tide of AmE. It may not be clear to these speakers, however, that they are sustaining BrE forms.

Social issues. (1) Stigmatized usages include 'dropping the *g*' in the words ending *-ing*, especially in *going* ('goin'), dropping the *t* in words like *just* ('jus'), and the use of the contraction *had've*, sometimes written 'had of' (*We would've helped you if you had've asked us*). (2) The trend away from Canadian Raising led by young women seems to indicate that standard AmE rather than standard CanE or standard BrE is becoming the prestige dialect. Jennifer Coates notes, 'it seems as though women are more sensitive to status-giving prestige norms, . . . while men are more sensitive to vernacular norms, which represent solidarity and values traditionally associated with masculinity' (*Women, Men and Language*, 1986). English Canadians have said and written relatively little about linguistic nationalism and in this they are different from Americans, Australians, Brazilians, Argentinians, and French Canadians: '[T]he normal and natural development of linguistic nationalism has apparently been blighted by the peculiar condition of Anglo-Canadian culture, caught between the Scylla of England and the Charybdis of the United States' (David Haberley, 'The Search for a National Language', *Comparative Literature Studies* 11, 1974, p. 87). However, it can be argued that linguistic nationalism is only 'normal' and 'natural' where its presence does not risk fragmenting the nation. CanE could be described as bland and Canadian attitudes to it as blighted, but CanE, like all varieties of English, is a practical response to a unique set of social, linguistic, and political pressures.

Conclusion. That Canada has had two official languages since its founding may explain why anglophone Canadians have by and large accepted bilingualism and multiculturalism as public policy. However, protest is mounting in New Brunswick and Ontario against this policy, especially by anglophone public servants who fear that their jobs will be classified as 'bilingual'. Heavy immigration (100,000 in 1985) is a commonplace of Canadian life and shows no sign of slowing. Immigrant varieties have developed, such as Toronto's *Italese*, an interlanguage resulting from three generations of contact between Italian and English. Currently, half the children in Vancouver schools and a quarter of those in Toronto schools speak English as a second language. This Canada has been described as a 'two-cultured, multi-ghettoed, plural community' (William Kilbourn, *Canada: A Guide to the Peaceable Kingdom*, 1970), where fascinating and unusual kinds of language change and accommodation are possible.

See ALLIANCE QUEBEC, AMERICAN ENGLISH, CANADA, CANADIAN BROADCASTING, CANADIAN DICTIONARIES, CANADIANISM, CANADIAN STYLE GUIDES, DIALECT IN CANADA, GENERAL CANADIAN, LANGUAGE POLICE, MARITIMES, MÉTIS (RED RIVER DIALECT), NASAL, NEWFOUNDLAND ENGLISH, OTTAWA VALLEY, QUEBEC, SOUTHERN ONTARIO. [AMERICAS, HISTORY, VARIETY]. M.F.

Avis, Walter S. 1972. 'So *Eh?* is Canadian, eh?', in *Canadian Journal of Linguistics* 17; reprinted in *Walter S. Avis: Essays and Articles*, ed. Thomas Vincent *et al.* Kingston, Ont.: Royal Military College, 1978.
—— 1973. 'The English Language in Canada: A Report', in *Current Trends in Linguistics* 10: 1, ed. Thomas A. Sebeok. The Hague: Mouton.
—— & Kinloch, A. M. 1977. *Writings on Canadian English, 1792-1975: An Annotated Bibliography.* Toronto: Fitzhenry & Whiteside.
—— *et al.* (eds.). 1967. *A Dictionary of Canadianisms on Historical Principles.* Toronto: Gage. Abridged paperback edition: *A Concise Dictionary of Canadianisms*, 1973.
Bailey, Richard W. 1982/1984. 'The English Language in Canada', in Bailey & Görlach (eds.), *English as a World Language.* Ann Arbor: Michigan University Press. Cambridge: University Press.
Chambers, J. K. (ed.). 1975. *Canadian English: Origins and Structures.* Toronto: Methuen.
—— 1981. 'Lawless and Vulgar Innovations: Victorian Views of Canadian English', in *Toronto Working Papers in Linguistics* 2. Toronto: Linguistics Graduate Course Union, University of Toronto.
Lougheed, W. C. (ed.). 1985. *In Search of the Standard in Canadian English.* Occasional Paper 1, Strathy Language Unit, Queen's University, Kingston, Ont.
—— 1988. *Writings on Canadian English, 1976-1987: A Selective, Annotated Bibliography.* Strathy Language Unit, Queen's University, Kingston, Ont.
McConnell, R. E. 1979. *Our Own Voice: Canadian English and How It Is Studied.* Toronto: Gage.
Pringle, Ian. 1985. 'Attitudes to Canadian English', in *The English Language Today*, ed. Sidney Greenbaum. Oxford: Pergamon.
Scargill, M. H. 1977. *A Short History of Canadian English.* Victoria, BC: Sono Nis.
—— 1988. 'The English Language', in *The Canadian Encyclopedia*, 2nd edition, pp. 709-10. Edmonton: Hurtig.

CANADIANISM [1870s]. A usage or custom special to or common in Canada, especially in language, such as the interjection *eh* in *He went into the store, eh, and saw this skidoo, eh,* and *riding* to mean 'political constituency'. Where English has Canadianisms, French has *canadianismes*. See CANADIAN DICTIONARIES IN ENGLISH, CANADIAN ENGLISH, -ISM. [AMERICAS, VARIETY, WORD]. T.MCA.

CANADIANISMS, DICTIONARY OF. See CANADIAN DICTIONARIES IN ENGLISH.

CANADIAN LANGUAGE ORGANIZATIONS. The bilingual nature of Canada has led to the development of many organizations associated with language. Several exist to promote English language rights in Quebec, such as *Alliance Quebec*, and similar organizations serve francophones outside Quebec, such as the *Fédération des francophones hors Québec* (Federation of Speakers of French outside Quebec). Some promote English nationwide, such as the *English Speaking Union of Canada*. Organizations for translators and interpreters include the *Society of Translators and Interpreters of Canada* (1957-71), renamed the *Canadian Translators and Interpreters Council/Conseil des traducteurs et interprètes du Canada* in 1971, and the *Literary Translators' Association/Association des traducteurs littéraires* (founded 1975). In 1977, *Canadian Parents for French*, a lobby group for bilingual education, was founded. The *Canadian Linguistic Association/Association canadienne de linguistique* was founded in 1954, and publishes *The Canadian Journal of Linguistics/La Revue canadienne de linguistique.*

Many writers' associations are active, including the *Playwrights' Union of Canada* (originally formed in 1972 as *Playwrights' Co-op*, then changed its name to *Playwrights Canada* in 1979 and merged with the *Guild of Canadian Playwrights* in 1984), the *League of Canadian Poets* (founded 1966), the *Writers' Union of Canada* (1973) for prose writers of trade books, the *Periodical Writers' Association of Canada* (1976), and the *Canadian Authors' Association* (1921). The *Writers' Union* led a campaign for Public Lending Right, successfully concluded in 1986, which compensates writers for the use of their books by libraries. Organizations concerned with the teaching of English literature include the *Association of Canadian University Teachers of English/Association des professeurs d'anglais des universités canadiennes (ACUTE/APAUC)*, the *Association for Canadian and Quebec Literatures/Association des littératures canadiennes et québécoises (ACQL/ALCQ)*, and the *Canadian Council of Teachers of English/Conseil canadien des professeurs d'anglais (CCTE/CCPA)*. Canadian book editors have long been frustrated by Canada's history of adhering to a mixture of British and American spelling, punctuation, and editorial practices. The *Freelance Editors' Association of Canada/Association canadienne des pigistes de l'édition (FEAC/ACPE)* was formed to deal with the resultant problems, and has produced a style guide. Literacy is a major concern in most modern nations, and Canada is no exception. The major private agencies working on the problem are *Frontier College* (founded 1899) and *World Literacy of Canada* (founded 1955).

Because of Canada's high rate of immigration, teaching English as a second language has always been a major concern of school boards and adult educators. In the 1970s, several provincial language organizations were founded, including *SPEAQ (La Société pour la promotion de l'enseignement de l'anglais, langue seconde, au Québec*: Society for the Promotion of the Teaching of English as a Second Language in Quebec). In 1978, the provincial ESL organizations came together to form *TESL Canada/Fédération TESL du Canada*, which publishes a quarterly, *The TESL Canada Journal/Revue TESL du Canada*. The Federal policy of multiculturalism was proclaimed in 1971 and in the Department of the Secretary of State there are a *Canadian Multiculturalism Council* and a *Multiculturalism Directorate*. Ontario's *heritage language* programme, designed to encourage the preservation of non-official languages in the province, was introduced in 1977, and similar programmes have been begun in Quebec, Manitoba, Alberta, British Columbia, and the Northwest Territories. See CANADIAN PRESS, CANADIAN STYLE GUIDES. [AMERICAS, LANGUAGE, MEDIA].   M.F.

CANADIAN LANGUAGES. Canada is an institutionally bilingual country, in which since 1969 Federal Government services have been available in English and French. The relationship between the two languages dominates the linguistic and often the political scene throughout the country. In the 1986 census, English was listed as the mother tongue of 61% (15.3m people) and French of 24% (6.2m people). However, English is spoken at home by many people for whom it is not a mother tongue, so that altogether some 16.6m people speak English and some 5.8m speak French at home. The proportion of francophones in Canada at large has been declining since 1951 (when they represented 29% of the population), but the proportion in the province of Quebec has remained stable at 81% while its anglophone population has dropped from 14% in 1941 to 10% in 1986. New Brunswick is the only officially bilingual province. Ontario and Manitoba provide some services in both languages. Since the passage of Bill 101 in 1977, French has been Quebec's official language, but anglophones are served by a school system, three universities, English-medium hospitals, and distinctive institutions. In the other provinces and territories, English dominates. English–French bilingualism has been increasing for at least 15 years (13.4% in 1971, 15.3% in 1981, and 16.2% in 1986), bilingualism being most common in Quebec (34.5%). Across Canada, more than 250,000 anglophone children are enrolled in French immersion programmes where all teaching, except for English studies, is done in French.

Of the 2.9m people (11% of the total) who in the 1986 census reported as their mother tongue languages other than the official languages, 2.1m listed European languages (Italian, German, Dutch, Portuguese, Polish, and Greek were most common), 634,000 Asian languages (Chinese being most common), and 13,000 languages outside these categories. The Native population (that is, people of indigenous descent) is currently estimated at 756,000 or around 3% of the total population: 331,000 Indians, 27,000 Inuit (speaking Inuktitut), and 398,000 Métis and people of mixed Native origin. Approximately 175,500 people reported one of the 53 indigenous languages as a mother tongue. The majority listed Algonquian languages (116,820 speakers) followed by Athapaskan or Dene languages

(17,080 speakers) and Inuktitut (22,210 speakers). The most stable language communities are Cree, Ojibwa, and Inuktitut. Many others are now spoken only by a few elderly people and will soon be extinct. Native Canadians have suffered from a long-established policy of assimilation through education that endangers their languages and has only been seriously challenged since the 1970s. As a result, they often speak an interlanguage between their own language and English and are not well disposed towards learning standard English. See AMERICAN LANGUAGES, GAELIC, HERITAGE LANGUAGE. [AMERICAS, LANGUAGE]. M.F.

CANADIAN LITERATURE IN ENGLISH. In

1857, the Reverend A. Constable Geikie argued that anglophone Canada's 'newspaper and other writers should abstain from the attempt to add new force to the English tongue by improving the language of Shakespeare, Bacon, Dryden and Addison'. However, in saying this, he was resisting a process of adaptation by an imported language to indigenous experience that was already well advanced. Canadian writing in English began with such works as Frances Brooke's *The History of Emily Montague* (1769), John Richardson's *Wacousta* (1832), and the sketches of Thomas McCulloch and Thomas Haliburton in the 1820s and 1830s. In addition, there were exploration narratives, travel books, and early immigrant journals, marking the beginning of the act of possessing through naming that Geikie feared would produce 'a language as unlike our noble mother tongue as the negro patua, or the Chinese pidgeon English' (in 'Canadian English', *Canadian Journal of Industry, Science and Art* 2, 1857).

Haliburton was the first Canadian writer to be widely identified as capturing a distinctive vernacular; his *Clockmaker* sketches presented Sam Slick of Slickville, Onion County, Connecticut, and introduced into literature scores of words and phrases like *upper crust, stick-in-the-mud*, and *large as life and twice as natural*. Haliburton was the first colonial to receive an honorary degree from Oxford (in recognition of his achievement in re-creating the dialect of a Yankee clock pedlar), and the award ironically anticipates the location of English-Canadian language and literature between the linguistic and literary empires of England and the US.

A literary Canadian English. The debate on the possibility of a distinctive Canadian style extends from the 1820s to the 1990s. Strong claims began with Charles Mair's generation in the 1880s and Roy Daniells in 1947 reflected the recurring concerns of impressionistic criticism in attempting to describe 'elements of style that

may safely be called Canadian'. He listed these as: 'No conscious Latinity, no marked or cumulative rhythm, no pronounced idiom or flavour in the diction, no hint of the grand manner or of rhetoric; on the contrary, a distrust of the sublime, the heroic and the pathetic. . . . Above all it is *wary* and exploring. Life is unpredictable; facts are strange things: the words must move humbly and alertly to adapt themselves to the matter, whatever it may be' ('Canadian Prose Style', *Manitoba Arts Review* 5, 1947). Two years later, Lister Sinclair described the literary CanE as characterized by 'the still small voice' of irony: 'our famous calculated diffidence can be used as the final stroke of irony to make our small voice influential' ('The Canadian Idiom', *Here and Now* 4, 1949).

Canadian literary voices gained unprecedented levels of attention if not influence in national and international contexts at the time of Canada's centennial in 1967. Change in educational, publishing, theatrical, and governmental institutions stemmed from and reinforced nationalist sentiment, including support for the development of an audience for a national literature in English. Margaret Laurence became a focal figure after the publication of *The Stone Angel* (1964), as she fulfilled her desire 'to take the language and make it truly ours, to write out of our own familiar idiom' ('Ivory Tower or Grassroots?', 1978). Al Purdy's poems were honoured for embodying 'in words, our historic modes of dwelling here . . . our native reflexes and tensions' (Lee, 1986, below). Concurrently, Margaret Atwood, Robertson Davies, and Alice Munro enjoyed unprecedented international publication and attention. There have, however, been reservations. Christopher Dean could find no evidence of 'a distinctive literary Canadian English' in a selection of short stories analysed in 1963 (*American Speech* 38), and more recently Robert Cluett, reporting on an analysis of texts by 53 Canadian writers included in the York University Computer Inventory of Prose Style, found little support for generalizations about 'a Canadian style'.

Nation and region. Throughout the 1970s and 1980s, literary criticism followed linguistic emphasis on regional dialects in placing increased emphasis on region rather than nation as cultural construct. The titles of Laurence Ricou's *Vertical Man, Horizontal World: Man and Landscape in Canadian Prairie Fiction* (1973) and Janice Kulyk Keefer's *Under Eastern Eyes: A Critical Reading of Maritime Fiction* (1987) suggest the perspective of scores of anthologies, articles, and books. Countering such an emphasis, however, is George Tilly's argument, based on a survey of 25 novels, that regional differences are less significant than differences between rural and urban speakers; he therefore calls for literary dialect studies based not on geography of region or nation but on an investigation of generational, class, and ethnic variations (dissertation: 'Canadian English in the Novels of the 1970s', York University, Toronto, 1980).

Contemporaneously, books, journals, and articles acknowledged the increasingly multicultural character of Canada, with titles including *Toronto South Asian Review* (1985), *Chilean Literature in Canada* (1983), and *Italian Canadian Voices* (1984). Increasingly, Canadians have become aware that a sense of literary nationality requires a recognition of internal cultural plurality. At the same time, Canadian writing in English has gained attention elsewhere in what Dennis Lee has called 'the recurrent process in which, language by language and country by country over the last sixty years, the hinterlands of empire have broken through to universal resonance by learning to speak local' (1986, below). [AMERICAS, LITERATURE].   L.M.

Cluett, Robert. 1990. *Canadian Literary Prose: A Stylistic Atlas*. Downsview, Ont.: ECW Press.

Keith, W. J. 1985. *Canadian Literature in English*. London: Longman.

Klinck, Carl F. (ed.). 1976. *Literary History of Canada*, 2nd edition. Three volumes. University of Toronto Press.

Lee, Dennis. 1986. 'The Poetry of Al Purdy: An Afterword', in *The Collected Poems of Al Purdy*. Toronto: McClelland & Stewart.

New, William H. 1988. *A History of Canadian Literature*. London: Macmillan.

CANADIAN PLACE-NAMES. There are some 300,000 place-names in Canada, reflecting the varied history of a huge territory inhabited, explored, and settled by many groups. Their main sources are Amerindian languages, Inuktitut, French, and English. Often names have been translated from one language to another or modified significantly to facilitate pronunciation.

Amerindian and Inuit. Place-names from aboriginal languages include *Canada* (from Iroquois *kanata* village), *Manitoba* (from Assiniboine *mini tobow* lake of the prairie, or Cree *manitowapow* strait of the spirit), *Ontario* (probably from *Onitariio* beautiful lake), *Quebec* (from Algonquian *Kebec* narrow passage, strait), *Saskatchewan* (from Cree *kisiskatchewani sipi* swift-flowing river), *Yukon* (from *yu-kun-ah* great river). Inuktitut names are now beginning to replace English place-names in the North: *Frobisher Bay* has become *Iqaluit* and *Resolute Bay* is *Kaujuitoq*. The names for the proposed divisions of the Northwest Territories are *Nunavut* (for the Eastern Arctic) and *Denendeh* (for the

Western Arctic), the first being from Inuktitut, the second from Dene. Chinook Jargon has provided the first elements in *Siwash Rock* (from French *sauvage*, a derogatory term for an Amerindian) and *Canim Lake* (from *canoe*), both in British Columbia. Place-names of Native origin may be orthographically French (*Chibougamau*, *Chicoutimi*, *Outaouais*, *Yamachiche*), English (*Shawinigan*), or neutral (*Ottawa*, *Yamaska*).

French. Place-names from French include: *Lachine*, Quebec (so called because early explorers thought they might be approaching China), *Montreal*, Quebec (Mount Royal: also the name in English of a town nearby), *Trois-Rivières*, Quebec (sometimes referred to as *Three Rivers*), *Sault Ste Marie*, Ontario (often shortened to *the Soo*, from *sault*, waterfall: St Mary Falls), *Tete Jaune Cache*, British Columbia (yellow head cache, where *cache* means a hidden food supply). Saints' names are particularly common in Quebec: *Saint-Chrysostome*, *Saint-Félix-de-Valois*, *Saint-Hyacinthe*. The name of a well-known French explorer appears in *Jacques Cartier Mountain* and of the commander of the French forces during the Seven Years' War in *Montcalm County*.

English. There are four broad categories of English place-names: (1) British place-names transferred to Canada: *London*, *Hamilton*, and *Kingston* (all in Ontario). (2) Those that honour individuals: royalty (*Queen Charlotte Islands* and *Victoria*, British Columbia, *Prince Albert*, Saskatchewan); early explorers (*Vancouver* and *Vancouver Island*, British Columbia); military and political leaders (*Wolfe Island*, Ontario, *Churchill Falls*, Labrador, *Lake Diefenbaker*, Saskatchewan); saints (*St. John's*, Newfoundland); literary figures (*Shakespeare* and *Haliburton*, Ontario). (3) Those that arise from frontier times: *Kicking Horse Pass* through the Rocky Mountains in Alberta, *Hell's Gate*, dangerous rapids on the Fraser River in British Columbia. (4) Descriptions: *Clear Lake*, *Rocky Mountains*, *Thunder Bay*.

Hybrids and translations. The island and province of Newfoundland (itself a name dating from 1502) has place-names deriving from many languages, reflecting the many groups that have fished in the region: from Portuguese, *Cauo de la Spera* (Cape Hope) and *Fogo Island* (from *fogo*, fire); from French, *Codroy River*, from nearby *Cape Ray*, once *Cap de Roy* (King's Cape). *L'Anse aux Meadows* may mean 'Bay of Meadows' or be from the French for 'Jellyfish Bay' (*L'Anse aux Méduses*). In Alberta, translations from local languages provide *Crow's Nest Pass* and *Medicine Hat*. In Quebec, such forms as *Sainte-Hélène-de-Kamouraska*, *Saint-Nazaire-de-Chicoutimi*, and *Saint-Prosper-*

de-Dorchester are the product of French–Amerindian and French–English mixing.

The names of anglophone towns in Quebec, especially in the Eastern Townships, reflect the two cultures: *Drummondville, Victoriaville*. The *Red River*, which flows through Winnipeg, Manitoba, is a translation of the French *Rivière Rouge*, in turn a translation of the Cree *Miscousipi* (Red Water River). The pronunciation of place-names varies. *Dauphin*, Manitoba, is locally pronounced to rhyme with *coffin* and *Bienfait* in Saskatchewan is pronounced 'Bean Fate'. Ironically, *Bay D'Espoir* (French: of hope) in Newfoundland is pronounced locally as if it were *Bay Despair*. Compare HOBSON-JOBSONISM. Unusual place-names include, east to west: *Witless Bay, Leading Tickles*, and *Joe Batt's Arm* in Newfoundland; *Ecum Secum* in Nova Scotia; *Saint-Louis du Ha! Ha!* and *Saint-Stanislas-de-Koska-de-la-Rivière-des-Envies* in Quebec; *Punkeydoodles Corner* in Ontario; *Flin Flon* in Manitoba; *Manyberries* in Saskatchewan; *Moose Jaw* in Alberta; *Woodfibre, Miocene, Skookumchuck, Point No Point* in British Columbia.

Toponymy. In 1897, the Geographic Board was established in an attempt to regulate place-names. Its successor is the Canadian Permanent Committee on Geographical Names, part of the Department of Energy, Mines, and Resources, which issues Canadian gazetteers. The main work of reference is William B. Hamilton's *The Macmillan Book of Canadian Place Names* (Toronto: Macmillan, 1983). See PLACE-NAME, TOPONYMY. [AMERICAS, NAMES].   M.F.

CANADIAN PRESS. In 1986, there were 110 daily newspapers in Canada, with a circulation of 5.6m (approximately 80% English, 20% French). Only the largest cities have more than one daily, although weekly community newspapers are common. One daily, the Toronto *Globe and Mail*, has a national edition. Four communications conglomerates own 67% of Canadian newspapers: Southam, Torstar, the Thomson group, and Maclean-Hunter. The major news agency, Canadian Press, is cooperatively owned by its users: 108 newspapers, the Canadian Broadcasting Corporation (CBC), and 320 privately owned broadcast outlets. Provincial press councils set guidelines for newspapers. The Canadian Daily Newspaper Publishers Association and the Canadian Community Newspaper Publishers Association, both in Toronto, provide support services for their members. The monthly *Maclean's Magazine*, founded in 1905 in Toronto, in 1978 adopted the format of *Time* and *Newsweek* when tax concessions were withdrawn for these US publications and became a weekly. Its publishers,

Maclean-Hunter, also bring out a French equivalent, *L'Actualité*. The Centre for Investigative Journalism, at Carleton University in Ottawa, is a national association of both print and broadcast journalists which promotes in-depth reporting in Canada. *The Canadian Newspaper Index* (Toronto: Micromedia, 1977–) indexes the Calgary *Herald*, Toronto *Globe and Mail*, Halifax *Chronicle Herald*, Montreal *Gazette*, Toronto *Star*, Vancouver *Sun*, and Winnipeg *Free Press*. See CANADIAN STYLE GUIDES, NEWSPAPER, PRESS. [AMERICAS, MEDIA].   M.F.

CANADIAN PUBLISHING. Publishing in Canada has always suffered from a small market, a large distribution area, and heavy competition from British and American books. Although Canadian publishers used to support their often unprofitable publication of Canadian books by acting as agencies for foreign presses, many American and British publishers now have branches in Canada. These publish few original Canadian books (in 1984, only 20% of the new titles in English), instead marketing textbooks and proven best-sellers. Canadian publishing therefore suffers from chronic unprofitability. In 1970, Ryerson Press (founded 1829 and a well-known publisher of Canadian literature) was sold to the US publisher McGraw-Hill and in 1971 the equally well-known McClelland and Stewart would have been sold to US interests if the Ontario government had not stepped in with a loan. These developments led to the institution of provincial and federal programmes that support the publication of Canadian authors and promote the sales of Canadian books at home and abroad. See CANADIAN DICTIONARIES, PUBLISHING. [AMERICAS, MEDIA].   M.F.

CANADIAN RAISING. See CANADIAN ENGLISH.

CANADIAN STYLE GUIDES. Canadian editors frequently use *The Chicago Manual of Style* (13th edition, 1982), although its rules often need to be adapted to the Canadian situation. For advice on Canadian issues, some use *The Canadian Press Stylebook: A Guide for Editors and Writers* (Toronto: Canadian Press, 1983), a guide for journalists, and *Caps and Spelling* (Canadian Press, 1985). The Toronto *Globe and Mail* and the Toronto *Star* also publish style guides. Recently, the Secretary of State produced *The Canadian Style: A Guide to Writing and Editing* (Toronto: Dundurn Press, 1985) designed for the use of public servants. The first stylebook intended primarily for book editors is *Editing Canadian English* (ed. Lydia Burton *et al.*, Vancouver: Douglas and McIntyre and the Freelance Editors' Association of Canada, 1987). It focuses on areas where Canadian editorial practice traditionally differs from both American and British usage. It covers not only spelling, punctuation, abbreviations, and the metric system, but also bias, documentation, copyright, and the use of French in an English context. There is a chapter on *Canadianization*: changing an American textbook so that it can be used in Canadian schools. For American and British equivalents, see HOUSE STYLE. [AMERICAS, STYLE, USAGE]. M.F.

CANON [Before 10c: from Latin *canon*, Greek *kanṓn* a measuring rod, rule]. (1) A decree of the Roman Catholic Church, part of its *canon law*. The gospels of the Bible are the *Canonical Gospels*, those accepted by the Church as authentic, as opposed to various *apocryphal gospels*. (2) An actual, supposed, or desired standard in art, life, and language: *the canons of good taste*. (3) The body of 'best' or 'classic' works of literature in a language: *the literary canon of English*. See BOOK, CANONICAL FORM, CLASSIC, COMMUNICATIVE SHIFT, ENGLISH LITERATURE, NORM, RHETORIC, RULE, STANDARD. [STYLE]. T.MCA.

CANONICAL FORM. The form chosen to represent especially the headword of an article in a dictionary. In English, many items have only one written form (*in, the, some, here, pre-, -ness*), but for others there is more than one possibility (*cat* or *cats, sing* or *sang, fast* or *faster*). By convention, dictionaries select in such cases the shortest form: the singular of nouns, the bare infinitive of verbs, the positive degree of gradable adjectives and adverbs. In cases of polysemy, a single form represents more than one word or lexeme (*crane* for both bird and the machine); in cases of homonymy, more than one article is headed by the same form (¹*bank* of a river, and ²*bank* for money). The form may be written in more than one way: *foetus/fetus, ice cream/ice-cream, USA/U.S.A.* If so, compilers choose one, typically the most common, but other factors may influence their choice, such as whether the dictionary is British (*aeroplane, colour*) or American (*airplane, color*), or whether one form, common or uncommon, has official status: *Muslim* preferred to *Moslem, Romania* to *Rumania*. The canonical form represents itself and its variants, and the variants may be given in the text of the article. On occasion, a double citation form may serve as headword: *foetus/fetus*. Variants may be headwords in their own right if alphabetical order places them far from the word that represents them; in such cases, the information given about them is likely to be a cross-reference: *fetus*, see FOETUS. The canonical form represents itself and any inflections: *cat* represents *cat, cat's, cats, cats'; sing* represents *sing, sings, singing,* *sang, sung.* It does not, however, represent derivatives: *sing* does not usually represent *singer*, which is entered either as a headword in its own right or as a *run-on entry* somewhere in the article for *sing*. Irregular inflections such as *sang* may be given with their headwords and may also be headwords with cross-references: '*sang*, past of SING'; '*sang*, see SING'. See CANON, DICTIONARY, ENTRY, HEADWORD. [REFERENCE, WORD]. R.F.I.

CANT [15c: from Latin *cantus* song: compare *canticus* singsong. Originally, the chanting of friars, then the singsong of beggars, then the language of members of the underworld]. The jargon of a class, group, or profession, often used to exclude or mislead others: a teenage gang member in Los Angeles saying that he was in his *hoopty* around *dimday* when some *mud duck* with a *trey-eight* tried to *take him out of the box* (he was in his car around dusk when a woman armed with a .38 calibre pistol tried to shoot him). Cant is a temporary form of language that changes quickly; when outsiders pick some of it up, the group evolves new usages. Expressions often move into the general language; cant terms that are now general slang include *moniker* name, *bilk* to swindle, *beef* a complaint/to complain, and *hit* kill. See ARGOT, JARGON, MEDICANT, SHELTA, SLANG. [STYLE, USAGE]. W.D.L.

CANTO [16c: Italian *canto* a song]. A chapter-like division of a long poem as employed by such Italian poets as Dante and Ariosto, consisting of a number of stanzas. Spenser in the 16c was the first to use cantos in English, in *The Faerie Queene*. Byron's *Don Juan* in the 19c was structured in the same way. [LITERATURE]. R.C.

CANTONESE. See BRITISH LANGUAGES, CHINA (CHINESE), HONG KONG, JONES (D.).

CANUCK. See ETHNIC NAME.

CAPE DUTCH. See AFRIKAANS, DUTCH, KITCHEN.

CAPITAL, also **capital letter** [14c in this sense: from Latin *capitalis* at the head, chief, foremost, from *caput/capitis* head]. A large letter such as *A, B*, as opposed to a small letter, *a, b*, so named because it can appear at the 'head' of a text, chapter, page, paragraph, sentence, or word. The written and printed form of English has two interlocking systems of letters: large letters, known variously as *capitals, upper-case letters, majuscules*, and small letters, or *lower-case letters, minuscules*. Not all written languages have such a system; Arabic and Hebrew have only one set of letters. Lower-case letters are revisions of the forms of Latin capitals, developed in the minuscule script of the Carolingian period in France (8–9c).

Capitalization. The consistent use of capitals in Western European languages, to begin the first word of a sentence and for the first letter of a proper name (for example, *John*, *Mr Smith*, *New York*), began in the late Middle Ages, and was not fully systematized in English until the end of the 16c. During the 17c and 18c, common nouns and other words were often capitalized, much like (though less consistently than) the capitalizing of common nouns in present-day German. This practice is now largely restricted to abstract nouns like *Liberty, Equality, Fraternity*; even then the use is often ironic, *truth* being usually less absolute and grand than *Truth*. The practice of capitalizing content words in the titles of books, book chapters, articles, etc., is well established, but is not followed in all systems of reference, so that although *Gone with the Wind* is the dominant usage, *Gone with the wind* is also found. Despite the expectation that there are or should be rules for capitalization, above all for proper nouns, conventions remain unstable: should/Should the first word in a clause that follows a colon be capitalized? In BrE, the practice is generally not to capitalize in such cases, whereas AmE tends to favour a capital. Is it *the Earl of Essex* or *the earl of Essex*? There is no absolute rule, but there is a consensus in printing styles for *Earl* when designating an actual title.

Additional uses. (1) To identify a word more closely with a particular ethnic or other source: *the Arabic language* (contrast *arabic numbers*); *the Roman alphabet* (contrast *roman numerals, roman type*). (2) To identify a word more closely with a particular institution or highlight a particular term, usage, etc.: *the State* as opposed to *the state*; *the Church* as opposed to *the church*; *Last Will and Testament* as opposed to *last will and testament*. (3) To give prominence to such special temporal usages as days of the week, months of the year, and epochs (*Monday, September, the Middle Ages*), and such institutional usages as certain religious terms (*God, the Mass*) and trade names (*Coca-Cola, Kleenex*). (4) In a series of *block capitals* or *block letters*, to ensure that a handwritten word or name is clear. Serial capitals used to represent stressed speech are a largely 19c development: ' "MISS JEMIMA!" exclaimed Miss Pinkerton, in the largest capitals' (W. M. Thackeray, *Vanity Fair*, 1847–8, ch. 1); Tweedledum, in Lewis Carroll's *Through the Looking-Glass* (1871, ch. 4), crying in a great fury, 'It's *new* . . . my nice NEW RATTLE!', where small capitals grow to full capitals, because his voice 'rose to a perfect scream'. (5) Initial capitals are widely used to highlight or dramatize

certain words: 'The first rule of politics is Never Believe Anything Until It's Been Officially Denied' (Jonathan Lynn & Antony Jay, *Yes Prime Minister*, 1986). (6) 'Internal' capitals have become fashionable in recent years, especially in computing and commerce, to indicate that in a compound or blend the second element is as significant as the first, as in *CorrecText, DeskMate, VisiCalc, WordPerfect*. Related word- and letter-play may also occur, as in *VisiOn, CoRTeXT*. Such a convention allows an unlimited range of visual neologism. See ALPHABET, ARCHETYPE, BINOMIAL, CASE², EARLY MODERN ENGLISH, LETTER¹, NAME, ONOMASTICS, PUNCTUATION, TECHNOSPEAK, UNCIAL. [TECHNOLOGY, WRITING]. W.W.B., T.MCA., R.E.A.

CAPTION [14c: from Latin *captio/captionis* taking, from *capere/captum* to take]. (1) A title or explanation, usually in the form of a short paragraph, of a picture, diagram, cartoon, or other illustration in a book, magazine, or newspaper. (2) A heading or title introducing a page, chapter, or article. (3) In law, the heading of a document, stating the place, time, and other details of performance, fulfilment, etc. (4) A title, text, or other statement superimposed on part of a motion picture or television or projected on to a screen while showing a film. See CARTOON, HEADING, LEGEND, TITLE. [MEDIA]. T.MCA.

CARDINAL VOWEL. See VOWEL.

CARET, also **caret mark** [17c: from Latin *caret* it lacks: compare STET]. A mark used by printers, editors, teachers, and others to indicate something missing from a line of text. In proofreading, the missing item is added in the margin; in correction, it is usually added above the point of omission. The caret was used in medieval manuscripts and has been employed by printers since the 15c. It has two forms: ∧ , ⋀ . See PROOF-READING. [TECHNOLOGY]. W.W.B.

CARETAKER LANGUAGE/SPEECH. See BABY TALK, CHILD LANGUAGE ACQUISITION, MOTHERESE.

CARIBBEAN [18c: from *Carib* an Amerindian people: compare CALIBAN. The islands were formerly known as *the Caribees*. Stress: 'Kari-BEE-an, Ka-RIB-i-an']. The name of both an arm of the Atlantic Ocean between North and South America and its islands, peoples, customs, and languages. Inter-island passages linking the Caribbean with the Atlantic include the Windward, Mona, and Anegada Passages. The region is marked by ethnic and cultural miscegenation due in the main to the development by various

European nations of plantation economies from the 17c, in which worked first Amerindians (Carib, Arawak), then prisoners from Europe and slaves from West Africa, then indentured East Indian labourers. Most Caribbean economies currently depend on agriculture (bananas, citrus fruits, cocoa, coffee, sugar, tobacco) and tourism, with some exploitation of minerals (bauxite, oil) and some manufacture.

See AFRICAN ENGLISH, AMERICA, AMERICAN[1], AMERICAN BLACK ENGLISH, AMERINDIAN, ANGUILLA, ANTILLES, ATLANTIC CREOLES, BAHAMAS, BAJAN, BARBADOS, BAY ISLANDS, BELIZE, BERMUDA, BLACK, BLACK ENGLISH, BLACK ENGLISH VERNACULAR, BLACK IRISH, BORROWING, BRATHWAITE, BRITISH BLACK ENGLISH, BRITISH EMPIRE, BROKEN, CALIBAN, CARIBBEAN BROADCASTING, CARIBBEAN ENGLISH, CARIBBEAN ENGLISH CREOLE, CARIBBEAN EXAMINATIONS COUNCIL, CARIBBEANISM, CARIBBEAN LANGUAGES, CARIBBEAN LITERATURE IN ENGLISH, CARIBBEAN PRESS, CAYMAN ISLANDS, CENTRAL AMERICA, COMMONWEALTH, COMMONWEALTH CARIBBEAN, CREOLE, CREOLESE, DICTIONARY OF BAHAMIAN ENGLISH, DICTIONARY OF JAMAICAN ENGLISH, DUB, EAST INDIAN, ENGLISH, DUTCH, FRENCH, GRENADA, GULLAH, GUYANA, INDIA, INDIES, JAMAICA, JAMAICAN CREOLE, JAMAICAN ENGLISH, LAMMING, MISKITO COAST CREOLE, MONTSERRAT, NAIPAUL, NATION LANGUAGE, NICARAGUA, PANAMA, PATOIS, PIDGIN, PORTUGUESE, PUERTO RICO, RAP, RASTA TALK, SAINT CHRISTOPHER AND NEVIS, SAINT LUCIA, SAINT VINCENT AND THE GRENADINES, SPANISH, TESD, TRINBAGONIAN, TRINIBAGIANESE, TRINIDAD AND TOBAGO, TURKS AND CAICOS ISLANDS, VIRGIN ISLANDS, WALCOTT, WEST AFRICAN PIDGIN ENGLISH, WEST INDIAN, WEST INDIES. [AMERICAS, NAME].   T.MCA., L.D.C.

CARIBBEAN BROADCASTING. The population of the Caribbean has greater access to radio than to any other mass medium; there is at least one radio station per country owned by the relevant government. In addition, many countries have privately owned stations, such as four in Barbados and three in the Bahamas. Antigua and Montserrat are the bases for regional transmitters of international broadcasting interests: in Antigua, there are relays for the BBC and Voice of Germany; in Montserrat, a relay for Radio Deutsche Welle. Other extra-regional services broadcasting in the region include Radio Canada International and the Voice of America. Television is less widespread but is growing rapidly through access to international satellites and the use of cable systems. In general, TV stations capable of generating their own programming are government-owned. There are several private companies that provide

satellite feed on a commercial basis. In Barbados, Jamaica, and Trinidad and Tobago, English Creole is used in advertising, light programmes, and call-in programmes, and St Lucia and Dominica make limited use of French Creole. Apart from news and features obtained from standard agencies, there is an increasing amount of regional programming by the *Caribbean News Agency* (*CANA*). See BROADCASTING, CARIBBEAN, MONTSERRAT. [AMERICAS, MEDIA].   L.D.C.

CARIBBEAN DICTIONARIES. The major published studies of varieties of CarE are the *Dictionary of Jamaican English* (1967, 1980) and the *Dictionary of Bahamian English* (1982). Two works in preparation are *The Dictionary of Caribbean English Usage* by Richard Allsopp and an untitled dictionary of Trinidadian and Tobagonian by Lise Winer. Glossaries and similar publications exist for individual countries, few claiming to be authoritative or exhaustive, some stating their fascination with the humorous and esoteric, many designed for the tourist market, and all valuable precursors to works of scholarship. In Barbados, Frank A. Collymore's notes began appearing in 1955. In their most recent form they are called *Notes for a Glossary of Words and Phrases of Barbadian Dialect* (Barbados National Trust, undated). The listed items vary in the extent to which they are specific to Barbados; some contain historical and etymological information while others do not; some carry citations or examples, while others offer only a brief gloss. *Trinidad and Tobago Dialect*, compiled and published by Martin Haynes (1987), *Coté ce Coté la: Trinidad and Tobago Dictionary*, compiled and published by John Mendes (1985), and *Creole Talk of Trinidad and Tobago*, compiled by Carlton R. Ottley (Victory Commercial, 1981), show a predilection for the quaint and humorous, use popular English spellings of Creole, and do not provide their criteria for inclusion. Pat Ryan's *Macafouchette: A Look at the Influence of French on the Dialect of Trinidad and Tobago* (Trinidad, 1985) lists items that she attributes to French via the Creole French of Trinidad. *What a Pistarckle: A Dictionary of Virgin Islands English Creole* by Lito Valls (St Johns, VI, 1981) also uses Anglicized spellings for Creole words, and identifies flora and fauna by their scientific names. The glossary in J. A. George Irish's *Alliouagana Folk* (Jagpi Publications, Montserrat, c.1985) also focuses on a Leeward Island Creole and uses popular spellings. Although there have been many studies of Guyanese Creole, little work has been done on its lexicon. John R. Rickford (ed.), *A Festival of Guyanese Words* (Georgetown: U. of Guyana, 1978) explores local vocabulary, but not in dictionary format. See DICTIONARY OF BAHAMIAN

ENGLISH, DICTIONARY OF JAMAICAN ENGLISH. [AMERICAS, REFERENCE].   L.D.C.

CARIBBEAN ENGLISH, short form *CarE*. A general term for the English language as used in the Caribbean archipelago and circum-Caribbean mainland. In a narrow sense, it covers English alone; in a broad sense, it covers English and Creole. The term is often imprecise, however, because of: (1) A long-standing popular classification of varieties of Creole as dialects of English, sometimes called *creole dialects* and *patois*. (2) The existence of a continuum of usage between English and Creole. (3) The use by scholars of the term *English* to cover both, as in the *Dictionary of Jamaican English* (1967, 1980) and the *Dictionary of Bahamian English* (1982). In order of decreasing specificity, the term embraces: (1) Regionally accented varieties of the standard language: standard Jamaican English. (2) Localized forms of English: Barbadian English. (3) Mesolects between English and Creole, as found in most communities. (4) Kinds of English used in countries where Spanish is official or dominant, such as the Dominican Republic, Nicaragua, and Puerto Rico. (5) Varieties of English-based Creole: Creolese in Guyana, Jamaican Creole, Sranan in Surinam.

Standard English. Although English is the official language of the Commonwealth Caribbean, only a small proportion of the nationals of each country speaks regionally accented standard English as a native language. Many, however, acquire it through schooling and taking part in activities in which its use is common and accepted. For such people, standard English is the register of formal communication, complemented by vernacular usage for other purposes. Conservative varieties of regional English have BrE as their reference norm, especially for writing and print, but the influence of the US mass media and tourism has made AmE a powerful alternative. Equally influential has been the attainment of independence by most regional territories and the national consciousness associated with it.

Localized English. In each country of the Commonwealth Caribbean there is a localized non-standard form of English whose prosodic and phonemic systems differ. In like fashion, vocabulary related to flora, fauna, local phenomena, and sociocultural practices varies from country to country. Such vocabulary is drawn variously from Amerindian languages such as Arawak and Carib, West African languages such as Ewe and Yoruba, European languages such as Dutch, French, Portuguese, and Spanish, and, as in Trinidad and Tobago, South Asian languages such as Bhojpuri and Hindi, as well as, predominantly, Creoles based on European lexicons

and with African substrates. Differences among CarE varieties are to some extent determined by the nature of the vernaculars with which they come into contact. In addition, three forces (operating in different ways in different countries) affect the degree of standardization of these forms: internationalization, regionalization, and indigenization.

Internationalization. The acceptability of the norms of BrE depends on sensitivities related to the colonial experience of influential groups in individual countries. Degree of comfort with AmE norms also varies, depending on the perception of the US as a benevolent or malevolent force. At the same time, there is a body of pressure for the unequivocal adoption of an accessible and familiar internationally recognized standard variety as a reference norm.

Regionalization. Pressures towards regionalization are stimulated by intra-regional travel, the spread of regional art forms (especially music), the sharing of a regional university (the U. of the West Indies), and the existence of a common examining council for secondary-level certification across the Commonwealth Caribbean. Procedures for marking scripts have exposed teachers to the written work of students in all parts of the region. Starting from 1977, the *Caribbean Examinations Council (CXC)* has been replacing the Cambridge Examination Syndicate as the certifying body for secondary education. Scripts are marked collectively by teachers from all parts of the region. The Council's guidelines have been established with significant sensitivity to localized forms of English, helping to modify teachers' perceptions of the acceptability of the forms with which they have become familiar. At the same time as they have recognized that no localized form merits greater respect than another, teachers have grown conscious of characteristics of English shared throughout the region. As a result, they have become more receptive to the idea of standards other than BrE and AmE.

Indigenization. Between 1962 and the early 1980s, most of the British Caribbean colonies became independent. This change has been associated with changes in the evaluation of local culture and institutions, including reassessment of Creole and other local speech forms. Positive evaluation of the vernaculars affects opinions about standardizing localized forms of English, and about the distinctness or 'purity' of a vernacular and the extent to which it should be preserved. It also increases the acceptability of code-switching and bidialectal expression, decreasing sensitivity to the limits of each variety. Generally, the result has been increasing indigenization of the localized form of English.

Mesolects. A *mesolectal* or *intermediate* variety is a form of speech lying between a localized English and a local Creole, arising from prolonged coexistence and the uneven penetration of English over several centuries of colonization. Such varieties are characterized by variation in the forms and structures used by the same speaker at different times and by different speakers on particular occasions. For example, in Trinidadian vernacular usage, the existential expression *it have* is equivalent to English *there is/are*, as in *It have plenty people in the park*. In the intermediate varieties of Trinidad, however, *they have* is used with the same meaning as both *it have* and *there is/are*, as in *They have plenty people in the park*. All three usages may occur in the speech of the same speaker depending on the level of formality or casualness of the context, or any one may be the preferred variant of different speakers.

English and Spanish. The term *Caribbean English* is also applied to varieties in the Latin countries of the region. There are two broad categories: (1) 'Foreigner' varieties, produced by people for whom Spanish is the primary language. This is especially the case in Puerto Rico, which, because of its close ties to the US, has AmE as the second language of the island. (2) Speakers of Creole in Colombia, Costa Rica, the Dominican Republic, Honduras, Nicaragua, and Panama, whose language is deemed English by opposition to Spanish rather than by congruence with English in its strict sense.

Creole. The final sense in which the term *Caribbean English* is used refers to the related English-based range of creoles throughout the region. These vernaculars are often referred to as variations of one form: *Caribbean Creole English*. They have traditionally been regarded as dialects of English, but are increasingly considered by scholars to be languages (*creoles*) or a single language with various forms (*Creole*) in their own right. There are close historical and linguistic links between the situation in and around the Commonwealth Caribbean and the pidgins and creoles of West Africa.

Pronunciation. (1) The varieties of Jamaica, Barbados, and Guyana are rhotic; the varieties of the Bahamas, Belize, Trinidad and Tobago, and the lesser Antilles are non-rhotic. (2) Rhythm tends to be syllable-timed. (3) There are fewer diphthongs than in RP: the distinction /iə/ versus /ɛə/ is neutralized in most varieties, so that *beer/bare*, *fear/fare* share the same vowels; in most acrolects, the equivalent of RP /eɪ/ in *face* is /e/, but in Jamaican and the varieties of the Leeward Islands it is /ie/; the vowel in such words as *goat* is generally /o/, but in Jamaican is /ʊo/. (4) Final consonant clusters tend to be reduced in all but the most careful speech, as in 'han' for *hand*. (5) There is a preference for a clear /l/ in such words as *milk, fill*, rather than the dark /l/ of RP.

Grammar. The syntax of CarE approximates fairly closely to general mainstream English. Special features include: (1) *Would* and *could* are common where BrE has *will* and *can*: *I could swim* I can swim; *I would do it tomorrow* I will do it tomorrow. (2) Where BrE has a simple past there is often a past historic: *The committee had decided* The committee decided. (3) *Yes-no* questions with a declarative word order and rising intonation are much commoner than the inversion of auxiliary and subject: *You are coming? Are you coming?*

Vocabulary. Regional usages include: (1) Local senses of general words: (Trinidad) *fatigue*, as used in *to give someone fatigue* to tease or taunt someone with a mixture of half-truths and imaginative fabrications; (general, as a noun) *galvanise* corrugated metal sheeting coated with zinc and used as roofing or fencing material; (Trinidad) *lime* to hang around, loiter without intent, be a casual observer of an event; (Trinidad and elsewhere) *miserable* mischievous; (Jamaica) *tall hair* long hair. (2) Local words: (Trinidad) *catspraddle* to send sprawling with a blow, to fall in an indecorous way; (Trinidad) *jort* a snack; (Trinidad) *touchous* touchy, short-tempered. (3) Loans from French Creole: *lagniappe* (shared with Southern AmE) something extra given by a vendor to a buyer for the sake of good will, a bonus; (Trinidad, St Lucia) *macafouchette* leftovers; (Trinidad) *ramajay* to warble, twitter, make an extravagant display. (4) Loans from local Spanish: (Trinidad, Barbados, and elsewhere) *alpargat(a)* a sandal with uppers made of woven rope-like material, canvas, or of intertwined leather thongs; (general) *parang* a term for a number of different musical rhythms, song types, and festivities associated with Christmas in Trinidad and parts of Venezuela (from *paranda*); (Jamaican) *fruutapang* breadfruit (from *fruta* fruit, *pan* bread); (Jamaican) *mampala* an effeminate man (from *mampolón* a common cock, not a fighting cock); (Jamaican) *scaveeched fish* (from *escabeche* pickled fish). (5) Words from West African languages: (general) *bakra, bukra, buckra* a white person; (widespread) *cotta, kata* a head-pad used under a load carried on the head; (widespread) *fufu* a dish made by pounding boiled plantains, yams, or cassava in a mortar to form a smooth, firm mass that may be cut and served. (6) Loan translations from West African languages: *sweet mouth* flattery, a flatterer; *eye-water* tears; *hard-ears* stubborn; *door-mouth* doorway, entrance to a building. See CARIBBEAN, CARIBBEAN ENGLISH CREOLE, ENGLISH. [AMERICAS, VARIETY]. L.D.C.

Alleyne, M. C. 1980. *Comparative Afro-American.* Ann Arbor: Karoma.

Bailey, B. L. 1966. *Jamaican Creole Syntax: A Transformational Approach.* Cambridge: University Press.

Bickerton, D. 1975. *Dynamics of a Creole System.* Cambridge: University Press.

Cassidy, F. G. 1961. *Jamaica Talk: Three Hundred Years of the English Language in Jamaica.* London: Macmillan.

Collymore, F. A. (No date). *Notes for a Glossary of Words and Phrases of Barbadian Dialect,* 5th edition. Bridgetown, Barbados: The Barbados National Trust. (First published 1955.)

Da Costa, J., & Lalla, B. (eds.). 1989. *Voices in Exile: Jamaican Texts in the 18th and 19th Centuries.* Tuscaloosa: University of Alabama Press.

Görlach, M., & Holm, J. A. (eds.). 1986. *Focus on: The Caribbean,* in the Varieties of English around the World series. Amsterdam & Philadelphia: John Benjamins.

Holm, J. (ed.). 1983. *Central American English.* Heidelberg: Julius Gross Verlag.

Le Page, R. B., & Tabouret-Keller, A. 1985. *Acts of Identity: Creole-Based Approaches to Language and Ethnicity.* Cambridge: University Press.

Rickford, J. R. 1987. *Dimensions of a Creole Continuum: History, Texts, & Linguistic Analysis of Guyanese Creole.* Stanford: University Press.

Roberts, P. A. 1988. *West Indians and their Language.* Cambridge: University Press.

CARIBBEAN ENGLISH CREOLE, also **Caribbean Creole English, Caribbean Creole, Creole English, West Indian Creole, Creole**. The technical term for an English-based creole or group of creoles in the Commonwealth Caribbean, the Samaná peninsula of the Dominican Republic, the coastal areas of Nicaragua and Costa Rica, the Bay Islands of Honduras, the Colombian dependencies of San Andres and Providencia, parts of Panama, and Surinam. Two major forms can be identified in Surinam (*Ndjuka, Sranan*); only in that country do varieties have specific names used by both speakers and researchers. In all other cases, speakers generally call their varieties dialects, such as *Jamaican dialect,* while scholars label each variety by its territorial name followed by *English, English-based,* or *English-lexicon,* such as *Antiguan English Creole, Barbadian English-based Creole, Trinidadian English-lexicon Creole.* These varieties are also commonly referred to by location alone (*Jamaican Creole*) or, when the location is apparent, as *Creole* (both with and without an initial capital). The range of usage is referred to as both *Creole,* when looked at collectively, and *Creoles,* when regarded as a group of vernaculars. Since not all varieties have been researched to the same extent, the assumption that there are as many distinct forms as there are territories is convenient rather than definitive. The settlement patterns of the region and later migratory movement suggest that there are fewer distinct forms

than locations. However, the absence of a regionally recognized standard reduces the perception of the unity of Creole, which is often currently discussed by scholars and others as a language in its own right, distinct from English. The unevenness of the research permits the continued use of a fragmentary and inconsistent labelling system.

History and development. Like most other such creoles, Caribbean English Creole is the outcome of contact among Europeans and West Africans in the course of European expansionism, the slave trade, and the colonization of the New World. The regional dialects of the English-speaking colonists were the dominant source of vocabulary for Creole before the 20c. More recently, standard varieties of English, propagated by contemporary mass media and the increased availability of schooling, have fed the expansion of the vocabulary. Large numbers of lexical items and phrases of West African provenance form part of the daily vocabulary. The grammatical structure of the group shows patterns that are characteristic of West African language families, patterns that are particular to creole languages as a whole, and features that appear to be restricted to the Caribbean Creole group.

Effects of contact. In most countries (excluding Surinam and the Latin American nations), the contact with English that produced Creole has persisted beyond its emergence, with a chain of associated results: (1) It has inhibited the evolution of widely recognized standard varieties within the group. (2) In its turn, the absence of one or more standards has made the language more permeable to influence from English than it might otherwise have been. (3) This permeability, combined with the prestige of English as a world language and its transmission through the official institutions of the societies concerned, has resulted in the evolution of varieties intermediate between the local variety of English and the prototypical variety of Creole. (4) The social stratification of these varieties is such that language use involves some fluidity of movement among the intermediate varieties. (5) The effect is to exaggerate the variation that one might normally expect in a coherent language variety and further inhibit the evolution and identification of a standard. The layering of varieties between local standard English and a creole is commonly described as a *post-creole (dialect) continuum.* Three main strata are recognized: the *basilect,* which refers to the prototypical creole variety, the *acrolect,* which refers to the variety most like the official standard version of English, and the *mesolect,* which refers to the set of intermediate varieties.

Features. Despite differences among varieties, Caribbean English Creoles share several defining characteristics: (1) Expressing tense, mood, and aspect mainly by pre-predicative particles: (Jamaican) *Im waak* He or she walked, He or she has walked, *Im a waak* He or she is walking, *Im bin waak* He or she walked, He or she had walked. (2) Marking noun plurals by postposed particles, not -*s*: (Jamaican, Guyanese) *di daag-dem* the dogs, (Trinidad) *di dog-an-dem* the dogs. (3) Using front-focusing structures to disambiguate or emphasize: (Trinidad) *Iz mi mʌdʌ tel mi du it* My mother (and not someone else) told me to do it; (Jamaican) *A tief im tief di gʋot* He stole the goat (he didn't buy it). (4) Reduplication in word-formation and for emphasis: (Jamaican) *poto-poto* slimy, muddy, *fenky-fenky* slight, puny, cowardly, fussy, *batta-batta* to beat repeatedly; (Guyanese) *tukka-tukka* a kind of plantain. (5) Differentiation of singular and plural second person, like archaic *thou* and *you*: (Barbados) *yu* versus *wʌnʌ*; (Trinidad) *yu* versus *all-yu*. (6) Possession shown by placing unmarked nouns side by side: (Trinidad) *mi fada kuzn hows* my father's cousin's house.

Social status and use. Creole is the preferred variety for informal and private communication, but yields to English in formal public settings. English, because of its strong association with educational systems and the official institutions of government and society, generally has higher prestige than Creole, but the latter enjoys increasing status as a sense of nationalism increases in various recently independent countries. The use of Creole for literature is increasingly common; it is the normal medium for popular drama and the lyrics of songs composed in local styles. The use of Creole in radio and television is most developed in Jamaica.

See ATLANTIC CREOLES, BRATHWAITE, CARIBBEAN, CARIBBEAN ENGLISH, CARIBBEAN LITERATURE IN ENGLISH, CREOLE, NATION LANGUAGE, NEW ORLEANS, RASTA TALK, WEST AFRICAN PIDGIN ENGLISH. [AMERICAS, VARIETY].   L.D.C.

CARIBBEAN EXAMINATIONS COUNCIL, short form *CXC*. See CARIBBEAN ENGLISH, EXAMINING IN ENGLISH.

CARIBBEANISM [Late 20c]. A usage or custom special to, or common in, the Caribbean and any of the languages of the region, such as *sweetmouth* for 'flatterer' in general Caribbean English and *poto-poto* for 'slimy' or 'muddy' in Jamaican Creole. See CARIBBEAN ENGLISH, CARIBBEAN ENGLISH CREOLE, -ISM. [STYLE, VARIETY, WORD].   T.MCA.

CARIBBEAN LANGUAGES. Many languages are or have been spoken in the islands and coast-lands of the Caribbean. They include European languages introduced from the late 15c, Creoles, and Amerindian languages. The European languages are *Danish* (the Virgin Islands, never widely used and no longer present), *Dutch* (The Netherlands Antilles), *English* (in many places, such as Barbados and Jamaica), *French* (in many places, such as Haiti and Martinique), and *Spanish* (in many places, such as Cuba and Puerto Rico). The Creoles have substrates from West African languages and are lexically based (in the main) on the European languages, and include *Papiamentu* (a Portuguese-based creole with Spanish and Dutch elements, in The Netherlands Antilles), *Jamaican English Creole* (or *Jamaican Creole English*), *Haitian Creole French* (or *Haitian French Creole*). Amerindian languages are spoken in the Caribbean regions of Central and South America, such as *Maya* in Belize and *Chibcha* in Nicaragua and Panama. In most Caribbean nations, there is a continuum from the standard varieties of the European languages to the most distinctive varieties of the local creole vernacular. Such creoles are increasingly regarded as languages in their own right and are often referred to collectively as *Creole*. See AMERICAN LANGUAGES, CARIBBEAN, CREOLE. [AMERICAS, LANGUAGE].   L.D.C.

CARIBBEAN LITERATURE IN ENGLISH.

The earliest example of writing in English about the Caribbean is Sir Walter Raleigh's *The Discovery of the Empyre of Guiana* (1596), an account of his search for El Dorado. Similar narratives on Caribbean subjects continued to be written, mainly by British authors, until the end of the 19c, when Creole (native-born) writers began to appear. These include poets such as Tom Redcam and J. E. Clare McFarlane of Jamaica, and Egbert Martin of Guyana reproduced the verse forms of Algernon Swinburne and Alfred Tennyson, as well as English Romantic poets of an earlier generation. Well into the mid-20c, the novels of H. G. DeLisser of Jamaica conveyed a mixture of adventure, terror, and romance that generally reflected standard Gothic elements in the fiction of British Victorian novelists. However, local manners, settings, idioms of speech, and modes of expression gradually asserted a distinctive Caribbean flavour that, by the 1950s, became evident in the work of such writers as George Lamming, Samuel Selvon, Roger Mais, and V. S. Naipaul, many of whom migrated to Britain to find an outlet for their writing.

Currently, there is a flourishing literature in most territories of the English-speaking Caribbean, not only in the larger islands such as Jamaica, Trinidad, and Barbados, but also in mainland territories like Belize and Guyana. The bulk of this literature is prose fiction, but there are many poets, of whom the most distinguished are Derek Walcott and Edward Brathwaite. Walcott is also known for plays such as *Dream on Monkey Mountain* (1967), *The Joker of Seville* (1974), and *O Babylon* (1976). Whether in fiction or non-fiction, poetry or drama, Caribbean writers in English are concerned with essential subjects: colonialism, cultural transplantation, racial and cultural diversity, and the struggle for national identity. Recurring themes are displacement and loss, rootlessness and alienation, exploitation and resistance. While most of their writing is in standard English, many writers employ Creole and Caribbean varieties of English, especially in dialogue and poetry. Creole dialogue has appeared in novels by DeLisser, Claude McKay, and such 1930s novelists as C. L. R. James, Alfred Mendes, and Ralph de Boissière. In 1949, Vic Reid wrote an entire novel, *New Day*, in a version of Jamaican English, and Samuel Selvon's novel *The Lonely Londoners* (1953) is narrated in a language based on Caribbean patterns. Caribbean literature in English is produced as much by Caribbean immigrants abroad as by people living in the region itself. In this sense, it has come full circle, being produced no longer by European visitors and settlers, but, at least in part, by Caribbean people or their children who have settled in Britain and North America. See BRATHWAITE, CARIBBEAN ENGLISH, COMMONWEALTH LITERATURE, ENGLISH LITERATURE, NAIPAUL, WALCOTT. [AMERICAS, LITERATURE, VARIETY].   F.M.B.

CARIBBEAN PRESS. There are newspapers in all the countries of the English-speaking Caribbean, but daily papers only in the larger countries, with three in the Bahamas, two in Barbados, three in Jamaica, four in Trinidad and Tobago, and one in Guyana. In the other countries of the region, newspaper publication is generally weekly and occasionally more frequent. In Trinidad and Tobago, there is a thriving popular tabloid press with publications ranging from three times a week to weekly. The proportion of trained journalists in the region is low and the quality of the press is variable. The daily press, except in Guyana, where it is state-owned, is held by private companies significantly linked with the business classes of the countries concerned. The less frequent publications are varied in ownership and include papers that are official organs of political groups and trade unions. There is some use of Creole in cartoons, political commentary, and fiction published by feature writers. The best-known and oldest papers are the *Daily Gleaner* of Jamaica, the *Trinidad Guardian*, the *Trinidad Express*, and the *Barbados Advocate*. See CARIBBEAN, NEWSPAPER, PRESS. [AMERICAS, MEDIA].   L.D.C.

CARICATURE [18c: through French from Italian *caricatura*, from *caricare* to load]. An exaggeration of physical appearance to create a ludicrous effect. Because such exaggeration can also be achieved verbally, the word has become a literary term: 'What Caricatura is in painting, Burlesque is in writing' (Fielding, *Joseph Andrews*, 1742). It appears in many genres, deriding individuals or groups. The fops of 17c Restoration comedy and the gossips in Sheridan's *The School for Scandal* (1777) caricature contemporary types. Shaw exaggerated the insularity of his pompous Englishmen, such as Broadbent in *John Bull's Other Island* (1904) and De Stogumber in *Saint Joan* (1923). In response to Smollett's complaints in *Travels through France and Italy* (1766), Sterne ridiculed him under a farcical but similar name: 'I popped upon Smelfungus again at Turin . . . and a sad tale of sorrowful adventures he had to tell' (*Sentimental Journey*, 1768). Some critics have objected that characters in Dickens and their ways of speaking are often too much like caricatures: ' "Under the impression," said Mr Micawber, "that your peregrinations in this metropolis have not as yet been extensive, and that you might have some difficulty in penetrating the arcana of the Modern Babylon in the direction of the City Road—in short . . . that you might lose yourself—I shall be happy to call this evening, and install you in knowledge of the nearest way" ' (*David Copperfield*, ch. 11). The librettos of W. S. Gilbert are in the same vein. He caricatured Oscar Wilde as 'A most intense young man, / A soulful-eyed young man, / An ultra-poetical, super-aesthetical, / Out-of-the-way young man!' See BURLESQUE, CARTOON, LAMPOON, PARODY. [LITERATURE, STYLE].   R.C.

CARLYLE, Thomas [1795-1881]. Scottish writer, editor, and social critic, born at Ecclefechan, Dumfriesshire, son of a stonemason, and educated at the U. of Edinburgh. He had intended to enter the ministry, but moved away from orthodox Christianity, becoming a teacher, then a writer. He moved to London in 1834, where he published *History of the French Revolution* (1837). His contrast between the 19c and an idealized Middle Ages influenced John Ruskin and William Morris. He came increasingly to look for the 'strong, just man' who could lead the country, and this drew him to edit the letters and speeches of Cromwell (1845) and write a life of Frederick the Great (1858-65). His prose is complex, often powerful and vivid, and at times difficult:

When, across the hundredfold poor scepticisms, trivialisms, and constitutional cobwebberies of Dryasdust, you catch any glimpse of a William the Conqueror, a Tancred of Hauteville or such like,—do you not discern veritably some rude outline of a true God-made King; whom not the Champion of England cased in tin, but all Nature and the Universe were calling to the throne? It is absolutely necessary that he get thither. Nature does not mean her poor Saxon children to perish, of obesity, stupor or other malady, as yet: a stern Ruler and Line of Rulers therefore is called in,—a stern but most beneficent *perpetual House-Surgeon* is by Nature herself called in. . . . Sweep away thy constitutional, sentimental, and other cobwebberies; look eye to eye, if thou still have any eye, in the face of this big burly William Bastard: thou wilt see a fellow of most flashing discernment, of most strong lion-heart (from *Past and Present*, 1843).

Carlyle's style was so distinctive as to acquire its own labels, *Carlylese* and *Carlylism*, associated with turgidity and the use of archaisms, Saxonisms, and Germanisms. His style, however, also exhibits the syntactic flexibility of English and its word-forming capacities. It helped to weaken the prestige of classical diction and open a new, experimental range for writers of prose. See index. [BIOGRAPHY, EUROPE, STYLE].   R.C.

CARROLL, Lewis [1832–98]. Pen name of *Charles Lutwidge Dodgson*. English mathematician and writer, born at Daresbury, Cheshire, the son of a clergyman, and educated at Rugby and Christ Church, Oxford, where he spent the rest of his life. He was a deacon in the Church of England, but did not become a clergyman. His most famous book, *Alice's Adventures in Wonderland* (1865), developed from a story he told one afternoon to the three daughters of the Greek scholar H. G. Liddell, Dean of Christ Church. Alice, named after one of them, continued her adventures in *Through the Looking-Glass* (1871). Carroll wrote other books for children, including a long poem 'The Hunting of the Snark' (1876). He published several mathematical works, but was not distinguished academically. He never married, and found pleasure in the company of little girls, with whom he lost his shyness. He was also an inventor of puzzles, games, ciphers, and mnemonics, and an amateur pioneer in photography. Carroll was a master of fantasy and his stories have their own logic. Young readers seem untroubled by such tensions and anxieties as forgetting one's name and calls for beheading offenders, while the adult reader enjoys the commentary on human absurdities and the manipulation of language. Carroll used the pun and coined neologisms, including what he called 'portmanteau words' like *chortle* (combining *chuckle* and *snort*). He played games with idioms, using such expressions as 'beating time'

(to music) in a literal sense. He reshaped such animals of fable or rhetoric as the *Gryphon*, *March Hare*, or *Cheshire Cat*, and invented such new ones as the *Bandersnatch* and the *Boojum*. As a parodist, he made nonsense poems out of well-known moral verses. His success as a children's author was aided by the illustrations of John Tenniel. Analysts of his works have made theological and psychoanalytical interpretations of his fantasies; students of language may find his genius more evident in Humpty-Dumpty's comment on people and words: 'The question is, which is to be master—that's all.' See index. [BIOGRAPHY, EUROPE, LITERATURE, STYLE].   R.C.

CARTOON [17c: from French *carton*, Italian *cartone* pasteboard, drawing paper, a drawing on such material, from *carta* paper, parchment]. Originally, and in the fine arts, a drawing on strong paper, usually a full-scale design to be executed in a fresco, an oil painting, a tapestry, a mosaic, or stained glass. For frescos and tapestries, the cartoons usually constitute a series of parts or frames, depicting a life (such as the frescos of St Francis at Assisi, probably by Giotto), or showing a series of events (as with the Bayeux Tapestry commemorating the Norman Conquest of England in 1066).

Graphic comedy. In 1841, a series of cartoons was prepared for paintings in the new Houses of Parliament in London. The magazine *Punch*, founded in the same year, took up the idea as follows: '*Punch* has the benevolence to announce that in an early number of his ensuing volume he will astonish the Parliamentary Committee by the publication of several exquisite designs, to be called Punch's Cartoons!' (24 June 1843). This development extended the term to mean a finished full-page illustration in a periodical, usually humorous and relating to current events, with the result that the term now commonly refers to drawings of this kind, of any size, and a *cartoonist* is the artist who provides them. Although cartoons need not use words, they are usually accompanied by a statement, often as a caption and sometimes as dialogue within the cartoon's frame or in the caption. Quotations are also common. Cartoons often mock and caricature prominent public figures and comment wryly on events and everyday life. They have been described as 'the slang of graphic art' by J. Geipel (*The Cartoon: A Short History of Graphic Comedy and Satire*, 1972), and as 'drawn humour' by W. Hewison (*The Cartoon Connection*, 1977).

Comments on language. Cartoons often comment on language itself: (Picture of) prim secretary to disconcerted boss, 'Did you particularly *want* that infinitive split?' Characters may have distinctive styles: for example, in *English Today* 6 (Apr. 1986), a cartoon accompanied an article dealing with *US English*, a campaign that seeks to amend the constitution and make English the official language of the US. The picture shows two supporters, one blue-collar, with a can of beer, the other an academic. Says blue collar: 'We don't gotta accept no t'reats to da Murrican langwidge!' Adds the academic: 'Affirmative. At this point in time the nation has to meaningfully reconceptualize its relationship with our primary communicative mode.'

Strip cartoons. The 20c *strip cartoon* or *comic strip* is a sequence of drawings usually presented as five or six frames in a horizontal set. They usually depict a series of events: humorous activities, an adventure or mystery story, or the activities of one or more stock characters, often serialized in periodicals (in a section, page, or part of a page set aside for this purpose, and referred to casually in AmE as *the funnies*). Leading comic strips are widely syndicated: for example, the UK series *Andy Capp*, by Reg Smythe, appears in some 1,600 newspapers in 57 countries (1,000 in the US alone), and every day an estimated 200m readers follow the career of its chauvinistic working-class 'hero'. Publications devoted to stories in strip-cartoon form were known first as *comic cuts*, then *comic books*, then *comics*. Characters in such works communicate in *balloons*, bubble-like zones near a character's head. When someone speaks, lines link mouth and balloon; when someone thinks, smaller bubbles link head and text, and the bubble becomes cloud-like.

Animated cartoons. The 20c *animated cartoon* is a motion picture consisting of serial drawings in frames, each slightly different from predecessor and successor; when the film runs, the speed of the passing frames creates the appearance of movement, allowing the characters to perform in a lifelike way. Many such cartoons portray adapted animals or fantasy people, such as Walt Disney's *Donald Duck* and *Snow White and the Seven Dwarfs*. Although commonly used for entertainment, especially for children, animated cartoons may also serve satirical ends, as with the cartoon version of George Orwell's allegory *Animal Farm*. Leading cartoon characters are copyrighted and have become at least as widely known as those of major folk-tales and children's literature, as with Disney's *Mickey Mouse* and Charles M. Schulz's beagle *Snoopy*.

Educational cartoons. Publishers of textbooks and works of reference sometimes use cartoons: for example, Snoopy and the children in Schulz's cartoon *Peanuts* are featured in Random House's *The Charlie Brown Dictionary* (1973).

This work, based on Wendell W. Wright's *The Rainbow Dictionary*, defines 2,400 words with the help of over 580 of Schulz's pictures: the definition of *bat* (with cartoon) runs: 'Beside Charlie Brown is his *bat*. A baseball bat is used to hit the ball in a baseball game. Why do you think Charlie Brown looks sad? Maybe he couldn't hit the ball with his bat.' The publishers rely on their young readers already knowing that Charlie Brown is one of life's losers. See CAPTION, CARICATURE, COMIC, HUMO(U)R, ICON, ONOMATOPOEIA, NEW YORKER, PUNCH. [EDUCATION, MEDIA, REFERENCE, STYLE, TECHNOLOGY]. T.MCA.

CASE[1] [12c: from French *cas*, Latin *casus* fall, translating Greek *ptôsis*]. A term for a set of forms for a noun, pronoun, or adjective in an inflected language, the choice of form depending on syntactic function. In Latin, the noun form *dominus* (lord) is in the *nominative case*, used when the word is the subject of the sentence, whereas *dominum* is *accusative*, used when the word is the direct object. A set of cases constitutes a paradigm for the class to which a word belongs: *dominus* is a masculine noun of the second declension, whose paradigm consists of 12 forms for six cases (nominative, vocative, accusative, genitive, dative, and ablative, each with singular and plural forms) that were regarded in classical times as 'falling' away from an upright nominative.

Case in Old English. Anglo-Saxon or Old English had the following cases for nouns, pronouns, and adjectives: *nominative, accusative, genitive, dative*, and to a limited extent *instrumental*. The equivalent of modern *stone* was masculine *stān* nominative and accusative cases (singular), *stānas* nominative and accusative (plural), *stānes* genitive singular (of a stone), *stāna* genitive plural (of stones), *stāne* dative singular (for a stone), *stānum* dative plural (for stones). See OLD ENGLISH[1].

Case in Modern English. The contemporary language has cases for nouns and pronouns, mainly the *common case* (*Tom, anybody*) and the *genitive* or *possessive case* (*Tom's, anybody's*). Potentially, countable nouns have four case forms: two singular (*child, child's*), two plural (*children, children's*). In regular nouns, these manifest themselves only in writing, through the apostrophe (*girl, girl's, girls, girls'*), since in speech three of the forms are identical. The genitive case is used in two contexts: dependently, before a noun (*This is Tom's/his bat*), and independently (*This bat is Tom's/his*). Most personal pronouns have different forms for the dependent and independent genitive: *This is your bat* and *This bat is* *yours.* The genitive case forms of personal pronouns are often called possessive pronouns. A few pronouns have three cases: subjective or nominative, objective or accusative, and genitive or possessive (see table).

Subjective	Objective	Genitive (1)	Genitive (2)
I	*me*	*my*	*mine*
we	*us*	*our*	*ours*
he	*him*	*his*	*his*
she	*her*	*her*	*hers*
they	*them*	*their*	*theirs*
who	*whom*	*whose*	—
whoever	*whomever*	—	—

The subjective is used when the pronoun is the subject of a finite verb: *I* in *I like strawberries.* The objective is used when the pronoun is the direct object (*me* in *The noise does not disturb me*), the indirect object (*me* in *She gave me her telephone number*), or the complement of a preposition (*The letters are for me*). When the pronoun is the subject complement, there is a divided usage: the objective is generally used (*It's only me*), but the subjective case occurs in formal style (*It is I who have the honour of introducing our guest speaker*). Except in formal style, *who* and *whoever* are generally used in place of *whom* and *whomever.* Compare the formal *Whom did you nominate?* and *For whom are you waiting?* with the more usual *Who did you nominate?* and *Who are you waiting for?* See ABLATIVE, ACCUSATIVE, APOSTROPHE[1], CASE GRAMMAR, CHOMSKY, DATIVE, GENITIVE, INSTRUMENTAL, LOCATIVE, NOMINATIVE, NOUN, OBJECT, SUBJECT, VOCATIVE. [GRAMMAR].   S.G.

CASE[2] [13c: from Middle English *cas*, from Norman French *cas(s)e*, Old French *chasse*, from Latin *capsa* a cylinder for holding scrolls]. (1) A term in bookbinding for a cover to be fitted to a book. However, a *cased* or *boxed edition* of a book is a copy fitted into a cardboard case for protection and display or as one of a set. (2) A printer's term for a tray of wood, metal, or plastic that has compartments for holding types. Such trays are usually sets of two: an *upper case* mainly for capital letters; a *lower case* mainly for small letters. These terms also refer to the letters themselves: capitals as *upper-case* (*letters*); small letters as *lower-case* (*letters*). See CAPITAL. [TECHNOLOGY].   T.MCA.

CASE GRAMMAR. A theory developed within generative grammar by the US linguist Charles Fillmore, *c.*1970. The theory was intended to capture the constant deep semantic relations found, especially for noun phrases, in different syntactic functions and employs the traditional term *case* to name such relations. In the sentences *I split the log with my axe, My axe split the log, The log split,* and *The log was split by my axe,* the semantic role of *the log* is patient (affected by the action) and that of *my axe* is instrument (used to perform the action). Influenced by formal logic, case grammar characterized the underlying structure of a sentence as having two parts: features such as tense, interrogation, and negation, which relate to the sentence as a whole; the verb and those arguments that accompany it, representing together the basic proposition denoted by the sentence. The arguments are expressed by noun phrases that have different semantic roles, such as *agent, patient, instrument.* These roles, termed *cases,* can be represented in constructions in various syntactic functions (as shown above). Although the insights of case grammar have been appreciated by linguists, the theory has not been further developed because of difficulties in determining and defining the set of cases, and because of problems in formalizing the model in a comprehensive description. References continue to be made to argument-like cases in grammars, but variations appear in the number and names of cases. Among the cases commonly referred to are: *agent, patient* (also *objective, affected*), *recipient, instrument, experiencer, source, goal, location/locative, path.* The term *case* derives from its use in inflectional languages for the variant forms of a word that relate to syntactic functions: such inflectional forms as nominative, accusative, and genitive in Latin. See ARGUMENT, CASE[1]. [GRAMMAR].   S.G.

CASSIDY, Frederic G(omes) [b.1907]. American linguist and lexicographer, born in Kingston, Jamaica, and educated at Oberlin College, U. of Michigan (Ph.D., 1938). An editor on the *Early Modern English Dictionary* (1931-7) and for briefer periods on the *Middle English Dictionary* and the *Linguistic Atlas of the Great Lakes.* This editorial work and the examples of Charles C. Fries and Albert H. Marckwardt helped shape his subsequent career. Appointed to the U. of Wisconsin (1939), he retired as Professor Emeritus (1978), but remains there as Editor-in-Chief of the *Dictionary of American Regional English* (*DARE*). Having codified American field practice in *A Method of Collecting Dialect* (1953), he turned his attention to dialect geography and language history. His *Jamaica Talk* (1961) provided an account of the English of his native land, and with Robert B. LePage he edited the *Dictionary of Jamaican English* (1967, revised 1980), a work on historical principles that incorporates evidence from spoken usage. In 1965, he secured financial support for the nationwide investigation that accumulated usages gathered by trained fieldworkers from 1,002 US communities. The findings, augmented with documentary examples, have begun to appear as *DARE* (1985-). See index. [AMERICAS, BIOGRAPHY, REFERENCE]. R.W.B.

CATACHRESIS [16c: through Latin from Greek *katákhrēsis* misuse. Stress: 'ka-ta-KREE-sis']. A traditional term for the mistaken use of one word for another, as in *Royal Anglican Regiment* for *Royal Anglian Regiment*. An actual or assumed mistake of this kind may cause confusion and resentment, and lead to controversy, as with the use of *disinterested* where *uninterested* might be more appropriate. Occasionally, catachresis can lead to the supplanting of one word by another: for example, *humble* for *umble* in the phrase *humble pie*. Such a pie was originally made from *umbles* (the innards of a deer) and was so recognized until the 19c. The *OED* records *humble pie* from 1648, and the figurative usage *eating humble pie* from 1830. In the 20c, only the figurative use occurs and there is therefore no confusion or resentment. By and large, catachresis arises when words are similar in form, as with *militate* and *mitigate* ('His book was always likely to be serious, which might have mitigated against a large sale,' *Sunday Times*, 17 Dec. 1989), or have a converse relationship, as with *learn* and *teach*, *imply* and *infer*, in which case one word may take over both senses (*Learn Yourself Scouse*: book title; *Are you inferring I don't know what I am doing?*). Confusion over such words can persist for centuries and is a popular topic in usage books and letters to editors. The term is neutral in philology but often pejorative in general use. See CONFUSIBLE, HOWLER, MALAPROPISM, MISTAKE, SEMANTIC CHANGE. [HISTORY, LANGUAGE, STYLE, USAGE]. T.MCA.

CATALECTIC. See TROCHEE.

CATALOGUE, also AmE **catalog** [15c: through French from Latin *catalogus*, Greek *katálogos* a counting up, register]. (1) A list or record, especially in the form of a book, leaflet, file, or sheaf of papers: *a sales catalogue*; *a mail-order catalog*. (2) Also *bibliographic catalog(ue)*. A list of the contents of a library or libraries, arranged according to various systems: for example, in the US, a *union catalog* (also *repertory catalog*), that contains bibliographic records indicating locations of materials in more than one library or in parts of libraries. Currently, British and American published books are registered in thematically ordered systems: in the UK, according to *British Library Cataloguing in Publications Data*; in the US, according to the *Library of Congress Cataloging in Publications Data*. Excerpted entries from both systems commonly

appear with the printing history on the copyright page in most relevant books. The French term *catalogue raisonné* refers to a (usually thematic) catalogue of books, paintings, etc., that has notes or commentary on the items listed. (3) Any list-like statement: *a catalogue of woes*. See BIBLIOGRAPHY, BRITISH LIBRARY, LIBRARY, LIBRARY OF CONGRESS, LIST, THEMATIC ORDER, TITLE, TITLE PAGE. [MEDIA, REFERENCE]. T.MCA.

CATAPHORA [20c: from Greek *kataphorá* a carrying forward, bringing down. Stress: 'ka-TA-fo-ra'. The adjective *cataphoric* dates from the 19c]. A forward reference in a text: the pronoun *she* is cataphoric in 'If *she* wants to, Nora can be charming.' Here, *she* substitutes for its antecedent *Nora*. The sentence exhibits cataphoric ellipsis, since *she wants to* is understood as *she wants to be charming*. Cataphora is less common than *anaphora*, in which the reference is backwards to a preceding part of the text. In broad terms, anaphora subsumes cataphora. Compare ANAPHORA. [GRAMMAR]. S.G.

CATASTROPHE. See DENOUEMENT, TRAGEDY.

CATCHPHRASE [1840s: a blend of *catchword* and *phrase*]. Also **catch phrase, catch-phrase**. A phrase that 'catches' one's attention, especially if often repeated and used as a slogan, as with 'Read my lips, no new taxes' (George Bush in his campaign for the US presidency, 1988). Some catchphrases are fashionable and ephemeral, others persist for years and may become idioms, such as *Follow that*, meaning 'Beat that' (dating from the 1950s), and *For my next trick* (followed by a pause, especially said by someone who has just botched something: dating from the 1930s patter of stage magicians). Advertisers and publicists try to create catchphrases, such as *Coke is it* and *the real thing* (advertising Coca-Cola). Sometimes they deliberately use special orthography, as in the British *Drinka pinta milka day* (advertising milk) and *Wotalotigot* (advertising the sweets called Smarties). See AMERICAN ENGLISH (THE STORY OF OK), CATCHWORD, DICTIONARY OF CATCH PHRASES, SLOGAN, TIMESPEAK. [MEDIA, STYLE]. T.MCA.

CATCHWORD [17c: a word that catches the attention]. (1) A memorable word or phrase, repeated by many people. (2) Also *headword*, *guideword, flagword, running head*. A word printed at the top of the page of a work of reference to indicate the first or last entry or article on a page; part of a series of such words intended to help users find what they want. (3) In printing, especially formerly, a device to help a binder assemble *signatures* (sets of pages) by inserting at the foot of each page the first word of the next. (4) Also *keyword*. In library science, a memorable or important term in the title, text, or abstract of an item being indexed and that is therefore used in the index entry. See CATCH-PHRASE, HEADWORD, KEYWORD, RUNNING HEAD, SIGNATURE. [MEDIA, STYLE, TECHNOLOGY].   T.MCA.

CATENATIVE [17c: from Latin *catena* a chain]. Arranged in a chain or series. See VERB. [GRAMMAR].   T.MCA.

CATHARSIS [18c: through Latin from Greek *kátharsis* purging, purifying]. (1) In literary theory, the cleansing or release of emotion through certain kinds of art. Tragic drama has traditionally been regarded as cathartic. (2) In psychiatry, a therapy that encourages the release of pent-up emotions, so as to achieve a temporary or permanent alleviation of nervous symptoms. See LITERARY CRITICISM, LITERATURE, POETICS, TRAGEDY. [LITERATURE].   T.MCA.

CAUSATIVE VERB. A verb that denotes causing something to happen. Such verbs are often formed from adjectives or nouns by means of causative suffixes: *harden* (to cause to become hard; to make hard), *purify* (to cause to become pure; to make pure), *harmonize* (to cause or create harmony; to make harmonious). Some linguists use the term to describe a variety of verbs where there is an underlying meaning of causation: *kill* (cause to die); *put, bring, take, send* (cause to move somewhere else); *burn*, as in *Alfred burned/burnt the cakes* (cause to burn). The term is also applied to the verbs *let, make, have*, and *get*. The first three can be followed by an object plus a bare infinitive, but *get* needs a *to*-infinitive: *You should let/make/have the children tidy their own rooms; get them to tidy things up. Have* and *get* can be followed by an object and a participle: *We soon had the car going again; we got it repaired.* These patterns, however, may also have a non-causative meaning: *I had my wallet stolen; You'll get people pestering you.* [GRAMMAR].   S.C., T.MCA.

CAWDREY, Robert. English schoolmaster (16–17c), from Oakham in Rutland, compiler of *The Table Alphabeticall* (1604), the first English dictionary, which briefly defined 2,560 'hard vsuall English wordes . . . gathered for the benefit & helpe of Ladies, Gentlewomen, or any other vnskilfull persons'. There were four editions to 1617. See index. [BIOGRAPHY, EUROPE, HISTORY, REFERENCE].   N.E.O.

CAXTON, William [*c*.1420–*c*.1491]. English printer, editor, and translator, who introduced printing to England in 1476, and published the first printed editions of Chaucer, Lydgate, Gower, and Malory. Nothing is known directly of his schooling; his father may have been a merchant, for by 1438 he was apprenticed to a leading member of the Mercers' Company. He was in Bruges in the Low Countries in 1450, where he became a leader of the English community and protégé of Margaret, Duchess of Burgundy. At her suggestion, he completed his first translation (from French), *The Recuyell of the Historyes of Troye* (1471). Wearied by copying, he went to Cologne to learn the art of printing introduced at Mainz *c*.1450, and the *Recuyell*, the first book printed in English, was published in 1476 at his press in Bruges.

Caxton set up the first printing house in England near the court and Westminster Abbey, just outside London. He published about 100 works, mostly in English and rarely in fashionable French or revered Latin. His first dated book was *Dictes and Sayenges of the Phylosophers* (1477). His patrons included kings, nobles, and wealthy merchants, who sometimes commissioned books, but the religious works which he published were probably the most widely read. Many of his publications were his own translations, but many were by English authors, such as Chaucer's *Canterbury Tales* (?1478) and Malory's *Morte Darthur* (1485). He sometimes set out his views on language and style in prologues and epilogues added to his publications. Best-known is the prologue to his translation of the French *Eneydos* (1490), where he confronted the difficult choice among late 15c styles: native 'olde and homely termes', courtly 'fayr & straunge termes', and 'comyn termes that be dayli vsed'. He pondered the variation of English in time ('our langage now vsed varyeth ferre from that which was vsed and spoken whan I was borne') and space ('that comyn englysshe that is spoken in one shyre varyeth from a nother'), weighty considerations to the publisher who, unlike a scribe who supplies a unique copy for his patron, sold his books nationwide.

For Caxton, Chaucer 'for his ornate wrytyng in our tongue may wel have the name of a laureate poete. For to fore that he by hys labour enbelysshyd, ornated and made faire our Englisshe, in thys royame was had rude speche & incongrue, as yet it appiereth by olde bookes whyche at thys day ought not to have place ne be compared emong to hys beauteuous volumes and aournate writynges.' Such stylistic concerns influenced Caxton's practice as an editor-publisher: he altered the text of 'beauteuous' Chaucer little, producing a second edition when his first proved to rest on an untrustworthy manuscript; but he 'enbelysshyd' passages in Malory that showed the influence of their 'olde and homely' original. Though his introduction of printing was epochal for English language and literature, his own style, even with regard to choice of words, was variable: Germanic when he had a Dutch source, Romance when it was Latin or French. He was ramshackle when unguided by a source, ad-libbing his spelling (*wrytyng/writynge, ornate/aournate*) and doubling and tripling his terms (*vsed and spoken, enbelysshyd, ornated and made faire*). Works on Caxton include: N. F. Blake, *Caxton and his World* (London: Deutsch, 1969) and Frieda E. Penninger, *William Caxton* (Boston: Twayne, 1979). See index. [BIOGRAPHY, EUROPE, HISTORY, MEDIA]. W.F.B.

CAYMAN ISLANDS. A British Caribbean dependency, consisting of the islands of Grand Cayman, Cayman Brac, and Little Cayman. Capital: Georgetown. Currency: the dollar. Economy: finance, tourism. Population: 16,677 (1979). Ethnicity: African and mixed. Languages: English (official), Creole, and Spanish. Visited by Columbus in 1503 but never settled by Spain; ceded to Britain in 1670. Colonized from Jamaica, and chose to remain a dependency when Jamaica became independent in 1962. See CARIBBEAN, ENGLISH. [AMERICAS, NAME, VARIETY]. T.MCA.

CBC, CBC ENGLISH. See CANADIAN BROADCASTING.

CBS. See AMERICAN BROADCASTING.

CEDILLA [16c: from Spanish *cedilla*, now *zedilla*, feminine diminutive of *zeda*, the letter *z*. Originally, a *z* was written after *c* to indicate that the sound it represented was 'soft'; later, the *z* was written underneath, where it developed the present shape]. A diacritic used in French under the letter *c* to indicate a soft pronunciation (/s/ not /k/): *Académie française, façade*. This use may or may not be carried over into English in a borrowed word: for example, both *façade* and *facade* occur. The cedilla is also used in Portuguese, Romanian, and Turkish. See DIACRITIC. [WRITING]. T.MCA., E.W.

CELT [17c: from French *Celte*, Latin *Celta*, from the Greek plurals *Kéltai, Keltoí*. The Greeks also used *Galátai* (in English *Galatians*), the Romans *Galli* (in English *Gauls*). Formerly pronounced mainly with soft *c*; currently mainly with hard *c*, as preferred by many Celts. The spelling *Kelt* is rare]. A member of an ethnic, linguistic, and cultural group once widespread from Anatolia to Ireland, now mainly in Brittany, Cornwall, Ireland, the Isle of Man, Scotland, and Wales, with a secondary presence in England, France, Portugal, and Spain, and, through emigration, in Argentina, Australia, Canada, New Zealand, and the US. Since classical times, the Celts have been widely regarded as a fair-skinned, fair- or red-haired, blue-eyed people, but many are dark-haired, with brown, green, or blue eyes and fair complexions. The latter are sometimes called *Black Celts*: compare BLACK IRISH. Celtic blood and red hair are traditionally associated with sharp and unpredictable tempers.

In classical times, the term referred to mainland Europeans, and when the word entered English it had only this sense, the English lexicographer Thomas Blount defining *Celt* as 'one born in Gaul' (*Glossographia*, 1656). The present-day use began in 18c French, in reference to Breton and Brittany, and was extended to cognate peoples as a single race and culture, a perception strongly tinged with 18-19c Romanticism. However, the peoples so identified share a variety of traditions and attributes that derive from and resemble those of the classical Celts: reputations for being proud, suspicious, flamboyant, and quarrelsome, for having vivid and often fantastic imaginations, for engaging in hyperbole and whimsy, and for a love of words, story, music, and liquor. A broad Celtic stereotype has come to underlie and reinforce the stereotypes of the Bretons, Cornish, Irish, Scots, and Welsh. In the history and mythology of Western Europe, the Celts are an ancient counterpoint to the Anglo-Saxons, often seen in contrast as stolid, reserved, deferential, and lacking in spontaneity.

See ANGLO-CELTIC, ANGLO-IRISH LITERATURE, ANGLO-SAXON, ANGLO-WELSH LITERATURE, AUSTRALIAN ENGLISH, BLACK IRISH, BLARNEY, BORROWING, BRETON, BRIT, BRITAIN, BRITANNIA, BRITISH, BRITISH LANGUAGES, BRITON, BRITTANY, BROGUE, BRYTHONIC, CANADIAN ENGLISH, CELTIC, CELTIC FRINGE, CELTICISM, CELTIC LANGUAGES, CELTIC TWILIGHT, CORNISH, CORNWALL, CUMBRIA, CUMBRIC, ENGLISH PLACE-NAMES, ERSE, EUROPEAN LANGUAGES, GAEL, GAELIC, GAELICISM, GAELTACHT, GIFT OF THE GAB, HIGHLAND ENGLISH, HISTORY OF ENGLISH, IRELAND, IRISH ENGLISH, IRISH GAELIC, IRISH PLACE-NAMES, ISLE OF MAN, LATIN[1], MCWORD, MANX, MARITIME PROVINCES/MARITIMES, NEWFOUNDLAND, PATRONYMIC, PICT, PICTISH, PLACE-NAME, PLAID CYMRU, SCOTLAND, SCOTS, SCOTTISH ENGLISH, SCOTTISH GAELIC, SCOTTISH LANGUAGES, SCOTTISH PLACE-NAMES, WALES, WELSH, WELSH LANGUAGE SERVICE, WELSH LANGUAGE SOCIETY, WELSH PLACE-NAMES, WILD IRISH. [EUROPE, HISTORY, NAME]. T.MCA.

CELTIC [17c: from French *celtique*, Latin *Celticus*. The spelling *Keltic* is rare]. (1) Of the Celts, their languages, and culture. (2) An inclusive term for the Celtic languages, particularly the

Common Celtic of ancient Europe and the British dialects of the first millennium AD. The term sometimes occurs in combinations: 'The Norman-Irish and the Celtic-Irish were drawn nearer to one another by common sorrows' (G. Bancroft, *History of the United States*, 1876). See CELT. [EUROPE, LANGUAGES, NAME].　　　T.MCA.

CELTIC FRINGE [1890s]. An informal and usually dismissive term for the Celtic regions of the British Isles, seen as peripheral and irrelevant; sometimes used by British journalists and politicians as a collective term for Northern Ireland, Scotland, and Wales, and perhaps the Isle of Man and Cornwall. Also formerly *the Celtic edge*. Compare CELTIC TWILIGHT. [EUROPE, NAME]　　　　　　　　　　　　　　　　　　　T.MCA.

CELTICISM [1850s]. The way of life or special interests of the Celts; a custom or usage, including a Celtic expression in a non-Celtic language, such as English *banshee*, from Irish Gaelic *bean sidhe* a fairy woman. See BORROWING, CELTIC LANGUAGES, -ISM. [EUROPE, STYLE, VARIETY, WORD].　　　　　　　　　　　　　　T.MCA.

CELTIC LANGUAGES, sometimes **Keltic languages**, and **Celtic**, **Keltic** when taken as a unity. A group of Indo-European languages, usually divided into: (1) *Continental Celtic*, a range of unwritten and now extinct languages spoken from around 500 BC to AD 500 from the Black Sea to Iberia, the best-known of which was *Gaulish*. (2) *Insular Celtic*, usually further divided into: *British* or *Brythonic* (from *Brython* a Briton) and *Irish* or *Goidelic* (from *Goidel* an Irishman: modern *Gael*). British and Gaulish were at one time a continuum of linked dialects. Philologists have referred to them as *P-Celtic* in contrast to Goidelic as *Q-Celtic*, on the basis of a sound shift of *q* to *p* which split an earlier tongue known as *Common Celtic*. The Gallo-British *p*-sound occurs in Old Welsh *map* son, *pen* head, and in Welsh *Prydain* Britain, while the Goidelic sound represented as *q* occurs in Gaelic *mac* son, *ceann* head, and in an ancient name for the Picts, *Cruithneach*, which may be a cousin of the name *British*. Currently, however, these terms are not generally used, Celticists arguing that a single sound shift, however important, should not serve as a label for such a complex division as that between British and Irish.

The long decline. In historical times, the British group has consisted of Welsh and Breton (which survive) and Cornish, Cumbric, and perhaps Pictish (which are extinct). Breton, though a language of France, has no links with Continental Celtic; it was taken to Brittany in the 5–6c by migrating Britons. The Irish group consists of

three languages or varieties of the same language: Irish and Scottish Gaelic and the extinct Manx Gaelic. During the first millennium AD, there were speakers of the British varieties in Ireland and speakers of the Irish varieties in Britain, including by the 6c the Scots: settlers from Ireland who in due course gave their name to their adopted country. Cornish and Manx are in limited use among local revivalists, but show no sign of significant resuscitation. The Celtic languages have been in decline for nearly two thousand years and most have vanished without obvious trace. The Continental languages survive only in place-names and Greek and Roman records. The Apostle Paul wrote in Greek to Anatolian Celts in his *Epistle to the Galatians*; by the time of this letter (1C AD), the Galatians appear to have largely given up their own language. The languages of Iberia and Gaul were replaced in the early Middle Ages by Romance languages and British gave way to English from the 5c onwards. In medieval Ireland, Scotland, and Wales, the indigenous languages were not at risk from Norse, Norman French, or English, but from the 16c Welsh and Gaelic have been in retreat before English and Breton before French. The last natural speaker of Cornish died in 1777 and of Manx in 1974. Welsh is the most viable of the survivors, with some half a million speakers (around 20% of the Welsh population). Irish Gaelic has some 100,000 speakers and Scottish Gaelic some 80,000 speakers.

Reasons for decline. The decline of these languages is a complex and often highly emotive issue. Efforts to slow or reverse their decline raise economic, educational, political, historical, and ethnic questions that relate to at least nine factors: (1) *Disunity* among the Celts in the face of colonization, cultural domination and assimilation, and the pressure of governments often regarded as alien and regarding Celts as alien. (2) *Loss of linguistic status* as English and French gained in strength and prestige. (3) *Shortage of reading material*, in tandem with the imposition of educational systems mediated by English and French. (4) *Lack of adequate instruction and backup*, even where a language has had official support, as in the Republic of Ireland and Wales. (5) *Loss of the language in religious life*, as in Scotland, under the influence of the Society for the Propagation of the Gospel (in English, with long-term Presbyterian resistance to translations of the Bible into Gaelic). (6) *Immigration* into Celtic areas by speakers of English and French, often to hold important posts and with little or no interest in the local language. (7) *Emigration*, often under pressure, as in the Irish famines and the Highland Clearances. (8) *The impact of the media*, especially in the 20c, with most or all newspapers, radio, cinema, and television in English or French. (9) *A sense of increasing irrelevance*, coupled with a general disdain for or indifference to Celtic speech, and assumptions of social and linguistic inferiority in the dominant culture that many Celts have slowly come to accept.

The question of 'linguicide'. These factors have promoted what some defenders of the Celtic languages see as a kind of linguistic murder. Although there has never been an official campaign to wipe out a Celtic language, Celtic communities have for centuries been officially and educationally neglected and their languages and literatures marginalized, especially in drives for national uniformity. Even where good will has existed, the positive results have been minimal, with the possible exception of Welsh. Even the backing of the government of the Irish Republic since the 1920s has failed to stop the decline of Gaelic, which has a belated co-official status with English. Overall, relations between the dominant culture and the Celtic-speaking communities in Britain have seldom been good. Welsh and Gaelic maintain only precarious holds as the circle of English continues to widen. In the process of that widening, however, Celtic substrates have developed in varieties of BrE and IrE used alongside the original languages or in areas where they were once extensive.

Celtic and Old English. The influence of Celtic on Old English appears to have been slight: 'The small number of Celtic words which found their way into the English language in earlier times has always been a cause of surprise to philologists' (Bernard Groom, *A Short History of English Words*, 1934). This early impermeability of English can be accounted for in at least three ways: (1) *A familiar environment*. The old and new environments of the Anglo-Saxons were much the same and therefore the vocabulary they brought from mainland Europe served them well in Britain. Unlike the British in Australia a thousand years later, they had no need to adopt local words for novel flora, fauna, and experiences: for almost everything they encountered they already had serviceable words. (2) *Little or no pidginization*. There appear to have been no contact languages or pidgins of Celtic and Anglo-Saxon through which infiltration could occur, as happened later with Norse and with Norman French. Any pidginization in Western Europe at the time appears to have been between popular Latin and local languages, not among local languages. (3) *The attraction of Latin*. The major cultural and religious influence of the time was Latin, with an equal impact on Celtic and Germanic. Speakers of both went to Latin for cultural and religious loanwords. It is

no more surprising therefore that Celtic did not influence Old English than that both Celtic and Germanic religion collapsed in the face of Christianization.

Celtic in English. In the course of the centuries, Celtic influence on English has been cumulative in four forms:

(1) *Loanwords*. Gaulish provided Latin with a number of loans, such as *carrus* a wagon, *carpentum* a light carriage, and *lancia* a long spear, from which are descended the English words *car, carry, carriage, chariot, charioteer, carpenter, carpentry, lance*, and *lancer*. From Insular Celtic there has built up over the centuries a set of words drawn from the main languages and linked with landscape and monuments, such as *ben, cairn, corrie, crag, crannog, cromlech, dolmen, glen, loch, menhir, strath, tor*: for further loans, see BORROWING.

(2) *Literary themes, styles, and names*. After the Norman Conquest of England in the 11c, Breton and Welsh users of Latin, French, and English spread Celtic themes and stories in the courts and monasteries of Western Europe. A key element in this dissemination was the *Matter of Britain*, whose original French form, *Matière de Bretagne*, indicates the link with Brittany as well as Britain. Foremost in this material are the legends of Arthur and his knights in which characters have such Frenchified and Anglicized Celtic names as *Arthur, Gareth, Gawain, Guinevere, Lancelot, Merlin*, and *Morgan*. Intricate Celtic styles and themes became interwoven with Christian, classical, and Germanic styles and themes in both pseudo-histories of Britain and romances of chivalry and the Grail. Celtic creativity in English has continued ever since: for example, in the 18c in MacPherson's *Ossian*, in the 19c in Scott's poems and novels, and in the 20c in James Joyce's novels and Dylan Thomas's poetry.

(3) *Place and personal names*. The foremost legacy of the Celts is names. Continental Celtic has left its place-names throughout Europe, most of them altered by other languages and many with such distinctive English forms as *Danube, Rhine, Rhone, Seine*. Some have regional connotations, such as the *-ac* names of France, several of which have uses in English: *Armagnac, Aurignac, Cadillac, Cognac*. Insular Celtic has provided such names as *Belfast, Cardiff, Dublin, Glasgow, London, York* for cities, *Avon, Clyde, Dee, Don, Forth, Severn, Thames, Usk* for rivers, and *Argyll, Cornwall, Cumbria, Devon, Dyfed, Glamorgan, Kent, Lothian* for regions. Personal names of Celtic origin or association are widely used, often without an awareness of their provenance: first names such as *Alan, Donald, Duncan, Eileen, Fiona, Gavin,*

Ronald, Sheila; patronymic and ethnic surnames in *mac/mc* (*MacDonald, McDonald*) and *O* (*O'Donnell, O'Neill*, sometimes dropping the *O* as in *Sullivan*), and such others as *Cameron, Campbell, Colquhoun, Douglas, Evans, Griffiths, Jones, Morgan, Urquhart*. A Common Celtic word for 'water' underlies such river-related names as *Aix-en-Provence, Axminster, Caerleon-on-Usk, Exmouth, Uxbridge*. It also underlies BrE *whisky* and IrE and AmE *whiskey*. These are shortenings of *whiskybae* or *usquebaugh*, from Gaelic *uisge beatha* (water of life, a calque of Latin *aqua vitae*).

(4) *Celtic varieties of English*. In varieties of English used in Ireland, the Isle of Man, Scotland, and Wales, there has been considerable influence from the local languages, which have served not only as sources of loans but also as substrates for the shaping of these varieties. In the case of IrE, such influence travelled across the Atlantic from the 16c onward to provide a major element in the English of Newfoundland, England's (and in a sense Ireland's) oldest North American colony.

See BRETON, CELTICISM, CORNISH, CUMBRIC, ENGLISH, ERSE, EUROPEAN LANGUAGES, GAELIC, HIGHLAND ENGLISH, INDO-EUROPEAN LANGUAGES, IRISH ENGLISH, IRISH GAELIC, ISLE OF MAN (MANX GAELIC), LATIN[1], NEWFOUNDLAND ENGLISH, OLD ENGLISH[1], PICTISH, SCOTTISH GAELIC, WELSH, WELSH ENGLISH. [EUROPE, HISTORY, LANGUAGE, NAME, VARIETY].   T.MCA.

Durkacz, Victor E. 1983. *The Decline of the Celtic Languages*. Edinburgh: John Donald.
Gregor, D. B. 1980. *Celtic: A Comparative Study*. Cambridge: Oleander Press.
Laing, Lloyd. 1979. *Celtic Britain*. London: Routledge & Kegan Paul.
Price, Glanville. 1984. *The Languages of Britain*. London: Edward Arnold.
Trudgill, Peter (ed.). 1984. *Language in the British Isles*. Cambridge: University Press.

CELTIC TWILIGHT [1893: from the title of W. B. Yeats's *The Celtic Twilight*, stories and poems based on Irish folk-tales]. An often dismissive term for the art, atmosphere, mist, and mysticism of the Celtic regions of Western Europe. Compare CELTIC FRINGE. [EUROPE, NAME].   T.MCA.

CENSORSHIP [16c]. The act or system of controlling, examining, and (if necessary) suppressing publications, theatrical presentations, films, letters, news, and other forms of communication and entertainment.

Censoring ideas. Historically, censorship has been more concerned with the suppression of language as a vehicle of ideas than with language

per se. In the Middle Ages, the Church exercised widespread control over reading and teaching: the Council of Paris (1210) prohibited the teaching of Aristotle's works on natural philosophy, because of their materialist emphasis. Within a century of the invention of movable type (*c*.1450), censorship of the printed word had become universal throughout Europe. The grounds for such censorship have changed during the intervening centuries. Initially, they were primarily ecclesiastical and theological, deriving from a desire to eradicate heresy and from the power struggles of the Reformation. With the increasing secularization of society, later motivations have included the upholding of public morality, the suppression of rival or inconvenient viewpoints, military emergency, the preservation of official secrets, and limiting broadcasting of 'bad language' and racial insult.

In earlier times in the West, censorship was imposed summarily and pre-emptively (especially in the case of plays) whereas in more recent times overt pressure has been increasingly superseded by self-censorship or by arbitration through professional bodies such as the Press Council in Britain. In many parts of the world, however, direct summary censorship continues. This may take the form of government scrutiny and 'guided reporting' (in Pakistan under the military dictatorship) or direct censorship of all media by the declaration of a state of emergency (in South Africa from June 1986). In Communist countries, fundamental criticism of the political system is not permitted, but overt censorship is rarely resorted to, since politically reliable editors have invariably been chosen.

Censoring language. Few categories of censorship are strictly linguistic, although there has long been a concern for balancing delicacy of expression against truthful reporting. In the 14c, Geoffrey Chaucer justified his use of 'broad' language as a mimetic necessity:

> Who-so shal telle a tale after a man,
> He moot reherse, as ny as ever he can,
> Everich a word, if it be in his charge,
> Al speke he never so rudeliche and large;
> Or elles he moot telle his tale untrewe,
> Or feyne thing, or finde wordes newe.
> He may nat spare, al-thogh he were his brother;
> He moot as wel seye o word as another.
>   (*The Canterbury Tales*, Prologue, 731–40)
> [*moot reherse* must repeat, *ny* near, *everich* every, *al speke he* even if he speaks, *rudeliche* rudely, *or elles* otherwise, *feyne* invent]

The printer and publisher William Caxton preferred to take the self-censoring route of euphemism, avoiding coarse language, as when he used *buttocks* for *arse* in his edition of Thomas Malory's *Morte Darthur* (1485). In so doing, he initiated a rigorous convention concerning language conceived as 'fit to print'. Subsequent Elizabethan injunctions against profanity on the stage prompted many minced oaths, such as *od/odd* (God), as in *Odsbodikins* (God's little body), and such contractions as *zounds* (God's wounds) and *snails* (God's nails). This use of phonetic erosion or adaptation to avoid a taboo term, has become an important general censoring device, evident in: *blooming*, *ruddy* (bloody); *sherbet*, *shoot* (shit); *flaming*, *flipping*, *freaking*, *frigging*, *effing* (fucking). This process of self-censorship is so general and common that for many people it is virtually unconscious.

Censoring the Bible. Although the papal censorship of texts, formalized in the *Index librorum prohibitorum* (the Index of Prohibited Books), had existed for centuries, Henry VIII of England was the first European monarch to limit the freedom of the press by issuing a list of banned books (1529), which included Thomas More's *Utopia* and the writings of Giordano Bruno in Italy. He prohibited (1538) the importation of books printed abroad in the English language, especially the translations of the Bible by William Tyndale and Miles Coverdale (both published on the Continent). These subsequently became the bases for the Great Bible of 1539 and the King James Bible of 1611: see BIBLE.

Censoring the theatre. The most enduring form of control, that over stage plays, began in England in the reign of Henry VII (1487-1509). All plays had to be registered or licensed prior to performance, enabling potentially subversive matter to be excised. In a proclamation of 1559, Elizabeth prohibited dramatic presentation of 'either matters of religion or of the governance of the estate of the common weale': the deposition scene in Shakespeare's *Richard II* was therefore expurgated from the first and second quartos (1597 and 1598). The performance of two satirical plays, *The Isle of Dogs* (1597) and *Eastward Ho!* (1605), led to authors and actors, including Ben Jonson, being sent to jail. The Licensing Act of 1737, by which virtually absolute powers were invested in the office of the Lord Chamberlain via 'the Examiner of the Stage', derived directly from attacks by the novelist Henry Fielding on the politician Robert Walpole, at the Little Theatre in the Haymarket earlier that year. Powerful initiatives to limit censorship were made in 1832 and 1843, resulting in the directive that the Lord Chamberlain was forbidden to withhold his licence unless on the grounds of 'the preservation of good manners, decorum or of the public peace'. Petitions by dramatic authors of note, made in 1865 and 1907, resulted in greater flexibility, but the responsibilities of the Lord Chamberlain for theatrical censorship were abolished only in 1968.

Censorship and obscenity. Censorship of fiction in Britain has in recent times focused largely on the question of obscenity, technically *obscene libel* or 'matter tending to deprave or corrupt', usually taken to mean the explicit depiction of sex and the use of 'dirty' or taboo words. These were the principal grounds for the suppression of D. H. Lawrence's novels *The Rainbow* (1915) and *Lady Chatterley's Lover* (1928), as well as of James Joyce's *Ulysses* (1922). They became the main issue in the trial of the unexpurgated edition of *Lady Chatterley's Lover* (*Regina v. Penguin Books Ltd.*) in 1960. In this test case the publishers were acquitted.

See ABRIDG(E)MENT, BOWDLERIZE, BRITISH PUBLISHING, COX REPORT, FIELDING, FREEDOM OF THE PRESS, OBSCENITY. [MEDIA].   G.H.

CENTRAL AMERICA. The isthmus between the land masses of North and South America. The dominant language of the region is Spanish, and such Amerindian languages as Maya and Chibcha are spoken. English is learned as a second or foreign language in most Spanish-speaking countries, is common in Panama because of links with the US, and is widely used in Costa Rica. It is the official language of Belize, an ex-British dependency. Communities speaking Caribbean Creole English are found in Honduras, Belize, Costa Rica, and Nicaragua; the Creole is sometimes referred to as *Central American English*. See BAY ISLANDS, BELIZE, CARIBBEAN CREOLE ENGLISH, CARIBBEAN LANGUAGES, CONTINENT, CREOLE, MISKITO COAST CREOLE, PANAMA. [AMERICAS, NAME, VARIETY].   T.MCA.

CENTRAL INSTITUTE OF ENGLISH AND FOREIGN LANGUAGES, short forms *Central Institute*, *CIEFL*. An Indian teaching and research institution established in 1958 in Hyderabad as the *Central Institute of English*. Its activities were expanded in 1972, when it was renamed, and in 1973 it gained university status. Initial planning involved the Indian government, the British Council, and the Ford Foundation. The CIEFL's objectives are to improve English teaching in India, to provide for the study of the language and its literature, to train teachers, to organize research and advanced courses, to hold examinations, to grant awards, to prepare textbooks, and to publish journals and periodicals. Since 1961, it has published the journal *The CIEFL Bulletin*, a newsletter, and a monograph series. See INDIAN ENGLISH[1]. [ASIA, EDUCATION, MEDIA].   B.B.K.

CENTRICITY [1820s]. The condition of being centred on one thing: *egocentric* centred on oneself; *ethnocentric* focused on a particular ethnic group. If something is *exocentric*, its focus is external; if *endocentric*, internal. When the norms of a language or a variety are set by another community, they are exocentric or *exonormative*: for example, the English of England as a standard for New Zealand. If a country has an endocentric or *endonormative* standard, it does not look elsewhere for justification of that standard: for example, the English of the US. See ANGLOCENTRIC, BRITOCENTRIC, ETHNOCENTRIC, EUROCENTRIC. [STYLE].   T.MCA.

CENTURY DICTIONARY, The, short form *CD*. An encyclopedic dictionary of English considered by many to be the finest ever produced in the US. The plans and preparations for the 1st edition (1889-91, 6 volumes) were supervised by William Dwight Whitney, assisted by Benjamin E. Smith, especially after Whitney's illness in 1886. Smith supervised subsequent editions after Whitney's death in 1894, including the supplements: *The Century Cyclopedia of Names* (1894) and *The Century Atlas* (1897). The *CD* was published by the Century Company, a publishing house which reprinted and sold Charles Annandale's 1883 enlarged edition of John Ogilvie's *Imperial Dictionary* (1850, 4 volumes), a British work based on Noah Webster's *American Dictionary of the English Language* (1828). The reprint was a success and the company engaged Whitney to undertake a similar American work. His intention, however, was to construct a dictionary 'designed to be a practically complete record of the main body of English speech from the time of the mingling of the old French and Anglo-Saxon to the present day, with such of its off-shoots as possess historical, etymological, literary, scientific, or practical value' (preface). After the 1st edition, the dictionary underwent a series of partial revisions which culminated in the retitled editions of *The Century Dictionary and Cyclopedia*. The 1901 edition included 10 volumes (vol. 9, *Names*; vol. 10, *Atlas*) and contained over 530,000 entries. The *OED* was at an early stage of publication when the *CD* appeared, and its editors relied heavily on the *CD*, especially for its unprecedented scientific and technical coverage. The *OED* editors cite the *CD* 2,118 times, for example for *Brazilian pebble, Holy Ghost pear, mud-lighter*. Other dictionaries that have used the *CD* include *The American College Dictionary* (1947), *The World Book Dictionary* (1963), and *The Dictionary of American English* (1938-44). *The New Century Dictionary of the English Language* (1st edition, 1927, 2 volumes, Appleton-Century-Crofts) claims a relation to the *CD*; though a much smaller work, it contains new definitions and illustrative quotations. *The New Century Cyclopedia of Names*

(1954, 3 volumes, Appleton), edited by Clarence Barnhart *et al.*, is a revision of volume 11 of the 1911 edition of the *CD*. See DICTIONARY, WHITNEY. [AMERICAS, REFERENCE].   R.W.B.

CEYLON, CEYLONESE. See SRI LANKA.

CHAMBERS, W. & R. A Scottish publishing company founded in 1819 in Edinburgh by William and Robert Chambers, sons of a bankrupt draper from Peebles. After finding work in bookselling, the brothers acquired a hand-operated printing press, the first product of which was an edition of *The Songs of Robert Burns*. In 1832, they launched the weekly magazine *Chambers's Journal*, which within a few years had a circulation of over 80,000. In 1834, they began a series of broadsheets on science, mathematics, history, geography, and literature under the title *Chambers's Information for the People*, which sold over 2m copies, followed by a low-priced *Education Course* of more than 100 titles. The avowed aim of being 'publishers for the people' led to *Chambers's Encyclopaedia*, which first appeared in 520 weekly parts (1859-68) and became a multi-volume work whose editions spanned a century. The first Chambers dictionary was A. J. Cooley's *Dictionary of the English Language* (1861), followed by James Donald's *Chambers's Etymological Dictionary* (1867) and *Chambers's English Dictionary* (1872). In 1901, the latter became *Chambers's* (later *Chambers*) *Twentieth Century Dictionary*, successively edited by Thomas Davidson, William Geddie, John Dickie, Agnes M. Macdonald, and Elizabeth M. (Betty) Kirkpatrick. With the edition of 1988, the earlier name was revived as *Chambers English Dictionary*, collectively edited by Catherine Schwarz, George Davidson, Anne Seaton, and Virginia Tebbit. The *CED*, with 1,792 pages, has a wider general coverage than most late 20c single-volume dictionaries (claiming 190,000 references and 265,000 definitions) and is noted for defining words in etymologically related entries, in which derivatives and compounds are listed under their base words: for example, *central, centralist, centric, centricity, centre fold,* and *centre of buoyancy* under *centre*. Its coverage includes the distinctive usages of the Bible, Spenser, Shakespeare, Milton, Burns, Scott, Dickens, and Twain, as well as many exotic and arcane items. It is the reference dictionary for Scrabble® in the UK, and is widely used by crossword enthusiasts. Other works of reference include *Chambers Biographical Dictionary* (1897; latest edition 1974), *Chambers Science and Technology Dictionary* (1940; latest 1988), and *Chambers World Gaz-*

etteer (1895; latest 1988). In 1989, Chambers was acquired by the Groupe de la Cité, a French publishing conglomerate that includes the imprints Larousse, Nathan, and Bordas. See BRITISH NATIONAL CORPUS, DICTIONARY, LEARNER'S DICTIONARY, SCRABBLE. [EUROPE, MEDIA, REFERENCE]. T.MCA.

CHANCERY STANDARD [1963: coined by Michael L. Samuels (*English Studies* 44) and developed in 1977 by John H. Fisher (*Speculum* 52)]. Also **Chancery English**. Terms for the 15c written usage of the clerks of Chancery in London, who prepared the king's documents. Before the 1430s, official records were mainly in Latin and French, but after that date mainly in an English based on the Central Midland dialect, with such usages as *gaf* (gave) not Chaucer's East Midland *yaf*, *such* not *swich*, and *theyre* (their) not *hir*. Until the end of the 15c, Chancery and the Exchequer built a foundation of written English that was developed by Caxton when he set up his press in Westminster in 1476. Over the years, printers replaced some features of Chancery usage with London equivalents, such as third person *-s* instead of *-th* (*hopes*, not *hopeth*), and *are* instead of *be*. See CAXTON, STANDARD ENGLISH. [EUROPE, HISTORY, VARIETY]. T.MCA.

CHANNEL ISLANDS, The French *Les Îles Anglo-Normandes* (the Anglo-Norman Islands). A group of British islands in the English Channel, closer to France than to England. The principal islands are Guernsey, Jersey, Alderney, and Sark. They are not part of the UK, but are an independent territory, the remnant of the English Crown's French possessions and the only part of the Duchy of Normandy to remain after 1204. Queen Elizabeth II is the islands' *Duke*, not Duchess. The islands are divided into the *Bailiwicks* of Guernsey and Jersey, with their own legal system and legislative assemblies. In each, the *Bailiff*, appointed by the Crown, presides over a Royal Court and an assembly known as *the States*. The island languages are English (dialect and standard), and a variety of French related to the Norman French once used in England, now in limited use. In the 19c, Georges Métivier wrote verse in the Guernsey dialect of French, and the Jersey dialect has a collection of stories by Georges le Feuvre and a *Dictionnaire jersiais-français* (1966) by Franck le Maistre. French is extinct on Alderney. See ENGLISH, FRENCH, NORMAN FRENCH. [EUROPE, HISTORY, NAME, VARIETY]. T.MCA., J.M.G.

CHAPTER [12c: a syncopation of *chapiter*, from Old French *chapitre*, earlier *chapitle*, Latin *capitulum* little head (of a plant, etc.), section of a book: compare CAPITAL, CAPTION, HEADING].

(1) A major division of a book or treatise, almost always numbered and often with a title of its own; by extension, any important new development or event: *a new chapter in the history of Europe*. (2) A division of a book of the Bible: *Second Epistle to the Corinthians, Chapter 22, Verse 2*. See BOOK, EPISODE, PARAGRAPH, TEXT. [WRITING]. T.MCA.

CHARACTER [13c: through Latin from Greek *kharaktēr* (the mark of) an engraving tool, stamp. Stress: the 16-17c often 'ka-RAK-ter'; currently 'KA-rak-ter']. (1) Archaic: an impressed or engraved mark. (2) A graphic sign or symbol, including one that is magical, mysterious, secret, exotic, etc.: *Chinese characters*. (3) Especially formerly: script, handwriting, print, alphabetic system: *written in a rough character, a universal character*. (4) A person created by a novelist, dramatist, or scriptwriter, such as 'Scarlett O'Hara' in Margaret Mitchell's *Gone with the Wind*. (5) In computing, one of a set of letters, digits, or other symbols that can be read, stored, or written and used to denote data; a representation of such a symbol by means of a number of bits, holes in punched tape, etc., arranged according to a code and taken as a unit of storage. See CHARACTERNYM, CHARACTER SET, CHINA, COMPUTING, JAPAN, KOREA, LETTER[1], SIGN, SYMBOL. [LITERATURE, STYLE, TECHNOLOGY, WRITING]. T.MCA.

CHARACTERNYM [20c: a blend of *character* and *-onym*]. A term for the name of a character in fiction, such as *Sherlock Holmes*, the name of Sir Arthur Conan Doyle's fictional detective. See ONOMASTICS. [NAME]. J.A.

CHARACTER SET [Late 20c]. A finite set of numbers, letters, punctuation marks, special symbols, and other representations formed from patterns of computer bits. The most common set is ASCII (American Standard Code for Information Interchange: pronounced 'Askey'), introduced in 1963 and defining 128 7-bit patterns, including 96 printable and 32 non-printing characters. Others are EBCDIC (Extended Binary Coded Decimal Interchange Code: pronounced 'Eb-see-dick'), used by IBM, and ISO7 (International Standards Organization 7-bit Code). A character set should include all symbols needed in a computer's applications: for example, for British computers the symbol £ is essential, but it is not often found in US displays and printers. The most complex sets occur in East Asian computers: for example, the 256 possibilities in an 8-bit byte are inadequate for the characters of Chinese and 16-bit representations are used instead. See CHARACTER. [TECHNOLOGY]. M.L.

CHARADE [18c: from French *charade* entertainment, from Provençal *charrado* chatting]. A parlour game in which participants try to guess a word by discovering its syllables. It was originally a written or spoken game in which syllables had to be guessed from clues, such as the rhyme in Austen's *Emma* (1816):

> My first doth affliction denote,
> Which my second was born to endure;
> My third is a sure antidote
> That affliction to soften and cure.

This leads to the answer *woe-man* (woman). Later, the charade (often referred to in the plural as *charades*, but treated as singular) became an acted game in which syllables are represented in mime or play-acting, or included in spoken dialogue. Such a charade is described in ch. 51 of Thackeray's *Vanity Fair* (1847–8). See MIME, WORD GAME. [WORD].   T.A.

CHAUCER, Geoffrey [1343?–1400]. Poet of Middle English and one of the foremost figures in English literature. No record remains of the education that gave Chaucer lifelong familiarity with Latin and several vernacular languages and literatures. However, as the son of a well-off London vintner, he had educational and social advantages that must have helped form his views. He may have attended the Inner Temple; by 1357, he was in the household of Edward III's daughter-in-law; in 1360, the king paid Chaucer's ransom after his capture by the French; by 1367, he had become a member of the king's household, and later he undertook many royal commissions to France, Spain, and Italy, some of them secret. In 1374, the king appointed him controller of the custom on wool, sheepskins, and leather in the Port of London, the first of several increasingly important offices he held by royal appointment. From 1374 onwards, he also received various grants and annuities from the Crown. He was elected Member of Parliament for Kent in 1386.

Works. Chaucer's first important poem appears to have been the *Book of the Duchess*, a memorial to John of Gaunt's first wife, who died in 1368 (though the poem may be several years later). Other major works were *The House of Fame* (1378–80), *The Parliament of Fowls* (1380–2), *Troilus and Criseyde* (1382–86), and *The Canterbury Tales*, some of them written earlier but assembled with others written c.1388–1400. In addition to these, Chaucer produced a great many translations, including a fragment of the *Romance of the Rose* (a version of the French *Roman de la Rose*), and a translation of Boethius's *De Consolatione Philosophiae* (On the Consolation of Philosophy). As a result, a French contemporary saluted him as a 'good

translator', the earliest explicit literary response to him. Though his official duties left many records, in his lifetime only Thomas Usk mentioned Chaucer's 'manly speech' (1385), and John Gower his 'glad songs', remarks that do not account for his later reputation as the founder of literary English.

Chaucer's language. The East Midland dialect of late 14c English, as Chaucer's works record it, differed from Modern English in structure, vocabulary, and especially spelling and pronunciation:

> 'So faren we, if I shal seye the sothe.'
> 'Now,' quod oure Hoost, 'yit lat me talke to the;
> Why artow so discoloured of thy face?'
> 'Peter!' quod he, 'God yeve it harde grace,
> I am so used in the fyr to blowe. . . .'
>
> (*Canon's Yeoman's Prologue*)

Spelling poses the chief obstacles for a modern reader, for whom the second line would end 'yet let me talk to thee'. Aloud the passage is likely to be more difficult still. Because of the great vowel shift, which began c.1400, the second line included words that sounded like *noo* now, *may* me, *toe* to, and *they* thee, the third line words that sounded like *whee* why, *saw* so, and *fahce* face. Chaucer's English also pronounced almost all the consonants, including the *l* in *talke* and the *r* in *harde*. His *yeve* is akin to modern *give*, which however descends from a different variety of Middle English: see CHANCERY STANDARD. The quotation contains other clues to Chaucer's pronunciation: he must have said *sothe* like *SAWthuh*, so when it rhymes with *to the*, we have evidence that the second line had eleven syllables, stressing *Now*, *Hoost*, *lat*, the first syllable of *talke*, and *to*. The same evidence also shows that *the* in the second line was a form of *thee* with a spelling to reflect the unstressed pronunciation *thuh*. Modern personal pronouns also have unstressed forms, but conventional spelling does not represent the *y'see* or *have 'em sent* of more informal writing. The grammatical forms of Chaucer's English in these four lines are familiar, except for *the* thee, *artow* art thou, and *thy*, which are no longer part of English outside of special, usually religious, contexts. Chaucer had some verb endings that no longer remain, such as the *-en* in *faren we*. Nowadays, the subjunctive construction *God yeve it* would be *May God give it*, to indicate a wish for the action. Cast in modern spelling and grammatical forms, Chaucer's vocabulary is rarely strange. Here, only *fare* get along, *sothe* truth, and *quod* said, are obsolete, though all were current in Chaucer's time and continued to appear in much more recent works than his. *Discoloured* is familiar, but was probably not so to Chaucer's first readers: it came into English only in the decade when he wrote this passage, as did much of his poetic vocabulary.

Chaucer's style. In pronunciation, grammar, and vocabulary, Chaucer was largely at one with his time and place, but in his use of these resources he was entirely singular. It was for his style that later centuries most admired him: William Dunbar called him 'rose of rethoris all' (the rose of all rhetoricians) and 'the noble Chaucer, of makaris flour' (flower of poets), William Caxton praised his 'crafty and sugred eloquence', and Edmund Spenser deemed him 'the well of English undefiled'. Certainly his style varied, from the monosyllabism of the passage above to Criseyde's noble protest:

What, is this al the joye and al the feste?
Is this youre reed? Is this my blisful cas?
Is this the verray mede of youre byheeste?
Is al this paynted proces seyd—allas!—
Right for this fyn? O lady myn, Pallas!
(Troilus and Criseyde, Book 2)

Like the earlier passage, these lines purport to be direct quotation of spontaneous speech, but here the poetry is marked with rhetorical figures: a repeated rhetorical question ('Is this . . . ?'), the anaphora varied at last with 'Is *al* this . . . ?', sarcasm ('my blisful cas'), alliteration ('paynted proces'), apostrophe ('O lady myn'), and more, just within these few lines. Chaucer's age respected and studied the 'arts of language': such rhetorical poetry was praiseworthy and often poetically effective. So Chaucer drew not only on traditional rhetoric but on traditional views of language itself: 'Eke Plato seith, whoso kan hym rede, / The words moote ben cosyn to the dede'. Elsewhere, he conveyed his own observations of language, that it varied in time ('Ye knowe ek that in forme of speche is chaunge / Within a thousand yeer': *Troilus and Criseyde*, Book 2, cf. Horace, *Ars poetica*) and that it varied in space, for in *The Reeve's Tale* he used dialect to portray two students from the North of England, including features of their grammar, pronunciation, and vocabulary, such as *gas* for southern *goeth*. The evidence of his ear for language variety is consistent with everything else we know about Chaucer, whom John Dryden called 'the father of English poetry'. See index. [BIOGRAPHY, EUROPE, HISTORY, LITERATURE, STYLE]. W.F.B.

Burnley, J. David. 1984. *A Guide to Chaucer's Language*. University of Oklahoma Press.
Eliason, Norman. 1980. *The Language of Chaucer's Poetry*. Anglistica 17. Copenhagen: Rosenkilde.
Elliott, Ralph W. V. 1974. *Chaucer's English*. London: Deutsch.
Howard, Donald R. 1987. *Chaucer: His Life, His Works, His World*. New York: Dutton.
Kerkhof, Jelle. 1982. *Studies in the Language of Geoffrey Chaucer*, 2nd edition. Leiden: Brill.
Sandved, Arthur O. 1985. *Introduction to Chaucerian English*. Cambridge: Boydell & Brewer.

CHAUCERIAN ENGLISH. See CHAUCER, MIDDLE ENGLISH.

CHAUCER SOCIETY. See FURNIVALL, OXFORD ENGLISH DICTIONARY.

CHAUVINISM [1860s: from French *chauvinisme*, after the Napoleonic soldier Nicholas Chauvin, whose excessive patriotism drew ridicule from exasperated comrades. After Napoleon's fall, the term was applied to the nostalgia of old soldiers for the days of Empire]. (1) Exaggerated and belligerent patriotism: the French equivalent of British *jingoism*. (2) Excessive loyalty to, or belief in, a cause or condition that includes prejudice against those who do not or cannot share it: *cultural chauvinism, religious chauvinism, scientific chauvinism*. Since the 1960s, the phrase *male chauvinism* has been applied by feminists to an assumption among some (or all) men that their interests should always be protected at the expense of women. The phrase *male chauvinist pig* (short form *MCP*) has been widely used for a man who behaves (or is considered to behave) towards women in a dismissive and patronizing way. The feminist writer Kate Millett (*Sexual Politics*, 1971) has pointed to an occasional *female chauvinism*. The term can also be used of prejudice in language: 'To imagine that some inherent literary superiority guarantees in perpetuity the present primacy of English is an exercise in linguistic chauvinism' (Jim McClelland, 'Why English may lose out to Esperanto', *Sydney Morning Herald*, 16 Apr. 1990). Compare IMPERIALISM, COLONIAL. See -ISM, SEXISM. [LANGUAGE, NAME, STYLE]. T.MCA.

CHEE-CHEE ENGLISH, also **chi-chi** [From *chi*, an interjection expressing disapproval in several Indian languages, comparable to English *fie*]. Also **Chee-chee twang**. Pejorative names for the speech of Anglo-Indians and other Eurasians in the Indian subcontinent, for whom *Chee-chees* is a disparaging ethnic name. See ANGLO-INDIAN, INDO-ENGLISH, TWANG. [ASIA, VARIETY]. B.B.K.

CHIASMUS [19c: through Latin from Greek *khiasmós* crossing, as in the lines of the letter X (khi). Stress: 'kye-AZ-muss'] Also **chiasm**. In rhetoric, an inversion of word order that creates a counterbalancing effect in the second of two linked phrases: 'One must eat to live, not live to eat' (Cicero); 'This man I thought had been a Lord among wits; but, I find, he is only a wit among Lords' (Samuel Johnson, of Lord Chesterfield, 1754). See ANTITHESIS, INVERSION. [STYLE]. T.MCA.

CHICAGO MANUAL OF STYLE, The. See HOUSE STYLE.

CHICANO [Early 20c: a clipping of Spanish *mexicano* Mexican. Used with or without an initial capital]. A name for a person of Mexican heritage in the US Southwest, first used by US-born Hispanics to refer, sometimes pejoratively, to recent immigrants from Mexico, as opposed to longer-established, more Americanized Hispanics known to Mexicans, also sometimes pejoratively, as *Pochos* (locals). *Chicano* later included all Mexican Americans. It became popular in the 1960s/70s, during the US civil rights movement, as a label to emphasize ethnic pride and the identity of Hispanics in the Southwest: not Spanish, Mexican, or American, but a unique combination. To some, the term implies militancy or radicalism; they therefore prefer *Mexican-American* or the more generic *Hispanic/hispanic*, *Latino/latino*. See CHICANO ENGLISH, SPANISH. [AMERICAS, NAME].   J.AM.

CHICANO ENGLISH, also **Mexican-American English**. English as used by Chicanos or Mexican-Americans. The term covers both English learned as a second language by people of Mexican-American heritage and the native English of speakers of Mexican-American background, both bilinguals and those who no longer speak Spanish. Both lack definitive descriptions. Differences from other varieties are due to at least four factors operating over several generations: interference from Spanish, learning errors that have become established, contact with other dialects of English, and independent developments. It is difficult to distinguish between contemporary and historical interference of Spanish in a community that includes first-generation learners, bilinguals of varying competence, and near-monolingual English-speakers of Hispanic descent. Typical phonological features are: the vowel sound of 'sheep' for 'ship'; the use of *s* for *z*, the *s* of *present* pronounced like the *c* of *decent*; confusion over *ch* and *sh*, as in *chip* and *ship*, and 'shicken' for *chicken*; the devoicing of final *d*, as in *hit* for *hid*; stress and intonation changes, such as *anticipáte* for *anticipate*, with an extreme rising tone; and a tendency towards a rising sentence-final intonation for statements. There are many borrowings from Spanish, such as *quinceañera* a special party for a 15-year-old girl, *comadre* godmother, *compadre* godfather. Mass nouns are often used as count nouns (*vacations* in *Next week we have vacations*, *applause* in *Let's have an applause for the speaker*, and *until* is sometimes used as a negative: *Is X here?—Until 3:00* (that is, *not* until 3:00). See: Fernando Peñalosa, *Chicano Sociolinguistics* (Newbury House, 1980), Joyce Penfield & Jacob L. Ornstein-Galicia, *Chicano English: An Ethnic Contact Dialect* (John Benjamins, 1985). See CHICANO. Compare SPANGLISH, TEX-MEX. [AMERICAS, VARIETY].   J.AM.

CHILD LANGUAGE ACQUISITION [Later 20c]. A term in linguistics for the process in which a child, in the course of normal development, learns a first language (or often, two or more languages). There are several methods for studying the subject. One strategy is to record samples of child speech and to analyse the emerging patterns of language which these samples display. Another is to set up experimental situations in which children are asked to carry out various tasks involving speech production or comprehension. Analysis is also carried out of the input language used by adults when they talk to children (*motherese* or *caretaker speech*) and of the nature of the interaction between them. The investigation may involve single children studied over extended periods of time (*longitudinal studies*) or groups of varying sizes, compositions, and ages studied at a particular point in time (*cross-sectional studies*).

Child development. It is commonplace to talk of 'milestones' in relation to child development in general, but this metaphor does not work as precisely for the development of speech. Sounds, grammar, vocabulary, and social linguistic skills are emerging simultaneously but at different rates, and significant progress can be made on several fronts in a matter of days. There are also many individual differences in the order of acquisition of specific features of language which need to be taken into account. However, most children appear to follow a similar path as they acquire sounds and grammatical structures, and broad similarities have been observed in relation to types of vocabulary and conversational skills. The aim of child language research is to explain the basis of this common order of emergence, allowing for the complex kinds of individual variation which are readily apparent.

Theoretical approaches. Several approaches have been applied to child language data. Certain features of the data seem to be the result of the children imitating what they hear in adult speech (for example, some of the early attempts at sound patterns, and the acquisition of new words), but very little of grammatical structure is learned by simple imitation. This was early noticed by researchers, who pointed out that child coinages such as *mouses* for *mice* or *goned* for *gone* could not have been produced through a process of imitation (for adults do not say such things), but must represent the child's own application of abstract rules already acquired. Furthermore, direct correction and coaching have very little effect, showing the important role of the child's own efforts. Various ways of explaining this internal ability were proposed, most notably Chomsky's argument that children must be credited with an innate *language acquisition device*: a set of outline principles about the way language is structured and a procedure for discovering the remainder. Investigators such as Piaget argued for the importance of relating the emergence of children's language to their underlying intellectual or cognitive development. Others stressed the importance of analysing the nature of the input presented to them by adult speakers. It is now apparent that each of these factors has a role to play in guiding the course of acquisition, but the nature of their interdependence is far from clear.

Stages of development. At a descriptive level, considerable progress has been made, especially for English, in establishing the order of emergence of sounds, grammatical structures, and (to a lesser extent) vocabulary, and determining the psycholinguistic principles involved. The focus has been on the earliest years, including the prelinguistic period of the first year. Between birth and 12 months, several stages can be detected in a child's emerging sound-producing and perceptual abilities, beginning with a range of basic biological noises reflecting such states as hunger, pain, discomfort, and contentment (0-8 weeks), and proceeding to a stage of cooing and laughing (8-20 weeks), vocal play (20-30 weeks), babbling (25-50 weeks), and the first melodically shaped utterances (9-18 months). At around a year, first words appear, though these are not easily identified with the words of the adult lexicon, but tend to have idiosyncratic meanings and to be used as primitive sentences (*holophrases*). *Dada*, for example, said with appropriate intonation and gesture, might mean 'There's daddy' or 'Where's daddy?' or 'Pick me up, daddy'. Moreover, the word *dada* might refer at this stage not only to the male parent, but also to the female parent, or to other adults, or to certain animals, or even to objects. From 12 months, an expressive vocabulary is acquired which by 18 months is usually around 50 words in size. By that time, children understand far more words than they produce: estimates suggest three or four times as many. In the next six months, expressive vocabulary approaches 200 words, and in the third year rapidly moves into the thousands. Detailed studies of the growth in vocabulary size in older children are as yet unavailable, though several studies have been made of the processes which seem to affect children's lexical progress, such as *over-extension* of meaning, as when *dog* is used for all animals, and *under-extension*, as when *dog* is used for one kind of dog only.

Pronunciation and grammar. Most research time has been devoted to the emergence of pronunciation and grammar. Children do not learn all their sounds in an identical order, but seem to share certain general tendencies. Most English consonants are acquired between the ages of 2 and 4 years. Moreover, within this sequence, certain important trends have been established. For example, consonants are more likely to be first used correctly at the beginnings of words, with final consonants emerging later. Several processes of simplifying pronunciation have been identified in early speech, such as the avoidance of consonant clusters (*sky* pronounced without the *s*), the dropping of an unstressed syllable (*banana* pronounced as *nana*), or the replacement of fricative sounds such as [f] and [s] by plosive sounds such as [p] and [t]: for example, *shoe* as /tuː/ and *fish* as /pɪ/. During the second year, some children make great use of a process of reduplication, with the different syllables of a word being pronounced in the same way, as when (in one child) *sister* became [sisi] and *mouth* became [muːmuː]. Patterns of intonation also develop in the early years (such as the difference between stating and questioning, using the melody of the voice only), but some of the more subtle intonation patterns are still being learned as late as the teenage years, such as the difference between *I THOUGHT it would rain* (and it has) and *I thought it would RAIN* (but it hasn't).

Grammatical patterns in the early years are fairly well established for English. A stage of single-word sentences appears from just before 12 months of age until 18 months, such as *bye*, *gone*, *teddy*, and *mama*. At around 18 months, children begin to put two words together, to make simple 'telegrammatic' sentences such as *dada bye*, *want car*, and *mine lorry*. Sentences increase in complexity during the third year, with more advanced features of clause structure being introduced. Clauses add extra elements, stabilizing word order, and developing a clearer subject-verb-object structure; and the hierarchical structure of a sentence develops, with phrasal complexity emerging within clauses, and ridding the sentences of their telegrammatic appearance. *My daddy do kick that ball* is a typical sentence for a 2-year-old. Each of the elements (subject, verb, object) appears as more than one word (a phrase), so that the sentence now has two layers of structure. By age 3, there is still greater complexity, in the form of linked sequences of clauses, using such words as *and*, *but*, *cos* (for 'because'), and *then*.

Narratives, sometimes of great length, now make their appearance. As sentence control develops, so more attention is paid to the more subtle aspects of grammar, such as the learning of the irregular forms of nouns, verbs, pronouns, and other parts of speech. At 3, most children are making errors in the use of certain pronouns (such as *me not like that mouse*); by 4, most such errors have been eliminated. During the early school years there are still several aspects of English grammar to be acquired, such as the rarer irregular forms, more complex patterns of sentence connection (such as the use of *although*), and the use of multiple subordinate clauses. There is evidence of grammatical development right through the primary school years until, as the teenage years approach, all that is left is the learning of more subtle aspects of grammatical style and the building up of vocabulary.

Other skills. The task of language acquistion requires more than the learning of the structural skills of sounds, grammar, and vocabulary. Children must also learn to *use* these structures appropriately in everyday situations. They need to develop conversational skills, the rules of politeness (such as when to say *please* and *thank you*), the correct use of forms of address, and how to make requests in a direct or indirect manner ('I was wondering if you could . . .'). Older children need to be able to handle such 'manipulating' features of language as *well, you know*, and *actually*, to learn to decode and use more subtle interactional features (such as sarcasm), and to cope with such stylistic differences as formal and informal speech. School brings an encounter with learning to read and write, though for many children considerable awareness of written language has come from reading materials at home. Finally, children have to develop a set of *metalinguistic* skills (the ability to reflect on and talk about language), through the use of a range of popular, semi-technical, and technical notions, such as *sound, word, page, sentence, capital letter*. The task of language acquisition is complex. The fact that it is largely complete by puberty makes it one of the most remarkable (if not *the* most remarkable) of all learning achievements.

See ANALOGY, BABBLING, BABY TALK, HALLIDAY, LANGUAGE LEARNING, LANGUAGE PATHOLOGY, PSYCHOLINGUISTICS, READING, SPELLING. [EDUCATION, LANGUAGE].   D.C.

Bennet-Kastor, T. 1988. *Analysing Children's Language*. Oxford: Blackwell.
Crystal, D. 1986. *Listen to your Child*. London: Penguin.
De Villiers, J. & P. 1979. *Early Language*. London: Fontana.
Fletcher, P. 1985. *A Child's Learning of English*. Oxford: Blackwell.
—— & Garman, M. (eds.). 1986. *Language Acquisition*. 2nd edition. Cambridge: University Press.
MacWhinney, B. (ed.). 1987. *Mechanisms of Language Acquisition*. Hillsdale, NJ: Lawrence Erlbaum Associates.
Wells, Gordon, *et al.* 1981. *Learning through Interaction: The Study of Language Development*. Cambridge: University Press.

CHINA. Official titles: Putonghua *Zhonghua Renmin Gongheguo*, English *People's Republic of China*. A country of East Asia. Capital: Beijing/Peking. Currency: the yuan (100 fen). Economy: mixed. Population: 1,084m (1988), 1,280m (projection for 2000). Ethnicity: 93% Han (ethnic Chinese) and 55 minorities, including Uighur, Tibetan, Manchu, Mongol, and Korean communities. Languages: Putonghua (official: see below), various Chinese dialects (see below), and various minority languages, including Uighur, Tibetan, Manchu, Mongol, and Korean. No Western language has established itself in mainland China as such, but English is used in Hong Kong and Portuguese in Macao (colonial territories leased in the 19c to Britain and Portugal), and English is the principal foreign language taught in China.

Chinese. Although Chinese is generally treated as a single language of the Sino-Tibetan family, with many dialects, it is more accurately described as a group of mutually unintelligible (though grammatically similar) languages that employ the same non-phonetic writing system. This group is usually described as the mother tongue of some 1,000m Han Chinese, a number taken to show, often in comparison with English, that more people speak Chinese than any other language. The main varieties of 'Chinese' (Cantonese, Hakka, Hsiang, Kan, Mandarin, Min, and Wu) are as distinct from one another as English from Danish or German. Cantonese, though traditionally described as a 'dialect', is a major language spoken by millions in China, Hong Kong, Malaysia, Singapore, and elsewhere in South-East Asia. It is often contrasted with *Mandarin* (*Chinese*), the range of dialects spoken in and around Beijing and, in its educated form, the traditional governing language of the Chinese Empire. Difficulties encountered by the BBC World Service when broadcasting in Chinese illustrate significant differences between Mandarin and Cantonese associated with writing as much as with speech:

Uniquely among the vernacular services, the BBC Chinese Section has to cope with two languages in one. In principle written standard Chinese is one language. In practice (quite apart from pronunciation problems), the differences between Cantonese and Mandarin can mean that scripts translated by Mandarin speakers may be difficult for Cantonese speakers to read for the microphone without recourse to the English original; and scripts translated by Cantonese speakers often present even more difficulty for speakers of Mandarin

(Rodney Mantle, 'Speaking with One Voice in Thirty-Seven Languages', *The Linguist* 29: 6, 1990).

The Chinese writing system is at least 2,000 years old. It consists of some 40,000 characters or ideograms, and is largely independent of sound, much as the numbers 1, 2, 3, 4, 5, etc., are language-independent and variously realized in different languages. Chinese characters have traditionally been written vertically and the columns read from right to left, but are often now written horizontally and read from left to right. In the People's Republic, a form of Mandarin has been developed as *Putonghua* (common speech), a unifying national standard and medium of instruction in schools that is written and printed in a simplified system of traditional characters (some 2,000 in number) and also, for certain purposes, in a system of romanization known as *Pinyin* ('phonetic spelling', from *pin* arrange, classify, *yin* sound, pronunciation).

Pinyin and Wade-Giles. The Pinyin system was introduced in 1958 and officially adopted in 1979. It differs significantly from the earlier system of romanization devised in the 19c by Sir Thomas Wade and adapted by Herbert Giles, and known as the *Wade-Giles system*. The following list has Wade-Giles first and Pinyin second in each pair: *Chou En-lai/Zhou Enlai, Mao Tse Tung/Mao Zedong, Nanking/Nanjing, Peking/Beijing, Sian/Xian, Soochow/Suzhou, Szechuan/Sichuan, t'ai chi ch'uan/tai ji quan, Teng Hsiao Ping/Deng Xiaoping*. The Beijing government prints all Chinese personal and place-names in the Pinyin style in its English-language publications and expects them to be used universally for diplomatic and official purposes and in the media. Pinyin is not, however, recognized as a replacement of Wade-Giles in Taiwan or by traditionalists outside the People's Republic, nor is it used in the People's Republic for everyday purposes. The use of Pinyin poses problems of distinguishing homographs, as in the 24 etymologically unrelated forms spelt *lian*. In traditional ideography, each of these has a distinct character. This problem may be circumvented with the use of the recently developed Monroe Keyboard used for word-processing, which types most Chinese characters in a small number of keystrokes and may make the use of Roman symbols less necessary.

Pidgin English. Contact between the English and Chinese languages dates from the establishment of a British trading post in 1640 in Guangzhou (Kwangchow, Canton), where *Pidgin English* developed in the 18c. This was a trade jargon of the ports, now known technically as *Chinese Pidgin English* and *China Coast Pidgin*. Influenced by an earlier *Cantonese Pidgin Portuguese* (used by and with the Portuguese traders who preceded the British), it developed into a lingua franca of the Pacific that influenced the pidgins of Papua New Guinea, the Solomon Islands, Vanuatu, Queensland, and elsewhere. With regard to its origin, the linguist Chin-Chuan Cheng notes: 'The Chinese held the British, like all "foreign devils," in low esteem, and would not stoop to learning the foreign tongue in its full form. The British, on the other hand, regarded the "heathen Chinee" as beyond any possibility of learning, and so began to modify their own language for the natives' benefit' ('Chinese Varieties of English', in Braj. B. Kachru (ed.), *The Other Tongue*, 1982). Pidgin spread when the Treaty Ports were established in China in 1843, but declined towards the end of the 19c as standard English began to be systematically taught in schools and universities. It is now extinct in the People's Republic and marginal in Hong Kong. The jargon, though a practical and useful medium, was generally looked down on; a disparaging term for it was *coolie Esperanto*. An example from its heyday is: *Tailor, my have got one piece plenty hansom silk; my want you make one nice evening dress.* See PIDGIN.

English in China. In the first half of the 20c, English was based on the British model and taught largely through literature. After the Communist regime established itself in 1949, the BrE model continued, not because of trade or imperial connections, but because the new educational policy was influenced by that of the Soviet Union, for which BrE was also the model. For many years China and the US had limited relations, and AmE has only recently become a possible target for learners. Currently, there is enormous interest in English in the People's Republic, with an estimated 250m people at various stages in learning the language. For most Chinese, English is the international language *par excellence*, but as Cheng (above) observes, use often includes 'identical or very similar expressions used in various publications. This tendency towards fixed expressions is also noticeable in spoken English. To an outsider, both spoken and written varieties appear stilted.' He calls this politicized style *Sinicized English*. Its exponents, especially in such official organs as the English edition of the *Beijing Review/Beijing Zhoubao* (formerly the *Peking Review*), have tended to lace their English with such loan translations from Putonghua as *running dogs* for 'lackeys' (from *zou gou*) and *capitalist roaders* (from *zou zi pai*). English used by speakers of any Chinese dialect anywhere, regardless of their political persuasion, is often informally referred to as *Chinglish*. Two recent works concerned with especially the teaching of English in China are: Donald J. Ford, *The Twain Shall Meet: The*

Current Study of English in China (Jefferson, NC, and London: McFarland, 1988), and Y. F. Dzau, *English in China* (Hong Kong: API Press, 1990).

English and Chinese. (1) *English in Chinese.* In the People's Republic, the influence of English on Chinese has been mainly lexical, and in particular a large number of technical terms. English has had a mild effect on the morphology of Mandarin/Putonghua, in that the formation of loans and loan translations (such as *modeng* modern, *moteer* model, *shehui* society, and *yuanliang* excuse) has meant an increase in polysyllables in a mainly monosyllabic structure. In syntax, translation from English and the study of English grammar appears to have led to an increase in passive usage entailing the co-verb *bei*: compare KOREA. (2) *Chinese in English.* The influence of Chinese on English at large has been almost exclusively lexical, with few items gaining additional senses beyond the originally borrowed meaning or being transferred out of their Asian semantic contexts. A few, like *tea*, have become international forms borrowed into languages around the world. Nearly 1,000 loans into English have been tabulated, such as *chow mein, ginseng, gung-ho, kaolin, kung fu, sampan, taipan, typhoon*: see G. Cannon, 'Chinese Borrowings in English', *American Speech* (Spring 1988).

See AMERICAN LANGUAGES, AUSTRALIAN LANGUAGES, BBC PRONUNCIATION UNIT, BORROWING, CANADIAN LANGUAGES, CHARACTER, CHARACTER SET, CLASSICAL LANGUAGE, DIALECT IN AMERICA, EAST ASIAN ENGLISH, HAWAII, HONG KONG, JAPAN, KOREA, LAMBDACISM, LATIN¹, LIBRARY OF CONGRESS, LINGUISTIC TYPOLOGY, MACAO, MALAYSIA, PIDGIN, Q, ROMAN, SINGAPORE, SINGAPORE ENGLISH, SOUTH-EAST ASIAN ENGLISH, TELECOMMUNICATIONS, TRANSLITERATION, WRITING. [ASIA, LANGUAGE, NAME].   G.C., T.MCA.

CHINA COAST PIDGIN. See CHINA, PIDGIN.

CHINESE PIDGIN ENGLISH. See CHINA, PIDGIN.

CHINGLISH. See CHINA, -GLISH AND -LISH.

CHINOOK JARGON, also **Jargon**. A pidgin language of the Pacific Northwest coast of North America. Its core languages were Chinook and Nootka, but just under half of its 700-word vocabulary derived from French and English: in Jargon, Hudson's Bay Company traders were *kin chotsch men* (King George Men). It may have originated before European contact in intertribal trade or later in the fur trade. At its peak in the later 19c, it had some 100,000 speakers

west of the Rockies from Alaska to California. From 1891 to 1904, Father J.-M. Lejeune published a weekly newspaper, *The Kamloops Wawa* (in Kamloops, British Columbia) in English and Jargon. Jargon was dying out by 1930 because of English-language schooling and is now extinct. However, words survive in such place-names as *Cultus Lake* (worthless lake) and *Skookumchuck* (strong, big, from Chahalis), and in AmE and CanE *potlatch* (gift-giving, from Nootka *patshatl*), *salt chuck* (ocean), and (*high*) *muckamuck* (a bigshot, from Chinook *hyas muckamuck* plenty to eat). People who fish in the ocean for sport are sometimes called *saltchuckers* or *chuckers* in British Columbia. See CANADIAN PLACE-NAMES, JARGON. [AMERICA, VARIETY].   M.F.

CHOMSKY, (Avram) Noam [b.1928]. American linguist and political writer, born in Philadelphia, Pennsylvania, and introduced to philology by his father, a scholar of Hebrew. At the U. of Pennsylvania he studied under the structural linguist Zellig Harris. After gaining his Ph.D. in 1955 (dissertation: 'Transformational Analysis'), he taught modern languages and linguistics at Massachusetts Institute of Technology, where he became full professor in 1961. He was appointed Ferrari P. Ward Professor of Foreign Languages and Linguistics in 1976. During this period, he became a leading figure in US linguistics, replacing a mechanistic and behaviouristic view of language (based on the work of Bloomfield) with a mentalistic and generative approach. His linguistic publications include: *Syntactic Structures* (1957), *Aspects of the Theory of Syntax* (1965), *Cartesian Linguistics* (1966), *The Sound Pattern of English* (with Morris Halle, 1968), *Language and Mind* (1968, 1972), *The Logical Structure of Linguistic Theory* (1975), *Reflections on Language* (1975), *Lectures on Government and Binding* (1981), *Barriers* (1986). His social, political, and economic works include: *American Power and the New Mandarins* (1969), *The Political Economy of Human Rights* (two volumes, 1979). *Language and Responsibility* (1979) combines his linguistic and social interests by exploring relationships among language, science, ideas, and politics.

Chomsky originated such concepts as *transformational-generative grammar* (*TGG*), *transformational grammar* (*TG*), and *generative grammar*. His definition of *grammar* differs from both traditional and structuralist theories, in that he is concerned not only with a formal descriptive system but also with the linguistic structures and processes at work in the mind. He sees such structures as universal and arising from a genetic predisposition to language. Features drawn from mathematics include *transformation* and *generation*. As proposed in 1957, *transformational rules* were a means by which one kind of sentence (such as the passive *The work was done by local men*) could be derived from another kind (such as the active *Local men did the work*). Any process governed by such rules was a *transformation* (in the preceding case the *passivization transformation*) and any sentence resulting from such rules was a *transform*. In Chomsky's terms, previous grammars had only *phrase-structure rules*, which specified how sentences are structured out of phrases and phrases out of words, but had no way of relating sentences with different structures (such as active and passive).

Such earlier grammars were also concerned only with *actual* attested sentences and not with all the *potential* sentences in a language. An adequate grammar, however, in his view, should *generate* (that is, explicitly account for) the indefinite set of acceptable sentences of a language, rather than the finite set to be found in a corpus of texts. *Aspects* (1965) presented what is known as his 'standard theory', which added the concepts *deep structure* and *surface structure*: deep or underlying forms which by transformation become surface or observable sentences of a particular language. In this theory, a passive was no longer to be derived from an active sentence, but both from a common deep structure which was neither active nor passive. Comparably, sentences with similar surface structures, such as *John is easy to please* and *John is eager to please* were shown to have different deep structures. The standard theory distinguishes between a speaker's *competence* (knowledge of a language) and *performance* (actual use of a language), Chomskyan grammar being concerned with competence, not performance.

Subsequent work has concentrated less on rules that specify what can be generated and more on *constraints* that determine what cannot be generated. The most definitive statement of his recent views is *Lectures on Government and Binding*, in which the theory is *GB theory*. Government is an extension of the traditional term whereby a verb governs its object, but for Chomsky prepositions may govern and subjects may be governed. Binding is concerned with the type of anaphora found with pronouns and reflexives, but the notion is greatly extended. The traditional notion of case is similarly used, though modified in that it need not be morphological. Such devices can be used to rule out ungrammatical sentences that might otherwise be generated. *Barriers* (1986) further extends GB theory.

Chomsky is widely considered to be the most influential figure in linguistics in the later 20c

and is probably the linguist best-known outside the field. His views on language and grammar are controversial and responses to them have ranged from extreme enthusiasm, sometimes verging on fanaticism, through a sober and reflective interest, to fierce rejection by some traditionalist, structuralist, and other critics. See index. [AMERICAS, BIOGRAPHY, GRAMMAR, LANGUAGE].   F.R.P., T.MCA.

CHORUS [16c: through Latin from Greek *khorós* dancers and singers in a group, dance]. (1) In ancient Greece, a lyric poem, usually part of a religious rite, sung by a group to the accompaniment of dancing. (2) In Greek drama, an ode or series of odes sung by a group of actors; the people engaged in such singing, who served as participants in, and commentators on, the action of the play. (3) A group of actors or a single actor, especially in Elizabethan drama, with a function similar to that of the Greek chorus; the part of the play so performed. (4) A company of dancers and singers, especially in a musical show. (5) A group of people singing in unison, sometimes complementing the singing of a solo performer; a piece of music for such a performance. (6) Part of a song that recurs at intervals, usually following each stanza; a refrain. (7) The speech, singing, shouting, etc. of a group of people, and the sound so uttered: *a chorus of catcalls*. See DRAMA, LYRIC, ODE, REFRAIN. [LITERATURE, SPEECH].   T.MCA.

CHRISTIAN NAME. See PERSONAL NAME.

CHURCHILL, (Sir) Winston (Leonard Spencer) [1874-1965]. British politician, statesman, writer, orator, historian, and painter; eldest son of Lord Randolph Churchill and his American wife, Jeannette ('Jennie') Jerome. He was born at Blenheim Palace and educated at Harrow School, of which he records that his weakness in Latin put him with the 'stupidest boys'. They learned 'to write mere English', and consequently 'I got into my bones the essential structure of the English sentence—which is a noble thing'. He passed from the Royal Military Academy at Sandhurst into the army, served in several imperial campaigns, and was war correspondent for the London *Morning Post* during the Boer War. He became a Member of Parliament (1901) and in a long career served in many offices, including Home Secretary (1910-11) and Chancellor of the Exchequer (1924-9). After a period out of favour, he became Prime Minister (1940) and war leader from crisis to victory. Defeated in the 1945 election, he was Prime Minister again (1951-5). Apart from public eminence, Churchill had a reputation as a writer and speaker acknowledged even by his political opponents, and which made evident his love of the language and its literature. His wartime speeches were rhetorical and passionate, inspired both country and Empire, and often drew on literary quotations, allusions, and cadences. He wrote one novel, *Savola* (1900), and a number of biographies, including those of his father (1906) and his ancestor John Churchill, first Duke of Marlborough (1933-8), and the autobiographical *My Early Life* (1930). He published two histories of his time, *The World Crisis* (1923-9) and *The Second World War* (1948-54), but his greatest literary achievement was *A History of the English-Speaking Peoples* (1956-8). He was awarded the Nobel Prize for Literature in 1953. Churchill's prose style is in the manner of Victorian historiography, notably that of Thomas Macaulay, and such a style is sometimes referred to as *Churchillian*. See index. [BIOGRAPHY, EUROPE, LITERATURE, STYLE].   R.C.

CINEMA. See MOTION PICTURE.

CIPHER, also BrE **cypher** [14c: from Medieval Latin *ciphra*, Arabic *ṣifr* empty, nothing, translating Sanskrit *śūnya* void. It is a doublet of *zero*, from Italian, from Medieval Latin *zephirum*, also from *ṣifr*]. (1) Rare: a synonym for *zero*; a term for an Arabic number or numbers; to use numbers for calculation. (2) Something or someone of no significance or importance; a nonentity (like zero or nothing). (3) A way of concealing a message, often by transposing or substituting letters; a secret way of writing, a code; a key to such a way of writing; secret writing generally, especially in the phrase *in cipher*; to write in, or convert into, cipher or code. A *cipher alphabet* lists the letters or other symbols used by a cryptographer to turn a message into a *ciphertext*. See CODE, CRYPTOGRAPHY. [LANGUAGE]. T.MCA.

CIRCUMFLEX [16c: from Latin *circumflexus* bent round, a loan translation of Greek *perispṓmenos*]. A diacritic placed over vowel symbols. It has three possible forms: angled (ˆ), rounded (ˆ), or waved (˜). In classical Greek, the circumflex marks a rise/fall in pitch; in French, it may indicate vowel quality (often due to the loss of a phoneme or syllable). It occurs in English only in unaltered loans from French: *gîte*; *dépôt* as opposed to *depot*. See ACCENT, DIACRITIC, SPELLING REFORM, TILDE. [WRITING].
                                    T.MCA., E.W.

CIRCUMLOCUTION [16c: from French *circonlocution*, from Latin *circumlocutio/circumlocutionis*, a loan translation of Greek *periphrasis* talking around]. Also **periphrasis**. In rhetoric, a wordy and indirect way of saying something, as when death in hospital is called *negative patient care outcome*. Such usage is often obscure, officious, pompous, authoritarian, and intimidating; the phrase *periphrastic usage* echoes the style it describes. In the novel *Little Dorrit* (1857: ch. 10), Dickens uses the word in the name of a government department: 'Whatever was required to be done, the Circumlocution Office was beforehand with all the public departments in the art of perceiving—How not to do it.' See EUPHEMISM, JARGON, LITOTES, PERIPHRASIS, PLEONASM, POETIC DICTION, POETRY, REDUNDANCY, TAUTOLOGY. [STYLE, USAGE].
                                         T.MCA.

CITATION [13c: from Latin *citatio/citationis* proclaiming, summoning, from *citare/citatum* to put in motion, call, summon (to a court), witness, quote]. (1) Reference to a rule, precedent, or text, especially for religious, legal, or linguistic purposes: *the citation of Biblical authorities*. (2) Quoting a passage from a text to support a fact, opinion, or policy: *the citation of written evidence*. (3) A phrase, sentence, or longer passage cited or quoted, especially to demonstrate or exemplify something: *legal citations*. (4) A specimen of language in use, especially as displayed in a dictionary or grammar book: *dictionary citations*. Linguistic citations provide evidence of the existence of an item or usage and may provide information about its origin, variant forms, references, use, frequency of use, distribution, and equivalents in other languages. They may be used overtly, as attributed examples in a work about language (such as the thousands of citations in *The Oxford English Dictionary*) or covertly, by influencing the form and content of the information in such a work, without themselves appearing in it (as with the *Collins English Dictionary*, the content of whose definitions derives from the study of textual citations kept on file). Citations are used in the preparation of grammars, dictionaries, usage guides, and language-learning materials. Two specialized works of reference, the *concordance* and the *dictionary of quotations*, are in effect arrays of citations: a Bible or Shakespeare concordance gives all the citations for each word used in the Bible or in Shakespeare's works, and a dictionary of quotations lists citations that have been selected from a variety of sources and entered under their authors' names. Compare ALLUSION, CONCORDANCE, QUOTATION. [REFERENCE, USAGE].   T.MCA., R.F.I.

CLASSIC [17c: from Latin *classicus* first in rank, from *classis* rank]. (1) Typical of the first and highest of a kind, reflecting established rules and styles in such areas as art, fashion, literature, and language: *a classic style, a classic dress, classic* *simplicity.* (2) A work of art that is simple, elegant, balanced, regular, and worth emulating, usually because it typifies or epitomizes the best of ancient Greek and Roman style. The works of some artists become classics in their own right: Dickens's major social novels, Carroll's *Alice* books, Orwell's dystopias. For an artist of classic stature, a single name is enough: *Homer, Goethe, Shakespeare.* The *classics* are an established canon of literary works: in the West, the major works of Greece and Rome, and the major works of such major languages as English, French, German, Italian, and Spanish. To *study Classics,* however, is to learn Latin and Greek, especially to university level. See CANON, CLASSICAL, CLASSICISM, ENGLISH LITERATURE. [EUROPE, LITERATURE, STYLE].   T.MCA.

CLASSICAL [16c: from Latin *classicus* first in rank, and *-al*]. Formative and normative. The classical culture of Europe is a synthesis of the cultures of ancient Greece and Rome. Elsewhere, the cultures of Sanskrit in India, Arabic at the time of Muhammad, and Confucian China are classical. If something Western is classical, it belongs to the *classical period* (Greece *c.*5c BC, Rome *c.*2c BC to 2c AD) or is part of a tradition that has evolved from those periods. The term is often contrasted with *Romantic* and when there has been a revival of interest the term *neoclassical* is often used. A *classical education* in the West is based on the study of Latin and perhaps Greek. The words *classic* and *classical* are sometimes synonymous: *classic(al) style.* See CLASSIC, CLASSICISM, ROMANCE, VERNACULAR. [EUROPE, STYLE].   T.MCA.

CLASSICAL COMPOUND, also **learned compound**. A compound word whose elements and pattern derive from a classical language, as in *agriculture* from Latin, *biography* from Greek. Two features distinguish such words from most vernacular compounds: further words can be derived from them, such as *agricultural(ly), agricultur(al)ist* and *biographical(ly), biographer*, and there are often suffix-related stress shifts in their derivational patterns, such as *ágriculture/ agricúltural, biógraphy/biográphical*, caused in these instances by the addition of *-(ic)al.* Because they have long been an international resource, such compounds are both part of English and other than English; in form, they range from the entirely English *dinosaur* to the Neo-Latinate *Tyrannosaurus.*

Origin. Such compounds derive from word-forming systems absorbed to varying degrees by many modern European languages. They have been in English since the Middle Ages, but did not become common until the influx of Neo-Latinisms during the Renaissance: *mystagogue*

1550, *androgyne* 1552, *troglodyte* 1555, *geographical* and *hydrographer* 1559. In adopting such words, English followed French rather than German, which tended to resist Neo-Latin compounds in favour of calques like *Landwirtschaft* for Latin *agricultura* and *Lebensbeschreibung* or *Lebensgeschichte* (description or history of life) for Greek *biographia* (although the term *Biographie* is widely used). In French, adoption was wholesale and adaptation minimal: *agricultura* and *biographia* became *agriculture* and *biographie.* From French, such items passed into English with little or no adaptation in spelling.

Nature. It is functionally unimportant whether a classical compound is first used in English, French, or any other language. The elements are international and the conventions for their adaptation well established. Greek elements are usually transmitted through Latin orthography. In this system, *k* usually becomes *c*: *cardiology*, not **kardiology* (but note *leuk(a)emia*, not **leuc(a)emia*, and both *leucocyte* and *leukocyte*). *R* with rough breathing becomes *rh* in French and English (*rhinocéros, rhinoceros*) or *r* in Italian and Spanish (*rinoceronte*). On occasion, a biological term may combine Greek and Latin: *Tyrannosaurus rex* (Greek 'tyrant lizard', Latin 'king') and *Oviraptor philoceratops* (Latin 'egg-snatcher', Greek 'lovable horned-face'). Some binomials contain information about people and places, such as *Albertosaurus sternbergi* Sternberg's Alberta lizard, and *Yangchuanosaurus shangyouensis* the Shanghai Yangchuan lizard. The classification for naturalists developed by such taxonomists as Carolus Linnaeus is an ad-hoc system that has its own fossils; it is as likely to mark ignorance as knowledge and to express subjective as objective comment. Linnaeus classified non-flowering plants as *Cryptogamia* (hidden marriage), because he did not know how they reproduced. When his successors discovered the processes involved, they left the name unchanged. When the British anatomist Richard Owen coined the name *dinosaur* ('terrible lizard', 1841) for the extinct reptiles whose skeletons were found in rock strata, Romanticism contributed more than science.

Uses and glosses. The compounds are part of technical usage and include the names of many scientific studies: *biology, cardiology, meteorology.* Such labels are often opaque and intimidating to people not trained in their use, with the result that, although tools of technical description, they have some of the features of a secret language. They may be difficult to pronounce, because of their length and suffix-related shifts in stress. Someone attempting an unfamiliar form can mispronounce it and retreat in confusion: for example, 'Tonight we have someone interesting to talk to you, folks. He's an orni-, an ornitho-, a birdman' (BBC disc jockey, live, 1970). The switch from *ornithologist* to *birdman* is part of a practice of explaining classical compounds by translation into everyday terms. Such glossing ranges from formal etymologies to informal paraphrases, as in: 'The name "echinoderm" comes from the Greek *echînos*, a hedgehog, and *dérma*, the skin'; 'The *Archaeopteryx*, whose name means "ancient wing" . . .'; 'the reptile subclass *Archosauria* (ruling lizards)'; 'Cosmology, the science of the universe'; 'Coprolites or fossilized excrement'; 'Cryptozoology, the quest for animals that scientists have yet to discover'.

Although such terms as *neurology* and *Archaeopteryx* are scientific, classical compounding is not confined to the sciences, and pre-dates scientific method. In divination, compounds based on *-mancy* are numerous, including: *necromancy* divination through talking to the dead, *nephelomancy* through observing clouds, *ophiomancy* by inspecting snakes, *pyromancy* by watching flames, *tyromancy* by examining cheese. Sometimes compounds are used to impress and lend a cachet, as in *cosmetology* the art of applying cosmetics. They have also been coined for facetious and satirical purposes, as with *odontopedology* the art of opening your mouth and putting your foot in it. Classical and vernacular elements combine to this end: *escapology* the carnival art of getting out of chains and cabinets, *kiddology* the art of kidding or conning people, *sudsology* the study of soap operas. See BINOMIAL NOMENCLATURE, COMBINING FORM, COMPOUND WORD, GREEK, INTERFIX, INTERNATIONAL SCIENTIFIC VOCABULARY, LATIN[1], NEO-LATIN, SUFFIX, WORD-FORMATION. [WORD].   T.MCA.

CLASSICAL ENDING. There are in English many nouns whose singular/plural contrasts derive from Latin and Greek, such as *stimulus/stimuli* (Latin: masculine), *formula/formulae* (Latin: feminine), *memorandum/memoranda* (Latin: neuter), *phenomenon/phenomena* (Greek: neuter). During the 16–19c, when writing was largely the concern of the classically educated, many such endings were retained as a matter of course. Some are universally used (*radius/radii*), some have become restricted to certain registers (*formulae* to scientific discourse, *formulas* gaining ground generally; *indexes* in books, *indices* in mathematics), and some have been considerably adapted (the singular *agendum* has disappeared and the former plural *agenda* has become a singular, with the non-classical plural *agendas*). Asymmetry is common: *campus* and *ultimatum* have the plurals *campuses* and *ultimatums*, not

campi and *ultimata*, while *desideratum* and *sanctum sanctorum* have the plurals *desiderata* and *sancta sanctorum*, not *desideratums* and *sanctum sanctorums*. Many would hesitate when choosing plurals for such words as *arboretum* and *thesaurus* (both classical and vernacular are possible).

Although contrasts such as Latin *addendum/addenda* and Greek *criterion/criteria* are maintained in academic and technical writing, *bacterium/bacteria* and *datum/data* pose problems. *Bacteria* is widely assumed to be collective, and *bacterium* and *datum* are so seldom used that they often raise doubts. *Data* is currently both plural ('The data are available') and collective ('How much data do you need?'), and is often therefore a controversial usage issue. *Curriculum* and *memorandum* have two plural forms: *curricula*, *curriculums* and *memoranda*, *memorandums*. The *medium/media* contrast is complex and extremely controversial. Among spiritualists, the plural of *medium* is *mediums*. In linguistics, it is both *media* and *mediums*. In the media, it is *media*, the singular *medium* often being overlooked, so that *media* is used as both plural ('the media are . . .') and singular ('the media is . . .'), with the occasional vernacular plural form *medias*: compare French *les médias*.

In the late 20c, traditional usage has declined as the number of people involved in technical and academic discourse has increased. Contrasting plurals are common: *cactus*, *formula*, *referendum* often have the technical plurals *cacti*, *formulae*, *referenda* and the popular plurals *cactuses*, *formulas*, *referendums*. Such usages as *a rock strata*, *a good criteria*, *this phenomena is widespread* all occur frequently, with the plurals *stratas*, *criterias*, *phenomenas*. They are disliked (often intensely) not only by purists but by many who consider themselves liberal in matters of usage. Purism, however, also has its barbarisms, such as the quasi-classical plurals *octopi* and *syllabi* for *octopus* and *syllabus*, competing with *octopuses* and *syllabuses*. (The Greek plurals for these words are, respectively, *octôpoda* and *sullabóntes*). See APPENDIX, MEDIA, MEDIUM, PLURAL, X. [GRAMMAR, USAGE, WORD].   T.MCA.

CLASSICAL LANGUAGE. A prestigious, often ancient language, such as Latin or Sanskrit, or a variety of a language, such as classical Greek. Such a language is usually learned formally, is often a yardstick against which other languages are measured, and may be a norm in terms of which they are described. Classical languages are often contrasted with *vernacular* languages, in a relationship of 'high' to 'low'. They have traditionally provided models for successor or dependent languages, especially for styles of verse and prose, literary genres, grammatical descriptions, pronouncements on usage, and philosophical and other texts. They have a body of literature, usually preserved in manuscript form and organized into a canon which may be scriptural (as with Sanskrit and Arabic), secular or secularized (as with classical Greek), or a mixture of these (as with Latin). The evaluation is often historical, made by later generations, and in many instances a certain period in the history of such a language has been regarded as a golden age.

Classical strata in non-classical languages. Generally, a classical language dominates a cultural area in which vernaculars are used. Because of this, elements of its vocabulary may be absorbed into a subordinate tongue, to form a more or less distinct 'high' stratum within it. Both learning the classical language and using its extension into a vernacular are often associated with prestigious systems of education in certain societies, such as Latinity in the public schools of England. After the invasion of the Persian Empire by Muslims from Arabia, Persian developed a learned stratum of Arabic, and in such languages as Hindi and Tamil there are Sanskrit strata. Both classical Arabic and Sanskrit have been associated with traditional forms of education. The Neo-Latin stratum of English developed during and after the Renaissance, largely as a response to the need for a prose capable of handling scholarship and science, traditionally the domain of Latin.

Dead language? There is a widespread view that to be truly classical, a language should be 'dead': that is, not passed on from parent to child within a community. Some classical languages, such as Latin and Sanskrit, have not been mother tongues for centuries, but this is not a universal feature of such languages. At one and the same time, Greek in various forms was the mother tongue of the Greeks, a Mediterranean lingua franca, and for the Romans a classical source of literary and rhetorical inspiration. In such situations, there has been a tendency to look to one variety of such a language as 'the best': that is, the properly classical and normative. In the case of Greek this was the educated Attic or Athenian variety.

A learned code. Because of centuries of standardization and veneration of literary usage, a classical language or a classicized variety of a language may split off from everyday use. Classical Latin split off from the 'vulgar' varieties of the Republic and the Empire, and Sanskrit split off from the Prakrits of northern India. When such a division occurs, the classicized medium becomes progressively less and less available as a mother tongue. It is instead perpetuated in script, print, and formal instruction as the learned code of an élite, taught by accredited masters. Latin became a 'high' language first through its literary and rhetorical tradition, then its association with Christian learning. Sanskrit and classical Arabic became 'high' languages primarily as the vehicles of religion. Mandarin Chinese became such a language because, especially in writing, it served to hold the Chinese Empire together for centuries, was associated with Confucianism and public examinations, and influenced such other cultures as the Japanese and Korean.

Classical English. English has within it a double classical inheritance, from Latin and from Greek through Latin. The standard language has two blended superstrates and is to some degree defined by their presence and use. After the Renaissance, English began to display classical tendencies of its own, when a 'refined' and 'elegant' standard was promoted by 17-18c writers who called themselves *Augustans* in imitation of the Augustan period in ancient Rome. Such writers and their associates set their own, especially literary usage above all other forms of the language and some campaigned for an academy and a dictionary that would enshrine classical norms. Samuel Johnson, however, found that he could not compile the kind of dictionary hoped for, and with the independence of the US a resistance to Augustan norms developed outside Britain. In 1828, the American writer John Neal observed:

For my own part . . . I never shall write what is now worshipped under the name of *classical* English. It is no natural language—it never was—it never will be spoken alive on this earth: and therefore, ought never to be written. We have dead languages enough now; but the deadest language I ever met with, or heard of, was that in use among the writers of Queen Anne's day (unpublished preface to the novel *Rachel Dyer*).

Nevertheless, present-day standard English has received a double legacy from the Augustans: (1) The variety known as the *King's/Queen's English*, associated with the public schools and the universities of Oxford and Cambridge. (2) The *print standard*, which, despite minor differences in spelling and some other conventions in BrE and AmE, was largely systematized in the 18c. In the late 20c, *standard English* has four quasi-classical features: it is a prestigious international medium; its literary canon is widely studied, including by many non-native speakers; its vocabulary is being drawn into 'vernaculars' throughout the world; and amid its varieties, the print standard serves as a canonical form, learned not at home but at school. It is not surprising, therefore, that for many people standard English is an object of some reverence, and that they wish to protect it from barbarians at its gates, as if it too were virtually a classical language.

See ACADEMY, ARABIC, ATTIC AND DORIC, ATTICISM, AUGUSTAN, BARBARISM, BIBLE, BIG WORD, BISOCIATION, CANON, CHINA (MANDARIN), CLASSIC, CLASSICAL, CLASSICAL COMPOUND, CLASSICISM, COMBINING FORM, DIGLOSSIA, ENGLISH LANGUAGES, GRAMMAR, GREEK, GREEK LITERATURE, INFLATED LANGUAGE, JAPAN, KOINÉ, LATIN[1], LATIN ANALOGY, LATINATE, LATINISM, LATINITY, LATIN LITERATURE, LATIN TAG, MODERN LANGUAGE, NEO-LATIN, PALI, POETIC DICTION, RECEIVED PRONUNCIATION, RHETORIC, ROMANTICISM, SANSKRIT, SOLECISM, STANDARD, STANDARD ENGLISH, THEMATIC VOWEL, TRISOCIATION, VERNACULAR. [AMERICAS, ASIA, EUROPE, HISTORY, LANGUAGE, STYLE]. T.MCA.

CLASSICISM [19c: from *classic* and *-ism* as in *euphemism*]. (1) Also *classicalism*. An attitude to language and literature found in many ages and cultures. In the West, it is based on respect for, and often veneration of, the models and achievements of Greece and Rome. Advocates of classicism value tradition and usually believe that written language should be governed by traditional, formal rules. They are generally conservative and often consider that contemporary culture cannot match the achievements of the ancients. They usually value regularity and simplicity of form, seek to maintain order and proportion, admire elegance and polished wit, encourage emotional restraint, and regard literature as an art at its best when paying close attention to technique. They are also often concerned for linguistic and cultural purity. In Britain, the period from 1660 to the late 18c was a time of *neo-classicism*. Its heyday was the early 18c, when writers thought of themselves as Augustans, in emulation of the age of Rome when Augustus was emperor. Pope's *Essay on Criticism* (1711) expounds the main tenets of the neo-classical school. In most respects, classicism is the antithesis of Romanticism. (2) A word or phrase of classical origin or inspiration: in the West, of Latin or Greek origin. In English, the majority of literary and technical terms are classicisms, such as *majority, literary, technical, term, classicism*. More noticeably classical are direct allusions and usages, whether loan-translated (*cleansing the Augean stables, cutting the Gordian knot, Beware the Ides of March, Let the buyer beware*) or borrowed (Greek *hapax legomenon, hoi polloi*, Latin *caveat emptor, Sic transit gloria mundi*).

See ATTICISM, BINOMIAL, CLASSIC, CLASSICAL, CLASSICAL LANGUAGE, -ISM, LATIN TAG, ROMANTICISM, SAXONISM, VERNACULARISM. [EUROPE, LITERATURE, STYLE]. R.C., T.MCA.

CLASSIFICATION OF LANGUAGES. There are three main methods of classifying language: *genetic, areal*, and *typological*: (1) A genetic classification groups together languages which are presumed to have arisen from a common source, such as the Romance languages. (2) An areal classification groups together languages sharing features which have spread by borrowing across a region, such as the Balkan language area, in which Albanian, Bulgarian, and Romanian all have the definite article attached after the noun, as in Romanian *munte-le* (mountain-the: 'the mountain'). (3) A typological classification divides languages into types based on shared properties which are not due to common ancestry or geographical contact, such as agglutinating languages. See LANGUAGE FAMILY, LINGUISTIC TYPOLOGY. [LANGUAGE]. J.M.A.

CLASSIFIED ORDER. See THEMATIC ORDER.

CLASSISM [1840s]. Behaviour and attitudes related to class: 'The same really contemptible feeling of class-ism, the curse of England and Englishmen, and of women also' (Samuel Bamford, *Passages in the Life of a Radical*, 1844); 'The user called another participant in the conversation "a classist" for arguing that (particular) middle class values and behaviors were superior' (*American Speech*, Summer 1988). Compare RACISM, SEXISM. [STYLE]. T.MCA.

CLAUSE [13c: from French *clause*, Latin *clausa*, the close of a sentence or formula]. In grammatical description, a sentence or sentence-like construction included within another sentence, such as *because I wanted to* in *I did it because I wanted to*.

Traditional kinds of clauses. (1) *Main clause*. A simple sentence consists of one main clause or principal clause: *I knew it. The computer industry is bursting with energy*. (2) *Coordinate clause*. In the following sentence, there are two main clauses, linked through coordination by *and*. Each is therefore a coordinate clause: *They milked the animals and then they made yoghurt, butter, and cheese*. (3) *Subordinate clause*. In the following sentence, there are two clauses, linked through subordination by *that*: *Some scientists argue that the earth's climate is changing*. In one contemporary analysis, the main clause includes the subordinate clause, and is the whole sentence, but in a traditional analysis the main clause is restricted to *Some scientists argue*. Two subordinate clauses may be coordinated (here with *and*): *We can see that the health of species is interconnected and that the human race is now in danger*. One subordinate clause may be subordinated to another, as in *I know that everybody believes that it is too late*. Both *that*-clauses are subordinate, but one of them (*that everybody believes that it is too late*) is superordinate to the *that*-clause within it (*that it is too late*). Some grammarians refer to a subordinate sentence or clause as being *embedded* within its *matrix sentence*.

Non-finite clauses. In some descriptions, the term *clause* is restricted to constructions whose verb is finite, as in the examples given so far. Other descriptions extend the term to sentence-like constructions that have a non-finite verb or no verb at all, both of which are phrases in traditional grammar. However, they are sentence-like because they can be analysed in terms of such elements as subject and object. In these more recent descriptions, the infinitive clause *to value two important pictures* in the sentence *She was asked to value two important pictures* can be analysed as having a verb *to value* and a direct object *two important pictures*, corresponding to the analysis of *She will value two important pictures*. Similarly, the verbless clause *obdurate as stone* in the sentence *Obdurate as stone, the man withstood all pleas* can be analysed as consisting of a subject complement, corresponding to the analysis of *The man was obdurate as stone*. In such a description, sentences are classified by form into three types: finite clauses; non-finite clauses (infinitive and participle clauses); verbless clauses.

Clauses and functions. Clauses can also be classified into three major types: *nominal* or *noun clauses*, *relative* or *adjective clauses*, and *adverbial clauses*. Nominal clauses have functions similar to those of a noun or pronoun, such as subject or object; for example, the nominal clause *that the spacecraft were too big* is subject in *That the spacecraft were too big was maintained by many critics* (compare *That view was maintained by many critics*) and object in *The committee stated that the spacecraft were too big* (compare *The committee stated that*). Relative clauses have a function shared with that of most adjectives, that is, modifying a noun; for example *that she was angling for a hereditary peerage* modifies *rumours* in *She denied rumours that she was angling for a hereditary peerage* (compare *malicious rumours*). *Adverbial clauses* have functions shared with those of most adverbs, such as modifying a verb, alone or with some other parts of the sentence, or the sentence as a whole; for example, the clause *if the organization is run by an amiable nonentity* in the sentence *The problems will prove insoluble if the organization is run by an amiable nonentity* (compare *in the circumstances*) and the clause *when the museum moves into the new centre* in the sentence *When the museum moves into the new centre it*

will organize scholarly exhibitions (compare *then*).

See ABSOLUTE CLAUSE, ADJECTIVE CLAUSE, ADVERBIAL CLAUSE, CLAUSE ANALYSIS, COORDINATE CLAUSE, COORDINATION, DISCOURSE ANALYSIS, MAIN CLAUSE, PARTICIPLE, PHRASE, RELATIVE CLAUSE, SENTENCE, SUBORDINATE CLAUSE, SUBORDINATION, SUPERORDINATE CLAUSE. [GRAMMAR] S.G.

CLAUSE ANALYSIS, also **general analysis**. A technique of formal grammatical analysis once common in schools in English-speaking countries and English-medium schools elsewhere. It involves the division of longer sentences into their constituent clauses: for example, the analysis of the complex sentence *When they arrived, they found that there was not enough food* into: *they found* (main or principal clause); *when they arrived* (subordinate adverbial clause of time, modifying the verb *found*); *that there was not enough food* (subordinate noun clause, object of the verb *found*). Such analysis was routine grammatical work in many secondary classrooms until the 1950s, but from the 1960s fell into disfavour. Most teachers and linguists currently present four arguments against such work: (1) It rests on a narrow theoretical base derived from the study of Latin, and ignores the range of types of clauses that can be identified in English. (2) It concentrates on only one aspect of grammar. (3) It is highly formal and remote from everyday language. (4) Most students did not respond well to it and many teachers did not like teaching it. As a result of the precipitous decline in teaching such analysis, students since the 1960s have generally had little organized instruction in sentence forms. Clause analysis continues to be favoured by many older, usually middle-class people, who argue that training in such analysis is useful in developing linguistic skills, especially in writing. Such groups as the Queen's English Society would like to see the teaching of clause analysis and parsing revived. See CLAUSE, PARSING. [EDUCATION, GRAMMAR]. T.MCA.

CLEAR *L*. See L-SOUNDS.

CLEFT SENTENCE. A construction in which a simple sentence is divided into two clauses so as to give prominence to a particular linguistic item and the information it carries. The sentence *On Monday the players objected to the delay* can be restated as any of three cleft sentences: (1) With the focus on the players: *It was the players who/that objected on Monday to the delay.* (2) With the focus on the delay: *It was the delay that the players objected to on Monday.* (3) With the focus on Monday: *It was on Monday that the players objected to the delay.* The first clause of a cleft sentence consists of *It*, a form of the verb *be*, and the focused item. The rest is a relative clause. A similar device is found in the *pseudo-cleft sentence*, where the subject is generally a *nominal relative clause*, the verb is a form of the verb *be*, and the focused item follows at the end: *What I badly need is a good rest* (based on *I badly need a good rest*). Unlike the cleft sentence, the pseudo-cleft sentence can have a verb (and other elements that follow it) as the focused item: *What we did was replace all the carpets*. Similar are sentences in which a pronoun or noun phrase with general reference is used instead of the nominal relative clause: *Something I badly need is a good rest*. *The thing we did was replace the carpets*. [GRAMMAR]. S.G.

CLERIHEW [20c: named after its inventor, Edward Clerihew Bentley]. A four-lined piece of light verse, in irregular metre, rhyming *aabb*:

Sir Christopher Wren
Said, 'I am going to dine with some men.
If anybody calls
Say I am designing St Paul's.'

As in this example, the first line is usually the name of a person, on whom the other lines make a comment. See VERSE. [LITERATURE]. R.C.

CLICHÉ, also cliche [1820s as a term in printing for a stereotype plate; 1890s as a term in the criticism of usage: from French *cliché* a stereotype or stencil. Compare BOILERPLATE, STEREOTYPE]. A usually pejorative general term for a word or phrase regarded as having lost its freshness and vigour through overuse (and therefore suggesting insincerity, lack of thought, or laziness on the part of the user). Many idioms and stock expressions are commonly called clichés: everyday phrases such as *all of a sudden, anything goes, strictly speaking*; whole or part proverbs such as *there's no smoke without fire, don't count your chickens*; similes such as *dead as a doornail, quick as a flash, avoid like the plague*; and fashionable usages such as *the name of the game, the bottom line*. In addition to its application to language, the term is widely used to refer to any social, artistic, literary, dramatic, cinematic, or other formula that through overexposure has, in the view of a commentator, become trite and commonplace.

Comments on clichés. Critics of the media often castigate as clichés 'tired expressions' produced under pressure by journalists and others writing against a deadline, and language teachers commonly deplore 'hackneyed usages' in the work of their students as marks of derivative ideas and sloppy presentation. Because such criticism is often scathing, usage guides generally offer advice on how to avoid (being accused of) using

clichés. For example, the *Longman Guide to English Usage* (Sidney Greenbaum & Janet Whitcut, 1988) describes them as 'substitutes for independent thinking and writing' and lists the following as 'always clichés': *in this day and age, each and every, for love or money, the calm before the storm, none the worse for wear, leave no stone unturned, explore every avenue, food for thought*. The compilers note, however, that 'a stereotyped expression may be justified as appropriate to the context' and advise the reader:

You should use your judgment, and not choose a cliché simply because it is the first thing that comes into your head.

The *Bloomsbury Good Word Guide* (ed. Martin Manswer, 1988) illustrates the term with such long-established phrases as *from time immemorial, as old as the hills, last but not least* as well as the more recent *at the end of the day, at this moment in time, keep a low profile*, and adds:

Not all fixed phrases are necessarily bad. Some clichés were quite apt when first used but have become hackneyed over the years. One can hardly avoid using the occasional cliché, but clichés that are inefficient in conveying their meaning or are inappropriate to the occasion should be avoided.

The cliché and originality. The use of the term *cliché* in the late 19c and throughout the 20c has been associated with a desire for originality of expression. Such a desire, however, is not much older than the term itself. Many stock expressions often currently described as clichés are part of a primarily oral process that facilitates fluency while speakers are thinking ahead to their next points or are wrestling with difficult ideas. Proverbs, because they are mnemonic formulas, help people pass on elements of oral tradition without needing or seeking to be novel or clever every time. Comparably, many common expressions derive from classical cultures (such as Greece and Rome) and much-admired texts (such as the Bible and Shakespeare's plays), and have become part of the language because they have long been highly valued, and acquire as a result a kind of proverbial status. Traditional approaches to education have also encouraged students to copy or quote the precise expressions of famous predecessors whenever possible rather than to seek to be original before they are ready. All such usages and formulas were admired precisely because they *were* unoriginal, and writers or speakers used them because they were familiar to their audiences. In such works as the Homeric epics, stock formulas served to maintain the rhythm of the verse and were mnemonically useful for performers and listeners alike. The phrase *rosy-fingered dawn* occurs so often in the *Odyssey* that a modern reader, accustomed to the idea of the cliché, might conclude that Homer was sloppy and unoriginal where in reality he was following the precise conventions of his craft. In making an assessment of various definitions of and comments on the cliché, *Webster's Dictionary of English Usage* (ed. W. Ward Gilman, 1989) observes:

We will offer only two suggestions. The first is that in all the use of *trite, overused, stale, outworn, threadbare* and such descriptors there is probably a connecting thread of meaninglessness. You might, then, want to base your notion of the cliché not on the expression itself but on its use; if it seems to be used without much reference to a definite meaning, it is then perhaps a cliché. But even this line of attack fails to separate cliché from the common forms of polite social intercourse. A second and more workable approach would be simply to call a cliché whatever word or expression you have heard or seen often enough to find annoying. Many writers, in fact, do seem to use some such rough-and-ready definition.

See BOILERPLATE, CONVENTION, FORMULA, HACK, HACKNEYED, IDIOM, JOURNALESE, METAPHOR, PLATITUDE, POETIC DICTION, PROVERB, QUOTATION, SHIBBOLETH, STEREOTYPE, STOCK, TIMESPEAK, TRITE, TRUISM. [LITERATURE, MEDIA, STYLE, USAGE]. T.MCA.

Bagnall, Nicolas. 1985. *A Defence of Clichés*. London: Constable.
Partridge, Eric. 1947. *A Dictionary of Clichés*. London: Routledge & Kegan Paul.
Rees, Nigel. 1984. *The Joy of Clichés: A Complete User's Guide*. London: Macdonald.

CLICK. See VELARIC.

CLIMAX [16c: through Latin from Greek *klîmax* a ladder]. (1) In rhetoric, an ascending series of words, ideas, or events, in which intensity and significance increase step by step: 'For want of a nail the shoe was lost; for want of a shoe the horse was lost; and for want of a horse the rider was lost' (Benjamin Franklin, *Poor Richard's Almanack*, 1758). (2) In drama, a crisis or moment of decision. In a five-act play, such as Shakespeare's, the climax usually occurs near the end of the third act. (3) In general usage, the highest or most intense point in an experience or series of events. By implication, anything following a climax is anticlimactic, but a work of literature, a drama, and life itself may sustain a series of minor and major climaxes. Generally, in the 20c, a play, novel, or film ends after its main climax. See ANTICLIMAX. [STYLE]. T.MCA.

CLINCH. See PUN.

CLIPPED [15c]. A non-technical term for a way of speaking English that is closely associated with the RP accent, with officers in the British Armed Forces, and with 'keeping a stiff upper lip' (remaining firm in the face of adversity). A clipped style is terse and tight-mouthed. See DIALECT IN NEW ZEALAND, KING'S ENGLISH, RECEIVED PRONUNCIATION (RP). [SPEECH, STYLE]. T.MCA.

CLIPPING [1930s in this sense]. Also **clipped form, clipped word, shortening**. An abbreviation formed by the loss of word elements, usually syllabic: *pro* from *professional*, *tec* from *detective*. The process is attested from the 16c (*coz* from *cousin* 1559, *gent* from *gentleman* 1564); in the early 18c, Swift objected to the reduction of Latin *mobile vulgus* (the fickle throng) to *mob*. Clippings can be either selective, relating to one sense of a word only (*condo* is short for *condominium* when it refers to accommodation, not to joint sovereignty), or polysemic (*rev* stands for either *revenue* or *revision*, and *revs* for the revolutions of wheels). There are three kinds of clipping:

(1) *Back-clippings*, in which an element or elements are taken from the end of a word: *ad(vertisement)*, *chimp(anzee)*, *deli(catessen)*, *hippo(potamus)*, *lab(oratory)*, *piano(forte)*, *reg(ulation)s*. Back-clipping is common with diminutives formed from personal names: *Cath(erine)*, *Will(iam)*. Clippings of names often undergo adaptations: *Catherine* to the pet forms *Cathie, Kate, Katie, William* to *Willie, Bill, Billy*. Sometimes, a clipped name can develop a new sense: *willie* a euphemism for penis, *billy* a club or a male goat. Occasionally, the process can be humorously reversed: for example, offering in a British restaurant to pay the william.

(2) *Fore-clippings*, in which an element or elements are taken from the beginning of a word: *(ham)burger*, *(omni)bus*, *(violon)cello*, *(heli)copter*, *(alli)gator*, *(tele)phone*, *(earth)quake*. They also occur with personal names, sometimes with adaptations: *Becky* for *Rebecca*, *Drew* for *Andrew*, *Ginny* for *Virginia*. At the turn of the century, a fore-clipped word was usually given an opening apostrophe, to mark the loss: *'phone, 'cello, 'gator*. This practice is now rare.

(3) *Fore-and-aft clippings*, in which elements are taken from the beginning and end of a word: *(in)flu(enza)*, *(de)tec(tive)*. This is commonest with longer personal names: *Lex* from *Alexander*, *Liz* from *Elizabeth*. Such names often demonstrate the versatility of hypocoristic clipping: *Alex, Alec, Lex, Sandy, Zander; Eliza, Liz, Liza, Lizzie, Bess, Betsy, Beth, Betty*.

Clippings are not necessarily uniform throughout a language: *mathematics* becomes *maths* in BrE and *math* in AmE. *Reverend* as a title is usually shortened to *Rev* or *Rev.*, but is *Revd* in the house style of Oxford University Press. Back-clippings with *-ie* and *-o* are common in AusE and NZE: *arvo* afternoon, *journo* journalist. Sometimes clippings become distinct words far removed from the applications of the original full forms: *fan* in *fan club* is from *fanatic*; BrE *navvy*, a general labourer, is from a 19c use of *navigator*, the digger of a 'navigation' or canal. See ABBREVIATION, APH(A)ERESIS, APOCOPE, APOSTROPHE[1], AUSTRALIAN ENGLISH, COMPOUND WORD, DIMINUTIVE, EPONYM, WORD-FORMATION. [NAME, WORD]. T.MCA.

CLOSE READING. In literary theory, a reading of a text that seeks the fullest possible understanding through study of all information relevant to it. The aim of the New Critics, following the theories of I. A. Richards and William Empson, was to produce such a reading by studying the linguistic features of a text in their relationships and ambiguities. They regarded matters external to the text as irrelevant, considering that the text contained in itself all that was needed for a good 'reading'. The approach was widely adopted in British and American higher and secondary education, and helped to develop interest in the language of literature. Compare EXPLICATION DE TEXTE. See LITERARY CRITICISM. [LITERATURE]. R.C.

CLUTTERING. See LANGUAGE PATHOLOGY.

COALESCENCE [16c: from Latin *coalescens/coalescentis* growing together]. In phonetics, a mutual assimilation of two sounds that results in a single sound: in BrE, /t/ and /j/ as in *tune* /tjuːn/ becoming /tʃ/ (as if 'tchoon'); /d/ and /j/ as in *due* becoming /dʒ/ (as if 'joo'). Such pronunciations have often been stigmatized, but the equivalent coalescence of /s/ and /j/ in *sugar*, becoming /ʃ/ ('shoogar'), is universally accepted. See ASSIMILATION. [SPEECH].
G.K., T.MCA.

COBBETT, William [1763-1835]. English soldier, politician, reformer, writer, editor, and grammarian. Born at Farnham, Surrey, son of a farmer, he joined the army and became a sergeant-major, but had to flee after bringing a charge of embezzlement against his superiors, first to France, then the US, where he wrote in defence of Britain under the pseudonym *Peter Porcupine*. When he returned in 1800, he was received with admiration, but was soon in trouble for expressing radical views. In 1810, he was imprisoned and fined after protesting about flogging in the army. He became Member of Parliament for Oldham in 1832. His most enduring book is *Rural Rides* (1830), an account of a journey through England. From 1802 until his death, Cobbett edited the radical journal *Political Register*, published at a price working-class readers could afford. Resisting the convention of editorial anonymity, he developed the *leading*

article or *editorial*. He started the reports of Parliament which became the official record, *Hansard*. His *English Grammar* (1818) was intended to help those seeking literacy through their own efforts. It was written in a prescriptive but friendly style as letters to his son. Hazlitt commented that he wrote 'plain, broad downright English'. [BIOGRAPHY, EUROPE, GRAMMAR, STYLE].
R.C.

COBUILD [1980s: an acronym for *Collins Birmingham University International Language Database*]. (1) A British research facility set up at the U. of Birmingham in 1980 and funded by Collins publishers with the aim of compiling works of reference and course materials for the teaching of English. Its director is John Sinclair, Professor of Modern English Language. The primary work of COBUILD has been the creation and analysis of a corpus of contemporary, mainly BrE texts, some recorded from speech. By 1985, this corpus had reached 18m running words, representing 260,000 word types, over half of which occur only once. Patrick Hanks, former project manager of the facility, has reported that 2% of the types (that is, 5,000 different spelling forms) account for 87% of the tokens. The implication is that 87% of all English texts comprises some 5,000 words, which could be presented in a basic dictionary as some 2,000 entries. Also in 1985, Sinclair began work on a *monitor corpus*, in which a constant flow of text runs through a suite of computer programs that assess word frequencies, usage patterns, and other occurrences. (2) An abbreviation and informal title for the *Collins COBUILD English Language Dictionary* (1987), a work derived from a study of the COBUILD corpus and primarily intended for foreign learners of English. It defines over 70,000 words, giving priority to the most frequent. Its definitions are generally supported by examples of usage taken from the corpus. See COLLINS, CORPUS, FREQUENCY COUNT, LEARNER'S DICTIONARY [COBUILD], VOCABULARY CONTROL. [EDUCATION, LANGUAGE]. T.MCA.

COCKNEY [14c: used with and without an initial capital]. A working-class Londoner, especially in the East End, and English as used by such a Londoner. Though often stigmatized as a gutter dialect, Cockney is a major element in the English of London, the core of a diverse variety spoken by some 7m people in the Greater London area.

Origins of the term. In Langland's *Piers Plowman* (1362), *cokeneyes* means eggs, apparently small and misshapen, as if laid by a cock. In Chaucer's *Canterbury Tales* (c.1386), the Reeve uses *cokenay* in the sense of a mother's darling or milksop. By the early 16c, country people had extended the term to people brought up in cities and ignorant of real life: 'This cokneys and tytyllynges [*delicati pueri*] may abide no sorrow when they come to age. In this great citees as London, York the children be so nycely and wantonly brought up that comonly they can little good' (Robert Whitinton, *Vulgaria*, 1520). By the early 17c, however, this expression of disdain for the city-bred young had narrowed to one place and one person: the 'Bow-bell Cockney' (1600) and 'our Cockney of London' (1611). In 1617, two definitions were written for the term in this sense:

A *Cockney* or *Cockny*, applied only to one borne within the sound of Bow-bell, that is, within the City of London, which tearme came first out of this tale: That a Cittizens sonne riding with his father into the Country asked, when he heard a horse neigh, what the horse did his father answered, the horse doth neigh; riding farther he heard a cocke crow, and said doth the *cocke neigh* too? and therefore Cockney or Cocknie, by inuersion thus: *incock*, q. *incoctus* i. raw or vnripe in Country-mens affaires (John Minsheu, *Ductor in linguas: The guide into tongues*).

Londiners, and all within the sound of Bow-bell, are in reproch called Cocknies (Fynes Moryson, *An Itinerary*).

A succession of stigmas has therefore been associated with the name from the start: odd egg, milksop, young city slicker, and street-wise Londoner. At the same time, the reference of *Cockney* moved from something new or young (an egg, a child) to a spoiled adolescent (city youth) to anyone of any age born in London within the sound of the bells of St Mary-le-Bow Church. With 'our Cockney of London', the other usages were forgotten and a stereotype developed of a breed with no interest in life beyond the capital: 'That Synods Geography was as ridiculous as a Cockneys (to whom all is Barbary beyond Brainford; and Christendome endeth at Greenwitch)' (Richard Whitlock, *Zootomia, or observations on the present manners of the English*, 1654).

Eighteenth-century Cockney. Comments on the usage of London Cockneys date from the 18c. After setting out the faults of the Irish, the Scots, and the Welsh, the London elocutionist John Walker noted in 1791: 'There are dialects peculiar to Cornwall, Lancashire, Yorkshire, and every distant county in England; but as a consideration of these would lead to a detail too minute for the present occasion, I shall conclude these remarks with a few observations on the peculiarities of my countrymen, the Cockneys; who, as they are the models of pronunciation to the distant provinces, ought to be the more scrupulously correct' (*A Critical Pronouncing Dictionary of the English Language*).

Walker lists four faults: (1) A habit among Londoners of 'the lowest order' of pronouncing words like *fists*, *posts*, *wastes* as two syllables, as if there were an *e* between the *t* and the *s*. (2) Not confined to the lowest order, 'the pronunciation of *v* for *w*, and more frequently of *w* for *v*' ('vine and weal' for *wine and veal*), which he called 'a blemish of the first magnitude'. (3) Not pronouncing *h* after *w*, so that 'we do not find the least distinction between *while* and *wile*, *whet* and *wet*, *where* and *were*, &c.' (4) 'Sinking the *h* at the beginning of words where it ought to be sounded, and of sounding it, either where it is not seen, or where it ought to be sunk. Thus we not infrequently hear, especially among children, *heart* pronounced *art*, and *arm*, *harm*.' He also notes that words like *humour* are pronounced as if written 'yewmour'. Even so, he concludes: 'Thus I have endeavoured to correct some of the more glaring errors of my countrymen, who, with all their faults, are still upon the whole the best pronouncers of the English language.'

Nineteenth-century Cockney. Cockney and London usage seem to have been synonymous for Walker. He makes no distinction between refined and unrefined usage in the capital apart from his reference to the lowest social order. In the 19c, however, the term was limited to those whose usage never served as a model for anyone. By the time of Shaw's play *Pygmalion* (1913), Cockney was generally regarded as debased language ('gutter Cockney') and Shaw's flower-girl Eliza Doolittle received far more help from the phonetician Henry Higgins than Walker felt his fellows needed. The speech of all classes of Londoner has changed greatly since Walker's time. In the process, one of his 'faults' has by and large become a feature of the standard spoken English of England: the /w/ in such pairs as *while*/*wile*: see W and WH-SOUND. Of the others, one remains a stigma, one has only recently disappeared, and the third vanished long ago but remains controversial. The dropping of aitches is widespread beyond Cockneydom and is generally considered substandard. There is, however, uncertainty about the extent to which aitches are sounded where they 'ought to be sunk': see AITCH, H. Pronunciations like 'fistiz' for *fists* continued into the 20c, but appear to have died out in the 1950s. The exchange of *v* and *w* has been the most controversial of Walker's shibboleths, commentators who deny that it ever occurred sometimes blaming Dickens for inventing it. He uses it copiously in *The Pickwick Papers* (1837), as part of the dialect of Samuel Weller, whose father calls him 'Samivel Veller':

'I had a reg'lar new fit o' clothes that mornin', gen'l'men of the jury,' said Sam, 'and that was a wery partickler and uncommon circumstance with me in those days. . . . If they wos a pair o' patent double million magnifyin' gas microscopes of hextra power, p'raps I might be able to see through a flight o' stairs and a deal door; but bein' only eyes, you see, my wision's limited' (ch. 34).

Walker, however, provides the proof that Sam's style of speech existed well before Dickens created him, but it appears to have been in decline when Dickens made it a literary stereotype, and had virtually disappeared by the 1870s, as noted by Shaw in an appendix to *Captain Brassbound's Conversion* (1900):

When I came to London in 1876, the Sam Weller dialect had passed away so completely that I should have given it up as a literary fiction if I had not discovered it surviving in a Middlesex village, and heard of it from an Essex one. Some time in the eighties the late Alexander Tuer called attention in the Pall Mall Gazette to several peculiarities of modern cockney, and to the obsolescence of the Dickens dialect that was still being copied from book to book by authors who never dreamt of using their ears, much less of training them to listen.

Twentieth-century Cockney. Currently, the term *Cockney* is applied to usage in the London area in a fairly free and easy way. There are, however, two broad perceptions: (1) That it is a range of usage centred on the East End of London, with fringe forms that shade out into the counties around the city, especially among the young. Here, the term refers to a widely diffused variety of working-class speech in south-eastern England. (2) That, in sociolinguistic terms, it is the basilect in a range of usages in which standard English with an RP accent is the acrolect. Here, Cockney is the core of working-class London speech and is not properly applied to the mesolects of the area, which may however have Cockney-like features. Whichever viewpoint is chosen, degrees of Cockneyhood are commonly perceived in the London area, according to such factors as class, social aspirations, locality, and education. The association with Bow bells is sometimes mentioned by inner Londoners with nostalgia. Few babies are now born near the Church of St Mary-le-Bow, and many who have in the past been born within the sound of its bells could never, because of their social class, have been Cockneys, except ironically. Cockney has long been associated with the East End and the inner suburbs of east London: Aldgate, Bethnal Green, Bow, Hackney, Limehouse, Mile End, Old Ford, Poplar, Shoreditch, Stepney, Wapping, and Whitechapel. Core Cockney is distinct from working-class usage south of the Thames in Bermondsey, Southwark, and Walworth. Like many varieties of English, it is most easily identified through its extreme forms. Like other stigmatized urban dialects, such as Brooklyn (New York), Glasgow, and Scouse (Liverpool), it is vigorous and influential, but generally viewed by both its speakers and outsiders as a liability for the upwardly mobile.

Pronunciation. The following features contribute to core Cockney speech: (1) *F and V*. Cockney differs from all other varieties of English in having /f/ for /θ/, as in 'firty fahsn' *thirty thousand*. This is matched medially by /v/ for /ð/, as in 'bovver' *bother*, 'muvver' *mother*. Initially, the sound is closer to /ð/ in such words as *this*, *these*, but pronunciations like 'vis' and 'vese' can be heard. *Everything, nothing, something* are pronounced 'evryfink', 'nuffink', 'sumfink'. A shibboleth for the *f/v* usage is *Firty fahsn fevvers on a frush's froat*. (2) *H-dropping*. Like many varieties of English in England, Cockney has no initial /h/ in words like *house* (*Nobody lives in them ouses now*), but sometimes adds /h/ for emphasis or as hypercorrection before initial vowels, as with 'hever' for *ever* (*Did you hever see the like?*). (3) *Diphthongs*. Cockney is well known for the elongation of its vowel sounds, often represented in print by several vowels together, as in Shaw's 'daownt' for *don't*. Distinctive diphthongs include /əi/ for RP /iː/ in *beet/seat*, /ai/ for RP /eɪ/ in *fate/great*, /ɒɪ/ for RP /aɪ/ in *high/why*. Conversely, the monophthong /aː/ serves where RP has the diphthong /aʊ/ in *about* 'abaht', *thousand* 'fahsn'. (4) *The glottal stop*. Use of the glottal stop for medial and final /t/, /kt/, and /k/, as in *but*, *butter*, *hectic*, *technical* ('tetnical'), and a glottalized /tʃ/, as in *actually* ('atshelly'): see GLOTTAL STOP. (5) *Linking R*. There is no postvocalic /r/ in Cockney, which like RP is non-rhotic: 'cah' for *car*, 'cahd' for *card*. Cockney shares the linking *r* used generally in south-east England, as in 'draw/r/ing room' for *drawing room*, 'Shah/r of Persia' for *Shah of Persia*: see LINKING R. (6) Syllable-final /l/ is vocalized as /w/: 'tewwim' for *tell him*: see L-SOUNDS.

Syntax and usage. (1) The grammar of Cockney is by and large 'general non-standard', with such usages as double negation (*There aint nuffink like it* There is nothing like it) and *done* and *seen* for *did* and *saw* (*I done it yesterday, I just seen er*). (2) Question tags are widely used to invite agreement or establish one's position: *I'm elpin you now, inneye?* I am helping you now, ain't I?— although I may not have helped you before or wanted in fact to help you at all; *Well, e knew all abaht it, dinnee?* Well, he knew all about it, didn't he?—Because he knew all about it, it's not surprising he did what he did. (3) The prepositions *to* and *at* are frequently dropped in relation to places: *I'm goin down the pub* I'm going down to the pub, *He's round is mate's* He is round at his friend's house, *They're over me mum's* They're over at my mother's.

Literary and stage Cockney. Since the time of Dickens, Cockney dialogue has often been included in otherwise standard texts. A fairly consistent sub-orthography has developed for it, such as *abaht* about, *Gawd* God, *larf* laugh, *muvver* mother, *orful* awful, *orl* all, with the apostrophe used to mark absent *h* as in *'abit* and absent *g*, signalling the pronunciation of *-ing* as syllabic /n/, as in *cuttin'* and *shoutin'*. Writers generally use just enough for flavour, along with typical expressions and a cocky, cheeky, or cheerful style, as in Rudyard Kipling's *The 'Eathen* (1892):

> The 'eathen in 'is blindness bows down to wood an'
> stone;
> 'E don't obey no orders unless they is 'is own;
> 'E keeps 'is side-arms awful: 'e leaves 'em all about,
> An' then comes up the Regiment an' pokes the
> 'eathen out.

Shaw employs a parallel stage Cockney for a similar burst of chauvinism in *Captain Brassbound's Conversion*:

> It gows agin us as Hinglishmen to see these bloomin furriners settin ap their Castoms Ahses and spheres o hinfluence and sich lawk hall owver Arfricar. Daownt Harfricar belong as much to huz as to them? thets wot we sy (Act I).

Allnutt, the mechanic in C. S. Forester's *The African Queen* (1935: ch. 2) is less orthographically assertive, but remains unequivocally a working-class Londoner:

> 'Why not?'
> 'Rapids, miss. Rocks an' cataracts an' gorges. You 'aven't been there, miss. I 'ave. There's a nundred miles of rapids down there. Why, the river's got a different nime where it comes out in the Lake to what it's called up 'ere. It's the Bora down there. That just shows you. No one knew they was the same river until that chap Spengler—'

Literary approaches to Cockney have generally been the work of middle-class non-Cockneys. Their conventions have, however, been both used and queried by Cockneys writing about their own speech, as in Barltrop and Wolveridge's *The Muvver Tongue* (1980):

> But the short ou of 'out' and 'about' is the chronically misrepresented Cockney vowel. For a hundred years there has been a convention of writing it as 'ah'. Shaw put 'baw ya flahr orf a pore gel' into Eliza Doolittle's mouth: 'rahnd the ahses' is the classic way of conveying East London speech. It is painfully wide of the mark. Whatever a Cockney's 'out' may be thought to sound like, it is not 'art'—which is what 'aht' would make it. The sound is a lengthened short u. It might be written 'uht', the u as in 'cut' but stretched out; more precisely, it is 'uh-ert'. The phonetic version of a Cockney's 'buy a flower off a poor girl' would be 'bah-eeya fluh-er orf a pore gel'. Practically any Cockney does this when he talks, but in a street vendor's chant it would become a flourish and almost musical.

Tone and rhetoric. A striking aspect of Cockney, especially when compared with RP, is its effusive range of tone and emotion. Barltrop and Wolveridge comment:

The East Londoner likes his utterances to be attention-catching whether they are plaintive, indignant, gloomy or humorous . . . Nagging, anecdote, giving opinions and even greeting a friend in the street are done with the same mobility of voice, to squeeze the utmost meaning out of them, and it is noticeable in ordinary conversation.

The devices of vigorous delivery include a wide range of tones, emphatic loudness, strong facial expression, and vigorous body language. There is in particular pitch prominence on content words (nouns, verbs, adjectives, adverbs) and their vowels are often stretched, as in *You ought to ave SEEEEN it—it was ever so GOOOOD*. In tandem, Cockneys are generally more uninhibited socially (laughing loudly, complaining vigorously) than middle-class Londoners, a feature which may have been influenced by Gypsies, Jews, and Irish in the East End.

Slang. Probably the best-known and most-discussed usage is *Cockney rhyming slang*, as in *Would you Adam and Eve it?* Would you believe it?, and *They had a bit of a bull and a cow* a row. It may have originated in thieves' cant, but its history is unclear and there is little evidence that it was ever widespread or extensive enough to be a code in its own right. If it was once so used by traders, entertainers, thieves, and others, the secret has been well kept. Such word-play was a fashionable game in the West End of London in the 1930s, and during and after the Second World War was disseminated by the media. Many of its usages have been spread by television: *Brahms and Liszt* pissed, drunk, in the 1970s TV comedy series *Steptoe and Son*, which also used *berk*, a clipping of *Berkeley/Berkshire Hunt* a cunt (whose first *OED* citation is 1936). Several rhymes for the same word may compete: *tea* is both *Rosy Lea* and *you and me*. *Bristol Cities* (titties) may have been media-inspired, traditional Cockney being *Manchester Cities* or *threepenny bits* (tits). Such slang has contributed to informal BrE at large such usages as *cobblers*, as an expression of scepticism from *cobblers' awls* balls, testicles, *butchers* from *butcher's hook* a look, *Jimmy Riddle* a piddle (an act of urinating), *rabbit on* for talking all the time, from *rabbit and pork* talk, *raspberry* for a derisive blowing sound with the lips (apparently from *raspberry tart* fart): see RHYMING SLANG.

Cockney slang includes: (1) Words from Romany: *chavvy* a child, *mush* a mate, buddy, *put the mockers on* to jinx. (2) Words from Yiddish: *gezumph/gazump* to swindle, *schemozzle* a disturbance, *schlemiel* a fool. (3) Minced oaths and euphemisms, especially relating to *God*: *Blimey* God blind me, *Cor* God, as in *Cor stone the crows*, *Gordon Bennett* (the name of an early 20c car-racing promoter) God. (4) Forces slang picked up in Asia: *ackers* money (probably from Arabic *fakka* small change), *bint* a girl (Arabic), *cushy* soft, easy, as in *a cushy billet* an easy job (from Hindi *khush* pleasure), *dekko* a look (from the Hindi imperative *dekho* look); *shufti* a look (Arabic), *doolally* (mad, from Deolali, a town in India where a British Forces mental hospital was located). (5) Abbreviations, sometimes with *-o* added (compare AusE slang): *aggro* aggravation (= aggression), *rarzo* a red nose (short for raspberry). (6) Back-slang: *yob* a boy, sometimes in the form *yobbo*. (7) Usage with run-together phrases that sound like, and are often written as, single words: *Gawdelpus* God help us, *Geddoudovit* Get out of it, *Gorblimey* originally 'God blind me', *Wotcha/Wotcher* What cheer (a once widespread greeting). Because of wartime contacts, National Service after the Second World War, and the media, many of these expressions are understood and often used throughout Britain.

Social issues. Core Cockney, fringe Cockney, and their neighbouring forms make up the most prominent and widely spoken urban dialect in Britain. It rests on an ancient working-class tradition and has had considerable media influence on BrE usage at large, especially in the London-based tabloid newspapers, and in radio and TV popular entertainment, such as the current BBC soap opera *EastEnders*. It remains, however, a stigmatized variety that attracts little academic attention and is often regarded as quaint and amusing. Barltrop and Wolveridge note:

We wanted to write for Cockneys as much as about them. The language is constantly shown as picturesque or comic, and almost invariably as inferior; it is taken for granted as coming from a people who do not know any better. We hope to persuade Cockneys as well as others that it is more than the equal of any other form of speech. . . . The Cockney does not have to define class—it defines him. While East Londoners are defined by the social system as are all other working people, they are resentful of it in a resigned sort of way and strongly conscious of 'Them and Us'. . . . Thus, speaking well—'talking posh'—does not make a great impression; it smacks of being the enemy's language.

The Cockneys share such sentiments with users of other working-class varieties that grew up with the Industrial Revolution. Like speakers of Scouse and Gutter Glasgow, they are embattled and often thumb a linguistic nose at the rest of the world. Cockneys have faced an extra stigma because they have often been seen as letting London down. Paradoxically, they are at the same time invoked with affection as a key element in defining the city. See AITCH, DICKENS, GLOTTAL STOP, LONDON, POSH, PYGMALION, SHAW. [EUROPE, VARIETY]. T.MCA.

Barltrop, Robert, & Wolveridge, Jim. 1980. *The Muvver Tongue*. London & West Nyack: The Journeyman Press.
Franklyn, Julian. 1953. *The Cockney: A Survey of London Life and Language*. London: Deutsch.
Matthews, William. 1938. *Cockney Past and Present*. London: Routledge.
Trudgill, Peter (ed.). 1984. *Language in the British Isles*. Cambridge: University Press.
Wells, John C. 1982. *Accents of English*. Volume 2: *The British Isles*. Cambridge: University Press.

COCKNEY RHYMING SLANG. See COCKNEY, RHYMING SLANG.

CODE [14c: through French from Latin *codex* a manuscript book (in which laws were recorded)]. (1) A system of words, letters, signs, sounds, lights, etc., that conveys information. (2) In cryptography, a system of letters or other signs that makes sense only to someone who already knows its *key* or *cipher*, and because of this can *encode* or *decode* a message. (3) In communication theory, conventions for converting one signalling system to another. (4) In sociolinguistics, a system of communication, spoken or written, such as a language, dialect, or variety. See CHARACTER, CIPHER, CODE-MIXING AND CODE-SWITCHING, COMMUNICATION, CONVENTION, CRYPTOGRAPHY, ELABORATED AND RESTRICTED CODE, REDUNDANCY. [LANGUAGE, MEDIA, STYLE]. D.C., T.MCA.

CODE-MIXING AND CODE-SWITCHING. Terms in sociolinguistics for language and especially speech that draws to differing extents on at least two languages combined in different ways, as when a Malay/English bilingual says: *This morning I hantar my baby tu dekat babysitter tu lah* (*hantar* took, *tu dekat* to the, *lah* a particle marking solidarity). A *code* may be a language or a variety or style of a language; the term *code-mixing* emphasizes hybridization, and the term *code-switching* emphasizes movement from one language to another. Mixing and switching probably occur to some extent in the speech of all bilinguals, so that there is a sense in which a person capable of using two languages, A and B, has three systems available for use: A, B, and C (a range of hybrid forms that can be used with comparable bilinguals but not with monolingual speakers of A or B). There are four major types of switching: (1) *Tag-switching*, in which tags and certain set phrases in one language are inserted into an utterance otherwise in another, as when a Panjabi/English bilingual says: *It's a nice day, hana?* (*hai nā* isn't it). (2) *Intra-sentential switching*, in which switches occur within a clause or sentence boundary, as when a Yoruba/English bilingual says: *Won o arrest a* *single person* (*won o* they did not). (3) *Inter-sentential switching*, in which a change of language occurs at a clause or sentence boundary, where each clause or sentence is in one language or the other, as when a Spanish/English bilingual says: *Sometimes I'll start a sentence in English y terminó en español* (and finish it in Spanish). This last may also occur as speakers take turns. (4) *Intra-word switching*, in which a change occurs within a word boundary, such as in *shoppā* (English *shop* with the Panjabi plural ending) or *kuenjoy* (English *enjoy* with the Swahili prefix *ku*, meaning 'to').

Borrowing and lending. Various grammatical constraints, some language-specific and some universal, have been proposed to account for code-switching and code-mixing, but none has so far proved free of exceptions. There is also some dispute about the extent to which borrowing can be distinguished from code-switching. Those who make such a distinction generally rely on criteria such as the degree of phonological, morphological, and syntactic integration undergone by the item in question. If there is full integration, the element can be regarded as a borrowing. In cases where closely related languages/varieties are in contact, compromise forms may emerge, as with Scots and ScoE, and it may not be possible to assign every word to one or the other variety/language, thus making the distinction between borrowing and code-switching tenuous. Panjabi/English bilinguals (among others from India and Pakistan) have created a set of mixed compound verbs: for example, *ple karnā* (play do), where *karnā* is a verb in the construction of many compounds; Panjabi uses the verb *khelnā* (to play). This process has resulted in parallel lexical sets in most of the Indian languages: for example, Hindi-Urdu/English *love karnā* (love do), Hindi/Sanskrit *prem karnā* and Urdu/Persian *mahabat karnā* all mean 'to make love'.

Names and attitudes: us and them. Some communities have special names, often pejorative or facetious, or both, for a hybrid variety: in India, *Hindlish* and *Hinglish* are used for the widespread mixing of Hindi and English; in Nigeria, *amulumala* (verbal salad) is used for English and Yoruba mixing and switching; in the Philippines, the continuum of possibilities is covered by the terms *Tagalog—Engalog—Taglish—English*, in Quebec, by *français—franglais—Frenglish—English*. Despite the fact that mixing and switching are often stigmatized in the communities in which they occur, they often serve such important functions as marking ethnic and group boundaries. Among minorities, the home language (*the 'we' code*) is used to signify in-group, informal, and personalized activities, while the other language (*the 'they' code*) is used to mark out-group, more formal, and distant events. Speakers use a change of language to indicate their attitude to what is being said. In the following, Panjabi marks the in-group and English the out-group among immigrants to the UK: *Usi ingrezi sikhi e te why can't they learn?* ('We learn English, so why can't they learn [an Asian language]?'). The switch emphasizes the boundaries between 'them' and 'us'.

Other reasons for switching include the prestige of knowing the out-group or dominant language, often a language associated with a religion, empire, education, and a wide sphere of operation and interest: for example, social status has long been marked among Hindus in India by introducing elements of Sanskrit and Pali into vernacular use and among Muslims by bringing in Arabic and Persian. In Europe, the same effect has been achieved by introducing elements of Latin and Greek. Today, social status is marked in India and elsewhere by introducing elements of English. It is not always the case that borrowing or switching occurs because speakers do not know the words in one or the other language. Widespread code-switching often indicates greater or less shift towards the more dominant of the two languages. Currently, English is the most widely used language in the world for mixing and switching. See Tej. K. Bhatia & William Ritchie (eds.), *Code-Mixing: English across Languages* (*World Englishes* 8: 3, special issue, 1989).

See AFFECTATION, ANGLIKAANS, BILINGUALISM, BISOCIATION, BORROWING, CODE, DIGLOSSIA, ENGLISH, ENGLISHIZE, FRANGLAIS, -GLISH AND -LISH, INTERLANGUAGE, LANGUAGE SHIFT, LOAN, MACARONIC, MULTILINGUALISM, PHILIPPINE ENGLISH, SOCIOLINGUISTICS, SPANGLISH, STYLE-DRIFTING. [LANGUAGE, STYLE, VARIETY]. S.R., B.B.K.

CODEX. See BOOK, CODE.

COGNATE [17c: from Latin *cognatus* born together]. Related by descent; one of two or more words so related, especially across languages. English *mother*, German *Mutter* are cognate words; English *five*, Latin *quinque*, Greek *pénte* are all cognates, descended from the common Indo-European ancestor **penkwe*. Cognates are more or less like each other in form, but need not have much in common semantically: English *silly*, German *selig* holy, blessed. On the other hand, English *ma*, Chinese *mu* (mother) are known to be cognates; though similar in form and meaning, they cannot (at present at least) be traced to a common source. German *Standpunkt* and its English calque *standpoint* are not usually called cognates, even when their elements are cognates: *Stand* and *stand*, *Punkt* and *point*. Pairs of cognates in a single language, such as English *regal* and *royal* (both ultimately from Latin) are called *doublets*. Cognates are easy to find in related (or cognate) languages such as English, German, Greek, and Latin, but unrelated languages may also have cognate items: the common ancestor of English *tea*, Malay *teh* appears to be *t'e*, from the Amoy dialect of Chinese. See CALQUE, DOUBLET, LOAN. [HISTORY, WORD].   R.F.I.

COGNATE OBJECT. A noun that functions as the object of a verb to which it is etymologically or morphologically related: *to sing a song, to tell a tale*. [GRAMMAR, STYLE].   T.MCA.

COGNITIVE CODE APPROACH/TEACH-ING. See LANGUAGE TEACHING.

COGNITIVE MEANING [Late 20c]. In linguistics and psychology, meaning that is related to intellect rather than emotion, in contrast with *affective meaning*. See CONNOTATION AND DENOTATION, SEMANTICS. [LANGUAGE].   T.MCA.

COHERENCE [16c, but 1970s in the second sense: through French from Latin *cohaerentia*, from *cohaerere/cohaestum* to cling together]. (1) The act or state of being coherent: that is, logically consistent and connected. (2) In linguistics, unity in a text or discourse, which makes sense because its elements do not contradict each other's presuppositions. *Surface cohesion* refers to the logical relations between clauses or segments of a text (such as time sequence and cause and effect); *situational coherence* refers to consistency in the structure of the information, its relation to general knowledge, and the appropriateness of a text. See COHESION, DISCOURSE ANALYSIS, TEXT. [LANGUAGE, STYLE, WRITING].
                                    M.MCC., T.MCA.

COHESION [17c, but 1970s in the second sense: from Latin *cohaesio/cohaesionis*, from *cohaerere/cohaestum* to cling together]. (1) The act or state of cohering. (2) In linguistics, the use of language forms to indicate semantic relations between elements in a discourse. *Grammatical cohesion* concerns such matters as reference, ellipsis, substitution, and conjunction; *lexical cohesion* concerns such features as synonymy, antonymy, metonymy, collocation, repetition, etc.; *instantial cohesion* concerns ties that are valid only for a particular text. Together, cohesion and register contribute to *textuality*, the sense that something is a text and not a random collection of sentences. See COHERENCE, COLLOCATION, DISCOURSE ANALYSIS, REGISTER, TEXT. [LANGUAGE, STYLE, WRITING].   M.MCC., T.MCA.

COINAGE [14c in general, 17c in this sense]. An invented word or phrase and the process of inventing it. Like *loan* and *borrowing*, the term *coinage* is based on an ancient analogy between language and money. The creation of words without the use of earlier words is rare: for example, *googol*, the term for the number 1 followed by a hundred zeros, or 10^{100}, introduced by the American mathematician Edward Kasner, whose 9-year-old nephew coined it when asked to think up a name for a very big number. See NEOLOGISM/NEOLOGY, ROOT-CREATION, WORD-FORMATION. [WORD].   J.A.

COLERIDGE, Herbert [1830–61]. English barrister and philologist, great-nephew of Samuel Taylor Coleridge, born in Hampstead in London, and educated at Eton and Oxford. He played a leading part in launching the project which became *The Oxford English Dictionary*. In 1857, the Council of the Philological Society appointed him with Frederick J. Furnivall and Richard C. Trench 'as a committee to collect unregistered words in English', with Coleridge as Secretary. In 1859, he was appointed Editor of the Society's new dictionary. Until his untimely death from tuberculosis, he promoted or executed several essential preliminary tasks, including drawing up lists of books for excerpting by volunteers, the compilation of a 'Glossarial Index to the Printed English Literature of the Thirteenth Century' (1859), and the preparation of some trial entries for the letter A. See index. [BIOGRAPHY, EUROPE, REFERENCE].   A.J.A.

COLERIDGE, Samuel Taylor [1772–1834]. English poet, critic, and philosopher, born at Ottery St Mary, Devon, son of a clergyman, and educated at Christ's Hospital and Cambridge. During his long friendship with William Wordsworth and his sister Dorothy, he visited Germany with them in 1798 and lived near them in Somerset and the Lake District. His poetry, mainly written between 1796 and 1802, includes 'The Rime of the Ancient Mariner', 'Kubla Khan', 'Christabel', and 'Dejection'. An addiction to opium contributed to his gradual estrangement from the Wordsworths. He emphasized imagination as a creative force and regarded language not as mechanical but as a product of imagination capable of organic growth. Coleridge's insistence on the philosophical importance of language and imagination makes him prominent in the history of poetics; his *Biographia Literaria* (1817) includes criticisms of Wordsworth's theory of poetic diction. He came to believe that everyday language was not always the best language for poetry, and regarded the discipline of metre as vital to it; prose was 'words in their best order—poetry, the *best* words in the best order'. He was a great purveyor of moral instruction, as in *Lay Sermons*. He planned the *Encyclopedia Metropolitana* (1818), an uncompleted thematic work of reference intended to eclipse the *Encyclopaedia Britannica*. Although often said to have dissipated his genius by personal weakness, he influenced Keats and Tennyson in poetry, Thomas and Matthew Arnold in education, and Broad Church leaders like Charles Kingsley and Frederick Maurice in theology. See index. [BIOGRAPHY, EUROPE, LITERATURE, REFERENCE]. R.C.

COLLECTIVE NOUN, also collective. A noun referring to a group of people, animals, or things, and occurring in the singular with a singular or plural verb: *army, audience, couple, family, government, group.* The plural use (*The majority are in favour*) is commoner and more acceptable in BrE than AmE, where the singular form (*The majority is in favour*) is preferred. The choice of singular or plural verb depends on whether the group is seen as a unit or as a group of entities. Co-occurring possessives and pronouns differ accordingly: *I was impressed by the audience, which was a distinguished one. I was impressed by the audience, who were all in their seats by 7.30.* When plural, collectives follow normal rules of concord: *The audiences this week have been small but appreciative.* Names of countries can be used as collective nouns for sports teams, in such headlines as *Pakistan build up a substantial lead, England look in good shape for Santander.* See SYNECDOCHE. Collective nouns are sometimes called *group nouns* and the collective label is sometimes applied to plural-only words such as *cattle, clothes, people, police,* although these are not collective nouns as such. There are many collectives in popular and technical use for naming groups of people, animals, or things. Some are familiar to most people, such as a *bench* of magistrates, a *flight* of stairs, a *flock* of sheep, a *swarm* of bees; others are less well known (and of uncertain provenance), such as an *exaltation* of larks and an *unkindness* of ravens. See NOUN. [GRAMMAR]. S.C.

COLLEGE ENGLISH ASSOCIATION, short form *CEA*. An American society founded in 1939 and concerned with scholarly, professional, and academic issues relating to English literary studies. It publishes two journals, *The CEA Critic*, which emphasizes scholarship, and *The CEA Forum*, which emphasizes professional and pedagogical concerns. [AMERICAS, EDUCATION, MEDIA]. J.A.

COLLEGIATE. See WEBSTER'S COLLEGIATE DICTIONARIES.

COLLINS. A Scottish publishing company founded in 1819 by William Collins, a Glasgow schoolmaster, to print and publish religious and educational books, including the Bible under licence. In the 20c, Collins have become known as publishers of dictionaries. The small *Gem English Dictionary*, first published in 1902, its early editions edited by Ernest Weekley, has been a perennial best-seller. In the 1970s, Jan Collins, after six generations one of the last members of the family who ran the business, organized the creation of a range of large practical dictionaries, starting with the *Collins Spanish Dictionary* (1971), *Collins-Robert French Dictionary* (1978), and *Collins German Dictionary* (1980). In these works, widely considered breakthroughs in bilingual lexicography, usage is recorded and translated in detail without noting too closely the authoritarian pronouncements of academies. Semantic distinctions are observed through 'sense indicators' that help the reader select the appropriate translation for polysemous words. Sensitive to register and context, the dictionaries provide plentiful examples: they moved beyond the reductionist approach of providing word-for-word translation equivalents. Next came the publication of the *Collins English Dictionary* (1979), editorial director Laurence Urdang, editor Patrick Hanks, a work similar in size, style, and content to US collegiate dictionaries, including significant people and places, definitions of many technical usages, and words from varieties throughout the world, as well as (in contrast to the traditions of Oxford and Chambers) placing the commoner meanings of words first rather than their chronologically earlier meanings. A second edition appeared in 1986 and a third in 1991. In 1989, Collins were taken over by News International Corporation. Amalgamated with the US publisher Harper & Row, they currently trade under the name *HarperCollins.* See AUSTRALIAN PUBLISHING, BIBLE, BILINGUAL DICTIONARY, COBUILD, LEARNERS' DICTIONARIES. [EUROPE, MEDIA, REFERENCE]. T.MCA.

COLLOCATION [17c: from Latin *collocatio/collocationis* a placing together]. (1) The act of putting two or more things together, especially words in a pattern, and the result of that act. (2) In linguistics, a habitual association between particular words, such as *to* with *fro* in the phrase *to and fro,* and the uses of *to* after *answer* and before *me* in *You'll answer to me* (as opposed to *You'll answer me*). In the phrase *Let's draw up a list,* the phrasal verb *draw up* is said to collocate with the noun *list;* one can *draw up a list of legal terms* but not **draw up legal terms* (although one can *list legal terms*). Collocation is basic to language. Its subtleties must be learned, and failure to get the collocations of English right is a major indicator of foreignness: for example, talking about *rotten* rather than *rancid butter*. The British linguist J. R. Firth encouraged the use of the term as one of a contrastive pair: *collocation* for semantic association, *colligation* for syntactic association. In current usage, however, *collocation* generally covers both types of association. Cohesiveness in semantics and syntax is a matter of degree. Idioms are holophrastic, usually fixed in form and used without recourse to the meanings of their elements: it can rain *cats and dogs*, but never *dogs and cats or *cats and cows. Even with idioms, however, there can be some leeway: for example, at least the three verbs *banging*, *hitting*, and *knocking* can occupy the slot in the idiomatic sentence *It's like ——— your head against a (brick) wall*. Collocations are more loosely associated than idioms: contiguously (as with *tortoise* and *shell* in *tortoiseshell*) or proximately (as with *cat* and *purr* in *The cat was purring*). When the elements of compound words collocate, they form new lexical items: *house* and *boat* coming together in both *houseboat* and *boathouse*, each with a distinct meaning and use. An item that collocates with another is its *collocate*. See HOLOPHRASE, IDIOM, PARADIGMATIC AND SYNTAGMATIC. [GRAMMAR, STYLE, WORD].   T.MCA., K.W.

COLLOQUIAL [18c: from Latin *colloquialis* conversational, from *colloqui* to speak together]. A semi-technical term for the vernacular form of a language (*colloquial Arabic*) or, sometimes mildly pejorative, for informal, everyday speech, including slang (*colloquial usage*). See COLLOQUIALISM, DEMOTIC, SLANG, VERNACULAR. [SPEECH, STYLE].   T.MCA.

COLLOQUIALISM [c.1800]. A semi-technical term, sometimes mildly pejorative, for informal speech generally and any expression that is typical of it, especially if regarded as non- or substandard: *ain't* in *He ain't comin'* (He is not coming); *gonna* in *They're gonna do it* (They are going to do it). See COLLOQUIAL, -ISM, VERNACULARISM. [SPEECH, STYLE, WORD].   T.MCA.

COLON [16c: from Latin *colon*, Greek *kôlon* a limb, part of a strophe, a clause, and the mark ending a clause]. The punctuation mark (:). It has an anticipatory effect, leading from what precedes to what follows. The following are the main uses: (1) To introduce a list of items: *You will need the following: a pen, pencil, rubber, piece of paper, and ruler*. (2) To introduce speech or quoted material, as a stronger alternative to the comma: *I told them last week: 'Do not in any circumstances open this door.'* (3) To lead or

'point' from one clause to another: from introduction to theme (*I want to say this: we are deeply grateful to all of you*); from statement to example (*It was not easy: to begin with, I had to find the right house*); from cause to effect (*The weather was bad: so we stayed at home*); from premiss to conclusion (*There are hundreds of wasps in the garden: there must be a nest there*); from statement to explanation (*I gave up: I had tried everything without success*). (4) To introduce an antithesis or highlight a contrast: *He died young: but he died rich*; *They spoke bitterly: and yet they were forgiving*. (5) To produce a staccato or paratactic effect, either by replacing a conjunction such as *but* (*I called: you did not answer*) or in a progression or sequence (*He arrived: he knocked at the door: we waited: he went away*). See CLAUSE, PUNCTUATION, SEMICOLON, SENTENCE. [WRITING].   R.E.A.

COLONIAL [18c AmE]. Of or relating to a colony or colonies: *the colonial spirit, a colonial administration, colonial life*. The usage is generally neutral, but has often implied a distinction between a superior Mother Country (England or Britain, France) and its inferior dependencies. In such a contrast, something produced for example in Britain (a *home product*) has been seen as better or more desirable than something produced in a colony (a *colonial product*). In 19c Australia and New Zealand, *colonial ale, colonial language, colonial tobacco* had a low value, but *colonial experience* was prized, suggesting self-reliance in a new environment and the quality most lacking in *the new chum* (a newly arrived British immigrant). The term *colonialism*, once positive in its association, is now, like *imperialism*, almost universally negative, and latter-day manifestations among Europeans and Americans are often referred to as *neo-colonialism*. The concept has been associated with the superiority of a *home* language, such as English or French, especially in its standard form, over the varieties common among *colonials*. The term has also been applied to styles of living, architecture, and the like, especially in the Thirteen Colonies which became the US (1776) and in Australia before Federation (1901). See BRITISH EMPIRE, HOME, IMPERIALISM, MOTHER COUNTRY, PROVINCIALISM. [AMERICAS, HISTORY, NAME, OCEANIA].   W.S.R., T.MCA.

COLOPHON [17c: through Latin from Greek *kolophōn* summit, crowning touch, finishing stroke]. (1) The inscription or device, sometimes emblematic or pictorial, placed at the end of a manuscript or book, containing the title, perhaps the subject, perhaps the author's name, the scribe's or printer's name, and the date and place of printing, etc. The work of the colophon is now generally performed by the *title page* of a book. (2) An emblem used as an identifying device on books, letterheads, etc., such as the Collins fountain (reflected in the name of the Collins 'Fontana' imprint). See IMPRINT, LOGO. [MEDIA, TECHNOLOGY]. T.MCA.

COMBINING FORM [Late 19c, coined for use in the *OED*]. In word-formation, a base designed to combine with another, either also a combining form or a free word: *bio-* with *-graphy* to form *biography*, *mini-* with *skirt* to form *miniskirt*. A vowel usually facilitates the combination: in *biography*, the Greek thematic vowel *-o-*, in *mini-skirt*, the Latin thematic *-i-*. This vowel is usually regarded as attached to the initial base (*bio-*, *mini-*) rather than the final base (*-graphy*, *-skirt*), but in Greek-derived forms it is sometimes shown as attached to the final base (*-ography*, *-ology*). If, however, the final base begins with a vowel (for example, *-archy* as in *monarchy*), the mediating vowel has traditionally been avoided (no **monoarchy*), but in recent coinages it is often kept and generally accompanied by a hyphen (*auto-analysis*, *bio-energy*, *hydro-electricity*, not **autanalysis*, **bienergy*, **hydrelectricity*).

Translation. There are hundreds of combining forms in English and other European languages. As traditionally defined, they cannot stand alone as free words, but there are many exceptions to this rule, and in the late 20c such forms are increasingly used independently: *bio* as a clipping of *biography*, *telly* as a respelt clipping of *television*. Most combining forms translate readily into everyday language, especially nouns: *bio-* as 'life', *-graphy* as 'writing, description'. Because of this, the compounds of which they are part (usually *classical* or *learned compounds*) can be more or less straightforwardly paraphrased: *biography* as 'writing about a life', *neurology* as 'the study of the nervous system'. Many combining forms are designed to take initial or final position: *autobiography* has the two initial or pre-posed forms *auto-*, *bio-*, and one postposed form *-graphy*. Although most occupy one position or the other, some can occupy both: *-graph* as in *graphology* and *monograph*; *-phil-* as in *philology* and *Anglophile*. Occasionally, the same base is repeated in one word: *logology* the study of words, *phobophobia* the fear of fear.

Preposed and postposed. Forms that come first include: *aero-* air, *crypto-* hidden, *demo-* people, *geo-* earth, *odonto-* tooth, *ornitho-* bird, *thalasso-* sea. Many have both a traditional simple meaning and a modern telescopic meaning: in *biology*, *bio-* means 'life', but in *bio-degradable* it telescopes 'biologically'; although *hypno-* basically means 'sleep' (*hypnopaedia* learning through

sleep), it also stands for 'hypnosis' (*hypnotherapy* cure through hypnosis). When a form stands alone as a present-day word, it is usually a tele-scopic abbreviation: *bio* biography, *chemo* chemotherapy, *hydro* hydro-electricity, *metro* metropolitan. Some telescoped forms can be shorter than the original combining forms: *gynie* is shorter than *gyneco-* and stands for both *gyn-ecology* and *gynecologist*; *anthro* is shorter than *anthropo-* and stands for *anthropology*. Forms that come second include: *-ectomy* cutting out, *-graphy* writing, description, *-kinesis* motion, *-logy* study, *-mancy* divination, *-onym* name, *-phagy* eating, *-phony* sound, *-therapy* healing, *-tomy* cutting. They are generally listed in dic-tionaries without the interfixed vowel, which appears however in such casual phrases as 'olo-gies and isms'.

Variants. Some combining forms are variants of one base. The Greek base *-graph-* underlies three combining forms in English: *-gram* something written or shaped, etc. (*telegram*, *hologram*), *-graph* something written or a piece of equipment (*autograph*, *polygraph*), *-graphy* the activity or business of writing, shaping, etc. (*telegraphy*, *holography*). Some are also free words, such as *mania* in *dipsomania* and *phobia* in *claus-trophobia*. Some are composites of other elements, such as *encephalo-* brain, from *en-* in, *-cephal-* head, and *-ectomy* cutting out, from *ec-* out, *-tom-* cut, *-y*, a noun-forming suffix.

Origins. In Greek and Latin grammar, com-bining bases usually require a thematic or stem-forming vowel. In *biography*, from Greek, the thematic is *-o-*; in *agriculture*, from Latin, it is *-i-*. In English, which does not inflect in this way and has no native thematic vowels, an element like *-o-* is an imported glue that holds bases together. Its presence helps to distinguish clas-sical compounds like *biography* and *agriculture* from vernacular compounds like *teapot* and *blackbird*. Generally, English has acquired its classical compounds in three ways: through French from Latin and Greek, directly from Latin and Greek, and by coinage in English on Greek and Latin patterns. An exception is *schizophrenia*, which came into English through German, and is therefore pronounced 'skitso', not 'skyzo'. The combining forms and the com-pounds built from them are as much a part of English as of Latin and Greek, and as much a part of French, Spanish, Italian, and any other language that cares to use them. They are an international resource.

The conservative tradition. From the Renaissance until the mid-20c, the concept of derivational purity has generally regulated the use of com-bining forms: Greek with Greek, Latin with

Latin, and a minimum of hybridization. *Biography* is Greek, *agriculture* Latin, but *television* is a hybrid of Greek *tele-* and Latin *-vision* (probably so coined because the 'pure' form *telescope* had already been adopted for another purpose). *Kiddology* facetiously combines vernacular *kid* and *-ology* to produce 'the science of kidding people'. Most dictionaries follow the *OED* in using *combining form* (*comb. form*) to label such classical elements, but the name is not widely known. In appendices to dictionaries and grammar books, combining forms are often loosely referred to as roots or affixes: 'a logo . . ., properly speaking, is not a word at all but a prefix meaning word and short for logogram, a symbol, much as telly is short for television' (Montreal *Gazette*, 13 Apr. 1981). They are often referred to as affixes because some come first and some come last, but if they were affixes, a word like *biography* would have no base whatever. While affixes are grammatical (like prepositions), combining forms are lexical (like nouns, adjectives, and verbs): for example, *bio-* translates as a noun (life), *-graphy* as a verbal noun (writing). They are also often loosely called roots because they are ancient and have a basic role in word-formation, but functionally and often structurally they are distinct from roots: the *-graph* in *autograph* is both a root and a combining form, while the *-graphy* in *cryptography* consists of root *-graph-* and suffix *-y*, and is only a combining form.

Contemporary developments. By and large, combining forms were a closed system from the 16c to the earlier 20c: the people who used them were classically educated, their teachers and exemplars generally took a purist's view on their use, contexts of use were mainly technical, and there was relatively little seepage into the language at large. However, with the decline of classical education and the spread of technical and quasi-technical jargon in the media, a continuum has evolved, with at least five stages:

Pure classical usage. In the older sciences, combining forms are generally used to form such strictly classical and usually Greek compounds as: *anthocyanin, astrobleme, chemotherapy, chronobiology, cytokinesis, glossolalia, lalophobia, narcolepsy, osteoporosis, Pliohippus, sympathomimetic.*

Hybrid classical usage. In technical, semi-technical, and quasi-technical usage at large, coiners of compounds increasingly treat Latin and Greek as one resource, to produce such forms as: *accelerometer, aero-generator, bio-prospector, communicology, electroconductive, futurology, mammography, micro-gravity, neo-liberal, Scientology, servo-mechanism, Suggestopedia.*

Hybrid classical/vernacular usage. In the later 20c, many forms have cut loose from ancient moorings: *crypto-* as in preposed *Crypto-Fascist* and *pseudo-* as in *pseudo-radical*; postposed *-meter* in *speedometer, clapometer*. Processes of analogy have created coinages like *petrodollar, psycho-warfare, microwave* on such models as *petrochemical, psychology, microscope*. Such stunt usages as *eco-doom, eco-fears, eco-freaks,* common in journalism, often employ combining forms telescopically: *eco-* standing for *ecology* and *ecological* and not as used in *economics*. In such matters, precision of meaning is secondary to compactness and vividness of expression.

Combining forms as separate words. In recent years, the orthography of many word forms has changed, usually without affecting pronunciation and stress. The same spoken usage may be written *micro-missile, micro missile, micromissile,* reflecting the same uncertainty or flexibility as in *businessman, business-man, business man*. When used in such ways, combining forms are often telescopic: *Hydro substation* Hydro-Electricity Board substation, *Metro highways* Metropolitan highways, *porno cult* pornography cult.

New combining forms. The mix of late 20c techno-commercial coinages includes three groups of post- and non-classical forms: (1) Established forms: *econo-* from 'economic', as in *econometric, Econo-Car, mini-* from 'miniature', as in *miniskirt, mini-boom, -matic* from 'automatic', as in *Adjustamatic, Instamatic, Stackomatic*. (2) Less established forms, often created by blending: *accu-* from 'accurate', as in *Accuvision, compu-* from 'computer', as in *Compucorp, docu-* from 'documentary', as in *docudrama, dura-* from 'durable', as in *Duramark, porta-* from 'portable', as in *Portacabin, Portaphone*. (3) Informal vernacular material in pseudo-classical form: *Easibird, Healthitone, Redi-pak, Relax-a-Cisor* (relax, exerciser). See BLEND, CLASSICAL/LEARNED COMPOUND, INTERFIX, INTERNATIONAL SCIENTIFIC VOCABULARY, THEMATIC VOWEL, WORD-FORMATION. [WORD].

T.MCA.

COMEDY [14c: from French *comédie*, Latin *comoedia*, from Greek *kōmōidia*, from *kômos* merry-making]. (1) A play performed on stage, as a motion picture, on radio, or on television that amuses and has a happy ending. (2) By extension, the element in drama, literature, and life that makes people laugh, and any event or series of events that causes amusement. Comedy as an art form has flourished in the major literary periods of Western culture, but has not commanded the same critical attention as *tragedy*. It has moments that threaten to turn to tragedy, but the audience accepts them in the certainty that all will be well. If tragedy purges the emotions by vicarious experience, comedy gives security by making harmless what could be frightening or embarrassing. In tragedy, divine or social rules are enforced; in comedy, they are suspended and dangerous consequences are averted. Comedy rests on human error, mistaken identity, awkward meetings, and verbal humour. In general, comic characters are less subtle and dignified than tragic characters, and do not develop much in the course of a play, book, or film.

In English drama, there are three broad types: (1) *Romantic comedy*, associated particularly with the 16c, especially the comedies of Shakespeare, dealing with young love, often in perils and difficulties, but ending with desired marriages. (2) *Satirical comedy*, mocking the follies and weaknesses of the age or of human nature, as in Ben Jonson's treatment of greed in *Volpone* (1605) and *The Alchemist* (1610). (3) *The comedy of manners*, requiring a sophisticated, urbane society, and deriving its humour from the constraints and evasions of social pressures and the complexities of intrigue: for example, Restoration comedy in the 17c, such later works as Wilde's *The Importance of Being Earnest* (1895), and in the 20c the works of Noël Coward and Alan Ayckbourn.

Traditionally, language in comedies is less elevated than in tragedies. Dialogue is usually in prose, with verbal tricks like puns and similes. It is quick and fluent, even humbler characters often being swift in repartee. There is little room for self-examination or general philosophy. Currently, the television *sitcom* (situation comedy), usually a series of episodes about characters in a given situation, has a strong farcical element, exaggerating the difficulties and embarrassments of everyday life. Subtler modern comedy has features of the theatre of the absurd, as in Tom Stoppard's *Rosencrantz and Guildenstern are Dead* (1966), or, as *black comedy*, has found humour in morbid or distressing subjects, like Joe Orton's *Loot* (1965) and *What the Butler Saw* (1969). See DRAMA, THEATRE/THEATER, TRAGEDY. [LITERATURE]. R.C.

COMIC [14c: from Latin *comicus*, Greek *komikós*, causing revelry: see COMEDY]. (1) Relating to comedy: *comic opera, comic actor*. (2) Also *comical*. Provoking amusement: *comic antics, comical situations*. (3) Also *comedian*. Someone who makes people laugh, either professionally or for fun. (4) Also *comic book*. A magazine containing comic strips. An expanded comic book, or work of fiction that is mostly cartoon-like drawings, is sometimes called (especially in AmE) a *graphic novel* or *graphic docudrama*. See CARTOON, DOCUDRAMA. [LITERATURE, MEDIA, STYLE]. T.MCA.

COMIC RELIEF [1810s]. An amusing scene, incident, or speech introduced into serious, tragic, or suspenseful drama to provide temporary relief from tension; anything similar in life. See COMEDY, COMIC. [LITERATURE]. T.MCA.

COMMA [16c: from Latin *comma*, Greek *kómma* a piece cut off, a phrase or group of words, a short clause in writing, the mark ending such a clause]. The punctuation mark (,), which has many uses and is highly flexible. Essentially, it gives detail to (especially longer) sentences and helps clarify their meaning. The comma is used: (1) To mark off elements in a sequence of words and phrases when there are no conjunctions or there is only a final conjunction: *Cats, dogs, rabbits, hares, squirrels, and hedgehogs*. (2) In pairs, to indicate an aside or parenthesis: *She is, you know, one of my best friends*. (3) To separate clauses of sentences: *If you want him to come, ask him yourself*. (4) To introduce direct speech: *She said, 'I'd rather not do it.'* (5) To clarify meaning and prevent ambiguity: *Cereals, orange juice, milk, bacon, and eggs*. The following sections provide detailed comment on these uses.

Commas with single words. (1) Adjectives before nouns are separated by commas unless there is a strong association between a noun and the adjective immediately preceding it: compare *an enterprising, ambitious person* and *a distinguished foreign politician*. When a conjunction such as *and* or *but* separates the adjectives, a comma is not used, but a pair of commas suggests an aside or gives emphasis: compare *a great and generous leader* and *a great, and generous, leader* (with spoken emphasis on *generous*). (2) With nouns, adverbs, and adjectives more generally, commas are normally used only with three or more words in sequence: *They spoke slowly, deliberately, and softly; We found guns, ammunition, and grenades; The children were happy, noisy, and overexcited*. (For the comma before *and*, see *serial comma*, below.) A comma marking off two such words conveys emphasis, as would a dash: *They spoke slowly, and deliberately*. (3) The same considerations apply to a sequence of verbs (*They arrived, shouted, and ran in*) and prepositions (*You will find it in, on, and under everything*). (4) *However* and *therefore* are often placed between parenthetical commas: *I do not, however, want you to go; We decided, therefore, to leave* (compare *We therefore decided to leave*). Parenthetical commas are optional with *moreover, nevertheless, unfortunately*, etc.

Commas with phrases. (1) Phrases such as *far and wide, by and large* are treated like single words:

They travelled far and wide through Spain; She was, by and large, very disappointed in the result. (2) Parenthetical commas may be used to highlight a phrase in much the same way as dashes and brackets, but form a less distinct break: *The witness, a middle-aged woman, then stepped forward*; *Their new song, 'Singing through my tears', was published this year.* (3) Commas are used to separate items in a list or sequence, as in cases already given. Usage varies as to the inclusion of a comma before *and* in the last item (*bring a chair, a bottle of wine, and a good book*). This practice is controversial and is known as the *serial comma* or *Oxford comma*, because it is part of the house style of Oxford University Press. It is often superfluous, and there are occasions when the sense requires it to be omitted, but on many occasions it serves to avoid ambiguity: *These colours are available: red, green, yellow, and black and white* as opposed to *red, green, yellow and black and white.* (4) Practice varies regarding introductory phrases. A comma is often but not always helpful, and the important point is to achieve a consistent and clear approach: *In the meantime, we must wait*; *In the circumstances, I will agree to your request*; *In 1939, he joined the army.* When there is an implied verb, especially *be*, a comma is usual (*Although ill, she managed to finish the work*; *Whatever the difficulties, we must keep trying*).

Commas with clauses. Commas are used in longer stretches of writing in the following ways:

(1) To separate two main clauses when emphasis or contrast is needed: compare *He woke up and immediately got out of bed* and *He woke up, and immediately got out of bed*: in the second example, the emphasis of sense is on the second clause, whereas in the first there are two more or less equal statements.

(2) To mark off the main clause of a longer compound sentence when the two parts are not close enough in meaning or content to form a continuous statement and are not distinct enough to warrant a semicolon. A conjunction such as *and*, *but*, *yet*, etc., is normally used: *The road runs through a beautiful wooded valley, and the railway line follows it closely.* It is usually considered incorrect to omit the conjunction: **I like swimming very much, I go to the pool every week* conventionally requires either the insertion of *and* before the second *I*, or the use of a colon or semicolon instead of the comma. However, there is no absolute rule: many writers place two short sentences together in this way when they wish to suggest a close tie between the sentences, are not subject to a publisher's house style, have a relaxed approach to punctuation, or are not certain about the use of commas and periods.

The practice is often adopted to represent disjointed speech or thought, as in: 'We didn't stay long, it gave me the creeps' and 'I made myself some food, gosh, I was hungry' (Somerset Maugham, *The Razor's Edge*, 1967). See PARATAXIS.

(3) Sometimes, to separate a subordinate clause from a main clause, especially when the subordinate clause comes first or when the sentence is long: *I decided to wait because I thought you would soon arrive* (comma optional before *because*); *Because I wanted to see them, I decided to wait* (comma usual); *However much you try, you will find it difficult* (comma usual). Use of a comma is especially common after a conditional clause which is placed first (*If you want to come, you must hurry*) but less common in short sentences in which it is placed second (*You must hurry if you want to come*: a comma before *if* in this example would give extra emphasis to what follows, in the manner of other examples given above). A comma is normally required when the subordinate clause is participial: *Feeling unwell, they decided to stay at home.*

(4) To separate a relative clause from its antecedent when the clause is giving incidental information rather than identifying the antecedent: compare *the car, which was standing in the road, was stolen* and *the car which was standing in the road was stolen.* In the first example, the position of the car is extra information that is not essential to the main sense; in the second, it identifies the car being referred to. See RELATIVE CLAUSE.

(5) A comma is often used to introduce direct speech in place of a colon (*I then said, 'Why don't you come in?'*), and is usual in resuming direct speech after a break, if the direct speech continues a sentence (*'Go away,' I said, 'and don't ever come back'*). See QUOTATION MARKS.

The clarifying comma. The comma is also used to prevent ambiguity or misunderstanding. If the comma is removed from the following examples difficulties may arise, at least for a moment: *With the police pursuing, the people shouted loudly*; *He did not want to leave, from a feeling of loyalty*; *However, much as I would like to, I cannot come.*

Other uses. The comma is also used in various ways not directly associated with punctuation, such as: (1) To indicate thousands in numerals, beginning from the right: *5,324,768.* (2) Traditionally, to separate a street number from the name of the road or street in addresses (a role that has diminished greatly in recent years): *24, High Street*, probably more commonly *24 High Street*. It has also traditionally been used to end each stage of an address, a practice that also appears to be obsolescent. (3) In letters, at the end of the initial greeting (*Dear James, . . .*;

Dear Mrs Taylor, . . .), and at the end of the concluding formula (*Yours sincerely,*). See OXFORD UNIVERSITY PRESS, PUNCTUATION, QUOTATION. [WRITING].   R.E.A.

COMMERCIALESE [1910]. A non-technical and usually pejorative term for an ornate style used in commerce and any example of such a style, including such expressions as *advise inform*, *as per* in accordance with, *be in receipt of* have received, *beg to* (*bring to your attention*) wish to (inform you), *re* with regard to, concerning. In the earlier 20c, many commercial expressions were ornate, inflated, and fawning (*your esteemed favour/order*, *your good self*), a style passed on to and maintained by many businesspeople throughout the English-speaking world and in some places virtually fossilized, as in: 'Sir—We are in receipt of your favour of the 9th inst. with regard to your esteemed order . . .'. See -ESE. [STYLE].   T.MCA.

COMMITTEE FOR LINGUISTICS IN EDUCATION. See BRITISH ASSOCIATION OF APPLIED LINGUISTICS.

COMMON [13c: through French from Latin *communis* sharing, common]. (1) Owned or shared by members of a community, general, public, free to be used by all: *common land, goods held in common, a common language, common English*. (2) Ordinary, familiar, everyday: *the common man, a common spelling mistake*. (3) Undistinguished, having no rank or status, not noble: *the common people*. Derivatives: *a commoner, the House of Commons*. (4) Cheap, inferior, low-class, unrefined, vulgar: *as common as muck, a common accent, very common English*. (5) In prosody, of a syllable: either long or short. (6) In grammar, not marked in any way: *a common noun* as opposed to *a proper noun*; *common gender* as opposed to masculine, feminine, or where applicable neuter. See COMMON NOUN, GENDER, NAME, PROPER, PROSODY. [GRAMMAR, SPEECH, STYLE].   T.MCA.

COMMON NAME. See NAME.

COMMON NOUN. A noun referring to anything or anybody as an example of what the word in question denotes (*an actor, the town, cheerfulness*), in contrast with a *proper noun*, which uniquely identifies and names, and begins with a capital letter (*London, China*). Grammatically, common nouns can be divided into countable and uncountable nouns. Semantically, common nouns can be classified as abstract and concrete nouns. See COMMON, NAME, NOUN, PROPER. [GRAMMAR].   S.C.

COMMONWEALTH [16c: originally the general good, similar to the older *common weal* or *commonweal* the public good, and equivalent to French *le bien commun*, both echoing Latin *res publica* the public thing/affair, from which the term *republic* derives]. (1) A state in which power is regarded as vested in the people: the republican *Commonwealth and Free State* of which Oliver Cromwell was Lord Protector (1649-60); *the Commonwealth of Australia/Dominica*. (2) A state of the US, especially Kentucky, Massachusetts, Pennsylvania, and Virginia, as in the formal title *the Commonwealth of Massachusetts*. (3) A territory part-integrated with the US: *the Commonwealth of Puerto Rico*. (4) (with *the*) In full *the British Commonwealth* (*of Nations*). An association of self-governing *dominions* of the British Empire owing allegiance to the Crown, as constituted by the Statute of Westminster in 1931, and including Australia, Canada, and New Zealand. (5) (with *the*) An association of states and their dependencies, comprising Britain and countries once in the Empire, as constituted by the Declaration of London in 1949. When this restructuring of the earlier Commonwealth was undertaken, it was agreed to drop 'British' and the concept of allegiance to the Crown, the monarch becoming symbolic head of the association. Its language is English and its aims are cooperation and understanding among nations.

As British colonies and protectorates gained independence in the decades after the Second World War, most became members of the Commonwealth. The organization has no constitution, no legal standing, and no legislative, executive, or judicial function. There are currently 49 members, whose combined population exceeds 1,000m. Every two years the heads of the Commonwealth meet for semi-formal discussions in a different venue. South Africa's membership lapsed in 1962, technically because it had become a republic and needed to have its new status confirmed, but in essence because of general disapproval of its policy of racial apartheid. Pakistan withdrew in 1972 after the admission to membership of Bangladesh (formerly East Pakistan). In 1965, a *Commonwealth Secretariat* headed by a *Secretary-General* was set up in London as a clearing-house for information of interest to members and a source of advice on technical cooperation. The *Commonwealth Institute*, founded in 1959 and based in London and Edinburgh, replaced the *Imperial Institute* founded in 1893. It promotes aspects of the culture and heritage of Commonwealth nations through exhibitions, conferences, the performing arts, educational courses, and library facilities. Its London premises, opened in 1962, provide a meeting-place for Commonwealth citizens. The Institute runs the Commonwealth poetry prize and organizes celebrations on *Commonwealth Day* (the first Monday in March). Its board of governors includes the high commissioners (ambassadors) in London of its member nations.

See (British dependencies asterisked) *ANGUILLA, ANTIGUA & BARBUDA, *ASCENSION (ISLAND), AUSTRALIA, BAHAMAS, BANGLADESH, BARBADOS, BELIZE, *BERMUDA, BOTSWANA, BRITISH EMPIRE, *BRITISH INDIAN OCEAN TERRITORY, BRUNEI, CANADA, *CAYMAN ISLANDS, CYPRUS, DOMINICA, EXAMINING IN ENGLISH, *FALKLAND ISLANDS, FIJI, GAMBIA, GHANA, *GIBRALTAR, GUYANA, *HONG KONG, INDIA, KENYA, KIRIBATI, LESOTHO, MALAWI, MALAYSIA, MALDIVES, MALTA, MAURITIUS, *MONTSERRAT, NAURU, NEWSPAPER, NEW ZEALAND, NIGERIA, PAKISTAN, PAPUA NEW GUINEA, SAINT CHRISTOPHER & NEVIS, *SAINT HELENA, SAINT LUCIA, SAINT VINCENT & THE GRENADINES, SEYCHELLES, SIERRA LEONE, SINGAPORE, SOLOMON ISLANDS, SRI LANKA, SWAZILAND, TANZANIA, TESL, TONGA, TRINIDAD & TOBAGO, *TRISTAN DA CUNHA, TURKS & CAICOS ISLANDS, TUVALU, UGANDA, UNITED KINGDOM (OF GREAT BRITAIN AND NORTHERN IRELAND), THE VANUATU, *VIRGIN ISLANDS (BRITISH), WESTERN SAMOA, ZAMBIA, ZIMBABWE. [AFRICA, AMERICAS, ASIA, EUROPE, HISTORY, NAME, OCEANIA].   T.MCA.

COMMONWEALTH CARIBBEAN. A collective term for Caribbean countries that are members of the Commonwealth and usually also those territories that continue to be dependencies of Great Britain. See CARIBBEAN, COMMONWEALTH. [AMERICAS, NAME].   T.MCA.

COMMONWEALTH LITERATURE, sometimes more broadly **Post-colonial Literature in English**. Terms for literature in English in the countries of the Commonwealth (usually excluding the United Kingdom). The term *Commonwealth Literature* is used in some centres of higher education to name courses covering literary works in territories that were once part of the British Empire, and may include for reasons of completeness countries that are not members of the Commonwealth, such as South Africa. Journals discussing this literature include: *World Literature Written in English* (based in North America, founded in 1962), *The Journal of Commonwealth Literature* (England, 1965), *The CRNLE Reviews Journal* (Centre for Research in the New Literatures of English, Flinders U., Bedford Park, South Australia, 1980). The literary journal *Ariel* (1962) devotes substantial space to the subject.

See AFRICAN LITERATURE IN ENGLISH, AUSTRALIAN LITERATURE, BRITISH EMPIRE, CANADIAN LITERATURE IN ENGLISH, CARIBBEAN LITERATURE IN ENGLISH, COMMONWEALTH, ENGLISH LITERATURE, INDIAN ENGLISH LITERATURE, JONES (J.), NEW ZEALAND LITERATURE, SOUTH AFRICAN LITERATURE IN ENGLISH, WORLD LITERATURE WRITTEN IN ENGLISH. [AFRICA, AMERICAS, ASIA, LITERATURE, OCEANIA, VARIETY].   G.D.K.

COMMUNICATION [14c: through French from Latin *communicatio/communicationis* making common]. A fundamental concept in the study of behaviour, whether by humans, animals, or machines, that acts as a frame of reference for the concept of *language*. Communication refers to the transmission of information (a *message*) between a source and a receiver, using a signalling system. In linguistic studies, both source and receiver are human, the system involved is a language, and the idea of response to feedback (a message) holds a central place. In theory, communication is said to have taken place if the information received is the same as that sent. In practice, we have to allow for all kinds of interfering factors (technically known as *noise*), which reduce the efficiency of the transmission, such as poor articulation or hearing, extraneous noise, and unconscious personal associations for words.

The study of human communication in all its modes is known as *semiotics*. Although in principle any of the five senses (six, if telepathy is conceded) can be used as a medium of communication, in practice only three (tactile, visual, aural) are implemented in both active (*expressive*) and passive (*receptive*) ways. Tactile communication involves touch (as in shaking hands, grasping someone's arm or shoulder, stroking, and punching) and the manipulation of physical distance and body orientation in order to communicate indifference or disagreement. The study of tactile communicative behaviour is *proxemics*. Visual communication involves the use of facial expressions (as in smiling, winking, and eyebrow flashing, which communicate a wide range of emotions) and gestures and body postures of varying levels of formality (such as waving, gesturing rudely, kneeling, bowing, blessing). Often, visual effects interact closely with speech: movements of the hands and head tend to coincide with points of greatest spoken emphasis, and may convey particular nuances of meaning not easy to communicate in speech (such as the drawing of inverted commas in the air to signal a special meaning). The study of visual non-verbal communicative behaviour is *kinesics*.

The chief branch of communication studies involves the oral-aural mode, in the form of speech, and its systematic visual reflex in the form of writing. These are the verbal aspects of communication, distinguished from the non-verbal (kinesic and proxemic) aspects, often popularly referred to as *body language*. A clear boundary needs to be drawn between these domains. The term *language* is usually restricted to speech and writing (and sign, in the case of deaf sign language), because these mediums of transmission display a highly sophisticated internal structure and creativity. Non-verbal communication, by contrast, involves relatively little creativity. In language, it is commonplace to find new words being created, and sentences varying in practically infinite complexity. In this respect, languages differ markedly from the very limited set of facial expressions, gestures, and body movements.

See (A)ESTHETICS, AMBIGUITY, ARGUMENT, ARTIFICIAL LANGUAGE, BIBLIOGRAPHY, BODY LANGUAGE, BOOK, CHILD LANGUAGE ACQUISITION, CINEMA, CLASSICAL LANGUAGE, CODE, COMMUNICATIVE SHIFT, COMPUTER, CONTEXT, CONVERSATION, DIALOG(UE), DISAMBIGUATE, FEEDBACK, FLUENCY, FORMULA, GESTURE, HANDWRITING, HUMO(U)R, INFORMATION, KNOWLEDGE REPRESENTATION, LANGUAGE, LANGUAGE SHIFT, LIBRARY, LINGUA FRANCA, LINGUISTICS, LITERACY, LOGIC, MEANING, MEDIA, MEDIUM, MESSAGE, MNEMONIC, MONOLOG(UE), MOTION PICTURE, NARRATIVE, NONSENSE, NUMERAL, ORACY, ORALITY, PARAPHRASE, RADIO, REDUNDANCY, REFERENCE, SEMANTICS, SEMIOTICS, SENSE, SIGN, SIGNAL, SIGN LANGUAGE, SPEECH ACT, STANDARD, STRUCTURALISM, STRUCTURE, STYLE, STYLISTICS, SYLLOGISM, SYMBOL, TECHNOLOGY, TEIL, TRANSLATION, USAGE, VERNACULAR, WORD, WRITING (WRITING SYSTEM). [LANGUAGE, MEDIA]. D.C.

Argyle, M. 1975. *Bodily Communication*. London: Methuen.
Barnow, Erik (ed.). 1989. *International Encyclopedia of Communications*. Four volumes. New York and Oxford: Oxford University Press.
Hinde, R. A. (ed.). 1972. *Non-Verbal Communication*. Cambridge: University Press.
O'Sullivan, T. (ed.). 1983. *Key Concepts in Communication*. London: Methuen.
Watson, J., & Hill, A. 1984. *A Dictionary of Communication and Media Studies*. London: Edward Arnold.

COMMUNICATION DISORDER. See LANGUAGE PATHOLOGY.

COMMUNICATIVE APPROACH. See LANGUAGE TEACHING.

COMMUNICATIVE COMPETENCE [1970s: associated with the US anthropologist Dell Hymes]. A term in sociolinguistics for a speaker's underlying knowledge of the rules of grammar (understood in its widest sense to include phonology, orthography, syntax, lexicon, and semantics) and rules for their use in socially appropriate circumstances. The notion is intended to replace Noam Chomsky's dichotomy of competence and performance. *Competence* is the knowledge of rules of grammar, *performance*, how the rules are used. Speakers draw on their competence in putting together grammatical sentences, but not all such sentences can be used in the same circumstances: *Close the window* and *Would you mind closing the window, please?* are both grammatical, but they differ in their appropriateness for use in particular situations. Speakers use their communicative competence to choose what to say, as well as how and when to say it. See COMPETENCE AND PERFORMANCE, LANGUAGE TEACHING. [LANGUAGE].   S.R.

COMMUNICATIVE SHIFT [1980s]. A radical change in the technology and practice of communication, such as the development of printing with movable alphabetic type in 15c Europe. There have been many such shifts, the most significant of which appear to be: the shift to speech (*c*.50,000–60,000 years ago); to script (*c*.5,500 years ago); to print (*c*.500 years ago); to the computer and screen (in the last 50 years or so).

The first shift. Little is known about how, when, and where people began to speak, but researchers generally agree that speech is a defining feature of the subspecies *Homo sapiens sapiens*, which has been in existence for at least 50,000 years. In relation to a human lifetime, the development of speech has been a long, slow process, but in evolutionary terms it is recent, brief, and swift. In its development, apparatus primarily used for breathing, eating, and drinking (the lungs, throat, mouth, and nose) has been adapted, along with the larynx, for a secondary purpose which did not displace but rather added to the various prior uses. Speech is both genetic and cultural: unimpaired babies have it as a birthright, but need priming and the opportunity to develop it. All later communicative shifts differ from speech in being cultural alone and requiring formal training in their use.

Storage speech. There is a considerable difference between everyday speech and the styles in which the lore of an oral community are preserved. The US classicist Eric Havelock has called such lore 'the tribal encyclopedia' (1963, below). To make such an encyclopedia possible, a subshift appears to have developed (perhaps *c*.15,000 years ago) through which the structured transmission from generation to generation of myth, genealogy, and other forms of orature became possible. This subshift into *storage speech* apparently consisted of styles and patterns in rhythm, rhetoric, narrative, plot, theme, and archetype, working together in performances that were similar but never identical. There was no 'original' form against which any performance could be checked, but performers may have by and large assumed that, however they might present a piece on a particular occasion, they were engaged in accurately providing an authentic statement.

Such 'storage speech' appears always to have been buttressed with mnemonic aids such as tally sticks, notched bones, strung beads, tapping, and vocal and instrumental music. Its genres have made the creation, retention, presentation, and assimilation of knowledge efficient and impressive, and because of it knowledge has been less at risk as it has passed from generation to generation. In developing and using such speech, individuals have served as living repositories who have shaped ('edited') their subject-matter not in introspective solitude but in the heat of performance (compare Albert Lord, 1960, below). In some societies, such performers have established castes with prestige and the power of monopoly, and sometimes with sacred status. The brahmins of India have traditionally been diviners, priests, and preservers of the *veda* (Sanskrit: knowledge) and as such have had the status of gods.

The second shift. The creation of writing can be compared to the control of fire, the domestication of animals, and the invention of the wheel. Unlike such advances, however, it has entailed adaptations of mind and body. The primary skills of mouth and ear are reinforced with secondary skills of hand and eye. Training in the two channels of communication gave scribes an extra grip on language which eventually made oral record-keeping archaic. In Sumer, Egypt, China, and India (3rd–2nd millennia BC), scribes became managers who engaged in land surveys, kept legal records, administered the state, and organized its wealth. The emergence of these activities, however, took time, and at first their work was mundane, as the British archaeologist Glyn Daniel has pointed out:

The earliest written documents of the Sumerians are not literature, they are not sagas or legends of creation. They are domestic or commercial documents such as lists of deliveries of bread and beer to various people, and lists of items delivered to temple and other officials
(*The First Civilizations*, 1968, p. 74).

Storage surfaces. The bards and minstrels in such newly literate societies had traditions of their own and appear at first to have paid little attention to script. Long before writing became flexible enough to handle their lore, they had developed genres and techniques which they jealously preserved. The ancient brahmins were slow to reinforce memory and chanting with script. In due course, however, and in ways which remain unclear, the transfer of storage speech to *storage surfaces* began, and with it the gradual adaptation of orature into literature. Early literary works like the Babylonian and Homeric epics did not emerge without precedents. They were the conversion of venerated and often sacred song (often regarded as divinely inspired) into signs on clay and papyrus. Their recording in writing was the beginning of a process which in due course relegated orality to a minor position in a world of 'letters'.

The alphabet. Between 1500 and 1000 BC, a subshift produced the first alphabet. This was a set of fewer than 30 phonic signs which competed with complex established systems: see ALPHABET. Yet it eventually became the world's most widespread writing system. In the process, it has provided languages such as English with expressions like *literacy, literally, literary, literature, man of letters*. In the first millennia of the second shift, a male minority looked after the business of script, recording matters of particular interest to them and their masters. Because most people were unable to read and write, non-literacy carried no stigma. Being literate, however, often inspired awe. Scribes were highly respected and sometimes regarded as magicians. When involved in religion and ritual, they became repositories of a special truth, known in Latin as *scriptura* (what is written) and in English as *Holy Writ*. Much of scribal culture has been influenced by hierarchies such as the Hindu brahmins, Christian priests, and Muslim mullahs. Although scribes have had many secular functions, the copying of tablets, rolls, and codices was often in the hands of clerics and clerks in monasteries and seminaries.

The third shift. Printing with movable type has been a major formative element in Western and Westernized society. One of the earliest industrial processes, it mechanized the production of texts that, before 1450, could only have been reproduced by a single scribe working alone or by a group receiving dictation in a scriptorium. Such copyists, while venerating accuracy and abhorring corrupt texts, often made troublesome mistakes. However, the invention attributed to the German metal-worker Johannes Gutenberg reinforced through the checking of proofs the ancient ideal of accuracy while at the same time providing copies of finished texts in numbers and of a quality that were at first hard to grasp. With the advent of such printing, the primary form of handwriting was adapted into a secondary process of 'machine-writing', through which the shapes of letters became guaranteed. Where finger, wrist, and eye had laboured before, the press offered an untiring mechanical rhythm that in due course downgraded script as script had earlier downgraded storage speech.

Print and language. The third shift has had a profound effect on language and people's attitudes to it. As Latin declined in Western Europe, such vernacular tongues as French and English (the national languages of powerful states) became major print languages, while others like Occitan and Scots did not, losing more and more ground in the contest for 'languagehood'. Type was a significant factor in the concept of a standard language: its hard-edged uniformity encouraged the idea of a parallel perfection in speech. Together with the usage of royal courts and the high literary styles inherited from Rome, print promoted a more normative ambition among the educated than had been possible in scribal times. As a result, Renaissance *orthography* ('proper writing', as exhibited in print) encouraged elocutionists in the 17–18c to aim for *orthoepy* ('proper speech'). In the process, the speech of the unlettered and uncourtly came to be perceived as barbarous and corrupt, like a poorly copied manuscript or a badly edited book.

New canons. In the age of print, oral traditions became even less significant, and by the 19c had dwindled to a folk art with some Romantic credentials. Like Latin in scribal times, major print languages have possessed the stamp of literary, scholarly, and administrative authority. Like Latin in former times, they are the primary means of instruction in schools, colleges, and universities, and everyone who passes through such institutions learns to a greater or less extent to conform to their norms. The canons of classical, scribal literature passed during the Renaissance to print languages with their aspiring national literatures. Scribal genres were adapted for print just as oral genres had earlier been adapted for script. Some, like the verse epic, flowered briefly in the new states (Dante's *Divina Commedia*, the *Lusiads* of Camoens, Milton's *Paradise Lost*), then fell into decline. New forms emerged, especially the prose romance which evolved into the 'novel'. Vernacular literary canons began to emerge in Europe at much the same time as printed vernacular versions of the Bible. A revived enthusiasm for the classics coexisted with a desire for courtly elegance and the refinement of the bourgeoisie. The golden ages of literature in the languages of several European states straddle the period of the Renaissance and the Reformation, when print was taking hold. These included the Elizabethan and Jacobean ages of English.

Type and typewriter. There have been a number of subshifts in the history of the printing press. Ways of making paper have changed and changes were made in the presses and in typography. One subshift, however, occupies a unique niche in the contemporary world. It came of age in 1868 in the US, when Christopher Latham Scholes patented the first workable model of the modern typewriter. The output of the typewriter, which personalizes printing, falls between longhand manuscript and letterpress product and has proved to be both utilitarian and romantic. In the workplace, it has been identified primarily with women trained in a new but subordinate kind of literacy, their roles comparable to those of medieval copyists. Journalists also used typewriters, but seldom learned to touch-type, by which 'failure' they paradoxically signalled that they were 'proper' writers, not copyists. The typing of such writers was not an end-product, but needed only to be adequate for processing into 'real' print. The gender and other tensions attaching to the typewriter continue to work themselves out in the early stages of the next shift.

The fourth shift. Although it is centred on electronics, this shift is a cluster of associated subshifts, of which four are *auditory* (telephone, telecommunications, radio, and audio-recording), six are *visual* (photography, basic cinematography, basic television, photocopying, video-recording, and the traditional computer), and five are *hybrid* (cinematography with sound, television with sound, video cassettes, some computers, and some applications of laser technology). With its beginnings in the later 19c, this massive shift has been happening faster and over a wider range of peoples, languages, territories, and belief systems than any previous shift. It is widely referred to as a *media revolution* and an *information explosion*, and has prompted the use of such distinctive terms as *media, multimedia,* and *hypermedia.* Like the shifts of the past, it has and will continue to have profound repercussions on language. Since English is the pre-eminent language of this shift, the repercussions will become apparent in English sooner than in most other languages. It is, however, a feature of this as much as earlier shifts that nothing is lost, although roles change. People still engage in oral performance and write with pens and pencils alongside the most sophisticated of computers and multimedia devices.

See BROADCASTING, CLASSICAL LANGUAGE, COMMUNICATION, COMPUTING, HYPERTEXT, INNIS, MCLUHAN, MOTION PICTURE, MULTIMEDIA, PRINTING, PUBLISHING, SCRIPT, SCRIPTURE, TEXT, TYPOGRAPHY. [HISTORY, LANGUAGE, LITERATURE, MEDIA, SPEECH, TECHNOLOGY, TELEPHONE, WRITING]. T.MCA.

Eisenstein, Elizabeth E. 1979. *The Printing Press as an Agent of Change: Communications and Cultural*

Transformations in Early-Modern Europe. Cambridge: University Press.

Goody, Jack. 1977. *The Domestication of the Savage Mind.* Cambridge: University Press.

—— 1986. *The Logic of Writing and the Organization of Society.* Cambridge: University Press.

—— 1987. *The Interface between the Written and the Oral.* Cambridge: University Press.

Havelock, Eric A. 1963. *Preface to Plato.* Harvard: University Press.

Kist, Joost. 1987. *Electronic Publishing: Looking for a Blueprint.* Bromley, Kent: Croom Helm.

Lord, Albert A. 1960. *The Singer of Tales.* Harvard: University Press.

McArthur, Tom. 1986. *Worlds of Reference: Lexicography, Learning and Language from the Clay Tablet to the Computer.* Cambridge: University Press.

McLuhan, Marshall. 1962. *The Gutenberg Galaxy.* London: Routledge & Kegan Paul.

—— 1964. *Understanding Media: The Extension of Man.* London: Routledge & Kegan Paul.

Ong, Walter J. 1977. *Interfaces of the Word: Studies in the Evolution of Consciousness and Culture.* Ithaca NY & London: Cornell University Press.

—— 1982. *Orality and Literacy: The Technologizing of the Word.* London: Methuen.

Parry, Milman. 1971. *The Making of Homeric Verse: The Collected Papers of Milman Parry,* ed. Adam Parry. Oxford: University Press.

Smith, Anthony. 1980. *Goodbye Gutenberg: The Newspaper Revolution of the 1980s.* Oxford: University Press.

COMMUNITY LANGUAGE [1970s]. In Britain and Australia, a term used by government officials, social workers, and others for a language used by immigrants, such as Hindi or Chinese: 'Today the term "Community Language" has become firmly established as a euphemism for low status languages of Britain' (Safder Alladina, *Language Issues* 1, Spring 1986). Compare HERITAGE LANGUAGE. [EUROPE, LANGUAGE, OCEANIA].   T.MCA.

COMPANION [13c: through French from Latin *companio/companionis* messmate, from *com-* together, *panis* bread]. A work of reference, usually arranged alphabetically, that is presented as a friend to be consulted whenever needed: *The Oxford Companion to the English Language*; *The Feminist Companion to Literature in English* (Batsford, 1990). Compare ENCYCLOPEDIA, GUIDE. [REFERENCE].   T.MCA.

COMPARATIVE DEGREE, also **degree of comparison**. The middle term in the three degrees of an adjective or adverb. With some exceptions (*better, worse, farther/further*), the comparative is formed by adding *-er* to shorter words (*kinder, faster*) and *more* to longer words (*more beautiful, more nervously*). Many words that inflect can also be modified by *more*: *commoner/more common*. [GRAMMAR].   S.C.

COMPARATIVE PHILOLOGY. The branch of philology that deals with the relations between languages descended from a common original, now generally known as *comparative linguistics*. See PHILOLOGY. [HISTORY, LANGUAGE].   W.F.B.

COMPARATIVE SENTENCE. A sentence containing two clauses joined by a two-part comparative element: *as . . . as* (*It's as big as a house*); *not so/as . . . as* (*It's not so/as good as it used to be*); *the same . . . as* (*It's just the same as it used to be*); *less/more . . . than* (*It's a lot less/more than I wanted to pay*); (*nicer/faster*) *. . . than* (*The car's faster than we expected*). [GRAMMAR].   S.C.

COMPARISON, Degree of. See COMPARATIVE DEGREE.

COMPETENCE AND PERFORMANCE [1965]. In linguistics, the distinction between a person's knowledge of language (*competence*) and use of it (*performance*). Performance contains slips of the tongue and false starts, and represents only a small sample of possible utterances: *I own two-thirds of an emu* is a good English sentence, but is unlikely to occur in any collected sample. The terms were proposed by Noam Chomsky in *Aspects of the Theory of Syntax*, when he stressed the need for a generative grammar that mirrors a speaker's competence and captures the creative aspect of linguistic ability. In *Knowledge of Language* (1986), Chomsky replaced the terms with *I-language* (internalized language) and *E-language* (externalized language). A similar dichotomy, *langue* and *parole*, was proposed by Ferdinand de Saussure (1915), who stressed the social aspects of *langue*, regarding it as shared knowledge, whereas Chomsky stressed the individual nature of competence. See CHOMSKY, COMMUNICATIVE COMPETENCE, ERROR ANALYSIS, GENERATIVE GRAMMAR, LANGUE AND PAROLE, MISTAKE. [LANGUAGE].   J.M.A.

COMPLEMENT [14c: from Latin *complementum* a filling up or completion]. A grammatical constituent that completes the meaning of a word. Broadly, complements can be found for every major word class: verbs (*in Canada* in *They live in Canada*); nouns (*of their debt* in *the payment of their debt*); adjectives (*that we're late* in *I'm aware that we're late*); adverbs (*for me* in *luckily for me*); prepositions (*our place* in *at our place*). Some grammarians use the term *complementation* for the constituent or the process of complementing the word. More narrowly, complements refer to constituents that complete the meaning of the verb, including direct objects (*their debt* in *pay their debt*), indirect objects (*me* in *Show me the way*), and adverbial complements (*at them* in *Look at them*). In an even more restricted use, two kinds of complements are recognized for verbs: (1) *Subject complements*, which follow the verb *be* and other copular verbs, *my best friend* in *Tom is my best friend*. (2) *Object complements*, which follow a direct object and have a copular relationship with the object: *I consider Tom my best friend*. *Complement clauses* are subordinate clauses that function as complements of a word: *that they were too noisy* in *She told them that they were too noisy*. The subordinator that introduces a complement clause is sometimes known as a *complementizer*: for example *that* in the sentence just cited. See PREPOSITION, VERB OF INCOMPLETE PREDICATION. [GRAMMAR].   S.G.

COMPLETE PLAIN WORDS, The. A book written by Sir Ernest Gowers, a senior British civil servant, the 1st edition published in 1954 by Her Majesty's Stationery Office. The book was based on two slimmer books that he wrote at the invitation of the British Treasury, *Plain Words* (1948) and *The ABC of Plain Words* (1951), which gave advice to civil servants on the writing of official English. *TCPW* became a classic guide to good writing and has been reprinted many times. It has attracted devoted followers, not only among civil servants in Britain and abroad, but also among others whose jobs require them to write in a formal style. There have been two subsequent editions. Both endeavoured to retain as much as possible of Gowers's original text and to follow the vitality and vigour of his style in the changes they introduced. Revisions were needed to take account of changes in the language or in the practice of writers. In addition, the writers introduced contemporary examples and references to replace those that seemed dated, and they discussed some recent trends in English. They also took the opportunity to improve the organization of the book. The 2nd edition (1973) was undertaken by Sir Bruce Fraser, another civil servant. The 3rd edition (1986) was the work of Sidney Greenbaum, Director of the Survey of English Usage at U. College London, and Janet Whitcut, an editor of the *Longman Dictionary of the English Language* (1984). All three editions have been published as Penguin paperbacks and the 3rd edition has appeared in the US as a hardback (David R. Godine, 1988). See EFFECTIVE WRITING, PLAIN, USAGE GUIDANCE AND CRITICISM. [MEDIA, STYLE, USAGE].   S.G.

COMPLEX PREPOSITION. See PREPOSITION.

COMPLEX SENTENCE. A sentence consisting of one main clause in which are embedded one or more subordinate clauses: *I know where she*

lives, in which *where she lives* is a subordinate clause. In *When I asked for his opinion, he said that he could not say anything at present*, there are two subordinate clauses: the *when*-clause and the *that*-clause. See SENTENCE, SUBORDINATION. [GRAMMAR].   S.G.

COMPLEX WORD. A word consisting of a base and one or more derivational elements: *unlikely* (*un-*, *like*, *-ly*); *vitality* (*vit-*, *-al*, *-ity*). In origin and structural type, there are four kinds of complex word in English: (1) *Vernacular*. Formed on 'native' principles, but including some long-established words of Latin, Greek, and French background: *darkness*, *womanhood*, *beefy*, *priestly*. Such words may have equivalents in the Germanic languages: English *unmanly*, German *unmännlich*. (2) *Romance*. Formed on Latinate principles. Many such words are structurally (though not phonologically) identical or similar in English and the Romance languages: English *impossible*, *discrimination*; French *impossible*, *discrimination*; Spanish *imposible*, *discriminación*. (3) *Greek*. Formed on principles adapted from classical Greek through Neo-Latin. Many such words are structurally similar in English and Greek: English *dogmatic*, *magnetism*, Greek *dogmatikós*, *magnetismós*. (4) *Hybrid*. A mix of the above: *uncreative* mixes vernacular *un-* with Latin *cre-* and *-ative*; *ethically* mixes Greek *eth-* and *-ic* with Latin *-al* and vernacular *-ly*. See COMBINING FORM, COMPOUND-COMPLEX WORD, DERIVATION, PREFIX, SUFFIX (SUFFIXES AND STRESS), WORD-FORMATION. [WORD].   T.MCA.

COMPONENT [1930s in this sense]. A term in linguistics for a part, particularly of a grammar, such as a *syntactic component*. See LEVEL OF LANGUAGE. [LANGUAGE].   J.M.A.

COMPONENTIAL ANALYSIS [1940s]. In linguistics, the analysis of aspects of language into contrastive components or distinctive features, such as *voiced/unvoiced* in phonology and *animate/inanimate* in lexicology. See SEMANTICS. [LANGUAGE].   T.MCA.

COMPOSITION [14c: through French from Latin *compositio/compositionis* something put together]. (1) The action, process, or art of composing especially pieces of music and works of literature. (2) An essay, usually short and written for training purposes, especially in school and usually in the English classroom. (3) A course in writing in a school or other educational institution. (4) The process of putting words and sentences together according to the traditional rules of grammar, style, and rhetoric. (5) An obsolete term for word-formation: 'Of some forms of composition, such as that by which *re* is prefixed to note *repetition*, and *un* to signify *contrariety* or *privation*, all the examples cannot be accumulated' (Johnson, preface to *Dictionary of the English Language*, 1755). See COMPOUND WORD, ESSAY, THEME, WORD-FORMATION. [STYLE, WORD, WRITING].   T.MCA.

COMPOUND-COMPLEX SENTENCE. A compound sentence in which at least one of the main clauses contains one or more subordinate clause. In the following sentence, the second main clause (after *and*) contains a subordinate *since*-clause: *Road-building in those mountains is dangerous and, since work began in 1968, hundreds of labourers have been swept away by landslides.* See SENTENCE, SUBORDINATION. [GRAMMAR].   S.G.

COMPOUND-COMPLEX WORD. A word whose structure is both complex and compound: *hot-bloodedness*, in which there are two base words, *hot* and *blood*, and two suffixes, *-ed* and *-ness*; *biographical*, in which there are two combining forms, *bio-* and *-graph* and a composite suffix *-ical*. Compare COMPLEX WORD, COMPOUND WORD. [WORD].   T.MCA.

COMPOUND   PREPOSITION.   See PREPOSITION.

COMPOUND SENTENCE. A sentence consisting of two or more main clauses. The clauses may be linked by a coordinating conjunction: *and* in *The power failed for the third time that day, and once again we sat in darkness.* There may be no connectives between them, as in *Smooth cotton sheets feel cold; fleecy blankets feel warm*; or they may be linked by a conjunct, as with *however* in *I telephoned at least ten times yesterday; however, the line was never free.* In speech, such compounding goes unnoticed; in formal writing, a semicolon (as here) is used to unite the two clauses. In more relaxed styles, a comma is used. A period is generally used when a clear-cut division is required, in which case the clauses are taken to be separate sentences. See COORDINATION, SENTENCE. [GRAMMAR].   S.G.

COMPOUND WORD, also **compound** [14c: from Middle English *compoune*, from Old French *compon(d)re*, Latin *componere/compositum*, to put together]. A word made up of two or more other words: *teapot*, from *tea* and *pot*; *blackbird*, from *black* and *bird*. Compound words occur in many languages. In German, they are conventionally written in solid form: *Eisenbahn* ('ironway') railway; *Eisenbahnknotenpunkt* ('ironwayknotpoint') railway junction. In Greek and Latin, they are typically joined by thematic vowels, such as the *-i-* of Latin *agricultura*, the *-o-* of Greek *biographia*. In French, one kind of compound has the form of a prepositional phrase: *pomme de terre* ('apple of earth') potato; *arc-en-ciel* ('arch in sky') rainbow. Another consists of a verbnoun phrase: *gratte-ciel* ('scrape-sky') skyscraper; *grille-pain* ('grill-bread') toaster. Such compounds occasionally occur in English; 'man of the church' matches *homme d'église*, and 'breakwater' matches *brise-lames*.

Compounds in English. The majority of English compounds fall into two types: (1) Vernacular compounds like *teapot* and *blackbird*, formed on principles typical of the Germanic languages. They are written in solid form, open form, or with hyphens. (2) Classical compounds like *agriculture* and *biography*, based on the compounding patterns of Greek and Latin. They are generally written in solid form. There are also some minor groups, such as those containing prepositions, in the French style: *commander-in-chief, man-at-arms, man of the church*. Grammarians generally treat the vernacular form as the compound proper. The classical compound belongs to a stratum of language which serves as an international resource on which many languages draw: see CLASSICAL COMPOUND. The status of vernacular compounds has traditionally been established through two criteria: how they sound and how they appear in writing and print. Because of this, they can be divided for practical purposes into *phonological compounds* and *orthographic compounds*.

Phonological compounds. In speech, most two-word compounds have a falling intonation and are stressed on the first word (*TEApot, BLACKbird*) or primary stress falls on the stressed syllable of the first word (*eMERgency plan, RePUBlican Party*). This pattern of stress and intonation usually serves to distinguish compounds from expressions which typically have equal stress on both elements: such adjectival phrases as *the white hóuse* (as opposed to *the WHITE House*) and nouns used attributively (*iron bridge*, as opposed to *IRONbridge*, the name of a town in England). Compound words, and phrases containing attributive nouns, generally have explanatory paraphrases: *teapot* a pot for tea; *iron bridge* a bridge made of iron. The following examples show differences in sound and meaning between compound and attributive usages (the compound first in each pair): *ORange juice* juice squeezed from oranges and *órange júice* juice that is orange in colour; *KEY position* the position of a key or keys and *kéy position* a position of great importance.

Adjective/noun combinations like *blackbird* are established as compounds both on the phonological criterion of stress and the semantic criteria of generic use and unique reference. *BLACKbird* has the stress pattern of *teapot* (distinct from the stress pattern of *a bláck bírd*) and serves as the unique generic name for all such birds. Colour adjectives often figure in such compounds (*blackboard, bluebird, brownstone, greenhouse, paleface, redcoat, redskin, whitecap*) as well as in place and personal names (*Blackburn, Greenland, Greystoke, Redpath, the White House, Whitehouse*).

Phonological and related factors become more intricate as structures containing compounds increase in length. In *car factory strike committee*, stress is placed on both *car* and *strike*. The group can be analysed as ((*CAR factory*) (*STRIKE committee*)), and paraphrased as a 'committee dealing with strikes in a factory that makes cars'. The compound *car factory* precedes the compound *strike committee*, and is therefore attributive. Such a combination is sometimes called a *double* or *multiple compound*. In principle, such groupings are indefinitely extensible: *Coventry car factory strike committee policy decision*, analysable as ((((COventry) (CAR factory)) ((STRIKE committee) (POLicy decision))), and paraphrased as a 'decision about policy made by a committee dealing with strikes in a factory that makes cars in Coventry'. In English, such expressions are not usually written as one word, as in German. Both languages, however, exploit very fully their capacity to form compounds and other multiple word groups.

Orthographic compounds. Traditionally, more attention has been paid to compounds on paper than to how they sound. In writing and print there are three forms: (1) *Solid compounds*, such as *teapot* and *blackbird*. (2) *Hyphenated compounds*, such as *body-blow, bridge-builder, mud-walled*. (3) *Open compounds*, such as *Army depot, coffee cup*. The conventions of solidity, hyphenation, and openness have tended to determine whether a word is considered a compound or not. Solidity and hyphenation endorse and reinforce compound status, visually distinguishing *a greenhouse* or *a green-house* from *a green house* (a house that is green). Although such distinctions can be valuable, they are not consistently applied: *Whitehouse* can be the name of a place or a family, but *the White House* in Washington is never **the Whitehouse* or **the White-house*.

In linguistics, the status of an item as a compound depends more on phonological than orthographic criteria, but in typography the orthographic forms have great importance. Even so, however, decisions about written compounds are more rule-of-thumb than rule, and fall into three groups: (1) Those made up of short words

and therefore likely to be solid: *teapot, blackbird*. (2) Those made up of constituents which would look strange when combined and are therefore likely to be open (*coffee cup* rather than *coffee-cup* or *coffeecup*) or hyphenated (*body-blow* rather than *bodyblow*). (3) Compound-complex words are usually hyphenated: *bridge-builder, mud-walled*. However, many items freely vary: *businessman, business-man, business man; wine bottle, wine-bottle, winebottle*. As a further rule of thumb, the older and shorter a noun/noun or noun/adjective compound, the more likely it is to be solid: *rattlesnake*. The newer and longer it is, the more likely it is to be open: *population explosion*. Beyond that, the traditional practice appears to be, 'When in doubt, use a hyphen'. However, the writing and printing of many compound patterns remain uncertain and idiosyncratic, except where a house style is firmly applied. The same writer may make the same compound solid in one place (*worldview*), hyphenate it in another (*world-view*), and open it up in a third (*world view*), sometimes within a few pages of each other.

Paraphrase patterns. Next to phonology and orthography, the most distinctive aspect of compounds is susceptibility to paraphrase. This exhibits a kind of covert syntax based mainly on prepositional phrases: the compound *teapot* can be paraphrased only as 'a pot *for* tea', not a 'pot *of* tea'. Similarly, an *armchair* is 'a chair with arms', a *flower pot* 'a pot for (holding) flowers', a *goatskin* 'the skin of a goat', and a *bank clerk* 'a clerk in a bank'. Innumerable semantic relationships of this kind occur among compounds, some easy to interpret in isolation, others dependent on context. *London goods*, for example, may be 'goods in London', 'goods for London', 'goods from London'. Paraphrasing is not, however, always straightforward, even when the context is clear. What paraphrase is best for *steamboat*: 'a boat that uses steam', 'a boat using steam', 'a boat driven by steam', 'a boat with a steam engine in it', or 'steam drives this boat'? Precise paraphrase is impossible, but imprecise paraphrases still work adequately, because the relation between *steam* and *boat* is clear enough. It is the same with *sheepdog* 'a dog that ? sheep', *silk merchant* a merchant who ? silk, *car factory* a factory ? cars, and *honey bee* a bee that ? honey.

Families of compounds. There are many sets of compounds based on the same word, such as *gunboat, riverboat, rowboat, steamboat*. In such sets, the second element is generic, but its relationship with each member of its set is likely to be different. A *steamboat* is a boat propelled by steam, but a *riverboat* is not a boat propelled by a river. It is a boat used on a river. A *houseboat* is neither a boat propelled by a house nor a boat used on or in a house, but a floating house in the form of a boat, or a boat in the form of a house, usually moored in one place. Analogous forms are unlikely. There is no *bungalow boat* or *mansionboat*, except for nonce or stunt purposes. A *gunboat* is a boat with one or more large guns on it, a *rowboat* is AmE for a boat that can be rowed, BrE equivalent a *rowing boat*. Such forms and relationships are legion, but native speakers generally have little difficulty with them. Similarly, they have no difficulty in distinguishing a *houseboat* from a *boathouse* or a *horse race* from a *racehorse*.

A continuum of analysability. Some compounds are easily analysable (like *teapot*), some less so (like *steamboat*), and others may need much more than a paraphrase formula. The *Collins English Dictionary* (1986) defines *limestone* as: 'a sedimentary rock consisting mainly of calcium carbonate, deposited as the calcareous remains of marine animals or chemically precipitated from the sea: used as a building stone and in the manufacture of cement, lime, etc.' *Lime* and *stone* figure quite modestly only towards the end of this description. Other compounds are thoroughly opaque, their forms offering so little help as to meaning and use that they must be treated as unanalysable wholes (sometimes called *holisms*). Although *cupboard* has something to do with cups and boards, neither helps in defining it, and *butterfly* has nothing whatever to do with butter or flies.

Compound names. Such holistic compounds include proper names like *Sutton* (a reduced version of 'South Town') and *Shakespeare* (who shook no spears). Words like these have unique references and histories and their elements make no contribution to their everyday use. Historical association has produced various more or less opaque everyday compounds formed from names, such as *Wellington boot* (a British rubber boot named after the Duke of Wellington) and *Balaclava helmet* (a knitted cap associated with Balaclava, first used by British soldiers in the Crimean War). Such compounds are readily clipped, to become *wellingtons* (or *wellies*) and *balaclavas*.

Compounds in context. The coinage and use of compound words often follow a pattern of development in texts and social situations, usually a sequence that reinforces certain usages and may precipitate others. A character in a story may be introduced as *a man with a red beard*, brought in again as *a red-bearded man* and then called *Redbeard*. This might be his only name in a story for children or it could be an epithet, like *Eric Redbeard*, in a historical saga. In the flow of a narrative, new information is placed in focus in

various ways. One such device is primary stress, already significant in compounds. It becomes particularly noticeable when texts containing patterns of compounding are read aloud, as in the following (each new focus italicized):

Let's have a little talk about *tweetle* beetles—
What do you *know* about tweetle beetles? Well . . .
When tweetle beetles *fight*, it's called a tweetle beetle *battle*.
And when they battle in a *puddle*, it's a tweetle beetle *puddle* battle.
AND when tweetle beetles battle with *paddles* in a puddle, they call it a tweetle beetle puddle *paddle* battle.
AND when beetles battle beetles in a puddle paddle battle and the beetle battle puddle is a puddle in a *bottle* . . .
they call this a tweetle beetle *bottle* puddle paddle battle *muddle*.

(from Dr Seuss, *Fox in Socks*, 1960)

Creative paradigms. Nonce and stunt compounds are often generated by social and linguistic circumstance. In the US television series *Hart to Hart* (1983), a character is asked: 'What's the matter, Max, you got heart-burn?' To which he replies, referring to a game of poker, 'Not only that—I got club-burn, diamond-burn, and spade-burn.' Comparably, *drug abuse* begets, as needs arise and similarities are recognized, such parallel forms as *alcohol abuse*, *child abuse*, *solvent abuse*, *spouse abuse*, *substance abuse*. Analogical paradigms of this kind are common.

Conclusion. Vernacular compounding is an open system. Users of English daily form and forget compounds in which words of vastly different pedigree and association come together. The following come from data collected in the 1980s: *ashram fashion*, *blimp patrol*, *energy vampire*, *herpes factory*, *karma debt*, *kitten juice*, *mistress bank*, *punctuality nut*, *Rebetika music*, *Stupor Bowl*, *time-womb*, *whale jazz*, *zombie powder*. Out of context, such forms may tax the ability to understand, but even in isolation items like *kitten juice* and *mistress bank* yield meaning, however bizarre and whether or not it is the meaning originally intended. For further discussion, see ABBREVIATION, CLASSICAL/ LEARNED COMPOUND, COMBINING FORM, EPONYM, FIXED PHRASE, NOUN INCORPORATION, PHRASAL VERB, PLURAL, RHYMING COMPOUND, WORD-FORMATION. [NAME, WORD].   T.MCA.

COMPREHENSIVE GRAMMAR OF THE ENGLISH LANGUAGE, short form *CGEL*. A major reference work on the grammar of standard English, by the British grammarians Randolph Quirk, Sidney Greenbaum, Geoffrey Leech, and David Crystal (as indexer), and the Swedish grammarian Jan Svartvik (published by

Longman, 1985, *c.*1,790 pages with a 110-page index). It succeeded and drew on an earlier reference work by Quirk, Greenbaum, Leech, and Svartvik: *A Grammar of Contemporary English* (*GCE*) (Longman, 1972, *c.*1,130 pages), and has been abridged in *A Student's Grammar of the English Language* (*SGEL*) by Greenbaum and Quirk (Longman, 1990).

Framework. The grammatical framework of *CGEL* is eclectic, drawing on the established tradition in scholarly grammars, such as those by Otto Jespersen and Hendrik Poutsma, and on various recent theoretical approaches, particularly aspects of the early stages of Noam Chomsky's *transformational-generative grammar* and of the work of Michael Halliday and his associates, often referred to as *systemic grammar*. The description in *CGEL* is a work of synthesis: it provides an account of the state of knowledge about English grammar at the time when the book was written, drawing on the research of the four authors as well as the contributions of scholars worldwide. Much of this research has used data from systematically compiled corpora, particularly the corpus of the Survey of English Usage, which includes spoken and manuscript material as well as printed works. An additional important source of data comes from the results of elicitation experiments.

Describing the standard language. *CGEL* is concerned primarily with the standard forms of AmE and BrE, and it notes differences between the two national varieties where these have been recorded. Within the standard language, it takes account of stylistic variation that correlates with distinctions between spoken and written English, level of formality, and such fields of discourse as literary, legal, and religious varieties. Notice is taken of divided usages, including disputed usages subject to controversy and prescription. Relative acceptability and relative frequency are recorded in general as well as specifically for references to national and stylistic variation. The central concern of *CGEL* is contemporary syntax, but syntactic form is related to syntactic and semantic functions. Other aspects of language are introduced for their association with syntax: intonation and punctuation, for the syntactic distinctions they signal; phonology and morphology, for inflections; morphology and lexicology, for multi-word units such as phrasal verbs; pragmatics, text linguistics, discourse analysis, and rhetoric, for the functions of sentences when uttered in context; language attitudes, as they affect syntactic choices.

In the language model presupposed, surface forms of syntax are related to meanings in the widest sense, including functions in discourse. Systematic correspondences are noted between structures where there is a constant meaning relationship between them, such as the correspondence between declarative and interrogative clauses. *CGEL* recognizes that grammar is an indeterminate system and that grammatical categories are not discrete. It therefore argues that there is no absolute distinction between coordinating and subordinating constructions, but a gradient in which there are central coordinators such as *and* and *or*, and central subordinators such as *if* and *although*, and conjunctions such as *but* and *for* that are intermediate in their status.

Background. At the time of writing the grammar, the authors were teaching at different universities: three in Britain, one in Sweden, and one in the US. They worked on their sections individually and revised drafts in the light of comments from co-authors and other readers. The final draft was written in the summer of 1983. *CGEL* is the culmination of collaboration on research and publication extending for 20 years. The general agreement between the authors on their approach to the description of English grammar reflects their association with the Department of English at U. College London and the Survey of English Usage. See SURVEY OF ENGLISH USAGE. [GRAMMAR]. S.G.

COMPUTATIONAL LINGUISTICS. The branch of linguistics which studies and creates formal descriptions of natural language that can be used by a computer to analyse the structure of a language. A computational description must be precise and comes as a formal grammar, a set of rules which describe the possible strings of elements in the language. In such descriptions, *generative grammars* produce sentences and *recognition grammars* parse them: that is, they work out and label the structures of the sentences which they are given. An important model is the *context-free grammar*, in which rules look like (1) NP—ART + NOUN, (2) NP—NP + PP, where the first rule says that a noun phrase (NP) may consist of an article followed by a noun, and the second that it may consist of a noun phrase followed by a prepositional phrase (PP). The left side of such a rule must be a single syntactic class.

Context-free grammars are computationally well understood and if English, the language most studied by such linguists, matched this model well there would be few problems. Unfortunately, it does not. Many words can function as both nouns and verbs (*function, set, turn*), and so it is not possible to assign them to only one word class. Faced with a string such as *my computer functions*, it is impossible to decide whether this will continue as *My computer functions are slow* or *My computer functions badly*. Even if the parts of speech are known, the grammar is ambiguous: *I saw the man with the telescope* could mean either that the speaker looked through a telescope or that the man seen was carrying a telescope. In more complex models, the left side of a rule may be a string of syntactic classes. These include *context-sensitive grammars* (in which the possible applications of a rule are restricted to certain contexts) and *transformational grammars* (in which phrases are reordered from a 'deep' *base* form to a *surface* form). Other more recent and currently favoured models include *lexical functional grammar, unification grammar*, and *government binding theory*.

Computational linguists also study semantics, especially to formalize the logical implications of sentences, as well as the relationships between successive sentences in a text, as in discourse analysis. In the absence of any evidence that supports one theory of grammar rather than another, such linguists turn to detailed studies of words and their frequencies, to avoid having to place too much emphasis on syntax as the central factor in the comprehension of language. Recent works on the subject include R. Grishman, *Computational Linguistics: An Introduction* (Cambridge: University Press, 1986), and K. Sparck-Jones and Y. Wilks, *Automatic Natural Language Parsing* (Chichester: Ellis Horwood, 1985).

See AMBIGUITY, CHOMSKY, COMPUTING, DISCOURSE ANALYSIS, GENERATIVE GRAMMAR, LINGUISTICS. [GRAMMAR, LANGUAGE, TECHNOLOGY]. M.L.

COMPUTERATE [1980s: a blend of *computer* and *literate*]. An occasional technical term for 'literacy' in the use of computers: 'That children leaving school should be literate and numerate has long been accepted . . . But it is essential that they are "computerate" also' (*Journal of the Royal Society of Arts*, 1981). See COMPUTER LITERACY. [TECHNOLOGY, WRITING]. T.MCA.

COMPUTERESE [1950s]. Also **computerspeak, computer lingo**. Non-technical, often pejorative terms for usage associated with computers, such as: (1) Strings of letters and words used in programming and processing: the command *copy c: adm1 a:*, meaning 'copy from c-drive to a-drive the first administrative file' (where the c-drive is a built-in hard disk and the a-drive contains an inserted diskette). (2) Terms like *mainframe*, defined as either 'the combination of central processor and primary memory of a computer system' or 'any large computer system' (*Oxford Dictionary of Computing*, 1986). (3) Casual expressions used by computer enthusiasts: *Give*

me your input on this Tell me what you think of this. See COMPUTER USAGE, TECHNOBABBLE. [STYLE, TECHNOLOGY, USAGE, WORD]. T.MCA., M.L.

COMPUTER LITERACY. Familiarity with, and ability to use, computers. Many universities, especially in the US, try to make all students *computer literate*, some faculties requiring them to buy computers on entry. The replacement of typewriters by word processors means that a basic level of such literacy is increasingly required in business and administration. In North America, the use of computers to send electronic mail and perform calculations is commonly expected from the computer literate, but not programming skills. See COMPUTERATE, COMPUTING, LITERACY. [TECHNOLOGY, WRITING]. M.L.

COMPUTER TYPESETTING. The production of printed matter by computer, usually by producing a master copy for offset reproduction. Starting in the 1970s, devices with film strips or film wheels, containing images of characters, were widely used to produce master copies on photographic film. More recently, the use of pre-made film images has given way to cathode-ray tubes which generate characters as requested. The use of film seems likely to become obsolete as laser printers become more widely available. The use of computers for typesetting is particularly helpful in revising texts and prepare indexes. See COMPUTING, LASER, TYPOGRAPHY. [TECHNOLOGY]. M.L.

COMPUTER USAGE, sometimes **Computer English**. The register of English associated with computer technology and electronic communication, for both professional and other purposes, such as: the creation, use, and maintenance of equipment; recreation, such as video games and electronic bulletin boards; the writing and transmission of electronic mail; the promotion of products; word processing, desktop publishing, and electronic publishing; and informal usage, including slang. Such usage has both lexical and syntactic aspects, including word-formation, semantic change, and distinctive prose styles.

Word-formation. (1) Compounds, such as *database* an organized store of information, *light pen* a light-sensitive rod for 'drawing' on screens or for reading data. (2) Fixed phrases such as *high-level language* an algebraic code with elements of natural language for operating computers, *mainframe* a very large computer system. (3) Abbreviations such as *ASCII* (pronounced 'Askey') for 'American Standard Code for Information Interchange', *CD-ROM* for 'compact disk read-only memory', *GIGO* for 'garbage in, garbage out', *WYSIWYG* or *wysiwyg* for 'what you see is what you get' (that is, a precise correspondence between what is on screen and what is printed out). (4) Blends, such as the programming languages *FORTRAN*, fusing '*for*mula' and '*tran*slator', and *LISP*, fusing '*lis*t' and '*processing*'. (5) Eponyms, such as *non Von Neumann architecture*, any architecture basically different from the style of computer specified by the US mathematician John von Neumann, and *Turing machine*, an imaginary computer with characteristics as stated by the UK computing pioneer Alan Turing. New concepts often develop on one base form: for example, the discussion of computers includes *hardware*, physical parts, and *software*, programs; from these such further terms have emerged as *courseware*, software for educational purposes, *firmware*, the code that turns programmers' instructions into directions to the wires and switches, and *bioware* and *liveware*, facetious terms for people.

Semantic change. The adaptation of meanings and uses from the language at large into computer usage (new uses for old words), from computer usage to the language at large (public uses for private 'jargon'), and from one register to another (such as from medicine to computer usage):

Specialization. New uses for old words: *architecture* the arrangement of complex hardware and software, *chip* a tiny wafer of silicon on which is engraved a minute circuit, *compiler* a program which translates computer languages into machine language, *document* as a verb, meaning 'write', *interface* (noun) a connection between devices which cannot otherwise communicate with each other, (verb) to provide or have such a connection, *library* a set of programs for common tasks, *mouse* (plural sometimes *mouses*) an electrical pointing device like a remote control used to move elements on the screen of a personal computer, *peripherals* ancillary devices that can be disconnected without interrupting normal work, *protocol* the rules by which two computers or programs communicate, *stack* a list of tasks a computer has to perform to execute a particular program, *turnkey* a system delivered to the customer ready to work immediately.

Generalization. Extended uses for 'computer jargon': *input* and *output* as nouns, as in *I didn't like his input to the meeting*, as verbs, as in *Can you input that again?—I didn't understand*, *bug* as in *directions for home brewing have been debugged so thoroughly they are foolproof*, *interface* as in *the interface between government bureaucracy and the average citizen*, *mode* as in *I attended the meeting in sponge mode* (I listened but said nothing), and *network* as in *to network* (to call around one's friends and colleagues).

Transfer. The term *virus* has been transferred from medical to computer usage, to mean a planted program that copies itself from machine to machine, causing trouble along the way by using up memory or corrupting or deleting files. Before this term became established, such a program was briefly known as *a Trojan horse* or *Trojan*.

Prose styles. The styles of computer usage are like those referred to pejoratively as *technospeak* and *agglomerese*. They engage in complex premodification with numbers, abbreviations, compound words, and attributive nouns, as in: *160KB/180KB single-sided diskettes*; *keyboard code page*; *a CloseSysWindow routine*; *the CONFIG.SYS DEVICE*; *CP/M or MS-DOS systems*; *the load-substitution (ldsub) command*. Punctuation exploits slashes, points, colons, parentheses, and capitals (including internal capitals). The following excerpts are representative:

Bit handling The facility provided in some programming languages to manipulate the individual bits of a byte or word. Operators provided usually include bitwise 'and' and 'or' between two bytes (or words), bitwise 'not' (inversion) of a single byte (or word), and circular shifts (part of definition: *Oxford Dictionary of Computing*, 1986).

Superfile VLDB runs equally well on a variety of media—Winchesters, WORM and CD-ROM. This makes it an ideal medium for the distribution of large databases. Southdata's MD Peter Laurie said: 'VLDB is excellent for the publication of huge amounts of data. Not only can end users look things up with spectacular speed, but they can also integrate data they buy with data they have collected themselves' (booklet: Southdata, London, late 1980s).

The *DoClose* routine that we looked at in the last chapter (Program 3.3) checks to see whether an application or a system window is active. If it's an application window, *DoClose* closes it by calling the routine *CloseAppWindow*, which we've already looked at (Program 3.4); if a system window is active, it calls the *CloseSysWindow* routine shown here as Program 4.7. This routine simply gets the reference number of the window's desk accessory from the *WindowKind* field (3.1.1) and calls the Toolbox routine *CloseDeskAcc* (4.5.2) to close the accessory, removing its window from the screen (Stephen Chernikoff, *Macintosh Revealed*, volume 2, 1985).

Most regular editing commands and keys may be used within a note input window. For example, you can underline, bold-face, right justify, or center text; insert phrases from a phrase library; move, copy, or delete text; move to the command line to execute a format command or to conduct a search or change (affecting the note input window only); and move the cursor by sentence, paragraph, etc. (Loren Siebert, *Nota Bene* reference manual, 1986, C2-6).

The density of terms in such passages tends to intimidate newcomers to the field and has prompted considerable dislike for instruction manuals and promotional literature. The problem is similar to that of any in-group (such as medical practitioners, physicists, or social scientists) seeking to communicate with the public at large. Currently, writers of computer-related manuals and other texts appear to need a more user-friendly interface. See COMPUTERESE, COMPUTING, REGISTER, WORD PROCESSOR. [STYLE, TECHNOLOGY, USAGE].   M.L., T.MCA.

COMPUTING [17c: from Latin *computare/computatum* to think, count]. The use of an electronic device that accepts data, performs mathematical and logical operations at speed on those data, and displays the results. Computers, although initially developed as calculating devices and open to a range of uses, have become central to communicative technology, and relate to language in at least three ways: they require their own artificial languages in order to function; their use has adapted natural language to new ends, such as the processing of texts by computer; and their users have developed their own registers for working with them and talking about them. Since the 1950s, these factors have developed explosively and are major influences on late 20c English, the language most closely involved in computing.

Nature. The present-day computer derives from British work during the Second World War on cryptographic machines and is the most recent in a line of calculating devices that includes the abacus, the Jacquard loom, Babbage's Analytical Engine, and Hollerith's tab-sorter. Its primary purpose has been to compute, not to compile or converse. There are two kinds of computer: *analog* and *digital*. Analog computers, related to the slide rule and tables of logarithms (and virtually obsolete), use the strengths of voltages to represent the size of numbers, whereas digital computers use electrical signals only in the on/off form. Holding up two fingers at a ticket office to indicate how many tickets you want is digital; holding your hands apart to indicate how big a fish you caught is analog. Currently, digital computers consist of four major parts:

A processor. Also *central processing unit* (*CPU*). The processor executes commands, performing arithmetical, logical, and manipulative operations on the data stored in the second part. Typically, computers execute more than one million instructions a second.

A memory. The information store. Most computers have at least two kinds of memory: primary and secondary. Primary memory is usually silicon chips, typically DRAM (dynamic random access memory) chips. 'Random access'

means that any part may be obtained immediately, as with a book that can be opened to any page. The process is fast, usually less than one microsecond to obtain an item of information. Secondary memory is usually magnetic disk, made of one or more platters rotating under a reading head. It is not random access: a particular part of the disk cannot be read until it rotates under the reading head, which usually takes several milliseconds. Storage is measured in *bytes*, one byte containing eight *bits*, and representing storage for one character in European alphabets.

Input/output equipment. This enables the user to get information into and out of the machine. The information is entered most commonly through a keyboard but also through removable disks, tapes, and other devices. Output goes to display screens, to printers (which produce text etc., usually known as *hard copy*), and also to disks and tapes.

Communications equipment. This permits a computer to 'talk' to other machines and to people located at a distance from it. The equipment includes *modems* (an acronym for '*mo*dulator *de*-*mo*dulators'), which connect computers by telephone line, and *networks* (including *LANs* or *local area networks*) to let machines talk at high speed to each other.

Computer programs. Since computers work very fast, they cannot be directed step by step. Instead, a script must be written out in advance for the computer to follow. The script typically contains sequences to be repeated, so that the script is much shorter than the operation as executed. The computer responds to *machine language*, which is binary code (strings of 0s and 1s), in which the operations are very simple (such as elementary arithmetic or moving one piece of data from one place to another). To write machine language by hand is tedious and error-prone. The scripts people write are now in higher-level languages called *computer programs* (BrE following AmE in this spelling, but AmE follows BrE in doubling the *m* in *programming*). A distinction is now universally made between the equipment as (*computer*) *hardware* and the programs as (*computer*) *software*. Most present-day computer users do not make their own programs, as was often the case in the early stages of software development, but use programs written by others, which are generally made available to them as commercial *software packages*.

Computer languages (also *programming languages, high-level languages*). Digital computers follow directions written in an often bewildering variety of artificial languages which provide precise specifications of operations to be done and the order in which they must be done.

Although strings of letters are used to name commands in these languages, they are quite different from natural language. Among other things, they must be logical and unambiguous: unlike people, computers do not know that the *and* in *I like bread and jam* means 'both together', while the *and* in *I like cats and dogs* does not imply that both must be present at once ('I like cats and I like dogs'). Computer languages usually provide an algebra-like notation for indicating mathematical calculations; typically, $a = b + c$ instructs the machine to add the values named by b and c together and call the result a. Particularly important is a way of specifying *control flow*: the order in which the instructions are to be executed. A person can be told, 'If you are late, if you can find a cab, take it; otherwise run', while a computer would not know whether the *otherwise run* instruction went with *if you can find a cab* or *if you are late* (that is, it might believe that it should run only if it were *not* late).

Compared with natural language, high-level computer languages normally have: (1) *Very short utterances*. While written English sentences might average 20 words in length, statements in programming language are typically only six items long. (2) *Large numbers of names for variables*. There are many labels for items whose value might change depending on the computation, with relatively few constant names for control, operators, etc. FORTRAN uses a dozen words like DO, READ, and GOTO for control. Even COBOL, which by computer standards has a great many reserved words, only has about 250. This is the reverse of natural English, in which proper names are rare and common nouns are the norm. (3) *Little syntactic variety*. The typical computer language at present has a grammar of about 100 rules, compared with thousands in a formal grammatical description of English. (4) *Very short words*. Most programmers save effort by giving variables names such as x, one or two letters long, and by using many abbreviations, such as *del* for *delete*. Sometimes their style can be compared to baby talk.

Specific languages. The many programming languages are divided into *business languages* (verbose, emphasizing simple operations on complex data) and *scientific languages* (terse, emphasizing complex operations on simple data). They often have distinctive histories and functions, and names of etymological interest. *ALGOL*, a language suitable for expressing algorithms, is widely regarded as the computational equivalent of Esperanto; it was created in 1960 by an international committee, and its name, a reduction of *Algorithm Language*, happens to be a homonym of the star *Algol*, which in Arabic means 'the ghoul'. *BASIC* is short for *Beginner's All-Purpose Symbolic Instruction Code*. The program so named was designed at Dartmouth College in New Hampshire in 1965 by J. Kemeny and T. Kurtz. It is often the first programming language learned and is similar to the *Basic* of *Basic English*, also an acronym. *ADA* was designed in a competition run by the US Department of Defense from 1974 to 1980, going through successive refinements with such names as *Strawman*, *Woodenman*, *Tinman*, and *Ironman*. The French computer scientist Jean Ichbiah led the winning team. It was named after Lady Ada Lovelace, the daughter of Byron and a supporter of Charles Babbage, the inventor of the Analytical Engine, an early mechanical digital computer. She is often called the first programmer.

Other names include: *APL*, short for *a programming language* and unrelated to the later *Apple* Computers; *COBOL*, short for *Common Business-Oriented Language*; *PASCAL*, named after the 17c French mathematician and philosopher Blaise Pascal; and *PROLOG*, short for *programmation en logique*. Many languages deal in special applications, such as *Nota Bene, Tex*, and *Scribe* for word processing, *AUTOCAD* for computer-aided design, *SIM-SCRIPT* for simulation, and *KEE* for knowledge representation. For some years, the goal of 'programming in English' (that is, using a more or less unrestricted subset of the natural language) attracted attention, but it has so far proved unattainable and is not the focus of mainstream work on the further development of computer languages.

The computer processing of text. Computers, among other things, are extensions of writing and print systems, and have therefore been used with greater or less success to do such things as evaluate, index, parse, translate, correct, and 'understand' text. When a suitably programmed computer is fed English, it can process it at several levels, but with decreasing competence as the task becomes more complex. The following sequence is typical:

The character level. Text can be entered into a computer by three means: *keying* it, typically into a word processor which will format the text (arranging the line lengths and character positions); *scanning* it, using a machine which transfers a paper version into an image followed by a program which looks at the image and tries to recognize the characters in it; *transferring* it electronically, typically by diskette or telephone, from another compatible computer. Transfer is the fastest and most accurate method, but currently the least used. When a cleanly typed or printed original is available, without too many fonts or typographic complexities, scanning is faster and easier than re-keying. Once the text is entered, computers can print it in a wide variety of typefaces, sizes, and page formats, using either a printer or a desktop publishing system.

The word level. A spelling checker can find some kinds of typing mistakes, usually by comparing words with a dictionary list and noting those that are not in that list. Programs can make word lists and concordances (lists of each word with some context before and after it). By noting the most frequent words in a document, and comparing the word frequencies in a particular text with the average word frequencies in English, a program can suggest words that might be used for indexing the document. The counting of relative word frequencies and comparison with word frequencies from a standard sample can also help in guessing the authorship of anonymous works or measuring the readability level of a text.

The sentence level. On the level of syntax, parsing programs can try to define the structure of sentences and relationships among words. See PARSING. This is typically done by applying grammar rules of the form 'a verb phrase may be a verb followed by an adverb'. Unfortunately many sentences are ambiguous. In the preceding sentence, a computer would not know whether *unfortunately* modified the verb (implying that it is sad that ambiguous sentences occur) or the adjective *many* (suggesting disappointment that ambiguous sentences are so frequent). Adding a comma after *Unfortunately* could, however, serve as a means of disambiguation. However, some kinds of grammatical and stylistic errors can be diagnosed, and grammar checkers and style checkers have become available to help in the writing of business letters and the propagation of Plain English.

The message level. At the level of word-and-sentence meaning, semantic analysis can map a sentence into a knowledge-presentation language. Some research projects have been able to take such sentences as *Which ships are in port?* and answer them by looking at a table of ship locations. However, such systems currently operate in strictly limited subject areas. Other applications of semantics include machine translation and direct generation of language by computers (that is, the computer produces text without human input).

The above levels of activity depend on computational linguists writing rules of analysis, accumulating a grammar of syntactic and/or semantic rules for such a language as English. An alternative strategy for processing written language, however, uses reference books: the use of a machine-readable dictionary or thesaurus may help a computer make reasonable guesses about which sense of an ambiguous word is intended in a particular context. Another strategy relies on the statistical properties of large corpora to determine word relationships. Such methods have allowed parsing without writing a grammar in advance, a higher quality of error correction in spelling, and the automatic recognition of phrases. However, they handle uncommon constructions less well than the grammar-based procedures handle them, and depend for their success on the fact that such constructions are uncommon.

The processing of speech. There are several goals in the use of computers to deal with spoken language. Although all of these apply to any natural language, the work done on English far exceeds that on any other language. The areas in which such work proceeds are *speech synthesis, speech recognition and comprehension, speaker verification*, and *speaker identification*.

Speech synthesis. The synthesis of speech entails turning text into sound signals: getting a computer to read aloud, formulating speech which can be adequately understood. There are two steps: translating standard written or printed language into a phonological sequence, and then pronouncing such a sequence. The translation can be done phoneme by phoneme, but if pronounced without rhythm and intonation, the result is monotonic, unnatural, and hard to understand. The interactions of syntax with rhythm and intonation to produce smooth speech are currently being studied. Pronunciation of isolated phonemes can be done well enough by such devices as DECTALK, which have either recordings of each phoneme or digital filters which generate them. Filtering can also be used to make smooth transitions between phonemes.

Speech recognition and comprehension. The recognition and comprehension of speech entails transcribing spoken English into printed English. Currently, it is possible to buy devices that recognize, with a few percentage errors, perhaps a hundred words spoken in isolation by a known speaker. The problems of dealing with a speaker for whom the device has not been trained, or partitioning continuous speech into words, are difficult and have not been solved.

Speaker verification. Verifying speakers entails checking by voice signal that people are who they claim to be. The frequencies characteristic of a person's voice (known as *formants*) are determined by the size and shape of the larynx and throat, and can be calculated from the recorded sounds. A computer can compare a speech sample presented by an individual with a recording of the same words made by the same person, and confirm that they are the same. Voices, however, are affected by colds and inflammation, and are therefore less precise than fingerprints.

Speaker identification. Identifying speakers entails finding out who people are by comparing their voices with stored samples. This is similar to verification, except that the task is not to compare with a single voice, but to compare with a choice of people, and without knowing what is being said, which is more difficult to achieve.

The general desire is a machine which can transcribe speech or spoken text into writing, but the hopes and promises of the 1970s have not been fulfilled. By contrast, simple speech synthesis is fairly common and both verification and identification are feasible if not yet in wide use. The numerous failures at speech understanding suggest that high-level linguistic processing and phonetics are needed to do it right. Similarly, the intelligibility of synthesized speech depends on prosody as well as individual phonemes: 'Take care of the sense, and the sounds will take care of themselves' (Lewis Carroll, *Alice's Adventures in Wonderland*, 1865).

See ALGORITHM, ARTIFICIAL INTELLIGENCE, BOILERPLATE, COMMUNICATIVE SHIFT, COMPUTATIONAL LINGUISTICS, COMPUTERATE, COMPUTERESE, COMPUTER LITERACY, COMPUTER TYPESETTING, COMPUTER USAGE, CONCORDANCE, CORRUPT, DESKTOP PUBLISHING, ELECTRONIC PUBLISHING, GRAMMAR CHECKER, HACKER, HYPERTEXT, ICON, INFORMATION (INFORMATION RETRIEVAL, INFORMATION TECHNOLOGY), KNOWLEDGE REPRESENTATION, MACHINE LANGUAGE, MACHINE TRANSLATION, NETWORK, NOTE, PARSING, PRINTING, REDUNDANCY, SERIAL, SPELLING CHECKER, STYLE CHECKER, WORD PROCESSOR. [LANGUAGE, MEDIA, SPEECH, TECHNOLOGY]. M.L.

Horowitz, E. 1983. *Programming Languages: A Grand Tour*. Rockville, Md.: Computer Sciences Press.

Illingworth, Valerie (ed.). 1983. 2nd edition 1986. *Dictionary of Computing*. Oxford: University Press.

Marcotty, M. W., & Ledgard, H. F. 1986. *The World of Programming Languages*. New York: Springer.

Miall, David S. (ed.). 1990. *Humanities and the Computer*. Oxford: Clarendon Press.

Raymond, Eric (ed.). 1991. *The New Hacker's Dictionary*. Cambridge (Mass) & London: MIT Press.

CONCEIT [16c: through French from Latin *conceptus* ('taken together') a thought]. (1) An elaborate, sometimes far-fetched literary image, as in the poetry of John Donne: see SIMILE. (2) A fanciful device or idea: 'The movie's central conceit is that in the golden age of Hollywood, the celebrated cartoon characters were as real as the other actors under contract to the big studios' (*Observer*, review of *Who Framed Roger Rabbit?*, 4 Dec. 1988). Compare DEVICE, IDEA, IMAGE. [LITERATURE, STYLE]. T.MCA.

CONCESSION [16c: through French from Latin *concessio/concessionis* giving way]. A grammatical relationship of contrast in which there is an implication of something unexpected. The relationship may be implicit in the content of two expressions that are juxtaposed: *The inhabitants were gentle, even friendly; underneath we sensed sadness*. The contrast may be made explicit by inserting the coordinating conjunction *but* before *underneath*: *The inhabitants were gentle, even friendly, but underneath we sensed sadness*. The unexpectedness may be made explicit by inserting concessive conjuncts (*yet, however, nevertheless*) or by subordinating the first clause and using a concessive subordinating conjunction to introduce it: *Although the inhabitants were gentle, even friendly, underneath we sensed sadness*. Clauses introduced by concessive subordinators such as *although, even though, though, while* are known as concessive clauses or adverbial clauses of concession. [GRAMMAR]. S.G.

CONCISE OXFORD DICTIONARY, short form *COD*. Perhaps the most famous of the smaller household dictionaries of BrE. It was conceived as a commercially more attractive derivative of *The Oxford English Dictionary*, although S–Z in the *COD* was written before the *OED* had reached that stage. The editors of the 1st edition (1911) were the brothers H. W. and F. G. Fowler, who had written a controversial usage manual called *The King's English* (1906). The influence of the *OED* on the *Concise* is apparent in the early editions and to a lesser extent in later editions, where the element of historical analysis is still marked. The *COD's* 'Fowlerian style' was analytical: idioms were distributed through entries as functions of word senses, etymologies were constructed element by element, and compound and derivative forms tended to be 'nested' under their base words. The editors abbreviated words and compressed information in a style they called *telegraphese*, with the definite and indefinite articles usually omitted. Prescriptivism has been avoided in all editions: the 2nd (1929) edited by H. W. Fowler alone (F. G. having died in 1918), the 3rd (1934) by H. G. Le Mesurier, who had corresponded with Fowler while serving in India, the 4th (1951) and 5th (1964) by E. McIntosh, a schoolmaster who introduced the space-saving swung dash, standing for the headword (retained in the next two editions), the 6th (1976) and 7th (1982) by J. B. Sykes, a physicist and translator, and the 8th (1990) by Robert E. Allen. The 6th was a far-reaching revision that drew on the *Supplement to the OED*. In the 7th, symbols were introduced to mark uses considered controversial or offensive, the closest the dictionary has come to prescriptivism. In the computer-based 8th, the original structure is largely discarded and many space-saving conventions have been abandoned, including the telegraphese. See AUSTRALIAN DICTIONARIES, DICTIONARY, NEW ZEALAND DICTIONARIES, OXFORD DICTIONARIES. [EUROPE, REFERENCE].   R.E.A.

CONCISE SCOTS DICTIONARY. See SCOTTISH DICTIONARIES.

CONCORD [13c: from Old French *concorde*, Latin *concordia* ('hearts together') harmony]. Also *agreement*. In grammar, the relationship between units in such matters as number, person, and gender: '*They* did the work *themselves*' (number and person concord between *they* and *themselves*); '*He* did the work *himself*' (number, person, and gender concord between *he* and *him*). Lack of standard concord occurs in sentences like *The books is on the table* and *I says do it but he don't do it*. Although ungrammatical in the standard language, such usage is consistent with the requirements of concord within some non-standard varieties.

Number and person concord. In standard English, number concord is most apparent between a singular or plural subject and its verb in the third person of the simple present tense: *That book seems interesting* (singular: *book* agreeing with *seems*) and *Those books seem interesting* (plural: *books* agreeing with *seem*). The verb *be* involves concord for the first person singular (*I am*, etc.) and uniquely among English verbs has different forms for singular and plural in the past (*was, were*). Number concord, requiring that two related units should both be singular or both be plural, can involve complements and objects: *That animal is an elk, Those animals are elks, I consider him a spoilsport, I consider them spoilsports*. Both number and person concord are involved in the use of pronouns and possessives, as in '*I* hurt *myself*' and '*My* friends said *they* were coming in *their* car'.

Singular *THEY*. Controversy surrounds the use of *they* as a third-person singular pronoun, in defiance of number concord. It is common after indefinite pronouns: *If someone puts themselves forward in showbiz, they should be prepared for exposure if they err* (*Observer*, 18 Dec. 1988). The practice is popular as a way of avoiding the alleged sexism of the traditional use of masculine pronouns and the awkwardness that often attends *he or she* phrases. It has a long history: 'Here nobody hangs or drowns themselves' (Horace Walpole, 18c). It can occur where a masculine or feminine word could be used: 'He

manages to think at least fifty years ahead, which for someone in their nineties is quite remarkable' (Prince Charles on the Earl of Stockton, *Daily Telegraph*, 22 Nov. 1985). Some grammarians claim that the usage is informal; others use it freely in their own formal writing: 'I have had a heart for years, but I would not know whether anyone else had a hole in theirs' (David Crystal, *Linguistics*, 1971).

Gender concord. This is an important part of the grammar of languages such as French or German, in which all nouns belong to a gender category, and articles and adjectives have to agree with them, as in the French *une petite plume* (a little pen), in which feminine agreement runs through the phrase, and *un petit livre* (a little book), in which the concord is masculine. In English, gender concord does not exist apart from personal and possessive pronouns, as in *Mary hurt herself badly in the accident but my father only broke his glasses*.

Notional concord. This stands in contrast to grammatical concord and means agreement by meaning rather than grammar, where the two are in conflict. In BrE, notional concord occurs when plural verbs are widely used with collective nouns: *The Opposition seem divided among themselves*; *The committee have decided to increase the annual subscription*. Some of the controversial uses of *they* can be accounted for in this way: *Everybody has left now, haven't they?* In both BrE and AmE, singular verbs are usual with apparently plural forms that are notionally felt to be singular, as in: *Fish and chips is no longer cheap*; '*The Grapes of Wrath*' *is a classic novel*; *$50 was a lot to pay*. Usage is divided in some areas. With various negative structures, some people favour grammatical, singular concord and others prefer notional, plural concord: *Neither John nor Mary knows about it* in contrast with *Neither John nor Mary know about it*, and *None of the bodies so far recovered was wearing a life-jacket* in contrast with *None of the bodies so far recovered were wearing life-jackets*.

Proximity concord. Clauses as subjects are usually treated as singular: *To err is human*; *That you don't agree upsets me*. With long noun phrases, the head word is relevant for number concord, as in *One of your friends is here*, not **One of your friends are here*, and *He is one of those people who always interfere*, not **He is one of those people who always interferes*, but in the heat of creation the concord in such constructions is often overlooked. In such cases, *proximity concord* operates, the verb agreeing with the nearest noun. It can also operate in awkward constructions like **Neither my sister nor I am going* and occurs in the traditional use of a singular verb after *More than one*, where both grammar and meaning require a plural verb: *More than one person has remarked on this strange fact.* See PLURAL. [GRAMMAR].　　S.C.

CONCORDANCE [14c: through French from Latin *concordantia* harmony: see CONCORD]. An alphabetical index of the principal words in a book, such as the Bible or the complete works of Shakespeare, with a reference to the passage or passages in which each indexed word appears. Using computer technology, a *concordancing program* can be applied to a text or corpus of texts so that a concordance of its words is produced. In the resulting display or printout, the words of the text are listed alphabetically in the centre of the screen or page, each token of occurrence of a word preceded and followed (usually with extra spacing) by its immediate co-text. See CORPUS, INDEX. [REFERENCE, TECHNOLOGY].
　　　　　　　　　　　　　　　　　T.MCA.

CONCRETE NOUN. See ABSTRACT AND CONCRETE, NOUN.

CONCRETE POETRY [1950s: a calque of both German *konkrete Dichtung* and Portuguese *poesia concreta*]. Poetry in which words and letters form significant visual shapes or patterns, either assembling words into an order that reflects the sense of the poem, or using them as much for appearance as meaning: for example, Ian Hamilton Finlay's pear-shaped poem made up of the repeated phrase *au pair girl*. The form arose independently in Brazil, Switzerland, and Sweden, but was foreshadowed by experiments with 'shaped poems' by the classical writer Simmias of Rhodes, such poets as George Herbert (16–17c), who wrote poems in the shape of wings or an altar, and the *calligrammes* of Guillaume Apollinaire during the First World War. Such 20c writers as Edwin Morgan, Ian Hamilton Finlay, and Dom Sylvester Houédard are considered to have brought dignity and wit to the genre. See POETRY, THOMAS, WORD GAME. [LITERATURE].
　　　　　　　　　　　　　　　　　T.A.

CONDENSED BOOK. A book whose text is a systematic and thorough abridgement of another, intended for readers who do not have the time or inclination to read the original in full: for example, the series known as the *Reader's Digest Condensed Books.* See ABRIDG(E)-MENT. [MEDIA].
　　　　　　　　　　　　　　　　　T.MCA.

CONDITION [14c: through French from Latin *condicio/condicionis* an agreement]. A grammatical relationship in which one situation is said to be dependent on another: in *He'll go if she goes*, his action is dependent on hers.

Expressing condition. There are various ways of expressing this relationship: (1) By a *conditional clause* introduced by the conditional subordinating conjunctions *if* and *unless*: 'Don't move *if it hurts*', where the prohibition depends on the fulfilment of the condition that it hurts. Other conditional subordinators include *as long as, assuming* (*that*), *provided* (*that*), *providing* (*that*), *supposing* (*that*), and (formal) *given that.* (2) Through two clauses linked by *and* or *or*, where the first clause is generally a directive and the second clause describes the consequence of obeying or disobeying the directive: 'Have a glass of water *and you'll feel better*' (If you have a glass of water, you'll feel better); 'Don't say anything or you'll be sorry' (Don't say anything. If you do, you'll be sorry). (3) Through conditional conjuncts such as *then* and *in that case*: 'Don't move, (*and*) *then you won't get hurt.*' These conjuncts can also be used as correlatives after subordinators: '*If I see her tomorrow, then* I'll give her your regards.' (4) Through generic nouns modified by relative clauses: 'Employers *who do not consult their staff* cannot expect cooperation from them' (If employers do not consult their staff, they cannot expect cooperation from them).

Kinds of condition. Conditions may be open or hypothetical. *Open conditions* are neutral: they leave open the question of the fulfilment of the condition. *Hypothetical conditions* imply that the fulfilment is doubtful or has not taken place. They have a past or past perfect in the conditional clause and a modal (usually *would*) in the past or past perfect in the main clause: '*If he had recognized us*, he would have spoken to us' (but he didn't recognize us); '*If he apologized tomorrow*, I would forget the whole thing' (but the expectation is that he won't apologize). The past subjunctive *were* is used (as well as the simple past *was*) in the singular first and third persons of the verb *be* in hypothetical conditional clauses: '*If I were a rich man*, . . . (but I am not)'; '*If your sister were here*, . . . (but she is not)'; '*If it were to rain*, . . . (but it is unlikely that it will rain).' In formal style, the relationship may be expressed by bringing the auxiliary or the subjunctive *were* to the front of the conditional clause and omitting the subordinator: '*Had it rained*, we would have gone to the museum'; '*Were I your representative*, I would protest vigorously'; '*Should you be interested*, I could let you have a ticket.' [GRAMMAR].　　S.G.

CONFUSAGE [1980s: on the analogy of *abusage*]. An informal, non-technical term for usage that confuses, such as doublespeak and gobbledygook, or results from confusion, such

as *militate* used where *mitigate* was intended. See
ABUSAGE, CONFUSIBLE, JARGON. [STYLE, USAGE].

T.MCA.

CONFUSIBLE, also **confusable** [1970s]. A
semi-technical term for one of two or more
words that are commonly or easily confused with
one another: *luxuriant* with *luxurious*; *they're*
with *there* and *their*. The British lexicographer
Adrian Room (1985, below) separates *confusibles* or 'lookalikes' such as *dominating* and
domineering from *distinguishables* or 'mean-
alikes' such as *faun* and *satyr*. At least seven
factors contribute to confusion: (1)
Homophony, in which words have the same
sound but different spellings and meanings: *slay*,
sleigh. (2) Homography, in which words have
the same spelling, but different sounds and
meanings: *wind* moving air, *wind* to turn or twist.
(3) Shared elements: *mitigate* and *militate* share
the same number of syllables, the same stress
pattern, and the same opening and closing syllables. (4) Transposable or exchangeable elements: *cavalry* and *Calvary*, *form* and *from*,
accept and *except*. Factors 3 and 4 become more
potent still when words have similar meanings
and uses: *affect* and *effect*. (5) Words mistaken
for phrases or vice versa: *already* and *all ready*.
(6) Semantic proximity: *baroque* and *rococo*,
nadir and *zenith*. Here, confusion may be encouraged by different but related applications of the
same terms by different people: *acronym* and *initialism*, *subconscious* and *unconscious*. Some
words are very different in meaning but sometimes displace one another because of close association: *acid* and *alkali*, *defendant* and *plaintiff*.
(7) Uncertainty arising from different uses in
different varieties of English: *biscuit* and *cookie*
in BrE and AmE. See CATACHRESIS, DOUBLET,
HOMONYM, MALAPROPISM, MISTAKE, SLIP OF THE
TONGUE, SPOONERISM. [STYLE, USAGE, WORD].

T.MCA.

Room, Adrian. 1985. *Dictionary of Confusing Words
and Meanings*. London: Routledge. A revision and
'enlarged blend' of two earlier works: *Room's Dictionary of Confusibles* (1978); *Room's Dictionary of
Distinguishables* (1981).
—— 1988. *Dictionary of Contrasting Pairs*. London:
Routledge.
Urdang, Laurence. 1988. *Dictionary of Differences*.
London: Bloomsbury.

CONJUGATION [15c: from Latin *coniugatio/
coniugationis* yoking together, from *iugum* a
yoke]. A paradigm, class, or table of verb forms
in such inflected languages as Latin and French,
where elements are distinguished from each
other by patterns of inflection relating to tense,
person, number. French has four regular conjugations, exemplified by *parler* to speak, *finir* to
finish, *recevoir* to receive, *vendre* to sell. These
verb classes conjugate differently, so that for
example the perfect tense (for the first person
singular) is respectively *j'ai parlé, j'ai fini, j'ai
reçu, j'ai vendu*. The term is relevant to the grammar of Old English, in which there were seven
conjugations of strong verbs, but not to Modern
English, although irregular verbs can be divided
into a number of pattern groups. See DECLEN-
SION, LATIN[1], PARADIGM. [GRAMMAR].   S.G.

CONJUNCT [15c: from Latin *coniunctus* joined
together]. (1) A sentence adverbial that has a
connective role: *therefore* in 'Our phone was out
of order; we *therefore* had a period of uninterrupted peace.' See ADVERBIAL. (2) A grammatical unit linked to other units through
coordination, that is, by means of *and*, *or*, or
but: the phrase 'the children and their parents'
contains two conjuncts: *the children* and *their
parents*. See COORDINATION. [GRAMMAR].   S.G.

CONJUNCTION [14c: from Latin *coniunctio/
coniunctionis*, translating Greek *súndesmos* joining together]. A part of speech or word class
used to connect words or constructions. The two
classes of conjunctions are *coordinating conjunction* or *coordinator* and *subordinating
conjunction* or *subordinator*: (1) Coordinating
conjunctions (chiefly *and*, *but*, *or*) connect units
of equal status and function: the two equal
clauses *They called me Ishmael, I didn't mind* in
They called me Ishmael, but I didn't mind; the
three equal adjectives *long, narrow, crooked* in
The street was long, narrow, and crooked. (2)
Subordinating conjunctions such as *because*, *if*,
although connect a subordinate clause to its
superordinate clause: *We did it because he told
us to*; *Take it if you wish*; *Although it was late,
they kept on working*.
  Two or more subordinate clauses can be connected with a coordinator: *Take it if you wish and
if no one else wants it*. The repeated subordinator
may be omitted, if there is no danger of misinterpretation: *I know that she wants it and he
doesn't*. The process of linking units by means of
coordinators is known as *conjunction, conjoining*,
and traditionally and most commonly *coordination*. The linked units that result are said to
be coordinated or coordinate: for example, a
coordinate clause. More recently, the units have
been called *conjoins* or in generative grammar
conjuncts. The process of linking units by means
of subordinators is usually termed *subordination*
or *embedding*. Both coordinators and subordinators may be reinforced by being combined
with correlatives, a term used both for the
reinforcing item and for that item and the
conjunction it accompanies. The principal correlative coordinators are *both . . . and* (*Both
Michael and Vivien were at my birthday party*),

either . . . or (*You can discuss it either with me or with the manager*), neither . . . nor (*Neither Jack nor Ava had the time to help me*). Correlative subordinators include as . . . as (*Derek is as fond of the grandchildren as Natalie is*), whether . . . or (*I'm not sure whether Ian or Carmel told me*), the . . . the (*The older I get, the less I worry*), and if . . . then (*If you tell Estelle, then she will tell Philip*). Although subordinators may consist of one word, as above, there are many complex subordinators of two or more words, such as *in order that, such that, as far as* (as in *as far as I know*), and *as if*. [GRAMMAR]. S.G.

CONNECTIVE [17c: from Latin *connectere/ connexum* to bind]. (1) A term that includes conjunctions (*and, but, if, because*) and conjuncts (*yet, nevertheless, on the other hand*) as units that connect linguistic units. (2) Also *linking verb*. A copular verb such as *be, seem*, and *become*. See ADVERBIAL, COPULA. [GRAMMAR]. S.G.

CONNOTATION AND DENOTATION [16c: from Latin *con-* together, and *de-* apart, and *notatio/notationis* marking]. Contrasting terms in linguistics. *Connotation*, also known as *affective meaning*, refers to the emotive and associational aspect of a term. *Denotation*, also known as *cognitive meaning*, refers to the direct relationship between a term and the object, idea, or action it designates. Connotation may be personal (stemming from experience, such as connotations of *swimming*, which one person may associate with recreation or training for competitions, another with fear of drowning) or common to a group (such as emotions raised by the name of a political leader). Denotation refers to the meaning of a word or expression in relation to everyday life and to other words and expressions: for example, colours can be described in terms either of wavelengths of reflected light or of such relationships as, in English, *red* with blood, *white* with snow, *green* with grass, *blue* with sea and sky. By virtue of their connotations, the same colours have further associations: *red* with anger or irritation, *white* with purity and innocence, *green* with inexperience or envy, *blue* with sadness and depression. See SEMANTICS, SENSE. [LANGUAGE, REFERENCE]. L.U.

CONRAD, Joseph [1857-1924]. British novelist, born in the Ukraine of Polish parents named Korzeniowski: perhaps the most famous example of English being acquired and used as a foreign language. In 1874, he joined the crew of a French ship. He learned English aboard British ships and became a British subject in 1886. After settling in England, he published *Almayer's Folly* (1895). Conrad's stories were often based on his experiences at sea, as in *Typhoon* (1901) and *The Nigger of the Narcissus* (1898). All his novels and stories have a strong narrative line and concern men under the strain of responsibility, as in *Lord Jim* (1900). His novella *Heart of Darkness* (1902) evokes unidentifiable terror and disquiet and expresses the tensions felt by the colonial European in Africa. Conrad employed retroaction and broken time sequence and often told his story through a detached but sympathetic narrator who offers comment without intrusion, as in: 'She was savage and superb, wild-eyed and magnificent; there was something ominous and stately in her deliberate progress. And in the hush that had fallen suddenly upon the whole sorrowful land, the immense wilderness, the colossal body of the fecund and mysterious life seemed to look at her, pensive, as though it had been looking at the image of its own tenebrous and passionate soul' (*Heart of Darkness*). See index. [BIOGRAPHY, EUROPE, LANGUAGE, LITERATURE, STYLE]. R.C.

CONSEQUENCES. A parlour game that has had a variety of forms since the 17c. Generally, one participant provides an adjective, another a man's name, another an adjective, and so on with a woman's name, a place where the two meet, what he says to her, what she says to him, the consequence, and what the world says. The participants do not know what the others have written. The amusement arises from the random juxtaposition of unlikely people, circumstances, and comments. It is a cooperative, not a competitive game, and in the 19c was a pastime through which the young could flirt without consequences. See WORD GAME. [WORD]. T.MCA.

CONSERVATIVE (ACCENT). See ADVANCED (ACCENT).

CONSONANT [From Old French *consonant* (Modern *consonne*), from Latin *consonans/ consonantis* sounding together (with a vowel)]. A speech sound distinct from a vowel (such as /b/ and /d/ in /bad/), and a letter of the alphabet that represents such a sound (such as *b* and *d* in *bad*). In general usage, a distinction between spoken consonants and written or printed consonants is not always made, but specialists seek to keep the two distinct. For some sounds and letters in English, the correspondence is straightforward and unequivocal, such as *d* and the alveolar plosive sound it represents. For others, correspondences are equivocal and can lead to uncertainty: for example, although the *c* in such words as *card, cord*, and *curd* has the 'hard' value /k/, and the *c* in such words as *cent* and *city* has the 'soft' value /s/, the *c* of *Celt* is /s/ for some, /k/ for others. In ScoE, it is always /s/ in the name of the football team *Glasgow Celtic*, but generally /k/ in such expressions as *the Celtic languages.*

Spoken consonants. In phonetics, consonants are discussed in terms of three anatomical and physiological factors: the *state of the glottis* (whether or not there is voice or vibration in the larynx), the *place of articulation* (that part of the vocal apparatus with which the sound is most closely associated), and the *manner of articulation* (how the sound is produced). Following this order, the sound /k/ can be described as a 'voiceless velar plosive', where *voiceless* refers to the state of the glottis, *velar* to the velum as the place of articulation, and *plosive* to the manner of articulation (the release of a blocked stream of air). The consonant system of English is conventionally presented on a grid with manner of articulation shown horizontally and place of articulation vertically. Voiced and voiceless pairs are in the same cells of the grid, with the voiceless member of each pair to the left (see table).

	Labial	Dental	Alveolar	Palatal	Velar
Plosive	p, b		t, d		k, g
Affricate				tʃ, dʒ	
Fricative	f, v	θ, ð	s, z	ʃ, ʒ	
Nasal	m		n		ŋ
Lateral			l		
R-sound			r		
Glides	w			j	(w)

Because of double articulation (pronunciation involving two places), /w/ occurs twice. The aspirate /h/ is distinct from the other sounds because it is a fricative formed in the glottis. The grid shows that only *obstruents* (stop and fricative consonants) enter into the voiced/voiceless distinction. Other sounds can be assumed to be voiced, so that /n/ for example can be described simply as an alveolar nasal.

Written and printed consonants. In the Roman alphabet as adapted for English, 21 letters are commonly described as consonants: that is, all save *a, e, i, o, u*. Positionally, they precede and/or follow the vowel in most syllables: *to, ox, cup, fen, him, jab, keep, queer, wig, veil, yes*. Most may be doubled (*ebb, add, cuff; dabbed, runner, selling*), but doubling of *k, v* is rare (*trekked, revved*), of *h, j, q, x* is abnormal (*Ahh, she sighed*), and none is doubled initially in native English words (but note *Lloyd* from Welsh, *llama* from Spanish). Many doubled consonants arise at the boundaries of affixes and roots, as with *abbreviation, accommodation, addition, affirmation, aggregation*, or before inflections, as

in *fitted/fitting, redder/reddest*. Consonants regularly occur in strings or clusters without intervening vowels: initially, as in *stain* and *strip*, finally, as in *fetch* and *twelfth*, medially, as in *dodging*. Many clusters are digraphs, such as the *ch* in *chin*, *sh* as in *she*, *th* as in both *this* and *thin*, and *ng* as in *sing*. In addition, English uses numerous other consonant digraphs that do not represent a sound in any straightforward way; some, like *ph* in *photograph*, are borrowed from other languages, while others, like *gh* in *though, trough* are native to English but have lost their original sound value.

The distinction between vowel and consonant sounds and symbols is by no means always straightforward, as can be seen from looking at aspects of the letters *j, v, w, y*. Until at least the 18c, *j* and *v* (now established as consonants) were widely regarded as variants of the vowels *i* and *u*. In the 17c, the English alphabet was considered to have 24 letters, not 26: *j* and *v* were sometimes referred to as *tayl'd i* and *pointed u*. The consonants *w* and *y* have some of the characteristics of vowels: for example, compare *suite/sweet, laniard/lanyard*. Phonetic analysis may class such letters as either *semi-consonants* or *semi-vowels*. Many uses of *y* parallel those of *i*: *gypsy/gipsy, happy/Hopi*. The consonants *l, m, n, r* also often have some of the qualities of vowels when used syllabically: *l* in *apple, m* in *spasm, n* in *isn't, r* in *centre*. In such positions, they are often pronounced with a schwa preceding their consonant value. Most consonant letters are sometimes 'silent': that is, used with no sound value (some having lost it, others inserted but never pronounced); *b* in *numb, c* in *scythe*; comparably with *handsome, foreign, honest, knee, talk, mnemonic, damn, psychology, island, hutch, wrong, prix, key, laissez-faire*. In general, consonant letters in English have an uncertain relationship with speech sounds.

See AFFRICATE, AITCH, ALPHABET, APPROXIMANT, ASPIRATE, CONSONANT CLUSTER, DIGRAPH, FRICATIVE, GLIDE, LETTER¹, LIQUID, L-SOUNDS, NASAL, OBSTRUENT, PLOSIVE, R-SOUNDS, SIBILANT, SILENT LETTER, SPEECH SOUND, SPELLING, STOP, SYLLABLE, VOICE, VOWEL, and letter entries for consonants. [SPEECH, WRITING].   G.K., C.U.

CONSONANT CLUSTER. A group of spoken or written consonants that come together at the beginning or end of a syllable, such as *br* in *bring*, *str* in *street*, *lfths* in *twelfths*. See CONSONANT, EPENTHESIS. [SPEECH, WRITING].   G.K.

CONSTITUENT [1930s in this sense]. In linguistics, a group of words that constitute a unit of syntactic structure. In the sentence *The owl has caught a mouse*, the elements *the owl, has caught, a mouse* are each constituents in a way that *owl has, caught a* are not. Constituents are layered one inside another, so that *has caught* and *a mouse* together form a larger constituent *has caught a mouse*. The breakdown of a sentence into its various layers is known as *constituent analysis*, and the result is usually displayed as a tree diagram (see diagram). Constituents are identified primarily by checking to see whether groups of words can be replaced by a single word: *has caught* can be recognized as a constituent largely because it can be replaced by *caught*, without altering the essential structure of the sentence. In cases where simple substitution fails to provide a clear-cut analysis, possible constituents are moved around, to see if they behave as a unit. In a sentence such as *The owl flew up the tree, flew up* might at first sight be a constituent, since it could be replaced by a word such as *climbed*. However, alteration of the order indicates that *up the tree* forms a constituent, since these words need to remain together in order to retain a well-formed sentence: *Up the tree flew the owl* is possible, but **The owl flew the tree up* is not. Constituent analysis differs from traditional grammatical analysis in that it attempts to identify patterns genuinely found in a language rather than imposing preconceived ideas about what grammarians think should be there. See STRUCTURAL LINGUISTICS. [GRAMMAR, LANGUAGE]. J.M.A.

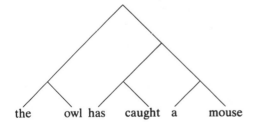

the   owl has   caught   a   mouse

CONTACT LANGUAGE. In sociolinguistics, a simplified variety of language that develops in situations where most speakers have no common language, such as ports, trading posts, plantations, and colonial garrison towns. It generally retains features of the varieties that contribute to it, usually local vernaculars and one or more languages brought by traders, settlers, soldiers, and missionaries. It may also draw on universal strategies for communicating without a shared language. See CONTACT VARIETY, FOREIGNER TALK, LANGUAGE LEARNING, LINGUA FRANCA, PIDGIN. [LANGUAGE]. S.R.

CONTACT LITERATURE. See CONTACT VARIETY.

CONTACT VARIETY. In sociolinguistics, a variety of a language, as for example English, that results from contact with other languages, usually in multilingual and multicultural contexts such as Africa and India. With the passage of time, the pronunciation, grammar, vocabulary, and discourse of such a variety become stable, but in forms that are not necessarily amenable to the standards and assumptions about usage in traditional English-speaking countries. The result of long-term contact is the *Africanization, Indianization*, etc., of English. When, for example, South Asian speakers of English ask *What is your good name?*, they are transferring an expression from another language into English. In many Asian, African, and European varieties of English, such 'interference' is evident in the use of syllable-timed rhythm as opposed to the stress-timed rhythm of English. In consequence, some researchers have called such forms of English *interference varieties*. Some are more institutionalized than others, and have developed *contact literatures* such as those of South Asia, West Africa, and the Philippines. These have slowly gained national and sometimes international recognition, as in the writings of Raja Rao in India and Chinua Achebe in Nigeria, and are now part of local literary tradition. The linguistic distinctiveness of such texts arises from a convergence of two or more distinct linguistic and literary canons. As they develop, English extends its sociocultural, historical, and literary contexts, a process that also entails an extension of the traditional literary, linguistic, and cultural canons of the language. Research into the literature of such varieties can provide insights into bilingual and multilingual creativity. See CONTACT LANGUAGE, INTERFERENCE, INTERFERENCE VARIETY. [LANGUAGE, LITERATURE, VARIETY]. B.B.K.

CONTEXT [14c: from Latin *contextus* woven together, from *texere/textum* to weave: compare TEXT]. (1) Also *co-text*. The speech, writing, or print that normally precedes and follows a word or other element of language. The meaning of words may be affected by their context. If a phrase is quoted *out of context*, its effect may be different from what was originally intended. (2) The linguistic, situational, social, and cultural environment of an element of language, an action, behaviour, etc. Technically, the occurrence of a word in a linguistic context is said to be determined by *collocational* or *selectional restrictions*: the use of *rancid* with *butter* and *bacon*, of *flock* with *sheep* and *birds*, of *pack* with *dogs, wolves*, and *cards*. Generally, such association is largely or wholly determined by meaning (*drink milk/beer, eat bread/meat*), but meaning can be affected by collocation: *white* as in *white wine, white coffee,* and *white people.*

Non-linguistic context is often referred to as *situation,* and meaning expressed in terms of context is *reference* (in contrast with *sense,* which exists in and among language elements regardless of context). To illustrate the meaning of *ram* by pointing to a picture or an animal is to use context, but to define it as *male sheep* in contrast with *ewe* is to do so by means of sense. While some scholars have argued that meaning *is* the use of language in context, others have excluded context from semantics mainly because it has proved intractable. Contextual analyses of meaning include the behaviourist approach of the US linguist Leonard Bloomfield, and *context of situation* or *situational context* as outlined by the UK linguist J. R. Firth, for whom context was a level of analysis with phonology, grammar, etc. He suggested that meaning at this level can be stated in terms of the relevant features of the participants, the relevant objects, and the effects of the verbal action. Although this is appropriate for such highly restricted language as the drill sergeant's command *Stand at ease!,* it is of little value for much of ordinary language, where the meaning of an utterance seldom has any direct relation to the contexts in which it occurs: for example, almost any subject might be discussed in a school classroom.

There are nonetheless many ways in which context does determine the choice of language. They include: (1) *Deixis.* Personal pronouns like *I* and *you* identify a speaker or writer and participants or non-participants in a discourse. Such locative markers as *this* and *that, here* and *there* identify the position of the speaker or writer in relation to other entities referred to. Such markers of time as *now, then, yesterday, tomorrow* identify time of speaking or writing and its relations to other events. (2) *Social relations.* Many usages depend on context, such as the French distinction of *tu* and *vous,* the honorifics of Japanese, and in English the language of politeness (*May I get you a drink? Would you like a drink?*), or the choice between *Shut up, Be quiet,* and *Would you please keep your voice down?* (3) *Features of style and register.* In such settings as a law court, the media, etc., usage depends on such contextual factors as age, sex, background, social class, and occupation. See DEIXIS, SEMANTICS, SENSE. [LANGUAGE, REFERENCE, STYLE]. F.R.P.

CONTINENT [14c: from Latin *continens/ continentis* holding together, containing]. (1) a major land mass, usually taken to be any of seven: *Africa, Antarctica, Asia, Australia, Europe, North America, South America.* However, the number may be reduced to five if, as continuous land masses, Europe and Asia are

treated as one (*Eurasia*) and North and South America as one (*the Americas*). Continents may or may not be regarded as including islands situated near them: for example, Tasmania, though part of Australia, is not part of the Australian land mass; Madagascar, Mauritius, and Seychelles may or may not be treated as African; Jamaica in the Caribbean is not usually considered part of North or South America, but is certainly in the Americas. The limits of a continent may be uncertain: for example, it is not clear whether North America reaches as far south as Panama or whether South America reaches as far north. The non-continental term *Central America* does, however, include Panama. (2) The term *the Continent* has long been used for the mainland of Europe as distinct from the British Isles, as in the apocryphal newspaper headline *Fog in Channel, Continent Isolated.* When, in November 1990, the first contacts were made between the two sections of the Channel Tunnel, French radio announced that 'Britain will no longer be an island' and the *Financial Times* in London ran the headline *Continent of Europe no longer isolated.* The term *Continental* generally refers to the mainland only (*Continental Europe*) and is a BrE name for someone from mainland Europe. (3) The term *the continental United States* is often used to distinguish the mainland states from the state of Hawaii, the Commonwealth of Puerto Rico, and other US territories. See AFRICA, AMERICA, ASIA, AUSTRALIA, EUROPE. [GEOGRAPHY, NAME]. T.MCA.

CONTINUANT. See APPROXIMANT.

CONTINUOUS [17c]. Also **progressive** [17c]. A verb form that basically denotes duration. In English, the contrast is between continuous (*She is repairing computers*) and non-continuous (*She repairs computers*). See VERB. [GRAMMAR]. S.G.

CONTRACTED FORM. See ENCLITIC, NEGATION, VERB.

CONTRACTION [14c: from Latin *contractio/ contractionis* a drawing together]. A reduction in form, often marked in English in writing and print by an apostrophe ('). There are five major types: (1) Auxiliary contractions such as *I've* I have, *he'll* he will, *somebody's* somebody is or has, *who'd* who had or would. (2) Negative contraction such as *isn't* is not, *don't* do not, *won't* will not. (3) Pronoun contraction of *us* in the first-person plural imperative *let's,* as in *Let's sit down awhile.* (4) Elisions, such as *C'mon* Come on, *bo'sun* boatswain. (5) Short forms used in note-taking, such as *runng* running, *dept* department. When elements are removed from inside a word or phrase, but nothing is taken from the end, a full point is often omitted. There is inconsistency in the use of some usually occupational titles, which may or may not have a point, depending on individual preference or house style, such as *Dr* or *Dr.* for *Doctor.* Although writers usually follow a convention or are required to do so by their publishers, the playwright George Bernard Shaw defied the use of the apostrophe for contractions, establishing a unique norm for his texts with such forms as *didnt, wouldnt.* Tradition favours the use of apostrophes in writing dialect, so as to mark deviation from the standard language, as in *li'l ole me* (little old me) in colloquial AmE and *Ah'm no' comin'* (I am not coming) in Scots. However, many late 20c dialect writers reject this convention, arguing that it downgrades the medium they have chosen to use and that for their purposes forms that may once have been contracted are not contractions at all. Writers of Scots, for example, might use an apostrophe when two words come together, but not for individual words, as in *Ah'm no comin.* See ABBREVIATION, ELISION, NEGATION, NOTE. [GRAMMAR, SPEECH, WORD, WRITING].   S.G., T.MCA.

CONTRASTIVE LINGUISTICS, also **contrastive analysis** [Mid-20c]. A branch of linguistics that describes similarities and differences among two or more languages at such levels as phonology, grammar, and semantics, especially in order to improve language teaching and translation. The study began in Central Europe before the Second World War and developed afterwards in North America.In the US in the late 1950s, Robert Lado proposed contrastive analysis as a means of identifying areas of difficulty for language learners that could then be managed with suitable exercises. Critics have pointed out that such areas of difficulty are already widely known and discussed by experienced professionals, and that, while headway has been made in analysing English, few other languages have been sufficiently studied to allow balanced comparison. Teachers, however, generally agree that mother tongue and target language merit comparison, many courses incorporate the results of contrastive study, and linguists involved in the area consider that the study is still in its infancy and continued research is likely to bear fruit.

In contrastive phonology, for example, descriptions of the systems of two or more languages may highlight gaps or non-correspondences among speech sounds: thus, a Japanese learner's pronunciation of *table* as /teburu/ can be accounted for as an approximation to /l/ in the form of the familiar flap /r/ and the replacement of the consonant cluster /bl/ by the familiar syllables /bu/ and /ru/.

In contrastive grammar, accounts of how words group into sentences may prove useful: for example, German students learning the interrogative patterns of English discover that auxiliaries are used rather than inverted word order (*Do you like . . .?* as opposed to *Magst du . . .?* 'Like you . . .?'). At the level of vocabulary, the difficulties of achieving word-for-word equivalence can be discussed for the benefit of compilers and users of bilingual dictionaries: for example, users of the *Collins–Robert French Dictionary* (1978), going from English to French, look up *flower* and get *fleur*, but going from French to English, look up *fleur* and get *flower*, *blossom*, and *bloom*; English *bloom* then leads to French *fleur, floraison* and *épanouissement*, while French *floraison* leads to English *blossoming* and *flowering.*

In discourse, much remains to be done to come to grips with such contrasts as genre conventions and register ranges, from differences in business cards and death notices to television newscasts and books of poems. A further area is the contrastive analysis of cultural beliefs, customs, and institutions, which could aid international interpretation and understanding. Systematic studies of cultural contrasts are rare and tend to cover limited domains, such as kinship terms and verbs of cooking. Whatever methods are pursued (self-observation, fieldwork, text comparison), the ultimate yardstick is the competence of the bilingual analyst, who must decide what features to contrast against what norms. Publications include Carl James's *Contrastive Analysis* (Longman, 1980) and Michael Swan & Bernard Smith (eds.), *Learner English: A Teacher's Guide to Interference and Other Problems* (Cambridge University Press, 1987). See ERROR ANALYSIS, FAUX AMI, LINGUISTICS, TEIL, TRANSLATION. [EDUCATION, LANGUAGE].   R.H.

CONTRASTIVE STRESS. See STRESS.

CONUNDRUM. See RIDDLE.

CONVENT ENGLISH. In former British colonies, an informal term for the kind of English acquired in schools and colleges founded by Christian missionaries. Despite the usual meaning of *convent*, the term extends beyond girls' schools run by Roman Catholic nuns to include all Christian educational institutions, most of which operate within a network of missionaries, local and foreign, who are involved in religion, education, and health care. In India, Sri Lanka, parts of Africa, and elsewhere, such schools date from the 17–18c; originally intended to provide a Christian education, they have become in recent decades increasingly secular. The model of Convent English is not specifically BrE or AmE, nor has the usage of school staff ever been homogeneous. In the past, European teachers were recruited not only from England, Ireland, Scotland, and Wales, but also from Belgium and other countries. In the Indian subcontinent, Convent English is associated with Anglo-Indian English (especially because of the existence of Anglo-Indian Christian schools), but is distinct from it. A 'convent-educated' person has a Westernized outlook, is generally comfortable with and fluent in English, and is likely to have an accent whose rhythm has been compared to the 'lilt' of Welsh speakers of English (with which, however, there is no apparent link). Extensive code-mixing with local languages occurs. In middle-class circles, Convent English is equated with modernity: in Indian matrimonial advertisements the woman sought is often described as a 'convent-educated bride'. See ENGLISH-MEDIUM SCHOOL. [AFRICA, ASIA, EDUCATION, VARIETY].

B.B.K.

CONVENTION [14c: through French from Latin *conventio/conventionis* a coming together, agreement]. A practice established by usage or agreement: writing from left to right in the Roman alphabet or from right to left in Arabic script; using an apostrophe in English to mark possession (*Mary's book*) and the omission of a letter (*isn't* for *is not*; spelling the 'same' word differently according to a national preference (AmE *color*, BrE *colour*) or a house style (*realise* rather than *realize*, or vice versa). Compare FORMULA, NORM, RULE. [STYLE]. T.MCA.

CONVERSATION [14c: from Latin *conversatio/conversationis* social intercourse, conversation, from *conversari* to associate with]. The most basic and widespread linguistic means of conducting human affairs. Because of the pervasive, everyday nature of conversing, its scientific study has proved particularly complex. It has been difficult to obtain acoustically clear, natural samples of spontaneous conversation, especially of its more informal varieties. When samples have been obtained, the variety of topics, participants, and social situations which characterize conversation have made it difficult to determine which aspects of the behaviour are systematic and rule-governed.

Conversational analysis. In recent years, research in *conversation analysis* (an aspect of discourse analysis) has shown that conversation is a highly structured activity in which people tacitly follow a set of basic conventions. Occasionally, however, the rules are made explicit, as when someone says 'Can I get a word in?' or 'Don't interrupt'. To have a successful conversation in the English-speaking world, several criteria need to be satisfied: for example, everyone must have one or more turns (opportunities to speak), with no one monopolizing or constantly interrupting. People need to have a sense of when to speak and when to stay silent, and also need to make their roles clear: speaking as a parent, friend, employee, etc. There is a great deal of ritual in conversation, as when people wish to join in (*Excuse me, but . . .*, *Could I just say that . . .*) or leave (*Well, that about rounds things up . . .*, *Hey, is that the time?*), change the topic (*that reminds me . . .*, *Speaking of Mary . . .*), or check on listeners' attention or attitude (*Are you with me?*, *Don't get me wrong . . .*). The subject-matter is an important variable, with some topics being 'safe' in certain social groups (in Britain, the weather, pets, children, and the locality), others more or less 'unsafe' (religious and political beliefs, questions of personal income such as *How much do you earn?*). There are usually some arbitrary divisions: for example, in Britain, it is polite to comment on the taste and presentation of a meal, but usually impolite to enquire after how much it cost.

Turn-taking. In conversation analysis, particular attention has been paid to the markers of conversational turns: how people know when it is their turn to speak. In formal dialogue, there are often explicit markers, showing that a speaker is about to yield the floor; in debate, the person in the chair more or less closely controls speakers' turns. In conversation, however, the cues are more subtle, involving variations in the melody, rhythm, and speed of speech, and in patterns of eye movement. When people talk in a group, they look at and away from their listeners in about equal proportions, but when approaching the end of what they have to say, they look at the listeners more steadily, and in particular maintain closer eye contact with those they expect to continue the conversation. A listener who wishes to be the next speaker may indicate a desire to do so by showing an increase in bodily tension, such as by leaning forward or audibly drawing in breath. In addition, there are many explicit indications, verbal and non-verbal, that a speaker is coming to an end (*Last but not least . . .*) or wishes to pass the conversational ball (*What do YOU think?*, looking with an expectant expression at another person).

Features of conversation. There are also several linguistic features that distinguish conversational style from other varieties of English. Speed of speech is relatively rapid: often over 400 syllables a minute, compared with a radio newsreading rate of around 200. There are many assimilations and elisions of consonants and vowels, such as the dropping of *t* in such words as *cyclists*, the reduction of *and* to *n*, or the compression of such auxiliary sequences as *gonna* and *wouldn'a'been*. It can be difficult to identify sentence boundaries in longer passages, because of the loosely structured narrative sequence (. . . *so I went out and got on a bus and found I'd left my purse in the house so I didn't know what to do and I hadn't any money and anyway* . . .). Informal discourse markers are common, such as *you know, I mean*, and *you see*. And there is a great deal of creativity in the choice of vocabulary, ranging from the unexpected coinage (*Don't be sad—be unsad*) and artificial accent (as in telling a joke about someone from a particular place not one's own) to the use of vague words (such as *thingummy* and *watchamacallit*). Publications include M. Stubbs, *Discourse Analysis* (Blackwell, 1983), and Ronald Wardhaugh, *How Conversation Works* (Blackwell, 1985). See DIALOG(UE), DISCOURSE, DISCOURSE ANALYSIS, KITCHEN-SINK DRAMA, PHATIC COMMUNION, REGISTER, REPETITION, SEXISM, TALK. [LANGUAGE, SPEECH, STYLE].   D.C.

CONVERSION [BrE: 1920s], **functional shift** [AmE: 1940s]. Also **zero derivation**. The use of a word normally one part of speech or word class as another part of speech, without any change in form: *access*, usually a noun, as a verb in *You can access the information any time*; *author* in *They co-authored the book*. Such shifts are impossible in highly inflected languages like Latin, which require a formal change, but are common in analytic languages like English. English *love* is both noun and verb, but in Latin the noun is *amor*, the verb *amare*. Conversion has for centuries been a common means of extending the resources of English and creating dramatic effects: 'The hearts that spaniel'd me at heels' (Shakespeare, *Antony and Cleopatra*, 4. 13). Etymologically, such words as *bang, crash, splash, thump* were once primarily nouns or verbs, but functionally they favour neither word class. The process has been described as derivation without a change of form (*zero derivation*), but because no new word is formed it can equally well be regarded as syntactic (many words are not tied to one grammatical role) or semantic (as a sense relation on a par with synonymy).

It is often said that 'there is no noun in English that can't be verbed': *bag* a prize, *doctor* a drink, *position* a picture with care, *soldier* on regardless. However, some factors appear to get in the way of complete freedom to convert: (1) *Morphology*. It is unlikely that such a verb as *organize* will shift, because of its verbal suffix: no **Let's have an organize*. (2) *Inertia*. Such a verb/noun contrast as *believe/belief* is unlikely to be overturned: no **This is one of my believes*. (3) *Utility*. In law, there may be no need for *jury* to be other than a noun: no **I've juried several times*. However, such a use cannot be ruled out.

Striking one-off shifts often occur in fiction and journalism: 'I decided she looked like the vamp in those marvellous Hollywood westerns, the lady who goes hipping and thighing through the saloon' (Susan Howatch, *The Wheel of Fortune*, 1984); 'A formidable battery of legal grandees m'ludded and m'learned friended it out before Mr Justice Butt' (J. Keates, *Observer*, 18 June 1989). 'DANGER contaminated sharps destroy by incineration' (instructions on a medical container: DRG Hospital Supplies, Bristol, England, 1989); 'Japanese advice columnists—mostly men—unrelentingly remind women readers of *gaman*, the tradition that women must endure their problems without complaint . . . "I suggested that she join a local women's group or start one," Mrs. Bottel recalls. "Many Japanese women want someone to encourage them to be their own person rather than '*gamaning*' their life away"' (Meredith F. Chen, *Christian Science Monitor*, 21-7 Nov. 1988); 'Relax, I'll Panasonic it' (ad, 1990). See SHAKESPEARE, WORD-FORMATION. [WORD].   T.MCA.

COOK ISLANDS. A self-governing dependency of New Zealand, which lies *c*.3,200 miles to the south-west of the 15 scattered islands. Capital: Avarua. Currency: the New Zealand dollar. Economy: farming and fishing. Population: 17,754 (1981). Ethnicity: *c*.82% Polynesian, 16% mixed, 2% European. Languages: English (official) and local Polynesian languages. Between 1888 and 1901, the islands were a British protectorate; in 1901, they became a New Zealand dependency; in 1965, they became self-governing. See ENGLISH, NEW ZEALAND, POLYNESIA. [OCEANIA, NAME, VARIETY].   T.MCA.

COOPER, Thomas [1517?-94]. English lexicographer, Bishop of Winchester, and Dean of Christ Church, Oxford, responsible for revising Sir Thomas Elyot's Latin-English dictionary (Bibliotheca Eliotae, 1548). His *Thesaurus linguae Romanae & Britannicae* (1565) was a standard dictionary for English readers of classical authors. It introduced such technical improvements as indications of pronunciation and the use of four type fonts into English lexicography from dictionaries of Latin with other vernaculars. It is a dictionary of Latin and English and a 'Historical and Poetic' dictionary drawn on by later lexicographers for classical names and etymologies. See ELYOT. [BIOGRAPHY, EUROPE, HISTORY, REFERENCE].   N.E.O.

COORDINATE CLAUSE, also **co-ordinate clause**. A clause connected to one or more other clauses of equal status. In the sentence *I telephoned twice, but no one answered*, the two coordinate clauses are connected by the coordinating conjunction *but*. See CLAUSE, CONJUNCTION, COORDINATION. [GRAMMAR]. S.G.

COORDINATION, also **co-ordination** [16c: from Latin *coordinatio/coordinationis* an arranging together]. In grammatical description, the process of connecting units of equal status and the resulting construction. Such units are usually connected by a coordinating conjunction (coordinator). *The houses and their occupants* is a noun phrase consisting of two coordinate noun phrases connected by *and*. There are three kinds of coordination, discussed in terms of *syndesis* (from Greek *súndesis*, binding together): (1) *Syndetic coordination*, in which a coordinator is used, as above. If three or more units are coordinated syndetically, it is usual to insert one coordinator only, before the final unit: *We visited Paris, Brussels, and Amsterdam*. (2) *Asyndetic coordination*, in which a coordinator is absent but can be inserted, as in *I came, I saw, I conquered*. (3) *Polysyndetic coordination*, in which the coordinator is inserted between every pair of units, for stylistic effect: *Within one year Susan was awarded a doctorate, and married Ted, and moved to the US*. See CONJUNCTION, HENDIADYS, SUBORDINATION. [GRAMMAR]. S.G.

COORDINATOR, also **co-ordinator** [20c in this sense]. A coordinating conjunction. See CONJUNCTION, COORDINATION. [GRAMMAR]. T.MCA.

COPPERPLATE, also **copper-plate**, **copper plate** [17c]. (1) A polished plate of copper on which a picture, a design, or writing may be engraved or etched for printing; a print or impression from such a plate; the general name for such work; to engrave or print from a copper plate. (2) A delicate style of handwriting with thicker and thinner lines, first developed for writing on copper plates, widely regarded as legible and elegant, and particularly favoured in the 19c. Special quills and later flexible nibs were devised to provide the pressure necessary to produce the characteristic line. See CALLIGRAPHY. [TECHNOLOGY, WRITING]. T.MCA.

COPROLALIA [1885: from French *coprolalie*, coined by Gilles de la Tourette, from Greek *kópros* dung, *lalia* talk]. The obsessive use of obscene language, for sexual gratification ('talking dirty') or because of a psychiatric disorder, such as Tourette's syndrome. See SCATOLOGY, SWEARING. Compare ECHOLALIA, GLOSSOLALIA. [STYLE]. T.MCA.

COPULA [17c: from Latin *copula* a tie, bond]. A verb that joins a subject to its complement. A term in the grammar of English for the verb *be*, but often extended to other verbs with a similar function. These *copular verbs* (also *linking verbs*) can be divided semantically into two types: (1) Those like *be* that refer to a current state: *appear, feel, remain, seem, sound*. (2) Those that indicate a result of some kind: *become, get* (wet); *go* (bad); *grow* (old); *turn* (nasty). *Be* is the copula that most often takes adverbial complements: *Maud was in the garden*; *Dinner is at seven*. All others take subject complements which characterize or identify the subject: *I felt cold*; *I felt a fool*. Compare VERB OF INCOMPLETE PREDICATION. [GRAMMAR]. S.C.

COPULAR VERB. See COPULA, VERB OF INCOMPLETE PREDICATION.

COPY [14c: from French *copie*, Latin *copia* ability, abundance]. Both an imitation or reproduction and material to be used in print or artwork (*advertising copy*). These opposed senses correspond to Latin *copia* as used in *habere copiam legendi* (to have the ability to read) and *facere copiam describendi* (to give the power to transcribe: 'to permit the reproduction of a text'). From them arose the medieval senses of *copia* as both a model for writing and a reproduction of that model. In English, the sense of copy as model continued into the 19c and is ancestral to the use of *copy* in printing and publishing: material prepared for publication, including editing by a *copy-editor* (also called a *sub-editor*, *copy-reader*). It is a negotiated document important for typesetting and proofreading, because it records changes agreed on before the work goes to press. See COPYBOOK, COPYRIGHT, EDITING, HARD COPY AND SOFT COPY. [MEDIA, TECHNOLOGY, WRITING]. W.W.B.

COPYBOOK [16c]. (1) Especially formerly, a book that contains models of handwriting or style that learners can study and copy. (2) A book that contains copies of documents. (3) Commonplace, stereotyped, or hackneyed: *copybook phrases*. See COPY, HACKNEYED, HANDWRITING, STEREOTYPE. [EDUCATION, STYLE, WRITING]. T.MCA.

COPY-EDITING. See EDITING.

COPYING. See PHOTOCOPYING.

COPYIST [17c]. (1) A person who makes copies, especially of manuscripts and other handwritten documents; a scribe. (2) An imitator. See COPY, COPYBOOK, SCRIBE. [WRITING]. T.MCA.

COPYRIGHT [18c]. The right to make copies of a literary, musical, or similar artistic work (the product of an original creative act: handwritten, typed, printed, taped, or electronically or otherwise stored), to license others to make such copies, and to exploit such a work for commercial and other purposes. Generally, works which have such a right are protected by *copyright law* during the lifetime of the *copyright holder*. Such a holder may be a person or an institution, and ownership of copyright is transferable; it can be sold either outright or as a limited licence, by dividing up *rights* that may be exclusive or non-exclusive, such as *film rights* and *translation rights*. See 'Notes on the History of English Copyright', Sir Frank MacKinnon, Appendix II, *The Oxford Companion to English Literature* (5th edition, ed. Margaret Drabble, 1985). For further discussion, see AMERICAN PUBLISHING, BRITISH PUBLISHING, WEBSTERS. [MEDIA, WRITING]. T.MCA.

COPYRIGHT PAGE. See FRONT MATTER, TITLE PAGE.

CORNISH [16c: from *Corn(wall)* and -*ish*: Celtic equivalents *Kernûak, Kernewek*]. (1) Of Cornwall and its people: *Cornish clay, Cornish pasty*. (2) The ancient Celtic language of Cornwall: 'In Cornwall is two speches: the one is naughty Englyshe, and the other is Cornyshe speche' (Andrew Boorde, *Introduction of Knowledge*, 1547). Information about early Cornish is scant; there are few texts, the major survivor being the *Ordinalia* (probably late 14c), a trilogy of verse dramas of 8,734 lines in all. The language began to decline during the Reformation, and its last known fluent speaker, Dolly Pentreath of the village of Mousehole, died in 1777. (3) Also *revived Cornish*. The partly artificial language administered by the *Kesva Tavas Kernewek* (Cornish Language Board), set up in 1967 'to promote the study and revival of the Cornish language'. This medium is sometimes referred to by scholars as *pseudo-Cornish*, and Glanville Price in *The Languages of Britain* (1984) calls it *Cornic*. The revival began with *A Handbook of the Cornish Language* (1904) by the Cornish nationalist Henry Jenner, followed by Robert Morton Nance's *Cornish for All: A Guide to Unified Cornish* (St Ives, 1929), Nance's dictionaries published by the Federation of Old Cornwall Societies, and A. S. D. Smith's grammar *Cornish Simplified* (1939). The revivalists claim that the traditional accent of English in Cornwall provides a key to Cornish pronunciation. The orthography was developed by Nance from the surviving texts, and vocabulary is extended by analogizing from Breton and Welsh and forming compounds from existing words. Price observes: 'It is rather as if one were to attempt in our present state of knowledge to create a form of spoken English on the basis of the fifteenth-century York mystery plays and very little else.' See ARTIFICIAL LANGUAGE, CELTIC LANGUAGES, CORNWALL, DIALECT IN AUSTRALIA. [EUROPE, LANGUAGES, NAME]. T.MCA.

CORNWALL [Before 10c: from Old English *Cornweallas* the 'Corn-welsh': Celtic equivalents *Kernóu* or *Pou Kernóu* (Latin *pagus Cornubii*, whence medieval Latin *Cornubia*). Compare the district of *Cornouaille* in Brittany, known in Breton as *Kernéô* and *Kerné*. Some derive the name from Celtic *corn(u)* horn, for the shape of the peninsula]. Official title *Cornwall and Isles of Scilly*. A county of England occupying the extreme south-western peninsula; the name of the tip, *Land's End*, matches *Finistère* in Brittany. Cornwall has long been considered the most remote and least English of the counties of England, romantically associated with tin mining, megaliths, smugglers, and wreckers. The names of five of the six districts formed in the restructuring of counties in 1974 are traditional Celtic: *Caradon, Carrick, Kerrier, Penwith, Restormel*. The sixth is *North Cornwall*. Although the region has been part of England since 815, many local people regard England as lying beyond the River Tamar.

Relics of the Cornish language are found in place and family names beginning with *pen* head, hill (*Pendennis, Penhale, Penzance*), *pol* pool, hole (*Polkerris, Polmassick, Polperro*), *porth* port (*Porthallow, Porthcothan, Porthcurno*), and *tre* farm (*Tremain, Tresillian, Trevelyan*). Where Brittany has *Mont-Saint-Michel*, Cornwall has *St Michael's Mount*. Both have many Celtic saints' names, and an epithet for Cornwall is 'the cornucopia of saints': *St Austell, St Buryan, St Columb, St Ewe, St Ives, St Just, St Levan, St Mawgan, St Newlyn*. A change of speech could formerly be heard at the county boundary, but Devon speech has encroached into the north-west about the River Bude. The rhotic usage of Devon is weakened in Cornwall, but not so much as formerly. The dialect is part of the West Country group, but because Cornish survived so long, local English developed as a language learned from foreigners, leading to many differences from Devon. In the dialect there are words wholly or partly derived from Cornish, such as *clicky-handed* left-handed (from *glikin*), *clunk* to swallow, and *whidden* runt or weakling (in a litter of piglets: from *gwyn* white). See BRITAIN, BRITTANY, CORNISH, ENGLAND, WEST COUNTRY. [EUROPE, NAME]. T.MCA., S.E.

CORPUS [13c: from Latin *corpus* body. The plural is usually *corpora*]. (1) A collection of texts, especially if complete and self-contained: *the corpus of Anglo-Saxon verse*. (2) Plural also *corpuses.* In linguistics and lexicography, a body of texts, utterances, or other specimens considered more or less representative of a language, and usually stored as an electronic database. Currently, computer corpora may store many millions of running words, whose features can be analysed by means of *tagging* (the addition of identifying and classifying tags to words and other formations) and the use of concordancing programs. *Corpus linguistics* studies data in any such corpus. Recent publications on corpora and corpus linguistics include: (1) *English Computer Corpora: Selected Papers and Research Guide*, eds. Stig Johansson & Anna-Brita Stenström: Berlin & New York, Mouton de Gruyter, 1991. (2) *English Corpus Linguistics: Studies in Honour of Jan Svartvik*, eds. Karin Aijmer & Bengt Altenberg: London & New York, Longman, 1991. (3) Articles in *English Today*: 'ICE: the International Corpus of English', by Sidney Greenbaum, 28, Oct. 1991: 'The Corpus Revolution', by Michael Rundell & Penny Stock, 30, July 1992. See BROWN CORPUS, BRITISH NATIONAL CORPUS, COBUILD, CONCORDANCE, KOLHAPUR CORPUS, SURVEY OF ENGLISH USAGE. [LANGUAGE, LITERATURE]. T.MCA.

CORRECT [14c: from Latin *correctus* (made) straight]. (1) In accordance with a standard, especially of artistic, literary, or linguistic style (and often synonymous with *proper*): *correct methods, correct spelling, correct usage.* (2) In accordance with fact, truth, and reason; free from error: 'Monsieur Misson has wrote a more correct Account of Italy than any before him' (Addison, preface to *Italy*, 1705). (3) Of persons, adhering to an acknowledged standard of behaviour, speech, writing, etc.: 'The best and correctest authours' (Johnson, 1736, quoted in Boswell's *Life*). (4) To set right, amend, mark or point out errors in (a text, essay, etc.); to rebuke, punish for faults of character or performance; to counteract and bring into line: 'So oft a daye I mote thy werk renewe / Hit to correcte and eek to rubbe and scrape' (Chaucer to his scribe Adam, *c.*1374); 'I praye maister Iohn Skelton . . . poet laureate in the vnyuersite of oxenforde, to ouersee and correcte this sayd booke' (Caxton, *Eneydos*, 1490). See CORRUPT, ERROR, ERROR ANALYSIS, ORTHOEPY, ORTHOGRAPHY, POLITICALLY CORRECT, PROOF-READING, STANDARD. [EDUCATION, STYLE, USAGE]. T.MCA.

CORRELATIVE [16c: from Latin *correlativus* related in a mutually supporting way]. A term for words that are part of the same construction but do not occur side by side. In *correlative coordination*, a correlative conjunction is reinforced by a word or expression that introduces the first coordinate unit: *and* reinforced by *both* in *Both Geoffrey and Marion were at my party*. Pairs of correlatives and correlative conjunctions used in this way are *both . . . and, either . . . or, whether . . . or, not only . . . but, neither . . . nor.* See CONJUNCTION. [GRAMMAR]. S.G.

CORRESPONDENCE COLUMN. See LETTER[2].

CORRUPT [14c: from Latin *corruptus* broken up, destroyed]. A text is considered corrupt if it does not conform to an acknowledged original; a usage is considered corrupt if it violates an actual or desired standard, as of orthography, typography, a house style, or an established convention. In a scribal culture, a flawlessly copied manuscript is the ideal, and careless copying or preservation is a grave disservice to society and truth. In medieval Europe, the concept of corrupt language was linked with the religious concept of a corrupt world and corrupt flesh, contrasted with the perfection and glory of God and Scripture. With the development of print during and after the Renaissance, the concept of a corrupt text was extended to spoken language, dialects being viewed as corruptions of ideal speech, inability or failure to follow educated usage becoming 'the corruption of ignorance' (Johnson, preface to *Dictionary of the English Language*, 1755). By extension, an electronically stored text is corrupt if human or mechanical fault has altered it. Without backup (secondary storage), it may be impossible to restore such a text, because like speech there is no original against which it can be judged. See CORRECT, MISTAKE, MUMPSIMUS. [MEDIA, STYLE]. T.MCA.

COUNCIL OF EUROPE. An organization of representatives of 21 western European states, founded in 1949 by ten founding members (Belgium, Denmark, France, Ireland, Italy, Luxembourg, the Netherlands, Norway, Sweden, and the United Kingdom) for the purpose of promoting European cooperation, protecting human rights, and fostering social and economic progress. Later members are: Austria, Cyprus, Germany, Greece, Iceland, Liechtenstein, Malta, Portugal, Spain, Switzerland, and Turkey. Its headquarters are in Strasbourg, France. It has created and administered a range of organizations concerned with such matters as law, crime, and local government, and including the *Council for Cultural Co-operation*, which has been responsible for a series of initiatives on second language teaching throughout the 1970s-80s.

A series of projects, known as the *Council of Europe Languages Projects*, was initiated in 1971 to improve the learning and teaching of European languages, under the direction of the

British applied linguist John L. Trim. They concentrated initially on an analysis of the needs of adult learners, the results becoming the content of syllabuses intended to serve as bases for a Europe-wide scheme. Learners are seen as needing to be able to express themselves in terms of certain *notions* and *functions*. The description of the notions and functions was undertaken for various languages. The first of these descriptions, for English, was by J. A. Van Ek. It was published in 1975 and extended as *Threshold Level English*, by J. A. Van Ek and L. G. Alexander (1980). The examples in the table illustrate some notions and functions as developed for the projects, and the distinction between items to be learned *productively* (P) and *receptively* (R).

Notions	Exemplification in English
Properties and qualities	
Existence	There is ... P
	There's no ... P
	Is there ...? P
	to exist P
Motion	to move P
	to stand still R
Length of time	for + NP (durational nouns) P
	since + NP (point of time) P
Quality, physical shape	round P
	square P
Visibility	(It) can (not) be seen R
	(I) can (not) see it P
Possessive relations	possessive adjectives: my, our, etc. P
	to have (got) P
	to own R
Functions	
Emotional attitudes	This is very nice/pleasant P
	I like + V-ing P
Moral attitudes, apologizing	I am very sorry P
	Sorry! P
	Please forgive me R

The threshold levels for the projects are not a syllabus or methodology as such, but a statement of content for a course design. The most recent project concerns teacher training. A set of principles has been proposed, in which language teaching should centre on the learner, not the teacher, be relevant to the learner's life, not remote academic goals, be part of permanent education, so that learning can be fostered at any time, be based as far as possible on participatory democracy, and be communicative, so that the language is learned socially rather than alone, and geared to learning-by-doing. Thousands of teachers have been involved in the projects, which have been influential in Europe and elsewhere. See ALEXANDER (L.), COMMUNICATIVE APPROACH, LANGUAGE TEACHING, THRESHOLD LEVEL, UNIT CREDIT. [EDUCATION, EUROPE].

P.S., C.J.B.

COUNTABLE AND UNCOUNTABLE. Contrasting categories of noun. A countable noun (also *count noun, unit noun*) can be both singular and plural, whether regular in form (*book/books, fox/foxes*) or irregular (*child/children, sheep/sheep*). In the singular, a countable noun cannot be used without a determiner or a possessive: *a book, one book, my book, that book, John's book*, but not **book* alone. An uncountable noun (also *non-count noun, mass noun*) has no plural forms, takes only a singular verb, and can occur without a determiner: *furniture* as in *The furniture has arrived* is uncountable, but *chair* and *table* as in *They bought some chairs and a table* are countable. Some words can be used both countably and uncountably: *wine*, as in *This is a splendid wine* and *Have some more wine*. Some words are normally countable or uncountable, but in certain contexts may have special uses: *money* is normally uncountable, even though one can count the thing to which it refers; the forms *moneys, monies* occur only in limited financial contexts. Many abstract nouns are uncountable, but not all uncountable nouns are abstract. In general, countable and uncountable are subcategories of common noun, but not all common nouns fit the categories: *scissors, trousers*, and other words for things consisting of two parts; *cattle, clothes* and other words that are plural only. Compare COLLECTIVE NOUN. [GRAMMAR].

S.C.

COUNTRY TALK. See KAMTOK.

COUNTRY-WESTERN, COUNTRY AND WESTERN. See DIALECT IN AMERICA, HILLBILLY.

COUPLET [16c]. A pair of verse lines that usually rhyme. A couplet may stand alone as a short stanza, but more often forms part of a sequence. Rhyming octosyllabic couplets appear in English in the 13c, when Old English alliterative verse was giving way to the syllabic verse of Norman French. In the 14c, Chaucer wrote much of *The Canterbury Tales* in iambic pentameter couplets; from its popularity for epic and heroic material, this form came to be called the *heroic couplet*. Shakespeare had sequences of heroic couplets in his early plays, and he and his contemporaries often used the device to mark the end of a scene:

> I goe, and it is done: the Bell inuites me.
> Heare it not, Duncan, for it is a Knell,
> That summons thee to Heauen, or to Hell.
> (*Macbeth*, 2. 1)

After the Restoration, the heroic couplet was

favoured from Dryden to the late 18c. Pope was its leading exponent, developing it to deadly effect in his satires. In *An Essay on Criticism* (1711), he comments in couplets on the hackneyed style of some contemporaries (with a triplet in lines 3–5):

> In the bright Muse, tho' thousand charms conspire,
> Her voice is all these tuneful fools admire;
> Who haunt Parnassus but to please their ear,
> Not mend their minds; as some to church repair
> Not for the doctrine, but the music there.
> These equal syllables alone require,
> Tho' oft the ear the open vowels tire; . . .
> Where'er you find 'the cooling western breeze',
> In the next line it 'whispers through the trees':
> If crystal streams 'with pleasing murmurs creep',
> The reader's threaten'd, not in vain, with 'sleep'.

The 18c heroic couplet is usually a *closed couplet*, in which the end of each pair of lines coincides with the end of a sentence or other strong syntactic pause. There is often a caesura in the middle of the line. By the end of the century, the heyday of the couplet had passed. Keats used it for *Endymion*, Byron for satire, but it was little used by the Victorians. In the 20c, poems in heroic couplets have been written by Rupert Brooke, Roy Campbell, and Robert Frost, among others. See END-STOPPED LINE. [LITERATURE]. R.C.

COVERAGE [1900s: AmE]. (1) The area covered by something, such as a broadcast or an insurance policy. (2) In the media, the range, prominence, space, and/or time given to an item of news or other topic. Among newspapers, coverage falls into two broad types: the *quality press* covers mainly world affairs with sober headlines, supporting photographs, and more or less prominent locations for major features on certain pages, while the *tabloid press* 'splashes' some stories on certain pages, especially the front page, often with sensationalizing headlines and photographs blown up and cropped for maximum impact. (3) In lexicography, the number of words, entries, senses, or other items included or claimed in a work of reference: for example, over 500,000 defined words in *The Oxford English Dictionary* (1989); over 350,000 entries in *The Random House Dictionary of the English Language* (1987); over 250,000 listed words in *Roget's Thesaurus* (Longman, 1987); over 75,000 definitions in *The Oxford Reference Dictionary* (1986); over 25,000 terms and 3,000 illustrations in *The Facts on File Visual Dictionary* (1988); over 10,000 quotations in the *Bloomsbury Dictionary of Quotations* (1987). See LEXICOGRAPHY, VOCABULARY CONTROL. [MEDIA, REFERENCE]. G.H., T.MCA.

COVERDALE, Miles [*c*.1488–1569]. English cleric and Bible translator, born in Yorkshire, educated at Cambridge, ordained in 1514, and influenced by Cambridge Protestant reformers. Bishop of Exeter (1551–3). He lived and worked in Germany, and may have helped Tyndale translate the Pentateuch. Coverdale produced the first complete printed Bible in English (1535) and helped produce the Great Bible (1539). On the accession of Edward VI, he returned to England, but under Mary lost his bishopric. He escaped to Denmark and may have taken part in preparing the Geneva Bible. After Mary's death, he settled in London, where he became renowned as a preacher. His Bible is largely from secondary sources such as Pagninus and Luther, but many of his renderings were retained in the Authorized Version and others were used in the 1549 and 1552 versions of the Book of Common Prayer and kept in the revision of 1662. These include the Psalms, Magnificat, and Nunc Dimittis. His version of the first lines of Psalm 23 runs: 'The Lorde is my sheparde, therefore can I lack nothyng. He shall feede me in a greene pasture; and leade me foorth beside the waters of comfort.' See BIBLE. [BIOGRAPHY, EUROPE, HISTORY]. M.LA.

COX REPORT. A report entitled *English for Ages 5 to 16*, published in 1989 in the UK for the Department of Education and Science on the teaching of English to pupils in England and Wales (but not Scotland and Northern Ireland) between the ages of 5 and 16, as part of the new National Curriculum. The committee which drafted the report was chaired by Professor Brian Cox of Manchester University, who had been a member of the committee that produced the Kingman Report (1988). However, whereas the Kingman Inquiry had to recommend a general model of the English language for teaching purposes, Cox was required to focus on how the teaching would be done. The Cox Report's recommendations reflected a compromise between concerns raised by the Kingman Inquiry regarding teaching a knowledge of language and the liberal consensus of many teachers of English. The recommendations were adjusted to the rigid format of the assessment model required by legislation relating to the National Curriculum established in 1987.

The report emphasized the subtlety of the process by which children acquire language and encouraged the use of English for a diversity of purposes. The role of wide reading and the centrality of literature in language development were also emphasized. At the same time, the report encouraged a sympathetic response to users of other languages in British society, but the successive levels of attainment proposed for the assessment of children's achievements reflected a monocultural rather than a multicultural view of English, with an expectation that the highest attainment would only be achieved by those using it for higher education, public speaking, or similar activities. The proposals were nonetheless widely reported as too liberal for the Secretary of State for Education. The National Curriculum Council, which was responsible for producing the version of the report to be used in schools (subject to parliamentary approval), attempted to add grammar in several places and make literacy more important than oracy, especially at the higher levels of schooling. Successive Secretaries of State also made pronouncements about the importance of spelling (associated with the view that reading should be taught primarily by the phonic method) in the assessment of all school subjects.

Because of concern about the level of knowledge of language on the part of teachers (who, at the secondary level, had mostly qualified with degrees in literature), the Cox recommendations were followed by a government-funded in-service training project known as *Language in the National Curriculum* or *LINC*, directed by Professor Ronald Carter of Nottingham University. However, the materials, due to be published by HMSO (Her Majesty's Stationery Office), were withdrawn in 1991 by ministerial order, and copyright was withheld for their commercial publication. Although precise reasons for these actions were not given, in the general view of the press they were a response to attempts by the writers of materials to situate language in social and political settings, and to 'downgrade' standard English in relation to the use of dialect. The writers also rejected phonics as a technique for teaching spelling. In the opinion of many observers, the long-standing conflict between the views of Conservative politicians on the role of language and those of linguists and educationists reached a new stage with an act of direct official censorship. See CURRICULUM, KINGMAN REPORT, MULTICULTURALISM. [EDUCATION, EUROPE]. C.J.B.

CPE. See CAMBRIDGE CERTIFICATE OF PROFICIENCY IN ENGLISH.

CRAIGIE, (Sir) William A(lexander) [1867–1957]. Scottish lexicographer and philologist, born in Dundee, and graduate in classics of St Andrews and Oxford. After four years teaching Latin at St Andrews, he joined the staff of the *Oxford English Dictionary* in 1897, becoming its third editor in 1901. Beginning with Q, he edited nearly a fifth of that work and a third of its 1933 *Supplement*. In 1905, he was appointed Taylorian Lecturer in the Scandinavian Languages at Oxford and in 1915 was elected to the chair of Anglo-Saxon (in addition to seven and a half hours' work each day on lexicography). From 1921, he collected quotations for his projected dictionary of Older Scots. In 1925, he became Professor of English at the U. of Chicago, to edit *The Dictionary of American English*, resigning his Oxford posts but not his *OED* editorship. For some years after this, Craigie was occupied simultaneously with three historical dictionaries and many other writings. After retiring in 1936, he worked on the US dictionary until its completion in 1944 and on the *Dictionary of the Older Scottish Tongue*, which he edited from 1925 to the completion of I in 1955, when he was 87. He was influential in establishing or launching the Frisian Academy (1938), the Anglo-Norman Text Society (1938), *The Anglo-Norman Dictionary* (1947), and the Icelandic Rímur Society (1947). A suggestion which he put forward in 1907 led ultimately to *The Scottish National Dictionary*, and he gave an address to the Philological Society in 1919 proposing the Period Dictionaries of English. See index. [AMERICAS, BIOGRAPHY, EUROPE, REFERENCE]. A.J.A.

CRANMER, Thomas [1489–1556]. English cleric, compiler of the Book of Common Prayer (1549 and 1552 versions) and Archbishop of Canterbury (1533–56); martyred at Oxford after recanting his Protestant faith then dramatically withdrawing his recantations. He was born at Aslockton, Nottinghamshire, and as a Cambridge scholar was drawn into the negotiations for the separation of Henry VIII and Catherine of Aragon. Cranmer was promoted to Archbishop with no earlier experience of public affairs. He was largely responsible for introducing the English Bible into parish churches in 1538. He drew up the Litany (1544), and the First and Second Prayer Books of Edward VI in 1549 and 1552 (the Book of Common Prayer). He also composed homilies or sermons which are still in print and the 45 Articles of Religion (later reduced to 39) defining Church of England doctrine. The 1549 and 1552 Prayer Books are considered almost entirely his work with material translated and/or adapted from earlier authors or of his own composition. Cranmer was in touch with all sorts and conditions of men and the language of the BCP reflects this, being explicitly designed to be 'understanded of the people'. See BIBLE, BOOK OF COMMON PRAYER. [BIOGRAPHY, EUROPE, HISTORY]. M.LA.

CREAK, CREAKY VOICE. See PITCH.

CREATIVE WRITING. (1) Imaginative writing, usually in the form of poetry, storytelling, and feature-writing for newspapers and magazines; imaginative fiction: 'But it's no good giving creative writing a monopoly on the benefits of intuition or giving nonfiction writing a monopoly on the benefits of conscious awareness. That's why I stress the intuitive processes in the first half of the writing cycle and conscious awareness or critical discrimination in the second half' (Peter Elbow, *Writing with Power*, 1981). (2) A course in writing imaginative fiction (especially for publication), usually conducted by tutors with some success in publishing their own work. Such a course may be provided at a school, college, or adult evening institute, or by correspondence course. (3) An approach to teaching writing in schools and colleges that emphasizes imaginative self-expression. It was the basis of a movement in teaching mother-tongue English that developed after the Second World War, and is particularly associated with Marjorie Hourd's *The Education of the Poetic Spirit* (London: Heinemann, 1949). Advocates of this approach have sought to encourage children's capacity to respond vividly and spontaneously, and convey such responses freely in their writing. They have, however, been accused of overemphasizing imagination and spontaneity at the expense of such pragmatic and communicative considerations as grammar, punctuation, and spelling. Evidence from assessment surveys in the 1970s suggests that there was a tendency to develop fictional and poetic rather than non-fiction writing in English classes. This distinction was blurred in the 1980s, teachers in all subjects generally agreeing that the boundaries between 'objective' and 'subjective' response in school writing need not be rigidly defined. Compare EFFECTIVE WRITING, FICTION. [EDUCATION, WRITING]. T.MCA, C.J.B.

CREOLE [16c: from French *créole*, Spanish *criollo*, Portuguese *crioulo*, from *criar* to nurse or breed, from Latin *creare/creatum* to beget]. A term relating to people and languages especially in the erstwhile colonial tropics and subtropics, in the Americas, Africa, the Indian Ocean, and Oceania. In Portuguese, *crioulo* appears to have referred first to an animal or person born at home, then to a black African slave in Brazil who was born in his or her master's house. In the 17–18c, particularly in the West Indies, the term could mean both a descendant of European settlers (a *white creole*) or a descendant of African slaves (a *creole Negro* or *Negro creole*). Later, the term came to apply also to life and culture in creole societies: for example, the (French) Creole cuisine of Louisiana. The intricacy of the term is captured by the comment of J. M. Ludlow: 'There are creole whites, creole negroes, creole horses, &c.; and creole whites are, of all persons, the most anxious to be

deemed of pure white blood' (*A Sketch of the History of the United States*, 1862). Since the later 19c, the term has extended to include a language spoken by creoles and has acquired a new sense in linguistics, associated with the development of pidgin languages.

Creole languages. In sociolinguistic terms, these languages have arisen through contact between speakers of different languages. This contact first produces a makeshift language called a *pidgin*; when this is nativized and becomes the language of a community, it is a creole. Such languages are often known locally as *pidgin* or *creole*, but may have such specific names as *Aku* in Gambia and *Papiamentu* in the Netherlands Antilles. They are usually given labels by sociolinguists that refer to location and principal *lexifier language* (the language from which they draw most of their vocabulary): for example, *Jamaican Creole*, in full *Jamaican Creole English* or *Jamaican English Creole*, the English-based creole spoken in Jamaica. *Haitian Creole French* is spoken in Haiti and is French-based. Creoles based on English, French, Spanish, and Portuguese occur in the Americas, Africa, and Asia. There are three Portuguese creoles in islands off the West African coast: Cape Verde, Annobon, and São Tomé. *Papiamentu* is the only such creole in the Caribbean, spoken by inhabitants of the Netherlands Antilles (Aruba, Bonaire, and Curaçao), with an admixture of Dutch. The Dutch-based creole *Negerhollands* (Black Dutch) is spoken by a small number of people in the Virgin Islands. Creoles not based on European languages can be found in parts of Africa (such as Swahili when used as a trade vernacular) and in Papua New Guinea (such as Hiri Motu).

Creole English. There are many English-based creoles. In West Africa, they include *Aku* in Gambia, *Krio* in Sierra Leone, *Kru English* in Liberia, and *Kamtok* in Cameroon. In the Caribbean and the neighbouring mainland they include *Bajan* in Barbados, *Creolese* in Guyana, *Miskito Coast Creole* in Nicaragua, *Sranan* in Surinam, *Trinbagonian* in Trinidad and Tobago, and the creoles of the Bay Islands of Honduras. In North America, they include *Afro-Seminole*, *Amerindian Pidgin English*, and *Gullah*. In Oceania, they include *Bislama* in Vanuatu, *Broken* in the Torres Straits, *Hawaii English Creole*, *Kriol* in Northern Australia, *Pijin* in the Solomon Islands, and *Tok Pisin* in Papua New Guinea. It has been argued that *Black English* (*Vernacular*) in the US has creole origins since it shares many features with English-based creoles in the Caribbean. In the UK, *British Black English*, spoken by immigrants from the Caribbean and their children, has features inherited from Caribbean English Creole.

Shared features. Typical grammatical features in European-based creoles include the use of pre-verbal negation and subject–verb–object word order: for example (from Sranan in Surinam) *A no koti a brede* He didn't cut the bread. Many use the same item for both existential statements and possession: for example, *get* in Guyanese Creole *Dem get wan uman we get gyal pikni* There is a woman who has a daughter. They lack a formal passive: for example, in Jamaican Creole no distinction is made in the verb forms in sentences such as *Dem plaan di tri* (They planted the tree) and *Di tri plaan* (The tree was planted). Creoles tend to have no copula and adjectives may function as verbs: for example, Jamaican Creole *Di pikni sik* The child is sick. Most creoles do not show any syntactic difference between questions and statements: for example, Guyanese Creole *I bai di eg dem* can mean 'He bought the eggs' or 'Did he buy the eggs?' (although there is a distinction in intonation). Question words in creoles tend to have two elements, the first generally from the lexifier language: for example, Haitian Creole *ki koté* (from *qui* and *côté*, 'which' and 'side') meaning *where*, and Kamtok *wetin* (from *what* and *thing*) meaning *what*. It has been claimed that many syntactic and semantic similarities among creoles are due to an innate 'bioprogram' for language, and that creoles provide the key to understanding the original evolution of human language.

Creolization. The process of becoming a creole may occur at any stage as a makeshift language develops from trade jargon to expanded pidgin, and can happen under drastic conditions, such as where a population of slaves speaking many languages has to develop a common language among slaves and with overseers. In due course, children grow up speaking the pidgin as their main language, and when this happens it must change to meet their needs. Depending on the stage at which creolization occurs, different types of structural expansion are necessary before the language can become adequate. In the case of Jamaican Creole, it is thought that a rudimentary pidgin creolized within a generation, then began to *de-creolize* towards general English. Tok Pisin, however, first stabilized and expanded as a pidgin before it became creolized; in such cases, the transition between the two stages is gradual rather than abrupt.

The term is also applied to cases where heavy borrowing disrupts the continuity of a language, turning it into a creole-like variety, but without a prior pidgin stage. Some researchers have argued that Middle English is a creole that arose from contact with Norse during the Scandinavian settlements (8–11c) and then with French after the Norman Conquest (11c). In addition to massive lexical borrowing, many changes led to such simplification of grammar as loss of the Old English inflectional endings. It is not, however, clear that these changes were due solely to language contact, since other languages have undergone similar restructurings in the absence of contact, as for example when Latin became Italian.

De-creolization is a further development in which a creole gradually converges with its superstrate or lexifier language: for example, in Hawaii and Jamaica, both creoles moving towards standard English. Following the creolization of a pidgin, a *post-creole continuum* may develop when, after a period of relatively independent linguistic development, a post-pidgin or post-creole variety comes under a period of renewed influence from the lexifier language. De-creolization may obscure the origins of a variety, as in the case of American Black English.

Conclusion. Pidgin and creole languages were long neglected by the academic world, because they were not regarded as 'real' or 'fully-fledged' languages, but their study is currently regarded as significant for general linguistics as well as the study of such languages as English. The study of pidgins and creoles has been rapidly expanding as linguists interested in language acquisition, language change, and universal grammar have taken more notice of them. Because these varieties arise and often expand rapidly, they provide an excellent testing ground for theories of historical change. Speakers must bring some general and possibly innate principles and strategies to bear on the task of learning to communicate under such circumstances. These languages have also attracted the attention of sociolinguists, owing to the amount of variation among them, and the study of such variation has had repercussions on the study of the totality of languages like English, in which variety is as much the norm as uniformity.

Since pidgins and creoles are generally spoken in Third World countries, their role and function are intimately connected with a variety of political questions concerned with national, social, and economic development and transition into post-colonial societies. Some countries give official recognition to pidgin and creole languages, among them Papua New Guinea, Vanuatu, and Haiti. In Haiti, the 1983 constitution declared both Haitian Creole and French to be national languages, but recognized French as the official language; in 1987, Creole was declared official too. The former Papua New Guinean Prime Minister, Michael Somare, has on occasion spoken abroad in Tok Pisin, even though he endorses the use of English for official purposes. Pidgin and creole languages also function as symbols of solidarity in many parts of the world where their use is increasing. In Haiti, it is often the case that to speak creole is to talk straight, while to speak French is synonymous with duplicity.

See ABORIGINAL ENGLISH, ACROLECT, AFRICAN ENGLISH, AFRO-SEMINOLE, AKU, ANGLO-DANISH, ATLANTIC CREOLES, BAHAMAS, BARBADOS, BASILECT, BELIZE, BISLAMA, BLACK ENGLISH VERNACULAR, BROKEN, CAMEROON, CARIBBEAN, CARIBBEAN ENGLISH CREOLE, CAYMAN ISLANDS, CENTRAL AMERICA, CREOLESE, CREOLOID, DIALECT, ENGLISH, FRENCH, GAMBIA, GHANA, GULLAH, GUYANA, HAWAIIAN ENGLISH, HAWAII CREOLE ENGLISH, JAMAICA, JAMAICAN CREOLE, JAMAICAN ENGLISH, KAMTOK, KRIO, KRIOL, KWEYOL, LECT, LIBERIA, MAURITIUS, MELANESIAN PIDGIN ENGLISH, MESOLECT, MISKITO COAST CREOLE, MONTSERRAT, NEW ORLEANS, NIGERIA, PAPUA NEW GUINEA, PIDGIN, PIJIN, SAINT CHRISTOPHER & NEVIS, SAINT LUCIA, SAINT VINCENT & THE GRENADINES, SAMANA, SIERRA LEONE, SOLOMON ISLANDS PIDGIN ENGLISH, SURINAM(E), TALK, TESD, TOK PISIN, TRINIDAD & TOBAGO, VANUATU, VARIETY, VIRGIN ISLANDS, WEST AFRICAN ENGLISH, WEST AFRICAN PIDGIN ENGLISH. [LANGUAGE, VARIETY].
S.R.

CREOLE CONTINUUM. See POST-CREOLE CONTINUUM.

CREOLE ENGLISH. See CARIBBEAN ENGLISH CREOLE, CREOLE.

CREOLESE [20c]. The everyday name for the English-based Creole of Guyana, the dominant vernacular of the country. It is locally preferred to *patois* and *creole*. See CARIBBEAN ENGLISH CREOLE, -ESE, GUYANA. [AMERICAS, VARIETY].   L.C.

CREOLIZATION. See CREOLE.

CREOLOID [1970s]. A term applied by sociolinguists to creole-like varieties such as *Singapore English*, where English acts as a superstrate ('high') language and a continuum of varieties develops between it and more basilectal ('low') varieties which reflect influence from speakers' native languages. [LANGUAGE].   S.R.

CRITICISM [17c: from *critic*, from Latin *criticus*, Greek *kritikós* skilled in judging, and *-ism*]. (1) The action, process, or result of passing judgement, evaluating, and/or analysing (someone or something), not in legal but in social, artistic, literary, linguistic, or similar terms; any instance of such judgement. In this sense, the term is usually neutral. (2) The action, process, or result of judging or assessing adversely and

severely, often with, or perceived as being with, the intention of finding fault and belittling; any instance of such judgement. The term is so powerfully negative in this sense that it often swamps the first sense, which may then need defending or protecting with the phrase *constructive criticism*, which indicates that any judgement is well meant. However, even the most constructive critics may find their comments unwelcome. (3) The study or investigation of documents and texts in order to establish such things as dates, origins, authenticity, content, style, and influence. Such work may be influenced by one or more method or theory of critical assessment. See (A)ESTHETICS, LITERARY CRITICISM, USAGE GUIDANCE AND CRITICISM. [LANGUAGE, STYLE].   T.MCA.

CROSS-REFERENCE, also **cross reference** [1800s]. Informal short form *x-ref*. A device for calling attention to another part of a text, corpus, or collection. If information is in another place than under the item consulted, a direct cross-reference is used; for example, in a British dictionary, the undefined entry *hematite* might have the cross-reference 'a variant spelling of *haematite*', 'see *haematite*', or simply '*haematite*'; in an American dictionary, *haematite* might be cross-referred to *hematite*, the main entry. If more information is available at another place, a 'see also' cross-reference (such as *see, see also, more at, q.v.*) might call the reader's attention to another entry or entries. Typographical marking may be used, especially for items in running text, such as small capital letters ('the Jacobins under Georges DANTON') or an asterisk before or after the word in question ('the Jacobins under Georges *Danton'). See HYPERTEXT, NOTES AND REFERENCES. [REFERENCE, TECHNOLOGY].   L.U.

CROSSWORD PUZZLE, also **crossword.** A puzzle in which the solver has to guess words from clues and write them in spaces on a chequered diagram which is usually square. The words are generally separated by black squares or by thick bars between squares. The pattern of black and white squares is usually symmetrical, so that the diagram looks the same if turned upside down. The clues are numbered and lead to interlocking words inserted in the appropriate numbered spaces. Crosswords are relatively recent and have developed from the *acrostic* and the *word square*. The earliest were diamond-shaped, such as that devised by Arthur Wynne for the *New York World* (21 Dec. 1913). The puzzles became a craze in the 1920s. In Britain, the first newspaper to have a crossword was the *Sunday Express* (2 Nov. 1924), followed by the *Sunday Times* (11 Jan. 1925) and *The Times* of London in 1930. The earliest crosswords had straightforward clues (usually simple definitions of words), but British puzzle-compilers like *Torquemada* (Edward Powys Mathers) and *Ximenes* (Derrick Somerset Macnutt), adopting names from the Spanish Inquisition, devised cryptic clues that use such devices as anagrams, ambiguity, abbreviations, reversals, and puns, often combining a literal clue with one that is disguised: for example, *Guide consumed our rice pudding* is a clue to *courier*, which means *guide* and is an anagram of *our rice*; *an English flower [4]* might be *rose*, but could be the River *Ouse* as *flow-er* (something that flows); *duck on the German river* is the River *Oder* (O, a duck in cricket, plus *der*, German for *the*). Crosswords have had little effect on English, apart from prolonging the life of such words as *dso* and *li*, which are useful to crossword-setters and are therefore retained in some dictionaries. See WORD GAME. [WORD]. T.A.

CROWN [18c in this sense]. A standard size of printing paper, 15 × 20 inches in Britain, 15 × 19 in the US, originally watermarked with the image of a crown. See BOOK, PAPER, QUARTO. [TECHNOLOGY]. T.MCA.

CRYPTANALYSIS. See CRYPTOGRAPHY.

CRYPTOGRAPHY [17c: from Greek-derived *crypto-* hidden, *-graphy* writing]. Both the study of secret kinds of writing (usually *codes* and *ciphers*) and ways in which they are used to send 'sensitive' messages between members of a group with information to protect. Technically, the term *encryption* [1940s] covers the conversion of a message from ordinary language into code (a process generally known as either *encoding* or *enciphering* and *encipherment*); the term *cryptanalysis* [1920s] refers to interpreting systems whose *keys* (means of encryption) are unknown (informally called *breaking* or *cracking* a code). The process of converting any code, known or unknown, into ordinary language is generally known as either *decoding* or *deciphering* and *decipherment*. When the words of a message are transformed into code, they become *codetext*, *ciphertext*, or a *cryptogram*; when a message is sent without encoding it is *cleartext* (referred to informally as *(sent) in clear*). When a coded message has been successfully decoded, the result is *plaintext/plain text*. A distinction may be made between cryptography proper, which involves changes in signs, and *steganography* [16c: from Greek *steganós* covered: also formerly a synonym of *cryptography*], which does not change the message but uses masking systems, such as invisible ink or microdots (see Fred B. Wrixon, *Codes, Ciphers, and Secret Languages*, Harrap, 1989). Word-play across languages,

with or without serious intent, has sometimes been used for cryptographic purposes: for example, when Sir Charles Napier conquered the Indian province of Sind in 1843, he communicated his victory with the one-word message *peccavi* (Latin: I have sinned). See CIPHER, CODE, KEYWORD, MESSAGE, PRIVATE LANGUAGE, RIDDLE. [LANGUAGE, WRITING]. T.MCA.

CRYSTAL MARK. See PLAIN ENGLISH.

CUED SPEECH. See SIGN LANGUAGE.

CULTIVATED [17c]. Of land, tilled and cared for; of people, their minds, and their manners, improved and refined by training or education: 'The prisoner is a well set-up and well-dressed man with a cultivated voice' (*Westminster Gazette*, 2 Jan. 1908). The term has often been used in relation to accents, RP being widely regarded as the most cultivated. It is used particularly of accents considered close to RP: *Cultivated Australian, Cultivated New Zealand*. See ACCENT, AUSTRALIAN ENGLISH, CULTURE, EDUCATED AND UNEDUCATED, NEW ZEALAND ENGLISH, RECEIVED PRONUNCIATION, REFINED. [OCEANIA, SPEECH, STYLE]. T.MCA., W.S.R.

CULTURA. A Latin American association that provides a cultural and linguistic link with the UK: for example, the *Instituto Cultural Anglo-Mexicano* in Mexico, the *Culturas Inglesas* in Brazil. Teaching English is the major activity of such associations, which work closely with the British Council on teaching programmes and the provision of native-speaking teachers. In Argentina, Chile, and Uruguay, teaching in the culturas to all levels of the Cambridge examinations is an adjunct to national provision for the training of EFL teachers. See BRITISH COUNCIL. [AMERICAS, EDUCATION]. W.S.

CULTURAL CRINGE. A phrase coined by the Australian literary critic A. A. Phillips (1900–85) to identify an alleged exaggerated and especially Australian deference to the cultural achievements of others, especially the English. [OCEANIA, STYLE]. W.S.R.

CULTURAL LITERACY. A phrase defined by E. D. Hirsch in the US as 'knowledge that enables a writer or reader to know what other writers and readers know within the literate culture' (*Reading, Writing, and Cultural Literacy*, 1983). From this viewpoint, literacy is a complex phenomenon related to the nature of texts and writing; the invention of alphabetic script 'externalized' memory and freed much of the mind for the development of analytic and abstract thought. Because writing provides the visual symbols of ideas, the interpretation of texts is bound by social norms and conventions concerning language use, strategies for evaluations of texts, and shared mental schemata. The texts in a cultural canon are selected as defining the cultural heritage of a people and are made the 'classic' foundation of decoding and interpretation by teachers. Training in literacy is then organized to foster the kind of thinking and problem-solving which these texts represent. Although the shared content of a literate culture changes over time, as individuals contribute new works and ideas, proponents of cultural literacy consider that mastery of grammatical rules, accepted knowledge, and tradition located in what Hirsch calls a 'permanent central core' enables members of a society to interact dynamically with each other and gain autonomy and power. Back-to-basics programmes, grammatical drills, and memorization of tropes are therefore supported as ways of fostering cultural literacy. See LITERACY. [EDUCATION, WRITING].

R.W.B.

CULTURE [15c: through French from Latin *cultura* tilling, cultivation. An obsolete sense in English meant 'worship, reverential homage': compare *cult*]. The first meaning of the term, tillage of the soil, continues in the sense of raising plants and animals (*bee culture*, *silviculture*) and in the scientific 'culturing' of micro-organisms and tissues. A sense of training (body, mind, ideas, tastes, or manners) underlies such phrases as *physical culture* and *a cultured manner*. A third sense, as in *twentieth-century Western culture*, refers to a social condition, level of civilization, or way of life, as also in the more focused terms *ancient Greek culture* and *Maori culture*. Language is generally considered part of culture in this sense. The scientist and novelist C. P. Snow defined 20c Western culture (implicitly associated with English) as in effect *two cultures*, the literary and the scientific, neither knowing much about the other: 'Those in the two cultures can't talk to each other' (*Two Cultures and Scientific Revolution*, 1959). It is not easy to separate *culture* as way of life or kind of society from *culture* as something possessed through social training or lacking because such training was not available or one failed to take advantage of it. The first sense is sociological: people *belong* to a culture. The second sense is social: people *have* or *lack* culture, much as they have or lack charm, good looks, and money. The antonyms *cultured/uncultured* are used only with the social sense, and are comparable to such pairs as *literate/illiterate*, *educated/uneducated*, which are also used sociologically. See BICULTURALISM, BOOK, CULTIVATED, EDUCATED AND UNEDUCATED, IMPERIALISM, LITERACY, MULTICULTURALISM. [EDUCATION, LANGUAGE, STYLE].

T.MCA.

CUMBRIA [Latin, from the Latinized Celtic *Cumbri*, a people of ancient Britain: cognate with Welsh *Cymru*. See WALES]. (1) A scholarly term for ancient south-west Scotland and north-west England from the Clyde across the Solway to the Eden, making up the British kingdoms *Strathclyde* and *Gododdin* to the north and *Rheged* to the south. The peoples of these kingdoms were known to the Welsh as the *gwyr y gogledd* (men of the north) and are sometimes called *the Northern Welsh*. (2) A county of north-western England since 1974, formed from the former counties of Cumberland and Westmorland, and Lancashire North of the Sands. It includes *the Lake District* or *Lakeland*, home of the poet Wordsworth. Cumbric was spoken there until the 11c, Anglian from the 7c, and Norse in the 9–11c. Local place-names reflect all three languages: Celtic as in *Culgaith* back wood, *Penrith* head of the ford, Old English as in *Broomfield* broom-covered field, *Rottington* farmstead of Rotta's people, Norse as in *Witherslack* wooded valley, *Haverthwaite* clearing where oats were grown, and (indicating that the Norwegians had come from Ireland and brought Irish people with them) *Ireby* farmstead of the Irishman.

The dialect of Cumbria is closely related to Scots and to the dialects from North and East Yorkshire northward. Westmorland speech has features in common with the north-western Yorkshire Dales, such as 'skyool' for *school* and 'gaa' for *go*. The dialect around Howden in East Yorkshire has more in common with that of Cumbria than with Wakefield, only 20 miles away in West Yorkshire. The speech of Lancashire North of the Sands is closer to Lancashire than to Lakeland; dialect boundary lines between North Midland and Northern (a bundle of isoglosses from the Humber to Morecambe Bay) cut across the area. Dunmail Raise, between Ambleside and Keswick, is said locally to be the linguistic boundary, and people north and south of the pass used to speak doubtfully of those who lived *ower t'Raise*.

The *Lakeland Dialect Society* was founded in 1939 to sustain interest in and use of the regional dialect. It publishes an annual journal whose poetry and prose attempts to display precise local usage with distinctive variants in spelling. The following examples, from a poem in North Westmorland dialect by Evelyn Metcalfe and a tale in North Cumbrian by Harold Forsyth, appeared in the 1990 journal:

> I like to hear t'auld sayins
> An teals fwok telt lang sen
> They mun herv lived, these caracters
> Beath women fwok an men.

[*t'auld* the old, *teals* tales, *fwok* folk, *telt lang sen* told long since/ago, *mun herv lived* must have lived, *beath* both]

Ther' wes yance a teal aboot a gadgie 'at stop't at a fillin stashin ta git fullt up wid petrol. Them wes t'days afoor this self-service carry-on, when t'garridge lad wad gie this windscreen a bit wipe an' axe if ther wes owt else he cud deu fer thee.

[*yance* once, *gadgie* car, *'at* that, *them wes* those were, *afoor* before, *wad gie* would give, *axe* ask, *owt* anything, *cud deu fer thee* could do for you]

The Society meets at various places in the county and holds an annual church service in dialect. See CUMBRIC, DIALECT IN ENGLAND, LANCASHIRE, NORSE, NORTHERN ENGLISH, YORKSHIRE. [EUROPE, NAME, VARIETY].   S.E., T.MCA.

CUMBRIC [1950s: from medieval Latin *Cumbria*; a term introduced by Kenneth Jackson and increasingly favoured by scholars in preference to the terms of wider reference *British*, *Brittonic*, *Brythonic*. See CUMBRIA]. A Celtic language, akin to Old Welsh, spoken in southern Scotland and north-west England until early medieval times. Although there are no extant texts, adaptations of oral Cumbric have survived in early Welsh poetry attributed especially to the bard Aneirin, including the elegiac *Y Gododdin*, recounting a defeat at the hands of the Angles, probably at Catterick in Yorkshire. The original may have been composed in the 6c in or near Edinburgh. Most relics of Cumbric are place-names such as *Pennersax* in Dumfriesshire, whose Welsh equivalent would be *Pen y Sais* Englishman's summit. Some commentators consider that garbled echoes of Cumbric survive in the *Cumbric Score* or *sheep-counting numerals*, numbers of a sort used in Cumberland and West Yorkshire by men counting sheep, women counting stitches, and children in games. A. J. Ellis published 53 versions of these in 1877–9, and Michael Barry 70 versions in 1969. In Borrowdale in Cumberland, 1–10 was *yan, tyan, tethera, methera, pimp, sethera, lethera, hevera, devera, dick* (Welsh is *un, dau, tri, pedwar, pump, chwech, saith, wyth, naw, deg*). 'Fifteen' was *bumfit* (Welsh *pymtheg*). The Score was acquired from informants at second hand; apparently, no one has ever been found actually using it. There are arguments for assuming that it was introduced into Yorkshire later than the medieval Welsh period. The issue may never be resolved, but it is often claimed as something that has lingered on for seven centuries after Cumbric became extinct. See BRITISH, CELTIC LANGUAGES, WELSH. [EUROPE, LANGUAGE].   T.MCA., A.J.A.

CURME, George Oliver [1860–1948]. American grammarian and philologist, born in Richmond, Indiana, and studied classics at Indiana Asbury U. and the U. of Michigan where, under the direction of Calvin Thomas and George A. Hench, he developed an interest in German and linguistic research. After further study at DePauw U. (MA 1885, D.Litt. 1908) and the U. of Berlin, he taught at Jennings Seminary in Aurora, Illinois, and studied grammar. He later taught at the U. of Washington (1884–6), Cornell College, Iowa (1886–96), and Northwestern U., Evanston, Illinois, from which he retired in 1934. He held a guest lectureship in German at the U. of Southern California (1934–9). Curme received an honorary doctorate from Heidelberg (1926) for his *Grammar of the German Language* (1905), which differed from previous works by stressing usage. His *Grammar of the English Language* (two volumes: *Syntax*, 1931; *Parts of Speech and Accidence*, 1935) was systematic and detailed: he listed nearly 300 irregular weak verbs in seven classes and another 100 strong verbs in a variety of classes and subclasses; in discussing variation, he noted the substitution of a personal for a possessive pronoun among some African-American speakers in the South: 'He rolls *he* eyeballs.' Such distinctions make his *Grammar* a major reference for the development of AmE syntax. He also wrote *College English Grammar* (1925) and *Principles and Practices of English Grammar* (1946). [AMERICAS, BIOGRAPHY, GRAMMAR].   R.W.B.

CURRICULUM [17c: from Latin *curriculum* ('a little run or runner') a race or chariot, a course, from *currere/cursum* to run: compare *cursum* running, a run or race, a course (the ancestor through French of English *course*)]. A programme of study at an educational institution, usually consisting of a group of related subjects. Although the terms *curriculum* and *syllabus* are often synonymous (*The school's English curriculum/syllabus*), *curriculum* often has a wider reach: for example, the widely used term *curriculum development* refers to research work in developing many courses of study; the term *syllabus development* is not so common, and if used is more likely to refer to work within one subject only. In 1987, the British Conservative government established a *National Curriculum* for England and Wales (but not for Scotland and Northern Ireland, whose educational systems are separate and autonomous). The most centralized plan in British educational history, this curriculum consists of ten subjects common to all primary and secondary schools: three *core subjects* (English, mathematics, and science) and seven *foundation subjects* (geography, history, technology, a foreign language at the secondary level, art, music, and physical education). Any other subjects offered at a school (such as additional languages) are extracurricular, even if catered for by public examinations. There are also four assessment stages: ages 5–7, 7–11, 11–14, and 14–16. The syllabus for each subject is proposed by a working party, after consulting the *National Curriculum Council*, which consists of fourteen people from education, industry, and commerce. As a core subject, English has attracted considerable attention since 1987, including two documents presented by government-appointed committees, the Kingman Report (1988) and the Cox Report (1989). See *A Guide to English Language in the National Curriculum*, ed. John Harris & Jeff Wilkinson (Stanley Thornes, 1990). See COX REPORT, KINGMAN REPORT, LANGUAGE TEACHING, TEACHING ENGLISH. [EDUCATION]. T.MCA.

CURSING. The invocation of supernatural power against someone or something, explicitly (*God damn you!*) or implicitly (*Damn you!*, *Curse them!*, *May he rot in Hell!*). Any entity with the power of speech may curse: God himself may invoke his own awful power. Not only can God curse man, but man can curse God: 'And sad Sir Balaam curses God and dies' (Pope, 1732). The tribulation conjured up by curses may or may not be specified, and ranges from death and damnation through excommunication to more mundane and trivial penalties. It was perhaps through invocation that cursing came also to mean expressing any sort of ill will. The progress from *God damn you/it!* to *Damn you/it!* to *Damn!* is straightforward, and when the *Damn!* stage is reached, both supernatural and object are implicit. Only one step further and *Damn!* serves less to direct ill will towards an object than to give vent to anger; it has changed from wish to exclamation. The expression is, however, still called a curse, as are exclamations like (*Oh*) *hell!* and (*Oh*) *shit!* and such insults as Timon and Apemantus hurl at each other: *Apemantus* Beast! *Timon* Slave! *Apemantus* Toad! *Timon* Rogue, rogue, rogue! (Shakespeare, *Timon of Athens*, 4. 3). The extension of cursing seems as old as its specific sense; the view that the specific sense came first is based more on logic than on philology, since according to the *OED* its source, late Old English *curs*, is of unknown origin. See SWEARING. [STYLE, USAGE]. R.F.I.

CURSOR. See KEYBOARD.

CURTAILMENT. See BEHEADMENT AND CURTAILMENT.

CUT-GLASS (ACCENT). See RECEIVED PRONUNCIATION.

CUT SPELLING [1970s: coined by the Australian psychologist Valerie Yule]. A truncated version of English traditional orthography (TO), intended as a means of reforming the spelling of the language; it is marked by the elimination of letters that are not needed to represent pronunciation. From her research, Yule concluded that, when redundant letters are removed from the spelling of words, the differences between such 'cut spelling' (CS) and TO are visually less disturbing for the reader than an orthography regularized on phonographic principles. Subsequent analysis by the British linguist Christopher Upward has shown that most of the letters amenable to cutting are of three types: (1) Letters irrelevant to pronunciation, such as *b* in *crumb*, *c* in *scissors*, *g* in *foreign*, *gh* in *haughty*, *h* in *rhyme*, *l* in *could*, *p* in *receipt*, *s* in *island*, *w* in *whore*. (2) Vowel letters representing schwa before *l, m, n, r* in weak syllables in longer words, especially the endings in such pairs as *principal/principle*, *assistant/consistent*, *stationary/stationery* and such individual words as *burglar*, *teacher*, *doctor*, *harbour*, *murmur*, *injure*, *martyr*, AmE *center*/BrE *centre*. In such words, the indeterminate letter can be removed, conforming to the TO patterns in *feeble, spasm, hadn't, centre*, which in CS appear as *feebl, spasm, hadnt, centr*. (3) One letter in double-consonant pairs, as in the doublets *abridge/abbreviate*, the alternants *wagon/waggon*, the variations AmE *traveling*/BrE *travelling*, and such words as *accommodation* when compared with cognates in other languages, such as Spanish *acomodación*; writers commonly experience difficulty in remembering which letters to double in such words as *embarrass* and *harass*, *commit* and *omit*. The omission of redundant letters as defined above produces various effects in written English, as shown and claimed in the following exemplifying text:

Th readr first has th impression of text containing misprints, but reading is not dificlt, words can be ritn fastr, and texts require less space. Numerus variant patrns for th same sounds ar reduced to ther comn letrs; consistncy is acheved by paring down to a standrd cor, rathr than by dislocating traditionl grafic forms. Som comn words wich confuse lernrs ar regulxrized, so that *ar* paralels *bar*, not *bare*, *wer* paralels *her*, not *here*, *huch* paralels *much*, and *tuch* ceses to resembl *pouch*. In adition, many spelings revert to ther erlir, simplr forms: *al, wel, ful* (again as in Chaucers day) mach th simplr forms found in th compounds *also, welcom, fulfil*, wile *receit* again machs *deceit, conceit*, and *det, dout* ar again ritn without *b* as wen they first entrd english from french. Many difrnces between AmE and BrE ar harmnized: *centr* for both *center* and *centre*, *harbr* for *harbor* and *harbour*, *travld* for *traveled* and *travelled*, *kidnapd* for *kidnaped* and *kidnapped*, wile shortr AmE forms prevail in *ax, catalog, esthetic, fetus, mold, mustache*, and shortr BrE forms in *fulfil, skilful* (text supplied by Christopher Upward, 1990).

Proponents claim that CS represents an optimal combination of familiarity, phonographic consistency, economy of effort, and historical and international compatibility. Unlike most proposals for reforming English spelling, CS does not reflect any one accent, as nearly all redundant letters are redundant in all accents. When a dilemma of accent does arise, CS prefers the more economical form, and not a particular accent: for example, it prefers AmE *fertl* to BrE *fertile*, BrE *secretry* to AmE *secretary*, EngE *mor* to Scots *more*, and ScoE *thot* to EngE *thaut* for *thought*. In recent years, the system has been developed within the Simplified Spelling Society as a practicable concept for regularizing the spelling of English. See SIMPLIFIED SPELLING SOCIETY, SPELLING REFORM. [WRITING].   T.MCA.

CYNIC [17c: from Latin *cynicus*, Greek *kunikós* doglike, perhaps from the gymnasium called the *Cynosarges* (White Dog) where the first Cynic teaching was done, perhaps from the Cynics' slovenly habits, perhaps both]. (1) A Greek philosopher of the school founded by Antisthenes, a pupil of Socrates. The Cynics advocated virtue as the only good and self-control as the only means of achieving it. They were noted for a 'snarling' contempt for wealth and self-indulgence. The ascetic Diogenes, a pupil of Antisthenes, reputedly lived in a tub. (2) Someone inclined to doubt the good intentions of the human race and to express that doubt with biting irony. Lexicographers have sometimes introduced cynicism into their definitions, as when Johnson defined a lexicographer as 'a harmless drudge' (1755). The term *cynic's lexicon* is sometimes given to collections of such sardonic comments: Shaw in 1916, 'Assassination is the extreme form of censorship'; Tom Wolfe in 1980, 'A cult is a religion with no political power' (both listed in Jonathon Green's *The Cynic's Lexicon: An Unashamed Collection of Utterly Amoral Advice*, Routledge, 1984). See BIERCE, IRONY. [REFERENCE, STYLE].   T.MCA.

CYPHER. See CIPHER.

CYPRUS. Official titles: Greek *Kipriaki Demokratia*, Turkish *Kıbrıs Cumhuriyeti*, English *Republic of Cyprus*. An island country in the Eastern Mediterranean, and member of the Commonwealth. Capital: Nicosia. Currency: lira/pound (100 senti/cents). Economy: mixed. Population: 686,000 (1988), 747,000 (projection for 2000). Ethnicity: 78% Greek, 18% Turkish, 4% Armenian, Maronite, and others. Languages: Greek, Turkish (both official), and English widely used. From the 16c, Cyprus was part of the Turkish Empire, was ceded to Britain in 1878, and became independent in 1960. The UK retains sovereignty over the military bases of Akrotiri, Dhekalia, and Episkopi. Since 1974, the republic has been divided into Greek and Turkish areas that have little direct contact with each other. See ENGLISH, GREEK. [ASIA, NAME, VARIETY].   T.MCA.

D

D, d [Called 'dee']. The 4th letter of the Roman alphabet as used for English. It originated in the triangular Phoenician symbol called *daleth* (akin to Hebrew *dālāh*, 'door'), which was altered by the Greeks to form their *delta* (*Δ*), and later rounded to form Roman *D*.

Sound values. In English, *d* normally represents the voiced alveolar plosive. However: (1) The boundary between *d* and its close phonetic neighbours *t* and *th* is sometimes breached. Formerly, for example, there was variation between *d* and *th*: *father* and *mother* were until the 16c written *fader* and *moder*; *burden* and *murder* were until the 19c written *burthen* and *murther*. After voiceless consonants (with the exception of /t/), the past-tense inflection *d* is pronounced /t/: *sacked, touched, stuffed, sipped, hissed, wished, earthed, waxed*. (2) In AmE and AusE, intervocalic /t/ is typically voiced to /d/, making homophones of such pairs as *Adam/atom, ladder/latter*, and *waded/waited*. (3) When the sound usually represented by *y* follows a *d*, the two sounds may merge to produce a *j*-sound /dʒ/: *grandeur, procedure*. This is acknowledged in the colloquial spellings of *Acadian, Barbadian, Indian, soldier* as *Cajun, Bajan, Injun, sojer*.

Double *D*. Two *d*s occur: (1) In monosyllables beginning with a vowel: *add, odd*. (2) In many disyllables after a stressed short vowel: *madden, meddle, midden, shoddy, muddy* (but contrast *shadow, medal, widow, modest, body, study*). (3) In monosyllables containing a short vowel when followed by suffixes: *bed, bedder, bedded, bedding*. (4) When the Latinate prefix *ad-* precedes a root beginning with *d*: *addition, address, adduce*.

Variations on -ED. The regular past-tense inflection adds *-ed* to the verb stem (*sail/sailed, stucco/stuccoed*), or *-d* if the stem already ends in *e* (*love/loved, hate/hated, free/freed, sue/sued, face/faced, rage/raged*). However, there is significant systematic variation in both spelling and pronunciation. There are also irregular past-tense forms, some using irregular *t* alongside regular forms with *d* (*costed/cost, smelled/smelt*), some with *t* and without an *ed* equivalent (*caught, felt, left, lost, put, spent*), some using only the *d* of the base form (*fed, found, shed, slid, stood*, etc.), and some introducing *d* in an irregular way (*fled, had, heard, made, paid, said, shod, sold*, etc.).

After a single vowel letter pronounced short in a stressed syllable, a final consonant is normally doubled when *-ed* is added: *bat/batted, fit/fitted, commit/committed, refer/referred* (contrast *headed, hatched*, with multiple vowel or consonant letters). Final *-ic* becomes *-ick-* when *-ed* is added: *picknicked, trafficked*. Final consonant plus *y* changes *y* to *i*: *carry/carried, deny/denied, pity/pitied* (contrast *convey/conveyed*). This rule results in the single homographic past form *skied* from *to ski* and *to sky*. Words of more than one syllable, not stressed on the final syllable, do not normally double the final consonant (*offer/offered*), but there are exceptions. In BrE, for example, there is a subrule that unstressed final *-el* becomes *-elled* (*travel/travelled*), to which *paralleled* is an exception, whereas AmE follows the general rule (*travel/traveled*). Similarly, BrE writes *kidnapped* and *worshipped* (but *galloped* and *gossiped*), while AmE may have *kidnapped* or *kidnaped* and *worshipped* or *worshiped*. There is some uncertainty with verbs ending in *-s*, BrE tending to double (*bus/bussed, bias/biassed, focus/focussed*) and AmE tending to stay single (*bus/bused, focus/focused*). Publishing houses may have their own preferences: Oxford University Press in Britain favours *biased, focused*. In AmE *benefited* is the only form used; in BrE, although it is the dominant form, *benefitted* also occurs.

THE CAPITAL LETTER						THE SMALL LETTER				
EARLY FORMS				CURRENT FORMS		EARLY FORMS			CURRENT FORMS	
Phoenician	Greek	Etruscan	Roman (Latin)	roman	italic	Roman cursive	Roman uncial	Carolingian minuscule	roman	italic
△	◁Δ	◖	D	D	*D*	Ⳇ	⳧	ⅆ	d	*d*

Indicators of pronunciation. (1) In the past tense of a regular verb whose stem ends in a /d/ or /t/, an unstressed (that is, centralized) vowel is heard before the final /d/: *needed, preceded, waited, hated.* The same is true of an adjective distinguished from a past participle: *an agèd man* as opposed to *aged 30*; *a learnèd professor* as opposed to *learned English quickly.* This distinction is sometimes required in poetry for metrical reasons, when the appropriate pronunciation can be shown by means of a grave accent or an apostrophe. So, in Shakespeare's *Hamlet, damned* has two full syllables in *smiling, damnèd villain* (1.5), but only one in *A damn'd defeat* (2.2). (2) If pronounced /t/, the inflection was formerly often written *t*: in early editions of Shakespeare, the phrase *untimely ripped* was spelt *vntimely ript.* (3) In the 18c, especially in private writing, the suffix *-d* was often preceded by an apostrophe to indicate an omitted silent *e* (*ask'd, pass'd, shew'd*).

Silent D. (1) In a few words, when *d* precedes or follows *n*, *d* is commonly no longer pronounced: *handkerchief, handsome*, and (with the exception of ScoE) *Wednesday.* (2) The *d* of the Latinate prefix *ad-* is silent before *j*: compare the pronunciations of *ajar* and *adjacent.*

Digraph DG. In the combination *dg*, the *d* serves to mark or emphasize the soft *j*-value of the following *g* (*badge, judge*: contrast *bag, jug*), and is the equivalent of doubling a single letter.

Epenthetic D. (1) A number of words have an epenthetic *d* after *n*: *thunder* (from Old English *thunor*: compare German *Donner*), and *jaundice, astound, sound*, from Old French *jaunisse* (Modern *jaunise*), *estoné* (Modern *étonné*), and *soner* (Modern *sonner*). (2) The *d* in *admiral, advance, advice* was inserted in Early Modern English in the belief that words like these were from Latin and should therefore contain the prefix *ad-*, although the forms in which they had come from French did not exhibit it: compare French *amiral, avance, avis.* Quasi-Latinate spellings with *d* became conventional, and pronouncing the *d* followed, even where the inserted letter was etymologically spurious: for example, *admiral* derives from Arabic *amir* (commander), and *advance* from Latin *abante* (from before: compare Italian *avanti*). *Advice* is from Old French *a vis* (abstracted from the phrase *ce m'est a vis*: It seems to me), which can ultimately be derived from Latin *ad visum.* See ALPHABET, APOSTROPHE[1], EPENTHESIS, G, GRAVE ACCENT, HARD AND SOFT, LETTER[1], SPELLING. [WRITING].

C.U., T.MCA., E.W.

DACTYL [14c: from Greek *dáktulos* a finger: that is, three joints counted from the knuckle]. A metrical foot of three syllables (– ∪ ∪): long/ short/short in quantitative metre, as in Latin; strong/weak/weak in accentual metre, as in the English words *butterfly* and *frequently.* It is rare in English, but was the metrical foundation of classical narrative verse, as in the dactylic hexameters of Homer and Virgil. Tennyson used the dactyl in 'The Charge of the Light Brigade' (1854):

$$- \cup \cup \quad - \cup \cup$$
/ Theirs not to / make reply, /
$$- \cup \cup \quad - \cup \cup$$
/ Theirs not to / reason why, /
$$- \cup \cup \quad - \cup \cup$$
/ Theirs but to / do and die . . .

The form sometimes occurs in short light poems, as in A. A. Milne's: 'Christopher Robin goes *hoppity hoppity*' (1924). See FOOT, METRE/METER, SCANSION. [LITERATURE]. R.C.

DAGGER. See OBELISK.

DANELAW [From Middle English *Dane-lawe*, Old English *Dena lagu* Danes' law]. Also **Danelagh, Danelaga.** The system of law in the part of England ceded to Danish invaders in 878, and the area itself, roughly north and east of a line from London to Chester. In the mid-10c, Scandinavian kings maintained a Norse-speaking court at York, but the ordinary population, English and Danish, seems to have developed a simplified language for use in their daily contact. In the later 10c, the kings of Wessex established overlordship over the Danish settlers, who however retained control of local affairs. William of Malmesbury declared (c.1130) that the language north of the Humber and especially at York 'sounds so harsh and grating that we southerners cannot understand a word of it' and blamed this on the presence of 'rough foreigners' (*De Gestis Pontificum Anglorum*, Book 3, Prologue). A few legal and technical terms have entered the English language from the administration of the Danelaw: *law, bylaw, outlaw, riding.* See ANGLO-DANISH, DANISH, NORSE. [EUROPE, HISTORY]. P.C.

DANGLING PARTICIPLE. See PARTICIPLE.

DANISH [Middle English variant of *Denish*, Old English *Denisc*]. A Germanic language spoken in Denmark, in parts of Schleswig (North Germany), and mostly as a second language in Greenland and the Faroe Islands. It has been historically influential on English and Norwegian. In the 9-11c, Old Danish (Norse) was used extensively in England, especially in the Danelaw. Danish influence survives in the general vocabulary of English (such as the *sk-* words *sky, skill, skin, skirt, scrape, scrub*) and the dialect vocabulary of northern England and Scotland (*gate/gait* a road, *sark* a shirt), as well as in the unusual feature that the words *they*, *their*, *them*, *though*, *both* are all Norse. Danish place-names are common in the Danelaw, especially those ending in *-by* (farm, town), such as *Grimsby*, *Whitby*. During the four centuries of Dano-Norwegian union, the language of Copenhagen became the model for both countries. For a century after the dissolution of the union in 1814, the written language of most Norwegians was virtually identical with Danish. See ANGLO-DANISH, BORROWING, CARIBBEAN LANGUAGES, DANELAW, EUROPEAN COMMUNITY, GERMANIC LANGUAGES, INDO-EUROPEAN LANGUAGES, NORSE, NORWEGIAN, SCANDINAVIAN LANGUAGES. [EUROPE, HISTORY, LANGUAGE]. P.C.

DARK L. See L-SOUNDS.

DASH [13c: perhaps echoing a striking or beating sound]. The punctuation mark (—), used to indicate pauses and asides; it occurs singly, or in parenthetical pairs when the main sentence is resumed after the pause: compare commas and brackets. The main uses are: (1) To indicate an additional statement or fact, with more emphasis than is conveyed by commas or brackets: *She is a solicitor—and a very successful one as well*; *They say that people in the north are more friendly—and helpful—than people in the south*. (2) To indicate a pause, especially for effect at the end of a sentence: *They all came to see him—the man they had admired*; *There is only one outcome—bankruptcy*. (3) To add an afterthought: *She wore a red dress—a very bright red*. In print, the dash is usually represented by an *em rule* (as in the preceding examples), although some styles favour the shorter *en rule* with a space on either side. An em rule is about twice the width of an en rule, and about three or four times the width of a hyphen. An unspaced en rule is often used as a link in cases such as *1944-80* and *the London-Brighton line*, where it is equivalent to *to*. In writing and typing, it is difficult to maintain any distinction in appearance between these three marks; few people attempt to do so in writing, but in typing some writers use a hyphen with spaces to left and right, or two hyphens together (with similar spaces). Dashes are also used non-punctuationally to stand for omitted letters, or for a whole word; for example a coarse word in reported speech: '*D—n you all,*' *he said*. The dash is sometimes used as a replacement for quotation marks (inverted commas) in printed dialogue; for example, in the work of James Joyce, who disliked what he called 'perverted commas':

> —Who is that? said the man, peering through the darkness.
> —Me, pa.
> —Who are you? Charlie?

> —No, pa. Tom.
> (*Dubliners*, 1914)

See ANACOLUTHON, APOSIOPESIS, ASIDE, DIALOG(UE), DOT, EM, EN, PARENTHESIS, PUNCTUATION, RULE. Compare HYPHEN. [STYLE, WRITING]. R.E.A.

DATA. See CLASSICAL ENDING, INFORMATION.

DATE [13c: through French from Latin *data* (feminine) given, from *data Romae* given at Rome]. The dating of years and centuries in English follows the Christocentric calendar, which assumes that Christ was born in the year 1. His birth year is, however, often taken to be the year 0, informally referred to as *the year dot*. Earlier years are marked BC or B.C. (short for *before Christ*) and later years may or may not be marked AD or A.D. (short for Latin *Anno Domini* in the year of the Lord, that is, the Christian Era). The closer to the present time, the less likely the use of the letters. Traditionally, *BC* follows and *AD* precedes the year: *200 BC, AD 200*, but currently both often follow: *200 BC, 200 AD*. Some non-Christians prefer the letters *BCE* or *B.C.E.* (*Before Common Era*) to *BC* and *CE* or *C.E.* (*Common Era*) to *AD*. There has been little if any international pressure to create a more neutral dating system. For dates of the Muslim calendar, the letters *AH* or *A.H.* are used, short for Latin *Anno Hejirae* (in the year of the Hejira, that is, the Muslim Era, sometimes taken to be English *after the Hejira*, and referring to the date of Muhammad's flight from Mecca to Medina, AD 622).

The ordinal dating of centuries is either the fuller *the nineteenth century* or the more compact *the 19th century*, and attributively either *a nineteenth-century novel* or *a 19th-century novel*. In a work of reference, a century may be abbreviated as *19th c* or, as in this volume, *19c*. The dating of decades is variously *the 1990s, the 1990's, the 90s, the '90s, the 90's, the Nineties, the nineties*. The conventions for writing dates for days differ in the UK and US. Distinctive British forms are *15th July 1990* and *15th July, 1990*. A distinctive American form is *July 9, 1990*. Both varieties use *15 July 1990*. When the date is given wholly in numbers, the differences become greater: (UK) day, month, year, *15-7-1990* (the month sometimes given in Roman numerals) or *15/7/90*; (US) month, day, year, *7-15-1990* or *7/15/90*. Confusion may occur with low numbers, as in *2-3-1990*, which in Britain is 'the 2nd of March 1990' and in America is 'February 3rd 1990'. Months with more than three or four letters are sometimes abbreviated, with or without a point (*Sep, Sep., Sept, Sept.*). Consistency and clarity are important in such matters as the dating of foods and medicines: many favour giving the month as a word or abbreviation rather than as a number. See NUMERAL. [WRITING].   T.MCA.

DATIVE CASE [15c: from Latin *casus dativus* the case for giving]. A term in the case system of Latin and other inflected languages. The dative is the form of nouns, adjectives, pronouns, and other words to which something is given (the recipient or beneficiary of an action). The same meaning is often expressed in English by the *indirect object*, which has sometimes been called the dative. In the Latin phrase *Deo optimo maximo* (to God best greatest: 'to God who is the best, the greatest'), the words *deus, optimus, maximus* are in the dative case. See CASE[1], OLD ENGLISH[1]. [GRAMMAR].   S.C.

DEAD LANGUAGE. See CLASSICAL LANGUAGE, GREEK, LANGUAGE DEATH, LATIN[1].

DEAD METAPHOR. See METAPHOR.

DECAY. See PROGRESS AND DECAY IN LANGUAGE.

DECLARATIVE [16c: from Latin *declarativus* for the purpose of making clear, ultimately from *clarus* clear]. A term for the grammatical mood through which statements are made, in contrast with *imperative, interrogative*, and *exclamative*. Although *declarative* is often used interchangeably with *statement*, it is useful as a means of distinguishing the syntactic form of a sentence from its function: for example, the sentence *You will do as I say* is declarative in form, but functions as a command; the sentence *You're not going to tell me?* is declarative in form, but in intent and intonation is a question. See INDICATIVE, MOOD. [GRAMMAR].   S.C.

DECLENSION [15c: from Old French *declinaison* from Latin *declinatio/declinationis* leaning over. In classical grammar, all other cases are presented as leaning over or falling away from an upright nominative case]. A term used to describe the case system of nouns and other words in Latin and other inflected languages, in which endings change according to syntactic function: *regina* (queen, nominative case: subject of the sentence); *reginam* (accusative case: object of the sentence); *reginae* (genitive case: of a queen, queen's), etc. Nouns in modern English change only when they become plural or possessive, and are not complex enough to be tabulated in declensions. If a word can be included in a declension, it can be *declined* and is *declinable*. If it is not, it is *indeclinable*. See CASE, CONJUGATION, LATIN[1], OLD ENGLISH[1], PARADIGM. [GRAMMAR].   S.C.

DECLINE. (1) See BOOK, DETERIORATION, DISEASED ENGLISH, LANGUAGE CHANGE, LANGUAGE DEATH, PROGRESS AND DECAY IN LANGUAGE, SEMANTIC CHANGE, USAGE. (2) See DECLENSION.

DECONSTRUCTIONISM. See LITERARY CRITICISM.

DECORATIVE ENGLISH [1980s]. Also **atmosphere English, ornamental English**. Nontechnical terms for English used as a visual token of modernity or a social accessory on items of clothing, writing paper, shopping bags, pencil boxes, etc., in advertising, and as notices in cafés, etc. The messages conveyed are 'atmospheric' rather than precise or grammatical, as in 'Let's sport violent all day long'. Use of decorative English appears to centre on Japan, but has spread widely in East Asia and elsewhere. On occasion, a succession of versions of the same message can become less and less intelligible while apparently continuing to achieve the desired effect: for example, the message on a sports jacket made in Hong Kong was *Never put off til tomorrow what you can do today. Let's sport.* On a jacket made in Guangzhou province, China, however, the message became *neveriputbofftlhtomorohowhatyoucnotforyaetspot*, while on one made further off in Guangxi province it became *nnehirpitothuihdronjfemtyouovhreuorhwhehpt* (cited by Mark N. Broad, ' "The Good Feeling of Fine": English for Ornamental Purposes', *English Today* 26, Apr. 1991). See JAPAN. [ASIA, STYLE].   T.MCA.

DECORUM [16c: from Latin *decorum* seemliness, propriety, the neuter form of *decorus* seemly, fitting]. (1) Suitability and seemliness, especially in social life: *a sense of decorum*. (2) In rhetoric, and by extension literature, drama, and art generally, the doctrine of style that should be appropriate to a subject, genre, situation, or audience. The term is traditionally associated with the proper choice and use of three classical styles: the *grand style*, the *middle style*, and the *plain style*. The successful juxtaposing of different styles in the same work, such as high tragedy and low comedy in a Shakespearian play, has discouraged use of the term. Compare APPROPRIATENESS. [STYLE].   T.MCA.

DE-CREOLIZATION. See CREOLE.

DEDUCTION. See LOGIC, SYLLOGISM.

DEEP STRUCTURE. See CHOMSKY, MODEL, TRANSFORMATIONAL-GENERATIVE GRAMMAR.

DEFINING RELATIVE CLAUSE. See RELATIVE CLAUSE.

DEFINING VOCABULARY. (1) The words used in the creation of definitions, especially in a dictionary. (2) Also *restricted defining vocabulary*. A restricted list of words used in writing definitions for especially learners' dictionaries, as in C. K. Ogden's *The General Basic English Dictionary* (1940), which uses only 900 words (the 850 words of Basic English and 50 international terms), and the *Longman Dictionary of Contemporary English* (1978, 1987), which uses the *Longman Defining Vocabulary* of permitted senses of 2,000 words, whose consistent application was checked by computer. Ogden's criterion for selecting his words was logical and semantic, and emphasized utility and coverage. More commonly, the criterion is high frequency, as in the American tradition of Edward L. Thorndike and the British tradition of Michael West, from whose *General Service List* (1953) the Longman list was developed. See BASIC ENGLISH[1], DEFINITION, FREQUENCY COUNT, GENERAL SERVICE LIST, LEARNER'S DICTIONARY, THORNDIKE, VOCABULARY CONTROL, WEST. [REFERENCE, WORD]. R.F.I.

DEFINITE ARTICLE. The technical term for the word *the* when introducing a noun phrase, as in *the telephone in my office*. *The* is also used, in a correlative pair, with a comparative adjective and adverb to introduce a clause: *The more I exercise, the healthier I feel.* For fuller discussion, see ARTICLE[1]. [GRAMMAR]. S.G.

DEFINITION [14c: through French from Latin *definitio/definitionis* fixing limits]. A statement of meaning, especially in a work of reference, ranging from a usually brief *dictionary definition* that gives the meaning of a word, to a usually lengthier *encyclopedic definition* that gives information about a person, thing, or topic: *The Concise Oxford Dictionary* (1976) defines the entry *oersted* briefly as 'unit of magnetic field strength'; *The Random House Dictionary* (unabridged, 1987) offers a more encyclopedic version: 'the centimeter-gram-second unit of magnetic intensity, equal to the magnetic pole of unit strength when undergoing a force of one dyne in a vacuum'. Formally, the term to be defined is the *definiendum* (Latin: that which requires defining) and the defining statement is the *definiens* (Latin: that which defines). Nouns and many verbs and adjectives usually receive full definition treatment especially in larger dictionaries. For practical purposes, it is not useful to distinguish between the meaning of a name for an object or idea and a description of the object or idea that a word refers to. A definition of *Grimm's Law* might logically be 'a phonological law formulated by Jakob Grimm', but such a definition is not particularly helpful. Dictionary users need detail, as in:

the statement of the regular pattern of consonant correspondences presumed to represent changes from Proto-Indo-European to Germanic, according to which voiced aspirated stops became voiced obstruents, voiced unaspirated stops became unvoiced stops, and unvoiced stops became unvoiced fricatives: first formulated in 1820-22 by Jakob Grimm, though the facts had been noted earlier by Rasmus Rask (*Random House Dictionary of the English Language*, 1987).

Frames of reference. Definitions depend on experience. A definition of *snow* is more easily grasped by someone who has seen snow, but people familiar with the many types of snow in Arctic regions might find a general definition inadequate. No definition can meaningfully convey the meaning of terms like *mauve, puce, beige*, or even, for someone whose culture fails to distinguish them, the difference between *blue* and *green*. To describe *green* as the colour of foliage and *blue* as the colour of a cloudless sky is meaningless to someone whose culture and language do not allow for such distinctions. For native speakers of the major Western languages, however, such variations present few problems; definitions of colours can compare a shade like *puce* to one likely to be familiar. A definer tries to temper the definiens to a user's *frame of reference*, which is impossible to anticipate accurately: those who seek a definition of a scientific term, though possibly naïve in the sciences, might be expert in another field; similarly, a scientist is unlikely to look up a scientific term in a dictionary, but might seek a definition for a term in an unfamiliar field.

Defining the obvious. Simpler terms are often the most difficult to define: tables appear in the physical world in many forms, are made of every conceivable rigid material, may be of almost any shape, size, or height, and may be supported by one or many legs or suspended from above by a rope, chain, or cable. Although it might be an exercise in ingenuity to write a definition of *table* that anticipates all of these manifestations, its usefulness is questionable, for people can be assumed to know what a table is. There are other senses (specific to jewellery, architecture, parliamentary procedure, etc.) that merit treatment, but omitting the basic definition from a general dictionary is unthinkable, despite the fact that it may never be needed. Early lexicographers solved the problem of 'obvious' words by a simple expedient: in his *Universal Etymological Dictionary* (1721), Nathaniel Bailey defined *cat* as 'a creature well-known', *bread* as 'the staff of life', and *five* as 'V or 5'.

Circular definitions. Within a particular discipline, definitions need to be sophisticated; the definition of *muon*, an atomic particle, employs *electron*, justifiably assuming that the user already knows the word. Even if that is not so, dictionaries generally define each of the words used in framing definitions, so that the meanings of unfamiliar words can be traced to simpler, more familiar concepts. If definitions fail to do this, they are *circular definitions*: *alligator* defined as a kind of *crocodile* and *crocodile* as a kind of *alligator*. In a monolingual dictionary, because the terms in the language are defined in terms of the language itself, all definitions must be ultimately circular; it is the responsibility of the lexicographer to ensure that the circles are as large as possible and that there are enough signals at various points on the circle that make immediate sense to the user.

Definition by synonym and paraphrase. Some dictionary definitions provide one word or a small set of words close in meaning to the definiendum: Robert Cawdrey's *Table Alphabeticall* (1604), the first dictionary of English, regularly used synonyms to explain hard Latinate words: '*abrogate* take away, disanull, disallow'; '*manuring* dunging, tilling'; '*prompt* ready, quicke'. Definition by synonym is often used for grammatical words such as prepositions and conjunctions, and for certain kinds of adjectives, adverbs, and verbs. Some definitions paraphrase compound words and phrases, so as to make the relationships among their elements easier to grasp: *toothbrush* explained in an EFL dictionary as 'a brush for the teeth', *goatskin* as 'the skin of a goat'.

Definition by genus and differentia. Many nouns, especially those for flora and fauna, belong to taxonomic categories, whose scientific names may help in distinguishing them from one another: the often confused words *tortoise* and *turtle* are defined in *Webster's Third International Dictionary* as, '*tortoise* . . . a reptile of the order Testudinata: TURTLE—used esp. of terrestrial forms', and '*turtle* . . . a reptile of the order TESTUDINATA—used esp. of the more aquatic and esp. marine members of the order; compare TORTOISE'. Here, identical initial wording establishes that the words belong to the same *genus*, while the information following the dash sets forth the *differentiae* (Latin: distinguishing features). The same approach, without the taxonomic terms, and often with inconsistency of presentation, is widely used to establish the difference between words or indicate specific attributes: '*daffodil* plant with a yellow flower and long narrow leaves, growing from a bulb', '*tulip* bulb plant with a large bell-shaped flower on a tall stem' (A. S. Hornby, *Oxford Student's Dictionary of Current English*, 1978). Here, both items are plants, differentiated from other plants by an association with bulbs, and differentiated from each other in terms of colour and leaves

for one, and flower shape and stem for the other.

Non-defining formulas. In some instances, words whose meanings are considered self-evident are not defined at all: adverbs formed by adding *-ly* to an adjective can often be understood to fit into the pattern 'in a . . . manner' ('*precisely*: in a precise manner'). Such words are often 'run on' (listed at the end of the entry for the word on which they are formed): for example, adjectives formed by adding a common suffix to a noun: *clown* n. . . . *clownish*, adj.; *heliograph* n. . . . *heliographic*, adj. Many words that are regularly formed with *co-*, *re-*, *un-*, *under-*, and other productive prefixes are often listed without comment at the bottom of pages in the appropriate sections of the book, on the assumption that users can draw the right conclusions about their meanings either from experience or from nearby words that are defined. In many dictionaries, the number of such run-on and listed entries may be as large as half the total number of words listed as 'entries' by the publisher. See DEFINING VOCABULARY, DICTIONARY, MEANING, SEMANTICS. [NAME, REFERENCE, WORD]. L.U., T.MCA.

DEFOE, Daniel [1660?-1731]. Sometimes *De Foe*. English journalist and novelist, born in London of Flemish descent, son of a chandler, and best known for the novel *Robinson Crusoe* (1719). He sympathetically represented nonstandard varieties of English in works like *Colonel Jack* (1722) and *A Tour thro' Somerset* (1724-7), but in *An Essay upon Several Projects* (1702) proposed that England emulate the Académie française with an academy appointed 'to encourage Polite Learning, to polish and refine the English Tongue, and advance the so much neglected Faculty of Correct Language, to establish Purity and Propriety of Stile, and to purge it from all the Irregular Additions that Ignorance and Affectation have introduc'd'. Like other proposals for such an academy, Defoe's concentrated on the literary language, and like them had no practical outcome. See index. [BIOGRAPHY, EUROPE, HISTORY]. W.F.B.

DEGREE [13c: from Old French *degré* rank, relation, from Latin *de-* down, *gradus* a step]. (1) A category for items of language used to express relative intensity: *very much*, of a verb in *I admire them very much*; *highly*, of an adjective in *highly intelligent*; *very*, of an adverb in *very often*; *big*, of a noun in *a big fool*; *dead*, of a preposition in *They're dead against it*. Such intensifiers or words of degree are used with other words that are *gradable* (that is, on a scale of intensity). They may indicate a relatively high point, as above, or a relatively low point: *slightly*, *somewhat*, *hardly*, *a bit*. (2) Three types of comparison applied to gradable adjectives and adverbs: to a high degree (*bigger, biggest*); to the same degree (*as big as*), and with a preceding negative (*not so big as*); to a lower degree (*less big, least big*). Non-extreme forms may be followed by comparative clauses: 'Jeremy is taller *than his parents* (*are*)'; 'Naomi is less tall *than Ruth* (*is*)'; 'Doreen is as tall *as Leslie* (*is*).' Higher-degree comparisons may be expressed by inflections (the absolute or positive degree *happy*, the comparative degree *happier*, and the superlative degree *happiest*) or periphrastically, in combination with *more* for comparatives (*more happy*) and *most* for superlatives (*most happy*). Monosyllabic adjectives (*young, sad, small*) generally take inflections, polysyllabic adjectives (*beautiful*) periphrastic *more/most*. Many disyllabic adjectives take either form: *commoner/ more common, commonest/most common*. Most adverbs allow only periphrastic comparison (*happily/more happily/most happily*), but a few are suppletive: *badly/worse/worst*; *well/ better/best*). See PERIPHRASIS. [GRAMMAR].　S.G.

DEIXIS [20c: from Greek *deîxis* display, reference]. In linguistics, the function of an item or feature that refers to relative position or location (*here, there*) and point of reference (*me, you, them*). *I* and *you* are deictic because they refer respectively to speaker and person spoken to. The third-person pronouns may be deictic (as in *Look at her!*). *This* and *these* are deictic when pointing to objects in closer proximity to the speaker, in contrast to *that* and *those* for objects further away. Temporal deixis may be expressed through tense (*I speak the truth, I spoke the truth*) and through adverbs (*now, then, today, yesterday, tomorrow*). Interpreting deixis in utterances depends on the situation: the *I* in *I spoke the truth* varies according to speaker, but the *she* in *She spoke the truth* has normally been identified in a previous verbal context. See CONTEXT, DEMONSTRATIVE, SEMANTICS. [GRAMMAR, LANGUAGE, REFERENCE].　S.G.

DELBRIDGE, Arthur [b.1921]. Australian phonetician and lexicographer, born in Sydney, New South Wales, and educated at the U. of Sydney and U. of London. He occupied the foundation chair of linguistics at Macquarie U., Sydney (1967-85). His publications include: *The Speech of Australian Adolescents* (with A. G. Mitchell, 1965) and *The Macquarie Dictionary* (1981), of which he was chief editor. He chaired the *Australian Broadcasting Corporation's Standing Committee on Spoken English* (1970-85). See index. [BIOGRAPHY, OCEANIA, REFERENCE]. W.S.R.

DEMONSTRATIVE [14c: from Latin *demonstrativus* showing]. A term used in association with pronouns and determiners as an adjective and a noun: *a demonstrative pronoun*; *three demonstratives in one sentence*. A demonstrative usage indicates relationships and locations, such as between *this* (near the speaker and perhaps the listener) and *that* (not near the speaker, perhaps near the listener, or not near either). See DEIXIS, DEMONSTRATIVE PRONOUN, DETERMINER. [GRAMMAR].　S.C.

DEMONSTRATIVE PRONOUN. A pronoun that shows where something is in relation to speaker and listener. Standard English has four demonstratives, paired and with number contrast: *this/these* here, *that/those* there. Some dialects have three (*this, that, yon/yonder*) and Scots has *this, that, yon/yonder* and its variant *thon/ thonder*. The sets of three are comparable to Latin *hic* this near me, *iste* that near you, *ille* that over there. For some grammarians, the term covers the demonstratives however used; for others, demonstrative pronouns ('I like *that*', 'Give me some of *these*') are distinguished from demonstrative determiners ('I like *that* one', 'Who are *these* people?'). See DEIXIS, DEMONSTRATIVE, PRONOUN. [GRAMMAR].　S.C., T.MCA.

DEMOTIC [1810s: from Greek *dēmotikós* of the people, popular, plebeian]. (1) Of ordinary people and everyday language: 'I had consciously decided to try to be more demotic in speech, to talk about the heave-ho rather than the proximate cause' (Alan Watkins, 'A Slight Case of Libel', *Observer*, 17 June 1990); 'The vocabulary of my space-age hooligans could be a mixture of Russian and demotic English, seasoned with rhyming slang and the gipsy's bolo' (Anthony Burgess, *Sunday Times*, 28 Oct. 1990). (2) Vernacular, colloquial, or informal as opposed to classical, literary, or formal: *Demotic Greek*. (3) Demotic or vernacular speech: 'Yet US attitudes to UK actors in popular television seem far more inflexible than any social structure yet devised. You won't hear British regional accents: *Minder* and *Auf Wiedersehen, Pet* would need subtitles over here. In the great republic, only British rock stars are allowed to speak in the demotic' (Mark Steyn, *The Independent*, 10 Nov. 1990). Compare COLLOQUIAL, VERNACULAR. [LANGUAGE, STYLE].　T.MCA.

DEMY [16c: from French *demi* from Late Latin *dimedius* half. Pronounced 'de-MY']. (1) A size of printing paper, $17\frac{1}{2} \times 22\frac{1}{2}$ inches (44.5 × 57.15 cm). (2) A British size of writing paper, $15\frac{1}{2} \times 20$ inches (39.4 × 50.8 mm). (3) A US size of writing paper, 16 × 21 inches (40.6 × 53.4 mm). (4) Also *demy octavo*. A book size, $8\frac{1}{2} \times 5\frac{1}{2}$ inches. (5) Also *demy quarto*. An especially British book size, $11 \times 8\frac{5}{8}$ inches. See BOOK, OCTAVO, PAPER, QUARTO. [TECHNOLOGY].　T.MCA.

DENOTATION. See CONNOTATION AND DENOTATION.

DENOUEMENT, also **dénouement** [18c: from French *dénouer* to untie, ultimately from Latin *nodus* a knot]. The resolution of a plot. In tragedy, the classical term is *catastrophe* (through Latin from Greek *katastrophḗ* overturning). In the denouement, mysteries are solved, errors rectified, misunderstandings explained, and rewards and penalties allocated. Such 20c dramatists as Samuel Beckett and Harold Pinter avoid a denouement and leave the end of a play open or ambiguous. See ANAGNORISIS, DETECTIVE STORY, PLOT. [LITERATURE].   R.C.

DENTAL [16c: from Latin *dentalis* of the teeth]. In phonetics, a term referring to sounds like /θ/ (the *th* in *thirty*) and /ð/ (the *th* in *those*), made with the tip of the tongue in the region of the upper front teeth. See ARTICULATION, LABIAL. [SPEECH].   G.K.

DEPENDENT CLAUSE. See SUBORDINATE CLAUSE.

DERIVATION [14c: from Latin *derivatio/derivationis* drawing or pouring off, from *rivus* a stream]. (1) A process through which one word, phrase, or sentence is formed from another: passive sentences (*They were met by a friend*) are often said to derive from active sentences (*A friend met them*). (2) A process by which the forms and meanings of words change over centuries: English *nice* derives from Latin *nescius*. (3) A process by which more complex words are formed from less complex words: *purification* from *purify* from *pure*. Although information about the history of words may help in analysing their current forms, there is no necessary link between a word's etymology and its current form and meaning: although *pure* has a close formal and semantic link with its ancestor, Latin *purus*, the tie makes no difference to how *pure* is used in English; present-day *nice* (meaning 'pleasant' and sometimes 'precise') has no obvious association in form, meaning, or function with its ancestor *nescius* (which meant 'ignorant').

Etymological derivation. The term *derivation* itself derives from an analogy between language and a river, in which later forms flow from earlier forms: *pure* from *purus*, *nice* from *nescius*. It has traditionally been assumed that Modern English flows from Old English, that elements in English flow from languages which were earlier and more prestigious (Greek and Latin) or had power and prestige at the time when English was developing (Latin and French), that Latin, Greek, and the Germanic languages flowed from still earlier

languages, and that studying the history of languages helps one appreciate this flow. Comparably, the inflected forms of words in declensions and conjugations 'fall' or 'flow' from primary forms: in Latin, from the *nominative* in nouns, the *masculine nominative* in adjectives, and the *infinitive* in verbs. Caution is often advisable when establishing the history of a word: although *outrage* seems to derive straightforwardly from *out* and *rage* (and mean anger beyond the normal), it actually comes from Old French *oultrage*: compare Italian *oltraggio*. The prior stage is however conjectural; philologists have reconstructed a Latin **ultraticum* as the common ancestor of *outrage*, *oultrage*, *oltraggio*. It resembles comparable established usages, but has never been found in a text. In English, assumptions that *rage* is part of *outrage* have affected the use and meaning of the word, and as a result the reinterpretation of *outrage* as *out* and *rage* together has become a factor in the 'story' of the word. As a result, although the sound and look of *outrage* are not helpful in deciding its origin, they are relevant in a consideration of current meaning and use.

Morphological derivation. Time is different in everyday word-formation. Derivational morphology has two aspects: static, when analysing internal arrangement, and dynamic, when considering how the more complex emerges from the less complex. In static terms, *transformation* can be analysed into three parts, *trans* + *form* + *ation* (prefix, base, suffix). In dynamic terms, analysis can establish stages through which words develop: for example, from *form* to *transform* to *transformation*. How long the process takes (centuries or seconds) is a secondary matter; once such a flow or pattern exists, users do not usually concern themselves with how long any element in the pattern has existed, and once they have become accustomed to a new derivative like *transformational*, they do not usually think about the flow that produced it. Although many complex words are derived along only one flow or path (as with *pure—purify—purification*), more than one may exist. The path for *transformation* could be either *form—transform—transformation* or *form—formation—transformation*. Whatever path is followed, a new base for another possible derivative is formed: *pure* the base for *purify* which is the base for *purification* which then leads to *purificational* and if so desired to **purificationalism*. Although there is no theoretical limit, in practice usefulness, comprehensibility, and pronounceability decide the cut-off points: **antipurificationalistically* is well formed, but not very useful.

See DERIVATIONAL PARADIGM, EPONYM, ETY-MOLOGY, FOLK ETYMOLOGY, INDO-EUROPEAN ROOTS, LONG WORD, MORPHOLOGY, ROOT-CREATION, SUFFIX, WORD-FORMATION, WORD ORIGINS. [HISTORY, WORD].   T.MCA.

DERIVATIONAL PARADIGM. In linguistics, a pattern displaying the morphological derivation of complex words, such as *knowledge— knowledgeable*, *sand—sandy—sandiness*. All such words have a basic underlying pattern or analogy: as *sandy* is from *sand*, so *cloudy* is from *cloud*, *rainy* is from *rain*, etc. When pairs of words overlap (*norm—normal* with *normal— normalize*), a derivational string is formed. A paradigm is machine-like and specific. When bases are fed in, only certain forms emerge: *cloud* does not beget **cloudal* like *normal*; *norm* does not produce **normy*, like *sandy*. In English, the abstract vernacular paradigm $X—Xy—Xiness$ underlies such actual strings as *sand—sandy— sandiness*. A comparable Latinate paradigm beginning $X—Xal—Xally$ generates twelve items from bases such as *centre*: *central, centrally, centralism, centralistic, centralistically, centrality, centralness, centralize, centralizing, centralized, centralizer, centralization*. Such systems have two aspects, actuality and potentiality: derivatives are either already in use or are available for use. Whether all the forms available in a paradigm are used is a social rather than a structural matter. See DERIVATION, NEOLOGISM, PARADIGM, SUFFIX. [WORD].   T.MCA.

DERIVATIVE [15c: from Old French *derivatif*, from Latin *derivativus* led off]. (1) A word or other item of language that has been created according to a set of rules from a simpler word or item. (2) A complex word: *girlhood* from *girl*, *legal* from *leg-* (law), *legalize* from *legal*. (3) Of an essay, article, thesis, etc., and usually pejorative: depending for form and/or inspiration on an earlier and better piece of work. See DERIVATION, PLAGIARISM. [STYLE, WORD].   T.MCA.

DEROGATORY [15c: from Latin *derogatorius* detracting, dishonouring]. Disparaging and offensive, a term often used in dictionaries (usually abbreviated to *derog*) to label expressions that intentionally offend or disparage: *skinny* when used instead of *thin*; *lanky* rather than *tall*; AmE *ass-hole* for someone considered stupid, mean, or nasty; ScoE *teuchter* for a speaker of Gaelic; *wog* used by whites of someone with a brown or black skin, and occasionally in England for the French ('The wogs start at Calais'). See ETHNIC NAME, PEJORATIVE. [REFERENCE, STYLE].   T.MCA.

DESCENDER. See ASCENDER AND DESCENDER.

DESCRIPTIVE AND PRESCRIPTIVE GRAMMAR. Contrasting terms in linguistics. A *descriptive grammar* is an account of a language that seeks to describe how it is used objectively, accurately, systematically, and comprehensively. A *prescriptive grammar* is an account of a language that sets out rules (*prescriptions*) for how it should be used and for what should not be used (*proscriptions*), based on norms derived from a particular model of grammar. For English, such a grammar may prescribe *I* as in *It is I* and proscribe *me* as in *It's me*. It may proscribe *like* used as a conjunction, as in *He behaved like he was in charge*, prescribing instead *He behaved as if he were in charge*. Prescriptive grammars have been criticized for not taking account of language change and stylistic variation, and for imposing the norms of some groups on all users of a language. They have been discussed by linguists as exemplifying specific attitudes to language and usage. Traditional grammar books have often, however, combined description and prescription. Since the late 1950s, it has become common in linguistics to contrast *descriptive grammars* with *generative grammars*. The former involve a description of linguistic structures, usually based on utterances elicited from native-speaking informants. The latter, introduced by Chomsky, concentrate on providing an explicit account of an ideal native speaker's knowledge of language (*competence*) rather than a description of samples (*performance*). Chomsky argued that generative grammars are more valuable, since they capture the creative aspect of human linguistic ability. Linguists generally regard both approaches as complementary. See CHOMSKY, COMPETENCE AND PERFORMANCE, DESCRIPTIVISM AND PRESCRIPTIVISM, GENERATIVE GRAMMAR, LINGUISTICS, STRUCTURAL LINGUISTICS. [GRAMMAR, LANGUAGE].   S.G., J.M.A., T.MCA.

DESCRIPTIVISM AND PRESCRIPTIVISM. Contrasting terms in linguistics. *Descriptivism* is an approach that proposes the objective and systematic description of language, in which investigators confine themselves to facts as they can be observed: particularly, the approach favoured by mid-20c US linguists known as *descriptivists*. *Prescriptivism* is an approach, especially to grammar, that sets out rules for what is regarded as correct in language. In debates on language and education, enthusiasts for one side often use the label for the other side dismissively. See AUTHORITY, CORRECT, DESCRIPTIVE AND PRESCRIPTIVE GRAMMAR, MIS-, RULE. [GRAMMAR, LANGUAGE].   S.G.

DESKTOP PUBLISHING [1980s: coined by Apple Computers]. Short form *DTP*. The formatting, graphic design, editing, and printing of texts using microcomputer equipment that fits on a desk. The term is a misnomer in that it is a form of printing, not publishing, but is now firmly established; because of the relationship between editing and design on one hand and printing and making copies on the other (often for immediate circulation), it highlights the revolutionary nature of the development. The essentials are a word-processor program with a formatter for typographic commands, and a laser printer. Various computer languages such as *Tex* and *Scribe* specify input. The processors that interpret these computer languages can hyphenate words and justify lines. Other languages, such as *Postscript*, control the printer, using operations that define character shapes and position the characters in a line. See COMPUTER TYPESETTING, COMPUTING, EDITING, PUBLISHING. [MEDIA, TECHNOLOGY, WRITING]. M.L.

DETECTIVE STORY, also, more literary, **roman policier** [French: police novel]. A novel of crime and detection, in which the detective is usually a private person with a less intelligent assistant. The genre began in French with the novels of Émile Gaboriau (1832–73) and in English with Edgar Allen Poe's *The Murders in the Rue Morgue* (1841). Charles Dickens and Wilkie Collins had police detectives among their characters, but the first great British fictional detective was Conan Doyle's Sherlock Holmes in *A Study in Scarlet* (1887). Later writers include Edgar Wallace, Dorothy L. Sayers, and Agatha Christie in the UK, and Raymond Chandler, Dashiell Hammett, Ellery Queen, and Erle Stanley Gardner in the US. The story may be a *whodun(n)it*, in which the mystery is resolved in a startling denouement (usually in front of the assembled suspects), or may show the unmasking of an already identified criminal. The form generally offers little scope for characterization, except of the detectives through a series of stories. Traditional British detective fiction tends to be elegant and mannered, while American detective fiction tends to be tough, and often explores the underside of society. Such novels often use colloquial dialogue and slang. The genre has been adapted to cinema and television with marked success. See DENOUEMENT, STORY. [LITERATURE]. R.C.

DETERIORATION [16c: from Latin *deterioratio/deteriorationis* getting worse]. (1) An emotive term for language change seen as evidence of linguistic and social decline. (2) Also *pejoration*. A category of semantic change, in which the meaning of a word or phrase depreciates with time: *crafty* once meant 'strong' and ciates with time: *crafty* once meant 'strong' and now means 'wily'; *cunning* once meant 'knowledgeable' and now means 'clever in a sly way'. See DISEASED ENGLISH, LANGUAGE CHANGE, PROGRESS AND DECAY IN LANGUAGE, SEMANTIC CHANGE. [HISTORY, STYLE]. T.MCA.

DETERMINER [1930s]. A word class (part of speech) that determines or limits a noun phrase, showing whether a phrase is definite (*the, this, my*), indefinite (*a, some, much*), or limiting it in some other way, such as through negation (*no* in *no hope*). Determiners include the articles and words traditionally classified as kinds of adjective or pronoun. They precede adjectives: *many clever people*, not **clever many people*; *my poor friend*, not **poor my friend*. Most words that function as determiners can be used alone as pronouns (*this* in *Look at this picture* and *Look at this*) or have related pronouns (*every/everyone/everything, my/mine, no/none*). Some grammarians regard as determiners such phrases as *plenty of . . .* in *We have plenty of money*.

Determiners can be subdivided into three groups according to their position in the noun phrase: (1) *Central determiners*. These may be articles (*a, the* in *a storm, the weather*), demonstratives (*this, those* in *this day, those clouds*), possessives (*my, your* in *my hat, your umbrella*), some quantifiers (*each, every, no, any, some* in *each moment, every day, no excuse, any help, some clouds*). Such determiners are mutually exclusive and contrast with adjectives, with which however they can co-occur: *the best weather, any possible help, no reliable news*. (2) *Post-determiners*. These are used after central determiners and including numbers (*two, first* in *those two problems, my first job*) and some quantifiers (*many, several* in *your many kindnesses, his several attempts*). (3) *Pre-determiners*. These are used before central determiners, mainly referring to quantity. They include: *all, both, half* (*all this time, both your houses, half a loaf*), *double, twice* and other multiplier expressions (*double the money, twice the man he was, once each day, six times a year*), fractions (*a quarter of the price*), and *such* and *what* in exclamations (*Such a waste of money!, What a good time we had!*).

They can also be divided according to the countability of the nouns they co-occur with: (1) With singular countable nouns only: *a/an, each, every, either, neither*. (2) With singular countable and with uncountable nouns: *this, that*. (3) With uncountable nouns only: *much* and *little/a little*, and usually *less, least*. (4) With uncountable and with plural countable nouns: *all, enough, more, most, a lot, lots of*, and the primary meaning of *some, any*. (5) With countable plurals only: *a few, few, fewer, fewest, both, many, several, these, those*, and numbers. (6) With most common nouns: *the, no,* the possessives *my, your,* etc., and some *wh*-words (*whose roll/rolls/bread, by which date, whatever food you eat*). See PART OF SPEECH. [GRAMMAR].   S.C.

DEVIANT [14c: from Latin *deviare/deviatum* to leave the path]. In linguistics, a unit of language is deviant if it does not conform to rules formulated in terms of data or native-speaker intuitions. A deviant unit is *ill-formed* and is generally marked by a preceding asterisk (**Dan does not be happy*). A form may be deviant in one variety of a language but *well-formed* in another: *selt* or *sellt,* the past form of *sell* in Scots, as opposed to *sold* in standard English. A form can be acceptable to most users of a language but be deviant in a particular analysis because the rules cannot be formulated to include it. Similarly, an unacceptable form can be well-formed because the rules as formulated cannot exclude it. Some linguists consider the term socially loaded, especially in favour of standard usage, and do not use it. Compare ACCEPTABILITY, FIGURATIVE LANGUAGE/USAGE, GRAMMATICALITY, NON-STANDARD, STYLE (DEVIATION). [GRAMMAR, LANGUAGE].   S.G.

DEVICE [16c in this sense: from Old French *devis* a plan, from Latin *dividere/divisum* to separate]. A linguistic or literary formula that produces an effect, such as a figure of speech (metaphor, metonymy), a narrative style (first-person, third-person), or a plot mechanism (flashback, flashforward). Compare CONCEIT, FORMULA. [STYLE].   T.MCA.

DEVIL'S DICTIONARY. See BIERCE.

DEVOICING. In phonetics, the process by which speech sounds that are normally voiced are made voiceless immediately after a voiceless obstruent: for example, the /r/ in *cream* /kriːm/ and the /w/ in *twin* /twɪn/. Voice is slow to build up at the onset of speaking and fades at the end, so that voiced obstruents (stop and fricative consonants) are partly or wholly devoiced in initial and final position, as with the initial and final /d/ in *dead* /dɛd/ when spoken in isolation. See VOICE. [SPEECH].   G.K.

DEVON. See WEST COUNTRY.

DIACHRONIC AND SYNCHRONIC [20c: from Greek *diá* through, and *sún* together, respectively, and *khrónos* time]. Contrasting terms in linguistics, which make a distinction between the study of the history of language (*diachronic linguistics*) and the study of a state of language at any given time (*synchronic linguistics*). Language study in the 19c was largely

diachronic, but in the 20c emphasis has been on synchronic analysis. The terms were first employed by the Swiss linguist Ferdinand de Saussure, who used the analogy of a tree-trunk to describe them: a vertical cut was diachronic, a horizontal cut synchronic. [HISTORY, LANGUAGE].
                                      J.M.A.

DIACHRONIC LINGUISTICS. See DIACHRONIC AND SYNCHRONIC, HISTORICAL LINGUISTICS.

DIACRITIC [17c: from Greek *diakritikós* distinguishing]. Also **diacritical mark**. In alphabetic writing, a symbol that attaches to a letter so as to alter its value or provide some other information: in French, the acute and grave accents over *e* (*é, è*); in German, the umlaut over *a, o, u* (*ä, ö, ü*); in Spanish, the acute accent over *o* (*nación*) and the tilde over *n* (*mañana*). Some languages that have adopted and adapted the Roman alphabet use diacritics to represent values not covered by the basic letters: Czech, Polish, and Croat use them with both vowel and consonant letters to distinguish Slavonic phonemes not found in Latin. Pinyin, the Romanized script for Chinese, uses them to represent distinctions in tone.

Advantages and disadvantages. Diacritics are economical, especially as alternatives to digraphs (two letters serving to represent a single sound). They can be written by hand, but are prone to distortion, misplacement, and omission in the heat of writing. In print, they have the disadvantage of requiring additional characters in a font: until the 1982 reforms, Modern Greek required 13 varieties of the letter alpha to allow for all possible combinations of diacritics, but since then only two have been retained; in Vietnamese, diacritics give the letter *a* 18 variants. This disadvantage is made worse by the limited number of characters on typewriters, whose keyboards were originally designed for English and may require a complex use of keys to add diacritics to letters. There may also be difficulties in using diacritics in electronic word processing.

Uses. (1) Diacritics were widely used by medieval scribes to form abbreviations by which savings could be made in the time needed for copying and the cost of parchment. An *m* or *n* might be represented by a macron above a preceding vowel (*poetā* for *poetam,* the accusative form of Latin *poeta,* poet). Omitted letters might be indicated by a suspension sign: the apostrophe in *M'ton,* short for *Merton.* (2) In handwriting, diacritics may serve to distinguish letters, if the grouping into separate letters of several successive vertical strokes (*minims*) is unclear: for example, the 15 strokes of handwritten *minimum.* In Russian, two similar letters can be distinguished with subscript and superscript bars, respectively, and in German a hook will often be written over *u* to mark it apart from an adjacent *n* or *m*. (3) A diacritic in one language and alphabet may sometimes be converted into a letter in another: for example, the Greek rough breathing or asper (ʽ) has been transcribed into Roman letters as *h* (Greek ῥυθμός becoming Latin as *rhythmus*, English as *rhythm*, and αἷμα becoming the *haema-* or *hema-* in *h(a)ematology*).

Diacritics in English. The use of diacritics is minimal in English. Native speakers of English, accustomed to a largely diacritic-free script, sometimes object to diacritics on aesthetic grounds, complaining that they defile otherwise plain print with untidy clutter. There is, however, a range of diacritical usage in or related to English, including two everyday marks with diacritical properties: the dot and the apostrophe. These are so much part of the writing system that they are seldom thought of as diacritical.

The superscript dot. The dot in lower-case *i* originally served to mark the stroke as a separate letter from adjacent minims. It was retained in *j* when that form became an independent letter. See I, J.

The apostrophe. Although it does not mark a particular letter, the apostrophe has two diacritical functions: indicating the omission of a letter (*o* in *hadn't*) and possession (singular *boy's*, plural *boys'*). In the First Folio edition of Shakespeare (1623), only omission is marked (*'tis; The Lawes delay*). The current applications became established in the 18c. See APOSTROPHE[1].

Foreign marks. The use of non-native diacritics is generally kept to a minimum in English. It is optional in such French loans as *café* and *élite* (with acute accents), and is provided in others where the writer and publisher consider the provision necessary for accuracy or flavour: for example, German *Sprachgefühl* (with umlaut).

Diaeresis. In addition to use as the German umlaut, diaeresis marks are sometimes used on the second of two vowels to show that they are to be spoken separately and not as a digraph: *daïs, naïve.* See DI(A)ERESIS.

Marks used in transliteration. An internationally agreed set of diacritics is standard in the academic transliteration of texts from such sources as Arabic and Sanskrit script, in which the strict values of the original symbols must be shown. See ARABIC, SANSKRIT.

Stress marks. Diacritics are widely used in dictionaries to mark stress. A stress mark is usually superscript vertical, but is sometimes oblique.

Traditionally, such a mark has come after a stressed syllable (*demand'*), but currently, in conformity with IPA practice, the mark generally precedes the stressed syllable (*de'mand*). Frequently, two marks are used: a superscript for *primary stress*, a subscript for *secondary stress*: *'photo‚graph*. Such marks may be used in conjunction with standard spelling, in respelling systems, and with IPA symbols. See STRESS.

Marks used in dictionaries. In addition to stress marks, diacritics of various kinds are commonly used as aids to pronunciation and word-division in dictionaries: for example, to mark vowel quantity (the 'long' vowel *ā* marked with a macron, the 'short' vowel *ă* marked with a breve) and to indicate syllabification, as with the medial dot in *bath·room*. See LONG AND SHORT, SYLLAB(IF)ICATION.

Diacritics as teaching tools. Systems using diacritics have been devised for teaching purposes in English: (1) John Henry Martin's *Writing to Read* (1986) encourages children to write English phonetically, representing the long values of the vowel letters with a macron, so that *mate, meet, might, moat, moot* can be written *māt, mēt, mīt, mōt, mūt*. (2) Thomas R. Hofmann advocates (1989) a system that adds diacritics to the conventional spelling of words to indicate the pronunciation of English vowels to foreign learners; he would annotate a sentence something as follows: *à lănguăge stūdĕnt mŭst fāce dĭfferĕnt prōnŭncîātiōns*.

See ACCENT, ACUTE ACCENT, APOSTROPHE[1], BREVE, CEDILLA, CIRCUMFLEX, DI(A)ERESIS, DOT, GRAVE ACCENT, I, INTERNATIONAL PHONETIC ALPHABET, J, MACRON, PHONETIC TRANSCRIPTION, POINT, TILDE, TRANSLITERATION, UMLAUT. [EDUCATION, WRITING]. C.U.

DIAERESIS BrE, **dieresis** AmE [17c: through Latin from Greek *diairesis* division]. A diacritic consisting of two points set over a vowel, as in *ä, ë*. In English, it indicates that a vowel that might otherwise be silent is to be sounded (as in *Brontë*) or that the second vowel of a pair is to be sounded separately (*naïve, coöperate*). Forms of spelling that might once have had a diaeresis or a hyphen are currently often written and printed without either: *Bronte, naive, cooperate*. See DIACRITIC, UMLAUT. [WRITING]. W.W.B.

DIAGONAL. See OBLIQUE.

DIALECT [16c: from French *dialecte*, Latin *dialectus*, Greek *diálektos* conversation, speech, debate, way of speaking, local language, style]. A general and technical term for a form of a language: *a southern French dialect; the Yorkshire dialect; the dialects of the United*

States; Their teacher didn't let them speak dialect at school, but they spoke it at home; It's a dialect word—only the older people use it. Although the term usually refers to regional speech, it can be extended to cover differences according to class and occupation; such terms as *regional dialect, social dialect, class dialect, occupational dialect, urban dialect,* and *rural dialect* are all used by linguists. In addition, the extracted element *lect* has become a term for any kind of distinct language variety spoken by an individual or group, with such derivatives as *acrolect* (a high or prestigious variety), *basilect* (a low or socially stigmatized variety), *mesolect* (a lect in a socially intermediate position between these two). See LECT.

Dialect, language, standard. Most languages have dialects, each with a distinctive accent, grammar, vocabulary, and idiom. Traditionally, however, dialects have been regarded as socially lower than a 'proper' form of the language (often represented as the language itself), such as *the King's* or *Queen's English* in Britain, and *le bon français* in France, or in general terms *the standard language.* Such a variety also has regional roots, but because it developed into the official and educated usage of a capital like London or Paris, it tends to be seen as non-regional, often as supra-regional, and therefore not a dialect as such. Certain processes create a social and linguistic distance between this variety and the dialects of a language: degrees of standardization in accent, grammar, orthography, and typography; its aggrandizement through the development of a literary canon and use as the medium of education and literacy; and social empowerment through its use by the governing, cultural, and scholarly élite. Many users of a standard variety have tended to look down on dialect speakers as more or less 'illiterate' and teachers have often sought to impose the standard throughout a country and eliminate or greatly reduce all other 'deviant', 'low', or 'vulgar' forms, with the occasional exception of some limited 'good' dialect. Such dialect is usually rural, seen as part of a romantic folk tradition or the vehicle of a favoured but unconventional writer (usually a poet, such as Robert Burns in Scotland). As a result of such factors, there is a long-standing tension among such words as *dialect, standard,* and *language.* See STANDARD.

A dialect continuum. During the 19-20c there has been considerable study of dialects in their own right and in relation to the standard variety of a language. As a result of this study, philologists and dialectologists generally regard a dialect as a historical subtype of a language and a language as the aggregate of the features of its dialects.

Within a language, there is usually a *dialect continuum*: speakers of Dialect A can understand and be understood by speakers of Dialect B, and C by B, and so on, but at the extremes of the continuum speakers of A and Z may be mutually unintelligible. The A and Z communities may therefore feel justified in supposing or arguing that A and Z are different languages. If politics intervenes and the speakers of A and Z come to be citizens of different countries (as with Spanish and Portuguese, or Swedish and Danish), the dialects may well be socially revalued as 'languages' (in due course with their own dialects and standard variety). Despite their differences, dialects have more shared than differing features, and those in which they agree (phonological, syntactic, lexical, idiomatic, etc.) serve as the defining core of a language, while the clusters of differences serve as the defining cores of the various dialects. Thus, a language X that has dialects A, B, C, D, E, may have 15 features, 12 of which are shared by A, B, C, 10 by B, C, D, 11 by B, D, E, and so forth. Perhaps only 8 features are common to all five. If they are, they form the core or common features of X, to which may be added additional features acquired through the conventions necessary for a standard language.

The evolution of dialects. Using a biological analogy, dialects can be described as the result of evolutionary speciation. The tendency of all languages to change in one detail or another and so develop dialects is restrained only by the need of communication between speakers, and so preserve a common core. Written forms, accompanied by the inculcation of a standard by the social and educational élites of a nation or group of nations, slow the process of change but cannot prevent it. Dialects are in fact often less changeable than the standard; their speakers tend to live in stable communities and to conserve forms of the language which are 'older' in terms of the development of the standard. Such a standard, however, is in origin also a dialect, and in the view of some linguists can and should be called the *standard dialect* (although for many this phrase is a contradiction in terms). Dialects prevail regionally while the standard is the usage of the nation at large, or at least of its most prominent and dominant representatives. As a consequence, many native speakers of a dialect may learn the standard as a secondary variety of their own language: see TESD.

The distribution of dialects. Geographically, dialects are the result of settlement history. As populations increase and spread out, they generally follow the natural features of the land. The sea and rivers serve as both boundaries and roadways. Lowlands tend to be settled first and mountains may separate groups of settlers. Dialect development can be understood to some extent in relation to topography: where populations can communicate easily, dialectal differences develop more slowly than where they lose immediate (or all) contact. An effective method of studying such matters is the science of *linguistic geography*. Individual features (sounds, words, grammatical forms, etc.) can be displayed on maps showing where one or another feature prevails in use and where competing forms are found. Lines on a *dialect map* outline the area within which any form is regularly used. Alternatively, the differing features may be shown on maps with dots or other symbols, giving a visual dimension to the data. Certain features of dialect can also be seen in relation to social factors not necessarily connected with geography. The type of language one speaks (a *social dialect* or *sociolect*) depends on community, family background, occupation, degree of education, and the like. Where a standard form has become established, the tendency is to consider it 'right' and to denigrate other varieties, whose only fault may be that they are out of style in the mainstream of a language. Distinctive dialects are most fully preserved in isolated areas (along sea coasts, on islands, in mountain areas) where they are little influenced by outsiders and the population is relatively self-sustaining. The dialects of large cities, however, run the social gamut of the language, with outside features being brought in and new features being created more or less continuously.

Autonomy and heteronomy. Max Weinreich's often-quoted dictum, 'a language is a dialect with an army and a navy', attests the importance of political power and the recognized sovereignty of a nation-state in the recognition of a variety as a language rather than a dialect. Situations in which there is widespread agreement as to what constitutes a language arise through the interaction of social, political, psychological, and historical factors, and are not due to any inherent properties of the linguistic entities referred to by such names as *English* and *French*. Jack Chambers and Peter Trudgill in *Dialectology* (1980) distinguish between *autonomous* and *heteronomous* speech varieties as alternative labels to *language* and *dialect*. A language is an autonomous speech variety which may have a number of other varieties heteronomous to it: that is, dependent on or subordinate to it. Relationships of autonomy and heteronomy may change, often in response to changing political fortunes and national borders. The language now called *Afrikaans* became autonomous when in the 1920s it was standardized and recognized as an independent

language rather than a dialect of Dutch. Conversely, a language variety may lose its autonomy, as Scots did, when it ceased to function as the standard language of the Scottish court after the Union of the Crowns with England in 1603.

See ACCENT, ACROLECT, AMERICAN DIALECT SOCIETY, BASILECT, CARIBBEAN ENGLISH, DIALECT IN AMERICA, DIALECT IN AUSTRALIA, DIALECT IN CANADA, DIALECT IN ENGLAND, DIALECT IN IRELAND, DIALECT IN SCOTLAND, DIALECT IN SOUTH AFRICA, DIALECT IN WALES, DIALECTOLOGY, DIALOG(UE), DIGLOSSIA, ELLIS, ENGLISH, ENGLISH DIALECT DICTIONARY, ENGLISH DIALECT SOCIETY, HISTORY OF ENGLISH, ISOGLOSS, LANGUAGE, LECT, LINGUISTIC ATLAS, LINGUISTIC/DIALECT GEOGRAPHY, MESOLECT, NON-STANDARD, ORTON, PATOIS, SOCIOLECT, SOCIOLINGUISTICS, STANDARD, STANDARD DIALECT, SUB-STANDARD, TESD, VARIETY, VERNACULAR, WRIGHT. [LANGUAGE, VARIETY].   F.G.C., S.R., T.MCA.

Cheshire, Jenny. 1982. *Variation in English Dialect: A Sociological Study*. Cambridge: University Press.
——, Edwards, Viv, Münstermann, Henk, & Weltens, Bert (eds.). 1989. *Dialect and Education: Some European Perspectives*. Clevedon & Philadelphia: Multilingual Matters.
Edwards, Viv, Trudgill, Peter, & Weltens, Bert (eds.). 1984. *The Grammar of English Dialect: A Survey of Research*. London: Economic and Social Research Council.
Hughes, A., & Trudgill, P. 1979/87. *English Accents and Dialects: An Introduction to Social and Regional Varieties of British English*. London: Edward Arnold.
Trudgill, Peter. 1975. *Accent, Dialect, and the School*. London: Edward Arnold.
——. 1986. *Dialects in Contact*. Oxford: Basil Blackwell.

DIALECTIC [14c: from Latin *dialectica*, Greek *dialektikḗ* (*tékhnē*) (the art or craft) of argument]. (1) Also *dialectical*. Relating to (the nature of) logical argument. (2) Also *dialectical*, and more commonly *dialectal*. Relating to dialect. (3) Logical argument, especially as a means of investigating or uncovering the truth of a theory or a point of view. (4) The association or interaction of ideas, forces, arguments, etc., that conflict and compete. (5) Often *dialectics* (with a singular verb). The arguments for *dialectical materialism*, especially as developed by Karl Marx, which begin from a position of accepting the fundamental priority of material existence. (6) In the philosophy of Immanuel Kant, a fallacious system of metaphysics that arises from attributing objective reality to one's perceptions of external objects. See ARGUMENT, LOGIC. [LANGUAGE].   T.MCA.

DIALECT IN AMERICA. While early travellers were inclined to praise the 'purity' and 'uniformity' of English in colonial North America, later visitors identified distinct dialects in the Yankee North and the plantation South. In modern times, a neutral spoken variety of AmE is widely held to be used by national news presenters, while broadcasters who deliver weather and sports information are likely to represent one or another localized variety, since their domains of reporting are less serious. In this lore, a kind of *Network Standard* is regarded as embodying prestige norms despite the evident regional features in the best-known news presenters. There is no evidence that listeners are much influenced by the linguistic style and preferences of these broadcasters. Ideas about varieties of AmE are remarkably consistent across communities. New Yorkers know that their English is regarded as 'unrefined' or 'rough' by people outside the City, but this realization has had only a minor influence on the New York dialect. Similarly, speakers from the Ozark mountains generally evaluate their speech as 'hillbilly' or 'poor', but most show little inclination to alter it, since the positive consequences of its local use outweigh these negative characterizations. Migrants to new areas may retain their home variety and, if there is a community to support it, that variety may pass from one generation to the next, as inland Northern has done in the larger cities of Georgia and Alabama, or as the sounds of eastern Kentucky have affected the speech of parts of Chicago and Detroit.

Americans tend to think that varieties of English are more determined by region than by any other factor that shapes usage, such as age, ethnicity, gender, and social class. A long-remembered radio programme of the 1950s, *Where Are You From?*, conducted by the linguist Henry Lee Smith Jr., sustained the idea that each region of AmE is highly distinctive. Scholars who have investigated the matter have been influenced by the theory of dialect geography formulated in the 19c by A. J. Ellis for England, by Jules Gilliéron and Edmond Edmont for France, and by Georg Wenker for Germany. As a result, investigations have presumed the idea of long-settled and stable regions, an idea appropriate for Europe but less apt to the more recent and fluid settlement patterns of the US. Even so, AmE dialects are conventionally treated under four broad geographical headings: North, Coastal South, Midland, and West. See AMERICAN ENGLISH, AMERICAN LITERATURE.

The North. The Northern dialect, stretching from New England and New York westward to Oregon and Washington, was shaped by migration from the 17c colonial settlements in Boston and New York. While the population of the region was greatly enlarged by waves of migration (in the 1850s from northern Europe, especially Scandinavia and Germany, in the 1890s from eastern and southern Europe, and in the 1930s from the American South), the northern metropolitan areas are relatively uniform (Buffalo, Cleveland, Detroit, Chicago, and Minneapolis). Both Boston and New York English have changed in ways not followed in their daughter cities to the west; despite their internal diversity, however, both Boston and New York remain distinctly Northern. See BOSTON, CANADIAN ENGLISH, NEW ENGLAND, NEW YORK.

Northern pronunciation. (1) The most noticeable difference within the region is that New York and New England east of the Connecticut River are non-rhotic areas, while the western portion of the North is rhotic. Linking *r*, common in many non-rhotic dialects of English, occurs in New England in expressions like *the idea/r of it*. (2) The Northern dialect lags behind Midland and Western varieties in the vowel merger that makes homophones of *cot* and *caught*: in New England, where the merger is beginning to occur, speakers select the first vowel; in the Midland and West, the second vowel is used for both. (3) *Grease* tends to rhyme with *lease* in the North and West, rhyming with *freeze* elsewhere. (4) In Northern speech, *matter* and *madder* are often near-homophones.

Northern grammar. (1) A distinctive syntactic feature is *all the* + an adjective in the comparative degree: *That's all the farther I could go* (That's as far as I could go). (2) *Dove* as the past tense of *dive* is apparently a North American invention by analogy with *drive/drove* and *weave/wove*. Widely attested in Northern and in CanE, *dove* is holding its own in its historic territory and spreading in AmE. (3) *Had ought* and *hadn't ought*, while more common in less formal contexts, are Northernisms for *ought* and *ought not*, though the usage has spread elsewhere: 'If you don't like people, you hadn't ought to be in politics at all' (Harry S Truman). (4) The Northern term *cellar* (basement) appears in a characteristic prepositional phrase *down cellar*: *Won't you go down cellar and get some potatoes?*

Northern vocabulary. Lexical usage provides the clearest evidence of the unity of the Northern region. In comparison to other varieties of AmE, Northern does not show many survivals of words or senses that have become archaic in BrE. The following terms are known elsewhere in the US and some are used for nationally distributed products, but they form a cluster that defines the Northern region: *American fries* boiled potatoes sliced and then fried in a pan, *bismark/danish* sweet pastry, *bitch* to complain, *bloodsucker* a leech, *cabbage salad* coleslaw, *comforter* a heavy quilt, *cowboy* a reckless driver, *grackle* a kind of blackbird, *ice-cream social* a gathering of people for refreshments, often to raise money for a worthy cause, *nightcrawler* a large earthworm, *pitch* the resin of coniferous trees, *sub(marine)* a sandwich prepared on a long roll, containing meat, cheese, and other ingredients, *sweet corn* maize grown for human consumption, *teeter-totter* a see-saw. Other languages have contributed to the Northern wordstock: *babushka* a head scarf (Polish and Russian), *cruller* a small fried sweet cake (Dutch), *frankfurter/forter, frankfurt/fort, frank* a cooked sausage, hot dog (German), *quahog* a thick-shelled edible clam (Narraganset), *schnozzle* nose (from Yiddish).

The Coastal South. Historically, the Coastal Southern dialect centres on the Atlantic port cities of the states of Virginia, the Carolinas, and Georgia, blending westward along the Gulf Coast into Texas. These areas are distinct both from the North and from their own hinterlands, whose dialect has conventionally been labelled *South Midland*. Coastal Southern was formed in a time of plantation and ranch agriculture, an economy that required large-scale operations, while the generally hillier interior regions were typified by villages and farms often close to the subsistence level. Plantation agriculture required an extensive labour force to grow rice, tobacco, and cotton, three early cash crops in America, and large numbers of Africans were enslaved to tend them. While the extent of African influence on Southern AmE remains a subject for debate, it is generally agreed that African influences remain in *Gullah*, a creole spoken on the offshore islands of South Carolina and Georgia. See APPALACHIAN ENGLISH, BLACK ENGLISH VERNACULAR, CAJUN, GULLAH, NEW ORLEANS, SOUTH (THE), SOUTHERN ENGLISH, SPANISH, TEXAS.

Southern pronunciation. (1) Coastal Southern is non-rhotic. While non-rhotic Northerners employ a vowel in place of historic *r* (in New England, seaboard New York, and New Jersey north of Philadelphia), many Southerners use the previous vowel alone, making *door* rhyme with *doe* and *torn* with *tone*. Linking *r* is rare. (2) The same tendency for diphthongs to become monophthongs is a related Southern feature, so that *hide* is a near rhyme of both *hod* and non-rhotic *hard*. On the other hand, Southern and Midland AmE add a vowel not used elsewhere in words like *loft* which results in a near rhyme with *lout*. (3) Some word-internal consonant clusters can be captured by such spellings as *bidness* (business) and *Babtist*

(Baptist). (4) Merger of vowels in *pin* and *pen*, *since* and *cents* (to the vowel of the first in each pair) is a Southern feature that is spreading elsewhere.

Southern grammar. (1) A feature of the region is *all the* + adjective in the positive degree: *That's all the fast I can run* (That's as fast as I can run). (2) Though more common in Black than White speech (and more common among men and the young), the use of invariant *be* is especially Southern: *She be here tomorrow*; *I be pretty busy*; *That land don't be sandy*. (3) Coastal Southern and Upper South are typified by double modals: *She might can do it*; *Could you may go?* (4) These areas also share a tolerance for *ain't* in informal contexts, though *ain't* is the universal shibboleth in AmE and especially stigmatized in the North. In the Coastal and Upper South, degrees of stigma attach to *ain't* increasingly from the set phrase *ain't I?*, to its use for *are not* (*They ain't here*), to its use for *have not* (*You ain't told us yet*).

Southern vocabulary. The complex settlement history of the South is evident in cultural and linguistic differences between the coastal plains and the hill country. Much of the distinctive coastal vocabulary consists of expressions that have become archaic in other varieties of English: *all-overs* feelings of uneasiness, *antigoglin* askew, slantwise, *(ap)preciate it* thank you, *bank* a storage heap of potatoes, other vegetables, or coal, *branch* a brook, stream, *carry* escort, *firedogs* andirons, *gullywasher* a violent rainstorm, *hand* a farm worker, *hull* the shell of a nut, *kinfolk* relatives, *lick* a sharp blow, *Scat!* Gesundheit! Bless you!, *slouch* a lazy or incompetent person, *squinch* to squint. Other languages have contributed to Southern: *hominy* hulled kernels of corn/maize, *terrapin* a turtle (the Amerindian languages of Virginia and used more in the South than elsewhere); *cooter* a turtle, *gumbo* soup thickened with okra pods (the languages of West African slaves); *armoire* wardrobe, *bayou* small creek or river, *jambalaya* a stew made with rice and various meats, *lagniappe* a small gift given by a merchant to a customer (the French of Louisiana). Farther west, there is Spanish influence: *arroyo* a brook or creek, *llano* an open, grassy plain, *riata* lariat, lasso, *vaquero* cowboy.

The Midland. Between Northern and Coastal Southern is a region that has been subject to much dispute. Some scholars have treated it as a unified area divided into North and South Midland; others emphasize its affiliation with its neighbours and describe it as *Lower North* and *Upper South*. The term *Midland* emphasizes the settlement pattern that flowed from Philadelphia in two directions: one, westward through

Pennsylvania into Ohio, Indiana, and Illinois; the other, south-west into the hill country of Kentucky, Tennessee, the interior of the Southern coastal states, Missouri, and Arkansas. The south-western direction of migration brought settlers into contact with the transportation routes northward from New Orleans along the Mississippi, Arkansas, and Ohio rivers, and these contacts left enduring traces on the dialect.

Midland pronunciation. (1) In common with other AmE dialects west of the Atlantic coast, Midland is rhotic. (2) Philadelphia, the only rhotic city on the Atlantic seaboard, is the focal area for Midland, and its dialect has traditionally influenced the hinterland, including Pittsburgh, Columbus, Indianapolis, Springfield, and St Louis. Thus, the boundary between the now obsolescent Northern pronunciation of *creek* (rhyming with *trick*) meets the Midland *creek* (rhyming with *seek*) along an east-west line running parallel to the Pennsylvania migration routes. (3) The merger of vowels in *tot* and *taught* begins in a narrow band in central Pennsylvania and spreads north and south to influence the West, where the merger is universal. (4) In the Ohio River valley westward to Missouri, the vowel of *itch* makes a near rhyme with *each*, so that *fish* and *television* have the sound of the vowel in *meek*. (5) Another Midland vowel is found in *bit* and *hill*, with a diphthong resembling the non-rhotic pronunciation of *beer*. That pronunciation is beginning to spread among younger speakers in the inland North.

Midland grammar. (1) Though increasingly archaic, *a-* prefixation to verbs ending in *-ing* is a well-known Midland feature: *She went a-visiting yesterday*; *They were a-coming across the bridge.* (2) The use of *anymore* in the sense of 'nowadays' (and without the requirement of a prior negative) is spreading to other regions from a Midland base: *My aunt makes hats all the time anymore*; *We use a gas stove anymore.* (3) Regions of the Midland influenced by the German settlements of east-central Pennsylvania employ *all* to refer to a supply of food or drink that has run out: *The pot roast is all* (elsewhere *all gone*).

Midland vocabulary. (1) Distinctive terms for this region include: *blinds* roller window shade, *fishing worm* earthworm, *mango* sweet or bell pepper, *woolly worm* a caterpillar. (2) As with the other regions, some formerly limited usages have come into more general use: *bucket* pail, *hull* to remove the outer covering of a bean, *off* as in *I want off at the next bus stop.* (3) The isolation of the southern part of the Midland area, its poor soil and chronic poverty, made it inhospitable to further migrants after initial settlement by Scots-Irish and Germans. Hence, few influences from other languages are apparent in the vocabulary, which is typified by relic forms and archaisms no longer found elsewhere in AmE: for example, *brickle* brittle, *donsie* sickly, *poke* sack, bag, *redd* to tidy up (all from Scots).

The West. The West was first settled by English speakers after the gold rush of the 1850s. Southern migration along the Butterfield Stage Route brought settlers from Missouri and Arkansas through central Texas, New Mexico, and Arizona, to California; the Santa Fe trail also originated in Missouri and reached southern California by a somewhat more northerly route. Northern trails and subsequently the railroad took settlers into the central valley of California and San Francisco through Nebraska, Wyoming, and Utah. The Oregon Trail and its successor railroad connected the northern tier of states to the Pacific Northwest. For historically minded dialectologists, initial investigations of the Western dialect region dwelt on the continuity of migration westward on the presumption that Northerners preferred the northern Pacific coast while Southerners were mainly attracted to the more salubrious climate in southern California. Thus, it was no surprise that such studies emphasized continuity: for example, *curtains* (roller window shades), a Northern term, appears more commonly from San Francisco northward; *arroyo* can be traced from Texas westward to Los Angeles, but does not extend north to San Francisco. What is missed by this approach is the fact that the West became a source of linguistic innovation spreading back to the longer-settled dialect regions. While it may have been a 'mixed' region in the past, California and the Pacific Northwest are now coming to be seen as a coherent dialect region in their own right.

Western pronunciation. In some respects, the West brings to completion processes begun elsewhere. The merger of the vowels of *Don* and *Dawn*, noted above, is virtually universal in the West, and its influence is spreading eastward. The vowel in such words as *measure* and *fresh* (which has the value of *bet* in much of the East) is increasingly given the sound of *bait*, so that *edge* and *age* have come to resemble each other. Though Westerners distinguish *seal* from *sill*, Easterners hear these as nearly identical (with the vowel of *sill* in both); as a result, outsiders regard the Western pronunciation of *really* as identical to their own pronunciation of *rilly*.

Western grammar. The fact that Western is the least intensively studied of AmE dialects may contribute to the lack of evidence for a distinctive grammar of the region. Subgroups within the region employ marked syntax: *We all the time used to go outside* (Hispanic-influenced English, East Los Angeles); *I been tripping for three weeks* (1960s San Francisco drug usage); *Moray eel you can spear it* (Hawaiian English); *Do you have any bets on?* (Las Vegas gambling talk); *Pete's wooding those trucks down* (logger usage, Pacific Northwest); *Here we shopping and went through the town to see things and places* (Apachean English of the Great Plains); *Like, no biggie* (San Fernando Valley teenage talk). All these examples suggest that grammatical variation in Western (as in other varieties of AmE) would profit from further study.

Western vocabulary. Some common Western terms are uncommon elsewhere except in reference to Western language or culture: *bar pit* a ditch by the side of an ungraded road, *bear claw* a large, sweet pastry shaped like a bear's paw, *bush pilot* a daring pilot of light aircraft used to reach remote Alaskan areas, *canyon* a steep-sided, narrow valley, *chesterfield* a sofa, *gunny sack* a burlap bag, *lower 48* used in Alaska to refer to the rest of the US, *lug* a field crate for fruit and vegetables, *parking* (*strip*) a band of grass between sidewalk and curb on a city street, *sourdough bread* bread started with a piece of fermented dough.

The most important foreign-language influence on Western is Mexican Spanish. Many borrowings are used mainly in southern California, Arizona, and New Mexico, but some are more widely known: *adios* goodbye, *adobe* sun-dried brick, *bronco* wild, mean, rough (from a wild or partly broken horse), *embarcadero* wharf, *hombre* guy, fellow, *Santa Ana* a seasonal hot, dry wind in southern California. Various terms for Mexican cookery were introduced into English elsewhere but are regarded as typical of the region and have widespread currency there: *carne seco* chipped beef, *frijoles* beans, *langosta* crayfish or spiny lobster, *tortilla* thin, round, unleavened bread. Other languages have contributed words to Western that have come to be known outside the region: *aloha* a greeting or farewell, *lei* a garland of flowers (Hawaiian); *chinook* a warm winter wind, *Sasquatch* (also called 'Bigfoot') a legendary hominid animal (Amerindian languages of the Pacific Northwest); *dim sum* meat-filled dumpling, *kung fu* a martial art (Chinese); *honcho* a strong leader, boss, *Nisei* a person of Japanese descent born or educated in the US (Japanese). See CHICANO ENGLISH, HAWAIIAN ENGLISH, SPANISH.

Influences on US dialects. The usage of all Americans, regardless of dialect, is influenced by social networks that include gender, age and peer group, social class, ethnic background, occupations, and recreations. Some distinctive varieties have gained national prominence, such as *Jewish English* through its use by entertainers and others. People who are not Jewish are likely to have at least a passive knowledge of it and a sprinkling of such loanwords as *chutzpah, schmaltzy, schmooze*. Other varieties present stereotypes, such as *Country-Western*, originating in the Appalachian and Ozark regions of the Upper South, which has become well known in the 20c through country-and-western music, associated movies, and radio communication among airline pilots, truck drivers, and others who imitate them. *Hispanic English* has been increasingly disseminated through popular culture and the media, though outsiders may not appreciate that many who speak it have little or no competence in Spanish. Refined Southern speech has been made internationally familiar in the models presented by films and plays, and a Texas style has become popular through Western films and the TV soap opera *Dallas. American Black English* has long created social solidarity among African-Americans and has been rendered (sometimes abusively) in popular entertainment. Such varieties, having national prominence, are available for imitation in dialect and ethnic jokes with enough shibboleths to identify the target group.

Other communities, though less widely known, exert similarly powerful constraints on their members and neighbours, for example the Finnish-flavoured English of northern Michigan; the German-influenced English spoken by the Amish and Mennonite communities of central Pennsylvania, Ohio, and Indiana; Native American or '*Indian*' English, especially in Arizona and New Mexico; the *Polish English* of north-eastern industrial cities like Buffalo and Detroit; the *Cajun English* of Louisiana, with its French and Caribbean-creole traces. Even a single community can develop a distinctive linguistic identity: between 1880 and 1920, Boonville, a small town in northern California, developed a thoroughgoing transformation of English known as *Boontling*, a lingo that made members of the community at once unintelligible to outsiders when they so wished and conscious of the importance of being Boonters. See BLACK ENGLISH VERNACULAR, INDIAN ENGLISH[2], JEWISH ENGLISH, PENNSYLVANIA DUTCH.

Regional markers. Varying preferences for synonyms help to distinguish the regions: *crawdad* is likely to occur in the Midland and west of the Appalachians, *crawfish* is used nationally but is most frequent in the South and West, and *crayfish* is common in the North. In the North, west of the Hudson River, people attend a *potluck*; to the east of the Hudson and in Midland and South, the same events are *covered dish luncheons/suppers*. People in the North and West are 'sick *to* their stomachs'; in Pennsylvania and southward along the Atlantic coast, they are 'sick *on* their stomachs'; along the Gulf Coast and in the Southwest they are 'sick *at* their stomachs'. Some of these are well-known markers of regional distinctions. Every American knows that many cultivated Southerners say *you-all* and less cultivated Northerners say *youse* for the plural of *you*. Carbonated soft drinks, whatever their trademarks, have regionally different names: *coke* or *dope* in the South, *cold drink* in the lower Mississippi Valley, *pop* in the interior of the North and West; *soda* in the Northeast; *tonic* in that part of the Northeast influenced by Boston. The varieties in which such usages occur are often described in terms of sound, sometimes pejoratively: Southerners *drawl*, New Yorkers are *nasal*, New Englanders speak with a *twang*. See DIALECT, DICTIONARY OF AMERICAN REGIONAL ENGLISH, LINGUISTIC ATLAS OF THE UNITED STATES AND CANADA. [AMERICAS, VARIETY].   R.W.B.

Carver, Craig M. 1987. *American Regional Dialects: A Word Geography*. Ann Arbor: The University of Michigan Press.
Kurath, Hans. 1949. Reprinted 1966. *A Word Geography of the Eastern United States*. Ann Arbor: University of Michigan Press.
—— & McDavid, Raven I. 1961. *The Pronunciation of English in the Atlantic States*. Ann Arbor: University of Michigan Press.

DIALECT IN AUSTRALIA. The English of Australia is considered to be regionally uniform, with no sub-dialects. Its homogeneity resulted from the mainly British origin of the population, the absence of enclaves (except for the now dispersed Cornish mining communities of South Australia), and mobility caused by the gold rushes and such seasonal occupations as shearing and cane-cutting. In recent years, some regional variation has been observed: for example, a red-skinned sausage may be a *polony* in Western Australia, a *fritz* in South Australia, and a *devon* in New South Wales. Calling a *utility truck* a *tilly* and a cocktail frankfurter a *cheerio* marks a speaker as coming from Queensland, while a *teacake* in NSW is a *Boston bun* in Victoria. Similarly, phonological variation is starting to emerge: speakers from Adelaide have a back variety of /uː/ before /l/ in words like *pool, school*, while most other speakers have a fronted /uː/. Melbourne speakers tend not to distinguish between /e/ and /æ/ before /l/ in words like *Melbourne, Allan, Ellen*. Sydney speakers tend to have a more centralized version of /ɪ/ than Melbourne speakers. There are two additional features: (1) Immigration in the later 20c has led to non-English-speaking communities and the English of many immigrants is often influenced by the patterns of these languages. This influence does not appear likely to carry over from one generation to the next. (2) Contact between Aborigines and Europeans has led to a number of pidgins and creoles, whose usage is often ranged along a continuum from standard AusE to forms unintelligible to non-Aborigines. See ABORIGINAL ENGLISH, AUSTRALASIAN ENGLISH, AUSTRALIAN ENGLISH, AUSTRALIAN PIDGIN, DIALECT. [OCEANIA, VARIETY].   W.S.R.

DIALECT IN CANADA. In the traditional view, the English of Canada has four major regional dialects: *Atlantic*, covering the Maritime Provinces (New Brunswick, Nova Scotia, and Prince Edward Island) and the island of Newfoundland as a distinctive sub-area; *Quebec*, with Montreal and the Eastern Townships as focal areas; the *Ottawa Valley*, adjacent to the federal capital, Ottawa; and *General Canadian*, from Toronto westward to the Pacific. More recent scholarship, however, regards 'General Canadian' as a class-based urban dialect of broadcasting and educated speech, and closer scrutiny invites a description of regional differences that mark the *West* (British Columbia), the *Arctic North* (the Yukon, Northwest Territories, northern Quebec, and Labrador), the *Prairies* (Alberta, Saskatchewan, and Manitoba), and *southern Ontario*. Variations from region to region include distinctive local words, many of which relate to local conditions and occupations: for example, in the West *boomsticks* 66-feet-long logs connected by *boom chains* to contain floating logs to be towed to a mill; in the Prairies *Calgary redeye* beer with tomato juice added, *stampede* a rodeo, *oil borer* (in contrast to *oil driller* in eastern CanE and in AmE); in southern Ontario, *reeve* the principal officer of a township; Ottawa Valley *snye* a side channel, especially one bypassing rapids (from French *chenail*); Quebec *whisky blanc* a colourless alcoholic drink (compare AmE *white lightning*); and Newfoundland, *outport* a coastal settlement other than the capital St John's. Many distinctive words have been borrowed from indigenous regional languages, such as: (1) *The West*. Loans from local Amerindian languages in the *Lower Mainland* area of British Columbia (the city of Vancouver and its hinterlands) are virtually unknown elsewhere in Canada or in the US: for example, *cowichan* a vividly patterned sweater, *kokanee* land-locked salmon, *saltchuck* ocean, *skookum* big, strong, *tyee* chief, boss. (2) *The Arctic North*. Loanwords from Inuktitut: for example, *angakok* a shaman, *chimo* a greeting, toast before drinking, *kabloona* a non-Inuit, a White, *ouk* a command to a sled-dog to turn right, *tupik* a tent of animal skins. (3) *The Prairies.* Loanwords from Cree, known only in the region: for example, *kinnikinik* a smoking mixture including sumac leaves and tobacco, *saskatoon* an edible berry and the shrub on which it grows, *wachee* a greeting (from Cree *wacheya*, from English *what cheer*). See CANADA, CANADIAN BROADCASTING, CANADIAN DIC-TIONARIES IN ENGLISH, CANADIAN ENGLISH, INUIT, MARITIME PROVINCES/MARITIMES, MÉTIS, NEW-FOUNDLAND, NEWFOUNDLAND ENGLISH, OTTAWA VALLEY, QUEBEC, SOUTHERN ONTARIO. [AMERICAS, VARIETY].   R.W.B., T.MCA.

DIALECT IN ENGLAND. In its primordial form on the European mainland and in its early stages in Britain (5–7c), English was a continuum of dialects whose traces survive only in texts. Present-day terms do not serve well in discussing the period: 'English' and 'German' now have different meanings and 'language' and 'dialect' inadequately describe the condition of Germanic speech when the Roman Empire was in decline. Until *c.*600, apparently all the tribes could understand each other: for example, on their way to convert the English in 597, the missionary Augustine and his companions engaged Frankish interpreters to help them. However, polarization was already taking place between the continental and insular Germans. the settlers in Britain developed their own usages and those on the mainland were absorbed into other spheres of linguistic growth: the Angles into Danish, the Saxons into Low German.

The Angelcynn. Around 730, the historian Bede called the invaders Angles, Saxons, and Jutes, but other evidence indicates that they also included Frisians and probably Franks. Once established, they called themselves the *Angelcynn* ('Angle-kin'), with *Englisc* as their common speech. The Angles settled in the Midlands and along the east coast, from somewhere north of the Thames to the Forth. The Anglian or Anglic dialects were *Mercian*, associated with the kingdom of Mercia and spoken from the Thames to the Humber, and *Northumbrian*, associated with the kingdom of Northumbria, and spoken from the Humber to the Forth. The Jutes settled in and near Kent, but the dialect for the region is known as *Kentish*, not *Jutish*. The Saxons settled around the Thames, the south, and the south-west: East Saxons in *Essex*, Middle Saxons in *Middlesex*, South Saxons in *Sussex*, and West Saxons in *Wessex*. Each group had its own usages, but *West Saxon*, the dialect of Wessex, became dominant and for a time served as the literary language. The early dialects continued into the period of Middle English,

many having undergone considerable change under the impact of the Danish settlements of the 8–9c.

Middle English dialects. By the 11c, the division of the island into the three domains of England, Scotland, and Wales had taken place and from that time forward the language developed with a border between the dialects of England and Scotland. The dialects of Middle English are generally classified as: *Northern*, both south and north of the border, the northern branch developing into Scots; *West Midland*, extending to the Welsh marches; *East Midland*, including East Anglia and the London area; *Southern*, extending west to Celtic Cornwall; *Kentish*, stopping short of the Isle of Wight. The social and literary standard form of English which slowly emerged after the Norman Conquest in 1066 was based not on the Southern but the East Midland dialect, with an increasing Scandinavian overlay.

Dialects and standard. With the introduction by Caxton of the printing press in London in 1476 a great boost was given to the speech of the capital. As the standard language evolved, writing in the other dialects of England rapidly came to an end. Regional speech, increasingly commented on as harsh and difficult to understand, came to be seen as the language of the lower classes; the 16c diarist John Aubrey, for example, pointed out that Sir Walter Raleigh rather surprisingly remained all his life a speaker of Devon dialect. Despite the powerful influence of print and the prestige of London, however, letters, manuscripts, public comment, and representations of dialect in novels all show that local speech continued among the lesser gentry and the upper middle classes until well into the 18c, and among industrialists, politicians, and other public figures from lower middle-class and working-class backgrounds until the present day.

Literary dialect and dialectology. Dialect was used by Shakespeare and others to depict various provincial and rustic characters, and a distinct-ive form of south-western speech began to de-velop as a stage country-bumpkin dialect: see MUMMERSET. From the 18c onward, novelists have sought to represent dialect, especially in conversation; exponents of dialect writing in England include George Eliot in *Adam Bede* (1859) and Thomas Hardy in the Wessex novels. See DIALOG(UE). Interest by scholars in the vari-eties of English grew at the beginning of the 17c and an early mention by Alexander Gil in his *Polychronicon* (1619) began a tradition of exam-ining and comparing dialect forms against stand-ard English. Although scholars realized that there was a historical development behind the forms of their speech, dialect speakers became increasingly identified as lower class. Throughout the 17-18c, interest in both standard and dialect varieties of English continued to grow. Many clergymen recorded the grammar and vocabulary of their parishioners, and a number of word lists and monographs of various kinds, often linked to descriptions of local industrial processes, began to appear. The *English Dialect Society* often published these as part of its work towards an English dialect dictionary.

The present day. Currently, there is a widespread belief that local dialect is dying out and to a certain extent this is true of vocabulary, but strong local pronunciation continues to be heard, in London as well as in the regions, and from the 1970s began to be used increasingly widely on radio and television: for example, in such dramatic series as *Coronation Street* (Manchester), *Crossroads* (Birmingham), *Auf Wiedersehen Pet* (Newcastle), *Bread* (Liverpool), and *EastEnders* (London). In such large cities robust local forms of pronunciation and grammar, with their own social varieties within an area, show little sign of diminishment. These forms continue to change and develop over generations; pronunciations show the sporadic influence of Received Pronunciation, a southern middle- and upper-class accent often described as the standard accent of England, but with considerable modification: for example, in Newcastle the traditionally developed /stiən/ and /stjen/ for *stone*, from a Middle English unrounded form /staːn/, can be heard alongside a loaned /støːn/ and /stəʊn/, developed from the more southerly Middle English /stoːn/.

See BIRMINGHAM (BRUMMIE), COCKNEY, CORNWALL, CUMBRIA, DIALECT, DORSET, EAST ANGLIA, EAST MIDLAND DIALECT, ELLIS, ENGLAND, ENGLISH DIALECT DICTIONARY, ENGLISH DIALECT SOCIETY, ENGLISH IN ENGLAND, GEORDIE, LANCASHIRE, LONDON, MIDLANDS, ORTON, RECEIVED PRONUNCIATION, SCOUSE, SKEAT, SOMERSET, WEST COUNTRY, WRIGHT, YORKSHIRE. [EUROPE, VARIETY]. T.MCA.

Trudgill, Peter. 1990. *The Dialects of England*. Oxford: Basil Blackwell.
Wakelin, Martyn F. 1972/7. *English Dialects: An Introduction*. London: Athlone.

DIALECT IN IRELAND. Because of the spread of education and the influence of the media, it is becoming increasingly difficult to subdivide the continuum of English found in Ireland. However, three main regional and several urban dialects can be distinguished. They are all rhotic, with a retroflex *r*, and share phonological features with AmE. The regional dialects are: (1) *Anglo-Irish*, used by the descendants of English settlers and found throughout the country with the exception of the most northerly counties. (2) *Ulster Scots*, in the northernmost counties, the speech of the descendants of 17c Protestant Scots settlers. (3) *Hiberno-Irish*, spoken by usually Catholic people whose ancestral tongue was Gaelic. In any region, Hiberno-English approximates to the dominant dialect, whether Anglo-Irish or Ulster Scots but, in the Gaeltacht and in less educated, rural usage, it displays a strong Gaelic substrate. Ireland has fewer urban dwellers than most Western European countries, but each city, including Armagh, Belfast, Cork, Derry, Donegal, Dublin, Galway, and Limerick, has its own forms and sphere of linguistic influence. See ANGLO-IRISH, BELFAST, DIALECT, DUBLIN, HIBERNO-ENGLISH, IRELAND, IRISH ENGLISH, ULSTER SCOTS. [EUROPE, VARIETY]. L.T.

DIALECT IN NEW ZEALAND. The English of New Zealand is considered to be regionally uniform, with no sub-dialects, but the subject has not been sufficiently researched to establish the matter firmly. Claims have been made, with varying degrees of conviction, that certain words occur only in certain regions. In Otago and Southland, a holiday home is a *crib*, elsewhere a *bach*. The words *chip*, *pottle*, *punnet* for a container for strawberries, and *half-G*, *flagon*, *peter* for a measure of beer, may be restricted to particular places. Some words of Scottish origin, such as *ashet* a meat-dish (from French *assiette*) are recorded only in Otago and Southland. *Couch grass*, the term in the North Island, is likely to be called *twitch* in the South Island. Some claim that a few words, such as *crib* a miner's lunch, a cut lunch, and *scunge* a miserly person, are used only on the West Coast of the South Island, but further investigation is needed to verify such statements. Despite the fact that many New Zealanders feel that there are regional differences in pronunciation (usually discussed in terms of *drawling* and *clipped tones*), the only such difference which can be reliably traced is the use of the *Southland burr*, the pronunciation of /r/ in words like *car, farm* in a shrinking area of rural Southland. There is a degree of mixing of English with Maori, especially among the Maori population, but this probably should not be counted as a separate dialect as such. The distinct variety commonly called *Maori English* is not spoken by all Maoris or exclusively by Maoris. Its main features are phonological rather than lexical, including voice quality and tendency to syllable timing. See AUSTRALASIAN ENGLISH, DIALECT, MAORI, MAORI ENGLISH, NEW ZEALAND, NEW ZEALAND ENGLISH. [OCEANIA, VARIETY]. RO.W.B., L.J.B.

DIALECT IN SCOTLAND. The dialects of Scots fall into four main regional groups:

(1) Those of the Northern Isles: see ORKNEY AND SHETLAND DIALECTS. (2) *Northern Scots*, from Caithness to Aberdeenshire and Angus. (3) *Southern Scots*, the Border districts of Roxburgh and Annandale, and Eskdale. (4) *Central Scots*, much of the rest of the Scots-speaking area, including the working-class dialects of Edinburgh, Glasgow, and other urban areas of Central Scotland. The working-class urban dialects are identified by both socially and regionally delimited features: see GUTTER SCOTS. The regional markers of the mainland dialects include:

Pronunciation. (1) The Northern use since the 15c of *f-* where other dialects have *wh-*, as in *Fa fuppit the fyte fulpie?* Who whipped the white whelp? (2) The different outcomes of the old front, rounded vowel *ui* /øː/ in such words as *guid* (good), *scuil* (school), *muin* (moon), *uise* (use: noun and verb), *puir* (poor), *shui* (shoe). In Angus and the Mearns in Northern Scots and in Southern Scots this pronunciation persists. In the rest of Northern, however, the original vowel has since the 16c been unrounded to *ee* /i/: *meen* moon, *eese* use (noun), *eeze* use (verb), *shee* shoe. In the Grampian Region, however, after *g-* and *k-* the outcome is *-wee-*, with *gweed* good, and *skweel* school, but *geed* and *skeel* further north. In much of the Central dialect, the results of a different and more recent unrounding are conditioned by the *Scottish Vowel-Length Rule*. In these dialects, SVLR long environments yield *ai* /e/: *pair* poor, *shae* shoe, *yaize* use (verb), but in SVLR short environments the outcome is an *i*-like vowel /ɪ/: *min* moon, *bit* boot, *gid* good, *yis* use (noun). (3) South-Eastern and Southern dialects have *twae, whae, away, whare, waken, waiter* for Western and Northern *twaw/twaa, whaw/whaa/faa, awa/awaa, whaur/whaar/faar, wauken/waaken, wauter/waater* (two, who, away, where, waken, water) on either side of a swathe of country from Musselburgh on the Firth of Forth to Gatehouse-of-Fleet on the Solway Firth.

Grammar. The grammar of the dialects of the far north and far south is more archaic, in retaining the old opposition between the present participle and the verbal noun in *He's aye gutteran aboot* (participle, with *-an*) and *He's fond o gutterin aboot* (verbal noun, with *-in* or *-een*) and, though now almost obsolete, except in Orkney and Shetland, traces of the pronoun system with *thou/thee/thy* as well as *ye/you/your*. The use of *on-, ohn-* /on/ as a negative with participles is now confined to the North-East (Grampian Region): *to haud her ohn kent at she had tint it* (to keep her 'not known'/ignorant that she had lost it); *Fa could be on lauch'n at that?* (Who could keep from laughing at that?).

Vocabulary. Of the innumerable local items of vocabulary in the mainland dialects, some result from the influence of Scandinavian in Caithness, such as *aikle* a molar tooth, *gilt* a large haystack, *roog* a peat store, *scorrie* a young seagull, *scroo* a stack. For the much larger number surviving in the dialects of the Northern Isles, see ORKNEY AND SHETLAND DIALECTS. Caithness also displays local Gaelic influence with *ask* a chain for tethering cattle, *brotag* a caterpillar, *buckie-faulie* a rose-hip, primrose, *cairie* a breed of sheep, *coachie* soft, spongy, *cown* to weep, *crellag* a bluebottle, *cyowtach* smart in appearance, and many others. Similar, but individually different, lists of Gaelic-derived words can be cited for other parts of the North, for the North-East, for Kintyre, and for the South-West, especially Galloway. Other variations result from the locally patchy effects of obsolescence and innovation, as with the words for 'soapy lather', for which the older *graith* is widely distributed in mainland Scotland, except the West (around Glasgow) and the South-West, where since the 18c it has been superseded by the newer *supples*. The dialects also display numerous, seemingly random or inexplicable, variations in words for everyday notions, like such synonyms for *mud* around the country as *dubs, gutters, glabber, clabber, glaur.*

Dialect literature. Written representations of local forms of Scots began appearing in the late 17c in distinctive adaptations of the traditional 'mainstream' orthography of Scots. The North-East in particular established its own regional standard in the 18c, and this has provided many works of note, such as William Alexander's novel *Johnny Gibb of Gushetneuk* (1871), the dialogue of which is in a subtly modulated rendering of Aberdeenshire Scots, and today in the poetry of Flora Garry and the descriptive prose of David Ogston. See DIALECT, DORIC, EDINBURGH, GLASGOW, HIGHLAND ENGLISH, LINGUISTIC SURVEY OF SCOTLAND, NORN, SCOTLAND, SCOTS, SCOTTISH ENGLISH, ULSTER SCOTS. [EUROPE, VARIETY].

A.J.A.

DIALECT IN SOUTH AFRICA. The usage of native speakers of English in South Africa varies more by class than region. In addition, English is the lingua franca of many millions for whom it is not the mother tongue, with the result that it exists in many forms: for example, the pronunciation of speakers of Afrikaans English shades from near-RP to Afrikaans, depending on education, experience, and rural or urban upbringing. In country schools, people of any race are rarely taught by a native speaker, with the result that they retain or acquire second-language characteristics. This is particularly the case for the Coloured community, urban and rural, for many of whom English is, as it were, a second first language. Those who use it in the workplace may use another language with children, older relatives, and in colloquial situations; many Coloured teachers who whenever possible use English because it is the prestige language do not acquire anything close to its prestige dialect. The opening of the private schools to all races in the last decade or more has given the children of wealthy Black, Coloured, and Indian families access to this dialect, but few others, including the majority of Whites, have the same opportunity. English in South Africa is spoken in many ways by far more non-native than native speakers; while it is stretching the term *dialect* to include the varieties they use, it is impossible in such a society to disregard them. See AFRIKAANS ENGLISH, DIALECT, SOUTH AFRICA, SOUTH AFRICAN ENGLISH, SOUTH AFRICAN INDIAN ENGLISH. [AFRICA, VARIETY].   J.B.

DIALECT IN WALES. Dialect differences in the Welsh language are to a large extent limited to variation in accents, the vocabulary having been standardized by literature, education, and the media. Dialects of English in Wales are as diverse as elsewhere in Britain. They vary in terms of pronunciation, grammar, and vocabulary, but can be broadly categorized as: (1) The English of people who are bilingual, Welsh/English, and whose English is strongly influenced by Welsh. (2) Dialects of English similar to those in neighbouring counties of England, and often sharing features, especially at the syntactic level, with other working-class BrE dialects. (3) Standard English with a Welsh accent. (4) Standard English with an RP accent. See DIALECT, WALES, WELSH, WELSH ENGLISH. [EUROPE, VARIETY].   L.T.

DIALECTOLOGY [1870s]. The study of dialects, that is, of variant features within a language, their history, differences of form and meaning, interrelationships, distribution, and, more broadly, their spoken as distinct from their literary forms. The discipline recognizes all variations within the bounds of any given language; it classifies and interprets them according to historical origins, principles of development, characteristic features, areal distribution, and social correlates. The scientific study of dialects dates from the mid-19c, when philologists using data preserved in texts began to work out the historical or diachronic development of the Indo-European languages. Their interest was etymological and systematic. Scientific phonetics and the principle that sound change was not erratic but followed discoverable rules or laws, were a basic part of the growth of dialectology.

Living dialects were seen to furnish a huge treasury of living data on phonology, lexicology, and other features of language that written texts could not furnish. The linguist's task was to gather, analyse, and interpret this living body of language. Dialectology is pursued through a number of methods; the American linguist W. Nelson Francis (*Dialectology*, 1983) describes the prevailing methods as traditional, structural, and generative.

In *traditional dialectology* the collection of data is the primary requirement. This entails fieldwork, the more detailed and massive the better, within the limits of practicability, and its presentation in the form of dictionaries, grammars, atlases, and monographs. This method Francis calls 'item-centered', emphasizing the individual datum and paying little attention to underlying system. In *structural dialectology*, the investigator seeks to find both the structure or system by which a dialect holds together or achieves synchronic identity and how it is changed by the introduction of any new feature. Since any change in the system affects every feature of it, it becomes in effect a different system, whose parts are, however, diachronically connected. There is a paradoxical element here which is partly due to difficulties of definition. In *generative dialectology*, the investigator holds that the language exists within the speaker as a competence which is never fully realized in performance. This competence, lying beneath actual language as it is produced (and as it is recorded by traditional dialectologists), works by a series of rules which transform it into actual speech. Thus, it is the dialectologist's task to find a basic system whose rules produce as economically as possible the surface structure of actual dialect. The complexities or variations within a language (its dialectal variants) may thus be traced back to a putative source form from which in the course of time they could by speciation have developed. However, without the mass of data which traditional dialectologists have furnished, theoretical systems could not have been either proposed or refined. See DIALECT, DIALECT IN ENGLAND, LINGUISTIC ATLAS, SOCIOLINGUISTICS. [LANGUAGE].   F.G.C.

Chambers, J. K., & Trudgill, Peter. 1980. *Dialectology*. Cambridge: University Press.
Fischer, Andreas, & Ammann, Daniel. 1991. *An Index to Dialect Maps of Great Britain*. Amsterdam & Philadelphia: John Benjamins.
Thomas, Alan R. (ed.). 1988. *Methods in Dialectology*. Clevedon & Philadelphia: Multilingual Matters.
Trudgill, Peter, & Chambers, J. K. (eds.). 1991. *Dialects of English: Studies in Grammatical Variation*. London & New York: Longman.

DIALOGUE, AmE also **dialog** [12c: through French from Latin *dialogus*, Greek *diálogos* a conversation, chat, debate]. A traditional semi-technical term for a conversation, especially if it is formal, or is presented in writing or print according to the conventions of drama and fiction.

Dialogue in drama. The playwrights of the Elizabethan and Jacobean periods (late 16c, early 17c) were the first to develop a full set of conventions for writing and presenting dialogue in English. Their use of dialogue, especially in blank verse, followed the classical tradition, in which speakers take turns to make lengthy, set-piece speeches, regardless of whether they are at ease in their homes or surrounded by enemies on the field of battle. Initial English attempts at dialogue did not therefore differ much from the stylized conversations of Homer's *Iliad*, except that at times the conversation of their characters could be short, sharp, and close to real life, as in Shakespeare's *Julius Caesar* (3. 2):

1st PLEBEIAN.
Me thinkes there is much reason in his sayings.
4th PLEBEIAN.
If thou consider rightly of the matter,
Cæsar ha's had great wrong.
3rd PLEBEIAN.   Ha's hee not Masters?
I feare there will a worse come in his place.
5th PLEBEIAN.
Mark'd ye his words? he would not take ye Crown,
Therefore 'tis certaine, he was not Ambitious.

Prose dialogue was often reserved for less elevated moments and characters in a play, such as the comic exploitation of kinds of English that were remote from the London stage, as with the Irishman Mackmorrice/MacMorris and the Welshman Fluellen in *Henry V* (3. 3):

GOWER. How now, Captaine *Mackmorrice*, haue you quit the Mynes? haue the Pioners giuen o're?
MACKMORRICE. By Chrish Law tish ill done: the work ish giue ouer. the Trompet sound the Retreat. By my Hand I sweare, and my fathers Soule, the Worke ish ill done: it ish giue ouer: I would haue blowed vp the Towne, so Chrish saue me law, in an houre. O tish ill done, tish ill done: by my Hand tish ill done.
FLUELLEN. Captaine *Mackmorrice*, I bessech you now, will you voutsafe me, looke you, a few disputations with you, as partly touching or concerning the displines of the Warre, the Roman Warres, in the way of Argument, looke you, and friendly communication: partly to satisfy my Opinion, and partly for the Satisfaction, looke you. of my Mind.

Prose was the common medium of drama by the end of the 17c, although Dryden and others wrote tragedies in heroic couplets. Prose was considered to be more realistic than verse and verse has never again been the principal medium of dramatic dialogue in English; the Romantic poets wrote verse plays not generally intended to be acted and there were minor revivals of poetic drama at the end of the 19c and in the

middle of the 20c. In 18c prose drama, the presentation of turn-taking continued in much the same classical style as the longer speeches of Hamlet and Othello: for example, the following excerpt from Sheridan's comedy, *The Rivals* (1775):

SIR ANTHONY. Why, Mrs. Malaprop, in moderation, now, what would you have a woman know?
MRS. MALAPROP. Observe me, Sir Anthony.—I would by no means wish a daughter of mine to be a progeny of learning; I don't think so much learning becomes a young woman; for instance, I would never let her meddle with Greek, or Hebrew, or Algebra, or Simony, or Fluxions, or Paradoxes, or such inflammatory branches of learning—neither would it be necessary for her to handle any of your mathematical, astronomical, diabolical instruments:— But, Sir Anthony, I would send her, at nine years old, to a boarding-school, in order to learn a little ingenuity and artifice. Then, sir, she should have a supercilious knowledge in accounts;—and as she grew up, I would have her instructed in geometry, that she might know something of the contagious countries;—but above all, Sir Anthony, she should be mistress of orthodoxy, that she might not misspell, and mis-pronounce words so shamefully as girls usually do; and likewise that she might reprehend the true meaning of what she is saying. This, Sir Anthony, is what I would have a woman know;— and I don't think there is a superstitious article in it.

Dialogue in novels. The conventions of dramatic scripts required each speaker to have a separate section, for easy consultation. The conventions of prose, as seen in the novels of the 17–18c, did not follow the theatre, but used long, unbroken paragraphs within which entire conversations could be set, as in Henry Fielding's *The History of Tom Jones* (1749):

"You don't imagine, I hope," cries the squire, "that I have taught her any such things." "Your ignorance, brother," returned she, "as the great Milton says, almost subdues my patience." "D—n Milton!" answered the squire: "if he had the impudence to say so to my face, I'd lent him a douse, thof he was never so great a man. Patience! An you come to that, sister, I have more occasion of patience, to be used like an overgrown schoolboy, as I am by you. Do you think no one hath any understanding, unless he hath been about at court? Pox! the world is come to a fine pass indeed, if we are all fools, except a parcel of roundheads and Hanover rats. Pox! I hope the times are a coming that we shall make fools of them, and every man shall enjoy his own. That's all, sister; and every man shall enjoy his own. I hope to zee it, sister, before the Hanover rats have eat up all our corn, and left us nothing but turneps to feed upon."—"I protest, brother," cries she, "you are now got beyond my understanding. Your jargon of turneps and Hanover rats is to me perfectly unintelligible."

In this style, such formulas as *answered the squire* and *cries she* were well established and considerable flexibility was available, as with the dramatists, to capture special kinds of speech. By the 19c, conversation was often still embedded in paragraphs, but a style similar to the dramatic script was beginning to open up these great blocks of print and speakers were often given paragraphs to themselves, turn for turn. Emily Brontë uses the 'open-plan' approach in *Wuthering Heights* (1847) in a passage that, like Shakespeare, uses dialogue to present dialect:

"Have you found Heathcliff, you ass?" interrupted Catherine. "Have you been looking for him, as I ordered?"

"I sud more likker look for th' horse," he replied. "It 'ud be to more sense. Bud, I can look for norther horse nur man of a neeght loike this—as black as t' chimbley! und Heathcliff's noan t' chap to coom at *my* whistle—happen he'll be less hard o' hearing wi' *ye*!"

By the end of the 19c, fictional dialogue had become more or less stable. Writers had become accustomed to paragraph-by-paragraph turn-taking and felt secure enough in their own and their readers' ability to move down a page of short paragraphs to dispense increasingly with such aids as *he said* and *she answered* in every paragraph. Novelists became more skilful in presenting the registers and varieties of speech; dialect, previously used mainly for comic or eccentric effect, was given by writers like Elizabeth Gaskell, George Eliot, and Thomas Hardy to serious and even tragic characters. From the late 19c to the present day, fictional conversation has generally been modelled closely on real life and used to exhibit characters' actions, styles, and attributes, as in this excerpt from Sir Arthur Conan Doyle's short story 'The Five Orange Pips' (in *The Adventures of Sherlock Holmes*, 1892):

'I owe you an apology,' he said, raising his golden pince-nez to his eyes. 'I trust that I am not intruding. I fear that I have brought some traces of the storm and the rain into your snug chamber.'

'Give me your coat and umbrella,' said Holmes. 'They may rest here on the hook, and will be dry presently. You have come up from the south-west, I see.'

'Yes, from Horsham.'

'That clay and chalk mixture which I see upon your toe-caps is quite distinctive.'

'I have come for advice.'

'That is easily got.'

'And help.'

'That is not always so easy.'

'I have heard of you, Mr. Holmes. I heard from Major Prendergast how you saved him in the Tankerville Club Scandal.'

'Ah, of course. He was wrongfully accused of cheating at cards.'

'He said that you could solve anything.'

'He said too much.'

'That you are never beaten.'

'I have been beaten four times—three times by men and once by a woman.'

Oscar Wilde exploited this swift-moving, pared-down style for the equally swift sallies and ripostes of the upper-class dinner party (as in chapter 17 of *The Picture of Dorian Gray*, 1891):

'Yesterday I cut an orchid, for my button-hole. It was a marvellous spotted thing, as effective as the seven deadly sins. In a thoughtless moment I asked one of the gardeners what it was called. He told me it was a fine specimen of *Robinsoniana*, or something dreadful of that kind. It is a sad truth, but we have lost the faculty of giving lovely names to things. Names are everything. I never quarrel with actions. My one quarrel is with words. That is the reason I hate vulgar realism in literature. The man who could call a spade a spade should be compelled to use one. It is the only thing he is fit for.'

'Then what should we call you, Harry?' she asked.

'His name is Prince Paradox,' said Dorian.

'I recognize him in a flash,' exclaimed the Duchess.

'I won't hear of it,' laughed Lord Henry, sinking into a chair. 'From a label there is no escape! I refuse the title.'

'Royalties may not abdicate,' fell as a warning from pretty lips.

'You wish me to defend my throne, then?'

'Yes.'

'I give the truths of tomorrow.'

'I prefer the mistakes of today,' she answered.

'You disarm me, Gladys,' he cried, catching the wilfulness of her mood.

'Of your shield, Harry: not of your spear.'

'I never tilt against beauty,' he said, with a wave of his hand.

'That is your error, Harry, believe me. You value beauty far too much.'

'How can you say that? I admit that I think that it is better to be beautiful than to be good. But on the other hand no one is more ready than I am to acknowledge that it is better to be good than to be ugly.'

'Ugliness is one of the seven deadly sins, then?' cried the Duchess. 'What became of your simile about the orchid?'

'Ugliness is one of the seven deadly virtues, Gladys. You, as a good Tory, must not underrate them. Beer, the Bible, and the seven deadly virtues have made our England what she is.'

Once such a flexible set of conventions was established, it became possible to experiment with other possibilities, in some cases abandoning entirely the system of quotation marks built up in the tradition of fiction and trying something closer to the unadorned dramatic script, as in James Joyce's *A Portrait of the Artist as a Young Man* (1916: ch. 5):

—Try to be one of us, repeated Davin. In your heart you are an Irishman but your pride is too powerful.

—My ancestors threw off their language and took another, Stephen said. They allowed a handful of foreigners to subject them. Do you fancy I am going to pay in my own life and person debts they made? What for?

—For our freedom, said Davin. . . . Ireland first, Stevie. You can be a poet or mystic after.

—Do you know what Ireland is? asked Stephen with cold violence. Ireland is the old sow that eats her farrow.

By and large, however, the experimentation has been less with quotation marks, turn-taking devices, and white space, and more with content: for example, in V. S. Naipaul's *A Flag on the Island* (1967), 'outlandish' speakers of English, remote descendants of Fluellen and Mack-morrice, turn up in a new guise. Fully conforming to the conventions he learned at school, Naipaul nonetheless uses the time-honoured techniques of English literary dialogue to make a point of his own about the trials of being a writer using a language with conventions far removed from everyday life:

'You know, I have been doing a lot of thinking. You know, Frankie, I begin to feel that what is wrong with my books is not me, but the language I use. You know, in English, black is a damn bad word. You talk of a black deed. How then can I write in this language?'
'I have told you already. You are getting too black for me.'
'What we want is our own language. I intend to write in our own language. You know this patois we have. Not English, not French, but something we have made up. This is our own. You were right. Damn those lords and ladies. Damn Jane Austen. This is ours, this is what we have to work with. And Henry, I am sure, whatever his reasons, is with me in this.'
'Yes,' Henry said. 'We must defend our culture.' And sadly regarding his new customers, he added: 'We must go back to the old days.' On the board outside Blackwhite's house there appeared this additional line: *Patois taught here.*

Writers of dialogue will always have the problem of accommodating the many sounds of English to the 26 letters of the alphabet. Deviant spelling and typographical contrivance are used to compensate for the inadequate and inconsistent relationship between the spoken and the written. Features of speech can sometimes be shown by such means, but usually they continue to be managed through such ad-hoc authorial formulas as *he stated emphatically*, *she whispered*, *Sabina said huskily*, and *Drake answered, slurring his words.*

See ASIDE, COCKNEY, CONVERSATION, DIRECT AND INDIRECT SPEECH, DRAMA, LANGUAGE TEACHING (SITUATIONAL), MONOLOG(UE), PARAGRAPH, PUNCTUATION, QUOTATION MARKS, SOLILOQUY, TALK, THEATRE OF THE ABSURD. [LITERATURE, SPEECH, STYLE, WRITING]. T.MCA., R.C.

DIAPHRAGM. See SPEECH.

DIARY [16c: from Latin *diarium* a daily allowance]. A day-by-day written account of (part of) someone's life, recorded soon after the events, usually at the end of the day. Many people keep diaries during their adolescent years, a practice which may be therapeutic. Famous diarists writing in English include Samuel Pepys (using a private code, 1660-9), John Evelyn (1620-1706),

and Fanny Burney (1768-1840). Such diaries can be valuable records of the life and language of their times. Diarists often use an abbreviated style, as with Pepys (1660):

January 1st. (Lord's Day). This morning (we living lately in the garret) I rose, put on my suit with great skirts, having not lately worn any other clothes but them. Went to Mr. Gunning's chapel at Exeter House, where he made a very good sermon. Dined at home in the garret, where my wife dressed the remains of a turkey, and in the doing of it she burned her hand.

Writers have often used the traditional diary or journal as a convenient narrative device: Daniel Defoe in *Robinson Crusoe* (1719), for the first year of life on the island; Bram Stoker in *Dracula* (1897), through the journals of four characters. A humorous account of suburban life in England is given by George and Weedon Grossmith in *Diary of a Nobody* (1892). Some public figures keep diaries which may eventually be published in diary or memoir form. A lightly cynical view of the practice is taken by Oscar Wilde's character Cecily Cardew, who describes her diary as 'simply a very young girl's record of her own thoughts and impressions, and consequently meant for publication' (*The Importance of Being Earnest*, 1895). The term is also used for a notebook of present and future engagements and a gossip column in a newspaper, usually published on a daily basis. See AUTOBIOGRAPHY, ELLIPSIS, JOURNAL, MEMOIR. [LITERATURE]. R.C.

DIASPORA [19c: through Latin from Greek *diasporá* scattering of seed, dispersion: Hebrew equivalent *galut* exile]. (1) (With an initial capital) the scattering of the Jews among the Gentiles in 586 BC, after the Babylonian Captivity. Diaspora Jews greatly outnumbered the Jews of Palestine even before the destruction of Jerusalem by the Romans in AD 70. (2) Jews living elsewhere than in Israel; the places where they live. (3) A mass migration, movement, or flight from one place to many other places; a group so dispersed: *the Armenian diaspora*. In the last sense, the term has been applied to languages as well as people: *the diaspora of English*. See AFRICAN, DIASPORA VARIETY, GEOGRAPHY, HISTORY OF ENGLISH, JEWISH LANGUAGES. [ASIA, EUROPE]. T.MCA.

DIASPORA VARIETY [1980s]. A term in sociolinguistics, a variety of a language spoken in any of a number of colonies or places of migration: a form of English in the Americas, Africa, Asia, and Australasia; a form of Hindi in the UK, the Caribbean, Fiji, and South Africa. See DIASPORA, VARIETY. [LANGUAGE]. T.MCA.

DIATRIBE [16c: through French from Latin *diatriba*, Greek *diatribē* a pastime, study, learned discussion, from *diatribein* to rub away (time, etc.)]. Originally a discourse, critical dissertation, and argument in the sense of presenting one's case. Currently, a discourse against someone or something, generally of a bitter nature. See ARGUMENT, DIALECTIC, POLEMIC. [STYLE]. T.MCA.

DICKENS, Charles (John Huffham) [1812–70]. English writer. Born in Portsmouth and moved to Chatham, then London. He became deeply unhappy when his father was imprisoned for debt and he worked for a time in a blacking warehouse. He became a Parliamentary reporter for the *True Sun* (1832), then the *Morning Chronicle* (1834), acquiring the knowledge of London that underlies his novels. *Sketches by Boz*, a series of commentaries on London life, appeared in various periodicals. It was followed by *Pickwick Papers* (1836), a comic episodic novel that made his name, and *Oliver Twist* (1837), a melodramatic tale of criminal life that established his success. In *David Copperfield* (1849–50), written in the first person, he put into fiction some of the bitterness of his early life. Earlier novels like *Oliver Twist* dealt with such specific social abuses as the workhouse, but his later novels took a more generally critical view of society. His fame was by then widespread, but his relationship with his wife Catherine (married in 1836) had steadily deteriorated and ended in 1858 with a separation accompanied by her accusations of infidelity. He increased both his income and popularity by public readings in the UK and US, but the strain was great and he died suddenly, leaving the novel *Edwin Drood* unfinished.

Characters and experiments. The strength of Dickens is his characters, particularly the comics and eccentrics, who live largely through their speech and through catchphrases that helped fix them for readers who met them in monthly serials. Their names are notable and often say something about their bearers: Mr Bumble the Beadle, the benevolent brothers Cheeryble, Thomas Gradgrind the Utilitarian, the fawning clerk Uriah Heep, the convict Abel Magwitch, Mr McChoakumchild the teacher, the amiable nurse Clara Peggotty, the impostor Mr Pumblechook, the miserly Ebenezer Scrooge. His place-names are also often suggestive: Blunderstone, Coketown, Dotheboys Hall, Eatanswill. Like Scott, Dickens worked dialect into his novels, particularly Cockney, for which he used idiosyncratic spelling that nonetheless conveyed the sounds and cadences of London, as for example the style, dialect, and accent of Mr Pickwick's servant Sam Weller:

'That a'nt the wost on it, neither. They puts things into old gen'lm'n's heads as they never dreamed of. My father, sir, wos a coachman. A widower he wos, and fat enough for anything—uncommon fat, to be sure.

His missus dies, and leaves him four hundred pound. Down he goes to the Commons, to see the lawyer and draw the blunt—wery smart—top-boots on—nosegay in his button-hole—broad-brimmed tile—green shawl—quite the gen'lm'n. Goes through the archvay, thinking how he should inwest the money—up comes the touter, touches his hat—"Licence, sir, licence?"—"What's that?" says my father.—"Marriage licence," says the touter.—"Dash my veskit," says my father, "I never thought o' that."—"I think you wants one, sir," says the touter' (*The Pickwick Papers*, ch. 10).

Dickens learned shorthand for his work as a reporter and had a good ear for slang and colloquialism, and was accused of coarseness by contemporary critics. His experiments in the presentation of material included setting a Parliamentary speech in musical notation and such non-traditional syntax and punctuation as:

Thomas Gradgrind, Sir. A man of realities. A man of facts and calculations. A man who proceeds upon the principle that two and two are four, and nothing over. Thomas Gradgrind, Sir—peremptorily Thomas—Thomas Gradgrind. With a rule and a pair of scales, and the multiplication table always in his pocket, Sir, ready to weigh and measure any parcel of human nature, and tell you exactly what it comes to. It is a mere question of figures, a case of simple arithmetic. You might hope to get some other nonsensical belief into the head of George Gradgrind, or Augustus Gradgrind, or John Gradgrind, or Joseph Gradgrind (all supposititious, non-existent persons), but into the head of Thomas Gradgrind—no, Sir! (*Hard Times*, 1854, ch. 1).

Poetic prose. Dickens's general style is usually powerful and persuasive in direct narrative and description. He convinces the reader by an accumulation of detail that can be extravagant to the point of absurdity, but makes its effect in his imaginary world. He can be tedious when expounding social ideas or unravelling mysteries and has features that seem uncongenial today, such as directly addressing the reader, moral commentary, sentimentality, and melodrama. His prose sometimes has an underlying rhythm close to blank verse, mimetic of sounds like the movement of coaches and trains. Some passages, with their non-classical punctuation, such as the opening of *Bleak House* (1852–3), have almost the quality of free verse:

LONDON. Michaelmas Term lately over, and the Lord Chancellor sitting in Lincoln's Inn Hall. Implacable November weather. As much mud in the streets, as if the waters had but newly retired from the face of the earth, and it would not be wonderful to meet a Megalosaurus, forty feet long or so, waddling like an elephantine lizard up Holborn Hill. Smoke lowering down from chimney pots, making a soft black drizzle with flakes of soot in it as big as full-grown snow-flakes—gone into mourning, one might imagine, for the death of the sun.

Stature. Like Chaucer and Shakespeare, Dickens is a giant of English literature, his work known as much through cinema and television as through his books themselves. On his contemporary significance, David Parker, Curator of the Dickens House Museum in London, has observed: 'For us Dickens stands where Homer did for earlier generations. We can no longer, without affectation, speak of the wisdom of Nestor, the beauty of Helen; we can, and we do, of a real Scrooge, a Micawberish attitude. Like Homer, Dickens gave us forms for the imagination, unconstrained by genre, affecting even the very language. Dramatizations of his novels were staged even before the final parts appeared, and the narratives he created now yield us, not only films and television serials, but also musicals, newspaper cartoons, Christmas cards, toby jugs, shop-window dressings, and annual festivals' (letter to the *Sunday Times*, 26 Feb. 1989). See index. [BIOGRAPHY, EUROPE, LITERATURE]. R.C.

Bentley, Nicholas, Slater, Michael, & Burgis, Nina. 1988. *The Dickens Index.* Oxford: University Press.
Brown, Ivor. 1963. *Dickens in his Time.* London: Thomas Nelson.
Giuliano, Edward, & Collins, Philip (eds.). 1986. *The Annotated Dickens.* Two volumes. London: Orbis.
Hibbert, Christopher. 1967. *The Making of Charles Dickens.* London: Longmans. New York: Harper & Row.
Mankowitz, Wolf. 1976. *Dickens of London.* London: Weidenfeld & Nicolson.
Wilson, Angus. 1972. *The World of Charles Dickens.* London: Secker & Warburg.

DICKINSON, Emily (Elizabeth) [1830–87]. American poet, born in Amherst, Massachusetts, daughter of a prominent lawyer and legislator, and educated at Amherst College and Mount Holyoke Female Seminary. She lived out her life in Amherst, an isolated village in the Connecticut River Valley with strong 17c Puritan beginnings: 'Amherst was famous for having more ministers per capita than any other town in the United States' (Jay Leyda, *The Years and Hours of Emily Dickinson*, 1960). She attended the First Church of Christ from early childhood until adulthood but, unlike other members of her family, resisted the periodic waves of revivalism that engulfed the town. She never formally professed membership in the First Church, but each week joined in singing the hymns of Isaac Watts, hymns in short, common, and long metre that haunted Dickinson all of her life and provided the understructure of fervent and homely piety on which she built her own witty, profound, and sometimes sceptical poems.

Dickinson's wide reading included Shakespeare, the Bible, 17c devotional prose and poetry, Dickens, the Brownings, the Brontës, George Eliot, and Ruskin; she also often used Noah Webster's *American Dictionary of the English Language* (1847). She loved words, Latinate and colloquial, abstract and concrete, often bringing them into startling juxtaposition. She rejected grammatical correctness and conventional punctuation to achieve powerfully elliptical talk on paper: for example, frequently using *dont* rather than *doesn't*, most notably in a poem that tells how the sudden death of a friend has stunned her:

It dont sound so terrible—quite—as it did—
I run it over—'Dead', Brain, 'Dead.'
Put it in Latin—left of my school—
Seems it dont shriek so—under rule.
    (no. 426, 1st stanza)

Dickinson's colloquialism here, the critic Brita Lindberg-Seyersted suggests, adds to the reader's awareness of the speaker's shock and pain, as niceties of speech and an orderly progression of ideas would not (*The Voice of the Poet: Aspects of Style in the Poetry of Emily Dickinson*, 1968). In another poem, Christ is presented in an unorthodox image as 'The Auctioneer of Parting' who shouts 'Going, going, gone' from the crucifix as he brings his hammer down. 'What is being knocked down from the cross . . . is death, the symbolic last "Parting" of all' (Charles Anderson, *Emily Dickinson's Poetry: Stairway of Surprise*, 1960), and the ensuing despair is that of lovers who have purchased from this auction a separation that brings everlasting pain. Her colloquialisms were smoothed away in the 1890s by her genteel New England editors (in versions still widely anthologized), but have been restored in Thomas H. Johnson's definitive edition, *The Poems of Emily Dickinson* (1955). The many biographical and critical studies of the poet and the recent formation of the *Emily Dickinson International Society* point to growing interest in a poet who used English in a profoundly American idiom. See index. [AMERICAS, BIOGRAPHY, LITERATURE]. B.L.

DICTATION [17c: from Latin *dictatio/dictationis* saying, asserting, dictating]. (1) Saying something formally and clearly, and at an appropriate speed, so that it can be written down by a copyist, student, or secretary, or recorded by a machine: *He started the dictation at 10 o'clock.* (2) Taking down what is dictated: *doing dictation, dictation exercises.* (3) The resulting text: *Can I see your dictation?* Someone who dictates notes, letters, etc., is a *dictater*, not a *dictator* (a distinction possible in writing and print but not in the normal rhythm of speech). In scribal societies, dictation was the only means by which multiple copies of a text could be made, and required great care and concentration on the part of both dictaters and copyists. The practice has been used in schools as a means of inculcating accuracy of spelling from the Middle Ages to the present day. In France, because of the complex subtlety of written French, *la dictée* continues to be of great general interest and often takes the form of competitions. In much of the English-speaking world, however, dictation has in recent decades largely dropped out of use as an educational tool. It continues to be widespread in the preparation of business and other formal correspondence, and appears likely to receive a new lease of life with the development and promotion of computers that can successfully recognize and transcribe the human voice. See CORRUPT, SPELLING. [EDUCATION, TECHNOLOGY, WRITING]. T.McA.

DICTION [15c: from Latin *dictio/dictionis* a speech, saying, word; speech, phrasing, delivery. See DICTIONARY]. (1) A way of speaking, usually assessed in terms of prevailing standards of pronunciation and elocution: *clear/slovenly diction*. (2) A way or style of using words and phrases, especially in a literary tradition: *aureate diction, poetic diction*. (3) The range of vocabulary used by a particular writer: *Shakespearian diction; the diction of Robert Burns*. See AUREATE DICTION, ELOCUTION, ORTHOEPY, POETIC DICTION, PRONUNCIATION. [SPEECH, STYLE]. T.McA.

DICTIONARY [16c: from Latin *dictionarium, dictionarius* a collection of *dictiones* sayings, words (a medieval book containing lists of words and phrases, however organized): see DICTION]. A generic name for a kind of reference book, usually a work devoted to the definition of words entered in alphabetic order, such as the *Collins English Dictionary*, but also including works of an encyclopedic nature, such as *The Oxford Dictionary of Natural History*. Such books are so closely associated with alphabetized entries that the phrase *dictionary order* is synonymous with *alphabetic(al) order*, but in fact since the Middle Ages many works called 'dictionaries' have been differently arranged, and a wide range of reference books, including thesauruses and gazetteers, are referred to for convenience as 'dictionaries'. Among the many kinds of dictionary, the commonest contrast is between *monolingual* or *unilingual dictionaries* that list and define the words of one language and *bilingual dictionaries* that offer the equivalents of Language A in Language B, and vice versa. In computing, the term refers to both a list of codes, terms, keys, etc., and their meanings, as used in computer programs, and a list of words (often drawn from a conventional dictionary) against which spellings can be checked.

Origins. The earliest known prototypes of the dictionary were West Asian bilingual word lists of the second millennium BC. They were Sumerian and Akkadian words inscribed in parallel columns on clay tablets in cuneiform writing and were organized thematically, like a thesaurus. Even after the invention of the alphabet later in the same millennium many centuries passed before alphabetic ordering became a common tool for organizing information. The lists came into existence because the Akkadians (Babylonians) had inherited through conquest the culture and traditions of Sumer and used the sets of signs as a means by which their scribes could learn what was, in effect, the classical language of writing. Over two thousand years later in medieval Europe, the same principle was used when scribes who spoke vernacular languages learned to read and write in Latin; the first European dictionaries were bilingual lists of (difficult) words of Latin explained in the vernacular of the learners in question: see GLOSS. A typical work that made Latin words accessible through English glosses was the *Promptorium parvulorum sive clericorum* (Storehouse for little ones or clerics) of Galfridus Grammaticus (Geoffrey the Grammarian), compiled around 1440.

The hard-word dictionaries. The need for a work in which harder English words were explained by easier English words arose in the late 16c. The first published dictionary of English was Robert Cawdrey's *Table Alphabeticall* (1604), which contained fewer than 3,000 'hard vsuall English wordes' listed alphabetically in roman type with the barest of explanations in black letter: *Dulcor*, sweetnesse; *Placable*, easie to be pleased. It was designed for quick consultation by 'Ladies, Gentlewomen, or any other vnskilfull persons', to help them understand and use foreign borrowings. It was followed by John Bullokar's *English Expositor* (1616), Henry Cockeram's *English Dictionarie* (1623), the first to be given that name, and Thomas Blount's *Glossographia* (1656), which had some 9,000 words, fuller definitions, and etymologies. Such works did not attempt to reflect the whole range of vocabulary in the age of Shakespeare and Milton. They were concerned only with 'hard words', the classical-based vocabulary of Renaissance English: they bristled with 'Terms of Art', the technical and semi-technical words coined by geographers, mathematicians, doctors, and others. They were highly derivative, drawing in particular on the older Latin-English dictionaries, and answered a real need: Cockeram went through 12 editions to 1670 and the last of many printings of Bullokar was in 1775.

The universal dictionaries. The hard-word tradition went on into the 18c in the work of John

Kersey and Nathaniel Bailey, and traces survive in such traditional works as the *Chambers English Dictionary* (1988). A novel approach emerged, however, in the *New World of English Words* (1658) by Edward Phillips, a nephew of Milton and a miscellaneous hack writer. His folio volume had its hard words, but was altogether grander and more inclusive. By the 5th edition in 1696, it had grown to about 17,000 items and in 1706 was revised and further enlarged by John Kersey. Nathaniel Bailey's folio *Dictionarium Britannicum* (1730) is in the same tradition but with a new emphasis on scientific and industrial matters: for example, with a page on *orrery*, and 17 items on the metal *lead*. With the publication of special works such as John Harris's *Lexicon Technicum* (1704), the need for such encyclopedic material in general dictionaries was already decreasing; when Samuel Johnson set his face against extraneous matter, a British tradition of dictionaries for words and encyclopedias for facts was established, although some later 18c works, such as Frederick Barlow's *Complete English Dictionary* (1772) and James Barclay's *Complete and Universal English Dictionary* (1774), continued to provide geographical and other non-lexical information.

The notion that a dictionary should as far as possible be an inventory of all the words of the language became established with Kersey's *New English Dictionary* (1702), which gave the dictionary a place in competition with spelling books as a quick look-up source. To begin with, little information was given about common words ('*To do*, or act, &c.' is the whole of Kersey's entry for that verb), but from this time forward the monolingual dictionary was of greater value to foreign learners of English. Since Elisha Coles's *English Dictionary* (1676), a sprinkling of the commoner dialect words, as well as some cant and flash terms, had come to be included in general dictionaries. With these, the need arose for more systematic usage labels to warn the reader of the status of such a word. Some obsolete items had been given a distinctive mark by Bullokar in 1616 and the uptake of 'old words' increased in the 18c, including legal items and literary archaisms drawn especially from Spenser and Chaucer. Bailey's *Universal Etymological English Dictionary* (1721) gave English a one-volume reference dictionary of some 40,000 entries that was strong on bookish and technical vocabulary, weak in definition and semantic coverage, up-to-date in spelling, and provided the accepted etymologies of its day. It was the standard dictionary of the 18c and was gradually updated and enlarged to some 50,000 entries through successive editions and reprintings to the 28th and last edition in 1800.

Johnson's dictionary. The *Dictionary of the English Language* (1755) by Samuel Johnson differs from the works of his predecessors in both scale and intention. On the model of the dictionaries of the French and Italian academies, he sought to encapsulate the 'best' usage of his day, and did this on the basis of over 100,000 quotations from Sir Philip Sidney in the 16c to his own time. In definition and the internal arrangement of entries Johnson also went beyond his rivals. Benjamin Martin, in his *Lingua Britannica Reformata* (1749), had been the first English compiler to mark off the different senses of words; by arranging his senses chronologically, Johnson enabled his readers to follow the evolution of each word and provided the foundation for the historical lexicography of the 19-20c. Johnson gave little attention to collocation, idiom, and grammatical information, although he provided a brief grammar at the front. In cases of divided or uncertain usage he provided a prescriptive comment (*governant*: 'a lady who has the care of young girls of quality. The more general and proper word is *governess*'). His dictionary enjoyed unique authority among successive generations of users in the matter of word choice and word meaning. In spelling, it represented a strongly conservative tradition, compared with which Bailey was progressive: *horrour, inferiour*, etc., where Bailey has *horror, inferior*, etc.

Pronouncing dictionaries. The provision of information about pronunciation developed in the later 18c. Johnson, following Bailey's second volume (1727) and Thomas Dyche's and William Pardon's *New General English Dictionary* (1735), marked only word stress. With an increasing concern for *orthoepy* (proper pronunciation), however, *pronouncing dictionaries* became established in the latter half of the 18c, of which John Walker's *Critical Pronouncing Dictionary of the English Language* (1791) was the foremost. Walker provided his pronunciations immediately after each headword, dividing each italicized word into its syllables and placing a superscript number over each vowel to indicate its value as specified in a list at the beginning of the book. The Walker pronunciations were effectively married with Johnson's definitions in many of the abridged versions of Johnson's Dictionary, which lasted well into the 19c.

A shift across the Atlantic. In 1828, Noah Webster, a publisher of school spelling books, created a new tradition and lent status to English as it was developing in North America with his *American Dictionary of the English Language*, which contained some 12,000 words not listed by Johnson and offered definitions of many words and concepts current in the New World.

Webster rejected many of the more conservative spellings in Johnson and established for AmE forms like *honor, color* (not *honour, colour*), a different pattern for spelling inflected forms (*traveler, traveling, traveled*, not *traveller, travelling, travelled*, etc.), and *-ize* for *-ise*. Some reforms were based on etymology (Latin *color, honor*) and some were phonetic (*-ize* for *-ise*). In 1790, Webster had been even more radical, urging in *A Collection of Essays and Fugitiv Writings* the elimination of all 'silent' letters and the regularization of spellings like *wur, breth, waz, tung* and *reezon*. One of his employees, Joseph E. Worcester, established his own dictionary-publishing venture in Boston, and produced in 1830 his *Comprehensive Pronouncing and Explanatory Dictionary*, which went through several editions (1846, 1855, 1860) and was closer to the Johnsonian tradition. In his preface to *A Universal and Critical Dictionary of the English Language* (1846), Worcester wrote of Johnson's *Dictionary*: 'No other dictionary has had so much influence in fixing the external form of the language, and ascertaining and settling the meaning and proper use of words. . . . His dictionary, from the time of its first publication, has been far more than any other, regarded as a standard for the language.' This view was shared by many in the US, especially by those who rejected Webster in favour of Worcester.

Other dictionaries by Worcester include *A Pronouncing, Explanatory, and Synonymous Dictionary of the English Language* (1855) and *A Dictionary of the English Language* (1860). Worcester died in 1865; although his heirs carried on, the competition from Webster's dictionaries proved too much, and the company failed. Webster died in 1843, but his son, William G. Webster, carried on, and in 1847, with Chauncey A. Goodrich of Yale, published a revised edition of the earlier work. Successive editions appeared in 1864 and 1890; in 1909 appeared a relatively large work, the 1st edition of *The New International Dictionary of the English Language*; a 2nd edition appeared in 1934, and a 3rd in 1961. The *Second Edition*, edited by William Allan Neilson, came to be regarded as the standard among dictionaries published in the US. Because of its descriptive approach (among other things), *Webster's Third* created even more consternation among conservatives in the mid-20c than Noah Webster's break with British tradition over a century earlier, and it failed to gain universal acceptance. See WEBSTER'S NEW INTERNATIONAL DICTIONARY.

Cross-fertilization. During the 19c, US and UK publishers often produced new dictionaries by adapting established works, sometimes without acknowledgement but often through agreements with the publishers of the existing works. Such cooperation could lead to a succession of related works over many decades. For example, the Scottish publisher Blackie selected the 1841 edition of Webster's *American Dictionary of the English Language* as the basis for a dictionary to be prepared by the mathematician John Ogilvie. This work, the *Imperial Dictionary, English, Technological, & Scientific*, was published in parts between 1847 and 1850. It was more encyclopedic than the *Webster* and greatly expanded the use of illustrative engravings. When Ogilvie died in 1867, Charles Annandale began to edit a revision, which was published in 1882–3. The illustrations were augmented, and the entry and definition coverage expanded to include Americanisms, slang, and colloquialisms. This series of dictionaries was successful in Britain, and the Century Company, an American publisher of the periodical *The Country Magazine*, published an edition for sale in the US. In 1882, Century put forward a plan for *The Century Dictionary*, to be based on the Annandale edition of Ogilvie, to which they had acquired the rights. As that work had been based, originally, on a Webster dictionary, ironic intricacies emerged concerning the ultimate basis of *The Century*, which was prepared during 1884–9 under the direction of William Dwight Whitney. This work, available in several editions (1889–1911), occupied ten quarto volumes. Though out of date, it is still widely regarded as a paragon of clarity and accuracy for its definitions and etymologies and as a model of design, production, illustration, typography, paper, printing, and binding. Several dictionaries have been directly or indirectly based on it, including *The American College Dictionary* (Random House, 1947), *The Random House Dictionary of the English Language* (1966), and the *Collins English Dictionary* (1979).

Popular and scholarly dictionaries. By the late 19c, the making of dictionaries of English had fallen into two broad types: general, usually single-volume works for the expanding community of the literate, such as *Chambers's English Dictionary* (1872), and scholarly dictionaries on philological principles, often multi-volume, concerned either with cataloguing distinct varieties in great detail, such as the *English Dialect Dictionary* (1898–1905), or with covering the entire language, such as the *New English Dictionary on Historical Principles* that emerged from plans made by the Philological Society in 1858 and ultimately became the *Oxford English Dictionary* (1st edition, 12 volumes, 1928; 2nd edition, 20 volumes, 1989). The family of Oxford dictionaries is closely related to the *OED* and combines the two types. Its general list is relatively recent, beginning in 1911 with the 1st edition of *The Concise Oxford Dictionary*, edited by the brothers H. W. and F. G. Fowler.

The dictionary industry. The number of dictionaries of English published in the 19–20c in Britain, America, and increasingly elsewhere is vast and varied. In terms of the size of books and the markets for which they are intended, they range from the great multi-volume works through the large 'unabridged' dictionaries and the single-volume desk and family dictionaries to the mid-range collegiate and concise editions, various school and pocket editions, down to a plethora of minis and micros. Leading publishers of dictionaries aim at bringing out and keeping up to date volumes at all or most of these levels, often presented in a standard livery with a logo that seeks to catch the eye. Beyond these mainstream products are a multitude of specialities, such as products for the fiercely competitive ELT market that has developed since the Second World War, the complex range of bilingual publications for English and the world's significant languages, and special-interest works relating to etymology and word histories, dialects and regional varieties, technical subjects, controversial usage, slang, and the vocabulary of subcultures. An awareness of the extent, diversity, and intricacy of the English-language dictionary industry can be gathered by consulting the entries listed below. In various ways, they represent the historical stages through which dictionaries and their users have passed: comparing English and other languages, looking for information on hard and exotic words, seeking reassurance about the 'proper' meaning and use of certain words, investigating the evolution of words, and seeking a precise fix on how a word or sense of a word is currently used.

See AUSTRALIAN DICTIONARIES, CANADIAN DICTIONARIES IN ENGLISH, LEXICOGRAPHY, NEW ZEALAND DICTIONARIES, OXFORD DICTIONARIES, PERIOD DICTIONARIES OF ENGLISH, REGIONAL DICTIONARIES OF ENGLISH, SLANG, SCOTTISH DICTIONARIES, SOUTH AFRICAN ENGLISH DICTIONARIES. For entries relating to specific dictionaries, dictionary-makers, and publishers, see REFERENCE. [WORD].　　　　N.E.O., L.U., T.MCA.

Bailey, Richard W. (ed.). 1987. *Dictionaries of English: Prospects for the Record of Our Language.* Ann Arbor: University of Michigan Press.

Burchfield, Robert (ed.). 1987. *Studies in Lexicography.* Oxford: University Press.

Hartmann, R. R. K. (ed.). 1986. *The History of Lexicography.* Amsterdam & Philadelphia: John Benjamins.

Ilson, Robert (ed.). 1986. *Lexicography: An Emerging International Profession.* Manchester: University Press.

Landau, Sidney I. 1984, 1989. *Dictionaries: The Art and Craft of Lexicography.* New York: Charles Scribner's Sons (1984). Cambridge: University Press (1989).

McArthur, Tom. 1986. *Worlds of Reference: Lexicography, Learning and Language from the Clay Tablet to the Computer.* Cambridge: University Press.

McDavid, Raven I., & Duckett, Audrey R. (eds.). 1973. *Lexicography in English.* Annals of the New York Academy of Sciences 211.

Stein, Gabriele. 1985. *The English Dictionary before Cawdrey.* Tübingen: Niemeyer.

DICTIONARY OF AMERICAN ENGLISH,

short form *DAE.* A historical dictionary of AmE in four volumes (1938–44), treating words and senses that originated in America, that are more common there than elsewhere in the English-speaking world, or that have some important connection with American life. The *DAE* was the first of the period and regional dictionaries intended to take up the exploration of English where the *OED* left off. Begun in 1925 by William A. Craigie, the *DAE* was published in fascicles beginning in 1936, the initial title page listing the editors as Craigie, James R. Hulbert, George Watson, Mitford M. Mathews, and Allen Walker Read. When the first volume appeared in 1938, the editors were listed as Craigie and Hulbert. Craigie's definition of the scope of the *DAE* limited it to words and senses illustrating 'the development of the country and the history of its people' in order to show how 'the language has been adapted to the country', as with *butte, confederacy, congress, federal, senate.* Words understood to be clearly of US origin were marked and the relationship of words to BrE or British colonial usage indicated. Slang after 1875, dialect words, CanE, and CarE were excluded, by editorial policy if not always in fact, and pronunciations were rarely given. The inclusion of words which had a 'greater currency' in the US than elsewhere, though narrowly conceived, was the principle of selection. See CRAIGIE, DICTIONARY, MATHEWS, PERIOD DICTIONARIES OF ENGLISH, READ, REGIONAL DICTIONARIES OF ENGLISH, WATSON. [AMERICAS, REFERENCE].　　　　R.W.B.

DICTIONARY OF AMERICANISMS, short

form *DA.* A dictionary compiled on historical principles, with entries selected to illustrate 'words and meanings of words which have been added to the English language in the United States', whether through coining, borrowing, or the adaptation of BrE words. Unlike the *Dictionary of American English,* which concluded its coverage at 1900, the *DA* presents entries and quotations to the time the work was being compiled. Its editor, Mitford M. Mathews, examined entries labelled *US* in the *Oxford English Dictionary* and the *English Dialect Dictionary* and found that many had not originated in AmE: for example *drummer* 'commercial traveller, travelling salesman'. He discovered that words and senses in BrE often had unsuspected American origins: for example, *stump* 'to campaign for election'. He also found that AmE borrowings from foreign languages were more numerous than previously suspected. Critics have suggested that the focus on origins gives a distorted picture of what kind of English was in use at a given time, but Mathews's emphasis on the sources of vocabulary has been repeated in many successor volumes. Resources for editing did not allow pronunciation variants to be investigated, but IPA pronunciations are given for borrowings from other languages into AmE. A small collection of entries were selected by its publisher, the University of Chicago Press, and issued as *Americanisms* (1966). See DICTIONARY, MATHEWS, REGIONAL DICTIONARIES OF ENGLISH. [AMERICAS, REFERENCE].   R.W.B.

DICTIONARY OF AMERICAN REGIONAL ENGLISH, short form *DARE.* The official dictionary of the American Dialect Society, published by the Belknap Press of Harvard University Press, Cambridge, Massachusetts. The first volume (1,061 pages) appeared in 1985; the second volume (1,175 pages) appeared in 1991; three others are in preparation, under Chief Editor Frederic G. Cassidy and Associate Editor Joan H. Hall, with a staff of 18. It is based at the U. of Wisconsin, Madison, and is supported mainly by the National Endowment for the Humanities, the National Science Foundation, and private foundations and donors. Volume I, covering the letters A, B, C, also includes an Introduction describing the purposes and methods of the *Dictionary,* with sections on the *DARE* maps and regional labels, the chief changes characterizing folk speech, present pronunciation in the US, the questionnaire used in field collecting, and the list of informants who answered it, with the location, type of community, age, degree of education, occupation, sex, and race of each. This information makes it possible for the reader to assess the responses as to both word usage and social status of the speaker; it also sharpens the lexicographer's ability to write accurate definitions and usage labels. Volume II covers the letters D to H. Volumes III–V will complete the alphabet and add the bibliography, summary of the field-collected data, comparative maps, indexes, and supplement (containing items that came in too late for inclusion in the main alphabet).

Typical full treatments of words and phrases entered in *DARE* include the form(s) of the entry, part of speech, pronunciation(s), spelling variants, etymology, region or locality of use,

usage notes, definitions, numbered senses, illustrative dated quotations, editorial notes, and cross-references. Besides the questionnaire responses, the database includes over 7,000 additional sources, oral and written, dating from the 17c. Standard words or senses and common etymologies are not treated, nor are technical words, cant terms, and slang. Included are folk terms and others that are in any way geographically or socially limited. 1,002 representative communities were investigated in the 50 states (1965–70), through direct interview by 80 fieldworkers. Informants were natives (or long-term residents) of their communities. The questionnaire includes 1,847 questions covering general concerns of daily life: 41 categories, ranging from concrete (dwellings, food, clothing, activities) to abstract (attitude, feelings, opinions), and some to investigate grammatical usages. Tape recordings, an important feature of fieldwork, furnish the basis for the pronunciations outlined in the Introduction. Pronunciations included in the entries are based on transcriptions by *DARE* or other fieldworkers. *DARE*'s contributions to lexicography include: (1) The use of maps that show where particular responses occurred (using an outline of the US that has been adjusted to reflect density of population rather than area. (2) The early use of computers to handle large amounts of alphabetical data. (3) The basing of both geographical and social usage labels on calculable data. With its detailed treatments presented in largely nontechnical terms, *DARE* is accessible to both linguists and general readers. See CASSIDY, DICTIONARY, REGIONAL DICTIONARIES OF ENGLISH, REGIONALISM. [AMERICAS, REFERENCE].   F.G.C.

DICTIONARY OF BAHAMIAN ENGLISH. The work of John A. Holm, with Alison W. Shilling (Lexik House, Cold Spring, New York, 1982), with a 35-page introduction containing notes on creole, its nature, origin, and history. The present-day Bahamian vocabulary, with its variations from island to island and among social groups, is comprehensively presented: the older components from a plantation society, correspondences with US and Caribbean usages, the African inheritance, and individual Bahamian differences. Notes on the current sociolinguistic situation and maps of related language types help to make the various interrelationships clear. The organization is alphabetic, interspersed with short articles covering topics that characterize the Bahamian scene which might otherwise not be understood by outsiders, such as bush medicine, festivals, folklore, obeah, and skin colour. The collection of information was done in eight major islands and further data were drawn from 320 printed sources, historical and contemporary. Pronunciation is shown phonemically and some attention is given to syntax. The African element in etymology is emphasized. Treatment is scholarly throughout and such technical terms as must be used are glossed for the general reader. See BAHAMAS, CARIBBEAN ENGLISH, DICTIONARY. [AMERICAS, REFERENCE].   F.G.C.

DICTIONARY OF CANADIANISMS. See CANADIAN DICTIONARIES IN ENGLISH.

DICTIONARY OF CATCH PHRASES, full title *Dictionary of Catch Phrases (British and American), from the Sixteenth Century to the Present Day.* A work by Eric Partridge, published in 1977 by Routledge & Kegan Paul (London) and Stein & Day (New York), with a 2nd (revised and augmented) edition edited by Paul Beale in 1985. A light-hearted, discursive dictionary, an offshoot of *A Dictionary of Slang and Unconventional English* (1937); its coverage of catchphrases is wider than those briefly entered in the *DSUE*; its bias, however, is still towards catchphrases of BrE, and most of those treated are of 19-20c origin. Partridge did not define a 'catch phrase' and so gave himself scope to include any informal phrase he wished: for example, *I'll have your guts for garters,* a threat in use since the early 17c; from colonial North America, *Don't take any wooden nutmegs* Don't let anyone cheat you. See CATCHPHRASE, DICTIONARY, DICTIONARY OF SLANG AND UNCONVENTIONAL ENGLISH, PARTRIDGE. [EUROPE, REFERENCE, STYLE, USAGE].   P.B.

DICTIONARY OF JAMAICAN ENGLISH. The first comprehensive treatment of the lexicon of a Caribbean area, with dated citations, following the method of the *OED.* It is the work of Frederic G. Cassidy and Robert Le Page, published by Cambridge University Press in 1967, and revised in 1980. It covers Jamaica alone, but the revised edition adds symbols indicating concurrent usage in Barbados, Belize, Guyana, Nicaragua, Surinam, and Trinidad. Etymology is given full attention in an area where the loan element includes Amerindian, French, German, Portuguese, Spanish, and a considerable West African infusion, carried as far as could be with languages at the time inadequately studied. Sources include not only printed material from 1655 onward, when the island was taken from Spain and English superseded Spanish, but many oral sources, especially interviews made throughout the island in 1952, following the methods of dialect geography. The lexicon covers the full range from basilectal creole to acrolectal standard Jamaican English. A unique feature is that words having established spellings are entered in capital letters while those only or chiefly used in speech are entered in lower-case phonemic letters. Included with a general introduction are lists of sources cited and a full linguistic introduction of 28 pages. See CASSIDY, DICTIONARY, JAMAICAN ENGLISH, REGGAE. [AMERICAS, REFERENCE].   F.G.C.

DICTIONARY OF MODERN ENGLISH USAGE, short forms *Modern English Usage, MEU.* The best-known usage manual of the 20c, compiled by H. W. Fowler and published by Oxford University Press in 1926, with a 2nd edition edited by Sir Ernest Gowers in 1965; a rewritten and alphabetically arranged version of Fowler's *The King's English* (1906). He dedicated it to the memory of his brother F. G. Fowler (d.1918) 'who shared with me the planning of this book, but did not live to share the writing'. At first to be called 'The Idiom Dictionary', it is the product of a far-reaching search for fastidious distinctions such as how *exterior, external, extraneous,* and *extrinsic* differ in meaning and use, and how apocope (*cinema* from *cinematograph*) differs from syncope (*pacifist* from *pacifistic*) and from aphaeresis (*special* from *especial*). Every major hazard in English usage was subjected to reanalysis and, where necessary, provided with sage qualifications or 'Keep Off' signs. *MEU* is a collection of articles arranged under both ordinary headings (*this, thistle, thither, -th nouns, those, though*) and idiosyncratic ones (*battered ornaments, out of the frying pan, sturdy indefensibles, swapping horses*). This work in particular has made the name *Fowler* as well known among those interested in usage and the language as *Johnson* and *Webster,* a point of reference for both those who venerate and those who regret what he has had to say. See FOWLER, GOWERS, KING'S ENGLISH (THE), USAGE GUIDANCE AND CRITICISM. [EUROPE, REFERENCE, STYLE, USAGE].   RO.W.B.

DICTIONARY OF NEWFOUNDLAND ENGLISH. See CANADIAN DICTIONARIES IN ENGLISH.

DICTIONARY OF PRINCE EDWARD ISLAND ENGLISH. See CANADIAN DICTIONARIES IN ENGLISH.

DICTIONARY OF SLANG AND UNCONVENTIONAL ENGLISH, short form *DSUE.* A work by Eric Partridge, published in 1937 in London by Routledge & Kegan Paul. The subtitle of the original work described its contents as: 'Slang, including the language of the underworld, Colloquialisms and Catch-phrases, Solecisms and Catachreses, Nicknames,

Vulgarisms, and such Americanisms as have been naturalized'. It built on more than 12 dictionaries of slang, beginning with Thomas Harman's *Caveat for Vagabones* (1567), and was based on Farmer and Henley's *Slang and Its Analogues* (seven volumes, 1890–1904). He added material from the *OED*, glossaries of contemporary slang from the 1930s onward, his observation of everyday common or specialized slang, and in due course notes from the worldwide network of correspondents that it brought into being. Its coverage was essentially the UK and Commonwealth. The *DSUE* was widely regarded as filling a lexicographical gap, because it treated four-letter words and sexual and scatological vulgarities that had previously been omitted by the *OED* and the general run of 'family' dictionaries. The obscenity laws of the time forbade the printing of such words in full; asterisks were therefore substituted for vowels in the two editions before the Second World War: 'c*nt. The female pudend'; 'f*ck. An act of sexual connexion'. Partridge noted in the preface: 'My rule, in the matter of unpleasant terms, has been to deal with them as briefly, as astringently, as aseptically as was consistent with clarity and adequacy; in a few instances, I had to force myself to overcome an instinctive repugnance.' By the 7th edition (1970), the book had become an institution and expanded to two (unstarred) volumes. In 1978, Partridge gave his notes for the 8th edition of *DSUE* to Paul Beale, who edited the two volumes back into one, as published in 1984. See DICTIONARY, PARTRIDGE, SLANG. [EUROPE, REFERENCE, USAGE].   P.B.

DICTIONARY OF THE OLDER SCOTTISH TONGUE. See SCOTTISH DICTIONARIES.

DICTIONARY RESEARCH CENTRE, short form *DRC*. A title for a lexicographical research centre established at an institute of higher learning, such as the DRC at the U. of Exeter in England (est. 1984), under the direction of Reinhard Hartmann, and the DRC at Macquarie U., Sydney, Australia (est. 1985), under the direction of Arthur Delbridge. The former has since 1987 run an annual training course for lexicographers and since 1989 created the (database) *International Who's Who in Lexicography*, and supports postgraduate work. The latter is developing a corpus of contemporary Australian texts, organizes a series of national conferences entitled *Style Council* (devoted to the discussion of standard spelling and punctuation), and supports masters courses in lexicography in the School of English and Linguistics. See AUSTRALIAN DICTIONARIES, DELBRIDGE. [EUROPE, OCEANIA, REFERENCE].   T.MCA., W.S.R.

DICTIONARY SOCIETY OF NORTH AMERICA, short form *DSNA*. An American and Canadian association founded in 1975, and concerned with lexicography, dictionary making, and dictionary use. It publishes a newsletter and the journal *Dictionaries*. Compare EURALEX. [AMERICAS, MEDIA, REFERENCE].   J.A.

DIGEST [16c in this sense: from Latin *digesta* a collection of laws or writings, the neuter plural of *digestus* divided, digested]. (1) A collection of writings on the same topic, especially if condensed and systematically arranged under special subheadings. (2) A summary of the kind that would appear in such a collection. See ABRIDG(E)-MENT, FACTS ON FILE, MAGAZINE, PERIODICAL, READER'S DIGEST. [MEDIA, WRITING].   G.H.

DIGLOSSIA [1958: a Latinization of French *diglossie*, from Greek *diglōssos* with two tongues: first used in English by Charles Ferguson]. A term in sociolinguistics for the use of two or more varieties of language for different purposes in the same community. The varieties are called *H* and *L*, the first being generally a standard variety used for 'high' purposes and the second often a 'low' spoken vernacular. In Egypt, classical Arabic is H and local colloquial Arabic is L. The most important hallmark of diglossia is specialization, H being appropriate in one set of situations, L in another: reading a newspaper aloud in H, but discussing its contents in L. Functions generally reserved for H include sermons, political speeches, university lectures, and news broadcasts, while those reserved for L include everyday conversations, instructions to servants, and folk literature.

The varieties differ not only in grammar, phonology, and vocabulary, but also with respect to function, prestige, literary heritage, acquisition, standardization, and stability. L is typically acquired at home as a mother tongue and continues to be so used throughout life. Its main uses are familial and familiar. H, on the other hand, is learned through schooling and never at home, and is related to institutions outside the home. The separate domains in which H and L are acquired provide them with separate systems of support. Diglossic societies are marked not only by this compartmentalization of varieties, but also by restriction of access, especially to H. Entry to formal institutions such as school and government requires knowledge of H. In England, from medieval times until the 18c, Latin played an H role while English was L; in Scotland, 17–20c, the H role has usually been played by local standard English, the L role by varieties of Scots. In some English-speaking Caribbean and West African countries, the H role is played by local standard English, the L role by English-based creoles in the Caribbean and vernacular languages and English-based creoles in West Africa.

The extent to which these functions are compartmentalized can be illustrated by the importance attached by community members to using the right variety in the appropriate context. An outsider who learns to speak L and then uses it in a formal speech risks being ridiculed. Members of a community generally regard H as superior to L in a number of respects; in some cases, H is regarded as the only 'real' version of a particular language, to the extent that people claim they do not speak L at all. Sometimes, the alleged superiority is avowed for religious and/or literary reasons: the fact that classical Arabic is the language of the Qur'ān endows it with special significance, as the language of the King James Bible, created in England, recommended itself to Scots as high religious style. In other cases, a long literary and scriptural tradition backs the H variety, as with Sanskrit in India. There is also a strong tradition of formal grammatical study and standardization associated with H varieties: for example, Latin and 'school' English.

Since the term's first use in English, it has been extended to cases where the varieties in question do not belong to the same language (such as Spanish and Guaraní in Paraguay), as well as cases where more than two varieties or languages participate in such a relationship (French, classical Arabic, and colloquial Arabic in *triglossic* distribution in Tunisia, with French and classical Arabic sharing H functions). The term *polyglossia* (a state of many tongues) has been used to refer to cases such as Singapore, where Cantonese, English, Malay, and Tamil coexist in a functional relationship.

See ARABIC, BILINGUALISM, BISOCIATION, CLASSICAL LANGUAGE, CODE-MIXING AND CODE-SWITCHING, DIALECT, STANDARD, TESD, VARIETY, VERNACULAR. [LANGUAGE, VARIETY]. S.R.

DIGRAPH [18c: from Greek *di-* twice, *graphḗ* writing]. A term in orthography for two letters that represent one sound, such as *th* in *this* and *sh* in *ashes*. If three letters together represent a single sound, they constitute a *trigraph*, such as *tch* in *catch* and *sch* in *schmaltz*. When letters form digraphs, they surrender their independent sound values so as to stand as a group for a single phoneme, usually because an alphabet has no letter to serve that purpose. In such cases, there may be some phonetic motivation in the combination (*sh*, *dg* roughly suggesting the sounds in *dash* and *dodge*), though this may have vanished as pronunciation has changed (for example, the *gh* in *tough* and *through*). Sometimes letters that happen to come together may

look like (and be mistaken for) digraphs: for example, the *t*, *h* in *posthumous* being interpreted as the *th* in *asthma*. Because English has more phonemes than letters, digraphs are used to represent sounds for which no original Roman letter would serve: for example, the initial sounds in *three* and *this* and the final sounds in *rich* and *ridge*. There is a greater degree of consistency in English in the use of consonant digraphs and trigraphs than in vowel digraphs.

Consonant digraphs. Most English consonant digraphs consist of a single letter followed by *h*, modelled on the Latin digraphs *ch*, *ph*, *th* used to transcribe the Greek letters chi, phi, and theta. Consonant digraphs include: *ch* as in *chair*, *charisma*, and *loch*; *sh* as in *shout*; *th* as in *three* and *these*; *wh* as in *whale*; *ph* as in *philosophy*; *gh* as in *tough* and *daughter*; *ng* as in *longer* and *singer*; *ck* as in *track*; *dg* as in *judge*. Although *zh* is not a conventional digraph in English, occurring mainly in loans from Russian (*Brezhnev*), it is well understood and is sometimes used to give a spelling pronunciation of a word (*measure* as 'mezher').

Vowel digraphs. Because the vowel sounds of English greatly outnumber the symbols available, digraphs are widely used to represent them. A few are fairly regular, such as *ai* in *fail*, *pain*, *maintain*, but most can represent several vowels (as with *ea* in *bead*, *bread*, *break*, *hear*, *hearse*, *heart*) and many vowels can be represented by a variety of digraphs (especially if 'magic' *e* as in *fate*, *eve*, *wise*, *rote*, *mute* is counted as the second element in alternative digraphs to those in *wait*, *eat*, *flies*, *oat*, *root*). Most problematic is the spelling of the long *e* sound, as in the patterns *be*, *bee*, *eve*, *leave*, *sleeve*, *deceive*, *believe*, (BrE) *anaemia*, (BrE) *foetus*, *routine*. Some digraphs representing a vowel combine vowel and consonant letters (*sight*, *sign*, *indict*), while others vary within the same root (*speak/speech*, *high/height*). In addition, vowel digraphs are well known for their use in a number of highly irregular, sometimes unique spellings, such as *quay*, *key*, *people*, *leopard*, *broad*, *brooch*, *blood*, *build*.

The digraphs Æ and Œ. The ligature digraph *æ* as in *Ælfric*, *Cæsar*, *encyclopædia* was originally used in Latin and adopted by Old English for the vowel in *hat* (*hæt*), often referred to as *ash*. It has been used in English, under the influence of Latin, to represent Greek *ai* as in *Æschylus*, *Æsop*, *anæmia*, *hæmorrhage*, now commonly *Aeschylus Aesop*, and BrE *anaemia*, *haemorrhage*. The AmE practice of simplifying *ae* to *e* is becoming general, as in *anemia*, *hemorrhage*, *encyclopedia*, *medieval*, but not **Eschylus*, **Esop*. The Latin ligature digraph *œ* represents Greek *oi* as in *Œdipus*, *amœba*, now commonly

Oedipus and BrE *amoeba, foetus*. The AmE practice of simplifying *oe* to *e* is becoming general, as in *ameba, fetus*, but not **Edipus*. In some words, the digraph (with or without the ligature) has long since vanished: for example, older *oeconomy* is now universally *economy*, and *ecology* has never been spelt **oecology*. See ASH, DIPHTHONG, GRAPH, LETTER[1], LIGATURE, SPELLING, and A, C, E, G, H, I, K, O, P, R, S, T, W. [WRITING].   C.U.

DIMINUTIVE [14c: from Latin *diminutivus* making less; cognate with *diminish*]. (1) An affix, usually a suffix, added to a word to suggest smallness (and, paradoxically, either affection or dismissal). In English, the diminutive suffix *-ling* is neutral in *duckling* little duck, affectionate in *darling* little dear, and dismissive in *princeling* little prince. Whereas the *-ette* in *cigarette* conveys smallness, in *usherette* it conveys femaleness and, generally, lesser status than *usher*. Compared with such languages as Spanish, English has few diminutives: *-ette* in *cigarette*; *-ie* in *hippie, lassie, Maggie*; *-let* in *booklet, starlet*; *-ling* in *darling, princeling*; *-y* in *Billy, honky, Tommy, Whitey*. (2) A name, usually a nickname or hypocorism, that suggests smallness, affection, dismissal, etc.: *Will, Willie, Willy* (and, in baby talk, the double diminutive *Willikins*) and *Bill, Billy* as short forms of *William*, and *willie* as a euphemism for the penis. See CLIPPING, L-SOUNDS, PET NAME, SCOTS, SEXISM, SUFFIX. [NAME, WORD].   T.MCA.

DIPHTHONG [15c: from French *diphthongue* (Modern *diptongue*), Latin *diphthongus*, Greek *diphthonggos* a double sound]. (1) In phonetics, a vowel that starts with one quality and moves in the direction of another quality, as in *toy*, which begins with the quality in *lawn* and moves towards the quality in *pin*. The combination is often described as a sequence of two vowels. There are several varieties of diphthong: wide and narrow; closing and opening; centring; falling and rising. A *wide diphthong* has a marked change in quality: in RP, the vowels in *high, how*, which move from open to close. A *narrow diphthong* has less movement: in RP, the vowel of *day*, which moves from half-close to close. The vowels of *weave, groove* are narrow diphthongs, because they move slightly within the close vowel area, but this movement is usually disregarded and they are treated as monophthongs. A *closing diphthong* ends closer than it begins, while an *opening diphthong* ends more open than it begins. The diphthongs of English tend to be of the closing type: in RP, *say, sigh, soy, so, sow*. A *centring diphthong* moves towards schwa: in RP, *here, there*. In rhotic varieties, this schwa is followed by an *r*-sound, but not in a non-rhotic variety like RP. A *falling diphthong* is stressed on the first element, and a *rising diphthong* is stressed on the second. The diphthongs of English tend to be of the falling type, with the exception of the vowel sound in *view*, which can be interpreted as rising. (2) Two closely associated letters, such as *ai* and *oy*, whether or not they represent a diphthong. Technically these are more accurately known as *digraphs*. See DIGRAPH, MONOPHTHONG, OLD ENGLISH[1], TRIPHTHONG, VOWEL. [SPEECH].   G.K., T.MCA.

DIRECT AND INDIRECT SPEECH, also **direct and reported speech**. Terms for kinds of grammatical construction in which reports are made of something said, written, or thought. Direct speech gives the exact words in the report, and in writing and print uses *quotation marks*, single as in '*I know the answer*,' *Jane said*, double as in "*I know the answer*," *Jane said*. Indirect speech conveys the report in the words of the reporter: for example, *Jane said that she knew the answer* (more formal), and *Jane said she knew the answer* (less formal). In direct speech, the reporting clause may appear initially (*He said, 'I'm finishing now and I'm going home'*), medially ('*I'm finishing now*,' *he said*, '*and I'm going home*'), or finally ('*I'm finishing now and I'm going home*,' *he said*). The reporting verb is sometimes put before the subject, particularly when it is *said* and the subject is not a pronoun: '*I'm finishing now*,' *said Andrew*. A wide range of verbs can be used to indicate the type of utterance or the way in which something is said (such as *answer, ask, comment, cry, ejaculate, enquire/inquire, exclaim, groan, growl, moan, murmur, mutter, note, observe, reply, respond, retort, scream, screech, shout, shriek, smile, whine, yell*) and an adverb may be added to evaluate the speaker's manner (such as *angrily, demurely, happily, mysteriously, radiantly, sadly, sweetly*). Some writers use such variants and additions liberally, others with great restraint.

In indirect speech, verbs are generally 'backshifted' in tense to align them with the time of reporting, and other changes, such as in pronouns and adverbials of time and place, are made for the same reason: *Doris told Robert, 'You can now watch television'* would possibly be reported as *Doris told Robert that he could then watch television*. This backshift relationship of verb tenses in the reporting and reported clauses is known as the *sequence of tenses*. Backshift, however, is optional when what was said applies equally at the time of reporting: *Benjamin said that he is/was coming over to watch television tonight*. Such traditional shifts are not, however, used in certain kinds of relaxed, colloquial reporting and storytelling: *Then he says he's coming and she says that he could come or not for all she cared.*

Apart from direct and indirect statements, there are: (1) *Direct and indirect questions*, the latter normally following the statement order of subject and verb: direct *'Do you understand?' she asked* becoming indirect *She asked if he understood*; direct *'Where has he gone?' I wondered* becoming indirect *I wondered where he had gone.* (2) *Direct and indirect exclamations*, as when direct *'What a clever boy you are!' David told his son* becomes indirect *David told his son what a clever boy he was.* (3) *Direct and indirect instructions*, such as direct *Jane said to Jenny, 'Phone me if you need any help'* becoming indirect *Jane told Jenny to phone her if she needed any help.* In such reports, care may sometimes be necessary to ensure that pronoun reference does not become unclear. Two variants of reported speech occur mainly in fiction: free direct speech and free indirect speech:

Free direct speech lacks a reporting clause to show the shift from narration to reporting; it is often used in fiction to represent the mental reactions of characters to what they see or experience. In the following extract from James Joyce's *Ulysses* (1922), Leopold Bloom reflects on what he sees as he walks along (italics not in the original have been added to mark the free direct speech):

By lorries along Sir John Rogerson's quay Mr Bloom walked soberly, past Windmill lane, Leask's the linseed crusher's, the postal telegraph office. *Could have given that address too.* And past the sailor's home. He turned from the morning noises of the quayside and walked through Lime street. By Brady's cottages a boy for the skins lolled, his bucket of offal linked, smoking a chewed fag butt. A smaller girl with scars of eczema on her forehead eyed him, listlessly holding her battered caskhoop. *Tell him if he smokes he won't grow. O let him! His life isn't such a bed of roses! Waiting outside pubs to bring da home. Come home to ma, da. Slack hour: won't be many there.* He crossed Townsend street, passed the frowning face of Bethel. *El, yes: house of: Aleph, Beth.* And past Nichols' the undertaker's. *At eleven it is. Time enough.*

Free indirect speech resembles indirect speech in shifting tenses and other references, but there is generally no reporting clause and it retains some features of direct speech (such as direct questions and vocatives). In this extract from the South African novelist Dan Jacobson's *A Dance in the Sun* (1956), Fletcher moves into free indirect speech in the course of a conversation with Frank (italics added):

He gave Frank the name of the house he had been in at school. He challenged Frank to look his name up in the school calendar, so that Frank would be able to see for himself the truth of what he was saying. *That was where he had learned what was right and what was not. It had not been his fault that his father had died and that the estate had been in disorder and that he had had to make his own way. But he had, and he had not done so badly either. But he was not a snob.* He repeated that he was not a snob, as though Frank had accused him of being a snob, as though Frank could see anything for him to be particularly snobbish about. *He was not a snob.* All he wanted was decency, decency, decency, he said.

See COMMA, CONVERSATION, DASH, DIALOG(UE), QUOTATION, QUOTATION MARKS, STREAM OF CONSCIOUSNESS. [GRAMMAR, SPEECH, USAGE, WRITING]
S.G.

DIRECT METHOD. See LANGUAGE TEACHING, METHOD.

DIRECT OBJECT. The person or thing affected by the action of a transitive verb. The direct object usually closely follows the verb ('I love *you*', 'Do *the work* now'), unless there is an *indirect object*, when the direct object comes second ('I've sent Audrey *a present*'). The expression 'affected by' has a range of meanings, referring also to things that only come into existence as a result of the action of the verb ('Then somebody invented *the wheel*') and objects of place ('She paced *the room*'). Although direct objects are typically nouns and pronouns, other structures can follow transitive verbs, and some grammarians analyse all the following constructions as direct objects: *that*-clauses ('He said *that he loved her*'); clauses beginning with *wh*-question words ('She explained *why the idea was impossible*'); various *-ing* and infinitive structures with or without subjects ('They both enjoy *dancing*', 'I can't bear (*you*) *to be unhappy*'). See OBJECT. [GRAMMAR].   S.C.

DIRGE [12c: from Latin *Dirige, (Domine)* 'Direct, (O Lord)', the opening words in the ecclesiastical Office of the Dead]. (1) An elegy often intended to be sung as a funeral song, like the Dirge in Shakespeare's *Cymbeline* (4. 2), and often set to mournful music. (2) Anything comparable. (3) A sung funeral service or office of the dead, especially in the Roman Catholic Church. Compare ELEGY, THRENODY. [LITERATURE]. R.C.

DISABILITY. See LANGUAGE HANDICAP.

DISAMBIGUATE [1960s: from *dis-* and *ambiguous*, and *-ate* as in *segregate*]. (1) To remove the ambiguity from a phrase, sentence, or text: 'In order to disambiguate the sentence "She lectured on the famous passenger ship," you'll have to write either "lectured on board" or "lectured about" ' (*Random House Dictionary*, 1987). (2) To determine in a word or phrase, etc., which of two or more possible senses is the right one: *disambiguating a line in a corpus (of words)*. See AMBIGUITY. [LANGUAGE, STYLE].　　　T.MCA.

DISCOURSE [14c: From French *discours*, Latin *discursus* a conversation, from *discurrere/discursum* to run around]. (1) A general, often formal term for a talk, conversation, dialogue, lecture, sermon, or treatise, such as John Dryden's *Discourse concerning the Original and Progress of Satire* (1693). (2) An occasional term for language and usage generally: *all human discourse; philosophical discourse*. (3) In linguistics, a unit or piece of connected speech or writing that is longer than a conventional sentence. See DISCOURSE ANALYSIS, METAPHOR, RHETORIC, TEXT. [LANGUAGE].　　　T.MCA.

DISCOURSE ANALYSIS [1960s]. In linguistics and semiotics, the analysis of connected speech and writing, and their relationship to the contexts in which they are used. Discourse analysts study written texts, conversation, institutionalized forms of talk, communicative events in general, and aspects of electronic text-processing. Early researchers included the structural linguist Zellig Harris in the US in the 1950s, at a time when linguistics was largely concerned with the analysis of single sentences. Harris was interested in the distribution of elements in extended texts and the relationship between a text and its social situation. In the 1960s, the American linguistic anthropologist Dell Hymes studied speech in its social setting (forms of address). The work of British linguistic philosophers such as J. L. Austin, J. R. Searle, and H. P. Grice was influential in the study of language as social action, through speech-act theory, conversational maxims, and pragmatics (the study of meaning in context) in general.

British discourse analysis. Research in the UK has been greatly influenced by the functional approach to language of M. A. K. Halliday, in turn influenced by the Prague School. His systemic linguistics emphasizes the social functions of language and the thematic and informational structure of speech and writing. Halliday relates grammar at the clause and sentence level to situational constraints, referred to as *field* (purpose of communication), *tenor* (relationships among participants), and *mode* (channels of communication). Also influential were John Sinclair and Malcolm Coulthard, who devised a model for the description of spoken interaction in school classrooms, based on a rank-scale of units of discourse, from larger stretches of talk termed *transactions* to individual *acts* of speech. Central to the Sinclair–Coulthard model is the *exchange*, the minimal unit of interaction. Other such work has dealt with doctor–patient talk, service encounters, interviews, debates and business negotiations, and monologues. Other work has related intonation to the structuring of topic and information, and to interaction. Such work follows structural linguistics in isolating units and framing rules for defining well-formed sequences. It also leans on speech-act theory.

American discourse analysis. Research in the US includes the examination of forms of talk such as storytelling, greeting, and verbal duels in different cultural and social settings (for example, the work of John Gumperz and Dell Hymes). The field often referred to as *conversation analysis* is also included under the heading of discourse analysis. Here the emphasis is not on models of structure but on the behaviour of participants in talk and on patterns recurring over a wide range of natural data. The work of E. Goffman, D. Sudnow, H. Sacks, E. A. Schegloff, and G. Jefferson is important in the study of conversational rules, turn-taking, and other features of spoken interaction. The description of turn-taking classically illustrates the approach. A set of rules or procedures is described for how participants manage their turns at speaking: speakers know when they may, without being seen to interrupt, take a turn at talk, and mechanisms exist for selecting who speaks next.

Generally, the basic unit of spoken discourse is the *adjacency pair*, a pair of utterances produced by different speakers, whose second member is constrained by the first: for example, in question–response and greeting–greeting. Adjacency pairs are an example of local management in talk. As well as strict adjacency, the description deals with embedding (*insertion sequences*) and with the larger-scale organization of openings and closings. Alongside the conversation analysts, in the sociolinguistic tradition, William Labov's studies of oral narrative have contributed to a more general knowledge of narrative structure. Such work has generated a variety of descriptions of discourse organization as well as studies of social constraints on politeness and face-preserving phenomena. These overlap with British work in pragmatics.

Text linguistics. Important in the development of discourse analysis is the work of *text grammarians*, mostly on written language. Such grammarians view texts as elements strung together in definable relationships. The *cohesion* of a text (the 'surface' marking of the semantic relations between its elements) is studied alongside the 'deep' or underlying logical and rhetorical relations between its elements, which account for its overall *coherence*. Such linguists as T. van Dijk, R. de Beaugrande, W. Dressler, M. A. K. Halliday, and R. Hasan have contributed in this area. Closely related to such work is that of J. Firbas and F. Daneš in the Prague School in the 1970s, with their interest in both *functional sentence perspective* (the relationship between units of information in utterances) and *theme-rheme* structures (showing the relationship between *themes* or clause-initial elements and *rhemes* or other elements in clauses), through which they have demonstrated that grammatical choice is dependent on discourse. There has also been research on anaphora, topic progression, and the discoursal significance of grammatical choices at clause level (such as tense, voice, aspect, and modality). Although discourse analysis is a wide-ranging and heterogeneous discipline, it is unified by interest in describing language 'above the sentence' and the contexts and cultural influences that motivate language in use.

See COHERENCE, COHESION, CONVERSATION, DISCOURSE, HALLIDAY, INFORMATION, LINGUISTICS, PRAGMATICS, SPEECH ACT, TEXT, THEME, TONE. [LANGUAGE, STYLE]. M.MCC.

Atkinson, J. M., & Heritage, J. (eds.). 1984. *Structures of Social Action: Studies in Conversation Analysis.* Cambridge: University Press.
Brown, G., & Yule, G. 1983. *Discourse Analysis.* Cambridge: University Press.
Coulthard, M. 1985. *An Introduction to Discourse Analysis: New Edition.* London & New York: Longman (first edition 1971).
Coupland, Nikolas (ed.). 1988. *Styles of Discourse.* London: Croom Helm.
de Beaugrande, R. & Dressler, W. 1981. *Introduction to Text Linguistics.* London: Longman.
Sinclair, J., & Coulthard, M. 1975. *Towards an Analysis of Discourse: The English Used by Teachers and Pupils.* Oxford: University Press.
Stubbs, M. 1983. *Discourse Analysis.* Oxford: Basil Blackwell.
van Dijk, T. A. 1985. *Handbook of Discourse Analysis.* 4 vols. London: Academic Press.

DISEASED ENGLISH [Late 20c]. An informal, non-technical, and highly emotive phrase used to express dismay at the state of the language, as in Kenneth Hudson's *The Dictionary of Diseased English* (1980), part of whose introduction runs: 'No language has better ingredients than English; no language has ever been more monstrously ill-treated and deformed by vandals and incompetents. The most beautiful instrument is always the most vulnerable to abuse and damage.' See ABUSE, (A)ESTHETICS, DETERIORATION, PROGRESS AND DECAY IN LANGUAGE. [STYLE]. T.MCA.

DISJUNCT. See ADVERBIAL.

DISORDER. See LANGUAGE HANDICAP.

DISTICH. See COUPLET.

DISTINGUISHABLE. See CONFUSIBLE.

DISYLLABLE [16c: from Greek *disúllabos* having two syllables]. Also **dissyllable**. A word of two syllables, such as *ago* and *depart*. See SYLLABLE. [SPEECH, WRITING]. T.MCA.

DITRANSITIVE. See DOUBLE ACCUSATIVE, TRANSITIVE AND INTRANSITIVE.

DIXIE [1850s AmE: from a minstrel song]. Also **Dixieland, Dixie Land**. An informal, affectionate name for the Southern states of the US, especially those that were part of the Confederacy. The term, first recorded in 1859, was spread just before the Civil War (1861–5) as part of the lyrics of the song 'Dixie's Land' or 'Dixie' by Daniel Decatur Emmett, an Ohioan. The lyrics run, in part, as follows:

> I wish I was in de land ob cotton,
> Old times dar am not forgotten.
> Look away, look away,
> Look away, Dixie Land.
> I wish I was in Dixie! Hooray! Hooray!
> In Dixie's land, we'll took our stand,
> To lib an' die in Dixie!
> Away, away,
> Away down South in Dixie.

Written as a 'hooray song' for use while minstrel performers paraded around the stage, it became a marching tune for the Confederate Army, was played during the inauguration of Jefferson Davis as president of the Confederate States (18 Feb. 1861), and is regarded as the unofficial anthem of the South (although often opposed by African Americans because of its association with segregation and the Old South). The earlier history and origin of the word are uncertain. Three imaginative theories are most often advanced, none supported by evidence: (1) That *dixie* is a diminutive of French *dix*, from ten-dollar banknotes issued in New Orleans with the word printed on them, *Dixieland* becoming the term for the area in which the notes circulated. (2) That *Dixie* is a hypocoristic shortened form of *Mason-Dixon Line*, the boundary between Pennsylvania and Maryland surveyed by Charles Mason and Jeremiah Dixon (1763–7), taken before the Civil War as the boundary between free and slave states and today as that between the North and the South. (3) That *Dixie* was the name of a slave-owner so generous that *Dixie's Land* became proverbial as a good place to be. Compare SOUTH. [AMERICAS, NAME]. J.A.

DOCUDRAMA [1960s: a blend of *documentary* and *drama*]. Also **drama documentary, dramadoc**. Sometimes **faction** [blending *fact* and *fiction*]. A television genre that combines drama and documentary. Viewers are informed in advance that the presentation is based on real-life events, but because the precise mix of fact and fiction is seldom immediately apparent the technique is controversial. See COMIC, DOCUMENTARY. [EDUCATION, MEDIA].   T.MCA.

DOCUMENT [15c: from Latin *documentum* that which teaches, warns, or serves as an example]. (1) A written or printed paper, often official, such as a passport or an invoice, that provides or serves as information or evidence. (2) Any written or printed item, such as a letter, article, or book, especially if it relates to fact rather than fiction. (3) A documentary. (4) In word processing, a text of any length and nature. See ARTICLE², BOOK, COPY, DOCUMENTARY, PAPER. [MEDIA, WRITING].   T.MCA.

DOCUMENTARY [18c in the general sense; 1920s in the media sense: from *document* and *-ary*: See DOCUMENT]. (1) Relating to a document or documents: *documentary evidence*. (2) In the media, relating to a motion picture, radio presentation, theatrical performance, or other work that is based on, re-creates, or 'documents' part of a person's life, an event or series of events, a period in history, etc., and such a work itself: *documentary television; a television documentary*. Documentaries are based closely on real life and usually on fact, but do not seek the kind of objectivity required by science; on the contrary, they are often intensely subjective, as for example a film about famine in Africa. The British film director and theorist John Grierson, the first maker of documentaries, referred to them as 'the creative use of actuality' to express a fuller truth. The line between fact and fiction in such work can easily be crossed. Documentaries often make use of such materials as diaries, letters, press reports, recorded interviews, and photographs. See DOCUDRAMA, DOCUMENT. [MEDIA, WRITING].   T.MCA.

DOG-, DOG [17c: suggesting contempt, as in obsolete *dogrime* filthy verses. Compare CYNIC, DOGGEREL]. An informal term added to the name of a language to show that it has been misused: ' "Nescio quid est materia cum me," Sterne writes to one of his friends (in dog-Latin, and very sad dog-Latin too)' (W. M. Thackeray, *The English Humourists of the Eighteenth Century*, 1853); 'They have been translated into a kind of academic dog-English' (*New York Times Book Review*, 22 Jan. 1961). *Dog Latin* refers to any kind of Latin regarded as inferior, and to any jargon or nonsense that resembles it, such as the humorous pseudo-motto *Non illegitimis carborundum* (Don't let the bastards grind you down) and the twist given to *De mortuis nil nisi bonum* (Speak only good of the dead) by the

British political theorist Harold Laski (mid-20c): *De mortuis nil nisi bunkum.* See GREEK, MOCK. [STYLE].   T.MCA.

DOGGEREL [14c: origin uncertain, but probably from *dog* and Old French *-(e)rel* as in *wastrel*, both suggesting contempt. Compare DOG-, CYNIC]. An informal term for both comic verse (especially if it has an irregular rhythm) and verse dismissed as crude or trivial: 'In doggrell Rimes my Lines are writ / As for a Dogge I thought it fit' (J. Taylor, *Dogge of Warre*, 1630). Doggerel can, however, serve as a vehicle for short, sharp, stinging comment: 'Illawarra, Mittagong, / Parramatta, Wollongong, / If you wouldn't become an orang-outang, / Don't go to the wilds of Australia' ('The Settler's Lament', in Stephen Murray Smith's *The Dictionary of Australian Quotations*, 1984). See VERSE. [LITERATURE, OCEANIA].   T.MCA.

DOMINICA. Official title *Commonwealth of Dominica.* A country of the Caribbean and member of the Commonwealth, situated between the overseas French departments of Guadeloupe and Martinique. Capital: Roseau. Currency: the East Caribbean dollar; the British pound and French franc are also used. Economy: tourism, agriculture. Population: 81,000 (1988). Ethnicity: African, mixed. Languages: English (official), French, and French Creole. Education: primary *c.*100%, secondary 20%, tertiary 2%, literacy 93%. The island was visited by Columbus in 1493, and was given its name because it was first seen on a Sunday (Latin *Dominica*, Lord's Day). In the early 18c, the French tried to settle the island, but it was declared neutral and returned to the Carib Indians in 1748. British planters with their African slaves settled it in 1763 and it became a British colony in 1805. Dominica became an independent republic in 1978. See CARIBBEAN, ENGLISH. [AMERICAS, NAME, VARIETY].   T.MCA.

DORIC [16c: from Latin *Doricus*, Greek *Dōrikós* Dorian]. In 1721, the Scottish poet Allan Ramsay compared his use of Scotticisms with the Doric dialect of the Sicilian Greek pastoral poet Theocritus (3-2c BC). In the 19c, British and especially Scottish writers began applying the term (referring to the supposedly rustic and uncultivated dialect of the Dorians of the Peloponnese) to 'broad' rural dialects in England and especially the Scottish Lowlands. In recent times, the people of north-eastern Scotland (the Grampian Region) have adopted the term for their own dialect. Elsewhere in Scotland, the term is used for any form of vernacular Scots. Generally it is favourable, *the Doric* being seen as rich, expressive, and rooted in tradition, whereas the *gutter Scots* of the cities is widely taken to have degenerated from 'the genuine Doric'. See ATTIC AND DORIC, GUTTER SCOTS, SCOTTICISM. [EUROPE, STYLE, VARIETY].   A.J.A.

DORSAL [16c: from Latin *dorsalis* relating to the back]. In phonetics, a sound made with the back of the tongue, such as the /k/ sounds in *kick*. See TONGUE. [SPEECH].   G.K.

DORSET. A county of southern England, regarded by many as the heart of the *West Country*, although others favour Somerset. Archaic dialect forms dating from Saxon times occur where the two counties meet: for example, the Old English first-person pronoun *ic* (pronounced 'itch': modern *I*) was heard in the 19c in what A. J. Ellis called 'the land of utch' (the area around Montacute in Somerset and stretching into Dorset). In the 1950s, fieldworkers for the *Survey of English Dialects* recorded *Udge am gwain* I am going. The Dorset dialect was made famous by the novelist Thomas Hardy, who usually portrayed the variety spoken by people who had received some schooling and were therefore influenced by the standard language. The philologist William Barnes wrote poetry in the dialect. See BARNES, ELLIS, HARDY, SOMERSET, WESSEX, WEST COUNTRY, Y-. [EUROPE, NAME, VARIETY].   S.E.

DOT [Perhaps from Old English *dott* head of a boil: compare Old High German *tutta* a nipple]. A small round mark, made or as if made by a pen or similar pointed instrument. The notational uses of the dot include: (1) As an element in a symbol, such as the Roman lower-case *i*, which is used as both a letter and a roman numeral. (2) As a diacritic: for example, in the transliteration of Sanskrit, the subscript dots in *Kṛṣṇa* (the scholarly form of the name *Krishna*) indicate a lingual pronunciation of the three marked consonants. (3) As an ancillary device in musical notation: placed after a note or rest, it indicates that the duration of the note or rest is increased by half as much again; placed under or over a note, it indicates that the note should be played staccato. (4) As one of two contrastive elements in Morse Code, in which Roman letters are variously represented by dots and dashes, such as · (E), – · (T), · – · (A), – · (N), – · · · (B), etc. See BRAILLE, DIACRITIC, POINT. [TECHNOLOGY, WRITING].   T.MCA.

DOUBLE ACCUSATIVE. A term taken from Latin grammar and used in connection with verbs that can take two nouns or pronouns in the accusative case: *Nihil nos celat* (Nothing us conceals-he: 'He conceals nothing from us'). In English, the term has been used in relation to

verbs taking both an indirect and direct object (sometimes known as *ditransitive* verbs), as in *Give me the book*. Here, both *me* and *the book* are objects of the verb, whereas in the equivalent sentence *Give the book to me*, the only object is *the book*. The phrase *to me* has traditionally been described as in the dative case and by some grammarians as the indirect object. See ACCUSATIVE CASE, DATIVE CASE. [GRAMMAR].   S.C.

DOUBLE ARTICULATION. (1) In phonetics, the production of a consonant which has two points of approximately equal maximum narrowing of the vocal tract: for example, /w/, which has a simultaneous narrowing at the lips and velum. See ARTICULATION. (2) In linguistics, duality in language: that is, the coexistence of systems like the two sides of a coin, the medium (either speech or writing) and the message (grammar and lexis). Compare LINGUISTIC SIGN. [LANGUAGE, SPEECH].   G.K., T.MCA.

DOUBLE-BARRELLED NAME. See PERSONAL NAME.

DOUBLE DUTCH [1870s: slang for something twice as hard as a language already considered difficult]. An informal term for unintelligible jargon, garbled speech, or language that is disliked because it is too technical or alien. Compare DOUBLESPEAK, JARGON. [SPEECH, STYLE].   T.MCA.

DOUBLE ENTENDRE [17c: from obsolete French, similar to *double entente*, whose present-day equivalent is *double sens* double sense/meaning. The phrase is often italicized]. An expression that can be understood in two ways, one of which has (often coarse) sexual connotations or implications; a risqué kind of *double meaning*: 'Another [advertisement] warned: "It only takes one prick to give you Aids." Although the accompanying photo shows a syringe about to be injected into an arm, the *double entendre* is obvious' (Michael Fumento, 'Is it a myth?' *Sunday Times*, 18 Mar. 1990). Compare AMBIGUITY, DOUBLE MEANING, FREUDIAN SLIP. [STYLE].   T.MCA.

DOUBLE GENITIVE. A term taken from Latin grammar and used in connection with a noun that is doubly possessed, using both *of* and either a possessive *s* or a possessive pronoun: '*Several neighbours of ours* were there', 'I've got an umbrella *of Rachel's*'. The first noun is normally indefinite (not **The neighbours of ours*) and the second is human and definite (not **an umbrella of a woman's*). The structure combines definiteness (*ours*, *Rachel's*) and indefiniteness (*several*, *an*) in a way not otherwise possible. The forms **several our neighbours* and **a Rachel's* *umbrella* are not possible. Compare also *a room of my own* but not **a my own room* Exceptionally, the first noun can have definite *this/these* (etc.) in front of it, but does not refer to one or some out of several, as in *That extraordinary voice of hers* (She has an extraordinary voice) and *Those unfortunate mistakes of Neil's* (Neil made those mistakes). [GRAMMAR].   S.G.

DOUBLE LETTER. See GEMINATION, and letter entries A–Z (excluding H, I, J, Q, X, Y).

DOUBLE MEANING. Ambiguity in a word or other expression, in which one sense is usually immediately apparent and relevant, while the other usually has a humorous, clever, cynical, or other implication: for example, the recent British advertising slogans *Running water for you* (Thames Water Authority) and *London Weekend Television—the best shows*. Compare DOUBLE ENTENDRE, IMPLICATION, SUBTEXT. See ABBREVIATION (SPECIAL EFFECTS), AMBIGUITY, PUN, RIDDLE. [STYLE].   T.MCA.

DOUBLE MODAL. See DIALECT IN AMERICA, SCOTS.

DOUBLE NEGATIVE. The use of two or more negatives in the same construction. There are two categories: (1) If the meaning is emphatically negative (*I never said nothing to nobody*), the construction is not part of standard English, though it is long-attested, and common in many varieties of the language. (2) If the meaning is rhetorically positive (*She is not unintelligent*: She is intelligent; *You can't not respect their decision*: You have to respect their decision; *Nobody has NO friends*: Everybody has some friends), the construction is part of standard English. Compare LITOTES. See NEGATION. [GRAMMAR].   S.G.

DOUBLE PASSIVE. The use of two passives together: *He was said to have been sacked*; *Their engagement is expected to be announced*; *Ten seamen are believed drowned*. The term is more commonly applied, however, to constructions considered clumsy: *The motorway is proposed to be built right across the valley*, rather than *It is proposed to build the motorway right across the valley* or *The Department proposes to build the motorway right across the valley*; *A protest meeting is hoped to be held soon* (= *It is hoped to hold a protest meeting soon*). [GRAMMAR].   S.C.

DOUBLE RHYME. See FEMININE ENDING.

DOUBLESPEAK [1971: coined in the US by the NCTE, blending *doublethink* and *newspeak*: see NEWSPEAK]. Language that diverts attention

from, or conceals, a speaker's true meaning, or from what is on the speaker's mind, making the bad seem good, and the unpleasant attractive or at least tolerable. It seeks to avoid, shift, or deny responsibility, and ultimately prevents or limits thought. Doublespeak can be discussed in terms of euphemism, bureaucratese, jargon, and inflated language. In 1984, the US State Department announced that in its annual reports on the status of human rights in countries around the world it would no longer use the word *killing* but instead the euphemism *unlawful or arbitrary deprivation of life*. The US Army, instead of referring to *killing the enemy*, often uses *servicing the target*. When asked why US military forces lacked intelligence information on Grenada before they invaded the island in 1983, Admiral Wesley L. McDonald replied: 'We were not micromanaging Grenada intelligence-wise until about that time frame.' In the doublespeak of jargon, smelling something is *organoleptic analysis* and a crack in a metal support beam is a *discontinuity*. In 1977, National Airlines called a crash of one of its airplanes an 'involuntary conversion of a 727', using a term of legal jargon as doublespeak to mislead its stockholders. In the doublespeak of inflated language, automobile mechanics are *automotive internists* and elevator operators are *members of the vertical transportation corps*. When a company 'initiates a career alternative enhancement program' it is laying off 5,000 workers. With global electronic communication, doublespeak spreads quickly within countries and around the world. The doublespeak uttered in one country moves quickly into the stream of information communicated to many other countries. It gains a certain legitimacy when used by public figures, especially leading political figures, and spreads by imitation. See DOUBLESPEAK AWARD, DOUBLE TALK, DOUBLETHINK, JARGON, NCTE, QUARTERLY REVIEW OF DOUBLESPEAK, -SPEAK. [STYLE, USAGE].   W.D.L.

Lutz, William. 1989. *Beyond Nineteen Eighty-Four: Doublespeak in a Post-Orwellian Age*. Urbana, Ill.: National Council of Teachers of English.
—— 1989. *Doublespeak: From Revenue Enhancement to Terminal Living*. New York: Harper & Row.
Rank, Hugh. 1974. *Language and Public Policy*. Urbana, Ill.: National Council of Teachers of English.
Rawson, Hugh. 1981. *A Dictionary of Euphemisms & Other Doubletalk*. New York: Crown.

DOUBLESPEAK AWARD. An ironic tribute established in 1974, and presented annually since then, by the Committee on Public Doublespeak of the NCTE. It is given each year to a person or organization in the US that has used public language that is, in the committee's judgement, deceptive, evasive, euphemistic, or self-contradictory. The Award is restricted to those uses of public language which have pernicious social, political, or economic consequences. The first winner of the Award was Colonel David Opfer, the Air Attache at the US embassy in Cambodia, who, after reporters revealed that American B-52 bombers had accidentally bombed and destroyed a Cambodian village, inflicting a large number of civilian casualties, said to the reporters: 'You always write it's bombing, bombing, bombing. It's *not* bombing. It's air support.' Other winners of the Award have included the nuclear power industry for using such terminology as *rapid oxidation* for fire, *energetic disassembly* for explosion, and *abnormal evolution* for accident, and the Pentagon for calling the neutron bomb a *radiation enhancement weapon*. See DOUBLESPEAK, GOLDEN BULL AWARDS, NCTE. [STYLE, USAGE].   W.D.L.

DOUBLET [14c: from Old French *doublet*, from *double*]. (1) One of two or more words derived from one source: *fragile/frail*, from Latin *fragilis*, the first directly, the second through Old French *frele*. Three such words are *triplets*: *cattle/chattel/capital*, from Latin *capitale*. Some doublets show little resemblance: *thesaurus/treasure*, from Greek *thesaurós* (a store), the first directly through Latin, the second through Latin then Old French *trésor*. Doublets vary in closeness of meaning as well as form: *guarantee/warranty* are fairly close in form and have almost the same meaning; *abbreviate/abridge* are distant in form but close in meaning (though they serve distinct ends); *costume/custom* are fairly close in form but distant in meaning, but both relate to human activities; *ditto/dictum* share only *di* and *t* and a common reference to language; *entire/integer* are so far apart that their shared origin is of antiquarian interest only. (2) A game invented in the 1870s by Lewis Carroll, in which a given word should be changed, letter by letter and always forming another word, into a second given word: for example, 'drive *pig* into *sty*' in the sequence *pig, wig, wag, way, say, sty*. Carroll called the given words *doublets*, the interposed words *links*, and the complete series a *chain*. See COGNATE, FRENCH, WORD GAME. [WORD].   T.MCA.

DOUBLE TAKE, also **double-take** [1930s AmE]. A second, usually surprised, response to a situation or statement, following close on a first inappropriate response, such as lack of interest. Such a response can occur in everyday life, but is particularly noted as a comic device: 'The only person who recognized the former President during our stroll together happened to be a friend of ours . . . who performed a double take worthy of the late Oliver Hardy' (*New Yorker*, 23 Nov. 1957). [STYLE].   T.MCA.

DOUBLE TALK, also **double-talk** [1930s: AmE]. (1) Also *Framis*. Patter that uses a mix of nonsense and real words. The US word buff Paul Dickson noted in 1982 that *Framis* is 'double-talk for double-talk', adding: 'Unfortunately, this form of talking does not enjoy the same popularity it did prior to and through World War II. Well done, it is a skilful blend of meaningful and meaningless words that when delivered leads the listener to think he is either hard of hearing or losing his mind. Or to be more to the point: a durnamic verbal juberance with clear mokus, flaysome, and rasorial overtones' (*Words*). (2) Deliberately ambiguous and evasive language. Compare DOUBLESPEAK, JARGON, PATTER, STUNT WORD, WORD SALAD. See AMBIGUITY, NONSENSE, TALK. [SPEECH].   T.MCA.

DOUBLETHINK [1949: coined by George Orwell in *Nineteen Eighty-Four*]. 'To know and not to know, to be conscious of complete truthfulness while telling carefully constructed lies, to hold simultaneously two opinions which cancelled out, knowing them to be contradictory and believing in both of them . . . Even to understand the word "doublethink" involved the use of doublethink' (Orwell). The paradox is expressed most succinctly in the novel in the three Party slogans: *War is Peace*, *Freedom is Slavery*, and *Ignorance is Strength*. The term is widely used to describe a capacity to engage in one line of thought in one situation (at work, in a certain group, in business, etc.) and another line in another situation (at home, in another group, in private life), without necessarily sensing any conflict between the two. See DOUBLESPEAK, PARADOX. [STYLE, USAGE].   W.D.L.

DOWN UNDER [1886: first used by the English traveller J. A. Froude]. An informal term for Australia and New Zealand perceived as the Antipodes of Britain and therefore as on the underside of the globe. Although in popular use among Australian service personnel during the First World War, it reflects a northern-hemisphere perspective and is seldom used by Australians and New Zealanders themselves: 'He was not handicapped by overbearing English mannerisms and a narrow English outlook, which the "down under" people dislike' (E. N. Speer, *Destiny*, 1934); 'I've got beyond the stage of imagining you are a lot of wild and woolly natives Down Under' (M. Sellars, *Carramar*, 1967); 'old fashioned northern hemisphere snobbery—the same attitude that applied to Australia the patronising term "down under" ' (*The Bulletin*, 12 Oct. 1974). [NAME, OCEANIA].   W.S.R.

DRAMA [16c: through Latin from Greek *drâma* action, play]. A form of literature intended for theatrical performance and written as prose or verse dialogue; a performance of this kind; anything in life that has similar attributes, such as confrontation, social tension, and great loss or great joy. Public rituals with dramatic implications date from the remotest times and formal drama has emerged in many parts of the world. In Western culture, it is one of the three literary genres developed by the Greeks: *drama*, *epic*, and (*lyric*) *poetry*. Drama was divided into *comedy* and *tragedy*, such further subdivisions as *farce* and *melodrama* being added much later. It differs from the other genres in that the dramatist's intention is fulfilled not by reciting or reading but by presentation with actors and theatrical devices. Although the words of a dramatic text remain the same, the effect of a play can vary greatly with different interpretations. Drama is therefore an oral and visual creation whose written form is first of all a preparation (*the script*), then an aid to performance (*an actor's lines*), and lastly a printed text (often with notes) for critical and educational scrutiny.

Classical and medieval drama. European drama has a less continuous history than epic and poetry; it has sometimes flourished and sometimes declined. The first surviving drama was in Greek, performed in Athens in the 5c BC: the work of Aeschylus, Sophocles, and Euripides (tragedy) and of Aristophanes (comedy). The main Latin contribution was the comedy of Terence and Plautus in the 2c BC. The later Roman Republic and the Empire produced no significant drama; Seneca (*c*.4 BC–AD 65) wrote tragedies based on the Greek model which were intended for reading to a select audience and not for the public stage. The later Roman theatre became increasingly devoted to elaborate and often decadent spectacle. The Christians opposed it and in the 6c the barbarian invasions brought it to an end. The revival of the theatre began in the 11c with the introduction of brief dramatized episodes into the Mass on the occasion of major festivals: see TROPE. These gradually developed into complete plays, performed in public places by the trade guilds and known as *mystery plays* or *mysteries* (Middle English *mistere* craft, from Latin *ministerium* service). In some towns, there was a cycle of dramatized stories from the Creation to the Last Judgement. These were succeeded in the 15c by *morality plays*, allegorical presentations of human virtues and vices in conflict. The best-known in English is the early 16c *Everyman*.

Modern European and American drama. The high point of drama in English came in the late 16c and early 17c, with such writers as Shakespeare, Marlowe, Jonson, and Webster. In the later 17c,

the Restoration theatre was mainly devoted to the witty and often scurrilous comedy of manners and intrigue. The French classical theatre had its great period at the same time, with the tragedies of Corneille and Racine, and the comedies of Molière. A long decline in Britain, briefly broken by the 18c comedies of the Anglo-Irish playwrights Oliver Goldsmith and Richard Sheridan, ended in a revival at the end of the 19c by the Irish dramatists Oscar Wilde and George Bernard Shaw, while the Irish national movement was the background of further work by W. B. Yeats, J. M. Synge, and Sean O'Casey. In England, prominent playwrights of the 20c include Noel Coward, Somerset Maugham, Terence Rattigan, John Osborne, David Storey, Arnold Wesker, Ann Jellicoe, and John Arden, and such experimenters in the *theatre of the absurd* as Harold Pinter and Samuel Beckett. The latter belongs as much to the French theatre, which has produced plays of challenge and questioning by Jean-Paul Sartre, Jean Anouilh, Jean Giraudoux, and Eugène Ionesco. Dramatists in the 20c US have looked at the predicament of modern humanity in a complex, pluralistic society, notably Eugene O'Neill, Tennessee Williams, and Arthur Miller. Some of the foremost modern plays are those of Henrik Ibsen in Norway, August Strindberg in Sweden, and Ivan Turgenev and Anton Chekhov in Russia, while in Germany, the expressionist Ernst Toller was followed by the influential Marxist dramatist Bertolt Brecht. All of these have been translated into and performed in English.

Times, tastes, and conventions. Dramatists are affected, like all writers, by the presuppositions and fashions of their time and place. Medieval drama derives from the prevailing popular Catholic Christianity, Elizabethan and Jacobean drama reflects contemporary views of status, honour, and revenge, Victorian drama displays the manners and attitudes of the new middle class. Conventions also affect the structure of plays. In the 16c and 17c, European drama was often obedient to the demand for the *three unities*, adding the unity of place to the unities of time and action attributed to Aristotle. Dramatists in English usually disregarded these restraints, supported the main plot with a sub-plot, and ranged widely through time and space. The practice of reading a play instead of seeing it produced is comparatively late; the majority of early plays were not printed, and the texts which appeared were often careless and poorly produced. When Jonson had his collected plays carefully printed as his *Works* (1616), he aroused some ridicule but helped establish the play as a literary text, probably influencing the publication of Shakespeare's plays in the First Folio (1623). The printed play became in its own right a branch of literature, with the result that theatrical and textual scholarship has been applied to the work of early dramatists. As time passed, playwrights gave more consideration to the reader. Stage directions evolved from laconic indications of entrances and exits to detailed descriptions of scenes and actions, including sketches of the appearance and nature of the characters. The effect is sometimes of an excerpt from a novel in the present tense. Shaw is notably full in his directions, and added detailed prefaces to explain the philosophy and polemics of his plays. Dramatists in general have become more self-explanatory and less inclined to entrust their work solely to the reactions of a live audience.

Constraints. Although great variety in dramatic structure is possible, most plays have a connected plot that develops through conflict to a climax followed by a resolution. Even when the story is known to the audience, the dramatist creates a mood of tension and suspense by the responses of characters to the changing situation. These factors apply in both tragedy and comedy. The suspense can be terrifying or mirthful and the resolution one of sadness or relief. Because the play is witnessed in short and continuous time, the dramatist needs to be economical, telescoping events that in reality would develop over a longer period and introducing meetings and juxtapositions that might seem remarkable outside the theatre. Divisions into acts and scenes may mark the passage of time and emphasize major developments. A play requires continuous action, not necessarily vigorous, but moving into new situations and relationships. Long set speeches and philosophical discourses are seldom effective, though dramatists such as Shaw have used them successfully.

Characterization. Although some types of drama, such as ritual performances and representations of myth, deliberately avoid a human focus, characterization is the device in most dramas. Characters may be depicted as great people, leaders of the community and powerful in its destiny, or, as is often the case in modern drama, as ordinary persons. They must be quickly presented to the audience and become familiar in a short time. They are created through the words they speak, their actions in the play, and what other characters report of them. Stage directions may aid the actor or the reader but in production there is no place for detached narrative or authorial comment. Leading characters are supported by minor roles, and the quality of a dramatist is shown partly by skill in making such roles credible and individual.

Dialogue. The medium of drama is dialogue, purporting to represent people communicating through speech. It varies as widely as other literary language, as in the following excerpts:

(1) Shakespeare, *A Midsummer Night's Dream*, 1. 1 (*c*.1598).

THESEUS. Now, fair Hippolyta, our nuptial hour
    Draws on apace. Four happy days bring in
    Another moon; but O, methinks how slow
    This old moon wanes! She lingers my desires
    Like to a stepdame or a dowager
    Long withering out a young man's revenue.
HIPPOLYTA. Four days will quickly steep themselves in night,
    Four nights will quickly dream away the time;
    And then the moon, like to a silver bow
    New bent in heaven, shall behold the night
    Of our solemnities.

(2) Oscar Wilde, *The Importance of Being Earnest*, 1 (1895).

ALGERNON. Why is it that at a bachelor's establishment the servants invariably drink the champagne? I ask merely for information.
LANE. I attribute it to the superior quality of the wine, sir. I have often observed that in married households the champagne is rarely of a first-rate brand,
ALGERNON. Good heavens! Is marriage so demoralizing as that?
LANE. I believe it *is* a very pleasant state, sir. I have had very little experience of it myself up to the present. I have only been married once. That was in consequence of a misunderstanding between myself and a young person.

(3) Terence Rattigan, *The Browning Version* (1948).

ANDREW. She's my wife, Hunter. You seem to forget that. As long as she wishes to remain my wife, she may.
FRANK. She's out to kill you.
ANDREW. My dear Hunter, if that was indeed her purpose, you should know by now that she fulfilled it long ago.
FRANK. Why won't you leave her?
ANDREW. Because I wouldn't wish to add another grave wrong to one I have already done her.
FRANK. What wrong have you done her?
ANDREW. To marry her.

Language. Early drama was written in verse, ranging from the poetry of ancient Greek tragedy and Shakespeare to the colloquial rhythms of the medieval mysteries and early Tudor comedy. The type of verse changes from one period to another. Blank verse was dominant in 16c and early 17c English drama, the heroic couplet in Restoration tragedy, and the alexandrine in French classical drama. Prose dialogue was also used by Shakespeare and his contemporaries, and by the end of the 17c was the normal medium for English drama. In the 20c, there was a revival of verse drama, for example by Yeats in Ireland, and T. S. Eliot and Christopher Fry in England. It was short-lived, however, partly through the decline of popular interest in poetry and partly through the failure of the dramatists to develop an idiom that could be sustained without becoming artificial and forced. Modern prose dialogue has tended to become more colloquial and naturalistic, in contrast to the stylized diction of early 19c prose drama. In the 20c, some writers have given close attention to specific dialects and registers: Synge listened to Irish peasant speech and Clifford Odets to conversation in New York bars. However, dramatic dialogue can never simply reproduce normal speech. The repetitions, hesitations, and redundancies of normal conversation would be intolerable on the stage. Nevertheless, dramatists like Harold Pinter and N. F. Simpson have developed the comic and sometimes disquieting qualities of apparently natural speech:

(4) N. F. Simpson, *One-Way Pendulum* (1959).

MABEL. It never seems to occur to her that a sedan chair would be far too heavy for her.
MYRA. It needs two in any case.
MABEL. Of course it does.
MYRA. One at the front and one at the back.
MABEL. She couldn't be in two places at once.
MYRA. And inside.
MABEL. And inside as well. It's too much for one person.

With allowance for convention and dramatic economy, the written dialogue of plays is a valuable record of speech in different periods. It covers a variety of class, regional, and social characteristics, reflects many emotions, and often includes the special expressions of sickness, intoxication, and madness.

Adaptations. Although drama is essentially an oral genre, writers may create a 'closet drama' designed to be read and not staged, as with Milton's *Samson Agonistes* (?1671), Shelley's *Prometheus Unbound* (1820), and Byron's *Marino Faliero* (1821), which was performed against his wish and of which he said: 'I have no view to the stage; in its present state it is, perhaps, not a very exalted object of ambition.' Performance combines aural and visual experience, but radio drama must depend on hearing alone, and television drama largely dispenses with the shared response of an audience in a theatre. Mime and silent cinema appeal solely to the visual sense. All such developments are variations on the fundamental traditional experience: being in the company of other spectators to hear words spoken by visible actors.

See BURLESQUE, CENSORSHIP, CHORUS, COMEDY, DENOUEMENT, DIALOG(UE), DOCUDRAMA, DOCUMENTARY, DOUBLE TAKE, DRYDEN, ELIZABETHAN, ENGLISH LITERATURE, ENGLISH STUDIES, EPIC, EPISODE, FARCE, FICTION, FILM, GENRE, IRONY, KITCHEN-SINK DRAMA, LITERARY, LITERARY CRITICISM, LITERARY THEORY, LITERATURE, LITERATURE IN ENGLISH, MASQUE, MEDIA, MELODRAMA, MONOLOG(UE), MOTION PICTURE, MOVIE, MUMMERSET, ORAL LITERATURE, ORATURE, PLAGIARISM, PLAY, POETIC JUSTICE, POETIC LICENCE/LICENSE, PUN, REPERTORY, RESTORATION, REVIEW, SERIAL, SERIES, SERMON, SHAKESPEARE, SHAW, SHERIDAN (R.), SOAP OPERA, SOCIAL REALISM, SOLILOQUY, STAGE, TALKIE, TELEVISION, THEATRE/THEATER, THEATRE OF THE ABSURD, TRAGEDY, TRAGICOMEDY, TROPE, WILDE. [LITERATURE, STYLE]. R.C.

Bentley, E. 1965. *The Life of the Drama*. London: Methuen.
Bigsby, C. W. E. 1982-5. *A Critical Introduction to Twentieth-Century Drama*. Three volumes. Cambridge: University Press.
Dawson, S. W. 1970. *Drama and the Dramatic*. London: Methuen.
Hayman, R. 1977. *How to Read a Play*. London: Eyre Methuen.
Kennedy, A. K. 1983. *Dramatic Dialogue*. Cambridge: University Press.
Nicoll, A. 1949. *World Drama*. London: Harrap.
Redmond, J. (ed.). 1979. *Drama and Society*. Cambridge: University Press.
—— (ed.). 1981. *Drama, Dance and Music*. Cambridge: University Press.
Vinson, J. (ed.). 1983. *Twentieth-Century Drama*. London: Macmillan.
Wells, S. 1970. *Literature and Drama*. London: Routledge & Kegan Paul.

DRAMATIC IRONY. See IRONY.

DRAVIDIAN ENGLISH [*c*.1960s]. English as used in southern India by speakers of Dravidian languages such as Kannada, Malayalam, Tamil, and Telugu. The degree of 'Dravidianness' depends on the speaker's educational background, social and professional status, and degree of exposure to established native and non-native varieties of English. In pronunciation, Dravidian English is marked by the substitution of retroflex for alveolar consonants in such words as *water* and *demon*, the gemination of intervocalic obstruent consonants (such as the *c* in *America*), and glides before non-low syllable-initial vowels, producing such forms as 'wold' for *old* and 'yelbow' for *elbow*. In grammar, it is marked by the invariant tag *isn't it?* (as in questions like *He is coming soon, isn't it?*) and clause-final *only*, as in *They lived like that only* (That is how they lived). Compare INDO-ARYAN ENGLISH. See GEMINATION, INDIAN ENGLISH[1], INDIAN LANGUAGES. [ASIA, VARIETY]. S.N.S.

DRAVIDIAN LANGUAGES. See INDIAN ENGLISH[1], INDIAN LANGUAGES.

DRAWL [16c: an intensive of *draw*, apparently introduced in vagabonds' cant. Compare Dutch *dralen* to loiter]. A non-technical term (verb and noun) for speech in which words are drawn out, especially prolonging vowels and final syllables. The term is often pejorative, suggesting that a speaker is affected or lazy: 'I never heard such a drawling-affecting rogue' (Shakespeare, *The Merry Wives of Windsor*, 2. 1, 1598); 'The clerks . . . in one lazy tone, / Thro' the long, heavy, painful page drawl on' (Pope, *The Dunciad*, 1728). Some accents are regarded as marked by drawling: *a southern drawl* (in the US). See ACCENT. [SPEECH, STYLE]. T.MCA., G.K.

DREAD TALK. See RASTA TALK.

DROPPING ONE'S AITCHES. See AITCH.

DRYDEN, John [1631–1700]. English poet, dramatist, and critic, born at Aldwinkle, Northamptonshire, and educated at Westminster School and Cambridge. He adopted the heroic couplet and helped make it the dominant metrical form for over a century. He made less use of enjambement and the caesura than Pope, as in his long satirical poems 'Absalom and Achitophel' (1681) and 'MacFlecknoe' (1682). His controlled and balanced rhythm, precision of attack, and presentation of characters combine to deadly effect, as in these comments on a contemporary in 'MacFlecknoe':

> Some beams of wit on other souls may fall,
> Strike through and make a lucid interval.
> But Shadwell's genuine night admits no ray,
> His rising fogs prevail upon the day.

Dryden wrote comedies and heroic tragedies, including *All for Love* (1678) in blank verse. He also contributed to the new style of expository prose, making it simple and flexible enough for any subject:

Virgil was of a quiet, sedate temper; Homer was violent, impetuous, and full of fire. The chief talent of Virgil was propriety of thoughts and ornament of words; Homer was rapid in his thoughts, and took all the liberties both of numbers and of expressions which his language and the age of which he lived allowed him. Homer's invention was more copious, Virgil's more confined; so that if Homer had not led the way, it was not in Virgil to have begun heroic poetry (Preface to *Fables Ancient and Modern*, 1700, ed. Douglas Grant, Dryden, 1955/85).

In his *Essay of Dramatick Poesy* (1668), he defends English drama and supports his argument by reference to specific works, also discussing such topics as the unities and the use of rhyme. Dryden was made Poet Laureate in 1668. See index. [EUROPE, LITERATURE, STYLE]. R.C.

DRY LITHO. See LETTERSET.

DUAL [16c: from Latin *dualis*, translating Greek *duikós* of two]. A term for the middle part of a three-part system of number in various languages, including classical Greek: *singular, dual, plural*. It marks nouns, adjectives, and pronouns for two as opposed to one or many. Old English had a dual in its system of personal pronouns: *wit* (we two), *ġit* (you two). In modern European languages, however, the dual has largely been subsumed into the plural. In English, dual meaning may be conveyed by *two* and by such phrases as *a couple (of), a pair (of)*. The term has been used in four other areas: (1) Where *both, either, neither* refer to two, in contrast with *all, several, none*, which when plural refer to three or more. (2) Prescriptively, in advocating '*between* two' and '*among* three or more'. However, *between* is widely used for three or more: *Flying between New York, Los Angeles, and Sydney*. (3) With regard to personal nouns of either sex (*foreigner, parent, teacher*) in contrast to gender-specific nouns like *daughter, schoolmaster*. (4) For *summation plurals* such as *scissors, binoculars, trousers, jeans, pyjamas/pajamas*, which refer to a tool, instrument, or article of clothing consisting of two parts. Here, number contrast is conveyed by *pair of*: *one pair of jeans, two pairs of jeans*. [GRAMMAR].

S.G., S.C.

DUB [20c: a clipping of *double*]. (1) To alter a soundtrack, as in *dubbing a film*, especially to re-express dialogue in a different language, or to use a different voice, series of sounds, etc.: *dubbing 'Gone with the Wind' into German; His voice was often dubbed for special effect*. (2) To alter a soundtrack by removing some parts and adding or changing others. *To dub in* means to add (music, speech etc.) to a film or tape: *They'll dub the songs in later*. (3) (Used especially of Afro-Caribbean disc jockeys speaking Creole) improvising against a soundtrack or a piece of recorded music. Dub is an especially Jamaican style of delivery that is associated with reggae and has spread in recent years to the UK, US, and West Africa. Performance poetry of this kind is called *dub poetry* and *toasting*; those who engage in it are *dub poets*. Compare RAP, REGGAE. See JAMAICAN CREOLE, RASTA TALK. [AMERICAS, STYLE]. T.MCA.

DUBLIN [From Gaelic *linn* pool, *dubh* black]. The capital of the Irish Republic, known in Irish Gaelic as *Baile Átha Cliath* Town of the Hurdle Ford, and home of more than a quarter of the Republic's 3.6m people. Dublin pre-dates the 9c Scandinavian settlements and some parts of the city have been English-speaking for almost 800 years. It is the birthplace of among others Jonathan Swift, Oliver Goldsmith, Richard Sheridan, Oscar Wilde, George Bernard Shaw, James Joyce, Sean O'Casey, Iris Murdoch, and Samuel Beckett. The speech of middle-class Dubliners is closer to RP than is any other variety of Irish speech, but it differs from RP in four ways: (1) It is rhotic, with a retroflex *r*. (2) The realization of /t, d, n/ is more dental than alveolar. (3) It has more aspiration in words like *part*, *tart*, *cart* (syllable-initial /p, t, k/). (4) The sounds *wh* and *w* are distinguished, so that *which/witch* are not homophones. This speech is the norm for the middle class throughout the Republic. The speech of working-class Dubliners has the following features: words such as *thin* and *this* sound like 'tin' and 'dis' ('Dere was tirty-tree of dem'); words such as *tea* and *peacock* sound like 'tay' and 'paycock'; in words like *fat* and *fad* there is often an *s*- or *z*-like hiss (/fatˢ/, /fadᶻ/: syllable-final affrication); in words such as *castle* and *glass* there is a front (short) /a/; in words such as *suit* and *school* there is a diphthong, so that for many people *suit/suet* are homophones; in words such as *but* and *hut* there is a centralized /u/; words such as *tie* and *buy* sound like 'toy' and 'boy'; the diphthong /æu/ occurs in such words as *how* and *mouse*, and in some pronunciations such words tend to be disyllabic; words such as *border* and *porter* tend to sound like 'bordar' and 'portar'. See IRISH ENGLISH. [EUROPE, NAME, VARIETY].   L.T.

DUMB SHOW. See MIME, MUMMERY.

DUMMY [16c: from *dumb* and *-y*]. (1) A pejorative term for a dumb person; someone with nothing to say, a stupid person, an imaginary player in a card game, a representation of a human figure, etc. (2) In printing and publishing, the representation or mock-up of a periodical, book, or other item planned for publication. (3) In computing, an instruction, address, or sequence of data that occupies space, either to regularize the position of other items or allow a later insertion to be made. (4) In grammar, an item that has little or no meaning but fills an obligatory position: prop *it*, which functions as subject with expressions of time (*It's late*), distance (*It's a long way to Tipperary*), and weather (*It's raining*); anticipatory *it*, which functions as subject (*It's a pity that you're not here*) or object (*I find it hard to understand what's meant*) when the subject or object of a clause is moved to a later position in the sentence, and is the subject in cleft sentences (*It was Peter who had an accident*); existential *there*, which functions as subject in an *existential sentence* (*There's nobody at the door*); the dummy auxiliary *do*, which is

introduced, in the absence of any other auxiliary, to form questions (*Do you know them?*). See ANTICIPATORY IT, CLEFT SENTENCE. [GRAMMAR, MEDIA, TECHNOLOGY].   S.G., T.MCA.

DURATION [14c: from Latin *duratio/durationis* the length of time something lasts]. In phonetics, the time (measured in centiseconds or milliseconds) taken to produce a sample of speech. See QUANTITY. [SPEECH].   G.K.

DURHAM BURR. See BURR, GEORDIE.

DUTCH [14c: from Middle Dutch *duutsch*, cognate with Old High German *diutisc* of the people (as opposed to Latin, the language of the learned) and German *Deutsch*. Speakers of Dutch refer to it as *Nederlands* of the low country]. The national language of The Netherlands, virtually identical with Flemish and ancestral to Afrikaans. Scholars use the term *Netherlandic* as a general and especially historical term for the varieties spoken in The Netherlands, Belgium, and north-western France. With English and Frisian, Dutch belongs to the Low German branch of the West Germanic group of Indo-European languages; all are structurally similar. Such words as *lip*, *maken*, *open*, *water* show that Dutch is closer to English than is German, whose equivalents are *Lippe*, *machen*, *offen*, *Wasser*. It was a major language of commerce in the 17c, and was established in North America (especially in the colony first known as New Amsterdam, then New York), in southern Africa (where *Cape Dutch* became Afrikaans), in the Caribbean region, and in Indonesia (formerly the *Dutch East Indies*). It has had an influence in Sri Lanka and, through early exploration, a role in place-name creation in Australasia (as in *Arnhem Land*, *Tasmania*, and *New Zealand*, named after the Dutch province of *Zeeland*). It has also had a strong influence on the formation of such creoles as Papiamentu in Curaçao (in the Dutch Antilles) and Sranan in Surinam.

Dutch and English. (1) *Dutch in English*. There was a considerable Low German influence on English from the later Middle Ages, through migration and commerce (especially the English wool trade with Flanders), as numerous Dutch nautical terms testify: *boom*, *deck*, *freebooter*, *sloop*, *smuggler*, *yacht*. Dutch was widely known in Europe in the 17c, when the first English–Dutch dictionaries appeared and such Dutch-derived artistic terms as *easel*, *etch*, *landscape*, *maulstick*, *sketch* were adopted into English. Later, many loans entered the language in the US: *boss*, *coleslaw*, *cookie*, *dope*, *poppycock*, *Santa Claus*, *snoop*, *spook*. (2) *English in Dutch*. Because of purist sentiment in the 16c and 17c, Dutch kept more of its Germanic character and resisted Latin more strongly than English did, but many Latinate words, such as *cruciaal*, *informatie*, and *educatie* (alongside Dutch *onderwijs*), are now entering Dutch from English, which has been the dominant foreign influence since the Second World War. English is now widely used for scholarly publishing in The Netherlands, is the first choice of foreign language in schools, and there is general exposure to it through the media, especially in TV from Britain. The effect is seen in borrowings (*management*, *research*, *service*), loan translations (*diepvries* deep freeze, *gezichtsverlies* loss of face, *gouden handdruk* golden handshake), changes in the meanings of established words (*controle* in the English sense as well as earlier 'check, supervision'), and idioms (*je nek uitsteken* to stick your neck out).

See AFRIKAANS, AMERICAN LANGUAGES, AMERICAN PLACE-NAMES, AUSTRALIAN PLACE-NAMES, BORROWING, BURGHER ENGLISH, CANADIAN LANGUAGES, CAPE DUTCH, CARIBBEAN LANGUAGES, DIALECT IN AMERICA, DOUBLE DUTCH, ENGLISH, EUROPEAN COMMUNITY, EUROPEAN LANGUAGES, FLEMISH, FRISIAN, GERMAN, GERMANIC LANGUAGES, HISTORY OF ENGLISH, INDIAN LANGUAGES, INDO-EUROPEAN LANGUAGES, INDO-EUROPEAN ROOTS, KITCHEN, LOW GERMAN, MALAYSIA, NEW ZEALAND, NEW ZEALAND PLACE-NAMES, NORSE, OLD ENGLISH[1], ORKNEY AND SHETLAND DIALECTS, PENNSYLVANIA DUTCH, SCOTS, SOUTH AFRICA, SOUTH AFRICAN ENGLISH, SOUTH AFRICAN LITERATURE IN ENGLISH, SOUTH AFRICAN PRESS, SPELLING REFORM, SRI LANKA, SURINAM(E), TELEPHONE COMMUNICATIONS. [AFRICA, AMERICAS, ASIA, EUROPE, LANGUAGE].   N.E.O.

DVORAK (KEYBOARD). See QWERTY.

DYNAMIC VERB. See STATIVE VERB.

DYSGRAPHIA [1930s: from the Greek elements *dys-* not, *-graph-* writing, *-ia* as in *aphasia*]. Also **agraphia**. A language disorder that primarily affects ability to write. It may be *developmental*, occurring in young children with no clear cause, or *acquired*, occurring in previously literate adults as a result of brain damage. Research carried out on adult patients shows several types of dysgraphic problem. In some cases, ability to spell is severely affected; in others, spelling is relatively intact, but spatial factors such as line direction, word spacing, and overall layout are disrupted. It is often associated with dyslexia. See DYSLEXIA, LANGUAGE PATHOLOGY. [LANGUAGE, WRITING].   D.C.

DYSLEXIA [1880s: from Greek elements *dys-* not, *léxis* word, *-ia* as in *aphasia*]. Also **alexia**. A language disorder that primarily affects the

ability to read and that can result in such written errors as 'saw' for *was* and 'dit' for *bit*. It may be *developmental*, occurring in young children with no clear cause, or *acquired*, occurring in previously literate adults as a result of brain damage. There are several types of acquired dyslexia, in which adults find themselves unable to read at all, or find difficulty with certain types of word, but most public attention has focused on children, where there has been considerable controversy over the nature of the problem. There are many children who, after only a short time at school, fail at the task of reading, writing, and spelling, despite normal intelligence, instruction, and opportunity to learn. Surveys of incidence vary greatly in their results, with the mean percentage of non-retarded children with reading difficulties often reaching 5%, and sometimes much larger. Boys outnumber girls in a ratio of at least 3 to 1. No medical, cultural, or emotional reason is available to explain the discrepancy between their general intellectual and linguistic abilities and their level of achievement in handling written language.

In an attempt to escape the originally medical connotations of the term, such children have in recent years been referred to as having a *specific learning disability*, and several terminological variants exist for the condition. The blighted school career of these children, where no one recognizes their handicap, has been well documented. Inability to read and regular failure at writing has a serious effect on their motivation to learn. Their poor writing and spelling tends to be viewed as a symptom of educational subnormality or lack of intelligence—or, if the child is known to be intelligent, leads to charges of laziness or 'not trying'. The question of causation has prompted great controversy. Candidate causes have included medical, psychological, and social factors, including problems of visual perception, memory, eye movement, verbal processing, and hemispheric dominance. The two traditional camps are those who favour a medical explanation (such as unstable eye dominance) as possible, and those who consider that social and psychological factors (such as a poor short-term memory) are critical. No single explanation fits the various symptoms. Individual case studies show that there is a variety of dyslexic syndromes, reflecting several possible causes, and requiring careful behavioural assessment and individual methods of teaching. Relevant publications include: M. Thomson, *Developmental Dyslexia* (London: Whurr, 1989), and F. R. Vellutino, *Dyslexia: Theory and Research* (Boston: MIT Press, 1979). See DYSGRAPHIA, LANGUAGE PATHOLOGY, READING. [LANGUAGE, WRITING].   D.C.

DYSPHASIA. See APHASIA, LANGUAGE PATHOLOGY.

DYSPHEMISM [19c: a blend of the Greek prefix *dys-* not, and *euphemism*. Stress: 'DIS-fe-mizm']. In rhetoric, the use of a negative or disparaging expression to describe something or someone, such as calling a Rolls-Royce a *jalopy*. A cruel or offensive dysphemism is a *cacophemism* (from Greek *kakós* bad: 'ka-KOFF-e-mizm'), such as using *it* for a person: *Is it coming again tonight?* See EUPHEMISM. [STYLE]. T.MCA.

DYSPRAXIA. See LANGUAGE PATHOLOGY.

E

E, e [Called 'ee']. The 5th letter of the Roman alphabet as used for English. It originated in the Phoenician consonant *hē*, which the Greeks adapted as E and called *epsilon* (that is, *E-psilón*, bare or simple *E*). The form was borrowed first by the Etruscans, then the Romans.

Sound values. The vowel letter *e* can represent a variety of sounds: (1) Short: *pet, very, herring, discretion*. (2) Long, as in stressed *be, he, me* and in *completion, region*. When unstressed, a shortened variant may be heard, as in *emit, acme*, and *the* before a vowel: *the apple*. (3) In RP, phonetically long and open, /ɛ/, before *r* in *there, where*. (4) In RP, long with a schwa glide before *r*: *hero, serious*. (5) In RP, often when stressed before *r* (unless followed by another vowel), the phonetically long, central sound in *her*: *infer, inferred, certain* (but not as in *peril*). (6) Schwa in unstressed syllables: *barrel, item, incident, robber*. In RP, there is sometimes a short *i*-sound, as in *emit, example, acme*; also (varying with schwa) in unstressed medial and final syllables (*packet, biggest*), especially in past participles (*admitted, waited*). (7) A long 'Continental' *e*, often with the sound of a long English *a*, in loans from French (*café/cafe, élite/elite, régime/regime, suède/suede, ballet, bouquet*), in Italian loans (*allegro, scherzo*), and in the Latin phrase *veni, vidi, vici* (I came, I saw, I conquered). (8) Exceptionally, *e* has the value of short *i* in *England, English, pretty*.

Digraphs. *E* is the first element in the following digraphs:

EA. With the values: (1) Long *e* as in *be: eat, sea, meat, defeat*. (2) Long *a* as in *chaos* in four words: *break, great, steak, yea*, and some Irish names such as *Shea, Yeats*. (3) Short *e* as in *pet* in 50 base words and many derivatives: *breath, health, measure*, etc. (4) Phonetically long and open before *r* in: *bear, pear, swear, tear, wear*.

(5) In RP, long *e* before *r*, with a schwa glide following: *ear, hear, near*. The same sound also arises when the *e* and *a* were formerly in separate syllables: *idea, real, theatre, European*. (6) In most accents, but not in ScoE, the vowel sound in *her* before non-final *r* in over a dozen words, including *early, earth, learn, pearl*.

EE. With the values: (1) Long *e* as in *be: eel, see, meet, proceed*. (2) In a few words, short *i* as in *din*: especially in AmE, but sometimes in RP *been* ('bin'); especially in RP, but sometimes in AmE, *breeches* ('britches'), and widespread in BrE *coffee* ('koffy'). (3) In RP, when followed by *r*, phonetically long with a schwa glide: *beer, cheer*. (4) In loans, a 'Continental' long *e* as in *matinée/matinee* (from French) and *Beethoven* (from German).

EI. With the values: (1) Long *e* as in *be: conceive, receive*, AmE *leisure*. (2) Long *a* as in *chaos* in about 40 common words: *eight, neighbour, reign, rein, veil, weigh*. (3) In some loans, more or less as *y* in *my*: from Germanic languages (*eiderdown, gneiss*); from Greek (*kaleidoscope, seismograph*). (4) Short *e* as in *pet: heifer, Leicester* ('Lester'), BrE *leisure*. (5) Schwa or unstressed *i* as in the second syllable of *victim: foreign, sovereign*. (6) Variation in *either/neither* between a long *i* and a long *e* sound, and in *inveigle* between a long *e* and a long *a* sound.

Note: EI and IE. The digraphs *ei* and *ie* (as in *receive* and *believe*) cause confusion in spelling. The dictum '*i* before *e* except after *c*' holds good for nearly all words where the sound is long *e* ('ee' as in *seen*), as with *conceive, deceive, perceive*. There are some exceptions with *ie* after *c* (such as *species*), and some words with *ie* after *c* where the pronunciation is not 'ee' (as with *ancient* and *glacier*). There are some 30 words with *ei* not after *c* but pronounced 'ee', such as *protein, seize, weird*.

THE CAPITAL LETTER

EARLY FORMS				CURRENT FORMS	
Phoenician	Greek	Etruscan	Roman (Latin)	roman	italic
ꓱ	ƎE	ꓱ	E	E	*E*

THE SMALL LETTER

EARLY FORMS			CURRENT FORMS	
Roman cursive	Roman uncial	Carolingian minuscule	roman	italic
ɛ	Є	℮	e	*e*

EU, EW, EAU. (1) The digraphs *eu* and *ew* generally have the value of *you*: *euphony, feud, queue; ewe, pewter, newt*. However, after alveolar and dental consonants, such as *n* in *new*, the vowel is often pronounced without the preceding *y*-sound in the US and in England in London and East Anglia ('noo'). After *j, l, r (jewel, lewd, rheumatism)*, the *y*-sound has generally ceased to be pronounced. (2) In *sew*, the *ew* has the value of long *o*, as it did for the pre-20c spelling *shew* for *show*. (3) In *-eur*, in loans from French, *eu* may have the stressed value of the sound in RP and AmE *her (connoisseur, saboteur)*, but in RP the *-eur* of *amateur* may be schwa. (4) In loans from French, the trigraph *eau* typically has a long *o* value (*bureau, plateau*), but in *bureaucracy* it has the short *o* of *democracy*, and in *beauty* has the same 'you' value as *eu* and *ew*: but see EAST ANGLIA. (5) In loans from German, *eu* has the value 'oi': *Freudian, schadenfreude*.

EY, EO. (1) The digraph *ey* has the values: long *a* in *chaos* in *they, convey, survey*; long *e* in *key*; and long *i* in *eye*. See Y. (2) The rare digraph *eo* has no single dominant value: short *e* in *jeopardy, Leonard, leopard*; long *e* in *people*; long *o* in *yeoman*.

Note. The letter combinations of the above digraphs also occur with separate, non-digraph values, as in *react, create, preexisting, deity, reinstate, reopen, reunite*.

Following E. In addition to the above, a following *e* has special functions that alter the value of a preceding letter: (1) When it directly follows another vowel letter, that letter has its long value: after *a* as in *maelstrom*, after *e* as in digraph *ee* (*wheel*), after *i* as in *tie, fiery* (despite *fire, wiry*), after *o* as in *toe*, after *u* as in *Tuesday*. These patterns occur less often in mid-word position, where the *e* may disappear before a suffix (*argue/argument, true/truly*) or where the letters may be pronounced separately (*diet, poet, duet*). Occasionally a following *e* indicates an anomalous digraph value which confuses learners: *friend, shoe*. (2) A word-final following *e* may serve to mark the distinction between the hard and soft values of the consonants *c, g*: hard in *music, dig*, soft with following *e* in *convince, urge*. Sometimes, it indicates a preceding long vowel at the same time: *face, page*. The *e* may be retained in an inflected form to avoid ambiguity (contrast *singing/singeing*), as well as exceptionally in *ageing* (although *aging* also occurs, especially in AmE, in which it is the preferred form). (3) After final *s*, *e* sometimes distinguishes a word that ends in voiceless *s* from a plural *s* that is pronounced /z/: contrast *dense, dens*. (4) After final *th*, *e* may distinguish a verb with voiced *th* from a noun with voiceless *th*: *sheath/sheathe, teeth/teethe, wreath/wreathe*, but not in

a mouth/to mouth. In *breath/breathe, cloth/clothe* the *e* may also mark a change in vowel quality.

Magic E. After consonants, final silent *e* may give a long value to a vowel immediately before the consonant. This practice arose with the change in value of the preceding vowel at the time of the Great Vowel Shift, after which the final *e* fell silent. Examples for each vowel are *take, eve, quite, hope, lute*. This usage, often referred to as *magic e* (perhaps so called because it operates, as it were, at a distance), also sometimes occurs after two consonants: *waste, change*. When a suffix beginning with a vowel (such as *-ing*) is added, the final *e* disappears, but the preceding vowel remains long: *desirable, hoping*. As a counterpart to this convention, a word with a short vowel and a single final consonant is required to double its consonant, so as to avoid confusion in such pairs as *planning/planing, hopping/hoping*.

Silent E. In many words, final *e* has no implications for pronunciation. It may silently mark a vowel that was once pronounced (as in *have*) or has been borrowed from French (as in *deplore, ignore*). In some combinations, it is a conventional device after certain consonants, especially *dg* and *v*, which do not usually occur in final positions in English: *judge, give*. In many words, a long *e* is indicated both by a digraph and by a final silent *e*: *receive, lease, needle*, BrE *meagre*. Some patterns with silent *e*: (1) After final /v/, particularly when the preceding vowel is short, in common monosyllables (*give, have, love*, contrast *shave, alive, move, rove*), in forms with *-lv, -rv* (*twelve, solve, carve, curve*, etc.), and with the suffix *-ive* (*active, motive*, etc.). (2) After *m, n* in some common monosyllables (*come, some, done, none, shone*, but contrast *company, home, son, on, tone*); similarly in some polysyllables (*cumbersome, destine, engine, discipline*, but contrast *random, mandolin, origin*). (3) In stressed vowel plus *-re* endings: *bore, core, more, restore* (contrast *abhor*); similarly in *are, were*. (4) After a short vowel and *-dg*: *badge, bridge, knowledge, porridge*. (5) In non-final position in *heart, hearth, hearken* (contrast *hark*), and *height* (not **hight*). (6) Medial *e* dropped in some words (*hindrance, disastrous*), but not in others (*preponderance, boisterous*). (7) In *-ate* endings of nouns and adjectives (all with a short vowel sound), but not verbs: contrast *a graduate/to graduate, moderate/to moderate*. (8) In *-ite*: *definite, favourite, opposite*. Contrast *calcite, Canaanite, Hittite* with *deposit, habit, benefit*. A similar contrast occurs between the unit of time *minute* ('minnit') and the adjective *minute* ('my-newt'). (9) After a consonant plus *l*, indicating that the *l*-sound is syllabic: *apple, steeple*.

A similar convention once applied to such words as BrE *centre*, in which the sound is now schwa. (10) In unstressed final *-ure*: *brochure*, *figure* (contrast *murmur*, *mature*).

Variations. The use of *e* frequently alternates with other letters or in certain cases is optional: *Latin and French prefixes.* (1) Historically, there has been some uncertainty in the spelling of words with the Latin prefixes *in-*, *dis-*, and their French equivalents *en-*, *des-*. Formerly, there was much free variation between *in-/en-* and *en-/des-*, as in *imploy/employ*, surviving in such pairs as *insure/ensure* (which are not strict synonyms), and BrE *dispatch/despatch* (AmE *dispatch* only), and *inquire/enquire* (in which there are slight differences in meaning in BrE, and AmE favours *inquire*). (2) A similar French/Latin variation is found between French-derived *letter*, *enemy*, *engineer* and Latin-derived *literal*, *inimical*, *ingenious*, and between *e* and *a* in the final syllable in pairs like *assistant/consistent*, *dependant/dependent*: see A.

Vowel variation. (1) *Agentives.* There is variation between *-er* and *-or* in the spelling of the agentive suffix in the words *adapter/adaptor*, *adviser/advisor*, *convener/convenor*, *imposter/impostor*: see O. Alternatives such as *briar/brier* also occur, as do such heterographs as *drier/dryer* and *friar/frier*. (2) *Endings in -y-.* The endings *-ie*, *-(e)y* may occur as alternatives: *bogie/bog(e)y*, *curtsy/curtsey*. The adjectival suffix *-y* normally entails omission of a final *e* in the base word (*race/racy*), but *holey* ('holey socks') and *gluey* are exceptions. Alternatives such as *bony/boney* and *stony/stoney* also occur, but without variation for comparatives and superlatives: *bonier*, *stoniest*. There is grammatical variation in the use of *e* when words ending in *-y* inflect to *-ie* (*city/cities*, *pity/pitied*), but alternatives arise with *honey*, *money* (*honied*, *monies* or *honeyed*, *moneys*). (3) *Morphological variation.* Varying vowel values between grammatically or derivationally related words are often reflected in a switch from a digraph or magic *e* to simple *e*: *deep/depth*, *sleep/slept*, *succeed/success*, *lead/led*, *leave/left*, *reveal/revelation*, *receive/reception*, *thief/theft*, *serene/serenity*. Elsewhere, however, *e* may be replaced by a different vowel altogether: *clear/clarity*, *compel/compulsion*, *desperate/despair*. In addition, a spelling change does not necessarily represent a change in sound (*height/high*, *proceed/procedure*, *speech/speak*), and sometimes a sound change is not reflected in a change of spelling: *deal/dealt*, *dream/dreamt*, *hear/heard*, *to read/he read*.

Omitting or retaining *E*. (1) The letter *e* may be optionally dropped or kept before the suffixes *-able*, *-age*, and *-ment*: *judgment/judgement*, *likable/likeable*, *lovable/loveable*, *milage/mileage*. (2) Adjectives ending in consonant plus *-le* lose the final *-e* when *-ly* is added: *able/ably*, *possible/possibly*, *probable/probably*, *simple/simply*. (3) While some nouns that end in *-o* add *-s* to form their plurals, others add *-es*, and others still vary, as with *pianos* (not *pianoes), *potatoes* (not *potatos), and both *ghettos* and *ghettoes*, often causing uncertainty. (4) The prefixes *for-/fore-*, *by-/bye-* are sometimes treated as interchangeable: *forego* is used with the meaning of both *to go before* and *to go without* (which strictly should be *forgo*); and both *by-law* and *bye-law* are found. (5) In some words initial *e* has been lost by aphaeresis: *squire* from *esquire*, *sample* from *example*, *state* from *estate*.

American and British differences. (1) BrE generally has *e* in *adze*, *axe*, *carcase*, *premise*, *programme*, *artefact*, and words of the type *analogue*, *catalogue*, while AmE commonly has *adz*, *ax*, *carcass*, *premiss*, *program*, *artifact*, and *analog*, *catalog*. BrE *to centre* has past tense *centred*, whereas AmE *to center* has *centered*. (2) In some words, where AmE follows a standard pronunciation for *e*, BrE gives it a value for *a*: *clerk*, *Derby*, *sergeant* (in which the pronunciation is the same as in the surnames *Clark*, *Darby*, *Sargent*). (3) Where AmE generally has *jewelry*, BrE generally has *jewellery*. (4) Where *e* in such words as *hostile*, *missile* has no value in AmE, in BrE it makes these words rhyme with *smile*. (5) BrE *whisky* contrasts with AmE and IrE *whiskey* as a generic name, but many people nonetheless keep the spelling *whisky* for the Scottish product and *whiskey* for the Irish and American products, regardless of the varieties of English they use. (6) In AmE, *story* and *stories* can mean both 'tales' and 'floors of a building', while in BrE they only refer to 'tales', the form for floors of buildings being *storey/storeys*. (7) Pronunciations differ for *lieutenant*: BrE 'leftenant', AmE 'lootenant'. (8) See also various points in the sections *Digraphs* (*EE* and *EI*), *Silent E*, and *Variations* above. See ALPHABET, LETTER[1], LONG AND SHORT, SPELLING. [WRITING].

C.U., T.MCA., E.W.

EAP, short for *English for Academic Purposes*. English taught to foreign learners who intend to follow courses of higher education in English. EAP courses provide instruction and practice in such matters as understanding lectures, taking notes, participating in seminars, using libraries and research facilities, writing essays and dissertations, and engaging in computing and word processing. They also often include aspects of social life in the host country and cultural differences between home and host societies. See ACADEMIC USAGE/ENGLISH, ASSOCIATED EXAMINING

BOARD, ESP, LANGUAGE TEACHING, TEFL. [EDU-CATION]. P.S.

EARLY ENGLISH. In philology and linguistics, a term that includes both Old English and Middle English and covers the first millennium of the language, c.450-1450. See EARLY ENGLISH TEXT SOCIETY, ENGLISH, MIDDLE ENGLISH, OLD ENGLISH[1], PERIOD DICTIONARIES OF ENGLISH. [HISTORY, VARIETY]. W.F.B.

EARLY ENGLISH TEXT SOCIETY, short form *EETS.* A society founded in 1864 by Frederick J. Furnivall to produce scholarly editions of English texts, with full glossaries and critical apparatus, ranging from the earliest Old English texts (including a facsimile of the *Beowulf* manuscript) to the 17c. The Society's publications provided important sources for the *OED.* See ARCHAISM, BEOWULF, EARLY ENGLISH, ELLIS, FURNIVALL, OXFORD ENGLISH DICTIONARY. [HISTORY, MEDIA]. R.C.

EARLY MODERN ENGLISH, short forms *EModE, eModE.* From one point of view, the earlier part of the third stage of a single continuously developing English language; from another, the first stage of a distinct language, Modern English, that evolved from an earlier language, Middle English. Scholars differ in deciding the best approximate date for both the beginning of the period (c.1450, c.1475, or c.1500) and its end (1660, the year of the Restoration of Charles II, or c.1700, a convenient point during the Augustan Age). In this volume, the span is c.1450-c.1700. EModE was an unsettled language whose great variability can be seen in the following excerpts of prose texts from the beginning, middle, and end of the period.

(1) *1490: William Caxton, printer.* The opening words of the Prologue to his translation of *The Aeneid*:

After dyuerse werkes made / translated and achieued / hauyng noo werke in hande. I sittyng in my studye where as laye many dyuerse paunflettis and bookys. happened that to my hande cam a lytyl booke in frenshe. whiche late was translated oute of latyn by some noble clerke of fraunce whiche booke is named Eneydos / made in latyn by that noble poete & grete clerke vyrgyle / whiche booke I sawe ouer and redde therin. How after the generall destruccyon of the grete Troye. Eneas departed berynge his olde fader anchises vpon his sholdres / his lityl son yolus on his honde.

(2) *1582: Richard Mulcaster, headmaster.* From ch. xiii of his textbook *The First Part of the Elementarie,* entitled 'That the English tung hath in it self sufficient matter to work her own artificial direction, for the right writing thereof':

As for the antiquitie of our speche, whether it be measured by the ancient *Almane,* whence it cummeth originallie, or euen but by the latest terms which it borroweth daielie from foren tungs, either of pure necessitie in new matters, or of mere brauerie, to garnish it self withall, it cannot be young. Onelesse the *Germane* himself be young, which claimeth a prerogatiue for the age of his speche, of an infinit prescription: Onelesse the *Latin* and *Greke* be young, whose words we enfranchise to our own vse, tho not allwaie immediatlie from them selues, but mostwhat thorough the *Italian, French,* and *Spanish*: Onelesse other tungs [. . .] will for companie sake be content to be young, that ours maie not be old.

(3) *1712: Jonathan Swift, clergyman and writer.* From 'A Proposal for Correcting, Improving and Ascertaining the English Tongue':

To examine into the several Circumstances by which the Language of a Country may be altered, would force me to enter into a wide Field. I shall only observe, That the *Latin,* the *French,* and the *English,* seem to have undergone the same Fortune. The first, from the days of *Romulus* to those of *Julius Caesar,* suffered perpetual Changes. and by what we meet in those Authors who occasionally speak on that Subject, as well as from certain Fragments of old Laws, it is manifest, that the *Latin,* Three hundred Years before *Tully* [Cicero], was as unintelligible in his Time, as the *English* and *French* of the same period are now; and these two have changed as much since *William the Conqueror,* (which is but little less than Seven hundred Years) as the *Latin* appears to have done in the like Term.

All three texts exhibit great differences in their written conventions. Sometimes these differences grew less over the centuries; for example, compare Caxton's spelling variants *lytyl* and *lityl* (little), Mulcaster's consistent *tung* and *young* (repeated in the same forms several times), and Swift's distinctly modern spelling. Where Caxton has *frenshe* and *destruccyon,* Mulcaster and Swift have *French* and Mulcaster has *prescription.* Sometimes, however, variability runs through the whole period: compare Caxton's nouns in lower-case roman letters (including most of his proper nouns) such as *fraunce, vyrgyle, anchises,* but excluding *Eneydos, Eneas, Troye*), Mulcaster's lower-case roman for common nouns but initial capitals and italic for proper nouns, and Swift's nouns all with initial capitals, the proper names set in italic. Punctuation achieved relative standardization during the period: for example, contrast Caxton's unfamiliar use of virgule (slash) and full point with the familiar uses of comma and full point by Mulcaster and Swift. A grammatical change that took place mainly in the 17c is shown where Mulcaster uses -*th* for the third-person singular of the verb (*it cummeth, it boroweth, which claimeth*) but Swift uses -*s* (*the Latin appears,* not *appeareth).

In general terms, EModE was marked by: (1) A major change in the vowel system of southeastern English: see GREAT VOWEL SHIFT. (2) The development of a single literary and administrative variety of the language that was later to be called 'standard English'. (3) The spread of English throughout Britain and Ireland and the beginning of the retreat of the Celtic languages of Wales, Ireland, the Scottish Highlands and Western Isles, Cornwall, and the Isle of Man. (4) The further spread of English to colonies in North America and the Caribbean, and to trading stations in Africa and Asia. (5) Massive lexical borrowing from other languages during the Renaissance and Reformation, especially from Latin and Greek for scholarly purposes, from Italian for literary and artistic purposes, and, particularly through Spanish and Portuguese, from sources beyond Europe. (6) The translation into English of many major foreign works, including a succession of versions of the Bible, classical Greek and Latin works, and contemporary writings from the European mainland. (7) The growth of a strong vernacular literature marked by the flowering of Elizabethan and Jacobean drama and the precursors of the novel.

See ADDISON, AUGUSTAN, AUREATE DICTION, BEHN, BIBLE, BOOK OF COMMON PRAYER, BRITISH EMPIRE, CAXTON, DRAMA, DRYDEN, EARLY MODERN ENGLISH DICTIONARY, ENGLISH, ENGLISH LITERATURE, EUPHUISM, GRAMMAR, GREAT VOWEL SHIFT, GREEK, HISTORY OF ENGLISH (AND CHRONOLOGY), HOLOFERNES, INKHORN TERM, ITALIAN, JACOBEAN, JONSON, LATIN[1], MIDDLE ENGLISH, MILTON, MODERN ENGLISH, MULCASTER, NOVEL, POPE, PORTUGUESE, PROSE, PUTTENHAM, REFORMATION, RENAISSANCE, RESTORATION, SHAKESPEARE, SPANISH, STANDARD ENGLISH, STEELE, SWIFT. [HISTORY, VARIETY].   T.MCA., W.F.B.

Barber, Charles. 1976. *Early Modern English*. London: André Deutsch.
—— 1987. 'Early Modern English, 1500-1700', in W. F. Bolton & D. Crystal (eds.), *The English Language*. London: Sphere.
Görlach, Manfred. 1991. *Introduction to Early Modern English*. Cambridge: University Press.

EARLY MODERN ENGLISH DICTIONARY, short form *EMED*. An unfinished dictionary of the period 1475-1700, of which no part has been published. In 1919, in his sketch of future historical dictionaries of English, William A. Craigie called the Tudor-Stuart era 'one of the most marvellous periods of the language' which required 'a dictionary which would be one of the greatest proofs of the wealth and dignity of the English language'. In 1928, Charles C. Fries was named editor-in-chief of the *Early Modern English Dictionary*. With Craigie's support, Oxford authorized the transfer of relevant citation slips to the U. of Michigan at Ann Arbor, where Fries assembled a staff and increased the collection from 2.3m to 4m specimens. A specimen entry for *sonnet* published in 1932 showed how *OED* coverage could be enhanced by more quotations and more detailed sense analysis, but the entry was seven times larger than that in the *OED*. In 1934, Fries began editing reduced entries for *L*, but even this would have resulted in a work equal in size to the *OED* rather than the planned 8,000 pages. In 1938, editing began at *A*. He estimated that the work would be finished in 1948, but war broke out in 1939, communication with Oxford became difficult, and the U. of Michigan decided that resources should be devoted solely to the *Middle English Dictionary*. The *EMED* was indefinitely postponed. In 1965, a proposal for a *Tudor Dictionary* was made by R. C. Alston and Bror Danielsson. Though their plan failed to find financial backing, it renewed interest at Michigan in the *EMED*. In the following decade, part of the collection was converted to a database of 1m words, available in microfiche and computer storage, and is now used worldwide by scholars concerned with the period. See EARLY MODERN ENGLISH, PERIOD DICTIONARIES OF ENGLISH. [HISTORY, REFERENCE].   R.W.B.

EARLY SCOTS. See SCOTS.

EAST AFRICA. See AFRICA, EAST AFRICAN ENGLISH.

EAST AFRICAN ENGLISH, short forms *EAE*, *EAfrE*. The English language as used in East Africa and associated parts of southern Africa, an outcome of European involvement since the 16c in Kenya, Malawi, Tanzania, Uganda, Zambia, and Zimbabwe. In these countries, English is taking its place as an African language in the registers of politics, business, the media, and popular culture. It includes an expanding body of creative literature, by such writers as John Mbiti (b.1931), Ngugi wa Thiong'o (b.1938), Peter Palangyo (b.1939), J. P. Okot p'Bitek (b.1931), and David Rubadiri (b.1930).

Background. When English was first used in East Africa, Swahili was already a regional lingua franca. Because of this, English came to be used as an additional language without any pidgin varieties. The contemporary choice of common language is most often between Swahili (with associations of informality) and English (with associations of formality and authority). The use of English, however, often depends on the attitudes of those being spoken to: there is a risk of causing offence by choosing English if the other people do not speak it, or Swahili, implying that they are uneducated. Linguistically mixed marriages (such as between a Luo and a Kikuyu) may make English the first language of some families. EAE is greatly influenced by such languages as Swahili at large, Kikuyu in Kenya, Chichewa in Malawi, Luo in Kenya and Tanzania, and Shona in Zimbabwe. Since these are related Bantu languages, they contribute to a common Bantu substrate, but even so the ethnicity of a speaker can be identified on the basis of pronunciation and lexical choices.

Pronunciation. (1) EAE is non-rhotic. (2) It has a five-vowel system, /i, ɛ, a, ɔ, u/. As a result, there are more homonyms in EAE than in WAE and English at large: 'bead' for *bead/bid*; 'bed' for *bade/bed*; 'bad' for *bad/bard/bird/bud*; 'bod' for *bod/board/bode*; 'pool' for *pool/pull*. (3) A vowel, usually close to schwa, is often inserted in consonant clusters: 'konəfidens' for *confidence*, 'digənity' for *dignity*, 'maggənet' for *magnet*. (4) Consonants are often devoiced: 'laf' for *love*, 'sebra' for *zebra*. (5) Homorganic nasals are introduced before stop consonants: 'mblood' for *blood*, 'ndark' for *dark*. (6) A distinction is not always made between *l* and *r* for speakers of some mother tongues: speakers of Lozi often use 'long' for *wrong*; in Bemba, the name for *oranges* is *(ma)olanges*.

Grammar. (1) Because many people are multilingual, code-mixing is common, as in the mixed Swahili/English sentence: *Ile accident ilitokea alipolose control na akaoverturn and landed in a ditch* (The accident occurred when he lost control and overturned and landed in a ditch). (2) The omission of either the comparative adverb (*more, less, worse,* etc.) or the correlative *than* in comparative constructions, sometimes with the addition of *and*: *This university is successful in its training program than yours*; *They value children than their lives*; *They would have more powder on the hand and in their faces.* (3) Use of the all-purpose tags *isn't it?* and *not so?*: *He came here, isn't it?*; *She is a married lady, not so?*

Vocabulary. (1) Loans from local languages: Swahili *boma* enclosure, administrative quarters, *duka* store, shop, *ndugu* brother, friend, *piripiri/pilipili* red-pepper sauce. (2) Loan translations from local languages: Kenya *clean heart* pure, *elephant ears* big ears (often of someone who does not listen), *word to come into one's throat* to have a word on the tip of one's tongue. (3) Extensions in the senses and uses of general words, many well established, some more or less ad hoc: *come with* (bring), as in *I will come with the kitenge* (I will bring the women's cloth: Swahili); *medicine* (medical), as in *She is a medicine nun*; *duty* (work), as in *He is at his duty now*. (4) Hybrid compounds and fixed phrases such as

magendo whisky black-market whisky (Swahili), *tea sieve* tea strainer. Occasionally, neologisms (some of them grandiloquent) are formed, such as *foodious* (gluttonous), *crudify* (to make crude), and *pedestrate* (to walk).

See AFRICAN ENGLISH, AFRICAN LANGUAGES, BANTU, KENYA, MALAWI, SWAHILI, TANZANIA, UGANDA, ZAMBIA, ZIMBABWE. [AFRICA, VARIETY].

C.L.N., L.T.

Bokamba, Eyamba. 1982. 'The Africanization of English', in B. Kachru (ed.), *The Other Tongue: English across Cultures*. Champaign: University of Illinois Press. Oxford: Pergamon.

Hancock, Ian F., & Angogo, Rachel. 1982. 'English in East Africa', in R. W. Bailey & M. Görlach (eds.), *English as a World Language*. Ann Arbor: University of Michigan Press. Cambridge: University Press.

Ngara, E. A. 1982. *Bilingualism, Language Contact and Language Planning: Proposals for Language Use and Language Planning in Zimbabwe*. Gwelo: Mambo Press.

Whiteley, W. H. 1969. *Swahili: The Rise of a National Language*. London: Methuen.

EAST AFRICAN EXAMINATIONS COUNCIL. See EXAMINING IN ENGLISH.

EAST ANGLIA. A region of England consisting of the counties of Norfolk and Suffolk, but also often taken to include Essex and parts of Cambridgeshire and Bedfordshire. It has two main urban areas, Norwich in Norfolk and Ipswich in Suffolk, which tend to influence the speech of the areas around them. The regional dialects belong to the Midland group, but are internally diverse: for example, Essex speech is closer to London varieties than are Norfolk and Suffolk speech. The so-called *singing Suffolk* accent has a wide pitch range and a high rising intonation at the ends of sentences. Many local accents are marked by a rhythm that tends to lengthen stressed vowels and to reduce or eliminate unstressed short vowels. Although many speakers are influenced by RP and media norms, some generalizations can be made of informal working-class speech: (1) It is non-rhotic. (2) Older, rural speakers tend to distinguish between the vowel sounds in words such as *game, grace,* and *tale* (with a long /e/) and words such as *bay, bait,* and *eight* (with /æɪ/ or /eɪ/). Younger speakers tend to use /æɪ/ or /eɪ/ for both. (3) Norfolk speakers in particular, especially older people, use two realizations for words that contain /əʊ/ in RP: words such as *bone* and *tone* have monophthongal /uː/ or a /ʊu/ diphthong, whereas words such as *bowl* and *tow* have /ʌu/. (4) Because of their use of /u/ for /əʊ/, some Norwich speakers have such homophones as *soap* sounding like *soup* and *boat* like *boot*. (5) The vowel sounds in words such as *bare* and *beer* are merged into /ɛ/ or /ɛə/, producing additional homophones. (6) Throughout the region, there tends to be no /j/ in words such as *dew*, *dune*. *Do* and *dew* are therefore often homophones. The pronunciation 'bootiful' for *beautiful* (with the /t/ often glottalized) is a regional shibboleth. (7) Word-initial /h/ tends to be preserved in Norfolk and Suffolk but not in Cambridgeshire or Essex. (8) Glottal stops are common throughout the area, including the towns; /hæʔ/ is a common pronunciation of *hat*. (9) In older, rural Norfolk speech, /l/ tends to be clear; elsewhere, the clear/dark distinction is similar to RP. (10) In casual speech, the unmarked verb form is often used with all subjects in the present tense: *I go*; *He go*. (11) *That* is often used rather than *it* in such greetings as *That's a cold day!*, *That's nice now*. (12) A feature formerly widespread but now recessive is conditional *do*: *They don't go there; do, they'd have a surprise* They don't go there; if they did, they'd get a surprise. (13) Some distinctive rural words can be found, such as *hodmadod/dodman* a snail, *fourses* a light afternoon meal (compare *elevenses*), and *neathouse*, a shed for *neat* (cattle). Scandinavian influence was once strong and can still be found, especially in northern Suffolk, where streams continue to be called *becks*. See ANGLIA, ANGLIAN, COCKNEY, DIALECT IN ENGLAND, MIDLAND, NEW ENGLAND. [EUROPE, VARIETY]. S.E., L.T.

EAST ASIAN ENGLISH. The English language as used in China, Hong Kong, Japan, Macao, South Korea, and Taiwan. Its functions vary from place to place and in no country is there a significant indigenous community of English speakers, although there are British and other expatriates in Hong Kong and the US has military bases in Japan and South Korea. Contacts from the 17c led to a number of pidgins, particularly *Pidgin English* used by and with British traders on the China coast and *Bamboo English* used by and with US soldiers in Japan, Korea, and Vietnam. Such forms are now virtually extinct, having given way to a range of English usually learned, in part at least, in school. Because of a tradition of teaching English formally through grammar, translation, and literature, spoken usage is often stilted and bookish. In recent decades, however, EFL techniques have made an impact, but differences in language type and in writing systems currently impede progress. All varieties look elsewhere for their model of English (for example to BrE in Hong Kong and to AmE in South Korea and Taiwan) and display in varying degrees the influence of mother tongues, as for example difficulty with /l, r/ among speakers of Chinese and Japanese. Nonetheless, it is likely that in the next decade

there will be an ever-increasing number of people (perhaps 300m) with varying competence in English, because of its position as an international medium. Borrowing from English into local languages is high. See CHINA, HONG KONG, JAPAN, JAPANESE PIDGIN ENGLISH, JAPLISH, KOREA, MACAO, PIDGIN. [ASIA, VARIETY]. J.P., H.W.

EAST INDIAN [16c]. (1) An inhabitant of the East Indies. (2) A Eurasian, especially of Indian and Portuguese origin, especially in Bombay and on the Malabar Coast of India. East Indians have tended to identify with the Anglo-Indian community, and to speak Anglo-Indian English. (3) In North America, an Indian from Asia as opposed to a *West Indian* or an *American Indian*. (4) Relating to the East Indies and any kind of East Indian. See ANGLO-INDIAN, CONVENT ENGLISH, EAST INDIES, INDIAN, WEST INDIAN. [ASIA, NAME]. T.MCA.

EAST INDIES. An archaic name for India and lands east of India, in contrast with the *West Indies*. When set up in 1600, the East India Company was known as *The Company of Merchants of London trading to the East Indies*. It traded with all south and south-east Asian lands, but in due course focused on India. An *East Indiaman* was a large sailing ship used for the 'East India' trade. The Dutch East India Company became interested in the Malay archipelago, where its colonies were known as *the Dutch East Indies*. These now constitute *Indonesia* (from Greek: the place of the Indian islands), a name that perpetuates the association with India. The same association occurs in *Indo-China*, a name for the lands (Cambodia, Laos, Vietnam) between India and China, once also known as *Further India*. See EAST INDIAN, INDIA, INDIES, WEST INDIES. [ASIA, NAME]. T.MCA.

EAST MIDLAND DIALECT. The dialect of the East Midlands of England, especially the dialect of Middle English from which present-day standard English is generally agreed to have emerged. See CHANCERY STANDARD, DIALECT IN ENGLAND, EAST ANGLIA, ENGLAND, MIDDLE ENGLISH, MIDLANDS, STANDARD ENGLISH, WYCLIF(FE). [HISTORY, VARIETY]. T.MCA.

ECHOISM [1880: coined by J. A. H. Murray, editor of the *OED*]. (1) A word that echoes a sound: *splash* echoing a liquid striking something or something striking liquid; *crunch* suggesting something brittle breaking into pieces. (2) An expression that echoes or alludes to another: the statement 'Marking T. S. Eliot's centenary, not with a whimper but a bang' (*Time*, 26 Sept. 1988) echoes and inverts Eliot's own lines 'This is the way the world ends / Not with a bang but a whimper' (*The Hollow Men*, 1925). Compare ALLUSION, ASSONANCE, ONOMATOPOEIA. See -ISM, ROOT-CREATION. [STYLE, WORD].   T.MCA.

ECHOLALIA [1880s: from the Greek-derived *echo* and *-lalia* speech]. The automatic repetition, usually without comprehension, of all or part of what someone has just said. Some echolalic speech can be heard in normal child language acquisition, especially during the first two years, but the notion is more commonly used as part of a description of various kinds of language handicap. Autistic and language-delayed children are sometimes echolalic, and the behaviour may be found in a range of adult conditions such as schizophrenia and aphasia. See LANGUAGE PATHOLOGY. Compare COPROLALIA, GLOSSOLALIA. [SPEECH].   D.C.

ECHO QUESTION. A question that, because of doubt, surprise, indignation, and the like, repeats part of a statement along with a stressed interrogative word: *Miriam did WHAT?*; *They're going WHERE?* [GRAMMAR].   T.MCA.

ECHO VERSE [16c]. Verse in which an element or elements at the end of a line are echoed, for humorous or ironic effect. In the 16c, Sir Philip Sidney wrote the poem 'Philisides', which opens: 'Fair rocks, goodly rivers, sweet woods, when shall I see peace? *Peace* / Peace? What bars me my tongue: Who is it that comes me so nigh? *I* / Oh! I do know what guest I have met; it is Echo. *'Tis Echo* / Well met Echo, approach: then tell me thy will too. *I will too.*' In the *Sunday Times* in 1831, the following couplet commented on the price of seats at the London Opera House (to hear *Orpheus*): 'What are they who pay three guineas / To hear a tune of Paganini's? *Pack o' ninnies.*' See VERSE, WORD GAME. [LITERATURE, WORD].   T.MCA.

ECLECTICISM [1820s: from Greek *eklektikós* choosing out]. (1) Taking material, ideas, etc., from different sources and putting them together for one's own purposes. (2) Also *the eclectic approach*. In language teaching, drawing on ideas and techniques from more than one source, such as grammar translation, the direct method, and audiolingualism. It is common in EFL/ESL teaching and ranges from principled choice to cynical or desperate pragmatism. See LANGUAGE TEACHING. [EDUCATION].   T.MCA.

ECLOGUE [15c: through French from Latin *ecloga*, Greek *eklogḗ* a selection]. A pastoral poem, often in the form of a soliloquy or a dialogue between shepherds. See PASTORAL. [LITERATURE].   T.MCA.

EDINBURGH [From Cumbric *Din-Eidyn*, from *din* fort, *Eidyn* perhaps a district, tribal, or personal name, Anglicized as *Edinburh*, with Old English *burh* (fort) replacing *din*, and Gaelicized as *Dun-eideann*, whence the modern alternative name *Dunedin*. Also eponymously associated with the 7c Northumbrian king Edwin, as in the 12c *Edwinesburch*, and referred to in the Middle Ages in Latin as *Castellum Puellarum*, Maidens' Castle, a name also associated with the Arthurian romances]. The capital of Scotland, population 438,000 (1986). Although the Scottish Parliament was abolished in the Act of Union with England in 1707, Edinburgh has remained the legal and administrative centre of Scotland, and the General Assemblies of the Church of Scotland and the Free Church of Scotland are held there. It houses the National Library of Scotland, the National Galleries of Scotland, and the Royal Museum of Scotland, and is host to the annual Edinburgh International Festival. The city has a high proportion of upper- and middle-class inhabitants, and an above average number of English residents. Local educated speech is more influenced by the norms of south-east England than elsewhere in Scotland. However, as part of the continuum of ScoE and Scots, vernacular speech is strong in working-class areas such as Leith and Gorgie and in the city's peripheral housing estates, showing variations due to dialect-mixing and nearby dialect boundaries.

Pronunciation. (1) Working-class Edinburgh speech shares features with Glasgow and other Central Scots dialects: for example, only the /o/ vowel in such pairs as *cloak*/*clock* and *road*/*rod*; /eː/ in *dae* do, *pair* poor; /ɪ/ in *buit* boot, *guid* good; /e/ in *breath*, *death*, *meal*; /i/ in *dead*, *deaf*, *swear*; initial /j/ in *yae* (adjective) one, *yin* (noun) one, *yins* (rhymes with *rinse*) once, *yaise* (verb) use, *yis* (noun) use. There are also the stigmatized glottalization of medial and final /t/ and the epenthetic vowels in 'girrul' for *girl* and 'fillum' for *film*. (2) Although most people have a falling final intonation for statements, some working-class speakers have a Glasgow-like fall followed by a low rise. (3) The combination *wa*- is /wɔ/ not /wa/ as in Glasgow: *want*, *warm*, *wash*, *water*. (4) The following both occur: *awaw* and *away* away, *twaw* and *tway* two, *whaur* and *whair* where (but only *whae*, *whase* who, whose). (5) *Make*, *take* also appear as *mak*, *tak*. (6) Where Glasgow has an unstressed word-final /ʌ/ as in *barra* barrow, Edinburgh has /e/, as in *barrie* barrow, *elbie* elbow, *fellie* fellow, *Glesgie*/*Gleskie* Glasgow, *lumbagie* lumbago, *awfie* awful, *carefie* careful, *moothfie* mouthful, *yisfie* useful. (7) The voiceless velar fricative /x/ may survive more strongly in Edinburgh than Glasgow, as in *richt* right, *strecht/strocht* straight. (8) Some speakers have 'terminal stress', whereby a normally unstressed final syllable is fully stressed, as in *Thát's áw-fie*, *véry clé-vér*, *He had a sáir áir-rúm* He had a sore/painful arm.

Grammar. (1) Some features said to originate in Glasgow also occur in Edinburgh, such as *youse/yese* (plural) you, and *youse-yins* (formerly *you-yins*: 'you-ones') you people. (2) The interrogative tags *eh?* and *Eh no?* are common, as in *Ye'll be wantin yer tea, eh?*, *Ye'll no be wantin any tea, eh-no?*, *Ye'll be wantin some tea, eh-no?* (3) The common pause-filler is *ken* (y'know), as in *Weel, ken, ye dinny pey, ken, for ti jist watch, ken* Well, y'know, you don't pay, y'know, just to watch, y'know. (4) The apologetic or depreciatory tag *like* is widely used, as in *Ah thocht ah heard ye greetin, like* I thought I maybe heard you crying, *Am ah gettin an invite, like?* Am I getting an invitation maybe?

Vocabulary. Local usages include *bairn* a child (where Glasgow has *wean*), *bunce* to share, *clipshear* an earwig, *dobbie/doobie* an idiot, *doddle* a lump of toffee, *guttie* a catapult/slingshot, *henner* a gymnastic feat, *hillan* a mound, hillock, *kip* a pointed hill, *lummie* a *lum* or chimney on fire, *mar oot* to score out, *poor-oot* a scattering of coins at a wedding, *swee* a swing.

Literary dialect. Much of Scotland's vernacular literature is by Edinburgh authors, mostly in literary Scots or in Lallans, but unlike Glasgow or Aberdeen, Edinburgh does not have a strong tradition of localized dialect writing. Among the sparse localized writings since the late 19c are pieces by the short-story writer Fred Urquhart (b.1912) and the poet and critic Alan Bold (b.1943), and the mixture of Lallans and everyday Edinburgh Scots in the poetry of Robert Garioch (1909–81). An example from Bold under the pseudonym Jake Flower is:

Ah havnae missed a day's work nigh on thirty year and ah've shifted some drink no danger. Ken? D'ye ken Bertie's Bar? D'ye no? Ye must ken Bertie's Bar, everybody kens Bertie's Bar. Ye cannae come fae Edinburgh if ye dinnae ken Bertie's Bar' ('Monologue', in *Scotia Review* 5, 1973).

See ATTIC AND DORIC, GLASGOW, GUTTER SCOTS, LALLANS, MORNINGSIDE AND KELVINSIDE, SCOTLAND, SCOTS, SCOTTISH ENGLISH. [EUROPE, NAME, VARIETY].   A.J.A.

EDITING [1780s: partly a back-formation from *editor*, partly from French *éditer*, ultimately from Latin *edere/editum* to give out]. To supervise or direct the preparation of text in newspapers or other periodicals, manuscripts and typescripts intended for publication as books, academic papers as published collections, the works of known writers in special collections (often with notes), and series of books or other documents. An *editor* is therefore someone with organizational and often managerial and policy-making responsibility for a publication or part of a publication or for aspects of the work of a publishing house. In addition, in the course of the 20c, the terms *edit*, *editing*, and *editor* have been extending their traditional areas of reference into broadcasting, motion pictures, audio- and video-recording, and computing.

Tasks. (1) Commissioning, assembling, and organizing material for publication and seeing it through preparatory stages such as galley and page proofs until *clean copy* (now often *camera-ready copy*) can be passed to the printer. (2) Assessing solicited or unsolicited material from writers to decide whether it conforms to the requirements and standards of a periodical or a publisher's list. (3) Adapting and revising material to meet general standards of clarity and efficiency and to fit the style of a periodical or publishing house, including ensuring the accuracy and appropriateness of punctuation, spelling, and other conventions. (4) Considering the most appropriate and effective layouts and graphics for the purpose in mind, often in recent years including the use of word-processing and desktop publishing equipment. (5) Preparing and/or planning supporting text of various kinds in newspapers or other periodicals (including editorial comment, lead-ins to articles, and notes), front and back matter, blurbs, etc. As necessary, all such work includes consultations with advisers and authors.

Types. In larger organizations and projects, tasks are usually divided among different kinds and levels of editor: an *editor-in-chief* with overall responsibility; a *managing editor* who looks after day-to-day administrative tasks; a *general editor* or *editor* who runs a particular operation; an *assistant editor* who does work allocated by the editor; a *commissioning editor* who looks for writers and projects for a publishing house (and may see them through to completion); an *associate editor* who works as a colleague alongside an editor, often for the duration of a particular project; a *consultant* or *consulting editor* who provides advice on request; a *copy-editor* or BrE *sub-editor*, who prepares final copy; and in newspapers and other periodicals such specialists as a *features editor*, *fashion editor*, and *sports editor*. See BLURB, BOWDLERIZE, CENSORSHIP, EFFECTIVE WRITING, EMENDATION. [MEDIA, WRITING]. T.MCA.

EDITION [16c: through French from Latin *editio/editionis* a publication: see EDITING]. (1) All copies of a book or other publication printed from one setting of type. (2) One in a series of printings of a book or other publication, each differing from its predecessors because of additions, corrections, excisions, etc.: *the 8th edition of the Concise Oxford Dictionary*. After several such issues, a work may become in effect a different book with the same title. (3) The form in which a work, especially of literature, is published: *an annotated edition of Dickens*. See CASE², IMPRESSION. [MEDIA, TECHNOLOGY].   T.MCA.

EDUCATED AND UNEDUCATED. Contrastive terms especially in sociology and linguistics, used to refer to people who have or have not had formal schooling (usually to at least the end of secondary or high school), and to their usage. The contrast is often used to suggest a continuum (*more educated/less educated*), and there are three broad approaches to its use: (1) That the terms are self-evidently useful and do not risk either the self-esteem of the people discussed or the reputation of those engaged in the discussion. (2) That they can sometimes be helpful but should be used with care, because they are at least as much social as scientific judgements. A precaution often taken is to place the terms in quotation marks: *an 'educated' speaker of English*. (3) That they are best avoided unless they can be rigorously defined for certain purposes, because they risk oversimplifying or distorting complex issues and relationships and may in effect be euphemisms for distinctions of social class. The contrast appears in some contexts to be stereotypical and patronizing, implying that people are performing on an unusual level: *Educated Indian English* (compare *Cultivated Australian*). The phrase *an educated accent* is widely used to denote the accent of someone educated to at least college level, often (for some of the time at least) at a private school, and implying (especially in Britain) that such an accent is not marked as regional, lower-class, or non-standard. See ACCENT, EDUCATED ENGLISH, STANDARD ENGLISH. [EDUCATION, STYLE, VARIETY].   T.MCA.

EDUCATED ENGLISH [20c]. Also **educated usage**. The usage of speakers and writers of English who have been educated at least to the end of secondary level. The term is sometimes used as a synonym for *standard English*: 'Social levels of English shade gradually into one another. But we can recognize three main levels. At the top is *educated* or *standard English*; at the bottom is *uneducated English*, and between them comes what H. L. Mencken called the *vernacular*' (W. Nelson Francis, *The English Language: An Introduction*, 1967). He adds: '*Uneducated English* is that naturally used by people whose schooling is limited and who perform the unskilled labor in country and city. Certain grammatical features,

such as the double or multiple negative are common to most regional varieties [of AmE].' See EDUCATED AND UNEDUCATED, GENERAL ENGLISH, STANDARD, STANDARD ENGLISH, VERNACULAR. [EDUCATION, STYLE, USAGE, VARIETY].   T.MCA.

EDUCATION [16c: from Latin *educatio/educationis* breeding, rearing, training, from *educare/educatum* to rear, train (animals, children), probably from *educere/eductum* to lead or draw out, bring up, rear]. (1) Obsolete: the nourishing and raising of an animal or a child: 'The people doe erre much about the education of children. I have seen some frequently give to their children strong Beere' (Robert Wittie, *Primrose's Popular errors*, 1651). (2) Obsolete: the process of bringing up young people to be conscious of their social station, manners and habits, and calling or employment: 'In the fyrste [volume] shall be comprehended the beste forme of education or bringing up of noble children' (Sir Thomas Elyot, *The boke named The gouernour*, 1521). (3) Formal schooling of the young in preparation for life, usually as a passage through various institutions set up for that purpose and arranged in the levels *primary* (around the ages 5–7 to around 11), *secondary* (from around 12 to 15–18), and *tertiary* (from 16–18 onward).

Background. Formal education in the Western style acquired its present form only in the last century, during which the concept and ideal of *universal education* has grown with the increasing complexity of society. With the development of institutions such as kindergartens and play groups for the early years, on the one hand, and further education and higher degrees for later adolescence and adulthood on the other, the concept of education has expanded so much as to be seen as virtually a lifelong process. The basic style and subject matter of Western education were, however, established over 2,000 years ago among the Greeks, in such philosophical communities as Plato's Academy in Athens and the scribal schools of Alexandria and other cities. These were followed first by the provision of tutors (often Greek slaves) for the privileged young in ancient Rome, then by medieval systems of training for mostly male recruits to the ecclesiastical and monastic communities of Christendom (and with them, from time to time, young people of noble background). Education retained a strong religious tinge until well after the Renaissance and Reformation, but particularly since the later 19c has become largely secular, somewhat less tied to the privilege of birth and wealth, and increasingly the responsibility of the state. Western-style education has spread to every corner of the earth and been taken up in varying degrees by most if not all non-Western cultures. In the 18-19c, this spread was influenced by Christian missionaries, but has also been facilitated by colonial and other governments, and has been accelerated by social, economic, and technological pressures.

Education and language. In most systems of Western and Westernized education, the skills of reading, writing, and arithmetic (*the three Rs*) have been basic. Such systems were once dominated by Latin, through which in addition grammar, logic, and rhetoric were taught. Until the late 19c, knowledge of contemporary foreign languages was regarded as a social 'accomplishment' rather than an essential part of a school's curriculum; all language teaching was prescriptivist, assuming a grammar based on firm rules and concentrating on a relatively fixed canon of literary texts both as source material and as models for composition. In the 20c, such assumptions have been increasingly disputed and greater language awareness has led to new, often experimental and controversial, approaches. Prescriptivism, however, is by no means dead. In contemporary educational practice, *oracy* as well as *literacy* is regarded as important, and a foundation of linguistic competence is taken to be essential for all subjects: that is, 'language across the curriculum', as recommended by the UK's Bullock Report in 1975.

Young people are currently introduced to many kinds of language material, including reports, advertisements, and technical instructions, as well as literature of various kinds. Free expression is encouraged in writing, rather than composition on a set theme with assessment based largely on correct syntax, spelling, and punctuation. Some educationists, however, consider that the processes of liberalism and liberation have gone far enough, and throughout the English-speaking world there appears to be an impulse towards basic knowledge and firmer standards (*back to the basics*). The teaching of foreign languages also looks to the living situation rather than a given literary corpus, with emphasis on the direct method and, wherever possible, complete immersion in the target language (especially by living among its speakers). Language in education has often been influenced by political factors: for example, Welsh was proscribed in the schools of Wales for a long time in the 19c, but is now part of their curriculum; the teaching of Basque was forbidden in Franco's Spain, but has since been encouraged. In the many countries with substantial ethnic minorities, decisions have to be taken about the status of the mother tongue in relation to the national language or language variety, as a result of which it has often been necessary to introduce specific teaching of the national medium as a 'second' (sometimes in effect a 'foreign') language.

Education and English. Although a general recognition of English as a significant literary language developed in the second half of the 16c, it was long before it was equally honoured in the educational systems of England and Scotland. The principal aim of education was for centuries to inculcate skill in Latin and to a lesser extent in Greek. The *grammar* of 'Grammar Schools' was Latin grammar, and the use of Latin continued at the ancient universities. Richard Mulcaster, who offered guidance in the basic teaching of English in *The First Part of the Elementarie* (1582), was exceptional among schoolmasters; John Brinsley made a plea for English teaching in 1627, but these lone voices were virtually unheeded. Thomas Sheridan in 1763 advocated the study of English grammar at the universities, but classics continued to dominate their curricula until well into the 19c. However, more attention was given to English in the Dissenting Academies for sons of nonconformist families, such as the Northampton Academy founded in 1729. Where English teaching developed, it was prescriptivist and based on formal grammars like those of Lowth and Murray.

The foundation of new universities in the 19c led to chairs and eventually whole departments of English. There was much concentration on Old English as giving a sound philological training; English literature was taught largely in historical terms, with major authors and defined periods. The grammar schools and public schools of England began to give attention to English: for example, at Rugby, Thomas Arnold laid emphasis on essay-writing in English. In 1868, the Taunton Commission on the endowed grammar schools recommended the teaching of 'modern' subjects, including English, a view endorsed and strengthened by later official educational reports in Britain. As late as 1886, Winston Churchill at Harrow was among those who 'were considered such dunces that we could only learn English' (*My Early Life*, 1930). The Victorian movement for popular education through Mechanics' Institutes and similar organizations gave some impetus to the study of English in circumstances where the traditional prestige of Latin and Greek did not come into the question.

By the beginning of the 20c, the teaching of English at all levels was established throughout the English-speaking world. A Board of Education report, *The Teaching of English in England* (1921), criticized the survival of old-fashioned approaches in both schools and universities.

Subsequently, the teaching of English has been influenced by wider understanding of the importance of language skills. In the schools, free composition and oral practice have largely taken the place of formal exercises. University departments of English have proliferated worldwide, the historical approach being superseded by practical criticism and personal response to texts. More recently, the abundance of rival theories of literary criticism has meant that a particular approach may be dominant in a department. Genre studies and work on writers outside the traditional canon are now almost universal. In addition, English is not always treated as a separate subject, but may be incorporated in *media studies* or *communication studies*, with wider attention to other forms of expression. See TEACHING ENGLISH. [EDUCATION, LANGUAGE].   R.C., T.MCA.

The education theme

A–C. ABERCROMBIE, ABRIDG(E)MENT, ADVANCED, ALEXANDER (L. G.), ANGLICIST, ANGLO-CHINESE SCHOOLS, APPLIED LINGUISTICS, APPROACH, ARGENTINA, ARNOLD (M.), ARNOLD (T.), ASSOCIATED EXAMINING BOARD, ASSOCIATION OF RECOGNIZED ENGLISH LANGUAGE SCHOOLS (ARELS), AUDIO-LINGUAL METHOD, AUDIO-VISUAL METHOD, BAAL, BARNES, BARNHART, BASCELT, BASIC ENGLISH, BBC ENGLISH[2], BEHAVIOURISM, BERLITZ, BONEHEAD ENGLISH, BRITISH ASSOCIATION FOR APPLIED LINGUISTICS, BRITISH ASSOCIATION OF STATE COLLEGES IN ENGLISH LANGUAGE TEACHING, BRITISH COUNCIL, BRITTON, BULLOCK REPORT, BUSINESS ENGLISH, CAMBRIDGE CERTIFICATE OF PROFICIENCY IN ENGLISH, CAMBRIDGE FIRST CERTIFICATE, CAMBRIDGE SYNDICATE, CAMBRIDGE UNIVERSITY PRESS, CARIBBEAN EXAMINATIONS COUNCIL, CARTOON, CENTRAL INSTITUTE OF ENGLISH AND FOREIGN LANGUAGES (INDIA), CHILD LANGUAGE ACQUISITION, CLAUSE ANALYSIS, COBBETT, COGNITIVE CODE TEACHING, COLLEGE ENGLISH ASSOCIATION, COMMONWEALTH, COMMUNICATIVE APPROACH, CONTRASTIVE LINGUISTICS/ANALYSIS, COPYBOOK, CORRECT, COUNCIL OF EUROPE, CREATIVE WRITING, CULTURE, CULTURA, CULTURAL LITERACY, CURRICULUM.

D–F. DIACRITIC, DIRECT METHOD, DOCUDRAMA, EAST AFRICAN EXAMINATIONS COUNCIL, ECLECTICISM, EDUCATED AND UNEDUCATED, EDUCATED ENGLISH/USAGE, EDUCATION, EDUCATIONAL TESTING SERVICE, EFL, EFL DICTIONARY, EFL GAZETTE, EIL, ELABORATED AND RESTRICTED CODE, ELEMENTS OF STYLE (THE), ELOCUTION, ELT DOCUMENTS, ELT PUBLISHING, ENCYCLOP(A)EDIA, ENCYCLOPAEDIA BRITANNICA, ENGLAND, ENGLISH AS A FOREIGN LANGUAGE, ENGLISH AS AN INTERNATIONAL LANGUAGE, ENGLISH AS A SECOND DIALECT, ENGLISH AS A SECOND LANGUAGE, ENGLISH FOR ACADEMIC PURPOSES, ENGLISH FOR CIVIL AVIATION, ENGLISH FOR GENERAL PURPOSES, ENGLISH FOR MARITIME COMMUNICATION, ENGLISH FOR OCCUPATIONAL PURPOSES, ENGLISH FOR SPECIFIC/SPECIAL PURPOSES, ENGLISH JOURNAL, ENGLISH-LANGUAGE EXAMINATIONS, ENGLISH LANGUAGE SCHOOL, ENGLISH LANGUAGE TEACHING, ENGLISH TEACHING FORUM, ENGLISH TODAY, ENGLISH WORLD-WIDE, ERROR, ERROR ANALYSIS, ESL, ESSAY, EUROCERT, EXAMINING IN ENGLISH, FAUX AMI, FEDERATION OF ENGLISH LANGUAGE COURSE ORGANIZERS, FEEDBACK, FLECO, FIRST CERTIFICATE IN ENGLISH, FIRST LANGUAGE AND SECOND LANGUAGE, FOREIGNER TALK, FORUM, FRAMEWORK, FREQUENCY OF OCCURRENCE, FREQUENCY COUNT, FRIES, FUNCTIONAL LITERACY.

G–O. GENERAL ENGLISH, GENERAL SERVICE LIST, HALLIDAY, HOME LANGUAGE, HORNBY, INITIAL TEACHING ALPHABET, INSTITUTE OF LINGUISTS, INTERFERENCE, INTERLANGUAGE, INTERNATIONAL ASSOCIATION OF TEACHERS OF ENGLISH AS A FOREIGN LANGUAGE, JAPAN, JESPERSEN, JMB TEST, JOINT MATRICULATION BOARD, KINGMAN REPORT, KOREA, LANGUAGE AWARENESS, LANGUAGE LEARNING, LANGUAGE PLANNING, LEARNER'S DICTIONARY, LIBRARY, LIBRARY LANGUAGE, LIMITED ENGLISH SPEAKER, LITERACY, LONDON CHAMBER OF COMMERCE AND INDUSTRY, LONGMAN, MACMILLAN, METHOD, MISTAKE, MNEMONIC, MONITOR MODEL, MULCASTER, MULTICULTURALISM, NATE, NATECLA, NATIONAL ASSOCIATION FOR THE TEACHING OF ENGLISH, NATIONAL ASSOCIATION OF TEACHERS OF ENGLISH AS A SECOND LANGUAGE, NATIONAL COUNCIL OF TEACHERS OF ENGLISH, NATURAL METHOD, NCTE, NEWBOLT REPORT, NOTIONAL-FUNCTIONAL APPROACH, NUCLEAR ENGLISH, O & C, ORACY, ORAL APPROACH, ORALISM, ORTHOEPY, OXFORD AND CAMBRIDGE SCHOOLS EXAMINATION BOARD, OXFORD DELEGACY.

T–Z. PALMER, PARSING, PASSY, PATTERN PRACTICE, PEDAGOGICAL GRAMMAR, PEDANT, PENGUIN, PITMAN (I.), PITMAN (J.), PITMAN PUBLISHING, POLITICALLY CORRECT, POPULAR, PRIMARY LANGUAGE AND SECONDARY LANGUAGE, PROFESSIONAL AND LINGUISTIC ASSESSMENT BOARD, PROFICIENCY, PROGRESS AND DECAY IN LANGUAGE, PUBLIC SCHOOL ENGLISH, PUBLIC SCHOOL PRONUNCIATION, QUILLER-COUCH, READER, READING, REDUCTIONIST LITERACY, RELC, REPERTOIRE, RESTRICTED LANGUAGE, RICHARDS, ROYAL SOCIETY OF ARTS, RSA, RSA (TEFL), SEASPEAK, SILENT WAY (THE), SIMPLIFIED READER, SITUATIONAL APPROACH, SOCIETY FOR PAKISTANI ENGLISH LANGUAGE TEACHERS, SPEAQ, SPEED READING, SPELT, STREVENS, STRUCTURAL APPROACH, SUGGESTOPEDIA, SURVIVAL LITERACY, SWEET, SYLLABUS, TEACHER TALK, TEACHING ENGLISH, TESD, TESL, TESL CANADA, TESOL, THORNDIKE, THRESHOLD, TOEFL, TRANSLATION, TRINITY COLLEGE LONDON, UCLES, UNIT CREDIT, UNIVERSITY OF CAMBRIDGE LOCAL EXAMINATIONS SYNDICATE, VOCABULARY, VOCABULARY CONTROL, WAYSTAGE, WEBSTER, WEST, WEST AFRICAN EXAMINATIONS COUNCIL, WOLLSTONECRAFT, WORD FREQUENCY (LIST), WORD LIST, WRENN.

EDUCATIONAL TESTING SERVICE, short form *ETS.* An autonomous US service founded in 1948 in Princeton, New Jersey, that provides school, professional, and English-language testing, including: (1) The *National Assessment of Educational Progress (NAEP)*, which monitors achievement at primary and secondary levels. (2) The *Graduate Record Examinations (GRE)*, which assess fitness for university. (3) The world's largest-entry EFL examination, the multiple-choice *Test of English as a Foreign*

Language (*TOEFL*), supplemented by *Tests of Spoken English* (*TSE*), a recorded-response test, and *Tests of Written English* (*TWE*), a free-writing exercise with elaborate team scoring. (4) The *Test of English for International Communication* (*TOEIC*), which uses the TOEFL format and specializes in business English. (5) *EUROCERT*, a system of certification organized in collaboration with the *National Institute of Educational Measurement* in the Netherlands and awarded for reaching passing scores in TOEFL, TSE, and TWE. See EXAMINING IN ENGLISH. [AMERICAS, EDUCATION].   W.S.

EFFECTIVE WRITING, also **good writing**. The ability to express oneself well in writing and print. Many successful writers have pointed out that writing well is a constant struggle ('the intolerable wrestle with words and meanings': T. S. Eliot, *East Coker*, 1940). There are no clear-cut, objective criteria for establishing a scale of effectiveness in writing for all purposes and occasions, but teachers at both school and college level, and writers of writing manuals, generally emphasize two levels of competence: (1) Ability with the basics of the written language: spelling, punctuation, grammar, and word use. (2) Awareness of the right style and rhetoric for the occasion and one's readership. The writers of four manuals that have been highly influential in the 20c offer their readers very similar 'core' advice on writing well:

Be direct, simple, brief, vigorous, and lucid . . . . Prefer the familiar word to the far-fetched. Prefer the concrete word to the abstract. Prefer the single word to the circumlocution. Prefer the short word to the long. Prefer the Saxon word to the Romance (H. W. & F. G. Fowler, *The King's English: The Essential Guide to Written English*, Oxford University Press: 1st edition 1906, 3rd edition 1931, most recent reprint 1990).

But the secret of good writing is to strip every sentence to its cleanest components. Every word that serves no function, every long word that could be a short word, every adverb which carries the same meaning that is already in the verb, every passive construction that leaves the reader unsure of who is doing what—these are the thousand and one adulterants that weaken the strength of a sentence (William Zinsser, *On Writing Well: An Informal Guide to Writing Nonfiction*, New York: Harper & Row, 2nd edition, 1980).

The golden rule is to pick those words that convey to the reader the meaning of the writer and to use them and them only. This golden rule applies to all prose, whatever its purpose, and indeed to poetry too (Sir Ernest Gowers, *The Complete Plain Words*, London: Her Majesty's Stationery Office, first published 1954, 3rd edition 1986; written primarily for British bureaucrats).

1. Place yourself in the background. 2. Write in a way that comes naturally. 3. Work from a suitable design. 4. Write with nouns and verbs. 5. Revise and rewrite. 6. Do not overwrite. 7. Do not overstate. 8. Avoid the use of qualifiers. 9. Do not affect a breezy manner. 10. Use orthodox spelling. 11. Do not explain too much. 12. Do not construct awkward adverbs. 13. Make sure the reader knows who is speaking. 14. Avoid fancy words. 15. Do not use dialect unless your ear is good. 16. Be clear. 17. Do not inject opinion. 18. Use figures of speech sparingly. 19. Do not take shortcuts at the cost of clarity. 20. Avoid foreign languages. 21. Prefer the standard to the offbeat (William Strunk & E. B. White, *The Elements of Style*, New York: Macmillan, 3rd edition, 1979: a list of the section-titles of ch. 5, 'An Approach to Style'.

Ability to write effectively is also commonly associated with the following points: (1) The habit of reading widely and a capacity to respond to established writers in terms not only of their surface messages but also their styles, subtexts, and allusions. (2) A willingness to fit the writing to the reader: 'You must give readers either the style or the content they want, preferably both' (Peter Elbow, *Writing With Power: Techniques for Mastering the Writing Process*, New York: Oxford University Press, 1981). (3) The capacity and willingness to undertake planning and research that involve drawing up schedules and agendas, making detailed notes, preparing interim résumés, framing proposals for publishers, employers, or others, and collating material in successive drafts. (4) The willingness, however painful, to seek and accept critical comment before the publication or circulation of one's material, and to live with adverse criticism afterwards. Established writers tend to be their own first and severest editors, with the aim of reducing the likelihood of changes imposed by their editors and negative comment from reviewers and readers. See BLAIR, COMPLETE PLAIN WORDS (THE), CREATIVE WRITING, DICTIONARY OF MODERN ENGLISH USAGE, ELEMENTS OF STYLE (THE), HOUSE STYLE, ORWELL, PLAIN ENGLISH, USAGE, USAGE GUIDANCE AND CRITICISM. [HISTORY, LITERATURE, STYLE, WRITING].   T.MCA.

Bailey, R. F. 1976. *A Survival Kit for Writing English*. Melbourne, Australia: Longman Cheshire.

Barnes, Gregory A. 1982. *Communication Skills for the Foreign-Born Professional* (Part III, 'Basic Principles in Writing English'; Part IV, 'Guidelines for Writing in the Professions'). Philadelphia: ISI Press (Institute for Scientific Information).

Byrne, Donn. 1988. *Teaching Writing Skills*. Harlow: Longman (for ELT teachers).

Casterton, Julia. 1986. *Creative Writing: A Practical Guide*. London: Macmillan.

Doherty, M., Knapp, Lee, & Swift, Susan. 1987. *Write for Business: Skills for Effective Report Writing in English*. Harlow: Longman (an ELT coursebook).

Ebbitt, Wilma R. & David R. 1990. *Index to English*, 8th edition (1st edition 1939). New York: Oxford University Press.

Ewing, David E. 1974/9. *Writing for Results: In Business, Government, the Sciences, and the Professions*. New York: John Wiley & Sons.

Gibson, Martin L. 1989. *The Writer's Friend: And a Companion for Copy Editors and Others Who Work with Publications.* Ames, Ia.: Iowa State University Press.

Johnson, David M. 1990. *Word Weaving: A Creative Approach to Teaching and Writing Poetry.* Illinois: NCTE.

Kaye, Sanford. 1989. *Writing Under Pressure: The Quick Writing Process.* New York: Oxford University Press.

Kent, Nigel (ed.). 1990. *The Student Writer's Guide: An A to Z of Writing and Language.* Cheltenham, UK: Stanley Thornes. First published 1989 by the Jacaranda Press, Australia.

McArthur, Tom. 1984. *The Written Word: A Course in Controlled Composition,* Books 1 & 2 (general and academic writing). Oxford: University Press (an ELT coursebook).

Petrovsky, Anthony R., & Bartholomae, David (eds.). 1986. *The Teaching of Writing* (85th Yearbook of the National Society for the Study of Education, Part II). Illinois: NCTE.

Pirie, David B. 1985. *How to Write Critical Essays: A Guide for Students of Literature.* London & New York: Methuen.

Rose, Mike, 1984. *Writer's Block: The Cognitive Dimension.* Illinois: NCTE.

Willis, Meredith Sue. 1984. *Personal Fiction Writing: A Guide to Writing from Real Life for Teachers, Students, and Writers.* Illinois: NCTE.

Young, Matt. 1989. *The Technical Writer's Handbook: Writing with Style and Clarity.* Mill Valley, Calif.: University Science Books.

Zinsser, William. 1983. *Writing with a Word Processor.* New York: Harper & Row.

EFL. See ENGLISH, TEACHING ENGLISH, EXAMINING IN ENGLISH, TEFL.

EFL DICTIONARY. See LEARNER'S DICTIONARY.

EFL GAZETTE. A monthly newspaper concerned with English as a foreign language, founded in 1977 by Colin Gordon, published from 1980 to 1987 by Pergamon Press, and since then by Loopformat, Wrights Lane, London. Distributed in 126 countries, it covers matters of professional interest in (T)EFL, (T)ESL, TEIL, TESOL, ELICOS, and ELT (see entries), including news, views, features, and reviews, and provides advertising space for language institutions, teacher-training courses, students' courses, recent publications in the field, and offers of employment. Individual issues often have a theme, such as learners' dictionaries or Business English, for features and advertisements. The *Gazette* also helps produce an annual *EFL Careers Guide,* covering such matters as entry into the profession, further qualifications, and conditions of work. [EDUCATION, EUROPE, MEDIA].   T.MCA.

EGYPT. See AFRICA, ARABIC.

EIRE [From Irish Gaelic *Eire* (genitive *Eireann,* dative *Eirinn*), from Old Irish *Eriu,* Old Celtic **Iveriu:* compare ERIN, HIBERNIA]. The Irish Gaelic name for Ireland. Its feminine gender may in part explain why Ireland is often referred to as female, sometimes an old woman, the *seanbhean bhocht* (old-woman poor: 'poor old woman'), sometimes a beautiful maiden, *Róisín Dubh* (rose-little dark: 'black-haired little Rose', or 'Dark Rosaleen' as in the title of a poem by J. C. Mangan, 1846). [EUROPE, NAME].   L.T.

ELABORATED AND RESTRICTED CODE. Terms introduced by the British sociologist Basil Bernstein in the 1960s, referring to two varieties (or *codes*) of language use, seen as part of a general theory of the nature of social systems and social rules. The *elaborated code* was said to be used in relatively formal, educated situations, permitting people to be reasonably creative in their expression and to use a range of linguistic alternatives. It was thought to be characterized by a fairly high proportion of such features as subordinate clauses, adjectives, the pronoun *I,* and passives. By contrast, the *restricted code* was thought to be used in relatively informal situations, stressing the speaker's membership of a group, relying on context for its meaningfulness, and lacking stylistic range. Linguistically it is highly predictable, with a fairly high proportion of pronouns, tag questions, and the use of gestures and intonation to convey meaning. The attempt to correlate these codes with certain types of social class background, and their role in educational settings (such as whether children who are used to restricted code would succeed in schools where elaborated code is the norm) brought the theory considerable publicity and controversy. See CODE, LEXICAL BAR, SOCIOLINGUISTICS. [EDUCATION, LANGUAGE].   D.C.

ELECTRONIC MAIL, also **E-mail, e-mail, Email, email**. The transmission of keyed messages from one computer to another through a network. E-mail uses digital transmission codes at almost the speed of a telephone call, even across oceans, but with the permanence of a letter, and does not require the simultaneous presence of both parties. The recipient can file the message electronically for later use, but incompatibilities between systems often make it complex to use. E-mail began in 1964, almost as early as the first computer time-sharing systems, and such networks as *BITNET, JANET,* and *UUCPNET* connect scientific and business groups around the world. See COMPUTING, FAX. [MEDIA, TECHNOLOGY].   M.L.

ELECTRONIC PUBLISHING [Late 20c]. A term referring to both the distribution of texts and other data using computer tapes, disks, and networks (usually as a commercial enterprise), and the use of computers to prepare printed materials. The widespread use of computers in typesetting and word processing means that electronic versions of most material composed today are in principle available, and can be distributed directly, rather than on paper, to those with equipment to read or print them out for themselves. There are several forms: (1) *On-line search*. Dialling a service permits access to material usually also available on paper. One command can search large volumes of material, such as journals of scientific abstracts, looking for a word or index term, then generating a list of such terms or printing out the texts in which they appear. Major vendors of such services include *Dialog Information Systems*, *Mead Data Central*, and *BRS*, all with files of billions of words of text. (2) *Disks and tapes*. CD-ROM disks, tapes, and diskettes permit people to read texts and data on their own terminals. Such data and texts are also available on paper, but can be searched faster with a computer, as for instance the *OED on CD-ROM*. The choice between dial-up and buying a copy is largely a matter of cost: the dial-up services can cost US$100 per hour, while CD-ROMs are a one-time purchase with a price of perhaps US$2000 each for a disk containing up to 100m words. (3) *Electronic distribution*. Distribution of information is often by means of *electronic bulletin boards*, where users post messages for others to read. Some of these are *moderated* (edited), others are unadapted and may contain quantities of extravagant matter. The *netnews* bulletin boards handle over 200,000 words a day written worldwide by users of the Unix system. Currently, although most material of value published electronically is also printed on paper for sale to customers, on-line use already contributes more than paper sales for some publications, and is growing fast. Computer storage is relatively cheap and the limits of size that constrain paper publication often do not apply. Electronic publication is widely preferred for searching data, and the development of high-quality screens may stimulate reading. See BRITISH LIBRARY, COMPUTER TYPESETTING, COMPUTING, PUBLISHING. [MEDIA, TECHNOLOGY].

M.L.

ELEGY [16c: from Latin *elegia*, Greek *elegeía oidé* a song of mourning. The term originally applied to a poem in *elegiac metre*, alternating hexameter and pentameter lines]. A poem of lamentation for the dead, with reflections on the departed life, often ending in a mood of calm and consolation; a poetic meditation on death, such as Gray's *Elegy Written in a Country Church-Yard*. Notable elegies include Milton's *Lycidas*, Shelley's *Adonais*, and Tennyson's *In Memoriam*. Some Old English poems such as *The Wanderer*, *The Seafarer*, and *The Wife's Complaint* are often called elegies; they are melancholy in tone, full of regret for the uncertainties of life and the loss of glory. See DIRGE, THRENODY. [LITERATURE].

R.C.

ELEMENTS OF STYLE, The, known informally as *the little book*. A short (85-page) prescriptive and proscriptive American work on prose style by William Strunk Jr., a professor at Cornell U. in New York State. It is widely considered a classic of its kind. Strunk used the text as teaching material from at least 1919, first publishing it in book form in 1935, with Edward A. Tenney. The later, better-known editions (Macmillan, 1959, 1972, and 1979) were revised and extended by E. B. White, a writer and former student of Strunk's. In his introduction, White refers to *Elements* as 'Bill Strunk's *parvum opus*'. There are five chapters to the Strunk and White editions: *Elementary rules of usage*; *Elementary principles of composition*; *A few matters of form*; *Words and expressions commonly misused*; and *An approach to style*. See EFFECTIVE WRITING, USAGE GUIDANCE AND CRITICISM. [AMERICAS, EDUCATION, STYLE].

T.MCA.

ELICOS, full form *English Language Intensive Courses for Overseas Students*. The common name in Australia for courses in English as a foreign language: 'All full time students enrolled at accredited Elicos centres . . . are legally entitled to take part time jobs for up to twenty hours a week—as long as it does not interfere with their studies' (*EFL Gazette*, Oct. 1990). The *ELICOS Association*, founded in the early 1980s, publishes a journal known first as the *TEA News* (1982-9), then the *EA Journal* (1990-). See TEFL. [EDUCATION, OCEANIA].

T.MCA.

ELIOT, T(homas) S(tearns) [1888-1965]. Anglo-American poet, playwright, and critic, born in St Louis, Missouri, and educated at Harvard, the Sorbonne, and Oxford. He settled in London where, after periods in teaching and banking, he joined the publishers Faber & Faber. His early poems were mostly short, but 'The Waste Land' (1922) made a more extended study of the state of England after the First World War. In 1927, he became a British subject and joined the Anglican Church. His faith appears in subsequent poetry, notably 'Ash Wednesday' (1930) and the 'Four Quartets' (1935-42). He brought contemporary colloquial language into verse and could convey nonstandard speech without deviant spelling:

When Lil's husband got demobbed, I said,
I didn't mince my words, I said to her myself,

HURRY UP PLEASE ITS TIME
Now Albert's coming back, make yourself a bit
smart.
He'll want to know what you done with that money
he gave you
To get yourself some teeth. He did, I was there.
You have them all out, Lil, and get a nice set,
He said, I swear, I can't bear to look at you.
(from *The Waste Land*, 1922)

He was, however, a learned poet whose allusions
can make reading difficult. His poetic style tends
to paradox, rhetorical questions, and a tentative
manner thinly veiling strong conviction, as in:

You say I am repeating
Something I have said before. I shall say it again.
Shall I say it again? In order to arrive there,
To arrive where you are, to get from where you are
not,
You must go by a way wherein there is no ecstasy.
(from *East Coker*, 1940)

As a critic, he emphasized the importance of
tradition in literature and society. Despite the
austerity of most of his work, he wrote a volume
of nonsense poems, *Old Possum's Book of Practical Cats* (1939), containing such whimsies as:

Jellicle Cats are black and white,
Jellicle Cats are rather small;
Jellicle Cats are merry and bright,
And pleasant to hear when they caterwaul.
Jellicle Cats have cheerful faces,
Jellicle Cats have bright black eyes;
They like to practise their airs and graces
And wait for the Jellicle Moon to rise.
(from 'The Song of the Jellicles')

Eliot's first play, *Murder in the Cathedral* (1935),
was produced in Canterbury Cathedral. He later
wrote for the commercial theatre, his greatest
success *The Cocktail Party* (1950). In 1948, he
received both the Order of Merit and the Nobel
Prize for Literature. See index. [AMERICAS, BIO-
GRAPHY, EUROPE, LITERATURE, STYLE].   R.C.

ELISION [16c: from Latin *elisio/elisionis* crush-
ing out]. In speech and writing, the omission or
slurring (*eliding*) of one or more vowels, consonants, or syllables, as in *ol' man* old man,
gonna going to, *wannabe* want to be, and the
usual pronunciation of *parliament* ('parlement').
Although in speech there is no direct indication
of elision, in writing it is often marked by an
apostrophe: *didn't* did not, *I'd've* I would have.
Elision is common in everyday speech and may
be specially marked in verse to ensure that readers keep the metre, as in *th'empire*. Foreign students often have difficulty coming to terms with
elisions created by the stress-timed rhythm of
English, which may make word sequences seem
nonsensical, *It is no good at all* sounding like
Snow good a tall. See APH(A)ERESIS, APHESIS, APO-
COPE, APOSIOPESIS, APOSTROPHE[1], ELLIPSIS, SYN-
(A)ERESIS, SYNCOPE, [SPEECH, STYLE].   T.MCA.

ELIZABETHAN [19c]. A term referring to the
reign of Queen Elizabeth I of England (1558-
1603), in which the vocabulary of English grew
rapidly through exploration, trade, translation,
scholarship, and literature. The period began
with questioning of the adequacy of English for
serious writing and by its end there was still no
grammar or dictionary. Yet it concluded with
such literary monuments as the works of
Spenser, Shakespeare, and Jonson. See AUREATE
DICTION, BIBLE, BLARNEY, CALIBAN, DRAMA,
EARLY MODERN ENGLISH, ENGLISH LITERATURE,
EUPHUISM, GENRE, HOLOFERNES, HUMO(U)R, INK-
HORN TERM, JACOBEAN, JONSON, LYLY, PROSE,
SHAKESPEARE, SONNET, SPENSER, TUDOR. Compare
VICTORIAN. [EUROPE, HISTORY, LITERATURE].
W.F.B.

ELLIPSIS [16c: from Latin *ellipsis*, Greek
élleipsis, coming short]. The omission of an element of language for reasons associated with
speech, rhetoric, grammar, and punctuation.
The omitted element can usually be recovered
by considering the context of what has been said
or written. In speech and writing, sounds and
letters are often left out of words: in the sentence
She said he'd come, he'd is elliptical for either *he
had* or *he would*. Such contractions are informal
and usually arise from speed of delivery, economy of effort, and the rhythm of the language:
see ELISION. At times, elliptical speech or writing
is so concise that listeners and readers must supply missing elements through guesswork or special knowledge, and if they cannot, they fail to
understand. Information can be left out or hinted at for reasons of style or discretion; in such
areas as politics, diplomacy, and negotiation,
remarks are often elliptical in nature and intent.

In grammar. Ellipsis is a common syntactic
device in everyday language: for example, the
full structure of the normal but elliptical sentence *Take another piece if you want to* is *Take
another piece if you want to take another piece*.
Here, the ellipsis depends on the words that precede it and is anaphoric: see ANAPHORA. In conversation, words may be omitted because they
relate to what someone has just said: *When can
I see you?—Tomorrow* (that is, *You can see me
tomorrow*). In *Those who can should pay*, the
elliptical *Those who can* depends for the interpretation *Those who can pay* on what follows
and is cataphoric: see CATAPHORA. Anaphoric
and cataphoric ellipsis are types of *textual ellipsis*, where the recoverability of the full structure
depends on what occurs before or after. It contrasts with *situational ellipsis*, in which recoverability depends on knowledge of the situational context (*Got any money?* may be *Have
you got any money?* or *Have they got any money?*),

and *structural ellipsis*, in which recoverability depends on syntax (the headline *Poll shows labour 10 points ahead* corresponds to the full *A poll shows that the Labour Party is 10 points ahead*). Another type, often used in making notes or writing a diary, is the telegraphic *Went out. Had a meal. Came home and watched TV. Then bed.*

Grammarians tend to restrict the notion of ellipsis to instances where the missing part can be recovered uniquely. *The patient she examined was still unconscious* is not therefore strictly elliptical, since several items may be inserted: *The patient that/who/whom she examined was still unconscious.* Similarly, in *Being taller than his brother, John could see over the wall, Being taller* cannot be expanded to a full form, though it can be interpreted as *Since he is taller* or *As he is taller*. Grammatical ellipsis is a device for achieving economy by avoiding repetition. It contributes to clarity and emphasis, and enables attention to be focused on important information. It shares these characteristics with pronouns and other forms of substitution such as the auxiliary *do* in *Marion liked the play as much as I did.*

In punctuation. In writing and print, ellipsis is the formal convention, in the form of three *ellipsis points* (. . .), for leaving out parts of quoted sentences and texts, while at the same time indicating that an omission has occurred: for example, the sentence *There has been, as far as we can tell, no loss of life* can be reduced in quotation to *There has been . . . no loss of life.* When ellipsis follows the end of a sentence, there are sometimes four points, consisting of a period to close the sentence and then three ellipsis points: for example, the sentences *We mustn't give in. What would be the point? We must go on!* can be reduced to *We mustn't give in. . . . We must go on!* Ellipsis points often serve, as does a dash, to leave a statement dramatically 'hanging in the air' (*The enemy slowly came nearer, then . . .*), after which there may be a new paragraph, a change of topic, or no further text. When points are used to suggest not an omission but a pause (*They left . . . rather quickly*), they are known as *points of suspension* or *suspension points*, and are not elliptical. Asterisks (***) are also sometimes used to mark omission, and a single asterisk is often used to replace a vowel in a taboo word (*c*nt*, *f*ck*); on such occasions, the asterisk serves as a kind of social ellipsis. See ARTICLE[1], PUNCTUATION, UNDERSTOOD. [GRAMMAR, STYLE, USAGE, WRITING].   T.MCA., S.G.

ELLIS, A(lexander) J(ohn) [1814–90]. English phonetician, dialectologist, and spelling reformer, born in London, and educated at Shrewsbury, Eton, and Trinity College, Cambridge. He was associated with Isaac Pitman in the creation of the shorthand system known as *phonotypy*, and in 1844 published *Phonetics: A Familiar System of the Principles of that Science.* Under the joint sponsorship of the Philological Society, the Early English Text Society, and the Chaucer Society, he undertook a historical study of pronunciation and published in 1869 the first volume of *On Early English Pronunciation*, a work intended to have four volumes, with some mention of modern dialects in about 30 pages in the fourth. However, on completion of the four volumes, these closing remarks grew into a fifth, published by the Early English Text Society in 1889 and entitled *The Existing Phonology of English Dialects.* The largest volume of all (835 pages), it described the contemporary situation throughout English-speaking Britain. Its data on regional pronunciations were in *glossic*, a phonetic notation of his own invention now generally considered unusable. The study covers 1,145 places in England, Wales, and Scotland, and uses information gathered by 811 informants; its main contribution has been to delineate dialect boundaries. Ellis also wrote treatises on the pronunciation of Latin and Greek, geometry, algebra, pitch, and musical scales. See index. [BIOGRAPHY, EUROPE, LANGUAGE, SPEECH].   S.E.

ELOCUTION [16c: from Latin *elocutio/elocutionis* speaking out]. The study and practice of oral delivery, including control of breath, voice, stance, and gesture (*Has he taken elocution lessons?*); the way in which someone speaks or reads aloud, especially in public (*flawless elocution*). An early meaning of the term was literary style as distinct from content, and relates to the Latin meaning of *elocutio*, one of the canons or departments of rhetoric. Elocution as training in how to speak 'properly' (as in *taking elocution lessons*) was a feature of education, particularly for girls, in the 18–19c; in Sheridan's play *The Rivals* (1775), Mrs Malaprop wished her daughter not to 'mis-pronounce words so shamefully as girls usually do'. Shaw, who gave an extended dramatic treatment to elocution in *Pygmalion* (1912), believed in the importance of speech training to the extent of adding to his will in 1913 a clause giving some of the residue of his estate to 'The substitution of a scientific training in phonetics for the makeshifts of so-called elocution lessons by actors and others which have hitherto prevailed in the teaching of oratory'. See ORATORY, ORTHOEPY, PERIOD, PHONETICS, PRONUNCIATION, PROSE, PUBLIC SPEAKING, PYGMALION, RHETORIC, SPEECH THERAPY TONGUE-TWISTER. [EDUCATION, SPEECH, STYLE].
T.MCA., R.C.

ELT, short for *English Language Teaching*. A British term for teaching English to non-native learners, often used in recent years either interchangeably with *EFL* (*English as a Foreign Language*) or as a cover term for EFL and *ESL* (*English as a Second Language*). Some commentators, such as Peter Strevens, have classified it as part of *FLT* (*Foreign Language Teaching*) in general. The term is not much used in North America, and tends not only to be the British term for the subject but also to be the term for the British approach to the subject. The organized teaching of English to foreign learners in England dates from the 16c. During the 17–19c self-instruction manuals were published throughout Europe to meet the needs of travellers and traders, and while mother-tongue teaching in the schools was bound up with parsing, translation, and literature, there was more emphasis in such books on immediate results and on oral rather than written production. The reform movement of the late 19c slowly moved foreign-language teaching both within and outside the formal systems of education towards a greater emphasis on speech and spontaneous use. It also represented a systematic attempt to derive methods of language teaching from the precepts of the developing science of linguistics.

As the language spread with general education and the evolution of the British Empire into the Commonwealth, ELT became a major element in the emerging post-colonial school systems. At first, syllabuses deriving from the teaching of English as a mother tongue predominated, with a strong literary emphasis, but the work of such 20c practitioners as Harold Palmer, Michael West, and A. S. Hornby built on the reformers' *direct method* and moved techniques away from traditional literature-based approaches. West concentrated on the use of graded vocabulary in reading programmes and Palmer and Hornby developed syllabuses based on limited ranges of grammatical structures. The work of West in India and Palmer and Hornby in Japan continued through teacher trainers like John Bright and Lionel Billows in East Africa until well after independence from colonial rule.

The British Council, from its foundation in 1934–5, played a significant role in ELT research and development throughout the world. British publishers throughout the years after the Second World War expanded their ELT production, and a superstructure of teacher-training courses, research programmes, and professional associations developed. The Institute of Education at the U. of London trained EFL teachers from 1932, and had a chair in the subject from 1948 (its chair in teaching English in Britain being founded in 1976). The School (later Department) of Applied Linguistics at the U. of Edinburgh

was founded in 1956, expressly to support high-level work in ELT, and the Association of Recognized English Language Schools (ARELS) was founded in 1960 to introduce professional controls on private English-language schools in UK.

Academically, the 1960s saw a swing away from work aimed at the Commonwealth, to free-lance and non-state-funded work throughout the world. The transfer of money to the Middle East resulting from the oil revolution of 1973 created a massive market for advanced education and thus indirectly for the English language that gave access to teachers and textbooks in major technical areas. English for specific purposes (ESP), providing access to academic English for education or job-specific English for training, became a major area of development. General English, at lower levels in the educational systems, was neglected in the 1970s until the desire to humanize what was perceived as an aridly scientific emphasis brought back into consideration many traditional practices such as literature teaching and translation. At the same time, approaches deriving from various psychological therapeutic models, such as the Silent Way, Counselling Learning, and Suggestopedia, became popular, particularly in the US, as another means of humanizing language teaching. While very different in the techniques and strategies adopted, these shared a concern to develop the full psychological potential of individual learners. A further psychological tradition reflected in more mainstream ELT is that of Second Language Acquisition research. The most ambitious theory of second-language learning from this tradition is Stephen Krashen's 'Monitor theory'. This asserts that language is typically acquired by unconscious and separate neurological processes from those used in formal learning, and that learning processes only come into play when conscious monitoring of language use is taking place. Consequently, Krashen places heavy emphasis on provision of reading or listening material ('comprehensive input') which is just beyond the reach of each learner, as a means of activating their language-acquiring capacities. This theory has been challenged by most applied linguists, but remains influential with language teachers.

In the 1990s, the relationship between language and personal identity is likely to become a major issue for ELT theory, as the social and cultural implications of the role of English as an international language are assimilated. See EXAMINING IN ENGLISH, LANGUAGE LEARNING, LANGUAGE TEACHING, TEACHING ENGLISH, TEFL, TEIL, TESD, TESL, TESOL. [EDUCATION].   C.J.B.

Harmer, Jeremy. 1983. *The Practice of English Language Teaching*. London & New York: Longman.

Howatt, A. P. R. 1984. *A History of English Language Teaching.* Oxford: University Press.

Seaton, Brian. 1982. *A Handbook of English Language Teaching Terms and Practice.* London: Macmillan.

ELT DICTIONARY. See LEARNER'S DICTIONARY.

ELT DOCUMENTS. A series of books on the theory and practice of English language teaching in a worldwide context. Started as a newsletter in 1971 by the British Council, it became a printed series in 1977, and was published commercially by Pergamon and later by Modern English Publications from 1983. Three issues are published a year, each being a collection of papers on a theme of contemporary interest, the aim being to bring together theorists and practitioners in ELT throughout the world. From 1990, the series has appeared simultaneously as a journal (*Review of English Language Teaching*) and as a series of books. See BRITISH COUNCIL, ELT. [EDUCATION, MEDIA].   C.J.B.

ELT JOURNAL. See IATEFL.

ELT PUBLISHING. A worldwide industry that produces and distributes materials for teaching and learning English as a foreign or second language at all educational levels, including textbooks, dictionaries, magazines, newspapers, readers, games, audio and video recordings, interactive video discs, and computer software. In addition, the ELT profession (teachers, teacher trainers, administrators, examiners, and related occupations) is served by a wide variety of books, journals, and newsletters. Whereas the first ELT books came into existence to facilitate contact between native speakers of English and others, in the late 20c the greater need is for English as the world's lingua franca used especially among non-native speakers, a development that has implications for both the content of materials in the 21c and the model(s) of English that will animate them. Where there are well-developed indigenous publishing industries, international publishers meet intense competition from materials specifically designed for local syllabuses and educational systems. To deal with it, they often form collaborative relationships with local publishers or establish branches with editorial offices to publish their own local materials.

The publishing of ELT texts dates from the mid-16c, when a manual to teach both English and French was published in Antwerp in 1553, as a response to the increasing role of English in European commerce. The oldest extant text for teaching English is Jacques Bellot's *The Englishe Scholemaister. Conteyning many profitable preceptes for the naturall born french men, and other straungers that haue their French tongue, to attayne the true pronouncing of the Englishe tongue* (1580), published in London to help French (Huguenot) refugees from religious persecution. The first ELT text published outside of Europe was *The Tutor, or a New English and Bengalee work, well adapted to teach the natives English, written and published by John Miller* (India, 1797), which was produced in response to a demand created by contacts between the British and the local population. ELT publishing grew with the spread of English in the 19c and earlier 20c and expanded enormously after the Second World War. Its foundations were laid by the language-teaching reform movement of the 1880s and in the early 20c when Daniel Jones produced three seminal works that are still in print in 1990: *The Pronunciation of English* (1909), the *English Pronouncing Dictionary* (1917), and the *Outline of English Phonetics* (1918). One of the first learner's courses to be successful internationally was Michael West's *New Method* grammar, practice books, and readers published by Longmans Green from 1938. In the same year the same publisher brought out the first level of C. E. Eckersley's *Essential English for Foreign Students.* This is one of the most successful courses ever produced and continues in use in some countries. These best-sellers, along with A. S. Hornby's *Oxford Progressive English Course for Adults* (1954), were overtaken by L. G. Alexander's *New Concept* series published by Longman from 1967.

In the 1970s-80s, leading ELT courses included: (UK) *Kernel Lessons Intermediate* by Robert O'Neill, Roy Kingsbury, and Tony Yeadon (Longman, 1971), *Strategies* by Brian Abbs and Ingrid Fairbairn (Longman, 1977), *Access to English* by Michael Coles and Basil Lord (Oxford, 1975), *Streamline* by Bernard Hartley and Peter Viney (Oxford, 1978), *Meaning into Words* by Adrian Doff, Christopher Jones, and Keith Mitchell (Cambridge, 1983), and *The Cambridge English Course* by Michael Swan and Catherine Walter (1984); (US) *Lado English Series* by Robert Lado (Regents, 1970), *New Horizons in English* by Lars Mellgren and Michael Walker (Addison-Wesley, 1973), *Intercom* by Richard C. Yorkey and others (American Book Company, 1977), and *Spectrum* by Donald R. H. Byrd and others (Regents, 1982). A special category is books and other materials to accompany radio and television courses, the most successful of which is the BBC's *Follow Me*, which has been watched by many millions throughout the world, including over 50m in the People's Republic of China. UK publishers became active in ELT before US publishers and continue to dominate the international scene, especially in reference books. While there is no significant learner's dictionary available from an American publisher, British publishers have published dictionaries keyed to both BrE and AmE. They include *The Oxford Advanced Learner's Dictionary* (1948, 1963, 1974, 1989), *The Longman Dictionary of Contemporary English* (1978, 1987), and *Collins COBUILD English Language Dictionary* (1987).

See ALEXANDER (L. G.), BBC ENGLISH[2], BRITISH COUNCIL, CAMBRIDGE UNIVERSITY PRESS, COBUILD, COLLINS, ELT, ELT DOCUMENTS, ENGLISH PRONOUNCING DICTIONARY, HORNBY, JONES (D.), LEARNER'S DICTIONARY, LONGMAN, OXFORD UNIVERSITY PRESS, PALMER, PUBLISHING, WEST. [EDUCATION, MEDIA].   A. DU P.

ELYOT, (Sir) Thomas [1499?-1546]. English statesman and scholar. In such works as *The boke named The gouernour* (1531), he held that though rhetoric made Latin and Greek style more eloquent, the structure of English made meaning clearer. Elyot sought to increase English vocabulary by borrowing from Latin, Greek, and French, in order to correct 'the insufficiencie of our owne langage'. When introducing new words, he often used them in explanatory pairs: *education or bringing up of children*; *explicating or unfolding*. Compare BOOK OF COMMON PRAYER. See index. [BIOGRAPHY, EUROPE, HISTORY].   W.F.B.

EM [18c: from the name of the letter M]. Also **mut, mutton**. A printer's term originally for the width of a piece of type bearing the letter 'm'. It is now used to mean: (1) A unit of horizontal measurement, variable according to type-size, and equal in width to the height of the typeface. An *em dash* is a dash one em long. A one-em space is often used as a paragraph indent, and the corresponding piece of blank metal type, with a square face measuring one em on each side, is an *em quad/quadrat*. (2) Also *pica em*. A fixed unit of measurement, equal to an em of 12-point type, used for example to express the width and depth of the print area on a page. See DASH, EN, PICA, RULE. [TECHNOLOGY].   T.MCA.

E-MAIL. See ELECTRONIC MAIL.

EMBEDDING [c.1960]. A term in generative grammar for the process by which one sentence is included by subordination within another (the *matrix* sentence). The sentence *Tom announced that they were engaged* is said to be derived from the matrix sentence *Tom announced (something)*, into which the complement clause *They were engaged* has been introduced by means of the complementizer *that*. [GRAMMAR].   S.G.

-EME [c.1950s: extracted from *phoneme, morpheme*, etc.]. In linguistics, a noun-forming suffix used in naming certain theoretical units of language, such as the *phoneme*, the minimal unit of phonology or speech sound, the *semanteme* and *sememe*, units of meaning, the *prosodeme*, a unit of rhythm, and the *tagmeme*, a unit of structure. Of the many units created in recent decades, most are restricted to specific theories and works, and have little current use. See LEXEME, MORPHEME, PHONEME. [LANGUAGE].   T.MCA.

EMENDATION [16c: from Latin *emendatio/ emendationis* removing faults]. The rewriting of a word, phrase, sentence, or text so as to correct or alter it or to give a (postulated) improved reading of a group of corrupted letters. See EDITING. [STYLE, WRITING].   T.MCA.

EMPHASIS [16c: through Latin from Greek *émphasis* showing, seeming, implying]. A use of language to mark importance or significance, through either intensity of expression or linguistic features such as stress and intonation. The classical sense of emphasis as something added to language survives in the phrases *add emphasis to* or *lay emphasis on*. It is generally achieved by any means that draws attention to a syllable, word, phrase, idea, event, or social situation, such as the increase of intensity and volume on *at once* when someone says 'Do it *at once!*' Here, print marks, by means of italics and an exclamation mark, what is achieved in speech by an increase in the volume of sound (usually accompanied by a change of expression).

In speech, writing, and print. (1) Spoken emphasis is usually achieved by changing style, pitch, tone, rhythm, stress, or any combination of these. Typically, people emphasize something by speaking more loudly or by shouting, but they can also be emphatic by speaking more quietly, intensely, clearly, quickly, or slowly. The normal rhythm of delivery can change so as to stress each word or syllable firmly and equally: *DO— IT—AT—ONCE*. Contrastive stress, involving rhythm and intonation, is commonly used to emphasize a word or point: *MARY should do it* (*not Joan*), *Mary SHOULD do it* (*and not avoid her responsibilities*), *Mary should DO it* (*rather than do nothing*). (2) Emphasis in writing is usually achieved by underlining or capitalizing words, and by using exclamation marks. In print, italics or other lettering are also used. The same word can therefore be emphasized as: 'Put the BOOK on the table', 'Put the *book* on the table', 'Put the book on the table.' A whole sentence can be emphasized as an order (*Put the book on the table!*), the exclamation mark implying anger, insistence, loudness, or any combination of these.

In grammar and style. (1) In its various emphatic uses the auxiliary verb is generally stressed. Prominent among them is contrastive emphasis on the positive or negative: *Why didn't you tell me?—I DID tell you*; *They say they've paid, but they HAVEn't.* The contrastive emphasis may be on tense (*Robert WAS—and still IS—a happy child*) or aspect (*She is living in Birmingham and HAS been for a long time*). The emphasis may, however, be non-contrastive, conveying emotion: *What HAVE you done?*; *Where ARE you going?*; *We ARE sorry*; *I DO like your hair.* The term *emphatic pronoun* refers to a reflexive pronoun used to emphasize a noun phrase, as in 'The town *itself* is very old' and 'Well, you said it *yourself*.' (2) A variety of devices alone or in combination serve to create emphases of style: a long sentence followed by a short sentence; a quiet tone followed by a loud tone; a dramatic pause; a change of direction; a deliberate omission; an unexpected silence; change in word order (*This I can do without* as opposed to *I can do without this*); repetition, especially towards a climax (*I want you to do it, I insist that you do it—and you'll do it NOW!*); figurative usage such as metaphor and rhetorical question (*Would you have believed he could design such a rhapsody in stone?*).

When a technique is overused or too many devices occur at the same time the result is *overemphasis*; when a technique is underused or too few devices occur the result is *underemphasis.* An intention to be emphatic is often introduced by such formulas as *I must emphasize that . . . , I cannot sufficiently emphasize that . . . , We lay emphasis here on . . . , I must stress that . . . , and This report underlines the fact that . . .*

See ALLITERATION, CAPITAL, EXAGGERATION, EXCLAMATION MARK, HYPERBOLE, INVERSION, LITOTES, MEIOSIS, REPETITION, RHYTHM, STRESS, UNDERSTATEMENT. [GRAMMAR, SPEECH, STYLE, WRITING]. T.MCA., S.G.

EN [18c]. Also **nut.** A printer's term originally for the width of a piece of type bearing the letter 'n', now used as a unit of horizontal measurement half the width of an *em*: see EM (sense 1). It approximates to the average width of the letters in a font, and is a useful basis for making rough calculations of the printed extent of a text. See DASH, PICA, RULE. [TECHNOLOGY]. T.MCA.

ENCLITIC [17c: from Greek *enklitikós* leaning on]. A word attached to a preceding word, sometimes in a reduced form: Latin *-que* (and) in *Senatus populusque Romanus* the Senate and the Roman people; in English, such contracted forms as *n't* in *didn't* and *'ve* in *could've.* Compare PROCLITIC. See NEGATION. [WORD]. T.MCA.

ENCRYPTION. See CRYPTOGRAPHY.

ENCYCLOPAEDIA, encyclopedia, also occasionally **cyclopaedia** [16c: from Latin *encyclopædia*, Greek *enkuklopaideia*, a form in manuscripts of Quintilian, Pliny, and Galen that is apparently a misreading of *enkúklios paideía* encircling training, well-rounded or general education: the circle of arts and sciences considered as essential to a liberal education, often later called *the liberal arts.* The common present-day spelling is *-pedia*]. (1) Formerly, a broadly based course of instruction in the classical style: 'The circle of doctrine [that is, learning] is in one worde of greke Encyclopedia' (Sir Thomas Elyot, *The boke named The gouernour*, 1531). (2) A work of reference containing a range of information in entry or essay form, such as *The Encyclopaedia Britannica*, whose 15th edition (1974 and annually updated) is an alphabetically organized general work in 32 volumes, and *The Cambridge Encyclopedia of Language* (compiled by David Crystal, 1987), a thematically organized work on one subject in one volume. Encyclopedias were until the end of the 18c regarded as a variety of dictionary, and currently some encyclopedic works are given that title: *The Oxford Dictionary of Natural History* (Michael Allaby, 1985). Conventional dictionaries that include elements of general information such as biographies and toponyms are known as *encyclopedic dictionaries* and sometimes announced as such: *The New Hamlyn Encyclopedic World Dictionary* (ed. Patrick Hanks, 1971), *The Oxford Encyclopedic English Dictionary* (eds. Joyce M. Hawkins & Robert Allen, 1991). See COMPANION, DICTIONARY, GUIDE, LIEBER. [REFERENCE]. T.MCA.

***ENCYCLOPAEDIA BRITANNICA*, The,** short forms *Britannica, EB.* The leading English-language encyclopedia, whose long and complex history (18-20c) illustrates certain patterns of development in educational publishing in the English-speaking world. It is published in Chicago with editorial advice from the faculties of the U. of Chicago and from committees drawn from the universities of Cambridge, Edinburgh, Oxford, London, and Sussex in the UK, and universities in Australia, Canada, Denmark, France, Germany, Italy, Japan, the Netherlands, and Portugal. It is currently in its 15th edition, with 32 volumes, and is promoted and marketed worldwide.

Scotland. The 1st edition of the *Britannica* was a British response to the *Encyclopédie* of Denis

Diderot. It was published as a partwork in Edinburgh (1768–71), edited by William Smellie, but the brainchild of the printer and book-seller Colin Macfarquhar and the engraver Andrew Bell. It was issued in full in three volumes entitled *Encyclopaedia Britannica: A Dictionary of the Arts and Sciences*, and was intended to cover the entire range of knowledge without the polemics of the French work. Its alphabetically ordered articles ranged from brief definitions (*Woman*. The female of man. See *Homo*.) to lengthy treatises (the longest, at over 75 pages, being *Law*, that is, Scots law). The modest success of the 1st edition led to a 2nd (1777–84) and a 3rd (1788–97), in the course of which it grew from three to ten to 18 volumes. From 1812 to 1827, the copyright was owned by the publisher Archibald Constable, who invested heavily in advancing its reputation for authority and scholarship. The 4th edition (1801–9) was the 3rd with two additional volumes, and the 5th and 6th (1815, 1820–3) were little different. While the 6th was in preparation, Constable engaged Macvey Napier to create a Supplement, which appeared in 12 half-volumes in 1815–24. Its contributors included James Mill, Walter Scott, Thomas Robert Malthus, and William Hazlitt. After Constable's death *Britannica* was acquired by Adam Black, whose firm published the 7th edition (1830–42), the first with an index; the 8th (1852–60), the first with contributions from American authors; and the 9th (1875–89), sometimes called the *scholar's edition*, which appeared in 25 volumes under the editorship of T. S. Baynes and then W. Robertson Smith, and which was the first to have an authorized US printing.

England and America. In 1901, the American businessmen Horace Hooper and Walter Jackson acquired the encyclopedia from A. & C. Black, and helped rescue *The Times* of London from financial difficulties through a heavily advertised promotion of a reprinted 9th edition. Hooper, Jackson, and the newspaper all profited from the 35-volume 10th edition (1902–3). In 1904, work on an 11th edition began, but before it was published (1910–11) the connection with *The Times* was ended and the U. of Cambridge agreed to act as the encyclopedia's sponsor. At this time, business operations began to shift to the US, first to New York, then Chicago. Editorial work was, however, based in London until the 1930s, under first Hugh Chisholm, then J. L. Garvin. The 12th and 13th editions (1921–2, 1926) comprised the reprinted 11th with three additional updating volumes. In 1927, work began on the 14th, which was to be a wholly new and different work. Financial difficulties, however, caused the *Britannica* to pass to the US

retailers Sears, Roebuck in 1928, the year before the 14th edition appeared. Soon after publication, the 14th was placed on a continuous revision programme, and from 1936 annually revised impressions were produced.

In 1943, Sears passed the encyclopedia to William Benton, an advertising executive who became a vice-president of the U. of Chicago, which had declined to take the *EB* itself. Benton remained owner and publisher until his death in 1973. Under his direction, the company produced the 54-volume *Great Books of the Western World* (1952), the annual *Britannica Book of the Year* (begun in 1938), the *Children's Britannica* (1960), and other works of reference. In 1974, the 15th edition was published, divided into three sections: the *Micropaedia* for short entries, the *Macropaedia* for in-depth articles, and the one-volume *Propaedia* (showing the arrangement of the work's themes). Annual revisions have continued, and a 1985 revision including two index volumes took the 15th edition to 32 volumes. In 1980, Doubleday and Britannica jointly produced the *Britannica Book of English Usage*, edited by Christine Timmons and Frank Gibney, which has sections on the contemporary language, origins, grammar, word-formation, spelling, pronunciation, words and dictionaries, the library, abbreviations, finer points of writing, letter-writing, and public speaking. Since 1981, the company has been owned by the William Benton Foundation of Illinois. See COLERIDGE (S.), ENCYCLOP(A)EDIA, MERRIAM-WEBSTER, WEBSTER'S NEW INTERNATIONAL DICTIONARY. [EDUCATION, HISTORY, MEDIA, REFERENCE, USAGE].

T.MCA.

ENDING. (1) A grammatical or derivational element at the end of a word: *-s* added to *horse* to form the plural *horses*, added to *sell* to form the third-person singular *sells*; *-ity* added to *central* to form *centrality*. Elements like *-s* are often referred to as *inflectional endings*. Elements like *-ity* may be referred to as *derivational endings*, but are more commonly known as *suffixes*. Inflectional endings may or may not be classed as suffixes. (2) Something that serves to end or close something else: for example, the closing words of speech or a novel, or the words or syllables at the end of a line of verse. See ADVERB, CLASSICAL ENDING, ENCLITIC, FEMININE ENDING, INFLECTION/INFLEXION, MASCULINE ENDING, PLURAL, SUFFIX. [WORD].

T.MCA.

ENDNOTE. See NOTES AND REFERENCES.

END-STOPPED LINE. A line of verse which ends at a point where a natural pause is likely in speech, as at the end of a clause:

> With every morn their love grew tenderer,
> With every eve deeper and tenderer still;

He might not in house, field, or garden stir,
But her full shape would all his seeing fill.
(John Keats, 'Isabella, or The Pot of Basil', 1818)

End-stopping is common in blank verse and in the heroic couplet. Compare ENJAMB(E)MENT. [LITERATURE].   R.C.

ENG [1950s: apparently by analogy with the names given to the letters *n* (enn) and *m* (emm). Compare *Ing*, the name of an ancient Germanic god and of a runic letter that has the same sound value]. Also **agma, angma** [19c: the Greek name for a velar nasal sound that was a value of the letter *gamma* in certain phonetic contexts]. Also less formally **tailed n, n with a tail**. The symbol ŋ, used in IPA and the pronunciation systems of some dictionaries for the voiced velar nasal consonant represented in English by the digraph *ng* as in *sing* /sɪŋ/. The form appears to date from the 17c, and was used by Isaac Pitman in 1845 with this value in his phonotypic alphabet. See ALPHABET, LETTER¹, NASAL. [SPEECH, WRITING].   T.MCA., E.W.

ENGALOG. See TAGLISH.

ENGLAND [from Old English *Englaland*, land of the Angles or English]. A kingdom that occupies the southern part of the island of Britain and is the historically primary home of the English language. Of it, the *Encyclopaedia Britannica* notes: 'Constitutionally, England does not exist. It is not mentioned in the title of the sovereign who rules "the United Kingdom of Great Britain and Northern Ireland and other Realms and Territories." Scotland, Wales, and Northern Ireland have certain governmental institutions of their own, but England . . . needs no special mention. Holding more than four-fifths of the population, however, England's dominance of the United Kingdom is beyond question' (1986).

The people of England are ethnically mixed, drawn from Germanic, Celtic, Scandinavian, Norman-French, and other European sources, with recent admixtures from colonial and ex-colonial territories in Africa, Asia, and the Caribbean. The country consists of regions that have distinctive histories and dialect forms: the *South-East*, centred on London; the *South-West*, including Cornwall, home of the last Celtic language of England; the *West Midlands*, centred on Birmingham; the *East Midlands* or *East Anglia*, considered to have provided the basic forms of present-day standard English; the *North-West*, including the cities of Liverpool and Manchester, and the county of Lancashire; the *North-East*, including the cities of Leeds and York, and the counties that once constituted the single county of Yorkshire.

Both the language and the English peoples pre-date the formation of the country. The various kingdoms of the Anglo-Saxon peoples extended to about the present national boundaries in the 9c. The unified kingdom was strengthened, somewhat ironically, by the Norman Conquest in 1066. Until the mid-15c, the kings of England had extensive territories in France, and it was only with their loss that a sense of English nationhood developed, coming to full flower in the 16c. Shakespeare's *King John* closes with the lines:

This England neuer did, nor neuer shall
Lye at the proud foote of a Conqueror,
But when it first did helpe to wound it selfe.

Such sentiments continued after the prolonged formation of the United Kingdom in the acts of union with Wales (1535), Scotland (1707), and Ireland (1801). Nelson sent his famous signal at Trafalgar, 1805: 'England expects that every man this day will do his duty', and popular songs like 'Send out the boys of the old brigade, who made old England free' prevailed into the 20c. Even at the present time, the name *England* is often applied loosely by the English, Americans, and many other nations to the whole of Britain: 'One of the stranger facts to emerge at the seminar was that German drama is more popular in the north of England than the south—or at any rate is more often produced there. Derby, Sheffield, Manchester, Edinburgh, Glasgow have a taste for Dorst, Fassbinder, Kroetz, Heiner Muller and Strauss that London lacks' (editorial notes, *The Author*, London, Summer 1990).

See ANGLES, ANGLIA, ANGLIAN, ANGLIC, ANGLICISM, ANGLICIZE, ANGLO-, ANGLOCENTRIC, ANGLOPHILE, ANGLOPHOBE, ANGLO-SAXON, BARNES, BBC ENGLISH¹, BIBLE, BRITAIN, BRITISH, BRITISH BROADCASTING, BRITISH EMPIRE, BRITISH PUBLISHING, CAXTON, CHAUCER, CORNISH, CORNWALL, DANELAW, DIALECT IN ENGLAND, DORSET, EAST MIDLAND DIALECT, ELIZABETHAN, ENGLISH, ENGLISH IN ENGLAND, ENGLISH LITERATURE, ENGLISH PLACE-NAMES, ENGLISHRY, GEORDIE, HEPTARCHY, HISTORY OF ENGLISH, HOME, HOME COUNTIES, IRELAND, JOURNALISM, JUTES, KENTISH, LANCASHIRE, LONDON, -MAN/WOMAN, MERCIA, MIDLANDS (THE), MOTHER COUNTRY, NEW ENGLAND, NORMAN, NORTHERN ENGLISH, NORTHUMBRIA, OLD COUNTRY, PUBLIC SCHOOL ENGLISH, RECEIVED PRONUNCIATION, SAXON, SCOTLAND, SCOUSE, SHAKESPEARE, SOMERSET, SYNECDOCHE, WALES, WESSEX, WEST COUNTRY, YORKSHIRE. [EDUCATION, EUROPE, LITERATURE].   R.C.

ENG LANG, ENG LANG AND LIT. The short forms (with or without points) of *English Language* and *English Language and Literature*, titles of certain traditional university courses: 'Those of us who have been in the Eng. Lang. and Lit. business for a long time will remember when academically "English language" meant the study of texts . . . before 1500 and "English literature" texts written after 1500: a distinction that has not entirely disappeared even today' (Raymond Chapman, *English Today* 23, July 1990). Compare ENG LIT. [LANGUAGE, LIT-ERATURE].   T.MCA.

ENGLAÑOL. See PUERTO RICO, SPANGLISH.

ENGLISH [From Old English *englisc, ænglisc*, from *Engle* the Angles]. (1) The name of a people (*the achievements of the English*); the adjective associated with that people and with its country, England (*English traditions*). (2) Short forms *E, E., Eng.* The name of a language originating in north-western Europe (*the history of English*); the adjective relating to it (*English dialects*). (3) Also *English language*. A course offered in schools, universities, and other institutions, whose aim is to provide students with knowledge about (and skills in the use of) the language, aspects of its literature, or both: *first-year English; English as a Foreign Language* (*EFL*); *English language teaching; English Language and Literature; Business English; remedial English.* (4) The adjective and noun used in Canada for speakers of English as opposed to French, regardless of ethnic origin: *differences between the French and the English; English Canadians*. In the article that follows, the first and second senses only are discussed. For the third sense, see TEACHING ENGLISH and ENGLISH LITERATURE. For the fourth, see ENGLISH CANADIAN.

The English. Early Germanic settlers in Britain were referred to in Latin as the *gens Anglorum*, which can be translated as both 'Angle race' and 'English people', and called themselves *Englisc/Ænglisc* or *Angelcynn* ('Angle-kin'). The name *Englisc* contrasted with the names of both Celtic and Scandinavian people in Britain: 'Nah naðer to farenne ne Wylisc man on Ænglisc lond ne Ænglisc on Wylisc' (Neither Welshman to go on English land, nor English on Welsh: ordinance); 'Gif Ænglisc man Deniscne ofslea' (If an Englishman kills a Dane: Laws of Aethelred, both citations from *c*.1000). However, by the time of the Norman Conquest, *English* was the name for all inhabitants of England, regardless of background. For many years after 1066, the Normans were commonly distinguished from their English subjects as *French*, a dichotomy sustained in state documents long after it ceased to mean much in social terms. By the 14c, *English* was again the name for all subjects of the king or queen of England, whatever their background, and has remained so ever since.

Ambiguity. A new uncertainty developed in the 16c. Wales was united with England in 1535 and the English and Scottish monarchies became one in 1603. The union of the parliaments of England and Scotland took place in London in 1707 and the state of Great Britain officially came into existence. Increasingly from these dates, the term *English* has been used in three ways: to refer to the people of England and matters concerning England alone; to refer to the people of England and Wales and matters concerning both; to refer to the people of Great Britain (England, Wales, Scotland, and varyingly all or part of Ireland), and matters concerning them all. Generally, the first usage prevails when Irish, Scots, Welsh, and English people are talking to or about each other, although English people are famous among the others for using their generic name to cover all four. When talking among themselves, through the media, and in international situations, many English people use *English* without specifying whether they are discussing themselves or all Britons and perhaps without being clear about the limits they intend. This is also often the case with Americans, mainland Europeans, and others:

'While Rafelson is a great admirer of Robert Redford, he did not think an American playing an aristocratic Englishman in "Out of Africa" worked. So he decided he wanted English actors and settled for two virtual unknowns. Patrick Bergin, like Burton, whom he plays, is Irish and the star of "Act of Betrayal," a recent mini-series about an Irish Republican Army informer. Iain Glen, a Scotsman, who plays Speke, was in the West End production of Tom Stoppard's "Hapgood" early last year' (in 'Quest for the Source of the Nile, on Film', *New York Times*, Feb. 1989).

The language. English is part of the Germanic branch of the Indo-European language family, along with, among others, Danish, Dutch, and German. Once confined to Britain, it is now used throughout the world. Its use and distribution can be discussed in various ways, including geographical distribution, status as an official or other language, and status as majority language or mother tongue (first language), alternative language, medium of education, second language, or foreign language. The territories in which English is a significant everyday language, in alphabetical order according to regions of the world, are:

Africa and the western Indian Ocean. Botswana, British Indian Ocean Territory, Cameroon, Ethiopia, Gambia, Ghana, Kenya, Lesotho, Liberia, Malawi, Mauritius, Namibia, Nigeria, Seychelles, Sierra Leone, Somalia, South Africa, Sudan, Swaziland, Tanzania, Uganda, Zambia, Zimbabwe.

The mainland Americas and the South Atlantic. Argentina, Ascension (Island), Belize, Bermuda,

Canada, the Falkland Islands, Guyana, Honduras, Nicaragua, Panama, St Helena, Surinam, Tristan da Cunha, the United States.

Asia. Bahrain, Bangladesh, Brunei, Cyprus, Hong Kong, India, Israel, Kuwait, Malaysia, the Maldives, Nepal, Oman, Pakistan, the Philippines, Qatar, Singapore, Sri Lanka, the United Arab Emirates, Vietnam.

The Caribbean. Anguilla, Antigua and Barbuda, Bahamas, Barbados, the Cayman Islands, Dominica, Grenada, Jamaica, Montserrat, Puerto Rico, St Christopher and Nevis, St Lucia, St Vincent and the Grenadines, Trinidad and Tobago, the Turks and Caicos Islands, the Virgin Islands (American and British).

Europe. The Channel Islands, Gibraltar, the Irish Republic, the Isle of Man, Malta, the United Kingdom (England, Scotland, Wales, Northern Ireland).

Oceania. Australia, the Cook Islands, Fiji, Hawaii (in the US), Kiribati, Nauru, New Zealand, Papua New Guinea, the Solomon Islands, Tonga, Tuvalu, Vanuatu, Western Samoa.

Official language. It is not always easy to establish whether English has a constitutionally endorsed status in the territories in which it plays a role. It might be expected to have such a status in the UK and the US, but does not; in both it is a *de facto* rather than a *de jure* official language, although in a number of US states it is formally endorsed as the official language: see ENGLISH LANGUAGE AMENDMENT. English has generally acquired legal status only when a government has concluded that explicit recognition is necessary, usually to establish it as a sole medium or a co-medium of administration and education. In the following countries, English has a statutory role: *Botswana* (with Setswana), *Cameroon* (with French), *Canada* (with French), *Gambia, Ghana, India* (with Hindi), *the Irish Republic* (with Irish Gaelic), *Lesotho* (with Sesotho), *Malawi* (with Chichewa), *Nigeria, Pakistan* (with Urdu), *Papua New Guinea* (with Hiri Motu and Tok Pisin), *the Philippines* (with Filipino), *Seychelles* (with Creole and French), *Sierra Leone, Singapore* (with Mandarin Chinese, Malay, and Tamil), *the Solomon Islands* (with Solomon Islands Pidgin English), *South Africa* (with Afrikaans), *Swaziland* (with Siswati), *Tanzania* (with Swahili), *Uganda, Vanuatu* (with French and Bislama), *Zambia, Zimbabwe.*

ENL, ESL, and EFL territories. The global distribution of English is often currently described in terms of English as a Native Language (ENL), English as a Second Language (ESL), and English as a Foreign Language (EFL):

(1) *ENL territories.* Most people in ENL territories have English as their first and often only language. There are two groups: (*a*) *English profoundly dominant:* Anguilla, Antigua and Barbuda, Ascension Island, Australia, the Bahamas, Barbados, Belize, Bermuda, Dominica, England, the Falkland Islands, Grenada, Guyana, the Isle of Man, Jamaica, Montserrat, Northern Ireland, St Christopher and Nevis, St Helena, St Vincent and the Grenadines, Trinidad and Tobago, the United States of America (but see next), the Virgin Islands (American and British). (*b*) *At least one other language significant:* Canada (French), Channel Islands (French), Gibraltar (Spanish), the Irish Republic (Irish Gaelic), Liberia (various Niger-Congo languages), New Zealand (Maori), St Lucia (Creole French), Scotland (Scottish Gaelic, and Scots if defined as a distinct language from English), South Africa (Afrikaans; various Bantu and Khoisan languages), Wales (Welsh). Some commentators argue that the US is, or will soon be, a member of this group, with Spanish as the other nationally significant language.

(2) *ESL territories.* Many people in ESL territories use English for various purposes, and in some English has an official, educational, or other role. English may be generally accepted or more or less controversial. The territories are: Bangladesh, Botswana, Brunei, Cameroon, Cook Islands, Fiji, Gambia, Ghana, Hong Kong, India, Kenya, Kiribati, Lesotho, Malawi, Malaysia, Malta, Mauritius, Namibia, Nauru, Nepal, Nigeria, Pakistan, Papua New Guinea, Philippines, Puerto Rico, Seychelles, Sierra Leone, Singapore, Solomon Islands, Sri Lanka, Swaziland, Tanzania, Tuvalu, Uganda, Vanuatu, Western Samoa, Zambia, Zimbabwe.

(3) *EFL territories.* The rest of the world. English may be more or less prestigious and more or less welcome in particular places. Many people learn it for occupational purposes and/or as part of education and recreation, at school or in college, or its acquisition may be casual and haphazard, in the family or the workplace, or on the street. Competence varies across a gamut from fluent to a smattering gleaned for limited purposes.

Provisos. These categories need to be buttressed by certain provisos regarding, among other things, the varieties of English used in ENL territories, the existence and use of related English-based creoles in both ENL and ESL territories, and the presence of communities of native speakers in some EFL territories. For example, the classification does not discriminate with regard to the nature and range of English within ENL nations. It does not cover such fundamentals as the historical and linguistic relationship between English and Scots in the UK, the relationship between standard English and Black English in the US, and the relationship between mainstream English and English-based creoles in West Africa and the Caribbean. In addition, although the categories allow for the coexistence of English with other languages in some territories, they do not discuss the influence of such languages on English or the influence of English on them, including code-mixing and code-switching between English and Gaelic in Ireland and Scotland, English and Welsh in Wales, English and French in Cameroon and Canada, and English and indigenous and other languages in Africa, South Asia, South-East Asia, and Oceania.

Although ENL countries like Jamaica and ESL countries like those in West Africa are kept apart by the categories, they share historically and structurally related English-based creoles that they use side by side with local forms of standard or standardizing English. Additionally, the classification does not cover the situation in such states as Papua New Guinea, the Solomon Islands, and Vanuatu, where local languages are used alongside standard English and the English-based creoles Tok Pisin, Pijin, and Bislama respectively. In some Commonwealth ESL countries, there are long-established native-speaking and quasi-native-speaking groups, such as in Hong Kong, India, and Kenya. In India, the precise numbers are unknown, but an estimate of 30m is widely accepted: that is, more users of English than in Canada. In some EFL countries, English is well established in groups of varying sizes: in Argentina, where Spanish is the national language, an English-speaking minority of some 100,000 people; in Portugal, a small but important enclave of English-speaking families who regard themselves as British and run the port wine industry.

History. The roots of English are in the coastal areas of what are now southern Denmark and north-western Germany. For some time after the settlement of peoples from this area in Britain, mutual intelligibility continued between settlers and home communities. With the passage of time, however, the varieties of each area developed differently, and English emerged as a distinct language in much the same way as Icelandic and Faroese, though on a far larger scale. Since the 19c, scholars have divided the Germanic language of Britain into four phases that cover some 1,500 years: *Old English c.*500–1050, *Middle English c.*1050–1450, *Early Modern English c.*1450–1700, *(Late) Modern English c.*1700 onward. Some scholars add an early stage, *pre-Old English* (before the first texts in Old English, and so before Old English properly so called), and some add a later stage, *World*

English (usually beginning during or after the Second World War).

The history of English can be discussed and described in at least three ways: (1) As one language changing over centuries, everything from pre-Old English to World English being 'the same' language. (2) As one language becoming another, showing how Old English (or Anglo-Saxon, so named to mark its distinctness) changed over centuries to become present-day English. (3) As a cluster of related forms of speech shifting historically and geographically to become another, larger cluster of related forms of speech, writing, and print generally subsumed under the umbrella term 'English'. This last approach focuses on variation within forms called for convenience 'Old English', 'Modern English', etc. The writers of histories of English differ in their emphases, 19c histories tending to favour the first and second approaches, 20c histories tending to favour the second and third.

Old English is unintelligible to a user of Modern English; anyone wishing to read *Beowulf* in the original must learn Old English in the same way as Latin and Greek. By the 15c, Middle English bore little resemblance to Old English, and a modern reader needs to come to terms linguistically and culturally with such works as Chaucer's *Canterbury Tales*. The language became more or less 'modern' in the late 17c and early 18c. The plays of the Elizabethan and Jacobean theatre and the poetry of Milton are therefore not easy to read or listen to: however much the work of Shakespeare is admired and performed, it lies at the edge of Modern English, requires interpretation, and may never be entirely understood by a present-day reader. Shakespeare, Jonson, Bacon, and the other eminent Elizabethans and Jacobeans were all dead before the present-day standard language began to develop in England, Ireland, Scotland, Wales, the American and Caribbean colonies, and in trading posts and settlements in Africa and Asia.

In the 18c, English became increasingly significant as a medium of science, technology, commerce, communication, education, and literature, with two focal points for the standard: the British Empire and the United States. By 1700, academics had come to prefer English over Latin as their medium of publication, and universities and schools throughout the English-speaking world had moved away from Latin as a primary medium of instruction. Increasing numbers of grammars and dictionaries (almost unknown before 1600) were devoted to the language, literacy grew, and in the 19c there was a boom in popular publishing. In the 20c, the growth of the language has continued beyond academia, in military alliances such as the *North*

Atlantic Treaty Organization (*NATO*), whose primary language is English, in the *European Community* (*EC*), for whom English is with French one of the working languages, in the *European Free Trade Association* (*EFTA*), whose official language is English although none of the member states are anglophone, and in communications, information technology, publishing, and popular culture. Because of the primary positions of the UK (especially in the 19c) and the US (especially in the 20c) in industrial development, economic enterprise, colonialism, and war, the international position of English has been increasingly secure since the mid-19c. See HISTORY OF ENGLISH.

Statistics. In the later 20c, non-native users of English have come to outnumber native users, partly because of the accelerating spread of the language, and partly because of increases in population and educational opportunities in many parts of the world. Estimates of the overall number of users of English relate to the three criteria of *English by birthright* (in the ENL territories in the 1970s estimated at *c*.300m people), *English through historical association* (in the ESL territories also *c*.300m), and *English through usually formal acquisition* (in the EFL territories *c*.100m). The total of *c*.700m was widely accepted in the early 1980s, but some linguists, for example David Crystal ('How Many Millions?—The Statistics of World English', *English Today* 1, Jan. 1985), have discussed doubling this total to *c*.1.4bn so as to bring in anyone who uses any kind of English, extended or restricted, 'correct' or 'broken'. It is probably safe to assume that by the end of the 1980s some 10% of the inhabitants of the EFL nations were usefully familiar with English, and that close to a billion people use it in varying degrees and for various purposes, in almost a 2-to-1 ratio of non-natives to natives.

Variety. The diversity of English has always been so great that efforts have often been made to distinguish between a 'proper' or 'correct' core, almost always a minority form associated with class and education, and other forms that are closer to or further away from that core, which is usually perceived as the standard language. There are four ways in which this kind of distinction has been made:

Language and dialect. The use of such terms as *language* and *dialect* for mutual definition is common to most European languages, but there is a paradox in how they are used and understood. Although a language is widely seen as being 'made up' of dialects, there is nonetheless in every language a single form held to be superior to all dialects: the social, literary, and educational standard. In this tradition, English paradoxically contains its dialects while standing apart from them. Linguists have sought to overcome the problem by treating standard English as another dialect, the *standard dialect*, whose generally assumed superiority and prestige are not attributable to intrinsic merit but rather to social utility. Because of its status, this dialect has diversified in ways that make it the only one that can be used in discussing such matters as philosophy, economics, and literature. However, although a perception of the standard as also being a dialect may be helpful in social and educational terms (making it first, as it were, among equals), tensions persist between speakers whose usage is judged (more or less) non-standard and those whose usages (more or less) fit the norm.

Language and lect. Sociolinguists have created such terms as *acrolect*, *mesolect*, and *basilect* from the root element of *dialect*. At first the terms referred, respectively, to the high, middle, and low forms of creole languages, when compared with the standard form of the language on which they are based: for example, the acrolectal form of Jamaican Creole is that form perceived by sociolinguists and others as closest to standard English, while its basilect is the form or forms farthest removed from Standard English, its mesolects jostling for space somewhere between. The terms have, however, been extended in recent years to refer to positions on the continuum of all relationships in any language complex. From this viewpoint, standard English is an acrolect in a firmament of other assorted lects.

Language and variety. In order to avoid the social and class implications of such terms as *dialect* and *lect*, scholars have in recent years often preferred the neutral term *variety*. Here, standard English is one variety among others (whether it is first among equals or unequals), and in turn has its own (sub)varieties. The standard and its varieties are used for one range of purposes, Scots, Cockney, and their equivalents and all their varieties for other purposes, and Jamaican Creole, Krio, and their equivalents and all their varieties for others still. By and large, this approach has proved useful and even emollient. *Variety* coexists with *dialect* and *lect* and enables diverse difficult issues to be examined and discussed in non-adversarial ways. It does not, however, change the general perception of one English that is, in effect, more equal than the others, an 'educated' variety that spreads into a vast periphery of other (usually 'uneducated') varieties.

The Englishes. The most radical departure in recent years looks at English not as singular but plural: in effect, a family like the Germanic languages. In such a view, the term 'English' has always covered more than one language: Old English different from Modern English; Scots different from English (both being Germanic languages as distinct as Dutch and Frisian in the Netherlands, or Dano-Norwegian and Nynorsk in Norway). In addition, Krio in Sierra Leone, Kriol in Australia, and Tok Pisin in Papua New Guinea, etc., are so different from the core that they are 'English-based' rather than 'English'. The commonest term for the plurality of English in Africa and Asia is the *New Englishes*, referring to varieties that have grown up in territories once controlled or greatly influenced by the UK and the US. A rarer and even more controversial expression in recent years has been the *English languages*, which places the main varieties of English on a par with such groups as the Romance languages and Slavonic languages.

A perilous extension of the discussion of kinds of English leads to such matters as *idiolect* (an individual's personal 'dialect') and asks: when is English really English? Every idiolect is unique, and people often need time to acclimatize linguistically one to another, for a variety of reasons such as geographical background, social background, education, ethnicity, world-view, occupation, interests, age, gender, skill with language, and personal disability (such as a speech impediment). Many kinds of more or less marginal usage occur every day: in code-switching, a mix of English and Hindi (or Spanish, or Tagalog, etc.) may be more English one moment, more Hindi the next; it is often hard to indicate precisely when speakers cross the border between two otherwise distinct languages, as for example English and French in Montreal, Quebec. One group of English-speakers may refuse to confer equivalent status on another ('*They* don't really speak English'), on weak grounds such as differences of accent or on strong grounds such as general unintelligibility. However, there is nothing new in this.

Diversity. Regardless of the terminology they might use, few scholars have supposed that there is only one monolithic English; rather, the problem has been how to reconcile one label with the many facets of the thing so labelled. English was diverse when it began and has continued to be diverse. Until the Union of the Parliaments (1707), the varieties used in England and Scotland were no less distinct than the different but closely related Spanish and Portuguese, but a consequence of the Union was the subordination of Scots (the English language of Scotland) to English (the English language of England) and a blurring of its ancient distinctness. In large part, the generic name *English* contributed to the assumption even among Scots that there was only one English language properly so called. In the same century, however, the American Declaration of Independence (1776) marked the creation of a new national and linguistic 'pole': a second national variety of the standard language that had been disconnected from London and the institutions of England. In the later 20c, Australia has begun to create the institutions of yet another national standard, while at the same time the concept of national standards has begun to spread: if there could be acknowledged varieties of the standard in two long-established autonomous nations, there could be further such varieties elsewhere.

National standards. The question has become: how many such standards are there (or can there be), and how do (or should) they relate to each other? In the last two decades, there has been a thoroughgoing reconsideration of the idea of a standard language or dialect or variety. Effectively, this is as much a political as a linguistic issue. In places once diffident about their English and accustomed to being patronized (such as Canada, India, Ireland, New Zealand, and Scotland), the possibility that they too either have or could have their own standard has led to such works as 'The Accents of Standard English in Scotland' (David Abercrombie, in *Languages of Scotland*, edited by A. J. Aitken and Tom McArthur, 1979) and *In Search of the Standard in Canadian English* (edited by W. C. Lougheed, 1985). Whereas few disagree that there is a national standard for the US and for England (or Britain), many are dubious about a standard Australian or an Irish standard, while others doubt that there is even such an entity as Indian English out of which a standard might grow. The debate proceeds, and institutions are emerging (linguistic surveys, dictionaries, publishers' house styles, centres of language study) that increasingly serve to reinforce and even extend claims that once seemed both radical and slightly absurd.

See ABORIGINAL ENGLISH, ACCENT, AFRICAN ENGLISH, AFRICAN LANGUAGES, AMERICAN ENGLISH, AMERICAN ENGLISH AND BRITISH ENGLISH, AMERICAN LANGUAGES, ANGLES, ANGLIAN, ANGLIC, ANGLICE, ANGLICISM, ANGLICIST, ANGLICITY, ANGLICIZE, ANGLIFY, ANGLIKAANS, ANGLO, ANGLO-, ANGLO ENGLISH, ANGLO-ENGLISH, ANGLO-INDIAN, ANGLO-IRISH, APPALACHIAN ENGLISH, ASIAN LANGUAGES, AUSTRALIAN ENGLISH, AUSTRALIAN LANGUAGES, BRITISH EMPIRE, BRITISH ENGLISH, BRITISH LANGUAGES, CANADIAN ENGLISH, CANADIAN LANGUAGES, CELTIC LANGUAGES, CHICANO ENGLISH, CODE-MIXING AND CODE-SWITCHING, COMMONWEALTH, CREOLE, EARLY MODERN ENGLISH, EAST AFRICAN ENGLISH, EAST ASIAN ENGLISH, ENGLAND, ENGLISH, ENGLISH ENGLISH, ENGLISHES, ENGLISHISM, ENGLISHIZE,

ENGLISH LANGUAGE AMENDMENT, ENGLISH LAN-
GUAGES, EUROPEAN COMMUNITY, EUROPEAN FREE
TRADE ASSOCIATION, EUROPEAN LANGUAGES,
FRANGLAIS, -GLISH AND -LISH, GRAMMAR, HAWAI-
IAN ENGLISH, HIBERNO-ENGLISH, HISTORY OF ENG-
LISH (WITH CHRONOLOGY), IMPERIALISM, INDIAN
ENGLISH[1], INDIAN LANGUAGES, INDO-EUROPEAN
LANGUAGES, INTERNATIONAL ENGLISH, IRISH ENG-
LISH, KING'S ENGLISH, LANGUAGE, MIDDLE
ENGLISH, NEW ZEALAND ENGLISH, NIGERIA,
NORTHERN IRISH ENGLISH, OLD ENGLISH[1], OLD
ENGLISH[2], PIDGIN, QUEEN'S ENGLISH, RECEIVED
PRONUNCIATION, RHYTHM, SCOTTISH ENGLISH,
SOUTH AFRICAN ENGLISH, SOUTH ASIAN ENGLISH,
SOUTH-EAST ASIAN ENGLISH, SPANGLISH, STAND-
ARD, STANDARD ENGLISH, TEACHING ENGLISH,
TEXAS, ULSTER ENGLISH, US ENGLISH, VARIETY,
WELSH ENGLISH, WEST AFRICAN ENGLISH, WORLD
ENGLISH. [AFRICA, AMERICAS, ASIA, EUROPE,
HISTORY, LANGUAGES, NAME, OCEANIA, VARIETY].
T.MCA.

Bailey, Richard W. 1991/2. *Images of English: A Cul-
tural History of the Language.* Ann Arbor: Michigan
University Press (1991): Cambridge: University
Press (1992).
—— & Görlach, Manfred (eds.). 1982. *English as a
World Language.* Ann Arbor: University of Michi-
gan Press. Cambridge: University Press.
Bolton, W. F., & Crystal, David (eds.). 1987. *The Eng-
lish Language.* London: Sphere Reference.
Bryson, Bill. 1990. *Mother Tongue: The English Lan-
guage.* London: Hamish Hamilton. New York: Wil-
liam Morrow.
Burchfield, Robert. 1985. *The English Language.*
Oxford: University Press.
Cheshire, Jenny (ed.). 1991. *English around the World:
Sociolinguistic Perspectives.* Cambridge: University
Press.
Crystal, David. 1988. *The English Language.* Har-
mondsworth: Penguin.
Fishman, Joshua A., Cooper, Robert L., & Conrad,
Andrew W. (eds.). 1977. *The Spread of English.* Row-
ley, Mass.: Nebury House.
Flaitz, Jeffra. 1988. *The Ideology of English: French
Perceptions of English as a World Language.* Berlin,
New York, Amsterdam: Mouton de Gruyter.
Görlach, Manfred. 1991. *English: Studies in Varieties
of English 1984-1988.* Amsterdam & Philadelphia:
John Benjamins.
Greenbaum, Sidney. 1985. *The English Language
Today.* Oxford: Pergamon.
Michaels, Leonard, & Ricks, Christopher (eds.). 1980
edition. *The State of the Language.* Berkeley, Los
Angeles, & London: California University Press and
the English-Speaking Union, San Francisco.
Quirk, Randolph, & Widdowson, H. G. (eds.). 1985.
*English in the World: Teaching and Learning the Lan-
guage and the Literatures.* Cambridge: University
Press.
Ricks, Christopher, & Michaels, Leonard (eds.). 1990
edition, *The State of the Language.* Berkeley, Los
Angeles, & London: California University Press and
the English-Speaking Union, San Francisco.

Trudgill, Peter, & Hannah, Jean. 1982. *International
English: A Guide to Varieties of Standard English.*
London: Edward Arnold.
Trudgill, Peter & Chambers, J. K. (eds.). 1991. *Dialects
of English: Studies in Grammatical Variation.* Lon-
don & New York: Longman.

Periodicals, etc.: see ENGLISH TEACHING FORUM,
ENGLISH TODAY, ENGLISH WORLD-WIDE, LAN-
GUAGE AND SOCIETY, VARIETIES OF ENGLISH
AROUND THE WORLD, VERBATIM, WORLD
ENGLISHES.

ENGLISH ACADEMY. See ACADEMY.

ENGLISH AS A FOREIGN LANGUAGE. See
TEFL.

**ENGLISH AS AN INTERNATIONAL LAN-
GUAGE.** See TEIL.

ENGLISH AS A SECOND DIALECT. See
TESD.

ENGLISH AS A SECOND LANGUAGE. See
TESL.

ENGLISH ASSOCIATION, The. An association founded in the UK in 1906 on the initiative of two schoolmasters, E. S. Valentine and
G. E. S. Coxhead, to further English studies in
education and 'to afford opportunities for
friendly intercourse and co-operation amongst
all who love our literature and language'. Prominent in its formation were Israel Gollancz,
scholar of Middle English and Shakespeare, and
first lecturer in English to be appointed at Cambridge, and the scholar and critic Andrew Bradley. It has sponsored lectures and conferences,
including since 1970 an annual conference for
students preparing for A-Level English: that is,
the Advanced Level of the General Certificate
of (Secondary) Education, a qualification for
entry to higher education. In collaboration with
various publishers, the Association has produced a number of anthologies and pamphlets,
Presidential Addresses, and, annually since 1910,
Essays and Studies, collections made by a different editor each year. The Association's main
publishing enterprise, annually since 1921, has
been the critical bibliography *The Year's Work
in English Studies (YWES).* See YEAR'S WORK IN
ENGLISH STUDIES. [EUROPE, MEDIA].   R.C.

ENGLISH CANADA. A collective term for
those provinces and territories of Canada in
which English rather than French is dominant:
'I question the political willingness of English
Canada to accept Quebec as we are' (Robert
Bourassa, premier of Quebec, *Time*, 9 July 1990).
See CANADA. [AMERICAS, NAME].   T.MCA.

ENGLISH CANADIAN. A term referring to linguistic background rather than ethnicity. Canadians who speak English usually refer to themselves simply as *Canadians*, and regard the term as inclusive, where francophone Canadians often find it exclusive: for example, in a book on 'Canadian' literature that does not mention works in French. As a result, in contexts where misunderstandings might occur, the contrasting terms *English Canadian* and *French Canadian* are generally used. See CANADIAN, ENGLISH (sense 4). [AMERICAS, NAME].   M.F.

ENGLISH DIALECT DICTIONARY, short form *EDD*. A dictionary of the dialects of English, especially in England, prepared under the auspices of the English Dialect Society, edited by Joseph Wright, and published by Oxford University Press (1898-1905) in six large volumes. The entries are complex and compact, making use of such abbreviations such as *Nhb.* for *Northumberland* and *Yks.* for *Yorkshire*. A word is described in terms of geographical distribution (such as *Sc. Nhb. Dur. Cum. Wm. Yks. Lan.*), its variant forms are given (such as *bahfam* and *bahfin* for the headword *bargham*, a horse-collar), brief definitions follow, then quotations in context from written sources (with an elaborate system of cross-referencing to the bibliography). After the *EDD* was published, the *OED* used it as source material for dialect words and early written citations. As part of the final volume, Wright prepared an *English Dialect Grammar*, seeking to cover the development of phonology and grammar from West Germanic to present-day dialects. He had, as a basis for his work, the publications of the English Dialect Society, the corpus of earlier works, published and unpublished, listed specifically for the project by W. W. Skeat, and the dialectological research of A. J. Ellis. He also dispatched to informants 12,000 copies of a questionnaire of some 2,400 items, giving them instructions on how to transcribe words phonetically. Various local groups were set up to assist. Wright and his wife Elizabeth Mary, once his student at Oxford, collated the material in the questionnaires and prepared it for publication in parts. The work was immense and the cost, which was largely borne by Wright himself, was helped by donations and public funds. His work, often criticized for what it does not contain, remains a landmark of dialect lexicography and both *Dictionary* and *Grammar* continue to be sources of information. See ELLIS, ENGLISH DIALECT SOCIETY, SKEAT, WRIGHT, YORKSHIRE. [EUROPE, REFERENCE].   S.E.

ENGLISH DIALECT SOCIETY. A society for the study of the dialects of England, formed in 1873 and dissolved in 1896. Its founder was Walter W. Skeat, Professor of Anglo-Saxon at Cambridge, who became its secretary and then its director. It published 80 works, mostly glossaries and grammars, and collected material for a dialect dictionary to complement the pronunciation work of A. J. Ellis. In 1886, Skeat launched a fund for such a dictionary, contributing a great deal of money himself to the project. In 1889, Joseph Wright began to edit the first collection for this work and appealed through newspapers and libraries for additional data. Over 600 people read material and collected and checked information. Helped by subscriptions, donations, and accommodation provided by Oxford University Press, Wright began in 1898 to publish in parts what became the *English Dialect Dictionary*. When the Society's aims had been achieved, it was dissolved. See AMERICAN DIALECT SOCIETY, DIALECT, ELLIS, ENGLISH DIALECT DICTIONARY, SKEAT, WRIGHT, YORKSHIRE. [EUROPE, MEDIA].   S.E.

ENGLISH ENGLISH [1800s]. English as used in England: 'Of the two hundred million people speaking English nearly seven-tenths live in the United States, and another tenth in the British dominions are as much influenced by American as English English' (*Spectator*, 5 Feb. 1943); 'Standard English English differs little from that used in Australia, New Zealand and South Africa' (Peter Trudgill, *Language in the British Isles*, 1984). The usage was rare until the 1980s, when, with its synonym *Anglo-English*, it began to be used in professional discussions of English. See ANGLO-ENGLISH, BRITISH ENGLISH, ENGLISH IN ENGLAND, STANDARD ENGLISH. [EUROPE, VARIETY].   T.MCA.

ENGLISHES. (1) [17c]. Archaic, plural of *an English*: English sentences to be translated into a foreign language, or English equivalents of foreign words: 'The first column contains some Englishes' (W. Walker, preface, *Dictionary of English Particles*, 1679). (2) [1980s]. Varieties of English collectively: 'Discourse analysis, non-native Englishes and second language acquisition' (title of a paper by Yamuna Kachru, in *World Englishes* 4: 2, 1985). The singular *an English* appears not (yet) to be common in the second sense, but comparable usages occur: 'There must . . . be provision for each English to have a distinctive lexical set that will express local cultural content' (Gerry Abbott, 'English across cultures', *English Today* 28, Oct. 1991). See ENGLISH, ENGLISH LANGUAGES, -GLISH AND -LISH, NEW ENGLISH, TEIL, WORLD ENGLISHES. [VARIETY].   T.MCA.

ENGLISH FIRST. See AMERICAN ENGLISH, ENGLISH LANGUAGE AMENDMENT.

ENGLISH FOR ACADEMIC PURPOSES. See EAP.

ENGLISH FOR CIVIL AVIATION. See AIRSPEAK.

ENGLISH FOR GENERAL PURPOSES. See GENERAL ENGLISH.

ENGLISH FOR MARITIME COMMUNICATIONS. See SEASPEAK.

ENGLISH FOR OCCUPATIONAL PURPOSES. See EOP.

ENGLISH FOR SPECIFIC/SPECIAL PURPOSES. See ESP.

ENGLISH IN ENGLAND, also **Anglo-English, England English, English English**. The English language as used in England. For many people in England and elsewhere, the terms *Anglo-English*, *England English*, and *English English* are tautologous and barbarous. It has seemed natural to them that, just as French is the language of France, so English is (and should be) the native language of the inhabitants of England. Other forms of the language have been used elsewhere, in some cases for many centuries, but they have been widely regarded in England as peripheral and in many cases deficient. In the late 20c, however, English in England is generally seen by scholars as one of many varieties that bear the name *English*, but because English English is, as it were, the parent stock it is often harder to discuss and describe than varieties that have added distinctive characteristics of their own. In the English of North America, parts of Africa, and South Asia, it is relatively easy to identify phonological, grammatical, and lexical features unique to certain varieties. It is less easy to say that a particular feature will be heard only or mainly in England.

A language without competition. Since the decline of French in the late Middle Ages, English in England has had no major competitor. English people have not shared the experience of the Celtic parts of Britain, where the presence of other vernaculars may affect the idiom even of those who do not speak them. Nor has there been resistance to the status of English, such as that which makes, the Irish writer James Joyce's character Stephen Daedalus think after speaking to an Englishman, 'My soul frets in the shadow of his language.' The language has never been officially standardized, but a typically English nostalgia for the past is reflected in attempts to fix one period as definitive. In the 18c, the best English was widely supposed to have been used in the 'Augustan' reign of Queen Anne (1702–14). Writers and scholars like Swift and Johnson sought to fix it, but at the same time there was strong and successful resistance to suggestions for an Academy on the French model. There continues to be a feeling that a certain type of English is the best, phrases like *the Queen's English*, *BBC English*, *Oxford English* suggesting that the ruling and cultural establishment has by right the correct usage.

Standard and accent. There is in England a degree of confusion between the terms *Standard English (SE)* and *Received Pronunciation (RP)*. Although SE is generally defined by linguists and teachers in terms only of grammar and vocabulary, and RP only in terms of accent, both are often used as virtual synonyms, and SE is often assumed to include (and require) RP. SE, however, can be and is spoken in many accents. RP emerged more slowly than SE; although regional accents were recognized and considered slightly comic or substandard as early as the 16c, generally dialect was not despised: Walter Raleigh spoke with a Devon accent and was an accomplished courtier and writer. It is not until the late 19c that the prestige of RP becomes apparent, with the desire to acquire it for the enhancement of status. SE is not a class usage, but RP is. Although it has considerable prestige value, RP is disliked and caricatured by many speakers with other accents. It is accepted without comment from a BBC newsreader, but is liable to arouse mirth or hostility when used by anyone suspected of shedding the local speech and 'talking posh'. See RECEIVED PRONUNCIATION.

The permutations of SE and RP are many. It is likely that an RP speaker will use SE in speech and writing. Most English people write SE, with occasional lapses in spelling and grammar. Many also speak SE, often with some mixture of regional words and idioms, ranging from an occasional item to full dialect. There has, however, been a steady decline in the degree of dialect differences from SE, accelerated over the last fifty years by media mainly purveying SE usage in RP voices. Dialect variation of lexis and syntax is less marked among younger people, but accents are still diverse. Some speakers in effect command two dialects, local for intimate uses and a version (among the many versions) of the national standard for more formal purposes. The increase of town populations has created marked differences between urban and rural dialects. In large conurbations, local forms which sometimes varied over even a small area have tended to lose their distinctiveness and merge into a more general and extensive type of speech. Pressures from the national educational system and the media have also acted to remove or reduce some of the more extreme variants. A large English town today will contain a variety of spoken English determined by social, educational, and generational factors, rather than the simpler division between educated speech and a fairly uniform local dialect which would until recently have been found in rural areas. The presence of immigrant groups has brought new forms of speech; the second generation usually acquires the local accent, but older speakers often keep distinctive features.

Defending the language. Strong feelings about the state of the language are made public in various ways. Among older middle-class users there is resistance to change and a freely expressed distrust of American and other influences. Resistance to an Academy has paradoxically resulted in unofficial watchdogs such as the *Society for Pure English*, founded in 1913, which carried on for many years a campaign against what it regarded as degenerate tendencies. Post-war exponents of 'U and non-U' (upper-class and non-upper-class usage) stigmatized certain words and idioms as 'common', and for a time in the 1950s the spotting of U and non-U terms was a kind of national game. The idea grew from an article by the linguist A. S. C. Ross, which suggested that the comparative levelling of outward signs of rank and wealth in post-war England had made linguistic usage a more important pointer. In 1979, taking a different tack, *Plain English Campaign* publicly destroyed government forms as the opening move in a crusade against officialese and obfuscation.

Changes. English in England appears to be losing many of its particularities. Traditionally, educated English people have separated *shall* for the first person and *will* for the second and third, and reversed them for special meaning or emphasis: *I shall come tomorrow; you shall go to the Ball.'* The immediate 'Have you (got) a pen?' has been distinguished from the more habitual 'Do you have a pen?' Similarly, the present perfect tense has been used for past states within a continuing time period: 'Have you seen him today?' as against 'Did you see him yesterday?' Modal verbs such as *would* and *might* have been used to express hesitation or extra politeness. *Would you care for some more tea?—If I might.* These and other features are still found with older speakers but seem to be declining, perhaps through the influence of AmE. Because so much is shared with other parts of the UK, and because there has been so much AmE influence in recent decades, it is probably true to say that

specifically English English is currently less distinctive within the British Isles than at any time in the past.

See ACCENT, AMERICAN ENGLISH AND BRITISH ENGLISH, ANGLES, ANGLO-, ANGLO-ENGLISH, ANGLO-SAXON, BIRMINGHAM, BRITISH ENGLISH, BRITISH LANGUAGES, BRUMMAGEM/BRUMMIE, BURR, CAXTON, CHAUCER, COCKNEY, CORNISH, CORNWALL, CUMBRIA, DEVON, DIALECT IN ENGLAND, DORSET, DURHAM BURR, EAST ANGLIA, EAST MIDLAND DIALECT, ENGLAND, ENGLISH, ENGLISH ENGLISH, ENGLISHRY, GEORDIE, HISTORY OF ENGLISH, HOME COUNTIES, JOHNSON, JUTES, KENTISH, KING'S ENGLISH, LANCASHIRE, LONDON, MERCIA, MIDDLE ENGLISH, MIDLANDS, MUMMERSET, NORTHERN ENGLISH, NORTHUMBERLAND BURR, NORTHUMBRIA, OLD ENGLISH[1], OXBRIDGE, OXFORD ACCENT, OXFORD ENGLISH, PUBLIC SCHOOL ENGLISH, QUEEN'S ENGLISH, QUEEN'S ENGLISH SOCIETY, RECEIVED PRONUNCIATION, SAXON, SAXONISM, SCOUSE, SHAKESPEARE, SOMERSET, WEST COUNTRY, YORKSHIRE. [EUROPE, VARIETY].   R.C.

Trudgill, Peter. 1984. 'Standard English in England', in Trudgill (ed.), *Language in the British Isles*. Cambridge: University Press.
Viereck, Wolfgang. 1985. *Focus on: England and Wales*, in the Varieties of English around the World series. Amsterdam & Philadelphia: John Benjamins.
Wells, John C. 1984. 'English Accents in England', in Trudgill (above).

ENGLISHISM [1850s: compare ANGLICISM]. Rare: (1) A habit or characteristic of the English; a policy pursued or favoured by, or typical of, the English: 'An Englishism which foreigners note' (*Indian Daily News*, 2 Oct. 1879). (2) An English-language word or other usage, occurring in another language: 'Whether in France or in French Canada, whether in Hebrew or in Yiddish, whether in Spain or in Spanish America, whether in Hindi, Indonesian, or Swahili—in every area and language the impact of English must be watched and regulated. At times the influence is disguised as "internationalisms," "Europeanisms," or "Westernisms," but in actuality it is more likely to be Englishisms than anything else' (Joshua A. Fishman, 'Sociology of English as an Additional Language', in Kachru (ed.), *The Other Tongue*, 1982). See ENGLISH, -ISM. [LANGUAGE, STYLE, WORD].   T.MCA.

ENGLISHIZE, also especially AusE & BrE **Englishise**. (1) [1850s: compare ANGLICIZE, ANGLIFY]. To make English in manner or in language: 'the Englishised Indian' (*Blackwood's Magazine*, 1922). (2) [*c*.1980s]. In linguistics, to adapt towards English, a term used to refer to the impact of English on other languages, especially in the noun form *Englishization*. The concept covers phonology, grammar, lexis, discourse, registers, styles, and genres, and relates to three major spheres of influence associated with the spread of the language: traditional areas of contact such as Europe, in which the languages are mainly cognate with English; areas in which English-speakers have settled or on which they have had a strong colonial influence, such as North America, the Caribbean, South Asia, South-East Asia, and parts of Africa; and such traditionally distinct areas as China, Japan, and Latin America. The most noticeable influence is lexical, manifesting itself mainly through *loanwords* (such as *hardwarowy* and *softwarowy* in Polish, and *hardver* and *softver* in Hungarian), *loan translations* (such as French *gratte-ciel* as a response to 'skyscraper' and *soucoupe volante* to 'flying saucer'), and *hybridizations* (such as Telugu *donga laysansu* illegal licence, and IndE *lathi charge* a charge, usually by policemen, in which *lathis* or metal-reinforced bamboo sticks are used). The Englishization of syntax takes many forms: for example, an increase in the number and use of phrasal verbs in the Scandinavian languages, the development of impersonal constructions in Indian languages (both Dravidian and Indo-Aryan), such as *suna gaya hai* it is heard, and the development of special passive forms, such as Korean *euihan* ('by'). In terms of literature, English provides a model for developing genres, such as the lyric in some Indian and Bantu languages. English has also contributed to thematic innovations, such as romanticism, social realism, and secularization. The massive present-day influence of English is reviewed in Wolfgang Viereck & Wolf-Dieter Bald, *English in Contact with Other Languages* (1986: Akadémiai Kiadó, Budapest, distributed by Palm & Enke, Erlangen, Germany). See CHINA, CODE-MIXING AND CODE-SWITCHING, ENGLISH, FRENCH, GAIRAIGO, GERMAN, -GLISH AND -LïSH, ITALIAN, JAPAN, KOREA, LOAN, SCANDINAVIAN LANGUAGES, SPANISH. [AFRICA, AMERICAS, ASIA, EUROPE, LANGUAGE, LITERATURE, OCEANIA, VARIETY].   B.B.K., T.MCA.

ENGLISH LANGUAGE AMENDMENT, short form *ELA*. A proposed amendment to the constitution of the US that would make English the official language of the republic. The aim of the proponents of ELA is to ensure that English retains its leading role in US society, especially in the face of actual or potential competition from Spanish. Despite a widespread assumption to the contrary, English has no official status in the US. For over two centuries, however, it has been the *de facto* national language which the vast majority of non-English-speaking immigrants have sought to adopt. In 1981, Senator Samuel Hayakawa, an American of Japanese background, introduced a constitutional amendment to make English the official language.

US English. Hayakawa did not succeed in his aim, but others have reintroduced the proposal, and following lack of action on his original measure he founded in 1983, with John Tanton, an organization called *US English*, to support and promote the cause. This is a nationwide, non-profit-making, non-partisan organization, currently with some 350,000 members and a board of advisers that includes the writers Jacques Barzun, Saul Bellow, and Gore Vidal, and the journalist Alistair Cooke. It promotes English as a common bond (a 'blessing' that integrates America's diverse population) and often refers to official French/English bilingualism in Canada as a source of disharmony that Americans should seek to avoid. In addition to its concern that English be made official, *US English* holds that every effort should be made, particularly through education, to assist newcomers to acquire English. At the same time, it rejects linguistic chauvinism, nativism, and xenophobia, encourages foreign-language study, supports individual and private rights to use and maintain languages other than English, and does not propose to prohibit forms of bilingual education intended to ease children into English ability.

Spanish. Both John Tanton and Linda Chavez (a former president of the organization) have explained why *US English* was founded when it was: in the past, of the many languages in or brought to the US, none had the capacity to threaten English. This state of affairs has changed, however, with the influx of Spanish-speaking immigrants, especially in such areas as southern Florida, the Southwest, and such large cities as New York. Members do not favour a change in bilingual education from the transitional (in which English replaces the mother tongue) to maintenance (in which a language like Spanish is retained alongside English). They also oppose the provision of bilingual Spanish/English ballots and comparable services.

Support. There appears to be considerable popular and political support for *Official English*, *English for US*, and *English First*, as the movement is variously called. A 'sense of the Senate' measure declaring English official has been passed three times in recent years as an attachment to immigration legislation. Such declarations do not, however, have the force of law. Seventeen states of the Union have made English their official language: Nebraska 1920, Illinois 1969, Virginia 1981, Indiana 1984, Kentucky 1984, Tennessee 1984, California 1986, Georgia 1986, Arkansas 1987, Mississippi 1987, North Carolina 1987, North Dakota 1987, South Carolina 1987, Arizona 1988, Colorado 1988, Florida 1988; in 1978, Hawaii made both English and

Hawaiian official. Legislation is pending or planned in Alabama, Maryland, Massachusetts, Missouri, New York, and West Virginia. Public-opinion polls in a variety of locations have also shown considerable support for English. Many have been relatively casual, often conducted by newspapers, radio, and television, but others have been taken by reputable survey organizations.

Opposition. *US English* has since the outset been subject to strong opposition. Many academics and ethnic leaders have seen it as a nativist organization that panders to the prejudices and entrenched attitudes of unilingual whites. Linda Chavez reports being called a fascist traitor to her own Hispanic heritage, and has been picketed at speaking engagements. A president of *La Raza* (a Hispanic political movement) compared *US English* to the Ku Klux Klan, and the journalist James Crawford has linked the group to allegedly racist funding agencies (through organizations called *US Inc.* and the *Federation for American Immigration Reform*, the latter also founded by John Tanton). These agencies include the Pioneer Fund, created in 1937 to promote 'racial betterment' through eugenics. Crawford has written about a leaked memorandum by Tanton which expresses fear of Hispanic control over America and lists such dangers as Roman Catholicism, large families, and a tradition of bribery. Linda Chavez resigned as president when she learned of this statement.

American organizations that have either explicitly or indirectly attacked *US English* and Official English include the *National Education Association* (a teacher's union), the *National Council of Teachers of English, Teachers of English to Speakers of Other Languages* (TESOL), the *Linguistic Society of America*, and the *Modern Language Association*. Many see it as promoting an English-only policy rather than simply Official English, despite claims to the contrary. Reaction has led to the *English Plus* pressure group (formed in 1987), which encourages Americans to be bilingual (English plus one or more other languages). It had its genesis in statements by the *Spanish-American League Against Discrimination* (*SALAD*: an acronym that implies disagreement with the traditional concept of the melting pot), and in 1987 established the *English Plus Information Clearinghouse* (*EPIC*), to canvass support and disseminate its views. Adherents to the idea of English Plus have proposed a constitutional amendment of their own: the *Cultural Rights Amendment*, which would give legal backing to the preservation and promotion of ethnic and linguistic diversity.

Conclusion. There is evidence that Hispanic immigrants tend, like others before them, to shed their original language so as to join the mainstream of American life. Such evidence of language shift does not, however, impress English-speakers in Miami or southern California who feel threatened by the powerful presence of an alternative language and culture. Similarly, despite disclaimers by *US English*, and its support for transitional bilingual programmes for adults, an impression of chauvinism among native speakers of English is being projected that arouses and reinforces old anxieties among non-English-speakers. Although the primacy of English in the US is hardly in doubt, people on both sides of the argument are likely to feel threatened for some time to come, whatever happens.

See AMERICAN ENGLISH, AMERICAN LANGUAGES, ENGLISH PLUS, OFFICIAL ENGLISH (MOVEMENT), SPANISH, US ENGLISH. [AMERICAS, LANGUAGE]. J.E.

Adams, Karen L., & Brink, Daniel T. (eds.). 1990. *Perspectives on Official English: The Campaign of English as the Official Language of the USA*. Berlin & New York: Mouton de Gruyter.
Baron, Dennis. 1990. *The English-Only Question: An Official Language for Americans?* New Haven: Yale University Press.
Daniels, Harvey A. (ed.). 1990. *NOT Only English: Affirming America's Multilingual Heritage*. Urbana, Ill.: National Council of Teachers of English.
Fishman, Joshua (ed.), with David F. Marshall. 1986. *Language Rights and the English Language Amendment*. Special issue of the *International Journal of the Sociology of Language* (no. 60). Amsterdam & New York: Mouton de Gruyter.

ENGLISH-LANGUAGE EXAMINATIONS. See EXAMINING IN ENGLISH.

ENGLISH LANGUAGES [1980s]. A phrase used by some linguists and other commentators to suggest that English is a group of languages (comparable to the Romance languages) rather than one language: 'What seems likely is that we shall have to use both models side by side, entirely consciously—aware that we already live, and to some extent always have lived, in a world where there are both an English language and a range of English languages' (Tom McArthur, 'The English Language or the English Languages?', in Bolton & Crystal (eds.), *The English Language*, 2nd edition, 1987); 'The European Society for the Study of English has been founded to encourage European understandings of English languages, literatures and cultures' (from a leaflet announcing the inaugural conference of the ESSE at the U. of East Anglia in England, Sept. 1991). See ENGLISH, ENGLISHES. [LANGUAGE, VARIETY]. T.MCA.

ENGLISH LANGUAGE SCHOOL. A school that specializes in the teaching of English, usually as a foreign language and outside the public system of education. Such schools can be found in many parts of the world, but the 1,000 or so in Great Britain are particularly well publicized. They cater for some 250,000 foreign students a year, usually providing short courses of typically three to ten weeks, especially in the summer. Most are operated for profit, but some are charitable foundations. Standards range from acknowledged probity and effectiveness to the brazen rip-off. See ARELS, CULTURA, ENGLISH-MEDIUM SCHOOL, TESL. [EDUCATION].   P.S.

ENGLISH LANGUAGE TEACHING. See ELT.

ENGLISH LITERATURE. An ambiguous term used and understood in at least five ways: as the literature of England, the literature of Great Britain (and Ireland) written in English, all literature in English (whatever the place of origin), a varying mix of all or any of these (depending on circumstance, preference, and emphasis), and any of these as a subject taught in schools and colleges.

The literature of England. In its first sense, English literature is on a par with other national literatures, such as Italian literature seen as the achievement and heritage of the people of Italy. This is the commonest sense of the term, widely used to contrast not only with Italian or French national literature but also with the national literature of the US, as in:

When we think of modern literature, we almost invariably associate it with national groups. English literature does not include American, and there is even hesitation in including Austrian literature under German. In the Middle Ages such national groups either did not exist at all or existed only in a rudimentary form. We can speak only of works written in a particular language
(W. T. H. Jackson, *Medieval Literature*, 1966).

The literature of Great Britain. In its second sense, the term refers to literature in English in the nation-state made up of England, Scotland, and Wales (and at certain times and in various ways all or part of Ireland), or of the British Isles:

For coherence, I have focused on the literature of the British Isles, and specifically of England—although with many necessary side glances at Scotland and Ireland
(Alastair Fowler, *A History of English Literature*, 1987).

This dimension is often inconsistently perceived and described: for example, Scottish writers like Walter Scott, John Buchan, and J. M. Barrie are included unreflectingly in lists, studies, and histories that do not precisely specify the 'Englishness' of the canon in question. This imprecision sometimes confuses the narrower heritage of England with the broader heritage of Britain and Ireland. The use of the term *British literature*, however, is complicated by the existence of literatures that are not in English (Gaelic, Welsh, Cornish, and Scots when defined as distinct from English). The term is, however, sometimes used in contrast with literatures in English elsewhere.

All literature in English. The third, non-national or supra-national sense includes the preceding and such terms as *African literature in English*, *American literature*, *Australian literature*, *Canadian literature in English*, *Irish literature in English*. It may or may not have a capital L. The sense dates from the 19c, with changing emphases:

Around 1900, not many literary historians in Europe or the United States would have been prepared to argue that there was such a thing as *an* American literature, or that the literature so far produced in America was worth an extensive analysis. Able American authors were conceded to exist. But they tended to be treated as men of individual merit—contributors (as Matthew Arnold saw it) to 'one great literature—English literature'
(Marcus Cunliffe, *American Literature to 1900*, 1986).

This literature of English at large is sometimes referred to as *literature (written) in English*, as in *The Cambridge Guide to Literature in English* (ed. Ian Ousby, 1988). It includes not only the British and American traditions, but also *Commonwealth literature*. The usage *world literature written in English* includes all literatures created in English and all literary works translated into English.

A mixture of senses. Because of the possible confusions and misunderstandings, resentment can arise among those interested in the literature and its description. Critics discussing such writers as Chinua Achebe, Robertson Davies, James Joyce, V. S. Naipaul, and Walter Scott, as part of 'mainstream' English literature with its supposedly 'universal' messages may or may not recall or appreciate that such writers have Nigerian, Canadian, Irish, Trinidadian, Scottish, or other dimensions as significant for their work as the English dimension of William Wordsworth and the American dimension of Mark Twain. Such problems arise partly from ambiguities inherent in the word 'English' itself and partly from distinctions and tensions among the peoples who use English, some of whom have no other language, some of whom are bi- or multilingual, and some of whom have seen English replace other languages important to them.

The development of English literature. Imaginative works have been written in English for over a thousand years, and, in historical terms, most of them are primarily the heritage of England. As with the language itself, such literature can be divided into Old, Middle, and Modern periods, the modern phase subdividing conveniently into compartments whose labels relate to monarchs (*Tudor, Elizabethan, Jacobean, Victorian*), cultural phases and assumptions (*Augustan, Romantic, Modernist*, etc.), centuries (*16c drama, the 18c novel*, etc.), and, most recently, varieties (*American literature, Indian English literature*, etc.).

Old English texts. Texts from Anglo-Saxon times survive in late manuscript form; their composition can seldom be certainly dated and their authorship is often unknown. They are among the oldest specimens of literature in a European vernacular. The longest and finest work, the heroic poem *Beowulf*, is known only in a manuscript of *c.*1000, and tells in alliterative verse a story concerning Germanic speakers of the Baltic, where the earliest forms of English originated. Like much other Old English poetry, it contains traces of oral creation. The heroic tradition includes *The Battle of Maldon*, written soon after the battle against the Danes (991) which it celebrates. There are also elegiac and reflective poems, including 'The Wanderer' and 'The Seafarer', that may date from the 7c.

Old English prose consisted of translations from Latin and such records as the *Anglo-Saxon Chronicle*, begun in 890 under the direction of King Alfred of Wessex and continuing until 1154. It records the principal events of contemporary history, and is an important witness to the development of English over the period. Most extant Old English literature is in West Saxon; few traces remain from the earlier Northumbrian, except such short pieces as the 'Hymn of Caedmon' (*c.*670). After the Norman Conquest (1066), English was subordinate to Latin as the language of learning and religion and the Norman French of court and government. Surviving manuscripts show that poems were being written in English from the 12c onwards; many are fragmentary, but there are lyrics and verse romances that attest to a vigorous culture, embodying pre-Conquest history and legends, as in the 13c poem 'Havelok the Dane'. Gradual changes in the language, and the adoption of rhymed metrical verse in place of the Old English alliterative measure, can be traced through the early medieval period. See OLD ENGLISH[1].

Middle English texts. In the 14c, English emerged as a new language with few inflections and a strong admixture of French vocabulary. Chaucer moved from a close imitation of French and Italian poetry to write the *Canterbury Tales* (*c.*1387), whose styles often vary according to

the teller of a tale. He wrote in the East Midland dialect, which in due course became the standard literary language. In the West Midland dialect, there was a revival of alliterative verse: Langland (14c) wrote *Piers Plowman*, a long moral and political allegory with glimpses of contemporary life; and an unknown poet or poets produced the allegorical *Pearl* and the romance *Sir Gawain and the Green Knight*. At the same time, vernacular prose was developing: mainly the 14c homiletic and theological work of Richard Rolle, John Wycliffe, and others.

Drama appeared in the mystery plays, whose extant cycles come mainly from the Midlands and the North of England, and provide evidence of the speech of the period. The Arthurian legends that had inspired many lays and romances were collected by Thomas Malory (15c) in *Morte D'Arthur*, whose prose style varies with the sources from which he draws but reflects a sense of assurance. The mystery plays continued to be acted into the 16c, but a new type, the allegorical morality play, in which characters are personified virtues and vices, was a precursor of later secular drama. The most noteworthy poetry of the 15c was Scottish, the work of James I (13-14c), Robert Henryson (15-16c), William Dunbar (15-16c), and Gavin Douglas (15-16c). See MIDDLE ENGLISH.

Tudor texts. In early Tudor England, the influence of the Italian Renaissance showed in the poetry of Thomas Wyatt and Henry Howard, Earl of Surrey, including the use of the sonnet. A rougher, more satirical native tradition was carried on by John Skelton (*c.*1460-1529), who praised and sometimes imitated earlier writers, while recognizing that their language was old-fashioned, at the same time regarding contemporary English as unstable and inadequate for a poet:

> Oure language is so rusty,
> So cankered, and so full
> Of frowards, and so dull
> That if I would apply
> To write ornately,
> I wot not where to find
> Terms to serve my mind.
> ('Phyllyp Sparowe', ?*c.*1508)

The printer William Caxton shared this concern. He was aware that printing made a standard literary language preferable and it was largely through the efforts of printers that written English had by the 17c become more uniform. In the later 16c, English came to be more fully accepted as a medium in which the traditional genres could be written, but many scholars distrusted its stability and continued to use Latin for their treatises. The vitality of Elizabethan writing owed much to both free borrowings from ancient and modern tongues and such inventive neologism as Spenser's *blatant* and *Braggadochio* (the character in *The Faerie Queene* from whose name *braggadocio* derives). Lyric poetry, especially in sonnet form, was written largely by courtiers and their dependants: for example, Philip Sidney, Walter Raleigh, and Spenser himself.

A tradition of stately religious prose, to endure for centuries, was begun with the Book of Common Prayer (1549, 1552) and the Authorized Version, the translation of the Bible approved by King James (1611), which built on earlier translations, notably those of Coverdale and Tyndale. The early Tudor writing of Thomas Elyot in *The Gouernour* (1531) and Thomas More in *Utopia* (translated from Latin by Robert Robinson in 1551) helped to prepare for original vernacular prose later in the century: romances, narratives of low life and the criminal underworld, treatises and pamphlets on the controversies of the age, and the philosophical and scientific writing of Francis Bacon, who used a succinct and familiar idiom in his *Essays* (1597–1626). Bacon was among the scholars who put more trust in Latin than in English: he wrote his *Advancement of Learning* (1605) in English, but later issued an expanded Latin translation, *De Augmentis Scientiarum* (1623).

Elizabethan and Jacobean drama. The supreme achievement of the late 16c and early 17c was drama performed by an organized profession in permanent theatres. The primacy of Shakespeare should not overshadow the work of his contemporaries: pioneers of a new type of dramatic tragedy that used neither Biblical nor classical subjects included Thomas Kyd and Christopher Marlowe (1564–93). Robert Greene and John Lyly wrote comedy and George Peele both tragedy and comedy. The greatest writer of comedy apart from Shakespeare was Ben Jonson. Jacobean drama was less vigorous, but notable writers included Thomas Dekker, George Chapman, John Marston, and Thomas Middleton. Francis Beaumont and John Fletcher wrote a type of romantic play combining tragic and comic elements which also emerges in Shakespeare's last works. The drama showed that literary English could be spoken effectively for public purposes, in blank verse and in prose. After the powerful tragedies of John Webster, however, drama became more formulaic and commercial until the theatres were compulsorily closed at the outbreak of the Civil War in 1642.

Royalists and Roundheads. In the first half of the 17c, a time of struggle between Parliament and King, lyrics in the classical manner of Jonson were written by Cavalier (Royalist) poets, among them Robert Herrick, Richard Lovelace, John Suckling, and Thomas Carew. A distinctive new kind of poetry was labelled *metaphysical* by Samuel Johnson from its concern with philosophical and theological issues. It is characterized by elaborate use of language with unexpected images and quaint conceits: elaborate and extended metaphors or similes. The leading metaphysical poet was John Donne, powerful in erotic and devotional poetry and using similar language and figures for both. Similar devotional poetry was written by George Herbert, Henry Vaughan, and Richard Crashaw. Andrew Marvell, who showed metaphysical qualities, began with Royalist sympathies but became a supporter of Cromwell. John Milton, regarded by many as the greatest poet of the century, was both Puritan and Parliamentarian, his early poetry (lyrical, pastoral, and elegiac) veiling his austerity in delicate, even sensuous language. His greatest work was the Christian epic *Paradise Lost* (1671).

The Restoration and the Augustans. The return of Charles II (1660) marked a new literary era. Prose was increasingly written for critical and informative purposes, with less of the polemical heat and idiosyncrasy of earlier religious and political controversy. The beginnings of the novel can be seen in the narratives of Aphra Behn and Daniel Defoe. John Bunyan in *Pilgrim's Progress* (1678, 1684) combined narrative art and allegory with Biblical themes and cadences. The old open-air theatres, closed through Puritan pressures in 1642, were reopened with indoor stages, presenting mainly witty and satirical comedies of manners, in prose that remained elegant even when its content was coarse and scurrilous. Dramatists included William Congreve, William Wycherley, John Vanbrugh, George Farquhar, and John Dryden, and in the 18c Oliver Goldsmith and Richard Sheridan.

For over a century after the Restoration, the heroic couplet was the dominant poetic form, which Dryden and Pope used to write largely satirical and polemical works. Because of its attention to classical principles and the craft of verse, the period has been called *neo-classical* or *Augustan*. However, the most important literary development of the 18c was neither poetical nor classical. Within a few decades, the novel was fully established, with the work of Samuel Richardson, Henry Fielding, Tobias Smollett, and Laurence Sterne. Continuous narrative, divided into long chapters and paragraphs, incorporated representations of speech from different registers, classes, and dialects, bringing the full resources of the language into literary use.

The Romantics. In the later 18c, neo-classicism slowly gave way to a *Romantic revival* that greatly influenced the arts throughout Western Europe. Although the idiom of Thomas Gray and William Collins was mainly Augustan, some Romantic tendencies appear in their poetry, especially in their treatment of the natural world. Similarly, Romantic freedom and sensibility are foreshadowed in the poetry of Robert Burns. Towards the close of the century, William Wordsworth called for simplicity in poetic language and usage closer to actual speech rather than to artificial *poetic diction*. Although neither Wordsworth nor his contemporaries Samuel Taylor Coleridge and Robert Southey fully achieved this aim, they opened the way to such powerful successors as Percy Bysshe Shelley, John Keats, and Lord Byron. Although primarily expressed in poetry, Romanticism also influenced other genres. It appears in the novels of Walter Scott, which helped to spread Romantic attitudes in the next generation.

The Victorians. During the reign of Queen Victoria (1837-1901), the novel was the foremost literary genre and poetry became less important. The syntax and orthography of standard written and printed English was now settled and its vocabulary was rapidly expanding under the influence of new inventions and ideas. As education expanded the reading public also increased. As an increasingly popular entertainment, the novel became more than ever an effective vehicle for argument and propaganda. Most Victorian writers were critical of their society and nearly all reforming movements had literary advocates. The early 19c novels of such writers as Walter Scott and Jane Austen showed little direct social concern, but by the mid-19c the problems following the Industrial Revolution were examined in the work of Benjamin Disraeli, Charles Dickens, Elizabeth Gaskell, the Bronte sisters, and W. M. Thackeray. The later novelists George Eliot, George Meredith, and Thomas Hardy found their themes in the changing pattern of life, particularly in the countryside, and in the impact of new beliefs and theories. The late 19c novel covered most aspects of contemporary life, and social and cultural anxieties were addressed by Thomas Carlyle, John Ruskin, Matthew Arnold, and William Morris. In many cases, the distinction between literary and non-literary texts was not always apparent, as essays, lectures, and works of criticism were often written in language as powerful and imaginative as that of many novels.

Poetry did not regain its former dominance. The influence of the Romantics was strong in the early poetry of Alfred Tennyson and Robert Browning, though both found their own idiom in which to express doubts and anxieties similar to those of the novelists. Matthew Arnold and

William Morris wrote both poetry and prose. Even poets like Dante Gabriel Rossetti, his sister Christina Rossetti, and Algernon Swinburne, who seemed removed from the conflict, wrote of public as well as private tensions. A new literary realism brought middle-class speech into writing and on to the stage. George Bernard Shaw restored intellectual and moral power to the drama and produced a rich variety of speech for his many characters, and his writing, among others, was influenced by growing interest in philology and phonetics, which helped to make writers and readers more aware of the workings of the language.

Modernism. The movement known as *Modernism* began in the first decade of the 20c and was a reaction against all aspects of *Victorianism*. Literary interest shifted from the external to the internal, to the psychology and motivation of characters and their roots in deeply shared experience, influenced by the theories of Sigmund Freud and Carl Gustav Jung, and the anthropological relativism of J. G. Frazer. Joseph Conrad, D. H. Lawrence, and E. M. Forster, among others, explored mind and feeling in fiction still largely conventional in narrative and dialogue. Virginia Woolf and James Joyce, however, experimented with the *stream of consciousness* to express a character's thoughts more directly. Poetry broke even more radically with the past, replacing traditional prosody with *free verse* and favouring the shorter poem with sharp, concrete imagery. The American-born T. S. Eliot became the most famous poet of the new style in England, while in Ireland W. B. Yeats started in Neo-Romantic vein but developed new verse styles for his own mythology, and Hugh MacDiarmaid in Scotland sought a renaissance of literary Scots in tandem with verbal experiment and socialist politics.

Much of the literature of the period was marked by a more colloquial and relaxed use of language. The magisterial tone and direct comment of 19c novelists changed into styles which allowed the reader a more open and less directed approach to the text. Scenes and topics once banned from literature were now admitted, with hitherto taboo words appearing in print and a more explicit presentation of sexuality and human differences. These traits increased in the years between 1918 and 1939, with a sense of the fragmentation of society and the dispersal of shared beliefs. Aldous Huxley and Evelyn Waugh wrote of the frenetic escapism of the years after the First World War. Under the threat of a second war, writers began to urge the need for commitment and political action, writers such as the poet W. H. Auden and the novelist George Orwell taking strong left-wing stances, while Graham Greene expressed a radical Roman Catholic point of view. All of them sought to make their work popular, using as appropriate to their genre the language of the thriller or the rhythm of popular dance music.

Postmodernism. After 1945, there was radical questioning of the basic savagery in human nature. William Golding, Iris Murdoch, Norman Mailer, and John Fowles brought this theme into fiction. The freedom to write explicitly of sex and violence was taken further. Drama and the novel now presented the human dilemma in terms influenced by French existentialist philosophy. The theatre of the absurd, with Samuel Beckett and Harold Pinter, took dramatic speech away from the communicative and naturalistic to the inconsequential. The term *Postmodernism* has been given to the extension of Modernism into a more radical questioning of the integrity of language and the uncertainty of all linguistic performance.

The language of literature. Although English literature has not been so detached from everyday usage as some literatures, it is closer to everyday life in the 20c than previously. The concept and practice of a 'high style', to be kept apart from common usage, has been steadily eroded; the idiom of speech has thoroughly penetrated the literary text and become the norm for those genres of cinema and television which have inherited so much from literature. The tradition has been public and responsible; few writers have taken a position of total withdrawal and alienation from society. The language has in all periods been a literary medium; conversely, literature has enriched the language with neologisms, allusions, and quotations. People regularly use literary quotations, often without knowing their origins: *to the manner born, not wisely but too well, what's in a name?* (Shakespeare); *a little learning is a dangerous thing* (Pope); *God tempers the wind to the shorn lamb* (Sterne); *a sadder and a wiser man* (Coleridge); *the female of the species (is deadlier than the male)* (Kipling); *some animals are more equal than others* (Orwell).

Literature in education. The academic study and examinable subject known as *English Literature* (short form *Eng Lit*) is comparatively recent. Appreciation of English as a literary language began in the late 16c, but literary works in the vernacular were valued mainly for recreation and moral instruction, while the classical languages and literatures continued to dominate education at every level. However, knowledge of English writers was gradually encouraged as a social accomplishment and a mark of breeding, especially among women, for whom a classical education was not usually available.

The dissenting academies. The first movement away from the classical monopoly in education came in the 17c, among the English Protestant dissenters, for whom texts in English served as sources for exercises in grammar and rhetoric. When the Act of Uniformity (1662) excluded dissenters from the universities, a number of clergymen dispossessed of their livings opened schools in their own houses, and after the restrictions were slightly eased by the Act of Toleration (1689), some of these schools developed into the *dissenting academies*, offering an alternative to the ancient universities. Their curricula were usually similar to those of Oxford and Cambridge in the study of the classical languages, but gradually broadened to include history, science, modern languages, and English literature. The Northampton Academy, founded by Philip Doddridge in 1729, was one of the first to teach English authors, and John Aikin lectured on Milton and 18c English poets at Warrington Academy, founded in 1757. The influence of those academies was widespread, not only in the UK but in many other parts of the English-speaking world.

The universities. The first chair of English Literature was in Scotland, at the U. of Edinburgh (1762), and was known as the *Chair of Rhetoric and Belles Lettres*. Its first occupant was the rhetorician Hugh Blair. This was followed in the 19c by the first colleges of the U. of London: U. College (1828) and King's College (1831). Chairs of English Literature were then created at Owens College, Manchester (1850) and at the U. of Glasgow (1862), after which the practice extended widely. In 1848, Frederick Denison Maurice and others founded in London the Queen's College for Women. Here, in 1848, Charles Kingsley, in his inaugural lecture as Professor of English, spoke of literature as suitable preparation for women's lives. In the US, the academic study of English literature was established in the early 19c. The first Boylston Professor of Rhetoric and Oratory at Harvard, in 1806, was John Quincy Adams (later US president). In 1851, Francis J. Child occupied the same chair as Professor of English.

Oxford and Cambridge were slow in taking the subject up, but when they did their prestige helped establish it firmly in the English-using world. At Oxford, English literature was offered in the pass degree in 1873 and the Merton Chair of English Language and Literature was created in 1885. After much controversy, the Oxford honours school of English was founded in 1894, its growth owing much to the work of J. C. Collins and W. A. Raleigh. At Cambridge, the Edward VII Chair of English Literature was first held in 1912 by Arthur Quiller-Couch. In 1917, it became possible to take English with another subject, for a degree, but English did not rank as a sole honours subject until 1926. However, Cambridge made up for this late start by its influence on literary criticism, notably through the work of I. A. Richards (1893-1979) and F. R. Leavis (1895-1978). There was considerable controversy about the study of early forms of the language, especially Old English, in an honours school of English, although Old English had been studied by some Oxford scholars since the 17c. A chair of Anglo-Saxon had existed at Oxford since 1849 and at Cambridge since 1878.

Literary scholarship. The growth of the study of English literature as an examinable university subject with its own departments was encouraged by three developments: an interest in the study of texts both as literary specimens and as philological evidence; a new appreciation of cultural history and an interest in the influence of the past on present conditions; the greater availability of inexpensively printed texts, especially of material previously available only in manuscripts and codices. The study and teaching of English literature has long been international. Early work in mainland Europe includes A. W. Schlegel's Romantic criticism in his *Über dramatische Kunst und der Literatur* (1809-11) and the *Shakespeare Commentaries* of Georg Gervinus in 1850 (translated into English in 1875). The Shakespeare Society, founded at Weimar in 1864, has brought out the *Shakespeare Jahrbuch* annually since 1865. Bernhard ten Brink, born in the Netherlands, became Professor of Modern Languages and Literature at Marburg in 1870 and at Strasbourg in 1873. He wrote on English philology and published *Chaucer-Studien* (1870) and *Geschichte der englischen Literatur* (1874). Universities in Commonwealth and other countries throughout the world have built up departments in which English literature is now taught and researched. At recent conferences of the Association of University Professors of English, the papers read have been divided almost equally between scholars from English-language countries and from others. Books and journals appear annually in countries where English is a second or foreign language and include, among many others, *Études Anglaises* (France), *Indian Journal of English Studies*, *Neuphilologische Mitteilungen* (Germany), and *Shakespeare Studies* (Japan).

Literature in the schools. Encouraged by growing interest at the university level, English literature was increasingly studied in the schools as a preparation for university and in its own right. As new universities and polytechnics were founded in Britain, many in the expansion of the 1960s, departments of English Literature multiplied. Fully established as a major university discipline by 1930, the subject filled much of the gap created by the slow decline in the study of classical languages and literatures. English Literature, often referred to simply as *English*, has become one of the most popular sixth-form subjects taken for the Higher Certificate of Education and its successor the Advanced Level of the General Certificate of (Secondary) Education (England and Wales) and as part of the Higher School Leaving Certificate (Scotland).

There have been many changes in the university teaching of English literature. Students in the first UK honours schools were examined on *period papers*, with concentration on major authors like Chaucer, Shakespeare, Milton, Pope, and Wordsworth as representatives of their times. These have been supplemented by *genre papers* and special areas such as women's writing, black literature, and regional varieties of literature around the world, with texts by living writers. There has been in recent years decreasing certainty about a canon of literature on which study should be based; texts not conforming to traditional literary criteria are often included in the English syllabus. In the past, the language element in an honours course meant mainly philology: the study of texts written before 1500. Currently, much attention is given to the language of literature as a whole, with stylistic analysis based on linguistic theory. Papers in aspects of general linguistics and semiotics can form part of an English degree whose main component is still literature.

Literature and the media. The cinema and television have used many works of English literature, including versions of plays and adaptations of novels: for example, BBC television has presented all of Shakespeare's plays in a five-year cycle and its serialized dramatizations of writers like Charles Dickens and Anthony Trollope have proved highly popular. English literature is now often taught as part of cultural and media studies. The *Centre for Contemporary Cultural Studies* at the U. of Birmingham in England and the *Centre for Critical and Cultural Theory* at University College, Cardiff, in Wales are representative of institutions in the UK and elsewhere in which literature is studied integrally with other media in relation to present-day life and thought.

Canons and classics. The literary texts of a language can be many things to many people; attitudes vary regarding the social and educational value or the appropriateness of certain texts and authors. Many people, whether or not they read acknowledged works of literature, regard them as a repository of 'good English' and as models for both the written and spoken language. The works form a canon (*the classics*), a greater or less knowledge of which is shared by the culturally literate. Historians, lexicographers, and other scholars, regardless of whether they share this view or gain aesthetic as well as academic satisfaction from their studies, find in the body of English literature a record of language usage over many centuries. Currently, many teachers and critics of English literature waver between a traditional aesthetic and value-laden approach to their subject and linguistic, Marxist, Freudian, postmodernist, feminist, or deconstructionist views of the inherited canon as texts to be dissected to provide proof of the rightness of a doctrine or reveal a writer's hidden agenda. They may seek at the same time to enlarge the canon by including overlooked writers (especially women) or adjust it by reassessing writers whom they see as overly revered: including Shakespeare.

See AFRICAN LITERATURE IN ENGLISH, AMERICAN LITERATURE, ANGLO-IRISH LITERATURE, AUGUSTAN, AUSTRALIAN LITERATURE, BLACK ENGLISH VERNACULAR, CANADIAN LITERATURE IN ENGLISH, CANON, CLASSIC, DRAMA, ENG LANG (AND LIT), ENGLISH, ENG LIT, FILIPINO LITERATURE IN ENGLISH, INDIAN ENGLISH LITERATURE, NEW ZEALAND LITERATURE, SCOTS LITERATURE, SCOTTISH LITERATURE, SOUTH AFRICAN LITERATURE IN ENGLISH. [AFRICA, AMERICAS, ASIA, EDUCATION, EUROPE, LITERATURE, MEDIA, OCEANIA, STYLE].

R.C.

Abrams, M. H. (ed.). 1987. *The Norton Anthology of English Literature*, 5th edition. New York & London: W. W. Norton.
Adams, Robert M. 1983. *The Land and Literature of England: A Historical Account*. New York & London: W. W. Norton.
Barnard, R. 1984. *A Short History of English Literature*. Oxford: Blackwell.
Bateson, F. W. 1934. *English Poetry and the English Language*. Oxford: University Press.
Bolton, W. F. 1967. *A Short History of Literary English*. London: Arnold.
Burgess, Anthony. 1958/74. *English Literature: A Survey for Students*. Harlow: Longman.
Chapman, Raymond. 1982. *The Language of English Literature*. London: Arnold.
Drabble, Margaret. 1985. *The Oxford Companion to English Literature*. Oxford: University Press.
Ford, Boris (ed.). 1983. *The New Pelican Guide to English Literature*. Nine volumes. Harmondsworth: Penguin.
Fowler, Alistair. 1987. *A History of English Literature: Forms and Kinds from the Middle Ages to the Present*. Oxford: Blackwell.
Groom, B. 1956. *The Diction of Poetry from Spenser to Bridges*. Oxford: University Press.
Ousby, Ian. 1988. *The Cambridge Guide to Literature in English*. Cambridge: University Press.
Sampson, G. 1941. *Concise Cambridge History of English Literature*. Cambridge: University Press.
Thornley, G. C., & Roberts, Gwyneth. 1984. *An Outline of English Literature*. Harlow: Longman.
Watson, G. 1962. *The Literary Critics*. Harmondsworth: Penguin.
Wynn-Davies, Marion (ed.). 1989. *Bloomsbury Guide to English Literature*. London: Bloomsbury.

ENGLISHMAN/WOMAN. See -MAN/WOMAN.

ENGLISH-MEDIUM SCHOOL. A school in which the medium of instruction is English, in a country in which English is not indigenous and may or may not have official or other status. Such schools are usually private and run on British or American lines. Many employ expatriate native speakers of English, but some, such as the Anglo-Indian schools in India, recruit almost entirely locally. Often, in addition to the teaching, the social and recreational life of the school is also carried on in English. In many cases, such institutions serve not only as centres of education but also as vehicles and symbols of social improvement or privilege for both the pupils and their families. In many countries, certain English-medium schools have great prestige, such as Mayo College and the Cathedral School (Bombay) in India. Compare ARGENTINA (BILINGUAL SCHOOL), CULTURA, ENGLISH LANGUAGE SCHOOL, HONG KONG (ANGLO-CHINESE SCHOOL). [EDUCATION]. T.MCA.

ENGLISH-ONLY MOVEMENT. A name given, in the main by their opponents, to groups that since the early 1980s have aimed at an amendment to the US constitution, making English the official language of the republic. Proponents refer to the movement as *Official English* and deny that they wish to restrict people's options to English alone. See ENGLISH LANGUAGE AMENDMENT. [AMERICAS, MEDIA]. T.MCA.

ENGLISH PALE. See PALE.

ENGLISH PLACE-NAMES. The place-names of England can be divided into seven primary chronological groups, according to the language or languages dominant when the names were first used: *Pre-Celtic, Celtic, Latin, Old English, Norse, Norman French, Modern English*. These groups are called 'primary' because there has been widespread adaptation and hybridization as older names have been adopted and adapted by later peoples to produce 'secondary' and further forms: for example, a Celtic settlement known to the Romans as *Eboracum* became Old English *Eforwicceaster*, then Modern English *York*; part of Roman *Letoceto* (from a Celtic source meaning 'grey forest') combined with Old English *feld* (open area) to become modern *Lichfield* in Staffordshire; *Lincoln* (now pronounced 'Linken') derives from Celtic *lin* (pool) and Latin *colonia* (colony).

Pre-Celtic and Celtic. The earliest inhabitants of Britain, before the Celts settled there around 500 BC, spoke a language or languages about which almost nothing is known. Pre-Celtic traces, however, may have been preserved in some otherwise unaccountable names, such as the rivers *Itchen, Soar, Tamar, Wey*; the meanings of such names are at best conjectural. The Celts of what later became England spoke an Indo-European language that is the ancestor of Welsh and is now generally known as *British* or *Brythonic*. It survives in many place-names, some of whose meanings are known, some open to various interpretations, some obscure. These include rivers (*Avon* 'river', *Severn* meaning unknown, *Thames* perhaps 'dark'), hills (*Malvern* bare hill, *Quantocks* edge, *Penkridge* chief ridge), forests (*Arden* steep place, *Chute Forest* wood, *Melchet Forest* bare wood), and settlements (*Dover* waters, *Andover* ash waters, *Wendover* white waters).

Latin. The Romans dominated Britain from the 1C to early 5C AD, but added few names of their own during their long occupation. Names directly derived from Latin, wholly or in part, include: *Catterick* in Yorkshire, from *cataracta* a waterfall; *Speen* in Berkshire, from *spinis* (ablative plural of *spina*) at the thorn bushes; *Faversham* in Kent, from *faber* a smith.

Latinized Celtic. Generally, the Romans Latinized local Celtic names, especially those of rivers, to provide names for their fortified settlements. Many of these names continue in use, particularly in combination with variants of Old English *ceaster* (from Latin *castra* a camp, walled town). Anglo-Saxon versions of Latinized Celtic provide the names of many English cities: *Doncaster* (from Romano-British *Danum*, referring to the river *Don*), *Dorchester* (from *Durnovaria* a fist fight, perhaps referring to local boxing contests), *Gloucester* (from *Glevum* bright), *Manchester* (from *Mamucium*, perhaps 'breast', referring to a nearby hill), *Rochester* (from *Durobrivae* bridge fort), *Winchester* (from *Venta* special place). Less regular *ceaster* names include: *Chichester* (Old English: Cissa's Roman fort, unrelated to the Romanized name *Noviomagus* new market), *Exeter* (from *Isca*, now the river *Exe*, the element *ceaster* being almost entirely lost). In the name *Chester*, the Roman name *Deva* (meaning 'goddess' and referring to the river now called *Dee*, on which the city stands) has not survived. Many names with long and complex histories have kept only a fragment of the original, as in *Rochester*, of which only the *ro* of *Durobrivae* survives.

Latin in Old English. Further place-name elements borrowed from Latin into Old English include: *camp* field (from *campus*), as in *Warningcamp* (Wærna's people's field); *port* port (from *portus*), as in *Portsmouth* (mouth of the port); *stræt* road (from *via strata* paved way), as in *Stratford*; *wīc* settlement, farm (from *vicus* settlement), as in *Warwick* (weir settlement). Two elements probably from Latin through British are *ecles* church (from Greco-Latin *ecclesia*), as in *Eccles*, and *funta* (from *fons/fontis* spring), as in *Havant* (Hama's spring).

Old English. The Anglo-Saxon settlers of the 5C and later both bestowed Germanic names and adopted Romano-British names as they spread across southern and south-eastern Britain. Old English place-name elements include: (1) *burh* fort, with the later variants *-bury* as in *Canterbury* fort of the Kentish people, *-borough* as in *Peterborough* St Peter's fort, *-brough* as in *Middlesbrough* middle fort, and *-burgh* as in *Bamburgh* Bebba's fort. (2) *dūn* hill (modern *down*, as in *the South Downs*), now *-don* as in *Faringdon* fern hill, *Huntingdon* (probably) Hunta's hill, *Swindon* swine hill. (3) *feld* open land, now *-field* as in *Macclesfield* Maccel's open land, *Petersfield* St Peter's open land. (4) *ford* river crossing, as in *Oxford* ford of the oxen, *Stamford* stony ford. (5) *hām* settlement, homestead (modern *home*) or *hamm* enclosure (modern *hem*), as in *Birmingham* settlement of Beorma's people, *Fareham* ferny homestead. (6) *stoc* place (modern *stock*), now also *-stoke*, as in *Basingstoke* place of Basa's people, *Woodstock* place in the wood. (7) *tūn* farm, village (modern *town*), now *-ton* as in *Eton* riverside farm, *Surbiton* southern barley farm. (8) *worth* enclosure, as in *Ainsworth* Ægen's enclosure, *Papworth* Pappa's enclosure.

In many Anglo-Saxon names of this type, the first element identifies a person, group, rank (such as *cyning* king, as in *Kingston* king's town) occupation (such as *prēost* priest, as in *Preston* priest's town), or the like, while the second indicates a settlement of some kind. Such individuals as Ægen and Pappa (above) were probably the original settlers. Most of the names are of men, but several places have women's names, such as *Bognor* Bucge's slope, *Edburton* Ēadburg's farm, *Kenilworth* Cynehild's settlement, and *Wilbraham* Wilburg's village. In some cases, it is difficult to say if an element is a personal name or a standard word, so that *Radford* could mean either 'Rēada's ford' or 'red ford'. The latter in this case is more likely, referring to the red soil of the ford, but *Reading* refers to a group (Rēada's people), as does *Hastings* (Hæsta's people).

Recent studies suggest that such names were among the earliest, the *-ham* names like *Bloxham* (Blocc's village) coming first, then the *-ingham* names (like *Birmingham*), then those in *-ing* and

-ings (*Reading* and *Hastings*). Not all names of this type contain a personal name, however, and some have either a river name as a first element, such as *Avening* in Gloucestershire (people by the Avon), or another topographical word, such as *Nazeing* in Essex (people by the spur of land). In some instances, *-ing* means 'place', as in *Clavering* in Kent (place of clover). This sense could also appear in some *-ington* names, so that *Whittington* could mean either 'farm at the white place' or 'farm of Hwīt's people'.

Some Old English place-name elements have a very precise meaning: for example, *ōra* usually denotes a flat-topped hill, as distinct from *dūn*, which is a rounded hill. The name *Bognor* (above) therefore relates not so much to the seashore of this coastal town as the flat-topped hills of the South Downs lying behind it. Similarly, *stōw*, as in *Padstow*, often means 'holy place', implying a place of worship or a church, in this case dedicated to St Petroc. Careful distinction is also needed between such similar elements as *hām* and *hamm* (above), either of which can give *-ham*. The latter implies 'hemmed-in land', such as a valley between hills on three sides or land in a river bend. *Southampton* contains *hamm*, so means 'farm on riverside land' (the city being located at the confluence of the Itchen and the Test), but *Northampton* has *hām*, so means 'northern home farm'. Again, certain Old English words can have apparently opposite meanings in place-names: for example, *lēah* (modern *lea*), which can mean either 'wood' or 'clearing', the latter having the sense 'meadow'. The appropriate sense can often be determined either by an examination of the local topography or by a consideration of the names of nearby places. If a name ending in *-ley* or *-leigh* is surrounded by a number of *-ton* names, it is likely to refer to an isolated wood, but if there is a cluster of *-ley/ -leigh* names, it indicates a number of clearings where people settled. Not surprisingly, *lēah* is frequently found in combination with the names of different kinds of trees, such as *Alderley*, *Ashley*, *Berkeley* birch-lea, *Elmley*, *Lindley* lime-lea, *Oakley*, *Thornley*. It can equally follow a personal name: *Dudley* Dudda's clearing, *Wembley* Wemba's clearing.

The division of England into shires (counties) mainly took place in the 9-10c, Old English *scīr* (literally 'office') denoting a defined region of jurisdiction. However, the counties called *Cornwall* and *Devon* derive from Celtic tribal names (respectively, the *Cornovii* and *Dumnonii*, in their Latinized forms), with Old English *walh* (foreigner) forming the latter half of Cornwall. See WALES. The earliest shires were in the kingdom of Wessex, and took their names from the local administrative centre, so that *Wiltshire* relates to *Wilton*, Hampshire to *Southampton*, and *Somerset* to *Somerton*. The name *Wessex* (West Saxons) did not survive as an administrative area, but the lesser kingdoms of *Essex* (East Saxons), *Middlesex* (Middle Saxons), and *Sussex* (South Saxons) in due course became counties. *Norfolk* (northern folk) and *Suffolk* (southern folk) were similar tribal districts, but not kingdoms, before they became counties. The element *-shire* can be added to many of the old county names, necessarily in such names as *Leicestershire*, *Yorkshire*, *Warwickshire*, optionally for *Devon*, but not to the *-ex* group, the *-land* group, or such distinctive names as *Cornwall* and *Kent*.

Old Norse. The next major settlers after the Anglo-Saxons were the Vikings from Scandinavia, during the 9-11c. Danish place-names fall generally within the area of eastern and northern England (the *Danelaw*), while Norwegian names are found mainly in the northwest. The commonest place-name element of Old Norse was *bý* (village, fortified place), as in *Corby* Kori's village, *Formby* Forni's village, and *Whitby* Hviti's village. In a few instances, the *-by* superseded *-bury*, as with *Rugby* (Hroca's fort), recorded in Domesday Book as *Rocheberie*. *Derby* (deer village) is a complete Old Norse replacement of Old English *Northworthy* (north enclosure). Another Scandinavian element is *-thorp* (village), implying a secondary settlement near a primary one. This is found only in Danish names and should be distinguished from its Old English equivalent *throp*. The theory that many Old Norse *thorp* names were formerly Old English *throp* names has not been conclusively proved. Most such names are in Lincolnshire and Humberside and refer to small villages, with the exception of *Scunthorpe* (Skúma's outlying settlement).

As with Old English names, many Old Norse names consist of personal and generic elements: for example, *Corby* (above). However, there are some names in which a Scandinavian personal name is followed not by Old Norse *-by* but Old English *-ton*. These are called *Grimston hybrids*, since the name *Grimston* (Grímr's village) is a typical example of forms in North Yorkshire. Places with names of this type would have had an Old English personal name replaced by a Danish name. A more general renaming is thought to have occurred with villages now called *Kirkby* and *Kirby* (church village), where Old Norse names have replaced Old English names. The East Midland shires came into existence at this time and, like the Saxon shires, took their names from their local administrative centres: for example, *Bedfordshire*, *Cambridgeshire*, *Derbyshire*, *Leicestershire*, *Northamptonshire*, and *Nottinghamshire*.

Norman French. The last major invasion of England was the Norman Conquest of 1066. From then until the late 14c, the language of government and of most of the clerical work of the kingdom was Norman French. Although by and large traditional place-names were left unchanged, some 'difficult' indigenous pronunciations were given a 'smoother' Gallic form: for example, 'hard' *ch* became 'soft' *c* in *Worcester*, *th* became *t* in *Turville*, *r* became *l* in *Salisbury* (earlier *Saresbury*), and *n* became *r* in *Durham* (earlier *Dunholm*). Where there was a consonant cluster, the Normans might simplify it, as in the county name *Salop*, Norman French for the *Shrop* in Old English *Shropshire*. Its county town *Shrewsbury* was *Scrobbesbyrig* before the Conquest. A famous instance of such Norman influence is *Cambridge*, originally *Grontabricc* (as if 'Grantabridge': compare the nearby village of *Grantchester*). The altered spellings are to be found primarily in Domesday Book, where they were made by Norman scribes.

The second contribution of the Normans was the addition of French manorial family names to many existing Old English names, as in *Bovey Tracy*, *Charlton Musgrove*, *Drayton Cerne*, *Littleton Panell*, *Melton Mowbray*, and *Stapleford Tawney*. These places are named respectively for Eva de Tracy, Richard de Mucegros, Henry de Cerne, William Paynel, Roger de Moubray, and Richard de Tauny. The Norman names in turn often developed from French place-names: for example, Roger de Moubray came from *Montbray*. Where the Normans gave names of their own, they were mainly evaluative, many based on Old French *beau*, *bel* (beautiful, fine), as in *Beaulieu* beautiful place, *Beaumont* fine hill, *Beachy Head* fine headland (with English *head* added later), *Belper* beautiful retreat, *Belsize* fine seat, *Belvoir* fine view. Other names include *Devizes* boundaries, *Fountains Abbey*, *Haltemprice* high enterprise (referring to the building of a monastery), *Malpas* bad step (that is, a difficult passage), *Pontefract* broken bridge, and *Richmond* strong hill. *Beaumont* in Essex is a deliberate improvement on the earlier *Fulepet* (foul pit).

Modern English. Place-names in what can be regarded as Modern English date from *c*.1500, and include: *Camberley*, from earlier *Cambridge Town* and -*ley* as in nearby *Frimley*, etc.; *Coalville*, from its colliery; *Devonport*, originally *Plymouth Dock*; *Maryport*, for the wife of its founder; *Nelson*, for Admiral Nelson's victory over the French at Trafalgar; *Newhaven* new harbour; *Peacehaven*, to mark the end of the First World War; *Peterlee*, a new town, for a local trades union leader; *Raynes Park*, for a local landowner, *Southsea*, for Henry VIII's 'south sea castle'; *Telford*, a new town, for the engineer Thomas Telford; *Tunbridge Wells*, for the nearby springs, discovered in 1606, with the spelling altered to distinguish it from nearby *Tonbridge*; *Waterlooville*, for Wellington's victory over Napoleon at Waterloo; *Westward Ho!*, for Charles Kingsley's novel. Most new towns, however, together with new counties and administrative regions formed as a result of local government reorganization in 1974 were given borrowed or revived historic names, such as the river names used for the new counties of *Avon*, *Humberside*, *Merseyside*, and *Tyne and Wear*.

A special type of modern name arises from *back-formation*, in particular that of a river named after the town standing on it. Well-known examples include the *Cam* after *Cambridge*, *Chelmer* after *Chelmsford*, *Chelt* from *Cheltenham*, *Rother* from *Rotherbridge*, and *Wandle* from *Wandsworth*. Such names were frequently devised by 16c map-makers and topographers and replace earlier names: for example, the *Rother* was earlier the *Shire*, and the *Mole* was the *Nymet*. Some well-known London districts have post-1500 names, such as *Barons Court*, *Camden Town*, *Earls Court*, *King's Cross*, *Pimlico*, *Swiss Cottage*, and *White City*, and similar names can be found in many cities. They often arise from a particular individual or building, or commemorate an event, such as London's *Maida Vale*, named after the battle of 1806 in which Sir John Stuart defeated the French in Maida, in southern Italy. See CORNWALL, PLACE-NAME. [NAME].   A.R.

ENGLISH PLUS. A pressure group formed in the US in 1985 to promote bilingualism and counter the drive by *US English* for an amendment to the constitution, making English the official language of the republic. The name means 'English plus one or more other language(s)'. See ENGLISH LANGUAGE AMENDMENT. [AMERICAS, MEDIA].   T.MCA.

ENGLISH PRONOUNCING DICTIONARY, short form *EPD*. A work of reference by the phonetician Daniel Jones, based on his *Phonetic Dictionary of the English Language* (1913). The *EPD* was published during the First World War by J. M. Dent (1917); it is one of the most influential ELT books ever published, is widely regarded as an institution, and is closely associated with the Department of Phonetics and Linguistics of U. College London, where Jones worked and where its revision has been maintained first by A. C. Gimson, then Susan Ramsaran. Revisions have appeared in 1924 (2nd edition: with supplement), 1926 (3rd: with revised introduction), 1937 (4th: enlarged and reset), 1940 (5th), 1944 (6th), 1945 (7th: with supplement), 1947 (8th), 1948 (9th), 1949 (10th), 1956 (11th: enlarged and reset), 1963 (12th: with supplement and phonetic glossary; with corrections and revisions by Gimson in the 1964 reprint), 1967 (13th: enlarged and reset), 1977 (14th: reset, with revisions and a supplement by Ramsaran in 1988). The dictionary is a pronouncing glossary that lists words and names in Roman letters followed by their equivalents (with variants, where appropriate) in a phonemic transcription that uses the International Phonetic Alphabet to represent RP as a pronunciation model. There is an account in the introduction of the model and the notation. The 14th edition contains over 59,664 items (44,548 words, 15,116 names) in the main list and over 1,000 in the supplement. See JONES (D.), PHONETIC TRANSCRIPTION, PRONUNCIATION MODEL, PUBLIC SCHOOL PRONUNCIATION, RECEIVED PRONUNCIATION. [EUROPE, REFERENCE, SPEECH]. T.MCA.

ENGLISHRY [13c: from Anglo-French *englescherie*, from early forms of *English* and *-ry*]. (1) The condition or fact of being English, especially in the obsolete legal phrase *Presentment of Englishry*, providing proof that a slain person was English, to escape the fine for murdering a Norman. (2) Englishness: 'Our Englishry is often a shallow veneer. Scratch a Teuton, and you find an O'Shaughnessy' (*Westminster Gazette*, 21 Sept. 1894); 'The high romance, the doggedness, the talent for nonsense that are still, to the connoisseur of Englishry, staples of life in this drab, unhygienic island' (*Times Literary Supplement*, 26 Sept. 1958). (3) Obsolete: an English population, community, area, or quarter: 'The English law made treasonable any marriage of the Englishry with persons of Irish blood' (John R. Green, *A Short History of the English People*, 1882). Compare IRISHRY, WELSHRY. [EUROPE, NAME]. T.MCA.

ENGLISH-SPEAKING UNION, short form *ESU*. A non-political and voluntary worldwide organization whose aim is 'improving understanding about people, international issues, and culture through the bond the English language provides'. It was founded in 1918, at the end of the First World War, by Sir Evelyn Wrench, an Englishman, Alexander Smith Cochran, an American, and associates from the British Isles, the US, the West Indies, and Australia. Under the chairmanship of Winston Churchill in the 1920s, it aimed at partnership between the UK, its self-governing dominions, and the US. The ESU is a confederation of national branches coordinated by a consultative International Council (formed in 1974) and a Commonwealth Board of Governors (since 1927). Its major divisions are the *English-Speaking Union of the Commonwealth* with 50 branches (headquarters in London, shared with the International Council) and the *English-Speaking Union of the United States* with 80 branches (headquarters in New York). There are ESUs or representatives in Australia, Bangladesh, Belgium, Canada, Finland, Germany, Ghana, Hong Kong, India, Malaysia, Mauritius, Monaco, New Zealand, Nigeria, Norway, Pakistan, Sri Lanka, Switzerland, the UK (England and Wales, and Scotland), and the US.

For the purposes of the English-Speaking Union, an English-speaker is 'anyone who uses English either as a mother tongue or as a second language or foreign language. . . . Equally valuable are the democratic values of individual liberty and free institutions which are the cultural basis of the language.' Its activities fall into four categories: educational exchanges, the creation of informed public opinion, fostering English as a means of international communication, and organized hospitality. It set up the conference that led to the creation of Seaspeak in 1980; has helped to run the BBC & ESU Language School in London for about 20 years; organizes annual public-speaking and Shakespeare competitions (national and international), and the annual *Duke of Edinburgh's English Language Book Competition* (started in 1978 and designed to find new ideas in the field of English language teaching). The ESU offers travel awards, scholarships, fellowships, and book and literacy programmes, and organizes conferences, seminars, lectures, and summer schools. The ESU of the Commonwealth publishes a quarterly newspaper and a journal. In the US, the San Francisco branch has sponsored the publication of *The State of the Language* (US publisher, the University of California Press; UK publisher, Faber), related collections of essays about English published in 1980 and 1990. Although the ESU's interest in the promotion of English and the maintenance of standards of usage is expressed through competitions and sponsored activities rather than examinations, it has been closely associated with attempts to simplify and rationalize EFL examinations by means of the *Framework Project*. This has set up a nine-point scale of English-language achievement into which existing tests have been fitted: see Brendan J. Carroll & Richard West, *ESU Framework: Performance Scales for English Language Examinations* (Longman, 1989). The ESU does not propose any kind of English as a norm, nor does it adopt any prescriptive position with regard to usage. See EXAMINING IN ENGLISH, FABER, SEASPEAK. [AMERICAS, EUROPE, MEDIA]. T.MCA., J.A.

ENGLISH STUDIES. A term for the academic study and teaching of English, often primarily literary but also covering the language, institutions, life, and culture of English-speaking areas, especially England, the UK as a whole, the US, all English-speaking North America, or (increasingly) the entire English-speaking world. Such studies may include aspects of linguistics, philology, literary criticism, semiotics, media, and the communication arts, a distinction sometimes being made between medieval language and literature and *Modern English Studies*. Further subdivisions are possible, depending on the model followed (such as transformational-generative grammar or systemic linguistics) and the level or branch studied (such as phonology, syntax, semantics, or dialectology). Thousands of people throughout the world are currently engaged in the systematic academic study of English: for example, there were in the late 1980s in the UK and Eire over 1,600 scholars in 71 institutions claiming English Studies (the vast majority) or Celtic Studies as their field: see bibliography below. Scholars of English are often consulted on practical issues, such as the framing of policies and recommendations regarding language teaching (as for example in the 1988 *Kingman Report* on the teaching of English in schools in England and Wales), or are asked to contribute to programmes aimed at codifying, comparing, and translating languages (especially in regions or situations where English is in contact with other languages). Their work may take the form of dictionaries, dialect atlases, phonetic guides, and pedagogical grammars, and their interests may be represented by regional, national, and international associations. The results of their research may be published in such periodicals as *The Review of English Studies: A Quarterly Journal of English Literature and the English Language* (Oxford University Press) and *English Studies: A Journal of English Language and Literature* (Swets & Zeitlinger BV, Amsterdam).

See AMERICAN DIALECT SOCIETY, AMERICANISTICS, AMERICAN SPEECH, ANGLICIST, APPLIED LINGUISTICS, AUSTRALIAN LANGUAGE RESEARCH CENTRE, CANADIAN LANGUAGE ORGANIZATIONS, CENTRAL INSTITUTE OF ENGLISH AND FOREIGN LANGUAGES (INDIA), DICTIONARY SOCIETY OF NORTH AMERICA, ENGLISH ASSOCIATION (THE), ENGLISH DIALECT SOCIETY (THE), ENGLISH LITERATURE, ENGLISH TODAY, ENGLISH WORLDWIDE, EUROPEAN ASSOCIATION FOR LEXICOGRAPHY (EURALEX), LANCASHIRE (DIALECT SOCIETY), LANGUAGE TEACHING, LINGUISTICS, LITERARY CRITICISM, MODERN LANGUAGE ASSOCIATION, NATE, NCTE, PHILOLOGICAL SOCIETY, REFERENCE GUIDE FOR ENGLISH STUDIES, SCOTS LANGUAGE ORGANIZATIONS, SOUTH AFRICAN LANGUAGE ORGANIZATIONS, TRANSLATION, VARIETIES OF ENGLISH AROUND THE WORLD, VERBATIM, WORLD ENGLISHES, WORLD LITERATURE WRITTEN IN ENGLISH, YEAR'S WORK IN ENGLISH STUDIES, YORKSHIRE (DIALECT SOCIETY). [EDUCATION, LANGUAGE, LITERATURE, MEDIA].   R.H., T.MCA.

Keeble, Neil H. (ed.). 1988. *Handbook of English and Celtic Studies in the U.K. and Republic of Ireland*. Stirling: University Press. Oxford: Basil Blackwell.
Lester, Geoffrey. 1987. *Handbook of Teachers of Medieval English Language and Literature in Great Britain and Ireland*. Sheffield: University Department of English Language.

ENGLISH TEACHING. See ELT, LANGUAGE TEACHING, TEACHING ENGLISH, TEFL, TESD, TESL, TESOL.

ENGLISH TEACHING FORUM, short form *Forum*. A quarterly journal for teachers of EFL/ESL, founded in 1963 and published by the USIA (United States Information Agency). Its first editor was Elizabeth Sadler (1965–75), and its present editor is Anne C. Newton. The *Forum* is distributed to teachers in 130 countries through the US Information Service and US embassies, and current circulation is some 120,000 copies. In some countries it is sold, in others it is free, and in the US it is available on subscription through the US Government Printing Office in Washington, DC. The journal consists mainly of articles from readers worldwide on methods, techniques, and ideas useful in the classroom, complemented by commissioned articles and editorial matter, including questions and answers about grammar, a vocabulary and idioms page, and a 'lighter side' with puzzles and humour. It is produced in-house on a Macintosh desktop publishing system. See UNITED STATES INFORMATION AGENCY. [AMERICAS, EDUCATION, MEDIA].   T.MCA.

ENGLISH TODAY, full title *English Today: The International Review of the English Language*. Short form *ET*. A quarterly founded in 1984 as a forum for the discussion of English throughout the world. Published by Cambridge University Press, it seeks to blend the styles of academic journal and popular magazine, including scholarly papers, news, reviews, letters to the editor, and such lighter features as word games and examples of neologisms. Contributors come from many professional and national backgrounds, and *ET* follows a policy of publishing their material in either BrE or AmE orthography and, within limits, the conventions a contributor needs in order to make a particular point (including kinds of reformed spelling). The Editor is Tom McArthur, the Consulting Editor David Crystal. The readership is drawn from professionals and amateurs, linguists and literary scholars, the media and publishing, and native and foreign users of the language. It is read in some 50 countries worldwide. Compare ENGLISH WORLD-WIDE, VERBATIM, WORLD ENGLISHES. See ETYMORPHS. [EDUCATION, EUROPE, MEDIA, VARIETY].   T.MCA.

ENGLISH WORLD-WIDE, short form *EWW*. A biannual scholarly journal concerned with varieties of English around the world. Founded in Germany in 1980 and originally published by Julius Gross, Heidelberg, it has since 1982 been published by John Benjamins, Amsterdam and Philadelphia. It is edited by Manfred Görlach, Professor of English at the U. of Köln, Germany. To date, *EWW* has published over 80 articles: 11 relating to Africa, 6 to Australasia, 3 to Canada, 12 to the Caribbean, 10 to England, 5 to Ireland, 6 to Scotland, 5 to South Asia, 6 to South and East Asia, 6 to the South-West Pacific, and 6 to the US, as well as 11 articles on general language topics and comparative regional studies. Dialects, pidgins, and creoles have been included. General topics include: English as an international language; the social significance of English; attitudes, evaluations, and domains associated with English; emerging standards and usage problems; types of texts and their uses in the media, in education, and in creative writing; interference and code-mixing. The review and notices sections have covered some 300 books. Compare ENGLISH TODAY, VERBATIM, WORLD ENGLISHES. See VARIETIES OF ENGLISH AROUND THE WORLD. [EDUCATION, EUROPE, MEDIA, VARIETY].   T.MCA.

ENGLISHY [1870s]. An informal term for anything especially ethnically English: 'such Englishy faces' (W. D. Howells, *Chance Acquaintance*, 1873); 'The English teacher [in Canada] needs much tact, for if she is suspected of being "Englishy", there will not be much reward of gratitude from the parents' (*Times Educational Supplement*, 26 Apr. 1930). Compare WELSHY. [EUROPE, NAME].   T.MCA.

ENG LIT, also **Eng. Lit.** [1850s]. The short form of *English Literature* as a subject taught in educational institutions, used formally as an official abbreviation, and informally and often wryly to refer to and comment on the subject, its teachers, and its students: 'Here, surely, are the makings of some future Ph D thesis: "The fictionalisation of Margaret Thatcher in popular literature, 1979–1992." No doubt some enterprising Eng Lit department will one day run a course on it' (Robert Harris, 'We are a heroine', *Sunday Times*, 8 Apr. 1990); 'We are so respectful of Eng. Lit. that it is startling to come on someone like Ober, who has ambled behind the scenery

with a flash-light' (Byron Rogers, reviewing William Ober's *Bottoms Up and Boswell's Clap* in: *The Times*, 25 Mar. 1990). See ENG LANG (AND LIT), ENGLISH LITERATURE, POTTER. [LITERATURE, NAME].   T.MCA.

ENIGMA. See RIDDLE.

ENJAMBEMENT BrE, **enjambment** AmE [19c: from French *enjambement* striding over, projecting, from *jambe* leg]. Syntax that runs over the end of a line of verse and reaches a pause within the next line, as in:

Deep in the seas, deep in the southern seas
The coral palace of Te Tuna lies
Beneath an ocean. Far above, the breeze . . .
    (Richard Adams, *The Legend of Te Tuna*, 1982)

The tension in verse between metrical and syntactic pauses is a source of pleasure for many readers of poetry and can be a challenge to reciters. End-stopping and enjambement work together to create a distinctive rhythm, especially in a long poem. Compare END-STOPPED LINE. [LITERATURE].   R.C.

ENTRY [13c: from Old French *entree*, Latin *intrata*, past participle of *intrare* to enter]. The text provided under a heading in a list, from a long article in an encyclopedia to a one-line item in an index, bibliography, telephone directory, almanac, chronology, account ledger, or other source, usually one in which the information is arranged in some systematic order. In terms of dictionaries, usage varies and is occasionally ambiguous. The main word, phrase, abbreviation, or alphanumeric symbol that appears flush left in alphabetical order in a general dictionary is sometimes called a *headword*, sometimes a *vocabulary entry* or *main entry*, sometimes an *entry*. The ambiguity arose because of the usage in US dictionaries. In 1934, the Department of Treasury (through which, at the time, governmental supplies were purchased) met with interested publishers to establish a standard system for assessing the amount of information contained in a dictionary. The system that they adopted used the term *entry* for each of the following categories of listed information:

(1) Each *headword* (or *vocabulary entry*) that has its own homograph number, each *change* in *part of speech*, each *inflected form*, each *idiom*, *phrase*, or *expression* (usually set off in bold type or in some other distinctive style) that has one or more definitions, each *run-in* (or *run-on*), that is, a word, shown at the end of a dictionary article, that consists of the headword with an added suffix that changes the headword into an adverb, adjective, or noun with obvious meaning, such as *-ly*, *-ive*, *-ness*, etc.

(2) *List words*, those words that many dictionaries merely list (without pronunciation, definition, or etymology) to show their spelling and give some credence to their existence, such as those with prefixes that modify their meanings to something obvious, like *re-, un-, under-, self-, super-, mis-*, etc. attached to words that are treated elsewhere.

(3) Each *variant spelling* that is not given its own headword treatment (because its spelling would place it, alphabetically, far from the preferred spelling form), like the form *esthetic* for *aesthetic*; and *hidden entries*, which are (usually) multi-word forms that are defined within a related entry but are not listed as headwords, as the hidden entry *regular hexahedron* under the entry for *hexahedron* in the *Collins English Dictionary*.

Because of the differences in the styles in which information is presented, there is considerable variation in the methods by which *entries* are counted. For example, *The Concise Oxford Dictionary* lists compounds formed with *off-* as the initial element (like *off-glide, off-key, off-line, off-load*, etc.) under *off*, while other dictionaries might give each its own headword status.

Owing to the influences of American lexicographical publishing practice, counting 'entries' in this way has been adopted by publishers (and lexicographers) in other countries, but the term almost always needs disambiguation. *The American College Dictionary* (New York, 1947) was advertised as containing 'more than 132,000 entries', but in fact contained about 75,000 headwords; *Webster's Third New International Dictionary* (1961), which, excluding *Addenda*, claimed some 450,000 entries (and includes in the count regular inflections of nouns, verbs, adjectives, and adverbs, rarely shown in other dictionaries), contains about 285,000 headwords. See CITATION, DICTIONARY, HEADWORD. [REFERENCE].   L.U.

EOP, short for *English for Occupational Purposes*. English taught to foreign learners with particular occupations. Students' needs range from being able to read manuals to conducting negotiations. Typical students are mature, employed, and without high expectations of themselves as language learners. They usually understand and accept the necessity of English and tend to be volunteers. Because the authenticity of teaching materials is paramount, there is generally collaboration between teachers and specialists when preparing them. See ESP, TEFL. [EDUCATION].   P.S.

EPANALEPSIS [16c: through Latin from Greek *epanálēpsis* taking up again. Stress: 'ep-a-na-LEP-sis']. In rhetoric, a word or phrase repeated like a refrain: 'Cannon to right of them / Cannon to left of them, / Cannon in front of them / Volley'd and Thunder'd' (Tennyson, *The Charge of the Light Brigade*, 1854). See ANADIPLOSIS, REFRAIN, REPETITION. [STYLE].   T.MCA.

EPANAPHORA. See ANAPHORA.

EPENTHESIS [17c: through Latin from Greek *epénthesis*, putting in. Stress: 'e-PEN-the-sis']. The insertion of a sound or letter into a word or phrase. An epenthetic vowel can be added to break up a consonant cluster, as in Hiberno-Irish 'fillim' for *film*. Such a vowel often has the value of schwa. An epenthetic consonant can be added through being near another: /p/ close in articulation to both /m/ and /t/, as with *empty* (Old English *ǣmtiġ*); /b/ close in articulation to /m/, as with *b* in *nimble* (Middle English *nemel*). In RP, epenthetic /r/ is typically added between words that end and begin with certain vowels: *Shah/r of Persia*. Epenthetic vowels are common in non-native forms of English, to handle consonant clusters not found in the speaker's first language, as in 'sakool' for *school* among Punjabi speakers of English and 'iskool' among Kashmiris. See APTRONYM, B, D, INTRUSIVE R, L, LINKING R, N, P, PARASITIC, PARTICIPLE, SOMERSET (BRISTOL L), SYLLABLE, T. [SPEECH]. T.MCA., G.K.

EPIC [16c: from Greek *epikós*, from *épos* speech, tale, song, epic poem/poetry; the term *epos* is sometimes so used in English]. (1) A long narrative poem usually divided into books or parts and generally mythic or religious in its theme. It tells a tale of great actions and events that are usually important to a nation or culture, whence the term *national epic*: Homer's *Iliad* in Greece, Virgil's *Aeneid* in Rome, Vyasa's *Mahabharata* in India, *Beowulf* in Anglo-Saxon England, and Milton's *Paradise Lost* in 17c England. The genre is sometimes divided into *natural* or *primary epic*, which is oral or close to oral in style, and *literary* or *secondary epic*, which is literary and intended for silent reading rather than singing, reciting, and listening. (2) By extension, a novel, motion picture, or other work conceived or created on a comparable scale: *Tolstoy's epic 'War and Peace', a Hollywood epic*. (3) The adjective for such a poem or any work or event compared to it; heroic, majestic: *an epic poem, an epic novel, an epic film, the epic events of 1989*. See BEOWULF, COMMUNICATIVE SHIFT, GENRE, HOMERIC SIMILE, MILTON, MUSE, NARRATIVE POETRY/VERSE, ORATURE, POETRY, SANSKRIT, SPENSER. [LITERATURE, MEDIA].   T.MCA.

EPIC SIMILE. See HOMERIC SIMILE.

EPIGRAM [15c: from French *épigramme*, Latin *epigramma*, Greek *epígramma* ('written on') an inscription]. A brief, witty observation about a person, institution, or experience. Originally only in verse, epigrams now include prose and spoken remarks. They make a point succinctly and may convey a paradox or the inversion of a hackneyed sentiment. A 16c example is Sir John Harington's 'Treason doth never prosper; what's the reason? / For if it prosper, none dare call it treason.' See SAYING, WILDE. [LITERATURE, STYLE]. R.C.

EPIGRAPH [17c: from Greek *epigraphḗ* inscription]. (1) An inscription on a building, wall, or the base of a statue. (2) A short quotation prefixed to a book, chapter, or other text and suggesting its theme. The use of epigraphs on title pages was common in the 16c. The custom was adopted by novelists and became fashionable in the 19c, when each chapter might be headed by a quotation from English or other literatures. Some writers invent their own epigraphs, giving them plausible sources: for example, Rudyard Kipling for each story in *Plain Tales from the Hills* (1888). See MOTTO, QUOTATION. [LITERATURE]. R.C.

EPILOGUE, also AmE **epilog** [14c: from Latin *epilogus*, Greek *epílogos* afterword]. (1) A term for both the speech by an actor at the end of a play and the actor delivering the speech. The form arose in Greece and was common in English plays, 16-18c, usually in verse but sometimes in prose. Rosalind in Shakespeare's *As You Like It* (c.1599) begins, addressing the audience: 'It is not the fashion to see the Ladie the Epilogue: but it is no more vnhandsome, then to see the Lord the Prologue.' (2) The concluding part of a literary work, such as a novel, or of a motion picture or television play, often serving to knit up loose ends in the plot or provide information about later events, and often specifically entitled 'epilogue'. See PLOT, PROLOG(UE). Compare APPENDIX, POSTSCRIPT. [LITERATURE, MEDIA]. T.MCA., R.C.

EPISODE [17c: from Greek *epeisódion* ('an entering-in') an addition, used especially for a section of a drama that carried part of the main action, originally one of a number of interludes inserted between odes sung by a chorus]. (1) A section or scene in a narrative, usually well developed in its own right and an integral part of the story line. (2) In motion pictures, radio, and television: one of the sequential productions that make up a serial or series. (3) By extension, an incident or event in a series of incidents or events. See CHAPTER, NOVEL, SERIAL, SERIES. [LITERATURE, MEDIA]. T.MCA.

EPISTLE. See LETTER².

EPISTOLARY NOVEL. See LETTER², NOVEL.

EPITAPH [14c: through French from Latin *epitaphium*, Greek *epitáphion*, from *epitáphios lógos* speech written over a tomb, funeral oration]. A commemorative piece in prose or verse on a tombstone or monument. Epitaphs were common in the Greek and Roman world, and the custom was taken into Christianity. British epitaphs were at their most elaborate in the 18-19c. Whereas some old epitaphs have charm and wit, the current fashion is a factual record and perhaps a Biblical text. A 17c epitaph prematurely composed for King Charles II by John Wilmot, Earl of Rochester, runs:

Here lies our sovereign lord the King
Whose promise none relies on;
He never said a foolish thing,
Nor ever did a wise one.

By and large, however, epitaphs are complimentary. As Johnson observed: 'In lapidary inscriptions a man is not upon oath.' Compare EULOGY. [LITERATURE, STYLE]. R.C.

EPITHET [16c: from French *épithète*, Latin *epitheton*, from the neuter form of Greek *epíthetos* put or added on]. (1) An expression added to a name as a characterizing description, before it in *glorious Devon*, after it in *Richard Crookback*, with a definite article in *William the Conqueror*, *Scotland the Brave*. (2) Also *Homeric epithet*, *poetic epithet*. A formulaic phrase containing an adjective and a noun, common in epic poetry: *grey-eyed Athene, rosy-fingered dawn, the wine-dark sea*. (3) A word or phrase that substitutes for another: *man's best friend* for *dog*, *the water of life* for *whisky*. (4) A word or phrase used to abuse and dismiss: *bastard, bugger, shit*, especially when used directly (*You shit!, You son of a bitch!*) or as a description (*The silly old cow!*). (5) Such a phrase as *that idiot of a lawyer* and *a devil of a doctor*. (6) An adjective or other descriptive word. See ANTONOMASIA, HYPALLAGE, SO(U)BRIQUET, SWEARING. [NAME, STYLE]. T.MCA.

EPITOME [16c: from Latin *epitome*, Greek *epitomḗ* ('cut on') an incision, cutting, abridgement. Stress: 'e-PIT-o-mi']. (1) Someone or something that represents a type or class, especially in a positive way: *She's the very epitome of good taste*. (2) Now rare: a condensed account or abstract of a text, discussion, etc. The verb *epitomize* is used with both senses: *to epitomize good taste* and less commonly *to epitomize an argument*. See ABRIDG(E)MENT. [STYLE, WRITING]. T.MCA.

EPONYM [19c: from Greek *epōnumos* named on]. (1) A personal name from which a word has been derived: *John B. Stetson*, the 19c US hatter after whom the *stetson* hat was named. (2) The person whose name is so used: The Roman emperor *Constantine*, who gave his name to *Constantinople*. (3) The word so derived: *stetson*, *Constantinople*. The process of *eponymy* results in many forms: (1) Such simple eponyms as *atlas*, which became popular after the 16c Flemish cartographer Gerardus Mercator put the figure of the titan Atlas on the cover of a book of maps. (2) Compounds and attributive constructions such as *loganberry* after the 19c US lawyer *James H. Logan*, and *Turing machine* after the 20c British mathematician *Alan Turing*. (3) Possessives such as *Parkinson's Law* after the 20c British economist C. Northcote Parkinson, and the *Islets of Langerhans* after the 19c German pathologist Paul Langerhans. (4) Derivatives such as *Bowdlerize* and *gardenia*, after the 18c English expurgator of Shakespeare, Thomas Bowdler, and the 19c Scottish-American physician Alexander Garden. (5) Clippings, such as *dunce* from the middle name and first element of the last name of the learned 13c Scottish friar and theologian *John Duns Scotus*, whose rivals called him a fool. (6) Blends such as *gerrymander*, after the US politician Elbridge Gerry (b.1744), whose redrawn map of the voting districts of Massachusetts in 1812 was said to look like a salamander, and was then declared a *gerrymander*. The word became a verb soon after. Works on eponymy include: Rosie Boycott's *Batty, Bloomers and Boycott: A Little Etymology of Eponymous Words* (Hutchinson, 1982) and Cyril L. Beeching's *A Dictionary of Eponyms* (Oxford University Press, 1988). See -ONYM, WORD-FORMATION. [NAME, WORD]. T.MCA.

EPSILON [From Greek *è psilón* bare or simple *e*]. Also **Greek e**. The fifth letter of the Greek alphabet: upper case *E*, lower case ε. Modified versions of the lower-case form have three further symbolic uses: in phonetics, the sign for Cardinal Vowel 3 in the IPA system (that is, the value of short *e* in the English word *net* /nɛt/); in mathematics, the sign either for set membership or for the representation of a quantity that is either very small or close to zero. See ALPHABET, E, LETTER[1]. [SPEECH, WRITING]. T.MCA.

EQUIVOCATION [14c: from Latin *aequivocatio/aequivocationis* having equal voices or meanings, roughly translating Greek *hōmonumía* the same name]. (1) Ambiguity and uncertainty that arise from unclear meaning. An equivocal usage can be interpreted, according to context, in two or more ways: for example, the ethnic name *Brit* may be pejorative (*Brits out!* in Northern Ireland), casual and neutral (*Lots of Brits do this*), or amiable (*Nice to see so many Brits in the States this year*). Because of such contextual variation, people can become uncertain about the basic connotations of such a usage, and correspondingly cautious in using it on any occasion. (2) Action taken to evade an issue, as when someone says, *Well, y'know, it takes all sorts to make a world*, and avoids assigning praise or blame. (3) Also *equivocatio*, in logic, the use of an ambiguous expression in one sense in one premiss and another sense in another premiss or in the conclusion of a syllogism: *Everybody needs to feel safe: insurance provides safety: so everybody needs insurance*. The equivocation lies in the meaning of *safe(ty)*. Compare AMPHIBOLY. [LANGUAGE, STYLE].

T.MCA.

ERIN [From the dative form of *Eire* as in *Bás in Eirinn* Death in Ireland: that is, May you be lucky enough to end your exile and die in Ireland]. A poetic name for Ireland, given currency by such popular songs as *Let Erin remember the days of yore*. [EUROPE, NAME]. L.T.

ERRATUM (SLIP). See PROOF-READING.

ERROR [13c: from Latin *error/erroris* going astray, from *errare* to wander, stray, err: compare *erratic*]. A mistake; a deviation from accuracy, correctness, or the truth; belief in something untrue or held to be untrue; a mistaken view; wrongdoing; (original) sin. This continuum of senses derives from the single metaphor of losing one's way or straying from the path (Biblically, of righteousness). It has at times made possible the association (strong or weak) of errors in using and learning a language with moral and religious shortcomings, especially in institutions that have interpreted teachings on sin, salvation, and education of the young with particular rigour. Compare CORRUPT. See ERROR ANALYSIS, EXAMINING IN ENGLISH, MALAPROPISM, MISTAKE, PROOF-READING, SLIP OF THE TONGUE. [EDUCATION, USAGE]. T.MCA.

ERROR ANALYSIS [1960s]. In applied linguistics, the study of patterns of error. Analysts have proposed six kinds of error, arising from inaccurate learning, inadequate teaching, wrong guessing, poor memory, the influence of the mother tongue, and the process of learning. In 1967, S. Pit Corder in the UK distinguished between a *mistake* (a flaw in performance: a casual breakdown in speech or writing) and an *error* (a failure in competence: a systemic fault). In this view, errors are part of the learner's *transitional competence*. In 1972, Larry Selinker in the US coined the term *interlanguage* for an inter-mediate state of knowledge of a language; a person's interlanguage develops through suc-cessive approximations to the target, starting with the dominance of the mother tongue and ideally ending in native-like fluency. Because many learners cease to develop beyond a certain point, their interlanguages are said to *fossilize* at various stages. See ERROR, INTERFERENCE, INTERLANGUAGE, LANGUAGE TEACHING, MISTAKE. [EDUCATION, LANGUAGE].   P.S., T.MCA.

ERSE [14c: a Scots variant of *Irish*, originally the term for Scottish Gaelic and its speakers. Compare INGLIS, IRISH, SCOTS]. A rare alternative name for Gaelic, used both neutrally and dis-missively. It is rarely used in Ireland, where it may be regarded as offensive. In the 18-19c, it was an English literary term for both Scottish and Irish Gaelic, and for this reason is sometimes thought to be the correct term. See GAELIC. [EUROPE, LANGUAGE].   T.MCA.

-ESE [From Old French *-eis* (Modern *-ais*, *-ois*) and cognate with Italian *-ese*, from Latin *-ensis* belonging to]. A suffix added to nouns and adjectives. Its primary use is the identification of nationalities, languages, and the like, as in *Chinese*, *Congolese*, *Japanese*, *Javanese*, *Viennese*, *Vietnamese*, but a significant sec-ondary use is the labelling of styles or registers of English. The primary use is neutral, but the secondary use is often pejorative, associated with individuals whose style is distinctive and idio-syncratic (*Carlylese*, *Johnsonese*), groups whose stylistic tendencies are seen as undesirable (*aca-demese*, *bureaucratese*), language varieties con-sidered deficient or peculiar (*Brooklynese*, *Pentagonese*), and the media and technology (*cablese*, *computerese*). Nonce and stunt cre-ations are common, such as *UNese*, a diplomatic style said to be used in the United Nations Organization. See ACADEMESE, AGGLOMERESE, AMERICANESE, AUSTRALIANESE, BROOKLYNESE, BUREAUCRATESE, CABLESE, CARLYLE (CARLYLESE), COMMERCIALESE, COMPUTERESE, HEADLINESE, JOHNSONESE, JOURNALESE, LEGALESE, NEW YORKESE, OFFICIALESE, SOCIOLOGESE. Compare -ISM, LINGO, -SPEAK, TALK. [STYLE, VARIETY, WORD].   T.MCA.

ESH [Probably 20c: blending the name of the letter *s* (ess) with the sound of the digraph *sh*]. In phonetics, an elongated form ʃ of the symbol *s*, that serves in IPA to represent the voiceless palato-alveolar central laminal fricative, a sound represented in English by the digraph *sh* as in *shape* and *rush*. The form was used by Isaac Pitman in 1845 with this value in his phonotypic alphabet. See ALPHABET, LETTER[1], LONG S. [SPEECH, WRITING].   T.MCA.

ESKIMO. See INUIT.

ESL. See ENGLISH, EXAMINING IN ENGLISH, TEACHING ENGLISH, TESL.

ESP, short for *English for Specific/Special Purposes*. The English language taught for professional, vocational, and other specified pur-poses. Originating in courses of business English for foreign learners, ESP developed in the 1960s in response to demands for courses geared to practical and functional rather than educational and cultural ends. Whereas general EFL/ESL teaching offers courses to schoolchildren and to adults of mixed ages and backgrounds, ESP addresses learners with a common reason for learning, such as the English of air traffic control or of dyestuff chemistry. Planning an ESP course starts with a *needs analysis*, to establish the limits of the language learners' needs. Courses and materials are then designed to teach all and only that subset of English. Success appears to depend on the quality of the needs analysis, the authenticity of the materials used, and the sens-itivity of the teacher to the maturity and status of the students. Although the development of such language teaching has been mainly in English, it is of growing importance for other languages as part of *languages for specific pur-poses* (*LSP*). A recent work on the subject is Pauline Robinson's *ESP Today: A Practitioner's Guide* (New York & London: Prentice Hall, 1991). Within ESP, there are further divisions: see EAP, EOP, LIBRARY LANGUAGE, TEFL. [EDU-CATION].   P.S.

ESPERANTO [1888: in Esperanto it means 'one who hopes' from Latin *sperare* to hope]. An arti-ficial language invented for universal use by the Polish oculist Ludwig Lazarus Zamenhof (1859-1917), and the most successful of such languages. His first publication was in Russian, *Mezh-dunarodnyy yazyk: predislovie i polnyy uchebnik* (An international language: introduction and complete manual, 1887), written under the pseudonym 'Doktoro Esperanto'. In 1905, he established the canonical form of the language in *Fundamento de Esperanto*. Because its struc-ture and vocabulary derive from the major Euro-pean languages, Esperanto is Indo-European, sometimes described as a planned pidgin of the Romance and Germanic languages (with Greek and Slavonic admixtures).

The word order is usually similar to English: *Rozo estas floro* A rose is a flower; *Rozoj estas floroj* Roses are flowers; *La besto estis kato* The animal was a cat. The grammar is inflectional, with a range of affixes: nouns in *-o* (*rozo* rose, *besto* animal), adjectives in *-a* (*bona* good, *forta* strong), plurals in *-j* (*bonaj rozoj, fortaj bestoj*), indicative forms of the verb in *-as* for the present tense, *-is* for the past, and *-os* for the future. The vocabulary is eclectic: *amiko* friend (from Latin *amicus*), *kaj* and (from Greek *kaí*), *havas* have, *jes* yes (from English). The spelling is phonetic, and stress in polysyllables is on the next-to-last syllable. Accents vary according to speakers' backgrounds. The extensive literature consists of both translations and original works. A representative sentence is: *Zamenhof arde deziris ke lia inventita lingvo fariĝu la dua lingvo de la mondo* Zamenhof fervently wished that his invented tongue would become the world's second language (from a bilingual text in *Time*, 27 July 1987).

Esperanto is promoted and regulated by the *Universal Esperanto Association*, which claims 10–15m users worldwide. Esperantists refer to it as a *planned language* and to the world's natural languages as *ethnic languages*. They argue that it takes far less time to become competent in Esperanto than in English and that it is a more efficient and fairer international medium. The British phonetician and Esperantist John C. Wells notes:

It is more efficient, because it is easier to learn (grammatically completely regular, no exceptions, regular spelling, virtually no idioms). It is fairer in that it is not the native language of any country or national group, so does not give enormous unjust advantage to the native English-speakers, which the adoption of English would. At most, one-tenth of the world's population speaks English as a first language: it is more equitable that everyone should learn a relatively easy second language (Esperanto) than that nine-tenths of the world should have to learn a relatively difficult one (English) (quoted in 'Bonvenon al Brighton', *EFL Gazette*, Jan. 1990).

In English, the term is sometimes used to refer to forms of expression that are international and/or artificial: 'Latin, the Esperanto of the Middle Ages and Renaissance' (*Westminster Gazette*, 1905); 'the special esperanto of *ciné-club* experts' (*Times Literary Supplement*, 1958). The name is also occasionally facetiously adapted: *Eurospeak Desperanto* a patois allegedly used by European Community bureaucrats; *Ozperanto* Esperanto in Australia. The extracted suffix *-anto* has a similar sense: *Euranto* a system of English spelt phonetically, proposed in the 1970s as the auxiliary language for the EC. See ARTIFICIAL LANGUAGE, BASIC ENGLISH, CHINA, COMPUTING, JESPERSEN. [EUROPE, LANGUAGE]. T.MCA.

ESSA AND ASSA. See SOUTH AFRICANISM.

ESSAY [16c: from French *essai* an attempt, from Late Latin *exagium*, ultimately from *exigere/exactum* to drive out, try, examine]. A piece of extended writing, usually in prose, ranging from set-piece exercises in school to university dissertations in the *belles lettres* tradition. At first, an essay was a piece of writing that lacked finish or polish: 'an irregular or undigested piece' (Johnson, *Dictionary*, 1755), but at an early date there developed the contrary notion of the finished product, with the result that an essay in its highest form is now expected to be reflective, elegant, and philosophical. Both term and form were borrowed from French after the publication of Michel de Montaigne's *Essais* (1580), translated by John Florio (1603, 1613); the first major essayist in English was Francis Bacon, who adopted a pithy, epigrammatic style, each piece usually dealing with one topic (*Essays*, 1597, 1612, 1625). The form is also associated with the periodicals written and edited by Steele, Addison, Goldsmith, and Johnson in the 18c, though Pope's *Essay on Criticism* (1711) and *Essay on Man* (1733–4) were in verse. The essay flourished in the 19c, with such writers as Lamb, Hazlitt, Dickens, Matthew Arnold, and Henry James, and in the earlier 20c, with Shaw, D. H. Lawrence, T. S. Eliot, and Orwell. Such contemporary stylists as Anthony Burgess, Paul Johnson, Bernard Levin, and Gore Vidal continue the tradition as a form of 'higher journalism'. Reviews in essay form are the primary feature of *The New York Review of Books* and *The London Review of Books*. Because of the number of essays annually written by students, as exercises in literacy and organizing one's thoughts, the genre is perhaps the most common prose form ever developed. Compare ARTICLE[2], COMPOSITION, MONOGRAPH, THEME, TRACT, TREATISE. [EDUCATION, LITERATURE, MEDIA, WRITING]. G.H.

ESTHETICS. See AESTHETICS.

ETH, also **edh**. In Old English, the letter *ð* or *ð*, used to represent both a voiced and an unvoiced apico-dental fricative (the *th* in both *these* and *three* in Modern English); in Modern Icelandic and IPA, the letter *ð*, used to represent a voiced apico-dental fricative (as in *these*). It originated in Old English as a crossed *d*. Its upper-case form is *Đ*. See ICELANDIC, LETTER[1], THORN. [SPEECH, WRITING]. T.MCA.

ETHNIC [18c: from Latin *ethnicus*, Greek *ethnikós* national, from *éthnos* people, tribe, nation. An obsolete sense in English is 'heathen, pagan']. An adjective referring to a community whose members share or appear to share certain features, such as distinctive origin, culture, religion, and/or language: *ethnic Italians in Toronto*, *ethnic Chinese in New York*. The term became widespread in the 1970s–80s as a means by which minority groups with such characteristics could be discussed in countries like the US and Canada. Such groups have often had special interests, needs, or aims: Vietnamese immigrants in the US requiring ESL classes, 'native' peoples in Canada seeking rights in a land in which they were once the sole inhabitants. Although the term serves principally to contrast such minorities with a 'mainstream' population, its use has prompted an awareness that everyone is in some sense ethnic. Defining *ethnicity* precisely, however, has proved formidable. There is no consensus among sociologists; many studies give no definition.

Common descent and kinship (actual or presumed) are usually taken to be central to ethnicity; it is, however, an involuntary matter, and one may or may not celebrate one's good fortune at having been born an X, especially where Xness results in persecution by or ridicule and disdain among Ys. In addition, patterns of thought and behaviour change over time, so that the practices of the sixth generation of Xs may be almost completely unlike those of the first, with which however a connection is felt and, for some Orthodox Xs, may be the most important thing in life. Although cultural content, geographical location, and language of daily use may change, some boundaries and some sense of 'groupness' can and often do persist for centuries, sometimes millennia. Objective boundary markers, such as language and culinary habits, are mutable, but ethnicity is felt as long as there are enough features at any time, even if only symbolic (such as the official use of Irish in the Republic of Ireland, or Highland Games as a point of focus in Nova Scotia, Canada). No single attribute is essential, except perhaps a conviction among enough members and enough others, identifying certain people as Armenians, Basques, Gaels, Gypsies, Jews, Latinos, WASPs, and so forth. *Ethnicity* would therefore seem to be membership of, or allegiance to, a group (large or small, dominant or subordinate) with which one has, or believes one has, or is believed by others to have, ancestral links. See AMERICAN LITERATURE, CULTURE, ETHNIC JOKE, ETHNIC NAME, INCLUSIVE LANGUAGE, RACISM, STANDARD. [LANGAUGE]. J.E., T.MCA.

ETHNIC JOKE. A joke turning on the alleged psychological and social characteristics of a particular nation or group, such as the Irish (for whimsical foolishness: 'The *Irish Times* published its £20,000 prize competition crossword today. For those who don't wish to take part, the answers are on page nine'), the Scots (for meanness: 'Whilst in London's West End tonight, a Scotsman died of starvation on the back seat of a Pay-as-You-Leave-Bus'), and the

Welsh (for quaintness and sentimentality: 'We'll take time out to meet Dai Evans, inventor of the Welsh boomerang. It doesn't come back, it sings about coming back'). All three jokes are from *The Two Ronnies*, a British TV comedy series in the 1970s-80s. The ethnic joke implies the superior stance of the casually mocking narrator, though it is well known that nations and communities often manufacture their own jokes and tell them among and against themselves. They may also tell jokes against subcommunities and subcultures: for example, the jokes told about the Irish are in turn told by the Irish about the inhabitants of Kerry, a southwestern county widely regarded as rustic. See ABERDEEN JOKE, ETHNIC NAME, HUMO(U)R, IRISH BULL, IRISH JOKE, JEWISH JOKE, JOKE, NEWFIE JOKE, SCOTTISH JOKE. [STYLE]. W.N., T.MCA.

ETHNIC NAME, also **ethnic label** and, when pejorative, **ethnic slur**. A nickname for someone from a particular nationality, race, community, or culture. The spectrum of ethnic names in English ranges from more or less affectionate nicknames (such as *Jock* for a Scotsman, as used in England) through relatively neutral terms (such as *Brit* for someone British) through the use in affectionate abuse of terms that can otherwise be offensive (such as *Limey* and *Yank* between American and British friends), to highly offensive racial and/or religious slurs used without restraint, such as *dago* for someone of Spanish, Portuguese, or Latin American background, and *Yid/yid* for someone Jewish.

Social and etymological categories. Ethnic names in English generally fall into three social categories: (1) For peoples (and their languages) outside the English-speaking world: *Frog/Froggie*, someone from France or who speaks French; *Kraut*, a German; *Polack*, a Pole; *Wop/wop*, an Italian. (2) For national and regional identities within the English-speaking world: *Limey*, especially in the US, for someone British; *Pom(mie)/pom(mie)*, in Australasia, for someone from England; *Newfie*, in Canada, for a Newfoundlander. (3) Groups marked as different by habitat, race, language, and/or religion: *Wog/wog* for an Arab, South Asian, or black African; *Yid/yid* a Jew. Such terms also generally fall into four etymological categories: (1) Taken from personal names already common in the group concerned: *Jock*, a common Scottish pet form of *John*; *dago*, from the common man's name *Diego* in Spanish. (2) Taken from names associated with the entire group: *Abo*, an abbreviation of *Aborigine*; *Newfie*, an abbreviation of *Newfoundlander*; *Yid*, a word already meaning 'Jew'. (3) Referring to something seen as characterizing the group in question, such as complexion (*Coloured* and *Negro/nigger*), food (*Frog* from the eating of frogs' legs in France; *Kraut* from the eating of *sauerkraut* in Germany), or an emblem (*Kiwi*, the name of a flightless New Zealand bird; *bogwog*, in which the element *bog* is associated with Ireland: whence 'an Irish wog'). (4) Formed as plays on words associated with the target group: *Pommy*, an abbreviation of *pomegranate*, in turn a play on *immigrant* (see below).

Once established, however, a name's origin is often lost to its users, with the result that etymologists may have difficulty tracing its provenance. Many ethnic names have uncertain or disputed etymologies, among them folk etymologies that may have been created as jokes: for example, *wog* has been explained as a pseudo-abbreviation of 'Westernized Oriental Gentleman' and, in the plural, as originally an official British acronym for 'workers on government service' in the Suez Canal area, who are said to have worn armbands emblazoned *WOGS*. Probably, however, *wog* is a clipping of *golliwog/gollywog*, the name for a soft cloth doll with a black face and fuzzy hair, taken in turn from the name of a doll character in *The Adventures of Two Dutch Dolls—and a Golliwog* (1895), a children's book by the US writer Bertha Upton, and illustrated by her sister Florence.

Some individual names. The terms listed below, drawn from all parts of the English-speaking world, have complex histories that variously illustrate the points made above:

Canuck [1820s: probably from Iroquoian *kanuchsa* someone in a *kanata* (village: compare CANADA), but possibly from Hawaiian *kanaka* man, through a pidgin used in the fur trade (in which Pacific Islanders were employed), and taken into French as *canaque*, perhaps being originally applied to French Canadian canoemen]. A nickname used informally and neutrally throughout Canada for a Canadian, but in the US Northeast referring pejoratively to French Canadians. In the 1900s, Emily Murphy, a feminist and the first woman magistrate in the British Empire, wrote under the pen name *Janey Canuck*. During the Second World War, when American comic books were not imported into Canada, Leo Bachle created the character *Johnny Canuck*, a hero who fought the Nazis single-handed.

Coloured BrE, *colored* AmE. (1) Having a skin other than white, and especially referring to someone either wholly black African in origin or part-European, part-African: 'Among the coloured circles of New Orleans' (Harriet B. Stowe, *Uncle Tom's Cabin*, 1850). (2) A person with such a complexion: 'A spot where fine young American coloureds can destroy themselves with female white trash' (C. MacInnes, *City of*

Spades, 1957). Although the term is currently regarded as offensive in the US, the organization for African-American civil rights continues to be known as the *National Association for the Advancement of Colored People* (*NAACP*). (3) Also *Cape Coloured/Colored*. In South Africa, terms (adjective and noun: formerly with initial capital letter) for a person of mixed African and European descent: 'The new house will contain 163 members, four of them representing the newly separate Coloured electorate in the Cape' (*New Statesman*, 12 Apr. 1958); 'the few Indians and Coloureds who also study there' (*The Times*, 30 June 1955). The term is widely disliked in South Africa, and is currently often printed lower-case and in quotation marks (*the so-called 'coloured' area*), but no serious alternative designation has emerged to date.

Honky [1940s: AmE, perhaps a variant of *hunky*, a nickname applied, usually disparagingly, to immigrants from east-central Europe: perhaps from *Hungarian*, with devoicing of /g/]. Also *honkey*. A black American slang term for a white person and white people collectively: 'Blacks should "beware of honkies bearing gifts"' (*Black World*, Mar. 1971); 'Mary forcefully shoved him away. "Split, honky, you smell"' (Bernard Malamud, *Tenants*, 1971).

Kaffir [17c: from Arabic *kāfir* ('one who denies'), an unbeliever, probably through Portuguese or Dutch]. Also formerly *Cafar*, *Caffer*, etc. (1) Originally, a non-Muslim, an infidel: 'He was to drive the English Caffers out of India' (T. Munro, letter, 1799); 'Being Mahommedans, they gave the general name of Cafer (Liar, Infidel) to all the inhabitants of the coasts of southern Africa' (A. Plumtre, *Liechtenstein's South Africa*, 1812). (2) In southern Africa, a European term for any black African, often used neutrally in earlier times, but generally disparaging, increasingly resented, and now an actionable insult in South Africa. (3) An element in compounds in South African English, now mostly obsolete or obsolescent: *kaffir beer* beer made by blacks from grain sorghum, now known as *sorghum beer*; *kaffirboom* (Afrikaans *-boom* tree) the coral tree (now its usual name); *kaffir sheeting* coarse white cotton cloth, sometimes euphemized as *K-sheeting*.

Limey [1880s: a clipping of *lime-juicer*, a slang nickname for an English or British sailor, because such sailors were required by law to drink lime juice aboard ship in order to ward off the disease scurvy. British ships were also called *lime-juicers* and *limeys*, because of this practice]. An often disparaging and offensive name used especially by Americans (but also in the recent past by Australians, New Zealanders, and South

African whites), for someone from Britain, especially England: 'Guy always plays up the limey accent when he's in the States' (D. Jordan, *Nile Green*, 1973).

Native [14c: directly from Latin *nativus* born in a place, from *natus* born, replacing Middle English *natif*, from French]. Formerly, people could be native to many things: a place, a condition of life (such as slavery), a sign of the Zodiac, or a characteristic (such as a mole). By the 18c, *native* as an adjective most commonly referred to being born in a place and as a noun was increasingly pejorative: 'superior to the rest of the odious natives in the neighbourhood' (Mrs Hervey, *Mourtray Farm*, 1800). In the 17c, the term began to be applied to the indigenous people of colonized territories, and this sense was dominant in the 19c and early 20c: 'Whether the native swaggers or cringes, there's always something behind every remark he makes' (E. M. Forster, *Passage to India*, 1924). In the 19c, Australia was for a time an exception, the term referring to a locally born white as opposed to an Aborigine, but Australians duly adopted the general use: 'The native is a strange child, and he needs sympathetic dealing . . . Make a boy laugh and you can do anything with him' (G. Page, *Jill on the Ranch*, 1921). Shaw played with the usage in *On the Rocks* (1934):

Sir Bemrose. If a Conservative Prime Minister of England may not take down a heathen native when he forgets himself there is an end of British supremacy.
Sir Arthur. For heaven's sake don't call him a native. You are a native.
Sir Bemrose (*very solemnly*). Of Kent, Arthur: of Kent. Not of Ceylon.

In 1948, the observation was made in *The Times Literary Supplement* (Oct.): ' "Native" is a good word that may not now be employed without giving deep offence.' In 1950, J. C. Furnas wrote sardonically: 'The meaning of "Native" can be approximated. It means: Darker. Productive of quaint handicrafts . . . Greedy for beads . . . and alcoholic drinks. Suspect of Cannibalism. Addicted to drum-beating and lewd dancing. More or less naked. Sporadically treacherous. Probably polygynous and simultaneously promiscuous. Picturesque. Comic when trying to speak English or otherwise ape white ways.' In 1988, the Afghan writer Idries Shah reversed the direction in *The Natives are Restless*, a book about Britain. Currently, the term is used with care, and the sense of 'born in a place' is strong again. There are, however, distinctive uses in various parts of the world. In the US, the term *Native American* has been widely promoted as a preferred term to *Amerindian*, (*American*) *Indian*, *Red Indian*, or *Redskin*. In Canada, the terms *Native Peoples* and *Native* are officially used for the original inhabitants of the land.

Negro [16c: through Spanish and Portuguese from Latin *niger* black]. A noun and adjective used generally and in anthropology until the late 20c for a member of various dark-skinned sub-Saharan peoples of Africa currently most commonly known as *black*, *Black*, *black African*, *Black African*, or *African*. Once common in expressions such as *American Negro* and continuing in *Negro spiritual*, the term is now generally disliked by Africans and people of African descent. Formerly, however, it was often used in a positive sense (and often in contrast to *black*, which was formerly considered pejorative). Such terms as *Negrophile* and *Negrophobe*, in use since the 17c, were at one time more or less neutral, like *Anglophile* and *Anglophobe*, but are now virtually obsolete, as is *Negroism*, a 19c AmE term for a social or linguistic usage typical of blacks and for the advocacy of equal rights for blacks, especially in the US.

Nigger [17c: from French *nègre*, Spanish *negro*, Latin *niger* black]. A word long used abusively or dismissively of any dark-skinned person: ' "You're a fool nigger, and the worst day's work Pa ever did was to buy you," said Scarlett slowly . . . There, she thought, I've said "nigger" and Mother wouldn't like that at all' (Margaret Mitchell, *Gone with the Wind*, 1936). The word continues to give offence, although some blacks, especially in the US, use it as a form of affectionate abuse among themselves. It has sometimes posed problems in the titling of books: for example, Agatha Christie's detective novel *Ten Little Niggers* (1939), whose title refers to a reductive rhyme in which one after another ten statuettes are broken, was not regarded as distasteful when it was published (at least among whites), but has since been renamed both *And Then There Were None* and *Ten Little Indian Boys*; the original name appears, however, to be in the process of rehabilitation. The title of Joseph Conrad's novel *The Nigger of the 'Narcissus'* has not been affected by changes in attitude and taste since it first appeared in 1897.

Paki [1960s: a clipping of *Pakistani*, plural *Pakis*]. Also *Pakki*, *Pakky*. A pejorative and offensive name used mainly in Britain and Canada for someone from Pakistan in particular and South Asia generally, or of such descent. It is usually applied to immigrants, especially in BrE *Paki-bashing* and CanE *Paki-busting*, compounds referring to physical attacks on South Asians, and in BrE *Paki shop*, a corner shop run by South Asians.

Pom, also *Pommie*, *Pommy* [c.1910]. An equivocal term used mainly in Australia and New Zealand for someone from England, especially an immigrant. It became popular in 1912, especially in the columns of the Sydney *Truth*. It is not, as is sometimes supposed, an acronym of *Prisoner of Her Majesty* or *Prisoner of Mother England*, but derives from word-play: *immigrant, jimmygrant, pomegranate, pommygrant, pommy, pom*. Of the fixed phrases *pommy bastard* and *whinging pom*, the first is often a term of affectionate abuse, the second is straightforwardly pejorative.

Sassenach [18c: From Gaelic *Sasunnach* English, Englishman, Englishwoman, from English *Saxon*]. An ethnic name formerly applied by the Highlanders of Scotland to the Lowlanders and the English (regarded as the same in race and language), and since the 19c commonly used more or less amiably by all Scots to refer to the English: *Next week the Scots take on the Sassenachs at rugby at Murrayfield.*

Teuchter [Origin uncertain: 'It seems to have come into oral currency about 1910 and to have been vaguely associated with Gaelic' (*Scottish National Dictionary*, 1931–76). Pronounced /'tjʊxtɪr/]. A disparaging term used by Lowland Scots to refer to a Highlander or Hebridean Islander, especially one who speaks Gaelic. In some places, it is applied by city people to any country person.

Yid [mid-19c: from Yiddish *yid* a Jew, from Middle High German *Jude*, Old High German *Judo*, Latin *Iudaeus*, Greek *Ioudaîos*, Hebrew *Yehudah* Judah (the ancient Jewish kingdom). Cognate with *Jew*. The first known reference in English is in the 1874 edition of John C. Hotten's *The Slang Dictionary*]. An ethnic slur applied to someone Jewish, although it derives from a Yiddish word that is in itself in no way pejorative.

Conclusion. Generally, ethnic names are restricted to informal and slang usage and ethnic slurs are associated with strong emotion and often unexamined bias on the part of the user. The degree of acceptability or unacceptability of such a name may change over the years, and from group to group. Sometimes, names that cease for a time to be used because of their derogatory associations are later revived with positive associations, as for example *Black/black* (see entry). See ABORIGINES, (A)ESTHETICS, AFRICAN-AMERICAN, AMERICAN ENGLISH, AMERICAN LANGUAGES, ANGLO, AUSSIE, BLACK, BRIT, CALIBAN, CHICANO, ETHNIC, ETHNIC JOKE, FANAKALO, GRINGO, HILLBILLY, JOHN BULL, KITCHEN, KIWI, MCWORD, MESTIZO, MÉTIS, MULATTO, NATIVE LANGUAGE, NATIVE SPEAKER, NATIVE USER, NATIVISM, NATIVIZATION, NICKNAME, PAKEHA, RACISM, UNCLE SAM, WASP, WHITE, YANK(EE). [AFRICA, AMERICAS, ASIA, EUROPE, NAME, OCEANIA, STYLE, USAGE, WORD].

T.MCA., M.F., W.B., W.S.R., A.J.A., S.S.

ETHNOCENTRIC [1900s]. (1) Centred on a particular ethnic community and its culture, language, etc., usually one's own and often in the belief that it is superior to all others. (2) Inclined to view other communities and cultures from the perspective or security of one's own, and therefore inclined to judge them by the norms or conventions with which one is familiar. See CENTRICITY, ETHNIC. [LANGUAGE, STYLE]. T.MCA.

ETHNOLINGUISTICS [1940s: a blend of *ethnology*, from Greek *éthnos* nation, *-logía*, study, and *linguistics*]. Also **anthropological linguistics**. A branch of linguistics that studies language and the part it plays in the life and culture of such groups as Amerindians, Australian aborigines, and minority (often immigrant) communities. See ETHNIC. [LANGUAGE]. J.E.

ETS. See EDUCATIONAL TESTING SERVICE.

ETYMOLOGICAL FALLACY. A term in linguistics for the view that the first recorded meaning of a word is or must be its correct meaning: 'bristling' as the 'true' meaning of *horrid* (the example given by Jeremy Warburg in 'Notions of Correctness', in R. Quirk, *Use of English*, 1962). It is a fallacy because the meanings of words change with time, so that *horrid* today has no semantic link with Latin *horridus* bristling, from which it derives. See ETYMOLOGY, ETYMON, FOLK ETYMOLOGY, LANGUAGE CHANGE, SEMANTIC CHANGE. [HISTORY, LANGUAGE]. T.MCA.

ETYMOLOGY [14c: from Greek *etumología*, from *étumon* true meaning of a word, and *-logía*, study]. Both the study of the history of words and a statement of the origin and history of a word, including changes in its form and meaning. The sense in which the 17c poet Milton used it ('Etymology, or right wording, teacheth what belongs to every single word or part of speech') is obsolete.

History. Classical Greek interest in words owed much to the development of alphabetic writing, in which they were laid out for inspection like merchandise. Early investigators of words included the Stoics of the 4c BC, who held that all languages were in a slow state of decline from erstwhile perfection. They therefore looked for the *etymon* or true first form of a word. Their pessimistic view survives among those who insist that the best writers are long dead, and their belief in etyma continues among those who argue that the original meaning of a word has current as well as chronological priority over any later senses it may develop. In Spain in the 7c, St Isidore of Seville compiled a 20-part encyclopedia called *Originum sive etymologiarum libri* (Books of Origins or Etymologies), more commonly known as the *Etymologiae*. He took the view that the essence of a word could be found associatively: the Latin *homo* (man), adjective *humanus*, derived from *humo* (from the soil), because God made man from clay. This view served a didactic and mnemonic end, and was influenced by Hebrew precedents in the Old Testament, in which words were accounted for through homonymic comparisons (Hebrew *adam* being both man and clay). Isidore's students of Latin remembered *cadaver* as a kind of theological acronym of *CAro DAta VERmibus* (flesh given to worms). Isidore appears to have sought to formalize what is now called *folk etymology*, in which associative guessing dominates. His ideological approach was not unique. In the 20c, it has been used by feminists reinterpreting *history* and *boycott* for propaganda purposes as *his story* and *boy cott*, so as to be able to formulate *herstory* and *girlcott*.

Isidore's views on etymology were affected by his belief that Adam and Eve spoke Hebrew in Eden and that the story of the Tower of Babel was literally true. This continued to be the majority view among scholars through the Middle Ages and the Renaissance and conditioned the research of such 18–19c enthusiasts as the Englishman John Horne Tooke and the American Noah Webster. Both were convinced that language was the product of historical development, but lacked a non-Biblical theory with which to transform traditional speculation into science. The many jugglers with words and letters led Voltaire to make an acid assessment of etymology as a science in which the vowels count for nothing and the consonants for very little. The study was transformed, however, by Sir William Jones and the comparative philologists, who depended on a painstaking analysis of textual evidence from many languages. As a consequence of their work, 20c etymology is part of historical linguistics.

Nature. Contemporary etymology is concerned with both fact and hypothesis. As with information in the fossil record of paleontology, what is known of the origin and development of a word or its elements is a matter of chance, since only the earliest recorded forms and meanings can be directly studied. Earlier forms reconstructed by means of this recorded evidence and the meanings assumed for such forms are hypothetical and need to be treated with caution. Where such forms are shown in writing or print, they are conventionally preceded by an asterisk (*) to mark their status. For English, such forms are usually those of the Indo-European root and its derivatives, or Romanic and Germanic roots.

Thus, the *-logy* part of the word *etymology* goes back to an IE root **leg-* (collect). Many words, however, cannot be taken so far back; the recorded evidence does not suffice, and so etymologists may tag a word 'o.o.o.' (of obscure origin) or 'origin unknown'.

Historical changes in meaning are unpatterned, because derivations are usually idiomatic; the meaning of the whole is not simply the sum of the meanings of the parts. The adjective *sedate* goes back to the Latin verb *sedare* (to settle: a person, a dispute, a war), which comes from the IE root **sed-* (sit); hence the basic meaning '(having been) settled'. The derived adjective *sedative* is then something that tends to settle someone. However, in Modern English, the adjective *sedate* means 'deliberately composed and dignified by one's own character or efforts', not (as *sedative* would suggest) 'stupefied by the effects of a drug'. The Modern English verb *sedate* is a back-formation from *sedative* and therefore draws on the meaning of *sedative* and not on the meaning of the earlier adjective *sedate*. The homonymic adjective and verb *sedate* share a common origin in IE **sed-*, but have developed such divergent meanings that the ancient adjective cannot suitably describe someone who shows the effects of the recent verb. As the 19c German philologist Max Müller wrote: 'The etymology of a word can never give us its definition' (1880).

It is therefore not surprising that the etymology of some common words reveals origins very unlike their modern form, meanings, or both. Thus, the four words *dough, figure, lady,* and *paradise* all derive in part at least from the IE root **dheigh-* (to knead clay). Three of these words specialize or narrow the *knead* part of that meaning and ignore the *clay* part: (1) *Dough* is something that is kneaded like clay. (2) *Figure* derives from Latin *figura*, which comes in turn from IE **dhigh-ūrā*, something formed by kneading or manipulation. *Feign, fiction,* and *effigy* are from the same root. (3) *Lady* derives from OE *hlāfdige*, composed of *hlāf* (loaf) and **digan* (knead). A lady was the member of the house who kneaded the loaf, and the *hlāford* (from which comes *lord*) was its guardian. Paradoxical developments of meaning attend the changes in *lady*. From one who kneads the dough it became both 'the chief female of the household' and hence the one least likely to deal with such chores. However, the fourth word specializes the *clay* part of the original meaning and ignores the *knead* part: *paradise*, originally an enclosed garden, from Indo-Iranian *pairi-daēza* (walled around), from *pairi* (around: compare *peri*scope) and *daēza* (wall, originally made of clay).

Even supposedly objective terms like numerals undergo change with the passage of time. Thus, although *only* was originally 'one-ly', it is now an adverb suitable for any quality or quantity, as in the etymological paradox 'only twelve'. *Combination* is now the mixture of any number of elements, but once it was only of *two* elements, its base being the Latin *bin-* as in *binary*. *Testimony* is from IE *tristi*, the '*third* (person) standing by', but is now evidence given by any person. *Quintessence* was once the *fifth* and highest essential element (in addition to earth, air, fire, and water), but is now simply the pure example of any thing or person. *September* was once the *seventh* month (Latin *septem*, seven), but is now the ninth; the other months from October to December follow the same pattern. *Dean*, now the head of a group, especially academic, of any number, was once specifically a group of *ten* (Greek *déka*, ten, as in *decathlon*); *decimate* once meant to reduce by a tenth (compare *decimal*), but now means to reduce by any substantial amount. *Quarantine* is now a sequestration of any length, but was once of *forty* days (French *quarante*).

Many of these semantic changes fall into discernible categories: *quarantine* results from *generalization*, while *paradise* results from *specialization*. Some arise from *melioration*, which elevates or improves the meaning, like *lady*, some from *pejoration*, which makes it less or worse than what it was, like *quintessence*, and some from *subreption*, which adapts it to a deceptively different use, like *September*. Sometimes it straddles two categories, as with *dean*, which is generalized as regards number of subordinates but specialized as regards their profession. Few words escape such changes, because change of form and meaning is inherent in language. Etymological study works at the level of the individual word, but with reference to more general rules of language change, the basic fact of language.

See BARNHART, BORROWING, CALQUE, CATA-CHRESIS, DERIVATION, ETHNIC NAME, ETY-MOLOGICAL FALLACY, ETYMON, ETYMORPHS, EXTENSION, FOLK ETYMOLOGY, FRENCH, GEN-ERALIZATION, INDO-EUROPEAN, INDO-EUROPEAN ROOTS, LANGUAGE CHANGE, LOAN, LOANWORD, NAME, ONIONS, OXFORD DICTIONARY OF ENGLISH ETYMOLOGY, PARTRIDGE, PERIOD DICTIONARIES OF ENGLISH, PHILOLOGY, RADIATION, REGIONAL DIC-TIONARIES OF ENGLISH, ROOT, SEMANTIC CHANGE, SKEAT, SPECIALIZATION, STEM, SUBREPTION, USAGE, WORD ORIGINS. [HISTORY, LANGUAGE, WORD].   W.F.B., T.MCA.

Barnhart, Robert K. (ed.). 1987. *The Barnhart Dictionary of Etymology*. New York: H. W. Wilson.
Heller, Louis, Humez, Alexander, & Dror, Malcah. 1984. *The Private Lives of English Words*. London: Routledge & Kegan Paul.
Hendrickson, Robert. 1987. *The Encyclopedia of Word and Phrase Origins*. New York: Facts on File.
Hoad, T. F. 1986. *Concise Oxford Dictionary of English Etymology*. Oxford: University Press.
Onions, C. T. (ed.). 1966. *The Oxford Dictionary of English Etymology*. Oxford: University Press.
Partridge, Eric. 1958. *Origins: A Short Etymological Dictionary of Modern English*. London: Routledge & Kegan Paul.
Ross, A. S. C. 1958. *Etymology*. London: Deutsch.
Skeat, Walter W. 1879-82. *Etymological Dictionary of the English Language*. Oxford: Clarendon Press.

ETYMON [16c: through Latin from Greek *étumon* essential meaning, from *étumos* true, actual. Plurals *etyma*, *etymons*]. (1) In the theory of language of the Stoic philosophers of ancient Greece, the true original form of which a current word is the degenerate descendant. (2) In philology, the earliest traceable form from which a later word is derived: for example, *rex/regis* (king) is the Latin etymon of English *regal*, while the Indo-European verbal root **reg-* (to move in a straight line, lead, rule) is the etymon of *rex/regis*, of Sanskrit *rājā*, and of the suffix *-ric* in *bishopric*. See ETYMOLOGY, INDO-EUROPEAN ROOTS, NOTATION, ROOT, ROOT-WORD. [HISTORY, LANGUAGE, WORD].   T.MCA.

ETYMORPHS [1989: a blend of *etymo(logy)* and *morph(ology)*]. A word game devised by the Australian writer and language teacher Ruth Wajnryb, a regular feature of the journal *English Today*. In it, a series of rare words is listed, each with four multiple-choice definitions and etymologies, only one of which is correct. For example, *ylem* is:

a ( ) The original matter from which the basic elements of the universe were formed after the Big Bang (Middle English from Greek *hyle*, wood, matter).

b ( ) Any of various kinds of hardwood used for props in mines, supports for jetties, piles, foundations, etc. (Old French from Greek *hylema*, hardwood).

c ( ) An acronym for Yankee Loyalists of Eastern Missouri, used during the US Civil War and still a term of abuse in some of the southern states (compare *wog*, short for 'worker on government service').

d ( ) A grey, green, or blue mineral consisting of aluminium silicate in triclinic crystalline form (named after the town of Ylem in Czechoslovakia).

The answer is (a). See CALL MY BLUFF, READER'S DIGEST, WORD GAME. [WORD].   T.MCA.

EULOGY [16c: from Latin *eulogium*, apparently a blend of *elogium* an inscription (on a tomb) and *eulogia*, from Greek *eulogía* praise]. A discourse in praise of a person living or dead; an oration at a funeral or memorial service. Milton's eulogistic sonnet 'To the Lord General Cromwell' (1652) celebrates a living hero: 'Cromwell, our chief of men, who through a cloud / Not of war only, but detractions rude, /

Guided by faith and matchless fortitude / To peace and truth thy glorious way hast ploughed.' Compare EPITAPH. [LITERATURE].   R.C.

EUPHEMISM [17c: from Greek *euphēmismós* speaking well (of something or someone)]. In rhetoric, (the use of) a mild, comforting, or evasive expression that takes the place of one that is taboo, negative, offensive, or too direct: *Gosh* God, *terminate* kill, *sleep with* have sex with, *pass water*, *relieve oneself* urinate. Official euphemism can prompt wry or rueful comment: 'To an observer of languages, it is interesting to note the new signification of the word *disperse*: that when a Black girl of fifteen is shot down she is said to be *dispersed*' (in *The Australian Race*, Melbourne, 1887, referring to an event in 1880). Official euphemisms can be circuitous and formulaic, as in the British announcement *a man is helping the police with their inquiries*, meaning 'a man has been detained by the police and may soon be charged'.

Arbiters of usage are generally severe on euphemism. Ronald Ridout and Clifford Witting in the UK (*The Facts of English*, 1964) claim that people 'commit a euphemism' when trying to hide something unpleasant, or when using a mild and indirect term: 'It is prudery or a false sense of refinement that causes us to use *paying guest* for *boarder* or *lodger*.' Fowler (*Modern English Usage*, ed. Gowers, 1965) notes: 'Its value is notorious in totalitarian countries, where assassination and aggression can be made to look respectable by calling them *liquidation* and *liberation*.' The US critic Joseph T. Shipley (*Dictionary of World Literary Terms*, 1977) considers euphemism 'the bane of much writing in the 20th c., esp. in the jargon language of sociologists, educationists and bureaucrats'. The US journalist Hugh Rawson, however, responds to euphemism as 'society's basic *lingua non franca* . . . outward and visible signs of our inward anxieties, conflicts, fears, and shames', and adds:

They cover up the facts of life—of sex and reproduction and excretion—which inevitably remind even the most refined people that they are made of clay, or worse. They are beloved by individuals and institutions (governments especially) who are anxious to present only the handsomest possible images of themselves to the world. And they are embedded so deeply in our language that few of us, even those who pride themselves on being plainspoken, ever get through a day without using them (*A Dictionary of Euphemisms*, below).

Because of its genteel associations, the term has itself been used euphemistically. In Edward Albee's *Who's Afraid of Virginia Woolf?* (1964), a guest has said that she would like to *powder her nose*. George responds with: 'Martha, won't you show her where we keep the euphemism?'

See ABUSE, CACOPHEMISM, DOUBLESPEAK, DYSPHEMISM, FIGURATIVE LANGUAGE/USAGE, GENTEELISM, -ISM, JARGON, MINCED OATH, NICENELLYISM. [STYLE].   T.MCA.

Allan, Keith, & Burridge, Kate. 1991. *Euphemism and Dysphemism*. New York: Oxford University Press.
Enright, D. J. 1985. *Fair of Speech: The Uses of Euphemism*. Oxford: University Press.
Holder, R. W. 1987. *A Dictionary of American and British Euphemisms*. Bath: University Press.
Rawson, Hugh. 1981. *A Dictionary of Euphemisms & Other Doubletalk*. New York: Crown.

EUPHONY [17c: from French *euphonie*, Latin *euphonia*, Greek *euphōnía* sounding good]. A pleasant, harmonious quality in speech. The perception of such a quality is partly physiological (soft, flowing, blending sounds are generally considered pleasanter than harsh, jangling, discordant sounds) and partly cultural (people tend to like sounds that they have been led to like). In English, euphony is often associated with long vowels, the semi-vowels or glides /j, w/, and the consonants /l, m, n, r/. All of these occur in the opening verse of Gray's 'Elegy Written in a Country Church-Yard' (1751):

The Curfew tolls the knell of parting day,
The lowing herd winds slowly o'er the lea,
The plowman homeward plods his weary way,
And leaves the world to darkness and to me.

Euphony can be achieved through the skilled use of a language's rhythms and patterns together with positive associations shared by performer and audience. These associations may relate to sound (preferred voice qualities and accents), allusion (oblique references to favoured or familiar poems, songs, etc.), and experience (bringing in positive images like spring, morning, youth, hope, love, and dreams). There may be agreement that X is *euphonious* and Y *cacophonous*, but people may differ as to just how and why this is so. Euphony in the sense of a greater ease in saying and hearing sounds has been cited as important in grammar and word-formation: as the reason for *an apple* rather than *a apple*, *Aren't I?* and not *Amn't I?*, *tobacconist* and not *tobaccoist*, *impossible* rather than *inpossible* or *unpossible*, and *calculable* rather than *calculatable*. In matters of this kind, however, analogy, convention, and phonology appear to be more significant factors. See (A)ESTHETICS. [SPEECH, STYLE].   T.MCA.

EUPHUISM [16c: from *Euphues*, the name of the hero of two prose romances by John Lyly, applied in 1589 to Lyly's style by the classicist Gabriel Harvey; from Greek *euphués* well-grown, fertile]. An ornate prose style, filled with classical and Biblical allusions, and rhetorical figures. Shakespeare emulated it in *A Comedy of*

Errors and parodied it in *1 Henry IV* (2. 5). In the following excerpt, Falstaff (Sir John Oldcastle) defends himself by pretending to be Prince Hal speaking on his (Falstaff's) behalf to the king:

But to say I knowe more harme in him then in myself, were to say more then I know: that he is olde the more the pittie, his white haires doe witnesse it, but that he is sauing your reuerence, a whoremaster, that I vtterlie denie: if sacke and sugar be a fault, God helpe the wicked; if to be olde and merry be a sin, then many an old host that I know is damnd: if to be fat be to be hated, then Pharaos leane kine are to be loued. No my good lord banish Haruey, banish Rossill, banish Poines, but for sweet Iacke Olde-castle, kinde Iacke Olde-castle, true Iacke Olde-castle, valiant Iacke Olde-castle, & therfore more valiant being as he is old Iacke Olde-castle,

Banish not him thy Harries companie,
Banish not him thy Harries companie,
Banish plumpe Iacke, and banish all the world.

Scott parodied the style through Sir Piercie Shafton in *The Monastery* (1820). Similar styles emerged at roughly the same time in other parts of Europe: for example, *Gongorism*, the style of the 17c Spanish poet Luis de Góngora y Argote. See AUREATE DICTION, HOLOFERNES, LYLY, PROSE. [STYLE, WRITING]. T.MCA.

EURALEX. See EUROPEAN ASSOCIATION FOR LEXICOGRAPHY.

EURASIAN [1830s: a blend of *European* and *Asian*]. (1) Relating to *Eurasia* (Europe and Asia together). Both terms are currently in vogue as a means of discussing the territories of the former Soviet Union: 'The evolution of a post-Soviet military establishment in Eurasia will mirror the redistribution of power among the former republics' (Igor Malashenko, 'The Eurasian Security Order' *Time*, 3 Feb. 1992); 'Eurasia is a challenging horse to ride. Gorbachev's business was to relax the reins, Yeltsin's is to pick them up' (Mark Frankland, 'Yeltsin sits astride Eurasia's wild horse', *Observer*, 2 Feb. 1992). (2) Of mixed European and Asian descent; a person of such descent. See ANGLO-INDIAN, BURGHER ENGLISH, EAST INDIAN, RACISM. Compare MESTIZO, MÉTIS, MULATTO. [ASIA, EUROPE, NAME]. T.MCA.

EURO- [1950s: a clipping of *European*]. A combining form for both (*Western*) *European* and the *European Community*: 'I hope *The European* will report the development of Europe in plain, unvarnished terms shorn of the Euro-jargon which so bedevils understanding' (Margaret Thatcher, in the first issue of *The European*, 11–13 May 1990); *Eurobonds go Euro-bust*, *Euro green year*, *Euro jobless figures* (headlines); *Euroforum* (the magazine of the European Commission in Brussels); *Eurobabble*, *EuroComm* *'88*, *Euro Disneyland*, *Eurodollar*, *Euro jungle*, *Euro-kids*, *Eurosclerosis*, *Euro-slang*, *Eurotunnel*, *Euroyen*. Word-play includes: *Eurocrat* a European bureaucrat, *Europhoria* European euphoria, *Europhonia* a scheme for a euphoniously multilingual Europe, *Eureka* the European Research Co-ordination Agency. The variant *Eur-* sometimes occurs: *Eurasia* the name of the combined land mass of Europe and Asia. See EUROCENTRIC, EUROSPEAK. [EUROPE, NAME].

T.MCA.

EUROCENTRIC [1960s]. Centred on Europe and its culture, languages, etc.: 'Precisely how an "Afrocentric and Latinocentric" approach to history would improve upon a Eurocentric one is unclear' (Jonathan Yardley, 'Temper This Eurocentrism', *Washington Post*, Apr. 1989). See CENTRICITY. [EUROPE, NAME]. T.MCA.

EUROCERT. See EDUCATIONAL TESTING SERVICE.

EURODICAUTOM, full title *European Automatic Dictionary*. A multilingual terminological database established in the late 1970s by the language and computer services of the European Community in Brussels, Luxembourg, and Strasbourg. Conceived as a workstation aid to EC translators, it is also offered on-line to other users. The term bank provides continuously updated information on technical terms and abbreviations (currently 430,000 and 110,000 respectively), including equivalents among the nine official languages. [EUROPE, LANGUAGE, REFERENCE]. R.H.

EUROLISH. See EUROSPEAK.

EUROPE [From Latin *Europa*, Greek *Eurōpē* name of a maiden carried west from Asia by the god Zeus]. A continent of the northern hemisphere, whose largest offshore islands are Britain, Ireland, and Iceland. Including the European states of the former USSR, the continent occupies 8% of the earth's surface and supports 25% of its population. The British generally refer to the mainland as both *Europe* and *the Continent*, a practice also occasionally adopted by Americans:

Averaged out over the population as a whole, the British adult receives some five items of direct mail each month—just half the average in Europe, and a mere one-tenth of what floods through the average US letterbox' (Alexander Garrett, 'Direct Mail: "To bin or not to bin" ', *Observer*, 28 Oct. 1990).

'I've just been in Europe.' The British still catch each other saying it when they get back from France or Germany—implying that their own country still does not belong to the same continent. (Anthony Sampson, *Newsweek*, 4 Dec. 1989).

Yet there is a residual hostility to Europe as well. It is English; the Scots and Irish have always had European ties and alliances. This is perhaps one reason the English fear Europe and the Europeans. (William Pfaff, 'Britain: Nearer the Edge in Tomorrow's EC?', Los Angeles Times Syndicate, Nov. 1989).

The terms *Europe* and *European* are often ambiguous. They may refer to all of Europe, the European Community, the mainland without the British Isles, or the mainland European Community without Britain (and perhaps the Irish Republic), as in the phrase *going into Europe*. Compare AMERICAN¹, ENGLISH (AMBIGUITY). [GEOGRAPHY, NAME].   T.MCA.

The Europe theme

A–B. ABERCROMBIE, ACCENT BAR, ADDISON, AELFRIC, AITKEN'S LAW, AITKEN'S VOWEL, ALBA, ALBION, ALFRED, AMERICAN ENGLISH AND BRITISH ENGLISH, ANGLES, ANGLIA, ANGLIAN, ANGLIC, ANGLICISM, ANGLICIST, ANGLICIZE, ANGLIFY, ANGLO, ANGLO-, ANGLO-AMERICAN, ANGLO-CANADIAN, ANGLO-CELTIC, ANGLOCENTRIC, ANGLO-DANISH, ANGLO-ENGLISH, ANGLO-FRISIAN, ANGLO-GAELIC, ANGLO-INDIAN, ANGLO-IRISH, ANGLO-IRISH LITERATURE, ANGLOMANIA, ANGLO-NORMAN, ANGLOPHILE, ANGLOPHOBE, ANGLO-SAXON, ANGLO-SAXON CHRONICLE, ARNOLD (M.), ARNOLD (T.), ARYAN, ATLANTIC, AUGUSTAN, AUNTIE (BEEB), AUSTEN, BARNES, BBC, BBC ENGLISH¹, BBC ENGLISH², BBC ENGLISH³, BBC PRONUNCIATION UNIT, BBC PUBLICATIONS, BEDE, BELFAST, BEOWULF, BERLITZ, BIRMINGHAM, BLACK, BLACK CELT, BLACK ENGLISH, BLACK IRISH, BLAIR, BLARNEY, BORROWING, BOSWELL, BRADLEY, BRETON, BRIDGES, BRIT, BRIT-, BRITAIN, BRITANNIA, BRITICISM/BRITISHISM, BRITISH, BRITISH ASSOCIATION OF STATES COLLEGES IN ENGLISH LANGUAGE TEACHING, BRITISH BLACK ENGLISH, BRITISH BROADCASTING, BRITISH COUNCIL, BRITISH EMPIRE, BRITISH ENGLISH, BRITISHER, BRITISH ISLES, BRITISH LANGUAGE, BRITISH LANGUAGES, BRITISH LIBRARY, BRITISH NATIONAL CORPUS, BRITO-, BRITOCENTRIC, BRITON, BRITTANY, BROAD SCOTS, BROGUE, BRONTË SISTERS, BRYTHONIC, BURGESS, BURNS, BUTLER.

C–D. CALEDONIA, CAMBRIDGE SYNDICATE, CAMBRIDGE UNIVERSITY PRESS, CAMDEN, CARLYLE, CARROLL, CAWDREY, CAXTON, CELT, CELTIC, CELTIC FRINGE, CELTICISM, CELTIC LANGUAGES, CELTIC TWILIGHT, CHAMBERS, CHANCERY STANDARD, CHANNEL ISLANDS, CHAUCER, CHURCHILL, CLASSIC, CLASSICAL, CLASSICAL LANGUAGE, CLASSICISM, COBBETT, COLERIDGE (H.), COLERIDGE (S.), COLLINS, COMMONWEALTH, COMMONWEALTH LITERATURE, CONCISE OXFORD DICTIONARY, CONCISE SCOTS DICTIONARY, CONRAD, COOPER, CORNISH, CORNWALL, COUNCIL OF EUROPE (LANGUAGES PROJECT), COVERDALE, CRAIGIE, CRANMER, CUMBRIA, CUMBRIC, DANELAW, DANISH, DEFOE, DIALECT IN ENGLAND, DIALECT IN IRELAND, DIALECT IN SCOTLAND, DIALECT IN WALES, DIASPORA, DICKENS, DICTIONARY OF MODERN ENGLISH USAGE, DICTIONARY OF SLANG AND UNCONVENTIONAL ENGLISH, DICTIONARY OF THE OLDER SCOTTISH TONGUE, DICTIONARY RESEARCH CENTRE, DORIC, DORSET, DRYDEN, DUBLIN, DUTCH.

E–H. EAST ANGLIA, EDINBURGH, ELIOT, ELIZABETHAN, ELLIS, ELYOT, ENGLISH, ENGLISH ASSOCIATION, ENGLISH DIALECT DICTIONARY, ENGLISH DIALECT SOCIETY, ENGLISH ENGLISH, ENGLISH IN ENGLAND, ENGLISHMAN/WOMAN, ENGLISHRY, ENGLISH-SPEAKING UNION, ENGLISH TODAY, ENGLISH WORLD-WIDE, ENGLISHY, ERIN, ERSE, ESPERANTO, ETHNIC NAME, EURALEX, EURASIAN, EURO-, EUROCENTRIC, EUROCERT, EURODICAUTOM, EUROPE, EUROPEAN (THE), EUROPEAN COMMUNITY, EUROPEAN FREE TRADE ASSOCIATION, EUROPEAN LANGUAGES, EUROSPEAK, EXAMINING IN ENGLISH, FABER, FACTS ON FILE, FA(E)ROESE, FIELDING, FLANDERS, FLEMISH, FOWLER, FRAMEWORK PROJECT, FRANGLAIS, FRENCH, FRISIAN, FURNIVALL, GAEL, GAELDOM, GAELICISM, GAELTACHT, GENERAL SERVICE LIST, GERMAN, GERMANIC LANGUAGES, GIBRALTAR, GLASGOW, GOTHIC, GOWERS, GREAT BRITAIN, GREEK, GREEK LITERATURE, GUTTER SCOTS, HALLIDAY, HARDY, HAZLITT, HEPTARCHY, HIBERNIA, HIBERNIANISM, HIBERNICISM, HIBERNO-, HIBERNO-ENGLISH, HIGHLAND ENGLISH, HOME, HOME COUNTIES, HORNBY, HOUSE STYLE.

I–M. IATEFL, IBERIAN LANGUAGES, INDO-BRITISH, INDO-EUROPEAN LANGUAGES, INDO-EUROPEAN ROOTS, INDO-GERMANIC, INGLIS, INGVAEONIC, INSTITUTE OF LINGUISTS, INTERNATIONAL ASSOCIATION OF TEACHERS OF ENGLISH AS A FOREIGN LANGUAGE, IRELAND, IRISH, IRISH BROADCASTING, IRISH BULL, IRISH ENGLISH, IRISHISM, IRISH JOKE, IRISHMAN/WOMAN, IRISH PRESS, IRISH PUBLISHING, IRISHRY, ISLE OF MAN, ITALIAN, ITANGLIANO, JACOBEAN, JAMIESON, JENNINGS, JESPERSEN, JEWISH ENGLISH, JEWISH LANGUAGES, JOHN BULL, JOHNSON, JOINT MATRICULATION BOARD, JONES (D.), JONES (W.), JONSON, JOYCE, JUTES, KENSINGTON, KENTISH, KERSEY, KINGMAN REPORT, KING'S ENGLISH, KING'S ENGLISH (THE), KING'S SCOTS, KIPLING, LALLANS, LAMB, LANCASHIRE, LATIN¹, LATIN², LATIN LITERATURE, LAW FRENCH, LAWRENCE, LEAVIS, LIEBER, LIMERICK, LINGUISTIC ATLAS, LINGUISTIC ATLAS OF ENGLAND, LINGUISTIC SURVEY OF SCOTLAND, LONDON, LONDON CHAMBER OF COMMERCE AND INDUSTRY, LONGMAN, LORIMER, LOWTH, LYLY, MACAULAY, MACDIARMID, MACMILLAN, McWORD, MAGAZINE, MALTA, MANX, MERCIA, MID-ATLANTIC, MIDDLE ENGLISH, MIDLANDS, MILTON, MORNINGSIDE AND KELVINSIDE, MULCASTER, MUMMERSET, MURISON, MURRAY.

N–R. NATE, NATECLA, NATIONAL ASSOCIATION FOR THE TEACHING OF ENGLISH, NATIONAL ASSOCIATION OF TEACHERS OF ENGLISH AS A COMMUNITY LANGUAGE, NEWBOLT REPORT, NORMAN FRENCH, NORN, NORSE, NORTH COUNTRY, NORTHERN ENGLISH, NORTHERN IRELAND, NORTHERN IRISH ENGLISH, NORTHERN ISLES, NORTHUMBRIA, NORWEGIAN, NOVEL, OLD COUNTRY, OLD ENGLISH¹, OLD ENGLISH², ONIONS, ORCADIAN, ORKNEY, ORKNEY AND SHETLAND DIALECTS, ORTON, ORWELL, OXBRIDGE, OXFORD ACCENT, OXFORD AND CAMBRIDGE SCHOOLS EXAMINATION BOARD, OXFORD DELEGACY, OXFORD DICTIONARIES, OXFORD ENGLISH, OXFORD ENGLISH DICTIONARY, OXFORD UNIVERSITY PRESS, PALE, PALMER, PARTRIDGE, PASSY, PATTER, PENGUIN, PHILOLOGICAL SOCIETY, PICT, PICTISH, PIOZZI (THRALE), PITMAN (I.), PITMAN (J.), PITMAN PUBLISHING, PLAID CYMRU, PLAIN ENGLISH (CAMPAIGN), POET LAUREATE, POLARI, POPE, PORTUGUESE, POTTER, PROTESTANT ASCENDANCY, PUBLIC SCHOOL ENGLISH, PUBLIC SCHOOL PRONUNCIATION, PUNCH, PUTTENHAM, QUEEN'S ENGLISH

SOCIETY, QUILLER-COUCH, QUIRK, RACISM,
REFORMATION, RENAISSANCE, RESTORATION, RICHARDS,
RICHARDSON, ROGET, ROMANI/ROMANY.

   S–Z. SCANDINAVIAN LANGUAGES, SCOT, SCOTCH,
SCOTCH-IRISH, SCOTIA, SCOTLAND, SCOTS, SCOTS
LANGUAGE ORGANIZATIONS, SCOTS LITERATURE,
SCOTSMAN/WOMAN, SCOTT, SCOTTICISM, SCOTTISH,
SCOTTISH DICTIONARIES, SCOTTISH ENGLISH, SCOTTISH
GAELIC, SCOTTISH JOKE, SCOTTISH LANGUAGES, SCOTTISH
LITERATURE, SCOTTISH PLACE-NAMES, SCOTTISH
PUBLISHING, SCOUSE, SHAKESPEARE, SHAW, SHELTA,
SHERIDAN (R.), SHERIDAN (T.), SHETLAND, SHETLANDIC,
SHETLAND NORN, SIDNEY, SKEAT, SLAVONIC LANGUAGES,
SLOANE RANGER, SMOLLETT, SOMERSET, SOUTHRON,
SPANISH, SPENSER, STANDARD BRITISH ENGLISH,
STANDARD ENGLISH ENGLISH, STEELE, STERNE,
STEVENSON, STRANG, STREVENS, SURVEY OF ENGLISH
DIALECTS, SURVEY OF ENGLISH USAGE, SURVEY OF
SPOKEN ENGLISH, SWEDISH, SWEET, SWIFT, TENNYSON,
TESD, TESL, THOMAS, TIMES (THE), TRENCH, TYNDALE,
UCLES, ULSTER, ULSTER ENGLISH, ULSTERMAN/WOMAN,
ULSTER SCOTS, UNIT CREDIT, UNITED KINGDOM,
VICTORIAN, WALES, WALIAN, WATSON, WEEKLEY, WELLS,
WELSH, WELSH ENGLISH, WELSH LANGUAGE SOCIETY,
WELSHNESS, WELSHRY, WELSH WALES, WELSHY, WESSEX,
WEST COUNTRY, WILDE, WILD IRISH, WILSON, WHITE
ENGLISH, WOLLSTONECRAFT, WOOLF, WORDSWORTH,
WRENN, WRIGHT, WYCLIF(FE), WYLD, YIDDISH, YOLA,
YORKSHIRE, ZETLAND, ZETLANDIC.

EUROPEAN, The, full form *The European: Europe's First National Newspaper*. A weekly English-language broadsheet newspaper founded in 1990, based in London, 50% in full colour, and aimed at a pan-European readership. Its founding publisher and editor-in-chief was the media tycoon Robert Maxwell, a British national of Czech origin; its first editor was Ian Watson, a Scot; and its staff and contributors are drawn from throughout the continent. After Maxwell's death in 1991, the newspaper was sold in early 1992 to the shipping and property magnate brothers, David and Frederick Barclay. Compare INTERNATIONAL HERALD TRIBUNE. [EUROPE, MEDIA].   T.MCA.

EUROPEAN ASSOCIATION FOR LEXICOGRAPHY, short form *EURALEX*. An association founded in 1983 to promote scholarly and professional activities related to lexicography. It holds an annual conference, publishes a *Bulletin*, and supports the *International Journal of Lexicography* (Oxford University Press) and *Lexicographica* (*International Annual* and *Series Maior*, Tübingen, Germany). Compare DICTIONARY SOCIETY OF NORTH AMERICA. [EUROPE, REFERENCE].   R.H.

EUROPEAN COMMUNITY, also **European Economic Community**. Short forms *EC*, *EEC*, *Europe*. An association of European countries, 12 in number in 1990: Belgium, Denmark, France, Germany, Greece, the Irish Republic, Italy, Luxembourg, the Netherlands, Portugal, Spain, and the United Kingdom. Its headquarters is in Brussels in Belgium, its Parliament mainly in Strasbourg, northern France, with some central institutions in Luxembourg. Its official working languages are English and French, and its official languages Danish, Dutch, English, French, German, Greek, Italian, Portuguese, and Spanish. All nine are used in EC meetings with simultaneous translation as a matter of course. Official documents must be published in all the official languages. In the period 1982–90, 40m ECUs (European Currency Units) were provided for EUROTRA automatic translation. There are between 30 and 40 minority languages, depending on definition, some of them varieties of official languages (such as Alsatian German in France), some unique (such as Breton in France and Basque in France and Spain). All member countries save Portugal have regional minority languages (such as Gaelic and Welsh in the UK). The *European Bureau for Lesser-Used Languages*, set up in 1982, represents all such languages but not the 'trans-European' minority languages Yiddish and Romany.

   English is increasingly the lingua franca. Representatives of smaller countries, such as Denmark and Greece, often give press conferences in English: 'The Danes are keener to speak English even than the British. . . . The Spanish on the other hand tend to talk French. On political subjects both languages are used in discussions. The French are very concerned to protect their language. But in more technical sectors—telecommunications or research for example—it is overwhelmingly English, as the technical vocabulary has developed on a more global basis' (Michael Berendt, *The Times*, 23 Oct. 1989). In Brussels, many shop signs and service notices are in English, Belgium's largest cash card is called *Mister Cash*, and its airline is officially known as *Sabena, Belgian World Airlines*; its in-flight signs are only in English and its in-flight magazine is mainly in English. In Belgium, a country often disturbed by tensions between speakers of Flemish and French, English is a neutral medium. British television is widely watched along the north-western European coast, and in the Netherlands interviews in English on national television are often not translated.

   While the aim of the Community is harmonization rather than homogenization, there is a strong EC-wide tendency towards greater use of English. Indeed, the results of any drive towards foreign-language learning may strengthen the already most prominent language: English is the first second language in all EC countries, including France. The breakup of the Eastern Bloc in the late 1980s may strengthen the position of German, which is widely used as a lingua franca and trans-European language in Eastern Europe; it is, with some 90m speakers in the region (77m within the EC), the largest single language bloc. At the same time, however, with the opening up of East European countries to the West in the late 1980s and early 1990s there has been a surge in demand for English courses and a decrease of interest in Russian, to the extent that in Hungary, for example, many schoolteachers of Russian are being retrained as teachers of English. [EUROPE, NAME].   T.MCA.

EUROPEAN FREE TRADE ASSOCIATION, short form *EFTA*. A free-trade association of European countries, six in number in 1990: Austria, Finland, Iceland, Norway, Sweden, and Switzerland (and Liechtenstein). Its headquarters are in Geneva, in Switzerland. Within EFTA, each nation retains its own trade policy towards non-members. When the group was formed in 1958, it also included the UK and Portugal, now members of the EC. English is the official language of EFTA, despite the fact that none of its present members has it as a mother tongue. Compare EUROPEAN COMMUNITY. [EUROPE, NAME].   T.MCA.

EUROPEAN LANGUAGES. The languages of Europe, most of which belong to the *Indo-European language family*. Exceptions are *Basque* (spoken around the southern shores of the Bay of Biscay, and apparently unrelated to any other language), and *Hungarian* and *Finnish* (members of the *Finno-Ugric language family*). Although *Turkish* is spoken in European Turkey (west of the Sea of Marmara), it is not usually considered a European language. Pragmatically, the term covers all long-established languages used in Europe, but not yet such immigrant languages of the 20c as *Arabic* in France, *Gujarati* in England, and Turkish in West Germany. Between the late 15c and 20c, many European languages have been carried to many parts of the world through empire-building, colonization, commerce, and Christian missionary work. In this diaspora, colonizing languages such as *Dutch, English, French, Italian, Portuguese, Russian,* and *Spanish* have predominated, but most other European languages have been carried in their wake: *Basque* to the northwestern US, *Scottish Gaelic* to Nova Scotia (Canada), *Ukrainian* to Manitoba (Canada), and *Welsh* to Argentina. English, Portuguese, and Spanish have become the foremost languages of the Americas; English, French, Dutch (in the form of *Afrikaans*), and Portuguese have become major languages of Africa; and English and French have become dominant in Oceania. In Asia, only Russian has succeeded as a settler language, spreading east from the Urals to the Kamchatka Peninsula to the north of Japan; English has been established as an official language of India, first Spanish then English have been important in the Philippines, and English is the primary language of Singapore. See BORROWING, BRETON, CELTIC LANGUAGES, DANISH, ENGLISH, FAROESE, FRISIAN, FRENCH, GAELIC, GEOGRAPHY AND GEOPOLITCS OF ENGLISH, GERMAN, GERMANIC LANGUAGES, GREEK, ICELANDIC, INDO-EUROPEAN, IRISH, ITALIAN, LATIN[1], MALTA, NORSE, NORWEGIAN, PORTUGUESE, ROMANCE LANGUAGES, RUSSIAN, SCANDINAVIAN LANGUAGES, SCOTS, SLAV(ON)IC LANGUAGES, SPANISH, SWEDISH, WELSH, WORLD LANGUAGE. [LANGUAGE].   T.MCA.

EUROSPEAK [1980s]. Also **Eurolish, Minglish**. Generally pejorative or facetious terms for kinds of English used in Continental Europe and especially the European Community: 'And as more and more magazines and newspapers view Europe as home territory, neologisms and borrowed words will undoubtedly emerge—as long as newspapers and magazines don't resort to bland Euro-speak' (*Journalist's Week*, 22 June 1990). See ESPERANTO, EURO-, -GLISH AND -LISH, -SPEAK. [EUROPE, VARIETY].   T.MCA.

EXAGGERATION [16c: from Latin *exaggeratio/exaggerationis* a heaping or piling up]. Presenting something as larger, greater, more important, or more awful than it is. See HYPERBOLE. [STYLE].   T.MCA.

EXAMINING IN ENGLISH. The formal testing of a student's command of English, usually in an educational institution or through a public system of evaluation and certification. Such testing dates from the mid-18c, when three necessary prior conditions had been fulfilled: (1) The standard language was increasingly widely taught in schools and had begun to be used as a vehicle for the testing of all school subjects. (2) A new educational tradition had developed, associated with the manufacturing and mercantile classes of Britain and America, an alternative to traditional Latin-medium or Latin-based education. (3) A network of institutions and administrators had begun to spread: for example, in Britain the Dissenting Academies and the Royal Society of Arts, which was founded in 1754 and conducted examinations in English before 1800.

British examinations. By the mid-19c, public examinations had become necessary for the recruitment of officials and others at home and abroad. In 1858, the report of a Civil Service Commission (set up to consider inefficiencies in the Crimean War and the problems of directly governing India) called for recruitment 'by public competition and not by private patronage' and for the provision of tests by the universities of Oxford and Cambridge of 'the elements of a plain English education'. Two bodies were set up, the *Oxford Delegacy* and the *Cambridge Syndicate*, which remain central to the British tradition of examining by independent bodies. Their establishment lent weight to the existing external examinations of the *University of London*, administered for its own matriculating purposes. In 1903 the *Joint Matriculation Board* and in 1953 the *Associated Examining Board* were added, and the five boards became responsible for officially recognized school-leaving examinations in England. More directly government-sponsored bodies were set up for the same purpose in Ireland, Scotland, and Wales. By the end of the 19c a range of school examinations had been established in Britain and parts of the Empire. These have been developed and refined throughout the 20c, under various names and with various emphases.

Commonwealth examinations. Within the Commonwealth there has been a process of devolution from British control, Australia, Canada, New Zealand, and South Africa having long had their own systems. In territories where English has second-language status the picture is complex. In some areas, links with UK examining boards have been retained, sometimes as the sole system of examination, sometimes alongside new indigenous systems. In India, there is a Council for the *Indian School Certificate Examination*, based on a grouping of English-medium schools and associated with the *Cambridge Overseas School Certificate*. A *West African Examinations Council* conducts school examinations in Ghana, Nigeria, Sierra Leone, and Gambia, in consultation with British boards (Cambridge and London) active in the area. London's influence continues to be strong for private candidates (adults seeking a second chance of education). An *East African Examinations Council* operates in Kenya, Uganda, Zambia, and Zimbabwe, associated with British boards (Cambridge and AEB). The Caribbean area has followed the same pattern, with the *Caribbean Examinations Council* established in consultation with British boards. Single-country examining authorities have been established, at first with British board sponsorship, in Hong Kong with London, and in Singapore and Malaysia with Cambridge. Smaller areas of UK influence, such as Malta, Cyprus, and the River Plate countries of South America, with their high level of second-language use, alternate between British or locally conducted school examinations and British-based EFL examinations such as Cambridge.

American examinations. State control of examining, closely linked to the systematic grading of classes, is a feature of US education that can be traced to the influence of the Enlightenment on the founders of the Republic. Each of the 50 states has its own educational system, of which testing is an integral part. In addition, decisions in many states are made by local school districts, as a result of which few useful generalizations can be made about examining in English for the whole country. Tests used for college admission in many parts of the nation are largely machine-graded, written and scored by such private bodies as the *College Entrance Examination Board* (with the *Scholarly Aptitude Test* or *SAT*), and the *American College Testing Program* (with the *American College Test* or *ACT*). Some students completing a first degree take the *Graduate Record Examination* (*GRE*) offered by *Educational Testing Service* (*ETS*) of Princeton, New Jersey, used by most US universities as one factor in admissions to postgraduate study. There is controversy over these standardized, multiple-choice tests of aptitude and the interpretation of their scores, and they are often said to be culturally biased or easier for those already accustomed to them. Despite such criticisms, they continue to be widely used, as one of a number of factors that include course grades, recommendations from teachers, application essays, and sometimes interviews: testing is less important as a determinant of the future of US students than in some other English-speaking countries.

Other countries. Local arrangements for the achievement and diagnostic testing of English in non-English-speaking countries follow the interests, needs, and resources of each country, varying from sophisticated provision for high levels of performance in northern Europe to more uncertain initiatives elsewhere, often linked with grammar–translation and literature-based approaches. Some countries have experimented in the teaching and testing of their own languages as foreign languages on EFL lines (for example, Swedish and Spanish), and have benefited from the resulting cross-fertilization in terms of local English teaching. Within Europe, the Cambridge examinations have achieved particular significance.

English as a native language. The broad target in examinations of English as a first language is a performance that meets the needs both of practical effectiveness and of conformity with agreed rules of syntax, vocabulary, and orthography, at a level associated with completion of a process of general education: that is, completion of an accredited school curriculum at 16, marked by a certificate that serves as a qualification for employment, vocational or other training, or higher education. The relevance of performance in public examinations to real-life social and communicative needs continues to be a matter of controversy, along with the general role and procedures of examining boards. Public examining has been criticized for institutionalizing an interlocking and educationally sterile system of teaching and testing, for the discouragement of cultural development through wider reading and writing, and for its tendency to concentrate on testable minutiae of vocabulary and usage. For testers, the problem has been one of reconciling the relative importance of the holistic and atomistic elements in a syllabus.

Directly analytical testing of orthography, vocabulary, and syntax has been generally abandoned in the later 20c, on the grounds that it does not predict effective communicative performance. The usual pattern of testing combines a form of global assessment (with a communicative or functional basis) and an objective mode based on reading comprehension. Attempts to maintain a constant standard, though procedurally successful because of the long experience of the boards and the paramount importance of consistency, are deeply affected by such wider issues as the level of tolerance of 'error' in examination scripts and linguistic factors in the teaching of general school subjects: the presentation of information in note form or in a subject-specific register, or in the formal prose associated with the humanities. Such factors have made for considerable uncertainty of aim and procedure in language testing throughout the English-speaking world, with an associated tendency to deflect problems by emphasizing either objectivity (in the narrow fields of usage and the comprehension of texts) or creativity (of a personal kind or in terms of literary appreciation).

English as a second language. One legacy of empire is the problem of variation between locally accepted but not mutually or internationally intelligible forms of English. Such local forms are often assisted by long association with a British-based, or British-developed, school examination structure that has not systematically addressed problems of variation. Second-language users have widely varying aspirations towards quasi-first-language status, with varied effects on linguistic conservatism, first-language influence, and the teaching styles favoured as appropriate and practicable in each area. There is little systematic knowledge of the elements of difference and little motivation to build examination syllabuses on an agreed corpus of these; instead, the assessment of free composition by non-local examiners for a British board remains a standard though uncertain procedure. Organized examining has to date failed to take significantly into account such broad developments as archaism of vocabulary in India and Pakistan, syllable-timing in English as spoken in Africa, and the movement towards the 'legitimization' of Creoles and Black Englishes. Although the pattern of centralized non-local examining is especially British, the problem of integrating second-language pupils and examination candidates into general educational systems is shared by English-speaking countries as a whole, sometimes shading off into wider aspects of sociolinguistic development and sometimes into the more clear-cut area of EFL. Teaching shows the effects of this confusion, as do the availability and content of tests.

English as a foreign language. A number of factors emerged in the 1960s as the basis for improvement in the testing of English as an international language, with its built-in emphasis on efficient communication. The post-war, post-colonial demand for an equalizing lingua franca, serving the needs of an era of unprecedentedly heightened communication, had increased interest in examinations available internationally, with heavy increases in entries and a heightened sense of involvement among teachers. The Cambridge examinations in particular, introduced in 1913 as a small-scale extension of the board's British and overseas school examining, but greatly expanded since 1945, came under critical review, with special emphasis on problems of culture bias in content and assessment, the testing of oral performance, and the general validity and reliability of tests. The Syndicate's links with specialized teaching, through the British Council and newly established university schools of applied linguistics (notably Edinburgh), made possible a research programme that resulted in a remodelling (1975) of the Cambridge syllabus. In this, the relative weighting given to objective/analytical and holistic/impressionistic elements was computer-controlled in a five-paper examination covering reading, writing, listening, and speaking, with such features as task-based composition, active and specific testing (through conversion or transformation exercises) of the candidate's grasp of language patterns, a substantial but contained element of objective testing, and the exclusion of culture-based elements such as literature, translation, and Brito- or Eurocentric texts and situations. The immediate popularity of the new syllabus, available at two established levels (Certificate Proficiency in English and First Certificate English) showed its relevance to international needs and its predictive accuracy, particularly at the lower level. Cambridge's position was further consolidated by the introduction of similarly designed elementary level tests from 1980, a further streamlining of the main CPE and FCE syllabus in 1984, and the taking over of responsibility for both the British Council's *English Language Testing Service* and the Royal College of Arts' range of examination schemes for EFL teachers. A number of other British and non-British examining bodies, of varying status and operational scope, also currently offer English language tests for the foreign learner. In the US, the ETS offers the *Test of English as a Foreign Language* (*TOEFL*), to measure the English-language ability of foreign students seeking admission to American universities.

See ARELS, ASSOCIATED EXAMINING BOARD, BRITISH COUNCIL, CAMBRIDGE CERTIFICATE OF PROFICIENCY IN ENGLISH, CAMBRIDGE FIRST CERTIFICATE, CENTRAL INSTITUTE OF ENGLISH AND FOREIGN LANGUAGES, CURRICULUM, EDUCATIONAL TESTING SERVICE, ELT, ENGLISH-SPEAKING UNION, FRAMEWORK PROJECT, LANGUAGE LEARNING, LANGUAGE TEACHING, TEACHING ENGLISH, TEFL, TEIL, TESD, TESL, UCLES. [AFRICA, AMERICAS, ASIA, EDUCATION, EUROPE, HISTORY, OCEANIA]. W.S.

EXCLAMATION [14c: through French from Latin *exclamatio/exclamationis* crying out]. (1) A sentence that conveys a strong emotion: *Please leave me alone!* (2) Also *exclamatory sentence*. A type of sentence, often verbless, that begins with *what* or *how* (followed by a noun phrase): *What courage! What a meal that was! How marvellous! How well they played!* See EXCLAMATION MARK/POINT, SENTENCE. [GRAMMAR]. S.G., T.MCA.

EXCLAMATION MARK, also AmE **exclamation point**. The punctuation mark (!). Its primary use is to show that a preceding word, phrase, or sentence is an exclamation or strong assertion: *Of course!*; *No!*; *I won't do it!*; *Yes, you are!* It indicates various emotions conveyed in the substance of the statement, such as surprise, disbelief, or dismay (*You're joking!*; *What a silly way to behave!*), wonder or admiration (*What a good idea!*; *Aren't they beautiful!*), personal feeling (*I love you!*; *I hate them!*); and pain or suffering (*Ouch!*; *I'm so miserable!*). It also indicates an instruction or command (*Go away!*; *Left turn!*). It is sometimes repeated in informal usage to express a specially strong exclamation (*What nonsense!!*) or added to a question mark to indicate a mixture of questioning and surprise, anger, etc. (*Did you say the house was tidy?!*). It is also used in round brackets/parentheses, as a kind of aside, to denote surprise or reserve about, or dissent from, what is stated: *They told us about the beauty(!) of the place*. See EXCLAMATION, PUNCTUATION. [WRITING]. R.E.A.

EXISTENTIAL SENTENCE. A sentence stating that something exists, usually consisting of *there*, the verb *be*, and an indefinite noun phrase: *There's a tavern in the town, There is hope for this mad world, There must be somebody we can ask*. Where more information follows (as in *There was an old woman who lived in a shoe, who had . . .*), *there* can be dispensed with (*An old woman lived in a shoe, who had . . .*). When *there* is used like this, as a prop subject, the newness of the information in the sentence is emphasized. That *there* is subject-like is shown by its use in question tags: *There's no problem, is there?* Existential *there*-sentences can also occur with some other verbs: *There came a big spider, and sat down beside her*; *There then began a time of great fear*. [GRAMMAR]. S.C.

EXONORMATIVE. See CENTRICITY, NORMATIVE.

EXPLETIVE [17c: from Latin *expletivus* serving to fill out, from *explere/expletum* to fill out]. (1) Originally, an expression used to fill out a line of verse or a sentence, without adding anything to the sense. (2) An interjected word, especially an oath or swearword. At the time of the Watergate hearings in the US in the 1970s, during the presidency of Richard Nixon, the phrase *expletive deleted* occurred frequently in the transcript of the White House tapes. The connection between original and derived meaning is caught in the *Longman Dictionary of Contemporary English* (1987), explaining the expletive use of *fucking* as an adjective in *I got my fucking foot caught in the fucking door*: it is 'used as an almost meaningless addition to speech'. Here, it is meaningless at the level of ideas but hardly at the level of emotion. See INFIX, SWEARING. [STYLE, USAGE]. R.F.I.

EXPLICATION DE TEXTE [French: textual explanation]. A term in literary theory for the close study and exposition of a text, paying attention to content, style, language, symbolism, and the relationships of part to whole. Compare CLOSE READING. [LITERATURE]. T.MCA.

EXPRESSION [15c: from Latin *expressio/expressionis*, a pressing out. Compare IMPRESSION, PRESS]. (1) The act, process, etc. of using language or some other medium of communication: *the expression of opinions*; *self-expression*. (2) An inclusive term for a word, phrase, form of words, idiom, usage, etc.: *archaic expressions in poetry*. [LANGUAGE]. T.MCA.

EXTENSION. See FIGURATIVE EXTENSION, SEMANTIC CHANGE.

EYE DIALECT [1925: first used in print by George P. Krapp, *The English Language in America*]. A term for how colloquial usage appears in print; spellings in which 'the convention violated is one of the eyes, not of the ear' (Krapp). Thus, spellings like *enuff* enough, *wimmin* women, *animulz* animals, indicate that those represented as using them are uneducated, youthful, rustic, or otherwise unlike the readership. In Krapp's definition, dialect writers use eye dialect not 'to indicate a genuine difference of pronunciation, but the spelling is merely a friendly nudge to the reader, a knowing look which establishes a sympathetic sense of superiority between the author and reader as contrasted with the humble speaker of dialect'. The term is sometimes extended to include both 'dialect' spellings and spellings based on pronunciation in a variety of English, as with *Kanajan* Canadian, *Murrican* American, *Strine* Australian. Many users, however, limit it to ' "spelling errors" that in fact reflect no distinctive phonological, lexical, or syntactic structure whatsoever' (Elizabeth C. Traugott & Mary L. Pratt, *Linguistics for Students of Literature*, 1980). Eye dialect is an important element in humorous dictionaries and glossaries which poke fun at varieties of English: *Awreddy* already (*Eh, Goondu!*, Singapore, 1982), *Baked Necks* bacon and eggs (*Lets Stalk Strine*, Australia, 1965), *Fairy Nuff* fair enough (*Bristle with Pride*, Bristol, England, 1987), *pannyhos* pantihose (*More How to Speak Southern*, US, 1980), *yidownsay* you don't say (*Ah Big Yaws*, South Africa, 1973). See DIALECT, HOBSON-JOBSONISM, KING'S ENGLISH, SPELLING. [STYLE, VARIETY, WRITING].   R.W.B.

EYE RHYME. In verse, the correspondence of written vowels and following consonants which may look as though they rhyme, but do not represent identical sounds, as in *move/love, speak/break*. Eye rhyme may be deliberate, but often results from a changed pronunciation in one of two words which once made a perfect rhyme, or rhyme in a non-standard variety of English, as in these lines by the Scottish general James Graham, Marquis of Montrose (1649): 'I'll tune thy elegies to trumpet *sounds*, / And write thy epitaph in blood and *wounds*.' In Scots, both italicized words have the same 'oo' sound. See RHYME. [LITERATURE].   R.C., T.MCA.

F

F, f [Called 'eff']. The 6th letter of the Roman alphabet as used for English. It originated in the Phoenician symbol *waw*, a vertical line forking at the top like *Y*, which was adapted by the Greeks into two letters: *F* (digamma: 'double gamma'), which represented the sound /w/, and *Y* (upsilon), which represented /u/. *Waw* was also the ancestor of *U, V, W*. *Digamma* was lost in classical Greek, which used *Φ* (phi) first for aspirated /p/, later for /f/. The Etruscans, then the Romans, gave *F* the value it has today in English: the voiceless labio-dental fricative, which has *V* as its voiced equivalent. In Old English, however, *f* was used for both voiceless and voiced consonants. Formerly, *of* was not distinguished in spelling from *off*: the *f* was voiced when the syllable containing it was unstressed, and voiceless when stressed, until the two came to be distinguished (*c.*16c) in spelling and meaning as *off/of*, the latter retaining the sound /v/. In ScoE, *of* and *off* are often homophones, both pronounced with /f/.

F/V alternation. There is sometimes an alternation between *f* and *v* in grammatically or etymologically related words. For example, the following nouns have singular *-f(e)*, plural *-ves*: *calf, elf, half, knife, leaf, life, loaf, self, sheaf, shelf, thief, wife, wolf*. In some cases, the plural may be either *-fs* or *-ves*: *dwarfs/dwarves, hoofs/hooves*. So engrained is the tendency to *f/v* alternation that *handkerchiefs, roofs* are often pronounced with /v/. Verbs from such nouns have *f* or *v*, but do not vary when inflected: *to knife/knifed, to halve/halved*. Other examples of *v/f* alternation include *believe/belief, leave/left, strive/strife, five/fifth, twelve/twelfth*. The *f/v* distinction in *fox/vixen* arises from the different dialects from which the words have been taken.

Double F. (1) Except in *if, of* and some loanwords, *f* is doubled in syllable-final position immediately after a single vowel letter that is pronounced short: *waffle, piffle, bailiff, cliff, scoff, stuff*. Single *f* occurs otherwise: *deaf, elf, beef, belief, dwarf, golf, loaf*. (2) There is doubling between vowels, especially to show the assimilation of the Latin prefixes *ad-, ob-, sub-*, as in *affair, offer, suffer*. An anomaly is single *f* in *afraid*, despite *ff* in the related *affray*.

F, GH, and PH. (1) In some common words, the digraph *gh* represents /f/: *cough, enough, laugh, rough, tough*. AmE does not make the BrE distinction between *draught/draft*, having *draft* for both. In BrE, a *draftsman* draws up the wording of documents and a *draughtsman* prepares technical drawings. See G. (2) The digraph *ph* represents /f/, generally in words of Greek origin: *photograph, philosophy*. See P. *F* has, however, varied historically with *ph* in some words: for example, with the revival of Greek learning in the 16c, *fantasy* began to be written *phantasy*, but in the 20c has reverted to *f*. Occasionally, words not derived from Greek have acquired *ph* in place of *f: nephew* was once written with both *f* and *v*. AmE *sulfur* retains the original Latin form, whereas BrE has *sulphur*; the AmE form is increasingly used internationally, as for example by pure and applied chemists. In commerce, a standard *ph* may be replaced by *f* in a trade name or for special effect, or both as with *fotopost* and *freefone*. See ALPHABET, LETTER[1], P, SPELLING. [WRITING].   C.U.

FABER. An English publishing company noted for its poetry, fiction, and drama. Faber & Gwyer was founded by Geoffrey Faber in 1925, with T. S. Eliot among the original working directors. Faber's list incorporated the books of The Scientific Press, a nursing publisher dating from 1892, of which he was briefly chairman. In 1929, the company was renamed Faber & Faber, and Eliot remained on the board until his death

THE CAPITAL LETTER						THE SMALL LETTER				
EARLY FORMS				CURRENT FORMS		EARLY FORMS			CURRENT FORMS	
Phoenician	Greek	Etruscan	Roman (Latin)	roman	italic	Roman cursive	Roman uncial	Carolingian minuscule	roman	italic
Ψ	ꓱF	ꓱ	F	F	*F*	ꜰ	Ꞙ	ſ	f	*f*

in 1965. Virtually all his poetry, criticism, and plays appeared under the Faber imprint, as did his quarterly review *The Criterion*. He was largely responsible for Ezra Pound, James Joyce, W. H. Auden, Louis MacNeice, and Stephen Spender becoming Faber writers. Later poets include Edwin Muir, Philip Larkin, Seamus Heaney, Ted Hughes, and Sylvia Plath. Lawrence Durrell, encouraged by Eliot, published *The Alexandria Quartet* (1957-60) with Faber, which also publishes the Nobel Prize winner William Golding, whose novel *Lord of the Flies* (1954) has sold millions of copies worldwide. Works on the English language include: *The Story of English*, by Robert McCrum, William Cran, & Robert MacNeil (with BBC Publications, 1986: the book of the TV series: see entry); the UK editions of *The State of the Language* (1980, 1990), ed. Christopher Ricks & Leonard Michaels (collections of articles first published by the U. of California Press jointly with the San Francisco branch of the English-Speaking Union); and John Honey's *Does Accent Matter?* (1989). See ELIOT, ENGLISH-SPEAKING UNION, STORY OF ENGLISH. [EUROPE, LITERATURE, MEDIA]. T.MCA.

FABLE [13c: from Old French *fable*, Latin *fabula* discourse, tale, plot]. A story illustrating a moral principle usually made explicit at the close by the narrator or one of the characters. In most fables, the protagonists are talking birds and animals whose words and actions reflect aspects of human behaviour. Such tales are often told to or written for children, but usually so that adults can also enjoy them; sometimes, when used for satirical purposes, they only appear to be for children. The most famous collection is attributed to the Greek slave Aesop (6c BC), their translations giving rise to familiar phrases like *sour grapes* and *a dog in the manger*, and to common perceptions such as the cunning fox and the industrious ant. Comparable fables, often with a strong humorous element, were common in medieval literature, including the Reynard the Fox series, Chaucer's *Nun's Priest's Tale* (14c), about the cock Chauntecleer, and Robert Henryson's *Morall Fabillis of Esope* (15c). In the 17c, Jean de la Fontaine retold in French fables from many sources and created a new interest shown in John Gay's *Fables* (1727, 1738). Joel Chandler Harris (1848-1908) wrote the 'Uncle Remus' stories of Brer Rabbit and his companions, in the black dialect of the southern US. There has been a revival of fables in the 20c, including David Garnett's *Lady into Fox* (1922), *Fables* by T. F. Powys (1929), and James Thurber's *Fables for our Time* (1940). The outstanding work, however, is George Orwell's *Animal Farm* (1945), a satire on the Soviet Union in the form of an animals' revolution in England. The fable form continues to be popular in children's literature, and a more modern related genre is the animated cartoon, especially in the US, with such characters as Tom and Jerry and Bugs Bunny. See BREWER'S DICTIONARY OF PHRASE AND FABLE. Compare ALLEGORY, LEGEND, MYTH, PARABLE. [LITERATURE]. R.C.

FACTS ON FILE. An American publishing company founded in 1940 and currently publishing from New York and Oxford (the British office being opened in 1984). The weekly *Facts on File World News Digest* was launched in 1941 and *Editorials on File*, a bimonthly selection of US newspaper editorials, was started in 1970. The company began to publish books in the 1970s, and titles on the English language include: *The American Literary Almanac: From 1608 to the Present* (1988), by Karen Rood; *American Literary Anecdotes* (1990), *British Literary Anecdotes* (1990), *World Literary Anecdotes* (1990), and *The Encyclopedia of Word and Phrase Origins* (1987), all by Robert Hendrickson; *The Facts on File Dictionary of 20th Century Allusions* (1990), by Sylvia Cole & Abraham H. Lass; *British English, A to Zed* (1988), by Norman W. Schur; *Last Lines: An Index to the Last Lines of Poetry* (1990), by Victoria Kline; *Kind Words: A Thesaurus of Euphemisms* (1990), by Judith S. Neaman & Carole G. Silver; *The Thesaurus of Slang* (1988), by Esther & Albert Lewin; and *The Dickson Baseball Dictionary* (1989), by Paul Dickson, covering many terms that have become a part of AmE general usage. The UK branch publishes the *Facts on File Visual Dictionary* (1988), by Jean-Claude Corbeil & Martin Manser (an 800-page illustrated thesaurus that provides terms relating to more than 3,000 depictable objects), *The Encyclopedia of Shakespeare* (1990) by Charles Boyce, and *The School Thesaurus* (1990) by Betty Kirkpatrick. [AMERICAS, EUROPE, MEDIA, REFERENCE]. T.MCA.

FALKLAND ISLANDS [1889: named by the British explorer John Strong after Viscount Falkland]. Also **Falklands**. A British dependency in the South Atlantic. Capital: Stanley. Population: *c*.1,800. Ethnicity: mostly British. Language: English, with a non-rhotic pronunciation. Argentina claims the islands under the name *Las Islas Malvinas*, from French *Les îles Malouines* (after Breton fishermen from Saint-Malo who once visited the area). See ARGENTINA, ENGLISH. [AMERICAS, NAME, VARIETY]. T.MCA.

FALLACY [14c, from Latin *fallacia* a trick, deceit, from *fallere/falsum* to trip (=cause to fall), deceive]. In general usage, a false and often deceitful idea, in logic, a line of reasoning (also known as a *paralogism*) that may seem valid but is not. Fallacies of discourse were first described in Greek and Latin, and many therefore retain their classical names, either uniquely or alongside a vernacular label. They include: (1) *Argumentum ad baculum* [Latin: argument backed by a stick]. Resorting to threat in order to have a point accepted. (2) *Argumentum ad hominem* [Latin: argument directed at the person]. Often called *ad-hominem argument* or an *ad-hominem attack*. Seeking to disprove a point by attacking the people making that point, either in terms of their character or by referring to their personal circumstances as an explanation of why a position has been adopted. (3) *Argumentum ad ignorantiam* [Latin: argument directed at ignorance]. Asserting that a proposition is true because it has not been proved false, or false because it has not been proved true. (4) *Argumentum ad populum* [Latin: argument directed at the people]. An appeal to popular opinion, bias, and inclination. (5) *Argumentum ad verecundiam* [Latin: shameful argument]. Appealing to an authority in one field regarding something in another field in which that authority has no more standing than anyone or anything else. (6) *Ignorantia elenchi* [Latin, Greek: ignorance of the conclusion]. While seeking to prove one proposition inadvertently proving something else, and therefore not sticking to the point. (7) *Non sequitur* [Latin: it does not follow]. A statement in which the premises of an argument do not lead to the conclusion provided. (8) *Post hoc ergo propter hoc* [Latin: after this therefore because of this]. Asserting that because A came before B, A caused B. See BEGGING THE QUESTION, EQUIVOCATION, ETYMOLOGICAL FALLACY, PATHETIC FALLACY, SYLLOGISM. [LANGUAGE, STYLE]. T.MCA.

FALSE ANALOGY. See ANALOGY.

FALSETTO. See PITCH.

FANAKALO, also **Fanagalo** [mid-20c: from Zulu, possibly *fana* resemble, appear, *ka* adverbial prefix, *lo* this, as in the phrase *khuluma fana kalo* speak in this way. Stress: 'fa-na-ka-LO', with Zulu /k/ resembling English /g/]. Also formerly and pejoratively *Mine Kaffir*. A pidgin language of southern Africa, used especially as a lingua franca in the mines, where it has been taught to facilitate communication between fellow workers and workers and employers. It has the basic sentence structure of English and vocabulary borrowed from especially black African languages (mostly Zulu), and from Afrikaans. It is strongly associated with discriminatory racial policies, is disliked by many Africans, and has been condemned by the National Union of Mineworkers as offensive and inadequate to its purpose. See RACISM. [AFRICA, LANGUAGE]. W.B.

FANTASY [13c: from Old French *fantasie*, Latin *phantasia*, Greek *phantasia* how things seem, what is sensed, appearance, apparition, imagination]. Both a story based on strange and wonderful happenings (the antithesis of realistic fiction) and the capacity to imagine vivid and unusual themes and images (as well as the themes and images themselves). The word has had a varied development. By the late 16c, *phantasie* or *fantasie* had come to mean in English a mental image without objective reality, as when Horatio believes the Ghost of Hamlet's father to be only 'fantasy' (Shakespeare, *Hamlet*, 1. 1). During the Romantic Movement (18-19c), it was used to describe writing connected with dreams, hauntings, and the supernatural, often in contrast to the more healthy and positive faculty of *imagination*.

Literature and fantasy. From the middle of the 19c, the term has denoted a literary genre that includes *The King of the Golden River*, by John Ruskin (1851), *The Rose and the Ring*, by W. M. Thackeray (1855), *The Water Babies*, by Charles Kingsley (1863), *Phantastes*, by George Macdonald (1858), the 'Alice' stories of Lewis Carroll (1865, 1871), the tales and poems of Edward Lear, and Frank Baum's *The Wonderful Wizard of Oz* (1900). Most of these works were intended for children but also appealed to adults. In the 20c, the genre includes C. S. Lewis's 'Narnia' books and science fiction such as *Perelandra* (1943), J. R. R. Tolkien's *The Hobbit* (1937) and the trilogy *The Lord of the Rings* (1954-5), and Mervyn Peake's *Titus Groan* trilogy (1946-9). Science fiction often has an element of fantasy in it, and the sub-genre *science fantasy* has flourished throughout the 20c, including Edgar Rice Burroughs's *Martian Tales* (from 1912) and Frank Herbert's *Dune* series (from 1965). Attempts to define fantasy precisely have not been successful and the name has been loosely applied to many works. It is, however, generally agreed that a fantasy is set in a world remote from ordinary experience, some or all of its characters are different from any known creatures, the fantasy world has its own rules and logic and is usually well ordered within them, and any everyday characters who get into this world have to conform to the new way of life. Conversely, fantastic creatures may enter the familiar world, and when they do so their powers often prevail, as in Rudyard Kipling's *Puck of Pook's Hill* (1906).

Literary dreams. The dream is a popular vehicle for fantasy, but despite its successful use in the Alice books and *Oz*, some critics object to it as a detraction from the verisimilitude which should accompany the fantasist's creation. Often characters reach the fantasy world through a magic entrance (the back of a wardrobe in the Narnia books) or a strange journey (the non-physical transference of Captain John Carter to 'the red planet' in the *Martian Tales*). In the new world, problems have to be overcome, and the characters return to their old life with a changed attitude. Fantasy may have a didactic purpose: a Christian message conveyed by C. S. Lewis, comparable to John Bunyan's *Pilgrim's Progress* (1678-84). Fantasy often conveys a sense of coming close to ultimate reality, with echoes of myths and legends or the evocative use of archetypal images such as mountain, cave, and sea. Death and rebirth are often symbolically encountered, along with the motifs of quest, rescue, and return: compare ARCHETYPE.

The fantastic. Even when fantasy carries a secondary message, it is different from *allegory*, which is more controlled and more directly corresponds with the familiar, from *ghost stories*, which show the supernatural impinging on the natural without creating a different world or world-view, from *science fiction* (as distinct from science fantasy), which is usually set in possible worlds, accessible through great but measurable distances of space or time, and from *utopias* and *dystopias*, which are often futuristic or based on a recognizably human community. The special name 'fantastic' has been given to stories which offer ambiguous interpretations between natural and supernatural happenings, such as *The Turn of the Screw* by Henry James (1898). Here, the new governess, who is the narrator, is uneasy about hints of a malign influence from a former governess and a manservant, both dead. Sitting by the lake, she sees a figure on the other side:

There was an alien object in view—a figure whose right of presence I instantly and passionately questioned. I recollect counting over perfectly the possibilities, reminding myself that nothing was more natural for instance than the appearance of one of the men about the place, or even of a messenger, a postman or a tradesman from the village. That reminder had as little effect on my practical certitude as I was conscious—still without even looking—of its having upon the character of the visitor. Nothing was more natural than that these things should be the other things they absolutely were not (ch. 6).

The language of fantasy. Fantasy must be logically developed, so that acceptance of an initial premiss allows the reader to enter fully into what follows. The narrative style should convey a credible story, even while normal expectations of narrative are being defeated. The use of familiar language to describe the unfamiliar requires skill in analogy and ingenuity in placing known features in new settings. Fantasy is marked by a

creative use of language. Strange creatures are given names like Carroll's *Jabberwock* and *Snark*, Lewis's *Sorns*, Burroughs's *Barsoomians*, and Frank Herbert's *Fremen*. Individuals receive exotic proper names like Peake's *Muzzlehatch*, Tolkien's *Gandalf*, and Burroughs's *Tars Tarkas, Jeddak of Thark*. Whole languages can be postulated, and specimens of them given, as Tolkien does with *Elvish* and other imaginary tongues. In the following excerpt, he blends Elvish names with a romantic medieval-cum-Biblical English:

Melian was a Maia, of the race of the Valar. She dwelt in the gardens of Lórien, and among all his people there were none more beautiful than Melian, nor more wise, nor more skilled in songs of enchantment . . . Elwë, lord of the Teleri, went often through the great woods to seek out Finwë his friend in the dwellings of the Noldor; and it chanced on a time that he came alone to the star-lit wood of Nan Elmoth, and there suddenly he heard the song of nightingales. Then an enchantment fell on him, and he stood still; and afar off beyond the voices of the *lómelindi* he heard the voice of Melian (*The Silmarillion*, 1977).

Fantasy adapts everyday language in two ways: (1) Through neologism, particularly in nonsense verse and the description of people, places, animals, objects, and customs. Lear's poems have given English *Pobble* and *Jumblies*, Tolkien's stories *hobbit* and *ent*. (2) Through the failure of language in the fantasy world. Alice passes through the 'wood where things have no names' and forgets her own. At the end of Lewis's *That Hideous Strength* (1945), the speech of some characters breaks down into incoherent sounds. Fantasy may also serve as a vehicle for commenting on language itself, as in Norton Juster's *The Phantom Tolbooth* (1961):

Above all the noise and tumult of the crowd could be heard the merchants' voices loudly advertising their products.
  'Get your fresh-picked ifs, ands, and buts.'
  'Hey-yaa, hey-yaa, nice ripe wheres and whens.'
  'Step right up, step right up—fancy, best-quality words right here,' announced one man in a booming voice. 'Step right up—ah, what can I do for you, little boy? How about a nice bagful of pronouns—or maybe you'd like our special assortment of names?'

Conclusion. At a safe remove from everyday life, literary fantasy can be a means of airing and dealing with anxieties and taboos, exploring imaginative and spiritual areas of experience, and also a context in which to experiment freely with the limits of language.

See ALLEGORY, FABLE, GOTHIC, NONSENSE, NONSENSE VERSE, NOVEL, ONOMASTICS, ROMANCE, ROOT-CREATION, SCIENCE FICTION. [LITERATURE, STYLE].   R.C., T.MCA.

FARCE [14c: from French *farce* stuffing, from *farcir*, Latin *farcire*, to stuff]. (1) Comedy in which the humour is often broad and unsubtle, designed to provoke continual laughter. In the 13c, the term referred to passages inserted into liturgy or liturgical drama (such as French in the Latin text of the Mass) and had a sense of the impromptu. Farce exaggerates such characteristics of comedy as coincidence, mistaken identity, embarrassment, and narrow escapes. Its often slapstick physical action and stock characterization help release anxiety and inhibition; its verbal humour is overt and transitory, and usually without wit. A farce may extend to a full-length play like *Charlie's Aunt* by Brandon Thomas (1892) or may be an ingredient in comedy proper, as with the farcical scenes in Shakespeare's *The Taming of the Shrew*. (2) By extension, absurdly futile proceedings; pretence or mockery: *This isn't a trial—It's a farce!* See HUMO(U)R. [LITERATURE, STYLE].   R.C.

FAROESE, also **Faeroese** [1850s]. The Germanic language of the Faroe/Faeroe Islands, a self-governing region of Denmark between Shetland and Iceland, first settled by the Norse in the 8c. It is similar to Icelandic and Norn, but whereas Norn gave way to Scots (17-18c), Faroese has survived, and acquired a written form in the 19c. Danish is taught on the islands as a second language. Despite their proximity, Faroese and English have had little impact on one other. See NORN, SCANDINAVIAN LANGUAGES. [EUROPE, LANGUAGE].   P.C.

FATHERESE. See MOTHERESE.

FAUX AMI [French: a false friend]. Also **false friend**. A term in language teaching for a word that has the same origin and general appearance as a word in another language, so that learners mistakenly assume that both have the same meanings and uses: English *deceive* to trick, French *décevoir* to disappoint. Such false friends are discussed by Philip Thody & Howard Evans in *Faux Amis and Key Words: A Dictionary-Guide to French Language, Culture and Society through Lookalikes and Confusables* (UK: Athlone, 1985; US: *Mistakable French*, Scribners), and Jacques Van Roey, Sylvaine Granger, & Helen Swallow in *Dictionnaire des faux amis, français-anglais* (Louvain, 1989: Éditions Duculot). Compare CONFUSIBLE, DOUBLET. See QUEBEC ENGLISH. [EDUCATION, LANGUAGE].   T.MCA.

FAX [Late 20c: a clipping of *(tele)facsimile*, with *cs* respelled as *x*]. A device for the digital transmission in facsimile form of documents, photographs, etc., and any communication sent by this means. A fax machine encodes images from paper, sends them over telephone wires to other machines with *fax numbers* as addresses, and

these then decode the signals and restore them to paper: 'The firm's primary fax, a Group III machine, has 100 telephone numbers in memory, a 50-page automatic feeder and is constantly in use. "We can have a three-dimensional sketch or a plan detail on a client's or builder's desk within two hours," Koppstein points out. "It's not unusual to have a portfolio of incoming and outgoing faxes contained in four or five volumes—several thousand faxes" ' (Martin Luray, 'Small-Business Fax', advertising section, *Newsweek*, 9 Dec. 1991). Faxing rapidly became during the 1980s a major international means of communication, primarily because the Japanese found it easier and more convenient to transmit sheets of signs in their traditional writing system than to recompose the text for other forms of electromagnetic transmission. See PHOTOCOPYING. [MEDIA, TECHNOLOGY].   T.MCA., M.L.

FCE. See FIRST CERTIFICATE IN ENGLISH.

FEATURE [14c: from French *faiture*, Latin *factura* making]. (1) In linguistics, a characteristic or component, often qualified by an adjective, as in *distinctive feature, semantic feature*. In phonology, a *distinctive feature* sets off one phoneme (distinctive sound) of a language from another: for example, the presence of the feature *voice* distinguishing /b/ from /p/ and /d/ from /t/. A *semantic feature* contributes an element of meaning to a word, such as the feature [female] in such words as *woman, mare* as opposed to [male] in *man, stallion*. (2) Also *feature film*. The main motion picture shown in a particular programme. (3) Also *feature article*. An article of general or specialist interest in a newspaper or other periodical, written by a *feature writer* and often edited by a *features editor* who looks after the *features pages*. (4) To make a feature of or give prominence to (something or someone), especially in the media or promoting a product: *The magazine features a different celebrity each week*. See ARTICLE², SEMANTICS. [LANGUAGE, MEDIA].   T.MCA.

FEEDBACK [1910s]. (1) In biology, a response within a system (a cell, organism, or population) that has an effect on the continued activity or productivity of that system. (2) In information theory, the use by a monitor of part of the output of a process to control or modify the input. (3) In education, the monitoring of a person's or group's performance, in which progress or nonprogress, etc., are noted and adjustments made appropriately in techniques and tactics. (4) In general usage, anything that feeds back into a system, such as the return of completed questionnaires in a survey which seeks opinions: *Our feedback suggests the original plan won't work*.

In educational terms, *positive feedback* is an increase in output that produces an increase in input (reinforcing a learner's ability and confidence) and *negative feedback* is an increase in output that produces a decrease in input (marking a lack of success and perhaps causing loss of morale). In engineering applications, however, positive feedback often leads to instability (such as the squeal when a microphone is too close to a loudspeaker it is driving and the amplification is too high), while negative feedback avoids this and produces stable and consistent systems. [EDUCATION, MEDIA, TECHNOLOGY]. M.L., T.MCA.

FELCO. See ARELS.

FEMININE [14c: from Old French *feminin* (Modern *féminin*), from Latin *femininus*, representing *genus femininum*, the translation of Greek *thēlukòn génos* the female kind]. A term relating to grammatical gender in nouns and related words. Words denoting female people and animals in such languages as French and Latin are usually feminine, but grammatical gender is not about sex: in the French phrase *la plume de ma tante*, the pen is as feminine as its owner. In English, the term is largely confined to personal pronouns (*she/her/herself/hers*), some nouns (*mare* in contrast to *stallion*), and some suffixes (*-ess* as in *hostess*). See GENDER, MASCULINE, SEXISM. [GRAMMAR]. S.C.

FEMININE ENDING. One or more unstressed syllables ending a line of verse. In rhymed verse, a line has a *feminine rhyme* if all sounds after the rhyming syllable are identical (*lending/bending*). A single extra syllable, as above, gives *double rhyme* and two extra syllables give *triple rhyme* (*garrison/caparison*). Double endings are generally used in English verse as occasional variants among *masculine endings*. The feminine ending can be used to suggest hesitancy, reflection, or deep feeling, as in the opening lines of Hamlet's best-known soliloquy:

> To be, or not to be, that is the question,
> Whether tis nobler in the minde to suffer
> The slings and arrowes of outragious fortune . . .
> (Shakespeare, *Hamlet*, 3. 1).

Such endings are more common in Italian and similar languages than in English. Compare MASCULINE ENDING. [LITERATURE]. R.C.

FEMINISM [1890s: from French *féminisme*, from Latin *femina* a woman, and *-ism(e)*]. A social philosophy concerned with the rights of women. Feminists generally consider women to be oppressed and in varying degrees alienated by a male-dominated society in which the use of language is anti-female. They argue that language favours men by helping to shape a society in which women are rendered subordinate and often taught to keep silent; when they speak, men often do not listen to them properly. In a radical feminist view, if society cannot change to accommodate both sexes equally, women will do their best to create their own society and their own kinds of language. This idea is explored by Suzette Haden Elgin in *Native Tongue* (Daw, 1984), which creates a world in which severely oppressed women rebel through an underground movement to make their own language, *Laadan*. In it, a distinction is made between *am* (love for blood kin) and *ashon* (love for kin of the heart), and prefixes at the start of sentences signal whether they are statements, promises, warnings, etc., making the language more explicit and avoiding possibly painful misunderstandings. See CHAUVINISM, COMPANION, FORM OF ADDRESS, GENDER BIAS, -ISM, LITERARY CRITICISM, SEXISM. [LANGUAGE, STYLE]. L.S.W., M.E.W.

FESTSCHRIFT [1890s: from German *Festschrift* ('festival writing') a commemorative volume]. A collection of academic papers to mark a special anniversary, such as the 65th birthday of a scholar. In addition to essays, such volumes often contain a summary of the career and a list of the publications of the honoured person. Two festschrifts in the field of English are *In Honour of Daniel Jones* (ed. David Abercrombie, 1964: 51 papers) and *Studies in Linguistics in Honor of R. I. McDavid* (ed. Lawrence Davis, 1972: 36 papers). [MEDIA]. R.H.

FICTION [14c: from Latin *fictio/fictionis* a shaping, from *fingere/fictum* to fashion]. A general term for something created by the human mind. It has three aspects, each with an appropriate adjective: (1) (Both countable and uncountable). Not fact, but an invention of some kind, sometimes a fabrication or lie. The detective Sherlock Holmes was an invention of the writer Arthur Conan Doyle, and as such is *fictitious*; no such person ever lived. (2) (Usually uncountable). Not fact, but still part of reality; imaginative narrative, often part of literature: *works of fiction* in contrast with *non-fiction*, especially in bookshops and libraries. Here the *fictional* Sherlock Holmes is a fact in the sense that a character with this name appears in certain stories and films, and can be discussed in much the same way as a historical person. (3) (Usually countable). A special kind of 'fact': a social and cultural construct, such as a *legal fiction* that helps in the administration of the law, *temporal fictions* such as the days of the week, and *geographical fictions* like the Equator. Such constructs are part of life; they are *fictive* or constructed, and include products of imaginative storytelling. Fictively, Sherlock Holmes and the Equator are on a par, the one influencing crime writers, criminologists, and enthusiasts for the detective story, the other affecting geographers and sailors. The fictive generally subsumes both the fictional and the fictitious. Fictitious reports and fictional plots and characters are constantly being created in a language like English. At a certain level of discussion the language is itself fictive: something created by the human mind within a cultural system so as to serve certain social ends. Compare FANTASY, MYTH. See NARRATIVE, NOVEL, ONOMASTICS, POETRY, POPULAR FICTION, ROMANTIC FICTION, SCIENCE FICTION, SOCIAL REALISM, STORY, VERSE. [LANGUAGE, LITERATURE]. T.MCA.

FICTIONARY. See CALL MY BLUFF.

FIELDING, Henry [1707-54]. English novelist and playwright, born in Somerset, and educated at Eton. He achieved early success in London as a comic dramatist. His most successful play, *Tom Thumb* (1730), was a burlesque of contemporary heroic tragedy. In 1736, he became manager of the New Theatre. His attacks on the royal family and Robert Walpole's government were a major reason for the passing of the 1737 Licensing Act, which imposed censorship of plays. Fielding turned to the practice of law, which he had studied for a time at Leiden, but was hampered by ill-health. The publication of Richardson's *Pamela* (1740-1) brought out a talent for parody in his *An Apology for the Life of Mrs Shamela Andrews* (1741). He continued to attack Richardson with *Joseph Andrews* (1742), his target the type of morality that equated virtue with a decorous marriage and paid excessive respect to outward forms of piety. *Tom Jones* (1749), which he described as 'a comic epic in prose', was disliked by the literary establishment, but gained a wide readership. Avoiding the epistolary style, he showed what could be done with continuous narrative, characters from many levels of society, and dialogue that included dialect: see DIALOGUE. The lowly hero Tom Jones, careless of conventional morality, introduced new frankness and breadth of vision to English letters. Fielding's legal career prospered; he became a magistrate and fought both the criminal underworld and the weaknesses of the legal system, using his legal experience in *Jonathan Wild* (1744). His last novel, *Amelia* (1752), showed signs of the failing health that caused his death on a visit to Lisbon. His *Journal of a Voyage to Lisbon* (1755) was published posthumously. See CENSORSHIP, NOVEL. [BIOGRAPHY, EUROPE, LITERATURE]. R.C.

FIGURATIVE EXTENSION, also **extension**. A process of semantic change in which a word gains further senses figuratively, especially through metaphor or metonymy. For example, the reference of *crown* has extended from a usually royal head-dress to royalty itself, to (among others) a coin with this symbol on it, to the part of the head where a crown rests, to the top of a hill or other such place, to the crest of a bird, to a crown-like award or honour, to the enamel-covered part of a tooth above the gum, and to a standard size of printing paper. See FIGURATIVE LANGUAGE/USAGE, SEMANTIC CHANGE, SLANG. [HISTORY, LANGUAGE]. T.MCA.

FIGURATIVE LANGUAGE, also **figurative usage** [14c: adjective from French *figuratif*, Latin *figurativus*, from *figura* a form, shape, device, or ornament: compare FIGURE OF SPEECH]. Language in which figures of speech such as metaphors and similes freely occur. In classical rhetoric and poetics there is an inherent contrast between *figurative* or ornamental usage on the one hand and *literal* or plain and conventional usage on the other; in this contrast, figures of speech are regarded as embellishments that deviate from the 'ordinary' uses of language. The 16c English rhetorician George Puttenham described the contrast as follows:

As figures be the instruments of ornament in euery language, so be they also in a sort abuses or rather trespasses in speach, because they passe the ordinary limits of common vtterance, and be occupied of purpose to deceiue the eare and also the minde, drawing it from plainnesse and simplicitie to a certain doublenesse, whereby our talk is the more guileful and abusing, for what else is your Metaphore but an inuersion of sence by transport; your allegorie but a duplicitie of meaning or dissimulation vnder couert and dark intendments? (*The Arte of Poesie*, 1589).

Puttenham implies here that there is a core of simple, literal language that can be distinguished from ornate, figurative language (which engages in a kind of unnatural double-dealing). There is, however, a paradox at the heart of the classical argument that Puttenham presents. The 18c Scottish rhetorician Hugh Blair touched on it when he wrote:

But, though Figures imply a deviation from what may be reckoned the most simple form of Speech, we are not thence to conclude, that they imply anything uncommon, or unnatural (*Lectures on Rhetoric and Belles Lettres*, 1784).

In this paradox, figurative language succeeds, somehow, in being both natural and unnatural at the same time.

From deviant to natural. The classical view was dominant at the end of the 19c, when the American rhetorician John F. Genung described figurative language as an 'intentional deviation from the plain and ordinary mode of speaking, for the sake of greater effect' (*Practical Elements* *of Rhetoric*, 1893). In the late 20c however, a change of approach was under way: for example, while referring to 'an intentional deviation from the normal' (in the traditional way), the American critic Joseph T. Shipley observed: 'Figures are as old as language. They lie buried in many words of current use. They are the backbone of slang. They occur constantly in both prose and poetry' (*Dictionary of World Literary Terms*, 1970). Two recent dictionaries demonstrate more explicitly a shift in the perception of the term 'figure of speech' away from linguistic deviance towards stylistic creativity, defining it as: (1) 'a form of expression (e.g. a hyperbole or metaphor) used to convey meaning or heighten effect, often by comparing or identifying one thing with another that has a meaning or connotation familiar to the reader or listener' (UK: *Longman Dictionary of the English Language*, 1984); (2) 'An expression, such as a metaphor or hyperbole, in which a nonliteral and intensive sense of a word or words is used to create a forceful, dramatic, or illuminating image' (US: *American Heritage Dictionary*, 1985).

Deciding where the literal ends and the figurative begins is notoriously difficult. There is no irreducible core of 'literal' language from which 'figurative usage' diverges. Rather, there is an easy movement between the one pole and the other: for example, behind such an everyday word as *brand* (in the sense of 'product' or 'trademark') is a history of burning that includes what was done to animals and slaves to mark them as property. The modern use of *brand* as 'product' is in effect a literal usage, yet its origin in branding-irons and the like is distinctly metaphorical and figurative. Similarly, behind the various *fields* in which scholars work lie the patches of land where farmers have 'literally' worked for millennia, and such a phrase as *electromagnetic field*, however mundanely literal it may be for physicists, depends for its creation on a comparable figurative shift: Puttenham's 'inuersion of sence by transport'.

Defining figures of speech. The precise definition of a figure of speech has proved to be as difficult as determining the limits of figurative usage. For centuries, rhetoricians have debated what each presumed figure refers to and how various figures relate to each other. As a result, *metaphor* in some approaches contains *metonymy*, in others does not, and *synecdoche* may or may not be a kind of metaphor or metonymy. As a result, in recent years attempts to arrange the figures hierarchically have been abandoned in favour of lists in which the main devices are presented each more or less in isolation, as stylistic equals, but perhaps with notes on celebrated doubts and

ambiguities about their precise natures and relationships. Classical rhetoric has tended to present figurative language as the concern primarily of poets, orators, critics, and language teachers, while conceding (usually in a brief aside) that everybody else uses it too and that the term therefore covers a universal practice in which sound, spelling, grammar, vocabulary, usage, and meaning are adapted to achieve special stylistic effects.

Kinds of figurative language. (1) Phonological figures include *alliteration*, *assonance*, and *onomatopoeia*. In his poem 'The Pied Piper of Hamelin' (1842), Robert Browning repeats sibilants, nasals, and liquids as he shows how the children respond to the piper: 'There was a ru*stling*, that seemed like a bu*stling* / Of merry crowds ju*stling* at pitching and hu*stling*.' Something sinister has started. (2) Orthographic figures use visual forms created for effect: for example, *America* spelt *Amerika* (by left-wing radicals in the 1970s and as the name of a movie in the 1980s), to suggest a totalitarian state. (3) Syntactic figures may bring the non-standard into the standard language, as in US President Ronald Reagan's 'You ain't seen nothing yet' (1984), a non-standard double negative used to project a vigorous, folksy image. (4) Lexical figures extend the conventional so as to surprise or entertain, as when, instead of a phrase like *a year ago*, the Welsh poet Dylan Thomas wrote *a grief ago*, or when the Irish dramatist Oscar Wilde said at the New York Customs, 'I have nothing to declare but my genius.' When people say that 'you can't take' something 'literally', they are generally referring to usage that challenges everyday reality: for example, through exaggeration (the *hyperbole* in 'loads of money'), comparison (the *simile* 'like death warmed up'; the *metaphor* 'life is an uphill struggle'), physical and other association (the *metonymy* 'Crown property' for something owned by royalty), and a part for a whole (the *synecdoche* 'All hands on deck!').

Puttenham divided figures into those that please the ear and the mind (or both), but to be effective, figurative usage does not need to please. The spelling *Amerikkka* has sometimes been used, especially in graffiti, to suggest that the Ku Klux Klan has great influence over how the US is governed. The usage is both imaginative and striking, but to many Americans it is very far from pleasing. The aim of all such usage is to make an impact: pleasing, shocking, political, social, etc. The ends of figurative language are achieved through repetitions, juxtapositions, contrasts, and associations, by violating expectations, by evoking echoes of other people, places, times, and contexts, and through novel, provocative imagery. When such usage succeeds, new expressions, concepts, and associations may be established in a language, as with *loads/tons of money*. When an expression succeeds so well that everyone adopts it, the result in due course is the opposite of what was first intended: a cliché from which the figurative power has drained away.

See ALLEGORY, ALLITERATION, ANACHORISM, ANACHRONISM, ANAPHORA, ANASTROPHE, ANTI-CLIMAX, ANTITHESIS, ANTONOMASIA, APOSTROPHE[2], BATHOS, CACOPHEMISM, CHIASMUS, CLICHÉ, CLIMAX, DYSPHEMISM, ECHOISM, EMPHASIS, EPANALEPSIS, EUPHEMISM, EUPHONY, EUPHUISM, FIGURE OF SPEECH, HENDIADYS, HOMERIC SIMILE, HYPALLAGE, HYPERBATON, HYPERBOLE, IMAGE, INNUENDO, INVERSION, IRONY, LITERAL, LITERARY TERM, LITOTES, MEIOSIS, METAPHOR, METONYMY, MIXED METAPHOR, ONOMATOPOEIA, OXYMORON, PARADOX, PARALIPSIS, PARALLELISM, PARONO-MASIA, PATHETIC FALLACY, PERSONIFICATION/PROSOPOPOEIA, PHRASAL VERB, PLAYING WITH WORDS/WORD-PLAY, POETIC DICTION, PROLEPSIS, PUN, REPETITION, RHETORIC, RHETORICAL QUESTION, SARCASM, SCHEME, SIMILE, STYLE, STYLISTICS, SYLLEPSIS, SYNECDOCHE, TRANSFERRED EPITHET, TROPE, UNDERSTATEMENT, ZEUGMA. [LANGUAGE, STYLE].   T.MCA.

Abrams, M. H. 1957. *A Glossary of Literary Terms*. New York: Holt, Rinehart & Winston.

Baldick, Chris. 1990. *The Concise Oxford Dictionary of Literary Terms*. Oxford: University Press.

Cuddon, J. A. 1991. *A Dictionary of Literary Terms and Literary Theory*. Oxford: Basil Blackwell. 3rd enlarged edition of *A Dictionary of Literary Terms*. London: André Deutsch, 1977, 1979; New York: Doubleday, 1977, 1980; Penguin, 1982.

Fowler, H. W. 1965. *A Dictionary of Modern English Usage*, 2nd edition revised by Sir Ernest Gowers. Oxford: University Press.

Fowler, Roger. 1987. *A Dictionary of Modern Critical Terms*, 2nd edition. London: Routledge & Kegan Paul.

Shipley, Joseph T. 1970. *Dictionary of World Literary Terms*, 3rd edition. London: Allen & Unwin.

Wales, Katie. 1989. *Dictionary of Stylistics*. London: Longman.

FIGURE OF SPEECH [1810s: a translation of Latin *figura orationis*, in turn a translation of the original Greek technical term *skhễma tễs léxeõs*]. A rhetorical device that achieves a special effect by using words in distinctive ways, such as *alliteration*, in which the same sound, especially an initial consonant, is repeated, as with /f/ in *life's fitful fever*, and *hyperbole*, in which one engages, usually deliberately, in unrealistic exaggeration, as in the informal phrase *tons of money* ('a great deal of money'). Here, a word usually associated with weights and measures has been moved out of context to refer to money, with which it is not normally associated. Devices traditionally regarded as figures of speech include: *alliteration*,

anachorism, anachronism, anticlimax, antithesis, antonomasia, apostrophe[2], assonance, bathos, cacophemism, chiasmus, climax, dysphemism, euphemism, hendiadys, hypallage (transferred epithet), hyperbaton, hyperbole, irony, litotes, meiosis (understatement), metaphor, metonymy, onomatopoeia, oxymoron, paradox, personification (prosopopoeia), prolepsis, pun (paronomasia), simile, synecdoche, zeugma (syllepsis) (for each of which there is a separate entry). See FIGURATIVE LANGUAGE/USAGE, INVERSION, PARALLELISM, PATHETIC FALLACY, PLAYING WITH WORDS/WORD-PLAY, POETIC DICTION, REPETITION, RHETORIC, SCHEME, STYLISTICS, TROPE. [LANGUAGE, STYLE].   T.MCA.

FIJI. A country in Oceania, consisting of some 330 islands. Capital: Suva. Currency: dollar (100 cents). Economy: mixed. Population: 700,000 (1988), 900,000 (projection for 2000). Ethnicity: 50% Indian, 45% Melanesian, 5% Chinese, European, Polynesian, and mixed. Languages: Fijian and English (both official), the Pacific languages Rotuman, Gilbertese, Tongan, and the Indian languages Gujarati, Tamil, Telugu. Education: primary 100%, secondary 40%, tertiary 5%, literacy 86%. Fiji was a British colony from 1874 to independence in 1970. Originally wholly Melanesian, the population became multiethnic through colonialism, especially the importing of plantation labourers from the Pacific islands and India. There are long-standing tensions between ethnic Fijians and the Indian community. The ethnically and linguistically distinct Rotumans are from an island administered by Fiji.

English in Fiji ranges from low-prestige varieties (the basilect) to a high-prestige variety (the acrolect). The language of education is standard English on a BrE model. A stable pidgin English did not develop, although some early plantation labourers knew Melanesian Pidgin English and later labourers arrived speaking a stable variety of the same pidgin, learned in Queensland. A pidginized Fijian was used on plantations. Features of local English include: (1) The focus marker *ga* (*You ga, you ga tell it* It's you who tells it) and the politeness marker *mada* (*Wait mada*). (2) Use of *one* as an indefinite article, as in varieties of IndE: *Tonight I'm going to one party*. (3) Use of *us two* as the first-person dual inclusive (myself and one other): *I can't give you us two's money because us two poor*. (4) The use of *fella* as the third-person pronoun with human reference: *Fella put that fella's hand in front* He put his hand in front. (5) Local words such as Fijian *tanoa* a bowl for making kava, and Hindi *roti* Indian flat bread. Such features as *us two* and *fella* are similar to those in Melanesian Pidgin English and indigenous languages; others are shared not only with pidgin and creole English but also with basilectal varieties of English as in Singapore, such as the use of *been* as a pre-verbal marker of past tense (*He been swear* He swore) and lack of copula (*That one nice house* That is a nice house). See ENGLISH, MELANESIA. [NAME, OCEANIA, VARIETY].   S.R., T.MCA.

FILIPINISM [1960s]. A linguistic usage specific to or typical of the Philippines, such as *Open the light* Switch on the light, *captain-ball* basketball team captain, and *viand* any dish eaten with rice. See -ISM, PHILIPPINE ENGLISH. [ASIA, VARIETY, WORD].   A.G.

FILIPINO [1890s: from Spanish, from *Las Islas Filipinas* the Philippine Islands]. (1) An inhabitant or citizen of the Philippines. The term is generic for all people in the Philippines, but *Filipina* is often used for women. (2) Relating to the Philippines: *Filipino languages*. (3) Also *Pilipino*. The co-official language (with English) of the Philippines, based on Tagalog. See AMERICAN LANGUAGES, HAWAII, PHILIPPINES, TAGALOG, TAGLISH. [ASIA, LANGUAGE, NAME].   T.MCA.

FILIPINO ENGLISH. See PHILIPPINE ENGLISH.

FILIPINO LITERATURE IN ENGLISH. The first notable work in English resulting from the intervention of the US in the Philippines in 1898 is Rudyard Kipling's poem 'The White Man's Burden'. Following the introduction of English-language education, however, Filipinos turned to literary expression in Kipling's language. Short stories appeared in college magazines from 1910 and the first novel in English, Zoilo M. Galang's *A Child of Sorrow*, was published in 1921. Since then, a considerable body of work in all literary genres has developed in a nation that regards itself as having the world's third largest English-speaking population. Creative writing in English perhaps suffered in the first 50 years from the language's association with material and social development, as opposed (in the minds of the intelligentsia at least) to Spanish as a cultural language. The effect can be seen in the functional quality of much English writing, artistry being subservient to social protest and bolstering national pride. This approach, championed by Salvador P. Lopez, was countered by another characteristic of Filipino writing in English: an 'art for art's sake' formalism developed by the poet José Garcia Villa. Other traits are: a tendency to sentimentality and romance (with roots in Spanish and indigenous traditions), a concern for identity in the face of colonial discontinuities and the blending of East and West, a focus on rural life (people against nature, village childhood, the pull to the city), dramatized questions of social justice, and the 'war of the sexes'.

The social phenomena having greatest impact have been the migration of Filipino workers to America, especially during the Depression, and the period of martial law under the Marcos regime (1972–86), although there has also been a lasting interest in historical reconstructions of the close of the Spanish period and the transition to American rule. In one picture of the development of English-language literature, three decades of apprenticeship led to a boom after 1930. The short story was the most notable development and is still the most popular and achieved form, with influences from Sherwood Anderson, Hemingway, Steinbeck, and Dos Passos; significant early writers include Arturo Rotor, Manuel Arguilla, and Francisco Arcellana. Poetry was mainly lyric and following models of Spanish devotional literature and English Romanticism, and was boosted by the success of Villa. Although interrupted by the Japanese invasion, literary output has continued steadily, social realism and romance being gradually supplemented by modernist experiments, international models, and the use of more colloquial language. Leading names include Linda Ty Casper, N. V. M. Gonzalez, Nick Joaquin, Bienvenido Santos, Edilberto Tiempo. Poets of note are Gemino Abad, Cirilo Bautista, Ophelia Alcantara Dimalanta, and Edith Tiempo. Drama in English has been overshadowed by vernacular productions and the flourishing Filipino film industry, but names of note in the English theatre are Alberto Floretino, Esla Coscolluela, Wilfrido Maria Guerrero, and Nick Joaquin.

The breeding ground for writers in English has always been the tertiary colleges and major universities; indeed, most of the writers are also teachers. They often edit magazines that serve as literary outlets and act as critics of each other's work. This has led to debate about the problem of establishing a solid literary tradition free of coterie biases. In the context of recovering a national cultural identity, writing in English has always been under attack from those advocating the primacy of vernacular expression. They argue that English is not only the tongue of foreign colonialists, but also the vehicle of a local élite, prone to ivory-tower irrelevance. Vernacular writing has been supported by recent generations of social activists; since the decline of English with post-war decolonization and the development of Filipino as a national language, it has given them access to the average Filipino worker. In turn, supporters of English claim that it is their natural means of expression, that language and culture do not work on one-to-one exclusivity, and that, as an international language, English offers access to world literary tradition and a protection against insularity. See

FILIPINO, PHILIPPINE ENGLISH, PHILIPPINES. [ASIA, LITERATURE, VARIETY]. P.SH.

FILM. See MOTION PICTURE.

FINGER SPELLING. See SIGN LANGUAGE.

FINITE [15c: from Latin *finitus* ended, limited]. A term for any occurrence of a verb inflected for grammatical features such as person, number, and tense. Compare FINITE VERB, INFINITIVE, NON-FINITE VERB. [GRAMMAR]. T.MCA.

FINITE VERB. A form of the verb with a distinction in tense: *likes, like, liked* are finite verbs in *Justin likes strawberry ice cream, Anne and Robert like my story,* and *David liked his wife's cooking.* On the other hand, *like, liked* are nonfinite in *Justin may like strawberry ice cream* and *David has always liked his wife's cooking,* since no tense contrast is possible in these sentences. Compare FINITE, INFINITIVE, NON-FINITE VERB. [GRAMMAR]. S.G.

FINNISH. See BORROWING, EUROPEAN LANGUAGES, SCANDINAVIAN LANGUAGES, URO-ALTAIC LANGUAGES.

FINNO-UGRIC LANGUAGES. See LANGUAGE, URO-ALTAIC LANGUAGES.

FIRST CERTIFICATE IN ENGLISH, short forms *FCE, First Certificate.* An EFL examination introduced by UCLES in 1939 (when it was called the *Lower Certificate*); the principal comprehensive test in English available internationally. See EXAMINING IN ENGLISH, UCLES. [EDUCATION]. W.S.

FIRST LANGUAGE, SECOND LANGUAGE, short forms *L1, L2.* Terms in applied linguistics and language teaching. The *first language* is the language in which learners are competent when starting a new language; the *second language* is another language that is being learned or has been learned to an adequate level. In many countries, a specific L2 is learned, usually at school, for national or international use. English is the second language for many purposes in such countries as India, Nigeria, and Singapore. An L1 may or may not be a learner's mother tongue, because a chronologically first language may not be the functionally first language of adulthood. Under certain conditions, such as migration, an original L2 may become a person's L1 or only language. See LANGUAGE TEACHING, MOTHER TONGUE, TEACHING ENGLISH. [EDUCATION, LANGUAGE]. P.C., T.MCA.

FIRST NAME. See PERSONAL NAME.

FIST HAND. See INDEX.

FIXED [17c in this sense]. Of a language: made uniform or standard, as in the definition of Latin as 'an Italic language spoken in ancient Rome, fixed in the 2nd or 1st century B.C., and established as the official language of the Roman Empire' (*Random House Dictionary,* 1987). The idea of 'fixing' or 'ascertaining' English was strong in the 18c, especially among such writers as Addison and Defoe. See ACADEMY, STANDARD. [USAGE]. T.MCA.

FIXED PHRASE. A phrase, often consisting of an adjective and a noun, which functions as a word, either with unique reference (*Red Ensign, Red Indian, Red Sea*) or as an idiom (*red herring, red tape*). The usual stress is level (*Réd Séa, réd tápe*) as opposed to initial emphasis in compounds (*REDcap, REDcoat*). Fixed phrases are common in technical usage: *adaptive radiation, chemical differentiation, natural selection, solar nebula, spontaneous generation.* The dividing line between a widely used ordinary phrase and a fixed phrase is not easy to determine. There are degrees of fixedness, depending on frequency of occurrence and people's perception of the usage. Darwin's phrase *natural selection* did not become fixed in the language at large for many years, but for Darwin, it was probably fixed from the moment of coinage. The line between fixed phrases and compound words is also not easy to draw. Linguists disagree as to whether the following are fixed phrases or compounds: possessive eponyms (*Parkinson's Law, Tourette's syndrome*), words linked by preposition (*brother-in-law, actor-cum-manager*), and emphatic expressions (*brute of a man, fool of a boy, hell of a time*). Fixed phrases are often incorporated into compounds: *red letter* in *red-letter day* (a *réd-LEtter dáy*), and ordinary phrases that have been incorporated into compound forms become fixed within them: *hot water* in a *hot-water system; quick action* in *quick-action glue.* See ADJECTIVE, HOLOPHRASE, PHRASE, TECHNOSPEAK. [GRAMMAR, WORD]. T.MCA.

FLAMING. See TECHNOLOGY.

FLANDERS. See FLEMISH.

FLAP, FLAPPED *R*. See R-SOUNDS.

FLASH. (1) An obsolete term for showy, vulgar usage defined in Dyche & Pardon's dictionary of 1735 as 'a Boast, Brag, or great Pretence Made by Spend-thrift, Quack, or Pretender to more Art or Knowledge than a Person has'; the cant of thieves, prostitutes, and vagabonds. See CANT,

ROMANI/ROMANY, SLANG. (2) Also *newsflash*, *news flash*. In journalism, a brief report sent by a wire service or announced on radio or television, that provides preliminary information about a story that has just 'broken'. For *flashback/flashforward*, see ANACHRONY. [MEDIA, STYLE].

T.MCA.

FLAT [13c: from Old Norse *flatr*, akin to Old English *flet*]. (1) (Of a sound, voice, or accent) lacking resonance and pitch variation; monotonous; not clear or ringing: 'Seemingly classless, with a flat, featureless accent and unimaginative style of dress, Mr. Major lacks flamboyance' (Barry James, on the British prime minister, *International Herald Tribune*, 28 Nov. 1990). (2) Of writing, unable to sustain interest; dull. See ACCENT, (A)ESTHETICS, NEW ENGLAND. [SPEECH, STYLE, WRITING]. T.MCA.

FLEET STREET. A street in London, running from Ludgate Circus to the Strand, and taking its name from the Fleet River; once known for its bookshops, more recently for its newspaper offices. The association of *the Street* (as it has been called) with journalism derives from the concentration of British mass-circulation newspapers and periodicals in the area at the turn of the 20c. By the 1920s, most national newspapers were located there. The name became a metonym for the Press, as in *Fleet Street is agog at the latest scandal*. The term has often implied a greater unity or consensus than existed, given the varied character of the British press. Since the departure of newspaper offices to other sites in London, beginning with *The Times* in 1986 and ending with *The Daily Mail* in 1989, the journalistic use of the name, though ongoing and widely used, has become anachronistic. Compare GRUB STREET. [MEDIA]. G.H.

FLEMISH [13c: from Middle Dutch *Vlaemsch* (Modern Flemish *Vlaams*)]. The Germanic language of Belgium, its standard form differing little from that of Dutch. It is often called a variety of Dutch, sometimes *Low Dutch* or *South Dutch*, or is described with Dutch as a variety of *Netherlandic*. With French, it is an official language of Belgium, spoken in the northern provinces. Flemish is closely associated with *Flanders*, an ancient region of Europe now divided among Belgium, the Netherlands, and France. In English, this name is associated with the trench battles of the First World War (*Flanders field*, *Flanders poppy*) and since medieval times with Flemish cloth and weaving (*Flanders flax*, *Flanders lace*). Contact between Flanders and Britain has been close, especially because its cloth industry once depended on English wool. Flemish weavers settled in England and

Scotland, sometimes with the surname *Fleming* (a native of Flanders). The Flanders link produced such loans as *cambric* a fine white linen or cotton (from Kamerijk or Cambrai, a town now in France), *dornick* a damask cloth (from Doornik or Tournai, a town in Belgium), and *spa* a place for taking the waters (from Spa, near Liège). The region was important in the development of printing: William Caxton lived there for many years, spoke Flemish, and in 1476 printed the first book in English at his press in Bruges: *The Recuyell of the Historyes of Troye*. See CAXTON, DUTCH, FRENCH, LOW GERMAN, SCOTS. [EUROPE, LANGUAGE, NAME].

T.MCA., N.E.O.

FLESCH READABILITY FORMULA, The, also **the Flesch Formula, the Flesch Reading Ease Test.** A technique for assessing the readability of texts, named after its American developer Rudolf Flesch (*The Art of Readable Writing*, Harper & Row, 1949), who based it on the tentative statistics (relating to estimates of decreasing sentence length since the 16c) of the literary critic L. A. Sherman (*Analytics of Literature*, Ginn & Co., Boston, 1893). The formula establishes first the average sentence length in words of any given text (which is then multipled by 1.015) and the number of syllables per 100 words (which is multiplied by 0.846). The totals are added, then subtracted from 206.8 to give a score for reading ease on a scale from 0 (practically unreadable) to 100 (easy to read). A score of 60 is taken to be plain English: about 20 words per sentence and 1.5 syllables per word. The *Reader's Digest* scores 65, *Time Magazine* 52, the *Harvard Law Review* 32. The scores translate into US school grades as 60-70 (8th-9th grade), 50-60 (10th-12th grade), 0-30 (college graduate level). Most US states require insurance documents to score between 40 and 50. Compare FOG INDEX. See STYLE CHECKER. [STYLE, WRITING].

T.MCA.

FLUENCY [16c: from Latin *fluens/fluentis* flowing, and *-cy* as in *currency*]. Smooth, rapid, effortless use of language. The concept is widely used in foreign-language teaching, where to be fluent means to have assimilated all or most of the sound patterns and grammar, and an appreciable level of vocabulary, and to be able to put these patterns into easy, appropriate use in conversation. In first-language use, it implies the ability to speak smoothly and continuously, and sometimes volubly and glibly. In the context of language pathology, it is a theoretical norm whose achievement is the goal of people handicapped by disorders such as stuttering. Although the concept has a ready intuitive plausibility, it is difficult to measure precisely, and there is controversy over how best to assess it in people learning a language. See COMMUNICATION, LANGUAGE PATHOLOGY. [LANGUAGE].   D.C.

FLYTAAL, also **fly taal, flaaitaal** [?1950s: from English slang *fly* cunning, smart, and Afrikaans *taal* language]. A versatile argot or street language among especially younger urban blacks in South Africa. It was originally based on Afrikaans and known as *tsotsi-taal* [1940s: from *tsotsi* thief, gangster], a term now disparaged because others besides tsotsis use the argot. It has increasingly shifted to using various African languages as its base, and includes a range of English loanwords. Its many names include *Town Talk* and in township slang *isicamto* and *isileng* [the latter from English *slang*]. It varies from area to area, as do the languages of its predominant loanwords and the inclinations of its speakers. Although formerly in-group slang, it is becoming more widely known and understood, and is appearing in dialogue in African literature and drama in English. Its vocabulary includes such former in-group words as: *sharp* good, right, *groove* enjoy, *dlas* house (from Zulu *idlala* temporary hut), and *dikota* marijuana/dagga (from Sotho *dikota* dry wood). Flytaal has many terms for money, clothing, and drugs, and many colourful modes of address, of which the most popular is *bra*/*bla* brother, often used as a title: *Bra Victor*. See SOUTH AFRICAN ENGLISH, TSOTSI-TAAL. [AFRICA, VARIETY].   J.B.

FOG INDEX, also **Gunning Fog Index**. An American technique for assessing the readability of texts, developed by Robert Gunning (*The Technique of Clear Writing*, 1968). For any text, a rating requires both average sentence length and percentage (calculated per 100 words) of 'foggy' words (that is, those with three or more syllables). For an average sentence length of 20 words and 10% 'fog', the rating is found by adding the 20 and 10 to get 30, then multiplying by 0.4, to get 12, a point on a scale in which 5 is very readable, 10 is becoming hard, 15 is difficult, and 20 very difficult. Such a check is part of the service provided by many computer style checkers. Compare FLESCH READABILITY FORMULA. See STYLE CHECKER. [STYLE, WRITING].   T.MCA.

FOLIO [16c: from the Latin ablative phrase *in folio* in a leaf, from *folium* leaf, used to refer to the format of a page]. (1) A piece of paper cut for use on its own, in a manuscript, or in a book. In this sense, a folio has two sides or pages: the upper or *recto*, and the *verso*. (2) A sheet of such paper folded to form two leaves: that is, four sides or pages. (3) The size of such a leaf, used to describe a format for manuscripts and especially early printed books. (4) A manuscript or book made up in such a format. A folio of this kind often consists of three or four sheets folded as a group to make six or eight leaves (12 or 16 pages) in a *quire*. If the sheets are large, the resulting book is very large: the 'elephant folio' edition of John James Audubon's *Viviparous Quadrupeds of North America* (1845-8) is sometimes mounted on wheels for easier consultation. A typical folio is 18 to 24 inches (45 to 60 cm) high by a foot (30 cm) or more in width. (5) A leaf of paper or parchment (as a sheet of manuscript or copy) numbered on one side only and abbreviated *fol.*, *fo.*, *f.*: *You'll find his comments on folio 316a.* (6) A page number in a book. (7) In legal usage, a unit of measurement of the length of documents, determined by the number of words, 72 or 90 in Britain and 100 in the US. See BOOK, FORMAT. [TECHNOLOGY].   W.W.B., T.MCA.

FOLK [From Old English *folc*]. (1) 'People as the carriers of culture, esp. as representing the composite of social mores, customs, forms of behavior, etc., in a society: *The folk are the bearers of oral tradition*' (*Random House Dictionary*, 1987). In this sense, the term is strongly associated with 19c Romanticism, in which the assumed honesty and innocence of country folk is contrasted with the sophistication and even degeneracy of the city dweller; country dialects have often been favourably compared with urban dialects that arose with the Industrial Revolution: see DORIC. (2) Attributive: relating to or originating among the (common) people: *folk art, folk dance, folk medicine, folklore, folktale.* In the use by scholars of such terms as *folk belief, folk etymology*, and *folk linguistics* there is often a dismissive quality implying that 'folk' movements inherently operate at a lower and therefore less significant level than the traditions to which the scholars themselves belong. See FOLK ETYMOLOGY, ORAL TRADITION, POPULAR, ROMANTICISM, SAYING. [LANGUAGE].   T.MCA.

FOLK ETYMOLOGY, also **popular etymology**. A term in linguistics for 'folk' or 'popular' theories (that is, the thoughts of ordinary, non-academic people) about the origins, forms, and meanings of words, sometimes resulting in changes to the words in question: *plantar wart*, a wart on the sole of the foot (from Latin *planta*), reinterpreted as *planter's wart*. See ETYMOLOGY, FOLK, POPULAR, WORD ORIGINS. [HISTORY, LANGUAGE, WORD].   W.F.B.

FONT, also **fount** [16c: from French *fonte*, from *fondre* to found (as in *foundry*), referring to the making of cast type]. A printer's term: (1) Technically, a uniform size of typeface, the term being applied both to the design of the type as metal or photographic image and to its form as received on a printed surface. (2) More loosely, a family of type, such as *Palatino, Bembo, Gill Sans*. Technically, a *9-point Baskerville* is a different font from a *72-point Baskerville*, but loosely the whole family of Baskerville type, regardless of size, is a font. Such a font can contain up to 275 *sorts* or individual characters, including accented letters, ligatured letters, abbreviations, etc. See DIACRITIC, POINT, TYPE-SETTING, TYPOGRAPHY. [TECHNOLOGY]. W.W.B.

FOOLSCAP [17c: from a watermark showing a fool's or jester's cap and bells]. (1) In Britain, a size of paper for writing, drawing, or printing, usually 17 × 13.5 inches (43 × 34 cm) when folded or cut. Abbreviated as *cap., fcp*. (2) In the US, a type of inexpensive lined, yellow writing paper (legal-size: 8.5 × 14 inches, 22 × 36 cm), bound in tablet form. (3) Also *foolscap octavo*. A book size, 4.25 × 6.75 inches (11 × 17 cm) untrimmed. (4) Also *foolscap quarto*. An especially British book size, 6.75 × 8.5 inches (17 × 22 cm) untrimmed. See BOOK, FORMAT, PAPER. [TECH-NOLOGY]. W.W.B., T.MCA.

FOOT. (1) In prosody, the traditional unit of metre, made up in English of strong and weak syllables in combinations such as *iamb* (weak/strong) and *dactyl* (strong/weak/strong). A line of verse usually consists of a series of the same kind of foot, but there are sometimes variations. Kinds of foot take their names from Greek pros-ody, the English pattern of stressed and unstressed syllables (*accentual metre*) replacing a classical pattern of long and short vowels (*quantitative metre*). The signs most commonly used to mark such syllables are the *macron* (‾) for strong or long syllables and the *breve* (˘) for weak or short syllables. Sometimes a *solidus* or *slash* (/) is used for strong and (×) for weak syllables, and sometimes there is only an acute accent for strong syllables. The commoner met-rical feet in English are the *iamb* (∪ -) as in *support, restore*, the *trochee* (- ∪) as in *danger, labour*, the *dactyl* (- ∪ ∪) as in *catapult, memory*, the *anapaest/anapest* (∪ ∪ -) as in *amputee, put it up*, and the *spondee* (- -) as in *green light, big town*. A line of verse is named from its pre-dominant foot and the number of feet within it: *iambic pentameter* five iambic feet per line; *dactylic hexameter* six dactyls per line. (2) In phonetics, a unit of speech that begins with a stressed syllable and continues to the next stressed syllable or the end of a tone group, whichever comes first. The sentence *Do not walk on the grass* contains three feet: //*Do not | walk on the | grass*//. Weak syllables are generally deemed to be trailing: that is, they follow a stressed syllable, so that *on the* is grouped with

walk in the foot / *walk on the*/. The exception is the case of one or more weak initial syllables, grouped rhythmically with a following stressed syllable: //*at the shop on the | corner*//. Some scholars suggest that such leading syllables fol-low an initial 'silent stress', a beat (×) that occurs before the utterance begins: // × *at the | shop on the | corner*//. As the examples show, foot division ignores grammatical boundaries. See AMPHIBRACH, ANAP(A)EST, DACTYL, IAMB(US), METRE/METER, PROSODY, RHYTHM, SCANSION, SPONDEE, STRESS, THESIS, TROCHEE. [LITERATURE, SPEECH]. R.C., G.K.

FOOTERS. See HEADERS AND FOOTERS.

FOOTNOTE. See NOTES AND REFERENCES.

FOREIGNER TALK. A term in linguistics and language teaching for the conventionalized and simplified kind of language used by many native speakers with foreigners who cannot speak their language, such as (with exaggerated pointing gestures) *Me help you, yes?* for *I am going to help you; is that all right?* It has a simple or non-existent morphology, more or less fixed word order, simple syntax, a small number of grammatical words, and little or no use of the copula: a complex sentence such as *I haven't seen the man you're talking about* could be reduced and simplified as *I no see man you say* or *That man you talk I not see*. Compare BABY TALK, TEACHER TALK. See PIDGIN, TALK. [EDUCATION, LANGUAGE, VARIETY]. S.R.

FOREIGNISM [1850s]. A foreign word or expression, as in the headline 'No more *Antagonismo*' (*Time*, 15 Aug. 1988). Foreign expressions in English (as opposed to *borrowings* or *loanwords* proper) are generally used for spe-cial effect, for 'local colour', or to demonstrate special knowledge. In print, they typically appear in italics and are usually glossed:

In the bazaars the shops were silently shuttered. In place of the turmoil of hawkers, scooters and vans pedestrians shrouded in the *phiran*, the long woollen winter coat, wandered or lounged in good humoured idleness, clutching under their wraps the *kongri*, a bas-ket containing an earthenware bowl full of hot charcoal to keep them warm ('Letter from Srinagar', *The Times*, 23 Jan. 1984).

Writers of fiction often dispense with italics, implying that in a given situation the unusual expressions are normal, whether or not the reader immediately understands them. A gloss may or may not be provided:

I am bawaji, the son of the son of and so on and so on of a bawaji; but as my bapaiji, my paternal grand-mother . . . recently said to me: You are a bawaji,

Hormusji, . . . but you yourself do not know what it means to be a bawaji. You should be ashamed (Boman Desai, *The Memory of Elephants*, 1988).

There tends to be a gradation in English from less to more foreign. French expressions range from the integrated (but variously pronounced) *garage* through *elite/élite* and *coup d'etat/état* to *fin de siècle* and *pâtisserie*. In such a spread, it is difficult to specify precisely where the 'properly' foreign begins: all the items are foreign, but some are more foreign than others, and more foreign for some than for others. Non-native words are used in English to a vast and unmeasurable extent. Many varieties of the language have everyday usages that in others would be foreignisms: Maori expressions in NZE, Hawaiian elements in AmE, and Gallicisms in the English of Quebec. Three works of reference that list foreignisms are: *A Dictionary of Foreign Words & Phrases in Current English*, by A. J. Bliss (1972), *Dictionary of Foreign Terms*, by C. O. Sylvester Mawson (revised by Charles Berlitz, 1975), and *Loanwords Dictionary*, by L. Urdang and F. Abate (1988). See ANACHORISM, BORROWING, HARD WORD, LOAN, LOANWORD, NATIVIZATION. [REFERENCE, STYLE, USAGE, WORD].

T.MCA.

FOREIGN USER [1970s]. A term in language teaching and applied linguistics for a non-native user of a language, in either or both speech and writing, as opposed to both *foreign learner* and *native speaker* and particularly in contrast to *native user*. It is common in discussions of English as a foreign language: 'What most learners really want is to be competent foreign users of the language, not cheap imitation native speakers' (John Shepherd, *EFL Gazette*, Oct. 1990). See NATIVE SPEAKER, NATIVE USER, TEFL. [EDUCATION].

T.MCA.

FORENAME. See PERSONAL NAME.

FORM [13c: from French *forme*, Latin *forma* mould, shape, beauty, translating Greek *eîdos*]. (1) Shape and appearance, as in *the human form*, *water in such forms as snow and ice*, and *the novel as a literary form*. (2) A prescribed or customary way of doing things, often with a ritualistic aspect, such as the form of words used in taking an oath. (3) A structured document containing usually numbered requests for information followed by spaces in which the information can be provided, often requiring a dated signature at the end: *a tax form, an insurance claim form*. (4) A master document used as a model or guide in framing similar documents for actual use. (5) A conventional way of proceeding, behaving, saying things, etc.: *forms of address*. In Anglo-Saxon cultures, the idea of socially *good* and *bad form*

('*It's bad form to do that, old chap*') is widespread, and often related to distinctions of class, especially in the UK. (6) A grade or class of pupils in a British secondary school. (7) In philosophy, the structure, pattern, or nature of a thing; for Plato it was also an idea (an abstract entity), for Aristotle it was what places a thing in its species or kind. (8) In logic, the abstract relations of terms in a proposition, and of propositions in a syllogism. (9) In linguistics, an inflected variant of a word: *men* as the plural form of *man*; *see*, *sees*, *saw*, *seen*, *seeing* as the forms of the verb *see*. (10) In linguistics, a category such as 'noun' when analysed in terms of structure (singular *man*, plural *men*) and function (subject and object of sentence). Items that share characteristics belong to the same *form class*: the forms *happy* and *careful* belong to the adjective form class. Criteria of form are used to identify units and classes of units. Words such as *man* and *information* are identified as nouns by the formal criterion (among others) that they can be the main words in a phrase that functions as the subject of a sentence (*man* in *That man looks familiar*) or as the object of a preposition (*information* in *This is for your information only*). The criterion may be negative: nouns, unlike most adjectives, do not have comparative and superlative forms: there are adjective forms *happier* and *happiest* alongside *happy*, but no corresponding forms for *girl*. In contrast, notional or semantic criteria identify units and classes by meaning: a noun defined as the name of a person, thing, or place; a verb as a doing word. While such criteria may adequately characterize central members of a class, they are not comprehensive. The notional definition of a noun does not cover such words as *action, existence, happiness, temperature* that belong to the noun form class on formal criteria. See FORMAT, FORM OF ADDRESS, FORMULA, FUNCTION, IDEA, MODEL, MORPHOLOGY, PARADIGM, SYLLOGISM. [GRAMMAR, LANGUAGE, WRITING].

T.MCA., S.G.

FORMAL [14c: from Latin *formalis* relating to form]. A term concerned with: (1) Structure and order: *a formal education, a formal garden, formal logic, formal grammar, formal as opposed to semantic criteria*. (2) More or less elevated and stylized ceremonial: *a formal dinner, formal dress, formal and informal meetings*. (3) Style and usage of a relatively elevated and impersonal kind: *a highly formal writing style*; '*receive*' a more formal word than '*get*'. See FORM. [GRAMMAR, STYLE].

T.MCA., S.G.

FORMAL LANGUAGE (1) Language that is formal and ceremonial. (2) A language designed for use in situations in which natural language is considered unsuitable, such as logic, mathematics, and computer programming. In such systems, the symbols and formulas stand in precise and unambiguous syntactic and semantic relation to specific referents or concepts. Compare ARTIFICIAL LANGUAGE, NATURAL LANGUAGE. [LANGUAGE]. T.MCA.

FORMAT [19c: from the Latin *formatus* shaped]. (1) The general appearance of a printed publication, including its type, paper, size, and binding. A broadsheet newspaper, a leather-bound octavo book, and a monthly magazine have very distinct formats. (2) An approximate indication of the size of a publication in terms of the number of times sheets of paper have been folded to make leaves: *folio, quarto, octavo, sixteenmo,* etc. (3) The style, plan, arrangement, presentation, etc., of a radio, television, or other programme. (4) The arrangement of data on magnetic tape, paper tape, drums, disks, etc., to comply with the input and output device of a computer. (5) To give a format to (something): *to format a book/diskette.* Compare FORM. See APPENDIX, BACK MATTER, BOOK, EDITING, EPILOG(UE), FRONT MATTER, GRAPHIC DESIGN, LANGUAGE TEACHING, LAYOUT, LINE, NEWSPAPER, PAGE, PAGINATION, PREFACE, PRELIM(INARIE)S, PROLOG(UE), SPACE, TEXT, TITLE, TYPOGRAPHY, WHITE SPACE. [TECHNOLOGY, WRITING]. W.W.B.

FORMATIVE [1870s as *formative element*]. (1) In philology, a derivational affix, especially one that determines part of speech or word class: *-ness* in *darkness,* forming a noun from an adjective. (2) In structural linguistics, a word-forming element: the prefix *un-* and suffix *-ly* in *unkindly.* (3) In generative grammar, a minimal unit of syntax: in *The dancers performed gracefully,* the formatives (joined by plus signs) are *the + dance + er + s perform + ed grace + full + ly.* Compare AFFIX, BASE, MORPHEME. [GRAMMAR, WORD]. T.MCA.

FORM OF ADDRESS. Any word, such as a name, title, or pronoun, that designates someone who is being addressed in speech or writing. Such forms of address may be built into the grammar of a language used (as with the French pronouns *vous* and *tu*), or may evolve as a range of titles, names, kinship terms, terms of endearment, and nicknames, all usually with an initial capital in English.

Pronouns. Some languages, such as Japanese, have elaborate systems of pronouns to mark the relationship between addresser and addressee. Some European languages have systems in which one pronoun (French *vous,* Spanish *Usted*) is used politely and formally among equals or by inferiors to superiors, and another

(French *tu,* Spanish *tu*), used informally and intimately among equals or by superiors to inferiors. In French, the verbs *tutoyer* (to call *tu*; to be on familiar terms with) and *vousvoyer* (to call *vous*; to be on formal terms with) derive from and refer to this system. General English once used pronouns in this way: in Shakespeare's *Tempest,* Prospero addresses his daughter Miranda with the intimate *th*-forms (*thou, thee, thy, thine*) and she addresses him with the respectful *y*-forms (*ye, you, your, yours*). In some circumstances, such as the wooing scene between Anne and Richard in *Richard III,* such pronouns are used to mark the changing relationships between speakers.

A continuum of usage. In addressing people, the two categories 'intimates/children/social inferiors' and 'acquaintances/elders/social superiors, etc.' are the poles of a continuum. At the intimately personal end, actual names may not be used at all; forms of address tend instead to be terms of endearment (*baby, darling, dear, dearie, honey, sweetie, sugar*) or expressions of derision (*dickhead, fishbreath, four-eyes, idiot, stupid*), usually hostile and dismissive, but sometimes affectionate. At the impersonal end, such forms of address as *sir* and titles (bare or with surname) may be used: *Excuse me, sir/Sir, Doctor (Kildare), do you have a moment, please?, Follow your orders, Captain (Bligh).* All the forms of address discussed below occur at various points on this continuum.

Names and titles. With the loss of its *th*-forms as living pronouns (except in North of England and Northern Isles dialect) and the extension of the *y*-forms to all uses, English has come to rely primarily on forms of address to convey nuances of relationship. The broad rule for forms of address is that those who are intimates address each other with given names such as *George* and *Sue* (and are 'on first-name terms'), whereas those who are acquaintances use a title and family name such as *Mr Jones, Mrs/Ms/Miss Smith* (and are 'on last-name terms'). Strangers in more or less formal situations use titles only (*Sir, Madam*). This rule has, however, many refinements and exceptions. In Britain, in the public (that is, private) schools, socially prestigious clubs, the armed services, and other groups, it has been common for males to address each other by surname alone (*Good to see you, Brown!,* or, affectionately, *Brown, my dear chap, it's good to see you!*), but this practice appears to be on the wane. In casual situations, men of all classes and backgrounds may employ strong, even taboo expressions affectionately, with *you,* as in *Come on, you old rascal/bugger, have another drink.*

Use of someone's given name (such as *Elizabeth*) when the person is commonly addressed by a diminutive (*Bess*) often signals formality, and, especially with a child, the possibility of a scolding. Between the unadorned given name and a title with a family name, a number of other uses are intermediate in formality but also restricted to certain groups. In the American South, the title *Miz* is spoken with a woman's first name as a respectful, but semi-familiar, form of address. Scarlett O'Hara in Margaret Mitchell's *Gone with the Wind* (1936) would have been *Miz Scarlett* to servants and slaves as well as to the family doctor. The mother of US president Jimmy Carter, a Georgian, was affectionately called *Miz Lilian* by many journalists, and the matriarch of the 1980s television soap opera *Dallas*, set in Texas, is *Miz Ellie* (*Ewing*).

Kinship usage. Within families, kinship terms are often used: (1) Formally, *Father, Grandfather, Grandmother, Mother*. (2) Very formally, especially in the British upper classes, especially in the 19c, *Mama, Papa* (stress on second syllable) or the Latin *Mater, Pater* (with English pronunciations, 'may-ter, pay-ter'). (3) Informally, with variations according to region and class, *Da/Dad,Daddy, Gramps/Grandad/Granda/ Grandpa, Gran/Grandma/Grannie, Ma/Mam/ Mom/Momma/Mum/Mammy/Mommy/Mummy, Pa/Pop/Poppa*. *Father, mother, brother, sister* have been extended beyond the family for religious purposes and to express fellowship. Within the family, especially in AmE, *Sister* has the short form *Sis*, *Brother* the occasional *Bro, bud(dy)* (extended into familiar use, mainly between men), and *brer*. *Cousin* in the past had the short form *coz*, often used by Shakespeare. Beyond the first degree of kinship or the direct line of descent, it is common to combine kinship term and given name: *Aunt*(*ie*) *Mary, Uncle Louis*, and especially in AmE *Cousin Jean*.

Nicknames. Used on an often close informal level, nicknames may be diminutives of given names that are relatively stable over years, or may be temporary monickers bestowed, changed, and dropped as the bearer moves from one group to another. A young male may be sequentially and colourfully called *Sewage, Fingers, Scar, Sunshine, Jay Eff* (his initials), or a chubby young female, by a process of association, *Pear, Persia, Iran, Irene, Irenebus*, and *Bus* (examples from Morgan, O'Neill, & Harré, *Nicknames*, 1979). Nicknames may be neutral (*Bill, Joanie*), admiring (*Refrigerator*, for a heavily built American football player), or stigmatizing (*Stinky*), and show a more intimate or immediate and often emotive relationship between addresser and addressee than if the bearer's ordinary name is used.

Titles with last names. At a markedly more formal and respectful level is the use of a title with the last name. The traditional set of such titles includes *Mr/Mr.* for men, *Mrs/Mrs.* for married women, *Miss* for girls and unmarried women, and *Master* for boys. The full form *Mister* (a variant of *Master*) is currently almost never used with the last name, but is a term of address to a stranger (*Mister, can you help me?*), usually considered a 'low' equivalent of *sir* (*Excuse me, sir, can you help me?*). Its short form in BrE is either *Mr* or more traditionally *Mr.*; in AmE, it is usually the latter. The conventions for *Mrs/Mrs.* are the same. Both *Mrs/Mrs.* and *Miss* are abbreviations of *Mistress*, a form once common (compare Shakespeare's *Mistress Quickly*, in *Henry V*), surviving into the late 20c in parts of Scotland, Northern England, and Ireland, and in the West Indies. The forms of address for married and unmarried women have been subjected to reassessment in recent years, especially by feminists, who have objected to the use of titles which announce a woman's marital status but not a man's. The forms have also been awkward because a woman's marital status may not be known to someone who needs to use a title when addressing or mentioning her. As an alternative, the form *Ms* (pronounced 'miz' like the Southern US form, but otherwise unrelated to it) has been adopted in recent years, first in the US, then elsewhere.

Professional titles. Certain professional titles may replace those just mentioned. In the US, physicians of all kinds and dentists insist on *Dr.* instead of *Mr.*, while in Britain *Mr/Mr.* is preferred by surgeons and dentists. The same title may be used in the US with the surnames of most holders of doctoral degrees (Doctor of Philosophy, Doctor of Education, etc.) who are practising academics, though not with those of non-academics; in Britain, anyone holding such a degree can use the title or not. In Britain, the academic title *Professor* (abbreviation *Prof.*) is restricted to holders of a professorial chair, while in North America generally any holder of a professorial rank (assistant, associate, or full professor) can use it. Consequently, most university-level teachers in the US and Canada are addressed and referred to as professors, while few in Britain and the Commonwealth are so addressed. In the military, titles for ranks are regularly used as forms of address: *Captain Bligh, some of the men would like to see you.* Similarly, titles for the clergy may be used in addressing them: *Father Brown, here is a mystery for you; Sister Bernadette, have you seen anything interesting lately?* In American law, judges are addressed as *Judge Bean* and lawyers as *Counsellor*, without surname (*Excuse me, Counsellor,* *but . . .*). In other branches of the US government, presidents, vice-presidents, senators, representatives (members of the House of Representatives, also called congressmen/women), governors, mayors, and assorted other office-holders are routinely addressed by their titles and surnames: *Senator/Mayor Smith, will you be running for office again?*

Royalty and nobility. In Britain, royal and noble titles have been in use since the Middle Ages, often involving complex conventions of address and precedence. A monarch is referred to as, for example, *King Edward* or *Queen Mary*, but is directly, formally, and traditionally addressed as *Your Majesty* (formerly also *Your Grace*); other royals are traditionally addressed as *Your Royal Highness*. At the present time, Queen Elizabeth and other royal ladies are addressed as *Ma'am*, male members of the royal household as *Sir*, without name. Members of the royal family are referred to as *His/Her Royal Highness*, often abbreviated to *H.R.H.*, especially in palace circles, without name (*H.R.H. would like . . .*). A lord is addressed either without name as *your lordship* (now restricted to use only by tradesmen or servants) or, in the case especially of a life peer in the House of Lords, as for example *Lord Bland*. The younger sons of dukes and marquesses are addressed as, for example, *Lord Henry*, distinguishing them by first name from relations with the same surname (*Lord Henry Barringby* from *Lord William Barringby*). A knight is addressed as, for example, *Sir Henry (Sherlock)*. The wives of both lords and knights are addressed and referred to as *Lady Bland* (matching *Lord Bland*), and *Lady Sherlock* (matching *Sir Henry Sherlock*). The daughters of dukes, marquesses, and earls are addressed as *Lady Jane* (matching *Lord Henry*). When the highly formal *Your Majesty, Excellency, Holiness, Eminence*, etc., are used, the style is usually oblique: *Would Your Majesty care to honour us with a few words?*

Bare titles. Use of a title without any name spans the continuum of familiarity and respect, but is the only possibility between strangers. The titles normally so used are *Sir, Madam/Ma'am*, which tend, however, to be restricted to use in more up-market shops, restaurants, and hotels, and as salutations in business correspondence. In response, customers might use *Miss* to a (younger) woman waiting on them; there is no corresponding standard term for a male, the older use of *boy* in such circumstances in the US and parts of Africa and Asia being no longer generally acceptable. The British upper classes would say *waiter* or *waitress* (or *young woman*), but not *Miss*. Certain occupational terms may be used without a name: *What do you recommend,*

Doctor?; *Nurse, could you get me an aspirin?*; *Yes, Sergeant*; *Father, bless me for I have sinned*; *It's so good of you to come, Vicar*; *Preacher, you had them in the aisles this Sunday*.

Informally, especially among working-class (BrE), blue-collar (AmE) groups, casual forms of address are common: (1) Male to male, *bud(dy)* in the US (especially to a stranger); *cock* among Cockneys in London (to an equal, including a stranger so perceived); *guv* among Cockneys, short for *governor* (to a social superior, including a stranger so perceived); *mac* in Scotland and parts of North America (to an equal, especially a stranger so perceived); *mate* in Britain, Australia, and New Zealand (to an equal, including a stranger so perceived); *pal* in North America and Scotland (to an equal, especially a stranger so perceived). (2) Female and male to female, *ducks* (singular use, in England, especially among Cockneys, to an equal, including to a stranger so perceived, with a camp variant *duckie*); *hen* (in Scotland, especially in Glasgow); *honey* (especially in North America, including to strangers), and its variant *hinny* in the North of England; *love* (especially in England, including to a male and a stranger, virtually regardless of social position).

Between strangers who are social equals, there are no polite forms of address in general use. Certain forms are used in limited circumstances, such as *Ladies and gentlemen*, the traditional opening of a formal speech, with less formal variants such as *Dearly beloved* (by clergymen), *Friends*, or such a formula as *My fellow citizens/Rotarians*. *Sir* and *Madam* (especially BrE) and *Ma'am* (especially AmE) are widely used as titles of respect, even for acquaintances, particularly those of more advanced years than the speaker, including in some traditional groups by children to any adult. In formal circumstances, in corresponding or with an audience, there are set forms for addressing royalty, titled persons, government office-holders, clergy, and others whose rank or function is deemed more important than their persons. The rules governing such forms of address are provided in guides to etiquette. See TITLE. [NAME].   J.A., T.McA.

FORMULA [16c: Latin, a fine form, small pattern, mould, rule, method, agreement, from *forma* shape, and *-ula*, a feminine diminutive suffix]. (1) A form or pattern of words prescribed by custom or authority, often with a ritualistic quality: *the use of dear and a name or form of address to start a letter.* (2) A convention or framework, such as the way in which the entries in this volume are shaped or *formulated.* (3) A form of words that reconciles differing points of view in an argument: *a peace formula.* (4) A repeatable phrase with a particular rhythm, such as the Homeric epithet *boôpis Hḗrē* (translated as *ox-eyed Hera*), which identifies and characterizes a goddess and fits easily into a line of dactylic hexameter verse. (5) In science and mathematics, a group of symbols and figures that serves to condense a principle or general statement, especially in algebra and chemistry. The adjective is *formulaic*. See ABBREVIATION, BIOGRAPHY, BOILERPLATE, CONVENTION, DEFINITION, FORM. [LANGUAGE].   T.McA.

FORTIS. See HARD AND SOFT, VOICE.

FORUM. See ENGLISH TEACHING FORUM.

FOUL LANGUAGE. Indecent or obscene words and phrases, such as four-letter words, such sexual slurs as *poofter* and *whore*, especially when used directly to refer to or address someone, and swearwords referring to hell and damnation, but not usually ethnic slurs or simple abuse. *Dickhead* is foul language, but *blockhead* and *nigger* are not. Someone *foul-mouthed* regularly uses foul language. See OBSCENITY, SWEARING. [STYLE, USAGE].   R.F.I.

FOUNT. See FONT.

FOUR-LETTER WORD. A word of four letters considered vulgar or obscene and referring to sex or excrement, such as (with varying degrees of offensive force) *arse, cock, crap, cunt, dick, fuck, piss, shit,* and probably *fart*. Such words are sometimes called 'Anglo-Saxon', although, of the above list, only *arse, cock,* and *shit* definitely derive from Old English. *Cunt, fart,* and *fuck* may, but firm evidence is lacking. *Dick* is a nickname for *Richard*, of uncertain age, while *crap* comes from Medieval Latin and *piss* from Old French. It is hard to trace the origins of such words because for long periods they have been banned from dictionaries. Although *fuck* appears in Florio's Italian-English dictionary (1598) and some taboo words were entered in 17-18c English dictionaries, they were usually not present in such works in the 19c and in the 20c before the 1960s. The phrase *four-letter* was first attested in print in 1923 and *four-letter word* in 1934. Such words are now usually entered in general dictionaries, with such labels or qualifications as 'usually considered obscene' or 'sometimes considered vulgar'. There are, in addition, some 'honorary' four-letter words, such as the five-letter but monosyllabic *prick, screw*. Learnèd words in the same area, such as *defecate, faeces, penis, urinate, vagina*, are not considered vulgar or obscene, but are euphemistic and/or technical. In English, there are no neutral terms for sex and excrement. Linguistic taboo makes four-letter words candidates for semantic extension and transfer: a *prick* is a man whom the speaker dislikes; *Shit!* and *Fuck!* are interjections of disapproval or dismay. The form *fucking* often has an emphatic function in casual but 'coarse' conversation: *I got my fucking hand caught in the fucking machine!* Slurs used in referring to people's sexuality (such as four-letter *poof, dyke*) are often felt to be closer to ethnic slurs (such as four-letter *dago, kike*) than to typical 'four-letter words'. The meaning of the phrase can be wryly extended, as in 'Work is a four-letter word'. See SWEARING, TABOO. [STYLE, WORD].   R.F.I.

FOWLER, H(enry) W(atson) [1858-1933]. English schoolmaster, lexicographer, and commentator on usage, born at Tonbridge, Kent, and educated at Rugby School and Balliol College, Oxford. He taught classics and English literature at Sedburgh School, then in north-west Yorkshire, now in Cumbria (1882-99), where he was variously described as 'lacking humanity', 'a first-rate swimmer, skater, and climber', and 'a stickler for etiquette'. There followed a period in London as a freelance writer and journalist, during which he wrote a number of works under pseudonyms, including *More Popular Fallacies*, by Quillet (1904), *Si mihi—!* by Egomet (1907), and *Between Man and Boy* by Quilibet (1908). He moved to Guernsey to join his brother, Francis George Fowler, and there, in two separate granite cottages in the parish of St-Peter-in-the-Wood, the brothers worked singly or together on several projects. Their translation of the works of the Greek writer Lucian of Samosata was published in 1905, and a book about good and bad English was eventually given the title *The King's English*. Though untrained in lexicography ('we were plunging into the sea of lexicography without having been first taught to swim') and with no satisfactory models before them except *Chambers Twentieth Century Dictionary* (1901), the brothers went on to edit *The Concise Oxford Dictionary* (1911), one of the most successful of 20c dictionaries.

After a brief adventure in the armed forces in France in 1915-16 ('performing only such menial or unmilitary duties as dishwashing, coal-heaving, and porterage'), they returned to England. F.G.F. died from tuberculosis in 1918 and H.W.F. carried on alone. First, he brought to completion a small dictionary derived from the *COD*. Known at the planning stage as 'The Shilling Dictionary' (referring to the price of pocket-sized dictionaries of the time), it was called *The Pocket Oxford Dictionary* when it appeared in 1924. The Fowlers declared at an early stage that the *COD* 'was found not to be easily squeezable' and they therefore adopted some unorthodox techniques in the pocket version. Thus, under *accelerando* a list was provided of all the main musical directions (*crescendo, diminuendo, pianissimo,* etc.), and under *paper* a list of paper sizes (*royal, octavo, crown quarto, demy, elephant,* etc.). H.W.F., as a member of the Society for Pure English, contributed numerous papers to its publications, including essays on *will/shall,* subjunctives, preposition at end, the split infinitive, *alright,* and nouns of multitude. His most famous work, *A Dictionary of Modern English Usage,* was published in 1926. The last years of his life were spent on an unfinished and unpublished dictionary, *The Quarto Oxford Dictionary,* which was to have been a 1,500-page dictionary of current English.

Fowler was a gifted amateur scholar. In what he called his 'lotusland' (Guernsey) and later at Hinton St George in Somerset, he remained essentially unaware of the linguistic controversies sweeping through the universities of Europe and the New World. He did not read the learned journals and books in which scholars like Ferdinand de Saussure, Leonard Bloomfield, Edward Sapir, and Otto Jespersen were propounding the doctrine of descriptive linguistics. His models were the classical languages of Greece and Rome, modified to suit the facts of the English language as he saw them. The responses of writers and scholars to his work have varied, journalists tending towards praise and even adulation, academic linguists towards caution and even reproof. Among reviews of the 1965 edition of *MEU*: 'a classic among English dictionaries' (*British Book News*); 'this literary goldmine' (*Medical News*); 'Mention of the names of Defenders of English brings me to Fowler, whose *Modern English Usage* made him the greatest champion and paladin of them all' (*Teachers' World*); 'Fowler was no great grammarian, still less a linguist in the modern sense' (Randolph Quirk); 'this guide is neither complete nor very systematic' (Yngve Olsson); 'Fowler's attitude is not a possible one for a good mind in the 1960's' (Barbara Strang); 'Who is Fowler to tell us what to say?' (Anthony Burgess). See index. [BIOGRAPHY, EUROPE, REFERENCE, STYLE, USAGE].   RO.W.B.

Burchfield, Robert W. 1979. *The Fowlers: Their Achievements in Lexicography and Grammar.* London: English Association.

Coulton, G. G. 1935. *H. W. Fowler* (Society for Pure English Tract 43). Oxford: Clarendon Press.

Gowers, Ernest A. 1957, *H. W. Fowler: The Man and his Teaching.* London: English Association.

FRACTURED ENGLISH. A facetious term for inadequate and amusing English as used by non-native speakers: *Teeth extracted by latest Methodists*; *Order your summers suit*; *Because is big rush we will execute customers in strict rotation*; *a town that has four thousand years of past historical.* The amusement is prompted by incongruity, and may be innocent or disdainful. In Britain, specimens of fractured English often feature in the media, especially after the holiday season, with invitations to send in specimens. Raconteurs may report usages faithfully, embroider them, or invent examples of their own. The following widely quoted item appears to have been lovingly polished: *When a passenger of foot heave in sight, tootle the horn. Trumpet him melodiously at first, but if he still obstacles your passage then tootle him with vigor.* Not all such usage is treated as amusing; language professionals draw attention to it from time to time to express their concern about the quality of English as a lingua franca. In the 1980s, the now-defunct UK *Translators' Guild Newsletter* had a section entitled 'Pitfalls and Howlers', drawing attention light-heartedly (but with serious intent) to such occurrences as this extract from a letter canvassing legal business: 'You are kindly informed that we are of the sincere and reliable attorneys who are undertaking the international business of same career in cooperation with associates/clients overseas from one country to another throughout the world.' Increasingly, however, non-idiomatic usage is quoted in the media without comment, as in: ' "We laugh when we hear all this," he said, "because we have no hostile intentions to do all this danger against him" ' (*International Herald Tribune*, 13 Jan. 1986). See BROKEN ENGLISH. [STYLE, VARIETY].
                                             T.MCA.

FRAMEWORK PROJECT, The. See ENGLISH-SPEAKING UNION.

FRAMIS. See DOUBLE TALK.

FRANCIZATION [Late 20c: from French *francisation.* Used with or without an initial capital]. Sometimes **Francicization**, with the verb *francicize.* A term in Canada for the conversion of texts and terminology (especially English) into French, and in Quebec for the conversion of the language of business and administration from English into French. See CANADA, QUEBEC. [AMERICAS, LANGUAGES].   T.MCA.

FRANGLAIS [1960s: a blend of *français* and *anglais*]. (1) An often pejorative term for French that contains many loans from English; it covers both the use of vogue words in the media and commerce and code-mixing and code-switching among bilinguals, especially in Canada. It was popularized by the French writer René Etiemble in *Parlez-vous franglais?* (1964), in which he condemned the spread of Anglo-Saxon culture and language since the Second World War. AmE rather than BrE was the target of Etiemble's criticism; imported US terms like *call-girl, coke, drugstore,* and *strip-tease* were seen as marks of Americanization. Etiemble's critique combines linguistic purism with a distaste for anything *yanqui* (*capitalisme yanqui, cancer yanqui, civilisation cocalcoolique*) and hostility to Europe's becoming *un protectorat yanqui.* His views have been widely discussed, and among the solutions offered are the Gallicization of Anglicisms and the more extensive use of native resources, including those of French outside France. Orthographic adaptation could turn the patently English *meeting, ticket, rocket* into a Gallicized *métingue, tiquet, roquette,* and loan translation could turn *surfing, flashback, script-girl* into *rase-rouleaux, retour en arrière, and secrétaire de plateau.* In Quebec, *franglais* belongs in a continuum of terms: *français, franglais, Frenglish, English.* (2) (Facetious). A hybrid medium developed by the English humorist Miles Kington in *Parlez-Vous Franglais?* (1981), which exaggerates the 'schoolboy' French of Britons abroad: 'Si vous êtes un first-time reader de Franglais, welcome! Franglais est comparativement painless et ne donne pas un hangover. En quantités judicieuses, il est mind-blowing. Ayez fun.' See ANGLIKAANS, CAMFRANGLAIS, FRENCH, SPANGLISH. [AMERICAS, EUROPE, LANGUAGE, VARIETY]. J.M.G., T.MCA.

FREE. See BOUND AND FREE, FREE VARIATION, FREE VERSE.

FREEDOM OF THE PRESS. The freedom of authors, journalists, and others to write what they wish and publishers and printers to produce and distribute it, within the limits of the laws of libel and defamation. Whereas the freedom of the press in the US is guaranteed by the First Amendment to the Constitution, the British press has never enjoyed such a right. Initially, in the time of the first printers in English, William Caxton and Wynkyn de Worde (15–16c), the press in England was unfettered, since it did not play a political or religious role, as was the case in the Reformation controversies on the Continent, but during the reign of Henry VIII strong repressive measures were taken against reformist works and unauthorized translations of the Bible. Penalties for unlicensed publication were severely physical in the 17c, and included cropping the ears (the epithet 'crop-ears' being especially associated with the opponents of Charles I), slitting the nose, and branding on both cheeks with the initials *S* and *L* for *seditious libeller*.

The stringent censorship imposed during the Civil War provoked Milton's *Areopagitica* (1644), a rhetorical plea for the freedom of the press which was deliberately issued unlicensed and unregistered: see POLEMIC. Since the lapsing of the Licensing Act in 1695, freedom of the Press has existed first in England, then in Britain at large (at any rate in principle), with the exception of censorship imposed on stage plays and in time of war. Stamp duty was, however, used as a vehicle of repression during the early 18c. Swift noted in 1712: 'All Grub Street is ruined by the Stamp Act.' Originally set up at one penny, the stamp duty was raised successively through the nervous years of the French Revolution, since newspapers were regarded as vehicles of turbulence. It was abolished in 1855. Marx's observation that 'The first freedom of the press consists in its not being a trade' emphasizes the point that certain economic constraints invariably curtail or compromise the freedom of the press. Partly because English-language newspapers have had a tradition of championing libertarian causes, they are often viewed with suspicion by governments and may therefore on occasion and in certain places operate under some degree of censorship and suppression. See CENSORSHIP, NEWSPAPER, PRESS. [MEDIA]. G.H.

FREE VARIATION. In linguistics, a relationship between the members of a pair of phonemes, words, etc., in which either can occur in the same position without causing a change of meaning: the initial vowels /i/ and /ɛ/ are in free variation in the pronunciation of *economics* ('eek-' or 'eck-') as are *up* and *down* in the phrasal verbs *slow up, slow down.* [LANGUAGE]. T.MCA.

FREE VERSE [20c: a loan translation of French *vers libre*]. Verse written without a regular metrical pattern, regarded as verse because of its rhythm and the use of such devices as imagery and concentrated language. *Vers libre* was developed by the late-19c French Symbolist poets J. Laforgue, A. Rimbaud, S. Mallarmé, and P. Verlaine, who influenced British and American poets of the next generation, especially those associated with the Imagist movement, such as T. E. Hulme, Richard Aldington, Hilda Doolittle, and Ezra Pound, who found other precedents in irregular forms of earlier English poetry, the King James Bible, and Japanese *haiku*. It became the dominant form of 20c poetry, as in D. H. Lawrence:

> And can a man his own quietus make with a bare
> bodkin?
> With daggers, bodkins, bullets, man can make
> a bruise or break of exit for his life;
> but is that a quietus, O tell me, is it quietus?
> ('The Ship of Death', 1929)

In sacrificing the discipline of traditional metre,

free verse gains a freedom of expression congenial to modern poets. The lines are divided by sense instead of metre, are usually variable in length, and without rhyme. A few poets, such as Walt Whitman, have combined free verse with rhyme, alliteration, and lines of equal length:

Wild, wild the storm, and the sea high running,
Steady the roar of the gale, with incessant undertone muttering,
Shouts of demoniac laughter fitfully piercing and pealing

('Patroling Barnegat', 1881)

Although free verse can accommodate good and even great poetry, it risks becoming formless and hard to distinguish from prose cut into lines. See DICKENS, ENGLISH LITERATURE, VERSE. [LITERATURE].   R.C.

FRENCH [Known to its speakers as *français*]. A Romance language of Western Europe, the official language of France and an official language of Belgium (with Flemish) and Switzerland (with German, Italian, and Romansch); spoken in Luxembourg, Andorra, Aosta in Italy, and the Channel Islands; during the 11–13c widely spoken in the British Isles. In the Americas, French is an official language of Canada (with English), the official language of the French island department of St Pierre and Miquelon (off Newfoundland), the French Caribbean island departments of Guadeloupe and Martinique, of French Guyana, and of Haiti, and is spoken in St Lucia, and Trinidad and Tobago. It is spoken in the US in Maine and Louisiana and among immigrants from Quebec in Florida. In Africa, it is the official language of Benin, Burkina Faso (Upper Volta), Burundi, Chad, Côte d'Ivoire, Gabon, Mali, Niger, Rwanda, Senegal, and Zaïre, and is widely used in Algeria, Egypt, Morocco, and Tunisia. In the Indian Ocean, it is the official language of the Comoros Islands, the Malagasy Republic, and the French island of Réunion, and is spoken in Mauritius. In Asia, it is spoken in Lebanon, and, to a lesser extent, in Cambodia, Laos, Vietnam, and the Indian territory of Pondicherry. In the Pacific, it is the official language of the French island of New Caledonia and is spoken in Tahiti, Vanuatu, and other islands. There are French pidgins and creoles in Africa, the Caribbean, and the Indian and Pacific oceans.

Origins and nature. Historically, the language is divided into Old, Middle, and Modern. Old French (OF) more or less coincides with Old English (OE) and early Middle English (ME). Middle French (MF) stretches from the 14c to c.1600. Geographically, French is traditionally divided into two areas: Northern French or the *Langue d'Oïl*, and Southern French or the *Langue d'Oc* (also *Occitan*). Oïl (from Latin *ille*

that) and *oc* (from Latin *hoc* this) are the words for *yes* in OF and Old Occitan. The northern tongue was influenced by Frankish, the Germanic language of the Franks, who gave their name to both France and French. The southern tongue is related to Catalan. Occitan (including *Provençal*) was a major medieval language, but declined after the annexation of the South by Paris and survives as a range of dialects, despite the efforts and literary success of the Provençal poet Frédéric Mistral (Nobel Prize, 1904). In medieval Europe, the northern language enjoyed great prestige, while in the 17–19c Modern French was a language of international standing, especially in diplomacy and culture. In 1637, the Académie française was founded with a view to fixing the standard language and keeping *le bon français* ('good French', based on court usage and 'the best writers') as pure as possible. The French Revolution in the late 18c promoted French as the language of national unity, the speaking of Basque, Breton, Alsatian, Flemish, and Corsican, etc., being considered unpatriotic. The Jacobin ideal of one standard national language was pursued by the founders of the modern educational system in the 19c, extended to French colonies around the world, and has continued into the 20c.

Protective laws, activities, and groups. In 1539, in the Ordinance of Villers-Cotterêts, King Francis I ordered the replacement of Latin by French as the language of law. In 1637, the Académie française was founded: see ACADEMY. In 1789, the Revolution linked the language to national unity and patriotism. In 1794, the Abbé Grégoire presented a report to the National Convention on the need and means to extirpate the patois and make standard French universal. In 1937, the *Office de la langue française* was formed by such linguists as A. Dauzat and F. Brunot. It disappeared after the German invasion, but was partially restored in 1957 as the *Office du vocabulaire français*, especially under pressure from Canadian francophones. In 1953, the *Défense de la langue française* was formed under the auspices of the Académie française. In 1964, René Etiemble published *Parlez-vous franglais?* (Paris: Gallimard): see FRANGLAIS. In 1966, the *Haut Comité pour la défense et l'expansion de la langue française* was formed, directly responsible to the Prime Minister of the Republic. In 1967, the *Association pour le bon usage du français dans l'administration* was formed, to regulate government language. In 1975, the Bas-Lauriol law was passed on the use of French only in advertising and commerce: in 1982, a government circular extended constraints to foreign exporters of goods destined for France. In 1977, *Loi 101/ Bill 101* was passed in Quebec, Canada, making

French the sole official language of the province, limiting access to English-medium schools, and banning public signs in other languages. In 1983, in France, a decree was passed requiring the use in teaching and research of terms made official by specialist committees. In 1984, the French *Haut Comité* was replaced by the *Commissariat général de la langue française*, to assist private groups and members of the public in the pursuit of violations of the Bas-Lauriol law.

Links with English. The *Chanson de Roland*, an epic poem about the Emperor Charlemagne's army in Spain in the 8c, was the first major literary link between Britain and France. The poem was sung by the Normans at the Battle of Hastings (1066) and the oldest surviving copy was discovered in Oxford in 1834. The first grammar of French was written in England, John Palsgrave's *Lesclarcissement de la Langue Françoyse* (1530). Borrowing in both directions has been continuous from the earliest times: French *bateau* from OE *bat*, Modern English *navy* from OF *navie*. The two languages came into close association in the mid-11c, especially through the Norman Conquest, after which Norman French was the socially and politically dominant language of England and a considerable influence in Wales, Scotland, and Ireland. By the time French died out as a British language, it had greatly altered and enriched English, and the fashion of borrowing from it continues to this day. Numerous conflicts, from the 14c Hundred Years War to the 18–19c colonial and revolutionary wars, did not prevent a mutual social and intellectual interest, accounting for Gallomania in Britain and Anglomania in France.

Because of its geographical position and cultural prestige, France has exported many words to its neighbours; of these, English has absorbed the highest proportion. As a result, hundreds of words have the same spellings in both languages, which also share a battery of Latin affixes. Before the Renaissance, prolonged contact with French had prepared English for an increased Latinization, just as French was itself re-Latinized. There is therefore a common Neo-Latin technical vocabulary: French *homicide* (12c) antedates English *homicide* (14c), but English *suicide* is recorded earlier (1651) than French *suicide* (1739), and *insecticide* is recorded as almost simultaneous in both (French 1859, English 1866). However, the Latinization has gone further in English than re-Latinization in French: *pedestrian* and *tepid* are closer to Latin than *piéton* and *tiède*, and such words as *abduct*, *connubial*, *equanimity*, *fulcrum*, *impervious*, *odium*, and *victor* do not occur in French. On the other hand, many words borrowed into French

from other Romance languages (especially Italian) have entered English in a more or less French form: *artisan*, *caprice*, *frigate*, *orange*, *picturesque*, *stance*, *tirade*.

French in English. Medieval loans from French have given English much of the look of a Romance language. The movement of French words into English was eased by cognates already present in OE. Thus, the OE verb *ceosan* accounted for the easy borrowing of *choose*. Similarly, OE *munt*, *nefa*, *prud*, *rice*, *warian* paved the way for *mount*, *nephew*, *proud*, *rich*, *beware* from OF. In English, Germanic and Romance cognates come together: the OF verb *spell* is related to the OE noun *spell*, OF *arm* the weapon extends OE *arm* the limb, and the late OE *arrow* is shot by an OF *archer* in a Norman French *garden* near an OE *yard*.

A hybrid vocabulary. The ancient closeness of the two languages has had peculiar effects: a young English *hare* is a French *leveret*, a young English *swan* a French *cygnet*, and a small English *axe* is a French *hatchet*. An OE stem can be used with a French suffix (*eatable*, *hindrance*) or vice versa (*faithful*, *gentleness*). The English *stool*, originally a chair (OE *stol*), gave way to the Norman French *chair*, and was demoted in size and usage. The animals tended by the Saxon peasantry retained English names like *calf* and *sheep*, while their meat when eaten in the Norman castles became French *veal* and *mutton*. Because of the long presence of the language in England, many French fossils survive in the strata of English: for example, an *s* lost by French is preserved in *bastard*, *beast*, *cost*, *custom*, *escape*, *establish*, *(e)state*, *false*, *honest*, *hostage*, *interest*, *master*, *paste*, *priest*, *scout*, *tempest*. In addition, because of the French connection, English is sometimes a twofold language in which people can *answer* or *respond* and *begin* or *commence* to seek *freedom* or *liberty*. Such pairs are near-synonyms, sometimes expressing stylistic differences like *kingdom/realm*, *sight/vision*, and *snake/serpent*. Others still are further apart in meaning, such as *ask/demand*, *bit/morsel*, *heel/talon*, and *illegible/unreadable*: SEE BISOCIATION, FAUX AMI.

Calques and doublets. French loan translations often lie beneath English expressions, as in *flea-market/marché aux puces*, *ivory tower/tour d'ivoire*, and *third world/tiers monde*. Romance word structure is still noticeable in *centre of gravity*, *chief of state*, and *point of view*. The word order is French in such forms as *Governor-General*, *poet laureate*, and *treasure trove*. Some idiomatic calques go back to OF (*to bear ill will* to *porter male volonté*) while others are from Modern French, such as *in the last analysis* (*en dernière analyse*) and *it goes without saying* (*ça va sans dire*). English contains many doublets of French provenance: *constraint/constriction, custom/costume, frail/fragile, loyal/legal, marvel/ miracle, poison/potion, sever/separate, straight/ strict.* In some cases, one of the elements does not exist in French (here the second of each pair): *allow/allocate, count/compute, croissant/ crescent, esteem/estimate, poor/pauper, royal/ regal, sure/secure.* In other cases, the same word may have been borrowed more than once, with different meanings and forms: *catch/chase, chieftain/captain, corpse/corps, forge/fabricate, hostel/hospital/hotel, pocket/poke/pouch, ticket/ etiquette, vanguard/avant-garde.*

English in French. Borrowing from English into French has been widespread for two centuries. However, when such borrowing takes place, special usages can develop. Thus, the role of a word may become specialized, a French *meeting* being political rather than general and an English *reunion* being for people who have not met for a long time (not general, like French *réunion*). Expressions may even swap roles, such as *savoir-faire* in English and *know-how* in French.

Loanwords. Waves of English words have been borrowed since the 18c, especially in: politics (*congrès, majorité, meeting, politicien, sinécure, vote*), horse-racing (*derby, outsider, steeplechase, sweepstake, turf*), sport (*baseball, basketball, football, goal, tennis*), railways (*bogie, condenseur, terminus, trolley, viaduc, wagon*), aviation (*cockpit, crash, jet, steward*), medicine (*catgut, pace-maker, scanner*), and social life (*bestseller, gangster, hot dog, leader, sandwich, strip-tease, western*). On occasion, English words can be Gallicized by adapting their forms and changing pronunciation and orthography: *boulingrin* bowling green, *contredanse* country dance, *paquebot,* packet boat, and *redingote* riding-coat. Borrowing of additional senses for existing French words also occurs: *environnement* (in the ecological sense), 'conviction *viscérale*', '*retourner* une lettre', '*délivrer* une carte d'identité', '*engagement* naval'. *Réaliser* and *ignorer* are now often used with their English meanings. Canadian French is especially open to such influences: 'la ligne est *engagée*'. Pseudo-Anglicisms have also arisen: *recordman* record-holder, *shake-hand* handshake, *tennisman* tennis player, and such forms in *-ing* as *footing* (recently replaced by *jogging*), and *lifting* (face-lift). French *dancing, parking, smoking* are reduced forms of *dancing hall, parking place, smoking jacket,* like *cargo, steeple, surf* (from cargo vessel, steeplechase, and surf-riding).

Loan translations. Calques conceal the English origin of certain French words: *cessez-le-feu* ceasefire, *franc-maçon* freemason, *gratte-ciel* skyscraper, *lavage de cerveau* brainwashing,

libre-service self-service, *lune de miel* honeymoon, *prêt-à-porter* ready-to-wear, and *soucoupe volante* flying saucer. However, native coinages expressing resistance to Anglicisms include *baladeur* Walkman, *cadreur* cameraman, *logiciel* software, *ordinateur* computer, and *rentrée* comeback. French *lift* was replaced by *ascenseur,* but only after the production of *liftier* liftman. The spread of the *-ing* suffix, however, has prevented *doping, kidnapping,* and *parking* from replacement by *dopage, kidnappage,* and *parcage,* and only in Quebec has *weekend* been overshadowed by *fin de semaine.* Loan translations also involve whole idiomatic expressions (such as *donner le feu vert* give the green light), especially in Canadian French (such as *manquer le bateau* miss the boat). As such, they can affect syntax (infuriating purists), as when adjectives are placed before rather than after nouns (such as *l'actuel gouvernement, les éventuels problèmes, les possibles objections*), and the passive voice is used with an unexpected verb (such as *Il est supposé savoir,* 'He is supposed to know', rather than *Il est censé savoir*).

A homecoming. Some argue that ancient exports coming back with a new sense should be welcomed into the language. This has already been the case for *budget, challenge, confort, intercourse, interview, nurse, partenaire, scout, sport,* and *toast.* Some words have come back with spellings unchanged since OF: *barge, label, maintenance, nuisance, partition, record, suspense,* and *train. Champion* has always existed in French, but its currently frequent use in connection with sports dates from the 19c. *Missile,* a 14c French borrowing from Latin, returned from English in 1960. This phenomenon is especially common in Canadian French, in which English *bargain, beverage, car,* and *county* account for the preservation of *barguigner, breuvage, char,* and *comté. Information* is more often used in Modern French because the traditional *renseignements* is not internationally understood.

The Anglo-Latinization of French. Few speakers of French are aware that *faisabilité* and *indésirable* come from *feasibility* and *undesirable* because these words are felt to be the normal derivatives of *faisable* and *désirable. Déforestation* and *reforestation* look so French that few complain about their use instead of *deboisement* and *reboisement. Sentimental* was first used in French by the translator of Sterne's *A Sentimental Journey through France and Italy* (1768). It sounded as French as *international,* coined in 1780 by Jeremy Bentham. 'Societé *permissive*' is easily associated by French-speakers with *permission.* Words coined in English from Latin in the 19c were absorbed into French (*exhaustif, sélectif, sélection, viaduc*) and the process continues. Thus, *crédible*, in competition with *croyable* as a recent loanword (1965), easily crept in because of its closeness to *crédibilité*. Until *c.*1950, French *forum* referred only to Rome, but now has the English meaning 'meeting-place for discussion, especially on television'. In such ways, French, the Trojan horse through which Latin entered the citadel of English, is being Latinized in its turn through English.

See ACADEMY, AFRICA, AFRICAN LANGUAGES, AMERICAN LANGUAGES, ANGLOPHONE, ARABIC, BEACH LA MAR, BISLAMA, BORROWING, BRETON, BRITTANY, CAJUN, CAMEROON, CAMFRANGLAIS, CANADA, CANADIAN ENGLISH, CANADIAN LANGUAGES, CANADIAN PLACE-NAMES, CARIBBEAN, CARIBBEAN LANGUAGES, CELTIC LANGUAGES, CHANNEL ISLANDS, CREOLE, DIALECT IN AMERICA, DICTATION, DOMINICA, DOUBLET, ENGLISH, FRANGLAIS, GAMBIA, GRENADA, HISTORY OF ENGLISH, KWEYOL, LAW FRENCH, LINGUISTIC TYPOLOGY, MAURITIUS, MIDDLE ENGLISH, NEWFOUNDLAND, NEW ORLEANS, NORMAN, NORMAN FRENCH, PALE, PASSY, PATOIS, PIDGIN, QUEBEC, ROMANCE LANGUAGES, SAINT LUCIA, TRINIDAD AND TOBAGO, VANUATU. [AFRICA, AMERICAS, ASIA, EUROPE, HISTORY, LANGUAGE]. J.M.G.

FREQUENCY COUNT. An attempt to discover the number of occurrences of particular units in particular contexts of language use, principally words in texts. Such counts have usually been undertaken to provide a statistical basis for word lists used in the teaching of subjects like shorthand and English as a foreign language. During the 20c there have been several large-scale frequency counts for English, particularly in the US under the inspiration of the psychologist Edward L. Thorndike, as in *The Teacher's Word Book* (1921). This was a list of 10,000 words that American children could expect to meet in their general reading. His list was derived from 41 different textual sources which provided 4m running words: 3m from the Bible and the English classics, 0.5m from letters, 0.3m from elementary school readers, 90,000 from newspapers, and 50,000 from general reading. The list was widely acclaimed as a breakthrough in the study and control of vocabulary and inspired many imitators and developers. It was considered a valuable objective measure of the appropriateness of vocabulary in schoolbooks and a basis for the construction of achievement tests in reading, spelling, and vocabulary. Although not so intended, it was also used as a basis for EFL word lists. One such list influenced by Thorndike was Michael West's *General Service List of English Words* (1953), which helped a generation of EFL lexicographers to develop the notion of a basic 'defining vocabulary'. The classic counts of the first half of the 20c were done with little or no mechanical assistance. More recently, the use of computers has made the gathering, analysis, and processing of data less laborious and time-consuming and has enlarged the body of texts (the corpus) which can be sampled in this way. Thus, the *Brown/Lancaster/Oslo/Bergen* corpus (started in 1967) has been used to confirm hunches about the predominance of certain features of writing, grammar, and semantics in particular varieties of English, and the Birmingham *COBUILD* corpus (started in 1980) has provided lexicographers with new information about collocation, grammar, and meaning on which to base their decisions on how to structure dictionary entries. See COBUILD, CORPUS, FREQUENCY OF OCCURRENCE, VOCABULARY CONTROL. [EDUCATION, LANGUAGE, REFERENCE, WORD]. R.H., T.MCA.

Francis, W. Nelson, & Kučera, Henry. 1982. *Frequency Analysis of English Usage: Lexicon and Grammar*. Boston: Houghton Mifflin.
Hindmarsh, Roland. 1980. *The Cambridge English Lexicon*. Cambridge: University Press.
Hofland, Knut, & Johansson, Stig. 1982. *Word Frequencies in British and American English*. Bergen: Norwegian Computing Centre for the Humanities. Harlow: Longman.
Sinclair, John M. (ed.). 1987. *Looking Up: An Account of the COBUILD Project in Lexical Computing*. London & Glasgow: Collins.

FREQUENCY OF OCCURRENCE. The number of times or the regularity with which something happens. Linguists and language teachers often take account of the frequency of occurrence of linguistic items and features. Geographic, socio-economic, and ethnic varieties of a language generally differ in the frequency with which choices are made rather than in the presence or absence of an item or feature: for example, the use of negative *too* in spoken Welsh English, as in *She won't do it, too* (as opposed to *either*). The same applies to stylistic variation in spoken and written language (ellipsis and contraction are, for example, more frequent in speech), such registers as legal language (which makes frequent use of compounds such as *hereinafter* and *thereof*), and religious language (with its use of *thou*-pronouns and corresponding verb forms), and in contrasts along the continuum from the most formal to the most casual (the choice of *furthermore* and *moreover* as opposed to *also* and *too*).

Language change commonly arises from the dominance of one variable over others and can often be observed through *frequency counts*. The characteristics of a genre, author, or work may be identified through the relative frequency of vocabulary items or grammatical features; this has been used to identify the disputed authorship of works and disputed passages in statements to the police. Information about frequency is commonly taken into account in selecting entries for dictionaries and ordering definitions within entries, as well as in grading material for learners of a language. Sociolinguists usually draw their evidence for relative frequencies from analyses of observed or elicited speech, sometimes incorporating the results in statements of probability. Some linguists have collected large corpora of written or spoken samples of a language, their frequency lists and studies of data made easier by computational processing. Recent experiments have obtained evidence of the perception of relative frequencies by eliciting judgements from native speakers: for example, of the relative frequencies of the subjunctive (*We urge that he give his reasons*), the *should*-construction (*We urge that he should give his reasons*), and the indicative (*We urge that he gives his reasons*). See CORPUS, FREQUENCY COUNT, VOCABULARY CONTROL. [EDUCATION, LANGUAGE]. S.G.

FREQUENTATIVE. See ITERATIVE.

FREUDIAN SLIP [1950s: after Sigmund *Freud*, the founder of psychoanalysis]. A term known technically in psychoanalysis as *parapraxis*: an unintentional mistake, usually in speech, that is held to reveal an unconscious (especially sexual) inclination or motivation: She *What would you like: bread and butter or cake?* He *Bed and butter.* In general use, the term often refers to any unintentional verbal slip. Compare SLIP OF THE TONGUE. [STYLE]. T.MCA.

FRICATIVE [19c: from Latin *fricare/fricatum* to rub]. In phonetics, a vocal sound made by bringing active and passive articulators close together, so that noise is generated as the airstream passes through the gap. The /f/ in *fee* is made by bringing the active lower lip close to the passive upper front teeth, and is a labio-dental fricative consonant. The /f/ and /v/ in *five* are the same kind of fricative; the first voiceless, the second voiced. Compare AFFRICATE. See CONSONANT. [SPEECH]. G.K.

FRIES, Charles C(arpenter) [1887-1967]. American grammarian and lexicographer, born in Reading, Pennsylvania, and educated at Bucknell U., where he was appointed to the faculty in 1911 to teach rhetoric and Greek. In 1914, he shifted from classics to English, and he gained his Ph.D. in 1922 with a study of *shall* and *will* in Renaissance English. He joined the English department at the U. of Michigan in 1921 and worked there until his retirement in 1958. He became editor-in-chief in 1928 of the *Early Modern English Dictionary*, and was an adviser to the Random House *American College Dictionary* (1948). Fries sought to describe English as it was rather than as it ought to be. In *American English Grammar* (1940), he investigated social-class differences through the study of letters written to a government agency. In defining the scope of this enquiry, he declared 'that there can be no "correctness" apart from usage'. A second descriptive work, *The Structure of English* (1952), drew on recorded telephone conversations; his innovative approach in that volume emphasized 'signals of structural meaning' that could be isolated and described from the stream of speech rather than from the 'ideas' expressed. A conviction that English should be described and learned through speech rather than writing shaped *Teaching and Learning English as a Second Language* (1945) and *Foundations of English Teaching* (1961). The methods he developed at the *English Language Institute*, which he founded at Michigan in 1941, influenced ESL teaching around the world and his conception of *pattern practice* shaped ESL teaching for a generation. He was senior author of the *Fries American English Series* (1952-6), among other ESL textbooks. After retirement, he turned his attention to reading instruction for native speakers and published *Linguistics and Reading* (1963) and *A Basic Reading Series Developed upon Linguistic Principles* (1963-5). See index. [AMERICAS, BIOGRAPHY, EDUCATION, LANGUAGE, REFERENCE]. R.W.B.

FRISIAN. A Germanic language spoken in coastal regions and islands in the north of The Netherlands and in neighbouring western Germany to the Danish border; the most closely related of the Continental languages to English. Some scholars have supposed the existence of an *Anglo-Frisian* language during the migratory period before the Anglo-Saxon tribes reached Britain in the 5c. The languages share common phonological features, such as: the initial consonant in English *cheese, church, chaff*, Frisian *tsiis, tsjerke, tsjef* (compare Dutch *kaas, kerk, kaf*, German *Käse, Kirche, Kaff*); a front vowel in English *sleep, sheep*, Frisian *sliepe, skiep* (compare Dutch *slapen, schaap*, German *schlafen, Schaf*); the loss of *n* in words such as English *goose, us*, Frisian *goes, ús* (compare Dutch *gans, ons*, German *Gans, uns*). The main variety is *Modern West Frisian*, spoken by some 400,000 people in and around The Netherlands province of Friesland. Since the 19c, Frisian has revived as a literary language. A movement seeking independence from the influence of the province of Holland has enhanced the legal status of Frisian and promoted its use alongside Dutch, especially in schools, where it was illegal until 1937. The *Frisian Academy* (founded in 1938) sponsors scholarly publications on Frisian history and culture, including a definitive historical dictionary. See CRAIGIE, DUTCH, GERMAN, INGVAEONIC, LOW GERMAN. Compare NORWEGIAN, SCOTS. [EUROPE, LANGUAGE].   N.E.O.

FRONT MATTER [1900s AmE]. Also **preliminaries, prelims**. A collective term for parts of a book or other publication that appear before the main text, such as the title page, copyright page, dedication, contents, preface, a list of abbreviations or illustrations, and the like. See BACK MATTER, FORMAT, TITLE PAGE. [MEDIA, TECHNOLOGY].   T.MCA.

FRUITY [17c]. (1) Like fruit; rich in flavour; excessively sweet; cloying and syrupy. (2) Of a usually male voice or accent: rich and deep, often ingratiating, with careful articulation and well-rounded vowels: 'Some minutes later a fruity voice caressed his ear. Albert Peasemarch's mentor, Coggs, had advised making the telephone-answering voice as fruity as possible in the tradition of the great butlers of the past' (P. G. Wodehouse, *Cocktail Time*, 1958). Compare PLUMMY. See (A)ESTHETICS. [SPEECH].T.MCA.

FRYE, Northrop [1912–91]. Canadian literary critic and clergyman, born in Sherbrooke, Quebec, and educated in Monckton (New Brunswick), at Victoria College in the U. of Toronto, at Emmanuel College (part of Toronto Theological College), and at Merton College, Oxford. He was ordained into the United Church of Canada but never held a church appointment. In 1939, he took up a post as lecturer in the Department of English at Victoria College, where he remained until retirement, with excursions to teach at Berkeley, Columbia, Cornell, Harvard, Oxford, and Princeton. His final appointment at Toronto was University Professor, a title reserved for professors of particular distinction. Frye's publications include: *Fearful Symmetry* (1947: a study of William Blake), *Anatomy of Criticism: Four Essays* (1957), *A Natural Perspective* (1965), *The Critical Path* (1971), *The Great Code: The Bible and Literature* (1982), *The Myth of Deliverance* (1983), and *Words With Power* (1990). Frye is noted for an approach to the theory of literature that emphasized modes (fictional and thematic), symbols (as motifs, signs, images, archetypes, and monads), myths (with apocalyptic, demonic, and analogical imagery, including the equations spring with comedy, summer with romance, autumn with tragedy, and winter with irony and satire). Inspired by Blake's view that the Bible was 'the Great Code of Art', Frye argued

that the Old and New Testaments are the basis on which the literature of Western civilization rests, and that without a knowledge of how this came about Western literature cannot be fully understood. See index. [AMERICAS, LITERATURE].

T.MCA.

FULL STOP. See PERIOD, POINT, PUNCTUATION.

FUNCTION [16c: through French from Latin *functio/functionis* performance]. (1) The role or activity appropriate to a person or thing; the contribution of an element in a system to the operation of that system as a whole. (2) In linguistics, the relation between linguistic units in a hierarchy: the adjective *large* functions as a modifier of the noun *house* in the noun phrase *that large house*, and in turn the noun phrase *that large house* functions as subject in the sentence *That large house belongs to Jill's parents*. In this sense, function contrasts with *form*. In a functional or relational grammar, the concept of function plays a dominant role. Extralinguistic aspects of language are also known as functions: in social contexts, relationships in different situations; in discourse, relationships in conversation; in pragmatics, the rules underlying the use of language in specific situations. Compare FORM. [GRAMMAR, LANGUAGE].   S.G., T.MCA.

FUNCTIONAL GRAMMAR. See HALLIDAY.

FUNCTIONAL LITERACY. A term initially defined for UNESCO by William S. Gray (*The Teaching of Reading and Writing*, 1956, p. 21) as the training of adults to 'meet independently the reading and writing demands placed on them'. Currently, the phrase describes those approaches to literacy which stress the acquisition of appropriate verbal, cognitive, and computational skills to accomplish practical ends in culturally specific settings. Although also labelled *survival literacy* and *reductionist literacy* because of its emphasis on minimal levels of competency and the preparation of workers for jobs, functional literacy is defended by proponents as a way to help people negotiate successfully in their societies. The notion of literacy as a utilitarian tool arose in 1942 when the US Army had to defer 433,000 draftees because they could not understand 'the kinds of written instruction . . . needed for carrying out basic military functions or tasks'. In 1947, the US Bureau of the Census began defining literacy quantitatively, describing anyone with less than five years' schooling as *functionally illiterate*. With the passing of the Adult Education Act of 1966, 12 years of education became the literacy standard in the US, while in Britain, the right-to-read movements of the 1970s characterized functional literacy as the ability to: (1)

read well enough to perform job activities successfully, and (2) understand printed messages. Over the decades, as societies have developed both technical innovations and new language formats and tasks, the definition of functional literacy has been modified to meet the changed demands. See ILLITERACY, LITERACY. [EDUCATION, WRITING]. R.W.B.

FUNCTIONAL SENTENCE PERSPECTIVE. See DISCOURSE ANALYSIS.

FUNCTIONAL SHIFT. See CONVERSION.

FUNK & WAGNALLS. An American publishing company based in New York City, incorporated by Isaac Kaufman Funk and Adam Willis Wagnalls in 1890. The company published inexpensive editions of standard works of reference and such books of general interest as *Hoyt's Cyclopedia of Practical Quotations*, *The Standard Encyclopedia*, *The Standard Bible Dictionary*, and *The Jewish Encyclopedia* (12 volumes). Their *Standard Dictionary of the English Language* (1893) was advertised on an unprecedented scale with full-page advertisements in 200 newspapers published on the same day in 32 states at a cost of $45,000. This expenditure alerted other publishers to the lucrative prospects of dictionary production. After Funk's death, the company continued to produce works of reference and acquired the US rights to the dictionaries of the British publisher Cassell. It was subsequently consolidated with Thomas Y. Crowell, which in turn became part of Harper & Row. In 1988, the firm was sold to Field Publications of Chicago. Its reference books are now sold mainly through direct-mail marketing and through grocery stores in one-book-a-week instalments. [AMERICAS, MEDIA]. R.W.B.

FUNK, Isaac Kaufman [1839–1912]. American editor, lexicographer, publisher, and spelling reformer. After studying for the Lutheran ministry in Springfield, Ohio, and working for 11 years (1861–72) as a pastor in Indiana, Ohio, and New York, he became editor of *The Christian Radical* in Pittsburgh, Pennsylvania. In 1876, he set up a printing house in New York City in which he was joined by his former schoolmate Adam Willis Wagnalls in 1877. In 1890, he began work on *The Standard Dictionary of the English Language* (1893). Assembling and directing a team of more than 740 editors, specialists, and readers, he sought to produce a dictionary which would provide essential information thoroughly and simply. In it, he placed current meanings first, obsolete and archaic meanings second, and etymologies last. Giving attention to pro-

nunciation, he represented each entry twice, once in a familiar key, then in a more precise one. He advocated spelling reform and was a member of the Simplified Spelling Board. On his death, his brother Benjamin Franklin Funk and later his nephew Charles Earle Funk continued his work by overseeing the production of the *Standard Dictionary* series and its abridgements, school, and pocket editions. See index. [AMERICAS, BIOGRAPHY, REFERENCE, WRITING]. R.W.B.

FURNIVALL, Frederick James [1825–1910]. English lexicographer, editor, and social reformer, born at Egham, Surrey, and educated at private schools in Surrey, at U. College London, and at Cambridge, then read law at Lincoln's Inn, London. He founded seven literary societies, including the *Early English Text Society* (1864) and the *Chaucer Society* (1868), and edited many medieval and Elizabethan texts and reprints, including Chaucer's *Canterbury Tales*. From 1853 till his death, he was secretary to the *Philological Society*. On the death in 1861 of Herbert Coleridge, he took over the editorship of the Society's dictionary (which became the *Oxford English Dictionary*), and continued the work of assembling its collection of quotations, with the help of many voluntary excerptors. He also set up the scheme of voluntary sub-editors to undertake preliminary analyses of the material, but his many activities gradually intervened and by 1874 work on the dictionary had lapsed. On the revival of the project under James Murray in 1879, Furnivall continued as a copious contributor to its store of quotations. See index. [BIOGRAPHY, EUROPE, REFERENCE]. A.J.A.

FUSIONAL [16c: from Latin *fusio/fusionis* a pouring, usually of molten metals]. In linguistics, a term denoting a language in which the grammatical units within a word (its morphemes) tend to be fused together, as in Latin *feminarum* of women, in which the ending -*arum* fuses the notions *possession, plural, feminine*. Many languages have some fusion: English *geese* ('goose' and *plural* together), *sat* ('sit' and *past* together), but in a language such as Latin this process predominates. See LINGUISTIC TYPOLOGY. [LANGUAGE]. J.M.A.

FUTHARK, FUTHORC, etc. See ALPHABET, RUNE.

FUTURE [14c: from French *futur*, Latin *futurus* about to be (a participle of *esse* to be)]. A tense contrasting with the present and the past. Traditionally, the *simple future* tense is *will* or *shall* followed by the infinitive: *will follow*. The *future continuous* or *future progressive* adds *be* followed by -*ing* participle: *will be following*. The *future* *perfect* adds *have* followed by the *-ed* participle: *will have followed.* The *future perfect continuous* combines the latter two: *will have been following.* Future time is also expressed by: *be going to* as in *Naomi is going to help Eliot;* the present progressive as in *I am playing next week;* the simple present as in *We leave for Paris tomorrow;* the use of *be to* as in *She is to be the next president of the company;* the use of *be about to* as in *It is about to rain;* the modal verb *can* as in *I can see you on Tuesday morning;* the phrase *be sure to* as in *They are sure to help us;* such verbs as *intend* and *plan* as in *I intend to vote for you.* See TENSE, VERB. [GRAMMAR].　　　　　　　　　S.G.

G

G, g [Called 'gee']. The 7th letter of the Roman alphabet as used for English. It primarily represents the voiced velar stop and was invented by the early Romans by adding a cross-bar to C, which represented the voiceless velar stop. In pre-Conquest England, a small g with a different shape from the Continental letter was used. This Insular g developed into ʒ, known as *yogh*. After the Norman Conquest (1066), both forms were used in English, g as it is today, ʒ either for the sound y, /j/, or for both a voiced and voiceless velar fricative. By the close of the Middle Ages, yogh was replaced by the digraph *gh*, as in *night* and *tough*: see *GH* (below).

Hard and soft G. In English, both g and c have inherited palatalized ('soft') values from the Romance languages, as in *cease, gem*, as opposed to the velar ('hard') values in *case, gun*. However, while the varied uses of c in English mostly derive from the Romance languages, many variations in the use of g are peculiar to English. It has three values: (1) The hard voiced velar stop: *got, gut, glut, grit, Gwen, argue, tug*. (2) The soft voiced palato-alveolar affricate /dʒ/, usually before *e, i, y* (*gem, gist, gymnast, rage, bilge, urge*). Especially in words of Germanic origin hard g can however also precede *e, i, y* (*begin, get, gig*), and very occasionally soft g precedes *a* or *o* (*gaol, margarine, mortgagor*). Rhyming words beginning with the sound of soft g are then commonly spelt unambiguously with j (*get/jet, gig/jig*), but *gill* remains ambiguous, having soft g when meaning 'liquid measure' and hard g for 'breathing organ of a fish' and Northern English 'stream'. (3) Some loans from French have kept the voiced palato-alveolar fricative value /ʒ/, as in *bourgeois*; this may be heard in *beige, genre, prestige, régime, rouge* and in some words ending in -*age* (*barrage, camouflage, fuselage, mirage*), including the AmE pronunciation of *garage*, with second-syllable stress.

Hard/soft variation. (1) One value of g may be replaced by another in derivatives, soft becoming hard in *allege/allegation, purge/purgative*, and hard becoming soft in *litigate/litigious* (but note *renege/renegade*, in which the g is always hard). The hard initial g of traditional BrE *gynaecology*, AmE *gynecology* is pronounced soft medially in *androgynous* and *misogyny*. (2) The hard-soft alternatives for g lead to uncertainty in its pronunciation in a number of words of classical origin: *hegemony* ('hedge-' or 'hegg-'?), *analogous* (hard as in *analogue* or soft as in *analogy*?), *pedagogical, longevity, longitude*.

Double G. (1) Normally hard as in *dagger* but exceptionally soft in *exaggerate* and BrE *suggest*. (2) Like many other consonants in monosyllabic words, g is doubled after an initial vowel (*egg*) but not after an initial consonant (*bag, leg, dig, fog, hug*), unless a suffix beginning with a vowel is added (*baggy, legged, digger, foggiest, hugging*). (3) Medial g in disyllables is commonly double after a short vowel: *haggis, trigger, nugget*. (4) The Latin prefixes *ad*- and *sub*- typically assimilate with roots beginning with g, causing g to double (*aggression, suggest*). AmE typically splits *gg* in *suggest*, speaking first hard g, then soft g ('sug-jest').

DG. The digraph *dg* is commonly a reinforced soft g (contrast *bad/bag/badge, bud/bug/budge*), but in unstressed final syllables the spelling of soft g has been uncertain: both *selvage/selvedge* are written today, and historically *colledge/knowledge, cabbach/spinach* could be spelt alike. The vowel preceding g in unstressed final syllables can vary as in *village, college, vestige*.

GH. The digraph *gh* causes difficulty. It is commonly a relic of a velar or palatal fricative that is preserved as a velar fricative /x/ in Scots, as in *bricht nicht* (bright night). (1) It is normally silent after *u* as in *taught, drought, naughty,*

THE CAPITAL LETTER

EARLY FORMS				CURRENT FORMS	
Phoenician	Greek	Etruscan	Roman (Latin)	roman	italic
			G	G	G

THE SMALL LETTER

EARLY FORMS			CURRENT FORMS	
Roman cursive	Roman uncial	Carolingian minuscule	roman	italic
ᛋ	ɕ	ᵹ	g	g

thought, though, through, thorough, bough, drought, and after i as in straight, weight, height, high, light, night. (2) It is pronounced /f/ in a few words such as cough, enough, laugh, rough, tough. (3) In the following place-names in England, each gh is different: Slough (rhymes with how), Keighley ('Keethley'), Loughborough ('Luff-'). (4) In hiccough, the gh was substituted for p (hiccup) in the mistaken belief that the word derived from cough. (5) It has disappeared in AmE draft, plow (formerly also used in BrE) and in dry, fly, sly, although preserved in the related nouns drought, flight, sleight. (6) It sometimes alternates with ch in related words: straight/stretch, taught/teach. (7) Occasionally, gh has been inserted by analogy with rhyming words even where no fricative had previously been pronounced: in delight (from Old French delit), by analogy with light, and in haughty from French haut, perhaps by analogy with high and naughty. (8) In loans from Italian, hard g is indicated by gh before e and i: ghetto, spaghetti, Malpighian; the form dinghy is similarly distinguished from dingy, with its soft g. (9) William Caxton's Dutch printers may have introduced Dutch gh in ghastly and ghost. (10) The gh in ghoul and yoghurt transliterates special Arabic and Turkish consonants respectively.

GU. (1) The French and Spanish practice of using gu to indicate hard g before e and i (guerrilla, morgue, disguise, guy) spread to some words of Germanic origin (guess, guest, guilt). The u in fatigue, however, no longer occurs in indefatigable. (2) BrE follows French in spelling Greek-derived final -ogue (analogue, catalogue), while AmE often removes the -ue (analog, catalog). (3) The gu in guarantee, guard was originally pronounced /gw/ in French, but as the u fell silent, it was dropped from the French spellings garantie, garde although preserved in English. The cognates warranty, ward derived from a different French dialect, and have kept the w in both sound and spelling. (4) The ambiguous sound value of gu is seen in its different pronunciations in guide, languid, (contrast languor, often pronounced with a /w/), ambiguity, and especially word-finally, as in ague versus plague. (5) The form tongue is an isolated anomaly.

NG. (1) Commonly a velar nasal, as in thing. It occurs almost only after short vowels: sang, length, sing, song, sung. In such disyllabic base words as anger, finger, hard g is normally heard after the nasal ('angger', 'fingger'). Finger/singer do not rhyme in most accents, but may do in the accents of parts of Midland and Northern England (both like finger) and in Scots (both like singer). (2) The possibility of soft g in the digraph ng may give quite different pronunciations to

parallel spellings: contrast hanged/changed, singer/ginger.

Silent G. In addition to silent gh, the letter g is silent: (1) Initially before n (gnarl, gnash, gnat, gnaw) and in (usually German or Greek) loans: gneiss, gnome, gnostic. (2) After a vowel before final m, in Greek forms (diaphragm, paradigm, phlegm), although the g is pronounced in derivatives (paradigmatic, phlegmatic). (3) Before final n in such Latinate forms as assign, benign, design, malign, impugn. This g effectively indicates a preceding long vowel (contrast sign/sin) and is sounded in some derivatives: malignant, signal. In such cases as align, campaign, the g has come from French, and is present in deign, though absent in cognate disdain. In foreign, sovereign, it has no etymological basis. In some French loans, gn is pronounced as n with a following y: Armagnac ('Armanyac'), cognac, poignant, soigné.

Other features. (1) There is variation between soft g and j in such names as Geoffrey/Jeffrey, Gillian/Jillian, Sergeant/Sarjent. Jelly, although cognate with gelatine, has become fixed with j. Jest and jester are etymologically related to gesture and gesticulate. The jib or projecting arm of a crane probably derives from gibbet, and gibe and gybe are often written jibe. The BrE alternatives gaol/jail exist for historical reasons: gaol from Norman French, jail from Central French. (2) Some words ending in dge in standard English (such as bridge, ridge) have Scots and Northern English variants in hard g (brig, rig). See ALPHABET, LETTER[1], HARD AND SOFT, SPELLING. [WRITING].   C.U.

GAEL [16c: from Scottish Gaelic Gaidheal, from Old Irish Gaidel, Goidel]. A person who speaks the Gaelic language: 'The Gael around him threw / His graceful plaid of varied hue' (Walter Scott, Lady of the Lake, 1810). See CELT. [EUROPE, NAME].   T.MCA.

GAELDOM [1860s: perhaps modelled on Gaidhealtachd]. The land, culture, and community of the Gaels: 'a Gael whose mind was nurtured in Gaeldom' (D. Corkery, Hidden Ireland, 1925); 'Scottish Gaeldom's great annual Festival [the Mod]'(Economist, 19 Oct. 1963). Compare GAELTACHT, IRISHRY. [EUROPE, NAME].   T.MCA.

GAELIC [16c: first used of the language in Scotland and its speakers]. (1) Of the Celts of Scotland, Ireland, and the Isle of Man, their languages, customs, etc.: Gaelic coffee, a Gaelic phrase book. (2) The English name for the Celtic language of Ireland (Gaeilge), Scotland (Gaidhlig), and the Isle of Man (Gaelg, Gailck); commonly pronounced 'Gay-lik' in Ireland, 'Gallik' in Scotland, where it is often referred to, especially by its speakers, as *the Gaelic* (*Does she have the Gaelic? Does she speak Gaelic?*). In Ireland it is generally known as *Irish*, and formerly in Scotland was referred to as both *Erse* and *Irish*: 'It is affirmed that the Gaelick (call it Erse or call it Irish) has been written in the Highlands and Hebrides for many centuries' (Boswell, letter to Johnson, 1775). Gaelic was the principal language of Ireland before and after Norse settlement in the late 8c and remained so until the 18c, after which it went into decline under pressure from English. It was taken to Scotland in the 3-5c and was the foremost language of the kingdom during the early Middle Ages. It dominated the Highlands and Western Isles until the late 18c, after which it also went into decline under pressure from English. It is the national language of the Irish Republic (co-official with English), spoken by some 100,000 and read by some 300,000 people; in Scotland it has some 80,000 speakers, mainly in the Hebrides and Glasgow. It died out as a natural language on the Isle of Man with the last native speaker, Ned Maddrell, in 1974, but revivalists sustain a version of it in an orthography distinct from the Irish and Scottish varieties. Gaelic was spoken widely in Canada and parts of the US in the 18-19c, but is now limited to a community of perhaps 5,000 in Nova Scotia, mainly on Cape Breton Island. See AUSTRALIAN LANGUAGES, BORROWING, CANADIAN ENGLISH, CELTIC LANGUAGES, ERSE, HIBERNO-ENGLISH, HIGHLAND ENGLISH, IRISH, IRISH ENGLISH, ISLE OF MAN, MACARONIC, SCOTTISH GAELIC, SHELTA, VOWEL HARMONY. [EUROPE, LANGUAGE].   T.MCA.

GAELICISM [1890s]. The way of life or special interests of the Gaels; a custom or usage, including a Gaelic expression in English: *banshee* from Irish *bean sidhe* a fairy woman; *loch* in ScoE, a lake. See BORROWING, CELTICISM, GAEL, GAELIC, -ISM. [EUROPE, VARIETY, WORD].   T.MCA.

GAELTACHT [1920s: from Gaelic *Gaidhealtachd*, a form also sometimes used in English, especially in Scotland]. An area in Ireland or Scotland where the Gaelic language is spoken: 'He who dwells in the Gaeltacht learns to relish the neat turn of phrase, the proverbial allusion, and the apt retort' (A. de Blácam, *Gaelic Literature Surveyed*, 1929). In Scotland, the term refers to one region; in Ireland, it is generally used for any one of several regions. See GAEL, GAELIC. [EUROPE, NAME].   T.MCA.

GAGE CANADIAN DICTIONARY. See CANADIAN DICTIONARIES IN ENGLISH.

GAIRAIGO [1980s: from Japanese, from *gai* outside, *rai* come, *go* language]. Words or expressions of foreign, especially European, origin in the Japanese language, borrowed from the 16c onwards, such as *tabako* tobacco (from Portuguese), *kōhī* coffee (from Dutch). The reopening of Japan to the West during the 19c led to the absorption of an unprecedented number of foreign terms, mainly from German, French, and English. Attempts to exclude such words followed growing resistance to imported culture during the 1930s, but since 1945 thousands of terms have entered the language, mainly from English. Borrowing from different European languages can have etymologically complex outcomes: *karuta* a type of playing-card (from Portuguese *carta*), *karute* a medical record (from German *Karte*), *arakaruto* à la carte (from French), and *kādo* identity, credit, greetings (etc.) card (from English *card*). Japanese use such terms freely in everyday conversation and writing, not always aware from which languages or expressions they derive. Non-Japanese may also fail to recognize loanwords because of adaptations in pronunciation, meaning, and/or form.

Writing, pronunciation, and meaning. Foreign words are readily taken into the written language by means of the phonetic script *katakana*. As its signs represent native syllables (such as *sa* and *ke*), transliteration almost invariably produces phonetic change. Most final consonants come to be followed by a vowel, and consonant clusters are often broken up: *erekutoronikkusu* electronics, *kurisumasu* Christmas, *purutoniumu* plutonium. Sounds that do not exist in Japanese are converted to the nearest Japanese syllables (*rajio* radio, *takushi* taxi, *chīmu* team, *tsuna* tuna, *rabu* love, *basu* bus, bath), or are represented by special katakana combinations created to allow foreign words to be expressed in a form closer to their original pronunciation. The endings *-ar* and *-er*, and final schwa are usually expressed as long *a*, as in *hanbāgā* hamburger. Loanwords may undergo semantic as well as phonetic change, as with *manshon* high-class block of flats (from *mansion*), *konpanion* a female guide or hostess (from *companion*), *sumāto* slim (from *smart*), *baikingu* buffet meal, smorgasbord (from *Viking*), *mōningusābisu* a set breakfast (from *morning* and *service*).

Abbreviation and combination. (1) Clippings are common: *terebi* television, *apāto* apartment building, *pāto* part-time work, *engējiringu* engagement ring, *masukomi* mass communication, *wāpuro* word processor: see ACRONYM. (2) Foreign words often combine with Japanese words: *haburashi* toothbrush (from Japanese *ha* tooth, English *brush*), *kuropan* black bread (from

Japanese for 'black' and Portuguese for 'bread'). (3) Words from different foreign languages can also come together: *rōrupan* bread roll (from English *roll* and Portuguese for 'bread'). (4) Two or more words from English are sometimes combined in new ways: *pureigaido* ('play guide') ticket agency, *bakkumirā* ('back mirror') rearview mirror. Such usages are known in Japanese as *wasei eigo* ('made-in-Japan English').

Functions and developments. (1) Foreign loanwords generally have a narrower range of meaning than the words from which they derive and their Japanese counterparts: for example, indicating Western style in *hoteru* hotel, *tīkappu* teacup. (2) Some loans are euphemisms, such as *shirubā* silver, used in certain expressions relating to old age. (3) New or imported goods or concepts are often described using loanwords from English: *fuirumu* roll of film, *puraibashī* privacy. (4) In general, gairaigo words have a modern, Western, and sophisticated image, sometimes competing with native equivalents: *depāto* (department store) has almost replaced the corresponding Japanese word. (5) English is tending to replace the combination of Chinese-derived root words as the main resource for describing new concepts and things: compare the older Chinese-derived *denwa* ('electric talk') for *telephone* and the more recent *terehon kādo* telephone card. (6) Many loans have endured for decades or centuries; others, such as *hai kara* ('high collar': meaning 'fashionable' in the Meiji era), have given way to new terms. (7) Loans are used especially in the media and to describe Western science, technology, ideas, arts, fashion, food, sports, leisure activities, and life-style. See JAPAN. [ASIA, LANGUAGE, WORD].   G.S.K.

GALLICISM [17c: from Latin *Gallicus* Gaulish, French, and *-ism*. Used with or without an initial capital]. A French word or phrase occurring in another language, such as *ancien régime*, *boutique, chanteuse, faux ami, a certain je ne sais quoi* in English. See FOREIGNISM, FRENCH, -ISM, QUEBEC. [STYLE, VARIETY, WORD].   T.MCA.

GALLEY Also **galley proof** [13c: from Latin *galea*, Greek *galaía* a long, low sea-going vessel. The printer's use may have arisen from a comparison between a tray of type and a ship packed with oarsmen, or such a tray may have resembled those used in a ship's galley (kitchen), also derived from *galaía*]. A printer's proof. Traditionally, a proof is 'pulled' from lead type set in a *galley tray* and printed in long single-column sheets. Usually, up to three octavo pages' worth of text is printed on one *galley slip*. Galleys are the first set of proofs to be read by a proof-reader and/or author. With computer typesetting, printed matter may come in galley form or be set immediately as pages. See PROOF-READING. [TECHNOLOGY].   W.W.B.

GAMBIA, sometimes **the Gambia**. Official title *Republic of (the) Gambia*. A country in West Africa and member of the Commonwealth. Capital: Banjul. Currency: the dalasi (100 butut). Population: 822,000 (1988), 1.4m (projection for 2000). Ethnicity: Mandinka, Fula, Wolof, Jola, Serahuli. Religion: 85% Muslim, 14% Christian. Languages: English (official), Arabic (especially in Quranic schools), the English-based creole Aku, and such indigenous languages as Fula, Mandinka, and Wolof. Education: primary 73%, secondary 21%, tertiary 1%, literacy 26%. Gambia became a British colony in 1807 and gained its independence in 1965. It occupies the banks of the Gambia River and, except for its short coast, is surrounded by Senegal, whose official language is French. In 1982, Gambia and Senegal formed the *Confederation of Senegambia*, bringing English, French, and the local languages into a relationship similar to that of Cameroon. See AFRICAN ENGLISH, CAMEROON, ENGLISH, KRIO, WEST AFRICAN ENGLISH, WEST AFRICAN PIDGIN. [AFRICA, NAME, VARIETY].
                    T.MCA.

GANDHI, Mohandas Karamchand [1869-1948]. Also **Mahatma Gandhi** (from Sanskrit *mahātmā* great soul), *Bapu* and *Bapuji* (from Hindi *bāpū* father, and *-ji* a suffix of respect and affection), and *Gandhiji*. Indian lawyer, politician, and religious leader, noted for his role in bringing the British Raj to an end and for his philosophy of non-violence (Sanskrit: *ahiṃsā*). After completing high school in Gujarat, he went to London in 1888 to study law and was called to the bar at Lincoln's Inn in 1891. As a lawyer in Natal in South Africa he organized a movement of passive resistance to the government to improve the lot of Indians living and working there. He returned to India in 1915 and entered politics in 1919, initiating a policy of non-violent resistance to British rule for which he adopted the yogic name *satyāgraha* (Sanskrit: insistence on truth). In 1924, he was elected president of the Indian National Congress, and until independence in 1947 led the opposition to the British in India. He was assassinated in 1948 by Nathuram Godse, a right-wing Hindu extremist.

Gandhi wrote extensively in Gujarati (his mother tongue), Hindi, and English; his autobiography *The Story of My Experiments with Truth* (1927-9) is widely regarded as a classic of its kind. He was the founder and editor of the weekly *Indian Opinion* (1903) in South Africa, and later wrote for *Young India* and other periodicals. He had strong opinions on the language issue in India, believing in instruction in and through the mother tongue, the use of Hindustani as a pan-Indian link language, and the use of two national scripts, Perso-Arabic and Devanagari. These positions did not receive much support, however, and were abandoned when the Constitution of India recognized Hindi in the Devanagari script as the official language and English as the associate official language. Gandhi regarded the educational system imposed by the British as 'unjust' and 'defective', because 'real education is impossible through a foreign medium' (an often quoted statement, source unknown). His comment on English in India in the 1920s was:

English is today studied because of its commercial and so-called political values. Our boys think, and rightly in the present circumstances, that without English they can not get Government services. Girls are taught English as a passport to marriage—I know husbands who are sorry that their wives can not talk to them and their friends in English. I know families in which English is being made the mother tongue. Hundreds of youths believe that, without a knowledge of English, freedom for India is practically impossible.... All these are signs for me of our slavery and degradation. It is intolerable to me that the vernaculars should be crushed and starved as they have been. . . . I do not want my home to be walled in on all sides and my windows to be stuffed. I want the cultures of all the lands to be blown about my house as freely as possible. But I refuse to be blown off my feet by any. . . . I would have our young men and young women with literary tastes to learn as much English and other world languages as they like, and expect them to give the benefits of their learning to India and to the world. But I would not have a single Indian to forget, neglect or be ashamed of his mother tongue, or to feel that he or she can not think or express the best thoughts in his or her own vernacular (*Young India*, 1919–22, pp. 482–4).

Further references by Gandhi to English are: 'English Learning' (in *Young India* 1: 6, 1921) and 'Evil Wrought by the English Medium' (in *The Modern Review*, Sept. 1925). See index. [ASIA, BIOGRAPHY].   B.B.K.

GATHERING. See QUIRE.

GEECHEE [19c: probably originally referring to a community along the *Ogeechee* River in Georgia, USA]. A name for Gullah, especially as spoken in Georgia: 'Among the negroes living on the Ogeechee River a patois, developed in ante bellum days, has persisted . . . [T]he "Geechee" negro speaks in a sort of staccato and always seems excited when talking' (*National Geographic Magazine*, Sept. 1926). See GULLAH. [AMERICAS, VARIETY].   T.MCA.

GEISEL, Theodor Seuss [1904–91]. Pen name *Dr Seuss*. American writer of children's books. He was educated in Springfield, Massachusetts, where his father was a part-time zoo-keeper,

then at Dartmouth College, New Hampshire, and the U. of Oxford, England. After a spell as an advertising copywriter, he began writing for children, bringing out his first book, *And to Think That I Saw It on Mulberry Street*, in 1937. His style differed sharply from the relatively bland and realistic readers of the period: 'If I start with a two-headed animal, I must never waver from that concept. There must be two hats in the closet, two toothbrushes in the bathroom and two sets of spectacles on the night table' (as quoted in *Time*, 7 Oct. 1991). In the 1950s, Geisel began to bring out a long and highly successful series of slender readers that employed the repetition of word types and groups, the use of nonsense words, and surreal drawings as aids in learning to read. His nearly 50 books, which have sold in hundreds of millions of copies, include *The Cat in the Hat*, *Fox in Socks*, *The Foot Book*, *How the Grinch Stole Christmas*, *The Lorax*, and *Yertle the Turtle*. The following extract is from *Green Eggs and Ham* (1960), where Sam-I-am is persistently pressing the 'hero' to try these culinary delights:

> Would you? Could you?
> In a car?
> Eat them! Eat them!
> Here they are.
>
> I would not,
> could not, in a car.
>
> You may like them.
> You will see.
> You may like them
> in a tree!
>
> I would not, could not in a tree.
> Not in a car! You let me be.
> I do not like them in a box.
> I do not like them with a fox.
> I do not like them in a house.
> I do not like them with a mouse.
> I do not like them here or there.
> I do not like them anywhere.
> I do not like green eggs and ham.
> I do not like them, Sam-I-am.

Henry Allen of the *Washington Post* (Sept. 1991) noted that the children in a Californian school once ate green eggs and ham *en masse* in honour of Dr Seuss's birthday, and asked, apropos of such well-established Seussian names as *the Grinch* and *the Lorax*: 'Has anyone since Lewis Carroll brought more evocative new words into the language?' See index. [AMERICA, EDUCATION, WORD].   T.MCA.

GEMINATION [16c: from Latin *geminatio/ geminationis* twinning]. (1) Doubling, duplicating, pairing, repeating, twinning. (2) In phonetics, the 'doubling' of a consonant sound (in effect, holding it for roughly twice the usual length), as in Italian, in which it is indicated in writing by double letters (*Anna, espresso*). Gemination does not occur in present-day standard international English, but did occur in Old English: contrast *biden* pronounced like 'bidden' and *biddan*, whose /d/ elements were like those in 'bid Den'. Speakers of languages in which gemination occurs may be tempted to carry it over into English because it has so many words spelt with double consonant letters. It is a feature in IndE, among speakers whose first languages are Dravidian. See DRAVIDIAN ENGLISH, INDIAN ENGLISH[1], OLD ENGLISH[1]. [SPEECH].   T.MCA.

GENAM. See GENERAL AMERICAN.

GENDER [14c: from Old French *gendre* (Modern French *genre*), from Latin *genus/generis*, translating Greek *génos* kind]. A grammatical distinction, in which such parts of speech as nouns, adjectives, and determiners are marked as masculine and feminine (as in French and Spanish), or masculine, feminine, and neuter (as in German, Latin, and Greek). In such languages, these parts of speech when being used together must agree in gender: the feminine endings in the Latin phrases *illae feminae bonae* (nominative: those good women), masculine endings in *illi viri boni* (nominative: those good men) and neuter endings in *illa oppida bona* (nominative: those good towns). Distinctions in grammatical gender match some but not all natural gender distinctions and extend them to many items which have no natural gender: French *une pierre*, a stone (feminine). There can sometimes be considerable discrepancies between grammatical and natural gender: German *das Mädchen* (the girl) and *das Kind* (the child) are both neuter.

In English, grammatical distinctions of gender are mainly confined to the third-person singular pronouns, *personal*, *reflexive*, and *possessive* (*she/her/hers/herself* versus *he/him/his/himself*). The term non-personal, rather than neuter, is usually preferred for *it/its/itself*. A contrast of personal and non-personal is also found with the relative pronouns *who/whom* versus *which*. *She/her* is widely used to refer to a ship or other means of transport (*She runs well before the wind*), to a country (*England will never forget those who gave up their lives for her*), and sometimes to machines (*She sounds rough; maybe the engine needs tuning*). A baby or young child (especially when the sex is not known) is sometimes referred to as *it*: 'You don't have to hit a child to abuse it' (charity advertisement). Plural *they/them* is genderless, being used for people and things. Its use with singular reference for people (*Ask anybody and they'll tell you*), a historically well-established usage which operates against the strict rules of concord, is common,

especially in spoken language, but arouses controversy and is considered a solecism by purists.

Some natural-gender distinctions between pairs of nouns show a derivational relationship (*bride/bridegroom, hero/heroine*), but most have no morphological connection (*father/mother, uncle/aunt, mare/stallion*). Some feminine endings are criticized as pejorative and sexist, especially by feminists: *authoress, poetess, usherette, stewardess* appear to be more disliked than *actress, waitress*. In recent years, conscious attempts have been made to use the unmarked or masculine term for both sexes: with little difficulty in such statements as *Emily Dickinson is a great poet*, more controversially in *She's a waiter/steward*. Such awkward usages are often avoided by neutral or unisex terms like *flight attendant*. There seems as yet to be no move to abolish such titles as *princess, duchess, countess*. Where terms exist that include *-man* (as in *chairman*), non-sexist alternatives like *chairperson, chair* are controversial and unstable, especially in the UK, although they are making some headway in the US. See COMMON, FEMININE, GENDER BIAS, MASCULINE, NEUTER, NOUN, PROPER. [GRAMMAR].   S.C.

GENDER BIAS. A term in sociology and women's studies for bias associated with sexual roles in society and gender terms in language. It extends the grammatical term *gender* to cover language-related differences in the behaviour of women and men and in perceptions of that behaviour. Such perceptions are expressed through casual stereotyping, as in: 'Well, she's supposed to be back by now but she's probably stopped off somewhere to gossip. You know how women are.' There are many such generalizations: for example, that the tone of women's voices is or should be *soft* and *feminine*, while men's tones are or should be *deep* and *masculine*; that in female gatherings (*hen parties*), voices are *shrill* or *cackling*; that women's intonation is often (like that of children) *whining* or *nagging*. In contrast, many men are said to sound *gruff*, speak *roughly*, and have *hard*, even *harsh* voices, and at times *bark out* commands.

Views of gender and language. Women and men have been stereotyped as using language in the following ways, among others: (1) Women tend to use such words as *adorable, cute, lovely, sweet* in describing people and objects and such vocatives as *my dear, darling, sweetie*. (2) Men tend to be more direct, less inclined to show their feelings, and more likely 'to call a spade a spade'. Tradition also requires them to be laconic: *men of few words; the strong, silent type*. (3) Women have often engaged in an 'overflow' of adjectives and adverbs, found in an extreme form in the usage of society women between the world wars: *My dear, it's just too simply wonderful to see you!* (4) Women are often eager to talk about feelings and emotions in a way thought of as 'gushing', while many men are almost tongue-tied in such matters. (5) Women frequently use *so, such, quite*: as intensifiers (*It's been so nice to see you again, and such a pleasure to meet the children— I'm really quite thrilled*), or as qualifiers (*Well, he's so, you know, so helpful, and it's such a shame he can't be here—I'm well, quite upset about it*). (6) Women are considered to be more polite, using phrases such as *could you please*, and more concerned about 'correct' and 'proper' grammar and pronunciation. (7) In conversations, women are said to be by turn insecure and hedging (as shown by tags such as *do you?* or *isn't it?*, and qualifiers such as *I think*) and overbearing, talking and interrupting more than men do. (8) Women's 'delicate sensibilities', especially in the middle classes, have traditionally kept them from using obscene or blasphemous language, and restricted its use by men in their presence. (9) Women are more likely to use polite euphemisms for topics such as death and sex. (10) Men typically talk about 'important', 'worldly' topics such as politics, sports, and war, whereas women's talk is 'trivial' and usually 'gossip'.

A masculine norm. There appears to be some basis in fact for some of these assumptions, but sorting out fact from unsupported stereotype is complex and much work remains to be done in this area. Overall, such stereotypes associated with women's speech tend to be viewed negatively even by many women. This generally negative judgement of women's styles of speech appears to be linked to lower social status in relation to men, but it is a circular question whether lower status leads to negative opinions or certain speech characteristics lead to lower status. For example, although behaviour such as a high rate of tag questions such as *isn't it?* may be more typical of women than men, it is also common among lower-status men speaking to higher-status men. Indeed, much language that is currently characterized as female may be more general, and may represent the language that any lower-status person might use in the circumstances.

One problem in assessing gender-linked speech patterns is that men's speech is typically taken as the norm against which women's speech is measured; alternatively, women's speech is ignored. For example, the filters on older traditional spectrographs, used to analyse physical properties of speech such as pitch, were based on male voice ranges; consequently, women's average higher-pitched voices (a result of generally smaller vocal cords) could not be clearly

displayed and were not studied by most researchers. Related to gender-linked speech patterns is a variety of speech sometimes used for identification and communication by some homosexual men. It is characterized in part by higher pitch, elongation of words, increased nasality, and specialized vocabulary, such as *queen* (any male homosexual, or one considered 'flamboyant' or 'effeminate') and *butch* (stereotypically or exaggeratedly masculine in appearance or behaviour), and the use of female pronouns to refer to men.

Social factors. Many factors affect language patterns, including topic, socio-economic class, degree of familiarity of the speakers, age, status, ethnicity, and degree of identification with mainstream social values. Both women and men often behave differently in same-sex and mixed-sex groups. In the latter, men tend to interrupt women (men with higher status doing it more often), have more turns at speaking, and speak more when taking those turns. In same-sex groups, participation is more balanced; in situations such as formal, male-dominated business conversations, it is closely related to rank and status. In addition, some speech and gender stereotypes are partly true: men do appear to use 'strong' words such as *damn* and *shit* more often and more publicly. Women, however, may also use them, especially with other women, and especially younger women in North America and Britain. Women may also express strong emotions with 'weaker' words (such minced oaths as *darn* for *damn* and *shoot* for *shit*), whereas men may use stronger words with less apparent emotion.

Recent studies suggest that in many situations, women seem to be more concerned than men about using educated language as a means of social mobility. The fact that so many teachers of especially younger children are women may also make their role as 'language correctors' more salient. This factor varies greatly with location, social class, and level of education: for example, many more British working-class men than women seem to use non-standard language as a badge of identity. Sometimes stereotyped behaviour appears to be gender-linked in terms of frequency, but other interpretations of its significance are possible: for example, tag questions such as *isn't it?* may indicate hesitancy, insecurity, or deference, but could also encourage conversation, in a non-aggressive way inviting the listener to respond. Such a strategy might be linked to women's greater use of minimal responses, such as *mmhm*, which indicate active listening, encouragement, or agreement. Both strategies can be characterized by hostile men as 'nagging' or 'pushing', if they are interpreted as inappropriate insertions in their conversation turn. Men's typically louder voices, less frequent uses of minimal responses, and greater use of obscenities can be seen as means of manipulating and dominating conversations. See FEMINISM, GENDER, GENERIC PRONOUN, INCLUSIVE LANGUAGE, SEXISM. [STYLE].   L.S.W., M.E.W.

GENDERLECT [1970s: a blend of *gender* and (*dia*)*lect*]. A term in sociolinguistics for a way of speaking taken to be characteristic of only one sex: 'Linguist Robin Lakoff has suggested that because their social roles are so different, men's and women's speech are almost different dialects ("genderlects")' (Mary Brown Parlee, 'Conversational Politics', *Psychology Today*, 1979). See GENDER, GENDER BIAS, LECT. [LANGUAGE, SPEECH, STYLE].   T.MCA.

GENERAL AMERICAN [1924: introduced by George P. Krapp in *The English Language in America*]. Short forms *GA, GenAm*. A term sometimes employed to refer to 'a form of U.S. speech without marked dialectal or regional characteristics' (*OED Supplement*) but one 'no longer in technical use' (*The Random House Dictionary of the English Language*, 1987). It was denounced by Hans Kurath in his review of Krapp's book, but has continued to be used in some scholarly and many popular treatments of AmE, often subtractively to refer to whatever is left once various 'regions' have been described: usually New England, New York, and Southern. Although there may have been some justification before 1945 for presuming uniformity elsewhere in the US, the term began to diminish in popularity once the complexity of AmE began to be understood. In revising Mencken's *The American Language*, Raven I. McDavid accounted for Mencken's use of the term by noting: 'In the last thirty years research for the L[inguistic] A[tlas] has shown that the so-called "General American" area is really made up of two major dialects' (1967). Some scholars outside the US continue to use the term, specifically to refer to a norm of pronunciation: for example, J. C. Wells, in both *Accents of English: Beyond the British Isles* (1982, p. 470) and the *Longman Pronunciation Dictionary* (1990). Robert Burchfield, editor of the definition in the *OED Supplement*, has declared that the kind of AmE taught to foreigners is a 'clinically analysed form of speech . . . not spoken by the majority of Americans' (1985). The history of the term is discussed by William R. Van Riper, 'General American: An Ambiguity' (1973), in *Dialect and Language Variation*, ed. Harold B. Allen & Michael D. Linn (Orlando: Academic Press, 1986). See AMERICAN ENGLISH, AMERICAN ENGLISH AND BRITISH ·ENGLISH, KRAPP, NETWORK STANDARD. Compare

GENERAL AMERICAN ENGLISH, GENERAL BRITISH, GENERAL CANADIAN. [AMERICAS, SPEECH, VARIETY]   R.W.B.

GENERAL AMERICAN ENGLISH. A term for the standard English of the US, usually intended to include pronunciation, grammar, and vocabulary: 'The educational system in the Philippines uses General American English as the norm' (regional seminar report by Philippines linguists, 1981). Compare GENERAL AMERICAN. [AMERICAS, VARIETY].   T.MCA.

GENERAL ANALYSIS. See CLAUSE ANALYSIS.

GENERAL AUSTRALIAN. A term, especially in linguistics, for the pronunciation used by most Australians. See AUSTRALIAN ENGLISH. [OCEANIA, SPEECH, VARIETY].   W.S.R.

GENERAL BRITISH. An occasional term in linguistics and language teaching for RP as the accent that represents BrE, used especially to contrast with *General American*: 'The British English form [in this dictionary] is that which has been called *Received Pronunciation* or *General British*' (*Oxford Advanced Learner's Dictionary of Current English*, 1974). See BRITISH ENGLISH, GENERAL AMERICAN, RECEIVED PRONUNCIATION. [EUROPE, SPEECH, VARIETY].   T.MCA.

GENERAL CANADIAN. A term, especially in linguistics, for the usage of a majority of Canadians (pronunciation, grammar, and vocabulary), especially from Ontario to the Pacific, traditionally considered one of four major dialects of Canada but increasingly regarded as a class-based urban dialect used for broadcasting and as an educational norm. See DIALECT IN CANADA. Compare GENERAL AMERICAN. [AMERICAS, VARIETY].   T.MCA.

GENERAL ENGLISH. (1) A non-technical term for English when the language at large is contrasted with a usage, variety, dialect, or register: *That's Cockney; it isn't general English.* (2) A semi-technical term for a course in English, usually as a mother tongue or in an English-medium school, within a framework of general education, usually teaching listening, speaking, reading, and writing. (3) In linguistics, a range of English that includes the standard but contrasts with specific accents and dialects. The British phonetician John C. Wells contrasts *General English* (capitalized) and *traditional-dialect* (lower case): 'Within General English . . . there are non-standard varieties in which one says *I couldn't see no one* and *Peter done it* rather than the standard *I couldn't see anyone* and *Peter did it*' (*Accents of English*, volume 1, 1982). (4) Also

English for General Purposes. A term in language teaching for a broadly based, usually long-term EFL or ESL course, in contrast to *English for Specific Purposes* (Business English, English for Medical Purposes, etc.). The assumption often underlies such courses that the learner should be offered 'the whole of' English. Compare ESP (ENGLISH FOR SPECIFIC PURPOSES), STANDARD ENGLISH, STANDARD GENERAL ENGLISH. [EDUCATION, VARIETY]. T.MCA., P.S.

GENERAL INDIAN ENGLISH. See INDIAN ENGLISH[1].

GENERALIZATION [17c]. A process of semantic change that widens the meaning of a word, phrase, or lexeme. In Middle English, *pigeon* meant a young bird, especially a young dove, but from the late 15c has come to refer especially to the whole family Columbidae. *Dove* is now generally used for a smaller variety of pigeon. Such shifts in meaning are usually slow and tendential rather than rapid and absolute. Early usages continue indefinitely alongside later changes that have become dominant, as was true of *pigeon* and *dove* in the 16c. In the process of change, terms may acquire further meanings within a set of words: the pigeon is not a symbol of peace and no one *dove-holes* information. See COMPUTER USAGE, SEMANTIC CHANGE, SLANG. [HISTORY, LANGUAGE, WORD]. T.MCA.

GENERAL NEW ZEALAND. A term, especially in linguistics, for the pronunciation used by most New Zealanders. See NEW ZEALAND ENGLISH. [OCEANIA, SPEECH, VARIETY]. T.MCA.

GENERAL SERVICE LIST, short form *GSL.* Full title *A General Service of English Words with semantic frequencies and a supplementary word-list for the writing of popular science and technology.* A word list compiled and edited by Michael West for use by ELT teachers and writers, published in 1953 by Longmans, Green & Co., and based on earlier work done by West and others as a result of the Carnegie conference on vocabulary selection held in New York in 1934, whose purpose was the selection of vocabulary as a stage in the teaching of English. It incorporated material from *A Semantic Count of English Words* by Irving Lorge and Edward L. Thorndike (1938). The *GSL* greatly influenced the choice of vocabulary for EFL course materials, graded readers, and dictionaries until the mid-1970s. An entry lists a word with its part of speech, its frequency position in a count of 5m running words, and the percentages of its major sense divisions in that count: for example, *game* N., 638, fun and games 9%, with the idea of competition 38%, a particular contest 23%, games as an athletic contest 8%, and sundries. See FREQUENCY COUNT, PALMER, THORNDIKE, VOCABULARY CONTROL, WEST. [EDUCATION, EUROPE, WORD]. T.MCA.

GENERATIVE [16c: from Latin *generativus* producing one's kind]. A term borrowed in the 1960s from mathematics into linguistics by Noam Chomsky. If a grammar is generative, it accounts for or specifies the membership of the set of grammatical sentences in the language concerned by defining the precise rules for membership of the set. The use of the verb *generate* in this sense (*The grammar will generate the following set of sentences*) is distinct from its general sense 'produce'. See GENERATIVE GRAMMAR. [GRAMMAR]. S.G.

GENERATIVE GRAMMAR. A grammar which precisely specifies the membership of the set of all the grammatical sentences in the language in question and therefore excludes all the ungrammatical sentences. It takes the form of a set of rules that specifies the structure, interpretation, and pronunciation of sentences that native speakers of the language are considered to accept as belonging to the language; it is therefore regarded as representing native speakers' competence in or knowledge of their language. A recent account of the development of generative grammar, both transformational and non-transformational, from the early 1960s to the late 1980s, is: Geoffrey Horrocks, *Generative Grammar*, Longman, 1987. See CHOMSKY, COMPETENCE AND PERFORMANCE, GENERATIVE, GRAMMATICALITY, TRANSFORMATIONAL-GENERATIVE GRAMMAR. [GRAMMAR]. S.G., T.MCA.

GENERIC [17c: from Latin *genus/generis,* translating Greek *génos* a kind]. (1) Belonging to or designating a genus (as opposed to a species) or a class, group, or kind. In semantics, a *generic term* includes other terms that belong in the same class: for example, *officer* includes *colonel*, *major*, *captain*, and *flower* includes *hyacinth*, *rose*, *tulip*: compare HYPERONYM. In law, a trademark ceases to be protected when it comes to be more widely used for, and understood as, a type rather than a brand: for example, the proprietary names *Hoover* for type of vacuum cleaner and *Xerox* for equipment that makes xerographic copies are, despite being trademarks, widely used for vacuum cleaners in general and xerographic copies of all kinds. When so used, especially as verbs, they are written without an initial capital (*to hoover; a xerox, to xerox*). In such uses the terms are in effect generic. When this happens, the mark is referred to as generic or *a generic*. (2) In grammar, a word is generic if it applies to both men and women. *He* has traditionally been considered a *generic pronoun*, but feminists among others object to both the classification and the usage. See BINOMIAL NOMENCLATURE, GENERIC PRONOUN, SEXISM, TRADEMARK. [LANGUAGE].

T.MCA.

GENERIC PRONOUN, also **common-gender pronoun, epicene pronoun**. A personal pronoun that includes both masculine and feminine, such as *u* in Persian (which translates *he* and *she*) and *they* in English, which does not distinguish gender. English does not have a singular equivalent for *u*, but the *he*-group of pronouns has traditionally been called generic, along with such words as *man* and *mankind*: 'Words importing the masculine gender shall be deemed and taken to include females' (from an Act of Parliament, London, 1850). The use of generic *he* is, however, often ambiguous, because it tends to identify masculine gender with the universally human and in the process appears to exclude or marginalize women. For these reasons, it has been challenged in recent years, especially by feminists. Generic *he* continues in use, but efforts have been made, with varying degrees of success, to circumvent it. These include (1) The use of *he or she*, which serves in limited contexts but becomes awkward in longer texts. (2) The use of composite *s/he*, which cannot be spoken, and composite *he/she* and *she/he*, in effect compound pronouns. (3) The use of *she* alone, often to make a sociopolitical point. (4) The reversal *she and he*, for similar reasons. (5) Generic *she* in texts and contexts where women are in the majority, such as books about teaching and secretarial work. (6) The use of *he and she* and *she and he* alternately, which may become forced in longer texts. (7) General *you* and *one*, which may alter the message. In AmE, the tradition of *one . . . he* (*When one does this, he finds . . .*), as opposed to BrE *one . . . one* (*When one does this, one finds . . .*) returns the user to the problem of generic *he*. (8) Plurals rather than singulars wherever possible: *the doctor . . . he* changed to *doctors . . . they*. This appears to be a widespread strategy to avoid the problem. (9) Rephrasing sentences so as to avoid pronouns completely, especially by using the agentless passive.

Singular *they*. The *they*-pronoun group is increasingly used in such singular constructions as: 'Anyone who wants to write non-sexist English will need to have their wits about them. They will need to be thick-skinned, too, for if they write sentences like my first one, they will hear criticism from those people who are upset by the use of the plural pronoun *them* with a singular pronoun like *anyone*' (Jenny Cheshire, 'A Question of Masculine Bias', *English Today*

1, Jan. 1985). The use of *they*-pronouns, as in *Everyone should bring their coats*, dates from the 16c, is widespread, is increasingly acceptable in informal BrE and AmE, and is increasingly common with 'dual gender' nouns such as *speaker*, *subscriber*. Singular usage occasionally includes *themself*, a form that dates from the 15c but has always been rare: 'I think somebody should immediately address themself to this problem' (A. Thomas Ellis, *The Times*, 9 Sept. 1987). If singular *they* continues to gain acceptance, *themself* may also become common, much as *yourself* became common with singular *you* in the 17c.

Artificial pronouns. In recent years, attempts to replace generic *he* have led to the invention of inclusive third-person pronouns. As members of a syntactic system, pronouns are normally slow to change; the last great adaptation was the 17c replacement of the *thou*-group with singular *you*. The coining of such new pronouns has met with responses varying from sober consideration through wry amusement to open ridicule. The first such pronoun appears to have been *thon*, created by Charles Converse of Erie in 1884, who described it as a contraction of *that one* and appears not to have been aware that demonstrative *thon* (that one over there) has long been used in Scots and Northern English. In *On Writing Well*, William Zinsser may have spoken for many when he commented: 'I very much doubt that thon wants that word in thons language or that thon would use it thonself. This is not how the language changes' (1980). Coinages (some serious, some tongue-in-cheek) include *co* (by the writer Mary Orovan), *e/ir* (by school organizers in Broward County, Florida), *et* (by Aline Hoffman of Sarnia, Ontario), *han* (by the business writer Audrie Stratford in King's Lynn, England), *hey* (by Ronald Gill of Derby, England), *hesh/hirm/hizer* (by Professor Robert Longwell, U. of North Carolina), *hir* (in a 1979 supervisors' guide for the American Management Association), *jhe* (by Professor Milton R. Stern, U. of Michigan), *mef* (by George Wardell of Reading, England), *na* (by the writer June Arnold), *per* (abbreviating *person*, by the writer Marge Pierce), *ws/wself* (by Dr John B. Sykes, editor, *Concise Oxford Dictionary*, 7th edition), and *ze/zon* (by Don Manley, Oxford). See GENDER BIAS, SEXISM. [GRAMMAR, STYLE, USAGE].

T.MCA.

GENERIC TERM. See GENERIC.

GENITIVE CASE [14c: from Latin *casus genitivus* the possessing case, from *gignere/genitum* to beget, produce]. A term marking possession and analogous relationships in the case system of Latin and other inflected languages. In the phrase *dies irae* days of wrath, *irae* is the genitive of *ira* wrath, anger. The term has been carried over into English grammar, but is not so common as *possessive*. See DOUBLE GENITIVE, GROUP POSSESSIVE/GENITIVE, SAXON GENITIVE. [GRAMMAR]. T.MCA.

GENRE [18c: from French *genre*, from Latin *genus/generis* kind, race: compare GENDER]. A term in literature and the arts for a particular type of performance, such as the novel or symphonic music. The genres of English literature derive from classical Greek theory, which divided literary works into three genres: *poetic, epic, dramatic*. Each of these divisions possessed a different narrative voice: in lyric poetry, the narrator is alone; in epic, narrator and characters speak; in drama, the characters alone speak. From the Renaissance to the Romantic period (16–19c), the classical genres and subgenres (usually known as *kinds*) were regarded in principle as fixed and virtually part of the natural order of things, with boundaries which should not be crossed. In practice, however, the Elizabethan dramatists frequently crossed them, mixing *comedy* with *tragedy* and high styles with low in one and the same play, as Shakespeare did in *Hamlet*. Although the neo-classical critics of the late 17c and the 18c wished to impose classical strictness, their view came to be regarded as prescriptive and restrictive. The growth of the *novel* in particular (an entirely non-classical genre, as the name implies) challenged assumptions about the immutability of types. The freer thinking of the Romantics and changes in knowledge about the physical world encouraged an awareness that such systems of classification were arbitrary and subject to change.

By the mid-20c, the concept of genre was largely out of favour among critics, because of the emphasis of the New Critics on the individual text. More recently, however, there has been a revival of genre theory, in which no single approach has been dominant. The early Formalists, such as V. Shklovsky (*Art as Device*, 1917) and O. Brik (*Rhythm and Syntax*, 1927), stressed the difference between poetry and narrative: in poetry, the opposition between poetical and practical language; in narrative, the presence of *fabula* (the basic story) and *syuzhet* (the formal devices of construction). The work of such linguists as Ferdinand de Saussure in Switzerland and Roman Jakobson (born in Russia) partly prepared the way for the French critic Roland Barthes and the Structuralists, for whom genre is a set of conventions representing the shared expectations of writer and reader, and changing from one period to another. Among individuals, the Canadian critic Northrop Frye (*Anatomy of Criticism*, 1957) has suggested that the categories *comedy, romance, tragedy, satire* correspond to archetypal human responses. Another approach, categorizing texts through a combination of *outer form* (such as metre, structure) and *inner form* (such as tone, attitude) was made by the former member of the Prague School, René Wellek (with A. Warren, *Theory of Literature*, 1949).

At the present time, literary scholars generally regard genre as something imposed, not inherent. It is convenient for analysis but has neither primal truth nor formal sanction. Like grammar, genre is held to be more descriptive than prescriptive. Though probably deficient in some respects, a description is likely to aid attempts to talk and write intelligently about literature. The integrity of a text demands respect, but family resemblances among texts justify grouping them together. In academic syllabuses, the teaching of genre courses in addition to, or instead of, period courses is common. The classical division (adapted as *poetry, fiction*, and *drama*) is often used, but there are new classifications such as *utopias* and *women's writing*, which usually adopt existing genres like the novel but have created new categories by dealing with subjects not generally found in earlier periods. Subgenres such as *lyric, Bildungsroman*, and *farce* are established terms of literary criticism. As further divisions emerge, it may be salutary to remember the categories of Polonius: 'tragedy, comedy, history, pastoral, pastoral-comical, historical-pastoral, tragical-historical, tragical-comical-historical-pastoral, scene individable or poem unlimited' (*Hamlet*, 2. 2). Traditional ideas about genre have affected literary language. The dominance of a genre in a period has led to the belief that the diction used in it is the 'right' or 'highest' form of literary expression. This has tended to inhibit experiment and to develop such narrow concepts as poetic diction. In the 20c, freedom to use all types of language in any genre has prevailed. Poetry in particular has accommodated colloquial words and idioms that would once have been considered ugly and unfitting, and many dramatists have tried to come as close as possible to the reproduction of actual conversation in their dialogue.

See ALLEGORY, AUTOBIOGRAPHY, BALLAD, BILDUNGSROMAN, BIOGRAPHY, BURLESQUE, COMEDY, DETECTIVE STORY, DIARY, DIRGE, DRAMA, ELEGY, EPIC, EPIGRAM, EPITAPH, FABLE, FANTASY, FARCE, FICTION, GENRE, HOMILY, HYMN, LAMPOON, LETTER[2], LIMERICK, LITERATURE, LYRIC, MEDIA, MEMOIR, NOVEL, NOVELETTE, NOVELIZATION, NOVELLA, ODE, PARABLE, PARODY, PASTORAL, POETRY, POLEMIC, PROSE, ROMANCE, SAGA, SATIRE, SERMON, SHORT STORY, SONNET, STORY, THRENODY, TRAGEDY, TRAGICOMEDY, VERSE. [LITERATURE, MEDIA]. R.C.

GENTEEL. See AMERICAN LITERATURE.

GENTEELISM [1900s: from *genteel*, from French *gentil* well-born, and *-ism*]. A semi-technical term for both genteel behaviour in using language and a word or phrase used for genteel reasons: 'By *genteelism* is here to be understood the substituting, for the ordinary natural word that first suggests itself to the mind, of a synonym that is thought to be less soiled by the lips of the common herd, less familiar, less plebeian, less vulgar, less improper' (H. Fowler, *Modern English Usage*, 1926). Such a substitution is *tummy* for *belly*. Genteelisms are generally euphemisms used for evasive 'polite' purposes, such as *bathroom, lavatory, powder room, restroom, toilet* for a place for urinating, defecating, and washing. See EUPHEMISM, -ISM, MINCED OATH, NICE-NELLYISM, POLITE. [STYLE, WORD].   T.MCA.

GEOGRAPHY AND GEOPOLITICS OF ENGLISH. The term *geography* refers to both the study of the planet and its major features. It came into English in the 16c, from Latin and ultimately Greek, at the time when European navigators were beginning to explore Africa and the New World. In the course of the long commercial and colonial diaspora that followed, a small number of Western European languages came to dominate vast areas of the world, two results of which were the major place of European terminology in international geographical studies and the spread of European-style place-names across the world. The Dutch, English, French, Portuguese, and Spanish languages were particularly prominent, along with classical Greek and Latin as used by scholars. Greek has provided such widely used names for geographical features as (in their English forms) *Antarctic, Antipodes, Arctic, Asia, Atlantic, Europe, ocean,* and *geography* itself, and Latin has provided terms for geographic concepts, such as *continent, Equator,* and *Tropic of Cancer,* and the universal naming suffix *-ia,* as found in *Albania, Kirghizia, Mongolia, Yugoslavia,* and *Zambia.* Work relating to geography, cartography, topography, toponymy, and oceanography undertaken in English absorbed names from many languages when the Royal Navy and other expeditionary groups were engaged in international surveying and mapping. At the same time, English-speaking settlers took names wholesale from the British Isles and put them to work in their new homes: for example, English *York* in American *New York,* and Scottish *Dunedin* (Celtic for *Edinburgh*) applied to a city in New Zealand. In addition, complex geographical labels have been synthesized in various

ways: for example, *the Gulf of Carpentaria* (Australia), is a term that both Latinizes the name *Carpenter* and embodies a formula 'the X of Y'. This formula was already used in such names as *the Bay of Biscay* and *the Isle of Mull.* Similarly, the phrase *Chesapeake Bay* spells an American Indian word in an English way and also applies the formula 'Y X', already used for *Galway Bay* and *Morecambe Bay.* Circumstance and convention have frozen such forms; there are, normally, no such alternative usages as **Carpentaria Gulf* or **the Bay of Chesapeake.*

Because of the European diaspora, English occupies in the late 20c a geopolitical position unique among languages past or present. The relationships between users of English and of other languages (always delicate, often explosive, sometimes tragic) include associations with: (1) Other languages in Europe, such as for centuries Welsh and Gaelic in Britain and more recently, with the development of Brussels as the administrative centre of the European Community, French and Flemish in Belgium. (2) Other European languages elsewhere, such as French in Canada and Spanish in the US. (3) Indigenous languages elsewhere, such as Aboriginal languages in Australia, Arabic in North Africa and West Asia, Bantu languages in Sub-Saharan Africa, Hindi-Urdu in the Indian subcontinent, Maori in New Zealand, and Tagalog in the Philippines. Relationships have been particularly acute where English has threatened the existence of another language, as with Gaelic in Ireland and Scotland and Algonkian or Hawaiian in the US, or has influenced its structures and vocabulary, as with (to a greater or less extent and in different ways) the languages of north-western Europe, and Korean and Japanese in East Asia. At the same time, relationships among the speech communities of World English add to the complexity: (1) Among dialect speakers within one country, as in England. (2) Among unilingual, bilingual, and multilingual users, as in Canada. (3) Between native and foreign users, as in the flux of international trade and travel. (4) In terms of the 'cultural cringe' of ex-colony towards mother country, as with Australia and New Zealand towards England or Britain. (5) Between creoles and standard forms, as in West Africa, the Caribbean, and Melanesia. (6) In the relationship between actual or potential national standards and an actual or potential international or supranational standard. Compare HISTORY OF ENGLISH. See ENGLISH.   T.MCA.

The geography theme.
AFRICA (with sublist of relevant entries), AMERICAS (with sublist of relevant entries), ARABIC, ASIA (with sublist of relevant entries), ATLANTIC, BANTU, BRITAIN,

BRITISH EMPIRE, CARIBBEAN, CHINA, COMMONWEALTH, CONTINENT, CREOLE, DIALECT, DIASPORA, DUTCH, ENGLISH, EUROPE (with sublist of relevant entries), FRENCH, GERMANIC LANGUAGES, HISTORY OF ENGLISH (AND CHRONOLOGY), IMPERIALISM, INDO-EUROPEAN LANGUAGES, INTERNATIONAL LANGUAGE, JAPAN, KOREA, LANGUAGE (with sublist of relevant entries), LINGUA FRANCA, LITERATURE (with sublist of relevant entries), NAME (with sublist of relevant entries), OCEANIA (with sublist of relevant entries), PIDGIN, PORTUGUESE, ROMANCE LANGUAGES, SPANISH, STANDARD, STANDARD ENGLISH, TEIL, TRANSLATION, VARIETY (with sublist of relevant entries), WORLD ENGLISH, WORLD LANGUAGE, WORLD LITERATURE.

GEORDIE [Late 18c: a diminutive of *George* favoured in the North of England and in Scotland, used as a nickname for miners, sailors, coal-boats in and from north-east England, and for Scots in Australia and New Zealand. In this instance, it is widely considered to derive from the name of George Stephenson, the Newcastle engineer who built the first successful steam locomotive in 1814, invented a miners' safety lamp in 1815, and became manager of the Stockton to Darlington Railway (the world's first public railway line) in 1821]. (1) A native of the North-East of England in and around the city of Newcastle upon Tyne (Tyneside), an area often referred to informally as Geordieland. (2) The variety of working-class speech in that area, deriving ultimately from Northumbrian, one of the three divisions of Old English, and in many ways closer to Scots than to Yorkshire dialect. (3) The term is often loosely applied to all people in the North-East of England and their speech. This can sometimes cause offence to non-Tynesiders, such as the people of Wearside and Middlesbrough.

Pronunciation. (1) Geordie is non-rhotic and the only urban accent of England in which initial *h* is not dropped. (2) The glottal stop occurs with /p, t, k/ in syllable-final position and sometimes initially before a weak vowel, as in *caper, city, local*. Phoneticians disagree as to whether the glottal stop precedes or follows the consonant. (3) There is a clear /l/ in all positions. (4) The uvular *r*, known as the *Durham* or *Northumberland Burr*, was once common but is now in decline, having been widely regarded and treated as a speech defect. The pronunciation of *r* is now generally dental, alveolar, or post-alveolar, but the burr has left a legacy in broad Geordie, in which certain vowels are pronounced as if still followed by the burr: *cure* as 'kyooah', *nurse* as 'noahss'. (5) Commonly, there is an /ɑː/ vowel in such words as *all, talk, walk, war*. Geordie *walk* sounds to non-Geordies like 'waak', and *work* like 'walk'. A joke recounts how a man went to his doctor because of a painful knee.

The doctor bandaged it and asked: 'Do you think you can walk now?' The man replied: 'Work? I can hardly walk!' (6) There is an /o/ or /oə/ in such words as *don't, goat, know, told*. (7) The vowel in such words as *down, town* ranges from the /u/ of Scots *doun, toun* to its RP value. (8) The closing vowel in words like *bonny* and *happy* is /i/ ('bonnee', 'happee'). (9) There is often a low rising tone in statements, making them seem tentative or like questions to non-Geordies.

Syntax, vocabulary, and usage. (1) A traditional *Aa* where standard English has *I* (*Aa doan't know*), comparable to *Ah* in Scots. (2) A traditional but now sporadic use of negative *-na* rather than *not* or *-n't*, as in *Aa canna bide yon chap* I can't stand that chap, comparable to Scots and Ulster Scots -nae/-na/-ny. (3) The form *diven't* is a traditional alternative to *don't*: *I diven't do nothin'* I don't do anything. (4) Common forms of address include *bonny lad* (to a man or boy), *bonny lass* (to a woman or girl), *hinny* (honey: to a woman, girl, man, or boy): *How there, bonny lass?* How are you, dear? (5) Geordie shares many words with Scots and ScoE: *bairn* child, *bonny* fine, good-looking (used of women and men), *canny* steady and cautious (but with a local nuance of good, kind, and gentle). See DIALECT IN ENGLAND, L-SOUNDS, NORTHERN ENGLISH, NORTHUMBRIA, SCOTS, YORKSHIRE. [EUROPE, VARIETY].   T.MCA.

GERMAN [Called by its speakers *Deutsch*: see DUTCH]. A Germanic language of Western Europe, the official language of Germany and Austria, and an official language of Switzerland (with French and Italian) and Luxembourg (with French). It is also spoken by communities in Belgium, Denmark, France, Hungary, Italy, Liechtenstein, Poland, Romania, and the Soviet Union, is widely used as a second language in Turkey and Yugoslavia, and is spoken in enclaves in North and South America, Africa, and Australia. With nearly 100m speakers, it ranks tenth among languages in world terms and first in Western Europe in numbers of native speakers. Because of close genetic links, German and English share many features, as seen in the sentence: *Für rund 95 (fünfundneunzig) bis 100 (hundert) Millionen Menschen ist Deutsch heute Muttersprache* (For around five and ninety to hundred million people is German today mother-speech: 'Today German is the mother tongue of about 95 to a 100m people'). The difference in word order is great, but a close match can be made with *für/for, rund/around, fünf/five, neunzig/ninety, hundert/hundred, Mensch/man, ist/is, Mutter/mother, Sprache/*

speech (with *million* as a shared Romance borrowing). German is structurally more complex than English, having inflectional endings for number, case, gender, person, tense, etc., and in this it resembles Old English more closely than Modern English. In its orthography, German gives an initial capital letter to its nouns, a practice common in English until the mid-18c.

Varieties. Historically, German has been an amalgam of dialects slow to develop a standard language. The continuum ranges from the geographically 'low' German dialect of Westphalia in the north-west (mutually intelligible with Dutch), through those of Lower and Upper Saxony, the Rhineland, and Franconia, to the 'upper' German varieties spoken in Bavaria, Switzerland, and Austria. The term *Plattdeutsch* (sometimes translated as 'Low German') is used for the 'broad' dialects in the north and west. *Schwyzertüütsch* is the common spoken German in Switzerland, a dialect more than most others in diglossic contrast with the written and printed language. The linguistic distinction between *Niederdeutsch* (Lower German) and *Oberdeutsch* (Upper German) covers the same continuum. It is usually traced to the Second Sound Shift in the 8c, in which the Southern dialects became phonologically distinct from the Northern, producing such South/North contrasts as *machen/maken* (make) and *Schiff/skip* (ship). Confusingly, the geographical term *Hochdeutsch* or High German is applied to the result of this sound change, so that the term can refer both to all the Upper German (that is, geographically 'highland' and Southern) dialects and to an idealized standard German language which is 'high' in the social sense.

Even then, however, the division into Lower and Upper/High German is not the whole story, as dialectologists and language historians generally recognize an intermediate variety: *Mitteldeutsch* (Central or Middle German) stretching from Cologne to Frankfurt and Leipzig. Observers can draw attention either to such Low/High contrasts as *Junge/Bub* a boy, and *Sonnabend/Samstag* Saturday, or such Low/Middle/Upper contrasts as *ik/ich/i* the pronoun *I*, and *Männeken/Männchen/Mandl* a little man. The contribution of the Central and Southern dialects to a common *Schriftsprache* (written or literary language) is often acknowledged, as is the fact that more recently a supra-regional *Umgangssprache* (colloquial semi-standard) has served to level out differences.

Tensions persist, however, between unifying and separatist tendencies. More than in English, orthographic conventions have been standardized, largely because of the influential *Duden* spelling dictionary (*Vollständiges ortho-* *graphisches Wörterbuch der deutschen Sprache*, Konrad Duden, 1880; *Duden*, vol. 1, *Die Rechtschreibung*, 19th edition, Bibliographisches Institut Mannheim, 1986). Local differences in pronunciation occur at all social levels and are often deliberately asserted to establish people's backgrounds. A single, supranational norm for pronunciation does not exist in German-speaking countries any more than in English-speaking countries, although 19c *Bühnendeutsch* (stage German) and 20c media and social mobility have promoted compromises between Lower/North and Upper/South German speech forms. While 'all German-language countries have problems or dilemmas concerning nationhood or ethnicity' (Michael G. Clyne, *Language and Society in the German-Speaking Countries*, Cambridge: University Press, 1984, p. xi), distinct varieties have emerged in East and West Germany (prior to reunification in 1990), Austria, and Switzerland, especially in vocabulary, which have been partly codified in 'national' dictionaries.

Historically, (High) German is divided into Old High German from AD 750, Middle High German from 1150, Early New High German from 1350, and New High German from 1650. The description and discussion of the language is further complicated by two factors: (1) The data of traditional dialectology as presented in such handbooks as the *DTV-Atlas* (1978) are often more than 50 years old. (2) Recent sociolinguistic studies are too limited or local to allow generalizations. In addition, there is a long-established equivocal relationship with loanwords (*Fremdwörter*: foreign words). Since the late 17c, these have often been resented and deliberately replaced with vernacular equivalents by purist grammarians: *Anschrift* for *Adresse*, *Bücherei* for *Bibliothek*, *Mundart* for *Dialekt*, *Stelldichein* for *Rendezvous*.

German in English. Over the centuries, many German words have found their way into English: for example, Low German *brake*, *dote*, *tackle* and High German *blitz*, *dachshund*, *kindergarten*: see BORROWING. Cultural acquisitions have been significant in such fields as food (*frankfurter*, *hamburger*, *hock*, *pretzel*, *sauerkraut*), mineralogy (*cobalt*, *feldspar*, *gneiss*, *quartz*), music (*glockenspiel*, *leitmotiv*, *waltz*), philosophy (*weltanschauung*, *zeitgeist*), and politics (*diktat*, *realpolitik*). Two powerful sources of borrowing in AmE have been such German settlers as the Pennsylvania Dutch (that is, *Deutsch*) and Yiddish-speaking Jewish immigrants.

English in German. Contacts between English and German have been on the increase since the early 18c, promoted by literary translation, diplomatic links, trade relations, language teaching, and the media. Loans have entered German from such fields as literature (*sentimental, Ballade*), sport (*boxen, Rally*), politics (*Hearing; Hochverrat*, from 'high treason'), and technology (*Lokomotive*, from locomotive engine; *Pipeline*). Resistance is no longer as vociferous as during the time of the *Sprachgesellschaften* (17c language societies) and the anti-foreigner propaganda of the Nazis in the 1930s. English usages are adopted and adapted as: loanwords (*babysitten* babysit), loan translations (*Beiprodukt* by-product), blends of loanword and loan translation (*Teamarbeit* team work), semantic transfer (*Schau* from 'show', in the sense of theatrical event), and loan creation (*Öffentlichkeitsarbeit*, 'work for the public', loosely based on 'public relations'). Most borrowing is at word level, but occasionally idioms or syntactic constructions are transferred, as in *grünes Licht geben* give the green light, *Ich fliege Lufthansa* I fly Lufthansa. The influence of English is strong in advertising (*High Life, Image*) and information science (*Compiler, Feedback*). In general, AmE has a greater influence than BrE.

See AMERICAN LANGUAGES, AUSTRALIAN LANGUAGES, AUSTRALIAN PLACE-NAMES, BORROWING, CAMEROON, CANADIAN LANGUAGES, DIALECT IN AMERICA, DUTCH, ENGLISH, EUROPEAN COMMUNITY, EUROPEAN LANGUAGES, FRENCH, FRISIAN, GERMANIC LANGUAGES, -GLISH AND -LISH, GOTHIC, INDO-EUROPEAN LANGUAGES, INDO-GERMANIC, LOANWORD, NAMIBIA, PAPUA NEW GUINEA, PENNSYLVANIA DUTCH, SPELLING REFORM, STANDARD, TANZANIA, TELECOMMUNICATIONS, YIDDISH. [LANGUAGES]. R.H.

GERMANIC LANGUAGES. A group of related languages including English, Dutch, Frisian, German, the Scandinavian languages (Danish, Faroese, Icelandic, Norwegian, Swedish), and a number of derived languages (Yiddish from German, Afrikaans from Dutch) as well as the extinct Burgundian, Gothic, Norn, and Vandal. In spite of a scholarly tradition going back at least to Jacob Grimm in the early 19c, some basic questions regarding these languages still await convincing answers: At what point in history and in what ways did a common *Proto-Germanic* break away from Indo-European? Do the various Germanic languages form a dialect continuum? How can they best be classified into regional and typological groups? On these issues, linguistic speculation needs the support of more cultural and historical data. What is certain, however, is the common heritage of, and mutual contact between, the Germanic languages, as shown in the table.

English	Dutch	German	Swedish
one	*een*	*eins*	*en*
two	*twee*	*zwei*	*två*
three	*drie*	*drei*	*tre*
come	*komen*	*kommen*	*komma*
day	*dag*	*Tag*	*dag*
earth	*aarde*	*Erde*	*jord*
hay	*hooi*	*Heu*	*hö*
live (verb)	*leven*	*leben*	*leva*
waterfall	*waterval*	*Wasserfall*	*vattenfall*
young	*jong*	*jung*	*ung*

See AFRIKAANS, ANGLE, ANGLIAN, ANGLO-DANISH, ANGLO-DANISH (PIDGIN), ANGLO-SAXON, ARYAN, CAXTON, CLASSICAL COMPOUND, COMPOUND WORD, DANISH, DUTCH, ENGLISH, FA(E)ROESE, FLEMISH, FRENCH, FRISIAN, GERMAN, GOTHIC, GRIMM'S LAW, HISTORY OF ENGLISH, ICELANDIC, INDO-EUROPEAN LANGUAGES, INDO-GERMANIC, INGVAEONIC, KURATH, LOW DUTCH, LOW GERMAN, MERCIA, NORN, NORSE, NORTHERN ENGLISH, NORTHUMBRIAN, NORWEGIAN, OLD ENGLISH¹, PRIMITIVE GERMANIC, REFORMATION, SCANDINAVIAN LANGUAGES, SCOTS, SWEDISH, VERNER'S LAW, WEST SAXON, YIDDISH. [HISTORY, LANGUAGE]. R.H.

GERUND [16c: from Latin *gerundium*, adapted from *gerendum*, the verbal noun of *gerere* to carry on, engage in]. A traditional term for a verbal noun, in English a word ending in -*ing*: *visiting* in *They appreciate my visiting their parents regularly*. Like a noun, it can be introduced by the genitive *my* (compare *my visit to their parents*), but like a verb it takes the direct object *their parents* (compare *I visit their parents*). In contrast, *visiting* is a noun derived from a verb in the less usual and more formal construction *They appreciate my visiting of their parents*. In the alternative common construction known as the *fused participle*, the -*ing* word is preceded by a non-genitive form: *They appreciate the neighbours visiting their parents regularly*. Some object to the non-genitive usage and avoid it, particularly in formal style, at least for names and pronouns, preferring *They appreciate Bill's visiting their parents* to *They appreciate Bill visiting their parents* and *They appreciate my visiting their parents* to *They appreciate me visiting their parents*. Some grammarians of English use the term *participle* to include the gerund. See VERBAL NOUN. [GRAMMAR]. S.G.

GESTURE [14c: from Latin *gestura* a way of acting or bearing oneself, from *se gerere/gestum* to bear or deport oneself, behave]. A bodily movement, especially of the hands and arms, which conveys a meaning, such as the use of two fingers to convey 'V for victory' (in one orientation) or in British usage an insult (in a different orientation). Such movements are almost always learned features of behaviour, but some are acquired at such an early age that they are often considered instinctive and universal, such as nodding or waving. The meanings and precise forms of such gestures are, however, subject to cultural variation: vertical nodding can mean *yes* in English but a similar movement of the head means *no* in Greek, and sideways nodding (similar to but not identical with shaking the head) can mean agreement in India. Gestures are a normal feature of communication, are relatively few in number, and are used to express a fairly constrained range of meanings. They should be distinguished from the more systematic and comprehensive use of hand movements in deaf sign language. See BODY LANGUAGE, COMMUNICATION, KINESICS, PARALANGUAGE, PROXEMICS, RHETORIC, SIGN LANGUAGE. [LANGUAGE]. D.C.

GHANA. Official title: *Republic of Ghana.* A country in West Africa and member of the Commonwealth. Capital: Accra. Currency: the cedi (100 pesewas). Population: 14m (1988), 20.2m (projection for 2000). Ethnicity: Akan, Mossi-Dagomba, Ewe, Ga-Adangme. Religions: 40% Protestant, 36% traditional, 13% Muslim, 11% Catholic. Languages: English (official), West African Pidgin English, and indigenous languages such as Ashanti, Ewe, Fanti, and Ga. Education: primary 74%, secondary 39%, tertiary 2%, literacy 54%. The region was under British influence from 1874, and present-day Ghana comprises the former British colonies of *the Gold Coast* and *Ashanti,* the protectorate of *the Northern Territories,* and the United Nations trusteeship of *British Togoland.* There is a cline of usage from English-based pidgin to the standard West African English of the media and such newspapers as the *Daily Graphic,* the *Ghanaian Times,* the *People's Evening News,* and *The Pioneer.* Ghanaian writers in English include C. Ama Ata Aidoo, Joseph W. Abruquah, Aye Kwei Armah, Kofi Awoonor, and J. Benibengor Blay.

Ghana has probably had more intimate and longer contact with English-speaking expatriates than any other West African country. The English established their first fort at Cormantine in 1631 and had four forts by 1670. English seamen and merchants and their local wives appear to have formed a nucleus of English-speakers in Ghana more than a century before the settlements in Liberia and Sierra Leone. Ghanaians have always prided themselves on the quality of their English. As Kofi Sey suggests: 'The linguist may be able to isolate features of Ghanaian English and describe them. But once these are made known to him, the educated Ghanaian would strive to avoid them altogether. The surest way to kill Ghanaian English, if it really exists, is to discover it and make it known' (*Ghanaian English: An Exploratory Survey,* London: Macmillan, 1973, p. 10). Localisms include: (1) Words and phrases found in other parts of anglophone West Africa: *balance* change (as in *The balance you gave me is not correct*), *chop box* food box (as in *Put the yam in the chop box*), *themselves* each other (as in *Those two really love themselves*). (2) Distinctive local usage, such as *an airtight* a metal box, *a cover shoulder* a kind of blouse, *enskin* to enthrone (a chief), *an outdooring* a christening ceremony. (3) Uncountable nouns often used countably: *equipments, furnitures.* (4) Hybrids of English and local words: *kente cloth, donno drum, bodom bead.* See ENGLISH, WEST AFRICAN ENGLISH, WEST AFRICAN PIDGIN ENGLISH. [AFRICA, NAME, VARIETY]. C.L.N., L.T.

GHOST WORD [1880s]. An item, especially in handwriting or print, that is taken to be a word but is not: 'We should jealously guard against all chances of giving any undeserved record of words which had never any real existence, being mere coinages due to the blunders of printers or scribes, or to the perfervid imaginations of ignorant or blundering editors' (W. W. Skeat, *Transactions of the Philological Society,* 1885-7). A classic 20c ghost word was described in 1976 by the US lexicographer Allen Walker Read: *Dord,* listed as a synonym of *density* in Webster's *Second International Dictionary* (1934). This error arose from misinterpreting 'D or d', used to show that *density* could be abbreviated as either *D* or *d.* The mistake was put right in the next edition, by which time, however, *Dord* had begun to haunt other dictionaries. Compare CORRUPT, MUMPSIMUS. [REFERENCE, WORD]. T.MCA.

GIBRALTAR [From Arabic *Jebel Tariq* Tariq's Mountain]. Also **the Rock of Gibraltar** or informally **the Rock.** A British colony and military base, a rugged peninsula on the south-west coast of Spain where Atlantic and Mediterranean meet as *the Strait(s) of Gibraltar.* Population: *c.*20,000. Ethnicity: *c.*14,000 Gibraltarians (of mixed southern European, North African, and British background), *c.*6,000 British (mainly Service personnel). Languages: English (official), Spanish widely spoken. The territory was ceded by Spain to Britain in 1713, and became a colony in 1830. A Legislative Council was established in 1950, becoming a *House of Assembly* in 1969. Spain disputes right of possession, but Gibraltarians generally regard themselves as British. The local English is non-rhotic. Standard English with an RP accent is the prestigious norm, while the speech of manual workers is influenced by Spanish, including a parasitic vowel before a word-initial cluster beginning with /s/, such as 'espoon' for *spoon* and 'estreet' for *street*. See ENGLISH, IBERIAN LANGUAGES. Compare MALTA. [EUROPE, NAME, VARIETY].　　　　　　　　　　T.MCA.

GIFT OF THE GAB [18c: probably from Scots *gob/gab*, slang for mouth, from Gaelic *gob* mouth]. An informal expression for effortless fluency that may include boasting and self-advertisement, often associated with the Celts and taken to be an asset for politicians, sales representatives, and confidence tricksters. Compare BLARNEY. [STYLE].　　　　　　　T.MCA.

GIFT OF TONGUES. See GLOSSOLALIA.

GIVEN NAME. See PERSONAL NAME.

GLASGOW [From Cumbric *glas* green, and probably *cau* hollow]. The largest city in Scotland and third largest in the UK, and centre of a large conurbation (population in 1986: 725,000). An important medieval burgh and cathedral city, its university founded in 1451, Glasgow from the 17c rapidly became Scotland's leading commercial and industrial centre, often referred to in the 19c and early 20c as the second city of the Empire. The Industrial Revolution brought a huge influx of immigrants from the Highlands and from Ireland. This has resulted in a large Roman Catholic minority and a Protestant/Catholic sectarian divide resembling that of Belfast. The decline of its heavy industries after the First World War has left high levels of unemployment. Though the slums for which the city was once notorious have since 1946 been largely cleared, the peripheral housing estates replacing them are mostly bleak and devoid of amenities. Throughout the 20c an artistic and literary centre, Glasgow was European City of Culture in 1990.

Like that of other Scottish regions, Glasgow speech is a continuum from the local accent of ScoE to the working-class vernacular. In origin a dialect of West Central Scots, Glasgow vernacular has been modified by the mixing of population since the early 19c, resulting in particular in the introduction of several features from Ireland. Like other urban Scots dialects, it has suffered some erosion of traditional vocabulary. Partly as a result of this, working-class speech, known variously as *Glasgow English, Glasgow Scots, Glaswegian, Glesca, Glasgow, Gutter Glasgow*, has since the 19c been the archetypical stigmatized Scots speech, commonly described as 'debased',

'hopelessly corrupt', or 'the language of the gutter'. In addition to the more or less localized features below, Glaswegian shares stigmatized features of working-class Scots generally, such as glottal-stop realizations of non-initial voiceless stops, use of past participles of verbs for past tenses and conversely, and multiple negation: see GUTTER SCOTS. For features shared with Edinburgh and other Central Scots dialects, see EDINBURGH.

Pronunciation. The first three items are well-known shibboleths. (1) Some speakers merge /er/ *air* with /ɛr/ *err*, as in *Merry* Mary, *ferr* fair. (2) Some speakers realize voiced *th* as /r/, as in *ra* for *the* (*ra polis* the police, *ramorra* tomorrow), *brurra* brother, *murra* mother. (3) In such words as *want, water, wash* the vowel is /a/, so that *patter* and *water* rhyme. (4) The words *away, two, who, whose, where* have an 'aw' sound: *awaw, twaw, whaw, whause, whaur*. (5) The /u/ of *blue, room* has a front, lowered realization, sometimes unrounded. (6) Unstressed final /ʌ/ appears in such words as *barra* barrow, *fella* fellow, *Glesca* Glasgow, *morra* morrow, *awfa* awful, *yisfa* useful. (7) As in Edinburgh, the enclitic negative is *-nae, -ny*, as in *cannae* can't, *dinnae* don't, whereas other dialects have *-na*. (8) /d/ is lost after /l/ and /n/: *caul* cold, *staun* stand, *roon* round, *grun* ground, *win* wind. (9) The form *wan* one, and the adding of a /t/ to *once* and *twice* may be from Ireland. (10) Except in shibboleths like *It's a braw bricht munelicht nicht* traditional Scots forms in /x/ are rare, although the usual ScoE velar fricative prevails in such words as *clarsach, loch, pibroch*. (11) Intonation is characterized by a predominant pattern of a markedly lowered pitch on the final prominence of the tone group, followed by a low rise, and in this position the final stressed vowel may be prolonged:

> ahm thaht depehhhhndint
> hingoanti ma vowwwwulz
> hingoanti ma maaaammi
> (Tom Leonard, 'Tea Time', *Intimate Voices*, New-castle: Galloping Dog Press, 1984)

Grammar. Well-known Glaswegianisms, some of which are spreading or have spread to Edinburgh, are: (1) *See* as a topic-defining word, as in *See me, see ma man, see kippers, we hate them.* (2) Of Ulster origin, plural-marked forms of the second-person plural pronoun: *youse, yese, yiz* you, also *youse-yins* you ones. (3) A stressed form *Ah'm ur* I am, *Ah'm ur gaun* I am going, *Naw, Ah'm urnae* No, I am not. (4) Certain reinforcing sentence tags: *Ye're drunk, so ye ur; Ah'm right fed up, so Ah am/so Ah'm ur; Ah felt terrible, so Ah did; Ah didnae touch nuthin, neither Ah did.* (5) Other tags: *annat*, as in *Aw thae* (all those) *punters wi the wings an haloes annat* (and that); terminal *but*, as in *Ah dinnae waant it but*.

Vocabulary. (1) Localisms include: traditional *dog* to play truant, *dunny* a basement, *ginger* a soft drink of any kind, *sherrickin* a public dressing down, *stank* a grating over a drain, *wallie close* the tiled entrance hall of a better-class tenement, *tummle yir wulkies* to tumble somersaults; more recent slang usages *bam, bampot, bamstick* idiot, *boggin, bowfin* smelly, *hairy/herry* and *hingoot* (hang-out) a girl (disparaging), *heidbanger/heidcase* a lunatic, *lumber* a pick-up, a boy/girlfriend, *brassie/riddie* a red face, a cause of shame, *malky* a weapon. (2) Glasgow Scots is also receptive to slang expressions of wider currency like *chib* a weapon, *nooky* sexual intercourse, *stocious* drunk.

Written dialect. From the 1960s writings in and about Glaswegian have included, as well as caricature by stage comics and by authors of joke and cartoon collections, much poetry, drama, and prose fiction that treats the variety seriously and with concern or indignation at its status. Part of this writing, in poetry or prose, consists of representations of local speech, some of this in an ostentatiously untraditional 'phonetic' and quasi-illiterate orthography, intended to emphasize the demotic character of the speech. An exaggerated variant of this orthography has been favoured by or for the comedians Stanley Baxter and Billy Connolly. Both variants sometimes run words together to achieve an exotic or comically grotesque effect. In Scottish writing, this style, which apparently originated *c*.1960, is all but unique to Glasgow. Some specimens:

Another interesting word heard in the discotheque is *jiwanni*. To a young lady a gentleman will make the request—*Jiwanni dance?* Should she find that he is over-anxious to ply her with refreshments she will regard him with suspicion and inquire—*Jiwanniget mebevvid?* *Jiwanni* in certain circumstances changes to—*Jiwanna*, used generally in conjunction with the word *beltoanramooth* (Stanley Baxter, *Parliamo Glasgow*, 1982).

[*Jiwanni* Do you want to, *Jiwanniget* Do you want to get, *mebevvid* me bevvied (me drunk: from *bevvy*, a clipping of *beverage*), *Jiwanna beltoanramooth* Do you want a belt (blow) on the mouth]

    ach sun
    jiss keepyir chin up
    dizny day gonabootlika hawf shut knife
    inaw jiss cozzy a burd.
    (Tom Leonard, from 'The Miracle of the Burd and
        the Fishes', *Poems*, 1973, Dublin: O'Brien)

[Ah, son. / Just keep your chin up. / Doesn't do going about like a half-shut knife. / And all just because of a bird (girl)]

'Heh,' goes Tommy, 'Ah'm gaun orr therr tae see aboot this. Wullie must be daft ur sumhin, shoutin at that f'lla. E'll get is heid done fur im.'—'Aye,' I says.

'Moan. Mibbe wull kin stoap im daein enihin stupit' (Alex Hamilton, from 'Gallus, did you say?', in *Three Glasgow Writers*, 1977, Glasgow: Molendinar Press).

[*gaun* going, *orr therr* over there, *sumhin* something, *f'lla* fellow, *heid* head, *fur* for, *moan* come on, *wull kin* we'll can (= double modal, we will be able to), *stoap* stop, *daein* doing, *enihin* anything]

Michael Munro's glossary *The Patter* (1985) and its sequel *The Patter Another Blast* (1988) are two out of several recent popular, half-comic works purporting to describe present-day Glasgow speech. A scholarly monograph is Caroline Macafee's *Glasgow* (in the *Varieties of English around the World* series: John Benjamins, 1983), with cassette accompaniment. See DIALECT IN SCOTLAND, EDINBURGH, GUTTER SCOTS, MORNINGSIDE AND KELVINSIDE, SCOTS, SCOTTISH ENGLISH. [EUROPE, VARIETY].   A.J.A.

GLIDE. In phonetics, such approximant sounds as the /w/ of *wet* and the /j/ of *yet*, which have no steady state even when pronounced in isolation. Whereas it is easy to say [s] and [m] and prolong them without a following vowel, [j, w] require a following vowel to glide into, such as schwa [wə, jə]. If they are artificially prolonged, they become vowels similar to the [uː] of *move* and the [iː] of *leave* respectively. The approximant *r* can also be regarded as a glide. Although they are vocalic, glides behave in a syllable as though they are consonants: the glides in *yak*, *wake*, *rake* belong to the syllable margin as do the consonants in *bake*, *sake*, *take*. In view of their intermediate status, glides are sometimes known as *semi-vowels*, sometimes as *semiconsonants*. See APPROXIMANT, CONSONANT, R-SOUNDS, SYLLABLE, VOWEL. [SPEECH].   G.K.

-GLISH AND -LISH [1970s]. Elements extracted from the word *English* and used to form blends with the names of other languages, so as to describe (often facetiously) the mixing of elements of English and the language in question: 'In an effort to stem the tide of "Arablish", Cairo's prestigious Language Centre has attempted to devise Arabic equivalents for expressions and terms which do not exist in the Koran' (*Johannesburg Star*, Aug. 1984). Since the 1970s, the formation and use of such words have been widespread; they include *Chinglish* for Chinese and English, *Gerlish* and *Deutschlish* for German and English, *Italglish/Italish* for Italian and English, and *Russlish* for Russian and English. See ANGLIKAANS, CAMFRANGLAIS, CODE-MIXING AND CODE-SWITCHING, ENGLISHES, EUROLISH, FRANGLAIS, HINDLISH/HINGLISH, INTERLANGUAGE, JAPANESE PIDGIN ENGLISH, KOREA, SINGLISH, SPANGLISH, TAGLISH, YINGLISH. [VARIETY].   T.MCA.

GLOSS [13c: from Latin *glossa*, Greek *glôssa/ glôtta* the tongue, a difficult word (needing explanation)]. (1) A note made in a margin or between lines, usually a word or phrase, explaining or translating a difficult word in a manuscript or other text. Such glosses have played an important role in the history of lexicography. Old English marginal or interlinear glosses of hard Latin words were collected in more or less alphabetical lists, known as *glossae collectae* (collected glosses) then *glossaria* (glossaries). These were ancestors of the first Latin–English dictionaries and ultimately of all English dictionaries. (2) Any definition, explanation, or interpretation of a word or phrase, especially if it is unusual or foreign. There is no etymological link between either of the above senses and *gloss* [of Germanic origin] meaning a surface lustre or glaze. However, casual usage may have brought the two together, especially in adding the negative sense of something superficial, deceptive, and perhaps artful, as in *glossing over someone's faults*, or in the phrase *not to put too fine a gloss on something* (not to interpret it too closely). If one *glosses* something, one adds a gloss or interpretation that may be accurate but could be deliberately misleading. Context usually serves to distinguish the possibilities. See GLOSSARY, LEMMA, LEXICOGRAPHY, RUBRIC. [REFERENCE, WORD].   T.MCA.

GLOSSARY [14c: from Latin *glossarium* a collection of glosses]. An alphabetical list of terms and explanations, often of a specialized or technical nature (*a glossary of computer terms*) or linked with a particular text (*a glossary of Indian words*, in a novel). Glossaries typically appear as appendices: a *Glossary of Selected Terms* in *Teaching English as a Foreign Language* (Geoffrey Broughton *et al.*, 1980). Here, the gloss of the term *aspect* begins: 'With time and mood, one of the grammatical categories of the verb'. None of the other senses of the word *aspect* (as in *several aspects of her character*) need be represented for the purpose of this work. A typical text-linked glossary is *How to Speak EastEnders: A Brief Glossary of Cockney Expressions* (Lionheart Television, 1988), prepared to acquaint US television viewers with usage in the British soap opera *EastEnders*. Here, the expression *knocked Ethel into a cocked hat* has the gloss 'upset, hurt, or worried Ethel'. See GLOSS, LEXICOGRAPHY. [REFERENCE].   R.F.I.

GLOSSOLALIA [19c: from Greek *glôssa* tongue, *lalía* talking]. Also **the gift of tongues, speaking in tongues**. A rapid, fluent burst of speech, usually unintelligible and delivered in a state of religious excitement. Such behaviour has been conceived as a sign of grace among early Christians, 13c Catholic friars, 18c Protestant Camisards, 17–18c French Catholic Jansenists, and 20c Pentecostalist Protestants. All have taken Acts 2: 3–4 of the New Testament, referring to events at the time of Pentecost, as their justification: 'And there appeared vnto them clouen tongues, like as of fire, and it sate vpon each of them. And they were all filled with the holy Ghost, and began to speake with other tongues, as the spirit gaue them vtterance' (Authorized Version, 1611). The apostle Paul claimed the ability (1 Corinthians 14: 14–19), but favoured brief, intelligible utterance to long, unintelligible outbursts. Glossolalia has been interpreted as both divine and satanic communication. In the West in recent centuries it has generally been seen as eccentric and dangerous, but in some evangelical movements the sounds are taken to be authentic. Psychologists have sought to account for them as the product of charlatanry, neurosis, psychosis, epilepsy, and hypnotic suggestion. There is no consensus. Compare COPROLALIA, ECHOLALIA. [LANGUAGE].
                        T.MCA.

-GLOT [From Attic Greek *glōttós* tongued: see GLOSS]. A combining form with the meaning 'having a language', as in *monoglot* having (only) one language (mono- or unilingual), and *polyglot* having many languages (multilingual). See DIGLOSSIA, LINGUAL, MONOGLOT, POLYGLOT. [SPEECH].   T.MCA.

GLOTTAL [1840s: see GLOTTIS]. In anatomy, relating to the glottis; in phonetics, articulated at the glottis. See GLOTTALIC, GLOTTAL STOP, GLOTTIS. [SPEECH].   T.MCA.

GLOTTALIC. [20c: from *glottal* and -*ic* as in *italic*]. In phonetics, an air-stream mechanism that uses the glottis. If the glottis is closed and the larynx raised, air will be forced out, producing *ejective* sounds. If the glottis is loosely closed (that is, in the position for *voice*), and the larynx is lowered, air will be sucked in, producing *implosive* sounds. Glottalic consonants are found in some African and Amerindian languages. Ejectives, which sound like plosives with glottal stops, occur occasionally in English for humorous purposes: for example, to mimic speech with relatively unaspirated stops, such as /t, p/ in *t'erribly t'erribly p'osh* RP. See GLOTTIS. [SPEECH].   G.K.

GLOTTAL STOP. In phonetics, a stop sound made by bringing the vocal cords tightly together, blocking off the air-stream, then releasing them suddenly. It occurs widely in the world's languages, including: (1) As an Arabic consonant, represented in script by the letter *alif* (and also by the sign *hamza*), and in Roman transliteration by the lenis symbol ' (or the apostrophe): *'akala* ate. (2) Comparably, as a consonant in Hawaiian: *a'o* to teach. (3) As a sharp 'attack' to an opening vowel in such languages as English and German, used by default when there is no consonant at the beginning of a syllable, as in forcefully saying *Anne, come here!* (4) In England and parts of Northern Ireland, as an accompaniment to the voiceless stops /p, t, k, tʃ/ in a stressed syllable. (5) Widely in BrE as an optional 'catch' between adjacent vowels, as in *co-opt, re-educate*. (6) As a substitute for post-vocalic /t/ in such accents as Cockney and Glasgow, in words like *better, butter*, a process known technically as *T-glottaling*. In all but the last of the above functions, the glottal stop is socially neutral, but in the sixth it is stigmatized. Because many users of English know the term only in this sense, the concept of the glottal stop has long been associated in the English-speaking world with slovenly, substandard speech. In its stigmatized use, it has been shown orthographically by means of an apostrophe (Glasgow, *be'ur bu'ur* better butter), in the 1950s by the Glasgow writer Cliff Hanley as a double colon (*be::er bu::er*), and in 1980 by the London writers Robert Barltrop and Jim Wolveridge by an exclamation mark (*be!er bu!er*). The IPA symbol is ʔ. See COCKNEY, GLASGOW, GLOTTAL, GLOTTIS. [SPEECH, STYLE].   G.K., T.MCA.

GLOTTIS [16c: through Latin from Greek *glōttís*]. In anatomy and phonetics, the space in the larynx between the vocal cords or folds. See GLOTTAL, GLOTTALIC, GLOTTAL STOP, LARYNX, VOCAL C(H)ORDS/FOLDS. [SPEECH].   G.K.

GOBBLEDYGOOK, also **gobbledegook** [1944: promoted by Maury Maverick, but probably an older slang term that echoes the sound of a turkeycock and combines *gob* mouth, *gobble* eat greedily, and *gook* a (foreign) speaker of gibberish: compare Scots *bubblyjock* turkeycock]. A pejorative and facetious term for pretentious and opaque jargon; inflated language. Maverick put it as follows: 'Just before Pearl Harbor, I got my baptism under "gobbledygook" . . . its definition: talk or writing which is long, pompous, vague, involved, usually with Latinized words' (*New York Times Magazine*, 21 May 1944). In Britain in 1979, Plain English Campaign was founded with the public shredding in London of official forms and a rampage along Downing Street by someone dressed as a monster called *the Gobbledygook*. In 1980, the National Consumer Council in the UK published a review of official forms under the title *Gobbledegook*. In 1986, the cover cartoon of *English Today* 5 showed a knight with *Plain English* on his shield facing a bloated dragon with *gobbledygook* written across its belly, over the caption 'Plain English Campaign'. PEC adopted the cartoon as a kind of logo. For examples of the kind of pretentious and opaque usage often classed as *gobbledygook*, see BAFFLEGAB, BUREAUCRATESE, DOUBLESPEAK, OBFUSCATION, OBSCURANTISM. For further general discussion, see JARGON, PLAIN, PLAIN ENGLISH CAMPAIGN. [STYLE].   T.MCA.

GODZONE [mid-19c: a clipping of *God's Own Country*, a term applied by British settlers to various territories]. An informal term for especially New Zealand and sometimes Australia: 'On warm summer evenings, when it is packed with Polynesians and the shops are livid with neon, it seems more like Asia than Godzone' (a comment on Karangahape Road, in *Auckland, their Auckland*, Lansdowne Press, 1983). [NAME, OCEANIA].   T.MCA.

GOLDEN BULL AWARDS. See PLAIN ENGLISH.

GONGORISM. See EUPHUISM.

GOOD ENGLISH. An informal term for English regarded as all or any of the following: well-spoken, well-written, well-constructed, fluent, effective, a mark of good breeding and social standing, a mark of good education. W. Nelson Francis observed in 1967: 'An expression like *I ain't got no time for youse* may be most effective in the situation in which it is used, and hence "good English" in the [sense of good communication]. But most people, including those who naturally speak this way, will call it "bad English" because grammatical features like *ain't*, *youse*, and the double negative construction belong to a variety of English commonly used by people with little education and low social and economic status' (*The English Language: An Introduction*). The term appears from time to time in the title of usage guides, in the sense of *good usage*: for example, Godfrey Howard's *A Guide to Good English in the 1980s* (London: Pelham Books, 1985). See BAD ENGLISH, STANDARD ENGLISH, WELL-SPOKEN. [USAGE, VARIETY].   T.MCA.

GOOD USAGE. See GOOD ENGLISH, USAGE, USAGE GUIDANCE AND CRITICISM.

GOOD WRITING. See EFFECTIVE WRITING.

GORDIMER, Nadine [b. 1923]. South African writer, born in Springs, Transvaal, and educated at a convent school until ten years old, after which, because of a heart ailment, she worked at home with tutors. She attended the U. of Witwatersrand for a year, but could not take a degree because she lacked formal entry qualifications. Gordimer began writing as a child, published her first short story at the age of 15, and her first novel, *The Lying Days*, in 1953. In addition to short stories in *The New Yorker*, other periodicals, and collected editions, her work includes the novels *A World of Strangers* (1958), *Occasion for Loving* (1963), *The Late Bourgeois World* (1966), *A Guest of Honour* (1970), *The Conservationist* (1974), *Burger's Daughter* (1979), *July's People* (1981), and *A Sport of Nature* (1987), and a study of black South African writers entitled *The Black Interpreters* (1973). She has been an outspoken opponent of apartheid concerned, among other things, with relationships between the races, the position and attitudes of white middle-class liberals like herself, and the future of South Africa. Gordimer won the UK's Booker Prize for *The Conservationist* in 1974 and the Nobel Prize for Literature in 1991: 'Her great achievement has been to give the world a reckoning of the terrible cost of racism to her country that goes beyond what journalism can relate' (*Time*, 14 Oct. 1991). See SOUTH AFRICAN LITERATURE IN ENGLISH. [AFRICA, BIOGRAPHY, LITERATURE]. T.MCA.

GOTHIC [17c: from Latin *Gothicus*]. (1) The extinct language of the Goths, the only documented member of the Eastern (or Gothic) branch of the Germanic language family. A small community of speakers survived in the Crimea until the 16c. It is known almost entirely from fragments of the 4c Gospels by Ulfilas, Bishop for it from Greek and runic. The Gothic for *Thy will be done, in heaven as on earth* (Matthew 6: 10) is *Waírþái wilja þeins, swē in himina jah ana aírþái* (May-it-happen the-will of-thine, as in heaven and on earth). (2) A type of fiction popular in the late 18c. When Horace Walpole wrote *The Castle of Otranto: A Gothic Story* (1764) he used the word to mean 'medieval' and placed a story of mystery and fear in a pseudo-medieval setting. The Gothic novel is characterized by sinister happenings and a sense of doom, sometimes supernatural, sometimes the product of wickedness. Its language is usually inflated and melodramatic. Gothic novels include Ann Radcliffe's *The Mysteries of Udolpho* (1794), Matthew Lewis's *The Monk* (1796), and Charles Maturin's *Melmoth the Wanderer* (1829). Jane Austen satirized the style in *Northanger Abbey* (1818). Writers who have used Gothic elements include Mary Shelley, Charles Dickens, Edgar Allen Poe, William Faulkner, and Iris Murdoch, and lineal descendants of the genre include the horror story and horror film.

(3) Also *gothic script, gothic black letter, black letter*. A family of heavy-script typefaces, whose three forms are based on medieval scripts: *Rotunda*, a rounded form used chiefly in the 15c; *Textura*, a regular type in England until the end of the 16c, currently used in newspaper titles and for pseudo-medieval purposes; *Bastarda*, a pointed version used for German. See FANTASY, GERMANIC LANGUAGES, ROMAN, ROMANTICISM, TEXT. [EUROPE, HISTORY, LANGUAGE, LITERATURE, TECHNOLOGY]. W.F.B., R.C., W.W.B.

GOVERNMENT [14c: from Old French *governer*, Latin *gubernare*, translating Greek *kubernân* to steer or direct]. The way in which the use of one word requires another word to take a particular form, especially in highly inflected languages. In Latin, prepositions govern nouns: *ad* is followed by an accusative of movement (*ad villam* towards the villa), *in* by either an accusative of movement (*in villam* into the villa) or an ablative of location (*in villa* in the villa). Though the concept is not strictly applicable to a mildly inflected language like English, prepositions require object pronouns where they exist: *of me* (not **of I*), *to them* (not **to they*), *for us* (not **for we*). The term is usually contrasted with *agreement* or *concord*, a condition in which two words interact. Some grammarians extend the term to the way in which some verbs require a particular preposition before a following noun phrase, as in 'We insist *on* seeing you tomorrow' and 'I will not compromise *with* them *on* a matter like this.' [GRAMMAR]. S.C.

GOWERS, (Sir) Ernest (Arthur) [1880-1966]. English civil servant and writer on usage, born in London, and educated at Rugby and Clare College, Cambridge, where he studied classics. He entered the Civil Service in 1903 and rose to become chairman of the Board of Inland Revenue. On his retirement in 1930, he was chairman of numerous official bodies and committees of inquiry. At the invitation of the Treasury (concerned at the obscure or convoluted style of many civil servants), he wrote *Plain Words: A Guide to the Use of English* (1948) and *The ABC of Plain Words* (1951). These were combined, with revisions, in *The Complete Plain Words* (1954). The books show his insistence on clarity, precision, and directness as essential for expository writing. Gowers's reputation as a sensible and sensitive authority on usage and style led to his being invited to revise Fowler's *Modern English Usage* (2nd edition, 1965). He received many public honours. See index. [BIOGRAPHY, EUROPE, REFERENCE, STYLE]. S.G.

GRADABLE. See ADJECTIVE, ADVERB, ANTONYM.

GRADED READER. See READER.

GRAFFITI [1850s: from Italian plural of *graffito* incised inscription, design, from *graffiare* to scratch, perhaps influenced by Latin **graphire* to write, from *graphium* stylus, from Greek *grapheîon* stylus, pencil: compare GRAPHIC]. (1) With a plural verb: markings and scribblings such as initials, slogans, kinds of verse, drawings alone or with captions, etc., often obscene, sometimes political, that are written especially in public places such as toilets, on walls, etc., using pen, pencil, sprayed paint, and the like. (2) With a singular verb: such markings as a whole or as a kind of genre or style of self-expression. The occasional singular *graffito* also has the archaeological sense of a drawing or piece of writing scratched on a wall. See LAMPOON, READ. [STYLE, WRITING].   T.MCA.

GRAMMAR [14c: from Anglo-Norman *gramere* and Old French *gramaire* (Modern *grammaire*), from a probable **gramadie*, from Latin *grammatica*, a clipping of *ars grammatica*, a translation of Greek *grammatikḗ tékhnē* the craft of letters, ultimately from *grámma* a letter. The Anglo-Norman variant *gramarie* had the senses grammar, occult learning, and magic. The Old French variant *gramoire* meant a book of magic (Modern *grimoire*). A Middle English variant *glomery* occurs in the phrase *Master of Glomery*, the title of an official of the U. of Cambridge who looked after its grammar school. A pupil there was a *glomerel* a little grammarian. The Scots variant *glamour* was first used in general English by Walter Scott in the 19c. It once meant a magic spell (*cast a glamour over someone*) and now means great but perhaps illusory charm. In 1789, Robert Burns wrote: 'Ye gipsy gang that deal in glamor, / And you deep read in hell's black grammar' (*Captain Grose's Peregrinations*)].

(1) The systematic study and description of a language, a group of languages, or language in general in terms of either syntax and morphology alone or these together with aspects of phonology, orthography, semantics, pragmatics, and word-formation: *universal grammar, comparative Indo-European grammar, Spanish grammar, the grammar of American English*. The study of the grammar of a language may be restricted to the standard variety or cover the standard and aspects of other varieties. Grammars of English have tended to deal mainly with either standard BrE or standard AmE, but in recent years have increasingly covered both main varieties, sometimes with notes on other varieties.

(2) A set of rules and examples dealing with the syntax and morphology of a standard language, usually intended as an aid to the learning and teaching of that language. A distinction is often drawn between *descriptive grammar*, which attempts to present an accurate description of the rules for actual usage, and *prescriptive grammar*, which prescribes certain rules for usage and often proscribes others. In practice, a *grammar book* or *grammar* may contain both kinds of rules. Prescriptive grammar is evaluative, distinguishing between *good grammar* (correct, approved usage) and *bad grammar* (incorrect, disapproved usage). A grammar may overtly or covertly downgrade regional and social dialects (implying that they either do not have 'proper' grammar or have no grammar at all). Such books have often been part of the equipment of formal education in Western countries and have tended to reflect (and endorse) middle-class values. As a result, reminders to offenders have often been couched in such terms as: *Mind your grammar—no double negatives!*

A distinction is often made between a *reference grammar* (intended, like a dictionary, for individual reference) and a *pedagogical grammar* (intended chiefly for class use under the guidance of a teacher). Reference grammars are structured primarily on linguistic principles, and are likely to have copious cross-references and an extensive index. Their contents are arranged primarily on linguistic principles, each topic being treated as comprehensively as possible for the size of the book. In pedagogical grammars, the material is presented and graded for ease of absorption in the learning of the language and/or learning about the language. They are divided into sections that can be assimilated within a normal class period by the students for whom the textbook is intended. They may also contain exercises, vocabulary lists, written dialogues, and reading passages.

(3) In linguistics, a term for the syntactic and morphological system which every unimpaired person acquires from infancy when learning a language: *a native-speaker's grammar*. In this sense, grammar is part of a Janus-faced psychological and neurological process: each person learns and uses a private system which blends into a social consensus. All speakers of a language like English 'know' this grammar in the sense that they use it to produce more or less viable utterances. Their knowledge is implicit, however, and it is not usually easy to think about and report on it. Formal education may help in some areas (especially in relation to literacy) and higher education in language studies may extend this ability, but the use of this natural grammar does not depend on the acquisition of descriptive or prescriptive grammar. English, for example,

was used for a thousand years before the first rudimentary grammar books were written, and no grammar book (however large) is ever fully comprehensive.

Classical grammar. The analytical study of language began in the second half of the first millennium BC in both Greece and India. In Greece, it began as the study of the written language, whereas in India it was concerned as much with the transmission of recited Sanskrit as with its written forms. The present-day study of grammar descends from the Greek tradition, in which it was linked with logic and rhetoric. Both Plato and Aristotle took a close interest in language and, among other things, helped provide the foundation for the discussion of the parts of speech. Grammar was first developed as a formal system, however, by Greek scholars in Alexandria (Egypt). The foremost of these was Dionysius Thrax, author of *Hē grammátikē tékhnē* (The Art of Letters: *c.*100 BC), a brief discussion in 25 sections on the nature of letters, syllables, words (according to form, function, and meaning), and sentences.

When Thrax wrote his treatise, students of reading and writing learned their letters in a strict order, aided by mnemonic hexameter verses. The letters were crucial for all learning, because each was simultaneously letter, number, and musical note. After their alpha-betas, students were taught syllables of increasing length, then simpler and more complex word forms, then specimen texts. In the texts of the period, there were no spaces between words, punctuation was meagre, and reading depended on a capacity to see patterns in the unbroken lines. Once this skill was acquired, an appreciation of the arrangement (*súntaxis*) of words was necessary, as well as their complex inflections, so as to see what was happening in a text. For this, the guidance in Thrax's treatise was crucial. It was in fact the prototype for grammars of all European and many other languages.

Thrax defined grammar as technical knowledge of the language of poets and writers. His interest did not extend to other kinds of Greek, to any other language, to language as a general phenomenon, or to spoken language except insofar as it might help in learning to write. It was the job of the *grammatikós* to use brush and papyrus, to copy and to edit, and, if fortunate and able enough, to analyse and improve the texts of such works as the epics of Homer. Writing was a mystery to the population at large, which associated scrolls with knowledge and power. As a result, in classical and medieval times, grammarians were sometimes taken to be sorcerers, but the craft was so laborious that the sorcerers' apprentices were often frustrated by

it. Ancient attitudes to grammar still survive: many people are in awe of it, know little about it, tend to fear or dislike it, often find it baffling and boring if exposed to it at school, and yet a minority is fascinated by it: a field in which precise scholarship and nit-picking pedantry have coexisted for centuries.

The Roman scholar Marcus Terentius Varro was a contemporary of Thrax's. Where the Alexandrian was brief, the Roman was copious, producing 25 volumes of *De lingua latina* (On the Latin Language). Of these, only Books 5-10 survive. Varro had studied the Greek debates on language, especially as to whether it was by nature regular or chaotic. See ANALOGY AND ANOMALY. He concluded that it is both regular *and* irregular, with a tilt towards the regular. He was the first comparative grammarian, looking at Latin and Greek side by side and, although he focused on writing, moved the discussion beyond it. Grammarians such as Varro converted the technical terms of Greek into Latin, and adapted Greek-based rules to serve their own tongue. A great advantage in describing Latin more or less in terms of Greek was the similarity of the two languages: both are highly inflected, with complex verb and noun structures. See PART OF SPEECH.

Medieval and Renaissance grammar. In the 4c, Aelius Donatus taught in Rome and wrote an elementary text known as the *Ars grammatica* (Art of Letters), the title a translation of Thrax's. He was the teacher of St Jerome, who translated the Bible into Latin, and was so influential that for a thousand years his name was given not only to a basic grammar book, but to any textbook or lesson. In Old French and Middle English, all of these were *donets*. In the 6c, a native of Mauretania, Priscianus Caesariensis (Priscian), taught in Constantinople and wrote the *Institutiones grammaticae* (Grammatical Foundations), the only complete surviving grammar of Latin. The texts of Donatus and Priscian became the basis of medieval grammatical studies, Priscian's texts being integrated into the framework of Scholastic philosophy in the 13c and 14c. It is a testimony to his importance that around 1,000 manuscripts of parts or all of his *Institutiones* survive. Just as Thrax focused on Greek, so medieval grammarians such as Peter Helias (12c) and Petrus Hispanus (13c) focused on Latin. However, as the Middle Ages gave way to the Renaissance, as printing spread, and as new nation-states became more conscious of their languages, grammarians in the mould of Varro began in the 16-17c to write descriptions of their own mother tongues by comparing them with the grammatical descriptions of Latin.

The first grammar of a modern European language described Spanish: Antonio de Nebrija's *Gramática de la lengua castellana* (Grammar of the Castilian language, 1492). The first grammar of French was written in England: John Palsgrave's *Lesclarcissement de la Langue Françoyse* (1530). An early grammar in one language but about another was in English: Richard Percivall's *Bibliotheca Hispanica, Containing a Grammar, with a Dictionarie in Spanish, English, and Latine* (1591). Like their predecessors, the creators of such works focused on the usage of the 'best' writers, establishing a tradition which lasted until the 19c and which still exerts considerable influence. Just as Thrax did not look beyond Greek and the medieval grammarians did not look beyond Latin, so the early modern grammarians hardly looked beyond a level of usage heavily influenced by Greek and Latin. On those occasions when they did so, they saw what seemed to be a barbarous mass of material that seemed to lack all grammatical order.

Early grammars of English. Most of the writers of grammars of English have been teachers, but some early grammars were written by men in other walks of life: in 1634, the playwright Ben Jonson wrote his *English Grammar*; in 1762, the Bishop of London, Robert Lowth, brought out *A Short Introduction to English Grammar*; in 1761 and 1762, the scientist Joseph Priestley, better known for discovering oxygen, published two grammars and a number of essays on language. James Harris, whose grammar appeared in 1751, was an amateur philosopher and a Member of Parliament. The American lawyer Lindley Murray grew rich outfitting the British troops who captured New York during the American Revolution, then retired to England and wrote a best-selling English grammar in 1795. In 1784, his compatriot Noah Webster turned to spelling, grammar, and lexicography as a last resort after failing to thrive as a lawyer or a teacher. Before 1800, at least 272 grammars of English were published and there have been countless since. From the 17c to the 19c, the vast majority of these works contained little more than Thrax's basic formula: lists of the letters and syllables of English, with comments on their pronunciation; definitions of the parts of speech illustrating their inflections; some elementary syntax, usually taught through the presentation of imprecise examples; and a section on punctuation and versification. Some grammarians have been speculative and philosophical in nature, in the late medieval tradition: James Harris in *Hermes* (1751) took language as something to be discussed and analysed rather than outlined for rote learning. Few attempted an exhaustive description of English. Goold Brown, in his encyclopedic *Grammar of English Grammars* (1851), refers to almost every extant treatise on English grammar, well-known or obscure, establishing himself as the grammarian's grammarian.

Latin and English. In the main, the aims of the grammarians were pragmatic and educational rather than philosophic: to introduce foreigners to English, to teach students their own language, or to prepare them for Latin. The early textbooks were influenced by the Latin grammar of William Lily (1540), grandfather of the dramatist John Lyly. Lily declined English nouns as if they were Latin. Just as a noun in Latin has a nominative (*dominus*), vocative (*domine*), genitive (*domini*), etc., so he had in English a nominative (*master*), vocative (*O master*), genitive (*of a master*), etc. Sometimes, even its indeclinable adjectives had their cases: nominative singular masculine *wise* and accusative feminine plural *wise*, etc. See CASE[1], DECLENSION. For centuries, English remained in the shadow of Latin and Greek as a school subject and as a vehicle of learning. Samuel Johnson shared the common 18c opinion that English was a copious and disorderly tongue which had only recently come under the sway of grammar. His own grammar fills 13 double-column folio pages in his two-volume dictionary. Of these pages, however, he devotes only 11 lines to syntax, explaining: 'Our language has so little inflection, or variety of terminations, that its construction neither requires nor admits many rules.' In his *Rudiments of English Grammar*, Joseph Priestley attributes this 'paucity of our inflections of words' to the barbarism of the Anglo-Saxons, from whom the language was inherited, 'the severity of whose climate, and difficulty of subsistence, left them little leisure for polishing, or indeed using, their language' (1761, p. v).

The rules of good English. So close-mouthed were the ancestors of English that, according to Johnson, the modern form of the language inherited only four syntactic rules: the verb agrees with its subject; adjectives and pronouns are invariable in form; the possessive noun is the genitive case; transitive verbs and prepositions take objects in the 'oblique' case. Priestley added four others: on pronoun agreement; on the concord of collective nouns (which may take a singular or plural verb); on ellipsis (most notably, deletion of the relative pronoun *that*); and on word order (adjectives precede nouns; subjects precede verbs, and objects follow verbs). It would not have been easy for anyone to learn English from such a grammatical basis, even when expanded to 21 rules of syntax in Lindley Murray's *English Grammar* (7th US edition, 1837). Most 18c and 19c grammarians were prescriptive in their approach, presenting grammar as the art or science of correct speech and writing. Although many paid homage to the dictum of the Roman poet Horace that usage is the norm by which correctness is judged, few believed that the speech and writing of masses or élite should constitute standard English. For them, instruction in correct English consisted largely in having students memorize and recite definitions and rules. Many texts were arranged as dialogues or catechisms to facilitate this task. More advanced texts allowed students to parse a sentence whose topic was morally uplifting. Examples from Murray include: *I learn; Thou art improved; The tutor is admonishing Charles.* Rosewell C. Smith, in his *English Grammar on the Productive System* (1843), emphasized the practical in his examples: *The business will be regulated; John is living within his income; He taught me grammar.*

The unpopularity of grammar. The grammarians' attitude toward language, combined with the mechanical instruction in grammar required by the texts, made the subject feared and despised by pupils and teachers alike. The 19c American commentator Richard Grant White, still smarting from a punishment he had received from his tutor many years previously for not knowing his grammar lesson, called grammar rules medieval. He preferred to criticize usage and particularly opposed the coining of new words. When grammar became a required subject in many US schools in the mid-19c, teachers objected that they knew no more about the subject than the students did. Since then, grammar has cycled in and out of favour in educational circles. In the early 1900s, progressive US educational groups called for an end to grammar instruction because it did not contribute to facility in writing. In Britain, the Newbolt Report (1921), which strongly favoured the teaching of English, advised against instruction in the science of language, because it interfered with the appreciation of literary art. In recent years, a conservative 'back-to-basics' movement in education, coinciding with a Conservative government, has encouraged a restoration of grammar drill as a way of solving the language problems of the schools in both the US and the UK.

Whether grammar has been in or out of favour, grammarians early on developed a negative image, both personally and professionally. Johnson called Harris a prig. Lowth was described as melancholy, and Lindley Murray was accused by his detractors of committing the errors he warned against. Although most dictionaries (with the exception of the *OED*) ignore this development, *grammarian* has come to mean someone whose concern for correctness in language is excessive or pedantic. According to Chambers' *Cyclopaedia* (1727-41, 1779-86), the formerly honourable title of *grammarian* had become a term of reproach: 'a person wholly attentive to the minutiae of language, industriously employed about words, and phrases; and incapable of perceiving the beauties, the delicacy, finesse, extent, &c of a sentiment'. Nowadays, not all students of grammar wish to be identified as grammarians. Serious academics who have produced comprehensive grammars of English, such as Otto Jespersen, formerly philologists, are now generally referred to as *linguists*.

Scholarly grammars of English in the twentieth century. There have been a number of 20c scholarly grammars of English characterized by a decidedly descriptive approach and a focus on syntax. The two largest works, both reference grammars, are by foreign speakers of the language. The Dutch grammarian Hendrik Poutsma published *A Grammar of Late Modern English* in five volumes at intervals (with revised versions of the first part) between 1904 and 1929. His grammar is historical (drawing on quotations from earlier periods) and comparative (contrasting the grammars of English and Dutch). The Danish grammarian Otto Jespersen produced his most important work, the seven-volume *Modern English Grammar on Historical Principles*, between 1909 and 1949. As the title indicates, Jespersen's grammar is also historical. This work continues to be consulted for its range of data and insights into grammatical phenomena.

The American structural linguist Charles C. Fries published two works on English grammar that influenced the teaching of English in schools in the US and elsewhere: *American English Grammar* (1940) and *The Structure of English* (1952). In 1972 and 1985, two large reference grammars were published by a team associated with the Survey of English Usage: the British scholars Randolph Quirk, Sidney Greenbaum, Geoffrey Leech, and the Swedish scholar Jan Svartvik: *A Grammar of Contemporary English* (1972) and *A Comprehensive Grammar of the English Language* (1985). Like the works of Fries, these are strictly synchronic. They take account of stylistic variation and the differences between BrE and AmE. Their derivatives are used in the teaching of English in universities and colleges throughout the world: *A University Grammar of English*, by Quirk and Greenbaum (1973), *A Communicative Grammar of English*, by Leech and Svartvik (1975), and *A Student's Grammar of the English Language*, by Greenbaum and Quirk (1990). In the last three decades there has been a noticeable increase in research publications (monographs and scholarly papers) on English grammar, stimulated by a ferment of ideas from competing theoretical approaches, the availability of several large corpora of English (now in computerized form, concordanced, and often grammatically coded), and the growth of importance of English as an international language. See ANALOGY AND ANOMALY, CASE, DESCRIPTIVE AND PRESCRIPTIVE GRAMMAR, PART OF SPEECH, PUNCTUATION. [GRAMMAR].

S.G., D.E.B., T.MCA.

The grammar theme

A–C. ABLATIVE ABSOLUTE, ABLATIVE CASE, ABLAUT, ABSOLUTE, ABSOLUTE CLAUSE, ABSTRACT AND CONCRETE, ACCEPTABILITY, ACCIDENCE, ACCUSATIVE CASE, ADJECTIVE, ADJECTIVE/ADJECTIVE CLAUSE, ADJUNCT, ADNOMINAL, ADVERB, ADVERBIAL, ADVERBIAL CLAUSE, ADVERBIAL PARTICLE, AELFRIC, AFFIRMATIVE, AGENT, AGENTLESS PASSIVE, AGRAMMATISM, AGREEMENT, ANALOGY, ANALOGY AND ANOMALY, ANAPHORA, ANIMATE NOUN, ANTECEDENT, ANTICIPATORY IT, AORIST, APODOSIS, APOSTROPHE[1], APPOSITION, APPOSITIVE CLAUSE, ARTICLE[1], ASPECT, ATTRIBUTIVE, AUXILIARY VERB, BARE INFINITIVE, BLOOMFIELD, CASE[1], CASE GRAMMAR, CATAPHORA, CATENATIVE, CAUSATIVE VERB, CHOMSKY, CLASSICAL ENDING, CLAUSE, CLAUSE ANALYSIS, CLEFT SENTENCE, COBBETT, COGNATE OBJECT, COLLECTIVE NOUN, COLLOCATION, COMMON NOUN, COMPARATIVE DEGREE, COMPARATIVE SENTENCE, COMPARISON (DEGREE OF), COMPLEMENT, COMPLEX PREPOSITION, COMPLEX SENTENCE, COMPOUND-COMPLEX SENTENCE, COMPOUND PREPOSITION, COMPOUND SENTENCE, COMPREHENSIVE GRAMMAR OF THE ENGLISH LANGUAGE, COMPUTATIONAL LINGUISTICS, CONCESSION, CONCORD, CONCRETE NOUN, CONDITION, CONJUGATION, CONJUNCT, CONJUNCTION, CONNECTIVE, CONSTITUENT, CONTINUOUS, CONTRACTION, COORDINATE CLAUSE, COORDINATION, COORDINATOR, COPULA, COPULAR VERB, CORRELATIVE, COUNTABLE AND UNCOUNTABLE, CURME.

D–H. DANGLING PARTICIPLE, DATIVE CASE, DECLARATIVE, DECLENSION, DEEP STRUCTURE, DEFINING RELATIVE CLAUSE, DEFINITE ARTICLE, DEGREE, DEIXIS, DEMONSTRATIVE, DEMONSTRATIVE PRONOUN, DEPENDENT CLAUSE, DESCRIPTIVE AND PRESCRIPTIVE GRAMMAR, DESCRIPTIVISM AND PRESCRIPTIVISM, DETERMINER, DEVIANT, DIRECT AND INDIRECT SPEECH, DIRECT OBJECT, DISJUNCT, DITRANSITIVE, DOUBLE ACCUSATIVE, DOUBLE GENITIVE, DOUBLE NEGATIVE, DOUBLE PASSIVE, DUAL, DUMMY, DYNAMIC VERB, ECHO QUESTION, ELLIPSIS, EMBEDDING, EMPHASIS, EXCLAMATION, EXISTENTIAL SENTENCE, FEMININE, FINITE VERB, FIXED PHRASE, FORM, FORMAL, FORMATIVE, FOWLER, FUNCTION, FUTURE, GENDER, GENERAL ANALYSIS, GENERATIVE, GENERATIVE GRAMMAR, GENERIC, GENERIC PRONOUN, GENITIVE CASE, GERUND, GOVERNMENT, GRAMMAR, GRAMMAR CHECKER, GRAMMAR-TRANSLATION METHOD, GRAMMATICAL CATEGORY, GRAMMATICALITY, GRAMMATICAL WORD, GROUP POSSESSIVE/GENITIVE, HALLIDAY, HANGING PARTICIPLE, HELPING VERB, HOLOPHRASE, HONORIFIC.

I–O. IMPERATIVE, INCEPTIVE, INCHOATIVE, INDEFINITE ARTICLE, INDICATIVE, INDIRECT OBJECT, INDIRECT SPEECH, INFINITIVE, INFIX, INFLECTED, INFLECTION/

INFLEXION, INFORMAL, INSTRUMENTAL, INTENSIFIER, INTERJECTION, INTERROGATIVE, INTRANSITIVE, INVERSION, IRREGULAR, IRREGULAR VERB, ITERATIVE, JESPERSEN, JONSON, LATIN[1], LINKING VERB, LOCATIVE, LOGIC, LONDON-LUND CORPUS, LOWTH, MAIN CLAUSE, MASCULINE, MASS NOUN, METANALYSIS, MILTON, MISRELATED PARTICIPLE, MODAL AUXILIARY, MODALITY, MODAL VERB, MODE, MODEL, MODIFICATION, MONOTRANSITIVE, MOOD, MORPHEME, MORPHOLOGY, MULTIPLE NEGATION, NAME, NEGATION, NEUTER, NOMINAL, NOMINALIZATION, NOMINATIVE ABSOLUTE, NOMINATIVE CASE, NON-COUNT NOUN, NON-DEFINING RELATIVE CLAUSE, NON-FINITE VERB, NON-RESTRICTIVE RELATIVE CLAUSE, NOUN, NOUN CLAUSE, NOUN-INCORPORATION, NUMBER[2], OBJECT, ONIONS, ONOMASTICS, ORTHOEPY, ORTHOGRAPHY.

P–Q. PARADIGM, PARADIGMATIC AND SYNTAGMATIC, PARATAXIS, PARENTHESIS, PARSING, PARTICIPLE, PARTICLE, PARTITIVE, PART OF SPEECH, PASSIVE (VOICE), PASSIVIZATION, PAST, PAST PARTICIPLE, PEDAGOGICAL GRAMMAR, PERFECT, PERFORMATIVE VERB, PERIODIC SENTENCE, PERIPHRASIS, PERSON, PERSONAL PRONOUN, PHILOLOGY, PHRASAL VERB, PHRASE, PHRASE WORD, PLUPERFECT, PLURAL, POLARITY, POP GRAMMARIAN, POSITIVE, POSITIVE DEGREE, POSSESSION, POSSESSIVE APOSTROPHE, POSSESSIVE CASE, POSSESSIVE PRONOUN, POST-DETERMINER, POST-MODIFICATION, POSTPOSITION, PRE-DETERMINER, PREDICATE, PREDICATIVE ADJECTIVE, PRE-MODIFICATION, PREPOSITION, PREPOSITIONAL ADVERB, PREPOSITIONAL VERB, PRESCRIPTIVE GRAMMAR, PRESCRIPTIVISM, PRESENT, PRESENT PARTICIPLE, PRETERIT(E), PRINCIPAL CLAUSE, PROGRESSIVE/CONTINUOUS, PROLEPSIS, PRONOUN, PROP, PROPER ADJECTIVE, PROPER NOUN, PROSCRIPTIVE, PROTASIS AND APODOSIS, PSEUDO-CLEFT SENTENCE, QUALIFY, QUANTIFIER, QUESTION, QUESTION TAG, QUIRK.

R–Z. RECIPROCAL PRONOUN, REDUPLICATION, REDUPLICATIVE, REFLEXIVE, REFLEXIVE PRONOUN, REGULAR, REGULAR VERB, RELATIVE CLAUSE, RELATIVE PRONOUN, RESTRICTIVE AND NON-RESTRICTIVE MODIFICATION, RESTRICTIVE AND NON-RESTRICTIVE RELATIVE CLAUSE, RULE, SAXON GENITIVE, SENTENCE, SENTENCE ADVERB, SENTENCE ADVERBIAL, SENTENCE FRAGMENT, SENTENCE STRESS, SENTENCE WORD, SIMPLE FUTURE, SIMPLE PAST, SIMPLE PRESENT, SIMPLE SENTENCE, SINGULAR, SPLIT INFINITIVE, STATIVE VERB, STEM, STEM FORMATIVE, STRONG VERB, STRUCTURE, STRUCTURE DEPENDENCE, SUBJECT, SUBJUNCTIVE, SUBORDINATE CLAUSE, SUBORDINATION, SUBORDINATOR, SUBSTANTIVE, SUFFIX, SUPERLATIVE (DEGREE), SUPERORDINATE CLAUSE, SUPPLETION, SURVEY OF ENGLISH USAGE, SWEET, SYNTAGMATIC, SYNTAX, TAG, TAG QUESTION, TENSE[1], THEMATIC VOWEL, THEME, THREE-PART VERB, TOPIC, TRANSFORMATIONAL-GENERATIVE GRAMMAR, TRANSITIVE AND INTRANSITIVE, TWO-PART VERB, UNATTACHED PARTICIPLE, UNCOUNTABLE NOUN, UNDERSTOOD, USAGE, UTTERANCE, VERB, VERBAL, VERBAL NOUN, VERBLESS SENTENCE, VERB OF INCOMPLETE PREDICATION, VERB PHRASE, VOCATIVE, VOICE, WEAK VERB, WHITNEY, WH-QUESTION, WH-SOUND, WORD, WORD CLASS, WORD-FORMATION, WORD ORDER, Y-, YES-NO QUESTION.

See also the grammar sections of entries for major varieties of English, such as CANADIAN ENGLISH.

GRAPH 451

GRAMMAR CHECKER. A computer program used in word processing to verify the grammatical correctness of what has been written. Such programs enforce such simple rules as number agreement between noun and verb and some of the overall requirements of sentence structure, such as that prepositions must have objects. A complete check on the entire grammar of English is not currently feasible. Grammar checkers are sometimes used in classrooms to help teach composition as well as by people writing letters and memoranda. Compare SPELLING CHECKER, STYLE CHECKER. [GRAMMAR, TECHNOLOGY]. M.L.

GRAMMAR-TRANSLATION METHOD. See LANGUAGE TEACHING.

GRAMMATICAL CATEGORY. In linguistics, a class of units such as *noun, verb, prepositional phrase, finite clause* and features such as *case, countability, gender, number*. These may in turn be subcategorized into kinds of noun, case, etc. Since nouns may be subclassified in various ways that do not coincide, they are said to be cross-classified in such pairs as *countable/uncountable, common/proper, animate/inanimate*. Grammatical units such as subject and object, which refer to functional relationships between the parts of a sentence or clause, are often termed *functional categories*. See PART OF SPEECH. [GRAMMAR]. S.G.

GRAMMATICALITY [1960s]. In linguistics, conformity to the rules of a language as formulated by a grammar based on a theory of language description. The concept became prominent with the rise of generative grammar in the 1960s, whose primary aim has been the construction of rules that would distinguish between the *grammatical* or *well-formed* sentences and the *ungrammatical, deviant,* or *ill-formed* sentences of a language. It is asserted that for most sentences the distinction is clear to the native speaker. For those where it is not clear, grammaticality will be determined by whether the sentences can be included under the rules distinguishing between the clearly grammatical and the clearly ungrammatical. If the rules of a grammar cannot be formulated so as to limit the number of possible coordinated phrases or clauses, the grammar will contain sentences that are unacceptable because of excess coordination: *If you eat without washing your hands, and if you drink too quickly, and if you go to bed late, and if you rise late, and if . . .*
  Consequently, grammaticality has been differentiated from *acceptability*, which is based on the judgements by native speakers as to whether they would use a sentence or would consider it correct if they met it. Judgements about what is acceptable may reflect views that a sentence is nonsensical, implausible, illogical, stylistically inappropriate, or socially objectionable. Many linguists believe that they can filter out such considerations in their investigations of the facts of language. Many also believe that they can rely on their own introspection to provide samples of clearly grammatical and clearly ungrammatical sentences that would be adequate for compiling and testing the rules. Others consider that the examination of large quantities of data stored and organized by means of computers can yield additional and more reliable information on what constructions are possible and which are central or peripheral to the language. A sensitive issue regarding grammaticality is variability within a language, for example the extent to which sentences are grammatical for one regional or social variety but not another, or indeed for one idiolect rather than another. Non-standard varieties of a language have their own grammars, which will resemble to a greater or less extent the grammar of the standard varieties, so that a sentence may be grammatical in one non-standard variety but ungrammatical in a standard variety, and vice versa. Some sociolinguists believe that linguists should have as their objective the compilation of *multilectal* grammar: a grammar that would take into account all variation within a given language. See ACCEPTABILITY. [GRAMMAR]. S.G.

GRAMMATICAL WORD. See WORD.

GRAMMATOLOGY [Late 20c: from Greek *grámma/grámmatos* letter, and *logía* study]. A branch of linguistics that studies the nature of writing and writing systems. Compare GRAPHOLOGY. [LANGUAGE, WRITING]. T.MCA.

GRAPH. (1) [1870s: short for *graphic formula*: see GRAPHIC]. A diagram that represents or displays a system of relations among two or more things by means of lines, dots, or bars. A common variety has an *X* or horizontal axis and a *Y* or vertical axis, and is used to display statistical information. A *line graph* displays the relationship of two sets of variables by means of a curve of distribution. A *bar graph* or *histogram* shows such relationships by means of adjacent columns of information that rise above or fall below the X axis or extrude horizontally from the Y axis. (2) [1930s: from Greek *graphḗ* writing]. A written or printed symbol for an idea, sound, or linguistic expression: see DIGRAPH, GRAPHEME. (3) Also *graf*. In journalism, an informal short form of *paragraph*. [TECHNOLOGY, WRITING]. T.MCA.

GRAPHEME [1930s: from Greek *graphē* writing, and *-eme* as in *phoneme*]. In linguistics, a minimal unit in a writing system, consisting of one or more symbols serving to represent a *phoneme*. Each grapheme is realized in writing or print by its *graphs*, such as the different ways of writing and printing an *a* or a *t*. An individual graph, when compared with another graph or representing a grapheme, is called an *allograph*. See -EME, GRAPH. Compare MORPHEME, PHONEME. [LANGUAGE, WRITING].   T.MCA.

GRAPHIC [17c: from Latin *graphicus* relating to painting or drawing, Greek *graphikós* able to paint or draw, from *gráphein* to write]. (1) In linguistics, relating to writing, as in *the graphic medium* (writing as a vehicle of language). (2) In mathematics, relating to diagrams and graphs, and especially to the determination of values or the solution of problems by means of measurement on diagrams and graphs. (3) Giving a clear, effective, and vivid mental picture: *a graphic description*. (4) Relating to the *graphic arts* (writing, lettering, printing, engraving, painting, drawing, etc.): *graphic design*. (5) A product of the graphic arts, such as a drawing or print; a device drawn, written, or printed on a surface. See CARTOON, GRAPH, GRAPHIC DESIGN. [MEDIA, WRITING].   T.MCA.

GRAPHIC DESIGN, also **graphics**. The visual effect of the layout of such artefacts as books, periodicals, pages, posters, leaflets, letterheads, and other graphics; the art of producing graphic layouts. See LAYOUT, SPACE. [MEDIA, TECHNOLOGY, WRITING].   T.MCA.

GRAPHIC MEDIUM. See GRAPHIC, MEDIUM.

GRAPHIC NOVEL. See COMIC.

GRAPHICS. See GRAPHIC DESIGN.

GRAPHOLOGY [1870s]. (1) The study and interpretation of handwriting so as to make observations on the character and abilities of the writer of a particular specimen. (2) A branch of linguistics that studies writing and print as systems of signs, and parallels *phonology* as the study of speech. Compare GRAMMATOLOGY, PHONOLOGY. See LEVEL OF LANGUAGE, MEDIUM. [LANGUAGE, WRITING].   T.MCA.

GRAVE ACCENT [From Latin *accentus gravis* a heavy tune. Pronounced 'grahv']. A diacritical mark over a letter as in French *è*: *première*, *siècle*. It is not usually retained when a word containing it is borrowed into English (*fin de siecle, premiere*), usually because it is not available on a keyboard or in type. Grave accents are, however,

sometimes applied to English words to mark such distinctions as the pronounced *e* of the second item of the pairs *aged/agèd, learned/learnèd*. In Shakespearian verse, the pronunciation of a normally silent *e* in *-ed* may be shown by a grave. The spelling is normal and unaccented in the prose of Lady Macbeth's *Out, damned spot!* (*Macbeth*, 5. 1), but Hamlet's verse shows the contrast between elision in *damn'd defeat* (*Hamlet*, 2. 2) and pronunciation in *smiling damnèd villain!* (1. 5). See ACCENT, D, DIACRITIC, LEARNED. [WRITING].   C.U.

GREAT AUSTRALIAN ADJECTIVE, also **Australian adjective**. An Australian name for the expletive *bloody*, although it is also widely used in BrE and NZE: 'I had once the curiosity to count the number of times that a bullock driver used this word in the course of a quarter of an hour, and found that he did so twenty-five times. I gave him eight hours in the day to sleep, and six to be silent, thus leaving ten hours for conversation. I supposed that he had commenced at twenty and continued till seventy years of age ... and found that in the course of that time he must have pronounced this disgusting word no less than 18,200,000 times' (A. Marjoribanks, *Travels in New South Wales*, 1847); 'The sunburnt —— stockman stood / And, in a dismal —— mood, / Apostrophised his —— cuddy; / "The —— nag's no —— good, / He couldn't earn his —— food, / A regular —— brumby"' (opening lines of '——: the Great Australian Adjective', W. T. Goodge, *Hits, Skits and Jingles*, 1899); 'Shootin' kanga-bloody-roos At Tumba-bloody-rumba' (W. N. Scott, *Complete Book of Australian Folk Lore*, 1976). See GREAT AUSTRALIAN SLANGUAGE, INFIX, TMESIS. [OCEANIA, STYLE].   T.MCA.

GREAT AUSTRALIAN SLANGUAGE [1890s]. Also **Australian slanguage**, sometimes **slangwidge**. Slang seen as pervading AusE; colloquial Australian: 'And our undiluted English / Is a fad to which we cling, / But the great Australian slanguage / Is a truly awful thing' (W. T. Goodge, *Hits, Skits and Jingles*, 1899); 'Actually, Australian slanguage is well stocked with words and phrases to describe those who are a bit slow off the mental mark' (*Weekend Australian*, 27 Aug. 1983). Compare GREAT AUSTRALIAN ADJECTIVE. See SLANGUAGE. [OCEANIA, STYLE].   T.MCA.

GREAT BRITAIN [16c: *Great* in the sense 'large', in contrast formerly with *Less Britain*, or Brittany]. A union of two kingdoms of Western Europe, occupying the island of Britain, and comprising England and Wales, and Scotland. Together with Northern Ireland, these constitute the *United Kingdom of Great Britain and Northern Ireland.* See BRITAIN, BRITANNIA, ENGLAND, NORTHERN IRELAND, SCOTLAND, UNITED KINGDOM, WALES. [EUROPE, NAME].   T.MCA.

GREAT VOWEL SHIFT. A sound change that began *c.*1400 and ended *c.*1600, changing late Middle English long, stressed monophthongs from something like the sounds of mainland European languages to those that they now have: for example, Middle English *fine* had an *i* like Italian *fino.* Words that entered English after the completion of the shift have often retained the original sound, as in *police*: compare *polite*, which entered earlier. In terms of articulation, the Middle English front vowels raised and fronted and the back vowels raised and backed; vowels already at the top became diphthongs with *ah* as the first element and the old vowel as the second, as in *fine* (see diagram). The shift marked a major change in the transition to Early Modern English, and is one reason why works of Geoffrey Chaucer and his contemporaries sound so unlike present-day English. *Chaucer's a* in *fame* sounded much like the *a* in present-day *father*, his *e* in *see* like the *a* in *same*, the *i* in *fine* like the *ee* in *fee*, the *o* in *so* like the *aw* in *saw*, the *o* in *to* like the *oe* in *toe*, and the *ou* or *ow* in *crowd* like the *u* in *crude.* See E, EARLY MODERN ENGLISH, LATIN[1], VOWEL SHIFT. Compare GRIMM'S LAW, VERNER'S LAW. [HISTORY, SPEECH].   W.F.B.

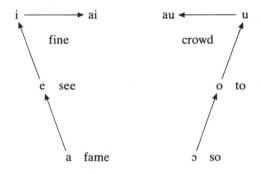

GREEK [Before 10c: from the Old English plural *Grecās*, Latin *Graeci*]. A language of southeastern Europe, a classical language of the Western world, and a member of the Indo-European language family. It is commonly divided into *Ancient* or *Classical Greek* (often thought of as a dead language) and *Modern Greek*, the language of Greece, Cyprus (with Turkish), enclaves in the Soviet Union and the eastern Mediterranean, and Greek and Cypriot immigrants in Australia, Britain, Canada, and the US. Greek has one of the longest unbroken linguistic traditions in the world, divided by scholars into six phases over *c.*3,500 years: (1) *Mycenaean*

Greek (14–12c BC) the language of Mycenae and Linear B writing. (2) *Archaic* or *Pre-classical Greek* (11–8c BC) the language of the Homeric epics, Hesiod, and the early lyric poets. (3) *Classical Greek* (7–5c BC), with several forms: Attic in Athens, Doric in the Peloponnese, Ionic in the Ionian islands and parts of Asia Minor, and Aeolic in Asia Minor, Thessaly, and Boeotia. (4) *Hellenistic Greek* (4c BC–4c AD), also known as *koinḗ*, the 'common language', a widely-used tongue of the Mediterranean and West Asia, a result of colonial settlement and the campaigns of Alexander the Great, one form of which was *New Testament Greek*, the language of the Gospels and St Paul. (5) *Byzantine* or *Romaic Greek* (5c–15c), the language of the Eastern Roman or Byzantine Empire. (6) *Modern Greek*, divided into *Demotic* or *Demotikí* (popular) and *Katharévousa* (purified, a classicized language of education). Since the early 1980s, a homogenizing Standard Modern Greek has developed, based on the usage of moderately educated people in the large urban centres of Greece.

Greek in English. The influence of classical Greek on English has been largely indirect, through Latin and French, and largely lexical and conceptual, with some orthographic and other effects. For speakers of English, Greek has been traditionally perceived as remote, esoteric, and yet worth a certain respect: compare the idiom *It's Greek to me* (I can't understand it) and the saying *The Greeks had a word for it* (expressing a traditional view of the richness of the language). Greek word-forming patterns, words, and word elements were adopted and adapted into Latin over *c.*1,500 years, and passed through Latin into many European and other languages, being used in the main for scholarly and technical purposes. The flow into English was at first limited and largely religious, such as Old English *cirice* and its descendant *church* (from *kūriakón dôma* the Lord's house). The significant influx was in the late Middle Ages and the Renaissance, as with *catalogue* 1460, *rhetorical* 1476, *stratagem* 1489, *psalmodize* 1513, *analytical* 1525.

Greek in Latin dress. The spelling of Greek words in English has been shaped by the orthographies of Latin and French: Greek *kalligraphia* becomes Latin *calligraphia*, French *calligraphie*, English *calligraphy.* Occasionally, however, a more Greek look survives: *kaleidoscope*, not **calidoscope*, *kinetic*, not **cinetic.* Synonymous variants sometimes occur: *ceratin*, *keratin*, both from *kéras* horn. Contrasts occur when a *k* survives in some usages but not in others: *ceratosaurus* horned lizard, *keratogenous* producing horny tissue; *cinematography* making moving pictures, *kinematograph* (obsolete) a film projector. Although most Greek personal and place-names have a Latinate look in English (*Achilles, Hercules; Athens, Crete*), they can, for literary and other purposes, take forms closer to the classical (*Akhilleus, Herakles*) or the modern (*Athinai, Kriti*). The use of *ph* as a marker of Greek words in Latin survives in English because it was favoured by French writers, the *ph* representing the Greek letter phi. English *philosophy* and French *philosophie* contrast with Italian *filosofia* and Spanish *filosofía*, which did not keep the Latinism: see F, P. English *neuralgia, neurosis* are closer to Greek than both French *névralgie, névrose* and Italian *nevralgia, nevrosi*, which have been influenced by the pronunciation of Modern Greek.

Hybridized Greek. Because it has been filtered into English through Neo-Latin, the Greek contribution has been liable to hybridization. However, because some loans (*diuretic, deontology, dogmatism*) are fairly close to their originals, and other forms are virtually identical with them (*diphtheria, dogma, drama*), the effects of Latinization and the easy creation of hybrids have tended to be overlooked. The words *rhetorical* and *analytical* are largely Greek, but they end with the *suffix -al, an adaptation of Latin -alis*. Scholars have tended to minimize such adaptations, because Latin and Greek were equally classical, sometimes discussing Greek as if it were a self-contained and pure source of technical vocabulary for English. Henry Bradley put it as follows:

So well adapted is the structure of the Greek language for the formation of scientific terms, that when a word is wanted to denote some conception peculiar to modern science, the most convenient way of obtaining it usually is to frame a new Greek compound or derivative, such as Aristotle himself might have framed if he had found it needful to express the meaning (*The Making of English*, 1904).

This is only partly true. A new formation is likely to be more Neo-Latin than classical Greek. It was circumstance rather than inherent worth that made Greek a prime source of terms for European academic discourse. Other classical languages, such as Arabic and Sanskrit, are comparably extensive in systems of word-formation exploited in their own scholarly traditions, but have had little impact on English because no such channels as Latin and French were open to them. Elsewhere, however, they have had a comparable impact. The word-creating capacity of Greek, while prodigious, is not unique; nor has it usually had a direct channel into the Western European languages. As a result, even the most rigorous scientific terminologies are hybrid, such as the names of the geological eras, created in English as an ad-hoc system unlikely to have been Aristotle's choice.

Part-Greek terminology. The names of the major eras of geology are Greek, labelled according to position in time: *Pal(a)eozoic* of old life, *Mesozoic* of middle life, *Cenozoic* of recent life. However, most of the terms for the periods into which the Paleozoic and Mesozoic divide are Latinate and none refers to time. Three refer to rocks in Wales (*Cambrian, Ordovician, Silurian*), one each to rocks in England (*Devonian*), Russia (*Permian*), Germany (*Triassic*), and France (*Jurassic*), and two to physical features (*Carboniferous* to coal, *Cretaceous* to chalk). The divisions of the Cenozoic, however, return to Greek and to time, marking vague degrees of recentness by turning the *cen(o)-* of *Cenozoic* into *-(o)cene*: *Paleocene* ancient recent, *Eocene* dawn recent, *Oligocene* few recent, *Miocene* less recent, *Pliocene* more recent, *Pleistocene* most recent, *Holocene* entirely recent. The mix of Greek, Latin, and English is marked in such subsidiary formations as *Early Prepaleozoic, Infracambrian, Eocambrian, Upper Silurian, Permo-Triassic*. Such a system, constructed to serve the ends of geology, is typical of how Greek is used in Modern English.

Dog-Greek? The subsystem of *-cene* terms did not endear its creator, the 19c Scottish geologist Sir Charles Lyell, to the English usage critic Henry Fowler, who makes the following comment under the entry *barbarism*: 'A man of science might be expected to do on his great occasion what the ordinary man cannot do every day, ask the philologist's help; that the famous *eocene-pleistocene* names were made by "a good classical scholar" shows that word-formation is a matter for the specialist' (*Modern English Usage*, ed. Ernest Gowers, 1965). More in sympathy with the needs and practices of scientists and engineers, the English philologist Simeon Potter noted that electricians have abstracted from *electron* a new noun-forming suffix *-tron*, for terms like *dynatron, kenotron, phanotron, magnetron, thyratron*. He observed: 'I once heard an unkind critic allude disparagingly to these neologisms as dog-Greek. To a lover of the language of Sophocles and Plato these recent coinages may indeed appear to be Greek debased. More appropriately, perhaps, they might be termed lion-Greek or chameleon-Greek. They are Neo-Hellenic in the genuine Renaissance tradition' (*Our Language*, 1950/66). Such flexible Greek is fully integrated into the vocabulary and word-formation of English: alone though Frenchified in *biosphere*, with Latin and again Frenchified in *bio-degradable*, and increasingly at ease with the vernacular in such forms as *bio-feedback* and *megabucks*.

See AUSTRALIAN LANGUAGES, BIBLE, BISO-CIATION, BORROWING, CANADIAN LANGUAGES,

CLASSICAL/LEARNED COMPOUND, CLASSICAL ENDING, CLASSICAL LANGUAGE, COMBINING FORM, COMPOUND WORD, CYPRUS, EARLY MODERN ENGLISH, EUROPEAN COMMUNITY, FIGURATIVE LANGUAGE/USAGE, GRAMMAR, GREEK, GREEK LITERATURE, INTERFIX, KOINÉ, LATIN[1], LATIN LITERATURE, LITERATURE, NEO-LATIN, PREFIX, RHETORIC, SUFFIX, WORD, WORD-FORMATION. [EUROPE, LANGUAGE].   T.MCA.

GREEK ALPHABET. See ALPHABET.

GREEK *E*. See EPSILON.

GREEK LITERATURE. Literature in Greek, both the surviving writings of archaic and classical Greece, and the entire body of writings from Homer to the present day. The Greeks were the first Europeans to use an alphabet, to theorize about language, and to frame language categories such as *ónoma* (name/noun) and *phrásis* (way of speaking, group of words). Most of the literary genres of the Western world were invented or formalized by the Greeks and many of the names they used have passed with only minor adaptation to many successor languages. Key literary words in English that are of Greek provenance (drawn variously from classical, Alexandrian, and Byzantine sources) include *anachronism, anthology, archetype, biography, catharsis, comedy, criticism, elegy, epic, euphemism, hubris, irony, lyric, metaphor, mythology, poesy, poetics, rhetoric, sarcasm, symbolism, tragedy.* Much of the matter of Greek literature emerged from the beliefs and rituals of pre-literate times, was classed as *múthos* (story) and *poíēsis* (making), and was analysed into three types: the *épos* (epic) of Homer and Hesiod; the *elegeiā* (flute song) and *lúra* (lyre song) of such poets as Sappho and Pindar; and the *dráma* (action) of such playwrights as Aeschylus and Aristophanes. All such works have served for centuries as Europe's literary templates. See ANAGNORISIS, CATHARSIS, COMEDY, DRAMA, ELEGY, EPIC, GENRE, HAMARTIA, HUBRIS, LATIN LITERATURE, LITERARY CRITICISM, LYRIC, MIMESIS, ODE, PASTORAL, POETICS, POETRY, TRAGEDY, TRAGICOMEDY. [EUROPE, LITERATURE].   T.MCA.

GREENGROCER'S APOSTROPHE. See APOSTROPHE[1].

GRENADA. A country of the Caribbean, and member of the Commonwealth. Capital: Saint George's. Currency: the East Caribbean dollar. Head of state: the British monarch, represented by a governor-general. Population: 102,000 (1988), 124,000 (projection for 2000). Languages: English (official), English Creole, French Creole. Education: primary *c.*100%, secondary 35%, tertiary 10%, literacy 98%. Columbus visited the island in 1498, in the mid-17c French settlers from Martinique ousted the Caribs, and the island was ceded to Britain in 1783. It was administered as part of the Windward Islands in 1833, became a colony in 1877 and independent in 1974, and was invaded by the US and some nearby nations in 1983 to remove a Marxist government. See CARIBBEAN, ENGLISH. [AMERICAS, NAME, VARIETY].   T.MCA.

GRIMM'S LAW. The first Germanic sound shift, a statement of the relationship between certain consonants in Germanic languages and their originals in Indo-European (IE), first described in 1818 by the Danish philologist Rasmus Rask (1787–1832) and set out in detail in 1822 by the German philologist Jacob Grimm (1785–1863). Greatly simplified, Grimm's Law states the regular changes in IE labials /p, b, f/, velars /k, g, h/, and dentals /t, d, θ/, as they developed in Germanic. Because English has words borrowed from Latin and Greek that retain the original IE sound, as well as words descended from Germanic that have the changed sound, it provides 'before and after' illustrations (see table).

	Sound shift	'Before'	'After'
Labials	p > *f*	*p*ed(al)	*f*oot
	b > p	la*b*(ial)	li*p*
	f > b	*f*und(ament)	bott(om)
Velars	k > h	*c*an(ine)	*h*ound
	g > k	*g*enu(flect)	*k*nee
	h > g	*h*ost(ile)	*g*uest
Dentals	t > th	*t*ri(ple)	*th*ree
	d > t	*d*uo	*t*wo
	th > d	*th*yr(oid)	*d*oor

In general, Grimm's Law holds that unvoiced IE stops became Germanic unvoiced continuants, that voiced IE stops became Germanic unvoiced stops, and that unvoiced IE continuants became Germanic voiced stops (see diagram). In the triangles, the change from IE to Germanic

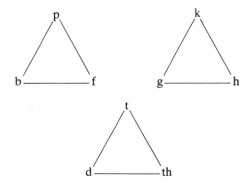

runs clockwise, the derivation of Germanic from IE anti-clockwise. See INDO-EUROPEAN LANGUAGES. Compare VERNER'S LAW, GREAT VOWEL SHIFT. [HISTORY, SPEECH].　　　　　W.F.B.

GRINGO [1840s: from Spanish 'foreign language, foreigner', probably from *griego* Greek: compare the English expression *It's all Greek to me*. Feminine: *gringa*. The alternative explanation, that the term derives from the first syllables of the song 'Green grow the Lilacs', popular during the US-Mexican War (1846-8), though attractive, appears to have no foundation]. A usually pejorative and dismissive ethnic name in Spain and especially Latin America for a foreigner, especially of American or sometimes British background. See ETHNIC NAME. [AMERICAS, NAME].　　　　　T.MCA.

GROUP POSSESSIVE, also **group genitive.** Terms for those occasions when the possessive apostrophe (*'s*) is added to a phrase rather than to the noun to which it logically relates: *The King of Thailand's visit* (not **The king's of Thailand visit*) or *the girl next door's bicycle*. See APOSTROPHE[1], POSSESSION, SAXON GENITIVE. [GRAMMAR].　　　　　S.C.

GRUB STREET. A street in London (renamed *Milton Street* in 1830), long associated with people who write for a living. The name now refers not to a location but to literary hack work, as professional writers often take on any kind of work in order to make ends meet. The sense of uninspired, hackneyed, commercial writing grew out of the association of name and place and was strong in the 17-18c. The poet Pope, who probably had a part in the short-lived satirical weekly *The Grub Street Journal* (1730-37), wrote:

> Not with less glory mighty Dulnes crowned
> Shall take through Grub Street her triumphant round;
> And her Parnassus glancing o'er at once,
> Behold an hundred sons, and each a dunce.
> (*The Dunciad*, 1728, iii. 135)

Johnson defined the term with self-irony as: 'Originally the name of a street in Moorfields much inhabited by writers of small histories, dictionaries, and temporary poems; whence any mean production is called *grubstreet*' (*Dictionary*, 1755). The expression is used in literary circles to denigrate and deplore commercialism. See FLEET STREET, FREEDOM OF THE PRESS, HACK. [LITERATURE, MEDIA].　　　　　G.H., T.MCA.

GUIDE [17c]. A book for beginners or those seeking help or reassurance; a manual or work of reference presented as if it were a person leading others through difficult country: *The Oxford Guide to the English Language* (1984); *The Cambridge Guide to Literature in English* (1988); *The Bloomsbury Good Word Guide* (1988). The term *guidebook* is commoner in general statements (*We need a guidebook*), while *guide* is commoner in the titles of such books. Compare COMPANION, MANUAL. See USAGE GUIDANCE AND CRITICISM. [REFERENCE].　　　　　T.MCA.

GUIDEWORD. See CATCHWORD.

GUJARATI, also **Gujerati.** An Indo-Aryan language of India, spoken by *c*.20m people in Gujarat, Bombay, and elsewhere in India, and by Gujaratis in Britain, East and South Africa, and elsewhere in the world. It is the state language of Gujarat, is one of the 15 major languages of India, and is written in modified Devanagari script, and its literary tradition dates from the 12c. See AFRICAN LANGUAGES, BRITISH LANGUAGES, EUROPEAN LANGUAGES, FIJI, GANDHI, INDIAN ENGLISH[1], INDIAN LANGUAGES. [ASIA, LANGUAGE].　　　　　Y.K.

GULLAH [Early 18c: speculatively linked with both the *Gola* of Liberia and the territory of *Angola*]. The name of a member of a black community in the Sea Islands and coastal marshes of South Carolina, Georgia, and north-eastern Florida, and of the English-based creole spoken by that community (also known as *Sea Island Creole*). Gullah is usually kept hidden from outsiders. It developed on 18c rice plantations after British colonists and their African slaves arrived in Charleston from Barbados in 1670, in an encounter among African languages such as Ewe, Hausa, Ibo, Mende, Twi, and Yoruba, the English of overseers from England, Ireland, and Scotland, and the maritime pidgin used in some West African forts and aboard slavers' ships. It shares many features with other Atlantic creoles, and is characterized by: (1) Distinctive words for tense and aspect: *He bin come* He came, He had come; *He go come* He will come, He would come; *He duh come* He is coming, He was coming; *He done come* He has come, He had come. *He come* may mean 'He came', 'He has come', 'He comes', but not 'He will come'. (2) Pronouns more inclusive than in general English: *He see um* He or she saw him/her/it; also *He see she* He saw her, and *He see we* He or she saw us. A pronoun usually has the same form whether subject or possessive: *He ain see he brother* He hasn't seen his brother, He didn't see his brother. (3) Subordinate clauses introduced by *say* (*Uh tell you say he done come* I told you that he has/had come), and by *fuh* (*Uh tell um fuh come* I told him/her to come). Both particles can be left out: *Uh tell you he done come; Uh tell um come*. There is a continuum between Gullah and local varieties of AmE: for example, from *He duh come* and *He duh comin* through *He comin* to *He's comin*. English words of African origin that may have come wholly or partly through Gullah include *goober* peanut (compare Kimbundu *nguba*), and *juke* bawdy and disorderly (compare Bambara *dzugu*, wicked), as in *juke house* brothel or cheap roadhouse, and *jukebox*. See AFRO-SEMINOLE, AMERICAN BLACK ENGLISH, ATLANTIC CREOLES, BAJAN, DIALECT IN AMERICA, GEECHEE, PIDGIN, TURNER (L.), WEST AFRICAN PIDGIN ENGLISH. [AFRICA, AMERICAS, VARIETY]. S.S.M.

GUNNING FOG INDEX. See FOG INDEX.

GUTTER [13c, from Norman French *goutiere*, equivalent to French *goutte* a drop (of water): compare SLOPPY]. (1) A channel for carrying off liquid such as rainwater on roofs or in streets. Because the gutters of streets are often foul, and beggars, derelicts, street urchins, and others have often been associated with them (*begging in the gutters*; *lying drunk in a gutter*; *a dirty little guttersnipe*), the term has come to be used, especially attributively, for kinds of language or things associated with language that belong or in someone's opinion ought to belong in the gutter: 'Each book I have written has brought a few letters and a certain percentage of reviews asking if it is really necessary for me to use so much "gutter" language' (Tabitha King, *Maledicta*, 1988–9). See GUTTER SCOTS, NEWSPAPER, YELLOW PRESS. [STYLE]. T.MCA.

GUTTER JOURNALISM/PRESS. See YELLOW PRESS.

GUTTER SCOTS. A pejorative term for urban working-class speech in Scotland. Sometimes *Scots* is replaced by a local name, such as *Gutter Glasgow*. It is identified by at least the following features, several of which are not confined to Scotland. (1) *The glottal stop*, realizing /t/ and less regularly /p, k/ as glottal plosives after vowels and /l, n, r/: *better*, *bottle*, *try to*, *quarter*, *tryin'* to, *shelter*, *keeping*, *working*. (2) Disyllabic forms with an intrusive vowel: 'girrul' *girl*, 'wurruld' *world*, 'fillum' *film*. (3) 'H-' for *th-* in 'hink' *think*, 'hing' *thing*, 'sumhn' *something*, 'nuhn' *nothing*, 'everyhn' *everything*. (4) A realization of *thr-* as 'hr-': 'hree' for *three*, 'hred' for *thread*. (5) Generalizing past participle forms as past tenses and vice versa: *Ah never done that*; *Ah seen im comin*; *Ah gien im aw Ah had* I gave him all I had; *Ah've swam further'n that*. (6) Other irregularities in verb morphology: *Ah seed im comin*; *Ah've brung ye some sangwidges*. (7) Multiple negation: *Ah dinna(e) waant nane* I don't want any. (8) *Never* used to negate one event: *Ah nivver done nothin* I didn't do that. (9) Double auxiliary *have*: *Ye'd've saw im if ye'd've came/If ye'd a came*. (10) *Here* as an exclamation of surprise: *And here! the shoap wis open efter aw*. (11) Repetition of reporting *say*: *He says tae me e says*, '*Ah'm no comin*'; *Ah says tae him Ah says*: '*Jis shut up!*' (12) Minced oaths as exclamations of surprise: *Jings* Jesus, *Crivvens* Christ, *Help ma Boab* (Help my Bob) Help me God. See EDINBURGH, GLASGOW, GLOTTAL STOP, SCOTS. [EUROPE, VARIETY]. A.J.A.

GUTTURAL [16c: from French *guttural*, Latin *gutturalis* throaty]. A general term for sounds made in or near the throat, such as the velar fricative in German *Achtung* and ScoE *loch*, the uvular *r* in Parisian French *derrière*, and the pharyngeal Arabic sounds known as '*ayn* and *ghayn*. The term is imprecise and little used by phoneticians. It is often used loosely when describing English spoken with a 'throaty' foreign accent: ' "I had some criticisms of my own education," he said in his slow guttural, uncompromised by 50 years of living and working in the USA' (referring to Bruno Bettelheim, *Observer*, 6 Sept. 1987). See ACCENT, ARABIC, BURR, PHARYNX, UVULA, VELUM. [SPEECH, STYLE]. G.K., T.MCA.

GUYANA. Official title: *Co-operative Republic of Guyana*. A country of the Caribbean coast of South America and member of the Commonwealth. Capital: Georgetown. Currency: the dollar. Economy: sugar, rice, bauxite, timber. Population: 820,000 (1988), 920,000 (projection for 2000). Ethnicity: 51% East Indian, 43% African, 4% Amerindian, 2% Chinese and Caucasian. Religions: 57% Christian, 33% Hindu, 9% Muslim. Languages: English (official), English Creole, Bhojpuri, Hindi, Urdu, Amerindian languages. Education: primary 90%, secondary 60%, tertiary 4%, literacy 96%. The region was sighted by Columbus 1498 and settled by the Dutch in the 16c. The Dutch colonies of Essequibo, Demerara, and Berbice were ceded to the British in 1815, and consolidated as *British Guiana* in 1831, with independence in 1966. The term *Guyanese English* is used, in opposition to *Creolese* or *Guyanese Creole English*, to refer to educated local usage. Its vocabulary contains items from Dutch (*paal* boundary mark, *stelling* wharf), Amerindian (*warishi* basket for heavy loads, *mashramani* celebration after cooperative work), and Indian languages (*sardar* field supervisor on a plantation, *dhan* rice paddy). See CARIBBEAN, CARIBBEAN BROADCASTING, CARIBBEAN DICTIONARIES, CARIBBEAN ENGLISH, CARIBBEAN ENGLISH CREOLE, CREOLESE, CARIBBEAN PRESS, ENGLISH, SURINAM(E). [AMERICAS, NAME, VARIETY]. T.MCA., L.D.C.

H

H, h [Generally called 'aitch', and sometimes 'haitch' in IrE and AusE]. The 8th letter of the Roman alphabet as used for English. It derives from the Phoenician consonant *heth*, ancestor of the Greek letter *eta* (H). The Romans adopted *eta* to represent the aspirate sound /h/.

Sound Value. In English, *h* represents a voiceless glottal fricative at the beginning of syllables before a vowel: *hat, behind, abhor, mishap*.

Silent H. (1) In syllable-final position, in exclamations such as *ah, eh, oh* and in such loans (usually Hebrew and West or South Asian) as *chutzpah, Jehovah, Messiah, Sara(h), howdah, veranda(h)*. (2) In words of Greek origin, after *r*: *catarrh, h(a)emorrhage, rhapsody, rhinoceros, rhododendron. Rhyme* (also *rime*) is so spelt by analogy with *rhythm*. (3) In *Thames, thyme*, and sometimes *Anthony*. (4) By elision after a stressed syllable (*annihilate, shepherd, Chatham*), and after *ex-* even at the onset of a stressed syllable (*exhaust, exhibit, exhort*). (5) In speech, commonly elided in *he, him, his, her* in unstressed positions, especially following a consonant: *What did 'e do; Tell us 'er name*. This elision affected the spelling and pronunciation of the Middle English pronoun *hit*, resulting in Modern English *it*. (6) After *c* in words of Greek and Italian origin, but indicating that the *c* is pronounced /k/: *archangel, archive, chemist, monarch, stomach, technical, chiaroscuro, scherzo*: and by analogy *ache*, modern spelling for earlier *ake*. (7) In words of Celtic origin, *ch* is generally pronounced /k/ (*clarsach, loch*), but in ScoE and often in IrE is a velar fricative /x/. English in England may have silent *h* in Irish names such as *Callaghan*, though in IrE and ScoE the *g* is generally silent. See C.

French H. Words derived from French vary in their use of *h*. Sometimes *h* has never been established in English: for example, *able* from Latin *habilis*, French *habile*. Sometimes *h* reached English, but has never been pronounced: *heir, honest, honour, hour*. Sometimes a silent French *h* has come to be pronounced in standard English: *horrible, hospital, host, hotel, human, humour, humble*. In some words *h* was introduced in English as in *hermit, hostage* (compare French *ermite, otage*), eventually coming to be pronounced. The *h* of *herb* is pronounced in standard BrE, but not in standard AmE.

Initial H. The uncertainty of initial *h* is shown in the controversy over the use of *an* before some words of French origin: *an heroic attempt* and *an historic occasion* as opposed to *a heroic attempt* and *a historic occasion*. Although it is now generally conventional to say *a hotel*, the form *an hotel* was once widespread and still occurs in England. In such cases, the *h* may or may not be pronounced in BrE (*an heroic attempt* or *an 'eroic attempt*) and is pronounced in AmE. This use of *an* before *h* is widely regarded as pretentious (especially when the *h* is pronounced), and has always been limited to words in which the first syllable is unstressed: no **an hopeless case* or **an hot day*.

H-dropping. Also *aitch-dropping*. In England and Wales there are several *h*-less accents, such as Cockney and Brummie, where the pronunciations *an 'orrible 'appening* and *an 'opeless case* are normal. In written dialogue associated with such accents, unpronounced *h* is represented, as here, by an apostrophe.

Digraphs. (1) *H* following some consonants may represent special joint values, as in the digraphs *ch, gh, ph, sh, th, wh*. See C, G, P, S, T, W. (2) This use of *h* was first established in Latin, which used *ch, ph*, and *th* for the Greek letters *chi, phi*, and *theta*. The digraphs *ch, sh* developed in English after the Norman Conquest. *Wh* arose analogic-

---

THE CAPITAL LETTER

EARLY FORMS				CURRENT FORMS	
Phoenician	Greek	Etruscan	Roman (Latin)	roman	italic
目	日H	日	H	H	*H*

THE SMALL LETTER

EARLY FORMS			CURRENT FORMS	
Roman cursive	Roman uncial	Carolingian minuscule	roman	italic
┗	h	h	h	*h*

ally by reversing Old English *hw*. *Gh* was introduced to represent the Old English palatal or velar fricative previously often spelt ʒ (yogh), itself going back to an old English *h*-form (old English *liht* becoming *liʒt* then *light*), and *th* was substituted for the Old English letters ð (eth) and þ (thorn): see ETH, THORN, YOGH. (3) *H* can be used in such digraphs because its usual value does not normally occur after consonants, except across syllable boundaries (see below).

Other features. (1) In some circumstances, ambiguity can arise regarding what may or may not be a digraph. Syllable boundaries may be unclear, so that the separate values of *sh* in *mishap* may be read together as in *bishop*. Uncertainty over syllable boundaries has influenced the spelling in *threshold* (contrast *withhold*). (2) The suffix *-ham* in place-names in England is often ambiguous in terms of pronunciation, the *h* being sometimes assimilated into a digraph (as in *Grantham*), sometimes not (as in *Clapham*). The spelling provides no guidance in such words. (3) In some languages, *h* can indicate aspiration of a preceding consonant (*bhakti, jodhpur, khaki*), but this use usually appears unmotivated to monolingual English speakers, who ignore it, especially in Indian usage (*bharat natyam, dharma, Jhabvala, Madhukar*) and often take aspirated *t* to be the conventional *th* digraph (*hatha yoga, Marathi*). See AITCH, ALPHABET, ASPIRATE, LETTER[1], SPELLING. [WRITING].   C.U.

HACK [17c: a clipping of *hackney* hired horse, hireling, prostitute: see HACKNEYED]. Someone who writes low-grade material for money, especially according to a formula; a literary or journalistic drudge. In the early 18c the term was associated with writing for book-sellers, and prompted the phrases *Grub Street hack, hack writer*, and *hack work*. The practice started in the 16c, when demand for plays outstripped supply and collaborative writing became common. Journalists currently use the term with self-mocking affection: *There were several hacks at the meeting.* See FORMULA, GRUB STREET. [MEDIA, WRITING].   G.H.

HACKER [16c: from *hack* to cut with heavy blows and a jagged effect]. (1) Someone or something that hacks or does things badly; formerly, by extension, someone who mangles words and meanings. (2) [1970s]. An informal term for an obsessive computer programmer who is constantly trying new things (tinkering or *hacking*), including seeking access to private systems (as an *electronic eavesdropper*) and planting destructive routines (*viruses*) in other people's programs. In the 1980s, for this reason, the term developed pejorative connotations. It is, however, used positively in both the title and the text of *The New*

Hacker's Dictionary (ed. Eric S. Raymond: MIT Press, 1991). This work discusses the jargon and slang of computer enthusiasts (which it sometimes refers to as *hackish*), with entries from *abend* (an 'abnormal end' in which a software program 'crashes') through *kluge up* ('to lash together a quick hack to perform a task') to *zork mid* ('the canonical unit of currency in hacker-written games). [MEDIA, TECHNOLOGY].

T.MCA., M.L.

HACKNEYED [18c: from *hackney* a hired horse or person, a drudge, a hired carriage (*hackney cab/carriage/coach*), from Old French *haquenée* an ambling horse of middle quality, considered especially suitable for women: compare HACK]. (1) Originally, of a horse or person: kept for hire as needed, and by implication not worth very much. (2) Used so often and indiscriminately as to have lost all freshness and interest, said especially of writing and expressions grown stale through overuse. See CLICHÉ, COPYBOOK, METAPHOR, STOCK, TRITE. [STYLE].   T.MCA.

HALF RHYME [19c]. Also **imperfect rhyme, near rhyme, oblique rhyme, off rhyme, slant rhyme**. Rhyme that does not meet the criterion of identity in stressed vowels and following sounds; the vowels may be different but followed by identical consonants (*wall/soul, made/ride*), or rhyming vowels may be followed by different consonants (*bake/mail, mock/long*). There may also be differences in vowels and consonants, but the sounds must be related enough to give a semblance of rhyme (*bit/bed; push/huge*). Half rhyme has been used by such 20c poets as Wilfrid Owen, W. B. Yeats, and W. H. Auden. Owen's 'Strange Meeting' begins:

It seemed that out of battle I escaped
Down some profound long tunnel, long since scooped
Through granites which titanic wars had groined.
Yet also there encumbered sleepers groaned,
Too fast in thought or death to be bestirred.
Then, as I probed them, one sprang up, and stared
With piteous recognition in fixed eyes,
Lifting distressful hands as if to bless.

Half rhyme can alleviate the comparative paucity of full rhymes in English. Poets have found it useful for common and important words for which the available rhymes have become predictable and hackneyed. It allows a wider choice, as in D. G. Rossetti's *The White Ship*:

And when to the chase his court would crowd,
The poor flung ploughshares on his road,
And shrieked, 'Our cry is from King to God!'

Some 20c poets have used forms of half rhyme which only lightly echo each other, with a result not readily distinguished from free verse, as in Dylan Thomas's:

The force that through the green fuse drives the flower

Drives my green age; that blasts the roots of trees
Is my destroyer.
And I am dumb to tell the crooked rose
My youth is bent by the same wintry fever.

By partly satisfying and partly frustrating expectation, half rhyme can have a vivid effect. BLANK VERSE, RHYME, VERSE. [LITERATURE].   R.C.

HALLIDAY, Michael A. K. [b.1925]. English linguist and grammarian, born in Leeds, Yorkshire, into an academic family; his father, Wilfred J. Halliday (1889-1975), after retiring as a headmaster, played a major part in compiling material for the North of England in Harold Orton's Survey of English Dialects. The younger Halliday studied Chinese language and literature at the U. of London and linguistics at graduate level, first in Peking and Canton, then at Cambridge (Ph.D. 1955, published as *The Language of the Chinese 'Secret History of the Mongols'*, 1959). In 1963, he was named to lead the *Communication Research Centre* at the U. of London, directing two influential projects: a description of scientific English, and a study of children's language that led eventually to the *Breakthrough to Literacy*, his method of teaching children to read. In 1965 he became Professor of General Linguistics at London, in 1970 Professor of Linguistics at the U. of Illinois in Chicago, and in 1976 Professor in the Department of Linguistics at the U. of Sydney, where he remained until retirement in 1987. In 1981 he gained the NCTE's Russell Award and in 1986 held the Lee Kuan Yew Distinguished Professorship at the U. of Singapore.

Halliday's contributions to the study of English have been varied. For the past quarter-century he has set the agenda for applications of linguistics, as proposed with Peter Strevens and Angus McIntosh in *The Linguistic Sciences and Language Teaching* (1964). His interests include first- and second-language acquisition, poetics, artificial intelligence, linguistic disorders, discourse analysis, text linguistics, semiotics, speech, and English grammar. In the last of these fields, contributions include *Intonation and Grammar in British English* (1967), *Cohesion in English* (1976, with Ruqaiya Hasan), and *An Introduction to Functional Grammar* (1985). The theory he espouses, currently known as *systemic grammar* and *systemic linguistics*, has an orientation towards applications. 'The value of a theory', he has declared, 'lies in the use that can be made of it.' The approach emphasizes the functions of language in use, particularly the ways in which social setting, mode of expression, and register influence selections from a language's *systems*: 'Meaning is a product of the relationship between the system and its environment.'

In his work on English texts, Halliday has asserted the unity of syntax and lexicon in a *lexicogrammar*, collapsing the usual distinction between grammar and dictionary. Meanings are expressed through three interrelated functions: the *ideational*, the *interpersonal*, and the *textual*. Messages combine an organization of *content* deployed according to the *expressive* and *receptive* needs of speaker/authors and listener/readers within conventions of discourse organization. Language users make a series of choices drawn from the meaning potential of their language as they express themselves; it is the task of the linguist to describe those choices as they are shaped by individual minds and social context. Many collections of Halliday's papers (sometimes including contributions by others) have been published. They include: *Halliday: System and Function in Language* (Oxford, 1976), *Language as Social Semiotic* (Arnold, 1978), *Readings in Systemic Linguistics* (Batsford, 1981), *The Semiotics of Culture and Language* (Pinter, 1984), *New Developments in Systemic Linguistics* (Pinter, 1987), and *Current Ideas in Systemic Practice and Theory* (Pinter, 1991). An analysis of his work has been prepared in the form of a thematic glossary with extended citations: *Terms in Systemic Linguistics: A Guide to Halliday* (St Martin's Press, 1980). At his retirement, he was presented with a two-volume festschrift: *Language Topics: Essays in Honour of Michael Halliday* (John Benjamins, 1987). See index. [AMERICAS, ASIA, BIOGRAPHY, EDUCATION, EUROPE, GRAMMAR, LANGUAGE, OCEANIA]. R.W.B.

HAMARTIA [1890s: from Greek *hamartia* fault, failure]. In traditional and especially classical drama, the *tragic flaw* that causes the death of the hero, such as Hamlet's indecision and Othello's jealousy. See POETICS, TRAGEDY. [LITERATURE].   T.MCA.

HAMITO-SEMITIC LANGUAGES, also **Afro-Asiatic languages, Afrasian languages, Semito-Hamitic languages**. A family of languages found throughout much of northern Africa and western Asia, whose parent language appears to have been spoken *c*.8,000-10,000 years ago in the present-day Sahara. It includes the *Hamitic language* group, containing such northern African languages as Amharic, Berber, and Hausa, and the *Semitic language* group, containing such West Asian languages as Arabic, Aramaic, and Hebrew. See AFRICAN LANGUAGES, ARABIC, ARAMAIC, ASIAN LANGUAGES, HEBREW, LANGUAGE FAMILY. [AFRICA, ASIA, LANGUAGE].   T.MCA.

HAND [From Old English]. (1) One of two organs of touching and holding, especially in primates. The opposability of thumb and fingers has been crucial in the emergence of *Homo sapiens* as a 'tool-using animal', including the development of writing. The hand has two basic functions: *prehensile* (gripping) and *non-prehensile*, with two grips, the *power grip* (as used with a club or sword) and the *precision grip* (as used to throw a ball or write with a pen or pencil). Non-prehensile functions include pushing, tapping, and typing. The term *handedness* refers to whether a person is predominantly *right-handed* (the majority of the human race, for whom most tools are designed), *left-handed*, or *ambidextrous* (a word whose origin in Latin proposes that both hands are 'right' hands). In many cultures, the right hand and right-hand side are associated with 'righteousness', 'dexterity' (Latin *dexter* right hand), white magic, handling food, and cleanliness, while the left hand and left-hand side are associated with evil, black magic, and sinister things (Latin *sinister* the left hand), with clumsiness or gaucheness (French *gauche* left), and with uncleanness, including toilet hygiene. The BrE dialect term *cack-handed* for 'left-handed' derives from *cack* excrement. Because of the prestige of the right hand, left-handed people in many cultures have been required or persuaded to write, however clumsily, with the right rather than the left hand. (2) Ability and style in handwriting: *She writes a beautiful hand.* (3) In grammar, the term *hand* occurs in two common figurative phrases associated with balancing statements: 'The Americans, *on the one hand*, want to develop the area, but the British, *on the other* (hand), want to leave it undisturbed.' See CALLIGRAPHY, LONGHAND, MANUAL, MEDIUM, SHORTHAND, SIGN LANGUAGE. [WRITING].   T.MCA.

HANDBOOK. See MANUAL, SAXONISM.

HANDEDNESS. See HAND.

HANDWRITING. See CALLIGRAPHY, HAND, WRITING.

HANGING PARTICIPLE. See PARTICIPLE.

HANLEY, Miles Lawrence [1893-1954]. American phonetician, born in Xenia, Ohio, and educated at Wittenberg College, Ohio State U., and Harvard (MA, 1927). From 1927, he amassed huge collections of written and recorded materials on the pronunciation of English (14-20c) which continue to provide data for researchers. Some of this material appeared in *Index to Rimes in American and English Poetry 1500-1900* (1959). He helped compile the *Linguistic Atlas of New England* (1934-40), helped prepare the *Linguistic Atlas of the United States and Canada* (1930-), served as phonetic adviser for

Webster's New International Dictionary (2nd edition, 1934), chaired the Committee on Pronunciation for the Thorndike-Century dictionaries (1934-46), and edited the synonyms and antonyms for the *American College Dictionary* and the *Thorndike-Barnhart Dictionary* (1944-8). [AMERICAS, BIOGRAPHY, REFERENCE, SPEECH].   R.W.B.

HAPA-HAOLE. See HAWAII PIDGIN ENGLISH.

HARD AND SOFT. (1) Qualities of the letters *c* and *g* that depend on whether they are pronounced like *k* or *s* in the case of *c* or like the *g* in *get* or the *j* in *jet* in the case of *g*. When hard, *c* and *g* are pronounced as velar stops, as in *cap/gap*; when soft, *c* is pronounced as a sibilant, *g* as an affricate, as in *cell/gell*. (2) Popular terms used to describe voice quality, a *hard* voice being forceful and likely to be reinforced by stop consonants (*Damn well tell him to come back tomorrow!*), a *soft* voice being gentle, perhaps kind and compassionate, and likely to be reinforced by sibilants, affricates, fricatives, and liquids (*Hush now; just leave it all to me*). Male voices are often stereotyped as 'hard' and 'rough', female voices as 'soft' and 'gentle'. (3) In phonetics, in the description of consonants, *hard* is an older term for *fortis* (articulated with considerable muscular tension or force of breath or plosion, as with the voiceless consonants of English, such as /p, t, k, s/) and *soft* for *lenis* (articulated with little tension, as with the voiced consonants, such as /b, d, g, z/). See (A)ESTHETICS, C, COMPUTING, G, GENDER BIAS, HARD COPY AND SOFT COPY, HYPHEN, PALATE, SEXISM, SPELLING, VOICE. [SPEECH, STYLE, WRITING]   T.MCA.

HARD COPY AND SOFT COPY [Late 20c: compare *hardware* and *software*]. Contrasting terms in computing and word processing: *hard copy* data in permanent form, printed out on paper by a printer attached to a computer; *soft copy* impermanent data displayed on a screen. Before the advent of computing, *hard copy* was copy ready for printing. See COMPUTING, COPY. [TECHNOLOGY].   T.MCA.

HARD HYPHEN. See HYPHEN.

HARD PALATE. See PALATE, SPEECH.

HARD WORD [17c]. A semi-technical term for a difficult word of foreign origin: *azimuth, hierophant, munificence, perigee, Vedanta*. Early English dictionaries especially in the 17c, that explained such exotic words by means of everyday words came to be known as *hard-word dictionaries*. See BIG WORD, CAWDREY, DICTIONARY, LONG WORD. [REFERENCE, WORD].   T.MCA.

HARDY, Thomas [1840-1928]. English novelist and poet, born at Higher Bockhampton, Dorset, where his father was a stonemason and small builder, and educated in Dorchester and articled to a local architect. In 1862, he moved to London and worked with the fashionable architect Arthur Blomfield, but because of poor health he returned to Dorset in 1867. Continuing to work in architecture, he also began to write and published *Desperate Remedies* (1871), a novel in the sensational manner popular at the time. With *Under the Greenwood Tree* (1872), he found his *métier*, and thereafter his best work dealt with rural life. He created the imaginary world of 'Wessex', based on Dorset and the surrounding counties, in which many of his locations are identifiable. He published 14 novels, including *The Mayor of Casterbridge* (1886), *Tess of the D'Urbervilles* (1891), and *Jude the Obscure* (1896), which was attacked for its attitudes to marriage and orthodox religion. Its reception was partly responsible for Hardy's decision to abandon novels and devote himself to poetry, which he had also been writing for many years. Several volumes of poetry appeared in the 20c, including a long verse-drama *The Dynasts*, set in the Napoleonic period. He received the Order of Merit in 1910.

More than simply a 'regional' writer, Hardy presented the life of the rural world in which he had grown up and preserved the image of a vanished way of life. He was concerned with relationships between men and women, with the frustrations of love and ambition, and the apparent chances and coincidences which shape people's lives. His style is uneven. He could write clear, strong prose and verse which convey the basic emotions and help to make him one of the few truly tragic English novelists. He could also become turgid and pretentious, too fond of abstruse words and elaborate phrases. Yet his power of description, the richness of his vocabulary, and the range of his allusions and imagery pervade his work. A major achievement is the use of dialect. He could capture the tones of Dorset speech, without the elaborately deviant spellings which make the Dorset poems of William Barnes difficult to read, but conveying the distinctive sounds as well as the words and grammar:

' 'Tis not to married couples but to single sleepers that a ghost shows himself when a'do come. One has been seen lately, too. A very strange one.'

'No—don't talk about it if 'tis agreeable of ye not to! 'Twill make my skin crawl when I think of it in bed alone. But you will—ah, you will, I know, Timothy: and I shall dream all night o't! A very strange one? What sort of a spirit did ye mean when ye said a very strange one, Timothy?—no, no—don't tell me.'

'I don't half believe in spirits myself. But I think it ghostly enough—what I was told. 'Twas a little boy that zid it' (from *The Return of the Native*, 1878).

Hardy used dialect for both tragic and comic episodes and varied its intensity to suggest the status of the characters and the degree of their relationship. He valued and defended the dignity of Dorset usage, which he saw not as a deviation from the national standard, but as a survival of the ancient speech of Saxon Wessex. See index. [BIOGRAPHY, EUROPE, LITERATURE, STYLE].   R.C.

HARSH. A pejorative non-technical term for accents and voice qualities regarded as grating on the ear. In the English-speaking world, such languages as Arabic and German as well as some accents of ScoE, northern England, and Northern Ireland have been described as harsh, principally because of sounds made at the back of the mouth, such as glottal stops, uvular *r*, and the velar fricative /x/ in German *Nacht* and Scottish *loch*. See ACCENT, (A)ESTHETICS, BURR, GUTTURAL, NEW ENGLAND, R-SOUNDS, VOICE QUALITY. [SPEECH, STYLE].   T.MCA.

HART'S RULES. See HOUSE STYLE, OXFORD UNIVERSITY PRESS.

HAUSA. See AFRICAN ENGLISH, AFRICAN LANGUAGES, CAMEROON, LINGUA FRANCA, NIGERIA.

HAWAII. An archipelago in the Pacific, since 1959 the 50th state of the United States. Capital Honolulu. Population: 0.96m (1980) (82% in or around Honolulu): Caucasian, Filipino, Japanese, Hawaiian, and other, no ethnic group forming a majority. The first people to reach the islands were Polynesian, over 1,000 years ago. The first European to visit the islands was the British explorer Captain James Cook in 1778, who named them the *Sandwich Islands*, after the Earl of Sandwich. The islanders were organized in a hierarchy of *alii* (nobles), *kahuna* (priests), and people, and were not united until 1810, when King Kamehameha I brought all the islands under his rule and encouraged trade with the US and elsewhere. The *alii* rejected their own system of religion and taboos *c*.1819, American Christian missionaries arrived in 1820, there was a brief British occupation in 1843, the monarchy was overthrown in 1893, and the islands were annexed by the US in 1898. Present-day Hawaii depends mainly on food production and tourism. A plantation system for sugar cane and pineapples was established in the 19c. Its expansion added to the native labour force thousands of workers from China, Korea, the Philippines, Japan, and elsewhere. By the start of the 20c, ethnic Hawaiians, through epidemic diseases and the increase in immigrants, accounted for less than 20% of the population. In the late 20c, there are fewer than 10,000 full-blooded Hawaiians, although there are many part-Hawaiians. Most ethnic Hawaiians now speak English or Hawaii Creole English rather than Hawaiian, though there are attempts to revive the language. Other languages spoken on the islands include Chinese, Japanese, Filipino, Korean, Portuguese, Samoan, and Spanish. English has been the language of education for well over a century and is the administrative and general language of the state. See HAWAIIAN, HAWAIIAN ENGLISH, HAWAII CREOLE ENGLISH, HAWAII PIDGIN ENGLISH, JAPANESE PIDGIN ENGLISH, POLYNESIA, UNITED STATES. [AMERICAS, NAME, OCEANIA]. T.MCA., S.R.

HAWAIIAN. (1) Relating to Hawaii. (2) Someone of indigenous Hawaiian background. (3) A native or resident of the US state of Hawaii, regardless of ethnic background. (4) A Pacific language belonging to the Malayo-Polynesian family and cognate with Samoan and Maori. It has eight consonants, /h, k, l, m, n, p, w/ and the glottal stop, and ten vowels /a, e , i, ɔ, ʊ/ (each long and short). Hawaiian words end in vowels (*lei, kahuna*), consonants are separated by vowels (*Kalakaua, Lapakahi*), and many words have no consonants at all (*aia* there, *oiaio* truly) or more vowels than consonants (*heiau* temple). Among the differences between Hawaiian and some other Polynesian languages are: /k/ for /t/ (*kapu* for *tabu*), /l/ for /r/ (*kalo* for *taro*), a glottal stop where some have /k/, marked in technical writing by a reverse inverted apostrophe (ʻ) and in general usage by an ordinary apostrophe (ʼ) (*muʻumuʻu* or *muʼumuʼu* for *mukumuku* shapeless, a loose-fitting woman's dress). The glottal stop is phonemic and therefore contrastive: *kaʻu* mine, *kau* yours. The sound written as *l* may have been close to /r/. When missionary printers standardized the language in Roman after 1820, they voted six to two in favour of *l*; when the personal name of King Kamehameha II was set in type, he preferred *Liholiho* to *Rihoriho*. Repeating a word base usually has a special meaning: *lau* leaf, *lau-lau* a bundle of food baked in leaves; *pai* slap, *paipai* to drive fish by slapping the water. Borrowings into Hawaiian have generally been adapted to its phonology: *hokela* hotel, *kelepona* telephone, *kula* school, *nupepa* newspaper, *pipi* beef, *puke* book, and such Biblical names as *Apikaila* Abigail, *Kaniela* Daniel, *Malia* Maria, *Kamaki* Thomas. Borrowings from Hawaiian into English are common locally but few in the general language: *aʼa* and *pahoehoe* lava which cools rough and smooth respectively, *ukelele/ ukulele* a jumping flea whose name was given to an adaptation of the Portuguese guitar. See BORROWING, DIALECT IN AMERICA, GLOTTAL

STOP, HAWAII, HAWAIIAN ENGLISH, MALAYO-POLYNESIAN LANGUAGES, MAORI. [AMERICAS, LANGUAGE, NAME, OCEANIA]. T.MCA.

HAWAIIAN ENGLISH. The English language as used in Hawaii. The distinctive features of Hawaiian AmE include words of indigenous origin, their combination with imported words, informal and slang expressions often incorporating elements of Hawaii English Pidgin/Creole, and unique expressions used in giving directions. Widely used words from Hawaiian include: *aloha* love, sympathy (a common form of greeting and farewell), *haole* originally any foreigner, now a Caucasian, *heiau* a traditional temple, *hula* a kind of dance (formerly usually sacred, now mainly performed for tourists), *kane* a man, *kapu* taboo, keep out, *lanai* a porch or patio, *lei* a garland of flowers, seeds, or shells (especially as a token of welcome), *mahalo* thank you, *mahimahi* a dolphin, *mahope* by and by, *pau* finished, *poi* a thick edible taro paste, *pupus* hors d'œuvres, *wahine* a girl, woman, wife, *wikiwiki* hurry up. Hybrid usages include: *the Ala Moana Center, an aloha party, Kalakaua Avenue, a lei-seller, the Kilauea Crater, the Kodak Hula Show, kukui nuts, the Waianae Coast, Waikiki Bar-B-Que House, the Waimea Arboretum.*

Hawaiian English mixes elements of AmE slang and informal usage with elements of Hawaiian, Hawaii English Pidgin/Creole, and other languages, as in: *ala-alas* balls (testicles), *brah* brother, *huddahead* (pejorative) someone from Japan or of Japanese background, *to cockaroach* to steal or sneak away with something, *da kine* that kind (*Wheah da kine?* Where's the whatsit?), *FOB* Fresh off the Boat, *haolefied* becoming like a haole, *JOJ* Just off the Jet, *kapakahi* mixed up (all from Douglas Simonson, *Pidgin to da Max*, Honolulu, 1981). Traditional terms of direction relate to geography, not points of the compass, as with *mauka* towards the mountains, *makai* towards the sea. On Oahu, these are combined with the names of two locations on the southern shore, *Ewa beach* and *Waikiki/Diamond Head*, as in: 'Go *ewa* one block, turn *makai* at the traffic light, go two blocks Diamond Head, and you'll find the place on the *mauka* side of the street' ('Which Way Oahu?', *National Geographic*, Nov. 1979); 'The ewa bound lanes of the H-1 Freeway airport viaduct were closed for hours' (*Honolulu Advertiser*, 27 Mar. 1990). Hawaiian journalists use localisms fairly freely, often with glosses: 'For 1,500 years, a member of the Mookini family has been the kahuna—priest—at an enormous heiau—temple—at Upolu Point in Kohala at the northern tip of the Big Island. For 1,500 years, no one in that unbroken kahuna line has spoken publicly about the family's sacred trust. Now Momi Mookini Lum, current kahuna nui of Mookini Luakini, has broken the silence' (*Honolulu Advertiser*, 4 May 1982). See AMERICAN ENGLISH, HAWAII, HAWAII CREOLE ENGLISH, HAWAII PIDGIN ENGLISH, MAORI ENGLISH, TESD. [AMERICAS, OCEANIA, VARIETY].   T.MCA.

HAWAIIAN PIDGIN. See HAWAII PIDGIN ENGLISH.

HAWAII CREOLE ENGLISH, also **Hawaii English Creole.** An English-based creole that developed for communication among a mixed population on plantations in Hawaii, a continuum from a low-status basilect to a high-status acrolect that has de-creolized. It retains features from the pidgin stage, such as the use of *bambai* (by and by: compare Tok Pisin *baimbai*) to mark future and hypothetical events: *Mai fada dem wen kam ova hia; bambai de wen muv tu Kawai* My father and the others came over here; then they moved to Kauai. The use of *wen* to mark the simple past is a more recent form taken from *went*. There is another, older form *bin* from *been* (compare Tok Pisin *bin*), as in *A bin go see mai fada* I went to see my father. Currently, many speakers use the English past tense auxiliary *had*. The use of *dem* (them) to mark plurals, as in *Stan-dem* Stan and the others, is found in other English-based creoles: for example, Jamaican Creole *Jan dem* John and the others. See CREOLE, HAWAII, HAWAIIAN ENGLISH, HAWAII PIDGIN ENGLISH. [AMERICAS, OCEANIA, VARIETY].   S.R.

HAWAII PIDGIN ENGLISH, also informally **Pidgin.** Although the term *Hawaiian pidgin* has been widely used to refer to the English-based pidgin and creole varieties used in Hawaii, some people of ethnic Hawaiian descent have objected to it because it suggests that Hawaiian rather than English was pidginized. The term *Hawaii Pidgin English* is now generally preferred among scholars and teachers. It may have been a pidginized version of Hawaiian re-lexified with English words and used by the Chinese plantation labourers who took over the cultivation of taro from native Hawaiians. This pidgin was originally known as *olelo pa'i'ai* (pounded but undiluted taro language) and is partially related to one of the earliest forms of English in the islands, *Maritime Pidgin Hawaiian*, which was used between Hawaiians and sailors and traders of various backgrounds, but principally from the US. During the development of a plantation economy in the later 19c, Hawaiians and English-speaking plantation owners communicated in so-called *hapa-haole* (half-foreign), probably foreigner talk rather than a pidgin. The crucial years for formation were 1890 to 1910, when most Chinese, Portuguese, and Japanese arrived. The initial pidgin was unstable and varied considerably, depending on the native language of the speaker. It became stable after the turn of the century, when pidgin-speaking immigrants married and brought up children using it as their primary language. At this stage, it was creolized and is now called *Hawaii Creole English*. See HAWAII, HAWAIIAN ENGLISH, HAWAII CREOLE ENGLISH, PIDGIN. [AMERICAS, OCEANIA, VARIETY].

S.R.

HAZLITT, William [1778–1830]. English essayist, critic, and journalist. Born in Maidstone, Kent, he grew up mainly in Shropshire. He attended a Unitarian training college, at first planning to become a clergyman like his father, but went to London to become a writer. There he met Coleridge and through him other writers. Hazlitt wrote and lectured on art, politics, and society, and was for a time a parliamentary reporter. His greatest influence was in dramatic and literary criticism. His publications include *Characters of Shakespeare's Plays* (1817), *Lectures on the English Poets* (1818), *A View of the English Stage* (1818), *Lectures on the English Comic Writers* (1819), and *The Spirit of the Age* (1825). He shared and promulgated the great Romantic enthusiasm for Shakespeare. Hazlitt was able to separate personal beliefs from literary judgement: for example, he disliked Scott's conservatism but admired him as a writer. He was one of the first to make a career of criticism, combining subjective personal judgements with a wide perspective of English literary history down to his own time. [BIOGRAPHY, EUROPE, LITERATURE].   R.C.

HEAD. See HEADING, RUNNING HEAD.

HEADERS AND FOOTERS [Late 20c]. Terms in word processing that identify information (codes, article titles, page numbers, persons' names) at the *head* (top) and *foot* (bottom) of a page. A *running header/footer* is text printed at the head or foot of every page. Compare RUNNING HEAD. [TECHNOLOGY, WRITING].   T.MCA.

HEADING [13c]. Also **head.** Words at the head (beginning) of a text, serving as a title for a page, section of a page, chapter, section of a chapter, article, section of an article, etc. A heading placed under another heading is a *subheading* or *subhead.* Compare CAPTION, HEADLINE, HEADWORD, MASTHEAD, RUBRIC, TITLE. [MEDIA, WRITING].   T.MCA.

HEADLINE [17c: probably from the headline on a sailing ship, a rope which held a sail tight to a spar or ran along the upper edge of a flag to strengthen it: compare MASTHEAD]. A heading, usually in large, heavy type, at the top of an article in a newspaper, magazine, or other publication, indicating the subject of the article.

Origin and development. At first, the *headline* was a printer's term for the top line of any page of print. In early journalism, it was not usually set apart from the rest of the copy by any typographical convention, but in the earliest surviving news pamphlet, issued by Richard Faques on the Battle of Flodden (1513), a rudimentary headline is separated from the main copy, being set above the woodcut depicting the battle. It runs: *In whiche batayle the Scottishe Kynge was slayne.* Although there are instances of headlines in the 17-18c, there was no continuous practice of headlining and many momentous events were not given this form of emphasis. Initially, headlines stayed within the boundaries of print columns. They were set out in 'steps' down the page, each set in different type and devoted to a different aspect of the story. In 1865, the *New York Herald* covered the assassination of President Lincoln with 17 such steps. The technique was used in Britain by Edward Levy Lawson, when he revived the *Daily Telegraph* in the 1860s, and by W. T. Stead, when he became editor of the *Pall Mall Gazette* in 1881. Present-day headlines (set across columns, brief, and often sensational) were an American innovation in the late 19c, part of the yellow journalism of the 'circulation war' between Joseph Pulitzer and William Randolph Hearst. By 1900, *banner headlines* (set in capitals) and *streamer headlines* (set in lower case) had been introduced.

Headlinese. Constraints on space affect the language of headlines, sometimes known (in its more extreme forms) as *headlinese*. It has developed from more or less conventional syntax to increasingly brief, generalized, powerful, and cryptic units. Particularly in the banner headlines of the tabloid press, the vocabulary has tended to consist of short, emotive, and suggestive words, often metaphors of violence, such as *axe, clash, cut, hit, oust, slam, slate,* and 'broad-spectrum' words such as *ban, bid, boost, call, curb, link, probe, riddle, scare, swoop, vow.* Since early headlines were set in steps or decks down the page, there was little constraint on vocabulary and it was possible for complex sentences to be broken up, as in this 17c instance:

Two Great
Battailes
Very Lately Fought
The one betwene Count Mansfield and Don
    Cordua the Spanish Generall,
since his arrival in Brabant wherein Don Cordua was
    defeated,

And the Duke of Brunswicke behaved himself most valiantly, having three horses slaine under him.
    (Weekly News, 2 Sept. 1622)

Words of 'high' register were once often on display, as in this series reporting Napoleon's defeat at the Battle of Leipzig:

Most Glorious News.
Bonaparte in Full Retreat, Cutting His Way
Towards The Rhine—
A Series of Sanguinary Battles.
Despatches From Lord Wellington.
Bonaparte's Utter Discomfiture.
    (Morning Post, 1813)

Such victories often unleash patriotic and emotive language, as in the following reference to the Relief of Mafeking, during the Boer War:

SHALL THEIR GLORY FADE?
HISTORY'S MOST HEROIC DEFENCE ENDS IN
    TRIUMPH
THE BOERS' LAST GRIP LOOSENED
MAFEKING AND BADEN-POWELL'S
    GALLANT BAND SET FREE.
    (Daily Express, 19 May 1900)

Layout and punctuation. Although, by and large, banner headlines continue to be popular, styles vary and many newspapers have sedate, largely lower-case styles: the *International Herald Tribune,* with initial capitals on main parts of speech (*For a Day, Pro Football Goes Global in Tokyo and London*); the *Independent,* with an opening initial capital, apart from proper names (*Sex abuse dispute children go home*). Punctuation, once the same as for prose, has been exploited in special conventions, notably among the tabloids: the exclamatiom mark used to generate interest (*MR K! DON'T BE SO BLOODY RUDE!*); the question mark implying speculation or doubt (*ELECTION PACT?*); both creating a visual shout (*Dogs! Dontcha hate 'em?!*). The comma is increasingly used for *and*: *PETROL, BUTTER PRICE HIKE; POUND'S FALL, PM TO ACT.* Conventional punctuation marks may be ignored: *I'm innocent says blast jet woman* (*Observer,* 6 Apr. 1986). Within a headline, quotes mark a statement or allegation from which the newspaper distances itself: *Union opposed to 'liquor police'* (Montreal *Gazette,* 14 Apr. 1983).

Style and syntax. Whereas the quality press tends to be relatively sober and restrained, using 'high' register and less immediately emotive words (*Uzbekistan Shocked by the Socialist Heroes Who Lived Like Lords:* IHT, 8 Oct. 1988), the tabloids prefer 'low', colloquial, often pejorative usage (*The Floozy, Fatso and the Fall Guy: Daily Mirror,* 8 Feb. 1989). Present-day usage tends to string terms together in concentrated (often opaque) sequences: *Fodor, Ex-Violin Prodigy, Starts Paying the Piper* (IHT, 7 Aug. 1989); *Gov't to up taxes on urban farm land* (*Japan Times,*

19 May 1987); *Fox on up up up* (*Observer*, 14 Aug. 1988). Such strings often entail heavy pre-modification (*Deadlock over Anglo-Irish EEC cash bid*: *Independent*, 9 Oct. 1986) and the completely pre-modified *STRIKE BAN SHOCK PROBE*. Abbreviations are common: *Gandhi Assails U.S. on Pakistani N-Arms* (*IHT*, 13 Sept. 1986).

Ambiguity and other effects. Dense headlinese often demands a second reading, because of strange combinations and unintended sense relations: *Payphone revamp plan to cost BT £23 million* (*Guardian*, 11 Mar. 1987); *Blue jean robbery victim legs it after trouser thieves* (Montreal *Gazette*, 30 Nov. 1982). Some headlines are ambiguous until the text has been read: *SLAVE ENDANGERED TREASURE, SAY DAM CRITICS* (Montreal *Gazette*, 25 Aug. 1982) refers not to a bondsman but to the Slave River in Alberta, a stretch of which is regarded as a treasure. The ambiguity can at times be funny: *WOMEN'S BODY SEEKS MEMBER* (Montreal *Gazette*, 30 July 1981); *Bill banning promotion of homosexuality founders* (*Independent*, 9 May 1987). Two possible readings can also serve to embarrass a newspaper: *AMNESTY CHAMPIONS TORTURED GIRL* (*Observer*, 13 Oct. 1985). Word-play is common (*Basquing in glory*: *Independent*, 11 June 1988, about holidays in the Basque Country); *SAVAGE DEFENCE* (*Guardian*, 20 Feb. 1986), with the text 'Obstetrician Wendy Savage yesterday attacked male colleagues' intolerance of differing childbirth methods.' Allusions and word-play are also common (*US poaches our eggheads*: *Observer*, 19 July 1987), as well as mixed metaphors (*Labour's last-ditch stand will go off with a bang*: *Independent*, 29 Nov. 1986). Occasionally, newspapers parody themselves with such attention-grabbers as *Sex-change bishop in mercy dash to Palace* (headline of article on headlines, *Observer*, 24 Mar. 1985). Relevant publications include: Harold Evans, *Newspaper Headlines* (Rinehart & Winston, 1973) and Heinrich Straumann, *Newspaper Headlines* (Allen & Unwin, 1935). See ACRONYM, ALLUSION, AMBIGUITY, HEADING, JOURNALESE, TIMESPEAK. [MEDIA, STYLE]. G.H., T.MCA.

HEADLINESE. See HEADLINE.

HEADWORD [1810s]. A main or key word set at the beginning of a line, list, or paragraph, sometimes used in contrast to *subword*, a word listed under it or included after it. The term is commonly used for the title of an article in a dictionary, also called a *main entry* (contrasting with a *sub-entry*). Headwords in works of reference function as both markers for finding articles and the topics of the articles themselves. In a dictionary, a headword with more than one spelling (*aeon, eon*) or form (*give, gives, giving, gave, given*) gets its primary article at the main spelling (*aeon*) or base form (*give*); other spellings or forms (*eon, gave*) may head secondary articles with cross-references to the primary article. A single spelling may represent more than one homonymous headword, so that articles may be distinguished by superscript numbers: ^1bear *n.*, ^2bear *v.*, or $bear^1$ *n.*, $bear^2$ *v.* Conversely, a single polysemous headword may have more than one sense: ^2bear *v. 1:* carry, *2:* give birth to. Furthermore, a headword may introduce an article giving information about other words and phrases containing it; thus, the article about *give* may include *giver* as a sub-entry. Because dictionaries vary in what they consider headwords, a phrasal verb such as *give up* is a headword in some dictionaries but a sub-entry at *give* in others, while a compound such as *blackbird* may be a headword, a sub-entry at *black*, or a sub-entry at *bird*, or both. See CANONICAL FORM, ENTRY, HEADING, KEY WORD, LEMMA. [REFERENCE, WORD]. R.F.I., T.MCA.

HEAVY. (1) A general term implying weight or excess (*heavy emphasis, heavy irony*) and dullness (*a heavy style*). (2) A semi-technical term for a stressed syllable in English and a syllable with a long vowel in Latin: *one heavy and two light syllables*. (3) An informal pejorative term for accents and voice qualities: 'Whether this was due to a foul-up in translation, a bad phone connection or the heavy accent of the translator is not known' (*Washington Post* editorial, Nov. 1985). Such heaviness may relate to low pitch, unfamiliar sounds, and voice quality, especially if foreign. Compare HARD AND SOFT, HARSH. (4) In the plural, an informal term in BrE for serious broadsheet newspapers: *the Sunday heavies*. See (A)ESTHETICS. [LITERATURE, MEDIA, SPEECH, STYLE]. T.MCA.

HEBRAISM [16c: from Greek *Hebraïsmós*]. An expression or construction typical of the Hebrew language, found in another language: in English *behemoth, cherub, leviathan, shibboleth* are Hebraisms. See HEBREW, -ISM, JEWISH ENGLISH. [ASIA, STYLE, VARIETY, WORD]. T.MCA., S.S.

HEBREW [Before 10c: Old English *Ebrēas*, Middle English *Ebreu, Hebreu*, from Latin *Hebraeus*, Greek *Hebraîos*, Aramaic *'Ibhraij*]. The Semitic language of the ancient Israelites and modern Israel, closely related to Aramaic and Phoenician, more distantly to Arabic. Hebrew is one of the oldest living languages, best known as the language of the Hebrew or Jewish Bible. In Biblical times, it was called *yehudit* (Jewish) and in post-Biblical rabbinic literature *lashon* *kodesh* (Holy Tongue). Scholars divide it historically into four phases: *Biblical Hebrew* (*c*.12c BC-*c*.AD 70), *Mishnaic Hebrew* (*c*.AD 70–500), *Medieval Hebrew* (6–13c), and *Modern Hebrew* (from the late 19c). The fourth phase is known to its speakers as *ivrit*, a revived form developed chiefly in Palestine by European Jewish settlers, especially after 1880. It became the predominant language of the state of Israel after 1948 and with Arabic is one of its official languages. It is often referred to as *Israeli Hebrew*. The alphabet consists of 22 letters, all consonants. Hebrew is written from right to left with or without vowel signs above and below the consonants. Currently, it has about 4m speakers, most of whom live in Israel.

Hebrew in English. (1) Because of the influence of Bible translations, there have been words and names of Hebrew origin in English since Anglo-Saxon times. They include *amen, babel, behemoth, camel, cherub, gehenna, leviathan, manna, rabbi, Sabbath, shekel, shibboleth*. (2) A number of religious and cultural terms were introduced during the Renaissance through the works of scholars, such as *Cabbala* 1521, *Talmud* 1532, *Sanhedrin* 1588, *Mishnah* 1610, *mezuzah* 1650. (3) Since the 19c, Yiddish has been an indirect source of Hebraisms, by and large colloquialisms such as *kosher* ritually fit, all right, satisfactory, legitimate, *mazuma* money, cash, *shamus* a policeman, detective, *chutzpah* impudence, gall, *goy* a gentile, *megillah* a long story. (4) During the 20c, terms from Modern Hebrew, used mainly by English-speaking Jews, include *kibbutz* a collective Israeli farming community, *hora* a Romanian and Israeli round dance, *moshav* a cooperative Israeli farming community, *sabra* a native-born Israeli, *aliya* Jewish immigration to Israel, *Knesset* the Israeli parliament.

English in Hebrew. The lexical and semantic influence of English on Israeli Hebrew has been considerable. During British rule in Palestine (1917–48), English was an official language. Following the establishment of Israel in 1948, the influence of English on Hebrew continued through American Jewish immigration, various English-language periodicals (notably the *Jerusalem Post*), and English-language motion pictures and television programmes (though most are subtitled in Hebrew). Generally, BrE is the dominant influence, as with *karavan* (a light mobile home) not AmE *trailer*, and *tships* (chips) not *french fries*, but AmE is becoming increasingly popular and includes such colloquialisms as *okey* OK, *hay* Hi, and *bay-bay* bye-bye. See ARAMAIC, BIBLE, HAMITO-SEMITIC LANGUAGES, ISRAEL, JEWISH ENGLISH, JEWISH LANGUAGES, S(C)HWA. [ASIA, LANGUAGE].   S.S.

HEBRIDEAN ENGLISH. See HIGHLAND ENGLISH.

HEINEMANN. A British publishing company founded by William Heinemann in London in 1890. He commissioned translations of foreign literature (including Zola, Maupassant, and Ibsen) and Constance Garnett's translations of Tolstoy, Turgenev, and Dostoevsky, on which Virginia Woolf observed: '[Her] translations were a crucial influence on the novel, for after reading *Crime and Punishment* and *The Idiot*, how could any young novelist believe in characters as the Victorians painted them?' (*Nation*, 1 Dec. 1923). Heinemann established an *International Library* series with translations from Norwegian, Russian, French, German, Spanish, and Italian authors, and a 15-volume study of foreign-language literature that included Arabic, Bohemian, Chinese, Hungarian, Japanese, and Sanskrit. The company introduced a British readership to the works of the American writers Henry James, Upton Sinclair, Jack London, and Stephen Crane, while maintaining a list of such British authors as Stevenson, Conrad, Wells, Galsworthy, Somerset Maugham, Kipling, and Lawrence. In 1912, Heinemann collaborated with the US publisher James Loeb in producing the *Loeb Classical Library* of Greek and Latin texts with parallel translations.

Despite difficulties for some years after Heinemann's death in 1920, the firm added to its list such authors as J. B. Priestley, Graham Greene, Noël Coward, John Steinbeck, the Australian novelist Henry Handel Richardson, and the Indian poet Sarojini Naidu. After the Second World War, the *New Windmill* series of reprints of older and modern classics was published, many adapted for children; by 1986, more than 300 titles had been published, with sales of over 20m copies to schools in Britain and abroad. The series introduced children to such writers as Doris Lessing, George Orwell, Henry James, H. G. Wells, and Ernest Hemingway. The *African Writers* and *Caribbean Writers* series published works in English by authors in developing nations, including such writers as Chinua Achebe and Ngugi wa Thiong'o, helping to maintain a tradition of written English where political changes might have threatened its survival. Heinemann has also published Anthony Powell (including the 12 volumes of the *Music of Time* sequence, 1951–75), Paul Scott (*The Raj Quartet*, 1966–75), Anthony Burgess, whose *A Clockwork Orange* (1962) introduced the futuristic Anglo-Russian vernacular called *Nadsat*, and Douglas Adams, whose *Hitch Hiker's Guide to the Galaxy: A Trilogy in Four Parts* (1979) has also had versions on radio and television. After several changes in ownership, Heinemann was taken over in 1985 by the Octopus Group, which merged with Reed International in 1987. See AFRICAN LITERATURE IN ENGLISH, BRITISH PUBLISHING. [EUROPE, MEDIA].   T.MCA.

HELPING VERB [19c]. An informal term for auxiliary verb, the class of verbs (such as *be*, *have*, *do*, *may*, *will*) that may combine with a following main verb to form a verb phrase, such as *is watching*, *has eaten*, *may have been playing*. See VERB. [GRAMMAR].   S.G.

HEMPL, George [1859-1921]. American philologist, born in Whitewater, Wisconsin, and educated at the U. of Michigan. After serving as a high-school principal in Michigan and Indiana and a lecturer in German at Johns Hopkins U., he spent several years at Berlin, Göttingen, Strasbourg, and Tübingen before receiving his Ph.D. at Jena (1889). Influenced by Eduard Sievers and Ernst Haeckel, he developed a scientific approach to language study. On his return to the US, he taught at Michigan (1889-1906), where in 1897 he became Professor of English Philology and General Linguistics. From 1907 until his death he was Professor of Germanic Philology at Stanford. Hempl's main interests were the etymology, meaning, usage, and pronunciation of early and modern English words. Many of his 150 scholarly works deal with the development of English sounds and phonological change, including *Old English Phonology* (1892) and *Chaucer's Pronunciation* (1893). As phonological editor for the Lippincott foreign-language dictionaries and the Hinds, Noble, and Eldredge Uniform International Dictionaries, he influenced the pronunciation of English learned by scholars throughout Europe by choosing his own rhotic pronunciation, an implicit statement that this was standard AmE rather than the non-rhotic pronunciation of Boston, New York, or Charleston. An advocate of spelling reform and a member of the *Simplified Spelling Board*, he used phonetic spelling in his correspondence and eliminated an unsounded final *e* from his own surname. Among the first researchers into AmE dialects, he collected a vast amount of material on vocabulary, usage, and pronunciation. He was president of the Modern Language Association (1903), the American Philological Association (1904), and the American Dialect Society (1901-5). [AMERICAS, BIOGRAPHY, LANGUAGE, SPEECH, WRITING].   R.W.B.

HENDIADYS [16c: from Latin *hendiadys*, Greek *hèn dià duoîn* one through two. Stress: 'hen-DIE-a-diss']. A term in rhetoric for equal words joined by *and*, instead of one word with a modifier (*nice and warm* rather than *nicely warm*), and similar words joined by *and* where

one might have been enough, usually for emphasis, sometimes for phonaesthetic effect (*gloom and doom*). [STYLE].   T.MCA.

HEPTARCHY [16c: from Latin *heptarchia*, from Greek *heptá* seven, *árkhein* to rule]. The seven kingdoms into which Anglo-Saxon England was apparently divided, 7-9c: the Angle kingdoms of Northumbria, Mercia, and East Anglia, the Saxon kingdoms of Essex, Sussex, and Wessex, and the Jute kingdom of Kent. See MERCIA, NORTHUMBRIA, WESSEX. [EUROPE, HISTORY].   T.MCA.

HERITAGE LANGUAGE [Late 20c]. In Canada, a language other than English and French officially recognized as culturally important to a national minority, whether it is indigenous (such as *Ojibwa* or *Inuktitut*) or immigrant (such as *Italian* or *Ukrainian*): 'The Modern Language Centre of the Ontario Institute for Studies in Education (OISE) is a major Research and Development Centre concerned with the theory and practice of second and heritage language learning and teaching' (advertisement, *TESL Canada Journal*, Nov. 1990). Compare COMMUNITY LANGUAGE. [AMERICAS, LANGUAGE].   T.MCA.

HETEROGRAPH. See HETERONYM, SPELLING.

HETERONYM [1880s: from Greek *heterónumos* other-named]. Also **heterograph**. A word that is spelt the same as another, but has a different meaning and often pronunciation. There are seven heteronyms in the following passage: 'Heteronyms must incense foreign learners! I can't imagine a number feeling than if they spent hours learning a common English word, a minute little word, then found a second meaning and pronunciation! Surely agape could not be a foreigner's emotion as he or she becomes frustrated with our supply textured English words, which, we must admit, can be garbage and refuse to be defined' (opening to 'Heteronyms', David Bergeron, *English Today* 24, Oct. 1990). A heteronym that is spelt the same as another word and has a different pronunciation is a *heterophone* (such as *bow* meaning 'knot' and *bow* meaning 'front of ship', and *number* meaning 'numeral', as opposed to *number* meaning 'more numb'). See HOMONYM, -ONYM, SPELLING. [WORD, WRITING].   T.MCA.

HETEROPHONE. See HETERONYM. Compare HOMOPHONE.

HIBERNIA [Probably a Latinization of *Iverna*, from Old Celtic *Iveriu, influenced by *hibernus* winter: compare EIRE]. A formal name for

Ireland. The adjective *Hibernian* is commoner: *the Ancient Order of Hibernians*, a Catholic men's association dedicated to preserving Irish traditions. [EUROPE, NAME].　　　　T.MCA.

HIBERNIANISM, HIBERNICISM. See IRISHISM.

HIBERNO- [1820s: from Latin *Hibernia* Ireland]. A combining form meaning *Irish*, as in *Hiberno-Celtic*, referring to the Celts of Ireland, and *Hiberno-English*, a form of IrE. See HIBERNIA. [EUROPE, NAME].　　　　T.MCA.

HIBERNO-ENGLISH. A variety of English in Ireland, used mainly by less educated speakers whose ancestral tongue was Irish Gaelic. It is strongest in and around the Gaeltachts (Irish-speaking regions) and in rural areas. It preserves certain Gaelic features in pronunciation, syntax, and vocabulary while at the same time many of its speakers approximate to the Anglo-Irish or Ulster Scots norms of the area in which they live.

Pronunciation. (1) Such words as *cat* and *garden* sound like 'kyat' and 'gyarden': initial /k/ and /g/ with a following semi-vowel /j/. (2) Such names as *Hugh* and *Hughes* sound as if they began with a 'ky'. (3) Such words as *true*, *drew* sound like 'threw' amd 'dhrew': dental rather than alveolar realizations of /t, d/. (4) In such words as *pine*, *time*, *come*, the opening consonant is aspirated, the /t/ in *time* sounding like a cross between *t* and the *th* in *three*: aspiration of syllable-initial /p, t, k/. (5) Some Gaelic rhythms include the use of an unstressed initial word in questions: *An' do you like it?*; *An' was it nice?* The unstressed word is usually *and*, but *well* and *sure* also occur. In Gaelic, questions normally begin with an unstressed element, which in the present tense is *an*: *An maith leat é? Do you like it?*

Grammar. Gaelic influence may be found in: (1) A preference for nominal structures: *Give her the full of it* Fill it; *He has a long finger on him* He steals. (2) Constructions with preposition and pronoun together: *His back's at him* He has a backache; *She stole my book on me* She stole my book; *I let a squeal out of me* I squealed. (3) Using *it* to foreground words and phrases: *It's a lovely girl she is now*; *It wasn't to make trouble I went.* (4) Foregrounding emphatic pronouns: *It's meself was the brave runner*, *It was himself I wanted.* (5) Differentiating singular and plural *you*: *You're dead bate, child*; *Yiz is dead bate, childer* You are dead beat (child/children). (6) Using forms of *be* to distinguish aspect: *She's a great wee help about the place*; *She biz a brave help when she comes*; *She doesn't be working all the time.* (7) Using *after* and *-ing* to indicate a recently performed action: *I'm after doing it this very minute.* (8) Using *a-* and *-ing* as a passive: *Where were you? You were a-looking* (being looked for) *this last hour and more.* (9) Using *and*, noun phrase, and *-ing* to show that two actions happen at the same time: *I went in and me trembling*; *In he walks and him whistling.* (10) Using traditional idioms: *She's as light on her foot as a cat at milking*; *There's a truth in the last drop in the bottle.* (11) Referring to God and religion: *In the name of God, did I rare an eejit?* (did I rear an idiot?). (12) Tending not to use *yes* and *no* in answering questions. Irish has no words for *yes/no* and many Irish people therefore tend to answer, for example, *Will you go?—I will*; *Is it yours?—It is not.* (13) Favouring emphatic forms such as *at all at all*, often rhythmic equivalents of Gaelic forms, such as *I'm not tired at all at all* (from *Níl mé tuirseach ar chor ar bith*). The emphatic *at all at all* also occurs in Highland English and the Canadian Atlantic provinces.

Vocabulary. Nouns retained from Irish often relate to food (*boxty* a potato dish, from *bacstaidh* mashed potato) and the supernatural (*banshee* a fairy woman, from *bean sidhe* a woman fairy). Others are: *kitter* a left-handed or clumsy person (from *citeóg*), *mass* respect (from *meas*), as in *I've no mass in them things now*, *smig* chin (from *smeig*), as in *It was a blow to the smig that felled him.* Gaelic influence on meanings can be seen in words such as *destroy* and *drenched*. These have the semantic ranges of their Gaelic equivalents *mill* to injure, spoil (*He has the child destroyed with presents*) and *báite* drenched, drowned, very wet (*You're drowned child. Get off you. There's not a dry inch to your clothes*). See HIGHLAND ENGLISH, IRISH ENGLISH, NEWFOUNDLAND ENGLISH. [EUROPE, VARIETY].　　　L.T.

HIGH AND LOW LANGUAGES. See CLASSICAL LANGUAGE, DIGLOSSIA, LECT.

HIGHLAND ENGLISH. The English language as used in areas of the Scottish Highlands where Gaelic was spoken until the late 19c or later, and the Hebrides or Western Isles, where many still have Gaelic as their mother tongue. The varieties of these two areas have also been distinguished as *Highland English* and *Hebridean English* (sometimes *Island English*). Since the late 17c, the majority of the inhabitants of the Highlands and Islands have learned standard English by the book, mostly from Gaelic-speaking Highland or Hebridean teachers, only some of whom had studied in Inverness or the Lowlands. The consequent influence of Gaelic is widespread, but most strongly marked among the bilingual speakers of the Isles. It varies in detail with the underlying Gaelic dialect and is also variously influenced from Lowland Scots. Some features, of grammar especially, from the Gaelic substrate are shared with Hiberno-English.

Pronunciation. (1) Corresponding to the opposition between voiced and voiceless stops in English, Gaelic opposes voiceless unaspirated to voiceless aspirated stops, and lacks voiced consonants opposed to /s/ and /ʃ/. This has led to 'reversal of voicing', as in 'chust' for *just*, 'pleashure' for *pleasure*, 'whateffer' for *whatever*, 'pring' for *bring*, and more rarely the converse, as in 'baratice' for *paradise*. These usages are shibboleths of Gaelic-influenced speech. (2) 'Pre-aspiration' of voiceless stops is widespread: the insertion of an /h/ before certain consonants, as in 'weeʰk' for *week*, 'haʰpen' for *happen*, 'abouʰt' for *about*. (3) The same consonants are aspirated word-initially: 'pʰig' for *pig*, 'tʰake' for *take*, 'kʰeep' for *keep*. (4) In the Hebrides, /l/ is commonly clear. (5) Many speakers pronounce vowels long that are short in ScoE generally: for example, in *bad, father, parlour, psalm, brainy, make, table, equal, heat, leak, weak, boat*. (6) As in the Lowlands and Ireland, some speakers realize such words as *film* and *worm* with epenthetic vowels: 'fillum' and 'wurrum'.

Grammar. The following features are characteristic: (1) Cleft sentences and other constructions with thematic fronting: *Isn't it her that's the smart one? Isn't she smart?*; *It's led astray you are by the keeping of bad company*; *From Liverpool he was writing*. (2) Simple verb tenses instead of perfect forms: *I'm a widow for ten years now*; *All my life I never went to the mainland*. (3) Progressive constructions: *Don't be learning bad English to the bairn*; *We were having plenty vegetables that year*; *If you can be waiting till the morning, our sale will be starting then*. (4) Distinctive modal usages in conditional and temporal clauses, including 'double *would*': *Try and get here before the rain will come*; *It's a poor crop we'll be having if there won't be more rain in it*; *If she would know about it, she would be over straight away*. (5) The formula *to be after doing* (something), replacing the regular perfect or past: *I'm after taking the bus* I have just taken the bus; *That's me just after cleaning it up* I've just this minute cleaned it up. (6) *Doesn't* in all persons and numbers: *I doesn't know*; *They doesn't bother*. (7) Non-reflexive use of *-self*: *It's glad I am to be seeing yourself*; *I'll tell himself you are here*; *Herself will not be too pleased at that*. (8) Sentence-initial *sure*: *Sure, it'll spoil the taste of it*. (9) Double plurals, especially where the plural is irregular: *Many peoples are coming every year*; *Three womens did the work*. (10) Singular forms for normally plural words: *She had a trouser on*; *He cut it with the scissor*. (11) Anticipatory pronoun constructions, especially in questions:

Who is he, the man? Did you see him, the minister? (12) Elliptical sentence responses replacing or supplementing *yes* and *no*: *Did Iain give you the letter?—He did*; *Is Morag coming?—She is not*; *Did you get the job finished?—Ay, we did/so we did*.

Vocabulary and idiom. In general, vocabulary is the same as in ScoE at large, and most people use such vernacular Scots words as *bairn* child, *brae* slope, *greet* weep, *oot* out, the negatives *no* (*He's no in*) and *-na* (*I canna say*), and *ay* yes. Many Gaelic words are freely used by Gaelic-speakers and some by non-Gaelic-speakers: *athair* father, *baile* village, *balach* lad, *bodach* old man, *bothan* shebeen, *caileag* young girl, *cailleach* old woman, wife, *duine bochd* poor fellow, *ropach* messy, *srúbag* a drink. Gaelic terms of address, vocatives, and salutations are common among Gaelic-speakers: *m'eudail, mo ghraid*, my dear, *A Chaluim* Calum!, *A Mhammi* Mummy!, *beannachd leat/leibh* goodbye, *oidhche mhath* good night, *tapadh leat* thank you; *slàinte, slàinte mhath, slàinte mhór* health, good health, big health (all three known and used throughout Scotland as toasts). English and Gaelic may be casually mixed: *Geordie m'eudail, come oot till ye see the ronnags* (stars); *I have the cadal-eunain* (pins and needles) *in my fingers*. The preposition *on* features in a number of idioms: *The minister has a terrible cold on him*; *That beast has a wild look on it*; *They're putting on him that he stole the sheep*; *It's on himself the stairn* (confidence) *is*.

Literary usage. In Lowland Scottish literature, a suspect tradition that dates from the mid-15c features such Highland shibboleths as the use of *she* and *her nain sell* (her own self) instead of the pronoun *I*: 'Her nainsell has eaten the town pread at the Cross o' Glasgow, and py her troth she'll fight for Bailie Sharvie at the Clachan of Aberfoil' (Walter Scott, *Rob Roy*, 1817, ch. 28). [Translation: I have eaten the town bread at Glasgow Cross and by my troth I'll fight for Bailie Jarvie at the Clachan of Aberfoyle.] Other representations display genuine Highland features, sometimes profusely, as in: 'I don't know what you'll get that you'll be foreffer in Iain Beag's shop. . . . The folk that will be gathering there on nights iss not the company I would be choossing for a son of mine' (Fionn MacColla, *The Albannach*, 1932; Reprographia, 1971). Compare HIBERNO-ENGLISH, ISLE OF MAN, WELSH ENGLISH. See GAELIC, SCOTTISH ENGLISH, SCOTTISH GAELIC. [EUROPE, VARIETY].　　A.J.A.

HILLBILLY, also **hill-billy,** formerly **hilly-billy** [1890s]. A generally condescending and offensive, but occasionally humorous term for a white person from a mountainous and rural ('back-woods') area in the south-eastern US. It is sometimes used in relation to varieties of English spoken by the mountain people of the Southeast. The term *hillbilly music* is sometimes used for the style more commonly known as *country and western (music)*. See APPALACHIAN ENGLISH, DIALECT IN AMERICA, SOUTHERN ENGLISH. [AMERICAS, NAME].   T.MCA.

HILL SOUTHERN. See SOUTHERN ENGLISH.

HINDI. An Indo-Aryan language, spoken by over 250m people in India and by Indians in Britain, Canada, Fiji, Guyana, South Africa, Surinam, Trinidad, the US, and elsewhere. Hindi is the official language of India, with English as associate official language, the state language of Bihar, Haryana, Himachal Pradesh, Madhya Pradesh, Rajasthan, and Uttar Pradesh, and one of India's 15 major languages. It is written in a modified form of the Devanagari script, and its literary tradition dates from medieval times. Hindi proper has three stylistic varieties: a Sanskritized variety used in higher law courts, administration, legislation, journalism, literature, philosophy, and religion; a Persianized variety used in lower law courts, in certain genres of literature, and in films; an Anglicized variety in day-to-day administration, on college campuses, and in scientific and technical registers. See BORROWING, BRITISH LANGUAGES, COCKNEY, CODE-MIXING AND CODE SWITCHING, FIJI, GUYANA, HINDI-URDU, HINDLISH/HINGLISH, INDIA, INDIAN ENGLISH[1], INDIAN LANGUAGES, MOTION PICTURE, SOUTH AFRICA, SOUTH AFRICAN INDIAN ENGLISH, SOUTH AFRICAN LANGUAGES, SURINAM(E), TRINIDAD AND TOBAGO. [ASIA, LANGUAGE].   Y.K.

HINDI-URDU. A composite name that emphasizes the common linguistic features of Hindi and Urdu, languages that have the same general pronunciation, grammar, and vocabulary, but differ in their script, Hindi being written in Devanagari, Urdu in Perso-Arabic. They differ largely because of politics and religion in the Indian subcontinent: Hindi generally favoured by Hindus, Urdu by Muslims. Hindi is the official language of India, Urdu the national language of Pakistan. Both have been extensively influenced by other languages, but whereas Hindi looks especially to Sanskrit for its technical vocabulary and literary conventions, Urdu looks especially to Persian and Arabic. Both have borrowed extensively from English. See HINDI, HINDUSTANI, INDIA, INDIAN LANGUAGES, URDU. [ASIA, LANGUAGE].   Y.K.

HINDLISH, also **Hinglish** [Later 20c: blends of *Hindi* and *English*]. Informal terms for a mixture of Hindi and English that includes such hybrid expressions as *city kotwali* (city police station) and *relgari* (railway train), and complete sentences such as *Mãĩ āp ko batātī huṁ, he is a very trusting person* I tell you, he is a very trusting person. See CODE-MIXING AND CODE-SWITCHING, -GLISH AND -LISH, HINDI, INDIAN ENGLISH[1]. [ASIA, VARIETY].   B.B.K.

HINDUSTANI. A demotic form of Hindi-Urdu that exhibits strong English influence. Although M. K. Gandhi advocated its adoption as the national language of India, and the Indian National Congress adopted it as the symbol of national unity in 1925, it never became a language of literature, academia, or journalism. After independence in 1947, it lost its status to Hindi in India and Urdu in Pakistan. See AMERICAN ENGLISH AND BRITISH ENGLISH, HINDI-URDU. [ASIA, LANGUAGE].   Y.K.

HIRI MOTU. An indigenous pidgin and lingua franca of Papua New Guinea, and a co-official language with Tok Pisin and English. It is based on the Austronesian language Motu, originally spoken around the Port Moresby area (now the National Capital District). A greatly reduced variety of Motu was employed on trading expeditions (*hiri*) along the Papuan Gulf. The language is used by some 10% of the people, mainly in Papua. It was once called *Police Motu*, because of its association with the colonial police force; it seems likely, however, that the lingua franca of this multilingual force was pidgin English and that a restructured and simplified Motu was used for dealing with the local people. See PAPUA NEW GUINEA/NIUGINI, TOK PISIN. [LANGUAGE, OCEANIA].   S.R.

HISPANIC [16c: from Latin *Hispanicus* Spanish. The first sense has an initial capital; the second may or may not]. (1) Associated with the languages and traditions of Spain and the Spanish-speaking countries of the world: *Hispanic civilization*. (2) A person of Spanish-language background in the US, long established in such states of the Southwest as New Mexico and Arizona, or of Cuban, Mexican, Puerto Rican, or other Caribbean or Latin American origin (*local Hispanics*); of anything associated with such a person (*hispanic cuisine*). See CHICANO, LATINO, SPANGLISH, TEX-MEX. [AMERICAS, NAME].   J.AM., T.MCA.

HISTORICAL LINGUISTICS, also **diachronic linguistics**. The branch of linguistics that deals with changes in language through time. Like philology, from whose later forms it is virtually indistinguishable, it studies language records, but may also include methods of synchronic linguistics in its approach to sounds, forms, meanings, or the social motivation of language change. See DIACHRONIC AND SYNCHRONIC, PHILOLOGY. [HISTORY, LANGUAGE].   W.F.B.

HISTORICAL SEMANTICS [20c]. In linguistics, the study of changes in meaning with the passage of time. See SEMANTIC CHANGE. [HISTORY, LANGUAGE].   T.MCA.

HISTORY OF ENGLISH. The history of a language can be an *internal history* (of linguistic categories such as sounds, structure, and vocabulary) and an *external history* (of geographical and social spread, attitudes toward the language, study of its features, and attempts at its regulation). Such a dual approach is useful so long as it does not ignore changes that overlap these categories, as when English borrowed heavily from French, in which attitudes (an external factor) influenced vocabulary (an internal feature). Internal linguistic change is often in the direction of greater diversity. Thus, a sound change may result not in one new sound pattern but in several: the *r* in *far*, which all speakers of English once pronounced, is now missing in some but not all varieties. Among those who pronounce this *r*, it may be trilled, tapped, retroflex, or some other variety; among those who do not, it may or may not reappear before a vowel, as in the phrase *far away*. Though linguistic change tends toward greater diversity, the change is generally regular. As a result, it is possible to state which geographical and social groups delete the historical *r* and in what linguistic contexts, beginning with the fact that none deletes it when it comes first, as in *raft*. See RHOTIC AND NON-RHOTIC.

Prehistory. Almost all knowledge of English before *c*.600 is hypothetical, a reconstruction based on later documents in English and on earlier documents in related languages. Scholars agree, however, that the ultimate origins of English, save for a few borrowed words, lie in Indo-European (IE), a postulated ancient language of uncertain location. It may have been spoken in north-eastern Europe or near the Black Sea between *c*.3000 and *c*.2000 BC and can now only be reconstructed from its descendants. The incremental changes that produced the obviously related English *daughter*, German *Tochter*, Armenian *dushtr*, Greek *thugátēr*, and Sanskrit *duhitár* (etc.) from a common original are still at work; thus, the English spelling *daughter* masks a variety of pronunciations including *DAWtuh* and *DAHdur*, in which only the initial sound remains the same. Some IE words have undergone changes so profound that the common origin is almost impossible to discern: English

father, Armenian *hayr*, Greek *patḗr*, and Old Irish *athir* do not look or sound as though they derive from the same original form. Similar divergence characterizes the structures and vocabulary of the languages descended from IE. See GERMANIC LANGUAGES, INDO-EUROPEAN LANGUAGES.

IE ceased to exist sometime soon after 2000 BC, having diversified into a number of increasingly distinct offspring as a result of migration and natural linguistic changes. One of these offspring is known to scholars as *Primitive Germanic*, which like the original IE has left no written records. It differed from the other languages descended from IE in certain sounds, features of structure (such as a simplified verb system including some verbs with a past tense like English -*d*), and a vocabulary that included some words not inherited from IE. The modern English sentence *Weapons grated against the ship* has only one word that is common to other languages derived from IE, *the* (related to Greek *tó*). However, it is distinctively Germanic in the remaining words (for which there appear to be no IE sources), in the *th* of *the*, and in the -*d* suffix of the verb. The Germanic-speaking peoples appear to have moved from the IE homeland to what is now Scandinavia and northern Germany, from which they later spread in several migrations, leaving a northern branch behind, creating a small eastern branch that included Gothic, and a much larger western branch, which was the source of German, Dutch, and English, among others.

Old English. Several migrating tribes from northern Germany reached Britain in the early 5c speaking the mutually intelligible dialects which in their new home are now called *Old English* (*OE*) or *Anglo-Saxon*. The first written form of the language was runic letters, replaced during the conversion to Christianity of the Anglo-Saxons after 597 by the Latin alphabet, which was adapted to serve OE, making use of some runic letters and some letter shapes used by Irish scribes. Although OE was used as a literary medium and was the language of the *Anglo-Saxon Chronicle*, it did not seriously rival Latin as an administrative or intellectual medium, and within a century of the Norman Conquest of 1066 it was dead. Like other early IE languages, it distinguished three grammatical persons, not only in the plural (as in modern English *we, you, they*) but in the singular (as in Early Modern English *I, thou, she/he/it*). It also distinguished three genders and five cases, categories that extended to the article, adjective, and noun. OE showed the effects of Grimm's Law in its consonants, such as *p* > *f*, IE **peku*-property (as in Latin *pecus*) becoming OE *feoh*, and *t* > *th*, IE **trei* three (as in Latin *tri-*) becoming OE *þrī*. A few items of OE vocabulary reflect its contact before the incursions into Britain with non-Germanic languages such as Latin (OE *mīl* mile, from Latin *millia* thousand), and later with Celtic and Norse, especially in place-names. Christianity brought further Latin influence both as a source (OE *nōn*, Latin *nona* the ninth [hour]) and as a model (OE *þrīnes*, Latin *trinitas* trinity). However, OE vocabulary expanded chiefly through compounding (OE *dæges-ēage* day's eye, daisy) and derivation (OE *hālgian* hallow, *hǣlan* heal, from *hālig* holy, from *hāl* hale, whole (whence also *hǣlþ* health)). There were also changes of meaning, as when OE *þrēat*, meaning 'throng', came to mean 'pressure', then *threat*. See ALFRED, NORSE, OLD ENGLISH[1].

Middle English. Many linguistic changes occurred in late OE, and in Middle English (ME) almost every feature of OE changed radically, so that though late ME such as Chaucer's usage remains intelligible now 600 years later, little or nothing of OE could have been intelligible to Chaucer only 300 years after the Norman Conquest. In structure, the elaborate system of cases, genders, and numbers vanished from the adjective and article, dwindled in the noun, and remained only in the personal pronouns. The form of verbs was less changed, though increasing numbers of 'strong' verbs like Modern English *drive* (past tense *drove*) joined the larger group of 'weak' verbs, like *climb* (past tense *climbed*); Chaucer has the strong past *clomb*. The modals *shall* and *will* (and their past tenses *should* and *would*) developed a use, almost unknown in OE, as expressions of the future.

ME dialects are more numerous than OE dialects, and unregulated spelling often reflects the variations: in the late 14c, *church* appears in the North of England and in Scotland as *kirk(e)* or *kyrk(e)*, in the South-East as *cherch(e)* and *chirch(e)*, in the South-West as *church(e)*, and in the Midlands as a mixture of these forms plus *chyrch(e)*. There were more works of literature, especially in the East Midland dialect, first largely through translation from Latin and French. A variety of ME flourished as almost a separate language (at least in political terms) in Scotland. Also known as Middle Scots, it was dominant over Gaelic at the court of the kings of Scots and had a literature that included both epic and lyric poetry. In addition, varieties of ME and Norman French were being spoken in Wales and Ireland: see INGLIS, OLD ENGLISH[2], SCOTS, YOLA.

The most striking internal development is vocabulary. Some personal pronouns changed, the feminine from OE *hē* to *she*, the plural from OE *hīe* to *they*, with eventually *them* and *their*.

More far-reaching, however, were the borrowings, mostly from French, that transformed English from an almost wholly Germanic language to a language of mixed Germanic–Romance composition. Chaucer makes more or less use of the new vocabulary as his verse and his subject require, so that in 'Bitwixen hem was maad anon the bond / That highte matrimoigne or mariage' (*Knight's Tale*, *c*.1390), the first line contains only words directly inherited from OE, while the second includes two synonymous borrowings from French. See BISOCIATION, CHAUCER, MIDDLE ENGLISH.

Early Modern English. From the Renaissance onwards, as the structure of the standard language stabilizes, comments about it become more frequent and external factors and influences become more marked and more important. In 1490, Caxton observed the changes in English since he was born, and its variation in the several parts of England. He felt unsure about the correct literary mixture of old native words and their new borrowed and scholarly counterparts, and his spelling was inconsistent. His own introduction of printing to England (1476), however, did much to spread the new features of English. Renaissance exploration added new words to the vocabulary. *Hurricano* appears in Shakespeare, but only in his last plays; the form shows that it came by way of Spanish, not directly from its West Indian origin, the Amerindian language Taino. Developments in the arts and sciences produced a huge influx of words, such as *sonnet* (from Italian via French) and *sextant* (from Neo-Latin). Exploration also enhanced the stature of English by establishing the language in new nations from Africa to the Americas. The Reformation provided a further impulse for translation, notable not only in the sequence of English Bible translations from Tyndale (1526) to the Authorized Version (1611), but also in the translation of Greek and Roman classics such as North's Plutarch (1579) and the translation of the masterpieces of the Continental Renaissance such as Hoby's *Machiavelli* (1561).

With the accession of the Tudors to the English throne (1485), the increase of national pride promoted greater confidence in the vernacular for original writing, often expressed with an exuberance of literary style, especially in the Elizabethan age. The range of the language was further enlarged when James VI King of Scots became James I of England in 1603. This event not only made possible the development of a standard language, especially in writing and print, throughout Britain and Ireland and later in North America and colonies elsewhere, but brought the King's English and the King's Scots together in one monarch. The outstanding symbol of this realignment into one variety of educated usage was the publication in 1611 of the Authorized Version of the Bible; see BIBLE. The forms of Renaissance English show the effects of the Great Vowel Shift, though it was still incomplete. The development of some features of structure, such as -s for -th (*hears* instead of *heareth*), led for a time to competition: Shakespeare used both, while the King James Bible used only -th. The preface to Johnson's *Dictionary of the English Language* (1755) and the American Declaration of Independence (1776) scarcely used the -th form, and both reveal that most other main features of Modern English structure were in place wherever English was used by the late 18c. However, pronunciation continued to change and diversify in the speech of all social classes and regional groups: Pope rhymed *tea* with *obey*, Johnson could find no certain authority for the sound of *sea*, and *break* still remains one of the few words with the old pronunciation of *-ea-*. The increasing uniformity of spelling, however, has tended to mask this diversity. See BIBLE, BORROWING, CAXTON, DICTIONARY, EARLY MODERN ENGLISH, GRAMMAR, SHAKESPEARE.

(Late) Modern English. In the 18c, the diaspora of English gained momentum. Not only was the language used almost everywhere in Britain and Ireland, to the increasing detriment of the Celtic languages, but the Crown gained Canada and India in competition with the French and supplanted the Dutch in colonizing Australia. In Britain and Ireland there had always been many subjects of the Crown for whom English was not the first or preferred language. Now, as English spread across the globe, large numbers began to use it as a second or learned it as a foreign language. In turn, English gained new vocabulary from languages throughout the world: words like Nahuatl *tomato*, Eskimo *kayak*, Hindi *chintz*, now so thoroughly assimilated that they retain no echoes of their exotic origins: see BORROWING. With increasing scope and variety came increasing attempts at regulation. In 1664, a committee of the recently formed Royal Society of London sought to propound a set of rules for English, and in 1712 Swift proposed an Academy comparable to the Académie française, 'for *ascertaining* and *fixing* our Language for ever'. Neither attempt succeeded. The English of Swift's day lacked the kind of reference books from which he had learned his Latin: the few grammars were sketchy and the dictionaries listed only the 'hard words' created by Renaissance borrowing and invention. In 1721, Bailey's dictionary made an attempt at comprehensiveness, and Johnson's dictionary in 1755 laid the foundation of modern lexicography, though it recorded little but the literary vocabulary, and none from its own day. In 1762 appeared Lowth's grammar, which set the tradition of concentration on 'errors' in usage, agreeing with Swift's opinions while finding fault with his grammar. See DICTIONARY, GRAMMAR.

The growth of natural science after 1800 produced numberless new theories and products, along with knowledge of new substances, processes, and ailments, all nameless. Many received names composed by analogy with their formulas (*carbon monoxide*); others were named for their discoverer (*Hansen's Disease*), by acronym (*AIDS*), or by classical borrowing (*rabies*, Latin for rage). The language of newer fields like computer science often gives technical meaning to familiar words: *Apple Mac, dumb terminal, mouse*. Among the new sciences was linguistics, the objective study of language. Emboldened by the achievements of philology in the first quarter of the 19c, scholars set aside such impressionistic views of language as Addison's that English was distinctively 'modest, thoughtful and sincere'. They also gave up culturally biased attempts to link Hebrew to Latin and Greek, and took account in their studies of non-Western languages such as Sanskrit. The publication of *The Oxford English Dictionary* under the leadership of J. A. H. Murray (1888-1933, with Supplements 1972-86, 2nd edition 1989) is a monument of late 19c linguistic science.

Close acquaintance with indigenous peoples of America, Africa, and Australia, and the two world wars of the 20c, confronted Europeans and Americans with languages wholly unrelated to theirs, forcing further reassessment of long-held views and diverting language study from the historical approach to the descriptive. Challenged by the growing mass of data, scholars turned to the theories underlying their work, especially influenced after 1957 by the theories of the American linguist Noam Chomsky. Parallel with growth in linguistic science has been the spread of electronic media, which has not resulted, as some had hoped or feared, in the extinction of variety. Mass education has likewise had little influence on internal developments in English. The citizens of English-speaking countries now number c.300m, while elsewhere at least another 400m use it or have learned it as a second language, and perhaps 1,000m others learn it as a foreign language. The Germanic dialects that migrated in the 5c to Britain have expanded into a 20c global common language. Compare GEOGRAPHY AND GEOPOLITICS OF ENGLISH. See ENGLISH, STANDARD ENGLISH. [HISTORY, VARIETY].   W.F.B.

Bailey, Richard W. 1991/2. *Images of English: A Cultural History of the Language*. US: Michigan University Press (1991). UK: Cambridge University Press.

Baugh, Albert C., & Cable, Thomas. 1978. *A History of the English Language*, 3rd edition. Englewood Cliffs: Prentice-Hall.

Bolton, W. F. 1982. *A Living Language: The History and Structure of English*. New York: Random House.

Burchfield, Robert. 1985. *The English Language*. Oxford: University Press.

Burnley, David. 1992. *The History of the English Language: A Source Book*. London & New York: Longman.

Claiborne, Robert. 1983. *Our Marvelous Native Tongue: The Life and Times of the English Language*. New York: Times Books.

Lass, Roger. 1987. *The Shape of English: Structure and History*. London: Dent.

Leith, Dick. 1983. *A Social History of English*. London: Routledge.

McCrum, Robert, Cran, William, & MacNeil, Robert. 1986. *The Story of English*. London: Faber; New York: Viking.

Pyles, Thomas, & Algeo, John. 1982. *The Origins and Development of the English Language*, 3rd edition. New York: Harcourt Brace Jovanovich.

Samuels, M. L. 1972. *Linguistic Evolution: With Special Reference to English*. Cambridge: University Press.

Strang, Barbara M. H. 1970. *A History of English*. London: Methuen.

Wakelin, Martyn F. 1988. *The Archaeology of English*. London: Batsford.

The history theme

A–D. ACADEMY, AELFRIC, AFRICA, AFRICAN ENGLISH, ALFRED, ALPHABET, AMERICA, AMERICAN ENGLISH, ANGLES, ANGLIAN, ANGLO-DANISH, ANGLO-SAXON, ANGLO-SAXON CHRONICLE, ANTIPODES, ARCHAISM, ARYAN, ASIA, ATTIC AND DORIC, ATTICISM, AUGUSTAN, AUREATE DICTION, AUSTRALIA, AUSTRALIAN ENGLISH, BARDOLATRY, BARNES, BEDE, BEOWULF, BIBLE, BIBLICAL ENGLISH, BISOCIATION, BLAIR, BLARNEY, BLUE-EYED ENGLISH, BOOK, BOOK OF COMMON PRAYER, BORROWING, BOSWELL, BRIT, BRITAIN, BRITANNIA, BRITISH, BRITISH BROADCASTING, BRITISH EMPIRE, BRITISH ENGLISH, BRITISH LANGUAGES, BRITISH LIBRARY, BRITON, CAMDEN, CANADA, CANADIAN ENGLISH, CATACHRESIS, CAWDREY, CAXTON, CELT, CELTIC LANGUAGES, CHANCERY STANDARD, CHANNEL ISLANDS, CHAUCER, CLASSICAL LANGUAGE, COGNATE, COLONIAL, COMMONWEALTH, COMMUNICATIVE SHIFT, COMPARATIVE PHILOLOGY, COOPER, COVERDALE, CRANMER, DANELAW, DANISH, DECAY, DEFOE, DERIVATION, DETERIORATION, DIACHRONIC AND SYNCHRONIC, DIALECT.

E–Z. EARLY ENGLISH, EARLY ENGLISH TEXT SOCIETY, EARLY MODERN ENGLISH, EARLY MODERN ENGLISH DICTIONARY, EDUCATION, ELIZABETHAN, ELYOT, ENCYCLOPAEDIA BRITANNICA, ENGLAND, ENGLISH LITERATURE, ETYMOLOGICAL FALLACY, ETYMOLOGY, ETYMON, EUROPE, EXAMINING IN ENGLISH, FIGURATIVE EXTENSION, FIXED, FOLK ETYMOLOGY, FRENCH, GENERALIZATION, GOTHIC, GREAT VOWEL SHIFT, GREEK, GRIMM'S LAW, HEBREW, HEPTARCHY, HISTORICAL LINGUISTICS, HISTORICAL SEMANTICS, HOBSON-JOBSON, INDIA, INDIAN LANGUAGES, INDO-EUROPEAN LANGUAGES, INDO-EUROPEAN ROOTS, INDO-GERMANIC, INGLIS, INGVAEONIC, IRELAND, IRISH ENGLISH, JACOBEAN, JOHNSON, JONES (W.), JONSON, JUTES, KENTISH, KUHN, KURATH, LANGUAGE, LANGUAGE CHANGE, LANGUAGE FAMILY, LATIN[1], LATIN ANALOGY, LEXICAL BAR, LITERATURE, LOAN, LOAN BLEND, LOAN TRANSLATION, LYLY, MACAULAY, MELIORATION, MERCIA, MIDDLE ENGLISH, MIDDLE ENGLISH DICTIONARY, MODERN ENGLISH, MULCASTER, NORMAN, NORMAN FRENCH, NORSE, OLD ENGLISH[1], OLD ENGLISH[2], OLD ENGLISH ANNALS, PALE, PEJORATION, PHILOLOGY, POPULAR ETYMOLOGY, PRIMITIVE GERMANIC, PUTTENHAM, RADIATION, REFORMATION, RENAISSANCE, RESTORATION, ROOT, ROYAL SOCIETY, RUNE, SAGA, SAXON, SCRIPTURE, SEMANTIC CHANGE, SHAKESPEARE, SOUTHRON, SPECIALIZATION, SPENSER, STORY OF ENGLISH (THE), SUBREPTION, SWEET, TRISOCIATION, TYNDALE, VERNER'S LAW, VICTORIAN, WESSEX, WILSON, WRITING, WYCLIF(FE), Y-.

A chronology of English

A selection of dates associated with the history and spread of the English language from Roman times to 1990.

55 BC Roman military expedition to Britain by Julius Caesar.

AD 43 Roman invasion of Britain under the Emperor Claudius, beginning 400 years of control over much of the island.

150 From around this date, with Roman permission, small numbers of settlers arrive from the coastlands of Germany, speaking dialects ancestral to English.

297 First mention of the Picts of Caledonia, tribes beyond Roman control, well to the north of Hadrian's Wall.

410 The Goths sack Rome.

436 The end of a period of gradual Roman withdrawal. Britons south of the Wall are attacked by the Picts and by Scots from Ireland. Angles, Saxons, and other Germanic settlers come first as mercenaries to help the Britons, then take over more and more territory.

449 The traditional date for the beginning of the Anglo-Saxon settlements.

450-80 The first surviving Old English inscriptions, in runic letters.

495 The Saxon kingdom of Wessex established.

500 The kingdom of Dalriada established in Argyll by Scots from Ireland.

527 The Saxon kingdoms of Essex and Middlesex established.

550 The Angle kingdoms of Mercia, East Anglia, and Northumbria established.

557 At the Battle of Deorham, the West Saxons drive a wedge between the Britons of Wales and Cornwall.

597 Aethelberht, king of Kent, welcomes Augustine and the conversion of the Anglo-Saxons to Christianity begins.

613 At the Battle of Chester, the Angles of Northumbria drive a wedge between the Britons of Wales and Cumbria.

638 Edwin of Northumbria takes Lothian from the Britons.

700 The first manuscript records of Old English from about this time.

792 Scandinavians begin to raid and settle in Britain, Ireland, and France. In 793, they sack the monastery of Lindisfarne, the centre of Northumbrian scholarship.

795 The Danes settle in parts of Ireland.

815 Egbert of Wessex defeats the south-western Britons of Cornwall and incorporates Cornwall into his kingdom.

828 Egbert of Wessex is hailed as *bretwalda* (lord of Britain), overlord of the Seven Kingdoms of the Angles and Saxons (the Heptarchy). England begins to emerge.

834 The Danes raid England.

843 Kenneth MacAlpin, King of Scots, gains the throne of Pictland.

865 The Danes occupy Northumbria and establish a kingdom at York. Danish begins to influence English.

871 Alfred becomes king of Wessex, translates works of Latin into English, and establishes the writing of prose in English.

886 The boundaries of the Danelaw are settled.

911 Charles II of France grants lands on the lower Seine to the Viking chief Hrolf the Ganger (Rollo the Rover). The beginnings of Normandy and Norman French.

954 The expulsion of Eric Blood-Axe, last Danish king of York.

965 The English invade the northern Welsh kingdom of Gwynedd.

973 Edgar of England cedes Lothian to Kenneth II, King of Scots. Scotland multilingual: Gaelic dominant, Norse in the north, Cumbric in the south-west, English in the south-east, Latin for church and law.

992 A treaty between Ethelred of England and the Normans.

1000 The approximate date of the only surviving manuscript of the Old English epic poem *Beowulf*.

1007 Ethelred the Unready pays *danegeld* to stop the Danes attacking England. In 1013, however, they take the country and Ethelred flees to Normandy.

1014 The end of Danish rule in Ireland.

1016–42 The reigns of Canute/Knut and his sons over Denmark, Norway, and England.

1051 Edward the Confessor, King of England, impressed by the Normans and with French-speaking counsellors at his court, names as his heir William, Duke of Normandy, but reneges on his promise before his death.

1066 The Norman Conquest. William defeats King Harold at Hastings, and sets in train the Normanization of the upper classes of the Britain Isles. England multilingual: English the majority language, Danish in the north, Cornish in the far south-west, Welsh on the border with Wales, Norman French at court and in the courts, and Latin in church and school.

1150 The first surviving texts of Middle English.

1167 The closure of the University of Paris to students from England accelerates the development of a university at Oxford.

1171 Henry II invades Ireland and declares himself its overlord, introducing Norman French and English into the island.

1204 King John loses the Duchy of Normandy to France.

1209 The exodus of a number of students from Oxford leads to the establishment of a second university in Cambridge.

1272–1307 The reign of Edward I, who consolidates royal authority in England, and extends it permanently to Wales and temporarily to Scotland.

1282 Death of Llewelyn, last native prince of Wales. In 1301, Edward of England's son and heir is invested as Prince of Wales.

1284 The Statute of Rhuddlan establishes the law of England in Wales (in French and Latin), but retains the legal use of Welsh.

1314 Robert Bruce reasserts Scottish independence by defeating Edward II at Bannockburn, an achievement later celebrated in an epic written in Scots.

1337 The outbreak of the Hundred Years War between England and France, which ends with the loss of all England's French possessions save the Channel Islands.

1343?–1400 The life of Geoffrey Chaucer.

1348 (1) English replaces Latin as medium of instruction in schools, but not at Oxford and Cambridge. (2) The worst year of the Black Death.

1362 (1) Through the Statute of Pleading, written in French, English replaces French as the language of law in England, but the records continue to be kept in Latin. (2) English is used for the first time in Parliament.

1384 The publication of John Wycliffe's English translation of the Latin Bible.

1385 The scholar John of Trevisa notes that 'in all the gramere scoles of Engelond, children leveth Frensche and construeth and lerneth in Englische'.

1400 By this date the Great Vowel Shift has begun.

1450 Printing by movable type invented in the Rhineland.

1476 (1) The first English book printed: *The Recuyell of the Historyes of Troye*, translated from French by William Caxton, who printed it at Bruges in Flanders. (2) Caxton sets up the first printing press in England, at Westminster. In 1478, he publishes Chaucer's *Canterbury Tales*.

1485 The Battle of Bosworth, after which the part-Welsh Henry Tudor becomes King of England. Welsh nobles follow him to London.

1492 Christopher Columbus discovers the New World.

1497 Giovanni Caboto (Anglicized as 'John Cabot'), in a ship from Bristol, lands on the Atlantic coast of North America.

1499 The publication of *Thesaurus linguae romanae et britannicae* (Treasury of the Roman and British Tongues), the first English-to-Latin wordbook, the work of Galfridus Grammaticus (Geoffrey the Grammarian).

1504 The settlement of St John's on Newfoundland as a shore base for English fisheries.

1507 The German geographer Martin Waldseemüller puts the name *America* on his map of the world.

1525 The publication of William Tyndale's translation of the New Testament of the Bible.

1534 Jacques Cartier lands on the Gaspé Peninsula in North America and claims it for France.

1536 and **1542** The Statute of Wales (Acts of Union) unites England and Wales, excluding Welsh from official use.

1542 Henry VIII of England proclaims himself King of Ireland.

1549 The publication of the first version of the Book of Common Prayer of the Church of England, the work in the main of Thomas Cranmer.

1558-1603 The reign of Elizabeth I.

1560-1620 The plantation of Ireland, first by English settlers and after 1603 also by Scots, establishing English throughout the island and Scots in Ulster.

1564-1616 The life of William Shakespeare.

1583 Sir Humphrey Gilbert establishes Newfoundland as England's first colony beyond the British Isles.

1584 The settlement on Roanoke Island by colonists led by Sir Walter Raleigh. In 1587, Virginia Dare born at Roanoke, first child of English parents in North America. In 1590, the settlers of Roanoke disappear without trace.

1588 The publication of Bishop Morgan's translation of the Bible into Welsh, serving as a focus for the survival of the language.

1600 English traders establish the East India Company.

1603 The Union of the Crowns under James VI of Scotland, I of England.

1604 The publication of Robert Cawdrey's *Table Alphabeticall*, the first dictionary of English.

1606 The Dutch explore northern New Holland (Terra Australis).

1607 The Jamestown colony in Virginia, the first permanent English settlement and the first representative assembly in the New World.

1608 Samuel Champlain founds the city of Quebec in New France.

1611 The publication of the Authorized or King James Version of the Bible, intended for use in the Protestant services of England, Scotland, and Ireland. A major influence on the written language and in adapting Scots towards English.

1612 (1) Bermuda colonized under the charter of the Virginia Company. (2) Traders of the East India Company establish themselves in Gujarat, India.

1614 King James writes in English to the Moghul Emperor Jehangir, in order to encourage trade with 'the Orientall Indies'.

1619 At the Jamestown colony in America, the first African slaves arrive on a Dutch ship.

1620 The *Mayflower* arrives in the New World and the Pilgrim Fathers set up Plimoth Plantation in Massachusetts. English is now in competition as a colonial language in the Americas with Dutch, French, Spanish, and Portuguese.

1622 Publication in London of the first English newspaper, *Weekly News*.

1623 Publication in London of the First Folio of Shakespeare's plays.

1627 An English colony established on Barbados in the Caribbean.

1637 (1) English traders arrive on the coast of China. (2) The Académie française founded

1640 An English trading factory established at Madras.

1647 The Bahamas colonized by settlers from Bermuda.

1652 The first Dutch settlers arrive in southern Africa.

1655 England acquires Jamaica from Spain.

1659 The East India Company annexes St Helena in the south Atlantic.

1660 John Dryden expresses his admiration for the Académie française and its work in 'fixing' French and wishes for something similar to serve English.

1662 The Royal Society of London receives its charter from Charles II. In 1664, it appoints a committee to consider ways of improving English as a language of science.

1670 The Hudson's Bay Company founded for fur trading in northern America.

1674 Charles II receives Bombay from the Portuguese in the dowry of Catherine of Braganza and gives it to the East India Company.

1687 Isaac Newton writes *Principia Mathematica* in Latin: see 1704.

1688 The publication of *Oronooko, or the History of the Royal Slave*, by Aphra Behn: one of the first novels in English, by the first woman novelist in English, based on personal experience of a slave revolt in Surinam.

1690 A trading factory established at Calcutta in Bengal.

1696 British and French colonists in North America in open conflict.

1697 The Boston clergyman Cotton Mather applies the term *American* to English-speaking settlers in the New World.

1702 Publication in London of the first regular daily newspaper in English, *The Daily Courant*.

1704 Isaac Newton writes his second major work, *Opticks*, in English: see 1687.

1707 The Act of Union, uniting the Parliaments of England and Scotland, creating the United Kingdom of Great Britain, but keeping separate the state religions, educational systems, and laws of the two kingdoms.

1712 (1) Jonathan Swift in Dublin proposes an English Academy to 'fix' the language and compete adequately with French. (2) In India, the Moghul Empire begins to decline.

1713 (1) At the Treaty of Utrecht, France surrenders Hudson's Bay, Acadia, and Newfoundland to the British. (2) Gibraltar is ceded to Britain by Spain.

1726 Ephraim Chambers publishes his *Cyclopaedia*, the first encyclopedia.

1731 The abolition of Law French in England.

1746 The Wales and Berwick Act, by which England is deemed to include Wales and the Scottish town of Berwick is incorporated into England.

1755 The publication of Samuel Johnson's *Dictionary of the English Language*.

1757 The East India Company becomes the power behind the government of Bengal.

1759 General James Wolfe takes Quebec for the British.

1759–96 The life of Robert Burns.

1762 The publication of Robert Lowth's *Short Introduction to English Grammar*.

1763 The French cede New France to Britain, retaining only St Pierre and Miquelon (islands off Newfoundland).

1768–71 The partwork publication in Edinburgh of *The Encyclopaedia Britannica*.

1770 Captain James Cook takes possession of the Australian continent for Britain.

1770–1850 The life of William Wordsworth.

1771–1832 The life of Sir Walter Scott.

1774 (1) The Quebec Act creates the British province of Quebec, extending to the Ohio and Mississippi. (2) The Regulating Act places Bombay and Madras under the control of Bengal and the East India Company becomes a kind of state.

1776 The Declaration of Independence by thirteen British colonies in North America and the start of the American War of Independence (1776–83) which created the United States of America, the first nation outside the British Isles with English as its principal language.

1778 Captain James Cook visits and names the Sandwich Islands (Hawaii).

1780–1800 British Empire loyalists move from the US to Canada.

1785 In London, the newspaper *The Daily Universal Register* founded. Renamed *The Times* in 1788.

1786 (1) Lord Cornwallis is appointed first Governor-General of British India. (2) A British penal colony is established at Botany Bay in Australia. In 1788, the first convicts arrive there.

1791 (1) The British colonies of Upper Canada (Ontario) and Lower Canada (Quebec) are established. (2) In London, the newspaper *The Observer* is founded, the oldest national Sunday newspaper in Britain.

1792 The first Europeans settle in New Zealand.

1794 The publication of Lindley Murray's *English Grammar*.

1802 The establishment of the British colonies of Ceylon and Trinidad.

1803 (1) The Act of Union incorporating Ireland into Britain, as the United Kingdom of Great Britain and Ireland. (2) The Louisiana Purchase, by which the US buys from France its remaining North American territories, and doubles its size.

1806 The British take control of Cape Colony in southern Africa.

1808 The establishment of the British colony of Sierra Leone.

1814 (1) The British annex Cape Colony. (2) France cedes to Britain Malta, Mauritius, St Lucia, and Tobago.

1816 The establishment of the British colony of Bathurst (the Gambia).

1819 (1) The establishment of the British colony of Singapore. (2) The US purchases Florida from Spain.

1820 Christian missionaries from the US visit Hawaii.

1821 American settlers arrive in the Mexican territory of Texas.

1828 The publication of Noah Webster's *American Dictionary of the English Language*.

1829 Australia becomes a British dependency.

1831 The establishment of the colony of British Guiana.

1833 (1) The abolition of slavery in the British Empire. (2) St Helena becomes a British colony.

1835 Thomas Macaulay writes the Minute on Education whereby the British rulers of India endorse English as a language of education for Indians.

1835–1910 The life of Sam Clemens (Mark Twain).

1836 Texas declares its independence from Mexico.

1839 The first Boer Republic is established in Natal, South Africa, after the Great Trek from the Cape.

1840 (1) The Treaty of Waitangi, by which the Maori of New Zealand cede all rights and powers of government to Britain. (2) The transportation of convicts to Eastern Australia is ended.

1841 (1) Upper and Lower Canada are brought together as British North America. (2) New Zealand becomes a British colony. (3) In London, the founding of the weekly magazine *Punch*.

1842 (1) The opening of Chinese ports other than Canton to Western traders, after the defeat of China in the Opium War. Hong Kong is ceded by China to Britain as a Crown Colony. (2) The Philological Society is formed in London.

1844 The first telegraph message transmitted, between Washington and Baltimore.

1845 Texas becomes a state of the United States.

1846 The British annex Natal but recognize the Transvaal and the Orange Free State as autonomous Boer republics.

1848 In the Treaty of Guadalupe Hidalgo, Mexico cedes vast western territories to the US.

1850 (1) Britain takes control of the Bay Islands of Honduras, an English-speaking enclave in Central America. (2) Legislative councils are established in Australia by British Act of Parliament.

1852 The publication of *Roget's Thesaurus*.

1853 (1) Japan is forced by Commander Matthew Perry of the US Navy to open its harbours to Western trade. (2) The transportation of convicts to Tasmania is ended.

1855 The government of the colony of New South Wales is established.

1856 The governments of the colonies of Tasmania and Victoria are established.

1856–1950 The life of George Bernard Shaw.

1857 The Sepoy Rebellion (War of Independence, Indian Mutiny) in India leads to the transfer of British India from the East India Company to the Crown.

1858 (1) The Philological Society passes a resolution calling for a new dictionary of English on historical principles. (2) Britain cedes the Bay Islands to Honduras.

1861 The establishment of the British colony of Lagos (Nigeria).

1862 The establishment of the colony of British Honduras.

1863 The establishment of the Cambridge Overseas Examinations.

1865 The abolition of slavery in the US, at the end of the Civil War. At the outbreak of the war there were over 4m slaves.

1867 (1) The Dominion of Canada is created, consisting of Quebec, Ontario, Nova Scotia, and New Brunswick. (2) Alaska is purchased from Russia by the US.

1868 (1) Transportation of convicts to Western Australia is ended. (2) In the US, Christopher Latham Sholes and colleagues patent the first successful typewriter.

1869 (1) Rupert's Land and the Northwest Territories are bought by Canada from the Hudson's Bay Company. (2) Basutoland becomes a British protectorate.

1870 Manitoba becomes a province of Canada.

1871 British Columbia becomes a province of Canada.

1873 (1) The formation of the English Dialect Society (dissolved in 1896). (2) Prince Edward Island becomes a province of Canada.

1874 The establishment of the British colony of the Gold Coast in West Africa.

1879 James A. H. Murray begins editing the Philological Society's *New English Dictionary on Historical Principles*.

1882–1941 The Life of James Joyce.

1884 (1) The Berlin Conference, in which European powers begin 'the scramble for Africa'. (2) Britain declares a protectorate over South East New Guinea. (3) The French, Germans, and British attempt to annex what shortly becomes the German colony of Kamerun. (4) Publication of the first fascicle, *A–Ant*, of Murray's dictionary (the *OED*).

1886 The annexation of Burma into British India and the abolition of the Burmese monarchy.

1888–94 The establishment of British protectorates in Kenya, Uganda, and Zanzibar.

1889 The formation of the American Dialect Society.

1895 The establishment of the British East African Protectorate, open to white settlers.

1898 (1) The annexation of Hawaii by the US. In 1900, it becomes a US territory. (2) Spain cedes the Philippines and Puerto Rico to the US. (3) Yukon Territory comes under Canadian government control.

1901 (1) The establishment of the Commonwealth of Australia as a dominion of the British Empire. (2) The first wireless telegraphy messages sent across the Atlantic by Guglielmo Marconi (Cornwall to Newfoundland). (3) The first film-show, in an arcade opened in Los Angeles, California.

1903 (1) A message from US President Theodore Roosevelt circles the world in less than 10 minutes by Pacific Cable.

1903–50 The life of George Orwell.

1905 (1) Alberta and Saskatchewan become provinces of Canada. (2) The first cartoon strip, 'Little Nemo', appears in the *New York Herald*.

1906 (1) The formation of the English Association. (2) The first full-length motion picture, *The Story of the Kelly Gang*. (3) the publication of the Fowler brothers' *The King's English*.

1907 (1) The establishment of New Zealand as a dominion of the British Empire. (2) The first regular studio-based radio broadcasts by the De

Forest Radio Telephone Company in the US. (3) The foundation of Hollywood as a film-making centre.

1910 (1) The establishment of the Union of South Africa as a dominion of the British Empire. (2) The first radio receivers made in kit form for sale in the US.

1911 The publication of the Fowler brothers' *Concise Oxford Dictionary*.

1913 (1) The formation of the Society for Pure English. (2) The first crossword puzzle published, in the *New York World*.

1914 (1) A third Home Rule Bill for Ireland passed by the British Parliament, but prevented from coming into operation by the outbreak of the First World War. (2) The German colony of Kamerun invaded by the French and British.

1915 The death of Sir James A. H. Murray, aged 78, having finished the section *Trink–Turndown* in the *OED*.

1916 (1) The Easter Rising in Dublin, an unsuccessful armed rebellion against the British, during which an Irish Republic is proclaimed. (2) The Technicolor process is first used in the film *The Gulf Between*, in the US.

1917 The publication of Daniel Jones's *English Pronouncing Dictionary*.

1918 (1) The formation of the English-Speaking Union. (2) The US War Industries Board declares moving pictures an essential industry.

1919 (1) The German colony of Tanganyika ceded to Britain. (2) The German colony of Kamerun divided between France (Cameroun) and Britain (Cameroon). (3) The publication of H. L. Mencken's *The American Language*.

1920 (1) The Partition of Ireland. (2) Kenya becomes a British colony. (3) The first public radio station set up by Marconi in the US.

1921 (1) A treaty between the United Kingdom and the Irish Free State, which accepts dominion status within the British Empire. (2) The first full-length 'talkie' *Dream Street* produced by United Artists, in the US.

1922 (1) The establishment of the British Broadcasting Company, renamed in 1927 the British Broadcasting Corporation (BBC). (2) The founding in the US of the monthly magazine *The Reader's Digest*.

1923 The founding of *Time* magazine in the US.

1925 (1) The borders of the Republic of Ireland and Northern Ireland established. (2) Afrikaans gains official status in South Africa. (3) The founding of the weekly magazine *The New Yorker*.

1926 The publication of Henry W. Fowler's *Dictionary of Modern English Usage*.

1927 (1) Fox's Movietone News, the first sound newsfilm, released in the US. (2) The first film with dialogue, *They're Coming to Get Me*, released in the US.

1928 The publication of Murray's Dictionary as *The Oxford English Dictionary*, 70 years after Trench's proposal to the Philological Society.

1930 (1) C. K. Ogden launches Basic English. (2) The first television programme with synchronized sight and sound broadcast by the BBC.

1931 (1) The British Commonwealth of Nations formed. (2) South Africa becomes a dominion of the British Empire. (3) The Cambridge Proficiency Examination held outside Britain for the first time.

1933 The publication of a supplement to *The Oxford English Dictionary*.

1934 The British Council created as an arm of British cultural diplomacy and a focus for teaching English as a foreign language.

1935 (1) The Philippines become a self-governing Commonwealth in association with the US. (2) The publication of the first ten Penguin paperback titles.

1936 The Republic of Ireland severs all constitutional links with Great Britain.

1937 (1) Burma is separated from British India and granted a constitution and limited self-rule. (2) In Wales, a new constitution for the National Eisteddfod makes Welsh its official language.

1938 Photocopying invented.

1942 The publication in Japan of the *Idiomatic and Syntactic English Dictionary*, prepared before the war by A. S. Hornby, E. V. Gatenby, and H. Wakefield.

1945 Japan is occupied by the Americans on behalf of the Allies.

1946 (1) The Philippines gain their independence from the US. (2) The French colony of Cameroun and the British colony of Cameroon become United Nations trusteeships.

1947 (1) British India is partitioned and India and Pakistan become independent states. (2) New Zealand gains its independence from Britain.

1948 (1) Burma and Ceylon gain their independence from Britain. (2) The dictionary of Hornby *et al.* is brought out by Oxford University Press as *A Learner's Dictionary of Current English*.

1949 (1) Newfoundland becomes a province of Canada. (2) Two New Guinea territories are combined by the United Nations as an Australian mandate: the United Nations Trust Territory of Papua and New Guinea.

1951 The launch of the first two working business computers: the LED in the UK and the UNIVAC in the US.

1952 Puerto Rico becomes a Commonwealth in association with the US.

1957 (1) The Gold Coast becomes independent from Britain as the Republic of Ghana. (2) Robert W. Burchfield is appointed editor of a new Supplement to *The Oxford English Dictionary*.

1957–63 The British colonies of Malaya and Borneo become independent and unite as Malaysia.

1959 Alaska and Hawaii become states of the US.

1960 Nigeria and French Cameroun become independent.

1961 (1) South Africa becomes a republic, leaves the Commonwealth, and adopts Afrikaans and English as its two official languages. (2) The British colony of Cameroon divides, part joining Nigeria, part joining the ex-French colony to become the Republic of Cameroon. (3) Sierra Leone and Cyprus gain their independence from Britain. (4) The publication of *Webster's Third International Dictionary*.

1962 Jamaica, Trinidad and Tobago, and Uganda gain their independence from Britain.

1963 (1) Kenya gains its independence from Britain. (2) The first protests in Wales by the Cymdeithas yr Iaith Gymraeg/Welsh Language Society, aimed at achieving fuller use of Welsh.

1964 (1) Malta, Nyasaland (as Malawi), Tanganyika and Zanzibar (as Tanzania), and Northern Rhodesia (as Zambia) gain their independence from Britain. (2) The publication in Paris of René Etiemble's *Parlez-vous franglais?*

1965 Gambia and Singapore gain their independence from Britain.

1966 Barbados, Basutoland (as Lesotho), Bechuanaland (as Botswana), and British Guiana (as Guyana) gain their independence from Britain.

1967 The Welsh Language Act gives Welsh equal validity with English in Wales, and Wales is no longer deemed to be a part of England.

1968 Mauritius, Swaziland, and Nauru gain their independence from Britain.

1969 Canada becomes officially bilingual, with a commitment to federal services in English and French.

1971 The invention of the microprocessor, a revolutionary development in computing.

1972 (1) East Pakistan secedes and becomes the Republic of Bangladesh. (2) Two feminist magazines launched: *Ms* in the US and *Spare Rib* in the UK.

1973 The Bahamas gain their independence.

1974 Cyngor yr Iaith Gymraeg/Council for the Welsh Language set up to advise the Secretary of State for Wales on matters concerning the language.

1975 (1) Papua New Guinea gains its independence from Australia. (2) The Bas-Lauriol law is passed in France, requiring the use of the French language alone in advertising and commerce.

1977 (1) The spacecraft *Voyager* travels into deep space, carrying a message in English to any extra-terrestrials. (2) In Quebec, Loi 101/Bill 101 is passed, making French the sole official language of the province, limiting access to English-medium schools, and banning public signs in languages other than French.

1978 The government of Northern Territory in Australia is established.

1980 The British government averts a fast to the death by Gwynfor Evans, leader of Plaid Cymru (Welsh National Party), by honouring election pledges to provide a fourth television channel using both Welsh and English.

1981 British Honduras gains its independence as Belize.

1982 The patriation of Canada's constitution. The Canada Act is the last act of the British Parliament concerning Canadian affairs.

1983 The publication of *The New Testament in Scots*, a translation by William L. Lorimer.

1984 The launch of the Apple Macintosh personal (desktop) computer.

1985 (1) The publication by Longman of *A Comprehensive Grammar of the English Language*. (2) The publication by Belknap Press of the first volume of the *Dictionary of American Regional English*. (3) The launch by Cambridge University Press of the quarterly magazine-cum-journal *English Today: The International Review of the English Language*.

1986 Showing by the BBC in the UK and public television in the US of *The Story of English*, a television series with both British and American backers, accompanied by a book, and followed by a radio version on BBC World Service.

1989 The publication of the 2nd edition of *The Oxford English Dictionary*, blending the first edition and its supplements.

HOBSON-JOBSON, full title: *Hobson-Jobson, a glossary study of colloquial Anglo-Indian words and phrases and of kindred terms, etymological, historical, geographical and discoursive*. A 1,020-page encyclopedic dictionary compiled by Henry Yule and A. C. Burnell, first published in 1886. A 2nd edition, edited by William Crooke, appeared in 1903 and was reissued in 1968 and 1985 by Routledge & Kegan Paul. It provides ethnographic, historical, and etymological information and discusses processes by which English was being indigenized in South Asia, including phonetic change (*apil* an appeal, *rasid* a receipt), semantic shift (*boy* a bearer, waiter), and hybridization (*brandy pani* brandy and water). In a foreword to the 1985 reprint, Anthony Burgess describes it as 'a reminder of how the tongues of India have modified the language of an invader'. See ANGLO-INDIAN, HOBSON-JOBSONISM. [ASIA, REFERENCE]. B.B.K.

HOBSON-JOBSONISM [1930s: from *Hobson-Jobson*, a 19c Anglo-Indian adaptation of the Shia Muslim cry *Yā Hasan! Yā Husain!*, used to mourn the deaths of Muhammad's grandsons]. The alteration of a foreign expression to fit the speech and spelling patterns of a borrowing language, usually English: for example, *Hobson-Jobson*, whose early versions include *Hosseen Gosseen* (1698) and *Hassan Hassan* (1773). Two comparable adaptations of Asian words are *Sir Roger Dowler* for the 18c Indian prince Siraj-ud-Dawlah and *juggernaut* for Sanskrit *Jagannātha* (Lord of the World, an epithet of the god Krishna). The term is rare, but the process common and ancient. It began in English with Celtic names: the town *Bathgate* in Scotland is from Cumbric words close to Welsh *baedd coed* (boar wood); Shakespeare in *Henry V* Saxonized *Llewelyn* to 'Fluellen'; in Ireland, the name *Baile na Dtulach* (Gaelic: town of the little hills) is Anglicized as *Ballynadolly*. In the 17c, *Hochheimer*, the name of a German wine, became *hockamore*, then *hock*. Settlers in North America changed Algonquian *pawcohiccora* to *pohickery* then *hickory*, *arahkun* to *raccoon*, *tamahaak* to *tomahawk*. At the turn of the 20c, Spanish *juzgado*, a tribunal, became *hoosegow*, an AmE slang term for a jail. The concept is sometimes called *the law of Hobson-Jobson*. See ANGLICIZE, ASSIMILATION, CANADIAN

PLACE-NAMES, EYE DIALECT, HOMONYM, -ISM. [ASIA, NAME, STYLE, WORD]. T.MCA.

HOLOFERNES [16c: from the names of a Biblical general and the theologian *Tubal Holofernes* in Rabelais' *Gargantua*, 1534]. The schoolmaster in Shakespeare's *Love's Labour's Lost* (1590s), often invoked as a symbol of pretentious learning: 'Constant reading of Greek and Latin bred a race of Holofernes pedants who preferred the Latin or Greek term to the English term' (Harold Whitehall, in L. F. Dean *et al.* (eds.), *The Play of Language*, 1971). In the following passage (5. 1), the curate Nathaniel and the pedant Holofernes amiably swap Latinisms:

NATHANIEL. I did conuerse this quondam day with a companion of the kings, who is intituled, nominated, or called, *Don Adriano de Armatho*.

PEDANT. *Noui hominum tanquam te*, His humour is loftie, his discourse peremptorie: his tongue fyled, his eye ambitious, his gate maiesticall, and his generall behauiour vaine, rediculous, & thrasonicall. He is too picked, to spruce, too affected, to od as it were, too peregrinat as I may call it.

NATHANIEL. A most singular and choyce Epithat.

PEDANT. He draweth out the thred of his verbositie, finer then the staple of his argument. I abhorre such phanaticall phantasims.

Compare AUREATE DICTION, EUPHUISM, INKHORN TERM/INKHORNISM, LYLY, MULCASTER, PEDANT. [LITERATURE, STYLE]. T.MCA.

HOLOPHRASE [19c: from Greek *hólos* whole, *phrásis* speech]. (1) A word functioning as a phrase or sentence: the imperative *Go!*; the drinking expression *Cheers!* (2) An idiomatic expression: *How do you do?*; *raining cats and dogs*. (3) A fixed phrase, a phrase word, or a sentence word: *natural selection, ungetatable, never-say-die-ism, happy-go-lucky* (*attitudes*). (4) A term in the study of child language acquisition for a short utterance that does not lend itself to syntactic analysis: *mama, allgone, doggie*. Such holophrastic utterances are typical of the first stage of language acquisition, and make sense only in the immediate situation: *doggie* as *Look at the doggie* or *That's a doggie* or *Bring me a doggie*. Compare BINOMIAL, FIXED PHRASE, IDIOM. [GRAMMAR, WORD]. S.G., T.MCA.

HOME [17c in these senses]. (1) Back to one's own country: 'A letter which was brought home by the last Indian fleet' (Samuel Purchas, *Pilgrimage*, 1614); 'Vauxhall car workers were shouting "Yankees go home!"' (*Guardian*, 9 June 1973). (2) The 'mother country' of an empire, especially England or Britain: 'The persons who sued for it will make application home for another [charter]' (1762: in B. Pierce, *History of Harvard*, 1833). The habit of referring to the UK as 'home' has persisted into the later 20c among older people in various places, as in these South African citations: 'My father called Britain "home" and my mother who had never seen it did likewise. But their children do not do so any more and their children's children have never done so' (A. Paton, *Towards the Mountain*, 1980); 'On one occasion X overplayed the English side to the point of saying she was planning a trip "home" in such a way as to suggest a girlhood spent in the British Isles. Her husband . . . asked with mock surprise, "Do you mean Rustenburg? Or Graaff-Reinet?" ' (F. G. Butler, *Bursting World*, 1983). The usage has been tenacious in Australia and New Zealand, but is dying out: 'The only really happy person on the deck . . . is a middle-aged Australian. . . . He has been saving for years for his trip Home. He wept when we . . . saw the green Cornish folds beyond, and wept again for the Isle of Wight and the Dover cliffs' (G. Johnston, *Clean Straw for Nothing*, 1969). See HOME COUNTIES, MOTHER COUNTRY, OLD COUNTRY. [AFRICA, ASIA, EUROPE, NAME, OCEANIA].   T.MCA., J.B., W.S.R.

HOME COUNTIES. The region around London, consisting of Buckinghamshire, southern Bedfordshire, eastern Berkshire, Essex, Hertfordshire, Kent, Middlesex, Surrey, and Sussex. The speech in its towns is dominated by that of London; many who live there commute daily to work in the capital. New towns built since 1945, such as Basildon, Harlow, and Slough, are heavily populated by former Londoners, with a resulting spread of Cockney-like accents. In many places, however, such as Kent and Sussex, local rhotic accents continue. The attributive use of the phrase (as in *a Home Counties accent*) relates only to RP and its speakers, the middle and upper classes: 'Ascot, Henley, Sunningdale, Glyndebourne and Wimbledon. The names are a roll call of the major sporting and cultural events in the summer calendar of the rich. They are all part of the regional identity. The Home Counties are not just a place. They are a way of life' ('Life in the Cocktail Belt', *The Geographical Magazine*, Oct. 1984); 'The Malaysian language contains many English words, but with the vowels changed, so that it sounds as if learned from the pre-war Home Counties. A taxi is a "teksi" and a club, "kelab" (pronounced "clab")' (Simon Hoggart, 'A Bit of Empire Blooms', *Observer*, 30 Dec. 1990). See COCKNEY, LONDON. [EUROPE, NAME].   T.MCA.

HOME LANGUAGE, also **language of the home**. A technical term for the language of the family as opposed to the *medium of instruction* in school: 'Persons who maintain or adopt English as their home language are 10 to 20 times more likely to leave Quebec for the other provinces than are persons whose home language is French' (Réjean Lachapelle, 'The Position of French Improves', *Language and Society* 32, Fall 1990). Educational organizers in English-speaking countries have tended to assume that the languages of school and home are the same, but this is not necessarily so, especially in areas of high immigration and those in which everyday usage differs from the standard. See MOTHER TONGUE, TESD. [EDUCATION, LANGUAGE].   P.C.

HOMEOTELEUTON [16c: from Latin *homoeoteleuton*, Greek *homoiotéleuton* having the same ending. Stress: 'ho-me-o-tel-YOU-ton']. Also **homoioteleuton**. (1) In rhetoric, the opposite of alliteration, in which several words in a series have the same closing sounds, as in *illustrious and industrious, ethical and practical*. (2) In writing and typesetting, an error in transcribing a text, in which a section is left out because two phrases, clauses, or sentences near each other end with the same word or phrase, causing the copyist or setter to think there is only one. [STYLE, WRITING].   T.MCA.

HOMERIC SIMILE, also **epic simile**. An elaborate simile of between two and 20 lines in length, freely used in the epics of Homer. In English, the narrative verse of Milton, Pope, and Arnold has been noted for its use. Typically, such a simile is framed by the formula (*just*) *as . . . so*:

But *as* a troop of pedlars, from Cabool,
Cross underneath the Indian Caucasus,
That vast sky-neighbouring mountain of milk snow;
Crossing so high, that, as they mount, they pass
Long flocks of travelling birds dead on the snow,
Choked by the air, and scarce can they themselves
Slake their parch'd throats with sugar'd mulberries—
In single file they move, and stop their breath,
For fear they should dislodge the o'erhanging snows—
So the pale Persians held their breath with fear
    (Matthew Arnold, *Sohrab and Rustum*, 1853; italics added)

Such similes have traditionally been associated with high or grand style. See SIMILE. [LITERATURE, STYLE].   T.MCA.

HOME SERVICE. See BRITISH BROADCASTING.

HOMILY [16c: from Old French *omelie*, Latin *homilia*, Greek *homīlía* a conversation, sermon. Adjective *homiletic*]. A story or lecture on a religious or moral theme. Two *Books of Homilies* (1547, 1563) were issued by the Church of England to ensure orthodox preaching and to promulgate 'godly and wholesome Doctrines, and necessary for these times'. See AELFRIC, SERMON. [LITERATURE, MEDIA].   R.C.

HOMOGRAPH [1800s: from Greek-derived *homo-* same, *-graph* something written, on the analogy of *homonym*]. A kind of homonym: one of two or more words that are identical in spelling but different in origin, meaning, and pronunciation, such as *entrance* (noun: stress on first syllable) a door, gate, etc., and *entrance* (verb: stress on second syllable) to put in a trance; *lead* (verb: rhyming with 'deed' to take, conduct, guide, etc., and *lead* (noun: rhyming with 'dead') a metal. See HOMONYM. [LANGUAGE, WORD, WRITING].   T.MCA., R.E.A.

HOMONYM [17c: from Latin *homonymum*, Greek *homōnumon* (a word) having the same name]. One of two or more words that are identical in sound or spelling but different in meaning. There are three kinds: those that sound and look alike (*bank*[1] a slope, *bank*[2] a place for money, and *bank*[3], a bench or row of switches); *homophones*, that sound alike but do not look alike (*coarse, course*); and *homographs*, that look alike but do not sound alike (the verb *lead* /liːd/, the metal *lead* /lɛd/). The occurrence of homographs is largely a matter of chance, although a tendency to assimilate the unfamiliar to the familiar is also a factor, as with *compound* (an enclosure, originally Malay *kampong*), and *pigeon* (as in 'not my pigeon', a variant of *pidgin*). Dictionaries distinguish homographs by means of superscript numbers preceding or following them, largely on the basis of etymology. The degree of separation in dictionaries usually depends on the extent to which variation in etymology is taken into account: for example, *bank* (slope) and *bank* (a place for money) are ultimately related, but have had sufficiently divergent routes on their way to English to warrant separate treatment. There are over 3,000 homographs in the *Concise Oxford Dictionary* (8th edition, 1990). James B. Hobbs, in *Homophones and Homographs: An American Dictionary* (McFarland, 1986), lists 600. See AMBIGUITY, CONFUSIBLE, HETERONYM, HOBSON-JOBSONISM, HOMOGRAPH, HOMOPHONE, JANUS WORD, POLYSEMY, SEMANTICS, SPELLING. [LANGUAGE, SPEECH, WORD, WRITING]. T.MCA., R.E.A.

HOMOPHONE [17c: from Greek-derived *homo-* same, *phonē* sound]. One of two or more words that are identical in sound but different in spelling and meaning: *beer/bier*, *there/their/they're*. The occurrence of homophones is largely a matter of historical chance, in which words with distinct meanings come to coincide phonologically: *byre* a cowshed, *buyer* one who buys. Homophones are sometimes the basis of conscious word-play, as in Thomas Hood's 'His death, which happen'd in his berth, / At forty-odd befell: / They went and told the sexton, and / The sexton toll'd the bell' ('Faithless Sally Brown', 1826). Words may be homophones in one variety of English but not another: *father/farther* and *for/four* are homophonous in RP, but not in AmE and ScoE; *wails/Wales* are general homophones; *wails/Wales/whales* are homophones for many, but not in IrE and ScoE. *Whether/whither* are homophones in Scotland, but not *whether/weather*, which are homophones in England. *The Dictionary of British and American Homophones* (Stephen N. Williams, Brookside, 1987) lists some 12,000 homophones. *Homophones and Homographs: An American Dictionary* (James B. Hobbs, McFarland, 1986) lists some 3,600 homophones. See HETEROPHONE, HOMONYM, HOWLER, PHONE, PUN. [LANGUAGE, SPEECH, WORD].   T.MCA., R.E.A.

HOMORGANIC [1850s: from Greek-derived *homo-* same, and *organic*]. A term in phonetics for two or more speech sounds that have the same place of articulation: for example, the bilabial consonants /p, b/, which are formed by using both lips. [SPEECH].   T.MCA.

HONDURAS. See BAY ISLANDS, BELIZE, CENTRAL AMERICA.

HONG KONG, also **Hongkong.** A British colony in East Asia. Currency: the dollar (100 cents). Economy: trade, finance. Population: 5.4m (1984). Ethnicity: 98% Chinese, 2% British and others. Languages: English, Cantonese (both official: the latter spoken by over 80% of the people), and other Chinese dialects. In 1842, by the Treaty of Nanking, Hong Kong Island was ceded to Britain; in 1898, the mainland New Territories were leased to Britain for 99 years. The colony was occupied by Japan in the Second World War. Under the Sino-British Declaration of 1974, Hong Kong will be restored to China in 1997, when the lease expires. English is important in Hong Kong for written and printed communication, as a lingua franca between Chinese and non-Chinese, and in international trade, but is not widely used as a spoken medium. Most primary education is in Cantonese, and secondary education is provided in *Anglo-Chinese schools* (in which English is the medium of instruction except for Chinese subjects) and *Chinese middle schools* (in which Cantonese is the medium except for English subjects). There are two universities, one English-medium, one Chinese-medium, and other mostly English-medium tertiary institutions. Of some 40 daily newspapers, two are in English: the *South China Morning Post* (circulation 101,000) and the *Hongkong Standard* (60,000), with a combined readership of *c.*400,000 (80% Chinese).

Hong Kong usage includes: (1) Words and phrases from Chinese: *dim sum* snacks served in Chinese restaurants, *fung shui* ('wind-water') geomancy used in deciding the sites, orientation, and design of buildings, *gweilo* ('ghost person') a European man, *gweipor* a European woman, *hong* a large usually long-established non-Chinese trading company, *mafoo* a stable hand, *pak choi* Chinese cabbage, *taipan* the head of a hong. (2) Loan translations from Chinese: *dragon boat* a long canoe-like boat raced at festivals, *snakehead* a smuggler of illegal immigrants. (3) Terms from other languages: *amah* (Portuguese) a maid, *godown* (Malay) a warehouse, *nullah* (Hindi) a watercourse, *shroff* (Arabic through Persian and Anglo-Indian English) a cashier in a government office. (4) Such abbreviations as *Exco* Executive Council, *Legco* Legislative Council, *HKCEE* Hong Kong Certificate of Education Examination, and *IIs* ('eye-eyes') illegal immigrants (often also called *illegals*). (5) Local uses of general words: *short week* a work schedule in which one works on Saturday morning only every second week, *triad* a secret criminal society. See CHINA, EAST ASIAN ENGLISH, ENGLISH, MACAO. [ASIA, NAME, VARIETY].

T.MCA, J.P., H.W.

Platt, John. 1982. 'English in Singapore, Malaysia and Hong Kong', in R. W. Bailey & M. Görlach (eds.), *English as a World Language*. Ann Arbor: University of Michigan Press; Cambridge: University Press.

Taylor, Andrew. 1989. 'Hong Kong's English Newspapers', *English Today* 20. Cambridge: University Press.

HONG KONG EXAMINATIONS AUTHOR-ITY. See EXAMINING IN ENGLISH.

HONORIFIC [17c: from Latin *honorificus* giving honour]. A particle, inflection, word, or phrase used to show respect for a person addressed or discussed, and perhaps also to mark the subordinate role or status of a speaker. The ancient contrast *you/thou*, in which singular *you* was used honorifically, died out in 17c standard English. Similar contrasts can be found in other languages: French *vous/tu*, Persian *shoma/to*, Spanish *usted/tu*. The honorific vocatives *sir*, *madam*, *miss* were common in conversation until the mid-20c, but are not now widely used: 'Were it not for imagination, Sir, a man would be as happy in the arms of a chambermaid as of a Duchess' (Samuel Johnson, 1778). *Sir* and *miss* are common when children address teachers. See FORM OF ADDRESS. [GRAMMAR, NAME, STYLE].   T.MCA.

HORNBY, A(lbert) S(idney) [1898–1978]. English grammarian and EFL teacher, born in Chester, and educated at U. College London. From 1923, he taught English in Tokyo, where he worked with Harold E. Palmer at the Institute for Research in English Teaching. After Palmer's departure in 1936, he became editor of the IRET *Bulletin*. In 1937, with E. V. Gatenby and H. Wakefield, he began work on a novel dictionary for foreign learners that would provide lexical, syntactic, and idiomatic information. It was completed in 1940 and published in 1942 in Tokyo by Kaitakusha, as *The Idiomatic and Syntactic English Dictionary*. When Hornby left Japan in 1939 he joined the British Council and after the war became editor of *English Language Teaching*. In 1948, the dictionary was reissued by Oxford University Press as *A Learner's Dictionary of Current English*. In 1963, its revision was retitled *The Advanced Learner's Dictionary of Current English*, the greatest commercial success in ELT publishing. Hornby also published *A Guide to Patterns and Usage in English* (1954). See index. [ASIA, BIOGRAPHY, EDUCATION, EUROPE].   P.C.

HOUSE [17c in such senses]. (1) A place of business (*a variety of mercantile houses, Shellmex House*); a commercial company (*the House of Fraser*). (2) A printing or publishing company *a printing house, a publishing house*. (3) Used attributively: *a house journal, house magazine, house organ*, names for a periodical issued to employees and associates of such a house. See HOUSE STYLE. (4) A theatre (*playhouse*) or cinema (formerly especially BrE *picture house*, AmE *movie house*) or more commonly its audience (*playing to a full house*) or a performance in such a place (*first house, second house*). See THEATRE/THEATER. [LITERATURE, MEDIA].   T.MCA.

HOUSE STYLE. A term for rules adopted to bring uniformity and consistency to printed material coming from one source, such as a government department, publishing house, newspaper, professional association, or commercial company. Such organizations usually find it necessary to have a policy for points of style and usage that arise in writing and printing, and occasionally in speaking. These include often delicate choices relating to: (1) Spelling variants: *inquire* or *enquire*, *judgement* or *judgment*, *matins* or *mattins*, *publicize* or *publicise*. (2) The spelling and pronunciation of foreign names: *Beijing* or *Peking*, *Marseilles* or *Marseille*, *Moslem* or *Muslim*. (3) Style in abbreviations, capitalization, etc.: *B.B.C.* or *BBC*; *the Company* or *the company*. (4) Contentious general usages: *the Arabian Gulf*, *the Persian Gulf*, or *the Gulf*; *Holland* or *The Netherlands*; *chair*, *chairman*, *chairperson*. (5) Contentious grammatical issues: *the management is/are*; *anyone . . . he* or *anyone . . . they*. (6) Use of double and single quotation marks: *He said, 'Tell us about it'* or *He said, "Tell us about it."* (7) Hyphenation or non-hyphenation: *dining room* or *dining-room; make-up* or *makeup.* (8) Compounding: *news letter* or *news-letter* or *newsletter.* (9) Inclusive language: *businessman* or *businesswoman,* or *businessperson;* generic *he* or *she* or *(s)he* or *he or she* or *she or he* or singular *they.*

In such matters, independent writers may find individual solutions on a longer- or shorter-term basis. Few such writers, however, are fully consistent in what they do and are often willing to alter their usages in relation to the expectations of publishers and markets or to have them altered by editors. This means that the evidence of usage in printed material is not necessarily that of the authors, especially in such areas as spelling and pronunciation. Published material associated with an organization, especially in the media, almost always becomes subject to standardization, so as to create a consistent and even authoritative image. Rules are formulated so that people know where they are, creating in effect 'localized' versions of a standard language (established, as it were, by small-scale 'academies'). If writers do not for any reason follow the rules, editors, sub-editors/copy-editors, printers, and proof-readers usually make the necessary changes (but even so some writers succeed in going their own way). Such rules make up a *house style,* often organized in a *style sheet, style guide,* or *style manual* for distribution and easy consultation. Such sheets, guides, and manuals usually become more consistent and detailed as time passes. They are usually available only within an organization, but may sometimes be more widely distributed or even published as commercial titles. This was the case with Ernest Gowers's *The Complete Plain Words* (1954), compiled for the benefit of British civil servants, and Keith Waterhouse's *Waterhouse on Newspaper Style* (1989), based on the house handbook for *Daily Mirror* journalists.

Great Britain. One of the most influential house styles in the UK is that of Oxford University Press, made publicly available in 1904 in the first published edition of *Hart's Rules* (see below), and in 1905 in the *Authors' and Printers' Dictionary,* ed. F. Howard Collins. The original material in the dictionary was not compiled systematically in the manner of an ordinary dictionary, but was accumulated over the years as an extended card index. Collins relied to a great extent on the *OED,* but often broke new ground where no previous guidance existed: for example, as to when to use initial capitals for words such as *Bible, Act of Parliament, New Year's Day, Squire.* Many of the rules that he formulated

have since become widely accepted in BrE. 'Collins', as the handbook became known, influenced the house style of *The Times* and other newspapers, as well as publishing houses and learned societies. The 11th edition of the dictionary (1973) was extensively revised and rewritten, and published in 1981 as *The Oxford Dictionary for Writers and Editors (ODWE,* 448 pp.), ed. R. E. Allen, D. J. Edmonds, and J. B. Sykes. As a guide to usage, it is offered in conjunction with *Hart's Rules,* a work first compiled by Horace Hart in 1893, primarily for printers. The Press made the 15th edition available to the public in 1904, and the 39th was published in 1983 (182 pp.), revised and extended so as to complement *ODWE.* In 1986, the Press published a third work, *The Oxford Spelling Dictionary* (299 pp.), compiled by R. E. Allen, which also gives word divisions. Whereas the dictionaries provide information on individual items (*focused* not *focussed, tumour* not *tumor*), *Hart's Rules* has three sections: Rules for Setting English, Spellings, and Rules for Setting Foreign Languages.

The United States. American style manuals tend to be more detailed and to cover more topics than their British counterparts. The most influential is *The Chicago Manual of Style* (U. of Chicago Press, 13th edition, 1982, 738 pp.). It covers book formats, manuscript preparation and copy-editing, proofs, rights and permissions, design and typography, composition, printing, binding, general points of style, punctuation, numbers, illustrations and captions, tables, documentation styles, bibliographic forms, note forms, and indexes. Many publishing houses and university presses use it as their principal reference. Based on the *Chicago Manual,* Kate L. Turabian's *Manual for Writers of Term Papers, Theses, and Dissertations* (U. of Chicago Press, 5th edition, ed. Bonnie Birtwhistle Honigsblum, 1987) is a shortened, specialized 300-page version. Academic associations publish manuals geared to various disciplines, whose styles (especially for documentation and citation) may vary greatly. In the humanities, *The MLA Style Manual* by Walter S. Achtert and Joseph Gibaldi (Modern Language Association of America, 1985, 271 pp.) is comprehensive and influential. It gives guidance in all matters of manuscript preparation and publication. The citation and documentation style it recommends (parenthetical documentation in the text keyed to a final list of references) has become the norm, replacing footnotes. A version for students is the *MLA Handbook for Writers of Research Papers* (MLA, 2nd edition, 1984, 221 pp.).

Comparable works for other disciplines are the *Publication Manual of the American Psychological Association* (American Psychological

Association, 3rd edition, 1983, 208 pp.) and the *CBE Style Manual* (by the Committee on Form and Style of the Council of Biology Editors, American Institute of Biological Sciences, 3rd edition 1972, 297 pp.). Short and specialized house styles are defined by most journals: for example, the 'LSA Style Sheet for Publications of the Linguistic Society' is printed annually in the directory issue of the *LSA Bulletin*, and a 'Style Sheet for Glossaries' presents the house style for dictionary format of *American Speech* (volume 45, 1970, pp. 141–51), the journal of the American Dialect Society. Most major newspapers have house styles, some of which are generally available and influential. *The New York Times Style Book for Writers and Editors* (ed. Lewis Jordan, McGraw-Hill, 1962, 124 pp.) and *The Washington Post Deskbook on Style* (ed. Thomas W. Lippman, McGraw-Hill, 2nd edition 1989, 249 pp.) are typical. Similar are works of news services, such as *The UPI Stylebook* (ed. Bobby Ray Miller, United Press International, 1977, 200 pp.) and *The Associated Press Stylebook and Libel Manual* (ed. Christopher W. French, Addison-Wesley, 1987, 341 pp.). These works are primarily alphabetical lists of problems with recommendations (comparable to *ODWE*, above), but may include general information on matters of special concern in reportage. A guide for US government publications, the *United States Government Printing Office Style Manual* (US GPO, 1984, 479 pp.), began in 1894 and is now in its 28th version. In addition to matters of general style, it gives attention to legal records, the *Congressional Record*, and other specialized government publications. It also includes information on the printed form of major foreign languages. A small supplement is devoted to *Word Division* (US GPO, 1987, 142 pp.).

See ACADEMY, AMERICAN DIALECT SOCIETY, AMERICAN SPEECH, AUSTRALIAN BROADCASTING, AUSTRALIAN ENGLISH, AUTHORITY, BBC ENGLISH[1], CANADIAN LANGUAGE ORGANIZATIONS, CANADIAN STYLE GUIDES, COMPLETE PLAIN WORDS, DICTIONARY OF MODERN ENGLISH USAGE, EDITING, LAYOUT, LINGUISTIC SOCIETY OF AMERICA, MODERN LANGUAGE ASSOCIATION, OXFORD UNIVERSITY PRESS, USAGE GUIDANCE AND CRITICISM, WEBSTER'S DICTIONARY OF ENGLISH USAGE. [AMERICAS, EUROPE, MEDIA, STYLE, USAGE, WRITING].

M.LA., J.A., T.MCA., R.E.A.

HOWLER [mid-19c: something that causes people to howl with laughter or pain]. An informal term for a mistake in the use of language that is likely to cause hilarity, such as confusion between homographs (*Tibetan llamas* rather than *lamas*), between similar words (*a virago of lies* rather than *farrago*), and between idioms (*If this is your first visit to our country, you are welcome to it*, where *you're welcome* was intended), and the misformation of sentences (*a specialist in women and other diseases*, said of a physician specializing in gynecology). Compare CATACHRESIS, CONFUSIBLE, FRACTURED ENGLISH, MISTAKE, SOLECISM. [STYLE].   T.MCA.

HUBRIS [1880s: from Greek *húbris* insolence, arrogance]. Sometimes *hybris*. The overweening self-confidence and ambition that leads in tragic drama to the ruin of its possessor. See POETICS, TRAGEDY. [LITERATURE].   T.MCA.

HUMOUR BrE, **humor** AmE [14c: through French from Latin *humor* moisture, body fluid, temperament]. Originally a mental disposition or temperament, fossilized in such forms as *good-humoured* and *ill-humoured*, humour is currently a disposition towards pleasantry, often realized in the enjoyment of anecdotes, jokes, puns, repartee, riddles, wisecracks, and witticisms. Not all humour is verbal, and by no means everything that is humorous is also witty, though humour and wit are customarily neighbours, humour relating to situations and wit to the sayings the situations evoke. Oscar Wilde's play *The Importance of Being Earnest* (1895) is humorous in its basic situation: Jack Worthing, the central figure, is a foundling, discovered in a handbag left in a cloakroom at Victoria Station in London. It is witty in the comments made by the characters: for example, Lady Bracknell, Jack's prospective mother-in-law, tells him that she cannot allow her only daughter to 'marry into a cloakroom and form an alliance with a parcel'. Some expressions of humour appear to be primordial and universal, a visceral drollery transcending languages, independent of cultures, exacting sympathy with elementary human fears, aspirations, placations, aversions. This wordless humour is often presented graphically, as in cartoons, but, as language becomes its mediator, humour becomes increasingly culture-dependent. The joke usually presupposes a social bond, joker and audience drawing freely on a stock of common knowledge involving a shared history, a familiar pattern of daily life, topical events, and popular assumptions and attitudes. Within this general societal humour there exist institutional types, associated with certain professions (the law, the Church) or social subgroups (children, the old, the family).

The linguistics of humour. What is called a *sense of humour*, as if it were a skill like ability in mathematics or music, is a complex effect of people's experience as members of a culture, a nation, and various kinds of community. It might more appropriately be called a 'sense *for* humour': an ability to judge the acceptability of humour in certain situations, and a willingness to regard the capacity to laugh and to evoke laughter as legitimate behaviour. In social terms, there are times when people are free to make jokes, times when they need to make jokes, and times when joking is inhibited or disallowed. In this respect, the study of humour and humorous language belongs in the branches of linguistics called *pragmatics* and *discourse analysis*. When humour is considered in its social setting, it seems clear that many jokes derive their force from the joker's readiness to challenge authority and institutional constraints, as in courtroom humour. There is the story of learned counsel who, by a slip of the tongue, refers to one of the defendants in a case as having been *drunk as a judge.* 'I believe the expression is *drunk as a lord,*' the presiding judge corrects him, upon which counsel, in gravely courteous acknowledgement, says, 'I am obliged to your lordship.' Here, the joke plays with the language of the English law court, in which 'learned counsel' (a lawyer) refers by convention to the judge as *m'lud* (my lord) or *your lordship*, and corrections or explanations are always acknowledged with the formal *I'm obliged*. The propriety of form, however, masks an improper motive: to subvert the dignity and authority of the judge, to whom learned counsel should defer in spirit as well as in words. In such ways, humour is often subversive.

The universal and the particular. The relationship between humour and society is obvious enough to prompt a common assumption, that particular societies, or nations, have symptomatic styles and preferences in humour. The assumption is challenged, however, by the fact that many jokes traverse the world and travel through time, as general comments on human nature and human thought, only modified in their presentation by local details of custom and setting. An ancient Roman joke tells how a man is accidentally knocked down in the street by a porter carrying a trunk. 'Look out!' says the porter. 'Why?' asks the victim, 'Is there another trunk coming?' This joke is an archetype with many subsequent realizations: for instance, in the slapstick film routines of workmen carrying planks that strike the same victim twice (one end at a time), or in the joke about the pedestrian run over by a motorist who stops, puts his vehicle into reverse, and runs over the unfortunate a second time. 'Does it hurt?' the motorist enquires, solicitously. 'Only when I laugh,' replies the sufferer. At one time this latter joke (a specimen of the so-called *sick jokes* that began to be popular in the late 1940s) was commonly quoted as a typical example of German humour; now, though it continues in circulation, with variations in the telling and sometimes with

elaborations that transform it into a *shaggy dog story*, it is no longer attributed to any national background.

There are two arguable cases. One asserts that humour is the peculiar product of the society in which it occurs, or (a lesser form of the same case) of the language in which it is expressed. The other maintains that humour is a property basic to human nature in all societies, and that local forms are only the product of transient fashions, time-bound pre-occupations, or shifts in social attitudes. If American humour is for many people very different from British humour, it may well be because Americans have been concerned with different social facts, and hence with the projection of a different social image. Nations in their humour tend to present themselves as they would wish others to see them; and if they mock themselves, contriving their own *ethnic jokes*, they mock themselves as they would prefer to be mocked.

Old and Middle English. As there are stereotypes of national humour with some support in cultural fact, so there are widely accepted if not wholly reliable notions about humour in former ages. England before the Norman Conquest, for example, is nobody's idea of a country full of wags and wisecrackers, though riddles existed and there is at least one sardonic joke in the epic of *Beowulf*, where a sea dragon is pierced by a warrior's arrow, and 'after that he didn't swim so well' (as the poet slyly comments). Medieval humour is commonly perceived as folky, robust, and 'Chaucerian': that is, much concerned with fornication, fraud, farting, booze, and bumfun. This view of Chaucer, based on tales like those of the Miller and the Reeve, or characters like those of the Host and the Wife of Bath, ignores the subtle laughter, the allusiveness, the parodic wit to be found elsewhere in *The Canterbury Tales* and in his other works. It represents, however, one constituent of a dual stereotype: in historical terms, humour is either 'popular', grounded in homely (not to say vulgar) situations and personalities, or 'intellectual', relying on the humorist's power of pointed appeal to an audience primed with the appropriate cultural and literary knowledge, listeners and readers who are socially adept and reasonably well acquainted with the skills of language and rhetoric. The stereotype might not bear close examination, but it persists in the common perception of 'broad' as opposed to 'sophisticated' humour.

The Elizabethans. The drama of the late 16c, with its puns and backchat, fosters the notion of an age in which humour is 'intellectual' and linguistic. 'To see this age!' says Viola in Shakespeare's *Twelfth Night*, 'A sentence is but a chervil [= kid, soft leather] glove to a good wit: how quickly the wrong side may be turned outward!' But while kid-glove badinage was undoubtedly a staple feature of the stage play, the drama reflected 'humour' in a more philosophical sense, the medieval 'humours' of character and temperament that in their more eccentric manifestations became the object of laughter. Elizabethan taste also ran to vulgar, knockabout, prat-falling humour. Bottoms, bawds, and beer mugs were as common as paronomasia and polysemy; if we moderns are inclined to stress the linguistic character in Elizabethan humour, it is perhaps because we regard that age as a time of peculiar triumph for the English language. Besides, while writings of one kind or another may reflect popular humour, they are by their very nature, as writing, disposed to give prominence to the calculations of wit, to a humour that is premeditated, educated, intellectualized.

The Augustans. Such is the case with the humour of the 18c, apparently given over (to judge by leading writers of the time) to political satire, social and moral commentary, urbane formulations, aphorisms, and epigrams: the verbal evidence of strong powers of mind. We have only oblique and fleeting reflections of what must have been a vigorous existence of tavern humour, street talk, and the racy jargon of villains and vagabonds. If challenged to invent an 18c joke, the modern reader would probably attempt some dapper, mordant witticism, pointedly framed, expressing a social or moral or political ideology. This is an incomplete and stereotyped view of the humour of the period. If there is a compendium of 18c humour in a literary source, it is Sterne's *Tristram Shandy* (1760-7), which wanders across every species and level of joke, from low to high to satirical to sentimental to crazy. Much 18c humour turns, no doubt, on assumptions about 'good sense', reasonable conduct, morality, and sociability, but there is also a vein of untrammelled fantasy which Sterne in particular exploits.

The Victorians. Humour in its social and historical manifestations is by turns dangerous and domesticated; dangerous when it appears to attack a political and institutional status quo, domesticated when it settles down to chuckling over the mores of an approved social order or the harmless oddities of stock figures and types: policemen, clergymen, urchins, schoolchildren, tramps, drunks, professors, artists, eccentrics. In the 19c, humour in England becomes deeply domesticated, and there is no better illustration of this than the history of the magazine *Punch*, which began life as a politically radical, antimonarchist journal with strong proletarian sympathies, but within two decades became a representative of the affluent middle class smirking indulgently at its own foibles, at its own establishment and its servants, at the oddities of the poor, and at the strange ways of foreigners. *Punch* represents a whimsical, smiling cosiness that generally pervades 19c literary humour: for example, in the essays of Charles Lamb and the novels of Dickens (though there are times when Dickens's humour borders on the dangerous). Even the mordant verbal humour of the Irish writer Oscar Wilde (1854-1900) could be tolerated and applauded by his British middle-class audiences, for as long as they could feel secure in their own values.

A province of this cosy, assured humour is the work of academic wits and parodists like Lewis Carroll. Carroll's work acquires its peculiar and enduring flavour from a surreal imagination, the sophistications of logic and reasoning (philosophers still use him as a source of playful illustrations), and, in keeping with the Victorian domestication of humour, an affectionately observant attitude to children, his primary audience. Children were also the intended auditors of Edward Lear, an artist of ability and an entertaining travel writer who is best known, however, for the collections of nonsense verse that may be said to have originated a strain of comic invention still evident in Anglo-American humour. (The humorous writings of Spike Milligan and the radio scripts of the company known as *The Goons* in the 1950s are recent developments of the 'queery-Leary' style.)

Humorists in North America in the late 19c and early 20c inherited and developed the Victorian tradition of domesticity, parody, and fantasy. The American Bret Harte and the Canadian Stephen Leacock were both fervent admirers of Dickens. Harte's jovially parodic *Condensed Novels* (1867), a brilliant spoof of Victorian fiction, set the pattern for the more elaborate exercise of Leacock's *Nonsense Novels* (1911). As a humorist with a reflective, moralizing bent, Leacock is a comic-aesthetic forerunner of both James Thurber and Garrison Keillor, whose *Lake Wobegon Days* (1986) echoes Leacock's *Sunshine Sketches of a Little Town* (1912).

Popular and subversive humour. Popular or working-class humour in 19c Britain was fostered by the pantomime, whose great star was Joe Grimaldi (1770-1837), and later by the music hall and the individual performer who combined the talents of clown, mimic, fool (in the Elizabethan sense), and ballad-singer. These personalities were the precursors of the stand-up comedians and club comedians of the 20c, and of the great comedians of the 'silent' film era,

Charlie Chaplin and Buster Keaton. Such performers have been in many cases the custodians of the counter-tradition of dangerous (irreverent, aggressive, satirical) humour, though their work is governed by the prudent perception of what pleases an immediate audience.

The media. The cult of the comic personality has been greatly promoted by the emergence of new forms of stage: radio, motion pictures, television. These media are notorious for their voracious consumption of performance material. Whereas a 19c music-hall idol could use the same routines for years, the media comedian must continually discard old material and evolve new routines generally produced by scriptwriters, who are generally highly competent but more or less anonymous journeymen, some however achieving popular distinction as literary artists in their own right. One instance is the American humorist S. J. Perelman (1904-79). In his day, he supplied comic material to the Marx brothers, who depended on film, but whose humour included, in wild diversity, elements that would have been recognizable to Chaucer, the Elizabethan clowns, Laurence Sterne, Victorian wits and parodists, double-talking music-hall comedians, and stand-up comics with their quickfire jokes and patter.

Conclusion. The history of humour is a parade of opposing tendencies: the popular as against the learned, the spoken as against the written, performing as against creating, dangerous as against domesticated. The further contrast of 'occupational' and 'incidental' might be added, because many examples of parodic or playful humour have been the by-products of writers engaged in serious literature scholarship: for example, T. S. Eliot's *Old Possum's Book of Practical Cats* (1939). Traditions in humour and humorous writing have, like other literary traditions, become many-stranded, as an attempt to tell the story of American humour would demonstrate. An account that included the predominantly 19c humorists Josh Billings (Henry Wheeler Shaw), Petroleum V. Nasby (David Ross Locke), Artemus Ward (Charles Farrar Browne), Mark Twain (Samuel Langhorne Clemens), Bret Harte, and Joel Chandler Harris (1848-1908), and the predominantly 20c figures O. Henry (William Sidney Porter), Damon Runyan, S. J. Perelman, Robert Benchley, James Thurber, and E. B. White, would have to consider traditions of anecdote, folk-tale, dialect, dialogue, monologue, rustic wiseacreage, urban wisecracks, slow, simple cunning and sudden cleverness, political engagement, regional pride, and metropolitan insouciance: all the European modes of humour translated and complicated in

a New World setting. Every humorist and every joke somehow manage to embody both the history and geography of laughter.

See ABERDEEN JOKE, ANECDOTE, ATTIC SALT, BADINAGE, BANTER, BIERCE (THE DEVIL'S DICTIONARY), BON MOT, BURGESSISM, BURLESQUE, CARROLL, CARTOON, COMEDY, COMIC, CYNIC, DOG-, DOG, ELIOT, EPIGRAM, ETHNIC JOKE, FARCE, FRACTURED ENGLISH, FRANGLAIS, IRISH BULL, IRISH JOKE, IRONY, JENNINGS, JEWISH JOKE, JOKE, JOYCE, LEACOCK, LIMERICK, NEWFIE JOKE, NEW YORKER, NONSENSE, NONSENSE VERSE, ONE-LINER, PARADOX, PATTER, PLAYING WITH WORDS/WORD-PLAY, POTTER, PUN, PUNCH, PUNCH LINE, REPARTEE, RIDDLE, SARCASM, SATIRE, SCOTTISH JOKE, TWO-LINER, WIT, WITTICISM, WORD GAME. [MEDIA, STYLE]. W.N.

Eastman, Max. 1921. *The Sense of Humour.* New York: Scribner.
—— 1936. *Enjoyment of Laughter.* New York: Scribner.
Farb, Peter. 1974. *Word-Play: What Happens when People Talk.* New York: Alfred Knopf.
Highet, Gilbert. 1962. *The Anatomy of Satire.* Princeton, NJ: Princeton University Press.
Muecke, D. C. 1970. *Irony.* London: Methuen.
Muir, Frank (ed.). 1990. *The Oxford Book of Humorous Prose: From William Caxton to P. G. Wodehouse.* Oxford: University Press.
Munro, D. H. 1951. *Argument of Laughter.* Cambridge and Melbourne: Cambridge University Press.
Nash, Walter. 1985. *The Language of Humour: Style and Technique in Comic Discourse.* London: Longman.
Sewell, Elizabeth. 1952. *The Field of Nonsense.* London: Chatto & Windus.

HUNGARIAN. See BORROWING, EUROPEAN LANGUAGES.

HUNT, (James Henry) Leigh [1784-1859]. English essayist and pioneer journalist, born Southgate, Middlesex, and educated at Christ's Hospital. In 1808, with his brother John, he began *The Examiner*, which became the principal defender of the younger Romantic poets, who were being attacked in other journals. It took a radical line in politics and in 1813 the brothers were fined and imprisoned for a libel on the Prince Regent. Hunt edited several other journals, in which he published work by Byron, Shelley, Keats, and Hazlitt. His *Critical Essays on the Performers of the London Theatres* (1808) are valued by theatrical historians. [BIOGRAPHY, EUROPE, LITERATURE, MEDIA]. R.C.

HYBRID [16c: from Latin *hybrida* offspring of tame sow and wild boar, Roman father and foreign mother, freeman and slave]. Also **hybrid word**. A word whose elements come from more than one language: *television* (from Greek *tele-*, Latin *vision*), *jollification* (from English *jolly*,

Latin -*ification*). Attitudes to hybrids have been influenced by views on propriety and aesthetics. Traditionally, they have been considered barbarisms; purists have assumed that just as Latin, Greek, French, and English are distinct languages, so elements from these languages within English should be distinct. Fowler's *Modern English Usage* (ed. Gowers, 1965) accepted that in English there are 'thousands of hybrid words, of which the vast majority are unobjectionable. All such words as *plainness* or *paganish* or *sympathizer* are hybrids technically, but not for practical purposes. The same is true of those like *readable*, *breakage*, *fishery*, *disbelieve*, in which an English word has received one of the foreign elements that have become living prefixes or suffixes.' Fowler, however, listed some 'words that may be accused of being misformed', through hybridization or bizarre combination, including: *amoral, automation, bi-weekly, bureaucracy, coastal, coloration, dandiacal, flotation, funniment, gullible, impedance, pacifist, speedometer*. He described them as an 'ill-favoured list, of which all readers will condemn some, and some all'. Some have not survived; others are now part of the language. Hybridization has grown steadily in the 20c, with such words as *genocide, hydrofoil, hypermarket, megastar, microwave, photo-journalism, Rototiller, Strip-a-gram, volcanology*. It is particularly common where English is used alongside other languages. See AFRICAN ENGLISH, BARBARISM, COMBINING FORM, INDIAN ENGLISH[1], SPELLING, SPELLING REFORM, THEMATIC VOWEL. [WORD].　　　　　T.MCA.

HYMN [Before 11c: from Latin *hymnus*, Greek *húmnos* a song in praise of a god or hero]. A poem on a sacred subject, usually Christian and intended for choral singing. Hymns were used in Christian worship from an early date in both Greek and Latin. Vernacular hymns were composed in Old and Middle English, but were not used liturgically. The Reformation, however, encouraged vernacular congregational singing. In England, metrical versions of the Psalms of the Old Testament of the Bible (*metrical psalms*) were generally used until the flowering of hymnology in the 18c, in which Charles Wesley and Isaac Watts were prominent. The Church of England, at first wary of hymns, gradually welcomed them. Leading Victorian hymnologists included John Henry Newman and John Keble. Popular evangelism in the later 19c included the US evangelists D. L. Moody and Ira D. Sankey and the foundation of the Salvation Army in Britain in 1878, resulting in vigorous hymns that often used militant language and imagery:

> Soldiers of the Cross arise!
> Gird you with your armour bright:

> Mighty are your enemies,
> Hard the battle ye must fight.
> （W. W. How, 1823-97)

The writer of hymns is constrained by requirements of doctrine and traditional language. A lack of fresh rhymes for the basic words of faith can lead to predictable repetitions, as in:

> Pleasant are thy courts above
> In the land of light and love;
> Pleasant are thy courts below
> In this land of sin and woe:
> O, my spirit longs and faints
> For the converse of thy saints.
> （H. F. Lyte, 1793-1847)

They also lead to half rhyme and eye rhyme, as in:

> Praise to thy eternal merit,
> Father, Son and Holy Spirit.
> （J. Cosin, 1594-1672)

> Come, ye thankful people, come,
> Raise the song of harvest-home.
> （H. Alford, 1810-71)

Many metrical forms have been used, but the need for what can be easily sung limits their range. Poems not originally intended for singing have been adapted from such poets as Herrick, Blake, Wordsworth, Tennyson, Kipling, and Clough. Poems set to music as hymns include Blake's 'Jerusalem', Tennyson's 'Strong Son of God, immortal love', and Clough's 'Say not the struggle naught availeth'. Hymn writing in the 20c often uses colloquial rather than formal language, as in:

> He's back in the land of the living,
> The man we decided to kill,
> He's standing among us, forgiving
> Our guilt of Good-Friday hill.
> He calls us to share in his rising,
> To abandon the grave of our past;
> He offers us present and future,
> A world that is open and vast.
> （Fred Kaan, b.1929)

See BIBLE, PSALM, QUATRAIN. [LITERATURE].　R.C.

HYPALLAGE [16c: through Latin, from Greek *hupallagé* exchange. Stress: 'high-PA-ladgy']. (1) Also **transferred epithet**. In rhetoric, an adjective or participle (an *epithet*) that qualifies not the appropriate noun but one associated with it: *What you need is a hot cup of tea* (that is, a cup of hot tea); *The prisoner was in the condemned cell* (the prisoner was condemned, not the cell). Such expressions as *a sleepless night, the forgetful snow* are hypallages, in that they shift the sleeping and forgetting from a person to something inanimate. See PERSONIFICATION. (2) The reversal of the expected syntactic or semantic relation between two words: *her beauty's face* for *her face's beauty*. [STYLE].　　　T.MCA.

HYPERBATON [16c: through Latin from Greek *hupérbaton* stepping over. Stress: 'high-PER-ba-ton']. In rhetoric, the inversion of the usual or logical order of words, usually for emphasis, as in *This I really have to see*. It is common in traditional verse ('High on a throne of royal state . . . Satan exalted sat': Milton, *Paradise Lost*, 1667), in colloquial usage (*Fred his name is*), and in ironical comment, especially in AmE under the influence of Yiddish (*For this I came so far?*). Compare HYSTERON PROTERON, INVERSION. [STYLE].　　　　T.MCA.

HYPERBOLE [16c: through Latin from Greek *huperbolé* flung too far. Stress: 'high-PER-bo-ly']. A rhetorical term for exaggeration or overstatement, usually deliberate and not meant to be taken (too) literally: 'At Nineveh alone—the greatest archeological discovery of all time—were found fifty thousand tablets' (R. E. Friedman, *Who Wrote the Bible?*, 1988); 'Old Celtic myths have been springing up around these hills and lakes since the very start of time' (Tom Davies, 'Home & Garden', *Times Saturday Review*, 18 Aug. 1990). Everyday idioms are often hyperbolic: *a flood of tears, loads of room, tons of money, waiting for ages, as old as the hills, having the time of one's life*. Their purpose is effect and emphasis, but frequency of use diminishes their impact. See EXAGGERATION. [STYLE].　　　T.MCA.

HYPERCORRECTION. (1) Over-correction resulting in usages that may be regarded as amusing, deplorable, and/or tokens of the insecurity that prompted it. In New York City, highly stigmatized pronunciations (represented in print as, for example, *Toity-Toid Street* for Thirty-Third Street) are popularly associated with Brooklyn (although they are widespread throughout the working class). Speakers who want to dissociate themselves from this accent often 'correct' all forms which contain *oi*, so that *toilet* becomes 'terlet' and *boil* becomes 'berl'. Having become aware of the stereotype, which suggests that *oi* is always an incorrect pronunciation of *er*, they try to eliminate it wherever it occurs. In cases like *terlet*, the resulting form is not only hypercorrect but non-existent in the speech they are trying to emulate. Such hypercorrections have often themselves become stereotypes and shibboleths. (2) A term used by some sociolinguists for instances in which speakers adopt forms closer to the standard than those they normally use. These forms are hypercorrect for such speakers, but exist normally in the speech of others: in New York City, the use of /r/ after vowels (as in *car, hurt*) has become the prestige norm and the working class tends to use /r/ more when speaking carefully, to such a

degree that they exceed the usage of the middle class. [EDUCATION, LANGUAGE].　　　S.R.

HYPERMEDIA. See HYPERTEXT.

HYPERONYM. See GENERIC, HYPONYM, SEMANTICS.

HYPERTEXT [1960s]. A term in computing for text made up of short units (typically a paragraph, or 24-line screen) between which the reader may jump using links assigned in advance. Unlike a book, in which the pages are in sequence, hypertext allows any of a number of pages to follow the one being read, and in any desired order. A hypertext system, such as *Apple Hypercard*, contains a great many *frames*, each of which normally contains one screenful of information. In each frame are several *buttons* or *arrows* which the reader can activate, and which call up another frame, in the same way as a cross-reference in ordinary text. Hypertext derives from an idea put forward in 1945 by the US computer designer Vannevar Bush; the term was coined by the US entrepreneur Ted Nelson. Brown U. in Providence, Rhode Island, has pioneered the use of hypertext in teaching, using its IRIS system, which includes pictures as well as text, in courses as diverse as English literature, anthropology, and cell biology. Such systems, which may include sound recordings, are known as *hypermedia*, and may include links between different sources and types of sources of information, such as continuous texts, dictionaries, and maps and illustrations of various kinds. See MULTIMEDIA, THEMATIC ORDER. [EDUCATION, MEDIA, TECHNOLOGY].　　　M.L., T.MCA.

HYPHEN [16c: from Late Latin *hyphen*, Greek *huphén* together, from *hupo-* under, *hen* one]. The punctuation mark (-), which has two main functions in present-day English: as a *link hyphen* (or *hard hyphen* in printing terminology), joining whole words or elements of words into longer words and compounds (*house-plant*, *Anglo-French*); as a *break hyphen* (or *soft hyphen*), marking the division of a word at the end of a line, especially in print (*divi-sion, liter-ature*).

The link hyphen. The use of the hyphen to mark compound words has existed in English since the 16c, and from an earlier date in various forms in words such as *to-day* and *with-out*. It has always been variable and unpredictable. In recent use, it appears to be diminishing in some circumstances: for example, when the elements of a compound are monosyllabic (*birdsong, eardrum, playgroup; lambswool*, formerly *lamb's wool*), in longer formations where the elements are regarded as closely associated (*businesswoman, nationwide*); where the two elements are regarded as having equal semantic weight, with the first acting as a modifier, forming a spaced pair (*road sign, snow goose*); and in prefixed forms such as *coordinate* and *reuse*. The absence of the hyphen in such cases is well established in AmE, and is becoming more common in BrE. The hyphen continues in BrE and AmE in both routine and occasional couplings when the elements seem to retain a stronger individual identity, and in ad-hoc formations: *boiler-room, filling-station*. In the second of these, *filling* is a noun ('a station for filling') and not a participle ('a station that fills'), which the absence of a hyphen might imply. Usage, however, is rarely consistent or completely logical in this regard. A hyphen is often retained to avoid awkward collisions of letters, as in *breast-stroke, co-worker*, and *radio-isotope*, but usage varies even in these cases, often in keeping the elements of compounds separate (*breast stroke, radio isotope*), and occasionally merging them (*breaststroke, radioisotope*).

The link hyphen also has a role in punctuation: (1) To establish such syntactic links as *truck-driver, labour-saving*, and *brown-eyed*. In the phrases *hard-covered books* and *French-speaking visitors*, the reference is to 'books with hard covers' and 'visitors who speak French'; here, hyphenation prevents misunderstanding and parallels the stress patterns of speech: *hárd-covered bóoks* and *Frénch-speaking péople* as opposed to *hard cóvered bóoks* and *French spéaking péople*. (2) To form expressions with a phrasal base, such as *drink-affected* (affected by drink), *weed-infested* (infested with weeds), and *panic-stricken* (stricken by panic). (3) To avoid ambiguity in *twenty-odd people* (compare *twenty odd people*). (4) To connect the elements of associated words used attributively as in *a well-known woman* and *Christmas-tree lights*, but not predicatively as in *the woman is well known* and *the lights on the Christmas tree*. (5) Connecting nouns in apposition that form a single concept, such as *city-state* (a city that is also a state) and *player-manager* (a manager who is also a player), and in units such as *passenger-mile* (a mile travelled by one passenger: a statistical usage). (6) Connecting elements to form words in cases such as *re-enact* (where the collision of the first and second *e* might be awkward), *re-form* (meaning 'to form again' as opposed to *reform*), and some prefixed words such as those in *anti-, non-, over-*, and *past-*. Usage varies in this regard, especially as between BrE and AmE. In AmE, solid forms such as *reenact* and *nonstandard* are common. In general terms, a great deal depends on how established and recognizable a formation is: when the second element begins with a capital letter, a hyphen is usual, as in *anti-Darwinian*. There are no hard-and-fast rules.

The break hyphen. The hyphen is used to divide a word at the end of a line, especially in print when words are spaced out to fill lines with justified margins. In handwritten texts, typed or word-processed material, and unjustified print, word-breaks can usually be avoided. In print, it has traditionally been a matter of pride with printers and publishers to ensure a careful division of words when line-breaks occur, taking account of the appearance and structure of the word. There are two basic approaches, *phonetic* (in terms of syllable structure) and *morphological* (in terms of word structure). Broadly, AmE favours a phonetic approach (preferring *trium-phant* to *triumph-ant*), while BrE has usually given greater weight to a morphological approach, although preferences are widely varied (*veg-etable, vege-table, ve-ge-table*). Newspapers in all English-speaking countries tend to produce word divisions that reflect neither criterion (such as *bat-hroom, se-arched, da-ily*), usually because the line-breaks in their computer typesetting programs are based on fairly crude principles such as division between two consonants. The traditional aim of word division at line-breaks is to distract the reader as little as possible: 'a brutish word-break is a frontal attack on the sensibilities of the ordinary reader' (Ronald McIntosh, *Hyphenation*, 1990). See COMPOUND WORD, DI(A)ERESIS, OBLIQUE, PHRASE WORD, PUNCTUATION, SENTENCE WORD, SYLLABICATION/SYLLABIFICATION. [STYLE, USAGE, WRITING]. R.E.A.

HYPONYM [1960s: on the model of *homonym, synonym*, using the Greek prefix *hypo-* under]. Also **subordinate term**. A word, phrase, or lexeme of narrower or more specific meaning that comes 'under' another of wider or more general meaning: for example, *rose* under *flower* ('a rose is a kind of flower', 'flowers include roses and tulips'). In this relationship, the word *flower* is a *hyperonym, generic term*, or *superordinate term*. Many hyponyms belong in groups, such as *carpet, chair, desk, table, rug, stool*, all of which are *co-hyponyms* of the hyperonym *furniture* ('a carpet is an item of furniture'). Hyponymic relations are often imprecise, unstable, and multidimensional, depending on both context and how relationships are analysed. The same word may be a hyponym of several superordinates: *axe* as 'kind of tool' and 'kind of weapon'; *weapon* also a hyponym of *tool* ('a weapon is a kind of tool'). *Battle-axe* is 'a kind of axe' and 'a kind of weapon', but is unlikely to appear under *axe* in the sense of 'a kind of tool'. *Rug* is in some contexts a synonym of *carpet* ('The cat sat on the rug/carpet'), in others a hyponym of *carpet* ('a rug is a kind of carpet'). See -ONYM, SEMANTICS, SENSE. [LANGUAGE, WORD]. T.MCA.

HYPOTAXIS [19c: through Latin from Greek *hupótaxis* under-arrangement]. A traditional term for *subordination*. See SUBORDINATION. Compare PARATAXIS. [GRAMMAR]. T.MCA.

HYSTERON PROTERON [16c: through Latin from Greek *hústeron próteron* the later first: that is, the cart before the horse]. (1) In rhetoric, a reversal of the expected order of words: *raining cats and dogs* changed for effect to 'raining dogs and cats'. (2) In logic, a fallacy in which the proposition to be proved is assumed as a premiss, or the conclusion comes before the premisses. Compare HYPERBATON, INVERSION. [LANGUAGE, STYLE]. T.MCA.

I

I, i [Called 'eye']. The 9th letter of the Roman alphabet as used for English. It originated in the Phoenician symbol *yod* (representing the sound of *y* in *yes*) which was adapted in Greek to a vertical line for the vowel called *iota*. This was adopted by the Romans as *I* with both long and short Latin vowel values, and also for the consonant value of *y*. In medieval times, a superscript dot was added to distinguish minuscule *i* in manuscript from adjacent vertical strokes in such letters as *u*, *m*, *n*. The variant form *j* emerged at this time and subsequently became a separate letter.

Sound values. It is difficult to fix a precise primary value for *i* in English. There is free variation between different values of *i* in the first syllable of words such as *digest, finance, minority, tribunal*. Elsewhere, there is a regular shift between related words: *child/children, five/fifth, crime/criminal, finish/final(ity), social/society, admire/admirable*. Variation in sound is overlaid by two uncertainties in spelling: except word-initially, both *i* and *y* can represent the same sound, even as alternatives: *gipsy/gypsy, siphon/syphon, laniard/lanyard, drier/dryer*. Many spellings are available for the one sound in the final syllables of *souvenir, Kashmir* (contrast *cashmere), cavalier, weir, musketeer, sincere, appear*. The result is a varied distribution of values, as follows:

Short I. (1) In most monosyllabic words before pronounced word-final consonants: *ill, in, is; bid, big, bit; which, sing, dish, with; fifth, milk, kiln, film, filth, wind* (noun), *link, hint, plinth, lisp, list*. However, long *i* occurs in this position in *pint, ninth* and *child, mild, wild* (but not *build, gild, guild*) and in *bind, find, kind, wind* (verb), etc. Short *i* occurs in *give, to live*, but long *i* in *dive, five, alive*. Similarly, short *i* occurs in *river, liver*, but long *i* in *diver, fiver*. (2) In most polysyllables before a doubled consonant (*bitter, bitty, cirrus, irrigate, immigrant*) and commonly before single consonants (*city, finish, spirit, river, consider, imitate, iridescent, limit, litigation, magnificent, ridiculous*). (3) Occasionally before a consonant and word-final *e* (*give, live, active, heroine, imagine, definite*), although *i* is normally long in this environment. (4) The sound of short *i* is often spelt with *y*, especially to represent the Greek letter upsilon, as in *myth, symbol*. Other vowel letters may also have this value: *e* in *pretty* and Greek-derived words such as *acme, catastrophe; o* in the plural *women; u* in *busy, business*. Certain unstressed vowels vary in pronunciation between short *i* and other values, especially schwa: *a* as in *furnace, cottage, e* as in *began, despair, hated, college, u* as in *lettuce, minute* (noun). (5) In RP, a modified short *i* occurs before single *r*, when *ir* is not directly followed by another vowel: *sir, stir, bird, girl, squirm, first, birth, circle, virtue*. The same modification occurs with the short values of *e, u, y*, producing the homophones *birth/berth, fir/fur*. (6) The letter *i* does not occur word-finally in traditional English spelling, its sound being represented by *y*, but such a short *i* or a lengthened variant (depending partly on accent) is found in some recent formations and loans: *taxi, safari, spaghetti*. A length distinction between this value and short *i* may be heard in *taxiing*, a distinction some speakers also make between the two vowels of *city*.

Long I. (1) Monosyllables and disyllables before one or sometimes two consonants preceding word-final *e: ice, tribe, wife, like, pile, time, fine, ripe, mire, kite, strive, size; idle, rifle, isle, title, mitre*. (2) In disyllabic verbs ending in a stressed Latin root, whose corresponding nouns often have short *i: ascribe/ascription, collide/collision, decide/decision, invite/invitation, provide/ provision, reside/residence*. (3) In monosyllables before: *-gh (high, sigh, fight, plight, height,*

THE CAPITAL LETTER

EARLY FORMS				CURRENT FORMS	
Phoenician	Greek	Etruscan	Roman (Latin)	roman	italic
𐤆	𐌓𐌉	𐌉	I	I	*I*

THE SMALL LETTER

EARLY FORMS			CURRENT FORMS	
Roman cursive	Roman uncial	Carolingian minuscule	roman	italic
I	J	ı	i	*i*

sleight, but not otherwise after *e*: (*weigh, sleigh, eight, freight*); *-ld* (*child, mild, wild*, but not *build, g(u)ild*); *-nd* (*bind, blind, find, grind, hind, kind, rind, wind* (verb); and in a single case each *-nt* (*pint*), *-nth* (*ninth*), and *-st* (*Christ*). Note also *whilst*. In monosyllabic and disyllabic roots, a following silent consonant sometimes signals the long value: *-g* (*align, benign, consign*), *-b* (*climb*), *-c* (*indict*), *-s* (*island, viscount*). (4) In many polysyllables with initial stressed syllables: *library, iron, island, item, final, libel, license, private, ivy, tidy* (but contrast *privy, city*). (5) The long value is not always stable: sometimes it remains in derivatives while losing stress (*final/finality, irony/ironic, library/librarian, virus/virology*), elsewhere becoming short while stress is retained (*arthritis/arthritic, bronchitis/bronchitic,* BrE *private/privacy*). (6) In initial stressed syllables directly followed by another vowel: *client, dial, diamond, diet, friar, ion, science, triangle, triumph*. The long *i* is kept when the stress shifts in derivatives: *science/scientific, triangle/triangular, triumph/triumphant*. (7) In some unstressed suffixes of Latin origin, such as *-ide* (*cyanide, sodium chloride*) and *-ite* (*Israelite, finite*, but optionally short in *plebiscite*). In other suffixes, usage varies. Long *i* occurs in *-ile* in BrE but generally not in AmE, which has a schwa or a syllabic consonant: *fertile, hostile, missile, volatile*. Long *i* occurs in such animal-related adjectives as *aquiline, bovine, equine*, but short *i* commonly in such general adjectives as *feminine, genuine, masculine* (although long *i* can also occur, especially in ScoE). Latin endings in *i* usually have long value (*alibi, fungi, termini*) as do Greek letter names (*pi, phi, psi, chi/khi*). (8) A unique spelling is *choir*, changed from *quire* to reflect its derivation from *chorus*.

Continental I. This is the 'ee' value of Middle English *i* before the Great Vowel Shift. It is found in recent loans from the Romance languages (*pizza, police, fatigue, routine, souvenir, mosquito*) and elsewhere (*bikini, kiwi, ski*). Japanese Romaji spellings also accord *i* this value: *Hirohito, Mitsubishi*. In final position in French loans, the *i* may be followed by a silent letter: *debris, esprit*. The spelling of this vowel sound in earlier French loans has been Anglicized as *ea* and *ee*: *league, esteem, canteen*. This value also occurs in native English words and older loans with the medial digraph *ie*: *field, fiend, frieze, grief, mien, piece, priest, shriek, siege*. A following *r* modifies this value in RP, but otherwise *bier, pierce, cashier* belong in this category. Occasionally the *ee* value of the *ie* may be shortened in speech to short *i*: *mischief*. The *ie* in *sieve* always has short value, and the *e* value in *friend* is exceptional.

Unstressed I. In unstressed position, *i* is commonly reduced to schwa, though in some accents, notably RP, tending towards its short value: *sordid, plaintiff, porridge, vestige, nostril, denim, raisin, tapir, premiss, limit, satirist, admiral, admiration*.

Silent I. (1) In the second written syllable of *business* and, for some people, in *medicine*. (2) Before another vowel in the unstressed syllables of *cushion, fashion, parishioner*, and commonly in *parliament*.

Variations. (1) The letters *i, y* were interchangeable in Middle English and remain so in several pairs of alternatives: short value (*gipsy/gypsy, lichgate/lychgate, pigmy/pygmy, sillabub/syllabub, silvan/sylvan*); long value (*cider/cyder, cipher/cypher, dike/dyke, siphon/syphon*); contrasting *ie* and *y* (*bogie/bog(e)y, caddie/caddy, pixie/pixy*). BrE *tyre* contrasts with AmE *tire*. However, these alternatives are distinct from such homophones as *calix/calyx, chili/chilly, die/dye*. (2) There is standard variation between *y* and *i* when a suffix is added to a word that ends in *y*: *happy, happier, happiest, happily, happiness; pity, pitying, pities, pitied, pitiable, pitiful*. However, *busy* keeps *y* in *busyness*, to distinguish it from *business*. Sometimes there are alternative forms (*drier/dryer*), or there is no *i* form (*slyness* only), or no *y* form (*gaily, daily*). The verbs *lay, pay, say* change *y* to *i* in their past tense only: *laid, paid, said*. The verbs *try, deny*, adopt *i* in *trial, denial*. (3) The digraph *ie* has the value of long *i* in open monosyllables: *die, lie, tie*. Nouns and verbs whose base form ends in *y* with the value of long *i* inflect with *ie* when followed by *s* and *d*: *try/tries, simplify/simplified*. (4) *I* replaces *e* when suffixes are added to base words ending in *-ce*: *face/facial, finance/financial, space/spacious* (but note *spatial*). For alternative spellings such as *despatch/dispatch, enquire/inquire* see under E. (5) Some Latin singulars ending in *-us* substitute *-i* in the plural (*fungus/fungi, radius/radii, terminus/termini*). This is sometimes optional (*cactuses, cacti*) and may include controversial usages such as *syllabuses, syllabi* (there being no justification in Greek or Latin for the form *syllabi*). Some Latin singulars ending in *-is* may change to plural *-es*: *axis/axes, basis/bases, oasis/oases*.

Other functions. (1) A following *i* may soften (that is, palatalize) the letters *c* and *g*: *electric/electricity, rigour/rigid*. (2) When a vowel letter follows, *i* may soften a preceding consonant, but lose its own sound value: for example, *c* sounding like *sh* in *racial, electrician, conscience, suspicion, conscious*. Similar palatalization occurs with *d* (*soldier*), *s* (*vision*), *ss* (*mission*), *t* (*nation*). (3) In a similar position, *i* is silent after (soft) *g*:

contagion, contagious, region, religion. (4) In the system of English personal pronouns, the capitalized letter *I*, spoken with a long value, represents the first person singular. To represent distinctive pronunciations, however, such as in Scots and Southern AmE, the form changes to *Ah.* See ALPHABET, HARD AND SOFT, J, LETTER[1], SPELLING. [WRITING].   C.U.

IAMB, also **iambus** [16c and 1830s: from Latin *iambus*, Greek *íambos* lame: that is, a weak step before a strong step. *Iamb* is pronounced 'I am' (stressing the first vowel, and with or without a closing /b/)]. A metrical foot of two syllables, short then long in quantitative metre, as in Latin, unstressed then stressed in accentual metre, as in English *begin* and *support.* The following lines of Gray's 'Elegy written in a Country Church-Yard' (1751) are in regular *iambic pentameter* (five iambs to the line):

$$\cup \; - \; \cup \; - \quad \cup \; - \; \cup \; - \; \cup \quad -$$
/The cur/few tolls / the knell / of par/ting day.
/The low/ing herd / wind slow/ly o'er / the lea.

The iamb is the most frequently used foot in English verse, in lines of various lengths, and is widely believed to fit the natural rhythm of the language. See FOOT, METRE/METER, SCANSION. [LITERATURE].   R.C.

IATEFL, short for *International Association of Teachers of English as a Foreign Language,* and pronounced 'Eye-a-teffle'. An association for teachers of English as a foreign or second language, founded in 1967 in London by William R. Lee, its chairman 1967-84. Its original name *Association of Teachers of English as a Foreign Language (ATEFL)* was changed in 1971. In 1989, it had 11 branches worldwide, 26 affiliated organizations (20 outside the UK), and a membership of 2,028 (60% outside the UK). The association is identified with the British tradition in EFL/ESL, and most of its members teach in such EFL countries as Germany, Italy, or Spain or such ESL countries as India, Nigeria, and Singapore. The association holds an annual conference and publishes the *IATEFL Newsletter.* With the British Council it sponsors the *English Language Teaching Journal (ELT Journal).* In 1990, a collection of articles from the journal was published as *Currents of Change in English Language Teaching,* ed. Richard Rossner & Rod Bolitho. Compare TESOL. See TEFL, TESL. [EDUCATION, EUROPE, MEDIA].   P.S., T.MCA.

IBERIAN LANGUAGES. The languages of the Iberian peninsula, consisting of: (1) The Romance languages *Castilian Spanish, Catalan* in north-western Spain and Andorra, *Gallego* in Galicia, and *Portuguese* in Portugal. (2) *Basque*

in Spain, a language apparently unrelated to any other in Europe, spoken along the eastern Bay of Biscay and in the western Pyrenees, as well as in neighbouring France. (3) *English,* used in Gibraltar since 1713, in recent decades among expatriate Britons in resorts for the retired along the Mediterranean littoral, and in the Douro valley of Portugal, among the long-established British families that make port wine. (4) *Arabic,* was widespread during the Middle Ages. See ARABIC, BORROWING, ENGLISH, EUROPEAN LANGUAGES, GIBRALTAR, PORTUGUESE, SPANISH. [EUROPE, LANGUAGE].   T.MCA.

IBO. See IGBO.

ICELANDIC [17c]. The Germanic language of Iceland. Old Icelandic embodies records of early Scandinavian literature, and some of its sagas refer to events in England and to early Scandinavian links with Britain. Modern Icelandic has two alphabetic letters, *thorn* [þ] and *eth* [ð], borrowed from Old English. A strong purist tradition attempts to exclude foreign influence, but the influence of English is increasing, especially on television. See BORROWING, CRAIGIE, ETH, SAGA, SCANDINAVIAN LANGUAGES, THORN. [EUROPE, LANGUAGE].   P.C.

ICON [16c: through Latin from Greek *eikōn* likeness, image]. Also **ikon.** (1) A picture or image, especially a saint painted on a wooden panel and venerated in Orthodox Christianity. If something is *iconic,* it represents something else in a conventionalized way, as with features on a map (roads, bridges, etc.) or onomatopoeic words (as for example the words *kersplat* and *kapow* in US comic books, standing for the impact of a fall and a blow). *Iconography* is: the study of imagery in the visual arts; symbolic representation through images; or a group or system of iconic representations. (2) An archetypal image: 'It is hopeless to retreat from the problem of racism to [Margaret] Mitchell's personal and Scarlett's fictional struggles against the role of the "icon" the "Southern Lady", a figure utterly entangled with the practice of slavery' (Patricia Storace, *The New York Review of Books,* 19 Dec. 1991). (3) A person regarded as embodying a certain quality, style, or attitude in a distinctive, often charismatic way: 'When Spike Lee, America's hottest black film director, decided to make a film about Malcolm X, the country's most controversial black icon, Hollywood sensed a blockbuster' (John Cassidy, *The Sunday Times,* 11 Aug. 1991). (4) A stylized symbol, especially in computing: a small image on a screen representing a function or an option, such as a paintbrush (representing and permitting a painting-like activity on screen) or a wastebasket (representing and permitting the erasure of material). Commonly, a program is started, a file obtained, etc., by pointing an arrow-like cursor at one icon in a menu-like group, generally using a hand-held mouse to move the cursor and activate the icon. Compare ARCHETYPE, IMAGE, SIGN, SYMBOL. See SEMIOTICS. T.MCA.

ICTUS [18c: Latin, a beat or stroke]. In prosody, the name for stress on a syllable in a line of verse (sometimes marked with an acute accent), and for the stressed syllable itself. The ictus usually coincides with normal speech stress, but pronunciation may be wrenched for effect, as with *missionary* in the 19c lines attributed to Bishop Samuel Wilberforce and less violently in *navy* in those of W. S. Gilbert:

> If I were a cassowáry
> On the plains of Timbuctoo,
> I would eat a missionáry
> Cassock, bands and hymn-book too.

> And I copied all the letters in a hand so free
> That now I am the ruler of the Queen's Navy.
> (W. S. Gilbert, *H.M.S. Pinafore*, 1878)

Historical changes in stress may cause ictus and ordinary pronunciation to conflict for a later generation, sometimes with an effect on rhyme, as at the ends of lines 2 and 4 in John Donne's 'The Funerall' (*c*.1605):

> For 'tis my outward Soule,
> Viceroy to that, which unto heaven being gone,
> Will leave this to controule,
> And keep these limbes, Her Provinces, from
> dissolution.

Donne's *dissolution* had five syllables, with a stress on the last. See ACCENT, METRE/METER, RHYTHM, STRESS, THESIS. [LITERATURE]. R.C.

IDEA [15c: through Latin from Greek *idéa* sight, shape, form, model. Cognate with Latin *videre* to see, Sanskrit *véda* vision, knowledge]. Something present in or perceptible to the mind. The Greeks took the concept of something seen and applied it metaphorically to something 'seen' with the mind's eye: that is, an *image*, as in *imagination*. In the philosophy of Plato (5/4c BC), the Ideas or Forms are perfect, abstract essences that lie 'behind' everyday existence; only they are real, and their reflections in this world are imperfect shadows. Generally, in current usage, an idea is less mystical and more immediate: an original thought or mental characterization with the potential of making things happen: for example, the conception of a wheel before the making of the first actual wheel. Compare ARCHETYPE, FORM, IMAGE. [LANGUAGE]. T.MCA.

IDEOGRAM. See WRITING.

IDIOLECT [1940s: from Greek *idios* personal, and *-lect* as in *dialect*]. In linguistics, the language special to an individual, sometimes described as a 'personal dialect'. See DIALECT, ENGLISH, LECT. [LANGUAGE]. T.MCA.

IDIOM [16c: from Latin *idioma*, Greek *idiōma* specific property, special phrasing, from *idios* one's own, personal, private]. Also (archaic) **idiotism**. (1) The speech proper to, or typical of, a people or place; a dialect or local language; the unique quality or 'genius' of a language: *classics in the Tuscan idiom*. (2) An expression unique to a language, especially one whose sense is not predictable from the meanings and arrangement of its elements, such as *kick the bucket* a slang term meaning 'to die', which has nothing obviously to do with kicking or buckets. In linguistics, the term *idiomaticity* refers to the nature of idioms and the degree to which a usage can be regarded as idiomatic. Some expressions are more holophrastic and unanalysable than others: for example, *to take steps* is literal and non-idiomatic in *The baby took her first steps*, is figurative, grammatically open, and semi-idiomatic in *They took some steps to put the matter right*, and is fully idiomatic and grammatically closed in *She took steps to see that was done*. These examples demonstrate a continuum of meaning and use that is true for many usages. No such continuum exists, however, between *He kicked the bucket out of the way* and *He kicked the bucket last night* (meaning 'He died last night'). Such idioms are particularly rigid: for example, they cannot usually be passivized (no **The bucket was kicked*) or otherwise adapted (no **bucket-kicking* as a synonym for *death*).

Creative adaptations. Although idioms are normally simply slotted into speech and writing, they are occasionally subject to creative wordplay. The phrase *on the other hand*, a convention in the presentation of contrasting information (*on the one hand, . . . on the other hand*), is radically adapted in the following statement, from an article about animals:

A female needs an area which will provide enough food and denning sites for raising kittens, even in a year when food is in short supply. On the other paw, a male has a very much larger home range, which usually overlaps with those of several females ('Just like Lions', *BBC Wild Life*, Jan. 1989).

The phrase *the tip of the iceberg* is similarly adapted in:

The Senate committee is also investigating charges that the Mafia had infiltrated the tribal bingo games in 12 of the 90 Indian reservations in America and skimmed $700,000 a year of the bingo profits. But this was just the tip of the teepee. Chief MacDonald managed to reduce the accumulated wealth of the Navajo nation from $100 million to a current pool of around $18 million ('Big Mac in heap big trouble', *Sunday Telegraph*, 12 Feb. 1989).

Spliced idioms. It is not unusual for even fluent speakers in the heat of conversation to blend or splice two idioms or collocations whose forms and meanings are similar. The following specimens were collected in the late 1980s: 'That seems an interesting step to go down' (splicing *step to take* and *road to go down*); 'He stuck his ground' (splicing *stuck to his guns* and *stood his ground*); 'Language plays a decisive factor here' (blending *is a decisive factor* and *plays a decisive role*); 'Bush did lance the bubble of damaging speculation' (blending *lance the boil* and *burst the bubble*).

See ALLITERATION, ARCHETYPE, BINOMIAL, CATCH PHRASE, CATCH WORD, CLICHÉ, COLLOCATION, FIXED PHRASE, HACKNEYED, HOLOPHRASE, IDIOTISM, METAPHOR, MIXED METAPHOR, PHRASAL VERB, PHRASE, PROVERB, QUOTATION, SAYING. [LANGUAGE, STYLE, USAGE, WORD, WRITING].

T.MCA.

Clark, John O. E. 1988. *Word Wise: A Dictionary of English Idioms*. London: Harrap.
Cowie, Anthony P., & Mackin, Ronald. *Oxford Dictionary of Current Idiomatic English*. 1975, volume 1: *Verbs with Prepositions and Particles*. 1983, volume 2 (with I. R. McCaig): *Phrase, Clause, and Sentence Idioms*. Oxford: University Press.
Gulland, Daphne M., & Hinds-Howell, David G. 1986. *The Penguin Dictionary of English Idioms*. Harmondsworth: Penguin.
Long, Thomas Hill (ed.). 1979. *Longman Dictionary of English Idioms*. London: Longman.
Manser, Martin. 1983. *A Dictionary of Everyday Idioms*. London: Macmillan.

IDIOTISM. See IDIOM.

IDYLL, also **idyl** [16c: from Latin *idyllium*, Greek *eidúllion* a little form. Pronounced both 'EYE-dil' and 'iddle']. (1) A work in verse or prose that describes pastoral scenes or events, usually simple, charming, and depicting happy people in beautiful rustic surroundings. (2) A time of great ('idyllic') pleasure, especially in the country or away from everyday life, often including a romantic affair. See PASTORAL. [LITERATURE].

T.MCA.

IELTS, full form *International English Language Testing System*. Also *the IELTS test*. A test of proficiency in English developed in the late 1980s for non-native speakers who wish to study at institutions of higher learning in English-speaking countries. In the UK, it replaces the *ELTS* (*English Language Testing Service*) of the British Council and is administered by UCLES; in Australia, it replaces the Government's *SST* (*Short Selection Test*) and is administered by the IDP (International Development Program of Australian Universities and Colleges). The test is scored in bands from 1 to 9, candidates receiving a result for each of the four skills (listening, speaking, reading, writing), averaged out to produce a final score. In most cases, a pass mark is 6 or 6.5. There are four modules, three academic (A for Physical Sciences and Technology, B for Medical and Life Sciences, C for Arts and Social Sciences) and a less demanding General Training or GT Module (highest band 6) for candidates seeking to enter secondary education or non-formal courses. See BRITISH COUNCIL, EXAMINING IN ENGLISH, UCLES. [EDUCATION, EUROPE, OCEANIA].

T.MCA.

IGBO, IBO. See AFRICAN ENGLISH, AFRICAN LANGUAGES, NIGERIA.

I-LECT. See RASTA TALK.

ILLITERACY [17c: from Latin *illitteratus* unlettered]. The inability to read or write, or the actual or perceived state of being uneducated or insufficiently educated. Social judgement is so powerfully built into the term *illiterate* that scholars now generally use more neutral terms, such as *non-literate* (for societies and individuals for whom literacy is not a relevant issue) and *pre-literate* (for societies and conditions before literacy emerged or was encountered and adopted). Formerly, the term *illiterate* was used to describe someone without book learning or a liberal education (especially in classical Latin and Greek), even though such a person could read in a vernacular language or handle accounts and correspondence. Expressing this view in his *Letters* (no. 152, 1748), Lord Chesterfield wrote: 'The word *illiterate*, in its common acceptation, means a man who is ignorant of those two languages', that is Latin and Greek. However, the word also carried the connotation of 'unpolished', 'ignorant', or 'inferior', as in 'the disadvantage of an illiterate education' (Edward Gibbon, *The Decline and Fall of the Roman Empire*, volume 2, 1781, p. 75).

Attitudes. As schooling moved away from the classical languages, the term came to mean inability to sign one's name (generally on a marriage or a census document) or to read a simple passage. Attitudes have been inconsistent: while works like Wordsworth's 'The Solitary Reaper' (1807) and Mark Twain's *The Adventures of Huckleberry Finn* (1885) have idealized the unlettered in comparison to the dishonest, weak-willed scholar, others have asserted: 'There is no manner of Competition between a Man of Liberal Education and an Illiterate' (Sir Richard Steele, *Tatler* 200, *c*.1710). The term *illiterate* has been widely used pejoratively for usage which, though literate, has not measured up to the standards or expectations of the person commenting. *Semi-literate* is similarly employed: 'an illiterate style', 'a semi-literate letter'. Because of the prestige of literacy and its influence on patterns of speech, some observers have attacked 'illiterate speech', and on occasion writers of guides to 'good' English have employed such phrases to persuade readers away from certain usages: 'The first principle of illiterate speech—emphasis by repetition—is evident not only in grammatical patterns but also in phraseology; the basement-level speaker frequently iterates an idea and then immediately reiterates the very same idea in slightly different words. He is not quite sure you will understand him until he has said a thing at least twice' (Norman Lewis, *Better English*, 1956).

Statistics. In recent years, the term has been used to describe the condition of people unable to cope with printed materials relevant to their needs (*functional illiteracy*) and people unacquainted with the canon and conventions of an educated populace (*cultural illiteracy*). Precise descriptions and accurate estimates of illiteracy of any kind in English-speaking countries are difficult to obtain because of a growing trend to differentiate between total or near illiteracy and functional illiteracy. Although UNESCO figures in 1983 indicated near-zero illiteracy in Western Europe and North America, levels are generally agreed to be much higher, owing to the underrepresentation of poor, minority, and immigrant groups in estimates. In the US, estimates have varied (depending on the criterion used) between 10% and 20% of the population (c.30m people). The 1981 Canadian census found that 22% or c.4m people over the age of 15 were 'functionally illiterate' and a fifth of these 'completely illiterate'. In Australia in the late 1970s, the figure was around 14%, or over 1m, and in the UK the most commonly cited figure in the 1980s was 3.5% or 2m, although a 10% estimate has also more recently been made. It is unlikely that any of these figures can be taken at face value, but they suggest perceptions of the problem.

Changing levels. Although illiteracy is not new, social changes have altered its significance. In the 1950s, the inability to read or write was not in itself detrimental to achievement, but in an increasingly technological society illiteracy usually limits employment and advancement. David Crystal has pointed out that, in the developed countries, it is becoming more rather than less difficult for 'illiterate' or 'semi-literate' people to achieve an acceptable standard of literacy:

A democratic society and a free press presuppose high general literacy levels. There are now more diverse and complex kinds of matter to read, and people are obliged

to read more if they want to get on. People who had achieved a basic literacy are thus in real danger of being classed as illiterate, as they fail to cope with the modern everyday demands of such areas as the media, business, bureaucracy, and the law. As a result of literate society continually 'raising the ante', therefore, the illiteracy figures rise, and the gap between the more and the less developed countries becomes ever wider ('Literacy 2000', *English Today*, Oct. 1986).

The inability to read and write not only prevents people from functioning fully within their communities, but also exerts an influence on national priorities and the use of human and material resources. See LITERACY, READING. [EDUCATION, WRITING].   R.W.B., T.MCA.

ILLOCUTION(ARY). See LOCUTION, SPEECH ACT.

IMAGE [12c: through Old French from Latin *imago/imaginis* likeness, statue, picture, idea, phantom, shadow: cognate with *imitate*]. (1) A likeness, in the form of a statue, drawing, painting, or photograph, or as seen in water, a mirror, or a polished surface. (2) The area of a printing plate that is reproduced on paper, etc. (3) Also *master image*. In photo-typesetting, the original representation from which a typeset character is reproduced. (4) A mental representation of something; an idea or conception. (5) In the media, advertising, politics, and the like, 'a body of impressions, feelings, or opinions regarding a company (*corporate image*) or other entity as held by its public' (Richard Weiner, *Webster's New World Dictionary of Media and Communications*, 1990). In this sense, a lack of fit is often cynically assumed to exist between public face and private reality, due to misperception or mispresentation. Consultants may be employed to provide a corporation with a fresh image: 'BT has been working with Wolff Olins, the leading corporate image-makers, for nearly two years, and asserts that a new image was needed to enable the company to be recognised as a "major global player".... The company's 92,000 public payphones will get new decals and its 90 shops will have to be changed, right down to the yellow door handles. More than 50,000 employees are likely to need new uniforms or "image clothing"' (Mark Skipworth on British Telecom, *Sunday Times*, 6 Jan. 1991). (6) In rhetoric and literary criticism, a figure of speech such as metaphor or simile: 'Marauders, bullies, thieves and plunderers ready to abuse those rules are never in short supply. In Churchill's vivid image, they move constantly through our common household, trying the doors to see whether they are locked' (E. M. Yoder, *International Herald Tribune*, 5 Sept. 1990). Such figures are collectively referred to as *imagery*; they may be single or composite, and are often extended through several complex sentences:

The English language is like a river—a mighty Amazon among rivers, springing from many sources and drawing nourishment from many tributaries. By the 8th century the main stream could be discerned in the Old English spoken by Anglo-Saxons. When we speak of *man*, *woman*, and *child*, of *bread* and *meat* we are using their tongue. The powerful tributary that came in from France after the Norman Conquest gave us *male*, *female*, and *infant*, and a host of other words including *crust* and *beef*. Latin, Old Norse, German, Arabic and many other languages all added their contributions. Downstream, the river broadened as it was joined by tributaries carrying the languages of science, technology, economics, sport, and other specialised areas of life. In recent years these streams have contributed words and phrases such as *quasar* and *quango*, *black hole* and *biodegradable*, *hang-gliding* and *hard-wired*. As the river flowed on, it branched into a delta, with channels carrying the varieties of Australia, New Zealand, India, South Africa, the Caribbean, Canada, the United States and others, along with the mother tongue down to the sea of world English (Robert Ilson, preface, *Reader's Digest Great Illustrated Dictionary*, 1984).

See ANALOGY, ARCHETYPE, CONCEIT, DEVICE, FIGURATIVE LANGUAGE/USAGE, FORM, ICON, IDEA, IMAGINATION, LOGO, METAPHOR, POETRY, ROMANCE, ROMANTICISM, SHAKESPEARE, SIMILE, TIMESPEAK. [MEDIA, STYLE, TECHNOLOGY].

T.MCA.

IMAGERY. See IMAGE.

IMAGINATION [14c: from Latin *imaginatio/imaginationis* forming images in the mind, fancy, fantasy]. The act or process of thinking in images and visions, often resulting in or expressed through art, literature, and figurative usage. The effects of imagination can be both positive and negative: 'Men may dyen of ymaginacion / So depe may impression be take' (Chaucer, *The Miller's Tale*, c.1386); 'The Imagination is one of the highest prerogatives of man. By this faculty he unites, independently of the will, former images and ideas, and thus creates brilliant and novel results' (Charles Darwin, *The Descent of Man*, 1871). See FANTASY, IMAGE, ROMANCE. [LITERATURE, STYLE].

T.MCA.

IMPERATIVE [16c: from Latin *imperativus* expressing a command, translating Greek *prostaktikē*]. The mood of the verb used to express commands ('*Go* away'), requests ('Please *sit* down'), warnings ('*Look* out!'), offers ('*Have* another piece'), and entreaties ('*Help* me'). Sentences with an imperative as their main verb require the person(s) addressed to carry out some action. Hence, the subject of an imperative sentence is typically the second-person pronoun *you*, which is however normally omitted, as in

'*Go* away', but appears in the emphatic 'You *do* as you're told!' First- and third-person imperatives refer to the doer of the action or the requirement to perform the action less directly: '*Let's* go now'; '*Someone close* the window'. See MOOD. [GRAMMAR].

S.G.

IMPERFECT RHYME. See HALF RHYME.

IMPERIAL [14c: from *imperialis* relating to empire]. (1) Relating to empire: *His Imperial Majesty*. See IMPERIALISM. (2) A size of printing or drawing paper, 22 × 30 inches (56 × 76 cm) in Britain, 23 × 33 inches (58 × 84 cm) in the US and Canada. (3) A book size made from this paper. See BOOK, PAPER. [TECHNOLOGY]. T.MCA.

IMPERIALISM [1850s]. A term relating to empires and their institutions and trappings. *Imperialism* and *imperialist* can be used neutrally, to refer to any empire or imperial institution. In the 19c, they were often used positively, with regard especially to the achievements and interests of the European mercantile empires. Currently, the terms are generally perceived as negative, under the influence primarily of Marxist critics of empire, bourgeoisie, and capitalism, and have been used to refer not only to overt empires such as that of Britain, but also to countries seen as more covertly (but equally nefariously) imperial, such as the US. However, in places where people have sought to get rid of foreign domination, both words have become little more than easy terms of abuse.

Imperial English. The domination and exploitation that are inherent in any empire often come to be associated with the imperial language, as with Latin in the Roman and English in the British Empire. Because of the complex social and emotional relationships within an empire, there is often a love/hate relationship between subject peoples and the élite that rules them and therefore also between those peoples and the language of their servitude. This is especially so where some local people receive preference because of their usefulness and loyalty, are privileged by visits to the 'mother country', and provide their children with education in schools whose medium is the imperial language. As a result, even after the immediate pressures of empire have gone, post-colonial societies find that they can live neither with nor without the imperial language.

Post-imperial English. In India, the Philippines, and many other countries, decades after independence English continues to dominate politics, education, technology, law, and business, evokes memories of colonialism, and imposes various strains on societies often divided on ethnic grounds as well as between a majority and an élite that has inherited many of the attributes and trappings of the erstwhile imperialists. Some Indians accuse Britain of ensuring that nearly 50 years after independence Indians must use English rather than an indigenous language to talk to other Indians. Philippine historians often accuse turn-of-the-century American military authorities of imposing English in order to keep Filipinos from communicating effectively in their own languages. Resentment against English-speaking political and economic élites easily translates into resentment against the language of post-imperial power. Class sentiments are therefore often displaced into linguistic attitudes. Political leaders may sometimes feel the advantage of easy access to a leading world language, but equally often are likely to envy such countries as Japan, Taiwan, and South Korea, whose economic success is associated with, if not actually attributed to, their linguistic nationalism. Intellectuals in post-colonial societies often see ex-imperial languages as preventing the intellectualization of vernaculars, much as Norman French in England first stunted then altered English. In a replay of the struggle of English to become a language of scholarship in a Latin-dominated world, national languages such as Malay and Filipino are deliberately being intellectualized by nationalist linguists and writers through expansions in words, styles, and domains (often drawing on the resources of English for this purpose, as English drew on Latin). In this struggle, the major field of combat is the school: for example, in the Philippines, the medium of instruction was predominantly English until 1974, when a Bilingual Education Policy (slightly revised in 1987) mandated the use of Filipino for some subjects, as well as local vernaculars at lower levels. By the late 1980s, leading universities were successfully expanding the number of subjects taught in Filipino.

Competitors with English. In some countries, English offers an escape route from ethnic conflicts: as a 'neutral' language in such countries as India, Nigeria, and the Philippines, it is said to be more widely acceptable than local alternatives. Nationalists argue, however, that there are often local languages that unify populations at least as well, and often in less psychologically damaging ways. An example is Filipino, despite resistance from northern Ilocanos and southern Cebuanos; it is now more widely spoken than English, Ilocano, or Cebuano. The success of the national varieties of Malay in Malaysia and Indonesia is also a case in point. Although English remains crucial to international trade and technology, Japanese currently outranks it in economic importance in Asia, despite the use

of Japanese as a short-lived imperial language during the Second World War. With Taiwan's expanding foreign investments, Mandarin Chinese has assumed increasing importance. The possibility of the Pacific Rim becoming 'the centre of the world' in the 21c might dislodge English as a second language from some of its post-colonial Asian strongholds, in favour of Japanese and Chinese (while it remains nonetheless the leading second language of the Chinese and Japanese themselves).

Cultural hegemony. It takes time for patterns of dominance to change, and it is not easy to assess the extent of the intellectual, social, and cultural hegemony exerted by a language like English. If the use of sexist or non-sexist expressions can indeed modify attitudes and behaviour towards women, one might then conclude that the use of a whole alien language can modify the attitudes and behaviour of an entire people: in 1973, at a conference in Nairobi on teaching literature, the Kenyan scholar Micere Mugo spoke of how reading the description of Gagool in Rider Haggard's *King Solomon's Mines* made her feel terrified of all old African women. Some non-native users of English advocate linguistic *détente*: watchful collaboration with a language only lately weaned, if weaned at all, from imperialism. They see the benefits of such collaboration in terms of a great good that is emerging from great ill, as English becomes the world's primary language. Other post-colonial observers, however, recall that to sup with the Devil one needs a long spoon. They warn against the linguistic unconscious of English, and that history's gift to the ex-colonial world may prove to be a Trojan horse. The Kikuyu writer Ngugi wa Thiong'o has described the predicament as follows:

The oppressed and the exploited of the earth maintain their defiance: liberty from theft. But the biggest weapon wielded and actually daily unleashed by imperialism against the collective defiance is the cultural bomb. The effect of the cultural bomb is to annihilate a people's belief in their names, in their languages, in their environment, in their heritage of struggle, in their unity, in their capacities and ultimately in themselves. It makes them see their past as one wasteland of non-achievement and it makes them want to distance themselves from that wasteland. It makes them want to identify with that which is furthest removed from themselves; for instance, with other people's languages rather than their own (*Decolonising the Mind*, 1986).

See ABORIGINES, ACHEBE, AFRICAN LITERATURE IN ENGLISH, BLACK, BLACK ENGLISH VERNACULAR, BRITISH EMPIRE, CALIBAN, CELTIC LANGUAGES, CHAUVINISM, CLASSICAL LANGUAGE, COLONIAL, CREOLE, DIASPORA, ENGLISH, GANDHI, GEOGRAPHY AND GEOPOLITICS OF ENGLISH, HOME, LATIN ANALOGY, MOTHER COUNTRY, NEHRU, NGUGI, PIDGIN,

RACISM, SOYINKA, STREVENS. [AFRICA, AMERICAS, ASIA, EUROPE, HISTORY].   I.R.C., T.MCA.

IMPLICATION [15c: from Latin *implicatio/implicationis* an interweaving]. (1) The act, process, or result of implying (indicating indirectly that something can or should be understood in a particular way). This can be done by such means as tone of voice, facial expression, or what one chooses to emphasize or omit. (2) In logic, the relation between two propositions or classes of propositions, so that one can be deduced from the other: the implication of the statements *All men are mortal* and *Socrates is a man* is that Socrates is mortal. See IMPLICATURE, LANGUAGE UNIVERSALS, LOGIC. [LANGUAGE].   T.MCA.

IMPLICATURE [20c]. A term in logic for potential inference that is not logically entailed by what is said: A, asked about B's intelligence, says *He dresses well*. The inference is that B is not intelligent. See IMPLICATION, INFERENCE, LOGIC, PRAGMATICS, SEMANTICS. [LANGUAGE].   T.MCA.

IMPRESSION [14c in first use, 16c in these senses: from Latin *impressio/impressionis* pressing on]. (1) The process or result of printing from type, plates, engraved blocks, etc. (2) A printed copy produced in such a way. (3) One of a number of printings of a book or other item made from the same type, etc., without alteration: *A best-seller in its twentieth impression in one year.* Compare COPY, EDITION, IMPRINT. [MEDIA, TECHNOLOGY].   T.MCA.

IMPRINT [14c: from French *empreinte*, from *empreinter*, Latin *imprimere/impressum* to press on (something)]. (1) A mark made by pressure. (2) In bibliography, the name of a book's publisher shown on its title page or elsewhere, usually with place and year of publication; such information in a bibliographic entry. (3) The printer's name and address as displayed on any printed matter. (4) In publishing, the name by which certain books are identified, as being published by a company or a subdivision of a company: for example, *Penguin (Books)* as the name for most books published by the company of the same name, but *Pelican (Books)* as the name for a list of scholarly works put out by the same company. The names of associated imprints are often similar, as with *Penguin, Pelican, Puffin (Books)*. Compare COLOPHON, IMPRESSION. [MEDIA, TECHNOLOGY].   T.MCA.

INCEPTIVE, also **inchoative** [17c, 16c: from Latin *inceptivus* and *inchoativus* starting]. An aspect of the verb in some languages, indicating the beginning of an action, and corresponding to *be about to* in English: *They're about to leave, so don't go away.* An inceptive or inchoative verb indicates that something is beginning: *darken* to grow dark, *thicken* to become thick. Here, *-en* is an inceptive or inchoative suffix. Compare CAUSATIVE VERB. [GRAMMAR].   S.G.

INCHOATIVE. See INCEPTIVE.

INCLUSIVE LANGUAGE, also **inclusive usage** [1980s]. Semi-technical terms for a use of language that includes rather than excludes particular groups, such as women and minorities: for example, the use of *humankind* or *people* rather than *mankind* or *men* when the whole human race is being discussed; the use of *Britain* rather than *England* when the entire UK is intended. See BIBLE, GENERIC PRONOUN, SEXISM. [STYLE].   T.MCA.

INCUNABLE, also **incunabulum** [19c: from the Latin plural *incunabula* swaddling clothes, beginnings, from *cunae* cradle]. A technical term for a book printed before 1501. See BOOK, LIBRARY OF CONGRESS. [TECHNOLOGY].   W.W.B.

INDEFINITE ARTICLE. In English grammar, the term for *a* and *an* when used to introduce a noun phrase: *a cup of coffee* or *an angry reply. A* occurs before consonant sounds (*a garden, a human, a use*) and *an* before vowel sounds (*an orange, an hour, an uncle, an MP, an SOS*). *An* is sometimes used before certain words beginning with an *h*, such as *an hotel, an historian*, particularly if the *h* is not pronounced. Some, however, pronounce the *h*, giving rise to controversy and being regarded by some others as slightly pretentious or precious. See ARTICLE[1], H. [GRAMMAR].   S.G.

INDENTING [18c: from *indent* to form a recess, a back-formation of *indented* having notches like teeth, from Latin *dens/dentis* tooth]. Also **indentation, indention**. The practice of setting a line of text further from the left margin than other lines, especially to start a paragraph. A poem or other block of text, especially a quotation, may also be indented so as to make it stand out from the surrounding text. Indenting is common in dictionaries and indexes, where it usually reverses the practice for text, effectively indenting every line except that of the headword. The space left by indenting is an indent(at)ion. See PARAGRAPH. [TECHNOLOGY, WRITING].   T.MCA.

INDEX [14c: from Latin *index/indicis* a pointer, guide. The plural is *indexes* for the linguistic senses, *indices* for the mathematical senses]. (1) A usually alphabetical list of words, names, topics, or other items, usually with the numbers of the pages of the book or books in which the items are mentioned. Indexes vary considerably in the amount of detail they include, and can be divided into separate lists of subjects, persons, places, etc., according to the requirements of the work in question. They are usually either part of the back matter of a book or in a special volume associated with a set of books. In research work, filing systems, and lexicography, *index cards* are often used to store information in a *card index*. (2) Any similar sequence of material in alphabetical or numerical order. (3) In computing, a value that identifies and locates an element in an array of data, or a table that contains such values. (4) Also *fist hand*. In printing, a sign in the shape of a hand with the forefinger (*index finger*) extended, used to point to a note, caption. (5) A sign, token, indicator: *Their clothes are an index of how rich they are.* (6) A list of publications or other material forbidden or restricted by a religion or political group (from the *Index Librorum Prohibitorum* Index of Prohibited Books, a list of books that Roman Catholics are forbidden to read, unless expurgated or with permission). (7) In mathematics, a number or formula expressing a property or ratio: *a cranial index, an index of intelligence.* (8) Also *index number*. In statistics, a quantity whose variation over a period of time measures change in an activity, process, etc. (9) Also *exponent*. In algebra, a number placed over and after another, showing the power to which it is to be raised, as in 2^{10} (two to the power ten). See CONCORDANCE, FOG INDEX, INDEXING LANGUAGE, KEYWORD, LIST, SEMIOTICS, SIGN, THESAURUS. [REFERENCE, TECHNOLOGY]. T.MCA.

INDEXING LANGUAGE. A restricted language with precisely defined terms for specifying meaning, used to make subject indexes to articles and books, etc., especially by computer. The compilation of large indexes depends on controlled registers from which the index terms are picked. Because ordinary English contains words with similar or overlapping meanings, different indexers may select different words for the same idea: for example, one using *track* where another uses *path*, forcing users to look in both places and work out any differences. Large indexing services recommend only specified terms and phrases in a vocabulary that defines the concepts to be used and the distinctions to be made among them. *MeSH* (Medical Subject Headings), a service run by the National Library of Medicine in Bethesda, Maryland, recommends that indexers avoid the generic term *vertebrate* and index the specific animal. Other terms may be indicated as *entry vocabulary*, with appropriate references to the standardized vocabulary, such as *cancer USE neoplasm*. The

index terms may also be arranged in a hierarchical structure to facilitate study of the term list. Indexing vocabularies are sometimes published as thesauri, such as *MeSH*, *ERIC* (Education Resources Information Clearinghouse), and *Inspec thesaurus* (for engineering). See CROSS-REFERENCE, INDEX, RESTRICTED LANGUAGE, THESAURUS. [LANGUAGE, TECHNOLOGY]. M.L.

INDIA [Through Latin from Greek *India*, from *Indós* the Indus, from Persian *hind*, Old Persian *hindu*, cognate with Sanskrit *sindhu*. These variants demonstrate the common origin of the terms *India*, *Sind* (a province of Pakistan), and *Hindu*. Old English used Latin *India*, but Middle English used French-derived *Ind* and *Inde*, words sometimes used in later poetry. The return to *India* in the 16c was part of the Latinization of English and may also reflect Spanish and Portuguese influence: see INDIAN, INDIES]. (1) Also *Hindustan*. A name originally restricted to the plain of the Indus but extended to include that of the Ganges and the peninsula to the south. (2) Also *the subcontinent* (*of India*). The South Asian land mass bounded to the north-west by Iran and Afghanistan, to the north by Tibet, and to the north-east by China and Burma. It covers the six mainland states of Bangladesh, Bhutan, India, Nepal, Pakistan, and Sikkim, and two island states of Sri Lanka and the Maldives. (3) Also *British India, undivided India*. Sometimes known institutionally as *the British Raj* (the British Realm). That part of the subcontinent once controlled by the British, made up of areas directly governed, such as the Bombay Presidency, and many indirectly controlled princely states, such as Gwalior and Jaipur. The name *undivided India* is retrospective, prompted by Partition in 1947. (4) Also officially *Bharat*, after a legendary Indo-Aryan people. Sometimes unofficially *Hindust(h)an*. The Republic of India, a South Asian nation and member of the Commonwealth. Capital: New Delhi. Currency: the rupee (100 paisa). Economy: mixed. Population: 813m (1988), 1,003m (projection for 2000). Ethnicity: 72% Indo-Aryan, 25% Dravidian, 2% Mongoloid, 1% others. Religions: 84% Hindu, 11% Muslim, 2% Christian, 2% Sikh, 1% Buddhist. Languages: Hindi (official), English (associate official), 15 national or major languages (including Hindi and English), and many ethnic languages. Proportion of population using major regional languages: 35% Hindi, 7% Bengali, 7% Marathi, 7% Telugu, 6% Tamil, 5% Gujarati, 5% Urdu, 4% Oriya, 3% Kannada, 3% Malayalam, 3% Punjabi, 1% Assamese, 1% Kashmiri. Education: primary 85%, secondary 35%, tertiary 10%, literacy 43%. The Republic was formed by the partition of British India into India and Pakistan in 1947. (5) Sometimes *the Indias*. From the 16c to the 18c, a name for the Americas and other places distant from Europe. The belief of Christopher Columbus in 1492 that he had reached India by a new western sea route was soon disproved, but the term lingered, as in the book title *A treatyse of the newe India, with other new founde landes and Ilandes* (Richard Eden, 1553). Unlike such names as *New England* and *New York*, however, the title *New India* did not endure.

See ANGLO-INDIAN, ARYAN, ASIA, BANGLADESH, BENGALI, CLASSICAL LANGUAGE, ENGLISH, GANDHI, GUJARATI/GUJERATI, HOBSON-JOBSON, INDIAN, INDIAN ENGLISH[1], INDIAN ENGLISH LITERATURE, INDIANISM, INDIAN LANGUAGES, INDIES, INDO-ANGLIAN, INDO-EUROPEAN LANGUAGES, INDO-GERMANIC, INDONESIA, KANNADA, MALAYALAM, MOTION PICTURE, NEHRU, NEPAL, PAKISTAN, PALI, PANJABI/PUNJABI, SANSKRIT, SCRIPTURE, SOUTH ASIAN ENGLISH, SRI LANKA, TAMIL, TELUGU/TELEGU, TESL, WEST INDIES. [AMERICAS, ASIA, NAME]. T.MCA.

INDIAN [From Latin *India* and *-an*]. (1) (A native or citizen) of India: *Indian customs*; *an Anglo-Indian accent*; *the Indian and Pakistani communities in London*; *Indians, Nepalis, and Pakistanis*. (2) (A member) of the indigenous peoples of the Americas: *an Indian reservation, the Sioux and Cherokee Indians*. From this sense, certain idioms have entered the language, such as *Indian corn, Indian file, Indian giver, Indian summer*, and some classicized place-names have emerged, such as *Indiana, Indianapolis*. This sense arose from a misunderstanding by Christopher Columbus and other 15-16c explorers of the western hemisphere, who believed that by sailing west they would reach India. When Columbus made landfall in 1492, he called the Caribs living on the island he named Hispaniola *Indios* (Indians). The usage persisted, with such adaptations as *North/South American Indian, Red Indian, Amerindian, West Indian*. In AmE, it has been syncopated to *Injun* (as in *Injun country* and the phrase *honest Injun*, meaning 'really, truly'). See ABORIGINES, EAST INDIAN, WEST INDIAN. [AMERICAS, ASIA, NAME]. T.MCA.

INDIAN BROADCASTING. See SOUTH ASIAN BROADCASTING.

INDIAN ENGLISH[1], short forms *IndE, IE.* Formerly also **Indo-English.** The English language as used in India. The term is widely used but is a subject of controversy; some scholars argue that it labels an established variety with an incipient or actual standard, others that the kinds of English used in India are too varied, both socially and geographically, and often too deviant or too limited, to be lumped together as

one variety. They also argue that no detailed description has been made of the supposed variety and that the term is therefore misleading and ought not to be used. However, the length of time that English has been in India, its importance, and its range, rather than militating against such a term, make the term essential for an adequate discussion of the place of the language in Indian life and its sociolinguistic context. An estimated 30m people (4% of the population) regularly use English, making India the third largest English-speaking country in the world. Beyond this number is a further, unquantifiably large range of people with greater or less knowledge of the language and competence in its use. English is the associate official language of India, the state language of Manipur (1.5m), Meghalaya (1.33m), Nagaland (0.8m), and Tripura (2m), and the official language of eight Union territories (at the time of writing): the Andaman and Nicobar Islands; Arunachal Pradesh; Chandigarh; Dadra and Nagar Haveli; Delhi; Lakshadwip; Mizoram; and Pondicherry. It is one of the languages of the *three language formula* proposed in the 1960s for educational purposes: state language, Hindi, and English. It is used in the legal system, pan-Indian and regional administration, the armed forces, national business, and the media. English and Hindi are the *link languages* in a complex multilingual society, in which English is both a *library language* and a *literary language*. The *National Academy of Letters/Sahitya Akademi* recognizes Indian English literature as a national literature.

History. The first speaker of English to visit India may have been an ambassador of Alfred the Great. The Anglo-Saxon Chronicle states that in AD 884, Alfred sent an envoy to India with gifts for the tomb of St Thomas. His name appears in one later record as Swithelm, in another as Sigellinus. After this, there was little if any contact until the 16c, when European commercial and colonial expansion began. In 1600, English traders established the East India Company, and in 1614 James VI wrote to the Emperor Jehangir, accrediting Sir Thomas Roe as ambassador to the Moghul court:

James, by the Grace of Almightie God, the Creator of Heauen and Earth, King of Great Britaine, France and Ireland . . . To the high and mightie Monarch the Great Mogor, King of the Orientall Indies, of Chandahar, of Chismer and Corazon . . . Greeting. We hauing notice of your great fauour toward Vs and Our Subiects, by Your Great *Firma* to all Your Captaines of Riuers and Offices of Your Customes, for the entertaynment of Our louing Subiects the English Nation with all kind respect, at what time soeuer they shall arriue at any of the Ports within Your Dominions, and that they may haue quiet Trade and Commerce without any kind of hinderance or molestation.

The use of English dates from the trading 'factories' started by the Company: Surat (1612), Madras (1639-40), Bombay (1674), Calcutta (1690). European traders at that time used a form of Portuguese, current since Portugal had acquired Goa in 1510. Missionaries were important in the diffusion of English in the 18c: schools such as St Mary's Charity Schools were started in Madras (1715), Bombay (1719), and Calcutta (1720-31). By the 1830s, an influential group of Indians was impressed with Western thought and culture, and its scientific advances, and wished to encourage the learning of English as a means through which Indians could gain a knowledge of such things. The Hindu social reformer Raja Rammohan Roy (1772-1833) wanted European gentlemen of 'talents and education to instruct the natives of India in mathematics, natural philosophy, chemistry, anatomy, and other useful sciences, which the natives of Europe have carried to a degree of perfection that has raised them above the inhabitants of other parts of the world'. In a long official controversy over the medium of education for Indians, the *Anglicists* supported the *transplant theory* and the *Orientalists* the *nativist theory*. Thomas B. Macaulay, a member of the Supreme Council of India, settled the question in favour of English in an official Minute (1835):

To sum up what I have said, I think it clear that we are not fettered by the Act of Parliament of 1813; that we are not fettered by any pledge expressed or implied; that we are free to employ our funds as we choose; that we ought to employ them in teaching what is best worth knowing; that English is better worth knowing than Sanscrit or Arabic; that the natives are desirous to be taught English, and are not desirous to be taught Sanscrit or Arabic; that neither as the languages of law, nor as the languages of religion, have the Sanscrit and Arabic any peculiar claim to our engagement; that it is possible to make natives of this country thoroughly good English scholars; and that to this end our efforts ought to be directed. . . . We must at present do our best to form a class who may be interpreters between us and the millions who we govern; a class of persons, Indian in blood and colour, but English in taste, in opinions, in morals, and in intellect. To that class we may leave it to refine the vernacular dialects of the country, to enrich those dialects with terms of science borrowed from the Western nomenclature, and to render them by degrees fit vehicles for conveying knowledge to the great mass of the population.

In 1857, the first three western-style universities were established at Bombay, Calcutta, and Madras. Allahabad and Punjab (the latter now in Lahore, Pakistan) were added by the end of the 19c. By 1928, English was accepted as the language of the élite, and after independence in 1947, its diffusion increased. However, because IndE is essentially a contact language, convergence with Indian languages and socio-cultural patterns have resulted in many processes of Indianization.

Variation. There are three major variables for IndE: proficiency in terms of acquisition; regional or mother tongue; and ethnic background. In IndE there is a cline from educated IndE (the acrolect) to pidginized varieties (basilects) known by such names as *Boxwalla(h) English, Butler English, Bearer English* or *kitchen English*, and *Babu English*. The regional and mother-tongue varieties are often defined with reference to the first language of the speaker (*Bengali English, Gujarati English, Tamil English*, etc.) or in terms of a larger language family (*Indo-Aryan English, Dravidian English*). In this sense, there are as many Indian Englishes as there are languages in India. There are, however, shared characteristics which identify IndE speakers across language-specific varieties. One variety, *Anglo-Indian English*, is distinctive, because it emerged among the offspring of British servicemen and lower-caste Indian women, and is sustained among other things by a nation-wide system of long-established English-medium private schools known as *Anglo-Indian schools*. Generally, however, when IndE is discussed, the term refers to the variety at the upper end of the spectrum, which has national currency and intelligibility and increasingly provides a standard for the media, education, and pan-Indian communication. In grammar and spelling, standard BrE continues to have influence.

Pronunciation. (1) IndE is rhotic, /r/ being pronounced in all positions. (2) It tends to be syllable-timed, weak vowels being pronounced as full vowels in such words as *photography* and *student*. Word stress is used primarily for emphasis and suffixes are stressed, as in *readiness*. Distinctive stress patterns occur in different areas: *available* is often stressed in the north on the antepenultimate, in the south on the first syllable. (3) The alveolar consonants /t, d/ are retroflex. (4) The fricatives /θ, ð/ are aspirated /t, d/, so that *three of those* sounds like 't^hree of d^hose'; /f/ is often pronounced as aspirated /p/, as in 'p^hood' for *food*. (5) In such words as *old, low* the vowel is generally /o/. (6) Among northern (Indo-Aryan) speakers, consonant clusters such as /sk, sl, sp/ do not occur in initial position, but have an epenthetic vowel, as in 'iskool' for *school* in the Punjab and 'səkool' in Kashmir. (7) The distinction between /v/ and /w/ is generally neutralized to /w/: 'wine' for both *wine* and *vine*. (8) Among southern (Dravidian) speakers, non-low initial vowels are preceded by the glides /j/ (as in 'yell, yem, yen' for the names of the letters *l, m, n*) and /w/ (as in 'wold' for *old* and 'wopen' for *open*). (9) South Indians tend to geminate voiceless intervocalic obstruents, as in 'Americ-ca'. Because gemination is common in Dravidian languages, double consonants in written English are often geminated: 'sum-mer' for *summer* and 'sil-lee' for *silly*. (10) Distinct kinds of pronunciation serve as shibboleths of different kinds of IndE: Bengalis using /b/ for /v/, making *bowel* and *vowel* homophones; Gujaratis using /dʒ/ for /z/, so that *zed* and *zero* become 'jed' and 'jero'; speakers of Malayalam making *temple* and *tumble* near-homophones.

A large number of IndE speakers, sometimes referred to as speakers of *General Indian English* (*GIE*), have a 17-vowel system (11 monophthongs and 6 diphthongs): /iː/ as in *bead*, /i/ as in *this*, /eː/ as in *game*, /ɛ/ as in *send*, /æ/ as in *mat*, /ɑː/ as in *charge*, /ɒ/ as in *shot*, /oː/ as in *no*, /ʊ/ as in *book*, /uː/ as in *tool*, and /ə/ as in *bus*; /ai/ as in *five*, /ɔi/ as in *boy*, /au/ as in *cow*, /iə/ as in *here*, /eə/ as in *there*, and /ʊə/ as in *poor*. See Bansal (1990, below).

Grammar. There is great variety in syntax, from native-speaker fluency (the acrolect) to a weak command of many constructions (the basilect). The following represents a widespread middle level (the mesolect): (1) Interrogative constructions without subject/auxiliary inversion: *What you would like to buy?* (2) Definite article often used as if the conventions have been reversed: *It is the nature's way*; *Office is closed today*. (3) *One* used rather than the indefinite article: *He gave me one book*. (4) Stative verbs given progressive forms: *Lila is having two books*; *You must be knowing my cousin-brother Mohan*. (5) Reduplication used for emphasis and to indicate a distributive meaning: *I bought some small small things*; *Why you don't give them one one piece of cake?* (6) *Yes* and *no* as question tags: *He is coming, yes?*; *She was helping you, no?* (7) *Isn't it?* as a generalized question tag: *They are coming tomorrow, isn't it?* (8) Reflexive pronouns and *only* used for emphasis: *It was God's order itself* It was God's own order, *They live like that only* That is how they live. (9) Present perfect rather than simple past: *I have bought the book yesterday*.

Vocabulary: loans. Loanwords and loan translations from other languages have been common since the 17c, often moving into the language outside India: (1) Words from Portuguese (*almirah, ayah, caste, peon*) and from local languages through Portuguese (*bamboo, betel, coir, copra, curry, mango*). (2) Words from indigenous languages, such as Hindi and Bengali. Some are earlier and more Anglicized in their spelling: *anna, bungalow, cheetah, chintz, chit/chitty, dacoit, dak bungalow, jodhpurs, juggernaut, mulligatawny, pice, pukka, pundit, rupee, sahib, tussore*. Some are later and less orthographically

Anglicized: *achcha* all right (used in agreement and often repeated: *Achcha achcha, I will go*), *basmati* a kind of rice, *chapatti* a flat, pancakelike piece of unleavened bread, *crore* a unit of 10m or 100 lakhs (*crores of rupees*), *goonda* a ruffian, petty criminal, *jawan* a soldier in the present-day Indian Army, *lakh* a unit of 100,000 (*lakhs of rupees*), *lathi* a lead-weighted stick carried by policemen, *masala* spices, *paisa* a coin, 100th of a rupee, *panchayat* a village council, *samo(o)sa* an envelope of fried dough filled with vegetables or meat, *Sri/Shri/Shree* Mr, *Srimati/Shrimati/Shreemati* Mrs. (3) Words from Arabic and Persian through north Indian languages, used especially during the British Raj: *dewan* chief minister of a princely state, *durbar* court of a prince or governor, *mogul* a Muslim prince (and in the general language an important person, as in *movie mogul*), *sepoy* a soldier in the British Indian Army, *shroff* a banker, money-changer, *vakeel/vakil* a lawyer, *zamindar* a landlord. (4) Words taken directly from Sanskrit, usually with religious and philosophical associations, some well known, some restricted to such contexts as yoga: *ahimsa* nonviolence, *ananda* spiritual bliss, *chakra* a mystical centre of energy in the body, *guru* a (spiritual) teacher (and in the general language a quasi-revered guide, as in *management guru*), *nirvana* release from the wheel of rebirth, *rajas* a state of passion, *samadhi* spiritual integration and enlightenment, *sattwa/sattva* a state of purity, *tamas* a state of heaviness and ignorance, *yoga* a system of self-development, *yogi* one who engages in yoga. (5) Calques from local languages: *dining-leaf* a banana leaf used to serve food, *cousin brother* a male cousin, *cousin sister* a female cousin, *co-brother-in-law* one who is also a brother-in-law.

Vocabulary: hybrids, adaptations, and idioms. The great variety of mixed and adapted usages exists both as part of English and as a consequence of widespread code-mixing between English and especially Hindi: (1) Hybrid usages, one component from English, one from a local language, often Hindi: *brahminhood* the condition of being a brahmin, *coconut paysam* a dish made of coconut, *goonda ordinance* an ordinance against goondas, *grameen bank* a village bank, *kaccha road* a dirt road, *lathi charge* (noun) a charge using lathis, *lathicharge* (verb) to charge with lathis, *pan/paan shop* a shop that sells betel nut and lime for chewing, wrapped in a pepper leaf, *policewala* a policeman, *swadeshi cloth* home-made cloth, *tiffin box* a lunch-box. (2) Local senses and developments of general English words: *batch-mate* a classmate or fellow student, *body-bath* an ordinary bath, *by-two coffee* (in the south) a restaurant order by two customers asking for half a cup of coffee each, *communal* used with reference to Hindus and Muslims (as in *communal riots*), *condole* to offer condolences to someone, *England-returned* used of one who has been to England, for educational purposes, a *been-to*, *Eve-teasing* teasing or harassing young women, *Foreign-returned* used of someone who has been abroad for educational purposes, *four-twenty* a cheat or swindler (from the number of a section of the Indian Penal Code), *head-bath* washing one's hair, *interdine* to eat with a member of another religion or caste, *intermarriage* a marriage involving persons from different religions or castes, *issueless* childless, *military hotel* (in the south) a restaurant where non-vegetarian food is served, *out of station* not in (one's) town or place of work, *outstation* (*cheque*) a cheque issued by a non-local bank, *prepone* the opposite of postpone, *ration shop* a shop where rationed items are available, *undertrial* a person being tried in a court of law. (3) Words more or less archaic in BrE and AmE, but used in IndE, such as *dicky* (the boot/trunk of a car), *needful* ('Please do the needful, Sri Patel'), *stepney* a spare wheel or tyre, and *thrice* ('I was seeing him thrice last week'). (4) The many idiomatic expressions include: *to sit on someone's neck* to watch that person carefully, and *to stand on someone's head* to supervise that person carefully; *Do one thing, Sri Gupta* There is one thing you could do, Mr Gupta; *He was doing this thing that thing, wasting my time* He was doing all sorts of things, wasting my time.

Usage. It is not easy to separate the use of English in India from the general multilingual flux. In addition to code-mixing and code-switching, other languages are constantly drawn into English discourse and English into the discourse of other languages, especially Hindi. In the English-language press, hybrid headlines are common: *JNU karamcharis begin dharna* (*The Statesman*, New Delhi, 12 May 1981), *Marathwada band over pandal fire* (*The Indian Express*, New Delhi, 9 May 1981), and *55 Jhuggis gutted* (*The Hindustan Times*, New Delhi, 3 May 1981). Matrimonial advertisements in the English-language press are equally distinctive: 'Wanted well-settled bridegroom for a Kerala fair graduate Baradwaja gotram, Astasastram girl . . . subset no bar. Send horoscope and details'; 'Matrimonial proposals invited from educated, smart, well settled, Gujarati bachelors for good looking, decent, Gujarati Modh Ghanchi Bania girl (25), B.A., doing her M.A. and serving'; 'Tall, beautiful, Convent educated girl between 18 and 21 Non Bharadwaj Vadama Brahmin required for well placed Air Force pilot

from a well-to-do and respectable family. Write with horoscope and particulars.'

Texts. The following excerpts demonstrate something of the variety to be found in IndE prose:

Thus the world's knowledge about India today is obtained overwhelmingly at one remove from people belonging to the Westernized and urban upper middle-class, who have become the heirs of British rule. For nimbleness of wit, plausibility, argumentative skill, and gift of the gab they are not surpassed by many people on the face of the earth. But in the very nature of things they are unqualified to give a full or fair view of what is taking place in the country. For one thing, they have their trusteeship of the people of India, which I look upon as their exploitation, to justify. This makes them prone to misrepresent and even to lie. But it would be a mistake to think that as a class they deceive intentionally. They are so completely imitative of the West, so dependent on current literature written in English, mostly by foreigners, for their knowledge of their own country, so ignorant about the original sources of knowledge, and so formed by their urban upbringing that the whole traditional and rural India remains outside their ken (Nirad C. Chaudhuri, Introduction, *The Continent of Circe*, 1965).

Mr G. D. Somani, president of the Bombay unit of the Sarvadaliya Goraksha Maha-Abhiyan Samiti, has urged the Government of India to 'amend the Constitution, if necessary' for a total ban on the slaughter of cows, bullocks and calves. He wanted the Centre to promulgate an ordinance, if it was not found possible to impose such a ban through legislation before November 20, 'Gopashtami Day'. . . . Mr Somani stated that the issue must be regarded as a national cause and not a communal one. He asserted that a total ban on cow slaughter would not involve any heavy economic burden (staff reporter, *Times of India*, Bombay, 26 Oct. 1966).

Even among us the regional, ethnic, economic variations are so many that a graduate in the English medium from Gauhati cannot be understood by or understand one from Gujarat or Gorakhpur, Kamarupa and Kerala and Kashmir are further apart today than when a smaller and conformist elite held sway just a quarter of a century ago. So spoken English is having its quietus administered by the bare bodkin of change. Written English is following suit. Let us then animadvert on Written English (V. Siddharthacharry, 'English Teaching in India,' *The Hindu*, Madras, 7 Aug. 1984).

'Bhai phor how long Gorement is elect?'
'Ujually phor phie years.'
'Whyphore ujually?'
'Becoss in some times, it is not so ujually.'
'What that means?'
'Bhai according to Constitution, when one is elect M.P. or MLA, seat is rejerve phor phie years, but nowadays all oph sudden MP or MLA sitting in one seat is getting tired.'
'Muss to be pheeling phie year hitch.'
'What that is?'
'Pheeling his to scratch.'
(from *Psst*, a satirical column in *The Current*, Bombay, in the 1960s, which regularly ended with

the slogan *Boycott British Language*. This example from a 1967 issue)

See ANGLO-INDIAN, BORROWING, CENTRAL INSTITUTE OF ENGLISH AND FOREIGN LANGUAGES, CODE-MIXING AND CODE-SWITCHING, DRAVIDIAN ENGLISH, HINDI, HINDI-URDU, HINDLISH/HINGLISH, HOBSON-JOBSON, INDIA, INDIAN ENGLISH², INDIAN ENGLISH LITERATURE, INDIAN-ISM, INDIAN LANGUAGES, INDIAN RECOMMENDED PRONUNCIATION, INDO-ANGLIAN, INDO-ARYAN ENGLISH, INDO-ENGLISH, KOLHAPUR CORPUS, L-SOUNDS, NIGERIA, PERSIAN, SANSKRIT, SOUTH AFRICAN INDIAN ENGLISH, SOUTH ASIAN ENGLISH. [ASIA, VARIETY].   B.B.K., T.MCA.

Bansal, R. K. 1990. 'The Pronunciation of English in India', in S. Ramsaran (ed.), *Studies in the Pronunciation of English: A Commemorative Volume in Honour of A. C. Gimson*. London: Routledge.

Kachru, Braj B. 1983. *The Indianization of English: The English Language in India*. Delhi: Oxford University Press.

—— 1986. *The Alchemy of English: The Spread, Functions and Models of Non-Native Englishes*. Oxford: Pergamon Press. Reprinted 1990: Urbana, University of Illinois Press.

Lewis, Ivor. 1991. *Sahibs, Nabobs and Boxwallahs: A Dictionary of the Words of Anglo-India*. Bombay: Oxford University Press.

Nihalani, P., Tongue, R. K., & Hosali, P. 1970. *Indian and British English: A Handbook of Usage and Pronunciation*. Delhi: Oxford University Press.

INDIAN ENGLISH². The English language as used by American Indians (Native Americans), especially in the US: 'It can be of social importance to a Native American to be competent in the variety of Indian English spoken in his community' (Dell H. Hymes, foreword to Ferguson & Heath (eds.), *Language in the USA*, 1981). See AMERICAN LANGUAGES, AMERINDIAN PIDGIN ENGLISH, DIALECT IN AMERICA, RED ENGLISH. [AMERICAS, VARIETY].   T.MCA.

INDIAN ENGLISH LITERATURE, short form *IEL*. Also, but now less common, **Indo-English writing, Indo-Anglian writing**. Literature in English written in India. The term *Anglo-Indian literature*, on the other hand, refers to the works of non-Indian, especially British writers, whose writing has India as a central theme, as with Rudyard Kipling's *Plain Tales from the Hills* (1888), *The Jungle Book* (1894), and *Kim* (1901), E. M. Forster's *A Passage to India* (1922-4), John Masters's *Bhowani Junction* (1954) and *The Venus of Konpara* (1960), and Paul Scott's *The Raj Quartet* (1966-75). IEL is established 'not only as an academic discipline in the universities but as one of our own literatures recognized by the Central Sahitya Akademi [National Academy of Letters] which has honoured our writers

in English like those in the regional languages' (C. D. Narasimhaiah, 1987, below).

The first extant works by Indians in English are Cavelly Venkata Boriah's *Account of the Jains* (1809) and Rammohan Roy's translations of four of the Upanishads (1816-20). Early attempts in creative writing include the work of two Bengali writers, Kashiprasad Ghosh's *The Shair and Other Poems* (1830) and Lal Behari Day's novel *Govinda Samanta: Bengali Peasant Life* (1874). Indianization has taken place not only in the themes of this growing body of writing, but also in its innovations of style and discourse, as in Mulk Raj Anand's *Untouchable* (1935) and *Coolie* (1936), Raja Rao's *Kanthapura* (1938), and G. V. Desani's *All About H. Hatterr* (1948). Political writing and journalism in IndE have played a vital role in India's national awakening and struggle for independence; writers in this area include Rammohan Roy (1772-1833), Mohandas K. Gandhi (1869-1948), Bal Gangadhar Tilak (1856-1920), and Jawaharlal Nehru (1889-1964). Although the literature has particularly and rather unexpectedly flowered since independence from Britain in 1947, controversy continues regarding the loyalty and identity of IndE writers.

The following is a representative list of writers: (1) Poets: Keki N. Daruwalla (b.1937), Kamala Das (b.1934), Toru Dutt (1859-77), Nissim Ezekiel (b.1924), Aurobindo Ghosh (1872-1950), Manmohan Ghosh (1869-1924), Arun Kolatkar (b.1933), Shiv K. Kumar (b.1937), Jayanta Mahapatra (b.1928), Sarojini Naidu (1879-1949), Pritish Nandy (b.1947), R. Parthasarathy (b.1934), and A. K. Ramanujan (b.1929). (2) Novelists, with representative works: Mulk Raj Anand (b.1905), *Across the Black Waters* 1940, *Lament on the Death of a Master of Arts* 1967; Bhabani Bhattacharya (1906-88), *So Many Hungers* 1947, *Who Rides a Tiger* 1954; Anita Desai (b.1937), *Cry, the Peacock* 1963, *Voices in the City* 1965; Manohar Malgonkar (b.1913), *A Bend in the Ganges* 1964; Kamala Markandaya (b.1924), *Nectar in a Sieve* 1954, *A Handful of Rice* 1966; R. K. Narayan (b.1906), *Swami and Friends* 1935, *The Bachelor of Arts* 1937, *The English Teacher* 1945, *Waiting for the Mahatma* 1955, *The Man-Eater of Malgudi* 1962; Raja Rao (b.1909), *The Serpent and the Rope* 1960; Nayantara Sahgal (b.1927), *Storm in Chandigarh* 1969, *Rich Like Us* 1985; Khushwant Singh (b.1915), *Train to Pakistan* 1956. (3) Critics, with representative works: Nirad C. Chaudhuri (b.1897), *The Autobiography of an Unknown Indian* 1951, *A Passage to England* 1960, *Continent of Circe* 1965; V. K. Gokak (b.1909), *English in India: Its Present and Future* 1964; K. R. S. Iyengar (b.1908), *Indian Writing in English* 1985;

C. D. Narasimhaiah (b.1921), *The Swan and the Eagle*, 1987.

IEL demonstrates the acculturation and nativization of English into Indian sociocultural and linguistic contexts; the Judeo-Christian tradition, the sociocultural contexts of Britain, and British literary traditions provide only a remote backdrop for IndE writers. Their credo was first articulated by the publisher and metaphysical novelist Raja Rao:

[T]he telling has not been easy. One has to convey in a language that is not one's own the spirit that is one's own. One has to convey the various shades and omissions of a certain thought-movement that looks maltreated in an alien language. I use the word 'alien,' yet English is not really an alien language to us. It is the language of our intellectual make-up—like Sanskrit or Persian was before—but not of our emotional make-up. We are all instinctively bilingual, many of us writing in our own language and in English. We cannot write like the English. We should not. We cannot write only as Indians. We have grown to look at the large world as part of us. Our method of expression therefore has to be a dialect which will some day prove to be as distinctive and colorful as the Irish or the American. Time alone will justify it (preface, *Kanthapura*, 1938).

See ANGLO-INDIAN, COMMONWEALTH LITERATURE, ENGLISH LITERATURE, GANDHI, INDIAN ENGLISH[1], INDO-ANGLIAN, INDO-ENGLISH, NAIPAUL, NEHRU, NOVEL. [ASIA, LITERATURE, VARIETY].   B.B.K., T.MCA.

Naik, M. K. 1982. *A History of Indian-English Literature*. Delhi: Sahitya Akademi.
Suleri, Sara. 1991. *The Rhetoric of English India*. Chicago: University Press.
Walsh, William. 1990. *Indian Literature in English*. London & New York: Longman.

INDIANISM [17c]. (1) An especially linguistic usage or custom peculiar to or common in India and IndE: *isn't it?* as a generalized question tag (*You are liking it here, isn't it?*); repeating a word for emphasis (*It was a small small box*; *Put put*; *Take take*). (2) Work on behalf of or enthusiasm for either India and Indians, or American Indians. -ISM. [ASIA, STYLE, VARIETY, WORD]. T.MCA.

INDIAN LANGUAGES. (1) The languages of the subcontinent of India or of the Republic of India. (2) Also *American Indian languages*. The languages of the indigenous peoples of the Americas, often referred to as (*American*) *Indians*: see AMERICAN LANGUAGES.

Indigenous languages. The languages of the Indian subcontinent are spoken by well over 1,000m people, in Bangladesh, Bhutan, India, the Maldives, Nepal, Pakistan, Sikkim, and Sri Lanka. Diaspora varieties of many of these languages are spoken in Africa, the Caribbean, Europe, North America, and South-East Asia. In genetic terms, they fall into four groups: *Indo-Aryan*, a subgroup of the Indo-Iranian branch of the Indo-European language family; the *Dravidian language family*; the Munda branch of the *Austro-Asiatic* language family; and the Tibeto-Burman branch of the *Sino-Tibetan* language family.

The Indo-Aryan languages. With Iranian and Greek, the Indo-Aryan languages have the longest unbroken traditions in the Indo-European language family. Their earliest speakers originated outside India, probably migrating from the north-west into the Indo-Gangetic plain in the late second millennium BC. The longest-established language is *Sanskrit*, the medium of the Vedas (the primary scriptures of Hinduism, probably composed c.1500-600 BC). A more cultivated form (7c BC onward) is known as classical Sanskrit. Indian literatures and grammatical traditions derive most of their conventions from the genres of Sanskrit and from Panini's Sanskrit grammar (c.350-250 BC). *Pali*, the classical language of Buddhism, emerged in the second half of the first millennium BC. Various ancient vernacular languages, related to Sanskrit and known as the *Prakrits* and *Apabhraṃśās* (c.600 BC-AD 1000), developed into such major languages as Assamese, Bengali, Gujarati, Hindi, Hindustani, Marathi, Nepali, Oriya, Panjabi, Sindhi, Sinhala, and Urdu, and such minor languages (often called dialects) as Awadhi, Bhojpuri, Braj, Magadhi, Maithili, Rajasthani, and Konkani. There are some 638m speakers of Indo-Aryan languages. It is difficult to decide the precise number of languages and dialects because there is often controversy over what constitutes a language: for example, the status of Punjabi and Rajasthani *vis-à-vis* Hindi. One non-Indian language, Romani, is Indo-Aryan in origin.

The Dravidian languages. The Dravidian group is located mainly in the peninsula and consists of four major languages, Tamil, Telugu, Kannada, and Malayalam, and several dialects or minor languages such as Toda, Kota, Kodagu, and Kui. The records of Tamil are of an age with those of the Indo-Aryan languages. A lone Dravidian dialect, Brahui, is located in the north, in Pakistan. There are some 110m speakers of Dravidian languages, all of which have been and continue to be heavily influenced by Sanskrit and other Indo-Aryan languages and have influenced them in turn.

Others. (1) The Munda languages are spoken by over 5m Adivasis (aboriginal people) in Andhra Pradesh, Bengal, Bihar, Madhya Pradesh, and Orissa. The best-known and most widely spoken language of this group is Santhali. (2) The

Tibeto-Burman languages are spoken by communities in the north-east and along the northern border of India. The best-known are Garo, Khasi, and Naga.

Immigrant languages. Five major exotic languages have been present for centuries in India, two Asian and three European. The Asian languages are Arabic and Persian, established through invasion, trade, and the influence of Islam, particularly during the Moghul Empire. The three European languages are English, French, and Portuguese, established during the European colonial diaspora (15c onward): English through the East India Company and the British Raj and spreading everywhere; French in the enclaves of Pondicherry and Chandernagore; Portuguese in the enclaves of Goa, Daman, and Diu. Dutch for a time had an influence in Sri Lanka. Of these languages, Persian and English have had the strongest impact, but only English has been constitutionally acknowledged (although its status as an Indian language remains controversial). It has been a language of empire and of resistance to empire, notably in the writings of Mohandas K. Gandhi and Jawaharlal Nehru.

See AFRICAN LANGUAGES, ASIAN LANGUAGES, BANGLADESH, BENGALI, BORROWING, BRITISH LANGUAGES, CARIBBEAN LANGUAGES, CLASSICAL LANGUAGE, DRAVIDIAN ENGLISH, FIJI, GUJARATI/GUJERATI, HINDI, HINDI-URDU, HINDUSTANI, IMPERIALISM, INDIA, INDIAN ENGLISH[1], INDO-ARYAN ENGLISH, INDO-EUROPEAN LANGUAGES, KANNADA/KANNARESE, MALAYALAM, MALAYSIA, MARATHI, NEPAL, PAKISTAN, PALI, PANJABI/PUNJABI, ROMANI/ROMANY, SANSKRIT, SINGAPORE, SINHALA, SOUTH AFRICAN LANGUAGES, SOUTH ASIAN ENGLISH, SRI LANKA, TAMIL, TELUGU/TELEGU, URDU. [ASIA, LANGUAGE].
Y.K., T.MCA.

INDIAN PRESS, The. The press of the Republic of India operates in over 92 languages: 14,531 newspapers and periodicals, comprising 929 dailies, 4,225 weeklies, and 9,299 others. Numerically, the state of Maharashtra (capital Bombay) has the largest number (2,057), followed by Uttar Pradesh (1,832), and Delhi (1,745). The English-language press has a major role, taking second place after Hindi (assessment of 1984), with 3,689 newspapers, the largest numbers being published from Delhi (1,065), Maharashtra (736), and West Bengal (392). The leading English dailies are: the *Times of India*, the *Statesman*, the *Hindu*, and the *Hindustan Times*. Other significant periodicals and magazines in English are: *India Today* (Delhi), *Sunday* (Calcutta), and *The Illustrated Weekly of India* (Bombay). Of the seven daily newspapers that

have been in existence for over a century, four are published in English: the *Times of India*, Bombay (1850), the *Pioneer*, Lucknow (1865), the *Mail*, Madras (1867), and *Amrita Bazar Patrika*, Calcutta (1868). Freedom of the press is watched over by the Press Council, established by Act of Parliament in 1965. The first English newspaper in India was published in 1780: the *Bengal Gazette* or *Calcutta General Advertiser*, a weekly owned and edited by an Englishman, James Augustus Hicky. The first Indian-owned English newspaper, also called the *Bengal Gazette*, was started by Gangadhar Bhattacharjee (1816). Two types of vernacular newspaper emerged in the 19c: those started by missionaries and those started by Indians. The Serempore mission founded the Bengali *Dig Darshan* (1818) and *Samchar Darpan* (1819), both monthlies, the missionaries cutting type for Indian languages. Rammohan Roy, considered the father of Indian journalism, started short-lived journals in English, Bengali, and Persian: *Brahman Sambādh* (1821), *Sambād Kaumudi* (1821), and *Mirāt-ul-Ākhbār* (1821) to counter the work of the missionaries. His action irritated the government and resulted in the Vernacular Press Act (1823), curtailing press freedom. Three English-language magazines helped initiate a pan-Indian political dialogue and demand for social change: G. A. Natesan's *Indian Review*, Ramanand Chatterjee's *Modern Review*, and Tej Bahadur Sapru's *Twentieth Century*. See NEWSPAPER, PRESS. [ASIA, MEDIA].
B.B.K.

INDIAN PUBLISHING. India is the third largest publisher of books in the world as well as in the English language. In terms of output, publishers in Hindi and English occupy the top position. During 1986-7, the export of publications of all kinds was worth Rupees 26 crores or c.$15m. Publishing houses number c.15,000, some 75% of whom are small; c.45% of titles are in English. Production and distribution are, however, often poor and print-runs low. The government has its own distribution network and the promotion and advertising of books is entrusted to its *National Book Trust* (established in 1957) and *Children's Book Trust*, agencies that do not yet operate strongly. In 1972, the Central Government in New Delhi established the *Raja Rammohan Roy Educational Resources Centre* with the aim of encouraging writing and the production of university-level teaching materials. It also publishes under the Indo-American, Indo-British, and Indo-Soviet textbook collaboration programmes, and has been designated as the national agency for the operation of the International Standard Book Numbering (ISBN) system. India is a member of the Bern Convention (1948) and the Universal Copyright Convention

(1952); the Copyright Act was amended in 1984 to check the widespread piracy of books. Paperback publication started in the 1960s: Penguin has an active publishing unit in New Delhi, and Hindi Pocket Books (New Delhi) has over 1,500 titles in English, Hindi, Urdu, and Punjabi. Textbooks have long been the most profitable sector, but in recent years comic books have become popular, including *Amar Chitra Katha* (India Book House) and *The Indrajal Comic* (Times of India). Indigenous English publishing faces competition from multinational companies such as Macmillan, Tata McGraw Hill, Prentice-Hall, and Oxford University Press. In order to support and encourage small publishing houses, the establishing of a Book Finance Corporation has been recommended. See *Directory of Publishers and Booksellers in India*, Delhi, 1986. See PUBLISHING. [ASIA, MEDIA]. B.B.K.

INDIAN RECOMMENDED PRONUNCIATION, also **Educated Indian English**. Short forms *IRP, EIE*. A standardizing model of pronunciation for teachers and students of English in India, described in *Indian and British English: A Handbook of Usage and Pronunciation* (Paroo Nihilani, R. K. Tongue, & Priya Hosali, Oxford University Press, India, 1979). In 1960, V. K. Gokak, Director of the Central Institute of English, in his presidential address to the 11th English Teachers' Conference in Delhi, urged an analysis of the speech of educated speakers of English, with a view to developing a norm for teaching. The IRP model develops this suggestion. It proposes a rhotic variety with the following vowels: /iː/ as in *seat*, /ɪ/ as in *sit*, /eː/ as in *say*, /e/ as in *cottage*, /ɛ/ as in *set*, /æ/ as in *sad*, /aː/ as in *part*, /ɒ/ as in *cot*, /ɔː/ as in *caught*, /ʊ/ as in *foot*, /uː/ as in *food*, /ə/ as in *bird* and the first syllable of *about*, /oː/ as in *coat*, /aɪ/ as in *kite*, /aʊ/ as in *house*, /ɔɪ/ as in *toil*, /ɪə/ as in *here*, /eə/ as in *air*, and /ʊə/ as in *poor*. The consonant /r/ is pronounced in all positions: *run, train, part, bird, here, air, poor*. For the sake of national and international intelligibility, the authors recommend that a distinction should be made clearly between /v/ and /w/ (so that *wine* and *vine* do not become homophones) and provide detailed advice on rhythm, stress, and intonation, urging that the tendency in IndE towards syllable-timing be resisted. A pronouncing dictionary of 2,000 words seeks to do for IndE what Daniel Jones's *English-Pronouncing Dictionary* did for RP. See INDIAN ENGLISH[1], PRONUNCIATION MODEL. [ASIA, SPEECH, VARIETY]. T.MCA.

INDICATIVE [16c: through French from Latin *indicativus* stating, a translation of Greek *horistikē*]. A term for the grammatical mood in which statements are expressed: the sentence *I saw her yesterday* is in the indicative (mood). The indicative is the most common mood in English, and is used for both statements (*She knew him*) and questions (*She knew him?*). However, these may imply meanings typically associated with the imperative (where both *I should like to borrow your pen* and *Can I borrow your pen?* are indirect requests) and the subjunctive (a wish in *God should bless you in all your works* or after expressions of request, necessity, and the like, as in *It is imperative that she answers our letter immediately*, where the subjunctive is an alternative). See DECLARATIVE, MOOD. [GRAMMAR]. S.G.

INDIES [16c: plural of *Indie* or *Indy*: see INDIA]. Formerly a name for both the mainland and islands of South and South-East Asia (in the 19c restricted to islands referred to as *the East Indies*) and for the Americas (in the 19c restricted to the islands of the Caribbean referred to as *the West Indies*). See EAST INDIES, INDIA, WEST INDIES. [AMERICAS, ASIA, NAME]. T.MCA.

INDIGENIZATION [1950s: from Latin *indigena* someone born in a place, and *-ization*]. In sociolinguistics, a process of change by which a transplanted variety of a language becomes established and in various ways different from the parent variety, as with English in Ireland. This happens partly through different internal changes in the parent and transplanted varieties and partly through contact between the transplanted variety and the new environment. English in North America and Australia adopted new terms for unfamiliar flora and fauna as well as cultural items from indigenous languages: AmE *hickory, tomahawk*; AusE *kangaroo, boomerang*. Indigenization can also occur when a population acquires the language of another (usually dominant) group, often under colonialism, as also in Ireland. If the local élite begins to use the colonial language, it may transfer features and sometimes norms from local languages to the colonial language, as with English in India, Singapore, and the Philippines. See LANGUAGE CHANGE, NATIVIZATION. [LANGUAGE]. S.R.

INDIRECT OBJECT. With verbs that can be followed by two objects, the indirect object typically comes immediately after the verb: *Audrey* in 'I've sent *Audrey* a present'; *his son* in 'He bought *his son* a ball'. It is typically animate and the recipient of the direct object. The same idea is often expressed by repositioning the recipient with a *to* or *for*: 'I've sent a present *to Audrey*'; 'He bought a ball *for his son*'. Grammarians differ about whether the noun in the prepositional phrases should be labelled indirect object. Occasionally, an indirect object is inanimate: 'Give the kitchen a coat of paint.' In such cases, usually idiomatic uses of common verbs, the same idea cannot usually be re-expressed with *to* or *for* (never **Give a coat of paint to the kitchen*). See DIRECT OBJECT, DITRANSITIVE, DOUBLE ACCUSATIVE. [GRAMMAR].

S.C.

INDIRECT SPEECH. See DIRECT AND INDIRECT SPEECH.

INDO- [From Greek *Indós* the River Indus]. A combining form for: (1) The River Indus: *the Indo-Gangetic plain*. (2) *India* and *Indian*: *Indo-Aryan, the Indo-European languages*. [ASIA, NAME].

T.MCA.

INDO-ANGLIAN [Perhaps late 19c; certainly 1930s: from *Indo-* and *Anglian*, and probably a playful reversal of *Anglo-Indian*]. An obsolescent term for Indian writing in English: *Anthology of Indo-Anglian Verse* (A. R. Chida, 1935); 'Authors such as R. K. Narayan, Dom Moraes, Balachandra Rajan (now called "Indo-Anglians") find their public in the West, rather than inside India itself' (*Times Literary Supplement*, 10 Aug. 1962). Compare ANGLO-INDIAN. See INDIAN ENGLISH LITERATURE. [ASIA, NAME].

T.MCA.

INDO-ARYAN. See INDIAN LANGUAGES, INDO-EUROPEAN LANGUAGES.

INDO-ARYAN ENGLISH [*c.*1960s]. A term in linguistics for English as used in India, Pakistan, and Nepal by speakers of Indo-Aryan languages such as Assamese, Bengali, Gujarati, Hindi, Marathi, Nepali, Oriya, Panjabi, and Urdu. Among its characteristics is an initial epenthetic vowel in words beginning with a consonant cluster ('iskul' for *school*, 'isteshan' for *station*) or such a vowel used as a means of simplifying such a cluster ('sekul' for *school*, 'sateshan' for *station*). In Assamese and Bengali English, /s/ is used for both /s/ and /ʃ/, in the Hindi area both /dʒ/ and /z/ are used for /dʒ/, and in Oriya English /ɪ/ is used for both /ɪ/ and /i/ (so that *sit*/*seat* are homophones). Compare DRAVIDIAN ENGLISH. See EPENTHESIS, INDIAN ENGLISH[1], INDIAN LANGUAGES. [ASIA, VARIETY].

B.B.K.

INDO-BRITISH. A term for matters concerning India and Britain, placing Indian interests first and avoiding the equivocal implications of *Anglo-Indian*, as in *Indian Words in English: A Study in Indo-British Cultural and Linguistic Relations* (G. S. Rao, 1954). See INDO-. [ASIA, EUROPE, NAME].

T.MCA.

INDO-ENGLISH [1890s]. An obsolete term for various kinds of English used in India. In 1891, Hugo Schuchardt used the German plural form, later translated as *Indo-Englishes*, as a cover term for the varieties *Butler English* in Madras, *Pidgin English* in Bombay, *Boxwal(l)a(h) English* among itinerant pedlars in northern India, *chee-chee* or *chi-chi English* among Eurasians, and *Baboo* (now *Babu*) *English* in Bengal (see *Beiträge zur Kenntnis das englischen Kreolisch III: Das Indo-Englische*, in *Englisch Studien* 15, 1891, translated by Glenn G. Gilbert as *Pidgins and Creole Languages: Selected Essays*: Cambridge University Press, 1980). In 1964, the Indian educationist and writer V. K. Gokak wrote: 'What I would call "Indo-English" literature consists of translations by Indians from Indian literature into English' (*English in India: Its Present and Future*, Bombay). Since then, the term has occasionally been used, like *Indo-Anglian*, for what is now generally called *Indian English literature*. See BABU ENGLISH, BOXWALLA(H) ENGLISH, BUTLER ENGLISH, CHEE-CHEE ENGLISH, INDIAN ENGLISH[1], INDIAN ENGLISH LITERATURE, INDO-, INDO-ANGLIAN. Compare ANGLO-ENGLISH. [ASIA, VARIETY].

B.B.K.

INDO-EUROPEAN LANGUAGES, The. The language family, or family of families, of which English is a member, along with other European languages such as French, German, Russian, and Spanish, and Asian languages such as Bengali, Gujarati, Hindi, and Persian, as well as the classical languages Greek, Latin, Pali, and Sanskrit. It constitutes the most extensively spoken group of languages in the world. The view that similarities among certain languages of Europe and Asia resulted from a common origin had attracted scholars for several centuries before the British scholar Sir William Jones suggested in 1786 that Sanskrit, Latin, and Greek shared features derived from 'some common source which, perhaps, no longer exists'. He guessed that the Germanic and even the Celtic languages had the same source. Within a century, the implications of Jones's suggestion had been studied in great detail and his postulated 'common source' is now called *Proto-Indo-European* (*PIE*) or simply *Indo-European* (*IE*).

Proto-Indo-European. PIE is considered to have vanished soon after 2000 BC without leaving written records. Many details, especially its sound pattern, remain the subject of debate, and new theories of the date and place of the original 'Indo-Europeans' and the nature of their diaspora continue to be proposed. Their assumed homeland is a place where words shared by IE languages would have had a use. The word for *fish* was common to them but not the word for *sea*, so the territory of the Indo-Europeans appears to have had bodies of water but not a coastline. They had horses and goats, and grain but not grapes. Such evidence seems to point to an area in the northern part of eastern Europe. The era of IE is usually dated from *c*.3000 BC until shortly after 2000 BC. Again, the evidence is chiefly archeological and linguistic, and the conclusions inferential: for example, horses and goats did not appear in the assumed homeland much before 3000 BC. The breakup of the community of original speakers of PIE can be dated from the earliest records in IE languages. Thus, elements of Mycenean Greek are preserved on tablets from 1600 to 1200 BC, so IE had given way to its successors by then, and probably a good deal earlier. Some recent theories push these dates earlier still, holding that archeological evidence for the gradual spread of farming from Greece across Europe and into Britain points to an IE origin in Anatolia (now eastern Turkey) as early as 6000 BC.

Features of Proto-Indo-European. Like all historical reconstructions, PIE is hypothetical, designed to explain the features of the IE languages which can be studied in written records or in their living spoken form. The forms of PIE words are known only indirectly from its reflection in the earliest written records in IE languages. So Sanskrit *ásmi*, Latin *sum*, Greek *eimí*, and Old English *eom* can best be explained by assuming a PIE form like **es-*, with a suffix related to modern English *me*: **esme*. The sum of such reconstructions is a language with many stop consonants, several similar to those of modern English, but also another set with a following aspirate: *bh, dh, gh, gwh*. IE had several varieties of the nasals *m* and *n*, the liquids *l* and *r*, and the glides *w*, *y*, and schwa. But it had only one unstopped consonant, *s*. The vowels were *a, e, i, o, u* in long and short forms. As reconstructed, PIE words take forms like **bhrāter* brother, **yeug-* to yoke, **wed-* wet, leading to English *water*, Latin *unda* (source of English *undulate*), Greek *húdōr* (source of English *hydrant*), and Russian *voda* (borrowed into English in its diminutive form *vodka*).

PIE verbs are thought to have followed an inflectional pattern similar to that of English *sing, sang, sung*, varying the vowel to indicate tense. Verbs also took an inflection to indicate person, number, and mood. All the major parts of speech were highly inflected, for three genders (masculine, feminine, and neuter), and for eight cases that defined the function of the word in the sentence much as the modern English *s* defines the difference between *The cat is John* and *The cat is John's*. Such inflections were chiefly suffixes, rarely prefixes, but both kinds of affix were used for word-formation. Compound words similar to modern English *Whitehouse* and *Longfellow* were common.

Indo-European culture. Language is a record of culture. Reconstructed IE records a polytheistic people with a northern farmer's awareness of annual cycles, names for the chief celestial bodies and phenomena, names too for the earth and its varieties, wet and wild. Trees, notably the birch and fruit trees, and the animals that lurked in them, such as wolf and beaver, occupied the IE landscape; fish swam in their inland waters, while above them flew several kinds of birds from sparrows to eagles. In the clearings were domestic animals, and the Indo-Europeans knew lice at close range. The family was a vital group, from father and mother to son and daughter, and their home was the village. A patriarchal society seems to be reflected in the prominence of names for male relatives. Weaving and pottery created products for home use, for barter, and for the socially important exchange of gifts that IE languages record in the words for *give* and *take*. It is probably as much this cohesive agricultural social structure as conquest that enabled the Indo-Europeans to spread out of their homeland into regions from Britain to India, although the ancient mythologies and stories of India, the Hittites, and Greece suggest a stratified society of priests, warriors, artisans, and farmers, in which warfare was common and honourable.

The Indo-European language families. PIE gave rise to several 'families', related by common descent from one or other early offshoot. These are often classified as *satem* or *centum* languages (according to the development of the IE word for *hundred* with a *k* sound as in Latin *centum* or an *s* sound as in Sanskrit *satem*). It was once thought that the *centum* group (including English and Latin) was western and the *satem* group (including Sanskrit) was eastern, but Tocharian, deciphered in this century, is the easternmost IE language, and it is a *centum* language. Three IE families are no longer represented among living languages: Venetic in Italy, Tocharian in Central Asia, and Anatolian in what is now eastern Turkey (once represented by Hittite). Not all members of the surviving families, moreover, are still living: Latin and Old English are dead languages. The ongoing IE language families are:

The satem languages. (1) Indo-Iranian, including modern Persian and such Indic languages as Bengali, Gujarati, and Hindi. (2) Thraco-Phrygian, perhaps represented by modern Armenian. (3) Illyrian, perhaps represented by modern Albanian. (4) Balto-Slavonic, including modern Bulgarian, Lithuanian, Polish, Russian, and Serbo-Croat.

The centum languages. (1) Celtic, including modern Breton, Irish Gaelic, Scottish Gaelic, and Welsh. (2) Germanic, including Danish, Dutch, English, German, and Swedish. (3) Hellenic, including modern Greek. (4) Italic, including Latin and its Romance descendants, such as French, Provençal, Italian, Spanish, Portuguese, Catalan, and Romanian. The Germanic family stems from an unrecorded offshoot of IE known as *Primitive Germanic.* The Germanic languages fall into three groups: (1) East Germanic, represented only by Gothic, which ceased to be spoken in the 16c. (2) North Germanic, represented by the Scandinavian languages. (3) West Germanic, represented by modern German, Yiddish, Dutch, Frisian, Afrikaans, and English.

By no means all early IE languages left written records. The Slavonic languages can be traced no further back than the 10c; the earliest records of Albanian are from the 15c. There is no record at all of Germanic before it subdivided into eastern, western, and northern groups; the earliest records, runic inscriptions from the 3c or 4c, are Scandinavian.

A double heritage. The contemporary English language has a native grammar and vocabulary that stem directly from its Germanic heritage, and a borrowed vocabulary from other, mainly IE, languages, notably Latin, its offshoots, and Greek. This double vocabulary provides alternatives like *brotherly* from Germanic and *fraternal* from Latin, with nuances of difference: see BISOCIATION. Literary style often exploits the duality: though Milton is considered a Latinate writer, the second line in his couplet 'But O, as to embrace me she inclined, / I waked, she fled, and day brought back my night' is composed only of Germanic words, contrasting with the borrowed 'embrace' and 'inclined' in the previous line.

The Indo-European diaspora. The terms *Indo-European* and the older *Indo-Germanic* and *Indo-Celtic* aptly described (at the time they were coined) the spread of the language families from India in the east to Britain and Iceland in the west. Exploration, migration, and colonialism have, however, taken the diaspora further afield: the Western IE languages English, Spanish, French, and Portuguese are now major languages not just of Europe but of the Americas, Africa, and even Asia, where English is the associate official language of India, and English and Spanish are used in the Philippines. Smaller populations speaking IE languages are everywhere, and IE languages such as French and English often serve as languages of accommodation between speakers of other languages. Because of such developments, the term *Indo-European* is

still historically, philologically, and taxonomically sound, but it has lost its geographical rationale.

See ARYAN, CELTIC LANGUAGES, DERIVATION, DUTCH, ENGLISH LANGUAGES, ETYMOLOGY, EUROPE, EUROPEAN LANGUAGES, FOLK ETYMOLOGY, FRENCH, GAELIC, GERMAN, GERMANIC LANGUAGES, GOTHIC, GREAT VOWEL SHIFT, GREEK, GRIMM'S LAW, HISTORY OF ENGLISH, INDIA, INDIAN LANGUAGES, INDO-EUROPEAN ROOTS, INDO-GERMANIC, IRISH, ITALIAN, JONES (W.), LANGUAGE, LANGUAGE FAMILY, LATIN[1], PALI, PHILOLOGY, PRIMITIVE GERMANIC, ROMANCE LANGUAGES, ROOT, ROOT-CREATION, ROOT-WORD, SANSKRIT, SCANDINAVIAN LANGUAGES, SPANISH, VERNER'S LAW, WELSH. [ASIA, EUROPE, HISTORY, LANGUAGE, NAME].   W.F.B.

Baldi, Philip. 1983. *An Introduction to the Indo-European Languages.* Carbondale: Southern Illinois University Press.
Lockwood, W. B. 1969. *Indo-European Philology.* London: Hutchinson.
—— 1972. *A Panorama of Indo-European Languages.* London: Hutchinson.
Mallory, J. P. 1989. *In Search of the Indo-Europeans: Language, Archaeology and Myth.* London: Thames & Hudson.
Renfrew, Colin. 1988. *Archaeology and Language: The Puzzle of Indo-European Origins.* Cambridge: University Press.
Stevenson, Victor. 1983. *Words: An Illustrated History of Western Languages.* London: Macdonald.

INDO-EUROPEAN ROOTS. The hypothetical forms and meanings of Indo-European (IE) words reconstructed by comparative philologists through comparison of living languages, the surviving records of their older forms, and dead languages. IE roots are usually printed with an asterisk (*) to show that they are unrecorded; many are also printed with a following hyphen (-) to indicate that an inflectional or derivational suffix follows. The form and meaning listed with a hypothetical root are those that plausibly explain the recorded forms and meanings; they are not primarily assertions about the details of the IE original, but statements about the relationship of extant words in IE languages that descended from it.

An IE root for *to fasten* appears to have had the forms **pag-* or **pak-*. It is the origin of Latin *pax* and hence of English *pacify, pacific,* and by way of French *paix,* of *peace* and *appease.* The sense development from **pak-* appears to arise from the figurative specialization 'fastening together (by means of treaty)'. From the same IE root came Latin *palus* (stake fastened in the ground), whence English *pole,* as well as *pale, impale,* and *palisade* through French, and *pawl* through Dutch. Three stakes fastened in the ground made an instrument of torture probably called *tripalium in Latin, from which comes French travailler (to work hard) and modern English travail and (from Middle English times when a trip was no pleasure) travel. One form of the root *pag- was the nasalized *pang-, which gave rise not only to the Latin source of modern English impinge and impact but also to Old English fang (that which is fastened upon: plunder). In Middle English, the meaning of fang was specialized to the plunder of an animal, its prey; in Modern English it has become the tooth by which an animal fastens onto its prey.

Latin also had the descendant of *pag- in pagus (staked-out boundary); a dweller within such a boundary was a paganus, a villager or rustic. The figurative sense gives us pagan directly from the Latin; the literal sense remains in peasant, from the same word by way of French. From pagus Latin also had pagina (little fastening), a frame onto which vines were fastened, and from those vines comes propagate by generalization, and propaganda (those things which are to be propagated) by metaphor; hence also a page, in which the columns of written text are like vines on a trellis. These examples illustrate some of the known outcomes of the IE root *pag- or *pak- in modern English. The reconstruction of the root takes into account not only these forms and meanings but such others as Greek pégnumi (to fasten or congeal: compare pectin). The examples trace the outcomes from their source; the reconstruction traces the source back from its outcomes. Such roots are listed and discussed in detail in the books listed below. See ETYMOLOGY, ROOT. [ASIA, EUROPE, HISTORY, LANGUAGE, WORD].   W.F.B.

Shipley, Joseph. 1984. The Origins of English Words: A Discursive Dictionary of Indo-European Roots. Baltimore: Johns Hopkins University Press.
Skeat, Walter W. 1879-82. An Etymological Dictionary of the English Language. Oxford & New York: Clarendon Press.
Watkins, Calvert. 1985. The American Heritage Dictionary of Indo-European Roots. Boston: Houghton Mifflin.

INDO-GERMANIC, also **Indogermanic**. An obsolete term succeeded by Indo-European. See ARYAN, INDO-EUROPEAN LANGUAGES. [ASIA, EUROPE, HISTORY, NAME].   W.F.B.

INDONESIA. Formal title: Bahasa Republik Indonesia, English Republic of Indonesia. A country in South-East Asia, whose main island areas are Sumat(e)ra, Java/Jawa, Kalimantan (two-thirds of Borneo), Sulawesi, and Irian Jaya (the western half of New Guinea). Capital: Jakarta. Currency: the rupiah (100 sen). Economy: mixed. Population: 172.9m (1988), 213.9m (projection for 2000). Ethnicity: largely of Malay origin, including 45% Javanese, 14%

Sundanese, 8% coastal Malays, 8% Balinese, Batak, Dayak, Madurese, Moluccan, etc., and 2% Chinese. Religions: 87% Muslim, 9% Christian, 2% Hindu, 1% other. Languages: Bahasa Indonesia/Indonesian, a form of Malay (the official and link language); Javanese, English, and Dutch widely spoken; many local languages, including Madurese and Sundanese; some Chinese. Education: primary 98%, secondary 39%, tertiary 7%, literacy 74%. Hinduism and Buddhism were once common, and Islam was introduced by Persian and Gujarati traders in the 14-15c. The Portuguese were the first Europeans to set up trading posts in the region, in the 16c, and were followed by the Dutch and English in the early 17c. When the Dutch had driven out the English, they set up the Dutch East Indies, which they controlled until the islands' independence in 1945-50. There were only two breaks in this long period of Dutch colonialism: during the Napoleonic era, when first the French then the British briefly occupied the islands, and the Second World War, when the Japanese held them (1942-5). On declaring their independence in 1945, the Indonesians rejected Dutch and made English the first foreign language of the new country. Since then, English has been the primary language of international relations and national development, especially in enriching Indonesian Malay. Around 80% of books imported since independence have been in English and thousands of private language schools offer EFL courses. English, especially AmE, has high status; its influence through books, magazines, films, tourism, and pop music is pervasive, and many educated people use it among themselves. In adding new words to Bahasa Indonesia, there appears to be a preference for English loans rather than Malay coinages: for example, efisien (efficient) rather than berdayaguna. Typical of the many words borrowed from English and other European sources into Bahasa are antena, baterai, biskuit, dokter, eklair (éclair), helikopter, interkom, kabin, karamel, kompas, mesin (machine), mesin-jet (jet engine), pelikan, pilot, radio, and stetoskop. See EAST INDIES, MALAY, MALAYO-POLYNESIAN LANGUAGES, RELC, SOUTH-EAST ASIAN ENGLISH, SPELLING REFORM. [ASIA, NAME, VARIETY].   T.MCA.

INDUCTION. See LOGIC.

INFERENCE [16c: from Latin inferentia a bringing-in, a reasoned conclusion]. Also **deduction**. In general terms, the process or result of drawing a conclusion. In logic, the process or result of deriving a conclusion from a set of premises, including a conclusion that is probable in relation to the premises. From the statements All men are mortal and Socrates is a man, one infers or deduces that Socrates is mortal. See LOGIC. [LANGUAGE].   T.MCA.

INFINITIVE [15c: from Latin *infinitivus* unlimited]. The non-finite verb that has the uninflected form of the verb: *be, say, dig, make*. The term may be used alone (the *bare infinitive*: *I made him tell the truth*) or preceded by *to* (the *to-infinitive*: *I asked him to tell the truth*). The bare infinitive is commonly used after a modal auxiliary verb (*be* after the modal *may* in *We may be late*) and after the auxiliary *do* (*I did answer your letter, They don't know the difference*). It is also found in the complementation of a small number of main verbs such as *have, let, make, see* and *hear* (*I had Tom paint the fence*; *The soldiers let us pass*; *They heard us leave*). In some instances, either type of infinitive may be used: *Steven helped Susan (to) teach the children good manners*; *What Sidney did was (to) help Justin with his homework*. The *to*-infinitive has a wider distribution as the verb in an infinitive construction: (1) It may be subject (*To meet you was a great pleasure*), though a variant with postponed subject is more usual (*It was a great pleasure to meet you*). (2) It may be the object in various types of verb complementation: *I hope to see Judith and Percy soon*; *I asked John and Joyce to come to my party*; *Jeffrey and Rosalind want me to be there*. (3) It may be introduced by a *wh*-word: *Anton and Stella asked me what to advise their elder son*. (4) It may function in various semantic classes of adverbial: *To set the alarm, press four digits*; *He grew up to be a fine man*; *To be frank, the meeting was boring*. See BARE INFINITIVE, SPLIT INFINITIVE, USAGE (CONTROVERSIES). [GRAMMAR].   S.G.

INFIX [1880s: from Latin *infixus*, from *infigere/infixum* to fasten in]. An element inserted into the body of a word so as to change its meaning or function: for example, in the Californian language Yurok, *-ge-* forms plurals (*sepolah* field, *segepolah* fields). There is no strict equivalent in English, but the following have been cited as kinds of infixation: (1) A recurring nonsense syllable in secret languages such as Turkey Irish (once used in and around New York City), in which *ab* comes before a spoken vowel, so that the sentence *Can you see me?* becomes *Caban yaboo sabee mabee?* (2) The opening up of polysyllables to make room for expletives: *abso-blooming-lutely, kanga-bloody-roo*. See AFFIX, GREAT AUSTRALIAN ADJECTIVE. [GRAMMAR, WORD].   T.MCA.

INFLATED LANGUAGE [Probably 17c, from which period *inflated* has been used to describe language, rhetoric, style, etc.]. A pejorative term for speech or writing that uses far more words

than necessary; bombastic, pretentious, and turgid language. See BOMBAST, DOUBLESPEAK, GOBBLEDYGOOK, JARGON. [STYLE].   T.MCA.

INFLECTED [14c: from Latin *inflectere/inflexum* to bend, alter, modify]. A term in linguistics for a language in which a word takes various forms, most commonly by alteration of an ending, to show its grammatical role: Greek *ho lúkos* the wolf (nominative case and subject of the sentence), *ton lúkon* the wolf (accusative case and object of the sentence). Languages vary in their degree of inflection. The Indo-European languages were originally highly inflected, as shown by the forms of nouns, verbs, and adjectives in Greek and Latin. See CASE[1], INFLECTION, LINGUISTIC TYPOLOGY. [GRAMMAR, LANGUAGE].   J.M.A.

INFLECTION, also especially BrE **inflexion** [16c: from Latin *inflectere/inflexum* to bend in, curve, modulate]. A grammatical form of a word. Some languages make more use of inflections than others: Latin is highly inflected for nouns, adjectives, pronouns, and verbs, whereas French is highly inflected for verbs but less so for other parts of speech. Generally, verbs inflect for *mood, tense, person, number*, while nouns and adjectives inflect for *number* and *gender*. Such inflections may involve affixes, sound and spelling changes (including stress shifts), suppletion, or a mixture of these. In English, there are relatively few inflections. Verbs inflect through suffixation (*look*/looks/looking/looked), but some irregular verbs have past forms that depart from the norm (*see*/sees/seeing/saw/ seen; *swim*/swims/swimming/swam/swum; *put* /puts/ putting/put). The verb *be* has eight forms: *am, are, be, been, being, is, was, were*. Nouns inflect for plurality and possession (*worker*/ workers/worker's/workers') and some adjectives inflect for their comparatives and superlatives (*big*/bigger/biggest). Seven pronouns have distinct object forms: *me, us, her, him, them, thee, whom*. See ACCIDENCE, CASE[1], ENDING, INFLECTED, STRONG VERB, WEAK VERB. [GRAMMAR].   S.C.

INFORMAL [16c: see FORMAL]. A term in linguistics for a situation or a use of language that is common, non-official, familiar, casual, and often colloquial, and contrasts in these senses with *formal*. Whereas *Would you be so good as to help me?* is highly formal, *Lend us a hand, would you?* is highly informal. [GRAMMAR].   S.G.

INFORMATION [14c: from Old French *informacion*, from Latin *informatio/informationis* an outline, idea, from *informare/informatum* to give a form to, describe]. (1) Originally, moulding the mind or character through instruction in knowledge of the kind that creates a preferred ideological 'shape'. (2) In general usage, a kind of knowledge obtained through direct experience, through study, by asking questions, or by consulting a *source of information*, such as a book, timetable, or teletext. (3) In information theory, the measure of probability that a particular message will occur. (4) In computing, data in a useful form, usually as output from a computer but also at any stage of processing: input, output, storage, transmission.

Matter, energy, and information. Whether brief and unimportant or complex and significant, information is a commodity. It can be: passed on or held back; bought, sold, or given freely; allowed to disappear or stored in various ways for future use. The provision and storage of information take many forms, pre-eminent among them natural language. Stores of information, whatever form they take, can be as important as material and energy resources. Some theorists consider that nature is more than matter and energy: 'To the powerful theories of chemistry and physics must be added a late arrival: the theory of information. Nature must be interpreted as matter, energy, and information' (Jeremy Campbell, *Grammatical Man*, 1982, p. 16). In this broad sense, information is a 'code' shared by matter, energy, genes, living systems, and both natural and artificial forms of language.

Information and its synonyms. It is not easy to distinguish such related terms as *data, information, knowledge, wisdom*, but the different qualities of understanding can, for limited practical purposes, be listed in a hierarchy from *data* at the lowest point, through *information*, to *knowledge*, to *wisdom* at the top. Such a hierarchy occurs in the lines of T. S. Eliot: 'Where is the Life we have lost in living? / Where is the wisdom we have lost in knowledge? / Where is the knowledge we have lost in information?' (Choruses from 'The Rock', 1934). *Data* are a collection of more or less isolated facts, such as daily temperatures. *Information* is data with a shape and a potential use, or is conclusions drawn from data, such as the average yearly temperature in London. *Knowledge* is applied and heightened information, such as an expert's awareness of the difference between summer and winter temperatures in London, of the average temperature difference between London and Madrid, and any consequences to be drawn from such information. *Wisdom* is still more general and valuable, such as the ability to draw conclusions about the nature of weather and why people respond to it the way they do. Computers are so good at processing data that they encourage relatively

low-level descriptions of the world. However, work in artificial intelligence tries to improve on this, seeking to upgrade data to the level of information or even knowledge.

Bits and bytes. In terms of information theory and computer technology, the unit of information and smallest unit of its storage is the *bit* (*b*inary dig*it*), a coinage of the US statistician John Tukey. A sequence of random choices of 0 and 1 (such as 101100101 . . .) contains one bit per symbol. 8 bits make a *byte* (and to continue the association, 4 bits are a *nibble*). Computer memories are measured in multiples of bytes: *megabyte* 1m bytes; *gigabyte* 1,000m bytes; *terabyte* 1,000,000m bytes. One bit provides a choice between two possibilities. Two bits provide a choice among four: 00, 01, 10, or 11. Similarly, n bits provide 2^n choices: 3 bits have 8 choices, 4 bits 16, and so on. Since there are 88 characters on a standard typewriter keyboard (44, with the shift key giving 88 possibilities), a minimum of 7 bits is required to store one character, since the next power of two above 88 is 2^7, or 128. For computer convenience, each character normally fills an entire 8-bit byte, wasting one bit. Just as characters can be made up of bits (8 bits each), so words, pictures, and sounds can be made up of characters. An average word is about 6 bytes (five characters plus the space after it), and a typical novel contains between 500,000 and 1,000,000 bytes. To record a voice takes between 1,000 and 20,000 bytes per second (depending on the quality sought), and a low-quality picture (TV resolution, black and white) is about 30,000 bytes. A high-quality picture needs about 1,000,000 bytes, although usually it can be compressed, by removing any redundancy, to not more than a tenth of that.

Information theory. Information scientists consider that the degree of information in a text is measured by the difficulty of guessing what comes next. The least information is conveyed when the next elements are highly predictable, the most when there is uncertainty. A predictable sequence such as *aaaa* . . . contains no information, because the listener knows what is coming next. However, such a varied sequence as *aaaazaaaz* is contrastive and contains a small amount of information, but if continued without variation also becomes predictable. Such a structure as *aazbaazbb* is more interesting because it carries more information in its contrasts and patterns. The mathematics of information are described by *information theory* (invented by the US mathematician Claude Shannon at Bell Laboratories). Shannon's experiments included covering up the last part of a message and asking people to guess the next letter. Information theory measures the capacities of communication channels and memories, and the amount of information required to convey certain kinds of messages. It relates the bandwidth or frequency range of a communications channel to the number of bits per second it can transmit. A typical telephone channel transmits frequencies between 300 and 3,300 hertz (cycles per second), and has a bandwidth of 3,000 hertz. Its ability to transmit information is limited by this bandwidth and by the signal-to-noise ratio (that is, the ratio of the loudest signals transmitted to the level of background noise), and is typically about 10,000 bits per second. By contrast a modern computer network operates at bandwidths of many megahertz and may transmit 50 megabits per second. Information theory describes the ways in which to represent either digital information on telephone channels designed to transmit sound, or the reverse: techniques for handling voice signals on digital channels. It also deals with suitable methods of coding for error correction. It explains how to introduce redundancy into messages so that they can be corrected if garbled without having to retransmit the entire message. See REDUNDANCY.

Information processing. The term information processing describes data processing (the processing of numbers) and the processing of texts, sounds, and images. It is a major industry which includes much of the work done with computers and communications. Computers, which began as cryptographic machines, now dominate both writing and printing. Similarly, branching out from their use in calculating artillery firing tables during the Second World War, they perform virtually all complex numerical calculations in developed countries, in particular those that make possible modern banking and credit systems. Their ability to manipulate data has made possible inventory control in businesses and reservation systems for airlines of a very high level of complexity.

Information retrieval. There are two aspects to information retrieval: the finding of information, especially by searching computer files, and the theory and practice of doing so. The files may belong to an individual or an organization or be a major commercial service, such as Mead Data Center's *LEXIS* system, which stores US legal decisions. There are two kinds of retrieval: (1) *Document retrieval*, in which the response to a query is a citation to a document or the document in which the information can be found. (2) *Fact retrieval*, in which the response is the provision of the specific answer to the query rather than a text containing the answer. The first is common, the second not yet practical. The major issue in computerized information retrieval is not mechanical manipulation of text,

but deciding which items to retrieve. Popular techniques include: (1) *Manual indexing*, in which people read material and assign terms from an *indexing language* to it. Queries are then phrased in terms of that language. (2) *Free-text search*, in which the computer looks for the words as written by the original author. (3) *Statistical* or *probabilistic retrieval*, in which the computer looks for the words believed (on the basis of the mathematical processing of the original words) to reflect the content of the query. (4) *Artificial intelligence techniques*, in which the computer attempts to translate both the query and the document into some kind of higher-level representation and then match these. This may involve parsing the sentences and attempting to match the structures with formal representations. Knowing that a meal has a cook, some food, and somebody who eats it, a computer might realize that *John ate Bill's omelette* does not necessarily mean that John stole Bill's food.

Retrieval systems are evaluated by measuring *recall* (the fraction of relevant material found by the search), and *precision* (the fraction of the material which is found that the user wanted to see). A search which operates at 80% recall has found four-fifths of what the user wanted. If it has 25% precision, every relevant document has been joined by three that are irrelevant. The ideal search would be 100% recall (everything important found) and 100% precision (everything found is important). Reality is more like 20–50% recall and 50–80% precision. Retrieval systems may be designed either for use by expert librarians, who then perform searches for the actual questioners, or for inquirers themselves. Typical queries involve Boolean operators, such as *and* (as in searching for 'Horowitz *and* language', to find items both written by Horowitz and dealing with language) and *or* (as in searching for 'Navajo *or* Hopi', to find items dealing with either group). In general, manual indexing picks up major concepts in documents, but requires the searcher to know the indexing language. Free-text search finds specific textual phrases or peripherally mentioned subjects. Retrieval systems are widely used in libraries, where on-line services such as Dialog Information Services in the US make available most major abstracting and indexing services together with current newspapers, standard reference works (*Books in Print*, encyclopedias, etc.), and some scholarly books. Extensions to retrieval systems are being studied, both to increase their scope of content and to boost the number of researchers using these systems directly rather than through library personnel. The original post-war goal of the US science administrator Vannevar Bush was to give each scholar a 'memex' desk-sized unit containing an entire library and all his and his colleagues' notes on it, accessible by keystroke ('As We May Think,' *Atlantic Monthly*, 1945). This unit is still being sought.

Information technology. There are two aspects to the term *information technology*: (1) The general term for the equipment used to store and process information: computers, copying machines, printing machines, communications gear, and other devices. (2) The general business of using and developing that equipment, including both hardware and software. Innovation and the immediate widespread dissemination of new devices and processes appear to be a built-in feature of the industry. Recent introductions include the *facsimile transmission machine* or *fax* and the *Winchester disk drive* (so named because the first of these had two 30-megabyte spindles which reminded the builders of the Winchester .30/.30 repeating rifle).

Conclusion. An increasing part of a modern economy is devoted to information: whenever people watch television rather than play a game or bake a cake, they substitute data for tangible objects. Information for the use of the average person is overwhelmingly either *language* (radio, audiotapes, books, periodicals) or *images* (television, cinema, videotapes, pictures in books and periodicals). An important property of such information is that it is cheap to copy. Unlike a traditional business where one- to two-thirds of the cost of an object relates to materials, hardly any of the cost of an information business is materials, most of the investment being concentrated on producing the first copy. This makes for economies of scale, as a result of which domination of this economy by the advanced countries is even more extreme than their domination of traditional industries concerned with matter and energy. This dominance includes the languages in which most information is conveyed. Since English is the foremost of the languages of the technology and the key language of computer science, the *information explosion* or *information revolution* seems set to ensure it an increasingly significant role. See MESSAGE, PROPAGANDA, REDUNDANCY, TELECOMMUNICATIONS. [LANGUAGE, MEDIA, TECHNOLOGY].   M.L., T.MCA.

INFORMATION EXPLOSION. See COMMUNICATIVE SHIFT, INFORMATION.

INGLIS [From 14c: from Old English *Englisc*. Pronounced /'ɪŋlɪz/ and /'ɪŋlz/]. The word for *English* in northern Middle English and Older Scots, used from the 14c by writers of Older Scots as the name of their language, which they saw as the same as the language of England. In the late 15c, such writers began using the

national name *Scottis* (pronounced /'skotɪs/ and /skots/) for the language of Lowland Scotland and both terms continued in use as more or less free alternatives, *Inglis* predominating. Sometimes, however, 16c Scottish writers used *Inglis* for the language of England alone:

> Lyke as in Latyn beyn Grew termys sum,
> So me behufyt quhilum, or than be dum,
> Sum bastard Latyn, Franch or Inglys oys,
> Quhar scant was Scottys.
>   (Gavin Douglas, Prologue to Book I, *Æneid*, 1513)

> [Just as in Latin there are some Greek terms,
> So it behoved me at times, rather than be dumb,
> Some bastard Latin, French or English to use,
> Where Scots was scant].

The term *Scottis* was opposed to *Sotheroun* or *Suddroun* (Southern: the English of England), a less ambiguous term than *Inglis*. Only from the early 18c was the present-day terminology consistently applied, *Scots* for the vernacular of the Scottish Lowlands and *English* for the language of England and the standard variety being imported into Scotland. See SCOTS, SOUTHRON. [EUROPE, HISTORY, LANGUAGES].   A.J.A.

INGVAEONIC, also **Ingweonic** [1930s: from Latin *Ingaeuones* a tribal name recorded by the Roman historian Tacitus, perhaps meaning 'people of (the god) *Ingwaz*' and linked with the origins of *English*]. The hypothetical language from which coastal West Germanic descended. Anglo-Frisian, the equally hypothetical ancestor of Old English, has been called an Ingvaeonic dialect. Compare LOW GERMAN. [EUROPE, HISTORY, LANGUAGE, NAME].   T.MCA.

INITIAL, also **initial letter, point** [17c: from Latin *initialis* first, from *initium* beginning]. (1) The first letter of a word, usually capitalized in a proper name: the *L* of *London*, the *G, B, S* of *George Bernard Shaw*. Since at least the Middle Ages, Europeans have signed documents with or been referred to by their initials alone: Queen Elizabeth the Second in the form *EIIR* (Latin: *Elisabetha Secunda Regina*). The practice of using initials or points in handwriting and print has encouraged the growth of such abbreviations as symbols, formulas, initialisms, and acronyms: for example, *a* stands, among others, for *acre* and *are* (units of land measurement); *e.g.* stands for Latin *exempli gratia* for the sake of an example; *BBC* for *British Broadcasting Corporation*; *NATO* for *North Atlantic Treaty Organization*. (2) The large ornamental letter at the start of a page or chapter, especially in an illuminated manuscript. See ACRONYM, FORMULA, INITIALESE, INITIALISM, INITIAL RHYME,

LETTER[1], PERSONAL NAME, POINT, PUNCTUATION. [NAME, WORD, WRITING]. T.MCA.

INITIALESE [20c]. An informal, sometimes pejorative term for a style that uses initials to economize in space, effort, and expense. It assumes familiarity on the part of readers or listeners and is common in classified advertisements, in which time names and stock phrases are reduced to letters with or without points: *tel* telephone; *Mon, Sept.*; *ono/o.n.o.* or nearest offer. The codes used in the personal ads of the *New York Review of Books* are: *B* Black, *Bi* Bisexual, *D* Divorced, *F* Female, *G* Gay, *J* Jewish, *JNR* Jewish no religion, *M* Male/Married, *NYC* New York City, *S* Single, *S/D* Single/Divorced, *W* White. To avoid ambiguity, *M*s are kept separate, as in *MWM* Married White Male. See AGGLOMERESE, -ESE, INITIAL. [STYLE, WORD]. T.MCA.

INITIALISM [19c]. Also **initial word**. An abbreviation that consists of the initial letters of a series of words, pronounced in sequence: *BBC* for *British Broadcasting Corporation*, pronounced 'bee-bee-cee'. A letter group such as *NATO*, pronounced as a word ('nay-toe') is commonly referred to as an *acronym*. Both initialisms and acronyms have word-like qualities and take affixes (*pro-BBC*, *non-NATO*, *ex-IBMer*); they are sometimes referred to jointly as *letter words* or *letter names*, and the acronym is regarded by some lexicologists as a kind of initialism. The pronunciation of initialisms is usually straightforward, but writing sometimes poses problems: formerly, points were the norm (*B.B.C.*), but currently an unpointed style prevails in data processing and in the Armed Services and increasingly in commerce, advertising, and publishers' house styles. Institutions often have preferences: *International Association of Physical Oceanography* is *I.A.P.O.* (pointed initialism), but *Global Geological and Geophysical Ocean Floor Analysis and Research* is *GOFAR* (unpointed acronym). Idiosyncratic usage is common: the *International Herald Tribune* prints *U.S.* for *United States* alongside *EC* for *European Community*. Although most names are upper case, there are such exceptions as the *Initial Teaching Alphabet* (or *initial teaching alphabet*), officially abbreviated as *i.t.a.* and *ita*. Sequences of letters created for other reasons are occasionally interpreted as initialisms: for example, the letters *SOS* were adopted as an international distress signal because they were easy to transmit in Morse code; they are, however, often said to stand for 'save our souls'.

See ABBREVIATION, ACRONYM/PROTOGRAM, INITIAL, LETTER WORD. [WORD]. T.MCA.

INITIAL RHYME. See ALLITERATION.

INITIAL TEACHING ALPHABET, short forms *i.t.a.*, *ita*, *I.T.A.*, *ITA*. A controversial adaptation of the Roman alphabet (sometimes called *an augmented Roman alphabet*) intended as an aid for children and adults learning to read and write English. It was devised in England in 1959 by Sir James Pitman, based on the *phonotypy* of his grandfather, Sir Isaac Pitman, and on the *Nue Spelling* of the Simplified Spelling Society. It has 44 lower-case letters, each with one sound value: see extract. The additional letters are adaptations of forms already occurring in traditional orthography (t.o.), such as the digraphs *au, ng, th*. When the function of a capital is needed, an i.t.a. letter is written or printed larger. When learners become proficient in reading i.t.a. they are expected to transfer easily to t.o. Teachers who use it see this transfer as a progression and not a process of relearning. The alphabet was adopted on an experimental basis by some schools in the UK in 1960 and the US in 1963, and Pitman set up i.t.a. foundations in both countries to administer its use. The British foundation closed from lack of funds, its work taken up in 1978 by the *Initial Teaching Alphabet Federation*, a group of experienced and enthusiastic teachers.

ꟷe iniɷial teꟷiꟷ alfabet is not an attempt at spelliꟷ reform ov ꟷe iꟷliꟷ laꟷwæj, but an iniɷial lerniꟷ mædium tu assist in ꟷe ackwisiɷon ov literasy skills. it can be uesd wiꟷ infants or adults and uꟷers hw hav prєviusly fæld. it bræks ꟷe lerniꟷ prosess dun intu stæjes, cœpiꟷ wiꟷ ꟷe difficultis ov spelliꟷ ᴡen confidens has ben aꟷєvd wiꟷ a consistent orꟷografy. it mæks for fast rædiꟷ ᴡiꟷ æds comprehenɷon.

The alphabet was tested for the U. of London by the researcher John Downing, whose report was favourable. His publications on the subject include *The Initial Teaching Alphabet* (Cassell, 1964), *The i.t.a. reading experiment* (Evans, 1964), *Evaluating the Initial Teaching Alphabet* (Cassell, 1967), *Reading and Reasoning* (Chambers, 1979). In 1975, the Bullock Report noted: 'It would appear that the best way to learn to read in traditional orthography is to learn to read in the initial teaching alphabet.' However, despite such conclusions and much initial interest, the mother-tongue English-teaching profession has since the 1970s massively ignored the alphabet, despite an increasing awareness of literacy problems in the English-using world. It continues, however, to be used on a modest scale in Australia, Canada, Malta, Nigeria, South Africa, Spain, the UK, and the US. Its advocates argue that it gives learners confidence and satisfaction, largely because of its consistency. Its opponents among spelling reformers consider it an unsatisfactory compromise through which the irregularities of t.o. are not removed but postponed. Its mainstream opponents see it as alien and confusing in appearance, expensive in terms of printing reading materials, uncertain in the ease with which transfer to t.o. occurs, and inconvenient in relation to the parallel process of teaching people to write. See BULLOCK REPORT, PITMAN (J.), READING, SIMPLIFIED SPELLING SOCIETY, SPELLING REFORM. [WRITING].   T.MCA.

INKHORN TERM, also **inkhornism, inkpot term** [16c: from *inkhorn, inkpot* containers for ink]. Archaic: an obscure and ostentatious word usually derived from Latin or Greek, so called because such words were used more in writing than in speech. Thomas Wilson observed in 1553:

Among all other lessons this should first be learned, that wee never affect any straunge ynkehorne termes, but to speake as is commonly received: neither seeking to be over fine nor yet living over-carelesse, using our speeche as most men doe, and ordering our wittes as the fewest have done. Some seeke so far for outlandish English, that they forget altogether their mothers language (*Art of Rhetorique*).

Among his examples of inkhornisms are: *revoluting; ingent affabilitie; ingenious capacity; magnifical dexteritie; dominicall superioritie; splendidious.* See ARCHAISM, AUREATE DICTION, HOLOFERNES, -ISM, PUTTENHAM, WILSON. [STYLE, WORD, WRITING].   T.MCA.

INNIS, Harold Adams [1894-1952]. Canadian economist and communications theorist, born in Otterville, Ontario, and educated at McMaster U., Hamilton, Ontario, and the U. of Chicago. He was head of the Department of Political Economy at the U. of Toronto from 1937 until his death. His early writing generally dealt with the importance of cod, lumber, railways, and fur to the Canadian economy, but later he studied the effects of systems of communication on culture and politics, publishing *The Bias of Communication* (1951) and *Empire and Communications* (1950). Innis felt that periods of shift such as from one medium to another (from oral to written, or manuscript to type) were likely to liberate thinkers from the mindset promoted by the dominant medium. His work influenced Marshall McLuhan. See index. [AMERICAS, BIOGRAPHY, MEDIA].   M.F.

INNUENDO [17c: from the ablative *innuendo* ('by nodding towards') of Latin *innuendum*, from *innuere* to nod. The term was first used to introduce a legal aside, in which a person was identified (usually as guilty) or a statement was explained (usually as defamatory). Plural *-does, -dos*]. A hint or oblique remark, often malicious. In Shakespeare's *Julius Caesar* (3. 2), Mark Antony speaks to the crowd after Caesar's death, adding such ironic innuendoes as 'For Brutus is an Honourable man, / So are they all; all Honourable men', and slowly turns the crowd against Caesar's killers. [STYLE].   T.MCA.

INSTITUTE OF LINGUISTS. A British organization set up in 1910 to promote the learning of languages, including English, for commercial and industrial purposes. The Institute provides examinations in English at five levels, from low basic to high professional. See EXAMINING IN ENGLISH. [EDUCATION, EUROPE, MEDIA].   W.S.

INSTRUMENTAL [13c: through French from Latin *instrumentum* a tool or means]. In some inflected languages, such as Russian, the case that expresses *by means of*; more generally, the concept expressed by such an inflection. The commonest English equivalent is a *with*-phrase: 'He fixed it *with a hammer*.' This may contrast with a human agent or other cause, often shown by a *by*-phrase: 'The work was done *by several people*.' However, to do something *by hand* is instrumental. Instrumental and agentive occur together in: 'He was hit *with a chair by a drunk man*.' See CASE[1], OLD ENGLISH[1]. [GRAMMAR]. S.C.

INSULT. See ABUSE, DEROGATORY, ETHNIC NAME, MALEDICTA, PEJORATIVE, SLUR, SWEARING.

INTENSIFIER [19c]. A word that has a heightening effect (*very* in *very large*) or a lowering effect (*slightly* in *slightly fat*) on the meaning of the word that it modifies. Words that can be modified in this way are said to be *gradable*. Intensifying adjectives modify nouns (*great* in *a great fool*). Intensifying adverbs mainly modify verbs (*greatly* in *greatly admire*), gradable adjectives (*extremely* in *extremely foolish*), and other adverbs (*somewhat* in *somewhat slowly*). Some intensifiers go with certain gradable words: *entirely* with *agree*, *deeply* with *worried*, *highly* with *intelligent*. See COLLOCATION, IDIOM. [GRAMMAR].   S.G.

INTERFERENCE [1880s in first sense, 1950s in the second]. (1) In broadcasting and telecommunications, disturbance in the transmission or reception of one set of signals, caused by the intrusion of another set of signals; signals or radiation that cause such disturbance; the unwanted sounds they produce. (2) In linguistics and language teaching, the effect of one language on another, producing 'instances of deviation from the norms of either language' (Uriel Weinreich, *Languages in Contact*, 1953). Interference occurs naturally in the speech of bi- and multilingual people and the efforts of learners of foreign languages. It affects all levels of language: accent, pronunciation, syntax, morphology, vocabulary, and idiom. Although it is natural, especially when speakers are tired, tense, excited, or distracted, it is often disapproved of in unilingual societies as a display of inadequate skill on the part of a foreign learner. See ERROR, ERROR ANALYSIS, INTERFERENCE VARIETY, INTERLANGUAGE, MISTAKE. [EDUCATION, LANGUAGE, TECHNOLOGY]. T.MCA.

INTERFERENCE VARIETY. In sociolinguistics, a variety of a language such as English that has been affected by close contact for a long period of time with one or more other languages, as in India (influenced for example by Hindi and Tamil), Africa (influenced by Yoruba and Swahili), and Singapore (influenced by Chinese and Malay). See CONTACT VARIETY, INTERFERENCE. [LANGUAGE, VARIETY]. B.B.K.

INTERFIX [1950s]. An element used to unite words and bases: the thematic vowels *-i-* in *agriculture*, *-o-* in *biography*, and *-a-* in *Strip-a-gram* are interfixed vowels; the middle words in *editor-in-chief*, *writer-cum-publisher*, *Rent-a-Car*, and *Sun 'n Sand* are interfixed words; *-ma-* and *-ummy-* in *whatchamacallit* and *thingamabob/thingummybob* are interfixed syllables. Such elements generally fit into the rhythm of the language as weak vowels and syllabic consonants. In late 20c English, thematic vowels proper sometimes overlap with such other interfixable elements as the indefinite article and the agentive suffix *-er*, as in: *megalith*, *megaton*, *aquaphobic*, *Linguaphone*, *Funarama*, *SelectaVision*, *Select-a-game*, *Post-a-Book*, *Porta-phone*, *Rent-a-car*, *Strip-a-gram*, *Pakamac*, *Comutacar*. Such coinages are often stunt words created as commercial names. In pronunciation, the *a*-element in all of these items is a schwa, but in many cases the function of the *a* is unclear: in *SelectaVision* it could be thematic like the *-e-* in *television*, a reduction of *-or* in *selector*, an indefinite article (*Select a vision*), or a mix of these. The range of such usages is large: (1) Like *-a-* in *megalith*: *Beat-A-Bug*, *Cup-a-Soup*, *gorillagram*, *Prismaflex*, *Relax-a-Dial*, *Rent-a-tux*. (2) Like *-e-* in *telephone*: *cineplex*, *Procretech*, *telecom*. (3) Like *-i-* in *carnivore*: *agri-biz*, *Chemi-Garded*, *Digipulse*, *flexitime*, *Healthitone*, *Multivite*, *Nutri-Time*, *VisiCalc*. (4) Like *-o-* in *cardiogram*:

biotech, *Dento-Med*, *Film-O-Sonic*, *Fotopost*, *Frig-O-Seal*, *FructoFin*, *Thermoshell*, *Tomorrow-vision*. (5) Like *-u-* in *acupuncture*: *Accu-Vision*, *CompuSex*, *Execu-Travel*, *Dentu Cream*. (6) Like *-y-* in *bathyscaphe*: *polywater*, *Skinnyvision*. See BLEND, COMBINING FORM, THEMATIC VOWEL. [STYLE, WORD]. T.MCA.

INTERIOR MONOLOGUE/MONOLOG. See MONOLOGUE/MONOLOG, STREAM OF CONSCIOUSNESS.

INTERJECTION [15c: through French from Latin *interiectio/interiectionis* something thrown in]. A part of speech and a term often used in dictionaries for marginal items functioning alone and not as conventional elements of sentence structure. They are sometimes emotive and situational: *oops*, expressing surprise, often at something mildly embarrassing, *yuk/yuck*, usually with a grimace and expressing disgust, *ow*, *ouch*, expressing pain, *wow*, expressing admiration and wonder, sometimes mixed with surprise. They sometimes use sounds outside the normal range of a language: for example, the sounds represented as *ugh*, *whew*, *tut-tut/tsk-tsk*. The spelling of *ugh* has produced a variant of the original, pronounced 'ugg'. Such greetings as *Hello*, *Hi*, *Goodbye* and such exclamations as *Cheers*, *Hurray*, *Well* are also interjections. See PART OF SPEECH. [GRAMMAR]. S.C.

INTERLANGUAGE [1920s]. (1) A language created for international communication, such as *Esperanto*, or used as a lingua franca in a particular region, such as Hausa and Pidgin English in West Africa. (2) In linguistics, a language intermediate between two or more other languages, generally used as a trade jargon, such as *Hindlish* in India and *Taglish/Mix-Mix* in the Philippines. (3) In language teaching and applied linguistics, the transitional system of a learner of a foreign language at any stage between beginner and advanced. See ARTIFICIAL LANGUAGE, CODE-MIXING AND CODE-SWITCHING, ERROR ANALYSIS, -GLISH AND -LISH, LANGUAGE LEARNING, PIDGIN. [EDUCATION, LANGUAGE]. T.MCA.

INTERLOCUTOR [16c: from the verb *interloqui/interlocutus* to speak between]. Someone who takes part in a conversation or a dialogue, or speaks to, banters with, or questions other people. *Interlocution* is a rare term for both conversation and alternate reading or speaking, as in making religious responses or reading alternate verses of the psalms. See LOCUTION. [SPEECH]. T.MCA.

INTERNAL RHYME. The use of rhyming words within a line of verse. The inner word may rhyme with the end of the line, as in W. S.

Gilbert's 'Then a sentimental *passion* of a vegetable *fashion*' (*Patience*, 1881), in which the effect is of two short lines written as one. However, internal rhyme may be independent of end rhyme, as in Swinburne's 'Sister, my sister, O *fleet sweet* swallow'. Medieval Latin *leonine verse* (composed in hexameters or elegiac couplets) employs internal rhyme, the word that precedes the caesura rhyming with the last word of the same line, as in, 'The fair breeze *blew*, the white foam *flew*' (Coleridge, 'The Ancient Mariner', 1798). See RHYME. [LITERATURE]. R.C.

INTERNATIONAL ASSOCIATION OF TEACHERS OF ENGLISH AS A FOREIGN LANGUAGE. See IATEFL.

INTERNATIONAL CORPUS OF ENGLISH. See SURVEY OF ENGLISH USAGE.

INTERNATIONAL ENGLISH [Late 20c: with or without a capital *i*]. The English language, usually in its standard form, either when used, taught, and studied as a lingua franca throughout the world, or when taken as a whole and used in contrast with *American English, British English, South African English*, etc., as in *International English: A Guide to Varieties of Standard English*, title of a work by Peter Trudgill and Jean Hannah (London: Edward Arnold, 1982) that reviews both standard and non-standard varieties worldwide. See ENGLISH, INTERNATIONAL LANGUAGE, STANDARD INTERNATIONAL ENGLISH, TEIL, WORLD ENGLISH. [GEOGRAPHY, VARIETY]. T.MCA.

INTERNATIONAL ENGLISH LANGUAGE TESTING SYSTEM. See IELTS.

INTERNATIONAL HERALD TRIBUNE. An English-language daily newspaper with an American background and house style, its head office in Paris, and 'The Global Newspaper' as its main slogan. It was founded in 1887 by James Gordon Bennett Jr. as the European edition of the *New York Herald*. Bennett pioneered the use of cables and radio to send news and, in Europe, the use of Linotype and colour comic strips. After his death and several changes of ownership, the newspaper became the European edition of the *New York Herald Tribune*, and when that paper closed in 1966 after a printers' strike it was maintained under its present name by the Whitney Communications Corporation, with the *Washington Post* and *New York Times* as co-owners and main sources of material. These newspapers became the sole owners in 1991. The 'Trib' is put together in Paris, printed by facsimile in Paris, London, Zurich, Hong Kong, Singapore, The Hague, Marseille, New York,

Rome, Tokyo, and Frankfurt, and sold through retail outlets and by postal subscription. Sales in 1964 were 52,578, in 1985 160,000, and the target for 2000 is over 200,000. Compare EUROPEAN (THE). See NEWSPAPER. [MEDIA]. T.MCA.

INTERNATIONAL LANGUAGE [Late 19c]. Sometimes **international auxiliary language**. A language, natural or artificial, that is used for general communication among the nations of the world: 'In the four centuries since the time of Shakespeare, English has changed from a relatively unimportant European language with perhaps four million speakers into an international language used in every continent by approximately eight hundred million people' (Loreto Todd & Ian Hancock, *International English Usage*, 1986); 'The success of English in its function as an international auxiliary language has often been regarded as a measure of its adequacy for the job' (Manfred Görlach, 'Varietas Delectat', in Nixon & Honey, *An Historic Tongue*, 1988). Compare LINGUA FRANCA, WORLD LANGUAGE. See BASIC ENGLISH, BROKEN ENGLISH, ESPERANTO, INTERNATIONAL ENGLISH, WORLD ENGLISH. [LANGUAGE]. T.MCA.

INTERNATIONAL LINGUISTIC ASSOCIATION, short form *ILA*. An American association formerly known as the *Linguistic Circle of New York*, founded 1943 by refugee linguists from the Société de Linguistique de Paris. It publishes the journal *Word*. [AMERICAS, LANGUAGE, MEDIA]. J.A.

INTERNATIONAL PHONETIC ALPHABET, short form *IPA*. An alphabet developed by the *International Phonetic Association* to provide suitable symbols for the sounds of any language. The symbols are based on the Roman alphabet, with further symbols created by inverting or reversing Roman letters or taken from the Greek alphabet. Such symbols are designed to harmonize as far as possible with standard Roman symbols, so as to fit as unobtrusively as possible into a line of print. The main characters are supplemented when necessary by diacritics. The first version of the alphabet was developed in the late 19c by A. E. Ellis, Paul Passy, Henry Sweet, and Daniel Jones from a concept proposed by Otto Jespersen. It has been revised from time to time, most recently in 1989 (see accompanying charts). The IPA is sufficiently rich to label the phonemes of any language and to handle the contrasts between them, but its wide range of exotic symbols and diacritics makes it difficult and expensive for printers and publishers to work with. As a result, modifications are sometimes made for convenience and economy, for example in ELT learners' dictionaries. Phoneme symbols are

CONSONANTS

	Bilabial	Labiodental	Dental	Alveolar	Postalveolar	Retroflex	Palatal	Velar	Uvular	Pharyngeal	Glottal
Plosive	p b			t d		ʈ ɖ	c ɟ	k g	q ɢ		ʔ
Nasal	m	ɱ		n		ɳ	ɲ	ŋ	N		
Trill	ʙ			r					R		
Tap or Flap				ɾ		ɽ					
Fricative	ɸ β	f v	θ ð	s z	ʃ ʒ	ʂ ʐ	ç ʝ	x ɣ	χ ʁ	ħ ʕ	h ɦ
Lateral fricative				ɬ ɮ							
Approximant		ʋ		ɹ		ɻ	j	ɰ			
Lateral approximant				l		ɭ	ʎ	ʟ			
Ejective stop	p’			t’		ʈ’	c’	k’	q’		
Implosive	ƥ ɓ			ƭ ɗ			ƈ ʄ	ƙ ɠ	ʠ ɠ		

Where symbols appear in pairs, the one to the right represents a voiced consonant.
Shaded areas denote articulations judged impossible.

used in phonemic transcription, either to provide a principled method of transliterating non-Roman alphabets (such as Russian, Arabic, Chinese), or to provide an alphabet for a previously unwritten language. The large number of diacritics makes it possible to mark minute shades of sound as required for a narrow phonetic transcription. The alphabet has not had the success that its designers hoped for, in such areas as the teaching of languages (especially English) and spelling reform. It is less used in North America than elsewhere, but is widely used as a pronunciation aid for EFL and ESL, especially by British publishers and increasingly in British dictionaries of English. The pronunciation in the 2nd edition of the *OED* (1989) replaces an earlier respelling system with IPA symbols. The IPA and other phonetic symbols are described in detail in *Phonetic Symbol Guide*, Geoffrey K. Pullum & William A. Ladusaw (U. of Chicago Press, 1986). See ALPHABET, ENGLISH PRONOUNCING DICTIONARY, INTERNATIONAL PHONETIC ASSOCIATION, LANGUAGE TEACHING, LEARNER'S DICTIONARY, PHONETIC TRANSCRIPTION, RESPELLING. [SPEECH, WRITING].

G.K., T.MCA.

INTERNATIONAL PHONETIC ASSOCIATION, short form *IPA*. An association that seeks to promote the science of phonetics and its practical applications. It was founded in 1886 in

VOWELS

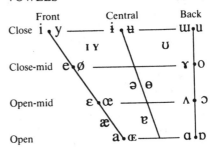

Where symbols appear in pairs, the one
to the right represents a rounded vowel.

France under the English name *The Phonetic Teachers' Association*, by a group of language teachers who used phonetic theory and transcription in their work. The journal *Dhi Fonètik Titcer* started in France in the same year, edited by Paul Passy and printed in English in a phonetic script; its name was changed in 1889 to *Le Maître phonétique*. At first, the Association was concerned mainly with phonetics applied to teaching English, but interest expanded with the membership to the phonetic study of all languages. It acquired its present name in 1897. Although the Association played an important part in the European movement for the reform of language teaching in the late 19c, it is now best known for its regularly revised alphabet. In addition to such occasional publications as *Differences between Spoken and Written Language* (Daniel Jones, 1948) and *The Principles of the International Phonetic Association* (Daniel Jones, 1949), which includes sample transcriptions of a large number of languages, the Association publishes *The Journal of the IPA*, which evolved from *Le Maître phonétique*. The current address of the Association is the Department of Linguistics & Phonetics, U. of Leeds, Leeds LS2 9JT, UK. See INTERNATIONAL PHONETIC ALPHABET, JONES (D.), LANGUAGE TEACHING, PASSY, PHONETICS. [MEDIA, SPEECH].

G.K., T.MCA.

INTERNATIONAL SCIENTIFIC VOCABU-LARY [1961: as used by Philip Gove, editor, *Webster's Third New International Dictionary*, 1961]. A term for the classically derived vocabulary of science common to such languages as English, French, and Spanish. In *Webster's Third*, the letters ISV mark words 'when their language of origin is not positively ascertainable but they are known to be current in at least one language other than English. . . . Some ISV words (like *haploid*) have been created by taking a word with a rather general and simple meaning from one of the languages of antiquity, usually Latin and Greek, and conferring upon it a very specific and complicated meaning for the purposes of modern scientific discourse.' Typically, an ISV word is a compound or a derivative which 'gets only its raw materials, so to speak, from antiquity'. Compare CLASSICAL/LEARNED COMPOUND, COMBINING FORM. [REFERENCE, WORD].

T.MCA.

INTERROGATION MARK/POINT. See QUESTION MARK.

INTERROGATIVE [16c: from Latin *interrogativus* questioning]. The grammatical structure through which questions are asked, and a term used in the classification of sentence types, in contrast with *declarative*, *imperative*, etc. It is often used interchangeably with *question*, but some grammarians keep interrogative as a category of form and question as a category of meaning, while others do the reverse. The sentence *Can I borrow your pen?* is interrogative in form, but is a directive in meaning, requesting the listener to lend the pen. See QUESTION. [GRAMMAR].

S.C.

INTERTEXTUALITY [mid-19c]. In literary criticism, the relationship between texts. The term is associated in particular with the French structuralist Julia Kristeva (b.1941), who regards every text as an *intertext* in a succession of texts already existing or yet to be written. They may be connected by citation or allusion: for example, T. S. Eliot begins 'The Journey of the Magi' (1927) with an extract from a sermon by Lancelot Andrewes (1555-1626). The relationship among texts may be through formal features, as in the succession of poets practising the sonnet, or the dominance of the heroic couplet from the late 17c to the end of the 18c. A writer may criticize and change the effect of an earlier text: for example, William Golding's *Lord of the Flies* (1954) 'subverts' the optimistic tone of R. M. Ballantyne's *The Coral Island* (1857), and makes use of the same or similar names for main characters. The following are contrastive excerpts:

The Coral Island. 'Now, then, Ralph and Peterkin,' said Jack, as we mingled with the crowd, 'it seems to me that the object we came here for having been satisfactorily accomplished, we have nothing more to do but get ready for sea as fast as we can, and hurrah for dear old England!'
'That's my idea precisely,' said Peterkin, endeavouring to wink, but he had wept so much of late, poor fellow, that he found it difficult; 'however, I'm not going away till I see these fellows burn their gods.'
Peterkin had his wish, for, a few minutes afterwards, fire was put to the pile, the roaring flames ascended, and, amid the acclamations of the assembled thousands, the false gods of Mango were reduced to ashes.

Lord of the Flies. Piggy wilted. Ralph took the conch from him and looked round the circle of boys.
'We've got to have special people for looking after the fire. Any day there may be a ship out there'—he waved his arm at the taut wire of the horizon—'and if we have a signal going they'll come and take us off. And another thing. We ought to have more rules. Where the conch is, that's a meeting. The same up here as down there.'
They assented. Piggy opened his mouth to speak, caught Jack's eye and shut it again. Jack held out his hands for the conch and stood up, holding the delicate thing carefully in his sooty hands.
'I agree with Ralph. We've got to have rules and obey them. After all, we're not savages. We're English; and the English are the best at everything. So we've got to do the right things.'

Some 20c writers have been overt with their intertextual references, as when Joyce imitates a succession of styles in English in the 'Oxen of the Sun' episode in *Ulysses* (1922). Christine Brooke-Rose's experimental novel *Thru* (1975) is rich in allusion to earlier works and presents a continual challenge of recognition to the reader. Some writers allude intertextually to their own work: Hardy introduces characters from *Far from the Madding Crowd* (1874) into *The Mayor of Casterbridge* (1886). In *The Sea, The Sea*

(1978), a novel that has many echoes of Shakespeare's *The Tempest*, Iris Murdoch has the narrator imagine a character who is an actress playing Honor Klein from her earlier novel *A Severed Head* (1961). These are specific and conscious references; intertextuality assumes that, as well as making its own unique reference, every text contains latent semiotic links with others. Compare ALLUSION, QUOTATION. See PASTICHE, TEXT. [LITERATURE, WRITING].   R.C.

INTERVOCALIC [19c]. A term in phonetics indicating that a consonant occurs between vowels: intervocalic /r/ in *merry* and /t/ in *butter*. See R, VOWEL. [SPEECH].   T.MCA.

INTONATION [17c: from Latin *intonatio/ intonationis* putting tone into (something), as in chanting plainsong, uttering musical notes, and modulating the voice]. The tone pattern of speech, produced by varying vocal pitch. Type and style of intonation are closely linked to patterns of rhythm and stress and cannot easily be described separately from them. See PROSODY, RHYTHM, STRESS, TONE. [SPEECH].   G.K.

INTRANSITIVE. See TRANSITIVE AND INTRANSITIVE.

INTRUSIVE L. See SOMERSET.

INTRUSIVE R. In some accents of English, including RP, an /r/ pronounced between the vowels /ɔ, ɑː, ə/ and a following vowel when there is no *r* in the spelling, as in *Australia/r and New Zealand, the India/r Office, draw/r/ing room*. Homophonic effects sometimes occur, as in *law and order/lore and order*. Occasionally, comment on the intrusion is humorous; in Britain, *Laura Norder* is a friend of the police and an advocate of strong government. The /r/ is in phonological terms an inherent feature of the accent in question, but because it sometimes has an orthographic form (as in *czar of Russia*) and sometimes does not (as in *Shah of Persia*), it has been widely stigmatized in the latter case as a sound that should not be there and that makes no sense. The /r/ is accepted in the first of these phrases but often rejected as non-standard in the second. However, its use continues regardless of approval or disapproval, and generally goes unnoticed among those speakers who do it. See LINKING R, RHOTIC AND NON-RHOTIC. [SPEECH, STYLE].   G.K., T.MCA.

INUIT, also **Innuit** [18c: from the Inuktitut word *inuit* people, plural of *inuk* person]. The name of a Native people of Canada, widely known as *Eskimo*. This name comes from Algonquian and means 'raw-meat eater'; the Inuit consider it pejorative, and their own name is now standard in Canada. Recent Canadian style guides recommend *Inuk* singular, *Inuit* plural. The language of the Inuit, *Inuktitut*, is often also called *Inuit*. See AMERICAN LANGUAGES, CANADIAN LANGUAGES, CANADIAN PLACE-NAMES. [AMERICAS, NAME].   M.F.

INVERSION [16c: from Latin *inversio/ inversionis* turning round]. Also *anastrophe* [16c: from Greek, turning back]. (1) Turning something round, as for example in English, when forming certain kinds of questions from statements, such as *Are you coming?* from *You are coming*, by inverting the order of *you are*. (2) In rhetoric, speech in which the normal word order of statements is turned round, usually for emphasis or to mark priority and eminence: 'To the Most High and Mightie Prince, Iames by the grace of God King of Great Britaine, France and Ireland, Defender of the Faith, &c. the Translators of the Bible wish grace, Mercie, and Peace through Iesus Christ our Lord' (dedication, the Authorized Version of the Bible, 1611). Fowler's *Modern English Usage* (ed. Gowers, 1965) states that such inversion has 'an essential place in the language', but adds that 'abuse of it ranks as one of the most repellent vices of modern writing'. Journalistic uses of inversion that are often regarded as vices include inverting verb and subject in reporting clauses that come before quoted statements: for example, *Says Darren Beagle, chief programmer at Megabux Inc.*, '*This is the breakthrough we've all been waiting for.*' See CHIASMUS, HYPERBATON, HYSTERON PROTERON, QUESTION, WORD ORDER. [GRAMMAR, STYLE, WRITING].   T.MCA.

IOTA [17c: through Latin from Greek *iôta*, from Semitic: compare Hebrew *yōdh* yod. A doublet of *jot*. Both words are commonly used to signify something small and trivial: *not an iota of proof*; *not a jot or tittle*]. The 9th and smallest letter of the Greek alphabet: upper case I, lower case ι. The term *iotacism* refers to considerable or excessive use of the letter *i* or any sound that *i* or *y* represents, as in *an itsy-bitsy, teenie-weenie bikini*. See ALPHABET, I, J, LETTER[1]. [SPEECH, WRITING].   T.MCA.

IPA, I.P.A. See INTERNATIONAL PHONETIC ALPHABET, INTERNATIONAL PHONETIC ASSOCIATION.

IRAQ. See ARABIC, ENGLISH.

IRELAND [Before 10c: from Old English *Iraland, Yraland*, from Gaelic *Eire*, English *-land*]. An island of Western Europe, often referred to as 'an island of the British Isles'

(*Longman Larousse*, 1968). However, many Irish people, especially in the Republic, consider this description inappropriate and offensive. In their view, Ireland is not, or should not be, in any sense 'British'. In the six counties of Northern Ireland, which is part of the UK, the term *British Isles* is generally accepted in Protestant communities, unless *British* is taken to be synonymous with *English*. The island was never invaded by the Romans, and after the decline of the Roman Empire became a centre of Christian culture that used both Gaelic and Latin. Irish clerics went as missionaries to the European mainland, where they were often known, and commemorated in place-names, as *Scoti* (Scots). Until the 8c, this name referred only to Irish people and settlers from Ireland in what later became Scotland. The long period of cultural, scholarly, and religious influence was brought to an end by two waves of Germanic invasion and settlement: the Norse (9–11c) and the Anglo-Normans (12c onward).

In 1171, Henry II of England declared himself Lord of Ireland, and in 1542 Henry VIII took the title King of Ireland, giving Irish chieftains such English titles as *Earl of Tyrone*. In 1603, the first British king, James VI of Scots and I of England, was declared King of Ireland, but Ireland was not formally joined to England and Scotland (as part of the UK) until 1803. Hostility between natives and early settlers was compounded after the Reformation by the enmity of Catholic and Protestant, especially when English and then Scottish Protestant settlers were 'planted' in Ireland as loyal supporters of the Crown, amid a largely resentful Celtic and Catholic majority. The history of Ireland from the 17c is dominated by a series of revolts against the *Protestant Ascendancy* imposed from London and the fight first for home rule then for outright independence. The struggle for Irish autonomy culminated in the Easter Rising (Dublin, 1916) and the partition of the island (1920), establishing the Catholic-dominated *Irish Free State* (1921), which became *the Irish Republic* (1949), and the Protestant-dominated six counties of *Northern Ireland*, part of the UK. In this province, also known loosely as *Ulster*, often violent hostility continues between loyalist Protestants who wish to sustain the British link and nationalist Catholics who seek a united Ireland. The Republic is 95% Catholic by religion and has two official languages, Irish Gaelic and English. Northern Ireland has since the 18c had a Protestant majority; currently, the population appears to be moving towards comparable numbers.

See ANGLO-CELTIC, ANGLO-IRISH, APPALACHIAN ENGLISH, AUSTRALIA, AUSTRALIAN ENGLISH, BELFAST, BLACK IRISH, BLARNEY, BROGUE, CANADA, CANADIAN ENGLISH, CELT, CELTIC, CELTIC LANGUAGES, DIALECT IN IRELAND, DUBLIN, EIRE, ENGLISH, ERIN, ERSE, GAELIC, GIFT OF THE GAB, HIBERNIA, HIBERNIANISM/HIBERNICISM, HIBERNO-ENGLISH, IRELAND, IRISH, IRISH BROADCASTING, IRISH BULL, IRISH ENGLISH, IRISH GAELIC, IRISHISM, IRISH JOKE, IRISH LITERATURE, IRISHMAN/WOMAN, IRISH PLACE-NAMES, IRISH PRESS, IRISH PUBLISHING, IRISHRY, LILT, LIVERPOOL, LONDON, NEWFOUNDLAND, NORMAN FRENCH, NORSE, NORTHERN IRELAND, NORTHERN IRISH ENGLISH, OLD ENGLISH[2], PALE, PROTESTANT ASCENDANCY, SCOT, SCOTCH-IRISH, SCOTLAND, SCOUSE, STAGE, ULSTER, ULSTER ENGLISH, ULSTER SCOTS, YOLA. [EUROPE, NAME]. T.MCA., L.T.

IRISH [Before 10c: from Old English *Irisc*, from *Iras* the people of Ireland]. (1) The adjective for Ireland, its people, languages, and traditions: *Irish Gaelic, the Irish language, the Irish Question, Irish whiskey.* Its nuances are varied, ranging from the sublime (*Irish patriot*) through such humorous and mischievous 'institutions' as the *Irish bull* and *Irish joke*, to facetious phrases like *Irish confetti* stones and bricks thrown as weapons, *an Irish hurricane* a flat calm with drizzling rain, *an Irish rise* a reduction in pay. Such expressions are sometimes deliberately used in Britain to express anti-Irish feeling. If something seems unusual, fey, or illogical, a common comment is: *That's a bit Irish.* (2) The Irish people: 'Other people have a nationality. The Irish and the Jews have a psychosis' (Brendan Behan, in *Richard's Cork Leg*, 1973). (3) Irish Gaelic: *In Connemara they speak Irish.* (4) The English language in Ireland: 'The *Irish* of the peasants, which is nothing but English Hibernicised' (*Westminster Review* 21, 1834). (5) Until the late 18c, the Scots, especially if Gaelic-speaking: 'We oft finde the Scots called Irishes, like as we yet term commonly our Highlandmen, in regard they speak the Irish language' (Spottiswoode, *History of the Church of Scotland*, 1655).

Irish and English. The relationship between the English and Irish languages is at least eight centuries old. In that period, the fortunes of both have waxed and waned, and the contacts have been complicated by conquest, rebellion, religion, ethnicity, immigration, emigration, politics, and education. As English has advanced and Irish retreated, it has been said both that English 'murdered' Irish and that Irish 'committed suicide' in the face of English. It is certainly true that the main reasons for the replacement of Irish by English are social and political rather than linguistic. They include: (1) The large-scale settlements begun in the 16c by the Tudors and reinforced by the Stuarts and

Cromwell in the 17c. (2) The penal laws of the 18c which reduced the native population to subsistence level and ensured that Irish was no longer the first language for those who hoped to improve their political or social position. (3) The introduction of National Schools in 1831, where English was the sole medium of instruction. (4) The years of famine in the mid-19c, which resulted in mass emigration and a belief that land and language were blighted.

The heyday of Irish. When in the 12c the Normans invaded Ireland, they found a secure language with strong and distinctive traditions. Speakers of Irish had Gaelicized not only the earlier people of the island and other Celtic settlers, but also later Pictish, Anglo-Saxon, and Norse settlers. The French, Flemish, Welsh, and English languages went to Ireland with the Normans and became in due course subject to pressure from Irish. Only within the eastern coastal region known as the Pale (see entry) did English maintain a fragile grip. Medieval statutes show both the power of Irish and a wish to protect English against it: in 1285, a letter sponsored by the Bishop of Kildare and sent to the king suggested that Irish-speaking clerics should not be promoted because of their wish to maintain their language, and in 1366, the Statutes of Kilkenny (written in French) enjoined the English to use English names, customs, and language. However, Irish encroached even at the highest levels: in the 14c, the Earls of Ormond and Desmond spoke Irish and the latter, although Lord Chief Justice, wrote Irish poetry.

The conquest of Ireland. In the 16c, the English defeated the Gaelic order in Ireland; land was confiscated and plantation schemes brought in large numbers of English and later Scottish settlers. From 1600, English grew in strength and by 1800 was regularly used by up to 50% of the population. However, such was the growth in population that on the eve of the famines of 1846-8 there were probably more Irish-speakers in absolute terms than at any previous time. What began with Tudor pronouncements became more and more part of the social tissue of the island. As the 19c famines and mass emigrations proceeded, English consolidated its position. The Catholic Church became more reconciled to it and wary of Protestant proselytism through Irish, a process started by Elizabeth. Political leaders such as Daniel O'Connell were more concerned with emancipation than language and a school system was established, managed by the Catholic clergy, that excluded Irish from the curriculum. The steady decline of Irish was abetted by a general,

pragmatic desire to acquire English. By the mid-19c, few Irish monolinguals were left and bilingualism had become a way-station on the road to English alone.

The Gaelic League. The founding of the Gaelic League in 1893 marked the start of the strongest wave of revivalist sentiment, which has endured in all its vicissitudes. Irish revivalism, an example of linguistic nationalism, arrived only when the language was already in grave peril. Its leaders were such Dublin intellectuals as Douglas Hyde and Eoin MacNeill, whose Irish was acquired rather than native. The movement largely failed to engage the support of the dwindling group of native speakers in the rural and impoverished *Gaeltacht*: an Irish-speaking area in the west that was idealized, romanticized, and kept at a safe remove. In addition, Irish was often linked with the strength of Catholicism, an association which permitted English to be depicted as the secular medium of a foreign culture, despite the fact that the Catholic Church promoted English even in Irish-speaking parishes.

Irish since independence. The Gaelic League had considerable success in fighting for Irish in schools and university but did not alter the language habits of the general population. When the Irish Free State was set up in 1921, Irish became a government responsibility. It was declared the national language, but accompanying the rhetoric was a serious and sometimes pessimistic concern for its fate. The government was often (and continues to be) accused of paying only lip service to revival. It entrusted the task to the schools and it is therefore in education that the most important action has taken place over the last 70 years, such as compulsory Irish classes and making the gaining of an overall secondary school leaving certificate dependent on passing Irish (a rule no longer in effect). However, these efforts have not reversed the long decline: Ireland is now an overwhelmingly English-speaking country in which only 1-2% use Irish regularly and, even in the Gaeltacht, many parents bring up their children in English. Given the strong social currents of English in everyday life, it is hard to see what more the schools could have done than apply a thin wash of Irish across the land.

Conclusion. Despite its decline, Irish has a special claim on the Irish. For some, it has symbolic value, like a flag; for others, it is the key to an ancient heritage. It is unlikely, however, that the language will ever again be a vernacular. Such recent trends as a growing demand in urban areas for Irish-medium education, though welcome to those concerned for Gaelic, are unlikely to make much difference. As in the Highlands and Islands of Scotland, the process of language shift has always been a symptom and a consequence of a larger contest between unequal forces. Actions on behalf of language are unlikely to succeed unless they are allied with a comprehensive unpicking and re-weaving of the forces affecting all social life in these countries, but the desire for such a development is not widespread. See BORROWING, CELTIC LANGUAGES, ERSE, GAELIC, HIBERNO-ENGLISH, SCOTTISH GAELIC, SHELTA. [EUROPE, LANGUAGES, NAME].

J.E., T.MCA.

IRISH BROADCASTING. Public service radio broadcasting began in the Republic of Ireland in 1926 in Dublin, with a second station in Cork in 1927 and a high-powered transmitter in 1933 in Athlone broadcasting nationwide. In 1938, these combined to become *Radio Eireann*. The television service was inaugurated in 1961 as *Telefis Eireann*. Following the Broadcasting Amendment Act of 1966, the corporate name *Radio Telefis Eireann (RTE)* was adopted. The norm for broadcasting in English has been educated Dublin speech, a variety close to RP but rhotic and with more varied intonation patterns. Developments include colour TV in 1971-3, an Irish-language radio service based in Galway in 1972, a second TV channel *RTE2* (subsequently *Network 2*) in 1988, and a second radio service, *Radio 2*, mainly for younger listeners, in 1979. RTE income is from licence fee and advertising. About 50% of all programmes are home-produced, often competing with programmes from the BBC and ITV in Britain. Home-produced programmes (current affairs, sport, light entertainment) command the highest figures. Following a period in the 1970s and 1980s when pirate stations were popular, an Independent Radio and Television Commission (IRTC) authorized the setting up of 24 independent radio stations. The Dublin-based Capital Radio and Century Radio went on the air in 1989, while RTE with Radio Luxembourg established a commercial long-wave radio channel, Radio Tara, broadcasting to Ireland and Britain. Mainstream British broadcasting can be picked up in Ireland. [EUROPE, MEDIA].   L.T.

IRISH BULL [18c: origin uncertain; perhaps from Old French *boul* deceit]. A statement containing or seeming to contain a contradictory proposition: *Childlessness is hereditary in their family*. The word *Irish* was not always prefaced to such apparent inconsistencies and paradoxes, but the practice was well established when Maria Edgeworth wrote her *Essay on Irish bulls* (1802). See BULL, IRISH JOKE. [EUROPE, STYLE].   L.T.

IRISH ENGLISH, short form *IrE*. The English language as used in Ireland. Scholars currently employ three terms to describe this variety: *Anglo-Irish, Hiberno-English,* and *Irish English. Anglo-Irish* is the oldest and has long been associated with the English language in Ireland, English people in Ireland, and British politics in Ireland, as a result of which it can be ambiguous and Irish people often dislike its use as a generic term. *Hiberno-English* avoids this difficulty and identifies English in Ireland with the people of Ireland, not with outsiders. The term *Irish English*, although to some ears whimsical and paradoxical, is less academic and opaque, is not likely to be misinterpreted, and fits into the set *American English, British English, Indian English*, etc. It is used here as the generic term for all kinds of English in Ireland.

The Germanic settlements. It is not certain when, how, or in what forms English was first heard and used in Ireland. Trading links have existed between Ireland and Britain for at least two millennia, but nothing is known about the contact languages used after the Old English dialects were established in Britain. Following the Viking invasions in the 9c, Danish and Norse settlements were established in the east and south of the island. In this way, Germanic dialects began to affect Irish Gaelic, especially in commerce, dress, and seafaring. In 1155, the English Pope, Adrian IV, granted Henry II of England permission to invade Ireland and bring about religious reforms. The subsequent invasion, launched from Wales, was a military success. The Treaty of Windsor suggests that, by 1175, half of Ireland was under Anglo-Norman control, and by 1250, almost three-quarters of the island had been divided into shires. The leaders of the invasion spoke French but the soldiers were Flemish, Welsh, and from south-west England. English was their lingua franca and became established in all large settlements, especially in an area around Dublin known as *the (English) Pale* and in the Baronies of Forth and Bargy in Wexford.

Gaelicization. Like the Vikings, the Anglo-Normans were absorbed into the Celtic way of life, slowly relinquishing their language and customs. Laws, such as the Statutes of Kilkenny (1366), tried to ensure that they would continue to speak English and use English-style surnames, but such laws were increasingly ignored, so that by 1500 Irish Gaelic had virtually replaced English even in the towns. The Reformation in England in the 16c reinforced the solidarity between the settlers (who remained Catholic) and their co-religionists, the Irish, further weakening the role of English in the island. The English of the Anglo-Norman settlers and their descendants came to be called *Yola* (a variant of *old*: see entry) and the settlers themselves became known as the *Old English* (see entry).

Language shift. The main forms of present-day IrE can be traced to the second wave of settlers. From the middle of the 16c, large numbers of English and Scottish *planters* settled in Ireland, creating communities (*plantations*) that preserved a separate identity from the native population, from whom they were marked out by language, religion, and culture. By the beginning of the 17c, Irish was still the most widely used language, but within 250 years a massive shift had occurred. The 1900 census records 21,000 monoglot speakers of Irish in the country (5% of the population). Today, the figure is zero, but some 100,000 people speak Irish as one of their mother tongues, the younger bilinguals showing English influence in their Irish, for example saying *Bhí siad uilig ólta* They were all drunk (*ól* drink; *ólta* drunk, used of liquids, not people) where older speakers would use the idiom *Bhí siad uilig ar meisce* (*ar meisce* intoxicated).

Kinds of Irish English. There are no dialect differences corresponding exactly with any county or other regional boundary in Ireland, but because of the different types of plantation, it is possible to distinguish three varieties of IrE: (1) *Anglo-Irish*, a middle- and working-class variety spoken over most of Ireland and deriving from the English of the 17c planters from England, modified by contacts with Irish, Ulster Scots, and Hiberno-English. (2) *Ulster Scots*, a variety of Lowland Scots spoken mainly in Antrim, Donegal, and Down, influencing all forms of northern speech. (3) *Hiberno-English*, the mainly working-class variety used by communities whose ancestral language was Gaelic. Because of their long association, the three varieties tend to influence and shade into each other in various complex ways.

Models of pronunciation. In pronunciation, three main models are followed: (1) *Received Pronunciation*. Two small groups of people have RP accents: men educated in England, especially in the public (private) schools, and some individuals in the media. (2) *Received Irish Pronunciation*. A rhotic accent and the prestige pronunciation of Radio Telefís Eireann (Irish Radio and Television). It is closer to RP than other varieties of Irish speech and is favoured by middle-class speakers of Anglo-Irish. (3) *Received Ulster Pronunciation*. In Northern Ireland, many broadcasters speak standard English with a regional accent and are more influential as models than speakers of RP.

Bilingual signs. Since the Irish Republic is officially bilingual, English appears widely with Irish on public buildings and signs, and on official forms and documents, as in the following pairs on notice-boards at Dublin Airport: *Shops/Siopaí, Bar/Beár, Snacks/Sólaistí, Post Office/Oifig an Phoist, Telephones/Telefóin, Information/Fiasrúcháin*. Both languages appear on most road signs, the English below and capitalized, the Irish above in smaller traditional letters, as with: *Cill Fhionnúrach* over *Kilfenora*, *An Carn* over *Carran*, *Baile Uí Bheacháin* over *Ballyvaghan*, and *Lios Dúin Bhearna* over *Lisdoonvarna*. In many instances, the English names are Anglicizations of traditional Irish names, and the two correspond closely; in others they are quite different, as with *Baile átha Cliath* (pronounced 'bla-clee') over *Dublin*.

See ANGLO-IRISH, BELFAST, DUBLIN, HIBERNO-ENGLISH, IRELAND, IRISH, L-SOUNDS, NEWFOUNDLAND ENGLISH, SCOUSE, ULSTER ENGLISH, ULSTER SCOTS. [EUROPE, VARIETY]. L.T.

Barry, M. V. 1981. *Aspects of English Dialects in Ireland*. Belfast: Institute of Irish Studies.
Bliss, A. J. 1979. *Spoken English in Ireland 1600-1740*. Dublin: Dolmen.
Gregg, R. J. 1985. *The Scotch-Irish Dialect Boundaries in the Province of Ulster*. Ottawa: Canadian Federation for the Humanities.
Harris, J. 1985. *Phonological Variation and Change: Studies in Hiberno-English*. Cambridge: University Press.
Hogan, J. J. 1927. *The English Language in Ireland*. Dublin: Educational Company of Ireland.
Jeffares, A. N. 1986. *Parameters of Irish Literature in English*. Gerrards Cross: Colin Smythe.
Joyce, P. W. 1910. *English as we speak it in Ireland*. Reprinted 1979, 1988. Dublin: Wolfhound Press.
Milroy, J. 1981. *Regional Accents of English: Belfast*. Belfast: Blackstaff Press.
O Muirithe, D. 1977. *The English Language in Ireland*. Cork & Dublin: Mercier Press.
Todd, L. 1989. *The Language of Irish Literature*. London: Macmillan.
—— 1990. *Words Apart: A Dictionary of Northern Ireland English*. Gerrards Cross: Colin Smythe.
Wagner, H., & O Boyle, C. 1969. *Linguistic Atlas and Survey of Irish Dialects*. Dublin: Institute for Advanced Studies.

IRISH GAELIC. See CELTIC LANGUAGES, GAELIC, IRISH.

IRISHISM [18c: from *Irish* and *-ism* as in *Scotticism*]. Also, though rare, **Iricism, Hibernianism, Hibernicism, Irishry**. An Irish usage, custom, or peculiarity, and especially a form of language regarded as quintessentially Irish, including shibboleths and stereotypes such as the exclamations *begorrah* and *bejabers*, and such expressions as *a broth of a boy* and *the top of the morning to you*, well known in Britain, North America, and Australia, but used by Irish people only when consciously speaking 'stage Irish' for amusement or as a parody. Phonological, syntactic, and lexical Irishisms occur in: *Divil the bit of a shtick could I find for to bate the baisht with* I couldn't find a stick to beat the animal with; *Will you be after havin a cup of tea?—I will, to be sure; Wasn't it herself broke the delph into smithereens?* Rhetorical Irishisms are often plays on words (*He's teetotally obsnorious*), malapropisms (*That man's a confederate liar, so he is*), or Irish bulls (*Nuns run in that family*). See IRISH BULL, IRISH ENGLISH, IRISH JOKE, -ISM, JOYCE. [EUROPE, STYLE, VARIETY, WORD].   L.T., T.MCA.

IRISH JOKE. A type of ethnic joke supposedly characterizing the habits and mentality of the Irish. Its target is often 'Irish logic', by which is meant a capacity to jump huge gaps or engage in creative paradox that is simultaneously foolish and wise: 'How d'you get to Killaloe?' enquires a traveller in a well-known two-liner. 'Ah now,' says Pat, 'I wouldn't be startin' from here.' See ETHNIC JOKE, IRISH BULL, IRISHISM. [EUROPE, STYLE].   W.N.

IRISH LITERATURE. See ANGLO-IRISH LITERATURE.

IRISHMAN/WOMAN. See -MAN/WOMAN.

IRISH PLACE-NAMES. The place-names of Ireland reflect linguistic and cultural contacts over 2,000 years. They include Gaelic (the majority), Scandinavian, Norman, and Anglo-Scottish influences during the Plantations, and are often hybrid or Anglicized in form.

Gaelic. (1) Settlements such as *baile* a town, *graig* a village: *Ballynadolly* in Antrim (from *Baile na Dtulach* town of the little hills), *Graigeen* in Limerick (*graig* and *ín*, a diminutive: little village). (2) Toponyms such as *clár, magh, réidh* a plain, which occur either on their own as in (*County*) *Clare* and *Moy* in County Tyrone, or in combinations such as *Macosquin* in Derry (*Magh Cosgrain* Cosgrain's plain), *Readoty* in Waterford (*Réidh Dóighte* burnt plain). *Coill* (a wood) occurs in *Kerrykyle* in Limerick (*Ceithre Choill* four woods). *Gleann* (a glen) appears in *Glennamaddy* in Galway (from *Gleann na Madaidhe* glen of the dogs). *Inis* and *oileán* (an island) occur in *Inishfree* in Donegal (*Inis Fraoch* heather island), *Illaunfadda* in Galway (*Oileán Fada* long island). *Tobar* (a well) appears in *Toberbilly* in Antrim (*Tobar Bile* well of the old tree). (3) Battles marked by such names as *Ballynarooga* in Limerick (*Baile na Ruaige* town of the rout), *Drumar* or *Drom Áir* in Monaghan (*drum* a ridge, *ár* slaughter), *Meenagorp* in Tyrone (*Mín na gCorp* mountaintop of the corpses: possibly as the outcome of an epidemic rather than a battle).

Names associated with Christianity include: *Knock* in Mayo (from *cnoc* a hill); *Donaghmore* (*Domhnach mór* great church); *Monasteranenagh* in Limerick (*Mainistear an Aonaigh* Monastery of the Fair); and one of Belfast's best-known streets, *Shankill* (*Seanchill* old church). Other names are pre-Christian, such as *Sheetrim* in Armagh (*Sidh Dhruim* fairy ridge), *Lough Gillagancan* in Donegal (*Loch Giolla gan Ceann* lake of the man without a head), *Boheraphuca* in Offaly (*Bóthar an Phúca* road of the Pooka, a supernatural being, cognate with Shakespeare's Puck).

Norse and Norman French. Viking names, found mainly around the coast, include those in *ford* a ford, as in *Longford, Waterford, Wexford, vig* a bay, as in *Wicklow, ey* an island, as in *Dalkey* (thorn island). *Leixlip* on the River Liffey was *Hlaxa Hlaup* (salmon leap). Relics of the Anglo-Norman invasion are few but include the Gaelicized *buirgéis* (a borough) in such names as *Borris* in Carlow and *Borrisnafarney* in Tipperary (*Buirgéis Fearna* borough of the alder trees). *Pomeroy* from a Norman family name (said to be from 'Pommes des Rois', king's apples). Influences from French can be seen in *Charleville* in Cork (named after King Charles II), *Jerpoint Abbey* in Kilkenny (from *Jeripont* Jeremiah's bridge), and *Powerscourt* in Wicklow.

The Plantations. Some names, introduced under the Tudors and the Stuarts, are English (*Greencastle* in Antrim, *Jamestown* in Leitrim, *Newcastle* in Tipperary), while others are Scottish (*Portmarnock* in Dublin, *Portstewart* in Derry, *Stewartstown* in Tyrone). Sometimes such place-names are associated with people (*Mountjoy* in Tyrone, *Nutt's Corner* in Antrim); occasionally, as in *Londonderry*, they are blends, here *London* with *doire* (oak-grove). Loyalists favour the London connection, while nationalists insist on Derry alone. Often, as with *Blackrock* in Dublin, names have been direct translations from Irish, here *Carraig Dhubh* (rock black). A number of hybrid Gaelic and English forms occur, including: *Ardmore Point* in Wicklow; *Glenshane Pass* in Derry; *Maguiresbridge* in Fermanagh; *the Mountains of Mourne* in Down. See PLACE-NAME. [EUROPE, NAME].   L.T.

IRISH PRESS. There are seven daily and two Sunday newspapers in the Republic, three dailies and two Sundays in Northern Ireland, and more than a hundred provincial newspapers. British newspapers are also widely read. The oldest newspaper in Ireland, *The Belfast Newsletter*, was started in 1757, has a daily circulation of over 44,000, and serves the Unionist community. *The Irish News*, also in Belfast, was started in 1855, has a daily circulation of over 42,000, and appeals mainly to Nationalists. The newspapers in Eire are read by all sections of the community. The main dailies are *The Cork Examiner* (established 1841, circulation over 58,000), *The Irish Times* (1859: 89,000), and *The Irish Press* (1931: 83,000). Magazines fall into the categories business (*Irish Business, Business Ulster*), general interest (*Ireland's Own, Ulster Tatler*), religion (*Caritas, The Church of Ireland Gazette, The Irish Catholic*), women (*Image, Women's Way*), and tourism (*Ireland of the Welcomes*). See NEWSPAPER, PRESS. [EUROPE, MEDIA].   L.T.

IRISH PUBLISHING. Although publishing in Ireland dates from the 16c in English and Irish, there has never been a strong tradition. The home market is small and foreign interest is limited, but since the 1950s there has been considerable expansion, with some 70 companies, including two in Northern Ireland, many operating as cottage industries. The main publishers are Dolmen Press (Port Laoise), Gill & Macmillan (Dublin), Mercier Press (Cork), Wolfhound Press (Dublin), Appletree Press (Belfast), and Blackstaff Press (Belfast). Publications include history, poetry, songs, fiction, and children's books, in both Irish and English. The need to exploit new technology to secure speedier production and larger readerships, especially outside Ireland, is appreciated, and was addressed in the 1988 report *Developing Publishing in Ireland* by the English consultancy firm Charles Pick. Its main recommendations were greater internationalization, changes in packaging, and possible amalgamations. Following this report, state agencies have been changing the system of funding to publishers and encouraging the sale of rights abroad. See PUBLISHING. [EUROPE, MEDIA].   L.T.

IRISHRY [14c]. Archaic: (1) A term for the Celtic people of Ireland, as contrasted with the *Englishry*, the English settlers: 'They that refuse to be under lawes are termed the Irishry, and commonly the Wilde Irish' (Philemon Holland, *Camden's Britain*, 1610). (2) A term for Irish character or nationality, or an Irishism. Compare ENGLISHRY, WELSHRY, WILD IRISH. [EUROPE, NAME].   T.MCA.

IRONY [16c: from Latin *ironia*, Greek *eirōneia* pretence, from *eirōn* a dissembler]. Also sometimes **antiphrasis** [16c: through Latin from Greek *antiphrasis* anti-speech. Stress: 'an-TI-phra-sis']. (1) In rhetoric, words with an implication opposite to their usual meaning. Ironic comment may be humorous or mildly sarcastic, as for example when, at a difficult moment, an act of kindness makes things worse, and someone says, 'Well, that's a *lot* better, isn't it?' Expressions *heavy*

with irony are often used to drive a point home: 'I'm really looking forward to seeing him, *I don't think*'; 'You're pleased to see me? *Pull the other leg/one* (*it's got bells on*).' In such usages, irony slides into *sarcasm*. (2) In general usage, incongruity between what is expected and what happens, and an outcome that displays such incongruity. The sentence adverb *ironically* is often used to draw attention to it: '*Ironically*, his kindness only made things worse.' In many instances, *ironically* serves virtually as a synonym of *paradoxically*. (3) Wry awareness of life's incongruity and irrationality. Irony as social comment is widely taken to work best without a fanfare.

Three kinds of irony have been recognized since antiquity: (1) *Socratic irony*, a mask of innocence and ignorance adopted to win an argument. Among the stock characters in early Greek comedy were two deceivers, the *eirōn*, a weak but wily underdog, who usually tricked the *alazōn*, a bombastic and stupid vagabond. In Plato's dialogues, Socrates often plays the *eirōn*, pretending ignorance and asking seemingly foolish questions so as to move a debate in the direction he wants. (2) *Dramatic or tragic irony*, a double vision of what is happening in a play or a real-life situation. In Greek tragedy, the characters were blind to fateful circumstances of which the audience was all too well aware, producing a privileged and often poignant appreciation of the plot. (3) *Linguistic irony*, a duality of meaning, now the classic form of irony. Building on the idea of dramatic irony, the Romans concluded that language often carries a double message, a second often mocking or sardonic meaning running contrary to the first. Such duality was labelled 'the Drie Mock' by the Elizabethan rhetorician George Puttenham (*The Arte of Poesie*, 1589).

In modern times, two further conceptions have been added: (1) *Structural irony*, a quality that is built into texts, in which the observations of a naïve narrator point up the deeper implications of a situation. In the stories of the English humorist P. G. Wodehouse (1917 onward), Bertie Wooster reports verbatim the smooth, deflating comments of his butler Jeeves without any indication that he has understood or even noticed what Jeeves 'really' says. (2) *Romantic irony*, in which writers conspire with readers to share the double vision of what is happening in the plot of a novel, film, etc. By the 17c and 18c, a refined ironic style was established in European writing, as when Henry Fielding interrupted the action in his novels to address his readers directly and comment on events. When engaging in this game, writers combine creative egotism with a suave and knowing self-mockery. By the 19c, critics had become adept at detecting and dissecting irony in literature and in life. The Danish philosopher Kierkegaard raised irony to the cosmic level when he proposed in 1841 that it was a way of viewing all existence, and some writers and critics have since implied that God is the greatest ironist of all. The phrase *irony of fate* suggests that, like drama, life treats people as if wryly mocking them, delivering at a strategic moment the opposite to what is deserved or at first seemed likely. See BIERCE, CYNIC, FIGURATIVE LANGUAGE/USAGE, SARCASM. [STYLE].

T.MCA.

IRREGULAR [14c]. A term for linguistic forms that are exceptional in that they cannot be predicted by general rules: *children* as the plural of *child*, because it is not formed, as most noun plurals are, by adding -*s*. See REGULAR, RULE. [GRAMMAR].

S.G.

IRREGULAR VERB. A verb that does not follow the general rules for verb forms. Verbs in English are irregular if they do not have a normal -*ed* form like *talked, walked*. The -*ed* form has two functions: past and past participle. In some irregular verbs, these functions are served by different forms. Contrast *He talked for a long time* and *He has talked for a long time* with *He spoke for a long time* and *He has spoken for a long time*. There are other kinds of irregularity: *shut* serves as base form and -*ed* form. Since for all verbs (regular and irregular) the -*s* and -*ing* forms are constructed from the base by regular rules, it is only necessary to cite the base, past, and -*ed* forms to characterize irregular verbs. These three are termed the *principal parts* of the verb and are always given in the order: base, past, -*ed* participle. Many irregular verbs exhibit changes in the middle vowel for one or both of the last two principal parts (*sing, sang, sung*) and have an -*en* inflection for the -*ed* participle (*speak, spoke, spoken*).

Forms of BE. The verb *be* is highly irregular, with eight forms: base *be*; present *am* (first-person singular), *is* (the -*s* form for third-person singular), *are* (second-person singular and all plurals); past *was* (first- and third-person singular) and *were* (second-person singular and all plurals); -*ing* form *being*; -*ed* participle *been*. The -*s* forms of *have, do, say* are irregular (*has, does, says*), though the irregularity in pronunciation is obscured by the spelling of *does, says*.

Modal verbs. The modal auxiliaries have a defective paradigm since they only have the base forms and irregularly constructed past forms (*can, could; may, might*). *Must* is further exceptional in having only the base form.

Irregular verbs in English. The accompanying table gives the principal parts for most irregular verbs, including common alternatives and differences between BrE and AmE. Generally, the alternatives are possible in both varieties, but the form labelled BrE or AmE is found especially in that variety.

Base	Past	-ed participle
awake	awoke, awaked	awoken, awaked
beat	beat	beaten, beat
become	became	become
bend	bent	bent
bet	bet, betted (*BrE*)	bet, betted (*BrE*)
bind	bound	bound
bite	bit	bitten, bit
bleed	bled	bled
blow	blew	blown
break	broke	broken
bring	brought	brought
build	built	built
burn	burnt (*BrE*), burned	burnt (*BrE*), burned
buy	bought	bought
catch	caught	caught
come	came	come
cost	cost	cost
creep	crept	crept
cut	cut	cut
deal	dealt	dealt
dig	dug	dug
do	did	done
draw	drew	drawn
dream	dreamt (*BrE*), dreamed	dreamt (*BrE*), dreamed
drink	drank	drunk
drive	drove	driven
eat	ate	eaten
feed	fed	fed
feel	felt	felt
fight	fought	fought
find	found	found
fit	fitted, fit (*AmE*)	fitted, fit (*AmE*)
flee	fled	fled
fly	flew	flown
forget	forgot	forgotten, forgot (*AmE*)
forgive	forgave	forgiven
freeze	froze	frozen
get	got	got, gotten (*AmE*)
give	gave	given
go	gone	went
grow	grew	grown
hang	hung	hung, hanged
have	had	had
hear	heard	heard
hide	hid	hidden, hid
hit	hit	hit
hold	held	held
hurt	hurt	hurt
keep	kept	kept
know	knew	known
lead	led	led
learn	learnt (*BrE*), learned	learnt (*BrE*), learned
leave	left	left
lend	lent	lent

Base	Past	-ed participle
let	let	let
lie	lay	lain
light	lit, lighted	lit, lighted
lose	lost	lost
make	made	made
mean	meant	meant
met	met	met
mistake	mistook	mistaken
put	put	put
read	read	read
rid	rid, ridded	rid, ridded
ride	rode	ridden
ring	rang, rung (*AmE*)	rung
say	said	said
see	saw	seen
sell	sold	sold
send	send	sent
set	set	set
shoot	shot	shot
show	showed	shown
shut	shut	shut
sing	sang, sung (*AmE*)	sung
sink	sank, sunk (*AmE*)	sunk
sit	sat	sat
sleep	slept	slept
smell	smelt (*BrE*), smelled	smelt (*BrE*), smelled
speak	spoke	spoken
spend	spent	spent
stand	stood	stood
steal	stole	stolen
stick	stuck	stuck
strike	struck	struck
swear	swore	sworn
swim	swam, swum (*AmE*)	swum
take	took	taken
teach	taught	taught
tear	tore	torn
tell	told	told
think	thought	thought
throw	threw	thrown
understand	understood	understood
upset	upset	upset
wake	woke, waked	woken, waken
wear	wore	worn
win	won	won
write	wrote	written

All new verbs in English are regular, as in *glitz, glitzed, glitzed*. Some irregular verbs also have regular forms: *sew, sewed, sewn* but also the regular *sew, sewed, sewed*. There are also some differences in irregular verbs between BrE and AmE: both *dived* and *dove* are found in AmE as pasts of *dive*, but only *dived* occurs in BrE. *Gotten* is used in AmE as an *-ed* participle in certain senses of the verb: *We've gotten more than we can use*, but not *We've got to do a lot better*. See CURME, STRONG VERB, T, VERB, WEAK VERB. [GRAMMAR].   S.G.

ISLAND ENGLISH. See HIGHLAND ENGLISH.

ISLE OF MAN [Before 10c: from Old Irish *Manu* and associated with the Irish sea god *Manannan*. Adjective *Manx*]. An island in the Irish Sea. Capital: Douglas. Population: 64,679 (1981). The island was ruled by the Welsh during the 6–9c, then by the Norse until Magnus King of Norway ceded it and the Hebrides to Alexander II of Scotland in 1266. Granted to the Earls of Derby in 1406, it passed to the Dukes of Atholl in 1736, and was purchased from them by the British government partly in 1765, wholly in 1832. The island has its own parliament, the *Court of Tynwald*, comprising the governor, the Legislative Council, and the elected *House of Keys*. Near the centre of the island is a circular artificial mound called *Tynwald Hill* where the acts of the Manx Parliament are proclaimed. Acts of the British Parliament do not generally apply to the Isle of Man, which has a high degree of autonomy.

Manx Gaelic (also *Manx*). This Celtic language is closely related to Irish and Scottish Gaelic. It was probably introduced in the 4c by Irish settlers and may have replaced an earlier language similar in structure to Welsh. In the 10–13c, Manx was influenced by Norse, especially in its lexicon, but continued to be the main language of the island until the end of the 18c, when English began to assume a dominant role. Ned Maddrell, the last surviving speaker of Manx, died in 1974. In his later years, he was curator of the preserved Manx village of Cregneish, and with some others was encouraged by members of the *Manx Society* to remember the language, much of which was then recorded. The Society has sought to sustain Manx as the second language of the island. The form now in use tends to be that of its classical literary period, the 18c, Anglicisms being replaced by coinages from Manx roots. It tends to be influenced in the spoken form by Irish Gaelic, since islanders can receive the Irish-language programmes of Radio Telefís Eireann. Texts in Manx, which has its own orthography, continue to be written and to be published by Yn Chesaght Ghailckagh, Douglas.

Manx English. Welsh and Scandinavian influence gave way in the later Middle Ages to a distinctive Manx dialect of English that has close links, especially in the south of the island, with varieties in Lancashire and shows substratum influence from Manx, modified over the centuries by the influence of Scottish and Irish Gaelic and of Welsh. The distinctive speech of the rural north is probably an older form. Although the Norse ruled the island until the 13c, their linguistic influence is limited to place-names such as *Jurby* and *Kirk Michael* and a few words such as *birk* (birch, as in Scots) and *slake* (to put out one's tongue). Manx English is non-rhotic, has /æ/ in both *glass* and *gas*, distinguishes between *wh* and *w* as in *which witch*, tends to replace /ŋ/ by /n/ in *-ing* words, and often has a glottal plosive for /t/ (especially before syllabic *n* as in *beaten, touting*). Syntactic influence from Gaelic is found in the use of such preposition and pronoun constructions as *They returned with money at them* and *put a sight on her* (visit her). The Gaelic influence is stronger in vocabulary and includes words associated with farming (*collagh* a stallion), food (*braghtan* bread and butter), the home (*chiollagh* hearth), and folk traditions (*crosh caoirn* a cross made from twigs or rushes and placed over a door). Until about 20 years ago, there was no general realization that some local words were from Manx roots. A recent surge in nationalism and in the use of revived Manx has made people more aware of the nature of the expressions they use. See CELTIC LANGUAGES, GAELIC, MANX. Compare CHANNEL ISLANDS, CORNISH, HIBERNO-ENGLISH, HIGHLAND ENGLISH. [EUROPE, NAME, VARIETY]. L.T., S.E.

-ISM [From French *-isme*, Latin *-ismus*, Greek *-ismós*]. A noun-forming suffix, three of whose uses relate to language: (1) Forming words for concepts, activities, and conditions: *agrammatism, behavio(u)rism, biculturalism, bilingualism, criticism, descriptivism, feminism, journalism, literary criticism, multiculturalism, multilingualism, nativism, obscurantism, plagiarism, prescriptivism, racism, romanticism, sexism, structuralism, symbolism.* (2) Forming linguistic and stylistic terms: *anachorism, anachronism, aphorism, archaism, atticism, barbarism, Burgessism, cacophemism, classicism, colloquialism, dysphemism, euphemism, euphuism, genteelism, initialism, localism, malapropism, mannerism, neologism, nice-nellyism, provincialism, purism, regionalism, Saxonism, solecism, spoonerism, syllogism, truism, verbalism, vernacularism, vulgarism, witticism.* (3) Forming words that identify usages as belonging to particular varieties of English: *Americanism, Anglicism, Australianism, Briticism/Britishism, Canadianism, Caribbeanism, Englishism, foreignism, Gaelicism, Gallicism, Indianism, Irishism, Latinism, New Zealandism, Scotticism, Yiddishism.* All the terms listed above have their own entries.

The three categories make up a continuum. Although *élitism* is usually an uncountable noun meaning 'a sense of (and desire to maintain) special status', it might be used countably: *an élitism* an élitist usage. Currently, *regionalism* means both 'a regional usage' and 'the inclination to think in terms of a region rather than a larger or smaller area'. A regionalism could be a usage

within a variety of Language X which might also be a borrowing from Language Y: Quebec English *professor* (a secondary-school teacher) is both a regionalism of CanE and a Gallicism. The suffix is widely used with considerable freedom and flexibility to label such regional or local usage, such as a *Newfoundlandism* or a *New-Yorkism*, and for nonce purposes, as in: (1) Robin White's *Men and Angels* (1961), where Sarojini Chellappa says: 'Cannot there be some verb to mean what we are doing? If one makes something, one is making. Why, if one is naked, cannot one be naking?'—'I hereby authorize a Sarojinism,' I said, 'a new word for the English language: the verb intransitive, to nake. Nake, naked, nade.' (2) Simon Hoggart's 'Bushism of the week', in the *Observer* magazine during 1989, referring to the usage of US President George Bush. When asked to comment on the fall of the Berlin Wall, Bush is reported to have said: 'I wouldn't want to say this kind of development makes things to be moving too quickly at all . . . so I'm not going to hypothecate that it may—anything goes too fast' (17 Dec. 1989). Compare -ESE, -SPEAK. See POLITICALLY CORRECT. [STYLE, WORD]. T.MCA.

ISOGLOSS [1890s: through German from Greek *isos* equal, *glôssa* tongue]. (1) In dialect geography, an area within which a feature is used predominantly or exclusively. Such a feature (phonological, morphological, syntactic, semantic, lexical, or other) usually contrasts with some similar feature in adjoining areas. Thus, some native speakers of English pronounce /r/ after a vowel, as in *barn, hard, car*, while others do not: in the US this postvocalic /r/ is normally present in the Chicago area but absent in the Boston area. Such distinct areas are isoglosses. (2) More commonly, the line on a dialect map which bounds the area of a certain usage. In England, an isogloss that stretches from the mouth of the Severn to Portsmouth separates the area of initial spoken /v/ from that of /f/, as in *vinger/finger*, *Vriday/Friday*, the *v*-forms being south-west of the line. Hans Kurath's *A Word Geography of the Eastern United States* (1949, fig. 2, p. 90) presents a series of isoglosses designating areas of the Atlantic states from New England to South Carolina and (fig. 5a, p. 93) a 'bundle' of isoglosses stretching across Pennsylvania, showing the strong boundary between North and Midland dialect features. No two isoglosses coincide exactly; there is always a transition area of partial overlapping. See DIALECTOLOGY. [LANGUAGE]. F.G.C.

ISOLATING. See ANALYTIC, LINGUISTIC TYPOLOGY.

ISRAEL. A country of West Asia. Capital: Jerusalem. Currency: shekel, plural *shkalim* (100 agorot). Economy: mixed. Population: 4.29m (1988), 5m (projection for 2000). Ethnicity: 83% Jewish, 16% Arab, 1% other. Religions: 83% Jewish, 13% Muslim, 2% Christian, 2% Druze. Languages: Hebrew, Arabic (both official), English widely used, and Yiddish, Russian, and other languages also used. Education: primary 95%, secondary 76%, tertiary 34%, literacy 88%. In 1922, after the collapse of the Ottoman (Turkish) Empire, the League of Nations gave Britain a mandate to govern Palestine and establish a Jewish national home there. In 1948, the British Mandate ended, and in the same year the state of Israel was created. English was used officially and for other purposes in Palestine during the Mandate, and its position, though no longer administrative, was to a great extent sustained in Israel by the settlement of many English-speaking Jews, especially from the US. See HEBREW, JEWISH ENGLISH, JEWISH LANGUAGES, YIDDISH. [ASIA, NAME, VARIETY]. T.MCA.

ita. See INITIAL TEACHING ALPHABET.

ITALESE. See CANADIAN ENGLISH.

ITALIAN [Called by its speakers *italiano*]. A Romance language, the official language of Italy and an official language of Switzerland, also spoken by Italian communities in Argentina, Australia, Britain, Canada, the US, Venezuela, and elsewhere. The term refers to both the standard and literary language in contrast to the many dialects and the entire complex of standard language and dialects, some of which are mutually unintelligible. In addition, some regional varieties, such as Friulian and Sardinian, are regarded as more or less distinct languages. Standard Italian is based on the medieval Tuscan dialect.

Italian in English. The influence of Italian on English is almost entirely lexical and has continued over many centuries. Since medieval times, Italian has had a strong influence on French, as a result of which many borrowings into English have had a distinctly Gallic aspect, as with *battalion* (16c: from *bataillon*, from *battaglione*), *caprice* (17c: from *caprice*, from *capriccio* the skip of a goat, a sudden sharp movement), *charlatan* (16c: from *charlatan*, from *ciarlatano*, from *ciarlare* to chatter), *frigate* (16c: from *frégate*, from *fregata*), *picturesque* (17c: from *pittoresque*, from *pittoresco*, with assimilation to *picture*), *tirade* (c.1800, from *tirade*, from *tirata* volley, from *tirare* to pull, fire a shot). Direct borrowings fall into four broad categories: (1) Terms from the centuries-old pan-European tradition of using Italian to discuss and describe music: for example, *adagio, alto,*

andante, arpeggio, bel canto, cello, coloratura, con brio, concerto, contralto, crescendo, diminuendo, divertimento, fortissimo, libretto, mezzo-soprano, pianoforte, pizzicato, scherzo, solo, sonata. (2) Comparable literary, architectural, artistic, and cultural terms, such as *canto, conversazione, cupola, extravaganza, fresco, intaglio, novella, palazzo, stanza, tarantella*. (3) Internationalized culinary terms, such as *lasagne, minestrone, mozzarella, pasta, pizza, ravioli, spaghetti, tagliatelle, vermicelli*. (4) A variety of social words, including *alfresco, bimbo, bordello, bravo, condottiere, confetti, fiasco, ghetto, gigolo, graffiti, imbroglio, mafia, piazza, regatta*. Some loans have adapted spellings, as with *macaroni* (Italian *maccheroni*, earlier *maccaroni*), *seraglio* (Italian *serraglio*, ultimately from Persian). In addition, some words have moved to a greater or less extent from their original area of application into wider use, as with *crescendo, extravaganza, piano, solo*. Italian singular/plural inflections usually apply among terms restricted to musical, cultural, and culinary registers (*concerto/concerti, scherzo/scherzi*), but English inflections apply in general use (*concerto/concertos, scherzo/scherzos*).

English in Italian. The influence of English on Italian is essentially lexical and relatively recent. Noticeable in the 1930s, it has accelerated greatly since the 1960s, encouraged not only by the growing international use and prestige of English, but also by the adoption after the Second World War of English (to replace French) as the first foreign language in schools. Recent borrowings, often described as contributions to *Itangliano* (highly Anglicized Italian), include: *baby, boom, boy, budget, cartoon, catering, ceiling, club, control system, deadline, dee-jay, designer, egghead, fifty-fifty, flash, girl, happiness, identikit, killer, lady, leader, life-saver, market, partner, shop, shopping, show, spray, staff, standard, stop, style, target, trekking, trend*. The assimilation and use of many borrowings resemble the processes by which English is absorbed into French, including: (1) The adaptation of words to fit the gender and inflectional systems: *un bluff* a bluff, *bluffare* to bluff; *uno snob* a snob, *snobbare* to snub; *handicappati* the handicapped. Compounds may be reversed to conform to Italian norms, *a pocket radio* becoming *un radio-pocket*. (2) The restriction and adaptation of senses: *un flirt* an affair; *look* used only as a noun; *un mister* a sports coach. (3) The clipping of compounds: *un full* a full hand (of cards); *un night* a night club.

See AFRICAN LANGUAGES, AMERICAN LANGUAGES, ARABIC, AUSTRALIAN LANGUAGES, BORROWING, C, CANADIAN ENGLISH (ITALESE), CANADIAN LANGUAGES, EARLY MODERN ENGLISH,

ENGLISH LITERATURE, EUROPEAN COMMUNITY, EUROPEAN LANGUAGES, FRENCH, GEMINATION, -GLISH AND -LISH, INDO-EUROPEAN LANGUAGES, ITALIC, ITANGLIANO, LATIN[1], LINGUISTIC TYPOLOGY, LITERARY CRITICISM, MACARONIC, MALTA, ROMANCE LANGUAGES, STANDARD. [EUROPE, LANGUAGE]. T.MCA.

ITALIC [16c: from Latin *Italicus* Italian]. Also **italic script, italic type, italics**. A slightly slanted letter form based on a style of handwriting favoured by Italian humanists; introduced into European printing in 1501 by the Venetian printer Aldo Manuzio (Aldus Manutius). Originally a separate typeface, italic has long been combined with roman as a marker for certain kinds of information in a text. In 16c English, it was often used for names and titles ('*Aristotle* wrote *De Caelo*'). Currently, it serves to highlight and emphasize titles, foreignisms, and words and phrases, and helps provide textual contrasts. Major quoted titles (books, plays, operas, films, musical compositions) are generally in italic (*The Wind in the Willows, King Lear, The Mikado, Gone with the Wind, William Tell*), but minor titles (poems in collections, articles in periodicals, or papers in scholarly works) are more commonly roman within quotation marks ('Ode to a Grecian Urn', 'Tense and aspect in Irish English'). The names in legal cases are also italicized: *Griffin* v. *Jones*. Italics are often used to mark exotic and unusual words in a text: 'Time to sit and think is a *sine qua non*', 'Japanese columnists remind women readers of *gaman*, the tradition that they must endure their problems.' Similarly, words are italicized so as to draw the reader's attention to them: '*castor*. A beaver hat', 'Ruskin called this attitude to nature *the pathetic fallacy*.' Italics highlight words which the writer wishes to emphasize, partially or fully: ' "Hel-*lo*!" said my aunt as I appeared' (H. G. Wells, *Tono Bungay*, 1908, Book 2, ch. 2); 'He won't; not that he's afraid; oh, no! he *won't*. Ha! ha!' (Charles Dickens, *The Pickwick Papers*, ch. 11). In addition, phrases and sentences used as examples of usage in dictionaries are usually italicized to contrast with definitions in roman, and similar uses occur in textbooks. Sometimes entire texts are set in italic, sometimes sections of texts (such as introductions, summaries, and lead-ins), sometimes italic and roman alternate contrastively: paragraphs in italic with commentary in roman, or vice versa; a letter read in a novel or a character's thoughts in italics while the mainstream is in roman. When manuscripts and typescripts are being prepared for publication and being proofread, single underlining is generally used to mark words and phrases to be italicized in print. See FOREIGNISM, PRINT, ROMAN. [TECHNOLOGY, WRITING].   W.W.B., T.MCA.

ITANGLIANO [1970s: a blend in Italian of *italiano* and *anglo*, on the analogy of *franglais*]. A non-technical term for Italian that contains many English expressions, apparently first used by Giacomo Elliot in the Italian-language publication *Parliamo Itangliano* (Milan, 1977). Elliot commented on 400 words and phrases (such as *know-how, management*, and *moonlighting*) used both in the export business and in business in Italy itself. The influx of English has been discussed in the media, including such serious journals of current affairs as *Europeo*, in articles with titles like 'Scusi, lei parla Itangliano?' (Excuse me, do you speak Itangliano?). The application of Italian phonology to English words can produce distinctive effects, such as the pronunciation of *puzzle* (noun) as 'pootzlay'. See ITALIAN. Compare ANGLIKAANS, CANADIAN ENGLISH (ITALESE), FRANGLAIS, -GLISH AND -LISH. [EUROPE, VARIETY].   T.MCA.

ITERATIVE [15c: from Latin *iterativus* happening again and again, from *iterum* again]. Also **frequentative**. Terms used to denote repetition and habituation in language. In Persian, iteration is expressed by the particle *hei: Khandidand* They laughed, *Hei khandidand* They kept on laughing. The English translation is also iterative, using the verb and particle *keep on*. There is only one iterative word element in English, the suffix *-le* in such verbs as *sparkle* to spark again and again, *suckle* to cause to suck again and again. In some *-le* words, the base may have little or no meaning but the iterative quality remains: *dazzle, drizzle, tingle, tinkle*. [GRAMMAR, WORD].   T.MCA.

-ITIS [Probably 20c: from the Greek feminine ending *-îtis*, as in *nósos arthrîtis* disease of the joints]. An informal suffix used humorously and pejoratively to suggest that certain behaviour is a disease: *exaggeritis* a habit of grossly exaggerating things, *smalltownitis* behaviour typical of a small town, such as minding your neighbour's business. It often forms nonce and stunt words associated with language: *telephonitis* using telephones too much. Compare -ESE. [STYLE].   T.MCA.

IYARIC. See RASTA TALK.

J

J, j [Called 'jay', rhyming with *say*, to match the pronunciation of *K*. In ScoE, often rhymes with *high*, to match the pronunciation of *I*]. The 10th letter of the Roman alphabet as used for English. Around the 13c, it developed as a graphic variant of *i*, including use as the last element of a Roman numeral, *iij* three, *viij* eight. Its status was uncertain for centuries. Lists published as recently as the early 19c did not always have *i* and *j* as separate letters of the alphabet. In print, the distinction was being made fairly consistently in lower case by 1630, though not in the first editions of Shakespeare. Introduced around 1600, upper-case *J* was not generally distinguished from *I* for another 200 years. See IOTA.

Sound value and distribution. (1) The standard value of *j* in English is the voiced palato-alveolar affricate /dʒ/, whose voiceless equivalent is spelt *ch*: contrast *jeep/cheap, Jews/choose. J, dg,* and soft *g* compete to represent this sound, as in *judge* and *gem. J* is not normally used at the end of a word or a stressed syllable. In this position, *ge* and *dge* are the rule, as in *rage* and *dodge*. The only exceptions are a small number of loanwords, such as *hajj/hadj* (pilgrimage) from Arabic and *raj* (rule, government) from Hindi. (2) There is a strong tendency for *d* followed by an *i*-glide (in words like *grandeur, Indian, soldier, endure*) to move to the value of *j*, prompting such non-standard spellings as 'Injun' for *Indian* and 'sojer' for *soldier*. (3) *J* occurs most often word-initially before *a, o, u,* a position in which *g* normally has its hard value: *jab/gab, job/gob, jut/gut*. (4) *J* does not normally feature in words of Old English origin, the digraph *dg* representing the sound medially and finally (*cudgel, bridge*), but some *j*-words (*ajar, jowl*) may be of Germanic origin.

Non-English influences. (1) French has given English many words with initial *j*: *jail, jaundice, jaw, jay, jealous, jeopardy, jet, jewel, join, jolly, journal, journey, joy, juice, jury, just.* (2) French *g* has been changed to *j* in *jelly, Jeffrey, jest* and possibly in *jib, jig*. The form *judge* (French *juge*) is an orthographic hybrid: initial French *j* and vernacular *dg* (marking a preceding short vowel). (3) Latin has contributed such words with initial *j* as *joke, jovial, jubilant, junior, juvenile*. (4) Other words with initial *j* tend to be exotic (*jackal, jaguar, jasmine, jerboa, ju-jitsu, jungle*), or recent, often AmE coinages (*jab, jam, jazz, jeep, jinx, jive,* and, with medial *j, banjo, hijack*). (5) Many proper names begin with *j*: *Jack, James, Jane, Janet, Jean, Jeffrey, Jim, Joan, John, Joseph, Julia*; as do the months *January, June, July*. (6) Medial *j* occurs commonly in Latinate roots after a prefix (*adjacent, conjunction, prejudice, reject, subjugate*) and such other Latinate words as *majesty, major, pejorative*. (7) Final *j* is rare, occurring only in such exotic forms as *raj* and *hajj/hadj*. (8) Since *j* differs in value in different languages, non-English values often occur in loans. The fricative of Modern French occurs in more recent loans (*bijou*) and in names (*Jean-Jacques*). German and some Slavonic languages pronounce *j* as a *y*-sound (*Jung, Janáček*). In Spanish *j* represents the voiceless velar fricative /x/ (*Jerez, Juan*), which may be represented by *h* in English (*marihuana*) or fall silent. (9) Currently, *g/j* alternate in *gibe/jibe* and in the cognates *jelly/gelatine* and *jib/gibbet*, as well as in the personal names *Jeffrey/Geoffrey, Jillian/Gillian*. See ALPHABET, G, I, IOTA, LETTER[1], SPELLING. [WRITING].   C.U.

JACOBEAN [18c: from Latin *Iacobaeus*, from *Iacobus* James]. A term for the reign of King James I of England (1603-25), excluding the earlier years of his reign as James VI King of Scots (1567-1625), when Elizabeth I was on the throne of England, and often taken to refer to the early 17c in the British Isles (*Jacobean*

THE CAPITAL LETTER						THE SMALL LETTER				
EARLY FORMS				CURRENT FORMS		EARLY FORMS			CURRENT FORMS	
Phoenician	Greek	Etruscan	Roman (Latin)	roman	italic	Roman cursive	Roman uncial	Carolingian minuscule	roman	italic
𐤆	⟨Ι	Ι	Ι	J	*J*	Ɉ	J	l	j	*j*

drama), and for a person of the period. During his reign the Pilgrim Fathers sailed to North America, the East India Company began to trade in India, the Authorized Version of the Bible was published, and Shakespeare wrote his last plays. The blend *Jacobethan*, coined in 1933 by the English poet John Betjeman, is sometimes used to cover shared aspects of both the Elizabethan and Jacobean periods: *Jacobethan prose*. Compare AUGUSTAN, ELIZABETHAN, RESTORATION. See BIBLE, BIBLICAL ENGLISH, EARLY MODERN ENGLISH, ENGLISH LITERATURE, INDIAN ENGLISH¹, IRELAND, PROSE, SHAKESPEARE. [EUROPE, HISTORY]. T.MCA.

JAMAICA. A Caribbean country and member of the Commonwealth. Capital: Kingston. Currency: the dollar (100 cents). Economy: agriculture, bauxite, tourism. Population: 2.26m (1988), 2.8m (projection for 2000). Ethnicity: 76% African, 15% mixed, 3% Caucasian, 3% East Indian, 2% Chinese. Languages: English, Creole. Education: primary 95%, secondary 58%, tertiary 6%, literacy 94%. The island was originally inhabited by Arawaks (*c*.7–10c), was visited by Columbus in 1494, and was colonized in 1509 by the Spanish, who in 1640 began to take African slaves there to work on the sugar plantations. The British occupied the island in 1655 and acquired it formally in 1670. Jamaica became independent in 1962. See ANTILLES, BAILEY (B.), BRATHWAITE, BRITISH BLACK ENGLISH, CARIBBEAN, CARIBBEAN ENGLISH, CARIBBEAN ENGLISH CREOLE, CARIBBEAN LANGUAGES, CARIBBEAN LITERATURE IN ENGLISH, CASSIDY, CAYMAN ISLANDS, DICTIONARY OF JAMAICAN ENGLISH, DUB, ENGLISH, JAMAICAN CREOLE, JAMAICAN ENGLISH, NATION LANGUAGE, RASTA TALK, REGGAE. [AMERICAS, NAME, VARIETY]. T.MCA.

JAMAICAN CREOLE, also **Jamaican English Creole, Jamaican Creole English, Jamaican.** The general and technical term for the English-based Creole vernacular of Jamaica. It has the most extensive and longest-standing literature and the widest media and artistic use of the varieties of Caribbean English Creole, and is the most fully studied. The wide appeal of Jamaican music, dub poetry, and Rastafarian religion has spread the vernacular throughout the Caribbean region as a widely heard (though frequently ill-understood) form of folk speech. Its influence is noteworthy in the UK, where it dominates other varieties of West Indian vernacular and has been a major factor in the evolution of British Black English. In the US, Jamaican immigrant communities have also retained linguistic characteristics related to continued use of the language.

Jamaican Creole is relatively well researched, particularly because of the presence in Jamaica

since 1948 of a campus of the U. of the West Indies. Detailed studies of phonology, grammar, lexicon, and social usage have been undertaken, including F. G. Cassidy, *Jamaica Talk: Three Hundred Years of the English language in Jamaica* (London: Macmillan, 1961) and G. Akers, *Phonological Variation in the Jamaican Continuum* (Ann Arbor: Karoma, 1981). Within Jamaica, consensus has evolved on its artistic value and on its distinctness from English, but despite this its use continues to be stigmatized and many literate Jamaicans do not value it. It is commonly viewed as an obstacle to education, an opinion actively countered by many who urge that the obstacle lies in failing to develop strategies for teaching English in the Creole environment. Because of the complex pattern of varieties between the English and Creole, Jamaica is often cited as a classic example of a *post-creole continuum* (see entry).

For those who have a command of both English and Creole, the one complements the other, English being more usual in formal public activity. Most of the population, however, use intermediate forms (mesolects). In radio and television, Jamaican is an established medium for advertisement, popular entertainment, and programmes with public participation. The news, however, is generally read in English. The use of Creole in newspapers is minimal, tending to be restricted to special columns. The *Dictionary of Jamaican English* (1967, 1980) has contributed to the stabilization of spelling in the press as well as to the readiness with which Creole is used by Jamaican writers. See BAJAN, CARIBBEAN CREOLE, CREOLE, JAMAICA, JAMAICAN ENGLISH, NATION LANGUAGE. [AMERICAS, VARIETY] L.D.C.

JAMAICAN ENGLISH, short form *JamE*. The English language as used in Jamaica. The term is used primarily to refer to the formal speech of educated Jamaicans, but has also been used to refer to Jamaican Creole in authoritative scholarly works, such as the *Dictionary of Jamaican English* (1967, 1980). It is the preferred variety of standard English within Jamaica and functions as the formal language of the society. See CARIBBEAN ENGLISH, JAMAICA, JAMAICAN CREOLE. [AMERICAS, VARIETY]. L.D.C.

JAMIESON, John [1759–1838]. Scottish lexicographer, born in Glasgow, and educated at the U. of Glasgow and U. of Edinburgh. A minister of the Secession Church and author of religious and antiquarian works, Jamieson also compiled *An Etymological Dictionary of the Scottish Language*, in two quarto volumes (1808), with a *Supplement* in two further volumes

(1825). See SCOTTISH DICTIONARIES, and index. [EUROPE, REFERENCE, VARIETY].   A.J.A.

JANGLISH. See JAPAN, JAPLISH.

JANUS WORD [20c: from Latin *Janus*, the god who faces both ways, and *word* as in *nonce word*]. A semi-technical term for a word with contradictory senses: *cleave* to split sharply (*cleave a skull*), to cling or stay close (*cleave together*). These usages arise from the convergence of distinct words: Old English *cleofan* and *cleofian* both developed into the single present-day form *cleave*. Sometimes, Janus words arise from diverging senses of the same word: *sanction* to approve (*sanction payment*), a punitive ban (*trade sanctions*). The Latin noun *sanctio* referred to a religious decree. See COPY, HOMONYM, POLYSEMY. [WORD].   T.MCA.

JAPAN [16c: Japan has been known to its people since the 7c as *Nippon* or *Nihon*, from Chinese-derived pronunciations of two characters meaning 'sun' and 'origin' (whence the epithet *Land of the Rising Sun*). Other Chinese readings of these characters gave rise to the form used by the 13c Venetian traveller Marco Polo, *Jipangu*, from which *Japan* appears to derive]. An island nation of East Asia. Capital: Tokyo. Currency: the yen. Economy: mixed. Population: 123.4m (1990), 130.8m (projection for 2000). Ethnicity: Japanese, with small Korean, Chinese, and Ainu minorities. Religion: Shintoist and Buddhist; less than 1% Christian. Language: Japanese (*Nippongo* or *Nihongo*). Education: primary and lower secondary 100%, upper secondary 95%, higher 35%, literacy 99%. Japan has borrowed culturally and linguistically from China (especially 6-9c), Western Europe (from the 16c), and the US (especially since 1945). The first contacts with European countries were with Portuguese merchants and Spanish Jesuit missionaries in the 16c; trade with The Netherlands and England was established in the early 17c. As a reaction against missionary activity, Japan discontinued contacts with all European nations except the Dutch until the 1850s, when US naval ships under Commander Matthew C. Perry forced a reopening to international commerce that led, after the Meiji Restoration of 1868, to rapid Westernization.

The Japanese language. Japanese shows some similarities to Korean and the Altaic languages. Although structurally and phonetically unrelated to Chinese, its writing uses borrowed Chinese characters, and a substantial portion of its vocabulary derives from their adapted Chinese readings (as with *Nihon*, above). Modern Japanese vocabulary contains native words (*wago*), words of classical Chinese origin (*kango*), and

mainly Western loanwords (*gairaigo*). Each type conforms to a pattern of open syllables, except syllabic /n/. Japanese is a syllable-timed language with a pitch accent. There are regional varieties, but standard Japanese (based on the Tokyo dialect) is understood throughout the country. Official research on the language is conducted by the *Kokuritsu Kokugo Kenkyujo* (The National Language Research Institute, established 1948), a department of the Ministry of Education, and language reforms are under the direction of the *Kokugo Shingikai* (National Language Council, established 1934). New compound words and recently adopted loans are listed and defined in the comprehensive annually updated lexicon *Gendai Yōgō no Kiso Chishiki* (Basic Information on Current Usage) and in large directories of general information, such as *Imidas*, whose name combines *imi* (meaning) and *dasu* (to take out) as well as being an acronym of the English title *Innovative Multi-information Dictionary Annual Series*. There are many dictionaries of loanwords, with headwords in katakana and explanations in Japanese, including the *Zukai Gairaigo Jiten* (Illustrated Loanword Dictionary, 3rd edition, Kadokawa, 1988, *c.*16,000 words) and *Katakana-go no Jiten* (Dictionary of Katakana Words, 1st edition, Shogakukan, 1990, *c.*20,000 words). Partly because of the emphasis on English/Japanese translation and reading comprehension in English-language education, one-way English-to-Japanese dictionaries are the best-selling type of dictionary in Japan. They include *Lighthouse* (Kenkyusha, 1st edition 1984) and *Progressive* (Shogakukan, 2nd edition 1990).

Writing. Japanese writing uses Chinese characters (*kanji*) and two native syllabic scripts (the *kana*: hiragana and katakana) derived from them. *Hiragana* is a cursive script used for writing grammatical elements and some native words, and is the main medium for young children's books. *Katakana*, a more angular script, is used principally for onomatopoeic native words and transcriptions of foreign words and names, including borrowings. Roman letters (*romaji*) are used for English and other European words in their original form, for loan material written as initials, for initials in foreign names, for Japanese words and names that may be read by non-Japanese (such as some company and product names), as a classifying device in some libraries, and for seating in some theatres and transport systems. *Hebon*, the standard system for Romanizing Japanese words, is named after the US physician and missionary J. C. Hepburn, who used it in the 1880s in his Japanese-English dictionary. It represents consonants according to English orthography, whereas official *kunrei* spellings are influenced by positions in the Japanese syllabary: compare *ta chi tsu te to* (Hepburn) with *ta ti tu te to* (kunrei). Long vowels are represented, for example, by *ā* in Hepburn, *â* in kunrei, or sometimes informally as, for example, *ah* or *aa*. Numbers are written in Chinese or Arabic symbols. Japanese scientific, technical, and official writing runs horizontally from left to right, whereas books, magazines, and newspapers generally run vertically, from top to bottom, and open from the right. Words in Roman script within vertical Japanese text are written on their side. Japanese English-language company names such as *National, Sharp, Citizen, Brother* are written in romaji and/or in katakana; Japanese-language company names are sometimes written in Roman letters, and Roman abbreviations of names from either language are common: *JAL (Japanese Air Lines), NEC (Nippon Electric Company), NHK (Nihon Hōsō Kyōkai).* Western-style shops, cafés, apartment blocks, and office buildings often have foreign names, such as the *Sunshine City* commercial building in Tokyo.

English in Japan. English has played an important role in the modernization of Japan, especially through the reading and translation of Western works. Calls by some radicals after the Meiji Restoration for English to be adopted as the national language, in order to promote Japan's development, were unsuccessful. During the 1920-30s, the EFL specialists H. E. Palmer and A. S. Hornby worked in Japan, the first as adviser to the Ministry of Education, with a special interest in oral methods and graded vocabulary lists, the second as one of the team which created *The Idiomatic and Syntactic English Dictionary*, first published in Tokyo (Kaitakusha, 1942), a work that evolved into the *Oxford Advanced Learner's Dictionary of Current English.* The majority of Japanese do not use English in everyday life, but recognize it as an important medium of international communication, especially for business and research. English as used by speakers of Japanese is characterized by the transfer of features from Japanese phonology, grammar, vocabulary, and discourse conventions: for example, difficulty in distinguishing between and pronouncing /l/ and /r/ (the nearest Japanese sound being between the two); the use of *yes* to express simple agreement with a statement or question; 'go to shopping' for *go shopping*; 'silent' used to translate *shizuka* (which has a wider meaning of 'silent, quiet, or peaceful'); the transfer to English of loan expressions from other foreign languages, as in 'I have an arbeit' (from the loan *arubaito* a part-time job, from German *Arbeit* work). For most Japanese, however, the term *Japanese English* is used, not to refer to the English spoken by Japanese, but as a translation of *wasei eigo* ('Made-in-Japan English'), a term referring to local expressions drawn from English but used in uniquely Japanese ways, such as *imējiappu* ('image up') meaning 'improving one's image': see GAIRAIGO.

English in the media. (1) *Newspapers and magazines.* Japan has four major English-language daily newspapers: the *Japan Times* (established 1897: 1990 circulation 75,000), the *Daily Yomiuri* (1955: circ. 55,000), the *Mainichi Daily News* (1922: 46,000), and the *Asahi Evening News* (1951: 33,000). All but the first are sister publications of Japanese-language newspapers. Magazines in English about Japan include the *Tokyo Journal* and *The Japan Quarterly*; the quarterly journal *Japan Echo* publishes English-language articles on Japan abridged and translated from Japanese-language journals. The *International Herald Tribune* and the Asian *Wall Street Journal* have presses in Tokyo, and the periodicals *Newsweek* and *Scientific American* have Japanese editions. (2) *Publishing.* Japanese publishers such as Tuttle, the Japan Times, and Kodansha International specialize in books on Japan in English; the latter has a 9-volume *Encyclopaedia of Japan* (1983). Large bookstores such as Kinokuniya and Maruzen stock a wide range of English-language books, and there are specialist English-language bookshops in main cities. Japanese scholars may publish some of their work in Japan or overseas in English. (3) *Motion pictures.* Foreign films are popular, and are shown under a katakanized or translated name, with their original soundtracks and Japanese subtitles. (4) *Television.* Imported feature films, serial dramas, and documentaries are usually dubbed in Japanese, but may have the original soundtrack also available on some radios and special 'bilingual' TV sets. Some daily, locally produced news programmes have an English-language translation which can be received on bilingual sets. Satellite TV is the major source of foreign TV broadcasts with their original soundtrack. (5) *Radio.* The Far East Network of the American Forces Radio broadcasts in English 24 hours a day, and can be received near US bases. Some local FM stations in the Tokyo area broadcast only in English. Radio transmissions in English are received from overseas: for example, from the Soviet Union on medium- and short-wave radio, and the BBC World Service and Voice of America on short-wave. (6) *Travel and tourism.* Announcements on airport buses, domestic flights, and *shinkansen* (bullet trains), and some sightseeing commentaries, are in Japanese and English, and place-names on railway platforms usually have Roman transcriptions.

Learning English. Some private kindergartens and elementary schools provide English instruction. Regular study normally begins in the first year of lower secondary school, and continues at least till graduation from upper secondary school. Traditional methods of language study, such as reading comprehension and grammar-translation, may be supplemented by oral work in the language laboratory and sometimes with native speakers, including those employed on the *JET* (*Japan English Teachers*) programme. Knowledge of English vocabulary and grammar is one of the important factors for selection of candidates to higher education, as the national examination for university entrance, and many individual entrance examinations, include an English language paper. The most popular non-compulsory private English-language examinations are those set by *STEP* (*Society for Testing English Proficiency*), authorized by the Ministry of Education and known in Japanese as *eigo kentei* or, for short, *eiken*. Some private universities and branches of US universities in Japan have English-medium courses. Tokyo and Osaka have public universities that specialize in foreign studies, and some technical colleges specialize in English-language instruction. There are also many language schools. The educational channel of Japanese TV broadcasts regular foreign-language-learning series, including English, and there is daily English-language instruction on the radio, teaching mainly colloquial AmE. Organizations for language teachers include the *Japan Association of Language Teachers* (*JALT*), which publishes *The Language Teacher* (monthly) and the *JALT Journal* (twice yearly), and the *Japanese Association of College English Teachers* (*JACET*).

English in Japanese. (1) *Loans.* English words are sometimes included in their original form within Japanese texts (for example, in advertisements and in some scientific writing), but are normally transcribed phonetically by katakana. This custom has assisted the entry into Japanese of loanwords (*gairaigo*) from English and other languages. There are over 1,000 such words in general use, and many thousands of scientific and technical borrowings: the *Kadogawa Gairaigo Jiten* (1969) defines some 25,000 such terms. For examples, see GAIRAIGO. (2) *Commerce and advertising.* Many modern Japanese products have English names written in their original form, often with katakana transcription, or only in katakana, and English words and phrases are often used in advertising to draw attention to the product, and give it an attractive, fashionable image.

Decorative English. English is ubiquitous as decoration on Western-style personal items such as clothes, fashion accessories, toiletries, and stationery. Goods for young people commonly feature popular characters such as Mickey Mouse, Alice in Wonderland, Snoopy, Beatrix Potter animals, and the local 'Kitty', often with related language, or bear English proverbs and inspirational mottos, such as *Let's sing a song with me!* Goods may be decorated with clippings or reproductions (not always accurate) from an English text, where the overall theme is appropriate but not the content, such as planting instructions accompanying a floral design. Decorative English is intended to be seen rather than read, the visual appeal of the foreign words taking precedence over their accuracy and appropriateness. The cosmopolitan form of the Roman script conveys a mood as much as a message, but the content may also embrace themes of youth, health, vitality, joy, and freedom (*for someone who seeks a long relationship with things nice*, on pocket tissues), or of romantic fantasy (*It's a romantic note book painted with a cute little cellophanetape*, on a notebook; *This case packs my dream and eyeglasses*, on a spectacles case; *tenderness was completed a pastel*, on a pencil box). English composed by Japanese for Japanese is often a literal translation of Japanese thoughts and expressions, ranging from the clearly recognizable (*enjoy superb combination of almond and chocolate*, on a chocolate wrapping) to the obscure (*Soft in one*, hair conditioner; *ReSpice Enjoy fashion life. Nice to Heart and Just Impression* and *The New York City Theatre District is where you can and us, anyone*, on casual bags). The decorative use of scripts is a cultural tradition in Japan. Since the Second World War, the English language has become strongly associated with American culture, and its use as part of the design of Western-style goods perhaps serves to reinforce their role as symbols of modernity and sophistication.

Japanese in English. Borrowing from Japanese into English began in the 16c; since then, there has been a small but steady flow of words related to Japanese life and culture, such as *bonze* 16c, *sake, shogun* 17c, *mikado, shinto* 18c, *geisha, jinricksha* 19c, *aikido, bonsai, origami, pachinko* 20c. Areas of special interest include: (1) The arts: *bonsai, haiku, ikebana, kabuki, kakemono, koto, Noh, origami, sumi-e, ukiyo-e.* (2) The martial arts: *aikido, bushido, judo, ju-jitsu* (*jiujitsu, jujutsu*), *kendo, sumo.* (3) Cuisine: *miso, nori, sashimi, satsuma, soba, sushi, tempura, tofu.* (4) Commerce: *zaibatsu, yen.* (5) Religion: *koan, shinto, zazen, zen.* (6) People: *geisha, issei, mikado, ninja, nisei, samurai, sansei, shogun, yakuza.* (7) Furnishings, clothes, etc.: *fusuma,*

futon, kimono, obi, shoji, tatami. (8) Entertainment: *enka, go, karaoke, nintendo, pachinko.*
(9) Language: *hiragana, kanji, katakana, kunrei.*
(10) Words taken from English, used in a special way in Japanese, and returned to English with their Japanese sense: *homestay* (from *hōmosutei*, from *home* and *stay*), *nighter* (from *naitā*, from *night* and *-er*), *salaryman* (from *sararīman*, from *salary* and *man*), and *wapuro* (abbreviating *word processor*). Such words have entered English in an adaptation of their Hepburn spellings, with long vowels not indicated by macrons: for example, *judo*, not *jūdō*. Early borrowings from Japanese, before systems of Romanization were established, particularly show modifications in spelling: for example, *soy* from *shōyu*, *tycoon* from *taikun*.

See ACRONYM/PROTOGRAM, AMERICAN LANGUAGES, BORROWING, CHINA, DECORATIVE ENGLISH, DIALECT IN AMERICA, EAST ASIAN ENGLISH, GAIRAIGO, JAPANESE PIDGIN ENGLISH, JAPLISH, KOREA, LIBRARY OF CONGRESS, LINGUISTIC TYPOLOGY, TELEPHONE, VOCABULARY. [ASIA, LANGUAGE, VARIETY].   G.S.K.

JAPANESE ENGLISH. See GAIRAIGO, JAPAN.

JAPANESE PIDGIN ENGLISH. An informal term applied, often pejoratively, to several varieties of English associated with Japan and the Japanese. They include: (1) A pidgin spoken from the early 20c by Japanese immigrants to Hawaii, and distinct from the other pidgins and creoles used in the islands. (2) Also *Bamboo English.* A pidgin used after World War II between some Japanese and the US occupation forces. American military involvement in other parts of East Asia later caused much of this pidgin to spread to other countries: for example, in Korea, the Philippines, Thailand, and during the Vietnam War, *mama-san* (Japanese: matron, especially one in charge of a geisha house, from *mama* mother, *san* honorific title) has been used to refer to any bar hostess, and *ichiban* (most, number one) means 'the best'. A humorous text in what was called *Korean Bamboo English* survives from the Korean War, apparently written by a US soldier. It blends elements of Japanese (and to a lesser extent Korean) with army slang, was published by Grant Webster in *American Speech* (1960), and begins:

Taksan years ago, skoshi Cinderella-san lived in hootchie with sisters, . . . ketchee no fun, hava-no social life. Always washee-washee, scrubee-scrubee, make chop-chop. One day Cinderella-san sisters ketchee post cardo from Seoul. Post cardo speakee so: one prince-san have big blowout, taksan kimchi, taksan beeru . . . Cindy-san sisters taksan excited, make Cinderella-san police up clothes.

(3) Also, loosely, *Japlish, Janglish, Japanized English.* The current use of some thousands of English words in daily speech in Japan, intended for use by Japanese among Japanese, and not for any attempt to communicate more easily with foreigners. Many of these are 'made in Japan' terms (*wasei eigo*), and are not transparent, phonologically or semantically, to native speakers of English: for example, *dokutā sutoppu* (doctor stop), a physician's prohibition on certain activities, such as smoking. The title of a recent best-selling novel, *Bājin Rodo* (Virgin Road), refers to the aisle a bride walks down in a church. The number of English-based vocabulary items has been steadily increasing since World War II. See GAIRAIGO, JAPAN, JAPLISH, LINGUA, PIDGIN. [ASIA, VARIETY].   J.S., T.MCA.

JAPLISH [1950s: a blend of *Jap(anese)* and *(Eng)lish*]. Also **Japalish** [perhaps to avoid the pejorative implication of *Jap* as an ethnic slur] and **Janglish** [playing on *jangle* discordant sound]. Informal terms, often wry, sometimes pejorative, for any mixture of Japanese and English. They may refer to Japanese spoken or written with an admixture of English or to English that shows Japanese influence: 'A great many Japanese speak English nowadays (or at least "Japlish", as the American colony calls it)' (*Harper's Magazine*, Jan. 1963); 'Japanese sometimes sounds like Japlish: *masukomi* for mass communications, *terebi* for television' (*Time*, 22 July 1966). See -GLISH AND -LISH, JAPAN, JAPANESE PIDGIN ENGLISH. [ASIA, VARIETY].   T.MCA.

JARGON [14c: from late Middle English forms *iargo(u)n, gargoun, girgoun* the twittering and chattering of birds, meaningless talk, gibberish, from Old French *jargoun, gargon, gergon.* Probably originally echoic]. An often pejorative general term for outlandish language of various kinds, such as speech perceived as gibberish or mumbo jumbo, slang, a pidgin language, or, most commonly, the specialized language of a trade, profession, or other group. The term is often associated with law, medicine, and the sciences: *technical jargon, scientific jargon.* To nonmembers of professional, occupational, and other groups, their usage is filled with terms and syntax that are not typical of general English and may therefore impede understanding among lay people, but to members of such a group, the usage is familiar and generally serves its purpose well. Because of ease and familiarity, however, they may use technical expressions and styles outside the group, either unthinkingly, because it seems best fitted for the topic in question, or on occasion to impress and even oppress.

Jargon as verbal shorthand. For those who understand it, jargon is a kind of shorthand that makes long explanations unnecessary. When used by the members of a profession or group, it can be an efficient and effective language. For physicians, the surgical removal of a gall bladder is a *cholecystectomy*. For lawyers, an *involuntary conversion* is loss or destruction of property through theft, accident, or condemnation, and *estoppel* means that a party is prevented by his or her own acts from claiming a right that would cause injury or loss to another party. Studies of surgeons have found that the jargon used during surgery improves the communication of factual information with brevity and clarity, and the legal profession has spent many years arriving at the strict definition of legal terms that inevitably entails jargon. In comparable ways, such new professions as the computer sciences have evolved a jargon which communicates technical ideas among members of the group, including such expressions as *dynamic random access memory*, *read only memory*, *core dump*, and *cache buffer*.

Jargon as group identification. Ability to understand and use the jargon of a group is a badge of identification: one belongs, and those who cannot use the jargon of the group do not, even if they possess other skills necessary for membership. In a sense, the ability to use the jargon indicates that the user is conforming to the norms of the group, as well as accepting and understanding the basic ideas, principles, and practices of the group. In addition, using jargon can lend an air of authority and prestige to those who use it, especially if the jargon is associated with a profession that enjoys a high social position. Its use identifies the user as (probably) a member of that profession and transfers (at least some of) the group prestige to the individual using the jargon.

The temptations of jargon. While jargon can and does have a legitimate function, it is probably more known for its abuse by people who use it to confuse, confound, needlessly complicate subject matter, and lend an air of importance and sophistication to their message and themselves. While doctors may easily understand *bilateral perorbital haematoma* a black eye, *agrypnia* insomnia, *cephalalgia* a headache, and *emesis* vomiting, patients rarely if ever understand such terms. Jargon also allows the speaker to make fairly simple ideas appear complicated, if not profound. It may sound more impressive to write that 'The argillaceous character of the formation is very prominent in some localities, although it is usually subsidiary to the arenaceous phase', rather than 'At some places the formation included considerable clay, but generally it is made up chiefly of sand.' The biologist writing that 'Although solitary under normal prevailing circumstances, raccoons may congregate simultaneously in certain situations of artificially enhanced nutrient resource availability' may have thought that jargon was more impressive than saying 'Raccoons live alone, but if you put some food out they will gather around it in a group.' Generally, when people use jargon not to communicate but to impress their audiences with their importance or the importance or complexity of their subject matter, or use it to announce membership in a group, communication suffers and the jargon can quickly degenerate into something close to the twittering of birds.

See ACADEMIC USAGE/ENGLISH, AGGLOMERESE, APHASIA, ARGOT, AUREATE DICTION, BAFFLEGAB, BOMBAST, BULL(SHIT), BUREAUCRATESE, CANT, CHINOOK JARGON, CIRCUMLOCUTION, COMPUTERESE, CONFUSAGE, DOUBLESPEAK, DOUBLESPEAK AWARD, DOUBLE TALK, DOUBLETHINK, -ESE, EUPHEMISM, GOBBLEDYGOOK, GOLDEN BULL AWARDS, HOLOFERNES, INFLATED LANGUAGE, INKHORN TERM, JIVE(TALK), JOURNALESE, LEGALESE, LEGAL USAGE, LINGO, MEDICANT, MUMBO JUMBO, NAUTICAL JARGON, NEWSPEAK, OBFUSCATION, OBSCURANTISM, OFFICIALESE, PACIFIC JARGON ENGLISH, PATOIS, PEDANT, PERIPHRASIS, PIDGIN, PLAIN ENGLISH, PLEONASM, PRIVATE LANGUAGE, PSYCHOBABBLE, REDUNDANCY, SLANG, SOCIOLOGESE, -SPEAK, TAUTOLOGY, TECHNOBABBLE, TRADE JARGON, VERBOSITY, WAFFLE, WRITING. [STYLE, USAGE].   W.D.L.

Green, Jonathon. 1984. *Newspeak: A Dictionary of Jargon.* London: Routledge & Kegan Paul.
Hudson, Kenneth. 1978. *The Jargon of the Professions.* London: Macmillan.
Miller, Don Ethan. 1981. *The Book of Jargon.* New York: Macmillan.

JENNINGS, Paul (Francis) [1918–90]. English humorist, born in Leamington Spa, Warwickshire, and educated at King Henry VII School, Coventry. While still in the Army during the Second World War, he began freelance writing for *Punch* and *The Spectator*, was a scriptwriter at the Central Office of Information (1946–7), an advertising copywriter (1947–9), and a columnist on *The Observer* (1949–66), after which he became an independent writer. Jennings's appeal resides in a gift for amiable fantasy and shrewd word-play, discerning the oddness, even lunacy, lurking under the commonplaces of middle-class English life. His humorous works include: *Oddly Enough* (1951), *Even Oddlier* (1952), *Oddly Bodlikins* (1953), *Next to Oddliness* (1955), *Model Oddlies* (1956), *Gladly Oddly* (1957), *Idly Oddly* (1959), *I Said Oddly, Diddle I?* (1961), *Oddles of Oddlies* (1963), *Oddly Ad Lib* (1965), *I Was Joking, of Course* (1968), *Just a Few Lines* (1969), *It's An Odd Thing, But . . .* (1971), *Britain As She*

Is Visit (1976), *The Book of Nonsense* (1977), *Golden Oddlies* (1983). By the early 1960s, his work had become sufficiently 'classic' for an anthology, *The Jenguin Pennings*, to be issued (1963). Other works include the novel *And Now For Something Exactly the Same* (1977), children's books (such as *The Great Jelly of London*, 1965), books about trains (such as *My Favourite Railway Stories*, 1982) and rural life (*East Anglia*, 1986). His prose is full of literary echoes and allusions, his light verse adroitly inventive. Jennings teased rather than satirized, in the English tradition of the kindly, comic observer, agreeably secure in his insecurity: 'I'm a perfectly ordinary, normal motorist. Never had a neurosis in my life. Happily married, fine kids, reasonable job. Car two-and-a-half years old and sound as a bell. But the more I drive these days the harder it is not to believe I am being followed. And preceded. Always by the same two men; the Man Behind and the Man in Front' ('Man in the Middle', from *I must have imagined it*, 1977). See SAXONISM. [BIOGRAPHY, EUROPE, STYLE].   W.N.

JERSEY. See CHANNEL ISLANDS, LATIN¹.

JESPERSEN, (Jens) Otto (Harry) [1860–1943]. Danish linguist and authority on language teaching and the grammar of English. Born at Randers, Jutland, he was educated at Frederiksborg School, Zealand, and at the U. of Copenhagen, where he began to study law but changed to languages, taking a degree in French, English, and Latin in 1887. To finance his studies he worked part-time as a parliamentary shorthand reporter. During a postgraduate year (1887–8), he went first to England, where he attended Henry Sweet's lectures on phonetics at Oxford and met James Murray and other scholars, then Germany, where he met the philologists Karl Brugmann and Eduard Sievers, then spent the spring of 1888 in Paris, discussing phonetics and language teaching with Paul Passy, after which, at the summer semester at the U. of Berlin, he attended Julius Zupitza's seminar on Chaucer and Julius Hoffory's lectures on Beowulf. Back in Copenhagen, he obtained a D.Phil. in 1891, and in 1893 was appointed Professor of English, a position which he held until his retirement in 1925.

While still an undergraduate, Jespersen made contact with some of the leaders of the Reform Movement of language teaching; he translated Felix Franke's book about the Movement's principles into Danish (1884) and wrote in Danish a grammar of English using the then revolutionary method of giving phonetic transcription (1885). He helped to form a Scandinavian society for language-teaching reform, named *Quousque*

Tandem [Latin: just how long], in 1886. In 1901, he published a book on language teaching, *Sprogundervisning* (revised edition, 1935), translated into English as *How to Teach a Foreign Language* (1904). In collaboration with a university colleague, he produced a set of school textbooks of English based on the ideas of the Reform Movement.

When Paul Passy in 1886 formed the organization that later became the International Phonetic Association, he was joined by Jespersen, who participated in the creation of the IPA system of notation. Jespersen later supplied phonetic transcriptions of the entries in Brynildsen's *English and Dano-Norwegian Dictionary* (1902–7), which was the century's first pronouncing dictionary. His main contribution to phonetics is a compendium originally published in Danish but issued in German in 1904, *Lehrbuch der Phonetic*, with its companion volume *Phonetische Grundfragen*. A book on the phonetics of Danish came in 1906 and one on the phonetics of English in 1912; the latter, originally written in Danish, was issued in an English translation in 1950.

Jespersen's publications on linguistics and grammatical theory are numerous, including: *Language* (1922); *The Philosophy of Grammar* (1924); *Mankind, Nation and Individual* (1925); *Analytic Syntax* (1937). His system of analysis of English grammar is explained briefly in *Essentials of English Grammar* (1933) and at greater length in his main work, *A Modern Grammar on Historical Principles* (seven volumes, 1909–49, the last completed by an assistant, Niels Haislund). Jespersen's theory has in part been superseded, but the mass of material that he collected and systematized retains its value. Volume 1 contains original views on the history of English sounds, including his account of the Great Vowel Shift (Jespersen's own term). His views on the general development of English are set out in *Growth and Structure of the English Language* (1905).

A vein of idealism pervades Jespersen's work. Language teaching to him was a means of bringing nations closer together. With the same object in mind he became actively involved in efforts to develop an international auxiliary language. In 1907, he helped create a reformed Esperanto called Ido, and in 1928 developed his own auxiliary language, Novial, in which he sought to apply a principle concerning simplicity in grammar and vocabulary which echoed the words of the English philosopher Jeremy Bentham: 'That international language is best which in every point offers the greatest facility to the greatest number.' Neither Ido nor Novial had any success. See index. [EDUCATION, EUROPE, GRAMMAR, LANGUAGE].   P.C.

JEWISH ENGLISH, short form *JE*. A collective term for several varieties of English spoken and written by Jews, marked by a range of lexical, grammatical, and other linguistic and paralinguistic elements. Though both concept and term are recent, JE has existed in one way or another as long as Jews have been speaking English. At present, the most common variety is an English influenced by Yiddish and Hebrew, used chiefly by Ashkenazim (Jews of Central and Eastern European origin or descent). This variety has introduced into colloquial AmE and BrE many neologisms, such as *maven, nebbish, nosh, shlep*. Other varieties include a Judezmo-influenced English used by Sephardim (Jews of Spanish origin or descent), a 19c variety of AusE, and a formal variety that uses general English words, such as *academy* for Yiddish-origin *yeshiva, skullcap* for Yiddish-origin *yarmulka* or Hebrew-origin *kipa, ritual bath* or *ritualarium* for Yiddish- or Hebrew-origin *mikva*. The term *Judeo-English* was formerly used to suggest a parallel with Jewish languages of the past whose vernacular names were commonly prefixed with *Judeo-*, such as *Judeo-Arabic* or *Judeo-Greek*. The name, like the combining form *Judeo-*, is now archaic, though the parallelism is valid. The following characteristics describe mainly the American Ashkenazic variety of JE.

Pronunciation. (1) The following features are traceable to Yiddish influence: the substitution of /ŋg/ for /ŋ/ in present participles and other words, such as *singing* and *singer*; a raising of /ɔ/ in words like *off, cough, soft*; over-aspiration of /t/; confusion of /s/ and /z/ in pronouncing the plural ending -*s* in some environments. Certain features of Eastern Ashkenazic New York City English of the immigrant generations (c.1880-1940) are still sometimes heard: pronunciation of such words as *circle, nervous, first* as if 'soikel', 'noivis', 'foist', and an intrusive /n/ in words like *carpenter* ('carpentner'), *painter* ('paintner'). (2) A widespread feature of Ashkenazic JE is replacement of Yiddish-origin word-final -*e* /e/, as in *pastrame, khale, shmate, tate, Sore* with -*i* /i/, as in *pastrami, khali* Sabbath loaf, *shmati* rag, *tati* daddy, *Sori* Sarah. (3) American Ashkenazic JE has numerous stylistic features, including those of pitch, amplitude, intonation, voice quality, and rate of speech, that reflect the influence of the Yiddish conversational style of the immigrant generations.

Grammar. (1) Yiddish and Hebrew loanwords are integrated into English in four ways: by dropping infinitive endings (*davn* pray, from Yiddish *davnen*) then giving the verb English inflections (*davns, davned, davning*); by replacing Yiddish and Hebrew plural forms (*shtetlekh*

small towns, *Shabatonim* Sabbath social gatherings) with English plurals (*shtetls, Shabatons*); by forming new derivatives with English affixes (*shleppy, shleppily, shleppiness, shleppish, shleppishly*); by extending the function of loans, for example, the Yiddish interjection *nebish* a pity, used (with the spelling *nebbish*) as an adjective meaning 'pitiful, unfortunate' (*a nebbish character*), and as a noun meaning 'unfortunate person, poor devil' (*What a nebbish he is!*). (2) Some verbs are used in a non-standard absolute way: *Enjoy, enjoy; Go figure; I'm entitled.* (3) The use of inversions for emphasis is common: *Shakespeare he is not; A roof over our heads we have.* (4) The use of Yiddish-origin constructions is frequent, and has spread into some forms of colloquial AmE: *I want you should do this; He is a boy is all* (that's all); *Don't be a crazy; Again with the complaints!* (complaining again); *Enough with the talk; Begin already!* (So begin!); *They don't know from nothing* (Don't know anything). (5) Similarly, Yiddish-origin idioms are often used, have spread into AmE at large, and are becoming increasingly widely used: *Get lost!; Eat your heart out; I need it like a hole in the head; I should live so long* (I would need to live a long time to see that); *You should be so lucky* (you are never going to be so lucky). (6) The use of rhetorical questions (usually calques from Yiddish) is frequent and similarly spreading: *Who needs it?; What's with all the noise?; So what else is new?; What's to forgive?* (7) Several Yiddish morphological forms have become common formatives: the dismissive *shm-* in hundreds of reduplications: *Oedipus-shmoedipus, rich-shmich, value-shmalue*; the agent suffix -*nik: beatnik, kibbutznik, peacenik, real-estatenik, spynik, noshnik, Freudnik*; the endearing diminutives -*ele* and -*l*, often appended to English given names (*Stevele, Rachele*), sometimes with a doubling of diminutives (*Debbiinkele, Samchikele*), sometimes with common nouns (*roomele, roomkele, boyele, boychickl, storele, storkele*).

Vocabulary. (1) There are thousands of Yiddish and many Hebrew terms used in English that relate to Jewish life: *shadkhn* a matchmaker, *hesped* a eulogy, *kanehore* preserve us from the evil eye, *halevay* would that it be so. (2) There are many compounds of Yiddish and Hebrew loanwords with English words: *matse balls* round dumplings, *shana tova card* a Jewish New Year card, *sforim store* a Jewish bookstore. (3) Lexical items formed from general English words: *Jewish Star, Hebrew School*. (4) Semantic shifts in English words, often due to homophony with terms of Yiddish: *learn* to study torah (the law), from Yiddish *lernen; give* to take, from *gebn*, as in *Give a look; by* with, from *bay*, as in *The money is by him.* (5) Informal abbreviations

for: vulgarisms of Yiddish origin (*TL* a syco-
phant, from Yiddish *tokhes leker* ass-licker);
pejorative terms with English components
(*JAP* Jewish American Princess); and Yiddish
and Hebrew expressions (*B'H* meaning *with
God's help*, *zal* an acronym meaning *of blessed
memory*).

Social issues. Speakers and writers of JE generally avoid terms with un-Jewish, especially
Christian connotations, such as: *Christian name*,
the preferred terms being *first name* or *given
name*; *AD* and *BC*, preferring *CE* for *Common
Era* and *BCE* for *Before the Common Era* (both
JE coinages); idiomatic expressions alluding to
Christian themes (*cross one's fingers, knock on
wood/touch wood, the gospel truth, Christ! Jeez!*);
terms with anti-Semitic denotations or connotations, such as *Hymietown* (New York City),
jew down (to bargain sharply with), *Shylock*,
and *Yid*.

Literary influence. JE has played an important
role in the works of many American, Canadian,
British, and South African Jewish writers,
among them Saul Bellow, Joseph Heller, Dan
Jacobson, Bernard Malamud, Mordecai Richler,
Philip Roth, and Israel Zangwill. The English
language in the hands of such writers takes on
many nuances reflecting their Jewish
background. Their writings are liberally
sprinkled with the Yiddish- and Hebrew-origin
loanwords and calques that characterize the
variety.

See ARABIC, ARAMAIC, BIBLE, DIALECT IN AMER-
ICA, DIASPORA, ENGLISH LANGUAGE, ETHNIC NAME,
GERMANIC LANGUAGES, HAMITO-SEMITIC LAN-
GUAGES, HEBRAISM, HEBREW, HYPERBATON,
ISRAEL, JEWISH ENGLISH, JEWISH JOKE, JEWISH
LANGUAGES, LETTER WORD, NEW YORK, PLURAL,
PUN, SCHWA/SHWA, SHIBBOLETH, SLAVONIC LAN-
GUAGES, SPANISH, YIDDISH, YIDDISHISM, YINGLISH.
[AMERICAS, EUROPE, VARIETY].   S.S.

JEWISH JOKE. An ethnic joke by or about
Jews, that deals mainly with stereotypes such
as mothers and in-laws, *shnorrers* professional
beggars, *shadkhonim* matchmakers, *shlemiels*
ne'er-do-wells, *leydigeyers* idlers, *luftmenshn*
impractical dreamers, and religious and communal functionaries such as rabbis, cantors, sex-
tons, ritual slaughterers, circumcisers,
synagogue presidents, and fund-raisers. Almost
any Jew who can be stereotyped is a natural
target: Conservative, Reform, Orthodox,
Hasidic, Lithuanian, Polish, millionaire, pauper.
While some of the types may be the targets of
anti-Jewish jokes, the quintessential Jewish joke
lacks malice. Its aim is to deflate, not destroy; it

does not reflect self-hatred but rather self-
mockery or self-irony. For example: a *luftmen-
sh*'s business card reads 'Psychologist and
Locksmith. Also caterer on weekends.' A miserly
rich Jew piously exclaims: 'If God doesn't give
to the poor, who am I to give?' A poor Jew
pleads with God: 'You help total strangers, so
why not me?' A young Jewish mother is asked
how old her two little sons are. 'The doctor',
she says, 'is four, and the lawyer is three.' Four
leydigeyers are sitting in a café. '*Oy*', groans one.
'*Oy vey*', says another. '*Nu*', says the third. 'Listen!' exclaims the fourth. 'If you men don't stop
talking politics, I'm leaving!' While the old Jewish jokes rooted in European life survive under
various disguises, the post-war period has introduced new topics (Americanization, Israel,
Soviet Jewry) and new targets (bar mitzvas, bat
mitzvas, the Catskill 'borscht belt' in New York
State). Jews still primarily make fun of themselves and their foibles. See ETHNIC JOKE, JOKE,
JEWISH ENGLISH. [STYLE].   S.S.

JEWISH LANGUAGES. A descriptive term for
the more than 30 languages spoken and written
by Jews in the course of their early wanderings
and eventual dispersion among the nations. The
two most widely known and investigated Jewish
languages are *Yiddish*, a Germanic language,
and *Judezmo* or *Ladino*, a Romance language
and the traditional language of Jews of Spanish
descent. Other Jewish languages of historical
importance include *Yavanic* or *Judeo-Greek*,
Yahudic or *Judeo-Arabic*, *Ebri* or *Judeo-Persian*,
Zarfatic or *Judeo-French*, *Italian* or *Judeo-
Italian*, and *Knaanic* or *Judeo-Czech*. As the
archaic names with the *Judeo-* combining form
imply, a Jewish language is a distinctively Jewish
form or correlate of a non-Jewish majority language. Thus, students of Jewish linguistics refer
to *Zarfatic* as the Jewish correlate of Old French,
Shuadit as the Jewish correlate of Old Provençal,
Gruzinic as the Jewish correlate of Georgian in
the Caucasus, and so forth.

The earliest Jewish language was probably a
variety of Canaanitic influenced by Aramaic,
used by the descendants of Abraham who settled
in Canaan. This developed into the classical
Hebrew of the Bible. The next most important
language was a Hebrew-influenced form of Aramaic used by the Jews of the Middle East after
the Babylonian Exile in the 6c BC. This became
the foundation of all succeeding Jewish languages: no Jewish language is known that has
not had at its core a Hebrew-Aramaic component. This component is not only found in the
lexicon of Jewish languages, but is usually integrated into their phonology, morphology, and
syntax. Typically, Jewish languages have served
as everyday means of communication within

Jewish communities and have often been used with only marginal awareness of the differences in pronunciation, vocabulary, grammar between them and the co-territorial languages of non-Jews. Though Jewish languages were usually written in Hebrew characters and read from right to left, they were considered by their users secular, temporary vernaculars, sharply distinguished from the sacred Hebrew tongue which was the medium in which most religious and communal matters, scholarly exchanges, and literary activities were conducted.

In this way, with no special significance attached to them, most Jewish languages have tended to be easily replaced by other languages acquired through immigration or conquest. This pattern of adoption and replacement characterized, for example, several Jewish languages that were precursors of Yiddish in western Europe. Yet for reasons that are not well understood, certain Jewish languages, including Yiddish and Judezmo, endured for an exceptionally long time. Some have had extensive literatures: for example, *Aramic*, the Jewish correlate of Aramaic, is the language of both the Babylonian and the Jerusalemite versions of the Talmud, each in its own dialect. *Yahudic* and *Ebri*, the Jewish correlates respectively of Arabic and Persian, produced many influential philosophical and scientific works throughout the Middle Ages. In modern times, Yiddish became the vehicle of a sophisticated and diversified literature that includes the classic works of Mendele Mokher Sforim, I. L. Peretz, Shalom Aleichem, and the Nobel Prize winner Isaac Bashevis Singer. The works of these and many other Yiddish writers have been translated into English. See ARAMAIC, ETHNIC NAME, HAMITO-SEMITIC LANGUAGES, HEBREW, ISRAEL, JEWISH ENGLISH, YIDDISH. [ASIA, EUROPE, LANGUAGE].

S.S.

JINGLE [14c: apparently echoic]. (1) A noise made by small bells, keys in a bunch, etc., intermediate between clinking and ringing; something that jingles. (2) The repetition of the same sound or a similar series of sounds, as in alliteration, assonance, or rhyme, and usually intended to have a pleasant effect: 'Milton often affects a kind of Jingle in his Words, as in the following Passages . . . "And brought into the World a World of Woe" ' (Addison, *Spectator* 297, 1717). The term has often been used pejoratively to suggest that certain verse is closer to doggerel than to poetry. (3) A short, catchy song, used in advertising, especially in radio or television commercials. See DOGGEREL, REPETITION, RHYME, SINGSONG. [STYLE].   T.MCA.

JIVE, also **jive talk.** (1) The slang or jargon associated in the earlier 20c with such African-American forms of music as jive (swing, jazz, etc.). (2) In the later 20c, an informal term for flattering, deceptive, exaggerated, meaningless talk, especially among black Americans (*Hey, don't give me that jive, man!*); double talk: 'Everything that we do must be aimed toward the total liberation, unification and empowerment of Afrika. Anything short of that is jive' (*Black World*, Oct. 1973). Compare BLARNEY, RAP. See TECHNOBABBLE. [AMERICAS, STYLE].   T.MCA.

JMB TEST. See JOINT MATRICULATION BOARD.

JOHN BULL [18c: from the chief character of John Arbuthnot's allegorical and satirical series of pamphlets advocating an end to war with France, the first of which was *Law is a Bottomless Pit, Exemplified in the Case of the Lord Strutt, John Bull, Nicholas Frog and Lewis Baboon: who spent all they had in a Law-suit* (1712). The whole series was called *The History of John Bull*, who is described as an honest, plain-dealing fellow, choleric, bold, quarrelsome, and fond of drinking. In the pamphlets, *John Bull* (England) and *Nicholas Frog* (the Dutch) engage in a lawsuit against *Lewis Baboon* (Louis XIV of France). They are represented by the attorney *Humphrey Hocus* (the Duke of Marlborough), and *Lord Strutt* is Philip of Spain]. An ethnic nickname for an Englishman, Englishmen collectively, Anglophiles, England, and Great Britain: 'John Bull was now an Imperialist, and dwelt very much abroad' (*Daily News*, 3 Jan. 1899). It is either neutral or mildly positive, and is closely linked to a cartoon figure, stout and striding out, with a ruddy face, a top hat, and the Union Flag for a waistcoat. The term *John-Bullism* was used in the 19c to signify the spirit of Englishness. In 1884, Leon Paul Blouet wrote *John Bull and His Island*, a book about Ireland; Bernard Shaw adapted it in 1904 as the ironic play *John Bull's Other Island*, written at the request of his fellow Irishman W. B. Yeats 'as a patriotic contribution to the repertory of the Irish Literary Theatre'. See ETHNIC NAME, -ISM. Compare UNCLE SAM. [EUROPE, NAME]   T.MCA.

JOHNSON, Samuel [1709-84]. English lexicographer, critic, poet, and moralist, who achieved through his *Dictionary of the English Language* (1755) and the model of his own writings pre-eminence in his lifetime as an authority on the language. Johnson was a voracious reader in classical literature and English from the earliest years in his father's bookshop in Lichfield, Staffordshire, and had a highly retentive memory. Such comprehensive scholarly works as his edition of Shakespeare (1765) and *The Lives of the English Poets* (1779-81) drew, like his Dictionary, on an encyclopedic knowledge of the authors of his age.

The Dictionary. This work, commissioned by a group of London book-sellers, was in part a response to a widely felt need in the late 17c and early 18c for stability in the language and for canons of correctness in usage. As a language of scholarly communication, English was seen to lack the permanence and concision of Latin, and the efforts of the French and Italian Academies in bringing about improvements in the vernacular were known and envied. Proposals, especially c.1660-1710, for establishing an English Academy to 'fix' the language had come to nothing, and the actor David Garrick's instant comment on the publication of the Dictionary that Johnson had 'beat forty French, and will beat forty more' accorded him the status of a one-man academy, and shows the readiness of his age to accept an arbiter of linguistic usage: Johnson himself had said 'it is more important for a law to be known, than for it to be right'.

Work on the Dictionary took eight or nine years, and was carried out mainly in the large garret at Johnson's house in Gough Square, London. He is thought to have used an interleaved copy of Nathan Bailey's *Dictionarium Britannicum* as a foundation word list and had the help of some half a dozen amanuenses, several of them Scots, who copied out the quotations which he had chosen. Johnson's perception of his task as a lexicographer changed while the Dictionary was in hand. When he published the *Plan of an English Dictionary* (1747), he saw himself as a verbal critic, condemning barbarous words and expressions, and guarding the purity of the language. But in the Preface (1755), he disclaimed that intention, saying that all the stubborn uncertainties of usage were not to be blamed on him, since his task was not to form, but merely to record the language. At the same time, he recognized that his dictionary could well have some effect on the language, though only through slowing down inevitable change, and minimizing undesirable developments ('It remains that we retard what we cannot repel, and that we palliate what we cannot cure').

Johnson's influence. The influence of his work on the development of the language has been widely assumed but cannot be proved and is difficult to assess. In particular, it is often held to have fixed English spelling; printers' spelling had, however, been established largely in the modern form before 1700, and where Johnson differed from it in his dictionary entries (as in words such as

logick and *errour*) his recommended form has often failed to survive. It is nonetheless likely that, through the countless abbreviated and miniature editions running well into the 19c, the Dictionary played a role in propagating a standard spelling among the less literate and in forming and restraining the writings of the educated. Earlier monolingual dictionaries were mainly concerned with 'hard' words: the bookish, Latinate, and technical vocabulary of Renaissance English. Except sometimes in providing etymologies, they were non-historical and paid little regard to literary usage. Johnson differed in seeking to illustrate the meanings of words by literary quotation. He favoured the usage of the preceding century, Shakespeare, Milton, and Dryden alone accounting for a third of all quotations. The arrangement of his citations is chronological, and Johnson commonly surpasses his predecessors in the elegance of his definitions: *enchant* 'to subdue by charms or spells'; *graceful* 'beautiful with dignity'; *insinuative* 'stealing on the affections'. It can be said that Johnson provided a powerful but conservative model of language usage for at least a century after his time. See index. [BIOGRAPHY, EUROPE, HISTORY, LITERATURE, MEDIA, STYLE].   N.E.O.

JOHNSONESE [1830s: coined by Thomas Macaulay]. An often pejorative term for the elevated style of Samuel Johnson. His leanings towards a Latinate vocabulary were remarked on in his own day (for example, by his biographer James Boswell). Thus, *repress the instantaneous motions of merriment* may be seen as a roundabout and obscure way of saying *stop laughing*. In his poetry, the Latinisms often lend compactness through sheer semantic weight ('The laureat tribe in venal verse relate / How virtue wars with persecuting fate'). The contortions of Latinity often quoted against him (as in the dictionary definition of *network* as 'any thing reticulated or decussated, at equal distances, with interstices between the intersections') are not typical of the work. See -ESE, JOHNSON, JOHNSONIAN, LATINATE. [STYLE]. N.E.O.

JOHNSONIAN [1780s]. A term applied to the style of Samuel Johnson or any style resembling it. His moralizing essays in *The Rambler* magazine (1750-2) best illustrate the style, not only in its long words, but in the antithetical balancing of phrases which often went with them: 'I could seldom escape to solitude, or steal a moment from the emulation of complaisance, and the vigilance of officiousness.' Johnson wrote in a century when English prose was becoming less formal; the subsequent rejection of his Latinate vocabulary reflected that change. See JOHNSON, JOHNSONESE. [STYLE].   N.E.O.

JOINT MATRICULATION BOARD. An examining board in England and Wales, founded in 1903, which operates the *General Certificate of Secondary Education* (*GCSE*) as part of the Northern Examining Group. It has examined largely in the area of its constituent universities: Birmingham, Leeds, Liverpool, Manchester, and Sheffield. Although it does not operate internationally, it has a *Test in English* (*Overseas*), popularly known as the *JMB Test*, for overseas applicants for degree courses. See EXAMINING IN ENGLISH. [EDUCATION, EUROPE].

W.S.

JOKE [17c: from Latin *iocus* a jest]. Something said or done to cause amusement: 'O Lord, we ken we hae sinned,' say the people in a Scots account of the Flood, 'but a joke can be carried too far.' A joke is a joke as long as two parties acknowledge it: reduce the number and it stops being funny. Children are adepts at the solipsistic joke; adults cannot easily understand why it is funny that Teddy has cornflakes for supper. Making or 'cracking' a joke requires certain well-established devices, such as, in English, a ritual announcement often containing the word *one*: 'Have you heard this one?'; 'I heard a good one yesterday'; 'Do you know the one about the actress and the bishop at Stonehenge?'; '. . . and there's the one about the politician and the performing seal'. Any such statement or question is a formulaic summons to laughter. Technically, jokes are like chess: there is a limited number of moves, but the variations and combinations are infinite. Old jokes may enjoy an extended span of life through variations on the original formula: 'Who was that lady I saw you with last night?'—'That was no lady; that was my wife.' This tired old two-liner picks up a little energy if recast: 'Who was that lady I saw you with last night?'—'That was no lady; that was your wife', or 'Who was that lady I saw you with last night?'—'If it was last night, that was no lady.' Jokes can be refurbished to suit the latest fashion, appearing and reappearing in different generic settings, as *doctor jokes, elephant jokes, red-white-and-blue jokes, sick jokes, waiter jokes*, and even *anti-jokes*, in which the joke is the absence of a joke. They can be attributed to diverse sources, from Geoffrey Chaucer to Groucho Marx, and can be supposedly typical of various races or communities.

The joke which purports to criticize racial or national defects and foibles, with malice or affection, is often of doubtful ethnicity. It can usually be transferred without loss of effect from one social context to another. An instance is the 'Irish joke' about the motor-cycle passenger who for protection against the wind puts on his overcoat back to front, then falls from the pillion on a bend near a village: 'Sure,' the villagers tell the ambulance men, 'wasn't he speaking and laughing till we got his head the right way round?' This is a jibe at Irish reasoning, but turns up in England as a 'West Country joke' about stolid yokels ('Oh, a-ar, 'e wurr foine till . . .': Ah yes, he was fine till . . .). Ethnic jokes are frequently invented and circulated by their supposed victims, amiably enough as a rule, though sometimes warning signals can be raised: 'What's red, white, and blue and washed ashore in Cumbria?' —'An Englishman who tells too many Irish jokes.' This two-liner has the substance of an ethnic joke, the form of a riddle, and the genus 'red-white-and-blue joke'. When the joke is 'on' somebody ('There was this Xman, see, and . . .'), some person or group has to suffer the consequences, which means that there are occasions when a joke is no joke. In the old ethnic jest about Scottish Calvinism, the preacher tells his trembling congregation that one day they will all burn in hell, and as they lie there in torment they will raise their eyes to heaven and cry, 'Lor-r-d, we didnae ken.' 'And then,' the preacher continues, 'Almighty God in his infinite mair-rcy will look doun upon ye and say, "Well, ye ken noo" ' (*ken* know, *noo* now).

See ABERDEEN JOKE, ANECDOTE, BON MOT, ETHNIC JOKE, HUMO(U)R, IRISH BULL, IRISH JOKE, JEWISH JOKE, JOKE TOWN, NEWFIE JOKE, ONE-LINER, ORAL TRADITION, POLITICALLY CORRECT, PUNCH LINE, SCATOLOGY, SHAGGY DOG STORY, TWO-LINER, WISECRACK, WITTICISM. [STYLE].   W.N.

JOKE TOWN [20c]. The name of a town that is considered inherently funny, usually a nearby, smaller town whose residents are regarded by those of its large neighbour as naïve, dull, comic, and the fit butt of humour. Most cities in the US have a neighbouring joke town: for example, the TV comedian Johnny Carson, who broadcasts from Los Angeles, makes jokes about *beautiful downtown Burbank*, and people in Gainesville, Florida, joke about *Micanopy* (pronounced 'mick-a-NO-pee'). [NAME].   J.A.

JONES, Daniel [1881-1967]. English phonetician, born in London and educated at Radley and University College Schools. He graduated in mathematics from King's College, Cambridge, in 1903, and received his MA in 1907, the year he was called to the Bar (Lincoln's Inn). However, he never practised law and, even during his legal training, spent time in Paris (part of 1905-6) studying phonetics under Paul Passy, whose niece he married in 1911. He gained an appointment in 1907 at U. College London, the year in which its Department of Phonetics was set up, and worked there for most of his life: as lecturer (1907-14), Reader (1914-21), Professor

(1921-49), and Emeritus Professor (1949-67). He was the leading British phonetician during the first half of the 20c and had a profound effect on the study of pronunciation (for example, as a member of the *BBC Advisory Committee on Spoken English* from its formation in 1926) and was in part responsible for the selection of *Received Pronunciation* or *RP* (which he named in the 1920s) as the norm for radio announcers. Jones collaborated with other scholars in compiling books on the pronunciation of several languages, including Cantonese (1912), Sechuana (now Setswana: 1916), Sinhalese (1919), and Russian (1923). The works for which he is best known are *An English Pronouncing Dictionary* (1917) and *An Outline of English Phonetics* (1918), both of which continue in revised editions. Jones spent most of his life working on phonetic transcription. He thought of the phoneme as a family of related sounds, and therefore differed from his contemporaries in the Prague School who defined it as a bundle of abstract distinctive features such as nasality, plosion, and voice. His views are summed up in *The Phoneme* (1950) and in his papers for the International Phonetic Association (of which he was secretary, 1928-49, and President from 1950), especially *The Principles of the International Phonetic Association* (1949). See index. [BIOGRAPHY, EUROPE, LANGUAGE, SPEECH].   L.T.

JONES, (Sir) William [1746-94]. British philologist and jurist, born in London of Welsh parentage, and educated at Harrow and University College, Oxford. His *Grammar of the Persian Language* (1771) was considered definitive for many years. He studied law and was called to the Bar in 1774, becoming a judge of the high court in Calcutta in 1783. His philological pursuits, interest in Indian legal literature (rare among Europeans of his time), and his liberal political outlook, introduced him to Indian languages, including Sanskrit. He founded the Asiatic Society in 1784, and in his presidential address of 1786 announced his view that 'the *Sanscrit* language . . . bear[s to Greek and Latin] a stronger affinity, both in the roots of verbs, and in the forms of grammar, than could possibly have been produced by accident; so strong indeed, that no philologer could examine them all three, without believing them to have sprung from some common source, which, perhaps, no longer exists. There is a similar reason, though not quite so forcible, for supposing that both the *Gothick* and the *Celtick* . . . had the same origin with the *Sanscrit*; and the old *Persian* might be added to the same family . . .'. By concentrating on systematic resemblances in the form of grammar, accepting that the common source no longer exists, and listing most of the chief language families that descended from that source, this statement embodies the founding principles of the historical study of the Indo-European languages. A recent study is: *The Life and Mind of Oriental Jones: Sir William Jones, the Father of Modern Linguistics*, by Garland Cannon (Cambridge University Press, 1990). See index. [ASIA, BIOGRAPHY, EUROPE, HISTORY, LANGUAGE].

W.F.B.

JONSON, Ben [1572/3-1637]. English poet, actor, dramatist, grammarian, and teacher, probably born in London, and educated at Westminster School. *Every Man in his Humour* (1598) was the first of several comedies, including *Volpone* (1605), *The Alchemist* (1610), and *Bartholomew Fair* (1614). His tragedies *Sejanus* (1603) and *Catiline* (1611) show a desire to respect the facts of Roman history and the conventions of classical drama not typical of contemporary dramatists. Jonson wrote masques for the Court, in collaboration with Inigo Jones; he also introduced the *anti-masque*, a comic prelude in contrast to the formal beauty of the masque. His contemporary prestige was high. He was esteemed as a witty conversationalist, and, although quarrelsome (he killed a fellow actor in a duel), he was convivial and generous. He admired Shakespeare, but could be critical of his work. James I gave him a pension that in effect made him poet laureate, although the title was not then official. His comedies were satirical and pessimistic, giving in blank verse a picture of London life that is vigorous and colloquial rather than beautiful. He caught speech, the technical terms of trades and sects, and named characters descriptively, such as Epicure Mammon, Zeal-of-the-land Busy. His lyrics departed from the prevailing Italian style and, although they used classical forms and allusions, were written largely in familiar everyday English:

> Though I am young, and cannot tell
> Either what Death or Love is well.
> Yet I have heard they both bear darts,
> And both do aim at human hearts.
> And then again I have been told
> Love wounds with heat, as Death with cold;
> So that I fear they do but bring
> Extremes to touch, and mean one thing.
> ('Death and Love')

Jonson disliked exaggerated style, said that Edmund Spenser 'writ no language', and avoided the elaborate conceits of John Donne. He influenced the Cavalier poets of the next generation, who were said to be 'of the tribe of Ben'. He also wrote an *English Grammar . . . for the Benefit of All Strangers, out of his Observation of the English Language now Spoken, and in Use* (published posthumously, 1640). He was

Professor of Rhetoric at Gresham College. See index. [BIOGRAPHY, EUROPE, GRAMMAR, HISTORY, LITERATURE].   R.C.

JORDAN. See ARABIC.

JOURNAL [14c: from Old French *jornal, jurnal* (Modern *journal*), from Latin *diurnalis* daily: compare DIARY]. (1) Originally, a daily record set down in a more elaborate form than a diary. Journals have always been, or purported to be, factual records, even in such literary forms as Daniel Defoe's fictional *Journal of the Plague Year* (1722). (2) In the 18c, a daily newspaper or periodical. Although this was the base of the 19c term *journalism*, as time passed such publications were less and less likely to be called journals. However, as late as 1903, Lord Northcliffe referred to *The Daily Mirror* in a letter as 'a new morning journal'. (3) Also *review*. In the 19c, a collection of related essays, published monthly or quarterly, the medium of respected intellectual comment in the humanities, the sciences, and current affairs: *Blackwood's Magazine* (Edinburgh, 1817), *The Edinburgh Review* (Edinburgh, 1802), *Quarterly Review* (?1809), *The North Briton* (1762), *London Magazine* (1817), and Charles Dickens's *Household Words* (1850). The content of such publications could, however, be varied: the first and the last of these journals serialized major new works of fiction. Only *Blackwoods* survives as a continuous series. The present *London Magazine* was started in 1954. (4) At the present time, the term has two main senses: the private record and the collected series of academic articles, as in *Journal of Linguistics* (Cambridge, 1965), *International Journal of Lexicography* (Oxford, 1988). See NEWSPAPER, PERIODICAL, REVIEW, SERIAL. [MEDIA].   G.H.

JOURNALESE [Late 19c: from *journal(ism)* and *-ese* as in *Japanese*]. A general, usually non-technical term for the way in which journalists write (and speak), or are thought to write (and speak). It is used both neutrally (referring to newspaper style at large) and more often pejoratively (implying that such a style is stereotyped, vulgar, and inclined to debase the language). The *Random House Dictionary* (1987) defines *journalese* as: '(1) a manner of writing or speaking characterized by clichés, occasional neologism, archness, sensationalizing adjectives, unusual or faulty syntax, etc., used by some journalists, esp. certain columnists, and regarded as typical journalistic style; (2) writing or expression in this manner: *Get that journalese out of your copy!* . . . *That word's not English—it's journalese.*'

Background. The characteristics of journalese arise from the nature of newspapers: ephemeral

sheets of paper printed and published to strict deadlines, kept resolutely up-to-the-minute, and designed to attract and stimulate readers whose attention spans, for various reasons, are likely to be short. The profession and the public share a certain cynicism about how this is done:

Journalists who reveal their occupation at parties are frequently greeted with the response: 'Oh, I always wanted to be a journalist. I was very good at English at school'. This invariably provokes a wry smile from the journalist, who knows that being good at English is very far down on the list of skills. The late Nicholas Tomalin, one of the *Sunday Times*'s top reporters, named the three prime qualities for success some years ago. They were, he said, a ratlike cunning, a certain plausibility and a little literary ability. That's still true. I studied English and Drama at university. The drama techniques have probably been of far greater use (Liz Gill, 'Journalese: The Inside Story', *English Today* 11, July 1987).

Technique. Working to a deadline and rendering complex issues into reports of the right length and style produce their own structures, short-cuts, and standards of excellence. When a story is too long for the space available, it is cut, usually from the bottom up. Because of this and the need to get the main points quickly to the browsing reader, reporters pack these points into the first paragraphs. If there is a picture, then the story may be little more than a caption to that picture; when the story is unaccompanied, it stands or falls by its opening statement: the introduction or *intro*. The first sentence is often the most difficult to write. There is a technique known as the *dropped intro*, in which the key statement is delayed for several paragraphs and comes as a punch line, but the danger of delay is that many readers will not persevere far enough to enjoy it. More time can be spent on the intro than on any other part of the article.

Stock expressions. Stories also use *colour*: striking words or graphic details that attract interest. Liz Gill notes:

I remember covering a murder case once in which an old lady was battered to death. As an agency reporter I was deputed by my colleagues to ring up the family of the dead woman for more details. They piled up their ten pences and waited outside the phone box. I spoke at some length to the relatives who, considering their grief, were helpful and patient. At the end of the conversation I came outside and relayed the quotes to the others. Satisfied they drifted away, all except one. When we were alone he whispered the vital question: 'Was she white-haired?' The questioner wanted to write something like: *White-haired granny Mrs X was yesterday found savagely beaten* . . .

Such a style may be praised for its terseness or deplored because it is cliché-ridden and inelegant. It is, however, as deliberate in its own way and for its own purposes as Homer's use of phrases like *grey-eyed Athene* or *cloud-gathering*

Zeus. It provides ways in which people can be recognized and pigeon-holed. The list of stock phrases includes: *bored housewife, broken-hearted clown, devout Catholic, distinguished surgeon, grieving widow*. See EPITHET. Comparably, especially in articles that strive for humour, words are used that relate to the characters or the occupations of the people concerned: when they face problems, teachers get *caned*, cooks are *browned off* or *burn with rage*, doctors might be *sickened*, butchers might be *beefing* about something, or *giving it the chop*.

Clichés. Many clichés and hackneyed expressions derive from or are favoured in newspaper writing, especially in relation to groups that can be stereotyped: *the beautiful people* (for the rich, well-dressed, and occasionally good-looking), *the ivory tower* (for the academic world: often concrete and plate glass), *the rat race* (competitive business), *the party faithful* (for loyal workers and voters for a political party), *mecca* (for any location attracting a particular group, other than for religious purposes, as in *fabulous, surfing mecca*).

Events and actions can be dressed with emotive and romantic words that add colour and are easily slotted into a report: such nouns as *burden, disaster, dream, fantasy, glamour, horror, nightmare, terror*; such adjectives as *amazing, bizarre, cataclysmic, devastating, heart-stopping, heart-warming, horrendous, moving, outrageous, scandalous, shattering, staggering*. Close to such stock words are such stock phrases as the now widely parodied *shock horror, street of shame*, euphemisms like *confirmed bachelor* (a homosexual man), *constant companion* (a lover), *fun-loving* (of a woman: sexually free-and-easy), *good-time girl, party girl* (a prostitute), *mystery girl/man* (someone the press is frantically trying to find out about). Certain syntactic forms also occur so regularly as to be clichés: *amid mounting* (*Amid mounting calls for his resignation, X has decided to tough it out*), appositional *many* (*firemen, many of them wearing masks; mothers, many with children in their arms*), *that was once* (*standing in the ruin that was once central Beirut*). There is a fine dividing line between the everyday sensationalism of popular and tabloid journalism and the parodies in such publications as the British satirical magazine *Private Eye*, which uses proletarianisms in such headlines as *The Royals, dontcha lovem!*

Special uses of words. Because they must be concise and make an immediate impact, journalists often use words in novel ways: (1) *Conversions*. Nouns are often put to use as verbs. Many of the first recorded instances of such changes have occurred in newspapers, especially in the US: *to interview, engineer, boom, boost, surge*. (2) *Attributives*. The use of nouns to qualify other nouns: *death* as in *death car, death ride, death ship*; *top* as in *top politician, top referee, top team*; *rescue* as in *rescue worker, rescue party, rescue team*; *community* as in *community leader, community problems, community relations*. (3) *Compounds*. Certain patterns are commoner in journalese than elsewhere, and may seem artificial because they are rare in speech: *litterbug, holidaymaker, roadhog*. (4) *Reduplicatives*. Such coinages often rhyme, lodge easily in the memory, and sometimes become catch-phrases: *the jet set* (the leisured class which travels frequently); *the brain drain* (exodus of academics), *culture vulture* (someone who indiscriminately 'consumes' culture). (5) *Archaisms*. Because they are short or perceived as popular, certain archaic words survive in newspaper usage: *agog, foe, hustings, scribe, slay*. (6) *Neologisms*. Journalists employ a variety of nonce and stunt forms, some of which are accepted in the language at large: *new-look, see-through, lookalike, lensman, weatherman, vocalist*. (7) *Kinds of modification*. Word combination often leads to strings of adjectives and attributive nouns, a style that began in *Time* magazine in the 1920s, with the aim of providing impact and 'colour'. They may be relatively short (*London-born disc jockey Ray Golding . . .*) or long enough to become self-parodies, either pre-modifying a name (*silver-haired, paunchy lothario, Francesco Tebaldi . . .*) or post-modifying it (*Zsa Zsa Gabor, seventyish, eight-times-married, Hungarian-born celebrity . . .*).

Immediacy of style. (1) *Short vernacular words*. Because of the need for conciseness and impact, journalists favour monosyllables and disyllables: *poll* for 'election'; *blast* for 'explosion'; *jobless* for 'unemployed'; *homeless* for 'destitute'. (2) *Emotive and inflated expressions*. The urge to promote excitement leads, especially in headlines, to such emotive and often inflated usage as: *fever* for 'excitement' (*World Cup fever grips Barcelona*); *rage* or *fury* for 'anger' (*Fury over Poll Tax*); *stricken* or *crippled* for 'disabled' (*stricken tanker adrift in Med*); *glory* for any sporting achievement (*glory day for Tottenham*); *storm* and *row* for 'controversy' (*storm over price-hikes; Cabinet row over inflation*). (3) *Quasi-illiterate usages*. For effect, some writers and publications, especially in Britain, favour eye dialect that suggests solidarity among philistines: *gonna, loadsamoney, showbiz, whodunnit, dontcha, wanna, wotalotigot*. (4) *Innuendo*. Especially in the tabloids, hints that are more or less explicitly muscular or sexual innuendo are often employed, especially as metaphors: *firm, harden, spurt, spill over, selling climax*. (5) *Allusive punning*. There appears to be a general increase in the use of a kind of punning allusion traditionally acceptable in US journalism but avoided in Britain: 'TV or Not TV' (*The Times*, 16 Oct. 1989); 'Moore's the pity', 'Know Your Rites', 'Heirs and Graces' (*The Listener*, 16 June 1988); 'Drapes of things to come', 'A test of skull on the Thames' (*The Times*, 26 July 1988); 'breaking into new arias' (*New Statesman*, 24 June 1988). See JOURNAL, JOURNALISM, PUN. [MEDIA, STYLE].   G.H., T.MCA.

JOURNALISM [Early 19c: from French *journalisme*. See JOURNAL]. The enterprise of producing newspapers and magazines (including reporting, writing, editing, photographing, and managing) as well as the styles of writing used in such publications. The term came into use some two centuries after the practice had started. From the 18c, there were basically two styles: the elegant and ornate 'high' style of Joseph Addison, Richard Steele, Samuel Johnson, and the other essayists, and the 'low' style of the so-called Grub Street hacks. Daniel Defoe is often regarded as the first journalist, as distinct from the man of letters. With the rise of the popular press in the 19c, the more fashionable alternative terms were the *higher journalism* (Matthew Arnold's term) and the *gutter press*. To a large extent these modes are perpetuated in the division of modern British journalism into the *quality press* and the *tabloids*. By the mid-19c, the term was starting to fall into disrepute, to imply rather superficial social and political commentary and a style which was less than exemplary. In England in 1879, George Eliot commented rather scornfully on 'Journalistic guides to the popular mind', while *journalese*, recorded from 1882, was defined by the *OED* c.1900 as ' "newspaper" or "penny-a-liner's" English'. The term *journalism* continues throughout the English-speaking world to retain a tinge of disapproval, and most of the epithets applied to the profession (such as *hacks, muckrackers, rat packs, reptiles, scribblers*) are uncomplimentary.

It was, however, from the early 19c to the First World War that journalism enjoyed its greatest influence. Editors were raised to virtually legendary status, their editorials or 'leaders' being regarded as models of stylistic elegance and political authority, with an impact on current affairs which has never been surpassed. Especially under the editorship of Thomas Barnes, *The Times* became such a powerful voice in Britain (promoting the Reform Bill and condemning the Corn Laws) that by 1829 it had earned the sobriquet *The Thunderer*. Among other prominent names are C. P. Scott of *The Manchester Guardian*, J. L. Garvin of *The Observer*, and W. T. Stead of the *Pall Mall Gazette*. Both

Samuel Coleridge and Benjamin Disraeli served as leader-writers for the *Morning Post*, which also published poems by William Wordsworth, Thomas Hardy, and Rudyard Kipling. Although editors are not so strongly associated with newspapers in the US as in the UK, the names of Ambrose Bierce, A. J. Liebling, H. L. Mencken, Lincoln Steffens, and Tom Wolfe are especially notable in American journalism.

Newspapers will do whatever is necessary to catch and hold readers at the level at which they operate. 'Serious' or 'quality' newspapers cater to a minority with a higher level of education and interest. This minority is willing to read lengthy articles and expects a quasi-literary quality in what it reads. 'Popular' newspapers are aimed at the un-literary majority in any area. Many of their readers have no special interest in language and little time or inclination for detail. They also often have a great interest in social events and sport, and in the human side of the entertainment business. There is therefore a greater emphasis on 'gossip' and 'inside stories' than in the 'heavies' (the serious papers), although these also carry more muted versions of the same thing, often in the form of reviews. Adapting to their markets, newspapers differ in physical terms (with preferred formats such as *broadsheet* or *tabloid*; preferred headline styles; longer or shorter stories and features) and in the linguistic style that appeals to their target readerships.

The tradition of trenchant freelance political journalism founded by Defoe and continued by John Wilkes in the 18c was maintained in the 19c by William Cobbett and Charles Dickens. In the 20c, the emphasis has moved from the editors who run newspapers to the enterpreneurs who own them, while new kinds of journalism have developed, contrasting *print journalists* with *radio journalists* and *television journalists*. See JOURNAL, JOURNALESE, NEWSMAGAZINE, NEWSPAPER, PRESS, QUALITY PRESS, TABLOID, YELLOW PRESS. [MEDIA, WRITING].   G.H.

Cranfield, G. A. 1978. *The Press and Society*. London: Longman.
Mott, Frank Luther. 1967. *American Journalism*. New York: Macmillan.
Smith, Anthony. 1980. *Goodbye Gutenberg: The Newspaper Revolution of the 1980s*. Oxford: University Press.
Waterhouse, Keith. 1989. *On Newspaper Style*. London & New York: Viking Penguin.
Williams, Raymond. 1975. *The Long Revolution*. Harmondsworth: Penguin.

JOYCE, James (Augustine Aloysius) [1882–1941]. Irish teacher and writer, born in Dublin, and educated at Jesuit schools and U. College, Dublin. He left Ireland in 1904 and, apart from a few brief visits, lived abroad for the rest of his life, mainly in Paris, Trieste, and Zurich. He supported himself for years by teaching English as a foreign language. Even after he achieved fame, he suffered from poverty and his eyesight steadily deteriorated. Despite his 'exile', Dublin was the background of all his work. He published a volume of poems, *Chamber Music* (1907), and his first important work was *Dubliners* (1914), a series of sketches of Dublin life rich in symbolism and giving an impression of inhibition and paralysis: some of the characters come to new understanding but seem unable to act and change their lives. These moments of revelation (called 'epiphanies' in the unfinished *Stephen Hero*) are important in *A Portrait of the Artist as a Young Man* (1916), an autobiographical novel that follows Stephen Dedalus until he rejects his background and goes abroad. A play, *Exiles* (1918), was not a notable success. Joyce's innovations emerge fully in *Ulysses* (1922). In episodes based loosely on the books of Homer's *Odyssey*, the novel follows Leopold Bloom through a whole day in Dublin. By representing events largely through Bloom's thoughts, Joyce broke away from the narrative tradition and allowed free association of impressions (*stream of consciousness*) to present the story. *Finnegans Wake* (1939) follows a night of dreams in the mind of H. C. Earwicker.

There is progression in style from the plain narrative of *Dubliners* to the dream sequence of *Finnegans Wake*. The use of the stream of consciousness begins with Stephen Dedalus, develops with Leopold Bloom, and becomes a prolonged inner monologue from Marion Bloom at the end of *Ulysses*; then follow the shifting patterns of Earwicker's dream. Aware of psychoanalysis, Joyce used free association and the prompting of unconscious desires to an extent that caused *Ulysses* to be banned as obscene. Behind his characters, he evoked themes and images from many sources, notably Homer, Shakespeare, Irish legends, and Roman Catholicism, whose influence he repudiated but never lost. His linguistic invention was prodigious and included such puns as 'half a league wrongwards' (for the Charge of the Light Brigade), such neologisms, often multilingual, as *mainhur* (a blend of 'mein Herr' and 'menhir'), and such comic assonances and blends as 'Dion Boucciacault' as *Dinosboozycough* and 'Pidgin English' as *pigeony linguish*. Other features are the writing of compounds as single words (*goathead, riverbed, streetorgan*), the use of dashes rather than quotation marks for direct speech (in the French style), and a section of *Ulysses* presented as a dramatic script. For *Finnegans Wake*, the hardest of his books to follow, he drew on many European tongues. It often suggests linguistic virtuosity for its own sake, but is built around recurring themes and has a quality

of 'word music'. Musical form underlies much of Joyce's writing and reflects his early home background. Widely considered the greatest 20c innovator in the language, he may be called a comic writer: causing laughter and presenting a basically affirmative view of humanity through looking clearly at its weaknesses. See index. [BIOGRAPHY, EUROPE, LITERATURE, STYLE]. R.C.

JUDEZMO. See JEWISH LANGUAGES, ROMANCE LANGUAGES, SPANISH.

JUNCTURE [14c: from Latin *iunctura* a joint]. In phonetics, the manner in which successive vowels and consonants are linked. Differences of juncture depend on syllable division, as with *nitrate* and *night rate*. In *nitrate*, close juncture runs the /t/ and /r/ together in one syllable. In *night rate*, the syllables belong to different words, normally kept apart by open juncture. However, when said quickly, the two forms have the same close juncture. The phrases *ice cream* and *I scream* are comparable in those accents in which both open with the same vowel. Juncture does not necessarily follow grammar: in *be/droom* and *bee/troot*, the open juncture comes before /d, t/ instead of after them, and the phrase *at all* is normally pronounced *a tall*. See SYLLABLE. [SPEECH]. G.K.

JUSTIFYING [18–19c in this sense]. A printer's term for making a line of type a certain length, normally by adjusting the space between words (but sometimes also between letters, especially in narrow measures), chiefly so that the lines of a column or page have straight margins on the right as well as the left. When this is done, the lines are said to be *justified*. When the margin is straight on the left and uneven on the right, the type is said to be *unjustified* or *ragged right*. Although a straight right margin may be pleasing to the eye, justifying sometimes reduces legibility, especially in narrow columns, and may lead to awkward word-divisions. See TYPOGRAPHY. [TECHNOLOGY]. T.MCA.

JUTES. According to the chronicler Bede (c.730), the name of a Germanic tribe which, with the Angles and Saxons, invaded Britain in the 5c and settled in Kent and part of the south coast, including the Isle of Wight. The Angles appear to have come from Schleswig and the Saxons from western Holstein and the north German coast from the Elbe westward. Since the Angles lived between the Saxons and the Jutes, the Jutes appear to have come from further north, probably the Jutland peninsula in Denmark, which may be named after them. See ANGLO-SAXON, KENTISH, OLD ENGLISH[1]. [EUROPE, HISTORY, NAME]. P.C.

K

K, k [Called 'kay', rhyming with *say*.] The 11th letter of the Roman alphabet as used for English. It originated in the Phoenician consonant *kap*, which was adopted as *kappa* for Greek. It reached the Romans via the Etruscans, but was little used in Latin, in which *C* and *Q* were preferred as symbols for the voiceless velar stop /k/. The transliteration of Greek *K* into *C* was standard: *comma* not *komma*, *Socrates* not *Sokrates*. When *c* acquired a soft value before *e* and *i* in later Latin and the Romance languages, *k* was available to represent hard *c* in those positions, and was so adopted by most of the Germanic languages. Old English, however, normally used *c* for /k/ (as in *cwic*, *cyning* for what later became *quick*, *king*), with *k* as an occasional variant. After 1066, under the influence of Norman-French spelling, both letters were widely used, but after a period of uncertainty (*could* being spelt both *coude*, *koude*) fairly distinct functions emerged for *c* and *k*, according to position and context.

Sound value and distribution. In English, *k* normally represents a voiceless velar stop, whose voiced equivalent is *g*. It is typically used: (1) Before *e*, *i*: *kennel*, *keep*, *kit*, *kind*, *sketch*, *skirt*, *skin*. It occurs more rarely before other vowel letters (chiefly after *s*) in long-established English words: *skate*, *skull*, *sky* (contrast *scale*, *Scot*, *scud*). (2) After a long vowel (*take*, *break*, *meek*, *like*, *soak*, *broke*, *duke*) as well as after *oo* (*book*, *cook*). Further syllables may follow (*naked*, *token*). (3) In conjunction with preceding *c* after a short vowel, *ck* having the function of a doubled *c* or *k*: *sack*, *wreck*, *lick*, *mock*, *duck*; *bracken*, *reckon*, *wicked*, *rocket*, *bucket*. (4) After other consonants which follow a short vowel (whose value may be modified and lengthened before *l*, *r*, *w*): *walk*, *whelk*, *folk*, *milk*, *hulk*, *frank*, *pink*, *lark*, *jerk*, *ask*, *desk*, *hawk*; *sparkle*, *whisker*.

Exotic and innovative usages. (1) Recently coined or borrowed words use *k* without positional restrictions: names for exotic creatures, such as *kangaroo*, *koala*, have *k*, not *c*, before *a*, *o*, and *yak*, *trek* lack the usual *c* between short vowel and *k*. (2) *K* may be doubled between vowels in such words as *yakkity-yak* and *trekking*. (3) For visual effect, *c* and *q* are sometimes changed to *k*: as trade names (*Kleenex*, based on *clean*) and businesses (*Kwik-Fit*, based on *quick*). The change may take place for facetious, humorous, or sinister purposes: *Krazy Kats*, *Ku Klux Klan*. (4) Foreign names commonly occur with *k* in untypical positions: *Kaiser*, *Kremlin*, *Kuwait*.

Digraphs. (1) *Ck* is not a digraph in the sense of a combination creating a new pronunciation, but is common after short vowels in vernacular words (*black*, not **blac* or **blak*), although the loanwords *bloc*, *chic*, and *dak*, *flak* occur. (2) *Kh* may constitute a digraph by representing a voiceless velar fricative /x/, rather as in ScoE *loch*, transliterating Russian *x* (*Kharkov*, *Khrushchev*) and similar sounds in other languages. However, in such words, the *h* is commonly ignored, and *kh* is pronounced as /k/: *khaki*, *khan*, *khedive*, *astrakhan*.

Silent *K*. (1) In Old and Middle English, initial *c* or *k* (like its voiced equivalent *g*) could be pronounced immediately before *n*: see OLD ENGLISH[1]. In this position, *k* has since fallen silent, but has been retained in writing in some twenty forms that include *knave*, *knee*, *knife*, *knot*, *knuckle*. This orthographic feature strikingly distinguishes several pairs of homophones: *knave/nave*, *knight/night*, *know/no*. (2) In isolated cases, *ck* or *k* has been assimilated or elided before another consonant, as in *blackguard* ('blaggard') and *Cockburn* ('Coburn').

Variations. (1) *K* is inserted before vowels in inflected forms and derivatives of verbs ending

THE CAPITAL LETTER						THE SMALL LETTER				
EARLY FORMS				CURRENT FORMS		EARLY FORMS			CURRENT FORMS	
Phoenician	Greek	Etruscan	Roman (Latin)	roman	italic	Roman cursive	Roman uncial	Carolingian minuscule	roman	italic
↓𐤊	𐤊K	𐌊	K	K	*K*	K	ʀ	k	k	*k*

in *c*: *bivouacked, picknicker, panicking* (but note *arced* not **arcked*, from *to arc*). (2) It occurs before *e* and *i* in place of a *c* in a related word or form: *cat/kitten, cow/kine, joke/jocular, curb/kerb, curfew/kerchief.* (3) It has been replaced in *ake*, which is now *ache*. (4) It has disappeared from *made*, which was formerly *maked.* (5) It no longer occurs in forms ending in *-ic*: *logic, music*, which were formerly *logick, musick.* (6) *Taken* has the poetic spelling *ta'en*, reflecting a common pronunciation in dialect in England and Scotland. (7) The letter *x* has replaced *cks* in *coxcomb* and *ck* in *coxswain*, while *bucksome* was one of many earlier forms of *buxom*. In India, it sometimes replaces the Romanized Sanskrit *ksh*, the names *Lakshman, Lakshmi* becoming *Laxman, Laxmi.* (8) For humorous, commercial purposes, such spellings as *socks* can become *sox*. (9) Alternations with *c* and *qu* in various combinations arise in loans from French: *block/bloc, manikin/mannequin, racket/racquet.* (10) BrE *barque, cheque, chequer, disc, kerb, mollusc, sceptic* are usually written *bark, check, checker, disk, curb, mollusk, skeptic* in AmE. However, some similar pairs of words are of distinct meaning and origin: *arc/ark, scull/skull.* See ALPHABET, C, LETTER[1], SPELLING, X. [WRITING]. C.U.

KAMTOK [1980s: a blend of *Cameroon* and *talk*. See TALK, TOK PISIN]. The English-based pidgin of Cameroon, widely used for at least 100 years. When the Germans annexed the region in 1884, they found it so well established as a lingua franca that they produced a phrase book in pidgin for their soldiers. Its speakers usually call it *pidgin* or *country talk* and linguists refer to it as *Cameroon(ian) Pidgin (English)*, but recently the media has begun to use *Kamtok*, to stress that it is local and useful, despite having no official status. It is the easternmost of a group of pidgins and creoles in West Africa that includes Gambian Aku (Talk), Sierra Leone Krio, Ghanaian Pidgin, and Nigerian Pidgin, and is a mother tongue on plantations, in some urban settlements, and in families where the parents speak different languages. It is, however, rarely if ever the only mother tongue. Kamtok has various forms, reflecting the age, education, regional provenance, mother tongue, and linguistic proficiency of its users. Its literary use is complicated by three different sets of orthographic conventions: semi-phonetic (*Wi di waka kwik kwik*), English-based (*We dee walka quick quick*), and French-based (*Oui di waka quouik quouik*). It has been used by the media, in Bible and other religious translation, and in creative writing, uses that may lead to standardization. It has relatively high prestige, and is preferred informally among Africans of different ethnic groups, ranking just below French and English as a vehicle for mobility from rural villages into modern urban life. Special varieties include *Grassfield* or, more usually, *Grafi* (among the Bamileke), *Pidgin-Maqueraux* (urban street slang), and an offshoot of Krio in Limbe (formerly Victoria) and in the African Baptist Church, in which Krio speakers played a prominent role in the 19c. The former British West Cameroon has extensive influence from Nigerian Pidgin and standard English, while in the east there is more influence from French.

Features. (1) *Pronunciation.* Kamtok is non-rhotic and syllable-timed. It has seven vowels /i, e, ɛ, a, ɔ, o, u/ and four diphthongs /ei, ai, au, oi/. General English central vowels are replaced, schwa becoming /a/ as in /fada/ for *father*, /ɜ/ becoming /ɔ/ as in /tʃɔs/ for *church*, and /ʌ/ becoming /a/ or /ɔ/ as in /graunat/ for *groundnut* and /bɔt/ for *but*. Centring diphthongs are reinterpreted, so that *beer* is /bia/, *air* is /ea/ or /e/, *sure* is /ʃua/. Consonant clusters tend to be simplified, as in /tori/ for *story*, /maʃ/ for *smash*, or to be broken up by an intrusive vowel, as in /sipia/ for *spear* and /sikin/ for *skin*. (2) *Grammar.* Plurality is assumed from context, as in *tu pikin* two children, or indicated by the third-person plural pronoun *dem*, as in *ma pikin dem* my children. Time and aspect are either deduced from the context or indicated by a number of auxiliaries: *a bin go* I went; *i go go* he will go; *we wan go* we almost went; *wuna di go* you (plural) are going; *yu sabi chop* you habitually eat. Adjectives and verbs are structurally similar: *a big* I'm big, *a waka* I walk, *a go big* I'll be big, *a go waka* I'll walk, *som big man* a big man, *som waka man* a walker. Serial verbs are widely used: *I ron go rich di haus kam* He ran as far as the house and came back. Questions are marked by intonation alone (*I no go kam?* Will he/she not come?) or by a question initiator followed by a declarative form (*Usai i bin go?* Where did he/she go?). (3) *Vocabulary.* Most Kamtok words are from English, but many have been widened in meaning: *buk* a book, letter, anything written; *savi buk* ('know book') educated. There are many loan translations from local languages: *krai dai* ('cry die') a wake or funeral celebration; *tai han* ('tie hand') meanness. Non-English vocabulary relates to culture and kinship: *ngɔmbi* a ghost, spirit of the dead, *danshiki* a tunic-like shirt, *mbanya* co-wife in a polygamous family, *mbombo* someone with the same name as someone else, *njamanjama* green vegetables. See CAMEROON, CAMFRANGLAIS, WEST AFRICAN PIDGIN ENGLISH. [AFRICA, VARIETY]. L.T., C.G.

KANAKA ENGLISH. See AUSTRALIAN PIDGIN.

KANNADA, also **Kannarese**. A Dravidian language of south India. It is spoken by some 37m people, and has a script based on southern Brahmi. Inscriptions in Kannada date from the 5c, and its grammatical tradition from the 11c. Kannada is one of the 15 major languages of India and the state language of Karnataka (formerly Mysore). Kannada literature has a close relationship with Sanskrit, from which, unlike Tamil, it has assimilated many words; Kannada writers exploit to the full the style range provided by borrowings from Sanskrit, Persian, and English. See BISOCIATION, DRAVIDIAN ENGLISH, INDIA, INDIAN LANGUAGES. [ASIA, LANGUAGE].   Y.K.

KELVINSIDE.   See   MORNINGSIDE   AND KELVINSIDE.

KENSINGTON [*c.*1900]. Also **Kensingtonian, Kensington Hay**. An affected or overly refined accent considered typical of the middle-class residents of the London borough of Kensington: 'Hilda had been deprived of her Five Towns [Staffordshire] accent at Chetwynd's School, where the purest Kensingtonian was inculcated' (Arnold Bennett, *Hilda Lessways*, 1911); 'her Kensingtonian "mothah and brothah" ' (*Times Literary Supplement*, 1936); 'the manner is brusque and voice exaggerated Kensington' (J. Lock, *Lady Policeman*, 1968). The phrase *Kensington Hay* satirizes both the affected pronunciation of 'high' as in *Kensington High Street*, and the aspirations of the speakers. Compare MORNINGSIDE AND KELVINSIDE, SLOANE RANGER. [EUROPE, SPEECH, VARIETY].   T.MCA.

KENTISH. A dialect of Old English, known in the 8c only from names in Latin charters but in the 9c as a language used for the charters themselves. It may have descended from the speech of the Jutes, who are said to have settled in Kent in the 5c. See DIALECT IN ENGLAND, JUTES, STRANG. [EUROPE, HISTORY, VARIETY].   T.MCA.

KENYA. Official titles: Swahili *Jamhuri ya Kenya*, English *Republic of Kenya*. A country of East Africa and member of the Commonwealth. Currency: the shilling/shillingi (100 cents/senti). Capital: Nairobi. Population: 23m (1988), 36m (projection for 2000). Ethnicity: Kikuyu, Luhya, Luo, Kalejin, Kamba, Kisii, Meru. Religions: Protestant 38%, Roman Catholic 28%, traditional 26%, Muslim 6%. Languages: Swahili (official), English (second), indigenous languages. Education: primary 69%, secondary 20%, tertiary 1%, literacy 59%. British control of Kenya was established by the Berlin Conference in 1885. The *British East African Protectorate* was established in 1895, opening the way to European settlers, especially in the area known as the *White Highlands*. In 1920, Kenya became a British colony. In 1944, African participation in politics was permitted. The Mau Mau rebellion lasted from 1952 to 1960 and Kenya gained its independence in 1963. English was the official language immediately after independence, but a constitutional amendment in 1969 instituted the use of Swahili in the National Assembly. In 1974, Swahili replaced English as the official language. At the time, President Jomo Kenyatta stated:

The basis of any independent government is a national language, and we can no longer continue aping our former colonizers. . . . I do know that some people will start murmuring that the time is not right for this decision; to hell with such people! Those who feel they cannot do without English can as well pack up and go (public address, Nairobi, 1974).

English is, however, the language of higher education and of professional and social status, used by most senior administrators and military officers. The 1967 curriculum focuses on mathematics, science, and English, which is valued as the language of modernity and mobility, often used to express authority, even at the family level, if the parents know it. The mixing of English, Swahili, and the indigenous languages is common. The first newspaper in Kenya was the *African Standard* (established in 1902), now known as the *Standard*. Other English-language publications are the *Daily Nation* (established in 1960) and the *Weekly Review*. Both the Voice of Kenya radio and Kenyan TV broadcast in English as well as Swahili. Contemporary writers include Ngugi wa Thiong'o (b.1938) and Mugo Gatheru (b.1925). In terms of its linguistic features, Kenyan English is usually considered part of East African English, but the authenticity and homogeneity of both the regional and the national variety are currently controversial matters in Kenya.

The following points can, however, be made with some confidence: (1) In pronunciation, Kenyan English is non-rhotic. (2) The fricatives /θ,ð/ are generally replaced by the stops /t,d/: 'tree of dem' for *three of them*. (3) Affricates tend to become fricatives: 'inrisht' for *enriched*, 'hwis' for *which*, 'jos' for *judge*. (4) The consonants /b, v/ are often devoiced: 'laf' for *love* and 'rup' or 'rop' for *rub*. (5) The sounds /f, p/ may be hypercorrected to their voiced counterparts, *laughing* and *loving* becoming homophones as 'lavin'. (6) Final -*l* is often deleted: 'andastandebu' for *understandable*, 'loko' for *local*, 'pipu' for *people*. (7) Usually uncountable nouns are often countable: *Thank you for your many advices*; *We eat a lot of breads*; *I held the child on my laps*; *A lady with big bums is attractive*. (8) The semantic range of some words has been extended: *dry* (of coffee) without milk or sugar, *medicine* chemicals, *hear* to feel (pain), to understand (language). (9) Loanwords and loan translations from indigenous languages are common: *panga* a machete, *sufuria* a cooking pot, *sima* cornmeal paste, *clean heart* without guile. Local usage is discussed in W. H. Whiteley, *Language in Kenya* (Nairobi: Oxford University Press, 1974). See EAST AFRICAN ENGLISH, NGUGI, SWAHILI. [AFRICA, NAME, VARIETY]. C.L.N., L.T.

KERSEY, John. 18c English lexicographer, credited with compiling *A New English Dictionary* (J.K., 1702), the first dictionary to include the ordinary words of the language, such as *apple*, *bold*, and *forget*. Where earlier dictionaries had concentrated on bookish hard words, the 1702 volume was aimed at those who needed a dictionary to learn to spell, and it boasted the inclusion of words 'now commonly used either in speech, or in the familiar way of writing letters'. In its patently defective definitions ('To *Flow*, as the Tide, &c.', 'A *Lurker*, in Corners'), the dictionary had much in common with the spelling books of the time, and the compiler quarried bilingual dictionaries for the common words he could not find elsewhere. In 1706, Kersey produced a thoroughly revised and much enlarged edition of the *New World of Words*, originally published by Edward Phillips in 1658. His *Dictionarium Britannicum* (1708), based on that work, was the first abridged dictionary of English. See DICTIONARY. [BIOGRAPHY, EUROPE, REFERENCE]. N.E.O.

KEY. See CODE, CRYPTOGRAPHY, KEYBOARD, KEYWORD, LEGEND, QWERTY, TYPEWRITER.

KEYBOARD [19c: compare *switchboard, signal board*]. A general and technical term for a complete set of keys on a musical instrument (accordion, organ, piano) and such printing equipment as typesetting machines, typewriters, and computers. On traditional typewriters, the keys are connected mechanically to pieces of type that strike ink through a ribbon on to the surface of a sheet of paper. In computing, the keys are square buttons set in a board that have no mechanical impact on a surface; instead, they transmit a signal to the computer's central processing unit. Such sets of keys include the letters of a variety of the Roman alphabet (as used for English, French, etc.) or comparable symbols in other systems.

Basic keys. English-language keyboards have 26 letters, ten numerical digits (0 to 9), punctuation marks, and a variable set of such marks as @, $, %, &, *, and +. A *shift key* doubles the function of the other keys by converting lower-case to upper-case letters and in some cases making

alternative symbols available. A *tab key* tabulates by locating the work at pre-set indentions. A (*space*) *bar* marks spaces between words. The *return* key brings the carriage of a typewriter back so that work can begin on the next line or, on a computer keyboard, opens a new line or executes a function or command. In addition to the basic alphanumeric keys, the keyboard of a computer has a number of cursor, command, and function keys.

Cursor keys. The *cursor* [Latin: runner] is a flashing symbol whose position indicates where one can work at any time on the screen. It can be moved around the screen by means of *cursor keys* that are located as a distinct group, as part of a numerical keypad, or both. They can also *scroll* up or down line by line through a file, bringing earlier or later parts of a text into view, or move screen-sized 'pages' or a whole document up or down through such functions as *page up, page down, home, end*.

Command keys. The set of *command keys* extends the functions of other keys. It includes *control* (short forms *c* or *ctrl*), which controls the function of another key, *alternate* (*alt*), which specifies an alternative function, and *escape* (*esc*), which indicates to the computer that any key pressed after it has a different function from before. They are like shift keys in typewriters, in that they double the functions of the other keys, and when used in combination can provide characters not visible on the keyboard, such as Greek letters. The *delete* key (*del*) erases material a word, a line, or a block at a time, depending on the specific instruction.

Function keys. The set of *function keys*, of which there are ten on most standard keyboards, usually placed above the other keys on the board, are operated either by themselves or with the command keys to give specific instructions to the computer. These functions vary from one program to another: for example, in WordPerfect, the key *F7* used alone saves (stores) text while one is working on it, whereas a combination of the shift key with F7 will begin a procedure for printing a document. In Nota Bene, F7 used alone will provide access to a number of 'windows' on which one can work on different texts or files simultaneously. In combination with control it will store specific words in an index.

Variety and complexity. Because of the variety of programs available, and the lack of a standard for functions and commands, the function arrangements of the keyboard must currently be relearned for each new word-processing program, and the training required for keyboarding is consequently highly specialized. This situation is made more complex by the sheer variety of specialized functions in the various programs, covering such things as typefaces, sorting, indexing, and layout. Because of this, the keyboard becomes the site of an extraordinary range of tasks and applications. A standard 84-character keyboard can now provide hundreds of different instructions to the processing unit of a computer.

Keyboarding. Because of the dominance of both typewriter and computer in the late 20c, a knowledge of the keyboard has become increasingly important in many occupations, and for many people ability to use a keyboard is part of literacy. The verb *to keyboard* applies to *keying in* data to a computer, and a person engaged in such work is a *keyboarder*. A satisfactory speed on a standard keyboard is 60 words per minute, but speeds of up to 149 words in sustained work have been recorded. A recent development has been the use of interactive computer screens as modified keyboards; touching the screen causes computers to receive information. Light pens and optical scanning devices have reduced reliance on keyboards and numerical keypads for inputting data, and separate devices for manipulating the cursor, such as the electronic mouse, the trackerball, and the slate (for handwriting), complement, extend, or replace the standard unit. See COMPUTING, DIACRITIC, QWERTY, TYPEWRITER. [TECHNOLOGY].   W.W.B.

KEYWORD, also key word [1850s]. (1) A word that serves as a crucial ('key') element in a usage, phrase, sentence, text, subject, concept, theory, or language: *A Dictionary of Key Words—800 key words that an intermediate student of English needs to know, because they cause difficulty, combine with other words to make new meanings, form the basic structures of English grammar, express ideas that are often needed* (Mary Edwards, 1985); *Keywords: A Vocabulary of Culture and Society*, by Raymond Williams (Fontana/ Croom Helm, 1976), a work in the form of a glossary of such words as *alienation, career, empirical, fiction, humanity, nationalist*, and *science*, described in the introduction as 'the record of an inquiry into a *vocabulary*: a shared body of words and meanings in our most general discussion, in English, of the practices and institutions which we group as *culture* and society'. (2) A significant word for a person or group: 'Self-reliance and self-care were the keywords' (Mary Kenny, 'Paying the Price of Feminism', *Sunday Telegraph*, 6 Nov. 1988). (3) A technical term for a term in a list through which it is possible to search an index, catalogue, filing system, or database: *For 'deponent', go to LANGUAGE then LATIN then GRAMMAR then*

VERB. (4) Also *catchword.* A term in library science for a memorable or important word or term in the title, text, or abstract of an item being indexed and therefore used in the index entry. (5) A term in cryptography for a word that is crucial in the enciphering or deciphering of a coded message. Compare CATCHWORD. [REFERENCE, WORD].   T.MCA.

KINESICS [1950s: from Greek *kinēsis* movement and *-ics* as in *economics*]. The study of body movements, gestures, and facial expression as forms of communication, sometimes regarded as a branch of *semiotics.* See BODY LANGUAGE, COMMUNICATION, GESTURE, SEMIOTICS. [LANGUAGE].   T.MCA.

KINGMAN REPORT. A British report on the teaching of English in England and Wales, presented in 1988 to the Secretary of State for Education by the Committee of Inquiry into Teaching of English Language under the chairmanship of Sir John Kingman. The Committee was asked to recommend a model to serve as a basis for training teachers in how the language works and to inform professional discussion, to consider how far the model should be made explicit to pupils, and to recommend what pupils should know about how English works. The model which it produced has four parts: the forms of the language; communication and comprehension; acquisition and development; historical and geographical variation. It has been criticized as a checklist of linguistic topics without an internal dynamic connecting the parts, or relating them to educational processes. Nonetheless, some of the Committee's arguments prepared the way for a greater emphasis on knowledge about language in the National Curriculum requirements for England and Wales (1989) than in previous curriculum discussion. See BULLOCK REPORT, COX REPORT, NEWBOLT REPORT, STANDARD ENGLISH, TEACHING ENGLISH. [EDUCATION, EUROPE].   C.J.B.

KING'S ENGLISH [16c: apparently by analogy from such expressions as *the king's coin*]. A traditional term in Britain that is earlier than, and more or less synonymous with, *standard English*: 'an old abusing of Gods patience and the Kings English' (Shakespeare, *The Merry Wives of Windsor*, 1. 4; 1598). It is altered to *the Queen's English* when the monarch is a woman: 'Plea for the Queen's English' (title of a work by Henry Alford, 1869, in the reign of Victoria). Formerly invested with considerable respect, the term has in recent years been used less reverently: for example, in *The Queen's English: High Taw Tawk Prawpah-leah* (ostensibly by Sir Vere

Brayne-d'Hemmidge and Lady Mayna Brayne-d'Hemmidge: London, Michael Joseph, 1985), the humorist Dorgan Rushton satirizes the accent technically referred to as 'advanced RP', mainly by means of eye dialect in which *shouting* is represented as 'shiteing', *family* as 'fear-mealy', and *taxi* as 'tex-yah'. The book comes with a bookmark to be gripped between the teeth as an aid to a 'proper' clipped articulation. See ADVANCED, CLIPPED, EYE DIALECT, KING'S ENGLISH (THE), LONDON, QUEEN'S ENGLISH SOCIETY, RECEIVED PRONUNCIATION, STANDARD, STANDARD ENGLISH. [EUROPE, STYLE, VARIETY].   T.MCA.

KING'S ENGLISH, The. A usage manual published in 1906 by the brothers Henry W. Fowler and Francis G. Fowler. It was aimed at writers who 'seldom look into a grammar or composition book', people who found grammars repellent because 'they must give much space to the obvious or the unnecessary', while composition books 'are often useless because they enforce their warnings only by fabricated blunders against which every tiro feels himself quite safe'. In 370 pages, the ten sections of *TKE* contain articles on vocabulary (concrete versus abstract words, malapropisms, loanwords, slang, etc.), syntax (relative pronouns, gerunds, *shall/will*, prepositions, etc.), what the Fowlers call 'Airs and Graces' (archaism, elegant variation, inversion, metaphor, etc.), punctuation, euphony, quotations and misquotations, meaning, ambiguity, and style. Most sections are supported by illustrative examples drawn from unfabricated sources, in particular from unspecified 19c works by Meredith, Thackeray, George Eliot, and others, and from Victorian or Edwardian issues (exact dates not specified) of *The Times*, *The Daily Telegraph*, and *The Guernsey Evening Press* (the brothers lived on Guernsey). At one stage, the work was to be called 'The New Solecist for literary tiros' (after *The Solecist* of the Greek rhetorician Lucian of Samosata, 2c) or 'The Book of Solecisms for journalists, novelists, & schoolboys'. More than any earlier usage book, *TKE* introduced a new national pastime—the hunting and exhibiting of solecisms. Henry was the *crème de la crème* of schoolmasters and with his brother Francis placed Britain, and soon English-speaking communities abroad, in a new schoolroom. Writers of English everywhere became aware of a voice commanding them to mend their ways. See DICTIONARY OF MODERN ENGLISH USAGE, FOWLER, KING'S ENGLISH. Compare AMERICAN LANGUAGE (THE). [EUROPE, REFERENCE, STYLE].   RO.W.B.

KING'S SCOTS. See SCOTS.

KIPLING, Joseph Rudyard [1865-1936]. English journalist, novelist, and poet. Born in Bombay, India. Went to England as a child in 1871 and, after five unhappy years with a family in Southsea, was educated at the United Services College. In 1882, he went back to India, where he worked as a journalist and became closely acquainted with both Indians and Anglo-Indians. Returning to England in 1889, he lived in London, then for a time with his wife's family in the US. He was a correspondent in the Boer War before settling in Sussex in 1902. Kipling was a prolific and a versatile writer, one of whose achievements was to gain some public respect for the despised professional soldier through a sympathetic presentation in fiction (*Soldiers Three*, 1890) and in verse (*Barrack Room Ballads*, 1892). In these works, and in stories about the East End of London, his reproductions of Cockney speech were painstaking but sometimes self-defeating through the density of deviant spelling and punctuation. Nevertheless, he caught the tones of colloquial speech there and elsewhere. In the novel *Kim* (1901), he sought to reproduce the various idioms of Indian speakers of English, including what is often called Babu English:

'Suppose we get into a dam'-tight place. I am a fearful man—most fearful—but I tell you I have been in dam'-tight places more than hairs on my head. You say: "I am Son of the Charm." Verree good.'
'I don't understand quite. We must not be heard talking English here.'
'That is all raight. I am only Babu showing off my English to you. All we Babus talk English to show off,' said Hurree, flinging his shoulder-cloth jauntily.

Some of his poetry caused offence then and later by his ardent support of imperialism, but there was a sombre and penitent tone in pieces like 'Recessional', which seems to show an awareness of the coming loss of British power:

Far-called, our navies melt away—
On dune and headland sinks the fire—
Lo, all our pomp of yesterday
Is one with Nineveh and Tyre!
Judge of the Nations, spare us yet,
Lest we forget—lest we forget!

His books for children are among his lasting successes: *The Jungle Book* (1894) tells of an Indian boy Mowgli brought up by wolves; *The Just So Stories for Little Children* (1902) are fables of how certain things happened in the world, such as 'How the Camel Got his Hump'; *Puck of Pook's Hill* (1906) embodies in simple tales and verses Kipling's love of England and its history; *Stalky and Co* (1899) is a period piece about late 19c boarding-school life. In 1907, Kipling was the first Briton to receive the Nobel Prize for Literature. He contributed to popular language, mainly through phrases from his verse: *the white man's burden*; *the female of the* species is more deadly than the male; you're a better man than I am, Gunga Din. The names of characters in *The Jungle Book*, such as Akela the chief wolf, have been used for leaders of the Wolf Cubs (or simply Cubs), junior members of the Boy Scout movement. See index. [ASIA, BIOGRAPHY, EUROPE, LITERATURE]. R.C.

KIRIBATI [Pronounced /kɪrɪbæs/]. Official title: *The Republic of Kiribati*. A country of Oceania and member of the Commonwealth. Capital: Tarawa. Currency: the Australian dollar. Population: 67,000 (1988), 90,000 (projection for 2000). Ethnicity: 90% Micronesian. Languages: Kiribati (Gilbertese) and English (both official). Education: primary 92%, secondary 15%, tertiary less than 1%, literacy 50%. Formerly known as the *Gilbert Islands*, and part of the British colony of the *Gilbert and Ellice Islands*, Kiribati gained its independence in 1979. See ENGLISH, TUVALU. [NAME, OCEANIA]. T.MCA.

KISETTLA, KISETTLER. See SWAHILI.

KITCHEN [19c]. A word used attributively and pejoratively for restricted, pidgin-like forms of their languages used by Europeans with servants and other menial workers in Africa and Asia in the 19c and earlier 20c. The term *Kitchen English* was common during the British Raj and continues to be used in South Asia for a minimal variety of English used by domestic servants to communicate with Europeans, and sometimes used in return by speakers of English. In southern Africa, the term *Kitchen Dutch* (Dutch *kombuis-Hollands*) was used in the 19c for the Dutch spoken by Cape Coloureds, and by English-speaking South Africans as a dismissive label for Afrikaans. *Kitchen Kaffir* was a mixture of indigenous and European languages used by employers with servants and in the mines. Some white South Africans continue to use the term to deprecate their lack of skill with indigenous languages: *Well, I muddle along with my dozen words of Kitchen Kaffir*. See AFRIKAANS, BEARER ENGLISH, BUTLER ENGLISH, ETHNIC NAME, PIDGIN. [AFRICA, ASIA, LANGUAGE, STYLE]. T.MCA.

KITCHEN-SINK DRAMA. A term used by critics for some plays written in the 1950s, because of an apparent excess of social realism and an emphasis on ugly and sordid aspects of life. It was applied particularly to British dramatists regarded as 'Angry Young Men' and women: John Osborne (b.1929), Arnold Wesker (b.1932), Anne Jellicoe (b.1927), Shelagh Delaney (b.1939). Their work was supported by the English Stage Company at the Royal Court Theatre, London, and defended by the critic Kenneth

Tynan (1927–80). It was widely hailed as a political protest against 'the Establishment' and a theatrical protest against the middle-class plays of Noël Coward (1899–1973) and Terence Rattigan (1911–77). Dramatically, its importance was less in content than in dialogue. The new dramatists broke away from the formal, educated speech used by their immediate predecessors, for whom dialect and non-standard usage was mainly confined to servants or comic characters. They gave the idioms and vocabulary of working-class speech to leading characters and sought to reproduce in their dialogue the hesitations, repetitions, and banalities of normal conversation. See CONVERSATION, DRAMA, GENRE. [LITERATURE]. R.C.

KIWI [Early 19c: from Maori, also *kiwi-kiwi*, *kivi*]. (1) The flightless and long-beaked New Zealand bird known to science as the *Apteryx*. (2) A slang term, originally either American or from New Zealand, applied since the First World War to a non-flying member of an air force. (3) An informal term for someone from New Zealand, originally especially a soldier or sportsman: 'New Zealand football representatives acquired the names *All Blacks*, *Fernleaves*, and *Kiwis*' (Sidney J. Baker, *The Australian Language*, 1945); 'It is hurtful to many Australians to see the Kiwis take all the credit for Antipodean anti-Pom feelings' (*The Times*, 17 June 1974); 'In the early 1970s, thousands of Kiwis took wing for the Australian good life and high wages' (*Observer*, 12 Aug. 1984). (4) An informal synonym for New Zealand English: 'We have exchanged Kiwi phrases over a few beers from time to time' (David McGill, *A Dictionary of Kiwi Slang*, 1988). (5) Also *kiwi fruit*, *kiwi berry*. An edible oval fruit originally native to Asia and known as the Chinese gooseberry (*Actinidia chinensis*) and now widely associated with New Zealand. (6) The short form of *Golden Kiwi*, New Zealand's national lottery: *He's just won the kiwi!* See ETHNIC NAME. [NAME, OCEANIA, VARIETY]. RO.W.B., L.J.B., T.MCA.

KNOWLEDGE REPRESENTATION [Late 20c]. A technical term for computer languages used for the formal representation of ordinary thought. Since at least the 17c, such philosophers as Gottfried Wilhelm von Leibniz in Germany and John Wilkins in England have sought a more precise way than natural language to describe precise thought. They saw that mathematicians were able to prove their statements, and hoped that a mathematical notation would make the same certainty and completeness possible in terms of general knowledge. The 19c philosophers Gottlob Frege in Germany and Charles Sanders Peirce in the US, and the 20c

British mathematician George Boole, developed notations for discussing logical ideas with formal methods. The advent of computers in the mid-20c offered the opportunity to reach such proofs and deductions automatically, and encouraged the hope of certainty and automaticity in ordinary reasoning. The US computer pioneer John McCarthy and co-workers encouraged the development of methods for knowledge processing on machines, along with such US logicians as Alonzo Church.

Frames. A typical device for knowledge representation is the *frame*, consisting of a head concept and a series of slots, each of which is a link to another concept serving in a particular role, such as *throw* linked to *the thrower, the thing thrown*, and *someone who is thrown to or thrown at*. These slots often match the roles listed in case grammar, such as *agent* or *object*, but some languages of knowledge representation are more expansive, and have hundreds of roles connecting concepts: distinguishing *time* into such details as *since* (starting at a point and continuing indefinitely) and *until* (from the beginning to a particular time). In addition to the slots which link to other concepts, some simple slots may contain local values, such as colour or weight. Some may also contain procedures (that is, computer programs), to be executed: the representation of *Take the next train to London* may require consulting a railway schedule to identify it.

Hierarchies. Another device is hierarchical structure, so that properties can be inherited downwards from level to level. Thus, at the bottom of the hierarchy, *canaries* are a subclass of *birds*, which are a subclass of *living things*, and the property *sings* is stored with *canary* (as a special attribute) while the property *flight* is associated with *bird* (as a general attribute). Unfortunately, the structure cannot always be a simple hierarchy with all higher-level properties inherited underneath, since ostriches are birds but do not inherit flight, and canaries also belong in the hierarchy of pets and inherit other properties from that heading. Lower-level slots may therefore contain entries that override values inherited from higher-level frames.

Language and mind. It is not known whether this sort of notation is a model for human thought. Most contemporary researchers assume that ordinary language is translated into something else inside the head, but nobody knows what. Studies of *facilitation* (the increase in speed in answering a question when a closely related question has been asked before) show relationships between words, but whether these are of the frame/slot type or hierarchical is impossible to say. Many think that ordinary language

at least limits and shapes thought, suggesting that even if thinking does involve other representations than language at least the labels on the categories resemble those of one's native language. See CASE GRAMMAR, HYPONYM, LEXICAL FIELD, SAPIR-WHORF HYPOTHESIS, SEMANTIC FIELD, SEMANTICS, THEMATIC ORDER. [TECHNOLOGY]. M.L.

KOINE, also **koiné** [1910s: from Greek *koiné diálektos* common usage]. (1) A variety of Greek that was the lingua franca of the eastern Mediterranean in Hellenistic and Roman times and the literary language between the heyday of Attic Greek (on which it was based) and the early Byzantine period: *c*.4c BC to 4c AD. It contained features of many dialects and one of its forms is New Testament Greek. (2) In sociolinguistics, any language or variety representing a compromise among dialects and providing communication across dialects. This may or may not involve a degree of simplification and is often part of standardization; some scholars call the initial stage in forming a standard language *koineization*. Koines include colloquial Arabic, Belgrade-based Serbo-Croat, the Popular or Vulgar Latin of the Roman Empire, medieval literary Italian, and Modern Israeli Hebrew, but few of these have all the formal and functional features of the original Koine. See CLASSICAL LANGUAGE, GREEK, LINGUA FRANCA, SOUTH AFRICAN LANGUAGES. [LANGUAGE]. T.MCA., S.R.

KOLHAPUR CORPUS, The. A computer corpus of written Indian English, compiled in the 1980s by Professor S. V. Shastri of the Department of English at Shivaji U., Kolhapur, Maharashtra. It consists of 1m words from 500 short texts published in 1978, covers 15 categories of prose-writing, and serves as material for such studies as code-mixing, modal verbs, and forms of complementation. Such research is linked with work on the *International Corpus of English* (*ICE*) at University College London. Work on a general service list of words is intended to lead to 'a modest dictionary of Indian English' (Shastri, *EFL Gazette*, Nov. 1990). See CORPUS. [LANGUAGE]. T.MCA.

KOREA [A name usually spelt *Corea* and occasionally *Korea* in the 19c, but fixed in the latter form during the Japanese occupation of the country (1910–45)]. A country of East Asia, currently divided into *North Korea* (1988, population 21.8m) and *South Korea* (42.3m). The Korean language, also spoken by communities in China (1.5m), Japan (1m), and the Soviet Union (0.4m), is agglutinative and usually regarded as a Uro-Altaic language. Ancient Korean was written in a script called *idu*, in which Chinese characters were used to represent Korean sounds as well as meanings (similar to the present-day Japanese *kanji*). In the 15c, an alphabet of 11 vowel and 17 consonant symbols (reduced later to 10 and 14) was devised and used for popular literature, while classical Chinese continued in use for official and scholarly purposes. Although banned during the last decade of the Japanese occupation, this system (known as *han-gul*, formerly *onmun* common script) was revived and is used on its own or, to a lesser degree, in a mixed script with Chinese characters read as Korean words. English has had a considerable influence on the structure of the modern language. Over the last 40 years, English has generally been assigned as many school hours as Korean for students aged 12–18, and is in the main an analytical grammatical exercise that has affected the study and use of Korean, resulting in adjustments made to some Korean constructions so as to align them more closely with English: for example, greater use of the optional plural particle *-tul*. Although this is not a strict equivalent of the English plural inflection *-s*, many think that it is or should be. Also under the influence of English and other Western languages, the convention of writing each word unit separately was adopted for Korean in the 19c, a procedure which has not been followed for Chinese and Japanese.

English was first taught in the 1880s by American teachers, when the royal government opened a school for the sons of the nobility. Around the same time, missionary schools began to provide instruction to commoners. During the occupation, Japanese teachers of English dominated the new school system and emphasized parsing. The end of the Second World War brought US soldiers to Korea, a fact which largely accounts for the dominance of AmE over BrE in Korea, but despite the importance of spoken English the emphasis on texts and grammatical analysis continued. English is widely regarded as highly subtle, its grammar subsumed under five basic structures, with such categories as the subjunctive mood and the future perfect progressive. When A. S. Hornby, who worked in Japan in the 1930s, classified English sentences into over 20 basic structures, many traditional teachers in both Korea and Japan were reluctant to base their English teaching on his system, or, for that matter, on any other contemporary system. After the war and partition, the need for English declined in North Korea but increased in the South, where it is the main foreign language. Almost all students have three years of it, and the 80% who attend high school have six years. There are many private English institutes, of which there are two sharply different kinds: one for students preparing for college entrance examinations, emphasizing parsing at deeper levels than in high school, and another for people who want to speak the language. Formal education rarely allows students to experience spoken English, and the minority who speak it generally say that they owe little to their schooling. The dismissive informal name *Konglish* has been used for non-standard usage by Koreans. Industrial expansion has been rapid in recent years and English is seen as vital for keeping pace with modern technology and for communication with trading partners, with the result that a reform of teaching methods is widely regarded as imperative. The influence of English is discussed in Sangsup Lee's 'The Subversion of Korean' (*English Today* 20, Oct. 1989). See AMERICAN LANGUAGES, CHINA, EAST ASIAN ENGLISH, HAWAII, JAPAN, LATIN[1], PARSING, TELEPHONE. [ASIA, LANGUAGE, NAME, VARIETY].

S.L., T.MCA.

KOREAN BAMBOO ENGLISH. See JAPANESE PIDGIN ENGLISH.

KRAPP, George Philip [1872–1934]. American linguist, born in Cincinnati, Ohio, and educated at Wittenberg College and Johns Hopkins U. (Ph.D., 1899). Krapp was one of several scholars at Teachers College and Columbia U. who in the early 20c became interested in a scientific study of grammar and usage, correctness and error. He published works on Anglo-Saxon manuscripts (*The Junius Manuscript*, 1931; *The Vercelli Book*, 1932; *The Paris Psalter and The Meters of Boethius*, 1932), medieval texts (*Troilus and Criseyde*, 1932), the historical development of English (*Modern English, Its Growth and Present Use*, 1909; *The Rise of English Literary Prose*, 1915), and English grammar (*Comprehensive Guide to Good English*, 1927; *The Knowledge of English*, 1927). Insistent that grammatical standards be based on the correct cultivated usage and social utility rather than on obsolete rules or literary tradition, he illustrated his research with first-hand observations. His most notable work, however, was the study of AmE. Bringing together data compiled by others as well as much original matter in *The Pronunciation of Standard English in America* (1919) and *The English Language in America* (1925, two volumes), Krapp carefully examined both those traditions and usages of BrE which had persisted in AmE and the US political movement toward a national linguistic standard. Basing his contentions on historical, scientific, and geographical records, he maintained that 'the Elizabethan quality in American English is not an inheritance but a development on American soil'. His theory concerning the progress of AmE was drawn from material previously overlooked, such as town records of colonial settlements, French gazetteers of the US, and name lists of college graduates. This work, regarded when it appeared as 'the most important scholarly study of American English yet published' (*American Speech*, 1934), incisively evaluated previous research and set the standard for subsequent treatments. See index. [AMERICAS, BIOGRAPHY, LANGUAGE, VARIETY].

R.W.B.

KRIO, also **Creo** [Mid-20c: an adaptation of *creole*. Compare CREOLE, KRIOL, KWEYOL]. An English creole spoken in Sierra Leone, which developed when freed slaves were transported from Britain and Nova Scotia to Freetown in 1787 and 1792. The Krios were Christian, often literate, and valued as teachers and clerks along the entire West African coast. Sizeable settlements were established in Gambia, Nigeria, Cameroon, and smaller settlements in Liberia and Ghana, and Krio had an influence on all West African pidgins and creoles, with the possible exception of *Merico* in Liberia. Krio is spoken as a mother tongue by some 250,000 people in and around Freetown and by many more Sierra Leoneans as a second language. It has a dictionary (*A Krio-English Dictionary*, ed. C. N. Fyle & Eldred Jones), and is probably the only standardized West African creole. It has been used for translating Shakespeare and parts of the Bible, and for plays, poems, and prose.

Features. (1) *Pronunciation.* Krio is non-rhotic, syllable-timed, and a tone language. It has seven monophthongs, /i, e, ɛ, a, ɔ, o, u/ and three diphthongs /ai, au, oi/. All vowels can be nasalized. Tone is significant, distinguishing grammatical as well as lexical meaning: for example, a customary low tone for auxiliaries becomes high for purposes of emphasis. (2) *Grammar.* There is little morphological variation, time and aspect being carried by pre-verbal auxiliaries, and plurality in the noun is either assumed or marked by *dɛm: I bin kil di arata dɛm kwik-kwik* He killed the rats quickly. Fluidity of word class is typical: Krio *plɛnti* can function as an adjective in *plɛnti pikin* plenty of children, as a verb *Pikin plɛnti* There are plenty of children, as a noun *Plɛnti pwɛl* Many are spoilt, and as an adverb *I gɛt pikin plɛnti* He has children in plenty. (3) *Vocabulary.* The majority of words derive from English: body parts such as *han* (hand, arm), *fut* (foot, leg), common verbs such as *bi, gɛt, go, kam, muf* (move), and auxiliaries *bin, de* (progressive), *kin, dɔn* (perfective), *nɔba* (negative perfective). English elements occur in many loan translations, such as *dei klin* (day clean: dawn), *drai ai* (dry eye: brave). There are also words

from African languages: *akara* (beancake, from Yoruba), *bundu* (camwood, from Mende), *jakato* (garden egg, from Wolof), *kola* (kola nut, from Temne), *nono* (buttermilk, from Mandinka). See AKU, GAMBIA, KAMTOK, SIERRA LEONE, WEST AFRICAN PIDGIN. [AFRICA, NAME, VARIETY].   L.T.

KRIOL [Mid-20c: an adaptation of *creole*. Compare CREOLE, KRIO, KWEYOL]. Also **Roper River Creole/Kriol, Roper Pidgin.** An English-based creole spoken mainly in northern Australia, from western Queensland, across the Barkly Tablelands and Roper River Basin throughout much of the top half of the Northern Territory and into the Kimberleys of Western Australia. A contact language between Aborigines and outside groups, it is now used in over 100 Aboriginal communities by more than 20,000 people, at least half of whom have it as their primary language. Kriol is a continuum of varieties, from *hebi Kriol* (heavy creole: the basilect) to *lait Kriol* (light creole: the acrolect). Speakers of hebi Kriol are mostly mother-tongue speakers of an Aboriginal language who use Kriol as a second language. Extreme lait Kriol includes virtually all the contrasts of mainstream English.

A word in Kriol may have several different pronunciations: *policeman* may be *balijiman* (basilect), *blijiman* (mesolect), *plisman* (acrolect). Most of the vocabulary is from English, in some cases with meanings altered to parallel the semantic range of equivalent words in Aboriginal languages: *kukwan* (from 'cooked one') means *ripe* as well as *cooked*. There are also some Aboriginal words: *munanga* a person of European descent. The grammar of Kriol shares some features with English-based pidgins and creoles in the Pacific: (1) The form of the transitive marker on verbs is *-im/-um*, as in *kilim* to hit, *kukum* to cook. Compare Tok Pisin *kilim, kukim*. (2) The use of *bin* as a completive auxiliary: *Ai bin rid det buk* I have read the book. Most of the limited Kriol morphology is associated with the verb and there are five prepositions which indicate grammatical relations: *blonga* (from 'belong'), as in *Aibin gibit im mani blonga daga* I gave him some money for food; *longa* (from 'long'), as in *Imbin bogi longa riba* He swam in the river. Other prepositions include *fo* for, *from* from, *garram* with, as in: *Olubat bin kaman from deya* They came from there; *Deibin hambagam mi fo daga* They pestered me for food; *Melabat kaan go garram yumob* We cannot go with you people. Kriol has a distinct orthography and a growing literature. In 1975, a school in Bamyili, where Kriol is a major language, was permitted to introduce it as the language of pre-school instruction. In 1979, permission was sought and obtained from the Northern Territory Department of Education for the introduction of a bilingual programme, despite opposition from those who did not consider Kriol a real language. See ABORIGINAL ENGLISH, AUSTRALIAN PIDGIN, CREOLE. [OCEANIA, NAME, VARIETY]. S.R.

KRU PIDGIN ENGLISH. See LIBERIA.

KUHN, Sherman McAllister [1907–91]. American philologist and lexicographer. Born on the South Dakota prairie and raised in the manses of villages which his father served as a Presbyterian minister, he was educated at Dubuque U. and Park College, became a high-school teacher of English, and attended summer school at the U. of Chicago, where he gained an M.A. in American literature (1933) and a Ph.D. in English linguistics (1936), the dissertation for which was *A Grammar of the Mercian Dialect* (published in 1938). Following military service as a cryptographer in World War II, he was appointed Associate Professor of English and Associate Editor of the *Middle English Dictionary* at the U. of Michigan. On the retirement of Hans Kurath in 1961, he was named Editor (and Professor) and continued in that post until retirement in 1983. While the Dictionary occupied most of his time, he continued to work on Mercian Old English and in 1965 published an edition of *The Vespasian Psalter*, a Latin text with an interlinear Mercian translation. At his retirement he was presented with a volume of his major papers (1939–79): *Studies in the Language and Poetics of Anglo-Saxon England* (1984). See MIDDLE ENGLISH DICTIONARY. [AMERICAS, BIOGRAPHY, HISTORY, REFERENCE]. R.W.B.

KURATH, Hans [1891–1992]. American dialectologist and lexicographer, born in Villach, Austria. When he graduated from the U. of Texas (1914), he was appointed an instructor in German at the same university. Because of anti-German sentiment following US entry into World War I, like many of his colleagues, he was not reappointed. He completed a doctoral degree at the U. of Chicago (1920), then worked at Northwestern U. (1920–7), the Ohio State U. (1927–32), and as Professor of Germanic Languages and General Linguistics at Brown U. (1932–46). In 1930, he was named director of *The Linguistic Atlas of the United States and Canada*. For this work he used methods established in the *Atlas linguistique de la France* (1902–10), for which fieldworkers selected and interviewed 'informants' long resident in their communities. The results were expected to show the survival or evolution of earlier pronunciations of English; older, rural speakers of

English descent were therefore dominant in the sample. Kurath later wrote: 'Without adequate phonic data no single dialect or idiolect can be adequately described; nor can its historical relation to its sister dialects or its parent dialect be traced in realistic fashion.'

Studies of the settlement history of selected communities, compiled as the work began in New England, were published in his *Handbook of the Linguistic Geography of New England* (1939). The findings themselves were published in 734 maps in three volumes in the *Linguistic Atlas of New England* (1939–43), which listed Kurath and his collaborators, Miles L. Hanley, Bernard Bloch, Guy S. Lowman Jr., and Marcus L. Hansen. Later fieldwork in England (1936–7), to illustrate the filiations of New England dialects, appeared as *The Dialectal Structure of Southern England: Phonological Evidence* (1970). Its co-author was Guy S. Lowman Jr., a student of Daniel Jones. Other segments of North America were assigned to other scholars and several of these regional studies are still in progress today. Kurath published summaries of investigations along the Atlantic seaboard: *A Word Geography of the Eastern United States* (1949) and *The Pronunciation of English in the Atlantic States* (with Raven I. McDavid Jr., 1961). He concluded his work in dialectology with two monographs: *A Phonology and Prosody of Modern English* (1964) and *Studies in Area Linguistics* (1972). From 1946 until retirement in 1961, he was Professor of English and Editor of the *Middle English Dictionary* at the U. of Michigan. Though work on the *MED* began in 1930, it had been suspended during World War II and no parts had been published. He issued the first fascicle in 1954. In amplifying coverage for Middle English in *The Oxford English Dictionary*, Kurath declared the contribution of the *MED* to be: 'Ample documentation of ME usage; full illustrations of regional and chronological variants in the quotations; adequate representation of all types of texts, literary, scientific, documentary, etc., in the quotations.' [AMERICAS, BIOGRAPHY, HISTORY, LANGUAGE, REFERENCE]. R.W.B.

KUWAIT. See ARABIC, ENGLISH.

KWEYOL [From French *créole*: see CREOLE; compare KRIO, KRIOL]. A preferred name in Dominica and St Lucia for the local French-based Creole, also called *patois*. The varieties on the islands are mutually intelligible with those in the nearby French departments of Martinique and Guadeloupe. See DOMINICA, PATOIS, SAINT LUCIA. [AMERICAS, LANGUAGE, NAME]. L.C.

L

L, l [Called 'ell']. The 12th letter of the Roman alphabet as used for English. It originated in the Phoenician letter *lamed*, adopted into Greek as *lambda* (*Λ*), which became the Roman letter *L*.

Sound value. (1) In English, the letter *l* represents a voiced alveolar lateral continuant, its articulation varying with accent and position: for example, in RP, a syllable-final velarization distinguishes the *l* in *pill* from that of syllable-initial *lip*. (2) A following *l* frequently gives a long value to the vowel letters *a, i, o*: *a* is like *aw* in *saw* (*all, fall, halt, talk, altercation, falsify*); *i* is like *y* as in *sky* (*child, mild, whilst*); *o* is like *owe* (*cold, poll, bolt, control*). However, pronunciation occasionally varies, as in such pairs as *holy/ holiday, Polish/polish*.

Double L. (1) In Middle English, final *l* in monosyllables after a single vowel letter was often single (*al, ful, wel*) but except in recent coinages like *nil, pal* it is now doubled (*all, bull, cell, fill, gull, hall, mill, pull, will*). In long-established compounds, however, such forms commonly have one *l*: *almost, also, although, until, welcome*, BrE *wilful*. Contrast standard *all right* and nonstandard but common *alright*. (2) Single *l* is usual when two vowel letters precede (*fail, haul, peel, coal, foul, tool*) or when *e* follows (*pale, while, pole, rule*). (3) Doubled *ll* usually signals a preceding short vowel: compare the related *vale/ valley*. The chief exceptions are monosyllables such as *roll*, the anomalous adverb *wholly, tulle* (derived from a French place-name), and *camellia*. (4) On the other hand, single *l* occurs medially after both short and long vowels: compare *balance/ballot, bilious/billet, chalice/ challenge, dolour/dollar, felon/fellow, gelatine/ jelly, military/million, palate/pallet, talent/ tallow, tranquillity/virility, valid/valley, vilify/ villain*. (5) Discrepancies: *tonsillitis* with *ll* and *colitis, poliomyelitis, diverticulitis* with *l*;

fusilier and *fusillade*; the pairs of alternates *colander/cullender, postilion/postillion, scalawag/ scallywag; belletristic*, in which the *ll* derives from the three *l*s in the phrase *belles lettres*. (6) The verb *to parallel* has the common inflected forms *paralleled, paralleling* and the less common and less accepted forms *parallelled, parallelling*. (7) An exotic *ll* occurs in Spanish loans (*llama, guerrilla*), but is pronounced /l/, not as /j/ as in Spanish. (8) Welsh *ll*, as in the names *Llandudno, Llangollen, Llewellyn*, represents an alveolar lateral fricative, and is usually pronounced /l/ by non-Welsh-speakers.

Doubling by affixation. (1) Inherited from Latin, when certain prefixes are assimilated: *ad-* (*allocation*), *con-* (*collocation*), and *in-* (*illustration, illegible*). (2) Inherited from Greek when the prefix *syn-* is assimilated: *syllable, syllogism*. (3) When *-less* attaches to a word ending in *l* (*soulless*) and when *-ly* is added to adjectives ending in *l*: *legally, coolly, beautifully*. Base words ending in *ll* (*fully*) and those ending in vowel plus *-le* normally add *-ly* (*palely, solely*); *wholly* from *whole* is anomalous. Base words ending in consonant plus *-le* replace the *e* with *y*: *able/ ably, simple/simply*. The adverb *supply* (in a supple manner) can be written *supplely* to avoid confusion with *to supply*, but there is only one form *multiply* for both adverb and verb. Adjectives ending in *-ic*, with the exception of *public*, add *-ally*: *automatically, basically*.

Syllabic L. The letter *l* can function syllabically, as in *table*, whose second syllable is pronounced /əl/, but in *tabling* the *l* loses its syllabic status and is the first consonant in a second full syllable. Many words have a separate vowel letter where schwa occurs in speech before final *l*, and there is no difference in pronunciation in: *bridal/bridle, cubical/cubicle, gamble/gambol*,

THE CAPITAL LETTER

EARLY FORMS				CURRENT FORMS	
Phoenician	Greek	Etruscan	Roman (Latin)	roman	italic
∠	↑∧	↵	↳L	L	*L*

THE SMALL LETTER

EARLY FORMS			CURRENT FORMS	
Roman cursive	Roman uncial	Carolingian minuscule	roman	italic
↿	L	(	l	*l*

idle/idol, mantel/mantle, metal/mettle (cognates), *muscle/mussel* (cognates), *naval/navel*. Such endings can constitute a spelling problem, as with *principal* and *principle*. Such surnames as *Liddell, Revell, Waddell* have either syllable stressed, according to owners' preference, leaving strangers who have only seen the name uncertain how to pronounce it. Certain adjectives derived from nouns with syllabic *l* contain a *u* that relates to the Latin origin of the words concerned: *constable/constabular, muscle/ muscular, scruple/scrupulous, table/tabular, triangle/triangular*. See SYLLABIC CONSONANT.

Epenthetic L. The letter *l* is epenthetic in *chronicle, emerald, participle, principle, syllable*. In *fault, falcon, realm* the *l* at one stage disappeared, but was restored. See EPENTHESIS, PARTICIPLE, SYLLABLE.

L and R. The sounds /l/ and /r/ are phonetically similar. The *l* in *belfry, marble, pilgrim* (cognate with *peregrine*), *plum* (cognate with *prune*), and *purple* evolved from *r*. *Glamour* derives from *grammar*, and the spelling *coronel* was replaced by French *colonel* in the 17c, although pronunciation still reflects the *r*. See L-SOUNDS, R-SOUNDS.

Silent L. (1) After *a*, before the consonant letters *f/v, k, m*: *calf/calve, half/halve, chalk, stalk, talk, walk, almond, alms, balm, calm, palm, psalm, salmon*. (2) After *o* before *k, m*: *folk, yolk, holm, Holmes* (contrast *film, helm*). (3) In *could, should, would*. (4) The vowel sound preceding *lk* (*chalk, folk*) is generally modified *a* or lengthened *o*, and in RP *a* is also lengthened before *lf, lm, lv* (*half, palm, calve*). Pronunciation may, however, be inconsistent, with *l* sometimes heard in *almond, calm, holm, palm*. (5) In some proper names, especially in England: always in *Alnwick* ('Annick'), *Lincoln* ('Linken'), generally in *Holborn* ('Hohben'). In most of the preceding words, *l* was once pronounced, but in *could* it was inserted unhistorically early in the 16c by analogy with etymological *l* in *should, would*, which was already silent. *Samon* was respelt *salmon* by reference to Latin *salmo*. Conversely, an *l* has disappeared from *as, each, which, much* (compare *also*, Scots *ilk, whilk, muckle*, and German *als, welch*).

British and American differences. (1) Some disyllabic verbs ending in *l* and with second-syllable stress are usually written with *l* in BrE, *ll* in AmE: *appal/appall, distil/distill, enrol/enroll, enthral/enthrall, instil/instill*. Others have a single *l* in both varieties: *control, compel, dispel, impel, repel, annul*. Inflected and some derived forms have *ll* in both varieties: *appalled, controlling, distillation, enrolling, installation* (but *enrolment, instalment* chiefly in BrE). (2) Verbs

ending in an unstressed vowel plus *l* (*to equal, travel, pencil*) normally double the *l* in inflected and derived forms in BrE (*travelled, travelling, traveller*), but not in AmE (*traveled, traveling, traveler*). BrE *callisthenics, chilli, councillor, counsellor, fulfil, jewellery, libellous, marvellous, skilful, tranquillity, wilful, woollen* correspond to AmE *calisthenics, chili, councilor, counselor, fulfill, jewelry, libelous, marvelous, skillful, tranquility, willful, woolen*. See ALPHABET, LETTER, SPELLING. [WRITING].   C.U.

L1, L2. See FIRST LANGUAGE AND SECOND LANGUAGE, LANGUAGE TEACHING.

LABEL NAME. See APTRONYM.

LABIAL [16c: from Latin *labialis* of the lip(s)]. A term in phonetics for a sound made with the lips or a lip, such as /p, f/. When both lips are used, the sound is *bilabial*: /p, b/. When the lower lip is raised towards the upper front teeth, the sound is *labio-dental*: /f, v/. [SPEECH].   G.K.

LABIO-DENTAL. See LABIAL.

LACONIC. See LACONISM.

LACONISM [16c: from Greek *lakonismós* favouring or imitating the people of Laconia in Greece: that is, the Spartans]. (1) A technical term for habitual brevity or terseness in speech: compressing as much as possible into as few words as possible; the art or habit of being *laconic* (saying as little as possible), as reputedly cultivated by the ancient Spartans. (2) A laconic remark. See MONOSYLLABLE. [STYLE].   T.MCA.

LADINO. See JEWISH LANGUAGES, ROMANCE LANGUAGES, SPANISH.

LALLANS, also **Lallan** [16c: a variant of Scots *lawland(s)* lowland(s)]. A name for the vernacular speech of Lowland Scotland from the 18c to the present day, adopted after the Second World War by poets of the Scottish Renaissance movement in preference to *Synthetic Scots*, a term coined in the 1920s for eclectic literary Scots. Following Hugh MacDiarmid's aim of restoring dignity and copiousness to Scots, they composed much of their poetry in this form, which hostile critics ridiculed as *Plastic Scots*. The following excerpt from MacDiarmid's 'The Eemis Stane' (*Sangschaw*, 1925) demonstrates its eclecticism, the entire first line, and the archaic words *eemis* and *yowdendrift*, being lifted from John Jamieson's early 19c *Etymological Dictionary of the Scottish Language*:

> I' the how-dumb-deid o' the cauld hairst nicht
> The warl' like an eemis stane
> Wags i' the lift;

An' my eerie memories fa'
Like a yowdendrift.

[*how-dumb-deid* (Jamieson) 'the middle of the night, when silence reigns; Ayrshire'; *cauld* (general) cold; *hairst* (general) autumn; *nicht* (general) night; *warl'* (general) world; *eemis* (Jamieson) insecurely balanced, toppling; *stane* (general) stone; *lift* (archaic) sky; *fa'* (general) fall; *yowdendrift* (Jamieson) 'snow driven by the wind']

Literary Lallans remains viable alongside other kinds of Scots verse and prose. It is a principal medium in *Lallans*, the journal of the Scots Language Society (1973–). See DORIC, LOWLAND SCOTS, SCOTS, SCOTS LANGUAGE ORGANIZATIONS. [EUROPE, VARIETY].   A.J.A.

LALLATION [17c: from Latin *lallare/lallatum* to sing the sound 'la-la' or a lullaby]. An obsolescent term in phonetics and speech therapy for the misformation of [l] or the pronunciation of [l] for [r]: 'The Popos and Dahomans have the same lallation as the Chinese, who call rum "lum" ' (R. F. Burton, *Dahome*, 1864). In the 1870s, the verb *to lall* was adopted, meaning to misform [l] and/or [r], often by substituting a [w] for either sound, as in 'weawy' for *really*, or a [j] for [l], as in 'yater' for *later*. Compare LAMBDACISM, RHOTACISM. See L-SOUNDS. [SPEECH].
                                            T.MCA.

LAMB, Charles [1775-1834]. English essayist, born in the Inner Temple, London, and educated at Christ's Hospital, where he was a contemporary of Coleridge. In 1792, he became a clerk in the London office of the East India Company, and worked there until retiring in 1825. He was temporarily mentally ill in 1795-6 and in 1796 his sister Mary killed their mother in a fit of madness. For the rest of his life, Lamb devotedly cared for her; they lived in various places in and around London. Lamb wrote some poetry, and two plays which had little success. His prose *Tales from Shakespeare* (1807), written with his sister, has remained popular, but not a similar work on Homer, *The Adventure of Ulysses* (1808). In 1808, Lamb published *Specimens of English Dramatic Poets who lived about the time of Shakespeare*, an anthology of extracts with commentaries which drew attention to neglected early dramatists. He wrote for a number of contemporary journals; his essay 'On the Tragedies of Shakespeare' examined characters in their own right apart from their dramatic function. A number of contributions to the *London Magazine* were published in 1823 as *Essays of Elia*; a second volume appeared in 1833. After Francis Bacon, Lamb is probably the most famous essayist in English. His work ranges from literary criticism, through accounts of experiences presented as autobiographical, to

humorous fantasies such as 'On the Origins of Roast Pork'. His tone is whimsical, his vocabulary sprinkled with archaisms, and his style frequently digressive, anacolutha indicated by dashes. His thought is seldom organized or his ideas continuous, but he lets his imagination range in a manner that reaches towards *stream of consciousness*. He set a pattern for the subjective type of essay associated in the 20c with writers like Robert Lynd and E. V. Lucas. See ANACOLUTHON, ESSAY. [BIOGRAPHY, EUROPE, LITERATURE, STYLE].   R.C.

LAMBDACISM, also **labdacism** [17c: from Latin *la(m)bdacismus*, Greek *la(m)bdakismós*, from *la(m)bda*, the 11th letter of the Greek alphabet]. A rare term in phonetics for great use of [l], its mispronunciation, or its substitution for [r], and for any example of this. Traditionally, Chinese speakers of English have been characterized as engaging in such lambdacisms as 'velly solly' for *very sorry*. Compare LALLATION, RHOTACISM. See L-SOUNDS. [SPEECH].   T.MCA.

LAMINAL [20c: from Latin *lamina* a thin plate]. A term in phonetics for the blade of the tongue and sounds made with it. The sibilants /s, z, θ, ð/ are usually made with the tip and blade together, raised to the alveolar ridge. See ALVEOLAR. [SPEECH].   G.K.

LAMMING, George [b. 1927]. Caribbean novelist, essayist, broadcaster, editor, poet, orator, born in Carrington Village, Barbados, and educated at Combermere School, Barbados. He taught at Mount Saint Benedict College, Trinidad, then migrated to England in 1950, where he became a book and film reviewer for the BBC, contributing to *Caribbean Voices* programmes in the 1950s and co-producing *New World of the Caribbean* (1956), a series of radio broadcasts of thematically arranged readings from West Indian novelists and poets. He was editor of the Guyana and Barbados Independence issues of *New World Quarterly*. His publications include: *In the Castle of My Skin* (1953), *The Emigrants* (1954), *Of Age and Innocence* (1958), *Season of Adventure* (1960), *The Pleasures of Exile* (1960), *Natives of My Person* (1972), *Water with Berries* (1972). Honours include a Guggenheim Fellowship (1955-6) and a Canada Council Fellowship (1962). Lamming is an activist in the causes of cultural sovereignty for small states, people's participation in decisions that affect their lives, and the responsibility of intellectual élites towards the societies that have engendered them. See CARIBBEAN LITERATURE IN ENGLISH. [AMERICAS, BIOGRAPHY, LITERATURE].   L.C.

LAMPOON [17c: from French *lampon*, perhaps from *lampons* let us drink: a refrain in popular songs]. A written attack on a person's character, ranging from graffiti to elegant composition and expressing a desire to wound publicly. Lampoons may occur in an extended satire, as with Dryden's presentation of the Duke of Buckingham as Zimri in 'Absalom and Achitophel' (1681), and Pope's attack on Addison as Atticus in 'An Epistle to Dr Arbuthnot' (1735). Verbal attacks on public figures have always been popular, and the UK magazine *Private Eye* (founded 1961) is a current specialist in the field. Television has added visual caricature, as in the British puppet show *Spitting Image*. See CARICATURE, PARODY. [LITERATURE].   R.C.

LANCASHIRE. (1) A north-western county of England whose name is historically associated with the city of *Lancaster* and the *Duchy of Lancaster* (which, unlike the *Duchy of York*, has no duke). It is administered from the city of Preston. (2) The dialect of the county, part of Northern English, and related to the Cumbrian and Geordie dialects to the north, and the Yorkshire dialect to the east, while also having features of the Midland dialect area. Some scholars give the town of Rawtenstall as the source of the alliterative 14c poem in North Midland dialect, *Sir Gawain and the Green Knight*. Although the Lancashire dialect is particularly associated with the cotton towns of the south-east, such as Burnley, Bolton, and Rochdale, it has many varieties, including the urban dialects of Manchester and Liverpool.

Pronunciation. (1) Lancashire shares many features of pronunciation with other Midland and Northern regions of England, accents ranging from the regional through the RP-influenced to RP. (2) Regional pronunciation is non-rhotic, except for a small and decreasing number of speakers in Rochdale, Accrington, and Preston. (3) Word-initial /h/ tends to be lost in frequently used words such as *house* and *hat*. (4) The same vowel /a/ is used for words such as *gas* and *grass*, *Sam* and *psalm*. (5) There is usually no distinction between the vowels in such words as *hoot* and *hut*, which are homophones pronounced /hʊt/. Among RP-influenced speakers, *book* is often pronounced /bʊk/, a usage that can be considered a shibboleth of Lancashire speech. (6) The long /u/ vowel is sometimes diphthongized in such words as *moon* /muən/ and *school* /skuəl/, especially to the north of Burnley. (7) There is a tendency to use the monophthongs /e, o, ɛ/ in words such as *take*, *soap*, *square*, where RP has diphthongs. (8) In the south, there is a tendency to round the /a/ vowel when it precedes a nasal, particularly /m/ and /n/ in words such as *ham* /hɒm/ and *hand* /hɒnd/. (9) Word-initial /l/ as in *land* and *look* is often dark, and the /l/ in *-ld* clusters is often lost, *old* and *cold* being realized as 'owd' /aud/ and 'cowd' /kaud/. (10) In words ending in /ŋ/ a final /g/ is sounded, as in 'long-g' /lɒŋg/ for *long*, 'sing-ging-g' for *singing*. (11) As in Welsh English, intervocalic consonants are sometimes lengthened in the south, making *chapel* sound like 'chap-pel' and *biting* like 'bite-ting'. (12) In the west, especially around Chorley and Southport, there has been a tendency to add a parasitic nasal after word-final plosives, as in *I've hurt my leg-n* and *They were but lad-ns* They were only boys. This feature is rare in the speech of people under 60.

Grammar. (1) There are many working-class structures such as multiple negation (*I haven't done nothing*), the use of *them* as a demonstrative adjective (*I don't talk to them people*), and the use of non-standard verb forms (*I seen, he done*). (2) In southern, rural Lancashire, 'aw' and '(h)oo' continue to be occasionally used for *I* and *she*: see verse below. In the south-east, *thou* and *thee* have been traditionally used, as in neighbouring Yorkshire, as a marker of intimacy and solidarity. However, the standard pronouns *I, she, you* are increasingly being used in all sections of society. (3) There is a tendency to drop the *to* in infinitive constructions, especially when the first verb ends in a *t*, as in *What d'you want do?* (4) The definite article is often reduced to /θ/ before both vowels and consonants: see verse below. (5) The negative modal verb *maun't* (mustn't) is sometimes used in rural areas, but the positive form *maun*, as used in Scots and in Northern Ireland, is rare. (6) As in many northern areas of Britain, such forms as *I've not seen it* are more widely used than *I haven't seen it*. (7) *Owt* (anything) and *nowt* (nothing) occur frequently, as in *I didn't say owt* and *He gave us nowt*. (8) *Right* and more recently *dead* and *well* are used as colloquial intensifiers, as in *We were right/dead lucky* and *They were well merry* (quite drunk).

Vocabulary. Lancashire shares many dialect words with other parts of northern Britain, including *elder* an udder, *freet* superstition, *fuddle* a drinking bout, *mither* to scold, and *oxter* an armpit. Items that do not occur elsewhere include *alicker* vinegar, *deggin'-can* watering can, *judy* a girl, *kay-fisted* left-handed, *maiden* a clothes-horse. However, most of these words are no longer widespread and are used only by old people, comedians, and dialectologists.

Literary Lancashire. The first well-known writer in dialect was John Collier (1708–86), a schoolmaster who lived near Rochdale and wrote under the pen name 'Tim Bobbin'. The most famous is an admirer of his, Edwin Waugh (pronounced 'Waff'), the son of a shoe-maker who became a journeyman printer and later a full-time writer (1817-90). He wrote, among other things, of the oppression of a work system that forced a father to leave home to gain employment. In the following lines, a woman 'reports' to her absent husband:

> When aw put little Sally to bed,
> Hoo cried, 'cose her feyther weren't theer,
> So aw kiss'd th'little thing, an aw said
> Thae'd bring her a ribbin fro' th'fair.
>
> An' aw gav' her her doll, an' some rags,
> An' a nice little white cotton-bo';
> An aw kiss'd her again, but hoo said
> 'At hoo wanted to kiss *thee* an' o.

[*thae* thou/you, *bo'* ball, *'at* that, *o* all]

Like other writers of dialect, Lancashire poets have tended to be obsessed with standard spelling and inclined to use apostrophes freely to mark 'lost' letters, some of which were not sounded in standard English either (as in *kiss'd*, above). Organized interest in the dialect centres on the *Lancashire Dialect Society*, founded in 1951 largely through the efforts of the late G. L. Brook, Professor of English Language at the U. of Manchester. The Society publishes an annual journal devoted to the academic study of, and writing in, the dialect. Past articles have covered such matters as inshore fishing terms, nicknames, and a survey of Lancashire bird names. The collection *Songs of the People*, edited by Brian Hollingworth (Manchester University Press, 1977), contains examples of conservative dialect usage. See CUMBRIA, DIALECT IN ENGLAND, ISLE OF MAN, MIDLANDS, NORTHERN ENGLISH, SCOUSE, YORKSHIRE. [EUROPE, VARIETY]. S.E., L.T.

LANGUAGE [13c: from Old French *lang(u)age*, from Latin *lingua* tongue]. (1) A human system of communication which uses structured vocal sounds and can be embodied in other media such as writing, print, and physical signs. Most linguists currently regard the faculty of language as a defining characteristic of being human. (2) A particular instance of this system, such as Arabic, French, English, Kwakiutl, Sanskrit, Swahili. (3) Any more or less systematic means of communicating, such as animal cries and movements, code, gesture, machine language, or metaphorically: the *language of dreams*; *the language of love*. (4) The usage of a special group, such as scientific language, technical language, journalese, slang. (5) Usage that is socially suspect, often with a modifier, as in *bad/foul/strong language*, but sometimes alone, as in *Mind your language!*

Students of language. Language is the concern of linguistics, the systematic or scientific study of language, and those who practice it are linguists. They do not, however, monopolize the study of language and languages, which takes various other forms. Many literary humanists, in particular, feel that objective analysis cannot replace the subjective insights of those steeped in literature; some deny or doubt the usefulness of linguistics.

The nature and properties of language. Language is a system in which basic units are assembled according to a complex set of rules. There is a major division between *natural language* (traditional human use of languages) and *artificial language* (devised languages like Esperanto; computer languages like BASIC). Human communication is multimodal, in that speech, gesture, writing, touch, etc., all interact. Language as such has the following properties:

(1) *A vocal–auditory channel.* This channel is often referred to as *the phonic medium*, that is, sounds produced by the vocal organs, which are then received by the ear.

(2) *Convertibility to other media.* Such media are writing and print (*the graphic medium*), sign language (a *visual medium*), and Braille (a *tactile medium*).

(3) *Use of arbitrary symbols.* There is no link in most words between the form used and the meaning expressed.

(4) *Duality or double articulation.* Language is made up of two layers: a layer of sounds, in which the units (phonemes) do not normally have meaning, but combine into another layer which does.

(5) *Interdependence.* Language can be regarded as an integrated structure in which the role of every item is defined by that of all the other items in the same system.

(6) *Open-endedness* (*productivity, creativity*). The number of utterances which can be produced is indefinitely large.

(7) *Displacement.* Language is used to refer to events removed in time and place, and to situations which never existed, as in lying and telling imaginative stories.

(8) *Continual change.* Language is always changing, and there is no evidence that overall progress or decay results from such change.

(9) *Turn-taking.* Spoken language involves structured interchanges in which people take it in turns to talk.

In addition to these features, there has in recent years been a search for universal characteristics which are somewhat more abstract. The difficulty of finding such universals has led to renewed interest in assigning languages to different types.

Language as a mental phenomenon. Language appears to be behaviour that is controlled by maturation, in that it is 'programmed' to emerge at appropriate stages in an individual's development, as long as the nervous system and the environment are normal. Some language disorders are environmental; others may be inherited. Language ability is believed by most linguists to be genetically in-built, at least in its broad outlines, though the nature and extent of the innate contribution is controversial. The mental aspects of language are the concern of *psycholinguistics*, which deals primarily with the acquisition, comprehension, and production of language. Some theoretical linguists also attempt to produce models of the human language faculty, though many of these are controversial. The link between language and thought is another contentious issue. Few linguists accept the claim that language determines thought, but many consider that language has some influence on the way a person thinks.

Language as a social phenomenon. The social aspects of language are the concern primarily of *sociolinguistics* and *anthropological linguistics*. There have been various attempts to define the sociocultural notion of 'a language'. Political and geographical boundaries do not necessarily coincide with linguistic boundaries, nor do ethnic names: many Belgians, for example, speak French. Different varieties of the 'same' language may be mutually incomprehensible even within the same country: in England, a Cockney accent may not be understood by someone with a Geordie accent. Linguists usually therefore regard a language as being defined by those who speak it: the many varieties of English used around the world are all defined as English because this is the language the speakers agree that they are speaking. A variety, however, may be regarded by its speakers as a distinct language if there is a strong literary, religious, or other tradition, as in the case of Scots.

Variation in a language. Within a language, there are subdivisions traditionally known as *dialects*, increasingly as *varieties*, which are most commonly geographical but may also be social. A dialect is more than a simple difference of pronunciation. In the British Isles, many people speak the same dialect of English, but with different accents. Sometimes, one dialect becomes socially prestigious and is adopted as the norm; it is then usually referred to as the 'standard' language. Social variation in language may be due to social class, ethnic origin, age, and/or sex, and within these, to the level of formality employed at any time. Sometimes this variation remains stable, but is often the forerunner of a change. Language shift usually appears as variation within a community, one variant increasing in frequency of use and in its distribution.

Languages in contact. The use of more than one language is common, particularly in frontier regions and in polyglot countries. Also common is the use of a restricted form of a language for a specialized purpose, such as the restricted variety of English used worldwide for air traffic control. Occasionally, formal and informal varieties of the same language may differ to such an extent that they are used virtually as different languages, as until recently in modern Greece. Sometimes, contact between languages may give rise to a system so different from the original(s) that it can no longer be regarded as the same language. A *pidgin* is a limited language system, with rules of its own, used for communication between people with no common language. A *creole* is a pidgin which has become the first language of a community. A *mixed language* is one in which elements from two or more languages have become so intertwined that it is unclear which is the 'basic' language.

The world's languages. There is no agreed figure for the number of languages spoken in the world today. Estimates cluster around 4,000–5,000, with a great deal of variation on either side. Some of the reasons for this uncertainty are: (1) From a linguistic point of view, some parts of the world remain unexplored, including areas where it is known that many languages are in use, such as New Guinea and Central Africa. The rate at which languages are dying, in the face of Western exploration, as in Amazonia, is an unknown factor. (2) Only after a great deal of linguistic enquiry does it become apparent whether a newly encountered community turns out to be speaking a new language or a dialect of an already 'discovered' language. (3) In some areas, it is not easy to decide on the status of what is spoken. Although normally those who can understand each other's spontaneous speech would be said to be speaking the same language, even if there were noticeable differences (as with AmE and BrE, or Cockney and West Country in England), in some places such relatively minor variants are considered important indicators of social, cultural, or political differences. In such cases, it proves necessary to talk of different languages, not different dialects. This has happened, for example, with Flemish and Dutch, Hindi and Urdu, and Swedish, Danish, and Norwegian. In these circumstances, a precise statement about the number of the world's languages is impossible to obtain. Similar differences are encountered when making estimates about the number of speakers of particular languages.

Language statistics. The following statistics are based on Crystal (1987, below):

(1) *Major language groups, with numbers of native speakers* (in descending order): 1 Indo-European 2,000m; 2 Sino-Tibetan 1,040m; 3 Niger–Congo 260m; 4 Afro-Asiatic or Hamito-Semitic 230m; 5 Malayo-Polynesian or Austronesian 200m; 6 Dravidian 140m; 7 Japanese 120m; 8 Altaic 90m (central Asia); 9 Austro-Asiatic 60m; 10 Korean 60m; 11 Tai 50m (Thailand); 12 Nilo-Saharan 30m; 13 Amerindian 25m; 14 Uralic 23m (Asia); 15 Miao-Yao 7m (Indo-China); 16 Caucasian 6m (Caucasus); 17 Indo-Pacific 3m (Papua New Guinea); 18 Khoisan 50,000 (southern Africa); 19 Australian aborigine 50,000; 20 Paleo-Siberian 25,000.

(2) *Major languages, with numbers of native speakers* (in descending order): 1 Chinese 1,000m (but see CHINA); 2 English 350m; 3 Spanish 250m; 4 Hindi 200m; 5 Arabic 150m; 6 Bengali 150m; 7 Russian 150m; 8 Portuguese 135m; 9 Japanese 120m; 10 German 100m; 11 French 70m; 12 Panjabi 70m; 13 Javanese 65m; 14 Bihari 65m; 15 Italian 60m; 16 Korean 60m; 17 Tamil 55m; 18 Telugu 55m; 19 Marathi 50m; 20 Vietnamese 50m.

(3) *Major languages and official-language populations* (the 20 main languages of the world according to aggregate populations of territories where they are official, in descending order): 1 English 1,400m; 2 Chinese 1,100m; 3 Hindi 700m; 4 Spanish 280m; 5 Russian 270m; 6 French 220m; 7 Arabic 170m; 8 Portuguese 160m; 9 Malay 160m; 10 Bengali 150m; 11 Japanese 120m; 12 German 100m; 13 Urdu 85m; 14 Italian 60m; 15 Korean 60m; 16 Vietnamese 60m; 17 Persian 55m; 18 Filipino/Tagalog 50m; 19 Thai 50m; 20 Turkish 50m.

[HISTORY, LANGUAGE]. J.M.A., D.C.

Campbell, George L. 1991. *Compendium of the World's Languages.* Volume 1: *Abaza–Lusatian*; volume 2: *Maasai–Zuni.* London & New York: Routledge.
Comrie, Bernard. 1987. *The World's Major Languages.* London: Croom Helm/Routledge.
Crystal, David. 1987. *The Cambridge Encyclopedia of Language.* Cambridge: University Press.
Ruhlen, Merritt. 1987. *A Guide to the World's Languages.* Volume 1: *Classification.* California: Stanford University Press.

The language and languages theme

Language and linguistics

A–C. ABERCROMBIE, ABSTRACT AND CONCRETE, ACCENT, ACCEPTABILITY, ACROLECT, ADVANCED, AGGLUTINATING, AGRAMMATISM, AMBIGUITY, AMERICAN DIALECT SOCIETY, AMERICAN LANGUAGE, ANALOGY, ANALOGY AND ANOMALY, ANALYTIC, ANGLICE, ANGLICITY, ANGLOCENTRIC, ANOMIA, ANTONYM, APHASIA, APPLIED LINGUISTICS, APPROPRIATENESS/APPROPRIACY, ARGUMENT, ARTIFICIAL LANGUAGE, ASSIMILATION, AXIOM, BABBLE, BABBLING, BABEL, BABY TALK, BAILEY (B.), BASE, BASILECT, BEGGING THE QUESTION, BICULTURALISM, BILINGUAL DICTIONARY, BILINGUALISM, BISOCIATION, BLACK, BLOOMFIELD, BODY LANGUAGE, BOLINGER, BORROWING, BOUND AND FREE, BRIDGES, BURGESS, CAMDEN, CARETAKER LANGUAGE, CATACHRESIS, CHAUVINISM, CHILD LANGUAGE ACQUISITION, CHOMSKY, CLASSICAL LANGUAGE, CLASSIFICATION OF LANGUAGES, CODE, CODE-MIXING AND CODE-SWITCHING, COGNITIVE MEANING, COHERENCE, COHESION, COLLOCATION, COMMUNICATION, COMMUNICATIVE APPROACH, COMMUNICATIVE COMPETENCE, COMMUNICATIVE SHIFT, COMMUNITY LANGUAGE, COMPARATIVE PHILOLOGY, COMPETENCE AND PERFORMANCE, COMPONENT, COMPONENTIAL ANALYSIS, COMPOUND BILINGUALISM, COMPUTATIONAL LINGUISTICS, COMPUTING, CONNOTATION AND DENOTATION, CONSTITUENT, CONTACT LANGUAGE, CONTACT VARIETY, CONTEXT, CONTRASTIVE LINGUISTICS/ANALYSIS, CONVERSATION, CORPUS, CREOLE, CREOLE CONTINUUM, CREOLIZATION, CREOLOID, CRITICISM, CULTURE.

D–G. DEAD LANGUAGE, DE-CREOLIZATION, DEDUCTION, DEEP STRUCTURE, DEIXIS, DESCRIPTIVE AND PRESCRIPTIVE GRAMMAR, DESCRIPTIVISM AND PRESCRIPTIVISM, DEVIANT, DIACHRONIC AND SYNCHRONIC, DIALECT, DIALECTOLOGY, DIASPORA, DIASPORA VARIETY, DIGLOSSIA, DISAMBIGUATE, DISCOURSE, DISCOURSE ANALYSIS, DOUBLE ARTICULATION, DYSGRAPHIA, ECHOLALIA, ELABORATED AND RESTRICTED CODE, ELLIS, -EME, ENGLISH LANGUAGE AMENDMENT, EQUIVOCATION, ERROR ANALYSIS, ETHNIC, ETHNOCENTRIC, ETHNOLINGUISTICS, ETYMOLOGICAL FALLACY, ETYMOLOGY, ETYMON, EURODICAUTOM, EXPRESSION, EXTENSION, FALLACY, FALSE ANALOGY, FATHERESE, FAUX AMI, FEATURE, FEMINISM, FICTION, FIGURATIVE EXTENSION, FIGURATIVE LANGUAGE/USAGE, FINGER SPELLING, FIRST LANGUAGE/SECOND LANGUAGE, FLUENCY, FOLK, FOLK ETYMOLOGY, FOREIGNER TALK, FORM, FORMAL LANGUAGE, FORMULA, FREE VARIATION, FREQUENCY COUNT, FREQUENCY OF OCCURRENCE, FRIES, FUNCTION, FUSIONAL, GAIRAIGO, GENDERLECT, GENERALIZATION, GENERIC, GESTURE, GIFT OF TONGUES, GLOSSOLALIA, GRAMMAR, GRAMMATOLOGY, GRAPHEME, GRAPHIC MEDIUM, GRAPHOLOGY.

H–L. HALLIDAY, HEMPL, HERITAGE LANGUAGE, HOME LANGUAGE, HOMOGRAPH, HOMONYM, HOMOPHONE, INDEXING LANGUAGE, INDIGENIZATION, INDO-EUROPEAN ROOTS, INDUCTION, INFERENCE, INFLECTED, INFORMATION, INTERFERENCE, INTERFERENCE VARIETY, INTERLANGUAGE, INTERNATIONAL LANGUAGE, INTERNATIONAL LINGUISTIC ASSOCIATION, ISOGLOSS, ISOLATING, JESPERSEN, JONES (D.), JONES (W.), KINESICS, KOINE, KOREA/KOREAN, KURATH, LANGUAGE, LANGUAGE ACQUISITION DEVICE, LANGUAGE AWARENESS, LANGUAGE CHANGE, LANGUAGE DEATH, LANGUAGE FAMILY, LANGUAGE LEARNING, LANGUAGE PATHOLOGY, LANGUAGE PLANNING, LANGUAGE POLICE, LANGUAGE RIGHTS, LANGUAGE SHIFT, LANGUAGE TEACHING, LANGUAGE TYPOLOGY, LANGUAGE UNIVERSALS, LANGUE AND PAROLE, LAPSUS LINGUAE, LATIN ANALOGY, LECT, LEVEL OF LANGUAGE, LEXEME, LEXICAL SEMANTICS, LEXICOLOGY, LEXICON, LINGUA FRANCA, LINGUAL, LINGUIST, LINGUISTIC, LINGUISTIC ASSOCIATION OF CANADA AND THE UNITED STATES, LINGUISTIC ASSOCIATION OF GREAT BRITAIN, LINGUISTIC ATLAS, LINGUISTIC ATLAS OF ENGLAND, LINGUISTIC ATLAS OF THE UNITED STATES AND CANADA, LINGUISTIC

GEOGRAPHY, LINGUISTICIAN, LINGUISTICS, LINGUISTIC SCIENCES, LINGUISTIC SIGN, LINGUISTIC SOCIETY OF AMERICA, LINGUISTIC SURVEY OF SCOTLAND, LINGUISTIC TYPOLOGY, LISP, LOGIC, LOW LANGUAGES.

M–Q. MCDAVID, MACHINE LANGUAGE, MACHINE TRANSLATION, MAKESHIFT LANGUAGE, MALAPROPISM, MALEDICTA, MARCH, MARGINAL LANGUAGE, MARKED AND UNMARKED TERMS, MARSH, MEANING, MEDIUM, MELIORATION, MESOLECT, MESSAGE, METALANGUAGE, MIME, MNEMONIC, MODEL, MODERN LANGUAGE ASSOCIATION, MORPHEME, MOTHERESE, MOTHER TONGUE, MULTICULTURALISM, MULTILINGUALISM, MULTIPLE MEANING, MYTH, NATIVE SPEAKER, NATIVE USER, NATIVISM, NATIVIZATION, NATURAL LANGUAGE, NONSENSE, NON-STANDARD, NORM, NORMATIVE, OBSCENE LIBEL, OFFICIAL LANGUAGE, ONOMASIOLOGY, ONOMASTICS, OPPOSITION, ORACY, ORTON, PANJABI, PARADIGM, PARADIGMATIC AND SYNTAGMATIC, PARALANGUAGE, PARALINGUISTICS, PARASITIC, PEJORATION, PHATIC COMMUNION, PHILOLOGICAL SOCIETY, PHILOLOGY, PHONEME, PHONEMICS, PHONETIC, PHONETICS, PHONOLOGY, PIDGIN, POLYGLOT, POLYSEMY, POLYSYLLABLE, POLYSYNTHETIC, POPULAR, POPULAR ETYMOLOGY, POST-CREOLE CONTINUUM, POUND, PRAGMATICS, PREDICATE, PREMISS/PREMISE, PRESUPPOSITION, PRETERIT(E), PRIMARY LANGUAGE AND SECONDARY LANGUAGE, PRIVATE LANGUAGE, PRONUNCIATION, PROPOSITION, PROXEMICS, PSYCHOLINGUISTICS, PSYCHOLOGY OF LANGUAGE, QUIRK.

R–Z. RACISM, RADIATION, RATIONALIZATION, READ, RECEIVED, REDUNDANCY, REGISTER, RELC, REPERTOIRE, RESTRICTED LANGUAGE, ROMAN NUMERAL, SAPIR, SAPIR–WHORF HYPOTHESIS, SCRIPTURE, SEMANTIC CHANGE, SEMANTIC FIELD, SEMANTICS, SEMASIOLOGY, SEMIOLOGY, SEMIOTICS, SENSE, SENSE RELATION, SEXISM, SEXUALITY AND LANGUAGE, SHAKESPEARE, SIGN, SIGNAL, SIGN LANGUAGE, SLIP OF THE TONGUE, SOCIAL DISTANCE, SOCIOLECT, SOCIOLINGUISTICS, SOPHISTRY, SPECIALIZATION, SPEECH, SPEECH ACT, SPEECH PATHOLOGY, SPEECH THERAPY, SPELLING, SPOONERISM, STANDARD, STANDARD DIALECT, STANDARD VARIETY, STEREOTYPE, STRANG, STRATHY LANGUAGE UNIT, STRUCTURALISM, STRUCTURAL LINGUISTICS, STRUCTURAL SEMANTICS, STRUCTURE, STRUCTURE DEPENDENCE, STYLE, STYLE DRIFTING, SUBREPTION, SUBSTRATE/SUBSTRATUM, SUBTRACTIVE BILINGUALISM, SUFFIX, SUPERORDINATE TERM, SUPERSTRATE/SUPERSTRATUM, SYLLOGISM, SYMBOL, SYMBOLISM, SYNCHRONIC, SYNONYM, SYNTAGMATIC, SYNTHETIC, TALK, TAUTOLOGY, TECHNOLOGY, THESIS, TONGUE, TOPIC, TRADE JARGON, TRANSLATION, TRANSLATION EQUIVALENT, TRISOCIATION, TURNER (G.), TURNER (L.), TYPE, TYPE AND TOKEN, TYPOLOGY OF LANGUAGE, UNILINGUAL, UNIVERSAL, USAGE, VARIANT, VARIETY, VERNACULAR, VERNACULARISM, VERNACULARIST, VOCABULARY, WHITE, WHITNEY, WHORF, WORD, WORD BLINDNESS, WORD-FORMATION, WORLD LANGUAGE, WRENN, WRIGHT.

Languages

Groups. AFRICAN LANGUAGES, AMERICAN LANGUAGES, ARTIFICIAL LANGUAGE, ARYAN, ASIAN LANGUAGES, AUSTRALIAN LANGUAGE, AUSTRALIAN LANGUAGES, AUSTRONESIAN LANGUAGES, BANTU, BRITISH LANGUAGES, CANADIAN LANGUAGE ORGANIZATIONS, CANADIAN LANGUAGES, CARIBBEAN LANGUAGES, CELTIC LANGUAGES, CLASSIFICATION OF LANGUAGES, DRAVIDIAN LANGUAGES, ENGLISH LANGUAGES, EUROPEAN LANGUAGES, FINNO-UGRIC LANGUAGES, GERMANIC LANGUAGES, HAMITO-SEMITIC LANGUAGES, HIGH AND LOW LANGUAGES, IBERIAN LANGUAGES, INDIAN LANGUAGES, INDO-EUROPEAN LANGUAGES, INDO-GERMANIC, JEWISH LANGUAGES, LANGUAGE FAMILY, LINGUISTIC TYPOLOGY, MALAYO-POLYNESIAN LANGUAGES, MODERN LANGUAGE, POLYNESIAN LANGUAGES, ROMANCE LANGUAGES, SCANDINAVIAN LANGUAGES, SCOTS LANGUAGE ORGANIZATIONS, SCOTTISH LANGUAGES, SINO-TIBETAN LANGUAGES, SLAVONIC/SLAVIC LANGUAGES, SOUTH AFRICAN LANGUAGE ORGANIZATIONS, SOUTH AFRICAN LANGUAGES, URO-ALTAIC LANGUAGES, WORLD LANGUAGE.

Individual languages. AFRIKAANS, ANGLO-DANISH, ANGLO-FRISIAN, ANGLO-GAELIC, ANGLO-LATIN, ANGLO-NORMAN, ANGLO-ROMANI, ANGLO-SAXON, ARABIC, ARAMAIC, BAHASA INDONESIA, BAHASA MALAYSIA, BENGALI, BRETON, BRITISH, BRITISH LANGUAGE, BRYTHONIC, CELTIC, CHINA/CHINESE, CORNISH, CUMBRIC, DANISH, DUTCH, EARLY MODERN ENGLISH, ENG LANG, ENG LANG AND LIT, ENGLISH, ERSE, ESPERANTO, FANAKALO/FANAGALO, FA(E)ROESE, FILIPINO/PILIPINO, FINNISH, FLEMISH, FRANCIZATION, FRANGLAIS, FRENCH, FRISIAN, GAELIC, GERMAN, GOTHIC, GREEK, GUJARATI/GUJERATI, HAUSA, HAWAIIAN, HEBREW, HINDI, HINDI-URDU, HINDUSTANI, HIRI MOTU, ICELANDIC, INGLIS, INGVAEONIC, IRISH, IRISH GAELIC, ITALIAN, JAPAN/JAPANESE, JUDEZMO, KANNADA/KANNARESE, KITCHEN, KOREA/KOREAN, KWEYOL, LADINO, LATIN[1], LAW FRENCH, LOW DUTCH, LOW GERMAN, LOWLAND SCOTS, MALAY, MALAYALAM, MALTA/MALTESE, MAORI, MARATHI, MIDDLE ENGLISH, MODERN ENGLISH, NORMAN FRENCH, NORN, NORSE, NORWEGIAN, OLD ENGLISH[1], OLD NORSE, PALI, PANJABI/PUNJABI, PAPUA NEW GUINEA, PENNSYLVANIA DUTCH, PERSIAN, PHILIPPINES, PICTISH, POLARI, POLISH, PORTUGUESE, PRAKRIT, PRIMITIVE GERMANIC, ROMANI/ROMANY, RUSSIAN, SABIR, SANSKRIT, SAXON, SCOTS, SCOTTISH GAELIC, SHELTA, SINHALA/SINHALESE, SPANISH, SWAHILI, SWEDISH, SYNTHETIC SCOTS, TAGALOG, TAMIL, TELUGU/TELEGU, TURKISH, URDU, WELSH, WELSH LANGUAGE SOCIETY, YIDDISH.

LANGUAGE ACQUISITION DEVICE, In

short form *LAD*. In linguistic theory, a genetic mechanism for the acquisition of language proposed by Noam Chomsky (*Aspects of the Theory of Syntax*, 1965). LAD was supposedly 'wired' with language universals and equipped with a mechanism which allowed children to make increasingly complex guesses about what they hear around them, aided by an in-built evaluation measure that enabled them to select the best grammar consistent with the evidence. It has, however, proved difficult to specify and test this theory, and Chomsky has abandoned it in favour of *parametric theory* (*Knowledge of Language*, 1986), which suggests that children are pre-programmed with some universals but only partially 'wired' with others. They have advance knowledge of certain basic language options, but have to discover by experience which occur in the language they are exposed to. In Chomskyan terminology, they know the parameters along which language can vary, but have to fix their values, perhaps by setting a 'switch' in one of two possible positions. According to this theory, languages are similar at an underlying level, even though on the surface they appear different. [LANGUAGE].   J.M.A.

LANGUAGE AND SOCIETY. A Canadian quarterly review published since the early 1980s by the Commissioner of Official Languages/ Commissaire aux langues officielles, Ottawa, one half in English, the other in French. In a style that has become standard for Canadian bilingual publications, each half is 'upside-down' in terms of the other, so that francophone and anglophone readers can read their section as the journal proper. Articles in English are translated for the French section, and vice versa, so that the content of each section is virtually identical. The review, distributed free of charge, is 'for all interested Canadians, and especially for social and political commentators, political and administrative leaders, educators and leaders in voluntary organizations, the private sector and linguistic communities. The review aims at reflecting the linguistic experience of Canadians and at keeping them informed of relevant major events and at encouraging dialogue' (from the masthead, Fall 1990). See CANADA. [AMERICAS, MEDIA].   T.MCA.

LANGUAGE AWARENESS. A term in language teaching and applied linguistics for the development of greater awareness among schoolchildren of the nature and purpose of language. Promoters of language awareness seek to apply the findings of linguistic research to education at large. Courses in Modern Languages and in English that are based on language awareness encourage awareness and appreciation of diversity among languages and varieties of languages. They seek to instil an appreciation of such matters as the mechanisms for speech, the nature of writing systems, and the historical development of language. Relevant publications include: Eric Hawkins, *Awareness of Language* (Cambridge University Press, 1984) and companion series of booklets for schools; B. Gillian Donmall (ed.), *Language Awareness* (National Congress on Languages in Education Reports & Papers 6, CILT, 1985); Paul Harvey, 'Language Awareness' (*English Today* 13, Jan. 1988). [EDUCATION, LANGUAGE].   T.MCA., C.J.B.

LANGUAGE CHANGE. The modification of forms of language over a period of time and/or physical distance. Such change may affect any parts of a language (pronunciation, orthography, grammar, vocabulary) and is taking place all the time. It may be abrupt (a change in spelling in a house style) or gradual (a slight change in the pronunciation of a vowel). In cases where language contact leads to pidginization, the changes are often rapid and abrupt. In other cases, change may spread so gradually through a community that it is hardly noticeable. Nevertheless, over time the cumulative effect of such changes may be great. During the past nine centuries, English has undergone more dramatic changes than any other major European language. As a result, Old English or Anglo-Saxon is not immediately accessible to the modern native English speaker in the way that Medieval Icelandic is to the modern Icelander. When people do notice change, their reactions are often negative: for example, to the use of *regime* in the sense of *regimen*, or *disinterested* to mean *uninterested*, and conscious attempts are made to resist it. These are usually not successful in the long term. However, deliberate attempts are sometimes made by social pressure groups or by governments to change aspects of a language or its use.

Sound change. Changes in pronunciation were a primary interest of 19c comparative philologists, who studied the historical relationships among groups of languages such as the Indo-European language family, which includes English, French, and German as well as Greek, Latin, and Sanskrit. The establishment of regular correspondences among sets of sounds enabled them to reconstruct genetic relationships and the shifts responsible for the present differentiation of languages and dialects: for example, a sound change which shifted /p/ to /f/ in some of the Indo-European languages accounts for some major differences between the Germanic and Romance languages. Compare the initial spoken consonant in Latin *pater* and Spanish *padre* with English *father* and German *Vater*. Many of these changes take a long time to complete and may never cover the entire range of a 'language'. Thus, one series of changes, the Great Vowel Shift, is responsible for the present-day pronunciations of English *house*, *mouse*, but has never affected Scots, in which the pronunciations are *hoose*, *moose*, as was true of all English before the shift occurred.

Grammatical change. Major changes in syntax and morphology have affected English over many centuries to the extent that speakers of Modern English are not able to understand Old English without training. The structure of Old English was more like Latin in that words had various inflectional endings to indicate their grammatical function. This situation has been much simplified: for example, the form of the definite article *the*, now invariant, once varied according to case, number, and gender, as in *se mona* (the moon: masculine, nominative, singular), *seo sunne* (the sun: feminine, nominative, singular), and *þæt tungol* (the star: neuter, nominative, singular). Word order in Old English was more flexible because grammatical relations were made clear by the endings: *Se hund seah þone wifmann* (The dog saw the woman) could also be expressed as *þone wifmann seah se hund*, because the inflected forms of the definite article make it clear that 'woman' is the direct object in both cases. In Modern English, however, grammatical relations are indicated largely by word order, so that *The dog saw the woman* and *The woman saw the dog* (compare Old English *Se wifmann seah þone hund*) mean two different things. Modern English has also lost its system of classifying nouns into three grammatical genders, as still occurs in German.

Lexical change. Such change is caused by both internal and external factors. Internal change can mean the adaptation of both the meanings and forms of existing words and phrases through such factors as assimilation, elision, and reduction, as with the conversion of *Saint Audries* in *Saint Audries lace* into *tawdry* (cheap and ill-made, originally referring to the quality of the lace sold at St Audrey's Fair in Ely, England). External change includes the borrowing of words, which may be occasional and minimal (as with loanwords taken into English from Turkish) or frequent and massive (as with the flow into English of French, Latin, and Greek words). All such acquisition results in the introduction of new vocabulary and sometimes new word structures and patterns of word-formation.

Conclusion. People often react negatively to change and regard it as due to ignorance, laziness, or sloppiness. This can be seen in the letters written to newspapers complaining that the contemporary uses of words like *disinterested*, *hopefully*, and *regime* are 'incorrect'. The spread of language change is basically a social phenomenon, as can be seen from recent sociolinguistic studies, which have shown that changes associated with prestige groups often have a greater chance of being adopted than others. Forms which from the point of view of one variety appear conservative may continue without comment in another, such as the use of *gotten* rather than *got* in *You've gotten more than you need*, which is conventional in Scots and in AmE, but is not now used in the English of England. Older forms may also survive in working-class non-standard speech (*hoose* in urban working-class Scots) and in informal styles (*workin* instead of *working* in many varieties), though sometimes older forms become restricted to formal or specialized contexts, as with the religious use of *brethren*.

See ETYMOLOGY, FRENCH, GREAT VOWEL SHIFT, GREEK, GRIMM'S LAW, INDO-EUROPEAN LANGUAGES, LANGUAGE PLANNING, LATIN[1], PHILOLOGY, PROGRESS AND DECAY IN LANGUAGE, ROOT, SEMANTIC CHANGE, SOCIOLINGUISTICS, USAGE, VERNER'S LAW. [HISTORY, LANGUAGE]. S.R.

LANGUAGE DEATH [1980s]. A term in linguistics for the extinction of a language: 'The present contribution is directed towards disseminating general information on the causes and effects of language shift. It is not a survey of all known cases of language contraction and death in eastern Africa' (Gerrit J. Dimmendaal, 'On Language Death in Eastern Africa', in Nancy C. Dorian (ed.), *Investigating Obsolescence: Studies in Language Contraction and Death*, Cambridge University Press, 1989). The associated term *language obsolescence* refers to a slow diminution in the number of users of a language. See CELTIC LANGUAGES (LINGUICIDE), CLASSICAL LANGUAGE (DEAD LANGUAGE). [LANGUAGE]. T.MCA.

LANGUAGE DISABILITY, DISORDER. See LANGUAGE HANDICAP.

LANGUAGE FAMILY. A group of languages which are assumed to have arisen from a single source: English, French, German, Greek, Persian, Russian, Sanskrit, and Welsh are all members of the Indo-European language family, and are considered to have descended from a common ancestor. Common ancestry is established by finding systematic correspondences between languages: English repeatedly has /f/ where Latin has /p/ in words with similar meaning, as in *father/pater*, *fish/piscis*, *flow/pluo* rain. It also often has /s/ where Greek has /h/, as in *six/héx*, *seven/heptá*, *serpent/hérpein* to creep. In addition, English and German compare adjectives in similar ways, as in *rich, richer, richest*: reich, reicher, reichste. These and other correspondences indicate that the languages are cognate (genetically related). Various related words can be compared in order to reconstruct sections of a hypothetical ancestor language. The purpose of such reconstruction is to enable ancient sound patterns and structures to be distinguished from more recent forms. The process of comparison and reconstruction is traditionally known as *comparative philology*, more recently as *comparative historical linguistics*. This process formed the backbone of 19c language study, though in the 20c it has become one branch among many. A 'family tree' diagram (not unlike a genealogy) is commonly used to represent the relationships between the members of a linguistic family, in which an initial parent language 'gives birth' to a number of 'daughters', which in turn give birth to others. This can be useful, but is rarely an accurate representation of how languages develop, since it suggests clean cuts between 'generations' and between 'sister' languages, and implies that languages always become more divergent. In fact, languages generally change gradually, and there is often considerable intermixing among those which remain geographically adjacent. Partly for this reason, their genetic classification (by language family) does not necessarily correlate with their classification by type.

See CLASSIFICATION OF LANGUAGES, HAMITO-SEMITIC LANGUAGES, INDO-EUROPEAN LANGUAGES, LANGUAGE CHANGE, LINGUISTIC TYPOLOGY, MALAYO-POLYNESIAN LANGUAGES, PHILOLOGY, SINO-TIBETAN LANGUAGES, URO-ALTAIC LANGUAGES. [HISTORY, LANGUAGE].   J.M.A.

LANGUAGE HANDICAP. See AGRAMMATISM, APHASIA, AUDIOBOOK, BRAILLE, DYSLEXIA, ECHO-LALIA, LANGUAGE PATHOLOGY, LISP, SIGN LANGUAGE, SLIP OF THE TONGUE, SPEECH PATHOLOGY, SPEECH THERAPY, STUTTERING/STAMMERING, TALKING BOOK, TESD.

LANGUAGE LEARNING, short form *LL.* In principle, the learning of any language; in practice, in language teaching, and applied linguistics, the term is usually limited to the learning of foreign languages. The psychological and neurological nature of such learning is not known, but some general statements can be made about its educational and social aspects. In broad terms, there are two kinds of foreign-language learning: *informal* ('picking a language up') and *formal* (taking an organized course).

The market-place tradition. Although not often discussed by applied linguists, the informal approach has been by far the commoner way of learning languages, especially among migrants, refugees, traders, sailors, soldiers, and the inhabitants of frontier settlements, garrison towns, and ports. This *market-place tradition* is primarily oral, usually haphazard, and part of a range of ad-hoc communicative strategies that include gesturing, drawing pictures, using interpreters, mixing elements from two or more tongues, and guesswork. The aim has seldom been to learn an approved or 'high' version of another language to the fullest possible extent, but rather to use language to get something else done ('to get by'). In the process, the boundaries between languages may not be well established. Code-mixing and code-switching are common, especially where people know two or more language systems fairly well. One result of the widespread need to communicate at this level has been what are variously known as *contact languages*, *make-shift languages*, *trade jargons*, and *inter-languages*, such as Bazar Malay, Chinook Jargon, Fanakalo, Lingua Franca, and Pidgin English. In course of time, under appropriate circumstances, some of these forms have evolved into new 'full' languages in their own right. In their early stages of stabilization and growth, such languages are known technically as *creoles*.

The monastery tradition. Because of its dominant position in most present-day societies, formal instruction in some kind of institution, in set periods of time, with one teacher and a class of learners in a room, has come to be seen as the 'proper' way to learn a language. Such formality, typical of present-day educational systems, is usually associated with certain assumptions about culture and utility: for example, it is traditionally applied more to prestige languages (such as French in Britain and English in France) than to minority or fringe languages (such as Welsh in Britain and Basque in France). In the Western world, the roots of formal learning of this type are classical, but the truly formative influence was the medieval training of religious novices in Latin as an international language. This *monastery tradition* favours rote learning associated with repetition, the study of canonical texts, and grammatical analysis. Though rigorous and demanding, and greatly valued by many people, it sits apart from the world, favouring abstraction and standardization. It distances learning from immediate need, demanding discipline (often, especially formerly, by coercion: learning Latin *sub virga* or 'under the rod') and motivation (or at least submission) on the part of students.

Attainment. Formal language learning is incremental. It is absorbed (or not absorbed) in doses, and runs from zero to whatever ceiling is reached. Progress is usually marked by a reduction of dependence on the teacher and changes in the kind of help needed. Such changes are gradual and occur at different rates for different people and in different aspects of learning. There are no easily displayed tokens of attainment, but administrators, teachers, and students need indicators of attainment, and for this purpose three levels are generally assumed: *beginner*, *intermediate*, *advanced*.

(1) *Beginner.* In the classroom, learning is at first by courtesy of the teacher. At first, beginners understand little and produce nothing, then gradually they understand individual words, fixed formulas, and disconnected items in speech

or text. There is often little creative scope, frustration is common, and regular praise and reassurance are essential. Translation is constant and often overt. Frequent, brief periods of reflection take place on differences between the two systems involved, such as between Italian *ragazza/ragazze* and English *girl/girls*, or on the fact that English nouns have no gender and therefore articles and adjectives do not change in their company: *a good mother, a good father* as opposed to French *une bonne mère, un bon père*. Generally, learning to understand (*receptive ability*) is faster than learning to express (*productive ability*). Performance is usually poor at this stage and dominated by the mother tongue.

(2) *Intermediate.* When learners begin to produce their own phrases and sentences they can use their own creativity in making mental connections (sometimes correct, often wrong, constantly developing) between items already encountered and partly learned. They make guesses, set up provisional theories about what things mean, or how they might be expressed, and modify them in the light of experience. Much of the learner's grasp of syntax is now established, though with gaps and shortcomings. Dependence on translation (spoken or mental) is less compulsive. Intermediates may feel the need for plenty of material, which confirms and consolidates what they know, speeding up recognition and comprehension, extending knowledge, and providing opportunities for reflection, rehearsal, practice, and use. Intermediate experience needs interest, variety, and relevance, without which learners become bored, but at the same time a balance is necessary between being starved and swamped. At this stage, many learners stop, their capacity fossilized at a point where they no longer find the target a challenge or cannot proceed further. For more motivated students, however, it is the level at which the *performance skills* (speaking and writing) improve rapidly, given opportunity, stimulation, and time for assimilation.

(3) *Advanced.* Learners at the advanced stage use their own creativity and need a new kind of help. They seek delicate discriminations of meaning, stylistic niceties, subtleties of culture and discourse, and greater acquaintance with the language. While encouraging such developments, teachers need to watch for idiosyncrasies and recurring errors, often due to carrying over features of the mother tongue into the target language. All going well, inner translation continues to decline and fluency, speed, and accuracy continue to develop. At this level, many learners achieve a close approximation to the skills of the native speaker of the target language.

Conclusion. The levels are not watertight. Individuals rise imperceptibly from one to the other, and may also slip back. Members of a class do not move forward uniformly, and the varying rates of fast, average, and slow learners may pose problems for teacher and students. Teachers, writers, and publishers often divide the levels into six: *absolute beginner, beginner-to-intermediate, lower intermediate, upper intermediate, early advanced, late advanced,* making it easier to structure courses and materials and conduct attainment tests. Although the marketplace and the monastery continue to be well-separated styles of language learning, there is a growing tendency to open the classroom door and let the world in, or take students out into that world to immerse them for a time in 'real' usage, before returning to the classroom for a time of consolidation. See BEHAVIO(U)RISM, CHILD LANGUAGE ACQUISITION, LANGUAGE, LANGUAGE TEACHING. [EDUCATION, LANGUAGE].

T.MCA., P.S.

Dakin, Julian. 1973. *The Language Laboratory and Language Learning.* London: Longman.
Ellis, Rod. 1985. *Understanding Second Language Acquisition.* Oxford: University Press.
Krashen, Stephen D. 1981. *Second Language Acquisition and Second Language Learning.* Oxford: Pergamon.
Spolsky, Bernard. 1989. *Conditions for Second Language Learning: Introduction to General Theory.* Oxford: University Press.
Stevick, Earl W. 1976. *Memory, Meaning and Method: Some Psychological Perspectives on Language Learning.* Rowley, Mass.: Newbury House.
Widdowson, Henry G. 1984. *Learning Purpose and Language Use.* Oxford: University Press.

LANGUAGE PATHOLOGY, also **speech pathology, communication disorders, logopaedics, phoniatry** (the various names are paralleled by such names for practitioners as *speech therapist, speech pathologist,* and *communicologist*). The study of disorders of spoken or written language, and the disorders themselves. Some scholars include disorders affecting ability to use sign language alongside those of speech and writing. Alternatives have been proposed to the term *pathology,* given the exclusively physical and medical application of its original use; *handicap, disorder,* and *disability* are three of the more widely used labels, though nuances differ: for example, 'disorder' implies a more severe disruption than 'disability'. There are two broad approaches to the subject:

(1) The medical model. This model examines pathologies of language in relation to their causes and physical symptoms. For example, the articulation of children born with a cleft palate is related to their abnormal anatomy and physiology, and to associated problems, such as reduced hearing in some cases. Other cases with medical antecedents include the language of deaf children, of children who have suffered brain damage, of aphasics, and of people whose vocal cords have been affected by growths or other conditions. Estimates vary, but about 40% of all pathologies can be related to medical causes. In the remaining cases, the reason for the problem is unclear; there is no obvious medical condition which could explain it, and the person affected seems within normal limits when subjected to medical tests. An appeal may be made to psychological, social, linguistic, and other factors, but it is difficult to arrive at a definite conclusion in such cases. These pathologies include cases of delayed language development, stuttering, abnormal voice quality, and linguistic problems associated with such conditions as hyperactivity, autism, and schizophrenia. In many cases, the combination of medical and other factors seems to be the only way of explaining the symptoms: for example, an abnormal voice quality may have begun as a physical problem, but if the speaker uses the voice professionally, anxiety may build up which in due course exacerbates the condition. Similar combinations of factors must operate to explain the remarkable variety of linguistic symptoms encountered in people who have the same medical condition: for example, a group of profoundly deaf children (all displaying the same levels of hearing loss) will manifest different kinds of language, depending on such factors as personality, intelligence, family background, memory and attention skills, and type of education.

(2) The behavioural model. Because medical factors can explain only a part of the problem, an alternative approach of a behavioural nature has been devised that looks directly at the linguistic symptoms and indirectly at the causes. It operates by taking a sample of language from the affected person, spoken or written, audio or video, of sufficient duration to represent the nature of the disorder. This sample is transcribed and analysed, so that the characteristics of the abnormal patterning become apparent. On the basis of this analysis, an assessment is made of the level of abnormality, and in association with non-linguistic factors (primarily, information obtained from psychological and medical tests) a diagnosis is made. Following this, recommendations are given for intervention, and a teaching programme outlined, to be implemented by speech therapists or other professionals. This kind of approach is essential in the case of language-disordered children, where there is often very little medical history and all one has to go on is the child's observed behaviour. It is also important in such cases as stuttering and lisping, where the original causative factors are usually obscure or unknown. The application of linguistics to the study of these problems is a relatively recent development known as *clinical linguistics*.

The communicative chain. Language pathologies are usually classified, using the medical model, in terms of interference with the normal communicative chain of events, involving input, central integration, and output. The chief disruption in input is deafness. Another problem arises when hearing is intact and the signal reaches the brain, but there are difficulties in decoding the signal. One such problem (*auditory agnosia*) is a failure to recognize the nature of incoming auditory stimuli: the sufferer is unable to recognize familiar sounds and cannot identify them in a consistent way. A further problem arises from brain damage which results in *receptive aphasia* (*receptive dysphasia*), an inability (mild, moderate, or severe) to comprehend grammar and vocabulary: a receptive aphasic hears incoming speech, but does not understand it. The converse problem is *expressive aphasia* (*expressive dysphasia*), an inability to produce the grammar and vocabulary of normal speech. Expressive aphasics know what they want to say, but are unable to formulate the sentences they need. The problem may be of varying severity. It is also possible for aphasics to be *globally* affected, with severe disruption of both receptive and expressive ability.

Damage to areas of the brain specifically concerned with language can produce other disorders. In particular, the ability to make voluntary movements of the vocal organs may be impaired, so that although the intention is present to produce a particular word, the wrong sounds are produced when the speaker attempts to say it. This disorder is known as *dyspraxia* or *apraxia*, often more specifically labelled *verbal* or *articulatory dyspraxia*. In such cases, there is no paralysis of the muscles controlling speech; in this respect, the disorder can be distinguished from *dysarthria*, which is a disorder arising from paralysis affecting the muscles controlling the vocal organs. The problem may be mild (as in a slight difficulty in lip movement), moderate, or severe (as in a major disruption to the functioning of the vocal cords, soft palate, and tongue). Other output problems include various disorders of fluency, which affect the ability of the speaker to control the timing and sequencing of sounds. *Stuttering* or *stammering* is the most widely recognized handicap here, but there is also *cluttering* (uncontrolled speed of speech). Speech can also be badly affected by such diseases as myasthenia gravis or Parkinson's disease and a wide range of problems can affect the vocal cords.

See AGRAMMATISM, ANOMIA, APHASIA, COPRO-
LALIA, DYSGRAPHIA, DYSLEXIA, ECHOLALIA, GLOS-
SOLALIA, LISP, LOGORRH(O)EA, NEUROLINGUISTICS,
SLIP OF THE TONGUE, SPEECH PATHOLOGY, SPEECH
THERAPY,   STUTTERING/STAMMERING,   WORD-
FORMATION (TOURETTE). [LANGUAGE].   D.C.

LANGUAGE PLANNING. The attempt to control the use, status, and structure of a language
through a language policy developed by a government or other authority. Normally carried
out by official agencies, such planning usually
passes through several stages: a particular
language or variety of a language is selected;
codification is undertaken to stabilize it, for
example by agreeing writing conventions for previously non-literate languages; the codified language is adjusted to enable it to perform new
functions, for example by inventing or borrowing scientific vocabulary; and mechanisms
are devised, such as teaching syllabuses and procedures for monitoring the media, to ensure that
the language is used in conformity with the
policy. This sequence is rarely appropriate for
English, whose dominant role in the world gives
it a unique position, but English is nonetheless
officially planned into national education systems in various ways. In Britain, Welsh has been
promoted through the National Curriculum in
Wales as a subject to be compulsorily learnt
within Wales, but is not compulsorily available
to Welsh speakers or others outside Wales. In
post-colonial nations the relationship of English
to indigenous languages is often carefully
defined: as the language of secondary and tertiary education in Tanzania while Kiswahili is
the national language; as an official language
recognized for legal purposes in India; as a library language in some subjects in some South
American universities. Planning policy may be
achieved through agencies at a number of levels
in a state hierarchy. Governments may define
their language policy throughout a country, min-
istries of education may define it within education, and institutions may contribute to planning
through their own policies: for example, in the
UK in the 1980s, local education authorities and
individual schools attempted to define the roles
of various especially migrant languages like Panjabi and Cantonese within particular regions or
institutions. Relevant publications include: John
Edwards (ed.), *Linguistic Minorities, Policies and
Pluralism* (Academic Press, 1984); C. Kennedy
(ed.), *Language Planning and English Language
Teaching* (Prentice Hall, 1989); James W. Tollefson, *Planning Language, Planning Inequality:
Language Policy in the Community* (Longman,
1991). See ACADEMY, FRANCIZATION, LANGUAGE
POLICE, LEXICAL BAR, LOGIC, SOCIOLINGUISTICS,
STANDARD. [EDUCATION, LANGUAGE].   C.J.B.

LANGUAGE POLICE [Late 20c]. Also **language cops, tongue troopers**. An informal,
emotive, and usually dismissive term in Canada
for the Quebec *Office de la Langue Française*,
which seeks to ensure compliance with the province's laws upholding the primacy of French:
'The Quebec language police have pursued and
punished a Ste-Anne-de-Beaupré motel owner
for having an "office" (a word used to describe
government services in Quebec) instead of a "ré-
ception," and charged a Hull restaurant owner
for using "dry gin" on his menu. "Brunch" and
"jogger" are allowed, but "essence," not "gasoline," should be sold. . . . The government's
tongue-troopers, after solemn deliberation,
recommended that a hamburger be called a
"hambourgeois" ' (Suzanne Zwarun, 'Language
Rights', *Chatelaine*, Feb. 1989). See QUEBEC.
[AMERICAS, LANGUAGE].   T.MCA.

LANGUAGE RIGHTS [1980s: on the analogy
of *civil rights, human rights*, etc.]. In linguistics
and in law as applied to language, the concept
that individuals and communities have certain
fundamental rights in relation to the language(s)
that they use or wish to use: 'The Supreme Court
of Newfoundland is of the view that it must be
more cautious interpreting legislative provisions
on "language rights" than those relating to
"legal guarantees" ' (Jacques Robichaud, 'Language Rights and the Courts', in *Language and
Society*, Ottawa, Spring 1988); 'Australia and
Yugoslavia are among the few countries that
have incorporated the principle of language
rights into official policy' (James W. Tollefson,
Planning Language, Planning Inequality, Longman, 1991). Compare LANGUAGE POLICE. [LAN-
GUAGE].   T.MCA.

LANGUAGE SHIFT [1960s]. A term in linguistics for a massive shift in use from one language to another, as in Ireland from Gaelic to
English (18–20c). In 1964, the US linguist Joshua
A. Fishman introduced the dual notion *language
maintenance and language shift* (*LMLS*) to discuss the situation of 'the minority language or
small national language faced by pressures
related to a much bigger national or international language'. To the latter, of which English is the pre-eminent example, he has given the
name *language of wider communication* (*LWC*):
see J. A. Fishman, *Language and Ethnicity in
Minority Sociolinguistic Perspective* (Clevedon &
Philadelphia: Multilingual Matters, 1989). See
BILINGUALISM, IRISH ENGLISH, LANGUAGE DEATH.
[LANGUAGE].   T.MCA.

LANGUAGE TEACHING, short form *LT*. In
principle, instruction in any language, under any
conditions, formal or informal; in practice, as

the term is commonly used among language teachers and applied linguists, instruction in a second or foreign language within a system of education, such as the institutionalized teaching of French in Britain and English in France. More specifically, the teaching of a mother tongue, home language, or national language may be referred to as *L1 teaching* (where L1 means *first language*) and the teaching of one or more other languages as *L2 teaching* (where L2 means *second language*).

L1 and L2 teaching. By and large, *L1 teaching* is that part of general education which deals with the transmission of a society's written culture and standard speech (which may or may not involve training in an approved accent). It usually includes instruction in aspects of a particular literature, and it has traditionally included explicit instruction in grammar, spelling, punctuation, and composition, matters that are currently controversial. *L2 teaching* for many centuries centred on acquiring a classical language, in Europe especially Latin, sometimes Greek or Hebrew, and elsewhere such languages as classical Arabic, Mandarin Chinese, and Sanskrit. In Britain, the teaching of a second vernacular (non-foreign) language has taken place, on a limited scale and mainly since the 19c, in Scotland and Wales, usually for those who have already had Gaelic or Welsh as their mother tongues, their general education proceeding in English as a second language which more often than not becomes their primary medium. Because there has been no significant other vernacular in England since Norman French in the 14c, L2 teaching in that country has generally been concerned with 'foreign' languages. The most powerful L2 tradition in England, and elsewhere in the English-speaking world, has usually been the teaching of French.

The literary method. Throughout Western history, literacy and education have run together. Only in the 20c has the technology of audio-recording allowed conversation to become an object of study. This change, along with a broad acceptance of democratic ideals in education as well as in politics, has made possible a vernacular rather than a classical education, or one that judiciously draws on both. For many centuries, language teaching in the European ('monastery') tradition of Christianity meant the teaching of the languages of religion, literature, and scholarship: Latin and to a limited extent Greek. In addition, in the Middle Ages in England, children of the aristocracy were taught Norman French, while English was a largely irrelevant vernacular. Although some attempt was made to teach spoken Latin (for example, in the English Abbot Aelfric's *Colloquy*, a conversation reader, *c.* AD 1000), learning centred mostly on a close acquaintance with the most highly valued literary texts. With the Renaissance and the Reformation, and the return of classical Latin as a model, the language largely ceased to be used in speech; thenceforth, the aim was written mastery, learners imitating the style of 'the classics', and being led away from the 'debased' styles of less highly regarded texts. The 'golden' texts of Cicero, Horace, and Virgil were accepted, while the base metal of Apuleius, Geoffrey of Monmouth, Petrarch, and other later Latin writers was ignored. The route to understanding lay through rote memorization of grammar and vocabulary and imitation that might or might not lead to creativity.

The grammar–translation method. Opposition to the literary tradition arose in and around Germany in the late 18c, with methods of teaching Latin and other languages that have in the 20c been given the name *the grammar–translation method/approach*. Reformers sought to organize and simplify the traditional exposure to texts by using specimen sentences and emphasizing practice by translating in both directions. Through translation of specially constructed sentences that were keyed to lessons centred on particular grammatical points, learners could be exposed to the grammatical and stylistic range of the target language in an economical and systematic way. The reform was not, however, complete, and for the next 200 years the grammar–translation method and the less systematic literary method coexisted and often blended.

The Reform Movement. Dissatisfaction with the practice of teaching modern languages by such text-based methods came to a head in the *Reform Movement* of the 1880s–90s, among scholars and teachers in Germany, Scandinavia, France, and Britain who were interested in the practical possibilities of a science of speech. It began with the publication in 1877 of Henry Sweet's *Handbook of Phonetics*. With its analyses and specimens of different sound systems, this book opened up the prospect of teaching speech systematically and escaping from the ancient dependence on texts. In 1882, the German phonetician Wilhelm Viëtor expressed the growing impatience in the pamphlet *Der Sprachunterricht muss umkehren* (Language teaching must start afresh), initially published under a pseudonym. Paul Passy in France is credited with inventing the term *la méthode directe* (*the Direct Method*) to sum up the aims of the reformers; other names are the *Natural Method*, *New Method*, and *Phonetic Method*.

Writing in *Transactions of the Philological Society*, Sweet continued to publish analyses of the sound systems of various living languages, adding in 1884 the paper 'On the Practical Study of Language'. In the same year, Felix Franke in Germany published *Die praktische Spracherlernung* (The Practical Acquisition of Languages), in which while acknowledging his debt to Sweet he emphasized, in addition to the use of phonetic transcription, the psychological aspect of learning, the importance of creating the right associations, of avoiding translation as much as possible, and of entering into the spirit of the community concerned. Later in 1884, Franke's book was issued in a Danish translation by Otto Jespersen. In 1885, Sweet published what for the reformers came to stand as the model textbook of English for a foreign learner, *Elementarbuch des gesprochenen Englisch*, aimed initially at a German-speaking public, but subsequently issued in an English version, *A Primer of Spoken English* (1890).

Phonetics. Early in 1886, under the leadership of Paul Passy, a group of teachers in France formed the *Phonetic Teachers' Association* and started a journal in phonetic script entitled *Dhi Fonètik Titcer*. At Jespersen's suggestion, membership was made international; he joined in May, Viëtor in July, and Sweet in September. This body in due course developed into the *Association Phonétique Internationale* (in English the *International Phonetic Association*, in German the *Weltlautschriftverein*), whose deliberations resulted in the IPA alphabet. In 1899, Sweet published *The Practical Study of Languages*. Two years later, Jespersen published his ideas in a book in Danish later issued in English as *How to Teach a Foreign Language* (1904). These complementary works by and large represent the Reform Movement, Sweet's concerned with principles, Jespersen's with classroom work. Their minor differences were typical of the movement as a whole.

The direct method. Reformers rejected the teaching of modern languages through grammatical paradigms, specimen sentences, and word lists. They wanted to base teaching directly on speech and to apply the results of phonetics in their courses so as to ensure sound pronunciation from the start. For the rest, they sought as close an approximation as possible to the way a child learns its first language. They adopted the principles of association, visualization, and learning through the senses, through pictures and through activity and play. They emphasized the learning of grammar by practice rather than precept, by making the responses to points of grammar automatic and unconscious. The mother tongue should be avoided as much as possible and translation reduced to a minimum. They held that learning a language in this way meant,

in effect, the absorption of another culture. It was generally agreed that professional language teachers should receive phonetic training, and that at the school stage the teacher should preferably be of the same language background as the pupils. The aim of the teaching should be successful use of the target language, actively and passively, but should not include translation.

The reformers' influence. The movement has had a varied impact in different parts of the world. In Continental Europe, it is generally considered to have led, virtually within a generation, to a marked improvement in spoken English and other languages, especially in Scandinavia, Germany, and the Netherlands. The principles and practices of the movement continue to have a strong influence. In Britain, influence has been limited in the teaching of modern languages in schools but considerable in the teaching of English as a foreign and second language. Two EFL pioneers particularly influenced by the movement were Harold E. Palmer, author of *The Oral Method of Teaching Languages* (1921), and Daniel Jones, compiler of the *English Pronouncing Dictionary* (1917). In the US, the movement had little success until the Second World War, although in 1914 Leonard Bloomfield had noted in his *Introduction to the Study of Language*: 'It is only in the last twenty-five years and in the European countries that success in modern-language teaching has ever been attained', adding that 'most of our practice is half a century or so behind that of the European schools.' Bloomfield's interest is reflected in his *Outline Guide for the Practical Study of Foreign Languages* (1942), the text that inspired both the massive US wartime programme of language teaching and post-war theories of teaching and learning.

The audio-lingual method. In the US in the 1950s there developed a movement based on the precepts of structural linguistics and behaviourist psychology and known variously as the *audio-lingual method* (*ALM*), *audio-lingual teaching*, *audiolingualism, the structuralist approach*, and *structuralism*. The ALM dominated the teaching of English as a second language in North America for some 25 years, and materials prepared by Robert Lado and others at the U. of Michigan were widely used there and elsewhere. Its content derived from an analysis of the phonemes, morphemes, and sentence patterns of the target language, and it sought to automate classroom activity through *pattern practice* drills (exercises in the repetition of specific kinds of phrases and sentences, with systematic changes intended to extend the learner's skills), taught by techniques of *mimicry and memorization* known for short as *mim-mem.*

The structural approach and the audio-visual method. The American audio-lingual method differed considerably from two European approaches with similar names: (1) The British *structural approach* of Harold E. Palmer and Michael West in the 1920s-30s, which augmented the direct method with graded grammatical structures, word lists, and readers. (2) The French *méthode structuro-globale* (in English usually called the *audio-visual method*), which developed in the 1960s and used a combination of textbooks, tape recordings, filmstrips, slides, and classroom presentation. Although it appeared to be the ALM with illustrations, the French method was technological, not ideological.

The situational approach. Almost from the start of the Reform Movement, practitioners used conversation readers in their teaching, often with texts in phonetic script, such as E. T. True and Otto Jespersen, *Spoken English* (1891) and H. Palmer and F. G. Blandford, *Everyday Sentences in Spoken English* (1922). In the 1960s-70s, many textbooks took such a practical approach further, grouping their teaching units around situational themes such as *At the Hairdresser* and *The Post Office.* The dialogues and narratives in the text derived from these settings, and teachers were expected to produce appropriate material to support action-based language use within the situation defined by the chosen topic. The strength of the topic was language appropriate to a situation, but its weakness, the difficulty of generalizing what is learned, led to its being used more in collaboration with other procedures than in its pure form.

The notional-functional approach. In the early 1970s there developed in Europe an approach to LT that focused on two kinds of semantic and performative criteria: *notions,* such as *time, place, quantity, emotional attitudes,* and *functions,* such as *describing, enquiring, apologizing, criticizing.* The introduction of such ideas has influenced subsequent syllabuses and coursebooks. However, courses whose content is entirely notional and functional are often difficult to teach and learn from, because some notions and functions presuppose a knowledge of grammar and vocabulary for which no provision may have been made. It is probable that no definitive list of notions or of functions exists or may even be possible, but the concept has proved useful. See COUNCIL OF EUROPE.

The communicative approach. In the 1970s-80s there developed in both Europe and North America an approach to foreign- and second-language teaching that drew on the work of anthropologists, sociologists, and sociolinguists. In many ways a lineal descendant of the direct method, it has concentrated on language as social behaviour, seeing the primary goal of language teaching as the development of the learner's *communicative competence.* In addition to formal linguistic knowledge, learners are considered to need both rules of use to produce language appropriate to particular situations, and strategies for effective communication. Partly through the influence of the *Council of Europe Languages Projects,* the movement at first concentrated on notional-functional syllabuses, which depended on analyses of semantic and functional categories of language use rather than on those of formal grammar. In the 1980s, however, the approach was more concerned with the quality of interaction between learner and teacher rather than the specification of syllabuses, and concentrated on classroom methodology rather than on content, which remained similar to that of situational and notional-functional course materials.

The cognitive code approach. This approach to language teaching, which developed especially in the US in the 1980s, advocates conscious (*cognitive*) awareness of the structure of the target language and argues that study of rules of pronunciation and grammar will give learners a practical command of that language. Some commentators see it as the *grammar-translation method* in a new form, others as essentially a rejection of behaviourism and the audio-visual method.

A plethora of methods. A wide range of approaches to L2 teaching are currently available, ranging from the *grammar-translation method* and the *communicative approach* (both 'mainstream', in the sense that they are used by large numbers of teachers) through the now less influential *audio-lingual method* or *structural method* with its behaviourist bias (favoured especially in North America in the 1950s-70s) to such radical 'fringe' approaches as Caleb Gattegno's *Silent Way* and Georgi Lozanov's *Suggestopedia.* The Silent Way seeks to give the learner maximum investment in the language-learning process, by reducing the spoken role of the teacher as much as possible. Highly formal charts for pronunciation and grammar, together with Cuisenaire rods for manipulation, provide the major teaching aids. Suggestopedia is based on the view that relaxation enables learners to exploit their capacities for language acquisition to the maximum degree. Emphasis is placed on comfortable surroundings, use of music and chanting, and trust in the authority of the teacher. Particularly used to assist memorization, the procedure relies on making language learning different from the stressful effort to produce appropriate communication for pre-defined needs. Conferences for EFL and ESL teachers currently provide sessions on a sometimes overwhelming array of methods and blends of methods, and a plethora of books describes the main varieties in detail or in overviews. *Holistic methods* emphasize putting the learner into a frame of mind for learning or developing the education of 'the whole person', and diminishing the teacher's appearance as an authority-figure. The *humanistic approach* similarly seeks to emphasize the shared interests and needs of teachers and students and provide a caring environment in which to learn. Many pragmatists, however, endorse no particular pedagogical or ideological position and are eclectic in their teaching, a style sometimes referred to as the *eclectic approach*. The ongoing debate testifies to the variety and vitality of the profession.

Public and community issues. LT requires today, in every country, deliberate policy decisions by government on such issues as: which language should be encouraged; how many teachers should be employed; what training teachers should be given; how they should be valued in terms of pay and conditions; what average class size should be supported and at what rate of intensity; what teaching resources and materials should be supplied; what support should be given to research and development; what the degree of direct government intervention should be, in such matters as setting a syllabus, prescribing books, and inspecting the teaching; what standards of achievement are desirable and hence what examinations and qualifications should be promoted. Community attitudes (friendly or hostile) towards particular peoples and their languages also strongly affect teaching, as do popular assumptions about how successful members of the community will be in learning languages: for example, compare expectations about whether the average citizen will learn at least one foreign language in The Netherlands and in Britain.

Teaching formats. A further aspect of the public and community dimension of LT is the educational format in which it takes place: in a teacher-led class in a school or college; through distance learning by correspondence or radio or television (with or without an element of face-to-face tutoring); in one-to-one contact between a teacher and a learner; in solitary, self-study learning; in 'immersion teaching' (for example, with immigrant children in Canada, where learners are immersed in an English-speaking or

French-speaking life instead of experiencing the target language only in timetabled class hours). Most of these formats are found in most countries; which one is being employed at a given time determines the different settings that will be necessary in the parameters of LT, in order to bring about effective LL. In addition, the ultimate aims of language teaching need to be clarified: whether it is part of general education, geared to instrumental needs such as the integration of immigrants into a particular society, or for such specific purposes as English for maritime communication (*Seaspeak*) or air traffic control (*Airspeak*).

Conclusion. Debates in L1 and L2 teaching in the 20c may be interpreted in terms of a tension between the *dual tradition* (the literary and grammar–translation methods) and the *reform movement* (the direct method and its various derivatives). The literary method has provided immediate contact with prestigious texts, serious subject matter, and a link with ancient traditions, while the various phases of grammar–translation have promised a less élitist approach, devising short-cuts to mastery of grammar or the social strategies necessary to become (more or less) part of the target-language community. Greater emphasis on writing or on speech has varied from time to time and place to place, but generally movements to renew or improve the effectiveness of teaching have consistently combined with movements to undercut the classical humanist traditions by appealing directly to usefulness. Reform movements have generally been equivocal about whether they are doing more efficiently the same things that previous traditions have done or whether they are subverting the previous traditions by changing the goals, substituting what any learner could do for what only a select few would wish to do. Each reform has therefore attracted adherents who imagined that they were undermining the values of previous education, together with those whose intention was to improve its effectiveness but not to question its goals.

See ALEXANDER (L.), APPLIED LINGUISTICS, APPROACH, BEHAVIO(U)RISM, BERLITZ, COMMUNICATIVE COMPETENCE, CONTRASTIVE LINGUISTICS/ANALYSIS, COUNCIL OF EUROPE, CURRICULUM, ECLECTICISM, EDUCATED AND UNEDUCATED, EDUCATION, ELT, ELT DOCUMENTS, ELT PUBLISHING, ENGLISH, ERROR ANALYSIS, FIRST LANGUAGE, FREQUENCY COUNT, GRAMMAR, HORNBY, HYPERCORRECTION, INTERLANGUAGE, INTERNATIONAL PHONETIC ASSOCIATION, JESPERSEN, JONES (D.), LANGUAGE LEARNING, LANGUAGE PLANNING, LEARNER'S DICTIONARY, MOTHER TONGUE, NATIVE LANGUAGE, NATIVE SPEAKER, NATIVE USER, NATURAL LANGUAGE, PALMER,

PASSY, PEDAGOGICAL GRAMMAR, PHONETICS, PRO-
NUNCIATION MODEL, READER, RECEIVED PRO-
NUNCIATION, STANDARD, STANDARD ENGLISH,
STANDARD LANGUAGE, STANDARD VARIETY,
STREVENS, SWEET, SYLLABUS, TEACHER TALK,
TEACHING ENGLISH, TEFL, TEIL, TESD, TESL, TESOL,
VIËTOR, VOCABULARY, VOCABULARY CONTROL,
WEST. [EDUCATION, LANGUAGE].

C.J.B., P.C., P.S., T.MCA.

Brown, H. D. 1987. *Principles of Language Learning
and Teaching*, 2nd edition. Englewood Cliffs, NJ:
Prentice Hall.

Brumfit, C. J., & Johnson, K. (eds.). 1979. *The Communicative Approach to Language Teaching*. Oxford:
University Press.

Christophersen, Paul. 1973. *Second-Language Learning*. Harmondsworth: Penguin.

Kelly, Louis G. 1969. *25 Centuries of Language Teaching*. Rowley, Mass.: Newbury House.

Lado, Robert. 1964. *Language Teaching: A Scientific
Approach*. New York: McGraw-Hill.

Littlewood, William. 1981. *Communicative Language
Teaching*. Cambridge: University Press.

McArthur, Tom. 1983. *A Foundation Course for Language Teachers*. Cambridge: University Press.

Nunan, David. 1991. *Language Teaching Methodology:
A Textbook for Teachers*. New York & London:
Prentice Hall.

Richards, J. C., & Rodgers, T. S. 1986. *Approaches and
Methods in Language Teaching*. Cambridge: University Press.

Rivers, Wilga M. 1972. *Speaking in Many Tongues:
Essays in Foreign-Language Teaching*. Expanded 2nd
edition 1976. Rowley, Mass.: Newbury House.

—— 1981. *Teaching Foreign Language Skills*. Chicago:
University Press.

—— 1983. *Communicating Naturally in a Second Language: Theory and Practice in Language Teaching*.
Cambridge: University Press.

Stern, H. H. 1983. *Fundamental Concepts in Language
Teaching*. Oxford: University Press.

Stevick, Earl W. 1982. *Teaching and Learning
Languages*. Cambridge: University Press.

LANGUAGE TYPOLOGY. See LINGUISTIC TYPOLOGY.

LANGUAGE UNIVERSALS, also universals of language.

Terms in linguistics for presumed universal properties of human language, sometimes
divided into: *absolute universals*, properties that
exist in all languages, and constraints that are
valid for all languages, and *statistical universals*,
properties that are likely to exist in languages.
Universals may exist independently or may be
implicational: if a language has X, then it will
have Y. The recent search for universals has had
two main sources of inspiration: Joseph Greenberg (1963, below) attempted to specify implicational universals relating to word order, while
Noam Chomsky (1965, below) argued that a
large proportion of language is genetically
inbuilt, and that this is likely to be reflected in
such universals. Initially, he hoped to find universals of two types: *substantive universals*, which
specify the substance out of which languages are
made, such as a universal set of possible sounds,
from which different languages select a subset;
formal universals, which specify that all languages must be arranged in accordance with
fixed principles: for example, words can only be
combined in certain prescribed ways.

When abstract properties common to all
languages proved hard to identify, researchers
gradually moved to a search for universal constraints, in an attempt to discover the bounds
within which human language operates. A common approach has been to study English in
depth, then to examine the extent to which
abstract constraints on English are observable
in other languages: starting with the sentence
Angela bought a duck and a parrot, it is possible
to form the related question: *What did Angela
buy?* It is not, however, possible to question only
part of the noun phrase at the end of the sentence
and say: **What did Angela buy a duck and?* or
**What did Angela buy and a parrot?* A similar
restriction against moving part of a noun phrase
seems to be valid for many, perhaps all,
languages. More recently, the failure to find a
sufficient number of convincing constraints has
led to an upsurge of interest in linguistic
typology, the attempt to find properties common
to groups of languages. Chomsky has also
revised his ideas about what may be universal.
He argues (1986, below) that a genetically inherited Universal Grammar (UG) involves some
fixed principles, supplemented by options which
have to be selected after exposure to a particular
language. See LANGUAGE ACQUISITION DEVICE,
LINGUISTIC TYPOLOGY. [LANGUAGE]. J.M.A.

Chomsky, Noam. 1965. *Aspects of the Theory of
Syntax*. Cambridge, Mass.: MIT Press.

—— 1986. *Knowledge of Language: Its Nature, Origin
and Use*. New York: Praeger.

Greenberg, Joseph H. (ed.). 1963. *Universals of Language*. Cambridge, Mass.: MIT Press.

—— Ferguson, Charles A., & Moravcsik, Edith A.
(eds.). 1978. *Universals of Human Language*. Four
volumes. Stanford: University Press.

LANGUE AND PAROLE

[Early 20c: French,
language and speech]. Contrasting terms in linguistics, proposed by Ferdinand de Saussure
(*Cours de linguistique générale*, 1915) to distinguish between the language system of a group
(*langue*) and instances of its use (*parole*) within
language in general (*langage*). See COMPETENCE
AND PERFORMANCE. [LANGUAGE]. J.M.A.

LANKAN ENGLISH. See SRI LANKA.

LAPSUS LINGUAE. See SLIP OF THE TONGUE.

LARYNX [16c: from Latin *larynx*, from Greek *lárunx*. Adjective: *laryngeal*]. An anatomical term for the modified upper part of the trachea (windpipe) of air-breathing animals. It is commonly known as the *voice box* in humans because of its importance in the creation of the voice. It contains the vocal cords or folds and influences voice quality. The front cartilage of the larynx is the *Adam's apple*, prominent in adult males. See GLOTTIS, VOCAL CORDS/FOLDS, VOICE, VOICE QUALITY. [SPEECH].   G.K.

LASER [1950s: an acronym, from *Lightwave Amplification by Stimulated Emission of Radiation*]. A general and technical term for a device that produces an intense and coherent beam of light. It has many uses in industry, medicine, and communication. When lasers scan written materials, the reflected images are transformed into electromagnetic data for storage. Such data can also be transferred back into light and used to create accurate images on paper. In the *fax* or *facsimile transfer machine*, a laser scans a document and translates the image into signals that can be sent by telephone to another machine that re-creates the image on a device resembling a photocopier drum, producing hard copy at the other end. Lasers are also used to generate typesetting images and, combined with the computer, allow for great flexibility in manipulating visual data. A *laser printer* translates encoded data from a computer into light impulses which are directed on to a small photocopying drum; the image is then transferred to paper. See FAX, PHOTOCOPYING. [TECHNOLOGY].   W.W.B.

LATE MODERN ENGLISH. See ENGLISH, MODERN ENGLISH, PERIOD DICTIONARIES OF ENGLISH.

LATERAL [16c: from Latin *lateralis* at the side(s)]. A term in phonetics for a vocal sound in which air gets round central blockage by the tongue by escaping round the sides. The only English lateral is /l/ as in *large, hollow, barrel*; Welsh has /ɬ/ as in *Llanberis, Llangollen*. See L-SOUNDS, WELSH. [SPEECH].   G.K.

LATIN[1] [Before 10c: from Latin *Latinus*, the adjective of *Latium* ('the broad place'), the region of the River Tiber and the Alban hills in west-central Italy, where the city of Rome was reputedly founded in 753 BC]. The classical and cultural language of Western Europe, a member of the Indo-European language family, and the precursor of the Romance languages. Latin does not have as long an unbroken tradition as Greek, but has existed for *c*.3,000 years, a period of time divided by scholars into four phases: (1) From an unknown date to around 5c BC, a western

Italic dialect dominated by Etruscan. (2) From 4c BC to 5c AD, the language of the Roman Republic and Empire, greatly influenced by Greek, with a literary standard and popular forms from which the Romance languages derive. (3) From 3c to 20c, the international vehicle of the Roman Catholic Church, and the learned language of Western Christendom. (4) Also *Neo-Latin, New Latin* (*c*.15c onward). The cultural medium of Renaissance and post-Renaissance Europe, rich in Greek borrowings.

Particularly since the Renaissance, Latin has also been the scholarly and literary seed-corn for the vernacular European languages. English has proved to be the most receptive among the Germanic languages to direct as well as indirect Latin influence, largely as a consequence of the Norman Conquest.

Nature and influence. Latin is a highly inflected language noted for conciseness of expression: for example, the one word *amābunt* translates the three English words *they will love*, while its passive form *amābuntur* translates *they will be loved*. For centuries, formal education in the British Isles has been closely associated with the teaching and learning of Latin. Especially in England, this training was provided in *grammar schools*, in which the term *grammar* was virtually synonymous with *Latin*. Such institutions in the 16c bear close comparison with 19-20c English-medium schools in such countries as India and Nigeria, and with contemporary grammar-based ways of teaching English in such countries as Japan and Korea. Both the terms and the style of the traditional grammatical study of English derive from Latin, and the formal analysis of English grammar widely taught until recent decades owes much to a Latin grammatical model derived in its turn from a Greek model.

Although in the later 20c there has been less interest in and emphasis on the learning of Latin in many school systems, its indirect influence remains great: Latin language and literature have had a pervasive influence over many modern languages and literatures, and the language continues to be taught in its classical form in many schools in Europe and throughout the European diaspora. Latin is often described as a 'dead' language, a metaphor which holds true in that it is well over a millennium since Latin was learned and used as a mother tongue. The concept of 'deadness' is, however, suspect in terms of the unbroken tradition of learning and using Latin, of scholarship in Latin and derived from Latin, and of the Latin loans in so many languages throughout the world. Much of the work done in Latin and the borrowing of lexical material from Latin took place long after it had ceased to be a language acquired by children from the community around them.

Latin and English. In the 4c, St Jerome's Vulgate Bible became the model for Christian writing in Latin. This model was further developed by St Augustine of Hippo (4-5c), a teacher of rhetoric, in works like *Civitas Dei* (The City of God). His example was followed in England by such scholars as Aldhelm (7c), Bede (7-8c), Alcuin (8-9c), and Aelfric (10-11c), while the translations from Latin into Old English by King Alfred of Wessex (9c) laid the foundation of early English prose writing. The fluid interplay of languages in Britain during the Middle Ages is illustrated by three events in the 12c, all associated with the cycle of mythic and legendary material known as the *Matter of Britain*. First, the Oxford cleric Galfridus Monemutensis (Geoffrey of Monmouth), an Englishman with Welsh and Breton connections, wrote the Latin prose work *Historia regum Britanniae* (History of the kings of Britain, *c*.1135). He claimed that he translated this work from a very old book 'in the British tongue': that is, in a form of Celtic similar to Welsh. The History begins with the settlement in Britain of a great-grandson of the Trojan hero Aeneas, whose name was Brutus and who purportedly gave his name to the island. It ends with the legendary King Arthur, a Celtic hero adopted by the Anglo-Normans. The History was then translated into French, and further romanticized, as the *Roman de Brut* (1155) by Wace, an Anglo-Norman from Jersey. This work then served as the source for the *Brut*, an alliterative poem in the late 12c by the Worcestershire priest Layamon, in what is now called Middle English. Layamon's work was the first appearance in English of the stories of Arthur, Lear, and Cymbeline.

Latin continued to be the primary language of scholarship until the end of the 17c. Such scholars as William Camden wrote by preference in Latin, considering that to use English was to write in sand, and for major contributors to the canon of English literature, such as John Milton, Latin was an essential professional tool. In the late 17c, Sir Isaac Newton chose Latin as the medium for *Philosophiae naturalis principia mathematica* (Mathematical principles of natural philosophy), better known as the *Principia* (1687), and this work was not translated into English until 1729. He chose Latin to ensure that the *Principia* would be widely read, but later wrote *Opticks* in English, its date of publication (1704) marking the point at which significant scholarly work began to appear in English first and, in due course, without any translation into Latin. Because of familiarity with the Classics, however, writers continued to evoke in English the images and phrases of ancient Rome, often only slightly adapted, and to allude fluently to topics that, until well into the 20c, their readership could generally grasp without editorial help. In addition, numerous Latin quotations and tags have enjoyed an extended life in English to the present day.

Anglo-Latin pronunciation. The pronunciation of Latin by speakers of English and the pronunciation of Latin words and tags used in English have had a turbulent history. In Anglo-Saxon times, the pronunciation of Latin had already been somewhat nativized, and after the Norman Conquest, when Latin was taught through the medium of French, it took on a French aspect: for example, both the *i* in *ius* and the *g* in *gens* were spoken as an affricate (the *j*-sound in *just* and *gent*). After the 13c, soft *c* was pronounced /s/, and long vowels were shortened before two or more consonants, as in *census* and *nullus*, much as in present-day English *census* and *null*. In the 14c, English began to take over as the medium of instruction for Latin, largely as a result of the work of the educational reformer John Cornwall, and remained the norm until the early 16c. Controversy was aroused throughout Europe, however, when in 1528 Erasmus published *De recta Latini Graecique sermonis pronuntiatione* (On the correct pronunciation of Latin and Greek). This work discussed the diverse national accents of Latin, forms of pronunciation that were often mutually unintelligible and could lead to confusion and derision at international gatherings. Erasmus proposed that they all be standardized on certain assumptions about classical Latin speech, such as the use of hard *c* and *g*, voicelessness in intervocalic *s*, and the maintenance of contrasts in vowel length.

Erasmian ideas were taken up at Cambridge by such radical young scholars as John Cheke and Thomas Smith, and met with great resistance. In 1542, a university edict forbade Erasmian pronunciation, with heavy penalties that included the beating of offending undergraduates and the expulsion of offending masters. According to Stephen Gardiner, the Chancellor who imposed the edict, speakers of Erasmian Latin were unintelligible to their elders. In 1558, the edict was repealed. The controversy, however, had been maturing while the Great Vowel Shift was taking place, and just as this shift was transforming the pronunciation of mainstream English (and creating many anomalies of spelling and pronunciation), so it also affected the pronunciation of Latin. For example, the Latin long vowels $\bar{a}$, $\bar{\imath}$, $\bar{e}$ acquired the values now found in the English words *same*, *fine*, *been*. A highly Anglicized, non-Erasmian

Latin became the norm in England from the later 16c to the earlier 20c.

Around 1870, a new reformed pronunciation was proposed at Oxford and Cambridge, but did not become widely used until the early 20c, and continued to be resisted until the outbreak of the Second World War. One outcome of the ancient tension between the native and the classical pronunciations has been a certain confusion regarding not only the pronunciation of Latin in its own right but also the pronunciation of some Latin elements in English. These include endings of words like *formulae* (whether to be 'ay' as in *say*, 'ee' as in *see*, or 'y' as in *try*) and *stimuli* (whether to be 'y' as in *try* or 'ee' as in *see*). Anglicization is, however, the norm for most everyday tags: for example, *tempus fugit* with a schwa for the *u* in *tempus*, and a soft *g*; *bona fide* with a long *o* and a schwa in *bona*, and *i* as in *hide* in *fide* (with the alternative pronunciations 'fidey' and 'fide' in both BrE and AmE). In Scotland, in contrast to England, there has been a strong historical preference for an Erasmian pronunciation, with full vowel values and hard *g* and *c*.

Latin in English. A large part of the lexicon of Latin has entered English in two major waves: mainly religious vocabulary from the time of Old English until the Reformation, and mainly scientific, scholarly, and legal vocabulary (slightly different in English and Scottish law), from the Middle Ages onwards. In the 17c, such makers of English dictionaries as John Bullokar deliberately converted Latin words into English, building on the already strong French component of the vocabulary so as to create a Latinate register of education and refinement. In it, words like *fraternity* and *feline* were set lexically and stylistically 'above' words like *brotherhood* and *cat*. These lexicographers' methods were straightforward: they turned the endings of Latin words into Anglo-French endings, a practice that has continued with minor modifications ever since: thus, *alacritas* became French-like *alacritie* (later *alacrity*), *catalogus* (Greek in origin) became *catalogue* (later *catalog* in AmE), *incantatio* became *incantation*, *onerosus* became *onerous*, *puerilis* became *puerile*, and *ruminare* (through its past participle *ruminatus*) became *ruminate*.

Such processes are so transparent to those with a knowledge of Latin morphology that they can usually without much difficulty identify relationships between basic Latin forms and words derived from them in languages like Spanish, French, and English. The majority of such forms are either verbal or nominal–adjectival, the verbal relating to the four Latin *conjugations*, the nominal–adjectival relating mainly to three of the five Latin *declensions*. Latin verbs are routinely listed with two canonical forms, the infinitive and the neuter of the past participle: *amare/amatum* to love (first conjugation); *monēre/monitum* to warn (second); *regere/rectum* to rule (third); *audīre/auditum* to hear (fourth). Latin nouns and adjectives are often listed using two categories of case (nominative for the subject of a sentence, genitive for possession): *regina/reginae* queen, *nigra/nigrae* black (both first declension); *dominus/domini* master, *ager/agri* field, *magnus/magni* great, *niger/nigri* black (all second); *rex/regis* king, *nobilis/nobilis* noble (both third).

The bulk of words in Latin-derived English words relate etymologically and structurally to these two broad types. For example, from the verb *cantare/cantatum* (to sing, usually with the form *-cent-* after a prefix) come such words as *cant, canticle, cantor, descant, incantation, accent, incentive, precentor, recant* (with *enchant, enchantment* through French, and *cantata, canto* through Italian). From *monēre/monitum* (to warn) come *monitor, admonish, admonition, admonitory, premonition*. From *agere/actum* (to do, act) come *agent, agency, agile, agility, agitate, act, actor, action, enact, exact, inaction, inactivity*. From *currere/cursum* (to run) come *current, currency, cursive, cursor, cursory, concur, incur, excursion, occurrence, precursor, recurrent*. From *claudere/clausum* (to close, with the forms *-clud-/-clus-* after a prefix) come *clause, include, exclude, preclude, seclusive, conclusion*. From *dominus/domini* (master) and *dominare/dominatum* (to master) come *dominion, dominate, domination, dominie, domineering* (through French and Dutch), *domain* (through French). From *caput/capitis* (head) come *capital, capitalism, capitalize, decapitate, decapitation* (and through French *cattle, chapter, chattel, chief*). From *avidus/avidi* (greedy) come *avid, avidity*; from *rigidus/rigidi* (stiff) come *rigid, rigidity*; from *audax/audacis* (bold) come *audacious, audacity*; from *ferox/ferocis* (fierce) come *ferocious, ferocity*.

In addition, many words that in Latin actually perform grammatical functions have been nominalized in English: *caveat* (beware) as a synonym for a warning, *floruit* (he/she flourished) to mark the period when someone was in his or her prime (usually when precise birth and death dates are not known), *imprimatur* (let it be printed) for someone's approval of a published text, *quorum* (of whom) the minimum number of people necessary for a committee or similar meeting, *tandem* (at length) for a bicycle built for two. Similarly, many phrases and sentences of Latin are perpetuated as tags and mottoes: *ad astra per aspera* to the stars through hardships (the motto of the US state of Kansas), *per ardua ad astra* through difficulties to the stars (the motto of the Royal Air Force); *habeas corpus* you may have the body (a technical term in law); *ipse dixit* he said it himself (as a sometimes caustic comment); *non sequitur* it does not follow (a name for a certain kind of logical fallacy). Further phrases have been abbreviated, and are part of the currency of everyday life, including writing: *AD* (for *anno Domini* in the year of the Lord, as part of calendar dating), *a.m.* (for *ante meridiem* before midday), *p.m.* (*post meridiem* after midday), *e.g.* (*exempli gratia* for the sake of example), *i.e.* (*id est* that is).

Currently, continuing a process of de-Latinization that has gathered momentum since the 18c (mainly because of the spread of literacy beyond the schools where Latin was a core subject), there is a tendency to translate such expressions into English (*time flies* rather than *tempus fugit*; *don't despair, don't give up* rather than *nil desperandum*), and to make Latin words more conventionally English: the plurals *cactuses* and *referendums* rather than *cacti* and *referenda*. In the train of such changes, and because the influence of Latin is still tenacious, there is often uncertainty and friction regarding usage: for example, in such vexed issues as the use of *data* and *media* as singular or plural nouns.

See ABBREVIATION, ABLATIVE ABSOLUTE, ABLATIVE CASE, ACCUSATIVE CASE, ANGLO-LATIN, BISOCIATION, BOG LATIN, BORROWING, CASE, CAWDREY, CLASSICAL COMPOUND, CLASSICAL ENDINGS, CLASSICAL LANGUAGE, CLAUSE ANALYSIS, COMPOUND WORD, CONJUGATION, COOPER, DATIVE CASE, DECLENSION, DERIVATION, DOG-, EARLY MODERN ENGLISH, ENGLISH, ENGLISH PLACE-NAMES, ETYMOLOGY, FOREIGNISM, FRENCH, FUSIONAL, GENITIVE CASE, GENRE, GRAMMAR, GRAMMAR–TRANSLATION METHOD, GREEK, HISTORY OF ENGLISH, INDO-EUROPEAN LANGUAGES, LATIN², LATIN ANALOGY, LATINISM, LATINITY, LATIN LITERATURE, LATIN TAG, LEXICAL BAR, LITERATURE, MOCK, NEO-LATIN, NOMINATIVE CASE, NOTES AND REFERENCES, PARADIGM, PART OF SPEECH, PIG LATIN, PLURAL, RHETORIC, ROMANCE LANGUAGES, SANSKRIT, SENTENCE, SPANISH, STANDARD, THIEVES' LATIN, VOCATIVE, VULGAR (LATIN), WORD, WORD-FORMATION. [EUROPE, GRAMMAR, LANGUAGE].   T.MCA.

LATIN² (1) A native or inhabitant of Latium in ancient Italy; an ancient Roman. (2) A member of any of the Latin peoples (that is, the speakers of Romance languages) both in southern Europe and elsewhere. (3) Relating to either of these, especially in Central or South America: *Latin America, the Latin republics.* Although the term is used to include the French and French-speaking people and the Italians, it is most usu-

ally understood to refer to speakers of Spanish and Portuguese in the New World, their cultures, languages, usages in English, etc. See AMERICAN¹, ANGLO, CHICANO, HISPANIC, LATIN¹, LATINO, PORTUGUESE, ROMANCE LANGUAGES, SPANISH. [AMERICAS, EUROPE, LANGUAGE, NAME].   T.MCA.

LATIN ANALOGY, The. A comparison between the prospects of late 20c English and the fate of Latin at the end of the Roman Empire, as in: 'One possible scenario for English as an international language is that it will succumb to the same fate as Latin did in the Middle Ages. That is, that the regional varieties will develop independently to the point where they become different languages rather than varieties of the same language' (Alan Maley, *English Today* 1, Jan. 1985); 'Small wonder that there should have been in recent years fresh talk of the diaspora of English into several mutually incomprehensible languages. The fate of Latin during and after the fall of the Roman Empire presents us with such distinct languages today as French, Spanish, Romanian, and Italian. With the growth of national separatism in the English-speaking countries . . . many foresee a similar fissiparous future for English' (Randolph Quirk, 'The English Language in a Global Context', in R. Quirk & H. G. Widdowson (eds.), *English in the World*, 1985).

The forms of the analogy. The comparison can be made in three ways: (1) Pessimistically, sometimes with apocalyptic overtones concerning 'the death of English as we know it'. Here, the breakup of Latin is presented as a dire warning to a careless world. (2) Optimistically, in the spirit of one-world liberalism, pointing to unity in diversity within 'the English languages'. Here, the breakup of Latin is seen as leading to the rich fabric of the Romance languages and the hybrid strength of English. (3) More or less neutrally and objectively, seeking as far as possible to establish the facts: whether Latin did break up and whether such an analogy is apt. Crucial to the discussion are the metaphors used in talking about change in Latin: for example, negative as in *broke up*, *disintegrated* and positive as in *gave birth to, was the mother language of.*

The evolution of Latin. The surviving evidence indicates that the everyday common language of the citizens of the Roman Empire was not the Latin used for literary, legal, and other such purposes. The populace at large used *Vulgar Latin* (*lingua Latina vulgaris*), the speech of the common people. This varied from region to region and coexisted with many vernacular tongues. The Romance languages derive from varieties of this Latin, such as *Gallo-Roman* in France, and not from the idiom of such aristocrats of literature as Cicero and Virgil. The history of the language of scholars and clerks was in fact different from that of the Latin of the people. It had a script standard that evolved from imperial through ecclesiastical Latin into the Neo-Latin of the late Middle Ages and Renaissance. This variety did not break up as such (although it developed markedly different national pronunciations), but continued as a unity because Europe was 'a morass of hundreds of languages and dialects, most of them never written to this day' (Walter J. Ong, *Orality and Literacy*, 1982). In this 'morass', Ong emphasizes, a single medium of religion, culture, learning, and diplomacy such as what he calls 'Learned Latin' was essential.

Learned Latin derived its power and authority from *not* being ordinary. Like Sanskrit in India, it was canonically fixed and honoured for that reason. It had no baby talk and colloquial usages, and could therefore serve as an elevated second language everywhere. Though variably pronounced throughout Europe, and a dynamic rather than a static medium, it was written for centuries in much the same way in every country. When printing was invented in the 15c, its written conventions helped establish the print standard followed in the European vernaculars. Latin was not a monolith that collapsed because people did not take proper care of it. Rather, in Iberia, one people's Latin evolved into forms called Spanish, Catalan, and Portuguese; among the Dacians, a Romanian complex emerged; among the Gauls and Franks, Gallo-Roman became Francien, then the standard form of French; and the many varieties of Italian developed in the home peninsula and adjacent islands. Central Sardinian or Logudorian was to remain the most conservative of the Romance languages. The historical record is incomplete, the processes were slow, and the outcomes so uncertain that it is only with hindsight that scholars can point to what appears to have happened. A textual Latin survived the changes in the oral Latins, which became in time distinct enough to be called separate languages. Among them, intelligibility varies not only from language to language but among the varieties (called dialects and patois) within each language.

The evolution of English. When this condition is compared to present-day English, the analogy takes on a different look. Many of the details of how the Romance languages emerged are missing, but it is currently possible to study what is happening to English, with its print standard, its national and regional varieties and subvarieties, and its pidgins and creoles. Standard English has much in common with Learned Latin: it is a minority form among the many forms of English, holding a metaphoric centre for purposes of education and communication, both nationally and internationally. The varieties of educated English usage around the world, buttressed by the print standard, are mutually intelligible, but many of the Englishes of the people are not. They appear to be about as mutually intelligible or unintelligible as the Latins of the late Empire, but, because of the power of mass communication, some of them may have become more mutually transparent than in the past and therefore less likely to part company in the future. In the case of some varieties, the status of separate language has long been discussed: Scots is for some a language, for others a dialect, for others something in between, and for others still sometimes a language and sometimes a dialect; Tok Pisin and other creoles are now generally described as 'English-based' rather than as kinds of English. If the Americans had so chosen, they could have called their language *American* and not *English* (and casually they often do), but the prognosis that one day AmE will become as distinct from BrE as Spanish is from Italian does not appear at present to have much foundation. See CLASSICAL LANGUAGE, CREOLE, LATIN[1], STANDARD, STANDARD ENGLISH. [HISTORY, LANGUAGE].   T.MCA.

LATINATE [1900s]. Relating to, derived from, or in the style of Latin: 'Who among us has not strained to decipher the Latinate crypticisms of a doctor's pronouncements?' (Don Ethan Miller, *The Book of Jargon*, 1981). The term is used for both words in which the Latin form has been retained (such as *formula, latex, mausoleum, stimulus*) and those in which adaptations have been made (such as *elucidate, legal, pungency, vociferous*). Texts in a language like English are Latinate if they adhere closely to the models of classical Rome. See AUREATE DICTION, DEFINITION, INKHORN TERM/INKHORNISM, JOHNSONIAN, LATIN[1], LATINITY. [STYLE].   T.MCA.

LATINISM [16c: from Latin *Latinismus* a Latin usage]. A Latin word or other element in another language: for example, in English the word *stimulus*, the phrase *non sequitur*, the sentence *Sic transit gloria mundi*, and the derivative *illegality* (from *illegalis*). The term is sometimes used pejoratively: 'The UGC report is a constipated sequence of Latinisms that would serve as a prize exhibit in any debate about the decline of the English language' (*Observer*, 12 Feb. 1989). See FOREIGNISM, -ISM, LATIN[1], LATIN TAG. [STYLE, WORD].   T.MCA.

LATINITY [17c: from Latin *Latinitas* 'Latin-ness']. (1) A Latin character or quality. (2) Familiarity with Latin and ease in its use: 'the Humanist traditions of Scottish Latinity' (George Davie, *The Democratic Intellect*, 1961); 'Latinity has largely vanished from the world. What people forget is how long it was kept up' (Tom Shippey, *London Review of Books*, 11 Oct. 1990). (3) A Latinate style, such as that of Samuel Johnson. Compare ANGLICITY. See JOHNSONESE, LATIN¹. [STYLE].   T.MCA.

LATIN LITERATURE. Literature in Latin, either the literary texts of the Roman Republic and Empire (3c BC-2c AD) or the entire body of writings in Latin from ancient Rome through the Middle Ages and the Renaissance, to works composed in Europe and elsewhere until at least the 18c. Just as Latin literature influenced later European vernaculars, so Latin was itself influenced by Greek literature. The oldest known Latin text (6c BC) is a four-word inscription in the Greek alphabet, and the first literary writer in Latin was Livius Andronicus (3c BC), a freed slave from the Greek colony of Tarentum in southern Italy, who, by translating Homer's *Odyssey*, set a precedent for the adoption of Greek genres into Latin and the loan translation of Greek words. The Romans adopted from the Greeks not only the three great genres (epic, drama, and lyric poetry), but also rhetoric and the writing of history and philosophy. To these they added satire and a forerunner of the novel. Among the most prominent Latin writers, Cicero developed an influential prose style, Livy adapted the historical prose style of Thucydides, Virgil became the Roman Homer, Caesar was an autobiographer and military propagandist, Catullus was a critic, Horace a poet, Ovid a mythologist, Pliny the Elder an encyclopedist, and Petronius Arbiter (the *Satyricon*) and Apuleius (*The Golden Ass*) kinds of novelist. All had a powerful and permanent effect on writing in the later languages of Europe. See ENGLISH LITERATURE, GREEK LITERATURE, LATIN¹. [EUROPE, LITERATURE].   T.MCA.

LATINO [1940s: from American Spanish, a special use of *Latino* Latin: see LATIN². Plural *Latinos*. Used both with and without an initial capital letter]. Someone of Latin-American background or descent, especially if Spanish-speaking and in the US. See CHICANO, HISPANIC, SPANGLISH, SPANISH. Compare LADINO, LATIN². [AMERICAS, NAME].   T.MCA.

LATIN TAG. A Latin phrase or other expression in English, such as *obiter dictum* ('a saying by the way') an incidental remark, *pro tem* (short for *pro tempore*) for the time being. Until the

mid-20c, Latin tags were widely used, intentionally or otherwise, as a mark of education, but in recent decades have grown less common (and often less understood) in educated circles, in which less common tags are often considered affected or unnecessary, even by those who know Latin. As a result, expressions like *Tempus fugit* are often loan-translated as 'Time flies'. Many tags are, however, firmly entrenched in everyday usage, whether in full or as abbreviations: in law (*de jure*, *habeas corpus*, *sub judice*), in medicine (*locum tenens*, *placebo*, *post mortem*), in logic (*argumentum ad hominem*, *non sequitur*, *reductio ad absurdum*), in administration (*ad hoc*, *quorum*, *sine die*), in religion (*Deo volente*, *Pax vobiscum*, *Requiescat in pace*), as sayings (*carpe diem*, *in vino veritas*), as set phrases (*mutatis mutandis*, *ne plus ultra*), as mottoes (*Nemo me impune lacessit*, *Semper fidelis*), and as academic footnotes and endnotes (*ibid.*, *op cit.*, *passim*). Some have passed into the language at large: as phrases (*bona fides*, *magnum opus*, *modus operandi*, *per annum*, *prima facie*, *quid pro quo*, *sine qua non*, *terra firma*, *vade mecum*), and as abbreviations (*a.m.*, *c.*, *cf.*, *e.g.*, *i.e.*, *p.m.*, *R.I.P.*). Works of reference list and explain such tags: for example, Eugene Ehrlich's *Nil Desperandum: A Dictionary of Latin Tags and Phrases* (Robert Hale, 1985). See ABBREVIATION, FOREIGNISM, LATIN¹, NOTES AND REFERENCES, TAG. [STYLE, USAGE].   T.MCA.

LAW FRENCH. A fossilized form of Norman French used until the 18c in the courts of England. In 1362, French ceased to be a language of pleading, but its legal use was not officially abandoned until 1731. Many archaic French usages continue in the legal usage of England, such as: *amerce*, *eyre*, *implead*, *jeofail*, *mainour*, *malfeasance*, *puisne*, *seisin*, *tort*. French word order is preserved in *attorney general*, *court martial*, *fee simple*, *heir male*, *letters patent*, *malice aforethought*. The names of most legal roles in English are French in origin, such as: *advocate*, *attorney*, *bailiff*, *coroner*, *counsel*, *defendant*, *judge*, *jury*, *plaintiff*. The same is the case with the names of many crimes (such as *arson*, *assault*, *felony*, *fraud*, *libel*, *perjury*, *slander*, *trespass*) and of legal actions, processes, and institutions (such as *bail*, *bill*, *decree*, *evidence*, *fine*, *forfeit*, *gaol/jail*, *inquest*, *penalty*, *petition*, *pillory*, *plea*, *prison*, *proof*, *punishment*, *ransom*, *sentence*, *suit*, *summons*, *verdict*). See NORMAN FRENCH. [EUROPE, LANGUAGE].   J.M.G.

LAWRENCE, D(avid) H(erbert) [1885-1930]. English writer and painter, born in Eastwood, Nottinghamshire, and educated at University College, Nottingham. He taught in Croydon for a time and published his first novel, *The White Peacock*, in 1911. His father was a coal-miner, his mother a former teacher who regarded herself as superior to her husband and his family. This and other family tensions, including Lawrence's attachment to his mother, were fictionalized in the novel *Sons and Lovers* (1913). In 1912, he eloped with Frieda, the wife of the lexicographer Ernest Weekley. She was German and during the First World War the couple fell under official suspicion. Resentment about this and the medical examination by which he was rejected for military service contributed to Lawrence's self-exile; after 1918 he never lived for long in England. His novels *The Rainbow* (1915) and *Women in Love* (1920) explored the theme of marriage and sexual attraction more frankly than had been customary in fiction, and aroused hostile criticism. Lawrence lived for some time in Mexico, the setting of *The Plumed Serpent* (1926). His last novel, *Lady Chatterley's Lover* (1928), was first published in Florence. He also wrote poetry and short stories. He died of tuberculosis in the South of France.

Lawrence suffered continually from charges of obscenity, both in his writing and his paintings, some of which were impounded at an exhibition in 1929. *Lady Chatterley's Lover* contained both direct descriptions of sexual intercourse and four-letter words, with the result that, although the novel had long been available in foreign editions, it had not been published in full in Britain. In 1960, however, Penguin books brought out an unexpurgated edition and was duly prosecuted under the Obscene Publications Act of 1959. Eminent witnesses gave strong opinions on both sides; the acquittal of the publishers, whether seen as a catalyst or a symptom, was significant in the new freedom of literary expression. Though some readers may find Lawrence distasteful and regard him as obscene or prurient, he pioneered explicit writing about sexuality and the use of words hitherto taboo in print. He was acquainted with Freudian psychology and used such theories to explore personal relationships. He has been accused of excessive earnestness about the need for individual fulfilment and of failing to see the humorous side of life. Lawrence was in many ways a late Romantic who obtruded his own views at a time when the withdrawal of the author was becoming characteristic of fiction. He was outstanding among 20c writers in describing the natural world, which he related to the feelings of his characters almost in the manner of the *pathetic fallacy*. In dialogue, he recorded the conversation of both simple and sophisticated people, and made considerable use of dialect without obscuring it by excessive deviation. Rather, he showed the nuances of intensity among different dialect speakers, such as Mr and Mrs Morel in *Sons and Lovers*. Some critics, including F. R. Leavis, have regarded him as the greatest British novelist of the early 20c. See index. [BIOGRAPHY, EUROPE, LITERATURE, STYLE].

R.C.

LAX. See VOWEL QUANTITY.

LAYOUT [1840s: AmE]. (1) A plan of a building, periodical, page, etc., showing how the parts contribute to the whole and relate to one another; the arrangement of the parts in such a building, periodical, page, etc. (2) How material is laid out in a book, magazine, newspaper, or other publication. (3) The process of making layouts in publishing, etc. (4) Also *spread*. In journalism, treatment of a subject that usually consists of a story or report, supplementary stories or data (often in *sidebars*: additional matter in marked-off columns or panels), and illustrations with captions (often called a *picture spread*). Such a layout usually extends over several columns or pages. See EDITING, GRAPHIC DESIGN, HEADLINE, PUBLISHING, SPACE, TYPOGRAPHY, WHITE SPACE. [MEDIA, WRITING].

T.MCA.

LEACOCK, Stephen (Butler) [1869–1944]. Canadian writer and humorist, born at Swanmoor, Hampshire, England, and educated at the U. of Toronto and the U. of Chicago (Ph.D., 1899). He taught Political Economy at McGill U. in Montreal (1901–36). His best-known works are *Sunshine Sketches of a Little Town* (1912), *Arcadian Adventures with the Idle Rich* (1914), stories like 'My Financial Career', 'Hoodoo McFiggin's Christmas', 'Boarding House Geometry', a travel book *My Discovery of England* (1922), and his memoir *The Boy I Left Behind Me* (1946). He comments on CanE: 'When I left Hampshire I spoke English. But I've lost it, and it might be too late to pick it up again' (in 'I'll Stay in Canada', *Funny Pieces*, 1936). He reveals typical Canadian linguistic self-deprecation when he notes: 'I myself talk Ontario English. I don't admire it, but it's all I can do: anything is better than affectation' ('Good and Bad Language', in *How to Write*, 1943). See index. [AMERICAS, BIOGRAPHY, STYLE].

M.F.

LEADING QUESTION [1810s]. A question phrased so as to prompt or suggest an answer: *How do you feel about such terrible behaviour?* as opposed to *How do you feel about behaviour of that kind?* The direction in which the question leads may be favourable or unfavourable for the person questioned. If used by a defending counsel in a court of law, it may serve to help the defendant, and therefore be objected to by the prosecution. Lawyers generally object to other lawyers 'leading the witness' when the direction does not suit their case. See LOADED LANGUAGE, QUESTION. [STYLE].   T.MCA.

LEAF [Before 10c: from Old English *léaf*]. The name of part of a plant extended to a sheet of paper or other material in a book or periodical, especially one of the folds of a larger sheet cut to size and containing two pages (*recto* and *verso*): 'Who so liste it nat yheere, / Turne ouer the leef, and chese another tale' (Chaucer, 'Miller's Prologue', *The Canterbury Tales*, c.1386). Such phrases as *take a leaf out of someone's book*, *turn over a new leaf* indicate the moral impact of books, especially scripture. See LEAFLET, PAGE. [TECHNOLOGY].   T.MCA.

LEAFLET [Late 19c]. (1) A small-sized leaf of paper or a sheet folded into two or more leaves but not stitched, and containing printed matter, often to be given away free as religious tracts, political pamphlets, and commercial advert- isements. (2) A pamphlet. See BOOKLET, LEAF, PAMPHLET. [MEDIA, TECHNOLOGY].   T.MCA.

LEARNED, sometimes, to avoid ambiguity, **learnèd** [14c: spoken as two syllables]. (1) Know- ing a great deal: *a learned scholar*. (2) Of the work of scholars and classical usage in English: *learned borrowings*; *the learned compounds of English*. See BIG WORD, CLASSICAL COMPOUND, CLASSICISM, LATIN ANALOGY. [STYLE].   T.MCA.

LEARNER'S DICTIONARY, also **English Learner's Dictionary, EFL dictionary, ELT dic- tionary**. A dictionary intended for the use of foreign- and second-language learners and printed entirely in English. For foreign learners of most languages, bidirectional bilingual dic- tionaries (Italian–English, English–Italian, etc.) have been the norm, but since the 1960s the pre- dominant type in TEFL and TESL has been a monolingual 'learner's dictionary', such as A. S. Hornby's *Advanced Learner's Dictionary of Current English* (Oxford University Press).

Origins. Although such dictionaries are products of the 20c, their roots lie in the Renaissance, when the vernacular languages of Europe were emerging from the shadow of Latin as the inter- national language of religion and scholarship. In the 15–16c, dictionaries of Latin were generally unidirectional and bilingual (listed Latin words glossed by vernacular words); in the 16c–17c, monolingual works began to appear, to help nat- ive speakers with difficult words in their own languages. Robert Cawdrey's *Table Alpha- beticall* (1604) was both the first dictionary of English and the first learner's dictionary of Eng- lish, its purpose being to explain 'hard vsuall

wordes' (mainly of Latin origin) through 'plain' everyday words. In the 18c, in addition to such standardizing works as Samuel Johnson's *Dic- tionary of the English Language* (1755), a number of pronouncing dictionaries appeared, such as John Walker's *A Critical Pronouncing Dic- tionary of the English Language* (1791), whose aim was to help the Scots, Irish, and Welsh, as well as English provincials and London Cockneys, to conform to the norms of the 'refined' English of the capital and the court.

Modern learner's dictionaries. In the late 19c, a reform movement in the teaching of foreign lan- guages discouraged direct translation and favoured the use of phonetic symbols to help learners with the pronunciation of English words. An outcome of this movement was the *English Pronouncing Dictionary* (1917) of Daniel Jones, in which a mix of everyday words, per- sonal names, and place-names was accompanied by phonetic transcriptions representing RP. Another outcome was the work, in the 1920s– 30s, of Harold E. Palmer (mainly in Japan) and Michael West (in Bengal and Britain), who pion- eered the arrangement of vocabulary in levels for such purposes as preparing graded and struc- tured readers. This led to the first learner's dic- tionaries proper, such as Michael West & J. G. Endicott, the *New Method English Dictionary* (Longmans Green, 1935). A parallel work, C. K. Ogden's *The General Basic English Dictionary* (1940), used the 850 words of Basic English as a defining vocabulary for over 20,000 words. The following sections describe the four major present-day learner's dictionaries.

The ALD. In 1937, Palmer's colleagues in Japan, A. S. Hornby, E. V. Gatenby, and H. Wakefield, began work on a dictionary which the publisher Kaitakusha brought out in Tokyo in 1942 as the *Idiomatic and Syntactic English Dictionary*. After the war, Oxford University Press reissued this work as *A Learner's Dictionary of Current Eng- lish* (1948). The 2nd edition was called the *Advanced Learner's Dictionary of Current Eng- lish* (*ALD, ALDCE*) (1963), the 3rd the *Oxford Advanced Learner's Dictionary of Current Eng- lish* (*ALD, OALDCE*) (1974), and the 4th the *Oxford Advanced Learner's Dictionary* (*ALD, OALD*) (1989). These constitute an international best-seller whose combined sales have exceeded 14m copies. The attractions of what is now often referred to as 'the Hornby dictionary' when it first came out were: (1) Headwords chosen because experienced teachers believed they were the most useful to foreign learners. (2) The omis- sion of archaic usage, historical and literary ref- erences, and etymology. (3) The provision of the pronunciation of each word in IPA transcription derived from Jones's *EPD*. (4) Meanings given in simple language, avoiding the often convoluted and Latinate constructions used in many mother-tongue dictionaries. (5) Meanings explained by definitions and specimen phrases and sentences to show the headword in use. (6) Grammatical information on every headword provided, including codes referring to the syntactic patterns of all listed verbs. (7) Illustrations providing further information and serving to break up the text. (8) Language-related appendices at the back of the book. For 30 years the *ALD* was unrivalled, accustoming teachers and learners to the existence of a non-historical, non-literary, learner-centred work of reference. It became a familiar tool of the trade for teachers in both EFL and Commonwealth ESL, but because of their BrE slant neither the *ALD* nor other subsequent learner's dictionaries became so well known in North American ESL teaching.

LDOCE. When the *Longman Dictionary of Contemporary English* (ed. Paul Procter) appeared in 1978, it was comparable to the *ALD* in size, layout, column style, and typeface, but differed in the following: (1) Headwords defined by means of a restricted defining vocabulary based on Michael West's *General Service List* (1953). (2) Grammatical information based primarily on *A Grammar of Contemporary English* (Randolph Quirk *et al.*, 1972) and provided as codes constituting a kind of distilled grammar of the language. (3) A Jonesian transcription similar to the *ALD* that provided AmE as well as BrE pronunciations. In 1974, Oxford had changed to a phonetic transcription in which there was no length mark (ː) with certain vowel symbols, disturbing many teachers worldwide. In 1978, Longman capitalized on the change, supplying length marks in their transcription.

CULD. In 1980, W. & R. Chambers published the *Chambers Universal Learners' Dictionary* (*CULD*). Similar in general style to the preceding and other such dictionaries, this work had small type, provided a limited range of grammatical information, had no pictures, and was marketed by a publisher not normally involved in ELT. Although provided with clear definitions, examples of usage, and a simplified 'broad' RP transcription by David Abercrombie, this work did not challenge Oxford or Longman.

COBUILD. In 1987, Collins published the *Collins COBUILD English Language Dictionary*, generally known as *COBUILD* (from *Collins Birmingham University International Language Database*). This was an innovative work with the following special features: (1) Meanings phrased not in elliptical dictionary style but as whole-sentence definitions in the style of teacher talk.

(2) Specimens of usage drawn directly from the Birmingham database and advertised as 'real English', sometimes amended for the sake of clarity. (3) Grammatical codes and semantic information listed in an 'extra column' (in effect as marginalia), so as not to clutter the text of the entries. (4) Superscript numbers added to the otherwise Jonesian phonetic transcription to indicate degree of weakness towards the central vowel /ə/, with the vowels of stressed syllables underlined (and reminiscent of the use of superscripts by Walker in the 18c).

Conclusion. Such dictionaries tend to mix simplicity (in definitions, specimens of usage, and language notes) with complexity (in the phonetic transcriptions and grammatical codes). As a result, despite their many innovations, a learner needs a good understanding of dictionary style, abbreviation, etc., to make good use of them. The direction of development appears, however, to be towards easier access and more lucid presentation. Such dictionaries have not only become a genre in their own right but have begun to influence the organization of mother-tongue dictionaries, often because many British lexicographers during the last two decades have worked on both kinds of book. A series of papers by authorities on such dictionaries is published as: *Learners' Dictionaries: State of the Art*, ed. Makhan L. Tickoo (SEAMEO Regional Language Centre, Singapore, 1989).

See BASIC ENGLISH[1], COBUILD, DEFINING VOCABULARY, ELT PUBLISHING, ENGLISH PRONOUNCING DICTIONARY, GENERAL SERVICE LIST, HORNBY, JONES (D.), LONGMAN, OXFORD DICTIONARIES, PALMER (H.), TEFL, TESL, WEST. [EDUCATION, REFERENCE]. P.S., T.MCA.

LEAVIS, F(rank) R(aymond) [1895-1978]. English critic, born and educated at Cambridge, where he became a Fellow of Downing College and later Reader in English. As a pupil of I. A. Richards, he learned the importance of close textual study and acquired a hostility to the 'literary history' approach of the previous generation of critics. He believed passionately in the importance of English studies as a civilizing influence in an increasingly technological mass culture and desired the emergence of an intellectual élite trained in English studies. His standards of judgement were rigorous and demanded deep seriousness in the approach to literature. Because his assessments were individual, his opponents accused him of an excessively empirical approach and a failure to establish a coherent theory of literature. In *New Bearings in English Poetry* (1932), Leavis was hostile to Victorian poetry and extolled T. S. Eliot, Ezra Pound, and other Modernists. In *Revaluation* (1936), he sought to trace the mainstream of

English poetry, praising Donne and Pope, among others, and attacking Spenser, Milton, and Shelley. In *The Great Tradition* (1948), he did the same for the novel, with enthusiasm for Austen, George Eliot, James, and Conrad. Leavis recognized writers like T. S. Eliot and D. H. Lawrence before they were widely accepted. He edited the critical journal *Scrutiny* (1932-53), whose contributors were known as *Scrutineers*. Critics often refer to his extensive influence as *Leavisism* and to the members of his 'school' as *Leavisites*. His prose style was forceful but not elegant and sometimes turgid to the point of obscurity. See index. [BIOGRAPHY, EUROPE, LITERATURE].   R.C.

LECT [1960s: extracted from *dialect*; ultimately from Greek *lektós* capable of being spoken]. A term in sociolinguistics for a speech variety; it is used relatively little on its own but often occurs in combination, as in *idiolect*. See ACROLECT, BASILECT, DIALECT, ENGLISH, GENDERLECT, IDIOLECT, MESOLECT, PRIVATE LANGUAGE (CRYPTOLECT), SOCIOLECT. [LANGUAGE].   T.MCA.

LEEWARD ISLANDS. See ANTILLES.

LEGALESE [1910s, on the analogy of *journalese*, etc.]. An informal, usually pejorative term for language that is typical of lawyers or that contains too much legal terminology: ' "It is highly probable, and more likely than not in the light of [the TV series] 'L. A. Law's' nationwide popularity, that one or more jurors viewed this segment and was impressed by or even discussed same among themselves," he argued in his best legalese' ('Role Models for Attorneys?', *International Herald Tribune*, 11 May 1990). See -ESE, JARGON, LAW FRENCH, LEGAL USAGE, REGISTER. [STYLE, USAGE].   T.MCA.

LEGAL-SIZE. A US and Canadian measurement of paper, approximately $8\frac{1}{2} \times 14$ inches (22×36 cm). Office equipment that is legal-size is made to take legal-size sheets. See LETTER-SIZE, PAPER. [TECHNOLOGY].   T.MCA.

LEGAL USAGE, also **legal English**. The register of the legal profession. The term covers the formulas and styles of both courts of law in all English-speaking countries and such documents as contracts and writs. In England, from the Norman Conquest in 1066 to the later 14c, the languages of law were French and Latin, and both have left their mark on the English which succeeded them, especially in such terms as *lien* (French 'binding, tie': a legal claim on someone's property to secure the payment of debt) and *habeas corpus* (Latin 'you may have the body': a writ requiring that someone be brought before a

judge or court, especially as a protection against that person's unlawful imprisonment). Legal usage in all English-speaking countries tends to be conservative, formal, syntactically complex, and often archaic, using expressions such as *aforesaid, hereinafter, thereto* that hardly occur in the language at large. Lawyers generally argue that the conventions and complexities of legal prose ensure that all possible contingencies are covered and ambiguities removed from documents on which legal decisions must rest. Critics reply that 'legalese' makes lawyers necessary as interpreters as well as counsellors, may obscure the implications of contracts and other documents, and often worries people unnecessarily. The first excerpt below is part of a traditional contract, the second the same material recast in 'plain' language:

GENERAL LIEN—The contractor shall have a general lien upon all goods in his possession for all monies due to him from the customer or for liabilities incurred by him and for monies paid on behalf of the customer, and if part of the goods shall have been delivered, removed or despatched or sold the general lien shall apply in respect of such goods as remain in the Contractor's possession. The Contractor shall be entitled to charge a storage charge and all other expenses during which a lien on the goods is being asserted and all these conditions shall continue to apply thereto.

Our right to hold your goods. We have a right to hold some or all of the goods until you have paid all our charges and other payments due under this contract. These include charges, taxes or levies that we have paid to any other removal or storage business, carrier or official body. While we hold the goods and wait for payment you will have to pay storage charges and all other necessary expenses. This contract will apply to the goods held in this way.

In recent years, campaigners for plain English have sought simpler contracts and in some cases 'translations' of difficult usage, so that the public can grasp the meaning and intent of documents couched in legal terms. In 1983, an English court ordered a law firm to pay £93,000 damages for unintentionally misleading a client by using 'obscure' legal language in a letter of advice; in the same year the report *Small Print* criticized the language and layout of many contracts and sought to show that clear presentation was not only desirable but also possible. See CHANCERY STANDARD, LAW FRENCH, LEGALESE, PLAIN ENGLISH, REGISTER. [STYLE, USAGE].   T.MCA.

LEGEND [14c: from French *légende*, Medieval Latin *legenda* (what is) to be read (as a religious lesson), from *legere/lectum* to read]. (1) Obsolete: a saint's life story, especially stressing miracles, read on his or her name-day; a collection of such accounts, such as *Legenda (Aurea)* or *The (Golden) Legend*, compiled by Jacobus de Voragine in Genoa in the 13c. (2) A traditional, unverifiable, usually fabulous story passed down (often orally) in a community, and widely accepted as in some sense true (*a national legend; the Legend of Robin Hood*); the body of such stories (*a hero in local legend*); a person who is the centre of such stories (*a legend in one's lifetime; a living legend*). (3) Obsolete: a roll, list, or record. (4) Rare: writing, as in 'a child's legend on the tideless sand' (Shelley, *Fragments*, 1822). (5) An inscription or motto on a coat of arms, a monument, a coin, or a medal, or under a picture. (6) A written explanation, often in the form of a headed table, chart, list, or key, on a map or accompanying an illustration. Compare BIOGRAPHY, CAPTION, FABLE, KEY, LEMMA, MOTTO, MYTH. [LITERATURE, WRITING]. T.MCA.

LEMMA [16c: from Latin *lemma* a theme, title, epigram, from Greek *lẽmma* something taken (as given), an argument, a title. Plural: traditionally *lemmata*, sometimes *lemmas*]. (1) In science, mathematics, and logic, a premiss or subsidiary proposition brought in, assumed, or demonstrated to help prove some other proposition (especially if taken from another field). (2) A heading or title that states the argument, theme, or subject of a piece of written work; the argument, theme, or subject itself. (3) A motto or legend below a picture. (4) A word or phrase that is glossed; a headword in a dictionary or other work of reference. In lexicography, the creation of a list of headwords is known as *lemmatization*. See GLOSS, HEADWORD, LEGEND, MOTTO, PROPOSITION. [LANGUAGE, REFERENCE, WORD, WRITING]. T.MCA.

LENGTH MARK. In phonetics, the mark (ː), used after a vowel to indicate that it is long, as when the RP pronunciation of *feast* is shown in IPA symbols as /fiːst/. For reasons of economy and simplicity, the colon (:) is often used instead: /fi:st/. Compare MACRON. See MARK, VOWEL QUANTITY. [SPEECH, WRITING]. T.MCA.

LENIS. See HARD AND SOFT, VOICE.

LEONINE VERSE. See INTERNAL RHYME.

LESOTHO. Official title: *Kingdom of Lesotho*. A country of southern Africa and member of the Commonwealth. Capital: Maseru. Currency: the loti (100 sente): plurals *maloti, lisente*. Population: 1.67m (1988), 2.3m (projection for 2000). Ethnicity: mainly Basotho. Religion: 45% Protestant, 40% Roman Catholic, 15% traditional. Languages: Sesotho and English (both official). Education: primary 85%, secondary 22%, tertiary 2%, literacy 35%. The first Bantu-speaking peoples arrived in the area in the 16c. In 1854, the territory was incorporated by the Boers into

the Orange Free State, but in 1869 became the British protectorate of *Basutoland*. The territory gained internal self-government in 1955 and independence as *Lesotho* in 1966. See AFRICAN LANGUAGES, ENGLISH, SOUTH AFRICA. [AFRICA, NAME, VARIETY]. T.MCA.

LETTER[1] [12c: from French *lettre*, Latin *littera* a shape or symbol used in writing]. An alphabetic symbol such as *A* or *a*, *B* or *b*. In writing based on the classical Roman alphabet, the separation of letters into *majuscules* (capital letters) and *minuscules* (small letters), the many variant alphabets (such as for English and Spanish), the typefaces available to them, and the distinctive joined letters of cursive handwriting have produced a wide range of letter forms.

Naming letters. In the Greek alphabet, each letter has a name that is not directly related to its sound value (*alpha, beta, gamma*, etc.), but this practice is not common in Roman-derived alphabets. The ways in which letters are referred to in English (*ay, bee, cee*, etc.) echo those of French, except that French *double-v* is English *double-u*, and the name of *y* may descend from the rounded Old English pronunciation of that vowel. Except for *h, w*, the names (*ay, bee, cee*, etc.) have a recognizable relationship with the sounds they commonly represent. The vowel letters are named by the long values in *mate, meet, might, moat, mute*, not the short values as in *pat, pet, pit, pot, putt/put*. Nine consonants in BrE and ten in AmE are named with a vowel after the sound value: with following *ee* in the case of *b, c, d, g, p, t, v* (and AmE *z*) and *ay* in the case of *j, k*. Six others are named with a preceding short *e*: *f, l, m, n, s, x*. The remainder (*h, q, r, w, y*, and BrE *zed*) have individual names. Teachers have often preferred not to use the names of letters when teaching children to read and write, but instead use the short values of the vowels and the immediate isolated sounds of the consonants, so as to make the relationship between sound and spelling as clear as possible. To make the task of learning easier, regularized letter names such as *fee, hee, lee, mee* or *eb, ed, eg*, or a schwa after the consonant sound have sometimes been used in teaching in the UK and the US. This may have been the origin of AmE *zee*. Even then, the alternative hard and soft values of *c, g*, whose names suggest only a soft value, can cause difficulty; beginning readers sometimes read *once* as 'onky' and *gone* as 'Joan'.

Letters as symbols. When letters are used as symbols they may operate alone, in sets, or in combination with words: (1) Alone: capitals *A, B, C*, etc., to mark an educational or other grade, *X* to indicate a mystery; small letters such as *a, x*, and *y* as used in mathematical expressions. (2) In sets: *zzz* in cartoons and elsewhere, to represent sleep; the thousands of letter-based abbreviations, such as *BBC, NATO, e.g., i.e.,* UN/U.N. (3) In combination with a word, as an abbreviation: BrE *L-plate*, where *L* means *Learner* (such plates being attached to the front and rear of motor vehicles); AmE *T-bill*, where *T* means *Treasury* (a reference to high-denomination promissory notes). (4) Combined with one or more words as part of a series: *B-movie* in the motion-picture industry; *C minor* in music. (5) Representing a shape: *X* in *Charing X* for the junction known as Charing Cross in London; *U-turn* a turn made through 180°. Some letters operate within established conventions, such as *A, B, C* and *X, Y, Z*, as the opening and closing letters of the Roman alphabet, often used to refer to sets of three things taken in order. *A to Z* means from the beginning to the end of something, such as a subject to be learned, while the Greek *alpha and omega* means the beginning and the end. The uses of letter symbols are complex and varied, and include: economy of expression in generalizing and in labelling, mnemonic aid, the replacement and augmentation of numbers, and special effects.

Economy of expression. Letters are widely used to form general statements abstracted from many specific instances, through such formulas as *How do we get from Point A to Point B?* and *Flight X is now boarding at Gate Y.* For some purposes, such letters form sets, as in *You need a minimum of BCC to get into the University of Wessex*, reference to examination grades. Letter symbols as compact labels are usually interim or temporary, such as *Factor S* used to name an element identified in research into *s*leep, but may become permanent, as with *X-ray*. Sometimes, such a letter combines with an initialism, as with the terms *UVA* and *UVB*, standing for *ultraviolet A* and *ultraviolet B* (types of solar radiation).

Mnemonic aids. The first letters of words and names in a list may be used acronymically to form a kind of name, such as *fonybas*, a mnemonic list of coordinating conjunctions (*for, or, nor, yet, but, as, so*), and *St Wapniacl*, once used to help US children memorize the departments of government in the order in which they were created (*State, Treasury, War, Attorney General, Post Office, Navy, Interior, Agriculture, Commerce, Labor*). Such usages may come in alliterative sets of three (*the three Bs* for *Bach, Beethoven, Brahms*), *the three Cs* for *cameras, computers, cars*), the words sometimes adapted to fit the idea and the rhythm (*the three Rs* for *reading, 'riting, 'rithmetic*).

Letters and numbers. Letters can be used instead of numbers (*A, B, C* for *1, 2, 3*), and in lists and classifications often occur with numbers, preceding as in *B-51, F-18* (types of US aircraft) or following as in *4A* (the top stream or track of the fourth year in a school). Such usages as *6(c)* indicate that the subsection headed *c* occurs in the section numbered *6* in a system or textbook. Letters are commonly used in such chemical formulae as *H₂O* for a molecule of water (based on the abbreviations used for the elements of the periodic table): H for hydrogen, 2 for the number of hydrogen atoms, and O for oxygen. Letter symbols used for listing can take on a life of their own and acquire grammatical attributes such as plurality and possession, as in: 'With totalitarian efficiency, the country's citizens had been classified as A, B or C, depending on whether they enthusiastically backed the regime, failed to demonstrate support for it, or opposed it; the Bs and Cs suffered economic reprisals' (*Los Angeles Times*, June 1983).

Special effects. Although all letters are available for use as special symbols, *K* and *X* have been particularly popular for such purposes. The uses of *K* include: an abbreviation meaning one thousand (from *kilo*), *10K* being 10,000 of a unit of currency; a token of alienness, as in *Amerika*, for the US conceived as dominated by Communists or Nazis; an eye-catching spelling for words in *q* and *c*, as with a company called *Kwik-Fit* and cartoon characters called *the Krazy Kids*. The uses of *X* include: a token for something unknown: *Mr X, Substance X, X-ray*; to represent *ex-*, as in *MX* for *missile experimental*, in *Xtra strong* and *X-ellent* (compare *D-grading* and *D-lightful*); for *Christ* in *Xmas*, representing the Greek letter *khi*; to signify censorship: *an X-rated movie*, not to be shown to minors; as the signature of an illiterate person; to mark a place on a map or where a signature should go on a paper (commonly called a cross and not necessarily identified as a letter); to represent a kiss, often in a series written in a letter.

Letters in word use and word-formation. Letter symbols are often attributive (*an A student, Type B behaviour*), and occur as abbreviations in compounds (*A-bomb, N-test* for *atomic bomb, nuclear test*). They may serve to emphasize significant words, whose full form may be taboo (*the F-word* for *fuck*), undesirable (*the big C* for cancer), or highly significant (*the big O* for the Olympics). Technical letter symbols in electrical engineering include *GeV* for *gigaelectron volt* and *TeV* for *teravolt*. Such symbols can include an ampersand: *R & D* for *research and development*. However, it may not always be easy to distinguish letter symbols from initialisms: in Britain, *ABC* may refer to the socio-economic classes A, B, C taken together; in the 1983 general election in

Canada, they meant *Anybody but Clark*; in Australia, they stand for the Australian Broadcasting Corporation; in Los Angeles, they have been used to mean *American-born Chinese*; in military terms, they mean *atomic, biological, chemical*.

See the entries for individual letters, A-Z, and ABBREVIATION, ACCENT, ACRONYM, ACUTE ACCENT, AGGLOMERESE, AITCH, ALPHABET, ASCENDER AND DESCENDER, ASH, CAPITAL, CONSONANT, DIACRITIC, DIGRAPH, DOUBLE LETTER, ENG, EPSILON, ESH, ETH, GOTHIC, GRAVE ACCENT, INITIAL, INITIALISM, INITIAL TEACHING ALPHABET, INTERNATIONAL PHONETIC ALPHABET, ITALIC(S), LETTER WORD, LITERAL, LONG S, MARK, MINIM, ORTHOEPY, ORTHOGRAPHY, ROMAN, SEMI-VOWEL, SERIF, SILENT LETTER, SPELLING, SPELLING REFORM, TECHNOSPEAK, THORN, TRANSLITERATION, TYPOGRAPHY, WORD, WRITING (SYSTEMS), YOGH. [TECHNOLOGY, WORD, WRITING].

C.U., T.MCA.

LETTER[2] [See LETTER[1]]. Also **epistle** [Through Old French from Latin *epistola*, Greek *epistolé* message, letter: now generally considered Biblical and/or pretentious]. A piece of writing addressed and usually sent to someone. Personal and official letters date from remote antiquity, as for example between Hittite and Egyptian rulers in the late second millennium BC. The letters of Cicero (106-43 BC) and the younger Pliny (AD 62-?112) are valuable records both of Latin prose and contemporary life. In England, the Paston Letters (15c) and Stonor Letters (14-15c) are similarly important for the study of their periods. Until the invention of the telegraph and telephone, letters were the commonest means through which people living at a distance from each other could keep in touch, and the 19c growth of national and international postal systems created a boom in letter-writing. Writing and reading letters became a major aspect of literacy after Rowland Hill introduced the penny post in Britain in 1840. Although with the spread of telephones the writing of personal letters and cards may have diminished, business letters remain a significant element of local and worldwide communication, whether posted or faxed.

Letters and literature. Literary compositions in the form of personal letters were popular in the 17-18c. The device was used mainly for the circulation of ideas and arguments, with the appeal of apparent direct address to the reader, as in Locke's *Letters on Toleration* (1689-92). Swift's *Drapier's Letters* (1724) were widely read and forced a change in government policy in Ireland regarding the grant of a private patent. Pope followed classical tradition in calling some poetic satires 'epistles', but indicates the contemporary

liking for the idea of the letter, as did the early newspaper *Dawks's News Letter* (1696-1716), printed to look as if handwritten. The most famous 18c political letters are the *Letters of Junius* (1769-72), pseudonymously attacking King George III and his ministers, and now usually attributed to Sir Philip Francis. Edmund Burke wrote several political letters, including *Letters on a Regicide Peace* (1796-7), which urged resistance to the French Jacobins. The use of letters in fiction was pioneered in the 16c by Lyly in *Euphues*, and taken up in the 18c by Richardson, who published *Letters to and from Particular Friends*, out of which grew the first major epistolary novel, *Pamela* (1740-1). This form of fiction was also practised by Smollett, Frances Burney, and, experimentally, by Austen, among others, but declined in vogue after the early 19c. It is now rare, but C. S. Lewis's *The Screwtape Letters: Letters from a Senior to a Junior Devil* (1942) uses the same technique. William Golding's *Rites of Passage* (1980) combines the epistolary and diary forms. Although often artificial in style, the epistolary novel combines personal narration by characters with multiple points of view.

Published letters. There have been many scholarly editions of letters not originally intended for publication, such as those of Horace Walpole, Byron, Keats, George Eliot, Henry James, Woolf, Shaw, and Tolkien. They reveal the lives and characters of their authors, often give insight into their literary methods, and show them using English in a more informal and personal manner. Newspapers, in addition to reportage, material from wire services, feature articles, and editorials, generally print letters from readers in their *correspondence columns*. Such letters cover a wide range of topics: commenting on material published in the newspaper and on general issues of the day, and raising matters of personal concern to the correspondent. On writers of letters to the editor, George Crabbe observed in his poem 'The Newspaper' (1785):

> These are a numerous tribe, to fame unknown,
> Who for the public good forego their own;
> Who volunteers in paper-war engage,
> With double portion of their party's rage:
> Such are the Bruti, Decii, who appear
> Wooing the printer for admission here;
> Whose generous souls can condescend to pray
> For leave to throw their precious time away.

If a paper war goes on too long, however, the editor is likely to intervene with the note: 'This correspondence is now closed.' Such letters often complain about language usage, a subject that sometimes stirs a treble portion of rage. See NEWSPAPER, NOVEL (EPISTOLARY), POSTSCRIPT, USAGE GUIDANCE AND CRITICISM. [LITERATURE, MEDIA, USAGE, WRITING].

R.C., T.MCA.

LETTERPRESS [18c]. (1) Also **relief printing**. Generally, the process of printing from raised type (letters in relief), as used from the mid-15c to the late 20c. Type and/or images cut in relief receive ink on their raised surfaces; the ink is then transferred by pressure to paper or some other surface. In general printing, letterpress has been superseded by photo-offset printing, except for large runs of newspapers and mass-market paperbacks; here, speed and volume require the durability of raised type made from photographic images transferred on to plastic cylinders, not from traditional lead typesetting. There are also some small private presses and specialist printers that continue to use letterpress. (2) Mainly in Britain, printed text as distinguished from illustrative material like drawings and photographs. See LETTERSET, PRINTING, PRINTING PRESS. [TECHNOLOGY]. W.W.B., T.MCA.

LETTERS. A former term for scholarship, especially in the classical languages, and for imaginative literature. The phrase *man of letters* originally denoted a scholar and later became the respectful title of a literary author. Carlyle spoke of the 'Hero as Man of Letters' in his lectures *On Heroes and Hero-Worship* (1840), with Johnson, Burns, and Rousseau as his examples. A Victorian monograph series on authors was called *English Men of Letters*. By the end of the 19c, the phrase generally referred to critics, essayists, and biographers. Now little used, the original meaning survives in the university degrees of M.Litt. and D.Litt. [Latin: *Litterarum Magister* and *Litterarum Doctor* Master and Doctor of Letters]. The title *litterae humaniores* [Latin: higher human letters] has been used in universities for study of the classics: originally, it distinguished secular from sacred texts. Compare BELLES LETTRES. See WRITER. [LITERATURE]. R.C.

LETTERSET [1962: a blend of *letterpress* and *offset*, a new term for the earlier *dry litho*]. A process of rotary printing that transfers the image from a 'wraparound' plate with letters in relief (as in *letterpress*) to an intermediate rubber roller or blanket cylinder then to the paper by offset techniques. See LETTERPRESS, PRINTING. [TECHNOLOGY]. T.MCA.

LETTER-SIZE. Mainly a North American measurement of paper, approximately $8\frac{1}{2} \times 11$ inches (22×28 cm). Letter-size equipment takes letter-size sheets. In recent years, US-style computer printouts in this size have made it more international. Compare LEGAL-SIZE. [TECHNOLOGY]. T.MCA.

LETTER WORD, also **letter name**. A word or name formed from the letters, usually the first letters, of several other words: *BBC* from British Broadcasting Corporation, *NATO* from North Atlantic Treaty Organization. It is a kind of abbreviation, with two forms: the *initialism* (*BBC* pronounced 'bee-bee-cee'); the *acronym* (*NATO*, pronounced 'Nay-toe'). The practice of forming words from letters is ancient. Medieval Jews formed personal names from the initials of a title, first name, and father's name: *Hida*, from *Hayyim Joseph David Azulai*. In medieval logic, letter words were used mnemonically to identify syllogisms (*Barbara, Bramantip, Celarent*), so as to help students remember and discuss the forms so labelled. See ACRONYM, INITIALISM, LETTER[1]. [NAME, WORD]. T.MCA.

LEVEL OF LANGUAGE. A term in (structural) linguistics. In the second quarter of the 20c, language was modelled by some linguists as a series of layers arranged one on top of the other, with units of sound (*phonology*) on the bottom layer, gathered into units of structure (*morphology*) above, which were then combined into larger grammatical units (*syntax*) above them, and, according to some, into units of meaning (*semantics*) at the top. The two lowest levels each had a unit of its own, formed with the suffix *-eme*: *phoneme* for phonology, *morpheme* for morphology. In some theories, this approach continued upwards with *lexeme* for an abstract lexical unit, and *tagmeme* sometimes used for syntax. The term has come into widespread, fairly loose usage to mean any one such layer: the phonological level, the syntactic level, etc. Originally, each level was studied independently of the others, at least in theory, and it was considered necessary to work from phonology upwards, finishing the study of one level before moving on to the next. A number of introductory textbooks of linguistics are organized in accordance with this model, which is still of value, although the strict separation of levels is no longer adhered to. In recent years, some linguists have tended to abandon the vertical 'layer cake' model in favour of a horizontal model with a *syntactic component* flanked by a *phonological component* on one side and a *semantic component* on the other. Syntax has this central role because it can be regarded as the component that links sound and meaning. See MODEL, MORPHOLOGY, PHONOLOGY, SEMANTICS, SYNTAX. [LANGUAGE]. J.M.A.

LEXEME [From Greek *léxis* speech, and *-eme*]. Also **lexical item, lexical unit**. In linguistics, a unit in the lexicon or vocabulary of a language. Its form is governed by sound and writing or print, its content by meaning and use. Thus, *penicillin* is the realization in print of a single English lexeme, while the nouns *crane* and *bank* represent at least two lexemes each: *crane* (a particular bird and a particular machine), *bank* (the shore of a river and a particular kind of financial institution). Most English dictionaries treat *crane n.* as a single headword with two senses (a case of polysemy) and *bank n.* as two headwords, each with at least one sense: a case of homonymy. Conventionally, a lexeme's inflections (such as *cranes, banks*) are considered variant forms, whereas such derivatives as *banker* are considered separate lexemes. In English as in other languages, lexemes may be single words (*crane, bank*), parts of words (*auto-, -logy*), groups of words (the compound *blackbird* and the idiom *kick the bucket*), or shortened forms (*flu* for *influenza*, *UK* for *United Kingdom*). See -EME, LEXICOLOGY, MORPHEME. [LANGUAGE, WORD].   R.F.I.

LEXICAL BAR [1980s: coined by the linguist David Corson]. A name for a perceived social, educational, and cultural barrier associated with a dual aspect of English lexis:

In English-speaking societies coincidences of social and linguistic history have combined to create a lexical situation that is unique among languages: most of the specialist and high status terminology of English is Graeco-Latin in origin and most of the less abstract terminology is Anglo-Saxon in origin. English in this respect, relative to other languages, has a fairly clear boundary drawn between its everyday and its high status vocabularies. This boundary is only contingent upon and reinforced by the etymological provenance of words, however; it is not erected by it. English etymology simply offers us a template for recognising more fundamental differences in conceptual frameworks. These more fundamental differences block high level interaction for some within the dominant culture. Once identified, though, these differences give us knowledge upon which we can base language planning policies in education to confront the social inequalities which are in part produced by the differences themselves. . . . The bar is partly a function of the historically introduced and social class-based orderings of society that are associated with the division of labour: It separates the lexes of the members of conservative peripheral social groups from the dominant and high status lexicon of the language (Corson, *The Lexical Bar*, Pergamon Press, 1985).

An illustration provided by Corson of the differences in the linguistic style of young people on opposite sides of the bar is:

I dunno, there's times when I think there are a few laws I'd like to stop but . . . don't know any I'd like to bring in (London poorer working-class 15-year-old).

I don't think I'd *introduce* many new ones but I would *abolish* quite a few (London upper middle-class 15-year-old).

An earlier work on the same theme is Victor Grove's *The Language Bar* (Routledge & Kegan

Paul, 1949). Compare ACCENT BAR. See BISOCIATION, DIGLOSSIA, DOUBLET, ELABORATED AND RESTRICTED CODE, PHRASAL VERB, SPELLING. [VARIETY, WORD].   T.MCA.

LEXICAL FIELD, also **lexical domain** and, if relatively small, **lexical set**. A group of words or lexemes whose members are related by meaning, reference, or use: for example, kinship terms, military ranks, colour words, and names for parts of the body. Some are hierarchically ordered (for example, ranks and taxonomies); some exhibit a part–whole relationship (*finger* and *toe* as parts of the hand or leg, and *hand* and *leg* as parts of the body); some occur in sequences or cycles (numbers, the seasons). Dictionary definitions of some items in the lexical field of animals might be *sheep* (an animal of a certain kind), *ram* (a male sheep), *ewe* (a female sheep). In such definitions, *sheep* is explained as a hyponym of *animal*, *ram* and *ewe* as hyponyms of *sheep*, while *ram* and *ewe* are also distinguished in terms of sex. Compare SEMANTIC FIELD. [WORD].   R.F.I., T.MCA.

LEXICAL ITEM. See LEXEME.

LEXICAL SEMANTICS [20c]. A term in linguistics for the study of the meaning of words, phrases, and lexemes, especially in sets rather than in isolation. See LEXICAL FIELD/SET, SEMANTICS. [LANGUAGE].   T.MCA.

LEXICAL SET. See LEXICAL FIELD.

LEXICOGRAPHY [17c: from Greek *lexikós* about words, and *-graphia* writing]. The procedure and profession of arranging and describing items of vocabulary in such works of reference as dictionaries, glossaries, thesauruses, synonym guides, usage guides, and concordances. Traditionally, lexicography has been of two kinds: *alphabetic lexicography*, the dominant form whose best-known product is the dictionary properly so called, and *thematic lexicography*, which arranges words by themes or topics, usually accompanied by an index, of which such a 'classified' work of reference as *Roget's Thesaurus* is a leading example. By and large, however, lexicography is taken to be a process of describing words in an alphabetic list, and most lexicographers work on dictionaries of a relatively standard kind. Equally traditionally, lexicography can be said to include the compilation not only of books about words (dictionaries, etc.), but also books about things (encyclopedias, etc.). Again, however, it is generally taken to centre on the making of wordbooks, which may be more encyclopedic (like many French and American works) or less encyclopedic (like many British works).

Products. The products of lexicography are varied. In terms of dictionaries proper, they range from the 20-volume *Oxford English Dictionary* and such large ('unabridged') one-volume US works as the *Webster's Third New International Dictionary* and the *Random House Dictionary of the English Language*) through the desk, family, or collegiate dictionary (such as *Chambers English Dictionary* and *Webster's Ninth New Collegiate Dictionary*), to the concise or compact (*The Concise Oxford Dictionary*), the pocket (*The Pocket Oxford Dictionary*), and even smaller works (the *Collins Gem* series). Lexicographic work may be monolingual (dealing in one language only), bilingual (with sections that define a language A in terms of another language B, and vice versa), or multilingual (in various ways covering three or more languages), and may be undertaken for general purposes or for (among others) small children, school and college students, or a range of other special-interest groups from musicians to word buffs. Whatever form they take, however, their compilation rests on the amassing and sifting of evidence about words and other expressions (for example citations from texts), and editorial guidelines as to what should be included, how it should be organized, and what special features (such as phonetics, etymologies, pictures, etc.) should be added.

Sources and coverage. All types of linguistic evidence are available to lexicographers, including introspection and discussion, the examination of pre-existing works of reference and other sources, and the formal use of survey questionnaires and citation corpora (both traditional, kept on cards, and electronic, stored in computer databases). Some classes of vocabulary item are normally excluded from most general dictionaries, but may appear in encyclopedic and specialist dictionaries, such as the binomial nomenclature of biology, the names of people, places, organizations, and events, proverbs, and quotations. After systematic exclusions are dealt with for the purposes of a general dictionary, what remains of the vocabulary is assessed for potential entries. Where large dictionaries seek to cover as much as possible, smaller dictionaries aimed at certain kinds of user have (often as the result of ad-hoc decision-taking) lists judged appropriate to their level. Specialist dictionaries have lists appropriate to their core topic (for example, *Brewer's Dictionary of Phrase and Fable*, *The Penguin Dictionary of Saints*, Fowler's *Dictionary of Modern English Usage*, Partridge's *Dictionary of Slang and Unconventional English*, etc.).

Dictionary information. Dictionaries generally give some or all of the following types of information in an order appropriate to the work in question: (1) Headword and any variants, sometimes with syllabication marked and homograph status indicated. (2) Pronunciation in a system of respelling or phonetic symbols. (3) Grammatical information and usage labels (often in the form of abbreviations or codes). (4) Number of senses as necessary. (5) Explanations proper. (6) Possible illustrative phrases or sentences. (7) Compounds, derivatives, phrasal verbs, and idioms (if not listed separately). (8) Etymology. (9) Points of usage. (10) Information about synonyms and antonyms. Dictionaries, however, are often characterized by the type of information on which they concentrate: for example, *The Oxford Dictionary of English Etymology* (1966, etc.), Daniel Jones's *English Pronouncing Dictionary* (1917, etc.), and in the study of English as a Foreign or Second Language such learner's dictionaries as the *Oxford Advanced Learner's Dictionary* (1948, etc.) and the *Longman Dictionary of Contemporary English* (1978, etc.).

Conventions. In presenting their information, most lexicographical works of reference (dictionaries, thesauruses, etc.) have two columns of densely organized information in small type. They use contrastive typefaces for distinct purposes, such as bold-face type for headwords, roman for definitions, italics for abbreviated codes and specimen words and phrases, and small capitals for cross-references. Square brackets may enclose special information, such as etymologies at the beginning or end of entries, while round brackets (parentheses) may add ancillary information in the body of the explanations. By and large, even when schools and colleges give students guidance on what to expect in a dictionary, the differences of format and emphasis from dictionary to dictionary are seldom discussed. As a consequence, for many people the complex layout of standard dictionaries may be intimidating. Thus, compounds may be main entries in one dictionary but sub-entries in another; abbreviations, word elements, biographical information, etc., may be in appendices at the back in one book, and interspersed through the main text in another.

Nowadays, lexicographers generally try to avoid unnecessarily cryptic abbreviations and conventions. However, some special conventions are necessary, if only to keep the size of the book within manageable proportions. Lexicographers are acutely aware of the importance of communicating with the user on the understanding of these conventions, which often involve knowledge of a limited number of facts and principles.

They often feel the need to develop strategies and techniques that encourage the user to become familiar with such matters, in order to get the maximum benefit from a work of reference. See DICTIONARY, LEXICOLOGY. [REFERENCE, WORD].

R.F.I., R.E.A.

Benson, Morton, Benson, Evelyn, & Ilson, Robert. 1986. *Lexicographic Description of English*. Amsterdam & Philadelphia: John Benjamins.

Burchfield, Robert (ed.). 1987. *Studies in Lexicography*. Oxford: Clarendon Press.

Hartman, R. R. K. (ed.). 1986. *The History of Lexicography*. Amsterdam & Philadelphia: John Benjamins.

Ilson, Robert (ed.). 1986. *Lexicography: An Emerging International Profession*. Manchester University Press, in association with the Fulbright Commission, London.

—— (ed.). 1987. *A Spectrum of Lexicography: Papers from AILA Brussels, 1984*. Amsterdam & Philadelphia: John Benjamins.

Landau, Sidney. 1984/9. *Dictionaries: The Art and Craft of Lexicography*. 1984, New York: Charles Scribner's Sons. 1989, Cambridge: University Press.

McArthur, Tom. 1986. *Worlds of Reference: Lexicography, Learning and Language from the Clay Tablet to the Computer*. Cambridge: University Press.

LEXICOLOGY [1820s: from Greek *lexikós* of words, *-logía* study]. An area of language study concerned with the nature, meaning, history, and use of words and word elements and often also with the critical description of lexicography. Although formerly a branch of philology, lexicology is increasingly treated as a branch of linguistics, associated with such terms as *lexeme*, *lexical field*, *lexical item*, *lexicon*, *lexis* (see entries), on the premiss that they offer (or could offer, if tightly defined and widely adopted) a more precise and useful basis for the study of language than imprecise terms such as *word* and *vocabulary*. [LANGUAGE, WORD]. T.MCA.

LEXICON [From Greek *lexikón* (*biblíon*) a word book, from *lexikós* concerning speech]. (1) A work of reference listing and explaining words: Henry G. Liddell & Robert Scott, *Greek-English Lexicon* (1843). A lexicon is usually a dictionary that deals either with a classical or scriptural language (a Hebrew lexicon) or a technical or facetious subject (Jonathon Green, *The Cynic's Lexicon: A Dictionary of Amoral Advice*, 1984). It may also, however, be a word list (Roland Hindmarsh, *The Cambridge English Lexicon*, 1980) or a thematic work of lexical reference (Tom McArthur, *The Longman Lexicon of Contemporary English*, 1981). The Greek-derived ending *-icon* is sometimes used as, or as if it were, a clipping of *lexicon*: *The Paradoxicon* (a collection of paradoxes, by N. Falletta, 1983) and *The Archaicon* (about archaisms, by J. E.

Barlough, 1974). (2) A term in especially American linguistics for the vocabulary of a language or sub-language, consisting of its stock of lexemes. Compare LEXIS. [LANGUAGE, REFERENCE, WORD]. T.MCA., R.F.I.

LEXIS [1960c: from Greek *léxis* speech]. A term in especially British linguistics for the vocabulary of a language or sub-language, consisting especially of its stock of lexemes. The term became popular because it is unambiguous, unlike its synonym *lexicon* (see entry), and is Greek in origin (fitting well with such other terms of Greek origin as *phonology* and *syntax*), in contrast with Latin-derived *vocabulary* (associated with Latinate *pronunciation* and Greco-Latin *grammar*). [LANGUAGE, WORD]. R.F.I.

LIBEL [13c: from Latin *libellus* a little book]. The publication of a false, defamatory statement likely to harm a person's reputation. In law, libel is a criminal offence; the intention of the defendant is immaterial, and it is the jury, not the judge, which decides whether the words are defamatory or not. See CENSORSHIP, FREEDOM OF THE PRESS, MALEDICTA, SLANDER. [MEDIA]. G.H.

LIBERIA [Early 19c: Latin, free place]. Officially *Republic of Liberia*. A country in West Africa. Capital: Monrovia. Currency: the dollar (100 cents). Population: 2.4m (1988), 3.5m (projection for 2000). Languages: English (official), and over 20 Niger-Congo languages, including Kru and Mande. Religion: 61% traditional, 29% Muslim, 10% Christian. Education: primary 76%, secondary 23%, tertiary 2%, literacy 35%. The region was mapped by the Portuguese in the 15c and later visited by the Dutch, British, and other Europeans looking for gold, spices, and slaves. The idea of a homeland for freed slaves was conceived by a group of US philanthropical societies, including the American Colonization Society, influenced by the British creation of Freetown in neighbouring Sierra Leone. Monrovia, named after President Monroe, was founded in 1822. The governors of Liberia were white Americans until Joseph Jenkins Roberts, a black born in Virginia, took over in 1841. He declared the *Free and Independent Republic of Liberia* in 1847. Freed slaves migrated from the US until the end of the Civil War in 1865, and black Americans have settled in small numbers ever since. After a coup in 1980, the US-style constitution was suspended and a People's Redemption Council established, with a new constitution in 1984. Civil war and inter-ethnic strife were widespread in the early 1990s.

Liberian English. Liberia is the only black African country in which English is a native language and the only country in Africa owing its

English more to the US than the UK. The variety originated first in contacts from the 17c between native speakers of BrE and AmE and such coastal peoples as the Kru (among whom English pidgins developed), and then in the settlement of repatriated blacks. Their descendants, known formally as *Americo-Liberians* and colloquially as *Mericos* and *Congos*, established and maintained the prestige of English and dominated Liberian society politically and economically, especially through the True Whig Party, until the 1980 coup, which was led by Samuel Doe, a non-Merico army sergeant. Sierra Leone Krio has had some impact on usage, and frequent travel to, and close political relations with, the US have given standard AmE and American Black English continuing prestige and influence. English in Liberia can be described in terms of an acrolect (high-prestige form), several basilects (low-prestige forms), and emerging mesolects (intermediate forms). *Standard Liberian English* is acquired through, and is a mark of, a high level of education, is heard on radio and television, and is the speech of those locally referred to as *civilized*. At the other end of the continuum, the basilects include *Kru Pidgin English* (the oldest pidgin), *Settler English* (formerly *Merico*), the everyday usage of the Americo-Liberian settlers (closely related to Southern US English before the Civil War), and *Liberian Interior English*, used mainly by speakers of Mande in the non-coastal areas. *Soldier English* is a pidgin used since the early 20c by and with non-English-speakers in the army, and *Vernacular Liberian English* includes urban and rural mesolects that compromise between the standard and non-standard varieties.

Features. The close historical link with AmE gives Liberian English its distinctiveness in relation to other West African varieties. Phonologically, the varieties range from a rhotic standard associated with AmE to non-rhotic pronunciations influenced by Kru and Mande. Grammatically, the mesolects and basilects have the following features: (1) Non-standard auxiliaries: *He done come* He has come; *A was not know* I did not know; habitual *do* as in *I do see boy all de time* I see the boy all the time; progressive *de* as in *I de go* I am going. (2) Uninflected verbs: *You see da man?* Did you see the man?; *A know dem* I knew them; *Dey kesh grahapa* They caught grasshoppers. The distinction between Settler English and Kru Pidgin can be seen in Settler *Da pekin cryin*, Kru *Di pekin de krai* (The child is crying), Settler *I ain see him*, Kru *A neva siam*. Distinctively Liberian words include: *bugabug* termite, *dumboy* boiled, pounded cassava, *favour* to resemble (compare AmE), *fresh cold* a runny nose, head cold, *groundpea*

peanut, groundnut, *jina* spirits, *kanki* measurement for rice (around two cups), *kwi* a foreigner, *outside child* a child acknowledged although born outside marriage, *sasse* cheeky, smart, sassy. Traditionally, the standard has been emphasized and the other varieties generally disparaged, but since the coup the compromise forms have begun to gain recognition in such public contexts as the media and informal greetings, as expressions of political and social solidarity. The mesolect in Monrovia is the centre of innovation, and is spreading throughout the country. Typically, the same kind of thing can be said at several different 'levels': acrolect *What you're saying, it's true, and I won't do it again*; mesolect *The thing you talking, that true, but I will not do it again*; basilect *The thing you telli me you no lie, but I can't do some again*. See AFRICAN ENGLISH, ENGLISH, WEST AFRICAN ENGLISH, WEST AFRICAN PIDGIN. [AFRICA, VARIETY].
L.B.B.

LIBRARY [14c: from French *librairie*, Latin *libraria* 'a book place', from *liber* book. Variously pronounced 'ly-brery', 'ly-bery', 'ly-bry']. (1) A collection of books, periodicals, and/or other materials, primarily written and printed, but increasingly in the 20c recorded on film or tape or kept in electronic storage. Libraries are sometimes commercial enterprises, but most often are public or institutional services that offer on-site reference and/or borrowing facilities. Larger libraries, such as the British Library and the Library of Congress (the national libraries of the UK and US respectively), may offer educational and cultural programmes, such as lectures and artistic performances, in addition to services more strictly related to information. *Librarians* work in libraries, *librarianship* is their profession, and *library science* is the study of the organization and administration of libraries and their services. (2) A series of books or other printed products, of the same type and with similar covers, usually dealing with related topics, such as *The Penguin Poetry Library*, which consists of works by major English-language poets. (3) In computing, a thematic collection of data or software. For further details, see BIBLIOGRAPHY, BOOK, BRITISH LIBRARY, CATALOG(UE), LIBRARY LANGUAGE, LIBRARY OF CONGRESS, SERIAL. [EDUCATION, MEDIA].
T.MCA., R.E.A.

LIBRARY LANGUAGE [1960s]. A language used for reference purposes in libraries, etc., especially for such subjects as engineering, medicine, and business: 'For a long time English will remain the most important library language for higher education in India and her window on the world' (Jamal Kidwai, *Times Educational Supplement*, 25 Oct. 1968). Compare ENGLISH

FOR SPECIFIC/SPECIAL PURPOSES, READING. [EDU-CATION, LANGUAGE, MEDIA].   T.MCA.

LIBRARY OF CONGRESS, short form *LC*. The library which serves the United States Congress in Washington, DC, founded in 1800 with a grant of $5,000. Many early LC materials were lost in a fire in 1814 during the bombardment of Washington by a British fleet. The collection was re-established through the acquisition of the library of Thomas Jefferson and has been expanding ever since. It is now the world's largest library, housing over 22.5m books and pamphlets, with more than 80.7m items in its collections. It serves in effect, though unofficially, as the national library of the US: the bulk of its funding comes from Congress and its librarian is appointed by the President, with the approval of the Senate. The staff of the LC provides research services to Congress, as required by law, as well as to the rest of the government and the general public.

Collections. Major collections include social and political science, US history and civilization, science and technology, aeronautical literature, music (including recordings), technical reprints, Chinese, Japanese, and Russian language books (the largest collections outside their respective countries), and the largest collection of incunabula in the western hemisphere. The Division of Motion Picture, Broadcasting and Recorded Sound, with over 250,000 reels, focuses on American films from 1914 to 1942. The special collections include the papers of many organizations (the League of Women Voters, the National Association for the Advancement of Colored People, the American Council of Learned Societies), most presidents, and other well-known Americans, such as Clara Barton, Alexander Graham Bell, Frederick Douglass, Felix Frankfurter, Benjamin Franklin, and Walt Whitman.

Services. Since 1870, the LC has been responsible for copyrights, and copies of all copyrighted materials must be deposited with it. It provides cataloguing services for libraries and publishes the *National Union Catalog* as well as specialized catalogues. It is responsible for the development of the Library of Congress classification scheme for books and subject headings for all printed matter; disseminates technical information on the preservation of books and manuscripts; and records books for the blind. Its *Center for American Folklife*, established in 1976, is charged with supporting, preserving, and presenting American folklife through exhibits, workshops, and archival presentation, including an extensive collection of early recordings on wax cylinders. The

Center for the Book, established in 1977, promotes reading as well as research and discussion about books and their production. The LC reading-rooms are open, free, to adult members of the public, though access to some collections is restricted to those with specific research purposes. The catalogue is now computerized. Some research services are also available by mail and phone, and some materials may be obtained through photo-duplication or through interlibrary loan. See BOOK, BRITISH LIBRARY, LIBRARY. [AMERICAS, MEDIA].   D.E.B.

LIEBER, Francis [1800–72]. American political scientist. Born in Berlin, he received his Ph.D. from the U. of Jena (1820). After participating in the Greek War of Independence (1822) and working as a library assistant in Italy (1823), he studied mathematics in Berlin and Halle. Unable to obtain employment in Germany because of his politics, he went first to England then the US, where he became Professor of History and Political Economy at the U. of South Carolina (1835–56) and Columbia (1857–64), before transferring to the School of Law at Columbia (1865–72). He continued to espouse often unpopular causes, including the establishment of AmE as an international language. As the first editor of the *Encyclopaedia Americana* (1829–33, 13 volumes), he explored the ways in which Americans viewed their speech and urged his contributors to study English outside Britain. He suggested that AmE be examined diachronically, first as a variety of BrE, then as a language form with its own varieties. Maintaining that understanding is primarily 'the art of finding out the true sense of words', he encouraged the description of AmE as used in specific contexts and criticized those who did not correctly delimit AmE contributions to the English lexicon.

Interested in language change and language maintenance, he kept notebooks (1849–51) focusing on interactions among speakers, interrelationships between writing and speech, and constraints on communication posed by differences in education and class. While recognizing the power of language as an instrument of nationalism, he advocated the right of linguistic minorities to maintain their first languages while adding English as a second. Suggesting that language shift and acquisition needed to be studied as processes of simplification and amplification, he kept records of his children's linguistic development as well as the development of children of slaves, and of Laura Bridgeman, a child born deaf and blind. Lieber's study of English in non-native contexts (found in collections of his letters, essays, addresses, and reminiscences) called attention to the ideology of languages and helped form the agenda for American linguistic research. [AMERICAS, BIOGRAPHY, EDUCATION, EUROPE, REFERENCE]. R.W.B.

LIGATURE [14c: from Latin *ligare/ligatum* to bind]. (1) A term in printing for two or more joined letters cast in the same piece of type: *æ* in *Cæsar*; *fl* in *florin*; *ffi* in *office*. Early typefaces had many ligatures, imitating connected letters in handwriting, but few are retained in contemporary English printed alphabets. Vowel ligatures such as *æ* are now commonly replaced by open *ae*, even when transcribing Latin, Latinized Greek, and Old English: *Caesar* not *Cæsar*; *Aeschylus* not *Æschylus*; *Aelfric* not *Ælfric*. (2) In phonetics, a mark like the slur in musical notation placed over or under a pair of symbols to show that they are spoken together: a͡ɪ, and a͜ɪ. Top ligature is favoured for letters with descenders, bottom ligature for letters with ascenders. Compare ASH, DIGRAPH. [SPEECH, TECHNOLOGY, WRITING]. W.W.B.

LIMERICK [19c: from the town of *Limerick* in Ireland]. A five-lined piece of light verse, rhyming *aabba*. The first two and the last lines should be anapaestic trimeter, with the third and fourth anapaestic dimeter, but the metre is often less regular. Traditionally, the name of a place or person is introduced in the first line and may be repeated in the last. The form is thought to derive from impromptu versifying about the inhabitants of a town or village, with the refrain 'Will you come up to Limerick?' Edward Lear made the form popular in the 19c, using it for nonsense verse. An anonymous limerick on the Theory of Relativity runs:

> There was a young lady named Bright
> Who could travel much faster than light.
> She started one day
> In a relative way
> And came back on the previous night.

The limerick's simple form and easy, swinging rhythm make it particularly suitable for humorous or scurrilous use and for taboo subjects. [EUROPE, LITERATURE]. R.C.

LIMITED ENGLISH SPEAKER, short form *LES*. A term in language teaching and applied linguistics for someone who speaks too little English for general purposes or only enough English for a particular purpose, such as hawking goods or acting as a tour guide. [EDUCATION]. T.MCA.

LINE [13c: from Old English *līn* flax (from Latin *linum* flax), influenced by Old French *ligne*, Latin *linea*, noun use of adjective *lineus* flaxen (also from *linum*). The concept of the line in writing derives from a plant fibre capable of being woven

into a pattern: compare TEXT, VERSE]. (1) A narrow, continuous mark made by a stick, plough, blade, pen, pencil, brush, etc., across a surface. (2) A similar feature of script and print, in which signs are arranged in sequence for the purposes of composing a text, usually straight and either vertical (as with Chinese characters) or horizontal (as in Western writing). Among literate people, the *linear* concept of language (both writing and speech) arises from this convention. Before the advent of writing, no poet could ever have 'recited a few lines (of verse)' or have conceived poetry in terms of lines. See ASCENDER AND DESCENDER, BREVE, DISTICH, HYPHEN, JUSTIFYING, LIST, MACRON, ONE-LINER, PRINTING, PUNCH LINE, STORY LINE, TRISTICH, TWO-LINER, TYPOGRAPHY, WIDOWS AND ORPHANS. [LITERATURE, TECHNOLOGY, WRITING]. T.MCA.

LINE BREAK, LINE-BREAK. See HYPHEN, JUSTIFYING, SYLLABICATION.

LINGO [17c: perhaps from Polari *lingo*, perhaps an adapted clipping of *lingua franca*]. An informal, slangy, usually dismissive term for: (1) A language that is perceived as strange and unintelligible: 'When men speak French, or any Outlandish Linguo' (J. Chubbe, *Miscellaneous Tracts*, 1770). (2) A hybrid patois, often as used in an area where different language groups meet: *Border Lingo*, a name for the mix of English and Spanish in Texas, also known as *Tex-Mex*. (3) An unusual way of speaking that is hard to follow; slang or jargon: 'Well, well, I shall understand your Lingo one of these days, Cozen; in the mean while I must answer in plain English' (William Congreve, *The Way of the World*, 1700); 'I have often warned you not to talk the court gibberish to me. I tell you, I don't understand the lingo' (Henry Fielding, *Tom Jones*, 1749). See JARGON, LINGUA, LINGUA FRANCA, PATOIS, TEX-MEX. Compare -ESE, -SPEAK, TALK. [LANGUAGE]. T.MCA.

LINGUA [17c: From Latin *lingua* tongue, mainly through Italian. Compare LINGUA FRANCA]. Obsolete: an informal term for a language or lingo: 'Was ever such a Beuk-learn'd Clerk / That speaks all linguas of the Ark?' (W. W. Wilkins, *Political Ballads*, 1678); 'Many of the women speak a little of the lingua called Chinese English, or, in the cant phrase, *pigeon*' (R. Tomes, *Americans in Japan*, 1857). See JAPANESE PIDGIN ENGLISH, LINGO, PIDGIN. [LANGUAGE]. T.MCA.

LINGUA FRANCA [17c: from Italian, language of the Franks. The plural is usually *lingua francas*, but sometimes Italian *lingue franche*]. (1) Originally, a name for the mixed language, based on Italian and Occitan (Southern French), used for trading and military purposes in the Mediterranean in the Middle Ages. (2) By extension, a semi-technical term for any additional (often compromise) language adopted by speakers of different languages, as a common medium of communication for any purposes and at any level. A lingua franca may be either a fully-fledged language (Latin in the Roman Empire, Hausa at the present time in West Africa), or a pidgin or creole (Tok Pisin in Papua New Guinea, Krio in Sierra Leone). A language may become somewhat reduced if it is widespread as a lingua franca (Swahili in East Africa). French served widely in Europe as the lingua franca of diplomacy in the 18-19c, and English now serves as a lingua franca in many countries with linguistically diverse populations (such as India and Nigeria) and for many purposes (as with the restricted variety Seaspeak, used by the world's merchant marine). See BUSINESS ENGLISH, EUROPEAN COMMUNITY, LANGUAGE LEARNING, LINGO, LINGUA, LINK LANGUAGE, PIDGIN, POLARI, SABIR. [LANGUAGE].   S.R., T.MCA.

LINGUAL [14c: from Latin *lingualis*]. (1) Relating to the tongue, as with a *lingual brace* in dentistry, which fits behind the teeth and is invisible when the wearer speaks or smiles, and a *lingual protrusion lisp*, a lisp caused by the tongue coming forward too far. (2) In phonetics, formed by (especially the tip of) the tongue, as with the consonants /d, t, n/; *a lingual sound*. (3) Relating to languages: *lingual skills*. The simple adjective is rare in this sense, but the combining form -*lingual* is common, as in *bi-*, *tri-*, and *quad-rilingual* able to use two, three, and four languages respectively. There are two terms for 'able to use (only) one language': the commoner *monolingual* (a hybrid form using Greek-derived *mono-* sole) and the etymologically more consistent *unilingual* (using Latin-derived *un-* one). The latter is common in CanE, under the influence of French *unilingue*. Compare -GLOT. See APICAL, BILINGUALISM, MULTILINGUALISM, TONGUE. [LANGUAGE].   T.MCA.

LINGUIST [16c: from Latin *lingua* tongue, language, and -*ist* as in *specialist*]. (1) Traditionally, someone who speaks a number of languages fluently and usually also works with languages (such as an interpreter or translator): *The Linguist*, the title of the journal of the *Institute of Linguists*, a UK-based organization for translators. (2) In the 20c, someone trained in linguistics, the science of language, and who may or may not be a linguist in the first sense. The term is often ambiguous; *linguistician* (coined in the 1890s) has been proposed from time to time as the 'proper' name for a student of linguistics.

It is, however, widely regarded as unwieldy and pretentious, and its main use is facetious (when, for example, scientific linguists poke fun at themselves) or pejorative (suggesting a new species of pedant): 'A "linguist" who isn't at least bilingual is no linguist at all. He's merely a linguistician' (Peter Fabian, *EFL Gazette*, Oct. 1990). [LANGUAGE].   T.MCA.

LINGUISTIC [1830s: from *linguist* and -*ic*]. A general-purpose adjective, meaning anything to do with language and linguistics: *linguistic skills*, *linguistic theories*. [LANGUAGE].   J.M.A.

LINGUISTIC ASSOCIATION OF CANADA AND THE UNITED STATES, short form *LACUS*. An American and Canadian association founded in 1974, and concerned with linguistics at large. It publishes an annual proceedings *LACUS Forum* and the journal *Forum Linguisticum*. [AMERICAS, LANGUAGE, MEDIA].
                    J.A.

LINGUISTIC ASSOCIATION OF GREAT BRITAIN, short form *LAGB*. An association founded in 1959 to promote the study of linguistics. It holds regular spring and autumn meetings and publishes the *Journal of Linguistics* (Cambridge University Press). See BRITISH ASSOCIATION FOR APPLIED LINGUISTICS. [EUROPE, LANGUAGE, MEDIA].   C.J.B.

LINGUISTIC ATLAS, also **dialect atlas.** A book of maps which show the distribution of language features over a chosen area, as an aid to visualizing the parts of that area where alternative or competing forms are in use: for example, *The Linguistic Atlas of England* (1978), *The Linguistic Geography of Wales* (1973). Phonological or lexical features are those most often mapped, but morphological, syntactic, and other features may be similarly displayed. The maps show, with conventional signs such as dots, circles, and triangles, the locations of features as used by native speakers. Ideally, the speakers are directly interviewed in their home communities and their responses immediately noted, but the data are sometimes gathered by postal enquiry. The linguistic atlas is a tool of dialectology. The first attempt to collect data massively was made by the German philologist Georg Wenker who, in 1876, sent out a series of literary sentences to 1,266 schoolmasters in the Rhineland, requesting them to convert the sentences to local dialect equivalents. Wenker later extended the work to cover all of Germany, but few maps were published. Unfortunately, many schoolmasters did not know phonetics and some did not know the local dialects. The results were not without value, but Wenker's method and maps were severely criticized and were superseded by the new 'direct' method of collecting used by Jules Gilliéron for the *Atlas linguistique de la France* (Paris: Champion, 1902–10), the first to cover an entire nation. Though postal enquiries are still in limited use, on-the-spot recording of local informants' speech currently prevails. Display of results on maps is slow, costly, and therefore limiting, but currently they provide the best direct image of variation within an area.

Linguistic atlases have been undertaken, though not many completed, for at least 30 provinces and many other areas of Europe and for more than 20 languages and regional dialects, with some beginnings in Africa, Asia, and South America (compare Sever Pop, *La Dialectologie*, 1951). In terms of English, atlases have been made for Scotland by Angus McIntosh (1952, *An Introduction to a Survey of Scottish Dialects*, U. of Edinburgh Press) and J. Y. Mather and H. H. Speitel (1975, 1977, 1986, *The Linguistic Atlas of Scotland*, 3 volumes, Croom Helm); for Wales by Alan R. Thomas (1973, *The Linguistic Geography of Wales*, U. of Wales Press), and for England by Harold Orton, Stewart Sanderson, and John Widdowson (1978, *The Linguistic Atlas of England*, Croom Helm). In North America, the overall project 'The Linguistic Atlas of the United States and Canada', for which fieldwork was begun in 1931, has been only partly achieved. Parts completed and published are: *The Linguistic Atlas of New England*, handbook and 3 volumes, by Hans Kurath (1939–43, Brown U.); *The Linguistic Atlas of the Upper Midwest*, 3 volumes, by Harold B. Allen (1973–6, U. of Minnesota Press); *The Linguistic Atlas of the Gulf States*, 3 volumes, with others in preparation, by Lee Pederson (1986–9, U. of Georgia). Supplementary publications covering other parts of the eastern states are: by Kurath (1949, *A Word Geography of the Eastern United States*, U. of Michigan Press); E. Bagby Atwood (1953, *A Survey of Verb Forms in the Eastern United States*, U. of Michigan Press); Gordon R. Wood (1971, *Vocabulary Change*, Southern Illinois U. Press). Field collecting has covered most of the US, especially east of the Mississippi. Almost all linguistic atlases are synchronic, but historical ones have been attempted, the most considerable being Angus McIntosh's pioneering work, begun in 1952 and published in 1986, *A Linguistic Atlas of Late Medieval English* (2 volumes, Aberdeen U. Press). See LINGUISTIC ATLAS OF ENGLAND, LINGUISTIC ATLAS OF THE UNITED STATES AND CANADA, LINGUISTIC SURVEY OF SCOTLAND. [AMERICAS, EUROPE, LANGUAGE, REFERENCE, VARIETY].   F.G.C.

LINGUISTIC ATLAS OF ENGLAND, short form *LAE*. An atlas of the dialects of England edited by Harold Orton, Stewart Sanderson, and

John Widdowson, published by Croom Helm, London, in 1978. Orton directed its preparation at the Institute of Dialect and Folk Life Studies, U. of Leeds, of which Sanderson was Director. The maps display selected material from the *Survey of English Dialects*, grouped according to phonology, lexis, morphology, and syntax. The phonological maps cover not only vowel differences but also variants in the pronunciation of such words as *tongue* with closing /g/ and *bacon* with /j/ after /b/ ('byacon'). The lexical maps show the distributions of such usages as *byre*, *cow-stable, mistal, neat-house, shippon* (dialect synonyms of *cowshed*) and *mowdy, mowdy-warp, want* (synonyms of *mole*). The morphological maps show the distribution of such forms as *he say* rather than *he says*. The irregularities of the verb *to be* are graphically shown, with occurrences of *I bin, I be, I are* rather than *I am*. Syntactic maps deal with such forms as *We put the light on* and *We put on the light*, which emerge as geographical distinctions. The *Atlas* is not exhaustive, and a corpus of material resulting from the Survey remains unresearched. See LINGUISTIC ATLAS, SURVEY OF ENGLISH DIALECTS. [EUROPE, REFERENCE, VARIETY].   S.E.

LINGUISTIC ATLAS OF THE UNITED STATES AND CANADA, short form *LAUSC*. The inclusive title for a series of affiliated investigations into North American dialects of English. Planning for an atlas project was begun by the Present-Day English Research Group of the Modern Language Association in the 1920s. The Linguistic Society of America, the American Council of Learned Societies, and the American Dialect Society supported the project, whose aim was to map linguistically the whole of English-speaking North America. The New England region was chosen for a pilot project, with fieldwork begun there in 1931. Under the editorship of Hans Kurath, that project was completed and published as the *Linguistic Atlas of New England* (*LANE*, 3 volumes in 6, Brown U., 1939–43, plus a *Handbook of the Linguistic Geography of New England*, 1939, 2nd edition AMS Press, 1973). By the time *LANE* was finished, however, it had become clear that North America was too large to be covered by a single team or project. Consequently, the original project was divided into a number of autonomous but loosely correlated regional dialect studies.

As fieldwork for the New England atlas was completed, that for a *Linguistic Atlas of the Middle and South Atlantic States* (*LAMSAS*) was begun and continued from 1933 to 1949. Originally separate projects for the Middle Atlantic (New York, New Jersey, Delaware, and Pennsylvania) and the South Atlantic (Maryland south to the north-east tip of Florida), the project was unified under the direction of Kurath; on his retirement, he was succeeded by one of the main fieldworkers, Raven I. McDavid Jr. Pending editing of the atlas, three interpretive volumes were published based on its field records and those of *LANE*: Hans Kurath, *A Word Geography of the Eastern United States* (U. of Michigan Press, 1949), E. Bagby Atwood, *A Survey of Verb Forms in the Eastern United States* (U. of Michigan Press, 1953), and Kurath & McDavid, *The Pronunciation of English in the Atlantic States* (U. of Michigan Press, 1961). Editing of the atlas proper is currently being done by William A. Kretzschmar Jr., at the U. of Georgia.

Work toward a *Linguistic Atlas of the North Central States* (*LANCS*) was begun by Albert H. Marckwardt in 1938. Fieldwork was carried out in Ohio, Indiana, Illinois, Kentucky, Michigan, Wisconsin, and portions of the Canadian province of Ontario. The field records are now stored at the U. of Georgia; the field records of both *LANCS* and *LAMSAS* are available on microfilm from the U. of Chicago. The second project to reach completion was *The Linguistic Atlas of the Upper Midwest* (*LAUM*), 3 volumes, U. of Minnesota Press, 1973-6), initiated in 1947 and edited by Harold B. Allen. The New England data had been published as large and costly hand-drawn maps; the Upper Midwest atlas used small maps as illustrations to a narrative exposition of the data, and included a variety of charts and tables. *LAUM* covers the states of Minnesota, Iowa, North and South Dakota, and Nebraska.

The Linguistic Atlas of the Gulf States (*LAGS*) began publication in 1986 (U. of Georgia Press), with second and third volumes appearing in 1988 and 1989. Several more volumes are in preparation. Edited by Lee Pederson of Emory U., this atlas covers the states of Florida, Georgia, Alabama, Mississippi, Tennessee, Louisiana, Arkansas, and eastern Texas. The data on which the atlas is based, including a concordance of all responses, is available on microfiche, and a computer program exists to map the information in complex combinations. In an independent study (*Vocabulary Change*, Southern Illinois U. Press, 1971), Gordon R. Wood covered much of the same geographical area using a lexical checklist distributed by mail. Dialect atlas studies west of the Mississippi, other than the Upper Midwest, are in various stages of progress. Although each of the published regional atlases has been in a different format and each project has had somewhat different emphases, all have been efforts to describe regional usage in a comparable way according to the age, sex, and social

group of speakers. In addition, there is a common core of items for which questionnaires seek to elicit terms. They are set forth by Alva L. Davis, Raven I. McDavid Jr., and Virginia G. McDavid, *A Compilation of the Worksheets of the Linguistic Atlas of the United States and Canada and Associated Projects*, 2nd edition (U. of Chicago Press, 1969) and Lee Pederson et al., *A Manual for Dialect Research in the Southern States*, 2nd edition (U. of Alabama Press, 1974). [AMERICAS, REFERENCE, VARIETY].

J.A.

LINGUISTIC GEOGRAPHY, also **dialect geography** [1920s]. The study of regional dialect variation. See DIALECT, ISOGLOSS, LINGUISTIC ATLAS. [LANGUAGE].　　　　T.MCA.

LINGUISTICIAN. See LINGUIST.

LINGUISTICS [1850s: from French *linguistique*, Latin *lingua* tongue, language]. The systematic study of language. Its aim is to look at language objectively, as a human phenomenon, and to account for languages as they are rather than to prescribe rules of correctness in their use. It therefore has a twofold aim: to uncover general principles underlying human language, and to provide reliable descriptions of individual languages.

History. Although the formal study of language dates from at least the middle of the first millennium BC in India and ancient Greece, the era of scientific language study is commonly dated from the end of the 18c, when English was discovered to have the same ancestor as a number of European and Asian languages. This discovery initiated at least a century of intense interest in comparative philology, which involved uncovering links between languages, writing comparative grammars of related languages, and reconstructing their common 'ancestors'. These activities stimulated a search for the mechanisms underlying language change. In the 20c, a change of emphasis occurred, largely through the work of the Swiss linguist Ferdinand de Saussure, sometimes regarded as 'the father of modern linguistics'. He advocated separating historical from synchronic aspects of language study. He argued that language at any point in time is an interlocking structure, in which all items are interdependent, an insight which is now taken for granted in linguistics and forms the basis of 20c structuralism. In the 1930s and 1940s, descriptive linguistics was developed largely in the US, as linguists sought to describe the fast-disappearing American-Indian languages, with Edward Sapir and Leonard Bloomfield being regarded jointly as the 'fathers of American linguistics'. Midway through the

20c, Noam Chomsky triggered another change of direction, when he instigated work in *generative linguistics*, a concern for the principles in the minds of speakers which could *generate* language (account for their knowledge of language in an explicit way).

Branches. Linguistics is a relatively young social science, in which there has recently been a massive expansion in almost all areas. It now comprises a large number of flourishing branches, several of them hybrids with other disciplines. Although *phonetics*, the scientific study of speech sounds, is usually regarded as an intrinsic part of linguistics, it is often taken to be a discipline in its own right, especially by phoneticians, who point to its 19c origins. Linguistics and phonetics together are therefore often referred to as *the linguistic sciences*. At its core, linguistics can be said to have three classic subdivisions: (1) *Phonology* the study of sound patterns; (2) *Morphology and syntax* the composition of words and sentences; (3) *Semantics* the study of meaning. Some linguists consider that morphology and syntax can be subsumed under the traditional term *grammar*; others argue that phonology, morphology, syntax, and semantics all constitute the grammar of a language. Each can be studied synchronically or diachronically (or both together) and the order in which they have been dealt with within a grammar has fluctuated over the years. In the last quarter-century, some previously fringe areas have become increasingly important, notably *pragmatics* the study of language usage, a topic which includes *discourse analysis*; *sociolinguistics* the study of the relationship between language and society; *psycholinguistics* language and the mind; *neurolinguistics* language and the brain; *linguistic typology* the analysis of languages into types; *computational linguistics* the use of computers to simulate language processes; *stylistics* linguistic analysis applied to literature and style; *applied linguistics* linguistics in relation to such practical activities as language teaching, lexicography, and speech therapy.

See ABERCROMBIE, AGGLUTINATING/AGGLUTINATIVE, AMERICAN DIALECT SOCIETY, AMERICAN SPEECH, ANALYTIC, APPLIED LINGUISTICS, APPROPRIACY, BILINGUALISM, BLOOMFIELD, BOLINGER, CASE GRAMMAR, CHILD LANGUAGE ACQUISITION, CHOMSKY, CLASSIFICATION OF LANGUAGES, CODE, COMMUNICATION, COMMUNICATIVE COMPETENCE, COMMUNICATIVE SHIFT, COMPARATIVE PHILOLOGY, COMPETENCE AND PERFORMANCE, COMPONENT, COMPUTATIONAL LINGUISTICS, CONSTITUENT, CONTRASTIVE LINGUISTICS/ANALYSIS, DESCRIPTIVISM AND PROSCRIPTIVISM, DIACHRONIC AND SYNCHRONIC, DIALECT, DIALECTOLOGY, DISCOURSE ANALYSIS, -EME,

ETHNOLINGUISTICS, FOLK ETYMOLOGY, FORM, FREE VARIATION, FUSIONAL, GENERATIVE GRAMMAR, GRAMMAR, GRAMMATOLOGY, GRAPHOLOGY, HALLIDAY, HISTORICAL LINGUISTICS, HUMO(U)R, IDIOLECT, INFLECTED, ISOLATING, JESPERSEN, KURATH, LANGUAGE, LANGUAGE CHANGE, LANGUAGE FAMILY, LANGUAGE UNIVERSALS, LANGUE AND PAROLE, LECT, LEVEL OF LANGUAGE, LEXEME, LEXICON, LINGUIST, LINGUISTIC, LINGUISTIC ATLAS, LINGUISTICIAN, LINGUISTIC SIGN, MCDAVID, MARKED AND UNMARKED TERMS, METALANGUAGE, MODEL, MORPHEME, MORPHOLOGY, MULTILINGUALISM, NATURAL LANGUAGE, NEUROLINGUISTICS, PARADIGMATIC AND SYNTAGMATIC, PARALINGUISTICS, PHATIC COMMUNION, PHILOLOGY, PHONEME, PHONETICS, PHONOLOGY, PHRASE, PRAGMATICS, PROGRESS AND DECAY IN LANGUAGE, PROXEMICS, QUIRK, REGISTER, SAPIR, SAPIR–WHORF HYPOTHESIS, SEMANTICS, SENTENCE, SOCIOLINGUISTICS, STRUCTURAL LINGUISTICS, STYLISTICS, SYNTAX, SYNTHETIC, TEXT LINGUISTICS, TRANSFORMATIONAL-GENERATIVE GRAMMAR, TYPOLOGY OF LANGUAGE, UTTERANCE, VARIANT, VARIETY, WHORF, WORD, WORD-FORMATION. [LANGUAGE]. J.M.A.

Classic texts

Bloomfield, Leonard, 1933. *Language*. New York: Holt, Rinehart & Winston.
Chomsky, Noam. 1965. *Aspects of the Theory of Syntax*. Cambridge, Mass.: MIT Press.
Jespersen, Otto. 1922. *Language: Its Nature, Development and Origin*. London: Allen & Unwin.
Martinet, André. 1970. *Éléments de linguistique générale*. Paris: Armand Colin.
Sapir, Edward. 1921. *Language*. New York: Harcourt Brace.
Saussure, Ferdinand de. 1916. *Cours de linguistique générale*. Édition critique préparée par Tullio de Mauro, 1972/8. Paris: Payot.

Recent overviews

Aitchison, Jean. 1987. *Linguistics*, 3rd edition. London: Hodder & Stoughton (Teach Yourself series).
Atkinson, Martin, Kilby, David, & Roca, Iggy. 1988. *Foundation of General Linguistics*, 2nd edition. London: Allen & Unwin.
Bright, William. (ed.). 1992. *International Encyclopedia of Linguistics*. 4 vols. New York & Oxford: Oxford University Press.
Brown, E. K. 1983. *Linguistics Today*. London: Fontana.
Chomsky, Noam. 1986. *Knowledge of Language: Its Nature, Origin and Use*. New York: Praeger.
Davis, Hayley G., & Taylor, Talbot J. (eds.). 1990. *Redefining Linguistics*. London: Routledge.
Fromkin, V., & Rodman, R. 1988. *An Introduction to Language*, 4th edition. New York: Holt, Rinehart & Winston.
Lyons, John. 1981. *Language and Linguistics: An Introduction*. Cambridge: University Press.
Malmkjær, Kirsten (ed.). 1991. *The Linguistics Encyclopedia*. London: Routledge.

Newmeyer, Frederick J. (ed.). 1988. *Linguistics: The Cambridge Survey*. Four volumes. Cambridge: University Press.

Traugott, Elizabeth Close, & Pratt, Mary Louise. 1980. *Linguistics for Students of Literature*. New York & London: Harcourt Brace Jovanovich.

Wallwork, J. F. 1969/85. *Language and Linguistics*. London: Heinemann.

Yule, George. 1985. *The Study of Language*. Cambridge: University Press.

LINGUISTIC SCIENCES. See LINGUISTICS.

LINGUISTIC SIGN [From French *signe linguistique*, as used by Ferdinand de Saussure]. A term in especially early 20c linguistics. Such a sign has two parts: a signifier (French *signifiant*), the form; something signified (*signifié*), what is referred to, the meaning. According to Saussure, language was a system of signs, in which each formed part of an interdependent whole *où tout se tient* (where everything holds together). He stressed the arbitrary nature of the sign, evidently covering two notions of arbitrariness: (1) That there is mostly no connection between the two parts of the sign: there is no intrinsic link between the sound sequence *cow* and the animal it refers to. This is accepted as a tenet of linguistics. Apparent exceptions, as with onomatopoeic words (*bang*, *coo*, *quack*) are relatively few and vary from language to language. In addition, sound symbolism, when a group of words in a language is characterized by a particular sound (such as *fl-* in English for *fl*ickering and *fl*uttering) is also language-specific and conventional. See PHON(A)ESTHESIA. (2) That each language cuts up the world in different, arbitrary ways. This viewpoint is controversial, as linguists are divided as to whether there is an underlying reality which is assembled differently by various languages, or whether the cutting up is as arbitrary as Saussure suggested. See SEMANTICS, SEMIOTICS, SIGN. [LANGUAGE]. J.M.A.

LINGUISTIC SOCIETY OF AMERICA, short form *LSA*. An American and Canadian association founded in 1924 'for the advancement of the scientific study of language' to support research and publication in descriptive and theoretical linguistics. It holds an annual meeting for the presentation of papers, sponsors in cooperation with various universities a summertime programme of courses and lectures bringing together students and teachers from all over the world, and publishes the journal *Language*. The LSA's *c*.7,000 members are mostly college and university teachers. [AMERICAS, LANGUAGE, MEDIA]. C.C.E.

LINGUISTIC SURVEY OF SCOTLAND. A survey instituted by the U. of Edinburgh in 1949, following preparatory work since 1935. It has two sections: Gaelic and Scots. The work of the Gaelic Section has been chiefly on dialect phonology and is yet to be published. In the main, the Scots Section has investigated the regional distribution of several hundred items of vocabulary (through postal questionnaires) and aspects of phonology (through interviews). The latter employ a 'polysystemic' approach to elicit systems of stressed vowels in distinct structural positions (before *t*, *h*, *d*, word-finally, etc.). A selection of findings was published in *The Linguistic Atlas of Scotland*, volume 1 (1975), volume 2 (1977), volume 3, *Phonology* (1986), edited by J. Y. Mather and H. H. Speitel. See LINGUISTIC ATLAS. [EUROPE, LANGUAGE]. A.J.A.

LINGUISTIC TYPOLOGY [20c]. Also **language typology, typology of language**. The classification of human languages into different types on the basis of shared properties which are not due to common origin or geographical contact. Linguistic typology therefore complements the long-established tradition of genetic classification, in which languages are assigned to a family on the basis of their presumed historical origin. The criteria used for dividing languages into types depend to some extent on the purpose of the classification, since a typology based on sound structure does not necessarily correlate with one based on word order. The most common classificatory criteria are morphological (word structure), syntactic (word order), and phonological (sound patterns), though recently a number of new criteria have been proposed, and there has been an increasing interest in the notion of implicational relationships: if a language has feature X, then it will also have feature Y.

Morphology. Investigation of the way in which different languages combine grammatical units (morphemes) within words is the longest-established aspect of typology. In the 19c, there was an attempt to assign languages to a number of basic morphological types, most commonly three, which divided languages according to the degree to which morphemes are fused together: (1) *Analytic or isolating languages*, in which each morpheme tends to form a separate word, as in Vietnamese *Com nâu ngoài troi ăn rât nhat* (rice cook out sky eat very tasteless: 'Rice which is cooked in the open air is very tasteless'). (2) *Agglutinating languages*, in which several morphemes are juxtaposed within a word, as in Turkish *adamlardan* (*adam-lar-dan*, man-plural-from: 'from the men'). (3) *Fusional languages*, in which morphemes are fused together within a word, as in Latin *servorum* (of slaves), where the ending *-orum* is a fusion of *possession*, *plural*, and *masculine*. In practice, few languages are pure types, since many use all three processes for handling morphemes, even though one favoured method tends to predominate. English has a tendency towards isolation (as in *I will now go out for a walk*), but both agglutination (as in *clever-ly* and *high-er*) and fusion (as in *gave*, in which *give* and *past* are fused) are also found.

Alternatively, languages may be classified morphologically according to the number of morphemes within a word: *analytic languages* (ideally, one morpheme per word, such as Vietnamese, with an estimated 1.06 morphemes per word) are opposed to *synthetic languages* (two or more morphemes per word, such as Sanskrit with an estimated 2.59 morphemes per word). The most extreme form of synthesis is found in a *polysynthetic* language, such as Inuit (Eskimo), which has an estimated 3.72 morphemes per word. On this scale, English comes out as mildly analytic with 1.68 morphemes per word. *Inflected languages* are a variety of synthetic language in which a word takes various forms, most usually by the addition of suffixes, which show its role in the sentence. Many languages have some inflection (such as English *boys*, *the boy's mother*, *play/played*) but in a highly inflected language, such as Latin, this process predominates. There are therefore two morphological scales, one which measures degree of fusion (*isolating— agglutinating—fusional*), the other degree of synthesis (*analytic—inflected—polysynthetic*). Since an isolating language is inevitably also an analytic language, English is at the low end of both scales.

Syntax. In the past quarter-century, basic word order has been the main criterion for classifying languages. In the early 1960s, it was observed that of the possible combinations of subject (S), verb (V), and object (O) within a sentence, only certain ones actually occur, and that these are not all equally likely. The commonest are those in which the subject comes first (SVO as in English, SOV as in Turkish), less common are those in which the verb comes first (VSO as in Welsh, VOS as in Malagasy), and least common are those in which the object comes first (OVS as in Hixkaryana, spoken in northern Brazil, OSV of which no sure example has yet been found). Many languages have mixed word orders, and not all languages have a firm order, so this classification has its flaws. However, English with its SVO structure, such as *The rabbit* (S) *gnawed* (V) *the carrot* (O), is a language with one of the two commonest word orders, even though some subsidiary orders are possible, such as *Up jumped the rabbit*.

The relative order of verb and object is often considered to be the most important from the point of view of typology, since not all languages express overt subjects. The main interest in classifying languages in this way lies in the *implicational* relationships, in that certain other constructions are statistically likely to occur in each type. A VO language, such as English, is likely to have prepositions rather than postpositions (such as *up the tree* rather than *the tree up), and auxiliaries before main verbs (such as *Bill may come* rather than *Bill come may). It is also likely to have relative clauses (beginning with *who/which*, etc.) after the noun they refer to, such as *The burglar who stole the silver escaped* rather than **The who stole the silver burglar escaped*. The general principle behind these observations appears to be a preference for consistency in the position of the *head* (main word) in any construction with regard to its *modifiers* (items attached to it): so a VO language such as English is a '*head first*' language and an OV language such as Turkish is a '*head last*' language.

A recent, controversial proposal by Noam Chomsky is that humans are genetically 'hardwired' with some universal features of language, but that these are supplemented with a number of options which have to be selected on the basis of exposure to a particular language: see LANGUAGE ACQUISITION DEVICE. The choice of one rather than another has complex ramifications throughout the language. Different language types are therefore the result of a number of fairly simple choices which are automatically available to humans. One proposal for such an option is between a *pro-drop language* (one which can optionally drop pronouns at the beginning of sentences, as in Italian *Io sono Italiano/Sono Italiano* (I am Italian/Am Italian) and one which does not usually do so, such as English. Pro-drop languages seem to behave somewhat differently over a range of constructions from languages which do not drop their pronouns.

Phonology. Phonological typology has received somewhat less attention, though some interesting work has been done on types of vowel system. In addition, a number of studies have proposed implicational hypotheses, such as if a language has fricative consonants, it will also have stop consonants. With regard to rhythm, some linguists divide languages into: (1) *Syllable-timed languages*, such as French and Japanese, in which the rhythm appears to be fairly even, with each syllable giving the impression of having about the same weight as any other. (2) *Stress-timed languages*, such as English and Arabic, in which stressed syllables recur at intervals. In recent years, a somewhat 'weak' version of this view has gained ground. The absolute division has been replaced by a sliding scale, in which there are few pure types, though many which can be placed towards one or the other end of the scale. There is no doubt that English is on the stress-timed end of the scale. Another distinction is sometimes made between *tone* or *tonal languages*, such as Mandarin Chinese, and *intonation or non-tonal languages*, such as English. In a tone language, the pitch level of any syllable is of critical importance, since words are sometimes distinguished from one another purely by the tone, such as Mandarin *ma* with level tone (*mother*), with rising tone (*hemp*), with a dipping tone (*horse*), and a falling tone (*scold*). In a language such as English, however, sentence intonation plays a crucial role, as in *You saw him!* versus *You saw him?*, where difference in meaning is signalled by the intonation.

Conclusion. Linguistic typology is a fast-expanding branch of linguistics and is consequently in a state of considerable flux and controversy. A wide range of criteria apart from those outlined above are currently under discussion, and it will be some years before reliable methods of classifying languages are established.

See AGGLUTINATING/AGGLUTINATIVE, ANALYTIC, CLASSIFICATION OF LANGUAGES, FUSIONAL, INFLECTING, ISOLATING/ISOLATIVE, LANGUAGE FAMILY, LINGUISTICS, POLYSYNTHETIC, RHYTHM, SYNTHETIC. [LANGUAGE].   J.M.A.

Comrie, Bernard. 1989. *Language Universals and Linguistic Typology*, 2nd edition. Oxford: Basil Blackwell.
Dauer, R. 1983. 'Stress-Timing and Syllable-Timing Reanalyzed', *Journal of Phonetics* 11.
Greenberg, Joseph H. 1960. 'A Quantitative Approach to the Morphological Typology of Language', *International Journal of American Linguistics* 26.
Hawkins, John A. 1983. *Word Order Universals*. New York & London: Academic Press.
Maddieson, Ian. 1984. *Patterns of Sounds*. Cambridge: University Press.
Mallinson, Graham, & Blake, Barry J. 1981. *Language Typology*. Amsterdam, New York, & Oxford: North-Holland.
Shopen, Timothy (ed.). 1985. *Language Typology and Syntactic Description*. Three volumes. Cambridge: University Press.

LINK HYPHEN. See HYPHEN.

LINKING R. In certain accents of English, including RP, /r/ pronounced between a word or syllable ending in the vowels /ɔː, ɑː, ə/ and a following vowel: the *r* in *beer and a sandwich, car engine*. See INTRUSIVE R, RECEIVED PRONUNCIATION, RHOTIC AND NON-RHOTIC. [SPEECH].
                    G.K.

LINKING VERB. See COPULA, VERB OF INCOMPLETE PREDICATION.

LINK LANGUAGE [1960s]. A semi-technical term for a language that allows communication between groups with no other common language: for example, Hindi in India, Swahili in East Africa, and forms of Malay in Indonesia and Malaysia. It may or may not be seen as neutral in relation to other languages used in a particular place. English serves as a link language in most of Africa and Asia: 'There has been a sort of political platform, that we should revert to Hindi as the national language, that English should not be given the importance it is. But if a thing is in force it is because it is needed. English is needed as a link language between the Indian states, and between the union government and the states' (Nayantara Sahgal, *South*, Aug. 1985). Compare LINGUA FRANCA. [AFRICA, ASIA, LANGUAGE].   T.MCA., B.B.K.

LINOTYPE [Late 19c: from *line o' type*, on the analogy of forms like *kilogram*]. The trade name of a typecasting and typsetting machine operated by keyboard, invented in the 1880s by the German-born US instrument maker Ottmar Mergenthaler. The name also refers to type produced by such a machine, which casts type from hot metal one line or slug at a time. When finished with, the slug is melted down and the metal used again. In such a process, if an error occurs the whole line has to be set again. It was widely used until the mid-20c, especially for printing newspapers. See MONOTYPE, TYPESETTING. [TECHNOLOGY].   W.W.B.

LIPOGRAM [18c: from *lipográmmatos* missing a letter]. A piece of writing constructed without using a particular letter of the alphabet. The omitted letter is usually a vowel. Thus, Ernest Vincent Wright's novel *Gadsby* (1939) and Georges Perec's *La Disparition* (1969) both avoid the letter *e*, the most commonly used letter in normal writing. A similar challenge is provided by the *univocalic*, which employs only one vowel, as in the verse: 'Persevere, ye perfect men, / Ever keep the precepts ten.' See WORD GAME. [WORD].   T.A.

LIQUID [14c: from Latin *liquidus* flowing, clear]. A term in phonetics for a frictionless approximant, especially an *r*- or *l*-sound. See APPROXIMANT, CONSONANT, L-SOUNDS, R-SOUNDS. [SPEECH].   T.MCA.

LISP [From Middle English *lipsen, wlispen*, from Old English *awlyspian*]. A minor abnormality of articulation that typically affects the /s/ phoneme in English, but which may also be heard on other sibilant sounds. Most commonly, the /s/ is replaced by a dental fricative /θ/, which remains when the rest of a child's pronunciation has moved on from the stage when such substitutions would be considered normal. It can be caused by physical or psychological factors, but often there is no apparent reason for it. See LANGUAGE PATHOLOGY, LINGUAL. [LANGUAGE]. D.C.

LIST [16c: from a Germanic source shared by Old English *līste* and French *liste*: the first sense relates to Old English, the second to Old French]. (1) (Obsolete or rare) the edge of a piece of cloth; a strip of cloth or paper; a line, band, stripe, mark, scar; a limit, boundary, region; a place of combat or competition (as in the idiom *to enter the lists*). (2) A connected sequence of items, as found in a dictionary, directory, or index: for example, of words (*a word list*), and of names, such as serving soldiers (*the active list*), members of an association (*a membership list*), and books (*a book list*). Written lists may run horizontally, filling each line in turn, or vertically, one item per line: 'Reassuring things, lists. They affirm that the blooming confusion of the universe can be reduced to a tidy vertical column. . . . Man is an inveterate listmaker. *I list therefore I am*' (Richard Stengel, *Time*, 31 Dec. 1990). The concept underlies most reference systems: for example, library catalogues, works of reference, databases, and thesauri. Informal lists usually exhibit some kind of ordering, especially the compiler's priorities, and their items are often numbered for easy reference; formal lists are usually *alphabetic* or *thematic*, or a mix of both. A *publisher's list* consists of the titles of books already or about to be published (*a spring/autumn list*); a *backlist* contains books in stock and therefore available for sale. Less obviously, listing is an inherent feature of language itself: whenever three or more words, phrases, clauses, sentences, etc., of the same type follow one another, they constitute a list. Compare ALPHABETIC(AL) ORDER, CATALOG(UE), INDEX, LINE, MARK, THEMATIC ORDER, THESAURUS. [MEDIA, REFERENCE]. T.MCA.

LIT CRIT. An informal, sometimes dismissive, clipping of *literary criticism* and *literary critic*: 'The lit crits argue that they are looking at the world in a new way, a way that requires the invention of a new language' (Richard Bernstein, '(Post)modern Lit Crit Positionality', New York Times News Service, July 1990). See LITERARY CRITICISM. [LITERATURE]. T.MCA.

LITERACY [1880s: from Latin *lit(t)eratus* lettered, able to read, learnèd]. The ability to read and write in at least one language. This ability developed in West Asia in the third millennium BC, when the Sumerians developed a system of symbols to record spoken language. They were followed by the Syro-Palestinians who, between 2000 and 1000 BC, introduced a consonantal script using a small number of signs, the precursor of the alphabet. During the same period, increasingly complex commercial, administrative, and religious structures and growing urbanization led to the invention of writing systems in such other regions as Egypt, India, and China. In ancient cultures, literacy was rare and specialized, and therefore a token of considerable learning. In more recent centuries, however, the term has often been interpreted minimally: as at least the reading and writing of one's name, anyone unable to do so being classed as *illiterate*. In the 20c, however, the ability to read and write has been delimited in many ways and *literacy* is often used interchangeably with *functional literacy*: the production and understanding of simple oral or written statements reflecting the social, economic, and educational conditions of a particular region. Yet the threshold of literacy is indeterminate, making exact measurements difficult or culturally variable. In 1965, at a world congress of ministers of education, UNESCO adopted the view that 'rather than an end in itself, literacy should be regarded as a way of preparing man for a social, civic and economic role that goes far beyond the limits of rudimentary literacy training consisting merely in the teaching of reading and writing' ('Literacy, Gateway to Fulfillment,' special issue of *UNESCO Courier*, June 1980).

Literacy in English. The earliest written English was the concern of a small minority of men, first in the runic alphabet, whose letters were carved on objects for both practical and ornamental purposes, then in the Roman alphabet introduced in Britain by Christian missionaries at the end of the 6c. Education remained for many centuries a province largely of the Roman Catholic Church and the need for reading and writing was not greatly extended until the introduction of movable type and inexpensive paper in the late 15c. This helped standardize written versions of English, expand the uses of literacy, and give reading and writing greater circulation among the populace. Determining who is literate and for what purposes has always been difficult. The collection of statistics tends to be confounded by the under-representation of people marginalized from the economic and political centres of a culture: for example, in censuses, by incomplete records, and by variable standards of what should be measured. Data such as signatures or court and ecclesiastical testimony have been used to estimate the degree of literacy in particular locales at particular times, but tend to depend on self-reports and minimal evidence; they give no account of such skills as comprehension of printed matter. Moreover, reading and writing have had different constituencies and uses during different periods. Thus, in the 17c Protestant communities of early New England, where male literacy was well above 60% by 1700, it was considered important to help women acquire reading skills for religious purposes but not writing because its 'commercial uses lay beyond women's traditional sphere of activity' (Clifford, 1984, below).

Ideology and literacy. Deliberately taught rather than acquired like speech, literacy has traditionally been seen as a commodity delivered through political, educational, and religious bureaucracies. Reading, writing, and counting at sophisticated levels continued to be reserved first for the clergy and then for the sons of the aristocracy and of wealthy merchants; the term *literacy* in its 15-18c usages was regularly associated with a classical education and with priestly or civic élites. The literacy needs of most people, however, have tended to be functional: the production of reports, accounts, journals, and letters, and in recent times the completion of forms. Institutional arrangements for instruction in literacy according to the British and American models have, until the 20c, generally been aimed at achieving low to moderate levels of literacy for large numbers of people and higher levels for smaller privileged groups. Educational developments in 18c Scotland, linked with Presbyterianism, were typical: while the literacy rate for adult males jumped from 33% in 1675 to 90% in 1800, the increase was due to emphasis on reading, memorization, and recall of familiar material; neither writing nor the application of knowledge was demanded (compare Stone, 1969).

Literacy, knowledge, and problem-solving. The association of literacy with the acquisition of theoretical knowledge and the development of problem-solving abilities was by and large a product of the Industrial Revolution and, prior to the 20c, was generally confined to centres of education in cities. Country schools, whose pupils were needed to work the land and whose instructors were not always professionally certified, generally offered training in basic skills rather than fluency in written language. Both in town and country, however, children were drilled first on letter names and sounds, then on syllables and words. During the 19c, many reform-minded educators stressed the need for comprehension of reading materials, asserting that encountering words in context would lead students to a more rapid acquisition of meaning

and a more appropriate use of emphasis and inflection. However, since lack of high-level literacy was regarded as neither degrading nor detrimental to economic or social advancement, 19c levels of literacy remained low while numbers of people described as literate grew.

During the 20c, attitudes to literacy have changed. School-based definitions of literacy and standards relating to year groups have been adopted in most English-speaking countries, as competency testing has replaced functional determinants. Paradoxically, because of heightened expectations and increased technological demands, many people who have exceeded traditional literacy criteria are now considered *semi-literate* or *functionally illiterate*. In addition, legislators, educators, and public activists throughout the English-speaking world have sought to broaden the social and personal dimensions of literacy through mandatory training in such things as *historical literacy* (awareness of the main outlines of history, especially as regards one's own country), *cultural literacy* (a knowledge of classical texts and great writers of one's own culture), *mathematical literacy* (also called *numeracy*), *symbolic literacy* (an appreciation of the value and use of symbols of various kinds), *media literacy* (familiarity with and a capacity to understand and to some extent evaluate the different media and what they provide), and *computer literacy* (familiarity with and ability to use a computer, without necessarily being able to write programs).

Conclusion. Literacy requirements, which often relate to and depend on such highly specific contexts as occupational need, continue to vary among social and economic groups, with low levels concentrated among the poor, the under-educated, and members of minority populations. Given the lack of contemporary agreement concerning its definitions and uses, literacy is best conceived as a continuum whose dissemination involves various kinds of behaviour at higher and lower levels, including reading, writing, speaking, listening, thinking, counting, coping with the demands of the state, of employment, and of social life. See COMMUNICATIVE SHIFT, COMPUTERATE, CULTURAL LITERACY, DYSLEXIA, FUNCTIONAL LITERACY, ILLITERACY, LETTER[2], ORACY, ORALITY, READING, SPELLING, SPELLING REFORM. [EDUCATION, WRITING].   R.W.B.

Bailey, Richard W., & Fosheim, Robin Melanie. 1983. *Literacy for Life: The Demand for Reading and Writing*. New York: Modern Language Association.

Cipolla, Carlo M. 1969. *Literacy and Development in the West*. Baltimore: Penguin.

Clanchy, M. T. 1981. 'Literate and Illiterate; Hearing and Seeing: England 1066-1307', in Graff (below).

Clifford, Geraldine J. 1984. 'Buch und Lesen: Historical Perspectives on Literacy and Schooling', in *Review of Educational Research* 54.

Eisenstein, Elizabeth. 1979. *The Printing Press as an Agent of Change: Communication and Cultural Change in Early-Modern Europe*. Cambridge: University Press.

Fries, Charles C. 1963. *Linguistics and Reading*. New York: Holt, Rinehart & Winston.

Graff, Harvey (ed.). 1983. *Literacy and Social Development in the West: A Reader*. Cambridge: University Press.

Lockridge, Kenneth A. 1974. *Literacy in Colonial New England*. New York: W. W. Norton.

Resnick, Daniel P. & Lauren B. 1977. 'The Nature of Literacy: An Historical Explanation', in *Harvard Educational Review* 47.

Stone, Lawrence. 1969. 'Literacy and Education in England 1640-1900,' in *Past and Present* 42.

LITERAL [14c: from Latin *lit(t)eralis* of letters]. (1) A term traditionally opposed to *figurative* and *metaphorical*. Although it is generally unrelated to letters, literacy, and literature, it suggests the influence of the letter as a measure of strictness and rightness: *the literal truth* is seen as being true in a basic and absolute way. If something is done *literally*, a person follows instructions 'to the letter' or 'word for word', without flexibility or imagination. Paradoxically, however, the adverb *literally* is often used to mean *figuratively*: 'And with his eyes he literally scoured the corners of the cell' (Vladimir Nabokov, *Invitation to a Beheading*, 1960). Compare PROSAIC. (2) A term in proof-reading for a misprint such as the substitution of one letter for another, the omission or addition of a letter, or letters transposed (for example, *parodixical, responsiblity, asssumed, phenonemon, prniter*). Usually such errors do not affect sense, but sometimes they do, causing confusion and misleading the reader. A famous literal in a 1922 edition of Hermann Melville's *White-Jacket* (1850: ch. 92) reads *soiled fish of the sea* for *coiled fish of the sea*. Critics have debated whether or not the slip improved the text. See FIGURATIVE LANGUAGE, MISPRINT, TYPOGRAPHICAL ERROR. [STYLE, TECHNOLOGY]. T.MCA., W.W.B.

LITERARY [17c: from Latin *lit(t)erarius* of letters, reading, and writing, from *lit(t)era* a letter]. (1) Of writing and especially literature: *literary language*. (2) Well-versed or engaged in works of literature: *a literary man*. (3) Having the style of literature, often to the point of affectation or stiltedness; bookish: *literary style, literary pretensions*. See LITERARY CRITICISM, LITERARY METHOD, LITERARY SCOTS, LITERARY STANDARD, LITERARY TERM, STILTED. Compare LETTER[1], LETTER[2], LITERAL. [LITERATURE, STYLE]. T.MCA.

LITERARY CRITICISM [19c]. Short form *lit crit*. The formal study, evaluation, and discussion of literary texts. Like any other subject, the critical analysis of literature requires a set of terms and usages through which discussion and instruction can proceed. Much of this metalanguage is traditional and dates from classical times: category terms such as *comedy, drama, epic, sonnet*; descriptive terms such as *anagnorisis, catharsis, hamartia, hubris*; rhetorical and stylistic terms such as *alliteration, irony, metaphor, simile*. Others have emerged in recent centuries, such as *denouement, imagery, pathetic fallacy, romanticism*; others still belong to the 20c, such as *deconstructionism, intertextuality, stream of consciousness, structuralism*. Although moral, social, political, and other issues may be introduced, criticism starts from the language of the original writer.

Origins. Western critical analysis began in classical Greece and was focused on poetry and drama. Plato (5-4c BC) did not place a high value on imaginative literature, which he saw as likely to present unedifying matters, inflame emotions, and harm the morality of the state, but his pupil Aristotle (4c BC) was the most important literary critic of the ancient world. Though incomplete, his treatise the *Poetics* established ideas that were influential for many centuries and still directly and indirectly influence critical thinking. Aristotle saw poetic composition as *mimesis*, an imitation or representation of life through the medium of words: art imitates life. The most detailed part of his treatise relates to tragic drama, which he presented as therapeutic, bringing the benefit of *catharsis*, a purgation or purification achieved by witnessing emotional events on the stage. He characterized the tragic hero as a noble person with a tragic flaw (*hamartia*) that proves fatal, as well as pride (*hubris*) that leads to a fall. Although the doctrine of the *three unities* (of time, place, and action) was later ascribed to him, Aristotle discussed only action, remarking that in tragedy the action usually took place within a period of 24 hours. Horace (1c BC) was the most important of the Roman critical writers. His ideas were largely derived from the Greek, but were expressed with Augustan vigour and enthusiasm. His *Ars Poetica*, written in hexameter verse, is not a systematic treatise but a set of maxims for success in writing poetry that emphasizes sincerity and attention to the best models from the past. Nothing certain is known about Longinus (1c AD), to whom the Greek text *Peri Hupsous* (On the Sublime) is attributed. This influential work relates poetic excellence to the profundity of writers' emotions and the seriousness of their thought. Plotinus (3c AD) provided a full statement of neo-Platonic thought, in which poets had a noble role, almost that of a second Creator, as their art ascends to the realm of the Platonic *Ideas* from which the world derives its being.

The Middle Ages and the Renaissance. In medieval Europe, assessments of literature were concerned principally with its moral value. The classical authors were distrusted for their paganism and valued more for their rhetorical advice than their literary views. Theories of poetry, like the *Poetria* of Jean de Garlande (mid-13c), discussed technique and the choice of appropriate style. Vernacular writing had little critical esteem before Dante Alighieri, in his unfinished *De vulgari eloquentia* (Of Common Eloquence, 1307), made a serious enquiry into the most suitable type of language for vernacular poetry. Giovanni Boccaccio advanced the importance of post-classical writing with his lectures on the writings of Dante (1373-4). The foundations of modern textual criticism were laid in *Miscellaneorum centuria* (A Century of Miscellanies) by the neo-Platonist Angelo Poliziano (1454-94, sometimes known in English as Politian), a dramatist and professor of Greek and Latin at Florence. The Renaissance revived interest in the classical critics. In the 16c, Julius Caesar Scaliger with his *Poetica* (Poetics) and Torquato Tasso with his *Discorsi* (Discourses) influenced writers and critics in England. Native English writers did not show a comparable concern for theory, although Geoffrey Chaucer in the 14c praised Dante, Boccaccio, and Petrarch as his masters and models, and took an adversely critical position towards some of the still popular but moribund poetic forms, parodying in *The Canterbury Tales* the ballad-romance style in his *Tale of Sir Thopas* and making his Parson dismiss alliterative verse ('I am a Southren man, / I can nat geste—rum, ram, ruf—by lettre'). William Caxton, as a printer, publisher, and editor, was anxious to develop English as a literary language.

Early English criticism. On the whole, the first approaches to literary criticism in England were conservative and legislative. They guided writers to emulate the classics, because English was regarded as not fully proved as a literary medium and therefore in need of judicious support. Thomas Campion in *Observations on the Art of English Poesie* (1602) asserted the supremacy of classical metres; he was answered by Samuel Daniel (1563-1619) in *A Defence of Rhyme* (1603), arguing on the basis of established practice and the nature of English: 'for as Greeke and Latine verse consists of the number and quantitie of sillables, so doth the English verse of measure and accent'. Philip Sidney wrote theoretical criticism in *The Defence of Poesie* (1579-

80, printed 1595), an analysis of poetic types based on ancient practice. Sidney thought little of contemporary English poetry and less of the new drama. George Puttenham stated some basic Elizabethan critical attitudes in *The Arte of English Poesie* (1589), in which he offered vernacular names for classical figures of rhetoric, such as 'the over reacher' for *hyperbole*. He ascribed to Sir Thomas Wyatt and Henry Howard Surrey the beginning of courtly poetry, after the rough work of John Skelton. By and large, although 'English' literary styles were developing, poets and critics alike continued to look primarily to classical and Italian sources for their inspiration.

Neo-classical criticism. In the 17c, simple appreciation of classical genres, motifs, and techniques gave way to a more descriptive and specific analysis of texts. From the Restoration to the late 18c, however, because of the prevailing spirit of neo-classicism, work in English was still generally constrained by classical standards. In most instances, the leading critics were also leading writers. As a consequence, John Dryden, himself a dramatist, treated English drama seriously in *Of Dramatick Poesie* (1668) and *Of Heroick Plays* (1672). Jonathan Swift, in *The Battle of the Books* (1697), satirized controversy between admirers of English writing and those who saw merit only in the classics. Thomas Rymer supported the ancients, denigrating Elizabethan and Jacobean drama in *The Tragedies of the last Age* (1678) and *A short View of Tragedy* (1692). John Dennis, an admirer of Longinus, replied in *The Impartial Critick* (1693). Alexander Pope wrote his major critical work in verse: his *Essay on Criticism* (1711) is legislative, advising poets and critics on virtues to cultivate (such as judicious assessment, 'Avoid extremes; and shun the fault of such / Who still are pleased too little or too much') and faults to avoid (such as hackneyed rhymes, 'the same unvaried chimes, / With sure returns of still expected rhymes'). The most influential critic in the later 18c was Samuel Johnson, the preface to whose edition of Shakespeare (1765) refutes insistence on the three unities in drama. His *Lives of the English Poets* (1779-81) exemplifies contemporary critical values and reflects some of his prejudices, including an attack on the Metaphysical poets. Neo-classical critics were prescriptive, regarding themselves as arbiters of public taste and guardians of the purity of English. Among them the novel attracted little serious critical attention in the 18c, Henry Fielding defending it as a 'comic epic in prose'.

Romantic criticism. Samuel Taylor Coleridge was the foremost among the Romantic critics of the late 18c and early 19c. He abandoned prescriptivism, to 'establish the principles of writing rather than to furnish rules how to pass judgement upon what has been written by others'. He cited specific texts mainly as illustrations of the poetic process, but wrote closely on Shakespeare, Milton, and others. William Wordsworth wrote little direct criticism apart from his theory of poetic diction in prefaces to *Lyrical Ballads* (1798, 1800, 1802). His concern with the language of poetry and its relationship to ordinary discourse anticipates some of the linguistic criticism of the 20c. In true Romantic spirit he wrote that 'poetry is the spontaneous overflow of powerful feelings: it takes its origin from emotion recollected in tranquillity'. William Hazlitt, among the first in the British Isles to make criticism a career, wrote reviews that were incisive in analysis and judgement. Charles Lamb, although an admirer of Coleridge, took the judgemental tone of Johnson towards what he saw as excess and indiscipline in writers of the 16c and 17c, but made a witty defence of Restoration drama.

Victorian criticism. In the Victorian period, the literary output, especially in fiction, was accompanied by a growth of periodical reviews, such as *Fraser's Magazine* (1830), *Saturday Review* (1855), *Cornhill Magazine* (1860), *Fortnightly Review* (1865). Matthew Arnold saw poetry as a spiritual force, a 'criticism of life' in an age of growing doubt and anxiety. His love of the Greek spirit and the austerity of its literature made him critical of much English poetry. Poetry, he considered, should be 'particular, precise and firm' and should appeal to 'those elementary feelings which subsist permanently in the race'. The claim he made for universality in particular texts has been challenged in 20c criticism. Many of the Victorian novelists commented on their art, notably Anthony Trollope in his autobiography; it was the American novelist Henry James who first attempted ordered criticism of the novel. He embodied his theories in his own fiction, while seeking to create a tradition of novel criticism. He emphasized form and design ('the figure in the carpet'), to be discerned in good fiction. He took his examples mainly from contemporary novelists, many of whom seemed to him to lack artistic discipline.

Early twentieth-century criticism. The development of English as an academic subject brought vigorous expansion in literary criticism. T. S. Eliot was influential as a critic, appealing to the tradition of past literature which must be respected by new writers ('the historical sense'), but without unthinking submission to the prescriptions of the past. Eliot was rigorous and selective in his judgements, admiring Elizabethan and Jacobean drama and Metaphysical poetry and disliking Romanticism. Other creative writers who wrote about the art which they practised were Virginia Woolf and E. M. Forster; the latter's *Aspects of the Novel* (1927) is a post-Jamesian attempt at a theory of fiction. The leading academic critics were I. A. Richards, who advocated a *practical criticism* that would concentrate on the text and its verbal nuances without preconceived ideas about the author; F. R. Leavis, who believed passionately in the civilizing influence of rigorous literary criticism in an age of technology and mass culture; and William Empson, whose *Seven Types of Ambiguity* (1930, revised 1947, 1953) explored levels of response to literary language and the verbal nuances open to individual readings. Whereas in the past critics had generally also been writers, the new academic status of literary critics meant that they were in the 20c increasingly commentators on literature with specialist assumptions and terminologies of their own.

New Criticism. Richards's practical criticism influenced both Empson and the *New Critics* in the US, who discountenanced the study of literature in terms of history, morality, or any purpose outside itself. New Criticism demanded close attention to the text itself and favoured the virtual exclusion of everything except the words on the page, including the author's life and interactions. Following the publication of J. C. Ransom's *New Criticism* (1941), it was dominant in critical circles in Britain and America for some twenty years. Other leading figures were R. P. Blackmur, A. Tate, and R. P. Warren. Although these critics differed in many respects, their collective influence struck at the roots of the idea of 'literary history' with its categorized authors and movements.

Russian Formalism. An earlier reaction against emphasis on content and 'message' appeared in Russia with the development of *formalism*; the name was first used by its opponents for its concentration on the formal pattern of sounds, words, and literary devices. The Russian Formalists regarded literature as a special use of language, which draws attention to its own distinctive features and thus distances or 'defamiliarizes' itself from the normal use of language referring to the external world. They considered that even mimetic realism uses language in a contrived and artificial way. All language is a medium infused with feeling and purpose by its users; literary writers have devices and techniques that make their work distinctive and that criticism should try to identify in a text. Features like metre, rhyme, and alliteration are thus essential qualities of literary language and not embellishments. The influence of the Formalists, particularly Roman Jakobson, has been considerable, even on those who challenged their approach. Jakobson left Russia in 1920 and continued the work of Formalism with the Prague School.

Structuralism. The Formalists were influenced by the theory of the Swiss linguist Ferdinand de Saussure, whose work was also seminal for the Structuralist movement, including Jakobson, Roland Barthes (1915-80), and Tzvetan Todorov (b.1940). They challenged the traditional mimetic theory, arguing that the important relationship is not with external reality but with recurrent elements in the code or 'system of signification' in a text. Language, in their view, is a first-order system that generates literature as a second-order system. Gérard Genette (b.1930) wrote: 'Literature has been regarded as a message without a code for such a long time, that it became necessary to regard it momentarily as a code without a message' (*Figures*, 1966: translated from the French). Structuralism demotes the individual author but considers that a distinct quality of *literariness* can be identified, even though non-literary elements appear in a text.

Deconstructionism or post-structuralism. A further retreat from tradition came with the Deconstructionist view of Jacques Derrida (b.1930) that literature continually subverts its own apparent claim to establish a definitive meaning. Literary and other uses of language are *logocentric* (focused on words), and imply that a self-certifying Platonic absolute does not exist. In the view of Deconstructionists, the reader plays a major part in producing meaning, and becomes in effect the creator of literary language. In the process, however, ultimate meaning is continually deferred, because every reader interprets every text differently. Derrida did not create a systematic critical theory but rather a number of close readings of texts to illustrate his approach. In the US, his followers include J. Hillis Miller (b.1928) and Paul de Man (1919-83). The term *post-structuralism* can also include recent developments in criticism based on the psychoanalytical theories of Sigmund Freud. Earlier critics found Freudian analysis a useful approach to the study of literature; the French critic Jacques Lacan (1901-81) held that the form as well as the content of linguistic expression was significant and revealed the individual struggle to come to terms with the world of language and meaning. *Marxist criticism*, emphasizing historical, social, and political influences on literature, was practised by a number of critics. The Hungarian critic Georg Lukács (1885-1971) considered that language is determined by the social background and ideological disposition of authors, many of whom have been proponents, consciously or otherwise, of a bourgeois world-view. All writers, especially those opposed to socialism, revealed inner tension in their work that transcended overt ideology: 'In every society the production of discourse is at once controlled, selected, organised and redistributed according to a certain number of procedures, whose role is to avert its powers and dangers' (Michel Foucault, 'The Discourse on Language', in *The Archaeology of Knowledge*, 1972).

Feminist criticism. The social and political movement for women's rights developed in the 19c and has become known as *feminism* in the later 20c. In the process, it has prompted an influential contemporary critical viewpoint among women, both as writers and critics. An early exponent of feminist criticism was Virginia Woolf in *A Room of One's Own* (1929). The principal lines of feminist criticism are women's freedom to write equally with men and to give full expression to their distinctive experience; a traditional predominance in literature of a male view of women; the implication that the standard reader is male creates sexist language, such as the use of male pronouns and *androcentric* words as generic terms (such as *he* for any human being and *mankind* for the human race). Feminist critics consider that literary language has expressed the dominance of the patriarchal society that shaped it and that traditional literary criticism has neglected female insights. Feminism has encouraged new women's writing, publishers with a special interest in women's writing, and the revival and reissuing of overlooked works by women in past centuries.

New Historicism. Marxist and feminist criticism, often working together, have challenged the exclusion of history as proposed and practised by the New Critics. Those critics who have revived a concern for literary texts as aspects of history belong to a movement known as *New Historicism*. They have moved from a Formalist approach to the examination of texts in relation to their historical background so as to gain insights into past societies, with their distinctive world-views. For the New Historicist, any text is open to scrutiny without 'privileging' one type over another, and particularly without giving special status to the traditional literary text or any canon of such texts.

Contemporary literary theory. The proliferation of critical schools, the mixing of their views and terms, and the plethora of works describing them can be bewildering for the student of literature, who may have first approached literary theory with the view that a literary text simply 'tells a story' about which there can or should be little disagreement. Critical theory is now a well-established academic subject and most critics are now trained professionals rather than (as in the 19c in particular) enthusiastic amateurs who wrote reviews for literary periodicals (although something of this broader humanist tradition survives in the book review sections of the 'quality' press, in which authors continue to comment on each other's works). Academic literary theory is currently in an unsettled state, with the possibility, as some see it, of becoming an end in itself (criticism for the sake of criticism) rather than as a means of understanding the literary heritage of a language or a society and a means of helping people select what they might most usefully read. Descriptive criticism is sometimes limited to texts that respond conveniently to a favoured approach. At the same time, however, variety and controversy have given vitality to literary studies and the study of literary language. Despite different and often warring ideological presuppositions, most critics currently give close attention to the details of literary language and use the insights of linguistics to identify and describe textual features. In addition, the metalanguage of criticism has added many new words and senses of words to the language of literary theory, including *foregrounding*, *gynocriticism*, *intertextuality*, *logocentricity*, *narratology*, *privileging*, and *subtext*. See (A)ESTHETICS, CRITICISM, ENGLISH LITERATURE, GENRE, MODERN. [LITERATURE]. R.C.

Barry, Peter. 1987. *Issues in Contemporary Literary Theory*. London: Macmillan.
Belsey, Catherine. 1980. *Critical Practice*. London: Macmillan.
Bergonzi, Bernard. 1990. *Exploding English: Criticism, Theory, Culture*. Oxford: University Press.
Booth, Wayne C. 1988. *The Company We Keep: An Ethics of Fiction*. Berkeley & Los Angeles: University of California Press.
Durant, Alan, & Fabb, Nigel. 1990. *Literary Studies in Action*. London & New York: Routledge.
Eagleton, Terry. 1983. *Literary Theory: an Introduction*. Oxford: Blackwell.
Fowler, Roger. 1973/87. *A Dictionary of Modern Critical Terms*. London: Routledge & Kegan Paul.
Jefferson, Ann, & Robey, David. 1982/6. *Modern Literary Theory: A Comparative Introduction*. London: Batsford.
Watson, George. 1964. *The Literary Critics: A Study of English Descriptive Criticism*. London: Chatto & Windus.
Wellek, René, and Warren, Austin. 1963. *Theory of Literature*. Harmondsworth: Penguin.

LITERARY ENGLISH. (1) See LITERARY STANDARD. (2) See ENGLISH LITERATURE, LITERATURE.

LITERARY METHOD. See LANGUAGE TEACHING.

LITERARY SCOTS. See SCOTS.

LITERARY STANDARD, also **Literary English**. A term used by Eric Partridge in the mid-20c for the English of literary prose:

'[It] lies beyond any matter of pronunciation, and is confined to written English,—and should it be used in speech, it is too bookish to be Received. Of Literary English—Literary Standard—it is necessary only to say that it is the more conventional, stylized, and dignified, more accurate and logical, sometimes the more beautiful form that Received Standard assumes, like evening dress, for important occasions; it is also more rhythmical and musical. The prose of Sir Thomas Browne, Gibbon, De Quincey, The Landors, Pater is in Literary English. With dialect, colloquialism, slang, cant, it has nothing to do unless they possess a long pedigree—and then only in rare instances' (*Usage and Abusage*, 1947, revised 1957).

See RECEIVED STANDARD AND MODIFIED STANDARD, STANDARD. [LITERATURE, STYLE, VARIETY].
                                            T.MCA.

LITERARY TERM. A term associated with works of literature. Its area of reference is imprecise: for example, in *A Dictionary of Literary Terms* (UK Deutsch, US Doubleday, 1977; Penguin, 1982), J. A. Cuddon lists ten overlapping categories for the inclusion of an expression: technical terms (such as *iamb*, *metonymy*), forms (*limerick*, *sonnet*), genres (*elegy*, *pastoral*), technicalities (*aesthetic distance*, *tenor and vehicle*), groups and schools (*Parnassians*, *Pre-Raphaelites*), well-known phrases (*pathetic fallacy*, *willing suspension of disbelief*), -isms (*naturalism*, *realism*), themes or motifs (*Faust*, *leitmotif*), personalities (*jongleur*, *villain*), and modes and styles (*irony*, *sentimental comedy*). Chris Baldick, however, in *The Concise Oxford Dictionary of Literary Terms* (1990), lists three overlapping categories for the exclusion of terms from his survey: too common (such as *anagram*, *biography*), self-explanatory (*detective story*, *psychological criticism*), and general (*art*, *culture*). See LITERARY, TERM. [LITERATURE, REFERENCE, WORD].
                                            T.MCA.

LITERARY THEORY. See LITERARY CRITICISM, LITERATURE.

LITERATURE [14c: partly through French *littérature* from Latin *lit(t)eratura* alphabetic letters, grammar, language study, learning, from *lit(t)era* letter.]. (1) Artistic creation through language and its products: *French literature*, *literature in English*. Although this is currently the major sense of the term, it was not in general use before the 19c. (2) The texts of a group or subject: *scientific and technical literature, the latest literature on computers*. Although this is currently the minor sense, it is the historically prior meaning of the term.

'Literary' literature. It is impossible to define the now primary sense of literature precisely or to set rigid limits on its use. Literary treatment of a subject requires creative use of the imagination: something is constructed which is related to 'real' experience, but is not of the same order. What has been created in language is known only through language, and the text does not give access to a reality other than itself. As a consequence, the texts that make up English literature are a part and a product of the English language and cannot be separated from it, even though there may be, especially in Britain, distinct university departments of English as 'language' and as 'literature'. Among the various ways of defining *literature* are to see it as an imitation of life, through assessing its effect on a reader, and by analysing its form.

(1) *The imitation of life*. Since at least the 4c BC, when Aristotle described poetry as *mimesis* (imitation), literature has been widely regarded as an imitation of life. The mimetic theory was dominant for centuries, only falling into disfavour in the late 18c with the rise of Romanticism, which took poetry to be essentially an expression of personal feeling. In the 20c, however, the idea of mimesis was revived by the neo-classical Chicago School of criticism.

(2) *Effect on the reader*. Reading literature is widely believed to develop understanding and feeling, by complementing the primary experiences of life with a range of secondary encounters. Although the experience of literature is not the same as 'real' experience, it can have an influence that extends beyond the period of reading. The response is inward and does not necessarily lead to physical movement or social action, although texts written as scripture or propaganda may have such results. In the 5–4c BC, Plato acknowledged the power of poetry, but distrusted its rhetorical effect and mythic quality. In the *Phaedrus*, he attacked the cultivation of persuasion rather than the investigation of truth, and in the *Republic* argued that, in an ideal state, poets would have no educational role. Aristotle, however, thought that the *catharsis* or purgation experienced in witnessing a tragic drama was beneficial. Generally, like Aristotle, critics have attached importance to the ethical purpose of literature and the morally uplifting value of 'the best' literature. The importance of moral values inculcated through reading the classics was emphasized in the 19c by Matthew Arnold and in the 20c by F. R. Leavis.

(3) *Analysing form*. A reader is unlikely to respond with interest to the discovery that a textbook is written in continuous prose, with paragraphs and chapters. This is simply the accepted mode of referential writing. However, confrontation with a sonnet or the structure of a novel raises questions about the author's choice of form, a choice often related to contemporary fashion as well as individual intention. The literary writer imposes on language a more careful ordering than the choice of words and syntax that accompanies general communication. The pattern is strong and overt in *verse*, less apparent but equally important in literary *prose*.

Identifying a literary text. Traditionally, literary texts have been easy to identify: an ode or a play is 'literary', but a menu or a telephone directory is not. There is, however, an indeterminate area of essays, biographies, memoirs, history, philosophy, travel books, and other texts which may or may not be deemed literary. Thomas Hobbes's *Leviathan* (1651) is commonly studied as a political text and John Bunyan's *Pilgrim's Progress* (1678–84) as a literary text, yet they share certain qualities, such as lively personifications; Bunyan creates Giant Despair and Little-faith, while Hobbes writes 'the Papacy is not other than the Ghost of the Deceased Roman Empire, sitting crowned upon the grave thereof'. As Edward Gibbon's *The History of the Decline and Fall of the Roman Empire* (1776–88) has grown less important as history, it has become more significant as literature. Many texts appear therefore to have literary aspects combined with other qualities and purposes, and ultimately individual or consensual choice must decide which has priority. Private and group judgement is also exercised in evaluative criticism. The word *literature* tends to be used with approval of works perceived as having artistic merit, the evaluation of which may depend on social and linguistic as well as aesthetic factors. If the criteria of quality become exacting, a *canon* may emerge, limited in its inclusions and exclusions, and the members of a society or group may be required (with varying degrees of pressure and success) to accept that canon and no other. Academic syllabuses for degrees in English have traditionally covered periods, focused on such well-established writers as Chaucer, Spenser, Shakespeare, Milton, and Wordsworth. Courses introduced more recently may include such topics as Women's Writing, with study of recent novelists like Doris Lessing and Margaret Atwood as well as Charlotte Bronte and Virginia Woolf, or Black American Literature, with James Baldwin and Richard Wright.

Literature and language. In the formative period of a written language, a successful literature may favour a particular dialect and contribute towards its becoming a national printed standard, in the case of English the East Midlands dialect from the 14c onwards. The prestige of literature can attract favour to an associated 'high style' that rejects aspects of common usage as vulgar. This favour prevailed for a time in some Continental European literatures, such as the *dolce stil* of 12c Italy and 17–18c classical French writing, but apart from the 18c cult of *poetic diction* has had little influence in the English-speaking world. Literature is an exceptional area of language use, which many people have regarded as the highest service to which language can be put and the surest touchstone of good usage. Its creation is dependent on the resources available to the author in any period, but those resources may be enriched and increased by a literary tradition in which quotations from and allusions to 'the classics' abound and many words have literary nuances. Writers have created such enduring neologisms as Spenser's *blatant*, Milton's *pandemonium*, and Shaw's *superman*.

The language of literature. In the 20c, much attention has been given to the language of literature and the question of whether there is in fact distinctively *literary language*. Many features thought of as literary appear in common usage. Metre and formal rhythm derive from everyday speech, words often rhyme without conscious contrivance, multiple meaning and word associations are part of daily communication, and tropes and figures of speech are used in ordinary discourse. However, literary language shows a greater concentration of such features, deliberately arranged and controlled. It may be said that communication is impossible without artifice, yet there is a difference between the colloquial simile that someone is 'as bold as brass' and T. S. Eliot's simile for the young man in *The Waste Land* (1922): 'One of the low on whom assurance sits / As a silk hat on a Bradford millionaire.' The difference lies not only in the originality and unexpected juxtaposition, but in the appropriateness of image to context, in the austere tone of the whole poem, in the evocation of a snobbish post-1918 attitude to men who had become rich through government contracts during the war, in the rhythm of the verse and the contemptuous sounds of the short vowels in the second line. Literary language makes us pause to consider, re-read, and assess in a way that would destroy the flow of other modes of communication.

Language in literature. Literary language may be drawn from any area or register of daily usage. Colloquialism, and dialect are used in fictional and dramatic dialogue, as in this passage from *Sons and Lovers* (D. H. Lawrence, 1913):

'But how late you are!'
'Aren't I!' he cried, turning to his father. 'Well, dad!'
The two men shook hands.
'Well, my lad!'
Morel's eyes were wet.
'We thought tha'd niver be commin',' he said.
'Oh, I'd come!' exclaimed William.

In James Joyce's *Ulysses* (1922), Leopold Bloom reads an advertisement in a newspaper:

What is home without
Plumtree's Potted Meat?
Incomplete.
With it an abode of bliss.

and incorporates the jingle into his stream of consciousness. The pattern of metre and rhyme may transform into poetry a statement which has neither rare words nor unusual syntax:

The lad came to the door at night,
When lovers crown their vows,
And whistled soft and out of sight
In shadow of the boughs.
(A. E. Housman, 'The True Lover', 1896)

Prevailing literary fashion may make literary language seem artificial without impairing comprehension:

If aught of oaten stop or pastoral song
May hope, chaste Eve, to soothe thy modest ear,
Like thy own solemn springs,
Thy springs and dying gales.
(William Collins, 1721–59, 'Ode to Evening')

Experiment and the personal vision may challenge the reader to make a new response to language and to accept T. S. Eliot's dictum that 'genuine poetry can communicate before it is understood':

Now as I was young and easy under the apple boughs
About the lilting house and happy as the grass was green,
The night above the dingle starry,
Time let me hail and climb
Golden in the heydays of his eyes.
(Dylan Thomas, 1914–53, 'Fern Hill')

These extracts are from texts commonly accepted as part of literature, yet, out of context, they seem to present irreconcilable differences. Every literary work must be seen in its totality as a unique creation, often connected by similarities with other texts but dependent on none for its validity. [HISTORY, LITERATURE]. R.C.

Blake, N. F. 1990. *An Introduction to the Language of Literature.* London: Macmillan.

Carter, Ronald. 1973. *Language and Literature.* London: Allen & Unwin.

Chapman, Raymond. 1973. *Linguistics and Literature.* London: Arnold.

Chatman, S. (ed.). 1971. *Literary Styles: A Symposium.* Oxford: University Press.

Davis, Philip. 1992. *The Experience of Reading.* London & New York: Routledge.

Page, N. (ed.). 1984. *The Language of Literature.* London: Macmillan.

Tambling, J. 1988. *What is Literary Language?* Milton Keynes: Open University Press.

The literature theme

A–E. AELFRIC, ALEXANDRINE, ALLEGORY, ALLITERATIVE VERSE, ANAGNORISIS, ANAPAEST/ANAPEST, ANGLO-INDIAN, ANTICLIMAX, ARCHETYPE, ASIDE, AUTOBIOGRAPHY, BALLAD, BALLADE, BARDOLATRY, BELLES LETTRES, BEOWULF, BIBLE, BLANK VERSE, BOOK OF COMMON PRAYER, BOUT-RIMÉS, BREVE, BURLESQUE, BUSH BALLAD, CAESURA/CESURA, CANTO, CARICATURE, CATASTROPHE, CATHARSIS, CENSORSHIP, CHARACTER, CLASSIC, CLASSICISM, CLERIHEW, CLICHÉ, CLOSE READING, COMEDY, COMIC, COMIC RELIEF, COMMUNICATIVE SHIFT, CONCEIT, CONCRETE POETRY, CORPUS, COUPLET, DACTYL, DENOUEMENT, DETECTIVE STORY/ROMAN POLICIER, DIALOGUE, DIARY, DIRGE, DISTICH, DOGGEREL, DOUBLE RHYME, DRAMA, DUB, DUMB SHOW, ECHO VERSE, ECLOGUE, ELEGY, ELIZABETHAN, ENG LANG/ENG LANG & LIT, ENGLISH LITERATURE, ENGLISH STUDIES, ENG LIT, EPIC, EPIGRAM, EPIGRAPH, EPILOG(UE), EPISTOLARY NOVEL, EPITAPH, ESSAY, EULOGY, EXPLICATION DE TEXTE.

F–N. FABLE, FANTASY, FARCE, FEMININE ENDING, FICTION, FILM, FOOT, FREE VERSE, GENRE, GOTHIC, GRUB STREET, HALF RHYME, HAMARTIA, HEAVY, HOLOFERNES, HOMERIC SIMILE, HOMILY, IMAGINATION, INITIAL RHYME, INTERTEXTUALITY, KITCHEN-SINK DRAMA, LAMPOON, LEONINE VERSE, LETTER[2], LETTERS, LIMERICK, LINE, LIT CRIT, LITERARY, LITERARY CRITICISM, LITERARY STANDARD, LITERARY TERM, LITERATURE, LITERATURE IN ENGLISH, LORIMER, LYLY, LYRIC, MACARONIC, MACDIARMID, MACRON, MAKAR, MAN OF LETTERS, MASCULINE ENDING, MASQUE, MATTER OF BRITAIN, MELODRAMA, MEMOIR, METRE/METER, METRICS, MIME, MIMESIS, MODERNISM, MONODY, MONOLOG(UE), MORALITY PLAY, MUMMERSET, MUSE, MYSTERY PLAY, MYTH, NARRATIVE POETRY, NARRATIVE VOICE, NARRATOLOGY, NOM DE PLUME, NONSENSE VERSE, NOVEL, NOVELETTE, NOVELIZATION, NOVELLA.

O–Z. OBLIQUE RHYME, OCTAVE, OCTET, ODE, OFF RHYME, ORAL LITERATURE, ORAL TRADITION, ORATURE, OTTAVA RIMA, PANTOMIME, PARABLE, PARODY, PASTICHE, PASTORAL, PATHETIC FALLACY, PATHOS, PEN NAME, PERIPETEIA, PINDARIC ODE, PLAY, PLOT, POET, POETIC DICTION, POETIC JUSTICE, POETIC LICENCE/LICENSE, POETIC PROSE, POETICS, POET LAUREATE, POETRY, POLEMIC, POPULAR FICTION, POST-MODERNISM, POST-STRUCTURALISM, PROLOG(UE), PROSE, PROSODY, PROVERB, PSALM, PYGMALION, QUATRAIN, QUIRE, REFRAIN, REPERTORY, REVIEW, RHYME, ROMANCE, ROMAN POLICIER, ROMANTICISM, SAGA, SATIRE, SCANSION, SCRIBBLER, SCRIPT, SERIAL, SERIES, SERMON, SESTET, SHORT STORY, SINGSONG, SLANT RHYME, SOCIAL REALISM, SOLILOQUY, SONNET, SPENSERIAN STANZA, SPONDEE, SPRUNG RHYTHM, STAGE, STANZA, STORY, STREAM OF CONSCIOUSNESS, TELEVISION, TERCET, TERZA RIMA, TEXT, THEATRE/THEATER, THEATRE OF THE ABSURD, THESIS, THRENODY, TRAGEDY, TRAGICOMEDY, TRILOGY, TRIOLET, TRIPLE RHYME, TRIPLET, TRISTICH, TROCHEE, TROPE, VERSE, VERSIFIER, VERS LIBRE, VOICE, WHODUN(N)IT, WORLD LITERATURE, WORLD LITERATURE WRITTEN IN ENGLISH, WRITER.

International varieties. AFRICAN LITERATURE IN ENGLISH, AMERICAN LITERATURE, ANGLO-IRISH LITERATURE, ANGLO-WELSH LITERATURE, AUSTRALIAN LITERATURE, CANADIAN LITERATURE IN ENGLISH, CARIBBEAN LITERATURE IN ENGLISH, COMMONWEALTH LITERATURE, FILIPINO LITERATURE IN ENGLISH, GREEK LITERATURE, INDIAN ENGLISH LITERATURE, IRISH LITERATURE, LATIN LITERATURE, LITERATURE, NEW ZEALAND LITERATURE, POST-COLONIAL LITERATURES IN ENGLISH, SCOTS LITERATURE, SCOTTISH LITERATURE, SOUTH AFRICAN LITERATURE IN ENGLISH, WELSH LITERATURE, WORLD LITERATURE.

Literary biographies. ACHEBE, ADDISON, ARNOLD (M.), AUSTEN, BEHN, BOSWELL, BRATHWAITE, BRIDGES, BRONTE SISTERS, BUNYAN, BURGESS, BURNS, BUTLER, CARROLL, CHAUCER, CHURCHILL, COLERIDGE (S.), CONRAD, DEFOE, DICKENS, DICKINSON, DRYDEN, ELIOT, FIELDING, GORDIMER, HARDY, HAZLITT, HUNT, JOHNSON, JONSON, JOYCE, KIPLING, LAMB, LAWRENCE, LEAVIS, MELVILLE, MILTON, NAIPAUL, NGUGI, ORWELL, PIOZZI (THRALE), POPE, POTTER, QUILLER-COUCH, RICHARDS, RICHARDSON, RICKERT, SCOTT, SHAKESPEARE, SHAW, SHERIDAN, SIDNEY, SMOLLETT, SOYINKA, SPENSER, STEELE, STERNE, STEVENSON, SWIFT, TENNYSON, THOMAS, TWAIN, TYNDALE, WELLS, WILSON, WOLLSTONECRAFT, WOOLF, WORDSWORTH, WYCLIF(FE).

LITERATURE IN ENGLISH [Late 20c]. A term used to circumvent the ambiguities in the term *English literature*, making it clear that the focus is on the language and not on England, as in the titles *The Cambridge Guide to Literature in English* (1988) and *The Feminist Companion to Literature in English* (Batsford, 1990). See ENGLISH LITERATURE. [LITERATURE].   T.MCA.

LITHOGRAPHY [18c: from Greek *lithós* stone, *graphía* writing]. A process of printing letters and images from a metal or stone surface, in which the surface to be printed is not raised, but a flat area is treated to hold ink in some places and reject it in others, some areas becoming *ink-receptive*, others *ink-repellent*. The antipathy of grease and water provides the basis of the lithographic process: a greasy image repels water but receives greasy ink, while a non-greasy area receives water but repels greasy ink. Only a greasy image is printed when the inked surface is pressed against paper or other material to receive the ink. The process, discovered almost by accident in 1798 by the Czech-born German playwright Alois Senefelder (who experimented with stone), has developed into a high-speed printing technology. See PHOTO-OFFSET PRINTING. [TECHNOLOGY].   W.W.B., T.MCA.

LITOTES [17c: through Latin from Greek *litotēs* meagreness. Stress: 'lie-TOE-teez']. In rhetoric, a positive and often emphatic statement made by denying something negative, as when

St Paul called himself 'a citizen *of no mean city*' (Acts 21: 39). Common phrases involving litotes include *in no small measure* and *by no means negligible*. See MEIOSIS. [STYLE].   T.MCA.

LIVERPOOL, LIVERPUDLIAN. See SCOUSE.

LOADED LANGUAGE. Biased and often emotive language, loaded like dice to favour the thrower. It may, among other things, be promotional and commercial (*New improved ZAPPO washes whiter than white!*) or social, political, and ideological (*They're taxing hardworking people to support idlers*; *There are too many foreigners getting into this country these days*). Compare PROPAGANDA. [STYLE].   T.MCA.

LOAN [19c in this sense]. An item of language given, as if by a lender, from one language to another, used both on its own and in such combinations as *loanword*, *loan translation*, *loan blend*, and *loanshift*. The commonest loans are single words: *pizza* (from Italian to English), *babysitter* (from English to French, German, and other languages). Once adopted, loans usually show some adaptation: in sound, French *garage*, variously pronounced in English; in form, English *night* taken into Italian as a clipping of *nightclub*; in grammar, English nouns borrowed into French and provided with a gender, *la babysitter* (feminine), *le golf* (masculine). Verbs adapt to the morphology of the borrowing language: in German, *babysitten* to babysit, past tense *babysittete*, past participle *gebabysittet*. See ASSIMILATION, BORROWING, CALQUE, CODE-MIXING AND CODE-SWITCHING, FOREIGNISM, LOAN BLEND, LOAN TRANSLATION, LOANWORD. [HISTORY, WORD].   S.R., T.MCA.

LOAN BLEND [mid-20c]. A usage that combines a foreign loan with a native form: *grüngrocer* in the German spoken in Australia, the first element German, the second English (from *greengrocer*); *Afrikanerdom*, combining *Afrikaner* (from Afrikaans) and the English suffix *-dom* as in *kingdom*. See BLEND, LOAN. [HISTORY, WORD].   S.R., T.MCA.

LOAN TRANSLATION [1930s] also **calque**. A compound or complex loan in which, rather than borrow an expression directly, speakers analyse the parts and replace them with similar native forms: AmE *skyscraper* adopted into French as *gratte-ciel* (scrape-sky), into German as *Wolkenkratzer* (cloud-scrape). See CALQUE, LOAN. [HISTORY, WORD].   S.R., T.MCA.

LOANWORD, also **loan-word, loan word** [1870s: from German *Lehnwort*]. A word taken into one language from another: in English, *garage* from French, *leitmotif* from German. Such words are, on the analogy of money, both 'loans' from Language A to B and 'borrowings' by B from A. Philologists use a three-word German system to discuss the process of lending and assimilation. *Gastwort, Fremdwort, Lehnwort.* A *Gastwort* (guest-word) is an unassimilated borrowing that has kept its pronunciation, orthography, grammar, and meaning, but is not used widely: for example, *Gastwort* itself, with /v/ for the *W* of *Wort*, a capital letter because it is a noun, and the alien plural *Gastwörter*. Such words are usually limited to the terminology of specialists and italicized and glossed when used. A *Fremdwort* (foreign-word) has moved a stage further. It has been adapted into the native system, with a stable spelling and pronunciation (native or exotic), or a compromise has been made by translating all or part into a native equivalent: for example, *garage* and *Lehnwort* itself (which has for general purposes been converted to *loanword*). A *Lehnwort* proper is a word that has become indistinguishable from the rest of the lexicon and is open to normal rules of word use and word formation. It is seldom possible, however, to separate the stages of assimilation so neatly: Russian *sputnik* and *glasnost* entered English virtually overnight, with immediate derivatives like *anti-sputnik* and *pre-glasnost*. Assimilation into a language as widespread as English occurs on three levels: local, national, and international. For example, such a Mexican-Spanish word as *taco* may remain local in AmE, used only along the US–Mexican border, then become national, then international. Such a process often takes years, leaving many loans drifting uncertainly. See ASSIMILATION, BORROWING, CALQUE, FOREIGNISM, LOAN, REGIONAL DICTIONARIES OF ENGLISH. [HISTORY, WORD].   G.C., T.MCA.

LOCALISM [19c]. An expression that belongs to a particular place or geographical variety of a language: for example, in Sierra Leone, *hot drink* means 'alcoholic beverage'; in ScoE, *loch* refers to a lake in Scotland, while *lake* is used for more general purposes. See -ISM, REGIONALISM. [STYLE, WORD].   T.MCA.

LOCATIVE [18c: from Latin *locativus* indicating place]. In some inflected languages, nouns have forms to show that they are the location of the action of the verb: Latin *domus* (house, home) has the locative *domi* (at one's house, at home). In English, such concepts are usually expressed with prepositions: *at home*, *to London*, *in New York*. In case grammar, English subjects and objects referring to place are sometimes said to be locative: *walls* in *The walls were running with water* (Water was running down the walls);

room in *She paced the room* (She went up and down the room). See CASE[1], CASE GRAMMAR. [GRAMMAR].   S.C.

LOCUTION [15c: from Latin *locutio/locutionis* (style of) speech, from *loqui/locutus* to speak]. (1) The act of speaking; utterance; speech as the expression of thought; (style of) discourse. (2) A formal, technical, sometimes pedantic term for an utterance, word, phrase, or idiom, especially if regarded as characteristic of a social or regional group: *Irish locutions*. (3) The base on which the British philosopher J. L. Austin coined a set of terms for the discussion of utterance and its consequences: 'The act of "saying something" . . . I call, i.e. dub, the performance of a locutionary act, and the study of utterances thus far and in these respects the study of locutions, or of full units of speech' (*How to Do Things with Words*, 1962/75, ch. 8). For Austin, a *locutionary act* is an act of speaking (a result of *locution*); an *illocutionary act* is an act of speaking that promises, requests, suggests, warns, etc. (a result of *illocution*); a *perlocutionary act* is an act that leads to an action of some kind on the part of a listener (a result of *perlocution*, an instance being *a perlocution*), such as laughing, complaining, or departing. 'He said that I should go' is locutionary; 'He argued that I should go' is illocutionary; and 'He convinced me that I should go' is perlocutionary. Compare ELOCUTION, INTERLOCUTOR. See SPEECH ACT. [LANGUAGE, STYLE].   T.MCA.

LOGIC [14c: from Latin *logica*, Greek *logikē tékhnē* the craft of speech]. In general usage, the process of reasoning and sound judgement, often taken to be the outcome of adequate education, an aspect of common sense, or both: *a logical decision*. In philosophy, the study and development of close reasoning, especially inference, traditionally the concern of logicians and mathematicians and currently important for computer programmers, computational linguists, and researchers into artificial intelligence. There are several kinds of logic, such as *formal logic* and *symbolic logic*, of philosophical systems that acknowledge its influence, such as *logical positivism*, and of techniques considered to incorporate logic, such as *logic arrays* and *logic circuits* in electronic technology.

Classical logic. The term *logikē* was coined by the Greek philosopher Alexander of Aphrodisias in the 3c, but systems of organized thinking had already developed well before this in Greece, India, and China. Western culture has inherited the Greek tradition mainly through Rome and the Arab world. In this tradition, logic is closely linked with grammar and rhetoric, and discussion of one often leads to discussion of the

others. Greek speculation appears to have begun with Thales (7–6c BC) and Pythagoras (6c BC), in the study of geometrical shapes and theorems, a discipline made possible by writing and scale drawing: for the Greeks, both reasoning and language were encompassed in the word *lógos*. From the philosopher Heraclitus (6–5c BC) to the early Christian era, the term also served to describe a rational principle considered to pervade the universe, and linked language and logic with God: 'In the beginning was the Word, and the Word was with God, and the Word was God' (The Gospel according to John, 1: 1, Authorized Version, in which *word* translates *lógos*).

The Greeks also contrasted *lógos* with *mûthos*, a term that encompassed words, speech, stories, poems, fictions, and fables. Plato (5c BC) in *The Republic* represented Socrates as wishing to exclude poetry from the proper education of the young, and after some 2,500 years, this viewpoint still carries weight: logic, science, and reason are commonly set on one side and poetry, art, and myth on the other. To make his case, however, Plato used many devices from poetry and rhetoric: he so structured his dialogues that Socrates always won, often with the help of poetic analogies such as the Simile of the Cave. His pupil Aristotle laid the foundations of logic proper, as the study of inference from *propositions* arranged as formal *arguments*. Sound arguments were taken to depend on two kinds of reasoning: *deduction* and *induction*. In deductive logic, well-framed propositions necessarily lead to a certain conclusion: for example, if Socrates is a man, and all men are mortal (propositions), then Socrates is mortal (conclusion). Inductive logic, however, draws analogies and deals not in certainty but in probability. A conclusion is drawn from a range of instances taken as evidence or justification for that conclusion: the sun has always risen in the east, all observers agree about this, all their lives they have seen it happening, and so (it is highly probable that) the sun will rise again tomorrow. There is, however, no proof or guarantee that it will do so. Because of such a marked difference, and because the scientific method during and after the Renaissance drew so heavily on induction, it was removed from logic proper. Deduction is now usually regarded as the concern of logicians and induction as the concern of scientists and statisticians.

Mind, brain, and logic. In the later 20c, the preeminence of sequential, propositional thinking has been challenged by such students of thinking as the Maltese psychologist Edward de Bono. He contrasts the *vertical thinking* of logic with the *lateral thinking* of creative minds, arguing:

Old style thinking insists on fixed concepts, certainties and absolutes. These are processed by means of traditional logic, and the answers are treated with the arrogance and dogmatism which always accompanies academic logic. There is nothing wrong with the logic as such, but the emphasis is on the perfection of the processing and not on the basic concepts used. Another important danger is the smugness that follows perfect logic and excludes the search for new ideas and better approaches (*Po: Beyond Yes and No*, 1972).

Recent neurological research indicates that, by and large, the hemispheres of the human brain have distinct functions: in the left (for most people) is the propensity for language, mathematics, and linear reasoning, in the right the propensity for visual, spatial, intuitive, and analogical skills, the hemispheres working together through their neural links. This discovery has prompted a re-examination of the roles and relationships of *lógos* and *mûthos*, suggesting that they may be partners rather than rivals. If this is so, creative thought may require both linear left and holistic right. In linguistic terms, logic is as likely in verse as in prose, and analogy and metaphor are as much the tools of philosophers and scientists as of bards and mystics.

Language and logic. Because logic and grammar developed together they have overlapping terminologies: both use the term *sentence*, and deductive logic consists of a *logic of propositions* (also called *sentential logic*) and a *logic of predicates* (also called a *logic of noun expressions*). Logicians, grammarians, and rhetoricians are all interested in such matters as ambiguity, fallacy, paradox, syntax, and semantics, and in such modalities as necessity, possibility, and contingency; linguists who are concerned with grammar, computation, and artificial intelligence take as much interest in logic as in natural language. Logicians and mathematicians have created systems that contain both sets of abstract symbols and the rules necessary for their combination and manipulation in strings. Such symbols, rules, and strings are often idealizations of elements in, or thought to be in, natural language (but isolated from such everyday factors as dialect variation, personal idiosyncrasy, figurative usage, emotional connotation, colloquial idiom, social attitude, and semantic change). When such a system of symbols is adapted to practical ends, however, as in computer technology and artificial intelligence, *pure logic* becomes *applied logic*, operating within a real machine intended to do real work in real time.

Grammar and logic. Although many logicians, grammarians, and linguists have been interested in a universal calculus of language (something that would transcend and dispense with the Babel of natural language or allow the dispassionate description of all language), they

have built their systems out of the natural languages that they know best: Greek for Aristotle and his disciples, Latin for medieval and Renaissance grammarians, and English for such present-day theorists as Noam Chomsky. Both prescriptive and descriptive grammarians of such Western languages as French and English have been influenced by logic and by the languages in which the principles of logic developed. Because it emerged in large part through the use and analysis of language, it has not been difficult to find quasi-logical patterns in language. Some analysts have been inclined to see logical orderliness either as inherent in language or as a reasonable goal of language planning, especially when a language is in the process of being standardized. Everyday language, however, has a persistent (even frustrating) tendency towards the illogical or non-logical, as for example in the use of double negatives (*I didn't do nothing*, which does not therefore mean 'I did something') and in idiomatic expressions (such as *it's raining cats and dogs*).

All analysts of language work towards orderliness, but some go further and engage in or recommend making certain aspects of language, such as the spelling of English, more 'regular' (that is, more rule-governed and therefore more logically consistent). They may also favour an artificial language such as Esperanto or Basic English that is (apparently) free from the illogic of natural language. Interest in such reforms has often gone hand in hand with particular conceptions of and assumptions about, progress, science, efficiency, education, literacy, and standards. Logic has therefore been used as a tool for both the description of natural language and its prescriptive improvement. In the development of the first grammars of English, the model was Latin and the analytical terms were Greek as used by the describers of Latin. Medieval and Renaissance models for vernacular prose as a vehicle of rational discourse were either Latin prose or vernacular prose written in the Latin style. Theories of sentences and parts of speech were those developed by classical grammarians and logicians, often the same people. The analysis of sentences into subjects and predicates, main and subordinate clauses, and the like, has paralleled the logician's view of propositions as the core of language and of binary division as a powerful conceptual tool.

The limits of logic. In the second half of the 20c, ancient practice has gained fresh impetus through the work of Noam Chomsky. Some features of his work are: (1) The definition of a language as a set of well-formed sentences, indefinite in number. (2) Abstract and diagrammatic analyses of sentences of standard written English. (3) The use of quasi-logical symbols such as S for sentence, NP for noun phrase, and VP for verb phrase, to sustain the analysis of such sentences. (4) Logical transformations performed on strings of symbols so as to produce further strings. (5) The creation of a generative grammar, that is, a set of explicit, formal rules that specify or generate all and only the sentences which constitute a language; in so doing, they are seen as demonstrating the nature of the implicit knowledge of that language possessed by an ideal native speaker-hearer. Such an approach has often been taken to be a break with the past, but is rooted in more than two millennia of logical and grammatical system-building. It remains a matter of debate whether natural language can be handled by linguistic theories that derive in the main from or are closely associated with aspects of formal logic. Natural language is a neural mechanism, apparently the result of genetic and social evolution. While it is sometimes regular, logical, and precise, it is as often irregular, non-logical, and imprecise, and oftener still a mix of the two. It blends intellect with instinct, logic with inspiration, and the standard with the varied. Logic is closely associated with language and with its description and discussion in literate societies. As such, it is an essential tool, but one cannot deduce from this usefulness that it is the sole or even primary means by which natural language can be understood.

See AMBIGUITY, AMPHIBOLY, ANALOGY, ANALOGY AND ANOMALY, APORIA, ARGUMENT, AXIOM, BEGGING THE QUESTION, CARROLL, CASE GRAMMAR, DIALECTIC, FALLACY, LEADING QUESTION, LETTER WORD, MEANING, METALANGUAGE, OPPOSITION, PREMISS/PREMISE, PROPOSITION, RATIONALIZATION, REFERENT, RHETORIC, SEMANTICS, SOPHISTRY, SYLLOGISM, TAUTOLOGY, THESIS, TYPE, TYPE AND TOKEN, USAGE. [GRAMMAR, LANGUAGE]. T.MCA.

LOGO [20c: a short form of either *logogram* or *logotype*]. A unique graphic representation of an institutional or other name (including trademarks and abbreviations). Logos like the penguin framed in an oval (Penguin publishers) or the ship in full sail (Longman publishers) serve as immediately recognizable symbols on books, vehicles, buildings, etc., and are meant, in addition, to sharpen the public image of the organization in question. Compare IMAGE, SYMBOL. See LOGOTYPE. [MEDIA, TECHNOLOGY]. T.MCA.

LOGOGRAM. See ALPHABET, WRITING.

LOGOPAEDICS. See LANGUAGE PATHOLOGY.

LOGOPHILE. See WORD BUFF.

LOGORRHOEA BrE, **logorrhea** AmE [1900s: from Greek *logós* speech, *rhoía* flow]. (1) A pathological need to talk. (2) A facetious term for talking and writing too much: 'an author suffering from acute logorrhoea' (*Daily Telegraph*, 5 Feb. 1970). See LANGUAGE PATHOLOGY, VERBOSITY. [STYLE]. T.MCA.

LOGOTYPE [1810s: from Greek-derived *logo*- word, speech, and *type*]. A single piece of type that bears two or more uncombined letters, a syllable, or a word. See LOGO, TYPE. [TECHNOLOGY, WORD]. T.MCA.

LONDON [Before 10c: from Romanized Celtic *Londinium*]. A city on the River Thames in southern England, the ancient capital of England and also the capital and seat of government of the United Kingdom of Great Britain and Northern Ireland. The city has experienced many languages: Celtic, the Latin of Roman Britain, Old English, Norman French, Middle and Modern English, and the languages of immigrants, diplomats, merchants, and visitors. It is, in the late 20c, one of the world's great cosmopolitan and polyglot cities, identified in particular with three varieties of English: *King's/Queen's English, BBC English*, and *Cockney*. The primacy of London (in England, in the United Kingdom, and in the British Empire) has in the past given a certain status to the language used there. However, the city did not play a major part in Old English culture until the reign of Edward the Confessor (1042–66). Prior to that period, Winchester to the south-west was the seat of the Saxon kings and West Saxon was the literary dialect. Through the medieval period, London grew in importance, and the triumph of Middle English over Norman French in the 14c gave preference to the variety of the East Midland dialect that was becoming current in London. The poet Geoffrey Chaucer, a Londoner of the time, generally used slightly older and more southern forms, with traces of Kentish.

Capital and provinces. The comparative stability of the Tudor period, with London as the seat of the royal court and major litigation, brought still greater regard for its superiority in language. In 1589, Puttenham advised the use of 'the vsual speach of the Court, and that of London and the shires lying about London with lx [sixty] myles, and not much aboue' (*The Arte of English Poesie*, 1589). The introduction of dialect speakers in drama, like Shakespeare's Welsh captain Fluellen and Scots captain Jamy in *Henry V*, and the use of 'stage southern' as affected by Edgar in *King Lear*, showed that Londoners were aware of their distinctive speech and amused by other varieties. The tendency is even more marked in later 17c comedy, in which country characters are differentiated by their speech: the restored Stuart court and the London location of groups like the new Royal Society made the city seem ever more significant than 'the provinces'. Discussions about the correct forms of English and the possibility of an Academy to regulate the language were carried on mainly by London speakers.

Perhaps because London usage was taken for granted by so many of the influential, there is not an extensive record of its nature before the 19c. When dialogue was written for plays or novels, only speakers of other dialects were marked by deviant spelling, the established orthography being used for the rest. The hymnographer Isaac Watts, in his *Art of Reading and Writing English* (1721), dismisses the 'dialect or corrupt speech that obtains in the several counties of England' and lists words that are written differently from 'their common and frequent pronunciation in the City of London'. He adds that 'there are some other corruptions in the pronouncing of several words by many of the citizens themselves' and cites among others *yourn* for 'yours', *squeedge* for 'squeeze', *yerb* for 'herb'. However, Samuel Pegge notes, in *Anecdotes of the English Language* (1803), words whose pronunciation 'is a little deformed by the natives of London'; as well as Cockney features like the confusion of /v/ and /w/, he mentions some that 'savour rather of an affected refinement' like *daater* for 'daughter' and *saace* for 'sauce'.

The greater mobility of the middle and late 19c, with increasing prosperity and concomitant confidence in other parts of Britain, helped bring other dialects into literary use for serious and even tragic as well as comic characters. The Brontes, Gaskell, and Hardy reminded readers that London was not the undisputed linguistic heart of England, and showed how Londoners might sound to those from other areas. Gaskell makes John Barton say, when he describes his visit to London for a Chartist meeting, that the policemen 'speak in a mincing way (for Londoners are mostly tongue-tied and can't say their a's and i's properly)' (in *Mary Barton*, 1848). In Hardy's poem 'The Ruined Maid', a country girl from Dorset marvels at the new and apparently refined speech of her friend, who has become a London prostitute and who observes, 'Some polish is gained with one's ruin.'

London English. True Cockney is relatively limited, though some of its features are shared by Londoners who are not themselves Cockneys. The double negative, found also in other parts of the country, is common in London. Some vowel and diphthong sounds, notably the nasalization of the diphthong /aʊ/ as in *now* and the changing of /ei/ to /ai/ which makes *paper* sound like *piper*, are frequently heard, as is the dropping of initial *h* (*We're 'appy to 'elp you*). Characteristics of neighbouring counties are heard in London, particularly in the outer suburbs, which have penetrated into what were once rural areas of Surrey, Kent, and Essex. It would be an acute or very bold observer who could guarantee to analyse all the features of speech among a random selection of Londoners, claiming, as Shaw's Professor Higgins did in *Pygmalion* (1913), to identify a person within a street or two. Shaw commented that 'Ladies and gentlemen in Southern England' pronounce *plum*, *come*, *humbug* as 'plam', 'cam', 'hambag', and in *Pygmalion* he makes Freddy Eynsford-Hill pronounce 'how do you do' as *ahdedo*.

The speech of educated Londoners is not necessarily to be equated with Received Pronunciation, but this is the model which has traditionally been followed by the 'upwardly mobile'. In many instances, however, there appears in the late 20c to be a levelling-out in the speech patterns of younger, educated Londoners of many backgrounds, including RP, into a distinctive accent and voice quality. Currently, however, the situation is complex, and London speech ranges from 'core' Cockney usage through a wide variety of intermediate forms to RP and forms of RP that some may regard as prestigious and others as affected or 'posh'.

The lexis and syntax of London English show few distinctive features. Immigrants in the 19c tended to remain in closed groups and in later generations to be absorbed into British society without adding new linguistic features to the extent that has happened in New York City. The immigrant influx in the second half of the 20c has been large, but has been shared with other parts of the country and such additions as have appeared have been disseminated by the media rather than localized. Londoners generally refer in an abbreviated or deictic form to topographical features which others would specify more fully, such as 'the Palace' (Buckingham Palace), 'the Abbey' (Westminster Abbey), 'the Elephant' (the Elephant and Castle, originally a public house, now used to refer to a major road complex and shopping area), 'the Palladium' (the London Palladium), but these are typical of local usage anywhere, magnified however by the significance of such landmarks simply because they are part of the topography of one of the world's best-known cities.

See BRITISH BROADCASTING, BRITISH EMPIRE, BRITISH LIBRARY, CAXTON, CHANCERY STANDARD, CHAUCER, COCKNEY, DIALECT IN ENGLAND, DICKENS, EAST MIDLAND, ENGLAND, ENGLISH IN

ENGLAND, ENGLISH PLACE-NAMES, FLEET STREET, HACK, HACKNEYED, HISTORY OF ENGLISH, HOME COUNTIES, JOHNSON, LONDON CHAMBER OF COMMERCE AND INDUSTRY, LONDON–LUND CORPUS, NASAL, PROVINCE, PUBLISHING, QUEEN'S ENGLISH, RECEIVED PRONUNCIATION, RHYMING SLANG, SHAKESPEARE, SHAW, STANDARD ENGLISH, UNITED KINGDOM. [EUROPE, VARIETY]. R.C.

LONDON CHAMBER OF COMMERCE AND INDUSTRY. Short form *LCCI*. A British organization concerned with the promotion of business, which conducts as part of its Commercial Education Scheme, begun in 1890 in collaboration with the London-based College of Preceptors, a range of examinations which link proficiency in English with office skills and related background knowledge. The LCCI's associations with foreign Chambers of Commerce have helped make these examinations popular in Europe and particularly in France. See EXAMINING IN ENGLISH. [EDUCATION, EUROPE, MEDIA]. W.S.

LONDON–LUND CORPUS. See SURVEY OF ENGLISH USAGE.

LONG AND SHORT Contrasting terms in prosody, orthography, and phonetics, used to discuss and mark the duration (or quantity) of speech sounds. In prosody, they refer to syllables and vowels; in orthography and related aspects of pronunciation, they focus principally on written vowels; in phonetics, they apply to spoken vowels and their written representations in IPA transcription. The three areas of application and their interrelationships are discussed below.

Prosody. Traditional prosodists have used the terms *long* and *short* primarily to contrast syllables, and to do this have placed marks above the vowels of those syllables. The practice began in the prosody of Latin and was applied to English during the Renaissance. Latin verse is quantitative, its rhythm established by the length of its syllables; if a syllable is long, it is marked by a macron over its vowel (*ā*), if short by a breve (*ă*): see BREVE, MACRON. English verse, however, is not quantitative but stress-related (accentual): syllables are not long or short, but *strong* (stressed, accented) or *weak* (unstressed, unaccented). Despite this difference, the early prosodists of the language applied the techniques of Latin scansion by analogy to English, marking the vowel of each strong syllable long and of each weak syllable short. In English metrical analysis, therefore, the macron and the breve serve to mark a rhythm quite distinct from that of Latin, and (despite the implications of their names and origins) they do not involve length. See SCANSION.

Orthography. In writing systems that use the Roman family of alphabets, the terms *long* and *short* relate to greater or less duration in spoken vowels: for example, in one form of written Maori, macrons are used to mark phonetically long vowels, while unmarked vowel letters are taken to be short: see MAORI. This practice derives from a long-established technique for indicating long and short vowels in Latin for educational and lexicographical purposes: for example, *lūminōsus*, the dictionary form of *luminosus*, is shown by macrons to have two long vowels. Short vowels are usually left unchanged (as in *bonus* in Latin, though not in English), but if clarification is required, a breve may be added over the vowel (*bŏnus*): see LATIN[1]. As with prosody, the contrast of long and short in Latin vowels was applied to the description of English, in whose earliest form, Old English, vowel pairs could usefully be described as long and short: see OLD ENGLISH[1]. By the time of Middle English, the vowel differences were no longer a matter of simple duration, but also of laxness or tenseness in the tongue: see MIDDLE ENGLISH. Later still, as Middle English became Modern English, the long, tense, and stressed vowels became subject to a major sound change that gave them their distinctive present-day values, some of which are not monophthongs but diphthongs: see GREAT VOWEL SHIFT.

Nonetheless, in traditional and popular accounts of English pronunciation and orthography, the ancient contrast between long and short vowels has been maintained, despite the wide phonetic gap between the two kinds of vowel. Thus, the six so-called 'long vowels' in *mate, meet, mite, moat, moot, mute* are often contrasted with the six 'short vowels' in *bat, bet, bit, hot, but, put*. Here, *mate* is said, for example, to contain a 'long *a*', in contrast with *bat*, which has a 'short *a*'. Such statements, often useful (sometimes even indispensable) in describing aspects of English spelling, are not accurate for Modern English in phonetic terms: for example, in *mate*, neither the /eɪ/ sound of RP nor the /e/ sound of ScoE is a 'long' version of the RP /æ/ or ScoE /a/ in *bat*. The differences in the two systems (the traditional and orthographic on the one hand and the phonetic on the other) make a consistent and clear discussion of English spelling and pronunciation difficult (as for example in the entries for the letters A, E, I, O, and U in this volume).

Phonetics. Phoneticians use the terms *long* and *short* to discuss only the degree of duration, greater or less, in a particular speech sound, usually a vowel. The relative value 'long' is shown by means of a *length mark* (ː) after a vowel symbol, as in /aː/, where unadapted /a/ is the unmarked short equivalent: see LENGTH MARK. Even so, however, a vowel sound referred to as having both a long and a short value is not necessarily always one vowel in qualitative terms: for example, in English, the *long i* represented by the IPA symbol /i/ and the *short i* represented by /ɪ/ are qualitatively as well as quantitatively different. In addition, each is a distinct phoneme: /hit/ (that is, *heat*), for example, is very different in sound and sense from /hɪt/ (*hit*). In dictionaries and other works intended for foreign learners of English, long *i* is often visually reinforced by a length mark, /iː/, as in /hiːt/: see LEARNER'S DICTIONARY. Sometimes, but not in English, quantitative difference alone can be phonemic: for example, contrast the long and short vowels in German *Bahn* (path, track) and *Bann* (magic spell). See COMMON, METRE/METER, QUANTITY, VOWEL, VOWEL QUANTITY. [SPEECH, WRITING].   T.MCA.

LONGHAND, also **long-hand** [17c]. Conventional handwriting, in which every word is written in full: *taking notes in longhand*; *a longhand report of what they said*. See HAND. Compare SHORTHAND. [WRITING].   T.MCA.

LONGMAN. The oldest commercial publishing house in Britain, founded in 1724 by Thomas Longman, son of a Bristol merchant. His business was conducted at the sign of the Ship and Black Swan in Paternoster Row in London, whence the company logo of a ship in full sail. After being owned by seven generations of the family, the company was acquired in 1968 by the Pearson Group, which has interests in publishing, information, and entertainment. Since 1969, only the name *Longman* has appeared on the company's publications, but earlier works have *Longmans* or *Longmans, Green & Co*, or, in the 19c, long lists of partners. The *Longman Group* is currently an international publisher in education (including ELT and works of reference), medicine, technology, and science, with an annual turnover close to £200m. The firm's premises in London, along with part of its archives, were destroyed by incendiary bombs in 1940. Modern records are kept in the library of the U. of Reading. Longman moved to Harlow in Essex in the 1960s.

Johnson and Roget. After acquiring the rights of the 4th edition of Bailey's *Universal Etymological Dictionary* (1728), Thomas Longman became one of five book-sellers who in 1746 signed a contract with Samuel Johnson for the compilation of *A Dictionary of the English Language* (published in two volumes in 1755). Thomas Longman II, the founder's nephew and heir, published later editions of Johnson's dictionary, as well as those of William Kenrick and Thomas Sheridan. His son, Thomas Norton Longman III, acquired sole rights to Johnson's dictionary in 1805; the company published the editions revised by H. J. Todd and R. G. Latham before bringing the series to an end in the 1880s. Longman also published Wordsworth and Coleridge, Disraeli, Macaulay, and Scott, and in 1852 brought out a first edition of 100 copies of Peter Mark Roget's *Thesaurus of English Words and Phrases*, which has been published by Longman ever since and has sold over 30m copies. The name *Roget* was registered in the UK in 1990 as a trademark belonging to Longman.

ELT and dictionaries. The firm has been active in Africa, the Caribbean, and West Asia, and in India as *Orient Longman*. Its extensive and often pioneering ELT publishing has included Michael West's New Method Readers (1920s), *New Method English Dictionary* (1935: the first specifically ELT dictionary), and *General Service List of English Words* (1952), C. E. Eckersley's *Essential English for Foreign Students* (1938), and L. G. Alexander's *New Concept English* (1967) and *Look, Listen and Learn* (1968–71). In 1978, the company published the *Longman Dictionary of Contemporary English* (ed. Paul Procter), an advanced learner's dictionary (2nd edition 1987, ed. Della Summers) with a defining vocabulary of 2,000 words. Its offshoots include the *Longman Dictionary of American English* (1983) and the *Longman Active Study Dictionary* (1983, 2nd edition 1991). It also provided material for the *Longman Lexicon of Contemporary English* (1981, ed. Tom McArthur), a thematic wordbook with semantic fields and contrastive definitions. The 1,876-page *Longman Dictionary of the English Language* (1984, 2nd edition 1991) is a substantial revision and Briticization of *Webster's New Collegiate Dictionary*, and has a range of offshoots. Current dictionaries benefit from one of the first UK computerized compiling systems, a collection of some 0.5m citation slips, and the Longman/Lancaster Corpus of 30m running words.

Language and literature. In 1795, Longman published Lindley Murray's *English Grammar*, which led the field until superseded by another Longman publication, Alexander Bain's *English Grammar* (1863). This tradition was revived in 1972 with *A Grammar of Contemporary English*, expanded in 1985 as *A Comprehensive Grammar of the English Language*, by Randolph Quirk, Sidney Greenbaum, Geoffrey Leech, and Jan Svartvik. Linguistics and phonetics are a significant part of the Longman list, including titles in the Longman Linguistics Library, edited by R. H. Robins, the English Language Series, edited by Randolph Quirk, and the *Longman Pronunciation Dictionary*, compiled by John C. Wells (1990). In the field of world literature in English, Longman is currently developing the Longman Literature in English series, edited by David Carroll and Michael Wheeler, whose sections include pre-Renaissance literature, poetry, drama, fiction, prose, criticism and theory, intellectual and cultural contexts, and national and regional literatures (such as American, Australian, Canadian, and Indian).

See ALEXANDER (L.), BAILEY (N.), BRITISH NATIONAL CORPUS, COMPREHENSIVE GRAMMAR OF THE ENGLISH LANGUAGE, DEFINING VOCABULARY, ENGLISH-SPEAKING UNION, GENERAL SERVICE LIST, IDIOM, JOHNSON, LEARNER'S DICTIONARY, LEXICON, PENGUIN, QUIRK, RECEIVED PRONUNCIATION, ROGET'S THESAURUS, WEBSTER'S COLLEGIATE DICTIONARIES, WEST. [EDUCATION, EUROPE, MEDIA]. T.MCA.

LONG S. Formerly, a variant of the lower-case letter *s* (roman form ſ, italic ſ) in initial and medial positions in words, such as *ſin* for *sin*, *ſleep* for *sleep*, *ſhall* for *shall*, *himſelf* for *himself*, *graſs* for *grass*, *thouſand* for *thousand*, *conſcience* for *conscience*, *poſſeſs* for *possess*. After 1800, the greater convenience of *s* for all positions prevailed, and ſ fell into disuse in English. In Germany and Austria, but not Switzerland, the variation survives vestigially in the combined ß (called 'eszett') for *ss* in most positions, as in *groß* (= *gross* big, great). See ALPHABET, ESH, LETTER[1]. [WRITING]. C.U.

LONG WORD [15c]. (1) Obsolete and only in the plural: a long speech or discourse: 'Dame what shall avaylle thenne Longe wordes?' (Caxton, *Dialogues*, c.1483). (2) A polysyllabic word, especially of Latin or Greek origin, and if uncommon and difficult to spell or pronounce, such as *diuretic* or *phantasmagorical*: 'He ain't like old Veal, who is always bragging and using such long words, don't you know?' (Thackeray, *Vanity Fair*, 1848). People often ask what the longest word in English might be, but the answer depends on what can be accepted as a word. Some chemical combinations have names of over 1,000 letters, but these are usually amalgams of combining elements rather than words in the commonly understood sense: for example, the full chemical name, 1,913 letters long, for *tryptophan synthetase A protein* (an enzyme with 267 amino acids) begins *methionylglutaminylarginyltyrosyl* . . ., and is listed in full in *Mrs Byrne's Dictionary* (1974). James Joyce invented several 100-letter words in *Finnegans Wake* (1939). Thomas Love Peacock's *Headlong Hall* (1816) describes the human body as *osseocarnisanguineoviscericartilaginonervomedullary* (51

letters). The longest word in the 1st edition of the *OED* is *floccinaucinihilipilification* (29 letters), 'the action or habit of estimating something as worthless', which the *Supplement* of 1982 topped with the lung disease *pneumonoultramicroscopicsilicovolcanoconiosis* (45 letters). This is longer than *supercalifragilisticexpialidocious* (34 letters), the title of a song in the film *Mary Poppins* (1964), and *antidisestablishmentarianism* (28 letters). The longest word in Shakespeare is the Latin *honorificabilitudinitatibus* (27 letters), used by Costard in *Love's Labour's Lost*. See BIG WORD, DERIVATION, HARD WORD, WORD-FORMATION. [WORD]. T.MCA., T.A.

LOOKALIKE. See CONFUSIBLE, FAUX AMI.

LORIMER, William Laughton [1885-1967]. Scottish classicist and translator, born at Strathmartine in Angus, educated at Dundee High School, Fettes College, and Oxford. He taught classics at U. College, Dundee, and the U. of St Andrews, where he became Professor of Greek in 1953. From 1946 until his death he contributed to the *Scottish National Dictionary*, and served from 1947 as member and later chairman of the Executive Council of the Scottish National Dictionary Association. He is especially remembered for his *New Testament in Scots*. Though completed shortly before his death in 1967, this work was not published until 1983, edited by his son R. L. C. Lorimer and published by the W. L. Lorimer Memorial Trust. The book was greatly acclaimed and republished in 1985 by Penguin Books. Lorimer was uniquely qualified for this project by his knowledge of Bible scholarship, the classical languages, several modern European languages and dialects, and a lifelong enthusiasm for literary and spoken Scots. To prepare the translation, made from the original texts, he studied versions of the Bible in many languages, including tongues of comparable status to Scots, such as Frisian and Rhaeto-Romansch. The special orthography is consistent and, to a greater extent than any translation in English, the *New Testament in Scots* employs a variety of styles to reflect those of the original. The translation is the greatest achievement of modern Scots prose. For an illustrative excerpt, see BIBLE. [BIOGRAPHY, EUROPE, LITERATURE]. J.D.M.

LOUISIANA. See AMERICAN PLACE-NAMES, CAJUN, DIALECT IN AMERICA, NEW ORLEANS, SOUTH (THE), SOUTHERN ENGLISH.

LOW DUTCH. See FLEMISH, LOW GERMAN.

LOWER CASE. In the present-day printed Roman alphabet, small letters of varying size, known as *lower-case letters*, as distinguished from capitals or *upper-case* letters. See CAPITAL (LETTER), CASE², LETTER¹, PRINTING. [TECHNOLOGY]. W.W.B.

LOW GERMAN. [1830s: a translation of German *Plattdeutsch*]. (1) Also *Plattdeutsch*. Dialects of German other than *High German* (*Hochdeutsch*), especially in Saxony and Westphalia: 'Then, too, *cambric, hawker, muff*, and *scone* found their way [into English] from Dutch and Low German' (Simeon Potter, *Our Language*, 1966). (2) All West Germanic languages except High German and English (that is, Dutch, Flemish, Frisian, and Plattdeutsch): 'Some [English words] may be of native origin, but their history is often obscure. They appear to be Low German in form, and to have been introduced from the Netherlands or Friesland or Hanover at various dates' (W. W. Skeat, *Etymological Dictionary of the English Language*, 1879–82). (3) Also sometimes *Low Dutch*. All West Germanic languages except High German, and including English: 'High German and Low German, the latter including certain German dialects, Dutch, Flemish, Frisian, and English in all the forms it has taken throughout the world' (Barbara Strang, *A History of English*, 1970, p. 405). Ambiguities arise because of the various applications of the term, as when in the same work Strang says: 'The debt of English to Low German (Dutch, Flemish, Saxon) chiefly reflects maritime relations' (p. 123). See GERMAN, INGVAEONIC, SAXON. [EUROPE, LANGUAGE]. T.MCA.

LOWLAND SCOTS, sometimes **Lowland Scotch**. A common name for the Scottish dialects of northern English that stresses both their location east and south of the Highland Line and their distinctness from the languages of the Highlands (*Gaelic* and *Highland English*). In the Middle Ages, Gaelic was known in Latin as *lingua Scotica* (the Scottish language) and some Gaels therefore claim that the Lowland tongue has usurped the name *Scots*. However, the usage dates from the 16c, and the 18c addition of *Lowland* serves to remove any ambiguity. See DORIC, INGLIS, LALLANS, SCOTS. [EUROPE, VARIETY]. A.J.A.

LOWLAND SOUTHERN. See SOUTHERN ENGLISH.

LOW LANGUAGES. See CLASSICAL LANGUAGE, DIGLOSSIA, VERNACULAR.

LOWTH, Robert [1710–87]. English clergyman and grammarian, born in Winchester, educated at Winchester School and New College, Oxford. Appointed Bishop of London in 1777, Lowth was a philologist 'more inclined to melancholy than to mirth', who believed that Hebrew was spoken in paradise. His *Short Introduction to English Grammar* (1762) became a standard textbook, and his name has become synonymous with prescriptive grammar. Lowth's reputation as a prescriptivist is not entirely deserved. Though he liberally illustrated his grammar rules with errors to be found in the English Bible and in standard authors, his approach to correctness was not invariably rigid and, like most grammarians, he described English as well as prescribing its rules. While Lowth advised against ending sentences with prepositions, he acknowledged the construction as 'an idiom, which our language is strongly inclined to'. Lowth also distinguished between *shall* and *will* as the future auxiliary, yet he noted that the pattern is a new one that took hold in the language after 'the vulgar translation of the Bible'. Lowth was convinced that English is rule-governed, and he defended the regularity and simplicity of the language against a tradition which viewed it as too primitive to possess any grammar at all. His model was Latin grammar, but he readily modified this to accommodate the idiosyncrasies of English. He also championed English language study in school, arguing that it facilitated the acquisition of the classics as well as the concept of universal grammar. See index. [BIOGRAPHY, EUROPE, GRAMMAR]. D.E.B.

L-SOUNDS. There are various ways in which the letter *l* is expressed in English. In phonetic terms, /l/ is made by raising the tongue tip to make and maintain central contact with the alveolar ridge, allowing air to escape round the sides. Variations can be made by changing the shape of the tongue behind the apical closure. A *dark l* [ɫ] is made by pulling the body of the tongue backwards, and a *clear l* [l] by pushing it up and forward towards the hard palate. Dark *l* is characteristic of the speech of northern England (excluding Geordie) and southern Scotland; clear *l* is characteristic of southern Ireland and India. Both types are heard in Northern Ireland and northern Scotland, and widely in AmE. In the speech of southern England and in varieties that developed from it, such as AusE, /l/ tends to be clear before the vowel in a syllable, as in *lick* /lɪk/, and dark after it, as in *kill* /kɪɫ/. As the tongue takes up the position for /ɫ/, a transitional schwa-like sound may be heard: /kɪəɫ/. Dark *l* may be accompanied by lip rounding, which often begins on the transitional vowel, making it sound more like /ʊ/, as in /kɪʊɫ/. The transitional vowel indicates that a dark *l* follows immediately, and the /l/ is in effect redundant. In some varieties, such as that of south-east England (in particular Cockney) and AusE, dark *l* is frequently vocalized (turned into a vowel), because the tongue tip does not make a central closure with the alveolar ridge. This 'l' therefore sounds like a back vowel or /w/: /kɪʊ/, /kɪw/ for *kill*. In NZE, where the influence of ScoE is strong, /l/ can be dark in all environments, but the clear/dark distinction as in RP is widespread. If, instead of maintaining central contact, the tongue strikes the alveolar ridge momentarily, or is held close to it, the result to the ears of native speakers of English is a kind of /r/. Some languages, such as Chinese and Japanese, have a single phoneme, in which the tongue contact is optional. When speakers of these languages speak English, they appear to mix up /l/ and /r/, as in the shibboleths of Chinese English *velly solly* (very sorry) and Japanese English *I rub you* (I love you). Many personal-name diminutives in English have *l* rather than *r*, as with *Hal* for *Harry*, *Del* for *Derek*, and *Tel* for *Terry*. See ALVEOLAR, APICAL, CONSONANT, LALLATION, LAMBDACISM, LATERAL, LIQUID, R-SOUNDS, SOMERSET. [SPEECH].

G.K., L.T.

LYLY, John [*c*.1554–1606]. English writer and Member of Parliament, born in Kent, and educated at Oxford and Cambridge. Known as 'the Euphuist', he was one of the first prose stylists to leave a lasting mark on the language. He wrote the two-part romance *Euphues, or the Anatomie of Wit* (1578) and *Euphues and his England* (1580), an early epistolary 'novel' with comments on religion, love, and style. His 'new English' favoured an ornate, classical style widely admired during the Renaissance and known to this day as *euphemism*: see entry. His prose comedies, performed by boy actors, include *Campaspe* and *Sappho and Phao* (*c*.1583), *Endimion*

(1586–7), and *Midas* (1589), and strongly develop dialogue. His popularity, however, was eclipsed by Shakespeare, Marlowe, and other playwrights, and he died in embittered poverty. See index. [BIOGRAPHY, EUROPE, HISTORY, LITERATURE, STYLE].

T.MCA.

LYRIC [16c: from Latin *lyricus*, Greek *lurikós*, of the lyre, referring to a poem sung to its accompaniment, especially as composed by Sappho, Pindar, and other poets *c*.7–6c BC. The Roman poets Catullus and Horace wrote similar poems, but to be read aloud rather than sung]. (1) Having the form and musical quality of a song: *lyric poetry* (contrasting with *narrative poetry*). (2) A usually short poem that expresses personal feelings, and may or may not be set to music: *a Romantic lyric*. The plural *lyrics* can refer to the words of a song, echoing the original Greek usage: *Who wrote the lyrics for that song?* In the Middle Ages and later, lyrical songs were written on many subjects and were often popular in style and content; they helped lay the foundations of English poetry, at times in the face of ecclesiastical disapproval. Such songs appear in Elizabethan and Jacobean plays, and on the Roman model lyrical poems were written to be read aloud or silently; they came to be regarded as essentially poems of personal feeling, and especially of love. The term was seldom further defined, and is used of almost any poem that is not clearly narrative, dramatic, or satirical. Although the lyric is usually short, the lyrical mood can extend into the ode and the elegy. The lyric has no prerequisite of form, metre, rhyme, or wording: a present-day lyrical poem may use colloquial and even coarse language. See CHORUS, GENRE, POETRY, VERSE, WORDSWORTH. [LITERATURE].

R.C.

M

M, m [Called 'em']. The 13th letter of the Roman alphabet as used for English. It originated in the Phoenician symbol *mem*, a zigzag line probably representing water (the word for which began with that letter: compare Hebrew *mayim* water). It was adapted by the Greeks as *mu* (*M*) and adopted with the same sound value by the Etruscans and the Romans.

Sound value The sound represented by *m* is normally a voiced bilabial nasal, but before /f/ the closure may be labio-dental rather than bilabial (*comfort*), and before /b, p/ an *n* may be pronounced /m/: *none better* ('numbetter'), *input* ('imput'). Assimilation of this kind helped turn the late Middle English phrase *in kenebowe* ('in keen bow', that is, in a sharp curve) into present-day *akimbo*.

Double M. (1) Final *m* is normally single in monosyllabic words: *am, aim, tame, rim, time, home, some, room, gum, fume, rhyme*. A suffix beginning with a vowel prompts *mm* after a short vowel (*jammed, brimming, drummer*), unless a silent consonant or final *e* in the base word intervenes (*thumbed, coming, damning*: contrast *damming*). (2) Medial *mm* normally signifies a preceding short vowel (contrast *comma/coma*), and also occurs in assimilations of Latin prefixes ending in *n*: *immaterial* (not *inmaterial*). Similarly, Greek *syn-* produces *mm* in *symmetry*. (3) *M*-doubling is inconsistent after short vowels, as shown by the pairs *camel/mammal, image/scrimmage, lemon/lemming*, prompting such common consequent misspellings as *accomodate, *ommit*.

Syllabic M The letter *m* can function syllabically, as in *rhythm, chasm*. See SYLLABIC CONSONANT.

Silent M. The *m* is silent in initial Greek-derived *mn-* (*mnemonic, Mnemosyne*), but is pronounced after a prefix (*amnesia*). See ALPHABET, B, EM, LETTER[1], SPELLING. [WRITING].   C.U.

MACAO, also **Macau**. An overseas province of Portugal close to Hong Kong. Population: *c.*260,000 (90% Chinese). Portuguese is the official language, Cantonese is generally spoken, and English is seen as vital for modernization, resulting in a growing demand for courses. Macao's private U. of East Asia, many of whose students are Hong Kong citizens, uses English as its medium of instruction. See CHINA, HONG KONG, PORTUGUESE. [ASIA, NAME].   J.P., H.W.

MACARONIC [17c: from Latin *macaronicus* and older Italian *macaronico* (modern *maccheronico*), from Greek *makaría* barley food. First recorded in the *Carmen macaronicum de Patavinis* (1490), popularized in the *Liber Macaronices* of the monk Teofilo Folengo (1517), who described his verses as literary macaroni: 'a gross, rude, and rustic mixture of flour, cheese, and butter']. (1) Burlesque verse in which Latin and vernacular words with Latin endings are mixed, such as the following lines attributed to William Drummond (1684): 'Maggeam, magis doctam milkare coweas, / Et doctam sweepare flooras, et sternere beddas' (Maggie, trained up in milking cows, sweeping floors, and making beds). (2) Serious vernacular verse in which Latin elements are incorporated into a native pattern of metre and rhyme. The practice predates the name, as for example mingled Latin and Old English at the conclusion of the late 9c poem *The Phoenix*. Macaronics of this kind were common in English when Latin was the language of learning, as in William Dunbar's 'Lament for the Makaris' (*c.*1507):

I that in heill wes and gladnes
Am trublit now with gret seiknes

THE CAPITAL LETTER

EARLY FORMS				CURRENT FORMS	
Phoenician	Greek	Etruscan	Roman (Latin)	roman	italic
⌇	MM	⋎	M	M	*M*

THE SMALL LETTER

EARLY FORMS			CURRENT FORMS	
Roman cursive	Roman uncial	Carolingian minuscule	roman	italic
⌒	ꟽ	ℳ	m	*m*

And feblit with infirmitie:
Timor mortis conturbat me.

[*heill* health, *wes* was, *trublit* troubled, *gret seiknes* great sickness, *feblit* enfeebled]

(3) Although the term usually refers to Latin and a vernacular together, macaronic verse is possible in principle between any two languages and any two varieties of a language: for example, in Scottish songs translated from Gaelic, the refrain and occasional phrases often remain in the original language. Comparably, there is sometimes a macaronic quality in the poetry of Robert Burns, vernacular Scots being mixed with Augustan English:

November chill blaws loud /lud/ wi' angry
   sough /sux/;
The short'ning winter-day is near a close;
The miry beasts retreating frae the pleugh /plux/;
The black'ning trains o' craws to their repose.
                 ('The Cotter's Saturday Night', 1786)

Compare CODE-MIXING AND CODE-SWITCHING. [LITERATURE, STYLE].   R.C., T.MCA.

MACAULAY, T(homas) B(abington) [1800–59]. British essayist, critic, poet, and historian, born in Rothley Temple, Leicestershire, son of the Presbyterian philanthropist Zachary Macaulay, who hailed from the Hebrides, had been governor of Sierra Leone, and opposed slavery. His mother was a Quaker and the daughter of a Bristol book-seller. At the age of eight he wrote 'The Battle of Cheviot', a romantic poem in the style of Sir Walter Scott. Macaulay was educated at a private school and Trinity College Cambridge, and intended a career in law, but an essay on Milton for the *Edinburgh Review* in 1825 brought him sudden fame and led to many subsequent articles. In 1830, he became Whig Member of Parliament for Calne in Wiltshire and helped pass the Reform Act of 1832. He became a member, then secretary, of the Board of Control that oversaw the work of the East India Company in India, and in 1834 went there to serve on the new Supreme Council of India. He played a part in the slow transfer of government from Company to Crown, and supported both freedom of the press and the equality of Indians and Europeans before the law. He set up a national system of education and in 1835 wrote the Minute that made English the subcontinent's future language of education: see INDIAN ENGLISH[1].

Macaulay returned to Britain in 1838, and began his *History of England*, which appeared in five volumes (1849–61) and covered only the period 1688–1702, yet was one of the best-selling books of the century in the UK and US and was translated into many languages. He was elected MP for Edinburgh in 1839 and 1852. In addition to holding major government offices, he wrote

copiously, including in 1842 the immensely popular *Lays of Ancient Rome*, which remained in use in schools well into the 20c. Although often criticized in his lifetime and later for shallowness, overconfidence (especially in the civilizing role of the Empire), narrowness of interests, and a tendency to glamorize history, Macaulay was markedly successful as a writer of popular history and criticism. His style was special pleading, not impartial assessment. Its emphatic manner and short sentences greatly influenced 'quality' journalism. He never married, was raised to the peerage in 1857, and died two years later from heart disease. See index. [ASIA, BIOGRAPHY, EUROPE, HISTORY, WRITING].   T.MCA.

McDAVID, Raven I(oor), Jr [1911–84]. American dialect geographer, born in Greenville, South Carolina, and educated at Furman U., completing a Ph.D. on Milton at Duke U. in 1935. McDavid came to an early appreciation of speech varieties and cultural stereotypes when he found 'speech correctionists' from outside his native region eager to alter his locally standard dialect. In 1937, he attended a summer school at the U. of Michigan where Bernard Bloch, a fieldworker for the *Linguistic Atlas of New England*, taught linguistic geography and selected him as an informant for the course. The excitement of dialect study that summer shaped his subsequent career. During World War II, along with other linguists he prepared language materials to assist in the war effort; his tasks included studies of Burmese and pedagogical tools to assist Italians learning English. In 1945, McDavid turned full-time to fieldwork for the *Linguistic Atlas of the Middle and South Atlantic States* (*LAMSAS*) under the general direction of Hans Kurath. He conducted several hundred field interviews recorded in precise phonetic transcription, not only in the South Atlantic region, but later in the Middle Atlantic and North Central States as well. McDavid joined the U. of Chicago in 1957 where he remained until retirement and beyond. When Kurath retired from active management of the *Linguistic Atlas* projects, McDavid became his successor. Editing *LAMSAS* and the *Linguistic Atlas of the North Central States* began under his direction and is continued today by his successors. With Kurath, he was co-author of the first comprehensive work drawing on *Atlas* files: *The Pronunciation of English in the Atlantic States* (1961). His abridgement and updating of Mencken's *American Language* (1963) renewed the popularity of that book. His many essays were revised and collected in two volumes: *Dialects in Culture* (1979) and *Varieties of American English* (1980). In 1972, his colleagues and former students published a congratulatory volume, *Studies in Linguistics in Honor of Raven I. McDavid, Jr.* See index. [AMERICAS, BIOGRAPHY, LANGUAGE, VARIETY].

R.W.B.

MacDIARMID, Hugh, pen name of *Christopher Murray Grieve* [1892-1978]. Scottish poet, critic, and polemicist, leader of the Lallans movement. Born and educated in Langholm, a Border town whose dialect and traditions contributed to the striking individuality of his poetic style, Grieve was a founder (1928) of the National Party of Scotland (expelled 1933) and a member of the Communist Party (expelled 1938, rejoined 1956). Although passionately committed to Scottish cultural and political nationalism, he was at first unconvinced of the viability of Scots for 20c poetry. He deplored the sentimentality of poets since Robert Burns and strongly disapproved of the North-East dialect writing of Charles Murray. His discovery of the extent and expressiveness of Scots vocabulary, however, particularly as recorded in Jamieson's *Etymological Dictionary of the Scottish Language* (1808), prompted him to experiment with a Synthetic Scots, first for short lyrics, then for extended metaphysical poem-sequences (most importantly *A Drunk Man Looks at the Thistle,* 1926) showing great linguistic virtuosity and an adventurous spirit of philosophical exploration not attempted in Scots poetry since medieval times. His omnivorous learning, social and political extremism, and exuberant fondness for linguistic effects formed an explosive and controversial poetic compound. His Scots is often difficult and challenging, but his success in revitalizing poetry in the language has been marked. In later life, he adopted English for equally experimental poetry, but other poets have continued his practice of writing effectively in Lallans. See index. [BIOGRAPHY, EUROPE, LITERATURE, VARIETY].

J.D.M.

MACHINE LANGUAGE [Later 20c]. Also **machine code.** A term in computing for information in a form which can be used by a machine such as a computer, in particular the system of numbers and/or instructions for the processing of data, usually by means of a binary code. Most programmers write in higher-level computer languages which are translated into a machine language to be executed by a *compiler* such as *Turbo Pascal,* designed for the language Pascal as used on IBM personal computers. Thus, a high-level language statement such as $x = x + I$ (add one to the variable x) must be turned into a three-instruction sequence: 'Load x from main memory into a central part of the processor; add one to that central item; store the result in the main memory location which holds the variable x.' See COMPUTING. [LANGUAGE, TECHNOLOGY].

M.L.

MACHINE-READABLE TEXT [Later 20c]. A term in computing for: (1) A text that can be read by a machine. (2) Such products of electronic publishing as information on magnetic tapes and laser discs. (3) Electronic versions of printed texts, created so that the material can be processed by computer in various ways and for various purposes. A machine-readable version of a large novel such as Herman Melville's *Moby-Dick* represents about a megabyte of computer storage. With machine-readable text, concordances can quickly be made for such a work, showing each occurrence of every word in context. Often, however, traditional texts are not available in machine-readable form. The availability of computer tapes or discs varies widely by subject and language: the entire corpus of classical Greek literature is available from the *Thesaurus Linguae Graecae* at the U. of Nancy in France, but English literature, being a much larger living tradition, is less well covered. There are, however, major archives, such as at Oxford in England, Brigham Young in Utah, and Lund in Sweden. The Oxford Text Archive serves as an international coordinating point for the effort to accumulate material in machine-readable form. See COMPUTING, TEXT. [TECHNOLOGY, WRITING].

M.L.

MACHINE TRANSLATION. Translation by computer. In 1949, the US mathematician Warren Weaver, reflecting on the wartime successes of computers at cryptography, proposed that they might be able to translate languages: 'It is very tempting to say that a book written in Chinese is simply a book written in English which was coded into the *Chinese code*' (in *Machine Translation of Languages,* ed. W. N. Locke & A. D. Booth, 1955, pp. 15-27). This suggestion stimulated research in the 1950s, which however found the problem too hard to solve with the technology then available. Word-by-word translation was tried first, but the result was confusing because of the many senses and therefore translations a word might have unless the context could be recognized by the machine. To go beyond word-by-word translation, it proved necessary to parse the languages concerned, something which depends on having a comprehensive description of those languages. Even with an adequate grammar, however, it is difficult for a computer to parse unambiguously, because it does not have a sufficient knowledge of the world that humans invoke intuitively when disambiguating such sentences as *I am going to run* (where *run* means either 'to move rapidly on foot' or, especially in AmE, 'to offer oneself for election'). Research was curtailed in the early 1960s and efforts have focused on creating aids for human translators, in particular word lists for special subjects. Some systems use a 'raw' translation which is then edited. It has proved possible to produce systems which operate well in limited areas, the best-known being a weather-report system designed in Canada by Ray Kittredge of the U. of Montreal (1974–6). Most researchers, however, consider that a fully automatic translation program for a wide subject area requires advances in computational linguistics rather than in technology. See COMPUTATIONAL LINGUISTICS, TRANSLATION. [LANGUAGE, TECHNOLOGY].   M.L., T.MCA.

MACHINE WORD [Later 20c]. A term in computing for a string of bits, characters, or bytes that is treated as one unit by a computer. [TECHNOLOGY, WORD].   T.MCA.

McLUHAN, (Herbert) Marshall [1911–80]. Canadian literary critic and communication theorist, born in Edmonton, Alberta, and educated at the U. of Manitoba (BA 1933, MA 1934) and the U. of Cambridge (BA 1936, MA 1939, Ph.D. 1943). In 1946, he began to teach literature at the U. of Toronto, where he met and was influenced by Harold Innis, and began the work on communication which led to the founding of the university's Centre for Culture and Technology, which he directed from 1963 until 1979. His publications include *The Mechanical Bride: Folklore of Industrial Man* (1951), *The Gutenberg Galaxy* (1962), *Understanding Media: The Extensions of Man* (1964), and *The Medium is the Message* (1967). In the 1960s, his controversial ideas about the impact of the media on the mind gained international currency. His phrase *the global village* and the aphorism *the medium is the message* have become part of the language. McLuhan postulated an oral tribal culture which involved all the senses, followed by a print culture (the Gutenberg galaxy), which favoured reason and sight, followed by a global village formed by television, which promoted a return to 'tribal' values. An account of his life and work is given by Philip Marchand in *The Medium and the Messenger* (New York: Random House, 1989) and a symposium on his theories has been edited by G. E. Stearn, *McLuhan Hot and Cool* (Harmondsworth: Penguin, 1968). See index. [AMERICAS, BIOGRAPHY, MEDIA].   M.F.

MACMILLAN. An international British-based publishing company that includes the London-based *Sidgwick & Jackson* and the paperback publisher *Pan Books*, and the New York-based *St Martin's Press* and *Stockton Press*; the original US house, now *Macmillan Inc.*, was sold in 1952 and is a separate organization. The company was founded in 1843 in London and Cambridge by the brothers Daniel and Alexander Macmillan, and remains a private company controlled by the Macmillan family trusts. The current president is the Earl of Stockton, grandson of Harold Macmillan, the British Prime Minister, who worked for the firm for many years. Macmillan publish across the spectrum: fiction; non-fiction; children's books; journals and magazines (including *Nature*, the leading international science weekly); reference books (including *The Statesman's Year-Book* and *The Macmillan Encyclopedia*); university, college, and school textbooks; academic, scientific, technical, medical, business, and management books; and ELT books. Macmillan authors include Kipling, Hardy, Tennyson, Yeats, and O'Casey, and well-known titles include Margaret Mitchell's *Gone with the Wind*, J. G. Frazer's *The Golden Bough*, and Lewis Carroll's *Alice in Wonderland*. See CARROLL, HARDY, KIPLING, TENNYSON. [EDUCATION, EUROPE, MEDIA].   T.MCA.

MACQUARIE DICTIONARY, The. See AUSTRALIAN DICTIONARIES.

MACRON [1850s: from Greek *makrón*, neuter of *makrós* large]. Also less formally **stroke, bar**. A traditional diacritic in the form of a horizontal bar over a vowel letter (ˉ), to show that it is long (as in some renderings of Latin and Maori words). From its use in classical scansion to indicate a long syllable, it has come to indicate in English scansion that the syllable in which it occurs is stressed (contrasting with the *breve*). Similarly, the macron has been used over vowel symbols in the respelling systems of English dictionaries and in teaching grammars to mark traditional 'long' vowels, which include diphthongs. See BREVE, LENGTH MARK, LONG AND SHORT, SCANSION. [LITERATURE, SPEECH, WRITING].   T.MCA.

McWORD [1983 AmE: coined by Paul Dickson on the analogy of *McMuffin*, *McChicken*, etc.: see below. The first element derives from Gaelic *mac* son of, as in many Scottish and Irish names, such as *Macintosh*, *Mackintosh*, *MacIntosh*, *McIntosh*, the Anglicized variants of *Mac an Toiseich* Son of the Chief]. An informal term for certain words beginning with *Mc* or *Mac*. The McDonald Hamburger company was set up in 1955 in Illinois by the entrepreneur Ray Kroc. Its leading product, the *Big Mac*, is accompanied by such other quasi-Scottish foodstuffs as *Chicken McNuggets* and *Egg McMuffin*. By analogy, Kroc's business has been referred to facetiously as a *McEmpire*, and related coinages suggest the quick, cheap, and superficial, as with *McFashion* pre-packaged clothing, *McPaper* (a dismissive name for) the newspaper *USA Today*, *News McNuggets* its news reports, *McLatin* classical studies made easy, and *McWar* 'a fast, cheap, well-packaged conflict that makes you feel good and doesn't cause indigestion' (*Independent Magazine*, 26 Jan. 1991). This range of McWords is distinct from another that emerged after an Apple personal computer (California, mid-1980s) was named after the Macintosh apple. This led to the short forms *Apple Mac* and *Mac*, names for software such as *MacWrite*, *MacPaint*, and *MacAuthor*, and periodicals with such names as *Mac World* and *The MACazine*. In computing, the *mac* prefix is neutral or positive. In the words based on *McDonalds*, the stress is usually on the syllable following *Mc*; in the computer words, *Mac* usually receives full stress.

Special uses of *mac* are older than hamburger franchises and personal computers. Because of the many *mac*-names, the patronymic element has long been used in Scotland as a casual form of address by one man to another whose name he does not know ('Hi, Mac, ye got the time?'); through emigration this usage spread to North America. In addition, someone with a *mac*-name may be referred to simply as *Mac* ('Where's Mac gone?'). The BrE abbreviations *mac* and *mack* stand for *mac(k)intosh*, the light raincoat invented by Charles Macintosh (d.1843). *Mac* also appears in the blend *tarmac*, short for the trade name *Tarmacadam* (after its inventor John McAdam, d.1836), and *CalMac*, the syllabic acronym for *Caledonian MacBrayne*, a Scottish ferry company. It also occurs in such facetious usages as *MacBeeb* (an informal name for the BBC in Scotland), *MacHISmo* (a stunt term protesting against Scottish male chauvinists), and *McYuppie* (a young Scottish urban professional). See PATRONYMIC. [AMERICAS, EUROPE, NAME, WORD].   T.MCA.

MAGAZINE [16c: from French *magasin* a store, shop, from Italian *magazzino* a storehouse, from Arabic *makhāzin*, plural of *makhzan* a storehouse. Figuratively developed in English as a storehouse of information: compare THESAURUS]. A publication issued periodically and intended for a wide circle of readers, usually bound in a paper cover, and typically containing articles, stories, poems, pictures, advertisements, etc. However specialized a magazine may be, there is always a suggestion of a miscellany about it. The first English publication to use the name, the *Gentleman's Magazine* (1731), described itself as 'a Monthly Collection to

Treasure up, as in a Magazine, the most remarkable Pieces on the Subjects abovemention'd'. Oliver Goldsmith may have summed up the objectives of the genre when he observed: 'It is the life and soul of a magazine never to be dull long upon one subject.'

British magazines. Until the late 19c, British magazines were predominantly literary and intellectual. Although the term is still used in such titles as *The London Magazine* or *Blackwood's Magazine*, which have maintained this characterization, the more serious publications in the field are now usually called *reviews* or *journals*. The more popular tone and format was announced with the appearance of George Newnes's *Tit-Bits from all the Most Interesting Books, Periodicals and Newspapers of the World* (1861). With increasingly sophisticated printing technology, the emphasis became pictorial rather than literary. There are now few British magazines which are purely verbal: indeed, some glossy magazines have 200-400 pages, of which over 50% may be devoted to consumer advertisements. Most serious ('heavy') British Sunday newspapers now incorporate such publications. When they first came out in the 1960s, they were known as *colour supplements*, but they are now promoted as magazines in their own right.

American magazines. The first US magazines, both published in 1741, were inspired by the *Gentleman's Magazine*. They were *The American Magazine, or A Monthly View of the Political State of the British Colonies* and Benjamin Franklin's *General Magazine and Historical Chronicle for All the British Plantations in America*. The first had three issues; the second, six. They were succeeded by a long line of short-lived magazines. Eventually some more enduring and influential publications appeared: *The North American Review* (1815), *The Saturday Evening Post* (1821), *Godey's Lady's Book* (1830), *The Knickerbocker* (1833), *New-Yorker* (1834), *Harper's New Monthly Magazine* (1850), *Atlantic Monthly* (1857), *Woman's Home Companion* (1873), *Ladies' Home Journal* (1883), *Good Housekeeping* (1885), *Collier's* (1888), *The Smart Set* (1890), *McClure's* (1892), *McCalls* (1897), *The Reader's Digest* (1922), *The American Mercury* (1924), *The New Yorker* (1925), *Life* (1936), and *Look* (1937). For the current scene, see AMERICAN PRESS.

American magazines have until recently served in lieu of national newspapers, providing a popular culture in which all could participate and a national perspective on issues which might otherwise have been left to merely local interpretations. In a nation the size of the US, in both area and population, such cultural binding served an important role in the history of the people. Magazines have provided their readers with literature, news, political commentary, muckraking, humour, entertainment, do-it-yourself guidance, social satire, titillation, and much else. The *National Era* in 1852 published Harriet Beecher Stowe's *Uncle Tom's Cabin* in serial form, struck a blow for the abolition of slavery, and helped provoke the Civil War. In 1870-1, *Harper's Weekly* led a successful attack on the Tweed Ring in New York's Tammany Hall. *McClure's* exposed the greed and exploitiveness of unrestrained capitalism. *The American Mercury* of H. L. Mencken and George Jean Nathan was the voice of iconoclasm, irony, scepticism, and cultural criticism of the 1920s.

Magazines, radio, and television. In the 20c, magazines have been a major growth area of popular publishing. Specialist magazines cater for every imaginable field and activity. In the UK, over 12,000 periodicals, magazines, bulletins, annuals, trade journals, and academic journals are published on a regular basis. There are some 40 women's magazines and over 60 dealing with particular sports, games, hobbies, and pastimes. Although some US magazines, such as the *Saturday Evening Post*, have succumbed to the competition of television, many continue to have enormous international circulations, *The Reader's Digest* over 16m, the *National Geographic* over 10m. For many people, magazines have been the most available and widely used form of continuing education, providing information about history, geography, literature, science, and the arts, as well as guidance on gardening, child-rearing, cooking, tailoring, home decoration, financial management, psychological coping, and conjugal adjustment.

Until the rise of television, magazines were the most available form of cheap, convenient entertainment in the English-speaking world. Radio served a similar function, but was more limited in what it could do. Magazines and television, however, both address the more powerful visual sense. During the third quarter of the 20c, coincident with a dramatic rise in the popularity of television, many general-interest, especially illustrated magazines went out of business. The shift in attention of a mass audience from reading such magazines to watching television has been a major factor in this decline, but it is an implicit tribute from television to the older genre that its programmes are generally organized in a similar format and content. See BROADCASTING, BULLETIN (THE), DIGEST, JOURNAL, JOURNALISM, NEWSMAGAZINE, NEWSPAPER, NEW YORKER (THE), PERIODICAL, PUNCH, READER'S DIGEST. [AMERICAS, EUROPE, MEDIA]. G.H.

MAGIC *E*. See DIGRAPH, E, VOWEL.

MAIN CLAUSE, also **principal clause**. A clause in a sentence to which other clauses are subordinated, and which is not itself a subordinate clause. In a simple sentence, the main clause is the entire sentence. In a compound sentence, there is more than one main clause. Complex sentences contain a main clause and one or more subordinate clauses. [GRAMMAR]. R.E.A.

MAINSTREAM [17c]. A term for the main element or direction in a society, activity, etc.: *the mainstream of American culture*; *mainstream British politics*. In the 1980s, the term came increasingly into use to contrast the standard or general form of a language with non-standard, especially minority forms: 'The rise of local varieties . . . or the generalization of imperfectly learned English . . . pours innovation back into the international mainstream of English' (R. W. Bailey & M. Görlach, Introduction, *English as a World Language*, 1982); '*slang*: informal language from mainstream English or non-technical subcultures (bikers, rock fans, surfers, etc.)' (Eric S. Raymond, *The New Hacker's Dictionary*, MIT Press, 1991). Compare GENERAL ENGLISH, STANDARD. [STYLE, VARIETY]. T.MCA.

MAJUSCULE AND MINUSCULE. See CAPITAL [LETTER].

MAKAR [14c: a translation of Greek *poiētḗs* maker (of poetry). Pronounced 'macker']. A term for a poet in Middle English and in Scots, as in William Dunbar's *Lament for the Makaris* (*c*.1507). Compare POET. [LITERATURE]. T.MCA.

MAKESHIFT LANGUAGE. A rudimentary form of language used for such purposes as trade among groups with no common language. Compare CONTACT LANGUAGE, MARGINAL LANGUAGE, PIDGIN, RESTRICTED LANGUAGE. [LANGUAGE].
S.R.

MALAPROPISM [19c: from *Mrs Malaprop*, a character in Richard Sheridan's play *The Rivals* (1775), from the French *mal à propos* inappropriate, and -*ism* as in *euphemism*]. An error in which a similar-sounding word is substituted for the intended one, a characteristic of the fictional Mrs Malaprop, who produced such errors as 'pineapple' for *pinnacle* ('He is the very pineapple of politeness!'), 'hydrostatics' for *hysterics* ('Oh! It gives me the hydrostatics to such a degree!'), 'interceded' for *intercepted* ('I have interceded another letter from the fellow!'). Such slips are sometimes divided into *classical malapropisms*, in which the mistakes are due to ignorance (as in the case of the self-educated Mrs Malaprop), and temporary *slips of the tongue*, in which the intended word is known by the speaker, but has been inadvertently replaced by another. Mrs Malaprop's mistakes are artificial and literary, but genuine errors of word selection in English show certain recurring characteristics: they come from the same word class (part of speech), tend to have similar beginnings and endings, and similar word rhythm, as with *magician* for musician, *competent* for confident, *anecdote* for antidote, *exhibition* for expedition. See CONFUSIBLE, DIALOG(UE), ELOCUTION, SLIP OF THE TONGUE. [LANGUAGE, NAME, STYLE]. J.M.A.

MALAWI. Official title: *Republic of Malawi*. A country of East Africa and member of the Commonwealth. Capital: Lilongwe. Currency: the kwacha (100 tambala). Population: 7.9m (1988), 11.6m (projection for 2000). Ethnicity: 99% indigenous (Chewa, Nyanja, Lomwe, Sena, Tombuka, Yao, etc.), 1% Asian, European. Religion: 40% Protestant, 30% traditional, 20% Roman Catholic, 10% Muslim. Languages: Chichewa, English (both official), and indigenous. Education: primary 46%, secondary 5%, tertiary 1%, literacy 49%. The first European contact was in 1859, by the Scottish missionary David Livingstone. In 1878, the *African Lakes Company* was established; in 1883, Britain appointed a consul to the Kings and Chiefs of Central Africa; the territory became the British protectorate of *Nyasaland*, which became independent in 1964 as Malawi. English is the principal link language and the language of education from the fourth year of school, and is used in the media. English-language newspapers include *The Daily Times*, the *Malawi News* (weekly, English and Chichewa), and *The Okini* (biweekly, English and Chichewa). See EAST AFRICAN ENGLISH, ENGLISH. [AFRICA, NAME, VARIETY]. C.L.N.

MALAY. An Asian language of the Western or Indonesian branch of the Malayo-Polynesian language family, used in the Malay Peninsula and many of the islands of Malaysia and Indonesia. The dialect of the southern peninsula is the basis of both *Bahasa Malaysia* and *Bahasa Indonesia*, the official languages of Malaysia and Indonesia respectively. Malay is spoken by some 60m people, many of whom use it as a second language for professional, academic, or other purposes. The two national standards use slightly different versions of the Roman alphabet and can also be written in Arabic script. *Bazaar Malay* is a pidgin used in markets and by servants. Currently, both national varieties are undergoing rapid lexical expansion, drawing especially on English for the vocabulary of technology. Loans from English into Bahasa Malaysia include: (loanwords) *ais* ice, *famili* family, *kempen* campaign, *oksyȧn* oxygen, *terompet* trumpet, *traktor* tractor, *variasi* variation, *wayar*

wire, *wiski* whisk(e)y, *zeng* zinc; (loan translations) *bulan madu* honeymoon, *meja bulat* round table, *papan hitam* blackboard, *pelum berpandu* guided missile, *pasar gelap* black market; (hybrids) *bom waktu* time bomb, *tenaga solar* solar energy, *antikerajaan* anti-government; (loans from trade names) *beraso* Brasso, *klorox* Chlorox, *termos* Thermos, *zeroks* Xerox. Such borrowing is discussed in detail in *The Influence of English on the Lexical Expansion of Bahasa Malaysia*, by Carmel H. L. Hsia (Dewan Bahasa dan Pustaka/Ministry of Education, Kuala Lumpur, 1989). See ARABIC, BORROWING, BRUNEI, INDONESIA, MALAYO-POLYNESIAN LANGUAGES, MALAYSIA, SINGAPORE. [ASIA, LANGUAGE]. T.MCA.

MALAYALAM. A Dravidian language of south India that branched from Tamil in medieval times. It is one of the 15 major languages of India and the state language of Kerala. Malayalam is written in a script based on southern Brahmi, and has a literary tradition dating from at least the 14c. It is spoken primarily by some 25m people in Kerala, Malaysia, and Singapore. The standard language is highly Sanskritized and also borrows from English. A style mixed with Sanskrit and known as *maṇipravālam* (rubies and coral) is unique to literary Malayalam. See BISOCIATION, BORROWING, DRAVIDIAN ENGLISH, INDIA, INDIAN LANGUAGES, TAMIL. [ASIA, LANGUAGE]. Y.K.

MALAYO-POLYNESIAN LANGUAGES, also **Austronesian languages**. A family of 300–500 languages, with a mainly insular distribution. The languages are found in Cambodia, Indonesia, Madagascar, Malaysia, Melanesia, Micronesia, the Philippines, Polynesia, Singapore, Taiwan, and Vietnam. Their speakers have come into contact with English in varying degrees since the 16c, with particular impact on Hawaiian, Indonesian, Malay, and Maori. See ASIAN LANGUAGES, BLOOMFIELD, HAWAII, INDONESIA, LANGUAGE, LANGUAGE FAMILY, MALAY, MALAYSIA, MAORI, MELANESIA, NEW ZEALAND, PAPUA NEW GUINEA, PHILIPPINES, SOLOMON ISLANDS, TAIWAN, VANUATU. [ASIA, OCEANIA]. S.R.

MALAYSIA [Until the 1960s, a term among geographers for all lands inhabited by Malays, including Indonesia and the Philippines; now largely restricted to one nation]. Formal title: *Federation of Malaysia*. A country of South-East Asia, a member of the Commonwealth, and a constitutional monarchy (a king being elected for five-year periods from among the sultans of the Malay states). Capital: Kuala Lumpur. Currency: rinngit (100 sen). Economy: mixed. Population: 17m (1988), 21m (projection for 2000).

Ethnicity: 47% Malay, 32% Chinese, 8% South Asian, 3% Iban, 3% Kadazan, 7% others. Religions: 53% Muslim, 25% Buddhist, Confucianist, and Taoist, 10% Christian, 8% Hindu, 5% traditional. Main languages: Bahasa Malaysia or Malay (the official language, link language, and medium of education), English (compulsory second language in education), Chinese (mainly Hokkien and Cantonese), Tamil, Punjabi, Iban. Education: primary 99%, secondary 53%, tertiary 6%, literacy 74%.

From the 16c, the British competed with Sumatran settlers, the Dutch, and the Portuguese for control of the Malay Peninsula. In 1826, Singapore, Malacca, and Penang were incorporated into the *British Colony of the Straits Settlements*, and from 1874 British protection was extended over the sultanates of Perak, Selangor, Negeri Sembilan, and Pahang, which became in 1895 the *Federated Malay States*. Further treaties were made with the sultans of Johor, Kedah, Perlis, Kelantan, and Terengganu, which were known as the *Unfederated Malay States*. After the Second World War, Singapore became a separate colony, Sarawak became a colony, the colony of North Borneo was formed, and the *Malay Union* created to unite the peninsular Malay states with the Straits Settlements of Malacca and Penang. Non-Malay opposition to this union led to the *Federation of Malaya* in 1948, which (after the defeat of a drawn-out Communist insurrection) gained independence in 1957. In 1963, when Sabah (North Borneo) and Sarawak joined the group, the *Federation of Malaysia* was formed. Singapore left the federation and became an independent republic in 1965. The Malay state of Brunei in Borneo also chose to remain distinct. See BRUNEI, ENGLISH, INDONESIA, MALAY, MALAYSIAN ENGLISH, SINGAPORE, SPELLING REFORM. [ASIA, NAME, VARIETY]. T.MCA.

MALAYSIAN ENGLISH.

The English language in Malaysia. The name *Anglo-Malay* has been used to describe the variety that emerged during colonial times among expatriates and a local élite, serving as the vehicle through which such words as *compound/kampong, durian, orang utan*, and *sarong* have passed into general English. Some English-medium schools were established in the 19c (in Penang in 1816, Singapore 1823, Malacca 1826, and Kuala Lumpur 1894), at the same time as Malay, Chinese, and Tamil schools were encouraged. Those members of the various ethnic groups who were educated in the English-medium schools came to use English increasingly in their occupations and their daily life; the 1957 census reported 400,000 people (some 6% of the population) as claiming to be literate in the language. When the British

began to withdraw in the late 1950s, English had become the dominant language of the non-European élite, and with independence became with Malay the 'alternate official language'. However, the National Language Act of 1967 established Malay (renamed *Bahasa Malaysia* in 1963) as the sole official language, with some exceptions in such areas as medicine, banking, and business. Among Malaysians, the term *Malaysian English* tends to refer to a more or less controversial variety that centres on the colloquialisms of those educated at the English-medium schools. Its essence is distilled in the cartoons of K. H. Boon in the *Malaysian Post*: 'Myself so thin don't eat, can die one, you know?'

English-medium education expanded after independence; there were close to 400,000 students in such schools when, in 1969, the Ministry of Education decided that all English-medium schools would become Malay-medium. By the early 1980s, the process through which Bahasa Malaysia has become the national language of education was virtually complete, but the shift prompted widespread concern that general proficiency in English would decline. To prevent this, English has been retained as the compulsory second language in primary and secondary schools. Some 20% of the present population (c.3.4m) understands English and some 25% of city dwellers use it for some purposes in everyday life. It is widely used in the media and as a reading language in higher education. There are seven English-language daily newspapers (combined circulation over 500,000) and three newspapers in Sabah published partly in English (circulation over 60,000). English is essentially an urban middle-class language, virtually all its users are bilingual, and code-switching is commonplace. Creative writers in English include Kassim Ahmad, Lee Kok Liang, and K. S. Maniam.

Features. (1) Malaysian and Singapore English have much in common, with the main exception that English in Malaysia is more subject to influence from Malay. (2) Pronunciation is marked by: a strong tendency to syllable-timed rhythm, and a simplification of word-final consonant clusters, as in /lɪv/ for *lived*. (3) Syntactic characteristics include: the countable use of some usually uncountable nouns (*Pick up your chalks; A consideration for others is important*); innovations in phrasal verbs (such as *cope up with* rather than *cope with*); the use of reflexive pronouns to form emphatic pronouns (*Myself sick* I am sick; *Himself funny* He is funny); and the multi-purpose particle *lah*, a token especially of informal intimacy (*Sorry, can't come lah*). (4) Local vocabulary includes: such borrowings from Malay as *bumiputera* (originally Sanskrit, son of the soil) a Malay or other indigenous person, *dadah* illegal drugs, *rakyat* the people, citizens, *Majlis* (from Arabic) Parliament, *makan* food; such special usages as *banana leaf restaurant* a South Indian restaurant where food is served on banana leaves, *chop* a rubber stamp or seal, *crocodile* a womanizer, *girlie barber shop* a hairdressing salon that doubles as a massage parlour or brothel, *sensitive issues* (as defined in the Constitution) issues that must not be raised in public, such as the status of the various languages used in Malaysia and the rights and privileges of the different communities; such colloquialisms as *bes* (from *best*) great, fantastic, *relac* (from *relax*) take it easy; and such hybrids as *bumiputera status* indigenous status, and *dadah addict* drug addict. See MALAY, SINGAPORE, SOUTH-EAST ASIAN ENGLISH. [ASIA, NAME, VARIETY]

P.H.L., T.MCA.

Asmah, Haji Omar. 1983. 'The Role of English in Malaysia in the Context of National Language Planning', in R. B. Ross (ed.), *Varieties of English in Southeast Asia*. Singapore: University Press, for SEAMEO Regional Language Centre.
Benson, Phillip. 1990. 'A Language in Decline? (Malaysian English)', in *English Today* 24, Oct. 1990.
Lowenberg, Peter H. 1986. 'Sociolinguistic Context and Second Language Acquisition: Acculturation and Creativity in Malaysian English', in *World Englishes* 5: 1.
Platt, John. 1982. 'English in Singapore, Malaysia and Hong Kong', in R. W. Bailey & M. Görlach (eds.), *English as a World Language*. Ann Arbor: University of Michigan Press. Cambridge: University Press.
—— & Weber, Heidi. 1980. *English in Singapore and Malaysia*. Kuala Lumpur: Oxford University Press.
Wong, Irene. 1981. 'English in Malaysia', in Larry E. Smith (ed.), *English for Cross-Cultural Communication*. New York: Macmillan.

MALDIVES, The. Official title: in Divehi *Divehi Jumhuriya*, in English *Republic of the Maldives/Maldivian Republic*. Also, especially formerly, *the Maldive Islands*. A country of 19 atoll clusters in South Asia, and member of the Commonwealth. Capital: Malé. Currency: rufiya (100 laari). Economy: mixed. Population: 200,000 (1988), 300,000 (projection for 2000). Ethnicity: mixed Sinhalese, South Indian, Arab. Religion: Sunni Muslim. Languages: Divehi (official), also called Maldivian, related to Sinhala and with a script derived from Arabic, and English, widely used in government and tourism. Education: primary 76%, secondary 29%, tertiary 1%, literacy 70%. From 1887 to 1965, the Maldive sultanate was a British protectorate. See ENGLISH, SINHALA/SINHALESE, SOUTH ASIAN BROADCASTING, SOUTH ASIAN ENGLISH. [ASIA, NAME, VARIETY].

T.MCA.

MALE BIAS. See GENDER BIAS.

MALEDICTA, full title *Maledicta: The International Journal of Verbal Aggression*. An American journal devoted to uncensored studies and glossaries of verbal aggression and abuse, curses, blasphemy, scatology, taboo language, exclamations, boasting, euphemism, terms of endearment, pet names, jargon, libel and slander, nicknames, slurs, stereotypes, racial and other names, the terminology of sex and body parts, proverbs and sayings, metaphors, similes, and comparisons, graffiti, satire and sarcasm, affixes, gestures, physical aggression, and murder and suicide. It was founded in 1977 in Waukesha, Wisconsin, by its editor and publisher Reinhold Aman, and appears more or less annually in a volume of c.300 pages, with subscribers in 71 countries: 'The journal's whimsical and humorous contributions, as well as its editor's personal engagement and verbal aggression against cowardly, repressed, and hypocritical establishment scholars are the major reasons why many of the latter ignore *Maledicta*. The uncensored presentation of so-called vulgar, obscene, and otherwise "sensitive" language material is another reason for establishment scholars to disdain *Maledicta* and to ignore the valuable linguistic corpus presented in its pages' (editor, personal communication, 1990). See SWEARING. [AMERICAS, LANGUAGE, MEDIA].

T.MCA.

MALTA. Official title: Maltese *Republika ta Malta*, English *Republic of Malta*. A Mediterranean island nation and member of the Commonwealth. Capital: Valletta. Currency: lira (100 mils or cents). Economy: mainly industry and tourism. Population: 360,000 (1988), 360,000 (projection for 2000). Religion: 98% Roman Catholic, 2% others. Languages: Maltese/Malti, English (both official, English the medium of education), and Italian. Maltese, a variety of Arabic with elements of several other Mediterranean languages, is the only Semitic language written in the Roman alphabet and used for official purposes in Europe. Education: primary 95%, secondary 76%, tertiary 20%, literacy 84%. Malta was a Sicilian dependency from the late 11c and was controlled by the Knights of St John from 1530. It was a French colony from 1798 and a British colony from 1802, becoming self-governing in 1921, then an independent monarchy (with the Queen as head of state) in 1964, and a republic in 1974, the last British troops being withdrawn in 1979. The use of English is widespread, especially in the cities. English-language newspapers include *The Democrat* (established in 1975) and the *Times* (1978). See ARABIC, ENGLISH. [EUROPE, LANGUAGE, NAME, VARIETY].

T.MCA., C.L.N.

MANCHESTER. See LANCASHIRE.

MANDARIN CHINESE. See CHINA, SINGAPORE.

MAN, ISLE OF. See ISLE OF MAN, MANX.

MANNERISM [18c]. A characteristic way in which a person behaves, consciously or unconsciously, occasionally or habitually. Mannerisms are often part of body language: for example, a gesture like frequently touching the hair or raising an eyebrow. When gestures or speech are *mannered*, however, they are stylized and affected. See AFFECTATION, BODY LANGUAGE, -ISM, REFINED. [STYLE]. T.MCA.

MANNER OF ARTICULATION. See SPEECH.

MAN OF LETTERS. See LETTERS.

MANUAL [14c: from Latin *manualis* that can be held in or done by the hand]. (1) Done or worked by hand (*manual labour*); related to the use of the hands (*manual dexterity*). (2) Also *handbook*. An instructional book suitable for holding in the hand, especially when working on a particular task: *a repair manual*; *a gunnery manual*; *a style manual*. (3) Also *manual typewriter*. A non-electric typewriter. Compare COMPANION, GUIDE. See HAND, MANUSCRIPT, TEXTBOOK, TYPEWRITER. [REFERENCE, TECHNOLOGY]. T.MCA.

MANUAL ENGLISH. See SIGN LANGUAGE.

MANUSCRIPT [16c: from Medieval Latin *manuscriptus* written by hand, from Latin *manu* by hand, *scribere*/*scriptum* to write]. Short form *MS* or *ms* (plural *MSS* or *mss*). (1) A handwritten document, especially one produced before the widespread adoption of printing. (2) The original text of an author's work, especially as submitted to a publisher. From the late 19c, the term has also been used to refer to typewritten documents (*a typed manuscript*); in the US in the 1890s, the term *typescript* was coined by analogy for a typed document. (3) Handwriting as distinguished from print (*notes in manuscript*); handwritten (*a manuscript poem on vellum*). The term *typescript* is used in the same way (*notes in typescript*; *a typescript poem*). See BOOK, HAND, MANUAL, SCRIPT, SCROLL, VOLUME. [TECHNOLOGY, WRITING]. T.MCA.

-MAN/WOMAN. Elements used in compounds to indicate that someone was born in a country or region: *Englishman*, *Scotswoman*, *Cornishman*, *Manxwoman*. Such usages appear to have originally been written separately (*Irish man*, *Welsh woman*), but are now solid, with stress on the first element, a practice that evidently began in the 15c. However, where a usage does not represent a traditional label, as with *a Glasgow man* (a man from Glasgow) or *a New York woman*, the place-names are used attributively, not as parts of compounds, and solid spelling is not used. The masculine form has traditionally been regarded as generic: that is, as including the feminine in general statements like *This is a matter of concern to all Englishmen*. Currently, this practice is resisted by feminists and others, along with such non-geographical terms as *chairman* and *fireman*. The forms *Scotsman/woman* can be shortened to the neutral *Scot*, widely preferred as a compact bias-free term, but most such terms cannot. The expressions an *Irisher* and an *Irish* (plural *Irishes*) were once common in Britain and Ireland, and the latter is still used in West Africa. See SEXISM. [NAME, WORD]. T.MCA.

MANX [16c: from Old Norse *manskr*, Middle English *Manisk(e)*, with *sk* metathesized to *x*. Compare dialect *aks* for *ask*]. (1) The adjective for the Isle of Man and its people, as in *Manx cat* a local breed of tailless domestic cat. (2) Also *Manx Gaelic*. The Celtic language of the Isle of Man. See GAELIC, ISLE OF MAN, METATHESIS. [EUROPE, NAME]. T.MCA.

MANX ENGLISH. See ISLE OF MAN, MANX.

MANXMAN/WOMAN. See -MAN/WOMAN, MANX.

MAORI [19c: from Maori, perhaps meaning 'the usual kind']. The name of the indigenous people (*tangata whenua*) of New Zealand and their language. Maori is spoken by about one-third of the approximately 300,000 Maori population. With such other languages as Hawaiian, Samoan, and Tongan, it is a member of the Polynesian branch of the Malayo-Polynesian language family.

Pronunciation. The Maori pronunciation of *Maori* has a long *a* /'maːɔri/, a usage which is fairly common in NZE alongside the traditional Anglicized /'maʊri/. No single dialect has emerged as the basis for a standard form of Maori. Tribal variation in pronunciation is shown in such pairs as *inanga/inaka* (a kind of fish), *mingimingi/mikimiki* (an evergreen shrub), and the place-name *Waitangi/Waitaki*. In each of these cases, /ŋ/ is a North Island equivalent of a South Island /k/. In words conventionally spelt with *wh* (*whare*, *kowhai*), some tribes use a sound approximating to /f/, others a sound approximating to /hw/. Maori has the consonants /p, t, k, m, n, ŋ, f, h, r, w/ and the five vowels /i, ɛ, a, ɔ, u/, which can be either long or short. It also permits a maximum of one consonant sound before any vowel. Consequently, loanwords from English may undergo considerable change: *sheep* to *hipi*, *Bible* to *paipera*, *London* to *Ranana*. The written consonant cluster *ng* is pronounced /ŋ/, as in *sing*, whether initial or medial. Maori *r* in many words corresponds to Hawaiian and Samoan *l*: *aroha*, Hawaiian *aloha* love; *whare*, Samoan *fale* house.

Writing. The language was unwritten before the arrival in the early 19c of British missionaries, who, in creating a written form for the language, did not always successfully equate its phonemes with the nearest equivalents in English. A major feature of their work was the decision that vowel length in Maori did not need to be reflected in spelling (although diacritical marks have since been optional). Some present-day scholars of Maori have adopted a system of doubling long vowels: *Maaori* instead of *Maori* or *Māori*; *kaakaa* instead of *kaka* or *kākā* (parrot); *kaakaapoo* instead of *kakapo* or *kākāpō*. However, since most printing of the language shows the older conventions, it seems likely that the missionaries' style will prevail.

Influence on English. All Maoris speak English, but few Pakehas (white New Zealanders) and a diminishing number of Maoris speak Maori with any fluency, although attempts are now being made to give greater prominence to Maori language and culture. From the beginning, European settlers adopted Maori names for physical features and tribal settlements, but such names came to be pronounced with varying degrees of adaptation. Thus, the place-name *Paekakariki*, pronounced /paɛˈkakariki/ by the Maoris, was Anglicized to /ˌpaɪkɒkəˈriːkiː/ and frequently reduced to the disyllabic /ˈpaɪkɒk/. The place-name *Whangarei* /ˈfaŋareɪ/ was Anglicized to /ˈwɒŋəˈreɪ/. Most of the Maori names for the distinctive flora (*kowhai, nikau, pohutukawa, rimu, totara*) and fauna (*kiwi, takahe, tuatara, weta*) were also adopted and varyingly adapted into NZE. The issue of how far English-speakers should attempt to adopt native Maori pronunciations of such words has, for many years, been a major point of linguistic discussion in New Zealand. Broadcasting now attempts, not always successfully, to use a Maori pronunciation at all times. Two features of colloquial NZE are frequently attributed to Maori influence: the use of the tag question *eh?* and plural *youse*. However, while these may have been encouraged by Maori structures, they are both found elsewhere in the English-speaking world.

Status. In the later 19c and early 20c, the use of Maori was officially discouraged in schools. Many Maoris concurred with this policy, seeing English as the language which was likely to give their children the greater advantage in later life.

In more recent times, there has been a resurgence in the use of Maori as a marker of ethnic and cultural identity. *Language nests* or *kohanga reo* have been established for pre-school children, and many Maori people aim at bilingualism. Although Maori has now been recognized as an official language in the courts, it is still too early to say what effect this growing recognition of Maori will have in the long term. See BORROWING, HAWAIIAN, KIWI, MACRON, MALAYO-POLYNESIAN LANGUAGES, NEW ZEALAND ENGLISH, NEW ZEALAND PLACE-NAMES, PAKEHA. [LANGUAGE, NAME, OCEANIA].   RO.W.B., L.J.B.

MAORI ENGLISH. A widely used term for a variety of NZE. Its features, however, remain poorly defined and to the extent that the variety is neither spoken by all Maoris nor exclusively by Maoris the label is misleading. It is spoken by pakehas (whites) in areas where there are many Maoris or as a means of showing solidarity with them. Maori English is primarily identifiable through voice quality and a greater tendency towards syllable timing than is normal in pakeha English. Certain vowel qualities appear to differ from those in standard NZE, but reliable descriptions are not yet available. In a survey of Maori schoolchildren by Richard A. Benton in 1963-4, it was found that they sometimes made no distinction between /ð/ and /d/, /θ/ and /t/, /s/ and /z/, /k/ and /g/, that /t/ and /d/ were sometimes interchanged, and that /ŋ/ was replaced by /n/. The use of the high-rise terminal intonation pattern for statements was also commented on. It is not clear to what extent these are maturational 'problems' and, if not, to what extent they also beset pakehas. The high-rise terminal is today widespread among pakehas, including the middle class, and variation between /ŋ/ and /n/ is a notorious shibboleth throughout the English-speaking world.

Similar problems arise in interpreting data on the grammar of Maori English. The above study mentions constructions such as *I went down the henhouse*, *Me and Bill went there*, *He learned me to do it*, all common non-standard forms in English elsewhere. It also mentions constructions that may be more representative of Maori English: *I went by my Auntie's*; *Who's your name?*; *To me, the ball*. Recent research shows some grammatical differences between Maori and pakeha speakers, such as the omission of *have* before some past participles and before *got to*. The use of the tag question *eh?* is stereotypical, but also occurs in other varieties of NZE and elsewhere. Typical vocabulary items include both Maori and non-Maori words: *kai* food, *fellers* /ˈfʌləz/ people, males (often in the vocative *you fellers*). There is another variety, mainly written and not usually called *Maori English*, in which far more Maori vocabulary is used. In it, the elements are neither italicized nor glossed: 'This indeed may be the nub from which this book gains perspective—that even after 145 years of Pakeha terms of reference, ka tu tonu the Maori. And so they should remain as yet to be consulted tangata whenua. Whether this book bears fruit will depend on a response to the kaupapa laid down on marae throughout Aotearoa at the feet of the manuhiri' (Philip Whaanga, *New Zealand Listener*, 5 Apr. 1986). The average pakeha New Zealander will not understand enough Maori to know precisely what is being said here. It is not clear whether the variety reflects code-switching in Maori speech or is a literary style that may provide a model for spoken usage. In either case, it seems to be a new development and may mean that a more prestigious kind of Maori English will soon emerge. See DIALECT IN NEW ZEALAND, MAORI, NEW ZEALAND ENGLISH. [OCEANIA, VARIETY].

L.J.B.

MARATHI. An Indo-Aryan language of India, spoken by some 50m people on the west coast of the peninsula and eastward across the Deccan, the state language of Maharashtra, and one of the 15 major languages of India. It is written in a modified version of Devanagari script and has a literary tradition dating from the 11c. Standard Marathi is based on the variety spoken in the city of Pune (formerly Poona). Structurally, Marathi is closer to the Dravidian languages than to any other major Indo-Aryan language. In the 17–18c, Marathi and Bengali absorbed the impact of Europeans, especially the British, earlier than other Indo-Aryan languages and led the way in the development of subcontinental vernacular literatures. See BORROWING, INDIA, INDIAN LANGUAGES, INDO-ARYAN ENGLISH. [ASIA, LANGUAGE].

Y.K.

MARCH, Francis Andrew [1825–1911]. American lexicographer and philologist, born in Sutton, Massachusetts, and educated at Amherst College, Massachusetts, where, influenced by Noah Webster and Webster's son-in-law, William C. Fowler, he developed an interest in philosophy and language. While teaching at Amherst, he studied law and was admitted to the New York Bar (1850). Ill-health forced him to abandon this career and resume teaching, at Lafayette College (1855–1904) where, despite invitations from better-known institutions, he remained for the rest of his career as chair of the Department of English Language and Comparative Philology (the first of its kind at any US institution). His method of research and instruction is delineated in *Method of Philological Study*

of the English Language (1865). Intrigued by historical grammar, March specialized in the study of early medieval English, producing *A Comparative Grammar of the Anglo-Saxon Language*, in which its forms are illustrated by those of the *Sanskrit, Greek, Latin, Gothic, Old Saxon, Old Friesic, Old Norse, and Old High German* (1870). Because of the scope and depth of his research, he is credited with laying the foundation on which subsequent English historical grammarians built. It was, however, his work in lexicography which earned him international attention. Having served as director of the American workers for the *OED*, he became consulting editor of the *Standard Dictionary* (1893-5, two volumes) and *A Thesaurus-Dictionary of the English Language* (1902, etc.). Active in the simplified spelling movement, he wrote one of the most widely reprinted texts on the subject, *The Spelling Reform* (1881). A member of many scholarly societies, he served as president of the American Philological Association (1873-4, 1895-6), the Spelling Reform Association (1876-1905), and the Modern Language Association (1891-3). [AMERICAS, BIOGRAPHY, LANGUAGE, REFERENCE].

R.W.B.

MARGIN [14c: from Latin *margo/marginis* a border: Compare MARK]. The space around the written or printed matter on a page, especially to left and right, and most particularly in English the left-hand margin: *He made notes in the margin*; *Don't start too close to the top of the page and leave a decent margin*; *Go in from the margin when you start a new paragraph*. The term *marginal note* refers to a single note in a margin and *marginalia* to marginal notes collectively. See GLOSS, INDENTING, LAYOUT, NOTES AND REFERENCES, SPACE, TYPOGRAPHY. [WRITING].

T.MCA.

MARGINAL LANGUAGE. A sociolinguistic term for a makeshift language arising through culture contact, where it is impossible or impracticable for the peoples concerned to learn each other's languages well. See CONTACT LANGUAGE, MAKESHIFT LANGUAGE, TRADE JARGON. [LANGUAGE].

S.R.

MARITIME PIDGIN, also **Nautical Jargon.** A trade jargon widely used by sailors, many of whom were multilingual, on European vessels from the 17c. Some scholars argue that it was passed on to others with whom the sailors came into contact, providing the origin of the European-based pidgins and creoles. Evidence can be found in the fact that most pidgins and creoles have a nautical element, though that should not be surprising since many of these languages are spoken in maritime areas. Not much support can be found for the so-called *nautical jargon theory* of the origin of pidgins, but the role of sailors in spreading linguistic features across vast areas accounts for some lexical similarities among such widely separated pidgins as *Hawaii Pidgin English*, *Chinook Jargon*, and *Eskimo Jargon*: for example, *kanaka* [Hawaiian: person, man] in Chinook Jargon and the English and French-based Pacific pidgins, and *kaukau* [from Chinese Pidgin English *chowchow*] in Eskimo Jargon and Hawaii Pidgin English. See JARGON, PIDGIN. [VARIETY].   S.R.

MARITIME PIDGIN HAWAIIAN. See HAWAII PIDGIN ENGLISH.

MARITIME PROVINCES, The, also **the Maritimes**. The Atlantic provinces of mainland Canada: New Brunswick, Nova Scotia (which includes Cape Breton Island), and Prince Edward Island. When Newfoundland is added, the collective term is *the Atlantic Provinces*. The regional accents of the Maritimes have features in common with Newfoundland and differ considerably from usage to the west; the urban accents of Fredericton, Halifax, and other centres of population are similar to inland urban CanE. The territory is roughly the region called *Acadian* by the French. It was also claimed by the English and settled by both in the 17c, changing hands several times until 1713, when it was ceded to Britain. A complex settlement history explains its variety of rural dialects, some of which were influenced by Acadian French, some by German (in Lunenburg County, Nova Scotia, settled in 1753), some by Gaelic (Cape Breton, settled 1802-28 by 25,000 Highlanders during the Clearances in Scotland), as well as various dialects of England. In 1783, the arrival of Loyalists after the American War of Independence almost tripled the English-speaking population.

The main differences between standard Canadian and the Maritimes appear to arise from the earlier settlement of the Maritimes (from 1713) than Ontario (from 1783), but it has also been suggested that they arise from the localities from which the Loyalists migrated. Most of the new arrivals in the Maritimes were from New England, while those moving into central Canada were primarily from further west and were the first settlers there. A well-known shibboleth of pronunciation is mentioned by a character in Margaret Atwood's *Lady Oracle* (1977): 'Being from the Maritimes, he said *ahnt* . . . whereas I was from Ontario and said *ant*.' Regional grammar includes the use of *some*, *right*, *real* as intensifiers: *It's some hot*; *It's right hot*; *It's real hot*. Regional vocabulary shares some terms with Newfoundland and some with New England, and includes: *banking* the storing of illegally trapped lobsters until the season

opens; *barachois* small ponds near the sea, held back by a narrow causeway, and by extension the causeway itself (from Canadian French *barachoix*, a sandbar; in Newfoundland, also a *barrasway*); *bogan* a backwater; *grayback* a large ocean wave; *make, make cod, make fish* to dry fish or cod; *malpeque* a famous oyster, from Malpeque Bay, Prince Edward Island; *sloven* a long low wagon with a specially low back axle, to make loading easier; *tern* a three-masted schooner. See CANADA, CANADIAN DICTIONARIES IN ENGLISH, DIALECT IN CANADA. [AMERICAS, VARIETY].   M.F.

MARK [From Old English *mearc* a sign, banner, dividing line, border: compare MARGIN]. (1) A visible impression or sign, such as a spot, line, cut, or dent. (2) A sign, usually a cross, in lieu of a signature made by someone who cannot write his or her name: *He made his mark at the bottom of the page*. (3) A symbol used in writing and printing to help in the organization of a text (*a punctuation mark*) or to identify a product and indicate ownership (*a trademark*). (4) A sign or token: *a mark of respect*. (5) An actual or figurative symbol used in rating ability, conduct, etc.: *a high mark in an exam*; *a black mark for poor behaviour*. (6) A norm or standard: *Their work isn't really up to the mark*. See DIACRITIC, EXCLAMATION MARK/POINT, INTERROGATION MARK/POINT, LENGTH MARK, LETTER[1], LIST, MARKED AND UNMARKED TERMS, PAPER (WATERMARK), PUNCTUATION MARK, QUESTION MARK, QUOTATION MARKS, SIGN, SIGNATURE, STANDARD, SYMBOL, TRADEMARK. [WRITING].   T.MCA.

MARKED AND UNMARKED TERMS [Originating in the work of the Russian linguist Nikolay Trubetzkoy (1890-1938) in relation to pairs of phonemes]. Terms in linguistics which designate a contrasting pair, one possessing a special 'mark', the other neutral: in *play/played*, *play* is unmarked and neutral, and *played* has the mark *-ed*. Similarly, *host* is unmarked, but *hostess* is morphologically marked for femaleness. The mark is not necessarily visible or audible: in the pair *horse/mare*, *horse* is the more general, unmarked term, while *mare* is marked for femaleness. In the pair *cow/bull*, *cow* is unmarked, while *bull* is marked for maleness. The terms are sometimes extended to wider, typological characteristics of languages, and also to social situations, to distinguish between normal (unmarked) behaviour and a less common variant. See MARK. [LANGUAGE].   J.M.A.

MARSH, George Perkins [1801-82]. American diplomat and philologist, born in Woodstock, Vermont, and educated at Dartmouth College. Marsh was a lawyer with a passionate interest in European languages and their history. While practising law in Burlington, Vermont, he published *A Compendious Grammar of the Old Northern or Icelandic Language* (1838), a translation of the innovative philological work of Rasmus Rask. A member of the US Congress (1843–9), he was later named the first US minister to the Kingdom of Italy, where he served from 1861 until his death. His *Lectures on the English Language* (1860) and *The Origin and History of the English Language* (1862) articulated for readers in the US and UK the newest discoveries of mid-19c literary and linguistic scholarship. His object in these books was to provide ordinary people such a facility in the mother tongue that they might take part 'in the never-ceasing dialogue, which, whether between the living and the living and the living and the dead, whether breathed from the lips or figured with the pen, takes up so large a part of the life of every one of us'. [AMERICAS, BIOGRAPHY, LANGUAGE].   R.W.B.

MASCULINE [14c: from French *masculin*, Latin *masculinus*, representing *genus masculinum*, the translation of Greek *arrhenikòn génos* the male kind]. A term relating to grammatical gender in nouns and related words, contrasting with *feminine* (as in French) and feminine and *neuter* (as in German and Latin). Words denoting male people and animals in such languages are usually masculine, but grammatical gender is not about sex: in French *le courage du soldat*, the courage is as masculine as the soldier. In English, the term is confined to personal pronouns (*he/him/himself/his*) and some nouns (such as *drake* in contrast with *duck*). See GENDER. [GRAMMAR].   S.C.

MASCULINE BIAS. See GENDER BIAS.

MASCULINE ENDING. A stressed syllable that ends a line of verse. If the line rhymes, the rhyme itself is called a *masculine rhyme*: *begun/sun, think/drink*. The masculine line has a tendency to be end-stopped and risks becoming monotonous. Compare FEMININE ENDING. [LITERATURE].   R.C.

MASQUE [16c: French *masque* mask]. A usually short dramatic entertainment with music and spectacle. It developed in Renaissance Italy and became a pastime of the English court and aristocracy in the late 16c and early 17c. It was usually presented by amateurs in disguise; at the end, the actors would reveal themselves and join the spectators in a dance. Plots were slight, often classical or allegorical. The dramatic element came to be increasingly subordinated to the musical and visual effects, which could be costly.

The form attracted poets rather than dramatists, though Jonson wrote court masques. Shakespeare introduced a masque-like interlude in *The Tempest* and there is a wordless masque in *Henry VIII*. Milton's *Comus* (1634), though described as a masque, is a pastoral play. See DRAMA, JONSON. [LITERATURE].   R.C.

MASS NOUN. See COUNTABLE AND UNCOUNTABLE.

MASTHEAD [18c: by analogy with the flag at the head of a ship's mast]. (1) A statement printed in each issue of a periodical, often in a column or special area on the contents or editorial page, providing such information as its name, founding date, motto or slogan, and editors' names. (2) Also *flag, nameplate, title*. The line of type for the name on the front of a periodical. (3) *The Masthead*: the title of the magazine for members of the *National Council of Editorial Writers* (of US newspapers). See PERIODICAL. [MEDIA, TECHNOLOGY].   T.MCA.

MATHEWS, Mitford McLeod [1891–1985]. American lexicographer, born in Jackson, Alabama, and educated at Southern U. He taught English and Latin in Alabama high schools until enrolling at the U. of Chicago in 1926. There he became William A. Craigie's student and research assistant, travelling to Oxford to select citations for the *Dictionary of American English* and assisting in Craigie's 1933 *Supplement* to the *OED*. In 1934, he enrolled at Harvard and completed the Ph.D. in 1936 with the dissertation 'Notes and Comments Made by British Travelers and Observers upon American English'. All the while, he worked as Assistant Editor of the *DAE* and, on its completion in 1944, was appointed as head of the dictionary department of the U. of Chicago Press, supervising, among other works, publication of the *Dictionary of the Older Scottish Tongue*. In 1951, Matthews published the *Dictionary of Americanisms* to bring the *DAE* up to date and provide more detailed analysis of words and senses originating in the US. Among his publications were: *The Beginnings of American English* (1931), *A Survey of English Dictionaries* (1933), *American Words* (1959), and *Americanisms* (1966), an abridgement of the *DA*. See index. [AMERICAS, BIOGRAPHY, REFERENCE].   R.W.B.

MATTER OF BRITAIN. See BRITAIN, CELTIC LANGUAGES, LATIN[1], ROMANCE, STANDARD, WELSH LITERATURE.

MAURITIUS. An Indian Ocean country and member of the Commonwealth. Capital: Port Louis. Currency: the rupee (100 cents). Head of state: the British monarch. Population: 1m (1988), 1.2m (projection for 2000). Ethnicity: 68% Indian (Indo-Mauritian), 27% African Creole, 3% Chinese. Religions: 53% Hindu, 30% Christian, 17% Muslim. Languages: English (official), a French-based creole called Morisiê, French, Hindi, Urdu, and Hakka Chinese. Education: primary 92%, secondary 51%, tertiary 3%, literacy 83%. A French colony from 1715 and a British colony from 1810, Mauritius gained independence in 1968. The Creole minority is descended from African slaves and French settlers, the Indo-Mauritian majority from indentured labourers brought to the islands by the British after the abolition of slavery in 1833. The mixture of influences is noticeable in place-names, such as the districts of *Rivière du Rempart, Pamplemousses, Flacq, Moka, Black River, Plaines Wilhems, Grand Port, Savanne.* Local newspapers print articles in English and French side by side. See BRITISH INDIAN OCEAN TERRITORY, ENGLISH, FRENCH. [AFRICA, NAME, VARIETY].   T.MCA.

MAXIM [15c: from Latin *maxima (propositio)* greatest proposition (in logic), axiom, feminine of *maximus* greatest, superlative of *magnus* great]. A statement that compactly expresses a general truth or principle; an axiom or aphorism, especially if pithy and moralistic; a rule or principle of conduct. See APHORISM, AXIOM, PROPOSITION, SAYING. [STYLE].   T.MCA.

MEANING [13c: from Old English *mænan* to have in mind, intend, signify. The obsolete phrase *a good meaning* had the sense of both 'a good intention' and 'a friendly disposition': compare *to mean well*]. (1) The purport or message conveyed by words, phrases, sentences, signs, symbols, and the like: '*Semantics' means 'the study of meaning'; A red traffic light means drivers have to stop and a green one means they can go.* (2) Signification, sense, interpretation, as in *The Meaning of Meaning,* the title of a book on semantics by C. K. Ogden & I. A. Richards (1923); any instance of these, as in *What is the meaning of the word 'semantics'?* (3) What a speaker or writer intends: *What do you mean?; They don't mean any harm.* For further discussion, see SEMANTICS, SEMIOTICS, SIGN, SIGNAL, SYMBOL. [LANGUAGE].   T.MCA.

MEDIA [1920s: short for **mass media**. In the later 20c, the usage has been increasingly perceived independently of the singular *medium,* and is often construed with a singular verb, like *data*: see MEDIUM, CLASSICAL ENDING]. A collective term for newspapers, broadcasting, and other vehicles of mass communication, often used attributively in such phrases as *Media Studies*

and *media education.* Traditionally, speech and writing have been regarded as information media ('Cogitations [are] expressed by the Medium of Words', Francis Bacon, *Advancement of Learning,* volume 2, 1605), but over the last century new systems of electrical and electronic communication have become capable of doing more than simply convey information from person to person; they serve to inform and entertain huge audiences, often hundreds of millions worldwide. Following the spread of television as a news medium, the Canadian communication theorist Marshall McLuhan fostered in the 1960s a radical and controversial perception of societies as shaped more by the style than the content of their media ('the medium is the message'). He divided media into two broad kinds: *hot* (high-definition media, such as radio or a photograph) and *cool* (low-definition vehicles, such as television or the telephone), a distinction based largely on the degree of visual definition inherent in each or the amount of data supplied by each. McLuhan argued that cool media had greater impact, since they encouraged, indeed required, greater audience participation. Furthermore, he saw the visual media as superseding the written media in modern times. One corollary of his basic distinction was that the term *medium* in its traditional sense was inadequate, since the media were not neutral, impassive agencies that transmit news and views but were themselves highly influential selectors, shapers, manufacturers, and even fabricators of news and views. The plural became institutionalized in the same way as *the press,* as a set of services that mould as well as interpret events. See MCLUHAN, MEDIUM. [MEDIA].
                                   G.H., T.MCA.

Bell, Allan. 1991. *The Language of News Media.* Oxford: Blackwell.

McLuhan, Marshall. 1964. *Understanding Media: The Extensions of Man.* New York: McGraw-Hill.

Masterman, Len. 1985. *Teaching the Media.* London: Comedia.

Turnstall, Jeremy, & Palmer, Michael. 1991. *Media Moguls.* London & New York: Routledge.

Watson, James, & Hill, Anne. 1984/9. *A Dictionary of Communication and Media Studies.* London: Edward Arnold.

Weiner, Richard. 1990. *Webster's New World Dictionary of Media and Communications.* New York: Simon & Schuster.

Winston, Brian. 1986. *Misunderstanding Media.* London & New York: Routledge & Kegan Paul.

The media theme

AUSTRALIAN LANGUAGE (THE), AUSTRALIAN LANGUAGE RESEARCH CENTRE, AUSTRALIAN NATIONAL DICTIONARY CENTRE, AUSTRALIAN PRESS, AUSTRALIAN PUBLISHING, AUTHOR, AUTHORIZED VERSION, BACK MATTER, BAILEY (N.), BALLAD, BASCELT, BBC, BBC ENGLISH[1], BBC ENGLISH[2], BBC ENGLISH[3], BBC PRONUNCIATION UNIT, BBC PUBLICATIONS, BEEB, BIBLE, BIOGRAPHY, BLURB, BOOK, BOOKLET, BRITISH LIBRARY, BROADCASTING, BROADSHEET, BROADSIDE, BROCHURE, BULLETIN, BULLETIN (THE), BY-LINE, BY-NAME, CABLESE, CALL MY BLUFF, CAMBRIDGE UNIVERSITY PRESS, CANADIAN BROADCASTING, CANADIAN LANGUAGE ORGANIZATIONS, CANADIAN PRESS, CANADIAN PUBLISHING, CAPTION, CARTOON, CATCHPHRASE, CATCHWORD, CAXTON, CENSORSHIP, CENTRAL INSTITUTE OF ENGLISH AND FOREIGN LANGUAGES, CHAMBERS, CINEMA, CLASSICAL ENDING, CLICHÉ, CODE, COLLEGE ENGLISH ASSOCIATION, COLLINS, COLOPHON, COMIC, COMMUNICATION, COMMUNICATIVE SHIFT, COMPLETE PLAIN WORDS, COMPUTING, CONDENSED BOOK, COPY, COPYRIGHT, CORRUPT, COVERAGE.

D–J. DESKTOP PUBLISHING, DIGEST, DOCUDRAMA, DOCUMENT, DOCUMENTARY, DUMMY, EDITING, EDITION, EFL GAZETTE, ELECTRONIC MAIL, ELECTRONIC PUBLISHING, ELT DOCUMENTS, ELT PUBLISHING, ENGLISH ASSOCIATION, ENGLISH DIALECT SOCIETY, ENGLISH LITERATURE, ENGLISH-ONLY MOVEMENT, ENGLISH PLUS, ENGLISH TEACHING FORUM, ENGLISH TODAY, ENGLISH WORLDWIDE, EPIC, EPILOG(UE), EPISTLE, ESSAY, EUROPEAN (THE), FAX, FEATURE, FEEDBACK, FESTSCHRIFT, FILM, FLASH, FLEET STREET, FREEDOM OF THE PRESS, FRONT MATTER, FUNK & WAGNALLS, GENRE, GRAPHIC, GRAPHIC DESIGN, GRAPHIC MEDIUM, GRAPHICS, GRUB STREET, GUTTER JOURNALISM/PRESS, HACK, HACKER, HEADLINE, HEAVY, HOMILY, HOUSE STYLE, HUMO(U)R, HYPERMEDIA, HYPERTEXT, IMPRESSION, IMPRINT, INDIAN PRESS, INDIAN PUBLISHING, INFORMATION, INFORMATION EXPLOSION, INNIS, INSTITUTE OF LINGUISTS, INTERNATIONAL ASSOCIATION OF TEACHERS OF ENGLISH AS A FOREIGN LANGUAGE, INTERNATIONAL HERALD TRIBUNE, INTERNATIONAL LINGUISTIC ASSOCIATION, INTERNATIONAL PHONETIC ASSOCIATION, IRISH BROADCASTING, IRISH PRESS, IRISH PUBLISHING, JAPAN, JOHNSON, JOURNAL, JOURNALESE, JOURNALISM.

L–R. LANGUAGE, LAYOUT, LEAFLET, LETTER[2], LIBEL, LIBRARY, LIBRARY OF CONGRESS, LINGUISTIC ASSOCIATION OF CANADA AND THE UNITED STATES, LINGUISTIC ASSOCIATION OF GREAT BRITAIN, LINGUISTIC SOCIETY OF AMERICA, LIST, LITERACY, LITERATURE, LONDON CHAMBER OF COMMERCE AND INDUSTRY, LONGMAN, McLUHAN, MACMILLAN, MAGAZINE, MALEDICTA, MASTHEAD, MEDIA, MEDIA LITERACY, MEDIA REVOLUTION, MEDIA STUDIES, MENCKEN, MERRIAM-WEBSTER, MODERN LANGUAGE ASSOCIATION, MONOGRAPH, MONTSERRAT, MOTION PICTURE, MOVIE, MULTIMEDIA, MUSE, NATE, NATECLA, NBC, NCTE, NETWORK, NEWS, NEWSLETTER, NEWSMAGAZINE, NEWSPAPER, NEW ZEALAND BROADCASTING, NEW ZEALAND PRESS, NEW ZEALAND PUBLISHING, OFFICIAL ENGLISH (MOVEMENT), ORALITY, OXFORD ENGLISH, OXFORD UNIVERSITY PRESS, PAMPHLET, PAPER, PENGUIN, PERIODICAL, PHILOLOGICAL SOCIETY, PHOTOCOPYING, PITMAN PUBLISHING, PLAGIARISM, PLAIN ENGLISH (CAMPAIGN), PLAY, PREFACE, PRELIM(INARIE)S, PRESS, PRINTING, PRIVATE EYE, PROLEGOMENON, PROLOG(UE), PROPAGANDA, PUBLISHING, PUNCH, QUALITY PRESS,

QUARTERLY REVIEW OF DOUBLESPEAK, QUEEN'S ENGLISH SOCIETY, RADIO, RANDOM HOUSE, READER'S DIGEST, REDUNDANCY, REVIEW, ROYAL SOCIETY, ROYAL SOCIETY OF ARTS.

S–Z. SCOSE, SCOTS LANGUAGE ORGANIZATIONS, SCOTTISH PUBLISHING, SCRIBBLER, SCRIBE, SCRIPT, SCRIPTURE, SERIAL, SERIES, SIMPLIFIED SPELLING SOCIETY, SLANDER, SLANT, SOAP OPERA, SOCIETY FOR PURE ENGLISH, SOUTH AFRICAN BROADCASTING, SOUTH AFRICAN PRESS, SOUTH AFRICAN PUBLISHING, SOUTH ASIAN BROADCASTING, SPEAQ, SPELT, STEELE, STORY, STORY LINE, STORY OF ENGLISH (THE), TABLOID, TALKIE, TALKING BOOK, TALKING HEAD, TALKING PICTURE, TECHNOLOGY, TELECOMMUNICATIONS, TELEGRAPHESE, TELEPHONE, TELEVISION, TESL CANADA, TESOL, TIME MAGAZINE, TIMES (THE), TIMESPEAK, TITLE, TITLE PAGE, UCLES, UNIVERSITY OF CAMBRIDGE LOCAL EXAMINATION SYNDICATE, VERBATIM, VOICE OF AMERICA, VOLUME, WEBSTERS, WELSH LANGUAGE SERVICE, WELSH LANGUAGE SOCIETY, WORLD ENGLISHES, WORLD LANGUAGE ENGLISH, WORLD LITERATURE WRITTEN IN ENGLISH, WRITING, YEAR'S WORK IN ENGLISH STUDIES, YELLOW PRESS.

MEDIA LITERACY. See LITERACY.

MEDIA REVOLUTION. See COMMUNICATIVE SHIFT.

MEDIA STUDIES. See EDUCATION, MEDIA.

MEDICANT [Late 20c: a blend of *medical* and *cant*]. An informal term for the jargon of the health professions that allows doctors and others to ease (often by means of euphemisms) some of the hard and unpleasant aspects of their work, to avoid responsibility, or to impress those who are not members of their group. In extreme medicant, especially in the US, patients do not die but *systems fail*, they have a *terminal episode*, or there is *negative patient care outcome*. Medical malpractice is a *therapeutic misadventure* or a *diagnostic misadventure of a high magnitude*. Patients are *compromised susceptible hosts* and ageing is *cell drop out* or *decreased propensity for cell replication*. Some US hospitals now call themselves *wellness centres* where patients can seek to *fulfill their wellness potential*. See CANT, JARGON. [STYLE, USAGE].   W.D.L.

MEDIUM [16c: from Latin *medium*, neuter singular of *medius* middle: see CLASSICAL ENDING, MEDIA]. (1) An intervening substance or process through which something else acts or travels, such as heat through glass. Language is often called *the medium of thought*. (2) In linguistics, a vehicle for the transmission of language, such as the *phonic medium* of speech (vibrations passing through air from mouth to ear), the *graphic medium* of writing (signs on surfaces created by the hand and interpreted by the eye), and *signing* (sign language for the deaf, involving hands, eyes, and space). See MEDIA, POETRY. [LANGUAGE, MEDIA].   T.McA.

MEIOSIS [16c: through Latin from Greek *meiōsis* lessening. Stress: 'my-OH-sis']. In rhetoric, a kind of understatement that dismisses or belittles, especially by using terms that make something seem less significant than it really is or ought to be: for example, calling a serious wound a *scratch*, or a journalist a *hack* or a *scribbler*. Compare LITOTES. [STYLE].   T.McA.

MELANESIA [From Greek *Melanēsia* place of black islands: that is, an archipelago inhabited by black people]. An island group in the southwestern Pacific Ocean. See BEACH LA MAR, BISLAMA, FIJI, HIRI MOTU, MELANESIAN PIDGIN ENGLISH, MICRONESIA, PAPUA NEW GUINEA, PIJIN, POLYNESIA, SOLOMON ISLANDS, TOK PISIN, VANUATU. [NAME, OCEANIA].   S.R.

MELANESIAN PIDGIN ENGLISH, also **Melanesian Pidgin**. The name commonly given to three varieties of Pidgin spoken in the Melanesian states of Papua New Guinea (*Tok Pisin*), Solomon Islands (*Pijin*), and Vanuatu (*Bislama*). Although there is a degree of mutual intelligibility among them, the term is used by linguists to recognize a common historical development and is not recognized by speakers of these languages. The development of Melanesian Pidgin English has been significantly different in the three countries. This is due to differences in the substrate languages, the presence of European languages other than English, and differences in colonial policy. In Papua New Guinea, there was a period of German administration (1884-1914) before the British and Australians took over. The people of Vanuatu were in constant contact with the French government and planters during a century of colonial rule (1880-1980) and for a time there was a condominium rule by the British and French; contact with French has continued after independence in 1980. However, Solomon Islanders have not been in contact with any European language other than English. See BISLAMA, ENGLISH, PIDGIN, PIJIN, TOK PISIN. [OCEANIA, VARIETY].S.R.

MELIORATION [17c: from Latin *melioratio/ meliorationis* making better]. Also **amelioration**. A process of semantic change in which there is an improvement or 'upward' shift in the meaning of a word: for example, *nice* has meant foolish, stupid (13-16c), lascivious, loose (14-16c), extravagant, elegant, rare, strange (15-16c), effeminate, shy, tender, slender, delicate, unimportant (16-17c), over-refined (17-18c), careful, precise, intricate, difficult, fastidious (16-19c), dainty,

appetizing (18-19c), refined, cultured, discriminating (17-20c), and agreeable, pleasant (18-20c). See PEJORATION, SEMANTIC CHANGE. [HISTORY, LANGUAGE].   T.McA.

MELODRAMA [19c: influenced by French *mélodrame*, from Greek *mélos* song, *drâma* action]. Originally, a play with music. Traditionally, a play in which plot and characters are exaggerated for effect. Early in the 19c, plays with musical accompaniment were staged to circumvent the restrictions on legitimate drama in London; these developed into a type of play, without music, in which the characters are stock types, totally good or bad, or providing comic relief. The plot usually centred on the perils of the heroine, pursued by the villain and eventually united with the hero; audience response (groans, sighs, shouted warnings, cries of condemnation) was part of the entertainment. Episodes were vigorous and sensational, emotions extreme, and overblown language (clichés like 'Curses, foiled again!' and 'Unhand me, villain!') was frequent. Dialogue was declamatory and subordinate to the plot. Some melodramas like *Sweeney Todd* and *Maria Marten* became classics of the popular 19c theatre. The 19c novel has touches of melodrama, such as Fagin in the condemned cell, in Dickens's *Oliver Twist*, and melodrama is a common element in motion pictures and television drama. The adjective *melodramatic* has come to apply to excessive emotions and reactions in life as well as in literature, drama, and the media. See DRAMA. [LITERATURE].   R.C.

MELVILLE, Herman [1819-91]. American novelist, storyteller, and poet. Born in New York City, he moved with his family to Albany, where his father died in 1832 shortly after the collapse of his business. His formal schooling ended, and after a variety of jobs he went to sea, spending four years whaling in the South Pacific. On his return, to Boston in 1844, he published six novels that drew on his experiences: *Typee* (1846), *Omoo* (1847), *Mardi* (1849), *Redburn* (1849), *White Jacket* (1850), and *Moby-Dick* (1851). Initial popularity waned, however, as he incorporated into *Mardi* and particularly *Moby-Dick* a mythic dimension. 'Dollars damn me', he wrote to Nathaniel Hawthorne while writing this book (which he dedicated to Hawthorne); 'What I feel most moved to write, that is banned,—it will not pay. Yet, altogether, write the *other* way I cannot. So the product is a final hash and all my books are botches.' The financial failure of *Moby-Dick* was followed by a land-based novel, *Pierre* (1852), which was an experimental personal fable and a satire on the literary profession, a series of magazine tales, the novels *Israel Potter* (1855) and *The Confidence-Man* (1857), and poetry that included *Battle-Pieces and Aspects of the War* (1866) and *Clarel* (1876), a narrative poem about a pilgrimage to the Holy Land. In his last years, he arranged for the private publication of two slender volumes of poems, *John Marr and Other Sailors* and *Timoleon*. He also returned to fiction and completed a short novel, *Billy Budd*, that was published posthumously in 1924.

At his death, Melville was largely forgotten in the US until British interest spurred belated international recognition, Oxford University Press publishing *Moby-Dick* in the World's Classics series in 1920, and Constable publishing in 16 volumes *The Works of Herman Melville* in 1922-4. Melville assimilates styles ranging from such classic texts as Shakespeare, the King James Bible, Robert Burton, Sir Thomas Browne, and John Milton, to the talk and songs that he listened to as a sailor. On his first voyage to Liverpool, young Wellingburgh Redburn tells of the singing that accompanies every nautical task:

Sometimes, when no one happened to strike up, and the pulling, whatever it might be, did not seem to be getting forward very well, the mate would always say, 'Come, men can't any of you sing? Sing now, and raise the dead.' And then some one of them would begin, and if every man's arms were as much relieved as mine by the song, and he could pull as much better as I did, with such a cheering accompaniment, I am sure the song was well worth the breath expended on it. . . . Some sea-captains, before shipping a man, always ask him whether he can sing out at a rope (*Redburn*, ch. 9).

Moby-Dick has a symphonic prose-poetry that conveys such mighty subjects as the Pacific Ocean:

To any meditative Magian rover, this serene Pacific, once beheld, must ever after be the sea of his adoption. It rolls the midmost waters of the world, the Indian ocean and Atlantic being but its arms. The same waves wash the moles of the new-built Californian towns, but yesterday planted by the recentest race of men, and lave the faded but still gorgeous skirts of Asiatic lands, older than Abraham; while all between float milky-ways of coral isles, and low-lying, endless, unknown Archipelagoes, and impenetrable Japans. Thus this mysterious, divine Pacific zones the world's whole bulk about; makes all coasts one bay to it; seems the tide-beating heart of earth. Lifted by those eternal swells, you needs must own the seductive god. bowing your head to Pan (*Moby-Dick*, ch. 3).

The grandeur of such prose contrasts with the colloquialism of the sailors, and of Ahab himself, capable both of quasi-Shakespearian soliloquizing and of salty nautical talk, as when he tells his men about the white whale:

'Corkscrew!' cried Ahab, 'aye Queequeg, the harpoons lie all twisted and wrenched in him; aye, Daggoo, his spout is a big one, like a whole shock of wheat, and

white as a pile of our Nantucket wool after the great annual sheep-shearing; aye, Tashtego, and he fan-tails like a split jib in a squall. Death and devils! men, it is Moby Dick ye have seen—Moby Dick—Moby Dick!' (ch. 36).

See index. [AMERICAS, BIOGRAPHY, LITERATURE, STYLE].   B.L.

MEMOIR [16c: from French *mémoire*, Latin *memoria* memory]. A written record of people and events as experienced by the author; a form of autobiography that gives particular attention to matters of contemporary interest not closely affecting the author's inner life. It is not a formal personal history, but an assembly of memories. Memoirs in the ancient world include Xenophon's *Anabasis* and Julius Caesar's *Commentaries*; among modern literatures, they are commonest in French, but English ranges from the 17c *Memoirs of Colonel Hutchinson* through Siegfried Sassoon's *Memoirs of an Infantry Officer* (1930) and Peter Wright's *Spycatcher* (1987). The memoir form has been a device for fiction, especially in the early novel: John Cleland's pornographic *Memoirs of a Woman of Pleasure* (1748-9) and Henry Mackenzie's sentimental novel *The Man of Feeling* (1771). See AUTOBIOGRAPHY, BILDUNGSROMAN, DIARY. [LITERATURE].   R.C.

MENCKEN, H(enry) L(ouis) [1880-1956]. American journalist and social critic, born in Baltimore, Maryland, and educated at a local private school and the Baltimore Polytechnic. He is remembered chiefly for his monumental work *The American Language* (*AL*, 1919), which was instrumental in establishing the scholarly study of English in the US. A lifelong resident of Baltimore, Mencken began writing for the city's newspapers in 1899 and continued doing so for most of his career. He was an iconoclast, noted for cynically witty essays in literary, social, and political criticism. Among his favourite targets were religion, the cultural barrenness of the American South (which he called 'The Sahara of the Bozart' (*beaux arts*)), the motives of politicians, and an English cultural tradition in America that he identified as puritanism. His terms for the stupid and gullible were *booboisie* and *Homo boobiensis*. Proud of his German ancestry, Mencken reacted strongly to the wave of anti-German feeling that swept the US during World War I. His unpopular position supporting Germany before US entry into the war, together with his strong opposition to President Woodrow Wilson's policies, made assignments scarce for several years. The result, however, was that Mencken had time to produce his *magnum opus*, *AL*.

Mencken's caustic journalism proved attractive to many who had become disillusioned after the war, with the result that his voice became central in American letters during the 1920s. He had achieved national prominence as early as 1908, when he became the drama reviewer of *The Smart Set: A Magazine of Cleverness*. He later co-edited that review (1914–23) with George Jean Nathan, bringing James Joyce, Aldous Huxley, and Somerset Maugham to US audiences, as well as publishing Sherwood Anderson, Willa Cather, F. Scott Fitzgerald, Eugene O'Neill, and Ezra Pound. In 1924, Mencken and Nathan started *The American Mercury*, a review that Mencken later continued to edit alone, focusing not on literature only but also on broad social commentary. For example, volume 13 (1928) contains articles by Vachel Lindsay on 'The Real American Language' and Bernard deVoto on 'English A', as well as work by James M. Cain, Zola Gale, and Sinclair Lewis. In the 1930s, Mencken's influence on the cultural scene declined, though he continued to write essays and to revise and expand *AL*.

Mencken was an autodidact whose interest in language led him to read widely and to collect citations of all aspects of AmE. His goal was to make the study of language accessible to the general reader. The 1st edition of *AL* claimed that Americans spoke a separate language of their own making that they could take pride in, not an imperfect imitation of the language of England. The language that he described as *American* was full of regional variation, new words borrowed from immigrant groups, figurative usage from such institutions as railroading and baseball, jaunty slang, and raucous vulgarisms. Americans in the era following World War I found in *AL* verification of their cultural independence as the US became an international power.

Incorporating new information from both scholars and general readers, Mencken brought out revised and enlarged editions of *AL* in 1921 and 1923. In 1925, he was instrumental in founding the journal *American Speech*, which he hoped would be sold at corner news-stands. Though the journal never attained such popularity, Mencken's publications and his personal encouragement influenced a number of scholars to turn their attention to the study of the English language in America. The 4th edition of *AL* (1936), along with two supplements (1945, 1948), is an unrivalled compendium of information about English in the US and its historical development before the mid-century. In later editions, Mencken abandoned his earlier thesis that BrE and AmE were developing as separate languages in favour of the view that they were merging, but with American as the dominant partner. Shortly after the publication of the second supplement in 1948, he suffered a stroke which left him unable to read or write. See index. See AMERICAN DIALECT SOCIETY, AMERICANISM, AMERICAN SPEECH. [AMERICAS, BIOGRAPHY, MEDIA, VARIETY].

C.C.E., D.E.B.

Adler, Betty. 1961. *HLM: The Mencken Bibliography*. Baltimore: Johns Hopkins Press.
Bode, Carl. 1969. *Mencken*. Carbondale: Southern Illinois University Press.
McDavid, Raven I., Jr. 1966. 'The Impact of Mencken on American Linguistics', in *Menckeniana*, Spring 1966, pp. 1–7.
Mencken, H. L. 1963. *The American Language*, 4th edition and supplements (abridged and augmented), ed. Raven I. McDavid Jr. New York: Alfred A. Knopf.

MENU [17c in its general sense: from French *menu* a detailed list, especially of dishes served at a meal in a restaurant, from *menu* detailed, from Latin *minutus* made small]. A display of options on a computer screen, that like a menu in a restaurant lets the user choose what to do next. A menu for choosing a type style might show for selection a series of names such as *Caslon, Helvetica, Times*, while an editing menu might show *abandon, information, layout, print, save*. Such displays save the user from having to remember or spell names and having to know which items are available with a program. A key or a cursor (on its own or controlled by a mouse) selects the desired item from the display. Software run by means of menus is said to be *menu-driven*. See COMPUTING, KEYBOARD, THEMATIC ORDER. [TECHNOLOGY]. M.L.

MERCIA [From Old English *Merce* Borderers]. A kingdom of the Angles, before the unification of England, occupying the Midland areas between the Welsh border and East Anglia, the Humber and the Thames. The zenith of Mercian power was in the 8c, when King Offa was treated virtually as an equal by the Frankish emperor Charlemagne. Later, Mercia was weakened by the assaults of the Danes and Wessex took its place as the leading Anglo-Saxon kingdom with the most prestigious dialect. Specimens of Mercian are preserved in royal charters, glosses on religious texts, and in bilingual Latin–English glossaries (8–10c). See HEPTARCHY, MIDLANDS, OLD ENGLISH[1]. [EUROPE, HISTORY, NAME]. T.MCA.

MERICO. See AMERICO-, LIBERIA.

MERRIAM-WEBSTER, originally known as the *G. & C. Merriam Company* of Springfield, Massachusetts. An American company publishing reference books and especially dictionaries descended from Noah Webster's *An American Dictionary of the English Language* (1828). Its origins can be traced to a family of bookbinders and printers in 1831. In 1843, after Webster's death, George and Charles Merriam secured publishing and revision rights to the 1841 edition of his dictionary. The brothers then pursued a vigorous commercial campaign, mostly against the publishers of dictionaries by Joseph Worcester, which resulted in the unrivalled success of their dictionaries until at least 1893. Part of their success arose from their ability to secure exclusive selling privileges to state and commercial institutions such as schools, newspapers, and legislatures. G. & C. Merriam pursued a policy of continual updating. Revised editions of the unabridged Webster appeared in 1847, 1864, 1890, 1909, 1934, and 1961. The rights to the abridged dictionaries were either retained by Merriam or farmed out to other companies, such as the American Book Company, which published school dictionaries. In addition to *Webster's New International Dictionary* and *Webster's New Collegiate Dictionary*, the company's publications include *Webster's New Dictionary of Synonyms*, *Webster's Biographical Dictionary*, *A Pronouncing Dictionary of American English*, *Webster's Thesaurus* (*School* and *Collegiate*), *Webster's New Geographical Dictionary*, *Webster's American Biographies*, *Webster's Sports Dictionary*, and *Webster's Dictionary of English Usage*. The G. & C. Merriam Company changed its name to Merriam-Webster Inc. with the publication of *Webster's Ninth New Collegiate Dictionary* (1983). The change reflects the descent of the company, which has been a subsidiary of Encyclopaedia Britannica Inc. since 1964. See DICTIONARY, WEBSTER, WEBSTERS, WEBSTER'S COLLEGIATE DICTIONARIES, WEBSTER'S DICTIONARY OF ENGLISH USAGE. [AMERICAS, MEDIA, REFERENCE]. R.W.B.

MERSEYSIDE. See SCOUSE.

MESOLECT [1960s: from Greek *mésos* middle, and *-lect* as in *dialect*]. The variety of language in a post-creole continuum intermediate between *basilect* and *acrolect*, often retaining semantic and syntactic features not found in the acrolect and tending to vary from speaker to speaker, such as between standard Jamaican English and Jamaican Creole. See DIALECT, LECT. [LANGUAGE]. S.R.

MESSAGE [13c: through Old French, probably from Popular Latin *missaticum something sent, from *mittere/missum* to send]. (1) A communication of any kind that contains information, news, a request, a command, or the like. (2) A communication seen as divine, mediated by a prophet or other messenger of a god or God. (3) The meaning, point, or moral of a work of art, parable, allegory, action, gesture, etc. (4) In computing and information science, one or more words regarded as a unit; a single group of characters (letters, numbers, symbols); a unit of information; a single transmission of data in one direction. See CODE, COMMUNICATION, CRYPTOGRAPHY, INFORMATION, MCLUHAN, MEDIUM. [LANGUAGE, MEDIA]. T.MCA.

MESTIZO [16c: from Spanish *mestizo* mixed, from Popular Latin *mixticius*, from *miscere/mixtum* to mix. The feminine *mestiza* is sometimes used: compare MÉTIS]. A non-technical term for a person of mixed ancestry, especially in Latin America (of a Spanish or Portuguese father and an Amerindian mother) and in the Philippines (of a Spanish father and a Filipino mother), and sometimes for an Amerindian who has adopted European ways and language. It has often been pejorative: 'Creoles and mestizes are for the most part too idle even to keep sheep' (Jagor, *Travels in the Philippines*, 1875). See RACISM. [AMERICAS, ASIA, NAME]. T.MCA.

METALANGUAGE [1930s: from Greek *meta-* beyond, and *language*]. A term in linguistics for language used to talk about language. In the sentence, 'In Early Middle English, the word *eyren* meant "eggs" ', the *object language* (the language under discussion) is Early Middle English, and the *metalanguage* is Modern English. In the sentence, 'In Danish there is an epistemic verb *burde* which satisfies the criteria of auxiliarity proposed above', the object language is Danish and the metalanguage is the register of linguistics in English. In the latter example, metalanguage is marked by a distinctive technical terminology: for example, *epistemic verb* and *auxiliarity*. The term *metalanguage* is also used to refer to symbolic systems that describe and discuss other such systems and in logic to refer to systems of propositions about propositions. The term is common in discussions of semantics and is often applied to specially constructed systems such as the formal logical system known as Montague grammar, devised by Richard Montague to represent linguistic semantics. The adjective relating to metalanguage is *metalinguistic*. [LANGUAGE]. J.M.A., T.MCA.

METANALYSIS [1914: from Greek *meta-* across, *análusis* loosening up. Coined by Otto Jespersen]. A technical term for a change in the way the elements in a phrase or sentence are interpreted and used, such as: Middle English *a naddre* reinterpreted as *an addre* (Modern *an adder*); Perso-Arabic *nāranj* becoming Old Provençal *auranja* then French and English *orange*, the /n/ being attracted to the article in both languages (but retained in Spanish *una naranja*).

On syntactic metanalysis, Jespersen notes: 'A good many sentences . . . are double-barrelled and present the possibility of a "metanalysis", by which "It is good for a man/not to touch a woman" may come to be apprehended as 'It is good/for a man not to touch a woman' (*Modern English Grammar*, volume 5, 1940, p. 308). [GRAMMAR, WORD].   T.MCA.

METAPHOR [16c: from Old French *métaphore*, Latin *metaphora*, Greek *metaphorá* a carrying-over, transfer]. A rhetorical figure with two senses, both originating with Aristotle in the 4c BC: (1) All figures of speech that achieve their effect through association, comparison, and resemblance. Figures like *antithesis, hyperbole, metonymy, simile* are all species of metaphor. Although this sense is not current, it lies behind the use of *metaphorical* and *figurative* as antonyms of *literal*. (2) A figure of speech which concisely compares two things by saying that one is the other. A warrior compared to a lion becomes a lion: *Achilles was a lion in the fight*. In such usages, the perception of something held in common brings together words and images from different fields: warriors and lions share bravery and strength, and so the warrior is a lion among men and the lion is a warrior among beasts.

Description. When introducing students to the idea of metaphor, teachers have generally adopted the approach of the Roman rhetorician Quintilian (1c AD), using the simpler figure simile (*He fought like a lion*) as a way in to the more complex metaphor (*He was a lion in the fight*). A typical definition on this principle is: 'A metaphor is like a simile condensed. In a simile the comparison is explicitly stated with the help of some such word as *like* or *as*, whilst in a metaphor the comparison is implied by an identification of the two things compared' (Ronald Ridout & Clifford Witting, *The Facts of English*, 1964). Such descriptions have helped generations of students recognize metaphors, but do not comment on the creative process at work. Aristotle provided a formula for creating metaphors which pointed to something inherent in all kinds of comparison. He proposed a ratio (*análogon*) of the type *A is to B, as X is to Y*, exemplified as *Life is to old age, as day is to evening*. This ratio demonstrated that *life* and *day* can come together because of a third shared factor, *time*. He then switched the second terms to get *A is to Y, as X is to B*, producing: *Life is to evening, as day is to old age*. Such a cross-over creates such phrases as *the evening of life* and *day's old age* (*Poetics*, 31. 11). Here, terms from distinct contexts are first aligned, then spliced, demonstrating the close relationship between metaphor and *analogy*. In 1936, the English critic I. A. Richards provided labels for the three aspects of metaphor implied by Aristotle: the original context or idea is the *tenor* of the metaphor, the borrowed idea is the *vehicle*, and the shared element the *ground*. In Aristotle's example, *life* is the tenor, *day* the vehicle, *time* the ground. Commentators, however, are not usually precise about where the metaphor proper resides: it is sometimes defined as the vehicle alone, sometimes as the combination of tenor and vehicle, and sometimes as tenor, vehicle, and ground together.

Range. Most commentators have been aware of how pervasive metaphor is. Quintilian considered it 'the commonest and by far the most beautiful' of figures, 'certainly so natural to us that even the uneducated unthinkingly use it a great deal' (*Institutio Oratoria*, 8). The Elizabethan critic George Puttenham treated metaphor (which he referred to as *transport*) as a literary matter, but through his examples showed that he recognized it as part of language at large:

And first, single words haue their sence and vnderstanding altered and figured many wayes, to wit, by transport, abuse, crosse-naming, new naming, change of name. This will seeme very darke to you, vnlesse it be otherwise explaned more particularly: and first of *Transport*. There is a kinde of wresting of a single word from his own right signification, to another not so naturall, but yet of some affinitie or conueniencie with it, as to say, *I cannot digest your vnkinde words*, for I cannot take them in good part: or as the man of law said, *I feele you not*, for I vnderstand not your case, because he had not his fee in his hand. Or as another said to a mouthy aduocate, *why barkest thou at me so sore?* (*The Arte of English Poesie*, 1589).

Metaphor is often used in naming and in extending the senses of words. Its capacity to name was exemplified in the US in 1966, when a group of black activists adopted the name *Black Panther*. At about the same time, people who disliked the police began calling them pigs. As a result, the sentence *Black Panthers hate pigs* could occur and be suitably interpreted in a context far removed from 'real' black panthers and pigs. In Orwell's *Animal Farm* (1945), pigs stand for Communist Party members, dogs for the police, and humans for the Russian *ancien régime*. Because of the meanings given to *pig* and *man*, the story's close is particularly potent as a comment on the fate of revolutions:

Twelve voices were shouting in anger, and they were all alike. No question, now, what had happened to the faces of the pigs. The creatures outside looked from pig to man, and from man to pig, and from pig to man again; but already it was impossible to say which was which.

Extended metaphors. Orwell's tale is an *allegory*, based on the *master metaphor* 'farm is to state as animals are to citizens', and its plot runs parallel to real life. The result of its use throughout a text is an *extended metaphor*, a device which can operate at many levels of speech and writing. The same imagery may run through a text, as a writer develops an analogy between the topic of immediate interest and another topic considered relevant and informative:

The architect delivers a number of completely impersonal plan drawings and typewritten specifications. They must be so unequivocal that there will be no doubt about the construction. He composes the music which others will play. Furthermore, in order to understand architecture fully, it must be remembered that the people who play it are not sensitive musicians interpreting another's score. . . . On the contrary, they are a multitude of ordinary people (S. E. Rasmussen, *Experiencing Architecture*, 1959).

Here, the writer splices architecture and music, so that tenor and vehicle run together through the whole paragraph. In the following text, the writer is more explicit, turning direct comparison into metaphor:

Can I compare Mrs Thatcher to a tomb-robber? Well, I can try. Nearly a decade ago, she broke through into the subterranean hall of sacred British assumptions. Her candle showed frowning idols towering in the shadows, each guarding its basin of gold, each inscribed with a curse on the violator. A thrill of fear must have run through her as she scooped the first handfuls of treasure: would the statues topple and crush her, or would the heraldic beasts leap at her from the darkness? But nothing happened. She took more. Still nothing. It was not long before she was striding about the tomb giving orders, as bull-dozers broke in and began to drag the colossi out into daylight and away to museums (Neal Ascherson, 'The Tomb-Robber of Downing St', *Observer*, 22 May 1988).

Metaphoric networks. In addition to this extension of a theme through a single discourse, networks of metaphor criss-cross language at large, especially in the form of idioms and sayings. In proverbs, similar advice may be proffered through different images: *A stitch in time saves nine, Look before you leap, Don't count your chickens before they're hatched, Don't cross your bridges before you come to them.* Idioms all drawn from the same source may reflect a significant element in a society and culture: for example BrE cricketing expressions, used to talk about arguments, contests, and life itself. A politician might *go in to bat* in the House of Commons, intent on *knocking the Opposition for six*, only to be *clean-bowled, stumped,* or *caught out* by an opponent. If people do things *off their own bat*, they do them without help from anyone else, and if they live to be a hundred, they *knock up their century*, in which case they have had *a (jolly) good innings.* The master metaphor animating such usages can be compactly expressed as: *Life is a Game of Cricket.*

Creative users of language can build up successions of linked metaphors in complex patterns. For example, in the *Rubáiyát of Omar Khayyám* (1859), Edward Fitzgerald equates life with a cup of wine and time with fire, clothing, and a bird, in the delicately ornate style of Persian poetry:

Come, fill the Cup, and in the fire of Spring
The Winter-garment of Repentance fling:
The Bird of Time has but a little way
To fly—and Lo, the Bird is on the Wing.

In the same poem, he extends one master metaphor through nine verses, in which God is potter and humankind his pots:

Shapes of all Sorts and Sizes, great and small,
That stood along the floor and by the wall;
And some loquacious Vessels were; and some
Listened perhaps, but never talked at all.

Said one among them—'Surely not in vain
'My Substance of the common Earth was ta'en
'And to this Figure moulded, to be broke,
'Or trampled back to shapeless Earth again.'

After a momentary silence spake
Some Vessel of a more ungainly Make;
'They sneer at me for leaning all awry;
'What! did the Hand then of the Potter shake?'

The universality of metaphor. Because metaphor is so pervasive in linguistic and cultural terms, it is often seen as central to thought and ordinary, non-literary language. In such speculation, the broader Aristotelian interpretation of metaphor is evoked. Language is seen as a system of symbols running parallel to reality, its purpose to blend form and meaning. All models of existence are associative make-believe: 'Existence is *like* X or Y', 'It is *as if* there were a Heavenly Father', or as T. R. Wright has put it: 'If narrative is the way we construct our sense of identity, metaphor is how we think, especially in areas in which we need to build our knowledge of the unknown by comparison with the known' (*Theology and Literature*, 1988). He adds that theology 'has always been irredeemably riddled with metaphor'. The Christian Gospels 'make Jesus repeatedly risk and often suffer the misunderstanding of the literal-minded', so that in Matthew (16: 6-7) the disciples say that they have no bread when Jesus warns them against accepting the leaven of the Pharisees, while in John (3: 4) Nicodemus wonders how a man can enter his mother's womb a second time so as to be 'born again'. Most religions and ideologies are imaginative in the shapes they lend reality, asserting in faith the virtues of Image X over Picture Y or Model Z. Wright considers that it is not so important to replace one metaphor with another ('addressing God continually as Mother instead of Father, She rather than He') as to

understand the processes involved in concretizing infinity and 'recognize the metaphorical status of all these terms'.

Dead metaphors. Whether such a status is recognized or not, metaphors and models tend to have a time of vigour, after which they may 'fade' and 'die'. Traditionally, those that have lost their force have been called *dead metaphors*; as such, they may still continue in service as *clichés* and *hackneyed expressions*. Many venerable metaphors have been literalized into everyday items of language: a clock has a *face* (unlike human or animal face), and on that face are *hands* (unlike biological hands); only in terms of clocks can hands be located on a face. Again, *decide* began as a metaphor, where Latin *decidere* meant *to cut through* something in order to achieve a conclusion or a solution. In their turn, *conclusion* and *solution* were once metaphorical (Latin *concludere* to shut up, and *solvere* to unfasten). The deadness of a metaphor and its status as a cliché are relative matters. Hearing for the first time that 'life is no bed of roses', someone might be quite swept away by its aptness and vigour.

See ALLEGORY, ANALOGY, CARTOON, DERIVATION, FANTASY, FIGURATIVE EXTENSION, FIGURATIVE LANGUAGE/USAGE, IDIOM, IMAGE, METONYMY, MIXED METAPHOR, MODEL, PERSONIFICATION/PROSOPOPOEIA, POETRY, PUN, SIMILE. [NAME, STYLE]. T.MCA.

Bartel, Roland. 1983. *Metaphors and Symbols*. Urbana: National Council of Teachers of English.
Brooke-Rose, Christine. 1958. *A Grammar of Metaphor*. London: Secker & Warburg.
Jakobson, Roman, & Halle, Morris. 1956. *Fundamentals of Language*. The Hague: Mouton.
Lakoff, G., & Johnson, M. 1980. *Metaphors We Live By*. University of Chicago Press.
Ortony, A. (ed.). 1979. *Metaphor and Thought*. Cambridge: University Press.
Nowottny, Winifred. 1962. *The Language Poets Use*. London: Athlone Press.
Richards, I. A. 1936. *The Philosophy of Rhetoric*. Oxford: University Press.
Ricœur, Paul. 1978. *The Rule of Metaphor*. Translated by Robert Czerny. London: Routledge & Kegan Paul.
Sacks, Sheldon (ed.). 1978. *On Metaphor*. Chicago: University Press.
Soskice, Janet M. 1985. *Metaphor and Religious Language*. Oxford: University Press.

METATHESIS [16c: through Latin from Greek *metáthesis* placing across. Stress: 'me-TA-the-sis']. The transposition of elements of language, usually two sounds and/or letters in a word: Old English *bridd* becoming Modern English *bird*, Middle English *Manisk* becoming Modern English *Manx*. Non-standard *aks* in *Don' aks me* metathesizes standard *ask*. Compare SLIP OF THE TONGUE, SPOONERISM, X. [STYLE]. T.MCA.

METCHIF PATOIS. See MÉTIS.

METER. See METRE.

METHOD [14c: from Latin *methodus*, Greek *méthodos* ('way across') a way, means]. A procedure for teaching and learning a language. The term became popular in the late 19c and for many decades it was incorporated (capitalized) into the names of particular procedures: *the Direct Method, the Berlitz Method, the Natural Method, the Oral Method, the Audio-lingual Method*. Proponents of 'Methods' have often presented them as sure-fire solutions. Since the 1960s, the initial capital has tended to be dropped (*the direct method, the grammar-translation method*) and the more tentative *approach* often used instead (*the situational approach, the humanistic approach, the communicative approach*). The terms are often interchangeable (*the direct approach, the situational method*), and many methods or approaches have names that do not incorporate either term: *cognitive code teaching, the Monitor Model, the Silent Way, Suggestopedia, Total Physical Response*. See APPROACH, LANGUAGE TEACHING, TEFL, TESL. [EDUCATION]. T.MCA.

MÉTIS [1810s: through French from Latin *mixticius*, mixed, from *miscere/mixtum* to mix. Compare MESTIZO, *miscegenate*]. Also **mixed-bloods**, and pejoratively **half-breeds**. Canadian names for individuals and communities of Amerindian and European descent (usually from European fur traders and Native women), especially those who settled in the 19c in the valleys of the Red, Assiniboine, and Saskatchewan rivers: French-speaking Roman Catholic Métis (also called *les bois brûlés*: burnt woods) and English-speaking Métis (also called *English half-breeds* or *Métis anglais*). The latter were usually descendants of Scots employed by the Hudson's Bay Company and if so were also called *Hudson Bay Scots* or *improved Scotsmen*. For some, the term *Métis* is properly restricted to the French group. In 1870, the Métis set up a provisional government in the Red River area under the leadership of Louis Riel. Troops were sent in by the federal government after the Métis tried and executed a government surveyor, and Riel fled to the US. After Manitoba joined Confederation in 1870, Métis interests were ignored in favour of the railways and new settlers; many moved to Saskatchewan, and the failure of their attempts to claim land there sparked the North-West Rebellion of 1885, again led by Riel. The Métis have founded various political and cultural organizations, mainly to pursue land claims, often in alliance with status and non-status

Indians. The Constitution Act of 1982 recognized them as an aboriginal people.

The word *Métis* is part of the general vocabulary of CanE, usually pronounced /'meti/ as in French, but in the Prairies sometimes as /'mɛtɪs/, while older Native people say it as 'metchif'. Pidgin languages spoken by the Métis were used in the fur trade, centred in the Red River Valley, now in the province of Manitoba. The best-known English-based dialect is *Bungee* (from Ojibwa *panki* a little), also known as the *Red River dialect*. Howard Adams has recalled: 'In all the twenty years I spent in my halfbreed home, a bed was known as a *paillasse* (*pa-jas*). Doughnuts made by Métis women were called "la bange" [French *beignet*]. . . . When I first went into mainstream society my Métis ways were ridiculed and my language of "Metchif patois", a combination of English, French, and Cree, was openly mocked' (*Prison of Grass: Canada from the Native Point of View*, 1975, p. 175). The writer Maria Campbell reported in an interview: 'We talk English, but we talk such a broken mixture of French, English, Gaelic and Cree, all mixed together' (to Doris Hills in 'You Have to Own Yourself', in *Prairie Fire*, 1988). [AMERICAS, NAME, VARIETY].   M.F.

METONYMY [16c: from Latin *metonymia*, Greek *metōnumia* change of name, cross-naming]. A figure of speech which designates something by the name of something associated with it: *the Crown* substituting for monarchy, *the stage* for the theatre, *the bottle* for alcoholic drink, *No. 10 Downing Street* for the British Prime Minister, *the White House* for the US President. A word used metonymically (*crown* or *bottle*, as above) is a *metonym*. Metonymy is closely related to and sometimes hard to distinguish from *metaphor*. It has sometimes been seen as a kind of *synecdoche* and sometimes as containing synecdoche. Both metaphor and metonymy express association, metaphor through comparison, metonymy through contiguity and possession. Many standard items of vocabulary are metonymic. A *red-letter day* is important, like the feast days marked in red in church calendars. *Red tide*, the marine disease that kills fish, takes its name from the colour of one-celled, plant-like animals in the water. The word *redcap* (a porter) originally referred to a piece of red flannel tied for visibility around the caps of baggage carriers at New York's Grand Central Station. On the level of slang, a *redneck* is a stereotypical member of the white rural working class in the Southern US, originally a reference to necks sunburned from working in the fields. Often the original metonymic connection is lost, but the term persists: the business of a *red light district*, a neighbourhood where prostitutes are

available, is usually carried out without the aid of brothels sporting actual red lights. Metonymy is a strategy commonly used to make sense of reference by association. In the sentence, 'I'm parked two blocks away in an illegal parking zone', the speaker uses the pronoun *I* to stand for his or her vehicle. Instances of such pragmatic metonymy do not involve additions to the vocabulary and usually pass unnoticed in conversation. See FIGURATIVE LANGUAGE/USAGE, METAPHOR, SLANG, SYNECDOCHE. [STYLE].   C.C.E.

METRE BrE, **meter** AmE [14c: from Old French *metre* (Modern *mètre*), Latin *metrum*, Greek *métron* a measure]. In music, the pattern of regular pulses and the arrangement of their parts, by which a piece of music is measured in terms of time (the number of beats to the bar); in prosody, a comparable stylized rhythm by which verse is measured in time (the number of feet to the line). The study of metre is known, especially in the US, as *metrics*. Two kinds of metre figure in the discussion of English verse: the *quantitative metre* of classical Greek and Latin, in which the length or quantity of a syllable depends on whether it contains a long or short vowel; the *accentual metre* of spoken English, in which accented, strong, or stressed syllables contrast with unaccented, weak, or unstressed syllables. Most of the terms used to discuss the metrical nature of English, such as *iamb* and *pentameter*, have been drawn from the classical tradition: such terms are understood quantitatively when applied to Latin and Greek, but accentually when applied to English. The labels for metres combine the name of a kind of foot, such as *iambic* or *trochaic*, with the number of feet in a line: *dimeter* for two feet, *trimeter* for three, *tetrameter* for four, *pentameter* for five, *hexameter* for six, and *heptameter* for seven. Combinations include *trochaic tetrameter*, *iambic pentameter*, and *dactylic hexameter*.

The distinctness of the two kinds of rhythm has not always been clear; under the influence of the classical languages 16c poets of English such as Spenser and Sidney attempted quantitative verse, without great success. Coleridge, Tennyson, and Bridges also experimented with quantitative metre, but English vowel quantity is too uncertain to produce consistent results. No major work of English poetry is quantitative. All Old English and some Middle English poetry was composed in *strong-stress metres*, in which only the stressed syllables are counted and the number of unstressed syllables is not fixed. The stressed words in such poems were also marked by alliteration. The metric conventions in some Middle English and most traditional Modern English poetry, however, fix the number of unstressed syllables. Few poems are entirely regular; syntactic or rhetorical demands for stress can cause breaks in the pattern adopted, affecting the regularity of the feet in which lines are arranged. See ACCENT, FOOT, PROSODY, RHYTHM, SCANSION. [LITERATURE]. R.C., T.MCA.

METRICS. See METRE/METER, PROSODY.

MEXICAN-AMERICAN ENGLISH. See CHICANO ENGLISH, SPANISH, TESD, TEXAS, TEX-MEX.

MICRONESIA [From Greek *Micronēsia* place of small islands]. A name for island groups east of the Philippines and north of the Equator, including the Mariana, Marshall, Caroline, and Gilbert Islands. See MELANESIA, POLYNESIA. [NAME, OCEANIA]. S.R.

MID-ATLANTIC. A term for kinds of English, especially accents, that have features drawn from both North AmE and BrE: 'It may be that one of the main influences on the speech of young people in Britain today . . . is the "mid-Atlantic" flavour of the accents in which many pop singers and pop music presenters speak or sing' (John Honey, *Does Accent Matter?*, 1989). See ATLANTIC. [AMERICAS, EUROPE, VARIETY]. T.MCA.

MIDDLE AMERICAN. See AMERICAN[1].

MIDDLE ENGLISH, short forms *ME*, *M.E.* From one point of view, the second stage of the single continuously developing English language; from another, a distinct language that evolved from Old English (OE) and slowly turned into Modern English (ModE). ME began when the linguistic effects of the Norman Conquest were complete (*c.*1150) and came to an end at the start of the period that scholars generally call Early Modern English (*c.*1450). Three features of ME contrasted with OE: a greatly reduced system of grammatical inflections; greatly increased lexical borrowing from other languages, in particular French and Latin; and a highly varied and volatile orthography. Surviving texts indicate that there was no uniform way of writing ME, and as a result texts are sometimes easy to read without much help, sometimes more difficult, and sometimes wellnigh impossible. The following sentence, from Chaucer's late 14c translation of Boethius, *De Consolatione Philosophiae* (*On the Consolation of Philosophy*: opening, Book I, prose VI), is representative:

First woltow suffre me to touche and assaye the estat of thy thought by a fewe demaundes, so that I may understonde what be the manere of thy curacioun?

Word for word in more or less modern usage, this sentence runs:

First wilt thou suffer me to touch and try the state of thy thought by a few demands, so that I may understand what be the manner of thy curation?

In more relaxed modern usage still, it might be:

First will you let my try the state of your thinking by asking a few questions, so that I can understand the way you cure people?

In the original sentence, many words have the same spelling (but generally not the same pronunciation) as ModE, and their meaning is often the same (*first, me, and, the, of, thy, thought, by, a, so, that, I, may, what, be*), some have a similar spelling (but not pronunciation) to present-day usage, and much the same meaning (*touche, estat, fewe, understonde, manere*), or similar spellings but rather different meanings and uses (*suffre, demaundes*), and some are variously alien at first encounter yet become less so after translation (*woltow, assaye, curacioun*). In terms of grammar, the most obvious difference between ME and strict standard ModE (as shown by means of this specimen sentence) is the loss of the second-person pronoun (*thou*, etc.) in everyday usage, though the form was present in Early ModE and continues to be widely and easily understood. Another is the loss of the subjunctive form as used in *so that I may understonde what be*. In terms of pronunciation, ME can very broadly be said to blend Germanic and Romance sound systems, words of Germanic origin being pronounced more or less with the values of Old English, words of Romance origin being pronounced more or less as in Norman French.

Background. As a spoken vernacular, ME was continuous with OE, but as a written medium it did not have the erstwhile autonomy or prestige of OE prose and verse. Instead, it competed unequally with Latin and French through most of its history. Latin was the dominant literary and ecclesiastical language in Europe long before the Norman Conquest and well into the Renaissance, while Norman French became after the Conquest the primary language of the cultivated classes of England, sharing with Latin high prestige in literature and administration; the legal profession in particular was permeated by French and Latin. As a result, English, the language of a conquered people, made scant literary and official appearance in documents during the two centuries after the Conquest, and no dialect had precedence over any other. In the 14c, Chaucer's much-admired contemporary John Gower wrote his vast poem *Confessio Amantis* (*The Lover's Confession*) in English (yet with a Latin title), but also wrote long poems in Latin and French. Such multilingual expertise was normal among the writers and scholars of the day.

Dialects. The four great dialect boundaries of OE developed in ME as follows: (1) The vast Mercian dialect area divided into East Midland and West Midland. (2) Kentish became part of a wider South-Eastern dialect to the south of the River Thames. (3) West Saxon, latterly the most prestigious OE dialect, especially for literature, shrank westward to become the South-Western dialect, which entirely lacked the prominence of its OE ancestor. (4) Northumbrian divided into the Northern dialects of England and the Lowlands of Scotland. Scholars generally refer to ME north of the border as Middle Scots, which developed its own courtly use and literature: see SCOTS. In addition to the growth of a separate national variety in Scotland, slowly spreading at the expense of Gaelic, ME was carried through invasion and settlement westward into Wales and Ireland. Although the city of London was close to the South-Eastern dialect, the distinctive usage of the capital towards the end of the ME period was primarily influenced from north of the Thames, by East Midland. It was the high form of this eclectic metropolitan variety that in due course became the primary source of modern standard English.

Pronunciation and spelling. (1) In the main, the sounds of ME were the same as those of OE, and for several lifetimes after the Norman Conquest the written language retained many of the characteristic features of OE orthography. In due course, however, script and style changed radically under the influence of Norman French, obscuring for later readers the continuity of the pronunciation system. Whereas OE spelling was relatively stable and regular, ME spelling varied greatly from place to place, person to person, and period to period, offering many variants for the same words: for example, OE *lēaf* (ModE *leaf*) became ME *lief, lieif, leif, lefe, leue, leeue, leaue*, etc. (2) The special OE letters ash (æ), wynn (*p*), yogh (ȝ), and eth (*ð*) went out of use early in the ME period; thorn (*þ*) remained longer and appears sporadically in early 15c Chaucer manuscripts. (3) The distinctive short and long vowel pairs of OE gave way to a system in which the lax or tense state of the tongue (and not the duration of the sounds themselves) distinguished such sounds as the /ɛ/ of *vers* (verse) from the /e/ of *wep* (weep). (4) Some ME sound changes altered vowel values, resulting for example in the present-day vowel differences between singular *child, staff* (a large stick) and plural *children, staves*. (5) The OE pronunciation of the first consonant in the initial cluster *cn-* (as in *cnāwan* to know) continued for centuries, though the new spelling was *kn-*. It died out only in the later stages of ME, leaving its mark, however, in contemporary spelling, as in *know*,

knee, knight (with their 'silent' fossil *k*). (6) Similarly, the voiceless velar or palatal fricative of OE (as in German *ach* and *ich*) continued in use for most of the period in England and continues to the present day in Scots. It has usually been represented in ModE by *gh*, leaving its silent fossils in such words as *dough, night, through, thought, thorough*. In Chaucer's line 'A knight ther was, and that a worthy man', *knight* (OE *cniht*) was pronounced /knɪxt/ or /knɪçt/. (7) Consonants coming between vowels were increasingly elided, with the result that many OE disyllables have been reduced to ModE monosyllables: for example, earlier OE *hlāfweard* ('loaf-ward') became later OE/early ME *hlāford* and *laford*, then 13c *louerd*, and 15c *lord*; OE *fuȝel* (bird) developed into 12c *vuhel*, 13c *fuwel*, 14c *fouxl* and *foul* (etc.), becoming 16c *fowle, foule* (etc.), and ModE *fowl*. (8) The voiced values /v/ and /z/ of the OE letters *f* and *s* became distinctive sounds in their own right, distinguished *fat* from *vat* and *seal* from *zeal*.

Grammar. (1) While the sound system of ME was relatively unchanged from OE, the inflectional system was greatly reduced, possibly because of close, long-term contacts between native OE speakers and first Danish- then French-speaking settlers. (2) The main classes of verb inflection survived, but the distinction in strong verbs between the singular and the plural of the past was on its way out in Chaucer's day: for example, for the verb *bind* (from OE *bindan* to bind), he had the past singular *bond* (from OE *band*) and past plural *bounde* (from OE *bundon*), but *bond* was soon to vanish as ModE *bound* took over both the singular and plural. (3) The occasional surviving inflectional suffixes for the plural and the infinitive in Chaucer's day likewise soon disappeared, and the four-case OE inflections for the noun were reduced to two (common and possessive) as in ModE. (4) The OE function words (pronouns and articles, conjunctions, prepositions, and auxiliary verbs) remained in ME and largely survive to the present day.

Vocabulary. (1) By and large, the everyday vocabulary of OE has survived into ME and ModE, as in the following sets, with OE first, then typical ME, then ModE: *bricg, bregge, bridge; fæstnian, festen, fasten; īegland, eland, island; langung, longinge, longing; nīwe, newe, new; strang, stronge, strong*. (2) As a result of the Norman Conquest and the great social and political changes that came in its wake, many OE words fell entirely out of use, often being supplanted by words of French provenance: for example, *eftsīð* was replaced by *retorn, retorne, retourne*, etc. (return), *eorlscipe* ('earlship') by *nobilite, nobylyte*, etc. (nobility), and *lārcwide* by *conseil, counseil,* etc. (counsel). (3) In the centuries immediately after the Conquest, English took on the basic forms and patterns of its present-day dual Germanic and Romance vocabulary: for example, native-based *freedom* as against French-based *liberty*; *hearty* versus *cordial*; *kingly* and *royal* (and also *regal*, directly from Latin); *knight* and *chevalier*, *knighthood* and *chivalry*; *lawful* and *legal*, *unlawful* and *illegal*, *unlawfulness* and *illegality*; *pig* and *pork*, *sheep* and *mutton*, *calf* and *veal*, *cow* and *beef*. See BISOCIATION, NORMAN FRENCH.

Intelligibility. ME words generally bear a fair resemblance to their present-day descendants, with the result that reading ME without help, though by no means always easy, is far simpler than reading OE: the OE sentence *Gemiltsa mīnum suna* (*c*.1000) is entirely foreign to speakers of ModE, but the ME equivalent *Haue mercy on my sone* (though only about 385 years more recent and with a distinctive pronunciation) shows its antiquity in only two small oddities of spelling. The grammatical functions signified by the suffixes on all three OE words in this sentence are gone; the grammatical function of *my sone* is indicated not by a case ending as in OE but by the preposition *on* (absent in OE); and the function of *haue* is indicated by word order. The OE word *gemiltsa* has vanished, replaced by a phrase composed of OE *haue* in its ME form, and ME *mercy*, borrowed from French. See CHAUCER.

Texts. The literary and other texts of ME vary greatly, dependent on the time and place of writing and often the individual orthographic inclinations of the writer: for further detail, see ENGLISH LITERATURE, PROSE. Below are three brief specimens. The first is from the 13–14c: the opening lines of an anonymous lyric poem. The second belongs to the late 14c, and is also anonymous: the work of a West Midlands poet that continues the alliterative verse patterns of OE. The third is from the 14c translation of a popular Latin work that provided the specimen sentence at the beginning of this entry.

(1) *Verse: Alison*

> Bytuene Mersh and Averil,
> When spray biginneth to springe,
> The lutel foul hath hire wyl
> On hyre lud to synge.
> Ich libbe in love-longinge
> For semlokest of alle thinge—
> He may me blisse bringe;
> Icham in hire baundoun.

TRANSLATION

> Between March and April,
> When the twigs begin to leaf,
> The little bird is free
> To sing her song.
> I live in love-longing

> For the seemliest of all things—
> She may bring me bliss;
> I am in her power.

(From *The Norton Anthology of Poetry*, coordinating editor Arthur M. Eastman, New York 1970, p. 5)

(2) *Verse: Sir Gawain and the Green Knight* (opening lines)

> Sithen the sege and the assaut was sesed at Troye,
> The borgh brittened and brent to brondes and askes,
> The tulk that the trammes of tresoun there wrought
> Was tried for his tricherie, the trewest on erthe.
> Hit was Ennias the athel and his highe kynde,
> The sithen depreced provinces, and patrounes bicome
> Welneghe of al the wele in the west iles.

TRANSLATION

> After the siege and the assault were ceased at Troy.
> The city crumbled and burned to brands and ashes,
> The man who the plots of treason there wrought
> Was tried for his treachery, the truest on earth.
> It was Aeneas the noble and his high race,
> Who after subjugated provinces, and lords became
> Wellnigh of all the wealth in the western isles.

(Adapted from the version in *The Norton Anthology of English Literature*, general editor M. H. Abrams, 5th edition, vol. I, New York, 1986, pp. 232-3)

(3) *Prose: Chaucer's translation of the* De Consolatione Philosophiae *of Boethius*

Allas! I, weping, am constreined to biginnen vers of sorowful matere, that whylom in florisching studie made delitable ditees. For lo! rendinge Muses of poetes endyten to me thinges to be writen; and drery vers of wrecchednesse weten my face with verray teres. At the leeste, no drede ne mighte overcomen tho Muses, that they ne weren felawes, and folweden my wey, *that is to seyn, whan I was exyled*; they that weren glorie of my youthe, whylom weleful and grene, comforten now the sorowful werdes of me, olde man (from the *Complete Works of Geoffrey Chaucer*, Oxford University Press, 1954).

[Glossary: *weping* weeping, *whylom* formerly, *delitable* delightful, *ditee* a ditty, song, *endyte(n)* to write, *verray* true, real, *tere* a tear(drop), *no drede ne mighte* (double negative) no dread might, *tho* those, *felawe* a companion, comrade, *folwe* to follow, *seyn* to say, *whan* when, *weleful* ('well-ful') prosperous, happy]

See ANGLO-IRISH, CAXTON, CHANCERY STANDARD, CHAUCER, EARLY ENGLISH, EARLY MODERN ENGLISH, ENGLISH, ENGLISH LITERATURE, FRENCH, GREAT VOWEL SHIFT, HISTORY OF ENGLISH (AND CHRONOLOGY), HUMO(U)R, LAW FRENCH, LONG AND SHORT, MIDDLE ENGLISH DICTIONARY, NORMAN, NORMAN FRENCH, OLD ENGLISH[1], OLD ENGLISH[2], PERIOD DICTIONARIES OF ENGLISH, PROSE, SCOTS, YOLA. [EUROPE, HISTORY, VARIETY].

W.F.B., T.MCA.

Brunner, Karl. 1970. *An Outline of Middle English Grammar*. Oxford: Basil Blackwell.

Cottle, Basil. 1969. *The Triumph of English, 1350-1400*, London: Blandford Press.

Jones, Charles. 1972. *An Introduction to Middle English*. New York: Holt, Rinehart & Winston.

Kurath, Hans, & Kuhn, Sherman M. (eds.). 1954- .
Middle English Dictionary. Ann Arbor: University
of Michigan Press.
Mossé, Fernand. 1952. *A Handbook of Middle English*.
Baltimore: Johns Hopkins University Press.

MIDDLE ENGLISH DICTIONARY, short
form *MED*. A dictionary on historical principles
now close to completion, covering the period
1100-1475. In his sketch of future dictionaries
(1919), William A. Craigie declared existing
accounts of Middle English vocabulary inadequate and envisaged a dictionary that would
encompass the 'marvellous richness and interest'
of both the language and 'the manners and customs of the time'. Though some earlier scholars
had gathered material for a planned Chaucer
dictionary, editing for a comprehensive *MED*
took place at Cornell U. under the direction of
C. S. Northup during 1925-30. The materials
were transferred in 1930 to the U. of Michigan
so that work might profit from editing then in
progress for the *Early Modern English Dictionary*. Soon thereafter, Craigie arranged for the
transfer to Michigan of the Middle English citations gathered for the *OED* in Oxford. A reading
programme (1930-4) led by Samuel Moore
increased the collection by 280,000 slips from
66,000 pages read or re-read from selected texts.
At the same time, a dialect census helped date
and localize manuscripts so that regional terms
could be identified and described. Following
Moore's sudden death, Thomas A. Knott
became editor (1935-45), though economic
depression and World War II made rapid progress impossible. In 1946, Hans Kurath became
editor and under his direction publication began
in 1954. On his retirement in 1961, responsibility
for the project was successively assigned to
Sherman M. Kuhn, John Reidy, and Robert E.
Lewis. The *MED* is rich in etymological discoveries; meanings are conveyed through Modern English translations, and brief encyclopedic
notes are appended to explain details of medieval
English technology, society, and culture. Like all
dictionaries on historical principles, the *MED*
provides abundant quotations to illustrate constructions and range of meanings. Issued in fascicles by the University of Michigan Press, the
MED is expected to reach completion in 1994.
See OXFORD DICTIONARY OF ENGLISH ETYMOLOGY,
PERIOD DICTIONARIES OF ENGLISH. [HISTORY, REF-
ERENCE].   R.W.B.

MIDDLE NAME. See PERSONAL NAME.

MIDDLE SCOTS. See SCOTS.

MIDLAND. (1) For the UK, see MIDLANDS. (2)
For the US, see DIALECT IN AMERICA.

MIDLANDS, The. A region of England often
associated with dialect and contrasted with *the
North* and *the South*. It is generally held that
there were five main dialect areas in medieval
England: *Northern, East Midland, West
Midland, Southern,* and *Kentish*. The Midland
group are described as having clearly defined
boundaries. They were found north of the
Thames and Severn and south of a line from the
mouth of the Humber to the west coast, south
of Heysham, and the line of the Pennines divided
the East Midland and West Midland areas.
Some dialectologists consider that such boundaries continue to be significant in contemporary
language research, others that the post-industrial
urban dialects of the cities of Birmingham, Wol-
verhampton, Leicester, and Peterborough now
exert greater influence than those of the rural
areas. Apart from speakers of RP, most people
in the English Midlands share features of pronunciation with speakers from the North rather
than the South. They often use /ʊ/ not /ʌ/ in
words such as *but, come, fun, some* (*put* and *putt*
being homophones), and use /a/ for the RP
sounds /æ/ and /ɑ/, so that the vowel sound is
the same in *bat* and *bath, lass* and *last, pat* and
path. The speech of the Midlands is not,
however, homogeneous. People in the West are
more likely to use /ŋg/ for /ŋ/ in words such as
singing /sɪŋgɪŋg/ and *tongue* /tʊŋg/, to use
/ɒn/, not /an/, in words such as *man* and *pan*,
and to be to some degree rhotic in words such
as *far* and *farm*. People in the north-east of the
region are generally likely to use /z/ in *us*, to
substitute /r/ for /t/ in *got a* ('gorra'), and to
use an alveolar tap for /r/ instead of the more
widely used post-alveolar approximant of RP.
See BIRMINGHAM, DIALECT IN ENGLAND, EAST
ANGLIA, EAST MIDLAND DIALECT, MERCIA.
[EUROPE, NAME, VARIETY].   L.T., S.E.

MILTON, John [1608-74]. English poet and
pamphleteer, born in London and educated at
St Paul's School and Cambridge. He travelled
abroad, mainly in Italy (1637-9). In the Civil
War, he supported the Parliamentarian side and
was Latin Secretary to the Commonwealth government afterwards. He became blind in 1651.
After the Restoration, he escaped reprisals and
lived quietly in London. His early poems, in Italian and Latin as well as English, included sonnets in the Italian form and the contrasting pair
'L'Allegro' and 'Il Penseroso'. He wrote a
masque, 'Comus' (1634), and a long elegy, 'Lycidas' (1637). During his years of public office,
he wrote polemical pamphlets in prose, notably
Areopagitica (1644), a plea for freedom of the
press. His greatest works are the 12-book *Paradise Lost* (1667), which established the use of

blank verse for English epic poetry, the four-book *Paradise Regained* (1671), and a Biblical tragedy in classical style, *Samson Agonistes* (1671). His style in both prose and verse is classical, often using borrowed words in their original Latin meanings: *admire* wonder at, *involved* wrapped in, *offend* harm, *fame* report, rumour. He also constructed his poetry in a Latinate style, as in the following extract, in which the main verb is delayed until the end of the sentence:

> Till, the signal given,
> Behold a wonder! they but now who seem'd
> In bigness to surpass Earths Giant Sons
> No less than smallest Dwarfs, in narrow room
> Swarm numberless.
>
> (from *Paradise Lost*, Book 1)

He also, however, used popular and dialect words and experimented with spelling, differentiating stressed and unstressed pronouns: *thir* unstressed, *their* stressed; *we* unstressed, *wee* stressed. He sometimes favoured pronunciation over tradition (*sovran* for *sovereign*), and indicated a syllabic consonant with an apostrophe (*forbidd'n*), and coined *pandemonium* ('place of all demons') as the name for Satan's palace in Hell. See index. [BIOGRAPHY, EUROPE, HISTORY, LITERATURE, STYLE].   R.C.

MIME [17c: from Latin *mimus*, Greek *mîmos* imitator: compare MIMESIS]. Acting without speech, depending on gesture, movement, and facial expression to convey feelings and actions. The mimed performance may be given by one actor or several working together. The mime was popular in the classical theatre, particularly in Rome. It appears in Elizabethan and Jacobean drama as the *dumb show*, prefiguring what is to be fully enacted later or giving a disguised message to characters in the play; the dumb show before the visiting players' performance in Shakespeare's *Hamlet* is a well-known example. Mimes were performed on the later English stage, and were popular in the 18c. The era of the silent film brought mime to a new level of sophistication, notably in the acting of Charlie Chaplin. Celebrated stage mimes in the 20c include the French actor Marcel Marceau, who combined clownish humour with an exploration of physical movement. Mime has enjoyed a new status in the second half of the 20c as an important aspect of contemporary theatre, perhaps reflecting a distrust of language and a clown-like view of the human situation.

Mime is a form of non-linguistic semiotics, distinct from systems like sign language for the deaf, which depend on an underlying language system and are not universally comprehensible. Much mimed action can be widely shared, such as shading the eyes to look into the distance.

Some gestures, however, like the 'thumbs up' of triumph, are limited to particular groups of speakers. Mime that is recorded in a text must be verbalized descriptively, as in printed editions of early plays, and may be interpreted in words by a character on the stage. Similar explanation will follow the more private entertainment of silent charades, which are also initially planned through the medium of language. Compare CHARADE, GESTURE, MUMMERY, SIGN LANGUAGE. [LANGUAGE, LITERATURE].   R.C.

MIMEOGRAPH [1880s, AmE: from Greek *miméomai* I imitate, and *-graph*. A trademark, 1903-48]. Short form *mimeo*. (1) Also especially BrE *duplicator*. A desk-size printing machine with an ink-loaded drum around which is wrapped a waxed stencil containing perforations made by handwriting or typing. As the drum is rotated by a handle, successive sheets of paper are fed to it, receiving impressions from the ink passing through the stencil. (2) A copy made by this means. See PRINTING. [TECHNOLOGY].T.MCA.

MIMESIS [17c: through Latin from Greek *mimēsis* imitation: compare MIME]. (1) In rhetoric, the imitation or reproduction of someone's supposed words, especially so as to represent his or her character and interests. (2) Mimicry. (3) The condition through which art and literature seek to imitate and represent life. See POETICS. [LITERATURE].   T.MCA.

MINCED OATH [Perhaps 16c: from *mince* to soften, suggesting both primness and indirectness. Compare a *mincing* walk and the idioms *not (to) mince words/matters*]. A semi-technical term for a swearword modified so as to be used without giving offence: *God* modified to *Gosh*, *shit* to *shoot*. Two forms of modification are common: (1) Creating a nonsense equivalent: *(by) God* becoming *(by) Golly/Gosh/Gum*; *Jesus* becoming monosyllabic *Gee* or disyllabic *Jeepers*, and *Jesus Christ* becoming *Jeepers Creepers*; *hell* becoming *heck*. (2) Substituting an everyday expression of similar sound and length, sometimes with an associated meaning, sometimes with no association whatever: *bloody* becoming *ruddy*; *damn (it)* becoming *darn (it)*; *fuck* becoming *flip*. See CENSORSHIP, EUPHEMISM, SWEARING, TABOO. [STYLE].   T.MCA.

MINIM [17c: from Latin *minimus* smallest]. In handwriting and calligraphy, a single downstroke of the pen, and, especially in Court hand or Secretary hand, the short downstroke in the letters *m*, *n*, *u*, etc. Compare ASCENDER AND DESCENDER, SERIF. [TECHNOLOGY, WRITING]. T.MCA.

MINIMAL PAIR. In phonetics, a pair of words that differ in one phoneme, such as *pin* and *bin* /pɪn, bɪn/ or *rich* and *wretch* /rɪtʃ, rɛtʃ/. *Sick* and *sink* are a minimal pair, the latter having an extra phoneme; *slink* and *shrink* are not minimal, as they differ in two phonemes. Minimal pairs are used in order to ascertain the phonemes of a language or dialect. Some differences are however phonetic rather than phonemic: for example, the differences in the vowels of *feed* and *feel* can be ascribed to the influence of the following consonants, and so the vowels are allophones of the same phoneme and not independent phonemes. The contrasting vowels of *bead* and *bid*, on the other hand, are in the same environment (in this instance, preceded by /b/ and followed by /d/), and must therefore belong to different phonemes. Pairs that are different in one dialect may be identical in another: for example, *cod* and *cawed* contrast in RP, but are identical in some Irish dialects. See OPPOSITION, PHONEME. [SPEECH]. G.K., T.MCA.

MINUSCULE. See CAPITAL (LETTER).

MIS- [A vernacular prefix as in *mistake*, associated with French formations in *més-*, as in *misadventure* (*mésaventure*). In Old and Middle English manuscripts, forms containing *mis-* were sometimes written as two words, sometimes as one; a hyphen was never used. From the 16c, the compounds have been printed as one word, with or without a hyphen, which is currently rare]. A prefix with such meanings as 'amiss', 'bad(ly)', 'wrong(ly)', 'improper(ly)', and 'mistaken(ly)', often used to identify error in the use of language: *mispronounce, misspelling, misrelated participle, misuse*. See MISPRINT, MISPRONUNCIATION, MISSPEAK, MISTAKE, MUMPSIMUS, QUOTATION. [STYLE, WORD]. T.MCA.

MISKITO COAST CREOLE, also **Miskito Coast Creole English, Nicaraguan English**. The language of the Creoles of the Miskito Coast (the Caribbean coast of Nicaragua and Honduras, named after Carib Indians known as Miskitos). Its focus is Bluefields, Pearl Lagoon, and Corn Island in Nicaragua and it is a second language of many Amerindian and Spanish speakers. It dates from the mid-17c and is similar to other varieties of Creole, but its vocabulary has been influenced by Spanish and Chibcha. See CARIBBEAN CREOLE ENGLISH, CENTRAL AMERICA. [AMERICAS, VARIETY]. L.C.

MISPRINT [15c]. Also *printer's error*. A mistake in printing, such as a missing letter, taken to be the responsibility or fault of the typesetter, editor, or publisher and not usually the writer.

A *misspelling* in print may or may not be a misprint. See BIBLE, LITERAL, MIS-, TYPOGRAPHICAL ERROR. [TECHNOLOGY]. T.MCA.

MISPRONUNCIATION [16c]. Wrong pronunciation, usually of a specific sound: for example, when a foreign learner of English says 'chilled' for *child* (on the analogy of *build* and *gild*); or, in the accentual pattern of a word, stressing *cement* on the first syllable and eliding the *t*, so that it sounds like *seaman* or *semen*. Within one language, what is correct in one variety may be incorrect in another: in most accents of English, the word *loch* (as in the name *Loch Lomond*) is a homophone of *lock*, but in ScoE it ends with the velar fricative /x/, as in German *ach*; most Scots regard the pronunciation 'lock' as incorrect, and many find it irritating. For foreign learners, the mispronunciation of English words may occur for systemic reasons, because of the phonology of their mother tongues, as with the tendency among German-speakers to devoice final voiced consonants:

At this point Nora appears to say: 'You vill not vont much, John, after the crap you had earlier!'
'Crap? . . . You don't talk about things like that in public, you know!'
There has, though, been a misunderstanding.
'I am talking about the crap you bought on the beach, John,' Nora explains.
'Oh, the crab!' Lydon realises. 'She's saying crab!'
(interview with the punk rocker Johnny Rotten/ John Lydon, *The Independent Magazine*, 27 Oct. 1990).

Among native speakers of English, the mispronunciation of a word or name usually arises from unfamiliarity, either because an item is exotic (as with 'makizmo' for *machismo*) or because it derives from Latin or Greek (as with 'fthizzis' for *phthisis*, usually pronounced 'thigh-sis' or 'tie-sis'). Many English words of classical origin have two or more possible pronunciations. Sometimes both or all the variants are accepted, as with 'hibbiskus' and 'highbiskus' for *hibiscus*, and with 'HEDGE-emony', 'heDGEMony', and 'heGGEMony' for *hegemony*. Sometimes one or the other is widely regarded as an error, as with *lamentable*, when stressed on the second syllable. See BBC PRONUNCIATION UNIT, ELOCUTION, MIS-, PRONUNCIATION. [SPEECH, USAGE]. T.MCA.

MISRELATED PARTICIPLE. See PARTICIPLE.

MISSPEAK [12c]. (1) Obsolete: to speak wrongly, improperly, and disrespectfully; to speak ill: 'I me repente if I mis spak' (Chaucer, *Troylus and Criseyde*, c.1374). (2) To speak, say, or pronounce something in an incorrect or inappropriate way: *I'm sorry; I misspoke that bit—*

I'll say it again. (3) Reflexive: to fail to convey the intended meaning: ' "The President," Ziegler said, "misspoke himself." He explained that [President Nixon] had noted his error in reviewing the transcript of the press conference' (*Harper's Magazine*, June 1973). See MIS-. [STYLE].   T.MCA.

MISTAKE [From Old Norse *mistaka* to err, miscarry]. A misapprehension of meaning or a fault in execution: 'Your whole letter is full of mistakes from one end to the other' (Lady M. W. Montagu to Lady Richmond, letter, 17 June 1717). Like Lady Richmond, everyone is at some time or other taken to task for committing an actual or perceived mistake. Following Chomsky (*Aspects of the Theory of Syntax*, 1965), mistakes can be divided into two types: *competence mistakes* (sometimes technically called *errors*), that arise from ignorance of or ineptness in using a language (as when an EFL learner says 'He no comes today' or a native user spells *receive* 'recieve'); *performance mistakes* (technically *mistakes*), where one knows what to say or write but through tiredness, emotion, nervousness, or some other pressure makes a slip of the tongue, leaves out a word, or mistypes a letter. People are particularly frustrated if a slip in performance is seen as a gap in their competence.

Native speakers, however, tend to get away with more slips than foreigners; in conversation, they can stop, start, change grammatical direction, mispronounce and then correct themselves, and so forth, without much or any censure, but a foreign user's shortcomings are on display all the time. Advanced users of a second language often appear to set themselves higher standards for that language than for their own, partly because they are more conscious of the mistakes they make in it. In educational circles, conservative teachers tend to treat mistakes as disease-like symptoms that need isolation through red ink. Radical teachers tend to overlook mistakes in the interests of good relations, students' confidence, and their ability to communicate and create. Neither extreme appears to be efficient in teaching the mother tongue or another language: the first intimidates and depresses, while the second may invite chaos. Since it appears to be inherent in the human condition to slip up in language as in other matters, a balance between correction and censure on the one side and turning a blind eye or a deaf ear on the other may be more productive.

See ACCEPTABILITY, ANALOGY, BAD ENGLISH, BARBARISM, CATACHRESIS, COMPETENCE, CONFUSIBLE, CORRECT, CORRUPT, DEVIANT, ERROR ANALYSIS, FREUDIAN SLIP, GHOST WORD, GOOD ENGLISH, GRAMMAR CHECKER, GRAMMATICALITY, HOWLER, LITERAL, MALAPROPISM, MIS-, MISPRINT, MISPRONUNCIATION, MISSPEAK, MISTAKE NAME, PLEONASM, PROOF-READING, SHIBBOLETH, SLIP OF THE TONGUE, SLIPSHOD, SLOPPY, SLOVENLY, SOLECISM, SPELLING, SPELLING CHECKER, SPOONERISM, STYLE CHECKER, TAUTOLOGY, TYPOGRAPHICAL ERROR. [EDUCATION, STYLE, USAGE].   T.MCA.

MISTAKE NAME [1970: first used by George R. Stewart in *American Place-Names* (New York: Oxford University Press)]. A place-name whose form has been modified as the result of a mistake in writing or reading it: for example, *Yolo* in California is of Amerindian origin, but *Tolo* in Oregon, which is said to have been named after it, has an erroneous substitution in the first letter. [NAME].   J.A.

MIXED METAPHOR. A feature of style in which unrelated and sometimes discordant metaphors occur together: 'The butter mountain has been in the pipeline for some time' (President of Farmers' Union, BBC1 news, 1987). The practice is widely regarded as a stylistic flaw caused by unthinkingly mixing 'clichés'. Although mixing metaphors is often ridiculed because of the amusing and distracting effects it can produce, the practice is commonplace and often goes unnoticed. It usually occurs when two or more figurative expressions that have become idiomatic are used together without considering how contact might 'reawaken' their images: 'On the basis that there is no smoke without fire, surely his hands cannot be completely clean?' (*Independent*, 9 Jan. 1988). See METAPHOR. [STYLE].   T.MCA.

MNEMONIC [18c: from Greek *mnēmonikós* of memory, mindful, from *mnémē* memory: see MUSE]. (1) Helping or intended to help the memory (*a mnemonic system*), and something that helps the memory (*acronyms used as mnemonics*). (2) In computing, a programming code that is easy to remember. The terms *mnemonics* and *mnemotechnics* refer to techniques that are intended to improve memorizing. See ABBREVIATION, ACRONYM/PROTOGRAM, COMMUNICATIVE SHIFT, LETTER[1], LETTER WORD, PROVERB, RHYME. [EDUCATION, LANGUAGE, TECHNOLOGY].   T.MCA.

-MO [18c: from the last syllable of the Latin singular masculine ablative phrase *duodecimo* (folded) in twelve parts]. A suffix used in printing and binding to help name certain book sizes. It is added to the number of leaves formed by folding a sheet of paper: *twelvemo* (*12mo*) rather than *duodecimo*, *sixteenmo* (*16mo*) rather than *sextodecimo*. It does not, however, replace *quarto* and *octavo* (no **fourmo* and **eightmo*). See BOOK. [TECHNOLOGY].　　　　　　　T.MCA.

MOCK [16c: attributive]. A term for something feigned: for training purposes (*a mock examination, a mock battle*); as a literary style imitating another, especially for humorous or satirical purposes (*mock-heroic poetry, a mock-romance*); as a style of any kind, but particularly in architecture, usually taken to be in poor taste (*a mock-Tudor mansion*); and as the deliberate, nonsensical, often disparaging imitation of a language (*a mock-Swedish accent, fluent mock-Welsh*). The term *mock Latin* refers to pseudo-Latin motto-like phrases whose humorous effect is achieved by adding a quick 'translation': *Non illegitimis carborundum* Don't let the bastards grind you down. Compare DOG-, DOG, PASTICHE. [STYLE].　　　　　　　　　T.MCA.

MODAL AUXILIARY. See MODAL VERB.

MODALITY [17c: from Latin *modalitas* the quality relating to manners, forms, and limits, from *modus* form, manner, limit: see MODE, MOOD]. In syntactic and semantic analysis, a term chiefly used to refer to the way in which the meaning of a sentence or clause may be modified through the use of a modal auxiliary, such as *may, can, will, must*. In a wider sense, the term is used to cover linguistic expression of these concepts other than through the modal auxiliaries: 'It will *possibly* rain later this evening'; '*I am sure* that the plane has landed by now'; '*You have my permission* to smoke now'; '*I am obliged to* go.' Adverbs such as *possibly, perhaps, probably, certainly* have been called *modal adverbs*, and such adjectives as *possible* have been called *modal adjectives*. The term is also extended to include the subjunctive mood and the past verb forms used to express hypothetical meaning (that is, that the situation is unlikely to occur or has not occurred): 'I wish I *knew* her'; 'If I *saw* him, I *would* recognize him'; 'If you *had said* that, I *would* not *have minded*.' In case grammar, *modality* refers to one of the two underlying constituents of sentence structure (the other being *proposition*). The modality includes those features that relate to the sentence as a whole, such as tense and negation. See MODAL VERB. [GRAMMAR].　　　　　S.G.

MODAL VERB, also **modal auxiliary, modal**. A verb, normally an auxiliary such as English *must* and *should*, used to express *modality* (see entry). In English, such verbs have largely replaced the subjunctive mood, and three kinds of modality can be distinguished for them: (1) *Epistemic modality*, which expresses a judgement about the truth of a proposition (whether it is possible,

probable, or necessarily true): *John may be in his office*. (2) *Deontic modality*, which involves the giving of directives (in terms of such notions as permission and obligation): *You must leave immediately*. (3) *Dynamic modality*, which ascribes such properties as ability and volition to the subject of the sentence: *I can come*. Often the same modal verb is used for more than one kind of modality: *may* for possibility (*It may rain tomorrow*) and permission (*You may smoke now*); *must* for necessity (*The plane must have landed by now*) and obligation (*I must go*).

Central and marginal modals. The central modal verbs are *can, could, may, might, must, shall, should, will, would*. The marginal modal verbs, sometimes called *semi-modal verbs*, are *dare, need, ought to, used to*. All share the following characteristics: (1) They are auxiliary verbs. (2) They have no third-person -*s* form: *She may go, They may go* (contrast *She goes, They go*). (3) They have no non-finite forms (no infinitive, -*ing* participle, or -*ed* participle), and therefore in standard English can appear only in initial position in the verb phrase, and cannot occur with each other (although 'double modal' forms such as *might could go* occur in some non-standard varieties, such as Southern US English). (4) All except *ought* and *used* are followed by the bare infinitive without *to*. (5) They have idiosyncratic semantic and formal features, affecting particularly their use in the past tense and in negation.

Kinds of modals. (1) Epistemic modals: *may* (*He may be at home*), *might* (*It might get too hot*), *must* (*It must be your sister on the phone*), *ought to* (*They ought to have heard by now*), *should* (*The show should be over soon*), *will* (*That will be the doctor*), *would* (*Who would have guessed he was so young?*). (2) Deontic modals: *can* (*You can leave now*), *could* (*Could I go now please?*), *may* (*You may smoke*), *might* (*Might we have another one?*), *must* (*You must be patient*), *need* (*You needn't say anything*), *ought to* (*I ought to write more often*), *shall* (*You shall have my resignation letter tomorrow*: a promise or a threat), *should* (*You should write more legibly*). (3) Dynamic modals: *can* (*Neil can drive a car*), *could* (*He couldn't drive at that time*), *dare* (*I daren't tell/don't dare tell my parents*), *shall* (*We shall allow no obstacle to impede our programme*), *will* (*I will stay as long as I wish*).

Future expressions. (1) *Shall* (with first-person subjects only, particularly in Southern England) and *will* (often contracted to '*ll*) express future time and are often said to comprise the future tense: *I shall be back next week*; *He will be here soon*. Other ways of expressing the future include the semi-auxiliaries (see below) *be going to* (*It's going to rain*) and *be to* (*She is to be married tomorrow*), the present continuous (*I'm leaving* *for New York next week*), and the simple present (*The plane leaves at noon*).

Marginal modals and semi-auxiliaries. *Dare, need, ought to,* and *used to* share most of the characteristics of modal verbs but are marginal for various reasons. Unlike the central modals, *ought* and *used* are followed by *to* and despite prescriptive objections often combine with *do* in negative and interrogative constructions, like a full verb: especially in England, *They didn't ought to say that* alongside the more traditionally acceptable *They oughtn't to say that*; *Did he used to play the violin?*, alongside the rare *Used he to play the violin?* *Used to* also differs semantically from central modals, since it conveys aspect (habitual situation) and not modality. In negative and interrogative contexts, *dare* and *need* may be either modals (*I daren't object*; *Need I say more?*) or full verbs with preceding *do* and following *to*-infinitive (*I don't dare to object* or the blend without the *to*, *I don't dare object*; *Do I need to say more?*). Elsewhere, they are full verbs: *I dare/dared to object*; *I need/needed to say more*. There are a number of semi-auxiliaries that express modal or aspectual meanings, such as *be able to, be about to, be bound to, be going to, have to, have got to.* They can be used as non-finite forms and are therefore convenient substitutes for modals in non-finite positions: for example, the use of *You may be able to see me tomorrow* instead of the impossible **You may can see me tomorrow*.

Negation. When a verb phrase containing a modal is negated, the negation applies in some instances to the modal and in other instances to the proposition: for example, the modal is negated in *You may not leave* (You are not allowed to leave), whereas the proposition is negated in *I may not be on time* (It is possible that I won't be on time). The difference may affect the choice of the auxiliary: for example, epistemic *must* (*It must be your sister on the phone*) usually forms its negative equivalent through *may not* for negating the proposition (*It may not be your sister on the phone*: It is possible that it is not your sister on the phone) and *can't* for modal negation (*It can't be your sister on the phone*: It is not possible that it is your sister on the phone).

Past tense. *Can, may, shall, will* have the past-tense forms *could, might, should, would.* These forms are chiefly used to express tentativeness or conditionality rather than past time, so that there is no time difference between *I may see you later* and *I might see you later*, or between *Can you pass the salt?* and *Could you pass the salt?* The past forms, however, are used for past time in indirect speech (*I may see you later* is reported as *She said that she might see me later*). There are no past forms for *must, dare, need, ought to.*

The epistemic modals indicate the past time of the proposition by using *have*: *Andrew may/might have been in his office*; *You must have seen them*; *They will/would have landed by now*. The deontic modals *ought to have* and *should have* express past obligation, usually with the implication that it was not fulfilled: *You ought to have phoned* (but you didn't); *They should have come in*. Dynamic *could* (was able to) and *would* (was willing to) are used for past time in negative contexts (*He couldn't type*; *They wouldn't help us*).

Would is commonly used in the main clause of a sentence expressing a hypothetical condition: *If I were you, I would buy it*; *If you had seen them, you would have been shocked*. Sometimes, in BrE, *should* is used with a first-person subject in place of *would*: *If I had seen them, I should have reported it*. *Would* and *should* appear in other hypothetical contexts: *I was at the demonstration, but it would take too long to tell you what happened*. *Should* may also appear after evaluative expressions (*It's odd that he should say that*; also *It's odd that he says that*) and expressions of necessity, intention, and the like (*We insisted that he should stay*). See AUXILIARY, DIALECT IN AMERICA, SCOTS, VERB. [GRAMMAR].

F.R.P., S.G.

Coates, J. 1983. *The Semantics of the Modal Auxiliaries*. London & Canberra: Croom Helm.
Palmer, F. R. 1979. *Modality and the English Modals*. London: Longman.
—— 1986. *Mood and Modality*. Cambridge: University Press.

MODE [13c: from French *mode*, Latin *modus* form, manner, limit. Compare MOOD]. A term in linguistics used in two ways: (1) As a synonym of *mood*. (2) To refer to the choice of features influenced by the purpose of an activity, including the format of presentation: *lecture mode*; *essay mode*. [GRAMMAR]. S.G.

MODEL [16c: from Old French *modelle* (Modern *modèle*), from Italian *modello* a small measure, something on a small scale]. A representation of something else, on a smaller and more manageable scale. It is either concrete (like a model boat), and matches the original in most details, or an idealization (like a mathematical model), which does not copy an original but seeks to represent its main features. The making of abstract models is an important part of theory-building, both on an informal level (using similes, metaphors, and analogies, as in the 19c view that languages are like living organisms) and on a formal level (in science and technology). Models give shape to concepts and systems that are otherwise hard to think about and work with, but, because they often rest on analogy (X is like Y), they are not always precise and are often deficient, especially in areas such as language. The model which the British librarian Peter Mark Roget used to create his *Thesaurus* (1852) was botanical, comparing relationships among words with the genera and species of living things. Words, however, are not discrete and organic entities like plants, and such a model, though useful in creating ordered lists, does not make an ultimate statement about the nature of the words so listed. Similar problems have arisen with the metaphor of language as a computer program. It may be useful to think of language in this way, but there is no evidence that the mind works like a digital computer.

Linguistics in the past two centuries has been heavily influenced by the *model* or mental picture of language assumed to be valid at a particular time. Over the years, such models have become increasingly detailed and explicit. In the 19c, language was often envisaged as a living organism which, like a plant or an animal, developed to maturity and then decayed. Under the influence of the Darwinian theory of evolution, the relationships among languages were also often described in terms of 'parent' languages giving way to 'daughter' languages, the whole presented in family-tree diagrams. In the first half of the 20c, this botanical model was complemented by a structural model, one version of which represented language as a series of relatively independent systems set one on top of the other in a box-like arrangement: see LEVEL OF LANGUAGE. Later, such an 'arrangement model' of language gave way to a 'process model' influenced by the theories of Noam Chomsky, who has taken syntax to be the basic component on which other language components such as phonology and semantics are dependent.

In Chomsky's classic transformational model of grammar (*Aspects of the Theory of Syntax*, 1965), a few syntactic rules in the *base* of the grammar provided a syntactic *deep structure* which was then elaborated by processes known as transformations in order to produce a *surface structure*. Semantics or meaning was dependent on the deep structure, while phonology or sound was dependent on the surface structure (see diagram). More recently, in *Knowledge of Language* (1986), Chomsky has envisaged a model of grammar which is less obviously directional, and which, as with a computer program, is composed of a series of modules, each of which is fairly simple in its general workings, but which becomes complex as it interacts with other modules. Compare ANALOGY, METAPHOR. [GRAMMAR, LANGUAGE].   J.M.A., T.MCA.

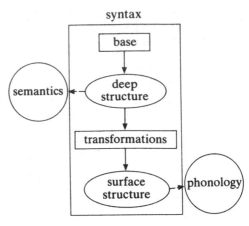

MODERN [16c: from Late Latin *modernus*, from Latin *modo* just now. In English, the Latinate sense of *modern* as 'at the time of speaking, writing, etc.', as in 'the first and modern President of the said Society' (charter, 1752) has long been obsolete]. (1) Of the present time (as contrasted with *ancient* and *medi(a)eval*); contemporary, up-to-date, recently developed or invented; not antiquated or obsolete. The concept of three ages, *Ancient, Medieval,* and *Modern* is essentially European; the *Modern Age* is not, however, young, being traditionally regarded by historians as beginning with the Renaissance and the Reformation in the 15-16c. It is associated with a change of mentality, considered by many traditionalists to be for the worse (by abandoning such things as classicism and medieval spirituality), by both social radicals and people of fashion as for the better (by embracing greater individualism, the scientific method, the concept of progress, the cult of the new and the original, and, increasingly, secular humanism). The attitude identified by the terms *modernity* and *modernism* looks to the future rather than the past as a source of inspiration and aspiration; it does not, in its purest form, depend on anything sanctioned or sanctified by tradition. Especially in art, architecture, and literature, modernists have sought to break sharply with practices that they see as bound to the past. However, many critics of art and literature towards the end of the 20c have in their turn reacted against modernism, seeing it as also having had its day, as belonging to the stultifying past. They discuss it in relation to *post-modernism*, a catch-all term for a range of recent cultural developments: see LITERARY CRITICISM. The use of *post-modern*, with its negative implications, adds to the difficulty of using the term *modern* objectively: in contexts in which it might mean 'at the present time' it may also be interpreted as meaning either 'and therefore better than in earlier times, states, and traditions' or 'and therefore suspect, because itself passé'. In this volume, the adjectives *current* and *present-day* are often therefore used instead, as in *current usage* and *present-day English*. (2) Used to identify the variety of a language in current use: for example, *Modern Greek* as opposed to *Classical* or *Ancient Greek*. In philology, it is the third of three terms for stages into which languages may be divided, as with *Old French, Middle French, Modern French*. (3) In printing, a term that designates a group of typefaces developed in the 18-19c, distinguished by flat serifs, increased contrasts between the thick and thin parts of the letters, and an effect of greater vertical emphasis. See MODERN ENGLISH, MODERN LANGUAGE. Compare CLASSICAL. [LANGUAGE, STYLE, TECHNOLOGY]. T.MCA.

MODERN ENGLISH, short form *ModE, MnE*. Also sometimes **New English**. (1) The third stage in the history and development of the English language, *c*.1450 to the present day, often divided into *Early Modern English* (*c*.1450-1700) and (*Late/Later*) *Modern English* (*c*.1700 to the present day). (2) Late Modern English treated as a fourth stage in the history and development of the language. See EARLY MODERN ENGLISH, ENGLISH, ENGLISH PLACE-NAMES, MODERN, MODERN LANGUAGE, PERIOD DICTIONARIES OF ENGLISH. [HISTORY, VARIETY]. T.MCA.

MODERN ENGLISH USAGE. See DICTIONARY OF MODERN ENGLISH USAGE.

MODERNISM. See ENGLISH LITERATURE, MODERN.

MODERN LANGUAGE [17c]. (1) A language used in recent times, in contrast to an ancient, classical, or medieval language: 'Our English Tongue . . . may be said to equal, if not surpass all other Modern Languages' (Edward Phillips, *The New World of English Words: or, a general dictionary*, ed. John Kersey, preface, 1706 edition). (2) (In the plural and often with initial capital letters) an area of linguistic study and a department in an educational institution devoted to it. Here, the phrase is generally taken to cover only the major living literary languages. In English-speaking countries, the term usually excludes English and includes only European languages, especially (for teaching purposes) French, German, Spanish, and Italian. Non-European languages are usually studied in other departments, such as *African Languages* and *Oriental Languages*. This is primarily because *modern* has long been used in Europe to contrast its own living indigenous languages with *Classical Languages* (Latin and Greek) or their own earlier forms, such as *Old French* and *Middle German*. Used attributively, the phrase may sometimes need disambiguating: 'In modern-language teaching, what is modern is the languages; in modern language teaching what is modern . . . is the teaching of languages' (R. B. Long, *The Sentence and its Parts*, 1961). See MODERN, MODERN LANGUAGE ASSOCIATION. Compare CLASSICAL LANGUAGE, ENGLISH STUDIES. [EDUCATION, LANGUAGE]. T.MCA.

MODERN LANGUAGE ASSOCIATION, short form *MLA*. The major professional organization of US college and university teachers of English and modern foreign languages, founded in 1883 to encourage the study of modern languages and literature at a time when the curriculum was dominated by Greek and Latin. Having grown to a membership of over 28,000, the MLA has for over a century held an annual meeting between Christmas and New Year's Day for the presentation of papers and the discussion of both scholarly and professional issues. Average attendance for the years 1983-7 was 8,500. The MLA is organized into 76 divisions and 32 discussion groups. Although most of them emphasize literary history and criticism, five divisions and three discussion groups focus on language: Linguistic Applications to Literature, Applied Linguistics, Language and Society, Language Change, and Language Theory; General Linguistics, Lexicography, and Present Day English. Among MLA publications is an annual bibliography, which includes English language and linguistics, and the organization's official journal, *PMLA* (the abbreviation being its only title). See MODERN LANGUAGE, STYLE CHECKER. [AMERICAS, LANGUAGE, MEDIA]. C.C.E.

MODERN SCOTS. See PERIOD DICTIONARIES OF ENGLISH, SCOTS.

MODIFICATION [15c: through French from Latin *modificatio/modificationis* setting limits]. A term for the dependence of one grammatical unit on another, the less dependent unit being delimited or made more specific by the more dependent unit: the adjective *good* modifying the noun *weather* in the phrase *good weather*; the noun *diamond* modifying the noun *mines* in *diamond mines*; the adverb *strikingly* modifying the adjective *handsome* in *strikingly handsome*. A distinction is made between *pre-modification* (modifying by preceding) and *post-modification* (modifying by following). In *diamond mines in South Africa*, *diamond* is a pre-modifier and *in South Africa* is a post-modifier. The example illustrates a phrase (here a prepositional phrase) used as a modifier (here a post-modifier of a noun). Clauses may also be modifiers in phrases, usually post-modifiers of nouns, such as the relative clause in 'the bag *that you are carrying*'. The dependence of a subordinate clause on its superordinate clause is generally not described in terms of modification: the subordinate clause in 'I know *that you are there*' is not said to be a modifier. Some grammarians, however, use the term *sentence modifier* for adverbials (including adverbial clauses) that express a comment on the sentence or clause: *fortunately* in '*Fortunately*, no one was hurt'; *in all probability* in '*In all probability*, it is closed by now'; the *since*-clause in '*Since you're here*, you may as well make yourself useful.' Although the distinction is obvious between such examples and clear instances of adverbials functioning as modifiers of verbs (such as 'The band is playing *too loudly*'), there is no agreement on how to draw the line between sentence modifiers and verb modifiers or on how many relational categories to establish for adverbials. [GRAMMAR].   S.G.

MODIFIED RP. See RECEIVED PRONUNCIATION.

MODIFIED STANDARD. See RECEIVED STANDARD AND MODIFIED STANDARD.

MONODY [16c: from Latin *monodia*, Greek *monōideía* a single song]. A song sung by one actor in a Greek tragedy; a musical composition for a single voice; a poem of lamentation. See ELEGY, THRENODY. [LITERATURE].   T.MCA.

MONOGLOT [1820s: from Greek-derived *mono-* single, *-glot* tongue, language]. (1) (Of a person) knowing only one language; (of a text) composed or available in only one language. (2) Someone who knows only one language well or at all, sometimes used dismissively by multilingual persons: 'Hands up, all you EFL monoglots, how many of you can function adequately in a foreign language? 20%? 15%? 10%? This, of course, is one of the real scandals of EFL . . . it is rather like being taught to drive by someone who has never learnt himself' (John A. Bishop, letter, *EFL Gazette*, Nov. 1990). See -GLOT, LINGUAL, POLYGLOT. [LANGUAGE].   T.MCA.

MONOGRAPH [1810s: from the Greek elements *mono-* single and *-graph* writing]. Earlier form *monography*. Originally, in natural history, a treatise on a species, genus, or group of plants, animals, or minerals. Currently, an academic treatise or paper on a single topic, accompanied by the full apparatus of notes, references, and documentation. Compare ESSAY. [MEDIA, WRITING].   T.MCA.

MONOLINGUAL. See LINGUAL.

MONOLOGUE, also AmE **monolog** [17c: from French *monologue*, 'one that loues to heare himself talke; or talkes very much about very little' (Randle Cotgrave, *A dictionary of the French and English tongues*, 1611), from Greek *monólogos* speaking alone]. (1) Obsolete: someone who does all the talking. (2) A scene in a play in which a character speaks by himself or herself (in contrast to *dialogue* and *chorus*). (3) A dramatic composition for a single performer; a kind of dramatic entertainment performed throughout by one person, a *monologist*, often humorous and presented with mock-solemnity; literary composition of this kind: *the art of monologue*. (4) A poem or other non-dramatic composition in the form of a soliloquy. (5) A long speech by one member of a group who is in effect 'hogging the conversation'. Many social dialogues can, however, in the nature of things contain stretches of monologue, and formal speeches are monologues in the sense that no immediate direct response is normally expected. *Heckling* a speaker at a meeting can, however, turn such solo performances into (more or less welcome) impromptu dialogues. (6) Talking aloud to oneself in private. (7) The solitary act of creative writing, the text serving as something 'overheard' by the reader. (8) In some novels, *interior monologue* is a spoken or written train of thought equivalent to the soliloquy of drama:

I knew it. I knew if I came to this dinner, I'd draw something like this baby on my left. They've been saving him up for me for weeks. Now, we've simply got to have him—his sister was so sweet to us in London; we can stick him next to Mrs Parker—she talks enough for two. Oh, I should never have come, never, I'm here against my better judgement, to a decision. That would be a good thing for them to cut on my tombstone: Wherever she went, including here, it was against her better judgement. This is a fine time of the evening to be thinking about tombstones. That's the effect he's had on me, already, and the soup hardly cold yet (Dorothy Parker, 1893-1967, in the short story 'But The One on The Right').

See ASIDE, CONVERSATION, DIALOG(UE), SOLILOQUY, STREAM OF CONSCIOUSNESS. [LITERATURE, SPEECH].   T.MCA.

MONOPHTHONG [17c: from Greek *monóphthonggos* a single sound]. In phonetics, a vowel whose quality is relatively constant, in contrast to a *diphthong* or *triphthong*. Some varieties of English have more monophthongs, some have fewer: in RP there are 12 (as in *see, sit, set, hat, arm, got, saw, pull, pool, cup, fur*, and the first syllable of *ago*); in ScoE there are 11, rather differently distributed (as in *say, see, sit, set, hat/arm, got/saw, so, pull/pool, cup/fur*, and the first syllables of *never, ago*). See DIPHTHONG, VOWEL. [SPEECH]. G.K.

MONOSYLLABLE [16c: from Late Latin *monosyllabus*, Greek *monosúllabos* one-syllabled]. Formerly also **monosyllabon**. A word of one syllable. 'Native' English is often said to be inherently monosyllabic ('Words monosillable which be for the more part our naturall Saxon English,' George Puttenham, *The Arte of English Poesie*, 1589), as opposed to polysyllabic Latinisms and other borrowings. Certainly, many common monosyllables are Germanic in origin (such as *am, be, can, dog, eye, fox, gun, hot, it, jump, key, leap, mum, nut, odd, pot, queen, run, say, two, up, vat, who, you*), but the same Germanic source also provides such poly-syllables as *cold-bloodedly* and *longwindedness*. The many monosyllables from non-Germanic sources include *act* and *flex* from Latin, *bloc* and *joy* from French, *crag* and *loch* from Gaelic, *gong* and *kris* from Malay, *steppe* and *tsar* from Russian, and *gene* and *zone* from Greek. A tend-ency to clip words does, however, provide some support for the idea of Anglo-Saxon *monos-yllabism* (addiction to monosyllables or the qual-ity of being monosyllabic), as with *cred* from the Latinate word *credibility*, *mob* from the Latin phrase *mobile vulgus*, and *zoo* from the hybrid Greco-Latin and vernacular *zoological gardens*. A person who is monosyllabic in style tends to be curt and keep to short words, especially simply *yes* and *no*. See CLIPPING, LACONISM, POLYSYLLABLE, SWIFT, SYLLABLE. [SPEECH, STYLE, WORD]. T.MCA.

MONOTONE [17c: from Latin *monotonus*, from Greek *monótonos* having only one tone]. Sustained level pitch. Whereas, in singing or chanting, such a pitch can be maintained over a syllable or group of syllables, in natural speech it is constantly moving. Speakers do not normally sustain a level pitch, and someone perceived as 'speaking in a monotone' is probably using a narrower pitch range than usual. See PITCH, TONE. [SPEECH]. G.K.

MONOTRANSITIVE. See TRANSITIVE AND INTRANSITIVE.

MONOTYPE [1890s: from Greek *mónos* single, *túpos* blow, impression. Compare LINOTYPE]. (1) The trade name of a typesetting and typecasting machine operated by a keyboard and devised in the 1880s/90s by the US lawyer and inventor Tolbert Lanston. (2) The type produced on this two-part machine. It first creates a perforated paper ribbon whose codes drive a metal type-caster, which rapidly and in serial order pro-duces single pieces of type from hot metal. Monotype was widely used until the mid-20c, especially for setting books. Linotype was also popular for this purpose in the US. (3) An unre-lated process by which prints are made from oil or ink paintings on glass and metal. See TYPE-SETTING. [TECHNOLOGY]. W.W.B.

MONTSERRAT. Officially *Colony of Mont-serrat*. Also *Emerald Isle*. A British dependency in the Leeward Islands. Capital: Plymouth. Cur-rency: East Caribbean dollar. Economy: tourism, agriculture. Population: 12,000 (1984). Ethnicity: African, European, and mixed. Lan-guages: English, Creole. Columbus named the island when he visited it in 1493, its terrain reminding him of Montserrat in Catalonia (from Latin *Mons Serratus* Saw-Toothed Mountain). In 1632, the island was colonized by English and Irish settlers from St Christopher, followed by more Irish from Virginia. Slaves from Africa began arriving in 1664. Although the French took the island for brief periods in 1664, 1667, and 1782, it remained British, but did not become a colony until 1871. In 1958, it became a member of the Federation of the West Indies, and did not seek independence on the dissolution of the Federation in 1962. The island's active volcanoes are known as *soufrières* (French: sul-phurous ones). The highest point, Chances Peak, rises above the Soufrière Hills in the south. The private radio service, Radio Antilles, broadcasts from the island to the Caribbean region in English. See BLACK IRISH, CARIBBEAN, ENGLISH. [AMERICAS, MEDIA, NAME, VARIETY]. T.MCA.

MOOD [16c: from French *mode*, Latin *modus* form, manner, limit, influenced by and assim-ilated to Old English *mōd*, later *mood*, feeling, disposition. Compare MODALITY, MODE]. In tra-ditional grammar, a term for a form of the verb that affects the general meaning of the sentence and for the sentence or clause type in which it occurs. Three moods are customarily recognized for English: the *indicative* (*God helps us*); the *imperative* (*Help us*); and the *subjunctive* (*God help us*). See IMPERATIVE, INDICATIVE, SUBJUNCT-IVE. [GRAMMAR]. S.G.

MOON TYPE. See BRAILLE.

MORALITY PLAY. See DRAMA, ENGLISH LITERATURE.

MORNINGSIDE AND KELVINSIDE. Accents of English in Scotland, named after middle-class districts of Edinburgh and Glasgow; in effect one accent, generally regarded as an affected, hypercorrect imitation of RP. In popular and literary caricatures since the 1940s, it is identified with two shibboleths in particular: a raised realization of the short, front vowel /a/, frequently represented as *e*, as in 'ectually' for *actually*; a single, narrowed realization of the ScoE diphthongs in *five*, *time* ('faive', 'taime'). The features come together in 'Eh'm quate well aware of thet fect' (Mrs M'Cotton, in Helen W. Pryde's *McFlannels United*, 1949). As a stigmatized stereotype, Kelvinside is on record since 1901, Morningside since the 1940s. The accent may have originated in 19c middle-class girls' private schools and seems not to be regionally restricted. Although the stereotype flourishes the accent may be dying out. The names are also used by speakers of the vernacular for any 'anglified' variety of ScoE, especially the near-RP speech of lawyers, architects, and other professional people. Other designations include (*to speak*) *pan loaf*/*haigh cless*, *tae pit oan the high pan* or simply *tae pit* (*it*) *oan* (to put on airs), and *to speak posh*. Compare KENSINGTON. See AFFECTATION, ANGLIFY, POSH, SCOTTISH ENGLISH. [EUROPE, VARIETY]. A.J.A.

MORPHEME [1890s: from French *morphème*, coined by analogy with *phonème*, from Greek *morphḗ* shape, form. See -EME, PHONEME]. In linguistics, a minimal unit of form and meaning. There are many variations in how the term is used and understood, arising in the main from a distinction between language as arrangement and language as process: (1) As proposed by the US structural linguist Leonard Bloomfield (*Language*, 1933), the morpheme is the unit of morphology and therefore grammatical. In this approach, language analysed as a static arrangement of data consists of minimal units of form and meaning, each of which can be physically identified. The sentence *The cats were sitting unhappily in the rain* is analysable into the morphemic string *the + cat + s + were + sit(t) + ing + un + happy + ly + in + the + rain*. The 8-word sentence consists of 12 morphemes, all of equal status. (2) As proposed by the French linguist Joseph Vendryes (*Le Langage*, 1921), the morpheme is one of two units, one grammatical, one semantic, and each in its own sense minimal. Language in this approach is the outcome of processes which may or may not all have observable forms, but which can be analysed as units of grammatical meaning (*morphemes*) and units of lexical meaning (for Vendryes *semantemes*, but now known as *lexemes*). Here, morphemes are the glue that holds lexemes together, and the specimen sentence can be analysed as: *the + CAT + s + (BE + past/plural) + SIT(T) + ing + un + HAPPY + ly + in + the + RAIN* (in which the lower-case items are morph-emes, the upper-case lexemes). The 8-word sentence in this analysis contains 8 morphemes and 5 lexemes.

There have been many variations on these themes. The US linguist Dwight Bolinger (*Aspects of Language*, 1968) divided Bloomfield's morpheme into a *system morpheme* (the glue) and a *source morpheme* (the content), while the French linguist André Martinet (*Éléments de linguistique générale*, 1970) subsumed Vendryes's morpheme and lexeme under a unifying unit the *moneme*. In this approach, the specimen sentence has 13 monemes divided into 8 morphemes and 5 lexemes. Currently, whatever the terms used, linguists tend to agree on three points: (1) Grammatical and lexical units need to be distinguished: for example, the two elements *cat* and *s* in the word *cats* are different aspects or levels of language. (2) Not all the features in a stretch of language are physically realized: for example, *cats* may exhibit a marker of plurality, but *sheep* does not. (3) One unit of form may serve more than one end: for example, *were* in the specimen sentence above combines *BE* and *past*. The traditional structuralist approach assumes that all the morphemes of a language can in principle be listed in a *morpheme inventory*, like a phoneme inventory, but because of the complexities involved, few such lists have been attempted and none exists for English.

In later structural linguistics, the *morpheme* has been defined as the abstraction behind a *morph* (a form that has semantic distinctiveness). It may subsume two or more *allomorphs*, morphs that have common semantic identity but differ in their pronunciation according to well-defined rules: for example, the prefixes *in-*, *im-*, *il-* are allomorphs of the same morpheme (in this case a negative prefix) in the words *insincere*, *impolite*, *illogical*, the choice of prefix being determined by the initial sound of the stem that follows the prefix. When it deals with morphs and morphemes, morphology is known as *morphemics*. See BLOOMFIELD, -EME, LEVEL OF LANGUAGE, LEXEME, MORPHOLOGY, PHONEME. [GRAMMAR, LANGUAGE, WORD]. T.MCA., S.G.

MORPHOLOGY [19c: from Greek *morphḗ* shape, structure, and -*logy* study]. In linguistics, the study of the structure of words, as opposed to *syntax*, the study of the arrangement of words in the higher units of phrases, clauses, and sentences. The two major branches are *inflectional morphology* (the study of inflections) and *lexical morphology* (the study of word-formation). See ACCIDENCE, DERIVATION, INFLECTION/INFLEXION, LINGUISTICS, LINGUISTIC TYPOLOGY, MORPHEME, SYNTAX, USAGE, VERB, WORD, WORD-FORMATION. [GRAMMAR, LANGUAGE]. S.G.

MORRIS, Edward Ellis [1843-1902]. Australian philologist, born in Madras, India, and educated at Oxford, England. He was appointed headmaster of Melbourne Church of England Grammar School in 1875 and held the chair of English, French, and German languages in the U. of Melbourne from 1883 until his death. His major publication was *A Dictionary of Austral English*. See AUSTRALIAN DICTIONARIES. [BIOGRAPHY, OCEANIA, REFERENCE].   W.S.R.

MOTHER COUNTRY [16c]. (1) Especially formerly, a person's native land; the country of origin of a person or a group. (2) More commonly, the country from which colonists have moved in order to establish a new settlement (for example, Greece, in ancient times the mother country of colonies around the coasts of the Mediterranean and the Black Sea), or the founding country of an empire (in more recent times, England or Britain, the mother country of the British Empire). The term was widely used until the 1960s/70s, often with sentimental affection, especially in Australia and New Zealand, after which it began to die out as memories of the Empire have faded. Compare HOME, OLD COUNTRY. See BRITISH EMPIRE, COLONIAL. [NAME].   T.MCA.

MOTHERESE [c.1960s]. A term used in the study of child language acquisition for the way mothers talk to their young children. Its features include simplified grammar, exaggerated speech melody, diminutive forms of words such as *doggie*, and a highly repetitive style. There is also a tendency to expand or comment on what the child has just said: when a child says *Castle down*, and the mother replies, *Yes, the castle's fallen down*. Although originally mothers were the focus of research study, similar conversational patterns have been observed in fathers' speech (sometimes referred to as *fatherese*) and in the speech of others who look after young children, such as grandparents and nannies (users of *caretaker speech*). These patterns, however, are not identical: for example, research indicates that fathers tend to be more intense and demanding in talking to young children, using more direct questions and a wider range of vocabulary. See BABY TALK, CHILD LANGUAGE ACQUISITION, -ESE. [LANGUAGE].   D.C.

MOTHER TONGUE. A general term for the language of the childhood home, learned 'at one's mother's knee', often used synonymously with *native language*. Although the implication is usually clear, there is no necessary connection between a child's use of language and the language of its mother: some children learn the language of a nurse or ayah first; a mother may talk to her child in a language not originally her own; the mother may be dead. The term is often used to mean a national language, such as French, whether or not it is the first or preferred language of all members of the nation, as with Basques and Bretons in France. Compare FIRST LANGUAGE/SECOND LANGUAGE, NATIVE LANGUAGE. See TONGUE. [LANGUAGE].   P.C., T.MCA.

MOTION PICTURE [20c]. Also technically **cinefilm**, informally (especially AmE) **movie**, (especially BrE) **film**. A series of sequentially ordered photographs or drawings (known as *frames*) recorded on one or more reels of film and projected at speed on to a screen by strong, focused light, giving an impression of natural motion. The pioneers of such strip pictures in the late 19c were Louis and Auguste Lumière with the *Cinématographe* in France, whose *La Sortie des ouvriers de l'usine Lumière* ('Workers leaving the Lumière factory', 1895) is regarded as the first successful motion picture, and Thomas A. Edison with the *Vitascope* in the US. Collectively, especially when considered as an art form, motion pictures are referred to as *cinema*, the art form being *cinematic art* or *cinematics*, and the process and technology *cinematography*. All words based on *cine-* have been inspired by the name chosen by the Lumières for their equipment (from Greek *kínēma* motion and *gráphein* to write). Public enthusiasm for filmshows, at first presented in music halls, fairgrounds, and the like, strong from the start, led to the development of specialized buildings called in the US first *nickelodeons* (shows priced at a nickel per person) then *movie theaters*, and in the UK *cinemas* and (formerly) *picture houses*.

In the first decade of the 20c, French production was pre-eminent, Charles Pathé building up the first film 'empire'. America, however, began to catch up, bringing out in 1906 the first full-length movie, *The Story of the Kelly Gang*; in the following year, film-making began in the Los Angeles suburb of Hollywood. In 1916, *The Gulf Between*, the first film in colour, was produced in the US, where movie-making benefited greatly from damage caused to the European film industry by the First World War. By 1918, when the US War Industries Board declared motion pictures an essential national industry, Hollywood with its system of *stars* (major actors and actresses) had come to dominate the international market and has remained dominant throughout the century. The first full-length 'talkie' (film with a soundtrack) was *Dream Street* in 1921; the first newsreel, Fox's Movietone News, appeared in 1927, the same year as the first film with fully developed dialogue, *They're Coming to Get Me*. On the coming of speech, and especially American speech, to the 'silver screen', *The Encyclopaedia Britannica* notes:

The silent film had been an international language; the talkies were a return to Babel. Hollywood's foreign market inevitably suffered, and talking films permitted a degree of revival in such film industries as those of Germany, France, and Italy. The international dominance of the United States, however, was not seriously or permanently affected. Hollywood's advantages were its vast domestic and foreign English-language audience, an unrivalled mastery of the techniques and marketing of films, and the ability to create and market star personalities of universal appeal (in the Micropaedia entry *motion picture*, 1986).

A major linguistic consequence of the international success of American films (in cinemas, on network television, or in videotaped versions) has been a diffusion of English to the world at large (whether or not films were subtitled and despite dubbing into other languages) and of AmE to the rest of the English-speaking world, especially informal usages such as *OK*, slang expressions such as *dough* for money, catchphrases like *Play it again, Sam* (associated with the actor Humphrey Bogart in the film *Casablanca*), and snatches from the lyrics of songs in musicals. Only one other national movie-making enterprise and with it one other language have attained anything close to the scale of Hollywood's success: Indian films with soundtracks in Hindi, produced in Bombay, whose industry has as a result of its success been nicknamed *Bollywood*. In addition to the mammoth American operation, English-language films with an international market are made in Britain, Australia, and Canada. See BROADCASTING, FEATURE, LIBRARY OF CONGRESS. [MEDIA] T.MCA., G.H.

MOTTO [16c: through Italian from Latin *muttum* sound, utterance. Plural: *mottos, mottoes*]. (1) Originally, a word or phrase attached to an emblem to emphasize or explain its symbolic importance. (2) A word, phrase, or sentence on a badge, banner, coat of arms, or the like, expressing an ideal, attitude, or guiding principle associated with the group, family, or organization to which it belongs. Mottos in English-speaking countries have often been in Latin (such as *Fide et opera* by faith and deeds, motto of Clan MacArthur) or in French (such as *Honi soit qui mal y pense* Shamed be he who thinks evil of it, motto of the Order of the Garter). (3) A proverb or pithy saying, especially if adopted as a rule of conduct: '*Never say die*', *that's my motto*. (4) A quotation set at the beginning of a book, chapter, or the like; an epigraph. (5) The doggerel lines in a paper cracker or the like. Compare EPIGRAPH, LATIN TAG, MAXIM, PROVERB, SLOGAN. [STYLE]. T.MCA.

MOUSE [1980s in this sense]. A term in computing for a device resembling a mouse, with an electrical lead as the tail, which is moved by hand on a surface such as a desktop. A rollerball in the mouse reads its motion and transmits it along the lead to the screen of a computer, where it influences the position and functions of a *cursor* (a movable point on the screen that indicates where one can type a letter or perform another function). See KEYBOARD. [TECHNOLOGY]. M.L.

MOUTH. See SPEECH.

MOVIE. See MOTION PICTURE.

MULATTO [16c: from Spanish and Portuguese *mulato*, a young mule. The feminine form *mulatta* sometimes occurs]. A general term for someone of mixed usually Caucasian and African ancestry, especially of a European father and an African mother. It is associated with the slave plantations of the New World, in which precise gradations of colour were marked; the offspring of a mulatto and a white was a *quadroon*, of a quadroon and a white an *octoroon*, etc.: 'A Mulatto woman, the offspring of a Spaniard and a negress, may give birth to a Morisco by uniting with a Spaniard' (Deniker, *Races of Man*, 1900). Until recently, a person in white society believed to have mixed ancestry was commonly said to *have a touch of the tar brush*. The term *mulatto* is sometimes intended neutrally ('92% African, 4% Caucasian, 4% Mulatto': population percentages in *South, 1990 Diary*) but has generally been dismissive: 'two woolly-headed poor little mulattos' (W. M. Thackeray, *The Newcomes*, 1854). Compare BLACK, CREOLE, MESTIZO, MÉTIS, RACISM, WHITE. [AMERICAS, NAME] T.MCA.

MULCASTER, Richard [1530?-1611]. English scholar, schoolmaster, author, and liberal educational theorist; the poet Spenser's headmaster at the Merchant Taylors' School in London and perhaps Shakespeare's model for the pedant Holofernes in *Love's Labour's Lost*. Mulcaster's *The First Part of the Elementarie* (1582) was the period's most significant pronouncement on English. It took an innovative stand in the movement on reforming spelling, issued the first call for a comprehensive dictionary of English, defended the right of borrowing words from other languages, and exhibited unlimited pride in English. He said that it is the learning in a language and not any inherent virtue that makes it esteemed, and English can be as learned and expressive as any: 'I loue Rome, but London better, I fauor Italie, but England more, I honor the Latin, but I worship the English.' Mulcaster's prose, which he admitted was difficult as befitting a scholar, is by turns witty and eloquent, exemplifying his confidence in the language. See index. [BIOGRAPHY, EDUCATION, EUROPE, HISTORY]. W.F.B.

MULTICULTURALISM [1960s]. (1) Also *cultural pluralism*. Sociological terms for the co-occurrence of many cultures (including hybrid forms) in one area, as in the cities of Auckland, Bombay, London, New York, Singapore, Sydney, and Toronto. (2) A sociopolitical policy of encouraging the coexistence and growth of several cultures in one place: 'A policy of multiculturalism within a bilingual framework commends itself to the government as the most suitable means of assuring the cultural freedom of Canadians' (*Daily Colonist*, Victoria, British Columbia, 9 Oct. 1971). The term *multicultural* is sometimes used as a synonym of *multiracial*: 'Although Britain has a multi-cultural society, where are the black faces among the television announcers, newscasters and sports commentators?' (*Daily Telegraph*, 20 July 1973). In recent years, the terms *multicultural, multiculturalism, multiculturalist*, etc., have been used, both positively and negatively, to identify and discuss a movement that confronts certain perceived biases in Western and especially US society, particularly in education and on college campuses: 'New York's state government voted last week to introduce multicultural history into its schools. The new syllabus, designed to reflect the multiracial make-up of the state, will emphasise the role of women and ethnic minorities, and play down the importance of those who have now been labelled Dwems (dead white European males), like Columbus, Jefferson, and Custer. The New York decision was the biggest victory yet for the "multiculturalists", an increasingly powerful group who believe the Anglo-Saxon tradition is a racist, sexist plot designed to preserve white male dominance' (John Cassidy, 'History turns its back on America's heroes', *Sunday Times*, 28 July 1991); 'It is in its most intense and extreme form . . . that multiculturalism is on its way to being a major educational, social and eventually political problem. This version is propagated on our college campuses by a coalition of nationalist-racist blacks, radical feminists, "gays" and lesbians, and a handful of aspiring demagogues who claim to represent various ethnic minorities' (Irving Kristol, 'The Tragedy of Multiculturalism', *Wall Street Journal*, 31 July 1991). See AUSTRALIAN ENGLISH, BICULTURALISM, CULTURE, MULTILINGUALISM, POLITICALLY CORRECT, RACISM, SEXISM. [AMERICAS, LANGUAGE, STYLE]. T.MCA.

MULTILINGUALISM [Mid-20c]. The ability to use three or more languages, either separately or in various degrees of code-mixing. There is no general agreement as to the degree of competence in each language necessary before someone can be considered multilingual; according to some, a native-like fluency is necessary in at least three languages; according to others, different languages are used for different purposes, competence in each varying according to such factors as register, occupation, and education. Where an individual has been exposed to several languages, as for example in India, Nigeria, or Singapore, one language may be used in the home, another professionally, another passively for listening or reading, another spoken but not written or read, and so forth. In a multilingual state, such as India, most individuals have a knowledge of several languages, but not uniformly nor in the same combinations across the nation: in Bombay, people may have a varying acquaintance with Marathi (the state language of Maharashtra), Hindi (the national official language), English (the national associate official language and an important language of business and culture in the city), and Gujarati (the language of two important minority groups, the Gujaratis and Parsis); in such a setting, few people are unilingual. BILINGUALISM, CODE-MIXING AND CODE-SWITCHING, LANGUAGE PLANNING, LINGUAL, MULTICULTURALISM, POLYGLOT. [LANGUAGE, STYLE]. T.MCA.

MULTIMEDIA [1960s: from *multi-* many, and *media*, plural of *medium*: see MEDIA]. A term, generally used attributively, for forms of educational, artistic, commercial, or other communication in which more than one medium is used simultaneously or in close association: *a multimedia rock festival*; *a multimedia publishing company*. A typical multimedia production is *The Hitch Hiker's Guide to the Galaxy* by Douglas Adams, which since 1979 has had a radio, a television, and a printed version. See BBC ENGLISH[2]. [MEDIA, STYLE, TECHNOLOGY]. T.MCA.

MULTIPLE MEANING. See MEANING, POLYSEMY, SEMANTIC CHANGE, SEMANTICS.

MULTIPLE NEGATION. See DOUBLE NEGATIVE, NEGATION.

MUMBO JUMBO [18c: of uncertain origin, but probably from Mandingo *mama dyumbo*, the name of a god, perhaps influenced by *mumble-jumble* to speak indistinctly and incoherently. In 1738, Francis Moore (*Travels into the inland parts of Africa*) reported among the Mandingo and other tribes 'a dreadful Bugbear call'd Mumbo-Jumbo, which is what keeps the Women in awe'. In 1799, Mungo Park (*Travels in the Interior of Africa*) reported 'A sort of masquerade habit . . . which I was told . . . belonged to Mumbo Jumbo . . . a strange bugbear employed by the Pagan natives in keeping their women in subjection', in effect a man grotesquely dressed up at night, with a rod to beat troublesome women]. (1) An object of superstitious awe or unintelligent veneration, such as an idol; foolish religious ritual or incantation. (2) Sometimes *mumbo* alone. Obscure, complicated, and confusing language: 'Mumbo jumbo developed by educators to confound the public in general and inquisitive parents in particular' (Mario Pei, *Words in Sheep's Clothing*, 1970); 'Labour's elected representatives mouth the mumbo-jumbo of capitalism: "The pound must be kept strong", "We must all buy British" ' (*The Times*, 14 Aug. 1975). Compare JARGON, NONSENSE. See REDUPLICATIVE. [AFRICA, STYLE].

T.MCA.

MUMMERSET [20c: a blend of *mummer*, one who mutters and murmurs, or takes part in a mime, and *Somerset*]. Also **Mummersetshire**. An imaginary rustic county of England and its dialect: 'Nowadays you can't be sure if they *are* eggs, even when somebody on television says they are in B.B.C. Mummerset' (C. Mackenzie, *Paper Lives*, 1966). This form of stage West Country is drawled and emphasizes retroflex /r/ ('Arrr, that'll be roit, zurr'). It replaces /s/ with /z/, /f/ with /v/ ('We ain't zeen 'im zince last Vroiday'), and uses special forms of *be* ('We be happy yere, bain't we?'). Comedians sometimes add pseudo-dialect words to the brew. See BURR, MUMMERY, SOMERSET, STAGE, WEST COUNTRY. [EUROPE, LITERATURE, VARIETY].

T.MCA.

MUMMERY [16c: from Old French *mommerie*: compare MUMMERSET]. (1) A performance of *mummers*, actors in a mime or dumb show, usually extravagant in style, in fancy dress, and masked. The word *mummer* has three meanings: one who mutters; one who 'keeps mum' (is silent or dumb); and one who is masked (from Old French *momeur*, from *momon* mask). The term *mumming* refers to the art and actions of mummers and also to indistinct or inarticulate speech (compare *mumbling*). (2) By extension, ridiculous ceremonial or play-acting, often applied dismissively to religious ritual. See MIME, MUMBO JUMBO, MUMMERSET. [LITERATURE, SPEECH].

T.MCA.

MUMPSIMUS [16c: from a once well-known humorous story told among others by Erasmus, of a semi-literate priest who had got into the habit of using in the Mass the nonsensical word *mumpsimus* (probably a textual corruption) in

the Latin phrase *quod in ore sumpsimus* (that we have taken up in the mouth). He doggedly refused to change when told of his error, saying: 'I will not change my old mumpsimus for your new sumpsimus']. Archaic: (1) An established reading of a text that is patently wrong but obstinately retained; an erroneous tradition blindly adhered to: 'Some be to styff in their old *Mumpsimus*, other be to busy and curious in their newe *Sumpsimus*' (Henry VIII, referring to religious reformation, in a Parliamentary speech, 24 Dec. 1545). (2) Stubborn persistence in using a mispronunciation, a misspelling, etc., when the fault has been pointed out. (3) One who persists in this; an ignorant and bigoted opponent of reform: 'other doctoures mumsimusses of diuinyte' (William Tyndale, *The practyse of prelates*, 1530). Compare CORRUPT, MIS-, MISPRONUNCIATION, NONSENSE. [STYLE, WRITING].

T.MCA.

MURISON, David Donald [b.1913]. Scottish lexicographer and philologist, born in Fraserburgh, Aberdeenshire, and educated at the U. of Aberdeen (from 1933) and Cambridge (from 1936). In the late 1930s, he was assistant to the Professor of Greek at Aberdeen. In 1946, he succeeded William Grant as Editor of *The Scottish National Dictionary*, the editing of which was then near the end of C. Murison completed the Dictionary some 30 years later, at a rate of progress high for a work of this kind, editing seven of the ten volumes. He has also produced many other scholarly writings on Scots, such as 'Linguistic Relationships in Medieval Scotland' (in *The Scottish Tradition*, 1974) and 'The Language of the Ballads' (in *Scottish Literary Journal*, Supplement 6, 1978), and several authoritative popular works such as *The Guid Scots Tongue* (1977) and *Scots Laws* (1981). Murison helped found and develop the study of Scots as an academic subject. During the 1960s, he lectured on Scots in the English Department of the U. of Aberdeen, and was Lecturer then Reader in Scots in the U. of Glasgow (1975-8). A festschrift in his honour, entitled *Scotland and the Lowland Tongue*, was edited by J. Derrick McClure (Aberdeen University Press, 1983). See SCOTTISH DICTIONARIES. [BIOGRAPHY, EUROPE, REFERENCE].

A.J.A.

MURRAY, Sir J(ames) A(ugustus) H(enry) [1837-1915]. Scottish lexicographer and philologist. Born in Denholm, Roxburghshire, he had no formal education after the age of 14, acquiring his erudition by private study. He moved from Hawick to London in 1864 in the hope that milder southern winters might help his first wife's health, but she died shortly afterwards. From 1870 to 1885, he was English master at

Mill Hill School in north-east London. He joined the circle of professional and amateur scholars who were establishing the scientific study of phonetics, Early English, and dialectology. From 1868, he was active in the Philological Society, and, urged on by F. J. Furnivall, produced several editions of Scots texts for the Early English Text Society. In 1873, he brought out *The Dialect of the Southern Counties of Scotland*, on which all subsequent work on the history and description of Scots has depended. His entry on the English Language in the 9th edition of the *Encyclopaedia Britannica* (1878) has long been regarded as a classic.

In 1876, Murray was invited by the publisher Macmillan to produce a major new dictionary of English. Although this proposal came to nothing, it reawakened the interest of Furnivall and others in the Philological Society's own lapsed project for a new historical dictionary. The upshot was its relaunching by Murray in 1879 at Mill Hill. With the help of hundreds of new volunteer excerptors, he augmented the collection of quotations (already over 2m on slips) assembled by Coleridge and Furnivall. At the same time, following the principles set out in R. C. Trench's paper of 1857, he laid down plan and methodology, after which, in the face of financial and other difficulties, he began to produce copy for *A New English Dictionary on Historical Principles* (later renamed *The Oxford English Dictionary*) at the remarkable rate of over 200 dictionary pages per year. In 1885, he gave up his part-time post at Mill Hill School and moved to Oxford to devote himself exclusively to the dictionary. He edited some 7,207 of its 15,487 pages, the remainder being divided among Henry Bradley, William Craigie, and Charles Onions. Because of the influence on later historical dictionaries of the methods he devised and of the editorial standard he set, and his own prodigious achievement as a dictionary compiler, Murray is widely regarded as the greatest ever lexicographer. His granddaughter, K. M. Elisabeth Murray, has written *Caught in the Web of Words: James A. H. Murray and the Oxford English Dictionary* (Yale University Press, 1977). See index. [BIOGRAPHY, EUROPE, REFERENCE].   A.J.A.

MUSE [14c, through French from Latin *musa*, Greek *moûsa*, also the source of *music* (through Latin *musica*, from Greek *mousikḗ tékhnē* the craft of the muse), and of *museum* (through Latin from Greek *mouseîon* the place of the muses). Often written with initial capital]. A classical female symbol of creative inspiration. In the mythology of the Greeks there appears originally to have been one muse, but various traditions list three, seven, or nine sisters born to Mnemosyne, the goddess of memory, and to Zeus. Homer invoked only one such unnamed 'goddess' at the start of both the *Iliad* and the *Odyssey*, and since his time many poems have begun with a so-called *invocation to the Muse*. The multiplication of muses suggests the development of an evolving taxonomy of the arts, each with a symbolic patron. The three muses were *Aoide* song, *Melete* meditation, and *Mneme* memory; the nine that the poet Hesiod claimed to have met were *Calliope*, the muse of epic poetry and foremost of them all, *Clio*, the muse of history, *Erato* of lyric poetry, *Euterpe* of music, *Melpomene* of tragedy, *Polyhymnia* of religious music, *Terpsichore* of dance, *Thalia* of comedy, and *Urania* of astronomy. Milton invoked a Christianized Urania, his 'Heavenly Muse', in *Paradise Lost* (1667), identifying her with the Holy Spirit that spoke to Moses. The term *the Muses* has been used to represent the liberal arts and *the Muse/muse* has referred to any source of inspiration: for example, the phrase *My muse was silent* might refer to a lack of ideas or to an inspiring woman who has nothing to say to the would-be poet. There have been many extensions of use, such as *a northern Muse* (Scottish poetic talent), *a crowned Muse* (King James I of England as literary patron), *a youthful muse* (the ability of a young, callow poet), and *the tenth Muse* (for a new kind of writing, such as both journalism and American literature in the 19c). Currently, the Muse is most commonly found in book titles, such as Stephen Potter's *The Muse in Chains* (1937), on the development of 'Eng. Lit.' as an academic subject, Herbert E. Read's *The Tenth Muse: Essays in Criticism* (1957), and Hugh Kenner's *The Mechanic Muse* (1987), a study of literature's response to technology. See IMAGINATION, MNEMONIC, POTTER. [LITERATURE, MEDIA].   T.MCA.

MYSTERY PLAY. See DRAMA, ENGLISH LITERATURE, TROPE.

MYTH [1820s: from Latin *mythos*, Greek *mûthos*, a story]. (1) A culturally significant story or explanation of how things came to be: for example, of how a god made the world or how a hero undertook a quest. As such, myth is opposed to *history*, in that it is usually fabulous in content even when loosely based on historical events. The term *mythology* refers both to the study of myth and a system of myths, such as *Greek mythology*. (2) A fictitious or dubious story, person, or thing: *That's a myth; it never happened*. Stories once regarded as true (and therefore not myths) may lose their power to convince (and be demoted to the status of myth), because other stories replace them (as pagan accounts of life were replaced by Christian accounts) or they are no longer considered relevant, credible, or useful. The adjectives *mythic* and *mythical* are synonymous, but *mythic* is often kept for the first sense of *myth* ('Mythic figures like Zeus and Heracles'; 'a story of mythic proportions') and *mythical* for the second sense ('the mythical land of El Dorado'). In classical Greece, *mûthos* was contrasted with *lógos*; both derive from verbs that translate as 'speak', but where *mûthos* subsumed poetry, emotion, and mythic thought, *lógos* subsumed prose, reason, and analytical thought. The present-day dichotomy between poetry, literature, and the humanities on the one hand, and reason, logic, analysis, and science on the other dates from the anti-mythic and anti-poetic stances adopted in the 5/4c BC by such philosophers as Plato. See ARCHETYPE, FICTION, LEGEND, LOGIC, RHETORIC. [LANGUAGE, LITERATURE]. T.MCA.

N

N, n [Called 'enn']. The 14th letter of the Roman alphabet as used for English. It originated as the Phoenician symbol *nun*, adopted by the Greeks as *nu* (*N*), a form which the Romans adopted in their turn.

Sound value. In English, the letter *n* represents a voiced alveolar nasal. Before a vowel, the sound-symbol correspondence is regular (*name, many*), but in loans from French a preceding medial *g* indicates a *y*-sound after the *n* (*cognac*: 'con-yack'). In French loans *n* may nasalize a preceding vowel, but have no clear sound of its own (*restaurant, lingerie*). Articulation may be affected by a following consonant: *b, p* may give the value of *m*, as in *inbred* ('imbred') and *input* ('imput'), and following hard *c, k, g, q, x* may produce a velar nasal 'ng': *zinc, increase, ink, sing, anger, concrete, congress, conquer, anxious*.

Double *N*. (1) In monosyllables following an initial consonant and vowel, *n* is normally single (*ban, can, fan, man, ran, tan, ten, tin, ton, tun*), with doubling before inflections beginning with a vowel (*bans, banned, banning*). *Nn* follows the initial short vowel in *inn, Ann*, but not in grammatical words (*an, in, on*). (2) In disyllables, after a short vowel, especially before -*er*, -*a*, -*y*: *manner, tenner, dinner, gunner; manna, henna; canny, tinny*. The pairs *dinner/diner, tinny/tiny* show the force of the doubling. However many other words do not observe this pattern: *any, canon* (beside *cannon*), *enemy, honour, linen, money, tenor*. A single *n* is usual before -*ish* (*banish, replenish, finish* (compare *Finnish*), *astonish, punish, Spanish*) and -*ion* (*companion, minion, pinion, onion, bunion*). Many such words derive from French, but do not follow modern French use of *nn/n*: *dîner, ennemi, étonner, honneur, manière, monnaie*. (3) With the Germanic prefix *un-* before *n* (*unnecessary, unnerved*) and Latin

prefixes ending in or assimilated to *n* (*annul, connect, innate, innocent*). (4) When the Germanic suffix -*ness* is added to words ending in *n*: *barrenness, openness* (but usually with a geminated or 'double' pronunciation). (5) In the comparative of adjectives ending in *n* following a short vowel if stressed (*thinner, thinnest*), but not if unstressed (*commoner, commonest*).

Syllabic *N*. The letter *n* may have syllabic value after alveolar consonants, as in the negative contractions *hadn't, isn't, mightn't* and the name *Haydn*. In similar environments, syllabic *n* can alternate with /n/ preceded by schwa. The schwa may, however, be spelt with a range of vowel letters: *beaten, raisin, fashion, cotton*. These variations can cause uncertainty: for example, in the endings -*ant*, -*ent*: *resistant, consistent*. See A, SYLLABIC CONSONANT.

Epenthetic *N*. Sometimes, an epenthetic *n* has been inserted in a word: *messenger, passenger*, from *message, passage* (compare French *messager, passager*). See EPENTHESIS.

Transfer. (1) Some nouns have lost an initial *n* that has been transferred to the indefinite article: *an adder* from *a nadder, an apron* from *a naperon, an umpire* from *a noumpere*. (2) Conversely, the *n* of *an* has sometimes been transferred to a following noun: *a newt* from *an ewt, a nickname* from *an ekename, the nonce* from *then anes*. See METANALYSIS.

Silence. (1) Word-final *n* is silent after *m* (*damn, hymn, autumn, column*), including inflected forms (*condemned, condemning*), but is pronounced in derived forms where a vowel follows (*autumnal, condemnation, hymnal, solemnity*). (2) *N* is sometimes preceded by a silent *g, k, p*: *gnat, feign, foreign; knit, know; pneumatic, pneumonia*. See G, K, P.

Other patterns. Many words in older English which ended in *n* (often an inflection) have lost

---

THE CAPITAL LETTER						THE SMALL LETTER				
EARLY FORMS				CURRENT FORMS		EARLY FORMS			CURRENT FORMS	
Phoenician	Greek	Etruscan	Roman (Latin)	roman	italic	Roman cursive	Roman uncial	Carolingian minuscule	roman	italic
ל	ᲧN	ᲧᲧ	N	N	*N*	ᴦ	N	ᴨ	n	*n*

the *n* with the inflection. Nevertheless, there are some pairs of words in which one member is without and another has kept the final *n*: *a/an*, *drunk/drunken*, *maid/maiden*, *my/mine*, *oft/often*, *ope/open*. One of the terms often has an archaic or poetic flavour: *maiden*, *oft*, *ope*. The inflectional function survives in the *olden* of *olden days/times*. See ALPHABET, EN, LETTER[1], SPELLING. [WRITING].   C.U.

NADSAT. See BURGESS.

NAIPAUL, (Sir) V(idiadhur) S(urujprasad) [b.1932]. Novelist, critic, essayist, reviewer, and broadcaster, of Indian background, born in Trinidad, and educated at Queen's Royal College, Trinidad, and Oxford. Widely travelled, he has regularly contributed to journals in the UK and US, and has been a Nobel Prize nominee. His works, mainly published in London by André Deutsch, include: *The Mystic Masseur* (1957), *Miquel Street* (1959), *A House for Mr Biswas* (1961), *The Middle Passage* (1962), *Mr Stone and the Knights' Companion* (1963), *An Area of Darkness* (1964), *A Flag on the Island* (1967), *The Mimic Men* (1967), *The Loss of Eldorado* (1970), *In a Free State* (1971), *The Overcrowded Baracoon* (1972), *Guerrillas* (1975), *India: A Wounded Civilization* (1977), *The Return of Eva Peron* (1980), *Among the Believers* (1981), *Finding the Centre* (1984), *The Enigma of Arrival* (1987, New York: Knopf), *A Turn in the South* (1987). Honours include the Trinity Cross (Trinidad and Tobago, 1989) and a knighthood. Further biographical details are provided in K. Jarvis, *V. S. Naipaul: A Selective Bibliography with Annotations, 1957–1987* (New Jersey: Scarecrow, 1989). See index. [AMERICAS, BIOGRAPHY, LITERATURE].   L.D.C.

NAME [From Old English *nama*, cognate with Latin *nomen* and Greek *ónoma/ónuma*]. A general, non-technical term for a word or phrase that designates a person (*woman*, *Helen*) an animal (*cat*, *Felix the Cat*), a place (*Helensburgh*, first a town in Scotland, then by commemorative extension a town in Australia), or a thing (the mineral *stone*, the subject or activity *electrical engineering*, the novel and motion picture *The Hound of the Baskervilles*). The same name may serve to designate more than one distinct though linked referent: for example, *Saint Helena* denotes both a saint and the island 'named' in her honour.

Common and proper names. Traditionally, names fall into two categories: (1) The *common name*, which designates a member of a class, such as *cat*, *tomcat*, *stone*, *rhinestone*, *verse*, *blank verse*. Generally, common names are written without initial capital letters. (2) The *proper name*, which

designates a specific entity: *Helen, Troy, Helen of Troy*; *Henry, Henry Smith, Henry VI* (both a person and a play). Generally, proper names are written with initial capital letters for each of their constituents, especially if they are nouns or adjectives: *Prince Hal, Blind Harry*. Occasionally, however, the capitals are dropped for effect, as in the name of the American poet *e. e. cummings* (1894-1962), and the names of some periodicals (such as the Australian literary magazine *overland*). Many common names that take the form of generic phrases that open with an embedded proper name, and therefore contain a capital letter, as in *Cheddar cheese, Siamese cat, Trojan horse, Wellington boot* See NOMENCLATURE, NOUN, TERM, TERMINOLOGY, WORD.

The study and classification of names. The descriptive and historical study of proper names is *onomastics*, and the study of common names (particularly as they form lexical systems or terminologies and vary from one group of speakers to another) is *onomasiology*. Proper names are distinguished, according to referent, as: personal names (*William Smith, Heather Gibson*); place-names (*Alice Springs, Chicago*); names of events (*Armageddon, the Boer War*); names of institutions (*the British Museum, the Library of Congress*); names of vehicles (*Ford, Pontiac; The Orient Express, the Queen Elizabeth II*); and works of art such as books and plays (*Pickwick Papers, Othello*), paintings (*the Mona Lisa, the Laughing Cavalier*), and musical compositions (*Eine kleine Nachtmusik, Finlandia*). Name study is logically a branch of linguistics, with an affinity to such other subjects as anthropology and topography, but in practice it is an independent discipline that combines the interests of philologists, linguists, historians, geographers, encyclopedists, sociologists, psychologists, genealogists, literary critics, and others. See FORM OF ADDRESS, ONOMASIOLOGY, ONOMASTICS, PERSONAL NAME, PLACE-NAME.

Associated meaning. The associations evoked by proper names may be either public (as with *Chernobyl*, a Ukrainian city associated throughout the world with a nuclear accident in 1986) or private (for example, someone associating the name *Rex* with pain and fear, because once bitten by a dog with that name). Public associations with some place-names are so strong that the names may come to be used in a sense that was originally no more than an association: for example, *Fleet Street*, a street in London, was until the late 1980s the location of many British newspaper offices, and came to mean, by metonymy, the British national press. It continues to be so used even though all London newspapers are now located elsewhere. Personal names often have both public and private associations that derive from particular individuals with those names: for example, *Mary* used to be, in the words of a popular song, 'a grand old name', the epitome of feminine virtue. Recently, however, it has been declining in popularity over much of the English-speaking world, and is now widely regarded as old-fashioned and pietistic. It may continue, however, to be used in certain families, for the sake of tradition, and may evoke the memory of a particular Mary whenever mentioned.

Name magic. In many societies, especially in the past, people's names have been regarded as closely linked with their owners' inmost natures. They are often intimately associated with those to whom they refer and in a non-rational way are considered to possess great power. Such names have often been conferred in special acts, such as the Christian rite of infant baptism, or such rites of passage as the taking of vows on entering a religious order, when monks and nuns give up worldly names along with worldly interests and assume new names to mark a new life. Giving and acquiring a personal name is a social act, once widely assumed to have a magical aspect: in ancient Egypt, for example, it was believed that to know someone's secret name gave one power over that person. The passing on of names within a family from one generation to the next is a long-established instance of what was once powerful word magic: a kind of time-binding by which ancestors are kept alive in their descendants.

Changing names. A change of personal name can be a powerful symbolic statement. In Western society, a woman once automatically adopted her husband's surname as her own, and socially used his full name instead of the names given to her at birth (as in *Mrs William Smith, née Heather Gibson*, where the French-derived *née* means 'born'). Current practice is variable. Generally, a compromise is achieved in the everyday form (*Mrs*) *Heather Smith*, where the personal first name is kept but the personal surname is changed. Especially in North America, the woman may keep her birth name, sometimes for professional purposes only, sometimes for all purposes (so that husband and wife may introduce themselves as *William Smith and Heather Gibson*). Occasionally, both partners will combine their surnames, as in *Heather and William Gibson-Smith*. Some committed feminists have dropped their family surnames altogether, and do not take a new one if married, since all such names are from the male line; instead, they may use a middle given name as surname (so that *Heather Rebecca Gibson*

becomes *Heather Rebecca*). A comparable reaction, especially in the US, is the dropping of traditional surnames by African-Americans who, seeing them as 'slave names', adopt instead African or Islamic names, as when the American boxer *Cassius Clay* became *Muhammad Ali*. See -ONYM. [NAME, WORD].   T.MCA.

Algeo, John. 1973. *On Defining the Proper Name*. Gainesville: University of Florida Press.

Davies, C. Stella, & Levitt, John. 1970. *What's in a Name?* London: Routledge & Kegan Paul.

Dickson, Paul. 1986. *A Collector's Compendium of Rare and Unusual, Bold and Beautiful, Odd and Whimsical Names*. New York: Delacorte.

Gardiner, Alan. 1954. *The Theory of Proper Names*, 2nd edition. Oxford: University Press.

Pulgram, Ernst. 1954. *Theory of Names*. Berkeley: American Name Society.

Sørenson, Holger Steen. 1958. *Word-Classes in Modern English with Special Reference to Proper Names*. Copenhagen: Gad.

—— 1963. *The Meaning of Proper Names*. Copenhagen: Gad.

The name theme

A–C. ABORIGINES, AFRICA, AFRICAN, AFRO-, ALBA, ALBION, AM-, AMER(I)-, AMERICA, AMERICAN[1], AMERICAN NAME SOCIETY, AMERINDIAN, ANGLIA, ANGLO, ANGLO-(ETC.), ANGLOMANIA, ANGLOPHILE, ANGLOPHOBE, ANGLOPHONE, ANGUILLA, ANTHROPONYMY, ANTIGUA AND BARBUDA, ANTILLES, ANTIPODES, ANTONOMASIA, AOTEAROA, APTRONYM, ARGENTINA, ATLANTIC, ATTIC AND DORIC, AUGUSTAN, AUNTIE, AUSSIE, AUSTRAL, AUSTRALASIA, AUSTRALIA, AUSTRALIAN, BAHAMAS, BANGLADESH, BARBADOS, BAY ISLANDS, BAYMEN, BBC PRONUNCIATION UNIT, BELFAST, BELIZE, BINOMIAL, BINOMIAL NOMENCLATURE, BLACK CELT, BLACK IRISH, BOTSWANA, BRETON, BRIT, BRITAIN, BRITANNIA, BRITISH, BRITISH INDIAN OCEAN TERRITORY, BRITON, BRUNEI, BURMA/MYANMAR, BUSH, BY-LINE, BY-NAME, CAJUN, CALEDONIA, CAMEROON, CAN-, CANADA, CANADIAN, CANADIAN PLACE-NAMES, CARIBBEAN, CAYMAN ISLANDS, CELT, CELTIC, CELTIC FRINGE, CELTIC TWILIGHT, CENTRAL AMERICA, CHANNEL ISLANDS, CHARACTERNYM, CHAUVINISM, CHICANO, CHRISTIAN NAME, CLIPPING, COLONIAL, COMMON NAME, COMMONWEALTH, COMMONWEALTH CARIBBEAN, COMPOUND WORD, CONTINENT, CORNISH, CORNWALL, CUMBRIA, CUMBRIC.

D–M. DEFINITION, DOMINICA, DORSET, DOUBLE-BARRELLED NAME, DUBLIN, EAST INDIAN, EAST INDIES, EDINBURGH, ENGLISH, ENGLISH CANADA, ENGLISH CANADIAN, ENGLISHRY, ENG LIT, EPITHET, EPONYM, ERIN, ESKIMO, ETHNIC NAME, EURASIAN, EURO-, EUROCENTRIC, EUROPE, FALKLAND ISLANDS, FIJI, FILIPINO, FIRST NAME, FLANDERS, FLEMISH, FORENAME, FORM OF ADDRESS, GAEL, GAELDOM, GAELTACHT, GAMBIA, GEOGRAPHY, GHANA, GIBRALTAR, GIVEN NAME, GODZONE, GREAT BRITAIN, GRENADA, GRINGO, GUYANA, HIBERNIA, HIBERNIANISM/HIBERNICISM, HIBERNO-, HILLBILLY, HISPANIC, HOBSON-JOBSONISM, HOME, HOME COUNTIES, HONG KONG/HONGKONG, HONORIFIC, INDIA, INDIAN, INDIES, INDO-, INDO-ANGLIAN, INDO-ARYAN, INDO-BRITISH, INDO-GERMANIC, INDONESIA, INGVAEONIC, INITIAL, INUIT, IRELAND, IRISH, IRISHMAN/WOMAN, ISLE

OF MAN, JAMAICA, JOHN BULL, JOKE TOWN, JUTES, KENYA, KIRIBATI, KIWI, KOREA, KRIO, KRIOL, KWEYOL, LABEL NAME, LATIN[1], LATIN[2], LATINO, LEEWARD ISLANDS, LESOTHO, LETTER WORD/NAME, LIVERPOOL/LIVERPUDLIAN, MACAO, McWORD, MALAWI, MALAYSIA, MALDIVES, MALTA, -MAN/WOMAN, MANX, MANXMAN/WOMAN, MAORI, MAURITIUS, MELANESIA, MERCIA, MESTIZO, METAPHOR, MÉTIS, MICRONESIA, MIDDLE NAME, MIDLAND, MIDLANDS, MISTAKE NAME, MONTSERRAT, MOTHER COUNTRY, MULATTO.

N–Z. NAME, NAMIBIA, NEW ENGLISH, NEWFIE, NEWFOUNDLAND, NEW ORLEANS, NEW YORK, NEW YORKESE, NEW YORRICAN, NEW ZEALAND, NEW ZEALAND PLACE-NAMES, NICKNAME, NIGERIA, NOMENCLATURE, NORTH AMERICAN, NORTH COUNTRY, NORTHERN IRELAND, NORTHERN ISLES, NORTHUMBRIA, OCEANIA, OLD COUNTRY, ONOMASIOLOGY, ONOMASTICS, ONOMATOPOEIA, -ONYM, ORCADIAN, ORKNEY, OXBRIDGE, OZ, PAKISTAN, PANAMA, PATRONYMIC, PEN NAME, PERSONAL NAME, PET NAME, PHILIPPINE, PHILIPPINES, PLACE-NAME, PLAID CYMRU, POLYNESIA, PROPER NAME, PROPER NOUN, PROTESTANT ASCENDANCY, PSEUDONYM, PUERTO RICO, RHODESIA, SAXON, SCOT, SCOTCH, SCOTCH-IRISH, SCOTCHMAN/WOMAN, SCOTS, SCOTTISH, SEYCHELLES, SHELTA, SHETLAND, SIERRA LEONE, SINHALA, SOBRIQUET/SOUBRIQUET, SOLOMON ISLANDS, SOMERSET, SOUTH (THE), SOUTH AFRICA, SOUTH AFRICAN PLACE-NAMES, SRI LANKA, SUDAN, SURINAM(E) SURNAME, SWAZILAND, SYNECDOCHE, TAGALOG, TALK, TANZANIA, TERM, TERMINOLOGY, TITLE, TOPONYM, TOPONYMY, TRADEMARK, TRADE NAME, TRIN(I)BAGONIAN, TRINIBAGIANESE, TRINIDAD AND TOBAGO, TRISTAN DA CUNHA, TSOTSI-TAAL, TURKS AND CAICOS ISLANDS, TUVALU, UGANDA, ULSTER, UNCLE SAM, UNITED KINGDOM, UNITED STATES, US/U.S., USA/U.S.A., VANUATU, VIRGIN ISLANDS, WALES, WALIAN, WASP, WELSH, WELSHMAN/WOMAN, WELSHNESS, WELSH PLACE-NAMES, WELSHRY, WELSH WALES, WELSHY, WESSEX, WEST COUNTRY, WESTERN ISLES, WESTERN SAMOA, WEST INDIAN, WEST INDIES, WEST OF ENGLAND, WEST SAXON, WILD IRISH, WINDWARD ISLANDS, YANK(EE), YORKSHIRE, ZAMBIA, ZETLAND, ZETLANDIC, ZIMBABWE.

NAMIBIA. A country of southern Africa. Capital: Windhoek. Currency: the rand (100 cents). Population: 1.3m (1988), 1.8m (projection for 2000). Ethnicity: 50% Ovambo, 9% Kavango, 8% Damara, 8% Herero, 5% Nama, 4% Caprivian, 3% Afrikaner, 3% San (Bushman), 2% German, 2% Basters, 5% mixed. Religion: 50% Protestant, 31% traditional, 19% Roman Catholic. Languages: English (official), Afrikaans, Damara, German, Herero, Kavango, Ovambo, Nama, etc. Education: primary 80%, secondary 60%, tertiary 3%, literacy 28%. Because of the Namib Desert, British and Dutch missionaries did not penetrate the region until the late 18c. The Germans colonized it as *German West Africa* in 1892–3, but lost it during the First World War to South Africa, which governed it from 1920 as *South West Africa*, under a League of Nations mandate. The United Nations sought to make it a trusteeship after 1946, but South

Africa refused to cooperate. In 1966, the UN mandate was withdrawn. In 1968, the territory's name became Namibia. South Africa governed the territory without international recognition until independence in 1990. English, Afrikaans, and German were all official until independence, when English was declared the sole official language. Afrikaans is, however, more widely used. See ENGLISH. [AFRICA, NAME, VARIETY].   T.MCA.

NARRATION [15c: from Latin *narratio/narrationis* telling, recounting: see NARRATIVE]. (1) The act, process, or result of narrating or telling; something narrated; the work of a *narrator*. (2) In classical rhetoric, the expounding of points or recounting of facts, the second of three stages in public speaking. (3) In the study of fiction, 'Narration is an aspect of the whole process of communication or discours(e) between author and reader, and between narrator and narratee. In critical studies and narratology it has involved the discussion of voices and points of view, of the different kinds and levels of narration (first person; third person, omniscient, etc.)' (Katie Wales, *A Dictionary of Stylistics*, 1989). In formal English, narration is usually in the past tense, but in informal and especially colloquial usage it is often in the present. See NARRATIVE, NOVEL, PLOT, RHETORIC, STORY, VOICE. [STYLE, WRITING].   T.MCA.

NARRATIVE [16c: from Latin *narrativus* suitable for telling, from *narrare/narratum* to tell, relate, ultimately from archaic *gnarus* knowing, practised, and cognate with Latin-derived *cognition*, Greek-derived *agnostic*, and vernacular *know*]. (1) The general or inclusive term for a story or account of any events or experiences, fact or fiction, long or short, detailed or plain. (2) The form that such a story takes, whether physical (a text or book) or a literary genre (epic or novel). (3) Without article: the process, art, or technique of narrating (telling a story): *the art of oral narrative; dramatic narrative*. (4) Relating to storytelling and the like: *narrative line; a narrative voice*. (5) In the fine arts, telling a story: for example, through sculpted forms or pictures (*narrative painting*). Compare DISCOURSE, PLOT, STORY, TEXT. See CHILD LANGUAGE ACQUISITION, NARRATION, NARRATIVE POETRY, NOVEL, STORY, VOICE. [STYLE].   T.MCA.

NARRATIVE POETRY, also **narrative verse.** Poetry or verse that tells a story. It ranges from such epics as Milton's *Paradise Lost* to the traditional ballad. Elizabeth Barrett Browning's *Aurora Leigh* (1857) is an 11,000-line story that Robert Browning called 'a novel in verse'. Narrative poetry differs from *lyric poetry* in content and authorial stance. See EPIC, GENRE, POETRY. [LITERATURE]. R.C.

NARRATIVE VOICE. See NARRATIVE, NOVEL, VOICE.

NARRATOLOGY. See PLOT, POETICS.

NARROW. See PHONETIC TRANSCRIPTION.

NASAL [14c: from Latin *nasalis* of the nose]. A term used generally and in phonetics for a speech quality influenced by air passing through the nose. When a nasal consonant is produced, the velum is lowered to allow air to pass out through nose as well as mouth: /m, n, ŋ/ as in *am, an, sing*. These consonants are generally referred to as *nasal consonants* or *nasals*. *Nasalization* is the production of resonance in the nose to accompany a speech sound, as in French *bon* but not *bonne*. English vowels may be partially nasalized when followed by a nasal consonant. Some accents of English are more nasal than others; some people's voices are said to sound nasal or are described as having a *nasal accent* or a *(nasal) twang*. Nasality is a feature of most varieties of AmE and CanE and some kinds of London English. It is the consequence of a setting of the velum which causes a degree of nasal resonance greater than the user of such a term as *twang* would consider normal. Reduced nasal resonance is also described as *adenoidal*. There is no fixed norm. See ACCENT, ARTICULATORY SET-(TING), ENG, LONDON, NEW ENGLAND, SCOUSE, TILDE, TWANG, VELUM. [SPEECH]. G.K.

NATE, full form *National Association for the Teaching of English*. The national professional organization of teachers of English in Britain, founded in 1963. It organizes an annual conference and a range of local meetings and workshops, and its publications include a newsletter and the journal *English in Education*. NATE grew out of the work of the *London Association for the Teaching of English*, and has concentrated on local groups and interest groups producing responses to specific problems: during the 1960s, for example, it advised the Schools Council on research in curriculum development, members contributing to projects on oracy, the development of writing abilities 11–18, teaching literature, and children as readers. Joint activities with US colleagues produced a statement of current views in John Dixon's *Growth through English* (Oxford University Press, 1967; 2nd edition 1975). The model outlined by Dixon was developed through the 1970s as NATE became increasingly concerned with English and those disadvantaged in society. In response to the Bullock Report, whose conclusions were much influenced by NATE members, 'language across the curriculum' became the concern of a number of conferences. In the same period, there was an increased interest in the role of language, in response especially to developments in sociolinguistics. In the 1970s–80s, NATE defended the achievements of English teaching against criticism and attack from various official and unofficial bodies. It gave substantial evidence to the Kingman Inquiry and to discussion on the National Curriculum for England and Wales, which was incorporated into the Education Act of 1988. Compare NCTE. [EDUCATION, EUROPE, MEDIA]. C.J.B.

NATECLA, full form *National Association for Teaching English and Other Community Languages to Adults*. An association founded in Britain in 1978 as *NATESLA* (*National Association of Teachers of English as a Second Language*), for teaching ESL to adults. It seeks to provide a professional forum for organizers and teachers of English and community languages to adults. It provides a network for training and the sharing of materials, and publishes a newsletter and the journal *Language Issues*. See COMMUNITY LANGUAGE. [EDUCATION, EUROPE, MEDIA]. C.J.B.

NATIONAL ASSOCIATION FOR TEACHING ENGLISH AND OTHER COMMUNITY LANGUAGES TO ADULTS. See NATECLA.

NATIONAL ASSOCIATION FOR THE TEACHING OF ENGLISH. See NATE.

NATIONAL COUNCIL OF TEACHERS OF ENGLISH. See NCTE.

NATIONAL CURRICULUM. See CURRICULUM.

NATIONAL LANGUAGE [20c]. A language officially designated the language of a nation or country, usually for cultural and/or ethnic reasons. Such a language may or may not be the *official language* of the country in question (that is, used in its government and administration): for example, in Botswana, the national language is Setswana, but the official language is English. Compare NATIVE LANGUAGE, OFFICIAL LANGUAGE. [LANGUAGE]. T.MCA.

NATION LANGUAGE [1980s]. A term coined by the poet and scholar Edward Brathwaite to present Caribbean Creole in a positive light, especially in its artistic and literary use (*History of the Voice: The Development of Nation Language in Anglophone Caribbean Poetry*, London: New Beacon, 1984). His concern has been to break away from the traditions of speakers of

English in the Caribbean and elsewhere. Although he develops his concept and examples in terms of English and the anglophone Caribbean, incidental remarks and references indicate that he applies the term to other creoles besides those based on English. He acknowledges the English lexical sources of Creole, but affirms the Africanness of its rhythms, experiential content, and personality, as well as its cultural links with West Africa. He opposes the term to *dialect*, whose pejorative connotations he sees as inappropriate and limiting. See BRATHWAITE, CARIBBEAN ENGLISH, CREOLE. [AMERICAS, VARIETY].

L.D.C.

NATIVE. See ETHNIC NAME.

NATIVE AMERICAN. See AMERICAN[1], AMERINDIAN, ETHNIC NAME.

NATIVE LANGUAGE [Since at least the 16c]. A general term often used synonymously with *mother tongue*. It dates from the Middle Ages, when it was widely believed that language is physically inherited, one's birth determining both language and nationality. Because of this association with birth and birthright and the confusion associated with the word *native*, some linguists consider that the term should, like *native speaker*, be avoided or used with caution in scholarly work. See ETHIC NAME, FIRST/SECOND LANGUAGE, MOTHER TONGUE, NATIVE SPEAKER. [LANGUAGE]. P.C.

NATIVE SPEAKER [Date uncertain: *native* used in this sense since at least the 16c]. A person who has spoken a certain language since early childhood: *A native speaker of French.* Native speakers are often appealed to, including by linguists, over questions of correct usage, because traditionally the language in which they are fluent has been regarded as their exclusive property. Some linguists, however, have in recent years argued that no one is 'born' into a language (as the etymology of the usage suggests) but acquires it from an environment that may in fact change in childhood, adolescence, or later, causing an individual to develop a second language into a medium as personal as the first (sometimes losing skills in the earlier 'mother tongue'). Whether such a *non-native speaker* is able to acquire the same command of the language as a native speaker is a much-debated question to which there is no simple answer. *Native* and *non-native* are not clear-cut homogeneous categories; each group comprises wide variations depending on such individual factors as regional or national origin, age of learning (for non-natives), degree of formal training, aspirations, and sense of identity. To avoid misleading associations with

birth, birthright, and claims of ownership, some scholars consider that the terms should be used with caution. See NATIVE LANGUAGE, NATIVE USER. [LANGUAGE, SPEECH]. P.C., T.MCA.

NATIVE USER [1970s]. A term increasingly used in language teaching and applied linguistics in preference to *native speaker*, to emphasize that language includes writing and print as well as speech. See FOREIGN USER, NATIVE SPEAKER. [LANGUAGE]. P.C., T.MCA.

NATIVISM [1840s] (1) Prejudice in favour of natives against foreigners, especially immigrants, usually due to fear and self-interest and associated with *ethnocentrism*, a preference for one's own kind, customs, language, etc. The newcomers most subject to nativism are those most easily distinguishable on racial, linguistic, religious, and other grounds and those who arrive during times of economic or social tension. An often-cited example is the anti-Catholic 'Know-Nothing' Party of the 1850s in the US, a response to large-scale Catholic immigration, particularly from Ireland. For a time it had considerable political clout and was a factor in the 1856 presidential election. Recent campaigns to make English the official language of the US have been interpreted as nativistic, with an anti-Spanish bias. As with 19c nativism, it comes at a time of change, and has widespread popular appeal. Nativist sentiment also often occurs among earlier immigrants against later immigrants. (2) The movement of an indigenous society back to its traditional culture or what is taken to be traditional culture after sustained and unsettling influence from outside pressures. Anthropologists regard such developments as the Native American Church among Amerindians and the cargo cults of Oceania as nativist. See CENTRICITY, ENGLISH LANGUAGE AMENDMENT, ETHNIC NAME. [AMERICAS, LANGUAGE]. J.E., T.MCA.

NATIVIZATION, also **nativisation** [1930s]. (1) The process by which a transplanted language becomes native to a people or place, either in addition to or in place of any language or languages already in use, as with English in Ireland and both English and French in West Africa. The process is often given a specific name, such as *Africanization* or *Indianization* (in the case of English), and takes place at every level of language, local users of that language developing, among other things, distinctive accents, grammatical usages, and items of vocabulary, such developments generally linked with their other or former languages. (2) The process by which a pidgin language becomes a creole, as with Tok Pisin in Papua New Guinea. (3) The process by which a foreign word becomes 'native' to a language, as in the various pronunciations of French *garage* in English. Compare ENGLISHIZE, INDIGENIZATION. [LANGUAGE].   B.B.K., T.MCA.

NATURAL LANGUAGE. A term in linguistics for language as it naturally occurs in humans. Compare ARTIFICIAL LANGUAGE, MACHINE LANGUAGE, METALANGUAGE. [LANGUAGE].   J.M.A.

NATURAL METHOD. See DIRECT METHOD, LANGUAGE TEACHING.

NAURU. Official title: *Republic of Nauru.* A country of Oceania, an island of 21 square miles, and member of the Commonwealth. Capital: Yaren district. Currency: Australian dollar. Economy: mainly mining and agriculture. Population: 9,000 (1988), 10,000 (projection for 2000). Ethnicity: *c.*58% Nauruan, 25% other Pacific Islanders, 8% Chinese, 8% Caucasian. Religions: 65% Protestant, 20% Roman Catholic, 15% others. Languages: Nauruan (official), English. Education: primary 100%, secondary 50%, tertiary 15%, literacy 99%. A German colony since the late 19c, Nauru became a League of Nations mandate in 1920 and later a UN trust territory administered by Australia, gaining internal self-government in 1966 and independence in 1968. See ENGLISH. [NAME, OCEANIA, VARIETY]. T.MCA.

NAUTICAL JARGON. See MARITIME PIDGIN.

NBC. See AMERICAN BROADCASTING.

NCTE, The, full form *National Council of Teachers of English.* The national professional organization of some 58,000 elementary, high-school, and college teachers of English throughout the US and Canada. Since its founding in 1911, the NCTE has sought to improve the teaching of English from kindergarten through college by sponsoring research projects, annual conferences, and workshops on special topics. Over 100,000 individuals and libraries subscribe to some or all of the nine NCTE journals: *Language Arts* (formerly *Elementary English*, devoted to language skills in the early years), *English Education* (concentrating on the nature of English teaching and the training and retraining of teachers at all levels), *English Journal* (containing short, illustrated articles on topics of general interest to secondary-school teachers), *College English* (mainly essays on topics of general professional interest), *Research in the Teaching of English* (reporting new research, summarizing trends in research, and publishing a continual annotated bibliography of current research on language and learning at all levels),

College Composition and Communication (providing articles about the history, theory, and sociopolitical implications of teaching writing in college as well as on research on the writing process and its relationship with other cognitive skills and forms of communication), *Teaching English in the Two-Year College* (directed at teachers of college freshmen and sophomores and focusing on the teaching of composition and literature), *Conference for Secondary School English Department Chairmen* (a source of information for administrators of high-school English programmes), and the *Quarterly Review of Doublespeak* (see entry).

Over the years, the NCTE has taken a particular interest in encouraging research and developing teaching materials about the language. Moving away from the strong grammatical and lexical prescriptivism that had characterized earlier generations of US teachers of English, in the 1930s the NCTE sponsored two works on usage: Sterling Leonard's *Current English Usage* (1932) and Albert Marckwardt and Fred Walcott's *Facts about Current English Usage* (1938). NCTE backing helped to publish Charles C. Fries's *American English Grammar* (1940). By 1949, interest in composition had grown so strong that the NCTE sponsored a special springtime conference that soon grew into the Conference on College Composition and Communication, now known almost exclusively by its acronym CCCC ('four cees'). During the 1960s, the emphasis was on dialects and NCTE published materials like the phonograph recording *Americans Speaking* and Roger Shuy's *American Dialects* (1967). In 1974, CCCC and NCTE adopted a controversial resolution entitled 'Students' Right to Their Own Language', affirming that 'teachers must have the experience and training that will allow them to respect diversity and uphold the right of students to their own language'. Responding to other societal issues that have consequences in the classroom, the NCTE published *Responses to Sexism* (1976) and *Sexism and Language* (1977) and adopted a non-sexist language policy for all NCTE publications and communications. In the 1980s, the NCTE provided through its meetings and special workshops a forum for discussing opening up the literary canon to include women and authors of various ethnic backgrounds. In 1991, the NCTE launched *The Council Chronicle*, a newspaper to be published five times per working year, in September, November, February, April, and June, as an exclusive benefit of membership. All activities are currently centralized at 1111 Kenyon Road, Urbana, Illinois, 61801. Compare NATE. [AMERICAS, EDUCATION, MEDIA].
C.C.E.

NDJUKA. An English-based creole of Surinam spoken since the 18c by the Eastern Bush

Negroes (the Aucan or Ndjuka and the Boni or Aluku). The language developed among runaways from plantation slavery. It is closely related to *Sranan* and to a limited degree mutually intelligible with it. Ndjuka is unusual among creoles in having its own syllabic writing developed by its speakers, a system with strong similarities to indigenous scripts of West Africa. See SRANAN, SURINAM(E). [AMERICAS, VARIETY, WRITING]. L.D.C.

NEAR RHYME. See HALF RHYME.

NEAR-RP. A term in phonetics and sociolinguistics for an accent of English considered close to but not identical with RP, even though speakers of such an accent and others hearing them may regard it as the same. See MORNINGSIDE AND KELVINSIDE, NEW ZEALAND ENGLISH, RECEIVED PRONUNCIATION. [SPEECH]. T.MCA.

NEGATION [14c: through French from Latin *negatio/negationis* denial]. A grammatical term for the process that results in changing a positive (affirmative) sentence or clause into a negative one: from *They came* to *They did not come*. This is sometimes known as a contrast in *polarity*. In English, a sentence is typically negated through the verb, by the insertion of *not* or its contraction *n't* after the first or only verb: *It is raining* becoming *It is not/isn't raining*. If an auxiliary verb is present, as with *is* in the above sentence, *not* follows it or *n't* is attached to it as an enclitic (*must not, mustn't*). If no auxiliary is present, then the relevant form of the auxiliary *do* (*do, does,* or *did*, according to tense and person) is inserted to effect the negation: *I know him* becoming *I do not/don't know him*.

Special cases. (1) The verb *be* is used in the same way when no auxiliary is present: *Justin was ill* becoming *Justin was not/wasn't ill*. (2) The verb *have* allows both alternatives, but in a variety of forms. The negation of *Benjamin has his own bedroom* can be *B. has not his own b.* (traditional BrE), *B. hasn't his own b.* (its informal variant), *B. has not got his own b.* (a current emphatic, especially BrE usage), *B. hasn't got his own b.* (its common, informal equivalent), *B. does not have his own b.* (a widely used formal, especially AmE usage), *B. doesn't have his own b.* (its common, informal equivalent). (3) See MODAL VERB [NEGATION].

Contracted forms. The contraction *n't* is typically informal, especially in speech, except when the negation is emphasized, as in a denial of something said before, in which case the full *not* is used and stressed. With many auxiliaries, there is often also a possibility of auxiliary contraction in informal English: *It isn't fair* or *It's not fair*

(more common); *He won't object* (more common) or *He'll not object*; *They haven't finished* (more common) or *They've not finished*.

Tag questions. When tag questions are used to invite confirmation, positive sentences are normally followed by negative tag questions (*David is abroad, isn't he?*) and negative sentences by positive tag questions (*David isn't abroad, is he?*). Positive sentences are sometimes followed by positive tag questions (*So David is abroad, is he?*), indicating an inference or recollection from what has been said. Occasionally, they suggest suspicion or a challenge: *So that's what Doris wants, is it?*

Expressions used with negation. Some expressions are found exclusively or typically in negative sentences: the *not . . . any* relationship in *Doris hasn't produced any plays*, contrasted with *Doris has produced some plays*; the *not . . . either* relationship in *David doesn't smoke a pipe, either* (in response to such statements as *John doesn't smoke a pipe*), contrasted with *David smokes a pipe, too* (in response to *John smokes a pipe*).

Negation other than through the verb. *No, not,* and other negative words may be introduced in order to negate a sentence: *Jeremy has no difficulties with this* (compare *Jeremy hasn't any difficulties with this*); *Ray said not a word to anybody* (compare *Ray didn't say a word to anybody*); *Maurice will never make a fuss, will he?* (compare *Maurice won't make a fuss, will he?*); *Nothing surprises them, does it?* (compare *There isn't anything that surprises them, is there?*); *Mervyn hardly ever makes a mistake, does he?* (compare *Mervyn doesn't ever make mistakes, does he?*).

Implied contrasts. The negative particle or word extends its scope over the whole or part of the sentence. The extent is manifested when expressions associated with negatives are present, as in the difference between *I didn't read some of the papers* (that is, I read others) and *I didn't read any of the papers* (that is, I read none). The *focus* of the negation (marked intonationally in speech) is the part of the sentence which presents a negative contrast: *Ted doesn't teach history* may imply that someone else does or that Ted teaches something else.

Double negation. Prefixes such as *un-* and *in-* make the word negative but not the sentence in which it is used: *unhappy* in *They are unhappy about their new house*; *insensitively* in *They spoke rather insensitively to him when he lost his job*. Such words may be combined with another negative to cancel out, to a large extent, the force of the negative prefix: *Jeremy was not unhappy*, meaning that he was fairly happy. See LITOTES. This type of double negation, which results in a positive meaning, is different from the kinds of *multiple negation* found in both general non-standard English (*I didn't see nothing*: I didn't see anything) and in some dialects (Glasgow *Ah'm no comin neer Ah'm no*: I am not coming neither I am not). Such usages are widely stigmatized and equally widely used. See DOUBLE NEGATIVE. [GRAMMAR].   S.G.

NEHRU, Jawaharlal [1889-1964]. Indian politician, lawyer, writer, born in Allahabad, the only son of Motilal Nehru and the father of Indira Gandhi, and educated at Harrow and Trinity College, Cambridge. He joined the Inner Temple in London in 1910 and became a barrister in 1912. Nehru took a great interest in Fabian socialism, but the greatest impact on his politics was made by Mahatma Gandhi, who nominated him as his political heir. Nehru was elected President of the Congress Party five times, and during 17 years as Prime Minister of India directed its foreign policy and its industrial and scientific growth. His extensive writings in English fall into three periods: mainly journalism (1920-8), when he wrote for such publications as *The Independent*, *Young India*, and *Modern Review*; a period when he was often imprisoned by the British (1928-42), when he wrote such works as *The Autobiography* (1936), *Glimpses of World History* (1934-5), and *The Unity of India* (ed. V. K. Krishna Menon, 1941); and his political heyday (1942-64), at the beginning of which he wrote *The Discovery of India* (1946). His works were exhilarating to many Indians and contributed towards an understanding of their past that differed from Western interpretation. Of himself, he is widely quoted as having observed, 'I have become a queer mixture of East and West, out of place everywhere, at home nowhere.' His 'prison writing' includes *Letters from a Father to His Daughter* (1930). In one of his last statements on the language question, Nehru touched on India's continuing love/hate relationship with English: 'It is not the fact that many people know English and learnt it, but it was a kind of fixation that English was a symbol of status, that a man who knew very indifferent English was somehow better than a scholar in our own languages. That was a fixation that was obviously most improper and most objectionable, and it had to be got rid of. I am not quite sure if we have got rid of it even yet. That has nothing to do with our liking English, considering it a very desirable language to learn and study. It is the mental attitude that is objectionable' (*Bulletin of CIEFL* 3, 1963). See index. [ASIA, BIOGRAPHY].   B.B.K.

NEO-CLASSICISM. See AUGUSTAN, CLASSIC, CLASSICISM, ENGLISH LITERATURE, LITERARY CRITICISM.

NEO-LATIN, also **New Latin.** A variety of Latin current during and after the Renaissance, especially in academic and scientific discourse. One of its features is a stratum of Greek associated with scholarly and highly technical usage. See BISOCIATION, CLASSICAL LANGUAGE, GREEK, LATIN[1]. [EUROPE, LANGUAGE].   T.MCA.

NEOLOGISM, also **neology** [18c: from French *néologisme* and *néologie*, both from Greek *néos* new, *lógos* word]. Terms used by students of language for a new word or sense of a word and for the coining or use of new words and senses. Most neologisms in English belong in the following categories: (1) Compounding: *couch potato*, someone constantly slumped on a couch watching television: *deep pocket*, a dependable source for financing; *teletext*, a computer-based news and information service transmitted by television; *video-conferencing*, a number of people taking part in a conference or conferences by means of video equipment rather than all meeting in one place. (2) Derivation: *yuppie*, formed from *yup*, the initial letters of the phrase 'young urban professional' by adding the suffix *-ie*; *yuppiedom*, the condition of being a yuppie, formed from *yuppie* by adding the further suffix *-dom*. (3) Shifting meaning: *spin*, a journalist's term for a special bias or slant given to a piece of writing; *necklace*, a name in South Africa for a tyre soaked in petrol, to be put round someone's neck and set alight. (4) Extension in grammatical function: the nouns *quest* and *necklace* (see preceding) used as verbs. (5) Abbreviation: in Stock Exchange usage, *arb* from *arbitrager* or *arbitrageur*, one who sells securities or commodities simultaneously in different markets to benefit from unequal prices; the computer acronym *GIGO*, meaning *garbage in, garbage out*. (6) Back-formation: *disinform* formed from *disinformation* (and not the reverse). (7) Blending: *harmolodic* mixing *harmony* and *melodic*; *orature* formed from *oral* and *literature*. (8) Borrowing: loanwords such as *glasnost* from Russian and *nouvelle cuisine* from French; calques or loan translations such as *found object* from French *objet trouvé*. (9) Very rarely, root-creation, or coinage from sounds with no previous known meaning whatever: *googol*, *Kodak* (both apparently formed *ex nihilo*).

New words are often the subject of scorn because they are new, because they are perceived as unaesthetically or improperly formed, or because they are considered to be unnecessary. They are, however, a normal part of language change; with frequent use and the passage of time they become unremarked items in everyday use, as can be seen from many of the items in the following representative decade-by-decade lists of neologisms coined between 1940 and 1990:

1940s. acronym, airlift, apartheid, atomic age, automation, baby-sit, bikini, blockbuster, call girl, circuitry, cold war, crash landing, debrief, declassify, doublethink, flying saucer, freeze-dry, genocide, gobbledygook, gremlin, guided missile, hydrogen bomb, nerve gas, petro-chemical, quisling, radar, snorkel, spaceship, starlet, tape recorder, task force, vegan, VIP, xerography, zero in.

1950s. A-OK, automate, beatnik, brainwashing, common market, cosmonaut, countdown, desegregation, discotheque, do-it-yourself, egg-head, hard sell, H-bomb, hotline, Kremlinology, LSD, McCarthyism, moonlighting, moonshot, Ms, name-dropping, nuke, overkill, panelist, paramedic, parenting, sci-fi, scuba, senior citizen, sex kitten, shopping mall, soft sell, space medicine, sputnik.

1960s. affirmative action, biodegradable, bionics, brain drain, cable television, counter-productive, cryonics, cybernation, disco, Euro-crat, Eurodollar, fast-food, genetic engineering, jet lag, microelectronics, microwave oven, plea-bargaining, pop art, postcode/postal code (BrE), quasar, reverse discrimination, sitcom, space shuttle, theme park, tokenism, under-achiever, uptight, ZIP Code (AmE).

1970s. boat people, bottom line, condo, corn row, downsize, ecocatastrophe, ecofreak, empty nester, flextime, gas guzzler, gasohol, hit list, junk food, Legionnaire's Disease, Mediagate, miniseries, nouvelle cuisine, petrodollars, shuttle diplomacy, supply-side economics, Watergate, Watergatology.

1980s. cash point, channelling, couch potato, Filofax, glasnost, golden handcuffs, golden handshake, golden parachute, gridlock, home shopping, kiss-and-tell book, necklacing, New Agers, perestroika, personal organizer, power breakfast, silent majority, telemarketing, whole-foodie, whoopie, yuppie, yuppiedom.

Publications that document neologisms include: *American Speech* (which has had a section called 'Among the New Words' since 1941); *The Barnhart Dictionary Companion* (since 1982); *The Barnhart Dictionary of New English since 1963* (1973), *The Second Barnhart Dictionary of New English* (1980); *The Third Barnhart Dictionary of New English* (1992); *Longman Guardian New Words* (1986); *12,000 Words: A Supplement to Webster's Third New International Dictionary* (1986); *Bloomsbury Neologisms: New Words Since 1960* (1991); *The Oxford Dictionary of New Words* (1991); *Fifty Years Among the New Words: A Dictionary of Neologisms, 1941–1991* (reproducing and extending the articles in *American Speech*, and published by Cambridge University Press, 1991). See ABBREVIATION, BACK-FORMATION, BARBARISM, BLEND, BORROW-ING, CAPITAL, COINAGE, NONCE WORD, NONSENSE VERSE, ROOT-CREATION, SEMANTIC CHANGE, TIME-SPEAK, WORD-FORMATION. [MEDIA, REFERENCE, STYLE, WORD].   J.A., T.MCA.

NEO-MELANESIAN. See TOK PISIN.

NEO-SOLOMONIC. See PIJIN.

NEPAL. A country in South Asia. Capital: Kathmandu. Population: 17.8m (1988), 24.1m (projection for 2000). Ethnicity: mainly Nepali and Tibetan. Religion: 90% Hindu, 5% Buddhist, 3% Muslim, 2% other. Languages: Nepali/Gurkhali (official), an Indo-Aryan language, the mother tongue of 58% of the people; other languages such as (Indo-Aryan) Bhojpuri and (Tibeto-Burman) Gurung; English, the primary foreign language, but more prevalent than this status suggests. Education: primary 55%, secondary 25%, tertiary 5%, literacy 26%. Although influenced by Britain and providing Gurkha soldiers for both the British and Indian armies, Nepal was never part of the British Empire. English in Nepal is unique in that it was introduced neither by colonization nor by missionaries. Until 1950, Nepal was a closed society ruled by hereditary prime ministers, but a tradition of English instruction came primarily from India, in whose universities most Nepalese teachers were educated. Since the 1960s, Nepal has had an open-door policy and English has become a major language of travel, tourism, and regional communication. In 1951, as part of a process of democratization, use of English in the media received some support. In 1985, there were 417 Nepali- and 32 English-language periodicals. English is widely used in advertising and there is a small body of creative writing. Radio and television have contributed to the diffusion of English and are used for teaching it. Code-mixing and code-switching with English are as common as in other parts of South Asia; Nepalese English has much in common with that of northern India. See ENGLISH, SOUTH ASIAN ENGLISH. [ASIA, VARIETY].   B.B.K.

NETHERLANDIC. See DUTCH, FLEMISH.

NETWORK [16c]. (1) A construct in which threads, wires, or other materials are arranged as or like a net; anything analogous (*a railway network, a police network*). (2) A communicative system that 'consists of linked dyads in which the *receiver* in one dyad is the *source* in the next. Such networks will vary in size and not all members . . . will necessarily have equal access to information or participation' (James Watson & Anne Hill, *Communication and Media Studies*, 1989). Such systems may have different structures, such as a *chain network* and a *circle network*. (3) A group of radio or television stations that are linked by wire or microwave relay so that they can broadcast programmes at the same times: 'The stations can be owned by a headquarters company—the network—that is the source of the programs or can be independent—an *affiliate* or *network affiliate*' (Richard Weiner, *Webster's New World Dictionary of Media and Communications*, 1990). The term *network identification* refers to the name or other signal used by such a network, usually at the beginning of each hour or programme: compare SIGNATURE. (4) In computing, a linked set of computers or computer systems that share programs, files, storage facilities, and peripheral devices. The constituents of a *Local Area Network (LAN)* are all in one place, such as a company or university, while those in a *Wide Area Network (WAN)* are dispersed and linked by telephone, radio, and/or satellite. The terms *to network* and *networking* relate to the design, construction, and operation of computer networks and any analogous way in which information and services may be shared among people with similar interests. See BROADCASTING, COMPUTING, NETWORK STANDARD. [MEDIA, TECHNOLOGY].   T.MCA.

NETWORK STANDARD. A variety of pronunciation supposedly favoured by radio and television announcers on US national network broadcasts, in effect a pronunciation without any features easily recognizable as characteristic of any region or social group. Thus, most Americans are rhotic (that is, they pronounce *r* where it is spelled); its non-pronunciation (except before vowels) is characteristic of eastern New England, New York City, and the South. Consequently, network standard is rhotic. Similarly, it neither diphthongizes the vowel of *caught*, as in the South, nor pronounces it long and tense, as in parts of the Northeast. On the other hand, in some regions of the US *caught* and *cot* are distinct in pronunciation (typically with a rounded vowel in the first and an unrounded vowel in the second); in other regions, they are homophonous. However, the different treatments of these words are not perceived as regional features by Americans; consequently, both options are appropriate for network standard. Because many national TV announcers have tried to avoid regionally identifying language, their homogenized speech has been given the name

Network standard. The word *standard* is, however, misleading because it suggests a more formally recognized variety than exists. Recently, moreover, there has been an increasing tendency in both the US and the UK to use regional accents on national broadcasts, so the bland pronunciation that inspired the term is less important than formerly. *Network standard* is the closest American analogue to British *Received Pronunciation*, but it is a distant one. It is best defined negatively as an AmE variety that has no regional features, does not mark class, is not learned collectively in childhood, and has never been institutionalized or set up as a pronunciation model. See DIALECT IN AMERICA, GENERAL AMERICAN, NETWORK, MODEL, STANDARD. [AMERICAS, SPEECH, VARIETY].   J.A.

NEUROLINGUISTICS [1960s]. A branch of linguistics that studies the neurological basis of language development and use, and constructs models of the way the brain controls the processes of speaking, listening, reading, and writing. Particular attention has been paid to the processes thought to underlie speech production: what kind of programming is it necessary to propose in order to explain the sequence and timing of articulation movements? Of central relevance to this approach are research findings in two main areas: (1) From the study of clinical linguistic conditions, such as aphasia, it is possible to construct hypotheses about the nature of the underlying system by looking at what happens to speech when it breaks down. (2) Hypotheses can be adduced from the study of everyday speech-production 'errors' in normal speech, such as slips of the tongue and hesitations. For example, based on the study of the distribution of tongue slips in a large corpus of speech data, it is possible to predict where they are likely to occur. In a sentence such as *I bought a POUND of MINCE / and a BOTTLE of GIN* (where / marks the intonation-and-rhythm boundary and capitals indicate the most strongly stressed), the more likely slips of the tongue are going to be between *pound* and *mince*, or between *bottle* and *gin*: in other words, *within* the intonation-and-rhythm units. Moreover, the initial sounds of the words are more likely to be affected. This kind of evidence can be used to support models of the way in which the brain processes speech: if slips tend to occur within intonation-and-rhythm units, this suggests that these units have a neuro-psychological reality as part of the programming mechanism for speech. See LANGUAGE PATHOLOGY, LINGUISTICS, PSYCHOLINGUISTICS, RHYTHM, SLIP OF THE TONGUE. [LANGUAGE].   D.C.

NEUTER [14c: from Old French *neutre*, from Latin *neuter* neither]. A term referring to grammatical gender in nouns and related words, contrasting with *masculine* and *feminine* in languages that have three genders such as German and Latin. Although there is some connection between natural and grammatical gender in such languages, a word which is grammatically neuter may be semantically quite different: in German *das Kind* (the child); *das Mädchen* (the girl). The personal pronoun *it* is sometimes said to be neuter in gender, but more accurately it is nonpersonal since it may be used to refer to animals and babies. See GENDER. [GRAMMAR]. S.C.

NEUTRAL VOWEL. See S(C)HWA.

NEWBOLT REPORT. A report on the teaching of English in England and Wales, presented to the Board of Education in 1921 by a committee chaired by Sir Henry Newbolt. Entitled *The Teaching of English in England*, the report argued that English was unduly neglected as a subject in many schools, and insisted that it should be built into the total educational experience. Cautiously rather than enthusiastically progressive, it covered the whole range of education, from elementary schools to universities, and argued that the understanding of literature should have a central role and that emphasis should be placed on teaching pupils how to form well-constructed arguments. See BULLOCK REPORT, KINGMAN REPORT. [EDUCATION, EUROPE]. C.J.B.

NEW CRITICISM. See LITERARY CRITICISM.

NEW ENGLAND. The name of the six north-easternmost states of the US (Maine, Vermont, New Hampshire, Massachusetts, Connecticut, and Rhode Island); the site of the second oldest permanent English settlement on the North American mainland. The New England colonies were populated by Puritans mainly from East Anglia, who came to the New World primarily for religious reasons. Because of their predominantly common origin and cultural unity, the New England settlers formed a more homogeneous community than did colonists elsewhere.

The Puritan inheritance. The character of the colonists was early famed for its seriousness, emphasis on the work ethic, and a social consciousness that sprang from the scriptural injunction to charity; this was, however, often expressed as a tendency to enforce their view of what is good on those who did not share it. The conflict between Puritanism and pleasure can be seen in much of American social life to the present day. Other aspects of the Puritan character, such as studiousness and intellectual mysticism, expressed themselves in the *New England Transcendentalists*, who blended German Romantic philosophy with ideas from Hindu philosophy. Ralph Waldo Emerson and Henry David Thoreau are the best-known embodiments of this merger of exotic East and Puritan West. New England has served as the school-house and conscience of the US. One of its most famous sons, Noah Webster, was a force in shaping the dictionary and schoolbook tradition of the country; today, his name has entered the lore of the nation as a synonym for dictionaries. One of its most famous daughters, Harriet Beecher Stowe, wrote a story, *Uncle Tom's Cabin* (1852), which so inflamed sentiment against slavery that it has been credited as a cause of the Civil War. New England's two greatest colleges, Harvard (founded 1636) and Yale (1701), became the models and source of teaching faculty for other institutions of higher learning throughout the nation.

Linguistic features. New Englanders are famed for laconism and a 'flatness' of accent. The terms applied popularly to present-day New England speech are often the same as those used in the 17c to characterize the language of the English Puritans: a nasal twang, high-pitched, harsh, and unmusical. In fact, however, New England is divided between two rather different dialects: *Eastern New England*, with Boston as its hub, and *Western New England*, which blends into upper New York State as the wellspring of the *Inland Northern* dialect that sweeps across the northern tier of states to the Pacific. One of the defining characteristics of these two dialects is their treatment of *r* when not followed by a vowel. Eastern New England is non-rhotic, articulating it much as British RP does, with a gliding vowel. Western New England, on the other hand, is rhotic, as is most of the US. In addition, present-day New England has had its Puritan roots considerably entangled with those of newer immigrants: French-Canadian, Italian, Irish, Greek, and many others, as well as Black in-migrants from the American South and yuppies from metropolitan New York. Even so, however, the old Yankee personality and the Puritan ethic vigorously survive. See BOSTON, DIALECT IN AMERICA, PURITAN, WEBSTER, YANK(EE). [AMERICAS, NAME, VARIETY]. J.A.

NEW ENGLISH [1980s: often plural]. A term in linguistics for a recently emerging and increasingly autonomous variety of English, especially in a non-Western setting such as India, Nigeria, or Singapore. Two works of the 1980s have had virtually the same title: *New Englishes*, ed. John Pride (US: Newbury House, 1982), and *The New Englishes*, by John Platt, Heidi Weber, and Ho Mian Lian (UK: Routledge & Kegan Paul, 1984). The term is sometimes used generically: 'The first documented evidence of the New English of Sierra Leone (NESL)' (Joe Pemagbi, 'Still a Deficient Language?', *English Today* 17, Jan. 1989). See -GLISH AND -LISH, ENGLISH, ENGLISHES, LYLY. [NAME, VARIETY].   T.MCA.

NEWFIE, also **Newf**. An informal name for a person born in Newfoundland and for the variety of English spoken there. See ETHNIC NAME, NEWFIE JOKE, NEWFOUNDLAND. [AMERICAS, NAME].   T.MCA.

NEWFIE JOKE. A joke about Newfoundlanders, a version of the ethnic put-down, that became popular in Canada in the late 1960s. Robert Tulk, a Newfoundlander, collected many of them (*Newfie Jokes*, 1971; *More Newfie Jokes*, 1972), including: 'What is black and blue and floats in the bay? A Mainlander, after telling a Newfie joke.' See ETHNIC JOKE. [AMERICAS, STYLE].   M.F.

NEWFOUNDLAND. (1) An Atlantic island of North America and England's first colony. The capital, St John's, was founded as a base for English fishermen in 1504 and Sir Humphrey Gilbert claimed the island in 1583. In 1855, it became self-governing, and in 1949, after two close votes, it was united with Canada. Its population in 1981 was 567,681. Its local nickname is *the Rock*. (2) A province of Canada from 1949, consisting of the island of Newfoundland and the adjacent mainland area known as Labrador. Its economy is mainly fishing, hydro-electricity, mining, oil, pulp, and paper. Its languages are English and French, and Amerindian languages in Labrador. See CANADA, CANADIAN, NEWF(IE), NEWFIE JOKE, NEWFOUNDLAND ENGLISH. [AMERICAS, NAME].   T.MCA.

NEWFOUNDLAND ENGLISH. The English language as used in the island and province of Newfoundland for almost 500 years, and the oldest variety in the Americas. It derives primarily from the speech of early settlers from the English West Country and later Ireland, and is the outcome of long, stable settlement and relative remoteness. The isolation, however, should not be overemphasized: 'The women in these communities were isolated, while the men were not, because they travelled to find seasonal work sealing, logging, and cod-fishing' (*Dictionary of Newfoundland English*, 1982). Many Newfoundland *townies* have features of pronunciation, grammar, and vocabulary that are distinct from the rest of Canada, and the varied dialects of the *baymen* are possibly the most distinctive in the country. Because of such factors,

the English of Newfoundland is something more than a dialect of CanE, and can be described as a variety with a standard and dialects of its own. Harold Paddock, in *Languages in Newfoundland and Labrador* (1982), delineates five main dialect areas on the island. In a survey by Sandra Clarke (reported in Paddock), the residents of St John's ranked six local accents in terms of prestige: first, BrE Received Pronunciation, then upper-class St John's Irish, Canadian Standard English, non-standard St John's 'Anglo-Irish', and a non-standard regional dialect of the southern shore.

Pronunciation. (1) Newfoundland speech is mainly rhotic. (2) There is English West Country influence in initial /v/ for /f/ and /z/ for /s/: 'a vine zummer' for *a fine summer*. (3) There is Irish influence in /t, d/ for /θ, ð/: 'tree of dem' for *three of them*. (4) Initial /h/ is unstable, sometimes added before the vowels of stressed syllables ('helbow' for *elbow*), sometimes dropped ('eel' for *heel*). (5) Final consonant clusters are often simplified: 'a soun in the loff' for *a sound in the loft*. (6) Certain vowel distinctions are commonly not made: *boy* is a homophone of *buy*, *speak* rhymes with *break* and *port* with *part*.

Grammar. Dialect usage includes: (1) The use of *is* or *'m* for present forms of *be*: *I is, you is, he is, we is, they is; I'm, you'm, we'm, they'm*. (2) The negative forms *baint'e* are you not, *I idden* I am not, *you idden* you are not, *he idden* he is not, *tidden* it is not (reflecting West Country influence). (3) Distinctive forms of *do, have, be*: They *doos their work*; I *haves a lot of colds*; It *bees cold here in winter*; Do *Mary work here?*; Have *she finished?*; 'Tis *cold here now*. (4) In some areas, an -*s* in all simple present-tense verb forms (*I goes, he goes, we goes*, etc.), distinguishing the full-verb use from the auxiliary use of *do, have*, and *be*. (5) Weak rather than strong forms in some irregular verbs: 'knowed' for *knew*, 'throwed' for *threw*. (6) Four variants for the perfect: *I've done, I've a-done, I bin done, I'm after doin*. (7) *He/she* as substitutes for inanimate countable nouns: *We'd have what we'd call a flake-beam, a stick, say, he'd be thirty feet long*. (8) In some areas, the form *un* or *ən* as a masculine pronoun and for *it*: *Tom kicked un* (the shovel). If, however, the shovel rather than the rake is stressed, *he* is used: *Tom kicked he*. (9) Some expressions of Hiberno-English origin: *It's angry you will be*; *It's myself that wants it*.

Vocabulary. (1) Expressions that are archaic or obsolete elsewhere: *angishore* a weak, miserable person (from Irish Gaelic *ain dei seoir*), sometimes transformed to *hangashore*; *bavin* brushwood used for kindling; *brewis* (from Scots, pronounced 'brooze') stew (applied to a mix of soaked ship's biscuits, salt codfish, and pork fat).

(2) Words for natural phenomena, occupations, activities, etc., such as terms for seals at various stages of development: *bedlamer, dotard, gun seal, jar, nog-head, ragged-jacket, turner, white-coat*. (3) A local word familiar elsewhere in Canada is *screech*, a potent dark rum (from Scots *screech* whisky). (4) A *livyer* (live here) is a permanent inhabitant, while a *come-from-away* (sometimes shortened to *CFA*) is an outsider or mainlander.   See CANADIAN DICTIONARIES, CANADIAN ENGLISH, DIALECT IN CANADA, IRISH ENGLISH, MARITIMES PROVINCES, WEST COUNTRY. [AMERICAS, VARIETY].   M.F.

NEW HISTORICISM. See LITERARY CRITICISM.

NEW LATIN. See NEO-LATIN.

NEW ORLEANS. A city in Louisiana whose distinctive variety of AmE is the result not only of the influence of its founders from Spain and France (who governed the region before the 19c) but also waves of migrants from Ireland, Germany, Italy, and most recently Vietnam. West African influence through pan-Caribbean creole is also apparent. The term *Creole*, as defined by local whites, applies to white descendants of early French or Spanish settlers. As defined by blacks, it applies to persons of Afro-French parentage. Both express 'authentic' local identity. Some of the dialect's characteristics come directly from French, either locally or from present and former French-speaking regions of the state, such as the obsolescent *banquette* for (AmE) sidewalk, (BrE) pavement, and the phrases *make the groceries* to shop for groceries, *make menage* to clean (the) house, and *save the dishes* to put the dishes away. The city has locally well-understood stereotypes based on race, class, and neighbourhood, though linguistic features criss-cross these in complex ways. Typical grammatical features include a widespread tendency to use *had* + past participle for the simple past (as in *Yesterday I had run into him*) and the tags *no* (as in *I don't like that, no!*) and the more widely current Coastal Southern *hear* (as in *I'm having another piece of pie, hear?*).

Yat. The most distinctive local variety is *Yat*, called by one observer 'the Cockney of New Orleans'. The name is said to derive from the greeting *Wha y'at?* 'What are you at?' Associated with such working-class districts as the Irish Channel and old Ninth Ward, it is also heard in other parts of the city and recently in some suburban *parishes* (government units in Louisiana that correspond to *counties* in much of the rest of the US). Outsiders confuse Yat with *Brooklynese*; its stereotypic features include such quasi-phonetic spellings as *berlin* boiling, *dat* that, *earl* oil, *mudder* mother, and *taught* thought.

Cuisine and Mardi Gras. The city has a varied cuisine with characteristic vocabulary, much of it from Louisiana French: *beignet* (pronounced 'bane yea') a square doughnut dusted with powdered sugar, *debris* pan gravy, *etouffee* stewed, *file* (pronounced 'fee-lay') thickener for soups and stews derived from young sassafras leaves, *jambalaya* a dish prepared with rice, seasoning, and meat or seafood, *praline* (pronounced 'prah-leen') a confection made with pecans and brown sugar, *sauce piquante* a condiment made from tomatoes and red pepper. Other terms are from English: *cajun popcorn* deep-fried crawfish/crayfish tails, *dirty rice* a spicy rice dish with chicken giblets, *king cake* a ring-shaped coffee cake traditionally served from Epiphany to Shrove Tuesday, *po' boy* a sandwich of the type known elsewhere in AmE as a *grinder*, *hoagie*, or *submarine*. Mardi Gras (Shrove Tuesday celebrated in Latin-American style) has a technical vocabulary emerging into national consciousness through US-wide television broadcasts of its elaborate parades: *krewe* an organization sponsoring a parade float, *trow* (throw) a trinket tossed by a parader to the streetside crowd, and *pair of beads* a necklace of plastic beads used commonly as a trow. See CAJUN. Compare BROOKLYNESE. [AMERICAS, NAME, VARIETY].   R.W.B.

NEWS [15c: from late Middle English *newis* (plural of *newe*), on the model of Old French *noveles* and Medieval Latin *nova*, plural of *novum* (something) new. Compare NOVEL, NOVELLA]. (1) Information about a recent event or events: *What's the latest news from China?* (2) The presentation of such information as reports by journalists and others in the media (print, radio, television, electronic, or other), often in a format described through a compound beginning with *news* such as *news broadcast, newscast, newspaper*, sometimes used as the title of a publication, column, or programme, such as *Newsweek, Newsday*, and *Newsnight*. See BULLETIN, FLASH, JOURNAL, NEWSLETTER, NEWSMAGAZINE, NEWSPAPER. [MEDIA].   T.MCA.

NEWSLETTER [17c]. A report or set of reports, usually printed as a leaflet or slim magazine, and issued periodically by or for an agency, club, group, company, or institution, to provide associates, members, employees, the media, and the like with information concerning relevant events, activities, and interests. See NEWS, NEWSPAPER. [MEDIA].   T.MCA.

NEWSMAGAZINE [1920s: combining *news* and *magazine*]. An illustrated, usually weekly magazine with reports and commentaries on events and issues of current interest. The genre began in the US, prompted by a lack of nationwide newspapers. The forerunner was, however, British: *The Illustrated London News* (founded 1842), which sought to present 'all the news in pictures' and (before the development of the half-tone photograph) used 32 woodblocks per issue. This tendency was followed by the *Penny Illustrated Paper* (1861), *The Graphic* (1869), the *Sketch* (1892), and the *Sphere* (1899). Of these, only the founder has survived, with difficulty. By contrast, the prominent US newsmagazines, *Time* (founded 1923) and *Newsweek* (founded 1933), have acquired an international readership and enjoy respective weekly circulations of nearly 5m and over 3m. There are specialized newsmagazines for such fields as business and science, and a variety of clones of *Time* have appeared in other countries, serving both English and other languages. See BULLETIN, MAGAZINE, NEWS, NEWSPAPER, PERIODICAL, TIME MAGAZINE, TIMESPEAK. [MEDIA]. G.H.

NEW SOUTH WALES PIDGIN ENGLISH.
See AUSTRALIAN PIDGIN.

NEWSPAPER [17c].
A publication issued at close, regular intervals, especially on a daily or weekly basis. It has large sheets and columns of text, usually interspersed with photographs, and commonly contains not only news but also comment, features, and advertisements (which are generally more important for the economic success of the publication than is the relatively small purchase price per copy).

History and nature. The genre originated in commercial (originally handwritten) *newsletters* made available at meeting-places such as coffee-houses and often consolidated into *newsbooks* or *news-pamphlets* (the first surviving example dated 1513). *Newspapers* or *news-sheets* appeared only sporadically, on an ad-hoc basis, in response to events of great importance. Regular news-sheets are recorded on the Continent from 1566, and Nathaniel Butter, a freeman of the Stationers' Company, is credited with the first regular series of newsbooks in England (1622-3). After these there appeared what were called *Intelligencers* and *Relations*, which announced their partiality in fairly direct terms: 'Mercurius Civicus. Londons INTELLIGENCER, or Truth Impartially related from thence to the whole kingdom, to prevent mis-information' (1643); 'An Exact and true Relation of the late Plots which were contrived and hatched in Ireland' (1641).

The first regular daily newspaper was Samuel Buckley's *The Daily Courant* (1702). This followed the abolition of censorship in 1695, after which the production of newspapers and periodicals increased dramatically. In many cases, they responded to a public thirst for 'news' with colourful, but unreliable, rumour, gossip, and 'eye-witness accounts'. The steady raising of the punitive Stamp Tax from 1*d.* to 4*d.* was intended to suppress both the 'gutter' and the radical press, and succeeded in this aim. The abolition of the tax in 1855 removed this restraint. With the great developments of printing technology achieved in the 19c, mass circulation, low-cost national newspapers became increasingly common. *The Daily Telegraph* (launched in 1855) was the first popular daily newspaper, while *The Daily Mirror* (1911-12) became the first British newspaper to achieve a daily circulation of 1m. Its success led the modern trend towards tabloid journalism. Many commentators on the modern British Press have detected a similarity between the divisions of the newspaper market and the class structure: the *quality press* catering for the élite, the *popular press* for the bourgeoisie, the *tabloid press* for the working class. Such divisions, however, do not apply to the American Press, where the main differences are between national and regional newspapers.

Sunday newspapers, the last genre to emerge, have become a significant institution in Britain. They initially encountered moral and religious objections, since only milk and mackerel were permitted to be sold on the Lord's Day. However, the first in the field, *Mrs E. Johnson's Sunday Monitor and British Gazette* (1779), proved so popular that by 1812 at least 18 Sunday papers were being published in London. The moral tone, initially high, has steadily declined in the case of the more popular publications, several being notoriously salacious and sensational, notably *The News of the World* (established 1843), which has long had the highest single circulation of the British press (currently over 5m). However, the 'quality' or 'heavy' Sundays, such as *The Observer* (1791), *The Sunday Times* (1822), and *The Sunday Telegraph* (1961), have a reputation for a high standard of comment on and analysis of current affairs. These were joined by the short-lived *Sunday Correspondent* (1989) and *The Independent on Sunday* (1990), making a combined circulation of some 20m. These papers have tended to increase in size, to the point that they divide, like many US newspapers, into sections and supplements covering business, sport, the arts, property, and a colour magazine.

The number of national newspapers published in the UK has declined steadily over the past half-century, since newspapers survive, not simply through readership, but as vehicles of advertising revenue. This means that they must cater for a particular segment of the advertising market. Consequently, it is possible for newspapers with large circulations, such as *Empire News, News Chronicle, The Graphic, Sunday Chronicle* (all of which had circulations of over 1.5m) to be closed through lack of advertising revenue. Others, like the *Morning Post* (1772–1937), have been merged with more successful operations, in this case *The Daily Telegraph* (1855). A new 'quality' daily newspaper *The Independent*, was launched in 1986. As a consequence of the increasing competition from radio and television, with their capacity for 'live' broadcast and virtually instant comment, newspaper circulations have declined, from over 25m in the late 1970s to 23m in the mid-1980s. Newspapers still retain a powerful influence, however, through their capacities for informed analysis and detailed comment, and as wielders of public opinion.

Format and content. The aims and formats of newspapers influence the ways in which editors, sub-editors, and journalists prepare and finalize *copy* for publication. Factors that constrain them include: immediacy and importance (influencing the position of a *story*, the most important being at the top of the front page, the least important 'buried' somewhere inside); type-sizes used for various purposes and levels of emphasis, ranging from headlines to small ads; distinctive arrangements of text in columns; limitations on space for copy in relation to the priority given to advertisements; and the pressure of recurring deadlines. In addition, there is a spectrum of locations and forms for separating or mixing *news* and *comment*, *stories* and *features*, as well as a range of departments or sections with their own editors, such as *news, features, letters to the editor, sports, entertainment, the arts, book reviews,* and *cookery*, depending on the profile of the readership on which the paper depends. All such factors in turn affect the styles in which journalists write, often lumped together as *journalese*.

Newspapers of the English-speaking world. Largely as a legacy of British colonialism and the Empire, there are well over 2,000 daily English-language newspapers worldwide (excluding international publications). The great majority of these are regional or city newspapers without national circulations.

The United Kingdom. The greatest concentration of newspaper readership per head of population is in the British Isles, where there are more than 25 national newspapers and 113 dailies in all, with a total circulation of 23m in the mid-980s, catering for a population of 56m (a ratio of 1 : 2.4). This market, more than any other, divides into quality and tabloid, the former often having an influence on political and social developments.

The United States. The earliest newspapers to be produced outside Britain were American. The first US newspaper, Benjamin Harris's *Publick Occurrences Both Forreign and Domestick* (Boston, 1690), was immediately suppressed by the British authorities. The first continuously published American newspaper was the Boston *News-Letter*, which first appeared in 1704, though it was superseded in influence by James Franklin's *New England Courant* (1729). Modern US newspaper readership is not as concentrated as in the UK, with 1,676 dailies generating a circulation of 63m catering for a population of 243m (a ratio of 1 : 4). Partly because of the size of the nation and its different time-zones, and partly because of its social diversity and political decentralization, there are few national papers, though the *Wall Street Journal* has four US editions as well as an Asian and a European edition (making a total combined circulation of nearly 2m). *The New York Times* (circulation over 1m) introduced a national edition in 1980. Others with a national readership are the *Washington Post, Los Angeles Times,* and the *Christian Science Monitor.*

The Commonwealth. The largest anglophone Black African country, Nigeria, has fourteen dailies (the *Daily Times* with a circulation of 400,000), while one of the smallest, the Gambia, has eight. In Zimbabwe and Zambia, both daily newspapers are English. In Australia, there are 63 daily newspapers generating a circulation of 4.8m for a population of 15m (a ratio of 1 : 3.1). Prominent among these are the *Sydney Morning Herald* (circulation 400,000) and the *Melbourne Age* (236,000). *The Australian* (135,000) is the only newspaper which can claim to have national status. Of New Zealand's 32 dailies, the *New Zealand Herald* is dominant (243,000). In Canada, the Toronto *Globe & Mail* (318,000) is the only English-language newspaper with national distribution out of 110 dailies which claim to reach 62% of the country's households. Hong Kong, with the highest news readership in Asia after Japan, has five English-language dailies, including the *South China Morning Post* (101,000) and the *Hongkong Standard* (60,000). In India, New Delhi has six, including the *Times of India* (175,000) and the *Navbharat Times* (294,000), both of which are published in other centres. Bombay also has the *Indian Express* (86,366), Calcutta the *Statesman* (223,000), Madras *The Hindu* (348,000). Other major newspapers within the Commonwealth are the Singapore *Straits Times* (281,000), the Kenya *Daily Nation* (148,000), and the Jamaican *Gleaner* (42,000).

Others. Elsewhere, significant numbers of English-language newspapers are to be found in South Africa, Sri Lanka, and the Philippines. Prior to its closure (by the management) in 1984, *The Rand Daily Mail* was South Africa's most respected and influential newspaper, mainly because of its opposition to the government. This role has largely been taken over by *The Cape Times* (circulation 75,000). The Johannesburg daily *The Star* has the largest circulation (200,000).

For further details of newspapers in particular countries, aspects of journalism and of newspaper usage, and other matters relating to newspapers generally, see AMERICAN PRESS, AUSTRALIAN PRESS, BROADSHEET, BULLETIN, CANADIAN PRESS, CARIBBEAN PRESS, EUROPEAN (THE), FLEET STREET, HEADLINE, HONG KONG, INDIAN PRESS, INTERNATIONAL HERALD TRIBUNE (THE), IRISH PRESS, JAPAN, JOURNAL, JOURNALESE, JOURNALISM, MAGAZINE, NEWS, NEWSLETTER, NEWSMAGAZINE, NEW ZEALAND PRESS, PAKISTANI ENGLISH, PRESS, QUALITY PRESS, SOUTH AFRICAN PRESS, SRI LANKA, TABLOID, TIMES (THE), USAGE, USAGE GUIDANCE AND CRITICISM, YELLOW PRESS. [MEDIA].　　　　　　　　　　G.H.

NEWSPEAK. A simplified artificial language based on English in George Orwell's novel *Nineteen Eighty-Four* (1949): 'Newspeak was the official language of Oceania and had been devised to meet the ideological needs of Ingsoc, or English Socialism. In the year 1984 there was not as yet anyone who used Newspeak as his sole means of communication, either in speech or writing' (Appendix: The Principles of Newspeak). Oceania has a team of Newspeak philologists 'engaged in compiling the eleventh Edition of the Newspeak dictionary'. Almost any Newspeak word could serve as any part of speech; hence the verb *think* did duty for the noun *thought*, and *Newspeak* replaced *Newspeech*. Affixes were common: *ungood*, *goodwise*. The regular *stealed* and *mans* replaced irregular forms like *stole* or *men*. Compounds were frequent: *doublethink*, *oldthink*, *Oldspeak* (standard English). Other words were telescoped: *Ficdep* Fiction Department, *Ingsoc* English Socialism, *Minitrue* Ministry of Truth.

Newspeak was intended not only to express but to form politically acceptable habits of thought, 'at least so far as thought is dependent on words'. It therefore excluded ambiguities and shades of meaning, along with words for unacceptable concepts like *honour* and *democracy*. Its ideological slant rendered it unable to express or translate such statements as the Oldspeak 'all men are created equal', because the concept of political equality was *crimethink*. For the same

reason, Newspeak readily expressed politically orthodox statements contrary to objective fact, such as 'Freedom is slavery'. Orwell's inspiration for Newspeak probably included the artificial languages in Jonathan Swift's *Gulliver's Travels* (1726), Evgeny I. Zamyatin's *We* (1920–1), C. K. Ogden's *Basic English* (1930), Aldous Huxley's *Brave New World* (1932), and H. G. Wells's *The Shape of Things to Come* (1933). For its features, he drew on standard English for compounding and changes of part of speech, the political propaganda of his day for the catchy slogan style, and the condensed syntax of telegraphic communication. *Newspeak* has become a term in the language at large for misleading (especially political) jargon, and is the source for a large number of words modelled on it, such as *nukespeak* and *teenspeak*. See BASIC ENGLISH[1], NOVEL, ORWELL, -SPEAK. [SPEECH, STYLE, VARIETY].　　W.F.B.

NEW SPELLING. See SIMPLIFIED SPELLING SOCIETY, SPELLING REFORM.

NEW YORK. A city and port at the mouth of the Hudson River, in the state of the same name: a major city of the US and of the English-speaking world, and the centre of one of the largest US urban areas. It occupies Manhattan and Staten Island, the western end of Long Island, and part of the adjacent mainland, and its conurbation extends into the states of New Jersey and Connecticut. It typifies the American concept of the melting-pot, having received through Ellis Island many waves of immigrants, especially from Europe and Latin America. Many languages are spoken in the city, which is the centre of a sub-dialect within the general Northern dialect area of AmE.

Pronunciation. (1) New York pronunciation has a long, tense, very round vowel in words like *caught*, and a long, tense, relatively high vowel in words such as *cab*. (2) Like eastern New England and the American South, it is a non-rhotic (non-*r*-pronouncing) variety and, also like eastern New England and some accents of England (including RP), it has the linking *r* and intrusive *r*. When a word ending in *r* (which would normally not be pronounced) is followed closely by a word beginning with a vowel, the linking *r* is sounded: *gopher* is pronounced 'gopha', but in *The gopher is lost* the *r* is pronounced. By analogy, an intrusive *r* occurs where it is not etymologically or orthographically justified: *sofa* rhymes with *gopher*, but in *The sofa/r is lost* an *r*-sound often intrudes. In contrast, the Southern US shares neither the linking nor intrusive *r*-sounds with the other non-rhotic varieties, indeed often losing an *r*-sound even between vowels, as in *ve'y* for *very* and *Ca'olina* for *Carolina*. Non-rhotic pronunciation differs widely in its prestige, depending on where it occurs. In the American South, *r*-lessness is a universal feature of many areas at all social levels. In New York City, on the other hand, it correlates strongly with class differences and has low prestige. In his investigations, William Labov found that *r*-pronouncing was more common among the employees of up-market department stores and shops than among those of businesses with merchandise of lower quality and prices. He also found more *r*-pronouncing in 'careful', self-conscious speech than in spontaneous dialogue. There is also an upper-class, old-family New York English, but it has been little studied and its features are not widely known.

Low prestige. New York English has low prestige even among its own speakers. Their reaction, which has been dubbed 'linguistic self-hatred', is not typical of many other areas, where the local speechways are usually regarded as indicating that the speaker is honest, friendly, sympathetic, intelligent, and reliable. New Yorkers' discomfort with their speech patterns may reflect the low regard the rest of the nation has for those patterns. It is, however, odd that the major city of the nation (its cultural and financial centre) should be low in linguistic prestige. In fact, the stereotype of New York English is the language of a lower socio-economic group, as though London English were to identify with Cockney usage, without the affectionate respect often accorded to it. See AMERICAN ENGLISH, BROOKLYNESE, DIALECT IN AMERICA, JEWISH ENGLISH, NEW ENGLAND, NEW YORKESE, NEW YORRICAN, RHOTIC AND NON-RHOTIC. [AMERICAS, NAME, VARIETY]. J.A.

Hubbell, Allan F. 1950. *The Pronunciation of English in New York City*. New York: Columbia University Press.
Labov, William. 1966. *The Social Stratification of English in New York City*. Washington: Center for Applied Linguistics.
—— 1972. *Sociolinguistic Patterns*. Philadelphia: University of Pennsylvania Press.

NEW YORKER, The. An American weekly magazine founded in 1925 by Harold Ross and known for its cartoons, essays, biographical studies, reports from abroad, and short works of fiction. Although associated through its title and style with New York City and an upper-middle-class metropolitan view of the world, the magazine has a nationwide readership devoted at least as much to its cartoons as its articles. Whereas the older British institutional weekly *Punch* has declined in sales, significance, and prestige in recent years, *The New Yorker* remains socially and commercially buoyant, with a circulation of *c*.600,000. It continues to be leisurely and literary, and apparently immune to the competition of television and pop culture, forces that have helped close a number of erstwhile rivals. A particularly conservative feature is the cover, which in each issue displays a single illustration unrelated to anything inside. Every February, however, as a matter of continuity, the cover features the character Eustace Tilley, an early American dandy, the magazine's trademark. *The New Yorker* comments wryly on the ways of the world, the denizens of bars, cocktail-party habitués, executives, fashionable folk, and life in New York's various communities. The cool put-down is common in its cartoons: (Intense woman to smug man) 'You remind me of why I found the Eighties wanting.' Literary contributors have included Truman Capote, John Hersey, Dorothy Parker, S. J. Perelman, Lillian Ross, Rebecca West, and E. B. White; cartoonists have included Charles Addams, Peter Arno, Roz Chast, Helen Hopkinson, Rea Irvin (creator of Eustace Tilley), Bob Mankoff, George Price, Saul Steinberg, and Jack Ziegler. James Thurber contributed both writing and cartoons. Charles Addams was the creator in its pages (1940s–50s) of the 'Addams Family', a group of ghoulish characters who subverted the idea of the family as the rock on which democracy and civilization are founded: Morticia to daughter Wednesday, complaining about brother Pugsley, 'Well, don't come whining to me. Go tell him you'll poison him right back' (1944). The family in due course moved from the pages of the magazine to become a cult TV series of the 1960s and in the early 1990s were revived in a motion picture. See MAGAZINE. Compare PUNCH. [AMERICAS, MEDIA]. T.MCA.

NEW YORKESE [1890s]. An informal and sometimes pejorative term for the speech of people in or from New York City. See BROOKLYNESE, DIALECT IN AMERICA, -ESE, NEW YORK. [AMERICAS, NAME, VARIETY]. T.MCA.

NEW YORRICAN [1980s: a blend of *New York* and *Puerto Rican*]. (1) Among Puerto Ricans, an informal, often pejorative term for Puerto Ricans living in New York City and for people who return to Puerto Rico from the New York area: 'The New Yorrican students . . . seem to have plenty to say about their island brethren. "A lot of snotty people," said one high school student at the Padre Juan Rulfo School in San Juan' (*International Herald Tribune*, 17 Feb. 1990). (2) In the form *Nuyorican*, the name given in 1975 by the Puerto Rican poet Miguel Algarín to a mixture of Spanish and New Yorkese, as in *Aquí your credito is good* Here your credit is good. See ETHNIC NAME, NEW YORK, PUERTO RICO. Compare SPANGLISH, TEX-MEX. [AMERICAS, NAME, VARIETY]. T.MCA.

NEW ZEALAND [17c: adapted from Dutch. The islands were first named *Staten Landt* by the Dutch explorer Abel Tasman, then *Nieuw Zeeland*, after the province of Zeeland]. In Maori, *Aotearoa* Land of the Long White Cloud. A country of the Southern Pacific and a member of the Commonwealth, comprising North Island, South Island, and many small islands. Capital: Wellington. Head of state: the British monarch represented by a governor-general. Population: 3.3m (1988), 3.6m (projection for 2000). Ethnicity: 88% European, 11% Polynesian (Maori and Pacific Islander, especially from Western Samoa, Niue, and Rarotonga). Languages: English, Maori (official in courts), and various Polynesian languages. Education: primary *c*.100%, secondary 85%, tertiary 35%, literacy 99%. The Maori people probably settled in the islands from the 9c. European settlers have been largely of British and Irish descent. The first European sighting was by Abel Tasman in 1642. The British explorer James Cook visited them in 1769, and the first European settlement was by sealers in 1792. When whaling stations were established and trade began with the colony of New South Wales in Australia, the territory became first a part of New South Wales, then a colony in its own right. In 1840, by the Treaty of Waitangi, the Maori ceded sovereignty to Great Britain, but disputes, especially over land, led to outbreaks of war (1860-70). The relationship between Maori and *Pakeha* (Europeans: a Maori term meaning *white, strange*) has been better than in many lands settled during the European diaspora, but continues to be uneasy, especially with regard to land ownership and the cultural and linguistic assimilation of the Maori. Ties between New Zealand and Britain have traditionally been strong, but New Zealanders increasingly see their future as a 'Euro-Polynesian' nation on the Pacific Rim.

See ANTIPODEAN ENGLISH, ANTIPODES, AOTE-AROA, AUSTRAL, AUSTRALASIA, AUSTRALASIAN ENGLISH, AUSTRALIAN ENGLISH, BURCHFIELD, DIALECT IN NEW ZEALAND, DOWN UNDER, ENGLISH, GODZONE, KIWI, MAORI, NEW ZEALAND BROADCASTING, NEW ZEALAND ENGLISH, NEW ZEALANDISM, NEW ZEALAND LITERATURE, NEW ZEALAND PLACE-NAMES, NEW ZEALAND PRESS, NEW ZEALAND PUBLISHING, OCEANIA, PACIFIC RIM, PAKEHA, PARTRIDGE, POLYNESIAN LANGUAGES. [NAME, OCEANIA]. T.MCA.

NEW ZEALAND BROADCASTING. New Zealand broadcasting has been subject to government regulation and involvement. Radio broadcasting in NZ began in 1921, and in 1925, the government-owned *Radio Broadcasting Company of New Zealand* was given permission to start broadcasts from Auckland, Wellington,

Christchurch, and Dunedin. In 1936, a Labour government made broadcasting more or less a government preserve, and set up the *New Zealand Broadcasting Service*, succeeded in 1962 by the *New Zealand Broadcasting Corporation*, which was also responsible for television. In 1977, the NZBC was replaced by the *Broadcasting Corporation of New Zealand*, controlling the two TV channels and *Radio New Zealand*. In 1988, BCNZ was split into *TVNZ* and *RNZ*, deregulation was promised, and Maori-language stations broadcast for the first time. RNZ controls not only the *National* and *Concert Programmes* (funded out of the broadcasting licence fee), but also commercial radio. *The New Zealand Listener* (published since 1939) is jointly owned by TVNZ and RNZ. In 1987, approximately 29% of TV programmes broadcast were NZ productions, the rest imported, mainly from the UK, US, and Australia. See BROADCASTING. [OCEANIA, MEDIA]. L.J.B.

NEW ZEALAND DICTIONARIES. The first NZ dictionary is shared with Australia: E. E. Morris's *A Dictionary of Austral English* (1898). After that, there were a number of school dictionaries and supplements to such dictionaries called *New Zealand* or *Australian and New Zealand*, mostly derived from Morris; the supplement to *Reed's School Dictionary* (1947) appears to be independent. In recent years, three pocket dictionaries have been edited to contain NZ material: the *Heinemann New Zealand Dictionary* (1979, revised 1989, ed. H. W. Orsman), *The New Collins Concise English Dictionary, New Zealand Edition* (1982, ed. I. A. Gordon), *The New Zealand Pocket Oxford Dictionary* (1986, ed. Robert Burchfield). The *Macquarie Dictionary* (1981, Australia) and *The Oxford English Dictionary* (2nd edition, 1989) both contain many NZ items. *The Dictionary of New Zealand English*, a major dictionary on historical principles (ed. H. W. Orsman), is close to publication. There are also several dictionaries of slang and colloquial NZE. The earliest, Sidney J. Baker's *New Zealand Slang: A Dictionary of Colloquialisms* (Whitcombe & Tombs, 1941) is thematic in form and discursive in style. Eric Partridge's *Dictionary of Slang and Unconventional English* (1937; 8th edition 1984, ed. Paul Beale) contains much specifically NZ material, reflecting Partridge's origins. Two recent works are *A Personal Kiwi-Yankee Slanguage Dictionary* by Louis S. Leland (John McIndoe, 1980) and *A Dictionary of Kiwi Slang* by David McGill (Mills Publications, 1988). See AUSTRALIAN DICTIONARIES, BURCHFIELD, DICTIONARY, PARTRIDGE. [OCEANIA, REFERENCE]. L.J.B.

NEW ZEALAND ENGLISH, short form *NZE.* The English language as used in New Zealand. English has been used in New Zealand for over 200 years, from the first visit of Captain James Cook and his English-speaking crew in 1769. He recorded in his diary some Maori words, such as *pah* (a fortified village) and on a later visit *pounamu* (greenstone or nephrite), that later became part of the vocabulary of all New Zealanders. However, a more realistic starting-point is 1840, when the Maori, inhabitants of the islands since the 9c, ceded *kawanatanga* (governorship, interpreted by the British as sovereignty) to the British Crown in the Treaty of Waitangi. From that time, settlers from the British Isles began to arrive in increasing numbers, bringing their regional modes of speech with them.

Australian and New Zealand English. Parallels are often drawn between AusE and NZE. Although the two varieties are by no means identical, they are often indistinguishable to outsiders. Some phoneticians consider that there is a social and historical continuum in which three varieties of pronunciation can be identified: *Cultivated New Zealand, General New Zealand,* and *Broad New Zealand.* If this is so, NZE is similar to AusE, in which these categories are generally established, but other phoneticians regard the matter as unproved. Many speakers of NZE share with many speakers of AusE and CanE the habit of using an upward inflection of the voice in declarative sentences, often considered by non-New Zealanders to produce a tentative effect, as if inviting confirmation of a statement. This intonational pattern, however, serves to check that someone is still following what one is saying. See AUSTRALASIAN ENGLISH.

Pronunciation. NZE is non-rhotic, with the exception of the *Southland burr,* the use by some speakers in Southland and Otago, South Island, of an /r/ in words like *afford* and *heart.* It is believed to derive from ScoE, since Otago was a predominantly Scottish settlement. It has been said that the norm of educated NZE is the Received Pronunciation of the BBC World Service. There are, however, relatively few RP-speakers in New Zealand, a larger proportion speaking what is now called *Near-RP.* Its consonants do not differ significantly from those in RP except that a *wh/w* distinction is often maintained in words like *which/witch.* In words like *wharf,* where no near-homonym *warf exists, aspiration is less detectable.

Features of General New Zealand include: (1) Such words as *ham, pen* perceived by outsiders as 'hem', 'pin'. (2) Centralization of short *i* to schwa: *ships* pronounced /ʃəps/ in contrast with General Australian /ʃips/. These usages are sometimes stigmatized in print as 'shups' and 'sheeps' respectively. (3) The maintenance of RP 'ah' in *castle* /kɑːsl/, *dance* /dɑːns/ by contrast with General Australian /kæsl, dæns/. (4) Schwa used in most unstressed syllables, including /əˈfɛkt/ for both *affect* and *effect,* and /ˈrʌbəʃ/ for *rubbish.* (5) A tendency to pronounce *grown, mown, thrown* as disyllabic with a schwa: 'growen', 'mowen', 'throwen'. (6) A distinctive pronunciation for certain words: *geyser* rhyming with 'riser', *oral* with 'sorrel'; the first syllable of *vitamin* like 'high', as in AmE and ScoE; the *Zea* of *Zealand* pronounced with the vowel of *kit.* Occasional pronunciations such as *basic* /ˈbæsɪk/ and *menu* /ˈmiːnjuː/ are also heard. (7) A tendency to diphthongize some long vowels, opening with a schwa, as in *boot* /bəuːt/ and *bean/been* /bəiːn/. (8) Lengthening of final -*y* in such words as *city, happy:* /ˈsətiː/, /ˈhæpiː/. (9) Full pronunciation of -*day* in *Monday, Tuesday,* etc. (10) A policy of the Broadcasting Corporation that words and place-names of Maori origin be pronounced by announcers as in Maori, rather than in Anglicized forms: *kowhai* not /ˈkəʊ(w)aɪ/ but /ˈkɔːfaɪ/.

Grammar. (1) Standard NZE is to all intents and purposes the same as standard BrE. However, the plural forms *rooves* and *wharves* are preferred to *roofs* and *wharfs,* and in spelling New Zealanders like Australians use -*ise* as in *centralise,* not -*ize.* Although -*ise* is common in BrE, -*ize* is widely used. (2) Nouns of Maori origin often appear in NZE, as in Maori itself, without a plural marker: *iwi* a tribe, as in *A Maori nation exists comprising various iwi* (not *iwis*); *marae* a courtyard of a meeting house, as in *Marae have always been open to all* (not *maraes*). The word *Maori* itself is now commonly spoken and written in plural contexts without a final -*s: the powerlessness which frustrates so many Maori.* Such usage is, however, currently controversial. (3) In recent works of literature, Maori speakers of non-standard English have begun to be portrayed, drawing attention to syntactic aspects of Maori English: *Here's your basket nearly finish* (Patricia Grace, 1986); *You big, brave fellow, eh?* (Bruce Mason, 1963).

Vocabulary. In the absence of a comprehensive dictionary of NZE on historical principles, the number of distinctive words cannot be estimated with any certainty, but the total is likely to be less than a third of the 10,000 claimed for AusE. This vocabulary falls into five classes: loanwords from Polynesian languages, words showing extension of or departure from the meanings of general English words, the elevation of regional BrE words into standard currency, loanwords from AusE, and distinct regional word forms. This vocabulary is distributed through all walks of life, but particularly in the language of farming, food production, government, local administration, education, and informal usage. In more detail, these are:

Loanwords from Maori. In addition to names of flora and fauna, there is an increasing number of Maori loanwords for abstract concepts and tribal arrangements and customs: *aue* an interjection expressing astonishment, distress, etc., *haere mai* a term of greeting, *iwi* a people, tribe, *mana* power, prestige, authority, *manuwhiri* a visitor, guest, *mauri* the life principle, *rahui* a sign warning against trespass, *tupuna* an ancestor. There are also some verbs, such as *hikoi* to march, *hongi* to press noses. Some Maori words have been Anglicized to such an extent that they no longer look like Maori words: *biddy-bid* a plant with prickly burrs (Maori *piripiri*), *cockabully* a small fish (Maori *kōkopu*), *kit* a flax basket (Maori *kete*).

Loanwords from Samoan. Samoan loanwords are not widely used by non-Samoan New Zealanders. They include: *aiga* an extended family, *fale* a house, *palagi* a non-Samoan, *talofa* a ceremonial greeting, and the returned loanword *afakasi* a half-caste.

Extensions and alterations. Adaptations of general English words include: *bach* a holiday house at beach (a clipping of *bachelor*), *creek* (also AusE) a stream, *crook* (also AusE) ill, *go crook at* (also AusE) to be angry with, *farewell* as in *to farewell someone* (also AusE) to honour that person at a ceremonial occasion, *section* a building plot, *tramp* to walk for long distances in rough country, hence *tramper* one who does this.

Standardization of British English dialect words. BrE dialect words promoted to standard, all also AusE, include: *barrack* to shout or jeer (at players in a game, etc.), *bowyang* a band or strip round a trouser-leg below the knee, to prevent trousers from dragging on the ground, *burl* a try or attempt, as in *give it a burl*, *chook* a chicken, fowl, *dunny* a lavatory, *larrikin* a hooligan, *lolly* a sweet of any kind, especially boiled, *Rafferty's rules* no rules at all, *smooge* a display of amorous affection, *wowser* a killjoy or spoilsport.

Loanwords from Australian English. Words acquired from AusE include, from the preceding section, *larrikin*, *Rafferty's rules*, and: *backblocks* land in the remote interior, *battler* someone who struggles against the odds, *dill* a fool, simpleton, *ocker* a boor, *offsider* a companion, deputy, partner, *shanghai* a catapult. However, many AusE words are not used in NZE, especially words of Aboriginal origin and words associated with the swagmen (old-time itinerant workers). Similarly, many NZE words are unknown in Australia, especially

words of Maori origin like the common fish names *hapuku*, *kahawai*, *tarakihi*, *toheroa*.

Distinct word forms. Regional coinages include compounds, fixed phrases, and diminutives: (adjective + noun) *chilly bin* a portable insulated container for keeping food and drink cool, *Golden Kiwi* the name of a national lottery, *informal vote* a spoiled vote (also AusE), *silver beet* seakale beet; (noun + noun) *Canterbury lamb* from the name of a province, *kiwifruit* the Chinese gooseberry; (diminutive suffix *-ie*) *boatie* a boating enthusiast, *postie* a person delivering post (shared with ScoE and CanE), *swannie* an all-weather woollen jacket (from the trademark Swanndri), *truckie* a truck-driver (also AusE), *wharfie* a waterside worker, stevedore (also AusE); (diminutive suffix *-o*, *-oh*): *arvo* afternoon, *bottle-oh* a dealer in used bottles, *compo* compensation, especially for an injury, *smoko/smoke-oh* a break from work for a rest, with or without a smoke.

English and Maori. The most significant social issue relating to language is the relationship between the European majority and the Polynesian minority. This includes issues such as the status of Maori as an official language on a par with English in the courts and the pronunciation of Maori words, including place-names, in English. See AUSTRALASIAN ENGLISH, L-SOUNDS, MAORI, MAORI ENGLISH, NEW ZEALAND, NEW ZEALANDISM, NEW ZEALAND LITERATURE. [OCEANIA, VARIETY].

RO.W.B., L.J.B.

Bauer, Laurie, 1986. 'Notes on New Zealand English Phonetics and Phonology', *English World-Wide* 7: 2. Amsterdam & Philadelphia: John Benjamins.
Bell, Allan, & Holmes, Janet (eds.). 1990. *New Zealand Ways of Speaking English*. Clevedon & Philadelphia: Multilingual Matters.
Burchfield, Robert. 1986. *The New Zealand Pocket Oxford Dictionary*. Auckland: Oxford University Press.
Deverson, Tony. 1989. *Finding a New Zealand Voice: Attitudes towards English Used in New Zealand*. Auckland: New House.
—— 1991. 'New Zealand English Lexis: The Maori Dimension', *English Today* 26, Apr.
Eagleson, Robert D. 1982. 'English in Australia and New Zealand', in R. W. Bailey & M. Görlach (eds.), *English as a World Language*. Ann Arbor: University of Michigan Press. Cambridge: University Press.
Gordon, Elizabeth, & Deverson, Tony. 1985. *New Zealand English: An Introduction to New Zealand Speech and Usage*. Auckland: Heinemann.
Turner, George W. 1966. *The English Language in Australia and New Zealand*. London: Longman.

NEW ZEALANDISM [20c: from *New Zealand* and *-ism* as in *Scotticism*]. A word, phrase, idiom, or other usage peculiar to, or particularly common in, New Zealand. Such expressions are drawn from the Maori language (*Pakeha* a white New Zealander, *tangi* a ceremonial funeral) or are adaptations of general English (*grass fence* a strip of long grass along an electric fence, a barrier to sheep even when the current is off, *sharemilker* a tenant farmer on a dairy farm who receives a share of the profits). See -ISM, MAORI, NEW ZEALAND ENGLISH. [OCEANIA, VARIETY, WORD].   T.MCA.

NEW ZEALAND LITERATURE. Arriving in Christchurch as an immigrant farmer in 1860, Samuel Butler was 'rather startled at hearing one gentleman ask another whether he meant to wash this year, and receive the answer "No" '. Butler soon discovered that a person's sheep were himself: 'He does not wash his *sheep* before shearing, *he* washes; and, most marvellous of all, . . . he "lambs down" himself.' Butler promptly turned this pragmatic settlers' language to literary purposes, creating in *A First Year in Canterbury Settlement* (1863) and later *Erewhon* (1872) a narrative language that intercuts between European cultivation and colonial earthiness. He could write of being 'stuck up' by a waterfall, and having to 'slew' it, in a spectacular gorge that he had just compared picturesquely to a street in Genoa. Most early New Zealand writing was in the spirit of dispossessed Tennysons, nostalgic for the old home or rhapsodic about the new. The best has a double-edged quality, like Butler's ironic utopia in *Erewhon*, or in poetry the mix of frontier ballad with literary verse by Blanche Baughan, or of intellectual and pastoral elements by Ursula Bethell (both early 20c).

The paradox of writing in English at the furthest possible distance from England became for such writers a source of energy, not loss. When Katherine Mansfield, a native of Wellington, reviewed from London Jane Mander's *The Story of a New Zealand River* (1920), she rebuked Mander for labouring to gloss words of Maori origin like *puriri* and *rimu*, preferring to weave threads of local diction and reference into her own stories set in New Zealand. Such local elements are the prime source of the mixture of mystical and domestic with which she invested 'my undiscovered country' in such works as 'Prelude' (1918) and 'At the Bay' (1921). The growth from a colonial to an independent culture has at times been controversial. Each new anthology seems to provoke dispute about the viability of an identifiable national literature in such a small and apparently 'English' country. There have, however, been distinctive characteristics. Between the wars, liberal-socialist realism prevailed, its emphases working-class, male, and outdoors. Its most sustained accomplishments were John Mulgan's *Man Alone* (1939), for years almost an archetype, and the vernacular narratives of Frank Sargeson, such as his stories *A*

Man and His Wife (1940) and the novel *I Saw in My Dream* (1949). A vigorous line of low-life ballads also emerged, nurtured by such mid-century poets as A. R. D. Fairburn, Denis Glover, and James K. Baxter. Literature has very largely stayed close to local realism and local speech, even in philosophical and religious poets and dramatists like Baxter and non-realist novelists like Janet Frame. The same is largely true of the ongoing effort to respond imaginatively to the country's awesome volcanic terrain.

New Zealand's remoteness, which might have caused self-absorption, has sharpened the national eyesight. There is a considerable literature in which life is observed from various oblique viewpoints: children, the old, and other marginal observers are the narrative voices of such notable fictions as Ian Cross's *Good Boy* (1958), Maurice Gee's *Plumb* (1978), and Janet Frame's *Owls Do Cry* (1957) and *Intensive Care* (1979). Semi-detachment is the nation's geographical and cultural situation. The Kiwi bombardier who provides the first level of narration in M. K. Joseph's European war novel *A Soldier's Tale* (1976) is witness, as New Zealanders have had to be in at least five wars, conflicts which involve them but are not theirs. The literature of New Zealand is therefore watchful and fairly muted. It is rarely exuberant, but the effort to connect the immediate and the inherited continues, in such different writers as Allen Curnow, the major contemporary poet, and Keri Hulme, whose *The Bone People* (1985) takes its strangeness from mixing intensely local ethnicity with gleefully eclectic bookishness: oral and literary cultures interact for her as they did for Butler. The emergence in the 1970s of a Maori literature in English has added a new dimension. Witi Ihimaera and Keri Hulme have transposed into English the sonorous spoken rhythms of Maori oratory. Patricia Grace has more subtly established the 'ways of talking' of her people, and has begun to adapt English prose fiction to Maori forms, rather than the other way round. This movement has been sympathetically received. See BUTLER. [LITERATURE, OCEANIA, VARIETY].   R.R.

NEW ZEALAND PLACE-NAMES. According to the New Zealand Geographic Board, the body charged by Act of Parliament with registering place-names, 58% of officially recognized names (including those of rivers and mountains) are of Maori origin, 42% of European origin. The breakdown between the two islands reflects the patterns of Maori and European settlement: in the North Island, 79% Maori, 21% European; in the South Island, 67% European, 33% Maori.

Maori. The longest officially recognized place-name is *Taumatawhakatangihangakouauo-tamateapokaiwhenuakitanatahu*, the name of a hill in southern Hawkes Bay, North Island. It means 'The hill on which Tamatea, circumnavigator of the land, played his kouau (flute) to his loved one'. In this name, the elements are clearly recognizable, but that is not always the case with Maori place-names, either because they have changed with time or have been altered by Europeans, as in *Amuri* from Maori *Haumuri* East Wind, and *Petone* from Maori *Pito-one* End of the Beach. Nevertheless, many Maori names can be understood, such as *Awakino* ('valley ugly') Ugly Valley, *Maunganui* ('mountain big') Big Mountain, *Waikaremoana* Great Lake of Rippling Water, *Waitangi* Weeping Water (that is, Waterfall).

European. While most European names are English (*Auckland*, *Christchurch*, *Wellington*), there are some from other languages, such as *Aiguilles Rouges* (French), *Dannevirke* (Danish), *Dunedin* (Celtic), *Franz Joseph* (Austrian), *New Zealand* (Dutch). Some English place-names reflect the experiences of early explorers, such as *Bay of Plenty*, *Cape Foulwind*, *Poverty Bay*, others commemorate people, such as *Clive*, *Greytown*, *Nelson*, *Onslow*, and many reflect the origins of the settlers, such as the Scottish *Aviemore*, *Bannockburn*, *Ben Lomond*, *Portobello*, *Roxburgh*. See PLACE-NAME. [NAME, OCEANIA].   L.J.B.

NEW ZEALAND PRESS. There is no national daily newspaper, the major dailies being associated with the four main centres of population: *The New Zealand Herald* (Auckland), *The Dominion* (Wellington), *The Press* (Christchurch), *The Otago Daily Times* (Dunedin). There are four other daily morning papers and over 20 daily evening papers, all regional. Some 80% of daily circulation is controlled by three major groups: New Zealand News, Independent News, and Wilson and Horton. Apart from the dailies, there are over 80 community newspapers and over 500 magazines, journals, and newsletters which accept advertising. See NEWSPAPER, PRESS. [MEDIA, OCEANIA].   L.J.B.

NEW ZEALAND PUBLISHING. There are over 300 publishers in NZ, some two-thirds of which are government departments, societies, and private organizations. Local companies include Cape Catley, Caxton Press, and John McIndoe, and the university presses of Auckland and Victoria (Wellington). In addition, large international companies such as Allen & Unwin, William Collins, Longman Paul, Macmillan, Octopus (Heinemann-Reed), Oxford University Press, Penguin, and Random Century are represented, all with specifically NZ as well as imported titles. Local publishing has increased its share of the NZ market from about 20% ten years ago to over 33% today, and includes many educational books. About 60% of those used in high schools are locally produced, while in primary schools the percentage is even higher. School texts have been important in the growth of publishing as an export industry: four NZ publishers export over 80% of their production to such countries as the UK, US, France, Spain, and Scandinavia, elementary teaching materials accounting for this percentage. In percentage terms, NZ book exports are second only to those from the UK, over 25% of local production being exported. See PUBLISHING. [MEDIA, OCEANIA].   L.J.B.

NGUGI WA THIONG'O, also written **Ngũgĩ**; formerly *James Ngugi* [b.1938]. Kenyan (Kikuyu) teacher, critic, dramatist, and novelist, born in Limuru, and educated in Kenyan schools and at Makerere U., Uganda, and Leeds U., England. His first works were in English, set against a background of social and political upheaval as Kenya moved towards independence from Britain in the 1950s and early 1960s. Ngugi's style has been described as Biblical in its purity, and expresses an African Marxist viewpoint. His writings in English include the novels *Weep Not Child* (1964), *The River Between* (1965), *A Grain of Wheat* (1967), and *Petals of Blood* (1977), and the plays *The Black Hermit* (1968), *This Time Tomorrow*, *The Rebels*, *The Wound in the Heart* (all 1970), and *The Trial of Dedan Kimathi* (1976, with Micere Mugo). When he completed *Petals of Blood*, he gave up English as the medium for his fiction, but continued to use it to translate his works and for non-fictional purposes. He argued that to provoke and cultivate the social and political reforms needed in Kenya requires novels and plays in the local languages. For this, his medium is Kikuyu (or Gĩkũyũ, as he writes the name). With Ngugi wa Mirii, he produced the play *Ngaahika Ndeenda* (1980), translated as *I Will Marry When I Want* (1982). It was immediately banned. In *Detained: A Writer's Prison Diary* (1981), he describes his one-year detention without trial in 1978. His Kikuyu novels are *Caitaani Mutharabaini* (1980), translated as *Devil on a Cross*, and *Matigari Ma Njiruungi* (1986), translated as *Matigari*. In these, Ngugi draws on oral traditions and tribal values to attack neocolonialism, and their apparently plain language is laden with aphorisms, symbols, and slogans. His works are widely read in Kenya by people far from the modern metropolitan centres. Ngugi discusses the language issue in *Decolonising the Mind: The Politics of Language in African Literature* (1986), a work dedicated to 'all those who write in African languages, and to all those who over the years have maintained the dignity of the literature, culture, philosophy, and other treasures carried by African languages'. He adds in the preface: 'If in these essays I criticise the Afro-European (or Eurafrican) choice of our linguistic praxis, it is not to take away from the talent and the genius of those who have written in English, French, or Portuguese. On the contrary I am lamenting a neo-colonial situation which has meant the European bourgeoisie once again stealing our talents and geniuses as they have stolen our economies.' In the same work, he says: 'This book . . . is my farewell to English as a vehicle for any of my writings. From now on it is Gĩkũyũ and Kiswahili all the way.' See index. [AFRICA, BIOGRAPHY, LITERATURE].

G.D.K., T.MCA.

NICARAGUA, NICARAGUAN ENGLISH. See CENTRAL AMERICA, ENGLISH, MISKITO COAST CREOLE.

NICE-NELLYISM, also **nicenellyism, nicenellieism** [1930s AmE: from *nice Nelly*, a disparaging name for a prudish woman or anyone considered to behave in a similar way. Used with or without capital letters for *nice* and *Nelly*]. (1) Excessive prudishness in speech or behaviour: 'Mr. Pyles attributes much of the nice-nellyism that blighted polite speech and writing during the nineteenth century to Webster's Puritan prudishness' (*New Yorker*, 18 Oct. 1952). (2) A genteelism: 'Nor is there an entry for *toilet* because Americans regard the word as indelicate and a shade vulgar but not as a subject of usage controversy, whereas some Britons use it as the most general word and others have distaste for it as what Americans call a nice-nellyism—a genteel euphemism' (John Algeo, reviewing *Webster's Dictionary of English Usage* in *English Today* 26, Apr. 1991). See EUPHEMISM, GENTEELISM, -ISM. [STYLE].

T.MCA.

NICKNAME [15c: from Middle English *a nekename*, metanalysis of *an ekename* an extra name: compare NONCE WORD]. An informal name used in place of, or together with, a formal name: for example, the short form *Ed* for *Edward*, or *Lefty* for someone left-handed. Nicknames are most common for persons, but are also used of places: *the Big Apple* for New York City, *the Smoke* for London, *Mile-High City* for Denver, Colorado, *the Eternal City* for Rome. Nicknames tend to suggest that their user is on familiar terms with the bearer of the name, although the familiarity may be equivocal (affectionate, disdainful, defamatory, even a mix of these). A common form of nickname is a modification of the formal name by clipping

alone (*Ed* for *Edward*), clipping and adaptation (*Ted* and *Ned*), clipping and diminutive suffix (*Eddy/Eddie, Teddy, Neddy*), sometimes with many variations (*Eliza, Liza, Lisa, Liz, Lizzie, Betty, Bess, Beth*, and *Betsy* for *Elizabeth*). On occasion, the modification can lead to an entirely different form, such as *Polly* from *Mary* and *Peggy* from *Margaret*. Another form of nickname is the descriptive epithet, on its own (*Shorty* for someone short, or ironically for someone tall; *chalky*, applied in BrE to someone whose surname is *White*; *Bluebeard*, someone with a beard dyed blue, or a menace to women, like the original holder of the nickname) or following the given name (*Ivan the Terrible, Richard Lionheart*). See EPITHET. Nicknames are informally given, as opposed to the ritual naming ceremonies typical of formal names, as in christening ceremonies or launching ships. They have, however, sometimes been adopted as regular names, as with such surnames as *Bright* and *Daft*. Relevant publications include: Jane Morgan, Christopher O'Neill, & Rom Harré, *Nicknames: Their Origins and Social Consequences* (Routledge & Kegan Paul, 1979), and Laurence Urdang, *Names and Nicknames of Places and Things* (US: Hall, UK: Grafton Books, 1987). Compare PET NAME, SO(U)BRIQUET. See FORM OF ADDRESS. [NAME].

J.A.

NIGER–CONGO LANGUAGES. See AFRICAN LANGUAGES, BANTU, LANGUAGE, LIBERIA.

NIGERIA. Official title: *Republic of Nigeria*. A country of West Africa and the most populous country in Africa. Capital: formerly Lagos; since 1991 Abuja. Currency: the naira (100 kobo). Population: 110.5m (1988), 162.5m (projection for 2000). Ethnicity: 21% Hausa, 21% Yoruba, 18% Igbo, 10% Fulani, 6% Tiv, 5% Kanuri, 5% Ibibio, 4% Edo, 10% others. Religion: 47% Muslim, 19% traditional, 17% Protestant, 17% Roman Catholic. Languages: English and the main languages of each state (official); the most widely spoken of the estimated 400 indigenous languages are Hausa (27%), Igbo (11%), Yoruba (18%); Nigerian Pidgin English, a widely used lingua franca. Education: primary 98%, secondary 29%, tertiary 3%, literacy 43%. English is the language of education after the first three years of primary school.

History. The Portuguese established the first trading posts along the Guinea coast in the 15c and various European nations traded in the area for gold, ivory, and slaves. British contacts with Nigeria go back at least to the 16c and varieties of English were sufficiently well established in coastal areas in the 18c for an Efik chief in Calabar to keep a diary, from which the following is an excerpt: 'about 6 am in aqua Landing with small Rain morning so I walk up to see Esim and Egbo Young so I see Jimmy Henshaw come to see wee and wee tell him for go on bord . . .' (D. Forde (ed.), *Efik Traders of Old Calabar: The Diary of Antera Duke*, 1956). British missionaries began to teach English in Nigeria during the first half of the 19c, but relations between Britain and parts of Nigeria were not formalized until 1861 when the settlement of Lagos was declared a colony. The Berlin Conference of 1885 recognized Britain's claim to the *Oil Rivers Protectorate* created in 1882 in the Niger delta area. This was enlarged and renamed the *Niger Coast Protectorate* in 1893. The *Protectorate of Southern Nigeria* and the *Protectorate of Northern Nigeria* were created in 1900 from territories controlled by the Royal Niger Company. These were amalgamated into the *Colony and Protectorate of Nigeria* in 1914. Nigeria became independent in 1960, a republic within the Commonwealth in 1961, and a federal republic in 1963.

English and Pidgin. A wide spectrum of English is used in Nigeria, including standard English whose spoken forms are influenced by various mother tongues, more general English whose structures are influenced by the mother tongues, the Indian English of many traders and teachers, and Nigerian Pidgin English, which is part of the continuum of West African Pidgin English and has many features in common with Krio in Sierra Leone and Kamtok in Cameroon. Pidgin is used throughout the country as a lingua franca. It is sometimes acquired as a mother tongue in such urban areas as Calabar and Port Harcourt, but almost always in conjunction with one or more local languages. It has many forms that reflect mother-tongue and English influence and, although a number of Pidgin dictionaries have been written and cyclostyled, it has not yet been standardized. It has been used in prose by many writers, including Chinua Achebe, and as a vehicle for poetry by Frank Aig-Imoukhuede and for drama by Ola Rotimi.

Pronunciation. (1) All varieties of Nigerian English are non-rhotic. RP is no longer the norm for the media, but continues to have prestige and to influence pronunciation. (2) There is a tendency towards syllable-timing that becomes more pronounced as one moves from standard English to Pidgin. Polysyllables tend to have all syllables equally stressed. (3) The central vowels /ə/ and /ɪ/ in RP tend to be replaced by /a/, /ɔ/, or /ɛ/, so that *but* can rhyme with *got* or in hypercorrect forms with *get*, and all three can occur in *church*. (4) There are fewer vowel contrasts in Nigerian English: often no distinction between *cheap* and *chip*, *caught*, *court*, and *cot*, *pool* and *pull*. (5) The diphthongs in RP *day* and *dough* tend to

become the single vowels /e/ and /o/; those in *hear* and *hair* tend to have the schwa replaced by /a/. (6) There are differences in the pronunciation of consonants in different parts of the country. The initial consonants in *thin* and *then* tend to be replaced by /t, d/ in Igbo and Yoruba-influenced English, and by /s, z/ in Hausa-influenced English. Igbo and Yoruba speakers tend to replace the final consonant /ʒ/ as in *rouge* by *sh* ('roosh'), while Hausa speakers often use /dʒ/ ('roodge').

Grammar. Educated Nigerians use standard forms especially in the written medium, but the following features are widely described as occurring in general Nigerian English: (1) Uncountable nouns are often treated as countable: *I had only fruits to eat*; *I am grateful for your many advices*. (2) Definite articles are sometimes used as if the rules of standard English have been reversed: *Lorry was overcrowded*; *What do you think of the Structuralism?* (3) The use of prepositions can differ from BrE and AmE norms: *He came to my office by four o'clock* (that is, at four o'clock); *She is the best teacher for our school* (in our school). (4) Phrasal verbs are sometimes used differently (as in *He couldn't cope up with any more money worries*) or drop their particles (*Pick me at the corner*: not *pick me up*). (5) The modal verbs *could* and *would* are often used instead of *can* and *will*: *He has assured me that he could come tomorrow*; *They say that he would be attending our next meeting. Will* is also sometimes used for *would*: *I will first of all like to thank you*. (6) *Themselves* is often used with *like/love* for *each other*: *The husband and wife loved themselves dearly*; *Why do they like themselves so much?*

Vocabulary. There are three groups of distinctive words in Nigerian English: (1) Borrowings from local languages and Pidgin: *danshiki* (Hausa) male gown, *oga* (Yoruba) master, boss, *obanje* (Igbo) spirit child, *dash* (Pidgin) to give, a gift. (2) Loan-translations from local languages: *have long legs* to exert influence, *throw water* to offer a bribe. (3) Items given local meanings or coined for local purposes: *come*, as in *I'm coming* I'll be with you soon, *You've come!* Welcome; *decampee* a person who moves to another political party; *hear* to understand, as in *I hear French*; *senior* elder, as in *senior sister* elder sister. See ENGLISH, WEST AFRICAN ENGLISH, WEST AFRICAN PIDGIN ENGLISH. [AFRICA, NAME, VARIETY]. L.T., T.MCA.

NOISE. See INFORMATION, SOUND.

NOM DE PLUME [1820s: from French, pen name]. A pen name or pseudonym. The expression was not approved in classical French, which preferred *nom de guerre* war name. Formerly widely used in English, the expression is now generally considered affected. See PEN NAME. [LITERATURE, WRITING]. R.C.

NOMENCLATURE [17c: from Latin *nomenclatura* a calling by name, list of names. Stress: on first or second syllable]. A system of names or terms, as used for any purpose but particularly an art or science. Compare TERMINOLOGY. See BINOMIAL NOMENCLATURE, TERMINOLOGY. [NAME, WORD]. T.MCA.

NOMINAL [15c: from Latin *nominalis* relating to a name or noun]. (1) Relating to nouns: *a nominal group*. (2) A noun or pronoun: *He* and *bridge* are the nominals in the sentence *He crossed the bridge*. (3) An adjective functioning as a noun: *the poor* (poor people); *the accused* (the accused person). The terms *nominal group* and *nominal clause* mean the same as noun phrase and noun clause. A nominal clause is a finite or non-finite clause that resembles a noun phrase in the range of its functions; for example, as the subjects of sentences, *That he can't lift his arm* in *That he can't lift his arm worries me*, and *Smoking cigarettes* in *Smoking cigarettes can cause cancer*. Compare ABSOLUTE ADJECTIVE, SUBSTANTIVE. [GRAMMAR]. S.C., T.MCA.

NOMINALIZATION [Mid-20c in this sense]. (1) The process or result of forming a noun from a word belonging to another word class: *writing/writings* and *shaving/shavings* derived from *white* and *shave* by adding *-ing*; *sanity* derived from *sane* by the addition of the noun-forming suffix *-ity*; *nominalization* derived from *nominalize* by adding *-ation*. (2) The process or result of deriving a noun phrase by a transformation from a finite clause: *their rejecting my complaint* or *their rejection of my complaint* from *They rejected my complaint*. [GRAMMAR]. S.G.

NOMINATIVE ABSOLUTE. See ABSOLUTE CLAUSE.

NOMINATIVE CASE [14c: from Latin *casus nominativus* the naming case]. A term in the case system of Latin and other inflected languages, typically marking a noun or pronoun as the subject of a sentence. The nominative is the citation form of nouns and pronouns listed in dictionaries and the first or top form in declension tables. *Marcus* is the nominative of the Latin name whose equivalent in English is *Mark*, and has the masculine nominative inflection *-us*. In English, the subjects of sentences have sometimes been described as nominatives. [GRAMMAR]. S.C.

NONCE WORD, also **nonce-word** [From Middle English *for the nanes*, metanalysis of **for then anes* for the one (thing), present-day *for the nonce* for the time being, for the work in hand: compare NICKNAME]. In medieval poetry, variants of the word *nonce* were used to complete lines, often plural and rhyming with *bones* or *stones*: 'Eneas hymself doun layd for the nanis, / And gave schort rest vnto his wery banis' (Gavin Douglas, *Æneis*, 1513). The term *nonce-word* was adopted in the preparation of the *OED* (1884) 'to describe a word which is apparently used only for the nonce'. From this usage have come by analogy such further forms as *nonce borrowing*, *nonce combination, nonce form, nonce formation, nonce meaning, nonce usage, nonce use* (all often hyphenated). Because of the special functions, ephemerality, and even eccentricity of such usages, it is not easy to exemplify them. Recent nonce occurrences, however, include the verb *to perestroik*, formed from the Russian loanword *perestroika* (for an illustrative quotation, see BACK-FORMATION), as if it were 'perestroiker' (one who perestroiks), and the noun *Excaliburger*, for a hamburger sold at Tintagel in Cornwall, a site associated with the legendary King Arthur, whose sword was called Excalibur. Although nonce forms are coined for the occasion and may never occur again or be used in another context, they sometimes become regular, widely used words, as with *mob* in the early 18c, clipped from Latin *mobile vulgus* (the fickle crowd). See BLEND, BUZZ WORD, -ITIS, NEOLOGISM/NEOLOGY, ROOT-CREATION, STUNT WORD. [STYLE, WORD]. T.MCA.

NON-COUNT NOUN. See UNCOUNTABLE NOUN.

NON-DEFINING RELATIVE CLAUSE. See RESTRICTIVE AND NON-RESTRICTIVE RELATIVE CLAUSE.

NON-FINITE VERB, also **nonfinite verb**. A form of the verb that does not display a distinction in tense, in contrast with *finite verb* (where there is a distinction between present tense and past tense: *hopes, hoped*). A non-finite verb is either an *infinitive* or a *participle*. There are two infinitives: the *to*-infinitive ('Estelle wants *to dance* with Matthew'); the *bare infinitive* ('Philip will *come* with Matthew'). There are two participles: the *-ing participle* or the *present participle* ('James is *playing* cards') and the *-ed participle* or (according to its function) the *past participle* or *passive participle* ('James has *visited* me recently'; 'Jane was *helped* by Jeremy'). See FINITE VERB, INFINITIVE, VERB [GRAMMAR]. S.G.

NON-RESTRICTIVE RELATIVE CLAUSE.
See RELATIVE CLAUSE.

NONSENSE

NONSENSE [17c]. Words or language with little or no meaning and perhaps an absurd or trivial quality: 'For learned Nonsense has a deeper Sound, / Than easy Sense, and goes for more profound' (Samuel Butler, *Genuine Remains of Samuel Butler*, published 1759); 'I daresay I shall go on scribbling one nonsense or another to the end of the chapter' (Walter Scott, letter, 1803). The form *non-sense* is occasionally used as a neutral antonym of *sense*: '[Lear's] non-sense is not vacuity of sense: it is a parody of sense, and that is the sense of it' (T. S. Eliot, *Music of Poetry*, 1942). The term is often attributive: a *nonsense book*, *nonsense verse*.

A *nonsense syllable* is formed by putting a vowel between consonants to produce a non-word, as in the sequence *dib, gib, kib, mib, pib, zib*, from which the forms *bib, fib, lib, nib* are excluded because they 'make sense' (that is, form known words or abbreviations). Nonsense syllables have often been used by psychologists in experiments that test memory and learning. The use of *nonsense words* is venerable: sometimes, like children's rhymes and folk expressions, they serve to fill out a phrase or a character (as with the giant who says *fee-fi-fo-fum, I smell the blood of an Englishman*); sometimes they garble words that once made altogether too much sense, like the references to plague behind *Ring-a-ring-a-roses, a pocket full of posies, hush-a, hush-a, all fall down*. Often, however, nonsense appears to be spontaneous and a matter of whimsy: for example, in 1862 the painter and poet Edward Lear wrote the following to his friend Evelyn Baring:

Thrippsy pillivinx,
Inky tinky pobblebockle abblesquabs?—Flosky!
Beebul trimble flosky!—Okul scratchabibblebongibo, viddle squibble tog-a-tog, ferrymoyassity amsky flamsky ramsky damsky crocklefether squiggs,
　　　Flinkywisty pomm,
　　　Slushypipp

The French linguist Jean-Jacques Lecercle draws attention to this letter in *The Violence of Language* (1990), saying first that it appears to be an incomprehensible hoax: 'The only surprise is that a man of 50 should still indulge in such childish games.' He notes, however, that the text is not entirely chaotic: it is English nonsense (not French), is laid out as a letter, suitably opens and closes, and is properly punctuated and (apparently) spelt. The words are clear-cut, some look credible, and here and there a bit of 'sense' creeps in (except that it may not be safe to assume that *ink, scratch,* and *tog,* or *-le* and *-y* are doing their usual jobs). Questions, exclamations, and statements also present themselves clearly, and so it is 'only' at the level of meaning that the system breaks down. Lecercle adds:

But perhaps I am looking for the wrong meaning. If I forget denotation and look for connotation, in other words if I go from semantics to pragmatics, the text as a whole acquires meaning. . . . We all have to write official letters, full of the expression of high-flown but empty feeling, of conventional phrases and clichés. . . . Hollowness, sometimes even hypocrisy, are the order of the day. Would not a semantically empty text, keeping only the pragmatic skeleton of a conventional letter, aptly embody the artificiality of such letters? Lear's meaning, if my hypothesis is correct, is satirical.

Lecercle draws this meaning almost painfully from Lear's text, his conclusion pointing to a distinctive feature of nonsense: that people often work on it, like a Delphic prophecy, to eliminate as much of the *non-* as they can.

Lear's interest in nonsense has been considerably enlarged throughout the world in the last decade, during which, especially in Japan, a kind of pseudo-English has begun to appear regularly on the packaging of goods, on T-shirts, and the like: *Joyful, let's dash in a sky* and *When I jumped far beyond your imagination, I found myself a gust of wind*. Such surreal snippets may now have become trendy in the English-speaking world. In 'English know-how, no problem' (an article in *The Independent on Sunday*, 9 Sept. 1990), the American writer Bill Bryson discusses such a 'message' on a British-made jacket seen in London: *Rodeo—100 per cent Boys for Atomic Atlas*. 'What', he asks, 'do these strange messages mean? In the literal sense, nothing of course. But in a more metaphoric way they do rather underscore the huge, almost compulsive, appeal of English in the world. It is an odd fact that almost everywhere on the planet products are deemed more appealing, and sentiments more powerful, if they are expressed in English, even if they make next to no sense.' See ACCEPTABILITY, BABY TALK, CUMBRIC, DECORATIVE ENGLISH, GRAMMATICALITY, JAPAN, MINCED OATH, MUMBO JUMBO, MUMPSIMUS, NONSENSE VERSE, TWADDLE, VERBALISM, WAFFLE. [LANGUAGE, STYLE].　　　　T.MCA.

NONSENSE VERSE

NONSENSE VERSE [Late 18c]. Light verse on improbable or fantastic subjects. The humour is usually emphasized by rare words, neologisms, and unexpected juxtapositions. Often intended for children, such verse also appeals to an adult sense of the ridiculous or whimsical. In English, the 19c writers Edward Lear and Lewis Carroll are its best known exponents. Carroll's poem 'The Hunting of the Snark' developed from a single line ('For the Snark *was* a Boojum, you see') that occurred to him while out walking one day in 1874. Whenever asked if the poem had allegorical, satirical, or other significance, he would answer, 'I don't know'. In the poem, Carroll is imprecise about the nature of Snarks, but makes it clear that Boojums are a kind of Snark, and a dangerous kind at that. The poem ends with the line out of which it first grew:

'It's a Snark!' was the sound that first came to their ears,
And seemed almost too good to be true.
Then followed a torrent of laughter and cheers:
Then the ominous words 'It's a Boo—'
Then silence. Some fancied they heard in the air
A weary and wandering sigh
That sounded like '—jum!' but the others declare
It was only a breeze that went by.

They hunted till darkness came on, but they found
Not a button, or feather, or mark,
By which they could tell that they stood on the ground
Where the Baker had met with the Snark.

In the midst of the word he was going to say,
In the midst of his laughter and glee,
He had softly and suddenly vanished away—
For the Snark *was* a Boojum, you see.

Nonsensical refrains are common in the traditional ballad and folk-song; they eke out the singer's material and allow audience participation:

Ha, ha! Ha, ha! This world doth pass
Most merrily I'll be sworn,
For many an honest Indian ass
Goes for a unicorn.
Fara diddle dyno
This is idle fyno.
(Christ Church manuscript, early 17c)

The language of nonsense verse ranges from the opaque and fanciful but often aesthetically pleasing ('Hi-diddle-diddle, the cat and the fiddle / The cow jumped over the moon'), to words on the edge of meaning that tell a not-quite story:

Long years ago
The Dong was happy and gay,
Till he fell in love with a Jumbly Girl
Who came to those shores one day.
For the Jumblies came in a sieve, they did,—
Landing at eve near the Zemmery Fidd
Where the Oblong Oysters grow.
(Edward Lear, 'The Dong with a Luminous Nose', 1877)

Successful nonsense verse must respect the structure and syntax of a language; comic neologisms need to be rooted in the familiar. In the opening lines of Carroll's 'Jabberwocky':

'Twas brillig, and the slithy toves
Did gyre and gimble in the wabe.

The reader can deduce that *toves* and *wabe* must be nouns, *slithy* an adjective and *gyre* and *gimble* verbs. See FANTASY, NONSENSE, VERSE. [LITERATURE].   R.C., T.MCA.

NON-SEXIST   LANGUAGE/USAGE.   See SEXISM.

NON-STANDARD, NONSTANDARD [1920s]. A term for usages and varieties that are not part of a standard language: such socially marked usages as *He ain't comin'*, *I seen him*; such regionally marked usages as *Ah dinnae ken* (Scots: I don't know); such regional varieties of English as Geordie in England and Brooklynese in the US. The term has three uses: as a neutral alternative to *sub-standard*; as one in a set of three (*standard, non-standard, sub-standard*); as a euphemism for *sub-standard*. It is not always easy to establish which use is dominant in particular texts and contexts. See STANDARD. [LANGUAGE, STYLE, USAGE].   T.MCA.

NON-U. See U AND NON-U.

NORFOLK. See EAST ANGLIA.

NORFOLK ISLAND. See PITCAIRNESE.

NORM [1810s: from Latin *norma* a rule, pattern, carpenter's square]. A standard, model, or average, often used of social behaviour and consensus in the use of a language: *deviations from the norm*; *linguistic norms*. See DEVIANT, NORMATIVE, REFERENCE NORM, REGULAR. Compare CANON, MODEL, RULE, STANDARD. [LANGUAGE, USAGE].   T.MCA.

NORMAN [13c: from Old French *Normant* (Modern *Normand*), from Teutonic *Northman*: compare Medieval Latin *Nort(h)mannus* and *Normannus*]. Noun and adjective for Scandinavian (mainly Danish) raiders who settled on the northern coast of France *c*.900, where they became Christians and gave up Norse in favour of French. In 911, the French king Charles the Simple made Hrolf the Ganger (Rollo the Rover) first Duke of Normandy (Latin *Northmannia*), a new province on the Lower Seine. The Normans are best remembered for Duke William's conquest of England: 'Apparently as the result of one day's fighting (14 October 1066), England received a new royal dynasty, a new aristocracy, a virtually new Church, a new art, a new architecture, and a new language' (R. H. C. Davis, *The Normans and Their Myth*, 1976). The Normans, however, also gained for a time the kingdom of Sicily, lands in southern Italy, and the principality of Antioch in the eastern Mediterranean, as well as having a powerful impact on Wales, Scotland, and Ireland. Normandy appears originally to have been the home of an aristocracy of Norse extraction and a general population of Celts and Franks; among William the Conqueror's followers were Bretons, Franks, Flemings, and Normans, all generally referred to as both *Norman* and *French*. In Ireland they were generally known as *English* and in Scotland as *French*. In England, their speech, *Norman French*, was the language of the court, the law, and literature until the mid-14c. Once in control of the country, the Normans compiled *Domesday Book* (1086), a comprehensive land record. Despite their enormous significance, however, by the beginning of the 12c they had disappeared as a distinct people, having merged into the communities on which they had imposed themselves. In England, they left a particular mark on the upper classes, many of whose members in the 20c continue to note that their families 'came over with the Conqueror'. See ANGLO-NORMAN, ANGLO-SAXON, BRETON, BRITTANY, CHANNEL ISLANDS, ENGLAND, ENGLISH, ENGLISH PLACE-NAMES, FRENCH, IRELAND, IRISH, IRISH ENGLISH, IRISH PLACE-NAMES, LATIN[1], NORMAN FRENCH, NORSE, Q, SCOTS, SCOTTISH LANGUAGES, SCOTTISH PLACE-NAMES, SPELLING, W, WALES, WELSH PLACE-NAMES. [EUROPE, HISTORY, NAME].   T.MCA.

NORMAN FRENCH. The variety of Old Northern French adopted in the 10c by the *Normans*, Norse settlers who gave their name to Normandy. It extended to England after the Norman Conquest in 1066. In its British context, it is often referred to as *Anglo-Norman*. Although native only to the aristocracy and their immediate retainers, Norman French was until the 13c dominant in England and important in Wales, Scotland, and Ireland. It influenced English and was in turn influenced by it, as well as by Central (Parisian) French, which as the language of the French court was considered more refined. In Chaucer's *Canterbury Tales* (14c), the Prioress is singled out as a speaker of English French: 'And Frensh she spak ful faire and fetisly, / After the scole of Stratford atte Bowe, / For Frensh of Paris was to hir unknowe.' By the end of the Hundred Years War (mid-15c), French was no longer a living tongue in England, although elements of it were preserved for centuries afterwards, as in *Law French*. Its last British remnant is in the Channel Islands.

Among the many Old French words in English, the oldest have a Norman French aspect (sometimes with doublets from Central French, shown in parentheses): (1) Hard *c* as opposed to *ch* as in *chair*: *caitiff, capon, car* (*chariot*), *carrion, carry, castle, catch* (*chase*), *cater, cattle* (*chattels*), *cauldron, decay, escape, pocket* (*pouch*). The Modern French equivalent is the *sh*-sound in *chateau*. (2) Hard *g* as opposed to *j* as in *James*: *gammon, garden, garter*. *Gaol* has a Norman French spelling but a Central French pronunciation, whence the alternative *jail*. The Modern French equivalent is the *zh*-sound in *jardin*. (3) A *w* as opposed to a *g(u)*: *ewer, reward*

(*regard*), *wage* (*gage*), *wait, wallop* (*gallop*), *ward* (*guard*), *warden* (*guardian*), *warranty* (*guarantee*), *warren, waste, wicket, wile* (*guile*), *wise* (*guise*). The Modern French equivalent is the *g(u)* in *garde, guichet*. (4) The *ch* in *chair, cherry, chisel, patch* (*piece*), etc. The Modern French equivalent is the *s*-sound in *cerise*. (5) The *sh* in *ashet* (ScoE), *brush, cushion, fashion, leash, mushroom, parish, push, usher*, etc. The Modern French equivalent is the *s*-sound in *façon, pousser*. *Sh* is notable in English verbs formed on Norman French verbs in *-ir*: *abolish, finish, perish, polish*. (6) The *qu* in *conquest* (but not *conqueror*), *enquire, quality, quarter, question, quit*, etc. The Modern French equivalent is the *k*-sound in *quitter*. (7) An *ai, ei*, or *ey* spelling (and an *ee* or *ay* pronunciation): *convey* (*convoy*), *deceive, faith, heir, leisure, prey, receive, veil*. The Modern French equivalent is the *wa*-sound in *loisir*. See ANGLO-NORMAN, CHANNEL ISLANDS, FRENCH, NORMAN. [EUROPE, HISTORY, LANGUAGE].   J.M.G.

NORMATIVE [1870s]. A term in linguistics and education for belonging to or serving to establish and maintain a norm, as in *normative grammar*. If a language, variety of a language, or culture depends for its norms on another community, it is *exonormative*; if it does not, it is *endonormative*. Most colonies and many post-colonial societies have exonormative rules: until recently AusE was exonormative in terms of BrE, but has in recent years become increasingly endonormative. See NORM, SOLECISM, STANDARD. [LANGUAGE, STYLE].   T.MCA.

NORN [First recorded *c*.1485 in Shetland: from Old Norse *norroena* (*mál*) or *norroent* (*mál*) northern (language), applied specifically to the language of ancient Norway and its colonies]. A variety of Norse once spoken in and around the Northern Isles of Scotland, and known as *Orkney Norn* and *Shetland Norn*. The name has also been recently applied to the Norse spoken in medieval Caithness on the mainland (*Caithness Norn*). Orkney and Shetland were settled in the 9c by Norse-speaking farmers, mainly from south-western Norway, who imposed their language on the local Pictish people. At about the same time there were settlements by Scandinavians in Caithness and in the West Highlands and Islands. But nowhere else in the British Isles apart from Orkney and Shetland did links with Scandinavia endure so long and leave such striking imprints on dialects, place-names, culture, and folk memory.

There was Scots influence in the family of the earls of Orkney from the 12c, but after the accession of the Lowland Scottish Sinclairs to the Earldom in 1379, and the pledging of Orkney and Shetland in 1468/9 by the King of Norway and Denmark to the King of Scots, the islands became dominated by Scots-speaking rulers, administrators, and clerics. From the 16c or earlier, Scots appears to have been the 'high' and Norn the 'low' language, and a probably common Scots attitude occurs in: 'Scho aundit in bitt, quhilk is ane Nourn terme and to [be] exponit into right longuag is alse mikill as scho did blaw her breath thairin' [Translation: She *aundit* [blew] into a *bitt* [bucket], which is a Norn term and to be expressed in proper language is as much as to say she blew her breath therein] (from *Orkney Witch Trial*, 1633, in *Register of the Privy Council of Scotland*, 2nd series, v. 545).

It has been conjectured that Norn was superseded by Scots in Caithness in the 15c and by Gaelic in the West Highlands and Islands in the 16c, but it appears to have endured to the later 18c in Orkney and perhaps into the 19c in Shetland. Garbled fragments (rhymes, proverbs, riddles, and snatches of songs) persisted in Orkney and especially Shetland folklore to the 20c (as late as 1958 on the island of Foula). The scanty earlier records reveal a language related to Faroese, but with a decaying inflectional system, as in this passage from the Lord's Prayer, as recorded by James Wallace in *Account of the Islands of Orkney* (1700): *Ga vus da on da dalight brow vora, firgive vus sinna vora, sin vee firgive sindara mutha vs* (Give us each day our daily bread, Forgive us our sins, as we forgive sins against us). The equivalent Old Norse was: *Gef oss dag um dag dagligt brauð vort, fyrirgef oss syndir várar, sem vér fyrirgef syndir i móti oss*. Local documents in Older Scots (from 1433) contain many administrative and legal terms of Norn origin, and court records (from the early 17c) introduce many originally Norn words, including: *galt* boar, *grind* gate, *heavie* straw basket, *row* to 'roo' or pluck (sheep), *spick* fat, blubber, *voe* inlet, *voir* springtime. Most of the 450 or so *noa* and other terms, constituting the former 'sea language' of Orkney and Shetland fishermen, are survivals of Norn. See FAROESE, NORSE, ORKNEY AND SHETLAND DIALECT, SCOTTISH PLACE-NAMES, SCANDINAVIAN LANGUAGES. [EUROPE, LANGUAGE].   A.J.A.

Barnes, Michael. 1984. 'Orkney and Shetland Norn', in P. Trudgill (ed.), *Language in the British Isles*. Cambridge: University Press.

Fenton, A. 1978. *The Northern Isles*, ch. 70: 'The Sea Language of Fishermen and the End of Norn'. Edinburgh: John Donald.

Jakobsen, Jakob. 1928/32. *An Etymological Dictionary of the Norn Language in Shetland*. London & Copenhagen: D. Nutt and V. Prior. (Reprinted 1985, Lerwick: Shetland Folk Society.)

Marwick, Hugh. 1929. *The Orkney Norn*. Oxford: University Press.

NORSE [16c: perhaps from Dutch *noorsch*, an obsolete variant of *noordsch* (modern *noords*) north. Compare Danish, Norwegian, Swedish *Norsk*]. Also *Old Norse*, *Scandinavian*, and (with particular reference to its use in England) *Danish*. The Scandinavian languages in an early, relatively homogeneous form. Old English and Old Norse were related to and to some extent mutually intelligible. Despite differences in grammar, communication appears to have been widespread, especially in the early Middle Ages when Danes settled in much of England and the country was ruled by Danish kings (1016-42). The numerous place-names in *-by*, *-thorp*, *-thwaite*, *-toft* testify to the density of the settlement known as the Danelaw. Many words were identical or similar in the two languages, such as *folk*, *hus*, *sorg* (sorrow), which were both English and Norse, and such correspondences as Old English *fæder*, *gærs/græs*, *wíf*, Old Norse *faðir*, *gras*, *víf* (father, grass, wife). Norse came to exercise a marked influence on English, especially when the Norman Conquest in the 11c broke the continuity of the Old English standard based on the West Saxon dialect. Norse influence has taken two forms: influence on English at large and influence on Northern English and Scots.

Influence on English at large. Much of the everyday vocabulary of English is of Norse origin: *call*, *cast*, *fellow*, *gape*, *happy*, *hit*, *husband*, *ill*, *leg*, *loose*, *low*, *sister*, *skill*, *skirt*, *sky*, *take*, *weak*, *window*, *wrong*. See BORROWING. Occasionally, both the English and the Norse form of the same word have survived as doublets: *shirt* (English), *skirt* (Norse). Norse borrowings include such legal and administrative terms as *hustings*, *law*, *bylaw*, *outlaw*, and *riding* (as in the North Riding of Yorkshire and as used in CanE for a parliamentary constituency), but the overwhelming majority of Norse words in English are general, everyday expressions, such as must have arisen from close social contact between the two peoples, an impression reinforced by the Norse origin of a number of English grammatical words: *they/their/them*, *though*, *both*. It is also possible that some syntactic structures common to Modern English and Scandinavian but unknown in other Germanic languages (such as *the house we live in*) had their origin in the Danelaw.

Influence on Northern English and Scots. A large number of Norse words which have not spread into English at large survive in the usage of northern England and Scotland: *gate* a street, *ken* to know (used in general English only in the phrase *beyond our ken*), *lake* to play, *neb* beak. Sometimes the Norse form is regional while a corresponding English form is standard: *garth/yard*, *kirn/churn*, *kist/chest*, *skell/shell*. In other cases of north-south doublets, both forms now belong to general English: *kirk/church, skirl/ shrill, screech/shriek.*

Conclusion. The extensive Norse settlements in the British Isles during the Viking age, followed by a long period of coexistence, have had a profound influence on English. Because of close kinship, Scandinavian influence is less immediately obvious than other foreign influences, yet it has altered basic vocabulary and grammar, and has permeated dialect usage even more than the standard language. In its origin and earliest form, English is classed with the West Germanic languages, a group which comprised the ancestors of Dutch, Frisian, and German, but a detailed comparison of the languages in their present form might place English nearer to the North Germanic group.

See ANGLO-DANISH, BORROWING, DANISH, ENGLISH PLACE-NAMES, IRELAND, IRISH, IRISH ENGLISH, IRISH PLACE-NAMES, NORMAN, NORN, NORTHERN ENGLISH, SCANDINAVIAN LANGUAGES, SCOTS, SCOTTISH PLACE-NAMES, WELSH PLACE-NAMES. [EUROPE, HISTORY, LANGUAGE]. P.C.

NORTH, The. (1) The northern part of a country: *Southern Italy is very different from the North.* The adjective is used contrastively with *South* in such national and regional names as *North Africa, North Korea, North Carolina (the United States), North Island (New Zealand).* (2) Also *the North Country.* The North of England, usually taken to include the traditional counties of Cumberland, Durham, Lancashire, Northumberland, Westmorland, and Yorkshire, and such cities as Leeds, Liverpool, Manchester, and Newcastle upon Tyne. (3) The North of Ireland, particularly Northern Ireland, a part of the UK, in contrast to the Irish Republic: *You're from the North, are you not?* (4) The area of the US to the north of the Ohio River, and especially the states that fought to maintain the Union in the Civil War (1861-5), usually also taken to include Maryland and Missouri. Compare SOUTH. See AMERICAN[1], CUMBRIA, DIALECT IN AMERICA, GEORDIE, LANCASHIRE, NORMAN, NORSE, NORTH AMERICAN, NORTH COUNTRY, NORTHERN ENGLISH, NORTHERN IRELAND, NORTHERNIZE, NORTHUMBRIA, SCOUSE, YANKEE, YORKSHIRE. [AMERICAS, EUROPE]. T.MCA.

NORTH AFRICA. See AFRICA, ARABIC.

NORTH AMERICAN. The adjective for North America and the name of a person born in North America, particularly the US and Canada. Canadians tend to use the term more than Americans, because it is inclusive and enables them to distinguish themselves from Americans: 'North Americans, when they read at all, prefer big, dumb, forgettable novels' (Crawford Kilian,

'Whatever Happened to Canadian Literature?', Toronto *Globe & Mail*, 24 Feb. 1990). Compare AMERICAN[1]. [AMERICAS, NAME]. T.MCA.

NORTH COUNTRY [13c: often capitalized and attributive]. (1) In general, the north of any country, but specifically England beyond the Humber: *a North Country story.* (2) The accent(s) and dialect(s) of the North of England: ' "If you borrow you make bad friends" — a flash of honest north country peeped through the trained accent' (C. Drummond, *Death at Bar*, 1972); '[The Lancashire singer] Gracie Fields reverts to the characteristic mixture of North Country, standard English and American overtones' (*The Times*, 30 Dec. 1974). See NORTHERN ENGLISH. Compare WEST COUNTRY. [EUROPE, NAME, VARIETY]. T.MCA.

NORTHERN. See DIALECT IN AMERICA, NORTH, NORTHERN ENGLISH.

NORTHERN ENGLISH. An occasional term for: (1) The Northumbrian dialect of Old English and its successor dialects in the North of England and in Scotland. (2) English as used in the North of England, sometimes extended to include Scots and ScoE. See CUMBRIA, DIALECT IN ENGLAND, GEORDIE, LANCASHIRE, LONG AND SHORT, L-SOUNDS, NORSE, NORTH COUNTRY, NORTHUMBRIA, SCOTS, SCOTTISH ENGLISH, SCOUSE, YORKSHIRE. [EUROPE, VARIETY]. T.MCA.

NORTHERN IRELAND. A part of the United Kingdom, consisting of the six north-easterly Irish counties Antrim, Armagh, Derry or Londonderry, Down, Fermanagh, and Tyrone. Northern Ireland in the geographical sense is usually referred to as *the North of Ireland* or *the North.* Paradoxically, Donegal, one of the most northerly counties in the island, is in the South: that is, it is part of the Irish Republic. See IRELAND, ULSTER, UNITED KINGDOM. [EUROPE, NAME]. T.MCA., L.T.

NORTHERN IRISH ENGLISH. English used in Northern Ireland, of which there are four varieties: (1) *Ulster Scots*, also known as *Scotch-Irish*, brought to the area in the 17c by Lowland Scots. It is the most northerly variety, found in Antrim, Down, Derry/Londonderry, and in eastern and central Donegal in the Irish Republic. (2) *Anglo-Irish* or *Ulster English*, introduced by 17c settlers from England. It stretches northward from Bundoran in the west to Dundalk in the east, has much in common with southern Anglo-Irish, and has been influenced by Ulster Scots. (3) *Hiberno-English*, influenced by Gaelic. It is most widely found in rural Armagh, Donegal, Fermanagh, and Tyrone. There is a further pocket in the Glens of Antrim, where Irish Gaelic was reinforced by Scottish Gaelic and survived into the 1940s. (4) The distinctive speech of Belfast. See ANGLO-IRISH, BELFAST, IRISH ENGLISH, L-SOUNDS, ULSTER ENGLISH, ULSTER SCOTS. [EUROPE, VARIETY].   L.T.

NORTHERN ISLES, The. The collective name for the island groups known as *Orkney* and *Shetland*. See NORN, ORKNEY AND SHETLAND DIALECT, SCOTLAND. [EUROPE, NAME].   T.MCA.

NORTHERNIZE AmE & BrE, **northernise** BrE & AusE [19c]. To make northern in respect of language, culture, character, etc.: '[George] Washington had, long previously to his death, . . . become perfectly Northernized' (*Charleston Mercury*, 21 June 1859). See NORTH. Compare SOUTHERNIZE. [VARIETY].   T.MCA.

NORTHUMBERLAND BURR. See BURR, R-SOUNDS.

NORTHUMBRIA [A Latinization of Old English *Northanhymbre* those north of the Humber]. A kingdom of the Angles before the unification of England, from the Humber to the Forth, formed through the union of *Bernicia* in the north and *Deira* in the south. In the 7c, especially under Edwin, its leadership was recognized by the other English kingdoms and its monasteries were in the forefront of European religious life. The Venerable Bede was a monk at Jarrow and the Lindisfarne Gospels demonstrate great skill in the illuminating of manuscripts. In the 9c the kingdom was overwhelmed by Danes and in the 10c the Scots (speakers of Gaelic) extended their border from the Forth to the Tweed, acquiring a province of speakers of Northumbrian English. In 944, when the last Danish king was expelled from York, Northumbria became an earldom of England. The Northumbrian dialect was ancestral to Northern English and Scots and is preserved in glosses on the Lindisfarne and other gospels, in manuscripts of Caedmon's *Hymn* and Bede's *Death Song* (8–9c), and in runic inscriptions (8–10c). See ANGLES, BEDE, GEORDIE, NORTHERN ENGLISH, RUNE, SCOTS. [EUROPE, HISTORY, NAME].   T.MCA.

NORTHUMBRIAN BURR. See BURR, R-SOUNDS.

NORWEGIAN [Called by its speakers *Norsk*]. The Germanic language of Norway. When differences began to appear in Old Norse (*c*.1000), the split was between *West Norse* in Iceland and Norway and *East Norse* in Denmark and Sweden. After the union with Denmark in 1387, written usage in Norway followed Danish,

and the speech of educated Norwegians became Danish with a local accent and Norwegianisms. The union was dissolved in 1814, there was for a time a looser union with Sweden, then in 1905 Norway became independent. The union with Denmark, however, has left a mark on the language of Norway. Throughout the 19c, most of the leading literary figures, including Henrik Ibsen, wrote in Danish with Norwegian features, and many had their books published in Copenhagen. They called their usage *Norwegian* (*Norsk*) or *Dano-Norwegian* (*Dansk-Norsk*).

Dano-Norwegian contrasts with a kind of Norwegian advocated from mid-19c by Ivar Aasen, a self-taught philologist and the son of a farmer, who had constructed a composite of various dialects that he called *Landsmaal* (country language). Speakers of Dano-Norwegian gave it a mixed reception, and a passage in Ibsen's *Peer Gynt* satirizes it as a 'primeval forest tongue'. Landsmaal, however, developed a literature and in 1885 was recognized as an official language to be taught in school alongside Dano-Norwegian, which came to be known as *Rigsmaal* (state language). Parents voted on the kind of Norwegian they wanted as their children's primary medium. The two terms, later spelt *Landsmål* and *Riksmål*, were replaced in 1929 by *Nynorsk* (Neo-Norwegian) and *Bokmål* (book language).

There have been three official language reforms, in 1907, 1917, and 1938, aimed primarily at bringing Bokmål closer to Nynorsk. Despite protests, the reforms have narrowed the gap, but differences remain and it is uncertain whether a *Samnorsk* (Pan-Norwegian) will develop. Since the Second World War, support for reform and for education in Nynorsk have declined, perhaps because of increased urbanization. Bokmål is the medium of most books and newspapers but lacks a firm standard. Educated Danes and Norwegians communicate with ease in speech and writing, but whereas before 1907 there was a common reading public, a novel or play in one country must now be 'translated' to succeed in the other. Compare FRISIAN, SCOTS. See BORROWING, NORN, NORSE, SCANDINAVIAN LANGUAGES, SPELLING REFORM. [EUROPE, LANGUAGE].   P.C.

NOTATION [16c: from Latin *notatio/notationis* a marking]. (1) Obsolete, but common in the 17c: the explanation of a word in terms of its actual or supposed etymology; the etymological or primary use of a word; its etymon. (2) Rare: the act or result of taking written notes. (3) A process or system of representing something audible or abstract by means of graphic symbols, such as *musical notation*, *phonetic notation*, or *mathematical notation*. See ETYMON, NOTE, NOTES AND

REFERENCES, PHONETIC TRANSCRIPTION, TRANSCRIPTION, TRANSLITERATION. [WRITING]. T.MCA.

NOTE [12c: through Old French from Latin *nota* a means of recognition, mark, sign]. (1) A graphic sign: *a musical note*. (2) A single tone of definite pitch, produced especially by a musical instrument, a bird, or a human voice when singing: *a musical note*. (3) A token of emotion, alarm, etc.: *sounding a note of caution*; *a note of reproach in one's voice*. (4) Importance: *a writer of note*. (5) A written record, usually brief and to the point: *to keep a note of what one spends*. A book used for such purposes is a *notebook* or a *notepad*; both words have been adopted as generic terms for small portable computers that can be used, among other things, for notetaking. (6) In the plural: a more or less informal memorandum or record, in greater or less detail, for any purpose, such as the written prompts used by someone giving a lecture or talk and the record kept of such a lecture by a listener (both called *lecture notes*). (7) A point to remember: *to make a mental note*; *taking note of what was needed*. (8) A comment added to a text, especially in a margin (*a marginal note*), or provided formally with a text (*scholarly notes*), especially as background or associated information, such as the name, etc., of an authority quoted or of a work cited. A work to which detailed notes have been added (especially in the margin) contains *annotations*, a point to which its title may refer: for example, *The Annotated Dickens* (Orbis, two volumes, 1986). (9) A brief statement that provides information in a concise form (such as a *usage note* in a dictionary), often one of several in a list (such as *study notes*). (10) In library science, an additional item of information included in a catalogue entry about a work, such as the series to which it belongs. (11) A short, informal letter: *a thank-you note*. See CONTRACTION, GLOSS, MARGIN, NOTES AND REFERENCES, USAGE GUIDANCE AND CRITICISM. [WRITING]. T.MCA.

NOTES AND REFERENCES. Additions to works of scholarship and science such as supplementary points of information and details of the sources to which writers have referred. There is no sharp distinction between the two categories: notes can consist of or contain references, and references may be annotated. Notes, however, are often more substantial than references (for example, in monographs), and tend to be either *footnotes* (at the bottom of a page) or *endnotes* (at the end of a chapter or entire work). *Sidenotes*, set in a margin, also sometimes occur. Scholarly notes are usually signalled by superscript numbers at appropriate points in a text, but such symbols as asterisks and obelisks

may be used instead for footnotes. References, on the other hand, tend to be listed in appendices whose titles and locations are usually given on the contents page of the work in question. The advantage of footnotes to the reader is ease of reference; the disadvantage to both reader and typesetter is that long notes are likely to run over to the lower part of the next page. The advantage of endnotes, especially for the printer and publisher, is that they are all arranged sequentially in one place, regardless of the length of individual notes. The disadvantage for the reader is that they are at a distance from the various parts of the text to which they relate, but this disadvantage may be lessened if the notes are so organized as to provide a linked set of supporting comments on the text. For texts which authors and publishers wish to keep free of superscript symbols, endnotes are keyed to such points of reference as page numbers or repeat identifying phrases from the text. All such addenda are generally kept as brief as possible, but endnotes can sometimes be in effect supplementary essays. Endnotes, bibliographies, lists of works referred to, and the like, are usually set in a smaller type-size than the main text. Footnotes, the compactness of which is especially desirable, may be set even smaller, several sizes down from the text type. Generally, the bulk of any set of notes and references is taken up by citations of the authors, titles, dates, etc., of publications. These may be presented in either of two ways: in note form, often in a *reference list*, such as 'See K. Wales, *A Dictionary of Stylistics*, 1989'; or in bibliographical form, such as 'Wales, K. 1989. *A Dictionary of Stylistics*. Harlow: Longman'. To save space, but also as a legacy from the days when Latin was the language of pan-European scholarship, authors and editors have tended to use, in texts and notes, Latin terms of reference, usually in abbreviated form and often printed in italic. The most common traditional usages are:

c., ca. Short for *circa* 'around': indicating an approximate date or figure, as in 'Chaucer was born *c.*1340' and '*c.*3m' (for 'around three million').

cf. Short for *confer* 'compare': inviting the reader to compare an entry, topic, or work with one or more others, as in '*cf.* Havelock, *Preface to Plato*', '*cf.* analogy, metaphor, simile'.

e.g. Short for *exempli gratia* 'for the sake of example': preceding an example of the point being discussed.

et al. Short for *et alii* (masculine), *et aliae* (feminine), *et alia* (neuter), 'and others': coming after the first of a list of names whose other elements the writer does not wish to provide or repeat: 'R. Quirk *et al.*, *A Comprehensive Grammar of the English Language.*'

etc. Short for *et cetera* 'and so on': used widely, both formally and casually, for more of the same: 'books, magazines, newspapers, etc.'

fl. Short for *floruit* 'flourished': indicating the period in which someone lived, usually because actual life dates are not known: 'Gautama the Buddha, *fl.* 6th century BC'.

ibid. Short for *ibidem* 'in the same place': referring the reader to a publication mentioned in an immediately preceding note: *Ibid.* p. 330.

id., ead. Short for *idem* 'the same man', *eadem* 'the same woman': used after the first reference in notes that have more than one reference to works by the same author, to save repeating the author's name.

i.e. Short for *id est* 'that is': used in running text to gloss or clarify a statement just made: '. . . the work of an *ovate*, i.e. a minor druid'.

loc. cit., l.c. Short for *loco citato* 'in the place cited': used in notes to indicate a passage already cited: 'Urdang, *loc. cit.*'

NB or N.B. Short for *nota bene* 'note well': used to call attention to something the writer considers important.: *NB* difficulties in dating such texts'.

op. cit. Short for *opere citato* 'in the work cited': used in notes to indicate reference to a publication already cited: 'Urdang, *op. cit.*, p. 18'.

passim 'here and there': used to inform the reader that the topic under discussion is treated in various parts of a cited publication: 'Chap. 5, *passim*' (that is, throughout Chapter 5), 'Chap. 5 *et passim*' (throughout Chapter 5 and elsewhere).

q.v. Short for *quod vide* 'which see': once a common device to indicate in passing that something is treated fully elsewhere, in its proper place: 'In 1792, the Jacobins under Georges Danton (*q.v.*) seized power' (that is, see the entry *Danton*). Plural *qq.v.*

sc., scil., scilicet. Adaptations of *scire licet* 'it is permitted to know' (understood as 'namely'): a reference in apposition that identifies a person or thing, as in 'Superman, *scil.* Clark Kent.'

sic 'thus': used parenthetically by writers and editors, especially in square brackets, to distance themselves from a dubious or erroneous usage, but also sometimes to draw attention to it, perhaps highlighting it in order to mock it: '. . . but they did not recieve [*sic*] the letter'.

s.v. Short for *sub verbo* or *sub voce* 'under the word/heading', 'under that word/heading': used in references to indicate the entry for a specified word in a dictionary, etc., as in 'see *OED* s.v. *camel*' or 'for the etymology of *camel*, see *OED* s.v.' Plural *s.vv.*

ut 'as': used in *ut infra* (as cited below) and *ut supra* (as cited above), to indicate that something has been or will be mentioned, discussed, etc.

vide, vid., v. 'see': used as a cross-reference, as in '*vide* hematite', and in running text to draw the reader's attention to a passage the writer considers relevant: referring to something preceding (*vide supra* see above, *vide ante* see before) or to something following (*vide infra* see below, *vide post* see after).

viz. Short for *videlicet* 'it is permitted to see' (understood as 'namely', 'to wit'): a reference in apposition that specifies examples or identifies a person or thing, as in 'The Magi, *viz.* Melchior, Caspar, and Balthazar'.

The organization and presentation of notes and references are discussed in: *Hart's Rules* (Oxford University Press, 1983); *The Chicago Manual of Style* (Chicago University Press, 1982); *The McGraw-Hill Style Manual* (1989); *The Canadian Writer's Handbook* (Prentice-Hall of Canada, 1980); *The Canadian Style* (Department of the Secretary of State, 1985); *Style Manual* (Australian Government Publishing Service). See ACADEMIC USAGE, APPENDIX, ASTERISK, BACK MATTER, BIBLIOGRAPHY, NOTE. [REFERENCE, WRITING]. T.MCA.

NOTIONAL–FUNCTIONAL APPROACH.

See COUNCIL OF EUROPE, LANGUAGE TEACHING.

NOUN

[14c: from Anglo-Norman *noun*, Old French *nun, num*, from Latin *nomen* name, translating Greek *ónoma*]. A part of speech or word class typically used in a variety of sentence functions such as subject and object, generally in combination with the definite or indefinite article and modifiers and traditionally regarded as 'naming' or identifying persons and things.

Form. In English, many especially monosyllabic nouns cannot formally be identified as such (*woman, girl, dog, cat, king, war*), whereas in some languages, such as Latin, they have distinctive endings (*femina, puella; canis, faelis; bellum*). Many polysyllabic nouns, however, are identifiable by suffixes used to derive nouns from other nouns or from verbs and adjectives: *-ing* (*farming, swimming*); *-er* (*dancer, writer*); *-ation* (*association, organization*); *-ity* (*morality, reality*); *-ness* (*darkness, kindness*); *-ism* (*humanism, racism*), *-ist* (*rationalist, socialist*).

Function. In a noun phrase, a noun functions as the main or only word which can be subject ('The *crew* boarded the vessel'), direct object ('They will clean up the *waste*'), indirect object ('I told the committee my *views*'), subject complement ('One fascinating discovery was a *musket*'), object complement ('Everybody thought her the best *candidate*'), adverbial ('We saw them last *night*'), complement of a preposition ('We did it for *Tony*'); modifier of another noun ('*income tax*').

Subclasses. There are a number of grammatical and semantic subclasses of nouns: common or proper (*Jane, Jeremy*); animate (*child*) or inanimate (*pencil*); abstract (*opinion*) or concrete (*glass*), countable (*student*) or uncountable (*information*). In the sentence *Pick up the book*, the noun *book* is common, inanimate, concrete, and countable. In the sentence *Barbara came too*, the noun *Barbara* is proper, animate, concrete, and in this instance uncountable. A noun may have one feature in one context and the opposite feature in another: *glass* is countable in *Have another glass of orange juice*, uncountable in *That dish is made of cut glass*.

Number. Countable nouns make a distinction between singular and plural in number. The distinction is generally indicated by a difference between singular and plural forms (*cat/cats, sample/samples, phenomenon/phenomena*).

Gender. English does not have gender classes of nouns as in Latin and German, but some nouns have male and female reference: *father, boy; mother, girl*. There are some pairs of nouns one of which has a suffix marking a male/female contrast: *host/hostess, hero/heroine, usher/usherette; widow/widower*). The gender reference of human nouns becomes manifest when *he* or *she* relates to the noun: *My neighbour said she/he wanted to speak to you*. Non-human animate nouns (and nouns relating to young children, depending on the circumstances) allow male, female, or non-sexual reference: *Don't touch the dog; he/she/it has fleas*.

Case. Old English had, like Latin, a complex case system for its nouns. Modern English, however, only makes two case distinctions: common case (*Tom*) and genitive case (*Tom's*). For regular plurals, the distinction is found only in punctuation, but not in pronunciation: *students/students'* (contrast *men* and *men's*).

See ABSTRACT AND CONCRETE, ANIMATE NOUN, CASE[1], COMMON NOUN, COUNTABLE AND UNCOUNTABLE, GENDER, NAME, NUMBER, OLD ENGLISH[1], PART OF SPEECH, PROPER NOUN, SUBSTANTIVE. [GRAMMAR].   S.G.

NOUN CLAUSE. See RELATIVE CLAUSE.

NOUN-INCORPORATION [Mid-20c]. A term in word-formation for the creation of a compound in which a noun is incorporated into a verb as its first element: *baby-sit, house-hunt, sleep-walk*. Such forms go back at least to the Middle Ages, as with *backbite* (*c.*1300) to bite someone on or behind the back. They are often nonce or stunt usages, sometimes with a touch of humour: *backseat-drive, ballroom-dance*. They generally have two sources: (1) Back-formation: *eavesdrop* from *eavesdropper*; *kidnap* from *kidnapper*; *mass-produce* from *mass production*; *window-shop* from *window-shopping*. (2) The conversion of a noun-noun compound to use as a verb: *fingerprint*, as in *fingerprinting suspects*; *scent-mark*, as in: 'How often a cat scent-marks varies according to how old it is' (*BBC WildLife*, Jan. 1989). See WORD-FORMATION. [GRAMMAR, WORD].   T.MCA.

NOVEL [16c: from Italian *novella* (*storia*) a little new (story). In the 14c, collections of stories in Italian and French, such as Boccaccio's *Decameron*, were known as novels. In the 17c, the term generally referred to romances of illicit love, and in the 18c, *history* was used for the long prose works (often in several volumes) that led to the modern novel in English]. A work of prose fiction, usually 30,000 to 100,000 words in length. The genre is recent compared with poetry and drama, but has antecedents in narrative verse and in the tales of every age and culture. Its connections with the *romance* are reflected in *roman*, the name for the genre in several European languages. The rise of the novel appears to owe much to the printing press and an increasing number of literate middle-class people (15–18c) with the time and money to devote to works of fiction.

Kinds of novel. The novel has tended to be realistic and to reflect contemporary life, with characters and concerns essentially of the urban middle class. However, the range of works that can be called novels is wide and no definition can cover them all. Some of these are, in rough order of their emergence: (1) The *picaresque novel*, relating in episodic form the adventures of an eccentric or disreputable hero: Cervantes's *Don Quixote* (1605), Smollett's *Roderick Random* (1748). (2) The *epistolary novel*, in which the story progresses in the form of letters and journals/diaries, popularizing the first-person style of narration: Richardson's *Pamela* (1741). (3) The *historical novel*, set in a period earlier than that of writing: Scott's *Waverley* (1814), whose action occurs in the Jacobite Rebellion of 1745. (4) The *regional novel*, set against the background of a particular area: Scott's *Rob Roy* (1817); Hardy's Wessex novels (1870s onward). (5) The *Bildungsroman* [German: novel of growth], the novel of development from childhood, a fictional autobiography: Dickens's *Great Expectations* (1861). (6) The *roman à thèse* [French: novel with an argument], the novel of social or political concern that emphasizes realism and seeks to influence changes in society:

Upton Sinclair's *The Jungle* (1906). (7) The *roman à clef* [French: novel with a key], in which the events are imaginary and real people are disguised as fictional characters: Aldous Huxley's *Point Counter Point* (1928). (8) The *roman-fleuve* [French: stream novel], in which a common theme or range of characters stretches across a number of novels: Anthony Powell's *A Dance to the Music of Time* (1951-75). Compare SAGA. (9) The *non-fiction novel*, in which living people and recent events are presented in the form of a story: Truman Capote's *In Cold Blood* (1979); Norman Mailer's *The Executioner's Story* (1965).

Style in the novel. The point of view of a story may be aided by *narrative voice*: a story can be told in the first person, in letters between characters, or by a detached narrator, *the third-person omniscient*. Unlike the theatre, encounter with the novel is usually solitary and silent, although reading aloud from novels was popular in the 19c. Apart from the linguistic experiments of a few 20c novelists like James Joyce, it is generally written in the accessible language of common usage, but more discursively than the tighter patterns of poetry and drama permit. Dialogue seeks to resemble real conversation and draws on all areas of the language, using dialects and registers as appropriate. The new style of post-Renaissance English prose, drawing on native patterns of the language, was better suited to telling a connected story than the attempts of earlier writers such as Lyly in *Euphues* (1578-80) to create an elaborate style with the classical periodic sentence and forms of rhetoric like extended similes.

The English novel. Antecedents of the novel include 16c romantic prose narratives such as Robert Greene's *Pandosto* (1588) and Thomas Lodge's *Rosalynde* (1590), and such tales of low life as Thomas Nashe's *The Unfortunate Traveller* (1594). 'Proto-novels' written after the Restoration by Aphra Behn, John Bunyan, and Daniel Defoe have a story rather than a plot, and relate a sequence of events with little change in the central characters. The novel proper begins in the 18c with Samuel Richardson, whose work was attractive to a middle class with increasing leisure and a relatively firm moral code. The rules of virtue rewarded and social morality upheld were largely accepted by novelists until the late 19c. They were partly contested by Henry Fielding, who praised honesty and generosity above forced obedience, and established the omniscient narrator who frequently comments on the action. Tobias Smollett developed the picaresque tradition, exploiting the humour and excitement of the less reputable section of society. He caught the tones

of uneducated speech, sometimes by deviant spellings. Laurence Sterne's *Tristram Shandy* (1759-67) has tricks of thought-representation and internal reference to the novel as a fiction which anticipate 20c developments.

The nineteenth century: Britain. The developing novel attracted many writers but there were few major novelists in the period between 1770 and 1830; in the Romantic revival, poetry was the dominant genre. Romantic interest in medievalism and in the supernatural combined to make the sensational Gothic type popular in fiction. Walter Scott raised the status of the more serious novel. He built up the tradition of the historical novel in a regional setting, often using dialect, especially in Scots, for the speech of his characters. Jane Austen observed upper-class society with irony and compassion; her conversations may seem formal to modern readers but they convey the feelings of real life. The Victorian period, however, was the great age of the novel in Britain, when writers benefited from growing literacy, cheaper production and distribution, and circulating libraries. Their strongly drawn characters and turbulent plots owe much to these libraries and to publication in serial form. In the early part of the 19c, the novel was often attacked as immoral, time-wasting, and creating falsehood, but gradually it came to be seen as a serious social and moral force. Charles Dickens wrote about the ills of society, but was above all an entertainer, mingling humour and pathos in narrative and dialogue with an ear for the comic potential of Cockney speech.

W. M. Thackeray had a different line of social comment in *Vanity Fair* (1847) and *Pendennis* (1848-50), satirizing the brittleness and insincerity in contemporary life. The Brontë sisters mingled realism and fantasy in novels that owed much to inspiration from Romantic and Gothic sources, but also expressed women's experience and frustrations. Like Elizabeth Gaskell in *Sylvia's Lovers* (1863), they followed Scott in using dialect for serious as well as comic speech. Still greater realism developed by the middle of the 19c. Anthony Trollope took a less sentimental view of the world than many predecessors in the Barsetshire novels of county life (1855-67), the Palliser novels of politics (1864-80), and in the broader social criticism of *The Way We Live Now* (1875). Realism mingled with sensation and crime in the novels of Wilkie Collins (*The Woman in White*, 1860) and Charles Reade (*Griffith Gaunt*, 1866). Naturalism never grew as strong in Britain as in France, but had a part in tales of urban poverty by George Gissing (*New Grub Street*, 1891) and George Moore (*A Mummer's Wife*, 1885), with scenes and dialogue that shocked many contemporaries. George Eliot (Mary Ann Evans) took up the challenges of new intellectual and religious movements, showing the nexus of human consequences in *Adam Bede* (1859) and *Middlemarch* (1871-2). The disquiet aroused by scientific and evolutionary discoveries influenced the work of George Meredith in *Beauchamp's Career* (1874-5) and Thomas Hardy, notably in *Tess of the D'Urbervilles* (1891) and *Jude the Obscure* (1896). The novel in 19c Britain gradually moved from simple representation to the use of imagery, symbolic themes, and different authorial stances: Samuel Butler used a detached first-person narrator for social criticism in *The Way of All Flesh* (1903) and Oscar Wilde combined witty dialogue with supernatural evil in *The Picture of Dorian Gray* (1890).

The nineteenth century: the United States. The American novel was established by the beginning of the 19c with the Gothic fiction of Charles Brockden Brown, including *Wieland* (1798) and *Edgar Huntley* (1799). An original tradition emerged with James Fenimore Cooper who, influenced by Scott, wrote of the expanding nation and contacts with the Indians. He produced over thirty novels, including *The Last of the Mohicans* (1826) and *The Deerslayer* (1841). Nathaniel Hawthorne wrote a different type of fiction; his *The Scarlet Letter* (1850) and *The House of the Seven Gables* (1851) are rich in symbolism and use narratives of ordinary life to allegorize contemporary attitudes and behaviour. Herman Melville, who admired Hawthorne's work, continued the allegorical approach in *Moby-Dick* (1851), sometimes seen as the archetype of the modern American novel in its sense of quest and wide horizons. However, the first linguistic break with British tradition was made by Mark Twain's *Tom Sawyer* (1876) and *Huckleberry Finn* (1884). Previous writers had generally followed the British literary pattern, but Twain used the forms and cadences of the American South and proved that North American English could provide its own literary idiom.

The twentieth century. The early 20c novel was influenced by new social attitudes and psychological insights. Henry James showed transition from the old to the new, particularly through the experiences of Americans in Europe. In Britain, D. H. Lawrence broke the Victorian taboo on depicting sexual relationships and advocated a new freedom and honesty in *Women in Love* (1920) and *Lady Chatterley's Lover* (1928). Closer attention to thought and motivation became characteristic of the novel, particularly through the technique known as *stream of consciousness*. Virginia Woolf used it in *Mrs Dalloway* (1925) and *The Waves* (1931), and James Joyce followed the free flow of characters' thoughts in *Ulysses* (1922) and dreams in *Finnegans Wake* (1939). In other respects there has been less technical innovation in prose fiction than in poetry. E. M. Forster wrote traditionally and with acute observation, in *Howards End* (1910) and *A Passage to India* (1924). In the US, the 20c brought revolt against what seemed the inhibiting restraints of the immediate past. Theodore Dreiser wrote with powerful and frank realism in *An American Tragedy* (1925), influencing the next generation of social realists like John Steinbeck, author of *Grapes of Wrath* (1939). A more restrained but incisive satirist of social limitations was Sinclair Lewis in *Babbitt* (1922). He received the Nobel Prize for Literature in 1930, the first American to do so. Ernest Hemingway's macho tales of adventure, such as *A Farewell to Arms* (1929) and *For Whom the Bell Tolls* (1940), won wide popularity. More recent tensions and achievements in American life are depicted by Saul Bellow (b.1915) and Norman Mailer (b.1923).

Science and fantasy. The growth of science inspired both popular science fiction and the scientific romances of H. G. Wells, such as *The Time Machine* (1895) and *The First Men on the Moon* (1901). Dystopian literature has included Aldous Huxley's *Brave New World* (1932) and George Orwell's *Nineteen Eighty-Four* (1949). Since 1945, darker visions of uncertainty and anxiety include William Golding's *Lord of the Flies* (1954), Iris Murdoch's *The Time of the Angels* (1968), and John Fowles's *The Magus* (1966). Although Orwell's dystopia discusses a new kind of English, Newspeak, the narrative language makes little use of it and follows traditional standard English, in contrast to the creation of a new futuristic kind of slang used by the narrator of Anthony Burgess's *A Clockwork Orange* (1962).

The English novel at large. From the 18c, the novel has gone with the language into all parts of the world. The literary and popular novels of the UK and US continue to dominate, but those of Australia, Canada, Ireland, and New Zealand are gaining international ground, followed by Black Africa, the Caribbean, the Indian subcontinent, and parts of Asia. Some of these newer traditions have roots in the 19c, others have begun in the 20c. For example, early Australian novels include Marcus Clarke's account of the convict settlements in *For the Term of his Natural Life* (1874), and the pioneers of the English novel in Canada were Thomas Haliburton (*The Clockmaker*, 1836) and John Richardson (*Wacousta*, 1832). In South Africa, the foremost 19c novelist in English was Olive Schreiner, whose *Story of an African Farm* (1883) includes a radical affirmation of feminism. In India, R. K. Narayan has created the town of Malgudi as the setting for such novels as *The English Teacher* (1945). West Indian novelists have written about life in both the Caribbean and England, including V. S. Naipaul's *Of Trees and the Sea* (1956) and E. Brathwaite's *To Sir with Love* (1959). In Nigeria, Amos Tutuola has used allegory in *The Palm-Wine Drinkard* (1952) and Chinua Achebe has written of the conflict of cultures and traditions in *Things Fall Apart* (1958). New Zealand novelists include Sylvia Ashton Warner (*Spinster*, 1958), Ruth Park (*Harp in the South*, 1948), and Janet Frame (*Owls Do Cry*, 1957). Although in the UK and US doubts are still expressed about the claims of certain territories to their own varieties of English, the success of novel-writing in those languages has greatly contributed to affirming their status.

Conclusion. Of all the genres, the novel appears to have covered the widest range of tastes and interests. Joyce and Woolf may be considered of high literary merit but be little read. For those who seek mainly entertainment or to pass the time on a journey, there is a stream of books whose authors find no place in mainstream critical studies of fiction. The line between the 'literary' and the 'popular' is not, however, always easily drawn. Dickens has delighted generations and his critical reputation has continued to grow; detective fiction is generally considered ephemeral, but the Sherlock Holmes stories of Sir Arthur Conan Doyle have become classics. The James Bond novels by Ian Fleming, such as *Doctor No* (1962) and *From Russia with Love* (1963), have all the ingredients of suspense, sex, and violence associated with the 'thriller', but have also been esteemed for their wit and elegant style and have received critical consideration. Graham Greene is treated as a serious novelist despite the fact that works like *Brighton Rock* (1938) and *Our Man in Havana* (1958) have much in common with the thriller. The ready transfer of both literary and popular novels to cinema and television, as single productions and as series, indicates qualities in the genre that do not depend, and never have depended, on academic approval.

See AFRICAN LITERATURE IN ENGLISH, AMERICAN LITERATURE, AUSTRALIAN LITERATURE, CANADIAN LITERATURE IN ENGLISH, CARIBBEAN LITERATURE IN ENGLISH, DETECTIVE STORY, ENGLISH LITERATURE, EUPHUISM, FANTASY, FICTION, FILIPINO LITERATURE IN ENGLISH, GENRE, GRAPHIC NOVEL, LYLY, NARRATIVE, NEW ZEALAND LITERATURE, NOVELETTE, NOVELIZATION, NOVELLA, POPULAR FICTION, SCIENCE FICTION, SHORT STORY, SOUTH AFRICAN LITERATURE IN ENGLISH, STORY, VOICE. [AFRICA, AMERICAS, ASIA, EUROPE, LITERATURE, WRITING]. R.C.

Allen, Walter. 1958. *The English Novel*. Harmondsworth: Penguin.
Bergonzi, Bernard. 1979. *The Situation of the Novel*. London: Macmillan.
Burgess, Anthony. 1967. *The Novel Now*. London: Faber.
Hawthorn, Jeremy. 1985. *Studying the Novel*. London: Arnold.
Kettle, Arnold. 1951-3. *An Introduction to the English Novel*. London: Hutchinson.
Lodge, David. 1966. *Language of Fiction*. London: Routledge.
Stevenson, Lionel. 1960. *The English Novel*. London: Constable.
Watt, Ian. 1963. *The Rise of the Novel*. Harmondsworth: Penguin.

NOVELETTE. See NOVELLA.

NOVELIZATION [1870s]. The conversion of a play, motion picture, or television film into a novel for sale to the general public. See NOVEL. [LITERATURE]. T.MCA.

NOVELLA [16c: from Italian *novella* a little new thing]. Originally applied to short narratives, such as the stories in Boccaccio's *Decameron* (1349-51), the term now refers to a work of prose fiction between the short story and the novel (around 12,000 to 30,000 words). Examples in English include Henry James's *The Turn of the Screw* (1898) and Joseph Conrad's *Heart of Darkness* (1902). The terms *long short story* and *short novel* are also used for literary works, while *novelette* usually describes a popular love story. See NOVEL, SHORT STORY. [LITERATURE]. R.C.

NUCLEAR ENGLISH. See NUCLEUS.

NUCLEUS [17c: from Latin *nucleus*, originally *nuculeus* ('little nut') a kernel]. (1) A part around which other parts are gathered; a core or kernel. The term *Nuclear English* has been used in recent years for a proposed 'core' language consisting of elements from natural English; in it, for example, such potentially ambiguous modal verbs as *can* and *may* would be replaced as appropriate by such paraphrases as *be able to* and *be allowed to*. Nuclear English would serve as the basis for purpose-built 'restricted' international varieties comparable to Seaspeak, the medium of worldwide maritime communication. (2) In phonetics, the central, most prominent part of a syllable, consisting of a vowel or vowel-like consonant, such as the [a] sound in *bat* or the [l] sound in *battled*. (3) In phonetics, the syllable that carries the tone change; the tonic syllable. See SYLLABLE, TONE. [SPEECH].   T.MCA.

NUMBER[1] [13c: from Old French *nombre*, Latin *numerus*]. A concept associated with quantity, size, measurement, etc., and represented by a word such as *three*, a symbol such as *3*, a group of words such as *eighty-three point five*, or a group of symbols such as *83.5*. Every number, regardless of the language in which it is expressed, occupies a unique position in a series, such as *3* in the series *1, 2, 3, 4, 5, . . .*, enabling it to be used in such arithmetical processes as addition, subtraction, multiplication, and division. There are two basic kinds of number in such languages as English and French: *cardinal numbers* (the term deriving ultimately from Latin *cardo/cardinis* a hinge: that is, something on which other things turn or depend), denoting quantity and not order (as in *1, 2, 3, 4*); and *ordinal numbers* (the term deriving ultimately from Latin *ordo/ordinis* order), denoting relative position in a sequence (as in *1st, 2nd, 3rd, 4th*). Grammatically, the number system of a language contrasts with its system of quantifiers: for example, *one house* with *a house*, and *two/three/forty people*, etc., with *some people*, *several people*, and *many people*, etc.

Numbers as words. A spoken number is a word or phrase in a language, but a written number may be realized as either a word or phrase or a symbol or groups of symbols, usually a *figure* such as *1, 2, 12, 21*. Written words are generally used for low numbers, from *one* to *ten* or *twelve* (as in the phrases *three blind mice*, *the seven wonders of the world*, and *the twelve signs of the Zodiac*). They are also often used for numbers up to *100* (with hyphenation for compound forms such as *twenty-one* and *eighty-three*) and for large round figures as in *a thousand years* and *four million visitors a year*. Words may or may not be used to express percentages, which may be given as *ten per cent*, *10 per cent*, or *10%*, depending on house style or personal preference. Most house styles and editors aim for consistency in whichever forms they have chosen.

Numbers as symbols. Arabic figures are commonly used for numbers above *ten* or *twelve* (as in *The ship sank with the loss of 18 lives*), before abbreviations (as in *8 pm* for *eight o'clock in the evening*, *7K* for *seven thousand*, and *3m* for *three million*), and for dates, addresses, and exact sums of money. Large numbers such as *118,985* are usually given as figures; when spoken, there is one significant difference between British and American usage: BrE always has *and* after *hundred*, as in *one hundred and eighteen thousand*,

nine hundred and eighty-five, while AmE generally does not, as in *one hundred eighteen thousand, nine hundred eighty-five*. In large numbers, commas are generally used after the figures representing millions and thousands (*1,345,905*), but spaces are also, perhaps increasingly, used for this purpose (*1 345 905*); commas or spaces may or may not be used for thousands alone (*2,345* and *2 345*), for which solid numbers are also common (*2345*). Telephone numbers are generally written with spaces between regional and local numbers (*0223 245999*), and reference numbers are generally solid (*N707096*). Plural *s* after a set of numbers is often preceded by an apostrophe, as in *3's and 4's* or *the 1980's*, but many house styles and individuals now favour *3s and 4s* and *the 1980s*.

Numbers in -illion. Formerly, BrE and AmE differed greatly in their use of numbers representing multiples of *million*: for example, in Britain, France, and Germany, *billion* was 'one million million', or 10^{12} (10 to the power 12), while in the US and Canada it was 'one thousand million' or 10^9. The North American equivalent to the British *billion* was the *trillion*. In the last decades of the 20c, however, the North American use has become universal, providing the set *million, billion, trillion, quadrillion, quintillion, sextillion, septillion, octillion, nonillion, decillion*. Generally, the higher numbers are little used or known, but ever-growing budgets coupled with inflation have in recent years brought *trillion* into increasingly common currency. Although, by and large, numbers in English leave little room for poetry or fantasy, the *-illion* pattern has prompted some word-play, especially in AmE, that makes use of various initial consonants and syllables: 'The savings-and-loan industry bailout, which as of yesterday afternoon was expected to cost taxpayers $752.6 trillion skillion, is now expected to cost $964.3 hillion jillion bazillion' (Dave Barry, 'Give or Take a Whomptillion', *International Herald Tribune*, 13 June 1990). The widely-used *zillion*, with its end-of-alphabet prefix, usually suggests the ultimate in facetious scale, but Barry's *ba-* adds even more force. See ALPHANUMERIC, COMPUTING, DATE, LETTER[1], NUMBER[2], QUANTIFIER, ROMAN NUMERAL, TECHNOSPEAK. [WORD].   T.MCA.

NUMBER[2] [13c: see preceding]. A grammatical category used in describing parts of speech that show contrasts of *plural, singular, dual*, etc. In English, the number system is basically a two-term contrast of singular and plural, shown in nouns and some pronouns and determiners, and to some extent in verbs. Even dual words, such as *both, either, neither*, take singular or plural verb concord: *both* taking the plural; *either*, *neither* usually taking the singular. English nouns, as far as number is concerned, can be divided into: singular only, plural only, and words that can be both. Singular-only nouns are: (1) Uncountable nouns which can occur with such uncountable-specific words as *much*, *little*: *much money*, *little sugar*. (2) Most proper nouns: *Edinburgh*, *the Thames* (in which other restrictions apply). Plural-only nouns are: (1) Countable: *people* in *six people*, but not in *the European peoples*. (2) Usually uncountable: *not enough clothes* (not **six clothes*); *many thanks* (not **five thanks*); *trousers* (*a pair of trousers* and not usually *three trousers*). The vast majority of countable nouns can be both singular and plural (*book/books*, *fox/foxes*, *mouse/mice*), but a few have no distinct plural form (as with *one sheep/three sheep*). Many nouns, however, have both countable and uncountable uses, in which case they may have a plural in some uses (*What an excellent wine/What excellent wines!*) but not in others (*I never drink wine*). Pronouns having distinct singular and plural forms include *personal*, *reflexive*, and *possessive*. Number contrast is neutralized with *you*, but the second-person reflexive forms distinguish *yourself* and *yourselves*. *Demonstrative* pronouns also have separate forms, singular *this*, *that* being used both with singular countable nouns (*this restaurant*) and with uncountable nouns (*this food*). Number contrast in verbs, except in the verb *be*, is confined to the distinct third-person singular tense form (*look/looks*). See CONCORD, NUMBER[1], PARTITIVE, PLURAL, PRONOUN, QUANTIFIER, SINGULAR. [GRAMMAR]. S.C.

NUMERAL [16c: from Latin *numeralis* relating to a number or numbers, from *numerus* a number]. A word or symbol, or a group of words or symbols, that represents a number. The two systems used for numbers in English are *arabic numerals* (ultimately of Indian origin), the major system, and *roman numerals*, the minor system. See NUMBER[1], ROMAN NUMERAL. [WORD]. T.MCA.

NUYORICAN. See NEW YORRICAN.

O

O, o [Called 'oh']. The 15th letter of the Roman alphabet as used for English. It originated as the Phoenician consonant symbol *ain*, representing a pharyngeal plosive (or 'glottal catch'). It had a roughly circular form and meant 'eye'. The Greeks adopted it as a vowel symbol, at first for both long and short values. Later, a letter *omega* (Ω) (that is *O-mega*, 'big O') was created for the long value, with O, known as *omicron* (that is, *O-micron*, 'little O'), kept for the short value. Latin took over only omicron, for both long and short values.

Sound values In English, as well as long, short, and digraph values, *o* has some irregular values, often overlapping with values of *u*. In some words, the letter *o* has a different value in different accents. Native speakers differ as to whether *log* and *dog* rhyme, whether *bother* has the vowel of *father*, whether *horse* and *hoarse* are homophones, and whether *your* is pronounced like *yore* or as *ewer*. The sound values are listed in the following paragraphs as *short O, word-final long O, pre-consonantal long O, O with the value of U, O and the inflections of DO*, and *O with doubled consonants*.

Short O. (1) In monosyllables before consonants, but not before *h, r, v, w, y*: *mob, lock, botch, odd, soft, log, dodge, doll, on, top, Oz*. The biblical name *Job*, however, has long *o*. (2) In polysyllables such as *pocket, soccer, biography, geometry*. (3) Before consonant plus *e* in *gone, shone*, in one pronunciation of *scone* (contrast *tone*), and before *ugh*, representing /f/, in *cough, trough*. (4) In RP and related accents, a lengthened variant of short *o* occurs before word-final *r* (*or, nor*), medially as in *corn, adornment*, and before final silent *e* as in *ignore*. The same value occurs as *oa* uniquely in *broad*, as *ou* in *ought, thought*, etc., and is sometimes heard (as it commonly was in old-fashioned RP)

instead of short *o* in *off, often, lost*, sometimes facetiously or mockingly rendered as *aw* in 'crawss' (*cross*), 'Gawd' (*God*); the poet John Keats, a Londoner, rhymed *crosses* and *horses*. This value is also spelt *au, aw*, as seen in the sets *sauce/source, fraught/fought/fort*. (5) In other accents, this distinction does not occur: in most Scottish accents, for example, the same vowel is heard in *cot, caught, ought*, and *sauce* does not rhyme with *source*. (6) In RP and related accents, the vowel sound in *word, work, world, whorl* is the same as that in *were*, and the set *whirled, whorled, world* is homophonous.

Word-final long O. (1) Standard long *o* occurs word-finally spelt simply as *-o* in the monosyllables *fro, go, so*, and in polysyllabic loans (*hero, piano, potato, radio, tomato, zero*), but in *lasso* final *o* usually has the value of long *u*. There is often uncertainty whether such loans form their plurals with *-s* (*armadillos*) or *-es* (*potatoes*) or optionally either (*lassos, lassoes*). Those ending in vowel plus *o* add *s*: *cameos, radios, duos*. Syllable-final long *o* is found in *coaxial, cloaca, oasis* (compare *coax, cloak, oats*), *poet, coerce, coeval*, etc. (2) The same sound occurs word-finally as *-oe* in the monosyllables *doe, foe, floe, hoe, sloe, throe, woe* and in some polysyllables (*aloe, felloe, oboe*), but *shoe, canoe* give *-oe* the value of long *u*. (3) Long *o* occurs as *-oh* in *oh, doh, soh*, as *-ough* in *dough, though* (but not other *-ough* words), and as *-ow* as in some 14 words: *bow, blow, crow, know, low, mow, row, show, slow, snow, sow, stow, tow, throw*. Of these, the forms *bow, row, sow* have different meanings (that is, are different words) when they rhyme with *how*. (4) The long-*o* value of the *-ow* ending occurs in disyllables of mainly vernacular origin, after *d* (*meadow, shadow, widow*), after *ll* (*gallows, swallow; bellow, yellow; billow, willow; follow, hollow*), after *nn* (*minnow, winnow*), and after *rr* (*arrow, barrow; borrow, sorrow; burrow,*

THE CAPITAL LETTER

EARLY FORMS				CURRENT FORMS	
Phoenician	Greek	Etruscan	Roman (Latin)	roman	italic
O	⊖O	O	O	O	*O*

THE SMALL LETTER

EARLY FORMS			CURRENT FORMS	
Roman cursive	Roman uncial	Carolingian minuscule	roman	italic
ʊ	O	o	o	*o*

furrow); and also in *window* (from a Scandinavian compound of *wind* + *eye*) and *bungalow* (from Hindi). (5) The diphthong value of final *-ow* (*now, vow*) is rare in polysyllables: *allow, endow*. (6) Some French loans have a final silent consonant after long *o*: *apropos, depot*. (7) Final long *o* may become *i* in the plural of Italian loans: *libretto/libretti, virtuoso/virtuosi*.

Pre-consonantal long O. (1) Simple *o* before *ld* (*bold, cold*), *lst* (*bolster, holster*), *lt* (*bolt, molten*), *ll* (*stroll, troll*), *lk* (*folk, yolk*). Sometimes also before final *st, th* (*ghost, most, past; both, sloth,* but contrast short *o* in *lost, cloth,* etc.). The anomalous long *o* in *only* contrasts with the related forms *one, alone, lonely*, which all have following *e*; however, a parallel may be seen in *nobly*. (2) Before a single consonant, with a following *a* or a magic *e* after the consonant: *soap, choke*. (3) Digraphs *ou* and *ow* often before *l* or *n* (*boulder, poultry, shoulder, smoulder; bowl, own, sown*), but contrast the diphthong value in *howl, down* and the more usual vowel spellings in *foal, sole, loan, tone*. Before *r* in RP, this value becomes that of *or* in *course, court, source*. (4) Uniquely as *oo* in *brooch* (contrast *broach*).

O with the value of U. (1) The letter *o* often has one of the values of *u*, phonetically central and short as in *but*, close and short as in *put*, or close and long as in *truth*. (2) The short *u*-value is common in monosyllables, especially before *n* (*son, front, monk, month, sponge, ton, tongue, won*), and in some words with silent *e* (*some, come, done, none, love, dove*). *One, once* contain the further anomaly of an unspelt initial /w/. The short *u*-value is heard before nasals, *l, r, th, v*, and *z* in such polysyllabic words as *above, accomplish, among,* BrE *borough, brother, colour, comfort, conjure, cover, dozen, dromedary, frontier, govern, Monday, money, mongrel, monkey, mother, nothing, onion, other, shovel, slovenly, smother, somersault, stomach, wonder*. Pronunciation varies, however: *Coventry, constable* occur in BrE with both short *o* and *u* values. This use of *o* for short *u* has been explained as a graphic device in Middle English to reduce the confusing succession of vertical strokes (minims) that would otherwise arise in manuscript in a word such as *money*. (3) Longer (close) values of *u*, as in *put* or *truth*, occur: with simple *o*, in *do, to, two, who, lasso*; with *o* before a consonant plus *e*, in *lose, whose, move, prove* (contrast *choose, booze, use, hose, drove*); with *oe* in *shoe, canoe*; in such special cases as *bosom, Domesday, tomb, whom, wolf, woman* (but *o* with the value of short *i* in the plural *women*), *womb*.

O and the inflections of DO. The forms of *do* are highly anomalous: the long-*u* value of *o* in *do*, the short-*u* value in *does* (contrast the plural of *doe*), and the long-*o* value of *don't*, matching *won't*.

O with doubled consonants. When followed by doubled consonants, *o* often has a short value, but before double *l*, whether final or medial, both values occur: *doll, loll,* but *poll, roll; dolly, follow,* but *swollen, wholly*. Doubled *l* in *holly* distinguishes its short *o* from the long *o* in *holy*. Many words with a short *o* preceding a single consonant, despite parallels with doubled consonants (*body/shoddy, proper/copper*) or with long vowels (*honey/phoney, hover/rover*). Other examples of single consonants after short *o* include *colour, holiday, honour, honest, money*. On the other hand, doubled *r* distinguishes short *o* in *sorry, lorry* from longer *o* in *story, gory*, though not in *historical*.

Digraphs. *O* is the first element in the following digraphs:

OA. The digraph *oa* has the values of: (1) Long *o* as in *no* (*soap, cloak*). (2) The open *aw*-sound before *r* in RP and related accents (*coarse, hoarse*).

OE. The digraph *oe* has the value of long *o* as in *no* (*woe, woeful*), or of *ee* in such Greek-derived forms as BrE *amoeba, foetus*, or of the first *o* in *colonel* in such German names as *Goethe* and *Goebbels*.

OI and *OY.* (1) The digraphs *oi* and (usually as a word- or syllable-final variant) *oy* are diphthongs: short *o* preceding short *i*, as in *boil, boy*. They are common in monosyllables and incorporate a glide before a vowel at a syllable boundary: *join, noise, voice, oyster, royal, voyage, buoyant*. (2) Rare final *oi* occurs in *borzoi* (from Russian) and *envoi* (Anglicized from French). (3) Special occurrences include: *porpoise, tortoise* with *oi* often reduced to schwa; a unique use in *choir* (rhyming with *friar* and *wire* and respelt from *quire*); in recent French loans, the value of /wa/ (*boudoir, reservoir*). (4) The *oi* combination is not always a digraph: compare *coin/coincide*.

OO. (1) The digraph *oo* is generally considered to have the value of long *u* as in *rule* (*booty, choose*), but with variation depending on accent. Exceptionally, it has the value of short *u* in *blood, flood*. (2) In RP and related accents, *oo* in some words is long *u* as in *truth* (*food, soon*), but elsewhere has the shorter *u* of *put* (*good, hood*) especially before *k* (*book, cook, look*). In *room*, both values occur in free variation. Similar variations occur before *r*: *door, floor, moor, poor*. (3) The form *too* developed in the 16c as a stressed variant of *to*; German has *zu* for both senses. (4) Occasionally, *oo* corresponds to French *ou* (contrast cognate *troop/troupe*), and *-oon* to French *-on* (*balloon/ballon*). (5) A few *oo* words are exotic: *bamboo* (probably Malay), *typhoon* (Chinese), *taboo* (Tongan). The digraph formerly occurred in *Hindoo*, now *Hindu*, and the alternative *tabu* exists for *taboo*. (6) *Zoo* is a clipping of *zoological garden*, but uniquely in *zoology* the second *o* functions simultaneously as part of the *oo* digraph and as a normal short *o*. (7) *Oo* becomes *ee* in the plural of *foot, goose, tooth*: *feet, geese, teeth*.

OU and *OW*. (1) The digraphs *ou* and (usually its word-final variant) *ow* can represent a diphthong, as in *cow, cloud, flour, flower*. Word-final *ou* occurs exceptionally in archaic *thou*, but *ow* is sometimes used medially. It is contrastive in *foul/fowl*, and is an alternative spelling in *to lour/lower* and formerly in *flour/flower*. (2) *Ou* has other values, as in *soul* (rhyming with *pole*), *sought* (with *bought*), *source* (with *course*), *soup* (with *loop*), *scourge* (with *urge*), and *touch* (with *hutch* and *much*). See U. (3) Final *-ow* as long *o* in *know* occurs in some 50 words as compared to some 15 with final *-ow* as in *bow, brow, cow, dhow, how, now*, AmE *plow, prow, row, sow, vow, wow, allow, endow*. (4) On its own, the form *wound* is ambiguous: the past tense of *to wind* has the standard diphthong value, but the noun has the value of *ou* in *soup*. (5) Exceptionally, *ow* has the value of short *o* in *knowledge, acknowledge*. (6) *Ou* becomes plural *i* in the plurals of such pairs as *louse/lice, mouse/mice*.

-OUGH. (1) Some *-ough* spellings have the standard value of *ou* (*bough, drought*, BrE *plough*). Variants are AmE *plow* and archaic *enow*, which was an alternative pronunciation of *enough*. (2) Other *-ough* spellings give *o* different values: short *o* in *cough, trough*; in RP, the *aw* sound in *ought, bought*; long *o* in *though*; schwa in *thorough, borough* in BrE, sometimes long *o* in AmE; and silent *o* in *tough, rough, through*.

O and schwa. (1) Unstressed *o* may be more or less reduced to the value of schwa, or elided altogether. In pronunciations of the word *police*, the full range can be heard, from long *o*, through short *o* and schwa, to zero value with initial consonants as in *please*. (2) There is also often variation between AmE, in which the *o* in *omit, cocaine, testimony, territory, phenomenon* (second *o*) may have one of its full values, and BrE where it is normally reduced. (3) Most typically, *o* (like other vowel letters) has the value of schwa after the main stress in polysyllables, especially in words ending in *l* (*petrol, symbol*), *m* (*fathom, bottom*), *n* (*cotton; cushion, fashion; ration*, and *-ation* words generally), *r* (*error, doctor*). (4) Homophones sometimes occur as a result of such reduction: *baron/barren, gambol/gamble, petrol/petrel, lesson/lessen, minor/miner*.

O and stress shift. In polysyllabic derivatives, the value of *o* may shift between long, short, and schwa (in unstressed position), as the spoken structure of the word changes: (1) *Atom* has schwa for its *o*, but in *atomic* has the short-*o* value. (2) *Colony* has the short o value for its first *o*, schwa for its second, but *colonial* has schwa for its first *o* and the long *o* value for its second. Such effects occur before suffixes like *-(i)al, -ic(al), -y, -ety*, as in *colony/colonial; atom/atomic; economy/economic(al); symbol/ symbolic; tone/tonic; geology/geological; photograph/photographer/photographic; proper/ propriety; social/society*. See SUFFIX.

Agentive *-or/-er*. The suffix *-or* is mostly used with Latin roots (*doctor, professor*), especially after verbs ending in *-ate* (*dictator, perpetrator*). It is normally pronounced with schwa, although occasionally the full value of *-or* is heard: *actor, vendor*. However, *-or* varies with *-er* in a number of patterns. BrE legal spelling may use *-or* where lay writing has *-er*: *grantor/granter*. A technical device may be distinguished by *-or* from a human agent with *-er*: *adaptor/adapter, conveyor/ conveyer*. In other cases, *-or* and *-er* are in free variation: *advisor/adviser, impostor/imposter, investor/invester*. *Caster/castor* sometimes differ in meaning, and *censor/censer* always do.

Silent *O*. (1) In *jeopardy, Leonard, leopard, people*, but the *o* in *yeoman* has long value and the *e* is silent. (2) The second *o* in *colonel*.

American and British differences. (1) The once widespread unstressed ending *-our* (as in *emperour*) has since the early 19c been increasingly rewritten *-or*: universally in *emperor, governor, horror, terror*, and in AmE in such forms as *ardor, behavior, candor, dolor, endeavor, favor, harbor, labor, odor, parlor, rigor, savior, vapor*. *Glamour* and *saviour* are, however, still widely written with *-our* in AmE. AmE has *o* in all derivatives, while BrE has *o* alone in many (*honorary, vaporise, vigorous*), but not all (*behaviourism, favourite, honourable, colourist*). In many rarer forms, such as *torpor* and *stupor*, *-or* is universal. (2) AmE writes BrE *amoeba, foetus, oesophagus. moustache* without the *o* and *manoeuvre* as *maneuver* (but note the common spellings *onomatopoeia, subpoena*). (3) Contrast AmE *mold, molt, smolder*, BrE *mould, moult, smoulder*. (4) AmE has *plow* for BrE *plough*. See ALPHABET, LETTER¹, SPELLING, [WRITING]. C.U., T.MCA., E.W.

O & C. See OXFORD AND CAMBRIDGE SCHOOLS EXAMINATION BOARD.

OATH [From Old English *āth*]. (1) A solemn pronouncement or pledge, as in taking an oath of allegiance, in Christian cultures often involving placing one's hand on a copy of the Bible and/or stating that God is one's witness at the time of swearing the oath. (2) By extension, a blasphemous, irreverent, or foul expression. See BLASPHEMY, MINCED OATH, SWEARING, SWEARWORD. [STYLE].   T.MCA.

OBELISK [16c: from Latin *obeliscus*, Greek *obeliskos* a small spit, small pointed pillar]. Also **dagger**. Printer's terms for a mark like a downward-pointing knife or needle (†), used to indicate a reference or annotation, especially a second footnote, in which case it follows the word, phrase, or sentence being marked in a text, and is repeated before the footnote or other reference. See ASTERISK, NOTES AND REFERENCES. [WRITING].   T.MCA.

OBFUSCATION [16c: from Latin *obfuscare/ obfuscatum* to darken, from *fuscus* dark]. A use of language that makes a subject obscure or difficult to understand, or complex to the point of confusion. The aim of obfuscation is to prevent communication, not to promote it. Government agencies often use such language. For example, in 1983 the US Department of Energy issued the following regulation: 'Nothing in these regulations precludes the secretary or his delegate from designating information not specifically described in this regulation as unclassified controlled unclear information.' Compare DOUBLESPEAK, JARGON, OBSCURANTISM. [STYLE, USAGE].   W.D.L.

OBJECT [14c: from Latin *obiectum* (something) thrown down, (something) presented (to the mind)]. A major functional element in the structure of clauses, present in any sentence with a transitive verb. With verbs that can have two objects, the *indirect object* generally refers to the recipient of what is denoted by the *direct object*. In *I sent my bank a letter* (Subject/ Verb/Object/Object), *my bank* is the indirect object, *a letter* the direct object. In the equivalent *I sent a letter to my bank*, some grammarians regard *to my bank* as also an indirect object. Pronouns in any object position must take their object forms, as with *I* and *they* in *Please send me them*. Despite the closer position of the indirect object to the verb in *I sent my bank a letter*, with most verbs it is the indirect object that is more easily omitted: *I sent a letter*, not **I sent my bank*. Exceptions include *pay* (*You can pay me*), *teach* (*She teaches the top class*), and *tell* (*You can tell me, if you wish*), where such direct objects as *the money*, French, and *the news* are omitted. In such constructions, some grammarians see the retained object as the direct object, while others see it as the indirect object. Compare SUBJECT. [GRAMMAR].   S.C., S.G.

OBLIQUE [15c: through French from Latin *obliquus* sloping. Pronounced 'obLEEK'. Once pronounced 'obLIKE']. Also **diagonal, oblique dash, oblique stroke, slash, solidus, virgule**. The punctuation mark (/), a forward-sloping line used in writing and printing. *Virgule* is the French term for *comma*; the virgule or oblique used in medieval English manuscripts and early printed works in black letter had more or less the value of a modern comma: see PROSE STYLE (Caxton). The mark was also once used as a precursor to the soft hyphen, to mark end-of-line word division. *Solidus* is Latin for 'shilling': in Britain, the name was extended to the mark used to separate shillings from pence in pre-decimal currency: 7/6 for *seven shillings and sixpence*. The device has six main uses: (1) To indicate vulgar fractions (23/24 for *twenty-three twenty-fourths*) and ratios (*miles/hour* for *miles per hour*). (2) As part of certain abbreviations and related symbols, such as *c/o* care of, *i/c* in charge, and the percentage sign %. (3) To mark the ends of lines of poetry when set in a prose text (as in *Tyger Tyger, burning bright | In the forests of the night*). (4) To unite alternatives as in *and/or, colour/color, his/her*, and *s/he* (for 'she or he'). (5) To indicate routes, as in *London/New York/San Francisco*. (6) In phonetics, to mark off phonemic transcription, as in /wik/, denoting the pronunciation of the words *week* and *weak*. The reverse oblique (\), known as a *back-slash*, is used mainly in computing: for example, in forming the elements of a filename, such as *NB\MAIN\OC\A\AB* (for 'Nota Bene, Main Directory, Oxford Companion, Letter A, Section AB'). See PHONETIC TRANSCRIPTION, PUNCTUATION. [TECHNOLOGY, WRITING].

W.W.B., T.MCA.

OBLIQUE RHYME. See HALF RHYME.

OBSCENE LIBEL. See CENSORSHIP, LIBEL.

OBSCENITY [17c: through French from Latin *obscaenus* ill-omened, indecent]. The use of language generally considered repulsive and indecent, and an instance of such use. Although reference to sex is central to obscenity, excrement is also included. See CENSORSHIP, SWEARING. [STYLE].   R.F.I.

OBSCURANTISM [1820s: from French *obscurantisme* what tends to obscure, conceal]. A deliberate use of language that is obscure, vague, or lacking in clear meaning. Politicians and others who seek to avoid specific statements often use this style of language. For example, at the height of US involvement in Vietnam, Governor Nelson Rockefeller of New York was asked his position on the war, and replied: 'My position on Vietnam is very simple. And I feel this way. I haven't spoken on it because I haven't felt there was any major contribution that I had to make at the time. I think that our concepts as a nation and that our actions have not kept pace with the changing conditions. And therefore our actions are not completely relevant today to the realities of the magnitude and the complexity of the problems that we face in this conflict.' See DOUBLESPEAK, JARGON, OBFUSCATION. [STYLE, USAGE].   W.D.L.

OBSTRUENT. See CONSONANT.

OCEANIA [19c: through Modern Latin from French *Océanie*, from Latin *oceanus*, Greek *ōkeanós* a vast stream believed to girdle the earth. Pronunciations: 'oh-she-AH-ni-a', 'oh-she-AY-ni-a', 'o-SHEE-ni-a']. (1) A general term for the islands of the Pacific Ocean, including Melanesia, Micronesia, and Polynesia, sometimes the Malay archipelago, and sometimes Australasia. The term is used in this volume to include Australasia but exclude the Malay archipelago, which is treated as part of Asia: see theme list below. (2) The name of a region of the world in George Orwell's dystopian novel *Nineteen Eighty-Four* (1949). See NEWSPEAK. [GEOGRAPHY, NAME].   T.MCA.

The Oceania theme

A–C. ABORIGINAL ENGLISH, ABORIGINES, ANGLO-CELTIC, ANTIPODEAN ENGLISH, ANTIPODES, AOTEAROA, ASSIMILATION, AUSSIE, AUSTRAL, AUSTRALASIA, AUSTRALASIAN ENGLISH, AUSTRALASIATIC, AUSTRAL ENGLISH, AUSTRALIA, AUSTRALIAN, AUSTRALIAN BROADCASTING, AUSTRALIAN DICTIONARIES, AUSTRALIAN ENGLISH, AUSTRALIANESE, AUSTRALIANISM, AUSTRALIAN LANGUAGE, AUSTRALIAN LANGUAGE (THE), AUSTRALIAN LANGUAGE RESEARCH CENTRE, AUSTRALIAN LANGUAGES, AUSTRALIAN LITERATURE, AUSTRALIAN NATIONAL DICTIONARY CENTRE, AUSTRALIAN PIDGIN, AUSTRALIAN PRESS, AUSTRALIAN PUBLISHING, BEACH LA MAR, BISLAMA, BLACKFELLA ENGLISH/TALK, BLUE-EYED ENGLISH, BROAD, BROKEN, BULLETIN (THE), BURCHFIELD, BUSH, BUSH BALLAD, COLONIAL, COMMONWEALTH, COMMONWEALTH LITERATURE, COMMUNITY LANGUAGE, COOK ISLANDS, CULTIVATED, CULTURAL CRINGE.

D–Z. DIALECT IN AUSTRALIA, DIALECT IN NEW ZEALAND, DICTIONARY RESEARCH CENTRE, DOGGEREL, DOWN UNDER, ELICOS, ENGLISH, ENGLISH LITERATURE, ETHNIC NAME, EXAMINING IN ENGLISH, FIJI, GENERAL AUSTRALIAN, GENERAL NEW ZEALAND, GODZONE, GREAT AUSTRALIAN, GREAT AUSTRALIAN ADJECTIVE, GREAT AUSTRALIAN SLANGUAGE, HALLIDAY, HAPA-HAOLE, HAWAII, HAWAIIAN, HAWAII CREOLE ENGLISH, HAWAII PIDGIN ENGLISH, HIRI MOTU, HOME, IELTS, KANAKA, KANAKA ENGLISH, KIRIBATI, KIWI, KRIOL, L-SOUNDS, MALAYO-POLYNESIAN LANGUAGES, MAORI, MAORI ENGLISH, MARITIME PIDGIN HAWAIIAN, MELANESIA, MELANESIAN PIDGIN ENGLISH, MICRONESIA, MORRIS, NAURU, NEO-MELANESIAN, NEO-SOLOMONIC, NEW SOUTH

WALES PIDGIN ENGLISH, NEW ZEALAND, NEW ZEALAND BROADCASTING, NEW ZEALAND DICTIONARIES, NEW ZEALAND ENGLISH, NEW ZEALANDISM, NEW ZEALAND LITERATURE, NEW ZEALAND PLACE-NAMES, NEW ZEALAND PRESS, NEW ZEALAND PUBLISHING, OCEANIA, OLD COUNTRY, OZ, PACIFIC JARGON ENGLISH, PACIFIC RIM, PAKEHA, PAPUA NEW GUINEA/NIUGINI, PAPUA NEW GUINEA PIDGIN, PARTRIDGE, PIJIN, PITCAIRNESE/PITCAIRN-NORFOLK CREOLE, POLYNESIA, QUEENSLAND CANEFIELDS ENGLISH/KANAKA ENGLISH, RACISM, ROPER RIVER CREOLE/ROPER PIDGIN, ROYAL SOCIETY, SCOSE, SOLOMON ISLANDS, SOLOMON ISLANDS PIDGIN ENGLISH (PIJIN), SOUTHLAND BURR, SOUTH SEAS ENGLISH/JARGON, STANDARD AUSTRALIAN ENGLISH, STRINE, STYLE COUNCIL, TEFL, TEIL, TESD, TESL, TOK BOI, TOK PISIN, TONGA, TORRES STRAIT BROKEN/CREOLE, TURNER (G.), TUVALU, VANUATU, WESTERN SAMOA.

OCTAVE. See SONNET.

OCTAVO [16c: from the Neo-Latin singular masculine ablative phrase *in octavo* in an eighth (of a sheet of paper)]. (1) Abbreviated *8°*, 8vo. A format for printed materials, for many centuries the commonest size for a printed book, made by folding a sheet three times, the folds creating a quire of eight leaves (16 pages). (2) The name for a book of this size. (3) Formerly, a size of cut paper 8 × 5 inches (20.3 × 12.7 cm). [TECHNOLOGY].   W.W.B.

OCTET. See SONNET.

ODE [16c: through French from Latin *oda*, Greek *aōidḗ* a song]. A long lyric poem that addresses a person, thing, or place, or celebrates a notable event. There are three principal forms in English: (1) *The Pindaric ode.* An elaborate Greek form imitating the style of Pindar (5c BC), who derived it from the *strophe, antistrophe,* and *epode,* the three movements of the dramatic chorus, which sang the strophe while dancing to the left, the antistrophe to the right, and the epode standing still. It has three stanzas, the first two identical in structure and without restriction of metre or length, the third taking a different structure. This sequence can be repeated several times to make a longer poem, as with Gray's 'The Progress of Poesy' (1754). (2) *The Horatian ode.* A form imitating the style of the Roman poet Horace. It keeps a constant stanza form throughout, often a quatrain rhyming *aabb* with the first two lines longer than the third and fourth, as in Andrew Marvell's 'Horatian Ode on the Return of Cromwell from Ireland' (1650). (3) *The irregular ode.* The most popular English form, introduced by Abraham Cowley in the 17c to imitate Pindar, but with greater freedom of structure; Wordsworth's 'Intimations of Immortality' (1807) is such a form. The ode, especially addressed to subjects in the natural world, was favoured by the 18c neo-classicists and, with new attitudes and style, by the 19c Romantics: Shelley's 'Ode to the West Wind' (1819), Keats's 'On a Grecian Urn' (1820) and 'To a Nightingale' (1820), and Allen Tate's 'Ode to the Confederate Dead' (1928). See CHORUS, LYRIC. [LITERATURE].   R.C.

OED. See OXFORD ENGLISH DICTIONARY.

OFFICIAL ENGLISH, also **Official English Movement.** Collective names for campaigning groups whose aim is an amendment of the US Constitution, making English the official language of the republic. The organization *US English* belongs within this grouping. See ENGLISH LANGUAGE AMENDMENT, ENGLISH-ONLY MOVEMENT. [AMERICAS, MEDIA].   T.MCA.

OFFICIALESE [1880s]. A style common in statements and texts issued by the official representatives of governments and large institutions, especially civil servants. The term is usually pejorative and the style is particularly criticized for obscure, polysyllabic, pompous, and/or pedantic usage. See BUREAUCRATESE, -ESE, JARGON. [STYLE, USAGE].   T.MCA.

OFFICIAL LANGUAGE. A language used for official purposes, especially as the medium of a national government. English is not the statutory or *de jure* official language of either the UK or the US, but is the *de facto* official language. It is, however, the sole statutory official language of Namibia; with French, it is one of the two statutory official languages of Canada; with Mandarin Chinese, Malay, and Tamil, it is one of the four statutory official languages of Singapore; and with Arabic, Chinese, French, and Spanish, it is one of the five statutory official languages of the Food and Agriculture Organization of the United Nations (FAO). See ENGLISH, NATIONAL LANGUAGE. Compare OFFICIAL ENGLISH (MOVEMENT). [LANGUAGE].   T.MCA.

OFF RHYME. See HALF RHYME.

OFFSET. See PHOTO-OFFSET PRINTING.

OLD COUNTRY, The. A term for Great Britain applied by settlers in the former dominions and surviving among older people as an affectionately sentimental term. In the heyday of the British Empire, such terms were used, often with affection and without affectation, by many people who did not hail from Britain, had never been there, and were never likely to go there. The expression is paralleled by *the old sod* for Ireland and *the old dart*, a term for Britain used in Australia and New Zealand, possibly formed

on an Essex dialect pronunciation of *dirt*. See HOME, MOTHER COUNTRY. [EUROPE, NAME, OCEANIA].   T.MCA., W.S.R.

OLD ENGLISH[1], short form *OE*, *O.E.* Also **Anglo-Saxon** (short form *AS*, *A.S.*). From one point of view, the earliest stage of the single continuously developing English language; from another, the language from which two other more or less distinct languages successively evolved, first Middle English (ME), then Modern English (ModE); from a third point of view, the common ancestor of English and Scots, the two national Germanic languages of Britain. OE was spoken and written in various forms for some eight centuries (5–12c). Although its texts are as unintelligible to present-day English speakers as Latin to speakers of French, even after modest exposure they can begin to make progress, as with the following (from the OE version of Bede's *Ecclesiastical History of the English People*):

Breten is gārsecges īegland, þæt wæs gēo geāra Albion hāten.

Translated word for word and with the same word order, this sentence runs:

Britain is sea's island, that was ago years Albion called.

Translated more freely, it is:

Britain is an island of the sea that was formerly called Albion.

In the original sentence, word order in the main clause is the same as in ModE, but in the subordinate clause differs markedly from it (with echoes of German). Some words are the same as or very like ModE words (*is*, *Albion*; *Breten*, *wæs*), some are further removed but easily identifiable after translation (*īegland* island, *geāra* years), and some are alien (*gārsecges* of the sea, *gēo* formerly, *hāten* called).

Background. Old English consisted of several West Germanic dialects taken to Britain from the north-western European mainland in the middle centuries of the first millennium AD. Germanic settlement was very limited during the late Roman period, but expanded greatly after the departure of the Romans in the early 5c. The language was never fully homogenized as a literary and administrative medium, but nonetheless made greater progress in this direction (despite the primacy of Latin) than most other European vernaculars. Writing in Latin in the 8c, the Northumbrian historian Bede identified the settlers of three hundred years earlier as three peoples, the Jutes, Angles, and Saxons; the Anglo-Saxon Chronicle, written entirely in OE from the 9c to the 12c, described year by year, from the settlers' point of view, the progress of various leaders and groups as they overcame the resistance of the Romano-Celtic Britons from the 5c to the 7c.

By the 8c, OE-speakers held territories roughly equivalent in size and distribution to the later kingdom of England. Four major varieties of the language can be distinguished in surviving documents: *Kentish*, associated with the Jutes, who probably migrated from what is now Denmark; *West Saxon*, in the southern region called Wessex, ultimately the most powerful of the Saxon kingdoms, whose founders originated in northern Germany; *Mercian*, the Anglian dialect spoken in Mercia, a kingdom stretching from the Thames to the Humber; and *Northumbrian*, the northernmost of the Anglian dialects, spoken from the Humber to the Forth. The Angles (in OE *Engle*) appear to have originated in Angeln, now in Schleswig, and gave their name to the language, *Englisc*, but it was the Saxons of Wessex who brought their dialect closest to a standard literary medium: see ALFRED. The last document in OE, an annal of the Anglo-Saxon Chronicle dated 1154, shows features of early Middle English, which was strongly influenced by the impact on OE of Danish during the 9–11c and Norman French from the 11c onward. The following sections, however, discuss OE without reference to such influences.

Pronunciation and spelling. OE had speech patterns similar to those of its fellow North Sea Germanic languages Old Frisian and Old Dutch. It was written first in runic letters then in an adaptation of the Roman alphabet that incorporated several such letters to represent distinctive OE sounds (see below).

Stress. In polysyllables, OE stress typically falls on the first syllable, as in ModE: *mórgen* morning, *séttan* to set. When the first syllable is a prefix, however, nouns and adjectives stress the prefix (*ándswaru* answer, *ándward* current, present), but verbs do not (*forgíefan* to forgive, *tōbérstan* to burst). Two prefixes are never stressed, whatever the part of speech: *be-* (*beswillan* to soak), and *ge-* (*gefrémed* done, from *fremman* to do; *gebólian* to tolerate, from *bólian* to endure; *gerégnad* ornamented).

Vowels. The monophthongs of OE consist of seven pairs of short and long vowels: (1) Short *a*, phonetically /a/, as in *nama* name; long *ā* /ɑː/, as in *stān* stone. (2) Short *æ* /æ/, as in *glæd* glad; long *ǣ* /æː/, as in *dǣd* deed. (3) Short *e* /ɛ/, as in *etan* eat; long *ē* /eː/, as in *hē* he. (4) Short *i* /ɪ/, as in *cwic* alive; long *ī* /iː/, as in *wīn* wine. (5) Short *o* /ɔ/, as in *god* god; long *ō* /oː/, as in *gōd* good. (6) Short *u* /ʊ/, as in *sunu* son; long *ū* /uː/, as in *nū* now. (7) Short *y* /y/, as in *cyning* king; long *y* /yː/, as in *ȳtmæst* utmost: compare French *tu* and *ruse*. The diphthongs of OE

consist of three pairs of short and long vowels in which the stress falls on the initial vowel: (1) Short *ea* /æa/, as in *eald* old; long *ēa* /æːa/, as in *ēast* east. (2) Short *eo* /ɛo/, as in *eorl* earl; long *ēo* /eːo/, as in *dēop* deep. (3) Short *ie* /ɪɛ/, as in *ieldu* age; long *īe* /iːɛ/, as in *hīeran* to hear.

Consonants. The consonants of OE are mostly the same as those of ModE. Differences include: (1) The pronunciation of all consonants in all written positions, notably /r/ and initial /g/ as in *gnagan* to gnaw, initial /k/ as in *cnēo* knee, initial /h/ as in *hlāf* bread, and initial /w/ as in *wrītan* to write. (2) Double letters represent geminated sounds (as in Italian): for example, OE *biden* and *biddan* differ phonetically in the same way as ModE 'bidden' and 'bid Den'. (3) Two consonants are absent from present-day mainstream English. The sound represented by non-initial *h*, as in *niht* night, is a voiceless palatal fricative (compare German *ich*) or a voiceless velar fricative (compare German *ach*, ScoE *loch*, Scots *nicht*). The sound represented by *g* after or between back vowels is a voiced velar fricative (compare one pronunciation of German *sagen* to say). Initial *h* has the same pronunciation as in present-day general English; *g* in other positions is as shown below in point 7. (4) There are several distinctive letters: *ash* (æ), *eth* (ð), *thorn* (þ), *wynn* (ƿ), *yogh* (ȝ). For details, see the entries for each. (5) The letters *f* and *s* each have voiceless and voiced values, the letters *v* and *z* not normally being used. Such words as OE *fæt* (fat) and *fæt* (vat) are therefore pronounced as homophones with either /f/ or /v/, according to dialect: compare present-day West Country speech in England. Similarly, thorn may represent either a voiceless /θ/ or a voiced /ð/: compare the current use of the digraph *th* in *three* and *these*. (6) The letter *c* is used as follows: before the 'hard' vowels *a*, *o*, *u*, *y* and all consonants, it has the value /k/, as in *cald* cold, *clipian* to summon, *cwic* alive, *cyning* king; before the 'soft' vowels *e*, *i*, it generally has the value /tʃ/, as in *ceaster* ('chester') town, *cirice* church. (7) Similarly, *g* is pronounced /g/ before *a*, *æ*, *o*, *u* and before consonants, as in *gāst* spirit, *god* god, *grim* fierce, and /j/ (as in ModE *yet*) before *e* and *i*, as in *gēac* cuckoo, *gif* if. (8) The letter combinations *sc* and *cg* are pronounced like *sh* and *dge* in present-day *shed* and *sedge* respectively: *scip* ship, *bricg* bridge.

Grammar. Textbooks of OE grammar distinguish eight parts of speech: nouns, adjectives, pronouns, verbs, adverbs, prepositions, conjunctions, and interjections. Unlike ModE, OE is highly inflected; the major aspects of its morphology are traditionally set out in paradigms, much as in textbooks of Latin, with declensions for nouns, adjectives, and pronouns, and conjugations for verbs. Its morphology and syntax are too extensive and complex to cover here; the following sections present only highlights.

Declensions. To discuss nouns, pronouns, and adjectives, grammarians of OE use the three categories number, gender, and case, with three subcategories for number (singular, sometimes dual, and plural), three for gender (masculine, feminine, and neuter), and four or five for case (nominative, accusative, genitive, and dative, the last serving an instrumental function for nouns, while there is a distinct instrumental case in certain parts of the declensions of adjectives and pronouns).

Table 1. *Declension of masculine weak noun* nama

	Singular	Plural
Nom.	*nama* (name: subject)	*naman* (names: subject)
Acc.	*naman* (name: object)	*naman* (names: object)
Gen.	*naman* (of a name, name's)	*namena* (of names, names')
Dat.	*naman* (to/for/with a name)	*namum* (to/for/with names)

Table 2. *Declension of masculine strong noun* stān

	Singular	Plural
Nom.	*stān*	*stānas*
Acc.	*stān*	*stānas*
Gen.	*stānes*	*stāna*
Dat.	*stāne*	*stānum*

The paradigm given in Table 1 shows the declension of nouns ending in *-an* (generally referred to as 'weak' nouns). In this case, the noun (*nama* name) is masculine. Table 2 shows the declension of a 'strong' noun: in effect, any form other than with *-an* endings. Here, for convenience of comparison, the noun is also masculine.

Table 3. *Declension of definite article* sē (*singular only*)

	Masculine	Feminine	Neuter
Nom.	*sē*	*sēo*	*þæt*
Acc.	*þone*	*þā*	*þæt*
Gen.	*þæs*	*þære*	*þæs*
Dat.	*þæm*	*þære*	*þæm*
Inst.	*þȳ*	*þære*	*þȳ*

Table 3 gives the declension for the singular only of the definite article (a subclass of pronoun also translated as *that*). In ModE, the definite article is invariable (only *the*), while the demonstrative pronoun has two forms (*that/those*); in OE, however, the forms varied through three

genders, two numbers, and five cases. The plural forms are simpler: nominative and accusative *þā* for all genders; genitive *þāra*; and dative *þǣm*. The OE for 'the/that name' as subject of a sentence is *sē nama*, as object is *þone naman*; 'the/those stones', as both subject and object, is *þā stānas*.

Conjugations. The tenses of the verb in OE are comparable to those of ModE, which contains remnants of the major distinction in OE verbs: between 'strong' and 'weak' forms. The main difference lies in the formation of the preterite (the simple past tense). The preterite of strong verbs is formed by changing the vowel of the root according to a series known as 'vowel gradation' (in ModE, for example, the change from *swim* to *swam*). The preterite of weak verbs is formed by adding a suffix containing *d* (as in ModE *walk* to *walked*). There are seven conjugations or classes of strong verbs and three of weak verbs. In Tables 4 and 5, the present and preterite paradigms of the indicative mood of the strong verb *bindan* (to bind) and of the weak verb *hīeran* (to hear) are set out for comparison.

Table 4. *Conjugation of strong verb* bindan, *indicative mood*

Person	Singular	Plural
	Present	
1st	*binde*	*bindaþ*
2nd	*bindest/bintst*	*bindaþ*
3rd	*bindeþ/bint*	*bindaþ*
	Preterite (with vowel change)	
1st	*band*	*bundon*
2nd	*bunde*	*bundon*
3rd	*band*	*bundon*

Table 5. *Conjugation of weak verb* hīeran, *indicative mood*

Person	Singular	Plural
	Present	
1st	*hīere*	*hīeraþ*
2nd	*hīerst*	*hīeraþ*
3rd	*hīerþ*	*hīeraþ*
	Preterite (with *d*-element)	
1st	*hīerde*	*hīerdon*
2nd	*hīerdest*	*hīerdon*
3rd	*hīerde*	*hīerdon*

Basic word order. (1) In phrases, adjectives and genitives generally precede nouns: *micel flōd* a great flood: *Westseaxna cyning* king of the West Saxons. Two coordinate adjectives are usually separated, one preceding and the other following the noun, after *and*: *gōda þēow and getrēowa* (good servant and faithful), good, faithful servant. Compare the fossilized ModE idiom 'twelve good men and true'. A title follows a proper name, the opposite of ModE: *Æþelred cyning* King Ethelred. (2) In sentences, inflection for case allows a certain freedom of word order, more or less as in Latin. There are, however, three common orderings in OE prose and verse: SV (Subject–Verb) and SVO (Subject–Verb–Object), as in *hēo beswāc hine* She betrayed him; S . . . V, especially in subordinate clauses, as in the clause which appeared above, *þæt wæs gēo geāra Albion hāten* (that was formerly called Albion); VS, which is used for both questions (*Hwǣr eart þū nū?* Where art thou now?) and statements, whether positive or negative (*Ne cōm se here* Not came the army: The army did not come).

Vocabulary. (1) The core OE wordstock was shared with the other West Germanic languages and like theirs was subject to the sound changes of Grimm's Law and Verner's Law (see entries). (2) Borrowing from non-Germanic languages was relatively rare, but there were significant loanwords from Latin and Greek. Some Latin words were acquired before the Anglo-Saxons settled in Britain, such as *strǣt* street (from *strata via* paved way) and *w(e)all* wall (from *vallum* rampart); others were borrowed afterwards, such as *fēfor* fever (from *febris*) and *mægister* master (from *magister*). Greek loans usually came through Latin, as with *biscop* (from *episcopus* from *episkopos*) and *scōl(u)* school (from *schola* from *skholḗ*). (3) Because of inflection, the structure of OE nouns, adjectives, and verbs differs greatly from that of ModE; for example, whereas ModE has one form *drink* for both noun and verb, OE has two, the noun *drinc* and the verb *drincan*. (4) Compound words were common, including as personal names: *Ælfred* Elf Council (original form of *Alfred*), *Æthel-dreda* Noble Strength (original form of *Audrey*), *bretwalda* ruler of Britain (a title for the foremost king of his time), *ealdormann* nobleman (ancestral form of *alderman*), *eallwealda* or *ælwalda* ruler of all, *Edwin* Prosperous Friend, *hēahgerēfa* high reeve (an official), *sǣweall* sea wall, *stormsǣ* stormy sea, *sweordbora* sword-bearer, *synnfull* sinful. (5) Derivation was also common: for example, with the prefix *be-* around, as in *berīdan* to ride around; with *for-* as an intensifier, as in *forlorenness* utter lostness, perdition; with *on-* un-, as in *onlūcan* to unlock; the suffix *-end* for an agent, as in *hǣlend* healer, saviour, *wīgend* warrior; *-ing* son of, as in *Ælfred Æþelwulfing*

Alfred son of Ethelwulf, *hōring* son of a whore, fornicator; and *-ig*, as in *cræftig* strong (the ancestral form of *crafty*), *hālig* holy. (6) A range of compounds and derivatives was created as loan translations of Latin terms, such as *tōcyme* (to-come) to match *adventus* (advent), *gōdspel* (good news: the ancestral form of gospel) to match *evangelium*, and *þrīnnys* (threeness) to match *trinitas* (trinity).

Texts. The literary and other texts of OE are among the oldest specimens of vernacular writing in Europe: see ENGLISH LITERATURE. Below are two brief specimens, with modern translations. The verse was committed to writing *c*.AD 1000 but was composed much earlier; its layout shows the typical OE metrical unit, the half-line. The prose represents the style of 10c Saxon annalists.

(1) Verse: Beowulf, lines 710–13

þa cōm of mōre	under misthleoþum
Grendel gongan;	Godes yrre bær;
mynte se mānscaþa	manna cynnes
sumne besyrwan	in sele þām hēan.
Wōd under wolcnum	to þæs þe hē wīnreced,
goldsele gumena	gearwost wisse
fǣttum fāhne.	

A CLOSE TRANSLATION

Then came out of the moorlands	beneath the mist-slopes
Grendel stalking;	he bore God's ire;
The evil one meant	of human kind
Someone to snare	in the high hall.
He went on under the clouds	till their wine-hall,
The gold-hall of men	he could clearly make out
plated in gold.	

A FREE TRANSLATION

Down off the moorlands' misting fells came
Grendel stalking; God's brand was on him.
The spoiler meant to snatch away
from the high hall some of the human race.
He came on under the clouds, clearly saw at last
The gold-hall of men, the mead-drinking place
nailed with gold plates.
(Michael Alexander, *Beowulf*, Penguin Classics, 1973)

(2) Prose: The Anglo-Saxon Chronicle (years 981, 982)

981. Hēr on þīs gēare wæs Sancte Patroces stōw forhergod, and þȳ ilcan gēare wæs micel hearm gedōn gehwǣ be þām scǣriman ǣgþer ge on Defenum ge on Wēalum.

982. Hēr on þȳs gēare cōmon ūpp on Dorsætum iii scypu wīcinga and hergodon on Portlande. þȳ ilcan gēare forbarn Lundenbyrig. And on þām ylcan gēare forþfērdon twēgen ealdormenn, Æþelmǣr on Hamtūnscīre and Ēadwine on Sūþseaxum.

A CLOSE MODERN RENDERING

981. [Here in this year] St. Petroc's, Padstow, was ravaged, and in the same year much harm done everywhere along the sea-coasts, in both Devon and Cornwall.

982. [Here in this year] Three ships of vikings came up into Dorset, and ravaged in Portland the same year. Also that year, London was burnt, and [in that same year] two ealdormen passed away, Aethelmaer in Hampshire and Eadwine in Sussex.

(Ann Savage, *The Anglo-Saxon Chronicles*, Phoebe Phillips, 1982)

See AELFRIC, ALFRED, ALLITERATIVE VERSE, ALPHABET, ANGLES, ANGLO-SAXON, ANGLO-SAXON CHRONICLE, ASH, BARNES, BEDE, BEOWULF, CASE¹, CELTIC LANGUAGES, DANELAW, DANISH, DERIVATION, DORSET, ENGLISH, ENGLISH LITERATURE, ENGLISH PLACE-NAMES, ETH, FRENCH, GERMANIC LANGUAGES, GRIMM'S LAW, HEPTARCHY, HISTORY OF ENGLISH (AND CHRONOLOGY), HUMO(U)R, ICELANDIC, INGVAEONIC, JUTES, MERCIA, METRE/METER, MIDDLE ENGLISH, NORMAN FRENCH, NORSE, NORTHERN ENGLISH, NORTHUMBRIA, PERIOD DICTIONARIES OF ENGLISH, PLAIN ENGLISH, PROSE, PURE, RUNE, SAXON, SAXONISM, SCANDINAVIAN LANGUAGES, SCOTS, STRONG VERB, THORN, VERNER'S LAW, WESSEX, WEST COUNTRY, WYN(N), Y-, YOGH, [EUROPE, HISTORY, VARIETY]. T.MCA., W.F.B.

Borden, Arthur R. 1982. *A Comprehensive Old-English Dictionary*. University Press of America.
Brook, G. L. 1955. *An Introduction to Old English*. Manchester: University Press.
Campbell, A. 1959/62. *Old English Grammar*. Oxford: University Press.
Campbell, James (ed.). 1982. *The Anglo-Saxons*. Oxford: University Press.
Clark Hall, J. R. 1960. *A Concise Anglo-Saxon Dictionary*, 4th edition with supplement by H. D. Meritt. Cambridge: University Press.
Davis, Norman. 1953 etc. *Sweet's Anglo-Saxon Primer*. Oxford: University Press.
Hamer, R. F. S. 1967. *Old English Sound Changes for Beginners*. Oxford: Basil Blackwell.
Mitchell, Bruce. 1985. *Old English Syntax*. Two volumes. Oxford: University Press.
—— & Robinson, Fred C. 1989. *A Guide to Old English*, 4th edition. Oxford: Basil Blackwell.
Quirk, R., & Wrenn, C. L. 1955 etc. *An Old English Grammar*. London: Methuen.
Toller, T. Northcote (ed.). 1898, 1921, 1972. *An Anglo-Saxon Dictionary Based on the Manuscript Collections of the Late Joseph Bosworth*. Oxford: University Press.

OLD ENGLISH². The first English settlers in Ireland, dating from the late 12c, and their language; in Irish Gaelic, they were known as *Na SeanGhaill* (The Old Foreigners). The term *Old English* was applied to them by later settlers, from the 16c onward: 'Howbeit to this day, the dregs of the old auncient Chaucer English are kept as well there [in Wexford] as in Fingall [North Dublin]' (Holinshed's Chronicle, 1586); 'Their advice was always prefaced by profuse professions of the traditional loyalty of the Old English community to the Crown' (R. F. Foster, *Oxford Illustrated History of Ireland*, 1989, p.

117). See IRISH ENGLISH, YOLA. [EUROPE, HISTORY, VARIETY]. T.MCA., L.T.

OLD ENGLISH ANNALS. See ANGLO-SAXON CHRONICLE.

OLDER SCOTS. See PERIOD DICTIONARIES OF ENGLISH, SCOTS, SCOTTISH DICTIONARIES.

OLD NORSE. See NORSE.

OMAN. See ARABIC, ENGLISH.

ONE-LINER. A joke compressed into a single sentence that both proposes and resolves the matter of the joke: for example, 'Karl Marx's grave—another Communist plot', punning on *plot* as both conspiracy and burial ground. See GRAFFITI, JOKE. [STYLE]. W.N.

ONIONS, C(harles) T(albut) [1873–1965]. English grammarian and lexicographer, born and educated at Birmingham where, at Mason College, he obtained an external degree from the U. of London. In 1895, he joined James Murray on the staff of the *Oxford English Dictionary* at Oxford, later worked for Henry Bradley (passing, as he put it, 'from the practical professional teacher to the philosophical exponent'), and in 1914 began independent editorial work on the section SUB–SZ, with his own assistants. He was also responsible for WH–WORLING and the letters X, Y, and Z. With W. A. Craigie, he co-edited the 1933 Supplement. His work on the *OED* overlapped with much else: preparing *An Advanced English Syntax* (1904); re-editing Emil Otto's *French Conversation Grammar* (1905) and J. Wright's *Elementary French Grammar* (1905); compiling *A Shakespeare Glossary* (1911); after William Little's death in 1922, completing *The Shorter Oxford English Dictionary* (1933); and editing with H. E. Berthon *Advanced French Conversation* (1924). As a Fellow of Magdalen College, Oxford, from 1923, he was involved in university teaching and its concomitants, including a revision of Henry Sweet's *Anglo-Saxon Reader* (1922, and later editions), a textual reconstruction of parts of the medieval poem *The Owl and the Nightingale* (1936), and numerous etymological or explanatory notes in learned journals and in the tracts of the Society for Pure English, on phrases like *distance no object* and topics like the fate of French *-é* in English. His crowning achievement and enduring monument is *The Oxford Dictionary of English Etymology* (1966), published posthumously and considered by many to be the standard work on the subject. His scholarly work and other activities, including his period as Director of the Early English Text Society (1945–57) and as editor of the journal *Medium Ævum* (1932-56), demonstrated the extent to which he was at home with all periods of the language. For much of his life, he was handicapped by a slight stammer. This endeared him to his friends and colleagues, as did his rueful reaction to the many people who pronounced his name as if it were spelt *O'Nions*. 'Pronounce it like the vegetable,' he would say. See index. [BIOGRAPHY, EUROPE, GRAMMAR, REFERENCE]. RO.W.B.

ONOMASIOLOGY [1930s: from Greek *onomasia* name, and *logía* speech or study]. The study of naming and of terminologies (systems of terms with related meanings) that vary geographically, socially, occupationally, or in other ways. In the UK, characteristic generic terms in street names are *avenue, close, crescent, drive, gardens, lane, mews, place, row, street, terrace*, but in the US are *avenue, boulevard, drive, place, street*. The adjective *onomasiological* is used in lexicography to describe and discuss works of reference such as thesauruses which proceed from concept to word, as opposed to *semasiological* works such as dictionaries which proceed from word to concept. See TERMINOLOGY. [LANGUAGE, NAME]. J.A., T.MCA.

ONOMASTICS [1930s: from Greek *onomastikós* related to names and naming]. The study of proper names, including their forms and uses, especially the names of persons (*Margaret, Thatcher, Margaret Thatcher*) and places (*Grantham, London, 10 Downing Street, the House of Commons*). Although a proper name may be given to anything, the *place-name* and the *personal name* have received most attention in onomastics. The study of place-names (*toponymy*) is closely allied to geography, history, and related disciplines. The study of personal names (*anthroponymy*) is related to genealogy, sociology, and anthropology. Another sub-discipline is *literary onomastics*, which examines the use of proper names in literature, and often focuses on the names of characters in fiction (*characternyms*). A primary requirement of onomastics is the clarification of certain basic terms relating to the concept *proper name*. In casual usage, proper names, proper nouns, and capitalized words are often taken to be the same thing. That assumption, however, can mislead, because the three expressions refer to three different things which partially overlap. A distinction between them is fundamental to onomastics and can be discussed in terms of semantics, grammar, and orthography.

Semantics. A proper name is often said to be an expression designating a particular person, place, thing, etc. That traditional characterization is useful in a rough and ready way, but poses two problems: (1) An expression like *the Prime Minister of the United Kingdom in 1989* designates a particular person, but would not usually be called a proper name. Some logicians have in fact so called it, because it does designate uniquely, but that is a technical, not an everyday, use of the term. (2) Expressions generally called proper names, such as *Margaret* and *Athens*, do not in fact designate particular persons. Many people have been and are now called *Margaret*, and in addition to the original Athens in Greece, many other locations now bear that name; in the US there are Athenses in Georgia, Ohio, and elsewhere.

What designates proper names semantically is not *what* they designate, but *how* they designate. *The Prime Minister of the United Kingdom in 1989* designates a particular person by describing characteristics that the person must have in order to be so designated, namely, 'holding the office of Prime Minister', 'holding that office in the United Kingdom', and 'holding that office in the year 1989'. On the other hand, the name *Margaret* designates any person who happens to be so called, without any characteristics being necessary. Even if no one has ever used the expression *the Prime Minister of the United Kingdom in 1989* to refer to Margaret Thatcher, she would still be the referent because she meets the characteristics specified in it. However, if a woman has not been named *Margaret* and no one has ever called her that, she cannot be so designated. Semantically, proper names are expressions used to designate a person, place, or thing that people have agreed to call by that name. It implies no characteristics beyond use of the name to designate its referent. The proper name *Margaret* serves to denote 'a person called Margaret' and nothing more.

Grammar. Most nouns in English are either countable (unit) or uncountable (mass) nouns. Countable nouns have plurals and denote individual items; when they are singular, they must be accompanied by a determiner and take modifiers denoting number: *a chair, many chairs*, but **chair* alone is normally ungrammatical. Uncountable nouns have no plural and denote a kind of thing; they may be used without a determiner and they take modifiers denoting amount: *furniture, less furniture, too much furniture*, but not in standard usage **a furniture* or **many furnitures*. Proper nouns are countable nouns, but are peculiar in that they are typically used (as most such nouns cannot be) in the singular without a determiner: *Margaret*, but also 'I know a *Margaret*' and 'There are many *Margarets* among my friends.' Most words that are semantically proper names are also grammatically proper nouns, but some proper names must be used with a determiner (generally *the*) in the singular: 'I live in *the Bronx* and have visited *the Argentine*', not 'I live in **Bronx* and have visited **Argentine*.' Conversely, some grammatically proper nouns are not semantically proper names. *Wednesday* is a proper noun because it is countable but can be used in the singular without a determiner: 'There are five *Wednesdays* in this month' and 'We will visit you on *Wednesday*.' However, *Wednesday* can also be defined as the middle day of the week: that is, the word is defined by characteristics that its referents have relative to other things in the world, and not merely by the fact that they are called by the name *Wednesday*. So most semantically proper names are grammatically proper nouns and vice versa, but not all.

Orthography. Most proper names are capitalized in English, and many capitalized words are proper names, but initial capitals are also used for a great many ordinary words, including common nouns, and so are not a precise guide to the 'properness' of a name. Specifically, words derived from or related to a proper name are usually capitalized. *Plato* and *America* are proper names and nouns and are capitalized. *Platonist* and *American*, however, are capitalized because derived from proper names but are not themselves proper, either semantically or grammatically: 'She is a *Platonist* and an *American*, one of *many Platonists* and *many Americans* in the world.' Compare the French *Platon*, *platonicien(ne)* and *Amérique*, *américain(e)*, in which capitals are not used for the derivatives. Some common names and nouns in English are capitalized out of respect: *Prime Minister* and *President* are frequently given 'honorary' capitals, although they are common names and nouns by both definition ('chief executive officer of a government') and grammar ('It is time to choose *a new Prime Minister/President*', not 'It is time to choose **new Prime Minister/President*').

Names and naming. Anything may have a proper name, as long as people have felt the need of designating the thing by an expression that simply names rather than specifies its characteristics. People are almost invariably named; indeed, a human being without a name would be socially and psychologically less than fully human. When the Hollywood Tarzan meets his mate, their first conversation establishes name: 'Me Tarzan, you Jane.' With that introduction, the ape-man becomes less ape and more man. Animals have names, provided they are pets or have otherwise individually captured human interest. When they do have names, they are typically personified, referred to by the pronouns *who* and *he/she* rather than *which* and *it*. Places

are named, but only if they are of such interest to human beings that a proper way of designating them is thought fit. Mount Everest is named, but a Himalayan peak of medium height may not be.

Things of various kinds may also have names, always providing that they have been singled out as the objects of particular interest. Constellations have names, often quite diverse; one group of stars whose unity is that they appear to observers on earth to be close to one another, as well as to the North or Polar Star, is called *Ursa Major, Charles's Wain, the Plough, the Big Dipper*, among other names. A clock may have a name (*Big Ben* in London) and so may a bell (*the Liberty Bell* in Philadelphia). Houses may have names, especially if they are grand: *Longleat* in the UK, *the White House* in the US. In Britain in particular, private homes may be named in addition to or instead of having street numbers, because of location (*Braeside*: the side of a brae or hill), sometime use (*The Barn*), or an association which the owners wish to project (*Ocho Rios*, linking the owners with a town in Jamaica), or to indicate, often jocularly, the owners' situation (*Dunromin*, a pseudo-Celtic name disguising 'done roaming', that is, retired). A named residence often has, or is assumed to have, a social cachet. In North America, it is chiefly vacation homes that are named, often poetically and jocularly (*Mountainview, Dew Drop Inn*).

Ships, smaller boats, trains, cars, and bicycles can be named. Names for larger vehicles, especially of public transportation, are for convenience of reference, but may also be romantically evocative: the trains known as *the Orient Express* (Paris-Istanbul), *the Flying Scotsman* (London-Edinburgh), *the Frontier Mail* (India: North-West Frontier-Delhi-Bombay). Names for smaller, personal vehicles are generally the result of imitation of the grander names and/or involve playful animism and personification: 'Old Bess needs her valves ground, but then she's 12 years old next month.' Parts of the body, especially the sexual organs, are sometimes named, especially the penis, with hypocorisms like *dick* and *willie*; the long-established full name for the penis, *John Thomas*, appears in D. H. Lawrence's *Lady Chatterley's Lover* (1928). Trees and rocks can be named: *General Sherman* is the name of a particularly old, large redwood tree in California; *Pilgrims' Rock* is the point at which the Pilgrim Fathers are said to have stepped ashore from the *Mayflower* in 1620. Musical compositions, ballets, paintings, sculptures, poems, plays, novels, and other works of art have names that are referred to as titles.

Fictional place-names. Of necessity, authors invent names for the locales of their stories: Shakespeare's *Forest of Arden* in *As You Like It*; Samuel Johnson's *Happy Valley* in *Rasselas*; J. M. Barrie's town of *Thrums*, in *A Window in Thrums*, based on his home town of Kirriemuir in Scotland; Sir Arthur Conan Doyle's *Grimpen Mire*, an imaginary marsh on Dartmoor in England, in *The Hound of the Baskervilles*; Sinclair Lewis's *Zenith*, an archetypal Midwestern American city; William Faulkner's *Yoknapatawpha County*, the site of much of his fiction; Garrison Keillor's *Lake Wobegon*, made famous in radio and print. Fantasy literature is rich in invented names, since the author of a work about an imaginary world is faced with the necessity of naming all its features. The English writer and philologist J. R. R. Tolkien's *Middle-Earth* cycle (*The Hobbit*, *The Lord of the Rings*, *The Silmarillion*, etc.) has been the subject of intense onomastic study, because of the large number of its names and Tolkien's skill in inventing them. The American science-fiction writer Ursula LeGuin has herself written about the naming process in literature, in *Language of the Night*, a collection of essays.

Characternyms. Whereas invented places and place-names are optional in literature, most writers invent characters and therefore personal names. The special feature of the *characternym*, however, is that it usually represents its bearer in some appropriate way: traditionally, a hero sounds dashing and aristocratic (*Mr Fitzwilliam Darcy*, in Austen's *Pride and Prejudice*, 1797), a heroine romantic (*Jane Eyre*, in the novel of the same name, by Charlotte Brontë, 1847), a villain nasty (*Mr Wackford Squeers*, the bullying headmaster in Dickens's *Nicholas Nickleby*, 1838-9). It has been common to provide characters with names that indicate or hint at their qualities: *Justice Squeezum* (in Fielding's *Rape upon Rape*, 1730), *Lady Sneerwell* (in Sheridan's *The School for Scandal*, 1777). Such names are allegorical, their intent made more or less obvious to the reader. In allegory proper, little subtlety or indirection is employed. Characters personify types and qualities, and are named appropriately: *Christian*, *Faithful*, *Giant Despair*, and *Mr Valiant-for-Truth* in Bunyan's *The Pilgrim's Progress* (1678). Allegorical usage survives in the 20c, as in the James Bond novels of Ian Fleming, in which an evil Chinese superscientist is *Dr No*, a character who loves gold is *Auric Goldfinger*, and a sexually vigorous woman pilot is *Pussy Galore*.

Writers, and novelists in particular, generally choose the names of their characters with care, to achieve the right connotative effect. When Margaret Mitchell was drafting her novel *Gone with the Wind* (1936), she first named her female protagonist *Pansy*, only later changing the name to *Scarlett O'Hara*. Although *Pansy O'Hara* captures some of the personality of the character, especially her youthful naïvety, it does not suggest the unconventionality and resourcefulness that she eventually shows. *Scarlett*, with its connotations of brightness, explosiveness, vigour, strength, and disdain for conventional morality, better suits the character. The two central characters of Thackeray's *Vanity Fair*, Becky Sharp and Amelia Sedley, could hardly have their names exchanged. Becky is the sharp dealer; Amelia is the better (ameliorated) of the two.

Associations and publications. In the US the American Name Society treats all branches of onomastics, holding several meetings a year and publishing a journal, *Names*. In Europe, the study is active through the journal *Onoma*, published by the International Committee of Onomastic Sciences at the International Centre of Onomastics in Leuven/Louvain, Belgium. An International Congress of Onomastic Sciences is held every few years. See ALLEGORY, APTRONYM, CHARACTERNYM, FANTASY, FICTION, -ONYM, SEMANTICS, TITLE, WORD. [LANGUAGE, NAME].

J.A.

ONOMATOPOEIA [16c: through Latin from Greek *onomatopoiia* making a name. Derived adjectives: both *onomatopoeic* and *onomatopoetic*]. A figure of speech in which: (1) Words are formed from natural sounds: *ping*, *cock-a-doodle-doo*, *rat-a-tat-tat*, *ding-dong*. (2) Words are used and sometimes adapted, including visually, to suggest a sound: *snow crackling and crunching underfoot*, *trrring* (of a bell), *R-r-i-i-p-p!* (of cloth tearing). In onomatopoeic usage, sound and sense echo and reinforce each other, often using alliteration and assonance; hence the alternative but more inclusive term *echoism*. Onomatopoeia is common: (1) In children's stories: *Only a bee tree goes, 'Buzz! Buzz!'* (2) In comic books and cartoons: *WHAM! POW! KERSPLAT! KABOOM!* (3) In the language of advertising: *All 3 Kodak disc cameras go bzzt, bzzt, flash, flash. One goes tick, tock, beep, beep. And anyone who gets one for the holidays will go oooooohh!* (4) When writers want to build up a phonaesthetic effect: 'The childhood dreams of . . . the grinning Fe-Fi-Fo-Fum giant swinging his axe . . . the slush-slurp of the Creature emerging from the Black Lagoon' (James Herbert, *Shrine*, 1983); 'The very words which define flatterers have a kind of onomatopoetic cringe: sneaking sycophants; fawning adulators; lickspittling toadies; crumb-catching crawlers' (*The Listener*, 2 July 1987). See ALLITERATION, ASSONANCE, ECHOISM, PHON(A)ESTHESIA. [NAME, STYLE].

T.MCA.

-ONYM [through Latin from Greek *ónuma*/ *ónoma* name]. A word base or combining form that stands either for a word (as in *synonym*) or a name (as in *pseudonym*). Words containing *-onym* have two kinds of adjective: with *-ous*, as in *synonymous* (having the nature or quality of a synonym: *synonymous words*) or with *-ic*, as in *synonymic* (concerning synonyms: *synonymic relationships*). The form *-onymy* indicates type, as with *synonymy* (the type of sense relation in which words have the same or similar meaning) and *eponymy* (the category of word-formation that concerns words derived from people's names). Because *-onym* begins with *o* (the commonest Greek thematic vowel, as in *biography*), the base form is sometimes taken to be *-nym*, an assumption reinforced by the initial *n* of the equivalent terms *nomen* in Latin and *name* in English. As a result, some recent technical terms have been formed on *-nym*: for example, *characternym* and *paranym*. See ACRONYM/ PROTOGRAM, ANTONYM, APTRONYM, CHARACTERNYM, EPONYM, HETERONYM, HOMONYM, HYPERONYM, HYPONYM, ONOMASTICS, PATRONYMIC, PSEUDONYM, RETRONYM, SYNONYM, TOPONYM. [NAME, WORD]. T.MCA.

OPPOSITE. See ANTONYM, SEMANTICS.

OPPOSITION [14c: from Latin *oppositio*/ *oppositionis* setting against, from *opponere*/ *oppositum* to place against, oppose]. (1) Opposing, especially through protest and criticism; being on the opposite side in an argument or debate, etc. (2) In logic, the relationship between two propositions in which the truth or falsity of one determines the falsity or truth of the other. (3) In linguistics, a functional contrast between partially similar elements in a language system: for example, between the meanings and uses of the negative prefixes *un-* and *non-* in *unprofessional* and *nonprofessional*, where *un-* is judgemental and *non-* is neutral. (4) In phonetics, the nature of the contrast between a pair of phonemes: for example, /t/ is a voiceless alveolar stop and /d/ is a voiced alveolar stop. The two consonants agree in place and manner of articulation, but fall into the opposition of voicing. See MINIMAL PAIR, PHONEME. [LANGUAGE, SPEECH]. T.MCA., G.K.

ORACY [1965: from Latin *os*/*oris* mouth, and *-acy* as in *literacy*]. The ability to express oneself (fluently) in speech: 'The term we suggest for general ability in the oral skills is *oracy*; one who has these skills is *orate*, one without them is *inorate*' (Andrew Wilkinson, *Spoken English*, 1965). Compare LITERACY. [EDUCATION, LANGUAGE, SPEECH]. T.MCA.

ORAL APPROACH. See LANGUAGE TEACHING.

ORALISM [1880s]. The theory, practice, or advocacy of education for the deaf mainly or exclusively through lip-reading, and training in speech production and the use of any residual hearing ability, instead of by signing. See SIGN LANGUAGE. [EDUCATION, SPEECH]. T.MCA.

ORALITY [17c]. (1) A term for the quality of being oral or a tradition that is entirely oral, especially as discussed in *Orality and Literacy*, by Walter J. Ong (1982). Ong distinguishes two kinds: *primary orality*, the condition of humankind before the invention and spread of writing, and *secondary orality*, a recent development associated with such inventions as the telephone, radio, and television. (2) In psychoanalysis, the condition of being oral: that is, in the stage of infantile psychological and sexual development in which pleasure is obtained from eating, sucking, and biting. Compare ORACY, ORATURE. [MEDIA, SPEECH]. T.MCA.

ORAL LITERATURE [20c]. A term in literary criticism for forms of oral art in societies with little or no recourse to writing that nonetheless have the same qualities as literary texts. Strictly speaking, the elements of the term are incompatible, because literature is fundamentally the outcome of writing and not of speech, but it is widely used and has proved convenient on the assumption that *literature* is an artistic enterprise whose nature is not confined to writing and print despite the fact that these are its main vehicles. The American scholar Walter J. Ong has, however, argued that it is a 'preposterous term' that continues to circulate 'even among scholars now more and more acutely aware how embarrassingly it reveals our inability to represent to our own minds a heritage of verbally organized materials except as some variant of writing, even when they have nothing to do with writing at all' (*Orality and Literacy*, 1982). See ORAL TRADITION, ORATURE. [LITERATURE, SPEECH]. T.MCA.

ORAL TRADITION. The tradition of passing on by word of mouth (from person to person and especially generation to generation) oral art forms such as poems, songs, chants, genealogies, and proverbs, often incorporating information of importance for culture and livelihood. Genres such as folk-tales and ballads, that are usually eventually written down and 'fixed' in particular forms, are usually the products of long-established oral traditions. In present-day literate societies, word of mouth sustains, among other things, an 'underground' tradition of taboo or *risqué* anecdotes, jokes, and limericks. See BALLAD, COMMUNICATIVE SHIFT, FOLK, JOKE,

ORALITY, ORAL LITERATURE, ORATURE, PROVERB, SAYING. [LITERATURE, SPEECH].   T.MCA.

ORATORY [16c: from Latin (*ars*) *oratoria* (the art of) speaking]. The art and practice of speaking in public, especially if intended to be eloquent and in the grand style of traditional rhetoric. See ELOCUTION, ORTHOEPY, PUBLIC SPEAKING, RHETORIC. [SPEECH, STYLE].   T.MCA.

ORATURE [1980s: from Latin *os/oris* mouth and *-ature* as in *literature*, or a syncopation of *oral literature*, coined quite separately at around the same time and for slightly different purposes in Kenya by Micere Mugo and in Canada by Tom McArthur]. An occasional technical term for the poetic, dramatic, and other oral genres and traditions of pre- or non-literate peoples, either before the invention of writing or in parts of the world that have maintained non-literate traditions intact, such as in Africa and South America: 'Like the ancient Hindus, the Greeks had vast and complex oral heritages that might more accurately be called their "*orature*", since the other term implies letters and literacy' (Tom McArthur, *A Foundation Course for Language Teachers*, 1983); 'In Kenya, English became more than a language: it was *the* language, and all the others had to bow before it in deference. . . . Orature (oral literature) in Kenyan languages stopped. In primary school I now read simplified Dickens and Stevenson alongside Rider Haggard' (Ngugi wa Thiong'o, *Decolonising the Mind*, 1986). Compare ORAL LITERATURE. See COMMUNICATIVE SHIFT, ORALITY, ORAL TRADITION. [LITERATURE, SPEECH].   T.MCA.

ORCADIAN [17c: from Latin *Orcades* the Orkney Islands]. (1) A person born or living in Orkney. The term is gender-neutral and appears to be gaining over *Orkneyman/Orkney man* and *Orkney woman*. See -MAN/WOMAN. (2) Relating to Orkney: *Orcadian dialect*. See ORKNEY. [EUROPE, NAME].   T.MCA.

ORGANS OF SPEECH. See SPEECH.

ORKNEY, sometimes **the Orkneys** (short for **the Orkney Islands**); *Orkney* is preferred by Orcadians. A group of islands off the northern coast of Scotland, constituting with Shetland the *Northern Isles*. Of the two, Orkney is closer to the mainland. Capital: Kirkwall. Population: 19,000 (1981). See NORN, NORTHERN ISLES, ORCADIAN, ORKNEY AND SHETLAND DIALECTS, SCOTLAND, SHETLAND. [EUROPE, NAME].   T.MCA.

ORKNEY AND SHETLAND DIALECTS. The dialects of the Northern Isles of Scotland: conservative varieties of Scots heavily influenced by the Norn which they superseded. The most similar mainland varieties are the most conservative of the Central Scots dialects: west Angus and east Perthshire.

Pronunciation. (1) Retention of the old front rounded vowel /ø/, written *ui*, *u-e*, or *ö*, as in *guid/gude/göd* and *scuil/scule/scöl*. (2) The preservation of the initial consonant clusters *kn-*, *gn-*, and *wr-*, as in *knee* /kniː/, *gnaw* /gnaː/, and *wrong* /wraŋ/. (3) Due to the Norn substratum: the stopping of the voiced and voiceless dental fricatives (*this* and *blithe* pronounced 'dis' and 'blide'; *three* and *earth* pronounced 'tree' and 'eart'); unvoiced realizations of /dʒ/ ('chust' for *just*). (4) Shetland tends to simplify /tʃ/ to /ʃ/: 'sheese' for *cheese*. (5) Shetland, like Icelandic, merges /hw/ and /kw/, in most localities as /kw/ (*white* pronounced 'quite'), but in south Mainland as /hw/ (*quite* pronounced 'white'), or with the sounds interchanged ('kweel' for *wheel*, 'hween' for *queen*).

Grammar. (1) Familiar *thou/thee/thy* alongside respectful *ye/you/your*. (2) Probably of Norn origin is the use of gender-marked personal pronouns, especially *he*, for weather, time, and other natural phenomena: *He was blaain a gale* It was blowing a gale; *Whin he begood tae flou, sheu set on an teuk brawly* When he [the tide] began to flow, she [the fish] set to and took (the bait) splendidly. (3) Commonly, perfective *be* rather than *have*: *I'm walked a piece the day* I've walked a long way today. (4) Limited use of simple inversion to form questions, as an alternative to the use of an auxiliary: *Whit tinks du?/Whit does du tink?* What do you think? and - a further example of Grammar (3): *Is du heard aboot yun afore?* Have you heard about that before? (5) Characteristic reflexive usages, especially in the imperative: *Heest dee!* Hurry up!; *Dip dee a meenit!* Sit down for a minute!; *A'll geng an rest me whin a'm pitten da bairns ta da scöl* I'll go and have a rest when I've put the children to school.

Vocabulary. (1) The vocabularies of the Northern Isles are distinct from those of other Scots dialects, mainly in their massive borrowing from Norn, of which over a thousand items survive. Typical examples of those in everyday use are: *benkle* dent, crumple; *frush* splutter, froth; *gaan* gawp; *glaep* gulp down, swallow greedily; *oag* crawl; *peedie* (Orkney)/*peerie* (Shetland) little; *roog* heap, pile; *skoit* peep, take a look; *smucks* carpet slippers; *spret* rip open, burst; *tirn* angry; *trivvel* grope, feel one's way. (2) Some words are structurally unusual for Scots, such as *andoo* to row a boat slowly against the tide, *brigdie/brigda* a basking shark, *fluckra* snow in large flakes, *glimro* phosphorescence (Orkney), *hyadens* animal carcasses (Shetland). (3) Some words fossilize Old Norse inflectional endings: the strong masculine -r in *ilder* fire (in the now-obsolete Shetland sea-language), *shalder* an oystercatcher; the weak masculine -i in *arvie* chickweed, *galtie* a pig, boar, *hegrie* a heron; the weak feminine -a in *arvo* chickweed, *shaela* hoar-frost (Shetland); the vocative in the former Birsay terms of address *gullie* to a man, *gullo* to a woman; and the gender distinctions in the Shetland sea-terms *russie* a stallion, *russa* a mare. (4) Some nouns contain the Old Norse suffixed definite article (*i*)*nn*: *croopan* trunk of the body, *fyandin* the devil (Shetland), *knorin* boat (Shetland), and the Shetland sea-terms *birten* fire, *hestin* horse, *monen* moon, and *sulin* sun. (5) Unique to Shetland, though now mostly archaic, are words borrowed from Dutch fishermen, who have visited Shetland since the 17c: *blöv* to die, *forstaa* to understand, *kracht* energy, *maat* a friend, *stör* a penny.

Literary texts. Both regions have dialect literatures that date from *c*.1880. There is considerable local interest in the native dialects, as shown in *The Orcadian* newspaper and articles in *The New Shetlander* magazine. The following are representative:

Orkney. So Geordie gleppid the last grain o tea ooto his cup and meed fir the byre. Noo Geordie was bothered sometimes wae a sore back when he waas been sta'an bent ower fir a while. So when he caam tae 'Reed coo', the bonniest and most litesome o aa the kye in Orkney, he glammed a haad o her yurrie waey his great knaves and keeled her ower i' the oddlar so he could milk her waeoot bendan doon too muckle (Karen Drever, Westray, *Geordie o Pizzlewusp*, first prize, dialect competition for under-16s, *The Orkney View*, Feb./Mar. 1989). [*glep* swallow, *grain* drop, *meed* made, *noo* now, *wae*(*y*) with, *waas been sta'an* had been standing, *coo/kye* cow/cows, *glam* grab, *haad* hold, *yurrie* udder, *knave* fist, *keeled her ower* threw her over, *oddlar* drain in a byre, *muckle* much. *Glep* and *oddlar* and probably *yurrie* are from Norn; *glam* and *knave* are Scots of Scandinavian origin]

Shetland. Twartree weeks later da story gaed roond at it wis a kist fae da Island a Hascosay, an it wisna a bonny story. Wan night lang fae syne a sailing ship had gone on a skerry in a storm dere an da men managed ta sweem ashore an wan o dem trailed his kist wi him an da folk on da Island cam doon ta da shoormel an murdered da whole lot an dis man wis sittin on his kist lid whin he wis struck doon (Joan M. Olsen, 'Da Hascosay Kist', *The New Shetlander* 168, Mar. 1989). [*twartree* two or three, *gaed* went, *at* that, *kist* chest, *fae* from, *wisna* was not, *lang fae syne* long ago, *skerry* reef, *shoormel* shoreline]

See DIALECT IN SCOTLAND, NORN, NORSE, ORKNEY, SHETLAND. [EUROPE, VARIETY].   A.J.A.

ORNAMENTAL ENGLISH. See DECORATIVE ENGLISH.

ORPHANS. See WIDOWS AND ORPHANS.

ORTHOEPY [17c: from Greek *orthoépeia* right speech, correct diction, from *orthós* right, *épos* speech: compare EPIC, ORTHOGRAPHY]. A term used mainly in the 17-18c for the part of grammar that deals with 'correct' pronunciation and its relation to 'correct' writing (*orthography*). The principles of orthoepy influenced a number of pronouncing (*orthoepic*) dictionaries of the time, such as William Kenrick's *A new Dictionary of the English Language: containing not only the explanation of words . . . but likewise their orthoepia or pronunciation in speech* (1773) and John Walker's *A Critical Pronouncing Dictionary of the English Language* (1791). Orthoepy, although primarily associated with elocution, is ancestral to phonetics and its application to language teaching, as in Daniel Jones's *English Pronouncing Dictionary* (1917). See COMMUNICATIVE SHIFT, CORRECT, ELOCUTION, ORTHOGRAPHY, PRONUNCIATION. [EDUCATION, GRAMMAR, SPEECH].   T.MCA.

ORTHOGRAPHY [15c: through French from Latin *orthographia*, Greek *orthographia* correct writing, from *orthós* right, straight, *graphós* writer]. (1) A term for correct or accepted writing and spelling and for a normative set of conventions for writing and especially spelling. In the 15-16c, there was considerable variety and uncertainty in the writing and printing of English. Advocates of standardized spelling emphasized the importance of regularization by referring to it as *trewe ortografye, trew orthographie*, etc. (2) The study of letters and how they are used to express sounds and form words, especially as a traditional aspect of grammar; the spelling system of a language, whether considered 'true' and 'correct' or not. In linguistics, however, the name for the study of the writing system of a language and for the system itself is more commonly *graphology*, a level of language parallel to *phonology*. The earlier, prescriptive sense of the term continues to be used, but the later, more neutral sense is common among scholars of language. The orthography of English has standardized on two systems, British and American. While far from uniform in either system, it allows for much less variation than is possible, for example, in the orthography of Scots. See ABBREVIATION, ACRONYM/PROTOGRAM, COMMUNICATIVE SHIFT, COMPOUND WORD, CORRECT, GRAMMATOLOGY, GRAPHOLOGY, NAME, ONOMASTICS, ORTHOEPY, SENTENCE, SHAKESPEARE, SIMPLIFIED SPELLING SOCIETY, SPELLING, SPELLING REFORM, TECHNOSPEAK, TRADITIONAL ORTHOGRAPHY, WORD. [GRAMMAR, WRITING].   T.MCA.

ORTON, Harold [1898-1975]. English dialectologist, born in Byers Green, County Durham, son of a village schoolmaster. His experience as an Army officer in the First World War and then as a student at Oxford (after being wounded and invalided out of the Army) impressed on him a form of speech that seemed to go against his passionate interest in dialect: while able to switch into the Durham dialect at any time, he was an ardent promoter of Received Standard. Orton studied under both Joseph Wright and Henry C. K. Wyld. From 1924 to 1928 he taught as Lektor in English at Uppsala, Sweden; returning to England, he was appointed at Armstrong College (the future U. of Newcastle), where he began his *Survey of Northumbrian Dialects*, which gave him grounding in field research. His monograph on Byers Green dialect was published in 1932 and during the 1930s he discussed with the Philological Society the possibility of a linguistic survey of England. He was lecturer in charge of the Department of English Language at the U. of Sheffield (1939-46). During the Second World War, he was seconded to work at the British Council as Deputy Director of Education and then Acting Director. After the war, he became Professor of English Language at the U. of Leeds where, at first with the collaboration of Eugen Dieth of Zurich, he set up a unit for the collection of material for a *Survey of English Dialects*. He retired from Leeds in 1964 and taught in various American universities, including Kansas, Michigan, and Iowa, working on a *Word Geography of England* (with Natalia Wright, Seminar Press, 1974). He also laid the basis for an archive of tape-recorded dialects kept at Leeds. The *Basic Material* for the Survey was published in 12 volumes (E. J. Arnold, Leeds, 1962-72) and *The Linguistic Atlas of England* in 1978. The completion of this mammoth work under his direction is the sole major piece of language research completed in England since the Second World War. See index. [BIOGRAPHY, EUROPE, LANGUAGE, VARIETY]. S.E.

ORWELL, George [1903-50]. Pen name of *Eric Arthur Blair*, English novelist, journalist, and political thinker. The adoption in 1933 of the pen name, taken from the River Orwell in East Anglia, marked his transformation from a member of the establishment of the British Empire into a social, political, and literary radical. He was born in Montihari, Bengal, India, the son of a British civil servant, and educated at Eton (where Aldous Huxley was one of his masters). From there he went in 1922 to serve in the Indian Imperial Police in Burma, but resigned because he disliked imperialism 'and every form of man's dominion over man'. In England in 1927, he became a reviewer and columnist, living for a

time in the poverty described in the 'documentary novel' *Down and Out in Paris and London* (1933). Six more works appeared before the Second World War: the novels *Burmese Days* (1934), *A Clergyman's Daughter* (1935), *Keep the Aspidistra Flying* (1936), *Coming Up for Air* (1939), and the non-fiction *The Road to Wigan Pier* (1937), *Homage to Catalonia* (1938). They range from reflections on his life in Burma and on class differences and unemployment in England to his experiences in the Spanish Civil War, in which he was wounded in the throat while fighting for the Republicans against Fascism. Orwell at first saw himself as an anarchist, then a socialist, but later sought to avoid political labels. He was opposed to totalitarianism in any guise. He died of tuberculosis, a disease from which he had suffered for many years. He is best known for his two post-war anti-totalitarian satirical novels, *Animal Farm* (1945) and *Nineteen Eighty-Four* (1949), the latter introducing the concept of *Newspeak*. From the same period comes the essay 'Politics and the English Language' (first published in *Horizon*, 1946), still frequently included in anthologies and widely admired for its advice on prose style.

Attitude to English. Like others of his time, background, and social position, Orwell was a polyglot: school Latin and Greek; school and colloquial French; Hindustani and Burmese as a police officer in Burma; Spanish as a soldier in Spain. He did not, however, accept contemporary standards for English; he often derided the variety of BrE common among his fellow Etonians, along with the variety employed on the BBC, seeing them as dangerous establishment tools. In its place, he advocated an artificial amalgam of lower-class varieties, including the *dropped aitch*, to be taught in schools. Orwell was not averse to the official promulgation of an invented variety of English. The Newspeak of *Nineteen Eighty-Four* is not, therefore, evil simply because it is artificial, but because its goals are untruth and mind control, and because its means to this end are the suppression of words for forbidden concepts (like *honour, justice*) and the ready conversion of parts of speech (like the verb *speak* as a noun, instead of *speech*). Orwell was in most ways a language conservative while he was a social individualist and a political adherent to 'democratic socialism', as he called it. His books sometimes champion those who speak non-standard English, but his essays severely oppose linguistic change and by implication condemn the diversity that change brings.

Rules for writing English. In 'Politics and the English Language', Orwell wrote that 'one can often be in doubt about the effect of a word or a phrase, and one needs rules that one can rely on when instinct fails. I think the following rules will cover most cases: (1) Never use a metaphor, simile or other figure of speech which you are used to seeing in print. (2) Never use a long word where a short one will do. (3) If it is possible to cut a word out, always cut it out. (4) Never use the passive when you can use the active. (5) Never use a foreign phrase, a scientific word or a jargon word if you can think of an everyday English equivalent. (6) Break any of these rules sooner than say anything outright barbarous.' The double implication (that half a dozen rules would 'cover most cases', and that all writers worthy of the name would agree about what was 'outright barbarous') reveals Orwell's conservative stand on the complexities of language variety. Hence, the adjective *Orwellian* can describe either the totalitarian political control that Orwell opposed, or the stringent linguistic standards that he advocated. See index. [BIOGRAPHY, EUROPE, LITERATURE, STYLE, WRITING].

W.F.B.

Bolton, W. F. 1984. *The Language of 1984: Orwell's English and Ours*. Oxford: Basil Blackwell.
Crick, Bernard. 1982. *George Orwell: A Life*. Harmondsworth: Penguin.

OTTAVA RIMA [19c: Italian, eighth or octave rhyme]. A form of stanza introduced into English in the 16c from Italian poetry by Sir Thomas Wyatt and at first used mainly in translations. It consists of eight iambic pentameters rhymed *abababcc* and has the effect of speed and vigour rather than dignity. Keats used it for a romantic story in 'Isabella, or The Pot of Basil' (1818). Its most successful extended use in English was Byron's 'Don Juan' (1819–24), where it proved effective for his wit and bravado:

What is the end of Fame? 'tis but to fill
A certain portion of uncertain paper:
Some liken it to climbing up a hill,
Whose summit, like all hills, is lost in vapour;
For this men write, speak, preach, and heroes kill,
And bards burn what they call their 'midnight taper',
To have, when the original is dust,
A name, a wretched picture and worse bust.

See RHYME, STANZA. [LITERATURE].

R.C.

OTTAWA VALLEY. A distinctive dialect region of Canada that extends along the Ottawa River from north-west of Montreal through the city of Ottawa and north to Algonquin Park. While the speech of the major towns is standard spoken CanE, that of the rural districts is strongly influenced by IrE, both from Ulster and the South, with small pockets of Lowland and Highland ScoE, and Gaelic, German, and Polish influence. The stereotypical feature of the accent is the local place-name *Carp* as /kærp/. Syntax includes *for to* as an infinitive complement: *Mary*

wants for to leave. Vocabulary includes (*cow*) *byre* a cowshed, cow barn, *moolie* a cow without horns, *snye* a channel (from French *chenail*), and *weight-de-buckety* or *weighdee* a teeter-totter, see-saw. See DIALECT IN CANADA. [AMERICAS, VARIETY].

M.F.

OVERSTATEMENT. See EXAGGERATION, HYPERBOLE.

OXBRIDGE [19c: a blend of *Oxford* and *Cambridge*. The term *Camford* is also occasionally used]. A composite name for the universities of Oxford and Cambridge and their shared traditions and characteristics, especially in contrast to other universities in England (often subsumed under the dismissive contrastive term *Redbrick*): 'Rough and ready, your chum seems . . . Somewhat different from your dandy friends at Oxbridge' (W. M. Thackeray, *Pendennis*, 1849); 'Oxbridge philosophers, to be cursory, / Are products of a middle-class nursery' (W. H. Auden, *Homage to Clio*, 1960); 'The prayer was often offered by a clergyman who read the liturgy with an Oxbridge accent even though he was a product of southern Ontario' (Toronto *Globe & Mail*, 1 July 1976). See CAMBRIDGE ENGLISH, CAMBRIDGE UNIVERSITY PRESS, OXFORD ACCENT, OXFORD ENGLISH, OXFORD UNIVERSITY PRESS. [EUROPE, NAME, SPEECH, STYLE].

T.MCA.

OXFORD ACCENT. A form of Received Pronunciation regarded as typical of faculty and students at the U. of Oxford, as opposed to the townspeople of Oxford. It was widely regarded, especially before the Second World War, as affected: 'It might be said perhaps that the "Oxford Accent" conveys an impression of a precise and rather foppish elegance, and of deliberate artificiality' (*Society for Pure English Tract* 39, 1934); 'The Sultan's manner is very deceptive. . . . His Oxford accent and his slang are all a sort of parody of our civilisation' (P. Dickinson, *Poison Oracle*, 1974). See AFFECTATION, OXFORD ENGLISH, RECEIVED PRONUNCIATION. [EUROPE, SPEECH].

T.MCA.

OXFORD ADVANCED LEARNER'S DICTIONARY OF CURRENT ENGLISH. See ELT PUBLISHING, HORNBY, JAPAN, LEARNER'S DICTIONARY, OXFORD DICTIONARIES, OXFORD UNIVERSITY PRESS.

OXFORD AND CAMBRIDGE SCHOOLS EXAMINATION BOARD, short form *O & C*. A joint examining body set up by Oxford and Cambridge universities in 1876 to examine the pupils of 'highest grade schools', separately from the pupils at schools emerging as a result of the Education Act of 1870. These are currently mainly the independent schools represented by the Headmasters' Conference. See EXAMINING IN ENGLISH, PUBLIC SCHOOL ENGLISH. [EDUCATION, EUROPE].   w.s.

OXFORD DELEGACY. A local examining body of England and Wales based on the U. of Oxford, founded in 1857 and responsible for school examinations in its own region and elsewhere. It operates currently as a member of the Southern Examining Group for the *General Certificate of Secondary Education* (*GCSE*). A written examination at two levels for foreign learners of English is conducted by the board, to complement the ARELS/FELCO oral examinations. Although primarily designed with students at local language schools in mind, it has been promoted overseas. See ARELS, EXAMINING IN ENGLISH. [EDUCATION, EUROPE].   w.s.

OXFORD DICTIONARIES. A range of English dictionaries published by the Oxford University Press, the first and greatest of which is *The Oxford English Dictionary*. The extensive investigation of printed sources of all kinds remains the main basis of this work, with electronic methods becoming increasingly important as a means of storing and applying the material obtained. At the heart of the Oxford family lie the scholarly works produced in the wake of the *OED*, but not to be overlooked is Joseph Wright's *English Dialect Dictionary* (1896-1905). Work on the *OED* began in 1879 when an agreement was signed between James A. H. Murray and the Clarendon (Oxford University) Press. It was soon realized, especially by Charles Cannan, Secretary to the Delegates from 1898, that Murray's materials and work could serve as sources for smaller and more profitable works, the first of which was the Fowler brothers' *Concise Oxford Dictionary* (1911). By the 1930s, the range included the *Pocket* (1924), the *Little* (1930), and the *Shorter Oxford English Dictionary* (1933), the last an abridgement of the *OED*. New editions of the smaller dictionaries appear regularly, and a revision of the *Shorter* is in progress.

More recently, the dictionaries have been augmented with works having a less formal presentation and style of definition, such as the *Oxford Paperback Dictionary* (1979), the first of its kind to include systematic advice on usage. Dictionaries dealing with special aspects of language include *The Oxford Dictionary of English Etymology* (1966), *The Oxford Dictionary for Writers and Editors* (1981), which sets out the OUP house style, and *The Oxford Spelling Dictionary* (1986). There are also dictionaries for foreign learners of English, notably the *Advanced Learner's Dictionary of Current English*, which first appeared in 1948, and dictionaries for children. To begin with, the smaller dictionaries were commissioned from outside editors such as the Fowlers; later revisions and new editions were done on the same basis. Editors had little if any direct contact with their users and it was the practice of the day for the publishers in Oxford to deal with correspondence from the public, consulting the editors as necessary.

In 1957, an in-house office was set up under the editorship of Robert W. Burchfield to produce a new *OED* Supplement, and this developed into an English Dictionaries department with Burchfield as chief editor until 1984. In addition to the *Supplement to the OED* (in four volumes, published 1972-86), the department has been responsible for new dictionaries and revisions of existing dictionaries, drawing on language data mainly in the form of several million citations of usage. ELT dictionaries, however, are published separately by the ELT Division. In recent years, there have been several adaptations of the smaller dictionaries to cater for English overseas, such as Australian, New Zealand, and South African editions of the *Pocket Oxford*, all produced by editors in or from the countries concerned.

In the 1990s, a chief concern is to develop dictionaries as computer databases, as editorial tools, and as marketable products. The interaction of computer methods and new approaches to the presentation of lexical information continues to influence developments in the compiling and revision of all the Oxford dictionaries.

See CONCISE OXFORD DICTIONARY, DICTIONARY, ENGLISH DIALECT DICTIONARY, FOWLER, LEARNER'S DICTIONARY, MODERN ENGLISH USAGE, MURRAY, OXFORD DICTIONARY OF ENGLISH ETYMOLOGY, OXFORD ENGLISH DICTIONARY, OXFORD UNIVERSITY PRESS, SKEAT, WRIGHT. [EUROPE, REFERENCE].   R.E.A.

OXFORD DICTIONARY FOR WRITERS AND EDITORS. See HOUSE STYLE, OXFORD DICTIONARIES.

OXFORD DICTIONARY OF ENGLISH ETYMOLOGY, short form *ODEE*. The last work of C. T. Onions, a co-editor of *The Oxford English Dictionary*, who died while the *ODEE* was going through the press. It was published in 1966, completed by G. W. S. Friedrichsen and R. W. Burchfield. The work was based on the *OED* and incorporated further research, notably from published parts (then A-F) of the *Middle English Dictionary*. A *Concise Dictionary of English Etymology*, edited by T. F. Hoad, was published in 1986. See ETYMOLOGY, ONIONS, OXFORD DICTIONARIES. [REFERENCE].   R.E.A.

OXFORD DICTIONARY OF QUOTATIONS.
See QUOTATION.

OXFORD ENGLISH [Early 20c]. (1) English spoken with an *Oxford accent*, widely considered, especially in the earlier 20c, to be 'the best' BrE usage, but also regarded by many as affected and pretentious. (2) A term used by Oxford University Press in recent years virtually as a trade name in the promotion of English-language reference books and ELT course materials. It also occurs in the title of *Oxford English: A Guide to the Language*, ed. I. C. B. Dear (1983). This work is presented as 'a guide to correct written and spoken English and an accessible introduction to the language in all its aspects'. It includes a range of essays on the written and spoken language, guides to proverbs, quotations, and writers, and to classical literature, and glossaries of technical terms (commercial and legal; scientific and medical; computing; literary). The Oxford editors R. W. Burchfield and E. S. C. Weiner write respectively on the history of the language and on aspects of word-formation, vocabulary, grammar, punctuation, and spelling. (3) A name for the teaching of English language and literature at the U. of Oxford: 'Meanwhile, what of Oxford, where the degree included a good deal of Old and Middle English, and literature stopped in 1830? Under the unadventurous guidance of George Gordon, Oxford English wanted no part in the Arnold–Newbolt–Cambridge line' (Bernard Bergonzi, *Exploding English*, 1990). See BBC ENGLISH[1], CAMBRIDGE ENGLISH, OXFORD ACCENT, OXFORD UNIVERSITY PRESS, RECEIVED PRONUNCIATION. [EUROPE, MEDIA, SPEECH, VARIETY].   T.MCA.

OXFORD ENGLISH DICTIONARY, short form *OED*. The foremost dictionary of the English language, initiated by the Philological Society as *The New English Dictionary on Historical Principles* (*NED*) and published by Oxford University Press, 1st edition 1928 (12 volumes, with later Supplements), 2nd edition 1989 (20 volumes). Shortly after its founding in 1842, the Philological Society appointed an 'unregistered words committee' to collect English words not listed in existing dictionaries, and its members, Herbert Coleridge, Frederick Furnivall, and Richard Chenevix Trench, came to the conclusion that a large new work was required. In 1857, Trench read two papers to the Society, jointly entitled 'On Some Deficiencies in our English Dictionaries'. They covered the need to find better ways to manage obsolete words, describe derivational families, provide accurate and dated citations, list important senses of words, distinguish synonyms, cover literary sources, and eliminate redundant material.

For Trench and his associates, a dictionary was a factual inventory rather than a tool for selecting only the 'good' words of a language (however decided); a lexicographer was therefore a historian rather than a moralist, judge, or teacher. An adequate dictionary of the language would record all possible words, much as the botanist Linnaeus had sought to record all possible plants. As a result of his recommendations, the Society passed resolutions in 1858 calling for a new dictionary 'on historical principles'. It would follow the lead established in Germany by the classicist Franz Passow and the philologists Jakob and Wilhelm Grimm. In 1812, Passow had recommended, for the compilation of a Greek lexicon, that definitions should be supported by textual citations organized chronologically, and in 1838 the brothers Grimm had begun the *Deutsches Wörterbuch*, aiming to cover all the words of German 'from Luther to Goethe'. The Society resolved in its turn to cover all the words of English from AD 1000 onward, their definitions emerging from citations garnered by volunteers in many countries reading thousands of texts.

Preparation. Coleridge, as first editor, supervised the work of two committees, one dealing with literary sources, the other with etymology, and looked after the submission of citations, a process facilitated by the recent development of a good international postal system. On his premature death in 1861 at 31, the editorship passed to Furnivall, who realized that an efficient system of excerpting was needed. This meant that for the earlier centuries printed texts had to be prepared of manuscripts not hitherto easily available; he therefore founded in 1864 the *Early English Text Society* and in 1865 the *Chaucer Society*, preparing editions of texts of general benefit as well as immediate value to the project. None of this work, however, led to compilation; it was entirely preparatory and lasted for 21 years. There were in the end some 800 voluntary readers. Their enthusiasm was enormous, but in a process which depended on paper and pen alone a major drawback was the often arbitrary choices made by the relatively untrained volunteers regarding what to read and select, what to discard, and how much detail to provide.

Compilation. The first editor properly so called was the schoolmaster James A. H. Murray. When appointed in 1879, he took over from Furnivall nearly two tons of material, mainly slips of paper. The Society and Murray entered into an agreement with the Delegates of the Clarendon Press, Oxford U., that the Press would publish the Society's *New English Dictionary on Historical Principles*, often also known as 'the Society's Dictionary' and 'Murray's Dictionary'.

It was agreed that the work would take ten years to complete, be published at intervals in fascicles, and in its final form would consist of four volumes of some 6,400 pages. Its aim was 'to present in alphabetical series the words that have formed the English vocabulary from the time of the earliest records (*c.* AD 740) down to the present day, with all the relevant facts concerning their form, sense-history, pronunciation, and etymology', but excluding words and meanings that did not survive the Norman Conquest in the 11c; it would include 'not only the standard language of literature and conversation, whether current at the moment, or obsolete, or archaic, but also the main technical vocabulary, and a large measure of dialectal use and slang' (preface, 2nd edition).

The editors. The Dictionary had four cooperating editors between 1879 and 1928, each working with a staff of about six assistants. The first fascicle of 352 pages (*a–ant*) was published in 1884. In the same year, Henry Bradley joined Murray as one of his assistants, and the project moved from Mill Hill School, where Murray had been a master since 1870, to Oxford. There the work continued in two separate locations. Murray and his assistants worked in the famous *Scriptorium* (a garden shed fitted with pigeon-hole shelving in his home at 78 Banbury Road); the teams of Henry Bradley, William Craigie, and C. T. Onions, at the Old Ashmolean building in Broad Street. There were many setbacks during the long period of compilation, including Murray's death in 1915 and Bradley's in 1923. One problem concerned balance between writers before and after *c.*1900. Whereas it was feasible to aim at including all the vocabulary of earlier writers (insofar as their works were accessible in reliable editions), the operation needed to be scaled down for the later period because of the proliferation of published work, especially newspapers and academic publications. The collecting process began to falter in the 1890s, by which time the main task of evidence-gathering was deemed to be over.

The First Edition. Although the project continued to belong officially to the Philological Society, its presence in Oxford and the expense of sustaining it tended to make it more and more an Oxford undertaking. In 1895, this was reflected by the appearance for the first time, above the title on the cover of the fascicle *deceit–deject*, the words *The Oxford English Dictionary*. The new name was more distinctive than the old but was only established slowly; in the early 20c, it came more and more into use and eventually supplanted the old. When, after 71 years of preparation, the complete work appeared in 1928, it was *The Oxford English Dictionary*, consisting of 12 volumes of 15,487 pages covering 414,825 words backed by 5m quotations of which some 2m were actually printed in the dictionary text.

The Supplements. In 1933, Craigie and Onions issued a *Supplement* of 867 pages, intended to include details of all words and meanings that had come into the language while the *OED* was in preparation, but it fell well short of that target. In 1933, the team was dispersed and the enterprise brought to a close for a quarter of a century. A new *Supplement* was set in hand in 1957, under the editorship of Robert W. Burchfield. This work followed the pattern of the original in taking approximately four times as long to compile as the initial forecasts suggested, and ending up as four volumes instead of the one proposed volume of 1,275 pages. *The Oxford English Dictionary Supplement* (*OEDS*) reached out to the vocabulary of all parts of the English-speaking world, approximate parity of treatment being given to the major forms of English in the United Kingdom, North America, Australia, New Zealand, and elsewhere. Volume A–G was published in 1972, H–N in 1976, O–Scz in 1982, and Se–Z in 1986. The independent existence of the *OEDS* was brought to a close by plans in the early 1980s for an electronic merging of the 12 volumes of the *OED* and the four volumes of the *OEDS*.

The Second Edition. Preparation for this began in 1983 and editorial work started the following year under the administrative direction of Timothy J. Benbow, and with John A. Simpson and Edmund S. C. Weiner as co-editors. An electronic system for integrating the original text and the supplements was created with help in the form of equipment and expertise from IBM (UK) Ltd. The U. of Waterloo in Ontario, Canada, helped develop the software for parsing the text, with a grant from the government of Canada. The project also received a grant from the UK Department of Trade and Industry. More than 120 keyboarders of International Computaprint Corporation in Tampa, Florida, and Fort Washington, Pennsylvania, USA, started keying in over 350m characters, their work checked by 55 proof-readers in England. There were four major changes to the text: Murray's system for indicating pronunciation was replaced by the International Phonetic Alphabet; all foreign alphabets except Greek were transliterated; the initial capital letter given for each headword was replaced by a system that reflected the normal facts of the language in respect to capitalization (for example, *American/amity*, *Lady day/lady-bird*); and important changes were made to the typographical layout. The two sets of information were merged in 1987, and some 5,000 additional modern words and meanings were inserted. This edition was published in 1989 in 20 volumes. It has 21,728 pages and contains some 290,500 main entries, within which there are a further 157,000 combinations and derivatives in bold type (all defined), and a further 169,000 phrases and undefined combinations in bold italic type, totalling 616,500 word forms. There are some 2.4m illustrative quotations, some 6m words of text, and over 350m characters. The electronic base takes up 540 megabytes of storage.

The electronic *OED*. The text of the First Edition was made available on CD-ROM in 1988, and a CD-ROM version of the Second Edition appeared in 1992. Its electronic text, which has the capacity of indefinite adaptation and extension, is structured in such a way that it can yield any desired combinatorial information, such as all entered words of Arabic origin, all words or meanings first recorded in the year 1819, or all the illustrative quotations cited in the *Dictionary* from the works of a given author. Such information was previously obtainable only through a laborious and time-consuming page by page search of the printed work.

See BRADLEY, BURCHFIELD, COLERIDGE (H.), CONCISE OXFORD DICTIONARY, CRAIGIE, DICTIONARY, EARLY ENGLISH TEXT SOCIETY, ENGLISH DIALECT DICTIONARY, FURNIVALL, LEXICOGRAPHY, MURRAY, ONIONS, OXFORD DICTIONARIES, OXFORD DICTIONARY OF ENGLISH ETYMOLOGY, PHILOLOGICAL SOCIETY, WATSON. [AMERICAS, EUROPE, REFERENCE]. RO.W.B., T.MCA.

Aarsleff, Hans. 1967. *The Study of Language in England, 1780-1860*. Princeton: University Press.

Landau, Sidney I. 1984. *Dictionaries: The Art and Craft of Lexicography*, New York: Charles Scribner's Sons.

McArthur, Tom. 1986. *Worlds of Reference: Lexicography, Learning and Language from the Clay Tablet to the Computer*. Cambridge: University Press.

Murray, K. M. Elisabeth. 1977. *Caught in the Web of Words: James A. H. Murray and the Oxford English Dictionary*. New Haven: Yale University Press.

Simpson, J. A., & Weiner, E. S. C. (eds.). *The Oxford English Dictionary*. 1989, 2nd edition, Introduction. Oxford: Clarendon Press.

OXFORD TEXT ARCHIVE. See MACHINE-READABLE TEXT.

OXFORD UNIVERSITY PRESS, short form *OUP*. A publishing business that is a department of the U. of Oxford. In 1636, Charles I granted a charter to the University to print books, although printing in Oxford dates from some 150 years earlier and the appointment of a 'Printer to the University' can be traced to 1584. The printing of books became better established in 1690, when the University was bequeathed a large collection of equipment and types by Dr John Fell (1625-86), Dean of Christ Church, to whom it had entrusted the exercise of its printing privilege some 18 years earlier. The University's role has been exercised since the 17c by the appointment of a board of delegates chosen from its members, with the Vice-Chancellor as ex-officio chairman. The main function of the Press has been to publish religious and learned books, including bibles and prayer books and books published under the academic imprint *The Clarendon Press*, named after Lord Clarendon (1609-74), whose works were its most profitable early publications. In more recent times, it has also produced an increasing number of general and non-specialist books, including novels, popular biographies and histories, general science and nature books, and books for children. Its profits are applied to financing scholarly books and large-scale publishing ventures, and it has the status of a charity.

The principal contribution of the Press to the study and use of English has been in its extensive list of language reference books, especially dictionaries and usage books of various kinds. The most notable and influential works are: *The Oxford English Dictionary* (1928, 1989); *The Concise Oxford Dictionary* (1911 and later editions); *A Dictionary of Modern English Usage* by H. W. Fowler (1926 and later editions), and A. S. Hornby's *Advanced Learner's Dictionary of Current English* (first published in 1948). The last of these is produced for foreign learners of English by the ELT Division (formerly a part of Overseas Education set up in the 1920s). The ELT and Education Divisions have produced a long list of dictionaries, usage books, and course books for students, children, and foreign learners.

At about the time James Murray and his colleagues were working on the early letters of *OED*, the University Printer Horace Hart (appointed in 1883) was applying rules of style to the printing of the Press's books. He codified these in a booklet entitled *Hart's Rules for Compositors and Readers at the University Press Oxford*, circulated in 1893, published in its 15th edition in 1904, and in its 39th edition in 1983 (with corrections, 1984, 1986, 1987, 1989). This, together with *The Authors' and Printers' Dictionary* of F. Howard Collins, first published in 1905 and from the edition of 1981 known as the *Oxford Dictionary for Writers and Editors*, embodies the Oxford house style. This evolved largely from the needs of editors and printers to produce consistently presented text. Its best-known and most controversial features are: the *Oxford comma* (also called the *serial comma*), occurring before the word 'and' in a list of items (as in *pens, pencils, and paper*); and the preference on carefully argued grounds for the letter *z* in verbs such as *generalize* (in which *-ise* is also possible), despite the strong counter-claims of BrE usage. The style is regularly revised: in 1978, for instance, full points were dropped from abbreviations such as *BBC* consisting entirely of capital initials. The publishing business has branches throughout the world (including New York, Toronto, Delhi, Bombay, Calcutta, Madras, Karachi, Petaling Jaya, Singapore, Hong Kong, Tokyo, Nairobi, Dar es Salaam, Cape Town, Melbourne, and Auckland), some of which publish in their own right. The UK business was consolidated in Oxford in 1976, and most of its London offices were closed. The printing business was largely closed down in 1989.

See AUSTRALIAN NATIONAL DICTIONARY CENTRE, AUSTRALIAN PUBLISHING, BBC PRONUNCIATION UNIT, BIBLE, BRITISH NATIONAL CORPUS, BRITISH PUBLISHING, DICTIONARY OF MODERN ENGLISH USAGE, ELT PUBLISHING, FOWLER, HOUSE STYLE, INDIAN PUBLISHING, KING'S ENGLISH (THE), NEW ZEALAND PUBLISHING, OXFORD DICTIONARIES, OXFORD ENGLISH, OXFORD ENGLISH DICTIONARY, QUOTATION, SOUTH AFRICAN PUBLISHING. [EUROPE, MEDIA]. R.E.A.

OXYMORON [17c: through Latin from the neuter form of Greek *oxúmōros* sharp and dull, pointed and foolish. Stress: 'awk-si-MO-ron']. A term in rhetoric for bringing opposites together in a compact paradoxical word or phrase: *bittersweet; be cruel to be kind; a cheerful pessimist*. The term is often used for social comment, both humorously or cynically (such as calling *military intelligence* a contradiction in terms) and dramatically, as in 'It has become an oxymoron to speak of the Lebanese nation' (Jim Hoagland, *The Washington Post*, Apr. 1989). [STYLE].

T.MCA.

OZ [1900s: an adaptation of the abbreviation *Aus.*, perhaps influenced by the US journalist Lyman Frank Baum's *The Wizard of Oz*, 1900]. An informal term relating to Australia: *a trip to Oz, the Oz Olympic team*. The usage may be neutral or pejorative. It is first recorded in 1908, but only became popular in the 1970s, probably as a result of its use as the title of a satirical Sydney magazine, and attracts such epithets as *the Land of Oz* for Australia. Compare AUSSIE. [NAME, OCEANIA]. W.S.R.

P

P, p [Called 'pee']. The 16th letter of the Roman alphabet as used for English. It originated in the Phoenician symbol *pe*, which was adopted by the Greeks as *pi* (*Π*), an earlier form of which the Romans adopted as *P*.

Sound values. In English, the letter *p* is normally pronounced as a voiceless bilabial plosive, as in *pip*. Phonetic variations in English include a less aspirated value after initial *s*, as in *spot*, and an unreleased plosive before other consonants, as in *slipped* (as opposed to the gently released *p* in *slipper*). In final position, spoken /p/ may or may not be released: *slip*, *snap*.

Double *P*. (1) Final *p* is normally single (*tap*, *step*, *tip*, *stop*, *cup*, *kidnap*, *worship*), the form *steppe* probably reflecting French or German spelling, as the original Russian has only single *p*. Monosyllables double the final *p* after a single short vowel before a suffix beginning with a vowel (*stopping*, *stopper*, *stopped*). Few polysyllables end in *p*; if they do, the *p* is generally not doubled before suffixes: *galloped*, *gossiping*, *syrupy*. However, BrE treats *kidnap*, *worship* as though based on monosyllables (*kidnapped*, *worshipping*), though AmE often follows the polysyllabic pattern (*kidnaped*, *worshiping*). (2) The doubling of medial *p* after stressed simple short vowels is inconsistent, as in the pairs *apple/chapel*, *pepper/leper*, *copper/proper*. In *coppice* there is doubling, whereas related *copse* has a single *p*. (3) When *p* is preceded by some Latin prefixes, it is doubled because of the assimilation of a consonant, as in *apparent* (ad-parent), *oppose* (ob-pose), *suppress* (sub-press).

Epenthetic *P*. (1) The nasal equivalent of *p* is *m*. The phonetic closeness of the sounds represented by these letters has prompted an epenthetic *p* after *m* in *empty* (earlier *emti*), and in the variants *sempstress/seamstress*, *Thompson/Thomson*, and *Hampstead/Hamstead* (part of London and part of Birmingham, respectively). (2) Phonetically, there may be the same epenthetic *p*-quality in *dreamt* ('drempt') as in *empty*. (3) The *p* in related forms such as *redeem/redemption*, *consume/consumption* has been carried over from Latin etyma.

***PH*.** (1) The digraph *ph* with the value /f/ originated as the Latin transcription of Greek *phi* (*Φ*), which originally had the value of a heavily aspirated /p/ (comparable to the sound in *uphold*). *Ph* pronounced /f/ occurs almost only in roots of Greek origin (*pharmacy*, *philosophy*, *photograph*), but has been adopted by analogy in occasional words of non-Greek derivation, such as *nephew* (compare French *neveu*, German *Neffe*), BrE *sulphur* (compare Latin and AmE *sulfur*). The *ph* in the name *Stephen* is pronounced /v/ and is alternatively *v* as in *Steven*. (2) *Ph* before *th* is often pronounced /p/, for example 'diptheria' for *diphtheria*, 'dipthong' for *diphthong*, 'opthalmic' for *ophthalmic*, and this leads to spellings without *h*. See F.

Silent *P*. (1) Initially, in words of Greek derivation before *n* (*pneumonia*), *s* (*psalm*), *t* (*pterodactyl*), producing combinations that, if pronounced, would be alien to English phonology. Middle English sometimes omitted *p* in *salme*, *salter*, but in Modern English it is seen in *psalm*, *psalter*, *pseudo-*, *psittacosis*, *psoriasis*, *psyche*, *Ptolemy*, *ptomaine*, etc. Of Gaelic origin, *ptarmigan* probably acquired its *p* by analogy with Greek derivations. (2) Occasionally, as when preceding a syllable beginning with its voiced equivalent *b*, the sound of *p* is assimilated, so effectively becoming silent, as in *cupboard* ('cubberd'), *raspberry* ('razb(e)ry'). (3) The *p* of *receipt* is an etymologically motivated insertion and was formerly often also inserted in *conceit* and *deceit*, but Samuel Johnson kept it only in *receipt* on grounds of common usage. (4) Silent

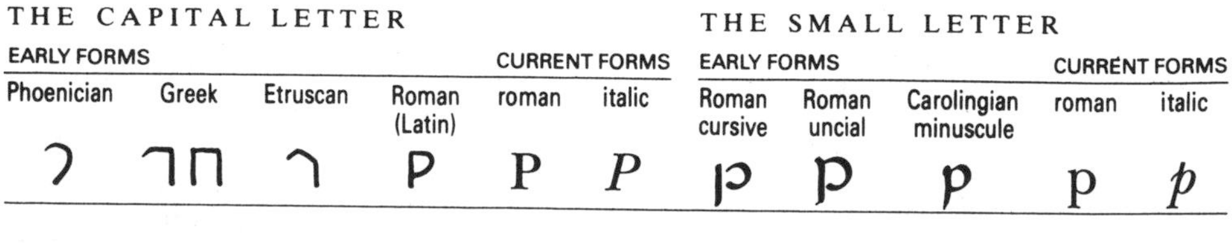
THE CAPITAL LETTER
EARLY FORMS
CURRENT FORMS
Phoenician
Greek
Etruscan
Roman (Latin)
roman
italic
THE SMALL LETTER
EARLY FORMS
CURRENT FORMS
Roman cursive
Roman uncial
Carolingian minuscule
roman
italic

p occurs in *sapphire*, whose first *p* was introduced to Middle English *safir* on etymological grounds. It also occurs in such French loans as *corps* and *coup*. (5) Whether *p* is pronounced after *m* in, for example, *empty, exempt, tempt, prompt, consumption* (as well as in *dreamt*) is unclear; at all events, the preceding bilabial *m* prepares the lips for *p* and is released as for /p/ with the following consonant. See ALPHABET, LETTER[1], SPELLING. [WRITING].　　　　　　　　　　　　　　　　C.U.

PACIFIC JARGON ENGLISH, also **South Seas English, South Seas Jargon, Jargon**. A trade jargon used by 19c traders and whalers in the Pacific Ocean, the ancestor of Melanesian Pidgin English. The whalers first hunted in the eastern Pacific but by 1820 were calling regularly at ports in Melanesia and took on crew members from among the local population. The sailors communicated in Jargon, which began to stabilize on plantations throughout the Pacific area after 1860, wherever Islanders worked as indentured labourers. See AUSTRALIAN PIDGIN, CHINA, JARGON, MELANESIAN PIDGIN ENGLISH. [OCEANIA, VARIETY].　　　　　　　　　　　　　　　　S.R.

PACIFIC RIM [Late 20c]. A collective term for countries around the Pacific Ocean, widely regarded in recent years as of great potential economic importance in the 21c. Throughout the area, English is the language of business and technology and the primary language of international communication. See AUSTRALIA, CANADA, CHINA, EAST ASIAN ENGLISH, HAWAII, HONG KONG, INDONESIA, JAPAN, KOREA, MACAO, MALAYSIA, MELANESIA, MICRONESIA, NEW ZEALAND, PAPUA NEW GUINEA, PHILIPPINES, POLYNESIA, SINGAPORE, UNITED STATES. [AMERICAS, ASIA, OCEANIA].　　　　　　　　T.MCA.

PAGE [16c: from French *page*, a reduction of *pagine*, from Latin *pagina* a vine trellis, column of writing, leaf, page, from *pangere/pa(n)ctum* to fasten, set]. (1) One side of a leaf or sheet of paper, especially in a book, pamphlet, newspaper, letter, etc. Technically, a page is either the *recto* side of a leaf (on the right as one looks at a book) or the *verso* (found when one 'turns the page'). (2) A leaf or sheet of paper. (3) In printing, the type as set up for printing a single page. (4) *Page* is often used as a verb, especially with prepositional and adverbial particles: if one *pages through* a book, one leafs through it; if one *pages up* or *pages down* on a computer screen, one shifts the displayed text up or down a screen at a time. If one *pages* a book, one paginates it (that is, provides the pages with numbers). See BOOK, LEAF, PAGINATION, PAPER. [TECHNOLOGY].　　　　　　　　　　　　　　　　W.W.B.

PAGE PROOF [1880s]. A typeset page of text ready to be proof-read. Traditionally, page proofs are a second stage in preparing printed text, after the *galley proofs* have been corrected and divided. With recent innovations, they are now often the first proofs seen by proof-reader or author, because typesetting equipment can now automatically divide material and provide running heads and page numbers. Page proofs are often divided into two stages: in Britain *proofs*, in North America *first pages*; then *revises* (first revise, second revise, etc.). See GALLEY, PROOF-READING. [TECHNOLOGY].　　　　W.W.B.

PAGINATION [1830s: from Latin *paginatio/paginationis* making pages: see PAGE]. Numbering pages in a book. The standard way is on both sides of a leaf, recto odd, verso even, a system that evolved in the 15–17c and the basis for finding information by means of indexes, contents lists, etc. (as opposed to such devices as paragraph and section numbers). The language of the text is located not by meanings or divisions in the text, but by spatial and material layout, which may change from edition to edition. See PAGE. [TECHNOLOGY].　　　　　　　　W.W.B.

PAKEHA [1810s: from Maori. Both with and without an initial capital letter. Plural: *pakehas, pakeha*]. A widely used name in New Zealand for a white person or a European, in contrast to *Maori*: 'Rua came from Taupo to the coastal district to work on the farm of a Pakeha' (R. Finlayson, *Brown Man's Burden*, 1938); 'Most damaging of all, the treaty [of Waitangi] failed to safeguard the standing of the Maori in their own country, for they have become an underdeveloped minority surrounded by pakeha affluence in a society where pakeha values have become the measure of all things. Cultural assimilation has been the 20th century norm— the whites providing the culture and the Maoris the assimilation' (Robert Macdonald, *Guardian*, 3 Mar. 1984). The term *pakeha Maori* has been used for a European who adopts the Maori way of life. See ETHNIC NAME, MAORI, NEW ZEALAND. [NAME, OCEANIA].　　　　　　　　　　　T.MCA.

PAKISTAN. Official title: Urdu *Islámi Jamhúriya-e Pákistán*, English *Islamic Republic of Pakistan*. A country of South Asia. Capital: Islamabad. Currency: the rupee (100 paisa). Economy: mixed. Population: 105.7m (1988), 150m (projection for 2000). Religion: 97% Muslim, 3% others. Ethnicity: 61% Panjabi, 21% Sindhi, 8% Pathan/Pashtun, 3% Baluchi, 3% Mohajir (Muslims who migrated from India in 1947–8), 2% Kashmiri. Languages: Urdu, English (both official), and such indigenous languages as Panjabi, Sindhi, Pashto, Baluchi, Kashmiri. English used as a second language by 2–3m people. Education: primary 49%, secondary 17%, tertiary 5%, literacy 25–30%. The name *Pakistan* (Urdu: Land of the Pure) was coined during the struggle for independence by Chaudhary Rahmat Ali and some other Muslim students at Cambridge in 1933. It is also an acronym of *Punjab, Afghania* (the North West Frontier), *Kashmir*, perhaps *Islam, Sind*, and the last syllable of *Baluchistan*. Before independence it was a collective term for the predominantly Muslim regions of British India. Mohammed Ali Jinnah's Muslim League adopted it in 1940, while bargaining for a separate Muslim state.

The Indian Independence Act of 1947 created two post-imperial states: India and Pakistan. In the first phase of its existence, Pakistan was a federation with two wings: *West Pakistan* in the north-west of the subcontinent (consisting of Baluchistan, North West Frontier, Sind, and West Punjab), *East Pakistan* in the north-east (consisting of East Bengal). In 1948, Pakistan occupied part of Kashmir, in the Indian state of Jammu and Kashmir, and called it *Azad Kashmir* (Free Kashmir). In 1956, Pakistan became an Islamic republic. In 1971, civil war in East Pakistan led to the independent state of *Bangladesh*. The influence of Islam, an uneasy relationship with India (including three wars since independence), close military ties with the US, and the alternation of military and civilian governments have been significant factors in the development of the country. See BANGLADESH, ENGLISH, INDIA, INDIAN LANGUAGES, PAKISTANI ENGLISH, PANJABI, SOUTH ASIAN BROADCASTING, SOUTH ASIAN ENGLISH, SPELT, TESL, URDU. [ASIA, NAME].   T.MCA.

PAKISTANI ENGLISH, short forms *PakE, PE*. The English language as used in Pakistan, a variety of South Asian English close to that of northern India. English has had co-official status with Urdu since independence in 1947, but the constitution of 1959 and the amendments of 1968, 1972, and 1985 recognize Urdu as pre-eminent and restrict the use of English, the aim being its eventual replacement. Both are minority languages. In 1981, the president appointed a study whose report recommended that 'Urdu should continue to be the only medium of instruction at the school level, with no exception' (1982), but that English and Arabic be introduced as additional languages from class six (sixth grade: age 11); a federal agency should ensure that the policy is implemented. English is an important medium in a number of leading educational institutions. It is the main language of technology, international business, and communication among a national élite, and a major element in the media. The constitution and the laws of the land are codified in English, and the *Pakistan Academy of Letters* recognizes works in English for its literature award. It also has a considerable influence on the vernacular languages; S. Hands notes that in personal interaction, 'the use of an English word is believed to add a note of refinement and elegance to conversation in the "lower" languages' (*Pakistan: A Country Study*, 4th edition, The American University, Washington, DC, 1983).

Pronunciation and grammar. (1) PakE is rhotic, tends to be syllable-timed, and shares many features with northern Indian English. (2) Some pronunciation features are typical of speakers of regional languages: for example, speakers of Panjabi have difficulty with such initial consonant clusters as /sk, sp/ (saying 'səport' and 'səkool' for *sport* and *school*); Urdu speakers also have difficulty with initial consonant clusters (saying 'isport' and 'iskool' for *sport* and *school*); Pashto-speakers have no such difficulty, but use /p/ for /f/ ('pood' for *food*). (3) Distinctive grammatical features relate to uses of the verb, article, relative clause, preposition, and adjective and verb complementation, all shared with IndE. Features of the indigenous languages influence use of English and code-mixing and code-switching are common, including among the highly educated.

Vocabulary. (1) Borrowings from Urdu and the regional languages: *atta* flour, *tehsil* district, *ziarat* religious place. (2) Loan translations from these languages: *cousin-brother*. (3) Terms shared with Indian English: *crore* ten million, *lakh* one hundred thousand, *-wallah* a word element denoting 'one who does something as an occupation', as with *policewallah*. (4) Hybrids of English and local languages: *biradarism* favouring one's clan or family, *gheraoed* surrounded by protesters in an office or similar place and unable to leave, *goondaism* hooliganism, thuggish behaviour. (5) English words, especially compounds, adapted for local use: *age-barred* over the age for (particular work), *load-shedding* intermittently shutting off a supply of electricity, *time-barred* referring to loss of validity after a specific period.

Media and literature. Pakistan has a strong English-language press. Most major cities have daily and weekly newspapers; in all, there are 20 dailies, 35 weeklies, 33 fortnightlies, 152 monthlies, and 111 quarterlies. They include *The Muslim, Daily News, Dawn, Morning News, Star, Pakistan Times* and *Khyber Mail*. Pakistani literature in English is developing in various genres and several writers have acquired national and international recognition, such as Ahmad Ali, Bapsi Sidhwa, Zulfikar Ghose, A. Hashmi, and Hanif Kureishi. The educated variety used by

Pakistan radio and television serves as the model for teaching and learning English throughout the country. The British connection has with the passage of time become fragile, as in other parts of South Asia; RP and other exonormative standards are used only for academic reference. See INDIAN ENGLISH[1], PAKISTAN, PANJABI, SOUTH ASIAN ENGLISH, SOUTH ASIAN BROADCASTING, URDU. [ASIA, VARIETY].   A.R.H., B.B.K.

Bansal, R. K. 1990. 'The Pronunciation of English in India', in S. Ramsaran (ed.), *Studies in the Pronunciation of English*. London: Routledge.

Baumgardner, Robert. 1990. 'The Indigenization of English in Pakistan', *English Today* 21, Jan. Cambridge: University Press.

Haque, A. R. 1983. 'The Position and Status of English in Pakistan', *World Language English* 2: 1. Oxford: Pergamon.

Hashmi, A. 1978, 1987. *Pakistani Literature: The Contemporary English Writers*. Islamabad: Gulmohar.

Rahman, Tariq. 1990. *Pakistani English: The Linguistic Description of a Non-Native Variety of English*. Islamabad: National Institute of Pakistan Studies, Quaid-i-Azam University.

—— 1991. 'The Use of Words in Pakistani English', *English Today* 26, Apr. Cambridge: University Press.

PALATE [14c: from Latin *palatum*]. An anatomical term for the roof of the mouth, behind the alveolar ridge, often described as having two parts: the *hard palate* (the roof of the mouth proper) and the *soft palate* (the *velum*). The adjective *palatal* is used to describe sounds made by raising the front of the tongue towards the hard palate. See ALVEOLAR, CONSONANT, VELUM. [SPEECH].   G.K.

PALE [14c: from Old French *pal*, Latin *palus* a pointed stake, fence: compare *impale*, *palings*]. A territory with distinct boundaries and distinctive laws, especially one in which a group of colonists maintains itself against alien pressures (as in Ireland) or one to which an oppressed group is confined (the *Pale of Settlement* to which Jews were restricted by law in 18-19c Russia). There have been three English Pales: in Ireland (12–16c), in France (the *Calais Pale*, 1347-1558), and briefly in southern Scotland (1545-9). In Ireland, the name was applied in the 14c to the area in which English rule was most secure. At its most extensive, it included Dublin, Kilkenny, Louth, Meath, Tipperary, Trim, Waterford, and Wexford, but by the later 15c had shrunk to Dublin, Louth, Meath, and Kildare. The Pale continued to diminish until the 16c conquest reversed the trend and the name became irrelevant. The term survives in such idioms as *beyond the pale* (beyond what is socially acceptable or considered decent). However, pales as such still exist; they include the British colonies of Gibraltar and Hong Kong, and until recently

West Berlin. See WILD IRISH. [EUROPE, HISTORY, NAME].   T.MCA.

PALI [17c: from Sanskrit *pāli* line of text, canon]. A scriptural language of Buddhism, a Prakrit (vernacular language) with a structure close to that of Sanskrit. A major collection of scriptures written down *c.*1c BC is known as both the *Tripitaka* and the *Pali Canon*. The Buddha's preference in the 6c BC for Prakrit rather than the Sanskrit of the brahmins crystallized Pali as the classical language of Theravada Buddhism in India, Burma, Cambodia, Laos, Thailand, and Vietnam. Pali and English are comparable in that both vernaculars developed international significance and regional varieties: the rise of Burmese Pali, Thai Pali, etc., can be compared with that of CanE and IndE, etc. The few Pali loanwords in English relate to Buddhism: for example, *dhamma* (religious law and duty) and *kamma* (action), cognates of Sanskrit *dharma* and *karma*. See CLASSICAL LANGUAGE, INDIAN LANGUAGES, PRAKRIT, SANSKRIT, SCRIPTURE, SINHALA. [ASIA, LANGUAGE].   T.MCA., R.S.

PALINDROME 17c: from Greek *palindromos* running back again]. (1) A word, phrase, or longer expression that reads the same backwards as it does forwards: for example, the words *level* and *noon*, and the phrases *Madam, I'm Adam* and *Able was I ere I saw Elba*. Palindromes range from the concise (*Sad? I'm Midas*) to the long-winded (*Live dirt up a side-track carted is a putrid evil*), from the clever (*A man, a plan, a canal—Panama!*) to the near-meaningless (*Harass sensuousness, Sarah*). The *OED* contains, among others, the palindromic words *Malayalam* (a language of South India) and *Ogopogo* (a Canadian water-monster). *Word palindromes* are sentences in which the order of the words can be reversed to read the same, as in *What? So he is dead, is he? So what?* and *Stout and bitter porter drinks porter, bitter and stout*. (2) Also *reversal*, *semordnilap* (a backward palindrome). A word that spells another word when reversed: for example, *doom*, *evil*, *warts*, and the trade names *Serutan*, *Trebor*. See REVERSAL, WORD GAME. [WORD].   T.A.

PALMER, Harold E. [1877-1949]. English language-teaching methodologist, born in London and educated privately in Hythe, Kent. In 1902, he went to teach at the Berlitz School in Verviers in Belgium, where he subsequently started his own experimental language school. He was closely associated with the International Phonetic Association and worked with the phonetician Daniel Jones at University College London after the outbreak of the First World War (1914). The lectures he gave were published as

The Scientific Study and Teaching of Languages (1917). His next work, *The Principles of Language-Study* (1921), related language-teaching methodology to psychology. In 1922, Palmer went to Japan to work for the Ministry of Education, a year later becoming director of the *Institute for Research in English Teaching* (*IRET*) in Tokyo. He developed teaching methods based on oral activity and vocabulary selection, in collaboration with A. S. Hornby and Michael West. His major concerns, teaching the spoken language, controlled vocabulary, and grammar based on the spoken language, laid the foundations for the distinctively British approach to EFL that dominated the years after the Second World War. See index. [ASIA, BIOGRAPHY, EDUCATION, EUROPE].   C.J.B.

PAMPHLET [15c: probably from 14c Anglo-Latin *panfletus*, French *pamphilet* and/or Dutch *panflet*, names given to a 12c romantic comedy in Latin verse called *Pamphilus* (named after its hero, in Greek the 'All-Beloved'). With *-et*, the name means 'the little thing about Pamphilus', extended to cover any light or brief publication]. A short and short-lived publication, usually with a paper cover. In the 15–16c, versions of romances, dramatic scripts, popular tracts, and newsletters were all called pamphlets. By the 17c, the word referred to controversial texts aimed at influencing opinion, a sense that has remained powerful, especially in *pamphleteer* (noun and verb). Polemical pamphlets were written and distributed for immediate ends, such as Milton's tracts and the satires of the Scriblerians (Pope, Swift, and others). Although apparently light, they often had more influence than larger works. Until the mid-20c, the pamphlet was a common medium of protest and propaganda. Currently, although the media generally leave little room for pamphlets, they continue to be used for social, political, and commercial messages. Where a state repressively controls publishing, pamphlet-style writing has been distributed through the underground system known as *samizdat* (Russian: self-published). Desktop publishing may offer a new lease of life. See BOOKLET, DESKTOP PUBLISHING, JOHN BULL, LEAFLET, NEWSLETTER, PRINTING, QUARTO. [MEDIA, TECHNOLOGY].   W.W.B.

PANAMA. Officially *República de Panamá*. A state of Central America. Capital: Panama City. Currency: balboa (100 centésimos); US dollar also legal tender. Economy: Canal services, petroleum products, sugar, coffee, cocoa, fruit. The US maintains a military and civilian presence in the Canal Zone, to protect and maintain the Panama Canal. Population: 2.3m (1988), 2.9m (projection for 2000). Ethnicity: 70% Spanish-Amerindian, 14% African, 10% Caucasian, 6% Amerindian. Languages: Spanish (official), English (a common second language because of US influence), and Chibcha. Education: primary 90%, secondary 59%, tertiary 26%, literacy 89%. The region was under Spanish control from 1538 to 1821, was part of Colombia until 1903, and with US backing has been a distinct entity ever since. See CARIBBEAN, CARIBBEAN ENGLISH CREOLE, CENTRAL AMERICA, ENGLISH. [AMERICAS, NAME].   T.MCA.

PANGRAM [1930s: from Greek *pan* all, *grámma* a letter]. A sentence or series of words that contains all the letters of the alphabet. The ideal pangram contains each letter only once, but it is difficult to compose a meaningful sentence of this kind. The nearest that seems possible is an enigmatic statement like *Quiz my black Whigs—export fund* or *Blowzy night-frumps vex'd Jack Q*. The most familiar pangram is *The quick brown fox jumps over the lazy dog*, which typists have traditionally used to check their typing of the alphabet, but it contains 35 letters. See QWERTY, WORD GAME. [WORD].   T.A.

PANJABI, also **Punjabi**. An Indo-Aryan language, indigenous in the Punjab, a region divided since 1947 between India and Pakistan. It is spoken by *c.*12m in India and *c.*40m in Pakistan, and by emigrants to the UK, Canada, Singapore, and the US. It is the state language of Punjab in India and is a regional language of Pakistan. It is the language of the Sikhs, whose multilingual scripture, the *Guru Granth Sahib* (compiled in 1604), includes its earliest literary works. Panjabi is written in two scripts, Lahanda and Gurmukhi, both derived from Brahmi. In grammar, it is similar to Hindi, of which some consider it a dialect. See CODE-MIXING AND CODE-SWITCHING, INDIA, INDIAN LANGUAGES, PAKISTAN. [ASIA, LANGUAGE].   Y.K.

PANTOMIME [16c: from Latin *pantomimus*, Greek *pantómimos* all-imitator]. (1) An actor in the Roman theatre who, with a triple-faced mask, mimed the parts in an acted fable. (2) A popular theatrical entertainment at Christmas time, derived from the 18c harlequinade, which had developed a set of stock characters and burlesque situations from the Italian *commedia dell'arte*. In the earlier 19c, pantomime proper emerged with a plot loosely drawn from a fairy tale or other story for children, as in *Cinderella, Dick Whittington, Aladdin*, and *Puss in Boots*. Pantomime includes song and dance, visual spectacle, and broad farcical humour, in a framework of romance and adventure in which good triumphs. A woman is cast as the hero or *principal boy* and a male comedian as the comic *dame*. Characters have been imported into traditional tales, such as the Widow Twankey in *Aladdin* (named from *twankay*, a variety of tea from China) and Buttons in *Cinderella*. The non-realist tradition of pantomime is reflected also in the language of the script, where prose is mingled with verse, usually doggerel with forced rhymes. A recent example is: 'Who may you be who makes so free with other people's poverty?'

The language may include attempts to match the pseudo-historical setting by occasional use of features like the second person singular (*thou, thee*, etc.), but jokes and catchphrases have a modern, and often local, reference. The combination of spoken dialogue with songs, dance, slapstick, and visual spectacle makes pantomime a popular form of 'total theatre'. It is mainly confined to the UK, though also performed in the US. The pantomime adapts texts, many of which first came through an oral tradition, and are probably more familiar today through the stage than through reading. The audience is encouraged to serve as a chorus, to hiss and boo the villain, and engage in exchanges with characters: *Actor*: 'Oh no, I didn't.' *Audience*: 'Oh yes, you did.' The colloquial BrE phrase *a proper pantomime* is used to suggest a chaotic and mismanaged situation: Compare FARCE. See DRAMA, MIME. [LITERATURE].   R.C.

PAPER [14c: from Anglo-Norman *papir*, Old French *papier*, Latin *papyrus*, Greek *pápuros*]. For about five centuries, the principal material for the recording and storage of written language. Paper is cheap, light, thin, and, depending on its manufacture and storage, relatively durable. It is made mainly from cellulose, and can in principle be produced from any kind of vegetable fibre. Linen, wood, flax, hemp, straw, and grasses of various kinds can all be ground down and cooked in a water base to produce a pulp that is then spread over a thin surface, pressed, and dried. Cotton blue jeans, properly prepared, make excellent paper.

Papyrus and paper. Although the term *paper* comes from the Greek *pápuros*, which may in turn come from an Egyptian original, there was no paper as such in ancient Mesopotamia (where clay tablets were used), in Egypt (where the reed *papyrus cyperus* was used for rolls), or in Greece and Rome (where papyrus and parchment predominated). The Egyptian technique of pressing together vertical and horizontal wet strips of fibre from the core of the papyrus plant shares with modern paper-making the bonding of cellulose, but was otherwise very different. Paper as such is believed to have originated in China.

About 200 BC, sheets were made from silk waste, then in AD 105 an official of the Imperial Court named Ts'ai Lun made a new kind of material from mulberry and other fibres, pieces of old fish net, hemp waste, and rags. Later, linen and cotton rags provided the base for this material, a technology which lasted virtually unchanged everywhere until the 19c. The first Western paper-making mill was established in Spain about 1150.

Paper and print. Paper did not immediately replace parchment as a writing surface, but by the mid-15c and the beginning of printing, it had become the standard surface for writing. Though the first mill in England was established at Hertford at the end of the 15c, most paper came from France or the Low Countries until the late 17c. The first paper mill in North America was founded in 1690 in Philadelphia. Clean rags of linen were placed in piles to rot, then stamped and cooked; a resulting watery pulp was taken up in screen-like moulds from which the water was drained with care; the damp sheets were transferred from the moulds and repeatedly pressed between felts for drying. The sheets were *sized* (coated with animal gelatin), so as to inhibit ink from bleeding into the paper. Woven into the mould was a *watermark*, a slightly raised wire design that registered on the sheet and could be seen in the final product. These watermarks were like trademarks and are now examined by scholars for evidence of the origin of sheets of paper or of the way a particular book was manufactured. Some of the watermarks were simple (a two-letter initial, a bull's head, a bunch of grapes); others (especially by the 18c) were elaborate heraldic designs. A variation on *mould paper* was introduced in the mid-18c; *wove paper* was made with fine screens and the lines of the watermark were eliminated.

Paper and pulp. At the beginning of the 19c, paper-making underwent some important changes. Machinery was developed that allowed the pulp to be picked up, formed, dried, pressed, and sized all in one linked procedure that produced a continuous roll or web at the end. The web could then be cut into sheets or fed directly into a web-fed press. Watermarks, especially useful in money to inhibit forgery, and even false wire lines can be introduced on this paper by the continuous action of a dandy roll (a light, open cylinder of wire gauze that smooths the wet pulp and impresses a watermark on it). At the same time, the increasing need for materials led to experiments, one result of which was the introduction of chlorine as an acidic bleach for the pulp. Another, from the mid-19c, was the adoption of wood pulp to replace linen.

Lignin and acid. Although wood pulp is a good source of cellulose fibre, it contains *lignin*, an impurity which can cause paper to degenerate. Airborne industrial pollutants such as sulphur dioxide are absorbed by lignin. In addition, the fibres of wood-based paper are much shorter than those of cotton or linen. Much modern paper therefore contains the seeds of its own destruction: the unneutralized acids, the residual lignin, and the quality of the fibre cause disintegration, especially under conditions of pollution. The paper loses its resiliency, becomes brittle, and finally falls apart. Millions of books produced since the mid-19c are subject to this steady decay. Newspapers, magazines, and mass market paperbacks (most of the latter held together by adhesives) begin to fall apart virtually from the moment they are manufactured. By contrast, in former times, the enemies of paper were fire, heat (cellulose needs some residual moisture), dampness (leading to fungus growth and internal rot), and general ignorance: how many early copies of Shakespeare's plays were used to wrap fish or wipe bottoms?

Acid-free paper. Early kinds of paper did not suffer from the problem of lignin and acid, and it is ironic that older books are likely to have a longer life than many recent publications. However, durable, acid-free papers are available and are increasingly used for books considered worth saving (although there may be disagreement about the criteria involved in selecting such books in advance). There are also procedures for the preservation of paper and some large libraries (notably the US Library of Congress) have undertaken huge and costly programmes of restoration of 19c materials.

Alternatives. The storage of books and other documents on microfilm is only a partial solution. The medium is changed and ancillary information lost: early texts contain evidence about their manufacture and provenance that is important to the scholar but is not preserved on film. Storage on laser disc, the dream of many librarians and certainly promising for information retrieval, removes the reader even further from the actual form of the original work. In addition to the matter of storage, with the development of word processing and databases, electronic equivalents to paper are now widely available, such as discs of various kinds, especially the CD-ROM (compact disc: read-only memory). These take up much less room and are not subject to the risks discussed above, but are dependent on a regular supply of electricity and can become subject to interference, such as through editing or computer viruses. Despite the great attraction of such devices, paper remains the primary medium for writing and printing, including computer printouts, and if anything the use of the 'electric word' has meant the consumption of more rather than less paper.

Properties. Paper is the vehicle for most writing, yet by and large only such professionals as designers, publishers, and printers pay much attention to its properties. These include: (1) *Permanence*: certain documents will have a predictably longer life than others. (2) *Toughness*: in relation to how often and in what way the document is handled. (3) *Weight*: especially in items sent by mail. (4) *Opacity*: whether show-through affects legibility. (5) *Folding capacity*: some papers, manufactured to be used flat, will crack on folding. (6) *Stiffness*: important for covers and for brochures that are to be displayed standing. (7) *Receptivity to writing materials*: pen, pencil, typewriter, and printing ink are all differently received by different surfaces and the paper should have proper and rapid absorption for the kind of ink used. (8) *Finish*: a heavily coated paper, useful for photographic images, can have a glare that makes it unsatisfactory for sustained reading of type. (9) *Sheet size*: careful estimation of final sizes, including trimming and folding, affects the sheet size to be chosen. (10) *Grain*: paper, especially made by machine, has a distinct grain; a book folded against this grain will be hard to close. (11) *Colour*: very few papers are a pure white and the shade of white influences legibility. See BOOK, CARTOON, CROWN, DEMY, DOCUMENT, FOLIO, FOOLSCAP, IMPERIAL, LEAF, -MO, PARCHMENT, PRINT, QUARTO, ROYAL, VELLUM. [MEDIA, TECHNOLOGY]. W.W.B.

Baynes-Cope, A. D. 1981. *Caring for Books and Documents*. London: British Museum Publications.
Gaskell, Philip. 1972. *A New Introduction to Bibliography*. Oxford: University Press.
Greenfield, Jane. 1988. *The Care of Fine Books*. New York: Nick Lyons Books
Hunter, Dard. 1947. *Papermaking: The History and Technique of an Ancient Craft*. New York: Alfred A. Knopf.

PAPERBACK. See BOOK, PUBLISHING.

PAPUA NEW GUINEA, also **Papua Niugini**. A state in the south-west Pacific, occupying the eastern half of the island of New Guinea and some 600 islands, the largest of which are New Britain, New Ireland, and Bougainville. Capital: Port Moresby. Population estimated in 1988 at 3,579,000, projected for 2000 at 4,600,000. Prior to independence in 1975, the southern half (Papua) was an Australian colony and the northern part (New Guinea) was administered by Australia under a mandate from the United Nations given after the First World War, when it ceased to be a German colony. The island of New Guinea was peopled by different waves of migrants, whose history is largely unknown. The terrain is rugged. Many villages have no road or river links with other settlements and some can be reached only by walking for up to two weeks. Travel by air is more important than by road. Port Moresby is not connected by road to any other urban area. The coastal population is thinly clustered in villages, but over one-third of the total population live in highland valleys. While settlement by Europeans has extended over a century, contact with many internal regions is fairly recent. Most of these communities were not known before 1930, when the discovery of gold encouraged further exploration. Even in the 1950s, Australian administrative patrols were still establishing contact with people in remoter areas. These conditions have fostered cultural and linguistic diversity; there are some 700–750 languages belonging to two families, Papuan and Austronesian, as well as an indigenous pidgin, Hiri Motu, and an English-based pidgin, Tok Pisin. Both serve as lingua francas and share official status with English. See ENGLISH, HIRI MOTU, MELANESIA, MELANESIAN PIDGIN ENGLISH, PIDGIN, TOK PISIN. [LANGUAGE, OCEANIA].   S.R.

PAPUA NEW GUINEA PIDGIN. See TOK PISIN.

PARABLE [13c: from Old French *parabole*, Latin *parabola*, Greek *parabolē* ('something cast alongside') an analogy, an extended simile]. A short narrative with an oblique style and a moral meaning, widely used by philosophers and religious teachers in antiquity. It generally uses plausible events and situations, of a kind familiar to listeners or readers, in order to present or illustrate a profound truth or teaching, and typically begins with a simile: 'The kingdome of heauen is like vnto a certaine King, which made a marriage for his sonne' (The Authorized Version of the Bible, 1611: Matthew 22: 2). Because of its very obliqueness, it may need an explanation afterwards, relating it part by part to aspects of the truth being imparted. The most famous parables are those of Jesus Christ recorded in the Synoptic Gospels which, through the King James version, have given English such phrases as *fall on stony ground* and *kill the fatted calf*; two of the best known, the Prodigal Son and the Good Samaritan, are not so named in the text but only in page headings. The parable differs from the *fable* in dealing with human beings and everyday events, and from *allegory* in having a single point of teaching and not a set of correspondences with the real world. See ALLEGORY, ANALOGY, BIBLE, BIBLICAL ENGLISH, FABLE, SIMILE. [LITERATURE].   R.C., T.MCA.

PARADIGM [15c: from Latin *paradigma*, from Greek *parádeigma* something set beside something else, a pattern, an example, a basis for comparison; stress: 'PA-ra-dime']. (1) In grammar, a set of all the (especially inflected) forms of a word (*write, writes, wrote, writing, written*), especially when used as a model for all other words of the same type. Paradigms serve as models for word forms in Latin and Greek (in which key words represent the patterns of numbered groups of nouns, adjectives, verbs, etc.) and to a lesser extent for such other languages as French and Spanish (principally for verbs). Their use is limited in English, because it is not a highly inflected language. See CONJUGATION, DECLENSION, DERIVATIONAL PARADIGM, SUFFIX. (2) In general usage, a model or stereotype, as in the phrase *a paradigm case*, a typical specimen of something. In such studies as the philosophy of science, comparative religion, and social science, a paradigm is an overriding viewpoint that shapes ideas and actions within a particular field or group. From time to time, a *paradigm shift* occurs, so that ideas and practices taken more or less for granted under the old paradigm are reassessed under the new. Such a shift occurred in the 16c when Copernicus claimed that the earth went round the sun, and in the 19c with Darwin's theory of natural selection. See ANALOGY, MODEL, OLD ENGLISH[1], PARADIGMATIC AND SYNTAGMATIC, STEREOTYPE, WORD-FORMATION. [GRAMMAR, LANGUAGE]. T.MCA., S.G.

PARADIGMATIC AND SYNTAGMATIC [17c and 20c: from Greek *paradeigmatikós* serving as a pattern, and *suntagmatikós* arranged together]. Contrasting terms in (structural) linguistics. Every item of language has a *paradigmatic relationship* with every other item which can be substituted for it (such as *cat* with *dog*), and a *syntagmatic relationship* with items which occur within the same construction (for example, in *The cat sat on the mat*, *cat* with *the* and *sat on the mat*). The relationships are like axes, as shown in the accompanying diagram.

		syntagmatic			
	The	cat	sat	on	the	mat.
paradigmatic	His	dog	slept	under	that	table.
	Our	parrot	perched	in	its	cage.

In this way, it is possible to build up a picture of the role of a linguistic item within a language at any level of structure and these relations of substitution and co-occurrence are crucial to linguistic analysis. Paradigmatic contrasts at the level of sounds allow one to identify the phonemes (minimal distinctive sound units) of a language: for example, *bat, fat, mat* contrast with one another on the basis of a single sound, as do *bat, bet, bit,* and *bat, bap, ban.* Stylistically, rhyme is due to the paradigmatic substitution of sounds at the beginning of syllables or words, as in: 'Tyger! Tyger! burning *bright* / In the forests of the *night.*' Syntagmatic relations involving sounds reveal the syllable and morpheme structure of the language concerned: the combinations *str, spr* as in *string, spring* are possible word beginnings in English, but *stl, sbw* are not (no *stling, *sbwing).

On the lexical level, paradigmatic contrasts indicate which words are likely to belong to the same word class (part of speech): *cat, dog, parrot* in the diagram are all nouns, *sat, slept, perched* are all verbs. Syntagmatic relations between words enable one to build up a picture of co-occurrence restrictions within syntax, for example, the verbs *hit, kick* have to be followed by a noun (*Paul hit the wall,* not *Paul hit), but *sleep, doze* do not normally do so (*Peter slept,* not **Peter slept the bed*). On the semantic level, paradigmatic substitutions allow items from a semantic set to be grouped together, for example *Angela came on Tuesday* (Wednesday, Thursday, etc.), while syntagmatic associations indicate compatible combinations: *rotten apple, the duck quacked,* rather than **curdled apple,* **the duck squeaked.* Frequent collocations are regarded as clichés: *furrowed brow, grin and bear it, good old days,* and as idioms when the meaning cannot be easily worked out from the component parts, as with *get the sack, kick the bucket, live on a shoestring.* See COLLOCATION, PARADIGM, SYNTAX. [GRAMMAR, LANGUAGE].   J.M.A.

PARADOX [16c: from Latin *paradoxum/ paradoxon,* from Greek *parádoxos* contrary to opinion or expectation]. A term in rhetoric for a situation or statement that is or seems self-contradictory and even absurd, but may contain an insight into life, such as *The child is father of the man.* Rationally, a child cannot be a father, but one can propose in this figurative way that the nature of one's early life affects later ideas and attitudes:

> My heart leaps up when I behold
> A rainbow in the sky:
> So it was when my life began;
> So it is now I am a man;
> So be it when I shall grow old,
> Or let me die!
> The Child is father of the Man.
> (Wordsworth, 'My Heart Leaps Up', 1807)

A series of paradoxical statements that involve antithesis, climax, metaphor, and repetition, opens Charles Dickens's *A Tale of Two Cities* (1859):

It was the best of times, it was the worst of times, it was the age of wisdom, it was the age of foolishness, it was the epoch of belief, it was the epoch of incredulity, it was the season of Light, it was the season of Darkness, it was the spring of hope, it was the winter of despair, we had everything before us, we had nothing before us, we were all going direct to Heaven, we were all going direct the other way. . . .

Some writers, such as Oscar Wilde, have made an art of the paradoxical and epigrammatic: for example, through the cynical Lord Henry Wotton, Wilde observed: 'Nowadays people know the price of everything, and the value of nothing' (*The Picture of Dorian Gray,* 1891). Compare ANTITHESIS, IRONY. [STYLE].   T.MCA.

PARAGRAPH [16c: from French *paragraphe,* Latin *paragraphus* and *paragraphum,* Greek *parágraphos* ('at the side of writing')]. (1) Formerly, a short, horizontal stroke below the beginning of a line in which a break of sense occurs; a passage so marked. (2) Currently, a piece of writing or print of variable length and having a variety of internal structures, arranged as a single block of text. It can contain only one sentence, but generally consists of two or more sentences presenting an argument or description. The beginning of a paragraph is usually *indented* in print, unless preceded by an interlinear space, but not always in handwriting or word processing, nor in display material. Sometimes, both indenting and extra line space are used to make each paragraph stand out strongly.

The layout of texts in European languages has changed considerably since the Middle Ages, when the paragraph was not a consistently organized unit of prose, and prose was not a highly developed form of writing. The development of printing in the 15c encouraged the use of paragraphs as blocks of lines that could be manipulated easily by the printer and helped break up the appearance of page after page of print. However, balance in the presentation of lines of print, whole pages, and the effect of the message has been a minor consideration in teaching composition and in the development of print. Nonetheless, the general view has arisen that just as a chapter (with or without a heading) is a section in the progression of an argument or a story, so within the chapter a paragraph (with or without a subheading) is part of the same orderly progression.

By and large, until the 19c, paragraphs tended to be long and to consist of periodic sentences, one period sometimes taking up a paragraph running over one or more pages. In manuals of instruction, however, especially where sections have been logically ordered (and numbered), paragraphs have tended to be shorter. The scripts of prose plays have always had marked-off sections opening with characters' names (on a par with verse drama). In novels and other works of fiction, along with the increasing use of separated-off dialogue (similar to the style of scripts), 19c writers reduced the lengths of their paragraphs, a process that has continued in the 20c, particularly in journalism, advertisements, and publicity materials, where paragraphs are often short and built out of sentence fragments. Writers of fiction often use the same effect to present swift action, changes in thinking, and the like.

Traditionally, teachers of composition have taught students to begin a new paragraph when beginning a new topic or subtopic in an essay or other piece of prose. The aim has been to produce logically ordered sentences, the first of which is a *topic* or *key sentence* that sets the scene. This ideal continues to be widely valued, but is not the only basis, or even a principal basis, on which paragraphs are constructed by professional writers. In the process of drafting their material, they may combine and recombine paragraphs. Two influences are: relationships with material in preceding and following paragraphs, and the 'eye appeal' of different lengths of paragraph arranged in relation to the size of page and typeface used. Paragraph construction is therefore as much a matter of layout and visual balance as of content and logical relationship between preceding or subsequent paragraphs. For purposes of highlighting or emphasis, longer paragraphs may be divided up, sometimes turning a proposed topic sentence into a *topic paragraph*. Paragraphs in academic works, works of reference, religious scriptures, specialist journals, consumer magazines, quality newspapers, and tabloid newspapers all follow different rules of thumb in their construction. See CHAPTER, COMPOSITION, DIALOG(UE), INDENTING, PERIODIC SENTENCE, PROSE, PUNCTUATION, SENTENCE. [STYLE, WRITING].   T.MCA.

PARALANGUAGE [1950s: from the Greek prefix *para-* alongside, and *language*]. Adjective **paralinguistic.** A term used variously in the study of human communication to refer to aspects of vocal or bodily expression that convey meaning, but in a less structured or systematic way than properties of speech as such. The main paralinguistic phenomena are: (1) Tones of voice, such as the nasal, breathy, and creaky vocal effects used to convey everyday emotions or to express social, psychological, or occupational states: for example, the flat tones of a person suffering from depression, the gruff tones of a drill sergeant. (2) Aspects of body language, such as gestures and facial expressions. The study of paralanguage is *paralinguistics.* See BODY LANGUAGE, COMMUNICATION, GESTURE, SPEECH-READING. [LANGUAGE].   D.C.

PARALINGUISTICS. See PARALANGUAGE.

PARALIPSIS, also **paraleipsis** [16c: through Latin from Greek *paráleipsis* leaving aside, omitting]. A rhetorical device in which something is emphasized by suggesting, often as if in an aside, that it is too obvious to discuss. In the Epistle to the Hebrews, St Paul says, 'And what shall I more say?', before proceeding for nine verses to say it. Some common phrases are paraliptic: *leaving aside, not to mention, to say nothing of, without considering, without taking into account.* [STYLE].   T.MCA.

PARALLELISM [17c]. A rhetorical device in which a formula or structural pattern is repeated, as in the Latin sequence *veni, vidi, vici* and its English translation *I came, I saw, I conquered.* It occurs in sayings and proverbs (such as *Now you see them, now you don't* and *Out of sight, out of mind*), and in verse and poetic prose ('My mother groaned, my father wept— / Into the dangerous world I leapt' (William Blake, *Songs of Experience*). Such balancing is common in both the titles and content of literary and other works: for example, Blake's *Songs of Innocence* and *Songs of Experience,* combined in 1794 as *Songs of Innocence and of Experience.* See ANTITHESIS, REPETITION. [STYLE].   T.MCA.

PARALOGISM [16c: from Latin *paralogismus,* Greek *paralogismós* ('something to the side of a statement') a defective argument]. False reasoning, an argument that violates the principles of logic, and a conclusion reached by such an argument. See FALLACY. [LANGUAGE].   T.MCA.

PARAPHRASE [16c: through French from Latin *paraphrasis,* Greek *paráphrasis* ('speaking alongside') saying the same in other words]. Also, more technically, *paraphrasis.* (1) The (more or less) free rewording of an expression or text, as an explanation, clarification, or translation: 'Paraphrase, or translation with latitude, where the author is kept in view . . ., but his words are not so strictly followed as his sense' (John Dryden, preface to his translation of Ovid, 1680). (2) An act or result of rewording, such as a simplified version of a legal document: a plain-English paraphrase of *The contractor shall have a general lien upon all goods in his possession for all monies due to him from the customer* is *We have a right to hold some or all of the goods until you have paid all our charges.* (3) To make a paraphrase; to translate or define loosely: the compound *teapot* can be paraphrased or explained by the phrase *a pot for tea* but not by *a pot of tea.* See COMPOUND WORD, DEFINITION, GLOSS, TRANSLATION. [STYLE, WRITING].   T.MCA.

PARASITIC [17c: from Latin *parasiticus,* Greek *parasitikós,* from *parásitos* ('feeding beside') one who eats at another's table (and pays for the food with flattery)]. (1) Relating to or characteristic of a parasite of any kind. (2) Also *excrescent* [17c: from Latin *excrescere* to grow out]. In phonetics and philology, terms referring to an 'added' sound or letter caused by the interaction or impetus of other sounds in a word: for example, the /t/ sometimes heard in *sense*, making it sound like *cents*. Many English words have sounds and letters that were once parasitic but are now considered normal, such as the *d* in *thunder* (Old English *thunor*) and the *e* in *flower* (Middle English *flour*). Such an added element is sometimes called a *parasite*. Compare EPENTHESIS. [LANGUAGE, SPEECH].   T.MCA.

PARATAXIS [1830s: through Latin from Greek *parátaxis* arrangement in order (of battle). Stress: 'pa-ra-TA-xis']. (1) Placing together phrases, clauses, and sentences, often without conjunctions, often with *and*, *but*, *so*, and with minimal or no use of subordination. A paratactic style is common in orature (oral literature) and in fast-moving prose, especially if intended for young listeners or readers:

Not always was the Kangaroo as now we do behold him, but a different Animal with four short legs. . . . He was grey and he was woolly, and his pride was inordinate: he danced on a sandbank in the Middle of Australia, and he went to the Big God Nqong. He went to Nqong at ten before dinner-time, saying: 'Make me different from all other animals; make me popular and wonderfully run after by five this afternoon.' Up jumped Nqong from his bath in the salt-pan and shouted, 'Yes, I will!' Nqong called Dingo—Yellow Dog Dingo—always hungry, dusty in the sunshine, and showed him Kangaroo. Nqong said, 'Dingo! Wake up, Dingo! Do you see that gentleman dancing on an ash-pit? He wants to be popular and very truly run after. Dingo, make him so!' (Rudyard Kipling, 'The Sing-Song of Old Man Kangaroo', *Just So Stories*, 1902).

(2) Punctuating two or more sentences as if they were one, as in *I came, I saw, I conquered* (translating Latin *Veni, vidi, vici*) and *Come on, let's get going!* See BIBLE, COMMA, COORDINATION, HYPOTAXIS, ORATURE. [GRAMMAR, STYLE, WRITING].   T.MCA.

PARCHMENT [13c: from French *parchemin*, Latin *pergamena*, from *Pergamena charta* a leaf or sheet from Pergamon, a Greek city in Asia Minor, where the material was developed as an alternative to papyrus after an embargo on its export from Egypt to Pergamon in the 3c BC]. Animal skin treated to make it suitable as a writing surface. Parchment was the commonest writing surface until the late Middle Ages, when it was replaced by paper. It was usually made from the skin of sheep or goats. If made from calfskin, it was *vellum* [from Latin *vitellinum*, from *vitellus* a calf]. Both terms, however, are applied to other

treated animal skins. The skin was soaked in lye or a similar corrosive to soften it and reduce and weaken the hairs, which were then scraped off. The skin was rinsed, stretched, and dried, scraped again, then rubbed with a pumice-stone for smoothness. Often it was treated with chalk to add lustre and further smoothness to the surface, then cut for folding into quires. Such a surface is durable and can be very thin and supple, but has always been expensive. A large parchment Bible, two feet high and a foot and a half wide, would consume a large herd of animals: 150 skins at one per folio to provide 300 leaves and 600 pages. Modern parchment is a vegetable product, usually an expensive cotton- or linen-based writing paper that imitates some of such qualities as heaviness, stiffness, and smoothness. See BOOK. Compare PAPER, VOLUME. [TECHNOLOGY].   W.W.B.

PARENTHESIS [16c: through Latin from Greek *parénthesis* ('a placing between') qualifying matter introduced into a passage and the device that marks it. Stress: 'pa-REN-the-sis'. Plural *parentheses* ('-seez')]. (1) In grammar, a qualifying, explanatory, or appositive word, phrase, clause, or sentence that interrupts a construction without otherwise affecting it. A written or printed parenthesis may be marked by pairs of commas, dashes, or round brackets/parentheses: *Our new manager (he has just this minute arrived) would like to meet you.* A spoken parenthesis has the same intonation as an aside. (2) In the plural, a name for round brackets: the general term in AmE, but a less common, more technical term in BrE (short form *parens*). The phrase *in parentheses*, however, refers to material within any pair of parenthetical marks: brackets, dashes, or commas. See ACADEMIC USAGE, ASIDE, BRACKETS, COMMA, DASH, PUNCTUATION. [GRAMMAR, STYLE, WRITING].   T.MCA.

PARLARY, PARLYAREE. See POLARI.

PARODY [16c: from Latin *parodia*, from Greek *paröidía* ('something sung alongside') a burlesque poem or song]. An amusing or mocking imitation of the style of a writer or speaker, usually requiring a basic parallelism of form and style and sudden unexpected twists, as in the second of the following stanzas:

Beneath these rugged elms, that yew-tree's shade
Where heaves the turf in many a mouldering heap,
Each in his narrow cell for ever laid,
The rude forefathers of the hamlet sleep.
(Thomas Gray, *Elegy Written in a Country Church-Yard*, 1751)

Here where the flattering and mendacious swarm
Of lying epitaphs their secrets keep,
At last incapable of further harm

The lewd forefathers of the village sleep.
(John Squire, in *Collected Parodies*, 1921)

Parody often emphasizes and exaggerates typical features of the original text or performance in order to make a point and, whether friendly or hostile, exploits any possible weakness. It is usually brief but may encompass a whole literary work: Henry Fielding parodied Samuel Richardson's *Pamela* (1740) in *Joseph Andrews* (1742), Jane Austen parodied the Gothic novel in *Northanger Abbey* (1818), and Kingsley Amis parodied the traditional bildungsroman in *Lucky Jim* (1954). The inconsequential arguments and failures of communication in plays like *Waiting for Godot* by Samuel Beckett (1955) and *The Caretaker* by Harold Pinter (1960) seem like parodies of plays by George Bernard Shaw, John Galsworthy, and others, which offered solutions to social problems through dramatic debate. Political or other styles of speech are often parodied on the stage or on television. Compare PASTICHE. [LITERATURE].   R.C.

PAROLE. See LANGUE AND PAROLE.

PARONOMASIA. See PUN.

PARSING [16c: from the verb *parse*, from Latin *pars/partis* a part, abstracted from the phrase *pars orationis* part of speech]. (1) Analysing a sentence into its constituents, identifying in greater or less detail the syntactic relations and parts of speech. (2) Describing a word in a sentence, identifying its part of speech, inflectional form, and syntactic function.

Traditional parsing. Parsing was formerly central to the teaching of grammar throughout the English-speaking world, and widely regarded as basic to the use and understanding of written language. When many people talk about formal grammar in schools, they are referring to the teaching of *parsing* and *clause analysis*, which virtually ceased in primary and secondary education in the English-speaking world in the 1960s, and in tertiary education has been superseded by linguistic analysis. The argument against traditional parsing is threefold: that it promotes old-fashioned descriptions of language based on Latin grammatical categories, that students do not benefit from it, and that it is a source of frustration and boredom for both students and teachers. The argument in favour of parsing is fourfold: that it makes explicit the structure of speech and writing, exercises the mind in a disciplined way, enables people to talk about language usage, and helps in the learning and discussion of foreign languages. A compromise position holds that the formal discussion of syntax and function can be beneficial,

but should take second place to fluent expression and the achievement of confidence rather than dominate the weekly routine.

Computational parsing. When a computer parses, it analyses a string of characters in order to associate groups in the string with the syntactic units of a grammar. Computers do this mostly for programming languages but also sometimes for English. Programming languages are defined by simple but precise grammars, and the translation of these languages into machine language requires knowing which rules apply to each statement. Typical grammars for computer languages take a few dozen rules and parse input at the rate of several seconds per statement. The grammars for such languages are designed to be unambiguous: only one 'parse' is possible for each statement. Computer scientists have often thought of applying similar techniques to natural language, but a language like English requires hundreds or thousands of rules, does not conform to the neat mathematical models that allow the rapid parsing of computer languages, often contains ambiguities, and has not yet been described in sufficient detail to be successfully parsed by a machine. See CLAUSE ANALYSIS, COMPUTING, KOREA. [EDUCATION, GRAMMAR, TECHNOLOGY].   T.MCA., M.L.

PARTICIPLE [14c: from French *participle*, with epenthetic *l*, from Latin *participium*, translating Greek *metokhḗ* a part-taking]. In grammatical description, the term for two non-finite verb forms, the *-ing* participle (known traditionally as the *present participle*) and the *-ed* participle (known traditionally as the *past participle* or *passive participle*).

The *-ing* (present) participle. This verb form ends with the inflection *-ing* and is used in combination with a form of the auxiliary *be* for the progressive continuous, as in: *am driving, was playing, will be going, has been talking*. It is also used as the verb in an *-ing* participle clause, as in: *Marvin and Jane liked playing with their grandchildren; Despite his protestations, Stanley was not averse to having a birthday party; John and Linda were happy to see Daniel behaving himself during the meal; After giving her lecture, Venetia had lunch with me at the College; The young man driving me to the shopping centre was Jeremy.*

The *-ed* (past) participle. This verb form ends with the inflection spelled *-ed*, *-d*, or *-t* for all regular verbs and many irregular verbs, but many irregular verbs form it with an *-en* or *-n* inflection (as in *stolen, known*) or with a change in the middle vowel (as in *sung*, in which case it is often identical with the simple past form, as with *sat*), or a combination of the two methods (as with *written*). The *-ed* participle combines with a form of the auxiliary *have* for the perfect: *has cared, had said, may have walked*. It combines with a form of the auxiliary *be* for the passive: *is paid, was told, are being auctioned, could have been seen*. It is also used as the verb in an *-ed* participle clause: *I had my study redecorated; Asked for his opinion, Ian was non-committal; Among the objects recovered from the ship was a chair stamped with the captain's initials*.

Attributive uses. Both participles may be used in the attributive position like an adjective, but only if the participle indicates some sort of permanent characteristic: *running water, the missing link, a broken heart, lost property*. The phrase *The Laughing Cavalier* is possible as the name of a picture (the man is laughing for all time), but **Who is that laughing man?* would be odd in most contexts. The *-ed* participle usually has a passive meaning (*listed buildings, burnt almonds, written instructions*), but may be used actively with some intransitive verbs (*an escaped prisoner*). Some participles that are not permanent enough to be used attributively alone are acceptable when modified (*their long-awaited visit*).

Participles and word-formation. There is a range of usage between participles which remain fully verbal (*running* in *swiftly running water*) and those that in some contexts are completely adjectival (*interesting* in *a very interesting idea*; *disappointed* in *a very disappointed man*). There are also some participle-like formations for which there are no corresponding verbs: *an unexplained discrepancy, an unconvincing narrative*, for which there are no conventional verbs **to unexplain* and **to unconvince*; *a bearded man, a forested hillside, a blue-eyed cat, a one-armed bandit*, common constructions which are aspects of word-formation rather than grammar.

Participial clauses. Traditionally known as *participial phrases*, such clauses function in various ways: (1) They can follow noun phrases (like abbreviated relative clauses): 'The train (which is) *now standing at Platform 5* is . . .', 'The food (that was) *served on the plane* was . . .'. (2) They can function rather like finite subordinate clauses, with or without a conjunction, and with various meanings, often of time ('*While running for the train*, he lost his wallet'), reason ('*Jostled by the crowd*, he did not really see what happened'), or result ('The train started suddenly, *throwing an elderly passenger to the floor*'). (3) They can follow an object + verb of the senses: 'We could all hear him *singing in the bath*'; 'He didn't see the soap *lying on the floor*.' Occasionally this multiplicity of functions may lead to ambiguity: 'I witnessed a sergeant push his way past supporters drinking openly in the

aisle' (letter in the *Daily Telegraph*, 27 May 1988).

The dangling participle. When a participial clause contains its own subject, it is called an *absolute clause*, as in '*Weather permitting*, we'll go sailing this weekend'. See ABOSLUTE, ABSOLUTE CLAUSE. When, as is more usual, such a clause does not contain a subject, it normally refers grammatically to the subject of the main clause: in 'I made my way, *depressed*, to the ticket office', it is clear who was depressed, and in 'The woman on the chair beside me was tipped on to my lap, *complaining all the time*' it is clear who was complaining (both from Colin Thubron, *Behind the Wall*, 1987). Failure to maintain such a clear relationship leads to the so-called *dangling, hanging, misrelated*, or *unattached participle*, as in: 'Her party was the first to discover that there were no sleepers left. The entire section had been booked. *Faced with a forty-four hour journey*, this was not good news' (Patrick Marnham, *So Far from God*, 1985).

Although 'misattached participle' would usually be an appropriate label, in the above example the participle does seem to hang in mid-air. It presumably refers to the author, but he has not mentioned himself for several sentences. With participles that attach themselves to the wrong noun, the effect may be momentarily confusing even if the writer's meaning is clear: '[Sir Mortimer Wheeler's] celebrity on television was so great that, *boarding an empty bus late one rainy night when in a white tie with rows of medals*, a conductress arranged with the driver to take him to the door of Wheeler's small house off Haymarket' (Anthony Powell, *To Keep the Ball Rolling*, 1982). Here, the meaning may be fairly obvious, but on first reading it is the conductress who boards the bus. In the following, it is a theory that is apparently called *locust bean* in the first example and the lines that apparently provided the clues in the second: 'Carob crops have been grown in the arid areas around the Mediterranean for centuries. *Known also as the "locust bean"*, one theory has it that these were the locusts on which John the Baptist is said to have survived while in the wilderness' (*Daily Telegraph*, 23 May 1986); '*By taking a great many such observations and analysing them statistically*, the lines gave crucial clues about the intervening space between us and quasars, and therefore of the early universe's history' (in 'Bonfire of the Cosmos', *Observer*, 16 Apr. 1989).

Sometimes, greater ambiguity results: '*Forced to sit on upturned buckets in front of fiercely glowing wood fires*, various friends of the President had pressed them to sample the young wine and the old' (Beryl Bainbridge, *Winter Garden*, 1980). On reflection, we may decide that it is the 'they' of the story who had to sit on the buckets, but it could be the President's friends. At other times, we are given absurd pictures: '*After travelling by road all day* . . . , the 123-room Sahara Palace is an air-conditioned all-mod-cons watering hole' (*Daily Telegraph*, 22 Sept. 1984); 'There, *coasting comfortably down the attractive green coastline*, the town of Malacca with its prominent hill was very evident' (Tim Severin, *The Sindbad Voyage*, 1982).

Participial prepositions and conjunctions. Apparent exceptions to the rule that participles should be properly attached are a number of participle forms that now function as prepositions, such as *following* in 'There was tremendous clearing up to do *following the storm*', and *including* in 'We all enjoyed ourselves, *including the dog*'; and participle forms that are now conjunctions, such as *providing* (*that*) and *provided* (*that*) in 'Everything will be all right, *providing/provided* you don't panic', and *given* in '*Given the difficulties*, I'd say it was a success.' See ENDING, GERUND, VERB. [GRAMMAR, STYLE, USAGE].   S.C., S.G.

PARTICLE [14c: through French from Latin *particula* a small part]. A word that does not change its form through inflection and does not fit easily into the established system of parts of speech. Among individual words commonly so classed are the negative particle *not* (and its contraction *n't*), the infinitival particle *to* (*to go*; *to run*), the imperative particles *do*, *don't* (*Do tell me*; *Don't tell me*) and *let*, *let's* (*Let me see now*; *Let's go*). There is also a set of adverbial and prepositional particles that combine with verbs to form phrasal verbs (*out* in *look out*; *up* in *turn up*) and prepositional verbs (*at* in *get at*; *for* in *care for*). The term *pragmatic particle* is sometimes used for words that play a role in maintaining discourse and are also known as *fillers* and *discourse markers*: *oh, ah, well, yes, no, actually, anyway*. See ADVERBIAL PARTICLE, PART OF SPEECH, PHRASAL VERB, PREPOSITION, PREPOSITIONAL VERB. [GRAMMAR].   S.G.

PARTITIVE [16c: from Latin *partitivus* relating to a part (not a whole)]. A grammatical term for constructions which are used to refer to a part of a whole (as opposed to all of it). In French, the preposition *de* often has a partitive function: *J'ai bu de la bière* (I drank of beer: 'I drank some beer', not all the beer or all possible beer). In such usages, *de* is *l'article partitif* (the partitive article). In English, the use of determiners like *some* (*I drank some beer*) is comparable. However, the term is usually restricted to countable nouns followed by *of*, used to ascribe quantity or quality to mainly uncountable nouns: *bit* in 'a bit of cheese'; *kind* in 'a kind of loving'. In

terms of quantity, there are four kinds of partitive nouns: general words that can go with many nouns (a *piece* of paper); nouns with specific collocations (a *lump* of sugar, a *loaf* of bread, a *blade* of grass); words for measures (a *pint* of milk, 50 *hectares* of land); parts of singular countable things (a *branch* of a tree, a *page* of a book). In terms of quality, there are three common partitives: *kind* (a kind of loving); *sort* (new sorts of experiments), *type* (some types of business). When used with *these*, *those*, two usages are common: traditionally approved concord (*these kinds of book*; *these kinds of books*), and a casual singular use (*these kind of books*). *Kind of* and *sort of* are extensively and informally used not only as part of a noun phrase but also adverbially to make statements less precise: *It's kind of nice to be here again*; *I was sort of sad to see them go*; *She was annoyed—a mountain of work left for her to do, kind of thing*. Because such usage is casual, colloquial, and often repetitious, people interested in precision widely condemn it as sloppy. A distinct orthography has developed, because of the prevalence of the usage and its controversial nature: *It's kinda nice*; *I was sorta sad*. This usage includes both the partitive *a cuppa tea*, *a pinta milk*, and their elliptical reduction in BrE to countable nouns ('Have another *cuppa*'; 'Have you had your daily *pinta*?'). The commercial slogan *Drinka pinta milka day* plays with partitives, orthography, and the strong-weak syllabic rhythms of the language. [GRAMMAR, STYLE].   S.C., T.MCA.

PART OF SPEECH [16c: a translation of Latin *pars orationis* a part or element of discourse, in turn a translation of the two Greek phrases *méros tês léxeōs* (Aristotle) and *méros lógou* (Dionysius Thrax)]. A grammatical category or class of words. Traditional grammars of English generally list eight parts of speech: *noun, pronoun, verb, adjective, adverb, preposition, conjunction, interjection*. The idea that there are, or should be, eight categories originates in a list made by the grammarian Dionysius Thrax, in Alexandria (*c*.100 BC). In the accompanying table, Thrax's parts of speech appear on the left, their Roman loan translations next, and the English terms on the right, each with the century in which it was first used.

The original eight categories were suited to the description of classical Greek. In Latin, however, there is no article, and its place in the list was taken by the interjection. Medieval grammarians altered the categories by, in effect, inventing the adjective and downgrading the interjection to make room for it. When the list was applied to English, the article proved useful again, but not as a major part of speech (because

Greek	Latin	English
ónoma	nomen	14c: noun
rhêma	verbum	14c: verb
—	adjectivum	14c: adjective
metokhḗ	participium	14c: (participle)
árthron	(articulum)	13c: (article)
antōnumía	pronomen	16c: pronoun
próthesis	praepositio	14c: preposition
epírrhēma	adverbium	16c: adverb
súndesmos	coniunctio	14c: conjunction
—	interiectio	15c: interjection

the English articles do not have complex forms like the Greek article), the participle became a subcategory of the verb, and the interjection regained its former status, so that there were eight parts once more.

The parts of speech are traditionally defined by a mixture of formal and notional criteria. This mixture has posed problems for 20c grammarians, and since the development of structural linguistics, many have come to prefer the term *word class*, for which the criteria are rigorously restricted to form alone. Some contemporary linguists and grammarians prefer to avoid the traditional term; others use it by and large in the same sense as word class, and treat the two as interchangeable. The contemporary categories, based on formal criteria and however named, are more numerous than the traditional parts of speech and can be subcategorized. In English, for example, grammarians recognize a class of *determiners* that introduce noun phrases, and subclasses of determiners include: the definite article *the* (*the weather*); the indefinite article *a/an* (*a pipe*); the demonstratives (*that painting*); the possessives (*our family*); and the indefinite pronouns (*some money*). Similarly, verbs may be distinguished as full verb and auxiliary verb, and within the auxiliary class there is the class of modal auxiliary or modal verb (*can, may, will*, etc).

See ADJECTIVE, ADVERB, ADVERBIAL, ARTICLE[1], AUXILIARY VERB, CONJUNCTION, DEMONSTRATIVE, DETERMINER, GRAMMATICAL CATEGORY, INTERJECTION, MODAL VERB, NOUN, PARTICIPLE, PARTICLE, POSSESSIVE PRONOUN, PREPOSITION, PRONOUN, VERB, WORD CLASS. [GRAMMAR].

S.G., T.MCA.

PARTRIDGE, Eric (Honeywood) [1894–1979]. New Zealand-born lexicographer, and writer on usage and other subjects, born in Waimata Valley, North Island, and educated in Australia. His studies at the U. of Queensland were interrupted by four years as a private in the Australian infantry during the First World War, in which he saw action at Gallipoli and the Somme. In the Second World War, though over military age, he again volunteered. After a spell as an army education officer he was invalided out, only to join the Royal Air Force, in which, after serving as a storeman, he became clerk to 'Writer Command', a group of writers including H. E. Bates, John Pudney, and W. Vernon Noble. The group was commissioned to publicize the Service. His military experiences, and encounters with all sorts and conditions of men, reinforced a lifelong interest in the underside of the language.

After graduating, he became a Queensland Travelling Fellow at Oxford. Having gained an MA and B.Litt. simultaneously there, he taught at the universities of Manchester and London, but boredom and dislike of lecturing made him found his own publishing firm, Scholartis, in 1927. He launched several young authors, including Norah Hoult, Gerald Hanley, H. E. Bates, and Norah James. Besides these and the reissue of a number of classics (some 90 titles in all), Partridge's most important publications were (with John Brophy) the discursive glossary *Songs and Slang of the British Soldier in the Great War* (1930) and his annotated version of *A Classical Dictionary of the Vulgar Tongue*, by Francis Grose (1931). Cecil Franklin, chairman of the London publishers Routledge & Kegan Paul, saw the potential of these works, and, when Scholartis closed because of the Depression in 1931, commissioned Partridge to produce a comprehensive dictionary of slang.

Published in 1937, *A Dictionary of Slang and Unconventional English* (see entry) was a worldwide success. It was followed by: *Usage and Abusage: A Guide to Good English* (1942); *Shakespeare's Bawdy* (1947); *A Dictionary of the Underworld* (1950); *Origins: An Etymological Dictionary of English* (1958); *A Dictionary of Catch Phrases* (1977: see entry); and over 20 other books of essays on language, some prescriptive, some descriptive. Partridge's influence has been twofold: generating curiosity about the language among its speakers in all walks of life; working for the adequate lexicographical coverage of colloquial and taboo usage, a procedure now, partly as a result of his influence, standard for major dictionaries. See index. [BIOGRAPHY, EUROPE, OCEANIA, REFERENCE, USAGE].   P.B.

Crystal, David (ed.). 1980. *Eric Partridge: In His Own Words*. London: Deutsch.

Partridge, Eric. 1929. *Frank Honywood, Private*. Reissued in 1987, with introduction and annotations by Geoffrey Serle. Melbourne: Melbourne University Press.

—— 1963. *The Gentle Art of Lexicography*. London: Deutsch.

PASSIVE VOCABULARY. See VOCABULARY.

PASSIVE (VOICE) [14c: from Latin *passivus* capable of suffering or being affected]. A grammatical term that contrasts with *active (voice)*: where the sentence *Helen met the visitors* is in the active voice, the sentence *The visitors were met by Helen* is in the passive voice. The American grammarian Dennis Baron (in 'Going out of style?', *English Today* 17, Jan. 1989) has argued that since the 1940s, especially in the US, writers of guides to good writing have increasingly urged their readers to avoid or minimize passive constructions: the passive voice has not only become associated with general wordiness and confusion but also, especially in its 'agentless' form, with evasiveness and deception, as in *The bombs were dropped on innocent civilians* (by whom?). In 1946, George Orwell, in his essay 'Politics and the English Language' (*Horizon*, vol. 13), proposed the principle 'Never use the passive where you can use the active.' However, as has often been pointed out, Orwell (like other commentators opposed to the passive) has nonetheless used it freely: for example, when in the same essay he says that in certain poor styles 'the passive voice is wherever possible used in preference to the active'.

Baron notes that critics who downgrade the passive apply to its use such adjectives as 'lazy', 'hazy', 'vague', 'distant', 'watery', and 'wordy'. He also draws attention to William Zinsser's observation: 'The difference between an active-verb style and a passive-verb style—in pace, clarity and vigor—is the difference between life and death for a writer' (in *On Writing Well*, Harper & Row, 1980). Opposition to the passive has been strong in recent years in two areas: among campaigners for plain English and in *style checkers*, word-processing aids to the editing of especially business documents. *Webster's Dictionary of English Usage* (1989), however, lists three situations in which the passive has generally been regarded as useful: (1) When the receiver of the action is more important than the doer, as in *The child was struck by the car*. (2) When the doer is unknown (*The store was robbed last night*), unimportant (*Plows should not be kept in the garage*), or too obvious to be worth mentioning (*Kennedy was elected president*). (3) In scientific writing, because it helps establish a tone of detachment and impersonality. The dictionary's entry on *passive* concludes: 'The point, finally, is that sentences cast in the passive have their uses and are an important tool for the writer. Everyone agrees you should not lean too heavily on passive sentences and that you should especially avoid awkwardly constructed passives. The few statistical studies we have seen or heard of indicate that you are likely to use the active voice most of the time anyway' (p. 721). See ACADEMIC USAGE, ORWELL, PASSIVIZATION, STYLE CHECKER, TENSE, VERB, VOICE. [GRAMMAR, STYLE, USAGE].   T.MCA.

PASSIVIZATION [1965: coined by Noam Chomsky]. (1) Turning an active sentence or clause into a corresponding passive sentence or clause: *Diana opened the door* becoming *The door was opened by Diana*. (2) The corresponding transformational rule formulated at the earliest period of generative grammar, intended to reflect the relationship of the two sentences and to derive the passive sentence from its basic active sentence. In effect, the rule moved the active object to subject position, moved the active subject into a *by*-phrase (which can be optionally deleted), and added the auxiliary verb *be* and (on the following main verb) the passive participle inflection (-*ed* in regular verbs). Passivization applies when the active sentence contains an object. If the sentence contains two objects (an indirect object followed by a direct object) each object may become the passive subject: the active sentence *Natalie showed Derek* [IO] *the photographs* [DO] becoming either *Derek was shown the photographs* (*by Natalie*) or *The photographs were shown to Derek* (*by Natalie*). Prepositional verbs, such as *look at* and *approve of*, often occur in the passive. The noun phrase following the preposition is the prepositional object and can often be made passive subject, the preposition being left 'stranded' at the end: *All the professors approved of the Provost's action* becoming *The Provost's action was approved of* (*by all the professors*). See PASSIVE (VOICE). [GRAMMAR].   S.G.

PASSY, Paul Édouard [1859-1940]. French phonetician and specialist in language teaching, the son of Frédéric Passy, co-founder of the International Peace League and first winner of the Nobel Peace Prize. Born at Versailles, he studied languages at the École des hautes études and chose to teach English as an alternative to military service. In 1886, he formed an organization of modern language teachers which was joined by Otto Jespersen, Wilhelm Viëtor, and Henry Sweet, and became the forerunner of the International Phonetic Association. Discussion resulted in the now widely used IPA system of phonetic transcription. Passy issued a journal, later called *Le Maître phonétique*, and wrote a number of manuals for the teaching of French and English for foreign learners. He appears to have been the first to use the term *Direct Method* (*méthode directe*) in a pamphlet written for the French Ministry of Education in 1899. He was referring specifically to the Reform Movement initiated by Viëtor and others, but the term has also been widely associated with the rather different method practised by the Berlitz schools. See index. [BIOGRAPHY, EDUCATION, EUROPE, SPEECH].   P.C.

PAST [13c: a variant of *passed*]. A term for a tense of the verb concerned with events, actions, and states that no longer occur. The *simple past* (or *preterite*) is regularly formed with *-ed* (*walked*). The complex past forms are: the *past continuous* (or *past progressive*) which combines a past form of auxiliary *be* with the *-ing* participle (*was walking*); the *past perfect* (or *pluperfect*), which combines auxiliary *had* with the *-ed* participle (*had walked*); the *past perfect continuous*, which combines these two (*had been walking*). Compare FUTURE, PRESENT. See PRETERITE, TENSE. [GRAMMAR].   S.G.

PASTICHE [18c: through French, from Italian *pasticcio*, from Vulgar Latin *pasticium*, pie. Cognate with *pasta*]. A text consisting wholly or largely of direct borrowings from one or more other works. Language, imagery, motifs, situations, and/or character-types may be derivative. It is different from *plagiarism*, which conceals borrowings in an attempt to deceive. Pastiche is closer to *parody*, with adherence to the exact forms of the orginal, and need not be humorous or derisive; indeed, pastiches are often sincere expressions of admiration for the original works. Used seriously, the term recognizes the totality of literature and illustrates in an extreme form the principle of *intertextuality*. The pastiche was largely out of favour after the Romantic quest for unique individual inspiration, but some 20c writers have used it to good effect. In *The Waste Land* (1922), Eliot included allusions and direct quotations from a variety of backgrounds: for example, nursery rhymes, Dante, Gérard de Nerval, Kyd, and the Upanishads, all within a few lines of each other. Some writers and topics have been particularly prone to pastiche, such as Conan Doyle's Sherlock Holmes stories and Ian Fleming's James Bond novels; demand for additions to the 'canon' appears to prompt such 'apocryphal' works, which seldom enjoy the prestige of the originals. The term is often used to imply a lack of originality and excessive dependence on previous writers. See INTERTEXTUALITY, MOCK, PARODY, PLAGIARISM. [LITERATURE, STYLE].   R.C.

PASTORAL [14c: from Latin *pastoralis* of shepherds and sheep]. A poem or other work about idealized rural life, sometimes 'contrasting its purity and innocence with urban corruption. The pastoral convention began with the *Works*

and Days of the Greek poet Hesiod (8–7c BC), and developed in the poems of the Sicilian Greek poet Theocritus (3c BC) and the *Eclogues* of Virgil (1c BC, which were widely read and imitated by poets of the Renaissance, first in Italy and later in England. A pastoral poem is sometimes called an *eclogue* or an *idyll*. Pastoral poetry in English began in the 16c: for example, Edmund Spenser's *Shepheardes Calender* and Sir Philip Sidney's prose romance *Arcadia*. Shakespeare adopted it in *As You Like It*, with an added sense of realism that shows the discomforts as well as the joys of the countryside. In the 18c, the pastoral was more artificial, as in the young Pope's *Pastorals*:

> First in these fields I try the sylvan strains,
> Nor blush to sport on Windsor's blissful plains:
> Fair Thames, flow gently from thy sacred spring,
> While on thy banks Sicilian Muses sing;
> Let vernal airs through trembling osiers play,
> And Albion's cliffs resound the rural lay.
> ('The First Pastoral, or Damon', 1709)

Pope further attempted pastoral poetry in *The Messiah* (1712), imitating Virgil's fourth *Eclogue* and drawing on the Book of Isaiah. The pastoral stories and imagery of the Bible, especially Psalm 23 and the idea of Christ as the Good Shepherd, have been influential on English pastoral. Other 18c pastoral poems include *The gentle Shepherd* (1715) by Alan Ramsay (1686-1758) and the *Persian Eclogues* (1742) of William Collins (1721-59). Samuel Johnson, however, thought poorly of the pastoral, both for its pictures of a golden age and also for its language:

Other writers, having the mean and despicable condition of a shepherd always before them, conceive it necessary to degrade the language of pastoral by obsolete terms and rustick words, which they very learnedly call Dorick. Without reflecting, that they thus become authors of a mangled dialect, which may as well refine the speech as the sentiments of their personage, and that none of the inconsistencies which they endeavour to avoid is greater than that of joining elegance of thought with coarseness of diction (*Rambler* 37, 1750).

Wordsworth called his tragic poem 'Michael' (1800) a pastoral, and present-day critics have used the word to describe any celebration of simple life or work written in a mood of escapism. However, the pastoral in English literature may also be seen as any work that reflects a love of the unspoiled country scene, occurring in novels well removed from the original tradition:

She was stronger, she could walk better, and in the wood the wind would not be so tiring as it was across the park, flattening against her. She wanted to forget, to forget the world, and all the dreadful, carrion-bodied people. . . . Little gusts of sunshine blew, strangely bright, and lit up the celandines at the wood's edge,

under the hazel-rods, they spangled out bright and yellow.
(D. H. Lawrence, *Lady Chatterley's Lover*, 1928).

In the ragged hedge on the opposite side the boughs of the elm trees swayed just perceptibly in the breeze, and their leaves stirred faintly in dense masses like women's hair. Surely somewhere nearby, but out of sight, there must be a stream with green pools where dace were swimming? . . . 'It's the Golden Country—almost,' he murmured.
(George Orwell, *Nineteen Eight-Four*, 1949).

The pastoral style has kept words like *glade*, *rill*, *swain*, *sward*, and *sylvan* in many people's passive vocabulary, and has fostered a certain sentimentality about sheep and shepherds. See POETRY. [LITERATURE, STYLE].   R.C.

PAST PARTICIPLE. See PARTICIPLE.

PAST PERFECT. See PERFECT, PLUPERFECT.

PATHETIC FALLACY [1856: coined by John Ruskin in *Modern Painters*]. A phrase associated with the figure of speech *personification*, a pejorative comment on the inclination common among poets to attribute human qualities to nature: *the spendthrift crocus*; *the cruel, crawling foam*. The term 'pathetic' refers to the arousal of feeling, not to pity. Ruskin coined it to comment on 'the difference between the ordinary, proper, and true appearance of things to us; and the extraordinary, or false appearances, when we are under the influence of emotion, or contemplative fancy'. He objected to such usage because, however attractive or dramatic it may be, it 'morbidly' imputes life and human intent to nature and is part of 'a falseness in all our impressions of external things'. See LAWRENCE, PATHOS, PERSONIFICATION. [LITERATURE, STYLE].
T.MCA.

PATHOS [16c: from Greek *páthos* feeling, suffering. Stress: 'PAY-thoss']. A quality in life, art, and language which evokes sadness, pity, or sympathy for loss. Its apt presentation in speech and writing is considered a figure of speech. Shakespeare uses pathos when in *Hamlet* the Queen reports Ophelia's death to Laertes:

There is a Willow growes aslant a Brooke
That showes his hore leaues in the glassy streame,
Therewith fantastique garlands did she make
Of Crowflowers, Nettles, Daises, and long Purples
that liberall Shepheards giue a grosser name,
But our cold maydes doe dead mens fingers call them.
There on the pendant boughes her cronet weedes
Clambring to hang, an enuious sliuer broke,
When downe the weedy trophies and her selfe
Fell in the weeping Brooke, her clothes spred wide,
And Marmaide like awhile they bore her vp,
Which time she chaunted snatches of old tunes,
As one incapable of her owne distresse,

Or like a creature natiue and indewed
Vnto that elament, but long it could not be
Till that her garments heauy with theyr drinke,
Puld the poore wretch from her melodious lay
To muddy death. (Act 4, Scene 7.)

When pathos slips into sentimentality, it evokes contempt as easily as it evokes compassion, whence the general contemporary meaning of *pathetic* (pitiable). Compare PATHETIC FALLACY. [LITERATURE, STYLE].   T.MCA.

PATOIS [17c: from Old French *patois* rustic speech, perhaps from *patoier* to handle clumsily, from *pate* paw (Modern *patte*). Pronunciation: 'patwa']. (1) A non-technical term for a dialect, especially if it has low status in relation to a standard, literary language: *peasants speaking a local patois*. Although it is strongly associated with French, the term has been used for such a variety of any language, often to suggest low, mixed usage: 'Alas cried she, in a *patois* dialect, between French and Spanish' (Charlotte Smith, *Ethelinde*, 1789); 'To ascertain that she had nothing *patois* in her dialect' (Hannah More, *Female Education*, 1799). (2) The slang or jargon of a particular group: *a criminal patois*. (3) A common name for a Caribbean creole, especially Jamaican Creole (usually without the definite article): 'She said something in patois and went on washing up' (Jean Rhys, *Voyage in the Dark*, 1934). The meaning varies according to location. In Dominica, St Lucia, Grenada, and Trinidad, it refers to the French-based Creole of the Lesser Antilles. In Guyana, the term is not popular, *Creolese* being preferred. In those countries where French-based Creole is the major vernacular (St Lucia and Dominica), there is a growing feeling that the term is pejorative and *Creole* or *Kweyol* is often used instead. Compare ARGOT, BRITISH BLACK ENGLISH, CANT, CREOLE, DIALOG(UE) (NAIPAUL), LINGO. See MÉTIS. [AMERICAS, STYLE, VARIETY].   T.MCA., L.D.C.

PATRONYMIC [17c: from Latin *patronymicus*, Greek *patrōnumikós* of the name of one's father]. A name derived from the name of a father or male ancestor. In English, such names are formed on a Germanic basis with *-son*, such as *Jackson* (Jack's son) and *Robinson* (Robin's son), or are Celtic in origin, including: Scottish and Irish clan names that begin with *Mac* or *Mc* (*MacGregor* or *McGregor* son of Gregor); Irish names that begin with *O* (*O'Neill* Neill's grandchildren); and Welsh names that begin with *ap* (*ap Huw* son of Hugh, Anglicized as *Pugh*). Originally, a patronymic referred to someone's immediate father; for some centuries, however, it has come to have an etymological rather than a personal significance. See MCWORD, -ONYM, PERSONAL NAME. [NAME].   T.MCA.

PATTER [14c: a clipping of Latin *Paternoster* Our Father (the name of a common Christian prayer), used as a verb meaning 'to gabble, recite quickly', then as a noun for any gabbling ritual or routine]. (1) Rapid, fluent speech that may or may not make sense or be sincerely intended, like someone going meaninglessly through a ritual learned by heart. (2) The stylized lingo of salesmen, hucksters, sideshow barkers, conjurors, and comedians: 'Look at these lovely hand-made shirts, I ask you, £60 a piece you'd pay in the shops for them, £60, but am I asking £50? Am I asking £40, or even £30?—no, I am not, Sir— I'm asking *only* £20 a piece for these lovely, these *beautiful* . . . Here, just feel the fabric, Madam, just feel it . . .'; 'Nothing up my sleeve, ladies and gentlemen, nothing down my trousers, and we take the bunny rabbit like so, you see—everybody see?—and—hey presto! No more bunny rabbit!' (3) Stylized dialogue, such as the rehearsed routines of stand-up comics, one of whom is the straight man (*A*), the other the funny man (*B*): *A* [pompously] Ladies and gentlemen, a little recitation . . . *B* [rushing on and interrupting] I say, I say, I say! *A* [in feigned irritation] What is it? Can't you see I'm giving a recitation? *B* [undeterred] I say, how d'you make a Swiss roll? *A* [with a sigh of resignation] Well, how *do* you make a Swiss roll? *B* Push him down a mountain! *A* [in a lordly and dismissive manner] I don't wish to know that—kindly leave the stage! (4) Especially in Glasgow in Scotland, words used with skill: *Ah like yur patter, Jimmy—yur patter runs like watter*. Someone fluent and garrulous, whether sincere or otherwise, is a *patter merchant*. From this usage, the term has been extended to Glasgow dialect, often called *the patter*. See BADINAGE, BLARNEY, GLASGOW, NONSENSE, REPARTEE. Compare RAP. [EUROPE, STYLE, VARIETY].   W.N., T.MCA.

PEDAGOGICAL GRAMMAR, short form *ped grammar*. A term in language teaching and applied linguistics for a book or set of books designed to help learners of a foreign or second language, or for a way of presenting grammar that is intended to help students. [EDUCATION, GRAMMAR].   T.MCA.

PEDANT [16c: through French from Italian *pedante* teacher, perhaps from Latin *paedagogare* to teach, from Greek *paidagōgós* teacher (of boys), pedagogue. When the word entered English, it was used in the sense 'teacher', but rapidly acquired its current sense]. Someone who uses language to display knowledge and learning, and overemphasizes minor points and rules, especially with regard to grammar and usage. A pedantic usage is often needlessly complicated and filled with specialized terms

designed to make the common or simple appear complex and difficult. Pedantry in writing is sometimes known as *academese* and *educationese*, a style commonly associated with scholarly articles: for example, from a review in 1972, 'Monod is constrained to use the word "telenomy," which stands for living "objects endowed with a purpose or project," and which includes the genetic replication of such purpose. Yet in no way is this to be confused with "teleology" *à la* Aristotle, or with final causation, and certainly not with "animism," which is the projection of organic telenomy into the universe itself.' See ACADEMIC USAGE, HOLOFERNES, JARGON, PURISM. [EDUCATION, STYLE, USAGE].   W.D.L.

PEJORATION [17c: from Latin *peioratio/ peiorationis* making worse]. A term in linguistics for the process of semantic change in which there is a depreciation or 'downward' shift in the meaning of a word, phrase, or lexeme: for example, Old English *cnafa* (boy: compare German *Knabe*) became Modern English *knave* someone dishonest; Latin *villanus* (a farm servant) became Middle English *vilain/vilein* (a serf with some rights of independence), then Modern English *villain* (a scoundrel, criminal). Some processes of pejoration have been extremely complex. For example, from the 15c to the 19c, *silly* meant holy, innocent, and piteous (as with the 'sely child' in Chaucer's *Prioress's Tale*); from the 16c to the 19c, it also meant helpless, defenceless, and weak (as in the once-common poetic phrase 'silly sheep'); from the 16c to the 18c it also meant simple, rustic, humble, and homely, then weak in the mind (19c); from the 16c to the 20c, it has meant foolish, absurd, and trivial. The old 'higher' senses of holy, innocent, piteous, and the more neutral senses of helpless, defenceless, weak, rustic, and humble, have all given way to the 'lower' senses of foolish and trivial. See MELIORATION, SEMANTIC CHANGE. [HISTORY, LANGUAGE].   T.MCA.

PEJORATIVE [19c: from French *péjoratif*, Latin *peiorativus* making worse, from *peior* worse. Stress: 'pe-JAW-ra-tiv'; formerly also 'PEE-jo-ra-tiv']. (1) A term in philology and semantics that refers to a complex word whose meaning is 'lower' than that of its base: *poetaster* a poor sort of poet; *princeling*, a minor or very young prince. (2) A term in linguistics and lexicography that refers to an expression, tone, or style that serves to devalue, disparage, or dismiss the subject being talked or written about: *illiterate* is pejorative when used to describe people who can read and write, but not to a level acceptable to the speaker (*What an illiterate scrawl!*); *Dago*, a pejorative nickname that distances and devalues people from or in Iberia and Latin America. Compare DEROGATORY, PEJORATION. [STYLE]. T.MCA.

PEN, PENCIL. See WRITING.

PENGUIN. A British company that publishes both paperback reprints and originals, founded in 1935 by Allen Lane with the aim of providing the general public with cheap editions of quality writing. Choosing the penguin as a 'dignified but flippant' symbol, Lane produced paperbacks at a fifth of the price of their hardback originals. No one expected him to succeed. Jonathan Cape, the first publisher to pass titles to Lane, in the firm expectation that he would fail, later said: 'You're the b—— that has ruined this trade with your ruddy Penguins' (Michael B. Howard, *Jonathan Cape, Publisher*, 1971). The first ten Penguins to be launched were colour-coded as biographies, detective stories, and novels, and included Dorothy L. Sayers's *The Unpleasantness at the Bellona Club* and Mary Webb's *Gone to Earth*. After a year, 3m books had been sold. In 1937, the *Pelican* imprint appeared, to pre-empt its use by rivals and as a vehicle for more serious books. The first Pelican was Shaw's *The Intelligent Woman's Guide to Socialism and Capitalism*. Between 1940 and 1950, the literary magazine *Penguin New Writing* was published; contributors included Graham Greene, George Orwell, and Tennessee Williams. In 1960, D. H. Lawrence's *Lady Chatterley's Lover* sold 2m copies in six weeks. In 1970, when Lane died, the company was taken over by Pearson Longman. In 1975, Penguin acquired the New York-based publisher The Viking Press, after which the joint name *Viking-Penguin* came into use, especially in the US. Penguin originals that deal with English include the *Penguin English Dictionary* (1965) and David Crystal's *Listen to Your Child* (1986). Pelican originals include Simeon Potter's *Our Language* (1950), F. R. Palmer's *Grammar* (1971), George W. Turner's *Stylistics* (1973), J. D. O'Connor's *Phonetics* (1973), and David Crystal's *The English Language* (1988). See CENSORSHIP, LAWRENCE. [EDUCATION, EUROPE, MEDIA]. T.MCA.

PEN NAME, also **pseudonym, nom de plume.** (1) A name assumed by a writer to conceal his or her real identity. The name may be obviously false, often with classical associations: for example, *Junius* in the 18c *Letters of Junius* (never definitively identified), *Elia* (Charles Lamb, 1775–1834), and *Palinurus* (Cyril Connolly, 1903–74). More commonly, however, it is a real name for an individual, such as *Hugh MacDiarmid* for Christopher Murray Grieve (1892–1978). Pseudonymity may be desired for many reasons. Academics wish to avoid confusion between their scholarly and lighter works: the 19c mathematician C. L. Dodgson who became *Lewis Carroll*; the 20c literary critic J. I. M. Stewart who has written detective novels as *Michael Innes*. In the 19c, a masculine pen name served to avert prejudice against women writers: Mary Ann Evans (1819–80), who wrote as *George Eliot*. Such adoptions and others like *Mark Rutherford* (W. H. White, 1831–1913), *Mark Twain* (S. L. Clemens, 1835–1910), and *George Orwell* (Eric Blair, 1903–50) have become the accepted names of the authors. (2) A comparable name in a newspaper or other periodical serving to identify a column written, at one time or successively, by several people, such as *Mandrake* in *The Sunday Telegraph* and *Pendennis* in *The Observer*. See CARROLL, MACDIARMID, ORWELL, QUILLER-COUCH, TWAIN. [LITERATURE, NAME, WRITING]. R.C.

PENNSYLVANIA DUTCH [1810s]. (1) With definite article: the rural religious community descended from Anabaptist Protestants from the Rhineland, South Germany, and Switzerland, who settled in the US state of Pennsylvania in the 17–18c, also known as *Mennonites* (from German *Mennonit*, after Menno Simons, a 16c Frisian religious leader) and *Amish* (from German *Amisch*, after Jakob Amman, a Swiss Mennonite bishop). (2) Their High German dialect, more accurately known as *Pennsylvania German*. The term *Dutch* is a variant of *Deutsch* (German) and has no direct link with either the Dutch or their language. The dialect is spoken mainly in the eastern part of the state and is strongly influenced by English, while the English used by 'the Dutchmen' is strongly influenced by the dialect, especially in word order and idioms. See AMERICAN ENGLISH, GERMAN. [AMERICAS, LANGUAGE, VARIETY]. T.MCA.

PERFECT [13c: from Latin *perfectus* fully done]. A term for an aspect of the verb concerned with completion. In the Slavonic languages, the *perfective* and *imperfective* are signalled by inflections on the verb, the perfective denoting the completion of the activity and the imperfective its non-completion. In English, the perfect (also sometimes termed the perfective) contrasts with the non-perfect, and is formed by a combination of the auxiliary *have* and an *-ed* participle: *present perfect* (*has/have discovered*); *past perfect* or *pluperfect* (*had discovered*); *present continuous progressive perfect* (*has/have been discovering*); *past continuous progressive perfect* (*had been discovering*); *future perfect* (*will have discovered*); *future continuous progressive perfect* (*will have been discovering*). In general, the perfect indicates a previous indefinite period within which the action of the verb takes place. For the present perfect, that period begins in the past and extends to the present: *I have lived in London since I was born* (until the present time); *She has broken her arm* (and the effect is still noticeable); *I haven't seen the film* (but may still do so). The past perfect indicates an action previous to another action within a past period: *Tom had not seen his parents since they were divorced*. The past perfect can also denote a past action (past before the past) without any aspectual force, in which case it is often replaced by the simple past: *After he (had) consulted his solicitor, Colin refused to sign the contract*. The future perfect refers to an event before a future event: *Pat will have finished her essay by the time we arrive*. See TENSE, VERB. [GRAMMAR].   S.G.

PERFORMANCE. See COMPETENCE AND PERFORMANCE.

PERFORMANCE VARIETY. See VARIETY.

PERFORMATIVE. See: (1) LOCUTION, SPEECH ACT. (2) PERFORMATIVE VERB.

PERFORMATIVE VERB [20c]. A term used in philosophy and linguistics for a type of verb (*apologize, forbid, inform, promise, request, thank*) that can explicitly convey the kind of speech act being performed. In saying *I apologize for my behaviour*, someone is making an apology, which could also be done in part at least without such a verb: *My behaviour was utterly deplorable*. Generally, the performative verb in such sentences is in the simple present active and the subject is *I*, but the verb may be in the simple present passive and the subject need not be *I*: *Smoking is forbidden; The committee thanks you for your services*. A test for whether a verb is being used performatively is the possible insertion of *hereby*: *I hereby apologize; The committee hereby thanks you*. In *hedged performatives*, the verb is present but the speech act is performed indirectly: in saying *I must apologize for my behaviour*, the speaker is expressing an obligation to make an apology, but implies that the acknowledgement of that obligation is the same as an apology. In contrast, *I apologized* is a report, and *Must I apologize?* is a request for advice. [GRAMMAR].   S.G.

PERIOD [16c: from French *période*, Latin *periodus*, Greek *períodos* ('way round') a round or length of time, cyclic recurrence, rounded sentence, from *perí* round, *hodós* way]. In the classical study of language, dominant in English during the 16–19c, the term for a sentence regarded as 'complete' because it is composed of a balanced group of main and dependent clauses.

If a period (also known as a *periodic sentence* or a *point*) was well formed, it was called *well-rounded* or *well-turned*: 'If you will not take this as an excuse, accept it at least as a well-turned period, which is always my principal concern' (Thomas Gray, letter to N. Nicholls, 1764). The term also applied, especially in the 16c, to a pause at the end of a spoken sentence: 'the longest Sommer hath his Autumne, the largest sentence his Periode' (Robert Greene, *Penelopes Web*, 1587). By the early 17c, it was being used, alongside *full stop* and *full point*, for the punctuation mark (.), which served to signal the closing pause. In elocution, this mark is associated with the silent counting of time: 'A Comma stops the Voice while we may privately tell one, a Semi-colon two; a Colon three; and a Period four' (John Mason, *An Essay on elocution*, 1748). The theory and practice of pauses associated with punctuation marks has lost most of its force in the 20c, but some teachers continue to use aspects of it, and when reading aloud many people pause for breath or effect at the end of sentences. Currently, *period* is the most widely used and understood term for the point at the end of a sentence: it is the dominant term in North America, but in the UK takes second place to *full stop*. Especially in colloquial AmE, the word *period* is often used as an interjection to indicate that someone has made a decision and has nothing more to say on the matter: 'I forbid them to go, period.' See DOT, ELLIPSIS, PERIODIC SENTENCE, POINT, PUNCTUATION, SENTENCE, STOP. [WRITING].   T.MCA.

PERIOD DICTIONARIES OF ENGLISH. The series of multi-volume historical dictionaries, one for each of several stages or periods in the history of English, proposed by William A. Craigie in an address to the Philological Society, 1919. In recent years, the term has been extended to any other dictionary of a period of English. Craigie's periods were: Old English, to 1150; Middle English, 1150–1500; Early Modern English, 1500–1700; Late Modern English, from 1700; Older Scottish, 1375–1700; Modern Scottish, from 1700. Work began in the 1920s on the *Middle English Dictionary* (1952–), which had reached *So* in 1989 (in 10 volumes of 80 parts), on *A Dictionary of the Older Scottish Tongue* (1931–) and *The Scottish National Dictionary* (1931–76), and *A Dictionary of American English* (1936–44). Craigie had regarded the Old English period as adequately covered by *An Anglo-Saxon Dictionary*, by Joseph Bosworth and T. N. Toller (1898) with *Supplement* by T. N. Toller (1921), a dictionary (with quotations) of 2,123 pages, but since 1969 an entirely new and exhaustive Old English dictionary has been in preparation at the U. of Toronto, based on a computer-readable version of the entire surviving corpus of the period (around 3m words of text); two parts, for C and D, have so far appeared on microfiche.

For the Tudor and Stuart period in England, preparatory work towards an *Early Modern English Dictionary* was carried out at the U. of Michigan (1928-39), resulting in a collection of over 3m quotations, and some trial entries, but was then suspended, pending completion of *MED*. For Late Modern English down to 1820 no separate dictionary is yet in view. However, because of its systematic excerption programme for 1820 onwards, the *Supplement to the Oxford English Dictionary* (four volumes, 1972-86), now incorporated into *The Oxford English Dictionary* (2nd edition, 20 volumes, 1989), fills the place of a period dictionary for recent English. All these works depend on vast collections of quotation-examples, comprehensively excerpted from the original texts: for example, *MED*, it is claimed, has over 3.5m quotations from over 3,000 original titles. From these quotations, the compilers substantiate each word's sense divisions and definitions and all other aspects of its history in copious arrays of dated and referenced quotations.

Previous period dictionaries have included, among others: for Old English, *Dictionarium Saxonico-Latino-Anglicum*, by William Somner (1659), and *A Concise Anglo-Saxon Dictionary for the Use of Students*, by J. R. C. Hall (1894); for Middle English, *A Dictionary of the Old English Language*, by F. H. Stratmann (1864-7, 1873, 1878), revised as *A Middle-English Dictionary*, by Henry Bradley (1891); for Older and Modern Scots, John Jamieson's *An Etymological Dictionary of the Scottish Language* (1808, 1825); and, for all periods, *The Oxford English Dictionary*. The new dictionaries, however, far surpass all of these in their exhaustiveness and precision, containing many words and usages previously unrecorded, and displaying innumerable details of meaning, collocation, formal history, and chronological, regional, and stylistic distribution previously unknowable, as well as much new encyclopedic information. See DICTIONARY, DICTIONARY OF AMERICAN ENGLISH, EARLY MODERN ENGLISH DICTIONARY, JAMIESON, MIDDLE ENGLISH DICTIONARY, OXFORD ENGLISH DICTIONARY, REGIONAL DICTIONARIES OF ENGLISH, SCOTTISH DICTIONARIES. [REFERENCE]. A.J.A.

PERIODICAL [*c.*1600: from *periodic* and *-al*: see PERIODIC SENTENCE]. A publication, especially a magazine or journal, that appears on a weekly, monthly, quarterly, or six-monthly basis, and is concerned as much with opinions, values, and theories as with news and other information. The first periodicals in English date from the early 17c and were varied in character. The scholarly variety contained philosophical essays and digests from recent books; a reformist strain offered studies under such titles as *The Night-Walker: Or Evening Rambles in Search After Lewd Women* (1696-7), which suggests a pornographic interest. The serious scientific periodical dates from 1665, the year in which the English *Scientific Transactions* and the French *Journal des Sçavans* first appeared. Defoe's *The Review*, offering commentary on political, social, and literary topics, was a prototype emulated by Steele's *Tatler* (1709-11), Addison and Steele's *Spectator* (1711-12), the *Examiner* (1710-11), and Johnson's *The Rambler* (1750-2). These were ephemeral, but were followed by the influential 19c journals. Currently, the terms *periodical*, *review*, and *journal* suggest a publication more serious and high-toned than a magazine. See BULLETIN, JOURNAL, MAGAZINE, MASTHEAD, NEWSPAPER, REVIEW, ROYAL SOCIETY, VOLUME. [MEDIA]. G.H.

PERIODIC SENTENCE [Late 19c: from French *périodique*, Latin *periodicus*, Greek *periodikós* coming round at intervals, cyclic, sentential, from *períodos* a cycle, sentence, and sentence. See PERIOD]. Also **period, point**. In traditional grammar, rhetoric, and composition, a complete sentence, usually characterized by an intricate relationship among its clauses. It is the classical 'rounded sentence', avowedly expressing a complete thought, adopted by writers in the European vernaculars from the prose stylists of Greece and Rome. The subordinate forms in a period are often nested one within the other, like Chinese boxes; in its most complex forms it can be cumbrous and hard to follow. Intricate periods were much used and admired until the late 19c. The following is a typical Augustan period, in which the first *who* is separated from its verb *had* by 51 other words:

This discovery was now luckily owing to the presence of Joseph at the opening of the saddle-bags; *who*, having heard his friend say he carried with him nine volumes of sermons, and not being of that sect of philosophers who can reduce all the matter of the world into a nutshell, seeing there was no room for them in the bags, where the parson had said they were deposited, *had* the curiosity to cry out, 'Bless me, sir, where are your sermons?'
(Henry Fielding, *Joseph Andrews*, 1742, italics added).

The period is unusual in present-day English, although it may occur in the language of the law and similar registers. When it occurs, it is usually designed to hold the reader in suspense as to the point being made. In the following, the serial descriptions ('Never to feel . . .; never to be able to . . .; to be aware of . . .') are concluded by an assertion ('whether or not . . .') in which the subject and negated verb are postponed to the very end:

Never to feel wholly what you wish to feel—and to wish it all the more intensely for that very reason; never to be able to believe in the veracity of whatever feelings you do have—and to make threatening gestures towards anyone who has his own doubts about them; to be aware of a sickening gap between assertion and inner state every time you open your mouth—not least when you open your mouth precisely to deny that there is such a gap . . . whether or not it is a crime to feel the 'throes' and 'pangs' of that kind of insincerity I do not know (Dan Jacobson, *Adult Pleasures*, 1988).

See PERIOD, POINT, SENTENCE. [GRAMMAR, STYLE, WRITING]. S.G., T.MCA.

PERIPETEIA. See PLOT, POETICS.

PERIPHRASIS [16c: through Latin from Greek *periphrasis* talking around. Stress: 'pe-RI-fra-sis']. In rhetoric, the use of more rather than fewer words, especially to talk about something in an indirect and circuitous way. The adjective *periphrastic* is used both directly in relation to this sense of periphrasis and to refer to the use of *more/most* for the comparative and superlative degrees of adjectives and adverbs, which is less compact than the use of *-er*, *-est*. See CIRCUMLOCUTION, DEGREE, TAUTOLOGY. [GRAMMAR, STYLE]. T.MCA.

PERIPHRASTIC. See DEGREE, PERIPHRASIS.

PERSIAN [Known to its speakers as *Fārsī*, from *Fārs*, the heartland province of the classical Persian Empire, known to the Greeks as *Persís* (Old Persian *Parsa*)]. An Indo-European language of West Asia, the official language of Iran, widely used in Afghanistan, culturally significant in West and South Asia, and noted for its literary and especially poetic tradition. Although a much older language, its development parallels that of English in several ways: (1) Scholars divide it, like English, into three stages: *Old Persian*, early first millennium BC to *c*.3C BC (written in cuneiform); *Middle Persian*, 3C BC to 9C AD (written in Aramaic script); and *Modern Persian*, 10C to the present day (written in Arabic script). (2) Modern Persian has lost most of the complex inflections of the older stages, much as Modern English has lost most of the inflections of Old English. (3) Just as English contains a vast lexical inheritance from Latin, Persian has absorbed, under the influence of Islam, a great number of Arabic loanwords. (4) Just as English has acquired many literary and rhetorical practices from Latin and ultimately Greek, Persian has acquired equivalent practices from Arabic and ultimately Greek. (5) Both have been widely used

in the Indian subcontinent and have greatly influenced its vernaculars. Used officially by the Moghuls (16–18c), Persian was the imperial language of India immediately before English.

Persian loanwords in English have usually been mediated by other languages, as with: (1) *Azure*, through Old French *azur*, through Arabic *al-lazward*, from Persian *lājward* or *lāzhward* lapis lazuli, the colour blue. (2) *Magic*, through Old French *magique*, through late Latin *magica*, from Greek *magikḗ* (*téknē*) magic (art), from *mágos* (Latin *magus*), from Old Persian *magu-s* a member of the priestly caste, perceived as a sorcerer. (3) *Khaki*, through military usage in Urdu from Persian *khākī* dusty, dust-coloured, from *khāk* dust. (4) *Paradise*, through French *paradis*, through Latin *paradisus*, through Greek *parádeisos*, from Old Persian *pairidaēza* enclosure, park, pleasure ground (used by Christians to mean both the Garden of Eden and heaven), from *pairi* around, *diz* to mould or form. (5) *Pilaf*, *pilaff*, *pilau*, *pillau*, *pilaw*, *pillaw*, *pilao*, *pulao* etc.: through the usage of a variety of languages and localities, such as Turkish *pilâv* and *pilâf* and Urdu *pilāo* and *palāo*, from Persian *pilāw* boiled rice (and meat). (6) *Turban*, through French *turban*, probably through Portuguese *turbante* (acquired in India), with an *l/r* change from Persian *dulband*. (7) In loanwords that have passed through Indian languages, the possessive linking vowel of Modern Persian (the *ezāfeh*) appears as *-i-*, as in *koh-i-noor/kohinoor*, the name of an Indian diamond in the British Crown Jewels, from Persian *kōh-i nūr* mountain (*kōh*) of light (*nūr*). See ARABIC, ARYAN, BISOCIATION, BORROWING, HINDI, HINDI-URDU, INDIAN LANGUAGES, INDO-EUROPEAN LANGUAGES, URDU. [ASIA, LANGUAGE]. T.MCA.

PERSON [12c: from Old French *persone*, Latin *persona* a mask (used in drama), a character acted, someone who has a role or legal status, a human being: compare PERSONIFICATION]. A grammatical and semantic category applying to pronouns and verbs and used in describing the roles of people and things.

Pronouns. In standard English, the first-person pronouns are the speaker(s) or writer(s) together with any others included in the plural (*I*, *me*, *we*, *us*). The second-person pronouns are the addressee(s) and possibly others in the plural (*you* and archaic singular *thou/thee*). The third-person pronouns are others being referred to (*she*, *her*, *he*, *him*, *it*, *one*, *they*, *them*). Melanesian Pidgin English makes a further distinction by having two words to correspond to *we*, one including speaker, listener, and possibly others (*yumi*: you-me) and one excluding the listener (*mipela*, me-fellow: 'me and someone else').

There can also be different words for *you*, implying greater or lesser degrees of intimacy or formality, as with French *tu/vous*, comparable to the archaic and dialectal English distinction *thou/you*. The distinctions of person are shown not only in personal pronouns but also in reflexive pronouns (*myself*) and possessive pronouns (*my, mine*).

There is no necessary correspondence between the grammatical and semantic category of person. In Spanish, the formal pronouns *usted/ustedes* (*you*, singular/plural) semantically address people but are grammatically third-person pronouns. *Usted* derives from an original *vuestra merced* (your grace), and parallels the highly formal convention in English in *Does His Majesty wish to leave?* (directly addressing the monarch) and *Does Madam wish to look at some other hats?* (addressed to a customer). Comparable usages in present-day English are the royal and editorial *we* and the generalized *you*. This use of *we* is semantically singular while grammatically plural, as in Queen Victoria's remark, 'We are not amused.' The generalized *you*, as in *You never can tell, can you?*, is second person grammatically but semantically includes others. Usage is sometimes ambiguous between the addressed and generalized *you*, prompting the question *Do you mean me or everybody?* Generic or inclusive *he* is a long-established usage in which the third-person masculine represents both man and woman (*Ask anybody and he'll give you the same answer*). Those who defend its use argue that sexist bias is not present in it or intended by it, and that the meaning is clear. Those who object to it argue that it misrepresents half the human race and reinforces male bias and social dominance. See GENERIC PRONOUN. In colloquial usage, *they* is often used instead (*Ask anybody and they'll give you the same answer*).

Verbs. In highly inflected languages like Latin, person is indicated in the verb itself: *amo* I love, *amas* thou lovest, *amat* he/she/it loves, *amamus* we love, *amatis* you (plural) love, *amant* they love. As a result, pronouns are used for other purposes, such as emphasis. In English, however, only the third-person singular of the present tense normally has a distinct form: *he loves*, *she likes*, *it does*. See PERSONAL PRONOUN, PRONOUN, VERB, VOICE. [GRAMMAR, STYLE]. S.C.

PERSONAL NAME. The proper name of a person, either inherited or given. Inherited personal names include *surnames* or *family names/last names*, and *patronymics* and *metronymics*. Given names include *forenames* (traditionally known in English as *baptismal names* or *Christian/christian names*), which may be *first names* or

middle names. In current usage, *baptismal name* seldom occurs, *Christian name* is less and less common (especially in official usage), and *forename, first name*, or *given name* are increasingly taking over, all used more or less synonymously. A *double-barrelled name* (BrE) combines two personal inherited surnames: *Boyd-Orr* and *Smith-Sykes*. Double given names occur: (1) in French (*Jean-Louis, Marie-Louise*), and are therefore common in Canada, and (2) in the American South (*Billy-Bob, Sue Ellen*).

Changing one's name. In most legal systems, provisions are made for individuals to change their names officially if they so wish: for example, in Britain by *deed poll*, a deed made by one party only. When people use names other than their given and inherited names, they may be doing so for professional purposes (a performer's *stage name*, a writer's *pen name*) or for socially dubious purposes (to avoid the police, the payment of debt, a spouse, etc.). In such cases, the new name is an *alias* (Latin: otherwise) and the police and other authorities may refer to someone as *John Smith aka/a.k.a. John Bland* where *aka* means 'also known as'.

Surnames. In Britain, surnames were uncommon before the 13c. They were originally epithets used to distinguish persons of the same given name, especially for legal purposes, and appeared earliest among the urban, moneyed classes with property to defend or bequeath. Surnames often indicated the occupation of the bearer (*Smith, Tailor*), place of habitation (*Lincoln, Washington*), appearance (*Black, Short*), character (*Fox, Goodfellow*), or father's name (*McDonald, Robertson*). The last are often called *patronymics*, although true patronymics, like those in Iceland (*Magnusson*, the son of Magnus) and Russia (*Ivanovich*, the son of Ivan) change with each generation, so that if such a system operated in English, the son of William Johnson would be Richard Williamson, his son Thomas Richardson, and so forth, as was once the case. Patrick Hanks and Flavia Hodges observe:

Surnaming crept northwards from Germany through Denmark and into Norway . . . in the 15th and 16th centuries. In Iceland, the traditional patronymic naming system has still not fully given way to hereditary surnames. Magnus Pálsson is Magnus the son of Pál, and his eldest son may well be called Pál Magnusson, preserving a traditional alternation that in some families goes back over a thousand years. His daughter would be, for example, Gudrun Magnusdottir. . . . The patronymic naming system still found in Iceland was common throughout Scandinavia until about two hundred years ago, and Swedish family histories still contain anecdotes about the incredulity and derision met by women who first called themselves Anna Andersson rather than Anna Andersdotter (1988, p. viii; below).

The parental feminine, the *metronymic*, is less common but was found in early Hindu culture, as when the epic hero Arjuna is called *Kaunteya* (son of Kunti).

Given names. In 20c English-speaking communities, these are often subject to fashions, so that the generation of a person can often be guessed from a first name. *Shirley* was popular in the 1930s because of the child actress Shirley Temple. Given names also vary between nations and social groups: *Giles* and *Nigel* are common middle-class names for men in England; *Alistair* and *Ian* are traditional Scottish men's names (Gaelic for *Alexander* and *John*); spelt *Alasdair* and *Iain*, they more fully reflect their origin. The Gaelic woman's name *Fiona* became popular in the middle classes of both Scotland and England and is no longer perceived as markedly Highland, while *Morag* is. The men's names *Chad*, *Earl*, and *Todd* are likely to be North American.

In some US families, there is a tradition of using a surname as a given name (usually a middle name). *John Foster Dulles*, a former US Secretary of State, and the ex-President *Richard Milhous Nixon* are instances. Such names are likely to be mistaken by people in Britain for double-barrelled names, and Dulles was often mistakenly referred to in the British press as *Mr Foster-Dulles*. Female double given names in the American South often follow a pattern in which the first name is the diminutive of a man's name and the second a one-syllable woman's name (*Bobby Sue, Johnny May, Jimmy Ruth*). Also Southern US is the use of invented names for both men and women, and such names are often androgynous in application: *Charleen, LaMoira, Shawanda*. The free invention of such names has been credited to the anti-pedobaptist culture of the area, where baptism occurs on conviction of faith, not as a christening service. Where the clergy has no part in naming, the fancies of the parents may run free. On the other hand, because of its Puritan tradition, older use in New England favoured such Old Testament names as *Hezekiah* and virtue names like *Prudence*.

Names and initials. The use of initials varies according to time and place. In the US, the traditionally favoured pattern for an official name is full first name and middle initial, as in *Dwight D. Eisenhower*. The use of both given names in full, as in *Richard Milhous Nixon*, seems 'showy', and the use of first initial and full middle name, as with *J. Danforth Quayle*, is widely considered pompous, and can lead to the middle name being used in full or short form as a first name, as in *Dan Quayle*. In the UK, custom allows for all of these, but has favoured both full forms without necessarily implying showiness, as in *Winston*

Spencer Churchill and *Arthur Conan Doyle*, and such double-barrelled forms as *Frank Mitchell-Hedges* and *Ivy Compton-Burnett*, which, because they require people to be addressed with both surnames, are widely viewed as 'posh' and pretentious. The predominant practice has been initials for both given names, as in *D. H. Lawrence*, *C. S. Lewis*, and *H. G. Wells*. There is a growing tendency on both sides of the Atlantic and in Australasia to use two names only, as in *Agatha Christie, Saul Bellow, George Bush, Norman Mailer, Margaret Thatcher*, often with the increased informality of President *Jimmy Carter* in the US and Prime Minister *Bob Hawke* in Australia. See INITIAL, PATRONYMIC. [NAME].   J.A., T.MCA.

Cresswell, Julia. 1990. *Bloomsbury Dictionary of First Names*. London: Bloomsbury.
Dunkling, Leslie. 1974, 1983, 1986. *The Guinness Book of Names*. Enfield: Guinness Books.
—— 1977. *First Names First*. New York: Universe Books.
Hanks, Patrick, & Hodges, Flavia. 1988. *A Dictionary of Surnames*. Oxford: University Press.
—— 1990. *A Dictionary of First Names*. Oxford: University Press.
Lawson, Edwin D. 1987. *Personal Names and Naming: An Annotated Bibliography*. New York: Greenwood.
Withycombe, Elizabeth G. 1977. *The Oxford Dictionary of English Christian Names*, 3rd edition. Oxford: University Press.

PERSONAL PRONOUN [17c]. A pronoun that refers mainly but not exclusively to a person or people, and that in many languages makes distinctions of person (often first, second, and third person), number, gender, and case. In English, most such pronouns distinguish subject and object case (*I/me, he/him, she/her, we/us, they/them*, and archaic *thou/thee*) and are the only words that do so (except for *who/whom* and *whoever/whomever*). Two pronouns, *you* and *it*, are without case distinction. In addition to its references to things, *it* can refer to information: *They're cheaper this week: I read it in the paper/ heard it on the radio*. *It* also has some purely grammatical functions, as in *It's raining, It's marvellous that you won*, and *I hate it when people shout*, in which it is known as *existential it*. The term personal pronoun is sometimes extended to cover *possessive pronoun*. See DUMMY, PERSON, PRONOUN. [GRAMMAR].   S.C.

PERSONIFICATION [18c: from Latin *personificatio* 'making' a person, loan-translating Greek *prosōpopoiía* making a mask, face, person]. In rhetoric, discourse in which animals, plants, elements of nature, and abstract ideas are given human attributes: 'bask in Heaven's blue smile' (Shelley). It has been regarded as both a figure in its own right and as an aspect of *metaphor* in which non-human is identified with human: 'Life can play some nasty tricks'. In classical Greek, a *prósōpon* was a face, mask, dramatic character, or person; in drama, an actor wearing a mask could represent an absent or imaginary person, a force of nature, an abstract quality, or an institution. The device called *prosopopoeia* was therefore both dramatization (putting imaginary speeches into the mouths of characters, human or non-human) and personification as understood today. It is common in verse: 'Slowly, silently, now the moon / Walks the night in her silver shoon' (Walter de la Mare, 'Silver', 1913). The representation of the moon as female is similar to the application of *she* to ships, cats, countries, and certain abstractions: 'He seems to want to destroy poetry as poetry, to exclude her as a vehicle of communication' (Eric A. Havelock, *Preface to Plato*, 1963); 'For most of her history, the Church's record with regard to sexuality . . . has been wretched' (*Independent*, 20 May 1988). In everyday idiom, the world is *Mother Nature* and necessity is *the mother of invention. Old Father Time* looks after the years, and the symbolism of a father-like God is traditional among Christians, Jews, and Muslims. In such imagery, human types and relationships have been projected on to the universe at large. See METAPHOR, PATHETIC FALLACY. [STYLE].   T.MCA.

PET NAME. An affectionate and usually intimate nickname, such as *Eddikins*, adding a second diminutive suffix to *Eddy*, short for *Edward*. It is often special or even unique to its referent, as used by parents and children, lovers, owners of pets, etc. Pet names may be used to achieve literary effects: for example, in Shakespeare's *Henry IV, Henry V*, part I, young Prince Henry (the future Henry V) is called *Harry* or, especially by his Boarshead Tavern companions, *Hal*, a form that symbolizes his roisterous youth. In *The Taming of the Shrew*, the shrew Katherine becomes by the end of the play plain *Kate*, perhaps punning on the obsolete term *cates* (delicacies to eat). See DIMINUTIVE, NICKNAME. [NAME].   J.A.

PHARYNX [17c: through Latin from Greek *phárunx*]. An anatomical term for the cavity of the upper throat through which air passes from the larynx to the mouth and nose. Sounds made in the pharynx are *pharyngeal*, such as the open back vowel of *palm* in RP and certain fricative consonants in Arabic. See ARABIC, GUTTURAL. [SPEECH].   G.K.

PHATIC COMMUNION [1923: from Greek *phatós* spoken: coined by the Polish anthropologist Bronisław Malinowski]. Language used more for the purpose of establishing an atmosphere or maintaining social contact than for exchanging information or ideas: in speech, informal comments on the weather (*Nice day again, isn't it?*) or an enquiry about health at the beginning of a conversation or when passing someone in the street (*How's it going? Leg better?*); in writing, the conventions for opening or closing a letter (*All the best, Yours faithfully*), some of which are formally taught in school. See CONVERSATION. [LANGUAGE, SPEECH, STYLE, WRITING].   D.C.

PHILIPPINE [1810s: adapted from Spanish *Filipino*]. Also *Filipino*. Terms relating to the people, islands, cultures, etc., of the Philippines: *Philippine languages, the Filipino capital Manila*. See FILIPINO, PHILIPPINES. [ASIA, NAME].   T.MCA.

PHILIPPINE ENGLISH, also **Filipino English**. The English language as used in the Philippines. The 1980 census counted the number of Filipinos with some competence in English as around 65%: some 35m people. Ability ranges from a smattering of words and phrases through passive comprehension to near-native mastery.

Background. Filipino experience of Western colonialism and its linguistic effects has been unique, in that there have been two colonizers in succession: Spain from the 16c and the US from 1898, when English arrived in the islands. It spread rapidly, to the detriment of Spanish, because it was the new language of government, preferment, and education. Incentives to learn English included recruitment into the civil service and study in the US. In 1935, US-educated *pensionados* (scholars) became leaders of the Senate and the House of Representatives as well as members of the cabinet. English was used universally in the elementary-school system set up by the colonial government, which brought in American teachers. Education was the last government department to be indigenized, with US superintendents still functioning under the Commonwealth government before the outbreak of World War II. In the Philippines there are some 85 mutually unintelligible though genetically related languages of the Malayo-Polynesian family, such as Tagalog, Cebuano, Ilocano, Hiligaynon, Waray, and Bicol. These languages of the home serve as substrates whose features have variously influenced the development of Philippine English.

Pronunciation. (1) Philippine English is rhotic, but the local /r/ is an alveolar flap, not an AmE retroflex. (2) It is syllable-timed, following the rhythm of the local languages; full value is therefore given to unstressed syllables and schwa is usually realized as a full vowel. (3) Certain polysyllables have distinctive stress patterns, as with *eligible, establish, ceremony*. (4) Intonation is widely characterized as 'singsong'. (5) Educated Filipinos aim at an AmE accent, but have varying success with the vowel contrasts in *sheep/ship, full/fool*, and *boat/bought*. (6) Few Filipinos have the /æ/ in AmE *mask*; instead, they use /ɑ/ as in AmE *father*. (7) The distinction between /s, z/ and /ʃ, ʒ/ is not made: *azure* is 'ayshure', *pleasure* 'pleshure', *seize* 'sees', *cars* 'karss'. (8) Interdental /θ ð/ are often rendered as /t, d/, so that *three of these* is spoken as 'tree of dese'.

Grammar. The following features occur at all social levels: (1) Loss of the singular inflection of verbs: *The family home rest on the bluff of a hill*; *One of the boys give a report to the teacher every morning*. (2) Use of present perfect for simple past (*I have seen her yesterday* I saw her yesterday) and past perfect for present perfect (*He had already gone home* He has already gone home). (3) Use of the continuous tenses for habitual aspect: *He is going to school regularly* He goes to school regularly. (4) Use of the present forms of auxiliary verbs in subordinate noun clauses rather than past forms, and vice versa: *He said he has already seen you* He said he had already seen you; *She hoped that she can visit you tomorrow* She hoped that she could visit you tomorrow; *He says that he could visit you tomorrow* He says that he can visit you tomorrow. (5) An apparent reversal of the norms for the use of the definite article: *He is studying at the Manuel Quezon University*; *I am going to visit United States*. (6) Verbs that are generally transitive used intransitively: *Did you enjoy?*; *I cannot afford*; *I don't like*.

Vocabulary and idioms. (1) Loans from Spanish: *asalto* a surprise party, *bienvenida* a welcome party, *despedida* a farewell party, *Don/Doña* title for a prominent man/woman, *estafa* a fraud, scandal, *merienda* mid-afternoon tea, *plantilla* faculty assignments and deployment in an academic department, *querida* a mistress, *viand* (from *vianda* provisions for a journey) a dish served to accompany rice in a Filipino meal. (2) Loans from Tagalog: *boondock* (from *bundok*) mountain (compare the AmE extension: *the boondocks*), *carabao* (from *kalabaw*) a water buffalo, *kundiman* a love song, *sampaloc* (from *sampalok*) the fruit of the tamarind, *tao* man (as in *the common tao*). (3) Loan translations from local usages: *open the light/radio* turn on the light/radio (also found in IndE), *since before yet* for a long time, *joke only* I'm teasing you, *you*

don't only know you just don't realize, *he is playing and playing* he keeps on playing, *making foolishness* (of children) misbehaving, *I am ashamed to you* I am embarrassed because I have been asking you so many favours. (4) Local neologisms: *aggrupation* (from Spanish *agrupación*) a group, *captain-ball* team captain in basketball, *carnap* to steal (kidnap) a car, *cope up* to keep up and cope with (something), *hold-upper* someone who engages in armed hold-ups, *jeepney* (blending *jeep* and *jitney*, AmE a small bus) a jeep converted into a passenger vehicle.

Written models. Because of the influence of reading and writing and the academic context in which English is learned, local speech tends to be based on written models. Filipinos generally speak the way they write, in a formal style based on Victorian prose models. Because of this, spelling pronunciations are common, such as 'lee-o-pard' for *leopard*, 'subtill' for *subtle*, and 'wor-sester-shire sauce' for *Worcestershire sauce*. Style is not differentiated and the formal style in general use has been called the *classroom compositional style*. When style differentiation is attempted there may be effects that are comical from the point of view of a native speaker of English: 'The commissioners are all horse owners, who at the same time will appoint the racing stewards who will adjudicate disputes involving horses. Neat no?' (from a newspaper column); 'Now the tandem [pair] is making its dreams come true, so it's not Goin' Bananas forever for Johnny' (from a gossip column).

Code-switching. A register has developed for rapport and intimacy that depends on code-switching between Filipino and English. It is largely confined to Metro Manila and other urban centres and used extensively in motion pictures and on television and radio as well as in certain types of informal writing in daily newspapers and weekly magazines. Examples:

(1) '*Peks man*,' she swears. '*Wala pang nangyayari sa amin ni Marlon*. We want to surprise each other on our honeymoon.' ['Cross my heart,' she swears. 'Nothing yet has happened between Marlon and me . . .'] (from a movie gossip column).

(2) Donna reveals that since she turned producer in 1986, her dream was to produce a movie for children: '*Kaya, nang mabasa ko ang Tuklaw sa Aliwan Komiks, sabi ko*, this is it. And I had the festival in mind when finally I decided to produce it. *Pambata talaga kasi ang Pasko*,' Donna says. ['That is why when I read the story "Snake-Bite" in the Aliwan Comic Book, I told myself, this is it. . . . Because Christmas is really for children] (from a movie gossip column).

Social issues. Philippine English is currently competing in certain domains with the rapidly spreading and developing Filipino, which is in a process of register-building sometimes called *intellectualization.* Filipino is not fully developed for academic discourse, especially in the sciences, and there is an ongoing debate on the use of Filipino instead of English for school work and official purposes. There is also conflict between the learning of Filipino for symbolic purposes and the learning of English for utilitarian, largely economic, purposes. The two official languages are propagated through a bilingual education scheme begun in 1974: mathematics and science continue to be taught in English although it is envisaged that when possible the teaching of these subjects at certain grade levels shall be in Filipino. The print media are dominated by English, but television, radio, and local movies are dominated by Filipino.

English in the Philippines shares patterns of development and constriction with English in Malaysia. From a situation similar to that of Singapore, where a premium is placed on learning English and using it extensively, the Philippines has now moved on to a stage at which English is used only in such domains as academic discourse and international relations. Philippine English has developed a vigorous literature. It is in the process of standardization, with a variety no longer marked by regional accents associated with regional languages, but a converging variety that originates in Manila. This form is propagated largely through the school system, the mass media, and tourism. Because of code-switching, it seems unlikely that a colloquial variety of English alone will develop. The future is open, without clear trends. On the one hand, code-switching may end up in code-mixing, resulting in a local creole. On the other hand, the need for international relations, the dominance of the print media, and the continued use of English in education may exercise a standardizing role, making it possible for the Philippine variety to be mutually intelligible with other varieties of English. It is also possible that the present system of bilingual education will be converted into a purely monolingual Filipino scheme in which English is taught as a foreign language and becomes available only to an élite.

See CODE-SWITCHING AND CODE-MIXING, FILIPINISM, FILIPINO LITERATURE IN ENGLISH, PHILIPPINES, RELC, SOUTH-EAST ASIAN ENGLISH, TAGLISH. [ASIA, VARIETY]. A.G.

Gonzalez, Andrew. 1982. 'English in the Philippine Mass Media', in John B. Pride (ed.), *New Englishes.* Rowley, Mass.: New Bury House.
—— 1985. *Studies on Philippine English.* Occasional Paper 39, SEAMEO Regional Language Centre, Singapore.
Kapili, Lily V. 1988. 'Requiem for English?', in *English Today* 16, Oct. Cambridge: University Press.
Llamzon, Teodoro A. 1969. *Standard Filipino English.* Quezon City: Ateneo de Manila Press.
Tinio, Rolando S. 1990. *A Matter of Language: Where English Fails.* Quezon City: University of the Philippines Press.

PHILIPPINES, The. Official titles: Filipino *Republika ng Pilipinas*, English *Republic of the Philippines*, Spanish *República de Filipinas.* A state of South-East Asia, an archipelago of more than 7,000 islands, including Luzon, Mindanao, Samar, Palawan, Mindoro, Panay, Cebu, Negros, and Leyte. Capital: Manila, on Luzon. Currency: the peso (100 centavos). Economy: mixed. Population: 59.5m (1988), 78.4m (projection for 2000). Ethnicity: mainly Malay, with many mixed descendants of Malays, Spanish, Chinese, and Americans, and a small Chinese community. Religion: 83% Roman Catholic, 9% Protestant, 6% Muslim. Languages: Filipino, English (both official), and local languages, including Cebuano, Tagalog, Ilocano, and Hiligaynon, with some Chinese and Spanish. Education: primary 95%, secondary 65%, tertiary 38%, literacy 88%. Ferdinand Magellan claimed the islands for Spain in 1521. The name *Philippines* derives from that given to the central island of Leyte in honour of Philip II of Spain. Spanish control lasted until 1898 when the islands were ceded to the US at the Treaty of Paris, after the Spanish–American War. The islands became a self-governing Commonwealth in 1935, were occupied by the Japanese during the Second World War, and gained their independence from the US in 1946. Since then, there have been periods of instability, including conflict between Muslims and Christians. See ENGLISH, FILIPINO, FILIPINO LITERATURE IN ENGLISH, PHILIPPINE, PHILIPPINE ENGLISH, TAGALOG, TELECOMMUNICATIONS, TESL. [ASIA, HISTORY, LANGUAGE, NAME]. T.MCA.

PHILOLOGICAL SOCIETY. A British society founded in 1842 for the study of comparative and historical philology. The main initiative came from Edwin Guest (1800–80), barrister and antiquary, who became its first secretary. Its inception was part of the growing but still largely amateur 19c interest in language study. Thomas Arnold, the headmaster of Rugby School, and his pupil and friend A. P. Stanley, later Dean of Westminster, were among its first members, joined a little later by F. J. Furnivall and J. A. H. Murray. A paper 'On some Deficiencies in our English Dictionaries', read to the Society by R. C. Trench in 1857, led in due course to the compilation of *The Oxford English Dictionary.* Papers read to the Society were published at first as *Proceedings* and later as *Transactions of the Philological Society.* This series continues, in accordance with the affirmation that the Society, 'while encouraging all aspects of language, has a particular interest in historical and comparative linguistics, and maintains its traditional interest in the structure, development, and varieties of modern English'. See COLERIDGE (H.), FURNI-VALL, LANGUAGE TEACHING, MURRAY, OXFORD ENGLISH DICTIONARY, PERIOD DICTIONARIES OF ENGLISH, PHILOLOGY, REGIONAL DICTIONARIES OF ENGLISH, SKEAT, TRENCH. [EUROPE, LANGUAGE, MEDIA].   R.C.

PHILOLOGY [14c: from French *philologie*, Latin *philologia*, Greek *philología* love of language]. The traditional study of language, especially of written languages in their cultural settings. The term first appears in English as in Chaucer's *Merchant's Tale*: 'Hold thou thy pees, thou poete Marcian, / That wrytest us that ilke wedding murie / Of hir, Philologye, and him, Mercurie.' Here, the pursuit of learning is presented by Marcianus Capella as the bride of the god of commerce. In 1623, Cockeram defined *phylologie* as 'loue of much babling', but its present-day uses in the English-speaking world date from another 17c meaning (Fuller's 'polite learning') and Johnson's narrower 18c meaning, 'grammatical learning'. In mainland Europe, the term has continued to be generously interpreted as the study of language, literature, and even national culture.

Method. Because philology deals with the relationship of languages, it is usually comparative; because these relationships evolve over time, it is typically historical. Languages appear to change in the direction of greater diversity: one language tends to be superseded by several; a written 'dead' language preserves evidence of the earlier forms from which 'living' languages developed. Thus, Latin *planctus* gave way to French *plainte* and Italian *pianto*; Latin *planus* to French *plain* and Italian *piano*. The descendants of the Latin words have diverged to the point that, though Italian is related to French, they are now foreign to each other, as is their common 'parent' to both. The changes, moreover, are regular: Italian reduces the Latin *-us* ending to *-o*, French reduces it to *-e* or deletes it entirely; Latin *a* becomes French *ai* and remains unchanged in Italian; and Latin *pl* becomes Italian *pi* and remains unchanged in French.

Not so regular is the change of meaning: Italian *piano* has at least one meaning ('soft' as opposed to 'loud') not in the related Latin or French. In the combination *piano e forte* (soft and loud), *piano* in due course became the name for a keyboard instrument, the *pianoforte*, more capable of dynamic variation than instruments like the harpsichord that came before it. By abbreviation, this new instrument is now usually called a *piano* in English and various other languages. The special meaning of the Italian phrase results from its cultural context and the distinctive feature of the instrument it names. The English word still names the same instrument, but the clipping discards 'and loud' from the original Italian phrase and hence becomes an arbitrary label and no longer a description. Over the centuries, philologists have learned to trace and tease out such facts and processes as these, and over the last century philology has concerned itself with all such changes and with the linguistic relationships they result in. In recent years, comparative philology and historical or comparative linguistics often merge in their pursuits.

Written documents provide the information needed for this study, but, by mapping such relationships, philologists can also reconstruct further relationships among stages of earlier languages that left no written records. Thus, philologists give the name *Germanic* to the language that is the source of English as Latin is the source of French; but Germanic, unlike Latin, vanished without leaving written testimony. Present-day understanding of the family of Indo-European languages therefore results from studies that systematically combine textual analysis and hypothetical reconstruction.

History. The ancient Greeks wrote about their own language, having little interest in comparing Greek with what they considered lesser (barbarian) languages. Roman writers, impressed by such thinking, undertook some comparisons of their Latin with Greek, for though not mutually intelligible, the two have many similarities of vocabulary (Latin and Doric Greek both have *māter* for mother) and of grammar (both have three grammatical genders and similar declensional systems). From such hints, some Roman writers concluded that Latin had descended from Greek, a view abandoned only with the development of comparative philology around 1800, which demonstrated that Greek and Latin descended collaterally from a putative common ancestor, Indo-European (IE).

In the Middle Ages, Latin ceased to be a spoken language, and the vernaculars descended from it, such as French and Italian, grew in prestige. Writers like Dante gave some consideration to the relationship among vernaculars and their kinship with Latin, that is, to comparative and historical concerns. Such consideration, aided from the Renaissance onwards by the publication of many early manuscript texts as printed books, yielded further knowledge of individual language families such as the Celtic and Germanic. But speculation concentrated on vocabulary and took no account of systematic relationships, and hence failed to discern larger 'genetic' connections. On the rare occasions where a common parent language was postulated, the language was (for cultural and even doctrinal reasons) usually Hebrew. As late as 1807, the writer Alexander Pirie could maintain that 'The originality of the Hebrew language being incontrovertible, nothing can be more natural than that all other languages should in some respects be derivatives.' Such arguments distracted from the successful study of IE, with which Hebrew has no genetic connection.

European imperialism put 18c scholars in touch with such Asian languages as Sanskrit, and in 1786 Sir William Jones announced his belief that the grammar of Sanskrit revealed its close affinity with Greek and Latin, suggesting the derivation of all three from 'some common source . . . which no longer exists'. Jones's belief, which served to unite previously fragmented studies of individual language families, underwent elaboration in the 19c, especially by F. von Schlegel, Franz Bopp, Rasmus Rask, and Jacob Grimm early in the century and later by A. F. Pott, K. Verner, Ferdinand de Saussure, K. Brugmann, and B. Delbrück.

These scholars concentrated on refining knowledge of the relationship of later languages (such as French and Italian) with their earlier written forms (such as Latin), the relationship of these earlier written forms (such as Latin and Sanskrit) with each other, and the relationship of them all with the unrecorded 'common source', whether the lost Germanic original of the Scandinavian, Gothic, German, and English languages, or the lost Indo-European original of Germanic, Latin, Greek, and Sanskrit. These relationships are usually set out in a form devised by A. Schleicher, resembling a genetic 'family tree' owing much to biological classification and Darwinism. The materials for establishing such a schematic form are the usual objects of language study: vocabulary, grammar (especially morphology), and sounds with their orthographic equivalents, as in the French and Italian words derived from Latin (above). However, vocabulary is at once the most tempting and the most treacherous evidence for the study, because, unlike sounds or grammatical forms, words readily migrate from one language to another.

Current status. Philology, as an ancient, evolving discipline, has to a great extent been eclipsed in the 20c by *linguistics*, which may be regarded as either an organic development out of philology or a rival to it. Many linguists, following Ferdinand de Saussure (the 'father of linguistics' who was himself trained in traditional philology), consider that philology has had little to say about languages as living systems of communication. In consequence, they generally prefer the synchronic study of spoken language to the diachronic comparison of words in texts, and have tended to regard philology as pre-scientific. Others have sought to bring elements of old and new together in panchronic studies that give equal importance to past and present. However regarded, philology (in association with traditional grammar and etymology) has built a formidable edifice which few scholars ignore when writing about or teaching the history of languages such as English.

See ETYMOLOGY, HISTORICAL LINGUISTICS, INDO-EUROPEAN LANGUAGES, JONES (W.), LINGUISTICS, MARCH, MARSH, MORRIS, MURISON, MURRAY, PHILOLOGICAL SOCIETY, POUND, SEMANTIC CHANGE, SEMANTICS, SKEAT, SWEET, TRENCH, [GRAMMAR, HISTORY, LANGUAGE].W.F.B.

Bynon, Theodora. 1977. *Historical Linguistics*. Cambridge: University Press.
Lockwood, W. B. 1969. *Indo-European Philology, Historical and Comparative*. London: Hutchinson.

PHONAESTHESIA BrE, **phonesthesia** AmE [1930s: through Latin from Greek *phōnē* voice or sound, *aisthēsis* feeling or perception]. Also *phonetic symbolism, sound symbolism*. Vocal sound that suggests meaning, as in onomatopoeic or echoic words like *cock-a-doodle-doo, cuckoo*. The term is often used to refer to the occurrence of the same consonant cluster in a series of words with similar meanings: *sl-* in *sleaze, slide, slime, slip, slope, sludge, slump, slurp, slurry*, suggesting downward movement and a rushing, sucking sound; *-sh* in *bash, dash, crash, flash, gush, hush, rush, splash, whoosh*, suggesting swift or strong movement. These clusters are sometimes referred to as *phon(a)esthemes*, two of which may occur in one word: *sl* and *sh* in *slash, slosh, slush*. Such phonetic and aesthetic elements, often used to effect in verse and rhetoric, are semantically imprecise, and do not necessarily apply to all the words of a certain type: *sleep* and *sleeve, dish* and *sash* do not normally have the same nuances as *slime* and *splash*. Compare ALLITERATION, ASSONANCE, ECHOISM, ONOMATOPOEIA, ROOT-CREATION. [SPEECH, WORD]. T.MCA.

PHONE [1860s: from Greek *phōnē* voice]. Also **speech sound**. In phonetics, an elementary spoken sound, the smallest segment of speech recognized by a listener as a complete vowel or consonant. Because all speakers sound slightly different, and any one speaker produces vowels and consonants differently on different occasions, the number of phones in a language is indefinitely large. They are grouped into a small number of *phonemes* or units of distinctive sound. See PHONEME, PHONOLOGY, SPEECH SOUND, TELEPHONE. [SPEECH].   G.K., T.MCA.

PHONEME [1890s: from French *phonème*, Greek *phŏnēma* a sound]. In phonetics and linguistics, the basic theoretical unit of distinctive sound in the description of speech, out of which syllables are formed, such as the three units /b, ı, t/ (consonant, vowel, consonant) in /bɪt/ (*bit*). The *OED* (1989) defines the phoneme as 'A phonological unit of language that cannot be analysed into smaller linear units and that in any particular language is realized in non-contrastive variants': see PHONE. The *Longman Dictionary of Applied Linguistics* (1985) defines the phoneme as 'the smallest unit of sound in a language which can distinguish two words', giving the examples *pan* and *ban*, that differ only in the contrast of the phonemic consonants /p/ and /b/, and *ban* and *bin*, that differ only in the phonemic vowels /æ/ and /ı/. The number of phonemes varies from language to language, and from variety to variety within a language. Any such number, as for example the 24 consonants and 20 vowels of RP, are known as a *phoneme inventory*. A *phone* is a realization in sound of a phoneme, and an *allophone* is one such realization among others: for example, English /n/ is normally alveolar, but is dental before the dental fricative /θ/ in *tenth* [tɛnθ]. There are no *minimal pairs* contrasting dental and alveolar [n], and so the difference is not phonemic: because of this, the two forms are said to be allophones of the same phoneme /n/. When allophones occur in different environments, only one ever occurring in one environment, they are said to be in *complementary distribution*. The term *allophone* is also used to include the *free variant*, a sound that can be substituted for another without bringing about a change of meaning. Examples include the various *r*-sounds of English and the use of the glottal stop as a variant of [t] in a word like *water*. See BLOOMFIELD, -EME, FEATURE (DISTINCTIVE FEATURE), JONES (D.), MINIMAL PAIR, PHONE, PHONETIC TRANSCRIPTION, PHONOLOGY. [LANGUAGE, SPEECH].   T.MCA., G.K.

PHONEMICS. See PHONEME, PHONOLOGY.

PHONEMIC TRANSCRIPTION. See PHONETIC TRANSCRIPTION.

PHONETIC [1820s: from Neo-Latin *phoneticus* (1797), Greek *phōnētikós* vocal, to be spoken]. (1) Relating to speech sounds and their production: *phonetic elements, phonetic change.* (2) Corresponding to or representing pronunciation in written or printed form: *phonetic as opposed to ideographic writing, a phonetic alphabet, a phonetic transcription, phonetic spelling.* (3)

Relating to phonetics: *phonetic training.* See PHONETICS, PHONIC. [LANGUAGE, SPEECH].
                                       T.MCA.

PHONETIC NOTATION. See PHONETIC TRANSCRIPTION.

PHONETICS [1830s]. The science or study of the sounds of speech. There three kinds: (1) *Articulatory phonetics*, the oldest branch of the subject, which investigates the ways in which sounds are made. Here, the phonetician is trained to recognize, produce, and analyse speech sounds. During the 20c, phonetics has developed as a laboratory subject, in which instruments are used to study the production of speech in the vocal tract: for example, by monitoring the positions and movement of organs, or breath flow and air pressure. Electropalatography uses an artificial palate to record, display, and store data on articulatory movements inside the mouth. (2) *Acoustic phonetics* is concerned with the study of the speech as heard: that is, its *waveform*. For the study of vowels and consonants, the waveform is presented as a spectrogram, on which sounds appear as recognizable visual patterns. For the study of intonation, the pitch, or more precisely the *fundamental frequency*, usually called *Fo* ('ef nought'), is extracted and displayed. A *speech workstation* is a machine, usually based on a computer, that analyses and displays speech, and allows the user to replay, edit, or annotate the waveform. (3) *Experimental phonetics* usually involves the manipulation of the waveform and makes psycho-acoustic tests to identify which aspects of sounds are essential for understanding, and for the recognition of linguistic categories. Major applications of phonetics have been made in such areas as language teaching, speech therapy, and automatic speech synthesis and recognition.

See ABERCROMBIE, ABLAUT, ACCENT, ADVANCED, AFFRICATE, AIR-STREAM MECHANISM, AITKEN'S LAW, AITKEN'S VOWEL, ALVEOLAR, APICAL, APPROXIMANT, ARTICULATION, ARTICULATORY SETTING, ASPIRATE, ASSIMILATION, BILABIAL, BLADE, BREATH, BREATH GROUP, BROAD, CLEAR L, CLICK, COALESCENCE, CONSONANT, CONSONANT CLUSTER, CONTINUANT, CONTRASTIVE STRESS, DARK L, DENTAL, DEVOICING, DIPHTHONG, DORSAL, DOUBLE ARTICULATION, DURATION, ELISION, INTERNATIONAL PHONETIC ALPHABET, INTERNATIONAL PHONETIC ASSOCIATION, JONES (D.), LABIAL, LABIO-DENTAL, LAMINAL, LANGUAGE TEACHING, LARYNX, LATERAL, LAX, LENIS, LINKING R, LIQUID, L-SOUNDS, MINIMAL PAIR, MONOPHTHONG, MOUTH, NARROW, NASAL, PALATE,

PHARYNX, PHONE, PHONEME, PHONEMICS, PHON-
EMIC TRANSCRIPTION, PHONETIC, PHONETIC NOT-
ATION, PHONETIC TRANSCRIPTION, PHONOLOGY,
PITCH, PLOSIVE, POSTVOCALIC, PRONUNCIATION,
PULMONIC, QUANTITY, RECEIVED PRONUNCIATION,
RETROFLEX, RHOTIC AND NON-RHOTIC, RHYTHM,
R-SOUNDS, S(C)HWA, SEMI-CONSONANT, SEMI-
VOWEL, SIBILANT, SOFT PALATE, SOUND, SPEECH,
STOP, STRESS, SUPRASEGMENTAL, SWEET,
SYLLABLE, TENSE, TONE, TONGUE, TRACHEA,
TRIPHTHONG, TUNE, UVULA, UVULAR R, VELAR,
VELARIC, VELUM, VOCAL, VOCAL CORDS, VOCAL
TRACT, VOICE, VOICE QUALITY, VOWEL, VOWEL
GRADATION, VOWEL HARMONY, VOWEL LENGTH,
VOWEL QUALITY, VOWEL QUANTITY, WEAK VOWEL,
WH-SOUND, and the pronunciation sections of
entries on major varieties, such as AUSTRALIAN
ENGLISH. [LANGUAGE, SPEECH].   G.K.

Abercrombie, D. 1967. *Elements of General Phonetics.*
  Edinburgh: University Press.
Catford, J. C. 1988. *A Practical Introduction to Phon-
  etics.* Oxford: University Press.
Clark, J., & Yallop, C. 1990. *An Introduction to Phon-
  etics and Phonology.* Oxford: Blackwell.
Hardcastle, W. J. 1976. *Physiology of Speech Produc-
  tion.* London: Academic Press.
Knowles, G. 1987. *Patterns of Spoken English.* Lon-
  don: Longman.
Ladefoged, P. 1962. *Elements of Acoustic Phonetics.*
  Edinburgh & London: Oliver & Boyd.
Roach, P. J. 1983. *English Phonetics and Phonology: A
  Practical Course.* Cambridge: University Press.
Wells, J. C., & Colson, J. 1971. *Practical Phonetics.*
  London: Pitman.

PHONETIC SYMBOLISM. See PHON(A)ES-
THESIA.

PHONETIC TRANSCRIPTION. A written or
printed representation of speech using a phonetic alphabet. Whereas, in standard orthography, the same letters can be used to represent
different sounds (the *y* in *sky* and *syrup*), and
different combinations of letters can be used to
represent the same sound (the *ee* of *meet* and the
ea of *meat*), a phonetic symbol always represents
the same sound, and a sound is always represented by the same symbol. Speech can be transcribed phonetically at different levels of detail
and accuracy. In general terms, there are two
kinds of transcription: (1) *Phonetic transcription*
proper, which draws on the total resources of a
phonetic alphabet to mark minute distinctions
in sound and places symbols in square brackets,
[t]. Such transcriptions are used especially to represent the usage of individual speakers, and are
informally known as *narrow transcriptions.* (2)
Phonemic transcription, which provides a symbol
for each phoneme in a text and places the symbols between obliques, as in /t/. Such transcriptions are used to represent an idealized

description of the system of a speech community.
It is the kind used in pronouncing dictionaries,
and is referred to informally as *broad
transcription.*

Contemporary phoneticians generally take
their symbols from the International Phonetic
Alphabet, but other symbols are also in use,
especially in North America. All such symbols
are mnemonic labels that ignore phonetic detail,
as when the initial consonants of *tea, two*, and
train are phonemically written /t/, even though
they are all phonetically slightly different. In
many cases, diacritics are added to phonemic
symbols to give further detail: for example, a
superscript *h* added to /t/ to indicate aspiration,
/tʰ/. A third kind of transcription is *prosodic
transcription*, for which there is no generally
agreed system of symbols. Its purpose is the representation of rhythm, stress, and intonation,
and it has elements in common with musical
notation. Generally, a text representing speech
is divided into its actual or probable tone groups,
the boundaries between groups being marked
with a bar (/), usually doubled to mark the end
of a major tone group (//), the rough equivalent
to a sentence. Next, the accented syllables are
identified, then the pitch contours associated
with these syllables are marked in.
See INTERNATIONAL PHONETIC ALPHABET, NOTA-
TION, OBLIQUE, PHONEME, PHONETICS, PROSODY,
TRANSCRIPTION. [SPEECH, WRITING].
                                    G.K., T.MCA.

PHONIATRY. See LANGUAGE PATHOLOGY.

PHONIC [1810s: comparable to French
phonique, ultimately from Greek *phōnḗ* voice].
(1) Relating to vocal sound: *phonic substance,
phonic vibrations.* (2) In phonetics, a term used
in contrast with *phonetic* to mean 'relating to
speech sounds': *the phonic medium, the phonic
method of teaching reading, a phonic reader* (a
book). (3) In physiology, relating to a nerve
centre that excites the organs of speech and to
vibration of the vocal folds or cords. Compare
PHONETIC. [LANGUAGE, SPEECH].   T.MCA.

PHONIC MEDIUM. See MEDIUM.

PHONICS [17c]. (1) An obsolete term for the
science of *phonetics.* (2) A method of teaching
reading and spelling based on the phonetic interpretation, element by element, of spelling, often
contrasted with the *look-and-say* method. See
PHONIC, READING, SPELLING. [EDUCATION, LAN-
GUAGE, SPEECH].   T.MCA.

PHONOGRAM. See WRITING.

PHONOGRAPHY [18c: from Greek *phōnē* voice, and *-graphy* writing]. (1) The art or practice of writing so as to represent sound as precisely as possible; phonetic spelling. The adjective *phonographic* is used to discuss the relationships between sound and writing. (2) The system of phonetic shorthand invented by Isaac Pitman in 1837 and so named by him in 1840. (3) A 19c term for recording sound by means of a phonograph recording machine. (4) A rare synonym for *phonology*. See SPELLING. [SPEECH, WRITING].   T.MCA.

PHONOLOGY [18c: from the Greek combining forms *phono-* sound, voice, and *-logy* study]. The study of sound patterns in languages, sometimes regarded as part of phonetics, sometimes as a separate study included in linguistics. Phonologists study both *phonemes* (vowels and consonants) and *prosody* (stress, rhythm, and intonation) as subsystems of spoken language. Phonological patterns relate the sounds of speech to the grammar of the language; a common 20c model has three levels or components: phonology, syntax, and semantics. Patterns that can be measured on laboratory instruments are generally regarded as part of phonetics, whereas phonological patterns tend to be more abstract and idealized. Until the 1960s, phonology was largely concerned with *phonemics*, the study of phonemes and phonemic systems, and often considered synonymous with it, especially in the US. Since then, however, attention has concentrated on the formulation of rules to account for sound patterns, its scope widening to include prosodic phenomena and patterns of connected texts. See COMPOUND WORD, LEVEL OF LANGUAGE, LINGUISTIC TYPOLOGY, MODEL, PHONEME, PHONETICS, PRONUNCIATION, PROSODY, SENTENCE, WORD. [LANGUAGE, SPEECH].   G.K.

PHONOTYPE [1830s]. (1) A character or letter of a phonetic alphabet. (2) Phonetic print or type. (3) To print in phonotype. A periodical of the 1840s associated with the work of Isaac Pitman was called *The Phonotypic Journal*, and systems of phonetic shorthand were for a time in the 19c widely referred to as *phonotypy*. Compare PHONOGRAPHY. See PITMAN (I.), SHORTHAND, TYPE. [SPEECH, WRITING].   T.MCA.

PHOTOCOPYING [1920s: from the Greek combining form *photo-* light, and *copy*]. Making a copy or copies of a sheet or set of sheets of writing or print, formerly by photographic or chemical means, currently by an electrostatic machine. Most photocopiers have the same basic technology. A sheet for copying is placed on a transparent surface. When the machine is activated and flashes, a reflected image of the sheet is received on a photo-sensitive drum which translates the image into positive and negative electrical fields. The drum picks up a *toner* (a bondable pigmented powder) which adheres to the electrical image. The toner image is transferred to paper fed for this purpose into the machine, is bonded to the paper by heat, and a virtual facsimile of the original emerges. Variations include multiple copying and reduction in image size. The electrostatic process is known as *xerography* [1940s: from Greek *xērós* dry, *graphía* writing] because unlike earlier methods no liquid is involved. The US company Xerox gained a major position in the manufacture and distribution of such machines, with the result that the trade name *Xerox* is widely applied to the copier, the verb *to xerox* to the copying process, and noun *a xerox* to the product. Until the advent of the laser, the photocopier was the most significant 20c advance in the reproduction of text and images. The ubiquitous copier has dramatically changed the way in which the written language is reproduced and stored and along with other reproductive media has challenged notions of copyright and the ownership of text that were formed in the heyday of the printing press. Compare FAX. See COPY, MIMEOGRAPH. [MEDIA, TECHNOLOGY].   W.W.B.

PHOTO-OFFSET PRINTING [1920s]. A form of lithography in which an image is *offset* or transferred from a laser- or photographically prepared lithographic plate to an intermediate surface (usually a roller in a printing press), then transferred from the roller to the surface to be printed on. Except for small runs of material reproduced by photocopying and large runs sometimes printed in a form of letterpress, photo-offset lithography is the commonest kind of printing in current use. See LITHOGRAPHY, PRINTING. [TECHNOLOGY].   W.W.B.

PHRASAL VERB [Early 20c: first used in print by Logan Pearsall Smith, in *Words and Idioms* (1925), in which he states that the *OED* Editor Henry Bradley suggested the term to him]. Also **verb phrase, compound verb, verb–adverb combination, verb–particle construction (VPC)**, AmE **two-part word/verb** and **three-part word/verb** (depending on number of particles: see below). A type of verb in English that operates more like a phrase than a word, such as *go up* (as in *The balloon went up*), *put off* (as in *Don't put it off any longer*), and *take down* (as in *That'll take him down a peg or two*). Such composites derive primarily from verbs of movement and action (*go, put, take*) and adverbial particles of direction and location (*up, off, down*). The base verbs are mainly monosyllabic and may underlie a range of phrasal verbs: for example, *get* underlying *get up, get down, get in, get out, get on, get off, get away, get back*. The combinations are used both literally and figuratively, and are often idioms or elements in idioms: *to get away with murder, to get on like a house on fire, to get back at someone, to get up to mischief.*

History. Although the phrasal verb has been present in English for many centuries, it has only recently been described in detail. Citations in the *OED* date from Middle English: for example, *turne aboute* 1300; *gon doun* 1388. They are common in Shakespeare: 'So long, that ninteene Zodiacks haue gone round' (*Measure for Measure*, 1603). Such verbs have often been used to translate Latin verbs (*to putte downe . . . calare, deponere: Catholicon Anglicum*, 1483) and to define verbs of Latin origin in English (*abrogate . . . take away*: Cawdrey, *Table Alphabeticall*, 1604). The 18c lexicographer Samuel Johnson was among the first to consider such formations seriously:

There is another kind of composition more frequent in our language than perhaps in any other, from which arises to foreigners the greatest difficulty. We modify the signification of many words by a particle subjoined; as to *come off*, to escape by a fetch; to *fall on*, to attack; to *fall off*, to apostatize; to *break off*, to stop abruptly . . . These I have noted with great care (Preface, *Dictionary of the English Language*, 1755).

Grammar. Grammarians have adopted two main positions with regard to the nature and use of phrasal verbs: (1) That the literal use of a form like *go up* is not a phrasal verb as such, but a verb operating with a particle: *The balloon went up into the air.* The term *phrasal verb* should properly be reserved for figurative and idiomatic uses: *The balloon went up* (= The crisis finally happened). Here, it is the holistic and semantic aspect of *go up* which is considered to identify the type, not syntax or morphology. (2) That the term covers both the literal and figurative/idiomatic uses and therefore includes syntax, morphology, and semantics: that is, both senses of *go up*, as above. This is the position adopted in the following review, which begins with a consideration of the grammatical aspects of phrasal verbs under three headings: transitivity and word order; particles functioning as adverbs and/or prepositions; and the position of adverbs.

Transitivity and word order. Phrasal verbs may be intransitive ('When they *went away*, she *got up* and *went out*') or transitive ('She *put* the book *down*, then *picked* it *up* again'). If the verb is transitive, the object can go before or after the particle without affecting meaning: *She put the book down, She put down the book.* If, however, the object is a pronoun, it comes between verb

and particle: *She put it down*, not **She put down it.* However, young children and occasionally adults for emphasis have been known to place the pronoun last: *Put down IT!*

Adverbial and prepositional particles. A sentence containing a verb followed by a prepositional phrase can usually (but not always) be shortened so as to turn preposition into adverb: *He carried the box up the stairs* becoming *He carried the box up* (stairs understood). If a further prepositional phrase is added, two particles (the first adverbial, the second prepositional) may occur in sequence: *He carried the box up to his room.* The syntactic relationships in such sentences can be shown by bracketing: (*He carried the chair up*) (*to his room*). Usage may appear inconsistent with regard to compound forms: *into*; *out of*; BrE *on to*, AmE *onto*; *off of*, non-standard in BrE, often standard in AmE. However, in terms of phrasal verbs, such usage is straightforward: the sentences *She took the books into the room, She took the books out of the room, She lifted the books on to/onto the table*, and *She lifted the books off (of) the table* all reduce to *She took the books in/out* and *She lifted the books on/off.* The particle *out* is followed in England by *of* in such sentences as *They looked out of the window*, but in AmE, CanE, ScoE the form is generally *They looked out the window.*

The position of adverbs. Adverbs often appear alongside the particles of phrasal verbs. With intransitive usages, the adverb can take any of the positions in: *He happily ran away, He ran happily away, He ran away happily*, the last probably commonest. With transitive usages, the adverb goes either before the verb or after the object or particle, whichever is last: *She eagerly picked the letter up, She picked up the letter eagerly, She picked the letter up eagerly, She picked it up eagerly*, no usage predominating, but in most contexts there are no such forms as **She picked the letter/it eagerly up.* (Note such relatively rare possibilities as *He pushed the letters clumsily through.*)

Adverbial particles. The particles commonly used are: *aback, about, ahead, along, apart, aside, around, away, back, beyond, down, forth, in, off, on, out, over, past, round, through, up.* The commonest are *down, in, off, on, out, up.* BrE favours *about* (*running about*), AmE (*a*)*round* (*running around*). A verb–particle combination may have: any of the meanings of the verb plus any of the meanings of the particle, and any meanings that emerge jointly in particular contexts, including a distinct figurative and often holistic meaning. For example: (1) The phrasal verb *get up* may be intransitive (*They got up*) or transitive (*Get them up*), may mean 'move from lower to higher' (*He got the child up on to the wall*), 'move from far to near' (*One of the other runners got up to him and passed him*), 'gather, accumulate' (*The engine got up steam*), 'organize, make' (*He can get up the plot of a new film in no time at all*), and something like 'put on special clothes' (*They got themselves up as pirates*). (2) The particle *up* can mean upward direction (*The smoke rose up*), approaching direction (*He swam up to the boat*), completion in the sense that nothing is left (*They used up all the oil*), completion in the sense that something is done as fully as possible (*They tidied the room up*), and emphasis (*Hurry up!*). It may also have several nuances, as with *Drink up!*, both completive and emphatic.

The use of phrasal verbs. Such verbs are often informal, emotive, and slangy, and may contrast with Latinate verbs, as in *They used up/consumed all the fuel*; *They gathered together/assembled/congregated in the hall*; *The soldiers moved forward/advanced*. *Putting off* a meeting parallels *postponing* it; *driving back* enemy forces *repels* them; *putting out* a fire *extinguishes* it; *bringing back* the death penalty *restores* it. However, such pairing often depends on context and collocation. In some cases, one phrasal verb may match several Latinate verbs: *bring back* = *restore* (the death penalty), *return* (money to someone), *retrieve* (a shot bird or animal from where it has fallen). In other cases, one Latinate verb may match several phrasal verbs: *demolish* matching *knock down, tear down, blow up* as variants in destructive style. It is sometimes possible to match the elements of phrasal verbs and Latinate verbs: *climb up* with *a/scend*, *climb down* with *de/scend*. See BISOCIATION.

Literal and figurative usages. The verb *bring in* is used literally in *The milkman brought in the milk*, figuratively in *The prime minister brought in a new policy*. Only in the second sense can *bring in* be matched with *introduce* (itself originally metaphorical in Latin): no *The milkman introduced the milk*, unless a joke is intended. Jokes and cartoons are often based on a deliberate confusion of phrasal-verb meanings: as when someone says, '*Put* the kettle *on*' (taken to mean heat some water in a kettle for tea), then notes with appreciation, 'Mmm, it suits you' (crossing over to *putting on* clothes and leaving the listener to imagine someone wearing a kettle). An artist might build a cartoon round the literal/figurative contrast in *Where did you pick up that idea?*, with someone searching through garbage for inspiration, and the headline *OIL WILL RUN OUT SOON* might be supported by a picture of barrels with legs leaving a room.

Derived phrasal verbs. In addition to the traditional combination of verb of movement plus directional particle, phrasal verbs are commonly created from adjectives, nouns, and Latinate verbs: (1) *From adjectives*. Basically, with *-en* verbs: *brighten/brighten up, flatten down/out, freshen up, harden off, loosen off/up, slacken off/up, smarten up, soften up, tighten up, toughen up*. Where verbs in *-en* cannot be formed (that is, from adjectives ending in *n, ng, m, l, r, th*, or a spoken vowel), the particle is added directly: *calm down* to become/make calm, *cool off* become/make cool, *even out* to become/make even, *tidy up* to make tidy. (2) *From nouns*. By telescoping an expression containing a phrasal verb and a special noun: *hammer out* encapsulating *beat out with a hammer*; *channel off* telescoping *carry or run off by means of a channel*; *brick up* meaning *close up with bricks*. Many phrasal verbs emerge in this way: *bed down, board up, book out, button up, dish out, fog up, gang up, hose down, iron out, jack up, mist up, saddle up, sponge down, wall in*. (3) *From Latinate verbs*. Particles are added, usually as completives and intensives, to two- and three-syllable verbs of Latin origin: *contract out, divide off/up, level off, measure off/out, select out, separate off/out*. Such usages are sometimes described as barbarous and pleonastic, but such criticism does not affect their widespread use.

Nouns from phrasal verbs. Two kinds of noun are formed from such verbs: (1) *The major pattern*. In speech, the level stress of *bréak dówn* changes to the compound stress of *BRÉAKdown*. In writing and print, nouns like this are either solid (*breakdown*) or hyphenated (*round-up*). The solid form is common when a usage is well established and is favoured in AmE. Hyphenation is common for newer usages and is favoured in BrE, in which a solid form may seem confusing or odd, especially when vowels come together: *cave-in* as *cavein*, *make up* as *makeup*. Typical nouns are: *blackout, breakout, break-up, build-up, getaway, get-together, hold-up, mix-up, sit-in, take-off, white-out*. (2) *The minor pattern*. By a process of inversion: when a disease *breaks out*, there is an *outbreak* of that disease. Again, compound stress occurs: *OUTbreak*. In writing and print, the presentation is usually solid. Typical nouns are: *input, onrush, outflow, output, overflow, overspill, throughput, upkeep, upsurge, uptake*. The contrasting patterns sometimes prompt different forms with different meanings: a *breakout* usually of people, an *outbreak* usually of disease and trouble; a *layout* in design and decoration, an *outlay* of money and goods; a *lookout* posted to observe, an *outlook* usually relating to weather, attitude, and prospects. Most phrasal nouns relate to situations. The few which relate to things and people tend to be dialectal, idiomatic, and slangy: BrE *layabout* someone who lays/lies idly about; AmE *dropout* someone who drops out of society or education;

write-off a car so badly damaged that it is written off the books of an insurance company; *blow-up* a photograph blown up like a balloon. As with the verb forms, phrasal nouns can run parallel with Latinate nouns that tend to be elevated, technical, and formal where the phrasal nouns are colloquial, informal, and slangy: *break-up/disintegration, checkup/examination, letdown/disappointment, let-up/relaxation, sellout/ betrayal, shake-up/ reorganization.*

Compounds and attributives. Phrasal nouns can occur in compound and attributive formations: (1) With the phrasal noun first: *blackout regulations, breakdown service, check-up period, getaway car, input time, overflow pipe, round-up time.* (2) With the phrasal noun second: *aeroplane take-off/airplane takeoff, traffic holdup, cholera outbreak, enemy build-up, population overspill, student sit-in.* (3) With the phrasal noun between other nouns: *cattle round-up time, truck breakdown service, population overspill problem.*

Phrasal-verb idioms. Idiomatic usages are usually colloquial and informal, more or less obvious figurative extensions of ordinary uses. Expressions used to gloss them are often more formal, less direct, and less emotive, as with: *bring down* or defeat (a government), *bring in* or introduce (a new law), *bring off* or clinch (a deal), *bring on* or encourage and train (a student), *bring out* or publish (a book), *bring up* or raise (a child); be *carried away* or overwhelmed (by one's emotions), *carry off* or win (a prize), *carry on* or continue (one's work), *carry out* or perform (one's duty), *carry through* or sustain (a project, to the end); a machine *coming apart* or disintegrating, a deal *coming off* or succeeding, work *coming on* or improving, soldiers *coming through* or surviving, something *coming up* or happening; *cutting back* or economizing (on expenses), *cutting down* or reducing (one's expenses), *cutting in on* or interrupting (a conversation), *cutting* people *off* or isolating them, *cutting* something *out* or excising or eliminating it; *getting down* or alighting (from a train), *getting* all the information *in* or collecting it, *getting on* or succeeding (in life), *getting off* or disembarking, or being allowed to go free, after an offence, *getting out of* or escaping from (a prison), and *getting out* or producing and publishing (a magazine), *getting up* or increasing (pressure), and *getting up* or rising from one's bed in the morning. Similar lists can be made for such other everyday verbs as *be, do, go, keep, make, pass, pull, put, run, set, take, turn.*

Phrasal verbs and prepositions. There is a continuum between the phrasal verb as described above and verbs followed by phrases in which the preposition may or may not be part of the phrase. A phrasal verb can be formed elliptically from a verb plus prepositional phrase (like *He took the box up* from *He took the box up the stairs*). A transitive usage may not be separable (like *pick up the book/pick the book up*), but may have distinct meanings depending on where the particle is placed (*get round someone, get someone round*). Particles may not be clearly either adverbial or prepositional, as with *off* in BrE *get off the bus* (compare widespread AmE *get off of the bus*). Some prepositions may be attached to verbs preceding them, usually for figurative reasons: where the sentence *He came across the street* is analysable as (*He came*) (*across the street*), the sentence *He came across an old friend* makes more sense as a phrasal form: (*He came across*) (*an old friend*), *come across* glossed as *meet by chance*. Some grammarians and lexicologists call a usage like *come across* a *prepositional verb*, because the particle is not adverbial but prepositional. Such a terminology, if extended, should turn phrasal verbs proper into 'adverbial verbs', but has not yet done so. Other commentators call the usage a *fused* or *non-separable phrasal verb*, because the preposition has been 'stolen' from its own phrase and fused with the preceding verb in an idiom. Others still consider some particles so equivocal that they are neither adverbs as such nor prepositions as such, but 'adpreps'. Usages include: *act for* represent, *bargain for* expect, *call for* demand, *come by* obtain, *get at* imply, *go for* attack. The issue is further complicated by occasions when the fusion occurs between a phrasal verb proper and a following preposition, as with *look down on* hold in contempt, *check up on* investigate, *go along with* accept, *face up to* confront, *look back on* recall, *look forward to* have good expectations of, *look up to* admire, *meet up with* encounter.

Stress. In normal speech, if no special emphasis is employed, the adverbial particle in a phrasal verb proper is stressed: *to pick úp a bóok/pick a bóok úp.* The preposition in a two-part fused (prepositional) verb is not usually so stressed: *They didn't bárgain for thát.* In a three-part fusion, the stresses combine the patterns: *to lóok UP to sómeone, lóok DOWN on sómeone.*

Productivity. Phrasal verbs have always been common, but have increased in number since the mid-19c and even more so since the mid-20c, especially in AmE. As a result, a number of dictionaries of phrasal verbs have been published since 1974 (see below) and increasingly dictionaries for both native and foreign users have given phrasal verbs main-entry or high secondary status. They are increasingly the subject of special attention in courses for foreign learners of English, and it was in this area that the category came of age as a distinct aspect of grammar, word-formation, and usage. See ADVERBIAL PARTICLE, POSTPOSITION, PREPOSITIONAL VERB, SLANG, WORD-FORMATION. [GRAMMAR, WORD].

T.MCA.

Bolinger, Dwight. 1971. *The Phrasal Verb in English.* Cambridge, Mass.: Harvard University Press.

Courtney, Rosemary. 1983. *Longman Dictionary of Phrasal Verbs.* Harlow: Longman.

Cowie, A. P., & Mackin, R. *Oxford Dictionary of Current Idiomatic English.* Volume 1: *Verbs with Prepositions and Particles.* Oxford: University Press.

McArthur, Tom, & Atkins, Beryl. 1974. *Collins Dictionary of English Phrasal Verbs and Their Idioms.* London & Glasgow: Collins.

Sinclair, John, & Moon, Rosamund. 1989. *Collins COBUILD Dictionary of Phrasal Verbs.* London & Glasgow: Collins.

Turton, Nigel D., & Manser, Martin H. 1985. *The Student's Dictionary of Phrasal Verbs.* London: Macmillan.

PHRASE [16c: from Latin *phrasis*, Greek *phrásis* speech, way of speaking]. (1) In general usage, any small group of words within a sentence or a clause, such as 'in general usage', 'small groups', and 'a clause'. Such a group is usually recognized as having a syntactic structure: groups like *usage any* and *or a* would not normally qualify as phrases. (2) In grammatical theory, a unit that does not have the structure of a sentence or clause, and cannot therefore be analysed in terms of subject, verb, and object. There are five types of phrase, named after their main word: *noun phrase* (*a very bright light*); *verb phrase* (*may be eating*); *adjective phrase* (*extraordinarily happy*); *adverb phrase* or *adverbial phrase* (*quite casually*); *prepositional phrase* (*in our city*). In traditional analyses, a phrase must consist of more than one word, as in the everyday use of the term, but in contemporary grammars one, two, or more words that function in the same way are all phrases. A noun phrase is therefore the subject of all three sentences '*The work* is in progress', '*Work* is in progress', '*It* is in progress'.

A phrase may have another phrase embedded in it: the prepositional phrase *for your information* contains the noun phrase *your information*; the noun phrase *a somewhat easy question* contains the adjective phrase *somewhat easy*. A phrase may also have a clause embedded in it: the noun phrase *the play that I saw last night* contains the relative clause *that I saw last night*. In most traditional grammars, constructions that do not have a finite verb are considered phrases, so that the infinitive construction '*To miss* the party would be a pity' and the participle construction in 'His hobby is *painting landscapes*' are phrases. In many contemporary grammars, these are regarded as clauses. In generative grammar, the term is treated even more widely: in 'I *know that they are waiting*' the verb phrase consists of everything but the subject *I*, since it is taken to include the complementaion of the verb, in this instance a *that-* clause. See BINOMIAL, CLAUSE, IDIOM, FIXED PHRASE, PHRASEOLOGY, PHRASE WORD, SENTENCE. [GRAMMAR].

S.G.

PHRASEOLOGY [17c: from the Neo-Greek *phraseología*, coined by the 16c German humanist Michael Neander. Stress: 'fraze-OL-o-jy'. If the classical Greek form *phrasilogía* had served as the source of the modern word, its form in English would have been **phrasilogy*]. A way of expressing oneself; the way in which words and phrases are used, especially by particular individuals or groups: *confused phraseology*, *legal phraseology*. Compare NOMENCLATURE, TERMINOLOGY. See PHRASE. [LANGUAGE, STYLE].

T.MCA.

PHRASE WORD. An occasional term in word-formation for a word formed from a phrase. There are at least six types: (1) Attributive phrase words, as italicized in '*a state-of-the-art* description' (more below). (2) Nouns followed by prepositions and other nouns, on the model of certain French compound words, as in *man-at-arms* and *tug-of-war* (more below). (3) Phrases turned into lexical bases by the addition of suffixes, as in *never-say-die-ism* and *state-of-the-artistry*. (4) Stunt formations of various kinds, such as *whodun(n)it*, the informal name for a murder mystery, and its derivative *whodunitry*, the activity of producing such books. (5) Such vague words as *whatchamacallit* and BrE *thingummyjig*, AmE *thingamajig*. (6) Phrasal verbs and their noun derivatives: *get together* ('They *got together* and discussed the matter'); *a get-together* ('I enjoy these family *get-togethers*').

Attributive phrase words. There are as many attributive phrase words as there are types of phrase. They are often based on idioms, proverbs, and common expressions (*run of the mill* in 'a *run-of-the-mill* TV show'), or cover a concept or situation ('the *arms-to-Iran-for-hostages-plus-money-for-the-"contras"* scandal'). Their orthography is diverse. They may be linked by hyphens, (which is probably the general rule) enclosed in quotation marks, capitalized, a mix of these, or left as straight phrases. In writing, an attempt is usually made to highlight such phrase words visually. In speech, they may be spoken quickly and deliberately as a unit. The lists which follow (taken from 1980s citations without major changes in their printed forms) cover the main types:

Noun-based. An able-baker-charlie-dog sequence; a Hound of the Baskervilles image; a 'Power of the Human Mind' theory; a plurality of wives revelation.

Verb-based. (1) *Infinitive*: a made-to-measure suit; ready-to-wear clothes; right-to-die legislation. (2) *Participial*: the 'standing up for America' syndrome; the having-your-cake-and-eating-it-too category; dyed-to-match co-ordinates; a producer-turned-network-executive. (3) *Modal*: a must-win context; more a will-try than a can-do situation.

Adjective-based. A 'best-buy' business computer system; 'good news, bad news' jokes; a 'good news' newspaper; odd-man-out tactics; blind-man's-buff diplomacy; stiff-upper-lip Brits; a happy-little-girl grin; a larger-than-life picture; a holier-than-thou approach.

Number-based. A seven-days-a-week service; a three-week vacation; a 40-pound weight; a three-year-old boy; a 1989 Audi Quattro.

Preposition-based. (1) *Preposition first*: behind-the-scenes information peddling; over-the-counter medication; round-the-clock surveillance. (2) *Preposition midway*: a back to the land movement; the signal-to-noise ratio; a rags-to-riches story; an Aid-to-El Salvador group; hole-in-the-corner affairs; a balance-of-payments problem; an end-of-May opening date; University of Utah doctors; an Equal-Time-for-God sermonette; a made-for-TV movie; a once-upon-a-time story; a heavy-on-the-tease-light-on-the-sleaze version.

Coordination-based. An 'accuse and demand' approach; a down-and-out alcoholic; a glass and aluminum sky-scraper; hit-and-run drivers; an open-and-shut case; protection and assassination rackets; a rock-and-roll eccentric; a 'them' and 'us' mentality; a tough-but-vulnerable look; a life-or-death decision.

Wh-words-based. You-know-who; a 'what-if' question; a what-went-wrong puzzle; how-to-massage books; some how-to stuff; that how-do-I-get-out-of-here feeling.

Negation-based. A no-man's-land; a no-win situation; a won't-go-away loneliness; a nobody-cares feeling.

Phrase words on the French model. One variety of French *mot composé* (compound word) is phrasal in form and joins nouns by means of a preposition: *pomme de terre* potato, *arc-en-ciel* rainbow. English acquired this pattern through Norman French: *editor-in-chief* (compare French *rédacteur-en-chef*). Common usages: *brothers-in-arms*, *cost of living*, *jack-in-the-box*, *man-at-arms*, *man-of-war*, *poet-in-residence*, *president-for-life*. Stunt variations include: *computer-on-a-chip*, *cynic-in-residence*,

hamburgers-on-the-hoof (beef cattle), *trainee-in-terror.*

See COMPOUND WORD, PHRASAL VERB, PHRASE, STUNT WORD, TIMESPEAK, VAGUE WORD, WORD-FORMATION. [GRAMMAR, WORD]. T.MCA.

PICA [16c: from Anglo-Latin *pica* a list of ecclesiastical rules, from Latin *pica* a magpie, because of its habit of picking up and keeping odds and ends. Pronounced: 'PIE-ka']. (1) A type-size equal to 12 point. (2) Also *pica em*. A printer's unit of linear measurement for areas of printed surfaces, based on the depth of pica-type and equal to 12 points (slightly less than one-sixth of an inch). (3) A 12-point type-size for typewriters, with ten characters to the inch. See EM, EN, TYPOGRAPHY. [TECHNOLOGY]. T.MCA.

PICT [From 3c Latin *Picti*, identified by Latin writers with the plural of *pictus* painted, but perhaps a native name, in Old Norse *Péttar*, earlier **Peht-*, Old English *Pehtas, Pihtas*]. One of the people of partly Celtic stock inhabiting Britain north of the Forth and Clyde during and immediately after Roman times, of whom there are some brief historical records and to whom are attributed the several hundred stone monuments known as *symbol stones*, found from Fife to Shetland. Many of the earlier Iron Age monuments found in parts of the same region, such as the defensive dry-stone towers known as *brochs* (in use 1c BC to 2c AD) and *souterrains* (underground passages, perhaps storehouses) are doubtless relics of ancestors of the Picts, including the people known to the Romans as *Caledonians*. As a separate nation the Picts virtually disappear from record shortly after their union with the Scots in the mid-9c, along with their language or languages and, largely, such customs as matrilineal succession. See CALEDONIA, PICTISH, SCOT. [EUROPE, NAME]. A.J.A.

PICTISH [17c, originally in Scottish writings: from *Pict*, on the analogy of *English, Scottish*, etc.]. (1) Relating to the Picts: *the Pictish question*. (2) The language of the Picts, whose principal records consist of a few early loanwords in Gaelic and, later, Scots and English, such as *mormaer* a high official, *davach* a land measure, *pett* a portion of land, and (of the same origin) *peat*, perhaps *mounth* a mountain range, some Caledonian and Pictish personal names (such as *Calgacus, Argentocoxos, Drostan, Gartnait, Nechton, Uurguist*), and some tribal and regional names (such as the Latinized *Cornavii, Decantae, Smertae*, the Scotticized *Buchan, the Mearns, Moray*, the place-names *Lossie* and *Orkney*, and a number of toponymic elements: see SCOTTISH PLACE-NAMES). Pictish appears to have been a P-Celtic language, similar to but not identical with Cumbric, possibly introduced from southern Britain or the European mainland in the first millennium BC. Until recently it has been accepted that the unintelligible inscriptions in Ogam writing on some 27 stone monuments and other Pictish objects are in a pre-Celtic non-Indo-European language whose speakers may also be the source of such non-Celtic Pictish customs as matrilineal succession and perhaps body painting or tattooing. Some place-names, such as ancient *Hebudae* or *Ebudae* (present-day *Hebrides*), *Spey* (a river), *Thule* (Iceland or Shetland), tribal names (*Caledonii*), and personal names (*Bargoit, Bruide, Derile, Itharnan, Spusscio*), whose origins and meanings are unknown, may also be relics of this aboriginal language. See BRITISH LANGUAGES, CELTIC LANGUAGES, PICT. [EUROPE, LANGUAGE, NAME].   A.J.A.

PIDGIN [1870s: widely considered to be from the Chinese pronunciation of *business*, also rendered as *pigeon*, as in *that's not my pigeon* (that's not my business or concern). Other suggested sources are Portuguese *ocupação* business, and *pequeno* small (suggesting baby talk), and Hebrew *pidjom* barter]. A term used in a general and a technical sense for a contact language which draws on elements from two or more languages: *pidgin Portuguese*; *a Spanish pidgin*.

The general sense. As generally understood, a pidgin is a hybrid 'makeshift language' used by and among traders, on plantations (especially with and among slaves of various backgrounds), and between Europeans and the indigenous peoples of Asia, Africa, and the Americas, especially during the heyday of European expansion (17-20c). Because the word has often been used and discussed pejoratively, it carries such connotations as 'childish', 'corrupt', 'lazy', 'inferior', 'oversimplified', and 'simple-minded'. The term has been extended with such a negative sense into wider use, as in 'writing pidgin Latin' and 'not satisfied with pidgin Marxism'. This view of pidgin languages has often appeared in works of reference, as in *Brewer's Dictionary of Phrase and Fable* (1965):

Pidgin-English. The semi-English lingua franca used in China and the Far East, consisting principally of mispronounced English words with certain native grammatical constructions. For instance, the Chinese cannot pronounce *r*, so replace it with *l*—*te-lee* for 'three', *solly* for 'sorry', etc.—and, in Chinese, between a numeral and its noun there is always inserted a word (called the 'classifier') and this, in Pidgin-English, is replaced by piece—e.g. *one-piece knifee, two piece hingkichi* (handkerchiefs). *Pidgin* is a corruption of *business*.

Etymologically, there appears to have been only one pidgin: *Pidgin English*, also known as *Business English, Pidgin-English, pidgin-English,*

Pigeon English, Pigeon-English, bigeon, pidgeon, pidjin, pidjun. This was a trade jargon used from the 17c onward between the British and Chinese in such ports as Canton. In 1826, B. Hall wrote: 'I afterwards learned that "pigeon", in the strange jargon spoken at Canton by way of English, means business'; in 1845, J. R. Peters noted: 'Pidgeon, is the common Chinese pronunciation of business'; and in 1872, A. D. Carlisle observed: 'The dialect . . . current between Englishmen and Chinamen . . . goes by the name of Pigeon-English' (*OED*). It should be noted, however, that *Chinese (Coastal) Pidgin English* or *China Coast Pidgin* is now a technical term referring to a contact language used between speakers of English and Chinese from the first half of the 18c until the early 1970s. See CHINA.

The technical sense. Sociolinguists in particular use the term to describe a phenomenon whose study has greatly increased since the Second World War. For them, a pidgin is a marginal language which arises to fulfil certain restricted communicative functions among groups with no common language. This more clinical approach now tends to predominate in works of reference, as in the *Concise Columbia Encyclopedia* (1983):

pidgin, a lingua franca that is not the mother tongue of anyone using it and that has a simplified grammar and restricted, often polyglot, vocabulary. An example is the pidgin English used in Far Eastern ports, principally for trading between the English and Chinese. The basic English vocabulary had Malay, Chinese, and Portuguese elements.

In sociolinguistic terms, there have been many pidgins and the process known as *pidginization* is seen as liable to occur anywhere under appropriate conditions. This process of simplification and hybridization involves reduction of linguistic resources and restriction of use to such limited functions as trade. The term is sometimes extended to refer to the early stages of any instance of second-language acquisition when learners acquire a minimal form of the target language often influenced by their own primary language. There is, however, some disagreement among scholars over the number of languages in sufficient contact to produce a pidgin. Some investigators claim that any two languages in contact may result in a degree of linguistic improvization and compromise, and so lead to pidginization. Such a viewpoint includes in the category of pidgin *foreigner talk* and other classes of makeshift and often transitory communication. Other investigators argue that only in cases where more than two languages are in contact do true pidgins spring up. In situations where speakers of more than two languages must converse in a medium native to none of them, the kinds of restructuring are more radical than in other cases and likely to be more durable.

The names given to pidgin languages by linguists refer to their location and their principal *lexifier* or *base language*: that is, the language from which they draw most of their vocabulary. *Papuan Pidgin English* therefore refers to the pidgin that is spoken in what was formerly the Territory of Papua, and that draws most of its vocabulary from English and is therefore an English-based pidgin; *Hawaii Pidgin English* is the pidgin English spoken in Hawaii. In addition and often prior to such academic names, pidgins may or may not be identified as such and often have specific names retained by scholars when discussing them, such as *Bazaar Hindustani/ Hindi*, *Korean Bamboo English*, *français petit-nègre*. Even after a pidgin develops into a *creole*, the name may continue to be used, such as *Roper Pidgin*, also known as *Roper River Creole*. A language may also have both pidgin and creole varieties, as with Tok Pisin in Papua New Guinea.

Features. A pidgin is characterized by a small vocabulary (a few hundred or thousand words) drawn largely from the superstrate language (that is, the language of the socially dominant group), together with a reduction of many grammatical features, such as inflectional morphology, as in Tok Pisin *mi kam* can mean 'I come', 'I am coming', 'I came', and *wanpela haus* means 'house' while *tupela haus* means 'two houses'. One source of grammar is the socially subordinate substrate language(s). Often though not always, where pidgins develop, one group is socially superior and its full language is more or less inaccessible to the other group(s), so that there is little motivation or opportunity to improve performance. Where the needs of communication are minimal and confined to a few basic domains such as work and trade, a casual and deficient version of language can be enough, as has been the case with *Kisettla* (settlers' language), the pidgin Swahili used between the British and Africans in Kenya. Many pidgin languages arose in the context of contact between European colonizers who enslaved or employed a colonized or transported population on plantations, in ports, in their homes, etc.

A notable feature of pidgins is lack of grammatical complexity; for this reason, they are often referred to at best as simple or simplified languages, at worst as bastardized or broken forms of another language. In popular accounts, simplicity is attributed to lack of grammar, but linguists agree that pidgins have a distinctive grammatical structure. The grammar of a pidgin language is constructed according to a principle which dictates that there should be a close relation between form and meaning. There is a tendency for each morpheme (or word element) to

occur only once in an utterance, and for it to have only one form. Non-pidgin languages generally have built-in redundancy and require the expression of the same meaning in several places in an utterance: for example, in the English sentences *One man comes* and *Six men come*, singular and plural are marked in both noun and modifier, and concord is shown in both noun and verb. However, the equivalents in Tok Pisin (Papua New Guinea Pidgin English) show no variation in the verb form or the noun: *Wanpela man i kam* and *Sikspela man i kam*.

Because they lack redundancy, pidgins depend heavily on context for their interpretation. Most pidgins have little or no inflectional morphology. Where English marks possession by adding *'s* (as in *John's house*), Tok Pisin has *haus bilong John*. Here, *bilong* has been taken from English, but has shifted its function from verb to preposition, and can be paraphrased as 'belonging to'. Pidgin languages tend to have only a small number of prepositions and they use them to mark a variety of grammatical relations which in other languages would be expressed by a much greater number of prepositions. Pidgins are highly regular and have fewer exceptions than many other languages, which makes them easier to learn. Another property is multifunctionality: the same word can function in many ways. In English, the word *ill* functions as an adjective (in *He is ill*, *an ill wind*). The corresponding noun is *illness*, derived by a regular process of word-formation. In Tok Pisin, however, the word *sik* can function as both noun and adjective: *Mi sik* I am ill; *Em i gat sik malaria* He has malaria. Pidgins may compensate for lack of vocabulary by circumlocution: in Tok Pisin, *Singsing taim maus i pas* to sing with the mouth closed (= to hum). Where English has *branch*, Tok Pisin has *han bilong diwai* hand of a tree.

In analysing the syntactic elements of pidgins, it is often impossible to separate the influence of substrate from superstrate language: as in the case of Tok Pisin, the influence of local languages from that of English. In Tok Pisin, the particle *i* is a so-called *predicate marker*, occurring in such sentences as *Ol man i kisim bigpela supia* (The men—predicate marker—got big spears). It is plausible to derive this marker from the use of resumptive pronouns in non-standard English, such as *he* as in *John, he got a new car*, as well as from similar syntactic patterns in Austronesian languages. Such a use of pronouns as predicate markers is widespread across pidgins, occurring in some of the French-based Indian Ocean creoles as well as in Chinook Jargon.

Classification. Pidgins can be classified into four types according to their development: jargon, stable pidgin, extended or expanded pidgin, and creole, each characterized by a gradual increase in complexity. (1) *Jargon.* In this stage, there is great individual variation, a very simple sound system, one- or two-word utterances, and a very small lexicon. Jargons are used for communicating in limited situations: trade jargons generally, and *Chinook Jargon*, a trade language spoken along the north-west Pacific coast of North America from the 18c. (2) *Stable pidgin.* This is more regular and more complex and there are social norms regarding its use, as with *Russenorsk*, a trade pidgin used in northern Norway by Russian merchants and Norwegian fishermen over some 130 years (1785–1917). Because the language was used for seasonal trade, it did not expand much structurally and had a core vocabulary of *c.*150–200 words. (3) *Extended* or *expanded pidgin.* Other pidgins, such as *Tok Pisin*, not only stabilized but expanded to become more grammatically complex, and to serve as well-established lingua francas, sometimes with official or other status. (4) *Creole.* At this stage, the pidgin is creolized: that is, it is acquired as a first language by children, particularly in urban areas. This is the stage of, for example, Tok Pisin in Papua New Guinea and Kriol (also known as Roper River Creole) in the Northern Territories of Australia. It is generally impossible to identify structural features which distinguish expanded pidgins from emerging creoles, since both exhibit increased structural complexity and share many features. The difference lies more in social use than in form.

Theories of origin. Various theories have been proposed to account for the origin of pidgin languages, and fall into three broad types: *monogenetic, polygenetic,* and *universalist.*

Monogenesis. This theory asserts a common origin for all European-based pidgins. Some monogenetic theorists claim that they all descend from a nautical jargon used for communication among sailors from different backgrounds. Others have argued that they descend from a 15c Portuguese pidgin which could in its turn have been a relic of *Sabir*, the lingua franca of the Crusaders and a Mediterranean trading language. It is claimed that this language was relexified (that is, renewed with vocabulary from different sources) as it came into contact with such other European languages as English and Dutch. Both the nautical-jargon and Sabir theories take as supporting evidence the fact that many pidgins share common words like *save* (to know: compare English *savvy*) and *pikinini* (child: compare English *piccaninny*). Both words are of Spanish/Portuguese origin, from *saber/sabir* (to know) and *pequeño* (small), and are widely used in English-based pidgins and creoles

in the Caribbean and Pacific. Such words could either have been directly inherited locally or transmitted from one location to another by sailors, who undoubtedly account for some of the lexical sharing across unrelated pidgins, although their role in the formation of stable pidgins was probably not great. However, it is difficult to account for the many differences among pidgins by appealing entirely to relexification, and neither approach explains the origin of the many non-European-based pidgin languages.

Polygenesis. This theory stresses distinctness and appeals to the influence of substrate languages, such as the influence of African languages in the formation of the Atlantic pidgins. According to one view, pidgins arise out of the imperfect learning of a model language by slaves or as a result of deliberate simplification, for example by Europeans in a master/slave relationship. There is evidence that the Portuguese taught a simplified version of their language to those they traded with along the west coast of Africa.

Universalism. This view argues for the universal nature of the social and psychological factors which occur in language contact. The *baby-talk theory* is based on the idea that certain systems of communication emerge in response to particular social and historical circumstances. There is evidence for this hypothesis in the fact that baby talk, foreigner talk, and pidgins show certain similarities of structure. Baby talk expressions such as *Daddy go bye-bye* are similar to the reduced versions of language used to address foreigners.

There is no doubt that the native languages of colonized, enslaved, and transplanted populations provided important input to pidgins, but there are also many features which can be explained only by reference to the superstrate languages of the colonizers, enslavers, and transplanters. At present, therefore, no single theory can adequately explain the origin of pidgin languages.

See ABORIGINAL ENGLISH, ACROLECT, AFRICAN ENGLISH, AKU, ANGLO-DANISH, AUSTRALIAN PIDGIN, BABY TALK, BASIC ENGLISH[1], BASILECT, BEACH LA MAR, BEARER ENGLISH, BISLAMA, BOX-WALLAH ENGLISH, BROKEN, BUTLER ENGLISH, CAMFRANGLAIS, CARIBBEAN ENGLISH CREOLE, CHINA, CONTACT LANGUAGE, CREOLE, FANAKALO, FIJI, FOREIGNER TALK, FRACTURED ENGLISH, FRENCH, HAWAII PIDGIN ENGLISH, INTER-LANGUAGE, JAMAICAN CREOLE, JAPANESE PIDGIN ENGLISH, JARGON, KAMTOK, KITCHEN, KOINE, KRIO, KRIOL, LECT, LINGUA, LINGUA FRANCA, LINGO, MAKESHIFT LANGUAGE, MARGINAL LANGUAGE, MARITIME PIDGIN, MELANESIAN PIDGIN ENGLISH, MESOLECT, NAUTICAL JARGON, PACIFIC

JARGON ENGLISH, PAPUA NEW GUINEA, PIDGIN, PITCAIRNESE, SABIR, SOLOMON ISLANDS PIDGIN ENGLISH, TALK, TOK PISIN, TRADE JARGON, WEST AFRICAN PIDGIN ENGLISH. [LANGUAGE, VARIETY].
S.R.

Holm, John. 1988/9. *Pidgins and Creoles*. Two volumes. Cambridge: University Press.
Hymes, Dell, (ed.). 1971. *Pidginization and Creolization of Languages: Proceedings of a Conference Held at the University of the West Indies, Mona, Jamaica, 1968*. Cambridge: University Press.
Mühlhäusler, Peter. 1986. *Pidgin and Creole Linguistics*. Oxford: Blackwell.
Romaine, Suzanne. 1988. *Pidgin and Creole Languages*. London: Longman.
Todd, Loreto. 1990. *Pidgins and Creoles*. 1st edition 1974. London & New York: Routledge.

PIG LATIN [1930s]. A private code or 'language' (especially among children), derived from everyday English by moving a consonant or consonant cluster from the beginning of a word to the end, usually followed by 'ay': *Eythay antcay eakspay igpay Atinlay* They can't speak pig Latin. When words begin with vowels, 'ay' is simply added: *Itsay oodgay* It's good. There are many variations. See PRIVATE LANGUAGE. [STYLE, VARIETY]. T.MCA.

PIJIN. See SOLOMON ISLANDS PIDGIN ENGLISH.

PILGRIM WORD. See BORROWING.

PINDARIC ODE. See ODE.

PINYIN. See CHINA, DIACRITIC, ROMAN.

PIOZZI, Hester (Lynch), also known as **Harriet Lynch Thrale, Hester Thrale Piozzi, Mrs Thrale,** née *Salusbury* [1763-1821]. British writer, born in Bodvel, Carnarvonshire, Wales. In 1763, she married Henry Thrale, a wealthy brewer. In 1765, she met Samuel Johnson, who in the following year, after a severe illness, spent much of the summer with the Thrales, after which he became virtually part of the family, living much of the time in their homes. Her husband died in 1781 and in 1784 she married, amid some social consternation, her daughter's music master, Gabriel Piozzi, and went with him to Italy. This development estranged her from Johnson in the closing months of his life. When she heard of his death in the same year, she compiled and sent to England material for *Anecdotes of the late Samuel Johnson, LL.D., during the last Twenty Years of his Life* (1786), a work that made her a rival of his friend and biographer James Boswell. After returning to England, she brought out a two-volume edition of *Letters to and from the late Samuel Johnson, LL.D.* (1788). Thousands of her letters have survived and her journal, kept

from 1776 to 1809, and given the name *Thraliana*, was edited in two volumes by K. C. Balderston (1942). She compiled the *British Synonymy* (1794), basing her sense discriminations on conversation rather than on textual evidence and noting that 'synonymy has more to do with elegance than truth'. Her style was light but trenchant:

ABANDON, FORSAKE, RELINQUISH, GIVE UP, DESERT, QUIT, LEAVE Of these seven verbs, so variously derived, though at first sight apparently synonymous, conversing does certainly better show the peculiar appropriation, than books, however learned; for whilst through them by study all due information may certainly be obtained, familiar talk tells us in half an hour—That a man FORSAKES his mistress, ABANDONS all hope of regaining her lost esteem, RELINQUISHES his pretension in favour of another; GIVES UP a place of trust he held under the government, DESERTS his party, LEAVES his parents in affliction, and QUITS the kingdom forever.

See index. [BIOGRAPHY, EUROPE, LITERATURE, REFERENCE]. T.MCA.

PITCAIRNESE, also **Pitcairn-Norfolk Creole.** The creole spoken by the descendants of the mutineers from HMS *Bounty*, who settled on uninhabited Pitcairn Island in 1790. There were 28 original inhabitants: nine mutineers led by Fletcher Christian, six Polynesian men and 12 Polynesian women from Tahiti, and one small child. For 33 years, the settlers lived in almost complete isolation. Half the Englishmen died within four years and all but one within ten years. Most Pitcairnese were moved permanently to Norfolk Island in 1856, where they are now outnumbered by settlers from mainland Australia. The English-speakers had the greatest influence on Pitcairnese, which draws most of its vocabulary from English. It is not clear to what extent pidginization and creolization played a role in its development, since the women presumably spoke Tahitian as well as rudimentary English to their children. Pitcairnese shares a number of features with other English-based pidgins and creoles. [OCEANIA, VARIETY]. S.R.

PITCH [12c: from Middle English *piche(n)* to throw, whence an act or place of pitching, a place where something happens, a high place or position, and a height or level from which to go up or down, as in music]. A term used generally and in phonetics for the level of the voice. Pitch depends on the frequency with which the vocal cords (or folds) vibrate to produce *voice*: the more rapidly, the higher the pitch perceived. When voices quaver, there is a fluctuation of pitch, especially in a *falsetto* (an especially male voice which is unnaturally high), the vocal cords having been greatly contracted. When a voice has a very low pitch, it is said to *creak*. *Creaky* *voice*, common among male RP-speakers, tends to occur at the end of a statement, as the voice falls low. *Pitch range* refers to the difference between high and low pitch. The greater the range, the greater the impression given of emotion. See ACCENT, TONE, VOICE. [SPEECH].

G.K.

PITMAN, (Sir) Isaac [1813-97]. English educational reformer, businessman, and inventor of the Pitman shorthand system. Born in Trowbridge, Wiltshire, the son of a hand weaver, he left school at 13 and served for a time as a clerk in a textile mill. He then trained as a teacher in 1831, taught as headmaster in various schools, and finally had a school of his own. Intrigued by John Walker's pronouncing dictionary and Samuel Taylor's shorthand, he developed a system of his own based on the representation of sound, described first in *Stenographic Sound-Hand* (1837), then in *Phonography* (1840). The latter was also called 'the Penny Plate' (because it was sent out by the new penny post) and was the world's first correspondence course. It was initially offered free of charge, a mark of Pitman's concern for 'educating anyone of any class from anywhere who could read and had the desire to learn' (Frances Moss, *Pitman: 150 Years of Innovation in Business Education*, 1987).

The system classifies speech sounds into groups, consonants being shown as strokes and generally paired (for example, a lightly written stroke for *f* and a heavier variant for *v*), vowels as dots and dashes, and abbreviations of consonant clusters (*str*), syllables (*der*), and affixes (*tion*) as circles, loops, and hooks. The system was refined through many editions, changes often causing confusion among users. The 10th edition of *Phonography* (1857) established the vowels as they have continued to be used, and the *New Era edition* (1922) contained extra devices for high-speed reporting at up to 250 words per minute. The Pitman system benefited from the spread of British imperial administration in the later 19c.

In 1843, Pitman set up his *Phonetic Institute* in Bath as a publishing house and marketing operation. His success in recording verbatim an anti-Corn Law speech by William Cobden gained converts to his system and in due course his shorthand was used for preparing Hansard, the official record of Parliament. He founded *The Phonotypic Journal* in 1840, which was for a time *The Phonetic Journal*, became *Pitman's Shorthand Weekly* in 1892, and *Office Training* in the 1930s. In 1870, *Pitman's Metropolitan College* opened, perhaps the first school of business education in the world, with a syllabus covering office routine, accounting and law, and shorthand and typing. In addition to being used

throughout the world for English, Pitman's system of shorthand has been adapted for such languages as Arabic, Dutch, French, German, Hebrew, Hindi, Japanese, Latin, Persian, Spanish, Welsh, and Tamil. His system of phonetic English spelling had little impact, however, although it served as the basis of the *Initial Teaching Alphabet*, devised by his grandson James Pitman in 1959. See index. [BIOGRAPHY, EDUCATION, EUROPE, WRITING].

T.MCA.

PITMAN, (Sir) (Isaac) James [1901-85]. English publisher and educational reformer, grandson of Isaac Pitman. He was born in London, and educated at Eton and Oxford, where he studied modern history. He played rugby for Oxford and for England, and was a noted boxer, runner, and skier. He joined his father Ernest and his uncle Alfred in the family business and was for a time headmaster of one of the Pitman's Colleges (in Maida Vale in the 1920s). He became chairman and managing director of Sir Isaac Pitman & Sons (*c.*1932), was Chairman of the Joint Examining Board (1935-50), a director of the Bank of England (1941-5), first Director of Organization and Method in the Civil Service (1943-5), President of the Society of Commercial Teachers (1951-5), and Conservative Member of Parliament for Bath (1945-64). In 1959, he published *The Ehrhardt Augmented (40-sound 42-character) Lower-Case Roman Alphabet* (in which *Ehrhardt* is the name of a typeface), which described a system that later became known as the *Initial Teaching Alphabet* (see entry), designed to help children learn to read more easily and successfully. Based on original work by his grandfather, it became a lifelong passion to whose promotion in the UK and elsewhere he contributed large sums of his own money, lobbying education ministers, school inspectors, and chief education officers, and attending conferences of teachers. His *Initial Teaching Alphabet Foundation* benefited from a large donation in the US, but disagreements led to litigation, and the movement lost momentum: 'Most teachers continued to prefer books in ordinary type. They never wholly believed claims that there were no difficulties in transferring from i.t.a. to traditional orthography' (Archibald Clark-Kennedy, obituary, *The Times*, 3 Sept. 1985). By the 1980s, the system had disappeared from most of the schools that had taken it up. See index. [BIOGRAPHY, EDUCATION, EUROPE, WRITING].

T.MCA.

PITMAN PUBLISHING. An English publishing company that has specialized in business education since it was founded by Isaac Pitman in 1837. Its materials for business and commerce include: training materials in shorthand, keyboarding, and office administration; textbooks for accountancy, finance, economics, and business management; reference works for managers; textbooks and professional books in information technology and computing; and multimedia instructional materials. The bestselling accountancy textbook *Business Accounting* by Frank Wood has sold 5m copies since 1967. The *Pitman Examinations Institute*, founded in Bath in 1885, examines in commercial and secretarial skills and includes a range of written and spoken examinations in English as a foreign language. The company has been involved in EFL teaching since 1914, when classes started at *Pitman's Central College* in London. In 1986, it conducted over 750,000 examinations, about half from overseas. Half of the Pitman publishing range is exported. A family firm for four generations, Pitman became a member of the Longman group in 1985. See BUSINESS ENGLISH, INITIAL TEACHING ALPHABET, PITMAN (I.), PITMAN (J.), SHORTHAND. [EDUCATION, EUROPE, MEDIA].　　　　T.MC.A

PLACE-NAME, also **place name, placename**. Technically **toponym**. The proper name of a locality, either natural (as of bodies of water, mountains, plains, and valleys) or social (as of cities, counties, provinces, nations, and states). In an island like Britain, settled by successive waves of peoples, the place-names embody its history. Celtic, Roman, Anglo-Saxon, Scandinavian, and Norman names vie with one another today as their name-givers did in past centuries. The elements that make up place-names reflect a polyglot heritage: *-coombe* from Celtic **kumbos* (Welsh *cwm*) for a hollow or small valley, as in *Cwmbrân* and *Cwm Rhondda* in Wales, *Coombe* and *High Wycombe* in southern England, and *Cumloden* and *Cumwhitton* in northern England. The variants *-chester* appear in *Chester* and *Manchester*, *-caster* in *Lancaster*, and *-cester* in *Cirencester* and *Gloucester*, and come from Latin *castra* (a military camp). Forms of the Old English *burh* (dative case *byrig*), a fortified settlement, appear in England as *-bury* in *Canterbury*, *-borough* in *Scarborough*, and *-brough* in *Middlesbrough*, and in Scotland as *-burgh*, in *Edinburgh* (with mainland European cognates in *Hamburg* in Germany and *Skanderborg* in Denmark). The Scandinavian *-by* (a farm or village) can be found throughout northern and eastern England, in such names as *Derby*, *Grimsby*, *Romanby*, *Walesby*, and *Whitby*.

In more recently settled English-speaking countries, names are often commemorative of places in the motherland, as with the city of *Boston* in Massachusetts in the US (after the town in Lincolnshire in England) and the town of *Hamilton* in Ontario, Canada (after the town near Glasgow in Scotland). They may also commemorate well-known people in the motherland or the new settlement: for example, the settlements and features called or incorporating the name of Queen Victoria in Cameroon (now Limbe), southern Africa, Canada, and Australia. Sometimes the names are simply descriptive, wherever they are found: *the Black Isle* a peninsula in Scotland, *North Island* in New Zealand, and *the Rocky Mountains* in the US and Canada.

Some place-names have two or more elements: a generic for the kind of place and a specific for a particular locale. The generic usually comes last, as in *Atlantic Ocean, British Isles, Malvern Hills, Madison Avenue, New York City*; sometimes, however, it comes first, as in *Cape St Vincent, Mount Everest, Lake Huron*; and sometimes the elements are joined by *of*, as in *Bay of Fundy, Cape of Good Hope, Gulf of Carpentaria*. Some names which might be expected to have a generic lack one: for example, *the Matterhorn, the Himalayas*. In a few instances, British and American practice differs: *River Thames* as against *Mississippi River*; *County of Warwick* and *Warwickshire* as against *Clinton County*, with *county* used attributively in Ireland, as in *County Clare* and *County Tyrone* (and in the one instance of *County Durham* in England).

See: (1) individual place-names, such as ALBION, AMERICA, BRITAIN, CALEDONIA, IRELAND (listed under NAME). (2) AMERICAN PLACE-NAMES, CANADIAN PLACE-NAMES, CARIBBEAN PLACE-NAMES, ENGLISH PLACE-NAMES, IRISH PLACE-NAMES, NEW ZEALAND PLACE-NAMES, SCOTTISH PLACE-NAMES, SOUTH AFRICAN PLACE-NAMES, WELSH PLACE-NAMES. (3) BRADLEY, JOKE TOWN, MISTAKE NAME, ONOMASTICS, PLURAL, TOPONYM, TOPONYMY. [NAME].　　　　J.A.

Cameron, Kenneth. 1988. *English Place-Names*, Revised edition. London: Batsford.

Ekwall, Eilert. 1960. *The Concise Oxford Dictionary of English Place-Names*, 4th edition. Oxford: University Press.

Field, John. 1980. *Place-Names of Great Britain and Ireland*. Newton Abbot: David & Charles.

―――― 1980. *Place-Names of Greater London*. London: Batsford.

Gelling, Margaret. 1984. *Place-Names in the Landscape*. London: J. M. Dent.

―――― 1988. *Signposts to the Past*. Chichester: Phillimore.

Hamilton, William B. 1978. *The Macmillan Book of Canadian Place Names*. Toronto: Macmillan.

Harder, Kelsie B. (ed.). *Illustrated Dictionary of Place Names: United States and Canada*. New York: Van Nostrand Reinhold.

Matthews, Constance M. 1972. *Place Names of the English-Speaking World*. London: Weidenfeld & Nicolson. New York: Scribner's.

Mills, David. 1991. *A Dictionary of English Place-Names*. Oxford: University Press.

Nicolaisen, W. F. H. 1976. *Scottish Place-Names*. London: Batsford.

Room, Adrian. 1983. *A Concise Dictionary of Modern Place-Names in Great Britain and Ireland*. Oxford: University Press.

—— 1986. *A Dictionary of Irish Place-Names*. Belfast: Appletree Press.

—— 1988. *Dictionary of Place-Names in the British Isles*. London: Bloomsbury.

—— 1989. *Dictionary of World Place Names Derived from British Names*. London: Routledge.

Stewart, George R. 1970. *American Place-Names*. New York: Oxford University Press.

—— 1975. *Names on the Globe*. Oxford: University Press.

PLACE OF ARTICULATION. See SPEECH.

PLAGIARISM [17c: from the obsolete noun *plagiary* kidnapper or a kidnapping, theft or a thief of ideas, from Latin *plagiarius* a kidnapper, literary thief, and *-ism*. In the cast of Richard Sheridan's play *The Critic* (1779) there is a dubious literary figure called Sir Fretful Plagiary]. The appropriation of someone's artistic, musical, or literary work for personal ends. Because most artists are affected by other artists, with all kinds of consequences in their work, it is not always easy to decide where legitimate influence ends and plagiarism begins. The term is usually reserved, however, for the flagrant lifting of material in an unchanged or only slightly changed form and its dissemination as the plagiarist's own work. In oral and scribal societies, most performers 'plagiarized', in the sense that they borrowed material but failed to identify their sources. It is unlikely, however, that this interaction was considered reprehensible. In addition, insofar as educational institutions invite students to model themselves on others, a degree of plagiarism and pastiche are built into the acquiring of creative skills. The concept of plagiarism as a serious legal offence became clear-cut with the growth of printing and the establishment of authors and publishers as people and institutions with property rights.

In recent years, a device for detecting plagiarism, primarily in scientific texts, has been developed by Walter Stewart and Ned Feder at the National Institutes of Health, Bethesda, Maryland, in the US. An optical scanner reads the suspect text into a computer programmed to divide it into overlapping strings of 30 characters, which are then checked against comparable strings in one or more texts relating to the same subject matter. Whenever exact matches occur, they are highlighted in boldface type. The procedure has been usefully employed in a number of cases of suspected misconduct. The creators of the device 'have learned . . . that plagiarism is rare; and that people who copy do so from obscure places and chiefly from dead authors' (*International Herald Tribune*, 8 Jan. 1992). See ALLUSION, COPYRIGHT, DERIVATIVE, PASTICHE, QUOTATION. [MEDIA, STYLE, TECHNOLOGY, WRITING].   T.MCA.

PLAID CYMRU [Pronounced 'Plied Kumry']. In English *Welsh Nationalist Party*. A political party founded in 1925 with the objective of self-government and dominion status for Wales and the preservation of Welsh language and culture. A referendum held in 1979 showed that 20% of Welsh voters favoured some form of political devolution within the UK. At the present time, the party seeks independence within the European Community. See WELSH LANGUAGE SOCIETY. [EUROPE, NAME].   T.MCA.

PLAIN [14c: through Old French from Latin *planus* flat, even, level, lowly, clear, intelligible, evident (all of which senses have carried over into English)]. A term for direct and unambiguous language: 'þis gospel telliþ a playen storie' (Wycliffe, of the New Testament, *c*.1380); 'Speketh so pleyn at this tyme, I yow preye, / That we may understonde what ye seye' (Chaucer, the Host speaking to the Clerk of Oxford in *The Canterbury Tales*); *The Complete Plain Words* (title of a British usage manual by Sir Ernest Gowers, 1954). *Plain* has been used since the late Middle Ages to contrast with *ornate, academic, technical, Latinate*, etc., and phrases such as *plain English, plain language, plain style* have been used to contrast with such expressions as *double Dutch, gobbledygook, jargon*, and *mumbo jumbo*. The contrast of *plain style* with other styles of language originates in ancient Greece and Rome, when rhetoric recognized three styles: the grand or high style, the middle style, and the plain or low style, each appropriate to certain audiences, occasions, and purposes. The grand declamatory style was suited to high themes, people, and occasions (with the risk of becoming grandiose), the moderate middle style was suited to instruction and education (with the risk of becoming bland or pedantic), and the simple style was suited to ordinary life and public speaking (with the risk of becoming coarse, colourless, or patronizing). During the Renaissance and Reformation (15–16c), styles tended to polarize between the classical, academic, and ornate on the one side and the popular, vernacular, and plain on the other, a division that mirrored religious disputes. Protestants, especially of the 'Low Church' in England, favoured *Puritan plain style* and Quaker *plain language* in their worship, speech, and writing. Both forms influenced the development of prose writing in the British Isles, North America, and elsewhere.

See AMERICAN LITERATURE, ANGLO-SAXON, COM-PLETE PLAIN WORDS, PLAIN ENGLISH, PLAIN LAN-GUAGE, RHETORIC, ROYAL SOCIETY, SAXONISM. [STYLE, USAGE].   T.MCA.

PLAIN ENGLISH [16c]. (1) English that is straightforward and easy to understand: 'Which ye shalle here in pleyne Englische' (*Chaucer's Dreme*, 1500); 'Conteyning and teaching the true vvriting, and vnderstanding of hard vsuall English wordes, borrowed from the Hebrew, Greeke, Latine, or French. &c. With the interpretation thereof by plaine English words, gathered for the benefit & helpe of Ladies, Gentlewomen, or any other vnskilfull persons' (Robert Cawdrey, subtitle to *A Table Alphabeticall*, 1604, the first English dictionary); 'A considerable body of information—central to the idea of plain English and derived from empirical research—has shown how a plain-English document stands out in sharp contrast to a fancy or rhetorical document' (James T. Dayananda, 'Plain English in the United States', *English Today* 5, Jan. 1986). (2) Blunt, no-nonsense language: 'If we double the thickness, the outside will be but one twenty-fifth as useful, or in plain English, nearly useless' (US government report, 1868). (3) Strong or foul language: 'With Princess Anne, who was apt to express herself in plain English when she found herself upside down in a water jump surrounded by clicking Nikons, there were some explosions' (Profile, *Observer*, 3 Sept. 1989). (4) In the later 20c, a term closely associated with an at-first diffuse but increasingly focused international movement against overly complex and mislead-ing, especially bureaucratic, usage: 'Award win-ners for plain English included the Association of British Insurers for the booklet "About insur-ance—some key facts"' (*Plain English Cam-paign Magazine* 26, June 1989).

Historical background. In the 17-18c, the British middle and upper classes generally favoured an ornate style of language, but towards the end of the 18c, as the Romantic movement and the Industrial Revolution gained momentum, this 'Augustan' style was modified by two concerns: for Wordsworth's 'language really used by men' and a general style that was serviceable rather than ornamental. Even so, however, English prose generally continued to be highly Latinate and often difficult and intimidating for people who, though they could read and write, had received little more than a basic education. For this and other reasons, purists and revivalists such as the dialectologist William Barnes advoc-ated the use of a more native or Germanic English, arguing for such words as *fore-elders* instead of *ancestors* and *birdstow* rather than *avi-ary*. This approach did not, however, necessarily

make usage clearer, because many Saxonisms, such as *hearsomeness* for *obedience*, were as difficult to learn and use as their classical equi-valents. A late form of purism or nativism found expression in the 1920s in C. K. Ogden's *Basic English*, which was intended to embody the vir-tues of plain usage; its vocabulary of 850 words is very largely Germanic. In the later 20c, however, advocates of a plainer English have not proposed the native rather than the Latinate, but rather avoiding any usage, whatever its source or inspiration, that confuses and misleads read-ers or listeners; the demonology of the plain Eng-lish movements includes such opponents as *bafflegab*, *gobbledygook*, *doublespeak*, and *psychobabble*.

Plain English movements. In recent decades there have been significant campaigns promoting plain English in both the UK and the US, with similar but smaller movements in Australia and Canada. The term *plain English campaign* (with the definite article) covers all drives towards the use of simpler language, especially in official, legal, and commercial writing (as in forms, con-tracts, business letters, and descriptions of prod-ucts) and medical usage (including labels on medicinal products). In the UK, campaigning tends to be from the bottom up, a grass-roots activism with some official support; in the US, it tends to be from the top down, especially government-initiated moves with popular approval. The name *Plain English Campaign* or *PEC* (without the definite article) stands for a pressure group in the UK that campaigns for plain English while also offering commercial and other services that help sustain its momentum and funds. These services provide a means through which government, business, and indi-viduals can obtain help in writing and checking plain-English texts (including forms and leaflets for public use) and document design that makes the transmission of information easier.

PEC was founded in 1974 by two campaigners in Liverpool. Chrissie Maher did not learn to read and write until she was 17, but once she had done so founded a community newspaper in 1971 to campaign for improved housing and amenities in the part of the city in which she was brought up. Martin Cutts studied psychology, English, and Italian at the U. of Liverpool and became a freelance journalist. Together, they edited *Liverpool News* (1974-6), a monthly news-paper for adults with reading difficulties, and in 1979 launched the Campaign with a public shredding of official forms in Parliament Square, London. PEC has since become, especially as a result of media interest, a national institution with considerable influence. In 1986, the found-ers reported: 'Today it is difficult to find a truly atrocious British government form being issued to the public. OUT are the acres of grey small print, the 60-word sentences, the endless use of that bureaucratic knee jerk, the passive verb. IN are forms that look good, read well, and even *save* money through their greater efficiency' (in Maher & Cutts, 'Plain English in the United Kingdom', *English Today* 5, Jan. 1986). In 1989, sponsored by the Midland Bank, PEC published *The Plain English Course*, a package of materials with which training officers in any organization might teach their staff how to write plain English. Currently, Maher directs PEC and Cutts runs *Words at Work*, one of whose proposals is a 12-point *Charter for Clear Legal English*.

In the US, plain-English initiatives have included: (1) In 1978, President Jimmy Carter's Executive Order No. 12044, that required regulations to be written in plain English (revoked in 1981 by President Ronald Reagan's Executive Order 12291). (2) In 1980, Secretary of Commerce Malcolm Baldridge's memo to staff requiring the use of plain English. (3) The *Document Design Center* in Washington, DC, created by the National Institute of Education, a federal research agency, to conduct research and training in the writing of simplified and well-designed documents, and to provide technical assistance on such matters. Publications by the Center include *Simply Stated*, a monthly newsletter on plain-English laws and document design (first issue, Nov. 1979), and *Guidelines for Document Design* (1981). (4) In 1978, a New York state law requiring that business contracts be written in plain language (since matched by a number of other states). (5) In 1983, a forum on the profitability of plain English sponsored by the Department of Commerce, its proceedings summarized in the brochure *Productivity of Plain English*. Participants in the forum set up the *Plain English Forum* (*PEF*), a group whose concern for promoting clear usage has included conducting 'plain English audits' for businesses and organizations.

Awards and endorsements. In the US, the Doublespeak Committee of the NCTE (National Council of Teachers of English) offers annual *Doublespeak Awards*, ironic tributes focusing on unsatisfactory and evasive language, especially as used by government (first awards, 1974). In the UK, PEC and the National Consumer Council present annual awards both to encourage organizations that have met their standards in the use of plain English and to draw critical attention to some that have not, by means of *Golden Bull Awards* for particularly unsatisfactory texts (first awards, 1982). PEC has also launched a scheme through which

organizations can seek an endorsement of the language and design used in their documents. This takes the form of the *Crystal Mark*, a logo-like symbol displayed on leaflets, products, and the like: 'The presence of the Crystal Mark shows that, in the opinion of Plain English Campaign, the document has reached a high standard of clarity in its language and layout. The Crystal Mark tells readers that the clarity of the document has been carefully examined by outside experts' (PEC leaflet, 1990).

See AUGUSTAN, BASIC ENGLISH, DOUBLESPEAK AWARD, LEGAL USAGE, ENGLISH, LEXICAL BAR, PASSIVE (VOICE), PLAIN, PLAIN LANGUAGE, PURISM, SAXONISM, STYLE CHECKER. [AMERICAS, EUROPE, MEDIA, STYLE, VARIETY, WRITING].   T.MCA.

Cutts, Martin, & Maher, Chrissie. 1986. *The Plain English Story*. Stockport, England: Plain English Campaign.

Gowers, Sir Ernest. 1954. *The Complete Plain Words*. London: H. M. Stationery Office. Pelican edition 1962. 2nd edition 1973. 3rd edition 1986, revised by Sidney Greenbaum & Janet Whitcut. Penguin edition 1987.

Roberts, Philip Davies. 1987. *Plain English: A User's Guide*. Harmondsworth: Penguin.

PLAIN LANGUAGE (1) Usage without social pretensions, overly complex structures, and such actual or supposed frills as poetic flourishes, foreignisms, and technical jargon: 'The mandate of the Joint Committee was to assess the use of English and French plain language in the legal profession' (Resolution M-08-91 on Plain Language Documentation, Canadian Bar Association, Feb. 1991). (2) Plain English: *Drafting Documents in Plain Language* (title of book published by the US Practising Law Institute, 1980). (3) The usage of the Protestant denomination known as the Quakers or Society of Friends (founded in the 17c), which favoured the use of *thou* and *thee* long after it ceased to be part of mainstream English, and referred to days of the week and months of the year as *First*, *Second*, etc., rather than the pagan *Monday*, *Tuesday* and *January*, *February*, etc. See PLAIN, PLAIN ENGLISH. [STYLE].   T.MCA.

PLAINTEXT, PLAIN TEXT. See CRYPTOGRAPHY.

PLAIN WORDS. See COMPLETE PLAIN WORDS, PLAIN.

PLANTATION SOUTHERN. See SOUTHERN ENGLISH.

PLATEN [15c: from Old French *platine* a chalice cover]. (1) A flat plate in a printing press for pressing the paper against the inked type or surface, to produce an impression. (2) A rotating cylinder used for the same purpose. (3) The roller of a typewriter, over which the paper passes and against which the keys strike. See PRINTING PRESS. [TECHNOLOGY].   T.MCA.

PLATITUDE [1800s: from French]. A commonplace statement or remark, especially if presented as though newly minted or uttered with an air of solemnity, as in 'I've said it before and no doubt I'll say it again: *There is no smoke without fire.* Someone who often 'mouths' platitudes is a *platitudinarian.* Compare CLICHÉ, PROVERB, TRITE. [STYLE].   T.MCA.

PLAY [From Old English *plega*]. (1) Light, free, and brisk movement (*sword play*; *a play of muscles*); space to move in (*an inch or more of play*); activity related to ideas, etc. (*a play of fancy*); exercise, sport, fun, pleasure, etc. (*children at play*; *word-play*; a play on words). (2) A dramatic composition written for performance in a theatre, on radio, and on television. During the 16–18c, the now archaic term *player* was a common synonym for *actor*. See DRAMA, PLAYING WITH WORDS, PUN, THEATRE/THEATER. [LITERATURE, MEDIA].   T.MCA.

PLAYING WITH WORDS, also **word-play**. Any adaptation or use of words to achieve a humorous, ironic, satirical, dramatic, critical, or other effect. Whereas a play *on* words is a pun, playing *with* words is verbal wit or dexterity at large and includes puns. One may play with the sound, spelling, form, grammar, and many other aspects of words: (1) *Sound.* 'Oh why can they not be made to see that all they have found is another man? A fellow man. A yellow man. A Jell-O man. A hollow man . . .' (Colleen McCullough, *A Creed for the Third Millennium*, 1985), alluding to T. S. Eliot's religious poem 'The Hollow Men' (1925). (2) *Spelling.* In 1653, Isaak Walton published *The Compleat Angler*, 'compleat' being his normal spelling for 'complete'. In 1987, Valerie Grove published *The Compleat Woman*, echoing Walton. In a review, Carol Rumens noted: 'Depicted on the back-jacket with her brood of four, Valerie Grove is clearly on her way to becoming compleat in her own right' (*Observer*, 18 Oct. 1987). (3) *Form.* Writing for the *New York Times* in 1988, William Safire referred to advertising usage as 'the work of the copywrongers . . . copywriters who make mistakes in grammar on purpose'. (4) *Grammar.* The British reference book *Who's Who* (founded 1849) contains biographies of 'people of influence and interest in all fields'. Its sister publication, *Who Was Who*, records the deceased. In 1987, a publisher brought out *Who's Had Who*, discussing known and alleged sexual relations

among the famous. (5) *All of language.* In *Ulysses* (1922), Joyce employs such expressions as *Lawn Tennyson, gentleman poet*, and *a base barreltone voice*. In *Finnegans Wake* (1939) he has *the hanging garments of Marylebone* and *all moanday, tearsday, wailsday, thumpsday, frightday, shatterday.* See BLEND, HUMO(U)R, NONCE WORD, NONSENSE, PLAY, PUN, TECHNOSPEAK, TIMESPEAK. [STYLE, WORD].   T.MCA.

PLAY ON WORDS. See PLAY, PLAYING WITH WORDS, PUN.

PLEONASM [16c: from Latin *pleonasmus*, Greek *pleonasmós* ('more-ness') excess, redundancy]. A traditional term for the use of more words than necessary, either for effect or more usually as a fault of style, and any instance of that use, as in: *Could you repeat that again?* rather than *Could you say that again?* or *Could you repeat that?*; *They both got one each* rather than *They both got one* or *They got one each*; *That's a more superior product* (*superior* already denotes 'more'); *It's a really new innovation* (an *innovation* is already *new*). Some common pleonasms attract little comment, such as *free gift* (gifts are by definition free) and *plans for the future* (plans cannot be about the present or past). Many famous writers have been pleonastic, including Shakespeare's double superlative 'The most unkindest cut of all' (*Macbeth*). See CIRCUMLOCUTION, PERIPHRASIS, REDUNDANCY, TAUTOLOGY. [STYLE].   T.MCA.

PLOSIVE [Early 20c: clipped from *explosive*, from Latin *explodere/explosum* to release with a noise like a clap]. In phonetics, a stop consonant that is released quickly, with a brief explosive sound known as a *release burst*. English voiceless plosives, such as /p, t, k/, are often followed by aspiration, particularly in IrE. The process is known as *plosion.* See ARTICULATION, CONSONANT. [SPEECH].   G.K., T.MCA.

PLOT [17c in this sense]. The narrative element in fiction and drama, whether in prose or verse. A plot is distinguished from a *story* by the causal quality which links episodes, reveals significances, and reaches a planned conclusion. The time sequence may be broken by a *flashback* to events preceding the narrative, or by glimpses of the future (sometimes called a *flashforward*), a device used by William Faulkner (1897-1962). A plot may be tightly structured, every detail contributing to the whole, as in classical Greek tragedy and the novels of Henry James (1843-1916), loosely structured, with some episodes not fully integrated (as in early Tudor comedy and the proto-novels of Aphra Behn and Daniel Defoe), or complex in structure, with two or more stories interacting while following their own course as plot and *sub-plot* (as in Elizabethan and Jacobean drama, 19c novels like Dickens's *Bleak House*, 1852-3, and George Eliot's *Middlemarch*, 1871-2). In the 20c, dramatists connected with Expressionism and the theatre of the absurd have rejected formal plot structure, in favour of an inconsequential series of episodes, emphasizing the non-logical world which they depict.

The classical theory of plot was based on Aristotle's study of *mythos* in his *Poetics*. He emphasized unity of action, requiring a single, continuous story with beginning, middle, and end. In the plot of dramatic tragedy, he identified *peripeteia* (the reversal of the protagonist's fortunes, usually from good to bad), *anagnorisis* (recognition of a change or of the real relationships among people, such as the revealing of a blood relationship), and *catastrophe* (final downfall or suffering, such as punishment for a transgression). A more recent influence on theory was the 'pyramid' of the German critic Gustav Freytag (1816-95), who in his *Technique of the Drama* saw the plot of a five-act play as a pyramidal shape with action rising to a climax and falling away (designated *introduction, complication, climax, resolution, catastrophe*). Although Freytag's stages can be precisely applicable to only a comparatively few plays, they can be useful descriptive terms for the analysis of the novel as well as drama.

In the 20c, there has been much interest in *narratology*, the study of the process by which a story becomes a plot. The Chicago Critics of the 1930s favoured a neo-Aristotelian approach; the Russian Formalists distinguished *fabula*, the simple chronological narrative, from *syuzhet*, the material organized into shape by a narrator; and the Structuralists examined plots as conventions for storytelling and tried to classify them on a linguistic model. The linguistic approach shows that plot cannot be separated from other elements in the text. Character and plot are connected: the responses and relationships of characters affect the course of the narrative and the demands of the plot direct the characters' fortunes. E. M. Forster, in *Aspects of the Novel* (1927), saw tension between plot and character with the result that 'nearly all novels are feeble at the end'. In novels and plays with a strong element of suspense and a mystery to be solved, character may indeed be subordinated to plot, with excessive use of coincidence and facts withheld from the reader. In general, however, plot criticism is an integrated part of textual study. See ANACHRONY, NARRATIVE, NOVEL, STORY, STORY LINE. [LITERATURE, WRITING].   R.C.

PLUMMY [18c]. (1) Full of or like plums. (2) A mainly 19c slang term for 'rich and desirable': *a plummy situation*. (3) An informal pejorative term for speech (especially the BrE accent known as 'advanced RP') considered to have a fruity, self-satisfied, and affected quality: 'It doesn't take a lexicographer's ear to notice that BBC English sounds less proper and plummy than it once did' (Vivian Ducat, 'Words from the Wise', *The Atlantic Monthly*, Sept. 1986); 'All India Radio—modelled on the BBC, even down to the plummy accents of its announcers' (*Daily Telegraph*, 1 Sept. 1970). See ADVANCED, (A)ESTHETICS, BBC ENGLISH[1]. Compare FRUITY. [SPEECH].   T.MCA.

PLUPERFECT [16c: from Latin *pluperfectum*, a syncopation of *plus quam perfectum* more than perfect]. A traditional term for the past perfect tense: *had come* in *Aren't they here? I thought they had come*. See PERFECT. [GRAMMAR].   S.G.

PLURAL [14c: from Old French *plurel*, from Latin *pluralis*, an adjective from *plus* more]. A term contrasting with *singular* (and *dual*) in the number system of a language. In English, it refers to 'more than one' (*one and a half hours*) as well as 'two or more' (*five hours*). Where there is a contrast with dual words such as *both* and *neither*, plurals refer to a minimum of three: *all her brothers*, *any of her brothers*, and *none of her brothers* entail that she has at least three. The word *every*, though it takes singular concord, also implies three or more. Although the principles for forming plurals in English are relatively simple, the history of the language has led to some complications.

Pronunciation. (1) The majority of countable nouns make their plurals by adding -s to the singular, except words ending in a sibilant, which add -es unless there is already an e in the spelling: *buses, ditches, wishes*; *bases, garages, judges*. The spelling -es is generally pronounced like *iz*, but the -s ending is pronounced in two different ways: usually an s-sound after a voiceless sound (*taps, cats, locks*), but a z-sound if the preceding sound is voiced (*tabs, cads, logs, boys, lines*). (2) Nouns ending in a consonant plus *y* usually change the *y* to *i*, and add -es (*mysteries, parties*), but proper nouns may retain the letter *y* (*the Henrys*; *the two Germanys*: but compare *the two Maries, the Ptolemies*) as do compounds with -by (*lay-bys, stand-bys*). (3) Some nouns ending in -o and generally of foreign origin simply add s (*photos, radios*), but others have -es (*heroes, zeroes*), and some have either (*mosquitos/mosquitoes*). (4) Nouns written with a final *f* or *fe* take regular or weak plurals (*cliffs*), irregular or strong plurals (*halves, knives*), or either (*dwarfs/dwarves, hoofs/hooves, scarfs/scarves*).

Compounds. Most compound nouns form their plurals in the usual way (*boyfriends, crime reporters, sit-ins*), but some pluralize both elements (*women pilots*). In traditional and rather formal usage, some pluralize the first element (*runners-up, courts martial, brothers-in-law*), but often they have a more colloquial alternative (*runner-ups, court martials, brother-in-laws*).

Place-names. Most place names ending in -*s* are singular: *Athens, Paris, Naples, the Thames, Wales.* Even names of countries which appear plural normally take singular concord (*The Netherlands/the United States is . . .*), although plural concord is possible if the meaning is, for example, a national or other comparable sports team (*The Netherlands are playing well*). However, mountain ranges and groups of islands are normally plural only: *the Himalayas/the Hebrides are . . .*

Plural-only usages. (1) Some plural nouns in -*s* have no singular form: *clothes, remains, thanks.* (2) Other plural-only words may appear to have singular forms, but these are either part of a singular/plural countable pair with a different meaning (plural only for *arms* meaning weapons, *arm/arms* for the parts of the body) or the singular form is an uncountable noun with a different meaning (*£500,000 damages* compared with *storm damage*). (3) Some words referring to tools and clothes with two parts are plural only (*scissors, tights*). The normal way of counting them is *a pair of scissors, two pairs of trousers*, etc.

Words ending in -s. (1) Although some singular words ending in -*s* add -*es* for plural (*buses, businesses*), others have the same form in both singular and plural: (BrE) *an innings, two innings* (compare AmE *an inning*), and *means* in *every means in my power, by all means, by no means.* (2) Some uncountable nouns end in -*s*, the best-known of which is *news.* Others include names of games (*billiards, bowls*) and words for subjects and sciences with an -*ics* ending (*mathematics, physics, politics*). (3) Some -*ics* words are singular or plural according to sense (*Economics is an arid subject; What are the economics of buying a house in Spain?*), while others give rise to uncertainty: *Metaphysics is/are too difficult for me.* In some cases, a singular may have been back-formed from the -*ics* form: *a statistic*, from *statistics.* (4) Diseases can give rise to doubt: *Measles is/are nasty; I had it/them as a child.* The feeling that an -*s* ending means a plural is strong, and even such countable nouns as *crossroads, headquarters, golf links* may be followed by a plural verb when the reference is to a single place: *The headquarters is/are in London.*

Other plural forms. (1) From Old English: *child/children, ox/oxen, man/men, woman/women,* *foot/feet, tooth/teeth, goose/geese, louse/lice, mouse/mice, penny/pence.* (2) 'zero' plurals (mainly with the names of animals) where singular and plural are the same: *one sheep/twenty sheep; a deer/some deer; a salmon/several salmon.* In the usage of hunters, the names of animals, birds, and fish are often singular in form: *went shooting lion; shot three buffalo.* The word *fish* has two plurals, one unchanged (*hundreds of dead fish*) and with a collective implication, the other regular (*lots of little fishes*) and implying individuals together. Zero plurals are common with measurements: *She only weighs 98 pound(s), though she is 5 foot/feet 5 inches; I'll take three dozen.* (3) Some plural-only words such as *cattle, clergy, people* (a plural of *person*, alongside *persons*), and *police.* (4) Some foreign plurals, such as *formulae, kibbutzim, mujahedin, phenomena,* and *radii.* The plural of French words ending in -*eau* may be written with an -*x* or an English -*s*: *chateaux, bureaus. Graffiti* is an Italian plural, but the singular *graffito* is rarely used in English.

Classical plurals. Latin plurals in English are: -*i* for words ending in the masculine inflection -*us* (*stimulus/stimuli*); -*ae* for singular words ending in feminine -*a* (*larva/larvae*); -*a* for words ending in neuter -*um* (*bacterium/bacteria*); -*ces* for words ending in -*x* (*appendix/appendices*). Greek plurals in English are: -*a* for words ending in neuter -*on* (*criterion/criteria*); and -*es* for words ending in -*is* (*analysis/analyses*). The situation with words of Latin and Greek origin which have kept their inflected nominative endings (*formula, memorandum, radius*) is complex and falls into three types: (1) With fully Anglicized plurals: *bonuses, rhinoceroses.* (2) Generally with classical plurals: *synthesis/syntheses, radius/radii, stimulus/stimuli.* (3) With two plurals, the classical for formal contexts and specialized meanings, the vernacular for informal and general use: *appendix* with *appendices* and *appendixes; cactus* with *cacti* and *cactuses; formula* with *formulae* and *formulas; referendum* with *referenda* and *referendums.* There is widespread uncertainty about words ending in -*a*, which may represent a Latin singular or plural or a Greek plural. In terms of their origin, Latin *agenda, data, media, strata* and Greek *criteria, phenomena* are plurals, but have to some extent been reclassified in English. In this matter, however, acceptability varies. *Data* is often an uncountable noun (*There isn't much data*), but use of *criteria, media* (press and television), *phenomena, strata* (level of society) as singular nouns is often stigmatized. See CLASSICAL ENDING, ENDING, S. [GRAMMAR, NAME]. S.C.

POCKET OXFORD DICTIONARY, The. See AUSTRALIAN DICTIONARIES, NEW ZEALAND DICTIONARIES, OXFORD DICTIONARIES, SOUTH AFRICAN ENGLISH DICTIONARIES.

POET [13c: from Latin *poeta*, Greek *poiētēs* a maker]. Someone who writes poetry. A contrast is often made between a *poet*, who writes verse regarded as high in quality, or at least adequate, and a *versifier*, whose work is thought not to merit the name *poetry*. The pejorative term *poetaster* (Greek: 'a poetling') has been in rare but continuous use since the 16c for someone considered even lower on the cultural ladder than a versifier. See MAKAR, POETICS, POET LAUREATE, POETRY, SEXISM, VERSE. [LITERATURE]. T.MCA.

POETIC DICTION. A term for a poetic style prevalent in the 18c and marked by some or all of the following features: fanciful epithets, such as *the finny tribe* for 'fish' and *feathered songsters* for 'birds'; stock adjectives and participles, as in *balmy breezes, purling brooks, honied flowers*; artificial and ornate usage, such as 'Hail, sister springs, / Parents of silver-footed rills' (Crashaw); classical references, such as 'Of Cerberus and blackest midnight born, in Stygian caves forlorn' (Milton); complex figures of speech, as in 'My love was begotten by Despair/ Upon Impossibility' (Marvell); archaism, as in 'and thither came the twain' (Tennyson); sentimentality, such as 'Absent from thee, I languish still' (Wilmot); unusual word order, such as 'This noble youth to madness loved a dame / Of high degree' (Dryden). The view that because poetry and prose have distinct conventions they should also have distinct styles and usages was favoured well into the 18c. In 1742, Thomas Gray wrote that 'the language of the age is never the language of poetry', a view challenged by Wordsworth (Preface, *Lyrical Ballads*, 1798), who argued against 'what is usually called poetic diction'. He considered that there should be no significant difference between the language of poetry and that of everyday life. However, despite an increasing 19-20c tendency to use similar styles and usages in poetry and prose, poetic usage continues to be widely regarded as more rarefied or 'flowery' than most kinds of prose. See DICTION, POETRY, WORDSWORTH. [LITERATURE, STYLE]. T.MCA.

POETIC JUSTICE [1678: coined by Thomas Rymer in *The Tragedies of the Last Age Considered*, a critical attack on Elizabethan drama. The concept dates from ancient Greece and is literary and dramatic]. The view that good is (or should be) rewarded and evil is (or should be) punished, in both fiction and real life; retribution should be fitting and ironically satisfying, in the spirit of *hoist with one's own petard*. Much traditional drama and literature is didactic and moralistic, with the aim of elevating the reader, such as *The Golden Ass* of Apuleius in the 2c and Samuel Richardson's *Pamela, or Virtue Rewarded* in 1740. Although the concept of poetic justice was effectively attacked by the French poet Pierre Corneille in 1660 and by Joseph Addison in English in 1711 (*Spectator* 40), it remains a strong thread in literature, drama, and social attitude. The happy ending in many novels and films owes much to the doctrine. See IRONY. [LITERATURE]. T.MCA.

POETIC LICENCE BrE, **license** AmE [18c]. Sometimes **dramatic licence/license, literary licence/license**. The traditional practice among poets, dramatists, and others of departing from conventional rules of form, fact, realism, logic, and the presentation of truth, for the sake of the effect to be gained. Such licence may entail exaggeration, shifts or collapses in time, the blending of two or more real people into one fictional character, or attributing specific words to someone who never in fact used them. Devices of this kind are accepted as part of the armoury of the artist, but dubious ploys are sometimes criticized as licence in the sense of excessive freedom. See POETRY. [LITERATURE, STYLE]. T.MCA.

POETIC PROSE. Prose that exhibits characteristics widely associated with poetry, such as vivid imagery and marked rhythms. Some regard such prose as unsatisfactory and even flawed (because prose is not poetry, and should not take on its trappings); others see it as an often effective medium for heightened emotion. See DICKENS, POETRY, PROSE, PURPLE PATCH. [LITERATURE, STYLE, WRITING]. T.MCA.

POETICS [18c: from Greek *poiētikós* of verse, from *poíēsis* making, poetry]. The study of the principles of poetry, as exemplified in the traditional genres of lyric, epic, and drama. The term originates in the *Poetics*, a treatise by Aristotle (4c BC) that has survived in fragmentary form. This work dominated Western criticism for centuries and did much to shape Neoclassical ideas in the 17c and 18c. It is the source of the principle developed by later critics as *the (three) unities* (of time, place, and action) and of such concerns as *catharsis* (the purging of the emotions through drama), *hamartia* (a tragic flaw), *hubris* (overweening pride), *mimesis* (imitation), and *peripeteia* (reversal of circumstances). Since the Renaissance, some British critics have propounded general ideas about poetry that have been influential in their time. Significant works include Philip Sydney's *Apologie for Poetrie* (1595), John Dryden's *Of Dramatick Poesie* (1668), William Wordsworth's

Preface to *Lyrical Ballads* (1801), and Percy Bysshe Shelley's *Defence of Poetry* (1821). In the 20c, I. A. Richards's *Principles of Literary Criticism* (1924) gave close attention to the process of reading, which has become a fundamental emphasis of modern theory.

The Russian Formalists, examining the specific techniques of literary language, sought a scientific basis for poetics in place of the traditional subjective aesthetic approach. The most influential 20c work has been done by critics who have tried to apply contemporary linguistic theories to literature and to 'construct a poetics which stands to literature as literature stands to language' (Jonathan Culler, *Structuralist Poetics*, 1975). The term *poetics* has been extended to cover all literary genres and in principle the search has been for a general theory of literature and not of poetry alone; in practice, the application has usually been to a specific genre. Structural linguistics, derived from a restatement of the work of the linguist Ferdinand de Saussure, is the foundation of much present-day work on poetics. In Saussurean terms, the concern of poetics with the method rather than the content of literary texts favours the *signifier* (that which serves as a sign) over the *signified* (that which is represented by a sign).

Roman Jakobson propounded a theory of *literariness* based on the occurrence of repetition, parallelism, and equivalence in texts. He also studied the formal patterning of sounds and prosodic features in his search for a general theory of poetry, sometimes proceeding through specific texts, as in his controversial close analysis of Shakespeare's Sonnet 129. Noam Chomsky's theory of grammar, which includes the *competence/performance* distinction, has been made the foundation for a *generative poetics*, in which it is suggested that the informed reader possesses a kind of *literary competence*, a sense of literary universals which makes the specific text accessible and allows detection of what is unacceptably 'deviant'. There has also been much interest in narrative structure; the work of the Formalist Vladimir Propp (*The Morphology of the Folk Tale*, 1928) was revised by Claude Lévi-Strauss and then by A. J. Greimas in the light of structuralist theory. Tzvetan Todorov's *Grammaire de Décaméron* (1969), although referring to a specific text, was intended as an attempt to create a *narratology* or science of narrative. In the latter part of the 20c, the tendency of literary criticism has been towards general theory and the formulation of an approach applicable to any text, poetry or prose.

See (A)ESTHETICS, CATHARSIS, CHOMSKY, COMPETENCE AND PERFORMANCE, DEVIANT, DRAMA, EPIC, GENRE, HAMARTIA, HUBRIS, LITERARY CRITICISM, LITERATURE, LYRIC, MIMESIS, PLOT, POETRY, STRUCTURALISM, STYLISTICS, TEXT, TRAGEDY, UNIVERSAL. [LITERATURE].   R.C.

POET LAUREATE [14c in the sense of 'acclaimed poet']. The official term for a poet appointed by the British Crown as an officer of the Royal Household, and for the appointment itself. *Laureate* refers to the classical custom of crowning a poet with a wreath of laurel. John Skelton was created such a laureate by the universities of Oxford (1490), Cambridge (1493), and Louvain (*c*.1491). Ben Jonson received a pension from James I, and William D'Avenant from Charles I, but John Dryden was the first to be called Poet Laureate. His successors include William Wordsworth (1770-1850) and Alfred, Lord Tennyson (1809-92). The Poet Laureate was once expected to write odes for the New Year and the sovereign's birthday; this duty was removed under George IV (1820), but Poets Laureate have generally continued to celebrate the principal royal and national occasions. Ted Hughes (b.1930) became Poet Laureate on the death of John Betjeman (1906-84). [EUROPE, LITERATURE].   R.C.

POETRY [14c: from Latin *poetria* the art of the poet, from Greek *poiētḗs* a maker]. Literary composition in verse form. It is often the case that to discuss a piece of work as poetry implies evaluating its quality, while to discuss it as verse relates to technique used in creating it. The terms, however, are blurred: the phrase *bad poetry* may refer to technique and the phrase *superb verse* may imply poetic excellence. In general, however, verse is the basis that supports a structure of sufficient quality to be called a poem.

The poetic medium. Poetry need not be written: early poetry was oral, transmitted and preserved through the mnemonic and performative skills of bards with no awareness of script or print. The written code accommodates poetry and adds the aesthetic effect of lines grouped on a page, or even of poems shaped in a visual pattern, like George Herbert's 'Easter Wings'. Other phonic features are added to the basic metrical pattern of verse, with or without rhyme. Thus, the sound of words may be directly onomatopoeic or may give a less overt effect of sound symbolism. Both are heard in Tennyson's 'Come Down, O Maid' (1847):

> The moan of doves in immemorial elms
> And murmuring of innumerable bees.

Slow or rapid movement can be suggested by a deliberate pattern of sounds and syllables as in Alexander Pope's *Essay on Criticism* (1711):

> When Ajax strives some rock's vast weight to throw,
> The line too labours, and the words move slow;

Not so, when swift Camilla scours the plain,
Flies o'er th'unbending corn, and skims along the main.

Alliteration is not a part of most modern verse structure, but has a tradition dating back to Old English. Many poets have made it a feature for rhetoric or emphasis. Imagery in poetry conveys ideas obliquely, drawing from almost any area of human experience to create a response more effective than direct exposition. Shakespeare makes frequent references to disease and corruption in *Hamlet* to suggest evil in the state of Denmark. In 'Dover Beach', Matthew Arnold likens his uncertainty and loss of faith to an ebbing tide. Images are often presented through figures of speech like simile and metaphor. These are also found in prose and to a lesser extent in everyday discourse. They are especially distinctive of poetry, however, because of their frequency and the stronger focus of attention given by verse forms.

The poetic message. The appeal of poetry is semantic as well as phonic. The poet has something to convey in language, which may range from the half-concealed situation in many of Shakespeare's sonnets, through Wordsworth's specific description and reflection of experience in 'The Daffodils', to the overt message of the 'Song of the Shirt' by Thomas Hood. In general, the poem gains by not being too explicit in its personal statement. The meanings and associations of a word may not be in harmony with its sound: although *paraffin* contains a pleasing phonemic sequence, it would not usually be regarded as a 'poetic' word; *equilibrium* refers to a good state of being but has not a traditional poetic sound. Polysemy, abundant in English, enriches poetic language, as when T. S. Eliot uses the theological and linguistic meanings of *word* to write of Christ in his nativity as:

The word within a word, unable to speak a word.
('Gerontion', 1920)

The pun is not currently in fashion for serious writing, but could once be used with telling effect:

Therefore I lie with her, and she with me,
And in our faults by lies we flattered be.
(Shakespeare, Sonnet 138)

The language of poetry. Concentration of special linguistic effects in a regular pattern tends to produce artificial diction. Rigid conventions about poetic usage have been less powerful in English than in some languages, but there have been times when poets have moved away from the familiar and everyday: particularly so in the 18c, with circumlocutions like *the finny tribe* for *fish* and *the bleating kind* for *sheep*. New generations of poets often demand a return to 'ordinary' language, as Wordsworth led the

Romantic reaction against 18c poetic diction with a call for 'a selection of the real language of men in a state of vivid sensation'. In the 1930s, the 'New Country' poets, such as W. H. Auden, Stephen Spender, and Cecil Day Lewis, wanted to write language that was accessible to ordinary people.

In the 20c, language has been accepted in poetry that would once have been considered too colloquial, commonplace, or even obscene, but this too can become mannered and removed from common usage. Poetry will always be to some extent artificial; selection and compression within the chosen form, even of free verse, distances the poem from daily usage. True poetry, however, is never entirely severed from the speaking voice; a certain latitude, however, sometimes called *poetic licence*, allows the poet to take liberties with language. In the classical set of genres, poetry was epic or lyric according to the degree in which the poet's direct voice was heard. Later theory has absorbed both genres under the general heading of poetry and added forms for specific purposes, such as elegy and pastoral. The frontier between poetry and prose is not always closely guarded or easy to delineate. If prose has a markedly high proportion of rhythm and other features associated with poetry, it is *poetic prose* or even *prose poetry*. An extended simile with imagery and careful choice of words can give poetic quality to a passage in a novel, as:

Her words faded. So a rocket fades. Its sparks, having grazed their way into the night, surrender to it, dark descends, pours over the outlines of houses and towers; bleak hill-sides soften and fall in.
(Virginia Woolf, *Mrs Dalloway*, 1925).

Some of the highest literary uses of English have been in poetry. Poets have wanted not only to create beauty but also to express themselves memorably; the attitudes, fashions, and beliefs of many periods are made permanent in poetry. It appeals to the senses as well as the intellect. Of the two, sensory attraction is the more important; without emotive beauty, versified philosophy has little to recommend it. Although a relatively objective metalanguage can be devised to describe and discuss poetry, individual response to it is necessarily subjective.

See ALEXANDRINE, ALLITERATION, ALLITERATIVE VERSE, AMPHIBRACH, ANAP(A)EST, ASSONANCE, BALLAD, BIBLE, BLANK VERSE, BOUTS-RIMÉS, BRIDGES, BURNS, BUSH BALLAD, C(A)ESURA, CANTO, CLERIHEW, COLERIDGE (S.), COMMUNICATIVE SHIFT, CONCRETE POETRY, COUPLET, DACTYL, DIRGE, DRYDEN, ELEGY, END-STOPPED LINE, ENGLISH LITERATURE, ENJAMB(E)MENT, EPIC, FEMININE ENDING, FOOT, FREE VERSE, GENRE, HALF RHYME, HYMN, IAMB, ICTUS, LANGUAGE, LIMERICK, LINE, LYRIC, MACARONIC, MAKAR, MASCULINE

ENDING, METRE/METER, MNEMONIC, MONODY, NARRATIVE POETRY, NONSENSE VERSE, ODE, PASTORAL, POET, POETIC JUSTICE, POETIC LICENCE, POETIC PROSE, POETICS, POET LAUREATE, POPE, PROSE, PROSODY, PUN, QUATRAIN, REFRAIN, RHYME, RHYTHM, SCANSION, SCOTT, SHAKESPEARE, SONG, SONNET, SPENSER, SPONDEE, SPRUNG RHYTHM, STANZA, STRESS, TERCET, THRENODY, TRIOLET, TRIPLET, TROCHEE, VERSE, WORDSWORTH. [LITERATURE].   R.C.

Adams, H. 1963. *The Contexts of Poetry.* London: Methuen.

Culler, J. 1975. *Structuralist Poetics.* London: Routledge & Kegan Paul.

Forrest-Thompson, V. 1978. *Poetic Artifice: A Theory of Twentieth-Century Poetry.* Manchester: University Press.

Hayden, J. O. 1983. *Inside Poetry Out: An Introduction to Poetry.* Chicago: Nelson-Hall.

Jones, R. T. 1986. *Studying Poetry.* London: Arnold.

Leech, Geoffrey N. 1969. *A Linguistic Guide to English Poetry.* London: Longman.

Levin, S. R. 1962. *Linguistic Structures in Poetry.* The Hague: Mouton.

Nowottny, Winifred. 1962. *The Language Poets Use.* London: Athlone Press.

Reeves, J. 1965. *Understanding Poetry.* London: Heinemann.

Riffaterre, M. 1978. *Semiotics of Poetry.* US: Indiana University Press. London: Methuen.

Skelton, R. 1971. *The Practice of Poetry.* London: Heinemann.

Williams, J. 1985. *Reading Poetry.* London: Arnold.

POINT [12c: from Old French, partly from *point* (a dot, mark, place, moment) and partly from *pointe* (a sharp end), both ultimately from Latin *pungere/punctum* (to prick, stab)]. (1) A sharp end to a blade, pencil, etc. (2) A moment (*At that point, she decided to leave*); a suggestion or recommendation, often one in a series (*He listed several points for discussion*). (3) The key element or moment in a story, argument, or joke: *He was interrupted so often he never got to the point*; *She just didn't get the point.* (4) The sign (.), in writing made with the point of a pen or pencil, known as a *period, full stop,* or *full point* when used to close a sentence that expresses a statement, including elliptical sentences and sentence fragments, as in: *They did not want to refuse. They didn't want to. On the contrary.* The point marks the close of, or elements in, many abbreviations (*Thurs., Gen., a.m., B.B.C.*) and follows initial letters, as with the *M* in *William M. Thackeray.* It is, however, increasingly omitted in initialisms (*BBC, GMT*), almost always omitted in acronyms (*Nato, yuppie*), and, especially in BrE, generally omitted in abbreviations such as *Mr* and *Dr.* A set of *ellipsis points* is used to mark gaps in writing, especially words omitted from a quotation, as in: 'All the business of war, and indeed all the business of life, is to endeavour to find out what you don't know' reduced to 'All the business of war . . . is to . . . find out what you don't know' (quoting the Duke of Wellington, *Croker Papers,* 1885). When such points are used to mark a pause, they are called *suspension points,* as in *Tell him, uh . . . to wait a moment.* (5) Also *decimal point.* The sign (.) or (·) used in decimal numbers, as in *2.22* or *2·22.* Compare the *decimal comma* in Continental European practice, as in *2,22.* (6) A periodic sentence. (7) In phonetics and orthography, a diacritical mark with various values: for example, in the modern transcription of Old English, sometimes placed above the letter *c* to indicate that it is pronounced 'ch' as in *church,* in such words as *ċild* (child) and *ċiriċe* (church). (8) One of the dots used in Braille and other systems of raised writing and printing for the blind. (9) A papermaker's term for a unit of measurement of the thickness of paper or card, equal to 0.001 of an inch. (10) A printer's term for the unit of measurement of type (0.0138 inches or 0.351 mm in the UK and US), first used as a standard (though of a slightly different size) in Continental Europe in the 18c, then in the English-speaking world at the end of the 19c. If type is set solid, with no extra spacing (*leading*) between the lines, it can be measured from the base of one line to the base of the next so as to get the size in points, such as *12-point Baskerville.* Typographic designers take account of the fact that different typefaces of the same *point size* will appear to be of different size when printed: for example, *11-point Bembo* is visually smaller than *11-point Times Roman.* See ABBREVIATION, ACRONYM, BRAILLE, DIACRITIC, DOT, ELLIPSIS, INITIAL, INITIALISM, PERIODIC SENTENCE, PUNCTUATION, SENTENCE, STOP, TYPOGRAPHY. [SPEECH, TECHNOLOGY, WRITING].   T.MCA., R.E.A., W.W.B.

POINT OF ARTICULATION. See SPEECH.

POINTS OF SUSPENSION. See ELLIPSIS, POINT.

POLARI, also **Palarie, Parlyaree, Parlary,** etc. [18c: from Italian *parlare* to talk]. A once-extensive argot or cant in Britain and elsewhere, among sailors, itinerants, people in show business (especially the theatre and circuses), and some homosexual groups. It survives as a vocabulary of around 100 words, some of which have entered general BrE slang: *mank(e)y* rotten, worthless, dirty (from Italian *mancare* to be lacking), *ponce* an effeminate man, pimp (from Spanish *pu(n)to* a male prostitute, or French *pront* prostitute), *scarper* to run away (probably from Italian *scappare* to escape, perhaps influenced by Cockney rhyming slang *Scapa Flow* go). A composite of different Romance sources, it was first taken to England by sailors, may derive ultimately from Lingua Franca, and has been called 'a secret language born out of oppression' (Peter Burton, in 'The Gentle Art of Confounding Naffs: Some Notes on Polari', *Gay News* 120, p. 23, 1979). A sample of present-day argot runs: 'As feely homies, we would zhoosh our riahs, powder our eeks, climb into our bona new drag, don our batts and troll off to some bona bijou bar' (Ian Hancock, 'Shelta and Polari', in P. Trudgill (ed.), *Language in the British Isles*, 1984) [*feely homies* young men, *zhoosh our riahs* fix our hair, *eeks* faces, *bona* nice, *drag* clothes, *batts* shoes, *troll* wander, *bijou* small]. See ARGOT, CANT, LINGO, LINGUA FRANCA. [EUROPE, STYLE, VARIETY]. T.MCA.

POLARITY [17c]. A term used in linguistics for the contrast between positive and negative in sentences, clauses, and phrases. [GRAMMAR].

S.G.

POLEMIC. [17c: from Latin *polemicus*, Greek *polemikós* warlike]. The art or practice of combative argument and controversy; a disputatious attack on the opinions, principles, beliefs, and reputation of a person or group. During the Middle Ages, the Renaissance, and the Reformation, polemical debate was primarily concerned with religious doctrine, theologians disputing in order to refute error. A leading polemic in English is John Milton's *Areopagitica* (1664), named after the Areopagus in ancient Athens, where debates were held. It is a speech against censorship, particularly of religious matter, and moves from an attack on the licensing of printed material to a plea for the freedom of speech, publishing, and ideas. See ARGUMENT, CENSORSHIP, DIALECTIC, DIATRIBE. [LITERATURE, STYLE].

T.MCA.

POLISH. See AMERICAN LANGUAGES, BORROWING, CANADIAN LANGUAGES, DIALECT IN AMERICA, INDO-EUROPEAN LANGUAGES, SLAVONIC LANGUAGES.

POLITE [15c: from Late Medieval Latin *politus* accomplished, refined, from *polire/politum* to polish]. (1) Showing good manners; civil: *a polite reply*. (2) (Often used of speech, usage, etc., especially 16–19c) refined, cultured, elegant: 'That they speke none englisshe but that which is cleane, polite, perfectly and articulately pronounced' (Sir Thomas Elyot, *The Governour*, 1531); 'Every polite tongue has its own rules' (Lyndley Murray, *English Grammar*, 5th edition, 1824). Compare CULTIVATED, EUPHEMISM, GENTEELISM, NICE-NELLYISM, REFINED. See (A)ESTHETICS. [STYLE]. T.MCA.

POLITICALLY CORRECT [c.1990]. Short forms *PC*, *P.C.* 'Marked by or adhering to a typically progressive orthodoxy on issues involving esp. race, gender, sexual affinity, or ecology' (*Random House Webster's College Dictionary*, 1991). The phrase is applied, especially pejoratively by conservative academics and journalists in the US, to the views and attitudes of those who publicly object to: (1) The use of terms that they consider overtly or covertly *sexist* (especially as used by men against women), *racist* (especially as used by whites against blacks), *ableist* (used against the physically or mentally impaired), *ageist* (used against any specific age group), *heightist* (especially as used against short people), etc. (2) Stereotyping, such as the assumption that women are generally less intelligent than men and blacks less intelligent than whites. (3) 'Inappropriately directed laughter', such as jokes at the expense of women, the disabled, homosexuals, and ethnic minorities. The abbreviation *PC* is also used as a term for people perceived as 'politically correct': ' "Community" is a rallying cry among PCs. They tend to use it. . . . as an all-purpose buzz word' (Mike Bygrave, 'Mind your Language', *Guardian Weekly*, 26 May 1991). Both the full and abbreviated terms often imply an aggressive intolerance on the part of PCs of views and facts that conflict with their 'progressive orthodoxy'. The Random House dictionary quoted above was accused by the reviewer Anne Hopkins ('Defining Womyn (and Others)', *Time*, 24 June 1991) of failing to 'protect English from the mindless assaults of the trendy' because its editors listed such usages as *chairpersonship*, *herstory*, *humankind*, and *womyn* alongside *chairmanship*, *history*, *mankind*, and *women*, thereby giving them, in the opinion of the reviewer, a respectability that they did not merit. Compare MULTICULTURALISM. See GENDER BIAS, RACISM, SEXISM, STEREOTYPE. [AMERICA, EDUCATION, STYLE]. T.MCA.

POLYGLOSSIA. See DIGLOSSIA.

POLYGLOT [17c: from Latin *polyglottus*, Greek *polúglōttos* many-tongued]. (1) Able to speak or write several languages; multilingual. (2) Containing, composed of, or based on several languages: *a polyglot Bible*. (3) Someone who is familiar with a number of languages. (4) A book, especially a Bible, with the same text in several languages. See -GLOT, LINGUAL, MONOGLOT, MULTILINGUALISM. [LANGUAGE]. T.MCA.

POLYNESIA [From Greek *Polunēsia* place of many islands]. A name for the island groups of the eastern and south-eastern Pacific Ocean, extending from New Zealand north to Hawaii and east to Easter Island. Compare MELANESIA, MICRONESIA. See BORROWING. [NAME, OCEANIA].

S.R.

POLYNESIAN LANGUAGES. See MALAYO-POLYNESIAN LANGUAGES.

POLYSEMY [1890s: from Neo-Latin *polysemia*, from Greek *polúsēmos* having many meanings]. Also **multiple meaning**. A term in linguistics for words or other items of language with two or more senses, such as *walk* in *The child started to walk* and *They live at 23 Cheyne Walk*. Such senses may be more or less distant from one another: *walk* (action), *walk* (street) are relatively close, but *crane* (bird), *crane* (machine) are much farther apart. It is generally agreed, however, that in each case only one word is being discussed, not two that happen to have the same form (to which the name *homonym* is given). Senses of the same word are seldom ambiguous in context, but the less specific the context, the greater the possibility of ambiguity: if someone who is looking at a picture says *What big cranes!*, it may not be immediately clear to someone who cannot see the picture whether the comment refers to birds or machines.

Polysemy and homonymy. There is an extensive grey area between the concepts of *polysemy* and *homonymy*. A word like *walk* is polysemous (*went walking, went for a walk, walk the dog, Cheyne Walk*), while a word like *bank* is homonymous between at least *bank* for money and *bank* of a river. Dictionaries usually put polysemous words with all their senses in one article and homonymous words in two or more articles, dividing each into senses and subsenses as appropriate. In doing this, lexicographers generally take the view that homonymy relates to different words whose forms have converged while polysemy relates to one word whose meanings have diverged or radiated. The way in which the dictionary has been organized may mean that words like *walk* and *crane* get a section each, or separate sections for their noun and verb uses. Although such decisions may be made for convenience of presentation, they have theoretical ramifications.

Polysemy in dictionaries. Just as homonyms like *bank*[1] and *bank*[2] are ordered in separate articles in dictionaries, so the separate senses are ordered inside an article. In the process of ordering, some senses may be treated as more distinct than others (technically, as lexemes), while others cluster as shades of meaning within one more or less delineated sense. The kinds of ordering include: (1) *Historical or etymological*, the older before the newer, a universal practice until the end of the 19c. (2) *Frequency*, the common before the

rare, the primary criterion in many 20c dictionaries. (3) *Logico-semantic*, the general before the specialized and the literal before the figurative, or some pragmatic mix of these. In the case of *walk*, verb precedes noun, and physical movement precedes place; in the case of *crane*, history, logic, and semantics combine to place the bird-sense before the machine-sense. See HOMONYM, JANUS WORD, POETRY, RADIATION, SEMANTIC CHANGE, SEMANTICS, SENSE. [LANGUAGE, REFERENCE, WORD].

T.MCA.

POLYSYLLABLE [16c: from Latin *polysyllaba* (*vox*) (word) of many syllables, from Greek *polusúllabos* many-syllabled]. A word with many syllables. Although words in English that have many syllables derive from many sources, the term is used especially of longer words of Latin and Greek origin, such as *polysyllable* itself. See DISYLLABLE, LONG WORD, MONOSYLLABLE, SYLLABLE. [LANGUAGE, SPEECH, WORD].

T.MCA.

POLYSYNTHETIC. See SYNTHETIC.

POP [1860s: a clipping of *popular*]. An informal term for popular culture and entertainment, as in *pop art, pop culture, pop novel, pop song, pop music*, and for pop music itself, as in *listening to pop* and *pop concert*. Since the Second World War, English has played a leading role in the global enthusiasm for American-style pop music: 'English pervades rock music the world over. In September, 11 of the top 20 LP's in Japan had English titles. West German rock songs average 56 English words a tune. And earlier this year a punk group in Spain called Asfalto released a record on learning English; it became a hit. Rock singers usually give the same reasons for singing in English: "I grew up listening to Neil Sedaka and the Beatles," says Yukihiko Takegawa, lead singer for the Japanese group Godeigo. "English was lyrics to me before it was a language." English also sounds better, says Bjorn Ulvaneus of the Swedish group ABBA. The words are shorter, the accent is not on the last syllable and it rhymes easily. Still, says Polish disc jockey Wojciech Mann, only one singer in a hundred understands the lyrics. "They just keep blubbering it out," he says. "It's a miracle how English fits that kinds of music" ' ('English, English Everywhere', section 'Pop Culture', *Newsweek*, 15 Nov. 1982). See POP GRAMMARIAN, POPULAR. [STYLE, VARIETY].

T.MCA.

POPE, Alexander [1688-1714]. English poet, born in London in a Roman Catholic family, and brought up at Binfield in Windsor Forest. He received little formal education, but his reputation was established by the craftsmanship of his *Pastorals* (1709) and by *An Essay on Criticism* (1711), which showed a neo-classical respect for the critical judgements of the ancient world. He was drawn into the literary circle that centred on Joseph Addison, whom he later attacked as 'Atticus' in the *Epistle to Dr Arbuthnot* (1735). His translations of the *Iliad* (1715-20) and *Odyssey* (1725-6) were couched in heroic couplets, a form over which no poet has achieved greater mastery, and were widely admired. Pope had an acute ear for the evocative and onomatopoeic qualities of English:

'Tis not enough no harshness gives offence,
The sound must seem an Echo of the sense;
Soft is the strain when Zephyr gently blows,
And the smooth stream in smoother numbers flows;
But when loud surges lash the sounding shore,
The hoarse, rough verse should like the torrent roar
When Ajax strives some rock's vast weight to throw,
The line too labours, and the words move slow;
Not so, when swift Camilla scours the plain,
Flies o'er th'unbending corn, and skims along the main.

(*An Essay on Criticism*)

He used the same metre in the satires, which attacked some of the leading writers and critics of his time: for example, in the first volume of *The Dunciad* (1728), he ridicules the Shakespearian editor Theobald. The savagery of much of Pope's writing may be partly attributed to his chronic ill health. *An Essay on Man* (1733-4) is, however, a theistic justification of the essential goodness of the universe. See index. [BIOGRAPHY, EUROPE, LITERATURE, STYLE]. R.C.

POP GRAMMARIAN [Late 20c: a clipping of *popular grammarian*]. A term, especially common in the US and often pejorative, for a writer on the English language with a wide readership, especially in a newspaper column, who adopts a prescriptive approach to language usage. It is sometimes used in tandem with *usage guru*, a term for a writer who tends to pontificate on points of usage. See POP, POPULAR. [GRAMMAR, USAGE]. S.G., T.MCA.

POPULAR [14c: from Latin *popularis* of the people: compare VULGAR]. (1) Relating to the people of a community (*popular elections*, in which every adult can vote) or the mass of the people, excluding the more privileged, highly educated, or aesthetically 'discerning' (*popular entertainment*, entertainment for mass consumption). Such terms as *popular fiction*, *popular newspaper*, and *popular romance*, as used by scholars and others (often neutrally, sometimes with condescension, sometimes dismissively), to refer to reading matter intended for 'ordinary' people, and therefore of a non-literary or sub-literary nature. In its positive sense, however, the term signals an interest in broadening the educated base of a community, as in such magazine titles as *Popular Science Monthly*. (2) Widely liked or approved: *a popular decision*. The second sense is commoner, and often impinges on the first, suggesting for example that popular elections are widely enjoyed. See POP, POP GRAMMARIAN, POPULAR FICTION. Compare FOLK. [EDUCATION, LANGUAGE, STYLE]. T.MCA.

POPULAR ETYMOLOGY. See FOLK ETYMOLOGY.

POPULAR FICTION Works of fiction written for popular consumption, and widely regarded by critics, teachers, and often the authors of such works themselves, either as without claims to being 'literature' or as a genre that cannot by its very nature aspire to the term: that is, the works are *sub-literary*. When the concept is seen as literary, however, the term *popular literature* is sometimes used instead (although for some the phrase may be seen as a contradiction in terms). In addition to such sub-genres as the *popular novel* and *popular romance*, such works have been associated in English since the 19c with a range of terms that usually distance them from the literary canon: for example, *dime novel* (AmE 1860s: a sensational and melodramatic adventure novel, usually a paperback, and sold for a dime), *penny dreadful* (BrE 1870s: such a novel sold for a penny), *shilling dreadful* or *shilling shocker* (BrE 1880s: a more substantial penny dreadful, sold for a shilling), *bestseller* (AmE 1880s: a high-selling book, often a popular novel), *thriller* (1880s: a novel, play, film, etc., that is full of excitement and suspense), *cliffhanger* (AmE 1930s: a melodramatic adventure series, in print or film, in which each instalment or chapter ends in suspense), *blockbuster* (1940s: an aerial bomb, then a book or film expected to have widespread and powerful appeal), *potboiler* (1860s: a run-of-the-mill work that sells steadily and was written to maintain a steady income), *bodice-ripper* or *bodice-buster* (later 20c: a Gothic novel or historical romance, usually paperback, with torrid scenes of sex and violence), and *airport novel* (1980s: a bestseller or blockbuster that sells in large quantities in airport bookshops).

Because works of fiction, popular or literary, usually have the same general features of style, structure, plot, and characterization, it is often difficult (if not impossible) to draw a firm line between the two. Rather than maintain the division between a 'higher' level of literary classics and a 'lower' level of ephemeral, popular works, some scholars regard all fictional genres as one, pointing to the fact that some works that are currently considered classics, such as the novels of Dickens, were once published in popular form, to popular acclaim, and for many years were not endorsed by the critical establishment. Unarguably, popular literature is more 'popular' in the sense of being more widely enjoyed and read than most classics: 'Surveys by Peter Man of Sheffield University show how little English "literature" plays a part in the lives of even the educated British public. . . . In light reading, crime novels, thrillers, westerns and romances dominate, as would be expected. Favourite authors include Alistair Maclean, Agatha Christie, James Herriot, Dennis Wheatley, Barbara Cartland, Hammond Innes and Jean Plaidy. Popular reading tastes rarely coincide with the established canon of what constitutes "literature". This can be gauged by the fact that the last four authors named do not even get a mention in Robin Myers' *A Dictionary of Literature in the English Language from Chaucer to 1940* (volume I) *and 1940-1970* (volume II), Pergamon. These volumes together list some 4,900 authors and 74,000 titles!' (Douglas Pickett, 'What is Literature—Established Canon or Popular Taste?', *English Today* 5, Jan. 1986). See DETECTIVE STORY, FICTION, NOVEL, POPULAR, ROMANCE, STORY. [LITERATURE].   T.MCA.

POPULAR PRESS. See NEWSPAPER.

PORTMANTEAU WORD. See BLEND.

PORTUGUESE [Called by its speakers *português*]. A Romance language of Western Europe, closely related to Spanish and the earliest of the major colonial languages originating in Europe. It is spoken by 135m people worldwide: in Europe, as the national language of Portugal (including the Azores and Madeira, islands in the Atlantic), with related Galician (*Gallego*), sometimes considered a dialect of Portuguese, sometimes a distinct language, in north-western Spain; in the Americas, as the official language of Brazil; in Africa, as the official language of Angola, Cape Verde, Guinea-Bissau, Mozambique, and Saõ Tomé and Príncipe; in Asia, as the official language of the Portuguese colony of Macao, near Hong Kong, and in ex-colonial territories such as Goa in India and East Timor in the Indian Ocean. It is also spoken by immigrant communities in Canada, France, the US, and elsewhere, and has given rise to or influenced pidgins and creoles in many parts of the world, such as a Portuguese creole in Cape Verde and Papiamentu in the Netherlands Antilles. Like Spanish, it was influenced by Arabic during the centuries of Muslim dominance in the Iberian peninsula. Portuguese mariners in the 15c were the first Europeans to explore the Atlantic coast of Africa and take the passage to Asia around the Cape of Good Hope. Portuguese settlers played a significant part in colonizing the northern part of South America and adjacent parts of the Caribbean. Although Portugal is the oldest ally of England (since the 14c), the impact of Portuguese on English has been slight. Loanwords (some of them undergoing adaptation) include *albino, auto-da-fe, ayah, caste, madeira, marmalade, molasses, palaver,* and *port* (wine). Many such words have reached English indirectly, as with *ayah* and *caste*, which are the outcome of Portuguese influence on English in India. Portuguese has also mediated words from other languages into English. *Albatross*, for example, is apparently an adaptation of obsolete *algatross*, a variant of *alcatras* (the frigate bird). This word in turn derives from Portuguese and Spanish *alcatraz*, a term applied variously to the frigate bird, pelican, gannet, and solan goose. Its origin is Arabic *al-ghaṭṭās* ('the diver': the white-tailed sea eagle), the substitution of *b* for *g* perhaps arising from an association with Latin *albus* white. See AFRICAN LANGUAGES, AMERICAN LANGUAGES, ARABIC, BORROWING, CANADIAN LANGUAGES, CREOLE, EARLY MODERN ENGLISH, ENGLISH, EUROPEAN COMMUNITY, EUROPEAN LANGUAGES, GEOGRAPHY, HAWAII, IBERIAN LANGUAGES, INDIAN ENGLISH[1], MACAO, PIDGIN, ROMANCE LANGUAGES, SPANISH. [AFRICA, AMERICAS, ASIA, EUROPE, LANGUAGE].   T.MCA.

POSH [1910s: perhaps from *posh*, the late 19c BrE slang name for a dandy, influenced by or identical with Romany *posh* half, meaning 'money' in 19c criminal cant. There appears to be no basis for the derivation from *port out(ward)*, *starboard home(ward)* abbreviated to *P.O.S.H.*, an apocryphal phrase for the cooler, more expensive berths on P & O (Peninsular & Orient) ships formerly travelling between the UK and India.]. An especially BrE slang term that in the earlier 20c meant 'splendid, wonderful, lavish, luxurious, fashionably smart, etc.' (*a really posh time, a posh London flat*) and in the later 20c has meant 'upper-class, wealthy, snobbish' (*a posh job with posh people*). It is widely used by the British to refer to uses of language that are regarded as snobbish or upper-class: *a posh accent*; *talking posh*. See RECEIVED PRONUNCIATION, U AND NON-U. [STYLE].   T.MCA.

POSITIVE [13c: from Latin *positivus* formally stated, definite]. (1) Also *affirmative* [15c: from Latin *affirmativus* making firm]. Terms for a sentence, clause, verb, or other expression that is not *negative*: *They are coming* as opposed to *They are not coming*. (2) A base form, as with the positive as opposed to the comparative or superlative forms of an adjective (*new* as opposed to *newer* and *newest*. See POLARITY, POSITIVE DEGREE. [GRAMMAR].   S.G.

POSITIVE DEGREE, also **absolute degree.** Terms for an adjective or adverb that is not marked for comparison (*new, happy, beautiful*), in contrast with the *comparative* (*newer; happier; more happy; more beautiful*) and the *superlative* (*newest; happiest, most happy; most beautiful*). See DEGREE. [GRAMMAR].   S.G., T.MCA.

POSSESSION [14c: from Latin *possessio/possessionis* holding (things) as property, occupancy]. The grammatical concept of one person or thing belonging to another, shown in English in four ways: (1) By verbs such as *have, own, belong to.* (2) By possessive pronouns that function as determiners: *my house.* (3) By the genitive or possessive case of nouns marked in writing by the possessive apostrophe: *John's book; The Smiths' farm.* (4) By the *of*-construction: *the end of the road.* These cover a wide range of meaning from practical ownership (*my clothes; I have a dog*) through kinds of association (*their parents; our country; Shakespeare's birthplace*), to more general and often figurative and idiomatic relationships (*have an appointment; a day's journey; a lover's quarrel; the story of his life*). The genitive is also used to introduce the subject of a gerund, as in *It's funny your saying that.* In some instances, a genitive and an *of*-construction are both possible, though not interchangeable in all contexts. The genitive construction is likeliest when the possessor is personal or at any rate animate, or is in some way perceived as having personal aspects: *Dr Johnson's house; a dog's breakfast; God's love; Scotland's national poet; the world's pressing needs.* The *of*-construction is preferred with things not considered capable of possessing anything: *the lid of a box* rather than *a box's lid.* See APOSTROPHE¹, GENITIVE CASE, GERUND, POSSESSIVE CASE, SAXON GENITIVE. [GRAMMAR].   S.C.

POSSESSIVE APOSTROPHE. See APOSTROPHE¹.

POSSESSIVE CASE [16c: from Latin *casus possessivus* the case that holds or possesses]. In the case system of Latin and other inflected languages, an alternative name for the *genitive.* In English, the term *possessive* refers to grammatical relations expressed through the preposition *of* and the apostrophe *s.* It is also a distinguishing label for certain kinds of parts of speech, such as possessive pronouns, which serve to indicate possession: '*my* house', '*your* car'. See APOSTROPHE¹, CASE¹, GENITIVE CASE, POSSESSION, SAXON GENITIVE. [GRAMMAR].   S.C.

POSSESSIVE PRONOUN. A pronoun which expresses possession. Strictly applied, the term covers eight items used independently, as in *The*

house is ours: mine, thine (archaic), *yours, his, hers, its, ours,* and *theirs.* More loosely, it includes eight items used attributively, as in *This is our house: my, thy* (archaic), *your, his, her, its, our,* and *their* (a set also labelled *possessive determiners* and *possessive adjectives*). The distinction between the two groups is the same as with any pronouns and determiners. Possessive determiners never take apostrophes: *its* is the determiner, while *it's* is short for *it is* or *it has.* See DETERMINER, PRONOUN. [GRAMMAR].   S.C.

POST-COLONIAL LITERATURES IN ENGLISH. See COMMONWEALTH LITERATURE, ENGLISH LITERATURE, WORLD LITERATURE WRITTEN IN ENGLISH.

POST-CREOLE CONTINUUM, also **creole continuum.** A chain of language varieties which arises linking a creole (also known as the *basilect*) to its superstrate language (also known as the *acrolect*) via intermediate varieties referred to collectively as the *mesolect*: for example, the Jamaican post-creole continuum, ranging from Jamaican creole proper to a Jamaican standard English based on standard BrE. The following are Guyanese English Creole forms for standard English *I gave him*: basilect *Mi gii am*; mesolect *A giv im*; acrolect, *A geev him.* The differences between coexistent varieties in such a continuum are generally greater than might be expected in a community with 'normal' processes of dialect formation, particularly in terms of the amount and degree of syntactic and semantic variation. A post-creole continuum may develop when, after a period of relatively independent linguistic development, a post-pidgin or post-creole variety comes under a period of renewed influence from the superstrate (the *relexifier language*, or principal source of vocabulary). This is generally described as *decreolization.* See CREOLE, LECT. [LANGUAGE, VARIETY].   S.R.

POST-DETERMINER. See DETERMINER.

POST-MODERNISM. See ENGLISH LITERATURE, MODERN.

POST-MODIFICATION. See MODIFICATION.

POSTPOSITION [16c: from *post-* after, and *position,* on the analogy of *preposition*]. (1) The use of words or other linguistic elements after the elements they modify or govern: for example, following the style of French, the adjective *martial* is postposed in *court martial* (not *martial court). (2) A part of speech, word class, or word element, that follows nouns and pronouns, to form a grammatical unit, as the equivalents of

English prepositions do in Hindi. Some grammarians have described the adverbial particles in English phrasal verbs (*off* as in *They took their hats off*) as postpositions, to emphasize their adverbial rather than prepositional role. Compare PREPOSITION. [GRAMMAR].   S.G.

POSTSCRIPT, formerly **post scriptum** [16c: from Latin *post scriptum* written afterwards]. Short form *PS*. (1) A sentence or paragraph at the end of a letter, after the signature, containing an afterthought or additional information. It is introduced by the letters *P.S.* or *PS*. A further postscript begins with *P.P.S.*, and so forth. (2) A paragraph at the end of any text, containing some appended matter. Compare APPENDIX, EPILOG(UE). [WRITING].   T.MCA.

POST-STRUCTURALISM. See LITERARY CRITICISM, STRUCTURALISM.

POSTVOCALIC [19c: from *post-* after, *vocalic* relating to a vowel]. A term in phonetics referring to consonants that occur after a vowel: postvocalic *r* in *work*. See R-SOUNDS, VOWEL. [SPEECH].   T.MCA.

POTTER, Stephen [1900–69]. English humorist and critic, educated at Westminster School and Merton College, Oxford, and author of the pioneering *D. H. Lawrence: A First Study* (1930) and several works on Coleridge, including *Coleridge and SIC* (1935). He had serious reservations, however, about the academic study and teaching of English, and in *The Muse in Chains: A Study of Education* (1932), made sport with 'the racket, the flummery, the techniques and gambits' in the teaching of what he called 'Eng. Lit.', an expression he claims to have invented. The identity of Potter the scholar is now generally lost in that of Potter the comic sage, author of *The Theory and Practice of Gamesmanship; or, the art of winning games without actually cheating* (1947), *Some Notes on Lifemanship, with a summary of recent researches in gamesmanship* (1950), and *One-upmanship: Being some account of the activities and teaching of the Lifemanship Correspondence College and of one-upness and gameslifemastery* (1952).

In these books, he makes fun of the flummery and gambits of scholars and the solemnities of sociologists. *Gamesmanship* (modelled on *sportsmanship*) refers to the *ploys* to which players may legitimately resort in trying to put opponents off their game: for example, coughing just as one's partner is about to tee off at golf. The principle extends to *lifemanship* and *one-upmanship*, the art of coming off best in life's little encounters: for example, If people talk of Moscow, you talk of Vladivostok, banking on the probability that

no one has been there; if the talk is of Italy, you confound the enthusiasts for Tuscany by saying, in response to any assertion, 'but not in the south'. These books caught the public fancy through their appeal to the everyman view of life as a series of minor competitions in which small face-saving victories are won by petty devices. Potter's choice of topics was typically English in his gravely systematic, quasi-scholarly analysis of trivia. Through his ploys he won for his coinages a place in the language: his own lifemanship might therefore be said to have left him *one up*. See MUSE. [BIOGRAPHY, EUROPE, LITERATURE, WORD].   W.N.

POUND, Louise [1872–1958]. American philologist and folklorist, born in Lincoln, Nebraska, and educated at the universities of Nebraska, Chicago, and Heidelberg (Ph.D., 1890). She became an instructor in English literature at the U. of Nebraska in 1894 and remained at that institution until her retirement 50 years later, becoming full professor in 1912. She was the first at the university to teach courses in American language and literature, and the most prominent woman academic during the first half of the 20c, when linguistics was establishing itself in the US and there was an unprecedented expansion in the observation and recording of American language and folkways. Throughout her career, she balanced research in the origins of English literary genres and the development of AmE. Her study of rhyme and stanza form in *Poetic Origins and the Ballad* (1921) disproved a commonly held belief in the cooperative origin of ballads.

Pound began her study of American speech as a student in George Hempl's Chaucer class at Chicago. Interested in those living American dialects that preserved many of the words, phrases, pronunciations, and intonations of late Middle English, she became an avid observer of language and a collector of its folklore, writing numerous articles on etymology, historical linguistics, and dialectology. As editor of the U. of Nebraska journal *Studies in Language, Literature, and Criticism* (1917–40) and adviser and contributor to *New England Quarterly, American Literature, Folk-Say, College English,* and *Southern Folklore Quarterly*, she traced the roots of American expression. Describing her work as a co-founder and main editor of *American Speech*, and acknowledging his indebtedness to her, H. L. Mencken wrote that she 'put the study of current American English on its legs' (*The American Language*, Supplement 1, 1962). Her dedication to the accurate recording of language was noted when she was elected 65th president of the Modern Language Association in 1955 at the age of 82, the first woman to hold the position. Pound considered that professional organizations could encourage research and teaching; she was president of the American Dialect Society (1938–42) and the American Folklore Society (1924–6), and active in the International Phonetic Association, the Linguistic Society of America, the Medieval Academy of America, and the Spelling Reform Association. See index. [AMERICAS, BIOGRAPHY, LANGUAGE, VARIETY].　　　　　C.C.E., R.W.B.

PRAGMATICS [1930s: from Greek *pragmatikós*, from *prâgma* matter in hand, action, on the analogy of *linguistics*]. A branch of linguistics which originally examined the problem of how listeners uncover speakers' intentions. It is sometimes defined as the study of 'speaker meaning', as opposed to linguistic meaning: the utterance *I'm thirsty* might need to be interpreted as *Go and buy me a drink* and should not necessarily be taken at face value as a simple statement. The term is usually attributed to the British philosopher Charles Morris (1938–71), who distinguished between *syntax* (the relations of signs to one another), *semantics* (the relations of signs to objects), and *pragmatics* (the relations of signs to interpretations). Recently, pragmatics has expanded into a wide and somewhat vague topic which includes anything relating to the way in which people communicate that cannot be captured by conventional linguistic analysis. Within pragmatics, *discourse analysis* (the study of language in discourse) has become a major focus of attention. See DISCOURSE ANALYSIS, LINGUISTICS, SEMANTICS, SPEECH ACT. [LANGUAGE].　J.M.A.

PRAKRIT [From Sanskrit *prākṛt* uncultivated, natural. Compare SANSKRIT]. (1) A collective term for the Middle Indo-Aryan languages from 600 BC to AD 110, sometimes called *the Prakrits*. This group is contrasted with both *Sanskrit*, the classical language of the Hindus, and *Pali*, a scriptural language of Buddhism that itself began as a Prakrit. The use of Prakrit in Sanskrit plays indicates a diglossic situation in which kings and officials used Sanskrit and women, children, servants, eunuchs, and the sick or insane used Prakrits. The extent of the influence of Prakrit on Sanskrit in grammar and literature makes it clear that the latter was not, as has often been suggested, a standard language kept pure and apart from other languages. The relationship between Sanskrit and the Prakrits can be compared to that of Latin and the Romance languages in Europe and standard English and many varieties of English around the world. See INDIAN LANGUAGES, PALI, SANSKRIT, VERNACULAR. [ASIA, LANGUAGE].　R.P., T.MCA.

PRÉCIS, also **precis** [18c: from French 'cut short', Latin *praecidere/praecisum* to cut down, shorten, the same source as *precise*. Pronunciation: 'PRAY-see'. Plural identical in spelling, but pronounced '-seez']. (1) A concise summary or abstract: *to make a précis of a report*. The term *précis-writing* has been commonly used in schools, especially in Britain, to refer to the teaching and practice of writing summaries. (2) To summarize: *to précis a report*. See ABRIDG(E)MENT, SUMMARY. [WRITING].　T.MCA.

PRE-DETERMINER. See DETERMINER.

PREDICATE [15c: from Old French *predicat*, Latin *praedicatus* made known]. A traditional grammatical term for a major constituent of the sentence, part of a binary analysis that divides the sentence into subject and predicate. In the sentence *Pat has joined our club*, *Pat* is the subject and *has joined our club* is the predicate. In both grammar and logic, the predicate serves to make an assertion or denial about the subject of the sentence. In some analyses, the predicate does not include optional constituents, so that *today* is not part of the predicate in *Pat has joined our club today*. [GRAMMAR, LANGUAGE].　S.G.

PREDICATIVE ADJECTIVE [19c]. Also **predicate adjective**. An adjective that occurs in the predicate: *silent* in *Eliot remained silent*; *uncomfortable* in *Naomi made her brother uncomfortable*. The adjective follows a linking verb (*remain, make*), and the relationship is with the subject (*Eliot*, who was silent), or the direct object (*her brother*, who became uncomfortable). Some adjectives can only be used predicatively: *asleep* (*The children were all asleep*, but not **the asleep children*); *aware* (*They were not aware of the danger*, but not usually **an aware person*). Increasingly commonly, the term *predicative adjective* is used to refer only to such adjectives, in contrast to *attributive adjective* (an adjective used before a noun). Some adjectives can only be used attributively: for example, *undue*, as in *undue pressure* (no **the pressure is undue*). See ADJECTIVE, ATTRIBUTIVE, COMPLEMENT, PREDICATE. [GRAMMAR].　S.G., T.MCA.

PREFACE [14c: from Medieval Latin *prefatia*, from Latin *praefatio/praefationis* something said beforehand, from *fari* to say, speak]. (1) Also *foreword, prologue*. A preliminary statement in a book, usually about one to three pages in length, by the author or editor, usually describing its nature, purpose, and scope. It may also acknowledge help, or there may be a separate *Acknowledgements* section for that purpose. (2) Anything similar, such as an opening speech, meeting, or prayer. See FRONT MATTER, PROLOG(UE), SAXONISM. [MEDIA, WRITING].　T.MCA.

PREFIX [14c: from Latin *praefixum* (something) fixed in front]. (1) A term in word-formation for an affix added at the beginning of a word or base to form a new word: *re-* added to *write* to form *re-write/rewrite*. (2) A general term for a word, letter, number, or other item placed before something else: the letter *A* in the sequence *A133*; the combining form *auto-* prefixed to *biography* to form *autobiography*.

Productivity. In word-formation, a prefix is *productive* when it contributes to the meaning of a word (the *un-* in *unhappy* having the meaning 'not') and can be added freely to other, comparable words (*unable, unkind*). It is *non-productive* when it occurs in a word but does not contribute to its meaning: *con-* in *condition*. The meaning of the word *condition* is unrelated to the union of *con-* and *-dition* and there is no independent base word **dition*. A prefix is *vestigial* when only a trace of it can be detected by scholars: the *s* of *spend*, which was once *expend*. The same prefix may be productive in some words (*dis-* in *disconnect, dislocate*), non-productive in others (*dis-* in *disaster, distribute*), and vestigial in others still (*sport*, once *disport*). There are 'twilight' states: *re-* when productive means 'again' (*re-do, reconnect*) and when non-productive (as in *remiss*) has no meaning, but in *rejuvenate, repair* the meaning 'again' is present even though the bases to which *re-* attaches (**juvenate, *pair*) are not independent words.

Provenance. The prefixes of English derive from: (1) Old English: *a-* in *asleep, be-* in *bespatter, un-* in *unready*. (2) French: *dis-* in *disappear, mis-* in *misgovern*. (3) Latin: *ante-* in *anteroom, in-* in *inactive, pre-* in *preconceive*. (4) Greek: *a-* in *amoral, anti-* in *anti-war, meta-* in *metaphysical*. Prefixes with different backgrounds can, however, fall into relational sets: vernacular *over-*, as in *over-sensitive* more sensitive than necessary or desirable; Latin *super-*, as in *super-sensitive* very sensitive (especially of instruments, film, etc.); Greek *hyper-*, as in *hypersensitive* excessively sensitive (especially to allergens). The negative prefixes of English form a range of usages that are sometimes irregularly paired (*ungrateful/ingratitude, unlikeable/dislike, unstable/instability*), are sometimes a source of confusion (*disinterested/uninterested*), and are sometimes delicately contrastive (*unmoral, immoral, amoral, non-moral*).

Pairing. In English, suffixes often occur in chains (such as the *-istically* in *characteristically*), but prefixes do not. They usually occur singly (*un-* in *unhappy, re-* in *re-write*), but sometimes occur in pairs: *un-, re-,* in *unremarried* not married again; *anti-, dis-,* in *antidisestablishment*. In these examples, both prefixes are productive (that is, *married* and *establishment* are independent base words), but pairing is commonly the addition of

a productive to a non-productive prefix: productive *in-* to non-productive *re-* in *irredeemable* (no **deemable*); *in-* added to *con-* in *inconclusive* (no **clusive*). Sometimes, the same prefix may be added twice, usually with a hyphen: *meta-metalanguage, re-reconstructed, co-conspirator* (the productive *co-* beside the non-productive *con-*). Very occasionally, a three-prefix chain occurs: *non-reproductive*, in which *non-* is fully productive, *re-* is partly productive (*reproduction* being more than an extension of *production*), and *pro-* is non-productive (no **ductive*). See COMBINING FORM, DIMINUTIVE, MORPHOLOGY, PRIVATIVE, PRODUCTIVE, SUFFIX, WORD-FORMATION. [WORD].   T.MCA.

PRELIMINARIES, PRELIMS. See FRONT MATTER.

PREMISS, also **premise** [14c: from Latin noun *praemissa*, from *praemissus* sent ahead (that is, preceding or leading to)]. In logic, a proposition that supports or helps to support a conclusion. Compare AXIOM. See LOGIC, PROPOSITION, SYLLOGISM. [LANGUAGE].   T.MCA.

PRE-MODIFICATION. See MODIFICATION, TECHNOSPEAK, TIMESPEAK.

PREPOSITION [14c: Middle English *preposicioun*, from Latin *praepositio*, a loan translation of Greek *próthesis* putting before]. One of the traditional parts of speech into which words are classified. It is a closed class, in that few new prepositions ever enter a language.

Kinds of preposition. (1) *Simple preposition.* Traditionally, the preposition proper: one- or two-syllable words, such as *at, from, through, without*. Many such words, however, also have adverbial roles: *up* is prepositional in *They took the boxes up the stairs*, adverbial in *They picked the boxes up/They picked up the boxes*. (2) *Compound preposition.* Two prepositions used together as one: *in* and *to* as *into*. Such forms are primarily conventions of writing and print and may vary according to the kind of English: BrE generally has *on to* and AmE *onto*. Forms like *into, on to/onto*, and *out of* are all compounds in speech, because of their rhythm and stress: the first preposition is stressed (*INto*), and the second is usually reduced. This point is reflected in the non-standard spelling of *out of* (*Will ya get outa here?*), where *a* stands for *of* reduced to schwa. (3) *Complex preposition.* A two- or three-word phrase that functions in the same way as a simple preposition: *according to*, as in *According to John, they are coming tomorrow*; *as well as*, as in *We're going as well as John*; *except for*, as in *They did everything, except for some work we'll* *finish tomorrow*; *in favour of*, as in *They voted in favour of the local candidate.*

Prepositions and complements. Unlike such major word classes as verbs and nouns, which have a more independent status, prepositions do not stand alone but need a *complement*. Typically, this is a noun or pronoun (*dawn* in *at dawn*, *you* in *after you*) but can be other parts of speech (*then* in *by then*, *short* in *in short*). Prepositions can also be followed by an *-ing* clause (after *of* in *A man has no reason to be ashamed of having an ape for his grandfather*) or by a *wh*-clause (*For what we are about to receive . . .*). They are not normally followed by *that*-clauses, although apparent exceptions are clauses introduced by complex conjunctions: *in that*, as in *The box was difficult to find, in that nobody knew where to look*; *except that*, as in *I wouldn't have gone, except that I'd promised*. Prepositions are not followed by *to*-infinitives, and there is a distinction between preposition *to* (as in *We look forward to seeing you/to your visit*, not **We look forward to see you*) and the *to* particle plus an infinitive (*We hope to see you soon*, not **We hope to seeing you soon*).

Semantics. In terms of meaning, prepositions range through various relationships: (1) Space and time, many being used for both: *at* in *They met at Heathrow Airport at six o'clock.* (2) Cause and purpose: *for* in *She did it for reasons of her own.* (3) Agent and instrument: *by* in *work done by an assistant*; *with* in *opened with a knife.* (4) The versatile *of*: possessive (*a friend of mine*, the *lid of the box*); assigning origin (*of royal descent*); indicating creation (*the works of Shakespeare*); referring to depiction (*a picture of Loch Fyne in winter*); indicating a subject of conversation (*telling them of his travels*); stating source and manufacture (*made of cotton*). (5) There are also many figurative meanings, such as the zeugma of *He left in a rage and a taxi.* (6) Normally, when the same preposition governs two consecutive phrases and has the same signification in both, it does not need to be repeated (*She works in London and Glasgow*), but on occasion, repetition is essential for the sake of clarity: *They lived in hope in Edinburgh* (because the significations are different: no **They lived in hope and Edinburgh*).

Usage: the ends of sentences. Because, in etymological terms, *preposition* means 'placing before', and Greek and Latin prepositions precede their complement, the classical prescriptive rule emerged for standard English that sentences should not end with a preposition. However, although English prepositions often do precede their complement, there are structures in which this is impossible (*What did you say that for?*; *What are you getting at?*) and some which have no grammatical complement (*The bed hadn't been slept in*; *It hardly bears thinking about*; *He's nothing to look at*). Traditionally, such usages have been described as more or less ungrammatical, often with the result that alternatives have been preferred or recommended (*Why did you say that?* instead of *What did you say that for?*). The resultant insecurity sometimes produces stilted inversions like *To whom do you think you are talking?* for *Who do you think you're talking to?* One such manoeuvre in a government report is said to have led Winston Churchill to make his famous marginal comment: *This is the sort of bloody nonsense up with which I will not put* ('bloody nonsense' often being changed to 'English' in quotations). With relative clauses, there are usually two positions for a preposition, the end position being less formal: *This is the house in which she lived* as against *This is the house (that) she lived in.* In using such constructions, both native and non-native speakers of English sometimes either forget the preposition (*He is the person you have to give it*, forgetting *to*) or repeat it (*He is the person to whom you have to give it to*).

Usage: prepositions and other parts of speech. Prepositions overlap with other parts of speech, especially adverbs and conjunctions. The grammatical classification of an item therefore often depends on use in context: in the sentence *Jack and Jill went up the hill*, *up* is a preposition, but in *They climbed up (and up)*, it is an adverb. Such adverbs are sometimes called *prepositional adverbs*, sometimes *adverbial particles*. In other instances, there are related prepositional and adverbial forms. In standard English in England, *out* is adverbial only (*I opened the window and looked out*), the related prepositional form being *out of* (*I looked out of the window*). However, in AmE and ScoE, *out* is both adverbial and prepositional (*I looked out the window*). *Near* (*to*) and *close* (*to*) function like prepositions, but are like adjectives and adverbs in having comparative and superlative forms, and can be modified by an intensifier: *He sat nearer* (*to*) *the fire/very near the fire*. Other prepositions overlap with conjunctions. The distinction is again one of usage and function: *We waited until she arrived* (conjunction plus clause), *We waited until her arrival* (preposition plus noun phrase). Some words are conjunctions, prepositions, and adverbs: *since* in *We haven't heard from him since he left* (conjunction); *We haven't heard since January* (preposition); *We haven't heard since* (adverb). At times, the distinction between preposition and conjunction is not easy to make and may lead to controversy, as with *as* and *than*. Depending on whether they are seen as conjunctions (needing subject pronouns) or prepositions (able to take object pronouns), in such comparisons as *I'm not as rich as she/her* and *He's taller than I/me* the first option may be viewed as correct (but stilted), the second as usual (but sometimes stigmatized).

Usage: like. Some people, regarding *like* as a preposition (*Do it like this*), object strongly to its use as a conjunction, as in *Do it like I told you*, rather than *Do it the way I told you*; *Like he said, it's good for you*, rather than *As he said, . . .*; *It's like he wanted to get away*, as opposed to *It's as if/though he wanted to get away*. These uses are, however, widespread. There are also some prepositions that introduce non-finite clauses but are never conjunctions, as with *on* in *On seeing us, he rushed away without saying a word.*

Marginal prepositions. These are words that have some of the characteristics of prepositions but also strong affinities with other word classes. They include some *-ing* and *-ed* forms which also have verbal use: *considering* (as in *Considering all the trouble he has caused, he should . . .*), *following, regarding, given, granted*. There are also such hard-to-classify words as *bar* (as in *all of them bar one*), *worth* (as in *It's worth much more*), and *minus* and *plus* (as in *minus four, plus ten*). *But* and *except* as prepositions can be followed not only by noun phrases (*There's nobody here but/except me*) but also by a bare infinitive (*They do nothing but complain*).

The prepositional phrase. This is a preposition and its complement together: *in the house; near the end*. Such a unit functions in different ways in a sentence: it can follow a noun in a noun phrase ('the man *in the white suit*'); it can follow particular verbs and adjectives ('Come and look *at my etchings*', 'Are you fond *of animals*?'); and it can function as an adverbial ('Put that thing *on the floor*'). This versatility sometimes leads to absurdity, when a prepositional phrase meant to have one function is misplaced and can be understood in another: *Staff are requested not to eat anything outside the canteen except for the duty telephone operator.* See next entries, and ADVERB, PHRASAL VERB, POSTPOSITION. [GRAMMAR, USAGE]. S.C., T.MCA.

PREPOSITIONAL ADVERB, also **adverb/ adverbial particle**. A term for an adverb that can also function as a preposition: *off* is a preposition in *It fell off the back of a truck*, but an adverb in *It was on a truck and fell off*. See PHRASAL VERB, PREPOSITIONAL VERB. [GRAMMAR]. S.C.

PREPOSITIONAL VERB. In one school of grammatical theory, the term for an often idiomatic combination of verb and preposition: *approve of* in *They fully approved of his actions*;

get at in *I really don't know what you are getting at*. Sometimes, such a verb is synonymous with a single verb: *come across* with *find* in *They came across the manuscript by accident*. The phrase that follows the preposition (*the children* in *Look after the children*) is a *prepositional object*. According to this view, some such verbs have two objects, one of them coming between the verb and the preposition: *blame on* in *Blame the noise on the children*. Other grammarians, however, argue that here the *on* is part of a traditional prepositional phrase. A *phrasal-prepositional verb* is a combination of a verb and two particles, the first an adverb, the second a preposition: *put up with*, meaning 'tolerate', as in *I can't put up with this noise any longer*. See PARTICLE, PHRASAL VERB. [GRAMMAR, USAGE]. S.G., T.MCA.

PRESCRIPTIVE GRAMMAR. See DESCRIPTIVE AND PRESCRIPTIVE GRAMMAR.

PRESCRIPTIVISM. See DESCRIPTIVISM AND PRESCRIPTIVISM.

PRESENT [13c: from Old French *present* (Modern *présent*), from Latin *praesens*, being at hand, immediate]. A term for the tense of the verb concerned primarily with events, actions, and states that apply at the time of speaking or writing (*The work goes on*), but also used to express future time (*We go to France tomorrow*), universal truths (in the simple present only: *Water is wet*), and past time in certain narratives, often of an informal or colloquial nature ('The narrative present': *He crosses the street and shoots them*). There are several types of present tense. The *simple present tense* has the form of the verb without inflections (*mention*) or with the third-person singular *-s* (*Everybody mentions his name*). The complex present tenses are: the *present continuous* or *present progressive*, which combines a present form of auxiliary *be* with the *-ing* participle (*is mentioning*); the *present perfect*, which combines a present form of auxiliary *have* with the *-ed* participle (*has mentioned*); the *present perfect continuous*, which combines these two (*has been mentioning*). Compare FUTURE, PAST. See TENSE. [GRAMMAR]. S.G., T.MCA.

PRESENT PARTICIPLE. See PARTICIPLE.

PRESS [c.13c, in the sense of an instrument that pushes hard: from Old French *presser*, Latin *pressare*, to keep pushing heavily on, frequentative of *premere* (past participle *pressus*), to push or rest heavily on]. A term with a range of loosely associated meanings. Primarily, it refers to the act of pushing hard and steadily and, because of its early application to the technology of movable type, has become closely associated with printing. Through the term *printing press* it has come to refer generally to newspapers and other print products, viewed collectively (*the popular press, the quality press, the tabloid press*), including their representatives *en masse* (*meet the press*). Finally, it has extended to news media in general, such as wire services and broadcasts on radio and television. Critical comment by reviewers employed by the media is commonly referred to as *a good/bad press*. The invention of the printing press (*c.*1450) had potent social and linguistic consequences. The new medium had the effect of concentrating powers of definition, controversial commentary, and authoritative statement into the hands of those who controlled the machines and the distribution of their products. The early presses were copiously used in the ecclesiastical controversies of the Reformation and the political ructions of the Civil War to generate pamphlets, translations of the Bible, and other matter considered subversive. The current sense of *the press* as the aggregate of newspaper coverage ('The press is full of the Watergate scandal') developed gradually through the 17–18c out of the phrase *the liberty of the press*, to the point where journalists and the business interests behind them were defined by Lord Macaulay as 'a fourth estate of the realm' (1828). The power of the press over social and political events is freely admitted and is the source of frequent comment. As the *Daily News* observed of developments in America in 1898: 'The yellow Press is for a war with Spain at all costs.' The emergence of 'press barons' such as W. Randolph Hearst and Joseph Pulitzer in the US, and Lords Northcliffe and Beaverbrook in the UK, has often occasioned the suspicion of possible indirect political influence by the press, as opposed to the kind of 'fearless exposure of the truth' often referred to technically as *investigative journalism*. See AMERICAN PRESS, AUSTRALIAN PRESS, CANADIAN PRESS, CARIBBEAN PRESS, INDIAN PRESS, IRISH PRESS, JOURNALESE, JOURNALISM, NEWSMAGAZINE, NEWSPAPER, NEW ZEALAND PRESS, SOUTH AFRICAN PRESS. [MEDIA, TECHNOLOGY]. G.H., T.MCA.

PRESUPPOSITION [16c: through French from Latin *praesuppositio/praesuppositionis* assuming beforehand]. (1) Supposing something in advance, with or without sufficient information. (2) An assumption of truth or rightness as a prerequisite to something else, usually a belief or an action. To believe in the Bible presupposes a belief in God, but a belief in God does not presuppose a belief in the Bible. (3) In philosophy, logic, and linguistics, the need for something to serve as a precondition so that a

statement can be true or false or a speech act successful. The question *Have you stopped smoking?* presupposes that the person asked has been smoking. See LOGIC, SEMANTICS, SPEECH ACT. [LANGUAGE]. T.MCA.

PRETERITE, also AmE **preterit** [14c: from Latin *praeteritus* gone by]. A traditional term for the simple past tense of the verb (such as *climbed* in *They climbed the hill yesterday*) and for a verb in this tense. See OLD ENGLISH[1], PAST, TENSE. [GRAMMAR]. S.G.

PRIMARY LANGUAGE AND SECONDARY LANGUAGE. Terms in applied linguistics and language teaching. The first language learned by a child is its primary language; all languages learned later are secondary languages. The primary language is commonly referred to as a *mother tongue* or *native language*, although one's primary language may not be the language of one's mother or of one's ethnic group or place of origin. See FIRST LANGUAGE/SECOND LANGUAGE. [EDUCATION, LANGUAGE]. P.S.

PRIMITIVE GERMANIC, short form *PG*. The modern name for the language, presumably never written and now lost, that became distinct from its parent Indo-European (IE) several centuries BC. It was superseded by the East Germanic, North Germanic, and West Germanic branches early in the Christian era. Stress in IE, which fell on different syllables according to inflection, much as in *Shákespeare/Shakespéarian*, in late PG became fixed on the first syllable of the word, as in *Bódley/Bódleian*. PG made elaborate use of case endings to signify the grammatical function of its nouns, adjectives, articles, and pronouns, much as modern English does with pronouns to mark the difference between 'The state is I' and 'The state is mine'. PG showed the effect of Grimm's Law (see entry), so that IE **pisk* appeared as PG **fiska*. It included, however, some vocabulary not common to the IE languages, such as **ertho* (earth). It also had a distinctive suffix to mark the past tense and past participle with a *d* sound as in *had*, and its system of verbal inflection was much simplified from that of IE. The distinctive vocabulary and simplified conjugational system suggest contact between speakers of PG and speakers of some non-IE language. See GERMANIC LANGUAGES, INDO-EUROPEAN LANGUAGES. [HISTORY, LANGUAGE]. W.F.B.

PRINCE EDWARD ISLAND ENGLISH, DICTIONARY OF. See CANADIAN DICTIONARIES IN ENGLISH.

PRINCIPAL CLAUSE. See MAIN CLAUSE.

PRINT [13c: from Old French *preinte, priente* the impression of a seal, etc., from *preindre* to press, from Latin *premere/pressum* to press]. (1) To create marks on surfaces by means of pressure, especially the reversed impressions made by imposing a seal on wax or pressing inked fingertips on paper; the outcome of such a process. (2) To write so that each letter of an alphabet is separate, without connecting lines (the opposite of writing *cursively*); the outcome of such a process. (3) Now rare: an instrument, machine, stamp, or die that makes an impression. (4) The result of impressing a design or other pattern on a surface: (on fabrics) *a cotton print*; (in electronics) *a printed circuit*. (5) The result of any process of making impressions on surfaces such as paper and parchment: *an artist's print*; *read the small print*; *out of print*. Language material produced by such a process is *printed matter*. (6) Formerly: a newspaper: 'I believe, Mr Puff, I have often admired your talents in the daily prints' (Richard Sheridan, *The Critic*, 1779). (7) A positive photographic image, in colour or black and white, produced usually on paper from a negative image on film. (8) In motion pictures and television, a copy of a film that is ready for showing. (9) An attributive term for printed publications such as newspapers and magazines, in contrast to radio and television: *a print journalist*; *the print media*. See PRESS, PRINTER, PRINTING. [TECHNOLOGY].   T.MCA.

PRINTER [15c]. (1) A person who produces printed matter of any kind. (2) A plate or image that prints a specific colour or image: *the yellow printer*. (3) A machine (not a printing press) that prints information: for example, a *teleprinter*, a device that records telegraphic or telexed messages (converting incoming signals to text); the *output device* attached to a computer to provide *hard copy* (a printed version of alphanumeric and graphic data). See COMPUTING, PRINTING. [TECHNOLOGY].   T.MCA.

PRINTER'S ERROR. See LITERAL², TYPOGRAPHICAL ERROR.

PRINTHEAD [Later 20c]. In typing and printers for word processors, a mechanical element such as a *daisy wheel*, *golfball*, or *thimble*, that imprints letters on paper. [TECHNOLOGY].   T.MCA.

PRINTING. The process, business, and art of producing standardized letters and texts, often accompanied by diagrams, pictures, and other addenda, by applying ink to paper and other surfaces so as to produce many copies of the same piece of work. Printing is often treated as an aspect or offshoot of writing, but differs from it in at least four ways: (1) Writing varies from person to person, but print retains invariant shapes regardless of who uses it. (2) Writing follows relatively informal rules of positioning and sequencing on paper, but printing keeps rigidly to such conventions as margin sizes, line spaces, number of lines per page, and type chosen for a project. (3) Where as writing is slow and produces approximate copies only through hand-copying or the use of carbon paper or photocopying, printing is rapid and produces identical copies in sequence until the process stops or ink and paper run out. (4) The legibility of handwriting varies, but the legibility of print is consistent.

Origins. The art of making inked reproductions from woodblocks and movable signs was developed in the 6–8c by the Chinese and Koreans. It is uncertain how the practice was disseminated from East to West. The Islamic world was not interested in printing, but reports that reached Europe of such an invention appear to have prompted speculation and experiment. The Western invention of printing from movable type is generally ascribed to Johann Gutenberg, a goldsmith from Mainz in Germany. Although scholars dispute the details of the early production of his press, the first dated item is a copy of a 42-line Bible, which a scribe finished *rubricating* (entering capitals and other matter) on 24 August 1456. There had been printing from woodblocks before Gutenberg. His genius was to perfect a number of separate but available technologies for printing from type. He appears to have devised a successful mould for casting regularly sized and spaced metal type, a heavy ink that would adhere to this type, and a variation of a press that would give an impression on paper. His 42-line Bible and other productions, far from being rudimentary initial experiments, are technically superior works of layout and typography.

Development. By the early 16c, printing and systems for distributing printed materials had spread throughout the main cities of Europe and stabilized. The English merchant William Caxton learned the art in Cologne and practised it in Bruges before setting up the first printing press in England, in Westminster in 1476. The first printing in India (by Portuguese Jesuits in Goa) was in 1556; in the North American colonies of England was in Boston in 1638; in French Canada in Quebec City in 1752; in Australia, 1796; in New Zealand, 1835. At first, printed materials imitated manuscripts in subject matter, design, and distribution, but printing gradually established its own conventions. By the 1520s, large numbers of relatively cheap, fairly rapidly distributed books had become available to an expanded reading public. The technology remained stable until the end of the 18c, though markets for printed matter grew, especially for journals and newspapers. Because of the quantities involved and the capital-intensive nature of the business, the early printing and publishing of books tended to be centralized. In Britain, in the early centuries of printing, the government encouraged centralization in London and the universities of Oxford and Cambridge, because printing and publishing could easily be controlled and censored from there. In the 19c, however, a great expansion took place because of the spread of education, large and small printers set up shop in many places, and publishers (becoming from the 18c steadily more distinct from printers) became established outside the major centres in England, Scotland, and Ireland. The technology also changed with new kinds of presses and, by the end of the century, with new systems for typesetting. In the 20c, there has been a pronounced shift towards general literacy and a vast provision of printed materials throughout the world and in particular throughout the English-speaking world.

Nature and impact. A printed book not only involves a different technology from a manuscript, but results in a different product. Whereas manuscripts were copied in very small quantities, early books were printed in editions that averaged 250 to 1,250 copies. In the late 20c, however, an academic book might have 1,500 copies and a best-selling popular paperback a first print-run of 250,000. This economy of scale means that material can be rapidly disseminated. In the early centuries of printing, pamphlets and other more ephemeral material, often religious or political, could present issues of immediate importance. Many debates in the Reformation took place in print and in England little pamphlet wars, such as the late 16c Marprelate Controversy (in which anonymous tracts, printed on a secret press, irreverently attacked bishops and defended Puritanism), set the stage for sustained radical writing during the following century. The quantity of books available helped increase the numbers of the reading public, which in turn increased the number of books and the importance of literacy as a social tool. Although writing and reading have been associated with a minority educated class, printers from Caxton onwards, and especially from the 19c onwards, have often tried to extend readership by publishing popular and entertaining works. Currently, most books in English are aimed at specific audiences, but some would-be bestsellers are directed at an undifferentiated mass of millions of potential readers. For newpapers and magazines, the size of the audience is greater still. Increasingly sophisticated textbooks, books

of self-instruction, and works of reference have also been a consequence of printing. Although rudimentary in the early centuries, they have become so refined that a surgeon can perform complex procedures based on text alone.

Printing and culture. Some scholars, following Harold Innis and Marshall McLuhan, suggest that print has created its own mental world, that it has been an agent of cultural change at a profound level. Although the attractiveness of such a theory may arise as much from a need to define literacy during a period of flux (the advent of cinematic and electronic media), the notion of a 'culture' associated with print bears cautious examination, especially in the way the press disseminates written language and at the same time changes it. Because of the nature of their work, printers affect the shape and style of printed matter. Traditional spelling and punctuation have been standardized by print and syntax and style influenced by it: see PUNCTUATION, SPELLING. The history of dictionaries and encyclopedias is closely bound up with the history of printing; a profound reliance on alphabetical order, though generated in the late Middle Ages, is basic to the culture of print: see DICTIONARY. The most pervasive text in English was once the Bible, but is now the telephone book. Although spoken English has retained its diversity, printed English shows less variation. Notions of correctness, for centuries part of the study of Latin manuscripts, have been passed on in the vernacular legacy of print; such notions spill over from print into speech, so that 'correct' speech follows bookish patterns.

See AMPERSAND, BACK-SLASH, BOOK, BOOKLET, BROCHURE, CAPITAL, CARET, CASE[2], COMMUNICATIVE SHIFT, COPY, CROWN, DEMY, DIAGONAL, DI(A)ERESIS, EDITION, EM, ERRATUM SLIP, FOLIO, FONT/FOUNT, FOOLSCAP, FORMAT, GALLEY, GATHERING, GOTHIC, HARD COPY AND SOFT COPY, HEADERS AND FOOTERS, IMPERIAL, IMPRESSION, INCUNABLE, ITALIC, KEYBOARD, LASER, LEAF, LEAFLET, LEGAL-SIZE, LETTERPRESS, LETTERSET, LETTER-SIZE, LIGATURE, LINE, LINOTYPE, LITERAL, LITHOGRAPHY, LOGO, LOGOTYPE, LOWER CASE, MIMEOGRAPH, MISPRINT, -MO, MONOTYPE, OBLIQUE, OCTAVO, OFFSET, ORTHOEPY, ORTHOGRAPHY, PAGE, PAGE PROOF, PAGINATION, PAMPHLET, PAPER, PARCHMENT, PHOTOCOPYING, PHOTO-OFFSET PRINTING, PICA, PLATEN, POINT, PRESS, PRINT, PRINTER, PRINTER'S ERROR, PRINTHEAD, PRINTING PRESS, PRINTOUT, PROOFREADING, PUBLISHING, PUNCTUATION, QUARTO, QUIRE, QWERTY, REAM, RECTO, ROYAL, RUNNING HEAD, SERIAL, SIGNATURE, SLASH, SOLIDUS, SPELLING, STET, TRANSCRIPTION, TRANSLITERATION, TYPE, TYPESETTING, TYPEWRITER, TYPOGRAPHICAL ERROR, TYPOGRAPHY, UPPER CASE,

VELLUM, VERSO, VIRGULE, WIDOWS AND ORPHANS, XEROGRAPHY. [MEDIA, TECHNOLOGY, WRITING].

W.W.B.

Eisenstein, Elizabeth. 1979. *The Printing Press as an Agent of Change: Communications and Cultural Transformations in Early-Modern Europe*. Two volumes. Cambridge: University Press.

Febvre, Lucien, & Martin, Henri-Jean. 1976. *The Coming of the Book: The Impact of Printing 1450-1800*. Translated by David Gerard. London: NLB.

Gaskell, Philip. 1972. *A New Introduction to Bibliography*. Oxford: University Press.

PRINTING PRESS [16c: combining *print* and *press*, both words deriving ultimately from one Latin verb, *premere/pressum*]. An apparatus for the production of printed matter, standard in form from the mid-15c to the early 19c: an upright wooden device supported by two main wooden beams which supported a screw mechanism holding a platen. The *platen* (a flat plate that presses paper against type) was lowered on top of packing that in turn covered paper resting on the surface of the inked type. Pressure exerted by the screw on the platen ensured that the surface of the paper was uniformly presented to the type. After the paper was printed on, the platen was raised, the bed of type was rolled out, the paper removed, fresh ink uniformly reapplied by dabbing the surface with large leather inking balls, new paper was inserted and lowered on to the type, and the bed rolled under the platen again for another impression. About 250 impressions per hour could be made. A quarto volume of 240 pages in an edition of 1,000 copies required 60,000 impressions: about 240 hours of work by two men (one inking, one working the press). Many printers had more than one press. In the early 19c, experiments were made with form and material. Iron presses were introduced which were more compact and durable and had more efficient hand-operated levers. Two innovations, however, greatly altered the speed and efficiency of presses: external power supply (steam, electricity), providing far greater energy than human operators, and *rotary presses* that allowed paper to pass between cylinders in continuous one-way movement rather than the constant traditional up and down. The fastest system is the *web-fed press* through which a single roll or web of paper runs over cylindrical surfaces to produce rapid printings in tens of thousands of impressions an hour. See DESKTOP PUBLISHING, LASER, PHOTOCOPYING, PRESS, PRINTING. [TECHNOLOGY]. W.W.B.

PRINTOUT [Later 20c]. A term in computing and word processing for the output of a computer through a printer attached to it (*a computer printout*), usually in the form of continuous fanfold sheets with perforated edges but also as single sheets fed in sequence into such a printer. Material printed out in this way usually has two qualities: *draft* and *letter quality*. See PRINTER. [TECHNOLOGY]. T.MCA.

PRINT STANDARD. See STANDARD ENGLISH.

PRIVATE LANGUAGE. Language used for private or in-group purposes; a particular language or variety of a language used for such purposes, such as adolescent *slang*, criminal *argot*, and technical *jargon*. A private language that is intended to be opaque to all or most outsiders is known technically as a *cryptolect* ('hidden dialect'). Such languages are difficult to study because they often change rapidly and investigators have difficulty gaining admission to the groups that use them. The *travellers* or *travelling people* of Europe and North America, a group that includes but is not limited to *Gypsies* or *Romanies*, use various cants and forms of Romani as a *language of the roads*, to mark their ethnic identity and exclude outsiders. The linguist Ian Hancock, of Romany descent, has reported on these cryptolects: for example, in 'Romani and Angloromani' (in P. Trudgill (ed.), *Language in the British Isles*, 1984).

In California, a more localized private language called *Boontling* (also *Boonville Lingo*) was used from the 1880s to the 1920s around Boonville in the upper Anderson Valley of Mendocino County in California. As the linguist Charles Adams (*Boontling: An American Lingo*, 1971) describes it, Boonville was at that time fairly isolated from the rest of the state, and local residents evolved the Boontling jargon to serve a variety of functions. Men used it as the secret language of sheep-shearing crews and baseball teams, from which women were excluded, though in practice women quickly learned it. Adults also used the jargon to keep discussions secret from children, though children also managed to work it out. Boontling was most effective in separating locals from outsiders, who could not easily fathom the altered pronunciations, abbreviations, and personal associations that formed the basis of Boontling. Among its evasive usages were: *burlap* (sometimes shortened to *burl*) to have sexual intercourse, *dreef* coitus interruptus, *keeboarp* premature ejaculation, *moldunes* breasts, *nonch harpins* objectionable talk, especially about sexual matters.

Perhaps the most common form of private usage in English occurs in families. Parents often coin private usages, such as nicknames and child-orientated euphemisms for bodily parts and functions, and adopt expressions used by their children when they were learning to speak. Twins are also sometimes credited with developing a private language that only they can understand. Family usages are often sustained for years without outsiders knowing much or anything about them. Perhaps the most opaque and isolated form of private language is that of schizophrenics. Although private language is widespread, no definitive study of the subject as a whole currently exists. A recent publication that deals, in popular form and format, with private usage in the home is Paul Dickson's *Family Words: The Dictionary for People Who Don't Know a Frone from a Brinkle* (Reading, Mass.: Addison-Wesley, 1988). *Frones* are particles that stick to plates; *brinkles* are marks on the face from sheets, a couch, etc., when one wakes up: compare BURGESSISM.

See ARGOT, BACK SLANG, CANT, COCKNEY, CRYPTOGRAPHY, DOUBLE DUTCH, DOUBLE TALK, INFIX, JARGON, PIG LATIN, POLARI, RHYMING SLANG, ROMANI, SLANG. [LANGUAGE, STYLE].

D.E.B., T.MCA.

PRIVATIVE [14c: from Latin *privativus* showing loss]. An element of language which expresses lack, privation, or negation: *un-* in *unhappy*, *-less* in *useless*. The terms *alpha privative* or *privative alpha* are used for the Greek prefix *a-* (*an-* before vowels and *h*), as in *atheism* (*a-the-ism* 'no-god-ness', a disbelief in God), *an(a)esthesia* (*an-aesthes-ia* 'no-feeling-ness', loss of sensibility), *anhydrous* (*an-hydr-ous* 'no-water-having', without water). [WORD]. T.MCA.

PROCLITIC [1840s: from Greek *proklitikós* leaning forward]. A monosyllable attached, usually in a reduced form, to a following word: *it* in *'twill* it will, *'twas* it was, *'twould* it would. Compare ENCLITIC. [WORD]. T.MCA.

PRODUCTIVE. A term in linguistics for the capacity of a word element or a word-forming paradigm to produce new words. The suffix *-ness* is productive because it can form many nouns on the same principle as *darkness* from *dark*, but the suffix *-ledge* is not, because it does not form new words on the same principle as *knowledge* from *know*. The productivity of some elements can be greater than others at particular times and in particular places. The combining form *megal(o)-* (as in *megalomania, megalosaurus*) is not highly productive, but its variant *mega-* (as in *megacycle, megawatt*) has been fashionable and prolific for decades, producing such technical usages as *megafrustule, megakaryocytic, megasporange, megasporophyll* and such informal, often stunt, expressions as *megabash, mega best seller, mega-city, megamachine, megamouthpiece, megastar, megatrend.* Some forms may be non-productive for decades or centuries, then become fashionable, then decline again. In the late 19c US, *-ine* was a popular feminine

suffix on the analogy of *heroine*, forming such words as *actorine, chorine, doctorine, knitterine, speakerine.* See PHRASAL VERB, PREFIX, SUFFIX, WORD-FORMATION. [WORD]. T.MCA.

PROFESSIONAL AND LINGUISTIC ASSESSMENT BOARD. A department of the General Medical Council in Britain that sponsors an English-language test designed as a qualification for medical practice in the UK by doctors who are not from the European Community and whose mother tongue is not English. See EXAMINING IN ENGLISH. [EDUCATION]. W.S.

PROFICIENCY. See CAMBRIDGE CERTIFICATE OF PROFICIENCY IN ENGLISH.

PROGRESS AND DECAY IN LANGUAGE. Two kinds of assumption are commonly made about languages: that they move from worse to better states (progress, amelioration); that they move from better to worse states (decay, deterioration). The Stoics of ancient Greece took the view that languages decay, whereas some social Darwinians in the 19-20c have held that languages improve as they evolve. A mixed viewpoint is also intermittently found: that some aspects of a language are deteriorating while others are improving. However, language change is an inevitable process and is the result of many factors, both linguistic and social. The interpretation of such change in terms of the improvement or deterioration of a language appears to be more a matter of social standpoint than linguistic observation.

Life cycles in language. In the 19c, it was widely believed in Western society that languages have a life cycle like animals and plants, in which they progress to a mature stage, then gradually decay. An inflected language such as classical Latin was a favoured example of a mature language, and English was thought by some to be in a state of disintegration because it was gradually losing its word endings ('English has no grammar'). This view, once held by scholars and lay people alike, is currently regarded as mistaken by most linguists. A later view, endorsed by Otto Jespersen, held that a fairly analytic language such as English represented the best and most evolved type of structure. This view is also now regarded as unfounded by most linguists.

States of language. There appears to be no reason for supposing that any one language is inherently superior to any other, either socially or structurally. Pidgins and creoles, which are languages in the process of development, are linguistically 'impoverished' in that they do not initially have the range of vocabulary and constructions found in 'full' languages. Some languages are widespread for political or social reasons, rather than because of any intrinsic superiority. Over the centuries, very different kinds of languages have held dominant cultural positions and had high prestige. See CLASSICAL LANGUAGE. Conversely, languages which decline and die out do so when they become subject to powerful social pressures, as with Gaelic, which has declined in Scotland because English has for many years been the dominant language of the United Kingdom.

The decline of English? The view that English is 'going to the dogs' is widely held, especially by older people with conservative views. It is frequently expressed in newspapers, both in letters to the editor and feature articles, which often assert that change arises from lack of care and proper education ('slovenly language', 'sloppy speech', 'illiteracy in the classroom'). The changes referred to, however, appear to be continuous and inevitable. Sometimes, changes occur which happen repeatedly in the languages of the world, such as loss of the final consonant in a word. At other times, the need to maintain patterns may cause large-scale restructuring: vowel changes in English obscured the connection between many singular and plural words, such as *cow/kine* and *brother/brethren*, so new plurals (*cows*, *brothers*) replaced the old ones. These either fell out of general use (*kine*) or acquired a specialized sense (*brethren*), though two of the old -*en* plurals remain in general use (*children*, *oxen*). At other times, changes take place under the influence of other languages, or other varieties of English: at an early stage, English borrowed numerous Latin words, and currently BrE is heavily influenced by AmE. In such changes, however, there is nothing either progressive or decadent. They simply occur.

Features of change. A social group with overt or covert prestige usually initiates a change, sometimes consciously, sometimes unconsciously, though it can only bring about an innovation that was liable to occur in any case. There are usually several directions in which a language can move at any one time, and social factors can push it towards one rather than another. Currently, BrE and AmE are adopting different paths over intervocalic /t/, which is inherently unstable. In a word such as *bitter*, the /t/ is increasingly being replaced by a glottal stop in BrE, but by /d/ in AmE, where the words *bitter* and *bidder* can be indistinguishable. Some people are indifferent to such changes. Others regard them as reprehensible and a symptom of a wider malaise in society, even though the changes are independent of social conditions. Disapproval of a change may therefore be more indicative of the disposition of the commentator than the state of the language. Such disapproval may, however, influence individuals in their response to changes, if they are aware of them. Occasionally, social pressure may postpone or reverse a change: for example, initial /h/ is an unstable element in some varieties of BrE, but is preserved by a popular belief that it is 'wrong to drop aitches'. See (A)ESTHETICS, LANGUAGE CHANGE, SEMANTIC CHANGE. [LANGUAGE].   J.M.A., T.MCA.

PROGRESSIVE, also **continuous**. Terms for a verb form that basically denotes duration. In English, the contrast is between progressive (*She is repairing computers*) and non-progressive (*She repairs computers*). The progressive is constructed in English by a combination of a form of the verb *be* and the -*ing* form of the following verb: *was talking, may be calling, has been seeing, is being investigated*. The English progressive is generally considered to be an *aspect* (the way in which the temporal situation is viewed by the speaker), as contrasted with a *tense* (the location of the situation in time). However, the marking of aspect is always combined with the marking of tense: *is reading* is present progressive; *was reading* is past progressive. See ASPECT, TENSE. [GRAMMAR].   S.G.

PROLEGOMENON. See PROLOG(UE).

PROLEPSIS [16c: through Latin, from Greek *prólēpsis* anticipation]. (1) A term in rhetoric for treating a future event as if it has already happened: *I'm dead—Get away before they kill you too!* (2) A debating device in which one raises an objection to one's own case before an opponent can do so: *I am well aware that the cost of the project is high, but consider the consequences of not going ahead.* (3) In traditional grammar, a structure anticipating another that comes later: *that old man* in '*That old man, I just saw him again.*' (4) Also *prochronism*. Assigning a person or event, etc., to an earlier period, usually by mistake; the representation of something in the future as if it already exists. Compare ANACHRONISM. [GRAMMAR, STYLE].   T.MCA.

PROLOGUE, also AmE **prolog** [13c: through French from Latin *prologus*, Greek *prólogos* ('fore-speech') introduction]. (1) Also *foreword, introduction, preface*, and most formally *prolegomenon*. A preliminary statement in a novel, long poem, treatise, or other text, that introduces its subject matter. In Chaucer's *Canterbury Tales* (14c), nearly all the tales told by the pilgrims are preceded by a prologue that in the setting of the pilgrimage to Canterbury prepares the reader for the tale in question; only three of the tales have no prologue of their own. The *General Prologue* to the whole work is one of the longest and best-known examples of the type in English. The plural *prolegomena* (sometimes with a singular verb) can name a preliminary academic treatise or paper, as in *Prolegomena to a Theory of Metaphor* (title). (2) An introductory speech, often in verse, that draws attention to the theme of a play; (archaic) the player who delivers this speech; an introductory scene that precedes the first act of a play. Compare EPILOG(UE). See PREFACE. [LITERATURE, MEDIA, WRITING].   T.MCA.

PRONOUN [16c: from Old French *pronom*, Latin *pronomen* a loan translation of Greek *antōnumía* before the name or noun]. A traditional part of speech that is typically used as a substitute for a noun or noun phrase. In contemporary grammatical theory, pronouns are sometimes viewed as a subclass of nouns. They constitute a closed class, in that few new pronouns ever enter a language.

Subclasses. There are eight subclasses: personal pronouns (*I, we, they*, etc.); possessive pronouns (*my/mine, our/ours, their/theirs*, etc.); reflexive pronouns (*myself, ourselves, themselves*, etc.); demonstrative pronouns (*this, that, these, those*); reciprocal pronouns (*each other, one another*); interrogative pronouns (*who, what*, etc.); relative pronouns (*who, that*, etc.); indefinite pronouns (*any, somebody, none*, etc.). Some forms belong to more than one subclass: *who* is an interrogative pronoun in *Who is that?* and a relative pronoun in *the child who did that . . .* Some may belong to other parts of speech: *any* is a pronoun in *Do you want any?* and a determiner (like the definite article, introducing a noun phrase) in *Do you want any money?* The possessive pronouns have two sets of forms: one strictly speaking a determiner (*my* in *You have my book*), the other a pronoun (*mine* in *That book is mine*).

Form. Some of the sets of pronouns have distinctions in person, number, case, or gender. Personal pronouns have distinctions in: person (*I, you, she*); number (*I, we*); gender (in the third-person singular only: *he, she, it*); case (subjective *I*, objective *me*). Possessives may be viewed as genitives of personal pronouns and make similar distinctions, as do reflexives (which do not have case). Demonstratives have distinctions in number (*this, that* versus *these, those*) and in physical or metaphorical distance (*this, these* are nearer to speaker than *that, those*). The reciprocals have genitives (*each other's, one another's*), as do the indefinites ending in *-body* and *-one* (such as *somebody's, anyone's*). Finally, the interrogatives and relatives have distinctions in gender (personal *who* and normally non-personal *what* for interrogatives, personal *who* and non-personal

which for relatives), and in case (subjective *who*, objective *whom*, genitive *whose*).

Function. In contemporary grammar, the pronoun by itself usually constitutes a noun phrase, though with certain restrictions some pronouns may be modified: *something colourful; those who know; what else*. As the main or only word in the noun phrase, it has the same set of syntactic functions as a noun. Many of the pronouns have important discourse functions. They contribute to cohesion in discourse by referring back to a previous unit in anaphora (*he* in *While Matthew was in Jerusalem, he joined a peculiar cult*) or forward to a subsequent unit in cataphora (*Although she is studying hard, Deborah finds time to help me*). Some of the pronouns are used in deixis to refer directly to persons or things in the situation of the discourse: *I* for the speaker or writer and *you* for the person or persons addressed, and *it* in *Pick it up* (where the thing referred to by *it* is not previously named). See DEMONSTRATIVE PRONOUN, GENDER, GENERIC PRONOUN, PART OF SPEECH, PERSON, PERSONAL PRONOUN, RECIPROCAL PRONOUN, REFLEXIVE PRONOUN, SHAKESPEARE. [GRAMMAR].   S.G., T.MCA.

PRONOUNCING DICTIONARY. See BBC PRONUNCIATION UNIT, DICTIONARY, ENGLISH PRONOUNCING DICTIONARY, ORTHOEPY.

PRONUNCIATION [15c: from Latin *pronuntiatio/pronuntiationis* delivering a speech]. (1) The act or result of producing the sounds of speech, including articulation, intonation, and rhythm. (2) The sound system of a language: *German pronunciation*. (3) An accepted standard of sound and rhythm for elements of spoken language: *the proper pronunciation of 'controversy'; the mispronunciation of vowels*. (4) The phonetic representation of a sound, word, etc.: see TRANSCRIPTION. Because of the vagaries of the spelling system of English, most larger dictionaries have since the 18c provided guidance on the pronunciation of words, usually immediately after the headword of an entry, and either in a system of *respelling* or, since the end of the 19c, in phonetic symbols. EFL learners' dictionaries published in the UK currently use the International Phonetic Alphabet to represent the phonemes of RP, an accent of England that has served as a *pronunciation model* (the target at which the learner aims) since the early 20c. Some learners' dictionaries provide AmE equivalents. Works that concentrate on pronunciation alone include Daniel Jones, *An English Pronouncing Dictionary* (*EPD*, 14th edition, revised by A. C. Gimson, 1977), and J. C. Wells, *The Longman Pronunciation Dictionary* (1990). In dictionaries for native speakers, respelling systems are generally preferred in the US, while in the UK publishers are currently divided, some favouring respelling, others (such as Oxford University Press) moving over to IPA symbols.

See: (1) ACCENT, ACRONYM, ARTICULATION, ARTICULATORY SETTING, BBC ENGLISH[1], BBC PRONUNCIATION UNIT, ELOCUTION, ENGLISH PRONOUNCING DICTIONARY, INTERNATIONAL PHONETIC ALPHABET, LEARNER'S DICTIONARY, MISPRONUNCIATION, ORTHOEPY, PHONETICS, PUBLIC SCHOOL PRONUNCIATION, RECEIVED PRONUNCIATION, RESPELLING, SHAKESPEARE, SPEECH THERAPY, SPELLING PRONUNCIATION, USAGE. (2) The pronunciation sections of entries describing major varieties of English, such as CANADIAN ENGLISH. [SPEECH]. G.K., T.MCA.

PRONUNCIATION MODEL. See MODEL, PRONUNCIATION.

PROOF-READING.
The reading of typeset or transcribed material (a *proof*) before it appears in its final printed form, to find and correct errors and make any necessary changes in presentation or content. Errors occur for many reasons (such as inattention, distraction, tiredness, misinterpretation, and mechanical failure) and can profoundly affect meaning: a *not* missing from a clause; *hate* spelled *ate*; a line, paragraph, or even page omitted; a word, phrase, or sentence misplaced or repeated. The so-called *Wicked Bible* (1631) reads 'thou shalt commit adultery' (Exodus 20: 14); another of 1682 reads 'if the latter husband ate her' (Deuteronomy 24: 3). Simple errors (*Germn* for *German*; *millenium* for *millennium*; *tendonitis* for *tendinitis*; *misssing* for *missing*) threaten meaning less, but too many of them may affect the reader's confidence in author and publisher.

Correcting proofs. Because of the complex nature of English orthography and the standard of accuracy demanded in cultural, educational, and publishing institutions, most readers expect printed material to be consistent in form as well as sound in content. Proof-reading is a stage in attaining that basic consistency. In the era of the hand-press (15–17c), when spelling was not entirely regular, many books were nevertheless proof-read with care. Errors were often corrected while the work was in press; the printers would 'pull' (print off) a sheet and continue working while the corrector scanned the proof. Errors such as broken type or missing words would be put right on the press and the printing resumed. This procedure for correction demanded that someone competent be nearby; authors were often at the printing house or small batches of proof were sent to them nearby for immediate attention. Corrected and uncorrected sheets are found mixed in single copies of old books. Responsibility for proof-reading changed when typesetting and printing became separate functions. Until the 1980s, the typesetter generally always read proofs, as did the author and the publisher's editor. Currently, in the context of computer typesetting, there is little significant proof-reading by typesetters. In addition, before the 18c, printers tended to be the custodians of spelling, and when dictionaries sought to standardize spelling from the 18c onwards printers continued to standardize other aspects of typeset presentation. In the 20c, however, this responsibility has passed to publishers.

Erratum sheets. Errors would also be caught after the book was completed. A list of *errata* (Latin: 'things that have wandered', mistakes) would be placed at the end of the book, with the understanding that the owner could enter the corrections where necessary. An *erratum sheet* or *slip* is still sometimes sent out, but the practice has become unusual. Errors are now commonly left until they can be fixed in a later printing, if at all. Sometimes, early publishers removed a whole leaf and replaced it with corrected matter, or pasted over the error with a small piece of paper containing the correction. Such changes are called *cancels* and in unusual instances still occur, most commonly when publisher's data have to be revised. Comments in errata sheets have sometimes been revealing. The poet Robert Herrick wrote in *Hesperides* (1648): 'For these transgressions which thou here see, / Condemne the Printer, Reader, and not mee.' Accusations, however, could as easily fly in the other direction: 'Good Reader the Authors coppy being not so legible as we could have wished, we were forc'd to transcribe it in his absence, and by this means these grosser escapes hapned' (Leonard Lichfield, printer of G. Ironside's *Seven Questions Disputed*, 1637). Such casting of blame continues to be common in private comment though it is rarely seen in print.

The persistence of error. Errors persist, even after reading by typesetter, proof-reader, and author, for two main reasons: (1) Translating visual into mental data, then into motor activity (the act of choosing the right piece of type or striking the right key on the keyboard) is fraught with difficulty, and an experienced proof-reader learns to watch for certain resulting kinds and patterns of error. (2) Most people do not read letter by letter but word by word or by groups of words at a time. Their eyes move across the page in short hops and words are identified in clumps, sometimes just by outline or even by what is expected to be there. Proof-reading, however, requires people to unlearn the habits appropriate to speedy consumption of material.

It is slower, identifying every letter form in the word, and requires steady attention to both the new and the original copy.

Proof-reading procedures. Many procedures for reading proof go to great lengths to break up normal reading habits. Some publishers recommend that a proof-reader be read to in a slow even tone by an assistant, or that the proof-reader read the material aloud to record his or her voice and then have the recorded voice played back while checking the text. Some present-day editors of early texts, for which accuracy is paramount, have gone so far as to read the material backwards; the normal habits of reading are then completely overturned. However, the drawback is exhaustion, one of the prime causes of inattention and error. The usual procedure is to read the proof against the copy as slowly as is needed to pay attention to every letter in every word and every mark of punctuation. Sometimes marking off the line of type with a ruler or strip of paper is helpful in isolating the visual field.

Spotting obviously misspelled words is easy. It is harder to pick up misspelled foreign words, unfamiliar and technical terms, missing items, confusible forms like *it's/its* or *personal/personnel*, mistakes that conform to a pattern (*futility* instead of *futurity*), and missing second members of pairs such as quotation marks and parentheses. By the time a work is in proof it is usually too late in terms of cost and schedule to make systematic alterations: for example, BrE spellings with *-our* for AmE *-or*. The point is to ensure that the chosen system has been consistently applied in preparing the text. Incorrect spacing, wrong type-fonts, and other typographical errors must also be seen and marked. In addition, proof-readers generally check end-of-line hyphenation, spacing, length of dashes, and other technical details. Bad word breaks at the ends of lines (*Oxf-/ord* for *Ox-/ford*) are often allowed by computer typesetting systems (although they are being increasingly eliminated), and must be watched for. Similarly, the inadequate entry or translation of computer printing codes can cause serious problems: neglecting the command to close a field causes all subsequent text to be set in the wrong typeface.

Proof correction. Traditionally, a proof-reader marks the errors and their corrections on a *galley proof*, using a highly standardized system of proof-reader's marks. While professional proof-readers are trained in the system, authors may sometimes be less knowledgeable or disciplined in using it. Some of the marks are centuries old, such as the *caret mark* (showing where something has to be inserted), a *circled dot* (to indicate a period), and the word *stet* (indicating that a

proposed correction is to be ignored). Two present-day systems are British Standard BS 5261: Part 2: 1976 and that laid out in the *Chicago Manual of Style* (13th edition, below). Once the corrections are entered in conformity with the system used, the proof is returned for *page proofs* or another set of galleys known as a *revised proof*. The corrections must then be double-checked to make sure that they have been entered properly and that new errors have not been entered with them. Error threatens every step of the way. See EDITING, GALLEY, PAGE PROOF, TYPESETTING. [TECHNOLOGY, WRITING].

W.W.B.

Butcher, Judith. 1975. 2nd edition 1981. *Copy-Editing: The Cambridge Handbook.* Cambridge: University Press.
Chicago Manual of Style, The. 1982. 13th edition. Chicago: University Press.
Gaskell, Philip. 1972. *A New Introduction to Bibliography.* Oxford: University Press.
Hart's Rules for Compositors and Readers. 1986. 39th edition. Oxford: University Press.
Simpson, Percy. 1935/70. *Proof-Reading in the Sixteenth, Seventeenth, and Eighteenth Centuries.* Oxford: University Press.

PROP. See DUMMY.

PROPAGANDA [18c: through Italian from Neo-Latin, from the phrase *Congregatio de propaganda fide* Congregation for propagating the faith, from *propagandus* requiring to be spread, from *propagare/propagatum* to reproduce (especially a plant by means of cuttings), spread; ultimately from *pro* forward, outward, and *pangere/pactum* to fasten, fix. Compare *dissemination*, from Latin *semen/seminis* seed. The usage derives from the work of the Congregation/College of the Propaganda (Latin name as above), a post-Reformation committee of cardinals founded in 1622 by Pope Gregory XV to oversee the foreign missions of the Roman Catholic Church: 'An Italian missionary of the Propaganda' (T. Hope, *Anastasius*, 1819). Many non-Catholics were suspicious of the aims and activities of the College, a factor that encourage negative nuances in the use of the word]. (1) Until the end of the 19c: an association, system, plan, or project for spreading a religion, ideology, doctrine, or practice. (2) In the 20c, in which the term has acquired increasingly sinister connotations: the systematic, often unscrupulous propagation of information and ideas by an interest group so as to encourage a desired response among as many people as possible, including the use of rumour, innuendo, disinformation, and smear campaigns against opponents. Governments, political parties, and other organizations have often used the mass media for propaganda purposes especially in wartime. For many years during the Cold War, in the decades following the Second World War, English was the major language of anti-capitalist propaganda issued by the Soviet Union and the People's Republic of China, because it was so widely understood. Both the British Council and the United States Information Agency (USIA) have been regarded in especially post-colonial countries as propaganda arms of the British and US governments respectively. Compare DOUBLESPEAK, DOUBLE TALK, DOUBLETHINK, EUPHEMISM, INFORMATION, INNUENDO, NEWSPEAK, TRACT. See BRITISH COUNCIL, UNITED STATES INFORMATION AGENCY, VOICE OF AMERICA. [MEDIA]

T.MCA.

PROPER [13c: from Old French *propre*, Latin *proprius* one's own, special]. A general term for what is right, suitable, or appropriate (*the proper clothes for the job*; *the proper technical term*; *proper conduct*), often implying a wish or need to 'do the right thing' socially (*They were always very proper in everything they did*; *Oh, it just wouldn't be proper to do that*). The term has sometimes been attached to groups and places: 'She was only a mild rebel: there was still too much of the Proper Bostonian in her' (J. Cleary, *High Road to China*, 1977). Traditionally, a *proper accent* has been the accent considered most suitable for polite, dignified, educated usage, among ladies and gentlemen: in England, Received Pronunciation. Such non-standard expressions as *He don't talk proper* have long been widespread, marking the social and linguistic gap between speakers of vernacular and standard English: 'Perhaps she'll 'ave another go at teachin' me to speak proper, pore soul' (Margery Allingham, *The Tiger in the Smoke*, 1952); ironically, 'How to talk proper in Liverpool' (subtitle of *Lern Yerself Scouse*, 1966, by Frank Shaw, Fritz Spiegl, & Stan Kelly). The term *proper English* is often used to mean *standard English*: 'Debates about the state and status of the English language are rarely debates about language alone. Closely linked to the question, what is proper English? is another, more significant social question: who are the proper English?' (publisher's statement opening Tony Crowley's *Proper English: Readings in Language, History and Cultural Identity*. Routledge, 1991). See (A)ESTHETICS, CORRECT, GOOD ENGLISH, STANDARD. Compare GENTEELISM. [STYLE].

T.MCA.

PROPER ADJECTIVE [Early 20c]. A traditional term for an adjective that derives from a proper noun and is written in English with an initial capital letter. It refers to a nationality (*American, Chinese*), a place (*Iberian, Parisian*), an ethnic or religious group (*Muslim, Roman*

Catholic), or an individual (*Churchillian, Byronic, Elizabethan, Kafkaesque, Napoleonic, Shavian*). [GRAMMAR].

S.C.

PROPER NAME. See NAME, ONOMASTICS, PROPER NOUN.

PROPER NOUN [15c]. A category of noun, distinguished on grammatical and semantic grounds from *common noun*, and written with a capital letter. Proper nouns are primarily names of persons (*John, Churchill*), places (*India, Edinburgh*), and various periods of time (*Sunday, August, Christmas*). Their reference is said to be unique in context and definite; sometimes *the* is used with the noun (*the Hague*), but most names are definite without requiring the definite article. Grammatically, indefinite *a/an* and most other determiners are not used with proper nouns, nor is there normally a singular/plural contrast: (*Mount*) *Kilimanjaro*, *the Matterhorn*, *the Seychelles*, but not **a Kilimanjaro*, **that incredible Matterhorn*, **a Seychelle*. There is, however, no clear demarcation between proper and common nouns, regardless of the initial capital. People can speak of *Churchills*, who could be members of the Churchill family, people with that surname, or people figuratively compared to Winston Churchill. See ANTONOMASIA. There might be *a different Churchill* (not Winston), *a Sunday in June*, *that memorable August*, *the Edinburgh of her childhood*, and so on. Here, for specific purposes, proper nouns have effectively been converted into common nouns. Common nouns can also on occasion behave like proper nouns, as in: *I do not fear you, Death*. See APOSTROPHE[2]. Nationality nouns (*Americans, a New Zealander, the Japanese*) lie on the borderline between proper and common nouns. Some grammarians distinguish the *proper noun* (a single noun like *London*; *the* and a single noun: *the Pennines*) from the *proper name*, a wider category which includes these and also such word groups as *the United States* (*of America*), *the Houses of Parliament*, *the Royal Navy*, *A Tale of Two Cities*, *The Concise Oxford Dictionary*. See NAME. [GRAMMAR].

S.C.

PROPOSITION [14c: from Latin *propositio/propositionis*, translating Greek *próthesis* a putting forward. Compare PROTASIS]. (1) Something proposed for consideration, acceptance, negotiation, discussion, or rejection. (2) In logic, an expression (couched in natural language or in symbolic form) that may be true or false: for example, the statement *I am hungry* is regarded as always expressing the same proposition no matter who produces it. See LEMMA, LOGIC, OPPOSITION, PREMISS, SEMANTICS, SYLLOGISM, THEME, THESIS. [LANGUAGE].

T.MCA.

PROSAIC [17c: from Latin *prosaicus* relating to prose]. In general usage, if something is *prosaic* it is dull and unimaginative. The conception of prose as the dull language of treatises took hold before the novel began to enliven writers' styles and give them qualities more commonly associated with poetry. See PROSE. [STYLE]. T.MCA.

PROSCRIPTIVE [18c: from Latin *proscribere/proscriptum* to display in writing, to publish (someone's name) as an outlaw]. A grammatical or other rule is proscriptive if it forbids the use of a particular feature of language on the grounds that it is incorrect or undesirable: proscribing the use of the verb *infer* in such a sentence as *What are you inferring?* and prescribing instead the verb *imply*. See DESCRIPTIVE AND PRESCRIPTIVE GRAMMAR. [GRAMMAR]. S.G.

PROSE [14c: through French from Latin *prosa* (*oratio*) direct or straightforward (speech), from *prosus* or *prorsus* direct, straight, contracted forms of *provorsus* or *proversus* (literally 'turned forward': compare VERSE). *Prosa oratio* was the Latin equivalent of Greek *pezós lógos* speech that goes on foot, as opposed to *émmetros lógos* ('measured speech') or verse, whose high prestige was reflected in the image of riding on horseback]. A form of written discourse based on the sentence and without the stylized patterning of *verse* (with which it often contrasts). A negative perception of prose, which has persisted from classical times virtually to the present day, sees it as a medium that lacks strong features and creative vigour: whence the use of *prosaic* to mean 'dull, commonplace, unimaginative'. This ancient perception has, however, diminished greatly in the 20c, in the course of which prose has become the dominant form of printed discourse and verse has become largely peripheral].

The term covers two kinds of procedure: employing physical features such as the non-metrical line, the paragraph, and sentence-based punctuation, and styles of discourse that serve narrative, expository, descriptive, persuasive, dramatic, and other ends. Prose writing is so similar in many ways to carefully organized speech, and the two have been linked for so long in the world of education, that prose is often thought of as simply speech transferred to paper: see SPOKEN PROSE. Everyday speech, however, is much less tightly structured than most types of prose, and its dynamics are quite distinct from those of formal writing. Colloquial English, for example, is not arranged according to the classical theory of the well-formed sentence ('a sentence is a complete thought'), long a key criterion for producing and evaluating prose. Such a criterion has been used by elocutionists and others in attempts to 'improve' speech, but without

great success: spoken usage that is too 'prosy' sounds artificial and perhaps pretentious. In the classical world, the study and use of prose were linked with rhetoric, grammar, and logic, but whereas the rhetorical tradition was oral in origin, the beginnings of grammar and logic lay in the use and study of writing. Lacking the mnemonic quality and often the histrionic roles of verse, prose has depended largely on writing (not oral delivery) for its transmission, and has come only within the last 300 years to serve as a regular vehicle for 'high' literary genres such as drama and the epic (the latter essentially in the form of the novel).

Kinds of prose. Because of its wide present-day use, prose ranges across many activities, including: the writing of technical instructions; the presentation of information in newspapers and other periodicals; legal, business, and other reports; personal letters; and the writing of fiction and drama. *Literary prose*, considered by many to be its highest form, shares with verse (despite the classical view) an intensification and stylization of rhythm and a greater than usual attention to rhetorical features and aesthetic factors such as euphony and assonance. Its status as prose is sustained, however, by the absence of recurring metrical patterns, however 'poetic' in form and content such texts may be. Many writers of literary prose have followed Aristotle's dictum that it 'must neither possess metre nor be without rhythm' (*Rhetoric*, 3. 8), and at times it can have a quality close to *free verse* or *blank verse*: see DICKENS. Just as the line of demarcation is not always easy to find between prose and verse, so there is no easy demarcation between one kind of prose and another. Prose discourses occupy a spectrum in which the extremes are easily identified: 'poetic' prose on one side, 'technical' or 'functional' prose on the other, with the middle ground often uncertain.

Prose and style. Although style is sometimes thought to reside only in 'good' literary writing (however judged), it is a factor in all writing; every specimen of prose from instructions on how to put together a piece of furniture to James Joyce's *Ulysses* has features that can be described, analysed, and evaluated by stylistic and aesthetic criteria. The evolution of Western prose has produced a variety of styles, often characteristic of a particular period, writer, or function. The traditional division of styles has been into *high, middle,* and *low,* according to the rhetorical principle of *decorum* (that the manner of writing should be adapted to subject and recipient). This socially ranked system, however, has not proved useful in contemporary analysis because it lacks objectivity (though it partly incorporates the present-day linguistic category of *register*: see entry). Like other Western European vernaculars, English developed in the shadow of Latin, and its models for prose were therefore Latinate, at first through translation, imitation, and experiment, later as a consequence of its hybrid inheritance. Because of the classical legacy (and despite specific differences), the prose styles of English have much in common with those of French, Italian, Spanish, German, and other languages also influenced by Latin models. It is possible therefore to talk of a broad European prose tradition of which English is part.

Old and Middle English prose. Old English prose writing was largely a matter of translation from Latin, as in the works of Alfred the Great (9c), but original vernacular prose was produced by such writers as Aelfric of Eynsham (10–11c) and the clerics who compiled the Anglo-Saxon Chronicle. By and large, the style is straightforward and unadorned. In the centuries immediately after the Norman Conquest (1066), the development of Middle English prose waited on the decline of French as the language of aristocracy and government and of Latin as the dominant language of religion and learning. There was therefore little demand for vernacular prose in the Middle Ages and as a result it was generally poorly structured in comparison with Latin. However, the vernacular sermon added persuasive rhetorical strength to some English prose texts, notably in the writings of John Wycliffe, Geoffrey Chaucer, Thomas Malory, and William Caxton.

The following excerpts are typically from translations, or associated with them: the Old English version of the Venerable Bede's *Historia Ecclesiastica Gentis Anglorum* (*Ecclesiastical History of the English People*, early 8c); Chaucer's rendering in the 14c of Boethius, *De Consolatione Philosophiae* (*On the Consolation of Philosophy*: 6c); and Caxton's prologue to the *Eneydos*, his version of a French version of Virgil's *Aeneid* (1490), which moved towards Early Modern English. The slashes (virgules) in Caxton's text were an experiment in punctuation, and are roughly equivalent to commas.

Old English. Breten is gārsecges īegland, þæt wæs gēo geāra Albion hāten: is gesett betwix norþdæle and westdæle, Germānie and Gallie and Hispānie, þæm mæstum dælum Eurōpe, micle fæce ongeān. þæt is norþ eahta hund mīla lang, and twā hund mīla brād. Hit hæfþ fram sūþdæle þā mægþe ongeān þe man hætt Gallia Belgica. Hit is welig, þis īegland, on wæstmum and on trēowum missenlicra cynna, and hit is gescrēpe on læswe scēapa and nēata, and on sumum stōwum wīngeardas grōaþ.

A close translation: Britain is a sea island, that was in former years called Albion: it is set between the north-parts and west-parts [that is, to the north and west] of Germany, Gaul, and Spain, the greatest parts of Europe, by much space opposite [that is, at a considerable distance]. It is north eight hundred miles long, and two hundred miles broad. It has on south-part the nation opposite that one calls Belgian Gaul. It is rich, this island, in fruit and trees of various kinds, and it is suitable for pastures of sheep and cattle, and in some places vineyards grow.

Chaucer. The poete of Trace, *Orpheus*, that whylom hadde right great sorwe for the deeth of his wyf, after that he hadde maked, by his weeply songes, the wodes, moevable, to rennen; and hadde maked the riveres to stonden stille; and hadde maked the hertes and the hindes to joignen, dredeles, hir sydes to cruel lyouns, *for to herknen his songe*; and hadde maked that the hare was nat agast of the hounde, which that was plesed by his songe: so, whan the moste ardaunt love of his wif brende the entrailes of his brest, ne the songes that hadden overcomen alle thinges ne mighten nat asswagen hir lord *Orpheus*, he pleynede him of the hevene goddes that weren cruel to him; he wente him to the houses of helle. And there he temprede hise blaundisshinge songes by resowninge strenges, and spak and song in wepinge al that ever he hadde received and laved out of the noble welles of his moder *Calliope* the goddesse; and he song with as mochel as he mighte of wepinge, and with as moche as love, that doublede his sorwe, mighte yeve him and techen him; and he commoevede the helle, and requerede and bisoughte by swete preyere the lordes of sowles in helle, of relesinge; *that is to seyn, to yilden him his wyf.*

Caxton. How wel that many honderd yerys passed was the sayd booke of eneydos wyth other werkes made and lerned dayly in scolis specyally in ytalye & other places / whiche historye the sayd vyrgyle made in metre / And whan I had aduised me in this sayd boke. I delybered and concluded to translate it in to englysshe And forthwyth toke a penne & ynke and wrote a leef or tweyne / whyche I ouersawe agayn to correcte it / And whan I sawe the fayr & straunge termes therin / I doubted that it sholde not please some gentylmen whiche late blamed me sayeng yᵗ in my translacyons I had ouer curyous termes whiche coude not be vnderstande of comyn peple / and desired me to vse olde and homely termes in my translacyons. and fayn wolde I satysfye euery man / and so to doo toke an olde boke and redde therin / and certaynly the englysshe was so rude and brood that I coude not wele vnderstande it. And also my lorde abbot of westmynster ded do shewe to me late certayn euydences wryton in olde englysshe for to reduce it in to our englysshe now vsid / And certaynly it was wreton in suche wyse that it was more lyke to dutche than englysshe I coude not reduce ne brynge it to be vnderstonden /

Elizabethan and Jacobean prose. In the 16c and 17c, more and more writers chose to develop English prose rather than continue with Latin. Although their prose still followed Latin models, it necessarily accommodated itself increasingly to such vernacular usages as the compound noun and the phrasal verb, as well as less formal syntactic constructions. Elizabethan prose often seems self-conscious in attempting to imitate

Latin, with the Roman lawyer and orator Cicero as the supreme model. Style was based on the periodic sentence, formal and ordered in structure, building to its climax before the full meaning is revealed. This apparent neo-classical artificiality tightened up the loose, rambling style of Middle English and took on a powerfully disciplined form in the preface to the Authorized Version of the Bible:

But how shall men meditate in that, which they cannot vnderstand? How shall they vnderstand that which is kept close in an vnknowen tongue? as it is written, *Except I know the power of the voyce, I shall be to him that speaketh, a Barbarian, and he that speaketh, shalbe* [sic] *a Barbarian to me.* The Apostle excepteth no tongue; not Hebrewe the ancientest, not Greeke the most copious, not Latine the finest. Nature taught a naturall man to confesse, that all of vs in those tongues which wee doe not vnderstand, are plainely deafe; wee may turne the deafe eare vnto them. The *Scythian* counted the *Athenian*, whom he did not vnderstand, barbarous: so the *Romane* did the *Syrian*, and the *Iew*, (euen S. *Hierome* himselfe calleth the Hebrew tongue barbarous, belike because it was strange to so many) so the Emperour of *Constantinople* calleth the *Latine* tongue, barbarous, though Pope *Nicolas* do storme at it: so the *Iewes* long before *Christ*, called all other nations, *Lognazim*, which is little better then barbarous. Therefore as one complaineth, that alwayes in the Senate of *Rome*, there was one or other that called for an interpreter: so lest the Church be driuen to the like exigent, it is necessary to haue translations in a readinesse. Translation it is that openeth the window, to let in the light; that breaketh the shell, that we may eat the kernel; that putteth aside the curtaine, that we may looke into the most Holy place; that remooueth the couer of the well, that wee may come by the water, euen as *Iacob* rolled away the stone from the mouth of the well, by which meanes the flockes of *Laban* were watered. Indeede without translation into the vulgar tongue, the vnlearned are but like children at *Iacobs* well (which was deepe) without a bucket or some-thing to draw with: or as that person mentioned by *Esay*, to whom when a sealed booke was deliuered, with this motion, *Read this, I pray thee,* hee was faine to make this answere, *I cannot, for it is sealed.*

A highly artificial but influential style was that of John Lyly, named *euphuism* from the hero of his prose romances. It was characterized by long periodic sentences, with abundant tropes and figures of rhetoric, classical allusions, and improbable analogies from the natural world. Shakespeare parodied it in *Love's Labour's Lost* (c.1595) and elsewhere: see EUPHUISM. A more restrained style, formal but somewhat less mannered, was achieved by Sir Philip Sidney in his *Arcadia* (1581) and *Defence of Poetry* (1579-80). The Elizabethans could also produce fresh colloquial prose, especially in controversies like the Marprelate pamphlets (1588-9) and in tales of low life like those of Robert Greene (1558-92) and Thomas Deloney (?1560-1600). The excitement of English as an emerging literary language in its own right brought exuberance to contemporary writing. Francis Bacon (1561-1626) criticized the tendency of the periodic style to mask sense with rhetoric. His own style was sometimes rhetorical, but produced greater simplicity, combined with balance and antithesis, in his *Essays* (1597-1625). In the early 17c, a preference for the Latin of Seneca and Tacitus rather than Cicero helped to bring more brevity and precision into English prose, as seen in the work of Thomas Overbury (1581-1613) and John Earle (?1601-1665), and in the learned, allusive prose of the *Anatomy of Melancholy* by Robert Burton (1577-1640).

Restoration and Enlightenment prose. The Restoration period saw the emergence of a distinctly native prose style, whose seeds were sown in the polemical writings of the Civil War. The new prose was simpler and less ornate, further from Latin syntax, more familiar in tone, though still polished and urbane. The beginnings of journalism strengthened the closer relationship between writer and reader; the political prose of Hobbes and the critical prose of Dryden are typical. Prose was increasingly used for instruction as well as for persuasion and entertainment. The members of the Royal Society (founded in 1662) were expected to prefer 'the language of artizans, countrymen, and merchants, before that of wits and scholars'. The polite, familiar style was further developed in the early 18c by Addison, Defoe, Steele, and Swift. The following is from Defoe's *An Essay upon Projects* (1697), relating to the establishing of an English equivalent of the Académie française (see ACADEMY):

I had the Honour once to be a Member of a small Society, who seem'd to offer at this Noble Design in England. But the Greatness of the Work, and the Modesty of the Gentlemen concern'd, prevail'd with them to desist an Enterprize which appear'd too great for Private Hands to undertake. We want indeed a *Richlieu* to commence such a Work: For I am persuaded, were there such a *Genius* in our Kingdom to lead the way, there wou'd not want Capacities who cou'd carry on the Work to a Glory equal to all that has gone before them. The *English* Tongue is a Subject not at all less worthy the Labour of such a Society than the *French*, and capable of a much greater Perfection. The Learned among the *French* will own, That the Comprehensiveness of Expression is a Glory in which the *English* Tongue not only Equals but Excels its Neighbours; *Rapin, St. Evermont,* and the most Eminent *French* Authors have acknowledg'd it: And my Lord *Ros-common,* who is allow'd to be a good Judge of *English*, because he wrote it as exactly as any ever did, expresses what I mean, in these Lines;

'*For who did ever in* French *Authors see*
The Comprehensive English *Energy?*
The weighty Bullion *of one* Sterling *Line,*
Drawn to French *Wire wou'd through whole* Pages shine.

And if our Neighbours will yield us, as their greatest Critick has done, the Preference for Sublimity and Nobeleness of Stile, we will willingly quit all Pretensions to their Insignificant Gaiety.'

'Tis great pity that a Subject so Noble shou'd not have some as Noble to attempt it: And for a Method, what greater can be set before us, than the Academy of *Paris*? Which, to give the *French* their due, stands foremost among all the Great Attempts in the Learned Part of the World.

With the rise of the essay and the novel in the 18c, prose took the assured and accepted place in literature that it already held in legal, commercial, and other uses. Critical responses, both casual and professional, which had previously been mainly confined to poetry, came to be applied to literary prose as well. In addition, a good prose style was considered a desirable accomplishment for the cultivated, and attention to models of 'good writing' in essays, letters, etc., became more and more a required part of education. However, in the late 18c there was a return to the periodic Latinate style. Johnson wrote with involved syntax and the frequent use of classical words, and Burke (1729-97) in political prose and Gibbon (1737-94) in historical prose followed a similar style. At the same time, a comparable prose was developing in North America, and is enshrined in the Declaration of Independence of 4 July 1776 (signed by John Hancock on behalf of Congress), which opens with the following statement:

When in the Course of human Events, it becomes necessary for one People to dissolve the Political Bands which have connected them with another, and to assume among the Powers of the Earth, the separate and equal Station to which the Laws of Nature and of Nature's God entitle them, a decent Respect to the Opinions of Mankind requires that they should declare the causes which impel them to the Separation. We hold these Truths to be self-evident, that all Men are created equal, that they are endowed by their Creator with certain unalienable Rights, that among these are Life, Liberty, and the Pursuit of Happiness—That, to secure these Rights, Governments are instituted among Men, deriving their just Powers from the Consent of the Governed, that whenever any Form of Government becomes destructive of those Ends, it is the Right of the People to alter or to abolish it, and to institute new Government (*A Declaration by the Representatives of the United States of America, in General Congress Assembled*, 4 July 1776).

Prose in the nineteenth century. This century brought as much variety and abundance in prose style as in other things. The reading public expanded on an unprecedented scale, the popularity of the novel in particular giving impetus to prose writing for entertainment and the growth of journalism making it a major vehicle of news and opinion. Although there are marked differences between the leading novelists of the period, they shared a desire to write accessibly and to keep the interest of the reader, who is addressed directly, as a friend. Narrative style became more assured in the hands of Austen, Dickens, Thackeray, Eliot, Hardy, and many other both 'literary' and 'popular' writers. A more didactic type of prose, designed to inform and convince, was practised by Arnold, Carlyle, Macaulay, and others. The following is from Macaulay's essay on Bacon, in the *Edinburgh Review* (1837):

Lady Bacon was doubtless a lady of highly cultivated mind after the fashion of her age. But we must not suffer ourselves to be deluded into the belief that she and her sisters were more accomplished women than many who are now living. On this subject there is, we think, much misapprehension. We have often heard men who wish, as almost all men of sense wish, that women should be highly educated, speak with rapture of the English ladies of the sixteenth century, and lament that they can find no modern damsel resembling those fair pupils of Ascham and Aylmer who compared, over their embroidery, the styles of Isocrates and Lysias, and who, while the horns were sounding and the dogs in full cry, sat in the lonely oriel, with eyes riveted to that immortal page which tells how meekly and bravely the first great martyr of intellectual liberty took the cup from his weeping gaoler. But surely these complaints have very little foundation. We would by no means disparage the ladies of the sixteenth century or their pursuits. But we conceive that those who extol them at the expense of the women of our time forget one very obvious and very important circumstance. In the time of Henry the Eighth and Edward the Sixth, a person who did not read Greek and Latin could read nothing, or next to nothing. The Italian was the only modern language which possessed anything that could be called a literature. All the valuable books then extant in all the vernacular dialects of Europe would hardly have filled a single shelf.

Carlyle wrote in an idiosyncratic and sometimes turgid style, but his vigorous use of 'Saxon' forms and his defiance of classical smoothness made him a strong influence on polemical prose: see CARLYLE. In addition, prose writing in English took firm root during this century in many parts of the world, particularly in the US but also in Australia, Canada, India, and New Zealand.

Prose in the twentieth century. More prose-writing in English has probably been published in this century than in all past centuries combined. Because, however, the quantities involved are so vast and the objectives and styles have been so varied, it is virtually impossible to make more than a few provisional general statements about 20c prose. It can, for example, be argued that there has been in literary and journalistic writing a move away from (often in tandem with a distaste for) the elevated literary and classical style, towards the more direct, immediate, and colloquial. In other areas, however, such as scholarly, scientific, medical, and legal writing, there continues to be an assumption that technical prose is necessarily complex and abstruse: see ACADEMIC USAGE, PLAIN ENGLISH. Despite the work of experimental stylists like Virginia Woolf and James Joyce, creative writing has on the whole become more functional rather than more artistic, and although the 'literary novel' continues to be distinguished from its 'popular' cousin, many writers with a distinct popular bent have from the mid-19c onward come to be regarded as classics in their own right and to be presented as such in university courses in English literature. By and large, although every kind of prose can be found in English in the late 20c, there is a general tendency towards factual and referential writing, favouring shorter sentences and a vocabulary as simple as the subject allows.

See ACADEMIC USAGE, AELFRIC, ALFRED, AMERICAN LITERATURE, BIBLE, CARLYLE, CAXTON, CHURCHILL, COMEDY, COMPOSITION, COMPUTER USAGE, CONVERSATION, DIALOG(UE), DICKENS, DISCOURSE, EARLY MODERN ENGLISH, ENGLISH LITERATURE, EUPHUISM, FREE VERSE, GRAMMAR, MACAULAY, NOVEL, OLD ENGLISH[1], ORWELL, PANTOMIME, PARAGRAPH, PERIODIC SENTENCE, PLAIN ENGLISH, POETIC PROSE, POETRY, PUNCTUATION, SENTENCE, SERMON, SPOKEN PROSE, TEXT, VERSE. [LITERATURE, STYLE, WRITING]. R.C., T.MCA.

PROSODY [15c: from French *prosodie*, Latin *prosodia*, Greek *prosōidia* towards (that is: relating to) song. Compare ACCENT]. (1) The theory and study of versification, concerned in English with rhythm and metre, rhyme, and the form of stanzas. Devices like alliteration, assonance, and onomatopoeia are sometimes regarded as part of prosody, but more usually as part of rhetoric. Prosody began as an attempt to classify and make coherent the practices of Greek and Latin poets; later, it supplied rules for European vernacular poets to follow, influencing poets' choice of form. Because features of stress, pitch, and quantity (which cause likeness or difference between syllables) do not operate equally in all languages, general theories of prosody are of limited value. In addition, change in politics and culture may affect prosody: for example, Old English alliterative verse became peripheral in the Middle Ages because of the dominance of French rhymed verse. The prestige of a system in one language may recommend its application to another; Latin prosody was long thought to be applicable to English, and classical names such as *iamb(us)* and *spondee* are still used for the principal metrical feet in English verse. Poets sometimes challenge the prosodic orthodoxy of their time by reviving old forms or by innovations of their own, as Gerard Manley Hopkins did with *sprung rhythm*. In the 20c,

there has been considerable questioning of traditional prosody by both poets and theorists, but although the use of free verse has increased and the regular older forms have been generally abandoned, no accepted new system has emerged. (2) In especially British phonetics, the area of phonology that goes beyond the study of phonemes to deal with such features as length, rhythm, stress, pitch, intonation, and loudness in speech. In American phonetics, this area is generally known as *suprasegmental phonology*. The study of prosody in verse has benefited from new knowledge about the characteristics of speech. See ALLITERATIVE VERSE, FOOT, METRE/METER, PHONETIC TRANSCRIPTION, RHYME, RHYTHM, SCANSION, SEMANTICS, STRESS, THESIS, TONE, VERSE. [LITERATURE, SPEECH]. R.C., T.MCA.

PROSOPOPOEIA. See PERSONIFICATION.

PROTASIS AND APODOSIS [17c: from Greek *prótasis* a putting or stretching forward, a proposition; *apódosis* a giving back, an answer. Stress: 'PRO-ta-sis', 'a-POD-o-sis']. A pair of contrasting grammatical terms. In a sentence, the *protasis* is the opening clause of two clauses and the *apodosis* is the closing or answering clause, as in the conditional sentence *If you come tomorrow* (protasis), *I'll help you look for them* (apodosis). However, the order of protasis and apodosis is often reversed: *I'll help you look for them, if you come tomorrow*. [GRAMMAR]. T.MCA.

PROTESTANT ASCENDANCY, The, also **The Ascendancy.** (1) The political and linguistic dominance in Ireland from the 16c to the 20c of a minority of English-speaking Protestants (descended from settlers from England and Scotland) over a majority of indigenous, originally Gaelic-speaking Roman Catholics. (2) The associated landed gentry of Ireland. See ANGLO-IRISH, IRISH ENGLISH. [EUROPE, NAME]. T.MCA.

PROTOGRAM. See ACRONYM.

PROVERB [13c: from Latin *proverbium* a saying supporting a point, from *pro-* on behalf of *verbum*, word]. A short traditional saying of a didactic or advisory nature, in which a generalization is given specific, often metaphorical, expression: *A stitch in time saves nine*, meaning that action taken now will prevent a small problem becoming larger. Proverbs are found in many languages and cultures. A common idea may be given different local references: English *carrying coals to Newcastle* equivalent to Greek *sending owls to Athens*. A collection of proverbs may come to be associated with a person famous for wisdom: the Book of Proverbs in the Bible was attributed to King Solomon and a Middle

English series of proverbs in verse was known as the *Proverbs of Alfred* (c.1180). Proverbial sayings were popular in the Middle Ages and treated as accepted wisdom. In the 16c and 17c, they were often used in literature, to support arguments and give emphasis to the author's views. Proverbs are quoted in the speech of literary characters. Chaucer's Pandarus says: 'It is nat good a slepyng hound to wake' (*Troylus and Criseyde*, iii. 110), the ancestor of 'Let sleeping dogs lie'. Shakespeare's Shylock says: 'Fast bind, fast find, / A proverb never stale in thrifty mind' (*Merchant of Venice*, 2. 5).

Proverbs are often of linguistic interest and may show lexical change. The saying 'Do not spoil the *hog* for a halfpennyworth of tar' is recorded in 1600, but changed to *sheep* in 1651 and *ship* in 1823. The mnemonic needs of oral transmission may appear in: *rhyme* 'Birds of a feather flock together'; *assonance* 'A stitch in time saves nine'; *alliteration* 'Look before you leap'. Two proverbs may seem contradictory when in fact they contain truths applicable to different situations: *Too many cooks spoil the broth* as against *Many hands make light work*. Proverbs in present-day usage may often be regarded as clichés, but their persistence indicates their sociolinguistic importance. Commonly, when they occur in informal conversation, only the opening phrase is used: *Well, a stitch in time, you know*; *Don't count your chickens* (before they are hatched). They are often used allusively, as in *the proverbial stitch in time*. Proverbs continue to be created: for example, the First World War saying *No names, no pack drill*, the more recent *If it ain't broke, don't fix it*, and the computer-related *Garbage in, garbage out*. The adjective *proverbial* may mean 'traditional' or 'characteristic': *the proverbial British stiff upper lip*. See ALLITERATION, METAPHOR, QUOTATION, SAYING. [LITERATURE]. R.C., T.MCA.

PROVINCE [14c: through French from Latin *provincia* a conquered territory outside Italy]. (1) An imperial territory: Spain as a province of the Roman Empire. (2) A territorial division in certain states, often originating as colonies of the British Empire: the provinces of Canada, such as Quebec and Newfoundland. (3) Although England is divided into counties, the phrase *the provinces* is used contrastively with *London*; theatrical groups often *tour the provinces* before putting on a show in the capital. The usage is often pejorative, suggesting that life and culture in the provinces are duller and less refined and desirable than in the metropolis. In this context, *provincial* as an adjective implies lack of sophistication, especially in accent, education, style, and usage; as a noun it labels someone from outside London who exhibits such a lack. See COLONIAL, HOME COUNTIES, LONDON, PROVINCIALISM. [STYLE]. T.MCA.

PROVINCIALISM [18c]. A usually pejorative term for a lack of social and linguistic sophistication regarded as typical of provinces and provincials, and for a word or other usage that is not accepted in the capital or the main cultural centre(s) of a nation. See PROVINCE, -ISM. [STYLE, WORD]. T.MCA.

PROXEMICS [1950s: from *prox(imity)* and *-emics* as in *phonemics*]. In psychology and linguistics, the study of the spatial arrangements people (and sometimes animals) need in their social activities and particularly for communication, including the social distances acceptable in face-to-face conversations in different cultures. See BODY LANGUAGE. [LANGUAGE]. T.MCA.

PSALM [From Old English *ps(e)alm*, Late Latin *psalmus*, Greek *psalmós* a plucking, a song sung to the harp, from *psállein* to pluck, pull: compare LYRIC]. A sacred song, especially one of the numbered songs in the *Book of Psalms* in the Bible. *Psalmody* is the act or art either of setting psalms to music or of singing psalms, and is a collective term for psalms and hymns. A writer of psalms is a *psalmist*. See BIBLE, HYMN. [LITERATURE]. T.MCA.

PSEUDO-CLEFT SENTENCE. See CLEFT SENTENCE.

PSEUDONYM [1840s: from Greek *pseudónumon* a false name]. An assumed name. The pseudonym taken by a writer is often called a pen name. See -ONYM, PEN NAME. [NAME]. R.C.

PSYCHOBABBLE [1977: from the title *Psychobabble: Fast Talk and Quick Cure in the Era of Feeling*, a book by the US journalist Richard D. Rosen: compare TECHNOBABBLE]. A form of jargon in which terms from psychology, psychiatry, psychotherapy, and related fields are used to impress the listener, give an appearance of scientific objectivity to mundane ideas, or inflate what someone has to say. According to Rosen, it is 'a set of repetitive verbal formalities that kills off the very spontaneity, candour and understanding it pretends to promote'. It is also part of the language of pseudo-science, using terms that sound scientific but may be meaningless, such as *polarity balancing manipulation*, *externalizing internals*, *meaningful interpersonal equilibrium*. A person engaged in psychobabble might seek 'ego reinforcement through consciousness raising by going where the energies are in my extrinsic peer group orientation'. See BABBLE, JARGON. [STYLE, USAGE]. W.D.L.

PSYCHOLINGUISTICS

PSYCHOLINGUISTICS [1930s: from Greek *psychē* mind, Latin *lingua* tongue, and *-istics* as in *statistics*]. The branch of knowledge which studies the mental aspects of language, especially its acquisition, storage, comprehension, and production. It is a branch of both linguistics and psychology, though their mode of study tends to differ: linguists usually draw inferences from observations of spontaneous speech, whereas psychologists mostly prefer to use controlled experiments. It overlaps with a wider, more general field known as the *psychology of language*, which includes the relationship of language to thought, and with an even wider one, the *psychology of communication*, which covers almost anything connected with communication, including its non-verbal aspects. Psycholinguistics, as the study of language and the mind, is usually distinguished from *neurolinguistics*, the study of language and the brain.

History. Useful observations about how the mind deals with language date from at least the end of the 18c, especially in the form of diary studies of child language. For example, the natural historian Charles Darwin reported on the linguistic progress of one of his children in the journal *Mind* (1877). The British psychologist Francis Galton is usually regarded as the first person to do psycholinguistic experiments, when he tried to probe his own and other people's word associations, for example, 'Tell me the first word you think of when I say *black*.' The results, he maintained, could 'lay bare the foundations of a man's thoughts with a curious distinctness' (*Inquiries into Human Faculty and its Development*, 1883).

Psycholinguistics remained a minor branch of psychology for the first half of the 20c, concerned with words rather than with sentence structure. Many people date psycholinguistics proper from the mid-1960s, when an upsurge of interest followed on from the work of Noam Chomsky, who argued that language was likely to be genetically programmed. Chomsky's ideas triggered an avalanche of work by both linguists and psychologists on child language acquisition, and also an interest in finding out whether his theory of transformational-generative grammar had 'psychological reality', in the sense of reflecting the way people store or process language. Much of this early work turned out to be somewhat naïve and had disappointing results. Because Chomsky repeatedly revised his theories, a number of psychologists decided that linguistic theory was too changeable to provide a secure basis for their work. The field has therefore become somewhat splintered, even though it continues to expand. Considerable progress has been made in major areas like child language acquisition, speech comprehension, and speech production.

Child language acquisition. Children all over the world show similarities in the way they acquire language, whose development appears to be maturationally controlled (pre-programmed to emerge at a particular point in development, providing that the environment is normal and the child unimpaired). Moreover, at each stage, child language is not just a substandard form of adult language, but an independent system with rules of its own. The nature of the genetic input is still under discussion, as is the question of how children abandon immature rules, such as *What kitty can eat?* for *What can kitty eat?*, since they are apparently impervious to direct corrections. See CHILD LANGUAGE ACQUISITION, LANGUAGE ACQUISITION DEVICE.

Speech comprehension. Understanding speech is now known to be an active rather than a passive process, in which hearers reconstruct the intended message, based on outline clues and their own expectations. This can be demonstrated by presenting them with a confusing sentence such as *Anyone who shoots ducks out of the line of fire* (Any person who uses a gun gets down quickly out of the line of fire). This is a so-called *garden-path sentence*, in which hearers are 'led up the garden path' (misled) as they try to impose their expectations of a subject–verb–object pattern on a sentence which requires a different interpretation. Further evidence of the active nature of comprehension comes from experiments with homonyms, such as *It's a rose/They all rose*, when all meanings of a linguistic form turn out to be briefly considered before the unwanted ones are suppressed.

Speech production. Producing speech is a complex procedure, in which future stretches of speech are prepared while others are being uttered, as shown by slips of the tongue such as *The curse has walked for you* (The course has worked for you). At the same time, more than one candidate is possibly being considered for each word slot: in an error such as *I looked in the calendar* (catalogue), the speaker has possibly activated several three-syllable words beginning with *ca-*, narrowed it down to those involving lists, then accidentally suppressed the wrong one. See MALAPROPISM, SLIP OF THE TONGUE.

Conclusion. The human mind is a highly powerful device which is thought to use a large amount of parallel processing, in that many processes are taking place at the same time. An important issue is to discover not only how the mind activates a required word or construction, but also how it suppresses the numerous alternatives which are subconsciously considered. See

BEHAVIO(U)RISM, CHILD LANGUAGE ACQUISITION, CHOMSKY, LANGUAGE PATHOLOGY, LINGUISTICS, PSYCHOLOGY OF LANGUAGE. [LANGUAGE, SPEECH].

J.M.A.

Aitchison, Jean. 1989. *The Articulate Mammal: An Introduction to Psycholinguistics*, 3rd edition. London: Unwin Hyman.

Clark, Herbert H. & Eve V. 1977. *Psychology and Language: An Introduction to Psycholinguistics*. New York: Harcourt Brace Jovanovich.

Ellis, Andrew, & Beattie, Geoffrey. 1986. *The Psychology of Language and Communication*. London: Weidenfeld & Nicolson.

Garnham, Alan. 1985. *Psycholinguistics: Central Topics*. London: Methuen.

PSYCHOLOGY OF LANGUAGE. A term sometimes used interchangeably with *psycholinguistics*, but more commonly to refer to a broader area than that covered by 'core' psycholinguistics. It is also sometimes used to mean *cognitive psycholinguistics* (based on inferences about the content of the mind) as opposed to *experimental psycholinguistics*. Somewhat confusingly, the terms *psycholinguistics* and *psychology of language* do not parallel the terms *sociolinguistics* (studied mainly by linguists) and *sociology of language* (the domain primarily of sociologists), since both linguists and psychologists perceive themselves as dealing with both types of study. See PSYCHOLINGUISTICS. [LANGUAGE].

J.M.A.

PUBLIC SCHOOL ACCENT. See PUBLIC SCHOOL ENGLISH, PUBLIC SCHOOL PRONUNCIATION.

PUBLIC SCHOOL ENGLISH [Probably early 20c: from the term *public school*, a loan translation of Latin *scola publica*, used at least since the 16c]. The English language as used in the public (in fact private) boarding- and day-schools of Britain, and especially England, the foremost of which are Eton, Winchester, Westminster, Harrow, Rugby, Charterhouse, and Shrewsbury ('the Seven Public Schools'). The variety is distinguished primarily by the so-called *public school accent* (known technically as *Received Pronunciation*) and to some extent by *public school slang*, which tends to vary from school to school. Originally, a public school was a *grammar school* founded or endowed for the use and benefit of the public, especially in the sense that the institution was under some kind of public management or control. Although this usage once contrasted with *private school* (a school carried on at the risk of its master or proprietors), the term has since the 19c been applied especially to those old endowed grammar schools that developed into large, fee-paying boarding-schools drawing pupils from all parts of the country and from abroad, and to other private schools established on similar principles. Traditionally, pupils in the higher forms were prepared mainly for the universities (especially Oxford and Cambridge) and for public service. Although still true to some extent, in recent years this has become less of a determining feature. See PUBLIC SCHOOL PRONUNCIATION, RECEIVED PRONUNCIATION, RECEIVED STANDARD AND MODIFIED STANDARD. [EDUCATION, EUROPE, VARIETY].

T.MCA.

PUBLIC SCHOOL PRONUNCIATION, short form *PSP*. The name chosen by Daniel Jones for the model of English in his *English Pronouncing Dictionary* (1917). In the edition of 1926 he changed it to *Received Pronunciation* (*RP*). See BBC ENGLISH[1], ENGLISH PRONOUNCING DICTIONARY, JONES (D.), PUBLIC SCHOOL ENGLISH, RECEIVED PRONUNCIATION. [EDUCATION, EUROPE, SPEECH].

T.MCA.

PUBLIC SPEAKING [18c]. Both the activity and the art of speaking in public, whether formally (such as giving an after-dinner speech) or in more informal situations, such as giving a talk or taking part in a discussion. In the 20c, as a name for the art, it has largely replaced the more traditional terms *oratory* (from Latin) and *rhetoric* (from Greek), the first of which tends to be kept for grand and eloquent public speech while the second is commonly used to mean 'the art of persuasion', both in speech and writing. Compare ELOCUTION, ORATORY, ORTHOEPY, RHETORIC. See QUOTATION. [SPEECH].

T.MCA.

PUBLISHING. [15c: from *publish*, from Old French *publier*, Latin *publicare/publicatum* to make available to the people, from *publicus* of or belonging to the people, done for the sake of or at the expense of the state (with the earlier forms *poblicus/poplicus/populicus*), from *populus* people]. The activity of making information widely available, especially as a commercial or official undertaking, and in the form of printed texts. In ancient Rome, literary and other works were 'published' by reading them aloud to an audience, a practice that continues in the tradition of the *public lecture*: that is, reading aloud from a script or notes and by this means disseminating one's views. Since the development of printing, however, the term has focused on the issuing (usually for sale to the general public) of books, periodicals, pamphlets, pieces of music, etc., or making something available in printed form, especially in a periodical: 'I shall here publish a short Letter which I have received from a Well-wisher' (Richard Steele, editor, *Tatler*, 115, 1709-10).

(1) For the history and current condition of publishing in the English-speaking world, see AMERICAN PUBLISHING, AUSTRALIAN PUBLISHING, BRITISH PUBLISHING, CANADIAN PUBLISHING, DESKTOP PUBLISHING, ELECTRONIC PUBLISHING, ELT PUBLISHING, INDIAN PUBLISHING, IRISH PUBLISHING, NEW ZEALAND PUBLISHING, SCOTTISH PUBLISHING, SOUTH AFRICAN PUBLISHING.

(2) For aspects of the history and nature of publishing, see AUDIOBOOK, AUTHOR, BALLAD, BIBLE, BOOK, BOOK OF COMMON PRAYER, BROADCASTING, BROADSHEET, BROADSIDE, BULLETIN, CENSORSHIP, COMMUNICATIVE SHIFT, COPYRIGHT, DICTIONARY, EDITING, FLEET STREET, FOLIO, FREEDOM OF THE PRESS, GRUB STREET, INFORMATION, JOURNAL, JOURNALISM, LIBRARY, MAGAZINE, MEDIA, NEWS, NEWSMAGAZINE, NEWSPAPER, PAMPHLET, PAPER, PERIODICAL, PRESS, PRINTING, PROOF-READING, READING, REFERENCE, REVIEW, TECHNOLOGY, USAGE GUIDANCE AND CRITICISM, WRITER, WRITING.

(3) For individual publishers and mass periodicals, see BBC PUBLICATIONS, BRITISH LIBRARY, CAMBRIDGE UNIVERSITY PRESS, CAXTON, CHAMBERS, COLLINS, ENCYCLOPAEDIA BRITANNICA, FABER, FUNK & WAGNALLS, HEINEMANN, INTERNATIONAL HERALD TRIBUNE, LIBRARY OF CONGRESS, LONGMAN, MACMILLAN, MERRIAM-WEBSTER, NEW YORKER, OXFORD UNIVERSITY PRESS, PENGUIN, PITMAN PUBLISHING, PUNCH, RANDOM HOUSE, READER'S DIGEST, TIME MAGAZINE, TIMES, WEBSTERS. [MEDIA].   T.MCA.

PUERTO RICO, formerly *Porto Rico*, a name still often used in the US. Official title: *Commonwealth of Puerto Rico*. The easternmost island of the Greater Antilles, between the Dominican Republic and the US Virgin Islands. Capital: San Juan. Currency: US dollar. Economy: textiles, clothing, electrical goods, petrochemicals, agriculture, tourism. Population: 3.2m (1980). Ethnicity: European, African, and mixed. Languages: Spanish (official), English widely used. Originally inhabited by Carib and Arawak Indians, the island was visited by Columbus in 1493 and was a Spanish colony until ceded to the US in 1898. In 1952, Puerto Rico became a semi-autonomous Commonwealth in association with the US; discussion as to whether the island should seek to become a state of the Union, become an independent nation, or maintain the status quo tends to dominate local politics. The English of Puerto Ricans at home and in the US ranges from that of the learner to the native speaker; like *Chicano English*, it presents difficulties in distinguishing the usage of individuals from that of groups. The American linguist Rose Nash has characterized Puerto Rican usage as ranging through four types: English comparable to standard usage in the US and other anglophone Caribbean communities; Spanglish, which adds Spanish to English, as in lexical code-switching ('He has that special *manera de ser*') and adaptations from Spanish ('Please *prove* the light', from *probar* to test; 'I *assisted to* the *reunion*', from *asistir* to attend, *reunión* meeting); *Englañol*, which adds English to Spanish, as in lexical code-switching ('Se solicitan dos *clerk typists*'), and is common among bilingual adults; Spanish comparable to standard usage elsewhere in Latin America. Puerto Rican English was prominent in the musical *Westside Story* (Broadway 1958, film 1961, lyrics by Stephen Sondheim, music by Leonard Bernstein), a contemporary version of Shakespeare's *Romeo and Juliet* set among teenage gangs in New York. See AMERICAN ENGLISH, CARIBBEAN ENGLISH, ENGLISH, NEW YORRICAN, SPANGLISH. [AMERICAS, NAME, VARIETY].

T.MCA., J.AM

PULMONIC [17c: from Latin *pulmo/pulmonis* lung]. An anatomical term used to refer to a stream of air produced by the action of the lungs. See AIR-STREAM MECHANISM. [SPEECH].   G.K.

PUN [17c: perhaps a slang clipping of obsolete *punnet* and *pundigrion*, or Italian *puntiglio*, a quibble. Puns also were formerly known as *clinches* and *quibbles*]. Also *paronomasia* [16c: through Latin from Greek *paronomasia*, adapting a name or word slightly. Stress: 'pa-ro-no-MAY-si-a']. (1) The conflating of homonyms and near-homonyms to produce a humorous effect: (in speech and writing) *Is life worth living?—It depends on the liver*; (in speech alone) *At his funeral, four of his drinking companions carried the bier/beer*. (2) A comparable play on words and phrases with similar sounds, sometimes requiring the (often forced) adaptation of one word or phrase to fit the other: *Life is such good pun*; *My wife's gone to the West Indies.—Jamaica?* (Did you make her?)—*No, it was her own idea.*

In scripture. In ancient times, puns were used to suggest deep truths. Especially in oral societies, sound was power, and similar sounds have often been taken to mean similar natures and origins. In the Book of Genesis, God takes some earth and from it makes a man. In Hebrew, the similarity of the word for *man* and *earth* (both represented in the name *Adam*) strengthened a belief that humanity was formed from clay. Such puns, however, are often lost in translation. One Biblical pun which has travelled well (though not into English) occurs in Matthew (16: 18), where Jesus says to his chief disciple: 'Thou art Peter (Greek *Petros*), and upon this rock (Greek *petra*) I will build my church.' Here, New Testament Greek could express a pun apparently first made in Aramaic with the word *kephas*, and French still expresses it with *pierre/Pierre*.

In drama and poetry. In the 16–17c, puns were common among dramatists and writers. In Shakespeare's *Romeo and Juliet*, when Mercutio is dying, he says, 'Ask for me tomorrow and you shall find me a grave man.' In *Macbeth*, when Lady Macbeth plans to incriminate King Duncan's attendants in his murder, she says: 'If he do bleed, I'll gild the faces of the grooms withal, for it must seem their guilt.' On this liberal approach to puns, Ernest Gowers has observed (in his 1965 edition of Henry Fowler's *Modern English Usage*: 'Now that we regard puns merely as exercises in jocularity, and a pretty debased form even of that, we are apt to be jarred by the readiness of Shakespeare's characters to make them at what seem to us most unsuitable moments.' In Shakespeare's time, however, few moments were unsuitable. The poet John Donne sustained the religious pun when he wrote in *Hymn to God the Father*: 'Thy Son shall shine as he shines now.'

Equivocal status. The pun lost status in English, despite (or perhaps because of) a wealth of homonyms and the pun's ability to create irony: an anti-Nazi looking at pictures of Hitler and Goering, and musing, 'Should one hang them or put them up against the wall?' In the 18c, Joseph Addison considered puns false wit, and increasingly since then critics have taken the same view. Currently, puns are widely considered so low a form of wit that they prompt a ritual groan, but despite this apparent disapproval the pun continues to thrive. Lewis Carroll used it widely and whimsically in his Alice books:

Here the Red Queen began again. 'Can you answer useful questions?' she said. 'How is bread made?'
'I know *that*!' Alice cried eagerly. 'You take some flour—'
'Where do you pick the flower?' the White Queen asked. 'In a garden or in the hedges?'
'Well, it isn't *picked* at all,' Alice explained: 'it's ground—'
'How many acres of ground?' said the White Queen. 'You mustn't leave out so many things'
(*Through the Looking-Glass*, 1872).

Despite their equivocal status, puns are common as a means of attracting attention in journalism and commerce: (1) In newspaper headlines: *Honoring a Pole Apart* (*Time*, Oct. 1980), on Nobel Prize winner Czesław Miłosz; *Rejoycing with the Ulysses set* (*International Herald Tribune*, 22 June 1984), on James Joyce's novel *Ulysses*; *Regimental ties* (*Observer*, 6 Oct. 1985), a title for reviews of military books. (2) In the names of businesses: *Lettuce Entertain You* (a restaurant); *Curl Up and Dye* (a hair stylist); *Drive Me Crazy Auto School* (in New York City); *Molly's Blooms* (a Dublin florist, playing on the name of the

Joycean character Molly Bloom). Part of the problem of the pun, however, is straining for effect, working with near-puns rather than with puns properly so called. Sometimes, however, a near-pun can be so stretched and distorted that it becomes a classic of its kind: as the woman said when she received greenery instead of flowers, 'with fronds like these, who needs anemones?' See CARTOON, DOUBLE MEANING, HUMO(U)R, PLAYING WITH WORDS, RIDDLE, WORD GAME. [STYLE].   T.MCA.

Culler, Jonathan (ed.). 1988. *On Puns: The Foundation of Letters*. Oxford: Basil Blackwell.
Hughes, Patrick, & Hammond, Paul. 1978. *Upon the Pun*. London: W. H. Allen.
Redfern, Walter. 1984. *Puns*. Oxford: Basil Blackwell.

PUNCH, full title *Punch, or the London Charivari*. A British weekly magazine founded in 1841 as a radical political journal enlivened by humorous writings and cartoons. The subtitle acknowledges as its model the Parisian journal *Charivari*, founded in 1832 as a vehicle of social satire, with each issue built round a large cartoon. Within a few decades, however, it had become the preferred reading of a conservative establishment that was inclined to view the rest of the world as either funny or presumptuous. Among its founders, who were mainly dramatists and journalists, were Henry Mayhew, Gilbert Abbott à Beckett, Douglas Jerrold, William Thackeray, and the illustrator Ebenezer Landells, who probably originated the idea. One of its major early illustrators, Sir John Tenniel, also did the drawings in Lewis Carroll's *Alice* books. The early issues were jointly edited; the first sole editor was Mark Lemon, a playwright and innkeeper whose pub, *The Shakespeare's Head* in Wych Street, was a salon for aspiring journalists. He edited the magazine until his death in 1870. The unchanging cover picture of *Mr Punch* lasted until 1949 and the puppet motif in various forms until 1969. The original was Richard Doyle's drawing of *Punchinello*, crooked, paunchy, nutcracker-jawed, capped and belled, with his dog Toby in slouch hat and ruff. There were precedents for this image in Abbott à Beckett's magazine *Punchinello* (1832) and Jerrold's *Punch in London* (1832), but Mayhew appears to have decided on the name while discussing the ingredients of a bowl of punch.

The volumes of *Punch* from 1841 to 1940 are an anthology of humorous assumptions about cabmen, clergymen, clubmen, Cockneys, country gentlemen, foreigners, Irishmen, Scotchmen, the labouring poor, social swells, soldiers, sweethearts, wives, and yokels. The captions of many cartoons have used eye dialect to point up accents, as when a farmer, proposing the health of the local squire, says: 'An' if a' squiears 'ud dew as our Squiear dew, there wudna be so many on 'em as dew as they dew dew!' (30 Dec. 1876). Such captions are now evidence of especially 19c usage: for example, in a cartoon by John Leech in 1857, portraying two London prostitutes, one asks the other: 'Ah! Fanny! How long have you been gay?', documenting a use of *gay* distinct from its present-day reference to homosexuality. Major serials in the magazine include Thackeray's *Book of Snobs* (1846-7), George and Weedon Grossmith's *Diary of a Nobody* (1852), and W. B. Sellar and R. Yeatman's antischolarly history of England, *1066 and All That* (1930), which gently ridiculed an evaluative style common among teachers: 'The Norman Conquest was a Good Thing, as from this time onwards England stopped being conquered and thus was able to become top nation'; 'Henry [ate] a surfeit of palfreys. This was a Bad Thing since he died of it.' In recent years, *Punch* experienced considerable financial losses and a great decline in subscribers, as a result of which it ceased publication in 1992. See CARTOON, HUMO(U)R, MAGAZINE. Compare NEW YORKER. [EUROPE, MEDIA, STYLE]. W.N., T.MCA.

PUNCH LINE [1920s: AmE]. The final sentence of a humorous anecdote, presenting the point of the story with a more or less powerful impact (its 'punch'). A Catholic known for his drinking asks his priest, 'Father, what's sciatica?' The priest, sensing an opportunity, describes sciatica as a foretaste of hell, specially visited on drunkards. 'Why do you ask?' he finishes, and the sinner replies (*punch line*), 'Because they're saying in the pub the Pope's got it.' See JOKE, LINE, STORY LINE. [STYLE]. W.N.

PUNCTUATION [16c: from Latin *punctuatio/punctuationis* making a point, marking with points, from *pungere/punctum* to pierce: compare POINT]. The practice in writing and print of using a set of marks to regulate texts and clarify their meanings, principally by separating or linking words, phrases, and clauses, and by indicating parentheses and asides. Until the 18c, punctuation was closely related to spoken delivery, including pauses to take breath, but in more recent times has been based mainly on grammatical structure. There are two extremes in its use: *heavy punctuation* and *light punctuation*. In the 18-19c, people tended to punctuate heavily, especially in their use of commas. Currently, punctuation is more sparing, but individuals and house styles vary in what they consider necessary; the same writer may punctuate more heavily or lightly for some purposes than for others.

Origins. In antiquity and the early Middle Ages, points were used, either singly or in combination, to separate sentences, or in some cases (such as Roman inscriptions) to separate words. Key figures in the development of punctuation up to 1600 are St Jerome in the 5c AD (in Latin translations of the Bible), Alcuin in the 8c (Anglo-Saxon tutor at the court of the Emperor Charlemagne, responsible for a new spelling and punctuation system for Biblical and liturgical manuscripts), two Venetian printers (grandfather and grandson) both named Aldus Manutius in the 15-16c (who developed a system using marks equivalent to the present-day period, colon, semicolon, and comma), and the Elizabethan critic George Puttenham (whose *Arte of English Poesie*, 1589, included advice on punctuation as a means of marking a text for sense and metre). The declamatory basis for punctuation was, however, replaced in the 17c by the syntactic approach of the playwright and grammarian Ben Jonson (incorporated posthumously in his *English Grammar* of 1640). Before the 17c, and especially in the work of William Caxton and other early printers, punctuation was haphazard and erratic, with little attention paid to syntax.

Terms and marks. Most of the principal terms and marks now in use in English date from the 15-16c, and some of the names are first attested in the writing of Puttenham or his contemporaries. Most are of Greek origin, and referred originally not to marks but to the sections of text that they marked off. For example, the terms *colon* and *comma* originally denoted the parts of a line or sentence in verse, not prose: a *kôlon* was at first a part of a strophe (a section of a poem), and only later came to refer, by analogy, to a clause in a sentence; a *kómma* (from *kóptein* to cut) was a 'piece cut off' (a short clause). The term *apostrophe* (from *apó* away, *stréphein* to turn) denoted a mark of 'turning away' (elision), and the term *hyphen* (from *huphén* in one) was used by the grammarians of Alexandria to denote a symbol that links elements meant to be read as one word. The use of the hyphen to divide words at the ends of lines of text dates from the 14c, and evolved from a marginal tick or check mark used to show that the final word of a line was not complete. Eventually, the terms for sections of text were transferred to the signs that mark the sections off one from another; no one now calls a phrase a *comma* or a clause a *colon*, nor do the marks now precisely relate to such segments of text. Generally, however, the historical connection continues.

Other terms are more recent and have superseded older equivalents. The Greek-derived *period* came to refer to a punctuation mark around 1600, another example of a term that originally referred to sentence structure (in this case, a complete sentence): see PERIOD[2]. The terms *stop* and *full stop*, for the same mark, date from about the same time: both occur in Shakespeare with reference to the ending of a speech or discourse: for example, in *The Merchant of Venice* (3. 1. 17), 'come, the full stop'. Earlier terms were *point* (found in Chaucer and still in use, especially in the terminology of printing) and the Latin *punctus*. *Full point* has also long been in use. Currently, *period* is the common usage in AmE and *full stop* in BrE. The term *question mark* has been used for less than a century: the earlier term was *mark/point of interrogation* (late 16c). It is a descendant of the *punctus interrogativus*, one of the marks found in 10–13c liturgical manuscripts, where it indicated inflection of the voice. The terms *mark/note of exclamation* and *semicolon* both date from the 17c. The term *dash*, which originally meant 'a blow', reached its present meaning in punctuation via the sense 'hasty stroke of the pen', often the case in writing. *Bracket* is not attested in this context until the 18c; the earlier term *parenthesis* (which continues in use, usually in the plural) generally refers also to the part of the sentence that the punctuation delimits, but in AmE is also used for what are in BrE called *round brackets*. The symbols now in use have evolved from many centuries of practice. The points derive from classical practice, the *comma* was a development of the late medieval *virgule* or *stroke* (/), also used as a separator, and the *semicolon* came into use in the Byzantine era; in Greek, it was and is used to mark a question.

Uses: linking and separating. Currently, punctuation serves to clarify the meaning of written language by marking strings of words into associated groups. It is based mainly on grammatical structure and has both a *linking function* and a *separating function*: linking in the listing use of commas, as in *They bought a newspaper, two magazines, and a cassette*; separating in the short sentences *We didn't know. But they knew from the start.*

Points and commas. The marks most commonly used are the point/period/full stop and the comma. These generally signal or establish boundaries, the period marking out sentences and the comma marking out associated words within sentences. The single comma may cause difficulty because it is a flexible and often optional mark and has applications that need to be weighed carefully in a specific piece of writing. Usage varies as to its inclusion in statements such as *a large, untidy house* and *a little black dog*: it is generally included when the notions underlying the words are of different kinds, as with *large* and *untidy* (whereas *little* and *black* go together in describing the type of dog in question). As a rule of thumb, if *and* can be inserted idiomatically between the adjectives, a comma tends to be used (*a large and untidy house*, therefore *a large, untidy house*); but if *and* cannot be so inserted, a comma is not used (**a little and black dog*, therefore *a little black dog*). Paired commas are more straightforward; they mark parenthesis in ways similar to dashes and brackets, although with less effect. Note the increased emphasis on the words 'and helpful' in the following:

(1) People in the north are more friendly and helpful than those in the south.
(2) People in the north are more friendly, and helpful, than those in the south.
(3) People in the north are more friendly (and helpful) than those in the south.
(4) People in the north are more friendly—and helpful—than those in the south.

Brackets often replace pairs of commas when the words marked off are added comment, especially explanation: *He is (as he always was) a rebel.* The following extract shows commas, brackets, and dashes used in one fairly long sentence:

The why and wherefore of the scorpion—how it had got on board and came to select his room rather than the pantry (which was a dark place and more what a scorpion would be partial to), and how on earth it managed to drown itself in the ink-well of his writing-desk—had exercised him infinitely.

(Joseph Conrad, *The Secret Sharer*).

Colons, semicolons, and dashes. The colon and especially the semicolon are often avoided in writing by hand because of uncertainty as to their precise uses, a view that they are rather formal and old-fashioned, and best left to certain kinds of printed text. In less formal writing, the dash is often a catch-all mark to take the place of both colon and semicolon, obviating the need to distinguish them or think about more subtle kinds of punctuation. They can be effective when used sparingly, in linking thoughts that go more closely together than separate sentences would allow and, in the case of the colon, in leading from one idea to its consequence or logical continuation, especially in the use of the colon at the end of a sentence, leading to a quotation or a list. The following sentences show how a semicolon can link two parallel statements, whereas a colon serves better when the intention is to lead from one thought to the next:

semicolon There was no truth in the accusation; it was totally false.
colon There was no truth in the accusation: they rejected it utterly.

Division into separate sentences, though grammatically satisfactory, implies a separateness (which the voice conveys with a longer pause) that is not always appropriate:

point There was no truth in the accusation. They rejected it utterly.

Compare the following, in which the second sentence is quite distinct:

There was no truth in the accusation. The other problem was why they had not been warned.

In the following extract, the semicolons provide continuity of thought in the first sentence, with distinctness in the short sentences that follow:

Her husband . . . was intent on listening to a Beethoven symphony on the gramophone and frowned across the room at Maggie to keep her voice down; he made an irritable gesture with his hand to accompany the frown; he was not in the least disenthralled with Maggie; he only wanted to savour the mighty bang-crash and terror of sound which would soon be followed by the sweet 'never mind', so adorable to his ears, of the finale. He was a sentimental man. Maggie and Mary lowered their voices.

(Muriel Spark, *The Takeover*).

Some writers, such as Henry James, are sometimes accused of overusing the semicolon, producing sentences that continue for half a page or more. In the following sentence, however, the colon and commas are effectively used:

The sense of the past revived for him nevertheless as it had not yet done: it made that other time somehow meet the future close, interlocking with it, before his watching eye, as in a long embrace of arms and lips, and so handling and hustling the present that this poor quantity scarce retained substance enough, scarce remained sufficiently *there*, to be wounded or shocked.

(Henry James, *The Golden Bowl*).

Without careful use of separating punctuation marks, the following, from the same source, would be almost unintelligible:

What had happened, in short, was that Charlotte and he had by a single turn of the wrist of fate—'led up' to indeed, no doubt, by steps and stages that conscious computation had missed—been placed face to face in a freedom that partook, extraordinarily, of ideal perfection, since the magic web had spun itself without their toil, almost without their touch.

Avoiding ambiguity. Punctuation also plays an important role in the avoidance of ambiguity or misunderstanding, especially by means of the comma (which separates) and the hyphen (which links), as in *They did not go, because they were lazy* as opposed to *They did not go because they were lazy*, in *twenty-odd people* as opposed to *twenty odd people*, and in sentences like *From then, on meeting a friend he would smile* as opposed to *From then on, meeting a friend was a great pleasure for him*. A carefully entered hierarchy of punctuation adds clarity to a long or complex sentence, as in the following:

I came out of the house, which lay back from the road, and saw them at the end of the path; but instead of continuing towards them, I hid until they had gone.

A period/full stop would also be possible here in the place of the semicolon, but it would break the continuity.

Hyphen and apostrophe: recent develoments. In everyday use and in ephemeral writing such as newsprint, punctuation is generally less precisely used than in more formal and permanent forms of writing and printing. The use of some marks is declining, especially the hyphen and the apostrophe. The hyphen is currently less common in forming compound words (such as *newspaper*, *worldwide*) and in separating vowels that may have the values of digraphs when placed together (as in *coordinate*, *makeup*). Arguably, the possessive apostrophe is needed only to distinguish number, as in *the girl's books* and *the girls' books*. In other cases, it could be (and increasingly is) dispensed with without any loss of clarity in such phrases as *Johns books* and *their mothers voice*; these are as comprehensible today as they were before the mark was introduced. It is also disappearing in names, such as *Smiths* and *Lloyds Bank*.

See APOSTROPHE[1], ASTERISK, COLON, COMMA, DAGGER, DIACRITIC, EARLY MODERN ENGLISH, EXCLAMATION MARK/POINT, FORMAT, FULL STOP, HEADLINE, INDENTING, INTERROGATION MARK/POINT, LAYOUT, OBLIQUE, PERIOD, QUESTION MARK, QUOTATION MARKS, RELATIVE CLAUSE, SEMICOLON, SENTENCE, SPACE, STOP, WHITE SPACE. [STYLE, WRITING].   R.E.A., T.MCA.

Allen, Robert E. (ed.). 1990. *Concise Oxford Dictionary*, 8th edition. Appendix: Punctuation Marks. Oxford: University Press.
Chicago Manual of Style, 13th edition. Ch. 5: Punctuation. Chicago: University Press.
McDermott, John. 1990. *Punctuation for Now*. London: Macmillan.

PUNCTUATION MARK [1850s]. Any one of a set of conventional marks or characters used in organizing written and printed language, such as a *comma* (,) or an *exclamation mark/point* (!). See MARK, PUNCTUATION. [WRITING].   T.MCA.

PUNJABI. See PANJABI.

PURE [13c: from Old French *pur*, Latin *purus* clean, plain, unmixed]. If something is pure, it is unadulterated, unmixed, untainted, clean, clear, intact, homogeneous, true, real, genuine. The adjective is used to describe such things as air, water, and food, and by extension language: 'An author of the Sixteenth Century would normally take pains to acquire the pure English of the Court and capital' (Bernard Groom, *A Short History of English Words*, 1965). See BARBARISM,

CORRUPT, HYBRID, PURISM, SOCIETY FOR PURE ENGLISH. [STYLE].   T.MCA.

PURE AUSTRALIAN. See AUSTRALIAN.

PURISM [18c: from French *purisme*]. Scrupulous observance of, or insistence on, purity or correctness in language and style, an attitude often considered by others as excessive. Purists may have specific plans for reforming languages in such areas as spelling, vocabulary, and grammar: for example, movements in English and German to get rid of foreign and especially Latinate borrowings, replacing them with native words, including archaic and dialect usages. This form of purism was prominent in English in the 16c and 19c, when *archaism* was also in vogue. One of the earliest English treatises on logic, Ralph Lever's *The Arte of Reason, Rightly Termed Witcraft* (1573), rejected Latinate terms in favour of a native technical vocabulary: in addition to *witcraft*, he coined among other terms *foreset* subject, *backset* predicate, *gainset* opposite, and *foresay* premiss/premise. In the 19c, the philologist William Barnes wrote an English grammar, the *Outline of English Speech-Craft* (1878), using invented vocabulary such as *thought-wording* proposition, *speech-thing* subject, and *timetaking* predicate. For everyday use, Barnes proposed hundreds of Saxonisms, including *cellar-thane* butler, *push-wainling* pram, baby carriage, and *tithe* decimate. Some words did catch on: the rhetorician John Earle (1890) credited the 19c movement with popularizing *open-mindedness, seamy, shaky,* and *unknowable*.

In present-day terms, purists are reformers who seek to root out presumed errors in grammar and usage and offer what they feel to be more correct alternatives. Some watch their own writing so carefully as to make it virtually unreadable, while others are so intent on uncovering other writers' mistakes that they commit the very errors they expose elsewhere. They usually object to the state of the language at a particular time and/or the direction in which it appears to be going, suspect and disapprove of new words or of old words with new meanings, insist on the literal meaning of words, and insist on logic in usage. In addition, they tend to see themselves individually as acting on behalf of an unclear ultimate authority. As a result, they may contradict one another: for example, in 1907, the American pronunciation expert Frank Vizately proscribed the common temporal phrase *a quarter of seven* on the grounds that it literally means 'one and three quarters': seven divided by four. He accepted only *a quarter to seven* as correct. Taking an opposite position on the issue, in the same year the grammarian Josephine Turck

Baker (*Correct English*, 1907), contended that since *to* is a preposition indicating 'direction toward', *a quarter to seven* is really 'one quarter of an hour in the direction of seven on the clock dial' (that is, 6.15), and mandated the form Vizately rejected. There are few self-confessed purists among the critics of the English language today; *purism* is generally a negative term, and by and large *purists* are regarded as hypercorrective extremists. It is not unusual, however, to find grammar and usage critics denying that they are purists while engaging in all the traditional forms of purism. See PLAIN, PURE. [STYLE].   D.E.B.

PURITAN, PURITAN PLAIN STYLE. See AMERICAN LITERATURE, BIBLE, ENGLISH LITERATURE, NEW ENGLAND, NICE-NELLYISM, PLAIN, ROYAL SOCIETY, THEATRE/THEATER. [HISTORY, STYLE].   T.MCA.

PURPLE PATCH [A translation of Latin *pannus purpureus* purple patch, a phrase used by the poet Horace to suggest a bit of imperial purple cloth sewn on to a commoner fabric]. Also **purple passage, purple prose**. A piece of writing marked by a florid, fanciful style:

There are few of us who have not sometimes wakened before dawn, either after one of those dreamless nights that make us almost enamoured of death, or one of those nights of horror and misshapen joy, when through the chambers of the brain sweep phantoms more terrible than reality itself, and instinct with that vivid life that lurks in all grotesques, and that lends to Gothic art its enduring vitality, this art being, one might fancy, especially the art of those whose minds have been troubled with the malady of reverie. Gradually white fingers creep through the curtains, and they appear to tremble. In black fantastic shapes, dumb shadows crawl into the corners of the room, and crouch there. Outside, there is the stirring of birds among the leaves, or the sound of men going forth to their work, or the sigh and sob of the wind coming down from the hills, and wandering round the silent house, as though it feared to wake the sleepers, and yet must need call forth sleep from her purple cave. (from Oscar Wilde, *The Picture of Dorian Gray*, 1890, ch. 11).

See EUPHUISM, POETIC DICTION, PROSE. [STYLE, WRITING].   T.MCA.

PUTTENHAM, George [1532-1600]. Elizabethan writer, the presumed author of *The Arte of English Poesie* (1589). This work reflected the late 16c confidence that English no less than Greek and Latin was 'significative' and so could serve for poetry; in it, Puttenham praised his poetic contemporaries. He defended the borrowing of foreign words when it was necessary and euphonious, but condemned it when the result was, in his view, a 'mingle mangle' of poetic vocabulary. However, he preferred vernacular compounding as a source for new words. He addressed an aristocratic but unlearned audience, and therefore insisted that English poetry must use the language of the court, not the inkhornisms of the universities, the ruralisms of the countryside, or the archaisms of Lydgate or Chaucer. See index. [BIOGRAPHY, EUROPE, HISTORY, STYLE].   W.F.B.

PYGMALION [The name of a legendary king of Cyprus who fell in love with a statue of Aphrodite, or, according to the Roman poet Ovid, fell in love with an ivory statue of his own making, expressing his ideal woman. The sculptor then prayed to Aphrodite for a wife like the statue, and the goddess accommodatingly brought it to life. At an unknown stage in the development of the story, *Galatea*, the name of a sea nymph, was given to the statue-woman. The Pygmalion theme has regularly recurred in English. The Elizabethan dramatist John Marston told the tale in *The Metamorphoses of Pigmalion's Image* (1598), the Victorian socialist poet William Morris included it in *The Earthly Paradise* (1868-70), and it was the subject of a comedy by W. S. Gilbert entitled *Pygmalion and Galatea* (1871)]. The title of a popular play by George Bernard Shaw (1912) that deals with the English language. It is generally classed as a romantic comedy but Shaw saw it as a didactic drama about the power of phonetics and the foolishness of contemporary social attitudes. It was first performed in German in Vienna in 1913, then in London in the original English in 1914, when it created a sensation because the phrase 'not bloody likely' occurs in Act 3. A result of this was the minced oath *not Pygmalion likely* and the use of the name to talk about swearing: 'The trouble really began when alderman Mrs. K. Sheridan was speaking about the council fleecing tenants and used a pygmalion word' (*The Times*, 28 Apr. 1960). The play recounts how Professor Henry Higgins (a character influenced in part by Henry Sweet) in order to win a bet trains the Cockney flower girl Eliza Doolittle to behave like a duchess, largely by teaching her 'to speak beautifully' in Received Standard pronunciation. In the play there is no cross-class romance between phonetician and pupil, but such a romance develops in a film version in 1938, of which Shaw approved; it is also strongly hinted at in the later musical based on the play, Alan Jay Lerner's *My Fair Lady* (1956) and the subsequent film (1964) starring Audrey Hepburn as Eliza and Rex Harrison as Higgins. Shaw also had a character called Pygmalion in the futuristic final part of *Back to Methuselah* (1921), a scientist who artificially creates a humanoid man and woman. The social and linguistic theme has been continued in the title and content of John Honey's *Does Accent Matter?—The Pygmalion Factor* (Faber, 1989). See ACCENT, COCKNEY, ELOCUTION, SHAW, SWEET. [LITERATURE, SPEECH].   T.MCA.

Q

Q, q [Called 'kew', rhyming with *few*]. The 17th letter of the modern Roman alphabet as used for English. It originated as the Phoenician symbol *qop*, which had the value of a voiceless uvular plosive: a *k*-like sound made well back in the mouth. It was initially adopted by the Greeks as *koppa*, to represent /k/ before a back vowel; but classical Greek preferred the letter *kappa*, the ancestor of *K*, and *koppa* fell into disuse. The Etruscans used three Greek letters, *gamma*, *kappa*, and *koppa*, for variants on /k/. *Koppa* was used specifically before /u/, a practice followed by Latin, which gave the letter its characteristic curved tail as *Q*. This letter was little used in Old English, which used the digraph *cw* in words now spelt with *qu*: *cwen/queen*, *cwic/quick*. French inherited the digraph *qu* from Latin, and after the Norman Conquest it was increasingly used in written English by French-influenced scribes, so that by 1300 *cw* had been supplanted. For a time, *qu* spread further, especially in Northern English, to words now spelt with *wh*. This pattern persisted longest in Scots, in which, for example, *what* was written *quhat* until the 18c, and *quh* survives in such surnames as *Colquhoun* ('Cahoon'), *Farquhar* ('Farker') and *Urquhart* ('Urkart').

Sound value and occurrence. (1) In English, *q* has the same value as *k* or hard *c*, and is generally followed by *u*, with the joint pronunciation /kw/: *quaint*, *quibble*. (2) Loss of /w/ in French led to spelling changes that obscure the common ancestry of such English/French pairs as *quash/casser*, *quire/cahier*. On the other hand, English has developed *qu* in words that in French had, and still have, *cu*: *esquire/écuyer*, *squirrel/écureuil*. (3) In English, *qu* typically occurs word-initially before *a, e, i, o* (*quack, quash, quail, quest, queer, quit, quite, quote*) and after *s* (*squat, squeal, squirrel*). (4) Medial *qu* also occurs: *adequate, banquet, equal, frequent, liquid,*

request. (5) When the Latin prefix *ad-* precedes *qu*, it is assimilated as *ac*: *acquaint, acquire, acquit*. However, initial *a* sometimes also precedes *qu* without *c* (*aquatic, aquiline*) with no distinction in pronunciation.

Exotic Q, QU. (1) Though rarely so used, *q* without *u* has the same value as *k* and as *c* before *a, o, u*. It is used as a transliteration of the Hebrew letter *qoph* and Arabic *qaf* (cognate with Phoenician *qop*), both uvular plosives given the value /k/ in everyday English: *Iraq, qaf, Qatar, Qur'ān* (Koran): see ARABIC. (2) In the Pinyin script for Chinese, *q* represents the *ch* sound in *cheese*, as in *Qian-long, Qin-huang-dao*: see CHINA. (3) Words that have entered English in recent centuries from Romance languages have mostly kept the value of *qu* as /k/: word-finally with *e* (*arabesque, grotesque, mosque, opaque, picturesque, unique*), medially (*bouquet, coquette, mosquito*), and occasionally initially (*quiche*, but not *queue*), especially in names (*Quezon City* in the Philippines). The recent French loan *questionnaire* is sometimes pronounced with /k/, but usually with /kw/ by analogy with the earlier loan *question*. *Quay* is an 18c respelling of *kay* or *key*, by analogy with French *quai*. There is an alternation between /kw/ in *conquest* (compare *quest, request*) and *liquid*, and /k/ in *conquer/conqueror* and *liquor*. (4) In the acronyms *Qantas* (Queensland and Northern Territory Aerial Services) and *QARANC* (Queen Alexandra's Royal Army Nursing Corps) the *q* is pronounced as /kw/, as if followed by a *u*: 'Kwontas', 'Kwarank'. (5) Forms with medial *cqu* pronounced /k/, include: *lacquer, lacquey* (now *lackey*), and *racquet* (also *racket*). (6) AmE generally has *bark, check, licorice* where BrE keeps the *q* in *barque, cheque, liquorice*. See ALPHABET, LETTER[1], SPELLING. [WRITING]. C.U.

QATAR. See ARABIC, ENGLISH.

....

THE CAPITAL LETTER						THE SMALL LETTER				
EARLY FORMS				CURRENT FORMS		EARLY FORMS			CURRENT FORMS	
Phoenician	Greek	Etruscan	Roman (Latin)	roman	italic	Roman cursive	Roman uncial	Carolingian minuscule	roman	italic
ϙ	ϙ ϙ	ϙ	૦	Q	*Q*	૪	q	q	q	*q*

QUAIR. See QUIRE.

QUALIFY [16c: from Latin *qualificare/ qualificatum* to say of which kind, from *qualis* of what kind]. A traditional term used to indicate that one grammatical unit depends on another: in the phrase *brave attempts*, the adjective *brave* is said to qualify the noun *attempts*; in traditional terms, the adjective indicates the 'quality' or nature of the noun. Contemporary grammars generally use the term *modify*. See MODIFICATION. [GRAMMAR].   S.G., T.MCA.

QUALITY PRESS, The. A mainly British term for newspapers considered authoritative, sober, and influential, and read by the middle and upper classes. The uppermost echelon of the Quality Press has traditionally been *The Times* (founded 1785), which was in its heyday a major national institution with quasi-official status. It was widely if facetiously asserted in the early 19c that Britain was ruled by *The Times* and that its editor was the most powerful man in the land. The *Morning Post* was, throughout its life (1772–1937), a 'society' paper, including such major authors as Coleridge, Disraeli, Hardy, and Kipling among its contributors and leader-writers. In the course of the 20c, other broadsheet newspapers, such as *The Guardian* (founded as *The Manchester Guardian* in 1821), *The Daily Telegraph* (1855), and *The Independent* (1986) have joined the category. Although the readership of the quality press has steadily declined to about 10% of newspaper readers, it remains socially and politically the most influential sector. See BROADSHEET, HEAVY, NEWSPAPER, PRESS, TABLOID, TIMES. [MEDIA].   G.H.

QUANTIFIER [20c: from *quantify* and *-er* as in *modifier*]. A category of determiner or pronoun used to express quantity. Most quantifiers have a limited distribution that depends on the countability of the nouns they relate to. *Many, a few, few,* and *several* relate only to plural countable nouns (*many newspapers, a few drinks, few people, several men*), in contrast to *much, a little,* and *little,* which relate to uncountable nouns (*much confusion, a little information, little news*). *Enough* can relate to both types of noun (*enough newspapers, enough information*), as can *some* and *any* (*some help, any houses*). However, *some* and *any* can also be used with singular countable nouns with non-quantitative functions: *Some chicken!* means 'What a poor chicken!' or 'What a wonderful chicken!', depending on tone and emphasis; *Any fool knows that* means 'There is nothing special about knowing that'. Distinctions in the use of certain quantifiers are contrastive and subtle: *few* newspapers (not many

newspapers), *a few* newspapers (some newspapers); *little* help (virtually no help at all), *a little* help (some help but not much). It is useful to treat *a few* and *a little* as distinct quantifiers and not simply as the indefinite article followed by *few* and *little*. Neither is used with a singular countable noun (*a few raisins, a little rice,* but not **a raisins,* **a rice,* **a few raisin,* *a little raisin). In addition, both *little* and *a little* have to be distinguished from the ordinary adjective *little* (small). Ambiguity is possible with nouns that can be both countable and uncountable: out of obvious context, *a little chicken* could mean either a small bird or a small quantity of the meat of a chicken.

Few and little have negative force, as is shown by the fact that, like negatives, they take positive question tags: *Few of us really think that, do we?* Contrast: *A few people believe that, don't they?* *Few* and *little* have comparative and superlative forms (*fewer, fewest; less, least*), while *much* and *many* share *more* and *most*. Traditionally, *fewer* and *fewest* have been described as modifying only countable nouns (*fewer houses, the fewest men possible*) and *less* and *least* as modifying only uncountable nouns (*less wine, the least fuel possible*), and many people regard this as the only acceptable usage in standard English. However, widely throughout the English-speaking world *less* and *least* are used with countable nouns (*less people, the least working hours*), regardless of criticism and in many instances without the least awareness of the basis for the criticism. *Much* tends to be non-assertive in informal English; it prefers negative or interrogative contexts: *We don't have much money, How much money do you need?* In affirmative statements, a quantitative phrase such as *a lot (of)* and *a great deal (of)* is often preferred: *That explains a lot (of what I've heard)* or *That explains a great deal* rather than *That explains much.* Quantifiers can be pre-modified by *very, so, too, as,* as in *very few people, so little help, too many cooks,* and *as much work as possible.* Some words and phrases used as quantifiers can also be used as intensifiers, as in: *much nicer; much less; many more; a little better; a lot older; a lot too old; a bit too much.* Some of these words are also used for duration and frequency: *We waited a little; They eat a lot.* This can lead to ambiguity; in *She eats a lot* and *He doesn't read much,* if the items are quantifying pronouns, the meaning is *a lot of food* and *a lot of books,* but if they are adverbs of frequency, the meaning is *She's constantly eating* and *He doesn't often read.* Compare NUMBER[1]. [GRAMMAR].   S.C.

QUANTITATIVE METRE/METER. See METRE/METER, QUANTITY.

QUANTITY [13c: from French *quantité*, from Latin *quantitas*, translating Greek *posótês* ('how-much-ness') amount]. In prosody and phonetics, a distinction between sounds and syllables based partly on duration (length). The concept has traditionally been important in discussing Latin vowels, whose values are either long or short; it is less important in English. The first syllables of such words as *thimble, bauble, table* tend to have greater duration than short syllables ending in a short vowel (the first syllables of *bubble, nibble*), on account of the durations of the vowels and consonants that they contain. Syllable duration is also conditioned by context, syllables being shortened when unstressed and lengthened in word-final position. All is relative: there are no fixed durations corresponding to 'long' and 'short' respectively. Longer syllables are more able to carry a pitch change or tone, and may for this reason be more likely to attract stress: the long second syllable of *arena* is stressed but the short second syllable of *cinema* is not. Partly because the concept of length is ill defined, and partly because other patterns are involved, some phoneticians consider it preferable to follow the example of the ancient Hindu grammarians and define quantity in terms of *weight* ('heavy' and 'light' syllables) rather than length. See DURATION, LONG AND SHORT, METRE/METER, RHYTHM, VOWEL QUANTITY. [SPEECH]. G.K.

QUARTERLY REVIEW OF DOUBLE-SPEAK. Begun in 1974 by the Committee on Public Doublespeak of the National Council of Teachers of English, the *Review* was originally titled the *Doublespeak Newsletter* and published irregularly. The title was changed in 1980 and a publication schedule of January, April, July, and October was instituted. Each issue has 12 pages and contains articles on and examples of doublespeak, book reviews, cartoons, and a bibliography of resources. The January issue carries the announcement of the winner of the annual Doublespeak Award and the winner of the annual George Orwell Award. The review is edited by William Lutz, and has over 7,000 subscribers in the US and 22 other countries. See DOUBLESPEAK, NCTE. [MEDIA, STYLE]. W.D.L.

QUARTO [16c: from the Latin ablative phrase *in quarto* in a quarter (of a sheet of paper)]. (1) Abbreviated as *4to, 4°*. A format for printed material, until recently commonly used for books, made up of gatherings or quires of sheets of paper (usually of crown or demy) folded twice to provide four leaves or eight pages. Quartos have usually been a fairly sturdy size, but many of Shakespeare's plays and similar 16–17c works were first published in quarto in pamphlet form.

(2) A size of cut paper 10 inches × 8 inches (25.4 cm × 20.3 cm). See FORMAT, PAPER. [TECHNOLOGY]. W.W.B.

QUATRAIN [16c: from French, from *quatre* four (from Latin *quattuor*), and *-ain* (from Latin *-anus*)]. A stanza of four lines, the most popular form in traditional English verse, probably because it does not require such repetition of rhyme as the sonnet or the Spenserian stanza, and allows for antithesis or parallelism. It can have any rhyme scheme or metre. The *heroic quatrain*, in iambic pentameter, rhyming *abab*, has been used by many poets, such as Thomas Gray, 'Elegy Written in a Country Church-Yard' (1751):

Let not Ambition mock their useful toil,
Their homely joys and destiny obscure;
Nor Grandeur hear with a disdainful smile
The short and simple annals of the poor.

The *ballad stanza* has alternate tetrameter and trimeter lines, rhyming *abcb* or sometimes *abab*; the latter is much used for hymns, where it is known as *common measure*, as in these lines by Isaac Williams (1802–65):

Still let me ever watch and pray,
And feel that I am frail;
That if the tempter cross my way,
Yet he may not prevail.

Other quatrains include the trochaic metre (rhyming *aabb*) used by William Blake:

When the stars threw down their spears,
And water'd heaven with their tears,
Did he smile his work to see?
Did he who made the Lamb make thee?
('The Tyger', 1794)

and the iambic tetrameter (rhyming *abba*) used by Alfred Tennyson:

Thy voice is on the rolling air;
I hear thee where the waters run;
Thou standest in the rising sun,
And in the setting thou art fair.
('In Memoriam', 1850)

Unrhymed quatrains are rare. Although usually part of a longer poem, the quatrain can stand alone as a vehicle for epigrams, epitaphs, and general observations. Compare COUPLET. See VERSE. [LITERATURE]. R.C.

QUEBEC, also **Québec**. The name of both the largest province of Canada (home of the largest French-speaking community in North America) and of its capital city (founded by Samuel Champlain in 1608). Out of a population of *c*.6m, 82% speak French, 16% English. Italian and Greek are prominent immigrant languages, and Cree and Mohawk are prominent indigenous languages. The first Europeans to settle in the region were the French in the 17c, and their colony was known as *Nouvelle France* (New France) until well into the 18c. In its heyday, the French empire in North America stretched from the valley of the St Lawrence down the Ohio and Mississippi rivers to the Gulf of Mexico, limiting British expansion west. In the late 20c, however, Quebec is the only politically significant French-speaking community in North America.

Quebec French. The French of Quebec descends from the speech of 17c Normandy and Picardy. Distinctive and varied, it has a broad form known as *joual* (pronounced 'zhwal': a variant of *cheval* horse). The traditional standard of education and the media has been that of Paris, often referred to as *le français international*. Local French of all varieties and most social levels has been stigmatized both in France and in Quebec as a patois marred by its accents, its archaisms, and its Anglicisms. As a result, many Québécois have had experiences similar to those reported by Léandre Bergeron, who in reaction treats the French of Quebec as in effect a distinct language:

'You don't speak *real* French in Quebec.' This often heard pronouncement, said either with scornful condescendence or, even worse, with matter-of-fact naiveté, has always struck me. What can you say to it? How can you reply to someone who rubs you off the map with one sentence? To make matters worse, we get this not only from English Canadians but from Frenchmen as well. The two main cultural influences in our lives tell us that the language our parents taught us was not a *real* civilized language, but a peasant patois, a primitive gibberish. . . . The fact is that the majority of the inhabitants of Quebec are no more French than the majority of the inhabitants of Canada are British. Most people in Quebec do not speak Parisian French any more than people in Canada speak London English (from the preface to *The Québécois Dictionary*, 1982).

Quebec English. British Empire Loyalists from the US, after the end of the War of Independence in 1783, were the first significant English-speaking settlers in Quebec. They founded the Eastern Townships south-east of Montreal. By 1831, anglophones of British descent were in the majority in Montreal itself, but an influx of rural francophones, who filled the ranks of the urban working class, had by 1867 reversed that trend. By 1981, 66% of the city's population was French-speaking. Such facts explain why English as used in Montreal (and more generally in Quebec) is not as homogeneous as other Canadian regional Englishes. Rather it exists as a continuum, from long-established unilingual anglophones broadly similar to anglophones in Ontario through bilinguals of various kinds to francophones using English as a second language. Until 1970, Montreal was the economic capital of Canada, but many controlling anglophone companies relocated, especially in Toronto, as a result of mounting separatist pressures

in the 1970s and early 1980s among the French majority and under the government of the secessionist Parti Québécois (1976-85).

Much has been written in French on the effects of English on French in Quebec. In such works, the dominating role of English in North America has generally been considered pernicious, and francophones have often been urged to *éviter les anglicismes* (avoid Anglicisms) and not *commettre un anglicisme* (commit an Anglicism) in their French. The French of Quebec and Canada as a whole, however, continues to be heavily influenced by both CanE and AmE, as for example the widespread use of *bienvenu(e)*, the equivalent of *You're welcome* (in response to *merci* thank you), rather than the *de rien* (It's nothing) of France. There has been little comparable concern in Quebec about the effects of French on English and there have been few studies of Quebec English. However, the research that has been done indicates that in Montreal, for socio-economic reasons, English was until *c.*1975 regarded in both communities as the language of prestige. In the last 15 years, however, under the impact of pro-French legislation, French has gained greatly in prestige. In addition, English in Montreal tends to favour the norms of AmE more than English in Ontario, and Montrealers are less likely to employ Canadian Raising in their speech.

The most marked feature of local English is the influence of French. Many expressions have simply moved into English, such as: *autoroute* highway, *caisse populaire* credit union, *depanneur* convenience store, corner shop, and *subvention* subsidy. Anglophones who speak French constantly use such loan expressions as: *give a conference* give a lecture (from *donner une conférence*), *sc(h)olarity* schooling (from *scolarité*), and *syndicate* a trade union (from *syndicat*). The Gallicisms of francophones when speaking English range from such easily grasped expressions as *collectivity* (for *community*) and *annex* (for the *appendix* to a document) to a commonplace misuse of *faux amis*, such as *deceive* in *I was deceived when she didn't come* (from *décevoir* to disappoint), *reunion* in *We have a reunion at 5 o'clock* (from *réunion* a meeting), and *souvenir* in *We have a good souvenir of our trip to Louisiana* (from *souvenir* a memory).

The battle of the signs. In 1977, the passing of Quebec's *Bill 101* (the *Charter of the French Language*) required among other things that public signs be in French only. This led to violations, especially in English-speaking areas of Montreal, and the imposition of much-resented fines. As part of the so-called 'battle of the signs', the English language rights group *Alliance Quebec* organized and financed the defence of five merchants accused of violating the law. The 'Chaussure Brown' case went to the Supreme Court of Canada, which in 1988 declared that the section of Bill 101 dealing with signs was unconstitutional. The Quebec government responded by passing a new law, *Bill 178*, which allows non-French signs inside stores but not outside (an ordinance mocked by some anglophones as 'the inside outside law'). To pass this law, the provincial government used a provision in the Canadian Constitution Act (1982: see below) that allows provinces to pass and enforce laws that contravene the constitution for periods of up to five years. In the furore that followed, three anglophone ministers resigned from Quebec's Liberal government. A subsequent election brought four new anglophones into the predominantly francophone legislature, all members of the *Equality Party*, founded to support minority language rights in Quebec. By and large, the province's francophones support the language law with its ban on non-French signs, while anglophones are either against it or ambivalent.

Quebec and the rest of Canada. In May 1980, a referendum was held in Quebec to decide whether the province would remain a part of Canada or seek a more independent status called *sovereignty-association*. The referendum rejected the latter option, opening the way for Ottawa to seek the *patriation* of the Canadian Constitution, the *British North America Act* of 1867. Renamed the *Constitution Act*, and incorporating a new *Charter of Rights and Freedoms*, the Act was 'brought home' from Britain in 1982. René Levesque, the separatist Parti Québécois premier at the time, was however the sole provincial premier to refuse to sign the national agreement to patriate the constitution.

In 1987, the *Meech Lake Accord* was worked out by the federal and provincial governments in an attempt to resolve the differences that led to this refusal and to establish a more generally acceptable association between Quebec and the rest of Canada. Robert Bourassa, the Liberal Party successor to Levesque as Quebec premier, put forward five requirements, among which was recognition of Quebec as a 'distinct society'. This point was accepted by the Prime Minister, Brian Mulroney, and all provincial premiers, although the premiers of several provinces had cited what they saw as Quebec's suppression of English language rights as a reason for resisting Quebec's demands. Once agreement was reached, the accord had to be ratified by every province by the agreed date of 23 June 1990. During the last-minute debate on the accord, however, the premier of Manitoba, Gary Filmon, insisted on holding hearings and on putting acceptance of the accord to a vote in his legislature. Elijah Harper, a Native member of the Manitoba Assembly, blocked debate until time ran out on the agreement, on the grounds that aboriginal rights had been inadequately served by the accord. The premier of Newfoundland, Clyde Wells, had insisted on presenting the accord to his legislature for a free vote, but, angered by federal pressure to ratify it before the deadline, adjourned his legislature without holding the vote. The deadline passed and because of the necessity for pan-Canadian agreement, the Meech Lake Accord died, throwing Canada into considerable uncertainty. As a result, the constitutional and emotional gulf between Quebec and the rest of the country remains unbridged. See ALLIANCE QUÉBEC, ANGLO, ANGLOPHONE, CAJUN, CANADA, CANADIAN ENGLISH, CANADIAN LANGUAGES, DIALECT IN CANADA, FRENCH, LANGUAGE POLICE, MÉTIS. [AMERICAS, VARIETY].

T.MCA., M.F.

QUEEN'S ENGLISH. See KING'S ENGLISH.

QUEEN'S ENGLISH SOCIETY. A nonprofessional association with charitable status formed in England in 1972 by Joe Clifton, an information scientist in the pharmaceutical industry. Originally known as the 'Society for the Protection of the Queen's English', it sought to attract the support of 'people who appreciate good English and wish to maintain the standard' (Society's public statement). Its primary concern is a 'decline in the standard of literacy . . . increasingly evident in the press, on radio and on television' (leaflet). The Society has lobbied the British government for a return to the teaching of formal grammar in schools. It publishes *Quest: Journal of the Queen's English Society*. See KING'S ENGLISH, PURISM. Compare SOCIETY FOR PURE ENGLISH. [EUROPE, MEDIA].   T.MCA.

QUEENSLAND CANEFIELDS ENGLISH/ KANAKA ENGLISH. See AUSTRALIAN PIDGIN.

QUESTION [13c: through French from Latin *quaestio/quaestionis* an occasion of asking]. In general usage, a form of language that invites a reply, marked in spoken English with specific patterns of intonation and in written and printed English by a closing question mark (?). In grammar, a term in the classification of sentences, referring to types distinguished by form and function from such other sentence types as *statement* and *command*. If the term is used functionally, sentences said with a rising intonation (*You don't believe me?*) can be included, while rhetorical questions (*How could I possibly forget!*) and exclamations in interrogative form

(*Isn't he lucky!*) are not. In formal terms, questions are of three main types:

Yes-no questions. Questions to which the answer could be a *Yes* or *No*, with or without further detail, as with *Did you telephone Robert?* Formally, they begin with a verb: *be, have,* or *do,* or a modal verb, followed by the subject: *Are you all right?*; *Do you understand?*; *Have you enough money?/Do you have enough money?*; *Will you telephone Robert?*; *Can I help you?* Their usual intonation pattern is a rising tone on and after the tonic syllable, but, when rhetorical or emphatic, they are said with a falling tone.

Wh-questions. Questions beginning with an interrogative word. With the exception of *how,* these all begin with the letters *wh-*: *who(ever), whom, whose, what(ever), which, when, where-(ver), why(ever)*: *Why did he leave and where has he gone?* Such questions are sometimes called *information questions* because they are seeking new information. They contrast with *yes-no* questions, but like them usually involve inversion of subject and verb. Their usual intonation pattern is a falling tone on and after the tonic syllable, but when rhetorical or emphatic are said with a rising tone.

Alternative questions. These offer a choice of answer: *Are you expecting Robert or his brother?*; *Shall I telephone or write?*; *Who are you expecting—Robert or his brother?* If the question begins with a verb, the usual intonation pattern is a rising tone on each of the alternatives before the last and then a falling tone on the last alternative. If the question begins with an interrogative word, the usual pattern is a fall on the first part, followed by the same pattern in the second part as for a question beginning with a verb.

Inversion. All three types generally involve inversion of the subject and an auxiliary or modal verb. This inversion applies also to questions containing *be* as the sole verb (*Are you ready?*) and in BrE sometimes to *have* (*Have you any wool?* as opposed to *Do you have any wool?* and *Have you got any wool?*). All other verbs use *do* if there is no auxiliary or modal: *Where does she live?*; *What did you do?* The only exception to this inversion rule is when *who, what,* or *which* is part of the subject. Contrast: *Who told you that?* (where *who* is subject) and *Who(m) did you tell?*

See BEGGING THE QUESTION, INTERROGATIVE, INVERSION, LEADING QUESTION, QUESTION MARK, QUESTION TAG, TAG QUESTION, TONE. [GRAMMAR].

S.C., T.MCA.

QUESTION-BEGGING. See BEGGING THE QUESTION.

QUESTION MARK, also especially AmE **interrogation mark, interrogation point**. The punctuation mark (?). Its primary use is to show that a preceding word, phrase, or sentence is a direct question: *Do you want more to eat?*; '*Why?*' *I asked*; *He's her husband?* It is not used in indirect speech, because a reported question is part of a statement: *I asked you whether you wanted more to eat.* The question mark is sometimes repeated in informal usage or followed by an exclamation mark/point in order to indicate a specially strong question (*What did you say??*; *What did you say?!*). It is also used, often in brackets, to express doubt or uncertainty about a word or phrase that immediately follows or precedes it: *Julius Caesar, born (?)100 BC*; *They were then seen leaving the house (in tears?) and walking away.* See MARK, PUNCTUATION, QUESTION. [WRITING].

R.E.A.

QUESTION TAG. A short question tagged on to the end of a statement (declarative sentence). Some languages have an invariable question tag that can be added to almost any statement: French *n'est-ce pas?* (isn't it?); Spanish *verdad?* (truly?). In IndE and some other varieties, *isn't it?* is used in this way (*You are going tomorrow, isn't it?*), while *yes* and *no* are used for confirmation (*You are coming, yes?*; *She is going there, no?*). In many kinds of English, an enclitic tag is used for confirmation and other purposes: *eh?* is a shibboleth of CanE and common in BrE (*You like that kind of thing, eh?*), and in some varieties of ScoE *eh no?* is common (*You're comin as well, eh no?—aren't you?*). Many AmE speakers use *huh?* or *uh?* (*You coming, huh?*). Other common informal tags are *right?* and *OK?* (*He'll be there, right? I'll see you soon, OK?*).

Standard English throughout the world requires the question tag to correspond to the subject and verb of the preceding sentence. Such tags consist of a single-word verb (*be* or *have* as main verbs, an auxiliary, or a modal) plus a subject pronoun, as in *It's a nice day today, isn't it?*, *You have enough books, haven't you* (especially BrE) and *You have enough books, don't you?* (especially AmE), *She went home last night, didn't she?*, and *You could help if you wanted, couldn't you?* Question tags are normally negative after a positive statement, and vice versa. When spoken on the rising tone of *yes-no* questions, they may genuinely be asking for information or be expressing surprise or uncertainty: *You're not going to tell them, are you?* However, tags are more usually spoken on the falling intonation of statements, to invite or expect agreement with the preceding statement: *Lovely day we're having, aren't we?*; *It's been a mild winter, hasn't it?* Question tags can also be used with imperatives: *Wait a minute, will you?*;

Send us a postcard, won't you?; *Let's go together, shall we?* Another possibility is for the tag to agree with a subordinate clause: *I don't think they'll come now, will they?*; *That's a nice mess you've got us into, haven't you?* Occasionally, a positive statement is followed by a positive tag, with a rising intonation. This may simply signify an inference or even a request for clarification (*He'll be 21 next year, will he?*), but the structure often suggests sarcasm or suspicion: *So he's innocent, is he?*; *It fell off the back of a truck, did it?* (implication: I doubt that very much). See QUESTION, TAG QUESTION. [GRAMMAR].   S.C.

QUIBBLE. See PUN.

QUILLER-COUCH, (Sir) Arthur (Thomas) [1863–1944] Pen name *Q*. English novelist, academic, journalist, and critic, born in Bodmin, Cornwall, and educated at Clifton and Oxford. His novels with a Cornish background include *Dead Man's Rock* (1887) and *Troy Town* (1888). He edited several anthologies for OUP, beginning with the *Oxford Book of English Verse* (1900). He was knighted in 1910. Quiller-Couch became the first King Edward VII Professor of English Literature at Cambridge (1912) and was influential in the development of the English Tripos. His inaugural lectures were published as *On the Art of Writing* (1916) and he was joint editor of the *New Cambridge Shakespeare* from 1921. Quiller-Couch did not practise the close critical scholarship of such younger teachers of 'Cambridge English' as I. A. Richards and F. R. Leavis. His contribution was a deep appreciation of English literature, which he saw as drawing its strength from classical rather than Anglo-Saxon influence. His views about good English were prescriptive; he made a forceful attack on official clichés and jargon. He had little interest in philology, but was concerned for the teaching of English at all levels. He served on a Board of Education committee in 1919 to investigate English in schools and wrote in 1920: 'The real battle for English lies in our Elementary Schools, and in the training of our Elementary teachers.' See index. [BIOGRAPHY, EDUCATION, EUROPE, LITERATURE].   R.C.

QUIRE [15c: from Old French *qua(i)er* (Modern *cahier*) a quire of six sheets, a copy-book, ultimately from Latin *quaterni* four at a time. A parchment folded four times was a *quaternion*]. (1) A set of four sheets of paper or other material doubled to form eight leaves and 16 pages, a common unit in medieval manuscripts. (2) Any similar collection or gathering of leaves, one within the other, in a manuscript or printed work. (3) A set of 24 or 25 sheets of paper, a 20th of a ream. (4) A set of all the sheets in a book, regardless of number. If a publication is available *in quires*, it consists of unbound sheets. (5) Also *quair*. An obsolete term for a pamphlet or small book in a single quire, usually a poem or tract: 'Heirefter followis the quair maid be King James of Scotland the first, callit the kingis quair' (MS Selden B24, *c*.1500). See FORMAT, PAGE, REAM, SIGNATURE. [LITERATURE, TECHNOLOGY].   W.W.B., T.MCA.

QUIRK, (Sir Charles) Randolph [b.1920]. British linguist. Born in the Isle of Man, he studied at U. College London, and was awarded the degrees BA, MA, Ph.D., D.Litt. from the U. of London. He was a lecturer in English at UCL (1947–52), Reader in English Language and Literature at the U. of Durham (1954–8), Professor of English Language at Durham (1958–60) and at UCL (1960–8), and Quain Professor of English Language and Literature at UCL (1968–81). He chaired a governmental Committee of Inquiry which reformed the training of speech therapists in the UK (HMSO, 1972), served as Vice-Chancellor of the U. of London (1981–5), as President of the British Academy (1985–9), was awarded the CBE in 1976, and was knighted in 1985. Quirk's scholarly activities cover a wide range of studies in the English language and related subjects. They include: the phonology, morphology, vocabulary, and syntax of Old English; editions of Old Icelandic texts; the language of Dickens and Shakespeare; the teaching of the English language; lexical studies of English in various periods; English as an international language; research and publications on modern English syntax.

He founded the *Survey of English Usage* in 1959, continuing as its Director until 1981 (see entry). At this research unit, he supervised the compilation and analysis of a corpus of spoken and written samples of the language used by adult educated native speakers of BrE. In association with researchers at the Survey, he developed techniques for eliciting usage and attitudes to usage. The analyses derived from the data in the Survey corpus and in elicitation experiments have resulted in numerous publications by Quirk himself and by scholars from all over the world, in particular the two major reference grammars on which he collaborated: *A Grammar of Contemporary English* (1972) and *A Comprehensive Grammar of the English Language* (1985: see entry). His approach to research has been theoretically eclectic and focused on the functions of language. He assigns priority to the meticulous examination of language data and to total accountability of the data. The pursuit of these priorities has induced him to assert the prominence of analogy and gradience in the functioning of the language system; language categories are viewed as overlapping rather than discrete, and peripheral subcategories or individual items are shown to share to varying extents the features of the central members of a category. In his view, the description of English must take account of the stylistic variation occasioned by the relationship between participants in a discourse, the medium, the educational and social standing of the participants, and the subject matter of the discourse. He envisages the English language as having a common core shared by regional and stylistic varieties.

Publications include: *An Old English Grammar* (with C. L. Wrenn, Methuen, 1955, 2nd edition 1957); *The Use of English* (Longman, 1962, 2nd edition 1968); *Systems of Prosodic and Paralinguistic Features in English* (with David Crystal, Mouton, 1964); *Investigating Linguistic Acceptability* (with Jan Svartvik, Mouton, 1966); *Essays on the English Language—Medieval and Modern* (Longman, 1968); *Elicitation Experiments in English: Linguistic Studies in Use and Attitude* (with Sidney Greenbaum, Longman, 1970); *The English Language and Images of Matter* (OUP, 1972); *A Grammar of Contemporary English* (with Sidney Greenbaum, Geoffrey Leech, and Jan Svartvik, Longman, 1972); *A University Grammar of English* (with Greenbaum, Longman, 1973; US title *A Concise Grammar of Contemporary English*, Harcourt Brace Jovanovich, 1973); *The Linguist and the English Language* (Edward Arnold, 1974); *A Corpus of English Conversation* (with Svartvik, Gleerups/Liber, 1980); *A Comprehensive Grammar of the English Language* (with Greenbaum, Leech, and Svartvik, Longman, 1985); *Words at Work: Lectures on Textual Structure* (Longman, 1986); *English in Use* (with Gabriele Stein, Longman, 1990), *A Student's Grammar of the English Language* (with Greenbaum, Longman, 1990). See index. [BIOGRAPHY, EUROPE, GRAMMAR, LANGUAGE]. S.G.

QUOTATION [15c: from Medieval Latin *quotatio/quotationis*, from Latin *quotare/quotatum* to distinguish by means of numbers, to divide into sections (chapters, verses, etc.), from *quot* how many. There is no connection between *quote* and the archaism *quoth* meaning 'said', which is the simple past of *quethe* to say, from Old English *cwethan*. The obsolete forms *cote, cott, coate*, as in 'He coateth Scriptures', are from French *coter*, also from *quotare*]. The act or practice of repeating a phrase, sentence, or passage from a book, speech, or other source, an occasion of doing this, and the words used: *a speech full of quotations*. The informal noun *quote* is also widely used, especially by journalists: *Can I have a quote on that? That's the quote of the week*. In classical and medieval times,

reciting and quoting were closely related; because books were rare and not always at hand when needed, it was necessary to memorize and be able to repeat large parts of important texts, especially scripture. Unlettered people, the vast majority, could only learn them if the literate could quote them *verbatim* (Latin: word for word). Preachers and orators would use and identify specific quotations for insertion in their sermons and speeches, to add weight and substance to what they said. When necessary, especially in matters of religion and law, texts would be produced, places of reference marked, and relevant sections read aloud or pointed out. Because of this, *quotation* also referred to the provision of references to parts of texts, to the listing of such references, and to copying out quotable excerpts by hand.

Quotation, plagiarism, allusion. The concept of quotation depends on identifying (briefly or in detail) the source to which reference is made and from which words have been taken. It also usually requires justification, explicitly stated or implicitly accepted: one quotes in order to substantiate a claim, bolster an argument, illustrate a point, demonstrate a truth, catch out an opponent, amuse an audience, or impress one's listeners or readers. A spoken quotation may be presented in a variety of ways: for example, with a lead-in that relates quotation to topic, followed by something on the person to be quoted, then the quoted matter itself, as in: 'Talking about the Canadian predicament, the former prime minister Mackenzie King put it this way: "If some countries have too much history, we have too much geography." ' Another possibility is: 'The humorist Stephen Leacock described the matter as follows in 1944: "In Canada, we have enough to do keeping up with two spoken languages without trying to invent slang, so we just go right ahead and use English for literature, Scotch for sermons, and American for conversations." ' The written forms used here to frame these quotations show how they are conventionally integrated into running text. Quotations in isolation, however, are usually set apart in paragraphs of their own, with plenty of white space, have the quoted matter first, then the name of the originator, often followed by such information as source and date, all of which may be presented in a variety of formats. For example:

Without quotation marks and with a dash, etc.
America is God's Crucible, the great Melting-Pot where all the races of Europe are melting and re-forming! - Israel Zangwill, *The Melting Pot*, 1908.

Without quotation marks and with parentheses, etc.
The most important thing to know about Americans— the attitude which *truly* distinguishes them from the

British and explains much superficially odd behaviour—is that *Americans believe that death is optional* (Jane Walmsley, 'A Native's Guide to Ameri-think', *Company*, Mar. 1984).

With quotation marks (British style), and both a dash and parentheses, etc.
'The Irish are a fair people—they never speak well of one another' - Samuel Johnson, quoted in James Boswell, *Life of Johnson* (1775, vol. 2, p. 307).

With quotation marks (American style), and both a dash and parentheses, etc.
"And while we don't exactly hate New Zealanders, we're not exactly fond of each other. While they regard us as vulgar yobboes, almost Yank-like, we think of them as secondhand, recycled Poms". - Phillip Adams, *The Age* (Melbourne: 18 June 1977).

If sources are not identified by such means as these, and the borrowed material is substantial and presented explicitly or implicitly as a writer's own, the person who does so may have engaged in *plagiarism*, the theft of someone else's words. If, however, the unassigned quotation is brief, appropriate to a situation, and belongs by more or less general agreement to a shared cultural tradition, it is neither quotation nor plagiarism, but *allusion*: the oblique and entirely legitimate reference to a source, part of whose effect is the pleasure (or frustration) listeners or readers feel as they identify (or fail to identify) the source in question. In addition, many expressions that belong entirely in the public domain, such as proverbs and idioms, may have a quotation-like flavour, or be quotations so often quoted that they have become detached from their sources. This is generally the case, for example, with *The pen is mightier than the sword*, a statement as proverbial as *A stitch in time saves nine*. It may be thought to have a Biblical or Shakespearian feel to it, but comes from the work of the 19c English politician, novelist, and poet Edward Bulwer-Lytton:

> Beneath the rule of men entirely great
> The pen is mightier than the sword.
> (*Richelieu, or the Conspiracy*, a play in blank verse, 1838, 2. 2)

Misquotation and non-quotation. Until the 20c, quotation was largely from written and printed sources; in recent decades, however, quotations have increasingly been taken from live performance, especially speeches and interviews, the taking of excerpts being done in shorthand or, more recently still, with the help of tape recorders. As a result, 'quotees' are increasingly aware of the risks of being *misquoted* or may take refuge from the consequences of what they have said by claiming that they were misquoted. People in the public eye may seek to establish ground rules for interviews and statements to the media: these range from the more informal *Don't quote me (on this)* to the more formal *This is off the record* and perhaps the requirement that a statement be *unattributed*, except perhaps to 'a usually reliable source'. Such requirements may or may not be respected; they may or may not even be meant to be respected, but intended instead to serve as an indirect way of gaining publicity.

The 'quotation industry'. Out of the tradition of quoting chapter and verse from the Bible, of quoting lines from great writers and orators, and of quoting the remarks of the famous, there has grown a minor industry that marshals and highlights the comments, aphorisms, quips, *bons mots*, and verbal *faux pas* of the celebrated, notorious, or fashionable. It includes: (1) The compiling and publishing of anthologies of observations by famous people, works promoted and purchased as a means through which public speaking may be enlivened ('quotes for all occasions') or readers can enjoy instances of language used to good effect. (2) Brief, topical features in newspapers and other periodicals with such names as *Quotes of the Week* or *They Said It*, listing significant, thought-provoking, egregious, or fatuous observations or remarks made by people currently in the limelight. The existence of such items not only requires journalists to find material to fill them but may prompt public or would-be public figures to formulate snappy one-liners that might be listed and attributed.

Books of quotations. Published collections of quotations take various forms. *The Oxford Dictionary of Quotations* was first published in 1941, with revised editions in 1953 and 1979; it lists people (such as Shakespeare and Shaw) and major authorless texts (such as the Bible) in alphabetic order, with the quotations under each heading numbered, identified, and keyed to an index listing words as topics, followed by brief contextualizing extracts, source name, page, and number. Within sections, the ordering is often but not always chronological: for example, Churchill is quoted as saying 'to jaw-jaw is better than to war-war' (in 1954, in Washington) a few lines above 'It is a good thing for an uneducated man to read books of quotations' (from *My Early Life*, 1930). *The Oxford Dictionary of Modern Quotations* (ed. Tony Augarde, 1991) has the same format. H. L. Mencken's *A New Dictionary of Quotations on Historical Principles from Ancient and Modern Sources* (Alfred A. Knopf, 1942) lists topics such as *advice* and *hell* alphabetically, with instances of what people have had to say about them. *Benham's Book of Quotations, Proverbs and Household Words* (Sir Gurney Benham, Harrap, 1948) has a number of themes: British and American authors, the Holy Bible, the Book of Common Prayer, Waifs and Strays (a miscellany), Greek Quotations,

Latin Quotations, Quotations from Modern Languages, and Proverbs. These are followed by an index of topics. Rhoda Thomas Tripp's *The International Thesaurus of Quotations* (Thomas Y. Crowell 1970, Allen & Unwin 1973, Penguin 1976) lists quotations under numbered topics such as *217 Deafness* and *663 Parenthood*, buttressed by three indexes: of authors and sources; of key words; and of categories and cross-references. The *Bloomsbury Dictionary of Quotations* (1987) follows the Oxford format while a spin-off *Bloomsbury Thematic Dictionary of Quotations* (1988), created by computerized rearrangement, lists the same information in a form similar to Mencken's, but with a keyword index. Manuals of public speaking often contain lists of quotations whose use might serve to 'make your speech sparkle'.

See ALLUSION, BIBLE, BOOK OF COMMON PRAYER, CARTOON, CITATION, COPYRIGHT, DIALOG(UE), DIRECT AND INDIRECT SPEECH, ELLIPSIS, ENGLISH LITERATURE, EPIGRAPH, PLAGIARISM, POINT, PROSE, PUNCTUATION, QUOTATION MARKS, QUOTE UNQUOTE. [REFERENCE, SPEECH, WRITING].

T.MCA.

QUOTATION MARKS [1880s]. Also less formally **quote marks, quotes**. In BrE also called **inverted commas** and informally **speech marks**. Punctuation marks used to open and close quoted matter and direct speech, either *single* (' ') or *double quotation marks* (" "). Double marks are traditionally associated with American printing practice (as in the Chicago style) and single marks with British practice (as in the Oxford and Cambridge styles), but there is much variation in practice; double marks are more often found in British texts before the 1950s, and are usual in handwriting. Quotation marks are a relatively recent invention and were not common before the 19c. Traditional texts of the Bible do not use them and do not suffer from the omission. Quotation marks can be untidy, especially in combination with other punctuation marks and when marks occur within marks. Some writers have therefore avoided them, notably James Joyce, who used dashes to introduce direct speech. Single quotation marks are tidier, less obtrusive, and less space-consuming than double marks, and for this reason are increasingly preferred in Britain and elsewhere in printing styles, especially in newspapers. The uses of quotation marks for direct speech, quoted material, and other purposes are discussed separately below; there is considerable overlap among the various categories.

Direct speech. Quotation marks indicate direct speech (that is, the words of a speaker quoted, more or less exactly) in such forms as BrE *He*

said, '*Come with me*' and AmE *He said, "Come with me*", and BrE '*Come with me,' he said* and AmE *"Come with me," he said*. The marks are normally placed outside other punctuation in sentences of direct speech, such as a final period or full stop, or a comma when the direct speech is interrupted:

BrE 'Go away,' she said, 'and don't come back.'
AmE "Go away," she said, "and don't come back."

In BrE, they are often placed inside other punctuation marks when they refer to a part of the sentence that is contained within the other marks, as in *When you said 'Go away', I was shocked*. In AmE, however, the quotation marks are normally placed outside other punctuation in all circumstances, as in *When you said "Go away," I was shocked*. Quotation marks are not used in indirect (reported) speech, except occasionally when the enclosed words are regarded as equivalent to a quotation, as in:

BrE He then declared that 'I was incompetent'.
AmE He then declared that "I was incompetent."

In BrE, the quotation marks are placed within other punctuation because the words referred to are a quotation within the structure of the whole sentence.

Opening marks are given when direct speech is resumed after an interruption such as a reporting clause, as in the examples above. Normally, a comma or other punctuation mark separates the ending or resumption of direct speech from its interruption:

BrE 'Certainly not,' he exclaimed. 'I would sooner die.'
AmE "Certainly not," he exclaimed. "I would sooner die."

Different practices have been advocated from time to time (for example by the Fowler brothers in *The King's English* of 1906), but the practice described here now prevails. In extended dialogue, the words of each speaker are normally given on a new line when the speaker changes: see DIALOG(UE). Speakers are often not named after their first appearance in a run of speech, except to describe some special feature or manner of speaking (as in *he exclaimed* or *she said proudly*). The first two illustrations are from BrE:

'Where is Joseph?'
'I don't know.'
'Why isn't he here?'
'I don't know.'
'You drove out with him last night.'
'Yes.'
'You returned alone.'
'Yes.'
'You had a rendezvous with the rebels.'
'You're talking nonsense. Nonsense.'
'I could shoot you very easily. It would be a pleasure for me. You would have been resisting arrest.'

'I don't doubt it. You must have had plenty of practice.'

(Graham Greene, *The Comedians*, 1960)

In more extreme cases, where several exchanges are going on at once, it can be difficult to follow the threads of the dialogue:

'Jean is here, sir,' said Alice, trying to hide Jean's confidential file under her mauve cardigan with the blue buttons.
'Hello, my dear young lady.'
'No, don't ring off, I haven't finished with you yet!'
'I had a lot of trouble, Alice. They said it wouldn't be ready till morning.'
'Have my seat, it's not awfully comfortable.'
'They distinctly said four-thirty. It's always the same. The more time one gives them the more unreliable they are.'

(Len Deighton, *The Ipcress File*, 1962)

The following is from AmE:

"He's a dear old friend," she said to Spizer. "We've known each other since we were kids."
"Childhood sweethearts?" Spizer said generously.
"No, just dear friends."
"I did have a dinner date with Marty," Martha said. "If you had only called."
"Not a word more," Spizer said. "I'm taking both of you to dinner. How many real friends do we have in this world? And you don't know," he said to Stephan, "how lucky you are."

(Howard Fast, *The Immigrants*, 1977)

Quotation marks are often omitted in *free direct speech*, in which the words of the speaker, often representing inward thought rather than actual utterance, are continuous with the surrounding text. In extended dialogue they are sometimes replaced by dashes introducing each change of speaker, a practice more common in Continental printing. Joyce favoured light punctuation and disliked quotation marks, calling them *perverted commas*. He therefore insisted on dashes, but his publishers did not always acquiesce.

Quotations. When quotation marks are used, as their name suggests, to indicate quoted material (words taken from another source in writing or print) they generally appear without any introductory conventions of the kind usual in direct speech:

BrE We then plan to visit the 'eternal city'.
AmE We then plan to visit the "eternal city."

Some of the uses given above for direct speech are often equivalent to quotation, and the boundary between the two uses is often indistinct. The position of the quotation marks in both BrE and AmE in relation to other punctuation follows the principles outlined above.

Headings and titles. Quotation marks are also generally used to designate cited headings and titles, which are in effect equivalent to quotations. Printing practice varies in this regard, italics being widely used to denote titles of books,

journals, and newspapers, and quotation marks to denote titles of individual articles or sections within larger works, as in: See Chapter 3, 'The Middle Ages', and J. Smith, 'Some Observations on Magic and Ritual in the Middle Ages', in *Journal of the Historical Society* 3 (1967), 6–16. In many scientific works, however, titles of papers are printed without quotation marks.

Highlighting. Quotation marks may also serve to alert the reader to a special or unusual word or use of a word, such as a foreign expression (as in *You need a lot of* 'savoir faire'), or to indicate a word or use that is not the writer's own (as in *Several* 'groupies' followed the band on their tour). The latter usage is often formally referred to as *scare quotes*, because the marks frequently serve as a warning to the reader that there is something unusual or dubious (in the opinion of the writer) about the quoted word or phrase. In conversation, speakers may indicate their use of such scare quotes by making finger movements that suggest quotation marks: see QUOTE UNQUOTE. This use is close to quotation, the implication being something like *Several groupies, as they are often called, followed the band on their tour.* The following extract from Howard Fast's *The Immigrants* (1977) further illustrates this usage, along with other features of AmE practice:

He was a self-styled "pioneer," which meant that with nine other young men, he was preparing to go to Palestine and become part of the tiny community that a handful of Jews had founded there. (In BrE, the punctuation would normally be *He was a self-styled* 'pioneer', *which meant that . . .*)

Special conventions. (1) When quoted material or direct speech extends continuously over several paragraphs, new paragraphs begin with opening quotation marks, and closing marks are given only at the end of the last paragraph. (2) When quoted material occurs within other quoted material, BrE and AmE adopt opposite conventions. The normal practice in BrE is to use single quotation marks in the first (enclosing) instance and double marks in the second (enclosed) instance: *He asked,* 'Have you seen "The Laughing Cavalier"?' In AmE, double marks are commonly used in the first instance and single in the second instance: *He asked,* "Have you seen 'The Laughing Cavalier'?" In both cases, the question mark comes after the marks that relate to the quoted names, and before the mark or marks that close the sentence of speech. See COMMA, CONVERSATION, DASH, DIALOG(UE), DIRECT AND INDIRECT SPEECH, FOREIGNISM, ITALIC, MARK, QUOTATION, QUOTE UNQUOTE. [SPEECH, STYLE, USAGE, WRITING]. R.E.A.

QUOTES, QUOTE MARKS. See QUOTATION MARKS.

QUOTE UNQUOTE. As a convention of dictation, a speaker may warn that a quotation is coming by saying *quote* and indicate that it has been completed by saying *unquote*. The usage has been carried over into conversation and public speaking: 'He expressed the personal opinion that the picture was quote great for America unquote' (Peter Ustinov, *Loser*, 1961). Here, the words are kept apart, but in a further development they come together as a phrase, *quote unquote*, used to indicate that what has just been said would be in quotation marks if written: 'If you're a liberal, quote unquote, they're suspicious of you' (*The Random House Dictionary*, 1987). The practice, in either form, distances speakers from words that they wish to emphasize are not their own. It is not unusual, in such cases, for speakers to raise their hands and twitch two curled fingers to represent quotation marks, with or without the spoken disclaimer. See QUOTATION, QUOTATION MARKS (HIGHLIGHTING). [SPEECH, WRITING].   T.MCA.

QWERTY [20c: a letter-name, from the first six letters in the second of the four rows (*qwertyuiop*) of keys on most typewriters. Compare *alphabet*, from the first two letters of Greek writing]. The standard keyboard configuration for typewriters and computers. Originally called the *Universal* system, it was one of many competing keyboard arrangements at the end of the 19c. It seems to have been devised by Christopher Letham Sholes in the late 1860s, and appeared on the first commercially sold typewriter, the Remington of 1873. Its chief competitor, the *Ideal* system, had the top row *dhiatensor*. The advantage of *qwerty* has not been speed (it tends to overwork the left hand with the frequently used letters *esatd*) but slowness; it forced operators of early machines to reduce speed so as to avoid jamming them. More ergonomically efficient mechanical systems exist, most notably the *dvorak* keyboard, which was developed by August Dvorak of the U. of Washington in the 1930s and was a serious rival to *qwerty* until rejected by the US government in 1956. It can give the skilled operator an increase of speed of up to 30%. A general replacement of *qwerty* would be expensive, yet computer keyboards can be easily restructured because there is no mechanical relationship between keystroke and letter. Though keyboards generally retain one key for one letter, more efficient keyboards such as are used for court reporting have a 'chord' system in which a small number of keys can be combined to produce a wide range of letters and stenographic marks. *Qwerty* is closely associated with English. French has an *azerty* system prompting the Gallic comment that only Anglo-Saxons would have their *Q* (*cul*) *dans le coin* (arse/ass in the corner). See KEYBOARD. [TECHNOLOGY].   W.W.B.

R

R, r [Called 'ar']. The 18th letter of the Roman alphabet as used for English. It originated in Phoenician and was adopted and adapted by the Greeks as *rho* (P). When the Romans adopted it, they adapted it further to distinguish *R* from *P*.

Sound values. In English, the letter *r* is pronounced in different ways in different accents, but normally has only one sound value in the speech of any individual. As well as occurring before and after vowels (*rear, roar*), *r* is also heard after initial consonants as in *brown, crown, frown, ground, proud, shroud, trout, thrown*, and after *s*+consonant as in *spray, stray, scream*. After a vowel, *r* may precede other consonants as in *barb, bard, dwarf, morgue, arc, ark, arch, barque, hurl, harm, barn, farce, hears, furs, burst, harsh, hurt, earth, serve, Xerxes, furze*. Final *r* cannot immediately follow a consonant in English as it does in Welsh (for example, *theatr*), but to form a syllable requires a vowel letter either after it (*acre*, BrE *theatre*) or before it (*later*, AmE *theater*).

Rhotic and non-rhotic. A major variation with implications for spelling concerns not how, but when, *r* is pronounced. The accents of English fall into two groups: *rhotic* or *r*-sounding accents (in which *r* is pronounced in all positions in *red, credit*, and *worker*) and *non-rhotic* or *r*-less accents in which *r* is pronounced only before a vowel (that is, in *rice* and *price*, but not in either position in *worker*). The presence or absence of /r/ in the pronunciation of words like *worker* has an effect on the pronunciation of preceding vowels. Rhotic speakers generally distinguish certain words which are homophones for non-rhotic speakers, such as *farther/father, iron/ion, tuner/tuna*. They do not, however, always distinguish words in the same way: for example, Scots and non-Southern Americans distinguish

sauce/source (homophones in RP) with different vowel sounds and different realizations of /r/. In some non-rhotic accents, final *r* is pronounced when the following word begins with a vowel ('linking *r*') and an unwritten /r/ ('intrusive *r*') is commonly pronounced in contexts like *Africa/r and Asia, law/r and order*, and *draw/r/ing*. See RHOTIC AND NON-RHOTIC, R-SOUNDS.

Rhotacizing and de-rhotacizing. Non-rhotic speakers often cannot tell from pronunciation when to put *r* in a word and when to leave it out, and are prone to misspellings such as *rhotacizing* (inserting an *r*) in *surport for *support*, and *de-rhotacizing* (removing an *r*) in *supprise for *surprise*. Some written forms reflect this ambivalence. *Marm* as a clipped form of *madam* reflects non-rhotic pronunciation and rhymes with *charm*, whereas the *r*-less spelling *ma'am* accords with both types of accent and can rhyme with either *calm* or *jam* (however pronounced). Paradoxically, the AmE vulgarism *He bust his ass* doubly de-rhotacizes *He burst his arse*, but is common in rhotic AmE speech. Poets on both sides of the Atlantic have sometimes exploited the non-rhotic pronunciation for the sake of rhyme, as in *crosses/horses* (Keats) and *quarter/water* (Longfellow). The insertion of a vowel after *r* in *alarum, chirrup, sirrah* (for *alarm, chirp, sir*) preserves (and emphasizes) the *r*-sound in non-rhotic speech.

Double R. (1) In word-final position, in some monosyllables when preceded by a single vowel: *err, purr, whirr* (also *whir*) (but contrast *blur, cur, her, slur, spur, stir* and note *bur/burr*). (2) Medially, in disyllables ending in -*y* (*carry, berry, lorry, hurry*) and -*ow* (*narrow, borrow, furrow*). (3) Some medial doubling derives from Latin: *error, horror, terror* and the root *terra* (Earth, land), as in *terrestrial, Mediterranean*. Double *r* can also be a consequence of the assimilation of

THE CAPITAL LETTER						THE SMALL LETTER				
EARLY FORMS				CURRENT FORMS		EARLY FORMS			CURRENT FORMS	
Phoenician	Greek	Etruscan	Roman (Latin)	roman	italic	Roman cursive	Roman uncial	Carolingian minuscule	roman	italic
𝈥	◁P	◁	P	R	*R*	⌒	R	┌	r	*r*

certain Latin prefixes to roots beginning with *r*: *ad-* in *arrive*, *con-* in *correct*, *in-* in *irremediate* and *irrigate*, *sub-* in *surreptitious*. (4) When suffixes beginning with a vowel are attached to stressed syllables ending in *r*: *blurred, averred* (contrast *severed*), *deferring* (contrast *suffering*), *referral, referrable* (optionally also *referable*, often with stress on the initial syllable: compare *reference*). (5) The discrepancy of *rr* in *embarrass*, but *r* in *harass* reflects French *embarrasser, harasser*. The *OED* attests variation in both words in English. (6) In some words, although doubling is obligatory in the source language, it is optional in English borrowings: English *garrotte/garotte*, *guerrilla/guerilla*, Spanish *garrote, guerrilla*.

Syllabic *R*. Difficulties in spelling arise from complex, unpredictable relationships between *r* and preceding unstressed vowel sounds and letters. Like the phonetically similar consonants *l, m, n*, the letter *r* functions in rhotic accents simultaneously as a spoken vowel and as a consonant (though less obviously in non-rhotic speech). The *r* is then syllabic, as in *acre*: see SYLLABIC CONSONANT. In non-rhotic accents, the *r*-sound has disappeared in these contexts, leaving schwa, with the result that pairs like *beater/beta*, *pucker/pukka*, *rotor/rota*, *peninsular/peninsula* are homophones in RP and similar accents. This syllabic *r* or the schwa which has replaced it may combine with a preceding long vowel or diphthong to form a single syllable, with the result that such words as *lair, layer* are homophones and rhyme with *mayor/mare* and *prayer*.

In *acre* (with 'magic' *e*), and BrE *centre*, AmE *center*, the schwa in non-rhotic pronunciation is represented by the *r* (the final *e* being silent). The effect is striking in inflected forms such as BrE *centred* (compare *entered*). Syllabic *r* creates uncertainty in spelling, because the schwa sound may be spelt with any vowel letter or several digraphs: *lumbar, cancer, nadir, rector, murmur, martyr, neighbour*. Pronunciation (especially in RP and related accents) is no guide; when in doubt, the less confident writer often settles on an *-er* form: **burgler* for *burglar*, **docter* for *doctor*.

The problem of spelling syllabic *r* (or final schwa) is compounded by numerous pairs of homophones: *altar/alter*, *auger/augur*, *calendar/calender*, *caster/castor*, *censer/censor*, *dollar/dolour*, *filter/philtre*, *fisher/fissure*, *friar/frier*, *hangar/hanger*, *lumbar/lumber*, *manner/manor*, *meddler/medlar*, *meter/metre*, *miner/minor*, *prier/prior*, *raiser/razor*, *rigger/rigour*, *roomer/rumour*, *sailer/sailor*, *sucker/succour*, *taper/tapir*, *tenner/tenor*. Homophone pairs in which the schwa + *r* sequence is medial pose

similar problems: *humerus/humorous*, *literal/littoral*, *savory/savoury*, *stationary/stationery*, *summary/summery*. Further problems for learners and weak spellers arise with words which have similar phonological but different orthographic patterns: *ministry/monastery*, *mystery/history*, *disparate/desperate*, *deliberate/elaborate*, *disastrous/boisterous*, *leprous/obstreperous*, *wintry/summery*.

Simple vowels before *R*. (1) The values of vowel letters before *r* are often modified. In monosyllables, if *a* and *o* precede *r*, they are lengthened: *star, hard, harm, barn, harsh, cart, carve; ford, torn*. However, *e, i, u, y* typically merge their values in RP to a lengthened schwa: *her, sir, cur, herd, turf, urge, irk, bird, curd, fern, turn, hurt, serve, myrrh*. The vowel digraphs *ea* and *ou* when followed by *r* may also have this value: *earn, journey*. These alternatives generate pairs of homophones: *berth/birth*, BrE *curb/kerb*, *earn/urn*, *fir/fur*, *heard/herd*, *pearl/purl*, *serf/surf*, *serge/surge*, *tern/turn*. Such long pronunciations also occur in the stressed final syllables of disyllables: *impart, suborn, concern, confer, concur*. However, when a *w*-sound precedes these vowel + *r* patterns, the values of *a* and *o* are commonly altered to those of *o* and *u* respectively, as in *dwarf* (compare *orphan*), *word* (compare *curd*), but not after silent *w* (*whore, sword*). (2) Especially in the accents of England, if an unstressed vowel between two *r*s is elided, single *r* may be heard as in *February* ('Febry', 'Febuary'), *library* ('libry'), *literary* ('litry'), *temporary* ('tempry').

Long vowels before *R*. The greatest complexity arises after long vowels or diphthongs, as a result both of the rhotic/non-rhotic split and of the effect of *r* on preceding vowels. When final silent *e* follows *r*, preceding vowels are typically long, but often modified: compare *hare/hate*, *here/eve*, *hire/hive*, *more/mope*, *lure/lute*. Different spellings for these vowels produce inconsistency in many common words: (1) *Pare* compared with *pair*, *pear* and contrasted with *bar* and anomalous *are*. (2) *Here* compared with *hear* and contrasted with *were, there, where* and the two pronunciations of *tear*. (3) *Fire* contrasted with *fiery, wiry*. (4) *Pure* compared with the varying value of *-ure* in *sure*. (5) *Sore, morning* are homophones of *soar, mourning* only in some accents. (6) The *-our* sequence is confused. The forms *-our* and *-ower*, as in *flour/flower*, may represent the standard value, but *course, court, four* have the vowel of *or* in RP; there is uncertainty about rarer words such as *dour, gourd*; and the common word *your* may be a homophone of *yore* or of *ewer*. In many non-rhotic accents, *sore/soar/saw* (but not *sour, sower*) are homophones. Similar variety prevails with the vowels in *moor/more/maw*. The oldest forms of RP, and many other accents, distinguish all three; others merge the first or last two; while recent RP and related accents merge all three.

Intervocalic *R*. In polysyllables, *r* between vowels may follow a short or long vowel: (1) Short *a, e, i, o, y* (not *u*) before *r* in stressed syllables: *arid, character, parachute, erudite, miracle, spirit, coracle, origin, courier, syrup, pyramid*. (2) Long vowels in stressed syllables: *area, parent, vary, hero, period, pirate, virus, story, floral, during, fury, spurious*. (3) The vowel before *rr* in the stressed syllables of polysyllables normally has the standard short value: *carry, barrier, error, ferry, mirror, stirrup, sorrow, hurry*. However, values differ between *warring/warrior*, the noun *furrier* and the comparative of the adjective *furry*, and between the verb *to tarry* and the adjective *tarry* from *tar*.

Distinctive combinations. (1) Initial *r* follows silent *w* in some words of Old English origin: *wrap, wraith, wreck, wriggle, write, wrong, wrought, wrung*. (2) The digraph *rh* occurs word-initially in Greek-derived words, representing classical Greek *r* with rough breathing ('hr'): *rhapsody, rhetoric, rhinoceros, rhododendron, rhubarb, rhythm*. In word-medial and word-final positions, the combination is *rrh*, following the classical Greek practice: *antirrhinum, catarrhine, diarrhoea/diarrhea, haemorrhage/hemorrhage, platyrrhine; catarrh, myrrh*. (3) *Rh* also occurs initially in Welsh names: *Rhoddri* (man's first name), *Rhondda* (place-name). (4) The combination *shr* and *sr* occur in IndE in Sanskrit loanwords such as the titles *Sri/Shri/Shree* and *Srimati/Shrimati/Shreemati*, as in *Sri* and *Srimati Gupta* (Mr and Mrs Gupta). (5) Initial *vr* occurs in *vroom* (the noise of a powerful engine revving).

Historical points. (1) There has been occasional variation between *r* and other alveolar consonants: *glamour* derives from *grammar; colonel* was formerly *coronel* (see L); the *rr* in *porridge* and single *r* in *porage* were originally the *tt* in *pottage*: compare SCOUSE. (2) The *r*-sound has disappeared in *speak* (compare German *sprechen*), in *palsy* (ultimately from Greek-derived *paralysis*), and in the colloquial forms *bust* for *burst, cussed* for *cursed*. (3) Sometimes, an *r*-sound has switched position with a following vowel, as in *burn/brand* and *work/wrought* (dating from Old English), *brid* (in Middle English) now *bird*; *r* occurring before the vowel in *three* but after it in *third, thirty*: see METATHESIS.

American and British differences. Variation in the use of *r* occurs between most BrE forms ending in consonant + *re* and their AmE equivalents, which are written consonant + *er*: BrE *calibre/*

AmE *caliber, centre/center, fibre/fiber, goitre/goiter, litre/liter, manoeuvre/maneuver, meagre/meager, metre/meter, ochre/ocher, reconnoitre/reconnoiter, sabre/saber, saltpetre/saltpeter, sceptre/scepter, sombre/somber, spectre/specter, theatre/theater*. However, no such difference arises after a long vowel + *c* or *g*: both varieties have the same spellings for *acre, lucre, mediocre*, and *ogre*. See ALPHABET, BURR, INTRUSIVE R, LETTER[1], LINKING R, RHOTACISM, RHOTIC AND NON-RHOTIC, R-SOUNDS, SPELLING. [WRITING].

C.U., T.MCA., E.W.

RACISM [1930s: from French *racisme*, from *race*, from Italian *razza*: of uncertain origin. The more recent form *racism* (favoured in AmE) contrasts with the older form *racialism* (1900s: formerly favoured in BrE); it appears to have become the standard international term: compare *sexism, ageism*]. (1) The theory, belief, doctrine, or prejudice which asserts that distinctive human characteristics and abilities, including language, are determined by race (especially as established through such broad physiological categories as *Australoid, Caucasoid, Mongoloid, Negroid*). Although often presented as scientific, especially in the 19c in the wake of Darwinism, such a theory, etc., serves to buttress the visceral assumption that one's own race is superior to all others. It may follow from this that one's own race therefore has, among other things, the right to control (and, when deemed necessary, enslave and even exterminate) people of races that are taken to be inferior or undesirable. A racist viewpoint figured in the arguments used to justify European imperial expansion and what Kipling called 'the white man's burden'; it was taken to the extreme by the Nazis during the Second World War (especially against Gypsies, Jews, and Slavs), and continues to underpin the concept of *white supremacy* among such groups as the Ku Klux Klan in the US. (2) Hatred and intolerance of, and discrimination against, people of another racial group or groups: 'Racism is an *ism* to which everyone in the world today is exposed' (Ruth Benedict, *Race: Science and Politics*, 1940); 'In the British sailors' reactions to the slaves . . ., the very existence of racism is as well documented as the difference in language' (J. L. Dillard, *Black English*, 1972).

Attitudes to and assumptions about race and language have been significant elements in many parts of the world where English has been used and distinctive varieties have developed: for example, in the UK, the US, parts of Africa, parts of Asia, and the Caribbean. For further discussions of racism and language, and in particular the English language, see ABORIGINAL ENGLISH, ABORIGINES, ACHEBE, AFRICAN LITERATURE IN ENGLISH, ANGLO-INDIAN, ARYAN,

BANTU, BLACK, BLACK ENGLISH, BLUE-EYED ENGLISH, BRITISH EMPIRE, BURGHER ENGLISH, CALIBAN, COLONIAL, CREOLE, EAST INDIAN, ETHNIC, ETHNIC JOKE, ETHNIC NAME, EURASIAN, FANAKALO, GORDIMER, IMPERIALISM, -ISM, MAORI, MESTIZO, MÉTIS, MULATTO, MULTICULTURALISM, NGUGI, PAKEHA, PIDGIN, POLITICALLY CORRECT, RASTA TALK, RED ENGLISH, SOUTH AFRICA, SOUTH AFRICAN LITERATURE IN ENGLISH, TESD, TESL, WHITE, WHITE ENGLISH. Compare CLASSISM, SEXISM. [AFRICA, AMERICAS, ASIA, EUROPE, LANGUAGE, OCEANIA, STYLE]. T.MCA.

RADIATION [16c: from Latin *radiatio/ radiationis* spreading out like rays of light]. In linguistics, a process of semantic change in which there is a multiplication in the senses of a word, phrase, or lexeme, whether within one language or across a number of languages. For example, in classical Greek, *pápuros* originally referred to a reed common in Egypt, used among other things for making into a writing surface. The word then came to refer to the writing material produced, and this is the dominant sense of the Latinate English word *papyrus*. In addition, *pápuros* has been adapted into other languages (into English as *paper*) without the original sense 'reed' and referring to writing material made from any source, whether reeds, cotton, linen, or wood pulp. In addition, the meaning of *paper* has radiated to include a written document or documents (from the 14c), a newspaper, a written or printed essay, a bill of exchange, and money (from the 17c), and a set of questions in an examination (from the 19c). See POLYSEMY, SEMANTIC CHANGE. As entries that themselves exemplify radiation, see READER, ROMANCE, THESIS. [HISTORY, LANGUAGE]. T.MCA.

RADIO. See BROADCASTING.

RANDOM HOUSE, short form *RH*. A US publishing firm based in New York City, with overseas divisions in the UK (Chatto & Windus, Century Hutchinson, The Bodley Head, Jonathan Cape), Australia, and New Zealand. The company was founded in 1927 by Bennett Cerf (president, 1927–66) and Donald Klopfer, from the earnings of their profitable 'Modern Library', a series of republished classics from Homer forwards. The firm's name comes from the idea that they would publish 'at random' whatever books struck them as worthwhile. Initially, RH printed US editions of literary properties owned by such British presses as Nonesuch, Golden Cockerel, Spiral, Fountain, and Shakespeare Head; by 1929, it had become the leading distributor of British books in the US. Following the economic collapse of 1930, RH established a trade division and, in 1934,

successfully brought suit to gain the right to publish a US edition of the previously banned *Ulysses* by James Joyce. After World War II, the company established a reference and textbook section to undertake the publication of *The American College Dictionary*, with Clarence Barnhart as general editor and Jess Stein as managing editor. For its foundation, RH secured the rights to use *The Century Dictionary*, *The New Century Dictionary*, and *The Dictionary of American English*; the *ACD* drew on the expertise of such US linguists as Kemp Malone (etymology), W. Cabell Greet (pronunciation), Leonard Bloomfield, Charles C. Fries (usage levels and dialects), and Allen Walker Read (BrE and AmE usage). Since the popular and financial success of the *ACD*, RH has continued to produce increasingly comprehensive English dictionaries and other wordbooks; in 1986, it published in computer form its *Dictionary* and *Thesaurus* through Reference Software, Inc. After merging with Alfred A. Knopf in 1960, RH was purchased by RCA (1966) and later by S. I. Newhouse's Advance Publications (1980). In 1988, RH acquired the Crown Publishing Group and sold its college and school divisions to McGraw-Hill. See AMERICAN PUBLISHING, BRITISH PUBLISHING, CARTOON, POLITICALLY CORRECT, RANDOM HOUSE DICTIONARY. [AMERICAS, MEDIA]. R.W.B.

RANDOM HOUSE DICTIONARY, full form *Random House Dictionary of the English Language*. Short form *RHD*. An American unabridged dictionary. Recognizing an opportunity in the national outcry against *Webster's Third New International Dictionary* (Merriam, 1961), Random House commissioned an expansion of its *American College Dictionary* (1947), with Jess Stein as editor-in-chief and Laurence Urdang as managing editor. The 1st edition appeared in 1966 and achieved immediate popularity in the 'large' dictionary market previously dominated by Merriam. Many features of the *ACD* were kept, such as biographical and geographical names in the main alphabet, senses ordered by contemporary frequency rather than historical development, and etymologies at the ends of entries. About two-thirds the length of *Webster's Third*, the *RHD* was promoted as a home reference work for non-specialists who could have an up-to-date large dictionary at a price below that of *Webster's Third*. Indirectly alluding to the defining practices of its major competitor, Stein declared that 'communication with the user' was 'a central concern' and wrote that 'we have tried to avoid ingeniously concise wordings that are meaningful only to the writer'.

To increase its appeal, the *RHD* included a 64-page atlas in colour and concise bilingual dictionaries of French, Spanish, Italian, and German. The first dictionary maker to employ computer-based editing and typesetting, RH produced a 'college edition' (1968) with Laurence Urdang as editor-in-chief and Stuart Berg Flexner as managing editor. Through access to computerized text archives, the *RHD* could claim to be 'the product of its editors' qualitative analysis and synthesis of more information on the words of English than has ever been collected for any dictionary of similar size'. In 1987, a 2nd edition of *RHD* appeared with Stuart Berg Flexner as editor-in-chief and Leonore Crary Hauck as managing editor. This edition claimed to add *c.*50,000 entries and 75,000 definitions; more encyclopedic material was included and most entries included dates indicating the time of first appearance of a word in English. In the usage note for *ain't*, the 2nd edition shows greater kinship with *Webster's Third* than with the *American Heritage Dictionary*: 'As a substitute for *am not*, *is not*, and *are not* in declarative sentences, AIN'T is more common in uneducated speech than in educated, but it occurs with some frequency in the informal speech of the educated, especially in the southern and south-central states.' See DICTIONARY, RANDOM HOUSE, RESPELLING, UNABRIDGED, WEBSTER'S NEW INTERNATIONAL DICTIONARY. [AMERICAS, REFERENCE].   R.W.B.

RAP [1960s: US black slang, an extension of the turn-of-the-century US slang term *rap* to talk, chat freely]. An informal term associated with inner-city neighbourhoods and popular radio and television, especially in the US: (1) To talk rapidly, rhythmically, vividly, and boastfully, so as to compete for prestige among one's peers and impress one's listeners. The verse of the American boxer Muhammad Ali (formerly Cassius Clay) is an early form of rapping: 'Only last week / Ah murdered a rock / Injured a stone / Hospitalized a brick / Ah'm so mean / Ah made medicine sick'. (2) The ritualized repartee of (especially young male) blacks, associated with the *hip* or *cool* street talk also known as *sounding*, *capping*, and *playing the dozens*, which includes assertions, taunts, and insults. Currently, rapping is closely associated with *hip hop*, a flamboyant youth style originating in the streets of the South Bronx in New York City in the early 1970s and including graffiti art, break-dancing, and Afrocentric ways of dressing. (3) To perform a rhyming, usually improvised monologue against a background of music with a strong beat: in a street, the music is usually from a portable radio/cassette-player (a *ghetto-blaster* or *boom box*); in a broadcasting studio, it is from a background of recorded music or is reduced to a heavy bass beat produced by a drum machine or synthesizer. (4) A song or poem performed in this way, the performer being a *rapper* and the overall effect being *rap music*. On television, the background may be a series of fragments of music or video scenes. Jon Pareles observes:

Ask most pundits about rap music, and they'll describe it as rude, jumbled noise. A few others may consider it million-selling post-modernism in audible form—songs as mix-and-match collages that treat the history of recorded music as a scrap heap of usable rubble and, often, trade narrative and logic for a patchwork of bragging, storytelling, speechifying and free-form rhymes. . . . It had to happen, sooner or later, that popular music would reflect the ubiquity of television—and it's true to American musical history that a black subculture picked up the new rhythms first. . . . To say that rap reflects television doesn't discount its deep roots in black culture; the networks didn't invent rap, ghetto disk jockeys did. Rap comes out of the storytelling and braggadocio of the blues, the cadences of gospel preachers and comedians, the percussive improvisations of jazz drummers and tap dancers. It also looks to Jamaican 'toasting' (improvising rhymes over records), to troubadour traditions of social comment and historical remembrance, and to a game called 'the dozens,' a ritual exchange of cleverly phrased insults. ('The Etymology of Rap Music', *The New York Times*, Jan. 1990).

Pareles considers that rap's chopped-up style reflects the impact of television, in which programmes are accompanied and interrupted by commercials, previews, snippets of news, and the like, as well as by using a remote control to 'zap' from channel to channel. He quotes as an example of this fragmentation the following lines from 'Bring the Noise', by Carlton 'Chuck D' Ridenhour of the group Public Enemy:

Bass! How low can you go?
Death row. What a brother knows.
Once again, back is the incredible the rhyme animal
the incredible D, Public Enemy No. 1
"Five-O," said, "Freeze!" and I got numb
Can I tell 'em that I never really had a gun?
But it's the wax that Terminator X spun
Now they got me in a cell 'cause my records,
they sell!
[*a brother* a fellow black man, *Five-O* a reference to the TV cop show *Hawaii Five-O*, *the wax* an LP record, *spun* played, *Terminator X* a disc jockey].

Word-play is prevalent not only in rap versifying but also in the names that performers give themselves: for example, alliterative forms that often focus on the consonants of *dee-jay* (short for 'disc jockey'), as in *Chuck D*, *Jazzy Jeff*, *LL Cool J*, and *Jam Master Jay*; coolness and hipness, as in *Ice T*, *Ice Cube*, *Kid Frost*, *Easy E*, and *Mellow Man Ace*; hyped-up menace, as in *Red Alert* and *Terminator X*; and an African connection, as in *Afrika Bambaataa* and *Queen Latifah*. Compare BLARNEY, DUB, JIVE, PATTER, REGGAE. See BLACK ENGLISH VERNACULAR. [AMERICAS, MEDIA, STYLE]. T.MCA.

RASTA TALK [1950s: a clipping of *Rasta-fari(an)*, from the Amharic title *Ras Tafari*, by which Prince Haile Selassie was known until 1930, when he became Emperor of Ethiopia; and *talk*. Used with or without initial capitals: see TALK]. Also **Rasta, Dread Talk, Iyaric, I-lect, the language/speech of Rasta(fari)**. The usage of the Rastafarian community in the Caribbean, UK, US, and elsewhere, derived from Jamaican Creole, with elements from the Old Testament of the Bible and the black consciousness movement. *Rastafarianism* (also *Rastafari, Rastafaria*; informal *Rasta, Ras*) originated among the poor in Jamaica in the 1930s. Haile Selassie is regarded as the incarnation of God (*Jah*), through whom, despite his death in 1975, the faithful of the black diaspora will be taken out of *Babylon* (the oppressive white power system) to the promised land of Ethiopia. Since the 1960s, young middle-class people have also been included among their number.

Rastas reject both standard English and Creole; their alternative usage emerged in the 1940s as an argot among alienated young men, became a part of Jamaican youth culture, and has been significant in the growth and spread of *dub* poetry and *reggae* music. A major syntactic difference from Creole is the use of the stressed English pronoun *I* (often repeated for emphasis and solidarity as *I and I*) to replace Creole *mi*, which is used for both subject and object. *Mi* is seen as a mark of black subservience that makes people objects rather than subjects. The form *I and I* may also stand for *we* and for the movement itself:

I and I have fi check hard . . . It change I . . . now I and I [eat] jus' patty, hardo bread, from Yard (*New York Magazine*, 4 Nov. 1973). [I was greatly affected . . . It changed me . . . Now I only eat patties, hard-dough bread, from Jamaica (a reference to Rasta vegetarianism).]

At the same time I fully know why leaders of societies have taken such a low view of I n I reality. They hold Rasta as dangerous to their societies (Jah Bones, 'Rastafari: A Cultural Awakening', appendix to E. E. Cashmore, *The Rastafarians*, Minority Rights Group Report 64, 1984).

Because of its significance as a mark of self-respect and solidarity, *I* often replaces syllables in mainstream words: *I-lect* Rasta dialect, *Iyaric* (by analogy with *Amharic*) Rasta language, *I-cient* ancient, *I-man* amen, *I-nointed* anointed, *I-quality* equality, *I-sanna* hosanna, *I-thiopia* Ethiopia. Other items of vocabulary are: *control* to keep, take, look after, *dreadlocks* hair worn long in rope-like coils (to signify membership of the group), *dub* a piece of reggae music, rhythmic beat, *queen* a girlfriend, *Rastaman* a male, adult Rastafarian, *reason hard* to argue, *sufferer* a ghetto-dweller, *trod* to walk away, leave, *weed*

of wisdom and *chalice* (by analogy with Holy Communion) marijuana, ganja (regarded as a sacred herb). Rasta word-play includes the etymology *Jah mek ya* (God made here) for *Jamaica*, and the adaptations *blindjaret* for *cigarette* (pronounced 'see-garet') and *high-erstand* in preference to *understand*. See Velma Pollard, 'Dread Talk—the Speech of the Rastafari in Jamaica' (*Caribbean Quarterly* 26: 4, 1980) and 'Innovation in Jamaican Creole: The Speech of Rastafari' (in Görlach & Holm (eds.), *Focus on the Caribbean*, John Benjamins, 1986). See AFRICAN, BLACK, DIASPORA, DUB, JAMAICAN CREOLE, RACISM, REGGAE. [AFRICA, AMERICAS, VARIETY].   T.MCA.

RATIONALIZATION [19c]. (1) The action or result of making something rational, intelligible, more efficient, etc. The running of a factory can be rationalized by reducing waste and over-manning. (2) The action or result of ascribing behaviour to causes that seem sensible and respectable, but are not the real reasons for the behaviour. Such reasons may be less sensible than they seem and even disreputable, and in the process of rationalization awkward facts and views may be ignored, concealed, or glossed over. See ARGUMENT, LOGIC. [LANGUAGE].T.MCA.

READ, Allen Walker [b.1906]. American lexicographer, born in Winnebago, Minnesota, and educated at the U. of Northern Iowa and the U. of Iowa. While teaching at the U. of Missouri, awarded a Rhodes Scholarship (1928–31) to Oxford. He was recruited shortly afterwards by William A. Craigie to assist in compiling the *Dictionary of American English* at the U. of Chicago, and served as a researcher and assistant editor (1932–8). In England on a Guggenheim fellowship (1938), he began work on a *Dictionary of Briticisms*, a project which is still under way. During World War II, he compiled a dictionary of military terms and in 1943 joined other US linguists in preparing language descriptions and materials, including dictionaries, to assist Americans abroad. These scholars, previously isolated across the country, set the tone for post-war linguistic inquiry; Read recalls the atmosphere at the Language Section of the War Department as 'crackling with innovation and fresh approaches'. In 1945, he joined Columbia U., where he became Professor Emeritus on his retirement in 1974. His monograph *Lexical Evidence from Folk Epigraphy in Western North America* (Paris, 1935) was a collection and interpretation of mostly obscene inscriptions in public conveniences; it was republished in less prudish times as *Classic American Graffiti* (1977). Best known to the public for his definitive investigations of the origins of *Dixie*, *O.K.*,

Podunk, and *Rebel Yell*, Read has traced the origins of hundreds of words and phrases; his findings have appeared in most histories of AmE in the past half-century. He has also contributed to place-name studies. Active in many learned societies, he has been president of the Dictionary Society of North America and the Linguistic Association of Canada and the United States. See index. [AMERICAS, BIOGRAPHY, LANGUAGE, REFERENCE].   R.W.B.

READER [From Old English *rædere* one who reads or advises]. (1) Someone who reads regularly, who is reading at a particular time, or who reads aloud to an audience. (2) In library science, someone who uses a library, whether or not for reading. (3) In full *publisher's reader*. Someone employed to assess material submitted for publication. (4) More commonly *proofreader*. Someone who reads the proofs of material about to be published. (5) Someone authorized to read Bible texts, lessons, etc., in church services. (6) Especially in Britain, the rank of a member of the teaching staff of a university between senior lecturer and full professor: *a Reader in English*. (7) A book intended to help someone learn to read: *an English reader*, *a first school reader*. Such readers may be written in restricted syntax and vocabulary (such as Ogden's Basic English or a set of graded structures and word lists as developed in the 1930s by Michael West), and are therefore referred to as *simplified readers*, *structural readers*, and *graded readers*. Some belong in series: for example, classic novels of English rewritten in a condensed and simplified form. (8) A book of writings on a particular theme (*a poetry reader*) or by a particular author (*a Kipling reader*). (9) A device that enlarges an image from a microform storage system so that it can be read on a screen. (10) In full *optical character reader*. Short form *OCR*. A device that reads data and programs, or information from an external medium, into the storage system of a computer. (11) The term *readership* can refer to the number of people regularly reading any publication, the status or profession of a professional reader, or the post of reader at a British university. See ABRIDG[E]MENT, BOOK, GEISEL, LITERACY, READING, WEST. [EDUCATION, WRITING].   T.MCA.

READER'S DIGEST. A monthly magazine founded in the US in 1922 by De Witt Wallace and Lila Acheson; currently one of the most widely read periodicals in the world. At first a digest of previously published articles on current affairs and human interest, it is now a general-interest magazine that also commissions its own material. Although primarily an English-language publication (including editions in Braille, large type, and cassette form), the *Digest* appears worldwide in 15 languages and 39 editions and has a circulation of some 30m. For many years, the English-language *Digest* has had two language-related features: a game at first called *It Pays to Increase Your Word Power*, now *It Pays to Enrich Your Word Power*, in which 20 words are listed with four definitions each, only one of which is correct; a section called *Towards More Picturesque Speech*, which gives examples of language play or colourful expressions submitted by readers who have made them up or culled them from other sources, such as *brain scanner* glossed as 'mind sweeper', and *snoring* as 'sheet music' (UK edition, Mar. 1989). The *Reader's Digest Association* also publishes books and recordings, sold mainly by mail order. These include home-study manuals and works of reference. The two-volume *Reader's Digest Great Illustrated Dictionary* (1984) is one of the ten largest 20c dictionaries of English; it is a British enlargement of the *American Heritage Dictionary*, and has served as the basis for two further US dictionaries: one by Reader's Digest, the other by Houghton-Mifflin (publishers of the *AHD*). There are two usage guides: the more descriptive American *Success with Words* (1983) and the more prescriptive British *The Right Word at the Right Time* (1985). Other works on language are *Write Better, Speak Better* (US 1972), the thesaurus-style *Family Word Finder* (US 1975, UK 1978), and the *Reverse Dictionary* (1989). See CONDENSED BOOK, DIGEST, MAGAZINE. [MEDIA, REFERENCE, USAGE].   T.MCA.

READING [From Old English *rædinge* reading, advice]. The process of extracting meaning from written or printed language: one of the four language skills (listening, speaking, reading, writing) and one of the two key aspects of literacy (reading and writing). The activity is of two kinds: *reading aloud*, so that others can hear (and benefit from) what is being read, and *silent reading*.

Reading aloud. People who are learning to read often read aloud, in order to relate what they see to the spoken language. Depending on the skill and confidence of the novice reader, this may be accompanied by tracing the line of text word by word with the index finger. In scribal societies, reading aloud appears to have been the norm, even for private, personal purposes. The shift to mature silent reading may have been encouraged by the advent of print, the spread of literacy, an awareness that reading aloud disturbs others within earshot, a view among teachers that saying (or muttering) what is being read indicates a low level of skill, and perhaps also appreciation of a silence that makes the message more personal. Reading aloud in public is an ancient practice that lies at the roots of publishing ('making public': see entry), and in many parts of the world continues to be an important means of disseminating information and educating the young. It includes *dictation* that is read out to be written down by students and *lecturing* from a prepared text at a pace that allows note-taking: compare French *lecture* (reading). Reading aloud well involves control of breath, voice, and body, a capacity to look up from a text and back without losing one's place, and, depending on subject and occasion, an element of drama and display. In public presentations, such reading has traditionally been from a document held in the hand or placed on a *lectern* (a special sloping surface that holds whatever is being read). On television, however, there is increasing use of an electronic prompting device (a *teleprompter* or trade name, an *Autocue*) placed between reader and audience. This enlarges the elements of a script line by line, so that someone may see it easily and use it without appearing (too obviously) to be reading.

Silent reading. Private reading is so basic a skill in present-day society that its nature is little discussed and its existence largely taken for granted. It differs from other forms of scanning one's surroundings by being focused, sustained, relatively disciplined, and accompanied by thinking about the meaning of what one sees. The concept of reading is often extended to other kinds of disciplined, reflective activity, such as 'reading' someone's face for a message, 'reading' a landscape for information, or asking *Do you read me?* (Have you understood me?) after sending a radio message. One can also 'read' semaphore signals at a distance, braille by touch, and Morse code by listening. The eye movements that occur in conventional reading consist of jerks and stops. Each jerk entails a change in focus, and is technically known as a *saccade* (from French: the jerk on the reins of a rider controlling a horse); each stop is a *fixation*, a moment of stability in which signals are transmitted from retina to brain. On average, readers make three or four fixations a second, and each may register several letters or several words, depending on such factors as distance from text, size and kind of lettering, and familiarity with language, orthography, and subject matter.

Readers use both visual and phonetic skills, combining a capacity to decipher writing and print letter by letter with an indirect awareness of the heard equivalents of what is graphically displayed. This cross-association of graphic and phonic symbols appears to be natural: readers may at any time audibly or inaudibly say a syllable or word so as to help grasp its nature, function, and meaning: in doing this, they may be returning to the historically and individually 'early' stage of moving the lips while interpreting the signs of the text. In this process, they are not usually put off by homophones, such as *right* and *write* or *dun* and *done*, which suggests that visual interpretation can function independently of phonetic backup. They may, however, be put off by homographs and polysemous words, such as the various uses of *bank* and *crane*. The fact that some people read so fast (over 500 words per minute) that they exceed the capacity of their phonetic backup to check what they are seeing is evidence for an element in reading that is not in any way tied to physical sound or 'sounds' in the mind.

Learning to read. There has long been controversy among teachers of reading over the primary means by which children learn (or should learn) to read. Attitudes and policies tend to vary between a *whole-language, whole-word, global, holistic,* or *look-and-say* approach on the one hand (in which words are minimal units to be learned as gestalts) and a *symbol-to-sound, code-based, atomistic,* or *phonic* approach (in which reading is like cracking a code that consists of correspondences between speech sounds and graphic symbols, with letters or *graphemes* as the prime units). Some teachers favour one approach over the other, while many favour a compromise that allows a judicious use of elements from both approaches. Some also make a distinction between a 'whole language' aproach in which children work from so-called 'real books' (as opposed to specially prepared readers) and the older 'look and say' method that is closely associated with readers, reading schemes, flash cards, and other aids. There is some evidence that concentrating on the atoms of reading in the early stages leads to a higher rate of word recognition later, followed by an expansion of global comprehension through the quality and interest of what is being read. It is also likely that strategies may differ depending on the writing system used: for example, learning to read the blend of logographic and syllabic signs used for Japanese may require a different approach from learning the set of signs used for such 'alphabetic' languages as Spanish, Italian, German and English.

Six stages? The American researcher Jeanne S. Chall (*Stages of Reading Development*, New York, 1983, and with Steven A. Stahl, 'Reading', *International Encyclopedia of Communications*, New York, 1989) has proposed that reading in

English proceeds through six (relatively idealized) stages, more or less as follows (with ages specific to educational experience in the US):

Stage 0: Pre-reading and pseudo-reading. Before they reach the age of 6, children are likely to 'pretend' to read, retelling a story when looking at the pages of a book that has already been read to them, increasingly naming letters, recognizing some signs, printing their own names, and playing with the general paraphernalia of literacy. This process develops naturally as a response to being read to by adults or older children who take a close and warm interest in that response. Most children at this stage can understand simple picture books and the stories read to them, but have a hazy perception of what reading really is.

Stage 1: Initial reading and decoding. Between 6 and 7, children may learn the relations between sounds and letters and between spoken and printed words, read simple texts containing short, high-frequency words that are spelt more or less regularly, and 'sound out' monosyllables. If they receive instruction in *phonics*, they are often read to from a level just above their own ability to read. Generally, their level of reading at this stage is well below their capacity to manage speech. Although it is not easy to quantify words known and used, Chall estimates that they can understand some 4,000 spoken words and some 600 written or printed words. A reading specimen of this stage is:

'May I go?' said Fay. 'May I please go with you?' (from *American Book Primer*).

Stage 2: Confirmation and fluency. Between 7 and 8, children may consolidate their skills, increasing their range of reading, their fluency, their general vocabulary, and their ability to decode the elements of words. Again, help may often include being read to at a level above their own ability. At the end of this stage, they can understand an estimated 9,000 spoken words and 3,000 written or printed words. A reading specimen of this stage is:

Spring was coming to Tait Primary School. On the new highway big trucks went by the school all day (from Ginn 720, Grade 2).

Stage 3: Reading for learning. Between 9 and 14, reading is no longer an end in itself but becomes a means by which further knowledge and experience can be gained. Use extends beyond the immediate subjects of school and includes textbooks, reference books, and periodicals (from comic books to newspapers and encyclopedias). Reading becomes part of a general experience of language that is likely to include explicit discussion of language skills, especially writing and spelling. At the beginning of this stage, listening comprehension of the same material is more effective than reading comprehension, but by the end the two are roughly equal. For some young people, reading may have edged ahead. Two reading specimens of this stage are:

She smoothed her hair behind her ear as she lowered her hand. I could see she was eyeing *beauty* and trying to figure out a way to write about being beautiful without sounding even more conceited than she already was (from Ginn 720, Grade 5).

Early in the history of the world, men found that they could not communicate well by using only sign language. In some way that cannot be traced with any certainty, they devised spoken language (from Book F, *New Practice Reader*, Graves *et al.*, 1962).

Stage 4: Multiplicity and complexity. From 14 to 17, if all has gone well, students are reading fairly widely from a range of increasingly complex materials, both narrative and expository, and varied in viewpoint. Such materials are both technical and non-technical, literary and non-literary, and may involve a parallel study of words and their elements. For poorer performers, listening and reading comprehension are about the same, but for stronger performers reading comprehension is better than listening comprehension, especially in technical subjects. A specimen for this stage is:

No matter what phenomena he is interested in, the scientist employs two main tools—theory and empirical research. Theory employs reason, language, and logic to suggest possible, and predict probable, relationships among various data gathered from the concrete world of experience (from A. B. Kathryn, 'College Reading Skills', in John & Mavis Biesanz (eds.), *Modern Society*, 1971).

Stage 5: Construction and reconstruction. Beyond 18, young adults should have developed the capacity to read for their own purposes, using their skill to integrate their own knowledge with that of others and to assimilate their experience of the world more effectively. In stronger performers, it is rapid and efficient, and serves as a basis for a lifetime of reading for personal and occupational purposes. Interested readers go beyond their immediate needs and in the writing of essays, reports, summaries, and other materials continue to integrate the four skills. A reading specimen for this stage is:

One of the objections to the hypothesis that a satisfying after-effect of a mental connection works back upon it to strengthen it is that nobody has shown how this action does or could occur. It is the purpose of this article to show how a mechanism which is as possible psychologically as any of the mechanisms proposed to account for facilitation, inhibition, fatigue, strengthening by repetition, or other forms of modification could enable such an after-effect to cause such a strengthening (from Edward L. Thorndike, 'Connectionism', *Psychological Review* 40, 1933).

Conclusion. The above stages resemble the developmental phases of the child's mind as proposed by the Swiss researcher Jean Piaget. They are both a generalization from objective study and an idealized assumption about an average child who progresses fairly smoothly through such stages in an English-speaking society that has an adequate educational system, without any significant social or personal problems. The order may be universal, but the age ranges will vary between individuals, cultures, and countries. Unfortunately, not all climb smoothly from the bottom to the top of this ladder and not all societies provide an adequate educational service. In addition, many competent readers might have serious difficulty with the specimen that Chall provides for Stage 5, many adequate readers with the specimen at Stage 4, and so on down the line to the large percentage of people whom English-speaking societies now recognize as *functionally illiterate*: that is, those who, for whatever reason, never managed to get successfully through Stage 1 or 2. Recent definitions of literacy have classed as illiterate all those who read less efficiently than they would like, including many who have moved well beyond Stage 2.

See BOOK, CHILD LANGUAGE ACQUISITION, DYSLEXIA, FRIES, HALLIDAY, ILLITERACY, LITERACY, PROSE, READER, SPELLING, WRITING. [EDUCATION].
T.MCA.

Anderson, Richard C., et al. 1985. Becoming a Nation of Readers. Washington, DC (national education report).

Chall, Jeanne S. 1967. Learning to Read: The Great Debate. New York: McGraw-Hill.

Crowder, Robert G. 1982. The Psychology of Reading. New York: Oxford University Press.

Department of Education and Science, UK. 1975. A Language for Life (the Bullock Report). London: Her Majesty's Stationery Office (HMSO).

Downing, John (ed.). 1972. Comparative Reading: Cross-national Studies of Behaviour and Processes in Reading and Writing. New York: Macmillan.

—— & Che Kan Leong, 1982. Psychology of Reading. New York: Macmillan.

Ellis, A. W. 1984. Reading, Writing and Dyslexia: A Cognitive Analysis. London: Erlbaum.

Kavanagh, J. F., & Mattingly, I. G. 1972. Language by Ear and by Eye: The Relationships between Speech and Reading. Cambridge, Mass.: MIT Press.

Meek, M. 1982. Learning to Read. London: Bodley Head.

Oakhill, Jane, & Garnham, Alan. 1988. Becoming a Skilled Reader. Oxford: Basil Blackwell.

Smith, Frank. 1971. Understanding Reading. New York: Holt, Rinehart, & Winston.

—— 1973 Psycholinguistics and Reading. New York: Holt, Rinehart, & Winston.

Thorpe, Dina. 1988. Reading for Fun: A Study of How Parents and Libraries Encouraged Children aged 9–12 to Read for Enjoyment. Bedford (UK): Cranfield Press.

REAM [14c: from Old French *raime*, Spanish *resma*, Arabic *rizmah* a bale]. A number of sheets of paper; 480 (a *short ream*) or 500 sheets (a *long ream*) or 516 (a *printer's ream* or *perfect ream*, allowing for waste). A short ream is equal to 20 quires of 24 sheets each, a long ream to 20 quires of 25 sheets each. The term has been extended to suggest large quantities of writing: *whole reams of argument*. [TECHNOLOGY].
T.MCA.

REBUS [16c: from French *rébus*, Latin *rebus* (ablative plural of *res* thing) by or with things]. A device that uses letters, numbers, or pictures to represent words: for example, *MT* used to mean *empty*; *B4* to mean *before*. The rebus is usually a puzzle that demands some lateral thinking to decipher it, as in *MIN* (half a minute), *CCCCCCC* (the Seven Seas), and *WORLAMEN* (World without end. Amen). The idea is as old as Egyptian hieroglyphics and came into English in the Middle Ages in heraldic devices and pictorial representations of names. In *The Spectator* (8 May 1711), Joseph Addison described a picture of a yew tree and berries surrounding a letter *N* to represent Mr Newberry. Rebuses are used mainly in children's puzzles (where an eye represents *I* and the number two stands for *to*), but can still be found in heraldry and on gravestones. See WORD GAME. [WORD, WRITING].
T.A.

RECEIVED [15c in this sense]. Accepted and approved: 'The appearance of Courtly Love has left an immense legacy of received ideas about sex and society' (J. Bayley, *Characters of Love*, 1960). When used of language, *received* usually refers to what is accepted and approved in educated, especially middle-class society: 'The tip of the tongue for received English is not so advanced towards the teeth or gums, as for the continental sound' (A. J. Ellis, *On Early English Pronunciation*, vol. 4, 1874). See RECEIVED PRONUNCIATION, RECEIVED STANDARD AND MODIFIED STANDARD, RECEIVED STANDARD ENGLISH, VERSION. [LANGUAGE].
T.MCA.

RECEIVED PRONUNCIATION. (1) [1820s: no initial capitals]. Pronunciation regarded as correct or proper, especially by arbiters of usage: 'the theoretically received pronunciation of literary English' (A. J. Ellis, *On Early English Pronunciation*, vol. 1, 1869); 'Edinburgh and Dublin have their received pronunciations' (Simeon Potter, *Changing English*, 1969). (2) [1920s: with initial capitals]. Short form *RP*. A term in phonetics, applied linguistics, and language teaching for the accent generally associated with educated BrE and used as the pronunciation model for teaching it to foreign learners. This accent has been referred to technically as *Received Standard English* (or *Received Standard*) and *Public School English* by Henry Cecil Wyld, *Public School Pronunciation* (*PSP*) by Daniel Jones, prior to using the term itself, *General British* in the *Oxford Advanced Learner's Dictionary* (3rd edition, 1974: in contrast to *General American*), *standard southern pronunciation*, and *standard* (*spoken*) *British English*. Since its initial description by Jones in the *English Pronouncing Dictionary* (*EPD*) in 1917, it has probably become the most described and discussed accent on earth.

Attitudes to RP. The terms *Received Pronunciation* and *RP* are not widely known outside the immediate circle of English-language professionals, but the form that they refer to is widely known as the spoken embodiment of a variety or varieties known as *the King's English*, *the Queen's English*, *BBC English*, *Oxford English*, and *Public School English*: see entries. It is often informally referred to by the British middle class as a *BBC accent* or a *public school accent* and by the working class as *talking proper* or *talking posh*. In England, it is also often referred to simply as *Standard English*. Its 'advanced' (that is, distinctive upper-class and royal) form is sometimes called *la-di-dah* (as in talking la-di-dah) or *a cut-glass accent*, especially if used by people judged as not really 'from the top drawer'. RP has been described by many of its users and admirers in the UK and elsewhere as the best pronunciation for BrE, for the countries influenced by BrE, or for all users of English everywhere. Americans do not normally subscribe to this view, but many of them admire RP as the representative accent of educated BrE while some associate it with the theatre and, in men, with effeminacy.

Many British people dislike Received Pronunciation, usually arguing that it is a mark of privilege and (especially among the Scots, Northern Irish, and Welsh) of social domination by the (especially southern) English. It has, however, a considerable gravitational pull throughout the UK, with the result that many middle- and lower middle-class people, especially in England, speak with accents more or less adapted towards it. These accents are therefore known among phoneticians as *modified regional accents* and *modified RP*. Comparable accents in Australia, Ireland, New Zealand, Scotland, South Africa, and elsewhere are often referred to as *near-RP*. It has always been a minority accent, unlikely ever to have been spoken by more than 3-4% of the British population. British phoneticians and linguists have often described it as a 'regionless' accent in the UK and especially in England, in that it is not possible to tell which part of the country an RP speaker comes from;

it is never, however, described as a 'classless' accent, because it identifies the speaker as a member of the middle or upper classes. Because it is class-related, it is socially and politically controversial and can lead to embarrassment when discussed.

General background. RP is often taken to have existed for a relatively long time, evolving from a prestigious accent well established in England by the 17c, when comparisons began to be made between the speech of the court and the nobility in London and that of their peers from the provinces. John Aubrey (*Brief Lives*, mid-17c) provides a hearsay report that Sir Walter Raleigh had a Devon accent till the day he died; Samuel Johnson in the 18c is on record as speaking with a Staffordshire accent. Although there was an increasingly homogeneous and fashionable style of speech in the capital in the 18-19c, little is known about it. It probably served in part at least as a model for the middle classes and may have been common at such ancient public schools as Eton, Harrow, Rugby, and Winchester, but there is no evidence that a uniform accent was used or promoted in these schools until the later 19c. However, by the beginning of the 20c, it was well established, and in 1917, at the height of the First World War, Jones defined his model for English as that 'most usually heard in everyday speech in the families of Southern English persons whose menfolk have been educated at the great public boarding-schools', and called it *Public School Pronunciation* (*PSP*).

The heyday of Empire, approximately 1890–1940, was also the high point of RP, which has been described by such terms as 'patrician' and 'proconsular'. Its possession was a criterion for the selection of young men as potential officers during the First World War and it has been the accent favoured for recruits to the Foreign Office and other services representing the British nation (largely drawn from the public schools, with a slight enlargement of the catchment area in recent years). Newcomers to the British establishment have tended to ensure that their children acquire RP by sending them to the 'right' schools or, especially in the past in the case of girls, to elocution teachers. In these schools the accent has never been overtly taught, but appears to have been indirectly encouraged and often promoted through peer pressure that has included mockery of any other form of speech. It has been the voice of national announcers and presenters on the BBC since its founding in the 1920s, but in the 1970s-80s there has been a move towards modified regional accents among announcers and presenters, and towards distinct (but generally modified) regional accents among presenters on popular radio channels and meteorologists and sports commentators on television.

Generalities and characteristics. (1) The description of RP in A. C. Gimson, *An Introduction to the Pronunciation of English* (Edward Arnold, 3rd edition, 1980) is widely regarded as standard. Its 4th edition (1990) has been revised by Susan Ramsaran. (2) RP is often used as a reference norm for the description of other varieties of English. An idealized representation has been available for this and other purposes for at least 20 years, with minor differences in the house styles of such publishers as Oxford University Press and Longman. A comparison between RP and 'GenAm' (General American) is a key element of John C. Wells's *Longman Pronunciation Dictionary* (1990). (3) RP differs little from other accents of English in the pronunciation of consonants, which are 24 in number. It is a non-rhotic accent that includes the linking/intrusive /r/ (widely noted in such phrases as *law/r and order*), which is not however taught as part of the EFL/ESL pronunciation model. (4) Wells (above) lists the following 22 basic values of RP vowels: /ɪ/ as in *kit, bid, hymn, intend, basic*; /e/ as in *dress, bed*; /æ/ as in *trap, bad*; /ɒ/ as in *lot, odd, wash*; /ʌ/ as in *strut, bud, love*; /ʊ/ as in *foot, good, put*; /iː/ as in *fleece, sea, machine*; /eɪ/ as in *face, day, steak*; /aɪ/ as in *price, high, try*; /ɔɪ/ as in *choice, boy*; /uː/ as in *goose, two, blue*; /əʊ/ as in *goat, show, no*; /aʊ/ as in *mouth, now*; /ɪə/ as in *near, here, serious*; /eə/ as in *square, fair, various*; /ɑː/ as in *start, father*; /ɔː/ as in *thought, law, north, war*; /ʊə/ as in *cure, poor, jury*; /ɜː/ as in *nurse, stir*; /i/ as in *happy, radiation, glorious*; /ə/ as in the first vowel of *about* and the last of *comma*; /u/ in *influence, situation, annual*.

Current situation. Although RP continues to be socially pre-eminent in Britain, and especially England, it has in recent years become less monolithic both phonetically and socially. Phoneticians recognize several varieties and also a generation gap. In the introduction to the 14th edition of the *EPD* (1977), Gimson noted of RP that its 'regional base remains valid and it continues to have wide intelligibility throughout Britain . . . [but there] has been a certain dilution of the original concept of RP, a number of local variants formerly excluded by the definition having now to be admitted as of common and acceptable usage. Such an extended scope of usage is difficult to define.' He retained the name, however, because of its 'currency in books on present-day English'. Even so, the observations of the phonetician David Abercrombie in 1951 still largely apply:

This R.P. stands in strong contrast to all the other ways of pronouncing Standard English put together. In fact,

English people are divided, by the way they talk, into three groups; first, R.P. speakers of Standard English—those [regarded as being] without an accent; second, non-R.P. speakers of Standard English—those with an accent; and third, dialect speakers. I believe this to be a situation which is not paralleled in any other country anywhere ('R.P. and Local Accent', in *Studies in Linguistics and Phonetics*, 1965).

RP and EFL. Because most British teachers of English have spoken with RP or modified-RP accents, overseas learners have until recently tended to assume that it is the majority accent of BrE. It retains its position as the preferred target for Commonwealth ESL learners, although in countries such as India and Singapore local pronunciations with a degree of prestige have emerged and may in due course replace it or operate alongside it. In EFL, it competes more and more with equivalent forms of AmE, but is strongly buttressed by the investment in RP made by British ELT publishers, especially in learners' dictionaries. It is generally selected as a matter of course as the reference norm for discussing spoken BrE (and often other varieties of English), as well as for such activities as automatic speech synthesis, but since most British people do not speak or even know RP as a coherent system, general statements about BrE keyed to Received Pronunciation can often be misleading and confusing.

See ACCENT, ACCENT BAR, ADVANCED (RP), AMERICAN ENGLISH AND BRITISH ENGLISH, AUSTRALIAN DICTIONARIES, AUSTRALIAN ENGLISH, BBC ENGLISH[1], BRITISH ENGLISH, CLIPPED, ENGLISH IN ENGLAND, ENGLISH PRONOUNCING DICTIONARY, INTRUSIVE R, IRISH BROADCASTING, LINKING R, JONES (D.), KENSINGTON, KING'S ENGLISH, LONDON, L-SOUNDS, NEAR-RP, NEW ZEALAND ENGLISH, OXFORD ACCENT, OXFORD ENGLISH, PLUMMY, PRONUNCIATION, PUBLIC SCHOOL ENGLISH, QUEEN'S ENGLISH, RECEIVED, RECEIVED STANDARD AND MODIFIED STANDARD, RECEIVED STANDARD ENGLISH, RESPELLING, RHOTIC AND NON-RHOTIC, R-SOUNDS, SCOTTISH ENGLISH, SLOANE RANGER, SOUTH AFRICAN ENGLISH, STANDARD, SWEET, TEFL, WELL-SPOKEN. [SPEECH, STYLE, VARIETY].

T.MCA., G.K.

RECEIVED STANDARD AND MODIFIED STANDARD. Contrastive terms proposed by Henry Cecil Wyld at the beginning of the 20c for two kinds of pronunciation in Great Britain:

It is proposed to use the term *Received Standard* for that form which all would probably agree in considering the best, that form which has the widest currency and is heard with practically no variation among speakers of the better class all over the country. This type might be called Public School English. It is proposed to call the vulgar English of the Towns, and the English of the Villager who has abandoned his native Regional Dialect *Modified Standard*. That is, it is

Standard English, modified, altered, differentiated, by various influences, regional and social. Modified Standard differs from class to class, and from locality to locality; it has no uniformity, and no single form of it is heard outside a particular class or a particular area.

(*A Short History of English*, 1914)

See ACCENT BAR, ORTON, PUBLIC SCHOOL ENGLISH, RECEIVED, RECEIVED PRONUNCIATION, RECEIVED STANDARD ENGLISH, STANDARD, WYLD. [SPEECH, STYLE, VARIETY].   T.MCA.

RECEIVED STANDARD ENGLISH [20c: introduced by Henry Cecil Wyld]. An occasional technical term for the accent of English generally referred to by phoneticians and EFL/ESL teachers as *Received Pronunciation*: 'Approximate pronunciations of OE vowels for those working without a teacher are given as far as possible in Received Standard English' (Bruce Mitchell & Fred C. Robinson, *A Guide to Old English*, 1964/1968/1989). Compare RECEIVED PRONUNCIATION, RECEIVED STANDARD AND MODIFIED STANDARD, STANDARD ENGLISH. [SPEECH, STYLE, VARIETY].   T.MCA.

RECIPROCAL PRONOUN. A term sometimes used for the compound pronouns *each other* and *one another*, which express a two-way interaction: *Romeo and Juliet loved each other/one another* (Romeo loved Juliet and Juliet loved Romeo). In meaning, reciprocal pronouns contrast with reflexive pronouns: *The Montagues and the Capulets loved themselves* (The Montagues loved the Montagues, and the Capulets loved the Capulets). Reciprocal pronouns are, however, like reflexives in not normally being used as subjects: no **They wondered where each other/one another was.* See PRONOUN. [GRAMMAR]
.   S.C.

RECTO. See PAGE.

RED ENGLISH [1960s: on the analogy of *Black English*]. A term for the English language as used by Native Americans ('Red Indians'): 'Joey Dillard and other linguists introduced the American public to "Black English," "Red English" (of American Indians), and Southern Appalachian English, and many people interpret this diversity as evidence of the decline and splitting apart of American English' (Charles A. Ferguson & Shirley B. Heath, Introduction, *Language in the USA*, 1981). Compare BLACK ENGLISH, BLUE-EYED ENGLISH, WHITE ENGLISH. See AFRO-SEMINOLE, AMERINDIAN PIDGIN ENGLISH. [AMERICAS, VARIETY].   T.MCA.

RED RIVER DIALECT. See MÉTIS.

REDUCTIONIST LITERACY. See FUNCTIONAL LITERACY.

REDUNDANCY [16c: from Latin *redundantia* excess, from *redundare* to overflow, from *re-* again, epenthetic *d*, and *unda* wave]. (1) In general usage, more of anything than is (strictly) needed, usually resulting from repetition or duplication; pleonasm or tautology. In the sentence *They also visited us last week too*, either *also* or *too* is redundant, because both words express the same idea. (2) Technically, both the repetition of information (or the inclusion of extra information so as to reduce errors in understanding messages) and part of a message which can be eliminated without loss of essential information.

Redundancy in language. Languages differ in the degree and kinds of redundancy they make use of: Latin syntax has a much higher level of redundancy than English syntax. In the sentence *Milites novi hodie venerunt*, as compared with its translation *The new soldiers came today*, plurality is marked three times in Latin (*-es* in *milites*, *-i* in *novi*, *-erunt* in *venerunt*) but only once in English (*-s* in *soldiers*). French often has greater redundancy in writing than in speech: in *Les nouveaux soldats sont venu aujourd'hui*, the plural is carried in speech by *les*, *sont* and in writing by *les*, *-x*, *-s*, *sont*. It is a feature of pidgin languages that redundancy is greatly reduced: in the English *Six men come*, plurality is marked by *six*, *men*, but in Tok Pisin, *Sikspela man i kam* ('six-fellow man he come') only *sikspela* indicates plurality.

Redundancy and style. It is a convention of English style that words should be varied rather than repeated: *It was a great enormous house, the biggest I've seen* rather than *It was a large large house, the largest I've seen*. Different phrasing is intended to decrease monotony and perhaps increase the amount of information conveyed. Repetition is, however, a common activity and has traditionally been justified as a rhetorical device, used for emphasis and the expression of emotion: see ANADIPLOSIS, REPETITION. It was lexically and grammatically redundant, but not emotionally so, for Shakespeare to have Lear say:

And my poore Foole is hang'd: no, no, no life?
Why should a Dog, a Horse, a Rat haue life,
And thou no breathe at all? Thou'll come no more,
Neuer, neuer, neuer, neuer, neuer.

(*King Lear*, 5. 3)

Redundancy and information. Redundancy can be described as the difference between the possible and actual information in a message. This difference may be repetition or other encodings beyond the minimal possible length. A message entirely without redundancy may contain the maximum amount of information, but cannot be corrected if it is corrupted in some way, because there is no 'spare' material to check with. In the Latin sentence above, three items would have to be lost before the plural message is lost. In the English equivalent, the loss of one *-s* would change the message drastically. To avoid misunderstandings, people generally repeat themselves more when speaking than writing. This corresponds to the greater possibility of error in listening than reading. A speaker in a noisy room will usually provide even more redundancy to help listeners recognize what is said.

Compression and abbreviation. Redundancy makes possible (and can be removed by) the compression of messages. The vowels can be removed from words, as in the advertisements *f u cn rd ts u cn gt a gd jb* (If you can read this you can get a good job) and *w big gdn, s/v* (with a big garden and a sea-view): see CONTRACTION. Shorthand systems work on the same principle of eliminating the non-essential, and such mechanized systems as Stenotype (a machine with a keyboard for recording proceedings, speeches, etc.) rely on the redundancy of natural language to produce shorter versions that can be translated back to conventional English. Compression is often used to shorten computer files by using the equivalent of a frequent-word table. A computer can look through a document, find the most common words, and have each replaced by a short code. If the ten digits (0 to 9) are almost never used in a document, but the words *language* and *English* are very frequent, the symbol *1* need no longer mean the digit, but could be used to abbreviate *language*, saving seven characters each time. Similarly, *2* could replace *English*, and *31, 32, 33* could replace the numbers *1, 2, 3*, and so on. If the text contained 1,000 instances of *language* and *English*, but only ten instances of *1, 2*, and *3*, it would be a total of 12,970 characters shorter as a result: 7,000 shorter from replacing *language*, 6,000 shorter from replacing *English*, and 30 longer from replacing the three digits. A more thorough version of this idea is the formal Lempel–Ziv algorithm, which usually shortens English to less than half its original length.

Code-breaking. Redundancy is of great value in code-breaking. By assessing the frequency of occurrence of letters in English (such as the commonness of *e*, the rarity of *z*), cryptographers can assign tentative values to certain symbols and so begin to break the code concerned. In a non-redundant system, all symbols would appear with equal frequency. English texts could be shortened by replacing all instances of *ee* with *z*, as in *I sz you have bzn to Grzce again*. No word would be misunderstood as a result. If this kind of substitution were continued until not only all letters but all letter patterns were equally

frequent, the crytographer would not be able to look for the repetitions of elements like *ed* or *th* that help break ciphers. As a result, an effective way to discourage code-breaking is, wherever possible, to compress the message first, disrupting the more obvious patterns.

Telecommunications and television. Sounds and pictures also contain redundancy, such as silences in conversations and areas of one colour in a painting. Each side of a telephone conversation is silent about half the time. By removing the silences, long-distance telephone calls are packed into fewer than the expected number of circuits by removing the redundant silence. A detector on each channel listens to the conversation, and on hearing no noise from one end, stops transmitting that conversation, switches in a different conversation, and sends an electrical signal on a separate channel, telling the switch at the other end of the conversation what has happened. That switch sends the sound it is now receiving to another conversation, and connects the current listener to silence. When it receives a signal from the detector that the original speaker has started talking again and which channel is being used for the resumed conversation, it switches the listener back to that channel. See ABBREVIATION, CODE, INFORMATION, PLEONASM, REPETITION, TAUTOLOGY, TELECOMMUNICATIONS. [LANGUAGE, MEDIA, STYLE, TECHNOLOGY].

M.L., T.MCA.

REDUPLICATION 16c: from Latin *reduplicatio/reduplicationis* doubling, folding]. The act or result of doubling a sound, word, or word element, usually for grammatical or lexical purposes. In classical Greek, grammatical reduplication serves to form the perfect of the verb, by means of a prefixed syllable that repeats the initial consonant: *lǔo* I loosen, *léluka* I have loosened. A mix of grammatical and lexical reduplication occurs in various languages: for example pluralizing in Malay *contoh* example, *contoh-contoh* examples, *raja* king, *raja-raja* kings. A word in which this process occurs is a *reduplication* or (more commonly) a *reduplicative*. In English, lexical reduplication is found: (1) In occasional borrowings, such as *beriberi*, a disease caused by deficiency of vitamin B$_1$ (from Sinhala, an emphatic doubling of *beri* weakness), and *ylang-ylang* or *ilang-ilang* the aromatic tree *Cananga odorata* (from Tagalog). (2) In echoic or otherwise phonetically suggestive words, such as *tut-tut/tsk-tsk*. In most cases, some elements contrast while others are repeated, as with *mish-mash* and *hanky-panky*. Such words are often informal and whimsical, with contrasts that affect vowels (*mishmash, pingpong, pitter-patter,* tick-tock, tittle-tattle) or consonants (mumbo-jumbo, niminy-piminy), the latter often involving an opening *h*-sound (hanky-panky, harum-scarum, helter-skelter, hocus-pocus, holus-bolus, hugger-mugger). Less precisely reduplicative resemblances occur in such words as *hunky-dory* and associations can be made between actions in such words as *walkie-talkie*. (3) In such occasional emphatic repetitions as *no-no* in the slang expression *It's a no-no* (It's something definitely not to be done). (4) In pidgin and creole usages, such as Tok Pisin *lukluk* to stare (from *look*) and *singsing* a festival (from *sing*), Kamtok and Krio *bɛnbɛn* crooked (from *bend*), and Kamtok and Nigerian Pidgin *katakata* confused (from *scatter*). See ALLITERATION, ASSONANCE, ECHOISM, EPANALEPSIS, HAWAIIAN, MALAY, RHYMING COMPOUND, SCOTS, SINGSONG, VAGUE WORD. [GRAMMAR, WORD]. T.MCA.

REDUPLICATIVE. See REDUPLICATION.

REFERENCE [16c]. (1) Referring to or mentioning someone or something, either directly or indirectly, and often in the form of an allusion or a quotation. (2) Also *objective reference*. In logic and linguistics, the activity or condition through which one term or concept is related to another or to objects in the world. (3) In sociology and psychology, the process by which, or the extent to which, people relate to elements in society as norms and standards for comparing such things as status and values. (4) An indication or direction in a text or other source of information to all or part of one or more other text, etc., where further, related information may be found. (5) The text or other source to which one is directed or referred. The term is often attributive in senses 4 and 5, as in *reference book*, *reference library*, *reference materials*. It may also be part of an *of*-phrase, as in *frame of reference*, *point of reference*, *work of reference*. (6) To provide a book or other source of information with references (*books that are all thoroughly referenced*) or to arrange (data, notes, etc.) for easy reference (*all the background material is referenced in an appendix*).

Reference materials have in the past depended mainly on surfaces that serve as receptacles of pictures and language symbols, from paintings on cliff faces, in caves, and on walls, through clay tablets and manuscripts of various kinds, to printed books and other products. Especially in the 20c, however, they have been extended to include audio- and video-recordings and electronically stored information on tape and disk. Distinct genres of reference book, such as the *atlas* for maps, the *dictionary* for words, the *directory* for a variety of general or specific information (such as names, addresses, and telephone numbers), the *encyclopedia* for facts and opinions, the *gazetteer* for geographical information, have emerged over many centuries, gaining their present-day forms especially in the expansion of book publishing in the 18–20c. See CROSS-REFERENCE, REFERENCE MARK, REFERENCE NORM, REFERENT, SEMANTICS. T.MCA.

The reference theme

A–C. ALLUSION, ALPHABETIC(AL) ORDER, AMERICAN COLLEGE DICTIONARY, AMERICAN HERITAGE DICTIONARY, AMERICAN SPEECH, ASTERISK, AUSTRALIAN DICTIONARIES, AUSTRALIAN NATIONAL DICTIONARY CENTRE, AUTHORS' AND PRINTERS' DICTIONARY, AVIS, BAILEY (N.), BARNHART, BIBLIOGRAPHY, BIERCE, BILINGUAL DICTIONARY, BRADLEY, BREWER'S DICTIONARY OF PHRASE AND FABLE, BURCHFIELD, CANADIAN DICTIONARIES, CANONICAL FORM, CARTOON, CASSIDY, CATALOG(UE), CAWDREY, CENTURY DICTIONARY, CHAMBERS, CITATION, COBUILD, COLERIDGE (H.), COLERIDGE (S.), COLLINS, COMPANION, CONCISE OXFORD DICTIONARY, CONCISE SCOTS DICTIONARY, CONCORDANCE, CONNOTATION AND DENOTATION, CONTEXT, COOPER, CRAIGIE, CROSS-REFERENCE, CYNIC.

D–F. DAGGER, DEFINING VOCABULARY, DEFINITION, DEIXIS, DEROGATORY, DEVIL'S DICTIONARY, DICTIONARY, DICTIONARY OF AMERICAN ENGLISH, DICTIONARY OF AMERICANISMS, DICTIONARY OF AMERICAN REGIONAL ENGLISH, DICTIONARY OF BAHAMIAN ENGLISH, DICTIONARY OF CANADIANISMS, DICTIONARY OF CATCH PHRASES, DICTIONARY OF JAMAICAN ENGLISH, DICTIONARY OF MODERN ENGLISH USAGE, DICTIONARY OF NEWFOUNDLAND ENGLISH, DICTIONARY OF PRINCE EDWARD ISLAND ENGLISH, DICTIONARY OF SLANG AND UNCONVENTIONAL ENGLISH, DICTIONARY OF THE OLDER SCOTTISH TONGUE, DICTIONARY RESEARCH CENTRE, DICTIONARY SOCIETY OF NORTH AMERICA, EARLY MODERN ENGLISH DICTIONARY, ENCYCLOP(A)EDIA, ENCYCLOPAEDIA BRITANNICA, ENGLISH PRONOUNCING DICTIONARY, EURALEX, EURODICAUTOM, EUROPEAN ASSOCIATION FOR LEXICOGRAPHY, FOREIGNISM, FOWLER, FREQUENCY COUNT, FRIES, FUNK, FUNK & WAGNALLS, FURNIVALL.

G–O. GAGE CANADIAN DICTIONARY, GHOST WORD, GLOSS, GLOSSARY, GOWERS, HANDBOOK, HANLEY, HARD WORD, HEADWORD, HOBSON-JOBSON, INDEX, INTERNATIONAL SCIENTIFIC VOCABULARY, JAMIESON, JOHNSON, JONES (D.), KERSEY, KEYWORD, KING'S ENGLISH (THE), KUHN, KURATH, LEARNER'S DICTIONARY, LEMMA, LEXICOGRAPHY, LEXICOLOGY, LEXICON, LIEBER, LINGUISTIC ATLAS, LINGUISTIC ATLAS OF ENGLAND, LINGUISTIC ATLAS OF THE UNITED STATES AND CANADA, LITERARY TERM, LONGMAN, MACQUARIE DICTIONARY, MANUAL, MARCH, MATHEWS, MERRIAM-WEBSTER, MIDDLE ENGLISH DICTIONARY, MODERN ENGLISH USAGE, MORRIS, MURISON, MURRAY, NEW ZEALAND DICTIONARIES, ONIONS, OXFORD ADVANCED LEARNER'S DICTIONARY, OXFORD DICTIONARIES, OXFORD DICTIONARY FOR WRITERS AND EDITORS, OXFORD DICTIONARY OF ENGLISH ETYMOLOGY, OXFORD DICTIONARY OF QUOTATIONS, OXFORD ENGLISH DICTIONARY.

P–Z. PARTRIDGE, PERIOD DICTIONARIES OF ENGLISH, PIOZZI (THRALE), POCKET OXFORD DICTIONARY,

POLYSEMY, QUOTATION, RANDOM HOUSE, RANDOM HOUSE
DICTIONARY, READ, READER'S DIGEST, REFERENCE,
REFERENCE BOOK, REFERENCE GUIDE FOR ENGLISH
STUDIES, REFERENCE MARK, REFERENCE NORM, REFERENT,
REGIONAL DICTIONARIES OF ENGLISH, RESPELLING,
ROGET, ROGET'S THESAURUS, SCOTTISH DICTIONARIES,
SCOTTISH NATIONAL DICTIONARY, SEMANTIC FIELD,
SENSE, SOUTH AFRICAN ENGLISH DICTIONARIES,
SYLLABICATION/SYLLABIFICATION, TERMINOLOGY,
THEMATIC ORDER, THEME, THORNDIKE, TOPIC, TOPICAL
ORDER, TOPONYM, TOPONYMY, TRANSLATION
DICTIONARY, TRENCH, TURNER (G.), UNABRIDGED,
URDANG, WATSON, WEBSTER, WEBSTERS, WEBSTER'S
COLLEGIATE DICTIONARIES, WEBSTER'S DICTIONARY OF
ENGLISH USAGE, WEBSTER'S NEW INTERNATIONAL
DICTIONARY, WEBSTER'S NEW WORLD DICTIONARY,
WEEKLEY, WHITNEY, WORCESTER, WORDBOOK, WORD
BUFF, WORK OF REFERENCE, WYLD, YEAR'S WORK IN
ENGLISH STUDIES.

REFERENCE BOOK. See REFERENCE.

**REFERENCE GUIDE FOR ENGLISH
STUDIES, A.** A 790-page single-volume annotated bibliography compiled by Michael J. Mar-
cuse (University of California Press, 1990). It
covers titles to the mid-1980s, and is intended
'to introduce and describe unfamiliar reference
sources that one may consult when dealing with
any reference question arising from current
teaching or research in any branch of English
studies. For these purposes, English studies are
defined as all those subjects and lines of critical
and scholarly inquiry presently pursued by members of university departments of English language and literature. Put more boldly, this work
aims to provide more help to more people than
any single reference guide we in English studies
have hitherto possessed.' The volume builds on
and extends prior American works in the field
of bibliography, relating in particular to literature. Its sections are: *A* General Works; *B* Libraries; *C* Retrospective and Current National
Bibliography; *D* Serial Publications; *E* Miscellany; *F* History and Ancillae to Historical
Study; *G* Biography and Biographical References; *H* Archives and Manuscripts; *I*
Language, Linguistics, and Philology; *K* Literary Materials and Contexts; *L* Literature; *M*
English Literature; *N* Medieval Literature; *O*
Literature of the Renaissance and Earlier Sev-
enteenth Century; *P* Literature of the Res-
toration and Eighteenth Century; *Q* Literature
of the Nineteenth Century; *R* Literature of the
Twentieth Century; *S* American Literature; *T*
Poetry and Versification; *U* The Performing
Arts—Theater, Drama, and Film; *W* Prose Fic-
tion and Nonfictional Prose; *X* Theory,
Rhetoric, and Composition; *Y* Bibliography; *Z*
The Profession of English. Compare YEAR'S
WORK IN ENGLISH STUDIES. See BIBLIOGRAPHY,
ENGLISH STUDIES. [REFERENCE].   T.MCA.

REFERENCE MARK [1850s]. Any of various
written or printed symbols, such as an asterisk
(*), an obelisk or dagger (†), or a superscript
number used to indicate that further information
is available in an end- or footnote, a bibliography, or another text. See ASTERISK, MARK,
NOTES AND REFERENCES, OBELISK. [REFERENCE,
WRITING].   T.MCA.

REFERENCE NORM [Late 20c]. A model for
the use of language, such as a standard variety.
In global terms, users of English tend to follow
one of two reference norms: Filipinos, for
example, have AmE as their reference norm,
while Indians tend to follow BrE. See AMERICAN
ENGLISH AND BRITISH ENGLISH, NORM, RECEIVED
PRONUNCIATION, STANDARD. [LANGUAGE, REF-
ERENCE].   R.F.I.

REFERENT [1830s]. (1) The object or event to
which a term or a symbol refers. The term *table*
has many referents, the majority of which have
a flat top and four legs. (2) In logic, the first
term in a proposition to which succeeding terms
relate. See SEMANTICS, SEMIOTICS, SENSE. [REF-
ERENCE].   T.MCA.

REFINED [16c: from *re-* and *fine*: compare
French *raffiner*, Spanish *refinar*]. (1) Purified,
freed from impurities: *refined iron*. (2) Characterized by fineness of feeling, taste, manners,
thought, and/or action (*refinement*); cultured,
civilized, well-bred; not vulgar or coarse: *refined
courtiers, a refined education*. (3) (Of language)
cultivated, polished, elegant: 'good Letters and
refined speech' (preface, Authorized Version of
the Bible, 1611); 'She spoke with a refined
accent' (George Eliot, *Felix Holt*, 1868). See
(A)ESTHETICS. Compare POLITE, PURE, STANDARD.
[STYLE].   T.MCA.

REFLEXIVE [16c: from Latin *reflexivus* bending back]. A term for a verb, pronoun, or construction that works on identity of reference
between two grammatical units, chiefly the subject and the object. In English, the relationship
is expressed by the use of *reflexive pronouns*. See
REFLEXIVE PRONOUN. [GRAMMAR].   S.G.

REFLEXIVE PRONOUN. A pronoun that
ends in *-self* or *-selves*. Such pronouns are used
when the direct and sometimes the indirect
object of a verb 'reflects' or refers back to the
subject: *I blame myself for what happened*; *They
have allowed themselves another week*. Occasionally, some other part of the sentence may
also reflect the subject: *She pulled the box
towards herself*. In standard English, a reflexive
pronoun cannot usually serve as the subject of a
sentence (no **Myself did it*), but especially in

Scotland and Ireland, under the influence of Gaelic, there is a mock-prestigious use of the third-person singular (*Is himself at home?*, *It was herself answered the phone*), deriving from usages that formerly referred to kings and chiefs: *Himself has eaten, the rest of the world may eat.* See PRONOUN, REFLEXIVE. [GRAMMAR].   S.C., T.MCA.

REFORMATION. The 16c religious movement that first sought to reform the Roman Catholic Church but ultimately resulted in the establishment of the Protestant churches. The ensuing theological polemic was voluminous (Edmund Spenser's *Faerie Queene*, I. i. 20, represents the dragon Errour spewing out 'vomit full of bookes and papers') and largely in the vernacular: John Wycliffe (*c*.1330–1384), a precursor of the Reformation, refused to use Latin, the traditional language of theological writing, and addressed the laity in English. His confidence in English led him to translate from Latin the first ever entire Bible to be published in a European vernacular. Later reformers often printed their works for wide distribution: in the five years before Martin Luther's 1522 translation of the New Testament, a third of all publications in German bore his name, and his High German became the literary standard throughout Germany. In England, reformers also renewed the study of Old English in an attempt to prove the continuity of the English church and its doctrines. In Scotland, there began an educational drive to make all citizens literate and able to read the Scriptures for themselves. Compare BIBLE, RENAISSANCE. See EARLY MODERN ENGLISH, MUMPSIMUS, WYCLIFFE. [EUROPE, HISTORY].W.F.B.

REFRAIN [14c: from Old French *refraindre* to break sequence, from Latin *refringere* to break up]. A sequence of words repeated throughout a piece of verse, usually at the end of a stanza but sometimes between lines. Common in ballads, folk-songs, and nursery rhymes, it breaks into the main course of the verse at intervals and sometimes suggests a stylized dialogue between solo voice and chorus. In effect, it eases the reciter's memory and allows participation by listeners. In printed texts it is often typographically highlighted, perhaps in italics or by indenting. In some forms, the refrain is cumulative, providing a chant-like framework for the entire piece. Short refrains are often nonsensical, doing little more than bear the melody of the line: Shakespeare's 'With a hey, and a ho, and a hey nonino' (*As You Like It*, 5. 3). In Hardy's 'Voices from things growing in a churchyard', each stanza ends with the thematic refrain 'All day cheerily, / All night eerily!'; in Yeats's poem 'The O'Rahilly', on a death in the Dublin rising, 1916, the refrain is oblique, asking 'How goes the

weather?' An extended refrain is often sung as chorus to a song, as in Robert Burns's 'Auld Lang Syne'. Compare CHORUS. [LITERATURE].

R.C.

REGGAE [1960s: probably from Jamaican Creole *rege(-rege)* rags, ragged clothes (referring to slum origins), perhaps with echoes of AmE *ragtime*, a term used to describe jazz]. Music with a heavy four-beat rhythm, with accents on one and three rather than two and four as in rock music. Reggae began in Kingston, Jamaica, and has cultural, social, and political implications in the Caribbean, UK, US, and elsewhere. The lyrics propose solutions to black problems ranging from social revolution to redemptionist prophecy, and are often a vehicle for Rastafarianism, as in:

> Babylon system is the vampire
> Sucking the children day by day.
> (Bob Marley, 'Babylon System', 1979).

> I hear the words of the Rasta man say
> Babylon your throne gone down, gone down.
> (Bob Marley and the Wailers, 'Rasta Man Chant')

Lyrics are sung in Jamaican Creole, Jamaican English, or a mixture of both, 'often expressing rejection of established "white-man" culture' (F. G. Cassidy & Robert Le Page, *Dictionary of Jamaican English*, 1980) and are 'a major, if not sole, source of information (or focal point of information) about Jamaica for North Americans' (Lise Winer, 'Intelligibility of Reggae Lyrics in North America: Dread ina Babylon' (in *English World-Wide* 11: 1, 1990). They are also sung in French in Quebec and Senegal, and in Hausa, Lingala, Soninke, and Twi in West Africa. See BLACK, DUB, JAMAICA, RAP, RASTA TALK. [AFRICA, AMERICAS].   T.MCA.

REGIONAL DICTIONARIES OF ENGLISH. Dictionaries which list and define words as used in a particular country, such as the *Dictionary of Jamaican English*, or part of a country, such as the *Dictionary of Newfoundland English*. Such dictionaries of English date from the 17c: for example, John Ray's *A Collection of English Words* (1674), which provided two alphabetic lists of words, one for the North and one for the South of England. Thomas Ruddiman's *A Glossary of Alphabetical Explanation of the Hard and Difficult Words* (Edinburgh, 1710) was keyed to Gavin Douglas's translation of the *Aeneid* into Scots (1553), and was the first to combine a regional perspective with a historical treatment of words. Various works explaining vocabulary used in areas of Britain followed these; the first to present an overseas variety as an independent entity was Noah Webster's *An American Dictionary of the English Language* (1828). This was followed by Henry Yule and A. C. Burnell's

Hobson-Jobson: A Glossary of Anglo-Indian Colloquial Words and Phrases (1886), E. E. Morris's *Austral English* (1898), and Charles Pettman's *Africanderisms* (1913). These works have an idiosyncratic charm; they count as the first extended efforts to record and define the distinctive vocabulary of parts of the British Empire.

In his address to the Philological Society (1919), William A. Craigie reflected on future dictionaries, suggesting that it was time to plan English lexicography beyond the long-contemplated *Supplement to the OED* (1933), which was intended only to correct errors and add new information. Dictionaries to follow should include not only 'period dictionaries' such as for Middle English but also 'regional dictionaries' such as for Scotland and the US. His definition of a regional dictionary appeared in the first part of the *Dictionary of the Older Scottish Tongue* (1931), in which he defined the scope of the work: 'the whole range of the Older Scottish vocabulary . . . down to 1600' and 'the history of the language to 1700, so far as it does not coincide with the ordinary English usage of that century'. From 1603, when Scotland and England acquired a common monarchy, Craigie takes 'ordinary English usage' to be normative and the English of Scotland as exceptional, and subsequent 'regional' dictionaries have tended to follow that principle, most limiting themselves to usage not identical to the standard English of England.

In the preface to his *Dictionary of American English* (1940), Craigie rejected as impracticable a comprehensive, historical dictionary of English as used in the US, and defined the scope of this 'regional' work to include: 'words and phrases which are clearly or apparently of American origin, or have greater currency here than elsewhere, but also every word denoting something which has a real connection with the development of the country and the history of its people'. Hence, the term *regionalism* came to be used for a 'word, phrase, or peculiarity of pronunciation which is not part of the standard language of a country' (*OED*, 2nd edition, 1989). Without necessarily addressing the presumption that educated BrE, particularly the variety used in England, is 'standard' and other varieties therefore in some sense 'peculiar', subsequent regional dictionaries have approached the issue of inclusiveness in three ways:

(1) The associationist approach. This approach parallels the *Dictionary of American English* in admitting entries that have some particular association with the region, even though they also appear in the English of England. *A Dictionary of Canadianisms* (Toronto: W. J. Gage, 1967) includes 'words and expressions characteristic of various spheres of Canadian life' without regard to their use elsewhere. The *Dictionary of Newfoundland English* (1982) includes coinages, survivals, and words and senses which have 'a distinctly high or general degree of use' there, and *The Australian National Dictionary* (1988) treats 'words and meanings of words which have originated in Australia, or which have a special significance in Australia because of their connection with an aspect of the history of the country'.

(2) The etymological approach. A more stringent definition of scope appears in *A Dictionary of Americanisms* (1951), which restricts inclusion to 'a word or expression that originated in the United States'. Similarly, the *Dictionary of Jamaican English* (1967, 1980) encompasses 'the English language in all the forms it has taken in Jamaica since 1655' which, in practice, means only borrowings, coinages, or sense developments entering English in Jamaica. Regional dictionaries of this type implicitly or explicitly acknowledge that the words and senses included are both distinctive and, from the Anglo-English perspective, alien. The *Dictionary of Bahamian English* (1982) focuses attention on 'words and expressions . . . which are not generally found in the current standard English of Britain or North America'; the *Dictionary of Prince Edward Island English* (1988) states forthrightly that it is 'a record of non-standard words as used, or once used, on Prince Edward Island'; *A Dictionary of South African English* (1987) defines its coverage as 'an unconventional part of the English vocabulary, namely that peculiar to or originating in South Africa'.

(3) The loanword approach. This approach describes words borrowed or adapted from a particular region of the world. Though there are many studies of the influence of various languages on English, only one dictionary has apparently been compiled so far on this basis: Gerard M. Dalgish's *A Dictionary of Africanisms* (1982), which lists words from African languages that appear in English.

Other regional dictionaries focus attention on subdivisions of the nation under scrutiny. Joseph Wright's six-volume *English Dialect Dictionary* (1898-1905) details usages according to the cultural geography of England. Frederic G. Cassidy's *Dictionary of American Regional English* (1985-), however, presents a more complex definition of 'regional', by including: 'Any word or phrase whose form or meaning is not used generally throughout the United States but only in part (or parts) of it, or by a particular social group' and 'Any word or phrase whose form or meaning is distinctively a folk usage (regardless of region).' In *DARE*, regions are not fixed but fluid and include social as well as geographical areas. Compare PERIOD DICTIONARIES OF ENGLISH. See DICTIONARY. [REFERENCE, VARIETY].

R.W.B.

REGIONAL ENGLISH LANGUAGE CENTRE. See RELC.

REGIONALISM [19c: from *regional* and *-ism* as in *Scotticism*]. A term in linguistics for a word or other usage belonging to a region, either of the world or a country. An *Americanism* is a regionalism of English in world terms, while a *Kentuckyism* or *New Yorkism* is a regionalism in US terms. See -ISM. Compare LOCALISM. [STYLE, WORD].

T.MCA.

REGISTER [1950s in this sense; 14c in origin, through French from Medieval Latin *registrum* a list or catalogue]. In sociolinguistics and stylistics, a variety of language defined according to social use, such as scientific, formal, religious, and journalistic. The term has, however, been used variously in different theoretical approaches, some giving it a broad definition (moving in the direction of *variety* in its most general sense), others narrowing it to certain aspects of language in social use (such as occupational varieties only). The term was first given broad currency by the British linguist Michael Halliday, who drew a contrast between varieties of language defined according to the characteristics of the user (*dialects*) and those defined according to the characteristics of the situation (*registers*). Registers were then subclassified into three domains: *field of discourse*, referring to the subject matter of the variety, such as science or advertising; *mode of discourse*, referring to the choice between speech and writing, and the choice of format; and *manner of discourse*, referring to the social relations between the participants, as shown by variations in formality. Compare DISCOURSE, CODE-MIXING AND CODE-SWITCHING, VARIETY. See CONTEXT, JARGON, RESTRICTED LANGUAGE, ROMANCE, USAGE. For details of some specific registers, see ACADEMIC USAGE, BIBLICAL ENGLISH, COMPUTER USAGE, JOURNALESE, LEGAL USAGE, TECHNOSPEAK. [LANGUAGE, STYLE, VARIETY].

D.C.

REGULAR [15c: from Old French *reguler* (Modern *régulier*), from Latin *regularis* according to rule]. A term in general use and in linguistics for items and aspects of language that conform to general rules. A *regular verb* in English has four forms, and the construction of three of those forms is predictable from the first (uninflected) form: *play, plays, playing, played*. On the other hand *speak* is an *irregular verb*. It has five forms, the last two of which are unpredictable:

speak, speaks, speaking, spoke, spoken. See ANALOGY AND ANOMALY, IRREGULAR, RULE. [GRAMMAR].

S.G.

REGULAR VERB. See REGULAR, VERB.

RELATIVE CLAUSE. In grammatical description, the term for a clause introduced by a relative word or a phrase containing a relative word. There are three types of relative clause: the *adnominal relative clause*; the *sentential relative clause*; the *nominal relative clause*.

The adnominal relative clause (also *relative clause, noun clause*). This clause modifies a noun, as in: (*the book*) *that I have just read*. It may be introduced by a relative pronoun such as *who, which, that*, or by a phrase containing a relative pronoun, such as *for which, to whom, in the presence of whom*, or by a relative adverb, such as *where, when*: (*the hotel*) *where he stayed*. Under certain circumstances, the relative pronoun may be omitted: (*the music*) *she composed*; (*the safe*) *I put the money in*. See RELATIVE PRONOUN. Adnominal relative clauses of the type (*She told me the reason*) *that they gave* are to be distinguished from the superficially similar appositive clause that also modifies a noun: (*She told me the reason*) *that they left*. The appositive clause is introduced by the conjunction *that*, which may sometimes be omitted: (*the reason*) *they left*. The difference between the two types of clause is that the appositive clause is complete in itself (*they left*, not *they left the reason*), whereas the relative clause requires the relative item to be present or to be understood, since it functions in the clause (*they gave that*, meaning *they gave the reason*). The relationship between a noun and its appositive clause differs from that between a noun and its relative clause in that it may be expressed by inserting the verb *be* between the two: *The reason is that they left*. Furthermore, the nouns that are modified by an appositive clause are restricted to a small set of general abstract nouns such as *fact, idea, news, report*.

Restrictive and non-restrictive clauses. The two major types of adnominal relative clauses are *restrictive relative clauses* and *non-restrictive relative clauses*. A *restrictive relative clause* (also *defining relative clause*) is a relative clause with the semantic function of defining more closely what the noun modified by the clause is referring to. In the sentence *My uncle who lives in Brazil is coming to see us*, the relative clause *who lives in Brazil* restricts the reference of *my uncle*. The restrictive modification would distinguish this uncle from any others who might have been included. A *non-restrictive relative clause* (also *non-defining relative clause*) adds information not needed for identifying what a modified noun is referring to. The sentence *My uncle, who lives in Brazil, is coming to see us* contains the non-restrictive relative clause *who lives in Brazil*. This clause provides information about the uncle, but his identity is presumed to be known and not to need further specification. Non-restrictive relative clauses are usually separated from the noun phrases they modify by parenthetical punctuation (usually commas, but sometimes dashes or brackets). In speech, there may be a pause that serves the same function as the parenthesis.

The sentential relative clause. This clause does not modify a noun. It may refer back to part of a sentence (*She exercises for an hour a day, which would bore me*: that is, the exercising would bore the speaker), to a whole sentence (*He kept on bragging about his success, which annoyed all of us*: that is, the continual bragging about his success annoyed everybody), or occasionally to more than one sentence (*I didn't enjoy the work. The weather was atrocious. I felt thoroughly homesick. And the locals were unpleasant. Which is why I have never been back there again*). *Which* is the most common relative word to introduce a sentential relative clause, sometimes within a phrase (*in which case, as a result of which*), but other relative expressions with this type of clause include *whereon, whereupon, from when, by when*.

Nominal relative clauses. In the adnominal and sentential relative clauses, the relative word has as *antecedent*, a word or longer unit to which the relative word refers back: in *the game which they were playing*, the antecedent of *which* is *the game*, since in its clause *which* substitutes for *the game* (they were playing the game). The relative word in the nominal relative clause has no antecedent, since the antecedent is fused with the relative: *I found what* (that which; the thing that) *you were looking for*; *He says whatever* (anything that) *he likes*. Because they are free of antecedents, such clauses are sometimes called *independent* or *free* relative clauses. See ADJECTIVE CLAUSE, CLAUSE, COMMA. [GRAMMAR].   S.G.

RELATIVE PRONOUN. A pronoun that alone or as part of a phrase introduces a relative clause: *who* in *the man who came to dinner*; *on whom* in *the woman on whom I rely*. The relative pronoun refers to an antecedent (*the man/who, the woman/on whom*), and functions within the relative clause: as subject in *who came to dinner*; as complement of a preposition in *on whom*. There is a gender contrast between the personal set of *who* pronouns and the non-personal *which* pronoun, and there are case distinctions in the *who* set: subjective *who(ever)*, objective *whom-(ever)*, genitive *whose*. However, except in a formal context, *who(ever)* replaces *whom(ever)*.

That can be used as a relative pronoun in place of *who, whom,* or *which*, except as complement of a preposition: *the woman who/that I rely on*, but only *the woman on whom I rely*. *That* can be omitted when functioning as object (*a man that I know; a man I know*), but not as subject (*a man that knows me*). The omitted pronoun is sometimes referred to as *zero relative*. See RELATIVE CLAUSE. [GRAMMAR].   S.G.

RELC, full form *Regional Language Centre*. An educational institution (headquarters, Singapore) of the *Southeast Asian Ministers of Education Organization* (*SEAMEO*), whose members are Brunei, Cambodia, Indonesia, Laos, Malaysia, the Philippines, Singapore, and Thailand, and associate members Australia, Canada, France, Germany, and New Zealand. RELC was founded in 1968 as the *Regional English Language Centre*, with the aim of improving the teaching of English as a second or foreign language in SEAMEO member countries. In 1977, its role was expanded to assist member countries in the development of all language education, and its full name was changed appropriately, while retaining the acronym. RELC assists member countries by providing training and study programmes that lead to postgraduate diplomas and degrees, and through research and development, regional seminars, publications, and information services. The annual *Regional Seminar* is well known and attracts scholars of international repute. RELC provides consultancy and advisory services and arranges exchange of personnel. Its publications include: two semi-annual periodicals, *RELC Journal* (language teaching and research in South-East Asia) and *Guidelines* (a magazine for classroom teachers); the *RELC Newsletter*; the *Annual Report*; a monograph series; an instructional series; occasional papers; and library and informational publications. The Library and Information Centre is a clearing-house of language-related information for the region. [ASIA, EDUCATION, LANGUAGE].   T.MCA.

RELIEF PRINTING. See LETTERPRESS.

RENAISSANCE [French: rebirth]. Also **Renascence** [From Latin *renascentia* rebirth]. The period of renewed influence of classical culture, beginning in 14c Italy and in England usually dated from about 1476 (the introduction of printing by William Caxton) or 1485 (the accession of the Tudors, culminating in the Elizabethan age). The close of the Renaissance in Britain is usually dated to the beginning or end of the Commonwealth (1649-60). Though the term (first used in English in 1840) inaccurately suggests an abrupt change from the culture of the Middle Ages, several 16c features increasingly distinguished Renaissance English from its medieval precursor: an enormous influx of new vocabulary; a characteristic exuberance of literary style; the impact of the Reformation, especially the increase of printed works in English and the consequent rapid growth of literacy; the increase of national pride and of confidence in the vernacular for serious writing; the spread of English in Britain and Ireland and to the New World; and the arrival of some features of English structure such as the verb suffix -*s* in place of older -*th* (*has* for *hath*, *goes* for *goeth*), so that Shakespeare can use both in a line like 'The ripest fruit first fall*s*, and so do*th* he'. Compare REFORMATION. See CAXTON, EARLY MODERN ENGLISH, ELIZABETHAN, JACOBEAN, LATIN[1]. [EUROPE, HISTORY]. W.F.B.

REPARTEE [17c: from French *repartie* retort, the feminine past participle of *repartir*]. A swift, sharp, and amusing reply, and conversation that is full of such replies. Repartee is counter-punching wit, the skill of the pointed, face-saving retort to language or behaviour that may lead to one's losing face: 'If you were married to me,' said Lady Astor to Winston Churchill, 'I'd put poison in your tea.' 'If I were married to you,' Churchill retorted, 'I'd drink it.' Repartee can be scripted (as when Shakespeare invents repartee for the fools and gentlefolk of his comedies), but it is generally taken to be spontaneous. The purport of repartee is to stop verbal aggressors in their tracks. Occasionally, the contest is friendly, and the contestants will make room for one another in the to-and-fro moves of a slanging match enjoyed by all, but more often repartee consists of the hostile move and the annihilating response. The huffy complaint, 'I didn't come here to be insulted' prompts the retort 'Where *do* you go to be insulted, then?'

The aggressor may devise a formula (such as 'Have you stopped beating your wife?') which appears to preclude effective retort. In such cases the one option for repartee is to return the challenge in the same form (such as 'Have *you* stopped making mischief?'), but this is unsatisfactory, and can only produce a Mexican stand-off, in which neither side dares fire. True repartee always beats the gunman to the draw. The image of the gunman is by no means amiss, since repartee is a kind of duelling, an activity displacing physical violence, which may follow, but as a rule only when one or other of the verbal duellists is humiliatingly dumbfounded. The scuffles of the schoolyard are often prefaced by crude exercises in repartee (*You're illiterate, see?—Well, you're illegitimate, see?*), in which the contestants work themselves up into a combative rage. More sophisticated practitioners,

for example among Cockneys, Glaswegians, Liverpudlians in Britain and urban blacks in America (with their verbal rituals of *sounding*, *signifying*, *capping*, and *the dozens*), win prestige for their successful recourse to the word that serves as counter-punch or knockout blow. See BADINAGE, BANTER, HUMO(U)R, PATTER. [STYLE]. W.N.

REPERTOIRE [1840s: from French *répertoire* notebook, catalogue, list of works, from Latin *repertorium* inventory. Compare REPERTORY]. (1) In general terms, a list or stock of works that can be performed by a theatrical or other group or of skills, techniques, and devices available to a performer or in an occupation. (2) In linguistics and language teaching, the range of languages or varieties that an individual speaker can command, especially to perform particular social roles. The term also refers collectively to the whole set of varieties within a speech community. Increasing one's linguistic repertoire is an index of growing fluency in a language. Foreign language learners at an elementary level have a limited repertoire of a single style. Advanced speakers have an ability to use and respond to several varieties, such as formal/ informal (in both speech and writing), regional, occupational, and other styles. In the case of bilingual or multilingual communities, speakers are able to choose between different languages in their repertoire (*code-switching*), which enables them to convey different kinds of social rapport and identity. See CODE, CODE-MIXING AND CODE-SWITCHING, DIGLOSSIA, REGISTER, VARIETY. [EDUCATION, LANGUAGE]. D.C.

REPERTORY [16c: from French *répertoire* a stock of plays, from Latin *repertorium* an inventory. Compare REPERTOIRE]. A theatre with a regular company and the resources to perform a variety of old and new plays, such as the Elizabethan theatres. Modern repertory developed in the late 19c, distinct from travelling companies and assembling a cast for a new production and disbanding it at the end of the run. In Britain, both the Royal Shakespeare Company and the National Theatre are repertories. See DRAMA, THEATRE. [LITERATURE]. R.C.

REPETITION [14c: through French from Latin *repetitio* a seeking again]. Doing, saying, or writing the same thing more than once. The recurrence of processes, structures, elements, and motifs is fundamental to communication in general and language in particular. Such repetition occurs at all levels, starting with rhythm. The distinctive rhythm of English derives from recurring syllabic stresses: *If whát/ you sáy/ is trúe/ I'd bétt/er gó*. Poetry intensifies such rhythms, iambic pentameter in particular formalizing the stress-timed rhythm of English: 'While thús/ I stóod,/ intént/ to sée/ and héar,/ One cáme,/ methóught,/ and whís/per'd ín/ my éar' (Pope, 1715). In addition, the repetition of shared sounds creates rhyme. These lines of Pope's have the rhyme pattern *aabb*: *hear/ear, raise/praise*. The use of poetic and rhetorical devices such as alliteration and assonance produces repetition of sounds and letters and other effects, as in the jingle-like:

> Nature, it seems, is the popular name
> for milliards and milliards and milliards
> of particles playing their infinite game
> of billiards and billiards and billiards
> (Piet Hein, *Grooks*, 1966)

Similarly, syntactic and rhetorical repetition can produce emphatic or climactic effects:

Lord Wilson's memoirs are not as dull as Lord Stockton's, nor as sad as Lord Avon's, nor as queer as Lord Bradwell's, but Lord! they are as worthless as any of them (*Independent*, 21 Oct. 1986).

In everyday conversation, people 'repeat themselves', often in slightly different ways, to ensure that the core of their message will not be missed. Such repetition spreads among several people in a conversation:

A: (Having just pulled a Christmas cracker, reads the riddle inside) Oh this one's awful. You won't want to hear this one. It's terrible.
B: Go on, let's hear it.
C: Yeah, let's hear it.
A: No, you won't want to hear it. I tell you, it'll make you ill.
C: Come on, let's all be ill together.
B: Yeah, let's hear it.
A: You really mean that. You want to hear it?
(cited by David Crystal, *English Today* 14, Apr. 1988)

Such repetition sustains conversation. It shows that the participants accept each other (whether they agree or not) and that they can create miniature dramas together. In formal writing, however, such repetition is generally avoided, both for the sake of economy and in favour of a tradition of 'elegant variation'. See ANADIPLOSIS, ANAPHORA, CONVERSATION, EPANALEPSIS, JINGLE, PARALLELISM, REDUPLICATION, TAUTOLOGY. [STYLE].   T.MCA.

REPORTED SPEECH. See DIRECT AND INDIRECT SPEECH.

RESPELLING, also **re-spelling.** (1) Spelling a word, etc., for a second time. (2) A lexicographical technique or system in which the pronunciation of English words is shown by means of a fixed set of letters and diacritics in which each letter unit has only one value: for example, *o* with the value in *hope* (usually regardless of accent variations). Most present-day respelling systems include the schwa or weak vowel [ə]. A dictionary that uses such a system not only describes it in detail in the introduction but also usually displays a set of key word-values at the bottom of each page, for easy consultation. In Britain, the key words of the *Chambers English Dictionary* (1988) are: *fāte; fär; hûr; mīne; mōte; för; mūte; mōōn; fŏŏt; dhen* (then); *el'əmənt* (element).' In the US, the key words (etc.) of *The Random House Dictionary* (1987), with the key letters in roman, are: 'a*c*t, c*ă*pe, d*â*re, p*ä*rt; s*e*t, ē*qual*; *if, ī*ce; *o*x, ō*ver, ô*rder, *oil, bŏŏk, bōō*t, *ou*t; *up, û*rge; *child, sing; shoe; thin, that;* zh as in *trea*sure*. ə = a* as in *alone, e* as in *system, i* as in *easily, o* as in *gallop, u* as in *circus*; ' as in *fire* (fī'r), *hour* (ou'r). l and n can serve as syllabic consonants, as in *cradle* (krād'l), and *button* (but'n).' The only current alternative to respelling is phonetic symbols, such as those of the International Phonetic Alphabet. IPA symbols representing the RP accent are standard in British learners' dictionaries and have become more common in recent years in British mother-tongue dictionaries: compare recent editions of *The Concise Oxford Dictionary*: the 7th in 1982 has respelling; the 8th in 1990 uses IPA. Respelling remains standard in the US. [REFERENCE, WRITING].   T.MCA.

RESTORATION, The. The period in the social, cultural, and literary history of England, Scotland, and Ireland from the re-establishment of monarchy in 1660 through the reign of Charles II (until 1685), and sometimes extended to include the reign of James II and VII (1685-8). The period was marked by a reaction, especially among the upper classes, to the puritanical austerity of the preceding years. The comedy of manners popular during this period is referred to as *Restoration comedy*. Compare AUGUSTAN, COMMONWEALTH, JACOBEAN. See COMEDY, DRAMA, EARLY MODERN ENGLISH, ENGLISH LITERATURE, PROSE. [EUROPE, HISTORY].   T.MCA.

RESTRICTED CODE. See ELABORATED AND RESTRICTED CODE.

RESTRICTED LANGUAGE [1960s]. A reduced form of a language: 'Some registers are extremely restricted in purpose. They thus employ only a limited number of formal items and patterns [and] are known as *restricted languages*' (M. A. K. Halliday *et al.*, *The Linguistic Sciences and Language Teaching*, 1964). Such a system is often artificial and highly specialized, created and used with a particular end in mind: for example, *Basic English*, limited in its syntax and lexis, but meant to be used as an international medium; *Seaspeak*, a form of English limited to specific procedures and terms, serving to facilitate the safe movement of shipping; *headlinese*, a register reduced in syntax and lexis, used to draw attention to news and other reports, and to indicate their content. See AIRSPEAK, ARTIFICIAL LANGUAGE, BASIC ENGLISH[1], CONTACT LANGUAGE, ELABORATED AND RESTRICTED CODE, HEADLINE, INDEXING LANGUAGE, JARGON, MAKESHIFT LANGUAGE, NATURAL LANGUAGE, NUCLEUS, PIDGIN, REGISTER, SEASPEAK. [EDUCATION, LANGUAGE, STYLE].   T.MCA.

RESTRICTIVE AND NON-RESTRICTIVE MODIFICATION. See ADJECTIVE.

RESTRICTIVE AND NON-RESTRICTIVE RELATIVE CLAUSE. See RELATIVE CLAUSE.

RETROFLEX [Early 20c: from Latin *retroflexus* bent back]. Sometimes *retroflexed*. A term in phonetics for sounds, especially /r/, made with the tip of the tongue curled back and raised towards the palate. These *r*-sounds occur in such rhotic varieties of English as AmE (non-Southern), CanE, IndE, IrE, and the accents of south-west England, in which postvocalic /r/ coalesces with a following alveolar consonant in words like *worse* and *hard*. The process is known as *retroflexion*. In the languages of the Indian subcontinent, retroflex consonants such as /t/ and /d/ are common and occur in South Asian English. See R-SOUNDS. [SPEECH].   G.K.

RETRONYM [1970s: from Latin *retro* backward, and Greek *ónuma* name]. A semi-technical term for (1) A phrase coined because an expression once used alone needs contrastive qualification: *acoustic guitar* because of *electric guitar*, *analog watch* because of *digital watch*, *manual typewriter* because of *electric/electronic typewriter*, *mono sound equipment* because of *stereo sound equipment*. Retronyms emerge when contrast becomes necessary: 'The fast food market is bucking a worldwide neurosis about health . . . What's new then? Well, a lot of money is being invested in the most declining market of all—what you might call slow food, the traditional sit-down restaurant' ('Burger Boredom', *Independent*, 24 Feb. 1990). (2) A word that spells another word backward: *warts*. See REVERSAL, -ONYM. [WORD].   T.MCA.

REVERSAL [20c in this sense]. Also **retronym**. Semi-technical terms for a word that spells another word backwards: *warts*. Accidental reversals are established words in both directions: *doom*, *straw*. Deliberate reversals form a new word: the trade name *Trebor*; the BrE slang *yob* ('a backward boy': a lout). Such reversals are sometimes used for effect in utopian and satirical writing, such as: (1) Samuel Butler's novel *Erewhon* (1872), which is set in a land where Victorian ideas and values are reversed. Crime is an illness, illness a crime. The local goddess *Ydgrun* reverses *Mrs Grundy*, a character in Thomas Morton's *Speed the Plough* (1798) and a symbol of rigid moral propriety. Erewhonians have such names as *Yram* and *Nosnibor*. To make the name of his land easier to read and say, Butler amended the strict reversal *Erewhon*. (2) *The Study of Man* (1936), a pseudo-academic paper by the US anthropologist Ralph Linton, which described the culture of the *Nacirema*, a people living between the Cree and the Yaqui Indians. In a sequel, 'Body Ritual among the Nacirema' (1965), Horace M. Miner added information about their culture hero *Notgnihsaw* and their temple, the *latipso*. See ANAGRAM, BACK SLANG, BUTLER, HYPALLAGE, PALINDROME, RETRONYM, SATIRE, WILDE. [WORD].   T.MCA.

REVIEW [16c: from French *revue* seen again]. (1) A general survey of any kind: *a review of recent events*. (2) An article, especially in a newspaper, magazine, or other periodical, that offers a critical assessment of a book, monograph, article, play (whether performed live, on radio, or on television), motion picture, or electronic product: *a book review*. In such contexts, the terms *reviewer* and *critic* are virtual synonyms. (3) A journal or magazine that prints only or mainly reviews: *a literary review*; *The Edinburgh Review*; *The New York Review of Books*. See ELT DOCUMENTS, ENGLISH TODAY, JOURNAL, MAGAZINE, PERIODICAL, QUARTERLY REVIEW OF DOUBLESPEAK, SCOTTISH PUBLISHING. [MEDIA, WRITING].   T.MCA.

REVIEW OF ENGLISH LANGUAGE TEACHING. See ELT DOCUMENTS.

REVISE. See PAGE PROOF.

***R*-FUL, *R*-FULL.** See R, RHOTIC AND NON-RHOTIC.

RHEME. See DISCOURSE ANALYSIS.

RHETORIC [14c: from Old French *rethorique* (Modern *rhétorique*), Latin *rhetorica*, from Greek *rhētorikḗ tekhnḗ* the craft of speaking, from *rhḗtōr* a speaker, orator]. (1) The study and practice of effective communication. (2) The art of persuasion. (3) An insincere eloquence intended to win points and get people what they want. All three senses have run side by side for more than 2,000 years. For many people who concentrate on the first sense, rhetoric is a deeply significant subject whose neglect impoverishes education and makes a high standard of literacy harder to attain. For others, who pay more attention to the second and particularly the third sense, it is generally specious and hypocritical (*empty rhetoric, mere rhetoric*). In the late 20c, rhetoric has an explicit and an implicit aspect. Explicitly, many 20c language professionals refer to rhetoric as archaic and irrelevant, while for some philosophers of communication and for many teachers of writing it is a significant and lively issue. In the latter circles, there is discussion of a 'new rhetoric' that blends the best of the old with current insights into the nature of communication. It is, however, an ironic measure of the centuries-old strength of rhetoric that many of its principles, concepts, and devices are implicit in Western society, taken as given by educated users of languages like English, French, and German. Terms like *analogy*, *antithesis*, *dialectic*, and *metaphor* had their beginning among the rhetoricians of ancient Greece, as did many of the techniques of courtroom argument, public speaking, advertising, marketing, and publicity. In such areas, the principles, terms, and practices of rhetoric are alive, and widely discussed, though not necessarily under the name *rhetoric*.

Origins. In ancient societies with no awareness of writing, the ability to speak informatively, cohesively, and memorably was essential and admired. In such societies, chiefs, bards, and seers used a variety of techniques to gain attention and ensure retention of information (in their own as well as their listeners' minds). Linguistic techniques included: rhythm; repetition; formulaic lists and descriptions; kinds of emphasis; balance and antithesis; ellipsis; and words and devices to evoke mental images. Generic shapes (genres) designed for the accurate retention and effective delivery of messages included: genealogy; praising and blaming; supplication and lamentation; proverbial expressions of wisdom; statements of law; threats and warnings; and other manoeuvres intended to influence and persuade.

Greek rhetoric. In the course of time, such techniques were organized into bodies of received knowledge. In some societies, they were largely a part of religious ritual, as in India; in others, such as Greece, they were part of the craft of speaking which in the 5c BC became the foundation of education in city states like Athens and Sparta. The story is told of exiles who returned to Syracuse, a Greek colony in Sicily, after the overthrow of a tyrant. Because they needed to organize their claims to appropriate land, they hired teachers to help them argue their cases, and, as a result, the craft of rhetoric emerged through pleading in the Syracusan court. Itinerant teachers known as *sophists* (wise ones) then taught this forensic art alongside logic, a subject which was associated with the new craft of writing. Rhetoric's foremost exponents and analysts were Gorgias, Isocrates, Plato (all 5-4c BC), and Aristotle (4c BC). Of their rhetorical works, however, only Plato's *Phaedrus* and Aristotle's *Rhetoric* have survived. As writing became commoner, elements of the oral craft were transferred to prose composition and efforts were made to harmonize the rules of speech and writing with those of logic. The devices of rhetoric, however, did not lose their links with poetry or their practical ties with the law. As a result, rhetoric came to be viewed in two ways: as the high moral and philosophical art of speech and writing, and as a low art of winning arguments and impressing the gullible. Because of the varied nature of their audiences, student orators were encouraged to study their listeners and adopt a suitable *rhetorical character* while arguing a case, shedding it afterwards like an actor's mask.

The five canons. Many manuals were compiled on the subject, such as the Latin treatise *Rhetorica ad Herennium* ('Oratory for Herennius': anonymous, 1c BC). These works usually listed five *canons* or *offices* of rhetoric, concerned with gathering, arranging, and presenting one's material. The names and nature of the canons, though generally unfamiliar nowadays as aspects of rhetoric, are by and large familiar in education, linguistics, philosophy, and general informed discussion. The canons are:

(1) Greek *heúresis*, Latin *inventio*. Finding or researching one's material. The speaker or writer assesses an issue, assembles the necessary material, and begins to work on the appropriate arguments.

(2) Greek *táxis*, Latin *dispositio*. Arranging or organizing one's material. Here, the orator puts the parts of the discourse in order, starting with the *exordium* or formal opening, then proceeding with the *narration*, including the division into various points of view, with proofs and refutations, and closing with the *conclusion*.

(3) Greek *léxis*, Latin *elocutio* or *educatio*. The fitting of language to audience and context, through any of three styles: the high-and-grand, the medium, and the low-and-plain (with examples of the good and bad applications of all three). Included in this 'style' section are the traditional rhetorical devices and figures of speech.

(4) Greek *hupókrisis*, Latin *pronuntiatio* or *actio*. Performance, including the arsenal of techniques to be used in proclaiming, narrating, or in effect acting. This aspect was concerned with

live audiences but also covered work on papyrus and parchment.

(5) Greek *mnémē*, Latin *memoria*. Training of the mind, to ensure accurate recall and performance in public assembly or court of law.

In addition, rhetoric was related to time. *Epideictic* or *demonstrative* discourse catered for the present time (in debate, during ceremonies, at commemorative events, etc.), *deliberative* discourse looked to the future (in planning and theorizing), and *forensic* or *judicial* discourse judged the past, especially in courts of law (in assessing guilt or innocence). In all such discourse, the speaker could appeal to *páthos* (the emotions, the heart), to *lógos* (reason; the head), and/or to *êthos* (character; morality). The five canons, three kinds of discourse, and three kinds of appeal reflect an enthusiasm for taxonomy often expressed through contentious and legalistic hair-splitting, which came to characterize the subject in the late first millennium BC.

Roman rhetoric. Republican Rome shared the Greek interest in debate and legal argument, and therefore considered rhetoric essential to public life. Classics like Aristotle's *Rhetoric* were augmented by the lawyer Cicero (2–1C BC), who produced among other works the *De inventione* (On Making your Case) and the *De oratore* (On Being a Public Speaker), and by Quintilian (1C AD), author of the *Institutio oratoria* or *Institutiones oratoriae* (Foundations of Oratory). The systematization of rhetoric served the Empire well, helping to develop Latin as a language of literacy throughout the dominions. Imperial Rome, however, generally discouraged free and democratic debate, with the result that style and effect became more important than integrity. The American commentator James J. Murphy has noted (1982, below):

At the heart of the Roman approach is the conviction that linguistic ability (*facilitas* is Quintilian's term) is a single, unitary human capacity, regardless of whether it is employed in reading or speaking or hearing or writing. Like a muscle, linguistic ability can be strengthened by purposefully stretching it into new uses, and, like a muscle, it can be reinforced by the repetition of varied uses. Thus, rewriting Greek prose into Latin verse exercises half a dozen specific abilities of form recognition and creativity.

Some of the schools in which this approach to rhetoric was taught outlived the Empire and survived into a new age, in which St Augustine of Hippo (4–5c) put it to work in the service of Christian doctrine.

Medieval and Renaissance rhetoric. Aristotle and Cicero had a profound influence on education in medieval Christendom. Through the works of Martianus Capella (5c), Cassiodorus (5–6c), and St Isidore of Seville (6–7c), their principles became part of Scholasticism, leading to the *trivium* (the three ways) of grammar, rhetoric, and logic-cum-dialectic, studied by aspirants to Latin learning and clerical orders. The trivium was the foundation for the *quadrivium* (the four ways) of arithmetic, geometry, astronomy, and music-cum-harmony. Together, these made up 'the seven liberal arts', the core programme of theocratic and general education. Cicero had been the first to use the phrase *artes liberales* (liberal arts), the model not only for medieval and Renaissance scholarly debate but for contemporary liberal arts colleges and degrees and the education they seek to provide. When the complete text of Quintilian was rediscovered in a Swiss monastery in 1416, it helped animate the revival of classical learning known as the Renaissance. Scholars like Peter Ramus (16c), however, saw rhetoric less as a way of developing speech than as a means of teaching writing, whose importance was much greater than in classical times, both to the Church and the new nation-states. The five ancient canons were reorganized, assigning *invention* and *disposition* to dialectic and largely ignoring *memory* (although learning by heart remained a prime element in education). Renaissance rhetoric served the growth of literacy in the vernaculars as well as Latin, focusing on composition, style, and the figures of speech.

Rhetoric and English. During and after the Renaissance, rhetoric dominated education in the humanities in England, Scotland, and France, remaining little changed until the later 19c. During this period, the ancient tension between 'good' and 'bad' rhetoric continued, as the following extracts indicate. The first, from *The Schoolmaster* (Roger Ascham, 1563), praises Cicero and everything Latinate; the second, from *Hudibras* (Samuel Butler, 1663) mocks the ornate and empty:

Ascham. There is a way, touched in the first book of Cicero *De oratore*, which, wisely brought into schools, truly taught, and constantly used, would not only take wholly away this butcherly fear in making of Latins but would also, with ease and pleasure and in short time, as I know by good experience, work a true choice and placing of words, a right ordering of sentences, an easy understanding of the tongue, a readiness to speak, a facility to write, a true judgment both of his own and other men's doings, what tongue soever he doth use.

> *Butler.* For rhetoric, he could not ope
> His mouth but out there flew a trope;
> And when he happened to break off
> In the middle of his speech, or cough,
> He had hard words ready to show why,
> And tell what rules he did it by.
> Else, when with greatest art he spoke,
> You'd think he talked like other folk;
> For all a rhetorician's rules
> Teach nothing but to name his tools.

The fragmentation of rhetoric that began in the Renaissance created whole new subjects in succeeding centuries. The third and fourth canons (*elocution* and *pronunciation*) became in the 18c courses in 'proper' speech, taught by actors like Thomas Sheridan and John Walker, both of whom published pronouncing dictionaries of English. At the beginning of the 17c, Francis Bacon initiated an interest in gesture, which was developed by John Bulwer in *Chirologia* ('the speech of the hand', 1644), which in turn prompted studies of gesture and body language by Charles Darwin and Alexander Melville Bell in the 19c and Edward T. Hall and Desmond Morris in the 20c.

During the 17–19c, the methods of Cicero and Quintilian were standard in British and American universities. Yet, while students learned the classical languages and their rhetoric, their teachers were often in the forefront of change to English. The Scottish scholar Adam Smith chose English rather than Latin when giving his lectures; his friend Hugh Blair was appointed to the first chair of Rhetoric and Belles Lettres at the U. of Edinburgh in 1762, the precursor of all chairs of English language and literature around the world. In 1806, the first Boylston Professor of Rhetoric and Oratory at Harvard, Massachusetts, was John Quincy Adams (later sixth US president). He was charged to instruct students in accordance with the models and exercises of Quintilian, but when Francis J. Child occupied the same chair in 1851, it was as Professor of English. In 18c society at large, issues of judgement and taste became more important than aesthetics and rhetoric, and among Romantics in the 18c and 19c freedom and feeling were more intriguing than discipline and refinement. As the 19c progressed, the ancient theorists became of less and less interest, except to classical scholars, and rhetoric became for many either the (empty) forms of public speaking or the study of writing and composition in schools. Some of the ancient aims and practices were, however, sustained in the debating societies of British universities and the departments of speech and public address in US colleges.

Conclusion. The ancient rhetoricians assumed that truth was absolute and separable from a text. Many 20c critics and scholars, however, see truth as relative and texts as self-contained objects whose 'truth' is re-made by every reader. The ancients regarded discourse as dynamic, embodying an intention and a design fitted to an audience, much as politicians and lawyers still see it. Many present-day literary critics, however, see discourses and especially texts as complete in themselves and distinct from their creators, the intention and ideas of the creator

having reduced importance or no importance at all if they are not directly shown in the text. The dynamic therefore lies not with the writer but with the reader, in the re-creation of meaning. The emphasis has accordingly been on structure, coherence, and interpretation rather than on creation and the techniques of dissimulation that may accompany it, except insofar as these can be deconstructed to reveal a variety of possible interpretations. Even so, classical rhetoric survives. It has given shape to much of the Western world's inheritance of oracy and literacy. Everyone who speaks and writes a Western language or any language influenced by the forensic and literary traditions of the West is willy-nilly affected by it. Anyone who speaks in public or writes for professional purposes engages in the processes first listed in the five canons. In journalism and publishing, on radio and television, in the theatre and cinema, the old names may or may not be known, but the tools continue to be used.

See ALLEGORY, ALLITERATION, ALLITERATIVE VERSE, ANACHORISM, ANACHRONISM, ANACOLUTHON, ANADIPLOSIS, ANALOGY, ANASTROPHE, ANTICLIMAX, ANTITHESIS, ANTONOMASIA, APORIA, APOSTROPHE[2], ARGUMENT, BATHOS, BELLES LETTRES, BIBLE, BLAIR, CACOPHEMISM, CHIASMUS, CIRCUMLOCUTION, CLIMAX, CLINCH, COMMUNICATION, COMMUNICATIVE SHIFT, DECORUM, DISCOURSE ANALYSIS, DYSPHEMISM, ECHOISM, ELLIPSIS, ELOCUTION, ELYOT, EMPHASIS, EPANALEPSIS, EPIC SIMILE, EPITHET, EUPHEMISM, EUPHONY, EUPHUISM, FIGURATIVE LANGUAGE/USAGE, GRAMMAR, HENDIADYS, HOMEOTELEUTON, HOMERIC SIMILE, HYPALLAGE, HYPERBATON, HYPERBOLE, HYSTERON PROTERON, INNUENDO, INVERSION, IRONY, JOURNALESE, LEGAL USAGE, LINGUISTICS, LITERARY CRITICISM, LITERATURE, LITOTES, LOGIC, MEDIA, MEIOSIS, METAPHOR, METONYMY, MIXED METAPHOR, ONOMATOPOEIA, ORATORY, ORTHOEPY, OXYMORON, PARADOX, PARALIPSIS, PARONOMASIA, PATHETIC FALLACY, PATHOS, PERIPHRASIS, PERSONIFICATION, PLAYING WITH WORDS, PLEONASM, POETIC DICTION, PROLEPSIS, PRONUNCIATION, PROSOPOPOEIA, PUBLIC SPEAKING, PUN, PUTTENHAM, QUIBBLE, REDUNDANCY, REPETITION, RHETORICAL QUESTION, SARCASM, SIMILE, SPEECH, SPEECH ACT, SPOKEN PROSE, STYLE, STYLISTICS, SYLLEPSIS, SYNECDOCHE, TAUTOLOGY, THESIS, TOPIC, TRANSFERRED EPITHET, TROPE, UNDERSTATEMENT, ZEUGMA. [STYLE].   T.MCA.

Bailey, Dudley (ed.). 1965. *Essays in Rhetoric*. Oxford: University Press.

Booth, Wayne C. 1983. *The Rhetoric of Fiction*, 2nd edition. Chicago: University Press.

Clark, Donald L. 1957. *Rhetoric in Greco-Roman Education*. New York: Columbia University Press.

Corbett, Edward P. J. 1965. *Classical Rhetoric for the Modern Student*. Oxford: University Press.

Freedman, Aviva, & Pringle, Ian (eds.). 1980. *Reinventing the Rhetorical Tradition*. Ottawa, Carleton University: Canadian Council of Teachers of English.

Horner, Winifred B. (ed.). 1980. *Historical Rhetoric: An Annotated Bibliography of Selected Sources in English*. New York: Hall.

Murphy, James J. 1974. *Rhetoric in the Middle Ages: A History of Rhetorical Theory from St. Augustine to the Renaissance*. Berkeley: University of California Press.

—— (ed.). 1982. *The Rhetorical Tradition and Modern Writing*. New York: Modern Language Association of America.

Nash, Walter. 1989. *Rhetoric: The Wit of Persuasion*. Oxford: Basil Blackwell.

Ong, Walter J. 1971. *Rhetoric, Romance, and Technology*. Ithaca: Cornell University Press.

Vickers, Brian. 1988. *In Defence of Rhetoric*. Oxford: University Press.

Woodson, Linda. 1979. *A Handbook of Modern Rhetorical Terms*. Urbana: National Council of Teachers of English.

RHETORICAL QUESTION [19c]. A question that expects no answer. The answer may be self-evident (*If she doesn't like me why should I care what she thinks?*) or immediately provided by the questioner (*What should be done? Well, first we should . . .*). The question is often asked for dramatic effect: 'GLENDOWER. I can cal spirits from the vasty deepe. / HOTSPUR. Why so can I, or so can any man, / But wil they come when you do cal for them?' (Shakespeare, *1 Henry IV*, 3. 1). Rhetorical questions are sometimes announced with such a phrase as *I ask you* (when nothing is in fact being asked): 'Garn! *I ask you*, what kind of a word is that? / It's Ow and Garn that keep her in her place, / Not her wretched clothes and dirty face' (Alan Jay Lerner, *My Fair Lady*, 1956). [STYLE].   T.MCA.

RHODESIA. A territorial name during the British colonial period in Africa, based on the surname of Cecil John Rhodes, a British mining magnate and adventurer. The one-time colonies of *Northern Rhodesia* and *Southern Rhodesia* are now the republics of *Zambia* and *Zimbabwe*. See EAST AFRICAN ENGLISH, ZAMBIA, ZIMBABWE. [AFRICA, NAME].   T.MCA.

RHOTACISM [Early 19c: from Latin *rhotacismus*, Greek *rhōtakismós* making a *rhō* or *r*-sound]. A special, excessive, or idiosyncratic use of /r/, such as *rolling one's rs* in a stage Scottish accent: 'Rotacism . . . a vicious pronunciation common in the northern parts of England' (Robley Dunglison, *Medical Lexicon*, 1855, referring to the uvular Northumbrian burr); 'The privileged families, with pronounced rhotacismus, are still there to help kill pheasants' (*Times Literary Supplement*, 11 Feb. 1977, referring to an /r/ pronounced like /w/). Compare BURR, GUTTURAL, RHOTIC AND NON-RHOTIC. See R, R-SOUNDS. [SPEECH, STYLE].   T.MCA.

RHOTACIZE, RHOTACISE. See R.

RHOTIC AND NON-RHOTIC. [Later 20c: from Greek *rhō*, the letter symbol for /r/, and *-tic* as in *neurotic*]. Terms in phonetics for two kinds of spoken English, a fundamental contrastive feature in the language. In one set of accents of English, *r* is pronounced wherever it is orthographically present: *red*, *barrel*, *beer*, *beard*, *worker*. Such a variety is variously known as *rhotic*, *r-pronouncing*, or *r-ful(l)*. In another set of accents, *r* is pronounced in syllable-initial position (*red*) and intervocalically (*barrel*), but not postvocalically (*beer*, *beard*, *worker*). In such positions it is vocalized (turned into a vowel) and not pronounced unless another vowel follows. Such a variety is variously known as *non-rhotic*, *non-r-pronouncing*, or *r-less*. The mainly rhotic and non-rhotic communities in the English-speaking world are: (1) *Rhotic*. Canada; India; Ireland; south-western England; Scotland; the northern and western states of the US apart from the Boston area and New York City; Barbados. (2) *Non-rhotic*. Black Africa; Australia; the Caribbean, except for Barbados; England apart, in the main, from the south-west; New Zealand; South Africa; the southern states, the Boston area of New England, and New York City vernacular speech; and Black English Vernacular in the US; Wales. Foreign learners from such backgrounds as the Romance languages and Arabic and those who have Network American as their pronunciation model tend to be rhotic. Foreign learners in Black Africa, and from China and Japan, as well as those who have RP (BBC English) as their model tend to be non-rhotic. See R, RHOTACISM, R-SOUNDS. [SPEECH].   G.K., T.MCA.

RHYME [13c, rival etymologies: (1) From Old French *ritme*, Latin *rhythmus*, *ritmus*, Greek *rhuthmós* flowing, acquiring a classical respelling in the 17c. (2) From Old French *rimer* to rhyme, Gallo-Romance *rimare to put in a row, Old High German *rīm* series, from *c*.1600 influenced by *rhythmus*. (3) A complex mix of both]. Also **rime**. A general and literary term for the effect produced by using words that end with the same or similar sounds: in the last stressed vowel (*fire/lyre/desire/aspire*) and in following vowels and consonants (*inspiring/retiring*; *admiringly/conspiringly*). Rhyme has been a major feature of English verse since the early medieval period and is widely regarded as essential to it, although a great deal of verse is unrhymed. Rhyme is a distinctive part of stanza form, but is also used in poems written in continuous couplets. The pattern of rhyme is commonly shown by using a letter to represent each terminal sound: a rhyming couplet is *aa* (*views/Muse*), a quatrain in which each alternate line rhymes is *abab* (*art/beat/heart/feet*). Rhyme can be a difficult constraint, but it provides form and can give prominence to words that express the theme or mood of the poem:

> How can I, that girl standing there,
> My attention fix
> On Roman or on Russian
> Or on Spanish politics? . . .
> And maybe what they say is true
> Of war and war's alarms,
> But O that I were young again
> And held her in my arms!
> (W. B. Yeats, 'Politics', 1939)

Such satisfaction of the expectation which the rhyme scheme arouses in the reader is a mark of the poet's skill. A predictable rhyme may disappoint expectation and trivialize a poem:

> I plodded to Fairmile Hill-top, where
> A maiden one fain would guard
> From every hazard and every care
> Advanced on the roadside sward.
> (Thomas Hardy, 'The Dear', 1901)

while an obviously forced rhyme damages the poet's artistic credibility:

> When it came to be known a whale was seen in the Tay,
> Some men began to talk and say
> We must try and catch this monster of a whale
> So come on, brave boys, and never say fail.
> (William McGonagall, 'The Famous Tay Whale', 1883)

The musical quality which resides in some combinations of sound is a matter of aesthetics and response to it can be subjective, but it is certainly part of the pleasure of rhymed verse. Rhyme has a strong mnemonic value and is used in educational mnemonics and advertising jingles as well as literary verse. English is poor in rhyme as compared with Romance languages like Italian and Portuguese and with Scots, enriched through its elided final consonants: *fa* and *a* (*fall* and *all*) rhyming with *blaw* and *snaw* (*blow* and *snow*). There is not, for example, a large range of rhymes for words as semantically important as *God*, *spirit*, and *life*; the frequent occurrences of such words in poetry eventually makes the chosen rhymes seem stale and predictable. This has made many poets favour simple rhyme schemes, or verse which is either unrhymed or includes unrhymed lines among rhymed ones. Changes in pronunciation can destroy rhyme: present-day readers may not respond well or at all to such earlier rhymes as *sounds/wounds*, *join/divine*. Conversely, the study of rhymes is a valuable aid in attempts to determine the pronunciation of former times. At any time, the validity of certain rhymes may be disputed, since pronunciation is not uniform: rhyming *morn* and *dawn* can seem reasonable to speakers of dialects that do not sound the *r* in this position, while rhotic speakers find it curious, disturbing, even displeasing. Despite the comparative paucity of rhyme in English, it can appear inadvertently in speech or written prose, when the effect is generally comic or inept (sometimes prompting the wry remark, 'I'm a poet, and I don't know it').

See ALLITERATION, ASSONANCE, BLANK VERSE, EYE RHYME, FEMININE ENDING, FREE VERSE, HALF RHYME, INTERNAL RHYME, JINGLE, MASCULINE ENDING, OTTAVA RIMA, POETRY, PROVERB, RHYMING COMPOUND, RHYMING SLANG, VERSE. [LITERATURE, SPEECH]. R.C.

RHYMING COMPOUND A compound word whose elements rhyme, such as *jet set*, *hotshot*, *sky-high*, *zoot suit*. See COMPOUND WORD, JOURNALESE, RHYME. [WORD]. T.MCA.

RHYMING SLANG. A form of slang that may have originated in the 18c, probably among the London Cockneys, as part of creative word-play and thieves' cant. It is unlikely, however, that there was ever a systematic code of rhymes used to create a private language. Rhyming slang was part of the general patter of traders and others, used as much for amusement as for secret communication. It was never a major feature of Cockney usage, and became more widely known through its use on radio and television. There are two stages in its formation and use:

(1) *Creating two-term phrases*. The effect depends on the creation of a binary expression that rhymes with a single everyday word: *apples and pears* with *stairs*, *ball of chalk* with *walk*, *bowl of water* with *daughter*, *Bristol City* with *titty*, *butcher's hook* with *look*, *trouble and strife* with *wife*. The rhyme need not be perfect and is sometimes based on an existing slang usage: *Lakes of Killarney/barmy*, *cobbler's awls/balls*, where *barmy* means 'mad' and *balls* stands for 'testicles' and by extension 'nonsense'.

(2) *Dropping the second term*. The second element in the pair may then be dropped: *Bristol Cities* becomes *Bristols*, as in *Get a load of those Bristols* (Just look at those breasts), *butcher's hook* becomes *butcher's*, as in *Take a butcher's at him* (Take a look at him), and *cobbler's awls* becomes *cobbler's*, as in *What a load of old cobblers* (What crap).

Rhyming slang may never have been limited to London and is found in other parts of the British Isles, in Australia, and in the US. It is, however, most commonly associated with London, at least as regards its origins, and much of its spread has been due to the broadcasting and other dissemination of Cockney and pseudo-Cockney usages. See COCKNEY, PRIVATE LANGUAGE, RHYME, SLANG. [STYLE].   T.MCA.

RHYTHM [16c: from Latin *rhythmus*, Greek *rhuthmós* flow]. (1) The flow and beat of such things as sound, melody, speech, and art. (2) In music, the arrangement of beats and lengths of notes, shown in notation as *bars* or groups of beats, the first beat of each bar carrying the stress. (3) In poetics, the arrangement of words into a more or less regular sequence of long and short syllables (as in the quantitative metre of Latin) or stressed and unstressed syllables (as in the accentual metre of English), and any arrangement of this kind. (4) In phonetics, the sense of movement in speech, consisting of the *stress*, *quantity*, and *timing* of syllables. The rhythm of a language is one of its fundamental features, acquired early by a child and hard for an adult to change. Its basis is pulses of air in the lungs: technically, in the pulmonic air-stream mechanism. Such a pulse or beat is produced by the intercostal respiratory muscles and is known as the *breath pulse*, *syllable pulse*, or *chest pulse*. This pulse serves as the basis for the syllable and a flow of such pulses creates the series of beats in the flow of syllables. Occasionally, a pulse can occur but be silent, as when someone says '*kyou* for *thank you*; this is technically referred to as *silent stress*. When a chest pulse has greater force, it produces a *stress pulse* whose outcome is usually a stressed syllable. Ordinary chest pulses occur at a rate of about five per second, stress pulses less frequently. David Abercrombie notes: 'These two processes—the syllable process and the stress process—together make up the pulmonic mechanism, and they are the basis on which the whole of the rest of speech is built' (*Elements of General Phonetics*, 1967, p. 36).

Stress-timed and syllable-timed languages. The two processes are coordinated in different ways in different languages, and the way in which they are combined produces a language's rhythm, which is fundamentally a matter of timing the pulses. In order to account for differences in timing among languages, a distinction is often drawn between *stress-timing* and *syllable-timing*, according to whether the foot or the syllable is taken as the unit of time. Broadly speaking, the languages of the world divide into *stress-timed languages* such as English, Modern Greek, and Russian, and *syllable-timed languages* such as French and Japanese; many languages, such as Arabic and Hindi, do not fit either category, and it is doubtful whether any language fits either category perfectly. In any language, timing is not

uniform throughout speech: it is affected by tone group boundaries, and slows down in final position. Nevertheless, the distinction is a useful pedagogical device: English learners of French can aim at syllable-timing, and French learners of English can aim at stress-timing. In some styles of delivery, including poetry reading and the recital of the liturgy, the rhythm appears more marked than usual. This is probably due to adjustments to the intonation (such as narrowed pitch range, and tones narrowed to the point where they become level) that background the intonation and leave the rhythm more prominent.

In a *stress-timed* rhythm, timing is based on stressed syllables that occur at approximately regular (*isochronous*) intervals: that is, the unit of rhythm known as the *foot* has about the same duration irrespective of the number of syllables it contains. According to this view, in the phrase //*dozens of*/ *old*/ *photographs*//, *dozens of* takes about the same time to say as *old*. In practice, such languages are not strictly isochronous, but rather tend towards it: the syllables of polysyllabic feet are compressed, and monosyllabic feet lengthened. A second feature of such languages is the reduction of unstressed syllables. This applies to the weak syllables of words and unstressed words. In a *syllable-timed* rhythm, timing is based on the syllable. This does not mean, however, that all syllables are equal in duration: they vary according to the vowels and consonants they contain. Syllable-timed languages lack the rhythmical properties of stress-timing: syllables are not compressed between stresses, and unstressed syllables are not reduced. Although syllable-timing is not used in native-speaker English (except occasionally for comic purposes), it is common in the kind of English spoken by people whose first language is syllable-timed, as is usual in Africa. The consequent lack of reduction might superficially appear to make speech clearer, but by obscuring the stress pattern it reduces the information normally carried by stress and reduces intelligibility. See LINGUISTIC TYPOLOGY, METRE/METER, S(C)HWA, SPELLING, SPRUNG RHYTHM, STRESS, SYLLABLE, TONE, WEAK VOWEL. [SPEECH].   G.K., T.MCA.

RICHARDS, I(vor) A(rmstrong) [1893-1979]. English critic and poet, born in Sandbach, Cheshire, educated at Clifton and at Magdalene College, Cambridge, and a teacher at Cambridge, Peking, and Harvard universities. His publications include three volumes of poetry, and three plays, the *Principles of Literary Criticism* (1924), and *Practical Criticism* (1929). In the last of these, he analysed the results of setting unascribed poems before students and seeking their opinions of them; cloaked in this anonymity, poets generally considered great were often poorly received and minor works highly praised. Richards attacked traditional literary criticism as vague and lacking in clear principles; his regard for irony and ambiguity, and his insistence on close attention to the text, had a profound effect on F. R. Leavis and William Empson in Britain and the New Critics in the US. He was interested in linguistic philosophy and in the teaching of English as a foreign language, collaborating with C. K. Ogden first on *The Meaning of Meaning* (1923), a classic text of semantics, then on the formulation of Basic English. See index. [BIOGRAPHY, EDUCATION, EUROPE, LITERATURE].   R.C.

RICHARDSON, Samuel [1689-1761]. English novelist. Born in Derbyshire. He moved to London at the age of 17 and was apprenticed to a stationer, in whose trade he prospered, acquiring his own business. He was asked to produce a manual of model letters for those with little skill in writing, and this gave him the idea of a novel written as a series of letters: *Pamela, or Virtue Rewarded* (1740), a story of the troubles and ultimate marital reward of a young woman who defends her virtue. It was followed by *Clarissa, or the History of a Young Lady* (1747-8) and by the story of a virtuous man, *Sir Charles Grandison* (1753-7). Richardson's novels were translated into several languages and won wide approval, although Henry Fielding disagreed and conceived *Joseph Andrews* (1742) as a parody of *Pamela*. Fielding may also have written an earlier anonymous parody: *An Apology for the Life of Mrs Shamela Andrews* (1741). The novels are long, with a message of rewards for good conduct and an ethic of success. The style is often heavy, but can be lively and straightforward. The conversations have a dramatic quality. The minute analysis of mood and motive, noting significance in the apparently trivial, foreshadows later fiction. The epistolary method helps in this; though artificial, it provides immediacy and a shifting narrative view. Richardson satisfied the taste of the rising middle class and is a key figure in the history of the English novel. See index. [BIOGRAPHY, EUROPE, LITERATURE, STYLE].   R.C.

RICKERT, Edith [1871-1938]. American philologist and author, born in Dover, Ohio, and educated at Vassar College, New York, and the U. of Chicago (Ph.D., 1899). As Professor of English at the U. of Chicago, she achieved a reputation as a Chaucerian scholar through years of research for a revision of the Chaucer *Life Records* and for *The Text of the Canterbury Tales, Studied on the Basis of All Known Manuscripts* (eight volumes, 1940), a landmark of US literary scholarship written with John Matthews Manly. *Chaucer's World* (1948), compiled from her research and edited after her death by her students, is a study of life in Chaucer's London. Rickert met Manly while working in the US War Department's ciphers and codes division during World War I. Their collaboration also resulted in a series of college textbooks including *Contemporary British Literature* (1921) and *Contemporary American Literature* (1922). These works helped to establish contemporary literature as an area of academic study at US universities. In *New Methods for the Study of Literature* (1927), she introduced linguistic methodology that entailed graphic and statistical methods for the representation of imagery, words, rhythm, and visual devices, as well as sentence and tonal patterns of literary language. Rickert also published works on research and writing, literary criticism, English romances and carols, and French literature. Her creative writing included the novel *Severn Woods* (1930), short stories, and children's literature. [AMERICAS, BIOGRAPHY, LITERATURE].   R.W.B.

RIDDLE [Probably related to Old English *ræd* a story, interpretation]. A statement or question that is intentionally worded in a puzzling or misleading way. The earliest English riddles were mystifying poems describing people or objects, as in the riddles of *The Exeter Book* (*c*.940). In translation, one such riddle runs: 'A moth ate words. That seemed to me, / when I heard of that strange happening, a curious event, / that the insect, a thief in darkness, devoured / what was written by some man, his excellent language / and its strong foundation. The thievish stranger was not / at all the wiser from swallowing those words' (as edited and translated by W. S. Mackie, 1934. The answer is a bookworm). Later versified riddles (often called *enigmas*) included poetry of quality, such as several poems by Sir Thomas Wyatt (16c) and Catherine Fanshawe's *'Twas whispered in heaven* (*c*.1814). Nowadays, riddles are usually *conundrums*, questions which use a pun or double meaning: *When is a door not a door?—When it's ajar; What dog keeps the best time?—A watch-dog*. In the 16c, conundrums were amusements for adults (as in Shakespeare's *The Merry Wives of Windsor*, where Slender wishes to impress Anne Page with some riddles), but are now generally thought appropriate only for children or inclusion in Christmas crackers. See DOUBLE MEANING, PUN, WORD GAME. [WORD].   T.A.

RIME. See RHYME.

R-LESS. See R, RHOTIC AND NON-RHOTIC.

ROCK, The. See GIBRALTAR, NEWFOUNDLAND.

ROGET, Peter Mark [1779-1869]. English physician and taxonomist, born in London, the son of John Roget of Geneva, a Calvinist pastor, and Catherine, daughter of the legal reformer Sir Samuel Romilly, of Huguenot origin. He was educated in a private school and at the U. of Edinburgh, where he graduated in medicine at the age of 19. Roget helped found the Manchester Medical School and created the North London Dispensary, to which he gave his services without payment for 18 years. He was actively involved in the founding of the U. of London, was the first Fullerian Professor of Physiology at the Royal Institution, contributed to the *Encyclopaedia Britannica* (6th and 7th editions) and to various other works, and wrote treatises on electricity and magnetism for the Society for the Diffusion of Useful Knowledge (of which he was a co-founder). Roget was secretary of the Royal Society and for 22 years (1827-49) edited its *Proceedings*. Among other activities and hobbies he invented a slide rule that measured the powers of numbers, experimented with a calculating machine, set chess problems for the *Illustrated London News*, and brought out in 1845 what was probably the first pocket chessboard. He retired from professional practice in 1840, and in 1849, at the age of 70, began to develop a project he had first worked on in Manchester in 1805: a thematic arrangement of words published in 1852 as *Roget's Thesaurus*. See next and index. [BIOGRAPHY, EUROPE, REFERENCE].   T.MCA.

ROGET'S THESAURUS, full title *Roget's Thesaurus of English Words and Phrases*. A work of reference by Peter Mark Roget, published in 1852 by Longman. Its aim was 'to supply, with respect to the English language, a desideratum hitherto unsupplied in any language; namely, a collection of the words it contains and of the idiomatic combinations peculiar to it, arranged, not in alphabetical order as they are in a Dictionary, but according to the *ideas* which they express' (original introduction). The *Thesaurus* has been revised many times, has sold over 30m copies worldwide in different editions, and has become an institution of the language. The words in *Roget* are arranged in listed sets like the genera and species of biology. The intention has not been to define or discriminate them, but to arrange them in synonymous and antonymous groups; it serves as both a word-finder and a prompter of the memory regarding words one knows but could not recall to mind.

The *Thesaurus* was sustained by the Roget family for three generations: Roget himself, a physician and librarian, brought out several revisions before his death in 1869, after which his son John Lewis Roget, a lawyer, continued the work (adding a word-index, which greatly aided use of the book, and a major revision in 1879) until his death in 1908, when his son Samuel Romilly Roget, an engineer, took over, providing a major revision in 1936. During Samuel's time as editor, the boom for crossword puzzles developed, creating a demand for the word-finder that neither his father nor grandfather could have predicted. He sold the rights to Longman in 1952, the year before he died. Since then there have been three revisions: by Robert A. Dutch (1962), Susan M. Lloyd (1982), and Betty Kirkpatrick (1987). There have been many changes between 1852 and 1987, but Roget's basic structure survives in the Longman work, whose latest edition is entitled *The Original Roget's Thesaurus* to disintinguish it from various adaptations by other publishers, especially alphabetic versions in the US.

The classification of the *Thesaurus* is hierarchical, with six major headings: *Abstract Relations, Space, Matter, Intellect, Volition, Affections*. In the 1982 and 1987 editions, *Affections* has been replaced by *Emotion, religion, and morality*. Each of these headings is further divided, *Abstract Relations* for example into: *Existence, Relation, Quantity, Order, Number, Time, Change, Causation*. Each subheading is further subdivided, *Existence* for example into: *Existence, Inexistence, Substantiality, Unsubstantiality, Intrinsicality, Extrinsicality, State, Circumstance*. At this third level come the specific sets of words, among which are italicized keywords preceded by numbers. These keywords, which were introduced by Dutch, serve as cross-references to sets elsewhere in the book. The following is the content and layout of part of set no. 1 in the 1987 edition:

existence, being, entity; absolute being, the absolute 965 *divineness*; aseity, self-existence; monad, a being, an entity, ens, essence, quiddity; Platonic idea, universal; subsistence 360 *life*; survival, eternity 115 *perpetuity*; preexistence 119 *priority*; this life 121 *present time*; existence in space, prevalence 189 *presence*; entelechy, realization, becoming, evolution 147 *conversion*; creation 164 *production*; potentiality 469 *possibility*; ontology, metaphysics; realism, materialism, idealism, existentialism 449 *philosophy*.

In addition to such thematic sets, which make up the bulk of the present-day book, a detailed index shows where a listed word may be found: for example, *existence* is shown as appearing not only in *existence* 1, but also in *presence* 189, *materiality* 319, and *life* 360. Longman claim that over 1.25m words are covered in the 1987 Kirkpatrick edition. Also in 1987, Bloomsbury (London) brought out a facsimile edition of the original *Thesaurus*, with an introduction by Laurence Urdang. See LEXICOGRAPHY, LONG-MAN, MODEL, ROGET, THEMATIC ORDER, THESAURUS. [REFERENCE, WORD].   T.MCA.

ROLL. (1) See SCROLL, VOLUME. (2) See R-SOUNDS.

ROMAJI. See JAPAN, ROMAN.

ROMAN [Before 10c: from Latin *Romanus*]. (1) Relating to Rome, its people, customs, empire, religion, etc. (*the Roman alphabet, a Roman holiday, the Roman Catholic church*); an inhabitant or citizen of Rome (*the ancient Greeks and Romans*). (2) Both with and without an initial capital: relating to the upright style of typeface that dominates the printing of texts in English (of which this volume is an example) and many other languages, and that derives from the letter shapes used in ancient Rome; Roman type or lettering: *a text printed in Times Roman; a mixture of Roman and Gothic; substituting italic for roman.* (3) Used of handwriting: round and bold, in the Roman style. (4) The Roman alphabet: *Malay can be written in both Roman and Arabic.* When the characters of another writing system are transliterated into Roman, they are said to be *Romanized* or, more commonly, *romanized.* Systems of romanization include *Wade–Giles* and *Pinyin* ('classifying sound') for Chinese and *Hepburn* and *romaji* ('Roman letters') for Japanese. See ALPHABET, ARABIC, CHINA, GOTHIC, ITALIC, JAPAN, LATIN[1], LETTER[1], TRANSLITERATION, TYPE, TYPEFACE, TYPOGRAPHY. [TECHNOLOGY, WRITING].   T.MCA.

ROMAN A CLEF. See NOVEL.

ROMAN ALPHABET. See ALPHABET, ROMAN.

ROMANCE [13c: from the Middle English noun *romaunce* Romanic language or a composition in such a language, from the Old French adjective *romanz/romans* Romanic, in turn from the adverb in the phrase *romanz escrire*, from Popular Latin *romanice scribere* to write in the Roman way (that is, in vernacular Latin). Compare Modern French *roman* a novel, and the *Romance languages*. The history of this word provides a striking example of semantic change from specific to general reference and from one to many senses].

Originally a book or narrative, usually in a Romance language, and especially one in which adventure, love, and chivalry are prominent, often with an accompaniment of magic and wonder. Medieval sources included garbled versions of classical myth and legend, Christian and Biblical story (including the so-called *Matter of*

Jerusalem), the legends of the Arthurian cycle (*the Matter of Britain*), and the deeds of Charlemagne and Roland (*the Matter of France*). An early example in English, where the form *romaunt* was commonly used, was the 13c verse poem *King Horn*. In the 14c, notable examples included *Sir Orfeo*, derived from the Orpheus story, and the Arthurian *Sir Gawain and the Green Knight*. The genre evolved into prose romances, such as Sir Thomas Malory's *Le Morte D'Arthur* (15c), Robert Greene's *Perimedes the Blacke-Smith* (1588), and Thomas Lodge's *Rosalynde* (1590), 'hatcht in the stormes of the Ocean, and feathered in the surges of many perillous seas'. Shakespeare based the plot of *The Winter's Tale* (c.1611) on Greene's *Pandosto: The Triumph of Time* (1588).

The classical and rationalist mood of the late 17c and 18c brought a more pejorative sense, in which a romance was remote from reality, gave false ideas about the world, and included personal fantasy verging on self-deception and the deception of others. John Evelyn writes of a knight who was 'indeed a valiant gentleman; but not a little given to romance, when he spoke of himself' (*Diary*, 6 Sept. 1651). This attitude later coexisted with the enthusiasm of the writers of the Romantic Movement for old stories as part of the medieval or Gothic revival: for example, Keats wrote:

> When I behold upon the night's starr'd face
> Huge cloudy symbols of a high romance
> (Sonnet: 'When I have fears', 1818)

With the rise of realism in the novel, a romance tended to be a less serious and more frivolous story, in which the writer's imagination played freely, especially on historical subjects. In the 20c, although the earlier meanings continue, in popular terms a romance is a story of love between a woman and a man, in which a happy ending follows a variety of vicissitudes. Such a tale is part of *romantic fiction*. Major writers of this genre include Georgette Heyer, Barbara Cartland, and Judith Krantz; many others write for such companies as Mills and Boon, as well as supplying short stories to weekly and monthly women's magazines. In addition, romantic motifs and formulas figure to varying degrees in many other genres, in print, in motion pictures, and on television. In colloquial usage, a romance is also a love-affair, with emphasis on its idyllic nature. Both these love-affairs and the stories that describe them contribute to the widespread concept *romantic love*, which for at least a century has had a pervasive influence on relations between the sexes in the Western and Westernizing world. In the 20c, a 'romantic' approach to life ranges from passive escapism into novels and films to an enthusiasm for 'real-life' adventures, quests, thrills, and passions for which the tradition of romance provides models that many find highly satisfying ('I'm a romantic at heart'). Because of the pervasiveness of romantic hopes or expectations, commercial advertising of consumer goods (from cosmetics and clothing to 'the holiday of a lifetime') commonly employ the images and language of romance:

New England quickly steals the heart. White clapboard houses clustering round a needle-spired church . . . forest-cloaked hills and mountainsides . . . cattle safe-grazing in green meadows . . . racing streams in whose waters trout grow sleek and fat . . . lakes of shining water . . . a rugged coastline of headlands, sheer sea cliffs and lonely, rocky coves that are home to lobster and clam. It's a land of endearing charm. Its people, independent, proud and warm of heart, love to share their rich heritage with visitors—and to feed them on waffles with local maple syrup, apple cider, blueberries, pumpkin pie and the finest, most succulent fresh lobster to be found anywhere (from 'See the Glory of New England in the Fall', *Woman and Home* for great-value holidays: a 10-night holiday for £799, *Woman and Home*, Mar. 1990).

To sell a particular vacation, this feature article seeks to cast a linguistic spell, romanticizing New England through such devices as metaphor, alliteration, emotive imagery, and colourful epithets, and suggesting that an experience of it is possible for surprisingly little outlay. Such 'applied romanticism' takes elements of a venerable and popular genre and puts them, often with considerable success, at the service not of kings but of commerce. Such writing is, however, no more contrived than the telling of the original romances; it serves an end, as they did. *Romanticism* as a concept, however, is one stage removed from *romance*: it consciously (sometimes cynically) chooses to invest life with the qualities of romance. Where romance is supposed to be spontaneous and free, the domain of the untrammelled spirit, romanticism is as deliberate as its opposite, *classicism*. In art and language, its forms are as well delineated as an Ionic column or an Augustan couplet. See CLASSICISM, GOTHIC, ROMANTICISM, SCIENCE FICTION. [LITERATURE, STYLE]. R.C., T.MCA.

ROMANCE LANGUAGES [From Medieval Latin *romancium/romancia* a Latin vernacular language, from *Romanicus* of Roman origin]. Sometimes **Romanic languages**. Languages descended from the Latin of the Roman Empire, such as French and Spanish.

Identifying the languages. The number of Romance languages varies according to the criteria used to establish them, such as: (1) Status as a national language, in which case there are five (French, Italian, Portuguese, Romanian, and Spanish/Castilian) or six if Romansch or Rhaeto-Romanic (a language of Switzerland) is included. (2) Possession of a literary tradition, in which case there are nine (the above, plus Catalan, Gallego (in Spain), and Occitan (including Provençal), in France). (3) Geographical or other distinctness, in which case there are 15 (the above, plus Andalusian (Spain), Friulian, Ladin (northern Italy), Sardinian and Sicilian (southern Italy), and Judeo-Spanish, also called Judezmo and Ladino (the Romance equivalent of Yiddish)). Extinct Romance varieties include Dalmatian (Yugoslavia) and Mozarabic (the language of Christians in Moorish Spain). There are also a number of Romance pidgins and creoles, including Haitian Creole French and Papiamentu, a mixed Portuguese-Spanish creole in the Netherlands Antilles. Romance languages are spoken by nearly 400m people and their creoles by nearly 6m more.

Origins and development. With the disintegration of the western Roman Empire (3-5c), forms of Vulgar or Popular Latin developed as the languages of many successor nations. In Italy, the transition was relatively straightforward, post-Latin varieties supplanting their closely related Italic predecessors, but elsewhere the success of the early Romance languages was largely at the expense of Celtic languages, especially in Spain and France. Germanic invaders of Italy, Spain, and France did not retain their own languages, and even as late as the 10c, Scandinavian invaders gave up Norse in favour of French when they settled what came to be known as Normandy. No Romance language developed in the Roman provinces of Britain, probably because Popular Latin was not so firmly established there, Celtic continued to be strong, and the language of the Anglo-Saxon settlers was little exposed to Latin influence before or after they left their homes on the north-western European coast. However, the many Latin loanwords in Welsh suggest that a Romance language might have developed in southern Britain if conditions had been more like those of Gaul and Spain.

Romance in English. The Germanic language of Britain developed largely free of Latin and of Romance influence until the 11c, when the Conquest of 1066 took Norman French across the Channel. For at least two centuries thereafter, a Romance language dominated social, political, and cultural life in much of the British Isles and had such an impact on the vocabulary and writing of English that, like Albanian and Maltese, English has been called a *semi-Romance language*; as Owen Barfield observed, 'the English language has been facetiously described as "French badly pronounced" ' (*History in English*

Words, 1962, p. 59). Because of the French connection and the associated influence of Neo-Latin, English shares with the Romance languages a vast reservoir of lexis, concepts, allusions, and conventions. The accompanying table (which could be greatly expanded) lists 20 everyday English words and their equivalents in French, Spanish, Italian, and Portuguese.

English	French	Spanish	Italian	Portuguese
art	art	arte	arte	arte
bandage	bandage	venda	fasciatura	venda
bed	lit	cama	letto	cama
date (fruit)	date	dátil	dattero	tâmara
eagle	aigle	águila	aquila	águia
garden	jardin	jardín	giardino	jardim
January	janvier	enero	gennaio	janeiro
February	février	febrero	febbraio	fevereiro
legal	légal	legal	legale	legal
magic	magie	magia	magia	mágico
mountain	montagne	montaña	montagna	montanha
oak	chêne	roble	quercia	carvalho
parcel	paquet	paquete	pacco	pacote
poor	pauvre	pobre	povero	pobre
price	prix	precio	prezzo	preço
question	question	pregunta	domanda	pergunta
round	rond	redondo	rotondo	redondo
solution	solution	solución	soluzione	solução
value	valeur	valor	valore	valor
war	guerre	guerra	guerra	guerra

The table shows not only the similarity (even visual identity) of many items, but also, roughly in proportion to the various vocabularies, certain patterns of dissimilarity. Three English words of non-Romance origin (*bed, garden, oak*) are included, one of which (*garden*) is an example of how, on occasion, Germanic words have been adopted into Romance. See BORROWING, CREOLE, EUROPEAN LANGUAGES, FRENCH, IBERIAN LANGUAGES, ITALIAN, LATIN[1], LATIN[2], LINGUA FRANCA, PIDGIN, POLARI, PORTUGUESE, SABIR, SPANISH. [LANGUAGE].   T.MCA., J.M.G.

ROMANI, also **Romany, Romanes** [*c*.1800: from Romani *Romani*, the plural of *Romano*, the adjective from *rom* a man, husband, Gypsy (a word also used in English, collectively as *the Rom* and attributively as in *the Rom people*), and *Romanes* (adverb) in the Romani way: probably from a source related to Sanskrit *ḍoma* a low-caste minstrel and dancer. The name *Gypsy/ Gipsy*, an adaptation of *Egyptian*, arises from the mistaken assumption (*c*.16c) that the Rom came from Egypt, whereas the original homeland of a major element in the community was northern India in the first millennium AD]. (1) A member of the Romani community, *c*.6–10m worldwide: 'The most frequent explanation which I was given by Gypsies [for the name] was: "We're Romanies 'cos we always roam"', (Judith Okely, *The Traveller-Gypsies*, 1983). (2) The originally Indo-Aryan language of the Gypsies, whose *c*.60 dialects vary greatly because of the community's wide dispersal and the impact of such languages as Persian, Greek, Hungarian, and English in places where Gypsies live or have lived. Most of the estimated 250,000 speakers of Romani are at least bilingual. In recent years, efforts have been made to create a standard written form for this largely non-literate language, in part so as to promote a stronger sense of ethnic identity among the Rom people. In Britain, there is a continuum of usage from a conservative inflected form called *Romnimos*, spoken by some 500 people mainly in Wales, to *Anglo-Romani, Angloromani, Anglo-Romany*, or *Romani English*, spoken by some 80,000 around the country, not all of them ethnic Gypsies. Anglo-Romani may contain more Romnimos or more English, depending on circumstances, and has often been regarded as a Travellers' argot: 'To patter romany, is to talk the gipsy flash' (James H. Vaux, *A new and comprehensive vocabulary of the flash language*, 1812). An excerpt from the New Testament in Anglo-Romani runs:

There was a rich mush with kushti-dicking purple togs. Every divvus his hobben was kushti. By his jigger suttied a poor mush called Lazarus. Lazarus dicked wafedi, riffly as a juk. He was ready to scran anything he could get his vasters on or kur it from the rich mush's table (The Gospel According to Luke, 16: 19–21, in *More Kushti Lavs*, the Bible Society, 1981) [*mush* man, *kushti* good, *dick* look, *divvus* day, *hobben* food, *jigger* door, *sutty* sleep, *wafedi* bad, *riffly* dirty, *juk* dog, *scran* eat, *vaster* hand, *kur* steal, *lavs* news].

Words from Romani borrowed into English tend to be slangy or informal; they include *mush* ('moosh': BrE slang) a friend, buddy, *nark* a (police) informer or spy (from *nāk* nose), and *pal* a friend. See Ian Hancock, 'Romani and Angloromani', in P. Trudgill (ed.), *Language in the British Isles* (1984). Compare SHELTA. See BORROWING, COCKNEY, EUROPEAN COMMUNITY, FLASH, INDIAN LANGUAGES, POLARI. [ASIA, EUROPE, LANGUAGE].   T.MCA.

ROMAN NUMERAL [18c]. A letter-like number used by the ancient Romans, part of a numeric system sustained, in both an upper- and lower-case form, to the present day as an alternative to arabic numerals, for such purposes as: showing numbers on buildings, etc. (upper case, as in *MDCVII*); representing the hours on clock faces (upper case); indicating the historical order of monarchs with the same name (upper case: *Henry VIII*, the eighth king of that name to rule England); enumerating items in lists and classifications (both upper and lower case, as in *III* and *iii*); and paginating the introductory pages in books (lower case, as in *xvi*). The basic symbols derive from the fingers and the hand, *I* (= 1) originating as a raised index finger, *V* (= 5) as the fingers of the hand spread, and *X* (= 10) as a stylized version of two hands together. The numbers from 1 to 10 are *I, II, III, IIII* or *IV, V, VI, VII, VIII, IX, X.* Two or more letter symbols together are to be interpreted according to two rules: (1) If a letter is immediately followed by one of equal or lesser value, the two are added: *XV* makes *15.* (2) If a letter is immediately followed by one of higher value, the first is subtracted from the second: *IV* makes *4.* The higher numbers are *L* (= 50), representing half of *C* (= 100) the first letter of *centum* (hundred), *D* (= 500), and *M* (= 1,000) the first letter of *mille* (thousand). The number *MDCVII* ('1,000, 500, 100, 5, 1, 1') stands for either *1,607* or the year date *1607.* A bar over a letter multiplies it by 1,000: a barred M is 1,000,000. The Roman system has no zero. See NUMBER[1]. [LANGUAGE, STYLE, WRITING]. T.MCA.

ROMAN POLICIER. See DETECTIVE STORY.

ROMANTIC FICTION. See ROMANCE.

ROMANTICISM [18c]. (1) Usually with an initial capital. A term referring to the ideas and attitudes of the *Romantic Movement* (late 18c, early 19c), a literary, artistic, musical, philosophical, and social movement which came as a reaction against 18c 'Augustan' neo-classicism and was linked with contemporary revolutionary and nationalist aspirations. In Britain, it covered two generations of writers, the first led by William Wordsworth and Samuel Taylor Coleridge, the second including Lord Byron, Percy Bysshe Shelley, and John Keats. The *American Romantic Period* occupied the mid-19c, with Henry Thoreau, Ralph Waldo Emerson, and Edgar Allen Poe. (2) Often without an initial capital. A general term suggesting romantic attitudes, ideas, ideals, and behaviour, especially when deliberately espoused as a way of life, style of writing, and the like.

Nature. In the 17c and early 18c, the term *romantic* was mainly pejorative, suggesting wild and disordered fancy. It came to be applied to landscapes and places appropriate to the old romances and passed from English, through French, into other European languages. Its first literary application was probably by Friedrich von Schlegel (1772-1829), an early German Romantic poet. Romanticism demands freedom in subject, form, and style: Coleridge saw poetry as shaped by the organic laws of imagination, not by external canons; Wordsworth believed that poetry should be 'the spontaneous overflow of powerful feelings'. Romantic literature is strongly personal and subjective. In it, the individual is of supreme importance, and feeling is superior to reason. The artist, especially the poet, has a high function, but may be driven by the opposition of society into becoming an outcast rebel. The lyric was the most favoured poetic form, but long poems were also attempted in emulation of the epics: for example, Wordsworth's autobiographical *Prelude* (1805, revised 1850). The period also produced the novels of Walter Scott and the prose of Coleridge and Thomas De Quincey.

Interests. Romantic writers were interested in the Middle Ages, a time regarded by neo-classicists as barbaric. Keats in 'The Eve of St Agnes' gave an imaginative medieval setting to a narrative love poem. The supernatural was a source of fascination often linked with medievalism, as in Coleridge's 'Christabel' and, in language rather than setting, 'The Rime of the Ancient Mariner'. Nature became a major theme, described in detail and valued as a source of moral lessons, with a fresh sense of rapport between humanity and the natural world, as in Wordsworth's 'Lines Written above Tintern Abbey'. Romantic writing, although sometimes melancholy and haunted, was optimistic about the human capacity for goodness and the hopes of a new age. There was admiration for the presumed innocence of children, peasants, and other peoples in their supposed natural ('savage') state.

Language. A revolt against poetic diction led to a desire for more simple style in poetry. Wordsworth proposed 'fitting to metrical arrangement a selection of the real language of men in a state of vivid sensation' (Preface to the 2nd edition of *Lyrical Ballads*, 1800). Romantic poetry is generally characterized by the use of familiar words with few distortions of syntax. The poetry of nature in particular moved far from 18c artificiality. Contrast Crabbe and Wordsworth:

When winter stern his gloomy front uprears,
A sable void the barren earth appears;
The meads no more their former verdure boast,
Fast bound their streams, and all their beauty lost.
        (George Crabb, 'Inebriety', 1775)

My heart leaps up when I behold
A rainbow in the sky:
So was it when my life began,
So is it now I am a man,
So be it when I shall grow old
Or let me die!
        (William Wordsworth, 'My Heart Leaps
                Up', 1807)

However, Wordsworth did not always follow his own theory, nor were the Romantic poets uniform in style. Coleridge's revolt was towards more solemn and incantatory diction, as in: 'Five miles meandering with a mazy motion, /

Through wood and dale the sacred river ran' (*Kubla Khan*, 1816).

Philology and folklore. A development linked with the enthusiasm for medievalry was an increased interest in earlier forms of English. A few scholars had studied Old English texts since the 17c, particularly at Oxford, but in general it was supposed that English had emerged gradually from a cruder form to reach its highest quality towards the end of the 17c. Regard for the past coincided with the new comparative philology of the early 19c. By the middle of the century, Benjamin Thorpe, who had studied with Rasmus Rask in Denmark, and J. M. Kemble, a pupil of Jacob Grimm in Germany, produced new editions of nearly all the extant Old English poetry. The work of the Grimm brothers on early Germanic folklore was entirely in tune with Romantic interest in the 'primitive', and was part of an enthusiasm for folk traditions which also influenced the development of dialectology.

Influence. Although the dominance of Romanticism was over by the mid-19c, it influenced the early work of the Victorian poets. In poetry, the early work of W. B. Yeats and in fiction the novels of D. H. Lawrence are late manifestations of 'the Romantic spirit'. Such writers have had a great influence over many popular novelists (including writers of historical fiction and kinds of fantasy), as well as dramatic presentations on the cinema and television screen. The importance to some Romantic writers of 'romantic' love has also influenced the growth of a formulaic popular *romantic fiction* written and read throughout the English-speaking world. See AUGUSTAN, CELT, CLASSICISM, ENGLISH LITERATURE, GOTHIC, LITERARY CRITICISM, ROMANCE. [LITERATURE].   R.C.

ROMANTIC MOVEMENT/PERIOD/ POETS/REVIVAL. See ROMANTICISM.

ROMANY. See ROMANI.

ROOT [16c in this sense]. (1) Also sometimes *radical*. In traditional grammar and philology, the element, often monosyllabic, left after all affixes have been removed from a complex word: *-ceive* in *receive, help* in *unhelpfully, act* in *reactivation*. A root may or may not be a word, and may have several forms and meanings the further back it is traced in a language or languages. Compare BASE. (2) Also *root-word*. A word that is ancestral to a present-day word: the Latin verb *decidere*, the root of the English verb *decide* and the French verb *décider*. Compare ETYMON, ROOT-WORD. The classical elements in the vocabulary of English have often been listed and discussed, especially in textbooks and dictionaries,

as 'Latin and Greek roots', sometimes in the first sense given here, sometimes in the second sense, sometimes as a mix of the two. Both senses of *root* arise from a comparison between languages and plants, in which older forms of language are seen as hidden in the soil of history, nourishing the 'word-plants' that flourish above ground. Philologists and etymologists are the gardeners who sometimes dig them up for inspection.

In linguistics, a distinction is generally made not only between the two senses of *root* (above) but also between the terms *root* and *base*. The Latin *nescius* is the root or source of English *nice*, but is not a root in the philological sense. Rather, it consists of two elements, *ne* not, *scius* knowing. Its form cannot be detected anywhere 'inside' or 'under' present-day *nice*, which serves as a base for the formations *nicety* and *niceness*. *Ne* is a particle that also appears in *neuter*, and *scius* is made up of a linguistic root *sci* and an inflectional ending *-us*. *Sci* is present in the Latin *scientia* and its English derivative *science*; it is ancient, being the Latin 'descendant' of the Indo-European root **skei* to cut, split. This 'deep' primordial root also appears to underlie Old English *scinu* (Modern English *shin*), Old High German *scina* needle, Old Irish *scian* knife, Greek *schizein* to split, and Latin *scindere* to cut. See BASE, ETYMON, INDO-EUROPEAN ROOTS, ROOT-CREATION, ROOT-WORD, WORD-FORMATION. [HISTORY, WORD].   T.MCA.

ROOT-CREATION. A term in word-formation for the creation of a new root, base, or simple word. The process is rare compared with compounding and derivation, and is divided into *motivated root-creation* and *ex-nihilo root-creation*. By and large, motivated root-creation (in which a reason can be given for the formation of an item) is ad-hoc and echoic, the new form resembling one or more pre-existing forms. As with *cuckoo*, the new form may represent a real or imagined sound: *zap* the noise made by a ray-gun, *vroom* the sound of a powerful engine. By retaining the consonants and varying the vowel, a word like *splash* can be adapted to *splish, splosh, sploosh, splush*. In addition, a new form may be a reversal, an anagram, or some other adaptation of a pre-existing form. In ex-nihilo root-creation, however, there appears to be no lexicological way of accounting for the formation of a word: it has no known precursors, as with the trade name *Kodak* (invented in the US in 1888 by George Eastman) and the number *googol* (invented on request by a 9-year-old boy).

Although rare in general usage, ex-nihilo forms are common in fiction, and especially fantasy, in which writers often seek to escape the bonds of their language: Robert A. Heinlein's

Martian word *grok* suggests empathy and understanding: 'the ungrokkable vastness of ocean' (*Stranger in a Strange Land*, 1961). When sets of words are coined in a fantasy, however, escape from some degree of motivation is unlikely: for example, in Edgar Rice Burroughs's adventure novel *Tarzan at the Earth's Core* (1929), the inner world of Pellucidar is peopled by such creatures as the anagrammatic *tarag* and *jalok* (variants of *tiger* and *jackal*), the *thag* (a primeval ox, echoing *stag*), the *sagoth* (a gorilla-like hominid, echoing and perhaps blending *savage* and *Goth*), the clipped *horib* (a snake-like being overtly referred to as *horrid* and *horrible*), and the perhaps ex-nihilo *gyor*, a triceratops found on the *Gyor Cors* (the Gyor plains, whose name has a reduplicative quality). Such creations are usually nouns, but any part of speech is possible:

They first repeated the word 'sak' a number of times, and then Tars Tarkas made several jumps, repeating the same word before each leap; then, turning to me, he said, 'sak!' I saw what they were after, and gathering myself together I 'sakked' with such marvelous success that I cleared a good hundred and fifty feet (Burroughs, *A Princess of Mars*, 1912, ch. 4).

Although such ad-hoc creations seldom move into the wider world, some occasionally do. J. R. R. Tolkien's *hobbit* (1937) appears to echo and blend *hob* a rustic, and *rabbit*. John Wyndham's *triffid* (1951) echoes the botanical term *trifid* cleft three ways. The limits of actual or apparent root-creation are hard to establish, because it shades into such conventional processes of word-formation as turning names into words (*Hoover* becoming *to hoover a rug*), blending (*smog* from *smoke* and *fog*), and abbreviation (*mob* from *mobile vulgus*). A classic clipping is *tawdry*, from *tawdrie lace* (16c), in turn from *Seynt Audries lace*, as sold at St Audrey's Fair at Ely in East Anglia (*Audrey* in turn being a Normanization of Anglo-Saxon *Etheldreda*). Such creations can reasonably be identified as 'roots' because they can and often do become the foundations of more complex forms, such as *hobbitomane*, *Hoovermatic*, *Kodachrome*, *mobster*, *smog-bound*, *tawdriness*, and *triffid-like*. See BASE, ECHOISM, FANTASY, NEOLOGISM, ONOMATOPOEIA, PHON(A)ESTHESIA, ROOT, WORD-FORMATION. [WORD].   T.MCA.

ROOT-WORD, also **root word**.

A term in word-formation for a word, usually monosyllabic, that is prior or ancestral to one or more other words: *blood* the root-word of *bloody*, *bloodily*, *bloodhound*, *bloodthirsty*, *bloodthirstiness*, *cold-blooded*, *cold-bloodedly*, *bleed*, *bleeds*, *bleeding*, *nose bleed*. The term belongs in a group of related and sometimes overlapping terms with *root*, *base*, and *simple word*, and implies that every language has a certain number

or range of basic words and word elements, often presumed to be known by every user and listed somewhere. Although the common, high-frequency words of a language can more or less be so listed, the 'root' material of a language or group of languages is more than simply common words, and is distinct from what can be listed as everyday vocabulary. No one knows all the root forms of English or can easily decide whether certain freshly encountered items are new, old, meaningful, or meaningless. Any of the following might be ancient or have just been coined: *grise*, *quetch*, *smidge*, *tleen*. Checking in a dictionary does not guarantee a clear-cut answer about whether they are words or not: even the *OED* does not list all the monosyllables of English.

Some things can, however, be said of these and similar items: for example, that *tleen* is odd, because /tl/ as an initial cluster is phonologically un-English. If it occurs, it ought logically to be a borrowing from such a language as Tlingit in Alaska (which it is not, having been coined for the purposes of this article). The others, however, are possible; in the *Chambers English Dictionary* (1988), *grise* is listed as an obsolete verb (to shudder), *quetch* as a variant of *quich* (Spenser: to stir, cognate with *quake*). *Smidge*, though unlisted, could be authentic, a cousin of *smidge(o)n* and *smit*, which *Chambers* lists. Although used here as a novel root-word, its absolute novelty cannot be guaranteed: it may exist or have existed, somewhere, for some purpose, public or private, at some time. Used widely enough (for example, as a noun meaning a small amount, or as a verb meaning to smear in dabs), *smidge* could acquire an everyday use. Such items as *grise*, *quetch*, and *smidge* conform to a pattern of what English words are like, in terms of syllable, sound, and spelling. Items like **tleen*, **pwrg*, and **xacs* do not. However, as loans like *axolotl* from Nahuatl, *cwm* from Welsh, and *tsar* from Russian indicate, alien structure is no bar to entry into English. See BASE, ROOT, ROOT-CREATION, VOCABULARY CONTROL, WORD-FORMATION. [WORD].   T.MCA.

ROPER RIVER CREOLE, ROPER PIDGIN.
See KRIOL.

ROTTEN ENGLISH
[1980s]. A term used by the Nigerian writer Ken Saro-Wiwa to describe the mixed variety of English that he uses in the novel *Sozaboy* ['Soldier Boy'] (1985). In his preface, he says: 'Sozaboy's language is what I call "rotten English", a mixture of Nigerian pidgin English, broken English and occasional flashes of good, even idiomatic English. This language is disordered and disorderly. Born of a mediocre education and severely limited opportunities, it

borrows words, patterns and images freely. . . . To its speakers, it has the advantage of having no rules and no syntax. It thrives on lawlessness.' An example in *Lomber Eighteen* (that is, 'Number' or Chapter 18):

To talk true, I was not thinking of all these things, I was just thinking of my mama and my young wife Agnes. If my mama die, what will I talk? If that sozaman have pregnanted my young darling or even sef killed her because she no gree 'am, what will I say? Ah, God no gree bad thing, God no gree bad thing. I must to find my mama and my wife. We must to all return to Dukana and build fine house to live inside.

Compare WEST AFRICAN PIDGIN ENGLISH. [AFRICA, VARIETY]. T.MCA.

ROUGH [From Old English *rūh*]. (1) Rude, unmannerly, impolite, uncouth: *rough words*. (2) (Of accents, voices, and sounds) discordant, jarring, grating, noisy, harsh: 'It requires very little skill to make our language rough' (Samuel Johnson, *Rambler* 92, 1751). See (A)ESTHETICS. [STYLE]. T.MCA.

ROYAL. See BOOK.

ROYAL SOCIETY, full name *Royal Society of London for the Promotion of Natural Knowledge.* The oldest continuously functioning scientific society in Britain and the world. It was founded in 1660 as the *Royal Society for the Advancement of Experimental Philosophy*, and granted royal charters in 1662 and 1663, when it acquired its present name. The Society arose out of small, informal groups that met from time to time to discuss scientific matters in the spirit of Francis Bacon; among its founding members were the architect Christopher Wren, the chemist Robert Boyle, and Bishop John Wilkins. Isaac Newton served as president from 1703 to 1727. In its origins, the Society was largely a Puritan venture; it therefore received little royal patronage or state support, and as a result enjoyed great freedom of expression and action (although members took care to exclude politics and religion from their discussions). In its early years, the Society showed a brief inclination to 'improve the English tongue, particularly for philosophic purposes', setting up in 1664 a committee with that end in view. Among its 22 members were the poets John Dryden and Edmund Waller, Bishop Thomas Sprat, and the diarist John Evelyn. However, the committee met only a few times and achieved nothing, despite considering a grammar of English and the omission of superfluous letters from the orthography. In his *History of the Royal Society* (1667), Sprat continued the discussion by arguing that the Society should require of its members 'a close, naked, natural way of speaking; positive expressions; clear senses; a native easiness; bringing all

things as near the mathematical plainness as they can; and preferring the language of artisans, countrymen, and merchants, before that of wits and scholars'. The Society took such matters no further, however, and this limited exercise was as close as England came to forming anything like the Académie française. The journal *Philosophical Transactions of the Royal Society*, begun in 1665, is one of the world's earliest periodicals; it was later complemented in the early 19c by *Proceedings of the Royal Society*, which was edited for many years by Peter Mark Roget, compiler of *Roget's Thesaurus*. Among its many projects, the Society sponsored the first scientific expedition to the Pacific, under James Cook, a venture that led directly to British settlement in Australasia and the spread of English among the Polynesians. See ACADEMY, ARTIFICIAL LANGUAGE, LONDON, ROGET. [HISTORY, MEDIA, OCEANIA]. T.MCA.

ROYAL SOCIETY OF ARTS, full form *Royal Society for the Encouragement of Arts, Manufactures and Commerce.* Short form *RSA.* A body founded in London in 1754 with a commitment to teach and test commercial skills, including proficiency in English. The Society conducted examinations for native and foreign users before 1800, and has been influential in the 20c in EFL and English for Adult Literacy and Immigrants. Since 1988, its EFL examinations have been administered internationally by the U. of Cambridge Local Examination Syndicate. These include examinations introduced in 1967 by the RSA examination board for teachers of English as a foreign language, leading to a certificate known as *Royal Society of Arts: Teaching English as a Foreign Language (RSA/TEFL)*. See EXAMINING IN ENGLISH, UCLES. [EDUCATION, MEDIA]. W.S.

RP. See RECEIVED PRONUNCIATION.

R-PRONOUNCING AND NON-R-PRONOUNCING. See RHOTIC AND NON-RHOTIC.

RSA, RSA/TEFL. See ROYAL SOCIETY OF ARTS.

R-SOUNDS. No other consonant of English is as variable as that represented by the letter *r*. Although /r/ is one phoneme in English, there are six ways in which it is pronounced: (1) *A post-alveolar approximant.* This is made by raising the tip of the tongue behind, but without touching, the alveolar ridge, the lips usually rounded, the lower lip brought close to the upper teeth. It is dominant in EngE and common in AusE and NZE. If the tongue movement is omitted, the result is a sound like /w/, suggested by (often facetious) spellings using *w* instead of *r*: *wound*

*and wound the wugged wocks the wagged wascal
wan*. This usage has been noted in EngE variously: as an aristocratic shibboleth, an affectation, and a speech defect. (2) *A retroflex*. If the
tip of the tongue is raised further and curled back
towards the palate, the result is a retroflex *r*. It is
dominant in the US, Canada, Ireland, and in the
south-west of England, and gaining ground in
Scotland. (3) *An alveolar flap*. If the tongue strikes
the alveolar ridge as the tip is lowered, the result
is a flapped *r*. This usage is characteristic of some
varieties of IndE. (4) *An alveolar tap*. If the tongue
strikes the ridge as the tip is raised, the result is a
tapped *r*. This usage is dominant in ScoE, common among older speakers of RP in England,
and typical of speakers of English in South Africa
of Afrikaans background. When used by RP
speakers in phrases like 'very American', Americans report hearing *Veddy Ameddican*. (5) *An
alveolar trill or roll*. If the tongue is held in such a
position that the air-stream causes it to vibrate
against the alveolar ridge, the result is a trill or
roll, a usage marked in Spanish by a double *r*
(contrasting *pero*, 'but', with *perro*, 'dog'). It is
widely regarded as a typically Scottish 'rolled r',
and is so promoted in stage and jocular stereotypes. (6) *A uvular* /r/. If the tongue is pulled
backwards towards the uvula, three kinds of *r*
can be made: a uvular approximant, a uvular
fricative, and a uvular trill (as in Parisian-French).
Small numbers of speakers with a uvular *r* can be
found in various parts of northern Britain, such
as north-east England (the *Durham* or *Northumberland burr*) and south-east Scotland (the
Berwickshire burr). See ALVEOLAR, BURR, CON-
SONANT, GEORDIE, INTRUSIVE R, LINKING R, LIQUID,
L-SOUNDS, R, RETROFLEX, RHOTACISM, RHOTIC AND
NON-RHOTIC. [SPEECH].   G.K., T.MCA.

RUBRIC [14c: from Latin *rubrica* red ochre, from
ruber red]. (1) A heading of part of a document,
written or printed in red or in special lettering, so
as to stand out; a word, phrase, sentence, or passage marked in such a way. (2) A direction for
the conduct of a Christian service, inserted especially in red in a liturgical book; a red-letter entry
of a saint's name in a Church calendar (whence
red-letter day). (3) A title or heading of a section
in a legal code, also originally in red. (4) A title,
category, procedure, protocol, explanatory comment, gloss, or instruction for an exercise in a
textbook or workbook. Compare GLOSS,
HEADING, TITLE. [WRITING].   T.MCA.

RULE [12c: Middle English *reule*, *riule*, from Old
French *riule*, from Latin *regula* a straight stick,
pattern]. (1) A principle that contributes to the
organization and control of a group, activity, system, etc., and has the backing of some kind of
authority. See AUTHORITY, CANON, CONVENTION,

NORM. (2) In language teaching and learning, a
formal statement about the use of an aspect of a
language, such as regular and irregular verbs in
French. Traditionally, such rules have often been
learned by heart. They are both prescriptive and
proscriptive. See ANALOGY AND ANOMALY,
DESCRIPTIVE AND PRESCRIPTIVE GRAMMAR, IRREG-
ULAR, REGULAR. (3) In linguistics, a formal statement of the relationship between structures or
units, such as the rules for forming plurals in
English. Such rules are intended to be descriptive:
explicit statements of how a language works (or
may work), representing procedures applied by
native speakers without conscious reflection when
they talk to each other. It is not always easy to
keep the first and second senses of the term distinct from the third sense. See DESCRIPTIVISM AND
PRESCRIPTIVISM. (4) In printing, a thin strip of
metal or its equivalent, used for printing a solid
or decorative line or lines. Such a line the length
of an em is an *em rule*, of an en, an *en rule*; such
rules are used in punctuation as longer or shorter
dashes. See DASH, EM, EN, REGULAR. [GRAMMAR].
                                    S.G., T.MCA.

RUNE [17c: (through Danish writers on antiquit-
ies) from the Old Norse and Icelandic *rún*, but
compare Old English *rún* a dark saying, secret,
mystery, letter, from which some commentators
directly derive the term]. A character in an ancient
script of 24 angular letters, usually cut on wood
or carved in stone, and known as either *the runic
alphabet* or *Futhark/Futhorc* (with or without an
initial capital: from the names of its first six
letters, regarded as equivalents of *f*, *u*, *th*, *a* or *o*,
r, and *k* or *c*). The origin of the script is uncertain;
most probably it was adapted by the Goths from
the Etruscan alphabet and later influenced by
Roman. It was used from the 3c to the 16/17c,
especially in Scandinavia, Iceland, and Britain, to
write Germanic languages. Runes, long regarded
as magical, have been used on monuments, in
charms, in fortune-telling (*casting the runes*), and
as decorative motifs. Each has a mnemonic name
beginning with the sound of the letter, such as
feoh (property) and *ūr* (bison) for the *f* and *u*
symbols. The letters *thorn* (thorn) and *wynn* (joy)
were added to the Roman alphabet for writing
Old English, and the runic name *æsc* (ash) was
given to the digraph *æ*. The term *runestaff* refers
to both a magic wand inscribed with runes and a
runic calendar or almanac. *Rune* may also refer
to something written in runes, to a saying or verse
with a cryptic meaning or used in casting a spell,
to a division of a Finnish poem, to a character in
comparable scripts (especially in fictional writings), and to anything perceived as similar:

In some English shires, if the house were sufficiently
eloquent, few would mind if its owner never spoke,
equipped as the English are to lip-read every last cornice

and swag, to read the runes from herbs and vegetable gardens, . . . and pronounce these trappings socially acceptable: or, disastrously, not' (Angela Lambert, 'Money may talk but the house says it all', *Independent*, 22 Dec. 1990).

Runic writings survive in *c*.4,000 inscriptions and some manuscripts. There were at least three varieties: *Early* or *Common Germanic/Teutonic*, before *c*.800; *Anglo-Saxon* or *Anglian*, in Britain, *c*.6–12c; and *Scandinavian* or *Nordic*, *c*.8–13c. The Common Germanic script had 24 letters, divided into three groups called *ættir* (eights). Anglo-Saxon added letters to represent sounds of Old English not present in the languages for which Common Germanic was used, and by the 10c had 33 letters. See ALPHABET, ANGLIAN, ASH, BRADLEY, GOTHIC, THORN, WYN(N). [EUROPE, HISTORY, WRITING].   T.MCA.

RUNNING HEAD, also **running title, running headline**. A heading at the top of every page or every other page of text, especially in a book. Compare HEADERS AND FOOTERS. See CATCHWORD. [TECHNOLOGY].   T.MCA.

RUSSIAN [Known to its speakers as *russkiy*]. The major language of the Slavonic branch of the Indo-European language family, the language of the Russian people and the state language of the former Soviet Union, written in Cyrillic script. It has *c*.150m native speakers, and at least another 50m inhabitants of the ex-Soviet territories, and others, use it as a second language. Although the vast majority of its speakers live in the successor States of the USSR, Russian is used internationally in economic, scientific, and military contexts, and in the United Nations Organization, where it is one of the six official languages. A thousand years or more ago, a relatively undiversified East Slavonic dialect, generally known as *Old Russian*, was spoken in and around the approximate area of present-day Western European Russia, the Ukraine, and Byelorussia. Out of it emerged the Russian, Ukrainian, and Byelorussian languages. An early form of standard modern Russian developed in the 16c, centred on the educated speech of Moscow, and was influenced from the 17c onward by other European languages, especially Dutch and French. It gained international status in the 19c because of the power of Imperial Russia and the achievements of such writers as Alexander Sergeevich Pushkin (1799-1837) and Lev Nikolaevich Tolstoy (1828-1910). The Revolution of 1917, which led to the creation of the Soviet Union, associated the language closely with the maintenance and spread of Communism.

Russian in English. The impact of Russian on English has been slight in comparison with that of French or Spanish, but many of its loanwords stand out because of their exotic spellings and connotations. Borrowings fall into two broad categories: (1) Traditional cultural expressions: *bors(c)h* a soup based on beetroot, *borzoi* (swift) a kind of hound, *czar/tsar* (from Russian *tsar'*, Old Russian *tsĭsarĭ*, Gothic and Greek *kaisar*, Latin *caesar*) emperor, king, *dros(h)ky* (from *drozhki*, diminutive of *drogi* à dray-cart or hearse) an open, four-wheeled carriage, *r(o)uble* (originally from *rubl'* a silver bar) the unit of Soviet currency, *steppe* (from *step'* lowland) a prairie, *troika* (threesome) a carriage drawn by three horses side by side, a group of three acting together, a triumvirate, *ukase/ukaz* an edict of the tsar, a decree or diktat, *vodka* (diminutive of *voda* water) an alcoholic drink. (2) Soviet and Communist usage: *gulag* (acronym of *Glávnoe upravlénie ispravítel'no-trudovy̆kh lagereĭ* Main Directorate of Corrective Labour Camps) a labour camp, especially for political prisoners, *kolkhoz* (from *kollektívnoe khozyáĭstvo* collective household) a collective farm. This group contains many expressions, including acronyms, coined in Russian from Latin and Greek: *commissar* (from *komissár*) a political officer; *agitprop* political agitation and propaganda (from the organization title *Agitpropbyuro*, from *agitatsiya* and *propaganda*), *apparat* party organization, *Comintern/Komintern* (from *Kommunistíchiskiĭ Internatsionál*) the Communist International organization (1919-43), *cosmonaut* (from *kosmonávt* 'universe sailor') a Soviet astronaut, *intelligentsia* intellectuals considered as a group or class.

English in Russian. The impact of English on Russian has been largely lexical, especially in the following areas, and has been increasing in recent years: (1) Sport and entertainment, etc.: *basketbol, chempion, futbol, kemping, khobbi* (hobby), *khokkey, kloun, klub, match, nokaut, ralli, rekord, sport, sportsmen, sprinter, striptiz, tent, yumor*. (2) Politics, management, etc.: *boykot, interv'yu, lider, miting, pamflet*. (3) Food and drink: *bifshteks, dzhin, grog, keks, puding*. (4) Transport, commerce, and travel: *konteyner, motel', tanker, tonnel'* or *tunnel', trauler, trolleybus*. (5) Culture and technology: *bitnik* (beatnik), *detektiv* (meaning also *detective novel*), *komfort, komp'yuter, lift, poni, radar, servis, toster*. See AMERICAN LANGUAGES, ASIAN LANGUAGES, BORROWING, BURGESS, EUROPEAN LANGUAGES, -GLISH AND -LISH, INDO-EUROPEAN LANGUAGES, JONES (D.), PAMPHLET, PROPAGANDA, SLAV(ON)IC LANGUAGES, SPELLING REFORM. [ASIA, EUROPE, LANGUAGE]. F.E.K., T.MCA.

S

S, s [Called 'ess']. The 19th letter of the Roman alphabet as used for English. It originated as the Phoenician symbol for a voiceless sibilant. The Greeks adopted it as the letter *sigma* (Σ), with lower-case variants according to its position in a word: medial (σ) and final (ς). The Etruscans and then the Romans further adapted the form to create S. A straightened lower-case variant (ſ), known as *long s* was used in script and (except in final position) in printing until the 18c.

Sound values: voiceless and voiced. (1) In English, the letter *s* represents a sibilant alveolar fricative, both voiceless /s/ and voiced /z/, that is sometimes palatalized. (2) Initial *s* is normally voiceless, and precedes vowels (*sat, sail, set, seat, sit, site, soon, soul, south*) and consonants (*scare, skill, slip, smith, snip, sphere, spit, squeal, still, svelte, swing*). (3) Final *s* in monosyllables is voiced in *as, has, his, is, was,* but not in *gas, yes, this,* nor in most accents after *u: us, bus, pus, thus*. Final double *s* is always voiceless: contrast *his/hiss*. (4) Certain common *s*-endings of Romance or Greek origin are voiceless (*-as* as in *atlas, -is* as in *cannabis, -os* as in *rhinoceros, -ous* as in *famous, -us* as in *terminus*), but final *-es* is typically voiced (*species, theses, Hercules*). (5) The Romance prefix *dis-* varies, with voicing in *disaster, disease* but not in *disagreeable, disgrace*. (6) The Germanic prefix *mis-* never has voiced *s: misadventure, mischance, misgovern, mishap, misspell*. (7) Between vowels, *s* is normally voiced: *bosom, busy, cousin, easy, feasible, hesitate, misery, peasant, poison, position, present, prison, reason, rosy, visit, weasel* (contrast *admissible, blossom, gossip, lesson, admissible, possible*). (8) Intervocalic *s* is voiceless in *basin, mason, sausage* (derived from earlier French *c*: compare Modern French *bassin, maçon, saucisse*), and usually also in *-osity* (*curiosity, luminosity*). (9) Greek-derived words commonly have voiceless medial *s: analysis, asylum, basalt,* *crisis, dose, episode, thesis* (but not *music, physics*). (10) After medial consonants *s* is usually voiceless: *balsam, arsenal, gipsy* but note *clumsy, crimson, damsel*. There is variation after *n: answer, ransom,* but *Kansas, pansy*. It is usually voiceless before voiceless medial consonants (*asphalt, basket, hospital, sister, whistle*), but otherwise voiced (*husband, wisdom, muslin, spasm, dismal*).

-CE, -SE, -ZE. (1) A final *e* sometimes distinguishes voiced and voiceless *s* (*tens/tense*), but the distinction is rarely reliable (contrast *chase/ phase*) compared with voiceless *-ce* (*hens/hence, advise/advice*) and voiced *-ze* (*dose/doze*). *Lens* is unusual: a voiced singular without final *e*. The cluster *-nse* usually has voiceless *s* as in *tense/ dense,* but note *cleanse*. The ambiguity of *-se* is not removed by contrasting forms with *-ce, -ze: since/rinse* both have voiceless /s/, while *fleece/freeze* are distinct. The dominant pattern of voiced or voiceless *-se* varies according to preceding vowel, but uncertainty is high after the long *e*-sound, as in *lease/please, geese/cheese*. (2) The pronunciation of *grease* (noun and verb) varies from accent to accent: /s/ in RP, /z/ commonly in ScoE, and regionally varied in AmE. (3) In *lose/loose* it is the consonant sounds that differ but the vowel spellings that vary. (4) Some words vary /s, z/ according to grammatical category, as in *close* (adjective and verb) and *house, use* (noun and verb) (*closest/closed, house/ houses/housed* and *useful/useable*), sometimes using *c* for the voiceless alternative or *z* for the voiced, as in *advise/advice, glass/glaze*. (5) AmE sometimes prefers *-se* for BrE *-ce*: AmE *defense, offense, pretense, practise, license, vise* (the tool), BrE *defence, offence, pretence, practice, licence, vice*. (6) *Erase, eraser, erasure* are normally voiced in BrE but voiceless in AmE.

THE CAPITAL LETTER						THE SMALL LETTER				
EARLY FORMS				CURRENT FORMS		EARLY FORMS			CURRENT FORMS	
Phoenician	Greek	Etruscan	Roman (Latin)	roman	italic	Roman cursive	Roman uncial	Carolingian minuscule	roman	italic
W	ϟΣ	⅂	S	S	*S*	ς	S	**S**	s	*s*

Palatalized S. (1) Before *i* or *u*, there are some common patterns of palatalization, with *s* pronounced *sh*, or, if voiced, *zh*. This arises by assimilation of a following *y*-sound, represented either by *i* or by *u* pronounced with an initial *y*-sound, as in *puce*, *pure*. Sometimes assimilation is incomplete, with *s* kept unpalatalized in careful speech: for example, /s/ in *issue* and /z/ in *casual*. Conversely, palatalization is sometimes extended to words like *assume* ('ashoom'). (2) Initial palatalized *s* is confined to *sugar*, *sure* (and the derivatives *assurance*, *insurance*), but palatalization is common before final unstressed vowels: geographical terms such as *Asia*, *Persia* are heard with both voiced and voiceless palatalized *s*. (3) Before final -*ion*, *s* is palatalized and voiceless after *l* or *n* (*impulsion*, *tension*), but has optional voicing after *r* (*version*, *immersion*, but not *torsion*), and regular voicing after vowels (*invasion*, *lesion*, *vision*, *erosion*, *fusion*). (4) Voiceless palatalized *s* after vowels is doubled: *passion*, *session*, *mission*, *concussion*: compare *Russian*, but unpalatalized *ss* in *hessian*. (5) Other endings preceded by palatalized *s* are -*ual*, -*ure*, voiced as in *casual*, *visual*, *usual*, *measure*, *leisure*, but voiceless in *fissure*, *censure*, *tonsure*, *sensual*. The list does not include -*ial*, before which the sibilant is written as *c* (*facial*) or *t* (*spatial*), for historical reasons.

Silent S. (1) Postvocalic *s* is often silent in French-derived words (*isle*, *apropos*, *chamois*, *chassis*, *corps*, *debris*, *fracas*, *precis*, *viscount*, *Grosvenor*, *Illinois*), or where inserted by false analogy with French: *island*, unrelated to *isle* (Middle English *yland*, etc.); *aisle* (compare French *aile*), which probably acquired its *s* by confusion with *isle*; *demesne*, cognate with *domain*. (2) Silent final *s* in French-derived words (*corps*, *fracas*) is often pronounced in the plural (*two army corps*, *frequent fracas*).

Double S. (1) *Ss* is normally voiceless (*pass*, *assess*, *dismiss*; *message*, *passage*, *possible*), but it is sometimes voiced in medial position (*brassiere*, *dessert*, *dissolve*, *hussar*, *scissors*, *possess*), and optionally in *hussy*. (2) In final position, *ss* typically occurs in monosyllables (*press*, *miss*, *loss*, *fuss*, *pass*), less often in polysyllables (*compass*, *embarrass*, *morass*), but commonly in the suffixes -*less* (*hopeless*) and -*ness* (*kindness*), derived from Germanic sources, and the suffix -*ess* (*hostess*, *princess*), derived from Romance sources. (3) The Latin prefix *ad*- becomes *as*- when assimilated to roots beginning with *s*: *assault*, *assemble*, *assimilate*, *assume*. (4) The prefixes *dis*-, *mis*- similarly produce *ss* when the following syllable begins with *s* (*misspell*, *dissatisfy*), but the *s* of *dis*- is assimilated into the digraph *sh* in *dishevelled* (formerly *discheveled*, etc.). (5) Some words optionally have double final *s* in their inflected forms: *biased/biassed*, *buses/busses*, *focusing/focussing*, *gased/gassed*. (6) *Ss* after a long vowel, as in *bass*, *gross* is rare, forms such as *face*, *dose* being more usual.

SC and SCH. The letter *s* occurs frequently with various values in conjunction with *c* and *ch*: *effervesce*, *schedule*, *scheme*, *scent*, *schism*, *schist*. See c.

SH. (1) The digraph *sh* represents a distinct English phoneme, a voiceless alveolar fricative /ʃ/, which mostly arose from palatalization of early *s*, whether in Old English or Old French. (2) Old English used *sc* rather than *sh*, *ship* being written *scip*, and *sh* only became general after *c.*1450, probably by analogy with other -*h* digraphs such as *ch*, *th*, *wh*. The evolution is demonstrated by such Old English and Middle English forms as *Englisc*, *Englisch*, *Englissche*, *Englisshe*. Nevertheless *sh* is most typically found in words of Old English origin: *shadow*, *shall*, *shape*, *shed*, *ship*, *shoot*, *shot*, *shut*, *fish*. (3) A French-derived palatalized *s* was frequently changed to *sh* as in *abash*, *anguish*, *ashet*, *brush*, *bushel*, *cash*, *cushion*, *fashion*, *leash*, *parish*, and verbs ending in -*ish* (*abolish*, *famish*, *finish*, *punish*).

ST. (1) The sequence *st* is sometimes pronounced as /s/, *ss/st* having the same value in *hassle/castle*, and *st* having different values in *whistle*, *pistol*. (2) The /s/ value of *st* occurs mainly before -*en* (*fasten*, *listen*, *moisten*) and -*le* (*castle*, *wrestle*, *thistle*, *jostle*, *rustle*), although elision of /t/ before *m* in *Christmas*, *postman* has the same effect.

Inflectional S. (1) Final *s* is commonly an inflection, as in the plural of most nouns (*year/years*), the third-person singular of the present tense of most verbs (*eat/eats*, *need/needs*), and in possessive forms with apostrophe (*my uncle's house*). (2) Inflectional *s* is normally voiced, as after all vowels and voiced consonants (*rays*, *skis*, *skies*, *rows*, *rues*, *bananas*, *purrs*, *paws*, *ploys*, *ploughs*, *ribs*, *rods*, *rugs*, *ridges*, *rolls*, *rims*, *runs*, *roars*, *races*, *roses*, *rushes*, *wreathes*, *arrives*, *boxes*, *razes*), but not after voiceless non-sibilant consonants (*tics*, *tiffs*, *treks*, *tips*, *cliques*, *sits*, *myths*). (3) Possessive *s* is similarly voiced, as in the pronouns *his*, *hers*, *ours*, *yours*, *theirs*, *whose*, but not *its* after *t*, and *is* is similarly devoiced in the contraction *it's*. (4) The use of the possessive apostrophe raises uncertainties when a noun ends in *s*. Personal names ending in *s* may add only an apostrophe (*Achilles'*), but *'s* is also common (*Achilles's*), while in set phrases the apostrophe may be dropped (*Achilles tendon*). The OED gives various conventions in plant names, such as *Venus's flytrap*, *Venus' hair*, *Venus looking-glass*. Fowler has suggested using only an apostrophe before *sake*, producing *for good-ness' sake*, and even *for conscience' sake*, but the practice is rare.

Singulars and plurals. (1) Noun plurals and verbs ending in a sibilant generally add *-es*: *lenses, buzzes, masses, foxes, wishes, touches, witches. Riches*, though a plural form, derives from singular French *richesse*. (2) Some names of diseases (*mumps, measles*) may be treated as plural, but *pox* (*smallpox, chickenpox*, etc.) functions as singular rather than as the plural of *pock* (its ultimate origin). (3) *Forceps, gallows*, and BrE *innings* may be singular or plural, although *gallows* was formerly plural. Fowler's *Modern English Usage* (1983) has recommended the plural *gallowses* if needed, and gives *inningses* as a BrE alternative to *innings* (compare AmE singular *inning*; plural *innings*, in baseball). (4) Tools with two arms (*pincers, pliers, scissors, shears, tweezers*) and garments with two legs (BrE *pyjamas*, AmE *pajamas, shorts, tights, trousers*) are grammatically plural, but semantically singular; plurality is expressed by preceding *pairs of*, and *-es* is never added: no **scissorses*. (5) Family names of Welsh provenance, such as *Jones* and *Williams*, add *-es* for their plural, but are sometimes written with an apostrophe even when not possessive: *the Williams'*. (6) Plurals are widely misspelt as possessives: for example, the so-called greengrocer's apostrophe: **6 apple's*: see APOSTROPHE[1], PLURAL. (7) For the pattern *half/halves*, see F. (8) For plurals of words ending in *o*, as in *potatoes, pianos*, see O. (9) For changing *y* to *ies*, as in *pony/ponies*, see I.

S/T variation. (1) Some variations of *s* and *t* have arisen in such related forms as *pretension/pretentious, torsion/distortion*. (2) S/t variation with corresponding changed pronunciation occurs in the endings *-sis/-tic* in sets of related words from Greek: *analysis/analytic(al), neurosis/neurotic, psychosis/ psychotic, synthesis/synthetic*. (3) The *-gloss/-glot* variation in *diglossia/glossary/glottal/polyglot* derives from dialect differences in ancient Greek. (4) Different derivational paths have been followed from Latin and/or French to English in the doublets *poison/potion, reason/ration*.

-IZE, -ISE. (1) Variation occurs between *s* and *z* in such words as *organise/organize, systematise/systematize*. Here the *-ize* ending reflects Greek origin, while *-ise* reflects the adaptation of some of these words during their passage through French, as in the verbs *organiser, systématiser*. (2) The *-ise* form is widespread in BrE and virtually universal in AusE, whereas the *-ize* form is universal in AmE, favoured in CanE, and is employed by some British publishers, such as Oxford University Press. (3) In BrE *-ize* is not used in some two dozen verbs based

on Latin roots, such as *advise, advertise, compromise, surprise*. In verbs with base nouns in *-lysis* (*analysis, paralysis*), BrE has *-lyse* (*analyse, paralyse*) and AmE *-lyze* (*analyze, paralyze*).

Lost letters. (1) An initial *s* in the Latin roots of some words has been assimilated by the prefix *ex-*, but appears after other prefixes, as in *exert/insert, exist/consist, expect/respect, expire/perspire, extinguish/distinguish, exult/result. S* has been similarly assimilated in *expatiate, exude*. (2) *X* has assimilated *s* from the now archaic forms *bucksome, cockscomb, pocks* in present day *buxom, coxcomb, pox*. (3) Some words that now begin with *s* have lost a preceding vowel by aphesis, although it may survive in cognates: *sample* from *example, squire* from *esquire, state* from *estate, story* from *history*. See ALPHABET, APHESIS, ESH, LETTER[1], LONG S, PALATE, SPELLING, VOICE. [WRITING].   C.U.

SABIR [1860s: from Portuguese *sabir* to know]. A name for the original *lingua franca*, the earliest known pidgin based on a European language. Its vocabulary is drawn mainly from the southern Romance languages, and it was used from the time of the Crusades (11–13c) until the beginning of the 20c for communication among Europeans, Turks, Arabs, and others in the Levant, and is believed by some scholars to have served as a base for the development of Atlantic and other pidgin languages first used by Portuguese sailors and traders and later by the British, Dutch, French, and Spanish. See LINGUA FRANCA, PIDGIN. [LANGUAGE].   S.R.

SAGA [Early 18c: from Norse *saga* what is said. Cognate with English *say*)]. (1) A medieval Icelandic prose narrative such as *Njáls Saga*, the story of a blood feud. Some sagas deal with history, others with legend, but all have a heroic outlook and emphasize family loyalty and personal honour. There is some saga-like material in the old English epic poem *Beowulf*. Snorri Sturlusson's saga *Heimskringla* (Circle of the World, *c*.1230) includes the reign of Canute and mentions Viking raids on England. In the anonymous *Gunnlaugs Saga* (late 13c), the hero visits the court of Ethelred the Unready and recites a poem in the king's honour. In this connection, the narrator explains that 'the language was then the same in England as in Norway and Denmark. But languages changed in England when William the Bastard won England.' This remark suggests that the passage of time had blurred the memory of the Danelaw. The English poet William Morris, who visited Iceland, collaborated in translating sagas and derived from them such poems as 'Sigurd the Volsung' (1876). (2) A generic term in the 20c for a long novel or series of novels, especially about a family. When

John Galsworthy named his series *The Forsyte Saga* (1922), he called the title ironic, but the usage caught on and is now widespread. Many *family sagas* have been written, such as Susan Howatch's *Penmarric* (1971), set in Cornwall (blurb: 'the saga of a family divided against itself'). Many such sagas are performed as television miniseries. (3) An informal term for a long and tedious personal story: *He told us the saga of how his marriage broke up.* [HISTORY, LITERATURE].   R.C., P.C.

SAINT CHRISTOPHER AND NEVIS, also St Christopher-Nevis, St Kitts and Nevis, St Kitts-Nevis. Official title: *Federation of St Christopher and Nevis.* A Caribbean country and member of the Commonwealth, consisting of St Christopher/Kitts, Nevis, and Sombrero. Capital: Basseterre. Currency: the East Caribbean dollar. Economy: sugar, vegetable oil. Head of state: the British monarch, represented by a governor-general. Population: 47,000 (1988), 55,000 (projection for 2000). Ethnicity: 94% African, 6% mixed. Languages: English, Creole. Education: primary 88%, secondary 60%, tertiary 5%, literacy 92%. In 1623, St Kitts became the first English colony in the Caribbean. Britain and France disputed control of the islands until in 1783 they became British under the Treaty of Versailles. They were united by the Federal Act of 1882 along with Anguilla. In 1980, Anguilla chose to remain a British dependency and in 1983 the other islands became independent. See ANGUILLA, CARIBBEAN, ENGLISH. [AMERICAS, NAME, VARIETY].   T.MCA.

SAINT HELENA, commonly written **St Helena**. A British dependency in the South Atlantic. Capital and port: Jamestown. Currency: the pound sterling. Administration: a governor and legislative council. Economy: fishing, agriculture, handicrafts, postage stamps; passenger and cargo services sail to the UK and South Africa; there is no airfield. Population: 5,500 (1984), a mix of European (mostly British), Asian, and African origin, known as *Yamstalks*. Religion: an Anglican majority. Sole language: English. When the Portuguese navigator João da Nova Castella discovered the island on 21 May 1502, he named it after the mother of the Roman emperor Constantine, the saint of the Eastern Church whose feast day it was. St Helena was a port of call for ships travelling to the East Indies, may have been occupied by the Dutch in the mid-17c, and was annexed and occupied by the East India Company in 1659. In 1873, nearly half the population was imported slaves. Its remoteness made it the choice for Napoleon's exile, 1815–21. By the later 1830s, the island was under direct British rule. In 1922,

Ascension Island was made a dependency, and in 1966 St Helena received a measure of autonomy. Local pronunciation includes: (1) Substitution of /w/ for /v/, so that *very* is pronounced 'werry'. (2) Replacement of /θ/ and /ð/ by /f/ and /d/, so that for example *bath* is pronounced 'baf', and *the* is 'de'. (3) Use of /ɔɪ/ for /aɪ/, so that *the island* is 'de oiland'. Special vocabulary includes: (1) Names for indigenous plants and animals, such as *gum wood, hog fish, old-father-live-forever, wire bird* (a small plover, the only native land bird). (2) Such usages as *jug up* to arrange flowers in a vase; *mug* a jug or pitcher for pouring; *make free with yourself* to take risks. Place-names on the island provide the contrast between the classical references in *Mount Actaeon* and *Diana Peak* and the more typically colonial *James Bay* and *Sandy Bay*. See ASCENSION (ISLAND), ENGLISH, TRISTAN DA CUNHA. [NAME, VARIETY].   J.B., T.MCA.

SAINT KITTS. See SAINT CHRISTOPHER AND NEVIS.

SAINT LUCIA, commonly written **St Lucia**. A Caribbean country and member of the Commonwealth. Capital: Castries. Currency: the East Caribbean dollar. Economy: agriculture, tourism. Head of state: the British monarch, represented by a governor-general. Population: 146,000 (1988), 200,000 (projection for 2000). Ethnicity: 90% African, 5% mixed, 3% East Indian. Languages: English (official), French Creole. Education: primary 79%, secondary 25%, tertiary 5%, literacy 78%. Columbus may have landed in 1502, and in 1605 and 1638 the English made attempts to colonize the island. In 1650, St Lucia, Grenada, and Martinique were purchased by two Frenchmen, after which ownership of St Lucia was disputed by England and France until in 1814 it became British by the Treaty of Paris. The island became independent in 1979. See CARIBBEAN, ENGLISH, FRENCH, WALCOTT. [AMERICAS, NAME, VARIETY].   T.MCA.

SAINT VINCENT AND THE GRENADINES, commonly written **St Vincent and the Grenadines**. A Caribbean country and member of the Commonwealth, including the islands of St Vincent, Balliceau, Bequia, Canouan, Isle D'Quatre, and Mustique. Capital: Kingstown. Head of state: the British monarch, represented by a governor-general. Currency: the East Caribbean dollar. Economy: agriculture. Population: 113,000 (1988), 135,000 (projection for 2000). Ethnicity: 65% African, 25% mixed, 4% East Indian. Languages: English (official), French Creole. Education: primary 90%, secondary 40%, tertiary 5%, literacy 85%. Columbus visited the area in 1498. Europeans could only settle in St Vincent after making treaties with the local Caribs. The British and French competed for the island until 1763, when it became British by the Treaty of Paris. In 1773, the Caribs agreed to divide the island with the British, but grew resentful and with French help rebelled in 1795. Most were deported in 1796 to islands in the Gulf of Honduras. St Vincent became part of the Windward Island colony in 1871 and the group became independent in 1979. See CARIBBEAN, ENGLISH. [AMERICAS, NAME, VARIETY].   T.MCA.

SAMANA, also **Samaná English**, **Samaná Creole English**. An offshoot of the English-based creole used on plantations in the southern US that was transplanted to the Samaná Peninsula of the Dominican Republic when blacks settled there in the 1820s. Currently spoken by some 8,000 people, Samaná English is much more de-creolized than the variety spoken in the Bahamas, despite the relative linguistic isolation of both groups. The Samaná-speakers were surrounded by a French colony (Haiti) and a Spanish colony (San Domingo), but remained isolated from such influences and from English-speakers until the 1930s. The type of English taken to Samaná and the extent to which it was de-creolized are issues debated by scholars; de-creolization may already have been far advanced in certain areas of the US before the breakup of the plantation system. This may be one reason why Samaná appears to be close to standard English. The present older generation were schooled mainly in English and some remain monolingual; most of their children, however, are bilingual in Spanish and English and have become more integrated into the Dominican Republic through intermarriage with Spanish-speakers. Spanish terms have been borrowed or calqued into Samaná: for example, *gain money* from *gañar dinero*. Compare GULLAH. See BLACK ENGLISH VERNACULAR, CARIBBEAN ENGLISH CREOLE. [AMERICAS, VARIETY].   S.R.

SAMIZDAT. See PAMPHLET.

SAMOA. See NEW ZEALAND ENGLISH, WESTERN SAMOA.

SANDALWOOD ENGLISH. See BEACH LA MAR.

SANSKRIT, also, especially formerly, **Sanscrit** [17c: from Sanskrit *saṃskṛta* put together, well-formed, perfected]. The dominant classical and scholarly language of the Indian subcontinent, the sacred language of Hinduism (with Pali) a scriptural language of Buddhism, and the oldest known member of the Indo-European language family. It is usually written in the Devanagari script, which runs from left to right. The major forms are *Vedic Sanskrit*, the medium of the Vedas and Upanishads (known as *daivī vāk* divine speech), and *Classical Sanskrit*, whose texts include the two epic poems, the *Mahabharata* (of which the *Bhagavad-Gita* is a section), reputedly by the poet sage Vyasa, and the *Ramayana*, reputedly by the poet sage Valmiki. The classical language was systematized by the grammarian Panini in the late first millennium BC. Much as Latin influenced European languages, Sanskrit has influenced many languages in South and South-East Asia. Since the 19c, it has also provided loans to European languages including English and French. The most apparent of these loans relate to religion, philosophy, and culture, such as *ahimsa*, *chakra*, *guru*, *karma*, *kundalini*, *mahatma*, *pundit*, *swami*, and *yoga/yogi*, but less direct loanwords in English (borrowed through other languages) include *carmine*, *cheetah*, *chintz*, *chutney*, *juggernaut*, *jungle*, and *jute*.

All major modern Indian languages (both Indo-Aryan and Dravidian) have a Sanskritized register, used in religious and secular contexts. Indian English, especially when concerned with Hindu religion and philosophy, also freely uses Sanskrit terms, and Indian literature in English makes use of such conventions from Sanskrit as repetition of main themes in paragraphs and an abundance of compounds and embedded clauses. Sanskrit words appear in English texts in two forms: fully Anglicized, as with the variants *pundit* and *pandit* (through Hindi *paṇḍit*); or, in scholarly writings, with various diacritics, following the conventions for transliterating Sanskrit into the Roman alphabet, as with *paṇḍita*. A representative scholarly text using full transliterations is:

In the *Bṛhad-āraṇyaka Upaniṣad* (3.9.1) we are told that, when Śākalya asked the sage Yājñavalkya what was the number of the gods, the sage gave a cryptic answer (Alain Daniélou, *Hindu Polytheism*, 1964).

Differences in meaning and use often match the different styles: for example, *paṇḍita* means a learned *brahmin* (or *brahman*, or *brāhmaṇa*); *pandit* may have the same meaning and is used as a title for such a person, as in *Pandit Nehru*; *pundit* may have the same meaning and use, but is more fully integrated into English, in which it commonly refers to an expert: 'Nobody dared to predict how long the financial upheaval would last, but every dealer and pundit agreed that it reflected international anxiety and not the economy' (*International Herald Tribune*, 22 Dec. 1990). Comparably, the term *guru* may refer to a Hindu teacher, a venerable spiritual leader, and any venerated sage or expert, as in the phrases *management guru* and *usage guru*. The extended non-Hindu senses of *pundit* and *guru* are often used in a tongue-in-cheek way, to suggest that there is something spurious or amusing about the persons so described. Most direct 20c borrowings do not, however, have such connotations, and some, such as Gandhi's *ahimsa* and *satyagraha*, currently have positive implications.

See ARYAN, BORROWING, BOSTON, CLASSICAL LANGUAGE, DOT, INDIA, INDIAN ENGLISH[1], INDIAN LANGUAGES, INDO-EUROPEAN LANGUAGES, JONES (W.), LINGUISTIC TYPOLOGY, PALI, PRAKRIT, ROMANI/ROMANY, TRANSLATION, TRANSLITERATION, WHITNEY. Compare ARABIC. [ASIA, LANGUAGE].   T.MCA., R.P.

SANSERIF, SANS SERIF. See SERIF.

SAPIR, Edward [1881–1939]. German-American linguist and anthropologist. Born in Lauenberg, Schleswig-Holstein. Emigrated with his parents to the US in 1886. Educated at Columbia U., graduating in 1904. His early work was on Germanic languages, but he soon came under the influence of the anthropologist Franz Boas, and turned to American Indian languages. Based in Ottawa, Canada, for 15 years, he produced works on Nootka and other Canadian Indian languages. In 1925, he moved back to the US, first to the U. of Chicago, then in 1931 to Yale as Professor of Anthropology and Linguistics. He wrote on a wide range of topics, but produced only one book, *Language: An Introduction to the Study of Speech* (1921). A selection of his best-known papers was published after his death as *Selected Writings of Edward Sapir in Language, Culture and Personality* (ed. D. G. Mandelbaum, 1949). Sapir and Leonard Bloomfield are often regarded as the fathers of American linguistics, even though their approaches differed considerably. Both can be regarded as proponents of structural linguistics, but, unlike Bloomfield, Sapir saw language as primarily a social phenomenon which must be considered within its cultural context. This led him to a view of *linguistic relativity*, the notion that 'human beings . . . are very much at the mercy of the particular language that has become the medium of expression for their society' (1929). See SAPIR–WHORF HYPOTHESIS. [AMERICAS, BIOGRAPHY, LANGUAGE].   J.M.A.

SAPIR–WHORF HYPOTHESIS, also **Whorfian hypothesis.** A term in linguistics for the proposition that thought and behaviour are influenced by the language spoken, promoted by the American linguists Edward Sapir and Benjamin Lee Whorf. In Sapir's words: 'The real world is to a large extent unconsciously built up on the language habits of the group. No two languages are ever sufficiently similar to be considered as representing the same social reality. The worlds in which different societies live are distinct worlds, not merely the same world with different labels attached' (1929, in *Selected Writings of Edward Sapir in Language, Culture and Personality*, ed. D. G. Mandelbaum, 1949). This assumption had considerable popularity in the 1930s and 1940s, when languages were believed to differ without limit, in unpredictable ways. Its influence decreased in the 1960s, primarily under the influence of Noam Chomsky, who directed attention to the possibility of language universals and the likelihood that language was genetically programmed. The views of Sapir and Whorf, however, were not as extreme as has sometimes been maintained. Neither of them argued for linguistic determinism (the belief that people are trapped in their languages), but both stressed linguistic relativity (the notion that different languages lead their speakers to different interpretations of the same physical evidence). These differences persist 'unless their linguistic backgrounds are similar, or can in some way be calibrated' (Whorf, 1940, in *Language, Thought and Reality*, ed. John B. Carroll, 1956).

Recent reassessments of the hypothesis suggest that Whorf misanalysed some of the data, particularly on the American Indian language Hopi. The supposed huge gap between the Hopi and Western conceptions of time has turned out to be largely a mirage: compare Ekkehart Malotki, *Hopi Time* (1983). However, psycholinguistic experiments show that linguistic boundaries have some influence on the behaviour of subjects when they are asked to make decisions about, for example, the closeness of colours to one another. The Mexican language Tarahumara has a single basic colour term *siyóname* covering both blue and green. An experiment was devised in which subjects were shown examples of three colours within the blue–green range, and asked to pick the two which were closest together. English-speakers were better at the task than Tarahumara-speakers, suggesting that separate names for *blue* and *green* had aided their performance, especially as Tarahumara-speakers scored similarly to English-speakers in other colour tasks (Paul Kay & Willett Kempton, 'What is the Sapir-Whorf hypothesis?', *American Anthropologist* 86, 1984). In general, it seems likely that habitual thought follows along the lines laid down by language, but that people are adaptable and can transcend their linguistic boundaries if they pause to reflect. [LANGUAGE].   J.M.A.

SARAMACCAN. A creole of Surinam whose vocabulary derives partly from Portuguese, partly from English; generally considered the oldest creole of Surinam and currently spoken by the *Central Bush Negroes* (the Saramaccans and the Matuari). It is important to both the study of Caribbean Creoles and theories of the origins and development of creoles with European lexicons. It developed among 17c runaway slaves who may have spoken a Portuguese pidgin in addition to their West African languages, and who came into brief contact with English in the plantations. They would, however, have escaped before contact with English affected their language to the same degree as those who developed *Sranan*. See CREOLE, NDJUKA, SRANAN, SURINAM(E). [AMERICAS, VARIETY]. L.D.C.

SARCASM [16c: from Latin *sarcasmus*, Greek *sarkasmós* tearing flesh, speaking bitterly]. A term in rhetoric and general use for sneeringly ironical remarks: 'Oh *yes*, we *know* how clever *you* are'; 'Well, Mr Know-it-all, what's the answer this time?' Sarcasm serves to taunt and deflate. It often stems from resentful and embittered insecurity, but is also used by people in authority (such as teachers and army instructors) as a means of marking and maintaining that authority. See BIERCE. Compare CYNIC, IRONY. [STYLE]. T.MC.A.

SATIRE [16c: from Latin *satira* medley, from *(lanx) satura* a full dish (of fruits offered to the gods). Associated from classical times with the Greek *sáturos* satyr, and with the chorus of satyrs in Greek *satyric drama*]. A literary attack through ridicule, irony, and parody, in verse or prose, and intended to arouse amused contempt for its target. Satire differs from denunciation or diatribe in its artistry and its desire to reform as well as discredit. It contrasts the actual with an existing or desired ideal and has an underlying moral stance in its exposure of weakness, vice, and folly. It may be directed against an individual, as in Dryden's 'MacFlecknoe, or A Satyr upon the True-Blew-Protestant Poet, T. S.' (attacking Thomas Shadwell, 1682), a group, such as the authors and critics ridiculed in Pope's *Dunciad* (1728), and humanity in general, as in Swift's *Gulliver's Travels* (1726). Satire can occur in any genre and has been practised in English in all periods, with such early exponents as Chaucer, Dunbar, and Skelton. There is a satirical element in Elizabethan drama, notably in Jonson. However, some 16c satirists regarded themselves as innovators, or as Joseph Hall put it:

> I first adventure, follow me who list
> And be the second English satirist.
> (Prologue to *Virgidemiae*, 1597)

The Augustan heroic couplet proved suitable for satire, especially as used by Pope:

> The Wit of Cheats, the Courage of the Whore,
> Are what ten thousand envy and adore!
> All, all look up with reverential Awe,
> At Crimes that 'scape, or triumph o'er the Law.
> ('Epilogue to the Satires', 1738)

Writers were influenced by such classical models as the amused and urbane *Horatian satire* (of the Roman poet Horace: as in Pope's 'Epistle to Augustus'), the more severe and harsh *Juvenalian satire* (of the Roman poet Juvenal: as in Johnson's 'London'), and *Menippean* or *Varronian satire* (of the Greek philosopher Menippus and his Roman imitator Varro), which used dialogue in a narrative framework (as in Thomas Peacock's *Headlong Hall*, 1816, and *Nightmare Abbey*, 1818). The poet Byron also used satire, as in 'English Bards and Scotch Reviewers' (1809). The Victorian novel contains satirical elements in its social criticism, particularly in Dickens, Thackeray, and Butler. In the 20c, satire has been used in drama by Shaw in *The Devil's Disciple* (1897) and *The Doctor's Dilemma* (1906), in verse by Roy Campbell, in 'The Georgiad' (1931) against the writers known as the Bloomsbury Group, and in novels by, among others, Aldous Huxley (*Antic Hay*, 1923), Evelyn Waugh (*Decline and Fall*, 1928), George Orwell (*Animal Farm*, 1945), and Joseph Heller, whose *Catch 22* (1961) is set in the US Air Force in the Second World War. From it has come the phrase *a Catch-22 situation*, one in which any move one makes will cause further problems. See BATHOS, BUTLER, CARICATURE, CHAUCER, DICKENS, DRYDEN, IRONY, JOHN BULL, LAMPOON, ORWELL, PARODY, REVERSAL, SCRIBBLER, SHAW, SWIFT. [LITERATURE, STYLE]. R.C.

SAXON [13c: through French from Latin *Saxo/Saxonis*, and parallel to the Old English form *Seaxan* (plural *Seaxe*), probably derived from *s(e)ax*, the name of a knife used by the Saxons]. (1) A member of a Germanic people that once lived near the mouth of the Elbe, and in Roman times spread across Germany from Schleswig to the Rhine. Some (*the Anglo-Saxons*: that is those who joined the Angles) migrated in the 5–6c to Britain; others (*the Ealdseaxe, Old Saxons*) became the founding people of *Saxony*, the name of a German territory that has changed its location and political standing several times over the centuries. (2) The dialects spoken by the Saxons in southern England, in *Essex* (home of the East Saxons), *Middlesex* (the Middle Saxons), *Sussex* (the South Saxons), and *Wessex* (the West Saxons). The term has sometimes been used instead of *Old English* and *Anglo-Saxon*, as the name of the language carried to Britain by the Angles and Saxons. (3) A native of Saxony. (4) The Low German dialect of Saxony. (5) An English man or woman, especially in medieval times, in contrast to *Norman*, and sometimes in more recent times in contrast to *Latin* and *Celt*. The term has also been used to contrast a Lowland Scot with a Highland Scot or *Gael*: see ETHNIC NAME [SASSENACH]. (6) Also *Saxon English, Saxon language*. Formerly, a name for native or vernacular English in contrast to French and Latinate usage: 'Our vulgar Saxon English standing most vpon wordes monosillable' (George Puttenham, *The Arte of English Poesie*, 1589). (7) Relating to any of the above: *Saxon traditions*. See ANGLES, ANGLO-SAXON, LOW GERMAN, SAXON GENITIVE, SAXONISM, WESSEX. [HISTORY, LANGUAGE, NAME]. T.MCA.

SAXON ENGLISH. See SAXON (6).

SAXON GENITIVE. A term for the forms of the possessive associated with the apostrophe (*boy's*, *boys'*), so called because, along with the plural ending, they are the only noun inflections surviving from Old English or Anglo-Saxon. This genitive is often described as a case form, but as it can be attached to phrases (*The King of Thailand's visit*; *somebody else's seat*), some grammarians argue against this view: see GROUP POSSESSIVE. The same meaning when expressed by an *of*-phrase is sometimes called the *of*-genitive: *the top of the hill*. The Saxon genitive can be used alone with a place reference: *See you at Tom's*; *I got it at the grocer's this morning*. Other usages include the *subjective genitive* (*the man's statement*, where the man made the statement); the *objective genitive* (*the group's leader*, where someone leads the group); and the *descriptive genitive* (*a moment's thought, a ladies' hairdresser, ship's biscuits, Parkinson's disease*), which shares some features with attribution and compound words. See APOSTROPHE[1], GENITIVE CASE, POSSESSION. [GRAMMAR]. S.C.

SAXONISM [18c: from *Saxon* and *-ism* as in *Scotticism*]. Also **Anglo-Saxonism**. A semitechnical term for: (1) The use of, and preference for, expressions of Anglo-Saxon origin. (2) A word or other expression of Anglo-Saxon origin or formed on an Anglo-Saxon or Germanic model, often contrasted with *classicism*, as in *foreword* with *preface*, *folkwain* with *omnibus*. Saxonisms are generally the outcome of a purist and nativist approach to the language. The aim behind many deliberately created forms has been to create compounds and derivatives to replace foreign borrowings; the device is rooted in the Old English practice of loan-translating Latin words: *benevolentia* as *welwilledness well-willingness*; *trinitas* as *thrines* threeness. Loan-translation was standard before the Norman Conquest, but was limited from the mid-11c by the predominance of French. Since the decline of French influence in the 14c, Saxonism has resurfaced only occasionally. In the 16c, it was a reaction to inkhorn terms; in his translation of the Bible, John Cheke used *hundreder* and *gainrising* instead of *centurion* and *resurrection*. In the 19c, it was prompted by comparative philology, when *folklore* and *foreword* (modelled on German *Vorwort*) were coined, *handbook* was revived to compete with *manual*, and *leechcraft* was preferred by Walter Scott to *medicine*. Dickens eulogized Anglo-Saxon times, when 'a pure Teutonic was spoken' (*Household Words* 18, 1858). The most enthusiastic 19c Saxonizer was William Barnes, who wished to turn English back into a properly Germanic language. Some of his coinages were structurally acceptable (*bendsome* for *flexible*, *folkwain* for *omnibus*), but others were awkward (*markword of suchness* for *adjective*). His work is now largely forgotten and where remembered is usually seen as quaint and unrealistic.

Currently, Saxonism occurs directly as a literary conceit and indirectly in campaigns for simpler English. In humorous writing, vernacular alternatives to established Romance words are coined and used for effect. In the magazine *Punch* in 1966, to celebrate the 900th anniversary of the Battle of Hastings, the humorist Paul Jennings wrote 'anent the ninehundredth yearday of the Clash of Hastings', and rendered Hamlet's most famous soliloquy into 'Anglish', beginning with:

> To be, or not to be: that is the ask-thing:
> Is't higher-thinking in the brain to bear
> The slings and arrows of outrageous dooming
> Or take up weapons 'gainst a sea of bothers
> And by againstwork end them?

In the word list of Basic English, C. K. Ogden showed a marked preference for vernacular over Romance and classical words. Campaigners for Plain English often urge people to avoid polysyllables and keep to everyday language, implicitly proposing a kind of Saxonism. In such movements, however, the main criterion is not linguistic pedigree but ease of communication. See AMERICAN LITERATURE, ANGLO-SAXON, CARLYLE, BARNES, BASIC ENGLISH, BLUE-EYED ENGLISH, BRIDGES, -ISM, PLAIN ENGLISH, PURISM. [STYLE, WORD]. J.M.G., T.MCA.

SAYING [13c]. An informal, general term for anything said, especially if it is brief and to the point; a pithy or concise observation that expresses folk wisdom that has been handed down orally, or represents a basic principle, fundamental teaching, or the like: *Time flies*; *It never rains but it pours*; *Honesty is the best policy*. In scribal times, when oral tradition was strong and printing had not yet developed, the imparting of education was often done through series of sayings that could be easily memorized. This has resulted in English in several more or less synonymous terms, mostly of classical origin, for kinds of short, instructional statement, such as *saying* (from Old English), *adage* (from Latin), and *aphorism* (from Greek). See ADAGE, APHORISM, APO(PH)THEGM, AXIOM, EPIGRAM, FOLK, MAXIM, METAPHOR, ORAL TRADITION, PROVERB, QUOTATION. [STYLE, WORD].   T. MCA.

SCANDINAVIAN LANGUAGES. A group of languages in northern Europe. Strictly speaking, *Scandinavian* relates only to the peninsula of Scandinavia (Norway and Sweden), but the term usually includes Denmark and sometimes Finland. The languages spoken in this area are the Germanic languages Danish, Norwegian, and Swedish and the Finno-Ugric languages Lappish and Finnish. In linguistics, the terms *Scandinavian* and *North Germanic* both refer to a subgroup of the Germanic language family. The languages of this subgroup are Danish (in Denmark, the Faroe Islands, and Greenland), Faroese (in the Faroe Islands), Icelandic (in Iceland), Norwegian (in Norway), and Swedish (in Sweden and Finland). The Scandinavian language Norn was spoken in Scotland until the 17-18c. Originally, there was little variation in Scandinavian, the common language of the Viking raiders and settlers of the 9-11c. At the present time, in Norway, Sweden, and Denmark, educated people seldom have difficulty in communicating across frontiers, speakers using their own languages. Icelandic and Faroese, however, are no longer immediately intelligible to other Scandinavians, even though they retain many features of original Scandinavian. The justification for regarding Danish and Swedish as distinct languages lies largely in their separate literary traditions, dating from the 16c. The distance between them is like that between standard English and Lowland Scots. The situation in Norway is more complex, but can also be compared to the linguistic situation in Scotland.

Scandinavian and English. During the early Middle Ages, the Viking invasions led to settlements in Britain and Ireland: in the Northern and Western Isles, the northern and western coasts of Scotland, parts of Ireland (including Dublin), the Isle of Man, and large parts of England, resulting in the Danelaw. As a consequence, Scandinavian was for several centuries a major language of Britain and Ireland, competing with Gaelic and English, on both of which it had a powerful impact. By 1200, however, Scandinavian (also referred to as Danish, Old Danish, Norse, Old Norse) had ceased to be spoken in England, but survived elsewhere: for example, as Norn in Orkney and Shetland. In England, the long period of contact and ultimate fusion between the Anglo-Saxon and Danish populations, especially north of a line between London and Chester, had a profound effect on English. More recently, Scandinavian influence has been slight and sporadic, in such loans as *ombudsman, ski, smorgasbord, tungsten*.

English and Scandinavian. English influence, for centuries slight, began to increase from *c*.1750, and in the 20c, especially since the Second World War, has become extensive in such fields as journalism, computer technology, and aviation, as well as in areas of life where American influence has been predominant: youth culture, leisure activities, sport, business, advertising. The influence is particularly noticeable in journalism. The impact of English includes: (1) Loanwords: nouns are the largest group, followed by verbs and adjectives. Before *c*.1900, borrowings usually conformed to local conventions (English *strike* became Danish *strejke*, Norwegian *streike*, Swedish *strejk*), but recent loans generally undergo little or no modification. (2) Loan translations: *blood bank* has become *blodbank*; *self-service* has become Danish and Norwegian *selvbetjening*, Swedish *självbetjäning*. Phrasal verbs are a feature of Scandinavian as well as English and loan translations have been increasing: Danish *tone ned* (tone down); Danish *ende op med*, Norwegian *ende opp med* (end up with). In addition, idioms like *drag one's feet* and *conspiracy of silence* have entered Scandinavian usage in translation. (3) Loan constructions: usages of the type *wall-to-wall carpets* and *lovely 20-year-old So-and-So* are no longer foreign to Scandinavian usage, although older people may object. (4) Semantic borrowing: the word for 'to sell' used in the sense 'to convince people of the worth of (a product, idea, etc.)'. (5) Vogue words from English competing with adequate existing terms: while *personlighed* or *personlighet* is usual, an advert for a new car might claim instead that it has *personality*. (6) Many existing borrowings from Latin have gained in frequency under the influence of their use in English: *status*; Danish and Swedish *kommunikation*, Norwegian *kommunikasjon*.

The above remarks apply to Denmark, Norway, and Sweden. In Iceland, English influence is felt on the colloquial level, but a purist tradition has kept the written language unaffected, neologisms being Icelandicized: *hamborgan* a hamburger. Recently, however, some authors have broken with the more extreme form of purism and English is making inroads in television. The Faroese situation is comparable. In Scandinavia proper, emphasis is placed on the teaching of modern languages and English is compulsory in all schools. Scholarly and scientific publications are often in English. University regulations usually allow doctoral theses to be submitted in English, German, or French as an alternative to a Scandinavian language, and English is a frequent choice. See ANGLO-DANISH, BORROWING, DANISH, FA(E)ROESE, GERMANIC LANGUAGES, ICELANDIC, INDO-EUROPEAN LANGUAGES, NORN, NORSE, NORWEGIAN, ORKNEY AND SHETLAND DIALECT, SAGA, SWEDISH. [EUROPE, LANGUAGE]. P.C.

SCANSION [17c: from Latin *scansio/scansionis* climbing, scanning a poem foot by foot, from *scandere* to climb]. The descriptive analysis of the metrical pattern of a poem. In English, this has traditionally been done by marking the stressed syllables in each line, dividing the line into feet by considering how these stresses are arranged, and from this identifying the poem's prevailing metre: for example, if the stress pattern of the syllables in a line is recurrently one weak one strong, one weak one strong, each foot is an *iamb* (∪-). If there are five such feet in a line, the line's overall metre is *iambic pentameter*. By showing each syllable as stressed (strong) or unstressed (weak) within its metrical foot, the structure of the whole poem can be indicated. The traditional notation in scansion marks stressed and unstressed syllables above the line. The examples below show three sets of conventions for analysing a line of iambic pentameter verse:

Using macron (-) and breve (∪):

∪ - ∪ - ∪ - ∪ - ∪ -
O thought/less mor/tals! e/ver blind / to fate

Using solidus or slash (/) and the symbol (×):

× / × / × / × / × /
O thought/less mor/tals! e/ver blind / to fate

Using acute accent (´) and breve (without marking the feet):

Ŏ thóughtlĕss mórtăls! évĕr blínd tŏ fáte

In order to identify its metrical rhythm, verse may be rendered in a stricter fashion than usual (often to the accompaniment of hand and head movements); for poet and audience, however, the overall effect of a poem is what matters, and its delivery requires more than the steady, stylized reproduction of perfect feet. Irregularities and changes are noted as each line of a poem is scanned. Thoughtful scansion, however, is pragmatic rather than rigid; very few poems show complete regularity of metre, and strict scansion can distort the stress demanded by normal pronunciation and syntax. If the metrical beat (*ictus*) does not coincide with the stress pattern of speech, it is better to show the difference than to make the verse seem dissociated from living language.

To catch the nuances of natural rhythm, some prosodists have devised more elaborate systems and attempted to show the degrees of emphasis on stressed syllables, a difficult task that results in mainly subjective judgements. Experiments in a pitch-based method of scansion, using a kind of musical notation, have not been successful. *Free verse* challenges the traditional method of scanning recurring metrical feet, and must be analysed through rhythm instead of regular metre. Scansion is an abstract process that is valuable as long as it remains descriptive and does not force an unnatural interpretation on a poem. Even a detailed and liberal scansion cannot indicate all the factors of pitch, loudness, timing, and rhetorical emphasis found in spoken recital or supplied by the silent reader; the poem is continually created in the tension between performance and scansion. See METRE/METER, PROSODY. [LITERATURE]. R.C.

SCARE QUOTES. See QUOTATION MARKS.

SCATOLOGY [1870s: from *skato-*, combining form of Greek *skôr* dung, shit, and *-logy* study]. (1) The scientific study of faeces for such purposes as medical diagnosis, the determination of diet, and the study of fossils. (2) A preoccupation with excrement and associated obscenity, often in writing or humour: *scatological jokes*. See COPROLALIA, OBSCENITY, SWEARING. [STYLE]. T.MCA.

SCHEME [16c: from Medieval Latin *schema*, Greek *skhêma* a form]. Also **figure**. An obsolete term in rhetoric for both an expression that deviates from the usual or natural through a change in sound, syntax, or through general arrangement (often with a pleasing effect), and the device or technique that makes such a change possible (turning the literal into the *schematic(al)* or *figurative*). Schemes include such devices as alliteration and assonance (that purposefully arrange sounds, as in *The Leith police dismisseth us*) and antithesis, chiasmus, climax, and anticlimax (that arrange words for effect, as in the cross-over phrasing *One for all and all for one*). See FIGURATIVE LANGUAGE/USAGE, FIGURE OF SPEECH, TROPE. [STYLE]. T.MCA.

SCHOLARLY APPARATUS. See ACADEMIC USAGE, NOTES AND REFERENCES.

SCHWA [Late 19c: from German *schwa*, from Hebrew *shwā*, from *shāw'*, emptiness. Hebrew grammarians traditionally mark consonants with signs referred to in Roman lettering as *sheva* or *shewa*. These signs indicate either no following vowel sound (*quiescent sheva*) or a following central vowel (*vocal or movable sheva*). There was nothing comparable in alphabets derived from Roman until the development of the International Phonetic Alphabet in the late 19c, when an inverted e was introduced to serve the same purpose as vocal sheva]. Also **shwa, neutral vowel, obscure vowel.** A term in phonetics for a central vowel sound represented by the symbol /ə/. To make a schwa in isolation, the tongue is neither pushed forward nor pulled back, neither spread nor raised nor lowered, and the lips are neither spread nor rounded: hence the term 'neutral'. Although not represented in the conventional alphabet, schwa is the commonest vowel sound in English. It typically occurs in unstressed syllables, and in the following list is shown for illustrative purposes as if it were an everyday letter: *əbove, əgain, səppose, photəgraph, scenəry, sofə*. It is often an ill-defined voice gap between consonants: for example, in *today* it is formed as the tongue moves away from the alveolar ridge on the release of /t/ and returns to form /d/ (*t'day*). Many languages do not have a neutral vowel, and this causes problems for foreign speakers of English from such backgrounds. However, another vowel may replace it: for example, the short /a/ of North Indian languages (as in the first vowel of *Punjab*) is used as a schwa in IndE, or the /a/ in many kinds of AfrE: *speaker* /spika/. Learners who have not had access to native-speaker English tend not to attempt a schwa at all, but to pronounce words more or less according to the vowel letters of the spelling. Their speech is therefore likely to be syllable-timed rather than stress-timed. See RHYTHM, SYLLABLE, WEAK VOWEL, VOWEL, VOWEL QUANTITY, and, in particular, the letter entries A, E, I, O, R, U. [SPEECH].

G.K.

SCIENCE FICTION [1850s: popularized in the 1920s by the US magazine editor Hugo Gernsback, regarded by many fans as 'the father of science fiction']. Short forms *sci-fi, SF*. Fiction inspired by the achievements and speculations of science. Gernsback's definition of an SF story was: 'a charming romance intermingled with scientific fact and prophetic vision' (editorial, *Amazing Stories*, 1926). Until recently, the genre was largely ignored or disdained by literary critics, but has begun to gain attention. It is increasingly studied as a genre in universities and schools and student anthologies are beginning to be published.

An early British term for the genre was H. G. Wells's *scientific romance*, applied especially to troubled works on the future of humankind, such as his *The Shape of Things to Come* (1933) and Aldous Huxley's *Brave New World* (1932). A term used in recent years, *speculative fiction*, seeks to improve the down-market image of the genre and distance it from the 'pulp magazines' edited by Gernsback and John W. Campbell, and from comic books and motion pictures replete with superheroes, little green men from Mars, and 'bug-eyed monsters'. Some writers have sought to stay close to the wellsprings of science, notably Isaac Asimov (US) and Arthur C. Clarke (UK).

However viewed, science fiction does not operate in a literary or linguistic vacuum: probably encouraged by such social forces as the Industrial Revolution, Darwinism, technological advance, and two world wars, as well as by 'hard' or 'soft' science, it demonstrates links with traditional philosophical and utopian writing as well as with allegory, satire, romance, and the Gothic novel. Related writing that does not attempt to follow science closely, but appears to be more concerned with aspects of myth, is known as *science fantasy*, while tales of adventure among the stars are often referred to, dismissively or affectionately, as *space opera*.

Themes, plots, and settings. Although SF themes, plots, and settings vary greatly, they tend to fall into three broad types: (1) Especially in British writing, accounts of a present time that slowly loses normality, as in H. G. Wells's *The War of the Worlds* (1898) and John Wyndham's *The Day of the Triffids* (1951). (2) Especially in American writing, accounts of future times and places often far from Earth, as in Ray Bradbury's *The Martian Chronicles* (1950) and the TV series, films, and books known collectively as *Star Trek* (1960s onwards), created by Gene Roddenberry. (3) Generally, accounts of alien worlds in some way reachable from this world, as in Conan Doyle's *The Lost World* (1912), located on a plateau in South America, and Edgar Rice Burroughs's *Pellucidar* (1915), the hollow interior of the Earth. Both of these worlds abound in prehistoric creatures.

Recent developments. Before the 1960s, science fiction readers were mostly young men, but women have in recent decades become more involved as both readers and writers. Leading women writers include Doris Lessing, Ursula Le Guin, and C. J. Cherryh. It can also be argued that science fiction as a genre was virtually created by Mary Shelley in *Frankenstein, Or The*

Modern Prometheus (1817). In recent years, not only have the boundaries of SF and other kinds of fantasy writing become increasingly indeterminate, but those between SF and 'straight' fiction have also grown less distinct. The genre has transferred spectacularly to motion pictures and television, particularly with special effects as exploited by the movie-makers Steven Spielberg and George Lucas. Such developments have also prompted multimedia sci-fi 'packages': for example, the humorous, satirical, and space-operatic 'trilogy in four parts', *A Hitch Hiker's Guide to the Galaxy* by Douglas Adams (1979 onwards), which has appeared in radio, television and print forms.

SF and English. Science fiction has been written in many languages, and from its inception in the 19c, French, with the seminal works of Jules Verne, has been a significant medium. In the late 20c, however, English appears to be the international voice of the genre: ' "The lack of broad vision in the novel tradition," declares Wolfgang Jeschke, the Munich writer and publisher, "makes science fiction possible and necessary." Although the venue is The Netherlands Congresgebouw in the Hague, and Jeschke is a German born in Czechoslovakia, he reads his speech in effortful but eloquent English. English may be the second language of Europe, but it is the first language, sometimes it seems the only language, of science fiction. Of nearly 3,000 SF fans, writers, editors and publishers attending the 48th World SF Convention a week ago, more than half were from Britain or America' (Colin Greenland, 'Millennial Visions', *Sunday Times*, 9 Sept. 1990).

See ANACHRONISM, FANTASY, FICTION, GOTHIC, MYTH, NOVEL, POPULAR FICTION, ROMANCE, ROOT-CREATION, WELLS. [LITERATURE].   T.MCA.

SCIENTIFIC USAGE/ENGLISH. See ACADEMIC USAGE/ENGLISH.

SCOSE [The acronym for *Standing Committee on Spoken English*]. See AUSTRALIAN BROADCASTING.

SCOT [From the Latin *Scotti*, *Scōti*, plural]. A native of Scotland. The name first appeared in late 4c Latin texts in reference to the Gaelic-speaking people of *Hibernia* (Ireland), but appears not to have been a native Irish tribal name. It was used by such Irish and English writers as Adomnán and Bede (7–8c) for the Irish, and its derivative *Scotia* or *Scottia* as an alternative to *Hibernia*. By then, however, as well as the people of Ireland, *Scot(t)i* included that part of the northern Irish tribe Dál Riata which had settled in Argyll by the end of the 5c. After

these *Scoti Britanniae* (Irish of Britain, as Adomnán and Bede sometimes called them) had come to rule their Pictish neighbours to the east (mid-9c), the names *Scot(t)i* and *Scot(t)ia* and their Anglo-Saxon renderings *Scot(t)as* and *Scotland* came by the 10c to apply to the entire kingdom north of the Forth. Until the 13c, these names did not apply to Strathclyde, Lothian, and Galloway to the south, and sometimes excluded Moray and Argyll to the north and west. By the mid-13c, however, they had begun to acquire their present-day wider sense. The plural has tended to be commoner than the singular, to which *Scotsman/Scotchman* and *Scotswoman/Scotchwoman* have been preferred. Currently, the singular is increasingly favoured because it is concise and avoids gender distinctions. See MAN/WOMAN, MÉTIS, SCOTCH, SCOTLAND, SCOTS. [EUROPE, NAME].   A.J.A.

SCOTCH. A late 16c contraction of *Scottish*, first in Early Modern English then in Older Scots. It ousted *Scottish* as the prevailing form in England. In Scotland, the native form *Scots* predominated until the 18c Anglicizing vogue *Scotch* became fashionable in both countries. In the early 19c, however, some Scottish writers were expressing doubts about it as a supposed innovation and returning to the more traditional *Scottish* and *Scots*, while others, such as J. A. H. Murray, editor of the *OED*, continued to use it. By the early 20c, disapproval of *Scotch* by educated Scots was so great that its use was regularly discountenanced by teachers, except for such entrenched phrases as *Scotch broth*, *Scotch mist*, *Scotch terrier*, *Scotch tweed*, *Scotch whisky*. In England and North America, *Scotch* has remained the dominant form into the late 20c, although awareness of middle-class Scottish distaste for it has been spreading. The *OED Supplement* (1982) reported that in deference to Scottish sensibilities the English have been abandoning *Scotch* for *Scottish* and less frequently *Scots*, and prefer *the Scots* to *the Scotch* as the name of the people. Paradoxically, for working-class Scots the common form has long been *Scotch* (sometimes written *Scoatch*) and the native form *Scots* is sometimes regarded as an Anglicized affectation. Compare SCOTS, SCOTTISH. See SCOTCH-IRISH. [EUROPE, NAME].   A.J.A.

SCOTCH-IRISH. The name of that part of the population of northern Ireland descended from the Scottish Presbyterian settlers of the 17c and later. From the 18c, it has been applied to the people of this background who migrated in large numbers to Pennsylvania and neighbouring regions of the US and later to Ontario and other parts of Canada. Since around 1950, it has also been applied by linguists to the variety of Scots spoken in northern and north-eastern Ireland, especially in Donegal, Derry, Antrim, and Down. The recent form *Scots-Irish* runs parallel with the increasing preference for *Scots* over *Scotch*: 'The ingrained hostility between the Catholic community and the Scots-Irish in Northern Ireland' (*The Listener*, 21 Dec. 1972). See APPALACHIAN ENGLISH, DIALECT IN AMERICA, SCOTCH, ULSTER SCOTS. [AMERICAS, EUROPE, NAME, VARIETY].   A.J.A.

SCOTCHMAN/WOMAN. See -MAN/WOMAN.

SCOTIA [Latin: Land of the Scots. See SCOT]. In present-day use, a formal and somewhat grand literary name for Scotland ('The halesome parritch, chief of Scotia's food': Robert Burns, *The Cotter's Saturday Night*, 1786), also sometimes used for fun ('Auld Scotia ma hame, hoo ye dirl in ma wame': Ebenezer McIlwham, pen name of Clifford Hanley, 'Caledonia', *c.*1975) [*halesome* wholesome, *parritch* porridge, *auld* old, *ma hame* my home, *hoo ye dirl in ma wame*, ambiguous: 'how you thrill in my heart' or 'how you upset my stomach']. Compare ALBA, CALEDONIA, SCOTLAND. [EUROPE, NAME].   A.J.A.

SCOTLAND [From Old English, Land of the Scots: see SCOT]. A kingdom in the island of Britain. The name, like its older Latin equivalent *Scotia*, first referred to Ireland, the home of the original Scots. By the 10c, the name was used of the realm of the Celtic kings of Scots, north of the Forth and Clyde, after which the original Irish association died out. From the 14c, *Scotland* has been the common name for the kingdom, its southern boundary virtually stable at the present border with England, the mouth of the Tweed and the Solway Firth. Other names for Scotland are *Alba*, *Caledonia*, *Scotia*: see entries. Since 1707, Scotland has been part of the United Kingdom. The mainland is divided into three regions: the *Highlands*, the *Lowlands*, and the *Southern Uplands*. The islands to the north-west are known as both the *Western Isles* and the *Hebrides*, and divide into the *Inner* and *Outer Hebrides*. The islands to the north are known as the *Northern Isles* and divide into two groups: *Orkney* and *Shetland*. Traditionally sources of tension in the lives of Scots include ancient rivalry and warfare with England (including a resentment of its wealth, influence, and political dominance), a long-standing mutual suspicion between Gaels (Highlanders and Hebrideans) and Lowlanders (on account of language and culture, and because the centres of power have been located in the Lowlands), and since the Reformation, antagonism between

Protestants (mainly Presbyterians) and Catholics (both among the Gaels and as immigrants from Ireland, especially in the 19c).

In 1503, James IV King of Scots married Princess Margaret of England, in the *Marriage of the Thistle and the Rose*. In 1603, James VI King of Scots became James I of England in the *Union of the Crowns*. In 1707, an incorporating (non-federal) union took place, the *Union of the Parliaments*, in which the Scots Parliament was dissolved and the English Parliament expanded as the British Parliament. In the Act of Union, both countries retained their separate legal and educational systems and national Protestant churches. There was massive unease in Scotland at the time of Union, in which there were elements of coercion and bribery; although an uncertain majority of Scots has generally supported the idea of Great Britain, waves of nationalist feeling recur, with demands ranging from home rule through federalism to independence. The Scottish National Party currently favours independence within the European Community.

See ABERDEEN JOKE, AITKEN'S LAW, AITKEN'S VOWEL, ALBA, ANGLE, ANGLIAN, APPALACHIAN ENGLISH, ATTIC AND DORIC, BIBLE, BRITAIN, BRITISH, BRITISH ISLES, BRYTHONIC, BURNS, CALEDONIA, CANADIAN ENGLISH, CELT, CELTIC, CELTIC LANGUAGES, CRAIGIE, CUMBRIC, DIALECT IN SCOTLAND, DORIC, EDINBURGH, ERSE, ETHNIC NAME, GAELIC, GEORDIE, GLASGOW, GREAT BRITAIN, GUTTER SCOTS, HEBRIDEAN ENGLISH, HIGHLAND ENGLISH, HISTORY OF ENGLISH, INGLIS, IRELAND, IRISH, IRISH ENGLISH, IRISH PLACE-NAMES, LALLANS, LINGUISTIC SURVEY OF SCOTLAND, LORIMER, LOWLAND SCOTS, MACARONIC, MAKAR, MORNINGSIDE AND KELVINSIDE, MURISON, MURRAY, NEAR-RP, NEW ZEALAND ENGLISH, NORN, NORSE, NORTHERN ENGLISH, NORWEGIAN, ORKNEY, ORKNEY AND SHETLAND DIALECTS, PICT, PICTISH, RHOTIC AND NON-RHOTIC, SCOT, SCOTCH, SCOTCH-IRISH, SCOTIA, SCOTLAND, SCOTS, SCOTS LANGUAGE ORGANIZATIONS, SCOTS LITERATURE, SCOTSMAN/WOMAN, SCOTT, SCOTTISH, SCOTTISH DICTIONARIES, SCOTTISH ENGLISH, SCOTTISH GAELIC, SCOTTISH LANGUAGES, SCOTTISH LITERATURE, SCOTTISH PLACE-NAMES, SCOTTISH VOWEL-LENGTH RULE, SHETLAND, SHETLANDIC, SMOLLETT, SOUTHRON, STEVENSON, TRISTAN DA CUNHA, ULSTER SCOTS, UNITED KINGDOM, ZETLAND, ZETLANDIC. [EUROPE, NAME].
                                              T.MCA., A.J.A.

SCOTS [Late 16c: a contraction of earlier Northern Middle English and especially Older Scots *Scottis* or *Scotis*, in contrast with the later English form *Scottish*]. (1) Relating to or characteristic of Scotland, its people, languages, culture, institutions, etc.: *Scots traditions, the Scots* *language*. Since the 15c, *Scots* (originally in Midland and Southern Middle English as *Scottes*, *Scotes*) has also occasionally been used in England. Although in certain uses (*Scots law*, *Scots Greys*, *Scots thistle*, *a Scots mile*, *a pound Scots*) the adjective has never gone out of favour, in other uses its popularity declined after the mid-18c in competition with *Scottish* and *Scotch*, reviving when *Scotch* fell into disfavour in the 19-20c. (2) A name for both Gaelic and the form of Northern English used in Scotland. The forms *Scottis*, *Scotis* and the Latin adjectives *Scotticus*, *Scoticus* down to the 15c applied only to Gaelic and its speakers and have occasionally been so used since. From 1494, the term was increasingly applied to the Lowland speech, previously known as *Inglis*, so as to distinguish it from the language of England. From then on, this was the regular application of the term, and until the early 18c *Scots* and *Inglis* or *English* were more or less interchangeable: 'They decided not to disjoin but to continue the Scots or English classe in the gramer school as formerly' (Stirling Burgh Records, 23 Aug. 1718).

The status of Scots. Scholars and other interested persons have difficulty agreeing on the linguistic, historical, and social status of Scots. Generally, it is seen as one of the ancient dialects of English, yet it has distinct and ancient dialects of its own. Sometimes it has been little more than an overspill noted in the discussion of English as part of the story of England. Sometimes it has been called the English of Scotland, part of general English yet often in contrast with it, and different from the standard English taught in Scottish schools. Sometimes, it has been called a Germanic language in its own right, considered as distinct from its sister in England in the same way that Swedish is distinct from Danish. In addition, in its subordinate relationship with the English of England, its position has been compared to Frisian in the Netherlands (dominated by Dutch) and Norwegian (once dominated by Danish). In *The Languages of Britain* (1984), Glanville Price notes:

In planning and writing this book, I have changed my mind four times, and, in the end, I devote a separate chapter to Scots not because I necessarily accept that it is a 'language' rather than a 'dialect' but because it has proved to be more convenient to handle it thus than include some treatment of it in the chapter on English.

Whatever it is, Scots is distinct enough to stand alone in this way. Despite the controversy, it has since the beginning of the 18c been the object of scholarly investigation and those scholars who have specialized in its study divide its history into three periods: *Old English* (to 1100); *Older Scots* (1100-1700), divided into *Early Scots*

(1100-1450) and *Middle Scots* (1450-1700); *Modern Scots* (1700 onwards).

The King's Scots. The first source of Scots dates from the 7c. It was the Old English of the kingdom of Bernicia, part of which lay in what is now southern Scotland: see NORTHUMBRIA. The second source was the Scandinavian-influenced English of immigrants from Northern and Midland England in the 12-13c, who travelled north at the invitation of the Anglo-Normanized kings of Scots. By the 14c, the variety of Northern English which had crystallized out of these sources (known to its speakers as *Inglis*) had supplanted Gaelic and Cumbric, languages formerly spoken in much of what is now Lowland Scotland, except in Galloway in the south-west, where Gaelic did not die out till the 17c. Throughout the rest of Lowland Scotland, all ranks, including the court and barons, who had formerly spoken Norman French, now spoke Inglis (known today as Older Scots). In Caithness, Orkney, and Shetland, however, the form of Norse known as *Norn* continued in use for some time. From the late 14c also, Latin began to be overtaken by Scots as the language of record and literature, a process well advanced by the early 16c, by which time the term *Scots* had joined *Inglis* as an alternative name for what had become the national language of Stewart Scotland.

Anglicization. By the mid-16c, Scots had begun to undergo the process of *Anglicization*, in which southern English word forms and spellings progressively invaded written and later spoken Scots. Among the conditions favouring this trend were the Scots' failure to produce a translation of the Bible in their own language and Protestant reliance (before and after the Reformation of 1560) on Bibles in English, so that the Biblical language of Scotland was English. By the late 16c, all Scots writing was in a mixed dialect, in which native Scots spellings and spelling symbols co-occurred with English borrowings: *aith/oath*, *ony/any*, *gude/good*, *quh-/wh-*, *sch-/sh-*, Scots *ei*, English *ee*, *ea*, with the English forms gradually gaining in popularity. Scots elements virtually disappeared from published writings in Scotland before the end of the 17c, except for some vernacular literature, mostly verse. The elimination of Scots from unpublished writings like local records took some decades longer. Scottish speakers were now coming into contact with spoken English of various sorts, notably Biblical English read or preached from Scottish pulpits and the English learned by the Scottish gentry on their visits to the English court and the Home Counties, following the Union of the Crowns (1603). Early in the 18c, Sir Robert Sibbald distinguished three sorts of Scottish speech: 'that Language we call Broad Scots, which is yet used by the Vulgar . . . in distinction to the *Highlanders* Language, and the refined Language of the Gentry, which the more Polite People among us do use'. That 'refined language', however, was no longer Scots but the ancestor of *Scottish English*.

Scotticisms. According to the Augustan ideals of good taste and propriety, shared by cultivated people in the 18c in both England and Scotland, the residue of Scots in the English of Scottish people was deplored as 'provincial' and 'unrefined'. This led many of the gentry and intelligentsia to try to rid themselves of all traces of their former national tongue by attending lectures on English elocution held in Edinburgh from 1748. In addition, from the late 17c they made great efforts to eradicate Scotticisms from their writing and speech. At the same time, the tongue 'yet used by the Vulgar' was regarded by the establishment as 'barbarous' and 'corrupt' and by the end of the 18c was thought by some to deserve 'total extinction' (John Pinkerton, 1786). Not all educated 18c Scots, however, accepted these propositions. From early in the century, a new literary Scots, which unlike most literary Middle Scots was based on up-to-date colloquial speech, burgeoned in the writings of Allan Ramsay (1686-1758) and some of his contemporaries, and such successors as Robert Burns. This led on to a stream of vernacular literature in Scots and was accompanied early in the 19c by a revival of interest in and approval of Modern Scots among the middle and upper classes, inspired to some extent by John Jamieson's *Etymological Dictionary of the Scottish Language* (1808). Scots was now generally accepted as a rich and expressive tongue and recognized as the 'national language', albeit (as had been repeatedly stated since 1763 or earlier) 'going out as a spoken tongue every year'.

Revival and survival. The need was now felt to record the old language before it was too late, as in Jamieson's dictionary, or to undertake the preservation or even restoration of Scots. In the 20c, this has manifested itself *inter alia* in the creation of Lallans or Synthetic Scots by the Scottish Renaissance writers from *c.*1920, and in a sustained output in recent decades of narrative, expository, and even some transactional prose in Scots, notably in the Scots Language Society's journal *Lallans* (1973-). From the early 18c to the present day, appeals in English prose or Scots verse have been made to Scots to speak their own language rather than Southron. Although these appeals have often been unheeded even by some of those who make them, all such activity has helped maintain the Scottish people's linguistic loyalty to their 'own

dying language' (Robert Louis Stevenson, 1887) and has helped to slow the drift away from native Scots elements at all levels of speech. But it could not reverse the trend which favours English as the language of power and prestige or restore the full Scots of a dwindling minority of rural speakers to its former central position. In its written form, even after its 20c renaissance, Scots remains restricted to a narrow sphere of literary uses and it makes only a marginal appearance in the written media, in comic strips, cartoons, and jokes (for example, in the enormously popular *Sunday Post*) and in couthy columns in the popular and local press. Full Scots is almost never heard on the broadcast media, though diluted varieties occur in a few popular television series. None the less, although English is dominant, the efforts of the elocutionists and the castigators of Scotticisms have not been especially effective: Scottish English remains permeated with features from Scots.

Scots and Northern English. Scots has many features of Northern English phonology, grammar, and vocabulary, which it shares with the contemporary dialects of northern England. However, because of the separation of the two kingdoms since early times, many of the characteristics of Scots extend only to the Border. What appears to be the most numerous bundle of dialect isoglosses in the English-speaking world runs along this border, effectively turning Scotland into a 'dialect island'.

Pronunciation. (1) Like other Northern dialects, Scots displays the results of many early divergences from the Midland and Southern dialects of Middle English: *hame, stane, sair, gae* as against *home, stone, sore, go*; *hoose, oot, doon, coo* as against *house, out, down, cow*; *baw, saut* against *ball, salt*; *gowd, gowf* as against *gold, golf*; *mouter* as against *multure*; *fou* as against *full*; and *buit, guid, muin, puir, dui* (or with some other front vowel, depending on dialect) as against *boot, good, moon, poor, do*: see DIALECT IN SCOTLAND. (2) Of the features largely exclusive to Scots (in Scotland and Ulster), the most pervasive is the *Scottish Vowel-Length Rule* (see entry), the most striking result of which is the split of Early Scots /iː/ into two phonemes in Scots and ScoE: /aɪ/ in *ay* (yes), *buy, alive, rise, tied*, and /əɪ/ in *aye* (always), *life, rice, bite, tide*. (3) The consonant system retains the Old English voiceless velar fricative /x/ in *teuch, heich* (equivalents of *tough, high*) and many other words (including such Gaelic loans as *clarsach, loch, pibroch*), and the cluster /xt/ in *dochter, nicht* (*daughter, night*). Such forms were once universal in English and have only become obsolete in Northern England in recent decades.

Spelling. By the late 14c, Older Scots was developing its own distinctive orthography, marked by such features as *quh-* (English *wh-*), *-ch* (English *-gh*), *sch-* (English *sh-*), and the use of *i/y* as in *ai/ay*, *ei/ey* to identify certain vowels: compare Scots *quheyll*, *heych*, *scheip*, *heid*, *heyd* with English *wheel*, *high*, *sheep*, *heed*, *head*. Following the Anglicization of the 16–17c, the literary Scots of Allan Ramsay and his contemporaries and successors in the 18c had discarded some of these forms but retained others, including *ei* as in *heid* (head), *ui* or *u–e* as in *guid/gude* (good), and *ch* as in *loch*, *thocht* (loch, thought). This orthography, however, was in the main an adaptation of English orthography to represent Scots, as is shown by the free use of apostrophes to mark 'missing' letters. Unlike English, but like Older Scots, it is tolerant of spelling variation, and attempts to regulate this, notably through the *Scots Style Sheet* of the Makars' Club (1947), have had only limited success. The *Concise Scots Dictionary* records many spelling variants, such as *breid*, *brede*, *bread*, *braid* (bread), and *heuk*, *huke*, *hook* (hook), and the larger Scots dictionaries record very many more.

Morphology. (1) The regular past form of the verb is *-it* or *-t/(e)d*, according to the preceding consonant or vowel: *hurtit*, *skelpit* smacked, *mendit*, *kent/kenned* knew/known, *cleant/cleaned*, *tellt/tauld* told, *deed* died. (2) Some verbs have distinctive principal parts: *greet/grat/grutten* weep/wept, *fesh/fuish/fuishen* fetch/fetched, *lauch/leuch/lauchen* laugh/laughed, *gae/gaed/gane* go/went, *gie/gied/gien* give/gave/given. (3) A set of irregular noun plurals: *eye/een* eye/eyes, *cauf/caur* calf/calves, *horse/horse* horse/horses, *coo/kye* cow/cows (compare archaic English *kine*), *shoe*, *shae*, *shee/shuin*, *sheen* shoe/shoes (compare archaic English *shoon*). (4) Nouns of measure and quantity unchanged in the plural: *four fuit* foot, *twa mile*, *five pund* pound, *three hunderwecht* hundredweight. (5) A third deictic adjective/adverb *yon/yonder*, *thon/thonder* (that and those there, at some distance): *D'ye see yon/thon hoose ower yonder/thonder?* (6) Ordinal numbers ending in *-t*: *fourt*, *fift*, *saxt/sixt*, etc. (7) Adverbs in *-s*, *-lies*, *-lin(g)s*, *gate(s)*, and *way(s)*, *-wye*, *-wey(s)*: *whiles* at times, *maybes* perhaps, *brawlies* splendidly, *geylies* pretty well, *aiblins* perhaps, *arselins* backwards, *halflins* partly, *hidlins* secretly, *maistlins* almost, *a'gates* always, everywhere, *ilka gate* everywhere, *onygate* anyhow, *ilkawye* everywhere, *onyway(s)* anyhow, anywhere, *endweys* straight ahead, *whit wey* how, why. (8) Diminutives and associated forms: in *-ie/y* (*burnie* small *burn* brook, *feardie/feartie* frightened person, coward, *gamie* gamekeeper,

kiltie kilted soldier, *postie* postman, *wifie* wife, *rhodie* rhododendron), in *-ock* (*bittock* little bit, *playock* toy, plaything, *sourock* sorrel) and chiefly Northern *-ag* (*bairnag* little *bairn* child, *Cheordag* Geordie), *-ockie*, *-ickie* (*hoosickie* small house, *wifeockie* little wife). Note the five times diminished *a little wee bit lassockie*.

Syntax and idiom. (1) Verbs in the present tense are as in English when a single personal pronoun is next to the verb; otherwise, they end in *-s* in all persons and numbers: *They say he's owre auld*, *Thaim that says he's owre auld*, *Thir laddies says he's owre auld* They say he's too old, etc.; *They're comin as weel* but *Five o them's comin*; *The laddies?—They've went* but *Ma brakes has went*. (2) *Was* or *wis* may replace *were*, but not conversely as in some Northern English dialects: *You were/wis there*. (3) The modal verbs *may*, *ocht to* ought to, and (except in Orkney and Shetland) *shall*, are rare or absent in informal speech, but occur in literary Scots. They are replaced respectively by *can*, *should*, and *will*. *May* and *shall* are similarly missing from most ScoE. (4) Scots, like Northern English, employs double modal constructions: *He'll no can come the day* He won't be able to come today, *Ah micht could come the morn* I might be able to come tomorrow, *Ah used tae could dae it, but no noo* I could do it once, but not now. (5) There are progressive uses of certain verbs: *He wis thinkin he wid tell her*; *He wis wantin tae tell her*. (6) Verbless subordinate clauses that express surprise or indignation are introduced by *and*: *She had tae walk the hale lenth o the road and her seeven month pregnant*; *He tellt me tae run and me wi ma sair leg* (and me with my sore leg). (7) Negation is mostly as in English, either by the adverb *no* (North-East *nae*), as in *Ah'm no comin* I'm not coming, or by the enclitic *-na/nae* (depending on dialect, and equivalent to *-n't*), as in *Ah dinna ken* I don't know, *They canna come* They can't come, *We couldna hae tellt him* We couldn't have told him, and *Ah huvna seen her* I haven't seen her. With auxiliary verbs which can be contracted, however, such as *-ve* for *have* and *-ll* for *will*, or in *yes-no* questions with any auxiliary, Scots strongly prefers the usage with the adverb to that with the enclitic: *He'll no come* rather than *He winna come*, and *Did he no come?* to the virtual exclusion of *Didna he come?* (8) The relative pronoun is *that* for all persons and numbers, and may be elided: *There's no mony folk (that) lives in that glen* There aren't many people who live in that glen. The forms *wha*, *wham*, *whase*, *whilk* (who, whom, whose, which) are literary, the last of these used only after a statement: *He said he'd lost it, whilk wis no whit we wantit tae hear*. That is made possessive by *'s* or appending an appropriate pronoun: *The man that's hoose got burnt*;

the wumman that her dochter got mairrit; the crew that thair boat wis lost. (9) Verbs of motion may be dropped before an adverb or adverbial phrase of motion: *Ah'm awa tae ma bed; That's me awa hame; Ah'll intae the hoose and see him.* (10) Like Northern English, Scots prefers the order *He turned oot the licht* to *He turned the light out* and *Gie me it* to *Give it me.*

Vocabulary. The vocabularies of Scots and English overlap, but Scots also contains words that are absent from the standard language, either shared with the dialects of Northern England, or unique to Scotland. Many words have wide currency and have strong emotive overtones for many Scots. The sources of the distinctive elements of Scots vocabulary include Old English, Old Norse, French, Dutch, and Gaelic.

Old English. (1) Not now shared with any dialect of England are such forms as: *but an ben* a two-room cottage, *but* the outer room, *ben* the inner room, *cleuch* a gorge, *haffet* the cheek, *skeich* (of a horse) apt to shy, *swick* to cheat. (2) Shared with (especially Northern) dialects of England: *bairn* a child, *bide* to stay or live (in a place), *dicht* to clean, *dwam* a stupor, *hauch* a riverside meadow, *heuch* a steep hill, *rax* to stretch, *snell* (of weather) bitter, severe, *speir* to ask, *thole* to endure. (3) Now in general or literary English: *bannock, eldritch, fey, gloaming, raid, wee, weird, wizened. Weird* and *fey* also have the original senses 'destiny' and 'fated to die'. *To dree yir ain weird* means 'to endure what is destined for you'.

Norse. The Scandinavian element, introduced by 12–13c immigrants from Northern England, is generally shared with the Northern dialects, but some words that are obsolete there survive in Scots and ScoE: *ain* own (*ma ain* my own), *aye* always, *big* to build, *blae* blue (whence *blaeberry*), *blether* to chatter, *brae* slope of a hill, *cleg* a gadfly, *eident* diligent, *ferlie* a wonder, *gate* a road (also in street names: *Gallowgate*, in Glasgow), *gowk* a cuckoo, *graith* equip, equipment, *kirk* church, *lass* a girl, *lowp* to jump, *lug* ear. This element includes the auxiliary verbs *gar* to make or cause to do (*It wad gar ye greet* It would make you weep) and *maun* must (*Ah maun find her* I must find her, and the proverb *He that will tae Cupar maun tae Cupar* Scots equivalent of 'A wilful man must have his way'). Most of this is also shared by the dialects of Shetland, Orkney, and Caithness, which have in addition their own distinct vocabulary descended from Norn.

French. Influence from French was first through the Anglo-Norman baronage of 12–13c Scotland and the Frenchified literary and fashionable culture of medieval Britain, then partly as a result of the *Auld Alliance* (Franco-Scottish Alliance, 1296–1560), and partly from Scots travelling and living in France and Switzerland in medieval and later times: (1) Shared with early English but surviving only in Scots: *causey* the paved part of a street (cognate with *causeway*), *cowp* to capsize or upset (from *couper* to cut, strike) *cummer* a godmother (from *commère*), *douce* (originally of a woman or manners) sweet (from *doux/douce*), *houlet* owl (from *hulotte*), *leal* (a doublet of *loyal* and *legal*), *tass/tassie* cup (from *tasse*). (2) Virtually exclusively Scots: *ashet* a serving dish (from *assiette*), *disjune* breakfast (from *desjun*, now *déjeuner*), *fash* to bother (from *fâcher*), *Hogmanay* (from Old French *aguillanneuf* a New Year's gift), *sybow/sybie* the spring onion (from Old French *ciboule*), *vennel* an alley (from Old French *venelle*). (3) Shared from the 17c with English: *caddie, croup* (the disease), *pony.*

Dutch. The population of medieval Scotland included Flemish landowners in the countryside, wool merchants, weavers, and other craftsmen in the burghs, and trade with The Netherlands dates from the same period. Borrowings from medieval Dutch or Flemish include: *callan* a lad, *coft* bought, *cowk* to retch, *cuit* an ankle, *groff* coarse in grain or quality, *howf* a favourite haunt, public house (from *hof* a courtyard), *loun* ('loon') a lad, *mutch* a kind of woman's cap, *mutchkin* a quarter of a Scots pint, *pinkie* the little finger (passed on to AmE), *trauchle* to overburden, harass. The words *croon, golf, scone* have been passed on to English at large.

Gaelic. (1) Early borrowings, from around the 12c to the 17c, many of which have passed on into English: *bog, cairn* a pile of stones as a landmark, *capercailzie* the wood grouse, *clachan* a hamlet, *clan, clarsach* the Highland harp, *cranreuch* hoar frost, *glen, ingle* a hearth-fire, *loch, partan* the common crab, *ptarmigan* an Arctic grouse, *slogan* originally a war cry, *sonse* plenty, prosperity (whence *sonsy* hearty, comely, buxom), *strath* a wide valley, *tocher* a dowry. (2) From the 17c onward, also often passing into English: *ben* a mountain, *brogue* a Highlander's shoe, *claymore* a Highland sword, *corrie* a cirque or circular hollow on a mountainside, *gillie* a hunting attendant, *golach* an earwig, *pibroch* solo bagpipe music, *sporran* a purse worn in front of a kilt, *whisky.* (3) From the late 19c onward: *ceilidh* ('cayly') an informal musical party, *Gaidhealtachd* the area where Gaelic is spoken, *slàinte* ('slanch') health and *slàinte-mhath* ('slanche-va') good health (said as a toast).

Latin. The distinctive vocabularies of education, the Church, and especially law in Scotland are largely Latin: see SCOTTISH ENGLISH. From the classroom a little schoolboy Latin has trickled into Scots since the 15c or earlier: *dominie* schoolmaster, *dux* best pupil in a school or a class, *fugie* a runaway, truant, *janitor* a school caretaker, *pandie* a stroke on the palm with a cane, etc. (from Latin *pande manum* stretch out your hand: also *palmie*), *vacance* vacation, holiday, *vaig* and *stravaig* wander aimlessly.

Echoisms, reduplicatives, and others. (1) Words of uncertain origin but with a distinct onomatopoeic element include: *birl* to whirl, *daud* a thump or lump, *dunt* a thump, *sclaff* to slap, *skrauch* and *skreich* to shriek, *wheech* to move in a rush, *yatter* to chatter. (2) Scots has many widely used reduplicative words, such as *argybargy* a dispute, *clishclash* and *clishmaclaver* idle talk, gossip, *easy-osy* easy-going, *eeksie-peeksie* six and half a dozen, *the hale jingbang* the whole caboodle, *joukerie-pawkerie* trickery, *mixtermaxter* all mixed up. (3) Combinations and fanciful formations: *bletherskate* an incessant talker, *camshauchle* distorted, *carnaptious* quarrelsome, *carfuffle* a commotion (passed into English), *collieshangie* a noisy squabble, *sculduddery* fornication (whence AmE *skullduggery*), *tapsalteerie* topsy-turvy, and *whigmaleerie* a trifle, whim.

Iteratives, intensives, and others. (1) Iteratives and intensives: *donner* to daze (whence *donnert* stupid), *scunner* to disgust, and someone or something disgusting (from the root of *shun*: also Northern English), *scowder* to scorch (cognate with *scald*), *shauchle* to shuffle, *shoogle* to joggle or shake. (2) Common words of various derivations, some obscure: *bogle* a ghost (perhaps of Celtic origin: note *tattie-bogle* 'a potato bogle', a scarecrow), *bonny* or *bonnie* handsome, beautiful (perhaps from French *bon* good), *braw* fine, excellent (perhaps a variant of *brave*), *collie* a sheepdog (now in general use in English), *couthy* homely/homey, congenial (from *couth* known: compare *uncouth*), *eerie* fearful, ghostly (now general), *glaikit* foolish (from *glaik* trick, deceit, flash), *glamour* a spell (now general, for a special kind of magic: a doublet of *grammar*), *gowkit* or *gukkit* foolish (perhaps from the *guk-guk* call of the *gowk* or cuckoo), *glaur* mud, *glower* to stare (now general), *gomerel* a fool, *gumption* get-up-and-go, guts (now general). (3) Recent creations: *bangshoot* caboodle (compare *jingbang*, above), *bletheration* foolish talk (see *blether*, above), *duffie*/*yuffie* a water closet, *fantoosh* flashy (probably a play on *fancy* and *fantastic*), *gallus* mischievous, *heidbanger* a madman, *high-heid-yin* ('high-head-one') boss, manager, *laldie* a thrashing, *multy* a multi-storey tenement, *sapsy* soppy, effeminate, *scheme* (clipping 'housing scheme') a local-authority housing estate, *skoosh* to gush, fizzy drink, *squeegee* askew.

Literary Scots. Already in Middle Scots, literary and official prose had grown archaic in comparison with contemporary speech, and spoken

innovations therefore largely fail to appear in writing, apart from comic verse and passages of quoted dialogue in law-court records. These last show novel forms such as *fow* for *full*, *mow* for *mouth*, *ha* and *gie* (later *hae* and *gie*) for *have* and *give*, and such new coinages as *glower* (to stare) and *glaikit* (foolish). The following passage illustrates polished 16c literary prose:

The samyn tyme happynnit ane wounderfull thing. Quhen Makbeth and Banquho war passand to Fores, quhair King Duncan wes for the tyme, thai mett be the gaitt thre weird sisteris or wiches, quhilk come to thame with elrege clething (from John Bellenden's translation, *c*.1531 of Hector Boece's Latin *Chronicles of Scotland*, 1527).

[Translation: At that time a wonderful thing happened. When Macbeth and Banquo were on their way to Forres, where King Duncan was at the time, they met by the roadside three 'sisters of fate' or witches, who approached them in unearthly (eldritch) garments.]

In the 20c, literary Scots of the variety that includes Lallans and the language of W. L. Lorimer's *The New Testament in Scots* similarly differs from colloquial varieties. It draws its typical word forms, vocabulary, and grammar from an archaic, more or less non-local, variety of Central Scots, retaining for example obsolete or obsolescent uses of modal verbs and negatives and such archaisms as *aiblins* perhaps, *descryve* describe, *leed/leid* a language, *lift* sky, *swith* quickly, and *virr* strength. It also sometimes employs a stilted, non-colloquial, English-like syntax. Occasionally, false analogies produce forms and usages that have no Scots pedigree: *ainer* an owner, *aipen* open, *raim* to roam, *delicht* delight, *tae* too (whose Scots equivalent is *owre*).

The following passages exemplify Modern Scots since the 18c, in works of wide currency within 'English literature':

O! 'tis a pleasant thing to be a bride;
Syne whindging getts about your ingle-side,
Yelping for this or that with fasheous din,
To mak them brats then ye maun toil and spin.
(Allan Ramsay, from the *The Gentle Shepherd*,
1725)

'Weel, weel,' said Mr. Jarvie, 'bluid's thicker than water; and it liesna in kith, kin and ally, to see motes in ilk other's een if other een see them no. It wad be sair news to the auld wife below the Ben of Stuckavrallachan, that you, ye Hieland limmer, had knockit out my harns, or that I had kilted you up in a tow'
(Walter Scott, from *Rob Roy*, 1817).

Faith, when it came there was more to remember in Segget that year than Armistice only. There was better kittle in the story of what happened to Jim the Sourock on Armistice Eve. He was aye sore troubled with his stomach, Jim, he'd twist his face as he'd hand you a dram, and a man would nearly lose nerve as he looked—had you given the creature a bad shilling or what? But syne he would rub his hand slow on his wame, *It's the pains in my breast that I've gotten again*;

and he said that they were fair awful sometimes, like a meikle worm moving and wriggling in there (Lewis Grassic Gibbon, from *Cloud Howe*, second in the trilogy *A Scots Quair*, 1932-4).

Conclusion. With its own history, dialects, and literature, Scots is something more than a dialect yet something less than a fully-fledged language. A wide linguistic distance lies between it and standard English, the poles of speech in most of Scotland. By and large, spoken and written Scots are difficult for non-speakers, and require an investment of effort. As a result, use of Scots in mixed company can make 'monolingual' English speakers feel excluded. In the larger European context, the situation of Scots resembles that of Frisian in the Netherlands, Nynorsk in Norwegian, Occitan in relation to French in France, and Catalan in relation to Spanish in Spain: see FRISIAN, NORWEGIAN. Scots is the substratum of general English in Scotland; most Scots use mixed varieties, and 'full' traditional Scots is now spoken by only a few rural people: see SCOTTISH LANGUAGES. None the less, despite stigmatization in school, neglect by officialdom, and marginalization in the media, people of all backgrounds have since the 16c insisted in regarding *the guid Scots tongue* as their national language, and it continues to play an important part in their awareness of their national identity.

See BORROWING, BRITISH LANGUAGES, BURNS, DIALECT IN SCOTLAND, DORIC, EDINBURGH, ENGLISH, GLASGOW, GUTTER SCOTS, HIGHLAND ENGLISH, INGLIS, LALLANS, NORSE, NORTHERN ENGLISH, NORTHUMBRIA, ORKNEY AND SHETLAND DIALECTS, SCOTLAND, SCOTS LANGUAGE ORGANIZATIONS, SCOTS LITERATURE, SCOTT, SCOTTISH ENGLISH, STEVENSON, ULSTER SCOTS, Z. [EUROPE, LANGUAGE, VARIETY].   A.J.A.

Aitken, A. J. 1984. 'Scottish Accents and Dialects', and 'Scots and English in Scotland', in P. Trudgill (ed.), *Language in the British Isles*. Cambridge: University Press.
—— & McArthur, Tom (eds.). 1979. *Languages of Scotland*. Edinburgh: W. & R. Chambers.
Graham, William. 1977. *The Scots Word Book*. Edinburgh: The Ramsay Head Press.
Kay, Billy. 1986. *Scots: The Mither Tongue*. Edinburgh: Mainstream.
MacLeod, Iseabail (ed.). 1990. *The Scots Thesaurus*. Aberdeen: University Press.
McClure, J. Derrick. 1988. *Why Scots Matters*. Edinburgh: The Saltire Society.
Murison, David. 1977. *The Guid Scots Tongue*. Edinburgh: William Blackwood.
Robinson, Mairi (ed.). 1985. *The Concise Scots Dictionary*. Aberdeen: University Press.

SCOTS-IRISH. See SCOTCH-IRISH.

SCOTS LANGUAGE ORGANIZATIONS. In addition to such university departments as Edinburgh's *School of Scottish Studies* (which includes the *Linguistic Survey of Scotland*) and Glasgow's *Department of Scottish Literature*, several voluntary bodies promote Scots. The *Scottish Text Society* (founded 1882) provides scholarly editions of (especially earlier) literature. Though with different aims, the publications of the *Scottish History Society* (from 1887) ensure the appearance of many works in Scots. The *Scottish National Dictionary Association* (founded in 1929) produces dictionaries of Modern Scots, based on original research on the language. From 1953 to 1976, the *Scottish Dictionaries Joint Council* oversaw the work of the *Scottish National Dictionary* and the *Dictionary of the Older Scottish Tongue* on behalf of the universities and other bodies; currently, as the *Joint Council for the Dictionary of the Older Scottish Tongue*, it continues to manage *DOST*. The *Saltire Society* was founded in 1936 to promote Scottish culture and has benefited Scots and Gaelic through its publications and public performances. The *Burns Federation* (founded 1885), with its annual journal *The Burns Chronicle*, carries out similar work. Since 1970, the *Association of Scottish Literary Studies* (*ASLS*) has published works of Scots literature and language. It publishes the *Scottish Literary Journal*, which includes an annual issue *Scottish Language*. The ASLS has a Language Committee and a Schools Committee. The *Scots Language Society* (founded in 1972 as the *Lallans Society*) supports the language and its literature, and publishes the magazine *Lallans*. See LALLANS, LINGUISTIC SURVEY OF SCOTLAND, SCOTS, SCOTTISH DICTIONARIES. [EUROPE, MEDIA].
                                      I.C.M.

SCOTS LITERATURE. Literature written in Scots, whose history falls into two periods: before the Union of the Crowns in 1603, when Scots was the accepted literary medium of non-Gaelic Scotland; after 1603, when literature in Scots as a literary language coexists and in some sense competes with standard English.

Before 1603. The period from 1376 to 1560 is considered the finest in the history of Scots literature. The language, with its large and varied vocabulary, allowed for a wide range of styles, exploited by such poets or *makars* as John Barbour (the epic poem *The Brus*, 14c), King James I (*The Kingis Quair*, 15c), Robert Henryson (*The Morall Fabillis, The Testament of Cresseid*, 15c), 'Blind Harry' (the epic poem *The Wallace*, 15c), William Dunbar (a varied output including religious, courtly, humorous, and satirical poems, 15-16c), Gavin Douglas (a translation of the *Aeneid*, 15-16c), and Sir David Lyndsay (poems including *Squyer Meldrum* and the play *Ane*

Satyre of the Thrie Estaitis, 16c). Scots prose never reached the same level of literary development, but the late 15c and the 16c produced some historical, theological, and polemical works. A short-lived poetic revival directed by James VI included experiments with French and Italian models.

After 1603. The 17c was a relatively barren period in Scottish letters. In the 18c, however, Allan Ramsay revived Scots poetry with a corpus of mainly comic and satiric verse and the pastoral drama *The Gentle Shepherd*. Robert Fergusson, Robert Burns, and Alexander Ross, among others, built on Ramsay's foundation to produce a varied and colourful poetry drawing on folklore as well as on the earlier literary tradition. The use of Scots for fictional purposes was developed in the late 18c and 19c by Walter Scott, John Galt, James Hogg, George Mac-Donald, Robert Louis Stevenson, and others. Stevenson, perhaps the foremost Scots poet since Burns, used an eclectic language that contrasted with a school of local dialect writing then emerging in the north-east, with William Alexander and (in the late 19c and early 20c) Charles Murray and Mary Symon among its practitioners. A revolution was effected in the 1920s by Hugh MacDiarmid, who used an eclectic literary dialect known as *Synthetic Scots* for a challenging, metaphysical poetry. His achievement launched a school of experimental poetry, among whose leading members were William Soutar, Sydney Goodsir Smith, Robert Garioch, and Alexander Scott. The distinctive North-Eastern dialect continued to produce poetry closely linked to the traditional life of the region. Other parts of the country, including Orkney and Shetland, have more recently developed traditions of local dialect writing. Stories and dramas in Scots, a vigorous school of writing in Glasgow working-class dialect, and a number of major literary translations, such as W. L. Lorimer's translation of the New Testament into Scots, are among recent developments.

See BURNS, DIALECT IN SCOTLAND, ENGLISH LITERATURE, GLASGOW, LALLANS, LORIMER, MACDIARMID, MAKAR, ORKNEY AND SHETLAND DIALECTS, SCOTS (LITERARY SCOTS), SCOTT, SCOTTISH LITERATURE, SMOLLETT, STEVENSON. [EUROPE, LITERATURE, VARIETY]. J.D.M.

SCOTSMAN/WOMAN. See -MAN/WOMAN.

SCOTT, Sir Walter [1771-1832]. Scottish poet, novelist, collector of ballads, and historian. Born in Edinburgh, he was partly brought up in the Borders, whose history and traditions were a fundamental influence. He was educated at the High School and U. in Edinburgh, and after training as a lawyer was appointed Sheriff-Depute of Selkirkshire in 1799. His first important published work was *Minstrelsy of the Scottish Border* (1802-3), an edited collection in three volumes of over 70 ballads. The tone and quality of ballad poetry influenced his series of narrative poems on Scottish historical themes, including *Marmion* (1808) and *The Lady of the Lake* (1810). However, his reputation rests mainly on his novels, of which many are set in 17-18c Scotland (including *Waverley*, 1814; *Old Mortality*, 1816; *Rob Roy*, 1817), but others have settings from various periods in the history of England (including *Ivanhoe*, 1819; *Kenilworth*, 1821) and France (*Quentin Durward*, 1823). His success as a novelist enabled him to purchase the estate of Abbotsford, in the Borders, on which he lavished much imagination and expense. In 1826, the collapse of the publishing company with which he was associated left him financially ruined; and the remainder of his life was spent, despite bereavements and deteriorating health, in heroic and ultimately successful efforts to redeem the company's debts by his writing.

By virtually inventing the historical and regional novel as genres, Scott exerted a profound influence on the subsequent course of literature throughout the world. His successors include not only English regional novelists such as the Brontë sisters and Thomas Hardy, but James Fenimore Cooper and Mark Twain, for example, in the US, and others in Australia, Canada, India, and elsewhere. His use of Scots for dialogue encouraged others to experiment with non-standard forms of English and to provide them with more or less consistent orthographies. His presentation of scenes and characters from Scottish history also made an enduring contribution to perceptions of Scotland both at home and abroad. His English vocabulary is ornamented not only with words taken from Scots but with a large number of archaisms from Spenser and Shakespeare, particularly in such fields as warfare, weaponry, horsemanship, and medieval architecture. His Scots dialogue is realistic and expressive, but the declining status of Scots in his time is suggested by the fact that most of his Scots-speaking characters belong to the lower orders or are associated with an age that was gone or passing when he wrote. See index. [BIOGRAPHY, EUROPE, LITERATURE]. J.D.M.

SCOTTICISM [17c: from Latin *Scotticus*, Scottish, and *-ism* as in *Anglicism*]. A feature of English peculiar to Scotland; a word or usage from Scots or related to Scotland that occurs in English at large or in any other language. The term has often been pejorative, especially in Scotland itself, where since the late 17c it has served to indicate a usage to be avoided for reasons of refinement at home and ease of communication abroad. As the Anglicization of Scots proceeded after the Union of the Crowns in 1603, Scottish writers began apologizing for, vindicating, or seeking English help in eradicating the Scots expressions which occurred in their writings. Published collections such as James Beattie's *Scoticisms arranged in Alphabetical Order, designed to correct Improprieties of Speech and Writing* (Edinburgh, 1787, 115 pp., *c*.500 entries) began appearing in 1752, continuing to the 20c. The general response to these collections has been mixed: (1) Some of the expressions warned against were eliminated from ScoE: *to come/sit into the fire*; the French-derived verb *evite* (to avoid). (2) Some have become (and may always have been) part of general English: *burial* for *funeral*; *come here* (18c refined usage in England preferred *come hither*); *close the door* (*shut* was preferred); *curt/curtly*; *greed*; *liberate* (*set at liberty* was preferred). (3) Many continue in present-day ScoE. With the return of Scots to respectability in the 19c, Scotticisms have lost much of their former odium, except for the shibboleths of *Gutter Scots*.

A distinction can now be drawn between *covert* and *overt Scotticisms*. Covert Scotticisms are characteristically Scottish expressions (though some are shared by other varieties, such as AmE) which speakers of ScoE use unselfconsciously, only slightly or not at all aware that they are not universal in English: *cast out* to quarrel, *cast up* to reproach, *handless* clumsy, *miss oneself* to miss a treat, *pinkie* the little finger, *give/get a row* to inflict/receive a severe reprimand, *sort* to mend, *stay* to live, reside, *swither* to hesitate between options. Overt Scotticisms make up a repertoire of hundreds of words, sayings, and idioms universally recognizable as Scots, which middle-class ScoE speakers sprinkle through their speech and to a less extent their writing, to claim membership of the in-group of Scots: *ay(e)* yes, *hame* home, *hoose* house, *ben the hoose* in(to) the inner part of the house, *bonnie* and *braw* good-looking, fine, *the craitur* ('the creature') whisky, *dreich* dreary (said of the weather, a sermon, etc.: Scots *gey dreich* pretty dreary), *kirk* church, *the auld kirk* ('the old church') whisky, *peelie-wallie* sickly, *wabbit* exhausted, *come into the body o' the kirk* to come forward and join the company, *it's back tae the auld claes and parritch tomorrow* back to old clothes and porridge (said on return from holiday), *keep a calm sough* to stay calm, *work for sweeties* to work for sweets or candy (that is, for a pittance). See GUTTER SCOTS, -ISM, SCOTS, SCOTTISH ENGLISH. [EUROPE, STYLE, VARIETY, WORD].   A.J.A.

SCOTTISH [From Middle English *Scottisc*, Old English *Scyttisc*]. Relating or belonging to Scotland, its people, institutions, etc., the most neutral and inclusive of the adjectives *Scottish*, *Scots*, *Scotch*. In the late 16c, as part of the Anglicizing fashion of the time, *Scottish* began to be used in Scotland as well as England as an alternative to *Scots*, which from the mid-18c it surpassed in popularity in most uses: *the Scottish Episcopal Church*, *the Scottish Language*, *the Scottish Office*, and in the title *The Scottish Monthly Magazine* (1836-7) as compared with *The Scots Magazine* (1739-). When, by the early 20c, *Scotch* had fallen out of favour in educated usage in Scotland, *Scottish* along with *Scots* superseded it in nearly all adjectival uses: for example, when the *Scotch Educational Department* had its name changed by Act of Parliament (1918) to the *Scottish Education Department*. Formerly used (since the 17c) in England and Scotland as a mass or collective noun, *Scottish* is virtually confined in Scotland to use as an adjective, unlike *Scots* or *Scotch*, as in 'Speak Scots/Scotch or whistle', 'the clannishness of the Scots/Scotch'. In expressions like these, *Scottish* is not now used. Compare SCOTCH, SCOTS. [EUROPE, NAME].
                                                    A.J.A.

SCOTTISH DICTIONARIES.

Since the 16c, Lowland Scotland has had a tradition of glossaries and dictionaries interpreting Scots to users of standard English, and since the mid-19c Scottish lexicographers have contributed significantly to a range of dictionaries of English.

The lexicography of Scots. The first substantial piece of Scottish lexicography was Sir John Skene's glossary of Scots law, *De Verborum Significatione: The Exposition of the . . . difficill wordes, contained in the . . . Actes of Parliament* (1597), but the foundation of the lexicography of the vernacular was Thomas Ruddiman's *A Glossary . . . of The hard and difficult Words in Gavin Douglas's Translation of Virgil's Aenis*, appended to his edition (1710) of Douglas (1513). This alphabetic glossary of *c*.3,000 entries, supported by Ruddiman's familiarity with local dialect and lore, was copiously supplied with references to the text, enabling words to be examined in their context. Following Ruddiman, it became usual to append a more or less alphabetical glossary, but mostly without text references, to any collection of Scots vernacular writing: for example, Burns's glossaries to the 1786 and 1787 additions of his *Poems*; until the late 19c, few or none of these have compared with Ruddiman for thoroughness. Another branch of Scottish lexicography (18-20c) was collections of Scotticisms: see entry. Following several abortive schemes to 'complete a Dictionary of words peculiar to Scotland' (Samuel Johnson to James Boswell, 1769), a full dictionary of Scots was realized in John Jamieson's *An Etymological Dictionary of the Scottish Language*, in two quarto volumes (1808), with a *Supplement* in two further volumes (1825). This was the first completed British dictionary to substantiate its definitions with accurately referenced quotations, usually in chronological order, and therefore the first dictionary on historical principles of any variety of English. In its original form or in re-editions or abridgements (the first his own abridgement of 1818), Jamieson's *Dictionary* was consulted as the authority on Scots vocabulary long after it had been superseded by the *Oxford English Dictionary* in 1928.

The 19-20c produced several one-volume dictionaries of Scots, mostly without quotations or references and with fairly brief definitions. The most important have been: *A Dictionary of the Scottish Language* (1818), by Ebenezer Picken; *Chambers Scots Dialect Dictionary* (1911), by Alexander Warrack; *The Scots Word-Book* (1977), by William Graham, containing an English/Scots section of *c*.5,000 entries, and a Scots/English section of *c*.4,500 entries; and the *Concise Scots Dictionary* (1985: see below). The appearance of numerous new and more reliable editions of early texts, the continued production (since Jamieson's time) of new dialect literature, and the copious body of new information on current oral dialect usage amassed by Joseph Wright for his *English Dialect Dictionary*, made possible the great advance over Jamieson achieved by the *EDD* and especially the *OED* in the coverage and description of Scots in every period. The *OED*'s etymologies are also incomparably more trustworthy than Jamieson's. One of its editors, W. A. Craigie, was the moving spirit behind the further progress of the lexicography of Scots.

Dictionary of the Older Scottish Tongue (short form *DOST*). This work is one of the Period Dictionaries of English and an exhaustive record of the vocabulary and usage of Older Scots, from its beginnings in the 12c to the end of the 17c. In his 1919 paper on the Period Dictionaries, W. A. Craigie proposed that he himself would undertake the dictionary of Older Scots, and in 1921 he began to collect the quotations for it. Editing began in 1925 and the first fascicle was published in 1931. By 1990, over two-thirds of *S* had been edited and 41 fascicles (comprising seven volumes, of nearly 5,000 pages) had been published to *ro*. *DOST* is an encyclopedic work, notable for quotations (the 21,000 or so main entries to *Ro* are illustrated by around 350,000

quotations) and for its editorial analysis by sense, spelling, and habitual collocation, manifesting at a glance the distributions of all these in time, region, and genre. Its editors have been W. A. Craigie (1921-55), A. J. Aitken (1955-86), J. A. C. Stevenson (1973-85), H. D. Watson (1983-), and Margaret G. Dareau (1984-).

Scottish National Dictionary (short form *SND*). This work, also one of the Period Dictionaries of English, provides a record of Scots from 1700 to the second half of the 20c. Unlike *DOST*, it records only those Scots words and uses, including those of Ulster and of Orkney and Shetland, which are not shared with general English or are not judged to be slang. Of Scots, however, it provides an exhaustive account, illustrated by quotations from over 6,000 source texts, supplemented by records of local oral use, partly from dialect studies, partly from local correspondents. The completed work, in ten volumes totalling 4,676 pages, contains around 20,000 main entries, illustrated by over 300,000 examples and references, more than half of which are quotations. Indications are given of the past and present regional and chronological distributions of each aspect of every word, and etymological notes cover much of the philological history of Scots. The accounts given of each alphabetical letter are unique and William Grant's *Historical Introduction* remains the clearest and most comprehensive survey of the main characteristics of the Scots dialects. The enterprise in effect began in 1907, with a suggestion from W. A. Craigie in a lecture he gave in Dundee. Dr William Grant, Lecturer in Phonetics, Aberdeen Teachers Training Centre, undertook to prepare a new dictionary of modern Scots. In 1929, the *Scottish National Dictionary Association* (*SNDA*) was formed to oversee the production of the dictionary. Grant brought out the first part in 1931, and by 1946, when he died at 83, he had carried the editing to near the end of *C*. His successor, David D. Murison, enlarged the collection of quotations, introduced new methods of collection and presentation, and completed the editing in 1976.

Concise Scots Dictionary (short form *CSD*). A one-volume dictionary with *c*.25,000 entries in 815 pages, edited by Mairi Robinson and published in 1985 by Aberdeen University Press. It resulted from a decision by the Council of the Scottish National Dictionary Association to produce a dictionary abridged from the *DOST* and *SND*. For the part of the alphabet not reached by the *DOST* at the time of editing the *CSD*, the main source for Older Scots was the *OED*. The *CSD* is unusual among concise dictionaries in showing the time span and dialect distribution of almost every meaning and form it records. It has etymologies and gives the pronunciation of every variant of every word, including obsolete words. In 1988, an abridged version appeared, *The Pocket Scots Dictionary*, and in 1990 a thematic consort to the *CSD*, *The Scots Thesaurus*, ed. Iseabail MacLeod, which defines 20,000 words in semantic fields from '*1* Birds, Wild Animals, Invertebrates' to '*15* Character, Emotions, Social Behaviour', and includes an English-into-Scots index.

The lexicography of English. Before the mid-19c, the contribution by Scots to general English lexicography was slight. The *Encyclopaedia Britannica* (1768–71) of three Edinburgh businessmen is in part a selective dictionary. Samuel Johnson, in the compilation of his *Dictionary* (1755), employed several Scots amanuenses, one of whom, Francis Stewart, collected specimens of cant and slang and explained words of gambling and card-playing. In his *Linguae Britannicae Vera Pronunciatio; or, a New English Dictionary* (1757), James Buchanan, a Scot who spent most of his life in London, made a modest improvement in the handling of indications of pronunciation; the schoolmaster William Perry, who made further improvements in the same direction in his *The royal standard English dictionary* (Edinburgh, 1775), though he lived in Scotland from 1774 or earlier and is often cited as an important 18c Scottish lexicographer, was apparently an Englishman.

John Ogilvie's *Imperial Dictionary, English, Technological and Scientific* (2 volumes, 1850) is notable as the completest dictionary of English to that date, as the first for over a century to use pictorial engravings to illustrate scientific and other terms, and as providing in many entries additional 'encyclopedic' description. This aspect was enhanced in the four-volume revised and much enlarged edition (1881–3) of another Scot, Charles Annandale. This formed the basis of the six-volume American *Century Dictionary* (1889–91), which was in turn the fountainhead of a succession of one-volume American and subsequently British dictionaries. Especially in the 20c, some of the most successful one-volume popular dictionaries of English have come from the Scottish publishing houses of W. & R. Chambers in Edinburgh and William Collins in Glasgow. Like most other British dictionaries, these differ from most American dictionaries and from Ogilvie in being without pictures. Collins too has earned a high reputation for its bi-directional dictionaries of English and various foreign languages. The Chambers flagship, its *Twentieth Century Dictionary* (1901), now renamed *Chambers English Dictionary* (1988), is noted for exhaustiveness of coverage and compactness of treatment and also for its unusually thorough

coverage of Scots usages and of English archaisms. However, the outstanding contribution by Scots to the general lexicography of the English language is that of the Scottish editors of and assistants to *The Oxford English Dictionary*, its *Supplements*, and *The Shorter OED*, most of all that of James Murray, who completed nearly half of the *OED*, and William Craigie, who edited a further fifth and also founded and co-edited the *Dictionary of American English*.

See CENTURY DICTIONARY, CHAMBERS, COLLINS, CRAIGIE, DICTIONARY, DICTIONARY OF AMERICAN ENGLISH, ENCYCLOPAEDIA BRITANNICA, JAMIESON, LEXICOGRAPHY, MURRAY, OXFORD ENGLISH DICTIONARY, PERIOD DICTIONARIES OF ENGLISH, REGIONAL DICTIONARIES OF ENGLISH, SCOTS, SCOTS LANGUAGE ORGANIZATIONS, SCOTTICISM, SCOTTISH ENGLISH, WATSON. [EUROPE, REFERENCE].

A.J.A.

SCOTTISH ENGLISH, short forms *ScoE, ScE.* The English language as used in Scotland, taken by some to include and by others to exclude *Scots*, or to include or exclude Scots as appropriate to particular discussions. When included, Scots is taken to be a northern dialect of English and part of the range of English found in Scotland. When excluded, Scots is taken to be a distinct language, still intact in literature and in the speech of some rural people, but otherwise now mixed with English from England. However the relationship is defined, Scots may be extolled or deplored, be a matter of indifference, or be an area of relatively dispassionate scholarly comment, and stands at the end of a social and cultural continuum from the language of official life and of education: standard English. Although for many the relationship between English and Scots is not clear-cut, most people are fully aware of the great differences at the poles of the continuum. Whatever the case, the traditional Scots usage of the Lowlands is distinct from *Highland English*, the English typically acquired by Gaelic-speakers in the Highlands and Islands. If Scots is excluded, ScoE can be defined as the mother tongue of a large minority of native-educated Scots (mainly the middle classes and those who have received a higher education) and the public language of most of the remainder (mainly the working class of the Lowlands). While most of its vocabulary and grammar belong to general English, ScoE has many features of Scots, which is the first language of its original speakers in the 17–18c and also of many people who today have English as their principal adult language, but occasionally revert to the Scots of their childhood.

Pronunciation. In many ways, the conservative ScoE accent is phonologically close to Scots, while in others it has departed from it.

Scots-based phonology. (1) The ScoE accent is rhotic, and all the vowels and diphthongs appear unchanged before /r/: *beard* /bird/, *laird* /lerd/, *lard* /lard/, *moored* /murd/, *bird* /bɪrd/, *word* /wʌrd/, *heard* /hɛrd/, *herd* /hërd/, *cord* /kord/, *hoard* /hord/. A distinction is made between the vowels in such words as *sword* /sɔrd/ and *soared* /sord/. Scots are widely supposed to trill the /r/, and many do, but majority usage is the alveolar tap in some phonetic environments and a fricative or frictionless continuant in others. There is a minority uvular *r* (see BURR) and retroflex *r* appears to be gaining ground in the middle class. (2) There are distinct phonemes in such words as *rise* and *rice.* The /aɪ/ diphthong occurs in *rise, tie/tied, sly, why* while the /ɔɪ/ diphthong occurs in *rice, tide, slide, while,* as well as in such borrowings from Scots as *ay(e)* always, *gey* very, *gyte* mad. (3) ScoE operates the Scottish Vowel-Length Rule: see entry. (4) There is no distinction between *cam* and *calm,* both having /a/, between *cot* and *caught,* both having /ɔ/, and between *full* and *fool,* both having /u/. (5) There is a monophthong in most regions for /i, e, o, u/ as in *steel, stale, stole, stool.* (6) The monophthongs and diphthongs total 14 vowel sounds, perhaps the smallest vowel system of any long-established variety of English. (7) ScoE retains from Scots the voiceless velar fricative /x/: for example, in such names as *Brechin* and *MacLachlan,* such Gaelicisms as *loch* and *pibroch,* such Scotticisms as *dreich* and *sough,* and for some speakers such words of Greek provenance as *patriarch* and *technical.* (8) The *wh-* in such words as *whale, what, why* is pronounced /hw/ and such pairs as *which/witch* are sharply distinguished. (9) In some speakers, initial /p, t, k/ are unaspirated.

Phonological options. (1) Vowels: *lodge* and *lodger* with /ʌ/ and not /ɔ/; *there* and *where* with /e/ and not /ɛ/. (2) Consonants: *length* and *strength* with /n/ and not /ŋ/; *fifth* and *sixth* with final /t/ and not /θ/; *raspberry* with /s/ and not /z/, *December* with /z/ and not /s/, *luxury* with /ɡʒ/ and not /kʃ/; *Wednesday* retains medial /d/. (3) Stress patterns: *tortoise* and *porpoise* with spelling pronunciation and equal syllabic stress; many words with distinctive stressing, such as *advertise, baptize, realize, recognize* and *adjudicate, harass, reconcile, soiree, survey* with the main stress on the final syllable, and *lamentable* and *preferably* on the second.

Non-Scots phonology. (1) Where many Scots speakers pronounce *coat* and *cot* with the same /o/ vowel, ScoE has /o/ in *coat* and /ɔ/ in *cot.* (2) Where some Scots speakers pronounce the vowel in *daughter* and *law* as /aː/ or /ɑː/, most educated ScoE speakers use /ɔː/, as in Central

Scots and Southern English. (3) Where in most Scots dialects the vowel in *bit, give* is open and more or less central, ScoE has a closer RP-like /ɪ/. A relic of the more open Scots vowel survives in the uniquely ScoE vowel /ë/ in the first syllable of *never* ('nivver', contrasted with *sever* and *river*): see AITKEN'S VOWEL.

Hybrid accents. The conservative accent just described is not the only accent of ScoE: (1) Especially in Edinburgh, in the group which includes lawyers, accountants, and architects, there exists a range of accents that to varying degrees incline towards RP. They date from the early 20c or earlier and their Scottishness is reduced by these main features: the addition of an RP-like /aː/ in such words as *calm, gather, value* contrasting with /a/ in *cam, bad, pal,* and /ɔː/ in *caught* beside /ɔ/ in *cot*; the merging of some or all of /ɪ, ʌ, ɛ, ë/ before /r/, in such words as *bird, word, heard,* and *herd* or *birth, worth, Perth,* and *earth,* usually with r-colouring; the sporadic or consistent merging of /ɔɪ/ and /aɪ/ under /aɪ/ in *tied/tide*; diphthongal realizations of /e/ as [ei] in *came,* and /o/ as [ou] as in *home*; and sporadic or consistent loss of pre-consonantal /r/ in such words as *farm, form, hard.* (2) Another hybrid, strongly stigmatized in the population at large, is a middle-class variety associated with both Edinburgh and Glasgow: see MORNINGSIDE AND KELVINSIDE. (3) Speakers of Highland English form a distinct community whose accents are influenced by Gaelic, including a tendency to lengthen vowels and devoice voiced consonants and aspirate voiceless ones, *just* sounding like 'chust', *big* like 'pick': see HIGHLAND ENGLISH.

Grammar. Features of present-day Scots grammar are carried over into ScoE: (1) *Modal verbs.* Many speakers do not use *shall* and *may* in informal speech, using *will* as in *Will I see you again?* and *can* for permission as in *Can I come as well?* and *might* or *will maybe* for possibility, as in *He might come later/He'll maybe come later. Must* expresses logical necessity as in *He must have forgotten, He mustn't have seen us,* but not compulsion, for which *have (got) to* are used, as in *You've (got) to pay.* Both *should* and *ought to* express moral obligation or advice, as in *You should/ought to try and see it,* but otherwise *would* is used where other BrE has *should,* as in *I would, if I was you* (not *I should, if I were you*). *Need to, use to,* and *dare to* operate as main verbs rather than auxiliaries: *He didn't need to do that; I didn't use to do that; She doesn't dare to talk back.* (2) *Passives.* The passive may be expressed by *get: I got told off.* (3) Certain verbs are used progressively, contrary to other BrE practice: *He was thinking he'd get paid twice; I was hoping to* *see her*; *They were meaning to come*. (4) *Negatives*. As with Scots *no* and *-nae*, ScoE *not* is favoured over *-n't*: *He'll not come* in preference to *He won't come*, *You're not wanted* to *You aren't wanted*, and similarly *Is he not coming? Can you not come? Do you not want it? Did he not come? Not* may negate a main verb as well as an auxiliary: *He isn't still not working?*; *Nobody would dream of not obeying*. (5) Verbs of motion elide before adverbs of motion in some contexts: *I'll away home then*; *The cat wants out*. (6) *The* is used as in Scots in, for example, *to take the cold*, *to get sent to the hospital*, *to go to the church*. (7) Pronouns in *-self* may be used nonreflexively: *How's yourself today? Is himself in?* (Is the man of the house at home?). (8) *Anybody, everybody, nobody, somebody* are preferred to *anyone, everyone, no one, someone*. (9) *Amn't I?* is used virtually to the exclusion of *aren't I?*: *I'm expected too, amn't I?*

Vocabulary and idiom. There is a continuum of ScoE lexical usage, from the most to the least international: (1) Words of original Scottish provenance used in the language at large for so long that few people think of them as ScoE: *caddie, collie, cosy, croon, eerie, forebear, glamour, golf, gumption, lilt, (golf) links, pony, raid, rampage, scone, uncanny, weird, wizened, wraith*. (2) Words widely used or known and generally perceived to be Scottish: *bannock, cairn, ceilidh, clan, clarsach, corrie, first-foot, glengarry, gloaming, haggis, kilt, pibroch, sporran, Tam o' Shanter, wee, whisky*. (3) Words that have some external currency but are used more in Scotland than elsewhere, many as covert Scotticisms: *bairn, bonnie, brae, burn, canny, douce, hogmanay, kirk, peewit* (the lapwing), *pinkie, skirl*. (4) General words that have uses special to ScoE and Scots: *astragal* a glazing bar on a window, *close* an entry passage in a tenement building, *stair* a flight of stairs, or a group of flats served by a single close in a tenement, *stay* to reside, *tablet* a variety of sweet, *uplift* to collect (rent, a parcel, etc.). (5) Scottish technical usages, many of Latin origin, especially in law, religion, education, and official terminology: *advocate* a courtroom lawyer (in England *barrister*), *convener* a chairman of a committee, *induction* of an ordained minister to a ministerial charge, *janitor* caretaker of a school, *jus relicti/relictae* the relict's share of a deceased's movable property, *leet* a list of selected candidates for a post, *procurator-fiscal* an official combining the offices of coroner and public prosecutor, *provost* a mayor, *timeous* timely. (6) Colloquial words used and understood by all manner of Scots and by the middle class as overt Scotticisms: *ach* a dismissive interjection, *braw* fine, good-looking, *chuckiestane* a pebble, *footer* to mess about, *gillie*

a hunting attendant, *girn* to whine, *glaikit* stupid, *haar* a cold sea-fog, *howf* a public house, *och* an interjection, *pernickety* fussy, *scunnered* sickened, *wabbit* tired out, *wannert* ('wandered': mad). (7) Traditional, sometimes recondite and literary, Scots words occasionally introduced into standard English contexts in the media, and known to minorities: *bogle* a phantom, *dominie* a schoolmaster, *eident* diligent, *forfochen* exhausted, *furth of* and *outwith* outside of, *gardyloo* the cry formerly used in Edinburgh before throwing slops from a high window, *hochmagandie* fornication, *leid* a language, *makar* a poet, *owerset* to translate, *Sassenach* an Englishman, a Lowlander, *southron* English, *yestreen* yesterday evening.

Conclusion. A feature of ScoE in its wider sense is the capacity and willingess to move, more or less consciously, and often for fun, from a more Scots to a more English way of speaking, employing differences in pronunciation, grammar, vocabulary, and idiom which add to the nuances of communication. Besides their use of overt Scotticisms as a token of national solidarity, the middle classes may also parade Scots (especially Gutter Scots and shibboleths) proudly, humorously, snobbishly, or patronizingly, according to inclination and circumstance. The working classes, for their part, sometimes send up people whom they consider snobbish, affected, or overly English in their ways by putting on 'anglified' speech.

See AITKEN'S LAW, AITKEN'S VOWEL, BRITISH ENGLISH, CODE-SWITCHING AND CODE-MIXING, DIALECT IN SCOTLAND, EDINBURGH, ENGLISH, GLASGOW, GUTTER SCOTS, L-SOUNDS, NORTHERN ENGLISH, R-SOUNDS, SCOTS, SCOTTICISM, SCOTTISH LANGUAGES, SCOTTISH VOWEL-LENGTH RULE, STYLE-DRIFTING. [EUROPE, VARIETY]. A.J.A.

Abercrombie, David. 1979. 'The Accents of Standard English in Scotland', in A. J. Aitken & Tom McArthur (eds.), *Languages of Scotland*. Edinburgh: Chambers.
Aitken, A. J. 1979. 'Scottish Speech: A Historical View with Special Reference to the Standard English of Scotland', in Aitken & McArthur (eds.) (above).
—— 1984. 'Scots and English in Scotland', in Peter Trudgill (ed.), *Language in the British Isles*. Cambridge: University Press.
McClure, J. Derrick. 1975. 'The English Speech of Scotland', *The Aberdeen University Review* 46.
Wells, John C. 1982. *Accents of English: The British Isles* (Scotland: pp. 393–417). Cambridge: University Press.

SCOTTISH GAELIC. The Celtic language of the West Highlands and Western Isles of Scotland. Gaelic-speaking Scots arrived from Ireland on the west coast of what is now Scotland in 3-5c AD. As they gradually gained power, their language spread throughout the country, though not the whole population; in the south-east, for example, it was probably used mainly among the ruling classes. With the increased influence of Northern English, the use and prestige of Gaelic began to decline and since the 12c there has been a gradual retraction. Political factors, social pressures, and educational policies have combined to threaten the language with extinction. In the later 20c, more positive attitudes have developed and efforts are being made to sustain Gaelic, encourage bilingual policies, and give it a valued place in school and pre-school education. Many, however, fear that these measures are too little too late. Gaelic is now used as a community language virtually only in the Western Isles. At the 1981 census, there were little over 80,000 speakers, with only a few hundred under the age of five and there are few monoglot speakers above this age.

Scottish Gaelic has an ancient literary tradition and paradoxically its literature flourishes in the 20c, with such poets as Sorley MacLean, Derick Thomson, and Iain Crichton Smith (also a novelist in English). The formal literature of the medieval period was shared with Irish Gaelic, the two cultures remaining in close contact until at least the 17c. Much poetry came from a bardic tradition of poets composing songs in strict metre in the service of their chiefs, a system which ended in the 17c. However, the 18c saw a golden age of less rule-bound poetry with a wide variety of subject matter: the songs of Donnchadh Bàn Mac-an-t-Saoir (Duncan Bàn Macintyre), Alasdair Mac Mhaighstir Alasdair (Alexander MacDonald), and Rob Donn continue to be sung, and the 20c flowering continues with a younger generation of poets. Public performance and composition are encouraged by the *National Mod*, an annual competitive festival of music and poetry organized by *An Comunn Gaidhealach/The Highland Association*, founded in 1891 to support the Gaelic language and culture and the Highland way of life. *Comunn na Gàidhlig* (the Gaelic Association) was set up in 1984 with the more specific aim of promoting the language.

There has been a considerable two-way traffic of words between Scottish Gaelic and Scots throughout the centuries, with some words making more than one journey across the linguistic boundary: for example, Gaelic *clann* (the children of a family) became older Scots and then English *clan* (a local or family group under a chief and having a common name), recently taken back into Gaelic in the latter sense. Gaelic has also influenced the pronunciation and syntax of English in Gaelic-speaking and recently Gaelic-speaking areas. Gaelic borrowings from English and Scots are numerous and increasing, especially in technical and administrative fields:

for example, *teilebhisean* television, *rèidio* radio, and *briogais* trousers (from Scots *breeks*). The influence of English on Gaelic syntax is considerable and rapidly extending, now that virtually all adult speakers are bilingual. Pronunciation has been less affected, but phonemic changes based on English or Scots are noticeable in the speech of children of Gaelic-speaking immigrants to the cities. More of these children now speak Gaelic, because of a recent increase in Gaelic playgroups and schools. The language is taught in three of the Scottish universities, two of which (Edinburgh and Glasgow) have a chair of Celtic.

See BORROWING, BRITISH LANGUAGES, CELTIC LANGUAGES, ETHNIC NAME, GAEL, GAELIC, GAELTACHT, HIGHLAND ENGLISH, IRISH, NORTHERN IRISH ENGLISH, SCOTS, SCOTTISH ENGLISH, SCOTTISH LANGUAGES, SCOTTISH LITERATURE, SCOTTISH PLACE-NAMES. [EUROPE, LANGUAGE]. I.C.M.

SCOTTISH JOKE. An ethnic joke that presents Scots as unredeemably mean: 'Whilst in London's West End tonight, a Scotsman died of starvation on the back seat of a Pay-as-You-Leave bus' (*The Two Ronnies*, 1978). See ABERDEEN JOKE, ETHNIC JOKE, JOKE. [EUROPE, STYLE]. T.MCA.

SCOTTISH LANGUAGES. Scotland's linguistic heritage is complex. In the Middle Ages, six languages were in regular use: *British* or *Brythonic* in Strathclyde, a Celtic language akin to Welsh and known among scholars as *Cumbric*; *Gaelic*, the majority language, a Celtic language originating in Ireland; *Inglis*, a variety of Northern English spoken in the Lowlands and later known as *Scots*; *Norn*, a form of Norse in the Northern Isles, the Western Isles, and the adjacent mainland; *Norman French* among the Normanized nobility; and *Latin* as an ecclesiastical, academic, and legal language. From the 16c, the English of England has been increasingly influential and of the early profusion only Gaelic and Scots survive. Gaelic is a distinct though dwindling language with its own literature, and there is controversy and even confusion over the nature of Scots: whether it is best described as a distinct language, a dialect of English, or in a half-way condition between the two. For some three centuries, a Scotticized standard English has been the language of official life, publishing, and in recent times the mass media. In private and informal speech, virtually all native-educated Scots (*c*.4.5m) operate within a variable range from the full Scots of some members of some farming, fishing, and former mining communities, through various mixtures of Scots and English, to a variety of ScoE, with such exceptions as bilingual speakers of Gaelic and

English. The remainder falls into two groups: an RP-speaking upper class and upper middle class (traditionally educated in England or in a number of private schools in Scotland, and generally using few Scotticisms), and immigrants from England, Ireland, or elsewhere (speaking with non-Scottish accents and a varying degree of assimilation to ScoE grammar and vocabulary). See BRITISH, BRITISH LANGUAGES, CELTIC LANGUAGES, CUMBRIC, GAELIC, INGLIS, LATIN[1], NORMAN FRENCH, NORN, PICTISH, SCOTS, SCOTTISH GAELIC. [EUROPE, NAME].   A.J.A., T.MCA.

SCOTTISH LITERATURE. Literature written in Scotland in any language, including Scots, English, Gaelic, Latin, and Cumbric (Brythonic), the only extant example of which is the late 6c poem *Y Gododdin*: the first surviving poem within what is now Scotland and also considered part of Welsh literature. The following article deals with writing by Scots in English; for other aspects of the literature of Scotland, see the list of entries at the end of the article. From the mid-16c, the combined influence of English-trained printers and widely disseminated works of theology in English (most importantly the Geneva Bible), led to a rapid assimilation of literary Scots to the orthographic, grammatical, and lexical canons of English. John Knox's *History of the Reformatioun within the realme of Scotland* (1587) shows a random mixture of Scots and English forms. The first major writer to adopt a virtually unmixed English for his work was the 17c poet and historian William Drummond of Hawthornden.

During the revival of Scottish artistic and intellectual activity in the 18c, English was the medium for all prose works on whatever subjects (for example, David Hume's philosophy, Adam Smith's economics, and James Hutton's geology), and for much of the poetry produced: such pseudo-Augustan works as William Wilkie's *Epigoniad* (1757), modelled on Homer, were preferred by critics to the more natural vernacular verse of Robert Fergusson. One of the most influential literary works of the century was James MacPherson's *Fingal, an Ancient Epic Poem, in Six Books* (1762), based loosely on early Gaelic tales and written in a highly poetic English prose. Purportedly based on the work of the Gaelic poet Ossian, it is now usually referred to as MacPherson's *Ossian*, and was a focus of controversy at the time. It was highly regarded by Hume, Smith, and the rhetorician Hugh Blair, by leading European writers, including Goethe and Schiller, and was one of Napoleon's favourite works. However, Johnson and other critics were doubtful about its authenticity and when asked to show the originals from which he had with considerable poetic licence claimed it

came, MacPherson produced fabrications. Whatever the morality of the episode, the bilingual author had succeeded in adapting and translating Gaelic tales and greatly influenced the Romantic Movement.

In this period, the question of how Scottish writers should express their national identities after the loss of independence in 1707, and the rival claims of Scots as the mother tongue and English as the language of formal education and social prestige, gave rise to a conflict which has never been resolved and which has informed much that is characteristic of Scottish literature to the present day. Many writers have used English for poetic or prose works on Scottish subjects: John Hume's *The Douglas Tragedy* (1756), Walter Scott's *Marmion* (1808) and other poems, James Thomson's *The City of Dreadful Night* (1874), and the novels of Neil Gunn. Others have sought a linguistic solution, employing an English coloured with the idiom, cadences, and to some extent vocabulary of one of the other languages of Scotland: South-West Scots in John Galt's *Annals of the Parish* (1821) and *The Provost* (1822), North-East Scots in Lewis Grassic Gibbon's *A Scots Quair* (1932-4), Gaelic and Highland English in Fionn Mac Colla's *The Albannach* (1932). Others again have produced work that is Scottish neither in subject matter nor language, and their Scottishness has to be identified on more subtle levels: much of the work of J. M. Barrie (drama), Edwin Muir (poetry), John Buchan and Eric Linklater (novels). The enduring sense of a Scottish identity, resisting submergence in the British state and transcending the strongly individual cultures of the regions of Scotland, has ensured the continuation and growth of a national literature. See ENGLISH LITERATURE, SCOTS (LITERARY SCOTS), SCOTS LITERATURE, SCOTTISH GAELIC. [EUROPE, LITERATURE].   J.D.M.

Bold, Alan. 1983. *Modern Scottish Literature*. London & New York: Longman.
Craig, Cairns (ed.). 1988– . *The History of Scottish Literature*. 4 vols. Aberdeen: University Press.
Watson, Roderick. 1984. *The Literature of Scotland*. Basingstoke: Macmillan.

SCOTTISH NATIONAL DICTIONARY. See SCOTTISH DICTIONARIES.

SCOTTISH PLACE-NAMES. The sources of the place-names of Scotland are diverse: the Celtic languages (British or Cumbric, Pictish, and Gaelic), the Germanic languages (Anglian, Norse, Scots, and English), and some others (pre-Celtic, French, etc.). Both hybridization and the Anglicization of non-English names occur.

Cumbric and Pictish. Many of the most ancient names are names of rivers: unexplained (*Spey*, *Ettrick*, *Tweed*), pre-Celtic (*Ayr*, *Nairn*), and Celtic (*Avon*, *Clyde*, *Dee*, *Don*). Both the Britons and the Picts spoke P-Celtic languages akin to Welsh. The Britons of Strathclyde and Lothian have bequeathed such Cumbric names as *Glasgow* green hollow, *Linlithgow* lake in the moist hollow, *Melrose* bare moor, and others containing such elements as *cair* fort (*Cramond* fort on the Almond River), *pen* head, end (*Penicuik* headland of the cuckoo), and *trev* homestead, village (*Tranent* village of the streams). Pictish has provided relatively few name elements; among them are *carden* thicket, as in *Kincardine* and *Pluscarden*, and *pett* a parcel of land, in some 300 names such as *Pittenweem* and *Pitlochry*. Some elements, such as *lanerc* glade (*Lanark*, *Lendrick*), are shared by both Cumbric and Pictish. Also Pictish is *aber* confluence, river mouth (*Aberdeen* Don mouth, *Aberfoyle* confluence of the sluggish stream), the P-Celtic equivalent of Gaelic *inver* (*Inverness* mouth of the Ness, *Inveraray* mouth of the Aray).

Gaelic. The most pervasive of the place-naming languages is Gaelic, the language of the original Scots from Ireland, who by *c*.500 had settled *Argyll* (coastland of the Gaels). Among the commonest Gaelic elements are *achadh* field (Scotticized as *ach-*, *auch-*, or, with the definite article in the genitive case, *Auchen*, *Achna*, as in *Auchmithie*, *Auchendinny*, *Achnasheen*), *baile* farm, village, town (Scotticized as *bal-*, as in *Balerno*, *Balfour*), and *cill* church, cell (Scotticized as *kil-*, as in *Kilbride*, *Kilmartin*). After the Gaelicization of Pictland and the annexation of Strathclyde and Lothian, Gaelic names spread throughout the country, from *Garvald* (rough brook) and *Glencorse* (glen of the river crossings) in the south-east to *Altnaharra* (brook of the wall) and *Dounreay* (fort by the broch) in the far north. They include the relatively Scotticized *Ardrossan* (headland of the little cape), *Arnprior* (prior's portion of land), *Achnasheen* (field of the storm), *Auchinleck* (field of the flagstone), *Cambuslang* (river-bend of ships), *Cumbernauld* (confluence of brooks). In the Highlands, Gaelic names tend to have more exotic spellings that often breach both Gaelic and Scots spelling rules, such as: *Achiltibuie* (? field of the yellow-haired lad), *Ardrishaig* (height of briars), *Drumnadrochit* (ridge of the bridge), *Tighnabruaich* (house on the bank). The names of mountains and other natural features often conform to Gaelic orthography: *Sgurr Domhnull* (Donald's hill), *Rubha Mòr* (big headland), *Loch an Eilean* (loch of the island).

Anglian. From the Northumbrian Angles, who settled in southern Scotland (Lothian) from the 7c, come such names as, in the south-east, *Whittinghame* (homestead of Hwīta's people), *Tynninghame* (homestead of the people by the River Tyne), *Haddington* (farm of Hadda's people), *Yetholm* (village near the gate or pass), *Polwarth* (Paul's enclosed farm), *Newbattle* (new house), *Hawick* (hedge farm), and in the south-west, *Whithorn* (white house), *Buittle* (house), *Prestwick* (priest's or priests' abode). Where Angle and Briton met, we have the hybrids *Edinburgh* (see EDINBURGH) and *Jedburgh* (fort on the Jed, formerly *Jed-worth*, with Old English *worth*, enclosed village, and a Cumbric river-name *Jed* (?)twisting river). Gaelic prefixes to Anglian names, as in *Bonjedward*, *Dalswinton*, *Tarbolton* signal the arrival, several centuries later, of Gaelic-speaking incomers.

Norse. From the 8c, the form of Norse known as Norn has covered the Northern Isles, and parts of Caithness, Sutherland, and Ross with such Scandinavian names as *Dingwall*, *Isbister*, *Kirkwall*, *Lerwick*, *Lybster*, *Papa Westray*, *Scalloway*, *Scapa Flow*, *Stromness*, *Sullom Voe*, *Thurso*, *Tingwall*, *Tongue*, *Wick*. Norse settlers of the same period in the Hebrides and the north-west mainland have left other names that were subsequently Gaelicized, as with *Uig*, *Mallaig*, originally with the same *vík* ending, for 'inlet, small bay', as in *Wick*, *Lerwick*; *Stornoway* in Lewis has the same element *vágr* (inlet, small bay) as in *Scalloway* and *Kirkwall*; similarly, *Shawbost*, with the element *bólstaðr* (homestead, farm), parallels *Isbister* and *Lybster*, and *Duirinish* and *Fishnish*, with the element *nes* (headland), echo *Durness* and *Stromness*. In the south-west, *Galloway* is named after the Gall-Ghàidhil (foreign Gaels), settlers of mixed Gaelic and Scandinavian stock from Ireland and the Hebrides, who appear to have been responsible for such 'inversion compounds' as *Kirkbride* and *Kirkoswald*, as compared with *Bridekirk* in Dumfriesshire and *Oswaldkirk* in Yorkshire; others are *Kirkcowan* and *Kirkcudbright* (pronounced 'Kircoobry'). In the same area, Cumbric, Gaelic, and Norse names co-occur: Cumbric *Penpont* and *Leswalt*, Gaelic *Ballantrae*, *Kilbride*, and *Stranraer*, Norse *Applegarth*, *Borgue*, *Gategill*, *Murraythwaite*, and *Tinwald*.

Norman, Scots, and English. There are some Norman French names, such as *Melville* (bad township), from the surname of Geoffrey de Melville, the 12c Norman owner, originally the name of a village in Normandy, and *Beauly* (pronounced 'Bew-lay'), once *Beau Lieu* (beautiful place). From the 12c, names in Early Scots spread beyond Lothian and include *Canonbie*,

Lamington, Neilston, Stewarton, and innumerable minor Lowland names: *Blackbogs, Broomielaw, Dyke, Fiddler's Flat, Newbigging, Skateraw, Skinfasthaven, Staneycroft, Threpeland, Windygates*. Some more recent names recall Hanoverian military outposts in the Highlands: *Fort William, Fort Augustus, Fort George*. Others commemorate a founder or a founder's wife or daughter (*Barbaraville, Bettyhill, Campbeltown, Fraserburgh, Grantown, Helensburgh*) or an event (several *Waterloos*) or memories of a residence abroad (*Lamancha*). Some have Biblical inspiration (*Canaan Lane, Joppa, Jordan Burn*) or are romantic or fanciful (*Beeswing, Comely Bank, Golden Acre*).

A mixed toponymy. Scottish toponymy is generally mixed, both linguistically and orthographically. The toponyms of the island of Skye, for example, include *Rubha Hunish, Kilmaluag, The Storr, Bernisdale, Portree, Kyleakin, Kyle of Lochalsh, the Cuillin Hills, the Crowlin Islands, Broadford, Teangue, the Sound of Sleat, the Point of Sleat, Loch Scavaig, Sgurr Alasdair, Idrigill Point, Macleod's Tables, Dunvegan, Dunvegan Head, Dunvegan Castle, Loch Bracadale, the Minch, the Little Minch*. North of Forth and Clyde, Gaelic predominates in the generic names for natural features: *ben/beinn* a mountain (*Ben Nevis, Beinn Dearg*), *glen/gleann* a narrow valley (*Glen Nevis, Glengarry*), *loch* a lake or arm of the sea (*Loch Ness, Loch Eriboll*), *strath/srath* a broad valley (*Strathearn, Strathmore*). In naming towns and villages at the head of a loch, Gaelic competes with a Gaelic/English hybrid: fully Gaelic *Kinlochleven, Kinlocheil*, and mixed Gaelic/English *Lochearnhead, Lochgoilhead*. Although *ben* dominates in the centre and north, in the south-east the Anglian *law* is common: *Broad Law, North Berwick Law, Traprain Law*. In the south and east, an arm of the sea may be a *firth*, of Norse origin, cognate with *fjord* (*the Solway Firth, the Firth of Clyde*). In one instance, in the far north, it is a strait: *the Pentland Firth*, between the mainland and Orkney. See CUMBRIC, EDINBURGH, GLASGOW, PICTISH, PLACE-NAME, SCOTLAND. [EUROPE, NAME].   A.J.A., T.MCA.

SCOTTISH PUBLISHING. Scotland has played a significant part in English-language publishing since the late 18c. Such companies as Constable and Oliver & Boyd were prominent in the early years of the 19c, based in Edinburgh, the most important centre of British publishing after London. Several publishers of the time produced magazines, the most prestigious of which were the Whig *Edinburgh Review* (1802-1929, originally published by Constable) and its Tory rival *Blackwood's Magazine* (1817, started by William Blackwood), which continued publication in one form or another until 1988. The brothers W. & R. Chambers played a significant role in the self-education movement of the early 19c, an important element in which was *Chambers's Journal* (founded 1832). In the 20c, publishing based in Scotland has been greatly diminished by increasing British centralization in London; as a result, many companies of Scottish origin, such as A. & C. Black and Nelson, have become prominent London publishers. Of the few firms that retained their Scottish base and gained in strength in 20c, William Collins was taken over by Rupert Murdoch's News International in 1988, and integrated with the US Harper & Row as Harper Collins; Blackie is the only long-established company of any size to remain independent. Both are based near Glasgow. W. & R. Chambers has since the mid-19c built up a worldwide reputation for its dictionaries of English and other reference books; it was taken over in 1989 by the French company Groupe de la Cité.

While the general picture has been one of retraction and withdrawal, there has been in recent decades an upsurge of smaller companies, some of which have supported Scottish language and literature: notably, in mid-century, William Maclellan and Macdonald & Co. Currently, contributions to Scottish culture in general and to literature in particular are being made by such newer firms as Aberdeen University Press, Canongate, John Donald, and Mainstream. Efforts are being made to reprint important works from the past, notably in Canongate's *Scottish Classics* series and Richard Drew's *Scottish Collection*. Apart from contributions by larger firms such as Oliver & Boyd (now owned by the Longman Group), publishing in Gaelic has generally been carried out by small companies, such as the Celtic Press in the 19c and Maclaren's in the 20c. At the present time, the publishers Acair (in Stornoway, Isle of Lewis) are supported by public funds in an effort to provide learning materials for Gaelic. Gairm in Glasgow publishes a wide variety of Gaelic books, including dictionaries, as well as a quarterly magazine of the same name. The *Gaelic Books Council/An Comunn Leabhraichean*, based in the U. of Glasgow, acts as a funding and encouraging body. Scottish publishing in general is supported by the *Scottish Arts Council*, which spends a higher proportion of its annual budget on literature than does the Arts Council of Great Britain. Since the 1970s, the *Scottish Publishers Association* has fostered cooperation among a growing number of Scottish companies. See BRITISH PUBLISHING, CHAMBERS, COLLINS, PUBLISHING. [EUROPE, MEDIA].   I.C.M.

SCOTTISH VOWEL-LENGTH RULE, short form *SVLR*. The name given by A. J. Aitken to the outcome of a 15-16c sound change, through which certain vowels of Scots and ScoE in Scotland and Ulster have no inherent length but are long or short according to following environment: long in stressed syllables before /r/, /v/, /ð/, /z/, and /ʒ/, before another vowel, before a morpheme boundary, and in certain other conditions; but short elsewhere. Thus, /i/ is long in *here*, *leave*, *see*, *sees*, in *idea*, in *agreed*, and in *feline*, but short in *beat*, *bead*, *feel*, *leaf*, *cease*, *greed*, and *feeling*. The vowels most regularly subject to the rule are: /i/, as shown above; /u/, which displays for example a contrast between *brewed* (with the vowel long before the morpheme boundary) and *brood* (with the vowel short), and, in many dialects, /e/, and /o/. Certain conservative Scots dialects have a vowel /ø/ that, in accordance with SVLR, is long in, for example, *do*, *poor*, and *use* (verb), and short in *boot*, *fool*, and *use* (noun). In the dialects of Central Scotland and Ulster Scots, this vowel has undergone an SVLR-conditioned phonemic split, so that *do*, *poor*, and *use* sound like 'day', 'pair', and 'yaize', whereas *boot*, *fool*, and *use* sound like 'bit', 'fill', and 'yis'. A similar split is responsible for the contrast between, for example, *alive*, *tie*, and *tied* (with the long diphthong /aɪ/), and *life*, *tide* (with the short diphthong /əɪ/). Other vowels in Scots and ScoE are not subject to the rule but have the same length in all environments: /ɪ/ as in *bit* and *fir*, and /ʌ/ as in *but* and *fur*, are short in all environments; certain other vowels, such as /ɑː/ or /ɔː/ in *saut* (salt), *law*, are in many dialects long in all environments. See AITKEN'S LAW, DIALECT IN SCOTLAND, SCOTS. [EUROPE, SPEECH].   A.J.A.

SCOUSE [From 18c *lobscouse*, a sailor's dish of stewed meat, vegetables, and ship's biscuit, not unlike Irish stew. *Lobscouser* was a slang name for a sailor. The terms *Scouse* and *Scouser* for someone from Liverpool seem to be recent, and probably arose because the city is a port and stew was a feature of the diet. The *OED* cites the *Southern Daily Echo* (1945), in which 'a scouse' is explained as 'a native of Liverpool where they eat "scouse" ']. (1) Also *Scouser*. A person born in the city of Liverpool, on the River Mersey, especially if from the working class. (2) The often stigmatized working-class speech of Merseyside. The accent combines features of Lancashire with varieties of English from Ireland and to a lesser extent from Wales, brought in by 19-20c immigration. Accents range from broad Scouse through modifications towards RP and RP itself in the middle and upper classes. Among the distinctive expressions in Scouse are *the Pool*, a nickname for Liverpool, and *Liverpudlian* (the

correct name for someone born in Liverpool, substituting *puddle* for *pool*). Non-Scousers, especially from north of the city, are sometimes called *woollybacks* (sheep), a nickname suggesting rusticity and lack of wits.

Pronunciation. Of the following features, 1-5 are widely regarded as shibboleths, especially when several occur together: (1) A merger of the vowels in such pairs as *fair*/*fur* and *spare*/*spur*, realized as an /eː/ or /ɜː/. (2) As in other parts of the north-west of England, syllable-final *-ng* is pronounced /ŋg/, as in 'long-g' for *long* and 'sing-ging-g' for *singing*. (3) The vowel in such words as *pin* and *sing* is pronounced /i/, so that they sound close to 'peen' and 'seengg'. (4) The sound /r/ may be either an alveolar continuant or an alveolar tap that is particularly distinct initially (*rabbit*, *run*), after stops and fricatives (*breathe*, *grass*, *three*), and between vowels (*carry*, *ferry*). (5) A /t/ between vowels is often replaced by /r/, sometimes shown in print as *rr*, as in 'marra' for *matter*: *What's the marra with you then?* In a publicity drive for the Liverpool clean streets campaign, litter was described as 'norra lorra fun'. (6) Some speakers, especially working-class Catholics of Irish background, replace /t, d/ with /θ, ð/, as in 'dese tree' for *these three*. *Month* may be pronounced 'muntth'. (7) In syllable-initial and syllable-final positions, a fricative can follow a stop, as in 'k/x/ing' for *king* (where /x/ represents the fricative in ScoE *loch*), 'me d/z/ad' for *my dad*, 'back/x/' for *back*, and 'bad/z/' for *bad*. (8) Scouse is often described as having a flat intonation, in effect a rise with a level tail where RP has a fall: in the statement *I don't like it*, it goes up on *like* then runs level, whereas RP starts going down on *like* and keeps going down. There is also a kind of fall in *yes-no* questions where RP would have a rise, so that in the question *Are you from Birkenhead?*, Scouse falls on *Birk* where RP rises. (9) Until recently it was possible to distinguish the speech of Irish Catholics from Protestant English through the pronunciation of some words; a double advertisement on local buses in the 1960s read on one side of the bus 'Treat us furly, travel early', on the other 'Treat us fairly, travel airly' (the latter denoting Irish-derived usage).

Adenoidal speech. The voice quality of speakers of Scouse has often been described as adenoidal, and phoneticians have speculated about the origins of such a feature. David Abercrombie, noting that children may acquire a quality of voice from others who have a problem, observes: 'A striking example . . . is afforded by some urban slum communities where adenoids, due doubtless to malnutrition and lack of sunlight, are prevalent, with their consequent effect on voice quality, but where people can be found with adenoidal voice quality who do not have adenoids—they have learnt the quality from the large number who do have them, so that they conform to what, for that community, has become the norm. . . . The accent of Liverpool seems to have had its origin in such circumstances' (*Elements of General Phonetics*, 1967). Gerald O. Knowles adds: 'In Scouse, the centre of gravity of the tongue is brought backwards and upwards, the pillars of the fauces are narrowed, the pharynx is tightened, and the larynx is displaced upwards. . . . The main auditory effect of this setting is the "adenoidal" quality of Scouse, which is produced even if the speaker's nasal passages are unobstructed' (in P. Trudgill (ed.), *Sociolinguistic Patterns in British English*, 1978). The effect is primarily achieved by the sustained closure of the velum or soft palate. See ACCENT, DIALECT IN ENGLAND, HIBERNO-, LANCASHIRE. [EUROPE, VARIETY]. T.MCA.

SCRABBLE [1930s: trademark of J. W. Spear & Sons plc]. A popular modern word game, invented by the American architect Alfred Butts and inspired by the crossword. His original game used letters printed on cardboard squares; later versions added a board of 225 squares and letters printed on plastic *tiles*. There are now versions for different languages. The English version is played by two, three, or four players, each using up to seven tiles at a time to make interlocking words on the board. Each tile bears a number indicating the score which can be made by that particular letter. Rare letters like J, Q, and Z have high values; common letters like E and S have low values. Some squares are *premium squares*, allowing double or triple scores for individual letters or for whole words. English Scrabble has 100 tiles, but sets in other languages have different numbers of tiles with different values, reflecting the distribution of the letters in those languages: German Scrabble uses 119 tiles, and players have eight tiles at a time. The British National Scrabble Championships started in 1970. See CHAMBERS, WORD GAME. [WORD]. T.A.

SCRIBBLER [15c: from *scribble* (apparently from Medieval Latin *scribillare*, a diminutive of *scribere* to write), and *-er*]. A dismissive term for someone whose handwriting is hurried and hard to read, or for a writer whose work is considered poor; sometimes also a tongue-in-cheek term for a journalist. In 1713, the name *the Scriblerus Club* (in which *scribbler* is turned into pseudo-Latin) was adopted by a group of conservative London writers, including John Arbuthnot and Alexander Pope, who wished to ridicule 'false tastes in learning'. To do this, they created *Martinus Scriblerus*, a pretentious 'modern' writer

whose memoirs they decided to write. Arbuthnot wrote most of the memoirs, and many of the pseudo-footnotes in Pope's later satire *The Dunciad* (1728-43) were signed *Scriblerus*: 'The Dunciad was . . . a declaration of war against the whole tribe of scribblers' (L. Stephen, *Pope*, 1880). Commentators have used the term *Scriblerian* to describe the Club members, their influence, and satire of a similar kind. Compare HACK, SCRIBE. [LITERATURE, MEDIA, WRITING]. T.MCA.

SCRIBE [14c: from Latin *scriba* a clerk]. (1) A copyist, especially of manuscripts before the invention of printing; a clerk or public writer, usually with official status, as in ancient Egypt, or with the right to copy, edit, and interpret scripture, as in ancient Israel. The term was used in English into the 18c for a secretary or note-taker. In recent years, scholars have come to refer to societies in which scribes were prominent as *scribal cultures*. (2) A tongue-in-cheek term often used by journalists to describe themselves. Compare HACK, SCRIBBLER, WRITER. See COMMUNICATIVE SHIFT. [MEDIA, WRITING]. T.MCA.

SCRIBLERIAN, SCRIBLERUS. See SCRIBBLER.

SCRIPT [14c: from Latin *scriptum* written]. (1) A collective term for the characters used in a writing system: *cuneiform script, Arabic script*. (2) Handwriting, especially if cursive or flowing: *Italic script*. (3) The text of a manuscript or other document. (4) The written or typed text of a play or motion picture, or radio or television broadcast. (5) In printing, a typeface that imitates handwriting. (6) To write a script for (a play, etc.) or to make arrangements for something: *They scripted the whole thing*. See COMMUNICATIVE SHIFT, CORRUPT, DRAMA, MANUSCRIPT, PARAGRAPH, PRINTING, SCRIBE, SCRIPTURE, TRANSCRIPTION. [LITERATURE, MEDIA, TECHNOLOGY, WRITING]. T.MCA.

SCRIPTURE [13c: from Latin *scriptura* writing]. A sacred text or texts (such as the Christian and Hebrew Bibles, the Qur'ān of the Muslims, and the Vedas of the Hindus), usually considered by adherents to originate in a form of divine inspiration or revelation. All scriptures compiled and edited in the first millennium BC or earlier appear to rest on an oral foundation which may have existed for centuries before being committed to writing. In the case of later scriptures, such as the New Testament and the Qur'ān, the length of time between the founding events and the creation of a canonical record has been shorter, but by and large the historical details are unclear. In linguistic terms, there are two traditions: those resistant to translation, insisting on the sacredness of the language in which the scriptures were first committed to writing (such as Islam and Hinduism), and those that encourage translation for missionary and other purposes, and do not consider the source language sacred as such (for example, Christianity and Buddhism). However, the Latin of the Vulgate Bible (based on St Jerome's translation of Hebrew and Greek) and the English of the Authorized Version (1611) have been to some degree elevated, but not to the exclusion of other languages. Similarly, the 'Biblical' style of the Authorized Version has been preferred by many over other (later) renderings in English.

Translating the Bible has often entailed the creation of writing systems for languages which did not possess them. The outcome has been the promotion of literacy in the languages concerned and, in such cases as Welsh and Icelandic, the creation of a vernacular Bible has served to strengthen the language in the face of pressure from other speech communities. The absence of a vernacular Bible has also been a factor in the decline of languages, because of their inability to form a stable and prestigious written or print standard, as with both Gaelic and Scots. Scripture, like other texts, has been affected by current media developments: for example, the UK audio-publisher Signal in 1986 made the Authorized Version of the Bible available in 15 volumes (each of four cassettes), totalling 87 hours of listening. The texts presented in this way were 'enacted' by 147 speakers; excerpts from them could be heard by telephoning a special number.

See ARABIC, ARAMAIC, BIBLE, BIBLICAL ENGLISH, CLASSICAL LANGUAGE, COMMUNICATIVE SHIFT, GOTHIC, GREEK, HEBREW, LATIN[1], LORIMER, PALI, PUN, SANSKRIT, SCRIPT, SERMON. [HISTORY, LANGUAGE, MEDIA, STYLE, WRITING]. T.MCA.

SCROLL [14c: from earlier *scrow*, from Anglo-French *escrowe*, perhaps from Medieval Latin **scroda*: compare Old High German *scrôt* a scrap]. (1) A roll of parchment, paper, or other material, especially with writing on it. Long scrolls or *rolls* are traditionally attached at one or both ends to spindles, from which they can be unrolled and on to which they can be re-rolled, more or less continuously, as they are read. The same principle is currently used for spools and reels of film and for audio/videotapes. (2) Verb: by analogy, in computing and word processing, to move (text, etc.) up or down on a screen by means of a cursor or function keys marked *page up* and *page down*, as if the screen were a scroll. See COMMUNICATIVE SHIFT, PAPER, PARCHMENT. Compare VOLUME. [TECHNOLOGY, WRITING]. T.MCA.

SEA ISLAND CREOLE. See GULLAH.

SEASPEAK [1980s]. Also **English for maritime communications**. The English of merchant shipping, a restricted language adopted in 1988 by the *International Maritime Organization* (*IMO*) of the United Nations for use in ship-to-ship and ship-to-shore communications as a necessary consequence of vastly increased shipping during the 1960s-70s. Two factors facilitated and encouraged the development of Seaspeak: the availability of Very High Frequency (VHF) radio-telephone began to make radio operators obsolete and ships' captains were able to send their own messages within a radius of 30 miles; following changes by many owners to flags of convenience, the distribution of nationalities of ships' officers gradually changed from 80% English-speaking and 20% other to 80% other and 20% English-speaking. The need for regularization of practices in one language and the training of officers in its use was therefore agreed, and English, already the language of civil aviation, was chosen by the IMO.

In 1982-3, Seaspeak was created by specialists in maritime communications and applied linguistics, working in Plymouth and Cambridge and funded by the UK government and Pergamon Press. It was made as concise and unambiguous as possible, was restricted to no more than two propositions in any message, allowed for constant checkback and confirmation, and made as few changes as possible to existing practice. The *SEASPEAK Reference Manual* by Weeks, Glover, Strevens, and Johnson (Oxford: Pergamon, 1984) was published after worldwide sea trials. In it, the *conventions* section regulates ways of speaking, such as the use of different frequencies, a required sequence of elements in identifying oneself, a list of commonly used seafaring abbreviations, and ways of speaking numbers, quantities, position, course, bearings, and expressions of time. The *procedures* section covers ways of establishing a conversation on VHF radio and different categories of communication, such as 'exchanges' and 'broadcasts'. The section *Major communication subjects* defines technical vocabulary and includes emergency, search and rescue, navigational dangers and instructions, meteorological reports, nonurgent medical information, ice conditions, anchor operations, tugs and towage, and cargo operations. The *messages* section contains the main linguistic innovation. Apart from special-format messages (as in stereotyped weather forecasts), all messages begin with a *message marker* that indicates the nature of what follows, such as advice, information, instruction, intention, question, request, warning, or a response to one of these. Below is a typical exchange, in which a ship called *Sun Dragon* calls up Land's End

Coastguard in England, to inform them of a change of plan:

Ship. Land's End Coastguard, Land's End Coastguard. This is Sun Dragon, Sun Dragon. Over.
Coastguard. Sun Dragon. This is Land's End Coastguard. Switch to VHF channel one-one. Over.
Ship. Land's End Coastguard. This is Sun Dragon. Agree VHF channel one-one. Over.
Coastguard. Sun Dragon. This is Land's End Coastguard on channel one-one. Over.
Ship. Land's End Coastguard. This is Sun Dragon. Information: I am returning to Mount's Bay. Reason: north-west gale and very heavy seas. Over.
Coastguard. Sun Dragon. This is Land's End Coastguard. Information received: you are returning to Mount's Bay. Reason: north-west gale and very heavy seas. Question: do you require assistance? Over.
Ship. Land's End Coastguard. This is Sun Dragon. Answer: no assistance required, thank you. Nothing more. Over.
Coastguard. Sun Dragon. This is Land's End Coastguard. Nothing more. Out.

Compare AIRSPEAK. See ENGLISH FOR SPECIAL PURPOSES, ENGLISH-SPEAKING UNION, RESTRICTED LANGUAGE, -SPEAK. [EDUCATION, VARIETY]. P.S.

SECONDARY LANGUAGE. See PRIMARY LANGUAGE AND SECONDARY LANGUAGE.

SECOND LANGUAGE. See FIRST LANGUAGE.

SEMANTIC CHANGE [Early 20c]. Also **semantic shift**. Change in the meanings of words, especially with the passage of time, the study of which is *historical semantics*. Investigators of changes in meaning have established a set of semantic categories, such as *generalization*, in which the meaning and reference of a word widen over the years (*pigeon* once meant a young dove and now means all members of the family Columbidae), and *specialization*, in which the meaning of a word narrows over the years (*deer* once meant any four-legged beast and now means only members of the family Cervidae). Such categories are not always sharply distinguishable; one may shade into another or develop from another. For example, before it meant a young dove, *pigeon* meant a young bird; it therefore specialized from young bird to young dove, then generalized from young dove to all dove-like birds. For scholarly convenience, the processes of semantic change are often described as if each operates alone, the 'story' of a word being told without bringing in too many other words. Such stories, however, are often complex and disseminate across whole networks of words. When a part of such a network is considered (such as the set of all barnyard fowls), many processes can be seen working together: the reference of one word widens while narrowing another (*chicken* generalizing to include

the meaning of *hen*), the reference widens in one period and narrows in another, sometimes establishing regional preferences (*cock* in BrE, *rooster* in AmE), and the reference extends figuratively (*chick* coming to mean a young woman) or idiomatically (*no spring chicken*), permitting a special use in one place but not another (in ScoE, *hen* as a term of endearment for women in and around Glasgow, comparable to *duck(s)* in parts of England). It has proved useful, therefore, to discuss semantic change in terms of webs of shifting forms and relationships rather than words on their own.

See BACK-FORMATION, CATACHRESIS, COMPUTER USAGE, CONVERSION/FUNCTIONAL SHIFT, DERIVATION, DETERIORATION, EPONYM, ETYMOLOGY, EUPHEMISM, EXTENSION, FIGURATIVE EXTENSION, FIGURATIVE LANGUAGE/USAGE, GENERALIZATION, HOMOGRAPH, HOMONYM, HOMOPHONE, JANUS WORD, LOCALISM, MELIORATION, METAPHOR, METONYMY, PEJORATION, PHILOLOGY, POLYSEMY, RADIATION, SEMANTIC FIELD, SEMANTICS, SPECIALIZATION, SUBREPTION, TOPONYMY. [HISTORY, LANGUAGE, WORD]. T.MCA.

SEMANTIC FIELD. A group, pattern, or framework of related words and word elements that covers or refers to an aspect of the world, such as colour words, culinary terms, military ranks, and the usage of sport. Many works of reference have been organized according to fields, from at least the time of Pliny the Elder's *Historia Naturalis* in AD 23-79. Recent works in English so organized are: *The English Duden: A Pictorial Dictionary* (1960), in 15 fields, the first of which, *Atom, Universe, and Earth*, is divided into such sub-fields as *Atom, Atmosphere, Astronomy, Meteorology*, each section consisting of a numbered list linked to a picture with numbered elements; *The Longman Lexicon of Contemporary English* (1981), organized in 14 semantic fields, the first of which, *Life and Living Things*, is divided into *Living creatures, Animals/mammals, Birds*, and *Kinds and parts of plants*, each group made up in turn of labelled lexical sets, usually of synonyms, antonyms, and associated words, defined together. There is no absolute list of such fields in any language, nor any fixed pattern or order in which a field or a set of fields may be presented. However, broad areas of experience can be isolated and structured in certain ways with certain ends in mind. They usually relate to such things as the world and its contents, human beings, and what human beings do. It is not known whether comparable structures exist in the brain. If they do, they are presumably multi-relational and far more fluid than anything so far attempted in printed or electronic form. Whether or not fields like *Kinds* of *Plants* and *Feelings and Sensations* have electrochemical correlates, they have a psychological reality in large part conditioned by culture. The presentation of such fields differs from age to age and place to place: a 9c Muslim list began with power and war and concluded with food and women; most European lists from the 7c to the 17c began with God and the angels. See LEXICAL FIELD, LEXICON, SEMANTIC CHANGE, SEMANTICS, SLANG, THEMATIC ORDER. [LANGUAGE, REFERENCE, WORD]. T.MCA.

SEMANTICS [1890s: from French *sémantique*, Greek *sēmantikós* significant, from *sêma* a sign]. The study of meaning. The term has at least five linked senses: (1) Sometimes *semasiology*. In linguistics, the study of the meaning of words and sentences, their denotations, connotations, implications, and ambiguities. The three levels or components of a common model of language are phonology, syntax, and semantics. (2) In philosophy, the study of logical expression and of the principles that determine the truth or falsehood of sentences. (3) In semiotics, the study of signs and what they refer to, and of responses to those signs. (4) In general usage, interest in the meanings of words, including their denotations, connotations, implications, and ambiguities. (5) Informally and often pejoratively, the making of (pedantic and impractical) distinctions about the meaning and use of words.

Background. The attempt to formulate a science of signs dates from the late 19c, when the French linguist Michel Bréal published *Essai de sémantique* (1897). He was interested in the influence of usage on the evolution of words and wished to extend the philological study of language (largely based on text and form) to include meaning. The historical study of meaning, however, is not currently central to the work of semanticists: see SEMANTIC CHANGE. Present-day semantic theory has developed largely from the later theories of the Swiss linguist Ferdinand de Saussure, who emphasized synchronic system and not diachronic evolution. Post-Saussurean semantics is the study of meaning as a branch of linguistics, like grammar and phonology. In its widest sense, it is concerned both with relations within language (*sense*) and relations between language and the world (*reference*). Generally, sense relations are associated with the word or *lexical item/lexeme* and with a lexical structure; their study is known as *structural* or *lexical semantics*. Reference is concerned with the meaning of words, sentences, etc., in terms of the world of experience: the situations to which they refer or in which they occur.

Semantic fields. One approach has been the theory of *semantic fields*, developed by J. Trier and W. Porzig in 1934. It attempts to deal with words as related and contrasting members of a set: for example, the meaning of English colour words like *red* and *blue*, which can be stated in terms of their relations in the colour spectrum, which in turn can be compared with the colour words of other languages. Thus, there is no precise equivalent of *blue* in Russian, which has two terms, *goluboy* and *siniy*, usually translated as 'light blue' and 'dark blue'. In Russian, these are treated as distinct colours and not shades of one colour, as users of English might suppose from their translation. See SEMANTIC FIELD.

Sense relations. In addition to semantic fields and lexical sets, a number of different types of *sense relation* have been identified, some traditional, some recent: (1) *Hyponymy*. Inclusion or class membership: *tulip* and *rose* are hyponyms of *flower*, which is their *hyperonym* or *superordinate term*. In its turn, *flower* is a hyponym of *plant*. In ordinary language, however, words can seldom be arranged within the kinds of strict classification found in zoology or botany: see BINOMIAL NOMENCLATURE. For example, there are arguments about whether rhubarb is a vegetable or a fruit, and whether the tomato is a fruit or a vegetable. (2) *Synonymy*. Sameness of meaning: *large* is a synonym of *big*. It is often maintained that there are no true synonyms in a language, but always some difference, of variety (AmE *fall*, BrE *autumn*), style (polite *gentleman*, colloquial BrE *chap*), emotive meaning (general *politician*, appreciative *statesman*), collocation (*rancid* modifying only *bacon* or *butter*). Partial or near synonymy is common, as with *adult*, *ripe*, and *mature*. (3) *Antonymy*. Oppositeness of meaning. There are, however, several types of opposite: *wide/narrow* and *old/young* are gradable both explicitly (X is wider than Y, A is older than B) and implicitly (a wide band is narrower than a narrow road). Such pairs allow for intermediate stages (neither wide nor narrow) and are antonyms proper. *Male/female* and *alive/dead* are not usually gradable and allow for no intermediate stage, except in expressions such as *more dead than alive*. Such pairs are *complementaries*. *Buy/sell* and *husband/wife* are relational opposites (X sells to Y and Y buys from X; only a husband can have a wife, and vice versa). Such pairs are *converses*. (4) *Polysemy* or *multiple meaning*. The existence of two or more meanings or senses to one word: for example, *flight* defined in at least six different ways: the power of flying; the act of flying; an air journey; a series (of steps); fleeing; a unit in an air force. (5) *Homonymy*. Words different in meaning but identical in form: *mail* armour, *mail* post. It is not always easy to distinguish homonymy and polysemy, and dictionaries rely partly on etymology to help maintain the distinction. *Ear* (of corn) and *ear* (the organ) are examples of homonymy, because etymologically the former derives from Old English *éar* (husk) while the latter derives from Old English *éare* (ear). See ANTONYM, HOMONYM, HYPONYM, -ONYM, POLYSEMY, SENSE, SYNONYM, SYNONYMY.

Componential analysis. An approach which makes use of semantic components was first used by anthropologists in the analysis of kinship terms. Componential analysis seeks to deal with sense relations by means of a single set of constructs. Lexical items are analysed in terms of *semantic features* or *sense components*: for example, such sets as *man/woman*, *bull/cow*, *ram/ewe* have the proportional relationships *man : woman :: bull : cow :: ram : ewe*. Here, the components [male]/[female], and [human] /[bovine]/[ovine] may account for all the differences of meaning. Generally, components are treated as binary opposites distinguished by pluses and minuses: for example, [+male] /[−male] or [+female]/[−female] rather than simply [male]/[female]. It has been argued that *projection rules* can combine the semantic features of individual words to generate the meaning of an entire sentence, and to account for ambiguity (as in *The bill is large*) and anomaly (as in **He painted the walls with silent paint*). There are complexities where the features are not simply additive but arranged in hierarchical structure: for example, in the proposal to analyse *kill* as [cause] [to become] [not alive]. It is controversial whether there is a finite set of such universal semantic components accounting for all languages and whether the components have conceptual reality.

Semantics and grammar. The meaning of a sentence is generally assumed to be derived from the meaning of its words, but it can be argued that we usually interpret whole sentences and that the sentence, not the word, is the basic unit of meaning, the meaning of words being derived from the meaning of sentences. This view is implicit in the referential theories of meaning discussed below. A distinction has been made by the British linguist John Lyons between *sentence meaning* and *utterance meaning*: sentence meaning is concerned with 'literal' meaning determined by the grammatical and lexical elements, unaffected by the context or what the speaker 'meant' to say.

Utterance meaning includes: (1) *Presupposition*. The statement *The king of France is bald* presupposes that there is a king of France, and the statement *I regret that Mary came* presupposes that Mary did come, but *I believe that Mary came* does not. What is presupposed in this sense is not asserted by the speaker but is nevertheless understood by the hearer. (2) *Implicature*. A term associated with H. P. Grice. The statement *It's hot in here* may imply the need to open a window, *I tried to telephone John yesterday* would normally suggest that I failed, and *I've finished my homework* (as a reply to *Have you finished your homework and put your books away?*) would suggest that the books have not been put away. Implicature is concerned with the various inferences we can make without actually being told, and includes presupposition. (3) *Prosodic features*. The use of stress and tone, as when *He SAW Mary this morning* means that he did not avoid her or telephone her, in contrast with *He saw MARY this morning*, rather than or in addition to anyone else. (4) *Speech acts*. Associated with J. L. Austin (*How to do Things with Words*, 1962). When a ship is launched with the words *I name this ship . . .*, the usage is not a statement of fact but an action. Similarly, *I declare this meeting closed* is the act of closing that meeting. Such speech acts, called *performatives*, cannot be said to be true or false. The notion of speech act can be extended to more common types of speech function: questions, orders, requests, statements, etc., and it is instructive to note that what appears to be a question may actually be a request: for example, *Can you pass the salt?*, where it would be inappropriate, though true, to reply *Yes, of course I can* without taking any action.

Reference. The place of reference in semantics is controversial. A problem with word meaning in terms of reference is that though words for objects may seem to denote, or refer to, objects (as with *stone* and *house*), other words (abstract nouns, verbs, and prepositions, etc.) do not seem to refer to anything. Many words are quite vague in their reference, with no clear dividing line between them (*hill/mountain*, *river/stream/ brook*), and may be used for sets of objects that are very different in appearance (*dog* and *table* covering a wide range of animals and pieces of furniture). Referential meaning (usually of words but also of sentences) is sometimes known as *cognitive meaning*, as opposed to *emotive* or *evaluative meaning*. In traditional terms, this is the difference between *denotation* and *connotation*. Since there are theoretical problems with the concept of referential meaning (which seems inapplicable to abstract nouns, verbs, etc.), some scholars prefer the terms *cognitive* and *affective*. Thus, the pairs *horse/steed*, *statesman/politician*, and *hide/conceal* may be said to have the same cognitive meanings, but different affective meanings.

Approaches to meaning. The American linguist Leonard Bloomfield regarded meaning as a weak point in language study and believed that it could be wholly stated in behaviourist terms. Following the Polish anthropologist Bronisław Malinowski, the British linguist J. R. Firth argued that *context of situation* was an important level of linguistic analysis alongside syntax, collocation, morphology, phonology, and phonetics, all making a contribution to linguistic meaning in a very wide sense. However, there have been few attempts to make practical use of that concept. Many scholars have, therefore, excluded reference from semantics. Thus, in transformational-generative grammar, the semantic component is entirely stated in terms of sense or semantic components, as described above in terms of componential analysis. Others have argued for a *truth-conditional* approach to semantics, in which the meaning of *bachelor* as 'unmarried man' is shown by the fact that if *X is an unmarried man* is true, then *X is a bachelor* is also true.

Pragmatics. Every aspect of meaning which cannot be stated in truth-conditional terms is *pragmatics*; the distinction is close to that of sentence and utterance meaning. But there are problems with this distinction and with the exclusion of reference. Thus, such deictic relationships as *here/there* and *this/that*, and words such as *today* and the personal pronouns, appear to contribute to sentence meaning, yet depend for their interpretation on reference, which varies according to the identity of speaker and hearer and the time and place of the utterance. See PRAGMATICS.

Conclusion. There can be no single, simple approach to the study of semantics, because there are many aspects of meaning both within language and in the relation between language and the world. The complexity of semantics reflects the complexity of the use of human language.

See AMBIGUITY, ANTONYM, BINOMIAL NOMEN-CLATURE, COGNITIVE MEANING, COMMUNICA-TION, CONNOTATION AND DENOTATION, CON-TEXT, DEFINITION, EQUIVOCATION, GRAMMAR, HOMONYM, HYPONYM, IMPLICATION, IMPLI-CATURE, LANGUAGE, LANGUAGE CHANGE, LEVEL OF LANGUAGE, LEXICOGRAPHY, LINGUISTICS, LOGIC, MEANING, NAME, ONOMASIOLOGY, ONO-MASTICS, POLYSEMY, PRAGMATICS, PROPOSITION, PROSODY, REFERENCE, RHYTHM, SEMANTIC CHANGE, SEMIOTICS, SENSE, SENSE RELATION, SIGN, SLANG, STRESS, SYMBOL, SYNONYM, SYNONYMY, TONE. [LANGUAGE]. F.R.P.

Hughes, Geoffrey. 1988. *Words in Time: A Social History of the English Vocabulary*. Oxford: Blackwell.
Kempson, Ruth M. 1977. *Semantic Theory*. Cambridge: University Press.
Lyons, John. 1977. *Semantics*. Cambridge: University Press.
—— 1981. *Language, Meaning and Context*. London & Glasgow: Collins (Fontana).
Ogden, C. K., & Richards, I. A. 1923. *The Meaning of Meaning*. London: Routledge & Kegan Paul.
Palmer, F. R. 1981. *Semantics*. Cambridge: University Press.
Ullmann, Stephen. 1957. *The Principles of Semantics*. Glasgow: Jackson. Oxford: Blackwell.
—— 1962. *Semantics: An Introduction to the Science of Meaning*. Oxford: Blackwell.

SEMASIOLOGY. See ONOMASIOLOGY, SEMANTICS.

SEMICOLON, also **semi-colon** [17c: from Latin *semi-* half, *colon*: see COLON]. The punctuation mark (;). Its main roles are: (1) To link statements that are closely associated or that complement or parallel each other in some way: *We will stay here; you may go.* In this role, it can link clauses (*they were poor; they had few clothes; they were often in despair*) or phrases or a mixture of phrases and clauses (*they had no money; nor any clothes; nor could they find work*). It marks antithesis, often with a word such as *and*, *but*, or *yet* to emphasize this: *They were poor; and yet they were happy.* Words such as *however*, *nonetheless/none the less*, and *moreover* are usually preceded by a semicolon when they begin a new statement: *books are cheap; moreover, they last a lifetime.* (2) To mark a stronger division in a sentence that is already punctuated with commas (*several people were still waiting, impatiently shuffling their feet, looking bored; but none of them, in spite of this, seemed willing to speak*). The semicolon is often avoided in ordinary writing, or replaced with a dash, because many users lack confidence in it. It is most often found in print. See COLON, PUNCTUATION. [WRITING].
R.E.A.

SEMI-CONSONANT. See CONSONANT, GLIDE.

SEMI-LITERATE. See ILLITERACY.

SEMIOLOGY. See SEMIOTICS.

SEMIOTICS [1870s: from Greek *sēmeiōtikós* observant of signs, from *sēmeîon* a sign. The adjective *semiotic* was coined by the English philosopher John Locke in the early 17c]. The study and analysis of signs and symbols as part of communication, as for example in language, gesture, clothing, and behaviour. Present-day semiotics arises from the independent work of two linguistic researchers, one in the US, the other in Switzerland. Charles S. Peirce (1834–1914) used the term to describe the study of signs and symbolic systems from a philosophical perspective, while Ferdinand de Saussure (1857–1913) coined *semiology* as part of his interest in language as a system of signs. The terms have generally been regarded as synonymous, and *semiotics* is better known, especially in the English-speaking world.

Semiotics is a comprehensive discipline, in that almost anything can be a sign: clothes, hairstyles, type of house or car owned, accent, and body language. All send messages about such things as age, class, and politics. Sign systems, however, are not peculiar to human beings: the study of animal communication by gesture, noise, smell, dancing, etc., is termed *zoosemiotics*, while the study of technical systems of signals such as Morse code and traffic lights is *communication theory*. In semiotics, the term *code* refers loosely to any set of signs and their conventions of meaning. Language represents a rich set of such codes, both *verbal* (in language proper) and *non-verbal* (in the paralanguage of facial expressions, body movements, and such vocal activities as snorts and giggles). The media provide visual and aural signals in photographs, radio and television programmes, advertisements, and theatrical performances. Literature is seen as a particularly rich semiotic field with such sub-disciplines as *literary* and *narrative semiotics*. Critical attention has come to focus not only on the codes themselves, but on the process of *encoding* and *decoding*. Readers, it is argued, do not simply decode messages, but actively create meanings: that is, they *re-code* as they read.

Peirce and Saussure were interested in the relationship between sign and *referent* (what a sign refers to). Although they both stressed that this relationship was essentially arbitrary, Peirce argued that different types of sign had different degrees of both *arbitrariness* and *motivation*. What he terms an *icon* is a highly motivated sign, since it visually resembles what it represents: for example, a photograph or hologram. His *index* is partly motivated to the extent that there is a connection, usually of causality, between sign and referent: spots indexical of a disease like measles; smoke indexical of fire; a stutter of nervousness. Peirce's *symbol* is the most arbitrary kind of sign: the word in language, the formula in mathematics, or the rose representing love in literary tradition. See CODE, ICON, LINGUISTIC SIGN, MIME, PARALANGUAGE, SEMANTICS, SIGN, SYMBOL. [LANGUAGE]. K.W.

Barthes, Roland, 1953. *Mythologies*. Paris: Seuil.
—— 1967. *Elements of Semiology*. London: Jonathan Cape.
Eco, Umberto. 1976. *A Theory of Semiotics*. Bloomington: Indiana University Press.
—— 1984. *Semiotics and the Philosophy of Language*. London: Macmillan.
Elam, Keir. 1980. *The Semiotics of Theatre and Drama*. London: Methuen.
Hawkes, Terence. 1977. *Structuralism and Semiotics*. London: Methuen.
Peirce, Charles S. 1931-58. *Collected Papers*. Eight volumes. Cambridge, Mass.: Harvard University Press.
Saussure, Ferdinand de. 1916. *Cours de linguistique générale*, ed. Charles Bally & Albert Sechehaye. Translated into English as *Course in General Linguistics*. 1975. London: Fontana.
Sebeok, T. A., Hayes, A. S., & Beaton, M. C. 1972. *Approaches to Semiotics*. The Hague: Mouton.
Tobin, Yishai. 1990. *Semiotics and Linguistics*. London & New York: Longman.

SEMITIC LANGUAGES. See ARABIC, ARAMAIC, HAMITO-SEMITIC LANGUAGES, HEBREW.

SEMI-VOWEL. See CONSONANT, GLIDE, VOWEL.

SEMORDNILAP. See PALINDROME.

SENSE [14c: from Latin *sensus* feeling, understanding]. A term whose meanings range from physical faculties (such as *the sense of sight*) through analogous faculties of mind or spirit (*a sense of humour*), intelligence (*Show some sense!*), and what is logical and proper (the opposite of *nonsense*) to meaning (*the sense of a text*) and the idea that many words have sub-meanings (*X used in the sense of Y; the various senses of the word 'make'*). Although people agree that words may have different 'senses', there is no agreed means of establishing just how many senses many *polysemous* (many-sensed) words have. The boundaries between senses are not always clear: a sense may be precise and restricted or vague and diffuse, and may be susceptible to analysis into more or less easily delineated *sub-senses*. Identifying a sense may depend on knowledge and experience, social and situational context, the reason for analysing a word, the policy used by compilers of a particular dictionary, the method of displaying words in that dictionary, the amount of detail to be provided, and different theories about what words are and of how they should be discussed and defined. As the accompanying table shows, dictionaries can differ considerably as to the main sense divisions

| Dictionary | Number of senses of: | | | |
| | *walk* | | *crane* | |
	noun	verb	noun	verb
CoED (1986)	15	11	4	3
LDEL (1984)	5	12	3	2
AHD (1985)	7	4	4	2
ChED (1988)	25	20	4	4

Key: CoED Collins English Dictionary, *LDEL* Longman Dictionary of the English Language, *AHD* American Heritage Dictionary, *ChED* Chambers English Dictionary.

of such words as *walk* and *crane*. See DICTION-
ARY, HOMONYM, MEANING, METAPHOR, NONSENSE,
POLYSEMY, SEMANTIC CHANGE, SEMANTICS. [LAN-
GUAGE, REFERENCE].   T.MCA.

SENSE RELATION. See SEMANTICS, SENSE.

SENTENCE [12c: through Old French from
Latin *sententia* a way of thinking, opinion,
judgement, used to translate the Greek terms
dóxa and *gnómē*]. The largest structural unit
normally treated in grammar. The sentence is
notoriously difficult to define; numerous definitions have been offered and found wanting. The
classical definition, that a sentence expresses a
complete thought, dates from the first Western
treatise on grammar, by Dionysius Thrax (*c.*100
BC), whose interest lay primarily in analysing,
using, and teaching written Greek. This traditional notional definition, however, only solves
the problem by transferring it: how does one
define a complete thought? Linguists and
anthropologists in the 19-20c, trained in the
Greco-Latin grammatical tradition and faced
with the analysis of previously unwritten Amerindian languages, have often noted how difficult
it is to establish the boundaries between what
might be words and what might be sentences in
some of those languages. Because of this, the
sentence as understood in the Western linguistic
tradition has not yet been unequivocally established as a universal of language.

The syntactic sentence. Formal definitions usually refer to the structural independence of the
sentence: that it is not included in a larger structural unit by such devices as coordination and
subordination. However, dependence is relative:
what are generally recognized as sentences may
be dependent to some extent on other sentences
through such devices as pronoun substitution
and connective adverbials: *therefore, however,
yet*. Elliptical sentences such as *Tomorrow* (in
answer to *When is your birthday?*) are clearly
dependent in some sense on linguistic context.
There are also problems in deciding the status
of formulaic utterances such as *Yes* or *Good
morning*, which in dialogue are complete in
themselves. Formal definitions may also refer to
the internal structures of sentences. Indeed, it is
possible to recognize as canonical sentences
those that conform in their structure to the normal clause patterns, such as subject-verb-direct
object. Other constructions would then be considered irregular or minor, and some (such as
Yes) perhaps not sentences at all.

The orthographic sentence. In written language,
sentence status is signalled by punctuation, primarily through the *period* (especially AmE) or *full

stop (especially BrE), but the orthographic sentence is not necessarily identical with the syntactic sentence: clauses separated by *semicolons*
or *colons* might well be analysed as independent
sentences, the punctuation reflecting the writer's
feeling that the sentences so linked are closer
semantically than the surrounding sentences. In
addition, in the prose of publicists and advertisers, traditional conventions for the organization of written sentences are routinely
abandoned, in order to highlight certain points:

Have a little pick-me-up before you get back to work.
Iberia's Business Class always welcomes you with a
glass of sherry. A taste of Spanish sunshine to whet
your appetite for the delicious meal ahead. And afterwards relax and take advantage of our unique, multilingual, on-board library. Efficient and professional
but warm and hospitable. That's how we think business
should be (advertisement, 1990).

The phonological sentence. Contemporary linguists tend not to worry over the definition of a
sentence. They assume that they can recognize
sentences, implicitly relying on their familiarity
with their orthographic forms. The spoken language, however, does not signal sentence boundaries. The syntax of speech, particularly in
spontaneous conversation, differs considerably
from the regularities of the written (particularly
printed) language in ways that have yet to be
fully investigated. Everyday conversation exhibits abundant hesitations, shifts in sentence construction, apparently incomplete structures, and
interconnections that are odd by the norms of
the written language. Most grammarians focus
on structures in the written language (and their
analogues in more or less formal speech) for the
data they use in constructing their grammars,
and if they turn their attention at all to samples
of speech tend to derive spoken structures from
what they consider to be fuller forms normal in
written texts. What constitutes a sentence in the
language should be (but does not appear to be)
of particular concern to generative grammarians
who view the goal of their grammar as accounting for all and only the sentences of the language.

Sentence structure. If the sentence is to constitute
a grammatical unit for the language as a whole,
then the orthographic sentence cannot serve as
that unit: speech signals do not correspond to
sentence punctuation, and punctuation only
crudely signals some elements of speech, such as
possible points for pausing or changing one's
tone. Instead, reference can be made to the relative independence of the unit and its internal
structure. A sentence may be viewed as a clause
complex, in which the parts are clauses linked to
each other by coordination and subordination.
From this viewpoint, the traditional *simple sentence* is indeed simple, because it consists of only

one clause, as in: *The governor of the prison negotiated with the prisoners throughout the day.* A *compound sentence* involves the coordination of two or more *main clauses* (each of which could constitute a simple sentence), linked by the coordinators *and, or, but,* as in: *The governor of the prison negotiated with the prisoners throughout the day and talks were continued into the night.* A *complex sentence* consists of one main clause within which there are one or more subordinate clauses: *The governor of the prison negotiated with the prisoners after police had seized control of the kitchen and food-store area.* The subordinate clause, here introduced by the subordinator *after,* can be moved to the front of the sentence, a typical property of subordinate clauses.

Further complexities are quite usual. A *compound-complex sentence* resembles the simple sentence in having more than one main clause, but in addition one or more of the main clauses contains one or more subordinate clauses: *A police officer said that the prison authorities could not confirm that there were bodies inside the prison, but he believed that there had been some deaths.* Here, the two main clauses are coordinated by *but,* the first main clause has a *that*-clause within which is embedded another *that*-clause, and the second main clause also contains a *that*-clause. It is further possible to recognize a *complex-compound* sentence (though the term is not often used), in which the one main clause contains two or more subordinate clauses that are coordinated: *The Home Secretary said that nine prisoners had been forcibly injected with drugs and that eight others had taken drugs voluntarily.* In this example, the two subordinate *that*-clauses are coordinated by *and.* The subordinate clause may be embedded in a phrase rather than directly in another clause, as in this example of a relative clause (introduced by *who*) that is embedded in a noun phrase: *Twelve prison officers who received minor injuries during the riot have all been discharged from hospital.*

All the examples of subordinate clauses given above have been *finite clauses,* but subordination may be effected through *non-finite clauses* and *verbless clauses.* In the next example, two coordinated participle clauses (which follow the comma) are subordinate to the main clause in this complex sentence: *The rioters have destroyed most of the ten wings of the prison, systematically smashing cells and setting fire to buildings.* In the example that follows, the *if*-clause is verbless: *If possible, prisoners will be moved to other prisons.*

Constituents of clauses. This structured account of sentences assumes the recognition of clauses. A clause consists of central and peripheral constituents, the first usually obligatory, the second optional. The central constituents are the *subject* (though generally omitted in imperative sentences) and the *verb,* as in *Nobody moved.* Other central constituents are *complements* of the verb: that is, elements that complete its meaning, such as the direct object *my typewriter* in *Somebody has taken my typewriter,* the indirect object *me* in *Derek gave me some books,* the subject complement *hungry* in *Jane is hungry,* the object complement *strong* in *I like my tea strong,* the adverbial complement *in the garage* in *The car is in the garage* and in *I put the car in the garage.* The peripheral or marginal constituents are mainly adverbials such as *incidentally, also,* and *last week* in *Incidentally, Derek also gave me some books last week,* and vocatives such as *Natalie* in *I like my tea strong, Natalie.*

Irregular structures. Some constructions are irregular in some respect, but are generally considered sentences or (if attached to a sentence) parts of sentences: (1) Certain types of subordinate clauses constitute independent exclamations: *That we should come to this! To think that I once helped him! If it isn't my old friend Jeremy! If only you had listened to me!* (2) Questions in which the phrases or subordinate clauses are introduced by interrogative words: *How about a kiss? Why all the fuss? What if they don't come? How come you're not ready yet?* (3) Such headings as *How to get help in an emergency; Where you should eat in Paris.* (4) Elliptical constructions such as *Serves you right* and *Never fails, does it?,* and elements of dialogue such as *A: Where are you? B: In the kitchen.* (5) Problematic sequences that cannot easily be analysed into clausal constituents appear in such contexts as labels, titles, warnings, and greetings: *Baked beans; The Department of English; Good morning; The police!; Thanks; Yes.* Conversations often contain such sequences as *That one. The big one. No, the one over there. Higher up. Yes. Beside the green jug,* which might as easily be written *That one—the big one—no—the one over there—higher up—yes—beside the green jug,* orthographically sidestepping the problem of deciding the status of the phrases in question. Such uncertain sequences are often referred to as *sentence fragments.*

Functional and syntactic categories. Sentences were categorized above by degree of internal complexity: *simple, compound, complex, compound-complex, complex-compound.* They are also commonly classified according to dominant function in discourse, as *declarative, interrogative, imperative,* and *exclamatory.* These functions are reflected in the four corresponding sentence types *statement, question, directive* (or *command*), and *exclamation.* In addition, sentences can be classified according to syntactic features that affect the sentence as a whole: *mood* (indicative, imperative, subjunctive), *voice* (active, passive), and *polarity* (positive, negative). Finally, they can be classified by the patterns of the central or kernel constituents that they exhibit: for example, *Subject–Verb–Direct Object (SVDO)*; *Subject–Verb–Subject Complement (SVSC)*.

See ADVERBIAL, CLAUSE, COLON, COMMA, COMPARATIVE SENTENCE, COMPLEMENT, COMPLEX SENTENCE, COMPOUND-COMPLEX SENTENCE, COMPOUND SENTENCE, COMPUTING, DISCOURSE, EXISTENTIAL SENTENCE, OBJECT, PARTICIPLE, PART OF SPEECH, PERIOD, PERIODIC SENTENCE, PHRASE, POLARITY, PREDICATE, PUNCTUATION, SEMICOLON, SENTENCE WORD, SIMPLE SENTENCE, STRESS, SUBJECT, TAG, VERB, VERBLESS SENTENCE, VOICE. [GRAMMAR, STYLE, WRITING]. S.G.

SENTENCE ADVERB, SENTENCE ADVERBIAL. See ADVERBIAL.

SENTENCE FRAGMENT. See SENTENCE.

SENTENCE STRESS. See STRESS.

SENTENCE TAG. See TAG.

SENTENCE WORD. An occasional term in word-formation for a sentence which serves as a word or part of a word, such as *never say die*, attributively in 'a *never-say-die* attitude', suffixed in *never-say-die-ism*, or as an often allegorical name: *Captain Never-Say-Die, Mrs Do-As-You-Would-Be-Done-By, She-Who-Must-Be-Obeyed*. The attributive use is the commonest. In writing and print, the constituents are often linked by hyphens (examples as collected in the 1980s): *an aren't-I-just-the-cutest-thing* smile; *a from-this-day-forward-I-have-no-daughter* scene; *her I-don't-understand-you* look. However, they may also come between quotation marks (*a 'print or shut down' ultimatum; a Toyota 'Drop Everything' Sales Event*), be capitalized (*the I Did It My Way approach*), or mix hyphens and capitals (*the great Support-Your-Local-Hostage binge*). Sentence words often begin with verbs in the imperative mood: *a Dial-a-Prayer service; a Rent-a-Car contract; a get-up-and-go Britain in place of a sit-back-and-wait-for-it culture*. Compare PHRASE WORD. [GRAMMAR, WORD]. T.MCA.

SERIAL [1830s: from Neo-Latin *serialis*: see SERIES]. (1) Occurring in a series (*serial polygamy*) or presented one part at a time (*a serial story in a magazine*). (2) A work that is published or broadcast in parts: *a weekly TV serial*. Included in the law of copyright are the *serial rights* to a book, film, etc. When a company obtains these

rights it can proceed to *serialize* the work in question. (3) In library science, a periodical such as a scientific journal, each part numbered and chronologically labelled: *International Journal of Lexicography*, Volume 3, Number 3, Autumn 1990. A *serial catalog(ue)* lists such publications, each of which usually has an *International Standard Serial Number (ISSN)*. (4) In computing, relating to the performance of data-processing operations in sequence: that is, *serial processing* as opposed to *parallel processing*. *Serial storage* is the recording of information in the order in which it is entered. Compare EPISODE, JOURNAL, PERIODICAL. [LITERATURE, MEDIA, TECHNOLOGY]. T.MCA.

SERIAL COMMA. See COMMA, OXFORD UNIVERSITY PRESS.

SERIES [17c: Latin *series* a row, chain, succession]. (1) A group, number, or set of usually similar things that occur or are arranged in sequence: *a series of events*; *the third book in the 'Patterns of English' Series*. (2) A number of related broadcast programmes (*a wild-life series*), or one programme in serial form, usually daily or weekly, with a specific format and theme or story-line, and a core group of performers, such as a TV *game show* or *situation comedy*. (3) In printing, all sizes of one typeface. See EPISODE, SERIAL, SOAP OPERA. [LITERATURE, MEDIA, TECHNOLOGY]. T.MCA.

SERIF [Early 19c: perhaps from Dutch *schreef* a written line, from *schrijven* to write]. Sometimes *ceriph*. A printer's and calligrapher's term for a small line used to finish off or ornament a main stroke of a letter. Some typefaces have serifs, others do not and are said to be *sans serif* (without serifs); there are therefore serif and sanserif typefaces. Compare MINIM. See TYPOGRAPHY. [TECHNOLOGY, WRITING]. T.MCA.

SERMON [12c: from Latin *sermo/sermonis* talk, discourse]. A discourse on a religious subject, usually delivered within corporate worship. Expositions of scripture took place in early Christian services; when Greek and Latin became archaic as liturgical languages, sermons were delivered in the vernaculars. Some Old English sermons are extant, notably by Aelfric (late 10c). Medieval sermons are among the earliest examples of original English prose. The Reformation in the 16c emphasized sermons that were often polemical. Leading English preachers of the 17c included Lancelot Andrews and John Donne. The growth of 18c nonconformity bred a line of famous preachers from John Wesley to Charles Spurgeon. John Henry Newman was an outstanding preacher of the 19c Oxford Movement. Many 19c preachers collected and published their sermons, usually edited to make them more conformable to the expectations of written English. Sermons in the 20c are less often published. They are usually shorter and less prominent in worship, though revivalists like Billy Graham have preached to vast crowds and US evangelists have adapted the sermon to television. It has also influenced the rhetorical style of Black American preachers and civil rights campaigners, such as Martin Luther King:

The battle is in our hands. I know some of you are asking today, 'How long will it take?' I come to say to you this afternoon, however difficult the moment, however frustrating the hour, it will not be long, because truth pressed to earth will rise again. How long? Not long, because no lie can live forever. How long? Not long, because you will reap what you sow. How long? Not long, because the arm of the moral universe is long, but it bends towards justice (in Montgomery, Alabama, 1965).

The sermon usually has dramatic qualities, and has been a means through which Biblical phrases have become part of the everyday idiomatic language of the English-speaking world. See BIBLICAL ENGLISH. Compare SCRIPTURE. [LITERATURE, SPEECH, STYLE].   R.C.

SESTET. See SONNET.

SETTLER ENGLISH. See LIBERIA.

SEXISM [1960s: on the analogy of *racism*]. A term used in feminist critiques of society and in general usage for: (1) Attitudes and behaviour based on traditional assumptions about, and stereotypes of, sexual roles in society and some gender usages in language. (2) Discrimination or disparagement based on a person's sex, especially when directed by men or society at large against women. In terms of language, sexism refers to a bias through which patterns and references of male usage are taken to be normative, superordinate, and positive and those of women are taken to be deviant, subordinate, and negative. Usage typically challenged as sexist includes: (1) *Man* used to refer to the human race in general (book title: *The Ascent of Man*) and to individuals (*What does the average man in the street think?*). Such neutral forms as *humankind* and *person* have been recommended in its place. (2) *Girl* used to refer to adult women (considered to be as demeaning as the use of *boy* for adult non-white males) and used attributively in such expressions as *girl athlete, girl reporter*. The use of such phrases appears to have declined in recent years. (3) *Lady* used to indicate a woman professional, as in *lady doctor* and *lady lawyer*, a genteelism that dates from a time when women

were rare in such professions and the few who did exist came from the upper and middle classes. (4) Naming that does not equally represent men and women, such as: *Professors Eliot, Goldstein, and Barbara Smith*. Many manuals of style now recommend strict parallelism: *Professors Eliot, Goldstein, and Smith* or *Professors Edgar Eliot, Sol Goldstein, and Barbara Smith*.

Non-sexist usage. Since the 1960s there has been strong social pressure from feminist and other groups, especially in North America, to make the use of English and other languages less biased against women. Some of these attempts have met with fairly widespread acceptance, while others have been resisted and appear to be regarded as too radical, or awkward, or unnecessary. An early change in the US (*c*.1970) was the coining of the abbreviated title *Ms* parallel to *Mr* in that it identifies gender but not marital status. This term is often used in public (such as in newspapers and the mail) in the way intended by feminists, but it has also often been used as a replacement of *Miss*, to designate an unmarried woman, while *Mrs* continues to designate a married woman (often because women and men wish to retain some such distinction). A more limited but definitive change occurred in 1979, when major tropical storms were no longer designated with female names alone, *Hurricane Harry* becoming as likely as *Hurricane Hazel*. This change has largely eliminated descriptions of 'temperamental' storms that 'flirt with the coast'. During the 1980s, increasing pressure against sexual discrimination in areas such as job advertisements and academic journals led to the development of guidelines for non-sexist usage, intended to help people avoid both explicit and implicit sexism in language. One such set of guidelines is *The Handbook of Nonsexist Writing* by Casey Miller and Kate Swift (Harper & Row, 1988). They cover such issues as not assuming that a doctor or other professional is always *he*, dropping such derivatives as *authoress, executrix*, and *usherette*, using neutral terms such as *draughter* for *draughtsman*, *chair* for *chairman*, *flight attendant* for *steward* and *stewardess*, and using *women* rather than *girls* for adults.

Radical coinages and adaptations. Many feminists consider that radical changes in the form of certain everyday words have psychological value, as with the conversion of *history* to *herstory*, which, they argue, presents a new perspective on and analysis of life and the processes with which the original words have generally been associated. *Herstory* focuses attention on the situation and accomplishments of women, seen as largely excluded from or marginalized in the 'his story' of male historians. The forms *womyn* and *wimmin* are seen as more detached from *man*, the origin of *woman* being *wifman*, meaning 'female human being' but easily interpretable as 'wife of a man'. Such usages are not currently widespread. Equally radical is the *reclamation* or *positive reinterpretation* of negative words for kinds of women, such as *crone, hag, witch*. Mary Daly and Jane Caputi's *Wickedary* (Boston: Beacon Press, 1987), for example, defines *revolting hag* as 'survivor of the perpetual witchcraze of patriarchy . . . [who has] Dis-covered depths of Courage, Strength and Wisdom in her Self'.

Generic male usages. Despite traditional assertions that such generics as *man* and *he* include *woman* and *she*, in practice the gender for many words is often specifically male, as in *refugees and their wives* (who are also refugees) and *When a bird isn't foraging, it's singing its heart out to advertise its territory, keep intruding males at bay and attract a female*. Both the *man in the street* and the *man of letters* are supposedly general, but the unacceptability of **She was a leading man of letters* and the non-use (or rarity) of *She was a leading woman of letters* demonstrate a primary and abiding male reference. A widely approved alternative to generic *he* (*Ask anyone and he'll tell you*) has not yet developed. The most common appears to be singular *they*, which has a long history of usage: *Ask anyone and they'll tell you*. *He or she* and to a less extent in writing *s/he* or *(s)he* occur, and sometimes *she and he*, but commentators generally recommend avoidance strategies, such as a shift to plural constructions.

Use of *person*. The neutral use of *person* in its own right and in compounds has made some progress: *anchorperson, chairperson, layperson, salesperson, spokesperson*, with the occasional successful plural *-people*: *business people, lay people, sales people, working people*. However, the usage is often mocked (*clergyperson, fisherperson, weatherperson*), and remains an uneasy term for many people. In two cases, especially in North America, the first element alone has had some success: *anchor, chair*. *Fisher* has not had much success, but *firefighter* has been used with some success instead of *fireman*. The term *layman* is widely used, especially in such phrases as *in layman's language*, but neutral *layperson/lay person* appear to have caught on for both religious and professional reference: plural *lay people*, religious collective *the laity*. The terms *non-specialist, non-professional* have been proposed for non-religious contexts. For many people, however, *person* remains an awkwardly formal and unwelcome intrusion in their lives, and of all the words associated with discussions of inclusive language has provoked the most jokes, as with *personhole covers, to person an*

assembly line, to personage a company, and *huperson beings*.

The feminine inanimate. Although standard English does not have gender for inanimate objects, female reference, such as the pronoun *she*, is often associated with things and qualities perceived as having 'female' characteristics. *Mother Nature* is associated with female fertility; *justice* and *liberty* are perceived as 'soft' and 'compassionate', as are women; boats and cars are seen as irrational, cranky, and dominated by men. Such associations may at times seem flattering, as in *She's got a beautiful stern*, but not when someone who is trying to start a motor is told to *give her a kick and she'll turn over*.

Lexical asymmetry. Male/female pairs of words are often asymmetrical: *governor* refers to a man with great power and position, *governess* to a woman employee with limited authority over children; *master* generally refers to a man who controls things (but may sometimes be a woman: *She's a master of the subject*), while *mistress* may refer to a powerful woman in charge of a house or college, but more often means a married man's kept lover (negative echoes from this sense often affecting the other). In some areas, however, female terms have not emerged, symmetrical or otherwise: the degrees of *Bachelor of Arts* and *Master of Arts*, once conferred only on men, are now conferred on both men and women without any such contrasts as **Spinster of Arts* or **Mistress of Arts*. In addition, although terms like *lady lawyer/doctor* are widely used, there has been no general move towards such forms as *doctorette, lawyeress*, instances of which are jocular and/or pejorative. The relative position of male and female in binomial phrases (such as *he or she, host and hostess, male or female, man and wife, men and women, men and girls, men and ladies, boys and girls*) gives primary status to males, the only exceptions being the chivalric *ladies and gentlemen* and the informal *mum/mom and dad*. Asymmetrical pairs are also common, with female terms as lower in status, as in *men and girls, men and ladies*. It is often also the case that pejorative terms are stronger when applied to women: *bitch* is seldom a compliment, whereas *bastard* (especially *old bastard*) can under some circumstances be intended as a term of respect or affection. Of similar positive status when masculine is *dog* (as in *you old dog!*, admiring a roué); when feminine in reference in AmE it means an ugly woman. *Witch* is almost always pejorative, whereas *wizard* is often a compliment.

Marked suffixes. In common with other European languages, English has traditionally indicated femaleness by the use of certain suffixes, indicating that the nouns to which they attach have traditionally been taken to refer only to men. The suffixes are: (1) -ess, as used in *actress, authoress, sculptress, waitress*. It is sometimes said to highlight women's accomplishments, but is often linked to roles presented as less significant than those of men, such as *manageress, poetess. Actress*, however, is widely used at the same time as the inclusive use of *actor* has gained ground, especially in the theatre. *Hostess* continues to be widely used, but because of its occurrence in such phrases as *bar hostess* it may decline, making way for inclusive *host. Jewess, Negress, Quakeress* are dismissive additions to often disparaging usages of *Jew, Negro, Quaker* and are not balanced by such creations as **Christianess, *Nordess, *Mormoness*. (2) -ette has three depreciative senses: small size (as in *cigarette, kitchenette*), artificiality (*leatherette*), femaleness and auxiliary status (*majorette, usherette, Jaycee-ette*). *Copette* is not as tough or reassuring an image as *cop*. The term *suffragette* is widely used to refer to activists at the turn of the 19–20c who sought votes for women. These women, however, called themselves *suffragists*. The better-known term was popularized by a largely hostile public and media, using a demeaning and dismissive suffix to disparage their goals. (3) -trix, as in the now rare *aviatrix*, has a limited use in legal language (for example, *executrix, testatrix*), and in the sado-masochistic term *dominatrix*. Such usages, however, mark females in these roles as unusual. (4) -ine is obsolete except for *heroine*.

Inclusive usage. The possibility of eliminating sexism from language involves the Whorfian hypothesis: not just that language is a reflection of the society which uses it, but that society is in part shaped by its language. If this is so, language change may bring about social change: children hearing constant references to *the doctor . . . he* may well assume that all physicians are or should be male. A consistent use of inclusive and non-sexist language might help change this perception. Male-based words appear to be increasingly challenged by both women and men. In many cases, they have been formally replaced by neutral terms: *chairman* by *chair, forefather* by *ancestor, headmaster* and *headmistress* by *head teacher, waiter* and *waitress* by *server, coed* by *student*. Asymmetrical words such as *mistress* in the sexual sense are being replaced by neutral terms such as *lover*. The replacement of *mother/father* by *parent*, unless gender-specific roles are involved, reflects some breakdown in socially stereotyping according to gender. *Steward* and *stewardess* have generally been replaced by *flight attendant*, although call buttons on aircraft continue in the main to show a female figure. In the case of *housewife*, on the

other hand, the male-oriented *househusband* seems to be integrated (sometimes mockingly) into both AmE and BrE, while *homemaker* appears to remain feminine in reference, and *home manager* has not gained acceptance. Common work terms can generally be neutralized without much difficulty: *manpower* can be changed to *personnel, work force*, or *workers*, and *man hours* to *operator hours*. Suffixes like -er in job titles such as *steelworker* and *bookkeeper* can be used to modify *longshoreman* to *longshoreworker* and *fisherman* to *fisher*, but often meet with ridicule. Many suggested changes raise further difficulties and have produced varied responses. Of the alternatives proposed for *chairman, chair* is comparable to *head* (of a department) and echoes the phrase *in the chair*. It is widely used in AmE. *Chairperson* is sometimes used more by, or referring to, women. The contrastive *Chairman/woman*, unlike *businessman/woman*, does not appear to work well. BrE tends to use *chairman* neutrally, with the contrasting forms of address *Mr Chairman* and *Madam Chairman*: not **Mr Chair, *Madam Chair*.

Feminist objections to inclusive usage. Some feminists have objected to the use of such terms as *faculty spouse, chair, lion* to neutralize the male-oriented *faculty wife, chairman, lioness*, on the grounds that they can hide information that is important to the cause of women's rights, such as the under-representation of women on university faculties and as controllers of committees, and the fact that female lions do most of the hunting. They argue that even if generic *man* ('When ancient man developed agriculture') is changed to *ancient people*, the new usage masks evidence that women were the earliest cultivators of plants. To say in the US that 'The fifteenth amendment ensured the voting rights of former slaves' hides the historical reality that this referred only to *men* who were former slaves.

See AMERICAN ENGLISH, BIBLE, FEMININE, FEMINISM, GENDER, GENDER BIAS, GENDERLECT, GENERIC, GENERIC PRONOUN, INCLUSIVE LANGUAGE, -ISM, -MAN/WOMAN, MASCULINE, PERSONIFICATION, POLITICALLY CORRECT, PRONOUN, SEXUALITY AND LANGUAGE. Compare CLASSISM, RACISM. [LANGUAGE, STYLE].   L.S.W., M.E.W.

Cameron, Deborah (ed.). 1990. *The Feminist Critique of Language: A Reader*. London & New York: Routledge.

Coates, Jennifer. 1986. *Women, Men and Language*. London: Longman.

Miller, Casey, & Swift, Kate. 1980/8. *The Handbook of Nonsexist Writing: For Writers, Editors and Speakers*. New York: Harper & Row.

Nilsen, Aileen Pace, *et al.* (eds.). 1977. *Sexism and Language*. Illinois: NCTE.

Spender, Dale. 1980. *Man Made Language*. London: Routledge.

Throne, B., & Henley, N. (eds.). 1975. *Language and Sex: Difference and Dominance*. Rowley, Mass.: Newbury House.

SEXTO. See SIXMO.

SEXUALITY AND LANGUAGE. The degree of ease with which people have spoken and written about sexuality in English has varied considerably by historical era, with such descriptive extremes as 'prudish Victorians' and 'modern permissiveness'. English has a well-documented history of delight in sexual topics, including dirty jokes, bawdy songs and limericks, and earthy elements in such works of literature as Chaucer's *Canterbury Tales*. A Shakespearean phrase for sexual intercourse, *the beast with two backs* (*Othello*, I. I. 107) is not used today but is probably recognizable in its context. However, Hamlet's command to Ophelia *Get thee to a nunnery* plays on a secondary slang meaning of *nunnery* as *brothel*, and the usage *to die* (slang for *to have an orgasm*) in *Much Ado About Nothing*, 5. 2. 99 ('I will live in thy heart, die in thy lap, and be buried in thine eyes') were obvious to contemporary audiences, but now need scholarly footnotes.

Literature containing sexual language or reference to aspects of sexuality has not always been readily available: for example, the explicit erotic poetry of the Scottish national poet Robert Burns was long published only in private editions. Censorship has often focused on particular sexual words, such as *fuck*, even when not used in a strictly sexual sense. Most controversy over sexuality in literature, such as in D. H. Lawrence's *Lady Chatterley's Lover*, is not over language but content: by and large, the detailed descriptions of sexual intercourse were more offensive than the use of *four-letter words*. Terms identifying or describing aspects of sexuality include names for body parts, sexual desire and activities, menstruation, pregnancy and birth, illness ('female complaints' and venereal disease), and prostitution. Such words can be placed along an overlapping continuum of acceptability: scientific-clinical, formal-neutral, child language, euphemism, slang, and taboo. Terms for parts of the body, for example, include as a group, more or less from the least to the most offensive, *vagina*, *privates*, *pussy*, *gash*, *cunt*. Words used to describe women sexually are often more negative and used more in abuse, than words that describe men in this way, both of women and men: for example, calling a woman a *cunt* is bad, calling a man a *cunt* is very bad, and both are stronger than calling someone a *prick*. Similarly, words for sexual activity often show a lack of parallel evolution. A woman can be called a *cock-teaser*, but there is no common equivalent for a man. A sexually active man with many partners is at worst a *womanizer*, but often publicly admired as a *stud*; a sexually active woman with many partners, although no longer generally considered *fallen*, is likely to be called *promiscuous*, a *tart* or a *whore*, and a *slut* or in BrE slang a *slag*.

Reluctance to talk about sexuality, because it is 'not nice' or at least 'private', is still strong. In certain groups, more open use began in the 'permissive' 1960s, in response to the women's liberation movement, the 'sexual revolution', increased attention to women's health issues, greater accessibility of birth control and abortion, and greater attention to sexually transmitted diseases. There has consequently been increased use in the media of formal terms, such as *sexually transmitted diseases* (instead of *venereal diseases*), *anal intercourse*, and *oral intercourse*. Many of the objections, particularly in the US, to sex education and awareness of the disease AIDS are linked to disapproval of their supposed encouragement of homosexual or non-marital sexual relations and the 'threat to family authority' that they may be thought to constitute. Thus, in many places, use of all informal, slang, or taboo terms (even for educational purposes) is forbidden. On television, some terms are not used at all and others only when children are presumed not to be watching. Advertisements for menstrual products can now mention *periodic flow*, for example, but advertising condoms, where permitted, uses indirect, non-specific, and euphemistic language such as references to 'protection'. See SEXISM, SWEARING, TABOO, VICTORIAN. [LANGUAGE, STYLE]. L.S.W., M.E.W.

SEYCHELLES. Official title: *Republic of the Seychelles*. A country of the western Indian Ocean and member of the Commonwealth, made up of over 100 islands. Capital: Victoria. Currency: the rupee. Population: 66,000 (1988), 75,000 (projection for 2000). Ethnicity: mixed African, European, Indian. Languages: Creole or Seychellois (French-based and spoken by around 95% of the population), English, and French (all official). Education: primary 92%, secondary 50%, tertiary 21%, literacy 75%. The islands were a French colony from 1768, a British colony from 1814, and became independent in 1976. The Seychellois are largely descended from French colonists and their freed African slaves, with smaller numbers of British, Chinese, and Indians. See ENGLISH. [AFRICA, NAME, VARIETY]. T.MCA.

SHAGGY DOG STORY [1940s: said to have begun as a species of joke about a talking dog]. A long, involved anecdote whose humour lies in its digressions and embroideries, the way it is told, and its long-delayed punch line. It is almost nihilistic in its pointlessness and the way in which it flouts the conventions of folk narrative. There is no easy sequence of 'once upon a time . . . then . . . next . . . in the end . . . and the moral is . . .'. The signal that the story has at last come to a point is usually a gleefully forced pun or play on words, as in the tale of the baron to whose castle gate one storm-lashed evening there comes a knight errant and his faithful hound. There is room within for only one stranger, and the baron, after giving the matter some thought, offers his hospitality to the dog. 'Would you turn a knight out on a dog like this?' cries the rejected traveller (playing on the idiom, 'I wouldn't turn a dog out on a night like this', with a cheerful disregard for the resultant collapse of logic and sense). This is the framework of the tale: its charm and torment lie in the detail, the development of inessentials, the loving exploration of narratological blind alleys, the excruciating relish of synonyms and stylistic curlicues, making the dog a *hound, a four-footed friend, a companion in many a time of trial.* Shaggy dog stories became popular after the Second World War and seem to be related to such other, more serious cultural developments as existentialism, *cinéma vérité*, and modernist fiction that does not put a construction on the events it describes but presents an undifferentiated report. However, the intricate, pointless tale is not exclusive to the 20c: a foremost example in English literature is Laurence Sterne's *Tristram Shandy* (1759-67), a 600-page rigmarole described at its conclusion as a story about a cock and a bull. Yesterday's cock and bull have become today's shaggy dog. See ANECDOTE, JOKE, PUNCH LINE, STORY. [STYLE].

W.N.

SHAKESPEARE, William [1564-1616]. English poet and playwright, the foremost figure in English literature and a primary influence on the development of especially the literary language. Knowledge of his life comes chiefly from documents unrelated to his career: records of his property transactions, his taxes, his occasional involvement in lawsuits. Other 'knowledge' derives from anecdotes, many set down long after his death, and biographical inferences from his writing.

Family and birth. Shakespeare's family goes back to the Warwickshire robber William Sakspere, whose hanging is recorded in the mid-13c. In the early 16c, Richard Shakespeare farmed as a tenant some three miles outside Stratford; his son John, a dresser of skins in Stratford, married his landlord's daughter Mary. John's growing prosperity is recorded not only in his real estate

purchases and in the expansion of his business into wool, timber, and barley, but also in a few brushes with the mercantile laws of his day. He rose nonetheless in the community, from Constable to Chamberlain and eventually to Mayor, though he apparently never learned to read and write: in surviving documents he signed with his mark. William, one of John and Mary Shakespeare's eight children, was baptized on 26 April 1564: it is only a guess that he was born on 23 April, St George's Day. The inscription on his tomb records his death on 23 April 1616, exactly 52 years later. No record of young William's education survives. The tradition, first set down in the early 18c, that says that he attended the Stratford 'free school', appears to be borne out by the thorough knowledge of Latin language and literature evident in his plays and poems. The same tradition says that his father's declining fortunes forced Shakespeare to quit school before he finished. He received special permission to marry Anne Hathaway in November 1582, when he was 18 and she was 26. Their daughter Susanna was born in May 1583; twins Hamnet and Judith were born in 1585.

Career. In 1592, the playwright Robert Greene alluded to another writer who 'with his *Tygers hart wrapt in a Players hide* . . . is in his owne conceit the onely Shake-scene in a countrey'. The allusion to *3 Henry VI* (1. 4. 137) and the pun on his name make it clear that Shakespeare was already in 1592 a prominent, if controversial, figure on the London theatrical scene. Within a few years, his pre-eminence was beyond controversy: in 1598, Francis Meres gave Shakespeare pride of place among the English dramatists he listed in *Palladis Tamia*, praising the 'sugred' sonnets and naming twelve plays composed in 'Shakespeares fine filed phrase'.

The plague forced the closing of London theatres from 1592 to 1594, years in which Shakespeare's non-dramatic *Venus and Adonis* and *The Rape of Lucrece* appeared. When the theatres reopened, Shakespeare wrote new plays, acted in some of Ben Jonson's, and, according to some traditions, in several of his own. He also became a part-owner of his theatrical troupe, the Lord Chamberlain's company. In the five years or so following, according to the conventional chronology, the phenomenally busy Shakespeare wrote eleven plays, the early sonnets, and *The Lover's Complaint*. His increasing success enabled Shakespeare to buy Stratford's second-largest house in 1597, when he was 33, and he continued to buy property in the town and in London as well until at least 1613. The list of property in his will makes impressive reading.

Shakespeare's company opened the Globe theatre in 1599. Queen Elizabeth died in 1603, and her successor James I pronounced Shakespeare's troupe his servants under the name the King's Men. The company often performed at court and, in 1608, took over the Blackfriars, a private indoor theatre. Shakespeare had written fewer plays since 1601, and seems to have stopped acting after 1607, perhaps because he was spending more time in Stratford. In 1613, he wrote his last play, probably in collaboration with Fletcher; in the same year, the Globe theatre burned down.

Works. Shakespeare's works do not survive in manuscript, and the copy that printers used was apparently not always his: some came from actors' reconstructions, some from the theatre company's prompt-books. Both scribes and printing-house compositors made occasional further alterations in the course of transmitting Shakespeare's text, including linguistic details such as punctuation, spelling, and grammatical inflections. Many of his works appeared in small separate editions known as 'quartos' during his lifetime; dates on the title page, or in the Stationers' Register, along with lists like Meres's, outline the chronology of Shakespeare's career. Some at least of the sonnets were already in circulation when Meres mentioned them over a decade before their 1609 publication, and some of the plays may likewise have been written and presented earlier than their publication. Several of the plays did not appear until the posthumous collected Folio edition of 1623, so the following chronology, though it reflects the preponderance of modern opinion, remains uncertain:
(1) Early works written before Shakespeare joined the Lord Chamberlain's company in 1594: *1 Henry VI, 2 Henry VI, 3 Henry VI, Richard III, Titus Andronicus, The Taming of the Shrew, Venus and Adonis, The Rape of Lucrece.*
(2) Works written between 1594 and the opening of the Globe in 1599: *Two Gentlemen of Verona, Love's Labour's Lost, Romeo and Juliet, Richard II, Midsummer Night's Dream, King John, Merchant of Venice, 1 Henry IV, 2 Henry IV, Much Ado About Nothing, Henry V*, the early sonnets, and *The Lover's Complaint.*
(3) Works written between 1599 and the acquisition of Blackfriars in 1608: *As You Like It, Twelfth Night, Hamlet, The Merry Wives of Windsor, Troilus and Cressida, All's Well That End's Well, Measure for Measure, Othello, King Lear, Macbeth, Antony and Cleopatra, Coriolanus, Timon of Athens*, the later sonnets, and *The Phoenix and the Turtle.*
(4) The last plays, written between 1608 and the burning of the Globe in 1613: *Pericles, Cymbeline, A Winter's Tale, The Tempest, Henry VIII.*

Language. The phrase 'Shakespeare's language' has come to mean both the state of English

around 1600 and Shakespeare's use of it. Both are topics in the following discussion of orthography, pronunciation and rhyme, syntactic structure, vocabulary and word-formation, linguistic variety, rhetoric, and pragmatics. In it, all the citations are from *Richard II* in the Quarto first edition (Q) of 1597, and comparisons with the Folio (F) of 1623. This concentration of examples from one play makes it easier to follow the passages cited, and gives an idea of the frequency of the features. Though no play embodies the full range of Shakespeare's linguistic ideas and practices, *Richard II* is notably concerned with the powers, limits, and dangers of language.

Orthography. The original editions of Shakespeare's works look very different from present-day orthography. They used no apostrophe for possessives; the occasional capitals on common nouns were more frequent in F than Q (for example, *violl* Q, *Vyall* F); and the letters *v* and *u* varied according to position rather than sound: *v* stood for both the *v*- and *u*-sounds when initial, and *u* stood for both when medial. Similarly, *i* stood for both *i* and *j* initially (*Iohn*). Other non-substantive variants included silent final *-e* (*robbes* 1. 3. 173 Q, *robs* F); this *-e* remains in conservative spellings like the surname *Clarke*.

Pronunciation and rhyme. The printed page best preserves features of vocabulary and structure; it preserves features of sound worst. Early editions of Shakespeare spelled the vowel in *band* and *bond* (5. 2. 65, 67) indifferently, and made no distinction between the consonants in words like *Murders* (1. 2. 21) and *Murthers* (3. 2. 40). Presumably, the spellings represented indistinguishable pronunciations. Q has *my owne* (1. 1. 133) but *thine owne* (1. 2. 35); where Q has *my honour* (1. 1. 191) and *thy oth* (1. 3. 14), F has *mine honour* and *thine oth*. The changes show that the matter of this historical *-n* before a vowel received editorial attention, but variations within Q indicate that the attention was not uniform. However, *sit* (1. 2. 47) in F differs from *set* in Q because the two words were commonly confused in the late 16c.

A rhyme such as John of Gaunt's *when/againe* (1. 1. 162-3) contrasts with the Duchess of York's *againe/twaine* (5. 3. 131-2), perhaps opportunistically making use of two current pronunciations, both still heard today. But the rhymes *teare* (verb)/*feare* (1. 1. 192-3) and *beare/heere* (5. 5. 117-18) reflect consistent pronunciation in both cases, as does *pierce/rehearse* (5. 3. 125-6) in Q, where F has the spelling *pearce* (from Old French *percer*) and the *-ea-* in *rehearse* looks back to a time when it was pronounced like the *-ea-* in *bear*. So too *happie hauens* (1. 3. 276) is a pun depending on a pronunciation of *heavens* implied by the *-ea-* spelling as in *bear*.

Much of the variation in spelling concerns the long vowels, which the Great Vowel Shift had left uncertain: for *yeeres* (1. 3. 159) in Q, F has *yeares*; but both have *yeeres* in line 171.

The rhyme *compassionate/late* (1. 3. 174-5) shows that the stress in the first word was fuller than at present, as with *loyaltie/lie* (1. 1. 67-8). But lack of stress and vowel reduction are implied in *a Gods name* (2. 1. 251), *Iohn a Gaunt* (1. 3. 76), *a dying* (2. 1. 90), where *a* means respectively 'in', 'of', and 'on'.

Syntactic structure. The structure of Shakespeare's Early Modern English is unlike present-day English. It seems familiar, however, because it is often studied, so its older features are overlooked, at least until they begin to cause difficulty. These features are, notably: word order; the polarity of adjectives and verbs; transitivity; subject-verb concord; negation and the use of *do*; relative pronouns and conjunctions; verb inflection; personal pronouns; and strong and weak verbs.

Word order. The sentence *My natiue English now I must forgo* (1. 3. 159-60) inverts typical English subject-verb-object word order from SVO to OSV, but is not ambiguous, because *I* is clearly the subject. However, there is structural ambiguity in *The last leaue of thee takes my weeping eie* (1. 2. 74): is *leaue* or *eie* the subject of *takes*? Shakespeare sometimes used the VS(O) order with the subjunctive verb for conditional clauses: *Holde out my horse* (2. 1. 300) means *If my horse holds out*, and *Put we our quarrell* (1. 2. 6) is a hortative order equivalent to *Let us put our quarrel to the will of heauen . . .*

Polarity. It *bootes thee not to be compassionate* (1. 3. 174) seems odd in part because *compassionate* now means *showing compassion*; for Shakespeare, it meant *seeking compassion*, and so the sentence translates as 'It won't help you to seek pity'. Similar instances of change in syntactic polarity are *pittifull = showing pity* (5. 2. 103), *fall = let fall* (3. 4. 104), *remember* (1. 3. 269) *= remind*, and *learne* (4. 1. 120) *= teach*.

Transitivity. A related feature is change in transitivity: *inhabit* (4. 1. 143) and *frequent* (5. 3. 6) are intransitive, while *Staies* for 'awaits' (1. 3. 3) and *part* for 'part from' (3. 1. 3) are transitive. The construction *Me thinkes* is impersonal, but Shakespeare could also write *I bethinke me* and *I had thought*.

Concord. His management of subject-verb agreement sometimes varied because the subject might be construed as either singular or plural: *this newes, these newes* (3. 4. 82, 100). Hence, *Reproch and dissolution hangeth ouer him* (2. 1. 258) is a singular verb following a double subject conceived of as a single entity.

Negation and the use of 'do'. Negatives like *I slewe him not* (1. 1. 133) avoid *do*, while *we do not vnderstand* (5. 3. 122) employs it; both are common in Shakespeare. The same is true of negative imperatives: *Call it not patience* (1. 2. 29), but *doe not so quickly go* (1. 2. 64). Multiple negations that retain negative sense are also common, though the Folio 'corrects' some of these: *Nor neuer looke vpon each others face, / Nor neuer write, regreete, nor reconcile* (1. 3. 185-6) Q becomes *Nor euer looke . . . Nor euer write . . . or reconcile* in F. Like negatives, questions can be formed with or without *do*: *Why dost thou say* (3. 4. 77), *what saist thou* (1. 1. 110).

Do also has an abundance of other uses: manage (*How shal we do for money*: 2. 2. 104); verb substitute (*let vs share thy thoughts as thou dost ours*: 2. 1. 273); idiomatically with *right* or *wrong* (*to do him right*: 2. 3. 137); idiomatically with *have* (*I haue to do with death*: 1. 3. 65); finish (*my life is done*: 1. 1. 183); with emphatic stress (*Yes . . . It doth containe a King*: 3. 3. 24-5).

Relative pronouns. Shakespeare will omit a relative pronoun for the subject of the clause where modern English omits it only for the object: *neare the hate of those loue not the King* (2. 2. 127), or use intricate subordination: *Hath causd his death, the which if wrongfully, / Let heauen reuenge* (1. 2. 39-40). He was no stickler for the use of *that* and *which* in restrictive and non-restrictive clauses, respectively: *the hollow crowne / That roundes* but *this flesh which wals about* (3. 2. 160-1, 167). He also used a variety of subordinating conjunctions: *for* (1. 1. 132) meaning 'as for', *for that* meaning 'because' (1. 1. 129) and 'in order that' (1. 3. 125), *for-because* (5. 5. 3) and *for why* (5. 1. 46), both meaning 'because'.

The endings -s and -th. The third-person singular indicative ending in Shakespeare's verbs could be either *-s*, as now, or the older *-th*. No meaning attached to the choice, so one line might include both: *Greefe boundeth where it falls* (1. 2. 58) F. But the forms of *do* and *have* were almost invariably *doth* and *hath*. The subjunctive mood, marked in the third-person singular present by the absence of a *-s* or *-th* ending, is often used in place of an auxiliary like *may* or *let*, and sometimes in combination with them: *O set my husbands wronges on Herefords speare, / That it may enter butcher Mowbraies breast: / Or if misfortune misse the first carier, / Be Mowbraies sinnes so heauy in his bosome / That they may breake his foming coursers backe* (1. 2. 47-51).

Pronouns. Shakespeare's English included the second-person pronouns *you* or *ye* and *thou*. Historically, they were plural and singular respectively, but *you* had come to be used as a formal or honorific alternative for the singular. In *Richard II*, some usages conform to this pattern: the Queen calls the gardener *thou* in 3. 4 and he calls her *you* in her presence; after she leaves he changes to a compassionately familiar *thou*. Likewise, the King regularly calls the disputants, his subjects, *thou* in the singular and *you* in the plural. Generally, they call him the respectful *you*, as Mowbray does at the beginning of his 'protest' speech (1. 3. 154-73); but by the end of the speech he has switched to *thou*. The change could arise from Mowbray's growing anguish, but other alternations between the two forms occur: in 1. 2, John of Gaunt usually calls the Duchess of Gloucester *you* (but *thee*: 1. 2. 57), while she consistently calls him *thou*; in 5. 5, the Groom calls the King *thou*, but the Keeper uses *you*.

Shakespeare's English lacked the possessive *its*; he sometimes used the uninflected *it*, sometimes the historical neuter possessive *his*: *what a Face I haue, / Since it is Bankrupt of his Maiestie* (4. 1. 266-7) F.

Strong and weak verbs. Among Shakespeare's weak verbs, the spelling often shows that the suffix *-ed* is not syllabic: *learnt* 1. 3. 159, *casde* 1. 3. 163. The suffix after *t* or *d* is, however, regularly syllabic: *blotted*. Both pronunciations accord with modern practice; unlike it, however, are words like *fostered*, which had three syllables. His strong verbs occasionally take unfamiliar forms in the past: for example, *spake* (5. 2. 12). Some forms of strong past participles are identical with the simple past: *broke* (5. 5. 43-8) F (*broken* 2. 2. 59 Q is extra-metrical, and F has *broke*), *shooke* (4. 1. 163) F, *spoke* (1. 1. 77) Q (*spoken* F). Others are archaic: *holp* (5. 5. 62), *eate* (5. 5. 85), *writ* (4. 1. 275) F.

Vocabulary and word-formation. Shakespeare's vocabulary is sometimes estimated at *c.*20,000 words. For it, he drew on Renaissance technical terms, derivations, compounds, archaisms, polysemy, etymological meanings, and idioms. *Richard II* abounds in technical terms, often words with specialized meanings distinct from their everyday use: in *That knowes no touch to tune the harmonie* (1. 3. 165), *touch* means 'fingering' and *to tune* means 'to play'. Suitably to the subject of the play, many technical terms are from the law or chivalry.

Conversion. Shakespeare is noted for verbal conversion such as *grace me no grace, nor vnckle me no vnckle* (2. 3. 86). Other examples include the verbs converted from nouns *refuge* (5. 5. 26), *twaine* (5. 3. 132), *priuiledge* (1. 1. 120), and *dog them at the heeles* (5. 3. 137).

Derivation. Shakespeare was also fecund with derivations, words created by the addition of a suffix, often in a new part of speech: the verb

'partialize' (1. 1. 120), from the adjective 'partial', a Shakespeare original as a transitive verb. In addition, every Shakespeare play makes concentrated use of some lexical field. Whereas in *Coriolanus* it is a lexical set centring on 'breath', 'voice', and 'vote', in *Richard II* it is a morphological set centring on privatives beginning with *un-*, like *vnfurnisht wals, / Vnpeopled offices, vntrodden stones* (1. 2. 68-9). Some of these appear nowhere else in Shakespeare, like *vndeafe, vnhappied*, and *vnkingd*.

Compounding. Lines like *My oile-dried lampe, and time bewasted light* (1. 3. 221) show Shakespeare's fondness for compounds: here, compounds formed on past participles. They are most often nouns, like *beggar-feare* (1. 1. 189), or adjectives, like the cluster *Egle-winged pride / Of skie-aspiring and ambitious thoughts, / With riuall-hating enuy* (1. 3. 129-31).

Polysemy. Shakespeare often used words in more than one meaning: *defend* (1. 3. 19) means 'protect', but in the previous line it means 'forbid'. His *recreant* (1. 1. 144) meant 'false to religion', but *caitiue recreant* (1. 2. 53) means 'captive coward', since *recreant* there is a figure of speech and means 'false to the religion of chivalry'.

Linguistic variety. The Welsh Captain in *Richard II* (2. 4) uses none of the regionalisms of Fluellen in *Henry V*, and lower-class characters like the Groom (5. 5) use none of the vulgarisms of the Carriers in *1 Henry IV*. At the level of dramatic idiolect, the play has no comic overreachers like Dogberry in *Much Ado About Nothing*, Mistress Quickly in *1 Henry IV*, the Gravedigger in *Hamlet*, or Holofernes in *Love's Labour's Lost*. Though the Queen refers to the Gardener's *harsh rude tong* (3. 4. 74), she seems to mean only the bad news he recounts: his speech is apparently quite standard. At least in this respect, *Richard II* is unlike other Shakespeare history plays such as *1-2 Henry IV*.

Rhetoric. Shakespeare was familiar with paradox and other figures of traditional rhetoric, for example *chiasmus* in *Banisht this fraile sepulchre of our flesh, / As now our flesh is banisht* (1. 3. 196-7); *the last taste of sweetes is sweetest last* (2. 1. 13); *Deposing thee before thou wert possest, / Which art possest now to depose thy self* (2. 1. 107-8). The last example also contains *paronomasia*; here, the pun is on *possessed* meaning both *having come into possession* and *unreasonably determined*. Richard comments on Gaunt's onomastic word-play, *Can sicke men play so nicely with their names?* (2. 1. 84), but Gaunt has already juggled *inspire* and *expire* (2. 1. 31-2), and urged his son to *Call it a trauaile that thou takst for pleasure* (1. 3. 262), playing on *travel* and *travail*. Even in prison, Richard replies to the salutation *Haile roiall Prince* with *Thankes noble peare: | The cheapest of vs is ten grotes too deare* (5. 5. 67-8), the royal being a coin worth ten groats more than a noble.

Imagery. Shakespeare's reputation has always rested more securely on another rhetorical figure: his images. Some of the images are submerged in a passing line: in *How high a pitch his resolution soares* (1. 1. 109), *pitch* is a technical term for the peak of a falcon's ascent before it plunges on its prey, so it forms an image with *soares* (and anticipates *Egle-winged pride* in 1. 3. 129). The three images of Mowbray's protest speech are more extended and more explicit: language is like a stringed musical instrument (1. 3. 162-5); the tongue is like a prisoner within the mouth (1. 3. 166-9); the breath of language is like the breath of life (1. 3. 172-3). The images form an increasingly ominous sequence from courtly entertainment to liberty to life. The most extended images are symbolic action like that of the literal gardeners, whose dialogue compares the commonwealth to a garden grown wild. When the Queen demands *Thou old Adams likenesse set to dresse this garden, | . . . | What Eue? what serpent hath suggested thee | To make a second fall of cursed man?* (3. 4. 73-6), her epithets revive John of Gaunt's proleptic comparison of England to *This other Eden* (2. 1. 42).

Allusion. Traditional rhetoric encouraged the invocation of authorities, in *Richard II* not the historical sources but other traditions that gave the historical action its meaning. Shakespeare made frequent use of proverbs: *Forget, forgiue* (1. 1. 156); *truth hath a quiet brest* (1. 3. 96); *There is no vertue like necessity* (1. 3. 278). But the greatest authority was the Bible: in 5. 5. 14-17, Richard deftly concords Matthew 19: 14 and 19: 24:

> set the word it selfe
> Against the word, as thus: Come little ones, & then
> againe
> It is as hard to come, as for a Cammell
> To threed the posterne of a small needles eie . . .

as he has already more daringly merged Matthew 26: 20-1 with Ecclesiastes 7: 28 in 4. 1. 169-71 F, in:

> Did they not sometime cry, All hayle to me?
> So Iudas did to Christ: but he in twelue,
> Found truth in all, but one, I, in twelue thousand,
> none.

Eloquence. Richard's fondness for such 'fine' language is often noted. He is also inclined to set his thoughts out in paratactic lists such as the seven parallel objects of 'Ile give', all beginning 'My':

> Ile giue my Iewels for a sett of Beades,
> My gorgeous Pallace, for a Hermitage,
> My gay Apparrell, for an Almes-mans Gowne,
> My figur'd Goblets, for a Dish of Wood,
> My Scepter, for a Palmers walking Staffe,
> My Subiects, for a payre of carued Saints,
> And my large Kingdome, for a little Graue
>
> (3. 3. 147-53)

Richard also composes poised hypotaxis, such as his verdict:

> For that our kingdomes earth should not be soild
> With that deare blood which it hath fostered:
> And for our eies do hate the dire aspect
> Of ciuill wounds plowd vp with neighbours swords,
> And for we thinke the Egle-winged pride
> Of skie-aspiring and ambitious thoughts,
> With riuall-hating enuy set on you
> To wake our peace, which in our Countries cradle
> Draw the sweet infant breath of gentle sleepe,
> Which so rouzde vp with boistrous vntunde drummes,
> With harsh resounding trumpets dreadfull bray,
> And grating shocke of harsh resounding armes,
> Might from our quiet confines fright faire Peace,
> And make vs wade euen in our kinreds bloud;
> Therefore we banish you our territories . . .
>
> (1. 3. 125-139)

If his eloquence often replaces action, it is nonetheless magisterial. But the play also undercuts the power of eloquence: following the Cardinal's eloquent speech, Northumberland comments *Well haue you argued sir, and for your paines, | Of Capitall treason, we arrest you heere* (4. 1. 150-1).

Pragmatics. Richard's language enforces his kingship: *How long a time lies in one little word. | Foure lagging winters and foure wanton springes | End in a word, such is the breath of Kinges* (1. 3. 213-15). Hence, his speeches are full of performatives: *The hoplesse word of neuer to returne, | Breathe I against him* (1. 3. 152-3). But Bolingbroke too (*With a foule traitors name stuffe I thy throte*: 1. 1. 44) and Mowbray (*I do defie him, and I spit at him*: 1. 1. 60) employ performatives, already signalling their traverse of the royal prerogative in the play's first scene. Richard interrupts Bolingbroke's procession to instruct his Queen *Tell thou the lamentable tale of me* (5. 1. 44) in future times, again transmuting physical action into speech. Richard's optimism about language, even in this moment of downfall, conflicts with the belief of others that language is at odds with both action and intention: rather than let his tongue recant, Bolingbroke would spit it in Mowbray's face, disabling his language and committing himself to incontrovertible action (1. 1. 190-3); the Duchess of York contradicts her garrulous husband because *His words come from his mouth, ours from our breast* (5. 3. 100). Shakespeare records lapses of language in the characters most involved in it: the Duchess of Gloucester, she of the great speech on the sons of Edward, falters a few lines later: *I shall remember more: Bid him, ah what? | With all good speede at Plashie visite* *me* (1. 2. 65–6); and York, whose mastery of language is his refuge from his inability to act, stumbles: *Come sister, cousin I would say, pray pardon me* (2. 2. 105).

Language and nation. The exchange of chivalric formulas and the reliance on legal terms in Act I witness the role of language as a civilized bond in *Richard II*. In this sense, language is like coin, the customary and authorized medium of exchange within a nation, as Richard acknowledges: *if my word be Sterling yet in England* (4. 1. 264) F, and as do lines like *to what purpose doest thou hoard thy words* and *the tongue's office should be prodigall* (1. 3. 253, 256). John of Gaunt's use of the comparison, however, delimits the currency of coin and language: *Thy word is currant with him for my death, / But dead, thy kingdome cannot buy my breath* (1. 3. 231–2). As Mowbray's protest speech shows, language equates not only with nationality but with life, for both take form in breath: abroad he will be without his native language, hence as good as dead. The report of Gaunt's death recalls Mowbray's imagery of language: *His tongue is now a stringlesse instrument, / Words, life, and al, old Lancaster hath spent* (2. 1. 149–50), as well as Gaunt's own: *Where words are scarce they are seldome spent in vaine* (2. 1. 7). The alterity of foreign languages reverses stable meanings. The Duchess of York begs Bolingbroke to *Say Pardon* for her son. But her husband, arguing against her, urges him to *Speake it in French, King say, Pardonne moy* (5. 3. 117), since the foreign phrase is a refusal. In the dangerous space that Shakespeare marks between the English *pardon* and the French lies the difference between their son's life and death, the empire of language. See index. [BIOGRAPHY, EUROPE, HISTORY, LANGUAGE, LITERATURE, STYLE]. W.F.B.

Abbott, E. A. 1872. Reprinted 1966. *A Shakespearian Grammar*. New York: Dover.

Blake, N. F. 1983. *Shakespeare's Language: An Introduction*. London: Macmillan.

Bolton, W. F. 1992. *Shakespeare's English: Language in the History Plays*. Oxford: Basil Blackwell.

Brook, G. L. 1976. *The Language of Shakespeare*. London: Deutsch.

Hulme, Hilda. 1972. *Yours that Read Him: An Introduction to Shakespeare's Language*. London: Ginn.

Hussey, S. S. 1982. *The Literary Language of Shakespeare*. London: Longman.

Macrone, Michael. 1990. *Brush up Your Shakespeare: An Infectious Tour Through the Most Famous and Quotable Words and Phrases from the Bard*. New York: Harper & Row.

Onions, Charles T. 1986. *A Shakespeare Glossary*, 3rd edition. Oxford: Clarendon Press.

Salmon, Vivian, & Burness, Edwina (eds.). 1987. *A Reader in the Language of Shakespearean Drama*. Amsterdam: Benjamins.

Schoenbaum, S. 1975. *William Shakespeare: A Documentary Life*. Oxford: University Press.

Spevack, Marvin. 1968–75. *A Complete and Systematic Concordance to the Works of Shakespeare*. Eight volumes. Hildesheim: Olms.

Wells, Stanley. 1986. *The Cambridge Companion to Shakespeare Studies*. Cambridge & New York: Cambridge University Press.

—— & Taylor, Gary. 1986. *William Shakespeare: The Complete Works* (separate volumes for modern and original spelling). Oxford: University Press.

——, with John Jowett & William Montgomery. 1987. *William Shakespeare: A Textual Companion*. Oxford: University Press.

SHAW, George Bernard [1856–1950]. Irish dramatist and critic. Born in Dublin. Educated at Wesley Connexional School. He moved to London in 1876, where he wrote five novels that had little success, was a music, art, and drama critic, and an early member of the Fabian Society. He found the contemporary English theatre trivial and remote from serious issues, and admired the Norwegian dramatist Henrik Ibsen's treatment of social problems; his first play, *Widowers' Houses* (1893), was an indictment of the profits made by slum landlords. Shaw began a long career as a playwright, controversial about specific issues and challenging the basic assumptions of his contemporaries, which sometimes brought conflict with theatrical censorship. Although polemical, his plays established him as the leading dramatist of his time by their humour, lively dialogue, and strong characterization. Shaw believed that, in order to survive, the human race must become more rational and better organized. He developed a philosophy of Creative Evolution, requiring cooperation with the Life Force, and against the mechanistic theory of Darwin he urged the power of human choice. His ideas on this subject appear in *Man and Superman* (1903), which emphasizes his belief in the creative strength of women, and *Back to Methuselah* (1921). Other plays are *Caesar and Cleopatra* (1898, the film 1945), *The Devil's Disciple* (1905), *Major Barbara* (1905, the film 1941), *Pygmalion* (1913, the film 1938), *Heartbreak House* (1919), *Saint Joan* (1923, the film 1956), and *The Apple Cart* (1929).

Shaw and language. In *Pygmalion*, the phonetician Henry Higgins teaches a Cockney girl to speak with an upper-class accent and adopt some social graces, then introduces her to smart society. Despite dramatic exaggeration, the play makes the point that in the stratified society of England powerful judgements of worth and suitability attached to accent and usage. Shaw's knowledge of phonetics and views on literacy led him to demand a rational system of spelling which would follow the sounds of English and reduce time wasted by traditional orthography. Having campaigned for spelling reform, he left a bequest for the establishment of a suitable new alphabet reflecting 'pronunciation to resemble that recorded of His Majesty our late King George V and sometimes described as Northern English'. A system was devised into which the play *Androcles and the Lion* (1912) was transcribed (published in 1962), but the project has had no further success.

Innovations. In his own work, Shaw adopted three innovations: (1) Some simplified spellings of the North American type, such as *cigaret, program, vigor.* (2) Omission of the apostrophe in contractions, as in *didnt.* (3) Spacing between letters for emphasis (*m u s t*). He complained that dialect speech could not be shown in writing without a phonetic system, but nonetheless used non-standard spelling for the purpose, as in: 'Aw knaow. Me an maw few shillins is not good enaff for you. Youre an earl's grandorter, you are. Nathink less than a anderd pahnd for you' (from *Major Barbara*) [*maw* my, *grandorter* granddaughter, *nathink* nothing, *anderd pahnd* hundred pounds]. Shaw was impatient of insistence on formal grammar and believed that a form of Pidgin English could become a world medium of communication. See index. [BIOGRAPHY, EUROPE, LITERATURE, STYLE]. R.C.

SHELTA, also **Shelter, Shelteroch, Sheldru** [*c.*1880s: origin uncertain]. An argot, derived from Irish Gaelic, used by Travelling People (*tinkers*) in Ireland and Britain. Many of its words are disguised through such techniques as back slang (such as *gop* kiss, from Irish *póg*) and altering the initial sounds of words (as in *gather* father, from Irish *athair*). The linguist Ian Hancock has described it ('Shelta and Polari', in P. Trudgill (ed.), *Language in the British Isles*, 1984) as having 'all the characteristics of an ethnic language'. The name appears not now to be used by its speakers, who call it *Gammon, Tarri,* or simply *the Cant* (perhaps from Irish *caint* speech: but compare CANT). It has also been referred to as *Bog Latin, Tinkers' Cant,* and *the Ould Thing.* There are two divisions, *Gaelic Shelta* (in Ireland and Scotland) and *English Shelta* (in England and Wales); although the influence of English in the latter is increasing, the varieties share a common core of some 2,000–3,000 Irish-derived words. *American Travellers' Cant* was originally also Shelta but is now largely Anglicized. BrE slang may have absorbed from Shelta such words as *gammy* lame (from *gyamyath*, Irish *cam*) and *monicker* name (from *munnik*, Irish *ainm*). English Shelta uses Irish-derived words in English syntax (as in *I korbed him so hard I broke his pi* I hit him so hard I broke his head) with Irish syntactic influence shown in some constructions (such as *Have you the feen's dorah*

nyocked? Did you take the man's bread?). See CANT, IRISH. [EUROPE, NAME, VARIETY]. T.MCA.

SHERIDAN, Richard Brinsley [1751–1816]. Anglo-Irish dramatist. Born in Dublin, son of Thomas Sheridan the actor and Frances Sheridan the novelist. Educated at Harrow in England. His first play *The Rivals* (1775) was a success at Covent Garden in London, and was followed in the same year by *St Patrick's Day* and an operetta *The Duenna.* In 1776, he became manager of Drury Lane theatre, and in 1777 wrote *A Trip to Scarborough* and his most popular play *The School for Scandal.* His dialogue avoided the stilted language, sentiment, and artificiality of much 18c drama. He satirized contemporary pretensions and intrigues; like Fielding, he extolled the worth of honesty and generosity above an outward piety that concealed hypocrisy. His observation was acute rather than wide-ranging and he recorded mainly the tones and usage of fashionable society. The term *malapropism* derives from his character Mrs Malaprop in *The Rivals,* who confused *pine-apple* with *pinnacle* and *allegory* with *alligator.* Sheridan became sole proprietor of Drury Lane in 1779 and wrote *The Critic,* but was becoming tired of the theatre and sought a career in politics. He was elected MP for Stafford in 1780, gained a reputation as a parliamentary orator, became a minister of the Crown, and gained the friendship of the Prince Regent and leading politicians. Drury Lane was found unsafe and demolished in 1792; the rebuilt theatre was destroyed by fire in 1809. Sheridan lost his parliamentary seat, was arrested for debt in 1813, and died in poverty. See index. [BIOGRAPHY, EUROPE, LITERATURE]. R.C.

SHERIDAN, Thomas [1719–88]. Anglo-Irish actor and elocutionist. Probably born in Dublin. Educated at Westminster School in London and Trinity College, Dublin. He acted in Dublin and at Drury Lane in London before becoming manager of the Dublin Theatre Royal. After a period of moving between the Dublin and London stages he settled in England as teacher of elocution. He travelled the country lecturing and became a respected member of London literary society. Sheridan's publications include *A Course of Lectures in Elocution* (1763) and *A Plan of Education for the Young Nobility and Gentry of Great Britain* (1769). In the latter, he describes his aim 'to establish a uniformity of pronunciation . . . in all quarters of the globe, where English shall be taught by this method, and to remain immutably so, whilst that language shall be spoken in any part of the earth'. His most ambitious work was his *General Dictionary of the English Language* in two volumes

(1780), in which he mainly followed Johnson's orthography while adding what he considered the correct pronunciation of each word. In the preface, he wrote of Queen Anne's reign as the golden age of spoken English, before the Hanoverian succession brought excessive French influence. He feared the decline of English into 'a mere jargon, which every one may pronounce as he pleases'. Sheridan was a leading exponent of 18c prescriptivism in pronunciation, believing in an ideal and correct state of usage to be defended vigorously. His writings preserve information about the fashionable speech of the period. In *Lectures on Elocution* he wrote: 'Spoken language is the gift of God, written the invention of men.' See index. [BIOGRAPHY, EUROPE, REFERENCE, SPEECH].   R.C.

SHETLAND, also, especially locally but now less commonly, **Zetland**. Sometimes **the Shetlands** (short for *the Shetland Islands*); *Shetland* is preferred by Shetlanders. A group of islands off the northern coast of Scotland, constituting with Orkney *the Northern Isles*. Of the two, Shetland is further from the mainland. Capital: Lerwick. Population: 27,277 (1981). See NORN, NORTHERN ISLES, ORCADIAN, ORKNEY, ORKNEY AND SHETLAND DIALECTS, SCOTLAND, SHETLANDIC. [EUROPE, NAME].   T.MCA.

SHETLANDIC, also **Zetlandic** [By analogy with *Icelandic*]. Of or characteristic of Shetland. The term, in general use in Shetland since at least the mid-19c, has since c.1950 been used to mean *Shetland dialect*: 'the present participle in Shetlandic' (John J. Graham, *The Shetland Dictionary*, Stornoway: Thule, 1979). See ORKNEY AND SHETLAND DIALECTS. [EUROPE, NAME].   A.J.A.

SHETLAND NORN. See NORN.

SHIBBOLETH [14c: from Hebrew *shibbōleth*, meaning uncertain, perhaps either 'stream in flood' or 'ear of corn'. The English use originates in the Bible, in the Book of Judges 12: 5–6, where Jephthah and the Gileadites defeat the Ephraimites at the River Jordan: 'And the Gileadites tooke the passages of Iordan before the Ephraimites: and it was so that when those Ephraimites which were escaped saide, Let me go ouer, that the men of Gilead said vnto him, Art thou an Ephraimite? If he said, Nay: Then said they vnto him, Say now, Shibboleth: and he said, Sibboleth: for hee could not frame to pronounce it right. Then they tooke him, and slewe him at the passages of Iordan: and they fell at that time of the Ephraimites, fourtie & two thousand' (Authorized Version, 1611)]. (1) A peculiarity of pronunciation that indicates someone's regional and/or social origins, such

as: *toity-toid* thirty-third, serving to identify someone from Brooklyn; *firty fahsn* thirty thousand, identifying a Cockney. (2) A style, expression, custom, or mannerism that identifies an enemy or someone disliked because of background, community, occupation, etc.: for example, extreme political slogans referred to as *Fascist/Commie shibboleths*. Usually, the disapproval runs one way, higher social Gileadites detecting and rejecting lower social Ephraimites, but the reverse is also possible, as when in Britain, in assessing the vowel sounds in *can't dance*, speakers who say 'cahn't dahnce' are often dismissed as toffs and snobs. Occasionally, the term is neutral (when referring to a favourite expression, piece of advice, or slogan, such as *Er, good, good!* or *The early bird catches the worm, y'know*) or positive (when it is a device through which members of a group can identify each other). See MARKED AND UNMARKED TERMS. Compare STEREOTYPE. [SPEECH, STYLE].   T.MCA.

SHORT. See LONG AND SHORT.

SHORTHAND [17c]. Also **stenography** [17c: from Greek *stenós* narrow, *-graphy* writing]. A method of writing rapidly by substituting special characters, symbols, and abbreviations for letters, words, or phrases, and used for recording the proceedings of legislatures and testimony in courts of law, dictation for business correspondence, and note-taking by journalists and others. Cicero's orations, Luther's sermons, and Shakespeare's plays were all preserved by means of shorthand; Samuel Pepys used it to keep his diary, Charles Dickens used it as a reporter in the London law courts and Parliament, and Bernard Shaw wrote his plays in it. There are two basic systems of shorthand: *orthographic*, based on standard letters, and *phonetic*, seeking to represent speech sounds directly. Also involved are the use of arbitrary symbols and abbreviations to facilitate speed, comparable to the use of & for *and* and *etc.* for *etcetera* in longhand.

The earliest attested shorthand appears to date from 63 BC. It was the system of *notae Tironianae* (Tironian notes) devised by Marcus Tullius Tiro, a learned freedman and friend of the lawyer and orator Cicero, and was used to record speeches in the Roman Senate. Tiro's system, which was cursive and orthographic, was used by Julius Caesar, taught in Roman schools, and continued in use for c.1,000 years. It influenced the first modern system, developed in England by Timothy Bright in his *Characterie: an Arte of Shorte, Swifte, and Secrete Writing by Character* (1588). Over the next 50 years some 13 orthographic systems were published, the best-known being Thomas Shelton's *Short Writing* (1626), which Pepys used. The Revd Phillip

Gibbs (1736) was the first to favour a phonetic system. The Industrial Revolution gave a strong boost to the quest for ever more efficient systems that were easy to learn, both in Britain and on the Continent.

In 1837, in England, Isaac Pitman launched his phonetic system, *Stenographic Sound-Hand*, which classified sounds in a scientific manner and introduced abbreviations for the sake of speed. Made up of 25 single consonants, 24 double consonants, and 16 vowel sounds, its principles include the use of the shortest signs for the shortest sounds, single strokes for single consonants, simple geometrical forms, and pairing consonants (one written more lightly, as for *f*, the other more heavily, as for *v*). Revised versions of this system are widely used throughout the English-speaking world and are predominant in Australia, New Zealand, and India. In 1888, in Scotland, the Irish-born John Robert Gregg published his *Light-Line Phonography*, a system that he took to the US where it became the dominant medium, although Pitman's Shorthand is widely used there and is predominant in Canada. Gregg Shorthand is also phonetic, but the characters are based on elements of ordinary longhand, vowels are shown by circles and hooks, and curving motions are used throughout to ease movement. It also employs abbreviations, blended consonants, and affix forms to enable the writer to gain speed. Systems developed in the 20c use longhand symbols for most or all letters, and include: *Baine's Typed Shorthand* (1917), *Speedwriting* (1923, 1951), *HySpeed Longhand* (1932), *Abbreviatrix* (1945), *Quickhand* (1953), *Stenoscript* (1955), and *Carter Briefhand* (1957). The advantages of orthographic systems are relative ease of learning and transcription, the disadvantage loss of speed; the advantages of phonetic systems are speed and ease of transcription, the disadvantage difficulty of learning. See ACRONYM, DICTATION, HAND, HANDWRITING, LONGHAND, PITMAN (I.), VOCABULARY CONTROL. [WRITING].   T.MCA.

SHORT STORY. A fictional narrative brief enough to be transmitted at a single hearing or reading. The form is ancient and examples of its popularity and success include *Aesop's Fables*, *The Arabian Nights*, and the medieval *fabliaux*, the stories in Boccaccio's *Decameron*, and Chaucer's *Canterbury Tales*. The literary short story dates from the 19c and was fostered by the rise of the novel and the growth of periodicals for leisure reading. It is found in all modern literary cultures and may range from some 500 words in a magazine to around 10,000 words; a longer story of less than novel length is a *novella*. Edgar Allen Poe defined it as 'a short prose narrative requiring from a half-hour to one or two hours

in its perusal' (review of *Twice-Told Tales* by Nathaniel Hawthorne, 1842). Despite its brevity, it shares with the novel such features as plot, characterization, and narrative point of view. It must, however, be succinct in presenting its basic intention: the plot cannot be elaborate, it is likely to begin near its climax, and is unlikely to continue long after the climax has been reached. The few characters are presented through dialogue and action rather than description and comment. Within these constraints, the interest may be primarily in the incidents (as with Poe's stories), in a surprise ending (as with Ambrose Bierce and 'O. Henry', the pen name of W. S. Porter), in the presentation of character (as by Anton Chekhov), or in the symbiosis of character and setting (as in James Joyce's *Dubliners*). Broadcasting has revived oral narration and television has encouraged dramatization (as with the short stories of Roald Dahl). The attraction of the form for readers is partly practical, as filling vacant time in waiting or travelling; there is also the satisfaction of encountering language carefully shaped to a purpose and giving a brief experience of an often unfamiliar aspect of life. See DETECTIVE STORY, NARRATIVE, NOVEL, STORY. [LITERATURE].   R.C.

SHWA. See SCHWA.

SIBILANT [17c: from Latin *sibilans/sibilantis* hissing]. In phonetics: (1) A consonant characterized by a hissing sound, such as the /s/ in *hiss* and the /z/ in *his*. (2) Relating to such a consonant: *sibilant sounds*. See CONSONANT. [SPEECH].   T.MCA.

SIC. See NOTES AND REFERENCES.

SIDEBAR. See LAYOUT.

SIDNEY, (Sir) Philip [1544-86]. English courtier, scholar, and author. In his *Apologie for Poetry* (1583?), Sidney held English the better for having a mixed vocabulary and simple grammar, and hence 'for the vttering sweetly and properly the conceits of the minde, which is the end of speech, that hath it equally with any other tongue in the world; and is particularly happy in compositions of two or three words together, neere the Greeke, far beyond the Latine; which is one of the greatest beauties can be in a language'. He opposed literary affectations like Spenser's archaisms and far-fetched vocabulary in the guise of eloquence. Among his many other accomplishments, his contemporaries praised the contributions of his style to literary English: Thomas Nashe said that Sidney was 'the first (in our language) . . . that repurified Poetrie from Arts pedantisme, and that instructed it to speake courtly'; Michael Drayton believed that his prose proved 'That plenteous *English* hand in hand might goe / With Greeke and Latine'; and Francis Meres claimed that English was 'gorgeouslie inuested in rare ornaments and resplendent abiliments by sir Philip Sidney'. See index. [BIOGRAPHY, EUROPE, HISTORY].   W.F.B.

SIERRA LEONE. Officially *Republic of Sierra Leone.* A country of West Africa and member of the Commonwealth. Capital: Freetown. Currency: the leone (100 cents). Population: 3.95m (1988), 5.4m (projection for 2000). Ethnicity: 34% Mende; the remainder including Temne, Kono, Fulani, Bullom, Koranko, Limba, Loko, Kissi, and Krios. Religions: 70% traditional, 25% Muslim, 5% Christian. Languages: English (official); Krio (an English-based creole), Mende, and Temne widely spoken. Education: primary 58%, secondary 17%, tertiary 1%, literacy 30%. The first Europeans to visit the area were Portuguese navigators and British slavers. In the 1780s, British philanthropists bought land from local chiefs to establish settlements for freed slaves, whence the name *Freetown.* In 1808, the coastal settlements became a British colony, and in 1896 the hinterland became a protectorate. Sierra Leone became independent in 1961 and a republic in 1971. The English of Sierra Leone is a variety of West African English; it is distinct from Krio, but the two shade into each other and into vernacular usage. English is the language of all education, all newspapers and magazines, 95% of television and cinema, and the medium for documenting local history and culture. It has such a high status that 'using an African language at a wedding reception or even a private party is unheard of, because it is considered a debasement of the value of the occasion' (Joe Pemagbi, 'Still a Deficient Language?—The New English of Sierra Leone', *English Today* 17, Jan. 1989). Its distinctive vocabulary includes: (1) Words derived from local languages: *agidi* a paste made from fermented cornflour, *bondo* a secret society for women, *fufu* grated and fermented cassava cooked into a paste and eaten with soup or sauce, *woreh* a cattle ranch. (2) Extensions of sense: *apprentice* a young man who loads and unloads vehicles, *bluff* to be elegantly dressed, to have a neat appearance ('She's bluffing today'), *cookery* cheap food eaten outside the home, *foolish* to make (someone) appear stupid ('The teacher was foolished'), *woman damage* money paid to a husband by another man as compensation for having a sexual relationship with his wife. See AFRICAN ENGLISH, ENGLISH, KRIO, LIBERIA, WEST AFRICAN ENGLISH. [AFRICA, NAME, VARIETY].   T.MCA.

SIGN [12c: noun use from Old French *signe*, Latin *signum* mark, sign, signal, image; verb use from *signare/signatum* to mark with a sign]. (1) Something that conveys meaning, such as an object, token, mark, image, movement, gesture, sound, event, pattern, and the like. Signs may be directly representational (as when a drawing of a hand points in the direction to be taken) or symbolic (as when a cross denotes Christianity and not the Crucifixion alone), but are often entirely arbitrary (such as letters standing for speech sounds, or in mathematics a *plus sign* and a *minus sign*). (2) A notice or other object that carries a name, etc. (as with a *shop sign* BrE, *store sign* AmE), names and directions (as with a *road sign*), a warning (as with a board marked *Danger*), etc. (3) Variously, by extension, a trace, symptom, omen, etc. (4) Verb senses include: to add one's signature to a document; to communicate by means of a sign or signs (*He signed that he wanted to leave*); to convey a message in sign language (*to sign the word 'friend'*). If one thing *signifies* another, it serves as a sign for it: for example, the symbol + signifying 'plus' in arithmetic. The act of signifying is *signification*; a term that is often used synonymously with 'meaning' and 'sense', and occurs in the discussions of students of semantics and semiotics. Compare SIGNAL, SIGNATURE, SYMBOL. See LINGUISTIC SIGN, SEMANTICS, SEMIOTICS, SIGN LANGUAGE. [LANGUAGE].   T.MCA.

SIGNAL [14c: from Medieval Latin *signale*, from Latin *signalis* of a sign]. (1) An object or action (often one of a set or series) intended to show, direct, warn, etc., such as a *distress signal*, indicating that people are in danger, a *hand signal*, such as raising one arm or waving both arms, a *traffic signal*, indicating when road-users must stop or go. (2) An electrical quantity or effect, such as a current, that can be varied to convey information: for example, in telephoning and when computers store data. (3) To communicate by means of signals, as with the flags used in sending *semaphore* messages (messages by means of handheld flags). See MESSAGE, SIGN, SYMBOL. [LANGUAGE].   T.MCA.

SIGNATURE [16c: from Latin *signatura* something marked]. (1) A name or mark placed on a surface, to show approval, agreement, authorization, source, etc.: *putting one's signature to a contract; an illegible signature on a letter.* (2) A feature or features, such as a musical motif, especially the *signature tune* of a group or a series on radio or television, or in biology and medicine a pattern of characteristics marking a formation or disorder. (3) Also *quire signature.* A mark (usually letters and numbers), with which a quire of pages has been signed, usually at the foot of the opening recto, to guide a binder in folding sheets and putting them in the right order. The signing is now often along the outer fold, which is hidden in the binding of the book. (4) Also *section*. A leaf or a quire so marked and folded for binding to form a book or periodical. (5) A booklet made from the first section of a large book, such as a dictionary or encyclopedia, as a specimen for promotional purposes. See BOOK, MARK. [TECHNOLOGY]. W.W.B.

SIGN ENGLISH, SIGNED ENGLISH. See SIGN LANGUAGE.

SIGN LANGUAGE [1840s]. (1) A means of communication using gestures, usually between speakers of different languages: *Plains Indian sign language*. (2) Also *sign*. A system of manual communication used by the deaf. It is widely believed that such sign languages consist of instinctive gestures that picture the world and are understood no matter which part of the world a signer comes from. This is not so: the signs are conventional movements that represent a range of meanings similar to those expressed by speech (including abstract notions), and differing widely between communities. There are two main types: *concept-based systems* used as natural languages; *language-based systems* often used when teaching deaf children to communicate. There are rules governing the way signs are formed and how they are sequenced, and people have to learn them, either as children (such as from deaf parents) or as adults (such as when working with the deaf). There are many thousands of signs in the leading sign languages.

When a sign language becomes widely used, it develops varieties similar to those in spoken language. Several 'mixed' varieties exist, where people use signs that show the influence of the speech of the community to which the signer belongs. Not only is it impossible for French and English signers to understand each other (without one person learning the other's sign), but there is little mutual comprehension between signers of *American Sign Language* (short forms *Ameslan*, *ASL*) and *British Sign Language* (short form *BSL*), because the sign vocabulary is different. However, both sign languages can be traced to the early 19c work of two educators of the deaf, Thomas Gallaudet in the US and Laurent Clerc in France. The signs express a range of meanings and nuances comparable to those expressed by spoken or written language. For example, time relationships can be expressed by dividing the space in front of the body into zones, such as further forward for future time and further back for past time. Personal pronouns can be distinguished using different spatial areas: *you* is front-centre and various

third-person forms are signed to the right and left. Use is made of repeated signs to convey such notions as plurality, degree, or emphasis. These signs are used simultaneously with other movements, such as facial expressions, eye movements, and shifts of the body: for example, questions can be signalled by a facial expression, such as raised eyebrows and a backwards head tilt. Fluent signing (between one and two signs per second) produces a conversational rate comparable to that of speech.

Sign languages within the community of English have been devised at various times to bring the signer into a close relationship with spoken or written English. These include: (1) *Finger spelling* (dating at least from the 19c), in which each letter of the alphabet has its own sign, using two hands in the British version and one hand in the American version. (2) *Cued Speech* (1966), a system of hand cues used alongside lip movements to draw attention to the phonemic contrasts in speech. (3) More complex systems that aim to reflect features of English grammar, including *Signed English* or *Sign English* (1966), *Seeing Essential English* (1969), *Manual English* (1972). See DUMMY, MEDIUM, MIME, MUMMERY. [LANGUAGE]. D.C.

Klima, E., & Bellugi, U. 1979. *The Signs of Language*. Harvard: University Press.

Kyle, J. G., & Woll, B. 1985. *Sign Language*. Cambridge: University Press.

Sacks, Oliver. 1989. *Seeing Voices: A Journey into the World of the Deaf*. Berkeley & Los Angeles: University of California Press. London: Picador (1990).

SILENT FILM/MOVIE. See MIME, MOTION PICTURE.

SILENT LETTER. A letter that is not pronounced, such as the *p* and *l* in *psalm*. With the exception of *f*, *j*, *q*, *r*, *v*, all consonant letters in English have no sound value in certain environments: *b* in *numb*, *c* in *scythe*, *d* in *handsome*, *g* in *foreign*, *h* in *honest*, *k* in *knee*, *l* in *talk*, *m* in *mnemonic*, *n* in *damn*, *p* in *psychology*, *s* in *island*, *t* in *hutch*, *w* in *wrong*, *x* in *prix*, *y* in *key*, and *z* in *laissez-faire*. See ALPHABET, B, D, E, G, H, K, L, M, N, P, R, S, SPELLING, SPELLING REFORM, T, W, X. [WRITING]. C.U.

SILENT READING. See READING.

SILENT STRESS. See RHYTHM.

SILENT WAY, The. See ELT, LANGUAGE TEACHING.

SIMILE [14c: from Latin *simile*, neuter of *similis* like]. A figure of speech, in which a more or less fanciful or unrealistic comparison is made, using *like* or *as*. *Some dogs are like wolves* is a prosaic or realistic comparison and therefore not a simile, but *The Assyrian came down like the wolf on the fold* (Byron) is a simile because the savagery is wolf-like, not the Assyrian, and neither savagery nor the Assyrian is physically like a wolf. Everyday usage is rich in similes, many of them idiomatic: (1) With *like*: *spread like wildfire, sell like hot cakes, run like the wind; like a bull in a china shop* (said of a clumsy, violent person), *like a fish out of water* (said of a person uneasy in an unfamiliar situation). (2) With *as . . . as*: *as thick as thieves* (of people cooperating closely), *as like as two peas* (of people or things virtually identical in looks), *as mad as a hatter* (of someone considered crazy), *as strong as an ox* (of someone very strong).

Most similes are brief, but *extended similes* take up many lines or sentences. The relationship between simile and *metaphor* is close, metaphor often being defined as condensed simile, that is, someone who *runs like lightning* can be called *a lightning runner*. Sometimes, simile and metaphor blend so well that the join is hard to find, as in: 'And hence one master-passion in the breast, / Like Aaron's serpent, swallows up the rest' (Pope, *Essay on Man*, 1732–4). A passage beginning with similes can turn into an extended metaphor, as in these verses of John Donne ('A Valediction: Forbidding Mourning', 1633; italics added):

> Our two souls, therefore, which are one,
> Though I must go, endure not yet
> A breach, but an expansion,
> *Like* gold to airy thinness beat.

> If they be two, they are two so
> *As* stiff twin compasses are two;
> Thy soul, the fixed foot, makes no show
> To move, but doth, if th'other do.

> And though it in the centre sit,
> Yet when the other far doth roam,
> It leans and hearkens after it,
> And grows erect as that comes home.

> Such wilt thou be to me, who must
> Like th'other foot obliquely run;
> Thy firmness makes my circle just,
> And makes me end where I begun.

Similes can draw in complex ways on immediate circumstance: 'Like light from a collapsing star, exhausted by the struggle against gravity, the thoughts of Stephen Hawking reach us as if from a vast distance, a quantum at a time. Unable to speak, paralysed by a progressive, incurable disease, the 46-year-old British physicist communicates with the world by a barely perceptible twitch of his fingers, generating one computer-synthesized word approximately every six seconds' (Jerry Adler, 'Reading God's Mind', *Newsweek*, 13 June 1988). See FIGURATIVE

LANGUAGE/USAGE, HOMERIC SIMILE, IMAGE, METAPHOR, PARABLE. [STYLE].　　　　T.MCA.

SIMPLE FUTURE. See FUTURE.

SIMPLE PAST. See PAST.

SIMPLE PRESENT. See PRESENT.

SIMPLE SENTENCE. A sentence that consists of one main clause and does not contain a coordinate clause or a subordinate clause: *The storm blew down several of my trees.* See SENTENCE. [GRAMMAR].　　　　S.G.

SIMPLE WORD. See WORD-FORMATION.

SIMPLEX. See WORD-FORMATION.

SIMPLIFIED READER. See READER.

SIMPLIFIED SPELLING SOCIETY, short form *SSS*. An association founded in Britain in 1908 with the aim of bringing about 'a reform of the spelling of English in the interests of ease of learning and economy of writing'. Its presidents have been predominantly philologists and linguists: W. W. Skeat (1908–11), Gilbert Murray (1911–46), Daniel Jones (1946–68), and Donald Scragg (from 1988). Others were the publisher and Member of Parliament Sir James Pitman (1968–72) and the psychologist John Downing (1972–87). Its officers have included the House of Commons Speaker Horace King, Archbishop William Temple, H. G. Wells, the industrialist Sir George Hunter, and the phoneticians David Abercrombie and A. C. Gimson.

A phonetic orthography. Between about 1915 and 1924, the SSS issued reading books in a phonetic orthography for learners in schools, such as *Nerseri Rymz and Simpel Poëmz: A Ferst Reeder in Simplifyd Speling*. Considerable success was claimed for them as a means of teaching literacy quickly and effectively. In 1923, the SSS sought to persuade the Board of Education to set up a committee to examine the possibilities of reform, but without success. A second approach was made in 1933, supported by over 900 university figures from vice-chancellors to lecturers, 250 MPs, 20 bishops, and ten teachers' organizations, but it also met with a refusal to entertain the question.

New Spelling. This failure led the SSS to concentrate on preparing a fully researched and revised version of the system it had previously advocated, a task undertaken by William Archer and Walter Ripman. The result was issued as *New Spelling*, a final edition (further revised by Daniel Jones and Harold Orton) appearing in

1948. Subsequent work was financed partly by a 1937 legacy from Sir George Hunter. Campaigning was renewed in Parliament by Mont Follick, an MP who twice promoted a Private Member's Bill (1949, 1953), the latter receiving a second reading and passing the committee stage. Official opposition, however, led to a compromise in which the government undertook no more than to facilitate research into the use of simplified spelling in schools. By way of research, the U. of London Institute of Education, the National Foundation for Educational Research, and the Association of Education Committees were, at first tentatively, concerned with school experiments in the early 1950s.

The initial teaching alphabet. By the end of the 1950s Sir James Pitman had evolved the *Initial Teaching Alphabet* (i.t.a), based on the Society's *New Spelling* system, but with new characters in place of digraphs. On his initiative and at his expense, i.t.a. was introduced in many hundreds of schools in the UK, US, Australia, and elsewhere. Its effects were researched by John Downing, who published his findings in *Evaluating the Initial Teaching Alphabet* (1967). Reformers argue that these findings confirmed previous experience: literacy skills were more successfully acquired in a phonographically regular system than in traditional orthography (t.o.). Organizational problems, however, led to rapid decline in the use of i.t.a in the 1980s. The i.t.a was controversial within the SSS, partly because of its unpopular new characters, and partly because it was a teaching medium and not the system for general use that the Society advocated.

Recent developments. In the 1970s–80s, the SSS broadened its interests and its worldwide links, initiating a series of international conferences and launching the *Journal of the Simplified Spelling Society*. In view of the non-acceptance of earlier reform proposals, the Society began to take up the ideas of Harry Lindgren in Australia and consider partial or staged reforms of t.o. as more practical and likely to overcome entrenched resistance. Three kinds of staged reform have so far been proposed: (1) The spelling of a single phoneme could be regularized, as with *e* in *eny*, *breth*, *frend*. (2) Problem graphemes such as *gh* could be regularized, producing forms such as *weit*, *dauter*, *tho*, *thru*, *cof*. (3) Redundant letters could be removed, as in *dout*, *principl*, *acomodate*, achieving far-reaching regularization with little disruption. In the late 1980s, the Society sought to influence British education policy by submitting statements on spelling problems to government committees inquiring into the future of English teaching. See CUT SPELLING, INITIAL TEACHING ALPHABET, PITMAN (J.), SPELLING, SPELLING REFORM. [MEDIA, WRITING].   C.U.

SINGAPORE [From Sanskrit *simha pura* city of the lion]. Official titles: English *Republic of Singapore*, Chinese *Hsin-chia-p'o Kung-ho-kuo*, Malay *Republik Singapura*, Tamil *Singapore Kudiyarasa*. A country in South-East Asia, and member of the Commonwealth. Capital: Singapore City. Currency: the dollar. Economy: mixed. Population: 2.6m (1988), 2.9m (projection for 2000). Ethnicity: 76% Chinese, 15% Malay, 7% South Asian, 2% others. Religions: 56% Buddhist and Taoist, 16% Muslim, 10% Christian, 4% Hindu, 14% other. Languages: English, Mandarin Chinese, Malay, Tamil (all official), with English the language of the law courts, government administration, and education. Singapore was originally part of the Sri Vijaya kingdom of Sumatra. Sir Stamford Raffles leased the island from the Sultan of Johore in 1819, and with Malacca and Penang it became in 1826 (under the East India Company) the *Straits Settlements*, which became a British colony in 1867. The island was taken by the Japanese in 1942 during the Second World War, became British again in 1945, obtained self-government in 1959, and was part of the *Federation of Malaya* from 1963 to 1965, when it became an independent state. In the early 1990s, it is a city state that, like Hong Kong, has raised its standard of living dramatically by becoming one of the most important financial, travel, and communications centres in South-East Asia. See MALAYSIA, SINGAPORE ENGLISH. [ASIA, NAME].   T.MCA.

SINGAPORE ENGLISH, informally **Singlish**. The English language as used in Singapore, a lingua franca influenced by Chinese and Malay that is fast acquiring a large community of native speakers. The English of Singapore serves as both a means of uniting the country and an international medium. In 1947, 31.6% of students in the colony were in English-medium schools; from 1987, English has been the sole medium of primary, secondary, and tertiary education in the republic. It is the main language of business and commerce, internally and externally, and has an influence extending well beyond the boundaries of the state. Educated Straits-born Chinese (locally known as the *Baba Chinese*) have traditionally used *Baba Malay* rather than a Chinese dialect, and currently tend to favour English over both Chinese and other languages. There are at least two forms of Singapore English: the standard variety, based on educated BrE spoken with an RP accent (used in textbooks and by the *Singapore Broadcasting Corporation*), and a colloquial variety whose forms range from a 'low' basilect strongly influenced by Chinese and Malay to a 'high' acrolect that blends with the standard.

Pronunciation. (1) English in Singapore is non-rhotic and generally syllable-timed. It places more or less equal stress on all syllables, usually with the final syllable of a tone unit somewhat lengthened. (2) Its intonation, often described as 'singsong', has many short tone groups; there is no contrastive stress. (3) Final consonants are often unreleased, resulting in glottal stops, as in /hɪʔ/ for *hit* and /stɛʔ/ for *step*. (4) Final consonant clusters are generally reduced to one spoken consonant, such as 'juss' for *just* and 'toll' for *told*. Often a Singaporean will say, for example, 'slep' or 'sleʔ', but write *slept*. Compare grammar point 1, below, on omission of *-s* and *-ed*. (5) The vowels in such words as *take, so,* and *dare* are often monophthongs: /tɛʔ/, /so/, /dɛ/.

Grammar. (1) There is a tendency to omit articles (*You have pen or not?*; *He went to office yesterday*), the plural inflection *-s* (*I got three sister and two brother*), the present-tense inflection *-s* (*This radio sound good*; *My mum, she come from China many year ago*), the past-tense inflection *-ed*/*-t* ('ask' for *asked*, 'slep' for *slept*; *He live there* for 'He lived there'), and the *be* before adjectives used predicatively (*This coffee house cheap*). (2) *Already* is used as a marker of completive aspect: *Eight years she work here already* She's been working here for eight years. (3) *Use to* occurs as a marker of habitual aspect: *My mother, she use to go to the market* My mother goes to the market. (4) *Would* is used for future events rather than *will*/*shall* or the present tense: *We hope this would meet your requirements* We hope this meets/will meet your requirements. (5) Direct and indirect objects are highlighted by being preposed: *This book we don't have*; *Me you don't give it to.* (6) The invariant tags *is it?* and *isn't it?* are common: *You check out today, is it?*; *They come here often, isn't it?* (7) There is a preference for *also* over *too*: *But we are supposed to learn Chinese also.* (8) There are various informal ways of checking that someone agrees or disagrees, or can or cannot do something: *Yes or not? Like it or not? Can or not? Enough or not? Got or not?* (9) Chinese particles, such as *lah* and *aa*, are a common means of conveying emphasis and emotion, in effect replacing the intonational features of mainstream English: for example, *lah* as a token of informal intimacy (*Can you come tonight?—Can lah/Cannot lah*); *aa* in yes-no questions (*You wait me, aa?* Will you wait for me?; *I come tonight, aa?* Should I come tonight?; *You think I scared of you, aa?*): compare MALAYSIA.

Vocabulary. (1) Words borrowed from regional languages: (Malay) *makan* food, as in *Let's have some makan*; (Hokkien Chinese) *ang pow* a gift of money, traditionally in a red packet (the meaning of the Hokkien words). (2) Non-English interjections include: *ay yaah!* suggesting exasperation; *ay yōr!* suggesting pain, wonder, or both; *ay yēr!* indicating a reaction to something unpleasant and perhaps unexpected; *che!* expressing irritation or regret. (3) Words of English with adapted meanings: *send* in the sense of 'take' (*I will send you home*); *open* meaning 'put on' (*Open the light*); *take* suggesting 'eat, drink, like' (*Do you take hot food? Do you like spicy food?*); *off* and *on* as verbs (*to off/on the light*); *off* as a noun, for time off (*We had our offs changed to Thursdays*). (4) Reduplicating of a word so as to intensify or emphasize a point: *I like hot-hot curries*; *Do you speak English?—Broken-broken.* (5) Formal and informal registers are less marked off from one another than in BrE, with the result that the highly colloquial and highly formal may co-occur: *her deceased hubby* rather than *her dead husband.* See CHINA/ MALAY, MALAYSIA, PHILIPPINE ENGLISH. [ASIA, VARIETY].   H.W., M.T., T.MCA.

Foley, J. (ed.). 1988. *The New Englishes: The Case of Singapore.* Singapore: University Press.

Fraser Gupta, Anthea. 1986. 'A Standard for Written Singapore English?', in *English World-Wide* 7: 1. Amsterdam & Philadelphia: John Benjamins.

Ho, Mian Lian, & Platt, John. 1991. *Dynamics of a Contact Continuum: Singapore English.* Oxford: University Press.

Platt, John. 1982. 'English in Singapore, Malaysia and Hong Kong', in R. W. Bailey & M. Görlach (eds.), *English as a World Language.* Ann Arbor: University of Michigan Press; Cambridge: University Press.

—— & Weber, Heidi. 1980. *English in Singapore and Malaysia.* Kuala Lumpur: Oxford University Press.

——, —— & Ho, Mian Lian. 1983. *Singapore and Malaysia,* in the Varieties of English around the World series. Amsterdam & Philadelphia: John Benjamins.

Tongue, R. K. 1974. *The English of Singapore and Malaysia.* Singapore: Eastern Universities Press.

SINGING SUFFOLK. See EAST ANGLIA.

SINGLISH. See -GLISH AND -LISH, SINGAPORE.

SINGSONG, also **sing-song** [17c]. (1) Formerly: a ballad or jingle; verse with (often monotonous) musical rather than poetic qualities: 'a beautiful legend; a nice sing-song to send men to sleep' (D. Jerrold, *St. Giles,* 1851); 'the despised melodrama, the sing-song of opera' (*Westminster Review,* 1833). (2) Informal BrE: the unrehearsed singing of popular songs; community singing: 'Wednesday was welfare. Ping pong night. Sing song night' (John le Carré, *Small Town in Germany,* 1968). The term *singsong girl,* used of especially Chinese women who sing, dance, and double as prostitutes, echoes China Coast Pidgin English. Compare *singsing*, a Papua New Guinea (Tok Pisin) term for an occasion of singing, dancing, and feasting. (3) A usually disparaging or condescending term for a rhythm or tone regarded as musical but monotonous and considered typical of certain accents, such as those of speakers of English in Wales and parts of Asia: 'A trace of Holyhead Welsh to his sing-song accent' (Ian Thomson, *Independent*, 29 Dec. 1990). In linguistics, the name *singsong theory* (originally used disparagingly by his critics) refers to the theory of the Danish linguist Otto Jespersen that language began as singing. See ACCENT, CANT, PHILIPPINE ENGLISH, REDUPLICATION, SINGAPORE ENGLISH, WELSH ENGLISH. [LITERATURE, SPEECH, STYLE].   T.MCA.

SINGULAR [14c: from Latin *singularis* one at a time, alone, single]. A term contrasting with *plural* and *dual* in the number system of a language and referring to one person or thing. In English, the term is often used to include uncountable noun usages like *love* and *wine* because they take singular verb concord, even though in other ways such nouns are different from singular countable nouns like *horse* and *stone*. Compare DUAL, PLURAL. [GRAMMAR]. S.C.

SINHALA, also **Sinhalese** and formerly **Singhalese, Cingalese**. An Indo-Aryan language spoken by over 10m people in Sri Lanka (formerly Ceylon) and on the Laccadive islands of India; in the Maldives, the variety known as Divehi has official-language status. Carried south with Buddhism by settlers from northern India *c.*5c BC, Sinhala was subsequently influenced by the Dravidian languages, especially Tamil, which is also spoken in Sri Lanka, by Pali, the sacred language of the local form of Buddhism, and to some extent by Sanskrit. Its earliest inscriptions date from *c.*200 BC, its present-day literary form from *c.*1250. The early literature is almost exclusively Buddhist, and, unlike in other parts of South Asia, mostly in prose. Sinhala is written in a distinctive syllabic script related to the scripts of the Indian languages. The arrival of Western powers in Sri Lanka led to the decline of the Sinhala literary tradition, which did not revive till the late 18c. The norms established for prose in the 13c, however, persist to this day. Modern Sinhala literature shows the influence of European literary traditions in addition to those of Sanskrit, Pali, and Tamil. There is currently a three-language policy in Sri Lanka for the use of Sinhala, Tamil, and English. See INDIAN LANGUAGES, MALDIVES, PALI, SANSKRIT, SRI LANKA. [ASIA, LANGUAGE].
   T.MCA., Y.K.

SINICIZED ENGLISH. See CHINA.

SINO-TIBETAN LANGUAGES. A family of tone languages in Central and East Asia. It includes most of the languages of China, the most prominent of which are Mandarin Chinese and Cantonese, and the Tibeto-Burman languages, among them Tibetan, Burmese, and various languages of Nepal. See ASIAN LANGUAGES, CHINA, INDIAN LANGUAGES, LANGUAGE FAMILY, LINGUISTIC TYPOLOGY (TONE LANGUAGES), NEPAL. [ASIA, LANGUAGE].   T.MCA.

SITUATIONAL APPROACH. See LANGUAGE TEACHING.

SIXMO [Probably 19c: from *six* and the suffix *-mo*, indirectly derived from *sexto*, from the Latin ablative phrase *in sexto* (folded) in six. See -MO]. Also *sexto*. Abbreviated *6mo*, *6°*. A book size obtained by folding a sheet of paper into six leaves or 12 pages; a book of this size. [TECHNOLOGY].   T.MCA.

SIXTEENMO [1840s: from *sixteen* and *-mo*, indirectly from *sextodecimo*, from the Latin ablative phrase *in sextodecimo* (folded) in sixteen]. Also *sextodecimo*. Abbreviated *16mo*, *16°*. A book size obtained by folding a sheet of paper into 16 leaves or 32 pages; a book of this size. See -MO. [TECHNOLOGY].   T.MCA.

SKEAT, W(alter) W(illiam) [1835-1912]. English clergyman and philologist, born in London and educated at King's College School, then Highgate, and at Christ's College, Cambridge, where he graduated in mathematics. He became a Fellow of the college in 1860, took holy orders in 1861, and became a curate at Godalming in the same year, but a serious throat illness cut short his career in the Church. In 1864, he took up an appointment at Christ's and began his study of Early English. In 1878, he became Professor of Anglo-Saxon at Cambridge. Skeat was typical of the generation of scholars that included F. J. Furnivall, J. A. H. Murray, and Henry Sweet (all members of the Philological Society), who promoted the collection and publication of texts (through the Early English Text Society and the Chaucer Society). They were concerned with the history of the language, its dialects, its cataloguing in works of reference, and such educational issues as spelling reform. He was founder and first director of the English Dialect Society in 1873, and edited a bibliography in preparation for the Society's *English Dialect Dictionary*, with the title 'A bibliographical list of works that have been published or are known to exist in MS, illustrative of the various dialects of English' (1873). His major publication was *An Etymological Dictionary of the English Language* (Oxford University Press, 1882, 1883, 1897, 1909), the fullest work of its kind at that time, with appendices of notes on the languages cited in the dictionary, canons for etymology, and suffixes, followed by prefixes, homonyms, doublets, Indogermanic (Indo-European) roots, and distribution of words borrowed into English according to language of origin. Other publications included: *Principles of English Etymology* (1891), *The Chaucer Canon* (Oxford, 1900), and *English Dialects from the Eighth Century to the Present Day* (Cambridge, 1911). See index. [BIOGRAPHY, EUROPE, HISTORY, REFERENCE].   S.E.

SLANDER [13c: from Middle English *s(c)laundre*, from Anglo-Norman *esclaundre* and Old French *esclandre*, from Latin *scandalum* a snare, cause of offence. A doublet of *scandal*]. A general and legal term for the uttering of a false and defamatory statement that injures someone's reputation. As distict from *libel*, which is written or printed, slander is oral. Though actionable, it is not a criminal offence, perhaps because strongly critical views may be uttered unguardedly on the spur of the moment, and are unlikely to reach a wide audience unless further broadcast. See LIBEL, MALEDICTA. [MEDIA].   G.H.

SLANG [18c: origin uncertain, perhaps from *sling* or a clipping that combines elements in such phrases as *beggars' language* and *rogues' language*]. An ever-changing set of colloquial words and phrases generally considered distinct from and socially lower than the standard language. Slang is used to establish or reinforce social identity and cohesiveness, especially within a group or with a trend or fashion in society at large. It occurs in all languages, and the existence of a short-lived vocabulary of this sort within a language is probably as old as language itself. In its earliest occurrences in the 18c, the word *slang* referred to the specialized vocabulary of underworld groups and was used fairly interchangeably with *cant, flash*, and *argot*.

Defining *slang*. The word is widely used without precision, especially to include informal usage and technical jargon, and the social and psychological complexities captured in slang vocabulary make the term difficult to define. For linguistic purposes, slang must be distinguished from such other subsets of the lexicon as *regionalisms* or *dialect words, jargon, profanity* or *vulgarity, colloquialism, cant*, and *argot*, although slang shares some characteristics with each of these. It is not geographically restricted (like BrE *lift*, AmE *elevator*), but is often regional (BrE *bloke*, AmE *guy*). It is not jargon (vocabulary used in carrying out a trade or profession), but it frequently arises inside groups united by their work: for example, such nontechnical vocabulary as the US Army phrases *chicken colonel* (full colonel) and *John Wayne* (used to describe exemplary military behaviour).

Although slang synonyms abound in the taboo subjects of a culture, not all slang terms violate social propriety; *Mickey Mouse* meaning 'easy' and *dough* for 'money' may be inappropriate in some contexts, but they are not usually offensive, although *Mickey Mouse money* may be used pejoratively of an unfamiliar or a disdained currency. Slang belongs to the spoken part of language, but not all colloquial expressions are slang: *shut up* for 'be quiet' would rarely be written except in dialogue, but it is not slang. *Cant* and *argot*, the specialized and sometimes secret languages of thieves and other groups which operate on the fringes of the law, have contributed many items to the general slang vocabulary of English: for example, *heist* for 'robbery' and *OD* for 'take an overdose (of drugs)'. Yet many slang words arise from the language of groups that have no association with the underworld, such as college students, sports fans, or enlisted personnel in the military. It is often the usage of the young, the alienated, and those who see themselves as distinct from the rest of society. People who at a formative stage belonged to a certain institution or milieu may continue to use the slang expressions of their group and generation for the rest of their lives.

Despite the difficulty of defining the term, slang does have some consistent characteristics. Foremost, taken as a whole, the slang vocabulary of a language is ephemeral, bursting into existence and falling out of use at a much more rapid rate than items of the general vocabulary. The slang of students can illustrate this. American college students who studied very hard in 1900 were known as *grinds* or *grubs*; in the 1980s, *grinds* were called *geeks*, and *grub* meant to kiss passionately. A tally of slang terms in use at the U. of North Carolina at Chapel Hill over a 15-year period (1972–87) showed a retention rate of less than 10%: the exclamation of approval *far out* was replaced by *awesome*, the all-purpose affirmative adjective *cool* yielded to *sweet*, and students stopped *cutting* classes and instead started *blowing them off*.

Transience. The rapid change characteristic of slang requires a constant supply of new words, sometimes replacing or adding to already established slang words, like a *waste case* for a 'drunk', and sometimes extending to new areas of meaning, like *jambox, ghetto blaster*, or *Brixton suitcase* for a portable stereo tape player. This makes novelty, or innovation, an often cited characteristic of slang and freshness a large part of its appeal. Yet some slang items have long lives. Thus, *bones* as slang for dice was used by Chaucer in the 14c and is still slang. But when slang items remain in the language for years, they often lose their slang status. Middle English *bouse* (now *booze*) persists in informal contexts, as does *pooped* (exhausted), first attested in the 16c. Still other slang items pass into the general vocabulary and bear little or no association with their earlier lives as slang: for example, *jeopardy* from gambling and *crestfallen* from cock-fighting have even acquired a learned tinge.

Sounds. Although, for the most part, slang items conform to the general constraints on sound combinations that govern English, the venture-some spirit behind much slang includes playing with sounds. Onomatopoeia accounts for many slang terms, including these for 'vomit': *barf, buick, earl, ralph*. Mock dialect and foreign pronunciations are sometimes the source for slang, as in *shoot the peel* (play basketball), an approximation of the Southern US pronunciation of 'pill', a reference to the round shape of the ball. Or *my feet are staying* (goodbye), a mock pronunciation of German *auf wiedersehen*. The American linguist Roger Wescott has noticed that some sounds appear to give words a slangier flavour, most noticeably: *z*, in words like *zazzy* from 'jazzy', *scuz* from 'scum', and *zap* from 'slap' or 'whap'; the replacement or addition of a vowel with *oo*, in words like *cigaroot* from 'cigarette', *bazooms* from 'bosom', and *smasheroo* from 'smasher'. Rhyming, however, is the favourite sound effect of slang, as in *brain drain* the loss of intellectual and educated people from a community because of a lack of opportunity, *boob tube* television, *frat rat* member of a US college fraternity, *groomed to zoom* dressed fashionably. The rhymers *par excellence* have been the Cockneys of London, who have developed an elaborate and colourful collection of slang terms based on rhyme. Straightforward examples are *trouble and strife* for 'wife' and *mince pies* for 'eyes', but most Cockney rhyming slang involves a shortening process in which the rhyme word is not expressed: *elephant* means 'drunk', from *elephant's trunk*; *plates* means 'feet', from *plates of meat*; and *Godfer* means 'child', from *God forbid*, which rhymes with 'kid'.

Word-formation. Slang items usually arise by the same means in which new words enter the general vocabulary: by recycling words and parts of words which are already in the language. Affixation allows limitless opportunities for open-ended sets like *megabucks, megabeers*, and *megawork* (for vast quantities of the item in question), or *bookage, fundage*, and *sleepage* (as collective terms, as in *I'm about to ask my folks for some major fundage*). Compounding makes one word from two: *airhead* AmE someone out of touch with reality, *homeboy* AmE a person from the same hometown, BrE a young man happy to stay with his parents. A currently productive process especially in AmE is the addition of a particle like *out, off*, or *on* to a noun, adjective, or verb, to form a phrasal verb: for example, *blimp out* to overeat, *blow off* (US college slang) to ignore, (British schoolboy slang) to fart, or *hit on* to make sexual overtures to. In slang, frequently used phrases and words are likely to be abbreviated, like *OTL* from *out to lunch* out of touch with reality, *VJ/veejay* from *video jock* an announcer for televised music videos, *obno* from *obnoxious*, and *Sup?* from *What's up?* Unlike the general vocabulary of the language, English slang has not borrowed heavily from foreign languages, although it does borrow from dialects, especially from such ethnic or special-interest groups which make an impact on the dominant culture as American Blacks or from a second language that is part of the culture, like Yiddish.

Semantics. The intricate interplay of exclusivity, faddishness, and flippancy which breeds and supports slang guarantees semantic and etymological complexity. Nevertheless, slang items often diverge from standard usage in predictable ways, especially by generalization and melioration. In generalization, a term acquires a wider range of referents: for example, in the 19c *dude* was 'a dapper man, a dandy' but in current US slang, via Black usage, it can be applied to any male. *Schiz out* is to have any kind of mental or emotional breakdown; it is not restricted to *schizophrenia*. Evaluative words in slang sometimes become so generalized in application that they lose specific meaning and retain only a value: for example, AmE *awesome, heavy, key*, and *solid*, BrE *ace, brill*, and *triff*, and *def* in both varieties, all mean 'worthy of approval'. Generalization often operates in conjunction with melioration, a process in which the connotations of a word become more favourable. Many words enter general slang from the taboo words of subcultures. Through increased use and broad application, they can lose their shock value and become more positive; the verb *jam* a century ago had specific sexual referents, but now means 'to dance, play music, have a good time, succeed'. Yet many words in slang remain negative, especially the large and constantly replenished set of epithets available at all time in slang: for example, the pejorative *boob, dork, dweeb, jerk, nerd, scuzbag, slimeball, wimp*.

Another characteristic of the semantics of slang is the tendency to name things indirectly and figuratively, especially through metaphor, metonymy, and irony. *Rack monster* exhaustion, *couch potato* one who lies around doing little except watch television, *coffin nail* a cigarette, are metaphors. *Brew* and *chill* (beer) take their meaning by association and are metonyms. Irony, in its simplest form, categorizes the tendency in slang for words to evoke opposite meanings: *bad, wicked, killer* can all mean 'good' when signalled with appropriate ironic intonation. The influence of semantic fields on productivity in slang is also important, as they provide an established framework to shape the form and meaning of new words. In English, the semantic field 'destruction' sets the pattern for the proliferation of terms for being drunk, such as *blitzed, bombed, fried, hammered, polluted, ripped, slammed, smashed, toasted, wasted*. Slang also often evokes meaning by drawing on the shared cultural knowledge of its users. Thus, calling a Ford automobile in the 1920s a *Henry* or a *Henrietta* alluded to automotive tycoon Henry Ford. The current verb *bogart* (to take an unfair share, originally of a marijuana cigarette) alludes to the American actor Humphrey Bogart's tough-guy image in films. *Midnight requisition* and *midnight supply company* (stealing) allude to military life.

Functions. The aim of using slang is seldom the exchange of information. More often, slang serves social purposes: to identify members of a group, to change the level of discourse in the direction of informality, to oppose established authority. Sharing and maintaining a constantly changing slang vocabulary aids group solidarity and serves to include and exclude members. Slang is the linguistic equivalent of fashion and serves much the same purpose. Like stylish clothing and modes of popular entertainment, effective slang must be new, appealing, and able to gain acceptance in a group quickly. Nothing is more damaging to status in the group than using old slang. Counter-culture or counter-establishment groups often find a common vocabulary unknown outside the group a useful way to keep information secret or mysterious. Slang is typically cultivated among people in society who have little real political power (like adolescents, college students, and enlisted personnel in the military) or who have reason to hide from people in authority what they know or do (like gamblers, drug addicts, and prisoners). With the possibility of instant and widespread communication, the group-identifying functions of slang for the population at large may be diminishing in favour of identification with a style or an attitude rather than with a group. If items like *low-life* and *sleaze* can be considered slang in the US, they are a kind of national slang and say little about group identification.

Slang lexicography. Because slang is usually considered a deviation from ordinary language, it has been little more than a curiosity in the scientific study of language. Nevertheless, a strong tradition in slang lexicography provides valuable data for analysing the workings of this often neglected portion of the language. Foremost among 20c slang lexicographers was the New Zealand-born writer Eric Partridge, an indefatigable collector of slang and of the unconventional kinds of vocabulary that demonstrate the ongoing vigour of the language. Recent lexicographical works include *The Thesaurus of Slang: 150,000 Uncensored Contemporary Slang Terms, Common Idioms, and Colloquialisms Arranged for Quick and Easy Reference* (Esther and Albert E. Lewin, Facts on File, 1988), which lists standard headwords in alphabetical order, each followed by an undiscriminated set of slang synonyms among which the reader may browse. For example, after the verb *converse* are listed *gab, rap, yack, chew the fat, rag around, modjitate, shoot the shit, schmoose, fold one's ear, bat the chat.*

Conclusion. People use slang consciously and unconsciously in the course of ordinary, everyday interaction. No arbitrary rules in grammar books make items of slang right or wrong, and, for the most part, current slang cannot be found in dictionaries, which are always engaged in catching up, and may never include certain terms, because they have proved to be highly ephemeral or are used in groups to which lexicographers have little or no access. Essentially, slang allows speakers the freedom to play with and enjoy the language, make words up, adopt new expressions indiscriminately, and use language for humour, irony, sarcasm, and irreverence. See ARGOT, BACK SLANG, BLACK ENGLISH VERNACULAR, CANT, CARTOON, COCKNEY, DICTIONARY OF SLANG AND UNCONVENTIONAL ENGLISH, FLASH, GREAT AUSTRALIAN SLANGUAGE, JARGON, NEW ZEALAND DICTIONARIES, PARTRIDGE, PATOIS, PHRASAL VERB, POLARI, RHYMING SLANG, SLANGUAGE, TIMESPEAK, USAGE. [LANGUAGE, STYLE].   C.C.E.

Berrey, Lester V., & Van Den Bark, Melvin. 1947. *The American Thesaurus of Slang.* With Supplement. New York: Thomas Y. Crowell.

Burke, W. J. 1939. *The Literature of Slang.* New York Public Library. (Reprinted 1965, Detroit: Gale Research.)

Chapman, Robert L. 1986. *New Dictionary of American Slang.* New York: Harper & Row, 1986.

Dumas, Bethany K., & Lighter, Jonathan. 1978. 'Is Slang a Word for Linguistics?', *American Speech* 53.

Farmer, John S., & Henley, William Ernest. 1890–1904. *Slang and its Analogues, Past and Present.* Seven volumes. London.

Mencken, H. L. 1963. 'American Slang', ch. 11 in *The American Language*, 4th edition, ed. Raven I.

McDavid Jr. & David W. Maurer. New York: Alfred Knopf.
Partridge, Eric. 1970. *Slang Today and Yesterday*, 4th edition. London: Routledge & Kegan Paul.
—— 1984. *A Dictionary of Slang and Unconventional English*, 8th edition, ed. Paul Beale. London: Routledge & Kegan Paul.
Thorne, Tony. 1990. *Bloomsbury Dictionary of Contemporary Slang*. London: Bloomsbury.

SLANGUAGE [Early 20c: a blend of *slang* and *language*]. A non-technical term for slang usage or a variety of language dominated by slang. In *The Slanguage of Sex: A Dictionary of Modern Sexual Terms* (1984), Brigid McConville and John Shearlaw define a slanguage as 'an underground language' of simile, metaphor, euphemism, and innuendo. Compare ARGOT. See GREAT AUSTRALIAN SLANGUAGE, NEW ZEALAND DICTIONARIES, SLANG. [STYLE].　　　T.MCA.

SLANT [15c: by aphesis from *aslant* sloping]. A term in especially journalism and advertising, through which the idea of obliqueness is extended to predisposition, bias, or distortion especially in a piece of writing: *There's always a political slant, even if he's writing about pet food.* Compare ANGLE, NEOLOGISM (SPIN). [MEDIA, STYLE, WRITING].　　　T.MCA.

SLANT RHYME. See HALF RHYME.

SLASH. See OBLIQUE.

SLAVONIC LANGUAGES BrE, **Slavic languages** AmE. A branch of the Indo-European language family spoken primarily by the Slav peoples of Central, Southern, and Eastern Europe. It is usually divided into *East Slavonic* (Russian, Ukrainian, Byelorussian), *West Slavonic* (Polish, Czech, Slovak, and Sorbian or Lusatian), and *South Slavonic* (Old Church Slavonic, Macedonian, Bulgarian, Serbo-Croat, and Slovene). Native speakers total some 300m. The approximate numbers of speakers of the larger languages are: Russian 150m; Polish 37m (with some 13m diaspora Poles in Western Europe, North America, and Australasia); Ukrainian 35m (with 600,000 in North America, two-thirds in Canada, and 100,000 in Poland); Serbo-Croat 12.5m; Bulgarian 8m; Byelorussian 7m. Slavonic languages also divide into those using the Roman alphabet (western and southern, including Polish, Czech, Slovak, and Slovene) and those using the Cyrillic alphabet (eastern and southern, including Russian, Ukrainian, and Bulgarian). Serbo-Croat uses both scripts, Serbs mainly Cyrillic, Croats mainly Roman. The classical language Old Church Slavonic, originally used by evangelists among the South Slavs, has had considerable influence on both the South and East Slavonic languages. The impact of the group on English has been relatively slight. Loanwords include: *mammoth* (from 17c Russian *mamot*), *mazurka* (from Polish, after a regional name), *robot* (from Czech, from the base of *robota* compulsory labour, and *robotnik* a peasant owing such labour), *samovar* (from Russian: 'self-boiling'), and *vampire* (through French from German from Serbo-Croat *vampir*). The especially AmE diminutive suffix *-nik* (mid-20c) is Slavonic in origin, and has entered English along two paths: from Russian, as in *sputnik* a space satellite, and through Yiddish, which adopted it from its Slavonic neighbours in Eastern Europe, as in *kibbutznik* one who lives on a kibbutz. The suffix as used in English refers to a person who exemplifies or endorses a way of life or an idea, as in *beatnik, no-goodnik, peacenik, refusenik*. It is often humorous or dismissive. Loans from English into the Slavonic languages have increased greatly in the late 20c, especially in such areas as sport (for example, Polish *faul* foul, *faulować* to cause a foul, *play-off, sprint, sprinter, tenis*) and high technology (Polish *bit, bajt, hardware* and *software*, and their adjectives *hardwarowy* and *softwarowy, interface, joystick, monitor*). See BORROWING, CANADIAN, CANADIAN ENGLISH, EUROPEAN LANGUAGES, INDO-EUROPEAN LANGUAGES, JEWISH ENGLISH (-NIK), RUSSIAN, YIDDISH. [EUROPE, LANGUAGE].　　　F.E.K., T.MCA.

SLIP OF THE TONGUE [Earliest *OED* citation N. Bailey, 1725: a loan translation of Latin *lapsus linguae*, earliest citation J. Dryden, 1667. Parallel usages are the now rare *slip of the pen* and *lapsus calami*]. An unintended mistake made in speaking, sometimes trivial, sometimes amusing: *This hasn't solved any answers* (rather than *problems, questions*), *a great floating lunk* (blending *lump* and *hunk*), *I want a thin chin . . . I mean, a thin cheese pizza.* Normal speech contains a fairly large number of such slips, though these mostly pass unnoticed. The errors fall into patterns, and it is possible to draw conclusions from them about the underlying mechanisms involved. They can be divided into: (1) *Selection errors*, where a wrong item has been chosen, usually a lexical item, as with *tomorrow* instead of *today* in *That's all for tomorrow.* (2) *Assemblage errors*, where the correct items have been selected, but they have been assembled in the wrong order, as in *holed and sealed* for 'soled and healed'. The former shed light on the organization of the mental lexicon, the latter on the preparation of chunks of speech for production.

Selection errors may involve: (1) Meaning: *crossword* instead of 'jigsaw'. (2) Sound: *cylinders* for 'syllables'. (3) Both of these: *badger* for 'beaver'. (4) Blends of two similar words:

torrible for 'terrible' and 'horrible'. Of these, errors in sound, usually called *malapropisms*, are probably the best known. Such errors suggest that meaning and sound are only partially linked in the mind, and also that the linking up involves the activation of a number of words which are similar to the target (the word sought). Among assemblage errors, common patterns are: (1) Anticipations, with a word or sound coming in too soon: *crounty cricket* for 'county cricket'. (2) Perseverations, with a word or sound repeated: *beef needle soup* for 'beef noodle soup'. (3) Transpositions, with words or sounds transposed: *to gap the bridge* for 'to bridge the gap'; *hole of rostess* for 'role of hostess'. The best-known of these are the sound transpositions called *spoonerisms*. These errors indicate that chunks of speech are pre-prepared for utterance, possibly in a tone group (a group of words spoken within the same intonation pattern), and that the activated words are organized in accordance with a rhythmic principle. Research is in progress in order to assess to what extent these findings are universal, or specific to the English language. See FREUDIAN SLIP, MALAPROPISM, MISTAKE, NEUROLINGUISTICS, SPOONERISM. [LANGUAGE, STYLE]. J.M.A.

Aitchison, Jean. 1987. *Words in the Mind: An Introduction to the Mental Lexicon.* Oxford: Basil Blackwell.

Boomer, Donald S., & Laver, John D. M. 1968. 'Slips of the Tongue', *British Journal of Disorders of Communication* 3, pp. 1–12. Also in Fromkin, below.

Fromkin, Victoria A. (ed.). 1973. *Speech Errors as Linguistic Evidence.* The Hague: Mouton.

SLIPSHOD [16c: originally meaning wearing ('shod with') slippers or loose shoes, and therefore down at heel]. A casual term often applied to speech and writing considered substandard and careless: 'The fashionable jargon of the day . . . seems to have been a sort of slipshod English, continually helped out with the newest French phrases' (Arthur H. Clough, *Poems*, 1861). See (A)ESTHETICS. Compare SLOPPY, SLOVENLY. [STYLE]. T.MCA.

SLOANE RANGER [1970s: a facetious blend of *Sloane Square* in London and *Lone Ranger*, the name of an American hero in Western films and cartoons]. An equivocal nickname for a young Englishwoman with an upper-class background and fashionable tastes, but otherwise conventional in outlook and ambitions. It is often extended, especially in the clipped form *Sloane* and the informal adjective *Sloan(e)y*, to anyone of the same class and type: 'The Sloane Rangers always *add tone*. They never put on prole accents, like self-conscious Oxford boys in the sixties' (P. York, in *Harpers & Queen*, Oct. 1975);

'In the circle of debutantes who used to be presented at court in the year of their "coming out" marked RP was commonplace, and since the ending of this social ritual in recent years, we have only to look at the Sloane Rangers for sounds which assure us that this special form of RP is alive and well and being passed on to a new generation of the socially privileged and those who try to identify with them' (John Honey, *Does Accent Matter?*, 1989); 'Also the voice had a hint of near-deb or off-Sloane Square: "The pollution of the ayah next ye-ah" ' (Edward Pearce, *Sunday Times*, 24 Sept. 1989). See MARKED AND UNMARKED TERMS, RECEIVED PRONUNCIATION (RP). Compare KENSINGTON, U AND NON-U. [EUROPE, VARIETY]. T.MCA.

SLOGAN [16c: from Scottish Gaelic *sluagh-ghairm* a war cry, from *sluagh* host, army, *gairm* a cry, shout. Formerly *slogurn, slughorn*, etc.]. (1) Obsolete: a battle or rallying cry of the Scots and Irish, usually the name of a leader or a place, or the motto of a clan. (2) A catchphrase shouted or exhibited by someone campaigning for a cause, or used in advertising and promotion, such as 'No more war' or 'Beer is best'. The regular use of such slogans is *sloganeering*, a common feature of politics. See ACRONYM, MOTTO. [STYLE, WORD]. T.MCA.

SLOPPY [18c: from *slop* mud, slush]. A casual term often applied to speech and writing considered substandard and careless: 'Too prone to indulge in sloppy English' (*The Academy*, 1881); 'Sloppy language makes for muddled thinking' (*The Right Word at the Right Time*, Reader's Digest, 1985). See (A)ESTHETICS. Compare SLIPSHOD, SLOVENLY. [STYLE]. T.MCA.

SLOVENLY [16c: from obsolete *sloven* a lazy, idle rascal, a term applied until the late 19c to careless writers]. A casual term often applied to speech and writing considered substandard and careless: 'When he gets into a sentence of five or six lines long, nothing can exceed the slovenliness of the English' (S. T. Coleridge, *Table Talk*, 1834). See (A)ESTHETICS, GLOTTAL STOP. Compare SLIPSHOD, SLOPPY. [STYLE]. T.MCA.

SLUR [15c: from Low German, to drag, trail]. (1) A semi-technical term for an indistinct sound or utterance that usually arises from two or more sounds being run together: *gonna* going to, *gotta* got to, *wannabe* want to be. Compare ELISION. (2) A non-technical term for a slighting and dismissive remark or reference. Linguistic slurs can, among other things, be racist and ethnic: an English-speaking person calling a German *a squarehead*, a French Canadian calling an English Canadian *une tête carrée* (a squarehead).

See ETHNIC NAME, FOUR-LETTER WORD. [SPEECH, STYLE].   T.MCA.

SMOLLETT, Tobias [1721–71]. Scottish surgeon and novelist, born near Dumbarton, and educated at the U. of Glasgow. After training as a surgeon in Scotland, he went to London in the vain hope of success in the theatre. He served in the navy as a surgeon's mate and later practised in London. His first novel *The Adventures of Roderick Random* (1747) drew partly on his experiences. A journey to Paris in 1750 gave him material for *The Adventures of Peregrine Pickle* (1751). His writing included a translation of *Don Quixote* (1755). In 1760, he was fined and imprisoned for publishing a libel on Admiral Knowles. He undertook a trip to Italy for the sake of his health and there wrote his last novel *The Expedition of Humphry Clinker* (1771). Smollett took a harsh view of the world and his picture of 18c life emphasizes sordid and cruel aspects that others refused to face. His love of controversy brought him into conflict with such contemporaries as Fielding. His influence on the course of the novel was considerable; he took many of his characters from disreputable society and presented them with a zest that verges on caricature yet remains credible. His narrative style is straightforward, sustaining the interest of picaresque stories that could easily have become diffuse. *Humphry Clinker* is a major example of the epistolary novel in English. He created vivid names for his characters, such as Commodore Trunnion and the schoolmaster Concordance, and portrayed dialect, registers, and the affectations of the newly fashionable, using deviant spellings for the usage of the uneducated, particularly in letters in *Humphry Clinker*. Dickens greatly admired his style. See NOVEL. [BIOGRAPHY, EUROPE, LITERATURE, STYLE].   R.C.

SMUT. An informal term for obscene language, on the analogy of something which smudges or stains, as in *There's too much smut on television nowadays.* See OBSCENITY, SWEARING. [STYLE, USAGE].   T.MCA.

SOAP OPERA [1930s: from a whimsical extension of *opera* to cover entertainments on US radio commercially sponsored by soap companies and aimed at housewives]. Informal short form *soap*. A usually long-running serial on radio or television that dramatizes the lives, problems, successes, and failures of a set of stock characters in stock situations, sometimes domestic, sometimes glamorous. Although the genre is usually dismissed by critics as trivial and escapist, it is a means by which information can be widely disseminated: for example, about family planning in developing countries. Major TV soap operas, such as the US series *Dallas* and *Dynasty* (mainly 1980s), the British *EastEnders*, and the Australian *Neighbours*, have been watched by millions around the world, the nature and doings of both characters and actors being widely discussed in the media and elsewhere. Some characters, such as J. R. Ewing in *Dallas* (played by Larry Hagman) and Alexis Colby in *Dynasty* (played by Joan Collins), have achieved virtually mythic proportions, comparable to the major characters of Disney and Hollywood. Compare MOTION PICTURE, MYTH, SAGA. See SERIES. [MEDIA].   T.MCA.

SOBRIQUET, also **soubriquet** [17c: from French *sobriquet*, earlier *soubriquet* a tap under the chin, a surname (often with a mocking quality)]. A nickname, originally a descriptive epithet used as a surname, such as *Plantagenet*, the name of a medieval dynasty of English kings, which may have come from the French *plante genêt* (the broom plant), because Geoffrey, Earl of Anjou, the founder of the line, used to wear a sprig of broom in his cap, or planted broom to improve his hunting covers. See EPITHET, NICKNAME. [NAME].   J.A., T.MCA.

SOCIAL DISTANCE. See PROXEMICS.

SOCIAL REALISM. An imprecise term for drama or fiction that tries to reflect life accurately. It excludes fantasy and romance, refuses to avoid the unpleasant, and is often inspired by a wish to expose injustice and encourage political action. Social realist novels were written in the late 19c and early 20c, by George Gissing, George Moore, Arnold Bennett, and Somerset Maugham. A similar approach was taken in the mid-20c by dramatists like John Osborne and Arnold Wesker. In novels and plays of this type, the dialogue reproduces everyday speech, warts and all. Social realism is distinct from *Socialist Realism*, a theory adopted by the Congress of Soviet Writers in 1934, which used drama to help audiences of workers understand Marxism. See DRAMA, FICTION. [LITERATURE].   R.C.

SOCIETY FOR PURE ENGLISH, The. A reforming society founded in England in 1913 by a number of writers and academics on the initiative of the poet Robert Bridges. The outbreak of the First World War impeded its development, but between 1919 and 1946 it carried on a campaign against what it regarded as degenerate tendencies within the language, mainly through a series of 66 *Tracts*, for many years printed and distributed by Oxford University Press. The terms *pure* and *tract* indicate the quasi-missionary approach adopted by Bridges and his associates. In Tract 21 (1925), which sets out the aims of the Society, Bridges indicated that by *pure* he did not intend *Teutonic* (that is, Germanic), an interpretation associated with the 19c reformer William Barnes, who had advocated a return to undiluted Saxonism. *Pure* was deliberately adopted 'as an assertive protest against that misappropriation of the term which would condemn our historic practice'. Bridges considered that the spread of English throughout the world was 'a condition over which we have no control', but one that 'entails a vast responsibility and imposes on our humanity the duty to do what we can to make our current speech as good a means as possible for the intercommunication of ideas':

That we did not of our own will or intention put ourselves in this predicament cannot excuse our neglect; nor in the exposure and trial that our language has to face can we honestly sustain our native pride in it, if, shutting our eyes to its defects, we refuse to accommodate it to the obvious needs of perspicuity and logical precision which are the essential virtues of any cultured speech. In certain respects the English language is in its present condition inferior to some of its rivals as a convenient carrier of thought; and it would be a disgrace to us if we made no effort to bring it up to the mark.

In addition to benefits gained from its intricate history, English 'carries many scars', some beyond remedy, others still capable of treatment. Bridges argued that 'we are the inheritors of what may claim to be the finest living literature in the world', and that steps should therefore be taken to ensure that the everyday language does not 'grow out of touch with that literature . . . so that to an average Briton our Elizabethan heritage would come to be as much an obsolete language as Middle English is to us now'. He saw as a special peril the scattering of speakers of English among 'communities of other-speaking races, who . . . learn yet enough of ours to mutilate it, and establishing among themselves all kinds of blundering corruptions, through habitual intercourse infect therewith the neighbouring English':

We can see this menace without any guess as to what may come of it, and in the United States, where it is most evident, it is natural that despair should encourage a blind optimism, expressed—as I redd[1] it in the *New York Times*—in some such jaunty phrase as this, that *the old Lady may be trusted to take care of herself.* But, whatever sort of speech might naturally arise, it is extremely unlikely that the unknown accidental linguistic profits would outbalance the calculable loss. [[1] I venture this spelling, long advocated by Henry Bradley and others, for the perfect of *read* and *spread*, like the use of *lead led, speed sped*, &c., the added *d* being the common sign of the perfect tense.]

Although the Society had only a slender influence on users of English beyond literary and philological circles, many of the views expressed by Bridges and his fellow members continue to be widely endorsed, especially by older members of the middle classes throughout the English-speaking world. They are from time to time restated by pressure groups with similar interests, such as the *Queen's English Society* in England in the 1980s, under the presidency of the writer and retired BBC broadcaster Godfrey Talbot, who echoes Bridges in writing:

Accost me as The Old-Fashioned Anglo if you like, but it appears to me that the Mother Tongue which half the world now uses is a cause for concern because while in demand overseas it is in decay at home, where increasingly it is both taken for granted and tainted. Restoration and repair are needed. Rarely has a rich inheritance been so undervalued as English today ('Protecting the Queen's English', *English Today* 11, July 1987).

Garland Publishing (New York & London, 1979) has produced a facsimile collection of the Society's *Tracts* (1-66) in seven volumes, with an introduction by Steele Commager of Columbia U., who calls them 'perhaps the most important, and certainly the most engaging, collection of essays devoted to the English language'. Contributors to the series included the English poet Lascelles Abercrombie, the Scottish lexicographer William Craigie, the English writer on language Bernard Groom, the Danish philologist Otto Jespersen, the US dialectologist Hans Kurath, and the Anglo-American essayist Logan Pearsall Smith.

See BRIDGES, PURE, PURISM, TRACT. Compare BAD ENGLISH, BARNES, CORRUPT, DISEASED ENGLISH, GOOD ENGLISH, PLAIN, PROGRESS AND DECAY IN LANGUAGE, QUEEN'S ENGLISH SOCIETY, SAXONISM. [MEDIA, USAGE, VARIETY].   T.MCA.

SOCIETY OF PAKISTANI ENGLISH LANGUAGE TEACHERS. See SPELT.

SOCIOLECT [1970s: a blend of *socio-* and *dialect*]. A social dialect or variety of speech used by a particular group, such as working-class or upper-class speech in the UK. See DIALECT, LECT. [LANGUAGE].   S.R.

SOCIOLINGUISTICS [1930s: from the combining form *socio-*, referring to society and sociology, and *linguistics*]. The scientific study of the social aspects of language. The relationship between language and society is complex and sociolinguistics reflects this complexity, encompassing many different activities which are social and linguistic to varying degrees: for example, the analysis of conversation focuses on language as used in social interaction.

Norms of speech. Conversation analysts deal with norms for the practice of conversation, including turn-taking, interruption, and silence.

They may also investigate relatively contentless but highly important conversational markers such as *well* and *anyway* which help to indicate the structure of conversations. A related area, the *ethnography of speaking*, notes that norms for how language is used vary from one society to another, and that, for instance, while English conversations do not normally contain silences of more than a few seconds, other cultures may permit much longer silences. Work in the ethnography of speaking is important for cross-cultural communication, where different attitudes towards language use can lead to misunderstanding and hostile ethnic stereotyping. This may be true even where both parties are native speakers of the same language: for example, Greek Australians are less likely to react favourably to humorous irony than are Australians of Irish origin.

Attitudes and expectations. Language attitudes of a different sort are the subject of the *social psychology of language*. This area of sociolinguistics investigates attitudes that people have to different varieties (accents, dialects, languages) and the way in which these attitudes influence perceptions of the characteristics and abilities of speakers. These attitudes are clearly social in origin: for example, speakers of the prestigious BrE accent known as Received Pronunciation are often perceived to be more competent and intelligent than speakers with regional accents, this view arising simply from the high social status of RP. Similarly, some accents of English are regarded as being more or less aesthetically pleasing than others. This, too, can be shown to be the result of the social connotations that different accents have for listeners. Americans, for example, do not find the accent of the West Midlands of England ugly, as many British people do, which has much to do with the fact that they do not recognize these accents as being from the West Midlands.

Accent, dialect, region, and class. The relationship between accent and dialect, on the one hand, and social class background on the other, is an issue of considerable sociolinguistic importance. For example, dialects and accents of BrE vary both geographically and socially. The high status of RP is traditionally associated with the British upper class and the public schools (a group of private boarding-schools), and, although often associated with southern England, it shows no regional variation. The further one goes down the social scale, however, the more regional differences come into play, with lower-class or 'broad' accents having many regional features. One of the major advances of modern sociolinguistics has been the introduction of quantitative techniques, following the

lead of the American sociolinguist William Labov, which enables investigators to measure exactly and gain detailed insight into the nature of the relationship between language and social class.

In a sociolinguistic study in Bradford, Yorkshire, Malcolm Petyt showed that the percentage of *h*s 'dropped' by speakers correlated closely with social class as measured by factors such as occupation and income. While lower working-class speakers on average dropped 93% of all *h*s in words like *house*, upper working-class speakers dropped 67%, lower middle-class speakers 28%, and upper middle-class speakers only 12%. This study provides information about the source of some of the language attitudes mentioned above. *H-dropping* is widely regarded in Britain as 'wrong'. Teachers and parents have often tried to remove this feature from children's speech, sometimes claiming that since the *h* appears in the spelling it must be wrong to omit it in speech. This is obviously a rationalization: no one makes this claim about the *h* of *hour*, or the *k* of *knee*. The real reason for this condemnation of *h*-dropping is its correlation with social class and its low social status.

Language change. Such quantitative techniques enable linguists to investigate some of the processes involved in language change. Large amounts of tape-recorded data (obtained in such a way as to ensure as far as possible that speakers are speaking naturally) can be used to plot the spread of changes through the community and through the language. For example, Labov was able in the 1960s to show that in New York City the consonant *r* was being reintroduced in the pronunciation of words like *form* and *farm* by comparing the number of *r*s used by older speakers to the number used by younger speakers. He was also able to show that this change was being spearheaded by speakers from the lower middle class, probably because saying 'forrm' rather than 'fawm' is considered prestigious (and therefore 'correct') in US society, and because speakers from this class are more likely to be both socially ambitious and insecure about the worth of their dialects.

Language planning. Sociolinguistics can be concerned with observing the details of individual behaviour in, for example, face-to-face conversation. It can also be involved in the larger-scale investigation of linguistic behaviour in communities the size of New York City. It can furthermore be concerned with the relationship between language and society in even larger-scale units such as entire nations. Sociolinguists working in areas such as the sociology of language and language planning are concerned with issues like the treatment of language minorities, and the selection and codification of languages in countries which have hitherto had no standard language. In nations such as Britain, Ireland, the US, Canada, Australia, and New Zealand, English is the majority language, in a relationship of dominance with numerically much smaller and officially much less well-supported languages, such as Gaelic and Welsh in Britain and Maori in New Zealand. Sociolinguists study such relationships and their implications for education. In the case of Britain, they also attempt to obtain information on more recently arrived languages such as Gujarati, Panjabi, Maltese, and Turkish. Elsewhere, they note that there are countries in which native speakers of English are in a minority, as in Nicaragua, Honduras, South Africa, and Zimbabwe.

Switching languages and styles. In multilingual situations, developments occur which are important for linguists, including the growth of pidgin and creole languages. Sociolinguists study the behaviour of bilinguals, investigating the way in which they switch from one language to another depending on social context. Speakers in all human societies possess large verbal repertoires, which may include different languages, different dialects, and different (less or more formal) styles. Varieties of language will be selected from this repertoire depending on features of the social context, such as the formality of the situation and the topic of conversation. Stylistic variation occurs in all English-speaking communities, signalled for the most part by vocabulary: for example, one might say *somewhat foolish* or *rather silly* or *a bit daft* depending on who one is talking to, what one is talking about, the situation one is in, and the impression one wants to create. Some English-speaking communities, like many Scots and members of overseas Caribbean communities, are *bidialectal*, having access to more than one dialect as well as different styles.

Conclusion. Sociolinguistics of all types is concerned with language as a social phenomenon. Some aspects of this subject may be more sociological in emphasis, others may be more linguistic. It is characteristic of all work in sociolinguistics, however, that it focuses on English and other languages as they are used by ordinary human beings to communicate with one another and to develop and maintain social relationships.

See ACCENT, CODE-MIXING AND CODE-SWITCHING, DIALECT, DIALECTOLOGY, LANGUAGE CHANGE, LANGUAGE PLANNING, LINGUISTICS. [LANGUAGE].   P.T.

Edwards, John. 1985. *Language, Society and Identity.* Oxford: Blackwell.

Gumperz, J. J., & Hymes, Dell (eds.). 1972. *Directions in Sociolinguistics: The Ethnography of Communication.* New York: Holt, Rinehart, & Winston.
Hymes, Dell (ed.). 1964. *Language in Culture and Society.* New York: Harper & Row.
Fishman, Joshua A. (ed.)1968. *Readings in the Sociology of Language.* The Hague: Mouton.
Labov, William. 1972. *Sociolinguistic Patterns.* Philadelphia: University of Pennsylvania Press.
Trudgill, Peter. 1983. *Sociolinguistics.* 2nd edition. Harmondsworth: Penguin.

SOCIOLOGESE [20c: from *sociology* and *-ese* as in *journalese*]. An informal, usually pejorative term for the style and register of sociologists, especially when addressed to or used by non-sociologists. Fowler's *Modern English Usage* (1965, edited by Ernest Gowers) refers in the entry *sociologese* to 'the harm that is being done to the language' and adds:

Sociology is a new science concerning itself not with esoteric matters outside the comprehension of the layman, as the older sciences do, but with the ordinary affairs of ordinary people. This seems to engender in those who write about it a feeling that the lack of any abstruseness in their subject demands a compensatory abstruseness in their language. Thus, in the field of industrial relations, what the ordinary man would call an informal talk may be described as *a relatively unstructured conversational interaction,* and its purpose may be said to be *to build, so to speak, within the mass of demand and need, a framework of limitation recognized by both worker and client.* This seems to mean that the client must be persuaded that, beyond a certain point, he can only rely on what used to be called self-help; but that would not sound a bit scientific.

Critics who condemn sociologese usually make a simultaneous plea for plain language, especially in speeches and texts addressed to the general public. The issue appears to be the need to fit register to audience and be clear in what one says and writes rather than the invasion of the language at large by the jargon of sociology. See ACADEMIC USAGE, -ESE, JARGON, PLAIN LANGUAGE, REGISTER, TECHNOSPEAK. [STYLE, VARIETY].
                                                    T.MCA.

SOFT. See HARD AND SOFT.

SOFT COPY. See HARD COPY AND SOFT COPY.

SOFT HYPHEN. See HYPHEN.

SOFT PALATE. See PALATE, SPEECH, VELUM.

SOFT SOAP. See SWEET TALK.

SOFTWARE. See COMPUTING.

SOLDIER ENGLISH. See LIBERIA.

SOLECISM, formerly **soloecism** [16c: from Latin *solæcismus,* Greek *soloikismós* what they do in Soloi, solecism]. A traditional term for the violation of good grammar and manners, and any instance of this, such as saying *I didn't do nothin'* instead of *I didn't do anything* (especially if done by someone who 'ought to know better'). In classical times, Athenian or Attic Greek was generally considered the best, but the usage of the Athenian colony of Soloi in Cilicia was considered such a disgrace that it came to represent bad grammar at large. In the 2c, Lucian of Samosata composed a manual of usage entitled *The Solecist*, to help people improve their style and usage. The term has often been used in tandem with *barbarism*, the perceived malcoinage and abuse of words. See ATTIC AND DORIC, ATTICISM, BARBARISM, BARDOLATRY, KING'S ENGLISH. [STYLE, USAGE].   T.MCA.

SOLIDUS. See OBLIQUE.

SOLILOQUY [16c: from Late Latin *soliloquium* an act of talking to oneself, from *solus* alone, *loqui* to speak]. A speech in which a dramatic character utters his or her thoughts aloud; it was particularly common and important in Elizabethan and Jacobean drama. It may inform the audience, offer self-revelation of motive, or put inner conflict into words. The convention of 'overhearing' a character's thoughts was accepted by 16c theatre audiences and continued until late in the 18c, when the development of realist drama put it out of fashion. The soliloquy has been revived by some 20c dramatists, notably Eugene O'Neill in *Strange Interlude* (1928). A soliloquy ends the first part of T. S. Eliot's *Murder in the Cathedral* (1935). Samuel Beckett's characters frequently soliloquize: *Happy Days* (1961) is a sustained soliloquy. Early soliloquies are in the same language as the dialogue, but modern dramatists have tried to reproduce the inconsequence of thought. The soliloquy is different from the *aside*, a short speech addressed to the audience in the presence of other characters, and from the *monologue*, which is a distinct genre. In film and television, the soliloquy has evolved into a technique managed through a *voice-over*, in which a character's thoughts are expressed by his or her voice while doing something in silence. See ASIDE, MONOLOGUE. [LITERATURE, SPEECH].   R.C.

SOLOMON ISLANDS. A country of Oceania due north of Vanuatu, a constitutional monarchy and member of the Commonwealth. Capital. Honiara. Population: 303,000 (1988), 417,000 (projection for 2000). Languages: English and Solomon Islands Pidgin (both official), and indigenous languages. The islands were a British colony from the late 19c, partly a German colony from 1885–1900, and became independent in 1978. See ENGLISH, MELANESIA, SOLOMON ISLANDS PIDGIN ENGLISH. [NAME, OCEANIA, VARIETY].   T.MCA.

SOLOMON ISLANDS PIDGIN ENGLISH, also commonly **Pijin** and technically **Neo-Solomonic**. A variety of Melanesian Pidgin English spoken in the Solomon Islands, in the south-western Pacific Ocean. It is closely related to Bislama in Vanuatu and Tok Pisin in Papua New Guinea. English is the official language of the Solomons, but Pijin is spoken by about half the population. In the early 1900s, copra plantations were established. The labourers employed there had also worked in Queensland and Fiji, where they had used pidgin English. The local variety stabilized early and several religious missions adopted it for use, though it never gained the status of Tok Pisin or Bislama. Throughout their post-colonial history, Solomon Islanders, unlike Papua New Guineans and Ni-Vanuatu, have never been in contact with any other European language but English. For this reason Pijin is closer than Tok Pisin to English and has less non-English vocabulary.

It is syntactically more elaborate than Tok Pisin, for example in having many more prepositions and a greater range of connectives, such as *so, bat, bikos* (so, but, because), as in: 'Mitufala jes marit nomoa ia so mitufala no garem eni pikinini iet. Mi traehad fo fosim haosben blong mi fo mitufala go long sip bat taem ia hemi had tumas fo faendem rum long sip bikos plande pipol wandem go-go hom fo Krismas tu' (from J. Holm, *Pidgin and Creole Languages*, volume 2, 1988, p. 536) [Translation: We've just got married only we haven't got any children yet. I tried hard to force my husband to go on the ship, but times were hard and we couldn't find room on board because plenty of people wanted to go home for Christmas too]. In this text, in addition to *so, bat, bikos, fo* (for) is used to introduce clauses. In cases like these, Tok Pisin would use *long* or *bilong*. See AUSTRALIAN PIDGIN, MELANESIAN PIDGIN ENGLISH. [OCEANIA, VARIETY].   S.R.

SOMERSET. The name of a south-western county of England and of its local speech, sometimes called *Somersetian* and occasionally referred to informally as *Zummerzet*. Many of its features are common to the entire West Country, but the diphthongs in such words as *cow, house* and *tail, came* are closer to RP than elsewhere in the region. The use of the voiced initial fricative in words such as 'zum' for *some* and 'varm' for *farm* is becoming rare in the towns. The influence of Bristol, the main city of the region (though since 1974 it has been in the new county of Avon), has helped mark off local speech from that of Devon and Dorset: a well-established feature in and around the city is a final or 'intrusive' -*l* in words that end in a weak vowel: 'areal' for *area*, 'cinemal' for *cinema*, 'Victorial Centre' for the *Victoria Centre*, a well-known shopping mall. The name *Bristol* institutionalizes the usage, having originally been *Bristow* (earlier *Bricgstow*, the holy place by the bridge). See DORSET, MUMMERSET, WEST COUNTRY. [EUROPE, NAME, VARIETY]. S.E.

SONNET [16c: from Italian *sonnetto* a little sound, a name at first applied to various short poems]. A lyric poem in 14 lines, usually of iambic pentameter. The Italian or Petrarchan sonnet, imitating the style of Francis Petrarch, was introduced into English in the 16c by Sir Thomas Wyatt. It consists of two parts: the *octave* or *octet*, rhyming *abbaabba*, and the *sestet*, rhyming variously but usually *cdecde*. The octave may pose a question that the sestet answers, or the octave may state one point of view and the sestet another. The Italian sonnet is difficult in English because it calls for repeated rhymes. Some poets have broken the Petrarchan rule by ending the sestet with a rhymed couplet; others have used *abbaacca* in the octave. Wyatt's contemporary Henry Howard, Earl of Surrey, devised the form known as the *Shakespearian sonnet*, rhyming *ababcdcd efefgg*. Shakespeare's 154 sonnets, generally considered the finest Elizabethan sonnets, were often devoted to love and have been arranged in a series, of which the following is no. 116:

Let me not to the marriage of true mindes
Admit impediments. Loue is not loue
Which alters when it alteration findes,
Or bends with the remouer to remoue:
O no, it is an ever fixed marke
That lookes on tempests and is neuer shaken;
It is the star to euery wandring barke,
Whose worths vnknowne, although his higth be taken.
Loue's not Times foole, though rosie lips and cheeks
Within his bending sickles compasse come,
Loue alters not with his breefe houres and weekes,
But beares it out euen to the edge of doome:
If this be error and vpon me proued,
I neuer writ, nor no man euer loued.

The sonnet fell largely into disuse after the Restoration of 1660, but was revived by the Romantics (especially Wordsworth) at the end of the 18c. Poets of the 20c who have written sonnets include W. H. Auden and Dylan Thomas. [LITERATURE]. R.C.

SOPHISTRY [14c: from Old French *sophistrie* (Modern *sophisterie*), Latin *sophistria* specious reasoning, from Greek *sophistḗs* a wise person, and pejorative -*ry* as in *palmistry*]. Reasoning

that seems sound but is misleading. The *sophists*, itinerant teachers in ancient Greece, were originally celebrated for their wisdom and rhetorical skills, but latterly widely regarded as intellectually suspect, in contrast with the *philósophoi* (lovers of wisdom), who seemed to be humbler about their knowledge. Anything *sophistical* is therefore plausible but dubious. Nowadays, *sophistication* means worldly wisdom, complexity, and refinement, but from the 14c to the 18c it meant hoodwinking people with sophistry: 'Hers were the acts of cunning practised upon fear, not those of sophistication upon reason' (Ann Radcliffe, *The Romance of the Forest*, 1791, ch. 3). Compare LOGIC. [LANGUAGE, STYLE]. T.MCA.

SORT. See FONT.

SOUND [13c: from Old French *son*, Latin *sonus*]. (1) In technical terms, vibrations that travel through the air at some 1,087 feet (331 metres) per second at sea level and are heard through their stimulation of organs in the ear. (2) A particular effect of such vibrations: *the sound of bells*; *a speech sound*. (3) In phonetics, the audible result of an utterance: *the b-sound in 'big'*. (4) To make or produce a sound: *The bells sounded across the valley*. (5) To indicate (something) through sound: *The bugle sounded 'lights out'*. (6) To say or utter: *Sound each letter clearly*. (7) To have an effect as sound: *Her voice sounded loud*. (8) To seem or appear, through what is said or written or how it is said or written: *You sounded unhappy last night*; *The report doesn't sound right*. (9) Although the nouns *sound* and *noise* can often be used interchangeably (*What was that sound/noise?*), *sound* usually relates to regular and harmonious vibrations, *noise* to irregular and discordant vibrations. See PHONETICS, SPEECH SOUND, TONE, VOICE. [SPEECH]. T.MCA.

SOUND SYMBOLISM. See PHON(A)ESTHESIA.

SOUTH, The. (1) The southern part of a country: *Northern Italy is very different from the South*. The adjective is used contrastively with *North* in such national and regional names as *South Korea*, *South Vietnam*, *South Carolina* (*the United States*), *South Island* (*New Zealand*), (*the state of*) *South Australia*. (2) The South of England, especially London and the Home Counties. (3) The South of Ireland, particularly the Irish Republic contrasted with Northern Ireland: *You're from the South, are you not?* It is a rather 'Irish' feature of the South that one of its counties, Donegal, is in the extreme north-west of the island. (4) The eleven states that formed the Confederacy during the American Civil War

(1861-5), consisting of the seven states of *the Deep South* (Alabama, Florida, Georgia, Louisiana, Mississippi, South Carolina, and Texas) and the four states of *the upper South* (Arkansas, North Carolina, Tennessee, and Virginia). In addition, border states that share some of Southern culture and history, including the holding of slaves, are often thought of as at least partly Southern: Delaware, Kentucky, Maryland, Missouri, and West Virginia. Despite internal differences, the people of the South are conscious of a cultural cohesion strongest in the Deep South. Most white Southerners trace their ancestry in the US to before 1800 and to English-speaking forebears from the British Isles. Their culture includes a romantic attachment to the past, allegiance to Protestant Christianity (accounting for the nickname *The Bible Belt*) and a belief in a class system based in part on ancestry. Black Southerners (many in fact of mixed descent) have their roots in West Africa, from which their ancestors were taken as slaves. Their culture also includes Protestant Christianity, and has shaped such pre-eminently American forms of music as jazz and the blues. About one-fifth of the population of the South is black, and the long and difficult relationship between the races has shaped the social, economic, educational, religious, and political institutions of the region. Historically more agrarian, poorer, and less educated than the North, the South has recently experienced a prosperity that has brought many outsiders to the region. Compare ASIA (EAST), NORTH, WEST. See AMERICAN LITERATURE, DIALECT IN AMERICA, DIXIE, SOUTHERN ENGLISH. [AMERICAS, NAME].

T.MCA., C.C.E., J.A.

SOUTH AFRICA. Official title: English *Republic of South Africa*, Akrikaans *Republiek van Suid Afrika*. Short form *RSA*. Black African activist name *Azania*. A state of southern Africa. Administrative capital: Pretoria. Judicial capital: Bloemfontein. Legislative capital: Cape Town. Population: variously estimated between 27m and 36m (late 1980s; average 31.5m); 44.6m (projection for 2000). Ethnicity: 70% black, 18% white, 9% Coloured (mixed), 3% Asian. Religion: 73% Protestant, 17% Roman Catholic, 2% Hindu, 1% Muslim; most blacks, whites, and Coloureds are Christian. Education: primary 75%, secondary 30%, tertiary 10%, literacy 65%. Languages: Afrikaans, English (both official); others include (black African) Zulu, Xhosa, South Ndebele, Sotho, Tswana, Siswati/Swazi, Tsonga, Venda, Shangaan (South African) Hindi, Tamil, Telugu, Urdu. The earliest inhabitants of the region appear to have been the San (better known as Bushmen) and the Khoi Khoi (traditionally but inaccurately referred to as

Hottentots). They are speakers of the so-called *Khoisan* languages, the term combining their names. The first Europeans to reach coastal southern Africa were the Portuguese in the late 15c. Dutch settlement began in 1652, followed by Huguenots in 1688, both of whom were well established when the British took the Cape in 1795. The Bantu peoples appear to have been moving from the north into the territories of the San and Khoi Khoi at about the same time as the Dutch began colonizing the same areas from the south. British settlers landed at Port Elizabeth in 1820 and settled in the Eastern Cape. To escape British control and keep their slaves after the abolition of slavery in the British Empire in 1833, many Dutch-speaking farmers (Boers) made the Great Trek beyond the Orange River. Their republic of Natal was established in 1839 and annexed by the British in 1846, but the republics of Transvaal (1852) and Orange Free State (1854) were left alone.

The rivalry of British and Boer was sharpened by the discovery of diamonds and gold, resulting in two wars (1880-1, 1899-1902), both won by the British without however settling any social and linguistic problems. In 1910, Cape Colony, Natal, Orange Free State, and Transvaal became provinces of the Union of South Africa, a dominion of the British Empire. In 1931, South Africa became independent within the Commonwealth and in 1961 became the Republic of South Africa, outside the Commonwealth. The National Party, dominated by the Afrikaner community, has governed since 1948, adopting a policy of *separate development* or *apartheid* (Afrikaans: separateness) among the various races: African, Asian, 'Coloured', and European. Voting rights were restricted to European South Africans until 1983, when some were extended to Coloureds and Asians. In the 1960s, the government created ten 'homelands' for the major African peoples, and blacks were classed as citizens of these 'homelands' rather than as citizens of the RSA: see BANTU. Bophuthatswana, Ciskei, Transkei, and Venda were declared independent between 1976 and 1981, but none has been recognized internationally. There has been both passive and guerrilla resistance by blacks to white rule, culminating in the declaration of a state of emergency in 1986. In the early 1990s, there were signs of possible reconciliation between the races and of social and political reform, including especially the dismantling of apartheid. The nature and use of the languages of South Africa are affected by the history and current social and political situation in the RSA.

At present black South African school pupils learn through the medium of their mother tongue for the first four years of school, with

English being introduced as one of their subjects. In the fifth year of school, English becomes the medium of instruction. The change happens abruptly in most cases, and there is a high failure and drop-out rate at this level. There is considerable debate about whether English should be introduced earlier or later; some advocate offering a choice of medium: mother tongue or English throughout school. The reasons against introducing English early are that there is a shortage of adequately trained primary teachers, and that many new concepts and skills are difficult in themselves, and having to grasp them through a foreign language makes them even more difficult. One reason given for introducing English early is that it has to be mastered at some time, and one might as well get on with it. Another is that local African languages do not always have terms for the concepts that have to be learned (such as multiplication and division in mathematics). In practice, teachers often teach in the mother tongue, simply borrowing English terms when necessary.

See AFRICA, AFRICAN ENGLISH, AFRICANISM, AFRICAN LANGUAGES, AFRIKAANS, AFRIKAANS ENGLISH, ANGLIKAANS, BANTU, BOTSWANA, DIALECT IN SOUTH AFRICA, DUTCH, ENGLISH, ETHNIC NAMES, FANAKALO, FLYTAAL, GERMANIC LANGUAGES, GORDIMER, LESOTHO, NAMIBIA, SOUTH AFRICAN BROADCASTING, SOUTH AFRICAN ENGLISH, SOUTH AFRICAN ENGLISH DICTIONARIES, SOUTH AFRICAN INDIAN ENGLISH, SOUTH AFRICAN LANGUAGE ORGANIZATIONS, SOUTH AFRICAN LANGUAGES, SOUTH AFRICAN LITERATURE IN ENGLISH, SOUTH AFRICAN PLACE-NAMES, SOUTH AFRICAN PRESS, SOUTH AFRICAN PUBLISHING, SWAZILAND, TSOTSI-TAAL. [AFRICA, NAME].   T.MCA.

SOUTH AFRICAN BROADCASTING. Broadcasting in the Republic of South Africa makes use of English, Afrikaans, and several African languages, and is almost entirely nationally controlled. Public radio transmissions were introduced in 1924, and the *South African Broadcasting Corporation* or *Suid-Afrikaanse Uitsaaikorporasie* was formed by Act of Parliament in 1936. *Radio South Africa* (English) and *Radio Suid Afrika* (Afrikaans) broadcast nationally, and *Radio RSA* broadcasts to other countries in English. There are also such regional and special-interest stations as *Radio Algoa* in the Eastern Cape, *Radio Metro* mainly for blacks, *Radio Lotus* mainly for Indians, *Radio 5* for all-day pop music, and *Radio Allegro* for classical music. There are also independently owned and operated stations such as *Radio 702* in Transvaal and *Capital Radio*, both broadcasting music, news, and interviews. Television was introduced in 1974 and operates from the SABC/TV Centre in Johannesburg, with the exception of 'Bop TV', the network based in Bophuthatswana (a black homeland), which can be picked up in some northern areas of the RSA. TV channels are nationally controlled with the exception of *M-Net*, a commercial network whose transmissions are scrambled and require a decoder and an independent subscription. The main SABC channel, *TV1*, is in English and Afrikaans, which are alternated at earlier and later times and days of the week. There are mixed-language early morning sessions and afternoon sessions for children. *TV2* and *TV3* serve the black community, generally using African languages and English. Certain times and frequencies are used for the transmission of the entertainment channel *TV4*. See BROADCASTING. [AFRICA, MEDIA].   J.B.

SOUTH AFRICAN ENGLISH, short forms *SAE*, *SAfrE*. The English language as used in the Republic of South Africa, the first language of *c*.10% (about 2.7m) of the total population of the RSA and its present black 'homelands'. About two-thirds of this 10% are white, and most of the rest Indian or 'Coloured' (mixed African and European descent). To a small but important African élite, English is a 'second first language', and it is spoken fluently by many Afrikaners. As a lingua franca, it is used with varying degrees of proficiency by millions whose mother tongue is not English. In 1990, with Afrikaans, it was one of the two principal official languages; a new 'language dispensation' appears likely in the near future. In the following discussion, South African English is distinguished from both *Afrikaans English* and black second-language varieties.

History. The Dutch settlement at the Cape dates from 1652. When the British seized the colony in 1795, they moved into a long-established Dutch-speaking community with its own culture, administration, and patterns of relationship with the black and Khoisan peoples of the subcontinent. The Dutch community was already diglossic, for example using standard Dutch for religious and governmental purposes and local varieties known variously as *Cape Dutch*, *colonial Dutch*, *South African Dutch*, or simply *the taal* ('the language') as dialects of 'hearth and home'. These were later, between 1875 and 1925, standardized as *Afrikaans*. Since the end of the 18c, many speakers of English in southern Africa have been in close contact with Dutch/Afrikaans people (with many intermarriages), and less closely with speakers of Bantu and Khoisan languages. Competent bilinguals (for example, in English and Dutch, or Xhosa and English) have been numerous and influential, and conditions have favoured complex code-mixing and code-switching. There is also a large body of published English writings by non-English authors ranging from the Tswana Sol Plaatje to the Afrikaner Andre Brink.

Pronunciation. (1) SAE is typically non-rhotic, but may become rhotic or partially so in speakers strongly influenced by Afrikaans English. These may have final postvocalic /r/ and a medial /r/ as trill or tap. Lanham has observed an initial obstruent (fricative) /r/, in such phrases as *red, red rose*, in older speakers in the Eastern Cape. (2) Variations in accent depend usually on education, social class, domicile (rural or urban), and accommodation to speakers of varieties different from one's own. (3) Conservative middle-class accents remain close to RP, though typically with the lowering and retraction (in certain phonetic contexts) of the vowel in RP *bit, pin* to a position approaching that of schwa /ə/, in varying degrees. The vowel of RP *goose* is often central rather than back. (4) Salient features of 'broader' accents include the following renderings: the vowel of RP *trap* as 'trep' (Afrikaans/Dutch and the southern Bantu languages lacking a vowel of the *trap* quality); the long back vowel of RP *car* in a higher and more rounded version as in the stereotype 'pork the car'; diphthong reductions as in *fair hair* as /feː heː/, and the vowel of RP *price* in a glideless or nearly glideless version, so that *kite* may resemble *cart*. (5) In a class of loanwords from Afrikaans, such as the interjection *ga* (/xa/) expressing disgust, and *gedoente* (fuss, bustle), most speakers use a borrowed velar or palatal fricative like the sound in ScoE *loch*. In another loan class, of words such as *bakkie* (light delivery van) and *pap* (porridge), there is a vowel between those of RP *but* and *hot*. The precise extent of Afrikaans influence on the sound system and other aspects of SAE is a matter of controversy. In many cases, such as the vowel of the *trap* class, there seem to have been convergent influences from English settler dialects, Dutch/Afrikaans, and in some cases African languages.

Grammar. The syntax of formal SAE is close to that of the international standard. Colloquial SAE, however, has many features, such as: (1) Sentence initiators such as affirmative *no*, as in *How are you?—No, I'm fine*, probably from Dutch/Afrikaans, and the emphatic *aikona* as in *Aikona fish* ('No fish today'), of Nguni (Bantu) origin. The common informal phrase *ja well no fine* (yes well no fine) has been adopted in solid written form as an affectionate expression of ridicule (*jawellnofine*) for broad SAE usage, and has served to name a South African television programme. (2) The suffixed phrase *and them*, as in *We saw Billy and them in town* ('Billy and the others'), a form found also in Caribbean varieties. (3) *Busy* as a progressive marker with stative verbs, as in *We were busy waiting for him*, and often with a non-animate subject, as in *The rinderpest was busy decimating their herds.* (4) The all-purpose response *is it?*, as in *She had a baby last week.—Is it?*, heard also in Singapore and Malaysia, but closely parallel in use to Afrikaans *Is dit?* (5) Extensive use of Afrikaans 'modal adverbs', such as *sommer* ('just') in *We were sommer standing around.*

Vocabulary. SAE has borrowed freely. A rough estimate of source languages for distinctively South African words is: Dutch/Afrikaans 50%, English 30%, African languages 10%, other languages 10%. The most recent years show an increasing proportion of items of English or African-language origin. Most of the SAE items best known internationally, such as *Afrikaner, boer, trek*, and *veld*, are of Dutch/Afrikaans origin. An exception is *concentration camp*, coined by the British during the second Anglo-Boer War. In most domains, such as landscape and topography, there is likely to be: (1) A high proportion of 'common words' borrowed directly from Dutch/Afrikaans, such as *drift* ford (1795), *kloof* deep valley or ravine (1731), *land* a cultivated stretch, usually fenced (from Cape Dutch), and *veld* open country (1835). (2) A number of 'English' items translated or partially translated from Dutch or Afrikaans, such as *backveld* back country, outback, from Dutch *achterveld*. (3) Some words of English origin that have acquired new senses, such as *location*, originally, as in Australia, an area allocated to white settlers, later 'a district set aside for Blacks', and still later 'a segregated urban area for Blacks', typically with strongly unfavourable connotations (as in 'the usual mess, the location, of sacking and paraffin tins': Dan Jacobson). In this sense, *location* has largely given way to the equally euphemistic *township*. (4) A sprinkling of items of African-language origin: for example, *karroo* semi-desert (Khoi, 1776), *donga* an eroded watercourse, usually dry (Nguni). (5) A few words reflecting South Africa's cosmopolitanism, past and present, such as *kraal* an African or Khoikhoi village, an enclosure for cattle (probably from Portuguese *curral*: compare Spanish *corral*).

Most topic areas reflect the wide range of peoples and cultures of past and present-day South Africa. Thus, among trees are the flowering *keurboom* (South African Dutch, 1731), the hardwoods *stinkwood* and *yellowwood* (translating Dutch *stinkhout* and *geolhout*) and *silver tree*, an English coinage dating from early travellers' accounts of the Cape (Dutch: *wittebome* white trees). Among living creatures are the antelopes *eland* (Dutch: elk), *kudu* (probably Khoisan), *impala* (Zulu), and *tssebe* (Tswana). Human types range from the *predikant* or *dominee* (Dutch/Afrikaans: minister of the Dutch Reformed Church) through the *sangoma* (Nguni: diviner) to the *ducktails* (Teddy boys) of the streets of the 1960s. Artefacts range from the traditional *kaross* (Khoisan via Afrikaans: skin blanket) through the *Cape cart* (mistranslating Afrikaans *kapkar* hooded cart) to the ubiquitous *bakkie* (from Afrikaans: basin or other container), a light truck, now a symbol of virile open-air life. Liquor ranges from traditional Nguni *tshwala* brewed with malted grain or maize (formerly *Kaffir beer*, now often *sorghum beer*) to the formidable *mampoer*, a brandy distilled from peaches and other soft fruits, prominent in the fiction of H. C. Bosman and now the focus of a cult of its own, possibly named after the Sotho chief Mampuru. *Mahog(a)* is brandy as served in township shebeens (many now legalized as *taverns*) and possibly from English *mahogany*. Foods include *boerewors* (Afrikaans: boer sausage), a centrepiece of a *braaivleis* (Afrikaans: barbecue), and *sosaties* (curried kebabs, probably from Malay). At outdoor parties, the focal dish may be *potjiekos* (Afrikaans), a stew with ingredients to taste, made in a three-legged pot over an open fire. African township culture has generated an enormous vocabulary that includes *matchbox* a small standardized dwelling, *spot* a shebeen or tavern, *boere* ('boers') the police, and *tsotsi* an African street thug (of uncertain origin). Much of the vast government vocabulary of apartheid remains in use, such as *group area* an area set apart for a particular racial group, and *resettlement*, sometimes forcible, of people into such areas. 'Resistance vocabulary' includes the rallying cry *Amandla* (*ngawethu*) 'Power (is ours)', from Nguni, and the more recent *Viva!*, perhaps from Portuguese-speaking Mozambique, *comrade* in the specialized sense of 'political activist, usually young' (but also as in *Comrade Slovo* or *Comrade Mbeki*), and *necklace* (execution by igniting a petrol-filled tyre hung round the victim's neck). Two items of special interest are *muti* and *larney*. The first, from Zulu, originally designated traditional African medicines and other remedies, but has passed into general white colloquial use as in *The pharmacist gave me a special muti for this. Lahnee*, of unknown origin, appeared first in IndE in general colloquial use, usually as *larney*, meaning 'smart, pretentious', as in *a hell of a larney wedding*.

See AFRICAN ENGLISH, AFRICAN LANGUAGES, AFRIKAANS, AFRIKAANS ENGLISH, ANGLIKAANS, BANTU, ENGLISH, FLYTAAL, SOUTH AFRICA, SOUTH

AFRICAN INDIAN ENGLISH, SOUTH AFRICAN LITERATURE IN ENGLISH, SOUTH AFRICAN PLACE-NAMES. [AFRICA, VARIETY].   W.B., J.B.

Branford, Jean. 1978, 1980, 1987, 1991. *A Dictionary of South African English*. Cape Town: Oxford University Press.
Lanham, L. W. 1982/4. 'English in South Africa', in R. W. Bailey & M. Görlach (eds.), *English as a World Language*. Ann Arbor: University of Michigan Press. Cambridge: University Press.

SOUTH AFRICAN ENGLISH DICTIONARIES. The first dictionary of South African English was *Africanderisms* (1913), compiled by the Methodist minister Charles Pettman, updated in 1934 by C. P. Swart in an unpublished thesis for the U. of South Africa ('Africanderisms: A Supplement') and in 1965, 1967, and 1970 by M. D. W. Jeffreys in *African Notes and News*. In 1968, the *Institute for the Study of English in Africa* began work towards a *Dictionary of South African English on Historical Principles*. In 1971, it published privately a sample of 50 historical entries called *Towards a Dictionary of South African English*, and in 1976, in a limited edition, *Voorloper* ('Forerunner': the term for a leader of a span of oxen), by J. D. Walker, P. M. Silva, and an editorial committee, a work of 921 pages. This was followed in 1984 by *Agterryer* ('After-rider': a mounted groom), a three-volume 1,638-page work by W. and J. Branford, M. Britz, and J. Pargiter, containing further entries. These, with further items still, constitute the basis for the *DSAE on Historical Principles*, to be published by Oxford University Press (UK) in the 1990s. The offices of the project are at Rhodes U., Grahamstown, Cape Province. A smaller work by J. Branford, *A Dictionary of South African English* (OUP SA), appeared in 1978, with revised editions in 1980, 1987, and 1991. It contains illustrative quotations and has become a generally used reference book, but is not intended as a substitute for the historical dictionary. OUP SA published in 1977 *A Dictionary of South African English Usage* by D. R. Beeton and H. Dorner, a prescriptive usage text combined with a largely biological vocabulary, and in 1987 a South African edition of *The Pocket Oxford Dictionary*, adapted with about 2,000 South African entries by W. Branford. See DICTIONARY. [AFRICA, REFERENCE].
   J.B., W.B.

SOUTH AFRICAN INDIAN ENGLISH, short form *SAIE*. English as used by South Africans of Indian background. In the province of Natal, where the majority of Indian South Africans live, SAIE is the first language of most under 40. The ancestral languages, chiefly Gujarati, Hindi, Tamil, Telugu, and Urdu, are in various stages of obsolescence 130 years after the first immigrations under indentureship in 1860. SAIE is not generally recognized as a variety in its own right, and in educational circles is stigmatized as poor English. It is a continuum from the low-prestige basilect of older people with little education to an acrolect used by some younger educated speakers that differs little from general South African English. Between these extremes is the mesolect, the usage of the majority. Indian influence is apparent in the syllable-timing of informal speech, retroflexion of /t, d/, especially at the ends of syllables (as in *but* and *bud*), and the replacement of /θ, ð/ by /t, d/. Parataxis is often favoured over hypotaxis (*I went to Derek—Derek filled that form in—he sent it*), topicalization is used for emphasis (*Only asthma I had*), and the word order of the Indian languages is sometimes used, as when kinship titles follow proper names (*Johnny Uncle, Meena Auntie*) and relative clauses precede the head noun of the main clause (*You can't beat Vijay's-planted tomatoes*: You can't beat the tomatoes which Vijay plants). Some lexical similarities with IndE suggest the 19c influence of teachers from India: *cousin-brother* a male first cousin, *further-studies* higher education, and the compounds *butter-bread* bread and butter, *curry-rice* curry and rice. Such similarities are not enough to suggest a simple process in which the English of the subcontinent was transplanted to Natal. Although the number of acrolectal speakers is increasing, there are few signs of merging with general South African English, partly because of past policies of segregation in housing and education. See AFRICAN LANGUAGES, INDIAN ENGLISH, SOUTH AFRICAN ENGLISH. [AFRICA, ASIA, VARIETY]. R.M.

SOUTH AFRICANISM [1970s]. A word or other expression that occurs in or is typical of the English of South Africa, such as the internationally known *laager* and *trek*, the local informal term *lekker* pleasant, excellent, delicious (as in *lekker sunshine* nice warm sunshine, and *the lekkerest ladies in London*), and the contrastive acronyms *ESSA* (English-speaking South African) and *ASSA* (Afrikaans-speaking South African). See -ISM, SOUTH AFRICAN ENGLISH. [AFRICA, STYLE, WORD]. T.MCA.

SOUTH AFRICAN LANGUAGE ORGANIZATIONS. The foremost language organizations in South Africa are the *Afrikaanse Academie*, with an authoritative role for Afrikaans similar to that of the Académie française, and the *Afrikaanse Taalkommissie* (Afrikaans Language Commission). There are no comparable organizations for English. *The English Academy of Southern Africa* (founded 1961), with members from all language groups,

is largely concerned with literary studies, but makes recommendations on style and punctuation for the guidance of teachers and others. It publishes the periodical *EAR* (an acronym for *English Academy Review*) and has a telephone service, *Grammar-Phone*, that answers questions on usage. The *South African Council for English Education* (*SACEE*) holds symposia and sponsors lectures on subjects relating to English language and teaching. The bilingual *Linguistic Association of Southern Africa/Linguistiese Vereniging van Suider Afrika* (founded in the 1970s) provides the broadest forum for linguists, but is not strongly supported by English-speaking academics, since many of them are not sufficiently bilingual. The Association publishes *Taalfasette* ('language facets'), in which some of its proceedings appear, and *The South African Journal of Linguistics*. The *South African Applied Linguistics Association* (*SAALA*) draws on a wider field and produces a quarterly newsletter. The *Names Society/Naamkundige Vereniging* (founded in the 1970s) is bilingual, has regular annual conferences, and publishes the journal *Nomina Africana* and the proceedings of major conferences. The *Institute for the Study of English in South Africa* (*ISEA*: founded 1965) is a research institute of Rhodes U., Grahamstown. Its interests have been: (1) The encouragement of South African literature, to which end it publishes *New Coin* (poetry by new writers) and *English in Africa* (a literary quarterly). (2) Running literary programmes for black children. This activity has become so large and complex that it is now separated off into what is known as the *Molteno Project*, named after the sponsors of the scheme. See SOUTH AFRICAN ENGLISH DICTIONARIES. [AFRICA, LANGUAGE]. J.B.

SOUTH AFRICAN LANGUAGES. The languages of South Africa consist of African languages and languages from Europe and Asia. In 1990, about four in every five South Africans were speakers of Bantu languages, though Afrikaans and English have substantial blocks of mother-tongue speakers. There are currently no reliable figures for language groupings in the total population (c.35.2m in 1987). Estimates are complicated by the problems of what, in a multidialectal society, constitutes a 'language', by governmental manipulations during the 'apartheid era', and by the lack of census language data since 1980. There are two major groups of Bantu-speaking peoples: *Nguni* and *Sotho-Tswana*. Nguni (perhaps 15m) includes over 6.5m speakers of *Zulu*, well over 6m of *Xhosa*, and (in the Republic) about 1m of *Siswati* (*Swazi*). Sotho-Tswana includes about 2m speakers of 'Southern Sotho', about 3m of *Tswana* (formerly called *Sechuana* or *Bechuana*), and about 3m of 'Northern Sotho'. The Nguni languages are largely mutually intelligible, as to a lesser extent are the Sotho–Tswana languages. A 'standardized Nguni' and a 'standardized Sotho', initially as written languages, are possible options for a post-apartheid society. Zulu is said to be used in some areas as a lingua franca, and there are many 'township colloquials', hybrid varieties in black urban areas such as *flytaal* and the 'Pretoria Koine'. The *Tsonga* group has about 1m speakers in the Republic, *Venda* about 0.5m. *Afrikaans*, Africa's only home-grown language of Germanic origin, has about 6m speakers, over half of them white and most of the rest Coloured; *English* has perhaps 3.5m, two-thirds white. Both are official, and widely used as second languages. The original languages of the Indian population (for example, the Dravidian languages Tamil and Telugu, and the Indo-Aryan languages Gujarati and Urdu) are rapidly giving way to English. The most important minority 'white' language is Portuguese. Khoisan languages (formerly called *Hottentot* and *Bushman*) are spoken by small groups in South Africa and by larger populations in Namibia, the largest being the Namas (*c*.45,000). See AFRICAN LANGUAGES, AFRIKAANS, ANGLIKAANS, BANTU, FANAKALO, FLYTAAL, NAMIBIA, SOUTH AFRICAN ENGLISH, TSOTSI-TAAL. [AFRICA, LANGUAGE].   W.B.

SOUTH AFRICAN LITERATURE IN ENGLISH.
Literature in English in South Africa originated during immigration from Britain in the 1820s to a former colony of The Netherlands, where Dutch, some Portuguese, and many indigenous languages were spoken. The cross-fertilization of the various languages characterizes the literature at large. Early prose writing was largely non-fictional: journalism, travellers' tales, and hunting romances that evolved into a tradition of fictional realism. First were the imperialist romances of Henry Rider Haggard, such as *Allen Quatermain* (1887), followed by a pastoral tradition whose leading writers were Olive Schreiner (*Story of an African Farm*, 1881) and Pauline Smith (*The Little Karoo*, 1925). Smith's work transfers into English the structures of Afrikaans, the language of her characters, a pattern followed by Herman Charles Bosman in *Mafeking Road* (1947) and others.

Race and politics. In the 20c, social realism has dominated in an increasingly politicized literature that, since the poetry of the 1820 settlers Thomas Pringle and Andrew Geddes Bain, has fostered a socially and racially liberal attitude. William Plomer's *Turbott Wolfe* (1929) was the first novel to use social realism as a mode of protest against repressive political practice. In the work of Alan Paton (*Cry, the Beloved Country*, 1948) the resonances of the Bible are consonant with the author's liberal humanist standpoint. Since the advent of apartheid in 1948, an awareness of the indignities suffered by non-whites under repressive Nationalist legislation has fuelled a committed literature among both white and black users of English, in which writers have sought to construct new forms to deal with a complex situation. From the 1960s, literature has tended to approach an African rather than a European consciousness, although such novelists as Nadine Gordimer (*The Conservationist*, 1974) and Dan Jacobson continue to use European models. White South African poetry, dominated at first by Roy Campbell (*Adamastor*, 1930) and more recently by Douglas Livingstone (*The Devil's Undertone*, 1978), has also tended to look stylistically to Europe though material is invariably local.

Black writing. Writing by blacks had been sparse, nurtured by church and mission schools and drawing heavily on British models, but in the 1950s writers associated with the black magazine *Drum*, centred in Johannesburg, were publishing material for readers in the townships. A new style developed: impressionistic, energetic, racy, though still complying with Anglo-American codes. In the late 1950s and 1960s, however, political protest and black writing were suppressed; many writers went into exile, where they continued to produce a largely poetical or autobiographical literature, such as Ezekiel Mphahlele's *Down Second Avenue* (1959). Oswald Mtshali's collection of poetry, *Sounds of a Cowhide Drum*, signalled the flowering of black poetry in the 1970s under the ideology of Black Consciousness. It became a matter of principle to reject Western culture, associated with the oppressor, to represent black standards, and to assist in consciousness-raising. Fostered by *Staffrider* magazine in Johannesburg, a new form of English emerged, especially among those whose facility in standard English had been destroyed by the policies of Bantu education, that uses *tsotsi-taal* (the lingua franca of the townships), the vernaculars, Afrikaans, Americanisms, and jazz rhythms. It also mingles epic and oral techniques in a rhetoric of resistance. In ideology and practice, it is similar to the radical poetry of West Indian immigrants in England, where much of the writing is conceived as performance. Some whites, such as the one-time political prisoner Jeremy Cronin, are involved in similar linguistic experimentation.

A vague middle ground. A parallel development has taken place in black theatre, especially since the non-racial Market Theatre opened in 1976, the year of the Soweto riots. Here is staged an indigenous dramatic form, with its roots in community theatre, giving the voiceless a voice. Athol Fugard, a leading white dramatist, has pioneered a new type of non-racial and politicized theatre based on US models but relying heavily on improvisation. It has been difficult for white, English-speaking writers to find an idiom to express their abiding sense of alienation and marginalization, trapped in a vague middle ground between the opposing nationalisms of blacks and Afrikaners and fearing a cataclysm. Recently, in what has been dubbed a *literature of disaster*, poets have turned for models to Italian, Russian, and South American poetry. In fiction and poetry, a movement led by J. M. Coetzee (*Waiting for the Barbarians*, 1980; *Foe*, 1986) looks outside the Anglo-African nexus, basing its work on the theories of post-structuralism and such non-British models as Albert Camus and Roland Barthes. See GORDIMER. [AFRICA, LITERATURE]. M.LE.

Chapman, Michael. 1982. *Soweto Poetry*. Johannesburg: McGraw-Hill.
—— 1984. *South African English Poetry: A Modern Perspective*. Johannesburg: Donker.
Christie, Sarah, Hutchings, Geoffrey, & Maclennan, Don. 1980. *Perspectives on South African Fiction*. Johannesburg: Donker.
Gordimer, Nadine. 1973. *The Black Interpreters*. Johannesburg: Ravan.
Gray, Stephen. 1979. *Southern African Literature: An Introduction*. Cape Town: David Philip.
Mphahlele, Ezekiel. 1962. *The African Image*. London: Faber.

SOUTH AFRICAN PLACE-NAMES. The place-names of South Africa reflect its complex multiracial and multilingual history. Their main sources are African languages, Afrikaans, and English.

African languages. Many place-names, especially in the west, are from the Khoisan (Bushman, Hottentot) languages, such as *Namib, O'Kiep, Garies, Nabapiep*. A major study of these names, known in Neo-Latin as *Toponymica Hottentotica*, has been made by G. S. Nienaber and P. Raper. There are many names from African languages, particularly Zulu names in Natal, such as the river *Amanzimtoti* (sweet water) and the hill *Majuba* (doves), the site of the battle of 1882, and the Cape Town township *Khayelitsha* (new home). The majority of new and relatively new place-names are of African-language origin. Several prefixes regularly appear in names, such as *Kwa-* (place of), as in *KwaZulu* (place of the people of heaven) and *KwaMashu* (Marshall's place), *e-* (on) as in both *Empangeni* and *Entabeni* (on the mountain), and *um-*, usually in the names of rivers, such as *Umfolozi, Umhlanga, Umkomazi, Umdhloti*.

Afrikaans. Various city names are associated with leaders of the Afrikaner community, such as *Pretoria*, after Andries Pretorius, and *Pietermaritzburg*, after the Voortrekker leaders Piet Retief and Gerrit Maritz. Several Afrikaans topographical elements appear regularly, such as *berg* mountain, *rand* ridge, *kloof* ravine, *krans* cliff, *hoek* angle, corner, *drift* ford, *baai* bay, *kop(pie)* hill(ock), *dorp* town, village, *stad* town, *burg* city. The English elements *-town, -ton*, and the French *-ville* are also found. The colours *groen, wit, swart, blou* (green, white, black, blue) and the names of animals and plants (such as *leeu* lion, *olifant* elephant, *baviaan* baboon, *eike* oak, *denne* pine) are also common. These combine with personal names and constitute an open system used to form new names, as in *Verwoerdburg, Groenkloof, Randburg, Denneoord*. Typical of older names are *Johannesburg, Krugersdorp, Venterstad, Spioen Kop* (Spy's Hill), *Witwatersrand, Buffelsbaai*, and *Waterkloof*, all of which show these same formatives and structure types.

English. Some well-known names are of English origin, such as the ports *Durban* (formerly D'Urban, commemorating a governor of that name), *East London*, and *Port Elizabeth*. *Cape Town* is a translation of *Kaapstad*; both names are used, the Afrikaans representing the earlier form. English place-names, such as *Grahamstown, George* (named after King George III), and *King William's Town*, are far outnumbered by those of the African languages and Afrikaans. See PLACE-NAME. [AFRICA, NAME]. J.B., W.B.

SOUTH AFRICAN PRESS. The first newspaper in South Africa was the bilingual English/Dutch *Cape Times Gazette and African Advertiser*, first published in 1800 by Messrs Walker & Robertson, a firm describing themselves as 'wholesale merchants, slave dealers and privateers'. The *Gazette* was taken over almost immediately by the government and became its official organ, ancestor of the present *Government Gazette*. In 1824 appeared the *South African Commercial Advertiser*, edited by John Fairbairn and Thomas Pringle, and the *South African Journal*, edited by Pringle. They were suppressed on the instructions of the Governor, Lord Charles Somerset, but a vigorous agitation won virtual freedom of the press in 1828. Many newspapers followed: *The Colonist* (1827-8), *The South African Quarterly Journal* (1829-31, 1833-4), *The Colonial Times* (1840), *The Cape Times* (1840, revived 1876), and *Sam Sly's African Journal* (1843). They included the *Grahamstown Journal* (1831), still published biweekly as *Grocott's Mail*, and the *Eastern Province Herald*

(1841). *The Friend of the Sovereignty* (1850), originally bilingual, is now *The Friend*. *The Star*, now Johannesburg's largest-circulation daily, began in Grahamstown as *The Eastern Star*, moving to the Rand in 1877. Most of these newspapers reflected, well into the 20c, the language and general stance of the British press of their day. Even the small-town *George and Knysna Herald* reads in its earlier issues much like *The Times* of London. Such newspapers indicate a high level of literacy and general culture, and many brought a close approximation to the British standard language into South African homes. A century later, in 1948, came the rise of the black and Indian press, mostly in English-language newspapers and magazines: *Drum*, *Golden City Post* (now *City Press*), *New Nation*, *Pace*, and the Indian *Graphic* and *Leader*. Their circulations and influence grew steadily in the 1970s and 1980s. They are important sources for many black items in the South African English vocabulary. See NEWSPAPER, PRESS. [AFRICA, MEDIA]. W.B., J.B.

SOUTH AFRICAN PUBLISHING. Long-established local houses include Juta's and Maskew Miller's, the latter now amalgamated with Longman. There are numerous private houses which have been in operation for many years: Howard Timmins; A. A. Balkema (also Utrecht); C. A. Struik, well known for a series of facsimile reprints of important works of Africana; David Philip, long-time specialist in South African material, literary and political; also more recently founded houses such as Ad Donker, Don Nelson, and the new Chameleon Press. Ravan Press is a house specializing in Black literature, or books of particular African interest, including literary collections from their journal *Staffrider*. Tafelberg Uitgewers/Publishers, one of the major Afrikaans houses, also publishes in English. Several overseas publishing houses have branches in SA, notably Oxford University Press, Harper Collins, and Longman. Others such as The Bodley Head, Heinemann, and McGraw-Hill have their sales distribution done for them through the agency of Oxford or some other house. See PUBLISHING. [AFRICA, MEDIA]. J.B.

SOUTH AMERICA. See AMERICA, AMERICAN LANGUAGES, ARGENTINA, CARIBBEAN ENGLISH, CARIBBEAN ENGLISH CREOLE, CONTINENT, CREOLE, CULTURA, FALKLAND ISLANDS, GUYANA, LATIN², PIDGIN, SURINAM(E).

SOUTH ASIAN BROADCASTING. All South Asian broadcasting, in Bangladesh, Bhutan, India, the Maldives, Nepal, Pakistan, and Sri Lanka, is currently government-controlled, with the exception of a private TV channel, *PTN*, in Pakistan, for news and entertainment. In India, however, there are proposals for an autonomous broadcasting corporation. English has a significant role as a link language, both internationally and across the regions of the larger countries. The first regional public radio service was set up in 1921 by the Bombay office of the *Times of India* newspaper, in collaboration with the government Posts and Telegraphs Department. This was followed by the radio clubs of Bombay, Calcutta, and Lahore (now in Pakistan). In 1926, the private *Indian Broadcasting Company* was authorized to set up medium-wave radio stations in Bombay and Calcutta, and provided a regular service until 1929. The government then set up the *Indian State Broadcasting Service* in 1930, and in 1935 Lionel Fielder from the BBC became the first controller of the renamed *All-India Radio* (*AIR*), 1936. Broadcasting became part of the *Department of Information and Broadcasting* in 1941. After independence in 1947, India and Pakistan divided the service between them, the Indian successor organization retaining the original name (since 1957 also known as *Akashvani*, Sanskrit for 'voice from space'). Indian television or *Doordarshan* (Sanskrit: 'distant vision') began as a UNESCO pilot project in 1959, with regular broadcasts in 1965 and colour in 1982. Pakistan by 1988 had 22 radio and TV stations. Television now covers 87% of the population and 47% of the total area of the country. The *Pakistan Broadcasting Corporation* (Islamabad) has daily broadcasts in over 20 languages (home service) and 15 languages (external service). The first TV station in Nepal began in March 1986, under the auspices of the *Nepalese Television Corporation*. *Radio Nepal* (Kathmandu) broadcasts on short and medium wave in Nepali and English. In Sri Lanka, an experimental TV station was started in 1979 by the *Independent Television Network* and was taken over by the government in the same year, as the *Sri Lanka Rupavahini Corporation* (*SLRC*). All the regional countries and therefore broadcasting services are multilingual and multicultural: for example, AIR broadcasts in 60 languages and dialects, its Kohima (Nagaland) station alone providing services in 12 dialects. Pakistan uses over 24 languages. In all the countries, English-language announcers generally use the educated form of the local variety. A relevant publication is P. C. Chatterji's *Broadcasting in India* (New Delhi, 1987). See BROADCASTING. [ASIA, MEDIA]. B.B.K.

SOUTH ASIAN ENGLISH, short form *SAE*. The English language as used in Bangladesh, Bhutan, India, the Maldives, Nepal, Pakistan, and Sri Lanka. The combined populations of these countries, projected as 1,400m in the year 2000, constitute almost a quarter of the human race. English is their main link language, largely as a result of British commercial, colonial, and educational influence since the 17c. Only Nepal, Bhutan, and the Maldives remained outside the British Raj. All South Asian countries are linguistically and culturally diverse, with two major language families, Dravidian and Indo-Aryan, a shared cultural and political history, common literary and folk traditions, and pervasive strata of Sanskrit, Persian, and English in language and literature. In 1600, Elizabeth I granted a charter to London merchants, giving them a monopoly of trade with 'East India'. The *East India Company* slowly expanded its influence in the Indian subcontinent, gaining control over the greater part of it by 1859, when it was replaced by direct British rule. Three factors operated in favour of the spread of English: the work of Christian missionaries; demand from local leaders for education in English, to benefit from Western knowledge; and a decision by the government of India to make English the official medium of education. Although the missionaries did not achieve the hoped-for mass conversions of Hindus and Muslims, their network of English-medium schools had a great impact and remains intact and successful (though largely secularized).

In 1835, Lord Macaulay wrote the Minute that led to the use of English as the language of education: see INDIAN ENGLISH[1]. The Minute divided the Administration, and that division and controversy has continued into the post-independent period of South Asian education and language policies. Macaulay's main opponent, H. T. Princep, considered the Minute 'hasty and indiscreet', and many South Asians believe that he was right. The political map of the subcontinent has changed drastically, but not the language policy. Before the Minute, each Indian state had its own policy for language in education: Hindi-Urdu, Sanskrit, and Persian were the languages of wider communication, and Hindus, Muslims, and Buddhists generally sent their children to their respective scriptural schools; afterwards, education in English was, even in Christian schools, increasingly secular and general, though with a bias towards English literature and European culture. In 1857, the three English-medium universities of Bombay, Calcutta, and Madras were set up. The new policy emphasized the use of vernacular languages instead of Sanskrit and Arabic, and indicated that English should be taught only where there was a demand for it. English continued as an important component of education, administration, and law, as well as among the educated élite across linguistic and political boundaries

until 1947, when the British left India. The diffusion and impact of the language has not abated since then; if anything, in its localized forms, the spread of English has increased both in its functional range and societal depth. There is a general educated South Asian variety of English used for pan-regional and international purposes. Its main characteristics in all the countries are those of educated IndE, with some national variations. Its use is influenced by three factors: level of education and proficiency; the user's first or dominant language (and the characteristics of the language family to which it belongs); and ethnic, religious, or other background. There is in effect a continuum from educated SAE (the acrolect) through such mesolectal varieties as *Anglo-Indian English*, *Babu English*, *Burgher English*, etc., to the basilects, such as the broken English of street vendors and beggars (*Bearer English*, *Boxwallah English*, *Butler English*, etc.).

See ANGLO-INDIAN, BABU ENGLISH, BANGLADESH, BEARER ENGLISH, BOXWALLA(H) ENGLISH, BRITISH EMPIRE, BURMA, BUTLER ENGLISH, CHEE-CHEE ENGLISH, CONVENT ENGLISH, DRAVIDIAN ENGLISH, ENGLISH-MEDIUM SCHOOL, GANDHI, HOBSON-JOBSON, INDIA, INDIAN ENGLISH[1], INDIAN ENGLISH LITERATURE, INDIAN LANGUAGES, INDO-ARYAN ENGLISH, INDO-ENGLISH, MALDIVES, NEHRU, NEPAL, PAKISTAN, PAKISTANI ENGLISH, SOUTH ASIAN BROADCASTING, SRI LANKA, TWANG. [ASIA, VARIETY].   B.B.K.

Aggarwal, N. K. 1982. *English in South Asia: A Bibliographical Survey of Resources*. Gurgaon, Haryana, India.

Kachru, Braj B. 1982. 'South Asian English', in R. W. Bailey & M. Görlach (eds.), *English as a World Language*. Ann Arbor: University of Michigan Press. Cambridge: University Press.

SOUTH-EAST ASIAN ENGLISH. English as used in South-East Asia falls into two broad types: second-language varieties in countries that were formerly colonies or protectorates of an English-speaking power (Britain in the case of Brunei, Malaysia, and Singapore; the US in the case of the Philippines); and foreign-language varieties in Cambodia/Kampuchea, Indonesia, Laos, Thailand, and Vietnam. In the first group, students in English-medium schools were not only taught English but learned other subjects through it; they were expected to use English in the playground, and there were often penalties for using anything else. Such education began with the establishment of the Penang Free School in 1816 and the Singapore Free School in 1823. English-medium education was the path to better-paid employment and in some cases to higher education leading to the professions. As a consequence, English became a prestige language among the élite. The greater the spread of

English and the more functions for which it could be used, the more it became indigenized. This is most apparent in Singapore where, since 1987, English has been the sole medium of education, and there are now native speakers of Singaporean English.

In formal situations, the English of educated Singaporeans is distinguishable mainly by accent, but in more informal situations an innovative use of words is noticeable, such as loans from Chinese and Malay and modifications in the meaning of English words. Grammatical structure shows the influence of local languages, especially Chinese dialects. In Malaysia, a similar type of English developed. In colonial times, most of the students at English-medium schools were Chinese, but since independence in the 1950s Malay-medium education has increased and Malay has become by far the main medium in primary schools and the only medium in secondary schools. English remains an important compulsory subject but its functions have greatly diminished. Brunei has a bilingual Malay and English education policy, earlier primary-school classes beginning with Malay alone, then an increasing use of English until in the senior secondary school English is the medium for 80% of class time.

English-medium education began in the Philippines in 1901 after the arrival of some 540 American teachers, not long after the defeat by the US of the former colonial power, Spain. English was made the language of education and with wider use became indigenized by the inclusion of vocabulary from local languages, the adaptation of English words to suit local needs, and the modification of pronunciation and grammar to produce a distinctively Philippine English. English was adopted for newspapers and magazines, the media, and literary purposes. After independence in 1946, the national language Tagalog (later called Pilipino) was made an official language along with English and Spanish. With increasing nationalism, the role of English diminished and in 1974 a bilingual education policy was implemented, with English as a school subject at primary level but as the medium for science and mathematics at secondary level. At tertiary institutions it remains the main medium of instruction. In the foreign-language countries, English has great importance as an Asian and international lingua franca, in tourism, a reading language for technical subjects, and a token of modernity. See BRUNEI, INDONESIA, MALAY, MALAYSIA, PHILIPPINES, RELC, SINGAPORE. [ASIA, VARIETY].   J.P., H.W.

SOUTHERN AFRICA. See AFRICA, SOUTH AFRICA.

SOUTHERN ENGLISH, also **Southern American English**. A collective term for the geographic and social varieties of English spoken in that part of the US roughly coextensive with the former slave-holding states: see SOUTH (THE). These varieties share the inclusive plural personal pronoun *y'all* (*Are y'all comin' tonight?*), the pronunciation of *greasy* with /z/, and the use of double modals like *might could* (*He might could come Friday*). Two of the major US regional dialect types, (*Coastal*) *Southern* and *South Midland*, cut across the vast territory in patterns following natural boundaries and settlement routes: (1) (*Coastal*) *Southern* (also *Lowland Southern, Plantation Southern*). Spoken along the Atlantic seaboard and westward across the lands of lower elevation with a predominantly agrarian economy once relying on slave labour. In this area, white and black speakers have traditionally shared many of its characteristics: a non-rhotic accent, a glide before /u/ in words like *news* and *Tuesday*, and the usages *tote* carry, *carry* escort, and *snapbeans* string beans. (2) *South Midland* (also *Appalachian, Hill Southern, Inland Southern*). Spoken in a region settled by the Scotch-Irish and Germans coming from Pennsylvania. It is rhotic, has a monophthongal /a/ in *nice time* ('nahs tahm'), and the usages *skillet* frying-pan, *poke* paper sack, and *green beans* string beans. Not all varieties of English spoken in the South fit easily into types: for example, the relic area of Tangier Island in the Chesapeake Bay; the English influenced by the creole Gullah around Charleston, South Carolina; and Cajun English in Southern Louisiana. In addition, non-rhotic appears to be losing out to rhotic pronunciation among the younger generation. For further details, see DIALECT IN AMERICA.

See AFRO-SEMINOLE, AMERICA, AMERICAN ENGLISH, AMERICAN PLACE-NAMES, APPALACHIAN ENGLISH, BLACK ENGLISH, BLACK ENGLISH VERNACULAR, CAJUN, CHICANO, CHICANO ENGLISH, GEECHEE, GULLAH, HILLBILLY, NEW ORLEANS, RHOTIC AND NON-RHOTIC, SOUTH (THE), SOUTHRON, SPANGLISH, TEXAS, TEXIAN, TEX-MEX, UNITED STATES. [AMERICAS, VARIETY].   C.C.E.

Fasold, Ralph W. 1981. 'The Relation Between Black and White Speech in the South', *American Speech* 56, pp. 163-89.

Feagin, Crawford. 1979. *Variation and Change in Alabama English: A Sociolinguistic Study of the White Community*. Washington, DC: Georgetown University Press.

McMillan, James B., & Montgomery, Michael. 1971. *Annotated Bibliography of Southern American English*. Miami: University of Miami Press.

Montgomery, Michael, & Bailey, Guy. 1986. *Language Variety in the South: Perspectives in Black and White*. University of Alabama Press.

Pederson, Lee A., McDaniel, Susan, Bailey, Guy, & Bassett, Marvin. 1986. *Linguistic Atlas of the Gulf States.* Volume 1: *Handbook.* Athens, Ga.: University of Georgia Press. Three volumes published to date.

SOUTHERNIZE AmE & BrE, **southernise** BrE & AusE [19c]. (1) To make southern in respect of language, culture, character, etc. (2) To apply linguistic and other norms, usages, and perspectives from the South of England to the North of England: 'Some of the poems bear traces of having been southernized from a Northern original' (preface, *Hymns to the Virgin and Christ,* c.1430, Old English Texts Society, 1867). (3) To apply the linguistic and other norms, usages, and perspectives of England to Scotland: 'When we Scots gather in groups now and again to succour Lallans and Gaelic, we do the succouring in a patently southernised style' (Tom McArthur, 'A Future for Scotland's Languages', *Scotsman,* 22 Feb. 1977). See NORTHERNIZE, SOUTH (THE), SOUTHRON. [VARIETY].

T.MCA.

SOUTHERN ONTARIO. Part of the Canadian province of Ontario considered as a dialect area that runs along the northern shore of the lower Great Lakes from Windsor on the Detroit River to Kingston at the eastern end of Lake Ontario. Because it is the most populous and wealthiest part of Canada, its usage preferences have generally been taken as normative for CanE and treated not as a 'dialect' but as the 'language'. Originally known as the colony of *Upper Canada* (contrasted with *Lower Canada* below the rapids at Montreal), southern Ontario came to dominate British North America after 1815 when its border with the US was ascertained. Neighbouring border cities, connected by road bridges across the waterway, are linguistically distinct despite shared broadcast media and regular travel from one country to the other: Sarnia (Ontario) and Port Huron (Michigan), Windsor and Detroit (Michigan), Port Erie and Buffalo (New York), Kingston and Watertown (New York). Though few in number, studies of these city pairs show that the linguistic boundary is as sharp as the political one: for example, CanE merger of the vowels of *Don* and *dawn* is restricted to the northern shore. Certain lexical usages of historical interest, relating to land surveys and political organization, are acknowledged as distinctive, and include: *concession* (from Canadian French) surveyed land subdivided into *ranges*; *continuation school* a secondary school; *crown land* publicly owned tracts of land available for purchase by settlers; *reeve* the principal officer of a township, municipality, or village; *riding* a parliamentary district (a term later applied to

electoral units elsewhere in Canada). However, contemporary differences between the usage of southern Ontario and the rest of Canada are less frequently acknowledged: for example, the *Survey of Canadian English* shows *eavestrough* ('channel along the eaves of a roof to catch rainwater and carry it away') as the term of choice for more than 95% of adults in Ontario, and is consequently given as normative in the illustration at *eaves* in the *Gage Canadian Dictionary* (published in Toronto). The synonymous *gutters,* however, is in increasing use among the young and is used by a majority in the Atlantic Provinces; in the *Dictionary,* it is treated as a subordinate entry glossed as 'eavestrough'. Similarly, *Gage* provides no usage label for *serviette* 'paper table-napkin', the word preferred to *napkin* by two-thirds of adults in the Atlantic Provinces and a plurality of younger Canadians in the Prairies and the West. All the quotations for *dew worm* 'earthworm' in the scholarly *Dictionary of Canadianisms* are from Ontario, but *Gage* identifies it not as *Ont.* but as *Cdn.* Were it not for the presumption that the dialect of southern Ontario is definitive for Canada as a whole, these expressions would be assigned a locality label. See CANADIAN DICTIONARIES IN ENGLISH, CANADIAN ENGLISH, DIALECT IN CANADA. [AMERICAS, VARIETY].

R.W.B.

SOUTH KOREA. See EAST ASIAN ENGLISH, KOREA.

SOUTHLAND BURR. See BURR, NEW ZEALAND ENGLISH.

SOUTHRON [Also *sutheroun, suddron,* etc.: Older Scots forms of *southern*]. (1) A Scots adjective and noun for the English and their language: 'Kepand na sudroun bot our awin langage' (Using no southern, but our own language: Gavin Douglas, Prologue to his *Aeneid,* 1513); the Catholic gibe of Ninian Winȝet at the Anglicizing Protestant John Knox: 'Gif ȝe, throw curiositie of nouationis, hes forȝet our auld plane Scottis quhilk ȝour mother lerit ȝou, in tymes cuming I sall wryte to ȝou my mind in Latin, for I am nocht acquyntit with ȝour Southeroun' (If you through eager seeking after new-fangled changes have forgotten our old, plain Scots that your mother taught you, in future I'll give you my opinions in Latin, for I'm not acquainted with your Southron: 1563). The expression *knap suddrone* (speak in an affected English fashion) was attributed to James V King of Scots by John Hamilton (1581). The term continues to the present day in Modern Scots, mostly in the *th*-spellings, as with Robert Burns's *Suthron.* (2) A person from the Southern states of the US: 'The

Southron was a better fighter than the Northerner' (*The North American Review* 126, 1878). (3) Anything southern; any southerner. See SOUTH. [AMERICAS, EUROPE, HISTORY, VARIETY].

A.J.A., T.MCA.

SOUTH SEAS ENGLISH, SOUTH SEAS JARGON. See PACIFIC JARGON ENGLISH.

SOYINKA, (Akinwande Oluwole) Wole [b.1934: pronounced 'Shoy-']. Nigerian and Yoruba playwright, poet, novelist, literary critic, translator, and commentator on African culture, born in Abeokuta, Western Region, and educated at the U. of Ibadan, Nigeria, and the U. of Leeds, England. He worked in London (1958-60), gaining experience in the theatre, and returned home to write and direct in 1960, the year of Nigeria's independence. He has taught in Nigerian universities and at Yale in the US, has worked on radio, television, and film, and has edited *Transition*, a leading African intellectual magazine. His work includes: plays, such as *The Lion and the Jewel* (1959), *The Bacchae of Euripides* (1973), and *Requiem for a Futurologist* (1984); novels, such as *The Interpreters* (1965) and *Season of Anomy* (1973); poetry, ranging from lyrics and epics, such as *Idanre and Other Poems* (1967) and *Ogun Abibiman* (1976), to political comment in *Mandela's Earth* (1988); literary criticism, illustrating his views on Yoruba culture, and African and European aesthetics and their cross-fertilization, in *Myth, Literature and the African World* (1976) and *The Critic and Society* (1980); autobiography, in *The Man Died: Prison Notes of Wole Soyinka* (1972), *Aké: The Years of Childhood* (1981), and *Ìsarà: A Voyage Around the Essay* (1990). Soyinka won the Nobel Prize for Literature in 1986. See index. [AFRICA, BIOGRAPHY, LITERATURE].

G.D.K., L.T.

SPACE [13c: from Old French *espace*, Latin *spatium* room, distance, interval, extent]. (1) A general term for an area of paper or other material that has been left blank, usually between letters or lines in a text. In a line of justified print the spaces between letters are the same but the spaces between words may vary. (2) A printer's term for any of the blank pieces of metal traditionally used to separate words and sentences. (3) A term in telegraphy for any interval in the transmission of a message when the key is not in contact. (4) A media term for the amount of page surface in a periodical or time in a schedule allowed for a story, article, programme, etc. See LAYOUT, TYPOGRAPHY, WHITE SPACE, WORD. [TECHNOLOGY, WRITING].

T.MCA.

SPANGLISH [1960s: a blend of *Spanish* and *English*, on the analogy of *franglais*]. An informal and often pejorative term, particularly common in North America, for: (1) Any of several mixtures of Spanish and English, ranging from extensive uses of loanwords and loan translations to code-switching among bilinguals. Occasionally, the term appears in Spanish as *el espanglish* and Spanish which is heavily influenced by English is sometimes known as *el englañol*. English-influenced Spanish is often referred to negatively in the US Southwest as *español mocho* (from *mochar* to cut limbs off trees) and *espäol pocho* (from Uto-Aztecan *potzi* short, tailless). (2) Less commonly, the slightly pidginized Spanish of some English-speakers, including *learner Spanish*. The term often refers broadly to non-standard Spanish which contains: (1) Loanwords from English, such as: *wachar* to watch, *pushar* to push. (2) Loan senses attached to traditional Spanish words, such as: *asistir* to assist, help, *atender* to attend (school). (3) Calques, such as: *llamar pa(ra) (a)trás* to call back (on the telephone). (4) Code-switching, such as *Sácame los files for the new applicants de alla!* (Get out the files for the new applicants from over there). A more precise terminology developed by Chilean linguist Lucía Elías-Olivares (1976) identifies standard Spanish, popular Spanish, mixed Spanish, *Caló*, and code-switching, to cover a continuum of varieties between Spanish proper and English proper. In this scheme, mixed Spanish contains extensive borrowings and calques, *Caló* is a mixed cryptolect descended in part from the traditional *germanía* (the argot of the Hispanic underworld) and associated in the main with adolescent boys in gangs, and code-switching is the rapid alternation of Spanish and English. Despite the apparent freedom with which they are used, lexical borrowing and code-switching are not random, but are closely related to syntactic structure. See CHICANO ENGLISH, -GLISH AND -LISH, PUERTO RICO, SPANISH, TEX-MEX. [AMERICAS, VARIETY].

J.AM.

SPANISH [Called by its speakers *español*]. A Romance language of Western Europe, spoken by c.250m people worldwide: the official language of Spain (including the Balearic and Canary Islands), and most of the nations of Central and South America: Argentina, Bolivia, Chile, Colombia, Costa Rica, Cuba, Dominican Republic, Ecuador, El Salvador, Guatemala, Honduras, Mexico, Nicaragua, Panama, Paraguay, Peru, Uruguay, Venezuela. In Paraguay, official status is shared with Guaraní, and in Peru, with Quechua, both Amerindian languages. Spanish is spoken in the US, especially in the Southwest (Arizona, California, New Mexico, Texas), Florida, parts of Louisiana, and such cosmopolitan cities as New York

City and Chicago, as well as in the Commonwealth of Puerto Rico. It has also been spoken on the Caribbean island of Trinidad and by Sephardic Jews in North Africa, Turkey, and the Balkans. In Africa, it is the official language of Equatorial Guinea and is spoken in parts of Morocco and in the Spanish coastal enclaves of Ceuta and Melilla. In Asia, it is spoken by a small minority in the Philippines. There have been Spanish creoles in Colombia, the Caribbean, and the Philippines.

Origins. Historically, Spanish evolved out of Late Vulgar Latin, with minor Germanic and major Arabic influence. Its history is divided into three periods: Old Spanish (c.750–1500), Renaissance Spanish (1500 to 1808, the beginning of the Napoleonic Wars in Spain), and Modern Spanish (since 1808). At the close of the Roman period (early 5c), the Iberian Peninsula was overrun by the Vandals and Visigoths, Germanic invaders who contributed such war-related vocabulary as *brida* (bridle), *dardo* (dart), *guerra* (war), and *hacha* (axe). During the Muslim period (711–1492), when much of the peninsula was held by Moorish rulers, Arabic loanwords were absorbed into the local post-Latin dialects, such as *aceituna* an olive, *ahorrar* to save, *albóndiga* a meatball, *alfalfa*, *algebra*, *alquilar* rent, *cifra* a cipher, zero, *naranja* an orange, *ojala* may Allah grant, may it happen, if only, some hope. This influx appears to have been made easy by the Christians who lived in Moorish territories: they were known as *mozárabes*, from Arabic *musta'rib*, Arabicized. Many of them were probably bilingual, speaking Arabic and the now-extinct variety of Spanish known as Mozarabic. The national epic, *El poema/cantar de mío Cid* (the Poem/Song of My Lord), in which the word *cid* is of Arabic origin (*as-sīd* lord), is from the period of the Reconquest.

Works of literature first appeared in Spanish c.1150 and a literary language was firmly established by the 15c. Three pivotal events all occurred in 1492: (1) 'The Catholic kings', Ferdinand and Isabella of Castile and Aragon, completed the reconquest of Spain by taking Granada, the last Moorish kingdom. (2) Christopher Columbus, acting on their behalf, sailed west to find China and India and instead discovered the Americas. (3) The first grammar of a modern European language was published, Antonio de Nebrija's *Gramática de la lengua castellana* (Grammar of the Castilian Language), duly followed by his dictionary and orthography. Spain became a world power and the centre of a vast empire. The standard language of Spain and its empire was based on Castilian (the dialect of Castile), and for this reason continues to be referred to in Spanish as both *castellano* and *español*. Other dialects, however, are also important, especially that of Andalusia ('land of the Vandals', long under Muslim control). Despite efforts made during the period in power of Generalissimo Francisco Franco (1939–75) to establish Castilian Spanish throughout the land, it is not the language of choice in all the regions of present-day Spain.

Spanish in the United States. Spanish has been spoken longer than English in what is now the US. Spanish settlement in San Agustin, Florida, dates from 1565, various areas in New Mexico were settled in 1598, and settlements in California were established from 1769 on. As the English-speaking US expanded, it incorporated territory originally held by Spain (Florida), France (the Louisiana Purchase), and Mexico (the Southwest, from Texas to California). Spanish was also incorporated into the US, by the addition of Texas in 1845 and the rest of the Southwest by the Mexican Cession in 1848. Although statehood for the Territory of New Mexico was delayed until 1912 at least partly because of a lack of English-speaking citizens, Spanish was later granted legal status there along with English. Puerto Rico became associated with the US in 1898 and currently has Commonwealth status, with Puerto Ricans holding US citizenship.

In recent years, immigration from Latin America has made Spanish the second most widely spoken language in the US. The influx of Cubans into Florida beginning in 1960 turned the Miami-Dade County area into a centre of Hispanic language and culture. In the Southwest, immigration from Mexico increased during and shortly after the Mexican Revolution (1912–15), after World War II, and in the 1980s. Immigration from Central America also increased rapidly in the 1980s. The increasing Hispanic population has given some areas outside the Southwest and Florida a decidedly Hispanic flavour, including the cities of New York and Chicago. In all areas, bilingual education has been implemented as a method for bringing new immigrants to fluency in English in the shortest time. In reaction, however, many (including some Hispanics and members of other immigrant groups) have supported the appeals of the organization US English, which advocates a constitutional amendment to declare English the official language of the country and seeks the elimination of bilingual education.

Spanish in English. Because of the reintroduction of Greek learning to Europe by the Arabs in Spain and then the great wealth and power of the new empire, 16c Spain was a major centre of learning. Spanish was a language of high prestige throughout Europe, and in late 16c England was the subject of a number of linguistic treatises, including Richard Percivall's *Bibliotheca Hispanica, Containing a Grammar, with a Dictionarie in Spanish, English, and Latine* (1591). The *Real Academia* (Royal Academy) was founded in 1713, on the model of the French Academy (1637), in order to *limpia, fija, y da esplendor* ('purify, fix, and lend splendour') to the language, the motto on the great seal of the Academy that appears on the spine and title page of all volumes of the Academy's dictionary.

The influence of Spanish on English at large has extended over centuries and been primarily lexical. Phonological and grammatical influences have occurred relatively rarely and recently in the Americas, and have been limited to particular regions and varieties. English shares with Spanish a large vocabulary derived from Latin, due especially to the impact of Norman French after the 11c Norman Conquest of England. During the 16–17c, a time of rapid colonial expansion among the seafaring nations of Europe, Spain and England were competing to amass empires and influence, and Spanish had its first direct impact. Loanwords of the 16c include the orthographically unadapted words *armada, cargo, desperado, flotilla, mosquito, mulatto, negro, pec(c)adillo, sombrero* and the adapted *ambush, cannibal, cask, cigar, comrade, jennet, parade, renegade, sherry*. Other loans have entered the language since then, such as unadapted *albino, flotilla, hacienda, mesa, plaza, siesta*, adapted *barbecue, caramel, cockroach, corvette, doubloon, escapade, guitar, jade, lime, maroon, picaresque, quadroon*. Some Spanish loans have Arabic origins, such as *alfalfa* (Arabic *al-fasfasah*), *alcazar* (Arabic *al-qasr* the castle), *alcove* (through French *alcôve*, from Spanish *alcoba*, from Arabic *al-qubbah* the vault). See ARABIC.

A wave of New World borrowings occurred in the 19c, mainly in the Southwest of the US, such as the unadapted *arroyo, bronco, cantina, corral, gringo, mesa, patio, rodeo, tequila*, and the adapted *alligator, buckaroo, chaps, lariat, mustang, ranch*. Many items borrowed from Spanish were through Spanish from indigenous Amerindian languages, such as *avocado, chocolate, coyote, peyote*, from the Aztec language Nahuatl. In the 20c, there has been a second wave throughout the US, related to the increase in Latin American immigration; loans include *contras, guerrilla, jefe, macho/machismo*, as well as such culinary terms as *burrito, chiles rellenos, flautas, frijoles, frijoles refritos, nacho, pan dulce, salsa, taco, tortilla*. See BORROWING.

English in Spanish. In recent decades, English has had a greater influence on Spanish than vice versa. This has happened wherever Spanish is spoken, but is particularly noticeable where

Spanish- and English-speaking communities live as neighbours (such as along the US–Mexican border) and where communities of speakers of one language have migrated to the territory of another (such as Puerto Ricans in New York City; British expatriate communities and facilities for holiday-makers along the Mediterranean littoral of Spain). Close contact between the two languages has produced hybrid forms, for which casual names have arisen: *Spanglish*, a term covering all forms of English influenced by Spanish and Spanish influenced by English, and the more particular *Tex-Mex* or *Border Lingo* along the Texas–Mexican border.

In general, the influence is lexical, especially in the borrowing and adaptation of technical and sporting terms. Many of these borrowings are accepted only grudgingly or until more Hispanicized equivalents are coined. Not all are current in all dialects, but are clearly favoured in contact dialects. Some expressions are borrowings, either unadapted or adapted, while others are Anglicisms in a more general sense: loan shifts resulting from English influence in the usage of traditional Spanish words, often cognates of English Romance-derived words. Examples of borrowings are: (in sport) *boxeo* boxing, *boxear* to box, *nocaut* a knockout, *noquear* to knock out, *jonrón* a home run, *jonronear* to make a home run, *fútbol, criquet, basquetbol*; (culinary) *cake/queque* a cake, *panqueques* pancakes, *(miel)maple* maple syrup, *bistec* a beefsteak, *cóctel* a cocktail, *hamburguesa*, a hamburger; (in politics) *agenda, boicot* a boycott, *boicotear* to boycott, *cartel, detective*; (in general usage) *bus, camuflaje, esmoking* a dinner jacket, tuxedo, *esnob* a snob, *esnobismo* snobbery, *jazz, jet, microchip, parquear* to park, *troca* a truck.

Loan shifts and translations may compete with established usages: the verbs *rentar* with *alguilar* (to rent) and *clarificar* with *aclarar* (to clarify); the nouns *elevador* with *acensor* a lift, elevator; *profesional* with *profesionista* a professional. They may also provide a new sense for a traditional word: *carácter*, in the theatre as opposed to *personaje*; *conductor*, of music as opposed to *director*; *década* for ten years as opposed to ten of anything; *educación* for schooling as opposed to manners. Sometimes they are entirely new: *perro caliente* a hot dog, *escuela alta* high school. Others, such as *filmoteca* a library of films, are loan blends.

See AFRICAN LANGUAGES, AMERICAN[1], AMERICAN ENGLISH, AMERICAN ENGLISH AND BRITISH ENGLISH, AMERICAN LANGUAGES, AMERICAN PLACE-NAMES, ANGLO, ARABIC, BORROWING, CARIBBEAN LANGUAGES, CHICANO, CHICANO ENGLISH, DIALECT IN AMERICA, EARLY MODERN

ENGLISH, ENGLISH LANGUAGE AMENDMENT, EURO-
PEAN COMMUNITY, EUROPEAN LANGUAGES, GIB-
RALTAR, HAWAII, IBERIAN LANGUAGES, JEWISH
LANGUAGES, PANAMA, PHILIPPINE ENGLISH, PHIL-
IPPINES, PORTUGUESE, PUERTO RICO, ROMANCE
LANGUAGES, SAMANA, SPANGLISH, SPELLING
REFORM, STANDARD, TEXAS, TEX-MEX. [AFRICA,
AMERICAS, ASIA, EUROPE, LANGUAGE].   J.AM.

-SPEAK, SPEAK [1949: from *Newspeak*, as
coined by George Orwell]. Both a combining
form and a word used informally (and often
pejoratively or facetiously) for the style of a
group or occupation, often regardless of whether
it is spoken or written. In a compound that contains *-speak*, the first element indicates either the
situation in which the style occurs (*adspeak*:
advertising) or what the user thinks of it
(*doublespeak*: a jargon intended to mislead).
There are three orthographic forms: (1) Solid:
*Aussiespeak, computerspeak, Femspeak, health-
speak, lewdspeak, modernspeak, moneyspeak,
nukespeak, pensionspeak, tycoonspeak, union-
speak.* (2) Hyphenated: *gay-speak, golf-speak,
management-speak, oblique-speak, Pentagon-
speak.* (3) Open: *art speak, estate-agent speak,
mandarin speak, political speak.* In terms of
structure, there are two extremes: (1) The first
element is monosyllabic like *new*, often a
clipping of a longer word: *bizspeak, Russpeak.*
(2) The first element is phrasal: *Hitch-Hiker's-
Guide-to-the-Galaxy-speak; medical and social
work 'speak'; Twentieth century era speak;
Womenslibspeak.* Occasionally, blending occurs,
as in *bureaucraspeak, litcritspeak, politspeak,
Shakespeak.* Such usages generally occur in
social and literary criticism: 'The aim of this
jargon-sodden Femspeak is to set up a myth of
women artists as a hated underclass' (*Time*,
15 Dec. 1980); 'It is customary to conclude
any piece about oblique-speak, jargon or
euphemisms by exhorting everyone to stop it and
return to the stern, plain language of our fathers'
(Katharine Whitehorn, *Observer*, 26 Oct. 1986).
See DOUBLESPEAK, NEWSPEAK, TECHNOBABBLE,
TECHNOSPEAK. Compare -ESE, -ISM, LINGO, TALK.
[SPEECH, STYLE].   T.MCA.

SPEAKING IN TONGUES. See GLOSSOLALIA.

SPEAQ. See CANADIAN LANGUAGE ORGAN-
IZATIONS.

SPECIALIZATION [1840s in this sense]. A process of semantic change in which narrowing
occurs in the meaning of a word. In Middle English, *deer* meant a four-legged beast (compare
Dutch *dier* and German *Tier*), but the early
restriction to one kind of animal (the family
Cervidae) has long since eclipsed the earlier

meaning. Such specialization is slow and need
not be complete; *fowl* is now usually restricted
to the farmyard hen, but it retains its old meaning of 'bird' in expressions like *the fowls of the
air* and *wild fowl* (compare Chaucer's 'Parlement
of Fowles' and German *Vogel*). See COMPUTER
USAGE, SEMANTIC CHANGE. [HISTORY, LANGUAGE,
WORD].   T.MCA.

SPEECH [From Middle English *speche*, Old
English *spēc*, a variant of *sprēc*, from *sprecan*
to speak, cognate with German *Sprache*, from
sprechen]. (1) The primary form of language; oral
communication in general and on any particular
occasion: *Most people are more fluent in speech
than in writing.* (2) A usually formal occasion
when a person addresses an audience, often with
the help of notes or a prepared text. (3) A way
of speaking, often involving a judgement of some
kind: *local speech, slovenly speech, standard
speech.* (4) The field of study associated with
speaking and listening: *the science of speech.*

Anatomy and physiology. Speech is possible
because of the development over millennia of
an appropriate physical system: the diaphragm,
lungs, throat, mouth, and nose, working
together. All such organs pre-existed the evolution of language and have such prior purposes
as breathing, eating, and drinking. With the
advent of speech, they continued to perform
these functions while becoming available for
additional uses, so that two systems (maintenance of the body and systematic communication) exist side by side. The diagram
overleaf displays the *organs of speech*. Vocal
sound becomes possible when a stream of air is
breathed out from the lungs and passes through
the larynx, then into and through the pharynx,
mouth, and nose. This sound may be *voiced* or
voiceless: that is, the larynx may vibrate or not.
Different sounds are made in the mouth by moving the lips, tongue, and lower jaw to change the
size and shape of the channel through which the
air passes. A *consonant* is made with a narrowing
of the channel, and the point of maximum narrowing is the *place* (or *point*) *of articulation* for
that consonant. The way in which this is done is
the *manner of articulation*. A *vowel* typically has
a wider channel than a consonant. Since it is
difficult to be precise about the articulation of
vowels, they are normally described by their
auditory quality. In discussing articulation,
phoneticians refer to an *articulator*, which may
be *active* (as with the lips and tongue) or *passive*
(as with the front teeth).

Place of articulation. For *bilabial* consonants,
the narrowing is achieved by bringing the lips
together. For *labio-dental* consonants, the active
articulator is the lower lip. In other cases, the

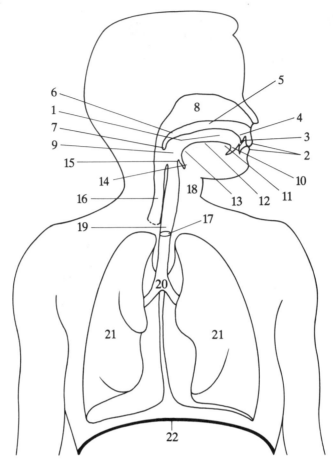

1 mouth (oral or buccal cavity)
2 lips
3 teeth
4 alveolar ridge
5 (hard) palate
6 velum or soft palate
7 uvula
8 nasal cavity

9 pharynx (pharyngeal cavity)
10 tip (of the tongue)
11 blade (of the tongue)
12 front (of the tongue)
13 back (of the tongue)
14 root (of the tongue)
15 epiglottis
16 *BrE* oesophagus,
   AmE esophagus

17 glottis
18 larynx and vocal
   cords/folds
19 trachea
20 bronchi
21 lungs
22 diaphragm

active articulator is part of the tongue, which is raised towards the passive articulator on the roof of the mouth: see table.

Sounds can be classified according to the active articulator, for example the tongue: *apical* sounds made with the tip (Latin *apex*); *laminal* sounds with the blade (Latin *lamina*); *dorsal* sounds with the back (Latin *dorsum*). *Retroflex* sounds are made with the tip of the tongue curled back behind the alveolar ridge towards the palate. However, the commonest classification is according to the passive articulator. This terminology assumes that the active articulator is

Articulator		Description	Examples
Active	*Passive*		
lower and upper lips	—	bilabial	/p, b, m/
lower lip	front teeth	labio-dental	/f, v/
tongue:			
tip	front teeth	dental	/θ, ð/
tip	alveolar ridge	alveolar	/t, d, s, z, n, l, r/
tip/blade	ridge/palate	palato-alveolar	/ʃ, ʒ, tʃ, dʒ/
front	palate	palatal	/j/
back	velum	velar	/k, g, ŋ/

the organ that lies opposite the passive articulator in the state of rest: for example, the passive articulator of a *dental* sound is the upper front teeth, and the active articulator is the tip of the tongue. If some other active articulator is used, it is specified explicitly: for example for /f, v/, the lower lip moves up to the upper teeth, and these sounds are *labio-dental*: see table. The *aspirate* /h/ is usually described as *glottal*. In English, /h/ is like a *voiceless vowel* in that there is no fricative-like narrowing in the mouth, so that the greatest point of narrowing is in the glottis. Most sounds have one place of articulation, but /w/ has a *double articulation*, being made by simultaneously rounding the lips and raising the back of the tongue towards the velum. It is thus both bilabial and velar.

Manner of articulation. This refers mainly to the degree of narrowing at the place of articulation of a sound. If the air-stream is blocked completely, the result is a *stop*, such as /b/, but if it is narrowed to the point where noise or *turbulence* is generated as air passes through the gap, the resulting sound is a *fricative* /v/. In the case of an *approximant* or *continuant*, the manner of articulation is more open, as with the /r/ of *rink* as compared to the /z/ of *zinc* (a voiced fricative). When a stop is released, the articulators move apart and necessarily pass through the degree of narrowing which produces fricative noise. A *plosive* is released quickly, whereas an *affricate* is released slowly:

plosives	/p, b; t, d; k, g/
affricates	/tʃ, dʒ/
fricatives	/f, v; θ, ð; s, z; ʃ, ʒ; h/

There are several types of approximant. The velum is normally raised to prevent air from entering the nose: a *nasal* is produced with the velum lowered. The air-stream normally passes centrally through the mouth: in the case of a *lateral*, the air escapes at the sides. The tongue normally offers a convex surface to the roof of the mouth: for an *r-sound*, the tongue surface is often hollowed out and the tip raised. A *glide* or *semi-vowel* is vowel-like and moves rapidly into the following vowel, and cannot be prolonged:

nasals	/m, n, ŋ/
lateral	/l/
r-sound	/r/
glides	/j, w/

Phoneticians conventionally describe consonants according to their articulation. See AIR-STREAM MECHANISM, CONSONANT, TONE, VOICE, VOWEL. [LANGUAGE, SPEECH]. G.K., T.MCA.

The speech theme

A–C. ABERCROMBIE, ABLAUT, ACCENT, ACCENT BAR, ADVANCED, AFFRICATE, AIR-STREAM MECHANISM,

AITKEN'S LAW, AITKEN'S VOWEL, ALVEOLAR, AMERICAN ENGLISH (PRONUNCIATION), AMERICAN ENGLISH AND BRITISH ENGLISH (PRONUNCIATION), ANACOLUTHON, APH(A)ERESIS, APHASIA, APHESIS, APICAL, APOCOPE, APPROXIMANT, ARTICULATION, ARTICULATORY SET(TING), ASH, ASIDE, ASPIRATE, ASSIMILATION, ASSONANCE, BABBLE, BABBLING, BABEL, BBC ACCENT, BBC ENGLISH[1], BBC PRONUNCIATION UNIT, BERWICKSHIRE BURR, BILABIAL, BLADE, BRAID SCOTS, BREATH, BREATH GROUP, BROAD, BROAD AUSTRALIAN, BROAD NEW ZEALAND, BROAD SCOTS, BROGUE, BROKEN, BROOKLYNESE, BURR, CANADIAN ENGLISH (PRONUNCIATION), CANADIAN RAISING, CARETAKER LANGUAGE, CLEAR L, CLICK, CLIPPED, COALESCENCE, COHERENCE, COHESION, COLLOQUIAL, COLLOQUIALISM, COMMUNICATIVE SHIFT (SPEECH), COMPUTING, CONSONANT, CONSONANT CLUSTER, CONTINUANT, CONTRACTION, CONTRASTIVE STRESS, CONVERSATION, CREAK/CREAKY VOICE, CULTIVATED.

D–L. DARK L, DENTAL, DEVOICING, DIALOG(UE), DICTION, DIPHTHONG, DIRECT AND INDIRECT SPEECH, DISYLLABLE, DORSAL, DOUBLE ARTICULATION, DOUBLE TALK, DURATION, DURHAM BURR, DYSPHASIA, ECHOLALIA, ELISION, ELOCUTION, EMPHASIS, ENG, EPENTHESIS, EPSILON, ESH, ETH, EUPHONY, FALSETTO, FLAP(PED) R, FOOT, FORTIS, FRICATIVE, GENDERLECT, GENERAL AMERICAN, GENERAL AUSTRALIAN, GENERAL BRITISH, GENERAL NEW ZEALAND, GLIDE, GLOTTALIC, GLOTTAL STOP, GLOTTIS, GREAT VOWEL SHIFT, GRIMM'S LAW, GUTTURAL, HANLEY, HARD AND SOFT, HARD PALATE, HARSH, HEAVY, HEMPL, INDIAN RECOMMENDED PRONUNCIATION, INTERNATIONAL PHONETIC ALPHABET, INTERNATIONAL PHONETIC ASSOCIATION, INTERVOCALIC, INTONATION, INTRUSIVE R, IOTA, JONES (D.), JUNCTURE, KENSINGTON, LABIAL, LABIO-DENTAL, LALLATION, LAMBDACISM, LAMINAL, LAPSUS LINGUAE, LARYNX, LATERAL, LAX, LENIS, LIGATURE, LINKING R, LIQUID, L-SOUNDS.

M–R. MINIMAL PAIR, MODIFIED RP, MONOLOG(UE), MONOPHTHONG, MONOSYLLABLE, MONOTONE, MOUTH, NARROW, NASAL, NATIVE SPEAKER, NEWSPEAK, NOISE, NORTHUMBERLAND/NORTHUMBRIAN BURR, NUCLEUS, ORACY, ORAL APPROACH, ORALISM, ORALITY, ORAL LITERATURE, ORAL TRADITION, ORATORY, ORTHOEPY, OXFORD ACCENT, OXFORD ENGLISH, PALATE, PARASITIC, PASSY, PHARYNX, PHATIC COMMUNION, PHON(A)ESTHESIA, PHONE, PHONEME, PHONEMICS, PHONEMIC TRANSCRIPTION, PHONETIC, PHONETIC NOTATION, PHONETICS, PHONETIC SYMBOLISM, PHONETIC TRANSCRIPTION, PHONIC, PHONIC MEDIUM, PHONICS, PHONOGRAPHY, PHONOLOGY, PHONOTYPE, PITCH, PLOSIVE, POINT OF ARTICULATION, POLYSYLLABLE, POSTVOCALIC, PRONUNCIATION, PROSODY, PSYCHOLINGUISTICS, PUBLIC SCHOOL ACCENT, PUBLIC SCHOOL PRONUNCIATION, PULMONIC, PUNCTUATION, PYGMALION, QUANTITY, QUOTATION, QUOTATION MARKS, QUOTE UNQUOTE, RECEIVED PRONUNCIATION, REPORTED SPEECH, RETROFLEX, R-FUL(L), RHOTACISM, RHOTIC AND NON-RHOTIC, RHYME, RHYTHM, RIME, R-LESS, ROLL[2], R-PRONOUNCING AND NON-R-PRONOUNCING, R-SOUNDS.

S–Z. S(C)HWA, SCOSE, SEMI-CONSONANT, SEMI-VOWEL, SHERIDAN (T.), SHIBBOLETH, SHWA, SIBILANT, SILENT STRESS, SINGSONG, SLUR, SOFT PALATE, SOLILOQUY, SOUND, SOUND SYMBOLISM, SOUTHLAND BURR, -SPEAK, SPEAKING IN TONGUES, SPEECH, SPEECH ACT, SPEECH DEFECT/DISORDER, SPEECH ORGANS, SPEECH PATHOLOGY, SPEECH-READING, SPEECH RECOGNITION

AND COMPREHENSION, SPEECH SYNTHESIS, SPEECH THERAPY, SPEECHWAY, SPELLING PRONUNCIATION, SPOKEN PROSE, STAGE, STAMMERING, STANDARD ACCENT, STOP, STRESS, STRESS-TIMING, STUTTERING, SUFFIX, SUPRASEGMENTAL, SURVEY OF SPOKEN ENGLISH, SWEET, SWEET TALK, SYLLABICATION/SYLLABIFICATION, SYLLABLE, SYLLABLE-TIMING, SYN(A)ERESIS, SYNCOPE, TAP/TAPPED R, TEACHER TALK, TENSE^2, TIP OF THE TONGUE, TONE, TONGUE, TONIC (SYLLABLE), TRACHEA, TRILL/TRILLED R, TRIPHTHONG, TUNE, TWANG, UNDERTONE, UTTERANCE, UVULA, UVULAR R, VELAR, VELARIC, VELUM, VERNER'S LAW, VOCAL C(H)ORDS/FOLDS, VOCAL TRACT, VOICE, VOICE BOX, VOICED AND VOICELESS, VOICE QUALITY, VOWEL, VOWEL GRADATION, VOWEL HARMONY, VOWEL LENGTH, VOWEL LIGATURE, VOWEL QUALITY, VOWEL QUANTITY, VOWEL SHIFT, WEAK VOWEL, WELL-SPOKEN, WHISK(E)Y VOICE, WH-SOUND, WINDPIPE, WORD ACCENT, WORD STRESS, WYLD.

SPEECH ACT. A term used by philosophers of language such as J. L. Austin, in *How to Do Things with Words* (1962), to refer to acts performed by utterances: for example, giving orders, making promises. In saying 'I name this ship the *Queen Mary*', one performs an act of naming; in saying 'I am sorry I offended you', one performs an apology. Such usages are *performatives*, as opposed to *constatives*, which are statements that convey information. *Speech act theory* distinguishes itself from conventional semantic theory by studying the effects of *locutionary acts* (utterances) on speakers and hearers rather than concerning itself with truth value; performatives in particular have no truth value. Speech acts are also known as *illocutionary acts* (that is, acts that occur in speech) and responses by hearers are *perlocutionary acts* (that is, acts that occur through or as a result of speech). There are many different kinds of speech act; John R. Searle (*Speech Acts*, 1979) recognizes five: (1) *Representatives*, where speakers are committed in varying degrees to the truth of the propositions they have uttered: swearing, believing, reporting. (2) *Directives*, where speakers try to get hearers to do something: commanding, requesting, urging. (3) *Commissives*, which commit speakers in varying degrees to courses of action: promising, vowing, undertaking. (4) *Declarations*, whereby speakers alter states of affairs by performing such speech acts as *I now pronounce you man and wife*. (5) *Expressives*, where speakers express attitudes: congratulating, apologizing. In order to be successful, speech acts have to meet certain *felicity conditions*: for example, a marriage ceremony can only be performed by someone with the authority to do so, and with the consent of the parties agreeing to the marriage. Speech acts may be direct or indirect: compare *Shut the door, please* and *Hey, it's cold in here*, both of which

are directives. See LOCUTION, SEMANTICS, UTTERANCE. [LANGUAGE, SPEECH, STYLE].   S.R.

SPEECH DEFECT/DISORDER. See SPEECH PATHOLOGY.

SPEECH ORGANS. See SPEECH.

SPEECH PATHOLOGY, also **speech and language pathology.** The study of disorders of speech. *Speech pathology* (practised by a *speech pathologist*) is the traditional name for the subject in many parts of the world (notably, the US) and reflects the early focus on handicaps of pronunciation in the development of the field. There is currently a trend to emphasize other aspects of linguistic disorder apart from pronunciation (such as grammar and vocabulary), other modalities of language (such as listening, reading, writing, and signing), and other professional activities than the diagnosis of pathology (such as teaching and therapy). For these reasons, there have been moves to replace the term by others thought to reflect more accurately the domain of the subject and the activities of its professionals, such as *language pathology and therapy*. The traditional name, however, retains considerable support. For further discussion, see LANGUAGE PATHOLOGY, SPEECH THERAPY. [LANGUAGE, SPEECH].   D.C.

SPEECH-READING [1890s]. (1) Interpreting speech by means of visual clues that accompany it, such as facial expressions, lip movements, and physical gestures. It may be attempted, more or less systematically, because people's speech is hard to hear or understand, listeners are hearing-impaired, or as part of the everyday processes of conversation, in which non-vocal signals assist comprehension. (2) Another name for *lip-reading*. See PARALANGUAGE. [EDUCATION, SPEECH].   T.MCA.

SPEECH RECOGNITION AND COMPREHENSION. See COMPUTING.

SPEECH SOUND [Perhaps mid-20c]. In phonetics, a general term for a (usually minimal) constituent sound in any flow of speech or in the vocal repertoire of a language; it may or may not be a member of the set of distinctive sounds of that language (a *phoneme*). See PHONE, PHONEME, SOUND. [SPEECH].   T.MCA.

SPEECH SYNTHESIS. See COMPUTING.

SPEECH THERAPY. The British term for the paramedical profession that diagnoses and treats disorders of speech; also known as *speech pathology*, especially in the US. The profession has hotly debated the appropriateness of the term in recent years, because of the implied limitation of their domain to speech (therapists deal also with problems of listening and to some extent of reading, writing, and signing) and also because the term *therapy* seems to exclude other aspects of their role (screening, assessment, and diagnosis). Although widespread dissatisfaction exists, the difficulty of finding a widely acceptable alternative has not been overcome, and the name continues to be the usual way of identifying this group in Britain and several other countries. See ELOCUTION, LANGUAGE PATHOLOGY, PHONETICS, SPEECH PATHOLOGY. [LANGUAGE, SPEECH]. D.C.

SPEECHWAY [Probably early 20c]. A term, especially in US dialectology, for a way of speaking shared by all or most of the people in a place and/or group: *the study of traditional American speechways*. [SPEECH]. T.MCA.

SPEEDHAND. See SHORTHAND.

SPEED-READING. Reading faster than the norm, especially by means of: disciplined skimming and controlled eye movements that take in whole phrases, clauses, and sentences; searching for main ideas and key words rather than giving equal attention to supporting detail; varying one's reading rate and attention to detail according to purpose; sensing the broad pattern of the developing text; and looking for, then concentrating on, the less predictable elements in the text. It is usually easier to speed-read a text that relates to a subject with which one is familiar than one that contains unusual grammatical constructions and specialized terms. See READING. [EDUCATION]. T.MCA.

SPELLER. (1) Someone who spells: *a good/poor speller*. (2) Especially in the US, a book that helps children learn to spell, usually through the provision of lists and exercises. The British equivalent is *spelling book*. (3) An informal name for a computer spelling checker. See SPELLING, SPELLING CHECKER, WEBSTER. [WRITING]. T.MCA.

SPELLING [14c: from Old French *espeller* (Modern *épeler*), probably from Germanic **spellōn*, ancestor of Old English *spel*, *spell* a magical incantation: compare *gospel* ('good spell', good news) and *spiel* extravagant talk (from German *Spiel*). In Middle English, *spelling* was a term for reading books and casting spells, and reading was formerly often called *spelling a book*]. The act, process, or system of relating speech sounds to letters and to the written form of words. The spelling system of an alphabetic language consists of the conventions by which its letters represent sounds and words

(*E-G-G spells egg*) and the way(s) in which words are spelt/spelled (*How d'you spell 'accommodation'—one m or two?*). Phoneticians describe the ideal relationship between sound and alphabetic writing as *phonographic*: letters indicate sounds and sounds indicate letters. As alphabets have evolved, however, they have been adapted in different ways to different languages, and the relationship is sometimes indirect and far from ideal. In French and English, whose orthographic traditions are ancient and intricate, the current situation is complex and often confused.

English spelling. The spelling of English has traditionally been discussed (and often taught) in terms of rules and exceptions. For example, the rule that the *ee* combination in *meet*, *sleep*, etc., stands for a single long /i/ sound, but the fact that the long /i/ sound can be represented in other ways, as in *be*, *sea*, *key*, *quay*, *ski*, *esprit*, *deceit*, *field*, *people*, *amoeba/ameba*, *aeon/eon*, *leave*, *these*. Similarly, there is a rule that *c* before *a/o/u* is hard (*cat*, *cot*, *cut*) but before *e/i* is soft (*cent*, *cite*), with such exceptions as *façade* on the one hand and a common pronunciation of *Celtic* on the other. Word forms that conflict with the phonographic principle are common: (1) Those with aberrant letter values, such as the *a* in *any*, the *e* in *sew*, the *g* in BrE *gaol*, the *gh* in *laugh*, the *l* in *colonel*, the *o* in *woman* and *women*, the *s* in *sugar*, the *x* in *xenophobia*, and the *z* in *schizophrenia*. (2) Those with silent letters, such as the *a* in *head*, the *b* in *thumb*, the *c* in *indict*, the *e* in *height*, the *g* in *foreign*, the *h* in *honest*, the *k* in *knee*, the *n* in *column*, the *p* in *ptarmigan*, the *t* in *castle*, and the *w* in *write*. (3) Those that carry over all or something of their non-English spelling from other languages, such as the *aa* in *bazaar* (from Persian), the *c* in *cello* (from Italian), the *dd* in *eisteddfod* (from Welsh), the *ch* and *y* in *chrysanthemum* (from Latinized Greek), the *chs* in *fuchsia* (from Latinized German), and the *j* in *marijuana* (from Spanish). A Dutch observer of English, Dr Gerard Nolst Trenité (1870-1946), wrote a wry poem on English spelling, entitled 'The Chaos'. It begins:

Dearest creature in creation,
Studying English pronunciation,
I will teach you in my verse
Sounds like corpse, corps, horse and worse,
It will keep you, Susy, busy,
Make your head with heat grow dizzy,
Tear in eye your dress you'll tear.
Queer, fair seer, hear my prayer,
Pray, console your loving poet,
Make my coat look new, dear, sew it!
Just compare heart, hear and heard,
Dies and diet, lord and word,
Sword and sward, retain and Britain,
(Mind the latter, how it's written).
Made has not the sound of bade;

Say, said, pay, paid, laid but plaid.
Now I surely will not plague you
With such words as vague and ague.

Although most of the letters of the alphabet have in isolation an unambiguous sound value, as represented in children's alphabet lists (*A is for Apple*, etc.), in the spelling of many words this correspondence does not apply (*A* is also for *above*, *all*, and *any*). Uncertainties run both ways: in interpreting the sound value of an unfamiliar written form and in determining the spelling of a word from its pronunciation. Learners sometimes mispronounce *gaol* as *gale* or *goal*, *misled* as 'myzled' or 'mizzled', and *archipelago* as 'ar-chip-elago' (compare *lumbago*), and adult native speakers are often unsure how to pronounce such words as *algae, fungi, hegemony,* and *lichen*. Common misspellings include confusion over silent letters (for example, 'figth' for *fight*), doubled consonants ('supprise' for *surprise*, 'accomodate' for *accommodate*, 'commitee' for *committee*, 'dissapear' for *disappear*), and the representation of the weak vowel schwa ('assistent' for *assistant*, 'consistant' for *consistent*, 'burgler' for *burglar*, 'docter' for *doctor*).

A hybrid system. The major elements in the creation of the present-day spelling of English have been the adaptation of the Roman alphabet to serve English, outside influences on that language, and the Great Vowel Shift. When the Roman alphabet was adopted as a medium for writing Old English, it was supplemented to cover sounds not present in Latin. The letters *ash, eth, thorn,* and *wynn* (along with *yogh*, a variant of Roman *g*) have not survived into Modern English, while the consonants *j, v, w* have been recent additions. Old English spelling appears to have represented pronunciation relatively consistently, but the Norman Conquest in 1066 introduced many Norman-French usages that conflicted with Old English tradition, such as the *qu-* in *queen* (Old English *cwēn*). Massive borrowing of Latin and Greek words (often through French or French spelling conventions) as well as the adoption of words from many other languages created a great variety of often conflicting spelling patterns. Many small sets of words with their own inherited patterns of letters emerged, such as the *kn-* group representing Old English *cn-* (such as *knave, knife, know*), the *gu-* group from Norman French (such as *guard, guide, guise*), the *-ence* group from Latin through French (such as *sequence, diligence, residence*), and the group of silent *p-* words from Greek (*pneumonia, pterodactyl, psychology*). The spelling of early loans conforms to what are now traditional 'native' patterns (*beef* from Norman French *boef* is like *keep* from Old English *cēpan*), but later loans have tended to keep their foreign forms (*rendezvous* French, *spaghetti* Italian, *yacht* Dutch). In the 15c the Great Vowel Shift changed the basic sound values of the language (compare Chaucerian with Modern pronunciations) and such ancient Germanic consonant sounds as the *k* and *gh* of *knight* were lost. Spellings often did not change to reflect these phonological developments. At the same time, writers inserted letters in a number of words on erroneous grounds of etymology, such as the *s* in *island* and the *gh* in *delight* by analogy with *isle* and *light*.

Fixed spellings. Before the spread of printing, publishing, and education, spelling reflected differences in individual and regional usage. The *OED* records, from the 9c onward, the following spellings of one word, only the last of which is now accepted: *myrʒe, murʒe, myriʒe, miriʒe, merʒe, meriʒe, murye, muri, murie, mury, miri, mirie, myry, miry, myrie, myri, mirrie, mirry, myrrie, myrry, mirre, meri, merey, merie, mery, merye, merrye, mere, meary, merrie, merry*. In 1586, Elizabeth of England wrote in a letter to James of Scotland *desiar* and *wold* and James in his reply wrote *desyre, desire* and *wolde, woulde*. As a consequence of the spread of printing and publishing (15c onward) and wider education in the vernacular, most common words had acquired their present-day fixed spellings by the 19c, with minor variations between BrE and AmE. Samuel Johnson's *Dictionary of the English Language* (1755) served as an authoritative work of reference. Until the late 18c, when AmE and BrE usage began to diverge, both members of such pairs as *center/centre, color/colour, magic/magick, plow/plough* were in general use. AmE usage followed Noah Webster's dictionary in 1829 in settling on the first in each of these cases. BrE usage, however, having favoured the second in each pair (as in Johnson's dictionary of 1755), continued with all but the *-ick* form as its standard practice, turning them into tokens of national distinctiveness. As a result, the most obtrusive differences between present-day American and British documents are their spellings.

A system of systems. Spellings became fixed in the 18c by a social consensus and not through the recommendation of an Academy or other institution. The result has been at the same time a lessening of variability and a fossilization of forms that came into existence in different times and places. These fossils occur, as it were, in orthographic strata: a vernacular substratum of Anglo-Saxon, Danish, and other Germanic material (and exotic material borrowed so early that it has come to look Germanic), a midstratum of Norman-French material, and a superstratum of nativized Neo-Latin (Latin and

Latinized Greek). The intricacies of this system of systems are so great that it is close to impossible to sort out its sets and subsets neatly, but literate users of English appear, by and large, to be aware (in functional, not etymological, terms) of the main patterns. These are amenable to several descriptions: a two-part contrast of Germanic and Romance (including Latinized Greek and ignoring the exotica); a five-part system of Germanic, French, Latin, Greek, and exotica; or a three-part system in line with the three major traditions of word-formation in English, Germanic, Latin, and Greek (Norman-French patterns variously affecting all three), representing a cline from the everyday to the highly technical. In addition to the core words that belong etymologically to each group there are many words that have crossed over from group to group or been drawn into a group from elsewhere, but what marks a group (among other things) is the distinctive pattern of its spellings, a limited selection of which are:

A vernacular-style spelling. (1) Syllable-initial sets of consonants: *kn-* with silent *k* in *knave, knee, knife, know, knuckle; sk-* in *skate, skill, skunk, sky.* (2) Syllable-final sets of consonants: *-sh* in *bash, mesh, dish, slosh, gush; -tch* in *batch, ketch, ditch, splotch, hutch; -ck* in *back, deck, tick, mock, suck; -le* in *cattle, kettle, sizzle, bottle, nuzzle; -ckle* in *crackle, heckle, sickle, grockle, knuckle; -dge* in *badge, hedge, midge, dodge, nudge.* (3) Prefixes: *a-* in *ablaze, aglow, alive, asleep; be-* in *become, believe, belong.* (4) Suffixes: *-ly* in *brotherly, kindly, lordly, northerly; -ness* in *darkness, lordliness, slimness, wetness; -y* in *sandy, slimy, wishy-washy.*

A Romance-style spelling. (1) Soft *c* and *g* before *e* and *i: cell, gelatin, decision, ginger.* (2) Prefixes (unaltered or assimilated): *ad-* in *admit, adopt, advise, allege, apparent; con-* in *conclude, commensurate, collection;* locative *in-* in *inherent, innate, instinct, investigate;* negative *in-* in *indecisive, inconclusive, ignoble, illiterate, impossible, irreversible; post-* in *post-date, postpone; pre-* in *prescribe, prevent; pro-* in *progress, provide.* (3) Suffixes: *-ity* in *adversity, centrality; -ion* in *addition, admission, condition, eruption, propulsion, segregation.*

A transliterated Greek-style spelling. (1) *Ch* with the sound value /k/: *chaos, archetype, orchid, cholesterol, monarch.* (2) Word-initial silent *m* and *p: mnemonic, psychology, pterodactyl.* (3) Use of *y* rather than *i: analysis, psychology, synthetic, syzygy.* (4) Use of *ph* rather than *f: amphibious, pharmacy, philosophical.* (5) Initial *rh* and medial and final *rrh* as in *rhetoric, rhythm, diarrh(o)ea, h(a)emorrhage, catarrh.*

Spelling and stress. English is a stress-timed language, but its written form does not show where the stress falls in polysyllabic words. The noun and adjective *present*, which are stressed on the first syllable (*présent*), have the same spelling as the verb, which is stressed on the second syllable (*presént*). English can, however, indicate stress when an unstressed vowel is spelt with a syllabic consonant and not a vowel letter: *apple, acre, hadn't,* and *spasm* show that the first syllable, with the vowel *a*, carries the stress, and not the second syllable, in which no vowel letter figures. In the weak syllables of the language (initial in *about, conspire, decide, persuade, remove,* final in *anthem, beggar, metal, phantom, worker*), the vowel is reduced in speech to a central weak quality (schwa) or is represented by a syllabic consonant. Unless one already knows the spelling of such unstressed or weak syllables, it is not easy to guess what it might be: compare *anthem/fathom, medal/model, principal/ principle.* In addition, patterns of stress associated with suffixes change the pronunciation of words without affecting spelling and without any indication of stress shift shown in writing, as in *átom/atómic, eléctric/electrícity, nátional/nationálity, phótograph/photógrapher/ photográphic.* Elsewhere, the stress shift is reflected in the spelling: *maintáin/máintenance, revéal/revelátion.*

Homographs and heterographs. Ambiguity of word form in English has three aspects: (1) *Homonyms,* words that have distinct meanings and are in origin unconnected, but have the same sound and spelling: *tender* as in *tender feelings, a locomotive tender,* and *to tender one's resignation.* In context, however, they seldom trouble the reader. (2) *Homophones* or *heteronyms/ heterographs,* words that have the same pronunciations but are differently spelt, of which there are over 600 sets in English. Phonologically they are *homophones,* orthographically *heterographs: pair/pare/pear, right/rite/write/ wright, cent/scent/sent.* Such forms are made possible by the many alternative sound-symbol correspondences in English. In reading, the different spellings prevent visual ambiguity, but for writing they require an effort of memorization and can lead to confusion, as when *flair* is written as *flare.* (3) *Homographs* or *heterophones,* words that have the same spelling but different pronunciations: *bow* for a violin, *bow* of a ship. These are ambiguous for readers but cause writers little trouble and are of two kinds: related and unrelated pairs. Related pairs include those that shift stress (*an insert/to insért*), introduce voicing (*a house/to house*), give an otherwise mute vowel full value (*aged, agèd*), and involve inflected forms (*bathing,* either from *bath* or *bathe*) and part-of-speech differences (*a live wire/to live nearby*). Unrelated pairs have usually resulted from accidental convergence: *axes* (plural of *ax(e)* or *axis*). Encounters with a member of such a pair can pose problems comparable to an optical illusion that can be interpreted in two ways: *bass, buffet, does, furrier, gill, lower, multiply, routed, sewer, skier, supply, tarry*. Such heterophones are not generally felt to constitute a problem, but some of the commoner pairs are easily misread: *lead, read, tear, wind, wound, bow, row, sow*.

The psychology of literacy. Because of the complexity of English spelling, psychologists, educationists, and linguists have long puzzled over the best way to teach it. It has become a widely held view that rather than seek sound–symbol correspondences, the spelling of words should be seen as forming a constellation of letters whose image is (or can be) more or less imprinted on the mind. Considered from this point of view, English spelling has been called *logographic*: not simply alphabetic, but with some of the qualities of Chinese writing; spellings such as *one* and *who* are read as wholes (gestalts), regardless of the implications of a letter-by-letter reading. Even a simple spelling such as *bad* triggers sound and meaning in a skilled reader's mind not by virtue of the letters alone but by global image, just like *one* and *who*. Proponents of such a 'look and say' approach to reading and writing consider that once these word-gestalts are imprinted on the mind, they can be read and written as easily as the spelling of a more directly phonographic language such as Spanish or Hungarian. Proponents of a 'phonic' approach (relating individual letters to sounds) as well as spelling reformers argue that it is precisely the difficulty of acquiring a separate mental image of so many English spellings that prevents a large number of people from reaching a functional level of literacy. The 'look and say' approach teaches quick recognition of familiar words, but can leave users helpless in the face of unfamiliar words if they do not know how to relate sounds and letters. While it is relatively easy to learn to read and write by a system of regular sound–symbol correspondences, the irregularities of English spelling make it difficult for many to master the unpredictable conventions of the written language.

See entries for individual letters, A–Z, and also ABBREVIATION, ACCENT, ACUTE ACCENT, AMERICAN ENGLISH AND BRITISH ENGLISH (SPELLING), ANGLIC, ASH, CIRCUMFLEX, CUT SPELLING, DIACRITIC, DIGRAPH, ENG, ETH, EYE DIALECT, GRAVE ACCENT, HETERONYM, HETEROPHONE, HOMOGRAPH, HOMONYM, HOMOPHONE, INITIAL, INITIALISM, INITIAL TEACHING ALPHABET, INTERNATIONAL PHONETIC ALPHABET, LETTER[1], LETTER WORD, LITERACY, NOTATION, ORTHOGRAPHY, PHONEME, PITMAN (I.), PITMAN (J.), PRONUNCIATION, PUNCTUATION, READING, RESPELLING, SHAW, SHORTHAND, SIMPLIFIED SPELLING SOCIETY, SPEEDHAND, SPELLING BEE, SPELLING CHECKER, SPELLING PRONUNCIATION, SPELLING REFORM, THORN, TRANSCRIPTION, UMLAUT, USAGE, WYN(N). [LANGUAGE, WORD, WRITING].

C.U., T.MCA.

Cummings, D. W. 1988. *American English Spelling.* Baltimore & London: Johns Hopkins University Press.

Gimson, A. C. 1980. *An Introduction to the Pronunciation of English*, 3rd edition. London: Edward Arnold.

Moseley, D., & Nicol, C. 1986. *The A.C.E. (Aurally Coded English) Spelling Dictionary.* Wisbech: Learning Development Skills.

Pitman, J., & St John, J. 1969. *Alphabets and Reading.* London: Pitman.

Scragg, D. G. 1974. *A History of English Spelling.* Manchester: University Press.

Vallins, G. H. 1954. *Spelling.* 2nd edition revised by D. G. Scragg, 1965. London: André Deutsch.

Wijk, Axel. 1959. *Regularized English.* Stockholm: Almqvist & Wiksells.

SPELLING BEE, also **spelling competition**. A contest or game in which players compete in the spelling of words whose difficulty increases as the game progresses, until one person is left as the winner. See SPELLING, WORD GAME. [WORD, WRITING].

T.MCA.

SPELLING CHECKER. Also **speller, spellcheck(er)**. A computer program that verifies the spelling in a text. It is often an adjunct to a word processor or to desktop publishing, and is usually based on the headword list of a published dictionary. Major word-processing programs such as *WordPerfect, WordStar 2000, Microsoft Word*, and *Multimate* contain a spelling checker, or one may be bought separately, such as *Turbo Lightning* or *Random House Proofreader*. Typically, such programs identify every word not in their source list. They detect finger slips and misspellings, but not the mind slips that confuse homonyms or violate grammatical agreement: that is, they detect non-words such as 'ther' for *there*, but not wrong words such as *their* for *there*. A more ambitious program may also make corrections, changing typed words which are not in its list to the closest match it has. When dealing with the text of dictation, phonetic representations are useful for guessing the word intended, and are incorporated into programs for people typing from phone lines (such as airline reservations clerks). Compare GRAMMAR CHECKER, STYLE CHECKER. See PROOF-READING, SPELLING. [TECHNOLOGY, WRITING].

M.L.

SPELLING PRONUNCIATION. Pronunciation based on the spelling of a word rather than on conventional speech, such as *often* pronounced with /t/. In a language such as Spanish, the patterns of whose speech and spelling correlate closely, the concept is unnecessary, but in English, in which correlations between spoken and written forms are often weak, the term labels a common, though often unevenly developed, phenomenon: for example, a number of English words that begin with *h*, such as *honour, honest, humble, human*, were borrowed from French with no /h/ in their pronunciation. While some, such as *honour* and *honest*, continue to be pronounced without /h/, others, such as *humble* and *human*, are now pronounced with /h/ to fit their spelling (except in such entirely aitchless varieties as Cockney); in standard BrE pronunciation, the /h/ is pronounced in *herb*; in AmE, it is not. In some cases, spelling pronunciation triumphs over erstwhile common pronunciations: in general usage, *waistcoat* is no longer pronounced 'weskit'. In others, when a word has been learnt only through reading, a spelling pronunciation may be used until the error is discovered: for example, that the *ch* of *archipelago* is pronounced /k/, not /tʃ/, and its closing syllables do not rhyme with *sago*. Spelling pronunciations can be invoked on an ad-hoc basis, to contrast words that are otherwise homophones: for example, by saying 'stay-shun-AH-ry' for *stationary* and 'stay-shun-ER-y' for *stationery*. Many place-names, especially in England, have both traditional and spelling pronunciations, such as *Cirencester*, whose pronunciations range from 'Sissiter' to 'Siren-sester'; *Gloucester*, however, perhaps because it is better known, has no spelling pronunciation; it is only 'Gloster'. See PRONUNCIATION, SPELLING. [SPEECH, WRITING].

T.MCA., C.U.

SPELLING REFORM. The planned alteration of the established alphabetic writing system of a language so as to remove or reduce elements taken to be sources of confusion and difficulty in learning and using that system. Spelling reform does not usually include such changes as the substitution of one writing system for another (as, for example, in 1928, when Arabic script was replaced by Roman for the writing of Turkish), changes in systems of non-alphabetic signs (as with the reform of Chinese characters begun in the People's Republic of China in 1955), or the readoption of earlier individual spellings (such as, in English, the spelling *fantasy* after some three centuries of *phantasy*, there being no general substitution of *f* for *ph* throughout the language).

Regulation and reform. Before the advent of printing in the 15c, European spelling conventions were not usually rigid and often reflected writers' accents and preferences. The concept of 'correct writing' (*orthography*) emerged partly because printers sought uniformity and partly from a Renaissance interest in word forms, but it was only gradually, over centuries, that the availability and example of dictionaries and the pressures of formal systems of education led individuals to strive to observe the conventions of print. Systematic changes in spelling have generally been the responsibility of language academies or government departments. Academies have been founded for Italian (1582), French (1634), Spanish (1713), and various other languages (but excluding English), to act among other things as authorities on orthography, and have strongly influenced the orthographic development of the languages over which they have presided. For example, the 1740 edition of the dictionary of the Académie française altered the spelling of 36% of French words, chiefly replacing mute *s* by acute and circumflex accents: for example, *estoit* by *étoit*, *boiste* by *boîte*. Similarly, in 1959, the Real Academia de la Lengua Española issued its *Neuvas Normas de Ortografía* (*New Norms of Orthography*), recommending that silent initial letters should be dropped: *psicología* could, for example, thenceforth be written *sicología*.

The German-speaking countries held a conference in 1901 to harmonize their spelling and eliminate redundant *h* in such words as *Thier, Thor, Thür*. In the Soviet Union after the 1917 Revolution, the new authorities removed four redundant letters of the Russian alphabet and curtailed the use of a fifth. In Malaysia and Indonesia in 1972, the two governments acted jointly to harmonize their previously British- and Dutch-derived writing systems. In the Low Countries in 1883, Dutch and Flemish spelling were harmonized, and in 1947 some double vowels were simplified and *sch* was replaced by *s*, *nederlandsch* for example becoming *nederlands*. In the 20c, spelling reform has most often been implemented by edict and through the schools. Government publications use the new forms and children grow up using them as the only forms they have been taught, while many adults continue with those they learned in childhood; as a result, in such situations, people's spelling may indicate their age group. Depending on the culture of the language and the political circumstances of such a change, reform may be smoothly adopted or encounter resistance; sometimes even a modest proposal for reform may be vigorously opposed. Successful reform usually presupposes either a very powerful central government with a strong ideological programme or agreement that existing spelling conventions are unsatisfactory.

Reforming English spelling. The orthography of English has never been subject to systematic official reform, and has seen few changes in 300 years. There appear to be two reasons for this: (1) *A hybrid orthography.* Written English emerged from the Middle Ages as a combined adaptation of two very distinct spelling systems, those of Old English and Norman French. Added to these disparate elements were important elements from other languages: first Scandinavian, then Latin and, with the Renaissance, Greek, to be followed in later centuries by further elements from other languages around the world. This mix made the phonographic basis of writing in English (the link between its sounds and its written symbols) less immediately apparent, and militated against the possibility of assimilating all the ingredients of the language into a phonographically consistent whole. The resulting diversity (and often confusion) were increased by the effects of changes in pronunciation, especially the Great Vowel Shift in the 15c, in response to which there were few changes in spelling.

(2) *The absence of an Academy.* No authority created or approved by the state took an interest in the writing systems, despite calls in the 17c and 18c for the establishment of an English Academy. The alternative institutions that established themselves were dictionaries, for BrE primarily Samuel Johnson's (from 1755) and for AmE primarily Noah Webster's (from 1828). Johnson's aim, however, was not to regularize but to 'adjust' what he saw as 'unsettled and fortuitous'; he was guided by etymology and usage, not by the phonographic principle of 'one letter, one sound', and considered that many irregularities were simply 'inherent in our tongue'. His intent was not to reform the writing system but, through the authority of his dictionary, to promote the notion of 'correct' spellings. Noah Webster was in part guided by the phonographic principle in making his reforms, and at one time advocated a radical break with BrE orthography; the conservative pressures of publishing, however, ensured that only a few of his proposed spellings were propagated (and increasingly widely accepted), and these constitute most of the characteristic present-day AmE forms: see AMERICAN ENGLISH AND BRITISH ENGLISH. Webster has been the only reformer whose ideas have had a lasting effect, and even that was limited and slow to spread.

Amenders and reformers. Many linguists and educationists have been concerned with ways of systematizing written English. Although there could be no reform before spelling became more or less fixed, many of the ideas that have dominated the spelling-reform debate were already under discussion in the 16c. For example, in 1568, Sir Thomas Smith called for consistency within an extended alphabet, including letters and diacritical marks from Old English and Greek; in 1569, John Hart called for the spelling of words strictly by their sound; in 1582, Richard Mulcaster appealed for stability based on consistency, analogy, and custom, and the recollection that 'letters were inuented to expresse sounds'. However, the schoolmaster Edmond Coote probably contributed most to the settling of English spelling in its present form through the 54 editions of his handbook *The English Schoole-maister* (from 1595 to 1737), which tended to avoid some of the redundant letters that were previously common.

Alexander Gil in 1619 and Charles Butler in 1633 advocated phonographic systems with the retention of Old English letters or the introduction of new letters (with some variation to mark etymology and distinguish homophones), but there was little serious advocacy of reform until 1768, when Benjamin Franklin assessed the needs of learners and poor spellers and devised an alphabet that did not use the letters *c, j, q, w, x, y* (which he considered superfluous) and introduced new characters for the vowels in *hot, up* and the consonants in *the, thin, -ing, she*. The scheme did not, however, receive much attention. A major 19c innovator was Isaac Pitman, who moved from the invention of his phonetic shorthand to the development of an extended alphabet called *phonotype* (see entry) or *phonotypy*. His emphasis on the need to encourage the education of the poor was echoed in Britain in the 1870 Education Act and led to a call by the National Union of Elementary Teachers in 1876 for a Royal Commission to consider spelling reform. The late 1870s saw the founding of spelling-reform associations on both sides of the Atlantic, whose memebers included Tennyson and Darwin. Such eminent philologists as Henry Sweet and Alexander Ellis in the UK and Francis March in the US experimented with reformed alphabets. In the 1880s, many students of the new science of phonetics were interested in the development of a phonetic alphabet not only for academic purposes but also as a possible precursor of a reformed spelling system for English.

New Spelling. At the beginning of the 20c, the cause of spelling reform was taken up for a time by the US President Theodore Roosevelt and sponsored by the industrialist and philanthropist Andrew Carnegie. In 1908, the British *Simplified Spelling Society* (*SSS*) was founded, chiefly with the aim of devising a reformed writing system based on the Roman alphabet, in the belief that such a development would stand a better chance of acceptance than a new alphabet. In 1948, the phonetician Daniel Jones and dialectologist Harold Orton published a system called *New Spelling*, the recommended orthography of the SSS, of which the following is a specimen:

We rekwier dhe langgwej as an instrooment; we mae ausloe study its history. Dhe presens ov unpronounst leterz, three or for diferent waez ov reprezenting dhe saem sound, three or for uesez ov dhe same leter: aul dhis detrakts from dhe value ov a langgwej az an instrooment.

New Spelling was accepted in 1956, with small amendments, by the *American Simplified Spelling Association*, was further developed and computerized by Edward Rondthaler in New York (1986), and was revised in the 1980s, its most recent form being published in the Society's Pamphlet No. 12, *New Spelling 90* (1991). It also provided the phonographic analysis on which Sir James Pitman based his *initial teaching alphabet* (*i.t.a.*) (1959). To date, however, the system has had little impact on the English-using world, and there appears currently to be little general interest in reform, and considerably less interest among langauge scholars than a century or even half a century ago.

A new alphabet. There have from time to time been attempts at radical change that go well beyond spelling reform proper into the creation and promotion of entirely new alphabets. Most prominently, a bequest from the dramatist and social reformer George Bernard Shaw financed a public competition in 1957-8 for the design of a new alphabet that would have at least 40 letters and no digraphs or diacritics. The winner of this competition, Kingsley Read (from Warwickshire in England), produced an alphabet that is utterly unlike Roman and has letters of four types: *tall* (those with ascenders), *deep* (those with descenders), *short* (those with neither ascenders nor descenders), and *compound* (combining basic symbols). In visual effect, the *Shaw Alphabet*, *Shaw's Alphabet*, or the *Shavian Alphabet*, as it is variously known, looks rather like the scripts used for the Dravidian languages of South India, with many gently curving characters. A bi-alphabetic edition of Shaw's play *Androcles and the Lion* was published by Penguin Books in 1962 to demonstrate the old and new orthographies side by side, the texts running parallel on facing pages. In it the Shaw Alphabet, though alien in its effect, proves markedly more compact and economical than the traditional system. To date, however, it has had no significant impact on the English-using world.

The contemporary situation. Recent thinking among spelling reformers stresses gradual rather than radical change, so as to ensure continuity of literacy, enable old and new to coexist, and limit the impact and scope of any one stage in reform: that is, evolution rather than revolution. Harry Lindgren in Australia, for example, proposes a multi-stage reform programme, each stage regularizing the spelling of a single phoneme. As a first stage, he suggests that the traditional short-*e* sound be written as *e*, as in *eny* 'any', *sed* 'said', *agenst* 'against', *bery* 'bury', *frend* 'friend', *hed* 'head'. Alternatively, rather than taking a rigid schema of sound–symbol correspondences as a starting-point, some reformers adopt a functional approach, asking what spellings would best suit the needs and abilities of users. One proposal suggests a first stage confined to removing the digraph *gh* in *though*, *caught*, etc. In addition, some reformers argue that by studying kinds of misspelling it is possible to identify the greatest difficulties among current spellings, and concentrate on regularizing them alone. The *Cut Spelling* proposal, for example, is based on the observation that many troublesome spellings involve letters that are superfluous in terms of pronunciation, and suggests that these be omitted, achieving greater ease of use and at the same time considerable economy of space (see CUT SPELLING).

Arguments about spelling reform. The idea of reforming the spelling of English has long been controversial, with arguments about the relative value of tradition and literacy, the practicalities of introducing change, and the specific changes that might be made. Opponents of reform often describe the rich variety of present spellings as a heritage not to be lightly discarded, while reformers attach priority to the actual or perceived needs of contemporary users. Orthographic conservationists point out that present spellings often reflect the history of words and their links across groups of words and with words in other languages, while reformers present a counter-list of historically inconsistent spellings and cite arbitrary variations both within English and from the spellings of other European languages. Conservationists object that radically changed spellings would seem alien to the older generation, while texts in the old spelling would seem alien to the young; the change-over would also, they say, create uncertainty and cost a great deal. Reformers reply that the present system has already alienated many, the spelling of earlier writers has in in any case been updated in various ways, and reform could potentially save money. Anti-reformers fear that interfering with an ancient, delicately balanced system might make learning not easier but more difficult, while many who have taught regularized spelling (such as teachers of the *initial teaching alphabet*) have argued that a more regular system is easier to learn. Resistance to the idea of change is often provoked by the disturbingly unfamiliar appearance of radically reformed spellings, such as *kof* and *skool* for *cough* and *school*, which for many people are both aesthetically displeasing and suggest semi-literacy.

Among the practical objections to spelling reform is the problem of coordinating reform worldwide in so widely used a language as English, as well as the fact that there is no consensus among reformers on the system to be introduced. Anti-reformers argue in particular that, if English spelling is directly to represent pronunciation, there is no serious answer to the question: if reform is to be phonographic, on which accent of English should it be based? To these points reformers reply that the traditional orthography of English is quite simply out of date and is demonstrably difficult both to learn and to use. Literacy, they maintain, is a precondition for individual, national, and international prosperity, and the present spelling system of the world's foremost language hinders the wider and fuller achievement of literacy in that language. As regards consensus and accent, they insist on the necessity of the major English-using communities getting together and discussing the problem, to find out what bases of agreement exist and to seek workable compromises, especially with regard to the phonemic analysis on which any international system might be built. Currently, there does not appear to be anything close to a meeting of minds in such matters.

See ANGLIC, CUT SPELLING, ELLIS, HEMPL, INITIAL TEACHING ALPHABET, INTERNATIONAL PHONETIC ASSOCIATION, JOHNSON, JONES, MARCH, ORTHOGRAPHY, ORTON, PITMAN (I.), PITMAN (J.), ROYAL SOCIETY, SHAW, SHORTHAND, SIMPLIFIED SPELLING SOCIETY, SPELLING, SWEET, WEBSTER. [WRITING]. C.U., T.MCA.

Abercrombie, David. 1981. 'Some Orthographic Experiments of the Last Four Centuries', in R. E. Asher & J. A. Henderson (eds.), *Towards a History of Phonetics*. Edinburgh: University Press.
Follick, M. 1965. *The Case for Spelling Reform*. London: Pitman.
Haas, W. (ed.) 1969. *Alphabets for English*. Manchester: University Press.
Pitman, J., & St John, J. 1969. *Alphabets and Reading*. London: Pitman.
Rondthaler, E., & Lias, E. J. (eds.). 1986. *Dictionary of American Spelling*. New York: American Language Academy (originally Simpler Spelling Association, then Phonemic Spelling Council, then American Language Academy; currently American Literacy Council).
Wijk, Axel. 1959. *Regularized English*. Stockholm: Almqvist & Wiksell.
Zachrisson, R. E. 1932. *Anglic*. Uppsala: University Press. Also College Park, Md.: McGrath Publishing (reprint 1970).

SPELT, full form *Society of Pakistani English Language Teachers*. A non-governmental organization set up in 1984 to improve the standard of English teaching and learning in Pakistan. It is a registered voluntary body with a national network in major centres. It provides a forum for teachers of English, disseminates current ideas and developments in ELT, provides in-service courses, seminars, and workshops, and develops national and regional resource centres. SPELT has monthly academic sessions and an annual seminar with international participation. A one-year Practical Teacher Training course (now recognized by the Royal Society of Arts) and a newsletter were introduced in 1985. See PAKISTAN. [ASIA, EDUCATION, MEDIA]. T.MCA.

SPENSER, Edmund [1552?-1599]. English poet, probably born in London, son of a clothmaker from Lancashire. He was educated as a 'poor boy' at Merchant Taylors' School in London and as a 'sizar' (a poorer student who did menial duties) at Cambridge, where he gained a wide knowledge of languages. In 1580, he was appointed secretary to Lord Grey of Wilton, Lord Deputy for Ireland. He grew attached to Ireland, but disliked its wildness and lack of law, and was involved in the plantation of English settlers in the province of Munster. His tract *A View of the Present State of Ireland* (1595-6) argued for firm measures in controlling the island, with gentleness only for those who submitted to English rule. He was granted considerable land and property, including Kilcolman Castle, County Cork (*c*.1588), and it was there that he completed his major literary work. His neighbour in Ireland, Sir Walter Raleigh, appears to have taken him to London to present the first sections of the epic *The Faerie Queene* to Elizabeth. In 1598, he was made Sheriff of Cork, but in the same year a rebellion broke out and his castle was burned. He returned to London with his family and with official letters about the state of Ireland, and died early the following year, perhaps as a result of his experiences.

Spenser was criticized in his own day for adopting an archaic style ('Spenser, in affecting the Ancients, writ no language': Ben Jonson, *Timber or Discoveries*, 1641), but has been recognized since then as a major influence on the language of English poetry. In imitating Chaucer, he extended the literary life of many Middle English archaisms, such as *dight* to adorn, *eke* also, *stour* conflict, *unneath* hardly, *whilom* formerly, and retained obsolete inflectional affixes for metrical purposes as in *eyen* eyes, *muchell* great, *to worken* to work, and especially in past participles with the *y-* prefix (*yclad*, *ywrought*). The liberal use of inverted word order ('Yet I am glad that here I now in safety am') helped with his elaborate rhyming patterns: see SPENSERIAN STANZA. Spenser's deliberately 'old' language served the purposes of pastoral in *The Shepheardes Calender* (1579), where it is often indistinguishable from ongoing dialect, and was used to evoke an idealized chivalric past in *The Faerie Queene* (1590–6), a work which served to vindicate Protestantism and glorify England. His poetry is full of etymological quibbles, puns, and verbal allusions which contribute to the patterning of this long allegorical poem in praise of Gloriana (Queen Elizabeth). Through later imitators and the Romantic poets, his language became a main source of English poetic diction. William Butler Yeats talked of his 'powerful and subtle language' and admiration of Spenser's verbal artistry has led to his being called 'the poet's poet'. See index. [BIOGRAPHY, EUROPE, HISTORY, LITERATURE]. N.E.O., T.MCA.

SPENSERIAN STANZA [1800s]. The form of stanza devised by Edmund Spenser for *The Faerie Queene* (1590–6), probably influenced by the *rhyme royal* used by Chaucer in *Troylus and Criseyde*, a seven-line stanza that rhymes *ababbcc*. The Spenserian stanza consists of eight lines in iambic pentameter followed by an alexandrine (a six-foot iambic line), rhyming *ababbabcc*, as:

> She also dofte her heavy habergeon,
> Which the faire feature of her limbs did hyde,
> And her well plighted frock, which she did won
> To tucke about her short, when she did ryde,
> She low let fall, that flowd from her lanck syde
> Downe to her foot, with carelesse modestee.
> Then to them all she plainly was espyde,
> To be a woman wight, unwist to bee,
> The fairest woman wight, that ever eye did see.

Other poets have written in Spenserian stanza, notably Keats in 'The Eve of Saint Agnes' and Shelley in 'Adonais'. See SPENSER, STANZA. [LITERATURE]. R.C.

SPLIT INFINITIVE. [Late 19c, as in: 'Are our critics aware that Byron is the father of their *split infinitive*? "To slowly trace", says the noble poet, "the forest's shady scene"' (*Academy*, 3 April, 1897)]. Also formerly **cleft infinitive**. A prescriptive term for an infinitive phrase such as *to cut* or *to enjoy* that has been opened up ('split', 'cleft') by the insertion of a word or phrase (especially an adverb), as in: '*to sharply cut* the federal deficit'; 'How *to actually enjoy* February'; 'encouraging more people *to, for example, park* their cars'; '*to one day do* my own elephant

study'. Long a major bone of contention among teachers, grammarians, and commentators on style and usage, the split infinitive in the last two decades has become a matter of minor concern. Many younger speakers and writers split or leave intact their infinitives without being aware that the matter was ever controversial. Probably the most famous split infinitive in the language is *to boldly go* (*where no man has gone before*), occurring in the opening voice-over of the US television series *Star Trek* (1960s), and subsequently often parodied. For further discussion of the controversy, see USAGE GUIDANCE AND CRITICISM. In addition, see DESCRIPTION AND PRESCRIPTION, INFINITIVE, USAGE. [GRAMMAR, STYLE, USAGE]. T.MCA.

SPOKEN PROSE [1959: coined by David Abercrombie]. A semi-technical term for prose presented as speech. Such prose is the spoken outcome of the lines of actors, the texts of public speakers, and the scripts of presenters on stage, screen, radio, and television. The term distinguishes all such speech from spontaneous, unscripted conversation. In 1957, T. S. Eliot argued (*On Poetry and Poets*) that the division of language into verse and prose was not enough; the need was for verse, prose, and 'ordinary speech'. Abercrombie proposed a fourfold division: verse, prose to be read silently, prose to be spoken aloud, and conversation:

Prose is essentially language organized for *visual* presentation. Eliot's point was that it is just as artificial to make characters on the stage speak prose as to make them speak verse, and the latter needs no more defending than the former. But there is another point to be made from what he said. Most people believe that *spoken prose* . . . is at least not far removed, when well done, from the conversation of real life. . . . But the truth is that nobody speaks at all like the characters in any novel, play or film. Life would be intolerable if they did; and novels, plays or films would be intolerable if the characters spoke as people do in life. Spoken prose is far more different from conversation than is usually realized (*Studies in Phonetics and Linguistics*, 1965).

Spoken prose is descended from drama, lecturing, and disputation, the recitation of more or less memorized public addresses, and the arguments of lawyers and orators whose craft originated in ancient Greece. Conversation is distinct from it, but the use of spoken prose has influenced educated and formal spoken usage. Speakers often use the same devices whether they are speaking spontaneously, using a script, or working from notes. See PROSE. [SPEECH, STYLE]. T.MCA.

SPONDEE [14c: from French *spondée*, Latin *spondeus*, from Greek *spondeîos poús* the foot of libation, referring to its use in melodies accompanying libations in classical times]. A metrical foot of two syllables, both long in quantitative metre, as in Latin, both stressed in accentual metre (– –), as in English. The normal stress of monosyllabic adjective and noun in English is spondaic: *good news, fine day*. In verse, the heavy effect of the spondee can be used to suggest weariness or depression, as in the following line from Tennyson, with its alternation of iambs and spondees:

∪ –   –   –   ∪ –   – –
The long / day wanes; / the slow / moon climbs.

The associated adjective is *spondaic*. See FOOT, METRE/METER, SCANSION. [LITERATURE]. R.C.

SPOONERISM [1890s: from the name of the Reverend W. A. Spooner (1844–1930), Dean and Warden of New College, Oxford, and *-ism* as in *euphemism*]. The transposition of the initial sounds of words, as in *ket of seas* (set of keys), *mit wunday* (Whit Monday). The eponymous Spooner was reputed to make errors of this type, and a number of utterances are quoted as 'original spoonerisms': *a well-boiled icicle* (a well-oiled bicycle), *a scoop of Boy Trouts* (a troop of Boy Scouts), and *You have hissed all my mystery lectures and tasted a whole worm*. It seems likely that these transpositions were exaggerated inventions by his students. In real life, transposed sounds often have some phonetic resemblance to one another, as in *slow and sneet* (snow and sleet). In addition, they can affect vowels, as in *cuss and kiddle* (kiss and cuddle) and the final sounds of words and syllables: *hass or grash* (hash or grass). They can also affect larger items, such as syllables and words: *mouth in her food* (food in her mouth), *to gap the bridge* (to bridge the gap). Such errors provide evidence of how speech is planned and produced. See SLIP OF THE TONGUE. [LANGUAGE, STYLE]. J.M.A.

SPREAD. See LAYOUT.

SPRUNG RHYTHM [1877]. A term used by the British poet Gerard Manley Hopkins to describe his innovative verse, which he derived from the strong-stressed metres of Old English poetry. His metre is different from the regular 'running rhythm' of alternating stresses and goes in 'jumps' of various occurrence. Each metrical foot begins with a stressed syllable that may be followed by one or more unstressed syllables, or may itself occupy the whole foot:

No worst, there is none. Pitched past pitch of grief,
More pangs will, schooled at forepangs, wilder wring.

Verse in sprung rhythm can be compelling and emphatic, especially when strong stresses appear in sequence. Hopkins used alliteration, assonance, and compound words to increase the effect.

Ezra Pound, T. S. Eliot, and other 20c poets have used it to vary the structure of free verse. See RHYTHM, VERSE. [LITERATURE]. R.C.

SRANAN, also **Sranan Tongo, Taki-Taki**. The major English-based creole of Surinam in South America, used as a lingua franca by the coastal population and influential among speakers of Ndjuka and Saramaccan. See BAJAN, SURINAM(E). [AMERICAS, VARIETY]. L.D.C.

SRI LANKA [1970s: from the Sanskrit and Sinhala name for the island, *Lanka*, preceded by the honorific *sri*. The Tamil equivalent is *Ilam/Eelam* or *Ilankai*. Arab traders used the name *Serendip/Serendib*. From the title of the Persian fairy tale 'The Three Princes of Serendip', the writer Horace Walpole in 1754 formed the noun *serendipity*, the faculty of happily discovering one thing while diligently looking for another, something that came naturally to the heroes of the tale. Both *Serendip* and *Ceylon* (the name used throughout the British colonial period) derive from Sanskrit *Simhala-dvipa* island of the Sinhala, a people known variously in English as *Sinhalese, Singhalese, Cingalese*, and *Ceylonese*]. Official title: Sinhala *Sri Lanka Janarajaya*, English *Democratic Socialist Republic of Sri Lanka*. A country of South Asia, and member of the Commonwealth. Capital: Colombo (or, more accurately since 1983, its suburb Sri-Jayawardenapura). Currency: the rupee (100 cents). Economy: mixed. Population: 16.6m (1988), 19.8m (projection for 2000). Ethnicity: 74% Sinhalese, 18% Tamils, 7% Moors/Muslims, 1% Burghers (Eurasians), Veddahs (aboriginals), and Malays. Religions: 69% Buddhist, 15% Hindu, 8% Christian, 8% Muslim. Languages: Sinhala, Tamil (both official, national languages), and English (often used in government and spoken by some 10% of the nation, including especially the Burghers). Education: primary 75%, secondary 30%, tertiary *c.*10%, literacy *c.*65%.

The mission schools. The first Europeans to visit the island were the Portuguese in 1505, who built a fort at Colombo. The Dutch forced them out in 1658, but failed to gain control of the whole island. The British defeated them in 1796 and established the colony of Ceylon in 1802, to which Tamil labourers were brought from south India to work on tea and coffee plantations. Ceylon became a Dominion of the British Empire in 1948 and the independent republic of Sri Lanka in 1972. Long-standing tensions between the majority Sinhalese and the minority Tamil community (concentrated in the north-east) led to civil strife in the late 1980s; many Tamils have sought to set up their own state. The history of English in Sri Lanka is closely linked with its communal problems. In 1799, the Revd James Cordiner went as chaplain to the British garrison in Colombo, becoming in due course principal of all the schools in the settlement. In 1827, the Christian Institution was set up by Sir Edward Barnes, the aim of which was 'to give a superior education to a number of young persons who from their ability, piety and good conduct were likely to prove fit persons in communicating a knowledge of Christianity to their countrymen'. Until about 1831, the teaching of English was in the hands of missionaries; when the government took control, there were 235 Protestant schools in the island, and until 1886 Christian schools and colleges predominated.

English in Sri Lanka. One result of the long-established tradition of such institutions was the emergence of two broad and at times hostile educated classes: an English-using and largely Christian minority and a Sinhala-educated majority, most of whom were Buddhists. Until 1948, three languages were used side by side, English, Sinhala, and Tamil. English served as the language of administration, the generally desired language of higher education, and a link language between the communities. In 1956, however, a socialist government replaced English with Sinhala, unleashing in the process a succession of riots that has not yet come to an end. The Sinhala-only policy resulted in 'the sharp cleavage between Sinhalese and Tamils, most of whom are monolingual in their own tongues and therefore have no means of communication with members of the other community' (Rajiva Wijesinha, *An Anthology of Contemporary Sri Lankan Poetry in English*, Colombo, The British Council, 1988). In recent years, a three-language policy has been proposed that provides for equality among Sinhala, Tamil, and English, and to some extent seeks to restore the position of English, whose role in the community was greatly reduced from the 1960s to the 1980s. English in Sri Lanka, sometimes referred to as *Lankan English*, has a range of subvarieties based on proficiency in its use and the language background of its users. In general terms, it is a subvariety of South Asian English, sharing many features with IndE. Sri Lanka has a number of daily and weekly English-language newspapers, including *Ceylon Daily News*, *Ceylon Observer*, *The Island*, *Sun*, and *Sunday Weekend*. There is a small body of creative writing, Sri Lankan prose writers including J. Vijayatunga, Punyakante Wijenaike, James Goonewardene, Raja Proctor, Rajiva Wijesinha, and Savimalee Karunaratne. Poets include George Keyt, Patrick Fernando, Lakdasa Wikkramasinha, Yasmine Goonaratne, Ashley Halpe, and Anne Ranasinghe. See ENGLISH, INDIAN ENGLISH[1],

SINHALA/SINHALESE, SOUTH ASIAN BROADCASTING, SOUTH ASIAN ENGLISH, TAMIL, TESL. [ASIA, NAME, VARIETY]. W.D., B.B.K., T.MCA.

STAGE [13c in general terms: from Old French *estage* (Modern *étage*), from Popular Latin **staticum* a standing-place, from *stare/statum* to stand]. The theatrical profession, metonymically named from the platform on which they usually stand to perform a play. The stage became an organized calling in England in the late 16c, with the establishment of permanent theatres. The *sharers* who divided the profits of the company often became prosperous, Shakespeare buying property in London and Stratford. Actors, however, were disliked by the authorities and classed as 'rogues and vagabonds' if they did not have royal or noble protection. For centuries, actors (and after 1660 actresses) were adulated by theatre-goers and despised by 'respectable' society. By the mid-19c, however, leading figures were accepted in literary and fashionable circles and Henry Irving's knighthood in 1895 confirmed the improved status of the profession. Stage usage that has extended into the language at large includes such stock phrases as *behind the scenes, the limelight, the show must go on, a stage whisper, taking one's cue*. There is also a popular sense of a register peculiar among actors: rhetorical, egocentric, and sprinkled with vocatives like *darling* and *laddie*. While such a style may have been affected in the 19c and earlier 20c, it is rare today. A significant aspect of theatrical usage has been accents and usages adopted on stage by actors unable to handle them well or constrained to exaggerate them. As a result, such comments are often made as '*Bejabers*' is stage Irish—no real Irish person says things like that. See DRAMA, IRISH ENGLISH, MUMMERSET, PLAY, THEATRE/THEATER. [LITERATURE, SPEECH, STYLE]. R.C., T.MCA.

STAMMERING. See STUTTERING.

STANDARD [12c: from Old French *estandard* (Modern *étendard*), Medieval Latin *standard(i)um, standardus*, from *extendere* to stretch out, and *-ard* as in *placard*: often associated with such ideas as *taking a stand, standing fast* (compare the Middle High German *stanthart*, suggesting 'stand hard')]. A prestigious and uniform variety of a language: *the literary standard, standard English*. The application of the term to language dates from the early 19c, when the idea of standard shapes, sizes, and measures and of commercial and manufacturing standards had become commonplace because of the Industrial Revolution. Since then, the concepts of a *standard language* (one with agreed norms and conventions) and a *language standard* (a level below which a 'cultivated' language should not fall) have been closely associated. For some, the expressions are two sides of the same linguistic coin: the standard is and should be the highest and best form of a language. For others, there is no necessary tie between the two: a standard language is an averaging-out of differences, neither higher nor better than any other variety of a language, and used with particular ends in mind. For others still, uncertainty may lead to ambivalence and confusion about the relative merit of standards and dialects. Dialect, colloquial usage, and slang are often lumped together, with greater or less discrimination, as *non-standard*, *substandard*, or *deviant* forms when judged against a dominant form that is taught in all schools and used by all major public and private institutions.

The king's standard. The earliest recorded use of the word was in the phrase *Battle of the Standard*, the name given to a defeat inflicted by the English on the Scots at Cowton Moor in Yorkshire in 1138. The English 'standard' in that battle was a ship's mast mounted on a mobile base, on which various flags were flown. When Richard of Hexham reported on the contest, he quoted a Latin couplet written for the occasion, which said in translation that this device was a standard because 'it was there that valour took its stand to conquer or die'. For many centuries afterwards, the primary meaning of *standard* was a flag or other object raised as a rallying point for armies and fleets: 'Then in the name of God and all these rights, Aduance your Standards, draw your willing Swords' (Shakespeare, *Richard III*, 5. 3).

A second meaning emerged in the 15c, referring (perhaps by extension from the flag) to a royal norm of weights and measures that would guarantee fair trading. Once officially approved, such a weight or measure was lodged where it could be consulted to verify other standard weights and measures: 'The sayd Burgese schall haffe ye standard . . . the qwhyche measures schuld agre with the kynges standard' (ordinance, *c*.1450). Such a sense lies behind phrases like *original standard* one from which others are copied and to which ultimate appeal must be made, *gold standard* gold used as a reservoir of value against which paper currencies can be measured, *standard atmosphere* a unit of atmospheric pressure, and *standard error* a measure of the statistical accuracy of an estimate. Ideas of firmness, uprightness, and centrality are found in other extensions of sense, such as an upright pole used as a support, a tall candlestick, a fruit tree trained to have an upright stem, a principle of honesty and decorum, and a level of excellence or quality, all of which have contributed to the

semantic complex in which the linguistic sense is embedded.

Standards and languages. In medieval times, the vernaculars of Europe were overshadowed by Latin, the language of scriptural truth, learning, and debate: the gold standard, as it were, against which base vernacular metal was judged. During the 12–16c, however, an accumulation of events and processes demoted Latin and promoted some vernaculars (such as Northern French over Occitan, the Romance language of southern France) and some varieties of some vernaculars (such as the East Midland dialect of English over other dialects). These events and processes were:

(1) *Ethnic and cultural unification.* Many groups using the same languages began to develop a firmer sense of unity. If the unity lacked political cohesion, as in Italy and Germany, linguistic refinement was fostered in certain cities and courts and through certain literary styles. If the unity was accompanied by political centralization, as in France, Spain, and England, linguistic refinement was fostered by a capital where the court resided. Such forms as Parisian French, Castilian Spanish, and the English of south-east England became the 'good' forms of those languages: that is, those drawn from or influenced by Latin. The presence of a strong, literate business class further enhanced the prestige and utility of metropolitan forms of speech and writing. See DIALECT.

(2) *The growth of vernacular literatures.* New literatures developed as counterpoints to Latin in such languages as Italian, Spanish, French, German, and English. They owed much to Latin and Greek in terms of the genres, formulas, and allusions available to them, but differed from them in being widely understood. They were able to exploit, among other things, popular epic cycles such as the *Matter of Britain* (Arthur, the Round Table, the Holy Grail) and the *Matter of France* (Charlemagne and Roland).

(3) *The invention of movable type.* The use of printing presses in the Rhineland from the mid-15c promoted standard letters, uniform formats and sizes of paper, and over time more regularized orthographies. The presses developed a greater influence over religious, literary, public, official, and educational language than scribes had ever had over the medieval and classical languages. In the case of English, Caxton and later printers, though at times anxious about their usages, built on a relatively stable written standard that had already been used for some decades by the clerks of Chancery when writing official documents.

(4) *The legacy of Latin.* During the Renaissance, the flow of elements of Neo-Latin (Latin with

admixtures of Greek) into the new 'high' forms of the vernaculars made them more effective as vehicles of learning and shed on them some of the lustre of the classics. This was particularly true of English, already receptive to the vocabulary of the Romance languages because of the impact of Norman French since the 11c.

(5) *Translating the Bible.* The questioning of the authority of the Pope and the Roman Catholic Church before, during, and after the Reformation also served to weaken the hold of Latin, the language of the Mass and of St Jerome's Vulgate Bible. In northern Europe in particular, the Bible in an élite ecclesiastical language ceased to be acceptable. When it was translated directly from the original Hebrew and Greek into such vernaculars as English, the variety used for the translation became privileged by that use, much as Latin had been privileged before.

Conclusion. The development of vernaculars such as French and English and of high forms of those vernaculars such as educated Parisian French and educated south-eastern English depended therefore on the existence of a royal court, a literature associated with that court, laws and ordinances promulgated by court and parliament, the aspirations of a growing middle class, increasing literacy in writing and print, and schools inspired by Latin and the grammatical descriptions of Latin. Such forms benefited from the sense of an educated and refined minority set by Providence over an uneducated and unrefined majority in town and country, a sense that continued uninterrupted from the Middle Ages to at least the American and French Revolutions in the late 18c.

See ACCENT, ACCEPTABILITY, AMERICAN ENGLISH, BAD ENGLISH, BIBLE, CANON, CHANCERY STANDARD, CLASSICAL LANGUAGE, CULTIVATED, DIALECT, EAST MIDLAND DIALECT, EDUCATED AND UNEDUCATED, EDUCATED ENGLISH, ENGLISH, FRENCH, GENERAL ENGLISH, GOOD ENGLISH, GRAMMATICALITY, GREEK, HISTORY OF ENGLISH, KOINE, LATIN[1], LITERATURE, MARK, NONSTANDARD, NORM, NORMATIVE, POSH, PRINTING, PROPER, RECEIVED, RECEIVED PRONUNCIATION, RECEIVED STANDARD AND MODIFIED STANDARD, REFINED, SCRIPTURE, STANDARD ACCENT, STANDARD AMERICAN ENGLISH, STANDARD AUSTRALIAN ENGLISH, STANDARD BLACK ENGLISH, STANDARD BRITISH ENGLISH, STANDARD CANADIAN ENGLISH, STANDARD CARIBBEAN ENGLISH, STANDARD ENGLISH, STANDARD ENGLISH ENGLISH, STANDARD GENERAL ENGLISH, SUBSTANDARD, TYPE, U AND NON-U, VERNACULAR, WESSEX. [LANGUAGE, STYLE, USAGE, VARIETY]. T.MCA.

Crowley, Tony. 1989. *The Politics of Discourse: The Standard Language Question in British Cultural Debates.* London: Macmillan.

John, Earl Joseph. 1987. *Eloquence and Power: The Rise of Language Standards and Standard Languages.* London: Frances Pinter.

Smith, Olivia. 1984. *The Politics of Language: 1791–1819.* Oxford: University Press.

STANDARD ACCENT [20c]. An accent that is (taken to be) standard for a language or variety of a language: 'The standard accent—the one that is regionless rather than regional—is the accent of a minority . . . and those who speak it are associated with high status, socially, politically and economically' (J. K. Chambers, in *In Search of the Standard in Canadian English*, 1986); 'It is crucial to realize that the direct ancestor of British English's present-day standard accent (RP) was not simply a particular regional one; it was also the property of a limited social group within that region' (John Honey, *Does Accent Matter?*, 1989). See ACCENT, STANDARD, STANDARD ENGLISH. [SPEECH]. T.MCA.

STANDARD AMERICAN [1947: proposed by Eric Partridge]. The standard English of the US: 'Standard English and Standard American are the speech of the educated classes in the British Empire and the United States' (*Usage and Abusage*, 1947, p. 304). Compare AMERICAN[2], STANDARD, STANDARD AMERICAN ENGLISH. [AMERICAS, VARIETY]. T.MCA.

STANDARD AMERICAN ENGLISH, also **American Standard English** [20c]. The standard English of the US: 'In many little ways standard American English is reminiscent of an older period of the language' (A. C. Baugh & T. Cable, *A History of the English Language*, 1978). See AMERICAN ENGLISH, STANDARD, STANDARD AMERICAN. [AMERICAS, VARIETY]. T.MCA.

STANDARD AUSTRALIAN ENGLISH, also **Australian Standard English** [20c]. The standard English of Australia: 'As the national variety of English in Australia, Standard Australian English ought to be used with confidence in Australia and overseas' (Joseph Lo Bianco, *National Policy on Languages*, Australian Government Publishing Service, Canberra, 1987). See AUSTRALIAN ENGLISH, STANDARD. [OCEANIA, VARIETY]. T.MCA.

STANDARD BLACK ENGLISH [1980s: coined by Orlando Taylor]. The standard English of black Americans: 'Taylor pointed to the fact that many educated African Americans speak "standard black English". They adopt the grammar of standard English, with all the necessary inflections, but do so with distinctive black English phonology' (John Baugh, personal communication, 1990). See BLACK ENGLISH, STANDARD. [AMERICAS, VARIETY]. T.MCA.

STANDARD BRITISH ENGLISH, also **British Standard English** [Late 20c]. (1) The standard English of the UK: 'The American pronunciation of *advertisement* . . . may have been current in standard British English . . . in the eighteenth century' (John Honey, *Does Accent Matter?*, 1989). (2) Received pronunciation: 'Far more marked is the social variation of speech patterns [in New Zealand] . . . New Zealand English may reasonably be divided into "broad", "general", and "conservative"—the last of which sets out to model itself on standard British English' (*New Zealand English* entry, The *Right Word at the Right Time*, The Reader's Digest Association, 1983); 'The onslaught against Standard British English as the most appropriate variety of spoken English for a foreign learner to study receives a new impetus with the publication of *Accent on Australia*' (Alan Thompson, *EFL Gazette*, Apr. 1986). See BRITISH ENGLISH, STANDARD. [EUROPE, VARIETY].
T.MCA.

STANDARD CANADIAN ENGLISH, also **Canadian Standard English**, short form *CSE* [Late 20c]. The standard English of Canada: 'Grammatical variants occur in Canada. Some of them are undoubtedly too regional or too colloquial (or both) to warrant a place in standard Canadian English, but such judgements cannot be made glibly' (J. K. Chambers, in *In Search of the Standard in Canadian English*, 1986). See CANADIAN ENGLISH, STANDARD. [AMERICAS, VARIETY].
T.MCA.

STANDARD CARIBBEAN ENGLISH, also **Caribbean Standard English** [Late 20c]. The standard English of the Caribbean/West Indies: '[The Caribbean Lexicography Project] is concerned with codifying the lexicon of those varieties of English spoken by educated West Indians. Its aim is to define a standard Caribbean English as a prestigious standard in its own right' (Donald Winford, 'The Caribbean', in *English around the World: Sociolinguistic perspectives*, ed. Jenny Cheshire, 1991). Subvarieties include *Standard Barbadian English*, *Standard Jamaican English*, and *Standard Guyana/Guyanese English*. See CARIBBEAN ENGLISH, STANDARD. [AMERICAS, VARIETY].
T.MCA.

STANDARD DIALECT [20c]. A term in linguistics for a part of a language traditionally equated with the language itself, and seen as the product of such 'refining' forces as use at a royal court, by the middle classes, and in literature, printing, publishing, and education. Because the standard has generally been set apart from and above *dialect*, the phrase *standard dialect* is sometimes used to indicate that, in linguistic

terms, it too can be regarded as a dialect, despite its special status: 'A grammar of present-day English is a grammar of a standard dialect of English, which is implicitly identified with the language as a whole' (Sidney Greenbaum, *Good English and the Grammarian*, 1988). See DIALECT, STANDARD, STANDARD LANGUAGE, STANDARD VARIETY. [LANGUAGE, VARIETY].
T.MCA.

STANDARD ENGLISH [19c: used with and without an initial capital *S*]. A widely used term that resists easy definition but is used as if most educated people nonetheless know precisely what it refers to. Some consider its meaning self-evident: it is both the usage and the ideal of 'good' or 'educated' users of English. A geographical limitation has, however, often been imposed on this definition, such as the usage of educated people in Britain alone, England alone, or southern England alone, or the usage of educated people in North America and Britain generally. Others still find standard English at work throughout the English-speaking world. For some it is a monolith, with more or less strict rules and conventions; for others it is a range of overlapping varieties, so that standard AmE is distinct from but similar to standard BrE. Although for some the term is negative, for most it appears to be either neutral or positive, referring to something important: 'Standard English (by whatever name it is known) is the variety of English that is manifestly recognised in our society as the prestigious variety' (Sidney Greenbaum, in *English Today* 18, Apr. 1989).

A minority form. Some commentators regard standard English as a convenient fiction, like the law; others see it as a thoroughly inconvenient fiction built on social élitism and educational privilege. Even the distinction in writing between *Standard English* with two capital letters and *standard English* with only one implies that the form may be viewed as more or less institutional. It is generally agreed that standard English contrasts (often strongly) with other kinds of English, but there is no consensus about the best way of describing and discussing this contrast: for example, as between 'standard' and 'dialect', 'standard' and 'non-standard', or 'standard' and 'substandard', or some mix of these. It is also usually agreed that standard English is a minority form. Some consider that this has always been so and probably always will be so; others see standard English as a social and political good to which all citizens of English-speaking countries have a birthright and/or should aspire; others again are less certain, or are hostile to the concept. The precise proportion of users of standard English to users of other kinds is not known, and may not be knowable; it is also seldom discussed. Even so, however, there appears to be a consensus that such a form exists, and serves (or should serve) as the basis for public and private education in English-speaking countries and in English-medium schools elsewhere.

A general definition. In everyday usage, *standard English* is taken to be the variety most widely accepted and understood within an English-speaking country or throughout the English-speaking world. It is more or less free of regional, class, and other shibboleths, although the issue of a 'standard accent' often causes trouble and tension. It is sometimes presented as the 'common core' (what is left when all regional and other distinctions are stripped away), a view that remains controversial because of the difficulty of deciding where core ends and peripheries begin. Linguists generally agree on three things: (1) The standard is most easily identified in print, whose conventions are more or less uniform throughout the world, and some use the term *print standard* for that medium. (2) Standard forms are used by most presenters of news on most English-language radio and television networks, but with regional and other variations, particularly in accent. (3) Use of standard English relates to social class and level of education, often considered (explicitly or implicitly) to match the average level of attainment of students who have finished secondary-level schooling.

A negative definition. In 'What *is* Standard English?' (*RELC Journal*, Singapore, 1981), the British applied linguist and language teacher Peter Strevens sought to establish the nature of standard English by saying what it was not:

(i) It is not an arbitrary, *a priori* description of English, or of a form of English, devised by reference to standards of moral value, or literary merit, or supposed linguistic purity, or any other metaphysical yardstick — in short, 'Standard English' cannot be defined or described in terms such as 'the best English,' or 'literary English,' or 'Oxford English,' or 'BBC English.'
(ii) It is not defined by reference to the usage of any particular group of English-users, and especially not by reference to a social class — 'Standard English' is *not* 'upper class English' and it is encountered across the whole social spectrum, though not necessarily in equivalent use by all members of all classes.
(iii) It is not statistically the most frequently occurring form of English, so that 'standard' here does not mean 'most often heard.'
(iv) It is not imposed upon those who use it. True, its use by an individual may be largely the result of a long process of education; but Standard English is neither the product of linguistic planning or philosophy (for example as exists for French in the deliberations of the Academie Francaise, or policies devised in similar terms for Hebrew, Irish, Welsh, Bahasa Malaysia, etc); nor is it a closely-defined norm whose use and maintenance is monitored by some quasi-official body, with penalties imposed for non-use or mis-use. Standard English evolved: it was not produced by conscious design.

A standard accent? In Strevens's view, the term *standard English* is valuable because it helps account for a range of distinctions and attitudes, offers a label for the grammatical and lexical components of the core taught to all students of the language, and constitutes the unifying element within the enormous diversity of the language. He argued strongly, however, that the standard applies to grammar, vocabulary, writing, and print, but not to accent (except as a pronunciation target in the teaching of English as a foreign language). However, although it is widespread among contemporary 'liberal' linguists, this view is relatively recent and is not universal. Use of the term to include, and specifically identify, an accent (and most commonly the accent known as *Received Pronunciation*) has long been common and continues in use: *US* 'The British version of standard English, RP, is the same for all speakers regardless of their place of origin' (W. Nelson Francis, *The English Language: An Introduction*, 1967); *UK* 'Both Chaucer and Shakespeare rhymed *cut* with our present-day (southern) standard English *put*' (John Honey, *Does Accent Matter?*, 1989). See RECEIVED PRONUNCIATION, RECEIVED STANDARD ENGLISH. The question of whether *standard English* does, can, or ought to include norms of speech remains the most controversial of the many difficult issues associated with the term.

An institutional definition. The Kingman Report on the teaching of English in England and Wales, submitted to the British government in 1988, began with a statement defining standard English that presented the variety as virtually limitless in its reach yet closely bound to one medium:

All of us can have only partial access to Standard English: the language itself exists like a great social bank on which we all draw and to which we all contribute. As we grow older, and encounter a wider range of experience, we encounter more of the language, but none of us is ever going to know and use all the words in the Oxford English Dictionary, which is itself being constantly up-dated, nor are we going to produce or to encounter all possible combinations of the structures which are permissible in English. . . . It is important to be clear about the nature of Standard English. It developed from one of the Middle English dialects (East Midlands — the dialect first printed by Caxton) to become the written form used by all writers of English, no matter which dialect area they come from. It is the fact of being the written form which establishes it as the standard. And it is the fact of being the written form which means that it is used not only in Britain but by all writers of English throughout the world, with remarkably little variation.

Standards and the standard. The figurative strength of the term *standard English* has been considerable. Just as there was at one time only one standard yard, kept in the capital as a measure against which all yards everywhere might be checked, so (by extension in the 19c) there was only one standard language, 'kept' in or near London for the 'same' purpose. Even after a war established the US as a separate centre of English, years passed before the British (and indeed many Americans) began to accept that government, writers, and publishers had set up a second centre and with it a second yardstick for the language. Even after 200 years, old ways of talking about the language die hard: 'The British are quick to point out how different American English is from Standard English' (Mandy Loader, *EFL Gazette*, Apr. 1990). Despite the time lag and the confusion of terms, however, there appears to be little doubt that since at least the early 19c two yardsticks have existed for English, and that in principle more are possible, if not already actual.

A standard of standards. Among the objective indicators that a language or a variety of a language has a standard form are such artefacts as grammars and dictionaries and such cultural achievements as a literary canon. It was taken to be proof positive of the success of French as a national and international language that by the end of the 17c it had all three. English had only achieved this status by the time the American colonies declared their independence. By the middle of the 19c, the US also had its grammars, its dictionaries, and its literary canon, although it took until the early 20c for many Americans to feel sure that 'American English' and 'American literature' were firmly established. In more recent times, Australia and Canada have produced national dictionaries and style guides, and have begun to acknowledge the extent and vitality of their literatures in English. In this, they appear to be experiencing afresh what happened in Britain and America. Some commentators favour the development and acceptance of various national standards: an indefinite number of distinct centres of gravity for a vastly complex world language. Others see such a plurality of 'Standard Englishes' as disruptive and disturbing. The paradox of the 1990s is the possibility that there can be, at one and the same time, a range of national standards and a single broadly recognizable international standard that subsumes them: a standard of standards. Even more than in the past, it is a creature born of consensus. See ENGLISH, STANDARD. [USAGE, VARIETY].   T.MCA.

STANDARD ENGLISH BRAILLE. See BRAILLE, STANDARD.

STANDARD ENGLISH ENGLISH, also **English Standard English.** The standard English of England: 'Standard English English is described, lexically, in the great dictionaries' (Peter Trudgill, 'Standard English in England', in *Language in the British Isles,* 1984). See BRITISH ENGLISH, ENGLISH ENGLISH, ENGLISH IN ENGLAND, RECEIVED PRONUNCIATION, STANDARD, STANDARD ENGLISH. [EUROPE, VARIETY].   T.MCA.

STANDARD GENERAL ENGLISH [1980s]. The standard form of English conceived as a non- or supra-regional language: 'Chapter 6 includes a discussion of the Scottish variety of Standard General English' (Peter Trudgill, Introduction, *Language in the British Isles,* 1984). See GENERAL ENGLISH, STANDARD, STANDARD ENGLISH. [VARIETY].   T.MCA.

STANDARD INTERNATIONAL ENGLISH [1980s]. Also **international standard English.** The standard form of English conceived as an international language; international English in its standard form: 'The relationship . . . is very complex, owing to the perception that Jamaican and standard international English are not really that different' (Lise Winer, 'Intelligibility of Reggae Lyrics in North America', in *English World-Wide* 11: 1, 1990). See INTERNATIONAL ENGLISH, STANDARD, STANDARD ENGLISH. [VARIETY].
                     T.MCA.

STANDARD LANGUAGE. A term for the form of a language used, for example, in general publishing, the news media, education, government, such professions as law and medicine, and by especially the middle classes: 'The existence of a standard language discourages further divergence, because many people try to make their usage more like the standard, especially if they wish to make their way in administration and government or are social climbers' (Charles Barber, *The Flux of Language,* 1965). See STANDARD, STANDARD DIALECT, STANDARD VARIETY. [LANGUAGE].   T.MCA.

STANDARD VARIETY [1980s]. A term in linguistics for the standard form of a language: '[T]he current national guidelines for examination in the English language do not require pupils to use the "standard" variety exclusively' (Tony Fairman, in *English Today* 17, Jan. 1989); 'The standard variety of British or American English would perhaps not have served this purpose. The language of Indian writing in English is the natural product of an alien medium in interaction and interference with native languages and native cultures' (R. R. Mehrotra, 'Indian Literature in English', in *English Across Cultures, Cultures Across English,* eds. Ofelia

García & Ricardo Otheguy, 1989). See STAND-ARD, STANDARD DIALECT, STANDARD LANGUAGE, VARIETY. [LANGUAGE].   T.MCA.

STANZA [16c: from Italian, standing, a stopping-place]. A group of lines in verse, forming a division of a poem. A poem usually keeps the same stanzaic form throughout, continuity being established by using the same metre, rhyme scheme, and number of lines. See BALLAD, OTTAVA RIMA, SPENSERIAN STANZA, TERCET. [LITERATURE].   R.C.

STATIVE VERB. A category of verb that contrasts with *dynamic verb* in the aspect system of a language, and relates to state and not action: in English, such verbs as *belong, love*. Syntactically, these verbs are used in simple rather than progressive tenses and generally not in the imperative (no *Belong!, but occasionally Love me!). Semantically, stative verbs refer to states of affairs (*belong, know, own*) in contrast to dynamic verbs that refer to actions (*buy, learn, jump*). In practice, the boundary between stative and dynamic verbs is sometimes fuzzy, and it is generally more useful to talk of stative and dynamic meaning and usage. In most varieties of English, some verbs are normally stative (therefore no *I am owning this car, *Know how to give first aid!), but others are partly stative and partly dynamic (no *She is liking to help people, but How are you liking your new job?; no *I am forgetting their address, but Forget it!). Some verbs belong to both categories but with distinct meanings, as with *have* in *She has red hair* and *She is having dinner*. In IndE, the stative/dynamic distinction described above is considered standard, but it is widely ignored, so that expressions like *I am owning this car* and *She is liking to help people* are commonplace. See VERB. [GRAMMAR].   S.C., T.MCA.

STEELE, (Sir) Richard [1672–1729]. Anglo-Irish essayist, dramatist, and journalist, born in Dublin and educated at Charterhouse and Merton College, Oxford. He joined the army and later obtained a court appointment, but his Whig principles led to loss of favour when the Tories came into power. Steele became MP for Stockbridge in 1713, but was expelled from Parliament for his pamphlet *The Crisis*, which favoured the Hanoverian succession. The accession of George I restored his fortunes and he was knighted in 1715. He showed a zeal to reform contemporary morals with the early treatise *The Christian Hero* (1701). He wrote several comedies, such as *The Conscious Lovers* (1722), often described as 'sentimental' because of their emotive appeals and rejection of Restoration bawdiness. In 1709, using the pseudonym *Isaac Bickerstaff*, he

started the periodical *The Tatler* with Addison, a contemporary at Charterhouse, followed by further collaboration in *The Spectator* (1711–12) and *The Guardian* (1713). Steele is generally thought inferior to Addison as an essayist, but he contributed greatly to the rise of journalism (particularly as a vehicle of political opinion) and his contemporary influence was considerable. He recognized the individual status and needs of women in society and created an imaginary woman editor 'Jenny Distaff' to introduce family interest. See index. [BIOGRAPHY, EUROPE, LITERATURE, MEDIA].   R.C.

STEM [Before 10c: from Old English *stemn, stefn*, probably cognate with *stand*. 17c in this sense]. Also *theme*. A term in grammar and word-formation for a root plus the element that fits it into the flow of language. Stems are basic to such inflected languages as Latin and rare in analytic languages like English. In Latin, the root *am* (love) and a thematic vowel *-a-* make up the stem *ama-*, to which appropriate inflections are added: *-s* in *amas* thou lovest, *-t* in *amat* he/she/it loves. The only stems in present-day English are acquisitions from Latin and Greek. Such stems have no syntactic role, but often decide the spelling and sometimes the pronunciation of derivatives: because *negative* and *auditory* derive from Latin *negare* to deny, *audire* to listen, their stems are *negat-* and *audit-*. Spellings like *negitive and *audatory are therefore not possible. Whereas the rhythm of Latin makes the quality and quantity of all stem vowels clear, the rhythm of English often does not do so, reducing the vowels to a schwa and therefore limiting sound/spelling correspondences. See STEM FORMATIVE, THEMATIC VOWEL. [GRAMMAR, WORD].   T.MCA.

STEM FORMATIVE. A term in linguistics for a word element that attaches to a root or base so that a suffix can be then added: the *-t-* added to *dogma* to produce the stem *dogmat-* in *dogmatic, dogmatism*. See STEM, THEMATIC VOWEL. [GRAMMAR, WORD].   T.MCA.

STENOGRAPHY. See SHORTHAND.

STEREOTYPE [18c: from Greek-derived *stereo-* solid, and *type*: compare CLICHÉ]. (1) A process for making metal printing plates in which a block of type is composed in, and cast from, a mould of papier mâché or other material; a plate made by such a process. (2) By extension, a stock concept, image, or type: *racial, ethnic, and sexual stereotypes*; *a stereotypical mean Scotsman*. Compare BOILERPLATE, QUOTATION, SHIBBOLETH, STOCK. [LANGUAGE, STYLE, TECHNOLOGY].   T.MCA.

STERNE, Laurence [1713–68]. Anglo-Irish novelist, born in Ireland and educated in Halifax, Yorkshire, and Jesus College, Cambridge. He was ordained into the Church of England, held several livings, and became a prebendary of York Minster. The first two volumes of *The Life and Opinions of Tristram Shandy* were published in 1759; further volumes appeared in 1761, 1765, and 1767. The book was not admired by Johnson and some other leaders of critical taste, but proved popular and made Sterne famous. His family life was not happy and his health became poor. He travelled abroad and lived for two years in France. A further visit to France in 1765 led to *A Sentimental Journey Through France and Italy* (1767), in which a first-person narrator 'Parson Yorick' (a character from *Tristram Shandy*) relates a series of humorous and bawdy episodes. The fashionable sentimentality of the time is mingled with admiration for French life and a mischievous sense of human absurdities. *Tristram Shandy* diverged from the course that the novel was taking with Fielding and Smollett. Purporting to tell the story of the narrator's life, it was an account of the eccentric Shandy family that did not follow a steady chronological course but was broken by digressions and reflections on numerous topics. By using rows of asterisks, typographical variations, and blank pages, Sterne draws attention to the artificiality of the novel and the lack of true relationship between life and book. He was influenced by Rabelais and by the philosopher Locke's views on the association of ideas. Sterne can be seen as the distant ancestor of the *stream of consciousness* in fiction. He wrote that 'writing, when properly managed, is but a different name for conversation'. Despite the deliberate disorder of his narrative, he created such memorable characters as Tristram's Uncle Toby, Corporal Trim, and Dr Slop. See index. [BIOGRAPHY, EUROPE, LITERATURE]. R.C.

STET [16c: the Latin phrase *stet* let it stand, from *stare/statum* to stand: Compare CARET]. In proof-reading, when something has been incorrectly marked to be changed, the original form can be kept by putting dots under the wrongly altered matter and writing *stet* in the margin. See PROOF-READING. [WRITING]. W.W.B.

STEVENSON, Robert Louis (Balfour) [1850–94]. Scottish writer, born in Edinburgh and educated at the U. of Edinburgh. He travelled frequently, attempting to improve his chronic ill health; he described early journeys in *An Inland Voyage* (1878) and *Travels with a Donkey in the Cevennes* (1879). He became famous with his first work of fiction *Treasure Island* (1883) and his popularity was upheld by novels with romantic themes and Scottish settings: *Kidnapped* (1886), *Catriona* (1893), and *The Master of Ballantrae* (1889). In a last search for health he settled in Samoa, where he was writing *Weir of Hermiston* at the time of death. Despite physical weakness, Stevenson was a prolific and versatile writer, from the simple diction of *A Child's Garden of Verses* (1885) to the strong prose that narrates the grim events of his last, unfinished novel. He took a detached attitude to the art of fiction, which he described as being 'to grown men what is play to the child', and critics in turn have not taken his work very seriously. He has, however, remained one of the most popular of late Victorian writers; *Treasure Island* in particular has delighted generations of children. For the speech of some of his characters, Stevenson used Scots:

'Aweel, Wully was unco' praying kind o' man; a dreigh body, nane o' my kind, I never could abide the sight o' him; onyway he was a great hand by his way of it, and he up and rebukit the Master for some of his on-goings. It was a grand thing for the Master o' Ballantrae to tak up a feud wi' a wabster, wasnae't?' (from *The Master of Ballantrae*, 1889).

Stevenson worked hard to achieve a style by imitation; he wrote, 'I have thus played the sedulous ape to Hazlitt, to Lamb, to Wordsworth, to Sir Thomas Browne, to Defoe, to Hawthorne, to Montaigne, to Baudelaire and to Obermann.' His chief contribution to current English comes from his novella *The Strange Case of Dr Jekyll and Mr Hyde* (1886), which tells how a man separates the good and evil sides of his nature: a disreputable or criminal life behind a façade of respectability is now called a *Jekyll and Hyde existence*. [BIOGRAPHY, EUROPE, LITERATURE, STYLE]. R.C.

STILTED [17c: 'on stilts']. A common term for artificial, pompous speech or writing that does not flow smoothly: 'There is a stiffness and stiltedness in the dialogue' (Edward Bulwer-Lytton, *Pelham*, 1828). Compare AFFECTATION, HYPERCORRECTION, LITERARY. [STYLE]. T.MCA.

STOCK [17c in this sense: always attributive]. Available for exploitation in acting, speaking, and writing, especially as part of a stock-in-trade of topics, arguments, plots, jokes, expressions, etc. (*a stock production, stock characters, stock responses*): 'If Agatha Christie works almost entirely with what the critics call "stock responses", she knows how to take advantage of our responding in a stock way to stock situations' (*The Times*, 20 Sept. 1975). A *stock expression* is a word or phrase that is often used and has therefore become commonplace and banal. Compare CLICHÉ, HACKNEYED, TRITE. See MELODRAMA. [STYLE]. T.MCA.

STOP. (1) [16c]. Also (*full*) *point, full stop, period.* The mark (.) at the end of a sentence: 'It is a sound principle that as few stops should be used as will do the work' (H. W. & F. G. Fowler, *The King's English*, 1906). See PERIOD, POINT, PUNCTUATION. (2) [Early 20c]. The word used in a cablegram/telegram to stand for a (full) stop or period: *ARRIVING LONDON AIRPORT FRIDAY 2200 HRS STOP WILL PROCEED STRAIGHT TO HOTEL STOP.* (3) [Early 20c]. In cryptography, a character representing a punctuation mark. (4) [17c]. Also *stop consonant.* In phonetics, a consonant sound made by momentarily blocking the air-stream. The two kinds of stop in English speech are the *plosive* (as in the *b*-sound of *bad*) and the *affricate* (as in the *ch*-sound of *choose*). See AFFRICATE, CONSONANT, GLOTTAL STOP, PLOSIVE. [SPEECH, WRITING].   T.MCA., G.K.

STORY [12c: from Anglo-French *estorie*, Latin *historia*, Greek *historía* learning by inquiry, history, from *histōr* a person who knows or sees. Where English generally keeps *story* and *history* separate, with distinct meanings, French retains the original Greek unity in *histoire*]. (1) A narrative, spoken or written, in prose or in verse, true or fictitious, related so as to inform, entertain, or instruct the listener or reader. A story has a structure that may be more or less formal, unfolds as a sequence of events and descriptions (even when devices like flashbacks alter the flow of time), and concerns one or more characters in one or more settings. (2) All such narratives: *long remembered in song and story.* (3) Also *story line.* The plot of a novel, narrative poem, drama, motion picture, etc.: *I liked the characters and the setting, but the story was unconvincing.* (4) An informal history: *the story of medicine.* (5) Informal: an account: *That's her story and she's sticking to it.* (6) Also *news story.* An account of events in a newspaper, etc. (7) A lie: *I'm afraid he's started telling stories again.* (8) Also *fabula.* In narratology (the literary study of narrative), the content rather than the form of a narrative. See ANECDOTE, DETECTIVE STORY, JOKE, LITERARY CRITICISM, NARRATIVE, PLOT (NARRATOLOGY), SHAGGY DOG STORY, SHORT STORY, STORY LINE. [LITERATURE, MEDIA, STYLE, WRITING].   T.MCA.

STORY LINE. The sequence or flow of events in a story: the unelaborated routine of the *plot,* as opposed to the *theme* that the plot treats. A common story line is *Boy meets girl—boy loses girl—boy finds girl,* and a twist in such a story line might be *girl meets boy—girl loses boy—girl finds another boy.* In some books, especially in the 18c and 19c, each chapter is preceded by a contents list that is in effect a story line: for example, in Chapter 10 of Jerome K. Jerome's

Three Men in a Boat (1889), *Our first night— Under canvas—An appeal for help—Contrariness of tea-kettles, how to overcome—Supper—How to feel virtuous—Wanted, a comfortably-appointed, well-drained desert island, neighbourhood of South Pacific Ocean preferred— Funny thing that happened to George's father— A restless night.* See LINE, STORY. [MEDIA, STYLE, WRITING].   W.N.

STORY OF ENGLISH, The. The name of a nine-part television series about the English language first broadcast in 1986 and of its companion book, published in the same year by Faber and BBC Publications. The dual project was created by the British novelist and publisher Robert McCrum, the British broadcaster William Cran, and the Canadian writer and broadcaster Robert MacNeil, anchorman of the US MacNeil-Lehrer Newshour. Their aim was to tell in a popular way 'the extraordinary tale of a language that came from nowhere to conquer the world'. Commenting on the democratic philosophy behind the project, McCrum observed in *English Today* (No. 6, Apr. 1986): 'Walt Whitman once wrote that English is "not an abstract construction of dictionary-makers but a language that has its basis broad and low, close to the ground"—and that, I suppose, would be a good epigraph for what we have done.' The title was used again for a radio series of 18 15-minute programmes, first broadcast on the BBC World Service in 1987. Created by the British linguists David Crystal and Tom Mc Arthur, working with BBC English by Radio and Television, it took up and extended many of the points covered in the TV series and book. *The Story of English* is the first international multimedia project devoted to the language. See FABER. [HISTORY, MEDIA].   T.MCA.

STRANG, Barbara M(ary) H(ope) [1925–82]. English linguist. Born Barbara Mary Hope Carr in Shirley, Surrey, she was educated at Coloma Convent in Croydon and King's College, London, where she researched the Kentish dialects for an MA thesis under Professor C. L. Wrenn. In 1950, she became a lecturer in English at King's College, Newcastle, then part of the U. of Durham and later reconstituted as the U. of Newcastle upon Tyne, in which she was Professor of English Language and General Linguistics (1964–82). Her major publications were *Modern English Structure* (1962/8) and *A History of English* (1970), one of the first such surveys to take account of the international spread of the language. It was also unique in working back from the present day and not forward from a relatively remote point in the past. *An Historic Tongue: Studies in Linguistics in*

Memory of Barbara Strang (ed. Graham Nixon and John Honey, Routledge, 1988) contains a biography and bibliography. See index. [BIO-GRAPHY, EUROPE, LANGUAGE].   T.MCA.

STRATHY LANGUAGE UNIT. A centre for research into English usage in Canada, established in 1981 by a bequest from the businessman J. R. Strathy to the Department of English of Queen's University, Kingston, Ontario. Its purpose is to 'stimulate interest in correct English' and produce 'an authoritative guide to correct written and oral communication in English within Canada'. The Unit has a corpus and bibliography of CanE, and publishes occasional papers, such as *In Search of the Standard in Canadian English*, ed. W. C. Lougheed (1985) and *The English Language as Used in Quebec*, by Tom McArthur (1989). The first director was W. C. Lougheed; the second and current director is Margery Fee. [AMERICAS, LANGUAGE].   M.F.

STREAM OF CONSCIOUSNESS [1890: used by William James in *Principles of Psychology*, to describe the waking process of continuous thought]. A literary term for a style that attempts to reproduce directly the often random thoughts, emotions, and impressions of a character. Examination of the inner worlds of characters is found in earlier writers, but the inception of the stream-of-consciousness technique is generally attributed to Édouard Dujardin in *Les Lauriers sont coupés* (1888). It appealed to Modernist novelists of the early 20c who were trying to remove direct authorial interference from the text; among its principal exponents were James Joyce and Virginia Woolf:

Joyce. Opening her handbag, chipped leather, hatpin: ought to have a guard on those things. Stick it in a chap's eye in the tram. Rummaging. Open. Money. Please take one. Devils if they lose sixpence. Raise Cain. Husband barging. Where's the ten shillings I gave you on Monday? Are you feeding your little brother's family? Soiled handkerchief; medicine bottle. Pastille that was fell. What is she? (*Ulysses*, 1922).

Woolf. But why should she invite all the dull women in London to her parties? Why should Mrs Marsham interfere? And there was Elizabeth closeted all this time with Doris Kilman. Anything more nauseating she could not conceive. Prayer at this hour with that woman. And the sound of the bell flooded the room with its melancholy wave; which receded, and gathered itself together to fall once more, when she heard, distractingly, something fumbling, something scratching at the door. Who at this hour? Three, good Heavens! Three already! (*Mrs Dalloway*, 1925).

Attention to the viewpoint of the character rather than the author, with attention to psychology and motivation, has been a feature of much 20c fiction. The realization of the stream of consciousness takes various forms: thoughts may be organized into the language of normal communication, or (as above) the free flow of associations and half-formed impressions may be presented in defiance of the regular syntax of prose. Concentration on unspoken inner experience is known as the *interior monologue*, a special form of the broader stream of consciousness that is projected into the outer world of the plot. See DIRECT AND INDIRECT SPEECH, ENGLISH LITERATURE, JOYCE, MONOLOG(UE), WOOLF. [LITERATURE, STYLE].   R.C.

STRESS [13c: a reduction of Middle English *destresse* (Modern *distress*), probably coalescing with a similar reduction of Old French *estrece/estresse* narrowness. Both terms are ultimately from Latin *stringere/strictum* to draw tight, and cognate with *stringent*, *strict*]. (1) In general usage, a word associated with emphasis, significance, tension, and strain. (2) Also *accent*. In poetics and phonetics, a term for the property by means of which syllables and words become *prominent*: that is, they are made to stand out from their background.

Phonetic prominence. Stress is not a single phonetic feature, stressed syllables having different kinds of phonetic prominence: (1) *Prominence of pitch*. A syllable is made prominent by a pitch movement on the syllable or by a pitch discontinuity involving a jump from the immediately preceding pitch. (2) *Prominence of duration*. Stressed syllables have full duration and may be prolonged, whereas unstressed syllables are likely to be shortened. (3) *Prominence of vowel quality*. Stressed syllables retain full vowel quality, whereas unstressed syllables may have weak vowels. (4) *Prominence of loudness*. Stressed syllables are generally said to be loud (although this is probably the least important kind of prominence for the recognition of stress in English). Stressed syllables with pitch prominence are said to be *accented* and a pitch contour or tone is associated with each accent.

Word stress. A property which makes some syllables in a word stand out. In writing and print, a stressed syllable is conventionally marked with the stress mark (') placed immediately before the syllable in phonetics and most contemporary dictionaries (but placed after it in many older works). The word 'foreign is stressed on the first syllable, and de'scribe on the second. Longer words may have two or more stresses, in which case the main stress is referred to as *primary stress* and others as *secondary stress*. Secondary stress is marked with the stress mark (‚). The word pho'tography has just one stress on the second syllable, but ‚photo'graphic has primary stress on the third syllable and secondary stress on the first, while 'photo‚graph has primary stress on the first syllable and secondary stress on the third.

It is rare for unrelated English words to be distinguished solely by stress, as in *be'low*, *'billow*. More commonly, related disyllabic words are stressed on different syllables, and the unstressed syllables may be reduced, for example, the verb *construct* is /kən'strʌkt/ and the noun *construct* is /'kɒnstrʌkt/. When a word is pronounced in isolation, it is treated as a tone group. The primary stress is the nucleus, and in isolation it is given a falling tone: ↓*foreign*, *de*↓*scribe*. A secondary stress before the primary stress is the onset, which normally takes a level tone: *photo*↓*graphic*. A secondary stress after the primary stress is an unreduced syllable in the tail of the tone group. See TONE.

Sentence stress. The process whereby some words in an utterance are made prominent while others remain in the background, as in: *THAT is the END of the NEWS*. In strict phonetic terms, *sentence stress* is a misnomer, as the domain of these patterns is not the sentence but the tone group. In general, lexical words (nouns, verbs, adjectives, adverbs in *-ly*) have sentence stress, unless they refer to information already provided, in which case the resulting pattern is *contrastive stress*. Grammatical words are more likely to be unstressed, and may be reduced to weak forms.

Contrastive stress. The process by which stress is used to imply a contrast, as in *MARY can go* (not Susan) and *Mary CAN go* (she is free to do so). A fall–rise tone with a wide pitch range is often associated with contrast: *I can't go on* ⌣ *MONday* leads to the implication 'but I can go some other day'. Whole words can be contrasted in a similar way in many languages, but English is unusual in that parts of words can be contrasted: *I wouldn't say she's an emplo*⌣*YEE she is actually an emploYER*. In such cases, the normal pattern of word stress is overridden. The term is also used to refer to a stress pattern relating a sentence to its context: without preceding information, the sentence *Ram's got a motorbike* is likely to be stressed on the first and last words, *RAM'S got a MOTorbike*. On the other hand, *RAM'S got a motorbike* belongs to a context where possessing a motorbike is already under discussion and *motorbike* is not given sentence stress because it is not in contrast with anything else (*bicycle*, *car*).

Stress and weak forms. The rhythm of English leads to special reduced forms in some monosyllabic grammatical words in unstressed contexts: in isolation, the words *an*, *from*, *his* are pronounced /æn, frɒm, hɪz/, but in context are usually reduced to /ən, frəm, əz/. The process of reduction includes replacing the vowel with a weak vowel, usually schwa, and dropping an initial /h/. If the vowel is lost altogether, the result is a contraction, represented in informal writing by an apostrophe replacing the missing vowel: *she's here*. Although a consonant may also have been dropped (for example, the *h* of *has* in *She's arrived*), this is not normally indicated. Weak forms are natural in all native varieties of English, even in slow, careful speech. This also applies to the dropping of /h/ from weak forms, which is different from the dropping of *h* from accented syllables, which is not normal in some varieties, such as RP, and is widely stigmatized in BrE.

Stress shift. It is a common feature of English that when derivative words are formed by means of certain suffixes, the (primary) stress shifts from a particular syllable in the base word to a new syllable in the derived word: *átom/atómic*, *cómplex/compléxity*, *devélopment/developméntal* (with appropriate adaptations in the fullness or weakness of the vowels). Such *stress shift* or *accent shift* occurs only in words of French, Latin, and Greek background, in terms of particular suffixes, such as *-ic*, *-ity*, *-al*, and not in words of vernacular Germanic background. See ACCENT, FOOT, ICTUS, MILTON, PHRASAL VERB, RHYTHM, SPELLING, SUFFIX, TONE. [SPEECH]. G.K.

STRESS MARK. See DIACRITIC, MARK.

STRESS SHIFT. See STRESS, SUFFIX.

STRESS-TIMING/TIMED. See RHYTHM.

STREVENS, Peter (Derek) [1922–89]. English phonetician, applied linguist, and language scholar, born in Norwich, and educated at Ackworth School, the U. of London, and U. of Cambridge. He lectured in phonetics at the U. College of the Gold Coast (1949–56), where he was a founding member of the faculty, and in phonetics and applied linguistics at the U. of Edinburgh (1957–61). He was Professor of Contemporary English, U. of Leeds (1961–4), and of Applied Linguistics, U. of Essex (1964–74); Secretary of AILA (1966–70), Chairman of BAAL (1972–5), Chairman of IATEFL (1983–6); a Fellow of Wolfson College, Cambridge (from 1976); and Director-General of the Bell Educational Trust (1976–88), a group of private language schools in southern England. His research interests included speech communication, language teaching technology, ESP, and TEIL. His publications include: *The Linguistic Sciences and Language Teaching* (with Michael Halliday & Angus McIntosh, 1964), *British and American English* (1972), *New Orientations in the Teaching of English* (1977),

Teaching English as an International Language (1980), *International English for Maritime Communication: Seaspeak* (jointly, 1984). Strevens saw his role as building language teaching in general and English-language teaching in particular into a confident profession that crossed international boundaries and linked scholarly work from diverse disciplines: 'He believed passionately in the beneficent influence of English as an international language. He was concerned that the pre-eminence of English should not be at the expense of quality nor lead to linguistic imperialism. It is significant that he was a founder member of the Association des Etats Generaux des Langues. In fact, he died while advising on the teaching of Japanese as a foreign language' (Alan Maley, *EFL Gazette*, Jan. 1990). See index. [BIOGRAPHY, EDUCATION, EUROPE].

T.MCA., C.J.B.

STRINE [1964: a syncope of *Australian*]. A non-technical word coined by Alistair Morrison, to represent an alleged Australian pronunciation of *Australian*. Writing under the pseudonym Afferbeck Lauder ('alphabetical order') and as Professor of Strine Studies at the University of Sinny (Sydney), Morrison published a series of humorous articles in the *Sydney Morning Herald*, some of which were later collected under the title *Let Stalk Strine* (Sydney, 1965). The series made much of such features as elision, assimilation, and metanalysis, as characteristic of Broad Australian: *Emma Chisit* How much is it?; *money* Monday; *ass prad* house proud; *tan cancel* town council. The term has had some local and international acceptance as a name for a stereotype of pronunciation and syntax (the 'style' of AusE). Examples like *Gloria Soame* (glorious home) and the title of a subsequent collection, *Nose Stone Unturned* (1966), indicate the importance of eye dialect in achieving the desired effect. See AUSTRALIAN ENGLISH, EYE DIALECT. [OCEANIA, VARIETY].

W.S.R.

STRONG LANGUAGE. A non-technical term for words and phrases often used to express strong feelings and opinions and capable of provoking a strong reaction, typically of shock or anger. Strong language that provokes shock includes bad language, blasphemy, foul language, four-letter words, obscene language, and taboo language. Typically, the usages in question are considered smuttily dirty or religious sensibilities are offended. Strong language that provokes anger includes cursing, expletives, and swearing. It is debatable whether strong language includes slurs such as *dyke, queer, wog*, and *Yid*. Nevertheless, the negative injunction 'Mind your language!' or simply 'Language!' (found especially in BrE rather than AmE and

meant to discourage strong, or at least bad, language) might be employed in response to slurs as well as to smut or abuse. See SWEARING. [STYLE].

R.F.I.

STRONG VERB. A term in the description of Germanic languages for a verb that indicates such differences as tense by modifying its vowels: English *ring, rang, rung*. In contrast, *weak verbs* add inflections: *play, play, played*. These terms are usually replaced in grammars of Modern English by *regular verb* (in place of *weak verb*) and *irregular verb* (in place of *strong verb*). In Old English, strong verbs could have as many as four different vowels, since the first- and third-person singular in the past differed from all the other past forms: compare *was* and *were* in the Modern English past of the verb *be*. An example from Old English is the verb *helpan*, with *e* in the present tense, but past *healp* (first- and third-person singular) and *hulpon*, and the past participle *holpen* (with the *-en* inflection found in some Modern English irregular verbs: *shaken, taken*). In Modern English, this verb has become weak (*help, helped*), a change that has affected many other strong verbs over the centuries, such as *climb, step, walk*. The strong verbs that have survived into Modern English seldom retain the original distinctions, and all (except the highly irregular *be*, with *was* and *were*) have lost the two forms for the past. In some Modern English verbs, the vowels of the past and the past participle have become identical (*sting, stung*), and in others all three forms are the same (*put*). Some originally strong verbs have regular variants (*swell, swelled*, or *swollen*). A few originally weak verbs have become strong, such as *wear, dig, fling*. Differences may occur between varieties: (1) *dive, dived* in BrE, but often *dive, dove* in AmE; (2) *sell, sold* and *tell, told* in standard English worldwide, but *sell, selt* and *tell, telt* in Scots. Occasionally, for facetious purposes, people play with strong forms: *I thunk very hard about it* and *Where were you brung up?* In general, new verbs in Modern English are regular; that is, formed on the pattern of weak verbs, the pronunciation of the *-ed* inflection as /(ə)d/ or /t/ varying systematically according to the immediately preceding sound. Verbs formed by prefixation or compounding usually take the same forms as the verbs on which they are based: *offset, babysit*, and (both regular and irregular) *deep-freeze*. Some phrasal verbs prefer a weak form (contrast *The car sped up the hill* and *The car speeded up*). See VERB, WEAK VERB. [GRAMMAR].

S.G.

STRUCTURAL APPROACH. See LANGUAGE TEACHING.

STRUCTURALISM [Early 20c]. A theory or method which assumes that the elements of a field of study make up a structure in which their interrelationship is more important than any element considered in isolation. Structuralist principles have been applied since the beginning of the 20c, primarily by francophone theorists, to various fields of interest: in linguistics, it is associated with the work of Ferdinand de Saussure in Switzerland and Leonard Bloomfield in the US; in anthropology, with Claude Lévi-Strauss in France; in literature and semiotics, with Roland Barthes in France; and in studies of history with Michel Foucault in France. Generally, structuralists follow de Saussure in emphasizing the arbitrary nature of the relationship between a sign (*le signifiant* the signifier) and what it signifies (*le signifié* the signified), and in treating objects of study (whether phoneme inventories, kinship groups, or texts) as closed systems abstracted from their social and historical contexts. See LANGUAGE TEACHING, LINGUISTIC SIGN, LITERARY CRITICISM, POETICS, SEMANTICS, SEMIOTICS, SIGN, STRUCTURAL LINGUISTICS, STRUCTURE. [LANGUAGE].   T.MCA.

STRUCTURAL LINGUISTICS. An approach to linguistics which treats language as an interwoven structure, in which every item acquires identity and validity only in relation to the other items in the system. All linguistics in the 20c is structural in this sense, as opposed to much work in the 19c, when it was common to trace the history of individual words. Insight into the structural nature of language is due to the Swiss linguist Ferdinand de Saussure, who compared language to a game of chess, noting that a chess piece in isolation has no value and that a move by any one piece has repercussions on all the others. An item's role in a structure can be discovered by examining those items which occur alongside it and those which can be substituted for it. The structural approach developed in a strong form in the US in the second quarter of the century, when the prime concern of American linguists was to produce a catalogue of the linguistic elements of a language, and a statement of the positions in which they could occur, ideally without reference to meaning. Leonard Bloomfield was the pioneer among these structuralists, attempting to lay down a rigorous methodology for the analysis of any language. Various Bloomfieldians continued to refine and experiment with this approach until the 1960s, but from the late 1950s onwards, *structural linguistics* has sometimes been used pejoratively, because supporters of *generative linguistics* (initiated by Noam Chomsky) have regarded the work of the American structuralists as too narrow in conception. They have argued that it is necessary to go beyond a description of the location of items to produce a grammar which mirrors a native speaker's intuitive knowledge of language. See BEHAVIO(U)RISM, BLOOMFIELD, COMPETENCE AND PERFORMANCE, LINGUISTICS, PARADIGMATIC AND SYNTAGMATIC, PHILOLOGY, POETICS. [LANGUAGE].   J.M.A.

Bloomfield, Leonard. 1933. *Language*. New York: Holt, Rinehart & Winston.
Newmeyer, Frederick J. 1986. *Linguistic Theory in America*, 2nd edition. New York: Academic Press.
Saussure, Ferdinand de. 1915/59. *Course in General Linguistics*. Translated by W. Baskin. New York: The Philosophical Library.

STRUCTURAL READER. See READER.

STRUCTURAL SEMANTICS. See SEMANTICS.

STRUCTURE [15c: from Latin *structura* something put together, from *struere/structum* to arrange, make, compose]. (1) A complex form seen as an arrangement of parts; a construction, organization, or system. (2) In linguistics, the pattern of organization of the elements and levels of a language, with such sub-patterns as *phonological structure*, *syntactic structure*, and *semantic structure*. See CHOMSKY (DEEP AND SURFACE STRUCTURE), LEVEL OF LANGUAGE, STRUCTURALISM, STRUCTURAL LINGUISTICS, STRUCTURE DEPENDENCE, SYSTEM. [LANGUAGE].   T.MCA.

STRUCTURE DEPENDENCE. In linguistics, the reliance of language on an intrinsic structure rather than on simple counting or recognition procedures. In the sentence *Alice saw the white rabbit*, speakers of English immediately know that the sequence *white rabbit* forms a chunk of structure for which there are no audible cues, and which can be manipulated in various ways: *A white rabbit was seen by Alice*; *Was it a white rabbit which Alice saw?* The US linguist Noam Chomsky has argued that this property of language is likely to be innate. See STRUCTURE. [GRAMMAR, LANGUAGE].   J.M.A.

STUNT WORD [Later 20c]. An informal term for a word created and used to produce a special effect or attract attention, as if it were part of the performance of a stunt man or a conjuror. All three such words in the following citation combine ordinary base words with Latinate suffixes to suggest pretentious immaturity: 'As they smoked and stuffed fat palatable bites of sandwich into their mouths, [the boys] would regard each other with pleased sniggers, carrying on thus an insane symphony of laughter: "Chuckle, chuckle!—laugh of *gloatation*." / "Tee-hee, tee-hee, tee-hee! . . . laugh of *titterosity*." / "Snuh-huh, snuh-huh, snuh-huh! . . .

laugh of *gluttonotiousness*" ' (Thomas Wolfe, *Look Homeward Angel*, 1929: italics added). Stunt words used to exhibit and practise spelling patterns are a feature of the children's books of Theodor Seuss Geisel (Dr Seuss): 'Did you ever have the feeling, / there's a WASKET in your BASKET? / . . . Or a NUREAU in your BUREAU? / . . . Or a WOSET in your CLOSET? / Sometimes I feel quite CERTAIN / there's a JERTAIN in the CURTAIN. / Sometimes I have the feeling / there's a ZLOCK behind the CLOCK. / And that ZELF up on that SHELF!/ I have talked to him myself' (from *There's a Wocket in my Pocket!*, 1974). The preceding examples derive from the work of individuals. Many stunt formations can, however, be the outcome of group effort relating to a shared theme, as for example acronyms and related forms based on the letters *y–p* (standing for 'young professional'), particularly fashionable in marketing and media circles in the 1980s, such as: *yuppie* (young urban professional), *yumpie* (young upwardly mobile professional), *yap* (young aspiring professional), *mumpie* (Malaysian yumpie), *McYuppie* (Scottish yuppie), *yucca* (young up-and-coming Cuban American), and *yuckie* (a yuppie who makes you sick). Compare BUZZ WORD, -ITIS, NEOLOGISM, NONCE WORD, NONSENSE VERSE. [STYLE, WORD].   T.MCA.

STUTTERING [16c: *stutter* from earlier *stut*. Compare Dutch *stotteren*]. A disorder of fluency in the use of language; also called (especially in the UK) *stammering* [before 10c, from Old English *stamerian*. Compare German *stammern*]. The primary symptoms are difficulty in controlling the rhythm and timing of speech, and a failure to communicate easily, rapidly, and continuously. Individual sounds may be abnormally repeated or lengthened, or fail to be released. Symptoms range from mild through moderate to severe. The cause is not known, but several genetic, physiological, and psychological factors have been implicated; in particular, stammerers are affected adversely by any increase in stress or anxiety: 'My own name is my hardest word. Too many big people have asked me, "What is your name, sonny?" I've had to say it too many times when I got into trouble. I've said it so often and stuttered on it so often that I almost think it should be spelled with more than one *t*, like T-T-Tommy' (in Charles Van Riper, *Speech Correction*, 1978). A number of treatments are available, which can help to alleviate the symptoms by bringing the stammer more under the speaker's control. Approaches used in speech therapy include the teaching of new techniques of speech production, such as slowed speech, in which the stammerers learn to slow their speech down to a rate of a syllable a second or less, then gradually speed up to achieve a rate which approximates to normal everyday speech. Another approach involves the wearing of acoustic devices that interfere with the normal process of feedback as stutterers listen to their own speech: for example, by playing high-frequency noise into their ears while they are talking. Of particular importance is the need to train stammerers to develop new attitudes to the task of becoming part of the everyday speech community. Many stammerers, because of their handicap, learn to live apart from normal social interaction, and develop a poor image of themselves as conversationalists. Using the telephone may be greatly inhibited or entirely avoided. A more positive self-image needs to be acquired, and opportunities to practise new-found skills in a supportive environment. Much contemporary therapy is based on such an approach. See LANGUAGE PATHOLOGY. [SPEECH].   D.C.

STYLE [14c: from Old French *stile*, *style*, from Latin *stilus* (variant *stylus*) a stake, pointed instrument for writing, way of speaking or writing. The spelling with a *y* derives from the mistaken belief that Latin *stilus* derived from Greek *stûlos* a pillar]. A general term that primarily means a way of doing things, with additional senses such as doing them appropriately, doing them well or badly, doing them in a distinctive way, or doing them in one of a number of ways. The term first referred in English to a writing implement, then to ways of using it, then to ways of doing virtually anything.

Linguistic style. It can be convenient, in synchronic terms, to think of linguistic style as an aspect of style in general: someone may write in an *ornate style*, speak in a *laconic style*, live in a *Tudor-style mansion*, dress in a *youthful style*, and have an *aggressive style* when playing squash. In all such cases, the way in which people do things can be seen to vary: from one medium to another (speech to writing), from one situation to another (formal to informal, legal to journalistic), and from one period or genre to another (Elizabethan to Romantic, prose to poetry, sonnet to ode). *Yours faithfully* is recognizably a formula of writing, *He's kicked the bucket* is a slangy equivalent of the euphemism *He's passed away*, and the following lines might at first possibly be prose, but soon resolve into verse: 'A thing of beauty is a joy for ever: / Its loveliness increases; it will never / Pass into nothingness' (Keats, *Endymion*, 1818). Although stylistic variation can be discussed in terms of groups, generations, movements, and the like, it is most apparent in terms of individuals. No two people have the same style in writing or playing a game; as Sir Thomas Browne put it in the 16c, *stylus arguit hominem* (style maketh the man). In the same way, for such 20c structural linguists as Ferdinand de Saussure, style in language was a matter of *parole* (individual performance) rather than *langue* (the collective system). Readers recognize distinctive authorial styles (the loose sentence structures and grotesque metaphors of Charles Dickens, the periodic sentences and abstract diction of Henry James) and also differences between the styles of writers at different points in their careers (the play of sound in Shakespeare's 'early style' in his comedies as distinct from the richly figurative style in his last plays).

Appropriateness. The definition of lingusitic *style* as a 'way' or 'manner' implies distinctiveness, that there are phonetic, grammatical, and lexical features which mark out a text, register, genre, or situation: for example, legalisms like the BrE *m'lud* (my lord: said to a judge); the often ambiguous ellipses of headlinese (*Defence cuts off agenda*); and the ways in which a secretary on the telephone handles different callers. In the study of literature, style is a matter principally of design and theme, but in the works of writers of usage manuals and style guides, it is a matter principally of layout and the physical appearance of a manuscript, typescript, or printed text. In both areas, however, a sense of *appropriateness* or *appropriacy* is crucial: that choices have been made or must be made that take into account situation, occasion, subject matter, and audience (readers, listeners, viewers). The notion of appropriateness appears in many definitions: in the 16c, Roger Ascham used the term *decorum*; in the 18c, Jonathan Swift used the phrase 'proper words in proper places'.

The idea of appropriateness has its origins in the canon of classical rhetoric known as *elocutio*. The three ways of speaking or writing were the *high* or *grand style*, the *middle style*, and *plain* or *low style*, all three of which were carried over into the European vernaculars. The grand declamatory style was associated with epic poetry and had Homer and Virgil as its models; it is well illustrated in English by Milton's *Paradise Lost* (1667). The restrained middle style was used in the main for education and edification; it was the basis of the English tradition of sermons from Aelfric in the 10c to Sir Thomas More in the 16c. The plain or low style was close to colloquial speech, used relatively simple vocabulary and syntax, and was the medium of popular entertainment in ballads and folk-tales. By and large, in both classical and English literature and oratory, the three styles have been points of reference rather than dogmatic categories, allowing for what 20c linguists call *style-switching*. Stylistic variability within broad generic frames

can be seen in, among many others, Chaucer's tales, Shakespeare's plays, and Dickens's novels.

Good style, bad style. Swift's definition of style as 'proper words in proper places' suggests approval, that styles can be evaluated, prescribed, and proscribed. In the 18c, the leaders of literate opinion were interested in elevating the literary language and promoting elegant and refined everyday usage among the upper and middle classes. They were by and large prescriptive, laying the foundation of attitudes to grammar, style, and usage which were not significantly questioned, particularly in educational institutions, until after the Second World War. Style in the evaluative sense tends to fall into two broad groups: 'good', 'rich', 'elegant', 'refined', 'careful', and 'precise' style and usage on the one hand, and 'bad', 'poor', 'crude', 'vulgar', 'sloppy', and 'slovenly' style and usage on the other. The latter has tended to be associated with colloquial, especially dialect, speech.

To be said to have 'style' is a high compliment similar to having 'class'; to be said to have 'no style (at all)' is a serious adverse judgement. The precise social, cultural, and psychological bases for such assessments of speech and writing (especially if part of a consensus) are by no means clear. They appear, however, to involve a mixture of criteria associated with *status* (usually educational, often social, sometimes economic), *ability* (in such matters as selection, structure, clarity, delivery, and wit), and *aesthetics* (in such matters as balance, elegance, and euphony). Literary and other critics of the use of language generally agree that 'good style' is difficult to describe and by no means a matter of general agreement, yet there is often something on which wide agreement is possible, with regard to the style and success of a writer or speaker, just as there is often a consensus about the style and success of an athlete or musician.

In more immediate matters, the 18c prescriptivists made specific decisions about what was and was not acceptable style in writing. For example, to repeat oneself was a mark of poor style, whatever the ancients and Shakespeare may have done. Writers were encouraged to seek 'elegant variation', especially in the use of synonyms and epithets: a *poet* in one line was a *bard* in the next, and *Shakespeare* in one line became the *Swan of Avon* in another. Similarly, variety of sentence types was encouraged, with a view to avoiding a succession of clauses linked by *and*. Such a paratactic style was associated with the childish and immature, despite the fact that it was typical of the grand style of Homer (though not of Milton). There are fashions in style as in clothes.

Style as deviation. Despite the frequency of the expression, it is difficult to imagine a text or discourse as having 'no style', whether the claim was typically dismissive or even a compliment. For the French critic Roland Barthes, the style of Albert Camus is 'degree zero writing', because it seems unmarked by idiosyncrasies of grammar and vocabulary. Yet even such an apparently 'unmarked' style is stylistically significant, by virtue of its apparent plainness: if there is a norm, and if such a style adheres strictly to that norm, then it is the normative style. In the 1960s, linguists tended to treat style as deviation, matching a text against the assumed norms of its genre or a perceived common core of language. They concentrated in particular on highly marked poetic idiolects like those of Gerard Manley Hopkins and e. e. cummings, because it was relatively easy to see where they departed from established convention: 'Our heart's charity's hearth's fire, / Our thought's chivalry's throng's Lord' (Hopkins, *Wreck of the Deutschland*, 1876). Some stylisticians have tended to regard style as decorative, to define it (as the Greeks and Romans defined figurative language) as something 'added' to an utterance. In this, they resemble Lord Chesterfield when, in a letter to his son in 1749, he wrote: 'Style is the dress of thought.'

Style as variation. Not only style, but language itself, can be regarded as the dress of thought. In the *elocutio* of classical rhetoric, style had to do with *verbum* (the word, in the sense of form and manner of presentation) and not with *res* (the thing, in the sense of content or matter). It has often been argued that style consists of saying the same thing in different words and ways: *Smokers are requested to occupy rear seats*; *Smokers please sit at the back*; *If you smoke, sit at the back*; *Smokers must sit at the back*; *Smokers at the back*. However, what is frequently debated in stylistics and literary criticism is the extent to which choice of synonym or syntactic structure involves an actual change of meaning. Notions of synonymy and paraphrase depend on what has been called the *dualist* view that the 'same' content can be expressed in different forms, against which *monists* argue that form and content are inseparable and that to change a form will produce a different meaning. In poetic language, with an aesthetic focusing on form, the monist argument is plausible: poetry is notoriously difficult to translate.

Conclusion. One way of reconciling the dualists and the monists would be to define *style* as 'different ways of saying not dissimilar things', or proposing that at times a monist view is useful, at times a dualist view. The term seems generally to depend on the concept of variation,

but within a set of more or less established conventions and genres that have been adopted for purposes which their target publics more or less appreciate. Depart too far from such common ground, as James Joyce did in *Finnegans Wake* (1939), and the public shrinks to a dedicated few who may or may not, with the author, prove to be in the vanguard of language and literature. Style is a matter of linguistic contrasts in contexts: one word set against another, one utterance against another, one text against another, one genre, *œuvre*, or period against another. [LANGUAGE, USAGE]. K.W.

Bally, Charles. 1909. *Traité de stylistique française*. Two volumes. Heidelberg: Carl Winters.
Enkvist, Nils E. 1973. *Linguistic Stylistics*. The Hague: Mouton.
Fish, Stanley E. 1970. 'Literature in the Reader: Affective Stylistics', in *New Literary History* 2.
Fowler, Roger. 1971. *The Languages of Literature*. London: Routledge & Kegan Paul.
—— 1986. *Linguistic Criticism*. Oxford: University Press.
Hough, Graham. 1969. *Style and Stylistics*. London: Routledge & Kegan Paul.
Leech, Geoffrey N., & Short, Michael H. 1981. *Style in Fiction*. London: Longman.
Spitzer, Leo. 1928. *Stilstudien*. Two volumes. Munich: Max Hueber.
—— 1948. *Linguistics and Literary History: Essays in Stylistics*. Princeton: University Press.
Turner, George W. 1973. *Stylistics*. London: Penguin.
Wales, Katie. 1989. *A Dictionary of Stylistics*. London: Longman.
Widdowson, Henry. 1975. *Stylistics and the Teaching of Literature*. London: Longman.

The style theme

A–C. ABERDEEN JOKE, ACADEMIC USAGE/ENGLISH, ACADEMY, ADAGE, (A)ESTHETICS, AFFECTATION, AGGLOMERESE, ALLITERATION, ALLUSION, AMBIGUITY, AMERICANISM, ANACHORISM, ANACHRONISM, ANACOLUTHON, ANADIPLOSIS, ANALOGY, ANAPHORA, ANASTROPHE, ANECDOTE, ANGLE, ANGLICITY, ANTICLIMAX, ANTIPHRASIS, ANTITHESIS, ANTONOMASIA, ANTONYM, APH(A)ERESIS, APHESIS, APHORISM, APOCOPE, APO(PH)THEGM, APORIA, APOSIOPESIS, APOSTROPHE², APPROPRIATENESS/APPROPRIACY, ARCHAISM, ARGOT, ARGUMENT, ASPIRATE, ASSONANCE, ATTIC AND DORIC, ATTICISM, ATTIC SALT, AUGUSTAN, AUREATE DICTION, AUSTEN, AUSTRALIANISM, AUSTRALIAN LANGUAGE, BABBLE, BABEL, BACK SLANG, BADINAGE, BAD LANGUAGE, BAFFLEGAB, BANTER, BAR, BARBARISM, BATHOS, BEGGING THE QUESTION, BIBLICAL ENGLISH, BIBLIOGRAPHY, BIERCE, BILINGUALISM, BISOCIATION, BLAIR, BLARNEY, BLASPHEMY, BLUE-EYED ENGLISH, BOILERPLATE, BOMBAST, BOMFOG, BON MOT, BOWDLERIZE, BRITICISM, BROCHURE, BROKEN, BULL(SHIT), BUREAUCRATESE, BURGESSISM, BUZZ WORD, CABLESE, CACOPHEMISM, CANADIANISM, CANADIAN STYLE GUIDES, CANON, CANT, CARIBBEANISM, CARICATURE, CARLYLE, CARROLL, CARTOON, CATACHRESIS, CATCHPHRASE, CATCHWORD, CELTICISM, CENTRICITY, CHARACTER, CHAUCER, CHAUVINISM, CHIASMUS,

CHURCHILL, CIRCUMLOCUTION, CLASSIC, CLASSICAL, CLASSICAL LANGUAGE, CLASSICISM, CLASSISM, CLICHÉ, CLIMAX, CLIPPED, COCKNEY RHYMING SLANG, CODE, CODE-MIXING AND CODE-SWITCHING, COGNATE OBJECT, COLLOCATION, COLLOQUIAL, COLLOQUIALISM, COMIC, COMMERCIALESE, COMMON, COMPLETE PLAIN WORDS (THE), COMPOSITION, COMPUTERESE, COMPUTER USAGE, CONCEIT, CONFUSAGE, CONFUSIBLE, CONRAD, CONTEXT, CONUNDRUM, CONVERSATION, COPYBOOK, CORRECT, CORRUPT, CULTIVATED, CULTURAL CRINGE, CULTURE, CURSING.

D–F. DASH, DECORATIVE ENGLISH, DECORUM, DEROGATORY, DETERIORATION, DEVIANT, DEVICE, DIATRIBE, DICTIONARY OF CATCH PHRASES, DICTIONARY OF MODERN ENGLISH USAGE, DISAMBIGUATE, DISCOURSE ANALYSIS, DISEASED ENGLISH, DOG-/DOG, DORIC, DOUBLESPEAK, DOUBLESPEAK AWARD, DOUBLETHINK, DRAMA, DRYDEN, DYSPHEMISM, ECHOISM, EDUCATED AND UNEDUCATED, EDUCATED ENGLISH/USAGE, ELEMENTS OF STYLE (THE), ELIOT, ELISION, ELLIPSIS, ELOCUTION, EMENDATION, EMPHASIS, ENGLISH LITERATURE, EPANALEPSIS, EPIC SIMILE, EPIGRAM, EPITAPH, EPITHET, EPITOME, EQUIVOCATION, -ESE, ESTHETICS, ETHNIC, ETHNIC JOKE, ETHNIC NAME, ETHNOCENTRIC, EUPHEMISM, EUPHONY, EUPHUISM, EXAGGERATION, EXPLETIVE, EYE DIALECT, FALLACY, FANTASY, FEMINISM, FIGURATIVE LANGUAGE/USAGE, FIGURE OF SPEECH, FIXED, FLASH, FOREIGNISM, FORMAL, FOUL LANGUAGE, FOUR-LETTER WORD, FOWLER, FRACTURED ENGLISH, FREUDIAN SLIP.

G–L. GALLICISM, GENDER BIAS, GENDERLECT, GENERIC PRONOUN, GENTEELISM, GIFT OF THE GAB, GOBBLEDYGOOK/GOBBLEDEGOOK, GOLDEN BULL AWARDS, GONGORISM, GOOD ENGLISH, GOOD USAGE, GOWERS, GREAT AUSTRALIAN ADJECTIVE, GREAT AUSTRALIAN SLANGUAGE, GUTTURAL, HACKNEYED, HARD AND SOFT, HARSH, HEAVY, HEBRAISM, HENDIADYS, HOBSON-JOBSONISM, HOMERIC SIMILE, HONORIFIC, HOUSE STYLE, HOWLER, IMAGE, IMAGINATION, INDIANISM, INFLATED LANGUAGE, INITIALESE, INKHORN TERM, INNUENDO, INTERFIX, INTRUSIVE R, INVERSION, IRISH BULL, IRISHISM, IRISH JOKE, IRONY, -ISM, -ITIS, JARGON, JENNINGS, JEWISH JOKE, JINGLE, JIVE (TALK), JOHNSON, JOHNSONESE, JOHNSONIAN, JOKE, JOURNALESE, JOYCE, KING'S ENGLISH, KING'S ENGLISH (THE), KITCHEN, LACONISM, LAMB, LATINATE, LATINISM, LATINITY, LATIN TAG, LAWRENCE, LEACOCK, LEADING QUESTION, LEARNED, LEGALESE, LEGAL USAGE/ENGLISH, LITERAL, LITERARY, LITERARY STANDARD, LITOTES, LOADED LANGUAGE, LOCALISM, LOGORRH(O)EA, LYLY.

M–Q. MACARONIC, MAINSTREAM, MALAPROPISM, MALE BIAS, MANNERISM, MEDICANT, MEIOSIS, MELVILLE, METAPHOR, METATHESIS, METONYMY, MILTON, MINCED OATH, MIS-, MISTAKE, MIXED METAPHOR, MOCK, MONOSYLLABLE, MULTICULTURALISM, MULTILINGUALISM, MULTIMEDIA, NARRATION, NARRATIVE, NEWFIE JOKE, NEWSPEAK, NEW ZEALANDISM, NICE-NELLYISM, NONCE WORD, NONSENSE, NON-STANDARD, NON-U, NORMATIVE, NOVEL, OATH, OBFUSCATION, OBSCENITY, OBSCURANTISM, OFFICIALESE, ONE-LINER, ONOMATOPOEIA, ORATORY, ORWELL, OVERSTATEMENT, OXYMORON, PARADOX, PARAGRAPH, PARALLELISM, PARAPHRASE, PARATAXIS, PARENTHESIS, PARONOMASIA, PARTICIPLE, PARTITIVE, PASSIVE (VOICE), PASTICHE, PASTORAL, PATHETIC FALLACY, PATHOS, PATOIS, PATTER, PEDANT, PEJORATIVE, PERIODIC SENTENCE, PERIPHRASIS, PERSON, PERSONIFICATION,

PHATIC COMMUNION, PIG LATIN, PLAGIARISM, PLAIN, PLAIN ENGLISH, PLAIN LANGUAGE, PLATITUDE, PLAYING WITH WORDS, PLAY ON WORDS, PLEONASM, POETIC DICTION, POETIC LICENCE/LICENSE, POETIC PROSE, POLARI, POLEMIC, POLITE, POLITICALLY CORRECT, POP, POPE, POPULAR, POSH, PRIVATE LANGUAGE, PROLEPSIS, PROPER, PROSAIC, PROSE, PROSOPOPOEIA, PROVINCE, PROVINCIALISM, PSYCHOBABBLE, PUN, PUNCH, PUNCH LINE, PURE, PURISM, PURPLE PATCH/PASSAGE/PROSE, PUTTENHAM, QUARTERLY REVIEW OF DOUBLESPEAK, QUIP.

R–Z. RACISM, RECEIVED PRONUNCIATION, RECEIVED STANDARD AND MODIFIED STANDARD, REDUNDANCY, REFINED, REGIONALISM, REGISTER, REPARTEE, REPETITION, RESTRICTED LANGUAGE, RHETORIC, RHETORICAL QUESTION, RHOTACISM, RHYMING SLANG, RICHARDSON, ROMANCE, ROMAN NUMERAL, ROUGH, SARCASM, SATIRE, SAXONISM, SAYING, SCATOLOGY, SCHOLARLY APPARATUS, SCOTTICISM, SCOTTISH JOKE, SCRIPTURE, SERMON, SEXISM, SEXUALITY AND LANGUAGE, SHAGGY DOG STORY, SHAKESPEARE, SHAW, SHIBBOLETH, SIMILE, SINGSONG, SLANG, SLANGUAGE, SLANT, SLIP OF THE TONGUE, SLIPSHOD, SLOPPY, SLOVENLY, SLUR, SMOLLETT, SMUT, SOCIOLOGESE, SOFT SOAP, SOLECISM, SOPHISTRY, SOUTH AFRICANISM, -SPEAK, SPOKEN PROSE, SPOONERISM, STAGE, STANDARD, STEREOTYPE, STEVENSON, STILTED, STOCK, STORY, STREAM OF CONSCIOUSNESS, STRONG LANGUAGE, STYLE, STYLE CHECKER, STYLE COUNCIL, STYLE-DRIFTING, STYLE GUIDE/MANUAL/SHEET, STYLISTICS, SUBSTANDARD, SWEARING, SWEARWORD, SWEET TALK, SWIFT, SYLLEPSIS, SYN(A)ERESIS, SYNCOPE, SYNECDOCHE, SYNONYM, TABLOID, TABOO, TALK, TAUTOLOGY, TECHNOBABBLE, TECHNOSPEAK, TELEGRAPHESE, THESIS, THIEVES' LATIN, TIMESPEAK, TMESIS, TOPIC, TRANSFERRED EPITHET, TRITE, TROPE, TURN OF PHRASE, TWADDLE, TWO-LINER, U AND NON-U, UNDERSTATEMENT, USAGE, USAGE GUIDANCE AND CRITICISM, VERBALISM, VERBICIDE, VERBOSITY, VERNACULAR, VERNACULARISM, VERNACULARIST, VERSION, VOGUE (WORD), VULGAR, VULGARISM, WAFFLE, WH-SOUND, WILDE, WILSON, WISECRACK, WIT, WITTICISM, WOOLF, WORD-MONGER, YIDDISHISM, ZEUGMA.

STYLE CHECKER. A computer program that tries to check the suitability of the style of a document in a word-processing system. The average style checker has two parts: one that looks for instances of listed items regarded as mistakes in style (such as overuse of *very* or of the passive voice); one that can compute certain properties of the document, such as reading level measured in terms of syllables per word and words per sentence. The program then warns the user about possible defects. Some checkers suggest ways of changing the document to eliminate the apparent problems. Programs referred to as 'style checkers' may incorporate spelling checkers and grammar checkers. A style checker commended by the Plain English Campaign in the UK is *Stylewriter: the Plain English Editor*, launched in Australia in 1988 and in Britain in 1989. A major style checker in the US is the

Modern Language Association's *Editor* ('a system for checking usage, mechanics, vocabulary, and structure'), launched in 1991. Compare GRAMMAR CHECKER, SPELLING CHECKER. See BRITISH NATIONAL CORPUS, FLESCH READABILITY FORMULA, FOG INDEX, PASSIVE (VOICE). [STYLE, TECHNOLOGY].   M.L., T.MCA.

STYLE COUNCIL. See DICTIONARY RESEARCH CENTRE.

STYLE-DRIFTING [1970s: coined by A. J. Aitken]. A term in linguistics for a phenomenon common in the Scottish and other similar speech situations, in which speakers modify their styles along a continuum from standard to non-standard or formal to informal, or both, in either direction, as in the following dialogue overheard in an Edinburgh restaurant: *A* 'Yaize yer ain spuin.' *B* 'What did ye say?' *A* 'I said, use yer ain spuin.' *B* 'Oh, use ma own spoon.' The modification is usually convergent (towards the style of another speaker, especially if this is more prestigious or formal than the drifting speaker's norm), but may be divergent (to express solidarity with the speaker's group and reject that of the interlocutor). Compare CODE-MIXING AND CODE-SWITCHING. [LANGUAGE, STYLE].   A.J.A.

STYLE GUIDE, MANUAL, SHEET. See HOUSE STYLE, USAGE GUIDANCE AND CRITICISM.

STYLE-SWITCHING. See STYLE (APPROPRIATENESS).

STYLISTICS [1840s: on the analogy of German *Stylistik* and French *stylistique*]. The branch of linguistics that studies style, especially in works of literature. Developing in Continental Europe in the late 19c out of comparative philology, it was greatly influenced by the work of both Charles Bally, a student of Ferdinand de Saussure, and Leo Spitzer, whose approach, known as *expressive stylistics*, was concerned with the expression or revelation of the 'soul' or personality of a writer. Currently, however, it is less orientated towards writer or speaker and more towards text and reader, reflecting changes in literary criticism, with which it has long been associated. The advent of the computer has given rise to both *computational stylistics* and *stylometry*, approaches in which (among other things) attempts are made to decide the authorship of disputed texts on the basis of key features in the writings of authors who may have been responsible for them. Stylistics became established in the UK and the US in the 1960s. It has drawn eclectically on the models and terminology of linguistics at large: on generative

grammar in the late 1960s, with a focus on 'deviant' usage, and more recently on discourse analysis and pragmatics. Stylistics used as a tool in EFL and ESL is known as *pedagogical stylistics*. See CRITICISM, DEVIANT, DISCOURSE ANALYSIS, LINGUISTICS, LITERARY CRITICISM, PHILOLOGY, POETICS, RHETORIC, SEMIOTICS. [LANGUAGE, STYLE].   K.W.

SUB-EDITING. See EDITING.

SUBHEADING, SUBHEAD. See HEADING.

SUBJECT [13c: from Latin *subiectum* grammatical subject, from *subiectus* placed close, ranged under]. A traditional term for a major constituent of the sentence. In a binary analysis derived from logic, the sentence is divided into *subject* and *predicate*, as in *Alan* (subject) *has married Nita* (predicate). In declarative sentences, the subject typically precedes the verb: *Alan* (subject) *has married* (verb) *Nita* (direct object). In interrogative sentences, it typically follows the first or only part of the verb: *Did* (verb) *Alan* (subject) *marry* (verb) *Nita* (direct object)? The subject can generally be elicited in response to a question that puts *who* or *what* before the verb: *Who has married Nita?—Alan.* Where concord is relevant, the subject determines the number and person of the verb: *The student is complaining/The students are complaining*; *I am tired/He is tired*. Many languages have special case forms for words in the subject, such as the *nominative* in Latin; and in English the subject requires a particular form (the *subjective*) in certain pronouns: *I* (subject) *like her, and she* (subject) *likes me.*

Kinds of subject. A distinction is sometimes made between the grammatical subject (as characterized above), the psychological subject, and the logical subject: (1) The *psychological subject* is the theme or topic of the sentence, what the sentence is about, and the predicate is what is said about the topic. The grammatical and psychological subjects typically coincide, though the identification of the sentence topic is not always clear: *Labour and Conservative MPs clashed angrily yesterday over the poll tax.* Is the topic of the sentence the MPs or the poll tax? (2) The *logical subject* refers to the agent of the action; *our children* is the logical subject in both these sentences, although it is the grammatical subject in only the first: *Our children planted the oak sapling*; *The oak sapling was planted by our children.* Many sentences, however, have no agent: *Stanley has back trouble*; *Sheila is a conscientious student*; *Jenny likes jazz*; *There's no alternative*; *It's raining.*

Pseudo-subjects. The last sentence also illustrates the absence of a psychological subject, since *it* is obviously not the topic of the sentence. This so-called 'prop *it*' is a dummy subject, serving merely to fill a structural need in English for a subject in a sentence. In this respect, English contrasts with languages such as Latin, which can omit the subject, as in *Veni, vidi, vici* (I came, I saw, I conquered: with no need for the Latin pronoun *ego*, I). Like prop *it*, 'existential *there*' in *There's no alternative* is the grammatical subject of the sentence, but introduces neither the topic nor (since there is no action) the agent.

Non-typical subjects. Subjects are typically noun phrases, but they may also be finite and nonfinite clauses: '*That nobody understands me* is obvious'; '*To accuse them of negligence* was a serious mistake'; '*Looking after the garden* takes me several hours a week in the summer.' In such instances, finite and infinitive clauses are commonly postposed and anticipatory *it* takes their place in subject position: '*It* is obvious *that nobody understands me*'; '*It* was a serious mistake *to accuse them of negligence.*' Occasionally, prepositional phrases and adverbs function as subjects: '*After lunch* is best for me'; '*Gently* does it.'

Subjectless sentences. Subjects are usually omitted in imperatives, as in *Come here* rather than *You come here.* They are often absent from nonfinite clauses ('*Identifying the rioters* may take us some time') and from verbless clauses ('New filters will be sent to you *when available*'), and may be omitted in certain contexts, especially in informal notes (*Hope to see you soon*) and in coordination (*The telescope is 43 ft long, weighs almost 11 tonnes, and is more than six years late*). See ANTICIPATORY IT, CASE, OBJECT, SENTENCE, WORD ORDER. [GRAMMAR].   S.G., S.C.

SUBJUNCTIVE [16c: from Latin *modus subiunctivus* subjunctive mood, from *subiungere/ subiunctum* to bind together]. A grammatical category that contrasts particularly with *indicative* in the mood system of verbs in various languages, and expresses uncertainty or nonfactuality. Some languages have a range of subjunctive tenses: Latin (*Caveat emptor*: Let the buyer beware); French (*Je veux que tu travailles,* literally 'I want that you should work', I would like you to work). There was such a system in Old English (*Ne hē ealu ne drince oþþ wīn*: Nor shall he drink ale or wine), but in Modern English there are few distinctive subjunctive forms and the use of the term is controversial. Grammarians have traditionally described English as if it had a subjunctive system comparable to Latin and French, with present and past subjunctive tenses. This approach poses problems, because the 'present' subjunctive is used in subordinate clauses referring to both present and

past time: *They are demanding that we pay now* and *They demanded that we pay there and then.* In form, this subjunctive is identical with the base of the verb (the bare infinitive), which means that, when the reference is to present time, it only differs from the indicative (except with the verb *be*) in the third-person singular: *We suggest that he leave soon* as against *They say he leaves at dawn tomorrow.* With past reference, the difference from the indicative is noticeable for all persons, as in *We suggested he leave.*

This subjunctive has three uses: (1) *Mandative.* Mainly in subordinate clauses, following a verb, adjective, or noun expressing a past or present command, suggestion, or other theoretical possibility: *I insist that she disband the team; It is essential that it be disbanded; She ignored his request that she disband the team.* When a negative is used with this subjunctive, it precedes the verb: *He requested that she not embarrass him,* except with *be* when *not be* and *be not* are both possible: *He was anxious that his name be not/not be brought into disrepute.* The mandative subjunctive is commoner in AmE than BrE, but appears to be on the increase in BrE. In both, but especially in BrE, it can be replaced by a *should*-construction or an indicative: *He requested that she should not embarrass him; He was anxious that his name was not brought into disrepute.* (2) *Conditional and concessive.* Sometimes formally in subordinate clauses of condition or concession: *If music be the food of love, play on . . .; Whether that be the case or not . . .; Though he ask a thousand times, the answer is still NO.* The alternatives are an indicative or a *should*-phrase: *If music is . . .; Though he should ask . . .* This usage does not extend to past time. (3) *Formulaic.* In independent clauses mainly in set expressions. Some follow normal subject-verb word order (*God save the Queen! Heaven forbid!*), while others have inversion of main verb and subject (*Long live the Queen!; Far be it from me to interfere*). *Come* plus a subject introduces a subordinate clause: *Come the end of the month, (and) there'll be more bills to pay.*

The 'past' subjunctive is now often called the *were*-subjunctive, because this is the only form in which there is a distinction from the indicative, and then only in the first- and third-person singular: *If I were you . . .* as opposed to *If I was you.* It is used with present and future (not past) reference in various hypothetical clauses, including condition: *If only I were young again; If he were asked, he might help; This feels as if it were wool; I wish she were here now; Suppose this were discovered; I'd rather it were concealed.* In popular and non-formal speech and writing, the *were*-subjunctive is often replaced by the indicative *was,* which brings this verb into line with other verbs, where the past tense is similarly used for hypotheses about the present and future: *If only I knew how*; *I'd rather you said nothing*. *Were* is, however, widely preferred in *If I were you* . . . In the fixed phrase *as it were* (*He's captain of the ship, as it were*), *were* cannot be replaced by *was*. The use of *were* instead of *was* to refer to a real past possibility is generally considered an over-correction: **If I were present on that occasion, I remember nothing of it*. This contrasts with the purely hypothetical past, *If I had been present* . . ., which strongly implies *but I was not*. See MOOD. [GRAMMAR].   S.C.

SUBORDINATE CLAUSE. A clause that cannot normally function independently as a sentence. Also *dependent clause*. See CLAUSE, SENTENCE, SUBORDINATION. [GRAMMAR].   T.MCA.

SUBORDINATION [17c: from Latin *subordinatio/subordinationis* under-arrangement, translating Greek *hupóstasis*]. In grammatical theory, a relationship between two units in which one is a constituent of the other or dependent on it. The subordinate unit is commonly a subordinate clause organized 'under' a superordinate clause. Such organization can be described in two ways: the subordinate unit as a constituent of the superordinate unit, and the subordinate unit as dependent on but distinct from the superordinate unit. In the sentence, *They did it when they got home*, the subordinate *when*-clause may be either a constituent of its superordinate main clause, which begins with *They* and is coextensive with the entire sentence, or dependent on a more limited main clause *They did it*. There is in principle no limit (apart from comprehensibility and practicality) to the subordination of clauses one under another. In the sentence, *They saw that I was wondering who had won the competition*, the subordinate *who*-clause is a constituent of or dependent on its superordinate *that*-clause (which ends with *the competition*), while the *that*-clause is also a subordinate clause, in turn a constituent of or dependent on its superordinate clause beginning with *They*. Subordinate clauses may also be constituents of or dependent on phrases: in *What's the name of the woman who's winning the competition?*, the *who*-clause modifies the noun *woman*.

Form. Traditionally, part of a sentence can only be classed as a subordinate clause if it contains either an identifiable or an 'understood' finite verb. In contemporary grammatical analysis, however, subordinate clauses may be classed as: finite ('I think *that nobody is in*'); non-finite ('He used to be shy, *staying on the fringes at parties*'); verbless ('She will help you, *if at all possible*'). Traditionally, the second category would be classed as a participial phrase and the third as a

clause with the verb 'understood' (*it is*). Finite subordinate clauses are usually marked as subordinate either by an initial subordinating conjunction (*after* in *He got angry after I started to beat him at table-tennis*) or by an initial *wh*-word that also functions within the clause (*who* in *Most Iranians are Indo-Europeans who speak Persian*, where *who* is the subject of the subordinate clause). These subordination markers sometimes introduce non-finite clauses (*while* in *I listened to the music while revising my report*), and verbless clauses (*if* in *If necessary, I'll phone you*).

Function. Subordinate clauses fall into four functional classes: *nominal, relative, adverbial, comparative*. Nominal or noun clauses function to a large extent like noun phrases: they can be subject of the sentence ('*That he was losing his hearing* did not worry him unduly') or direct object ('He knew *that he was losing his hearing*'). Relative or adjective/adjectival clauses modify nouns: the *that*-clause modifies *star* in 'She saw a star *that she had not seen before*.' Adverbial or adverb clauses function to a large extent like adverbs: the adverb *there* could replace the *where*-clause in 'You should put it back *where you found it*.' Comparative clauses are used in comparison and are commonly introduced by *than* or *as*: 'The weather is better *than it was yesterday*'; 'The weather is just as nice *as it was yesterday*.'

All such clauses occur in complex sentences. Subordination contrasts with *coordination*, in which the units, commonly the clauses of a compound sentence, have equal status: the clauses joined by *but* in *We wanted to visit the cathedral first, but the children wanted to see the castle straight away*. Sentences in which both subordinate and coordinate clauses occur are compound-complex sentences: with *before* and *but* in *We wanted to visit the cathedral before we did anything else, but the children wanted to see the castle straight away*. See CLAUSE, COORDINATION, SENTENCE. [GRAMMAR].   S.C.

SUBORDINATOR. See CONJUNCTION.

SUBREPTION [16c: from Latin *subreptio/subreptionis* a snatching away]. A process of semantic change in which a shift in a word's reference takes it away from its strict etymological and structural meaning: for example, the use of *September* and *October* (in Latin, the seventh and eighth months of the year: *septem* seven, *octo* eight) for the ninth and tenth months of the year. See SEMANTIC CHANGE. [HISTORY, LANGUAGE].   T.MCA.

SUBSCRIPT [18c: from Latin *subscriptus* written beneath]. (1) Also *inferior*. Written below:

subscript numbers. (2) Also *inferior, subfix*. A character, letter, or symbol written or printed next to and partly or wholly below another, usually in a smaller size. In the chemical formula H_2O, the number 2 is a subscript. Compare SUPERSCRIPT. [TECHNOLOGY, WRITING].   R.E.A.

SUBSTANDARD, also **sub-standard** [20c: *standard* and *sub-* as in *subnormal*]. A semi-technical term for usage that is not standard or correct: *He ain't done nothin'*; *I don't got no money*. A variety of speech may also be so labelled: 'St. Mary's Lane, Lewes, is called "Simmery Lane" in local sub-standard speech' (*English Studies* 45, 1964). The term has often been used academically, without necessarily intending a negative judgement: 'In such communities the nonstandard language can be divided, roughly, to be sure, and without a sharp demarcation, into *sub-standard speech*, intelligible at least, though not uniform, throughout the country, and *local dialect*' (Leonard Bloomfield, *Language*, 1933). Many linguists and teachers object to this use, arguing that in such phrases as *substandard housing* the term means 'of poor or low quality' and that usage referred to in the same way is perceived in the same way. They consequently prefer the term *nonstandard*. See DEVIANT, NON-STANDARD, STANDARD. [STYLE].   T.MCA.

SUBSTANTIVE [14c: from Latin *nomen substantivum* a name of a thing, a substantive noun]. A grammatical term that in the Middle Ages included both noun and adjective, but later meant noun exclusively. It is not usually found in later 20c English grammars. In such languages as Latin and French, the equivalent terms serve to distinguish the use of Latin *nomen*, French *nom* (etc.) as 'name' from the grammatical use as 'noun', a distinction which is unnecessary in English. However, the term has been used to refer to nouns and any other parts of speech serving as nouns ('the substantive in English'). The adjective *local* is used substantively in the sentence *He had a drink at the local before going home* (that is, the local public house). See NOUN. [GRAMMAR].   S.C., T.MCA.

SUBSTRATE [16c: from Latin *substratus* spread or laid under]. Also **substratum** [16c]. A language or aspect of a language which affects another usually more dominant language, often where the speech of a colonized people influences the superimposed language of the conquering group: for example, the syntax of Gaelic providing the model for the IrE construction *I am after eating my dinner* (I have eaten my dinner) in the English of bilingual English/Gaelic-speakers and of some unilingual English-speakers. Compare SUPERSTRATE. [LANGUAGE].   S.R.

SUBTEXT, also **sub-text.** (1) [18c]. A text that is placed in a subordinate position below another, especially on the same page. (2) [1940s: a translation of Russian *podtekst*]. In literary theory, a theme or viewpoint that underlies a text or activity, is often at odds with the apparent meaning of what is going on, and reflects a significant though not immediately obvious truth: 'We are not against a translation being given [on television by means of voice-overs], but the original language should be clearly audible rather than faded out. Not only would language students gain, but the implied sub-text—that foreign languages are of secondary interest and importance—would receive a long overdue challenge' (letter, *Independent*, 19 Jan. 1991). Compare CONTEXT, TEXT. [WRITING].   T.MCA.

SUBTRACTIVE   BILINGUALISM. See BILINGUALISM.

SUBWORD. See HEADWORD.

SUDAN, also **the Sudan.** Official title: English *The Republic of Sudan*, Arabic *Al Jumhurīyat as-Sūdān*. A country of north-eastern Africa. Capital: Khartoum. Currency: the pound. Population: 23.9m (1988), 33.7m (projection for 2000). Ethnicity: 55% Arab, 35% African (Dinka, Lokuta, Nuer, Shilluk), 10% Nubian. Religions: 70% Muslim, 25% traditional, 5% Christian. Languages: Arabic (official), Nubian, and other indigenous languages. Education: primary 50%, secondary 19%, tertiary 2%, literacy 31%. In the early 19c, the northern Sudan was controlled by Egypt. In 1899, the entire region became a condominium of Britain and Egypt (the *Anglo-Egyptian Sudan*), and in 1956, it became independent. The division between Arab and Nubian Muslims in the north and pagan and Christian societies in the south has been an ongoing source of unrest. English was widely used in the 19c and earlier 20c, but currently has no official status. Of all the African nations colonially associated with Britain and English, Sudan has had least interest in maintaining the language, although English is more attractive to the non-Muslim south than to the Arabic-using north. See AFRICAN ENGLISH, ENGLISH. [AFRICA, NAME, VARIETY].   T.MCA.

SUDRON, SUTHRON. See SOUTHRON.

SUFFIX [16c: from Latin *suffixum* (something) fixed after or under, from *sub-* under, *figere/fixum* to attach]. An affix added at the end of a word, base, or root to form a new word: *-ness* added to *dark* to form *darkness*; *-al* added to *leg-* to form *legal*. Two distinctions are usually made: (1) Between a derivational suffix proper, such as

-*ness* and -*al*, which creates derivative words, and an inflectional *ending*, such as -*s* added to form the plurals of nouns, which changes the inflection of a word. (2) Between a *productive suffix*, which actively forms words (-*ness*: *darkness*, *newness*, *quaintness*, *wordiness*) and a *nonproductive suffix*, which does not (-*ledge*: *knowledge*). There is a continuum from the highly through the mildly and rarely productive to the dormant and dead, and usage can vary according to time and place: the suffix -*y* has generally been added to vernacular nouns to form adjectives (*ease/easy*, *oil/oily*, *rain/rainy*) with some disyllabic bases (*paper/papery*, *powder/powdery*). In the 20c, however, -*y* has increasingly been added casually and often for nonce purposes to longer bases (sometimes with idiosyncratic or debatable spellings), including compounds and classical words: *air-hostessy*, *chocolat(e)y*, *dry-biscuity*, *garden-y*, *idiomaticky*, *linguisticky*, *pizzazzy*, *statusy*, *teenagey*, *uppercrusty*, *warm-bready*.

Origins. In 1882, the philologist Walter W. Skeat noted: 'The number of suffixes in Modern English is so great, and the forms of several, especially in words derived through the French from Latin, are so variable that an attempt to exhibit them all would tend to confusion' (*Etymological Dictionary of the English Language*). The diversity of the backgrounds from which the suffixes of English have been drawn, the different periods in which they have entered the language, and the different processes involved all contribute to the complexity of the subject. Most suffixes, however, fall into one of three groups:

(1) *Vernacular.* Suffixes in the main from Old English and other Germanic tongues: -*ish* as in *childish* is from Old English and is cognate with German -*isch* as in *kindisch*.

(2) *Romance.* Suffixes that have come especially from Old French and Latin: -*al* as in *legal* and *natural* derives either directly or through Old French from Latin -*alis* as in *legalis* and *naturalis*, and is cognate with the Modern French forms -*al* in *légal* and -*el* in *naturel*.

(3) *Greek.* Suffixes that have come mainly through Neo-Latin and French: -*oid* as in *anthropoid* and *steroid* is from the combining form -(*o*)*eidḗs* as in *anthrōpoeidḗs* (human-like), and is cognate with French -*oïde* as in *anthropoïde*) and Spanish -*oide(o)* as in both *antropoide* (adjective) and *antropoideo* (noun).

Some suffixes fall into more or less parallel sets according to use and background; for example, three suffixes for causative and inceptive verbs: vernacular -*en* (*harden* to make or become hard), Latinate -*ify* (*purify* to make or become pure), and Greek -*ize* (*systematize* to make or become systematic). The conditions for using such

suffixes are strictly circumscribed: no **hardize*, **puren*, **systemify* (although the third is conceivable, on the model of *humidify*). Great variation is possible in a single form or group of related forms, as with the Latin form whose masculine is -*arius*, feminine -*aria*, neuter -*arium*. This has entered English in at least four ways: original forms unchanged, as in *denarius*, *urticaria*, *aquarium*; as the genderless -*ary* in *aviary*, *honorary*, *primary*, *salary*; as French -*aire* (contrast *legionnaire/legionary*, *commissionaire/ commissioner*); in the complex forms -*arian* in *disciplinarian*, -*arious* in *hilarious*. In Latin, -*arius* was close to -*aris* (as in *similaris*, English *similar*); many words, especially from French, that contain the element -*ar*- derive from either -*arius* or -*aris*. In addition, a part of a word may look as though it contains a member of the -*ar*- group but does not, as with *barbarian*, whose division is *barbar/ian*, not **barb/arian*.

Functions. The functions of a suffix are: to form a noun, adjective, or verb from another noun, adjective, or verb, in such patterns as noun from verb and verb from adjective; to provide a more or less clear-cut element of meaning in the complex word so formed: when -*y* is added to *rock*, an adjective is formed from a noun and the meaning of the phrase *a rocky coastline* can be paraphrased as 'a coastline made up of rocks/ covered with rocks/with a rock-like aspect'. Some suffixes function in isolation (for example, -*ard* in such words as *communard*, *drunkard*); no other element attaches to these words except the plural -*s* (but note *bastardy*). Others belong in sets, both associatively (-*ist*, -*ism*, -*ize*) and cumulatively (-*ist*, -*istic*, -*istical*, -*istically*). Such a cumulative set forms a *derivational paradigm*, a pattern whose potential can be exploited as needed. There are some 14 patterns of cumulative suffixation in English. Of these, four are vernacular and ten Neo-Latin, sometimes blending Latin and Greek: (pp. 1003–5). The vernacular paradigms belong to the language at large, while the Neo-Latin paradigms tend to be limited to educational, technical, and scientific registers. Such paradigms indicate a higher level of regularity in English suffixation than is often supposed to exist, but for every more or less regular system there are many incomplete or idiosyncratic arrangements in all areas and levels in which suffixes are involved. For example:

(1) *Vernacular.* The nouns *sand*, *milk* provide the usually literal *sandy* and *milky*, but the nouns *brain*, *hand* provide *brainy* and *handy*, which are figurative and do not refer directly to brain or hand.

(2) *Latinate.* The noun *nation* is the base of the adjective *national*. The noun *nationality* is formed from it, but not usually the noun

nationalness. Compare the noun *use*, the etymological base of the adjective *usual*, which has little to do with using things. From it, *usualness* is formed, but not **usuality*.

(3) *Greek*. The adjective *syllogistic* derives from the noun *syllogism*, not from **syllogy*, but *eulogistic* currently derives from the noun *eulogy*, not *eulogism*. Where *biology* begets *biological* and not **biologistic*, *eulogy* begets *eulogistic* and not in present-day English **eulogical*.

Gradations of meaning and use. Suffixes display all kinds of relationships between form, meaning, and function. Some are rare and have only vague meanings, as with the *-een* in *velveteen*. Some have just enough uses to suggest a meaning, as with *-iff* in *bailiff*, *plaintiff*, suggesting someone involved with the law, and *-ain* in *captain*, *suzerain*, suggesting someone with power. Some may be rare and apparently inert, yet come to life when needed: the Greek suffix *-ad* marks a nymph (*dryad*, *oread*), a number group (*monad*, *triad*), an epic (*Iliad*, *Dunciad*), and an activity occurring on an epic scale (*Olympiad*). Few nymphs and number groups are now created, but the recent *Asiad* as the name for pan-Asian games indicates that *-ad* is still available for epic events, at least in the context of athletics.

Thematic groups. The major semantic groups of suffixes and suffix-like elements are listed, with examples of their use, in the groups below. The same element or a variant of an element may appear in more than one group, because many elements have more than one meaning and use. No attempt is made to signal the degree of productivity of any suffix listed.

Forming agents, people, instruments (feminine forms marked with an asterisk). *-ad** naiad, *-aire* legionnaire, *-al* general, *-an* human, Cuban, sacristan, *-ant* claimant, *-ar* beggar, *-ard* sluggard, *-ary* fritillary, legionary, *-ast* enthusiast, *-aster* usageaster, *-ate* affiliate, magistrate, *-ator* aviator, *-atrix** aviatrix, *-ean* epicurean, *-ee* employee, *-eer* engineer, *-ener* sharpener, *-ent* resident, *-er* mixer, runner, *-ess** hostess, *-ete* athlete, *-ette** usherette, *-i* Pakistani, *-ian* Australian, electrician, historian, simian, *-ic* cleric, stigmatic, herpetic, syphilitic, *-id* aphid, druid, *-ier* soldier, fusilier, *-iff* plaintiff, *-ifier* humidifier, *-ile* hostile, *-ine** actorine, *-ion* hellion, *-ist* cyclist, mentalist, semanticist, *-ister* chorister, *-ite* ammonite, Hittite, Thatcherite, *-ive* captive, *-izer/iser* atomizer, *-oid* anthropoid, *-oon* octoroon, *-or* actor, *-ot* pilot, *-ote* zygote, *-ster* youngster, *-yst* analyst.

Forming objects, items, concepts, substances (scientific usages marked with an asterisk). *-a** lava, ammonia, *-ad** monad, *-ade* fusillade, lemonade, *-al** methylal, *-alia** mammalia, *-ane** methane,

-ar* pulsar, *-ary* capillary, *-ase** oxidase, *-asm* orgasm, *-ate** nitrate, *-eme** phoneme, *-ene** benzene, *-ese* manganese, *-iac* ammoniac, *-ian* obsidian, *-id* plasmid, *-ide* cyanide, *-il* fossil, *-in* insulin, protein, *-ine* caffeine, cocaine, plasticine, *-ino* neutrino, *-ism* organism, *-ite* dynamite, phosphite, *-ma* magma, *-mo* sixteenmo, *-ode** electrode, nematode, *-oid* alkaloid, *-ol** glycerol, *-oma** carcinoma, *-ome** genome, *-on** photon, *-one* silicone, *-ose** glucose, *-tron* cyclotron, *-um* platinum, *-us* phosphorus, *-yl** methyl, *-yne** alkyne, *-ysm* aneurysm.

Forming states, conditions, situations, and instances. *-acy* accuracy, *-age* baggage, blockage, wharfage, *-al* renewal, *-ale* morale, *-ance* clearance, *-ancy* occupancy, *-asm* enthusiasm, *-ation* communication, *-dom* kingdom, serfdom, *-efaction* liquefaction, *-ence* munificence, *-ency* consistency, *-erie* lingerie, *-ese* journalese, *-hood* adulthood, *-iasis* elephantiasis, *-ics* statistics, *-ie* bonhomie, *-ification* purification, *-ing* running, bridge-building, swimming pool, *-ion* junction, fusion, *-ism* Darwinism, euphemism, *-ition* tradition, *-itis* arthritis, telephonitis, *-ity* nudity, formality, humanity, ferocity, *-ization/isation* atomization, *-ledge* knowledge, *-ment* development, *-ness* darkness, *-or/our* color, labour, *-osis* osmosis, psychosis, *-red* hatred, *-ship* chieftainship, hardship, *-sis* synthesis, *-sy*[1] minstrelsy, *-sy*[2] epilepsy, *-th* warmth, *-tude* magnitude, *-ure* debenture, departure, *-ution* distribution, *-y* infamy.

Forming groups, collections, and classifications. *-a* arthropoda, *-acea* cetacea, *-aceae* rosaceae, *-age* assemblage, *-alia* marginalia, *-ana* Americana, Shakespeariana, *-aria* filaria, *-ata* chordata, *-dom* Christendom, *-hood* brotherhood, *-ia* amphibia, bacteria, *-iana* Darwiniana, *-idae* Formicidae, *-ilia* reptilia, *-ish* the British, *-kind* humankind, *-oidea* Crinoidea, *-ry* circuitry, peasantry, *-ship* readership.

Forming places, lands, locations, and institutions. *-a* Cuba, Java, hacienda, veranda, *-ada* Nevada, *-ades* the Cyclades, *-aea* Judaea, *-age* hermitage, vicarage, *-ain* Britain, *-aine* Aquitaine, *-alia* Australia, *-an* the Vatican, *-ana* Montana, *-ania* Romania, *-any* Brittany, *-arium* aquarium, *-ary* aviary, formicary, *-ate* caliphate, emirate, *-ea* Judea, *-ery* monastery, nunnery, rookery, *-ia* India, Somalia, *-iana* Louisiana, *-ides* the Hebrides, *-ory* dormitory, priory, observatory, *-um* asylum, mausoleum, Elysium, *-y* county, Italy.

Forming national and ethnic types and associations. *-ad* nomad, *-al* Oriental, Vandal, *-alian* Australian, *-an* American, Cuban, Moroccan, *-ard* Savoyard, *-arian* Bavarian, *-ch* French, *-ck* Canuck, Polack, *-ean* Galilean, *-ee* Chinee,

Maccabee, Shawnee, Yankee, -*er* Londoner, Icelander, islander, villager, westerner, -*ese* Chinese, Japanese, Viennese, Congolese, -*i* Iraqi, Pakistani, -*ian* Brazilian, Canadian, Romanian, -*ic* Asiatic, -*ie* Scottie, townie, -*ish* British, Yiddish, -*ite* Hittite, Manhattanite, -*ot* Cypriot, Epirot, -*s(e)* Erse, Scots, -*tch* Dutch, -*wegian* Glaswegian, Norwegian, -*x* Manx, -*y* gypsy, Romany, Taffy.

Forming adjectives. -*able* teachable, -*aire* doctrinaire, -*al* doctrinal, ducal, incremental, royal, -*alian* Episcopalian, -*alic* vocalic, -*an* human, -*ane* humane, -*ant* concomitant, radiant, -*ar* solar, -*arian* vegetarian, -*aric* velaric, -*ary* arbitrary, -*astic* enthusiastic, -*atic* dramatic, phlegmatic, -*eal* laryngeal, -*ean* subterranean, -*en* brazen, golden, drunken, priest-ridden, -*ent* current, nascent, -*erly* southerly, -*ern* southern, -*ernal* fraternal, -*ernmost* southernmost, -*esque* Bunyanesque, grotesque, -*e(u)tic* phonetic, therapeutic, -*iac* cardiac, -*iacal* maniacal, -*ial* circumstantial, colonial, residential, -*ian* draconian, -*iar* peculiar, -*ible* tangible, -*ic* civic, comic, -*ical* ethical, heretical, -*id* horrid, -*il* civil, -*ile* fertile, -*ine* adamantine, feminine, -*ique* oblique, -*ish* owlish, sevenish, greenish-yellow, -*itic* arthritic, -*ly* princely, yearly, -*mental* incremental, developmental, -*oidal* adenoidal, -*ory* inflammatory, -*sy* cutesy, tricksy, -*uble* voluble, -*ular* granular, molecular, -*y* naughty, sandy, tidy, worthy.

Forming verbs of causation and inception. -*ate* accentuate, -*efy* liquefy, -*en* harden, -*esce* effervesce, -*ify* purify, -*ize/ise* atomize.

Forming diminutives and hypocorisms. -*cle* tabernacle, icicle, -*er(s)* champers, rugger, soccer, -*ette* cigarette, -*ie* Jackie, lassie, -*ikin(s)* mannikin, sleepikins, -*ipoo* drinkipoo, -*let* leaflet, -*ling* darling, duckling, -*nik* beatnik, peacenik, -*o* arvo, cheapo, journo, reffo, -*ock* hillock, -*ola* granola, payola, -*ula* uvula, -*ule* granule, molecule, -*ulus* cumulus, -*y* Molly, Tommy.

Suffixes and stress. Many suffixes of Latin and Greek origin trigger a shift in stress (technically, *stress shift* or *accent shift*) when added to polysyllabic bases: for example, -*ity* attracts stress to the syllable preceding it (*cómplex/compléxity*). No vernacular suffixes cause stress shift, nor do all classical suffixes do so: for example, there is no shift in the vernacular set *shárp/ shárpen/shárpener*, nor in the Romance set *devélop/devélopment*, but a shift occurs when this set is extended with -*al*: *devélopment/ developméntal*. In terms of stress shift, there are three groups of suffixes:

(1) *Vernacular: no shift.* Suffixes and compounding elements which do *not* cause stress shift: -*dom* kingdom, -*ed* salted, red-haired, -*en* darken, -*er* writer, -*erly* easterly, -*ern* northern,

-*erner* westerner, -*ernmost* southernmost, -*ful* hopeful, -*fulness* truthfulness, -*hood* adulthood, -*iness* dirtiness, -*ing* startling, soap-making, -*ish* roundish, -*ishness* reddishness, -*less* useless, -*lessness* meaninglessness, -*let* leaflet, -*like* stone-like, -*liness* loneliness, -*ling* hireling, -*ly* womanly, -*ness* darkness, -*ship* readership, -*y* sandy.

(2) *Romance and classical: no shift.* Suffixes and compounding elements which do *not* cause stress shift: -*able* breakable, -*age* marriage, -*al* renewal, -*ant* dependant, -*ar* similar, -*ary* legionary, -*cy* accuracy, normalcy, -*ible* incorrigible, -*ion* attention, -*ism* Darwinism, -*ist* socialist, -*ite* meteorite, -*ive* suggestive, -*ment* development, -*or* dictator, -*ure* fixture. Although they do not themselves affect stress, they may occur in composites which do, such as -*ability*, in which the -*ity* attracts the stress to the syllable preceding it: *téachable/teachability*.

(3) *Classical: causing shift.* The lists indicate the form which the shift takes when the words containing the suffixes are pronounced in isolation. Minor changes relating to primary or secondary stress may occur in the flow of longer utterances. When the suffix is attached, stress falls: (*a*) on the only syllable of the suffix: -*ee* referée, refugée, -*eer* auctionéer, enginéer, -*ese* Japanése, Vietnamése, -*esque* picturésque, Junoésque, -*ette* cigarétte, usherétte. (*b*) on the first syllable of a composite suffix with two syllables: -*ation* commendátion, degradátion, transformátion, -*ition* compositíon, definítion, edítion, -*ution* dissolútion, revolútion, -*atic* dogmátic, systemátic, -*etic* energétic, pathétic, -*iety* sobríety, socíety, -*mental* developméntal, experiméntal, -*ental* continéntal, -*ential* presidéntial. (*c*) one syllable before the (composite) suffix: -*an* subúrban, -*ian* Canádian, -*ial* torréntial, -*eal* larýngeal, -*ual* resídual, -*ify* humídify, -*ic* económic, históric, -*ical* económical, histórical, -*ity* compléxity, informálity. (*d*) two syllables before the suffix: -*al* colónial, indústrial, -*ar* molécular, rectángular, -*ize* decéntralize, réalize, -*ous* censórious, labórious.

See ABBREVIATION, ADJECTIVE, AFFIX, CAUSATIVE VERB, COMPLEX WORD, DIMINUTIVE, INCEPTIVE/INCHOATIVE, PRODUCTIVE, SEXISM, STRESS, WORD-FORMATION. [GRAMMAR, LANGUAGE, SPEECH, WORD]. T.MCA.

Paradigms of suffixation

In the following 14 derivational paradigms (see SUFFIX, functions), X stands for a base that fits a paradigm. If the words shown as products of a paradigm are marked (*), they are no more than potential, no attested use of such words having been found by 1990. They may well be impossible for various reasons, both structural and semantic. Although the tables are relatively detailed, some of their information remains implicit, such as:

(1) The precise kinds of base feeding into particular paradigms. In principle, all verbs feed into Paradigm 1, producing the appropriate derived forms, subject to such factors as irregularity and strong-verb forms, spelling, pronunciation, comprehensibility, and practicality. For many Latinate verbs, there is a subparadigm in which *Xer* becomes *Xor*: act/actor, not act/*acter.

(2) The kinds of paraphrase that suggest the meanings of derivatives. Every form produced in a paradigm can be interpreted by means of a paraphrase such as: *climber* someone who is climbing (at a particular time) or climbs (as a pastime, occupation, etc.); *centrality* state or condition of being central.

(3) What happens if a prefix is added to a base or derivative. Prefixes enter the system at any appropriate point: *non-* may be added in Paradigm 5, so that *central* becomes *non-central*, after which the paradigm continues to produce words beginning with *non-* as long as they meet the tests of comprehensibility and practicality: *non-centralitarian* is improbable, but not impossible.

The 14 paradigms represent a core of productive suffixial patterns available in present-day English, despite the existence of many 'rogue' items that do not successfully fit into the appropriate system. There are other such paradigms, as for example the *-able/-ible* paradigm (*teach/teachable/teachability*) and the *-ment* paradigm (*develop/development/developmental*), but they are excluded for reasons of space or because of the complexities involved in their description.

(1) Words from basic verbs

X > Xer
  > Xing
  > Xed

climb	climber	run	runner
	climbing		running
	climbed		ran

(2) Words from basic adjectives

X > Xly
  > Xness
  > Xie
  > Xish > Xishness
  > Xen > [P1]

dark	darkly	
	darkness	
	darkie	
	darkish	*darkishness
	darken	[darkener darkening darkened]
red	redly	
	redness	
	*reddie	
	reddish	reddishness
	redden	[*reddener reddening reddened]

(3) Words from basic animate nouns

X > Xhood/Xdom/Xship
  > Xly   > Xliness
  > Xish   > Xishly
           > Xishness

child	childhood	
	childly	*childliness
	childish	childishly
		childishness
king	kinghood/kingdom/kingship	
	kingly	kingliness
	*kingish	*kingishly
		*kingishness
woman	womanhood	
	womanly	womanliness
	womanish	womanishly
		womanishness

(4) Words from basic inanimate nouns

X > Xy > Xily
        > Xiness

dirt	dirty	dirtily	water	watery	*waterily
		dirtiness			wateriness

(5) Words containing -al (but excluding P8)

X > Xal > Xally
         > Xalism > [P13]
         > Xality > Xalitarian
         > Xalness
         > Xalize > [P12]
                   > [P1]

centre	central	centrally	
		centralism	[centralist
			centralistic
			centralistically]
		centrality	*centralitarian
		centralness	
		centralize	centralization
			[centralizer
			centralizing
			centralized]

leg- legal legally
            legalism [legalist
                          legalistic
                          legalistically]
            legality *legalitarian
            legalness
            legalize legalization
                          [legalizer
                          legalizing
                          legalized]

Note. When *l* occurs in the base (as in *pole* and *sol-*), *-al* becomes *-ar* (*polar*, *solar*) and the paradigm continues in the same form.

(6) Words containing *-an* (especially geographical uses)

X > Xan > Xanism > Xanist
            > Xanness
            > Xanize > [P12]

Africa African Africanism Africanist
                    Africanness
                    Africanize [Africanization
                                    Africanizer
                                    Africanizing
                                    Africanized]

India Indian Indianism Indianist
                  Indianness
                  Indianize [Indianization
                                Indianizer
                                Indianizing
                                Indianized]

(7) Words containing *-id, -ile, -ine, ous*

X > Xid > Xidly
      Xile Xilely
      Xine Xinely
      Xous Xously
            > Xidity
            Xility
            Xinity
            Xosity
            > Xidness
            Xileness
            Xineness
            Xousness

---

luc- lucid lucidly
            lucidity
            lucidness
fert- fertile fertilely
            fertility
            fertileness
femin- feminine femininely
            femininity
            feminineness

visc- viscous viscously
            viscosity
            viscousness

(8) Words containing *-ic*

X > Xic > Xical > Xically
      > Xicity
      > Xicness

---

history historic historical historically
            historicity
            historicness
irony ironic ironical ironically
            *ironicity
            ironicness
symbol symbolic symbolical symbolically
            symbolicity
            symbolicness

(9) Words containing *-ion* and *-ive*

Xion > Xional > [P5]
        > Xive > Xively
                  > Xivism > [P13]
                              > Xivity
                              > Xiveness

---

predict prediction *predictional
            predictive predictively
                          *predictivism
                          *predictivity
                          predictiveness
*receive reception *receptional
            receptive receptively
                          *receptivism
                          receptivity
                          receptiveness
select selection selectional
            selective selectively
                          selectivism [*selectivist]
                          selectivity
                          selectiveness

(10) Words based on *-ics*

X > Xics > Xicist/Xician
      > Xicize > [P12]
      > Xic > Xical > Xically

---

eth- ethics ethicist
            ethicize *ethicization
            ethic ethical ethically
polit- politics politician
            politicize politicization
            politic political politically

(11) Verbs in *-ify*

X > Xify > Xification > Xificational/Xificatory
> [PI]

class	classify	classification	classificational/atory [classifier classifying classified]
ver-	verify	verification	verificational/atory [verify verifying verified]

(12) Verbs in *-ize*

X > Xize > Xization
> [PI]

creole	creolize	creolization [*creolizer creolizing creolized]
maximum	maximize	maximization [*maximizer maximizing maximized]
Stalin	Stalinize	Stalinization [Stalinizer Stalinizing Stalinized]

(13) Words based on *-ism* (uncountable)

X > Xism
> Xist > Xistic > Xistically

commun-	communism		
	communist	communistic	communistically
Darwin	Darwinism		
	Darwinist	Darwinistic	*Darwinistically
Narcissus	narcissism		
	narcissist	narcissistic	narcissistically

(14) Words based on *-ism* (countable)

X > Xism
> Xistic > Xistically

euphem-	euphemism	
	euphemistic	euphemistically
Spooner	Spoonerism	
	*Spooneristic	*Spooneristically

SUFFOLK. See EAST ANGLIA.

SUGGESTOPEDIA. See ELT, LANGUAGE TEACHING.

SUMMARY [15c: from Latin *summarius* highest, chief, main, from *summus* highest. Compare Latin *summa* a synthesis of all that is known about something, such as the *Summa theologica* of St Thomas Aquinas]. (1) (Now rare) containing the chief or essential points: *a summary journal*; *summary aphorisms*. (2) Concise, brief; stated or done very quickly: *summary proceedings*; *summary justice*. (3) A comprehensive and usually brief abstract or digest of a text or statement. See ABRIDG(E)MENT, ABSTRACT, PRÉCIS. [WRITING].   T.MCA.

SUPERLATIVE (DEGREE). In grammatical theory, the third degree of an adjective or adverb. This is usually formed either by adding *-est* to the uninflected positive or absolute form of shorter words (*kindest, fastest*) or by putting *most* before longer words and adverbs (*most extraordinary, most quickly*). Irregular superlatives include *best* and *worst*. See ADJECTIVE, ADVERB, COMPARATIVE DEGREE, DEGREE POSITIVE. [GRAMMAR].   S.C.

SUPERORDINATE CLAUSE. In grammatical analysis, a term for a clause that contains another clause. In *It was raining when I left home*, the sentence constitutes a superordinate clause, since it contains a subordinate *when*-clause. In *I think it was raining when I left home*, the clause beginning with *it* remains superordinate to the *when*-clause, but is at the same time subordinate to the superordinate clause that constitutes the sentence. See CLAUSE, SUBORDINATION. [GRAMMAR].   S.G.

SUPERORDINATE TERM. See HYPONYM, SEMANTICS.

SUPERSCRIPT [16c: from Latin *superscriptus* written above]. (1) Also *superior*. Written above: *superscript numbers*. (2) Also *superior*. A character, letter, or symbol written or printed next to and partly or wholly above another, usually in a smaller size. The main applications of superscripts are: to denote footnotes, both at the note itself and the point in the text to which the note refers; to identify homographs in a dictionary or glossary (bat^1 the animal, bat^2 the implement); in mathematics and science, to denote various functions of numerals, especially the power of a number (10^3 representing $10 \times 10 \times 10$); in bibliographies, to denote an edition of a work cited (CAH^2 identifying the 2nd edition of the *Cambridge Ancient History*), and in bibliographical collation to indicate the number of leaves in a gathering of a book. (3) Formerly, a *superscription*, such as a postal address at the beginning of a letter. Compare SUBSCRIPT. See DIACRITIC, HOMONYM, NOTES AND REFERENCES. [TECHNOLOGY, WRITING].   R.E.A.

SUPERSTRATE [1980s: from Latin *superstratus* spread or laid above]. Also **superstratum** [1800s]. A language or aspect of a language which affects another less prestigious or socially and culturally dominated language: for example,

Latin or French influencing Old and Middle English; English influencing many of the indigenous languages of Africa and Asia. Compare SUBSTRATE. [LANGUAGE].   S.R.

SUPPLETION [13c: from Latin *suppletio/suppletionis* making complete]. A term in linguistics for a situation in which a form in a grammatical paradigm bears no family resemblance to the base form: for example, *went* in *go/goes/going/went/gone* and *better* and *best* in *good/better/best*. Suppletive forms are common in irregular usage in many languages. [GRAMMAR].   S.G.

SUPRASEGMENTAL. A term in phonetics and linguistics, used especially in the US to refer to features of stress and intonation. Structural linguists adopted this term because in their notations, the features were marked on paper 'above' (*supra-*) the morphological features (*segments*) of an utterance. In Britain, the equivalent term is *prosodic*. See PROSODY. [SPEECH].   T.MCA.

SURFACE STRUCTURE. See CHOMSKY, MODEL, TRANSFORMATIONAL-GENERATIVE GRAMMAR.

SURINAM, also **Suriname**. Officially *Republic of Surinam*. A state of the Caribbean coast of South America. Capital: Paramaribo. Currency: the gulden (guilder). Economy: agriculture, mining. Population: 399,000 (1988), 508,000 (projection for 2000). Ethnicity: 45% African (including 10% Morron, Bosneger, or Bush Negro), 34% East Indian, 16% Javanese, 3% Amerindian, 2% Chinese. Religions: 27% Hindu, 25% Protestant, 23% Roman Catholic, 20% Muslim, remainder traditional beliefs. Languages: Dutch (official), Sranan and other Creoles, English, Hindi, Javanese. Education: primary 98%, secondary 66%, tertiary 3%, literacy 90%. The first European settlers in the area were British from Barbados in 1651, but the Dutch gained the territory in 1667 in a swap that gave Nieuw Amsterdam (to become New York) to Britain. After this, the colony became *Dutch Guiana*. The British held it again (1799-1818) during the Napoleonic wars. The colony became independent as Surinam in 1975. It is remarkable for its variety of English-based creoles: *Ndjuka, Saramaccan,* and *Sranan* or *Taki-Taki*. See BEHN, CARIBBEAN ENGLISH CREOLE, ENGLISH, NDJUKA, SARAMACCAN, SRANAN. [AMERICAS, NAME, VARIETY].   L.D.C.

SURNAME. See PERSONAL NAME.

SURVEY OF ENGLISH DIALECTS. A survey of the dialects of England directed by Harold Orton and published under his editorship in twelve volumes by E. J. Arnold, Leeds, from 1962 to 1972. In the 1930s, Orton engaged in discussions with European and American colleagues on a project that would lead to a *Linguistic Atlas of England*, but the plan did not mature until after the Second World War, when he re-established contact in 1946 with Eugen Dieth at Zurich. They spent several summers preparing, testing, and revising a survey form duly published in 1952 by the Leeds Philosophic and Literary Society. This questionnaire differed from others before it in being not simply a worksheet setting out items to be collected but also presenting some 1,300 questions to be asked in such a way that later reviewers of the material would know how it had been gathered, and so that the questions would be seen to have avoided planting a pronunciation or a word in the minds of informants. These were to be older people born and living in the 313 areas surveyed. Since the survey was largely rural, the questions were mainly based on agricultural topics. The aim, however, was not simply to elicit farming vocabulary but to gain samples of every conceivable realization of the development of vowels and consonants from earlier English forms, as well as giving a comprehensive view of differences in morphology and syntax in contemporary dialect.

The first full-time fieldworker was Peter Wright (1949-52), the second Stanley Ellis (1952-9), assisted by graduate researchers who included some American Fulbright Scholars. With the help of W. J. Halliday, a retired headmaster active in the Yorkshire Dialect Society, three volumes of material for the North of England and the Isle of Man were published in 1962, material for the rest being published over the next ten years. Co-editors with Orton, after Halliday in the North, were P. M. Tilling for the East Midlands, Michael V. Barry for the West Midlands, and Martyn Wakelin for the South. Publication was in pages of phonetic answers to the questionnaire, presented under the heading of each question. Orton supervised the preparation of the *Linguistic Atlas of England* from Survey materials, but its publication came after his death in 1978. See DIALECT, LINGUISTIC ATLAS OF ENGLAND, ORTON. [EUROPE, VARIETY].   S.E.

SURVEY OF ENGLISH USAGE, short form *SEU*. A survey founded by Randolph Quirk in 1959 at the U. of Durham, England. It was moved to permanent premises at U. College London in 1960, when Quirk became Professor of English Language there. He remained its Director until 1981. The present Director is Sidney Greenbaum, who assumed the position in 1983, when he succeeded Quirk as Quain Professor of English Language and Literature.

Aim. The aim of the Survey is to provide the resources for accurate descriptions of the grammar available to, and used by, adult educated native speakers of BrE. It was assumed that grammarians cannot rely simply on their own knowledge to provide the grammatical data that are at the disposal of speakers of English in a range of stylistic contexts. The major activity of the Survey was therefore the collection and analysis of representative samples of spoken and written BrE. A subsidiary activity was the development and administration of experiments eliciting use and judgement among native speakers. The elicitation tests supplemented corpus data on features that were in divided use or that were infrequent in the corpus, such as the choice of the subjunctive, the *should*-construction, or the indicative after verbs such as *demand* and *recommend*; the normal positions of different types of adverbials; the verbs that collocate with such intensifiers as *badly* and *entirely*.

fiction, news reports, legal and administrative documents.

Analysis of the Corpus. In its original form the Corpus was and is available in photocopied booklets and slips. Each slip (6 × 4 inches) contains 17 lines, including four lines of overlap with preceding and following slips to provide context. For each collected feature there is one slip that is marked for that item. The Survey has collected 65 grammatical features (such as adverbs, names, negation, direct speech); over 400 specified words or phrases that were felt to have grammatical significance (such as *a*, *is*, *could*, *not*, *and*, *in spite of*); for spoken texts, about 100 prosodic features (such as rising and falling tones) and paralinguistic features (such as laughing, sobbing); and for written texts, all punctuation marks. The slips are in specified drawers of filing cabinets in text order. Scholars from many parts of the world visit the Survey's premises at UCL to consult the files.

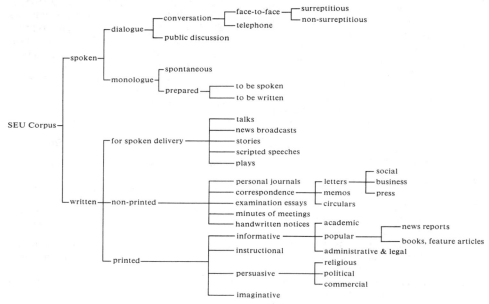

Content of the Corpus. The Corpus consists of 200 samples ('texts'), each of 5,000 words, for a total of one million words. The texts cover a wide range of subject matter, situations, and degrees of formality. The 100 spoken texts comprise face-to-face conversations and telephone coversations, discussions, interviews, broadcast commentaries, lectures, demonstrations, sermons, committee meetings, and dictations. The 100 written texts comprise: scripted material that was read aloud, such as drama and news broadcasts; manuscript material, such as social and business letters; printed publications, such as learned and popular books on various topics,

The London–Lund Corpus. In 1975, the Survey of Spoken English was established by Jan Svartvik at Lund University in Sweden with the aim of transferring the Survey spoken texts to machine-readable form. This version of the spoken texts reduces the amount of detailed information in the Survey transcriptions by omitting some of the original prosodic features and all the paralinguistic features. The 87 Survey spoken texts (all that had by then been processed at the Survey) became available in machine-readable form for distribution in the early 1980s. This set of texts is called the *London–Lund Corpus* because it derived from the Survey Corpus in London and was computerized at Lund University. A selection of 34 texts of face-to-face conversations, totalling some 170,000 words, has been published in *A Corpus of English Conversation*, edited by Jan Svartvik and Randolph Quirk (Lund: Gleerup, 1980). The Lund Survey of Spoken English has since been engaged in developing a semi-automatic, interactive system of grammatical tagging that can be used primarily for research into the interrelationship of grammar and prosody.

Survey corpus: status and plans. In 1989 (30 years since its founding), the Survey completed the collection of its 200 texts, the transcription of its spoken material, the computerization of the remaining 13 spoken texts (which have been added as a supplement to the original London–Lund corpus), and (with financial assistance from IBM and practical assistance from Geoffrey Kaye, an IBM researcher) the computerization of the 100 written texts. For copyright reasons, the written texts must be consulted at the Survey premises. The whole corpus is being provided with an interactive concordance browser, which allows the user to request concordance lines for any lexical string and to gain access for any line to the full preceding and subsequent contexts. A program is being applied that automatically assigns word-class tags to every word. Plans include applying a program for automatic parsing of sentences, and processes for the digitization of sound recordings. These analyses will be available on the interactive concordance browser.

Survey publications. Numerous books and articles have drawn on data from the Corpus (including its computerized spoken texts in the London–Lund Corpus) and from the results of experiments conducted at the Survey or by associates of the Survey. Prominent among them are two major reference works: *A Grammar of Contemporary English* (Longman, 1972) and *A Comprehensive Grammar of the English Language* (Longman, 1985), both by R. Quirk, S. Greenbaum, G. Leech, and J. Svartvik. Two advanced-level textbooks based on the 1972 reference grammar are used in universities and colleges throughout the world: *A University Grammar of English*, by Quirk and Greenbaum (Longman, 1973; US title *A Concise Grammar of Contemporary English*, Harcourt Brace Jovanovich, 1973) and *A Communicative Grammar of English*, by Leech and Svartvik (Longman, 1975). An advanced-level textbook based on the 1985 reference grammar has also been published: *A Student's Grammar of the English Language*, by Greenbaum and Quirk (Longman, 1990). A select bibliography of other books using Survey data appears below.

International Corpus of English (short form *ICE*). In 1988, Greenbaum initiated discussions on a proposal for an International Corpus of English that will be available for distribution on computer disks. The collection of texts began in 1990. At the time of writing, research teams participating in the project are drawing on English used in Australia, Canada, East Africa (Kenya, Tanzania, Zambia), Hong Kong, India, Jamaica, New Zealand, Nigeria, the Philippines, Singapore, the UK, and the US. Supplementary projects deal with translations into written English and English used in international spoken communication, and English in teaching material for learners of the language. The national corpora will each contain one million words and will be compiled and analysed in similar ways. The texts in the supplementary corpora will be drawn from varieties similar to those in the national corpora. The Survey will be providing the UK component. The ICE project will facilitate comparative studies of national varieties of English, including the English used in countries such as India and Nigeria where English is primarily a second language. The Survey component will also provide the means for investigating recent changes in the language through a comparison with the Survey corpus. See CORPUS, GRAMMAR OF CONTEMPORARY ENGLISH, QUIRK. [EUROPE, GRAMMAR, USAGE]. S.G.

Akimoto, M. 1983. *Idiomaticity*. Tokyo: Shinozaki Shorin.
—— 1989. *A Study of Verbo-Nominal Structures in English*. Tokyo: Shinozaki Shorin.
Altenberg, B. 1987. *Prosodic Patterns in Spoken English*. Lund: University Press.
Bäcklund, I. 1984. *Conjunction-Headed Abbreviated Clauses in English*. Uppsala: Almqvist & Wiksell.
Bald, W. D., & Ilson, R. (eds.). 1977. *Studies in English Usage: The Resources of a Present-Day English Corpus for Linguistic Analysis*. Frankfurt: Lang.
Bublitz, W. 1988. *Supportive Fellow-Speakers and Cooperative Conversations*. Amsterdam: John Benjamins.
Carvell, H. T., & Svartvik, J. 1969. *Computational Experiments in Grammatical Classification*. The Hague: Mouton.
Coates, J. 1982. *The Semantics of the Modal Auxiliaries*. London: Croom Helm.
Crystal, D. 1969. *Prosodic Systems and Intonation in English*. Cambridge & New York: Cambridge University Press.
Granger, S. 1983. *The 'be' + Past Participle Construed in Spoken English with Special Emphasis on the Passive*. Amsterdam: North-Holland.
Greenbaum, S. 1969. *Studies in English Adverbial Usage*. London: Longman.
—— 1991. 'ICE: the International Corpus of English', in *English Today* 28, Oct. Cambridge: University Press.
Lipka, L. 1972. *Semantic Structure and Word-Formation: Verb-Particle Constructions in Contemporary English*. Munich: Fink.

Mair, C. 1990. *Infinitival Complement Clauses in English*. Cambridge: University Press.

Palmer, F. R. 1979. *Modality and the English Modals*. London: Longman.

Rusiecki, J. 1985. *Adjectives and Comparison in English: A Semantic Study*. London: Longman.

Stenström, A.-B. 1984. *Questions and Responses in English Conversation*. Malmö: Liber.

Svartvik, J. 1966. *On Voice in the English Verb*. The Hague: Mouton.

Taglicht, J. 1984. *Message and Emphasis: On Focus and Scope in English*. London: Longman.

Thavenius, C. 1983. *Referential Pronouns in English Conversation*. Lund: Liber.

Tottie, G., & Bäcklund, I. 1986. *English in Speech and Writing: A Symposium*. Uppsala: Almqvist & Wiksell.

SURVEY OF SPOKEN ENGLISH. See SURVEY OF ENGLISH USAGE.

SURVIVAL LITERACY. See FUNCTIONAL LITERACY.

SUSPENSION POINTS. See ELLIPSIS.

SWAHILI [Early 19c: from Arabic *sawāḥilī* coastal, bordering, from *sāḥil* coast, edge]. Also **Kiswahili, KiSwahili,** formerly **Swahilese.** A Bantu language spoken as a mother tongue or a second language in the East African mainland and islands, from Lamu Island in Kenya in the north to the southern border of Tanzania, and west to Zaïre. It may have arisen from a Bantu language pidginized through contact with Arabic. As a language of trade, it spread inland from the coast during the 19c. It is the official language of Kenya and Tanzania and a lingua franca in Uganda and Zaïre. Arabic has provided many loanwords, and the earliest Swahili literature, from the 18c, is in Arabic script. Its most important varieties are: *Kiunguja* or *KiUnguja* in Zanzibar and mainland Tanzania, *Kimvita* or *KiMvita* in Mombasa and other areas of Kenya, and *Kiamu* or *KiAmu* on Lamu and in adjacent coastal areas. Early literature consisted of local narratives, Arabic tales, and translations of European writers. The British colonial administration in the 1930s encouraged the development of standard Swahili from Kiunguja and literary Swahili is a strong medium for East African literature. The body of work reflects colonial and post-colonial experience, as in James Mbotela's historical novel *Uhuru wa Watumwa* (Freedom for the Slaves, 1934) and the work of the poet and novelist Shaaban Robert. Swahili nouns are divided into classes according to the grammatical prefixes they take. Such prefixes also bring verbs, adjectives, demonstratives, and possessives into concord with the subject of a sentence: for example, in *Watu wetu wale wakubwa wamekuja* (Those big people of ours have come), *watu* is the plural of *mtu* (person), and other words harmonize by beginning with *wa*. Comparably, *mbenzi* is a rich person (who owns a Mercedes-Benz), plural *wabenzi*. In the proverb *Kidole kimoja kikiumia vidole vingine vitoa damu* (If you hurt one of your fingers, the others will bleed), *ki* in the first clause marks singular concord, while *vi* in the second marks the plural. Swahili is one of the few indigenous black African rivals to English. Because it is used over such a wide area, it tends to be ethnically neutral. See AFRICAN ENGLISH, AFRICAN LANGUAGES, AGGLUTINATING, ARABIC, BANTU, EAST AFRICAN ENGLISH, KENYA, TANZANIA, UGANDA. [AFRICA, LANGUAGE]. T.MCA.

SWAZILAND. Officially: English *Kingdom of Swaziland*, Siswati *Umbuso weSwatini*. A country in southern Africa, between South Africa and Mozambique. Administrative capital: Mbabane. Legislative capital: Lobamba. Currency: lilangeni (100 cents), plural *emalengeni*. Population: 738,000 (1988), 1.1m (projection for 2000). Ethnicity: Swazi 90%; Nyasa, Sotho, Zulu 7%; European and mixed 3%. Religions: 49% Protestant, 43% traditional, 8% Roman Catholic. Languages: Siswati or SiSwati (also known as Swazi, the Zulu form of the name) and English (both official). Education: primary 85%, secondary, 40%, tertiary 3%, literacy 68%. The Swazi occupied the territory in the early 19c, in competition with the Boers. Their autonomy was guaranteed by Britain, but the territory was administered by the Boer province of Transvaal until 1903, when it came under the British governor of Transvaal, then a province of the Union of South Africa. Independence was gained in 1968. See ENGLISH, SOUTH AFRICA. [AFRICA, NAME, VARIETY]. T.MCA.

SWEARING. A term that refers to both taking an oath and using language that is regarded as foul, abusive, and profane. In Macaulay's *Lays of Ancient Rome* (1842) are the lines: 'Lars Porsena of Clusium / By the Nine Gods he swore / That the great house of Tarquin / Should suffer wrong no more.' When he swore this oath, Lars Porsena invoked the punishment of the gods on himself if he should fail to help the house of Tarquin. Similarly, when people in a Christian culture swear on the Bible to tell the truth in court, they assume that God will punish anyone who then lies, quite apart from the legal consequences of 'being forsworn' (*perjury*). When people swear something or swear to do something, for example on their honour, they pledge that honour as a security to be forfeited if forsworn. When the ringleader of a plot swears fellow conspirators to secrecy, or the Chief Justice of the US Supreme Court 'swears in' a new president, a binding oath is administered. To 'swear off' smoking is to take an oath to stop smoking and to 'swear by' the *OED* is to have great faith in it. Oaths sworn to a god or God are solemn matters, but over the centuries have passed from being ritual formulas to being exclamations. The negative aspect of oath-swearing (retribution) allows other kinds of negatively charged language to be called *oaths*, and their exclamatory use to be called *swearing*. The extension of these notions from *By God!* through *Hell!* and *Shit!* to *You son of a bitch!* is striking but not surprising; the last three can be called both *oaths* and *curses*, and the activity in general can be called *cursing and swearing*. The notion of cursing has undergone a similar development: solemn cursing invokes supernatural retribution on someone or something the curser holds odious. By swearing an oath, Lars Porsena invited the punishment of the Nine Gods on his own head. He might equally well have urged them to punish the offending Romans by cursing the Romans in their name.

See ABUSE, (A)ESTHETICS, ANGLO-SAXON, AUSTRALIAN, AUSTRALIAN LANGUAGE, BAD LANGUAGE, BLASPHEMY, CENSORSHIP, COPRO-LALIA, CURSING, DEROGATORY, DICTIONARY OF SLANG AND UNCONVENTIONAL ENGLISH, ETHNIC NAME, EUPHEMISM, EXCLAMATION, EXPLETIVE, FOUL LANGUAGE, FOUR-LETTER WORD, GRAFFITI, GREAT AUSTRALIAN ADJECTIVE, INFIX, LANGUAGE, MALEDICTA, OATH, OBSCENITY, PARTRIDGE, PEJOR-ATIVE, PLAIN ENGLISH, PYGMALION, READ, SCAT-OLOGY, SLANG, SLUR, SMUT, STRONG LANGUAGE, SWEARWORD, TABOO, VULGAR, VULGARISM. [STYLE, USAGE].   R.F.I.

SWEARWORD. A non-technical term for a word or phrase that is obscene, abusive, and socially offensive. Swearwords are usually associated with the genitals and sexual activity (*cunt, fuck, prick*), excrement (*crap, shit*), or religion (*Jesus Christ!*), and may combine elements from each area (*fucking shit, fucking hell*). Conceptions of what is or is not, should or should not be, a swearword have varied over the years. In the 19c, *damn* was widely regarded as a swearword, but is nowadays generally considered mild because, by and large, religious topics such as heaven and hell are no longer taken as seriously as in the past. See SWEARING. [STYLE].   T.MCA.

SWEDISH. A Germanic language spoken in Sweden and parts of Finland, where it is an official language together with Finnish. In comparison with Danish and Norse, it has had relatively little historical contact with or impact on English, but in the late 20c English has begun to have a considerable impact on Swedish. See BORROWING, SCANDINAVIAN LANGUAGES. [EUROPE, LANGUAGE].   P.C.

SWEET, Henry [1845-1912]. English philologist, phonetician, and grammarian. Born in London, and educated at King's College School, London, he matriculated in 1864 at the U. of Heidelberg, where he gained experience of German philological method. After a spell in a commercial office he entered Balliol College, Oxford, in 1869, acquiring a fourth-class degree in 1873 because of interests not directly related to his courses: in 1871, while still an undergraduate, he edited King Alfred's translation of the *Cura Pastoralis* for the Early English Text Society, his commentary laying the foundation of Old English dialectology. Further works on Old English include: *An Anglo-Saxon Reader* (1876); *The Oldest English Texts* (1885); *A Student's Dictionary of Anglo-Saxon* (1896). He has been described by C. L. Wrenn as 'England's greatest Anglo-Saxonist' (in *Transactions of the Philological Society*, 1946).

Having failed in his candidacy for the Merton Chair of English at Oxford in 1885, Sweet concentrated on other interests. In 1877, he had published *A Handbook of Phonetics*, which attracted attention among scholars and teachers of English on the Continent. He followed it with *Elementarbuch des gesprochenen Englisch* (1885), adapted as *A Primer of Spoken English* (1890). This was the first scientific description of educated London speech, the accent later known as Received Pronunciation. Sweet used phonetic script throughout this work, including specimens of connected speech in transcription. By emphasizing the spoken language and the use of phonetics he was a pioneer in language-teaching methodology. His views on the subject were set out in *The Practical Study of Languages* (1899). His last book on English pronunciation was *The Sounds of English* (1908). Other interests to which Sweet gave attention in later life were the historical development of the sounds of English (*The History of English Sounds*, 2nd enlarged edition, 1888), the theory and philosophy of grammar (*A New English Grammar, Logical and Historical*, 1892-8), and comparative philology, including the relationship between Indo-European and other language families (*The History of Language*, 1900).

In 1901, Sweet was again unsuccessful in an application for a professorship at Oxford, this time the Chair of Comparative Philology that had become vacant on Max Müller's death. Instead, he was offered a Readership in Phonetics, which he accepted and held until his death. To outsiders, including admirers on the Continent, his failure to gain appropriate academic recognition at Oxford seemed incomprehensible.

Those familiar with the local scene knew of a clash of personalities, with faults on both sides. Sweet's own behaviour was at times 'almost suggestive of nascent "persecution-mania" ' (Wrenn, above). After his death, his widow told Jespersen that she had tried to persuade the Clarendon Press to publish her husband's autobiography. The Press had refused on the grounds that it contained libellous attacks on persons still living. Jespersen read it in the spring of 1914 and found it a moving *document humain* which threw light on much in Sweet's character. The manuscript has since disappeared. Bernard Shaw, who knew Sweet personally and regarded him as a man of genius, writes in the preface of *Pygmalion* about his 'Satanic contempt for all academic dignitaries and persons in general who thought more of Greek than of phonetics'. The play's Professor Higgins, he says, is not a portrait of Sweet: 'With Higgins's physique and temperament Sweet might have set the Thames on fire.' There are, however, 'touches of Sweet in the play'. In 1984, a society was formed in Oxford to promote the study of the history of linguistic thought, and named the *Henry Sweet Society*. Its membership is international. See index. [BIOGRAPHY, EDUCATION, EUROPE, GRAMMAR, HISTORY, SPEECH].   P.C.

SWEET TALK [1920s]. An informal term for cajolery or 'soft soap' (smooth, slick, persuasive talk). *To sweet-talk* (*people*) is to use cajoling words to persuade them: compare *to soft-soap* (*someone*). In Black English Vernacular and West African Pidgin English, *sweet talk* covers everything from flattery to fluent, well-chosen expressions. See TALK. [SPEECH, STYLE].   T.MCA.

SWIFT, Jonathan [1667–1745]. Anglo-Irish clergyman and satirist, born in Dublin, and educated at Trinity College, Dublin. After a time as secretary to the diplomat Sir William Temple, he returned to Ireland, where he was ordained in 1694. During a second period in Temple's service, he wrote *The Battle of the Books* (1697), ridiculing the critical debate between the 'ancients' and the 'moderns', and *A Tale of a Tub* (1704), which satirized contemporary religious disputes. Although he received a prebend at St Patrick's Cathedral in Dublin, Swift spent much of his time in the London literary world. The Whig Government's tolerance of dissenters made him a Tory supporter and propagandist. His *Journal to Stella* (1710–13), a sentimental correspondence with Esther Johnson, was written in an infantile language of his own devising. In 1713, he became Dean of St Patrick's. Anger at the Whig treatment of Ireland drove him to write defences of Irish rights, including the *Drapier's Letters* (1724) and *A Modest Proposal*

(1729). His most famous work, *Gulliver's Travels* (1726), satirized both contemporary and universal follies under the guise of a seaman's visits to various imaginary countries, among them *Lilliput*, a land of tiny people, and *Brobdingnag*, a land of giants.

Swift's contributions to English include these names and their adjectives, *Lilliputian* and *Brobdingnagian*. Swift expressed strong opinions in the contemporary debate about good English; his *Proposal for Correcting, Improving and Ascertaining the English Tongue* (1712) assigns the best English to the period from the accession of Elizabeth Tudor to the beginning of the Civil War in 1642, after which came corruption. He particularly disliked fashionable slang words, and practices such as the clipping of words, as when *physiognomy* became 'phi(z)' and *mobile vulgus* ('the fickle crowd') became 'mob': pronouncing the first syllable in a word that has many, and dismissing the rest; such as *phizz, hipps, pozz, rep*, and many more; when we are already overloaded with monosyllables, which are the disgrace of our language' (*Tatler*, 1710). His humorous *Complete Collection of Polite and Ingenious Conversation* (1738) is a valuable record of contemporary speech. Swift's prose style is plain, deceptively simple, and incisive in the command of irony. He also wrote poetry, much of it satirical, and some of it revealing his feelings of disgust with the human body. In his later years, his mind was affected by illness, but the view that he died insane is not now generally held. See index. [BIOGRAPHY, EUROPE, LITERATURE, STYLE].   R.C.

SWUNG DASH [1950s]. A name for the tilde (~) when used in dictionaries as a space-saving device: in an entry for *house*, ~*boat* stands for *houseboat* and ~ *style* for *house style*; in an entry for *hero*, ~*es* stands for *heroes*. The device is common in bilingual dictionaries, when it is generally called a tilde, and has been extensively used in Oxford dictionaries. The name *swung dash* first appeared in the introduction to the 4th edition of the *Concise Oxford Dictionary* (1950), the first edition to use it. It has been disappearing from recent editions of Oxford dictionaries, including the 8th edition of the *COD* (1990). See CONCISE OXFORD DICTIONARY, DASH, TILDE. [TECHNOLOGY, WRITING].   R.E.A.

SYLLABARY. See ALPHABET, JAPAN.

SYLLABIC ACRONYM. See ACRONYM, TELESCOPING.

SYLLABICATION, also **syllabification**. The division of a word into syllables: either phonologically, in terms of speech sounds, or orthographically, in terms of letters. In orthographic syllabication, there may be correspondences with spoken syllables (*native* into *na·tive*) and/or with elements of morphological and etymological significance (*nat·ive* from Latin *natus* born, and *-ive*). The two kinds of division do not always correspond. Neither syllable boundaries in speech nor morphological/etymological elements are always clear-cut, and the fact that the same word may be pronounced differently in different varieties of English can mean a different number of syllables and different syllable boundaries: *medicine* generally pronounced with two syllables in BrE and three in AmE. Nevertheless, orthographic syllabication is straightforward in many words, as with the division of *postman* into *post·man*, which satisfies phonetic, morphological, and etymological criteria in both BrE and AmE. Such a word as *structure* is more problematic; both BrE and AmE phonology dictate *struc·ture*, while morphology and etymology require *struct·ure*. It has been claimed that when such a conflict occurs, AmE favours the phonetic and BrE the morphological and etymological. Rules for syllabication are given in various style manuals: for BrE, *Hart's Rules for Compositors and Readers at the University Press Oxford* (1893, 39th edition, 1983); for AmE, *The Chicago Manual of Style* (13th edition, 1982). The syllabication of individual words is routinely provided in the headwords of AmE dictionaries, less often in BrE dictionaries, unless they are EFL learners' dictionaries or mother-tongue dictionaries influenced by American practice (with AmE syllabication sometimes shown for BrE). Some dictionaries, such as *Webster's Ninth New Collegiate* and the *Oxford Advanced Learner's*, show only those syllable boundaries where a word can be divided at the end of a line (*gar gan tuan*); others, such as the *American Heritage* and the *Longman Dictionary of Contemporary English*, show all boundaries (*gar gan tu an*), whether or not they can serve as end-of-line divisions. The second policy is probably more frequent than the first. See HYPHEN, SYLLABLE. [REFERENCE, SPEECH, WRITING].   R.F.I.

SYLLABIC CONSONANT. See SYLLABLE, and the letter entries L, M, N, R.

SYLLABLE [14c: from Anglo-Norman *sillable*, Old French *sillabe*, Latin *syllaba*, Greek *sullabḗ* taken, brought, or put together]. The smallest unit of speech that normally occurs in isolation, consisting of either a vowel alone (as in the pronunciation of *ah*) or a combination of vowel and consonant(s) (as in the pronunciation of *no*, *on*, and *non*). Some consonants can be pronounced

alone (*mmm*, *zzz*), and may or may not be regarded as syllables, but they normally accompany vowels, which tend to occupy the central position in a syllable (the *syllabic position*), as in *pap*, *pep*, *pip*, *pop*, *pup*. Consonants occupy the margins of the syllable, as with *p* in the examples just given. A vowel in the syllable margin is often referred to as a *glide*, as in *ebb* and *bay*. *Syllabic consonants* occur in the second syllables of words like *middle* and *midden*, replacing a sequence of schwa plus consonant; here, the time needed to pronounce the schwa is transferred to the following consonant: for example, in the pronunciation /'mɪdl̩/ for *middle* and /'mɪdn̩/ for *midden*. As the examples show, a syllabic consonant is marked phonetically with a subscript vertical dash (̩). See L, M, N, R.

The structure and arrangement of syllables vary from language to language: for example, in English a syllable can begin with /tr/ and /tw/ but not /tl/ (*tree* and *twee*, but not *tlee), while in another language initial /tl/ may be unexceptionable: for example, among speakers of Tlingit, an aboriginal language of Canada and Alaska. There may also be variations among varieties of the same language: for example, in mainstream English the initial clusters /fr/ and /sl/ occur (*from* and *slow*), but not /vr/ and /zl/, but such pronunciations as 'vrom' and 'zlow' are shibboleths of the West Country dialects of England. However, an unusual syllabic sequence is not necessarily difficult to say: initial /vr/ is easily pronounced in the unique word *vroom* and /zl/ in the Polish loanword *zloty*.

A syllable standing alone is a *monosyllable*, and may be a word in its own right, as with *a*, *an*, *big*, *cat*, *no*, *the*, *yes*. A word containing many syllables is a *polysyllable* or *polysyllabic word*, such as *selectivity* and *utilitarianism*. A *disyllable* or *disyllabic word* has two syllables, a *trisyllable* or *trisyllabic word* has three.

See BREVE, DISYLLABLE, FLESCH READABILITY FORMULA, FOG INDEX, FOOT, HYPHEN, JUNCTURE, MACRON, METRE/METER, MONOSYLLABLE, POLYSYLLABLE, RHYTHM, ROOT WORD, SCANSION, SYN(A)ERESIS, TONE. [SPEECH].   G.K., T.MCA.

SYLLABLE-TIMING/TIMED. See RHYTHM.

SYLLABLE WORD [1980s]. An occasional term in word-formation for a word formed from syllables or syllable-like elements drawn from two or more other words: *sial* from the first syllables in *silicon* and *alumin(i)um*. Compare ACRONYM, LETTER WORD, MONOSYLLABLE, SYLLABLE. [WORD].   T.MCA.

SYLLABOGRAM. See WRITING.

SYLLABUS. See CURRICULUM, LANGUAGE TEACHING.

SYLLEPSIS. See ZEUGMA.

SYLLOGISM [14c: from Latin *syllogismus*, Greek *sullogismós* a thinking out]. (1) A piece of deductive reasoning, from the general to the particular. (2) A subtle, sophisticated, and misleading argument. (3) In logic, an argument usually containing three categorical statements or *propositions*, the first the *major premiss/premise*, the second the *minor premiss/premise*, the third the *conclusion*, as in: *All men are mortal* (major): *Socrates is a man* (minor): *therefore Socrates is mortal* (conclusion). By applying the minor to the major premiss, a valid conclusion is reached. In such a syllogism, there is also a *major term* (mortal), a *middle term* (men), and a *minor term* (Socrates). The middle term connects the major and minor terms, but is absent in the conclusion. An invalid syllogism may arise for many reasons, such as the inaccurate framing of the major premiss, as in: *All birds fly: ostriches are birds: therefore ostriches fly*. This syllogism is false because ostriches do not fly and yet are birds. The fallacy of the *undistributed middle* (*term*) occurs when the middle term refers only to some members of the class which it designates, as in: *All birds fly: a bat flies: therefore a bat is a bird*. The syllogism is false because not all flying things are birds. The fallacy of the *missing middle* (*term*) occurs when no such term appears in the premisses, as in: *All birds fly: a bat is a mammal: therefore a bat does not fly*. This is false because there has been no discussion of what mammals may or may not do. On occasion, word-play can be introduced into a syllogism, as in: *All sovereigns are made of gold: a king is a sovereign: therefore a king is made of gold*. Because of the multiple meaning of *sovereign*, there are four terms in this 'syllogism', not three. See EQUIVOCATION, FALLACY, LOGIC, PREMISS/PREMISE. [LANGUAGE]. T.MCA.

SYMBOL [15c: partly through French *symbole* from Latin *symbolum*, Greek *súmbolon* ('put together') a mark, token, or sign]. (1) Something that represents something else, such as a drawing of a heart pierced by an arrow (standing for romantic love). Symbols arise from association; in this instance, the heart has traditionally been regarded as the seat of emotion and especially of love (as opposed to the head, the seat of reason), while the arrow indicates being stricken or wounded (especially by Cupid, the Roman god of love). In principle, anything can symbolize anything else, temporarily or permanently, especially something concrete or material used to represent something abstract or non-material, if an association can be formed between them: for example, a river symbolizing the flow of life; a circle symbolizing completion; a light symbolizing God. A word, phrase, image, character in a story, etc., may, in addition to its immediate nature and purpose, have symbolic status: for example, in Orwell's allegory *Animal Farm* (1945), the dogs symbolize the police in a repressive state. Religions, mythologies, works of literature, etc., have distinctive *symbol systems* that believers, investigators, and readers seek to interpret, develop, and benefit from. In the discussion of art, literature, language, etc., the term *symbolism* may refer to symbolic meaning as a whole, to the use of symbols, or to the disposition to invest things with symbolic meaning. (2) A mark, figure, character, etc., alone or in combination, that serves to designate something else, such as *x* as used in algebra to stand for an unknown number, or the chemical formula O, representing oxygen. Compare ARCHETYPE, CHARACTER, ICON, IMAGE, LOGO, SIGN. See LITERACY, NOTATION, SEMIOTICS. [LANGUAGE, WRITING]. T.MCA.

SYMBOLISM. See SYMBOL.

SYNAERESIS, AmE also **syneresis** [16c: from Latin *synaeresis*, Greek *sunaíresis*, a taking together. Stress: 'si-NEH-ri-sis']. In poetics and phonetics, the collapsing of two syllables into one: in verse, *thou see-est* becoming *thou seest* (pronounced like 'thou ceased') and *The Almighty* becoming *Th'Almighty*. This occurs when the first syllable ends and the second begins with a vowel. It is common in everyday usage, as when the last syllables of *familiar* ('fa-mí-li-ar') are merged in 'famílyer'. In some words, the merger becomes fixed: for example, although in the past *righteous* had three syllables ('ry-te-ous'), there can now only be two ('ry-chous'). In some kinds of English, a stressed diphthong merges with a following schwa: for example, in varieties of RP sometimes regarded as affected, where *flower pot* sounds like 'flah pot' and *lawnmower* like 'lawn-myrrh'. [SPEECH, STYLE]. G.K., T.MCA.

SYNCHRONIC. See DIACHRONIC AND SYNCHRONIC.

SYNCOPE [16c: through Latin from Greek *sunkopḗ* a cutting off. Stress: 'SING-ko-py']. A traditional term for contraction in the middle of a word through the loss of a sound or letter, commonly marked (especially in verse) by an apostrophe: *ever* reduced to *e'er*, *even* to *e'en*, *taken* to *ta'en*. The process or act of making such a contraction is *syncopation*. See ELISION, STRINE. [SPEECH, STYLE]. T.MCA.

SYNECDOCHE [14c: through Latin from Greek *sunekdokhē* gathering together. Stress: 'sin-EK-doh-ky']. In rhetoric, a figure of speech concerned with parts and wholes: (1) Where the part represents the whole: 'a hundred *head* of cattle' (each animal identified by head alone); 'All *hands* on deck' (the members of a ship's crew represented by their hands alone). (2) Where the whole represents the part: '*England* lost to *Australia* in the last Test Match' (the countries standing for the teams representing them and taking a plural verb).

Synecdoche is common in the use of geopolitical terms, often leading to confusion, ambiguity, and resentment: (1) When *Russia* and *Russian* were formerly used for *Soviet Union* and *Soviet*, the names of a part were used for a whole. In the process, offence was often given to such non-Russians as the Armenians, Estonians, and Georgians. (2) The names *America* and *American* have been transferred from a whole (the Americas) to a part (the United States of America). On occasion, Canadians and Latin Americans may be unsure about what is intended when these names are used, especially by US citizens, and may resent any limitation or centrality implied. (3) In the usages *Anglo-*, *England*, and *English*, a part (England) is often used for a whole (the island of Britain; the United Kingdom of Great Britain and Northern Ireland), often distressing the Scots, Welsh, and Northern Irish. Such usages tend to reflect historical patterns of power. See COLLECTIVE NOUN, METONYMY. [NAME, STYLE].   T.MCA.

SYNONYM [15c: from Latin *synonymum*, Greek *sunōnumon*, neuter of *sunōnumos* having the same name, from *sun* together and *ónoma/ónuma* name]. A word that means the same as another. Linguists and many writers agree that there is 'no such thing as a synonym', though the reasons for their opinions may differ. Linguists maintain that no two words have the same distribution, frequency, connotation, or language level; the reasons given by others are often vague, but in essence focus on differences in connotation, or reactions evoked in the reader or hearer by alternative words for the same thing. It is therefore perhaps best to say that a synonym is a word that shares the same denotation with another word. Notwithstanding disputes over the validity of the concept, there is a substantial body of published information containing synonym lists and studies, and it has become standard practice among dictionary publishers to include some of that information in general dictionaries.

Synonyms in dictionaries. Many present-day dictionaries, particularly those of 'college size'

in the US, include as an attraction information about synonyms in either or both of two different forms: a simple list of synonyms may be shown at the end of a given entry, usually identified with one or more specific definitions; in some dictionaries, longer treatments called *synonymies* or *synonym studies* offer discussions in which various nuances of application are discriminated, often with illustrative examples. Thus, *The Random House College Dictionary* contains synonym studies at *male* (for discriminations between *male* and *masculine*) and at *persuade* (for a discussion of *persuade*, *induce*, and *convince*). This entry also has a short list of synonyms: *urge*, *influence*, *entice*, *impel*. A more subtle use of synonyms can be seen in some dictionaries, in which many definitions consist largely or entirely of one-word equivalents for the headwords. In many cases, however, lexicographers resort to the use of a string of synonyms in place of an explanatory form of defining. Dubbed 'scatter-gun defining' by Clarence L. Barnhart, it was widely used in *Webster's Third New International Dictionary* (1961), as in the definitions for *lurking*: 1 *CONCEALED, LATENT* . . . 2 *PERSISTENT, LINGERING*. It is more often used to supplement an explanatory definition, as in *Webster's Third*: for example, *luxuriant* 1 (a) yielding or capable of yielding abundance: *FRUITFUL, PRODUCTIVE* . . . (b) characterized by abundant growth: *LUSH, FLOURISHING*. The synonyms were capitalized to indicate that they were defined elsewhere in the book.

The synonym dictionary. Scores of books, ranging in length from a few thousand words to almost a million, are available for those who seek an alternative word or one that cannot be readily brought to mind but is close in meaning to one thought of. Such sources are useful as a 'promptory': a means for reminding users of words that have slipped their minds. Selecting an unfamiliar word from a synonym list, however, may lead to an inappropriate choice, either because the word chosen is less formal or more formal, less technical or more technical, or less common or more common than the other words in the text. Generally, synonym books are arranged in alphabetical or thematic order. In alphabetical order, a given entry may be followed by several numbered listings of synonyms, corresponding, more or less, to the several sense discriminations of the headword and to its different parts of speech. For example, the entry for *obedient* might have one set of synonyms for one sense (such as 'compliant, acquiescent') and another for another sense (such as 'servile, obsequious'); *object* is likely to have several sets of synonyms for the noun and several for the verb. Reflecting the view that there are no 'true' synonyms in the language, the choices listed vary considerably in length and precision: shorter books may list alternatives that hew more closely to the meaning of the headword; longer books may list such words first, then (after a break of some sort, like a semicolon) go on to list words and phrases that are farther afield in meaning, on the assumption that the user, who might have only a vague notion of the word being sought, should be offered as wide a selection as possible. Most such books offer no guidance as to the syntactic or idiomatic usage of the synonyms listed and only sparse information concerning their language level (whether they are formal, slang, taboo, technical, etc.). A few give illustrative examples for each listing, showing the headword in a context in which the listed synonyms are more or less substitutable. Alphabetically arranged synonym dictionaries often tend to be repetitious, a typical example being the entries for *ailment, malady, illness, sickness, complaint, disease*, etc., each of which lists all the others. Because of the structure of the book, a certain amount of repetition is unavoidable, but it does tend to make such books appear to contain far more than they do.

The thesaurus. The term *thesaurus* is commonly associated with the *Thesaurus of English Words & Phrases* (1852) by Dr Peter Mark Roget (1779-1869), in which the author created a metaphysical structure of the universe and listed words in categories within each part of the system. Modern editions of Roget, which retain the original hierarchical system, exhibit the expansion needed to allow for the great number of words added during the past century or so, particularly in the sciences and technology. It is doubtful that many users of *Roget's Thesaurus* pay much attention to its structure: most resort to the index to find the word for which they seek alternatives, either synonyms or antonyms. While a virtue of the arrangement is that a given word is listed only once for each of its senses, the index is as long as the book. The large number of editions in which versions of the *Thesaurus* are available attests to its continued popularity. See ANTONYM, BINOMIAL NOMENCLATURE, BISOCIATION, DEFINITION, -ONYM, ROGET'S THESAURUS, SEMANTICS, SYNONYMY, THESAURUS. [LANGUAGE, WORD]. L.U.

SYNONYMY [17c: from Latin *synonymia*, Greek *sunōnumia* ('name-togetherness') possession of the same name or meaning, from *sun* together, *ónoma*/*ónuma* a name]. (1) Equivalence in meaning, as with *enormous* and *immense*, both having the general sense 'very

big'. Such equivalence may be precise, as is generally the case with these adjectives, or may be relative, as with *big* and *large*: the phrases *a big house* and *a large house* may communicate the same idea of size, but in *That was a big help* and *He was in large part to blame for what happened*, the two words are not interchangeable. (2) The study of words of similar meaning. (3) In biology, an annotated list of the scientific names for a taxonomic group. (4) A set, list, system, or book of synonyms. There have been many such works since the 18c, including books that seek through short essays to make discriminations among the members of sets of words. One of the earliest of these in English was Hester Thrale Piozzi's *The British Synonymy* (1794), which set the style for later works of the same kind: see PIOZZI. George Crabb brought out in 1816 a detailed work entitled *English Synonyms Explained in Alphabetic Order*, containing etymologies, citations, and discursive personal comment, and in 1851 Elizabeth Jane Whately published *A Selection of English Synonyms*, arguing that words in need of discrimination are not synonyms as such but 'pseudo-synonyms'. Since the mid-19c, alphabetically ordered synonymies are usually called dictionaries, and include Richard Soule's *A Dictionary of English Synonyms* (1871, revised by A. D. Sheffield, 1937: lists only), *Webster's New Dictionary of Synonyms* (ed. Rose Egan, 1968: largely with discriminating statements and described on the cover as a 'thesaurus'), and the *Longman Synonym Dictionary* (ed. Laurence Urdang, 1979: without discriminations but with usage labels). See SYNONYM, THESAURUS. [REFERENCE, WORD]. T.MCA.

SYNOPSIS [17c: through Latin from Greek *súnopsis* an overview, a shared view. The *Synoptic Gospels* of the New Testament (Matthew, Mark, and Luke) are so called because they make similar statements about the life of Christ]. (1) A set of headings or statements that summarizes a text, formerly often placed at the beginning of chapters in books: 'A conference betwixt an angler, a falconer, and a hunter; each commending his recreation' (the synoptic title of the first chapter of Izaak Walton's *The Compleat Angler* 1653). (2) A brief, condensed list or statement of the elements of a topic; the contents page of a book or periodical is in effect a synopsis of what it contains. (3) A summary of the plot of a novel, play, motion picture, or the like. See ABRIDG(E)MENT. Compare ABSTRACT, LIST, SUMMARY, TITLE. [WRITING]. T.MCA.

SYNTAGMATIC. See PARADIGMATIC AND SYNTAGMATIC.

SYNTAX [16c: from Latin *syntaxis*, Greek *súntaxis* (things) drawn up together, arranged in order]. A term in general use and in linguistics for the study of the ways in which words combine into such units as phrase, clause, and sentence. The sequences that result from the combinations are referred to in linguistics as *syntactic structures*. The ways in which components of words are combined into words are studied in *morphology*, and syntax and morphology together are generally regarded as the major constituents of *grammar*, although in one of its uses, *grammar* is strictly synonymous with *syntax* and excludes morphology. In models of language description that are divided into levels of analysis or components, the syntactic level or component is contrasted with the phonological and semantic levels or components. Syntactic descriptions do not usually go beyond the level of the sentence, though they may deal with relationships between sentences such as are signalled by a pronoun (*it*, *them*) or a conjunct (*therefore*). See COMPONENT, LEVEL OF LANGUAGE, LINGUISTIC TYPOLOGY, MORPHOLOGY. [GRAMMAR].　　S.G.

SYNTHETIC [17c: from Greek *sunthetikós* put together, combined]. A term in linguistics for a language in which words tend to be composed out of two or more grammatical units (morphemes), as in Latin *amabamus* (we loved), which combines 'love', *past, first person, plural*. English has such synthetic words as *distrustful* (distrust-ful), *unfindable* (un-find-able), and *repainted* (re-paint-ed). The notion of synthesis applies to the number of morphemes involved rather than the method by which they are combined. When many are combined, a language is known as *polysynthetic*, for example Siberian Yupik, with such words-cum-sentences as *angyaghllangyugtuq* (*angya-ghlla-ng-yug-tuq*, boat-*argumentative*-acquire-*desiderative-third singular*, He wants to get a big boat). See LINGUISTIC TYPOLOGY. [LANGUAGE].　　J.M.A.

SYNTHETIC SCOTS. See LALLANS, SCOTS.

SYSTEM [17c: from Late Latin *systema*, Greek *sústēma* ('a standing together') a whole formed of various parts]. (1) An orderly complex of elements and patterns constituting a functioning whole: *a system of currency*; *a transport system*; *a system of philosophy*; *a language system*. If approaches or people are *systematic*, they proceed in an orderly way, step by step; if a theory or an approach is *systemic*, it arises from or relates to a particular system or to certain assumptions about systems: *systemic grammar*. (2) In computing, a working combination of hardware, software, and other devices. Compare NETWORK, STRUCTURE. See HALLIDAY. [LANGUAGE, TECHNOLOGY].　　T.McA.

SYSTEMIC GRAMMAR/LINGUISTICS. See HALLIDAY, SYSTEM.

T

T, t [Called 'tee']. The 20th letter of the Roman alphabet as used for English. It originated as the Phoenician symbol *taw*, which the Greeks adopted and adapted as *tau* (T), which was in turn adopted by the Etruscans and then the Romans as *T*.

Sound value. In English, the letter *t* represents a voiceless alveolar plosive stop, produced by the release of breath blocked by the tongue being placed against the roof of the mouth behind the front teeth. The aspiration of /t/ is slight after *s*, the *t* in *stub* being less forceful than in *tub* and rather resembling /d/. Before another stop, or *m*, or in syllable-final position, *t* may occasion no audible release of breath, as in *hatpin*, *atmosphere*, *Wait!* Before syllabic *l*, *n*, and (in rhotic accents) *r* the breath may be released nasally (*bitten*) or past the sides of the tongue (*little*) or its tip (*falter*).

Glottalized T. In some accents, especially in Britain, the tongue may not touch the roof of the mouth, the *t* being spoken as a glottal stop, as for example in London and Glasgow working-class pronunciations of *a bit of butter*: see GLOTTAL STOP.

Voiced T. The letter *t* may be voiced almost as /d/ following a stressed vowel and before a second vowel. This pronunciation is typical of AmE and AusE, making virtual homophones of such pairs as *atom/Adam*, *latter/ladder*, *waiting/wading*, *writing/riding*. It is also heard sporadically in BrE, especially in certain rapid colloquial expressions, such as *I'd better go*, *get out*, and *not a hope*.

Palatalized T. (1) When *t* is palatalized before *u*, it represents the affricate otherwise spelt *ch* as in *church*: before *-ure* (*capture, culture, fracture, legislature, picture, temperature*), before *-ual* (*actual, intellectual, perpetual*), and in some other environments (*century, fortune, statue, virtue*). Compare palatalized *d, s, z* in *verdure, closure, seizure*. (2) This affricate value also occurs before *i* in the ending *-stion* (*question, digestion, combustion*) and in *Christian*, and before *e* in *righteous*. However, in precise, conservative speech, the value of *t* in such words may be /t/ followed by a *y*-sound rather than /tʃ/. (3) Elsewhere, when followed by unstressed *i* and another vowel, *t* is commonly palatalized to produce the voiceless palato-alveolar fricative *sh*-sound. This value of *ti* is found in such words as *inertia, patient, ratio, nasturtium*, and the proper names *Domitian, Horatio, Titian*, but particularly in the endings *-tial* (*palatial, essential, initial, partial, potential, presidential, substantial*), *-tious* (*conscientious, superstitious, vexatious*), and the hundreds of *-tion* words (*association, completion, discretion, ignition, motion, solution*). Some of these also have a preceding consonant: *action, infarction, mention, adoption*. In words ending in *-tiate*, etc., the *i* usually remains syllabic: *negotiate, substantiate*. (4) Uniquely, *equation* may be heard with *zh*, rhyming with *invasion*. Occasionally, some of these words are pronounced carefully with non-palatalized *t* heard as /s/: *inertia, negotiate*.

Double T. (1) Syllables containing a stressed short vowel double a final *t* before a suffix that begins with a vowel: *mat/matted/matting, bet/betting, fit/fitted/fitter/fittest, rot/rotted/rotting, cut/cutting/cutter, regret/regretted/regretting* (contrast *wait/waited/waiting, visit/visited/visiting*). *Format* commonly has *formatted/formatting*, while *benefit* is found with *benefited/benefiting* and, less commonly, *benefitted/benefitting*. (2) Disyllables commonly have medial *tt* following a stressed short vowel: *batter, better, bitten, bottle, butter*. (3) *T* is doubled when the Latin prefix *ad-* is assimilated to a stem beginning with *t*: *attain, attend, attract*. (4) Some cognate words vary

THE CAPITAL LETTER						THE SMALL LETTER				
EARLY FORMS				CURRENT FORMS		EARLY FORMS			CURRENT FORMS	
Phoenician	Greek	Etruscan	Roman (Latin)	roman	italic	Roman cursive	Roman uncial	Carolingian minuscule	roman	italic
+	XT	T	T	T	*T*	ϲ	T	ᴄ	t	*t*

in their doubling: *Britain/Brittany, catty/ caterwaul, letter/literate, matter/material*. (5) Few words other than proper names end in *tt*: *watt* originated in the proper name *Watt*; *matt*, *nett* are alternatives for *mat* (not shiny), *net* (not gross); *mitt* is a clipped form of *mitten*; *putt* originated as a Scottish variant of *put*; *butt* (noun) may have retained double *t* so as to be distinguished from *but*.

Inflectional *T*. (1) Regular verbs form their past tense with -(*e*)*d*, but many irregular verbs use *t*: *deal/dealt, feel/felt*. (2) Some have alternative forms, especially in BrE (*burnt/burned, learnt/ learned, spoilt/spoiled*), the *t*-versions often being favoured as adjectival forms (*burnt papers, badly learnt lines, spoilt food*). (3) Some reduce a doubled consonant before *t*: *smelt/smelled, spelt/spelled, spilt/spilled*, and formerly also *past/passed*. (4) Some shorten their stem vowel (but not its spelling) before *t*: *dreamt/dreamed, leant/leaned, leapt/leaped*. (5) Many shorten sound and spelling before *t*: *cleave/cleft, creep/crept, feel/felt, keep/kept, kneel/knelt, leave/left, lose/lost, shoot/shot, sleep/slept, sweep/swept, weep/wept*. (6) Some substitute -*t* for final -*d* in their root: *bend/bent, build/built, gild/gilt* (also *gilded*), *gird/girt* (also *girded*), *lend/lent, rend/rent, send/sent, spend/spent*. (7) Some make more substantial changes to the vowel and/or final consonant of the stem in adding -*aught* or -*ought*: *beseech/besought, bring/ brought, buy/bought, catch/caught, seek/sought, teach/taught, think/thought*. (8) Some have stems with final -*t* which is preserved without inflection in all tenses: *burst, cast, cost, cut, hit, hurt, let, put, quit, set, shut, slit, split, thrust*. (9) Some change their stem-vowel, but not final *t*: *fight/fought, light/lit, meet/met*.

Epenthetic *T*. (1) The letter *t* and sound /t/ have sometimes intruded in words originally without them: *peasant, tapestry* (from French *paysan, tapisserie*). (2) In *against, amidst, amongst, betwixt, whilst, t* has arisen parasitically, perhaps by analogy with the superlative inflection of adjectives: see PARASITIC.

Silent *T*. (1) In word- and syllable-final position in loans from French, both early and recent: *ballet, beret, bouquet, buffet, cabaret, chalet, crochet, croquet, depot, mortgage, parquet, potpourri, trait, valet*. (2) Elided after *s* following a stressed vowel: before /l/, especially in the terminal syllable -*le*, in *castle, nestle, pestle, trestle, wrestle, bristle, epistle, gristle, mistletoe, thistle, whistle, apostle, jostle, throstle, bustle, hustle, rustle*; before /n/, especially the terminal element -*en*, in *chasten, hasten, fasten, christen, glisten, listen, moisten*; and in isolated words such as *Christmas, postman, waistcoat*. (3) Elided

after *f* in *soften* and often in *often*. (4) In *boatswain*, the elision is reflected in such alternative spellings as *bo's'n, bosun*. (5) The historical function of *t* before *ch*, typically after short vowels as in *match, fetch, pitch, botch, hutch*, is the equivalent of doubling a simple letter, but is in present-day English redundant. The redundancy is particularly apparent in *ditch/rich, hutch/much*.

Variations. Some variation occurs between *t* and other letters in related words, as between *benefit/beneficial, space/spatial, extent/extend/ extension* (contrast *retention*).

TH. This digraph is regularly used to represent a common, characteristically English phoneme, the dental fricative, both voiced /ð/ as in *this* and voiceless /θ/ as in *thin*. Sometimes related forms vary: voiceless *smith*, but voiced *smithy*. In Old English, the sounds were represented interchangeably by the runic letter *thorn* (þ) and *eth* (ð), a modification of the letter *d*. A relic of thorn occurs in the form *Ye* for *the* in 'old' inn and shop signs, such as *Ye Olde English Tea Shoppe*, the *y* being a corruption of handwritten þ. English borrowed the digraph *th* from Latin, where it served to transliterate Greek *theta* (θ); *th* superseded other symbols for the dental fricative following the advent of printing. See ETH, THORN. In Modern English *th* occurs in common words of Old English origin and in many, usually technical, words of Greek origin. The *h* is ignored in the pronunciation of a small number of words: *thyme, Thomas*, in BrE but not necessarily in AmE in *Thames* (for example, the Thames River in Connecticut has a spelling pronunciation), and usually in *Anthony, Esther*. *Th* may be silent in *asthma, isthmus, clothes*. *Th* in *north, south* is commonly omitted in nautical language: *nor' nor' east, sou'wester*. The form *good-bye* also arose from the omission of *th*, being a clipping of *God be with ye*.

Voiced *TH*. (1) Initially in many grammatical words: *than, that, the, thee, their, them, then, thence, there, these, they, thine, this, thou, though, thus, thy*, but contrast *through*, in which the following *r* may have prevented the voicing of the *th*. (2) Medially: *bother, brother, father, further, gather, hither, leather, mother, northern, rather, smithy, southern, weather, wether, whether, whither, wither, withy, worthy*, but contrast *brothel* and the derived forms *healthy, wealthy*. (3) Some nouns voice final *th* in the plural (*baths, mouths, truths, youths*) but not in the corresponding inflected BrE verb *baths*. (4) A following final *e* indicates a voiced *th*, a long preceding vowel, and usually a verb form (contrast *breath/breathe*): *bathe, clothe, lathe, lithe, loathe, seethe, sheathe, soothe, swathe, teethe,* *wreathe, writhe,* but *to mouth, to smooth* lack final *e.*

Voiceless *TH.* (1) Initially, in lexical words: *thank, thatch, theft, thew, thick, thimble, thin, think, third, thirst, thistle, thong, thorn, thorough, thought, thousand, thrash, thread, threat, three, thresh, thrift, thrill, throat, throb, throes, throng, throttle, throw, thrush, thrust, thud, thumb, thump, thunder, thwack, thwart.* (2) Finally, in both lexical and grammatical words: *bath, birth, both, breath, broth, cloth, dearth, death, earth, filth, forth, froth, girth, health, hearth, heath, loath, mirth, month, moth, mouth, north, oath, path, smith, south, stealth, tooth, truth, wealth, worth, wrath, youth,* but contrast voiced *smooth* and *booth* with either pronunciation (but historically voiced). *Th* is voiced in the derivatives *mouths, northerly, southerly.* The word *with* is variable. (3) In Greek-derived words: *antithesis, epithalamium, hyacinth, pathos, theatre/theater, theme, theory, Theseus,* but not in *rhythm.*

Morphological *TH.* The ending *-th* was formerly a present-tense verb inflection (for example, *maketh* for Modern English *makes*), and occurs as the ordinal ending for numerals (*fourth, fifth, twentieth, hundredth, thousandth,* but with written assimilation of preceding *t* in *eighth,* from *eight*). It creates abstract nouns from several common adjectives often suggesting measurement: *breadth, depth, length, strength, warmth, width* (but only *t* after *gh* in *drought, height, sight*). See ALPHABET, LETTER[1], SPELLING. [WRITING]. C.U., T.MCA., E.W.

TABLOID [1900s: from *tabl(et)* and *-oid*]. A newspaper with pages half the size of broadsheet and usually five columns wide. The term was coined in the pharmaceutical industry, to describe a concentrated form of pill; the journalistic sense was used by Lord Northcliffe, in the UK, to describe the new, half-size *Daily Mirror* (which he re-launched in 1904), to imply that it was a concentrate of good things for its readers (and much better than the old *Mirror,* launched as a 'paper written by gentlewomen for gentlewomen'). The term currently means a newspaper of this size, written in a popular and sensational style, sometimes crudely infringing on personal privacy. The tabloids now occupy 60% of the British newspaper market. In addition to *The Daily Mirror* (circulation over 3m), the category includes *The Sun* (circulation 4m), *The News of the World* (circulation 5m), and *The People* (circulation nearly 3m). The reputation of the tabloids has, however, declined. Even among the tabloids the term is one of condemnation: 'He went public in a sleazy tabloid' (*Daily Mirror,* 9 Feb. 1989). The term *tabloid journalism,* first recorded in 1901, was originally complimentary, referring to a concentrated and compressed news-style, but has come to denote journalism which is unashamedly sensationalist and profits by appealing to the lowest instincts. The term *tabloidese* is used, often pejoratively, for the style used in tabloids or any similar style. Typical tabloid coverage has been criticized as mainly concerned with 'skin' or 'tit and bum' (especially through scandalous revelations and revealing photographs, as for example the so-called 'page 3 girl' in Britain). See JOURNALESE, JOURNALISM, NEWSPAPER, QUALITY PRESS. [MEDIA, STYLE]. G.H.

TABOO [1770s: from Malayo-Polynesian, both Fijian *tabu* and Tongan *tapu,* consecrated or limited to a special use, and therefore prohibited]. In language terms, something taboo is not to be mentioned, because it is ineffably holy or unspeakably vulgar. The taboo is enforced by religious or social convention rather than by statute: it may be illegal to reveal official secrets, but it is not taboo to do so. English Puritanism caused such words as *God* to be banned on the stage during the early 17c and references to *Hell* have also often been reproved. It is not easy to distinguish between taboo matters and taboo words. Sex and excrement are, or have been, taboo topics in English and other languages, and many of the words relating to these topics have been stigmatized as *bad language, foul language,* or *four-letter words.* They have been in effect banned in polite conversation, in writing, and especially in print; though occasionally recorded in earlier dictionaries, they were not entered in such works *c.*1760–1960. When taboo subjects must be broached, the techniques for doing so include:

Truncation. Taboo words can be amended both in writing (by a dash as in *G-d* and asterisks as in *f**k*) and in speech (by using the letter *p,* usually spelt *pee,* for *piss*). The Biblical Third Commandment enjoins believers not to take God's name in vain; in Orthodox Judaism, this has come to be interpreted so strictly as to preclude writing out *God* in full; the resulting form *G-d* exhibits a process of abbreviation like that through which *Mister* became *Mr.*

Adaptation. Because of a combination of the sense of taboo and the need for expletives, taboo words when used as exclamations have been adapted and softened so as to be less direct, sacrilegious, and offensive: *(by) God!* becomes *(by) Gosh!* and *(by) Golly!, Jesus!* is shortened to *Gee!* and adapted to *Gee-whiz!,* and *Gee-whiz!,* *Christ!* becomes *Crikey!, Crimey!,* and *Cripes!,* and *Jesus Christ!* becomes *Jeepers Creepers!* and

Jesum Crow!, *Damn* (*it*)*!* becomes *Darn* (*it*)*!*, *Damnation!* becomes *Tarnation!*, *Hell!* becomes *Heck!*, and *Fucking hell!* becomes *Flipping heck!* See MINCED OATH.

Substitution. Taboo expressions can be replaced with other words through euphemism, as with *make love* for 'have sex', and through the use of elevated technical terms, such as *coitus/coition* and *sexual intercourse*. In dealing with smuttier topics, users of English often find that there is no neutral phraseology available. Furthermore, the substitute for a taboo word can itself become socially awkward if its referent remains taboo: *intercourse* is avoided by some people in any of its other uses because of its sexual use. The notion of taboo has come to be extended, at least for humorous and facetious purposes, to refer obliquely to any topic likely to be controversial, cause envy, etc. Politics and religion may be taboo subjects in certain places; death, money, and details of one's personal life in others. The interaction of taboo and euphemism occurs in late 20c combinations of a capital letter such as *L* with *-word*, as in *the L-word* (liberal) and *the N-word* (nigger), on the analogy of *the F-word* (fuck). Such phrases use only 'the initial letter of a word under real or pretended taboo' (J. & A. Algeo, *American Speech*, Winter, 1988). See ELLIPSIS, NAME (NAME TABOOS), SWEARING, VICTORIAN. [STYLE].   R.F.I.

TAG [20c in this sense]. A term in linguistics for several types of structure in which one or more words are tagged on to a clause or sentence, including: (1) *Continuation tags*. Words and phrases used as shorthand at the end of a list: *etc.*; *and so on*; *and so forth*. (2) *Questioning and commenting tags*. Questions, questioning words, and commenting words that can be added to statements are common in formal conversation: 'She's pretty, *don't you think?*'; 'It's more acceptable in the north, *wouldn't you say?*'; 'He's disappeared, *do you mean?*'; 'You'll pay me back tomorrow, *OK?*'; 'It's difficult, *I suppose*'; '*You know*, it can't be easy for her.' Such forms can usually be rearranged as standard questions and statements: *Don't you think she's pretty?*; *I suppose (that) it's difficult.* (3) *Focusing and emphasizing tags*. These usually restate the subject and sometimes the verb: 'She's amazing, (*is*) *my grandmother*'; '*My grandmother*, she's amazing'; 'She's amazing, *she is*'; 'She comes here often, *does Joan*' (a usage common in the North of England). (4) *Additions, alternatives, and responses*. These characteristically consist of one or two introductory words plus auxiliary and subject (or subject and auxiliary): 'She refused, *and so did I*'; 'She wouldn't agree, *nor would my grandfather*'; 'I've been there before, *but she*

hasn't'; 'You surely wouldn't tell them. *Or will you?*'; 'So she's been there before?'—'*Yes, she has.*' Some grammarians also classify as tags the subject + verb (or verb + subject) in reported speech: ' "That's amazing," *he said.*' The commonest use of the term is, however, in *question tag* and *tag question*. See LATIN TAG, NEW ORLEANS, QUESTION TAG, TAG QUESTION. [GRAMMAR].   S.C.

TAGALOG [Stress: 'ta-GA-log']. (1) A Malayan people of the island of Luzon, the largest ethnic group of the Philippines and the majority population of Manila, the capital. Most are farmers, but the importance of Manila has given urban Tagalogs a leading position in manufacturing, business, and the professions. (2) A Malayo-Polynesian language of the Philippines, one of the major indigenous languages, the mother tongue of some 10m Filipinos, and the basis of the official and national language referred to as both *Filipino* or *Pilipino*. See BORROWING, FILIPINO, PHILIPPINES, TAGLISH. [ASIA, LANGUAGE, NAME].   T.MCA.

TAGLISH [1960s: a blend of *Tagalog* and *English*]. Also **Mix-Mix**. A half-serious name given to a mixture of Tagalog and English, as used in the Philippines and particularly in Manila and the island of Luzon: 'Pwede kayong magbayad three months after arrival. Pwede pang i-extend up to two years ang payment. At sa pinak-amababang interest rate pa' (quoted by Lily V. Kapili, *English Today* 16, Oct. 1988) [Translation: 'It is possible to pay three months after arrival. It is possible to extend payment up to two years. And the interest rate is the lowest.' *Pwede* is from Spanish *puede* it is possible]. The Philippine continuum between full English and full Tagalog is covered by the terms *English, Taglish, Engalog, Tagalog*. See -GLISH AND -LISH, PHILIPPINE ENGLISH, TAGALOG. [ASIA, VARIETY].   T.MCA.

TAG QUESTION. A grammatical term for a statement with a *question tag* added at the end, turning it into an actual or apparent question: *They're coming here next week, aren't they? You really shouldn't do that, should you?* See NEGATION, QUESTION TAG, TAG. [GRAMMAR]. S.C.

TAILED N. See ENG.

TAIWAN. See CHINA, EAST ASIAN ENGLISH.

TAKI-TAKI. See SRANAN.

TALK [12c: cognate with *tale*]. (1) Speech or conversation, especially of an easy, informal kind: *a fireside talk/chat*. (2) An informal account, speech, or lecture: *a short talk on local radio*. (3) A conference or negotiating session: *peace talks*. (4) Rumour, gossip: *There's been talk about big changes here*; *It's the talk of the town*. (5) Empty speech: *a lot of idle talk*. (6) A way of talking or speaking, usually embracing what one talks about: *teacher talk* the usage of teachers in the classroom; *chalk and talk* an informal term for teaching methods that do not use complex technology; *small talk* trivial news and gossip. The term is informal in such forms as *country talk* and *local talk*, and pejorative in such forms as *nigger talk*. (7) A variety or dialect, especially if not taken too seriously or low in prestige: *Bungo Talk* 'country bumpkin' speech in Jamaica; *Creole Talk of Trinidad and Tobago* (title of a book, 1980): see CARIBBEAN DICTIONARIES. This sense has long been associated with English-based pidgins and creoles; the word has been adopted and adapted, usually in the written form *tok*, in various names, such as *Kamtok* in Cameroon and *Tok Pisin* in Papua New Guinea. It may also occur in such pidgin and creole usages as *tumantok* ('two-man talk') a tête-à-tête. (8) Sound that approximates to speech, whether produced by an animal, an infant, or a machine: *baby talk*. Compare -ESE, LINGO, -SPEAK. See ABORIGINAL ENGLISH, AKU (TALK), BABY TALK, DOUBLE TALK, FLYTAAL, FOREIGNER TALK, KAMTOK, RASTA TALK, SRANAN/ TAKI-TAKI, SWEET TALK, TALKING BOOK, TALKING HEAD, TEACHER TALK, TECHNOBABBLE, TOK PISIN. [LANGUAGE, NAME, SPEECH, STYLE]. T.MCA.

TALKIE. See TALKING PICTURE.

TALKING BOOK [1930s]. A phonograph record or tape recording of the entire text of, or excerpts from, a book, magazine, or other publication, made especially for the blind. See TALK. Compare AUDIOBOOK. [MEDIA]. T.MCA.

TALKING HEAD [1960s]. (1) A slang expression for a close-up television picture of someone talking, usually for some time, especially in a talk show or a documentary. (2) By extension someone whose talk is empty and pretentious. See TALK. [MEDIA]. T.MCA.

TALKING PICTURE [1900s]. Informal short form *talkie*. Especially formerly, a motion picture with synchronized sound. See MOTION PICTURE. [MEDIA]. T.MCA.

TAMIL. A Dravidian language of south India, comparable to Sanskrit in its antiquity and textual traditions. It is written in a derivative of the southern Brahmi script (*c*.250 BC) and its literary and grammatical works date from the same period. Tamil is one of the 15 major languages of India and the state language of Tamilnadu. Its speakers number some 50m and constitute a significant minority in Malaysia, Singapore, and Sri Lanka, all of which recognize it as one of their official languages. The Tamil community distinguishes between Brahmin and non-Brahmin dialects on the one hand, and a High variety (*centamil*) and Low variety (*kontuntamil*) on the other. Modern standard Tamil is based on the High non-Brahmin dialect of central Tamilnadu. Speakers are loyal to their heritage, and do not tolerate borrowing from either Sanskrit or English for modernization, though mixing with English is fairly common in colloquial High Tamil. See BORROWING, DRAVIDIAN ENGLISH, FIJI, INDIA, INDIAN ENGLISH[1], INDIAN LANGUAGES, MALAYALAM, MALAYSIA, SINGAPORE, SINHALA, SOUTH AFRICA, SRI LANKA. [ASIA, LANGUAGE]. Y.K.

TANZANIA [20c: a blend of *Tanganyika* and *Zanzibar*, with *-ia*. Usual stress: 'Tan-zan-EE-a']. Official title: English *United Republic of Tanzania*, Swahili *Jamhuri ya Mwangano wa Tanzania*. A country of East Africa and member of the Commonwealth. Capital: Dodoma. Currency: the shillingi or shilling (100 senti or cents). Population: 24.8m (1988), 36.8m (projection for 2000). Ethnicity: 97% black African (Chaga, Luo, Makonde, Masai, Nyamwezi, etc.), 2% Arab, 1% other. Religions: 40% Christian, 35% Muslim, 25% traditional. Education: primary 65%, secondary 3%, tertiary below 1%, literacy 85%. The Germans colonized Tanganyika from the late 19c until in 1920 it became a League of Nations mandate and later a United Nations trust territory administered by the British. Zanzibar was a British protectorate from 1890 to 1963. The territories united on independence in 1964. English was a joint official language with Swahili until 1967. This political empowerment of Swahili improved its prestige in relation to English and other indigenous languages. English continues to be important for higher education, media, and international relations, while Swahili has taken over roles in pre-college-level education and internal government and business. A number of loans associated with administration, politics, etc., have passed from English into Swahili, such as *parliament, president, capitalism*. The *Daily News* (established 1930) is the major English-language newspaper. Creative writing in English is represented by writers such as novelist Peter Palangyo (b.1939).

Tanzanian English shares many features with Zambian English: see ZAMBIA. Devoicing of word-final /b, v/ is common ('laf' for *love*), and /f/v/ may alternate ('lavin' for *laughing*). Mass or singular nouns may be construed as plurals (*behaviours, breads*). Borrowings from indigenous languages are frequent, and may become standardized as marking the Tanzanian variety: *sufuria* cook-pot, *pole* (an expression of sympathy), *foforu car* fancy car. Some typical local usages are: *Thank you for your postcard extended to us recently*; *We were happy to learn* (hear) *from you*; *Please inquire if she had the mails* (got the letters); *I decided to mail* (write) *you*. Code-mixing, particularly Swahili/English, is common: *Ile accident ilitokea alipo-lose control na aka-overturn and landed in a ditch* The accident occurred when he lost control and overturned and landed in a ditch. Here, mixing includes putting Swahili prefixes on English stems, as with *alipo-lose*. See: Josef Schmied, 'Attitudes towards English in Tanzania', *English World-Wide* 6: 2 (1985); Casmir M. Rubagumya (ed.), *Language in Education in Africa: A Tanzanian Perspective* (Clevedon & Philadelphia: Multilingual Matters, 1990). See EAST AFRICAN ENGLISH, ENGLISH, SWAHILI. [AFRICA, NAME, VARIETY].   C.L.N.

TAP, TAPPED *R*. See R-SOUNDS.

TAUTOLOGY [16c: from Latin *tautologia*, Greek *tautología* repeating what has been said, from *tautó* the same, from *tò autó* the (thing) itself]. (1) Also *pleonasm*. A term in rhetoric for unnecessary and ineffective repetition, usually with words that add nothing new: *She was all alone by herself*; *Me myself personally*. Many tautological (or tautologous) expressions occur in everyday usage. The tautology in some is immediately apparent: *all well and good*; *to all intents and purposes*; *cool, calm, and collected*; *free, gratis, and for nothing*; *ways and means*. In others, it is less obvious, because they contain archaic elements: *by hook or by crook*; *a hue and cry*; *not a jot or tittle*; *kith and kin*; *null and void*; *part and parcel*; *rack and ruin*; *weird and wonderful*; *without let or hindrance*. (2) In logic, a compound proposition that is always true: *A or not-A*, as in *Either it is raining or it is not raining in Dublin today*. Compare CIRCUMLOCUTION, PLEONASM, REDUNDANCY. [LANGUAGE, STYLE, USAGE].   T.MCA.

TEACHER TALK. A semi-technical term in educational research and applied linguistics for the characteristic (often simplified) style of speech of teachers. In general terms, this may be prompted by the social setting of the classroom, with repetition, rephrasing for the sake of clarity, and patterns of stereotyped interaction with learners, such as question, response, and evaluation. For teachers of English as a foreign language, speech may be slower and clearer than is usual, avoiding and minimizing elided usages such as *must've/musta* and *'sno good y'know*, repeating the same thing in several ways, and using expressions particularly associated with education, classrooms, and textbooks. See TALK. [EDUCATION, SPEECH].   C.J.B., T.MCA.

TEACHING ENGLISH, also **teaching of English** and **English teaching**. General, non-technical terms for the work of teachers of English, whether with children, adolescents, or adults, and whether as a first, second, foreign, or additional language. However organized, whatever the aim, and whatever the methods used, such teaching currently proceeds on a scale well beyond that of any other language past or present, and approached only (in a more restricted geographical area) by Putonghua in the People's Republic of China. In language teaching and applied linguistics, and increasingly in education generally, the teaching of English is divided into five categories, each with its own tradition, terminology, perspective, theory, practice, publications, organizations, and conferences. They are:

(1) Teaching English as a Native Language. Also *Teaching English as a Mother Tongue* and *Teaching English as a First Language*. In the English-speaking world, the teaching of children, adolescents, and adults in institutions of primary (elementary), secondary, and tertiary (higher) education, and of adults in continuing education, including literacy programmes. *English* is often used as a shorthand (but sometimes ambiguous) term for the teaching and study of both language and literature, being understood as meaning mainly language at the primary level, both at the secondary level, and at the tertiary level literature (perhaps with traditional philology), language (usually the modern language), or sometimes both. In recent years, however, there has been a tendency in secondary schools, universities, and other institutions to reduce the possibility of ambiguity by distinguishing 'English Language' and 'English Literature' clearly as the names of the courses, the subjects of degrees, and subjects for examination. The term *ENL countries* ('ee-en-ell': English as a Native Language) refers to those territories in which English is the first, and for many the only significant, language, such as Australia, anglophone Canada, Britain, the Irish Republic, New Zealand, and the US.

(2) Teaching English as a Second Language. Short form *TESL* ('tessle'). (1) The teaching of English in countries where the language is not a mother tongue but has long been part of the fabric of society, usually for imperial and colonial reasons in the relatively recent past, either as a lingua franca or a medium of education, or both. The term *ESL countries* ('ee-ess-ell') refers to those territories in which English has a statutory role such as (co-)official language or medium of education, but is not generally used in the home, such as India, Nigeria, and Singapore. (2) The teaching of non-English-speaking immigrants to ENL countries. The comparable term *TESOL* ('tee-sol': *Teaching English to Speakers of Other Languages*), originally used in North America primarily for the teaching of immigrants, is now used worldwide in both senses. See TESOL, TESL.

(3) Teaching English as a Foreign Language. Short form *TEFL* ('teffle'). (1) The teaching of English in countries where it is of interest and/or importance but is not or has not been until recently a local medium of communication or instruction, such as Japan, Saudi Arabia, and Sweden. In the late 20c, the term *EFL countries* ('ee-eff-ell') refers in effect to the rest of the world. (2) Providing courses in ENL countries for visiting students from EFL countries. Another term used principally for this category, especially in Britain, is *English language teaching* or, more commonly, *ELT* ('ee-ell-tee'). See ELT, TEFL.

(4) Teaching English as an International Language. Short form *TEIL* ('teel', 'tee-ee-eye-ell'). Teaching English as a global lingua franca, making people aware in the process of the worldwide role of the language and the problems that derive from or are related to that role. EIL ('ee-eye-ell') embraces all countries, learners, and users (ENL, ESL, and EFL), its proponents arguing that native users of English need as much consciousness-raising with regard to an adequate international use of the language as those who learn it as a second or foreign language. They also argue that the more English becomes institutionalized as the world's main medium of international expression the more native and non-native users will need to learn to acclimatize to each other's ways of using it. See TEIL.

(5) Teaching English as a Second Dialect. Short form *TESD* ('tezd', 'tee-ee-ess-dee'). Teaching the standard language to speakers of non-standard varieties of English, such as a dialect (Scouse in the UK, Appalachian in the US) or a creole (Nation Language in Jamaica or any Caribbean Creole in the UK). Here, the term *English* is restricted to a use traditionally given to it (usually implicitly) by many educationists and grammarians: the language of professional and business people educated to college level or its equivalent and of the major media: that is, the standard language, dialect, or variety. Both term and abbreviation have been modelled on the labels of the preceding three categories. To make their standpoint clear, however, some proponents of TESD use the term *Standard English as a Second Dialect* (short form *SESD*) to present standard English as one dialect among many, and not as a specially prestigious entity in its own right. See TESD.

Mother-tongue English teaching. In all ENL countries, the educational profession in general and a significant part of the interested public regard good English teaching (whatever 'good' is taken to mean) as fundamental to all schooling at all levels, and as an essential underpinning for students' later lives. Despite the often acrimonious debate that follows from close concern for the language and how it is taught, it is widely accepted that the roles of the people teaching English are so different at the three educational levels that in fact there is no such thing as a 'typical' teacher of English for all seasons:

(1) In primary schools, because of the nature of the work, most teachers teach English along with everything else that the children learn. Such teachers are not so much English specialists as educational generalists who integrate the key elements of elementary English teaching (such as listening, speaking, reading, and writing) into the whole fabric of the child's experience at school.

(2) In secondary schools, again because of the nature of the work, most teachers are (at least ideally) specialists in different subjects or groups of subjects. However, while English specialists have an obviously central role, the others are also in a serious sense teachers of English (whether they wish to see themselves in that light or not), because the language is the medium through which they work. When for example science teachers introduce new terms, indicate how the notes of an experiment should be kept, or discuss relevant texts, they are providing instruction in the register of scientific and technical English, something that is not usually the concern of the English specialist.

(3) In tertiary institutions, teachers are not only (at least ideally) 'general' specialists in 'English', but also teachers and researchers in sub-specialities of their own, such as the Victorian novel, Creole Studies, Media Studies, or aspects of grammatical or literary theory. As a result, the precise nature of a degree course in English often rests not only on an understanding among the teachers and administrators of what must or should be covered as a foundation, but also on a supplement of courses arising from the special interests and inclinations of the staff available at any time in a department.

The secondary-school teacher of English. Although it is relatively easy to specify what is going on at the primary and tertiary stages, it is difficult to be clear about the precise nature and aims of the work done in the middle years. As a result, the secondary level tends to receive more critical attention from the public than the others. The two professional comments that follow, on the nature of the teacher's work at this level, demonstrate the burden that English-speaking societies have long placed on the secondary specialist. The first quotation is from the US in 1965, the second from the UK in 1991, both periods of vigorous and controversial debate:

The United States, 1965. Like any other professional person, the professional English teacher is one who has been trained, or has trained himself, to do competent work. For him professional competence should mean, at the minimum: a college major in English or a strong minor, preparation sufficient to qualify him to begin graduate study in English; systematic postcollegiate study, carried on privately or in a graduate school; a reading command of at least one foreign language, ancient or modern; a deep interest in literature, old and new, and a solid set of critical skills; the ability to write well and the habit of writing, whether for publication or not; a knowledge of the development of the English language and familiarity with recent work in linguistics; a desire not simply to know but to impart knowledge; skill in the handling of instructional problems and knowledge of the research concerning them; an unflagging interest in the processes by which the young learn to use language effectively and richly (from *Freedom and Discipline in English*, the Report of the Commission on English, chaired by Harold C. Martin of Harvard University, College Entrance Examination Board, New York, 1965).

The United Kingdom, 1991. English teachers are asked to cover a wide spectrum. In addition to the fundamentals of reading, writing, listening, speaking and spelling required by the National Curriculum [for England and Wales, 1987 onward], they usually teach drama and media studies and are expected to show greater interest in the whole child than many other subject specialists. Most children probably write more prose, and certainly compose more poetry in school than many of their parents. Hence the joke: 'Don't look out of the window or she'll make you write a poem about it.' Both science and English are important subjects in the curriculum, but if something goes amiss in adult life, then it is more likely that blame will be attached to English teachers than to science teachers. In the Sixties, Andrew Wilkinson drew attention to this wide role when he described several models of English teaching, ranging from 'proof reader', which involved meticulous correction of every spelling and punctuation error, to 'Grendel's mother, guardian of the word-hoard', the person with the awesome responsibility of keeping alive and enhancing the nation's cultural heritage. Fortunately, English teachers are among the best qualified academically to undertake such an assignment. Analysis of graduate recruits to teaching shows that English, history and modern languages entrants have more firsts and upper seconds than in any other subject (from 'Peace in the Civil English War', Schools Report, *Observer*, 22 Sept. 1991, by Ted Wragg, head of the School of Education, Exeter University, England).

Society and the teacher. In the last analysis, however, all teachers involved in English, primary or secondary, are regarded as responsible for the quality of the language skills of young people when they leave school. If employers and politicians, among others, complain (rightly or wrongly) about falling standards, the spotlight is turned on these teachers and their trainers, and on the theories that underpin their practices. It often seems to the professional English teacher that in public discussions of English teaching everyone has a view of how things should be done, where there might be caution in the expression of opinions about the teaching of mathematics or science, or about the work of lawyers and doctors. In public debate, there is often an elemental polarization: between conservatives who consider that changes in ways of teaching grammar and spelling (among other things) are symptomatic of a more general social decay, and radicals who consider that progress will never be made until the outdated methods favoured by the conservatives are utterly uprooted. As is often the case in other areas, most teachers are located at neither end of the spectrum, but are somewhere in the middle, where efforts can be made to unite, as judiciously as possible, the most effective aspects of the old and the new.

See BULLOCK REPORT, CHILD LANGUAGE ACQUISITION, CLAUSE ANALYSIS, COX REPORT, CREATIVE WRITING, CURRICULUM, EDUCATION, EFFECTIVE WRITING, ELT, ENGLISH, ENGLISH LITERATURE, ENGLISH STUDIES, EXAMINING IN ENGLISH, GRAMMAR, KINGMAN REPORT, LANGUAGE AWARENESS, LANGUAGE LEARNING, LANGUAGE TEACHING, LITERACY, LITERATURE, NEWBOLT REPORT, PARSING, READING, RHETORIC, SPELLING, SPELLING REFORM, TEIL, TESD, TESL, TESOL, WRITING. [EDUCATION]. T.MCA.

Currie, William B. 1973. *New Directions in Teaching English Language*. London: Longman.
Howatt, A. P. R. 1984. *A History of English Language Teaching*. Oxford: University Press.
Jones, Michael, & West, Alastair (eds.). 1988. *Learning Me Your Language: Perspectives on the Teaching of English*. London: Mary Glasgow Publications.
Michael, Ian. 1987. *The Teaching of English: From the Sixteenth Century to 1870*. Cambridge: University Press.
Strevens, Peter. 1977. *New Orientations in the Teaching of English*. Oxford: University Press.

TECHNICAL TERM. See TERM, TERMINOLOGY.

TECHNOBABBLE [1980s: a combination of *techno-* as in *technology* and *babble*. Compare PSYCHOBABBLE. See BABBLE]. An informal term for the use or overuse of technical jargon. John A. Barry in the introduction to *Technobabble* (MIT Press, 1991) says that 'the word connotes meaningless chatter about technology' but 'is also a form of communication among people in the rapidly advancing, computer and other high-technological industries'. As an example he gives: *This paper-based, productized module is designed to support the robust implementation of a friendly, context-driven interface between the developer and the end-user* (a facetious description of his own book). In his glossary, he provides five near synonyms for the term: *compuspeak, computalk, tech speak, techno-talk,* and *technojive*. Compare COMPUTERESE, TECH-NOSPEAK. [STYLE, TECHNOLOGY, WORD]. T.MCA.

TECHNOLOGY [17c: from Latin *technologia*, Greek *tekhnología* systematic study, from *tekhné* craft, and *logía* speech, study]. The methods, knowledge, and theory needed to create and maintain tools and other types of equipment, and such tools, etc., viewed collectively: *science and technology, clay-and-cuneiform technology in ancient Mesopotamia, courses in computer technology*. Technology relates to language in two ways: (1) Pragmatically, by providing aids to communication, such as: the clay tablet and the reed stylus, used for cuneiform writing (*c*.3,500–500 BC); pen, ink, and parchment, especially as used in bound codices, the beginning of the world's book culture (*c*.300 BC–AD 1500); printing presses with movable type (developed in the 15c); the typewriter, with keys, platen, and inked ribbon (since the late 19c); and the word-processing computer, with keyboard, screen, and peripherals (a product of the late 20c). (2) Terminologically, requiring large numbers of words and phrases for naming and discussing tools, products, and processes, such as *amniocentesis, CAT scan, mammography, radiography, scalpel,* and *surgery* in the language of medical technology, and *CD-ROM, compact disk, laser printer, microfloppy, telephone,* and *television* in the language of the technologies of communications and computers.

Technology and language. Technologies of various kinds have played a fundamental part in creating and preserving language artefacts that can be read years, centuries, or even millennia later. The transmission of information over time is impossible without the use of physical equipment such as paper, pens, pencils, scrolls, books, audio- and video-tapes, and computer storage media, and of the varied conventions that govern their use, such as writing in one direction (horizontally, from right to left or left to right; vertically, from top to bottom), and a more or less closed set of devices for presentation and punctuation, such as spacing and points. The technology needed to create, use, and maintain language-related equipment often dictates the kinds of linguistic convention used with such

equipment: for example, the flag positions used in sending a semaphore message; the dots and dashes of alphabet-related Morse code flashed by heliograph or tapped out in telegraphy. At other times, attempts to address the needs of the user lead to a particular kind of linguistic expression, such as the raised dots of the Braille system by which the blind can read special kinds of printed matter.

Standardization, fossilization, and change. Since the 15c, the technology of printing, which underpins the production of all books and periodicals, has encouraged the relative standardization of type and orthography throughout the world and also, in some languages, the fosilization of forms more closely associated with past than present linguistic situations, as with the retention in French of verbal endings long since gone from the spoken language, such as the *-ent* inflection in *ils aiment* (they love), and the *-gh* digraph in the English words *bough, dough,* and *tough*. In the earlier 20c, the emergence of radio broadcasting tended to disseminate, endorse, and lend prestige to certain educated accents of English, such as Received Pronunciation as used by the BBC and the accent widely associated with Network English in the US. In the later 20c, a global market in films, television programmes, and print products (with a common technological denominator in their use of photography) has affected national and regional language usages within the English-using world, especially in speech, orthography, and vocabulary: for example, the extensive distribution of American material in the UK and British material in the US, which has led to the adoption of Americanisms in the UK and to a lesser extent Briticisms in the US. A small indicator of technology-related exchange appears in the terminology of the computer industry: the BrE use of the AmE spelling *program* (not *programme*) and the AmE use of the BrE spelling *programming* (not *programing*). Such recent technological developments as personal radio transmitter-receivers and electronic mail also offer scope for innovation in the use of language: for example, a truck-driver using citizens' band radio in the US can talk and listen to many other people, all using the conventions, codes, and slang of CB radio; similarly, the use of telephone answering machines has meant distinctive new speech conventions, and sending messages by electronic mail has created an exchange of screen-borne or printed-out messages whose conventions lie somewhere between those of letter-writing and making a telephone call. The entries in the technology theme discuss such relationships between technology and language. [LANGUAGE, MEDIA]. M.L., T.MCA.

The technology theme.

ALGORITHM, ALPHABET, ALPHABETIC(AL) ORDER, ALPHANUMERIC, ARTIFICIAL INTELLIGENCE, ARTIFICIAL LANGUAGE, ASCENDER AND DESCENDER, ASCII, AUDIOBOOK, AUTHORS' AND PRINTERS' DICTIONARY, BACK MATTER, BAR, BIT, BLACK LETTER, BOILERPLATE, BOOK, BOOKLET, BRAILLE, BRITISH LIBRARY, BROADCASTING, BROADSHEET, BROADSIDE, BROCHURE, BYTE, CARET, CARTOON, CASE², CATCHWORD, CHARACTER, CHARACTER SET, COLOPHON, COMMUNICATIVE SHIFT, COMPUTATIONAL LINGUISTICS, COMPUTERATE, COMPUTER LITERACY, COMPUTER TYPESETTING, COMPUTER USAGE, COMPUTING, CONCORDANCE, COPPERPLATE, COPY, CROSS-REFERENCE, CROWN, CURSOR, DATA, DEMY, DESKTOP PUBLISHING, DICTATION, DUMMY, DVORAK, EDITION, ELECTRONIC MAIL, ELECTRONIC PUBLISHING, EM, FAX, FEEDBACK, FIST HAND, FOLIO, FONT/FOUNT, FOOLSCAP, FORMAT, FRONT MATTER, GALLEY, GATHERING, GOTHIC, GRAPHIC DESIGN, GRAPHICS, HARD AND SOFT COPY, HART'S RULES, HEADERS AND FOOTERS, IMAGE, IMPRESSION, IMPRINT, INDEX, INDEXING LANGUAGE, INFORMATION, INTERFERENCE, ITALIC, JUSTIFYING, KEYBOARD, KNOWLEDGE REPRESENTATION, LASER, LEAF, LEAFLET, LEGAL-SIZE, LETTER¹, LETTERPRESS, LETTERSET, LETTER-SIZE, LIGATURE, LINE, LINOTYPE, LITERAL, LITHOGRAPHY, LOGO, LOGOTYPE, LOWER CASE, MACHINE LANGUAGE, MACHINE-READABLE TEXT, MACHINE TRANSLATION, MACHINE WORD, MANUAL, MANUSCRIPT, MASTHEAD, MIMEOGRAPH, MINIM, MISPRINT, MNEMONIC, -MO, MODERN, MONOTYPE, MOUSE, MULTIMEDIA, NETWORK, OBLIQUE, OCTAVO, OFFSET, PAGE, PAGE PROOF, PAGINATION, PAMPHLET, PAPER, PARCHMENT, PARSING, PEN, PHOTOCOPYING, PHOTO-OFFSET PRINTING, PICA, PLAGIARISM, PLATEN, PUNCTUATION, PRESS, PRINT, PRINTER, PRINTHEAD, PRINTING, PRINTING PRESS, PRINTOUT, PROOF-READING, QUAIR, QUARTO, QUIRE, QWERTY, REAM, RECTO, REDUNDANCY, RELIEF PRINTING, ROMAN, ROYAL, RUNNING HEAD/TITLE, SAN SERIF, SCRIPT, SCROLL, SERIAL, SERIES, SERIF, SEXTO, SIGNATURE, SIXMO, SIXTEENMO, SPACE, SPELLING CHECKER, STEREOTYPE, STYLE CHECKER, SUBSCRIPT, SUPERSCRIPT, SWUNG DASH, TECHNOBABBLE, TECHNOLOGY, TECHNOSPEAK, TELECOMMUNICATIONS, TELEGRAPHESE, TELEPHONE, TELEPRINTER, TELEVISION, TEXT, THEMATIC ORDER, TRANSCRIPTION, TRANSLITERATION, TYPE, TYPEFACE, TYPESCRIPT, TYPESETTING, TYPEWRITER, TYPOGRAPHICAL ERROR, TYPOGRAPHY, UPPER CASE, VELLUM, VERSO, VOLUME, WHITE SPACE, WIDOWS AND ORPHANS, WORD PROCESSOR, WYSIWYG, XEROGRAPHY.

TECHNOSPEAK [1980s: a blend of *technology* and *Newspeak*]. An informal term for a prose style used by high-technology industries, their associated media, and the marketing and publicity groups that surround them, as in: 'LISA lookalike systems, such as VisiCorp's VisiOn software, require a massive 256K bytes of Random Access Memory and a 5 megabyte hard disc capable of storing five million characters of information' (*Observer*, 7 Aug. 1983); 'Elegant, innovative and Inphone at its most ingenious, the Versatel features press-button dialling

incorporated in the sleek lines of the handset' (*Inphone Info*, 1980s ad, British Telecom); 'Three modes of operation are provided: voice-activated-mode (VOX), press-to-talk (PTT) and call. With the selector switch set on VOX, the Easy Talk will automatically transmit whenever you talk' (*Motorcyclist*, Feb. 1984). There are at least ten identifying features: (1) The use of letter symbols, initialisms, and acronyms: *K*, *PTT*, *LISA* (local integrated software architecture). (2) Number-and-letter groups: *256K*. (3) Blends: *SELECTaCOM*, *Versatel*. (4) Vogue usages: *info*, *mega*. (5) Compounds: *lookalike*, *press-button*. (6) Fixed phrases: *hard disc*, *Random Access*. (7) Word-play: *LISA lookalike*, *VisiOn*. (8) Novel orthography: *SELECTaCOM*, *VisiCorp*. (9) Heavy pre-modification: *Advanced Videotech Bike-to-Bike Intercom*, *LISA lookalike systems*. (10) A generally dense presentation. The style invites parody: '*Megaforce* is a movie for mini-minds set at maxi-gullibility and zero-taste' (Montreal *Gazette*, 29 June 1982). See ACRONYM, AGGLOMERESE, BLEND, COMBINING FORM, COMPUTERESE, INTERFIX, LETTER¹, -SPEAK, TECHNOBABBLE, VOGUE (WORD). [STYLE, TECHNOLOGY, WORD]. T.MCA.

TEFL, short for *Teaching English as a Foreign Language*. Also *EFL* alone. The teaching of English to learners in or from countries where it has not been traditionally used. The terms (T)EFL, (T)ESL, and TESOL all emerged after the Second World War, and in Britain, no distinction was made between (T)EFL and (T)ESL before 1950, both being subsumed under *ELT* (*English Language Teaching*). *EFL* and *TEFL* are usually pronounced 'ee-eff-ell' and 'teffle'. Informally, someone engaged in TEFL is a *TEFLer*.

Background. The teaching of English as a foreign language has been common since at least the mid-19c, and for most of that time was comparable to the teaching of any other foreign language. However, with the explosion in the importance of English since the Second World War, teaching it to foreign learners has been so institutionalized that it has acquired a distinct name and acronym. Traditionally, such teaching has been mainly in the care of local teachers at the secondary and tertiary levels in such countries as France and Germany. It has been primarily cultural, more or less on a par with learning a musical instrument. In EFL, however, the teaching has mainly social and economic importance, and such cultural aspects as literature have a secondary role. The focus of (T)EFL is largely on everyday communication, business, and access to English-medium education. In such work, the place of native-speaking teachers has become significant, particularly in privately run schools and colleges. Currently, in Britain, EFL is largely a private, often entrepreneurial activity, ranging from well-established and respected institutions to 'cowboy' outfits. Rates of pay for teachers are generally low, conditions of service vary, and the quality of teaching varies with them.

Current situation. Between 1960 and 1990, as demand for courses in Britain steadily increased, TEFL became a significant earner of foreign currency. Some 1,000 private language schools, mainly in southern England, provide short courses for some 250,000 students a year, mostly young adults. A wide range of course materials, published and unpublished, has been produced to cater to this demand and the needs of learners elsewhere. There has been a great increase in radio and TV courses and the provision of examinations and certificates of attainment. The British Council is closely involved in EFL, providing scholarships for foreign students to attend courses or obtain higher degrees in applied linguistics and EFL/ESL. Organizations include the *Association of Registered English Language Schools* (1960) and the *International Association of Teachers of English as a Foreign Language* (*IATEFL*) (1971). Associated publications include the *ELT Journal* and *EFL Gazette*. Teachers at British language schools were at first mainly graduates in English Literature, usually without training as language teachers. In the 1970s–80s, however, there has been a move towards professionalization. Centres for research and development in applied linguistics and EFL/ESL have been established in such universities as Edinburgh, Lancaster, and Reading, strengthening the academic base of the profession and helping to provide teachers with an awareness of the theory and practice of foreign-language teaching.

Principles. EFL, as represented by the major language schools and the universities in Britain, generally aims at a working command of the spoken and written language. Methods tend to be eclectic and the range of materials wide, generally emphasizing fluency and accuracy. Features of grammar are explained after rather than before being used. The explicit teaching of grammar is not dominant and most teachers do not consider that command of the language is a consequence of knowing a set of rules. The four skills of listening, speaking, reading, and writing are by and large taught in an integrated way. Classroom activity varies, and pair work, group work, tasks, and projects are all favoured. Reading and writing tend to be taught with practical aims in mind: letters, reports, notes, instructions, stories. Many teachers create their own materials as a supplement to, or a substitute for, published

courses, which are available in great variety. By and large, teaching techniques are flexible, varying according to a student's level of attainment (beginner, intermediate, advanced) as well as the aims of the course and students' hopes and expectations.

EFL and FLT. Despite its international predominance, EFL is only one among many kinds of *foreign-language teaching* (*FLT*). With common origins in the direct method of the late 19c, EFL and other FLT began to diverge about 1960, but have recently begun to come together again. The source of the divergence was greater demand for English than any other language, creating resources for developments in theory, methodology, and materials, and strengthening the academic basis for EFL, largely through a coming together of applied linguistics and descriptive studies of the contemporary language. Since the mid-1970s, the Council of Europe has helped integrate EFL and the teaching of other European languages.

See ELICOS, ELT, ENGLISH, EXAMINING IN ENGLISH, LANGUAGE LEARNING, LANGUAGE TEACHING, RECEIVED PRONUNCIATION, ROYAL SOCIETY OF ARTS, TEACHING ENGLISH, TEIL, TESD, TESL, TESOL. [AFRICA, AMERICAS, ASIA, EDUCATION, EUROPE, OCEANIA].   P.S., T.MCA.

Doff, Adrian. 1988. *Teach English: A Training Course for Teachers.* Trainer's handbook and teacher's workbook. Cambridge: University Press.
Hubbard, P., Jones, Hywel, Thornton, Barbara, and Wheeler, Rod. 1983. *A Training Course for TEFL.* Oxford: University Press.
Strevens, Peter. 1977. *New Orientations in the Teaching of English.* Oxford: University Press.

TEIL, short for *Teaching English as an International Language.* Also *EIL* alone. A term in language teaching and applied linguistics for teaching the use of English between or among speakers from different nations. Such persons may be native speakers (such as Americans and Britons who may not always understand each other well), non-native speakers (such as Thais dealing with Arabs or Mexicans dealing with Japanese), or native speakers and non-native speakers (such as Americans dealing with Hungarians, or Ethiopians dealing with Australians). The term differs from both *TEFL* and *TESL* in that native speakers are also seen as needing help in cross-national and cross-cultural communication, rather than as representing the norm at which non-natives should aim. It is assumed in TEIL that English belongs to all of its users (whether in its standard or any other form), and that ways of speaking and patterns of discourse are different across nations.

Communication and miscommunication. Problems of interpretation are especially likely to occur when native and non-native users are communicating, or when one non-native is communicating with another. In many instances, miscommunication is often linked to two mistaken and often unconsidered assumptions: (1) Someone with a native or native-like control of pronunciation, grammar, and vocabulary has no cross-national communication problems, or should not have such problems. (2) The ways of speaking and patterns of discourse of all fluent speakers of English are similar. TEIL stresses that a good command of English is helpful for efficient international communication but is not enough, because information and argument are structured differently in different nations, and topics of conversation, speech acts, expressions of politeness and respect, irony, understatement and overstatement, and even uses of silence are different in different nations. People using English in an international context could benefit from knowing more about such things.

Englishes. Practitioners of EIL do not usually claim that English is or should be the universal language, and recognize the roles of other languages. They note, however, that English is the most frequently used international medium, but argue that international communication in English cannot be reduced to the limited range of material and communication patterns that characterize ESL and EFL. Practitioners do not usually claim that more people should use English or that if everyone used the same language, the world would be a better place. The term *Englishes* is often used when discussing EIL, because it describes the functional and formal variation in the language and its acculturation in Africa, Asia, the Caribbean, and Oceania, as well as its traditions in the UK, the US, Ireland, Australia, Canada, and New Zealand.

Teaching. The goal of TEIL is to increase proficiency when using English across nations. Its students are both native and non-native speakers of English, and its concerns are intelligibility, comprehensibility, and interpretability. These concerns are not speaker- or listener-centred, but are shared by both speaker and listener; international communication is interactional, and meaning must be negotiated. Students are exposed to varieties of English from many different parts of the world and are encouraged where appropriate to become proficient users of their own country's educated variety. Cultural information is not limited to native English-using countries, but is given for countries in all three of Braj B. Kachru's English-using circles: the *Inner Circle* (the traditional English-speaking countries), the *Outer Circle* (the countries where English is developing new varieties), and the *Expanding Circle* (countries in which the use of

English is increasing). A discussion of the subject is provided in Peter Strevens, *Teaching English as an International Language* (Oxford: Pergamon, 1980). See ENGLISH, ENGLISHES, INTERNATIONAL LANGUAGE, TEACHING ENGLISH. [AFRICA, AMERICAS, ASIA, EDUCATION, EUROPE, OCEANIA, VARIETY].   L.E.S.

TELECOMMUNICATIONS. See TELEPHONE.

TELEGRAPHESE [Late 19c]. An informal term for the concise expression achieved in telegraphic messages: *Arriving Monday 1800 Heathrow Sheila*, which condenses *I will be arriving on Monday at 1800 hours at Heathrow Airport, London: (this note is from) Sheila*. Such concision risks ambiguity and even wilful misinterpretation: a cable is said to have been sent by a movie agent who wanted to know Cary Grant's date of birth; it read HOW OLD CARY GRANT, and received the reply from Grant himself OLD CARY GRANT FINE HOW YOU. In the first edition of the *Concise Oxford Dictionary* (1911), H. W. and F. G. Fowler noted: 'If common words are to be treated at length, and their uses to be copiously illustrated, space must be saved both by the curtest possible treatment of all that are either uncommon or fitter for the encyclopaedia than the dictionary, and by the severest economy of expression— amounting to the adoption of telegraphese— that readers can be expected to put up with.' Recent editions of the *COD* have relaxed this policy. See CABLESE, CONCISE OXFORD DICTIONARY, -ESE. Compare TELESCOPING. [MEDIA, STYLE, WORD].   T.McA.

TELEPHONE [1820s: from Greek *tele-* afar, *phōnē* voice, a term with various applications in the 19c, including to what are now known as the foghorn, the megaphone, the speaking tube, and a system of signalling by musical notes. The invention of Bell's *Electrical Speaking Telephone* in the 1870s fixed the term in its present-day use]. Short form *phone*. An electrical instrument or process for the conversion, transmission, reception, and reconversion of especially acoustic signals such as the human voice by wire or by a combination of wire and radio. The inventor of the first successful telephone, the Scottish audiologist Alexander Graham Bell (1847-1922), had been trained by his father, Alexander Melville Bell, in elocution and the written representation of sound. After the family moved to Canada in 1870, the younger Bell continued his father's work there and in the US, teaching speech phonetically to the deaf and seeking to create an electric hearing instrument for their benefit. In 1876, before he was 30, he had patented a device with much more extensive applications and implications. In 1877, he formed the *Bell Telephone Company*, since 1900 known as the *American Telephone & Telegraph Company* (*AT&T*). By 1887, there were over 150,000 telephones in the US, 16,000 in the UK, 9,000 in France, and 7,000 in Russia; by 1987, the number of telephones throughout the world was reckoned in hundreds of millions. Links across continents and oceans by short-wave relay were established by the 1920s, and in 1956 the first transatlantic cable was laid from Scotland to Newfoundland to Nova Scotia.

Telephone voices, formulas, and procedures. Use of the telephone has led to various adapted styles of speech, necessary because people cannot see each other when talking. In its earlier period, because of cost, communication tended to be brief and direct, sometimes borrowing from radio such expressions as *roger* (meaning 'message received and understood'). As the telephone became part of everyday life, and less expensive to use, speaking through it has become closer to normal face-to-face conversation, and may include an unconscious use of gestures and expressions that the listener never sees. The inability of the listener to perceive any such paralinguistic aids to speech makes it necessary, however, for the speaker to be precise, to repeat points in order to be fully understood, to avoid silences because these are not understood or may be misunderstood, and to repeat what the other person has said to confirm that the message has been successfully communicated. Speakers may also make a list of notes before a phone call, and summarize the main points made in the call before ending it. In business, secretaries and receptionists are expected to have a good *telephone manner*; their styles of speech often exhibit features valued in traditional elocution, such as clarity, restraint, and refinement, and they often use politeness formulas intended to impress callers and safeguard people not on the line: *I'm afraid Mr Smith is in conference at the moment; could you call again later?/if you can let me have your number he'll call you back the moment he's free/but he'll be glad to know you called and will get in touch as soon as he can.*

Uses and services. The ease with which the telephone makes immediate contact (often interrupting and taking precedence over face-to-face discussions in progress when it rings) has prompted a range of developments, from *telemarketing* (using the telephone for commercial research and promotion) to obscene and abusive calls (especially by men to women, and accompanied by 'heavy breathing'). In recent years, technological additions have included the

(*telephone*) *answering machine*, which invites speakers to ad-lib to a tape recorder and enables receivers of calls to monitor such messages without revealing their presence, and the *modem* (an acronym for *modulator/demodulator*), a device that converts digital to analog signals and vice versa, passing them along a telephone line from computer to computer. Services offered by *telecom* (telecommunications) companies range from dialling special numbers for the time or such services as *Dial-a-Prayer* or *Dial-a-Song*, to encyclopedic numbered services in which a customer dials for specific taped information about, for example, aspects of health. Emergency services include numbers for the police, fire, and ambulance, *helplines* for people in distress (such as victims of assault or those considering suicide), and *hotlines* (for information relating to particular critical needs, usually associated with disasters, but including *grammar hotlines* that offer advice on linguistic usage). Radio broadcasting has also been made more open to public involvement by programmes referred to as *phone-ins* or *call-ins*, in which commentators, celebrities, and experts talk over the radio with individuals who are telephoning them. *Teleconferencing*, in which several people can link up by telephone, and take turns in a discussion, has also become common.

Telecommunications. Activity associated with telephone use has grown so greatly since the Second World War that it is now generally known as *telecommunications*, the transmission of information (words, sounds, or images) over often great distances primarily by telephone but also by telegraph, radio, and television. Over the last decade there has been at least a sixfold increase in international telephone communication. In the late 1980s, to measure the flow of this traffic, Gregory Staple and Mark Mullins of the *International Institute of Communications* in London devised a statistical unit called the *minute of telecommunication traffic* or *MiTT*, which measures contact by voice, fax, or data transmission on public circuits. Their survey showed that, in gross terms, Americans are the primary users of telephones, clocking up 5.3bn MiTTs in 1988. However, a comparative measure of MiTTs per 1,000 people in a given territory showed that in 1988 Hong Kong led the field with 56,296 units (one-third to China), followed by Singapore, Canada, the Netherlands, and West Germany. On this scale, the US ranked ninth, with 21,839 units per 1,000 (a fifth to Canada, a tenth each to Britain and Mexico, then 7% to West Germany and 4% to Japan). The next six receivers of US calls, around 2–3% each, were France, Italy, South Korea, the

Dominican Republic, Colombia, and the Philippines. In return, nearly three-quarters of South Korea's outward calls and half of Taiwan's went to the US and Japan, while Singapore spent the same proportion, around 13%, on each of Indonesia, Hong Kong, Japan, and the US. Europeans mainly called each other, except for the British, who made more than a fifth of their calls to the US. Such links are axes of influence and interdependence, and provide a means of mapping global relationships, in which English appears to have a major share. See COMMUNICATIVE SHIFT, REDUNDANCY, TELEPHONE. [MEDIA, SPEECH, TECHNOLOGY]. T.MCA.

TELEPRINTER. See PRINTER.

TELESCOPING [1870s: *telescope* as a verb]. The contraction of a phrase, word, or part of a word, on the analogy of a telescope being closed: *biodegradable* for *biologically degradable*; *sitcom* for *situation comedy*. There are two main processes: (1) Adapting classical combining forms through reducing the first word in a compound or fixed phrase: when *biologically degradable* is telescoped to *biodegradable*, *bio-* refers not to life alone but to biology; when *telephone communications* is reduced to *telecommunications*, *tele-* refers to the whole technology of remote communication. (2) Creating syllabic acronyms like *sitcom* and blends like *smog*. The reduction of a series of words to some of their component syllables (or syllable-like elements) creates such new usages as *sitrep* for *situation report*, *Saceur* for *Supreme Allied Commander Europe*, and *NAVFORKOR* for *Naval Forces Korea*. Such forms are common in military, industrial, and technical usage. Some options are more telescopic than others. The computer language *SNOBOL* comes from the capitalized elements of *StriNg Oriented symBOlic Language*. A possible letter acronym would be *SOSL* and syllabic acronyms *Sorsyl* and *STORSYMLANG*. However, a variety of factors, such as convenience, ease of memorization, suitability of meaning, and whimsy, all contribute to the form finally adopted. See ABBREVIATION, ACRONYM. Compare TELEGRAPHESE. [WORD]. T.MCA.

TELEVISION. See BROADCASTING, MEDIA.

TELUGU, also **Telegu**. A Dravidian language of south India with some 52m speakers. It is one of the 15 major languages of India and the official language of the state of Andhra Pradesh. Written in a script based on southern Brahmi, it has a literary tradition that dates from the 11c, though inscriptions dating from the 7c point to an earlier development of the language. Telugu, unlike Tamil, is tolerant of borrowings from

Sanskrit, and like Tamil has diglossic variation between a High (*grānthika*) and Low (*vyāvahārika*) variety, with the modern standard based on the High variety. See DRAVIDIAN ENGLISH, FIJI, INDIAN LANGUAGES, SOUTH AFRICA. [ASIA, LANGUAGE]. Y.K.

TENNYSON, Alfred (Lord) [1809–92]. English poet, born in Somersby, Lincolnshire, and educated at Trinity College, Cambridge. His early life was saddened by family difficulties and the death in 1833 of his close friend A. H. Hallam. He published his first volume of poetry, in collaboration with his brothers, in 1827; subsequent volumes in 1830, 1833, and 1840 gained him the status of a major poet, and in 1850 he was appointed Poet Laureate on the death of Wordsworth. *In Memoriam* (1850), his elegy for Hallam, was widely acclaimed and helped to bring him the favour of the widowed Queen Victoria. He was made a peer in 1884. His mature work included the long poem *The Princess*, with a portrayal of university education for women, and successive pieces on the Arthurian legends, collectively titled *Idylls of the King*. He continued to publish poetry to the end of his life and also wrote several plays in verse, of which *Queen Mary* (1875) was the most successful. Tennyson's reputation, high in his lifetime, was being challenged before the end of the 19c. Later, he suffered partly from critics' preference for Browning as a precursor of Modernism. He was a spokesman of the Victorian era, expressing its doubts and self-division in *Maud*, its optimism tinged with anxiety in *Locksley Hall*, and its bellicose patriotism in *The Charge of the Light Brigade*. The *Idylls of the King* expressed 19c idealization of the Middle Ages as a period of faith and chivalry. In them, he used such archaisms as *elfin*, *thrall*, *whate'er betide*, and the *-eth* ending of the verb. Tennyson had a fine ear for English word music; he used the full resources of the language in rhyme, rhythm, and alliteration and was a bold metrical experimenter as well as using blank verse and other traditional forms. His dramatic monologues are stately, lacking the colloquial quality that Browning gave to his speakers. His 'Lincolnshire Farmer' poems are in the dialect he heard in his early years. General educated usage includes such Tennysonian phrases as *theirs not to reason why*, *the old order changes*, and *ring out the old, ring in the new*. See index. [BIOGRAPHY, EUROPE, LITERATURE]. R.C.

TENSE[1] [13c: from Old French *tens* (Modern *temps*), from Latin *tempus* time]. The grammatical category, expressed in forms of the verb, that locates a situation in time. In English, tense must be expressed in all finite verb phrases. It is marked by the choice of the first or only verb in the verb phrase: *play* versus *played*; *has played* versus *had played*; *will play* versus *would play*; *is playing* versus *was playing*. Since contrasts in number and person, where they apply, are also marked on the first or only verb, these choices combine with tense: present *I/They play* versus present *She plays*; present *I am/She is* versus present *We/They are*; past *I/She was* versus past *We/They were*. By definition, non-finite verb phrases do not have tense marking. There is also no tense choice for the imperative ('*Play* harder') or the subjunctive ('We insisted that he *play* harder').

Tense in English. In terms of morphology, English has only two tenses, the present or non-past (*take/takes*) and the past (*took*). The paradigm is extended by the use of the auxiliaries *be* and *have*: *be* followed by the present participle forms the progressive or continuous (*is taking*); *have* followed by the past participle forms the perfect (*has taken*). Although these are traditionally known as tenses, recent terminology refers to them as *aspects* (such as progressive aspect) and (for the perfect) *phase*. All three features can be combined: *had been taking* is past, progressive, and perfect. The passive voice is formed within the same paradigm, by *be* followed by the past participle, but is not a tense. The sequence of the auxiliaries is fixed: *have + be +* present participle, *be +* past participle, with the full verb in final position and a modal verb preceding all other auxiliaries: *may have been taken*.

The simple present. With dynamic verbs, this tense expresses habitual activity and 'timeless truths': *He goes to London every day; Water boils at 100 Celsius.* In commentaries, demonstrations, and performatives, it serves to report events simultaneous with the speech event: *He passes the ball to Smith, and Smith scores; I take three eggs and beat them in this basin; I name this ship 'Fearless'.* With static verbs, it refers to a present or timeless state: *It contains sugar; Air consists of oxygen and other gases.* With private verbs (of sensation, mental processes, etc.) it expresses how things are: *I smell something burning; I think he'll come.* In statements about the future, it shows that events have been arranged: *We fly to Paris tomorrow.* In literature and conversation, as the *historic present*, it reports past events dramatically and dynamically: *He comes up to me and says . . .* With verbs of communication, it states or informs: *The Bible says . . .; John tells me that he is going to Spain.*

The simple past. Generally, this tense refers to events, habitual activities, and states in the past: *I talked to my brother this morning; The Normans conquered England in 1066; He went to London every day; It contained sugar.* In the 'sequence of tenses' rule in reported speech, it restates the present tense of the original utterance: 'He likes chocolate' as reported in *She said he liked chocolate.* However, the present tense may be retained if the state of affairs being reported is covered by the time of speaking: *John said he likes chocolate.* It is used to express unreality, especially in unreal conditional sentences (*If John came, Mary would leave;* compare *If John comes, Mary will leave*), with wishes and recommendations, etc. (*I wish I knew; It's time we went*), and for tentativeness or politeness (*Did you want to talk to me?*). This accounts for some of the uses of the modal forms *might, could,* and *would,* as in: *Might they want to see her?; Would you like us to come?*

The progressive. The present progressive is most commonly used to indicate an event in progress at the time of speaking: *He's reading a book.* With the past progressive, the time of the continuous event is often explicitly shown to overlap a point of time or another briefer event: *I was reading at ten o'clock/when he arrived.* In contrast, the simple past would suggest that the event was subsequent to the point of time or other event: *When he arrived, I left.* In standard English, static and private verbs are non-progressive, in that they do not usually occur in the progressive, the simple present being used instead (no **I am loving you,* no **I'm thinking he will come,* although such usages occur in varieties of IndE and PakE). There are a number of verbs with inherent duration which may be used in the non-progressive form, even if the duration is clearly indicated: *I worked all morning; She slept for eight hours.* The progressive may indicate: (1) Incompletion: *I was painting the house this morning* versus *I painted the house this morning.* (2) Simple futurity, especially with verbs of motion: *I'm flying to Paris tomorrow.* (3) Limited duration of habitual activities or with non-progressive verbs: *We're eating more meat now; We're living in London these days* (compare *We live in London*). (4) Sporadic repetition: *My car's always breaking down* versus *My car always breaks down when I forget to service it.*

The perfect. The non-progressive perfect refers to an event in the past with current relevance: *I've broken the window* indicates that I broke the window and that the window is probably still broken; *I've seen John* might suggest that I have told him what I intended to, or that he is now nearby. It is also used with *just* for events in the immediate past: *I've just seen him.* The progressive perfect relates to activity beginning in the past and continuing up to the present, or, for past-tense forms, to a point of time in the past: *I've been reading for two hours; I'd been reading for two hours when he arrived.* It may also indicate continuous activity in the past with current relevance: *Someone's been moving my books—they are no longer where I left them.* The present perfect is not normally used with past-time adverbials: no **I've broken the window yesterday.* The simple past is often used in AmE where BrE uses the perfect: (1) BrE *Have you washed your hands?*, AmE *Did you wash your hands?* (2) BrE *Have you done it yet?*, AmE *Did you do it yet?* There is, however, wide variation in the use or non-use of the perfect in AmE.

The future. Traditionally, grammarians have taught that English has a future tense formed with *shall* and *will*, *shall* being used with first-person subjects (*I shall be happy to see her*) and *will* with the others (*She will be happy to come*). However, *will* is also commonly used with first-person subjects (*I will be happy to see her*) to indicate futurity, though conversely *shall* is not used in the same way with the other persons (no **She shall be happy to come*). The view that *will* and *shall* mark the future tense is widely held and often strongly asserted, but there are three arguments against it: (1) Morphologically, there are only two tenses, present and past; to talk about the future tense is to confuse time marking with grammatical tense. (2) *Will* and *shall* are formally modal verbs, and should be handled in the modal system, not the tense system. (3) *Be going to* is as good a candidate for the marker of the future tense as *will* and *shall*.

In the majority of instances, *will* and *shall* express a conditional future and are the forms used in the apodosis of future conditionals (the part without *if*): *If you ask them, they will do it. Be going to* indicates an envisaged progression towards a future event: *It'll cost me a lot of money* may imply 'if I buy it', whereas *It's going to cost me a lot of money* suggests that the decision to buy has been made. There are two arguments in favour of treating *will* and *shall* as markers of the future tense: (1) Future tenses in other languages also often express conditional futures. This is not unexpected, since the future is not factually known as the present and past are, and it is not surprising, therefore, if the future tense in English is marked by modal-type verbs. (2) *Will* and *shall* function in some ways more like tense markers than modal verbs, particularly in that they cannot be marked independently from the main verb for negation, as most modal verbs can. Thus, there is only one negative of *You will see him tomorrow* (*You will not/won't see him tomorrow*), as there is only one negative of *You saw him yesterday* (*You did not/didn't see him yesterday*), but there are two negatives of *He may be in his office*: (1) *He can't be in his office* (It is not possible that he is in his office). (2) *He may not be in his office* (It is possible that he is not in his office). See MODAL VERB, VERB. [GRAMMAR]. F.R.P., S.G.

TENSE[2]. See VOWEL QUANTITY.

TERCET [16c: from Italian *terzetto* a little third]. A stanza of three lines, usually rhyming *aaa*; an unrhymed tercet or *tristich* is rare. The lines may be of equal lengths (Robert Herrick's 'Upon Julia's Clothes', 17c) or of varying lengths (Richard Crashaw's 'Wishes to his Supposed Mistress', 17c). A more elaborate form is *terza rima* (third rhyme), in which the tercets are linked by a continuing rhyme scheme, *aba bcb cdc*. This is the form of Dante's *Divina Commedia*, was first used in English in the 16c by Sir Thomas Wyatt, and is well known in Shelley's 'Ode to the West Wind' (1820; italics added):

O wild West Wind, thou breath of Autumn's *being*,
Thou, from whose unseen presence the leaves *dead*
Are driven, like ghosts from an enchanter *fleeing*.

Yellow, and black, and pale, and hectic *red*,
Pestilence-stricken multitudes: O *thou*,
Who chariotest to their dark wintry *bed*

The wingèd seeds, where they lie cold and *low*,
Each like a corpse within its grave, *until*
Thine azure sister of the Spring shall *blow*

Her clarion call o'er the dreaming earth, and *fill*
(Driving sweet buds like flocks to feed the *air*)
With living hues and odours plain and *hill*.

The tercet is not easily sustained in English, which lacks the Italian facility for rhyme, but terza rima can have a compelling effect as expectation is continually drawn forward to the next stanza. See VERSE. [LITERATURE]. R.C.

TERM [12c: from Old French *terme*, Latin *terminus* a limit, boundary]. A word, phrase, or a sense of a word or phrase, that has a particular (often unusual) meaning because of the context in which it is used. In the context of botany, for example, the term *ivory* refers to the hard endosperm of the *ivory nut*; in metal-working, the term *pig* means a mould for casting metals. Typically, a term names something within a specialized field: *hysterectomy* is a medical term and *morpheme* is a term in linguistics. Such terms as *hysterectomy* and *morpheme* are generally referred to as *technical terms* in their appropriate fields. See GENERIC TERM, LITERARY TERM, NAME, TERMINOLOGY. [WORD]. T.MCA.

TERMINOLOGY [18c: from Latin *terminus* a limit or boundary, and Greek *logia* study]. (1) The vocabulary of a specialized field as contrasted with the general vocabulary of a language. There is, however, no clear dividing line between general and specialist vocabulary: for example, a common, everyday word can have a technical application, such as *pig* in the senses 'a mass of metal such as iron, copper, or lead when cast into a simple shape' and 'the mould for such casting'. Conversely, there is nothing to prevent a technical term from being used in the general vocabulary: for example, *neon*, the name for a rare gas, as in *neon sign*. Many technical usages are composites in form. They may be: complex, as in *cooperativity* (a kind of molecular interaction in biochemistry) and *luxulianite* (a rare form of granite, named after the village of Luxulyan in Cornwall); compound, as in *scabbard fish* (a spiny-finned fish of the family *Trichiuridae*) and *oxidation-reduction* (a reversible chemical process involving the transfer of electrons); and fixed phrases, as in *fatty degeneration* (in pathology, the abnormal formation of globules of fat within body cells). In technical terms, especially of the noun–noun variety, there is often a close semantic link between concept and form, as with *pipe/exhaust pipe, brake/cantilever brake*. Such usages may or may not seem immediately transparent to lay people and in composites the meaning is usually much more than the sum of the parts involved.

(2) The study of how technical terms are formed, used, and codified. In traditional lexicography, technical usage has been listed thematically or alphabetically, either in standard or specialized works, usually by the same definers as work on the rest of the language. A current approach, however, has been to design specialized encyclopedic glossaries, in which the close link between concept and term is established by the coordinated effort of several experts in the subjects concerned. National and international standards institutions work to achieve agreed multilingual equivalence between standardized terms. Large international bodies such as UNESCO and NATO have special terminology bureaux, often in conjunction with translation services and computer centres: for example, the European Community's *EURODICAUTOM* (*European Automatic Dictionary*).

(3) Also *terminography*. The theory and practice of compiling specialist dictionaries in fields like engineering and medicine. Such works tend to be classified or thematic rather than alphabetic; are often concerned with meanings and concepts rather than with word forms; may relate to or result from the deliberate standardization of terms within a field; and can be multilingual as well as monolingual. An example is the trilingual dictionary *The Machine Tool*, compiled by the Austrian terminologist Eugen Wüster (London: Technical Press, 1968), which follows guidelines established by a United Nations committee. Terminography has benefited greatly from the use of computers, but further progress depends on agreement about relationships between concepts and terms and the willingness of institutions to pool their databases.

See BINOMIAL NOMENCLATURE, DEFINITION, DICTIONARY, ENTRY, GENERIC TERM, HEADWORD, INFORMATION, INTERNATIONAL SCIENTIFIC VOCABULARY, JARGON, LEXICOGRAPHY, LEXICON, LEXIS, LITERARY TERM, NOMENCLATURE, ONOMASIOLOGY, REGISTER, VOCABULARY. [NAME, REFERENCE, WORD]. R.H., T.MCA.

Aitchison, Jean, & Gilchrist, Alan. 1972. *Thesaurus Construction: A Practical Manual*. London: ASLIB.
Felber, Helmut. 1984. *Terminology Manual*. Paris: UNESCO (UNISIST Programme). Vienna: INFOTERM.
Picht, Herbert, & Draskau, Jennifer. 1985. *Terminology: An Introduction*. Guildford: University of Surrey, Department of Linguistic and International Studies.

TERZA RIMA. See TERCET.

TESD, short for *Teaching English as a Second Dialect*. Also *SESD* (*Standard English as a Second Dialect*). The teaching of national or international standard English to speakers of non-standard dialects or varieties, on the principle that the standard will be additional to, rather than a replacement of, the kind of English already used. There are four kinds of non-standard variety: (1) Regional and class dialects, such as Cockney and New Yorkese. (2) Varieties influenced by other languages, such as Hispanic English and Malaysian English. (3) Creoles, such as Krio in Sierra Leone and Jamaican Creole English. (4) Vernaculars with distinctive histories, such as Hawaiian English and Black English. Such varieties have traditionally been regarded as bad or broken English, often by their own speakers as well as others; they tend to be associated with lower-class and/or lower-prestige ethnic, racial, political, and economic groups. Speakers of these varieties have been and often still are assessed at school as deficient in verbal and cognitive skills, as deaf, as learning-disabled, and as educationally or psychologically disturbed, whereas the significant difference lies in a use of language with which their teachers may be unfamiliar and for which they have not been prepared.

Britain, Canada, and the United States. In Britain and Canada, the movement against ethnic and linguistic prejudice has focused in the main on immigrant Afro- and Indo-Caribbean students. In the US, the focus has largely been on students of African-American background, and to a much lesser extent students of Hispanic background. In Canada and the US, some attention has been given to students in Native communities as well. In Britain, an important catalyst for change was a book by Bernard Coard in 1971 (see below), together with rising linguistic nationalism in the Caribbean, and increasing tolerance for and interest in regional and class dialects. In North America, such sociolinguists as William Labov (see below), William Stewart, and J. L. Dillard claimed both social and linguistic validity for these language varieties. Feeling towards their own language usage was often positive within the communities concerned, but parents and teachers also stressed the need for students to succeed in the kind of English (the standard variety) recognized as prestigious and useful by schools, business, and the community at large.

The TESD approach. The approach is based on an acceptance of language variation of all types, as exemplified in Mike Raleigh's *The Languages Book* (below) and the Open University packet *Every Child's Language* (Open University, Milton Keynes, 1985). It is often contrastive, examining the grammar and vocabulary of different varieties, emphasizing variation and situational appropriateness in language, and using culturally and linguistically appropriate materials. Unlike ESL students, ESD students generally have a high comprehension and even production of standard English; similarities and overlaps yield positive progress in the beginning, but ESD students reach humps or plateaus which involve core differences between varieties. For example, in standard English *She does wait for the bus*, the auxiliary *does* indicates emphasis; in Trinidadian usage, however, *does* shows habitual action (she waits every day). Throughout the Caribbean, *hand* refers to the whole physical area covered by standard *hand* and *arm*. In Black English, the 'invariant *be*' denotes habitual or ongoing action (*We be playing after school* We play after school every day), and *it* denotes presence (*It ain't nobody there* There isn't anyone/anybody there).

Features such as different vocabulary and pronunciation are generally recognized, even if they are not understood, but differences in prosodic features, such as intonation and stress patterns, may be neither recognized nor understood. Features of discourse, such as patterns of turn-taking in conversation, are not commonly recognized as legitimate differences among varieties of English. For example, children who speak Black English, Caribbean Creole, or Hawaiian English tend to categorize many questions from adults as 'scolding', to which the

proper response is silence, while not looking directly at the questioner; in standard English, such questions may indicate adult interest, but always require a verbal response while looking directly at the questioner's face. All such linguistic and social differences may cause confusion for teacher and student, with the result that responses to difficulties may be misinterpreted as misbehaviour or stupidity. Students may also have low motivation; many perceive themselves as already speaking English, and some may not want to identify with mainstream English and its speakers.

General issues. Current issues in TESD are linguistic, social, and political. There continues to be a widespread opposition to overtly anti-racist education and to devoting special attention to groups perceived as educationally and socially marginal. There is also often a lack of awareness of teaching methods that can be helpful with such students. Some educators consider that the particular difficulties for learners who already know some kind of English are unimportant or too subtle; there have always been such problems and in many generations of dialect speakers and immigrants many people have overcome them. Even where teachers and administrators are sympathetic to the principles involved, they may see TESD as legitimating 'substandard forms' and delaying students' progress, a view also held by some parents of these students and the community groups with which they identify. Some attention to language is usually part of programmes focused on 'academic skills upgrading'. In the US, most work specifically directed at language is on an individual teacher, school, or business level. Some national organizations have addressed this area: for example, TESOL's *Standard English as a Second Dialect* Interest Section and newsletter, now defunct because of lack of continued widespread participation, and the NCTE black caucus, which primarily addresses literary concerns. Despite years of attention, both positive and negative, there is little cohesiveness to this area in the US.

A landmark in the US was the 'King' decision in Ann Arbor, Michigan, in 1979, in which the court required the local Board of Education to provide teachers with the best 'existing knowledge' to help them realize educational goals, specifically in reading. Programmes specifically addressing African-American students and Hawaiian English speakers in the US have had varying degrees of success. Some programmes exist for students of English Caribbean background (for example, in Toronto, Ontario, and in Hartford, Connecticut); Caribbean students, however, are often perceived as not numerous enough in any area to justify special courses, or are lumped in with ESL or special education students. Attention to language in these groups has often been overshadowed by emphasis on social, economic, and disciplinary factors. Little formal research has been done specifically on ESD, particularly in primary and secondary schools, or in literacy classes. The lack of consensus on this topic may stem from the complexity of the problems that children from such backgrounds face. Some observers feel that the language issue is used as a smokescreen to avoid dealing with such larger and more important issues as low socio-economic status, minority racial status, and the need to upgrade academic skills in both teachers and students.

See TEACHING ENGLISH, TEFL, TESL, TESOL. [AMERICAS, EDUCATION, EUROPE, OCEANIA]. L.W.

Coard, Bernard. 1971. *How the West Indian Child is Made Educationally Sub-Normal in the British School System*. London: New Beacon.
Coelho, Elizabeth. 1988. *Caribbean Students in Canadian Schools*. Toronto: Carib-Can.
Labov, William. 1972. 'The Logic of Nonstandard English', in *Language in the Inner City*. Philadelphia: University of Pennsylvania Press.
Raleigh, Mike (ed.). 1981. *The Languages Book*. London: Inner London Education Authority English Centre.
Sato, Charlene. 1989. 'A Nonstandard Approach to Standard English', *TESOL Quarterly* 23: 2.

TESL, short for *Teaching English as a Second Language*. Also *ESL* alone. The teaching of English to non-native learners in countries where it has an established role, such as India, Nigeria, and Singapore, and to immigrants to English-speaking countries, such as Australia, Canada, the UK, and the US. The terms (T)EFL, (T)ESL, TESOL emerged after the Second World War, and in Britain, no distinction was made between (T)ESL and (T)EFL before 1950, both being subsumed under *ELT* (*English Language Teaching*). *ESL* and *TESL* are usually pronounced 'ee-ess-ell' and 'tessel'. The terms apply in particular to two types of teaching that overlap but are in many ways distinct: *Commonwealth ESL* and *Immigrant ESL*.

Commonwealth ESL. In this sense, ESL is a major activity in many non-white countries of the Commonwealth, especially where English is official and/or a language of higher education and professional opportunity. It has been largely confined to school-age pupils, often in English-medium schools, and methods have been influenced by developments in language education and methodology generally, especially since the Second World War. It relates in the main to work undertaken not in Britain itself (apart from courses for teacher trainers), but in such countries as India, Nigeria, and Singapore. It assumes that the learners will encounter English outside the classroom and expects to achieve adequate levels of ability. By and large, emphasis on the acquisition of BrE Received Pronunciation has declined and an educated local accent and pronunciation are often the acknowledged target. An English-language examination is usually part of the school-leaving qualifications and teacher training is usually the responsibility of departments and colleges of education. Most teachers have a degree, and the emphasis in their training is on classroom techniques rather than linguistic theory. British EFL and Commonwealth ESL have much in common.

Immigrant ESL in North America. The teaching of ESL for immigrants to the US and Canada has a different tradition. It is concerned principally with adults and the need for learners to be integrated into local life. Waves of immigrants since 1945, especially from Asia and Latin America, have created a great demand. Local communities, particularly in the larger cities, offer adult courses and make provision for non-English-speaking children in schools. Many universities have instituted MA courses in related subjects and created centres for teaching and for research and development. In addition, many countries have looked to the US and Canada for assistance with teacher training. Some universities have therefore set up links with centres in other countries, and a number of in-country projects in English-language training and teacher education have been undertaken in such countries as Peru, the Philippines, and Thailand, with help from such bodies as the Ford Foundation or with government sponsorship. Because many US immigrants are refugees, their ESL teacher may be the only representative of society they can relate to without arousing their fears of authority. This gives a quality of social service to much North American ESL, especially in larger cities, and has led to characteristics not found elsewhere: (1) A sense among teachers that their students need special care because of past or present experiences, resulting in efforts to establish warm relationships in the classroom. (2) The promotion by some teachers of holistic methods that link a concern for the student as a whole person to the teaching of ESL. Such teachers typically have an MA degree in which linguistics and research figure prominently. While practical training is included, classroom methodology is usually secondary to academic content.

Immigrant ESL in Britain. Immigrants to the UK are in the main from Commonwealth countries, principally the West Indies and West Africa (where English and English-based creoles are spoken), Uganda (mainly South Asian traders), South Asia (Bangladesh, India, Pakistan, Sri Lanka), and Hong Kong, where English is widely used in the community. ESL work includes both school-age children and adults, including literacy for women. ESL teachers are mainly teachers of the mother tongue who have received special in-service training. How much and how effective this training is depends on where they work; the London and Birmingham areas currently provide the most thorough training. Because many people of West Indian background speak standard West Indian English in addition to English-based creoles, they have been classified as speakers of English rather than as second-language learners, a factor that can lead to the disregarding of language issues in schools where standard English is the expected norm. Until the mid-1980s, ESL was often taught in separate classes or language centres (where the numbers justified such provision). However, this procedure came to be widely regarded as divisive, even racist, as it cut ESL learners off from the rest of the curriculum. After a court case by the Commission for Racial Equality in 1986, integrated classes became the norm, requiring ESL to become an element in the training of all teachers rather than the concern of only a few. ESL classes are also provided for adults in further education colleges, and by a range of voluntary groups providing individual home-based teaching. Increasingly, ESL teachers have concerned themselves with political issues arising from the status of many learners. In the 1980s, activists from minority groups became increasingly involved, determined to associate language learning more strongly with minority rights. The successive renamings of one association from *Association for Teaching of English to People of Overseas Origin (ATEPO)* to *National Association for Multiracial Education* to *National Anti-Racist Movement in Education* (both *NAME*) illustrate this shift.

See ELT, ENGLISH, ENGLISH TEACHING, LANGUAGE LEARNING, LANGUAGE TEACHING, TEFL, TEIL, TESD, TESOL. [AFRICA, AMERICAS, ASIA, EDUCATION, EUROPE].   P.S., T.MCA., C.J.B.

Bright, J. A., & McGregor, G. P. 1970. *Teaching English as a Second Language.* London: Longman.
Brumfit, C. J., Ellis, R., & Devine, J. (eds.). 1985. *ESL in the United Kingdom.* Oxford: Pergamon.
Finocchiaro, Mary. 1974. *English as a Second Language: From Theory to Practice.* New York: Regents.
Murphy, Edna (ed.). 1990. *ESL: A Handbook for Teachers & Administrators in International Schools.* Clevedon & Philadelphia: Multilingual Matters.

TESL CANADA. See CANADIAN LANGUAGE ORGANIZATIONS.

TESOL, short for *Teaching English to Speakers of Other Languages.* A professional association for teachers of English as a second language, founded in the US in 1966, and the especially US name for teaching English as a second or additional language, especially to immigrants in English-speaking countries. The organization was at first focused on North America, but in the 1970s–80s became increasingly international. Its core membership at June 1990 was some 16,000 individuals, but as an association of associations, with 70 affiliates worldwide, it represents an additional 26,000 English-teaching professionals. Its stated aim is 'to strengthen the effective teaching and learning of English around the world while respecting individuals' language rights. To this end, TESOL, as an international professional association: supports and seeks to inspire those involved in English language teaching, teacher education, administration and management, curriculum and materials design, and research; provides leadership and direction through the dissemination and exchange of information and resources; and encourages access to and standards for English language instruction, professional preparation, and employment.' TESOL is governed by an Executive Board elected by the membership to represent the affiliates, the 16 special-interest sections, and the membership at large. The Board is headed by a President who holds office for one year.

TESOL's major public activities are an annual conference of about 6,000 participants, usually held in March in either the US or Canada, and a Summer Institute of six to eight weeks, usually in North America but occasionally in Europe. Ongoing activities are supported by six standing committees: professional standards, sociopolitical concerns, publications, awards, nominations, and rules and resolutions. In addition to books and policy statements, publications include *TESOL Quarterly* (a journal presenting mainly research papers), *TESOL Matters* (a bimonthly medium for news of the organization and the profession at large), and *TESOL Journal* (a quarterly featuring practical concerns). The last two replaced the *TESOL Newsletter*, which ceased publication in 1990. TESOL also publishes a directory of professional preparation programmes in the US, a membership directory, and reference texts. Its 16 interest sections publish newsletters representing such interests as elementary education, applied linguistics, computer-assisted language learning, programme administration, video, and materials writers. TESOL has a mutual recognition agreement with the *International Association of Teachers of English as a Foreign Language*, is represented on the Executive Committee of the *Fédération Internationale des Professeurs de Langues Vivantes*, and has observer status as a non-government organization at the United Nations in New York. Its headquarters are at 1600 Cameron Street, Suite 300, Alexandria, Virginia, USA.

See ELT, ENGLISH TEACHING, IATEFL, LANGUAGE LEARNING, LANGUAGE TEACHING, TEACHING ENGLISH, TEFL, TEIL, TESD, TESL. [AMERICAS, EDUCATION, MEDIA].   C.J.B.

TEXAS [19c: from Caddo *techas* allies, friendship]. A state of the US Southwest, bordering on Mexico to the south. Its first European colonizers, in the 18c, were speakers of Spanish, and until 1836 the region was part of Mexico. Until the 1870s, there was some debate as to whether a citizen of the state was a *Texan* or a *Texian* (the latter formed by eliding the *c* of *Texican*, a prior term created by analogy with *Mexican*). Although *Texan* won, the earlier variants continue in use, generally for facetious and humorous purposes, as in *Kin Ah Hep You to Talk Texian?* (title of an article about Texas usage: Robert Reinhold, *New York Times*, July 1984). The clipping *Tex* has been used as a nickname (for example, the cowboy *Tex Ritter*) and as a combining form (as in *Tex-Mex* and the town *Texarkana*, on the border with the state of Arkansas). The terms *Texas English*, *Texas*, and *Texian* refer to English as used in the state. The variety is Southern and stereotypically features a twang and a drawl: that is, it is slightly nasal and vowels are elongated into diphthongs which can be shown in eye dialect as *hee-ut* hit, *ray-ud* red. Some diphthongs, however, are rendered as single vowels, most noticeably so that *white* is a homophone of *watt*, *oil* of *awl*, *wire* of *war*. The phrase *the oil business* sounds like 'the awl bidness' and *barbed wire* like 'bob war'. Several vowels are shifted from standard AmE usage, so that *rate* is nearly homophonous with *right* and *star* approaches *store*. Texas English is not homogeneous and shows some variety between East Texas (where phonology and lexicon show greater affinity with Southern usage) and West Texas (where they are somewhat more Midlands and Western). A growing Hispanic population may produce a distinct variety, *Chicano English*, and forms of mixed English and Spanish are already identified by the terms *Spanglish* and *Tex-Mex*. Immigrants from other areas of the US have imported their own speech characteristics or have failed to adopt the Texas variety. Cliff's Notes, the publisher of guides to students, published in the late 1970s a series of six booklets by Jim Everhart with the grandiose title *The Illustrated Texas Dictionary of the English Language*. See AFRO-SEMINOLE, DIALECT IN AMERICA, SOUTHERN ENGLISH. [AMERICAS, VARIETY].   J.AM.

TEXIAN. See TEXAS.

TEX-MEX [1940s: a rhyming blend of *Texas* and *Mexico*]. An informal and occasionally pejorative term for: (1) Anything considered to be a combination of Texan and Mexican, most commonly in food, cultural traditions, and language, especially along the common 1,200-mile border. (2) Anything of Mexican origin found in Texas or along the border, presumed by most North Americans to be not as good as the purely Mexican. Tex-Mex food includes *enchiladas, frijoles refritos* with *salsa picante* (refried beans with a piquant sauce), and *tacos*, prepared in the Northern Mexican style. In music, it refers to Northern Mexican *ranchera* music adapted to modern themes, North American life, use of some English, and electronic instrumentation. In politics, the *pachanga* (a gathering featuring food, drink, and speeches) is an important Tex-Mex event. In language, the term refers to any of several varieties of Spanish (also sometimes referred to as *Border Lingo*) that may or may not show English influence, including code-mixing with English by Spanish-speakers:

Husband. ¿Que necessitamos? Wife. Hay que comprar pan, con thin slices. [to sales clerk] ¿Donde está el thin-sliced bread? *Clerk.* Está en aisle three, sobre el second shelf, en el wrapper rojo. *Wife.* No lo encuentro. *Clerk.* Tal vez out of it (from Lorraine Goldman, 'Tex-Mex', *English Today* 5, Jan. 1986) [Translation: *H.* What do we need? *W.* We have to buy bread, with thin slices. Where's the thin-sliced bread? *C.* It's in aisle three, on the second shelf, in the red wrapper. *W.* I can't find it. *C.* Maybe we're out of it].

The term is also sometimes used for a more or less pidginized variety of Spanish spoken by non-Hispanics. See SPANGLISH, SPANISH, TEXAS. [AMERICAS, VARIETY].   J.AM.

TEXT [14c: from Old Northern French *tixte*, *texte*, Latin *textus* something woven, a tissue, version, style, from *texere/textum* to weave. Compare *textile, texture*]. (1) A continuous piece of writing, such as the entirety of a letter, poem, or novel, conceived originally as produced like cloth on a loom: *the text of Caesar's 'De Bello Gallico'*. (2) The main written or printed part of a letter, manuscript, typescript, book, newspaper, etc., excluding any titles, headings, illustrations, notes, appendices, indexes, etc. (3) The precise wording of anything written or printed: *He didn't keep to the text*; *the definitive text of James Joyce's 'Ulysses'*; *the most authoritative text of Homer's 'Odyssey'*. (4) A theme or topic, especially of a religious nature and related to a topic or statement in the Bible: *The pastor chose as his text the Sermon on the Mount*. (5) A book prescribed as part of a course of study; a textbook: *the prescribed texts for the exam*. (6) In printing, type as opposed to white space, illustrations, etc. The term is also sometimes a synonym for *Gothic* lettering. (7) In linguistics, a unit of writing or speech, especially if composed of more than one sentence and forming a cohesive whole. (8) In literary criticism, a piece of writing complete in itself and forming the subject of analytical study. (9) In computing, words displayed on a screen or printed out as hard copy. Traditionally, *text* as a concept has suggested something fixed and with a quality of authority about it not unlike scripture. Electronic and laser technology, however, has made the concept more fluid:

Text derives originally from the Latin word for weaving and for interwoven material, and it comes to have an extraordinary accuracy of meaning in the case of word processing. Linkage in the electronic element is interactive . . . With economical and virtually invisible storage of multiple versions of documents, the whole notion of an original text shifts. In magnetic code there are no originals (Michael Heim, *Electric Language: A Philosophical Study of Word-Processing*, 1987, pp. 160 ff.).

Under such conditions, the product of script and print begins to combine in new ways its potential for fixity with the dynamism until recently associated only with speech.

See BOOK, BRAILLE, CHAPTER, COHERENCE, COHESION, COMPUTING, CONTEXT, CRYPTOGRAPHY (CIPHERTEXT, CLEARTEXT, PLAINTEXT), DISCOURSE, DISCOURSE ANALYSIS (TEXT LINGUISTICS), HYPERTEXT, INTERTEXTUALITY, LINE, LITERARY CRITICISM, MACHINE-READABLE TEXT, PARAGRAPH, PRINT, PRINTING, PROSE, SUBTEXT, TEXTBOOK, VERSE. [LITERATURE, TECHNOLOGY, WRITING]. T.MCA.

TEXTBOOK [Early 18c]. A book written for and used by students as a standard work in a particular subject or as a source of information and exercises, activities, projects, etc., intended to help the user develop specific skills. When used attributively, it suggests something suitable for inclusion in such a work: *a textbook case*. See BOOK, TEXT. [MEDIA, TECHNOLOGY]. T.MCA.

TEXT LINGUISTICS. See DISCOURSE ANALYSIS.

THEATRE BrE, **theater** AmE [14c: from Latin *theatrum*, Greek *théatron*, from *theâsthai* to behold]. A place where drama is performed. The term, like *stage*, is metonymically extended to drama itself, regarded as presentation rather than text. Basically, a theatrical performance requires only a place where actors can be seen and heard by an audience; the rest is embellishment. A play is a cooperative effort, newly created at every performance and subject to varieties of interpretation. A vital element is the sympathy between actors and audience, which has varied historically with theatrical and other conditions: for example, Greek theatres were large

and the performance stylized, with masked actors, but plays were part of religious festivals and based on myths shared by the whole community. The new beginning of European drama in the medieval mystery plays brought the theatre into the streets, with performances on movable stages surrounded by spectators, who were in sympathy with the religious themes of the plays. The first permanent theatres in the 16c evolved from improvisations in the halls of great houses and the yards of inns. The Elizabethan stage was an open platform, with the audience close to it on three sides of a protruding 'apron', in a daylight performance. When the English theatres were closed by the Puritans at the beginning of the Civil War in 1642, the relationship between the stage and the audience was destined to change. The new theatres after the Restoration of 1660 were indoors, with proscenium arch, front curtain, and artificial lighting. Contact with the audience was not entirely lost at first, but over the next two centuries the separation gradually increased: the proscenium or forestage was brought forward until the apron at the front was lost and the play was viewed in a picture-frame effect. Better lighting (first gas then electricity) gave a brilliant stage and a darkened auditorium.

Actors and audiences. Changes in the cohesion of society have tended to make the theatre a spectacle rather than an experience: Drama draws people together and, when it can be based on common assumptions, reflects the concerns of the community. Greek and medieval drama enacted contemporary religious beliefs. The Elizabethan playwrights were sure of an audience generally united in religious and secular attitudes and, in theory if not in practice, a common sense of morality. In a plural society of many ideologies, and with a wide choice of theatrical entertainments, the theatre occupies a different role. Audience and actors can never be totally distanced from each other, even on radio and television; the audience colludes in the illusion of the play and suspends its realistic perception for the time of enactment. Even today, the unpredictable differences between audiences can markedly effect a live performance. A feeling of participation is essential, though repartee across the footlights is generally confined to the pantomime and music hall. The present-day tendency is to return to a wider playing-space: for example, performances at the Royal Shakespeare Theatre, Stratford, and the Barbican Theatre, London, take place on stages without the proscenium arch. Some dramatists have invited the audience to feel the importance of issues in the play and to make a decision about them; this approach has been taken by Bertolt

Brecht (1898-1956) in Germany and Clifford Odets (1906-63) in the US. Brecht wanted the spectator not to merge in a collective audience but to respond individually and apply problems being acted out in the play to the present world. Songs, chorus characters, and direct homily invite such identification in plays like *The Good Woman of Setzuan* (1938) and *The Caucasian Chalk Circle* (1941). Odets used naturalistic dialogue and direct address to draw the audience into the stage situation. In *Waiting for Lefty* (1935), the actors created the atmosphere of a trade union meeting so successfully that the question from the stage, 'Well, what's the answer?' produced cries of 'Strike!' from the audience.

Theatrical language. The structure of the theatre has its effect on dramatic language. Asides and soliloquies, accepted on the open stage with a visible audience, seem artificial when spoken into the darkness, and have largely gone out of fashion. Shared beliefs produce shared imagery and phraseology which can make dramatic dialogue communicate more easily. Both dramatists and actors must always be sensitive to the speech community to which they belong, combining dramatic economy and emphasis with naturalism. The language of early plays, perhaps strange in lexis and syntax, is usually delivered today in a comparatively familiar and conversational manner that would make older styles of acting appear flamboyant. Descriptions of actors in earlier centuries record rhetorical delivery and ample gesture which would have removed the stage more radically from common experience than the later development of naturalism in acting. There appear always to have been degrees of 'theatricality'; the advice to the players that Shakespeare puts in Hamlet's mouth satirizes the style evidently associated with the rival company of Henslowe. Response to the directly spoken word is not a priority in a late 20c culture whose education is centred in book, screen, and image; because of this, live theatre remains significant as a linguistic resource with its roots in more directly oral times.

See ASIDE, CENSORSHIP, DIALOG(UE), DRAMA, ENGLISH LITERATURE, GENRE, HOUSE, JONSON, MONOLOG(UE), MUMMERSET, PLAY, SCRIPT, SHAKESPEARE, SHAW, SHERIDAN (R.), SOLILOQUY, STAGE, THEATRE OF THE ABSURD. [LITERATURE].   R.C.

Banham, Martin (ed.). 1988. *The Cambridge Guide to World Theatre*. Cambridge: University Press.
Braun, E. 1982. *The Director and the Stage*. London: Methuen.
Brockett, O. G. 1979. *The Theatre: An Introduction*, 4th edition. New York: Holt, Rinehart, and Winston.
Burton, E. J. 1962. *The Student's Guide to World Theatre*. London: Jenkins.
Hatlen, T. 1962. *Orientation to the Theatre*. London: Peter Owen.
Morrden, E. 1981. *The American Theater*. Chicago: University Press.
Nicoll, A. 1962. *The Theatre and Dramatic Theory*. London: Harrap.
Simon, E. 1982. *The Ancient Theatre*. London: Methuen.

THEATRE OF THE ABSURD. Drama that depicts life as basically meaningless and inconsequential. It attracted a number of dramatists in the middle decades of the 20c, expressing feelings of loss and alienation that had been explored philosophically by the French existentialists. The leading writers in English have been Samuel Beckett (1906-89), Harold Pinter (b.1930), and, in lighter vein, N. F. Simpson (b.1919). Beckett's *Waiting for Godot* (1954) came to typify a movement that, after some initial incomprehension, was accepted as making serious dramatic statements of human tensions:

VLADIMIR. That passed the time.
ESTRAGON. It would have passed in any case.
VLADIMIR. Yes, but not so rapidly.
(*Pause.*)
ESTRAGON. What do we do now?
VLADIMIR. I don't know.
ESTRAGON. Let's go.
VLADIMIR. We can't.
ESTRAGON. Why not?
VLADIMIR. We're waiting for Godot.
ESTRAGON (*despairingly*). Ah!

Dialogue is disjointed, often failing to keep the normal 'turns' of conversation, and digressing into apparent irrelevance. It suggests that real speech itself is often more discursive than is generally supposed. Banalities and clichés appear as the only available verbal response to serious situations. A theatre built on the impossibility of effective communication would seem paradoxical, but has produced some powerful drama. See DIALOG(UE), THEATRE. [LITERATURE].   R.C.

THEMATIC ORDER, also **classified order, topical order**. The ordering of information according to themes or topics, as in a classified index or a thematic encyclopedia. Works ordered in this way may or may not also use alphabetic order: for example, in *Roget's Thesaurus* there is a non-alphabetical and numbered set of categories, alphabetic order appearing only in the index; some works alphabetize their themes, but may use chronological or other order within them, as in the *Bloomsbury Thematic Dictionary of Quotations* (1988); others may thematize their contents and use numbered illustrations and lists in their sections, as in the *English Duden: A Pictorial Dictionary* (1960). In many works of reference, a thematic system of defining entries in sets underlies the alphabetic order in which the entries are finally published, as in this volume. Such an arrangement is implicit in any work with consistent and widespread cross-referencing. See ALPHABETIC(AL) ORDER, CATALOG(UE), CROSS-REFERENCE, HYPERTEXT, LEXICOGRAPHY, LEXICON, MENU, THESAURUS. [REFERENCE]. T.MCA.

THEMATIC VOWEL, also **thematic**. In an inflected language like Greek or Latin, the vowel which adheres to a root or base, to form its stem or theme. This vowel then usually controls the inflectional and derivational affixes attaching to it: for example, in the Latin verb *amare* (to love), the base is *am*, the thematic vowel *-a-*, and the stem *ama-*. The vowel appears in all or most of the other inflected forms and derivatives of a thematic group; for the *amare* group (the first conjugation of Latin verbs), *a* appears throughout the imperfect tense: *amabam, amabas, amabat, amabamus, amabatis, amabant*. A selection of Latin words formed by means of thematic *-i-* is shown in the accompanying table.

Base	Thematic vowel	Addition	Outcome
aud (hear)	*-i-*	*o*	*audio* (I hear)
		ens	*audiens* (hearing)
		tor	*auditor* (hearer)
agr (field)	*-i-*	*cola*	*agricola* (field-tender)
		cultura	*agricultura* (field-tending)
hort (garden)	*-i-*	*cultura*	*horticultura* (garden-tending)

Thematic vowels from Greek and Latin are common in English, often serving to mark sets or families of words: (1) *Latin*, *-a-* as in dict*a*te/dict*a*tor, negoti*a*te/negoti*a*tor/negoti*a*ble, aud*a*cious/aud*a*city, ten*a*cious/ten*a*city; *-e-* as in compl*e*te/compl*e*tion, conveni*e*nt/conveni*e*nce, Ven*u*s/ ven*e*real, larynx/laryng*e*al; *-i-* as in aud*i*t/aud*i*ence/aud*i*tion, agr*i*culture/hort*i*culture, minister*i*al, president*i*al, space/ spat*i*al; *-o-* as in atr*o*cious/atr*o*city, fer*o*cious/fer*o*city; *-u-* as in resid*u*e/resid*u*al, use/ us*u*al, vac*u*ous/vac*u*ity, ambig*u*ous/ambig*u*ity, ac*u*puncture/ac*u*pressure; *-y/i-* as in colon*y*/ colon*i*al, Ital*y*/Ital*i*an/Ital*i*anate, audit or*y*/ audit or*i*um. (2) *Greek*, *-a-* as in dogm*a*/ dogm*a*tism, theme/them*a*tic; *-e-* as in frenzy/ fren*e*tic, phon*e*tic/phon*e*mic; *-eu-* as in hermen*eu*tic/pharmac*eu*tical; *-i-* as in arthr*i*tis/ arthr*i*tic, bas*i*s/bas*i*c, cris*i*s/crit*i*c/crit*i*cism; *-o-* as in astr*o*physics/astr*o*physicist, b*i*ography/ b*i*ographical, hypn*o*sis/hypn*o*tic/hypn*o*tism, neur*o*sis/neur*o*tic. See COMBINING FORM, INTERFIX, STEM. [GRAMMAR, WORD]. T.MCA.

THEME [13c: from Old French *te(s)me* (Modern *thème*), Latin *thema*, Greek *théma* something put down, proposition: compare THESIS. In the 16–17c, often spelt *theam*]. (1) Sometimes, more formally, *thema* (plural *themata, themas*). A topic for a discourse, discussion, composition, sermon, or meditation; a unifying or dominant idea, motif, or field; in music, a principal melody. (2) (Now especially AmE) an exercise written on a given subject, especially in school: *an English theme*. (3) In classical grammar, either the part of a word left when all endings and affixes are removed (the root), or the first-person singular present indicative of a verb, such as Latin *amo* (I love). (4) Also *thema*. In philology, the inflectional base or stem of a word, to which other elements (thematic vowels and consonants; inflections) are added: for example, in Greek, the root *lip* underlies the present theme *leip* to which the inflection *ein* is added to form the present infinitive of the verb *léipein* (to leave). (5) Also *topic*. In some linguistic analyses, that part of a sentence or utterance which expresses what is being talked or written about (often carried over from the preceding context), as opposed to the *rheme* (1890s: from Greek *rhéma* something said, verb, predicate), also called the *comment*, that part which provides new information. Anything pertaining to a theme or thema is *thematic*. See DISCOURSE ANALYSIS, STEM, THEMATIC ORDER, THEMATIC VOWEL, TOPIC. [GRAMMAR, REFERENCE, WORD, WRITING]. T.MCA.

THEME AND RHEME. See DISCOURSE ANALYSIS, THEME.

THESAURUS [19c: through Latin from Greek *thēsaurós* a store(house), treasury, repository. There are currently two plurals: traditionally *thesauri*, more recently and less formally *thesauruses*. See DOUBLET]. (1) A work of reference presented as a treasure house of information about words, such as Thomas Cooper's bilingual dictionary, the *Thesaurus Linguae Romanae et Britannicae* (1565), and the thematic *Roget's Thesaurus of English Words & Phrases* (1852). (2) A work of reference containing lists of associated, usually undefined, words (such as synonyms) arranged thematically, in the style of *Roget's Thesaurus*. (3) A work of reference containing such lists but presented alphabetically, such as *The New Roget's Thesaurus in Dictionary Form* (ed. Norman Lewis, Putnam's, 1961), *The New Collins Thesaurus: A Creative A–Z Wordfinder in Dictionary Form* (1984), and *The Oxford Thesaurus* (ed. Laurence Urdang, 1991). (4) In information technology, an alphabetic index list of key terms, through which information of a specialist nature (such as terms used in a particular industry) can be retrieved from a database. In such a thesaurus, terms are commonly linked associatively by cross-reference through such relations as synonymy and antonymy. (5) In word processing, a stored list of synonyms and antonyms, to be consulted in the preparation of texts, and provided as a service comparable to a spelling checker. See FACTS ON FILE, LEXICOGRAPHY, LEXICON, MARCH, ROGET, ROGET'S THESAURUS, SLANG, SYNONYMY, THEMATIC ORDER. [REFERENCE].   T.MCA.

THESIS [14c: through Latin from Greek *thésis* setting down, something set down or put in place, a lowering (of the voice). Plural: *theses*]. (1) In classical prosody, setting down the foot or lowering the hand when beating time; in Greek, the half of the metrical foot in which the voice falls; the part of a foot that bears the ictus; an accented syllable. In music, the downward stroke in conducting; the downbeat. The opposite of the thesis is the *arsis* (14c: through Latin from Greek *ársis* raising): raising the foot or hand; the half of the foot in which the voice rises; an unaccented syllable; the upward stroke in conducting; an upbeat. Among later Latin writers such as Priscian (*c*.500 AD), however, the relationship was reversed: *thesis* became the lowering of the voice on an unaccented syllable while *arsis* was its raising on an accented syllable, from which developed the use of *thesis* for an unaccented and *arsis* for an accented syllable. The terms have often been used in these latter senses in discussing Old English prosody. Because of the confusion, however, both terms were virtually abandoned in the 19c, perhaps encouraged by the awkwardness of the plural form of arsis: *arses*. (2) In logic and rhetoric, a proposition to be considered or defended; a statement, assertion, or tenet. In rhetoric, its opposite is *antithesis*. In the dialectic of the German philosopher G. W. F. Hegel, a *thesis* or proposition is contradicted by an *antithesis* or opposing proposition, after which at a higher level thesis and antithesis are resolved by a *synthesis* of opposites. (3) A theme for an educational exercise, or more commonly, especially in BrE, a dissertation supported by original research, presented in order to obtain a usually higher university degree: *a doctoral thesis*. Compare ANTITHESIS, ICTUS, PROPOSITION, THEME. See ACCENT, FOOT, PROSODY. [LANGUAGE, LITERATURE, STYLE].   T.MCA.

THIEVES' LATIN, also **Thieves' cant.** Archaic terms for the language of criminals: 'A very learned man [who] can vent Greek and Hebrew as fast as I can Thieves' Latin' (Walter Scott, *Kenilworth*, 1821). Compare ARGOT, CANT, SLANG. [STYLE].   T.MCA.

THOMAS, Dylan (Marlais) [1914-53]. Welsh poet and journalist, born in Swansea, son of an English master at Swansea Grammar School, where he was educated. After working as a local reporter, he followed a career of journalism, broadcasting, and writing in London. His early volumes *Eighteen Poems* (1934) and *Twenty-Five Poems* (1936) gained attention, and with *Deaths and Entrances* (1946) he came to be regarded as a leading poet. His poetry deals with nature, sex, time, and death. He wrote strongly rhythmic free verse, using traditional devices of alliteration and internal rhyme with novel collocations and compounds; he liked to present startling paradigmatic choices in seemingly familiar phrases ('happy as the grass was green', 'once below a time', 'a grief ago'). He rewrote many times before publication. Although he did not speak Welsh, forms of Welsh poetry influenced his work. Thomas took care with the appearance of words on the page, occasionally elaborately shaping poems in the style of George Herbert (17c). He also wrote a number of short stories, many autobiographical. His radio play *Under Milk Wood* (1954), later presented on the stage, is a portrait of life in a Welsh village painted with the idiom of South Wales:

Me, Mrs Dai Bread One, capped and shawled and no old corset, nice to be comfy, nice to be nice, clogging on the cobbles to stir up a neighbour. Oh, Mrs Sarah, can you spare a loaf, love? Dai Bread forgot the bread. There's a lovely morning!

Although some critics dismissed him as lacking content and needlessly obscure, Thomas was an influence on young 'neo-romantic' poets in the 1940s. He died in the US after one of many heavy drinking bouts. See index. [BIOGRAPHY, EUROPE, LITERATURE].   R.C.

THORN [From the Old English mnemonic name þorn]. The name of a runic letter and its manuscript and printed form þ, used in Old and Middle English for voiced and voiceless *th*. In late medieval times, its form became similar to, and in some handwriting identical with, *y*, with the result that *ye*, *yis*, *yat*, etc., were used (well into modern times) as variants of *the*, *this*, *that*, etc.: the origin of *ye* for *the* in such phrases and names as *Ye Olde Englishe Tea Shoppe* (often facetiously pronounced 'ye oldy Englishy tea shoppy'). The character has sometimes been used in phonetic transcriptions for the sound of voiceless *th*, now more commonly represented by the IPA symbol /θ/. See ETH, LETTER[1], RUNE, T. [WRITING].   E.W.

THORNDIKE, Edward L(ee) [1874-1949]. American psychologist and lexicographer, born in Williamsburg, Massachusetts, and educated at Wesleyan U., Connecticut, and Harvard. He won a fellowship to Columbia, where he studied with the psychologist James McKeen Cattell and the anthropologist Franz Boas, from whom he acquired a lifelong interest in the quantitative treatment of psychological data. His doctoral dissertation *Animal Intelligence* (1899) implied that the mind was not a separate entity but a total response of the organism to the environment. Influenced by the writing and teaching of William James, he spent his life educating teachers and school administrators, particularly at Teachers College, Columbia (1899-1940). Through his lectures, research, and publications (in particular *Educational Psychology*, three volumes, 1921), he popularized the use of fact-finding, statistics, and experimental techniques in education. His research on stimulus-response and transfer of learning had a major impact on English-language instruction in US schools for both native and second-language speakers. Thorndike suggested that conditioned responses account, in part, for word meaning in everyday life and maintained that words which occur frequently in contiguity come to be associated with each other and function as a class. The meaning of a word could therefore be described as a 'habit bond'. To demonstrate his contention that the frequency of a word's usage was related to the recognition of its meaning on the part of the learner, Thorndike prepared with Irving Lorge several lists of the most commonly used English words (published as *The Teacher's Word Book* series, 1921, 1931, 1944) which were used by editors of elementary school readers and ESL texts to select vocabulary for their publications.

Applying the results of his research on language and learning, Thorndike influenced the design, order, and writing style of *The Thorndike Junior Dictionary* (1935) and *The Thorndike Senior Dictionary* (1941), on which he collaborated with Clarence Barnhart. The definitions and illustrative sentences in these dictionaries emphasized what he held to be the ultimate aims in education: happiness, appreciation of beauty, utility, and service. The entry on *eugenics* reads:

the science of improving the human race. Eugenics would apply the same principles to human beings that have long been applied to animals and plants, and develop healthier, more intelligent, and better children; science of improving offspring.

To help users of the dictionaries with spelling, he entered important variant spellings in their alphabetical positions, and followed each spelling with the definition(s) associated with it. He excluded the history of words and word origins from his school dictionaries on the basis that such facts 'are valuable for students who have certain special abilities and interests and knowledge of foreign languages; but there are

relatively few such students in the present population of high schools, and even of colleges' (Preface, *TSD*, 1941). Although many of his opinions were controversial, his influence was widespread. He produced more than 500 works, including *Reading Scales* (1919), *The Thorndike Test of Word Knowledge* (1922), and *Teaching English Suffixes* (1941), and served as president of the New York Academy of Sciences and the American Psychological Association. See index. [AMERICAS, BIOGRAPHY, EDUCATION, REFERENCE].

R.W.B.

THRALE, (Mrs) Hester. See PIOZZI.

THREE-PART VERB. An alternative name, especially in the US, for a type of phrasal verb, also especially in Britain called a *phrasal-prepositional verb*, that consists of a verb plus an adverb plus a preposition: *look forward to, put up with.* See PHRASAL VERB, PREPOSITIONAL VERB. [GRAMMAR].

S.C.

THRENODY [17c: From Greek *thrēnōidía* song of lamentation]. Also **threnode**. An ode, song, or speech expressing grief and loss. See ELEGY. [LITERATURE].

R.C.

THRESHOLD LEVEL, The. The name of certain specifications for a survival level of language competence, developed by the Council of Europe in the 1970s and adopted as a basis for English-language examining by several British examining boards: for example, in the Preliminary English Test (PET) of the Cambridge U. Local Examination Syndicate. See COUNCIL OF EUROPE, UCLES. [EDUCATION].

W.S.

TILDE [1860s: from Spanish *tilde*, from Latin *titulus* superscription; cognate with French *titre*, English *title*: see TITLE. Stress: 'TIL-day']. A diacritic (˜) placed over *n* in Spanish (as the *ñ* in *señor*), to indicate a palatalized nasal sound (sometimes rendered into English as a depalatalized *ny*, as in *canyon*, from *cañon*), or over a vowel in Portuguese (as in *são* saint), to indicate nasality. (2) A symbol used in mathematics to indicate equivalency or similarity between two values, and in logic to indicate negation. (3) A swung dash. See DIACRITIC, CIRCUMFLEX, SWUNG DASH. [WRITING].

T.MCA.

TIME MAGAZINE. An American weekly newsmagazine founded by Henry R. Luce and Britton Haddon in 1923 and published by *Time Inc.*, one of the largest magazine publishers in the world (headquarters New York). *Time* is sold in six regional editions based on the same core format and content: the US, Canada, Latin America, Asia, the South Pacific, and 'the

Atlantic' (Europe, Africa, and West Asia). Its English-language circulation is around 5m and there are several foreign-language editions. Sister publications include *Fortune* (founded 1930), *Life* (founded 1936, discontinued 1972, revived in a different format 1978), *Sports Illustrated* (1954), *Money* (1972), *People* (1974), and *Discover* (1980). There is also a significant book-publishing group, centred on *Time-Life* Books, which was set up in 1960 and publishes book series and single titles in 30 languages, and including *Little, Brown & Company* and *Book-of-the-Month Club*. A video-publishing group includes the pay-television system *Home Box Office* (*HBO*) and the cable-TV operation *American Television & Communications Corporation*. The format and style of the newsmagazine has led to such rivals as *Newsweek*, and many imitative periodicals in many languages. See AMERICAN PRESS, MAGAZINE, NEWSMAGAZINE, TIMESPEAK. [AMERICAS, MEDIA].   G.H., T.MCA.

TIMES, The, sometimes referred to as *The Times of London, The London Times*. Britain's oldest, best-known, and most influential newspaper, founded in 1785 by John Walter as *The Daily Universal Register* and renamed *The Times* in 1788. His son, John Walter II, made it the country's leading newspaper, independent of government and with its own news-gathering service. In 1805, he published the first news of the Battle of Trafalgar. Under the editorship of Thomas Barnes (1817–41), the influence of the newspaper grew and it was nicknamed *The Thunderer*; under his successor John Thaddeus Delane, who edited it until 1877, it became in effect the nation's newspaper of record and the voice of the British establishment, at times almost a partner in government. Delane hired the first war correspondent, William Howard Russell, to cover the Crimean War (1853–6). The British government's first knowledge of Russia's peace proposals came through the pages of *The Times*. During the editorship of George Earle Buckle (1854–1935), because of overspending and the publication of what proved forged letters (attributed to the Irish political leader Charles Parnell), *The Times* experienced a serious loss in reputation and circulation. To counter this, it entered into an agreement to advertise and sell the 9th and 10th editions of the *Encyclopaedia Britannica*. In 1906, the press tycoon Alfred Harmsworth (Lord Northcliffe) bought the paper, and during the editorship of Geoffrey Dawson (from 1912 to 1919) ground was regained. Dawson quarrelled with Northcliffe and left, but returned after his death. He edited the paper from 1922 to 1941 with considerable success until his advocacy of appeasement towards the Nazis brought discredit on both him

and *The Times*. The Astor family owned the paper from 1922 to 1966, after which it was acquired by Lord Thomson of Fleet. In 1981, after four years of industrial strife, the Thomson Organization sold it to the Australian media tycoon Rupert Murdoch. Despite its vicissitudes, *The Times* continues to be a national institution to which its *leaders* (editorials), court circular (of the activities of the royal family), letter page, personal column, crossword, law reports, obituaries, and book reviews all contribute. In 1822, the companion *Sunday Times* was published, and in 1902 a weekly literary supplement, *The Times Literary Supplement* (*TLS*). More recently, two educational supplements have been added: *The Times Education Supplement* (*TES*) and *The Times Higher Education Supplement* (*THES*). It has 'lent' its name to many newspapers in the English-speaking world, including *The New York Times, The Los Angeles Times, The Times of India*, and *The Straits Times* in Singapore. See CROSSWORD PUZZLE, NEWSPAPER. [EUROPE, MEDIA].   T.MCA.

TIMESPEAK, sometimes **Timese** [Later 20c: see -SPEAK, -ESE]. An informal term for the style of the writers of *Time Magazine* and similar newsmagazines. Often pejorative, it identifies a homogenized, racy, digest-like prose in which the following often overlapping features are prominent: (1) Heavy pre-modification, in such phrases as 'Surgeon Barnard's cardiologist colleagues', 'William Littlewood, 69, aircraft engineer and longtime (1937-1963) vice president of American Airlines', 'Black Power Proselyter [*sic*] Stokely Carmichael'. (2) A wide-ranging, often whimsical vocabulary that uses such pseudo-archaisms as *atop*, *afoul*, and *awry*, such recherché terms as *bravura* and *quondam*, such slang terms as *glitz(y)*, *miffed*, *natty*, and *wacky* (often in formal contexts), such neologisms as the blend *shopaholic*, the compound *sweetspeak*, the derivative *hippiedom*, and such phrase words as 'Johnson's *close-to-the-vest* method' and 'the ebullient, inexhaustible, *larger-than-life* campaigner'. (3) A mix of registers, especially in headlines, as in 'Welcome to the Champs des Yobs', 'First-Class Philippic', 'hell-driving citizenry', 'A back-slapping braggart with the laugh of a hyena and the implacable euphoria of a lobotomy patient'. (4) Word-play, again common in headlines: 'Call it Politics Lite, with lots of froth and little annoying substance'; 'Turning Swords into Trade Fairs'; 'Once and Future Champ'; 'Tressed to the Nines'. (5) Current clichés, catchphrases, and buzz words worked into the copy, often in adapted form, as when the name of the popular film *Fatal Attraction* was exploited in a feature on European road safety entitled 'A New Summer of Fatal Traction'

(*Time*, 15 Aug. 1988). (6) An enthusiasm for sharp images: 'Ambulances scream to multiple pileups', 'vacationers of the white-knuckle variety', 'Once the precinct of elegant stone edifices, Paris's finest shops and stateliest homes, the Champs has become a chrome-and-glass jumble, a jangle of outlets for *le fast food*, neon signs and porn emporiums' (*Time*, 15 Aug. 1988). See HEADLINESE, JOURNALESE, -SPEAK, TIME MAGAZINE. [AMERICAS, MEDIA, STYLE]. G.H.

TINKERS' CANT. See CANT, SHELTA.

TIP OF THE TONGUE. See SPEECH, TONGUE.

TITLE [From Old English *titul*, from Latin *titulus* label, superscription, title. Compare TILDE]. (1) The name of a book, poem, picture, piece of music, or the like; a heading in a book or periodical, or of an article, chapter, or section in a text. A title that comes under another is a *subtitle*; when a story gives its name to an entire collection, it is the *title story*; when a catalogue provides only the titles of works, it is a *title catalog(ue)*; when a title is given to a work, the preferred verb in BrE is *entitle* (*a novel entitled 'Bleak House'*), in AmE is *title* (*a novel titled 'Gone With the Wind'*). The conventions for entitling texts vary from language to language and age to age: for example, it was common in Latin and in 16–17c English to begin with a focusing word or phrase, as in Caesar's *De Bello Gallico* ('On the War in Gaul') and Locke's *Essay Concerning Human Understanding* (1690). Formerly the titles and subtitles of books, etc., often occupied several lines, in effect offering more than one title, as in: *Encyclopaedia Britannica, or a Dictionary of Arts and Sciences, compiled upon a New Plan* (1768–71). Currently, they tend to be short and to the point, as in: *The Hutchinson Encyclopedia* (1988). (2) An additional name gained through inheritance, attainment, rank, or office, either permanently or for a given length of time, such as the *sir* in *Sir Arthur Conan Doyle*, the *lord* in *Alfred Lord Tennyson*, the *captain* in *Captain Ahab*, and the *president* in *President Bush*. (3) A championship in sport (*winning the top golf title, title-holder*); an established or recognized right to something (*Do they have title to the money?*); in law, a legal right of possession (*a title to a piece of land, title deeds*). (4) Usually plural: written matter inserted into a film or programme, such as a list of *credits* (names of actors, administrators, etc.); (also *subtitles*) superimposed on motion pictures and television presentations, brief text in a language other than that of the performance. See CAPTION, COLOPHON, FORM OF ADDRESS, HEADING, HEADLINE, RUBRIC, TITLE PAGE. [MEDIA, NAME]. T.MCA.

TITLE PAGE [17c]. The page at the beginning of a book that indicates the title and any subtitle, the name or names of any authors or editors, etc., brief publication information (such as publisher's name and location), and perhaps date of publication. Further information on copyright, printing history, British and American library cataloguing, name and location of printer, etc., appears on the *copyright page* (the verso of the title page). See BOOK, FRONT MATTER, TITLE. [MEDIA, TECHNOLOGY]. T.MCA.

TMESIS [1600: through Latin from Greek *tmêsis* a cutting]. The insertion of one word into another: for example (archaic) *work* in *what work soever he may do* instead of *whatsoever work he may do*; (current) *bloody* and *blooming* for emphasis in *every-bloody-where* and *abso-blooming-lutely*. See GREAT AUSTRALIAN ADJECTIVE, INFIX. [STYLE, WORD]. T.MCA.

TOEFL. See EDUCATIONAL TESTING SERVICE, EXAMINING IN ENGLISH.

TOK BOI. See TOK PISIN.

TOK PISIN [Late 19c: from English *Talk Pidgin*. Pronounced 'tock pizzin']. Also **Tok Boi, Pidgin**. Technically, **Papua New Guinea Pidgin**, and, especially formerly, **Neo-Melanesian, Neomelanesian, Melanesian pidgin**. Names for the English-based lingua franca of Papua New Guinea (PNG), officially named *Tok Pisin* in 1981. It descends from varieties of *Pacific Jargon English* spoken over much of the Pacific during the 19c and used as a lingua franca between English-speaking Europeans and Pacific Islanders. It was learned by Papua New Guineans on plantations in Queensland, Samoa, Fiji, and in PNG itself. Typically, male workers learned the pidgin and took it back to the villages, where it was passed on to younger boys. Tok Pisin crystallized in the New Guinea islands and spread to the mainland *c*.1880. Although a by-product of and sustained by colonialism, it quickly became more than a means of communication between the local people and their European colonizers. It has become the most important lingua franca for PNG and is now being acquired by children as a first language. In sociolinguistic terms, Tok Pisin is an expanded pidgin currently undergoing creolization. It now has more than 20,000 native speakers and some 44% of the population of 3.5m claim to speak it. There has been considerable discussion as to whether it should become the national language of PNG. Currently, it has official status with English and another pidgin, Hiri Motu, which is largely restricted to the Papua area, and only about 9% of the population speak it.

Grammar. Many structural traits have been transferred from indigenous languages. Even where items derived from English are used to express grammatical categories, their patterns and meanings often follow structures in the substrate languages. For example, in most if not all of the Melanesian languages and in Tok Pisin, but not in English, there is a distinction between inclusive and exclusive first-person plural pronouns. The speaker of Tok Pisin distinguishes between *we* (speaker and person or persons addressed), and *we* (speaker and another or others, excluding anyone addressed). Where English has only *we*, Tok Pisin has inclusive *yumi* (from *you* and *me*) and exclusive *mipela* (from *me* and *fellow*). Although the lexical material used to make the distinction is from English, the meanings derive from categories in Melanesian languages. The element *-pela* (fellow) serves additional grammatical ends as a suffix marking attributives: *gutpela man* a good man; *naispela haus* a nice house; *wanpela meri* a woman. In the pronoun system, it appears as a formative in the first- and second-person plural, *mipela* (*we* exclusive) and *yupela* (*you* plural).

Vocabulary. There are five sources of words: (1) English, which makes up most of the approximately 2,500 basic words: *mi* I, *yu* you (singular), *askim* a question, to ask, *lukautim* to take care of. (2) German, because of the German administration of the northern part of New Guinea (1884-1914): *rausim* to get rid of, *beten* to pray. (3) Spanish and Portuguese words are widely found in European-based pidgin and creole languages and also occur in Tok Pisin: *save* to know (from *sabir/saber*), *pikinini* a small child (from *pequeño*, small). (4) Polynesian languages: *kaikai* food, *tambu* taboo (from *tabu*). (5) Indigenous PNG languages: *kiau* an egg (from Kuanua, a language of East New Britain, which played an important part as a substrate language). In some cases, Tok Pisin expressions have been borrowed into the varieties of English used by expatriates in PNG: *going finish* (from *go pinis*), as in *going finish sale* a sale of household goods held when people leave for good.

Traditionally, Europeans have regarded Tok Pisin as a bastardized form of English. In it, some everyday vulgar words have taken on different and socially neutral meanings: *baksait* (from *backside*) the back rather than the buttocks; *as* (from *arse*) the buttocks, but extended to refer to the base or foundation of anything, as in *as bilong diwai* (the base or foot of a tree) and *as bilong lo* (the reason or cause of a law); *bagarap* (from *bugger up*) used as noun and verb, as in *Em kisim bagarap* (He had an accident) and *Pik i bagarapim gaden* (The pig ruined the garden); *sit* (from *shit*), as in *sit bilong paia* (shit

belonging to fire: ashes); *bulsitim* (from *bullshit*) to deceive. The Tok Pisin word for excrement is locally derived: *pekpek*. Some European dictionary-makers, often missionaries, have often gone to some length to invent respectable etymologies for such words. Tok Pisin has other terms of abuse often quite different from or completely unrelated to English: *puslama* (sea slug) for a lazy person; *tu kina meri* (where *kina* is a unit of currency and *meri* means 'woman') for a prostitute. Accounts by Europeans often contain concocted versions of pidgin expressions, such as the alleged circumlocution for piano. A. Deiber, a German traveller in the south Pacific, wrote in 1902: 'All in all the black does not lack a sense of humour. His description of the first piano brought to the German South Seas is also delightful. It was a Papuan who, horrified, told of big fellow box, white fellow master fight him plenty too much, he cry (of the box which the white man beats so much that it screams).'

Status and functions. Tok Pisin has undergone structural and functional expansion. Although English is the official medium of education, Tok Pisin is used in a variety of public domains, not only in political debates in the House of Assembly (where it is the preferred medium), but also in broadcasting and journalism, and for all its new functions it has drawn heavily on English. So much English has been borrowed into the language, particularly by educated urban speakers, that there are now two main varieties: urban pidgin and rural or bush pidgin. There are also a number of registers, such as *tok piksa* (talk picture), a way of speaking in similes and metaphors, and *tok bokkis* (talk box), a way of giving words hidden meanings. Most of the printed material in Tok Pisin until recently has been religious, centred on a translation of the Bible. Since 1970, there has been a weekly newspaper in Tok Pisin called *Wantok* (one talk: one language), a word used to refer to members of one's own clan group. The use of Tok Pisin for literary purposes is becoming more common. See CREOLE, MELANESIAN PIDGIN ENGLISH, PACIFIC JARGON ENGLISH, PAPUA NEW GUINEA, PIDGIN. [OCEANIA, VARIETY]. S.R.

TONE [13c: from French *ton*, Latin *tonus*, from Greek *tónos* tension, sound, tone]. A term used generally for musical and vocal pitch and quality, and in phonetics and linguistics for a level or contour of *pitch*, the quality or choice of which is known as *tonality*. Specifically, tone is a *pitch contour* that begins on an accented syllable and continues to the end of a *tone group*: that is, up to but not including the next stressed syllable. Simple tones move only in one direction: *fall* and *rise*. In English, these tones suggest finality, the fall frequently occurring at the end of a statement, the rise at the end of a *yes-no* question. The compound tones *fall-rise* and *rise-fall* are non-final, suggesting that the speaker has not yet finished (see below).

Tone group and breath group. Normal speech does not consist of unorganized strings of words, but stretches of words in the utterance of which breath and tone are integral parts. The *breath group* is a group of words uttered on a single breath, after which the speaker either stops speaking or draws breath to continue. This group may or may not correspond to phrases and sentences as recorded in writing or print, and will consist of one or more further groups of words organized in terms of tone. Such a further group is a *tone group* or *tone unit*. Major tone groups correspond more or less closely to sentences of prose, while minor tone groups (those which phoneticians have analysed in particular detail) are phrasal or lexical. The division of tone groups in speech is analogous to punctuation in writing, and in historical terms the conventions of punctuation have by and large arisen as attempts to reflect on a surface such aspects of speech as tones and pauses for breath or effect: see PUNCTUATION. Where a punctuation mark like a period or a comma is appropriate in writing, a tone-group boundary is usually appropriate in speech. However, the reverse is not true: if a spoken text is written down, the position of many tone-group boundaries cannot be marked by punctuation.

The constituents of the tone group. The nature of the tone group relates to the natural rhythm, stress, and intonation of English. Each group contains one or more stressed syllables known as the *nucleus*, the *tonic syllable(s)*, or the *tonic(s)*: for example, the capitalized syllables in *YES* and in *OH YES it is*. The nucleus is often assumed to be the most prominent syllable in the tone group, but this is not always the case. Any syllables following the nucleus form the *tail*: for example, *it is* in *Yes it is*, *-shire* in *YORKshire*. If there is more than one stressed syllable, the first is referred to as the *onset*: the *OH* in *OH YES it is*, the *NEW* in *NEW YORK is big*. The term *head* is used for a group of syllables beginning with the onset up to but not including the nucleus. Any weak syllables preceding the onset are generally known as the *prehead*: for example, *she* in *she WON'T*. A combination of prehead, nucleus, and tail occurs in *TasMAnia*. The end of a major tone group is typically marked by a pattern indicating finality: for example, a fall in pitch to close a statement. Non-final minor tone groups are often marked by levelling off in the pitch contour, or by a rise in pitch: for example, in a list-like series, with a fall on the closing item.

Individual tones. There are five tones in English: the falling tone or fall, the rising tone or rise, the rise-fall, the fall-rise, and the level tone: (1) The *fall* moves from a higher to a lower pitch, and there are two subtypes. A *low fall* is used to end statements, give orders, ask non-emphatic *wh*-questions, and ask emphatic and rhetorical *yes-no* questions. The *high fall* is used in contrastive stress: for example, in *John loves Mary* it is on *John* if he is being contrasted with *Bill*, on *loves* if it is contrasted with *hates*, and on *Mary* if she is contrasted with *Helen*. (2) The *rise* moves from a lower to a higher pitch, and there are two subtypes. The *low rise* is used for incomplete statements (often signalling an intention to continue speaking), in listing (until the end, when the tone falls), for requests, and in expressions of politeness and interest. The *high rise* occurs in asking non-emphatic *yes-no* questions, echo questions, and emphatic *why*-questions. (3) The *rise-fall* moves from a lower to a higher pitch, then back. It is like the fall, but more emphatic or exclamatory, and may also express disagreement and irony. It is rare in RP, but common in some other varieties, such as WelshE, IrE, and IndE. In varieties which do not use it much, its actual or apparent overuse can suggest naïvety, unwarranted enthusiasm, and a patronizing attitude. (4) The *fall-rise* moves from a higher to a lower pitch, then back. It may express assertion and contradiction. (5) The *level tone* is one in which the 'slope' of the pitch movement is not enough for it to be classed as a rise or a fall. Its functions are similar to those of the rise. See INTONATION, MONOTONE, PITCH, RHYTHM, SYLLABLE. [SPEECH]. G.K.

TONGA. Official title: *Kingdom of Tonga*. A country in Oceania and member of the Commonwealth, consisting of 170 islands due south of Western Samoa. Capital: Nuku'alofa. Currency: pa'anga (100 seniti). Economy: agriculture, fishing, industry, tourism. Population: 98,000 (1988), 110,000 (projection for 2000). Ethnicity: 98% Tongan. Languages: Tongan, English (both official). Education: primary 100%, secondary 70%, tertiary 5%, literacy 90%. Tonga was a British protectorate from 1900 until independence in 1970. See ENGLISH. [NAME, OCEANIA, VARIETY]. T.MCA.

TONGUE [From Old English *tunge*, cognate with Dutch *tong* and German *Zunge*]. A flexible mass of tissue attached to the lower back of the mouth of most vertebrate animals; an aid to chewing and swallowing, the organ of taste, and an important component in the articulation of speech. Words for 'tongue' in many languages stand for speech itself. English has a number of words and phrases of different origin which do this: *language*, through French *langue*, from Latin *lingua*, tongue; *linguistics*, directly from Latin; *polyglot* and *isogloss*, from the Greek *glṓssa*, tongue; the phrases *mother tongue*, *foreign tongue*, and the Biblical *gift of tongues*; such idioms as *Has the cat got your tongue?* (said to someone who will not speak), *to bite one's tongue* (to remain silent despite provocation), *it's on the tip of my tongue* (I know it but I can't quite recall it), *Hold your tongue* (Be quiet).

In terms of anatomy and phonetics, the tongue has five parts: the *tip* (*of the tongue*), the *blade* (*of the tongue*), the *front* (*of the tongue*), the *back* (*of the tongue*), and the *root*, which lies not in the mouth but in the pharynx. Sounds made at the tip (the 'apex' of the tongue) are *apical*. The blade is immediately behind the tip, lies opposite the alveolar ridge of the upper mouth when the tongue is in a state of rest, and sounds made with the blade (Latin *lamina*) are *laminal*. The area behind the blade is the front, which lies opposite the hard palate when the tongue is in a state of rest, and sounds made with the front are *palatal*. The back of the tongue lies opposite the soft palate or velum when the tongue is in a state of rest, and sounds made with the back include *velar consonants* and *back vowels*. See APICAL, GLOSSOLALIA, LINGUAL. [LANGUAGE, SPEECH].   G.K., T.MCA.

TONGUE-TWISTER [1890s]. A sentence, phrase, or rhyme that is difficult to pronounce, especially when said quickly. The difficulty is usually caused by alliteration: the presence of similar-sounding consonants interspersed with a variety of vowels, as in *Peter Piper picked a peck of pickled pepper* and *The Leith police dismisseth us*. Such tongue-twisters may be accidental or deliberately used for especially comic effect, such as Shakespeare's: 'Whereat, with blade, with bloody blameful blade, / He bravely broach'd his boiling bloody breast' (*A Midsummer Night's Dream*, 5 : 1 : 145-6). They became particularly popular in the 19c as rhymes designed to cause pronunciation problems and elocutionists used examples like *Truly rural* and *She sells sea-shells on the sea-shore* to improve enunciation. See ALLITERATION, ALLITERATIVE VERSE, ELOCUTION, WORD GAME. [WORD].   T.A.

TONIC (SYLLABLE). See TONE.

TOPIC [16c: from Latin *topica*, Greek (*tà*) *topiká* (title of a philosophical work by Aristotle, *The Topics*) things that pertain to *tópoi* places, categories (particularly *koinoì tópoi* commonplaces, shared or general categories)]. (1) In traditional rhetoric, a field of considerations from which arguments can be drawn; a heading under which arguments may be organized. (2)

The subject of a discourse, essay, treatise, speech, etc.: *religious topics*; *a topic of conversation/for discussion*. (3) A theme or heading: *a subject arranged according to topics and subtopics*. (4) In linguistics, an item serving as the subject or focus of a sentence or utterance. The process by which any such item is given prominence is called *topicalization*. (5) The adjective *topical* refers to: formerly, a locality (*topical gods*); in medicine, a part of the body (*topical application of a powder*); in classification, headings or themes (*topical order*); in general usage, something of current interest (*topical events*). See PARAGRAPH, THEME. [GRAMMAR, LANGUAGE, REFERENCE, STYLE].   T.MCA.

TOPICAL ORDER. See THEMATIC ORDER.

TOPONYM [1890s: from Greek *tópos* place, *ónoma/ónuma* name]. A place-name, such as *London, New York, the North Sea, the Bay of Fundy, Mount Everest, Kilimanjaro*: See PLACE-NAME, TOPONYMY. Although not toponyms properly so called, many nouns have toponymic origins and/or associations, such as *champagne* from Champagne in France, *gin* from Geneva in Switzerland, *calico* from Calico in India, *muslin* from Mosul in Iraq. Such words are often associated with trade and food. Their categories appear to be: (1) *Simple words.* The name, usually with a small initial letter, used as a noun and perhaps with some adaptation: *cashmere* (sometimes *kashmir*) a kind of wool associated with Kashmir in India; *port* a fortified wine from *Oporto* in Portugal; *tweed* (probably from *tweel* twill, but influenced by the name of the River Tweed) a kind of cloth associated with Scotland. (2) *Fixed phrases, compounds, etc.* Special developments from toponyms proper, such as *Loch Ness Monster* from *Loch Ness*, a lake in Scotland. Fixed phrases whose attributive element is a toponym (or its derivative) may lose both the capital letter and the last element: *a Balaklava helmet* becoming *a balaklava*; *an Alsatian dog* (a dog from Alsace) becoming *an Alsatian*. The practice is common in naming breeds of animal: for example, *Guernsey cattle* becoming *Guernseys*. Occasionally, a fixed phrase such as *Cheddar cheese* becomes the base for further fixed phrases: for example, *Canadian cheddar cheese, Scottish cheddar*. (3) *Clippings.* Examples include *gin* from *Geneva*, and *Champ*, the informal name for a monster said to live in *Lake Champlain* in the US. Some clippings involve the diminutive *-ie*: *Nessie* for the *Loch Ness Monster*, and *Chessie* for its supposed equivalent in *Chesapeake Bay*. Some words, though originally toponymic, are more properly *eponyms* (coined from personal names and titles drawn from place-names): for example, *cardigan*, the knitted garment named after J. T. Brudenell (b.1797), the 7th Earl of Cardigan. Compare EPONYM. See -ONYM. [REFERENCE, WORD].   T.MCA.

TOPONYMY [1870s: from Greek *tópos* place, *-ōnumia* naming]. The system of place-names of an area or a language; the study of such place-names. A place-name within such a system is a *toponym*. Toponymic study covers the type of referent, etymology, and structure of the name. The broadest division among types of places named is between natural features of the landscape and political divisions. Natural features include bodies of water (oceans, seas, gulfs, lakes, ponds, rivers, streams, swamps) and land masses (continents, peninsulas, islands, shores, mountains, hills, plateaus, canyons, valleys), including areas characterized wholly or in part by their flora (deserts, plains, forests). Political divisions are: nations; states and provinces; counties and other districts; cities, towns, and other settlements; neighbourhoods and streets. Structures like bridges and buildings may be thought of as either places or things.

The etymology of toponyms treats the sources from which the names have been derived and the process of their creation. Particularly, it treats the languages from which the names come, as well as whether the names echo other place-names, or honour the names of persons, or commemorate events, or describe the locale, or have various other origins. British toponymy has focused mainly on the language of the etyma of names, whether Celtic, Roman, Anglo-Saxon, Scandinavian, or Norman, and is thus aligned with antiquarianism. Toponymy in other English-speaking countries concentrates instead on the type of etymo-referent, that is, whether the place is named for a person, another place, etc. This difference correlates with a difference in time depth of names in Britain and other anglophone nations. In structure, many place-names consist of two terms: a generic and a specific, as in *the Firth of Forth*, the generic *Firth* naming the type of place and the specific *of Forth* narrowing it. Such names are typically endocentric constructions, with the generic as head and the specific as modifier.

Names of bodies of water tend to have both terms, although the generic is often omitted in practice, especially when the resulting name is still distinctive: *the Atlantic* (*Ocean*), *the* (*English*) *Channel*, *the Great Lakes*, *the North Sea*, *the Mediterranean* (*Sea*). The order of the generic and the specific is partly a matter of language variety, with BrE favouring the order generic-specific in some river names (*River Thames, River Clyde*) whereas AmE prefers specific–generic (*Thames River, Colorado River*). Names of other sorts of referent vary in the frequency with which

they include a generic. Names of countries commonly lack a generic (*Brazil, France, Japan, New Zealand*), even if a generic is part of the official name of the land (*The United States of Brazil*). Some nation names have a generic as an integral part: *the United Kingdom, the United States,* or may even use the generic alone: *the States,* as a short form for *the United States of America. Great Britain* is an endocentric construction without a generic, a minor pattern seen also in *the Lesser Antilles* and *the Outer Hebrides.* See AUSTRALIAN PLACE-NAMES, CANADIAN PLACE-NAMES, ETYMON, -ONYM, PLACE-NAME, TOPONYM. [NAME, REFERENCE].   J.A.

TORRES STRAIT BROKEN/CREOLE. See BROKEN.

TOWN TALK. See FLYTAAL.

TRACHEA [14c: from Latin *trachea*, Greek *trākheîa* (*artería*) rough (passage). Stress: 'tra-KEE-a']. An anatomical term for the tube carrying air to and from the lungs, commonly known as the *windpipe.* [SPEECH].   G.K.

TRACT [15c: apparently a clipping of Latin *tractatus* treatment; cognate with *treat, treatise*]. An essay of an instructional or propagandistic kind, often in pamphlet form and on a religious topic: *Tracts for the Times* (also *the Oxford Tracts, the Tracts*), a series of theological pamphlets (1833–41) started by John Henry Newman. Any similar work may be described as 'a tract for the times'. See SOCIETY FOR PURE ENGLISH. Compare ESSAY, PAMPHLET, PROPAGANDA, TREATISE. [LITERATURE, MEDIA].   T.MCA.

TRADE JARGON [1930s]. Also *trade language* [1950s]. A semi-technical term for a minimal language used by people with no common language, as a means of communication for trading purposes, such as *Chinook Jargon* and *Trader Navajo* in North America. Such languages do not generally stabilize and expand. See JARGON, PIDGIN. [LANGUAGE].   S.R.

TRADEMARK, also **trade mark, trade-mark,** [16c]. (1) A sign or name that is secured by legal registration or (in some countries) by established use, and serves to distinguish one product from similar brands sold by competitors: for example, the shell logo for *Shell,* the petroleum company, and the brand name *Jacuzzi* for one kind of whirlpool bath. Legal injunctions are often sought when companies consider that their sole right to such marks has been infringed; the makers of *Coke, Jeep, Jell-O, Kleenex, Scotch Tape,* and *Xerox* have all gone to court in defence of their brand (or proprietary) names:

see WEBSTERS. Although companies complain when their trademarks begin to be used as generic terms in the media or elsewhere, their own marketing has often, paradoxically, caused the problem: 'Most marketing people will try hard to get their brand names accepted by the public as a generic. It's the hallmark of success. But then the trademarks people have to defend the brand from becoming a generic saying it is unique and owned by the company' (trademark manager, quoted in *Journalist's Week*, 7 Dec. 1990).

There is in practice a vague area between generic terms proper, trademarks that have become somewhat generic, and trademarks that are recognized as such. The situation is complicated by different usages in different countries: for example, *Monopoly* and *Thermos* are trademarks in the UK but generics in the US. Product wrappers and business documents often indicate that a trademark is registered by adding *TM* (for 'trademark') or *R* (for 'registered') in a superscript circle after the term, as with *English Today*™, *Sellotape*®. The term usually differs from *trade name* [first used *c*.1860s] by designating a specific product and not a business, service, or class of goods, articles, or substances: but some trademarks and trade names may happen to be the same. Everyday words of English that were once trademarks (some now universal, some more common in one variety of English than another, some dated, all commonly written without an initial capital) include *aspirin*, *band-aid*, *cellophane*, *celluloid*, *cornflakes*, *dictaphone*, *escalator*, *granola*, *hoover*, *kerosene*, *lanolin*, *mimeograph*, *nylon*, *phonograph*, *shredded wheat*, *zipper*. Trademarks facing difficulties include *Astroturf*, *Dacron*, *Formica*, *Frisbee*, *Hovercraft*, *Jacuzzi*, *Laundromat*, *Mace*, *Muzak*, *Q-Tips*, *Scotch Tape*, *Styrofoam*, *Teflon*, *Vaseline*, *Xerox*. The inclusion of such names in dictionaries, even when marked 'trademark' or 'proprietary term', indicates that their status has begun to shift. Trademark names used as verbs are a further area of difficulty, both generally and in lexicography. One solution adopted by publishers of dictionaries is to regard the verb forms as generic, with a small initial letter: that is, *Xerox* (noun), but *xerox* (verb). (2) A mark or feature characteristic of, or identified with, a person or thing: *That slow drawl is his trademark*. See GENERIC, NAME (TRADE NAMES). [NAME, WORD].

T.MCA.

TRADE NAME. See NAME, TRADEMARK.

TRADITIONAL-DIALECT. See GENERAL ENGLISH.

TRADITIONAL ORTHOGRAPHY [20c]. Usual short form *t.o.* A term used especially by spelling reformers for the conventional orthography of standard English, usually in contrast to proposed replacements. See INITIAL TEACHING ALPHABET, ORTHOGRAPHY, SPELLING REFORM. [WRITING]. T.MCA.

TRAGEDY [14c: from Latin *tragoedia*, *tragedia*, Greek *tragōidía* goat-song. The connection with goats is obscure: a goat may have been the prize for a winning play, the reference may be to the figures of goat-like satyrs associated with rural festivals, or actors may have worn goat-like masks]. Drama dealing with serious themes, ending in the suffering or death of one or more of the principal characters. The main influence on European ideas of tragedy is Aristotle's *Poetics*, based on the Greek drama of the 5c BC. Aristotle defined tragedy as 'the imitation of an action that is serious and also, as having magnitude, complete in itself' (translation I. Bywater). The tragic hero should be of high worth or standing, but not perfect: a tragic flaw, weakness, or transgression (*hamartia*) or an excess of arrogant ambition (*hubris*) leads to downfall. The effect of the inevitable disaster (*catastrophe*) on the spectators is the purgation or cleansing (*catharsis*) of the emotions of pity and terror through what they have seen.

History. Greek tragic drama proper begins with Aeschylus (525-456 BC), who added a second actor to the existing dialogue between an actor and the leader of the chorus. His plays, which include the *Oresteia* trilogy on the family of Agamemnon, are notable for their insistence on wisdom through suffering and the long retribution for *hubris*. Sophocles (496-406 BC) introduced a third actor and gave more attention to the inner struggles and personal choices of the characters. His *Oidipous Túrannos* (*Oedipus Rex*, Oedipus the King) exemplifies Aristotle's theory of tragedy; Oedipus, removed from his parents in infancy, unwittingly fulfils the prophecy that he will kill his father and marry his mother. He becomes king of Thebes but his *hamartia* is at last revealed in a terrible moment of *anagnorisis* (discovery). He tears out his eyes and the *catastrophe* is complete when he goes into a disgraced exile. Euripides (480-406 BC) further emphasized the element of moral doubt and took a more sceptical attitude towards the official religion, in *Medea* and *Alcestis*; his plays show a new concern for the position of women in society. In Rome, Seneca (*c*.4 BC-AD 65) wrote verse tragedies on subjects of Greek mythology. His rhetorical and often bloodthirsty plays were intended for reading rather than performance, but their rediscovery and translation in the

16c had an influence on the development of Elizabethan and Jacobean stage drama.

Aristotle's criteria do not fit every example of tragedy, but they remain useful, particularly in explaining why people benefit from watching in a theatre events that would be distressing or intolerable in life. The word has been applied at different periods to various types of literature. In the Middle Ages, tragedy was the narrative of an individual fall from high position: 'Of him that stood in greet prosperitee / And is y-fallen out of high degree / Into miserie, and endeth wreccedly' (Chaucer, *The Monk's Prologue*). There is much sorrow and suffering in the medieval mystery plays, but as representations of the Christian story they cannot be reckoned tragic. Dramatic tragedy in England developed in the 16c, reaching its height in the last decade and the beginning of the 17c. The influence of Seneca is seen in the many tragedies of revenge, usually with supernatural prompting, of which Thomas Kyd's *Spanish Tragedy* (1592) is the prototype and Shakespeare's *Hamlet*, the most famous and complex.

The archetypal Renaissance tragic hero, filled with fatal *hubris*, appears in Christopher Marlowe's *Tamburlaine* (c.1587) and *Dr Faustus* (1604). It is not, however, possible to fit the leading figures in the tragedies of Shakespeare and his contemporaries into a single mould. *Macbeth* raises different questions from *King Lear*, and both differ from Webster's *Duchess of Malfi*: the avenger in *Hamlet* is the hero who engages our sympathy, but Webster's Duchess is the victim and her brothers who work revenge on her are the villains; Lear is redeemed and brought to humble self-knowledge by suffering, but Macbeth dies still defiant. The Renaissance hero, unlike the Greek, is seldom wholly ignorant of the situation and a strong *anagnorisis* is rare, though it is found in *Othello*. The sense of fate and retribution remains, but there is more concern with the freedom of individual action. Inexorable suffering as the consequence of action is an Aristotelian characteristic that remains.

High or aristocratic tragedy did not survive in English beyond this period; domestic tragedy, however, dealing with humbler people, was written in the early 17c and again in the 18c. Many 20c plays are serious and moving, but critics dispute whether they are tragedies in the classical sense, especially as the effects of social problems and personal inadequacy largely replace the mythic conflict of good and evil. A play like Arthur Miller's *Death of a Salesman* (1949) may be reckoned a tragedy of the common man. Eugene O'Neill adapted classical themes in *Mourning Becomes Electra* (1931), J. M. Synge used Irish legends, and Samuel Beckett dramatized the inarticulacy of alienation.

Language. Traditionally, the language of tragedy has been elevated, as befitting great events and noble characters. It was considered a fit vehicle for the 'high style' of literature and rhetoric and was originally always in verse, even when dealing with humbler people in plays like the anonymous *Arden of Feversham* (1592). George Lillo's *The London Merchant* (1731) is one of the few early examples in English of a prose tragedy of ordinary life. In English, a grand style in prose tends to sound artificial and stilted when it is spoken in the form of a dialogue, especially in 19c melodrama. Modern serious dramatists write dialogue in the common register, with the greater economy and precision which is customary in dramatic speech. Sean O'Casey raised the everyday speech of Dublin to tragic grandeur. Tennessee Williams and Arthur Miller successfully used natural-sounding American speech. Dramatists in the *theatre of the absurd* have come closer to the inconsequential features of daily speech, but it may be disputed whether their work, though powerful and moving, can be called tragic.

Although tragedy is a dramatic form, its qualities are readily acknowledged in fiction, as in the 'tragic' quality of Thomas Hardy's novels, exemplified in the combination of character and circumstances which leads to the downfall of Henchard in *The Mayor of Casterbridge* (1886) and the execution of Tess in *Tess of the D'Urbervilles* (1891). The use of such words as *tragedy*, *tragic*, and *tragically* in relation to public or private misfortune in life is as old in English as the dramatic form itself; although it departs from Aristotelian technicalities, it expresses feelings of loss, horror, sympathy, and awe comparable to those which prompted the original development of dramatic ritual in ancient Greece. The styles in which journalists have reported on disastrous events have been significant in extending the reference of such words; in their reports, the vocabulary of tragedy relates to deep distress and misfortune without any necessary moral concomitant. See COMEDY, DRAMA, THEATRE OF THE ABSURD, TRAGICOMEDY. [LITERATURE]. R.C.

TRAGICOMEDY [16c: from Latin *tragicomoedia*, syncope of *tragicocomoedia*]. Drama that mixes elements and styles of tragedy and comedy. Dramatists have sometimes ignored the rigid theoretical distinction made in classical Greece between the two types. The Roman playwright Plautus called his *Amphitryon* a *tragicomedia* because noble and divine persons appeared in comic situations. The Renaissance dramatists, particularly in England, used considerable freedom, including noble and humble characters in the same play, introducing comic scenes into tragedy, or even pairing a tragic plot with a comic sub-plot, as Middleton and Rowley did in *The Changeling* (1622). The name is given particularly to Jacobean plays with romantic and exciting plots in which disaster threatens but is diverted into a happy resolution. This form was written by Beaumont and Fletcher, as in *A King and No King* (1611), and by Shakespeare in such late plays as *Cymbeline* (c.1610) and *The Winter's Tale* (c.1611). Critics were divided about the propriety of the form; Sidney castigated plays which were 'neither right Tragedies, nor right Comedies' (*An Apologie for Poetrie*, 1597-80), but Dryden approved the effect of 'a Scene of Mirth mix'd with Tragedy' (*Of Dramatick Poesie*, 1668). Plays that provoke amusement yet end tragically have been common since the 19c, and many are currently written for the cinema, radio, and television. See COMEDY, DRAMA, TRAGEDY. [LITERATURE].   R.C.

TRANSCRIPTION [16c: from Latin *transcriptio/transcriptionis* writing 'over' (from one text to another)]. The act or result of writing or printing material already available in some other form, especial recorded oral matter such as courtroom speech, office dictation, phonetic data, and linguistic fieldwork. Transcribing involves the visual or aural interpretation of the matter, its mental processing, and the motor activity of copying by hand or with type. Errors can occur at any stage: a monk might misread a word; a secretary might not be able to decipher the boss's handwriting; a keyboarder might strike the wrong key; a phonetician might enter the wrong symbol. Even if the matter is clearly set out, the eye can err: *eye-skip* causes the transcriber to jump from a word in one line to the same word three lines lower; misrecognition turns a badly written word like *Munby* into *Meenby*; a tendency to banalize turns the unfamiliar *Foresman* into the everyday *Foreman*; mistyping turns *heart* into *heat*. The mind can also work on the material, substituting for what is in the text an item that the transcriber thinks is there. Such problems have long been known to scholars of manuscripts and other documents, who try to work their way back to an original from the evidence of an error. Compare NOTATION, PROOF-READING, TRANSLITERATION. [TECHNOLOGY, WRITING].   W.W.B.

TRANSFERRED EPITHET. See EPITHET, HYPALLAGE.

TRANSFORMATIONAL-GENERATIVE GRAMMAR, short form *TG*. In theoretical linguistics, a type of generative grammar first advocated by Noam Chomsky in *Syntactic Structures* (1957). Since then, there have been many changes in the descriptive apparatus of TG. Common to all versions is the view that some rules are transformational: that is, they change one structure into another according to such prescribed conventions as moving, inserting, deleting, and replacing items. From an early stage of its history, TG has stipulated two levels of syntactic structure: *deep structure* (an abstract underlying structure that incorporates all the syntactic information required for the interpretation of a given sentence) and *surface structure* (a structure that incorporates all the syntactic features of a sentence required to convert the sentence into a spoken or written version). *Transformations* link deep with surface structure. A typical transformation is the rule for forming questions, which requires that the normal subject-verb order is inverted so that the surface structure of *Can I see you later?* differs in order of elements from that of *I can see you later*. The theory postulates that the two sentences have the same order in deep structure, but the question transformation changes the order to that in surface structure. Sentences that are syntactically ambiguous have the same surface structures but different deep structures: for example, the sentence *Visiting relatives can be a nuisance* is ambiguous in that the subject *Visiting relatives* may correspond to *To visit relatives* or to *Relatives that visit*. The ambiguity is dissolved if the modal verb *can* is omitted, since the clausal subject requires a singular verb (*Visiting relatives is a nuisance*), whereas the phrasal subject requires the plural (*Visting relatives are a nuisance*). See CHOMSKY, GENERATIVE GRAMMAR. [GRAMMAR].   S.G.

TRANSITIVE AND INTRANSITIVE [16c and 17c: from Latin *transitivus* passing across]. A transitive verb (*enjoy, make, want*) is followed by an object (*We enjoyed the trip*; *They make toys*; *He's making progress*), or is preceded by its object, in such questions as *What do you want?* Such verbs are not normally found in the forms *We enjoyed*, *They make/He's making*, *Do you want?* In this, they contrast with *intransitive* verbs, which do not have objects: *They shouted*; *He's fallen down*; *She hurried home*. Many verbs can, however, be both transitive and intransitive: *He is playing (football)*; *She hurried (the children) home*; *He ran (a good race)*. Some grammarians divide transitive verbs into: *monotransitive verbs*, which take one object (*She ate the apple*); *ditransitive verbs*, which take two objects (*Give a dog a bad name*); *complex transitive verbs*, which take an object and a complement (*Paint the town red*). [GRAMMAR].   S.C.

TRANSLATION [14c: from Latin *translatio/translationis* what is carried across, from *trans* across, *ferre/latum* to carry. A doublet of *transfer*]. The restatement of the forms of one language in another: the chief means of exchanging information between different language communities. Translation is a fundamental yet often overlooked element in life and has played a decisive part in the development of languages like English, especially by promoting the flow of ideas and the spread of the literary forms in which they have been expressed: for example, Homeric poetry from ancient Greece and the Bible translated from Hebrew and Greek. As the Canadian historian of translation Louis Kelly has observed, 'Western Europe owes its civilization to translators' (1979). Translation derives from the universal need for mediation between speakers and writers of different languages. It depends on bilingual competence, and five distinctions are commonly made when discussing it, none of which represent absolute positions, but rather end-points in an appropriate continuum:

(1) *Translating and interpreting*. Written translation can be distinguished from oral translation or interpreting, which came first, as for example in military and diplomatic exchanges. However, because of its relative permanence and lasting influence on the transmission of culture and technology, written translation has traditionally been considered more important. Whereas such translation usually allows time for reflection and redrafting, professional interpreting does not usually allow time to think about alternatives. It takes two forms: *simultaneous interpreting* (at international conferences, etc.) and *consecutive interpreting* (in court, at diplomatic gatherings, in business transactions, etc.).

(2) *Word-for-word and free translation*. Languages do not match neatly in the way they form messages. Depending on the level at which translation equivalence can be established (word with word, phrase with phrase, word with phrase, etc.) translations can be *literal* (that is, one-to-one at the level of words), or *free* (restatement of the message regardless of formal correspondence).

(3) *Literary and technical translation*. Depending on the type of discourse translated, a distinction is often made between literary translation (of aesthetic, imaginative, fictional texts) and technical translation (of workaday, pragmatic, non-fictional texts). However, boundary lines between them are sometimes difficult to draw, as in the translation of religious texts such as the Bible (which is currently available in over 2,000 languages). Such a text may contain both literary and other passages: for example, the drama of the Book of Job and the listing of laws in Leviticus.

(4) *Professional and pedagogical translation*. Depending on the context and the practitioner, a distinction can be made between translation as a vocation or trade (working for a client) and translation as an exercise in the process of language learning (working for a teacher). It has been argued that traditional grammar-translation tasks in school do not constitute a suitable training for translating as such; they have also, however, been widely believed to have value as an analytic discipline on a par with playing chess.

(5) *Human and machine translation*. The high cost of professional translating and interpreting has encouraged institutional investment in experiments with large-scale electronic translation and dictionary systems. Fully automatic translation of high quality seems still to be a long way off, but some computer manufacturers are currently offering PC workstations for ordinary translators which provide assistance with word processing and the making of glossaries.

Target and source. The intricacies of translation can be considered in terms of communication within a single language. This is usually more or less unimpeded, provided that both the sender and the receiver share and understand any dialects involved, and the channels (mouth and ear; eye and text) allow unbroken transmission. When sender and receiver do not speak the same language or dialect, translators/interpreters can mediate, if their bilingual and bicultural competence is sufficient to convert the message in Language A (*the source language*) into a more or less equivalent message in Language B (*the target language*). This is a big 'if': the translator must be skilful enough to understand the text in the source language (*receptive phase*), find suitable equivalences (*code-switching phase*), and then produce an appropriate version within the norms of the target language (*productive phase*). The success of the mediation depends on the completion of the three phases. Each phase requires a range of skills haphazardly present in all bilingual speakers and capable of being honed to a professional standard in training schools and through experience, aided by such tools as bilingual dictionaries.

The spectrum of translation. At its widest, the process of restatement from one language into another can include both *transliteration* (transfer from one writing system to another) and the range of options from strict word-for-word literalism to free adaptation. The following excerpts, all from *The Bhagavad-Gita* (Book 2, verse 22) illustrate, more or less, the whole spectrum.

(1) *The source*. The original Sanskrit verse, printed in the Devanagari script:

वासांसि जीर्णानि यथा विहाय
नवानि गृह्णाति नरोऽपराणि
तथा शरीराणि विहाय जीर्णा-
न्यन्यानि संयाति नवानि देही

(2) *Transliteration*. The Sanskrit verse, printed in a variety of the Roman alphabet:

vāsāṁsi jīrṇāni yathā vihāya
navāni grhṇāti naro 'parāṇi
tathā śarīrāṇi vihāya jīrṇāny
anyāni saṁyāti navāni dehī

(3) *Word-for-word literalism*:

clothes worn-out just-as casting-off
new-ones takes a-man others
in-the-same-way bodies casting-off worn-out
different-ones takes-on new the-embodied.
  (Tom McArthur, *Yoga and the Bhagavad-Gita*, Thorson, 1986)

(4) *A close blank-verse translation*:

As leaving aside worn-out garments
A man takes other, new ones,
So leaving aside worn-out bodies
To other, new ones goes the embodied (soul).
  (Franklin Edgerton, *The Bhagavad Gītā*, Harvard University Press, 1944)

(5) *A close translation in prose*:

As a man casts off his worn-out clothes and takes on other new ones, so does the embodied (self) cast off its worn-out bodies and enters other new ones.
  (R. C. Zaehner, *The Bhagavad-Gītā*, Oxford University Press, 1969)

(6) *A freer translation in prose*:

Just as a person casts off worn-out garments and puts on others that are new, even so does the embodied soul cast off worn-out bodies and take on others that are new.
  (Sarvepalli Radhakrishnan with Charles A. Moore, in *Indian Philosophy*, Princeton University Press, 1957).

(7) *A free 'Biblical' prose translation*:

As a man leaves an old garment and puts on one that is new, the Spirit leaves his mortal body and then puts on one that is new.
  (Juan Mascaró, *The Bhagavad Gita*, Penguin, 1962)

(8) *A free colloquial version*:

You know how easily a man changes his clothes; in the same way this inner something casts off its old worn body and takes on a new one.
  (Tom McArthur (above), 1986)

For specimens of translations of two verses of the Bible over some six centuries of English, see BIBLE.

The subtleties of translation. Below are four lines from the German poet Johann W. von Goethe's fourth 'Mignon's Song' (in *Wilhelm Meisters Lehrjahre*, 1795). They are followed by three translations into English and a brief comment.

Kennst du das Land, wo die Zitronen blühn,
Im dunkeln Laub die Gold-Orangen glühn,
Ein sanfter Wind vom blauen Himmel weht,
Die Myrte still und hoch der Lorbeer steht . . .?

(1) *Literary translation*:

Know'st thou the land where lemon trees do bloom,
  [earlier]
citron-apples bloom,
  [later]
And oranges like gold in leafy gloom;
A gentle wind from deep blue heaven blows,
The myrtle thick, and high the laurel grows?
  (from Thomas Carlyle's *Wilhelm Meister's Apprenticeship and Travels*, 1824/7)

(2) *A translation set to music*:

Knowst thou the land in which the citrons grow,
And oranges in golden splendour glow,
A gentle wind is breath'd from azure skies,
The myrtle bends, and proud the laurels rise?
  (from H. Stevens, *Beethoven: 67 Songs with Piano Accompaniment*, 1949)

(3) *A 'prose' translation*:

Do you know the land where the lemons blossom?
Where golden oranges glow among the dark leaves,
a soft breeze blows from the blue sky,
and the still myrtle and the tall laurels grow?
  (from S. S. Prawer (ed.), *The Penguin Book of Lieder*, 1964)

Carlyle's rhymed version captures the essential grammatical, semantic, and cultural associations, although in a second version he changed part of the first line; he may have been aware of the parallel line 'Know ye the land where the cypress and myrtle', from Byron's *Bride of Abydos*, 1813. Stevens's adaptation produces a translation which can be sung to Beethoven's setting, retaining all the features of form and content. Prawer's translation, which accompanies Hugo Wolf's setting of the song, ignores formal features, including singability, in line with the purpose of the book: that is, to provide a non-literary guide for listening to German art songs.

Translation and publishing. Much of the world's publishing depends on translation, although the centrality of the translator's role is often only minimally indicated in the credits of particular works. Thousands of translators and interpreters around the world continue to perform essential tasks in often less-than-ideal conditions. Professional bodies such as the *Institute of Translating and Interpreting* (*ITI*), the *American Translators Association* (*ATA*), the *International Federation of Translators* (*FIT*: French acronym), and the *Association Internationale des Interprètes de Conférence* (*AIIC*) represent their interest nationally and internationally. By the early 1970s, close to half of the world's book production was made up of translations, the chief source languages being English, French, Russian, German, Spanish, and Italian, the chief target languages German, Russian, Spanish, English, Japanese, and French. The main text categories are literary works and material from the social and applied sciences, with Vladimir Ilyich Lenin, Karl Marx, Jules Verne, and Enid Blyton as the top-ranking authors. Because of worldwide demand for translation of all kinds, the 20c has been referred to as 'the age of translation'.

See AELFRIC, ALFRED, BIBLE, BILINGUAL DIC-TIONARY, CODE-MIXING AND CODE-SWITCHING, COMBINING FORM, CONTRASTIVE LINGUISTICS, EURODICAUTOM, OLD ENGLISH, TERMINOLOGY, TRANSCRIPTION, TRANSLATION EQUIVALENT, TRANSLITERATION. [EDUCATION, LANGUAGE]. R.H.

Bassnett-McGuire, Susan. 1991. *Translation Studies: Revised Edition*. London: Routledge. Original edition, 1980. London & New York: Methuen.
Hutchins, William J. 1986. *Machine Translation: Past, Present, Future*. Chichester: Ellis Horwood.
Kelly, Louis G. 1979. *The True Interpreter: A History of Translation Theory and Practice in the West*. Oxford: Basil Blackwell.
Larson, Mildred L. 1984. *Meaning-Based Translation: A Guide to Cross-Language Equivalence*. Lanham: University Press of America.
Newmark, Peter. 1988. *A Textbook of Translation*. New York: Prentice Hall.
Periodicals
Babel: The International Journal of Translation (Amsterdam, since 1955).
The Bible Translator (Reading, since 1950).
Meta: Journal des Traducteurs/Translators' Journal (Montreal, since 1956).
Target: International Journal of Translation Studies (Amsterdam, since 1989).

TRANSLATION DICTIONARY. See BILIN-GUAL DICTIONARY.

TRANSLATION EQUIVALENT. An expression from a language which has the same meaning as, or can be used in a similar context to, one from another language, and can therefore be used to translate it: for example, English *I don't understand*, French *Je ne comprends pas*, Italian *Non capisco*, Modern Greek *Dhen katalaveno*, Japanese *Wakarimasen*. Achieving such correspondences involves special bilingual skills to cope with the tendency among languages to 'lack of fit' (technically, *non-isomorphism* or *anisomorphism*). Thus, the source-language expression may be a single word, a phrase, or a sentence within a text, but its target-language equivalent may have to be rendered at a different level: for example, the English idiom *It's pouring (with rain)* cannot be translated word-for-word into German, but the meaning can be redistributed as *Es regnet in Strömen* (It rains in streams). Most bilingual speakers can supply examples of such equivalents, and bilingual dictionaries codify them in bulk, but it is the job especially of the translator and interpreter to decide whether a particular expression is a fitting match for a particular passage. A number of complex strategies are needed to find translation equivalents, ranging from literal procedures such as direct transfer, substitution, and loan translation to devices of free translation such as transposition, adaptation, and circumlocution (which aim to find the closest functional equivalent). The literal approach can work well when language pairs have a similar structure: for example English and German with *mother/Mutter, Mother's Day/Muttertag*: but see FAUX AMI. The free style, however, is demanded even in similar languages whenever anything close to idiom occurs: *mother country/Heimat* (homeland), *motherfucker/Saftsack* (juicebag), *necessity is the mother of invention/Not macht erfinderisch* (need makes inventive). [LANGUAGE].   R.H.

TRANSLITERATION [1860s: from Latin *trans-* across, *lit(t)era* a letter, and *-ation*]. The action, process, or result of converting one set of signs to another, usually involving at least one set of alphabetic letters. Where two writing systems have a common base, such as for Polish and English, which use variants of the Roman alphabet, transliteration is unnecessary, despite differences in sound–symbol correspondence. Transliteration becomes necessary when the systems differ greatly. Such differences range along a continuum, from the somewhat similar (Roman and Cyrillic), through the significantly dissimilar (Roman alphabet, Arabic script), to the utterly different (Roman alphabet, Japanese syllabaries and ideograms). Transliteration became important in the 19c, when European scholars wished to find Roman equivalents for the writing systems of various 'exotic' languages. As a result, there are systems of Roman transliteration (each more or less standard for its purposes) for Arabic, Chinese, Greek, Japanese, Persian, Russian, Sanskrit, and Tamil, among others. Conversion to Roman requires, in varying degrees, diacritics and special symbols for sounds or practices that have no equivalent in any prior Roman system. See ACUTE ACCENT, ALPHABET, ARABIC, CHINA, GREEK, JAPAN, NOT-ATION, ROMAN, SANSKRIT, TRANSCRIPTION. [TECH-NOLOGY, WRITING].   T.MCA.

TRAVELLER'S CANT. See SHELTA.

TREATISE [14c: from Anglo-French *tretiz*, ultimately Latin *tractare/tractatum* to handle, treat]. (1) Formerly, a story, narrative, description, or work of literature. (2) A text, usually longer than an essay, but usually similar in style, that treats a subject in a formal, methodical, scholarly manner. The literary term *treatise poem* was coined by C. S. Lewis (*The Allegory of Love*, 1936) for 18c poems intended to instruct and edify the reader. Compare ESSAY, NARRATIVE, STORY, TEXT, TRACT. [LITERATURE, WRITING]
T.MCA.

TRENCH, Richard Chenevix [1807-86]. Anglo-Irish clergyman, poet, and philologist; Dean of Westminster (1856-63), Archbishop of Dublin (1863-84). Born in Dublin. Educated at Twyford School in Hampshire, at Harrow, and at Cambridge. His many publications include the popularizing works *The Study of Words* (1851) and *English, Past and Present* (1855). In 1857, Trench joined the Philological Society and in the same year read to its members two papers 'On Some Deficiencies in our English Dictionaries', dealing especially with inadequacies in the treatment of word histories. At the same time, he indicated the principles which a more perfect dictionary might follow, along lines laid out by the German classicist Franz Passow in 1812 and demonstrated by H. G. Liddell and Robert Scott in their *Greek-English Lexicon* (1843). The immediate effect was to crystallize the plans which Trench, Herbert Coleridge, Frederick Furnivall, and others in the Philological Society had been developing for a new dictionary of English on historical principles. A longer-term effect was the influence the papers exerted on the aims and practice of those who eventually brought the *Oxford English Dictionary* into being. See index. [BIOGRAPHY, EUROPE, REFERENCE]. A.J.A.

TRILL, TRILLED *R*. See R-SOUNDS.

TRILOGY [17c: from Greek *trilogía* three-part discourse]. A sequence of three literary works linked by a common set of characters; originally three related tragedies performed at the festival of Dionysus in Athens. Trilogies are not common in English, though there are examples of a single sequel to a novel and, especially in the 20c, the novel sequence or *roman fleuve*. Eugene O'Neill (1888-1953) derived his dramatic trilogy *Mourning Becomes Electra* (1931), set in the aftermath of the American Civil War, from the *Oresteia* of Aeschylus. Evelyn Waugh (1903-66) wrote a trilogy of novels about the Second World War (*Sword of Honour*, 1965) and Joyce Cary (1888-1957) produced two trilogies, one on the life of a politician and the other of an artist. The name is sometimes applied to three works

with a common purpose but without necessary continuity of characters or action, like the three political novels of Benjamin Disraeli (1804-81) (*Coningsby*, 1844; *Sybil*, 1845; *Tancred*, 1847). The name is often incorporated as part of the title of three novels: *The Deptford Trilogy* of Robertson Davies (*Fifth Business*, 1970; *The Manticore*, 1972; and *World of Wonders*, 1975). [LITERATURE]. R.C.

TRINBAGONIAN, also Trinagonian, Trinibagonian [20c: blends of *Trinidad* and *Tobago*, and *-ian*. Compare TANZANIA]. Non-technical terms, used largely on an experimental basis by the local media, as composites to refer to the two-island nation, its people, and their Creole vernacular(s). The need for such a composite arises from the clumsiness of using the phrase *Trinidadians and Tobagonians* to refer to citizens and as a general-purpose adjective in a situation where it is no longer politic to subsume Tobago (the smaller island) and its residents under Trinidad or Trinidadian. The terms are more commonly written than spoken and have limited acceptance. Compare TRINIBAGIANESE. [AMERICAS, NAME, VARIETY]. L.D.C.

TRINIBAGIANESE [1970s: a blend of *Trinidad* and *Tobago*, and *-ese* as in *Japanese*]. A non-technical name for the Creole vernacular(s) of Trinidad and Tobago, coined by C. R. Ottley and used in his *Creole Talk of Trinidad and Tobago: Words, Phrases and Sayings Peculiar to the Country* (1971). See -ESE, TRINBAGONIAN. [AMERICAS, NAME, VARIETY]. L.D.C.

TRINIDAD AND TOBAGO. Official title: *Republic of Trinidad and Tobago*. A Caribbean country and member of the Commonwealth, consisting of the two major islands at the southern end of the Lesser Antilles, close to the South American coast. Capital: Port of Spain. Currency: the dollar. Economy: mixed. Population: 1.23m (1988), 1.4m (projection for 2000). Ethnicity: 41% African, 40% East Indian, 17% Afro-Indian. Religions: 36% Roman Catholic, 23% Hindu, 13% Protestant, 6% Muslim. Languages: English (official), English Creole, and some Bhojpuri, Hindi, French, and Spanish. Education: primary 91%, secondary 76%, tertiary 4%, literacy 96%. Both islands were visited by Columbus in 1498. The Spanish settled in Trinidad in the 16c and the island was periodically raided by the French, British, and Dutch. In 1802, it was ceded to the British under the Treaty of Amiens. Tobago, after being colonized by Dutch, British, and French settlers, became a British colony of the Windward Islands group in 1814. It was administratively linked with Trinidad in 1899 and the joint territory became independent in 1962.

The term *Trinidadian English* refers to the variety of English used for formal communication by educated speakers of Trinidad and Tobago. Its lexical distinctiveness derives from the use of Spanish and of a French-based Creole before the arrival of English speakers, as well as from the influence of East Indian languages dating from the earlier 19c. Its phonetic characteristics result from pressure from the Trinidadian and Tobagonian English-based creoles with which it coexists. See CARIBBEAN, CARIBBEAN BROADCASTING, CARIBBEAN DICTION-ARIES, CARIBBEAN ENGLISH, CARIBBEAN ENGLISH CREOLE, CARIBBEAN PRESS, ENGLISH, FRENCH, NAIPAUL, TRINBAGONIAN, TRINIBAGIANESE. [AMERI-CAS, NAME, VARIETY]. T.MCA., L.D.C.

TRINITY COLLEGE LONDON. An examining body founded in 1873 primarily for music, but with a wide range of examinations in Spoken English as a Foreign or Second Language. [EDU-CATION]. W.S.

TRIOLET [17c: from French, a little trio]. An eight-lined piece of verse, rhyming *abaaabab*. The first line is repeated as the fourth, and the first two lines are repeated as the seventh and eighth, as in this example by Thomas Hardy:

At last one pays the penalty—
The woman—women always do.
My farce, I found, was tragedy
At last!—One pays the penalty
With interest when one, fancy-free,
Learns love, learns shame . . . Of sinners two
At last *one* pays the penalty—
The woman—women always do!

There is no set metre and the lines are usually short. The repeated lines can be so presented as to change their significance and allow the writer to exercise ingenuity in structure and connection. See VERSE. [LITERATURE]. R.C.

TRIPHTHONG [16c: from French *triphtongue*, Latin *triphthongus*, Greek *triphthonggos* a triple sound]. (1) In phonetics, a vowel that starts with one quality, moves through another, and ends in a third: that is, a sequence of three vowel sounds together, such as those of *fire* and *flower*. In rhotic varieties of English, these three vowel sounds are always followed by an *r*-sound, /ˈfaɪər, ˈflaʊər/; in non-rhotic varieties, they are not, /ˈfaɪə, ˈflaʊə/. (2) By analogy, three letters together, whether or not they represent a triphthong; technically, a *trigraph*, such as the *eau* in *plateau*. See DIGRAPH, DIPHTHONG, MON-OPHTHONG, RHOTIC AND NON-RHOTIC, VOWEL. [SPEECH, WRITING]. T.MCA.

TRIPLE RHYME. See FEMININE ENDING, TRIPLET.

TRIPLET [17c: from *triple* and *-et* as in *couplet*]. (1) In verse, another name for a tercet, but often applied to the insertion of *triple rhyme* into a sequence of heroic couplets:

Chiefs shall be grudged the part which they pretend,
Lords envy lords, and friends with every friend
About their impious merit shall contend.
(John Dryden, *The Medal*, 1682)

Restoration and Augustan poets used the triplet, sometimes with an alexandrine as the third line, to make a strong emphasis or to come to a definitive point in a long poem. Compare TRISTICH. (2) One of three words in a language like English, all derived from the same ancestral word, such as *cattle, chattel, capital*, all ultimately from Latin *caput/capitis* head. See DOUBLET. [LITERATURE, WORD]. R.C.

TRISOCIATION. See BISOCIATION.

TRISTAN DA CUNHA, short form *Tristan*. A British dependency in the South Atlantic. Main settlement: Edinburgh. Economy: mainly fishing (especially rock lobsters) and Tristan stamps. Language: English. Administration: an *Island Council* and an elected *Chief Islander*. The Portuguese discovered St Helena and the Tristan Archipelago in 1506 and the British occupied Tristan in 1816 during the exile of Napoleon at St Helena. In 1961, the islanders were evacuated after a volcanic eruption, but returned in 1963. The people, among whom there are only seven surnames, number some 350. Their speech is thought to have elements in common with Highland English. Distinctive features include: (1) An intrusive initial /h/: 'highland happle' for *island apple*. (2) Such words as *first, herb* pronounced 'farst', 'harb'. (3) Tense and possessive inflections often dropped and *is* often omitted. (4) Such usages as *plant in* (intransitive) to plant potatoes, *the sea put up bubbles* the sea grew (too) rough (for fishing), and *eastings* and *westings*, to indicate which way the island is circled. (5) The term *gulch* is common, as are such complex place-names as *Down-where-minister-pick-up-his-things*, *Ridge-where-the-goat-jump-off*, and *Blackinthehole Hill*. The island has a monthly newspaper, *Tristan Times*, produced by roneo and free to all households. Unique features of local life include *Queen's Day*, a patriotic festival, and *fishing days* regulated by the sounding of *the gong* by the Chief Islander. See SAINT HELENA. [AFRICA, NAME, VARIETY]. J.B.

TRISTICH [19c: from Greek *tri-* three, *stikhos* a row, line, verse]. A stanza or poem consisting of three lines. See TERCET. [LITERATURE]. T.MCA.

TRITE [16c: from Latin *tritus* worn, common, from *terere/tritum* to rub, wear away: compare *detritus*]. Worn out by repetition; stale, hackneyed, commonplace: *a trite adage*; *trite phrases*. Compare HACKNEYED, STOCK. See CLICHÉ. [STYLE]. T.MCA.

TROCHEE [16c: from French *trochée*, from Latin *trochaeus*, Greek *trokhaîos* (*poús*) running (foot)]. A metrical foot of two syllables, long then short in quantitative metre, as in Latin, stressed then unstressed in accentual metre (–◡), as in the words *open* and *better*. In English verse, the trochee is often used as a variation in iambic lines. It is generally avoided at the end of a line, where it disturbs the rhythm. A trochaic line often omits the last syllable, to give a masculine ending. Such a line is *catalectic* (Greek, *katalēktikós* incomplete) and the foot in question is a *catalectic foot*, as in the opening lines of Blake's 'The Tyger' (1794):

– ◡ – ◡ – ◡ — ◡
Tyger! Tyger! burning bright
In the forests of the night.

See FOOT, IAMB(US), METRE/METER, SCANSION. [LITERATURE]. R.C.

TROPE [16c: from Latin *tropus*, Greek *trópos* a turn, manner, style]. (1) Also *turn of phrase*. In rhetoric, both an expression that deviates from the natural and literal through a change in meaning, often with a pleasing effect, and the device or technique that makes such a change possible. For the Roman rhetorician Quintilian, tropes were metaphors and metonyms, etc., and figures (*figurae*) were such forms of discourse as rhetorical questions, digression, repetition, antithesis, and periphrasis (also referred to as *schemes*). He noted that the two kinds of usage were often confused (a state of affairs that has continued to the present day). In the 18c, the term became associated with over-ornate style and fell into disrepute when a plainer style came to be preferred. As a result, what were once known as tropes and figures are now generally called *figures of speech* or, more broadly still, *rhetorical devices*. (2) A musical adornment in medieval Christian liturgy that included dialogue and increased the popular appeal of the services. The expansion and elaboration of one particular trope, the Latin dialogue *Quem quaeritis?* (Whom do you seek?), part of the Introit of the Easter Mass, is generally regarded as the beginning of medieval drama. See FIGURATIVE LANGUAGE/USAGE, FIGURE OF SPEECH, SCHEME. [LITERATURE, STYLE]. T.MCA.

TRUISM [Early 18c]. A self-evident (and usually trivial) truth, and the inclination to make such statements; a comment (considered) so obviously true that it does not need discussion, such as *We cannot live without food, you know*. The term is often a neutral synonym of *cliché* and *platitude*. See -ISM. [STYLE]. T.MCA.

TSOTSI-TAAL, also **tsotsi taal** [1940s: perhaps from *tsotsi* a flashily dressed African street thug, from *potso-tso* stove-pipe trousers, possibly an Africanized adaptation of the AmE rhyming compound *zoot-suit*; and Afrikaans *taal* language]. An argot or street language among the members of young black urban gangs in South Africa: 'Black lawyers are required to be fluent in English, Afrikaans, Latin, Zulu, Venda and Tsotsi-taal whose vocab changes annually from place to place and depending on which gangs are in power' (O. Musi, *Drum*, Jan. 1987). See FLYTAAL, SOUTH AFRICAN LITERATURE IN ENGLISH. [AFRICA, NAME, VARIETY]. T.MCA.

TUNE. See INTONATION, RHYTHM, TONE. [SPEECH].

TURKISH. See AFRICAN LANGUAGES, AGGLUTINATING, ARABIC, BORROWING, EUROPEAN LANGUAGES, LANGUAGE, LINGUISTIC TYPOLOGY, URO-ALTAIC LANGUAGES, VOWEL HARMONY.

TURKS AND CAICOS ISLANDS. A British Caribbean dependency, consisting of two groups of 30 islands and cays forming the south-east end of the Bahamian archipelago. Capital: Grand Turk. Currency: the US dollar. Economy: tourism, fishing. Population: 7,413 (1980). Ethnicity: African, mixed. Languages: English (official), Creole. In 1765, the islands were formally linked with the Bahamas, then in 1848 with Jamaica. When Jamaica became independent in 1962, the islands were again associated with the Bahamas, then in 1972 became a British colony by local choice. See CARIBBEAN, ENGLISH. [AMERICAS, NAME, VARIETY]. T.MCA.

TURNER, George William [b.1921]. Australasian linguist and lexicographer, born in Dannevirke, New Zealand, and educated at the U. of New Zealand and U. College London. He was trained as a librarian before being appointed to the English department of the U. of Canterbury, New Zealand. He held a readership in English at the U. of Adelaide, Australia, from 1965 until his retirement in 1986, and was elected a Fellow of the Australian Academy of the Humanities in 1974. His publications include *The English Language in Australia and New Zealand* (1966), *Stylistics* (1973), a revision of Grahame Johnston's *Australian Pocket Oxford Dictionary* (1987), and an annotated edition of the novelist Joseph Furphy's *Such is Life* (forthcoming). See index. [BIOGRAPHY, LANGUAGE, OCEANIA, REFERENCE]. W.S.R.

TURNER, Lorenzo Dow [1895-1972]. American linguist, born in Elizabeth City, North Carolina, and educated at Howard U. and Harvard U., with a Ph.D. at the U. of Chicago (1926). His dissertation was *Anti-Slavery Sentiment in American Literature Prior to 1865* (published 1931). Turning his attention to the history of English, Turner became the first African-American member of the Linguistic Society of America. He studied at the School of Oriental and African Studies, U. of London, to test his conviction that AmE showed greater linguistic influence from Africa than had hitherto been supposed. His findings appeared in a series of articles beginning in 1941 and culminating in *Africanisms in the Gullah Dialect* (1949). In this volume, he traced to West African sources usages common in the Sea Islands of South Carolina and Georgia. Using a form of the protocol developed for the *Linguistic Atlas of the United States and Canada*, Turner secured the cooperation of Gullah-speakers where others had failed. Almost alone in his field, Turner demonstrated the importance of African languages for the understanding of AmE. In 1951, Raven I. McDavid Jr. and Virginia Glenn McDavid noted that his work was 'perhaps the greatest single contribution to an intelligent reappraisal of the relationships between white and Negro speech' (in 'The Relationship of the Speech of American Negroes to the Speech of Whites', *American Speech* 26, p. 11). Moving from a professorship at Fisk U. in Nashville to Roosevelt U. in Chicago, Turner published a series of textbooks on Sierra Leone Krio for the use of Peace Corps volunteers. In 1969, he was elected to the Hall of Fame of the city of Chicago. His surviving papers, audio-recordings of Gullah, and correspondence are maintained at the Herskovits Library of African Studies, Northwestern U., Evanston, Illinois. [AFRICA, AMERICAS, BIOGRAPHY, LANGUAGE, VARIETY]. R.W.B.

TURN OF PHRASE. See TROPE.

TURN-TAKING. See CONVERSATION.

TUVALU. A country of Oceania and member of the Commonwealth. Capital: Funafuti. Currency: the dollar (Australian dollar also legal tender). Economy: fruit, fishing. Population: 8,500 (1988), 11,000 (projection for 2000). Languages: Tuvaluan, English (both official). Education: primary 100%, secondary 18%, tertiary 5%, literacy 70%. Formerly known as the *Ellice Islands* and part of the British colony of the

Gilbert and Ellice Islands, Tuvalu gained its independence in 1978. See ENGLISH, KIRIBATI. [NAME, OCEANIA, VARIETY]. T.MCA.

TWADDLE [17c: originally slangy, perhaps a variant of *twattle*, blending *twiddle* and *tattle*]. Senseless, silly, trifling talk or writing; commonplace nonsense; drivel, rubbish. Compare WAFFLE. [STYLE]. T.MCA.

TWAIN, Mark [1835-1910]. Pen name of *Samuel Langhorne Clemens*. American author, born in Florida, Missouri. A few years after his birth, the family moved to Hannibal, a village beside the Mississippi River. He had little formal schooling and went to work as a printer's apprentice soon after his father's death in 1847. When his brother Orion started a newspaper, young Sam went to work for him and wrote his first humorous sketches for the paper. He left Hannibal at 18, to travel as a journeyman printer, but his greatest ambition, fulfilled for several years until the outbreak of the Civil War closed shipping on the Mississippi, was to be a steamboat pilot. He produced a series of articles, 'Old Times on the Mississippi', in which he laid the groundwork for Huckleberry Finn's account of his adventures along the river. Mark Twain's ability to record with fidelity and insight the varied languages of the people he met was a central feature of his art. In *A Tramp Abroad* (1880), an illiterate miner tells a story about the animals and birds he has encountered in his solitary labours, and whose language (he has persuaded himself) he can understand. Here Jim Baker reflects on the unreliable grammatical usage of some of these creatures:

I've noticed a good deal and there's no bird, or cow or anything that uses as good grammar as a bluejay. You may say a cat uses good grammar. Well, a cat does— but you let a cat get excited once; you let a cat get to pulling fur with another cat on a shed, nights, and you'll hear grammar that will give you the lockjaw. Ignorant people think it's the *noise* which fighting cats make that is so aggravating but it ain't so; it's the sickening grammar. Now I've never heard a jay use bad grammar but very seldom, and when they do, they are as ashamed as a human, they shut right down and leave.

A special satiric target was pretentious language. In the following sample of an 'absurd mixture of elegant and vernacular styles' (from *The Gilded Age*, 1873), David R. Sewell has highlighted the clash of styles by putting markedly 'genteel' expressions in italics, non-standard or regional usages in boldface. A woman with newly acquired wealth and status is speaking:

I should think so. Husband says Percy'll die if he **dont** have a change, and so I'm going to **swap round** a little and see what can be done. I saw a lady from Florida last week and she recommended Key West. I told her

Percy couldn't *abide* winds, as he was *threatened with a pulmonary affection*, and then she said try St. Augustine. It's a **awful** distance—ten or twelve hundred miles, they say—but then in *a case of this kind* **a body cant stand back for trouble**, you know (as quoted in Sewell, *Mark Twain's Language: Discourse, Dialogue, and Linguistic Variety*, 1987).

In *The Adventures of Huckleberry Finn* (1885), Mark Twain, speaking through the voice of a semi-literate runaway boy, evokes the mythic greatness of the river and universal truths about mankind. 'The beauty of Huck Finn', says Perry Miller, 'is that the boy sees all there is to see about human depravity, violence, skulduggery, as well as virtually all which is noble, lovely, self-sacrificing, and that he tells about both without yielding to florid language.' Miller cites a passage that conveys the beauty and mystery of a dawning day on the Mississippi, as seen by Huck:

Not a sound anywhere—perfectly still—just like the whole world were asleep, only sometimes bullfrogs a-cluttering maybe. The first thing to see, looking away over the water, was a kind of dull line—that was the woods on t'other side; you couldn't make nothing else out; then a pale place in the sky; then more paleness spreading around; then the river softened up away off, and warn't black any more, but gray; you could see little dark spots drifting along ever so far away—trading scows, and such things; and long black streaks—rafts; sometimes you could hear a sweep screaking; or jumbled-up voices, it was so still, and sounds come so far; and by and by you could see a streak on the water which you know by the look of the streak that ther's a snag in a swift current which breaks on it and makes that streak look that way; and you see the mist curl up off the water, and the east reddens up, and the river, and you make out a log cabin in the edge of the woods, away on the bank on t'other side of the river, being a wood-yard, likely, and then the nice breeze springs up, and comes fanning you from over there, so cool and fresh and sweet to smell on account of the woods and flowers; but sometimes not that way, because they've left dead fish around, gars and such, and they do get pretty rank; and the next you've got the full day, and everything smiling in the sun, and the song-birds just going it! (ch. 19).

Miller's observation about this passage sums up the dimensions of Twain's achievement: 'Several dawns break over Walden Pond, and in *Moby-Dick* the sun rises over the Pacific Ocean; but had the plain style ever before so woven together the mystery and the depravity? Surely not in any American writing!' (*Nature's Nation*, 1967). See index. [AMERICAS, LITERATURE]. B.L.

TWANG [16c: probably echoic like *bang, ping*, suggesting both plucking a string and a ringing sound]. (1) Also *nasal twang* and (obsolete) *twang of the nose*. A nasal way of speaking attributed to English Puritans in the 16/17c: 'To make incoherent Stuff (seasoned with Twang and Tautology) pass for high Rhetorick' (Robert South,

Sermons, 1661); 'odious as the nasal twang heard at conventicle' (William Cowper, *The Task*, 1784). (2) A distinctive accent or voice quality: 'You talk very good English, but you have a mighty Twang of the foreigner' (Farquhar, *The Beaux Stratagem*, 1707); 'You must not be too near them or you will hear the Cockney twang' (*Good Words* 12, 1883). See ACCENT, CHEE-CHEE ENGLISH, NASAL, NEW ENGLAND, PURITAN. [SPEECH]. T.MCA.

TWO-LINER. A joke in two parts, such as a question and an answer, a riddle and its resolution, a statement and a response, a proposition and an added comment. The first line 'plants' the joke, establishing the reference that is playfully exploited in the second line: 'The meek shall inherit the earth'—'But not its mineral rights' (see the Bible, Matthew 5: 5); 'Waiter, what's this fly doing in my soup?'—'It looks like the breast-stroke, sir.' See JOKE. [STYLE]. W.N.

TWO-PART VERB. An alternative name, especially in the US, for a phrasal verb or prepositional verb that consists of a verb and one particle: *grow up, look at*. See PHRASAL VERB. [GRAMMAR]. S.C.

TYNDALE, William [*c*.1492–1536]. English cleric, Bible translator, and Protestant martyr. Born in Gloucestershire, he studied at Oxford and probably Cambridge, was ordained in 1521, and entered a Gloucestershire household as chaplain/tutor, where he resolved to translate the Bible and issued a challenge to a local priest: 'If God spare my life I will cause that the boy that drives the plough shall know more of the scripture than thou.' He preached and wrote in London before moving to Germany, where his New Testament was printed in Worms (1524–5), with a later revision printed in Antwerp (1534). Copies smuggled to England were rigidly suppressed. He also translated the Pentateuch and Jonah, and possibly other parts of the Old Testament, after contact with Jews at Worms in Germany. He was betrayed to officials of the Holy Roman Emperor in Antwerp and was strangled and burned as a heretic at Vilvorde, near Brussels. Besides Bible translation, Tyndale wrote English expositions and treatises including 'Obedience of a Christian Man' and 'Parable of the Wicked Mammon'. His original work shows scholarship and literary ability; his Biblical translation was deliberately homely and without pedantry, yet was assured and with some happy renderings of Hebrew idiom, as in the phrases *for ever and ever, to die the death, a man after his own heart, apple of his eye*, which have passed into general English usage. The work fulfilled his aim of appealing to all classes in English society and formed a basis for most subsequent renderings, including the Authorized Version. His translation was reissued in modern spelling as *Tyndale's New Testament*, with an introduction by David Daniel (Yale University Press, 1989). See index. [BIOGRAPHY, EUROPE, HISTORY, LITERATURE].   M.LA.

TYPE [15c: from Latin *typus* a figure, image, bas-relief, ground plan, from Greek *túpos* a blow, impression of a seal, stamp on a coin, mould, replica, image, shape, model]. (1) A kind, class, group, or character: *a type of book*; *the right type (of person) for the job*. When people or things are typed, they are categorized or classified. (2) In logic and linguistics, the general form of a word, symbol, or expression, as opposed to any instance or occurrence of that word, symbol, or expression: see TYPE AND TOKEN, WORD. (3) In traditional printing, a small individual rectangular block of hard material (sometimes wood, usually metal, generally lead), with a letter or character reversed in relief on its face; such pieces collectively; the marks or impressions made with ink by such pieces on surfaces like paper. (4) Analogous marks produced without impact, such as through photocopying and heat transfer, and electronically on screens. (5) If text is typed, it is printed by means of a typewriter or more recently by computer technology that imitates the typewriter: laser printer, dot printer, etc. See COMMUNICATIVE SHIFT, STANDARD, TYPE AND TOKEN, TYPEFACE, TYPESETTING, TYPEWRITER, TYPOGRAPHY. [LANGUAGE, TECHNOLOGY]. T.MCA.

TYPE AND TOKEN. In statistical and related contexts, a *type* is a generic form and a *token* is any instance of that form. Thus, the word *love*, when cited as a lexical item, is a type. If that word occurs 14 times on a page, each of those forms is its token; there are therefore 14 tokens of the type *love* on the page. In addition, the variant (usually inflected) forms of a word are also counted as tokens: if therefore there were also 7 occurrences of *loves* and 7 of *loved*, these would constitute a further 14 tokens, making 28 in all. In addition, if *lover* were also regarded for the purposes of the count as a form of *love*, and there were 2 occurrences of that form, there would be a grand total of 30 tokens of the type *love* on the page. See GENERIC, TYPE. [LANGUAGE, WORD].   T.MCA.

TYPEFACE [1900s]. Also **face**. The printing surface of a piece of type and the style, design, and sometimes size of the character formed by the printing surface. There are many kinds of typeface, usually divided into *body type* or *text faces*

for the printing of standard text, such as *Baskerville, Bembo, Bodoni, Caledonia, Century Schoolbook, DeVinne, Electra, Garamond, Janson, Melior, Optima, Plantin, Times Roman,* and *display type* or *display faces* for the printing of titles, headings, advertisements, etc., such as *Avant Garde, Friz Quadrata, Futura, Helvetica Heavy, Italia, ITC Franklin Gothic, Palatino, Serif Gothic, Stymie*. Compare FONT, ROMAN. [TECHNOLOGY].   T.MCA.

TYPESCRIPT. See MANUSCRIPT, SCRIPT.

TYPESETTING. The setting of type for printing. Procedures for setting type remained standard from the time of Gutenberg (mid-15c) to the late 19c; type was cast in metal, character by character, from moulds. Thousands of pieces of this type were arranged letter by letter in two cases, one for the capitals (the *upper case*, so called because of its usual position on the workers' sloping bench) and another for the smaller letters (the *lower case*). The man who set the type (the *compositor*) would pick up one piece of type at a time and line the pieces up in an adjustable frame (a *composing stick*). When some lines of such type had been assembled, they were put in a tray (a *galley*) before the mass of lines was arranged into pages and made ready for printing. Hand typesetting was slow, even when done by skilled workers: some 2,500 pieces of type (including spaces) in an hour was fast. By the late 19c, a number of mechanical inventions served to speed the process up. On these, an average skilled worker could set some 10,000 characters in an hour. In the 1960s, *phototypesetting* was introduced, in which images of the letters were projected through to photosensitive paper. *Photo-offset* plates would then be created from these images. Earlier with the cathode-ray tube and now with the laser, images can be created directly on to plates for printing. Verbal and visual electronic data can be manipulated by laser and computer in extremely subtle ways, but the danger of rapidly succeeding technologies is that refinements essential for the legibility of printed text can be neglected. See LINOTYPE, MONOTYPE, PRINTING, TYPOGRAPHY. [TECHNOLOGY].   W.W.B.

TYPEWRITER [1860s AmE: a term applied at first to both the machine and the person using it. The term *typist* was first used from the 1880s and took several decades to become established]. A machine for writing mechanically, using the letters and characters of traditional printing. Such a device for stamping letters through an inked ribbon on to paper was first thought of in the early 18c, and working machines were known by the early 19c, but the typewriter as such was established in the later 19c. It revolutionized office life and, even more than the printing press in the 15c, contributed to the replacement of scribes, copyists, and many of the traditional functions of clerks. The invention of a workable typewriter is usually credited to the American journalist Christopher Latham Sholes, who, with a group of co-inventors, produced a series of models, the first of which was patented in 1868. Their invention was sold to the gunmakers E. Remington & Sons, who produced a machine with a QWERTY keyboard for commercial sale in 1873. Mark Twain bought one and noted: 'It piles an awful stack of words on one page. It dont muss things or scatter ink blots around. Of course it saves paper' (his first typed letter, 1873).

The first typewriters wrote only in capitals, but a shift key (to allow both upper- and lower-case letters) was introduced by Remington in 1878. One result of their use was the complaint that typewritten letters were insulting. An early objection ran: 'I do not think it was necessary then, nor will be in the future, to have your letters to me taken to the printers, and set up like a handbill. I will be able to read your hand-writing and am deeply chagrined to think you thought such a course necessary.' By the 1920s, however, the manual typewriter was thoroughly accepted and had a smooth, efficient action. Electric typewriters were attempted at the turn of the 20c and were first made available by the International Business Machine Company. The *golfball* typing head is usually associated with IBM machines of the 1960s onwards, but Thomas Edison had already described a work-able model in the 1870s, and such devices as the *daisy wheel* are also 19c technology reapplied to modern machines.

Although the word-processing computer shows signs of replacing the typewriter, various generations of these machines continue to be used by the million throughout the world, and manufacturers continue to refine the technology, often in combination with word processing in various kinds of electronic typewriter. The print-ers used with computers (dot-matrix and laser printers) use a technology that render the type-stamping mechanical typewriter archaic. Yet the typewriter set the stage for the computer and its keyboard has been retained for computer pur-poses. It established the widely held view that typed material has precedence over handwritten material. The typewritten document has less individuality than the handwritten script, and may have had some influence on style of verbal expression, especially in the usage of business and government offices. The decline of hand-writing as a widely practised art may well be due to the dominance of the typewriter. See BRAILLE,

COMMUNICATIVE SHIFT, DIACRITIC, KEYBOARD, MANUAL, QWERTY, TYPE. [TECHNOLOGY]. W.W.B.

TYPOGRAPHICAL ERROR, short form *typo.* An error in setting type, in typing, and in key-boarding. Such an error is easy to make in the process of transcribing manuscript or typescript into print and can be easy to miss in proof-reading. The word *typo* usually refers to a minor error, but typographical error can range from missing out a letter to omitting or transposing pages, or entering the wrong word: *Judas* for *Jesus* (in John 6: 67) in three Bibles published by the same printer, Robert Barker, between 1608 and 1611. Compare LITERAL, MISPRINT, MISTAKE. [TECHNOLOGY]. W.W.B.

TYPOGRAPHY [17c: from Latin *typographia*, from Greek *túpos* type, and -*graphia* writing]. The art and design of typeset material. Most literate people are so accustomed to text that they are almost oblivious to the effects of layout and type design on their reading. Their concern is usually limited to the size of page and type, but such matters as length of line, space between lines (leading), size of indentation, thickness and opacity of paper, and shade and reflectivity of ink are all important in typography, which involves every aspect (sometimes in the most minute detail) of the presentation of text.

Legibility. The ease with which a text can be read is the first concern of the typographer, and is not a simple concept. What is legible under certain conditions for certain readers is not necessarily legible for others. Moreover, the rules of typo-graphic legibility for books does not hold true for other forms of reading: an elegant book roman, such as Baskerville, displayed on a screen or used in a traffic sign can be hard to read because the thin areas of the shaped letter become lost in definition by the screen or over distance. Even though there is considerable dis-agreement over what is most legible for the typography of reading-matter in quantity, there are some generally accepted central principles:

(1) *Kinds of type.* Plain serifed roman is easier to read than sanserif type or any variant form of a typeface (italic, condensed, solid capitals, expanded). Even boldface, which is easier for some, does not significantly enhance legibility for most readers. Serifs (the brackets and feet found on traditional typefaces) create a flow from one letter to the next. Sanserifs (which lack these elements) do not sit so tightly together and are not weighted heavily along the base line of the type. They can be perfectly readable in small quantities, but generally need more leading and the type areas have to be smaller. Italics,

which have greater flow than romans, run narrowly together and are therefore less legible in quantity.

(2) *Spacing*. There should in a full typeset page be more apparent space between the lines than between the words. The words should be set fairly tightly, and should never (as is common with some computer typesetting) be letterspaced: spaces introduced between the letters of the words to break up the 'fit' of the letters (type characters for reading are designed to fit snugly together so that the words can be recognized almost by their outline). Gaps between words can create vertical lines or *rivers* running up and down the page; these are distracting and break the left-to-right movement of the eye. The problem of spacing is especially apparent in typewritten material where the strong vertical orientation of single-spaced typewritten material resists (sometimes imperceptibly) the horizontal movement of the eye.

(3) *Line*. The type line should be about ten to twelve words long, with a minimum of seven words. The eye may become lost in a page with longer lines. A newspaper column, meant to be scanned as much as read, may successfully be narrower than the type area of a standard book.

These rules for legibility are constantly broken. The designer of a text for children, a popular magazine or newspaper, or various forms of advertising wants effects different from the kind of legibility thought suitable for continuous prose. No one would want an index or telephone book set ten or twelve words across, because the information is scanned vertically, then horizontally, not read sequentially. Typography, like most applied arts, is on the whole conservative: one may imaginatively stretch the limits of the normal, but beyond a certain point legibility (based on conventions previously learned by readers) must be acknowledged.

White space. Above all, typography is the art of using space intelligently. Few readers see the *white space* (empty areas) on a page. Yet for the designer this space is as essential as the black of the letters. It is basic to the way information is structured visually: on a microscopic level, the empty holes in type (*counters*) influence their legibility, and space between words is a key marker for meaning and governs the way people read. Empty space can be used to organize data, as in paragraph indentations, the small blanks that separate entries in a dictionary, the gaps between columns of numbers, or the spaces that signal the end of a section or a chapter. Graphs and other displays of information are places where verbal and numerical data intersect in spatial configurations.

Margins. Another significant empty space in a page is the margin. In a paperback novel, outer margins are sacrificed for a larger type-size, but in a work of reference wider margins may be kept for ease in consultation. The *gutter* of a book (the internal margins running down the centre of the opening) is often misunderstood by the inexperienced designer: a book can be rendered almost unusable by a narrow gutter, because the binding must then be constantly forced so as to get at the text. This is especially troublesome with so-called *perfect-bound* books, in which the leaves are held together only by flexible adhesive.

Layout grids. Type areas, margins, headings, the placement of illustrations, and so on are often governed by *grids*: areas of space that are in predetermined relationships. The grid layout is most apparent in a newspaper, with its often highly structured arrangement of advertisements, columns, spreads, illustrations. Such a grid creates expectations and guides our consumption of information and language. A simpler grid structure is used in the layout of books. Early printed books sometimes show a sophisticated use of the double grid space created by an opening of two facing pages (a two-page spread) where the relations of margins and type space are sometimes derived from mathematical harmonies such as the Golden Section. The grid is especially important in magazines and books that use illustrations.

In determining the architecture of a book or other printed document, one may analyse a design in terms of the related elements of letter, line, page, and whole work. Decisions regarding each aspect are controlled by the nature of the text and by the cost of creation, materials, and promotion. The large quantity of material in a work like *The Oxford Companion to the English Language* requires a smallish type and a two-column page format. The type will be chosen for maximum legibility in a small size. Running heads, essential in an alphabetic work of reference, must also be of a clear size. White space is especially important as a means of marking of entries and sections. The book is organized both to be consulted and browsed in, and must look like other Oxford Companions. All the decisions for typographic design, down to the use of small capitals for cross-references and the style of numbers, are marked on a specification sheet which guides the typesetter, who will enter codes into the electronic text. The elements of design, while to some extent predetermined by a standard layout, may vary from other Companions for a variety of reasons specific to the subject in question: this is a Companion to a language, not to music or the mind.

See EDITING, EM, EN, FONT/FOUNT, GOTHIC, GRAPHIC DESIGN, ITALIC, JUSTIFYING, LAYOUT, LETTER[1], LINE, MARGIN, PICA, PRINTING, ROMAN, SPACE, TYPE, TYPEFACE, TYPESETTING, TYPEWRITER, TYPOGRAPHICAL ERROR, WHITE SPACE. [TECHNOLOGY]. W.W.B.

Baudin, Fernand. 1989. *How Typography Works (And Why It Is Important)*. London: Lund Humphries.

Gerstner, Karl. 1974. *Compendium for Literates: A System of Writing*. Translated by Dennis Q. Stephenson. Cambridge, Mass.: MIT Press.

McLean, Ruari. 1980. *The Thames and Hudson Manual of Typography*. London: Thames & Hudson.

Reynolds, Linda. 1979. 'Legibility Studies: Their Relevance to Present Day Documentation Methods', in *Journal of Documentation* 35: 4, pp. 307-40. Also in *Information Design*, ed. R. Easterby & H. Zwaga. 1984. Chichester: John Wiley.

Spencer, Herbert. 1969. *The Visible Word*. London: Lund Humphries.

Tschichold, Jan. 1967. *Asymmetric Typography*. New York: Reinhold.

Tufte, Edward R. 1983. *The Visual Display of Quantitative Information*. Cheshire, Conn.: Graphics Press.

Williamson, Hugh. 1983. *Methods of Book Design*, 3rd edition. New Haven: Yale University Press.

TYPOLOGY OF LANGUAGE. See LINGUISTIC TYPOLOGY.

U

U, u [Called 'you']. The 21st letter of the Roman alphabet as used for English. It originated in the Phoenician consonant symbol *waw*, the common ancestor of the letters *F, U, V, W, Y*. The Greeks adopted *waw* as *upsilon* (*Y*, lower case *v*), which the Romans took from the Etruscans as *V*. The distinction in English between *u* as vowel and *v* as consonant was not made consistently in print until the 17c. Previously, the distinction tended to be positional, not phonological, with *v* used word-initially and *u* medially: *vnder, liue*. Until the 19c, some dictionaries listed *u* and *v* together rather than successively, or *v* before *u* in the alphabet. The use of *V* for *U* has survived into the 20c for some lapidary inscriptions: the BBC's *Bush House* in London has *BVSH HOVSE* carved over the entrance.

Sound values. (1) Formerly, the common feature in the pronunciation of *u*, *v*, *w*, was lip movement: lip-rounding is a feature of the back vowel in *put* and *truth* and the front vowel in French *tu*; /v/ is a labio-dental consonant; /w/ is a labial semi-vowel. In Modern English, French *u* has been Anglicized as a diphthong with a preceding *i*-glide (*music, argue*) and *u* commonly represents /w/ before a vowel after *g*, *q*, and *s* (*anguish, quiet, persuade*). (2) Beside these traditional values of *u*, most English accents have a further value. By the 17c, a vowel shift in southern England had changed the *put*-value of *u* in many words to a new sound, now heard in most accents, but not in the accents of the English Midlands and North. This is the value of *u* in *but* (except for the North of England), which today no longer rhymes with *put* and involves no lip-rounding. (3) In general pronunciation, the letter *u* spells four distinct vowel sounds, as in *but, put, truth, music*, as well as the /w/ in *quiet*, etc. The four vowel sounds will be referred to below as the values *but-u, put-u, truth-u, music-u*.

Long and short *U*. The four vowel values can be grouped into long and short pairs: *but-u* and *put-u* are short, *truth-u* and *music-u* are long. Like the long and short values of the other vowel letters, short and long *u* alternate in related words: *assumption/assume, humble/humility, judge/judicious, number/numerous, punish/punitive, reduction/reduce, study/student*.

Variation in values. The four values are not consistently distinguished. Scots typically do not distinguish *put-u* and *truth-u*, and AmE often gives a *truth-u* to words pronounced with *music-u* in RP: AmE *duty* rhyming with *booty*, RP *duty* rhyming with *beauty*. This change occurs only after alveolar consonants: /d, l, n, r, s, t/. Because the *but/put* split did not take place in the Midlands and North of England, *but/put* rhyme in the accents of these regions. This non-distinction of *but-u* and *put-u* has often been stigmatized as non-standard, while their occasional reversal (*butcher* being pronounced with *but-u* rather than *put-u*) is considered to be hyper-correction towards RP. Variation between *truth-u* and *music-u* is not always regional, the distinction generally being blurred after *l, s*, as when *lute/loot* may or may not be pronounced as homophones, and *sue/suit* may in BrE have either long value of *u*.

Although four possible vowel values in many accents make *u* a complex letter (with division into short and long realizations, and with variation between these values), a particular value is generally apparent from the environment. *U* is normally short except syllable-finally, and *truth-u* only arises after certain consonants.

Other spellings. The values of *u* have common alternative spellings. As a result of vowel shifts or spelling changes, patterns have arisen with the sound values of *u* in *but, put, truth*, but using *o* (*son, wolf, do, move*), or *oe* (*does, shoes*), or *oo*

THE CAPITAL LETTER						THE SMALL LETTER				
EARLY FORMS				CURRENT FORMS		EARLY FORMS			CURRENT FORMS	
Phoenician	Greek	Etruscan	Roman (Latin)	roman	italic	Roman cursive	Roman uncial	Carolingian minuscule	roman	italic
Y	ЧY	Y	V	U	*U*	u	u	u	u	*u*

(*blood, good, food*), or *ou* (*touch, could, youth*). Similarly the sound of long *u* is commonly spelt *ew* (*crew, dew, few, newt, pewter, steward*); arguably *w* should be seen here as a positional variant of *u* (compare *few/feud*).

But-*U* (short). Short *u* occurs before final consonants and (usually multiple) medial consonants: initial *u* in words of Old English origin (*udder, ugly, under, up, us, utter*, and the negative prefix *un-* as in *unborn, uneventful*); before two consonants in some non-English words (*ulcer, ultimate, umbilical, umpire*); in monosyllables ending in a consonant letter (*tub, bud, cuff, mug, luck, cull, bulk, hum, sun, bunk, cup, bus, just, hut*); in short-vowel monosyllables ending in silent *e* (*budge, bulge, plunge*). A few monosyllables contain *put-u* (see below), and the *truth-u* in *truth* itself (and also in *Ruth*) is an exception. In polysyllables, *but-u* usually precedes two consonants, either doubled (*rubble, bucket, rudder, suffer, nugget, sullen, summer, supple, hurry, russet, butter*) or as a string (*publish, indulgent, number, abundant*). Words ending in *-ion* similarly have short *u* before two consonants: *percussion, convulsion, compunction, destruction, assumption*, but long *u* before a single consonant in *confusion, evolution*. Exceptions to these patterns include long *u* in *duplicate, lucrative, rubric* and as indicated by final magic *e* in *scruple* (contrast short *ou* in *couple*); short *u* before a single consonant in *study* (contrast *muddy, Judy*) and in *bunion* (contrast *trunnion, union*).

Put-*U* (short). The lip-rounded *put-u* occurs in a few words, especially after the labial consonants *b, p*, and before *l*: *bull, bullet, bulletin, bullion, bully, bush, bushel, butcher, cuckoo, cushion, full, pudding, pull, pullet, pulley, pulpit, push, puss, put, sugar*. *Muslim* is heard with both *but-u* and *put-u*. *Put-u* is nevertheless not a rare sound in English, being also spelt *ou* in the common *could, would, should*, and frequently *oo*, as in *foot, good*.

Truth-*U* and Music-*U* (long). Long *u* (whether *truth-u* or *music-u*) occurs in polysyllables before a single consonant with following vowel: contrast *fundamental/funeral* and the patterns in *cucumber, undulate*. Long *u* occurs in: *alluvial, deputy, educate, fury, ludicrous, lunar, peculiar, refusal, ruby, rufous, ruminate, superb*. In final closed syllables, long *u* is usually shown by magic (lengthening) *e*: *amuse, flute, fume, huge, prelude, puce, puke, pure, refute, rude, rule, ruse, tube, tune*. In accordance with the above patterns, the monosyllabic prefix *sub-* has *but-u* (*subject*), but disyllabic *super-* has long *u*. In most circumstances, long *u* is *music-u*, the initial *i*-glide being assimilated to produce *truth-u* only after certain consonants. *Music-u* is therefore found word-initially before a single consonant, especially in

derivations from the Latin root *unus* (one), as in *unicorn, unify, union, unity, universe*. Other cases include *ubiquitous, urine, use, utility*. *Music-u* follows consonants as in *ambulance, acute, confuse, coagulate, music, annual, compute, enthuse, revue*, and in RP but commonly not in AmE as in *duke, tube*. Both *music-u* and *truth-u* are heard after *l, s* (*lute, suit*). *Truth-u* occurs after *r, sh* (including the affricate *j*) and is explicit in *yu: truth, prune, Shute, chute, Schubert, June, jury, yule*. In an unstressed medial syllable, 'long' *music-u* tends in fact to be a rather short vowel: contrast *deputy, educate* with *despite, duke*.

Final *U*. Syllable-final *u* is pronounced long. Word-finally, it has an additional silent *e* in long-established English words (*argue, continue, due, rue*), although this commonly disappears before suffixes (*argue/argument, continue/continual, due/duty, true/truth*). Final *u* occurs without following *e*, particularly in recently formed or borrowed words: *emu, flu, guru, Hindu, jujitsu, menu*. Long *u* also arises syllable-finally before a vowel (contrast *annul, annual*): *dual, suet, fluid, fluoride, vacuum*.

***U* before *R*.** Before *r* with no following vowel, RP gives *u* the same value as *e* or *i* before *r*: *fur, hurt, nurse, absurd, purchase, concur* (compare *her, sir*). When a vowel follows, *u* is long (*rural, bureau, during*), but is modified with the hint of an inserted schwa (*cure, pure, endure; rural, bureau, during*). Like other multiple consonants, *rr* normally induces a preceding *but-u*: *burrow, current, flurry, furrier* (noun): but the adjective *furry* retains the value of *u* of its base form *fur*, and its comparative *furrier* is then a homograph of the noun *furrier* with its *but-u*.

***U* and schwa.** Like all vowel letters in English, *u* when unstressed in fluent speech may lose distinctive value, being reduced to schwa: initially (*until, upon*), before a stressed syllable (*suggest, surround*), and after the main stress especially before *l, m, n, r, s* (medially, as in *faculty, calumny, voluntary, Saturday, industry*, and in final syllables *awful, difficult, autumn, album, minimum, museum, tedium, vacuum, murmur, injure, circus, radius*). In some words, *u* is reduced to schwa while retaining the preceding *i*-glide of *music-u*: *century, failure*. In *lettuce* and in the noun *minute, u* is commonly reduced to schwa, and in RP to the value of short *i*. The adjective *minute* has *music-u*.

Assimilation. Phonetically, *music-u* is a diphthong consisting of a glide *i*-sound followed by *truth-u*, but in fluent speech the glide often affects the value of a preceding consonant, sometimes being assimilated with it entirely, as when *duty, tune* are spoken as 'jooty', 'choon' (typically not in North America), and *casual, picture* are spoken as 'kazhel', 'pikcher'. Such assimilation is usual before the suffixes -*ual*, -*ure* after *d, s, t, z*: *gradual, casual, mutual; verdure, closure, picture, azure*. The assimilation with initial *s* in *sugar, sure* is of such long standing that the *s* is perceived as having an abnormal value. For some speakers, the tendency extends to *assume* and *presume* spoken as 'ashoom', 'prezhoom'.

Semi-vowel *U*. (1) The value of *u* as a semi-vowel occurs commonly in words of French derivation and typically after *g* (*distinguish, guava, language, sanguine*), *q* (*quash, quail, quest, quit, quiet, quote, acquaint, equal, loquacious*), and *s* (*suave, suede, suite, persuade*). (2) In similar contexts, however, *u* may have its full vowel value: contrast *suite/suicide*. (3) Some words with initial *qu* are of Old English origin, having changed their spelling after the Norman Conquest from *cw*- to *qu*-: *cwen, cwic* now written *queen, quick*.

Silent *U*. (1) Especially in words of French derivation: after *g* (where it serves to distinguish hard and soft *g*: *page/vague*), as in *vague, fatigue, vogue, fugue*, and after *q*, as in *opaque, technique, mosquito*. (2) In initial *qu* (*quay, queue*) and in *conquer* and often *languor*, although pronounced /w/ in *conquest, languid*. (3) Elsewhere, *u* is inserted only to preserve the hard value of preceding *g*: *Portugal/Portuguese* (see G, Q). (4) Although apparently part of a digraph, *u* is effectively silent in *gauge, aunt, laugh*, BrE *draught* (compare AmE *draft*), *build, cough, trough, though*, BrE *mould, moult, smoulder* (compare AmE *mold, molt, smolder*), *boulder, shoulder, soul, buoy* (especially BrE), *buy*. Although *u* is silent in *biscuit, circuit*, it arguably indicates preceding hard *c* (contrast *explicit*). It is optionally silent in *conduit*.

Digraphs. *U* often has the secondary function of indicating a modified value for a preceding letter. For the digraph *au* (as in *taut*) and *ou* (as in *out*), see A, O respectively. *Eau* in *beauty* has the value of *music-u*. For final *eau* (*bureau*, etc.), see E. The main digraphs having one of the four sound values of *u* are:

EU. (1) The digraph *eu* regularly represents *music-u*, especially in words of Greek derivation (*Europe, eulogy, pseudo-, neurotic*), but occasionally elsewhere (*feud*). (2) In *sleuth*, the *eu* represents *truth-u*, as does *oeu* in BrE *manoeuvre* (AmE *maneuver*).

OU. (1) The digraph *ou* has one of the values of *u*, except when it is used as a standard digraph for the diphthong in *out* and for long *o* as in *soul*. See O. The spelling *ou* sometimes derives from French, and sometimes represents earlier pronunciation with a long vowel. (2) It represents *but-u* as in *country, couple, cousin, double, southern, touch, trouble, young*, with following

/f/ spelt -*gh* as in *enough, rough, tough*, and in BrE *courage, flourish, nourish*, AmE giving this -*our*- the value as in *journey*. (3) It represents *put-u* in *could, should, would* and *truth-u* in *ghoul, group, soup, through, uncouth, wound* (noun), *youth* and also in such recent French loans as *boulevard, bouquet, coup*, BrE *route* (in AmE often homophonous with *rout*), *souvenir, tour, trousseau*. (4) It represents modified *u* before *r*: *courteous, courtesy* (compare cognate *curts[e]y*), *journal* (cognate *diurnal*), *journey, scourge* (compare *urge*).

UE, UI. The combinations *ue* and *ui* usually indicate long *u*: *Tuesday, juice, sluice, bruise, nuisance, cruise, fruit, suit, pursuit, recruit*. The *i* is redundant when the word already ends in *e*: compare *reduce/juice, ruse/bruise*. In the verbs related to *suit, pursuit*, the *i* is replaced by *e*: *sue, pursue*.

Variations. (1) Historically, there has been variation of spelling and pronunciation, especially between *u* and *o*: in the cognates *custom/costume, ton/tun, tone/tune*. See O. One factor may have been a need to distinguish the vertical strokes or minims of *u* from the vertical strokes of adjacent letters in Middle English manuscripts; hence Middle English *sone* rather than *sune* for Old English *sunu* and Modern English *son*. (2) Similarly, *w* may sometimes have been used to avoid confusion of *u/v* (contrast *coward/cover* and French *couard*), or to distinguish homophones (*foul/fowl*), or even meanings of the 'same' word, such as the recent differentiation of *flour/flower*. (3) In general, *ou* occurs medially (*house, though*) and *ow* more often finally (*how, throw*), before vowels (*tower*), and before *l* (*howl, bowl*), *n* (*clown, sown*), and *d* (*crowd*). However, the choice between *ou, ow* is often arbitrary, as in the cognates *noun/renown*. (4) For AmE -*or*, BrE -*our*, see O. (5) The number *four* loses *u* in the derivative *forty*, though not in *fourteen*. See ALPHABET, CLASSICAL ENDING, LETTER[1], SPELLING, V, W. [WRITING].

C.U., T.MCA., E.W.

U AND NON-U [1954: abbreviations of *Upper class* and *Non-Upper class*, coined by the philologist A. S. C. Ross]. Upper-class and non-upper-class usage, linguistic and social: terms first used by Ross for academic purposes and popularized through inclusion in *Noblesse Oblige* (1956), edited by Nancy Mitford, a work whose lists of expressions that served as social clues inspired over the next few years a search for further U-isms and non-U-isms: 'In this article I use the terms *upper class* (abbreviated: U), *correct, proper*, . . . to designate usages of the upper class; their antonyms (*non-U, incorrect, not proper*, . . .) to designate usages which are not upper class' (A. S. C. Ross, *Neuphilologische Mitteilungen* 55, 1954); '*Fault, also, Balkans* are pronounced by the U as if spelt *fawlt, awlso, Bawlkans*' (Ross, in *Noblesse Oblige*); ' "I don't think he's really U, though, do you?"—"Oh no. Shabby genteel, maybe" ' (Alison Lurie, *Love and Friendship*, 1962); 'He had spoken with a distinct English accent. Very U indeed' (D. Bennett, *Jigsaw Man*, 1977); 'The Wicked Queen said "Mirror, mirror, on the wall", instead of "Looking glass, looking glass, on the wall" . . . So the Wicked Queen exposed herself as not only wicked but definitely non-U' (Frederic Ogden Nash, *You can't get there from here*, 1957). [STYLE, VARIETY].   T.MCA.

UCLES, short for *University of Cambridge Local Examination Syndicate.* Also informally *the Cambridge Syndicate, the Syndicate.* A local examining body based on the U. of Cambridge and established in 1858. It is responsible for schools examinations in England (as a member of the Midland Examining Group), for the *General Certificate of Secondary Education (GCSE),* and individually for the *General Certificate in Education at Advanced Level.* The strong involvement of UCLES in overseas examining dates from *c.*1870 with the *School Certificate* and examining in English as a foreign language from 1913, with the *Certificate of Proficiency in English.* See CAMBRIDGE CERTIFICATE OF PROFICIENCY IN ENGLISH, CULTURA, EXAMINING IN ENGLISH, FIRST CERTIFICATE IN ENGLISH, IELTS, ROYAL SOCIETY OF ARTS. [EDUCATION, EUROPE, MEDIA].   W.S.

UGANDA. Official title: *Republic of Uganda.* A country of East Africa and member of the Commonwealth. Capital: Kampala. Currency: shilling (100 cents). Population: 16.2m (1988), 23.6m (projection for 2000). Ethnicity: 18% Baganda, 14% Banyoro, 10% Bagisu, 8% Banyankole, 8% Turkana, 8% Iteso, 7% Bachiga, 7% Lango, 4% Acholi, 3% Karamajong, 13% others. Religion: 33% Protestant, 33% Roman Catholic, 18% traditional, 16% Muslim. Languages: English (official), Swahili, and Luganda and other indigenous, mainly Bantu, languages. English is the language of education, government, and the media, including the leading newspaper, the *Uganda Times.* Education: primary 54%, secondary 10%, tertiary 1%, literacy 58%. Uganda was visited by Arab traders in the 1830s, by the British explorer Captain John Speke in the 1860s, and in 1888 granted by the Crown to the Imperial British East Africa Company. In 1893, the Company withdrew and the territory was administered by a commissioner, the kingdom of Buganda becoming a British Protectorate in the same year. Between 1900 and 1903, treaties with the four Ugandan kingdoms resulted in the entire territory becoming a protectorate. Uganda gained its independence in 1962. The English of Uganda is a variety of East African English. It is non-rhotic and tends to be stress-timed. Because local Bantu languages generally have only two fricatives, /f, s/, the other English fricatives tend to be obscured: 'sooeh' for *sure,* 'ferry' for *very.* Many do not distinguish *r* and *l:* 'rorry', 'lolly', and 'rolly' are all variants for *lorry.* There are fewer consonants in the vernaculars than in English and consonant clusters are managed by means of an epenthetic vowel ('sitring' for *string*) or by reducing the cluster (in various ways: for example, 'lents' or 'lenss' for *lengths*). See BANTU, EAST AFRICAN ENGLISH, ENGLISH, SWAHILI. [AFRICA, NAME, VARIETY].
                              C.L.N., L.T.

UK, U.K. See UNITED KINGDOM.

ULSTER. The name of one of the four historic provinces of Ireland, also applied to Northern Ireland, which covers less territory. It is associated with the Celtic epic cycles of Cúchulain and Finn MacCumhail and with the Scots who went from Ireland in the 6c to settle in the west of what later became Scotland. There are nine counties in Ulster proper, six in Northern Ireland (Antrim, Armagh, Derry, Down, Fermanagh, Tyrone) and three in the Irish Republic (Cavan, Donegal, Monaghan). During the English conquest of Ireland, Ulster was the most rebellious province and was therefore more heavily 'planted' (settled) than Connaught, Leinster, and Munster, creating the *Ulster Plantation* of Protestant English and Scots. It is the most linguistically varied region of Ireland: Gaeltacht areas in Donegal; Hiberno-English communities especially in Fermanagh and Tyrone; Ulster Scots especially in Antrim and Down; Anglo-Irish especially in the south; RP speakers among the Northern Ireland Ascendancy (landed gentry). See BELFAST, HIBERNO-ENGLISH, IRELAND, NORTHERN IRELAND, PROTESTANT ASCENDANCY, ULSTER ENGLISH, ULSTER SCOTS. [EUROPE, NAME].   L.T., T.MCA.

ULSTER ENGLISH. English as used in any part of the historic province of Ulster, which includes Northern Ireland and three counties of the Irish Republic. See NORTHERN IRISH ENGLISH, ULSTER. [EUROPE, VARIETY].   T.MCA.

ULSTERMAN/WOMAN. See -MAN/WOMAN.

ULSTER SCOTS. A variety of Scots spoken in the north of Ireland, mainly in parts of Antrim, Derry, Donegal, and Down, but influencing all varieties of speech in Northern Ireland and adjacent parts of the Irish Republic. The extent of

Ulster Scots in a person's speech is related to region, education, and social position. The lower down the social ladder, the more likely is the speaker to roll the /r/ in words such as *war* and *work*; lose the postvocalic /l/ in words like *fall* and *full* (*fa*, *fu*); rhyme *die* with *me* ('dee'), *dead* with *bead* ('deed'), *home* with *name* ('hame'), *now* with *who* ('noo'); and use the voiceless velar fricative in the pronunciation of *Clogher*, *laugh*, *trough* (like ScoE *loch*). The phonological similarity between Ulster and Lowland Scots is reinforced by vocabulary, although many traditional words are in decline. Words shared by the two communities include *ava* at all, *bairn* a baby, child, *brae* a hill, steep slope, *firnenst* in front of, *greet* to cry, *ken* to know, *lum* a chimney, *message* an errand, *nor* than, *oxther* an armpit (Scots *oxter*), *peerie* a spinning-top, *tae* to. Two distinctive grammatical features are the negatives *no* (*We'll no be able to come*; *Do ye no ken who A mean?*) and -*nae/ny* added to auxiliary verbs (*A didnae think he would do it*; *Ye canny mean it*), and the demonstratives *thon* yon, *thonder* yonder (*Thon wee lassie's aye bonny*; *Thonder he is*). Ulster Scots has had a literary tradition since the peasant poet James Orr in the 18c. G. F. Savage-Armstrong and Adam Lynn have used it in the 20c. It has also been used for prose, especially for comic purposes, by writers such as W. G. Lyttle in the novel *Betsy Gray* (1888). The following passage is from Savage-Armstrong's poem 'Death and Life' (1901):

> 'Puir Wully is deed!'—'O, is he?'
> 'Ay, caul' in his coffin he's leein'!'
> 'Jist noo A em muckle tae busy
> Tae trouble me heed about deein';
> There's han's tae be got fur the reapin'
> We're gaun tae the wark in the murn;
> An' A'm thinkin' the rain 'ill come dreepin',
> The-night, an' destroyin' the curn.'

[*puir* poor, *deed* dead, *caul'* cold, *leein'* lying, *jist noo A em muckle tae busy* just now I am much too busy, *me heed* my head, *han* hand (worker), *gaun tae the wark* going to work, *murn* morning, *dreepin* dripping/dropping, *the-night* tonight, *curn* corn]

See BELFAST, IRISH ENGLISH, NORTHERN IRELAND, NORTHERN IRISH ENGLISH, SCOTCH-IRISH, SCOTS, SCOTTISH VOWEL-LENGTH RULE, ULSTER. [EUROPE, VARIETY]. L.T.

UMLAUT [1830s: German, from *um* around (signifying making a change), *Laut* sound]. A diacritic placed over a vowel in some languages to mark a modification in quality: in German, the *a* in *Mann* modified in the plural *Männer* (compare English *man/men*). The symbol originated in German as a superscript *e*. In English, the umlaut is sometimes rendered by a following *e*: *Duesseldorf* for *Düsseldorf*. See ABLAUT, DIACRITIC, DI(A)ERESIS. [WRITING]. C.U.

UNABRIDGED. (1) [16c]. Not shortened: *an unabridged dictionary*. (2) [mid-19c: AmE]. A dictionary that has not been shortened but is as comprehensive as constraints of size, effort, and expense permit: 'You small boy there, hurry up that "Webster's Unabridged"!' (Oliver Wendell Holmes, *The Professor at the Breakfast-Table*, 1860); *The Random House Dictionary of the English Language: Second Edition, Unabridged* (title, 1987). See ABRIDG(E)MENT, RANDOM HOUSE DICTIONARY, WEBSTER'S NEW INTERNATIONAL DICTIONARY. [REFERENCE]. T.MCA.

UNATTACHED PARTICIPLE. See PARTICIPLE.

UNCIAL [17c: from Late Latin *unciales* (*litterae*), from *uncialis* relating to a twelfth part, weighing one-twelfth of a *libra* (pound), from *uncia* a twelfth part. The words *inch* and *ounce* also derive from *uncia*]. (1) Relating to an inch or ounce; divided into twelve parts; based on a duodecimal numbering system. (2) Relating to a form of majuscule writing with unjoined and generously curved or rounded letters that are faster to write than standard Roman capitals. Uncial writing was used chiefly for Greek and Latin manuscripts *c*.3-9c, and characterized much early Christian writing. The minuscule letters of the English Carolingian style were developed from uncial and 'half-uncial' forms. Half-uncial was the hand used in writing the Book of Kells, a Latin work that is displayed in the library of Trinity College, Dublin. The term is also applied to letters of a similar type, whether or not they are capitals in form. The original relationship of letters to weights and sizes is unclear: they may at first have been an inch high or large enough to suggest the comparison, or the word may have originally been *uncinales* hooked, bent. (3) An uncial letter (*written in uncials*); uncial writing (*Irish uncial*, *Roman uncial*); an uncial manuscript; a large or capital letter. See CALLIGRAPHY, and the uncial letters shown beside the letter entries (A, B, C, etc.) in this volume. [WRITING]. T.MCA.

UNCLE SAM [During the War of 1812, a jocular expansion of the initials *U.S.*]. A personification of the United States, its government, or its people. By the mid-19c, the figure now associated with the name (a tall, gangling man with long white hair and chin whiskers, dressed in striped trousers, a tailcoat, and a tall hat with stars) had begun to appear in cartoons and by 1870 had been popularized by the cartoonist Thomas Nast. The figure of Uncle Sam is derived partly from two earlier personifications, *Brother Jonathan* and *Yankee Doodle*, and like them is historically associated, by name and appearance, with New England, although few present-day Americans make the association. Compare JOHN BULL. [AMERICAS, NAME].   J.A.

UNCOUNTABLE NOUN. See COUNTABLE AND UNCOUNTABLE.

UNDERSTATEMENT [19c]. A semi-technical term for saying less than one might or saying something less forcefully than one might; any occasion of doing this. Understatement is often used as a kind of emphasis in reverse, especially in BrE: *We're (quite) pleased* (said when something has been an outstanding success and jubilation would be appropriate). See LITOTES, MEIOSIS. [STYLE].   T.MCA.

UNDERSTOOD. A traditional term for a word or words not present but required in interpreting a construction: the subject *you* is 'understood' in the order *Go away* (You go away); auxiliary and subject *have you* in *Got any cake?* (Have you got any cake?); auxiliary *is* in *Anybody in?* (Is anybody in?). See ELLIPSIS. [GRAMMAR].   S.G.

UNDERTONE [18c]. Both a continuous low or subdued tone, whether of a voice (*conversing in undertones; chanting a dirge in an undertone; a wheedling undertone*) or a sound (*the faint undertones of insects' wings*), and an underlying quality, especially of feeling (*an undertone/undercurrent of resentment in their arguments*). Speaking in an undertone is comparable to whispering, especially so as to make asides and private comments to a neighbour while someone is speaking normally, giving a talk, or the like; its effect is often to make such a speaker irritated or nervous. Compare ASIDE, TONE. [SPEECH].   T.MCA.

UNILINGUAL. See LINGUAL.

UNIT CREDIT. An examination system testing one portion of the syllabus at a time, with accumulative certification. As a language examination, the concept was introduced by the Council of Europe in 1976, as part of their *Threshold* and *Waystage* specifications. Applications in the field of English as a Foreign Language (EFL) include the RSA/UCLES examination in the *Communicative Use of English as a Foreign Language*, the UCLES *Diploma of English Studies*, and the UCLES *Cambridge Examination for English Language Teachers*. See COUNCIL OF EUROPE, EXAMINING IN ENGLISH. [EDUCATION, EUROPE].   W.S.

UNITED ARAB EMIRATES. See ARABIC, ENGLISH.

UNITED KINGDOM, The. Full form *The United Kingdom of Great Britain and Northern Ireland*. Short form *the UK*. A country of Western Europe, also known as *Great Britain* or *Britain*. It is a monarchy consisting of the formerly separate kingdoms of England and Scotland, the principality of Wales, and the province of Northern Ireland, is a member of the Commonwealth, and has various dependencies around the world, such as Anguilla in the Caribbean, Gibraltar in the Mediterranean, and until 1997 Hong Kong in East Asia. Capital: London. Currency: the pound sterling (100 pence). Economy: mixed. Population: 56.96m (1988): 73% English, 10% Scottish, 5% Welsh, 4% Irish, 2% Caribbean, 2% South Asian, Chinese, Cypriot; 2% foreign nationals. The projection for 2000 is 57.5m. Religions: 59% Protestant (including 49% Anglican, mainly in England, 4% Presbyterian, mainly in Scotland, and 1% Methodist), 28% non-professing, 10% Roman Catholic, 2% Muslim, 1% Jewish, Hindu, Sikh. Languages: English is the national language, Welsh is spoken in Wales, Gaelic in parts of Scotland, and many other languages variously throughout the country (and especially in London): see BRITISH LANGUAGES. Education: primary 97%, secondary 89%, tertiary 22%, literacy 99%. See AMERICAN ENGLISH AND BRITISH ENGLISH, ANGLO-, BRIT, BRITAIN, BRITANNIA, BRITICISM, BRITISH, BRITISH EMPIRE, BRITISH ENGLISH, BRITISHER, BRITISH PUBLISHING, BRITON, COMMONWEALTH, DIALECT IN ENGLAND, DIALECT IN SCOTLAND, DIALECT IN WALES, ENGLAND, ENGLISH, GREAT BRITAIN, HISTORY OF ENGLISH, JOURNALISM, LITERACY, LONDON, NEWSPAPER, NORTHERN IRELAND, SCOTLAND, SPELLING, TELEPHONE, TESD, TESL, ULSTER, WALES. [EUROPE, NAME].   T.MCA.

UNITED STATES. In full *United States of America*. Short forms *US, USA*. A republic of North America, comprising 50 states (49 continental states, made up of the 'lower 48' contiguous states and Alaska, and Hawaii). There are also: a capital territory (the District of Columbia, comprising the city of Washington and its immediate environs); the US Virgin Islands and the Commonwealth of Puerto Rico in the Caribbean; and various dependencies elsewhere, such as islands of the Pacific. Capital: Washington. Currency: the dollar (100 cents). Economy: industrial, agricultural, services, tourism. Population: 245.2m (1988), 262.7m (projection for 2000). Ethnicity: 83% Caucasian (including 5% Hispanic), 11% African-American, 1% Amerindian, 1% Asian, Polynesian, Inuit, Aleut. Religions: some 40% non-professing, 33% Protestant, 22% Roman Catholic, 2% Jewish, 2% Orthodox, 1% other. Languages: English in general and governmental use (the *de facto* but not *de jure* official language); many other languages. See AMERICAN LANGUAGES. Education: primary 99%, secondary 95%, tertiary 57%, literacy 99%. See AMERICA, AMERICAN ENGLISH, AMERICAN ENGLISH AND BRITISH ENGLISH, AMERICANISM, AMERICAN LITERATURE, AMERICAN PLACE-NAMES, AMERICAN PRESS, AMERICAN PUBLISHING, AMERINDIAN, DIALECT IN AMERICA, ENGLISH, ENGLISH LANGUAGE AMENDMENT, SPELLING, TELEPHONE, TESD, TESL, TESOL, UNCLE SAM, UNITED STATES ENGLISH. [AMERICAS, NAME].   T.MCA.

UNITED STATES ENGLISH, also **US English, USE.** An alternative term for *American English,* the English language as used in the United States of America. The term is used especially by those who wish to make a clear distinction between US and Canadian usage or avoid the ambiguities inherent in the word *American.* The difficulty arose because the name *United States of America* has no simple and natural adjectival form; citizens of the land early solved the problem for their own purposes by adopting *American* from the last word of the country's name, an adjective already used for the western hemisphere and in colonial times for its English-speaking settlers. See AMERENGLISH, AMERICAN[1], AMERICAN ENGLISH, AMERICAN ENGLISH AND BRITISH ENGLISH, AMERICAN LANGUAGE, NORTH AMERICA. [AMERICAS, VARIETY].   J.A., T.MCA.

UNITED STATES INFORMATION AGENCY, short form *USIA.* An agency of the US government. The USIA is a descendant of the Office of War Information (1941–6). It was separated from the Department of State in 1953 to oversee international information and cultural programmes. It supervises the Voice of America, the Worldnet satellite television system, and the Fulbright scholarships. Its overseas arm is the *United States Information Service* (short form *USIS*), which operates 204 posts in 127 countries. It is charged with strengthening foreign understanding and support of US policies and actions, advising US government officials on the impact of foreign opinion, and administering international cultural exchanges. See VOICE OF AMERICA. Compare BRITISH COUNCIL. [AMERICAS, MEDIA].   D.E.B.

UNITED STATES INFORMATION SERVICE. See UNITED STATES INFORMATION AGENCY.

UNITIES, THREE. See LITERARY CRITICISM, POETICS.

UNIVERSAL. See LANGUAGE UNIVERSALS.

UNIVERSITY OF CAMBRIDGE LOCAL EXAMINATION SYNDICATE. See UCLES.

UNIVOCALIC. See LIPOGRAM.

UNMARKED TERM. See MARKED AND UNMARKED TERMS.

UPPER CASE. A technical term for capital letters or majuscules (that is, letters larger in size and form than *lower-case letters*), so named because they were stored in the upper of the two cases used by compositors when setting type by hand. See CAPITAL, CASE[2], TYPESETTING. [TECHNOLOGY].   W.W.B.

URDANG, Laurence [b.1927]. American lexicographer, born and educated in New York, including B.S. and postgraduate work at Columbia U., New York, as a student of the French linguist André Martinet and the American linguist Allen Walker Read. He taught English and general linguistics at New York U. (1955–60) before becoming Director of the Reference Department at Random House (1957–69). He was Managing Editor of the *Random House Dictionary of the English Language—Unabridged Edition* (1966), and Editor-in-Chief of the *College Edition* (1968), pioneering the application of computers to lexicography. He then set up his own company, *Laurence Urdang Inc.,* offering consultancy services to publishers in the preparation of reference books and to publishers and compositors in automatic typesetting and the use of computers in the compilation of reference books. In 1970, he was asked by Jan Collins, Managing Editor of Collins Publishers, to prepare a 'college-type' dictionary for the British market. This led to the establishment of a company, *Laurence Urdang Dictionaries,* in Aylesbury, Buckinghamshire, which undertook the work on the *Collins English Dicitonary* (1979). An ancillary company, *Laurence Urdang Associates, Ltd.,* was organized to research, compile, design, typeset, and produce other reference works, while Laurence Urdang Inc. in the US was expanded in the mid-1970s to undertake reference-book preparation for American publishers.

Between 1975 and 1987, the three companies produced more than 125 dictionaries, encyclopedias, indexes, and other kinds of reference materials under his direction, mainly for British and American publishers. These include: *New York Times Everyday Reader's Dictionary of Misunderstood, Misused, Mispronounced Words* (NY Times Books, 1972, 1985); *Official Associated Press Almanac* (1972, 1973, 1974); *CBS News Almanac* (1975, 1976, 1977); *Basic Book of Synonyms and Antonyms* (New American

Library, 1978, 1985); *Longman Dictionary of English Idioms* (Longman, 1979); *Synonym Finder* (US: Rodale, 1978; UK: Longman, 1988); *-Ologies & -Isms* (Gale, 1978, 1981, 1986); *Urdang Dictionary of Current Medical Terms* (UK: Oxford/Corgi, 1980; US: Wiley/Bantam, 1981); *Macmillan Encyclopedia* (1981); *Allusions—Cultural, Literary, Biblical, and Historical: A Thematic Dictionary* (Gale, 1982, 1986); *Idioms & Phrases Index* (3 volumes: Gale, 1983); *Loanwords Index* (Gale, 1983); *Slogans* (Gale, 1984); *Mottoes* (Gale, 1986); *Dictionary of Differences* (UK: Bloomsbury, 1988; US: *Dictionary of Confusable Words*, Facts on File, 1988); and *The Oxford Thesaurus* (1991). He is founder and editor of *Verbatim, The Language Quarterly*, and of Verbatim Books, which publishes popular and scholarly books about language. See index. [AMERICAS, BIOGRAPHY, REFERENCE]. T.MCA.

URDU [18c: from Persian *zabān-i-urdū* language of the camp, from Turkic *ordu* camp, whence also Russian *orda* clan, crowd, troop, Polish *horda*, and English *horde*. Compare *the Golden Horde*, a Tatar tribe in Central Asia, 14-15c]. An Indo-Aryan language of the Indian subcontinent, associated with the Moghul Empire, in which Persian was the court language. It is used especially by Muslims and written in a variant of the Perso-Arabic script. Closely related to Hindi, Urdu has a similar pronunciation and grammar but a more heavily Persianized and Arabicized vocabulary. It is the national language of Pakistan and is its co-official language with English. In India, it is the state language of the state of Jammu and Kashmir, and associate state language of the state of Uttar Pradesh. It is spoken as a first language by c.30m and as a second language by c.100m people in India and Pakistan, and some thousands of people of Indo-Pakistani origin in Fiji, Guyana, South Africa, the UK, and the US. The literary tradition of Urdu dates from the 16c in the Deccan (South India). By the 18c, the centre had shifted north, and present-day literary Urdu was fashioned in Delhi and Lucknow in India and in Karachi and Lahore in Pakistan. See BANGLADESH, HINDI, HINDI-URDU, HINDUSTANI, INDIA, INDIAN LANGUAGES, PAKISTAN, PERSIAN, SOUTH AFRICA. [ASIA, LANGUAGE]. T.MCA., Y.K.

URO-ALTAIC LANGUAGES, also **Ural-Altaic languages**. A proposed family of languages made up of the *Uralic languages*, comprising the Finno-Ugric group (which includes Finnish, Estonian, and Hungarian in Europe) and Samoyed (in Europe and Asia), and the *Altaic languages*, comprising the Turkic, Mongolian, and Tungusic languages, spoken from south-eastern Europe to the northern Pacific coast of Asia. Korean and Japanese are sometimes tentatively included in the family. See BORROWING (TURKISH/TATAR, TUNGUS, FINNISH, HUNGARIAN), EUROPEAN LANGUAGES, JAPAN, KOREA, SCANDINAVIAN LANGUAGES, TURKISH. [ASIA, LANGUAGE]. T.MCA.

US, U.S. See USA.

USA, U.S.A. The abbreviation for both *United States Army* and *United States of America*, a full name that is typical of formal or ritualistic contexts and therefore likely to sound pompous in other situations. Just as the name of the country is usually clipped to *United States*, so the abbreviation *US* is more neutral than *USA*. The latter is used in some contexts (for example, as an abbreviation in formal contexts or in the name of the newspaper *USA Today*, where it makes a memorable rhyme), but its use generally implies a sense of patriotism, as in the Bruce Springsteen song title 'Born in the USA'. The fuller abbreviation *US of A* is either jingoistic or humorous. See UNITED STATES. [AMERICAS, NAME]. J.A.

USAGE [13c: an adoption of Old French *usage*, corresponding to medieval Latin *usaticum*, from Latin *usus* use]. (1) In general terms, the customary or habitual way of doing something; what is done in practice as distinct from principle or theory; an instance or application of this, a customary practice, as in religion, commerce, military matters, and diplomacy. (2) In linguistic terms, the way in which the elements of language are customarily used to produce meaning; this includes accent, pronunciation, spelling, punctuation, words, and idioms. It occurs neutrally in such terms as *formal usage, disputed usage,* and *local usage*, and it has strong judgemental and prescriptive connotations in such terms as *bad usage, correct usage, usage and abusage,* and *usage controversies*.

History. The first citation of the term *usage* in the *OED* in a linguistic sense is from Daniel Defoe in 1697, referring to the proposed English Academy to monitor the language, on the model of the Académie française: 'The voice of this society should be sufficient authority for the usage of words.' Before the 17c, the concept of usage or custom in English was hardly known: individuals spoke and wrote largely as they wished, and each printer had his own conventions. During the 17-18c, however, writers and leaders of society were concerned to codify the language in grammars and dictionaries, usually drawing on principles established in Latin and Greek. Defoe, Swift, Pope, and others held the view that usage should be monitored; but this notion failed along with the attempt to set up an Academy, and guidance about usage became largely the concern of teachers, publishers, and self-appointed usage guardians.

The present-day scholarly concept of usage as a social consensus based on the practices of the educated middle class has emerged only within the last century. For many people, however, the views and aims of the 17-18c fixers of the language continue to hold true: they consider that there ought to be a single authority capable of providing authoritative guidance about 'good' and 'bad' usage. For them, the model remains that of Greek and Latin, and they have welcomed arbiters of usage such as Henry Fowler who have based their prescriptions on this model. In spite of this, and although public opinion responds to arguments that the language is in decline, no nation in which English is a main language has yet set up an official institution to monitor and make rules about its usage. New words, and new senses and uses of words, are not sanctioned or rejected by the authority of any single body: they arise through regular use and, once established, are recorded in dictionaries and grammars. This means that, with the classical model of grammar in rapid decline, the users of English collectively set the standards and priorities that underlie all usage.

Standard usage. Guidance tends to centre on *standard English*, a form assumed to be shared, used, and accepted by educated speakers throughout the English-speaking world, despite great variety in accent, grammar, and vocabulary; it is based partly on intellectual argument and partly on received opinion. Standard usage is taught in schools on the assumption that students should speak and write English that is acceptable across a broad spectrum of society. The forms of standard usage correspond to the major national standards of English, such as those of BrE, AmE, and AusE. In Britain, and especially England, correct usage has long been identified with the form of the language in use among the educated middle and upper classes in southern England, and surveys carried out in the US also suggest a class orientation. In both countries, a desire for guidance tends to predominate among the linguistically less secure, especially the lower-middle classes, while demands that 'good' usage be maintained may come from all levels of society, but particularly from those who feel secure in the prevailing standard forms and look to authorities on usage as much for reassurance and support as for guidance. Guidance is therefore based on what is thought to be acceptable to educated users of English, and is often reinforced by the institutional authority associated with a famous scholar or publisher (Webster, Fowler, Merriam Webster, and the like).

Criteria for criticism. Criteria traditionally invoked in the criticism of usage include analogy (or precedent), logic, etymology (usually Greek and Latin, rarely Germanic), and questions of taste and social acceptability:

Analogy. Reference to analogy is the most influential criterion, because analogy underlies the working of all language. Often, proponents of a particular usage tend to choose the analogies that suit their preference: for example, the stress patterns *conTROversy* and *forMIDable* are widely deplored and *CONtroversy* and *FORmidable* favoured, following the analogy of *MAtrimony* and *MANageable* rather than *orTHOgraphy* and *aMENable*. *KiLOmetre/kiLOmeter* follows the analogy of *speeDOMeter* rather than that of *KILogram* and *CENTimetre/CENTimeter*. Inflection also follows analogy: reference to two *Germanies* follows the example of *Ptolemies* and *Maries* and the behaviour of countable nouns in -*y* generally, but the form *Germanys* also occurs. See ANALOGY.

Logic. Appeals are regularly made to logic: for example, in determining what a group of words ought to mean from its constituents. Such appeals work when logic and standard usage happen to coincide, but can often fail because the use of language is not always amenable to logic: for example, *Aren't I* as a tag question is widely regarded in BrE as the proper form, and *Amn't I*, though eminently logical, is discounted as childish, while *ain't I* is considered either slovenly or archaic. The double negative, as in *I didn't do nothing*, has been condemned since the 18c solely on the ground that two negatives make a positive; before the 18c, the logic worked the other way in regarding the succession of negatives as cumulative in effect. Similarly, the grammatical treatment of collective nouns (*committee, government*, etc.), if based on logic, should require a singular verb, but usage often favours a plural verb to emphasize the collective sense of the word: *The committee have not yet reached agreement*.

Etymology. Appeals made to etymology to defend the language against change rarely satisfy by themselves, because they fail to recognize the independent development of words: for example, Latinate words such as *formula* and *stadium* have vernacular plurals *formulas, stadiums* that are often rejected by purists in favour of *formulae, stadia*, as if origin should be the predominant consideration. These are, however, adopted words, and may be treated on the analogy of words in English rather than Latin; *ultimatum* is so treated and few propose *ultimata* as a plural rather than *ultimatums*.

Personal preference. Criteria based on intuition, personal preference, or what one thinks educated users prefer, are common and may be supported by appeals to such further criteria as euphony ('*Biofeedback* sounds ugly and clumsy'), good taste ('No literate person says *irregardless* and *for free*'), and chauvinism ('Our language is rich enough; it doesn't need words like *chutzpah* and *shlep*'). Attitudes towards, and avoidance of, clichés such as *conspicuous by one's absence* and *at the present time* are a highly subjective matter that belongs in this category.

For all these reasons, it is difficult to evaluate usage objectively. In the view of linguists and lexicographers, evaluation must depend on sound evidence of what constitutes current established use; if not, it tends to become an argument for individual custom or preference. Establishing current majority usage is not as straightforward as it sounds, even in the age of mass media, because it rests on the need to be sure of what constitutes currency and majority. Until the development of databases, scholarly evidence consisted of collections of citations, generally from printed sources. Depending on the range of sources studied, the evidence has tended to have a literary or formal bias; usage criticism based on it does not therefore take adequate account of ordinary English spoken and written in everyday communication. Even computer corpora are collected mainly from the language in print, although conversational texts do exist, notably in the Survey of English Usage at University College London, which aims at a million words available for on-line analysis. Grammars based on this kind of evidence have been published, but in general the traditional sources of usage prevail.

Usage controversies. There are always issues of special concern; these do not, however, remain constant. The split infinitive has been a controversial matter since the 18c, but is now of less importance; ending a sentence with a preposition was once considered a grave offence in formal writing, but is now generally accepted as a common feature of informal usage. Other controversies prove to be ephemeral, usually overwhelmed by the weight of actual usage: for example, *nice* was once strongly deplored in the now dominant sense 'agreeable', 'pleasant', in favour of the sense 'precise'. On the other hand, the double or multiple negative has long been deplored and is generally still regarded as uneducated, although it is used by many speakers of English throughout the world. A good example of the unpredictable and often capricious nature of usage controversies is the current issue of *hopefully* as a sentence adverb: *Hopefully, it won't rain tomorrow.* Well-established uses of other words as sentence adverbs, such as *Clearly,*

there is no case to answer, and *Generally, the weather is fine in July,* are by contrast hardly noticed. So a particular use has been singled out for disapproval while others like it are passed over, and this is typical of many controversies. Usage controversies fall into several categories, with some overlap: *pronunciation,* including accent, stress, and the relationship of sound to spelling; *grammar,* including collocation, concord, and word order; *spelling and morphology,* including problems of inflection and confusable words; and *vocabulary,* especially with regard to the choice and meaning of words.

Pronunciation. Most pronunciation controversies concern *stress,* such as the examples *controversy* and *formidable* mentioned above. An older example is *abDOMen* (the second syllable stressed and pronounced like *dome*), now resolved in favour of *ABdomen.* Other current examples are *dispute* (where stress on the first syllable of the noun is deprecated but common), *harass* (where the same applies in BrE to stress on the second syllable; this, however, is standard in AmE), and *kilometre,* which is pronounced in AmE and increasingly in BrE with stress on the second syllable, by (false) analogy with *speedometer* and related words. Problems also arise with vowel quality in words like *deity, spontaneity* and *homograph, homosexual.* In general preferences are based on what educated speakers are thought to prefer. The pronunciation of foreign words also causes difficulty, as with *garage* and *apartheid.* Recourse is often had to the pronunciation in the original language, but this can be a misleading criterion because the original pronunciation is usually based on rules and procedures that are inherently different from the phonology of English. Examples of loanwords now fully absorbed phonetically into English are *cadet* and *coupon*; sometimes a 'foreign' pronunciation is revived, as with *turquoise* and *valet.*

Grammar. Two grammatical categories account for a high proportion of disputes: *collocation* (the constructions with which words are assembled into phrases and sentences), and *concord* (the way in which words of one part of speech agree with others). Among the most troublesome collocational issues is the word that follows *different.* In recent years, advice in usage guides has moved from prescribing *from* exclusively (as the traditionally preferred educated usage) to allowing and even advocating *from, to,* and *than.* The evidence suggests that *different than* is now the majority usage in North America, *different to* the majority usage in Britain, while *different from* retains a powerful influence on more conservative speakers and writers. This is because, with a classical model, *different* is seen as an extension of *differ,* and thought to require the same construction (*differ from*, and so *different from*). The same classical model applies to the construction required with *none*. Traditionally, *none* has been taken to represent *no(t) one* and should therefore be followed by a singular verb, as in *none of them is here* rather than *none of them are here*. This position is not, however, supported by actual usage over several centuries nor by many current usage guides, which advocate a choice of singular or plural according to sense: *none of them are here* when the sense is collective, *none of them is here* when the emphasis is on individuals.

Many grammatical problems have to be seen in the context of *register* or the kind of language being used. In formal English, especially in literature and official documents, grammar is usually given a higher value than idiom and ease of communication; in informal English, especially everyday speech, established custom is more predominant, because fluent and easy communication is the main consideration. None the less, the more prescriptive guidance on usage still tends to give insufficient weight to this factor. Especially relevant are problems of word order, where there is less scope or need for precision in ordinary spoken English. The position of *only* has been the subject of much comment over many years. In formal and precise English the difference between *I only found them by chance* and *I found them only by chance* may be significant, but in speech it matters less, because intonation will usually clarify the sense.

Spelling and morphology. The role of usage in spelling is complex, and forms the basis on which dictionaries assess and record variants and state preferences, as well as the basis of approved practice in matters such as inflection and hyphenation, where English is unpredictable. The eighth edition of the *Concise Oxford Dictionary* (1990) records many changes in hyphenation practice, including *benchmark*, *birdsong*, *figurehead*, *lawbreaker*, and *scriptwriter*, all previously hyphenated. These changes have been made on the basis of usage, and there is no theory of hyphenation beyond what is discernible in the evidence. This shows, in particular, that there is an increasing tendency to put two single-syllable elements together as single words, as with *benchmark* and *birdsong*. In other cases, practice varies and defies attempts at classification. The rules of *inflection* are also based on established practice, which is unpredictable, as in the matter of doubling a final consonant in forms such as *budgeted* and *travelled* (but *paralleled*). On the other hand, usage has to be critically assessed and tempered by considerations such as analogy and patterns of form. Variant spellings are not admitted in dictionaries simply on the grounds that they are known to be used; that would admit forms such as *accomodate and *mischievious, which are regarded as incorrect. They are rejected because they do not have sufficient authority in sources deemed to conform to standard English. On the other hand, Samuel Johnson's deviant spelling *despatch* for *dispatch* was established by its inclusion in his dictionary, and rapidly confirmed by usage afterwards. Borderline cases are *alright* (for *all right*; compare *altogether*, *almighty*), *nearby* (still resisted in its one-word form, especially as an adverb), and *onto* (resisted in printed BrE, despite its frequency in casual use, the analogy of *into*, and its standard use in AmE).

Vocabulary. There is a long-established, widespread belief that words have a 'true' meaning, usually based on etymology. If this were so, the earliest senses of all words would be the only proper senses: a *camera* would denote a room, not a machine, and a *doctor* would be a learned person, not a physician. Change in the meaning of words is the signal most clearly discernible to ordinary users that the language is changing. This is generally recognized and accepted as a historical phenomenon when the results are convenient to present-day users, but change as it happens is often resisted: *anticipate* in the sense 'expect', *aggravate* in the sense 'annoy', and *transpire* in the sense 'happen' (all disapproved of in current guidance on usage). Resistance is particularly strong where change occurs, or is perceived as occurring, in confusable words, such as *disinterested* (impartial) and *infer* (deduce). The senses just given are regarded as standard, while other senses (uninterested, imply) are often deprecated, despite equally sound historical credentials. Maintaining the distinctions between *disinterested* and *uninterested* and *infer* and *imply* is considered useful, in the same way as preserving the distinct senses of *childish* and *childlike*, *alternate* and *alternative*, and *regretful* and *regrettable* is useful. Usage guidance also deals with more accidental confusions of unrelated words, such as *sinecure/cynosure* and *prevaricate/procrastinate*. In all these cases, the purpose is to retain a distinction in the interests of clear meaning, and this is arguably the most sound basis on which any usage guidance relating to words can depend.

Social and cultural factors in usage. An important element of usage is the degree of social acceptability of certain terms and uses; these vary from age to age, and are matters of social or moral concern rather than of linguistic correctness. In the 16c, titles and forms of address such as *gentleman*, *master*, and *woman* had to be used with care because of the sensitivities arising from social status. *Chinaman*, once standard, is now regarded as offensive, as are *Eskimo* and *Mohammedan*. The preferred terms are now *Chinese*, *Inuit*, and *Muslim*. A far-reaching contemporary concern arises from the feminist movement and its wish to avoid the perpetuation of sex-based prejudice in language: for example, in the titles *Mrs*, *Miss*, relating to marital status. The neutral replacement *Ms* was originally based on the prescription of a social group on moral grounds, was taken up by some style guides in the US, and came to be widely endorsed as socially convenient. Such prescription succeeds only rarely. Despite the invention of a variety of experimental forms, there is still no widely agreed gender-neutral third-person pronoun to replace generic *he* or stand for the often awkward *he or she*. In informal spoken English, and in some written English, the plural form *they* has emerged (or re-emerged, having been common though non-standard since the 16c) to fill the need, as in *If anyone calls, tell them to come back later*. Received opinion may regard this as bad grammar, but it shows that as grammar changes with usage a new model of grammar has to emerge. See USAGE GUIDANCE AND CRITICISM. [GRAMMAR, LANGUAGE, STYLE, USAGE].   R.E.A.

Crystal, David. 1984. *Who Cares about English Usage?* London: Penguin.

Fowler, Henry W. (ed. Sir Ernest Gowers). 1965. *A Dictionary of Modern English Usage*. 2nd edition. Oxford: University Press.

Gilman, E. Ward (ed.). 1989. *Webster's Dictionary of English Usage*. Springfield, Mass.: Merriam Webster.

Leith, D. 1983. *A Social History of English*. London: Routledge.

Milroy, James, & Milroy, Lesley. 1985. *Authority in Language*. London: Routledge.

Nash, Walter. 1986. *English Usage*. London: Routledge.

Orwell, George. 1946. 'Politics and the English Language', in *Collected Essays, Journalism and Letters* (Vol. iv, ed. S. Orwell & I. Angus). London: Secker & Warburg (1968).

Partridge, Eric. 1942. *Usage and Abusage: A Guide to Good English*. London: Hamish Hamilton.

Quirk, Randolph. 1968. *The Use of English*. 2nd edition. London: Longman.

Todd, Loreto, & Hancock, Ian. 1986. *International English Usage*. London: Croom Helm.

The usage theme.

ABBREVIATION, ABUSAGE, ACADEMIC USAGE, ACADEMY, ACCENT, ACCENT BAR, ACCEPTABILITY, ACRONYM, ADVERBIAL, (A)ESTHETICS, AFFECTATION, AMERICAN HERITAGE DICTIONARY, AMERICAN LANGUAGE (THE), APOSTROPHE[1], APPROPRIATENESS/APPROPRIACY, AUTHORITY, BAD ENGLISH, BAD LANGUAGE, BAFFLEGAB, BARBARISM, BLASPHEMY, BULL(SHIT), BUREAUCRATESE, CANADIAN STYLE GUIDES, CANT, CATACHRESIS, CIRCUMLOCUTION, CITATION, CLASSICAL ENDING,

CLICHÉ, COMPLETE PLAIN WORDS (THE), COMPUTER USAGE, CONFUSAGE, CONFUSIBLE, CORRECT, CURSING, DANGLING PARTICIPLE, DICTIONARY OF CATCH PHRASES, DICTIONARY OF MODERN ENGLISH USAGE, DICTIONARY OF SLANG AND UNCONVENTIONAL ENGLISH, DIRECT AND INDIRECT SPEECH, DOUBLESPEAK, DOUBLESPEAK AWARD, DOUBLETHINK, EDUCATED ENGLISH, ELEMENTS OF STYLE (THE), ELLIPSIS, ENCYCLOPAEDIA BRITANNICA, EXPLETIVE, FIXED, FOREIGNISM, FOUL LANGUAGE, FOWLER, GENERIC PRONOUN, GOLDEN BULL AWARDS, GOOD ENGLISH, GOOD USAGE, GRAMMAR, JARGON, LATIN TAG, LEGALESE, LEGAL USAGE, MEDICANT, MISTAKE, NON-STANDARD, NORM, OBFUSCATION, OBSCURANTISM, OFFICIALESE, ORWELL, PARTICIPLE, PARTRIDGE, PASSIVE, PEDANT, PLAIN, POP GRAMMARIAN, PREPOSITION, PSYCHOBABBLE, QUOTATION MARKS, READER'S DIGEST, SMUT, SOCIETY FOR PURE ENGLISH, SOLECISM, SPLIT INFINITIVE, STANDARD, SURVEY OF ENGLISH USAGE, SWEARING, USAGE, USAGE GUIDANCE AND CRITICISM, WEBSTER'S DICTIONARY OF ENGLISH USAGE, WH-SOUND.

USAGE GUIDANCE AND CRITICISM. The concept of usage and usage criticism in English dates from the 17c, when the first grammars of the language were written by William Bullokar (1586), Ben Jonson (1640), John Wallis (1658), and others. A more critical approach to the use of English emerged with literary figures such as John Dryden, Joseph Addison, Richard Steele, and Jonathan Swift. Bishop Robert Lowth's *Short Introduction to English Grammar* was published in 1762; it attempted to show that good use of language could be determined by the application of rules, and it became the largely unacknowledged source of the better-known work of Lindley Murray, an American grammarian who lived in England and wrote the school grammars *English Grammar*, *English Exercises*, and others, published from 1795 onwards. Robert Baker's *Reflections on the English Language* (1770) was one of the earliest works that would now be regarded as a usage book. The genre developed in the 19c, with Henry Alford (Dean of Canterbury) in Britain, author of *A Plea for the Queen's English* (1864), and Edward S. Gould (*Good English*, 1867), and Richard Grant White (*Words and Their Uses*, 1870) in America. Since the turn of the century, usage criticism in print has proliferated, in the form of reference books, usually arranged alphabetically as dictionaries, and columns on language in newspapers.

Another strand of usage criticism is represented by George Orwell. Explicitly in a number of essays, and implicitly in his novel *Nineteen Eight-Four* (1949), Orwell criticized language use that he saw as artificial and bureaucratic, and remote from the language of ordinary people. In his view, it had the effect of confusing and obscuring rather than communicating effectively, for example by writing 'in my opinion it is a not unjustifiable assumtion that . . .' instead of 'I think . . .'. He was not attempting to set standards of ordinary usage, but was condemning authoritarianism, seeing misuse of standard English as its instrument. This theme has also been pursued—though not with the same political implications—by Ernest Gowers and Ifor Evans (see below), and others, and in the work of societies promoting the cause of 'plain' or 'direct' English. See PLAIN ENGLISH, SOCIETY FOR PURE ENGLISH.

British usage books. The most famous and controversial British usage book is H. W. Fowler's *A Dictionary of Modern English Usage* (1926), in which he developed ideas presented earlier in the thematically organized *The King's English* (1906). *MEU* is a blend of prescription, tolerance, and idiosyncrasy, and was the first usage book of its kind to be organized as a dictionary, thereby departing from the traditional codified grammar. It was also the first to include the name *usage* in its title. Fowler wrote about what he thought usage should be, not about what it was, and his evidence, as far as can be judged from the citations in the book, was selected to show where he thought users of English went wrong. None the less, it is to Fowler's credit that he avoided (especially misplaced) pedantry, as in his article on the *split infinitive*. The book was published in a second edition in 1965 with revisions by Sir Ernest Gowers, a senior civil servant who twenty years earlier had attempted to persuade the British Civil Service to avoid pretentious and often incomprehensible jargon in *Plain Words* (1948), in later editions *The Complete Plain Words*. Other works on usage include Eric Partridge's *Usage and Abusage* (1942, with many revisions), B. Ifor Evans's *The Use of English* (1949), G. H. Vallins's *Good English* (1951) and *Better English* (1953), Logan Pearsall Smith's *Words and Idioms* (1925), A. P. Herbert's *What a Word* (1935), and Ivor Brown's *Words in Our Time* (1958) and other works. Current guides include Martin H. Manser's *Bloomsbury Good Word Guide* (1988), Sidney Greenbaum and Janet Whitcut's *Longman Guide to English Usage* (1988), *The Oxford Guide to English Usage* (1983), and John O. E. Clark's *Word Perfect* (Harrap, 1987).

Today, no major British reference publisher can afford to lack a usage guide, and some boast several, each with its own philosophy and style. In some cases, guidance is associated with a publisher's *house style*, as in *The Oxford Dictionary for Writers and Editors* (1981), a work largely concerned with spelling and hyphenation. Most current usage manuals are written by grammarians and lexicographers in alphabetical format and concentrate their advice on specific points, usually with made-up examples of use; an exception is *The Oxford Miniguide to English Usage* (1983), which organizes its material into thematic sections covering grammar, vocabulary, etc., and bases its advice on usage exemplified by established writers, mostly of fiction. None of these, however, has attained the level of authority achieved by Fowler and by Partridge.

American usage books. Usage criticism in the US has tended to be in the conservative, prescriptive tradition of Lindley Murray, whose works remained in print to the end of the 19c. Standard works include Bergen and Cornelia Evans's *A Dictionary of Contemporary American Usage* (1957), Wilson Follett's *Modern American Usage* (1966), which derives its format and approach from Fowler and Fowler's US adaptation by M. Nicholson as *A Dictionary of American English Usage* (1957), and William and Mary Morris's *Harper Dictionary of Contemporary Usage* (1975, 1985), which drew on a usage panel of 166 consultants. A recent work that examines a wide range of issues, quoting extensively from printed sources, is *Webster's Dictionary of English Usage* (1989). H. W. Horwill's *Modern American Usage* (1935; 2nd edition, 1944) is primarily intended to help Britons with AmE, and Norman W. Schur's *British English A to Zed* (1987) is intended to help Americans with BrE.

Usage criticism in newspapers. Usage criticism and guidance is provided on a regular basis as a column in newspapers and other periodicals. The doyen of usage columnists in the US in the late 20c is William Safire of the *New York Times*, whose articles are widely syndicated. American journalism has also been the foundation of systematic usage and style guides, notably Theodore Bernstein's *The Careful Writer* (1965) and William Strunk Jr. and E. B. White's *The Elements of Style*, known affectionately as 'the little book' (3rd edition, 1979; earlier editions 1959, 1972). In Britain, Philip Howard in *The Times*, John Silverlight in *The Observer*, and Robert Burchfield in *The Sunday Times* have a more limited following, often seeming to entertain and inform the converted rather than advising the doubtful. A feature of some columns is a response to queries from readers, on which the columnists provide personal comment along with quotations from dictionaries and usage guides.

Usage panels and usage notes. Current general dictionaries of English often include usage notes attached to individual entries. The first such work to employ a team of advisers was the Random House *American College Dictionary* (1947). The practice was extended by Houghton Mifflin in the *American Heritage Dictionary*

(1969), whose usage notes were compiled from replies to questionnaires from a panel of consultants including linguists, writers, journalists, and broadcasters. The results are often colourful and distinctive, as at *hopefully*: 'this usage is by now such a bugbear to traditionalists that it is best avoided on grounds of civility, if not logic' (2nd edition, 1982). The editor of the *AHD* was William Morris; with Mary Morris he took the panel approach further in the *Harper Dictionary of Contemporary Usage* (above), in which a range of controversies was treated with reference to the opinions of panellists, often quoted in full or given statistically. The panellists included writers, journalists, broadcasters, and academics, with many famous names among them, such as Isaac Asimov, W. H. Auden, Saul Bellow, Anthony Burgess, Alistair Cooke, Walter Cronkite, Jessica Mitford, and William Zinsser. The method affords flexibility, with different levels of usage distinguished. Panellists' comments are varied and colourful: 'The English language is the finest tool for communication ever invented. Since it is used indiscriminately by hundreds of millions, it is no wonder that it is badly misused so often' (Isaac Asimov); 'The English language began to curl up and die, instead of being regenerated, sometime after the Second World War, until now it has become like, wow!, you know' (Douglas Watt). The use of usage notes is now common in dictionaries on both sides of the Atlantic, for native speakers and foreign learners alike.

Kinds of guidance. The nature, style, and content of the guidance provided by usage guides over the years is illustrated in the following sequence of advice and comment on a classic controversy, the *split infinitive*: 'to boldly go' as opposed to 'boldly to go' and 'to go boldly'. The comments range from 1851 to 1983.

Of the infinitive verb and its preposition *to*, some grammarians say that they must never be separated by an adverb. It is true, that the adverb is, in general, more elegantly placed before the preposition than after it; but, possibly, the latter position of it may sometimes contribute to perspicuity, which is more essential than elegance (Goold Brown, *The Grammar of English Grammars*, US, 1851).

A correspondent states as his own usage, and defends, the insertion of an adverb between the sign of the infinitive mood and the verb. He gives as an instance, '*to scientifically illustrate*'. But surely this is a practice entirely unknown to English speakers and writers. It seems to me, that we ever regard the *to* of the infinitive as inseparable from its verb, and when we have a choice between two forms of expression, 'scientifically to illustrate', and 'to illustrate scientifically', there seems no good reason for flying in the face of common usage (Henry Alford, *A Plea for the Queen's English*, UK, 1864).

If you do not immediately suppress the person who takes it upon himself to lay down the law almost every day in your columns on the subject of literary composition, I will give taking up the *Chronicle*. . . . Your fatuous specialist . . . is now beginning to rebuke 'second-rate newspapers' for using such phrases as 'to suddenly go' and 'to boldly say'. I ask you, Sir, to put this man out . . . without, however, interfering with his perfect freedom of choice between 'to suddenly go', 'to go suddenly' and 'suddenly to go' (George Bernard Shaw, in a letter to the *Chronicle*, UK, 2 Sept. 1892).

A constant and unguarded use of it is not to be encouraged. . . . On the other hand, it may be said that its occasional use is of advantage in circumstances where it is desired to avoid ambiguity (C. T. Onions, *An Advanced English Syntax*, UK, 1904).

The English-speaking world may be divided into (1) those who neither know nor care what a split infinitive is; (2) those who do not know, but care very much; (3) those who know and condemn; (4) those who know and approve; and (5) those who know and distinguish. . . . Those upon whom the fear of infinitive-splitting sits heavy should remember that to give conclusive evidence, by distortions, of misconceiving the nature of the split infinitive is far more damaging to their literary pretensions than an actual lapse could be. . . . The attitude of those who know and distinguish is something like this: We admit that separation of *to* from its infinitive . . . is not in itself desirable, and we shall not gratuitously say either 'to mortally wound' or 'to mortally be wounded'; but we are not foolish enough to confuse the latter with 'to be mortally wounded', which is blameless English. . . . We will split infinitives sooner than be ambiguous or artificial; more than that, we will freely admit that sufficient recasting will get rid of any split infinitive without involving either of those faults, and yet reserve to ourselves the right of deciding in each case whether recasting is worth while (H. W. Fowler, *A Dictionary of Modern English Usage*, UK, 1926).

The name is misleading, for the preposition *to* no more belongs to the infinitive as a necessary part of it, than the definite article belongs to the substantive, and no one would think of calling 'the good man' a split substantive (Otto Jespersen, *Essentials of English Grammar*, UK, 1933).

(1) There is no doubt that the rule [against the split infinitive] at present holds sway, and on my principle the official has no choice but to conform (Ernest Gowers, *Plain Words*, UK, 1941). (2) A friend whose opinion I value has reproached me for this. . . . I ought, he tells me, to have the courage of my convictions. I ought to say about the split infinitive . . . that it is right for the official to give a lead in freeing writers from this fetish. . . . My friend may be right. Rebels will find themselves in good company (Ernest Gowers, *The Complete Plain Words*, UK, 1954).

Avoid the split infinitive wherever possible; but if it is the clearest and the most natural construction, use it boldly. The angels are on our side (Eric Partridge, *Usage and Abusage*, UK, 1947).

The temptation to split an infinitive is extremely rare in spoken English, because the voice supplies the stress needed by the unsplit form or conceals by a pause the awkwardness of the adverb placed before or after. It is in written work that splitting is called for, and desk sets should include small hatchets of silver or gold for the purpose (Wilson Follett, *Modern American Usage*, US, 1966).

The split infinitive is another trick of rhetoric in which the ear must be quicker than the handbook. Some infinitives seem to improve on being split, just as a stick of round stovewood does (Strunk & White, *The Elements of Style*, 3rd edition, US, 1979).

It is often said that an infinitive should never be split. This is an artificial rule that can produce unnecessarily contorted sentences. Rather, it is recommended that a split infinitive should be avoided by placing the adverb before or after the infinitive, unless this leads to clumsiness or ambiguity. If it does, one should either allow the split infinitive to stand, or recast the sentence (E. S. C. Weiner, *The Oxford Miniguide to English Usage*, UK, 1983).

Conclusion. With the current proliferation of usage books, publishers will need to strike a balance between two kinds of authority: that based on received opinion (backed up by their name and the names of their authors) and that derived from intellectual argument. This argument will in its turn depend on a model of English grammar that has yet to evolve.

See (A)ESTHETICS, COMPLETE PLAIN WORDS (THE), CRITICISM, DICTIONARY OF MODERN ENGLISH USAGE, ELEMENTS OF STYLE (THE), FOWLER, GOWERS, KING'S ENGLISH (THE), WEBSTER'S DICTIONARY OF ENGLISH USAGE. [GRAMMAR, MEDIA, REFERENCE, STYLE, USAGE].

R.E.A.

USAGE GURU. See POP GRAMMARIAN.

US ENGLISH. (1) An occasional term for the English language as used in the US. See AMERICAN ENGLISH, UNITED STATES ENGLISH. (2) The name of an organization formed in 1983 to promote an amendment to the US constitution making English the official language of the republic. See ENGLISH LANGUAGE AMENDMENT. [AMERICAS, VARIETY].   T.McA.

USIA, USIS. See UNITED STATES INFORMATION AGENCY.

UTTERANCE [15c: from *utter*, from Middle Dutch *ūteren* (Modern *uiteren*) to show, make known, speak, probably introduced as a term of commerce: compare the archaic sense *utter* to put on the market, dispose of by sale]. (1) Speech; the power of speech; an act of uttering or saying; something uttered or said; a word, phrase, sentence, etc., especially taken in isolation. (2) In linguistics, a term for something spoken that is more or less equivalent syntactically to a written or printed sentence. See SEMANTICS, SENTENCE, SPEECH ACT. [GRAMMAR, SPEECH].   T.McA.

UVULA [14c: Latin, little grape]. The anatomical term for the soft, fleshy protuberance at the back of the mouth, hanging down from the velum. The adjective *uvular* describes sounds made by raising and retracting the tongue towards the uvula: for example, the uvular fricative /r/, the *r grasseyé* of Parisian French. See ORGANS OF SPEECH, R-SOUNDS. [SPEECH].

G.K.

UVULAR *R*. See BURR, R-SOUNDS, UVULA.

V

V, v [Called 'vee']. The 22nd letter of the Roman alphabet as used for English. It originated, along with *F, U, W, Y,* in the Phoenician consonant symbol *waw*, which the Greeks adopted first with the form *V,* then as *Y* (called *upsilon*: that is, *Y-psilón*, bare or simple *Y*). The Etruscans and then the Romans adopted the first symbol. In Latin, *V* was a vowel letter, but in Romance languages such as French and Italian its value before a second vowel evolved to the modern consonantal pronunciation /v/. Until the 17c, *v* was ambiguous in English, capable of representing the sounds of both *u* and *v*. Further ambiguity arose with the introduction of the letter *W*, which originated as *VV*. This prevented the doubling of *v* in the same way as other consonants are doubled in English, except in such rare and recent forms as *revving/revved*.

Sound value. (1) In English, *v* nearly always represents a voiced labio-dental fricative. It occurs word-initially (*valley*), medially (*even*) and finally, usually supported by a following *e* (*active, drove; rev*). (2) Over centuries, there has been a tendency for medial *v* to become a vowel or disappear: *hawk* from Old English *heafoc*, the *f* pronounced /v/, *head* from Old English *heafod*, *curfew* from Anglo-Norman *coeverfu*, *kerchief* from Old French *cuevre-chef*, *lady* from Old English *hlæfdige*, *laundry* from Old French *lavandier*, *lord* from Old English *hlaford*, *manure* from Anglo-Norman *mainoverer*, *poor* from Middle English *povere*. (3) The once colloquial and now poetic forms *e'en, e'er, ne'er, o'er* mark the omitted *v* with an apostrophe.

Word-initial *V*. (1) In Old English, initial /v/ did not generally occur, and therefore *v* was not written word-initially. Latin *vannus* was for example respelt *fan*, and most words currently spelt with initial *v* are of later Romance derivation: *vacant, vaccine, vague, vain, valley, value,* *valve, vanish, vapour, vary, vase, vassal, vault, vegetable, vehicle, vein, velvet, venom, vent, verb, vermin, very, vest, veto, vex, vibrate, vice, victory, view, vigil, vigour, vile, village, vine, viola, virgin, virus, vision, vital, vivid, vocal, volley, volume, vomit, vortex, vote, vowel, vulgar.* (2) Exceptions have arisen from dialects in which *f-* became *v-* (*vane, vat, vixen*) or are exotic loans (*vaishya, Valhalla, Vanuatu, Viking, Vladimir, voltaic*). (3) *V* does not normally occur syllable-initially before other consonants, *vroom* representing a conspicuous break with customary spelling patterns.

Word-final *V*. (1) Except for a few modern slang or clipped forms such as *lav, rev, spiv, gov, luv, v* does not occur as a final letter in English. (2) Where /v/ occurs as a final sound, as in *have, give, live, love,* the present spelling became fixed before the final *e* fell silent. Although final *e* may indicate a preceding long vowel (*save, eve, dive, rove*), that vowel value is often already indicated by a digraph (*waive, leave, sleeve, receive, believe, groove*), or a modified value is indicated by *r* (*starve, swerve, curve*), and the final *e* again serves simply to camouflage final *v*.

Double *V*. Medial *v* is found equally in words derived from Old English and Romance sources: *anvil, envy, heavy, marvel, over.* Because *vv* was already adopted as an early form of *w*, English did not double *v* even to indicate a preceding short vowel, as is common with other consonants (compare *comma/coma*), and ambiguity as to the length of a preceding vowel letter resulted. The spelling gives no indication of the differing vowel values in: *having/shaving, seven/even, driven/enliven, hover/rover, lover/mover.* More recently coined words not normally used in formal prose are under no such inhibition: *bovver, navvy, revving, skivvy* are all written with double *v*.

THE CAPITAL LETTER						THE SMALL LETTER				
EARLY FORMS				CURRENT FORMS		EARLY FORMS			CURRENT FORMS	
Phoenician	Greek	Etruscan	Roman (Latin)	roman	italic	Roman cursive	Roman uncial	Carolingian minuscule	roman	italic
Y	ꟼY	V	V	V	*V*	u	Y	u	v	*v*

Miscellaneous. (1) *V* does not normally occur after *u*, since until *u* and *v* were regularly distinguished, the sequence *uv* could equally be read as *vu*, *vv*, *uu* (but note for example *uvular*). A preceding *u*-sound is therefore commonly written *o*, as in *dove*, *love*, *glove*, *move*, *cover*, *discovery*. However, a modern mock-spelling such as *luv* for *love* doubly flouts the conventions, with preceding *u* and final *v*. (2) In the 16c, *nevewe* was respelt *nephew*, and now usually has a spelling pronunciation with /f/ (but compare French *neveu*). Similarly, *Stephen/Steven* are variants, both with a /v/ pronunciation, and etymological variation between *b* and *v* occurs in *devil/ diabolical*. (3) Oral variation between *v/w* formerly occurred in Cockney: Sam Weller in Dickens's *Pickwick Papers* (1836–7) spells his name *Veller*, and his father refers to the letter *v* as *we*. See ALPHABET, COCKNEY, F, LETTER[1], SPELLING, U, W. [WRITING]. C.U., T.MCA., E.W.

VAGUE WORD [1980s]. An occasional semi-technical term for a word of imprecise reference, such as *thingummy*, *widget*. There are two broad types: (1) Fillers for moments of haste or forgetfulness: *Put the thingummy on the whatsit.* They are usually casual, often have whimsical spellings, and may be regionally distinct: BrE *doodah*, AmE *doodad*. They may be: phrase words based on a question (*whadyamecallit*, *what's-his-name/face*, *whatsit*, *whoosis*), variants of *thing* (BrE *thingie*, *thingummy*, BrE *thingummybob* AmE *thingamabob*, BrE *thingummyjig* AmE *thingamajig*, AmE *thinkumthankum*, *chingus*, *dingbat*, *dinglefoozie*, *dingus*, *ringamajiggen*, *ringamajizzer*, *majig*, *majigger*), extensions of *do* (*doings*, *doodah/doodad*, *doflickety*, *dofunnies*, *doowillie*, *doowhistle*). (2) Pseudo-technical but usefully non-specific terms: *Suppose you suddenly need 50,000 widgets.* They tend to be plays on numbers (*umpteen*, *zillion*), reduplications of *so* and *such* (*old so-and-so*, *such-and-such a person*), forms containing *g*- and *j*-sounds that suggest a tool or piece of equipment (*gadget*, *gidget*, *gimmick*, *gismo*, *gizwatch*, *goofus*, *gubbins*, *jiggus*, *widget*), or made up of 'rustic' nonsense syllables: *boozenannie*, *hootmalalie*, *oojah*, *wingdoodle*. Virtually by definition, all such words are open to improvisation and miscegenation. See NONSENSE, NUMBER. [WORD]. T.MCA.

VANUATU. Official title: *Republic of Vanuatu.* A country of Oceania and member of the Commonwealth, consisting of twelve main islands and 70 islets. Capital: Port-Vila. Currency: vatu (100 centimes). Economy: agriculture, fishing. Population: 142,000 (1988), 198,000 (projection for 2000). Ethnicity: 91% Melanesian (known as *ni-Vanuatu*), 3% French, 3% Polynesian. Languages: English, French, Bislama (all official), and ethnic languages. Education: primary 86%, secondary 11%, tertiary 2%, literacy 30%. Until 1980 known as the *New Hebrides*, jointly administered since the late 19c by Britain and France. See BEACH LA MAR, BISLAMA, ENGLISH, FRENCH, MELANESIAN PIDGIN ENGLISH. [NAME, OCEANIA, VARIETY]. T.MCA.

VARIANT [14c: from Latin *varians/variantis* changing (in colour, etc.). Compare VARIETY]. (1) Different in some aspects while the same or similar in others: *a variant reading of a text*; AmE *color* and BrE *colour* are *variant spellings* of the same word, each conforming to different national norms. (2) A similar but distinct form: the words *despatch* and *dispatch* are *spelling variants*, the first common in BrE, the second common in AmE; the Scots word *warsle* can be regarded as a variant of standard English *wrestle*. Compare VERSION. [LANGUAGE, VARIETY]. T.MCA.

VARIETIES OF ENGLISH AROUND THE WORLD, short form *VEAW*. A series of scholarly studies of the English language, edited by Manfred Görlach (first at the U. of Heidelberg then at the U. of Köln, Germany) and from 1979 to 1982 published by Groos (Heidelberg), thereafter by John Benjamins (Amsterdam & Philadelphia). The constituent titles are intended as both reference books and teaching manuals for use in departments of linguistics and English. Topics include dialects, registers, national forms of English, and pidgins and creoles. There are two subseries: (1) The *Text Series*, each title illustrating the range of English in an area by means of texts. Volumes include: *Cameroon* (Loreto Todd, 1982), *Central American English* (John Holm, 1982), *Glasgow* (Caroline Macafee, 1983), *Singapore and Malaysia* (John Platt, Heidi Weber, & Mian Lian Ho, 1983), and *The Southwest of England* (Martyn F. Wakelin, 1986). Individual volumes contain: introductions to the social history of the communities concerned, to attitudes, norms, and social and regional variations; selected and annotated texts; bibliographies and glossaries. Most are accompanied by cassettes linked to texts in the books. (2) The *General Series*, which contains collections of scholarly articles, revised dissertations, bibliographies, and other material for academic research and teaching. Volumes published to date include: *The Standard in South African English and its Social History* (L. W. Lanham & C. A. MacDonald, 1979, 1984), *Issues in English Creoles: Papers from the 1975 Hawaii Conference* (ed. R. R. Day, 1980), *A Bibliography of Writings on Varieties of English,*

1965–1983 (ed. Wolfgang Viereck, Edgar W. Schneider, & M. Görlach, 1984), *Focus on: England and Wales* (ed. W. Viereck, 1985), *Focus on: Scotland* (ed. M. Görlach, 1985), *Dialect and Accent in Industrial West Yorkshire*, (K. M. Petyt, 1985), *Chicano English: An Ethnic Contact Dialect* (J. Penfield & J. Ornstein-Galicia, 1985), and *Focus on: The Caribbean* (ed. M. Görlach & J. Holm, 1986). See ENGLISH WORLDWIDE. [VARIETY].   T.MCA.

VARIETY [16c: from Latin *varietas/varietatis* diversity, from *varius* speckled, diverse]. A term in sociolinguistics for a distinct form of a language:

Let me give some recent examples where the word *English* is preceded by an adjective or noun to designate a specific 'variety': American English, Legal English, Working-class English, Computer English, BBC English, Black English, South Asian English, Queensland Kanaka English, Liturgical English, Ashkenazic English, Scientific English, Chicago English, Chicano English (Randolph Quirk, 'Language Varieties and Standard Language', *English Today* 21, Jan. 1990).

Varieties fall into two types: (1) *User-related varieties*, associated with particular people and often places, such as *Black English* (English as used by blacks, however defined and wherever located, but especially African-Americans in the US) and *Canadian English* (English as used in Canada: either all such English or only the standard form). In this sense, the term *variety* is similar to but less likely to carry emotive and judgemental implications than *dialect, patois,* etc.: compare the phrases *speaking the local patois* and *speaking the local variety*. (2) *Use-related varieties*, associated with function, such as *legal English* (the language of courts, contracts, etc.) and *literary English* (the typical usage of literary texts, conversations, etc.). In this sense, the term *variety* is conceptually close to *register* and in practice is a synonym of *usage*, as in *legal usage, literary usage*. See REGISTER, USAGE.

Users and uses of English can be characterized in terms of variation in region, society, style, and medium. Regional variation is defined in terms of such characteristics as phonological, grammatical, and lexical features, as when *American English* is contrasted with *British English*: see AMERICAN ENGLISH AND BRITISH ENGLISH. Social variation represents differences of ethnicity, class, and caste, as in *Black English* and *Chicano English* in the US, *Anglo-Indian English* in India, and *Hiberno-English* in Ireland: see entries. Stylistic variation is defined in terms of situation and participants (such as formal versus informal usage, colloquial versus literary usage) and function (as with *business English* and the restricted variety known as *Seaspeak*): see entries. Variation according to medium is defined in terms of

writing, speech, and the use of sign language for the deaf (where there are, for example, differences between American and British practices).

In discussing English at large, the term *variety* permits the identification of differences without pre-empting the argument in favour of one or other set of such differences: for example, standard usage is no more or less evidence of a 'variety' than non-standard usage, and non-standard forms need not be approached as 'deviations' from a norm. In order to describe regional varieties of English, the Indian scholar Braj B. Kachru has proposed a model consisting of three concentric circles: inner, outer, and expanding. The *Inner Circle* contains territories where English is the primary or *native* language. To it belong such varieties as *American English* and *New Zealand English*. The *Outer Circle* refers to territories colonized by Britain (such as India, Nigeria, and Singapore) and the US (such as the Philippines). In it can be found such institutionalized and increasingly autonomous *non-native* varieties as *Indian English* and *Philippine English*. The *Expanding Circle* contains those countries not colonized by Inner Circle nations: that is, the rest of the world. To it belong such *performance varieties* as *German English* and *Indonesian English*. For further discussion, see DIALECT, ENGLISH. [LANGUAGE, VARIETY].   T.MCA.

The variety theme

A. ABERDEENSHIRE DIALECT, ABORIGINAL ENGLISH, AFRICAN ENGLISH, AFRICANISM, AFRIKAANS ENGLISH, AFRO-SEMINOLE, AGGLOMERESE, AIRSPEAK, AKU (TALK), AMERENGLISH, AMERICAN[2], AMERICAN ENGLISH, AMERICAN ENGLISH AND BRITISH ENGLISH, AMERICANESE, AMERICANISM, AMERICAN LANGUAGE, AMERICAN LANGUAGE (THE), ANGLIAN, ANGLIC, ANGLICISM, ANGLICIZE, ANGLIFY, ANGLIKAANS, ANGLO-DANISH, ANGLO ENGLISH, ANGLO-ENGLISH, ANGLO-GAELIC, ANGLO-INDIAN, ANGLO-IRISH, ANGLO-SAXON, ANGUILLA, ANGUISH, ANTIGUA AND BARBUDA, ANTIPODEAN ENGLISH, APPALACHIAN ENGLISH, ARGENTINA, ASCENSION (ISLAND), ATLANTIC CREOLES, AUSTRALASIAN ENGLISH, AUSTRAL ENGLISH, AUSTRALIAN, AUSTRALIAN ENGLISH, AUSTRALIANESE, AUSTRALIANISM, AUSTRALIAN LANGUAGE, AUSTRALIAN LANGUAGE (THE), AUSTRALIAN PIDGIN, AVIATION ENGLISH.

B–C. BABU ENGLISH, BAHAMAS, BAJAN, BAMBOO ENGLISH, BANGLADESH, BARBADOS, BASIC ENGLISH[1], BAY ISLANDS, BBC ENGLISH[1], BEACH LA MAR, BEARER ENGLISH, BELFAST, BELIZE, BERMUDA, BIBLICAL ENGLISH, BIRMINGHAM, BISLAMA, BLACK ENGLISH, BLACK ENGLISH VERNACULAR, BONEHEAD ENGLISH, BOSTON, BOTSWANA, BOXWALLA(H) ENGLISH, BRITICISM, BRITISH ENGLISH, BRITISH INDIAN OCEAN TERRITORY, BRITISH LANGUAGE, BROAD SCOTS, BROKEN, BROKEN ENGLISH, BROOKLYNESE, BRUMMAGEM/BRUMMIE, BRUNEI, BUNGEE, BURGHER ENGLISH, BUSINESS ENGLISH, BUTLER ENGLISH, CAJUN, CAMBRIDGE ENGLISH, CAMEROON, CAMEROON(IAN) PIDGIN, CAMFRANGLAIS, CANADIAN ENGLISH,

CANADIANISM, CARIBBEAN ENGLISH, CARIBBEAN ENGLISH CREOLE, CARIBBEANISM, CARIBBEAN LITERATURE IN ENGLISH, CAYMAN ISLANDS, CELTICISM, CENTRAL AMERICA, CHANCERY STANDARD, CHANNEL ISLANDS, CHEE-CHEE ENGLISH, CHICANO ENGLISH, CHINOOK JARGON, CODE-MIXING AND CODE-SWITCHING, COMMONWEALTH LITERATURE, CREOLE, CREOLE ENGLISH, CREOLESE, CUMBRIA.

D–G. DEVON, DIALECT, DIALECT IN AMERICA, DIALECT IN AUSTRALIA, DIALECT IN CANADA, DIALECT IN ENGLAND, DIALECT IN IRELAND, DIALECT IN SCOTLAND, DIALECT IN SOUTH AFRICA, DIALECT IN WALES, DIASPORA VARIETY, DIGLOSSIA, DISCOURSE, DISCOURSE ANALYSIS, DOMINICA, DORIC, DORSET, DUBLIN, EARLY ENGLISH, EARLY MODERN ENGLISH, EAST AFRICAN ENGLISH, EAST ANGLIA, EAST ASIAN ENGLISH, EDINBURGH, EDUCATED AND UNEDUCATED, EDUCATED ENGLISH, ENGLISH, ENGLISH IN ENGLAND, ENGLISHES, ENGLISH IN ENGLAND, ENGLISH TODAY, ENGLISH WORLD-WIDE, -ESE, EUROSPEAK, EYE DIALECT, FALKLAND ISLANDS, FIJI, FILIPINISM, FILIPINO LITERATURE IN ENGLISH, FLYTAAL, FOREIGNER TALK, FRACTURED ENGLISH, FRANGLAIS, GAELICISM, GALLICISM, GAMBIA, GEECHEE, GENERAL AMERICAN, GENERAL AMERICAN ENGLISH, GENERAL AUSTRALIAN, GENERAL BRITISH, GENERAL ENGLISH, GENERAL NEW ZEALAND, GHANA, GIBRALTAR, GLASGOW, -GLISH AND -LISH, GRENADA, GULLAH, GUTTER SCOTS, GUYANA.

H–L. HAPA-HAOLE, HAWAIIAN ENGLISH, HAWAIIAN PIDGIN, HAWAII CREOLE ENGLISH, HAWAII PIDGIN ENGLISH, HEBRAISM, HIBERNIANISM/HIBERNICISM, HIBERNO-ENGLISH, HIGHLAND ENGLISH, HILL SOUTHERN, HINDLISH/HINGLISH, HISTORY OF ENGLISH, HONDURAS, HONG KONG, INDIAN ENGLISH[1], INDIAN ENGLISH[2], INDIAN ENGLISH LITERATURE, INDIANISM, INDIAN RECOMMENDED PRONUNCIATION, INDONESIA, INTERFERENCE VARIETY, INTERNATIONAL ENGLISH, IRISH ENGLISH, IRISHISM, ITALESE, ITANGLIANO, JAMAICA, JAMAICAN CREOLE, JAMAICAN ENGLISH, JAMIESON, JAPAN, JAPANESE PIDGIN ENGLISH, JAPLISH, KAMTOK, KENSINGTON, KENTISH, KENYA, KING'S ENGLISH, KIWI, KOREA, KOREAN BAMBOO ENGLISH, KRAPP, KRIO, KRIOL, LALLANS, LANCASHIRE, LESOTHO, LIBERIA, LINGUISTIC ATLAS, LINGUISTIC ATLAS OF ENGLAND, LINGUISTIC ATLAS OF THE UNITED STATES AND CANADA, LITERARY STANDARD, LIVERPOOL/LIVERPUDLIAN, LONDON, LOWLAND SOUTHERN.

M–O. MCDAVID, MACDIARMID, MAINSTREAM, MALAWI, MALAYSIA, MALDIVES, MALTA, MANCHESTER, MANUAL ENGLISH, MAORI ENGLISH, MARITIME PIDGIN, MARITIME PIDGIN HAWAIIAN, MARITIME PROVINCES, MAURITIUS, MELANESIAN PIDGIN ENGLISH, MERICO, MERSEYSIDE, METCHIF PATOIS, MÉTIS, MEXICAN-AMERICAN ENGLISH, MID-ATLANTIC, MIDDLE ENGLISH, MIDLAND, MIDLANDS, MISKITO COAST CREOLE, MODERN ENGLISH, MONTSERRAT, MORNINGSIDE AND KELVINSIDE, MUMMERSET, NAMIBIA, NATION LANGUAGE, NAUTICAL JARGON, NEW ENGLISH, NEWFOUNDLAND ENGLISH, NEW ORLEANS, NEW SOUTH WALES PIDGIN ENGLISH, NEWSPEAK, NEW ORLEANS, NEW YORK, NEW YORKESE, NEW ZEALAND ENGLISH, NEW ZEALANDISM, NEW ZEALAND LITERATURE, NICARAGUAN ENGLISH, NIGERIA, NORTH COUNTRY, NORTHERN, NORTHERN ENGLISH, NORTHERN IRISH ENGLISH, NORTHERNIZE, NUCLEAR ENGLISH, OLD ENGLISH[1], OLD ENGLISH[2], OTTAWA VALLEY, OXFORD ENGLISH.

P–R. PACIFIC JARGON ENGLISH, PAKISTANI ENGLISH, PAPUA NEW GUINEA PIDGIN, PATOIS, PATTER, PENNSYLVANIA DUTCH, PHILIPPINE ENGLISH, PIDGIN, PIG LATIN, PIJIN, PITCAIRNESE/PITCAIRN NORFOLK CREOLE, PLAIN ENGLISH, PLANTATION SOUTHERN, POLARI, POP, POST-CREOLE CONTINUUM, POUND, PRINT STANDARD, PUBLIC SCHOOL ENGLISH, PUERTO RICO, QUEBEC, QUEEN'S ENGLISH, QUEENSLAND CANEFIELDS ENGLISH/KANAKA ENGLISH, RECEIVED PRONUNCIATION, RECEIVED STANDARD AND MODIFIED STANDARD, RED RIVER DIALECT, REGIONAL DICTIONARIES OF ENGLISH, REGISTER, ROPER RIVER CREOLE, ROTTEN ENGLISH.

S. SAINT HELENA, SAMANA, SANDALWOOD ENGLISH, SARAMACCAN, SCOTS, SCOTS LITERATURE, SCOTTICISM, SCOTTISH ENGLISH, SCOTTISH LITERATURE, SCOUSE, SEA ISLAND CREOLE, SEASPEAK, SETTLER ENGLISH, SEYCHELLES, SHELTA, SIERRA LEONE, SIGN(ED) ENGLISH, SINGAPORE ENGLISH, SLOANE RANGER, SOCIETY FOR PURE ENGLISH, SOCIOLOGESE, SOLDIER ENGLISH, SOLOMON ISLANDS, SOLOMON ISLANDS PIDGIN ENGLISH, SOMERSET, SOUTH AFRICAN ENGLISH, SOUTH AFRICAN INDIAN ENGLISH, SOUTH ASIAN ENGLISH, SOUTH-EAST ASIAN ENGLISH, SOUTHERN ENGLISH, SOUTHERNIZE, SOUTHERN ONTARIO, SOUTHRON, SOUTH SEAS ENGLISH/SOUTH SEAS JARGON, SRANAN, SRI LANKA, STANDARD, STANDARD AMERICAN, STANDARD AMERICAN ENGLISH, STANDARD AUSTRALIAN ENGLISH, STANDARD BLACK ENGLISH, STANDARD BRITISH ENGLISH, STANDARD CANADIAN ENGLISH, STANDARD DIALECT, STANDARD ENGLISH, STANDARD ENGLISH ENGLISH, STANDARD GENERAL ENGLISH, STRINE, SUDAN, SUDRON/SUTHRON, SURINAM(E), SURVEY OF ENGLISH DIALECTS, SWAZILAND.

T–Z. TAGLISH, TAIWAN, TANZANIA, TEXAS, TEXIAN, TEX-MEX, TOK BOI, TOK PISIN, TONGA, TORRES STRAIT BROKEN/CREOLE, TOWN TALK, TRIN(I)BAGONIAN, TRINIBAGIANESE, TRINIDAD AND TOBAGO, TRISTAN DA CUNHA, TSOTSI-TAAL, TURKS AND CAICOS ISLANDS, TURNER (L.), TUVALU, U AND NON-U, UGANDA, ULSTER ENGLISH, ULSTER SCOTS, UNITED STATES ENGLISH, US ENGLISH, VANUATU, VARIANT, VARIETIES OF ENGLISH AROUND THE WORLD, VARIETY, VIRGIN ISLANDS, WELSH ENGLISH, WEST AFRICAN ENGLISH, WEST AFRICAN PIDGIN ENGLISH, WEST COUNTRY, WESTERN SAMOA, WEST INDIAN CREOLE, WORLD ENGLISH, WORLD ENGLISHES, WRIGHT, YIDDISHISM, YINGLISH, YOLA, YORKSHIRE, ZAMBIA, ZIMBABWE.

VELAR. See VELUM.

VELARIC [20c: from *velar* and -*ic* as in *italic*]. A term referring to an air-stream mechanism used for making click sounds. The velaric mechanism involves raising the back of the tongue to make contact with the velum, and then sliding the tongue back, sucking air into the mouth: for example, in the sound conventionally written *tut-tut*/*tsk-tsk*, the 'gee up' sound used with horses, and the pecking kind of kiss. In English, clicks are not strictly regarded as part of the language, but in such African languages as Xhosa (South Africa), they are consonants. They can appear in the English used by speakers of such languages when including words from their own languages in their conversation. [AFRICA, SPEECH]. G.K.

VELLUM. See PARCHMENT.

VELUM [18c: from Latin *velum* an awning, sail, veil]. Also *soft palate*. The soft part of the roof of the mouth, behind the *hard palate*. There are two adjectives: *velar*, for the velum itself and sounds made by raising the back of the tongue towards the velum; *velaric*, referring to a stream of air. See AIR-STREAM MECHANISM, ARTICULATION, VELARIC. [SPEECH]. G.K.

VERB [14c: from Latin *verbum* word]. A class of words that serve to indicate the occurrence or performance of an action, or the existence of a state or condition: in English, such words (given here in the infinitive with *to*) as *to climb, to cultivate, to descend, to fish, to laugh, to realize, to walk*. Although many verbs in English have the same base form as nouns (*climb, fish, hound, love, walk*), they are morphologically and syntactically a distinct word class and one of the traditional parts of speech. There are two main types: *full verb, auxiliary verb*. In terms of form, full verbs divide into *regular* and *irregular verbs*. Auxiliaries may be further divided into *primary auxiliaries* (*be, have, do*) and *modal auxiliaries* or *modal verbs* (*may, can, will, shall, must, ought to, need, dare*).

The morphology of regular verbs. Regular verbs have four forms used in the *verb phrase*: (1) The base form, for example *walk*, used for the present tense with all persons (except third-person singular) as subjects, for the imperative, and (usually with *to*) for the infinitive. (2) The *-s* form *walks*, used for the present tense with third-person singular subjects. (3) The *-ing* form, that is, the present or *-ing* participle, *walking*. (4) The *-ed* form, for both past tense and the past or *-ed* participle, *walked*. There are some spelling conventions associated with these forms, especially: (1) The doubling of the final consonants before *-ing* and *-ed* after a stressed syllable (*beg/begging/begged*) and, in BrE, of final *-l* and some other final consonants (*travel/travelling/travelled, worship/worshipping/worshipped*). (2) The dropping of final *-e* before *-ing* and *-ed* (*like/liking/liked*), except for the *-ing* forms of *dye* (*dyeing*), *hoe* (*hoeing*), some verbs ending in *-nge* (*singeing*), and optionally in *ag(e)ing*. (3) The addition of *e* before *-s* after sibilant consonants (*pass/passes*) and final *-o* (*go/goes*). (4) The change of *-y* to *-ie* before *-s* and to *-i* before *-ed* (*carries/carried*). The *-s* form is usually pronounced /z/ after sibilants (*miss/misses*) and voiced sounds (*tab/tabs*), and /s/ after all other voiceless sounds (*fit/fits*). The *-ing* form usually has its spelling pronunciation, but is also widely pronounced as if it were *-in* (sometimes shown with an apostrophe, as in *huntin', shootin', and fishin'*). The *-ed* form is pronounced as /ɪd/ or /əd/ after *d* and *t* (*pat/patted*), as /d/

after all other voiced sounds (*save/saved*), and as /t/ after all other voiceless sounds (*pack/packed*).

The morphology of irregular verbs. The *-s* forms and *-ing* forms are regular except that the *-s* form of *say* is usually pronounced 'sez'. Many irregular verbs distinguish the past tense and participle (*take/took/taken*), but others do not distinguish one (*come/came/come*) or both (*hit/hit/hit*) from the base form. Many have a vowel change in either or both of the past tense or participle (*swim/swam/swum*), and may have an *-n* or *-en* ending for the past participle (*broken, driven, shaken*). There are seven main classes: (1) The past tense and participle are identical, but either the suffix is optionally devoiced and spelt with *-t* (as in *burn/burnt : burned*) or a final *-d* is changed to *-t* (as in *send/sent*). *Make/made* is idiosyncratic, but may be included here as it does not distinguish the two forms. (2) The past tense and participle are identical, the suffix usually devoiced, a vowel change occurring in the spoken form though not always shown in the spelling (as in *keep/kept, mean/meant, sell/sold*), but in BrE the forms *dreamt, leant, leapt* often occur, whereas in AmE only *dreamed, leaned, leaped* occur. Some forms are even more irregular with loss of final consonants (*teach/taught*). (3) The past participle has an *-(e)n* suffix (*show/showed/shown*) and in a few cases a vowel change (*shear/sheared/shorn*). (4) There are both an *-(e)n* suffix for the past participle and vowel changes of many kinds in either or both forms (*steal/stole/stolen, grow/grew/grown, bite/bit/bitten*). (5) Both forms are identical with the base form (*hit/hit/hit*). (6) There is a vowel change (not always shown in the spelling), no suffix, and the two forms are identical, but always pronounced and usually written differently from the base (*feed/fed/fed, read/read/read, dig/dug/dug, shoot/shot/shot*). (7) There is no vowel change, no suffix, and the two forms are different (*sing/sang/sung*). With a small number of verbs, the past participle is the same as the base form (*come/came/come*). See IRREGULAR VERB, for list.

The morphology of auxiliaries. *Be, have*, and *do* function not only as auxiliaries, but also as full verbs. The only morphological difference is that, except for *be*, the auxiliaries do not have the full range of non-finite forms (the infinitive and the participles). *Be* has eight different forms: in the present tense, *am* with first-person singular subjects; in the present tense, *is* with third-person singular subjects; in the present tense, *are* with the other pronouns; in the past tense, *was* with singular subjects; in the past tense, *were* with plural subjects and also with *you* when used in the singular; a present participle *being*; a past participle *been; be* itself, used as the infinitive and imperative. *Have* has an irregular *-s* form, *has*, and a past-tense *had*; the past participle *had* occurs only as a form of the full verb. *Do* has an irregular *-s* form in speech only (*does*), a past-tense form *did*, and a past participle *done*, but only the finite forms occur as auxiliaries. The present participles *being, having*, and *doing* are regular.

The modal auxiliaries have only one present-tense form, the base form (there is no *-s* form). Only *may, can, will, shall* have past-tense forms *might, could, would, should*, though these are not regularly used for the expression of past time: see MODAL VERB. Many of the auxiliaries have contracted forms: *'m* (*am*), *'s* (*is* or *has*), *'re* (*are*), *'d* (*had* or *would*), *'ll* (*will*). These are reflected in speech by 'weak' forms, but there are other weak forms not shown in the spelling, such as /wəz/ for *was*. Except for *am* and (usually) *may*, there is a full set of written contracted negative forms: *isn't, aren't, wasn't, weren't, can't, couldn't, mightn't, won't, wouldn't, shan't, shouldn't, mustn't, oughtn't, needn't, daren't.* These reflect speech, but not all the changes from the spoken forms are fully indicated by the spelling (for example, the omission of *t* in *mustn't*); especially in the English of England and of South Africa, the distinctive vowel of *can't*; the nasalized vowel and no /n/ in AmE *can't*.

The syntax and semantics of auxiliaries. The primary auxiliaries *be* and *have* mark aspect, phase, and voice (see TENSE) and the modal auxiliaries function in the modal system (see MODAL VERB). A striking feature of the auxiliaries, which can be used as a criterion for recognizing them, is that there are four environments in which they alone of English verbs can occur: (1) Negation: *He isn't coming, He can't come,* but not **He comesn't* or in contemporary English **He comes not.* (2) Inversion of the subject: *Is he coming?, Can he come?* but not in contemporary English **Comes he?* (3) In reduced clauses: *Yes, he is* and *Yes, he can* as replies, but not normally *Yes, he comes* as a reply to such a question as *Is he coming?* (4) Emphatic affirmation: *He IS coming, He CAN come* as confirmation of doubting questions or remarks. Where an auxiliary verb is not required by the semantics (to mark aspect, voice, or modality), *do* is used, functioning as an 'empty verb': *He doesn't/didn't come, Does/did he come?, Yes he DOES/DID, He DOES/DID come.* However, *be* and *have*, even when used as full verbs, occur in these four environments without *do: He isn't very happy, Have you any money?— Yes, I HAVE, He IS very unhappy,* though *have* is also used with *do*, especially in AmE: *Do you have/Have you got any money?—*

No, I don't have any money, Do you have any money?— Yes, I do/I DO have some money.

Active and passive. The passive is formed with *be* plus the past participle and involves placing the object of the active sentence in subject position and putting the subject after the verb, preceded by *by* (*John saw Mary* becoming *Mary was seen by John*). The function of the passive is to bring the object of the active sentence into focus, and not merely to remove the subject from focus, but frequently to omit it altogether, especially if it is unimportant or unknown. Constructions of the latter type are agentless passives: *Mary was seen.* The meaning is otherwise unchanged. With a small number of verbs it is the traditional indirect object that is placed in subject position (*The boy was given a book by the teacher*), but it can be argued that this is an interpretation derived from Latin. The corresponding active sentence is *The teacher gave the boy a book,* in which there is no formal evidence that *the boy* is an indirect rather than a direct object. Some prepositional objects are also placed in subject position: *The woman looked after the old man* becomes *The old man was looked after by the woman; No one has slept in the bed* becomes *The bed's not been slept in.* Here, *look after* and *sleep in* are treated as if they were single-word verbs. A few verbs appear not to be used in the passive, such as *resemble, have, hold* (in the sense of 'contain'), and *marry* (in the sense of 'wed': *Mary was married by John* is only possible if John is a priest or official and not the husband).

The syntax of full verbs. There are seven major clause types into which a full verb can enter, their constituents being S for subject, O for object, C for complement, and A for adverbial. They are: (1) SV: *The smoke disappeared* (intransitive verbs). (2) SVO: *The boy broke the window* (transitive verbs). (3) SVC: *The child seems happy.* (4) SVA: *My home is in London.* (5) SVOO: *The teacher gave the boy a book* (ditransitive verbs). (6) SVOC: *Her success made her happy* (ditransitive verbs). (7) SVOA: *The girl put the book on the table.* A verb may belong to more than one of these classes. For example, *get* belongs to all but the first: *get a present, get angry, get into difficulties, get someone a present, get one's hands dirty, get someone into a business.*

Minor categories. There are various minor categories of verbs, such as *catenative verbs*, so named because they form a 'chain' with another verb: *He keeps singing; She persuaded him to come.* They may be classified in two ways: (1) In terms of the form of the non-finite verb: infinitive without *to* (*He helped clean up*), infinitive with *to* (*He wants to come*), present participle (*She keeps talking*), or past participle (*He got hurt*). (2) In terms of whether there is a noun phrase between the two verbs or not: *He made them come, He wants them to come, She kept them talking, He had them punished.* Where there is no intervening noun phrase, the subject of the main verb functions as the subject of the subordinate verb: *John wants to come* refers to John's coming. Otherwise, the intervening noun phrase has that function: *John wants Mary to come* refers to Mary's coming. *Promise* is an exception: *I promised John to come* relates to my coming, not John's. The intervening noun phrase may or may not also function as the object of the main verb (*I persuaded John to come* versus *I wanted John to come*), where the meaning is that I persuaded John, but not that I wanted him. Syntactically, the difference is shown by the passive (which moves the object of the main verb to subject position): *John was persuaded to come*, but not **John was wanted to come.* Many verbs belong to more than one of these classes: *He wants to come, He wants them to come, He wants it done.* An idiosyncratic class contains verbs like *seem* and *happen*, the verbs with voice neutrality: *John happened to meet Mary* becoming *Mary happened to be met by John.* Another category is *need* and *want*, where the present participle, in contrast with the infinitive, has a passive meaning (*They need/want watching* versus *They need/want to watch*). Further categorization of full verbs can be made in terms of the type of finite subordinate clause that may follow them, for example, *say, announce*, etc., followed by a *that*-clause: *They said that they would do it.*

See ACTIVE (VOICE), ADVERB, ADVERBIAL, AGENTLESS PASSIVE, ASPECT, AUXILIARY VERB, BARE INFINITIVE, CAUSATIVE VERB, CONCORD/ AGREEMENT, COPULA, DANGLING PARTICIPLE, DECLARATIVE, FINITE VERB, FUTURE, GERUND, GRAMMAR, HELPING VERB, IMPERATIVE, INCEPTIVE/INCHOATIVE, INDICATIVE, INFINITIVE, INTERROGATIVE, IRREGULAR VERBS, MODALITY, MODAL VERB, MOOD, NEGATION, NUMBER^2, OBJECT, PARTICIPLE, PART OF SPEECH, PASSIVE (VOICE), PASSIVIZATION, PAST, PERFECT, PERFORMATIVE VERB, PERSON, PHRASAL VERB, PHRASE, PLUPER-FECT, PREPOSITIONAL VERB, PRESENT, PRETERIT(E), PROGRESSIVE/CONTINUOUS, REFLEXIVE, REGULAR, SENTENCE, SPLIT INFINITIVE, STATIVE VERB, STRONG VERB, SUBJECT, SUBJUNCTIVE, TENSE^1, THREE-PART VERB, TRANSITIVE AND INTRANSITIVE, TWO-PART VERB, VERB, VERBAL, VERBAL NOUN, VERBLESS SENTENCE, VERB OF INCOMPLETE PREDICATION, VERB PHRASE, VOICE, WEAK VERB, WORD. [GRAMMAR]. F.R.P.

Palmer, F. R. 1988. *The English Verb*, 2nd edition. London: Longman.
Quirk, R., Greenbaum, S., Leech, G., & Svartvik, J. 1985. *A Comprehensive Grammar of the English Language.* London: Longman.

VERBAL [15c: from Latin *verbalis* to do with words]. (1) Relating to words or consisting of words, often in contrast to something else: *verbal ability*; *a verbal protest*, as opposed to a protest in writing; *a verbal distinction*, as opposed to a distinction in reality. (2) Relating to the verb: *verbal as opposed to nominal elements of syntax*; *a verbal noun*. (3) Also *deverbal*. Derived from a verb: *a verbal noun, a deverbal adjective.* [GRAMMAR, WORD]. T.MCA.

VERBALISM [18c]. (1) A verbal expression; a word, phrase, or sentence. (2) Wording or phrasing. (3) A word, phrase, or sentence with an adequate form but little or no meaning. (4) Emphasis or overemphasis on words rather than what they refer to. (5) Being too verbal; wordiness. Someone either good with words or more concerned with words than with ideas or reality is a *verbalist*. Compare VERBIAGE, VERBOSITY, WORD-MONGER. [STYLE, WORD]. T.MCA.

VERBAL NOUN. A category of non-countable abstract noun derived from a verb, in English by adding the suffix *-ing*. Like the verb from which it derives, it refers to an action or state: *writing* in *The writing has taken too long*; *hearing* in *His hearing is defective.* Verbal nouns are frequently combined with the preposition *of* and a noun phrase that corresponds to the subject or object in a clause: *The grumbling of his neighbours met with no response* (compare *His neighbours grumbled*); *His acting of Hamlet won our admiration* (compare *He acted Hamlet*). Verbal nouns contrast with *deverbal nouns*, that is, other kinds of nouns derived from verbs, such as *attempt, destruction*, and including nouns ending in *-ing* that do not have verbal force: *building* in *The building was empty.* They also contrast with the *gerund*, which also ends in *-ing*, but is syntactically a verb. See GERUND, NOUN, VERBAL. [GRAMMAR]. S.G.

VERBATIM. See QUOTATION.

VERBATIM, Full title *Verbatim, the Language Quarterly.* An international periodical dealing with language in general and the English language in particular, founded in 1974 by its editor and publisher, the American lexicographer Laurence Urdang. Its stated purpose is to inform, amuse, and entertain a readership in 80 countries that includes linguists, translators, language teachers, writers, and members of the public. A typical issue contains several articles, a number of reviews of specialized and popular books (including dictionaries), correspondence, short humorous pieces, brief commentaries on etymology, grammar, usage, style, meaning, etc., a cryptic crossword puzzle, a word game, and, till it was discontinued in 1989, a catalogue offering many language and reference books. Till 1989, $2,500 in prizes in the *Verbatim Essay Competition* was offered. In that year it was replaced by the *Verbatim Award*, an annual donation of £1,500 in grants administered by EURALEX, 'for the pursuit of scholarship in lexicography'. See EURALEX, URDANG. [AMERICAS, MEDIA].　　　　　　　　　　T.MCA.

VERBIAGE [18c: from Latin *verbum* word, and *-age* as in *foliage*]. (1) An overabundance of words: 'The Homeric phrase is thus often muffled and deadened by Pope's verbiage' (Sir Leslie Stephen, *Alexander Pope*, 1880). (2) Rare: the wording of a document. Compare VERBALISM, VERBOSITY. [STYLE, WORD].　　T.MCA.

VERBICIDE [19c: from Latin *verbum* word, and *-cide* as in *regicide*]. An emotive non-technical term for: (1) Someone who 'kills' words: 'It is this laziness in speaking which makes [people] grow up habitual verbicides' (letter to the *Melbourne Argus*, 10 Jan. 1894). (2) The act or process of destroying or perverting the meaning and value of a word or words: 'The verbicidal impulses of Pentagonese' (*The Times*, 27 Mar. 1985). [STYLE, WORD].　　　　T.MCA.

VERBLESS SENTENCE. A term in some grammatical descriptions for a construction that lacks a verb but can be analysed as consisting of grammatical units functioning as subject, object, etc., as in: (1) Elliptical responses: *Who took my pencil?—Sam*; *Where did they go?—Straight home*. (2) Questions: *What about another drink?*; *Why no mail today?* (3) Commands: *Inside, everybody!* (4) Idiomatic usage: *The sooner, the better*. Subordinate verbless constructions, traditionally called phrases, often now called clauses, are also common: 'I can help you *if necessary*'; '*Though in great pain*, they struggled on.' See CLAUSE, SENTENCE. [GRAMMAR].　　S.G.

VERB OF INCOMPLETE PREDICATION. A traditional term now usually replaced by *copular verb* or *linking verb*, the most frequent being the copula *be* as in 'Justin *is* intelligent'. Such verbs have been so called because the main meaning of the predication is conveyed by the complement required to 'complete' the meaning of the verb. Other copular verbs (with possible complements) are: *become* (*mature*); *seem* (*tired*); *remain* (*my friend*); *go* (*mad*); *grow* (*old*); *appear* (*the best choice*); *taste* (*good*). See COPULA, PREDICATE, VERB. [GRAMMAR].　　S.G.

VERBOSITY [16c: from Latin *verbositas*, from *verbosus* full of words]. The use of more words

than necessary, especially Latinate words intended to impress. The British politician Benjamin Disraeli (1878) illustrated the style ironically by calling his rival William Gladstone 'a sophistical rhetorician, inebriated by the exuberance of his own verbosity'. Compare CIRCUMLOCUTION, JOHNSONESE, VERBALISM, VERBIAGE. [STYLE, WORD].　　　　　　　　　　T.MCA.

VERB-PARTICLE CONSTRUCTION. See PHRASAL VERB.

VERB PHRASE. (1) Also *verbal phrase*. In traditional grammar, a term for the main verb and any auxiliary or combination of auxiliaries that precedes it: *can spell*; *may have cried*; *should be paid*; *might have been transferred*. (2) In generative grammar, a term roughly equivalent to the traditional *predicate*. It includes the traditional verb phrase with (at least) any complements of the verb, such as the non-bracketed parts of the following sentences: (*They*) *have understood his intention*; (*Susan*) *was very patient*; (*My parents*) *promised me a computer*; (*We*) *haven't been to Paris*. See NOUN (FUNCTION), PHRASE, VERB. [GRAMMAR].　　S.G.

VERNACULAR [c.1600: from Latin *vernaculus* domestic, indigenous, native, from *verna* a home-born slave, native: compare CREOLE, *native* (see ETHNIC NAME)]. (1) Occurring in the everyday language of a place and regarded as native or natural to it: *vernacular usage*, *expressions vernacular to English*. The term is used contrastively to compare the mainly or only oral expression of a people, a rural or urban community, or a lower social class (*a vernacular Indian language*, *a vernacular poet*, *vernacular West Country English*, *vernacular Glasgow*) with languages and styles that are classical, literary, liturgical, or more socially and linguistically cultivated and prestigious (*a classical Indian language*, *Augustan English*, *liturgical usage*, *standard English*, *polite Glasgow*). (2) Such a language or variety: *speaking* (*in*) *the vernacular; written in the Yorkshire vernacular*. The term is used across the judgemental spectrum, from the warm approval of 'vernacularists' through the more or less neutral usage of linguists to a traditionally casual and dismissive attitude among many writers and teachers. (3) Relating to the plain standard style or variety of a language as opposed to more ornate, pedantic, classical, or complex styles and varieties; such a style or variety: *What's that in the vernacular?* (4) Relating to any medium or form that reflects indigenous and usually simple style, or popular as opposed to sophisticated taste: *vernacular architecture*. (5) Relating to the common name of a plant or animal, as opposed to its name in Latinate scientific nomenclature; such a name. See BINOMIAL NOMENCLATURE, BLACK ENGLISH VERNACULAR, CLASSICAL, CLASSICAL LANGUAGE, COLLOQUIAL, DEMOTIC, DIALECT, LITERARY, PLAIN, STANDARD, TESD, VERNACULARISM, VERNACULARIST. [LANGUAGE, STYLE]. T.MCA.

VERNACULARISM [1840s]. (1) A vernacular or native word or saying. (2) Use of a vernacular, a native language, etc.: 'If Rome not merely allows, but authorises such vernacularism, who can forbid us to employ our own Ecclesiastical English?' (*Ecclesiologist* 11, 1850, p. 176). See ATTICISM, CLASSICISM, COLLOQUIALISM, -ISM, VERNACULAR, VERNACULARIST. [LANGUAGE, STYLE, WORD]. T.MCA.

VERNACULARIST [1860s]. (1) A person who advocates the use of a demotic, regional, or working-class language or dialect, who speaks and/or writes it, or advocates its use instead of a classical, standard, literary, liturgical, or other form: 'There was ample material ... in the industrial struggle with which Clydeside was so familiar, which in the hands of a Vernacularist of genius could produce a play so striking as "Strife" ' (*Glasgow Herald*, 27 July 1926); 'Creosote bush, which the Spaniards call *hedonillo* but the American vernacularists termed "little stinker" ' (*Saturday Review*, 4 Dec. 1974). (2) Of any such person, tendency, fashion, or movement: 'Mr St John Stevas's Latin is not good . . ., but that is a venial sin in these vernacularist days' (*Observer*, 25 Apr. 1982). See VERNACULARISM. [LANGUAGE, STYLE]. T.MCA.

VERNER'S LAW. A statement of the evolution of certain consonants in Germanic languages, already affected by Grimm's Law; see entry. It was made in 1875 by the Danish philologist Karl Verner. Greatly simplified, Verner's Law holds that Primitive Germanic voiceless fricatives (such as *s*) were voiced (in this case, to *z*) when the immediately preceding vowel did not carry the chief word-accent. Because the past plural and past participle were stressed on the suffix but other parts of the verb were stressed on the root syllable, some portions of the original conjugation met these conditions and others did not; hence the Law is sometimes called *Grammatical Sound Change*. The consonants that changed in accordance with Verner's Law underwent further changes; thus, when original *s* became *z*, it usually went on to become *r*, and the voiceless *th* sound (as in *thought*) voiced by Verner's Law (as in *though*) went on to become *d*. Analogy levelled out many of these effects, but modern English still has *dead, sodden, (for)lorn, rear, were*, and (*Val*)*kyrie*, all affected by Verner's

Law, alongside the related *death, seethe, lose, raise, was*, and *choose*, which were unaffected by it. Compare GREAT VOWEL SHIFT, GRIMM'S LAW. [HISTORY, SPEECH]. W.F.B.

VERSE [Before 10c: from Old English *fers*, from Latin *versus* a turn of the plough, furrow, line of writing, from *vertere* to turn: compare LINE, PROSE]. (1) Language in metrical form. (2) Poetry, especially when contrasted with prose. (3) A particular metrical structure, such as iambic or trochaic verse. (4) A stanza or other short division of a poem, as in *a poem of four verses*. (5) One of the small sections into which the Bible is divided: *chapter and verse*; *Chapter 23, Verse 2*. In this article, the first two senses predominate.

Structure. The succession of syllables gives natural rhythm to speech through stress, vowel quantity, and pitch. Verse builds on this rhythm, organizing it into stretches of speech with recurring syllabic patterns. Such stretches have traditionally been written as sequences of lines, with the result that the expression *a line of verse/poetry* is used in discussing all such works, whether oral or written. Metre, the measured use of vocal rhythm, remains fundamental to verse, its basic pattern generally enhanced by such other features as rhyme, alliteration, and the repetition of words or phrases; verse draws on the natural resources of language, but imposes organization not found in common discourse. There may be regularity or variation in the length of lines, stanzas, or verse paragraphs, and the discourse can be brief or extended for thousands of lines. As an oral conception, verse depends on the repetition of sound effects. Many cultures without a written language have or have had verse, often in elaborate forms. Written verse is therefore a translation from the oral to the written code, in which a literate society reinterprets verse as a written form whose pattern is 'heard' imaginatively in silent reading or re-expressed orally in various ways, through reading aloud or recitation from memory. Written verse, however, adds an element of graphic design, in the appearance of the line on the page, no longer mechanically constrained by the width of the paper but displaying conscious choice of a linguistic unit: see CONCRETE POETRY.

Differences between languages produce differences in verse. Greek and Latin verse is quantitative; the metrical structure of the line depends on the duration of the syllables, determined by rules concerning individual vowels and their combination with consonants. English verse is based on syllabic stress, although there have been experiments with quantitative metres.

These were most frequent in the 16c when classical influence was strong. Thomas Campion defended classical metres in *Observations on the Art of English Poesie* (1602); his argument was countered by Samuel Daniel in *A Defence of Rhyme* (1603). Campion practised his own principles by writing in classical forms. His 'English elegeick' uses alternative iambic and trochaic quantitative lines:

> Constant to none, but euer false to me,
> Traiter still to loue through thy faint desires,
> No hope of pittie now nor vain redresse
> Turns my griefs to teares, and renu'd laments.

Later poets experimented with classical forms. The effect is usually forced if it is maintained through a long poem. A successful example is A. H. Clough's *The Bothie of Tober-na-Vuolich* (1848), written in hexameters:

> Great was the surprise in college at breakfast, wine and
> supper,
> Keen the conjecture and joke; but Adam kept the
> secret.

Terms like *iambic pentameter* have long been accepted as appropriate for the stress-based metres of English verse-making. English is not rich in rhymes, as compared with some Romance languages. Forms like *terza rima* are difficult to sustain, writers in English usually preferring simple schemes with frequent changes of rhyme. Strong initial consonants made alliteration a feature of Old English verse, and response to alliteration has survived in modern English. However, many of the forms and terms of Latin and Greek have been successfully adapted to English versification, as in: 'I hear lake water lapping with low sounds by the shore' (W. B. Yeats, 'The Lake Isle of Innisfree').

Rhythm and syntax. The effect of verse is to draw attention to the manner as well as the matter of the discourse. The flow of language is not simply an extension in time but becomes consequential and fulfils an expectation of recurrence. There is a doubleness about it, the first rhythmic structure working with a second syntactic structure that is necessary to give meaning. The needs and aims of the two systems may coincide, metre and rhyme demanding pauses that are in harmony with the demands of syntax, as in:

> Little Jack Horner
> Sat in a corner
> Eating his Christmas pie
> (from a nursery rhyme)

or enjambement can make the two systems coexist in tension:

> At the round earth's imagined corners, blow
> Your trumpets, Angels, and arise, arise
> From death, you numberless infinities
> Of souls, and to your scatter'd bodies go.
> (John Donne, *Holy Sonnets*, 7)

The functions of verse. In traditional literary criticism, the terms *verse* and *poetry* are not synonymous, although in everyday usage the two are often treated more or less as synonyms. Critics usually see verse as technique, not art: to call a composition 'verse' is generally descriptive, not evaluative, and the decision to make verse does not always produce poetic quality. The term *verse* is sometimes used to imply that, in a critic's opinion, some poems do not deserve to be called poetry, and the terms *versifying* and *versifier* have been used pejoratively to suggest inferior work. However, poetry is written in verse and cannot be fully discussed without attention to its technical aspect. Verse stands in opposition to prose, and thus makes poetry also different from prose. When someone speaks of 'poetic' prose, the phrase suggests either that certain features of poetry have moved away from their natural form of expression into prose, where they are essentially alien, or that the creative writer is free to move elements traditionally identified with one type of expression into the other. Verse is not used only for poetry. Its patterning gives it a strong mnemonic value which is essential in a non-literate society and remains useful in a literate one. The oral origins of early written verse can often be detected by the presence of repeated formulas and stock phrases which aid the mnemonic effect of the metre. There are charms and riddles in Old English, as well as heroic poetry. Spells, charms, weather-lore, and useful information are passed on and remembered in aphoristic verse:

> Thirty days hath September . . .

> Red sky at night, shepherd's delight,
> Red sky in the morning, shepherd's warning.

Mnemonic verse can also have a more formal pedagogic value:

> In fourteen hundred and ninety-two
> Columbus sailed the ocean blue.

Conclusion. The contemporary world is rich in verse. Popular songs continue the tradition of songs and ballads with (often meaningless) refrains that allow the audience to participate. Children make up jingles about people and places as well as repeating traditional nursery rhymes. Advertisers use the power of verse and, through commercial media, have adapted orality and combined it with the pictorial, so that advertising jingles have, while they last, a role comparable to the nursery rhyme. Verse can be spontaneous or planned, ephemeral or enduring. How it works is described by *prosody*, which discerns and states the patterns. In addition, contemporary linguistic study can aid understanding of how verse works, especially within the field of *stylistics*, pointing out how verse serves to isolate and emphasize such features of everyday language as rhythm and tone, figurative usage, grammatical form, and the meanings of words. See POETRY, PROSODY, STYLISTICS. [LITERATURE]. R.C.

Fraser, G. S. 1970. *Metre, Rhyme and Free Verse*. London: Methuen.
Leech, G. N. 1969. *A Linguistic Guide to English Poetry*. London: Longman.
McAuley, J. 1966. *Versification*. Michigan State University Press.
Shapiro, K., & Beum, R. 1965. *A Prosody Handbook*. New York: Harper & Row.

VERSIFIER. See POET.

VERSION [16c: through French from Latin *versio/versionis* a turning (a sense taken into English, but now obsolete), a translation. Compare TROPE, VERSE]. (1) A rendering of a text or the like, especially by translation (the *Authorized Version* of the Bible, published in 1611; an *English-language version* of a work created in another language) or after the passage of time (*a modern version of an old song*). (2) An account or report of something when compared with one or more other accounts or reports of the same thing: *There are at least three versions of this story*; *Each side has its own version of what happened*. A *generally received version* of something is the one that most people accept. Compare VARIANT. [STYLE]. T.MCA.

VERS LIBRE. See FREE VERSE, VERSE.

VERSO. See PAGE.

VICTORIAN [1870s]. (1) Relating to the reign of Queen Victoria (1837–1901): *Victorian literature, Victorian values*. The period was highly significant in the history of England, of Britain, and of the British Empire; it is noted for its industrial, commercial, technological, and cultural vigour, for the expansion of British influence throughout the world, and for the attendant spread of the English language and British conceptions of education in Africa, the Americas, Asia, and Oceania. Attitudes and viewpoints that can be classified as 'Victorian' are generally considered not to have been restricted to Britain and its Empire, but to have been widespread in the rest of Europe, in the US, and elsewhere, and to have survived the death of Victoria herself, who was often considered to be their embodiment. There was, for example, a widespread taboo in English and other languages against both the use of strong language and direct references to sexuality in print and in the middle-class drawing-room. Subsequent views of the era have varied: some have looked back on the period as a time of unsurpassed visionary optimism and admirable moral rectitude; others, however, have seen it as a time of strict, stifling, bigoted, and often hypocritical narrow-mindedness; still others have focused on the struggle between social reformers and liberal thinkers and an entrenched élite regarded as self-serving exploiters of the people and the natural world (both at home and in the colonies). The collective term *Victoriana* covers the objects, institutions, and attitudes of the period: 'The dear old Princes Theatre . . . a perfect specimen of Victoriana' (*Lancashire Life*, Mar. 1978); 'The terrifying Victoriana within' (Ngaio Marsh, *Final Curtain*, 1947). The term *Victorianism* refers to the attitudes and style of the era, and to anything that characterized it. (2) A person who lived during, or was born in, the Victorian era: *Eminent Victorians* (title of a collection of biographical essays by G. Lytton Strachey, 1918). Compare AUGUSTAN, ELIZABETHAN, JACOBEAN, RESTORATION. See ARNOLD (M.), BIOGRAPHY, BRITISH EMPIRE, BRONTË, CARLYLE, CARROLL, DICKENS, ENGLISH LITERATURE, HARDY, HUMO(U)R, IMPERIALISM, LITERARY CRITICISM, MACAULAY, NOVEL, PUNCH, ROMANTICISM, TENNYSON. [EUROPE, HISTORY, STYLE]. T.MCA.

VICTORIANISM. See ENGLISH LITERATURE, VICTORIAN.

VIETNAM(ESE). See AMERICAN LANGUAGES, JAPANESE PIDGIN ENGLISH, LINGUISTIC TYPOLOGY.

VIËTOR, Wilhelm [1850–1918]. German phonetician and authority on language teaching methodology. Born at Kleeberg (Hesse-Nassau), Germany, he trained as a teacher of English. He taught German in schools in England (1872–4) and was Lecturer in German at U. College, Liverpool (1882–4). His pamphlet *Der Sprachunterricht muss umkehren* (Language Teaching Must Start Afresh), published in 1882 under the pseudonym Quousque Tandem (Latin: Just how long), initiated the Reform Movement for language teaching in Germany and neighbouring countries (whose other leading members were Otto Jespersen, Paul Passy, and Henry Sweet). Viëtor was Professor of English Philology at the U. of Margburg from 1884 until his death. His works include *Elemente der Phonetik des Deutschen, Englischen und Französischen* (Elements of German, English and French Phonetics, 1884) and *Die Methodik des neusprachlichen Unterrichts* (Modern Language Teaching

Methodology, 1902). See LANGUAGE TEACHING. [BIOGRAPHY, EDUCATION, EUROPE]. P.C.

VIRGIN ISLANDS. Caribbean dependencies of Britain and the US in the Lesser Antilles. The economies of both depend largely on tourism, their currencies are the US dollar, and their languages English and Creole. The *British Virgin Islands* consist of four large islands (Tortola, Virgin Gorda, Anegada, Jost Van Dyke) and numerous small islands, with their capital Road Town on Tortola. The Dutch settled the islands in 1648 and gave way to British planters in 1666. They became part of the colony of the Leeward Islands in 1872 and a separate colony in 1956. The *US Virgin Islands* (official title *Virgin Islands of the United States*) consist of more than 50 neighbouring islands formerly known as the *Danish West Indies*, the three main islands being St Croix, St Thomas, and St John. Capital: Charlotte Amalie, on St Thomas. Population: 95,591 (1980). Ethnicity: mainly African, many from other Caribbean territories, with 10% US Caucasian, 5% European. In 1671, the Danish West Indies Company colonized St Thomas and St John and in 1733 bought St Croix from France. The islands were Danish for 200 years, with a short break in Napoleonic times. The US purchased them in 1917 as part of a strategic passage to the Panama Canal and they are an unincorporated territory of the US, with a republican-style democracy. See CARIBBEAN, ENGLISH. [AMERICAS, NAME, VARIETY]. T.MCA.

VIRGULE. See OBLIQUE.

VOCABLE [16c: from Latin *vocabulum* a little voice, a bit of language, a word, a vowel]. A rare term for a word, common among 18c Scottish writers. See VOCABULARY. [WORD]. T.MCA.

VOCABULARY [16c: from Latin *vocabularium* a list of *vocabula* words. The medieval *vocabularium* was a list of Latin words to be learnt by clerical students. It was usually arranged thematically, with translation equivalents in a vernacular language]. A traditional term with a range of linked senses: (1) The words of a language: *the vocabulary of Old English*. The general vocabulary of a language is sometimes called its *wordstock* and is generally referred to by linguists as its *lexicon* or *lexis*. (2) The words available to or used by an individual: *a limited French vocabulary*. (3) The words appropriate to a subject or occupation: *the vocabulary of commerce*. (4) A word list developed for a particular purpose: *Use the vocabulary at the back of the book*; *a dictionary with a restricted defining vocabulary*. (5) A list or set of code words, gestures, symbols, styles, or colours.

Specialized vocabularies in a language. The vocabulary or lexicon of a language is a system rather than a list. Its elements interrelate and change subtly or massively from generation to generation. It increases through *borrowing* from other languages and through *word-formation* based on its own or borrowed patterns. It may decrease or increase in certain areas as interests change. Whole sets of items may vanish from general use and awareness, unless special activities serve to keep them alive. For example:

(1) *A vocabulary of carving.* There was in 16c England a set of verbs for carving kinds of game, fish, and poultry, which included *allaying a pheasant*, *barbing a lobster*, *chining a salmon*, *fracting a chicken*, *sculling a tench*, and *unbracing a mallard*.

(2) *A vocabulary of falconry.* Until at least the 17c, the names of birds classed as hawks and used in falconry included *falcon*, *gerfalcon*, *jerkin*, *tassel-gentle*, *laner*, *laneret*, *bockerel*, *bockeret*, *saker*, *sacaret*, *merlin*, *jackmerlin*, *hobby*, *jack*, *steletto*, *waskite*, *eagle*, *iron*, *goshawk*, *tarcel*, *sparhawk*, *musket*, *French Pye* (from Izaak Walton, *The Compleat Angler*, 1653). Few people would currently class an eagle as a kind of hawk.

(3) *A vocabulary of coaches.* In the 19c, there were many terms for horse-drawn vehicles, including *brougham*, *buckboard*, *buggy*, *cabriolet*, *carriage*, *chaise*, *coach*, *coupé*, *droshky*, *gig*, *hackney* (*carriage*), *hansom* (*cab*), *jaunting/jaunty car*, *landau*, *stagecoach*, *tonga*. The use of horse-drawn vehicles has steeply declined, but many such words are kept alive in historical novels and films, some refer to vehicles still in use in certain places, and some have moved into the vocabulary of rail travel and the automobile.

There is a present-day Japanese parallel to the carving verbs of Tudor England. Whereas, in English, people *put* their clothes *on* (whatever form the clothes take), Japanese has a set of verbs of dressing that differentiate kinds of clothing: to put on a kimono is *kimono-o kiru*, to put on a hat *oshi-o kaburu*, to put on shoes *kutsu-o haku*, to put on gloves *tebukuro-o hameru*, to put on a muffler *erimaki-o suru*, to put on a hairpiece *heapisu-o tsukeru*. Typically, the verb *kiru* collocates with kimonos, cloaks, slips, blouses, and clothing in general, *kaburu* collocates with words for headgear and face coverings, *haku* with footwear and items for the lower body and legs, *hameru* with gloves, rings, and bracelets, *suru* with headbands, scarves, and wrist-watches, and *tsukeru* with wigs, false eyelashes, hearing aids, ear-rings, brooches, medals, perfumes, and powders (from A. E. Backhouse, 'Japanese Verbs of Dress', *Journal of Linguistics* 17: 1, 1981).

Distinctive vocabularies across languages. Just as the vocabulary of a language changes from age to age, so the vocabularies of different languages are distinct in their systems, uses, and references. There may be some close translation equivalents among several languages, but items and arrangements of items in one language may have no precise parallel elsewhere, because the culture in which the vocabulary has evolved rests on unique needs, interests, and experiences. As the American anthropologist Stephen Tyler has put it:

The people of different cultures may not recognize the same kinds of material phenomena as relevant, even though from an outsider's point of view the same material phenomena may be present in every case. For example, we distinguish (in English) between dew, fog, ice, and snow, but the Koyas of South India do not. They call all of these *mancu*. Even though they can perceive the differences among them if asked to do so, these differences are not significant to them. On the other hand, they recognize and name at least seven different kinds of bamboo, six more than I am accustomed to distinguish (*Cognitive Anthropology*, 1969).

The vocabulary of English. Historically, the word-store of English is a composite, drawn in the main from the Indo-European language family. There is a base of Germanic forms (mainly Old English and Old Norse) with a superstructure of Romance, mainly from French and Latin, with a technical stratum contributed by Greek (mainly through Latin and French): see BISOCIATION. In addition, there are many acquisitions from languages throughout the world. Because of such a complex background, and because dictionaries and other resources state that they list thousands of headwords and other items, the question often arises: *How many words are there in the English language?*

No easy answer is possible. In order to reach a credible total, there must be agreement about what to count as an item of vocabulary and also something physical to count or to serve as the basis for an estimate. Counting words (however defined) is wearisome, complex, and difficult, and experience suggests that no matter how well organized the count there can never be enough data to ensure completeness. There are at least five reasons for this: (1) There is no corpus available in a countable form which represents the whole language. (2) Even if there were, it would only indicate what was available at the time the count started. It would therefore be a static assessment of a dynamic process. (3) The result of the counting would consequently be out of date before the counting was completed. (4) Even with careful safeguards, the total reached would be different for each counter. In practice, counters tend to interpret instances differently and so count items in different ways. (5) The

administrative work needed to homogenize the efforts of the counters would be formidable and time-consuming, making the survey even more out of date by the time it appeared.

Points 4 and 5 can be demonstrated by means of one example: the *-ing* form in *running* and *walking*. There are three ways to handle this suffix in a word count: (1) Count every item containing *-ing* as a distinct word. (2) Omit every item, treating *-ing* as an inflected form of the verb, like *runs* and *walks*, and therefore a matter of grammar, not lexis. (3) Count only some instances, like *clearing* and *drawing*, because these are used as distinct nouns with the plurals *clearings* and *drawings*, and ignore the rest. Whatever decision is taken significantly affects the outcome, because there are as many *-ing* forms as there are such verbs as *run* and *walk*. If Solution 3 is chosen, it poses further problems, because in the corpus to be counted will appear citations like *rustlings and twitterings among the trees*. If *rustling* and *twittering* are taken as distinct words on this occasion, how will the counters handle the fact that many *-ing* forms can be so used, even if they are not recorded in the corpus?

In effect, the overall vocabulary of English is beyond strict statistical assessment. Nonetheless, limited counts take place and serve useful ends, and some rough indications can be given about the overall vocabulary. The *Oxford English Dictionary* (1989) defines over 500,000 items described as 'words' in a promotional press release. The average college, desk, or family dictionary defines over 100,000 such items. Specialist dictionaries contain vast lists of words and word-like items, such as the *Acronyms, Initialisms & Abbreviations Dictionary* (Gale, 1989), which contains over 450,000 accredited abbreviations. When printed material of this kind is taken into account, along with lists of geographical, zoological, botanical, and other usages, the crude but credible total for words and word-like forms in present-day English is somewhere over a billion items.

Individual vocabularies. No one person can know, use, or imagine the entire available lexical resources of English. Many people are, however, curious about either how many words they or someone else knows, or what the 'average educated person' might be supposed to know and use. When such questions arise, they raise issues comparable to those of the vocabulary at large. Even in the case of writers whose texts are available for analysis, different totals emerge: the vocabulary of Shakespeare's works is variously listed as *c.*25,000 (Simeon Potter, *Our Language*, 1966), *c.*30,000 words (Robert McCrum *et al.*, *The Story of English*, book, 1986), and *c.*34,000

(J. Barton, in McCrum *et al.*, *The Story of English*, TV series, episode 3, 1986). Such totals apparently depend on what has been counted and the information passed on is a very rough approximation.

It is not unusual, however, to find assertions that the average person makes use of, for most purposes, fewer words than Shakespeare: perhaps 15,000 items. If, however, the count starts with the *c.*3,000 words in lists used for the early stages in the learning of English as a foreign language, such a total is soon exceeded simply by adding compounds, derivatives, phrasal verbs, abbreviations, and fixed phrases commonly associated with those *c.*3,000 words. For example, words formed on *run* alone include *runner, running, run in, run out, run on, run off, run up, run down, runway, gun-runner*, all with meanings and uses that qualify them as distinct words. All or most of such items are well within the range of most users of English educated to around 16–18 years of age. A crude extrapolation of 10 × 3,000 suggests that such people are familiar with some 30,000 such items, or twice the above estimate. Bringing in many everyday words not in the basic 3,000, and applying the same multiplier, soon takes the average person to double or treble this number without discomfort, every personal 'list' of words and word-like items differing from every other.

Active and passive vocabulary. When teachers and linguists discuss the words people know, a distinction is commonly made between an *active* or *productive vocabulary* (what one can use) and a *passive* or *receptive vocabulary* (what one can recognize). The passive vocabulary is larger than the active, and the dividing line between the two is impossible to establish. All such terms and statements founder on the rock of what is meant by 'word' and 'vocabulary'. Lexical skills go well beyond the simplicities of printed words with white space on either side. These skills include knowledge of the *senses* of words. To take this knowledge into account would multiply what an individual knows many times over, because common words like *head* and *foot* have over a dozen important senses each, and many nuances. A person who 'knows' 50,000 'words', each with an average of five clear-cut senses, is actively or passively acquainted with 250,000 nuggets of lexical information. Such an estimate, however crude it may be, is decidedly impressive.

See: (1) DEFINING VOCABULARY, FREQUENCY COUNT, LEXICON, LEXIS, TERM, TERMINOLOGY, USAGE, VOCABULARY CONTROL. (2) The vocabulary sections of entries for major varieties of English, such as CANADIAN ENGLISH. [EDUCATION, LANGUAGE, WORD]. T.MCA.

VOCABULARY CONTROL. A term in applied linguistics for the organization of words into groups and levels, especially as the outcome of frequency counts and in the form of word lists intended to help in writing, reading, and learning languages. An early approach in English was made by Isaac Pitman (*Phonotypic Journal*, Oct. 1843), making available to stenographers a list of words 'showing how often each occurs in 10,000 words, taken from 20 books, 500 from each'. This served as a guide in selecting what he called *grammalogues* (words such as *and*, *the*, and *of*, that can be written in shorthand as single symbols). A later approach in German, also with stenographers in mind, was made by F. W. Kaeding, who counted 11m words from a variety of texts, providing the results in alphabetic lists that showed the frequency of occurrence of each item (*Häufigkeitswörterbuch der deutschen Sprache*, 1898). Since the beginning of the 19c, the organization of English vocabulary has been undertaken mainly to improve reading skills and make learning the language easier. For details of such work, see BASIC ENGLISH, COBUILD, DEFINING VOCABULARY, FREQUENCY COUNT, GENERAL SERVICE LIST, LEXICON, READER, THORNDIKE, WEST.

Counting words and creating word lists is a complex task, and for useful results requires an initial conception of 'word' for the purpose in hand. Problems regarding what to count as a word include: (1) The orthographic problem of spelling variants such as *colour* and *color*. (2) The homonymic problem of identical forms such as *bear* (animal) and *bear* (carry). (3) The homographic problem of identical forms such as *wind* (air on the move) and *wind* (to turn, twist). (4) The phonological problem of statistics relating to spoken (and informally written) language (do items like *'ll* and *n't* count as *will* and *not*, are they special events to be counted on their own, or are they parts of units like *I'll* and *didn't*, to be counted separately?). (5) The morphological problem of the forms of *be* (are *be*, *am*, *art*, *is*, *are*, *was*, *were* different words or realizations of the same word?). (6) The lexical problems of counting compounds and distinguishing them from attributive forms (is a *key decision* one word or two, in the same way that a *keyhole* or *key-hole* or *key hole* is one word?). (7) The statistical problem that, even granted that there is a utilitarian solution to the preceding problem, should the count include only agreed compounds or both compounds and their elements (so that for *keyhole* one counts *keyhole*, *key*, *hole*)? (8) The grammatical problem of particles and prefixes (does one count the *up* in *put up* with alongside the *up* in *up the hill*, and with the *up* in *uproot*?). (9) The onomastic problem of personal and place names (are *Manchester*, *Manila*, and *Manitoba*, etc., to be counted as words simply because they appear in texts?). (10) The polysemic problem of deciding whether to count *fire* in a grate and *fire* at an artillery range as the same or a different word. (11) The lexicographical problem of how to describe and list the findings of any such survey, so that people of different experience can see and appreciate what has been counted. After all of these, there are two further problems: how to train the personnel and program the computer so that such highly sophisticated work can be brought to a successful conclusion. Anyone taking part in such work usually ends up with a cautious respect for words. See ATTRIBUTIVE, COMPOUND, HOMONYM, ONOMASTICS, POLYSEMY, TYPE AND TOKEN, VARIANT, VOCABULARY, WORD-FORMATION. [EDUCATION, REFERENCE, WORD].

T.MCA.

VOCAL CORDS, also **vocal chords, vocal folds**. Anatomical terms for folds inside the larynx, stretching from front to back, which control the flow of air from the trachea or windpipe into the pharynx, mouth, and nose. When muscular action pulls them apart a voiceless sound is produced, such as /s, t/. When they are held loosely together, air passing through forces them to vibrate, producing voiced sounds, such as /z, d/. See VOICE. [SPEECH]. G.K.

VOCAL FOLDS. See VOCAL C(H)ORDS.

VOCAL TRACT. A term in anatomy and phonetics for the area of the mouth and throat from the lips to the larynx, used in the production of speech. [SPEECH]. G.K., T.MCA.

VOCATIVE [15c: from Latin (*casus*) *vocativus* the naming case]. (1) Also *vocative case*. A term in the case system of Latin and other inflected languages, in which it marks the form of address for a noun or other word. The vocative of *dominus* occurs in the question *Quo vadis, Domine?* (Whither goest thou, Lord?). The element *O* was formerly regarded as marking the vocative in English: 'O Caesar, these things are beyond all use' (Shakespeare, *Julius Caesar*, 2. 2). See CASE. (2) In contemporary grammar, the function of a name or noun phrase used to attract attention, start a letter, or show the speaker's relationship to the person addressed: *Waiter, can we have the bill/check, please?*; *I'm sorry, darling*; *Fred, what's the time?*; *The gloves are in the next section, madam*. See FORM OF ADDRESS. [GRAMMAR, NAME]. S.C.

VOGUE, especially as used in **vogue word** [16c: from French *vogue* rowing, course, success, from Italian *voga* rowing, fashion, from *vogare* to row, go well]. If something is *in vogue*, it is fashionable and widely used for a time. Linguistic usages can be as much in vogue as clothes or ideas: 'Pox on your Bourdeaux, Burgundie . . . no more of these vogue names . . . get me some ale' (Howard & Villiers, *Country Gentleman*, c.1669). *Vogue word* is a semi-technical term, and the terms *vogue name*, *vogue phrase*, *vogue term*, *vogue usage* all occur. When usages are taken up by journalists, publicists, and media celebrities, they quickly become fashionable and may prompt analogue forms: for example, *junk food* leading to *junk bonds*, *junk mail*, *junk fax*; *marathon* leading to *beg-a-thon*, *readathon*, *telethon*; *sit-in* leading to *be-in*, *love-in*, *teach-in*; *the F-word* (fuck) prompting *the L-word* (liberal), *the T-word* (tax), the *W-word* (wimp). Common sources of vogue expressions include: (1) Technology: *interface*, *input*, *downtime*, from the use of computers. (2) Advertising and publicity: *bottom line*, *targeting*, *yuppie*. (3) Medicine, health care, social science, and accompanying social comment: *aerobic*, *battered wives syndrome*, *executive stress*, *fitness freak*, *Type-A personality*, *workout*. Compare BUZZ WORD, KEYWORD, NONCE WORD. [STYLE, WORD]. J.A., T.MCA.

VOICE [13c: from Anglo-Norman *voiz*, *voice*, Old French *vois*, *voiz* (Modern *voix*), from Latin *vox/vocis* a sound, tone, cry, voice, word, saying, sentence]. A term that refers to four aspects of language, of which the first two concern sound, the third is grammatical, and the fourth literary. The distinctions are illustrated in the phrases *a high-pitched voice* (general usage), *a voiceless consonant* (in phonetics), *the passive voice* (in grammar), and *narrative voice* (in literary theory).

Voice as vocal sound. The typical sound of someone speaking, the product of the vibration of the vocal cords, the resonant effect of the pharynx, mouth, nose, and tongue, the effect of rhythm and pitch, and such qualities as huskiness and throatiness. Individual voices differ, but the voices of members of certain groups have common features: adult male voices are usually 'deeper' (have a lower pitch) than women's and children's voices; the voices of people from the same region and/or social group usually share features of a particular accent. Kinds of voice can be categorized according to musical register: *a tenor voice*, *a falsetto voice*. Figuratively, the concept of voice extends to such things as: the words that someone utters (*the voice of experience*); the opportunity to say something (*have a voice in a decision*); being able to express a point of view (*to voice an opinion*); kinds of sound (*the voice of the wind in the trees*). See SOUND, TELEPHONE, VOICE OF AMERICA, WHISK(E)Y VOICE, WHITE VOICE.

Voice in phonetics. The buzzing sound made in the larynx by the vibration of the vocal cords or folds. In terms of this vibration, sounds are said to be *voiced* or *voiceless*. Voiced sounds such as /b, d, g, z/ are made by bringing the vocal folds close together so that the air stream forces them to vibrate as it passes through the glottis. This action reduces the amount of noise generated in the mouth for obstruents (stop and fricative consonants). Voiced obstruents are therefore said to be *lenis* (weak). Voiceless sounds such as /p, t, k, s/ are made by pulling the folds apart to allow the air to pass through unimpeded and increase the amount of noise generated in the mouth for obstruents. Voiceless obstruents are therefore said to be *fortis* (strong). The difference between voice and voicelessness can be checked by holding the larynx and saying *zzzz* and *ssss* in alternation, feeling vibration then lack of vibration. See ARTICULATION, DEVOICING, HARD AND SOFT, PITCH, SPEECH, VOICE QUALITY.

Voice in grammar. A category that involves the relationship of subject and object in a sentence or clause. In English, the contrast is between *active voice* and *passive voice*, affecting both the structure of the sentence and the form of the verb: *Susan chose the furniture* is an active sentence whose corresponding passive is *The furniture was chosen by Susan*. The active object (*the furniture*) is identical with the passive subject, while the active subject is incorporated in a *by*-phrase (*by Susan*). The two sentences have the same truth value, though there are differences in style and emphasis, in that passives are usually more formal than actives and the end of a sentence or clause tends to have the greatest emphasis. The *by*-phrase is often omitted from the passive sentence, especially in technical writing, producing an *agentless passive*. The passive verb adds auxiliary *be* to the corresponding active verb, and is followed by the passive participle of the main verb (*-ed* in regular verbs): active *washes, washed, was washing, has washed*; passive *is washed, is being washed, was washed, was being washed, has been washed*. The distinction between active and passive applies only when the verb is transitive, since only a transitive verb can be accompanied by an object. Typically, the active subject is the doer of an action (*Ted* in *Ted was repairing the computer*), whereas the passive subject (like the active object) is the person or thing affected by the action (*the computer*). See PASSIVE (VOICE), PASSIVIZATION.

Narrative voice. A term in literary criticism for the person who 'speaks' in a story, either a narrator who represents the author ('third person': the *implied author* or *omniscient narrator*) as in novels by Fielding and George Eliot, or who is represented by a character ('first person'), as in

Defoe's *Robinson Crusoe* or Swift's *Gulliver's Travels*. Within a narrative, other 'voices' may be heard in dialogue, in direct speech, and in some works of fiction several first-person voices may take up the same story from different perspectives, as in Susan Howatch's *The Wheel of Fortune*. The concept of narrative voice can become problematic in 'indirect' modes of speech presentation. In indirect speech and free indirect speech the voice is predominantly the (third person) narrator's, but the style may be coloured by the voice of the character whose words are being reported. Compare:

direct speech He said, 'I'll cough up the cash tomorrow.'

indirect speech He said (that) he would cough up the cash the next day.

free indirect speech He would *cough up* the cash *tomorrow.*

In the free indirect style (without the reporting clause *He said*), although the main voice is the narrator's, the perspective is predominantly the character's. See DIRECT AND INDIRECT SPEECH, NARRATION. [GRAMMAR, LITERATURE, SPEECH].

G.K., S.G., K.W., T.MCA.

VOICE BOX. See LARYNX, SPEECH.

VOICED AND VOICELESS. See VOICE.

VOICE OF AMERICA, short form *VOA*. Begun in 1942 under the Office of War Information, the VOA first broadcast in German to occupied Europe. Funded by Congress and charged from the outset with the delicate task of reporting the news objectively while representing US policy overseas, the VOA has often been subject to political pressure. After World War II, the VOA, as a division of the US State Department, broadcast news and anti-communist propaganda to audiences in Eastern Europe, the Soviet Union, and the People's Republic of China. Its signals were frequently jammed. In 1953, the VOA was purged as a result of Senator Joseph McCarthy's blanket accusation that the US State Department was riddled with traitors who were soft on communism. The new VOA was transferred to the newly formed *United States Information Agency* (*USIA*), where it has remained, though not always comfortably. The VOA charter lays down a strict policy of objective reporting of verified news and its broadcast manual has always carefully separated news from editorializing. However, the agency still has difficulty juggling the potentially conflicting roles of newscaster and diplomatic representative, and VOA broadcasts are still charged by their critics with being too pro- or anti-American. The VOA currently broadcasts in more than 40 languages, producing 160 hours of programming per day for a world audience of 120m, mostly educated, urban, politically aware young adults. A subsidiary, Radio Marti, has broadcast to Cuba since 1985. Although the News Division remains VOA's primary focus, and attracts the greatest number of listeners, the VOA also promotes US cultural interests through feature programmes on American history, science and agriculture, jazz and rock music, interviews with celebrities, and commentaries on English vocabulary. Special English broadcasts of news and features (including adaptations of short stories by American writers) are aimed at learners of English and are read at a slower pace using a simplified vocabulary of 1,500 words, short, active sentences, and few numbers or technical terms. See PROPAGANDA. [AMERICAS, MEDIA]. D.E.B.

VOICE QUALITY. The characteristic sound of the voice brought about by the mode of vibration of the vocal cords or folds. Differences in the degree and manner of glottal closure distinguish *modal voice* and *whisper*, and *breathy voice* and *whispery voice*. The quality of the voice also depends on the degree of tension in the larynx and pharynx, and on the vertical displacement of the larynx: a raised larynx produces a thin tense voice, and a lowered larynx a booming 'clergyman's' voice. Apart from distinguishing voiced and voiceless sounds, voice quality does not make linguistic contrasts, but conveys information about the speaker. Languages and dialects have characteristic voice qualities; personal voice quality enables a listener to recognize a particular individual. The quality of someone's voice also conveys emotions and attitudes. See ACCENT, ARTICULATORY SET(TING), VOICE. [SPEECH]. G.K.

VOLUME [14c: through French from Latin *volumen/voluminis* a coil, roll (of sheets of papyrus or parchment, usually wound on a spindle)]. (1) (Obsolete) a roll or scroll of written work. (2) (Obsolete) especially in 17-19c poetry, the coils of a serpent or the winding of a stream ('Her twisting volumes and her rolling eyes': Pope, *Thebais*, 1703). (3) A collection of written or printed sheets bound to form a book. The terms *Sacred Volume* for the Bible and *Christian Volume* for the New Testament were common in the 18-19c. The phrase *to speak volumes* (to say a great deal, to be expressive or meaningful) is a figurative extension of this sense. (4) A book in a set or series, usually large in size, such as the volumes of an 18-19c novel, a large dictionary, or an encyclopedia (*Volume II of the OED*); a set of issues of a periodical, usually covering one year and sometimes kept in a special binding (*The 1970 volume of American Speech*). (5) Bulk or quantity, as in a large book, object, or mass of material: *Volumes of smoke/water poured from the hole*; *They received volumes of mail*. (6) A total amount: *The volume of sales was down last year*. (7) In physics mathematics, quantity measured in cubic units: *They measured the volume of water displaced*. (8) The power or tone of a singing voice or a musical instrument. (9) The degree of loudness in a machine that gives out sound, such as a radio or music centre: *Turn the volume down*. See BOOK, PARCHMENT, PERIODICAL, ROLL, SCROLL. [MEDIA, TECHNOLOGY, WRITING]. T.MCA.

VOWEL [14c: from Old French *vouel*, a variant of *voyel* (Modern *voyelle*), from Latin *vocalis* (*littera*) vocal (letter), a letter representing uninterrupted voice or breath]. A term in general use and in phonetics for both a speech sound that is distinct from a consonant (also *vowel sound*) and the letter of the alphabet that represents such a speech sound (also *vowel letter*). In general usage, the distinction between vowels in speech and writing is not always clearly made, but linguists and phoneticians seek to keep the two kinds of vowel distinct.

Vowel sounds. Phonetically, a vowel is a speech sound characterized by voicing (the vibration of the larynx) and by absence of obstruction or audible friction in the vocal tract, allowing the breath free passage. The quality of a vowel is chiefly determined by the position of the tongue and the lips: see VOWEL QUALITY. Vowel sounds divide into *monophthongs* (single vowel sounds that may be long or short), *diphthongs* (double vowel sounds formed by gliding from one vowel position to another), and *triphthongs* (triple vowel sounds formed by gliding from one through another to a third vowel position). See entries. The human speech mechanism is capable of producing a wide range of simple and complex vowel sounds. As with consonants, however, in each language (or language variety) a particular range of vowels is used: for example, in standard Parisian French, there are 12 non-nasal and 4 nasal monophthongs (16 vowel sounds in all); in BrE, the basic vowel system of RP has 12 monophthongs and 8 diphthongs (20 vowel sounds in all) while the basic vowel system of ScoE has 10 monophthongs and 4 diphthongs (14 vowel sounds in all).

Vowel letters. The five classic vowel letters of the Roman alphabet are *a, e, i, o, u*, to which *y* is usually added; apart from its syllable-initial role as a semi-vowel or semi-consonant in words like *year*, *y* functions in English largely as an alternative vowel symbol to *i*. Phonetically, the letters *w* (as in *win*) and *y* (as in *year*) are articulated similarly to vowels, but positionally they function as consonants, initiating syllables and introducing vowels: compare *wear/bear* and *year/fear*. Phonetically, too, the liquid consonants written as *l, r* and the nasal consonants written as *m, n* have some of the characteristics of vowels (such as continuous non-fricative voicing), and when used syllabically (as in the pronunciations of *apple, spasm, isn't, centre*) they in effect represent a preceding schwa vowel sound in addition to their own sound value.

Whereas the five classic vowel letters match the five vowel phonemes of a language like Spanish, they are insufficient to distinguish the much larger number of vowel phonemes of English. When unaccompanied by another vowel letter, the five letters usually have a basic 'short' sound value in medial position in English words (as in *pat, pet, pit, pot, putt/put*), but in some words (such as *yacht, pretty, son, busy*) their values are aberrant, and in certain environments, such as after /w/ and before /l, r/, they are commonly modified (as in *was, word, all, old, far, her, fir, for, fur*). For each of the short values there is a corresponding 'long' value which formerly (before the Great Vowel Shift of the 15c) was close to the short value, but is today in varying degrees removed from it (and is not the 'long' value as understood in phonetics). The present-day long values are as heard in *mate, meet, might, moat, mute*. Native speakers perceive the long values as intimately associated with the short values; the two often alternate in related words (as in *sane/sanity, abbreviate/brevity, five/fifth, depose/deposit, student/study*) and the long values are heard as the names of the letters themselves (heard as *ay, ee, eye, oh, you*). See LONG AND SHORT.

The spelling of the long values of the vowels is varied and unpredictable: for example, Edward Rondthaler and Edward J. Lias (*Dictionary of American Spelling*, 1986) list 114 alternative spellings for the five sounds. These include single graphemes (units of writing), as in *mind, post, truth*, digraphs as in *leave, sleeve, receive, believe*, and longer graphemes as in *beau, queue*. Some of these longer graphemes include consonant letters (as in the *eigh* of *weigh* and the *et* of *ballet*) that are in effect constituents of vowels. Highly characteristic of English vowel spellings is the 'magic' *e* placed after a consonant, which has the effect in Modern English of showing the long value of a preceding vowel, as in *mate, mete, mite, mote, mute*. In addition to these parallel sets of short and long vowels corresponding to *a, e, i, o, u*, English also needs to spell several vowel sounds for which alternative pairs of digraphs are widely (but not consistently) used according to position: for example, initial and medial *au, eu, ou, ai, oi*, but final *aw, ew, ow,*

ay, oy (contrast *fault/flaw, feud/few, count/cow, rain/ray, coil/coy*). A corollary of the many alternative spellings for the same vowel sound is the many alternative pronunciations that may be required for the same vowel letters: for example, *ea* is pronounced in nine different ways in *eat, threat, great, react, create, pear, hear, heart, hearse*.

Unstable pronunciation of vowel letters. The pronunciation of vowel letters varies between communities and individuals, and within the speech of individuals. Variation between communities includes the tendency of BrE to reduce words such as *secretary, monastery, dormitory* to rhyme with *ministry*, while in AmE the penultimate vowel letter usually receives full value. Within Britain, different speech communities vary in the distinctions they make between the values of *u*. In England, Northern English does not distinguish the vowel sounds of *putt* and *put*, and many East Anglians pronounce *beauty* like *booty*; in ScoE, no distinction is made between the vowel sounds of *pull* and *pool*. Variation between individuals occurs when some give the first vowel of *either* the long value of *e* and others give it the long value of *i*. In addition, unstressed vowels may vary from occasion to occasion, formal, careful speech being more likely to give vowels their full orthographic value while fluent, conversational speech is more likely to reduce them to schwa or elide them altogether: *February* may have each letter pronounced explicitly, or be reduced in various ways, including in BrE 'Febry'.

See A, ABLAUT (VOWEL GRADATION), ACCENT, AITKEN'S VOWEL, ALPHABET, APHESIS, CONSONANT, DIACRITIC, DI(A)ERESIS, DIGRAPH, DIPHTHONG, E, ELISION, EPENTHESIS, GREAT VOWEL SHIFT, I, LETTER[1], LIGATURE, LONG AND SHORT, MONOPHTHONG, O, RECEIVED PRONUNCIATION, RHYTHM, S(C)HWA, SCOTTISH VOWEL-LENGTH RULE, SPELLING, STRESS, SYLLABIC CONSONANT, SYLLABLE, TRIPHTHONG, U, UMLAUT, VOWEL HARMONY, VOWEL LENGTH, VOWEL QUALITY, VOWEL QUANTITY, VOWEL SHIFT, W, WEAK VOWEL, Y. [SPEECH, WRITING].   C.U., G.K.

VOWEL GRADATION. See ABLAUT.

VOWEL HARMONY. A distinctive phonological patterning in which the vowels in a word share certain features. As in Irish Gaelic, they may all be front vowels (*cipiní* sticks, *teilefís* television), open vowels (*balla* wall, *hata* hat), or back vowels (*lúdrú* buffeting, *solus* light). Vowel harmony is found in Gaelic, Turkish, Hungarian, Finnish, and many West African vernaculars, but not in mainstream English. In Kamtok (Cameroonian Pidgin English), however, the same vowel may appear in adjacent syllables (*palava* talk, *pikin* child, *potopoto* mud, muddy), and when different vowels occur in adjacent syllables, a fixed pattern of exclusion is followed (for example, *i* cannot be followed by *e*, producing *witi* with, and not *wite). See ANGLO-IRISH, KAMTOK. [SPEECH].   L.T.

VOWEL LENGTH. See LONG AND SHORT, VOWEL QUANTITY.

VOWEL LIGATURE. See LIGATURE.

VOWEL QUALITY. A term in phonetics for the property that makes one vowel sound different from another: for example, /iː/ as in *sheep* from /ɪ/ as in *ship*. The quality of a vowel is determined by the position of the tongue, lips, and lower jaw, and the resulting size and shape of the mouth and pharynx. Vowels are classed as *close* or *open* (in British terminology) and *high* and *low* (in American terminology) according to whether the tongue is held close to the roof of the mouth or low in the mouth. They are classed as *front* or *back* in both terminologies according to whether the body of the tongue is pushed forward or pulled back. They are classed as *rounded* or *spread* according to the shape of the lips: for example, the /iː/ in *sheep* is a close front spread vowel, the /ɪ/ in *ship* a semi-high front unrounded vowel.

Cardinal vowels. While this general classification provides an approximate description of vowel quality, it is not sufficient to define all the vowels in a system such as English. Some vowels can only be defined in relation to other vowels: for example, /ɛ/ in *bet* is intermediate between close /ɪ/ in *bit* and open /æ/ in *bat*. The most widespread method of dealing with relative vowel quality is based on the system of *cardinal vowels* devised by Daniel Jones. These vowels are used as reference qualities for the vowels of all languages. The eight primary cardinal vowels are shown in Fig. 1.

Cardinal [i] is produced with the body of the tongue held forward in the mouth, and with the tongue surface as close as possible to the palate without generating turbulence (which would turn it into a consonant). Cardinal [ɑ] is produced with the body of the tongue held back in the mouth, and with the root of the tongue as close as possible to the back wall of the pharynx, again without generating turbulence. The remaining cardinal vowels are placed at equidistant points on the lines from [i] to [ɑ]. The system of cardinal vowels provides a means of describing vowel sounds, as shown in Fig. 2.

Cardinal [i] has spread lips; from [i] to [ɑ] the vowels become less spread and progressively more lip neutral. From [ɑ] to [u] they are

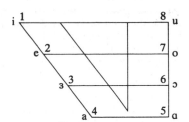

FIG. 1

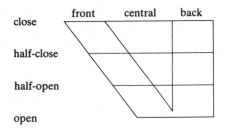

FIG. 2

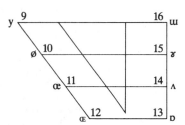

FIG. 3

progressively more rounded, and [u] is fully rounded. For ease of reference, the cardinal vowels are numbered anti-clockwise (counterclockwise) from 1 to 8. The statement 'a vowel in the region of cardinal 2' is equivalent to 'a vowel in the region of [e]'. Both refer to a 'half-close front spread vowel'. Most vowels in most languages combine lip spreading with frontness, and rounding with backness, as in the primary cardinal vowels, but this is not always the case. *Secondary cardinal vowels* have the lip positions reversed from those of the primary cardinals, the first five being rounded and the last three spread. These cardinal vowels are numbered anti-clockwise from 9 to 16: see Fig. 3.

See VOWEL, VOWEL QUANTITY. [SPEECH].   G.K.

VOWEL QUANTITY. A term in phonetics and poetics for the length of a vowel, usually indicated in phonetic transcription by a length mark [ː] or a colon [:] after a vowel, as in /aː/. Vowels so marked have in general greater duration than the same vowels with no such mark. Vowels so marked are described as *long*, and unmarked vowels are *short*, a distinction known as *vowel* *length*: see LONG AND SHORT. However, the measurable duration of vowels depends also on at least two other factors: (1) Vowel height, in terms of the position of the tongue. Open vowels as in *ban* /ban/ or *balm* /bɑːm/ are longer than close vowels as in *bin* /bɪn/ or *beam* /biːm/. (2) Environment, in terms of preceding and following sounds. Vowels are shortened before some consonants and lengthened before others, for example /uː/ is longer in *move* /muːv/ than in *boot* /buːt/. These factors have different weightings in different varieties of English, and contribute to the variety of rhythms in English. In many varieties, short vowels may have greater duration than long vowels: for example, /a/ in *jazz* may be longer than /iː/ in *sleep*. To avoid the confusion, some phoneticians consider it preferable to treat the length mark as a mark of quantity rather than duration, and refer to 'heavy' and 'light' vowels. If a vowel has sufficient duration, as in *halve* /hɑːv/, there is time for the organs that form it to move into their target positions and remain there briefly before moving to the next target. Such a vowel is described as *tense*. If the vowel is too short, the organs have to leave the target as soon as they reach it, and in extreme cases (for example, in *six* /sɪks/) may not reach the target at all. Such a vowel is described as *lax*. In view of the time required to move to more peripheral vowel positions, tense vowels tend to be peripheral and lax vowels closer to *schwa*, the neutral or central vowel. If an English word ends in a vowel, then the vowel must be either heavy (that is, it is either marked with a length mark or is a diphthong) or reduced: for example, *me* /miː/, *day* /deɪ/, *banana* /-nə/. See LENGTH MARK, VOWEL, VOWEL QUALITY. [SPEECH].   G.K.

VOWEL SHIFT. A term in philology and phonetics for a process under which a set of vowels undergoes changes. The term *Great Vowel Shift* is used for a number of long-term changes which affected the English vowel system during the 15c–17c. In this shift, the long vowels in *reed*, *rood* changed from [eː, oː] to [iː, uː], and close vowels became diphthongs, the vowels in *five*, *house* changing from [iː, uː] to [aɪ, aʊ]. The degree to which vowels have shifted varies from one variety of English to another: for example, conservative dialects of Scotland, Ireland, and the North of England retain a monophthong [eː, oː] in words like *raid*, *road*, whereas these vowels have generally become diphthongs elsewhere, as in RP [eɪ, əʊ]. See ABLAUT, GREAT VOWEL SHIFT, VOWEL. [SPEECH].   G.K., T.MCA.

VULGAR [14c: from Latin *vulgaris* common, from *vulgus* the people]. A non-technical term that has moved from a neutral and general to a pejorative meaning. Formerly, it referred to ordinary life and ordinary people, as opposed to an upper-class or educated minority. *Vulgar Latin* was the everyday Latin of the Roman Empire and, until the 19c, European vernacular languages were referred to as *vulgar tongues*. Concomitantly, a sense of coarseness and lack of breeding and culture developed, associated with the 'lowest orders' of society, and now dominates, particularly with reference to language: *a vulgar remark*. See PARTRIDGE, RECEIVED STANDARD AND MODIFIED STANDARD, SWEARING, VERNACULAR, VULGARISM. [STYLE].   T.MCA.

VULGARISM [17c]. A coarse expression, especially when used in elevated discourse or on formal occasions: for example, *fart* appearing in an academic treatise or *crap* said loudly at an elegant dinner party. It is a vulgarism if a sailor or a saint says *You're pissed* to someone who is drunk, but in the case of the sailor it provokes less comment. See VULGAR, -ISM. Compare SWEARWORD. [STYLE, WORD].   T.MCA.

W

W, w [Called 'double-you']. The 23rd letter of the modern Roman alphabet as used for English. The Romans had no letter suitable for representing the phoneme /w/, as in Old English, although phonetically the vowel represented by *v* (as in *veni, vidi, vici*) was close. In the 7c, scribes wrote *uu* for /w/, but from the 8c they commonly preferred for English the runic symbol *wynn* (*þ*). Meanwhile, *uu* was adopted for /w/ in continental Europe, and after the Norman Conquest in 1066 it was introduced to English as the ligatured *w*, which by 1300 had replaced *wynn*. Early printers sometimes used *vv* for lack of a *w* in their type. The name *double-u* for double *v* (French *double-v*) recalls the former identity of *u* and *v*, though that is also evident in the cognates *flour/flower, guard/ward, suede/Swede*, and the tendency for *u, w* to alternate in digraphs according to position: *maw/maul, now/noun*.

Sound value. In English, *w* normally represents a voiced bilabial semi-vowel, produced by rounding and then opening the lips before a full vowel, whose value may be affected.

Vowel digraphs. (1) The letter *w* commonly alternates with *u* in digraphs after *a, e, o* to represent three major phonemes. Forms with *u* typically precede a consonant, with *aw, ew, ow* preferred syllable-finally: *law, saw, taut; dew, new, feud; cow, how, loud*. (2) When the preceding vowel opens a monosyllable, silent *e* follows the *w*: *awe, ewe, owe* (but note *awful, ewer, owing*). (3) Word-finally, *w* is almost always preferred to *u* (*thou* is a rare exception), but *w* occurs medially quite often (*tawdry, newt, vowel, powder*), and the choice of letter may be arbitrary (compare *lour/lower, flour/flower, noun/renown*). (4) In some words, digraphs with *w* have non-standard values: *sew, knowledge, low*. Final *-ow* with its non-standard value in *low*

occurs in nearly four times as many words as the standard value in *how*. (5) In the name *Cowper*, *ow* is uniquely pronounced as *oo* in *Cooper*. (6) Final *w* in many disyllables evolved from the Old English letter *yogh* (*ʒ*) for *g*, as in *gallows, hallow, tallow, bellows, follow, harrow, borrow, morrow, sorrow, furrow* (compare German *Galgen, heiligen, Talg, Balg, folgen, Harke, borgen, Morgen, Sorge, Furche*).

WH. (1) The digraph *wh* occurs word-initially, and in ScoE, IrE, often in AmE, and among some RP speakers it has the once universal voiceless, aspirated pronunciation often represented as /hw/, sometimes as /ʍ/: *whale, wharf, what, wheat, wheel, wheeze, whelk, when, whelp, where, whet, whether, which, while, whimper, whip, whirl, whisker, whistle, white, whither, whorl*. Such forms were mostly spelt *hw* in Old English. The *h* in *whelk* appears to be a late insertion. (2) Several common parallel spellings without *h* are homophones for speakers who do not make the *w/wh* distinction: *whale/wail, where/ware, whet/wet, whether/weather, whey/way, which/witch, whig/wig, while/wile*. See WH-SOUND.

Silent W. (1) Initial *w* fell silent before *r* in the 17c, but is written in *wrack, wraith, wrangle, wrap, wrath, wreak, wreath, wreck, wren, wrench, wrest, wrestle, wretch, wriggle, wright, wring, wrinkle, wrist, writ, write, writhe, wrong, wrote, wroth, wreak, wrought, wrung, wry*. The form *awry* derives from *wry*. (2) The *w* in *two, who, whose, whom* is thought to have fallen silent under the rounding influence of the following *u*-sound, while the *w* in *whole* (cognate with *hale, heal*) and *whore* was added in the 15c under the influence of dialects in which a *w*-sound arose before the vowel *o* (as in the pronunciation of *one*). This was once the case with *whoop*, which now has the optional pronunciations 'hoop' and '(h)woop'. A modern instance of adding an

THE CAPITAL LETTER

EARLY FORMS				CURRENT FORMS	
Phoenician	Greek	Etruscan	Roman (Latin)	roman	italic
Y	ҺY	Y	V	W	*W*

THE SMALL LETTER

EARLY FORMS			CURRENT FORMS	
Roman cursive	Roman uncial	Carolingian minuscule	roman	italic
	Ա		W	*w*

etymologically inappropriate *w-* occurs when Greek-derived *holistic* (compare *holocaust, holograph,* from *hólos* entire) is spelt *wholistic,* on the assumption that it derives from *whole.* (3) Medial *w* has fallen silent after *s* in *answer, sword,* and after consonants when initiating unstressed final syllables in English place-names: *Chiswick* ('Chizzik'), *Norwich* ('Norritch', 'Norridge'), *Southwark* ('Suthark'), *Welwyn* ('Wellin'). This *w* has also fallen silent in nautical usage, with adapted spellings *bosun, bo's'n* for *boatswain,* and *gunnel* for *gunwale.* (4) In informal or non-standard, often archaic, speech, *w* is elided in *allus* always, *forrad* forward, *ha'p'orth* halfpennyworth, *summat* something. (5) *Will, would* lose *w* when they assimilate to preceding pronouns, as in *he'll, I'll, it'll, he'd, I'd.*

Variations. (1) The sound /w/ has other spellings. Because lip-rounding is a feature of most pronunciations of *u,* /w/ is spelt *u* in some words, chiefly of French derivation, after *g, q,* and *s,* as in *languish, question, quiet, suite, persuade.* (2) Recent French loans may keep the French *oi* for the sound /wa/: *boudoir, memoir, repertoire, reservoir, soirée,* a pattern which may have influenced the respelling of *quire* as *choir* in the late 17c. (3) A change of pronunciation has given an unspelt initial /w/ to *one, once,* but not to their cognates *only, alone.* (4) *R* is sometimes spoken /w/. This has long been regarded as a shibboleth of some kinds of BrE upper-class accents and may occur in the speech of small children and in imitation of such speech (*Weally weally big!*), and in defective articulation. It is sometimes referred to as *rhotacism.* (5) Historically there has been some parallel development of Anglo-Norman spellings with *w* and French spellings with *g: ward/guard, warranty/guarantee* (compare French *garde, garantie*), *reward/regard, -wise/guise.* See A, ALPHABET, E, H, I, LETTER[1], O, RHOTACISM, SPELLING, WH-SOUND. [WRITING]. C.U.

WAFFLE [Late 19c: formerly Scots and Northern English, from obsolete *waff* to yelp, and *-le*]. Also **woffle.** An informal especially BrE term for rambling, uninformative, and boring talk or writing, and for talking and writing in such a way: 'I under-estimated his shrewdness . . . I thought he was waffling' (Laurence Meynell, *Bandaberry,* 1960). The comment *waffle* or *Stop waffling* is a common note by teachers in students' essays. Compare TWADDLE. [STYLE].
T.MCA.

WALCOTT, Derek Alton [b.1930]. Caribbean poet, playwright, and critic, born on St Lucia, and educated at St Mary's College, St Lucia, and U. College of the West Indies, Mona, Jamaica (1950-3). He has taught at Grenada Boys' Secondary School, St Mary's College, St Lucia, and Jamaica College, and has been a feature writer for *Public Opinion,* Jamaica (*c.*1956), and the *Trinidad Guardian* (1960-8). He went to Trinidad in 1957, having been commissioned to write *Drums and Colours,* an epic drama for the 1958 West Indian Festival of Arts, and in 1958 was awarded a Rockefeller Foundation Fellowship to study theatre in New York. In 1959, he founded the *Little Carib Theatre Workshop* (later known as the *Trinidad Theatre Workshop*), whose company toured the West Indies and Canada. His publications include: *25 Poems* (Bridgetown, 1948), *Epitaph for the Young* (Bridgetown, 1949), *Poems* (Kingston, 1951), *In a Green Night* (London: Jonathan Cape, 1962), *Selected Poems* (New York: Farrar Strauss, 1964), *The Castaway and Other Poems* (Cape, 1965), *The Gulf and Other Poems* (Cape, 1969), *Dream on Monkey Mountain and Other Plays* (New York: Farrar, Strauss, & Giroux, 1970), *Another Life* (Cape, 1973), *Sea Grapes* (Cape, 1976), *The Joker of Seville* and *Oh Babylon* (Farrar, etc., 1978), *The Fortunate Traveller* (Farrar, etc., 1981), and *The Arkansas Treatment* (Farrar, etc., 1987). Honours include the Royal Society of Literature Award, the Hummingbird Medal Gold (Trinidad), the Guggenheim Award, and Honorary Member of the American Academy of Arts and Literature. Walcott has observed: 'You start off as a colonial writer, you get promotion to Commonwealth writer, West Indian writer, then maybe to the international club by the people who run this thing called English literature. The horrific thing for them is that English literature is out of their control' (quoted in 'Conquering English', *South,* July 1988). See CARIBBEAN LITERATURE IN ENGLISH. [AMERICAS, BIOGRAPHY, LITERATURE]. L.D.C., T.MCA.

WALES [From Old English *Wealas,* plural of *Wealh* foreigner, Welshman. Welsh equivalent: *Cymru,* from Celtic *Cumbroges* compatriots. Pronounced 'Kumry']. A principality in southwestern Britain and part of the United Kingdom. Capital: Cardiff. Economy: mixed. Population: 2.8m (1981). Languages: English (*c.*100%), Welsh (some 25%). Education: mainly in English, with some state-supported Welsh-medium schools. In classical times, the region was part of the general Celtic culture of northwestern Europe, strongly influenced by Rome during the four centuries in which southern Britain was a province of the Roman Empire. After the expansion of the Anglo-Saxons (5-9c), Wales was the sole surviving autonomous Celtic territory in southern Britain; for centuries its peoples warred among themselves and with the English, Irish, Norse, and Danes. In the 8c, to strengthen the defence of the Welsh Marches, King Offa of Mercia built a wall from the Dee to the Wye, which came to be known as *Offa's Dyke*. In the 9c, Rhoddri Mawr (Rhoddri the Great) united the country for the first time since the Romans.

In 1282, during the invasion of Edward I of England, the last native Welsh prince, Llewelyn ap Gruffydd, was killed. In 1301, Edward's son was crowned *Prince of Wales*, a title since borne by most of the eldest sons of English, later British, monarchs. Wales may be regarded as England's first colony, and served almost immediately after the Norman Conquest as a springboard for the invasion and settlement of Ireland. The part-Welsh nobleman Henry Tudor became Henry VII of England in 1485 and Wales was effectively incorporated into England in the Acts of Union of 1535 and 1543, English becoming the language of administration, education, and trade. Although there was a body of Welsh law, the *Cyfraith Hywel* (Law of Howel), it had been increasingly superseded by English law from the 13c and after the Union the law of England was applied throughout the country.

The distinctness of Wales has survived integration, but the dominance of England and English, and the ambiguous status of Wales (administratively united with, but psychologically distinct from, England) have created a tension that centres particularly on whether, to be truly Welsh, one must know Welsh. Unilingual English-speaking people born in Wales do not regard knowledge of Welsh as a criterion of Welshness, and may resent the assumption that it can or should be. Wales is known for: song and poetry in both languages, including the male-voice choirs that originated in the English-speaking south during industrialization in the 19c; *eisteddfodau* (arts festivals) in Welsh; nonconformist Protestantism ('the chapel'); a tradition of radical politics; and a passion for rugby football that transcends language. The principality has in effect an Anglo-Celtic culture that blends ancient tradition with local forms of a language and institutions that were once alien, but have long since been thoroughly digested.

See ANGLO-WELSH LITERATURE, BRITISH, BRITON, BRYTHONIC, CELT, CELTIC, CELTIC LANGUAGES, CORNWALL, CUMBRIC, ENGLISH, ENGLISH PLACE-NAMES, HISTORY OF ENGLISH, PATRONYMIC, PLAID CYMRU, SCOTLAND, SCOTTISH LITERATURE, SCOTTISH PLACE-NAMES, THOMAS, WALES, WALIAN, WELSH, WELSH ENGLISH, WELSH LANGUAGE SERVICE, WELSH LANGUAGE SOCIETY, WELSH LITERATURE, WELSHMAN/WOMAN, WELSHNESS, WELSH PLACE-NAMES, WELSHRY, WELSH WALES, WELSHY. [EUROPE, NAME].   T.MCA.

WALIAN [1890s: from *Wales* and *-ian*]. An element in the compounds *North Walian* and *South Walian*, referring respectively to North Wales and South Wales and serving to name people from these regions: 'He was a Methodist preacher, though he was a South Walian' (*Wales*, Aug. 1894); 'the stern North Walian' (D. E. Allen, *British Tastes*, 1968). See WALES, WELSH. [EUROPE, NAME].   T.MCA.

WASP [1950s: an acronym for *White Anglo-Saxon Protestant*]. An informal, sometimes pejorative term for what is widely thought to be the dominant cultural group in the US. Hispanics in the Southwest talk about *Anglos* (English-speakers) and African Americans about *whitey* or *Mr Charlie* (whites); but *Wasp* refers particularly to whites of English (or at least not notably other ethnic) origin who are mainline Protestant in church affiliation. From the insect may come associations of irritability, annoyance, and pettiness. Wasps are thought to set the standards, including those for language, in the US. See ETHNIC NAME, WHITE. Compare ANGLO. [AMERICAS, NAME].   J.A.

WATERMARK. See PAPER.

WATSON, George Marr [1876–1950]. Scottish lexicographer and author of the *Roxburghshire Word-Book* (1923), an account of the vocabulary of his native county. Apprenticed as a printer and self-educated, Watson is typical of the learned sub-editors on whom the success of the major historical dictionaries of English has depended. Brought to Oxford in 1907 by his fellow Borderer James Murray, Watson worked for 20 years preparing *OED* entries for the volumes N to W. Under the editorship of William Craigie, he worked (1927–37) on the *Dictionary of American English*. A memorial notice declares: 'Service in the First World War did not interrupt his work, for he continued to read the proofs of the *Dictionary* even in the trenches.' In recognition of his work, Oxford awarded him an honorary MA in 1933. See DICTIONARY OF AMERICAN ENGLISH. [BIOGRAPHY, EUROPE, REFERENCE].
                                              R.W.B.

WAYSTAGE. See COUNCIL OF EUROPE.

WEAK FORM. See STRESS.

WEAK VERB. In the traditional description of Germanic languages, a verb that indicates such meaning differences as tense through the addition of inflections: Modern English *play*, *played*. In contrast, strong verbs modify their vowels: *ring*, *rang*, *rung*. The terms are usually replaced in grammars of Modern English by *regular verbs* (in place of weak verbs) and *irregular verbs* (in place of strong verbs). See STRONG VERB, VERB. [GRAMMAR].   S.G.

WEAK VOWEL. In phonetics, a vowel that normally occurs only in unstressed syllables. There are two weak vowels in English: schwa /ə/, as in the unstressed syllables of *above* and *sofa*, and short *i* /ɪ/, as in the unstressed syllables in RP *example* and *Sophie*. See S(C)HWA, VOWEL. [SPEECH].   G.K.

WEBSTER, Noah [1758-1843]. American teacher, writer, editor, lexicographer, lecturer, and lobbyist, born in West Hartford, Connecticut, educated at Yale College (1778), and admitted to the bar (1781). His best-known works, *The American Spelling Book* (the 'Blue-Back Spelling Book', 1783) and *An American Dictionary of the English Language* (1828), greatly contributed to lessening US dependence on British models of the standard language. His career as a schoolmaster led to the publication of *A Grammatical Institute of the English Language*, which included *The American Spelling Book* (1783), a grammar (1784), and a reader (1785). The speller was particularly popular, notably for its moral and patriotic flavour as opposed to the religious orientation of earlier texts. The grammar, influenced by Robert Lowth and in subsequent editions by John Horne Tooke, was less popular; it was criticized for being too advanced for schoolchildren and for overemphasizing elocution. Webster's achievement with *A Grammatical Institute* was in separating spelling, grammar, and reading into individual texts, a strategy which may have influenced other textwriters to stage the learning process for children. His vigorous lobbying to protect his work from piracy led to the institution of the first federal copyright laws in 1790.

Webster also wrote essays on educational reform. His *Letters to a Young Gentleman Commencing His Education* (1802) shows his desire to 'delight and allure' students by emphasizing science and reason rather than philosophy and religion. His celebration of the beauty and regularity of English is notable as his emphasis on civic responsibility. Webster's lexicographical career began with the compilation of *A Compendious Dictionary* (1806), which was marked by innovations in spelling and by adherence to New England educated speech for pronunciation. Public criticism of the innovations eventually led to the 'dictionary wars' in which Joseph Emerson Worcester, who favoured BrE norms, led the opposition. Webster modified his stance in *An American Dictionary of the English Language* (1828, 1840), and considered its etymologies to be the most important aspect of his

work. He adhered to the Biblical account of the origin of languages, claiming that all languages derived from 'Chaldee'. The inclusion of technical terms and an attempt at precision in definitions distinguished this dictionary, but few Americanisms were included.

Some of Webster's recommendations for spelling reform, suggested as early as his *Dissertations* (1789), survived modification in later editions of his texts. The principles behind his reforms were analogy, etymology, reason, and usage. He was most concerned about superfluous letters and indeterminate sounds and characters. Although most of his early suggestions were retracted, the US spelling of such words as *honor, center, defense, public* can be attributed to his choice of them rather than *honour, centre, defence, publick*. He recognized that language influences people and he sought to ensure that American texts reflected American values as he understood them. His greatest achievement was probably his influence rather than the scholarship of his works. His view that 'the process of a living language is like the motion of a broad river which flows with a slow, silent, *irresistible* current' (*Letters*, 369) prefigured attitudes of later language scholars. Although traces of his social, religious, and regional affiliations are evident in all his work, his adoption of current educated usage as standard was an advance in lexicography. See index. [AMERICAS, EDUCATION, REFERENCE, WRITING].
                                              R.W.B.

Leavitt, Robert K. 1947. *Noah's Ark, New England Yankees, and the Endless Quest*. Springfield, Mass.: Merriam.

Shoemaker, Ervin C. 1936. *Noah Webster, Pioneer of Learning*. New York: Columbia University Press.

Skeel, Emily E. F. 1958. *Bibliography of the Writings of Noah Webster*. New York Public Library.

Warfel, Harry R. 1936/66. *Noah Webster, School Master to America*. New York: Octagon Books.

WEBSTERS. An informal American term for dictionaries and related works. The first dictionary referred to in this way was George & Charles Merriam's 1847 edition of Noah Webster's *An American Dictionary of the English Language* (1828) and the name was later used for the Merriam editions of 1847, 1864, and 1890, the last entitled *Webster's International Dictionary*. Because of the popularity of these works, when the copyright of the 1847 edition (registered under the name *An American Dictionary of the English Language*) expired, several companies published dictionaries with *Webster's* in their titles and sold them cheaply. Some were photolithographed with various additions to and deletions of material from that edition. G. & C. Merriam sued for damages in several states. In

1917, it was determined by federal court decision that Merriam did not own exclusive rights to the name *Webster* and that, after the expiration in 1834 of the 1806 copyright on Webster's *Compendious Dictionary*, anyone could publish a 'Webster' dictionary. It was recognized, however, that by 1904 the name had acquired a 'secondary meaning', designating the Merriam dictionaries. To protect this interest, other publishers were required to distinguish their dictionaries from those of G. & C. Merriam; refrain from using the Merriam 'open book' logo on advertisements, circulars, letterheads, etc.; attach printed slips to title pages notifying the purchaser if the publication was a reprint of an earlier edition (1892); distinguish their company on the dictionary covers (1908); and disclaim any relationship with G. & C. Merriam (1909). Merriam, however, was burdened with the responsibility of proving financial losses incurred by other publishers' practices (1909, 1911, 1912). In the litigation with the Ogilvie and Saalfield companies, Merriam objected to their use of the description 'authentic Webster'. Until legally restrained, Saalfield published a desk dictionary called *Webster's Intercollegiate*. However, Merriam was not able to convince others of its exclusive right to the name and the claim was repeatedly rejected by the courts. The name is therefore in the public domain: since 1953 Simon & Schuster have published a desk dictionary, *Webster's New World Dictionary of the American Language*, which does not contain the legal disclaimer of affiliation with the Merriam–Webster line and is obviously distinct in its appearance and editorial content. See MERRIAM–WEBSTER, WEBSTER. [AMERICAS, MEDIA, REFERENCE]. R.W.B.

WEBSTER'S COLLEGIATE DICTIONARIES. A line of best-selling desk dictionaries produced by Merriam–Webster, Springfield, Massachusetts. The first *Collegiate* (1898) was compiled to be used by college students, taking its place in a series of abridgements intended to serve students from primary to university level. However, it was soon dubbed 'the busy man's dictionary', indicating its general usefulness. Subsequent editions appeared in 1910, 1916, 1931, 1936, 1946, 1963, 1973 (which sold over 11m copies) and 1983 (the 9th Edition, with almost 160,000 entries based on a file of some 13m citations). The dictionaries, in addition to detailed coverage of pronunciations, spellings, word senses, and common synonyms, are known for their encyclopedic appendices, covering foreign words and phrases, biographical and geographical names, US and Canadian colleges and Universities, signs and symbols, and a style manual. The 9th Edition added the dates of first entry

words into the language (where well substantiated) and usage notes at the ends of entries subject to controversy. The term *collegiate* is now used to describe not only the Webster products but similar desk dictionaries produced by other publishers. See MERRIAM–WEBSTER, WEBSTERS. [AMERICAS, REFERENCE]. R.W.B., T.MCA.

WEBSTER'S DICTIONARY OF ENGLISH USAGE, short form *WDEU*. A 978-page guide to disputed points of usage, edited by E. Ward Gilman and published in 1989 by Merriam–Webster. A typical entry defines and describes the history of a dispute, gives citations as illustrations, summarizes what usage critics have said, analyses present usage on the point (drawing on Merriam's file of 14m citations), and lays out options of use with the probable consequences of choosing one over the other. See PASSIVE, USAGE GUIDANCE AND CRITICISM. For an example of the *WDEU*'s editorial comment, see CLICHÉ. [AMERICAS, REFERENCE, USAGE]. J.A.

WEBSTER'S NEW INTERNATIONAL DICTIONARY. The descendant of Noah Webster's *An American Dictionary of the English Language* (1828) and the most comprehensive English-language dictionary currently published in the US. The 1961 edition, known as *W3* and published by Merriam–Webster, treats nearly 0.5m words. Since its appearance, Webster's dictionary has undergone five complete revisions and appeared in eight editions. After Noah Webster's death in 1843, the Merriam brothers secured the publishing and revision rights from his heirs and from J. S. & C. Adams of Massachusetts, which had published a commercially unsuccessful version of the 2nd edition (1840). The Merriams produced a 3rd one-volume edition (1847) edited by Chauncey A. Goodrich, Noah Webster's son-in-law. The 4th edition (1864) and all subsequent editions were completely revised. Officially entitled *An American Dictionary of the English Language*, the 4th edition was popularly known as *the Unabridged*. It was edited by Noah Porter, later president of Yale. A German scholar, C. A. F. Mahn, so thoroughly revised the etymologies that the dictionary took undisputed lead over the remaining and waning popularity of Joseph Worcester's rival works.

The 5th edition (1890), also edited by Porter, was titled *Webster's International Dictionary* in recognition of the company's market, which had expanded to Britain and the British colonies, continental Europe, and Asia. A supplement followed in 1900. What was in fact the 6th edition was marketed as the first of a new series: *Webster's New International Dictionary of the*

English Language (1909), edited by William Torrey Harris and F. Sturges Allen. Its 2nd edition (the 7th in line) was *W2* (1934), edited by William Allan Neilson and Thomas A. Knott. The *W3* (1961; 8th in line) was edited by Philip B. Gove. The development of the unabridged dictionary has been toward more precise etymology, more thorough description of the sounds of the language, and more generous inclusion of the technical and specialized lexicon of English, and away from an encyclopedic and prescriptive vision of the work of the lexicographer.

Controversy. The publication of *W3* sparked one of the most intense debates about lexicography and word usage since the Webster–Worcester dictionary wars. Gove eliminated the labels 'colloquial' and 'informal', which had often been interpreted as pejorative. Instead, he carefully defined usage labels to identify cultural dimensions (*nonstandard, substandard, slang*), temporal dimensions (*archaic, obsolete*, with 1755 as the pivotal date), and spatial dimensions (geographical labels like those in regional atlases). Overall, fewer labels were used. The debate aroused a controversy over the alleged 'permissiveness' of the dictionary. Through reviews and editorials, many critics deplored what they regarded as an abdication of the dictionary's responsibility to foster good English. Most knew little of the long-standing tradition in English lexicography of describing the language as actually used and were distressed to find *ain't* included, even with the explanation 'though disapproved by many and more common in less educated speech, used orally in most parts of the U.S. by many cultivated speakers esp. in the phrase *ain't I*'.

Research by the linguist E. Bagby Atwood had, in 1953, determined that one-third of 'cultured informants' in the coastal Southern speech area employed *ain't I*: 'informants in the South seem to be least inhibited about the use of *ain't*, those in Rhode Island and the New York City area, most inhibited'. Since an overwhelming number of the reviewers were from New York City or influenced by its intellectual climate, their shock at the 'permissive' description in *W3* might have been foreseen. The controversy mirrored deep-seated attitudes and biases concerning linguistic correctness and cultural changes reflected in AmE usage. One unhappy critic, Jacques Barzun, named the dictionary 'the longest political pamphlet ever put together' (1963). Supporters, defending the editorial policy of *W3* and the ideas which had influenced it, pointed out that, for those who wished it, information about usage could be gleaned from other features of the entries: synonyms, usage notes, illustrative quotations, and labels. An anthology of the many editorials, reviews, and periodical essays commenting on *W3* is *Dictionaries and THAT Dictionary: A Case Book of the Aims of Lexicographers and the Targets of Reviewers*, ed. James Sledd and Wilma R. Ebbitt (Scott Foresman, 1962).

There were, however, other criticisms of *W3* even by those who were generally satisfied with it. 'Permissive' was a charge levelled at the dictionary for the inclusion of many words outside educated usage and for the citations taken from popular mid-20c US culture. Other critics charged that it was mainly a tool for the language scholar and did not adequately serve the public. Thus, the Merriam lexicographers chose to increase the number of minutely described pronunciation variations provided for headwords. The entry for *a fortiori* contained 132 theoretically possible variations. Other complaints concerned some of the space-saving decisions, such as the use of symbols instead of repetitions of entry words and the use of lower case for all entry words except *God* and trademarks. Still others complained about the small size of type, the numerous spelling variants supplied, allegedly unsystematic categorizations of definitions, and such extended definitions as definition 2b of *hotel*:

a building of many rooms chiefly for overnight accommodation of transients and several floors served by elevators, usu. with a large open street-level lobby containing easy chairs, with a variety of compartments for eating, drinking, dancing, exhibitions, and group meetings (as of salesmen or convention attendants), with shops having both inside and street-side entrances and offering for sale items (as clothes, gifts, candy, theater tickets, travel tickets) of particular interest to a traveler, or providing personal services (as hairdressing, shoe shining) and with telephone booths, writing tables, and washrooms freely available

The American Heritage Publishing Company tried to buy out the G. & C. Merriam Company in order to rescue the Webster line from 'sabotage in Springfield'. The company was ultimately sold to Encyclopaedia Britannica Inc. in 1964 and there has been no fourth (or ninth) unabridged since. See AMERICAN HERITAGE DICTIONARY, MERRIAM–WEBSTER, RANDOM HOUSE DICTIONARY, UNABRIDGED, WORCESTER. [AMERICAS, REFERENCE].   R.W.B.

WEBSTER'S NEW WORLD DICTIONARY, short form *WNWD*. A work published in 1951 by the World Publishing Company of Cleveland, Ohio, in a two-volume *encyclopedic edition*, followed in 1953 by a single-volume *college edition*. The latter, edited under the supervision of Joseph H. Friend and David B. Guralnik, was claimed to be the largest of the US desk dictionaries, treating 142,000 words. The senses of entries were in chronological order of development (as in the *Webster's Collegiate* series), and biographical and geographical names were included in the main alphabet (as in the *American College Dictionary*). A *second college edition* appeared under Guralnik's editorship in 1970, with a supplementary pronunciation key (a *phonoguide*) in the form of a small recording. A five-pointed star was used to indicate words and senses added to English in the US, information provided by Mitford M. Mathews, editor of *A Dictionary of American English*. World Publishing was purchased in 1980 by Simon & Schuster (New York), but its offices remained in Cleveland, and updates of the *New World* have continued on a biennial schedule. In 1989, a revised *third college edition* was issued under the editorship of Victoria Neufeldt. The dictionaries in this series are unusual in giving etymologies for place-names. [AMERICAS, REFERENCE].

R.W.B., J.A.

WEEKLEY, Ernest [1865-1964]. English lexicographer and writer, born in London, and educated at Cambridge, London, Paris, and Berne. From 1898 till 1938, he was Professor of French at U. College, Nottingham. His publications include *The Romance of Words* (1912), *The Romance of Names* (1914), *Surnames* (1916), *An Etymological Dictionary of Modern English* (1921), *Words Ancient and Modern* (two series: 1926, 1927), and *Words and Names* (1932). See COLLINS, LAWRENCE. [BIOGRAPHY, EUROPE, REFERENCE].

T.MCA.

WELLS, H(erbert) G(eorge) [1866-1946]. English writer, born in Bromley, Kent, and educated at Midhurst Grammar School and, after work as a draper's apprentice and an assistant teacher, at the Normal School of Science in London. His long and varied writing career began with *The Time Machine* (1895), followed by a number of other scientific romances. Some, like *The War in the Air* (1908), were prophetic works of science fiction; others, like *The Island of Doctor Moreau* (1896), were fantasies that obliquely commented on contemporary life. His combination of scientific and literary interests made these novels seem real. Wells's sense of social concern led him to join the socialist Fabian Society in 1903 and is apparent in such novels as *The History of Mr Polly* (1910) and *Tono Bungay* (1909). These, written with humorous social realism, indicted the waste and hypocrisy he discerned in Edwardian England. *Ann Veronica* (1909) portrayed the struggle for women's emancipation and suffrage. After a political novel, *The New Machiavelli* (1911), he turned to polemical and informative writing, such as the vast *Outline of History* (1920). By the time of his death, however, he had lost faith in human progress. Wells did not see the novel as important and preferred to be regarded as a reporter rather than an artist. He recorded life among shop-keepers, clerks, and teachers, represented Cockney and other uneducated forms of the speech of southern England (such as Miriam's 'Elfrid' for 'Alfred' in *Mr Polly*), and was skilful with the conversation of scientists and professionals. In *The Shape of Things to Come* (1933), he imagined a world free from conflict in which English would be an international medium capable of expressing previously inaccessible ideas. This book, like *The Invisible Man* (1897), reached a wider audience through its filmed version. In 1938, Orson Welles's radio adaptation of *The War of the Worlds* (1898) in New York caused widespread panic when people believed that an actual Martian invasion was under way. See index. [BIOGRAPHY, EUROPE, LITERATURE].

R.C.

WELL-SPOKEN, also **wellspoken** [15c]. A general term for speaking clearly, politely, elegantly, etc.: 'He is wel spokyn in Inglyshe, metly wel in Frenshe' (*Paston Letters*, 1476); 'A very well-spoken, genteel, shrewd lady' (Jane Austen, *Persuasion*, 1816); 'It is still common in Britain for job advertisements to specify "well-spokenness", which implies clarity of articulation and a restricted range of accents which certainly excludes any broad regional or social accent' (John Honey, *Does Accent Matter?*, 1989). See ACCENT. [SPEECH].

T.MCA.

WELSH [From Old English *Wilisc, Wylisc, Welisc, Wælisc*, from *Wealh, Walh* a foreigner, slave, Briton, equivalent to Middle High German *Walch* and German *Wahle* a Celt, Roman, foreigner, and Old Norse plural *Valir* Gauls, Frenchmen. The English adjective corresponds to Middle High German *walh-, wälhisch, walsch* and German *wälsch, welsch*, used to describe the Romans, Italians, and French, and Dutch *waalsch* Walloon. By the 16c the major form was *Welsh* or *Welch*, supplanting such earlier variants as *Welische, Welsc, Walsshe*, and *Walsh*, which however survives as a family name, like the Scottish name *Wallace*, which derives from Anglo-French *Waleis. Welch* survives in *Royal Welch Fusiliers*, with the same pronunciation as *Welsh*.

(1) An adjective relating to Wales and its people, also used elliptically for the nation: *the Welsh*. The Anglo-Saxon original referred to the Britons in general, seen as foreigners and slaves, but by the 12c it had been generally restricted to Wales proper, its people, their language, customs, etc., largely losing the original connotations: 'Sir, there is a fray to be fought, betweene Sir Hugh the Welch Priest, and Caius

the French doctor' (Shakespeare, *Merry Wives of Windsor*, 2. 1, 1598); 'All the water in Wye, cannot wash your Maiesties Welsh plood out of your pody' (Shakespeare, *Henry V*, 5. 1, 1599). It commonly occurs in such compounds as *Welsh dresser, Welsh terrier, Welsh rabbit/rarebit.*

(2) The Celtic language of Wales, known to its speakers as *Cymraeg*. Welsh and Breton are the only surviving members of the ancient British or Brythonic subdivision of the Celtic language family. The original British language was highly inflected, but its descendant, Modern Welsh, has lost some of these inflections. Once the principal language of Wales and a literary language since the 6c, Welsh has been in decline since the accession of the partly Welsh Henry Tudor (Henry VII) to the English throne in 1485. There are now few monolingual speakers of Welsh, and some 500,000 of the people of Wales are bilingual: that is, 25% of the population. The condition of Welsh at the end of the 20c is relatively stable, and it is being learnt by non-Welsh-speaking Welsh people and others, including immigrants from England. It is taught in all schools and is a medium of instruction in some. In the northern county of Gwynedd it is a language of local government and appears with English on road signs. Language activists, however, consider that much remains to be done.

The spoken language consists of several dialects, and has had a significant influence on the English language as used in Wales, but has had little impact on English at large. The most characteristic sounds of Welsh are the voiceless alveolar lateral fricative (spelt *ll* as in *Llanelli*), the voiceless alveolar roll /ɽ/ (spelt *rh* as in *Rhondda*), and the velar fricative (represented as in Scots and German by *ch*, as in *Llywarch*). As in all Celtic languages, grammatical mutations occur, as in the noun *ci* (dog), where the initial sound is affected by the modifier, as in *dy gi* your dog, *fy nghi* my dog, *ei chi* her dog, and *tri chi* three dogs. See AUSTRALIAN LANGUAGES, BORROWING, CELTIC LANGUAGES, CORNISH, CUMBRIC, LINGUISTIC TYPOLOGY, WALES, WELSH ENGLISH, WELSH LANGUAGE SERVICE, WELSH LANGUAGE SOCIETY, WELSH LITERATURE. [EUROPE, LANGUAGE, NAME]. T.MCA.

WELSH ENGLISH. The English language as used in Wales. The term is recent and controversial. According to G. Williams (quoted in Coupland, 1990, below), 'establishing "Welsh English" or even discussing its possible existence is a political act', invoking 'distinctions such as that between "the state" (and its language—necessarily English), and "the region" (and its subordinate variety of the state language—Welsh English)'. English is, however, the majority language of Wales, and as in other parts of the English-speaking world, a concise term such as *Welsh English* (analogous to, among many others, *Canadian English* and *South African English*) appears unavoidable. It is increasingly applied by sociolinguists to a continuum of usage that includes three groups of overlapping varieties of English: those influenced by the Welsh language, those influenced by dialects in adjacent counties of England, and those influenced by the standard language as taught in the schools and used in the media. The influence of Welsh is strongest in the northern counties (sometimes referred to as *Welsh Wales*), where Welsh/English bilingualism is most commonly found; it is weaker in mid-Wales, and weakest in the south, but even in such southern cities as Cardiff and Swansea the influence of Welsh is present.

Origins. It is not certain when speakers of an English dialect arrived in Wales, but it seems probable that Mercian settlers were in the Wye valley by the 8c, when King Offa built his Dyke. In the winter of 1108-9, Henry I established a group of Flemish settlers in Pembrokeshire and it is likely that there were English-speakers among that group. Other English settlements grew up in the 12-13c in the Gower Peninsula, the Usk valley, and in the towns of Beaumaris, Caernarfon, and Harlech in the north and in the southern towns of Brecon and Carmarthen. Since most trade was in the hands of the English, the earliest regular Welsh users of English were almost certainly traders: see WALES.

Pronunciation. Accent varies according to region, ethnicity, and education. RP is spoken mainly by English expatriates and its influence is strongest in the south-east. The following generalizations refer to the English of native Welsh people: (1) Speakers of Welsh are often described as having a lilting or singsong intonation in their English, an effect created by three tendencies: a rise-fall tone at the end of statements (where RP has a fall); long vowels only in stressed syllables, the vowels in the second syllables of such words as 'increase and 'expert being short; reduced vowels avoided in polysyllabic words, speakers preferring, for example, /tɪkɛt/ for *ticket* and /kɔnɛkʃɔn/ for *connection*. (2) Welsh English is usually non-rhotic, but people who regularly speak Welsh are likely to have a postvocalic *r* (in such words as *worker*). (3) The accents of South Wales are generally aitchless. In North Wales, word-initial /h/ is not usually dropped, partly because it occurs in Welsh. (4) There is a tendency towards the monophthongs /e/ and /o/ and away from the diphthongs /eɪ/ and /əʊ/ in such words as *late* and *hope*. (5) The vowel /a/ is often used for both *gas* and *glass*. (6) Schwa is often preferred to /ʌ/ in such words as *but* and *cut*. (7) Diphthongs are often turned into two syllables with /biə/ for *beer* becoming /bijə/ and /puə/ for *poor* becoming /puwə/. (8) There is a preference for /u/ over /ju/ in such words as *actually* /aktuali/ and *speculate* /spɛkulet/. (9) The inventory of consonants is augmented from Welsh by the voiceless alveolar lateral fricative /ɬ/ (spelt *ll* as in *Llangollen*), the voiceless alveolar roll /ʧ/ (spelt *rh* as in *Rhyl*), and the voiceless velar fricative /x/ (spelt *ch* as in *Pentyrch*). (10) In many parts of the south, /l/ tends to be light and clear in such words as *light* and *fall*; in the north, it tends to be dark in both. (11) The voiced plosives /b, d, g/ are often aspirated in initial position, as with /bʰad/ for *bad*, often heard by non-Welsh people as 'pad'. The voiceless plosives /p, t, k/ are often aspirated in all positions, as with /pʰɪpʰ/ for *pip*. Consonants between vowels are often lengthened, as in /mɪsːɪn/ for *missing*, and /apːiː/ for *happy*. (12) The *-ing* participle is often realized as /ɪn/, as in /dansɪn/ for *dancing*. (13) There is a tendency, especially in the north, to substitute /s/ and /ʃ/ for /z/ and /ʒ/, so that *is* becomes 'iss' and *division* 'divishon'. (14) The *-y* ending in words such as *happy* and *lovely* is realized by /iː/: 'appee', 'lovelee'.

Grammar. (1) Working-class users of English in Wales tend to use the following constructions, also found elsewhere in the UK: multiple negation (*I 'aven't done nothin' to nobody, see?*); *them* as a demonstrative adjective (*them things*); *as* as a relative pronoun (*the one as played for Cardiff*); non-standard verb forms (*She catched it, The coat was all tore*); *'isself* for *himself* and *theirselves* for *themselves* (*'E done it 'isself and they saw it for theirselves*); the adverbial use of an adjective (*We did it willin'*: that is, willingly); the addition of *-like* at the end of phrases and sentences (*'E looked real 'appy-like*); and the use of the *-s* verb ending with all subjects in the present (*I goes to school an' they goes to work*). (2) Non-standard forms reflecting an influence from Welsh include: *do/did* + verb, to indicate a regularly performed action (*He do go to the rugby all the time; He did go regular-like*); foregrounding for emphasis (*Goin' down the mine 'e is* He is going down the mine; *Money they're not short of* They aren't short of money); *there* and not *how* in exclamations (*There's lovely you are!*); untransformed embedded sentences, especially after verbs of saying and thinking (*I'm not sure is 'e in* I'm not sure if he's in); the overgeneralization of the question tag *isn't it?* (*We're goin' out now, isn't it?*); occasional *yes* replacing a positive question tag (*You're a teacher, yes?*); *will* and not *will be* (*I'm not quite ready, but I will soon*); and *too* for *either* (*I don't like it.—I don't like it too*). (3) *Look you* (you see) is often

regarded as a shibboleth of Welsh English in such sentences as *Tried hard, look you, but earned nothin'*. *See* is also often used: *We were worried about 'im, see*. The non-use of the subject pronoun is also characteristic of Welsh-influenced English: *Saw 'im, bach. Saw 'im yesterday*.

Vocabulary. (1) Words drawn from Welsh generally relate to culture and behaviour: *carreg* a stone, *clennig* a gift of money, *eisteddfod* (plural *eisteddfodau*) a cultural festival, *glaster* a drink of milk and water, *iechyd da* ('yachy da') good health (a salutation or toast, from *iechyd* health, *da* good); the use of *bach* and *del* as terms of affection: *Like a drink, bach? Come near the fire, del*. (2) Words that are shared by Welsh English and dialects of England include: *askel* a newt, *dap* to bounce, *lumper* a young person, *pilm* dust, *sally* willow, *steam* a bread-bin. (3) General English words with local extensions of meaning include: *delight* a keen interest, as in *She's gettin' a delight in boys*; *lose* to miss, as in *'Urry or we'll lose the train*; *tidy* good, attractive, as in *Tidy 'ouse you've got, bach*. (4) The form *boyo*, from *boy*, is common as both a term of address and reference, and is sometimes negative in tone: *Listen, boyo, I've somethin' to tell you; That boyo is not to be trusted*.

Social issues. There seems to be little or no stigma attached to the use of Welsh English in Wales, as compared with, for example, Gutter Scots in Scotland, or Brummie in Birmingham. Experiments reported in 1975 suggest that speakers of Welsh English are positively viewed in the principality. There is, however, considerable tension with regard to the use of the Welsh language, especially in schools and the media, and this can affect attitudes to English. Many consider that education should be bilingual, so that all Welsh people have access to Welsh as their 'national' language; others, however, including some parents originally from England, feel that bilingualism in schools puts an unnecessary strain on children, and do not necessarily regard Welsh as part of their patrimony. See BRITISH ENGLISH, WALES, WELSH, WELSHNESS. [EUROPE, VARIETY].   L.T.

Bellin, Wynford. 1984. 'Welsh and English in Wales', in P. Trudgill (ed.), *Language in the British Isles*. Cambridge: University Press.

Coupland, Nikolas (ed.). 1990. *English in Wales*. Clevedon & Philadelphia: Multilingual Matters.

Russ, Charles V. J. 1982. 'The Geographical and Social Variation of English in England and Wales' (section: 'English in Wales'), in R. W. Bailey & M. Görlach (eds.), *English as a World Language*. Ann Arbor: University of Michigan Press. Cambridge: University Press.

Thomas, Alan. 1984. 'Welsh English', in Trudgill (above).

Viereck, Wolfgang. 1985. *Focus on: England and Wales*, in the Varieties of English around the World series. Amsterdam & Philadelphia: John Benjamins.
Wells, John C. 1982. *Accents of English*, vol. 2, pp. 377–92. Cambridge: University Press.

WELSH LANGUAGE SERVICE, in Welsh *Sianel Pedwar Cymru*. Short form *S4C*. A bilingual television network set up in Wales in 1980, broadcasting since 1982 on the fourth British TV channel. It is administered by the Welsh Fourth Channel Authority on behalf of the Independent Broadcasting Authority, and is funded through advertising, levies on independent TV companies, and a BBC contribution. S4C transmits English-language items from the UK Channel Four service and programmes in Welsh made by the BBC and Harlech Television, providing about 22 hours of Welsh-language material per week, mostly at peak viewing, 7–9 p.m. The service is a response to pressure for a Welsh-language TV service. See BRITISH BROADCASTING, PLAID CYMRU, WELSH, WELSH LANGUAGE SOCIETY. [EUROPE, MEDIA].　　　　　　　　　T.MCA.

WELSH LANGUAGE SOCIETY, in Welsh *Cymdeithas yr Iaith Gymraeg*. An organization formed in Wales in 1962 to promote the Welsh language. Although a militant element in the Welsh nationalist movement, its primary role is linguistic, its demands including bilingual road signs and official forms, and a separate television channel for Welsh. Its methods include demonstration, civil disobedience, and selective law-breaking, such as painting out English-only road signs and the non-payment of broadcasting licence fees. Militants from time to time damage property, such as television transmitters and the holiday homes in Welsh-speaking areas of people living in England. If the perpetrators are caught, the ensuing court appearances are used to raise demands for trials conducted in Welsh. The activities of the society evoke a mixed response in Wales and little attention elsewhere. There has been some reaction to the society's demands, with bilingual signs in some areas, some bilingual forms made available in the 1970s as a result of the Welsh Language Act of 1967, and the creation in 1980 of a bilingual TV service. See WELSH, WELSH LANGUAGE SERVICE. Compare PLAID CYMRU. [EUROPE, LANGUAGE, MEDIA].　　　　　　　　　T.MCA.

WELSH LITERATURE. Either literature written in the Welsh language or the literature of Wales, whether in Welsh, Latin, or English. Artistic performance in Welsh dates from the 6c, the earliest surviving texts relating to oral composition in the 5c in Cumbric, the long-extinct Welsh-like language of what is now the Scottish Lowlands: see CUMBRIC, SCOTTISH LITERATURE. The bardic period began with the legendary poets Aneurin, Taliesin, Myrddin (Merlin), and Llywarch Hen, and is marked by strict rhyme and metre in heroic and elegiac works. The *Mabinogion* of *c*.1060, however, is a prose narrative about Celtic gods and heroes. Such early works had a disproportionate impact on the literature of Western Europe and are the primary source of the *Matter of Britain*: accounts of Arthur, the Round Table, and the Holy Grail, written in Latin, French, English, and German: see BRETON, LATIN[1]. Towards the end of the Middle Ages, the poetic style became more relaxed and the topics more varied, and prose works were concerned mainly with the law and storytelling. In the 16c, the translation of both the Bible and the Book of Common Prayer into Welsh strengthened the position of the language, and the Renaissance encouraged a brief revival of classical Welsh verse forms. The tradition, however, declined because of its formalism and the strength of English, especially among the gentry as patrons of the arts.

In the 18c, the Morris brothers (Lewis, Richard, and William) preserved medieval texts and encouraged poets to use the ancient metres. A neo-classical school was started by Goronwy Owen, whose verse was modelled on the bards. The *Cymmrodorion Society* was established by the Welsh in London as a centre of literary studies, cooperating with the *Cymreigyddion Society* and *Gwyneddigion Society* in Wales to encourage the revival of *eisteddfodau* or poetic assemblies. As a result, the *National Eisteddfod* was revived in the early 19c. At this time, lyrical hymns and religious verse were popular, as well as ballads that used *cynghanedd*, a complex traditional blend of accentuation, alliteration, and internal rhyme. The modern period of literature in Welsh began in the late 19c with the establishment of the U. of Wales, a federal institution with campuses throughout the country. Current writing encompasses all the genres of Western literature. See ANGLO-WELSH LITERATURE, WALES. [EUROPE, LITERATURE].　　　　　　　　　T.MCA.

WELSHMAN/WOMAN. See -MAN/WOMAN.

WELSHNESS [17c]. The quality of being Welsh, often debated on the basis of whether it is necessary to speak the Welsh language in order to be properly Welsh: 'In spite of the strangeness, the *Welshness*, of Pontypool, [he] had been disappointed to find that it was not *in* Wales' (Amelia H. Stirling, *Life of J. H. Stirling*, 1912). See WELSH. [EUROPE, NAME].　　　　　　　　　T.MCA.

WELSH PLACE-NAMES. The place-names of Wales are mainly from the Welsh language, most of them providing a topographical or historical description. Other languages that have shaped Welsh place-names are Norse, Norman French, and English.

Welsh. River names are among the oldest and are usually descriptive, such as *Gele* blade (that is, straight and shining), *Taff* water, *Ystwyth* winding. Names associated with heights are also frequent: for example *Carnedd Llywelyn* Llywelyn's burial mound, *Moelfre* bare hill, *Mynydd Du* black mountain. Some names, especially in the south-east, date from Roman times, notably *Caerleon* fort of the legion, referring to the Second Legion stationed at *Isca Silurum* '(place on the river) Usk of the Silures (a Celtic tribe)', and *Caerwent* fort of Venta (the Roman *Venta Silurum*). Common Welsh words occurring in place-names are: (1) *aber* river mouth, as in *Abergavenny* mouth of the Gefenni, *Aberystwyth* mouth of the Ystwyth. (2) *caer* fort, as in *Caernarvon* fort in Arfon, *Caerphilly* Ffili's fort. (3) *cwm* valley, as in *Cwmbran* valley of the (river) Bran, *Cwmfelin* valley of the mill. (4) *din* fort, as in *Dinas Powys* fort of Powys, *Dinefwr* fort of the yew. (5) *llan* church, as in *Llandaff* church on the Taff, *Llanfair* Mary's church. (6) *llyn* lake, as in *Llyn Fawr* big lake, *Llyn Glas* green lake. (7) *maen* stone, as in *Maentwrog* stone of Twrog, *Penmaenmawr* head of the great rock. (8) *nant* stream, as in *Nantgaredig* gentle stream, *Nantyglo* stream of the coal. (9) *pen* head, end, as in *Penarth* head of the promontory, *Penrhyndeudraeth* headland of the two beaches. (10) *rhos* moor, as in *Rhosgoch* red moor, *Rhosllanerchrugog* moor of the heather glade. (11) *tref* farm, homestead, town, as in *Tregarth* ridge farm, *Tremadoc* Madoc's farm. (12) *pont* bridge, as in *Pontnewydd* new bridge, *Pontypridd* bridge by the earthen house. (13) *porth* port, harbour, as in *Aberporth* harbour mouth, *Porthcawl* harbour of the sea kale. Both *pont* and *porth* entered Welsh from French (see next).

Norse and Norman French. Norse raids on the coasts of Wales in the 9–10c have left some Scandinavian names as a legacy, especially for islands: *Anglesey* Ongull's island, *Bardsey* Bardr's island, *Caldy* cold island, *Ramsey* wild garlic island, *Skokholm* block island, *Skomer* cloven island. Also Norse in origin are the names of the towns *Fishguard* fish yard, *Milford Haven* harbour of the sandy inlet, and *Swansea* Sveinn's sea (place). The Normans invaded Wales in the 11c and left such names as *Beaumaris* beautiful marsh, *Grosmont* big hill, *Malpas* bad passage, *Montgomery* (castle of Roger of) Montgomery.

English. Edward I of England conquered Wales in the 13c, leaving many of the names that are still in use today. Sometimes the present name has evolved as an Anglicization of the Welsh:

Cardiff for *Caerdydd*, *Carmarthen* for *Caerfyrddin* fort of the seaside stronghold, *Denbigh* for *Dinbych*, *Lampeter* for *Llanbedr* Peter's church. In other instances, the name was English from the first: *Chepstow* market-place, *Haverfordwest* western goats' ford, *Holyhead* holy headland, *Knighton* knights' settlement, *Newport* new port, *Presteigne* priests' household, *Welshpool* Welsh pool (that is, on the Welsh side of the border), *Wrexham* Wryhtel's pasture, *Snowdon* snow-covered hill (the name of the highest mountain in Wales, recorded as early as the 11c). Most English names are found close to the border, although a pocket of such names is notable in the south-west. This region, on the Gower peninsula and in the south of the former Pembrokeshire, has been predominantly English-speaking since the 12c, when the Welsh were driven out, and is still known as 'Little England in Wales'. Examples of names in the area are *Cheriton* church settlement, *Middleton* middle settlement, and *Newton* new settlement.

In the 18c and early 19c, several villages arose with Biblical names, based on the names of the Nonconformist chapels that were the focal points of the communities. They include *Bethel*, *Bethlehem*, *Carmel*, *Hebron*, and *Salem*. Most are small, but *Bethesda* in Gwynedd, North Wales, grew into quite a large town because of its slate quarries. The industrial development of South Wales in the 19c, and especially its coal mines, led to the giving of a number of modern names, often those of mine-owners, forgemasters, and other entrepreneurs. They include *Griffithstown*, *Treharris*, *Trelewis*. *Tredegar* is also in this category, after the title of Sir Charles Morgan, created Baron Tredegar in 1859, the title deriving from his family seat.

English and Welsh. The present names of the Welsh counties were introduced in 1974 on the reorganization of local government, and are mostly revivals of territorial names: *Clwyd* hurdle (a river name), *Dyfed* territory of the Demetae (a Celtic tribe), *Gwent* special place, *Gwynedd* territory of Cunedda (an ancient chief), *Powys* province. The older county names date from the 13c, and were based on the chief town of the region, as with *Breconshire, Cardiganshire, Montgomeryshire, Pembrokeshire*. Today, most places with names of non-Welsh origin have their own unrelated name in Welsh, such as: *Abergwaun* mouth of the river, for *Fishguard*; *Caergybi* Cybi's fort, for *Holyhead*; *Trefaldwyn* Baldwin's homestead, for *Montgomery*. *Snowdon* is *Yr Wyddfa* the cairn place, and *Swansea* is *Abertawe* mouth of the (river) Tawe. See CORNWALL, PLACE-NAME. [NAME].   A.R.

WELSHRY [14c]. A now rare term for Welsh people, a part of Wales where Welsh is used, an area where Welsh people live, and Welsh descent: 'This Shere is taken to be devided into two partes, that is to the Englishrie, and Welshrye' (G. Owen, *Pembrokeshire*, 1603). Compare ENGLISHRY, IRISHRY. [EUROPE, NAME]. T.MCA.

WELSH WALES. An informal term for the parts of Wales (the north-west and central west) where the Welsh language, culture, and traditions are strongest: ' "The Vale of Glamorgan is legally Wales, isn't it, though no one speaks any Welsh here?"—"Quite right . . . This is Wales, if not Welsh Wales" ' (G. Daniel, *Welcome Death*, 1954). See WALES, WELSHNESS. [EUROPE, NAME]. T.MCA.

WELSHY [18c]. (1) Welsh-like: 'Then we get towards a wild and Welshy country' (*Bentley's Miscellany*, Jan. 1848). (2) An informal name for someone Welsh: 'You'd think I was a Welshy by my name, Gwen Evans, but I'm a proper Cockney' (E. Coxhead, *One Green Bottle*, 1951). Compare ENGLISHY. [EUROPE, NAME]. T.MCA.

WESSEX. (1) The kingdom of the West Saxons, whose foremost king was Alfred the Great and foremost scholar Aelfric. Before their time, the dialect was unrecorded, but from the 9c records are abundant, including the Parker Manuscript of the Anglo-Saxon Chronicle, manuscripts of Alfred's own translations, Aelfric's works, the West Saxon Gospels, and many royal documents. (2) A fictional region of England in the *Wessex novels* of Thomas Hardy, roughly corresponding to the old kingdom, and centred on Dorset. See AELFRIC, ALFRED, ANGLO-SAXON, ANGLO-SAXON CHRONICLE, DIALECT IN ENGLAND, HARDY, OLD ENGLISH[1] WEST COUNTRY. [EUROPE, HISTORY, NAME]. T.MCA.

WEST, The [Usually with an initial capital]. (1) The western part of a country: *The West of Ireland.* The adjective commonly contrasts with *East*, as in *West Africa, West Asia*, but note *Western Europe*, not usually **West Europe. West Virginia* contrasts as the name of a US state with *Virginia* alone, and is very different from *western Virginia*. (2) Also *the West Country*. The West of England, especially the counties of Somerset, Devon, and Cornwall: see WEST COUNTRY. (3) The West of Scotland, especially around Glasgow. (4) The area of the US west of (especially, the Mississippi River, including in particular the Great Plains, the Rocky Mountains, and the Pacific Coast, and associated with 'western' films and novels, 'country and western' music, and the myth of the cowboy: *the wild and woolly West; the fastest gun in the West; the Old West.* Subdivisions of the American West are: *The Midwest/Middle West*, including among

others the states of Illinois, Indiana, Minnesota, and Ohio; the *Southwest*, including Texas, Arizona, and New Mexico; the (*Pacific*) *Northwest*, including Idaho, Washington and Oregon. See DIALECTS OF AMERICA (THE WEST). (5) The non-Communist countries of Europe and the Americas, and their allies, as opposed to *the East*, a term referring to the former Soviet Union, its former Eastern European satellites, and China. (6) Also *the Western world*, sometimes *the Occident*. The part of the world traditionally understood to be where the sun sets, as opposed to *the East* or *Orient*, where it rises. The term focuses primarily on Western Europe and North America, and has strong cultural and economic connotations. It is an emotive term long associated with empire (*western imperialism*) and industry (*western technology*). Because of the widespread influence of Western countries in recent times, it is geographically elastic: 'New Zealand [has] transformed itself from the West's first and most protective welfare state into its most deregulated economy' (*Time*, 16 Dec., 1991); 'The request comes amid an unusually high level of tension over technology between the West's two biggest economic competitors. American corporate executives and members of Congress have complained that Japan has acted as a sponge for technologies developed in the United States' (*International Herald Tribune*, 1 June 1990). New Zealand, in the southern hemisphere, is here described as Western because it was heavily settled by the British; Japan, in East Asia (and 'the Land of the Rising Sun'), is called Western because of the success of its deliberate policy of Westernization. The implication of these citations is that 'the West' grows as its impact on the non-Western world increases. Compare ASIA, NORTH, SOUTH. See DIALECT IN AMERICA, IMPERIALISM, WEST COUNTRY, WESTERNIZE. [AMERICAS, ASIA, EUROPE]. T.MCA.

WESTERNIZE AmE & BrE, **westernise** BrE & AusE [19c: with and without an initial capital]. To make western in culture, character, language, etc., usually in terms of *the Western World* (see WEST, sense 6): 'Some of the nations of the East, notably Japan, are rapidly westernizing' (L. F. Ward, *Pure Sociology*, 1903). Westernization has in the 19-20c been a worldwide process, a leading feature of which is the use of Western languages, as with French in North Africa and English in India, or of elements from such languages: for example, the absorption of general English words into Japanese and of its technical terms into Malay. Compare NORTHERNIZE, SOUTHERNIZE. [AMERICAS, ASIA, EUROPE]. T.MCA.

WEST, Michael [1888-1973]. English language teacher and lexicographer, educated at Oxford before joining the Indian Education Service. In 1923, he was commissioned to carry out a major examination of bilingualism that resulted in the report *Bilingualism, with Special Reference to Bengal* (1926). Basing his argument on an analysis of the needs of learners, he concluded that reading should have a prominent place in bilingual education. The rest of his life was devoted to exploring the implications of that idea in materials and theoretical analysis. The *New Method Supplementary Readers*, based on controlled vocabulary, were produced by Longman under his editorship, and he convened the 1934 *Carnegie Conference on Vocabulary Selection* in New York which eventually led to *The General Service List of English Words* (1953), providing the ELT world with a minimum vocabulary based on frequency statistics. He also published widely in the teaching of oral language, writing, and methodology. See index. [ASIA, BIOGRAPHY, EDUCATION, EUROPE]. C.J.B.

WEST AFRICA. See AFRICA.

WEST AFRICAN ENGLISH, short forms *WAfrE, WAE*. English as used in West Africa, the official language of Nigeria, Ghana, Sierra Leone, Gambia, and Cameroon. It is typically acquired as a second, third, or fourth language, and the line between English as used by a small élite and the more general West African Pidgin English is difficult to draw. Speakers in the five countries generally understand each other well, but there are differences inside and between countries. WAE is non-rhotic, and /r/ is often trilled. Intonation is influenced by the tonal systems of West African languages, and because there is a tendency towards syllable-timing, the schwa in unstressed syllables is usually replaced by a full vowel, as in 'stu-dent' and 'quiet-ness' for *student* and *quietness*. The consonants /θ, ð/ are generally realized as /t, d/, *three of these* being pronounced 'tree of dese'. Such words as *gush* and *fur* sound like *gosh* and *for*, and the vowel sounds of *bake* and *toe* are commonly the single vowels /e, o/, not diphthongs as in RP. Grammar is generally the same as standard BrE, but such constructions occur as *a country where you have never been there* and *He is an important somebody*. Regional vocabulary includes: loans from local languages, such as *buka* a food stand (from Hausa), and *danfo* a minibus (from Yoruba); compounds of English and vernacular words, such as *akara ball* a bean cake, and *juju music* a kind of music; loan translations and adaptations of local usages, such as *bush meat* game meat, and *father* and *mother* used for relatives, as in *He is staying with his fathers* (He is staying with relatives of his father); and local

extensions of general English words, such as *corner* a curve in a road, *go slow* a traffic jam, *to wet plants* to water plants. See AFRICAN ENGLISH, AFRICAN LANGUAGES, AFRICAN LITERATURE IN ENGLISH, CAMEROON, CARIBBEAN ENGLISH, ENGLISH, GAMBIA, GHANA, LIBERIA, NIGERIA, SIERRA LEONE, WEST AFRICAN PIDGIN ENGLISH. [AFRICA, VARIETY]. S.S.M.

WEST AFRICAN EXAMINATIONS COUNCIL. See EXAMINING IN ENGLISH.

WEST AFRICAN PIDGIN ENGLISH, also **Pidgin English, Pidgin.** Short form *WAPE*. A continuum of English-based pidgins and creoles from Gambia to Cameroon, including enclaves in French- and Portuguese-speaking countries. Among its varieties are *Aku* in Gambia, *Krio* in Sierra Leone, *Liberian Settler English* and *Liberian Pidgin English*, *Nigerian Pidgin English*, and *Kamtok* or *Cameroon Pidgin English*. It originated in the 16c in contacts between West Africans and British sailors and traders. Its varieties are more or less mutually intelligible, and there is a complex continuum from constructions close to standard English to those far removed from it. WAPE is located midway between West African English and vernaculars spoken natively by those of its users for whom it is an additional language; some speakers, especially in cities, do not speak an African vernacular. Syntactic features of the variety farthest from standard English and with the lowest status (the basilect) are similar to those of the New World creoles, prompting researchers to speak of a family of 'Atlantic creoles' that includes WAPE, Gullah, Bahamian, Jamaican, Trinidadian, and Belizean. Tense and aspect are non-inflectional: *bin* denotes simple past or past perfect (*Meri bin lef* Mary left, Mary had left), *de/di* the progressive (*Meri de it* Mary is eating, Mary was eating), and *don* the perfective (*Meri don it* Mary has eaten, Mary had eaten). Depending on context, *Meri it* means 'Mary ate' or 'Mary has eaten' and *Meri laik Ed* means 'Mary likes Ed' or 'Mary liked Ed'. Adjectives are used without a copula when predicative: *Meri sik* Mary (is) sick. In *Meri de sik* Mary is falling sick, the progressive *de* marks transition into the condition of being sick. See AFRICAN ENGLISH, CREOLE, GHANA, KAMTOK, KRIO, LIBERIA, NIGERIA, PIDGIN, ROTTEN ENGLISH, WEST AFRICAN ENGLISH. [AFRICA, VARIETY]. S.S.M.

WEST COUNTRY, also **West of England, South-West.** A region of England with imprecise boundaries but generally agreed to centre on Avon, Devon, Dorset, Gloucestershire, and Somerset ('the cider counties'). Wiltshire and parts of Hampshire are sometimes included, as is Cornwall because of its location and despite its Celtic background, distinctive and controversial Cornish language, and dialect of English influenced by Cornish. The range of accents in the West Country extends from broad in the working class and in rural areas through accents modified towards RP in the towns and the lower middle class to RP proper in the middle and upper classes. Local speech is rhotic, with a retroflex /r/ in such words as *rap*, *trip* and *r*-coloured vowels in such words as *car*/*cart*. Postvocalic /r/ is widely retained in such cities as Bristol and Exeter, despite the influence of RP, which is non-rhotic. In other cities, such as Plymouth and Bournemouth, rhoticity varies. Traces of variable *r*-pronunciation are found as close to London as Reading in Berkshire.

Pronunciation. For many people in Britain and elsewhere, traditional West Country has become stereotyped as rustic. Two particular shibboleths are associated with 'yokels' leaning on gates and sucking straws: a strong West Country burr, as in *Arrr, that it be* Yes, that's so; voiced initial fricatives, as in *The varmer zeez thik dhree-vurrow plough* The farmer sees that three-furrow plough. The stage accent known as *Mummerset* has long exploited these features. Shakespeare appears to have been the first to use a special spelling for it, as when Edgar in *King Lear* (4. 5), disguised as the peasant Tom a Bedlam, says 'Chill not let go Zir, without vurther 'cagion' (I'll not let go, sir, without further occasion). Although the accent is now largely confined to the west and south-west, it was once common across England south of a line from the Severn to the Thames. The current boundary is a line from the Severn round Gloucestershire, including the Forest of Dean on the other side of the river, round the north-east boundary of Wiltshire, and passing through Hampshire to the sea around Portsmouth. West Country rhotic pronunciation is widely considered a survival of the /r/ of Old English. It turns preceding alveolar sounds into post-alveolars, resulting in a burr that contrasts strongly with RP, and is often remarked on as a pleasing feature of West Country; it is similar to the Irish /r/ and that of many parts of the US. Another local feature is an initial /w/ in such words as *old* and *oak*, giving 'wold' and 'woak'. Before /ɔɪ/, a /w/ may also occur, as in 'bwoys' for *boys*. In a stretch of country from the Somerset coast to the sea in Dorset there is an *h*-sounding area; elsewhere in the West Country, initial *h* is not pronounced.

Grammar. Forms of grammar associated with traditional West Country speech are generally regarded as working-class and rural. They include: (1) The use of *thick* or *thicky* /ðɪk(ɪ)/ as a singular demonstrative, with *they* as plural:

thick man that man, *they houses* those houses. (2) Present and past participles often preceded by *a-*, as in *a-goin*, *a-done*. (3) The use of periphrastic *do*, as in *He do go every week* He goes every week, *They do be ard-workin*. (4) The present tense of the verb *be* has been regularized to a single form that is still widely used: *I be, you be, he be, she be, we be, you be, they be*. (5) The negative *baint* is widely used: *I baint* I am not, *baint I* am I not, *ye baint* you aren't, *baint ye* aren't you, *they baint* they aren't, *baint they* aren't they.

Vocabulary. (1) Many West Country words are now restricted to part of only one county. Words formerly well known include: *fardel* a burden, *lew* dry, *mazzard* a black cherry, *truss* a bale (of hay), *tiddly* to do light housework. (2) In *The Grockles' Guide: An Illustrated Miscellany of Words and Phrases of Interest and Use to 'Voreigners' in Somerset* (Jeremy Warburg & Tessa Lorant, Thorn Press, 1985), the following are listed, among many others, as current: *anywhen* any time, *aps* a boil, *backalong* homeward (*I'll be doddlin backalong*), *brize* to bring pressure to bear on (*I'm goin to brize down on thik*), *caddle* a muddle or difficulty, *chammer* to chew noisily, *chatter*, *chatterbag* a gossip, *clumble-fisted* awkward with the hands, *combe* (pronounced 'coom') valley, *emmet* an ant, small fly, *gert* great, large, *jibber* a restless horse, *leary* hungry, tired, thin, empty, *mugget* the intestines of a young heifer or sheep, *pissabed* the dandelion, *quirk* to moan, whine, complain, *rafty* rancid, off, crafty, *randy* a party (*on the randy* out to enjoy oneself), *rozzum*/*ruzzum* a tall tale, *scrumpy* farmhouse cider, *somewhen* some time, *teddy* a potato, *verdic* a viewpoint, opinion (compare *verdict*). The term *grockle* for a holiday-maker or tourist is of uncertain origin and apparently recent, its first *OED* citation being 1964.

Literary West Country. Most admired among West Country writers is Thomas Hardy, who in numerous novels attempted to represent the speech of rural men and women. His written dialect varies according to the speaker. Tess, the heroine of *Tess of the d'Urbervilles* (1891), although a peasant, had received some education and so had a regional accent, some local words, but more or less standard grammar. Hardy himself says of her: 'The dialect was on her tongue to some extent, despite the village school: the characteristic intonation of that dialect for this district being the voicing approximately rendered by the syllable UR, probably as rich an utterance as any to be found in human speech.' The dairy maids, on the other hand, use such forms as *zid* (saw), *hwome* home, and *I be, so be you*.

The 19c philologist and language reformer William Barnes wrote poetry in the Dorset dialect:

> Then they took en in hwome to his bed,
> An' he rose vrom his pillow no mwore.
> Vor the curls on his sleek little head
> To be blown by the wind out o' door.
> Vor he died while the hay russled grey
> On the staddle so leately begun:
> Lik' the mown-grass a-dried by the day—
> Aye! the zwath-flo'r's a-killed by the zun.
> ('The Child and the Mowers')
>
> [*en* him, *staddle* lower part of a stack of corn, *zwath* swath, a line of mown crops]

The novelist and playwright Eden Philpotts (1862–1960), most of whose novels are set on Dartmoor, also wrote dialect poetry:

> Then old man's talk o' the days behind 'ee,
> Your darter's youngest darter to mind 'ee;
> A li'l dreamin', a li'l dyin'
> A li'l lew corner o' airth to lie in.
> ('Man's Days')

More recently, representations of Cornish dialect have appeared in the historical *Poldark* novels of Winston Graham, often for comic relief and to point up differences between the common people and the gentry:

> 'Nay, *nay*, sur, I never heard such words out of me mouth! Yer worship, I never thought upon no such thing. Tedn fair, tedn just, tedn *right*.'
> 'This statement, I would remind you, Paynter, was made before witnesses and signed with your mark. It was read over to you before you signed.'
> 'Well, I'm 'ard of hearing,' said Jud, staring barefaced at the counsel. 'Tes more'n likely they mistook what I did say an' I mistook what they did say. Tes more'n likely, that's for certain' (*Jeremy Poldark*, 1961).

The *Devon Dialect Society* was started in the early 1980s and received support from Radio Devon and local newspapers. For a time it had a strong membership, work went forward on tape-recorded memories of local speech, and an annual journal similar to those of the Northern dialect societies was published from 1983. There were members from many parts of England and as far away as Newfoundland and Japan. The constitution was, however, 'temporarily suspended' in the late 1980s. See: Martyn F. Wakelin, *The Southwest of England*, in the Varieties of English around the World series (John Benjamins, 1986). See BARNES, BURR, CORNISH, CORNWALL, DIALECT IN ENGLAND, DORSET, ENGLISH IN ENGLAND, HARDY, MUMMERSET, NEWFOUNDLAND ENGLISH, SOMERSET, Y-. [EUROPE, NAME, VARIETY].
S.E., T.MCA.

WEST COUNTRYMAN/WOMAN. See -MAN/WOMAN.

WESTERN. See DIALECT IN AMERICA, WEST.

WESTERN ISLES, The, also **the Hebrides.** The islands off the north-western coast of Scotland. See HIGHLAND ENGLISH, SCOTLAND, SCOTTISH GAELIC. [EUROPE, NAME].   T.MCA.

WESTERN SAMOA. A country of Oceania, a monarchy, and member of the Commonwealth. Capital: Apia. Currency: tala (100 sene). Economy: agriculture, timber. Population: 168,000 (1988), 197,000 (projection for 2000). Ethnicity: 90% Polynesian, 7% mixed, 1% European. Languages: Samoan, English (both official). Education: primary 100%, secondary 40%, tertiary 5%, literacy 97%. A German colony from late 19c, Western Samoa was a League of Nations mandate in 1920, and later a United Nations trust territory administered by New Zealand, gaining its independence in 1962. [NAME, OCEANIA, VARIETY].   T.MCA.

WEST INDIAN, occasionally **Westindian.** (1) Relating to the West Indies. (2) Someone born in the West Indies or of West Indian descent. Self-identification as a West Indian is most common when natives of the region find themselves in some other part of the world. The term usually includes the peoples of the former British islands and of Guyana, and usually also Belizeans, and may include the peoples of the French islands (Martinique and Guadeloupe), Haiti, and the Netherlands Antilles, but usually not those of the Spanish-speaking Caribbean. The term stands in opposition to *Caribbean*, which is usually seen as geographical. See ANTILLES, CARIBBEAN, EAST INDIAN, INDIAN, WEST INDIES. [AMERICAS, NAME].   L.D.C.

WEST INDIAN CREOLE. See CARIBBEAN ENGLISH CREOLE.

WEST INDIES, The. An ambiguous traditional term used in its widest geographical sense to refer to the islands of the Greater and Lesser Antilles, excluding the Bahamas. At mid-century, it was used to designate the *Federation of the West Indies*, a union of British possessions excluding Guyana and Belize. The union lasted from 1958 to 1962. Residents of the region use the term to refer to countries that were former members of the union and are now linked in a loose common-market arrangement called the *Caribbean Community* (*Caricom*). It also refers to the cricket team that draws its players from ex-members of the Federation and Guyana, and occurs in the official title of the regional *University of the West Indies*. See EAST INDIES, INDIA, INDIES, WEST INDIAN. [AMERICAS, NAME].   L.D.C.

WEST OF ENGLAND. See WEST COUNTRY.

WEST SAXON. See WESSEX.

WH-ADVERB. See ADVERB.

WHISKY VOICE, also **whiskey voice.** A hoarse voice associated with sustained heavy drinking: 'The women in the souk, with those long red finger-nails and blue hair in bandanas and those cracked whiskey voices' (John Updike, *Coup*, 1978). In phonetic terms, it combines the features voice, creak, and whisper. See VOICE. [SPEECH].   T.MCA.

WHITE [From Old English *hwit*; akin to *wheat*]. (1) The colour of milk, snow, a fleecy cloud, the crests of waves, etc. Technically, the colour called *white* is not part of the spectrum, but arises from the reflection or emission of most of the rays of light all together; most so-called 'white' colours are shades of grey. (2) Having such a colour: *white clothes*; *a white Christmas*. (3) (Of hair) without pigment: *an old man with a white beard*. (4) (Of sound and other kinds of radiation) mixed like the elements of white light, often heard as a background to other sounds (for example, as hiss on a telephone line), making specific sounds hard or impossible to hear or detect: *white noise, white sound*. A *white voice*, however, translating Italian *voce bianca*, is a singing voice that lacks *dark* emotional 'colour', such as provided by vibrato. (5) (Used variously of food and drink) *white bread*, made from highly refined flour, as opposed to *brown bread*; *white wine*, yellowish in colour, in contrast to *red wine*; especially in BrE *white coffee*, which has milk or cream in it, as opposed to *black coffee*, which does not. (6) (Both adjective and noun) in politics, usually opposed to *red*, ultra-conservative, anti-revolutionary, royalist: *White Russians*; *fighting for the Whites*. (7) Spiritually pure; used with good intentions; respectable: *white magic* as opposed to *black magic*; *a white lie*; 'It is I whose duty it is to see that your name be made white again' (Anthony Trollope, *Orley Farm*, 1862). (8) (With and without an initial capital letter) marked by the slight skin pigment typical of people of European/Caucasian origin: *the white races*; *the White Dominions*; *white blood*. The ethnic slur *poor white trash/folks* has been used by American blacks and whites in the 19-20c for white people of few means and low social standing: 'I wouldn't do my hair in a three strand braid on no account; it is too poor-white-folksy for me' (*Harper's Magazine*, Aug. 1864). (9) (With and without an initial capital letter) a white person, often referred to especially in the US as a Caucasian: *South African Whites*; *poor whites*; *clubs operating a whites-only policy*. The ethnic nickname *Whitey* for a (usually male) Caucasian is common among African-Americans. (10) (Originally AmE, informal, now obsolescent) honourable, in a manner once avowedly expected by whites of whites, as in the phrases *That's real white of you* and *I mean to act white by you*: 'There ain't a whiter man than Laramie Jack from the Wind River Mountains down to Santa Fe' (*Century Magazine*, Feb. 1890). (11) Limited, restricted to, or typical of white people: *a white neighbourhood*; *White English*; 'A couple who affected sophisticated white manners and even spoke English with an almost white accent' (J. McClure, *Artful Egg*, 1984). (12) (Used of white people) very pale because blood has left the face: *white with rage/terror*. (13) Usually in plural only, a blank space in printing. (14) Verb, also *white out*. A printer's term for making part of a page white by leaving blank spaces and whitening areas of artwork. In general usage, however, to *white (something) out* means to cover errors in a text with white correction fluid, or to censor text by covering it with white ink. See ANGLES, BLACK, RACISM, WASP, WHITE ENGLISH, WHITE SPACE. [LANGUAGE, TECHNOLOGY, VARIETY].   T.MCA.

WHITE ENGLISH. [Late 1980s]. The English language as used wholly or mainly by white people, especially in the US and UK: 'We saw a very good foreign film here the other night, one of those coming-of-age movies in exotic settings. The people were attractive, likable types trying to survive in a hostile environment. The language was a little hard to follow, but the customs and costumes were interesting in a kind of National Geographic way. It was called "Boyz N the Hood" and it was set in a place called South-Central Los Angeles. The film is the work of a gifted 23-year old black man named John Singleton—from the hood. That's "neighbourhood" in white English' (Richard Reeves, Universal Press Syndicate, July 1991). See BLACK ENGLISH, WHITE. [AMERICAS, EUROPE].   T.MCA.

WHITE SPACE [1840s]. A term in printing, editing, and design for the area left free of text and illustrations on a page, poster, etc. The use of white space as part of the layout and appearance of published material is considered important by graphic designers and is a factor that often affects the readability and attractiveness of a publication. See GRAPHIC DESIGN, LAYOUT, SPACE, TYPOGRAPHY, WHITE (13, 14). [TECHNOLOGY, WRITING].   T.MCA.

WHITE VOICE. See WHITE.

WHITNEY, William Dwight [1827-94]. American orientalist, grammarian, and lexicographer, born in Northampton, Massachusetts, and educated at Williams and Yale

Colleges. His older brother, Josiah (later a geologist at Harvard), had studied in Germany and brought home, among other works, Bopp's *Sanskrit Grammar*, which William enthusiastically studied. He enrolled at Yale in the Sanskrit course of Edward E. Salisbury, then the only trained US orientalist, and in 1850 went to Germany, spending three years studying with Weber, Bopp, and Lepsius in Berlin and Roth in Tübingen. On his return, Salisbury resigned in Whitney's favour and provided the funds for his salary. He edited Sanskrit texts and wrote his *Sanskrit Grammar* (1879), still standard in US universities. Two compilations of lectures (*Language and Study of Language*, 1867; *The Life and Growth of Language*, 1875) were published in many editions and attracted a wide public to developments in philology and linguistics. These works earned the notice of Ferdinand de Saussure and influenced 20c structuralism. Whitney's contribution to studies of English arose from an extramural appointment at the Sheffield Scientific School in New Haven, where he taught English, German, and French. For each language he published a grammar; his *Essentials of English Grammar* (1877) went through 18 editions before 1903. Its distinguishing features included his restriction of tenses to two, present and past, a syntactic definition of *verb* in place of the 'wholly erroneous' notional and Latin-based definitions in schoolbooks, and a method of 'diagramming' sentences to show a constituent's role in larger constructions. His work is among the first school grammars to show the influence of 19c linguistic ideas, above all Bopp's scepticism about unquestioningly following the ancient grammarians. Whitney contributed to *Webster's New International Dictionary* (1864) and edited *The Century Dictionary*. See index. [AMERICAS, ASIA, BIOGRAPHY, GRAMMAR, LANGUAGE, REFERENCE]. R.W.B.

WHODUNIT, whodunnit. See DETECTIVE STORY.

WHORF, Benjamin Lee [1897–1941]. American amateur linguist. Born and raised in Winthrop, Massachusetts. Educated as a chemical engineer at Massachusetts Institute of Technology. He became a fire-prevention officer, a career he continued throughout his life, in spite of being offered academic posts. His interest in linguistics began in his mid-twenties, when he studied Maya writing. In his thirties, he was profoundly influenced by the work of Edward Sapir, and also by his own study of Hopi, an American Indian language of Arizona. In his own work, he also noted the uses and effects of particular words, for example that factory workers used the word *empty* to mean 'empty of liquid' when gasoline cans were still full of combustible fumes, and he advocated the use of *flammable* as a warning rather than *inflammable*, because the prefix *in-* was often taken to mean 'not'. From study and personal experience, he formed the opinion that people's language profoundly affected their behaviour and world-view. In particular, he argued that speakers of European languages envisaged concepts of space and time differently from speakers of Hopi. He claimed that 'formulation of ideas is not an independent process . . . but is part of a particular grammar. . . . We dissect nature along the lines laid down by our native languages' (1940). This view is known as the *Whorfian hypothesis* or the *Sapir-Whorf hypothesis* (see entry). Whorf's best-known papers were collected and published after his death under the title *Language, Thought and Reality: Selected Writings of Benjamin Lee Whorf* (ed. John B. Carroll, 1965). [AMERICAS, BIOGRAPHY, LANGUAGE]. J.M.A.

WHORFIAN HYPOTHESIS. See SAPIR-WHORF HYPOTHESIS, WHORF.

WH-QUESTION. See QUESTION.

WH-SOUND. In phonetic terms, the voiceless counterpart of /w/. The distinction between /hw/ and /w/ in such pairs as *whales/Wales* and *which/witch* was once universal in English and is currently a matter of controversy and sometimes confusion. In Old English, *h* could precede *l*, *n*, *r*, *w*, as in *hlāf* loaf, *hnecca* neck, *hwa* who, and was pronounced in each case. Only the /hw/ now survives, normal in IrE and ScoE, widespread in AmE and CanE, and common among older speakers of RP. The Old English written sequence *hw* was reversed to *wh* in the Middle Ages to align it with the other *h*-patterns (*ph*, *th*, *ch*, *sh*). In the process, an anomalous *w* was added in such words as *whole* (Old English *hāl*), *whore* (Old Englsh *hōre*), while *whelk* (Old English *weoloc*) acquired a superfluous *h*. In Older Scots and formerly in Northern English, the /hw/ sound was distinctively represented as *quh*: *quhat* what, *quhilk* which. In *who, whom, whose*, *w* rather than *h* has fallen silent. The presence of *wh* can cause spelling difficulties for speakers who do not distinguish /hw/ and /w/: *wen for *when*, *wheather for *weather*, *whent for *went*. Some speakers in England use /hw/ as a self-consciously 'correct' pronunciation in which overcompensation produces, for example, **the Prince of Whales*. See DIALECT IN SCOTLAND, W. [SPEECH, STYLE, USAGE]. G.K., C.U., T.MCA.

WIDOWS AND ORPHANS [Apparently 20c in this sense]. Terms in printing. A *widow* is an excessively short line of type, usually at the end of a column or paragraph; more specifically, a short concluding line of a paragraph that appears on its own at the *top* of the following page. An *orphan* is the first indented line of a paragraph or other short line found at the *bottom* of a page, with the rest of the related material on the following page. Both are considered typographically unattractive and are usually eliminated at the proofing stage by changing the number of lines per page or by otherwise adjusting the page make-up. See LINE. [TECHNOLOGY].

W.W.B.

WILDE, Oscar (Fingal O'Flahertie Wills) [1854–1900]. Irish writer, born in Dublin, and educated at Trinity College, Dublin, and Magdalen College, Oxford. He had early success in London as a wit, poet, and exemplar of the *Aesthetic movement*; he was satirized by W. S. Gilbert in *Patience* (1881): see CARICATURE. His comedies of manners, such as *Lady Windermere's Fan* (1892), were theatrical successes, with the mannered but witty style of dialogue that had already appeared in his novel *The Picture of Dorian Gray* (1891). Capacity for more serious social thinking was shown in *The Soul of Man under Socialism* (1891). During the run of his most successful play, *The Importance of Being Earnest* (1895), he began a suit for criminal libel against the Marquis of Queensberry which resulted in his own prosecution and imprisonment for homosexual offences. After his release in 1897, he lived in France, where he wrote of his prison experiences in *The Ballad of Reading Gaol* (1898), often quoted in the campaign for the abolition of capital punishment, and *De Profundis* (posthumously published in 1905). Despite their apparent superficiality, Wilde's comedies addressed the follies and pretences of contemporary life and recorded the mood and idiom of fashionable London in the last decade of the 19c. He was a master of epigram ('a cynic is a man who knows the price of everything and the value of nothing') and the unexpected reversal of clichés ('her hair has gone quite gold with grief'; 'work is the curse of the drinking classes'). See index. [BIOGRAPHY, EUROPE, LITERATURE, STYLE].

R.C.

WILD IRISH. A term formerly used by the English for the Irish who lived beyond the Pale: 'Irland is deuyded in ii. partes, one is the Engly[sh] pale, & the other, the wyld Irysh' (Andrew Boorde, *The breviary of healthe*, *c*.1547). After the 16c conquest, the term was applied to the *mere Irish* (mere meaning *pure* here), considered less civilized because they spoke Gaelic, did not conform to English norms, were Roman Catholics, and were not (particularly) loyal to the Crown. However, *wild* has also been used positively in Ireland: by Lady

Morgan in her novel *The Wild Irish Girl* (1806), to mean free, unfettered, and natural; in the phrase *the Wild Geese* (17–18c Jacobite Irish soldiers of fortune) and the song *The Wild Colonial Boy*, set in Australia. See BLACK IRISH, IRISHRY, PALE. [EUROPE, NAME].

T.MCA., L.T.

WILSON, Thomas [1525?–1581]. English government official and author of *Logique* (1552), which he claimed to be the first work of its kind in English, and *The Arte of Rhetorique* (1553, 1560), which was not the first manual of rhetoric in English but was among the most influential of the period. He condemned such affectations as unnecessary borrowing, archaizing, and *inkhorn terms*, and included a parody of pedantic writing, noting 'I know them that thinke Rhetorique to stande wholie vpon darke wordes, and hee that can catche an inke horne terme by the taile, him they coumpt to be a fine Englisheman, and a good Rhetorician.' See index. [BIOGRAPHY, EUROPE, HISTORY, STYLE].

W.F.B.

WINDPIPE. See SPEECH, TRACHEA.

WINDWARD ISLANDS. See ANTILLES.

WISECRACK [1910s: AmE slang, related to meanings of *crack* as conversation and loud, boastful talk]. Also **crack**. A brief witticism, generally facetious, aggressive, or disparaging: for example, a hungry diner in an expensively fashionable and snobbish restaurant, contemplating a very thin serving of very thin soup, says: 'Waiter, take this plate away, it's wet.' See BISOCIATION, JOKE. [STYLE].

W.N.

WIT [Before 10c: from Old English *wit*, *gewit*, cognate with German *Witz*, Old Norse *vit*, the mind, conscious thought, thinking, knowing, wisdom, as fossilized in such expressions as *use your wits*, *lose one's wits*, *at one's wits' end*, *witless*, *unwitting*, *nitwit*]. In current usage, quickness of mind and ability in pointed verbal humour. Lord Chesterfield's smart comment on the placing of Beau Nash's (full-length) portrait between the busts of Newton and Pope significantly twins *wisdom* and *wit*: 'The picture plac'd the busts between, / Adds to the thought much strength; / Wisdom and Wit are little seen, / but Folly's at full length.' This quatrain, originally by Jane Brereton (1685-1740), is itself a witticism embodying a definition of the role of wit in all ages: to *add to the thought much strength*.

Not everything that is witty is by the same token funny. Jonathan Swift's remark that 'We have just enough religion to make us hate, but not enough to make us love one another' (*Thoughts on Various Subjects*, 1727) is far from humour but close to wit. The thought takes added strength from a formulation that points the antitheses of 'just enough . . . not enough', and 'love . . . hate'. Paraphrase, however faithful to the content, would destroy the witty form: 'Our religion is not strong enough, because it only makes us hate rather than love each other.' Witty sayings in general follow a well-accentuated design. It is often said that 'Brevity is the soul of wit', but a better version might be 'Design is the test of wit', with a rider that economy is the test of design. The stylistic designs characterizing wit's brevity are often rhetorical schemes of parallels and antitheses, such as 'Truth is never pure, and rarely simple' (Wilde, *The Importance of Being Earnest*, 1895). Other recurrent forms are the definition and the quasi-philosophical proposition:'It is a truth universally acknowledged, that a single man in possession of good fortune, must be in want of a wife' (Austen, *Pride and Prejudice*). Such schemes are the structural foundation of literary wit, in prose or verse. The wit structure provides an expandable frame for the development of the witty image, as in this sentence from Edith Wharton's story *Xingu* (1916): 'Her mind was an hotel where facts came and went like transient lodgers, without leaving their address behind, and frequently without paying for their board.'

Ability to create appropriate linguistic frames is only one aspect of the power of wit; a complementary aspect is the understanding of semantic categories and the possibility of juxtapositions that are both novel and revelatory. This perception is the source of figures of speech, such as puns and metaphors, and also of discursive modes like irony and paradox. Essentially, it is the perception of concord within semantic dissonance, and vice versa. Wit is therefore a central element in satire and polemic, genres which require the pointed representation of ideas in conflict or the arbitrary yoking of discrete notions, and in this satirico-critical role takes on a colouring not only of humour but also of aggression: 'Mr X was a little out of his shallows', declares a television critic. This punning and metaphorical play on *shallows* as opposed to *depths* is witty. It would probably be said by anyone who has formed an opinion of Mr X to 'add to the thought much strength'. What is added, however, is cruel, and wit can be unabashedly cruel when wisdom is overwhelmed by the impulse to raise a laugh or make an impression. See ATTIC SALT, HUMO(U)R, JOKE, WITTICISM. [STYLE].   W.N.

WITTICISM [17c: from *witty*, coined by John Dryden on the analogy of *criticism*, blending English and Greek]. A witty remark. Like aphorisms, witticisms are brief utterances that neatly encapsulate a perception, an argument, an analysis. Common forms include the definition *An X is Y* ('A mistress is something between a mystery and a mattress') and quasi-syllogisms like Wilde's 'All women become like their mothers. That is their tragedy. No man does. That is his' (*The Importance of Being Earnest*, 1895). Witticisms of the definitional kind occur in such cynics' lexicons as Ambrose Bierce's *The Devil's Dictionary*:

Bride, *n.* A woman with a fine prospect of happiness behind her.

Backbite, *v.t.* To speak of a man as you find him when he can't find you.

Such witticisms are *constructed*, thought out at leisure, while others, often more striking for that reason, are *elicited*, in response to a some kind of conversational 'feed' or even as a consequence of the witty person's self-priming. This process of elicitation suggests an affinity of the witticism and the riddle, the witticism often assuming the function of the riddle's pay-off line. Wilde mimics the process: 'What is a cynic?'—'A man who knows the price of everything and the value of nothing' (*The Picture of Dorian Gray*, 1891). A kind of spontaneous riddling appears in the following exchanges among guests in a TV chat show: *Host* But now, what's all this about 'secondhand food'? *First guest* Well, I'm calling it 'secondhand food'. *Second guest* [incredulously] You mean regurgitated? *Third guest* Oh, I did hope you wouldn't bring that up.

Unlike its parent terms *wit* and *witty*, the word *witticism* can have a pejorative colouring, as a vehicle for jeering or disparaging, and is occasionally stigmatized as 'cheap'; cheap witticisms, like cruel wit, arise when the passion to score a point ignores the moderating influences of reason, justice, and tact. However, the effect of a disparaging witticism can always be nullified by repartee: the Oxford wit who remarked that 'Learning at Cambridge is a closed book' (alluding to that university's coat of arms) was answered with, 'Yes, but yours is always open at the same page' (alluding to the Oxford arms). See BIERCE. Compare BON MOT, EPIGRAM, HUMO(U)R, -ISM, WIT. [STYLE].   W.N.

WOLLSTONECRAFT, Mary [1759-97]. English writer and worker for women's rights. Born in London, she spent an insecure childhood with her prodigal father. In 1780, she and her sister opened a school in London. She published *Thoughts on the Education of Daughters* (1787) and a novel, *Mary* (1788). She spent some time in Ireland as a governess, and after returning to London published *A Vindication of the Rights of Man* (1790) as a riposte to Edmund Burke, then *A Vindication of the Rights of Women* (1792).

After an unhappy liaison with an American, Gilbert Imlay, she married William Godwin in 1797. She died soon after the birth of their daughter Mary, who married the poet Shelley and wrote the novel *Frankenstein*. Wollstonecraft argued that it was the social system and not any basic difference between the sexes that forced women into subordinate status. Although generally considered subversive and unwomanly, her works were well received by radicals and she laid the foundation for later suffragism and feminism. [BIOGRAPHY, EDUCATION, EUROPE].   R.C.

WOOLF, Virginia [1882–1941]. English novelist, born in London, daughter of Leslie Stephen, the first editor of the *Dictionary of National Biography*. Through her brothers, she was drawn into the circle of writers, painters, and critics who came to be known as *the Bloomsbury Group*. They included Lytton Strachey, Roger Fry, Clive Bell (who married her sister Vanessa), and Leonard Woolf (whom she married in 1912). Her first novel, *The Voyage Out* (1915), had few technical innovations, but foreshadowed some of her later approaches to fiction. In *Jacob's Room* (1922) she made a break from the contemporary novel whose attention to externals she attacked in her essay 'Mr Bennett and Mrs Brown' (1923). *Mrs Dalloway* (1925) and *To the Lighthouse* (1927) established her as a leading practitioner of the *stream of consciousness* in fiction. She concentrated on the inner life of thought and motivation, using indirect narrative through the viewpoint of individual characters. She did not take the flow of free association and incomplete expression of ideas as far as Joyce did in *Ulysses*, but *The Waves* (1931) presented a story of six lives through sequences of shared and separate experience. Woolf used more traditional techniques in *Night and Day* (1919) and *The Years* (1937); *Orlando* (1928) is a lively excursion through English history in a pastiche of styles from different periods. Her last novel, *Between the Acts* (1941), partly returned to her earlier style; it was published after she committed suicide while suffering from the depression that had afflicted most of her adult life.

For Woolf, the novel was an impressionistic record of individual experience rather than a mimetic picture of society: 'Life is a luminous halo, a semi-transparent envelope surrounding us from the beginning of consciousness to the end' ('Modern Fiction', 1919). Her characters live between past and present, finding some of their strongest experiences in moments of recall. Her descriptive passages were often poetic, in balanced and rhythmic prose with extended similes; the passages describing the changing aspects of the sea in *The Waves* are notable examples:

The sun rose. Bars of yellow and green fell on the shore, gilding the ribs of the eaten-out boat and making the sea-holly and its mailed leaves gleam blue as steel. Light almost pierced the thin swift waves as they raced fan-shaped over the beach. The girl who had shaken her head and made all the jewels, the topaz, the aquamarine, the water-coloured jewels with sparks of fire in them, dance, now bared her brows and with wide-opened eyes drove a straight pathway over the waves.

Woolf was an acute literary critic, particularly of women writers; her essays were collected in *The Common Reader* (1925, 1932). From 1917, she and her husband ran the Hogarth Press, which published many leading contemporary writers, including Katherine Mansfield and T. S. Eliot. Woolf was a strong feminist and has been highly esteemed by recent feminist criticism. She was anxious to present the feminine view of life which literature had generally neglected and was among the first to suggest that language has been shaped by men: 'It is useless to go back to men writers for help, however much one may go to them for pleasure . . . [They] never helped woman yet, though she may have learned a few tricks of them and adapted them to her use. The weight, the pace, the strikes of a man's mind are too unlike her own for her to lift anything substantial from him successfully . . . A book is not made of sentences laid end to end, but of sentences built, if an image helps, into arcades of domes. And this shape too has been made by men out of their own needs for their own uses' (*A Room of One's Own*, 1929). See index. [BIOGRAPHY, EUROPE, LITERATURE, STYLE].   R.C.

WORCESTER, Joseph E(merson) [1784–1865]. American scholar and lexicographer. His first publications included *A Gazetteer of the United States* (1818) and *Elements of History, Ancient and Modern* (1826), which were used as textbooks. His lexicographical career began with an 1828 abridgement of Samuel Johnson's *Dictionary of the English Language* that included John Walker's *Key To The Classical Pronunciation of Greek, Latin, and Scripture Proper Names*. In 1829, he published an abridgement of Noah Webster's *American Dictionary of the English Language* which included a synopsis of words pronounced differently by various orthoepists as well as Walker's *Key*. Worcester published *A Comprehensive Pronouncing and Explanatory Dictionary* in 1830, with subsequent editions in 1835, 1855 (with a new title), and 1860. The appearance of this work marked the beginning of the so-called 'dictionary wars'. Worcester was a linguistic conservative who used the speech of London as his standard and was not a spelling reformer; he also cited British writers in his illustrative material. Webster advocated spelling reform, current American usage, and cited many American writers. Webster later retracted some of his more unusual spelling proposals, such as *tuf* tough, *dawter* daughter, *fateeg* fatigue, while Worcester became more lenient towards some widely accepted American pronunciations and in his abridgement of Webster's dictionary modified some words even more than Webster, such as *gold* to rhyme with *fold*, not *fooled*, and *medicine* to a three-syllable pronunciation. The publication in Britain in 1853 of *A Universal and Critical Dictionary* (1st edition, 1846) intensified the 'war'. In the preface, Worcester had denied basing his dictionary on Webster's book. The British publisher, however, omitted that disclaimer and to increase sales put on the title page the statement that Worcester's dictionary 'was compiled from the Materials of Noah Webster'. The ensuing pamphlet war carried out by Webster's publishers lasted into the 1860s. Among the innovations attributed to Worcester are: the introduction of synonyms into dictionaries, the inclusion of given names and their etymologies (1855), and pictorial illustrations (1860), all of which were included in his *Dictionary of the English Language* of 1860. See index. [AMERICAS, BIOGRAPHY, REFERENCE].   R.W.B.

WORD [Cognate with German *Wort* word, Greek *(w)eírein* speak, Latin *verbum* word, Sanskrit *vrátam* command]. A fundamental term in both the general and technical discussion of language. The entry on *word* in the *OED* (2nd edition, 1989) displays its senses under the three headings used in 1927 by C. T. Onions:

(1) *Speech, utterance, verbal expression*, divided into eleven sense groups: speech, talk, utterance; a speech, an utterance; speech as distinct from writing; verbal expression as contrasted with thought; contention, altercation; a report, news, rumour; an order, request; a promise, undertaking; a declaration, assertion; an utterance in the form of a phrase or sentence, a saying or proverb; a divine communication, scripture, and Christ.

(2) *An element of speech*, a single twelfth sense initially defined as: 'a combination of vocal sounds, or one such sound, used in a language to express an idea (e.g. to denote a thing, attribute, or relation), and constituting an ultimate minimal element of speech having a meaning as such'. This technical definition is followed by the seven sense groups: a name, title, idea, term; engraved or printed marks on surfaces; in contrast with the thing or idea signified; the right word for the right thing; a telegraphic message; a mathematical sequence; a string of bits in a computer.

(3) *Phrases*, a heterogeneous collection of such usages as *take a person at his word*, *in so many words*, *word of honour*, and *by word of mouth*.

Other dictionary definitions. The technical definition provided above comes twelfth in the order of *OED* senses because the dictionary was compiled on historical principles. Most 20c dictionaries are, however, synchronic and tend to place their equivalent of the technical sense first. The following selection of primary definitions of *word* is drawn from recent editions of two American and two British works:

(1) *Webster's Ninth New Collegiate Dictionary* (1984): 'a speech sound or series of speech sounds that symbolizes and communicates a meaning without being divisible into smaller units capable of independent use'.

(2) *American Heritage Dictionary* (1985): 'a sound or a combination of sounds, or its representation in writing or printing, that symbolizes and communicates a meaning and may consist of a single morpheme or of a combination of morphemes'.

(3) *Collins English Dictionary* (1986): 'one of the units of speech or writing that native speakers of a language usually regard as the smallest isolable meaningful element of the language, although linguists would analyse these further into morphemes'.

(4) *Chambers English Dictionary* (1988): 'a unit of spoken language: a written sign representing such an utterance'.

Literacy and the word. The earliest known word study in the Western world took place in ancient Greece. Latin words were later analysed in terms of Greek words, the model being adapted in minor ways to fit a second but similar language, and since then the classical analysis, adapted and refined for other languages, has evolved into a model through which Western scholars analyse all languages. In Greece, word study was an inseparable part of the study of texts, which had been prompted by the invention of script. Prior to that, *name* was a more clearly delineated concept than *word*, which was rather imprecisely associated with *speech* (apparently the meaning of **wer*, the Indo-European root underlying Latin *verbum*, Sanskrit *vrátam*, and English *word*). In oral communities, there appears generally to be no great interest in separating out 'units' of language, a lack of delimitation carried over into the early stages of alphabetic writing, in which letters followed each other in lines without spaces to separate off what are now perceived as 'words'. Spaces between groups of letters became important as the conventions of writing evolved. In alphabetic systems, spaces are now universal and as a result literate people learn to recognize 'words' as visual rather than auditory units. In a real sense, the first orthographers of a language make the decisions about how words are to be perceived in that language.

The idea that marks on a surface might also relate to speech only slowly emerged from (and coexisted with) the earlier view of words as speech itself, not elements of speech. This ancient lack of distinction between *word* and *language* continues, as in Bernard Groom's comment:

To the imaginative writer, and especially to the poet, language is a medium for self-expression. Hard and unyielding up to a point, words can none the less be so manipulated as to bear the impress of a particular mind (*A Short History of English Words*, 1934).

Children learn about words while learning to write, become more or less comfortable with 'the written word', and may later assume that words as they are written automatically have a place as theoretical units of both speech and script. Grammarians, philologists, and linguists, all the legatees of the Greeks, have tended to focus on words as visual entities even when analysing sound, for which phoneticians developed a special alphabet. The place of the word as an ultimate unit of language has not, however, been easy to find, with the result that many 20c linguists have found it necessary to look elsewhere for key units of language: 'below' the word among phonemes and morphemes or 'above' it in sentence and discourse.

The word in different languages. The nature of words varies from language to language: *amaverunt* is one word in Latin, but cannot be translated into one word of English (in which it means either *they loved* or *they have loved*). It is a verb with a root *am-*, a thematic vowel *-a-*, a marker of the perfect tense *-v-*, and a complex inflectional ending *-erunt*. The English verbs that translate it have different tenses (simple past *they loved*, present perfect *they have loved*) and bear not the slightest resemblance to the structure of their Latin equivalent. Different from both English and Latin, Swahili has a primary verb form such as *kuta* (meet). The forms *kutana* ('meet each other') and *kutanisha* ('cause to meet each other') may be conceived as either variations of *kuta* or as distinct words. In effect, the conception 'word' is determined afresh within the system of every language, and as a result the word-as-element-of-speech is language-specific, not language-universal. The various kinds of language have their own broadly similar words, but even so there is variation from language to language inside a category: for example, among Romance languages between French and Spanish.

Eight kinds of word. Despite such complications, however, certain features are more or less true for many if not all languages. Eight such features are fundamental to English and each has its own 'word':

The orthographic word. The word understood in terms of alphabetic or syllabic writing systems: a visual sign with space around it. It may or may not have a canonical form: in the 14c, before print encouraged standardization, *merry* was also spelled *myry*, *myrie*, *murie*, and *mery*. On occasion, the orthographic word has canonical forms for different varieties within English: BrE *colour* and AmE *color* ('the same word' in two visual forms).

The phonological word. The word understood in terms of sound: a spoken signal that occurs more commonly as part of a longer utterance than in isolation and is subject to rhythm. Traditional spoken English is a series of stressed and unstressed syllables which behave in more or less predictable ways: where an experienced listener hears *It's no good at all* being pronounced in a relaxed, informal way, a foreigner may hear *Snow good a tall*. In the flow of speech, words do not have such distinct shapes as on paper, and syllable boundaries do not necessarily reflect grammatical boundaries: the phrases *a notion* and *an ocean* are usually homophonic and only context establishes which has in fact been said.

The morphological word. The word in terms of form lies behind both the orthographic and the phonological word: *big* has a spelt-out realization *b-i-g* and a spoken realization /bɪg/, but is independent of both, because it can be expressed in either medium and also in sign language. This entity is capable of realization in different 'substances'; it is distinct from such spelt-out variants as *colour* and *color* as well as from the innumerable ways in which African, American, Australian, Caribbean, English, Irish, Scottish or other people may say 'colo(u)r'. However, all such users have it in common and it is the basis of such further forms as *colourful* and *discoloured*.

The lexical word (also called a *full word*, *content word*, *lexeme*, *lexical item*). The word in terms of content relates to things, actions, and states in the world. It is usually realized by one or more morphological words, as when *do*, *does*, *doing*, *did*, *done* are taken to be five 'versions' of the one verb DO. Lexical words are generally fitted into the flow of language through such mechanisms as *affixation*, *suppletion*, *stress shift*, and *vowel change*, all of which have morphological and other effects. The set of such words is always open to new members, and in English embraces nouns, verbs, and adjectives, and other parts of speech when they behave like nouns, verbs, and adjectives, as in 'But me no buts'. Lexical words may be simple in structure (*cat*, *mouse*), or composite (*cold-bloodedness*, *incomprehensible*, *teapot* blackbird, Commonwealth, stamp collector, put up with, natural selection, Parkinson's disease).

The grammatical word (also called a *form word, function word, structure word,* and in some theories a subvariety of *morpheme*). The word in terms of syntactic function contrasts with the lexical word and is an element in the structural system of a language. It serves to link lexical words. In English, conjunctions, determiners, interjections, particles, and pronouns are grammatical words. They occur frequently and have their own semantic systems, as with such particles as *up* and *down*, which relate to position, direction, space, and time. In principle, such words are a closed set to which new items are seldom added. As lubricants, grammatical words are like affixes: the *out* in *throw out* is like the prefix *e-* in *eject*; the *before* in *before the war* means the same as *pre-* in *pre-war*. They can also function like affixes, as in *he-man* and *yes-man*.

The onomastic word. The word in terms of naming establishes special, often unique reference: the difference between *Napoleon* and *emperor*. It may be simple like *Smith* or complex like *Smithsonian*. Names may be motivated, like *Sitting Bull* (a Sioux name derived from an omen involving a bull buffalo) or conventional, like *Smith* today (though not in the Middle Ages, when the name was occupation-based). Although such words are lexical, they are not usually listed in dictionaries and may or may not be relevant in encyclopedias. They are often regarded as apart from normal vocabulary, though they too have to be learned.

The lexicographical word. The word in terms of dictionaries is usually presented in an alphabetic setting. Many dictionaries have an entry *did* as the past of *do*, an entry *them* as the object form of *they*, and so on, with cross-references to the representative form. There are therefore two kinds of entry: anything the compilers think anyone might look up, and the *citation forms* under which definition proceeds. The conventional citation form for nouns is the singular (unless a word is always plural) and for the verb is the bare infinitive (unless the verb only occurs as a participle, or is a modal verb).

The statistical word. The word in terms of occurrences in texts is embodied in such instructions as 'Count all the words on the page': that is, count each letter or group of letters preceded and followed by a white space. This instruction may or may not include numbers, codes, names, and abbreviations, all of which are not necessarily part of the everyday conception of 'word'. Whatever routine is followed, the counter deals in tokens or instances and as the count is being made the emerging list turns tokens into types:

for example, there could be 42 tokens of the type *the* on a page, and 4 tokens of the type *dog*. Both the tokens and the types, however, are unreflectingly spoken of as words.

Other 'words'. In addition, there is a large number of more or less common expressions, some technical, some semi-technical, some general and casual, all specifying kinds of words and word-like units. They fall into overlapping groups that include: (1) Terms in which *word* appears, such as: *base word, buzz word, compound word, long word, root word*. (2) Terms based on the suffix *-ism*, such as: *Americanism, Australianism, burgessism, malapropism*. (3) Terms based on the combining form *-onym*, such as: *antonym, aptronym, characternym, eponym, hyponym, synonym*. (4) Terms that relate to form more than meaning, such as: *abbreviation, acronym, complex word, compound word, initialism, portmanteau word*. (5) Terms that relate to meaning more than form, such as: *antonym, burgessism, eponym, hard word*. (6) Terms that relate to social usage, such as: *anagram, buzz word, confusible, loan(word), malapropism, nonce word, palindrome, stunt word, vogue word*. All such terms fit in various ways and at various levels into the model of the word presented above. Those with their own entries in this volume are shown in the theme list below.

Words as clusters. Because of its many dimensions, the concept 'word' is more like a cluster than an atom. On the level of theory, the cluster contains the kinds of words discussed above. On the level of practical activity, people 'know a word' not simply when they can use and understand a single item but when they know a range of variation and practices associated with it: for example, to know the word *know* entails knowing how to say, hear, read, and write its various forms and extensions, fitting them into phrases and sentences (*knows, knowing, knew, known*), relating the simple to the complex (as in *knowledge, knowledgeable, unknowing, unknowable, unknowably, unknown*), relating these to such compounds as *knowhow* and *know-all*, managing idioms (*y'know, in the know, know the ropes, know what's what, know a thing or two*), using and grasping senses, expressions, and collocations (*knowing someone or something, knowing how to do something, knowing better*, and even *knowing 'in the Biblical sense'*). This cluster, with its clear centre and hazy periphery, shares semantic space with other clusters cited as the words *understand, perceive, grasp*, and *fathom*. All operate within a system whose size and complexity defy comprehensive description, but without being beyond the reach of the everyday user of the language. [LANGUAGE, WORD].

T.MCA.

The word theme

A–D. ABBREVIATION, ACRONYM, ACROSTIC, ADAGE, AFFIX, AFRICANISM, AMERICANISM, ANACHORISM, ANACHRONISM, ANAGRAM, ANGLICISM, ANTIGRAM, ANTONYM, APTRONYM, ATTRIBUTIVE NOUN, AUSTRALIANISM, BACK-FORMATION, BASE, BEHEADMENT AND CURTAILMENT, BINOMIAL, BINOMIAL NOMENCLATURE, BISOCIATION, BLEND, BORROWING, BOUND AND FREE, BOUT-RIMÉS, BURGESSISM, BUZZ WORD, CALL MY BLUFF, CALQUE, CANADIANISM, CANONICAL FORM, CARIBBEANISM, CELTICISM, CHARADE, CLASSICAL COMPOUND, CLASSICAL ENDING, CLIPPING, COGNATE, COINAGE, COLLOCATION, COLLOQUIALISM, COMBINING FORM, COMPLEX WORD, COMPOSITION, COMPOUND-COMPLEX WORD, COMPOUND WORD, COMPUTERESE, COMPUTING, CONFUSIBLE, CONSEQUENCES, CONTRACTION, CONVERSION, CROSSWORD PUZZLE, DEFINING VOCABULARY, DEFINITION, DERIVATION, DERIVATIONAL PARADIGM, DICTIONARY, DIMINUTIVE, DISTINGUISHABLE, DOUBLET.

E–K. ECHOISM, ENTRY, EPONYM, -ESE, ETYMOLOGY, ETYMON, ETYMORPHS, FILIPINISM, FIXED PHRASE, FOLK ETYMOLOGY, FOREIGNISM, FORMATIVE, FOUR-LETTER WORD, FREQUENCY COUNT, FREQUENTATIVE, FUNCTIONAL SHIFT, GAELICISM, GAIRAIGO, GALLICISM, GENERAL SERVICE LIST, GENTEELISM, GHOST WORD, GLOSS, HARD WORD, HEADWORD, HEBRAISM, HIBERNIANISM, HOBSON-JOBSONISM, HOLOPHRASE, HOMOGRAPH, HOMONYM, HOMOPHONE, INDO-EUROPEAN ROOT, INFIX, INITIAL, INITIALESE, INITIALISM, INKHORN TERM, INTERFIX, INTERNATIONAL CORPUS OF ENGLISH, INTERNATIONAL SCIENTIFIC VOCABULARY, IRISHISM, -ISM, ITERATIVE, JANUS WORD, KEYWORD.

L–S. LATINISM, LEMMA, LETTER², LETTER WORD, LEXEME, LEXICAL FIELD, LEXICOGRAPHY, LEXICOLOGY, LEXICON, LEXIS, LIPOGRAM, LITERARY TERM, LOAN, LOAN BLEND, LOAN TRANSLATION, LOANWORD, LOCALISM, LONG WORD, MACHINE WORD, MCWORD, -MAN/WOMAN, METANALYSIS, MIS-, MONOSYLLABLE, MORPHEME, NAME, NEW ZEALANDISM, NICE-NELLYISM, NOMENCLATURE, NONCE WORD, NOUN-INCORPORATION, NUMERAL, -ONYM, PALINDROME, PANGRAM, PHON(A)ESTHESIA, PHRASAL VERB, PHRASE WORD, PILGRIM WORD, PLAYING WITH WORDS, POLYSEMY, POLYSYLLABLE, PORTMANTEAU WORD, POTTER, PREFIX, PRIVATIVE, PROCLITIC, PRODUCTIVE, PROTOGRAM, REBUS, REDUPLICATION, REDUPLICATIVE, REGIONALISM, RETRONYM, REVERSAL, RHYMING COMPOUND, RIDDLE, ROGET'S THESAURUS, ROOT, ROOT-CREATION, ROOT-WORD, SAXONISM, SAYING, SCOTTICISM, SCRABBLE, SEMANTIC CHANGE, SEMANTIC FIELD, SEMORDNILAP, SENTENCE WORD, SOUTH AFRICANISM, SPELLING, SPELLING BEE, STEM, STEM FORMATIVE, SUBWORD, SUFFIX, SUPERORDINATE TERM, SYLLABIC ACRONYM, SYLLABLE WORD, SYNONYM.

T–Z. TECHNOBABBLE, TECHNOSPEAK, TELEGRAPHESE, TELESCOPING, TERM, TERMINOLOGY, THEMATIC VOWEL, THEME, TMESIS, TONGUE-TWISTER, TRIPLET, TRISOCIATION, TYPE AND TOKEN, VAGUE WORD, VERBAL, VERBALISM, VERBICIDE, VERBOSITY, VERNACULARISM, VOCABLE, VOCABULARY, VOCABULARY CONTROL, VOGUE, VULGARISM, WORD ACCENT, WORDAGE, WORD BLINDNESS, WORDBOOK, WORD BUFF, WORD CLASS, WORD-FORMATION, WORD LIST, WORD-LORE, WORD-MONGER, WORD ORDER, WORD ORIGINS, WORD PROCESSOR, WORD SALAD, WORDSMITH, WORD SQUARE, WORD STRESS, WORDS WITHIN WORDS, WORD WORD, YIDDISHISM.

WORD ACCENT. See STRESS.

WORDAGE [1820s]. Words taken collectively, or a quantity or total of words in a book or other document. [WORD]. T.MCA.

WORD BLINDNESS [1880s]. A non-technical term for *dyslexia*. See DYSLEXIA. [LANGUAGE, WORD]. T.MCA.

WORDBOOK also **word-book**, **word book**. [16c]. An occasional, usually informal term for a dictionary or other work that presents and defines words. It is sometimes used by lexicologists as a generic term covering the *dictionary* (taken to be primarily arranged in alphabetic order), the *thesaurus* (taken to be primarily arranged in thematic order), and works with any other organizing principle, such as frequency of occurrence or pictures. See ALPHABETIC(AL) ORDER, DICTIONARY, THEMATIC ORDER, THESAURUS, VOCABULARY. [REFERENCE, WORD]. T.MCA.

WORD BUFF [20c]. An informal term for someone more than usually interested in words. The English word buff Ivor Brown observed that the 'snatchers and hoarders of birds' eggs and of flowers first create a scarcity, then hunt down the rareties. To hunt words is to do no trespass' (*A Word in Your Ear*, 1942). The American collector Paul Dickson has added: 'I am a word collector. I approach my collecting with a zeal that borders on the compulsive' (*Words*, 1982). A formal and (often jocularly) pretentious synonym for 'word buff' is *logophile* (from Greek *lógos* speech, *philos* friend, lover). The word buff's enthusiasm, obsession, or 'vice' is consequently known as *logophilia*. [REFERENCE, WORD]. T.MCA.

WORD CLASS [1920s], also **grammatical category**. Terms in linguistics for a category of words that have been grouped together because they are similar in their inflection, meaning, functions, or a combination of these. Many linguists prefer the term to *part of speech*, which has traditionally been used for a more limited set of classes that are less rigorously defined. Others use the three terms as synonyms. See PART OF SPEECH. [GRAMMAR, WORD]. S.G.

WORD DIVISION, word-division. See HYPHEN.

WORD-FORMATION [probably 19c]. (1) The formation of longer, more complex words from shorter, simpler words. (2) The formation of all words, simple or composite, from more basic elements of language. (3) The study of the formation of words. In the West, the analysis of word form began in classical Greece and passed in due course to Rome. Philosophers including Plato and Aristotle and grammarians including Dionysius Thrax and Terentius Varro developed the study of the ways in which words were formed as a part of grammar, founding a long and subtle tradition that was inherited and extended by 19c comparative philology and 20c linguistics. The classical study was based only on Greek and Latin words, and contrasted *simple word* and *complex word*. The simple word was discussed either in terms of its *root* (a basic element without adaptations or inflections), such as Greek *log*, whose core meaning was 'speech', or as a *root word*, consisting of a root, stem, and inflection (in most cases cited in standard forms, such as the nominative singular for nouns), such as Greek *lógos* (speech, word) and Latin *verbum* (word, verb). The complex word was discussed in terms of two processes or categories: (1) *Derivation*, in which affixes and inflections could be added to a root, as with *logikós*, an adjective formed from *lógos*, and *verbalis*, an adjective formed from *verbum*. (2) *Composition*, in which two or more roots could be combined, with appropriate affixes and inflections added, as with the nouns *biología* and *biologistẽs*, formed from *bíos* (life) and *lógos*, and *agricultura*, formed from *ager* (field) and *cultura* (cultivation).

Contemporary terms. The classical description was somewhat modified when transferred to English. The concept *root* has continued in use, but in the 20c has been increasingly replaced by *base* when discussing non-historical processes. A *root word* is usually called either a *simple word* or a *simplex*. The classical 'complex' forms divide into *complex words* and *compound words*, the formation of complex words being *derivation* and of compound words being formerly called *composition* but now usually *compounding*. Derivation is the process by which the word *unfriendly* is built up from the simple word or free base *friend*, and *illegality* is built up from the bound base *-leg-* (from Latin, meaning 'law'). Compounding is the process by which the vernacular compound *teapot* is formed from the simple words *tea* and *pot* and the classical compound *biography* is formed from the combining forms *bio-* and *-graphy*. Although derivation and compounding account for a large number of the composite word forms of English and other languages, they do not cover everything. As a result, at various times further descriptive categories have been added, such as *conversion* or *functional shift*, *back-formation*, *phrasal verb*, *blend*, *abbreviation*, and *root-creation*. Sometimes, specific word-formational terms have lagged behind an awareness of the distinct forms actually occurring in a language: although, in English, verb forms like *put up* and *put up with* have been discussed since at least the 18c, the name *phrasal verb*, by which they are now most commonly known, was not applied to them until the early 20c.

In more detail, these categories are: (1) *Conversion or functional shift*, the process by which words extend their grammatical function: for example, from verb to noun (*run* in *go for a run*), and from noun to verb (*position* in *positioning people*). (2) *Back-formation*, the creation of a simpler or shorter form from a pre-existing more complex form: *edit* from *editor*, *intuit* from *intuition*. (3) *Phrasal verb*, a class of verb followed by an adverbial and/or prepositional particle: *put up* provide a bed for, *put up with* tolerate. (4) *Blend*, the outcome of a process which collapses two words into one: *breakfast* and *lunch* into *brunch*; *electro-* and *execute* into *electrocute*. (5) *Abbreviation*, the shortening of words and phrases, in three basic forms: the *initialism*, a set of letters pronounced as such and standing for an idea, group, or institution (*BBC*, pronounced 'bee-bee-cee', for *British Broadcasting Corporation*); the *acronym*, a set of letters pronounced as a word (*NATO*, pronounced 'Nay-toe', for *North Atlantic Treaty Organization*); the *clipping*, a short form created by removing one or more syllables (*pro* for *professional*, *phone* for *telephone*, *flu* for *influenza*). Blends are often closely involved with the processes of abbreviation. (6) *Root-creation*, the formation of new roots or bases, which tend to be *echoic*, where a form resembles one or more pre-existing forms (*cuckoo*, *splish*: sounds of nature), or *onomastic*, deriving from names (*atlas* from the name of the mythical titan; *gin* from the city of Genoa). See relevant entries (as listed at the end of this article).

Word-formation clusters. In accordance with need, social context, and formational patterns, clusters of derivatives, compounds, and other usages develop around words and bases. The noun *wolf*, for example, is the focus of a wide range of expressions: (1) Compounds like *prairie wolf* and *timber wolf* kinds of wolf, *wolf dog* the offspring of a wolf and a dog, *wolfhound* a dog that hunts wolves, *wolf-fish* a fish in some way like a wolf, *wolf spider* a spider that hunts its prey like a wolf, *wolfsbane* a poisonous plant, *wolf child* a child brought up by wolves, *wolfman* a man who can turn into a wolf, *wolf pack* a pack of wolves, *wolf note* a discordant note in music, *wolf whistle* a whistle of sexual admiration, *she-wolf* a female wolf, *werewolf* (from German) someone who can become a wolf. (2) Derivatives like *wolfer/wolver* a hunter of wolves, *wolf-like* and *wolfish* like a wolf, *wolfishly* its adverb, *wolfishness* the quality of being wolfish, *wolf down* to swallow food like a wolf, *wolverine* a large weasel-like animal with wolf-like attributes. (3) Fixed phrases like *Tasmanian wolf* a wolf-like animal in Tasmania, *lone wolf* a person who does things alone. (4) Idioms and sayings such as *cry wolf, keep the wolf from the door, be a wolf in sheep's clothing, throw someone to the wolves.*

Although the *wolf*-cluster exhibits the range of word-forming potential, it is an ancient and diffuse system whose members cover many contexts. As such, it does not illustrate the vigour of present-day word-formation, which can be seen in a recent more or less 'nonce' cluster based on the name *Tourette*. In 1885, the French neurologist Georges Gilles de la Tourette described a nervous condition marked by tics, jerks, grimaces, curses, mannerisms, imitative actions, and antic kinds of humour. This became known as *Gilles de la Tourette Syndrome*, then as *Tourette's syndrome*, often further shortened to *Tourette's*. When describing people with Tourette's, the American neurologist Oliver Sacks has used the following derivations, compounds, and other forms: (1) Nouns: *Tourettism* the syndrome and its effects, *motor Tourettism* the physical aspect of the syndrome, *mental Tourette's* the psychological aspect, *Tourette* a symptom of the syndrome, *Touretter* someone with the syndrome, *Tourette's Syndrome Association* a proper name, *TSA* its initialism, *Tourettoma* a figurative mind-tumour, *super-Tourette's* a powerfully destructive variety, *super-Touretter* one who has it, *Tourette psychosis* 'an identity frenzy', *Tourettesville* the nickname of the town of LaCrete in Alberta, Canada, many of whose Mennonite inhabitants have the syndrome, *Grandma Tourette* the nickname of a matriarch of the town. (2) Adjectives, adverbs: *Tourettic* (formal) pertaining to the syndrome, *Tourettically* its adverb, *Tourette-like* like the syndrome, *Touretty* (informal) showing symptoms, *Tourettish* (informal) relating to the syndrome, *Tourettishly* its adverb. (3) Verb forms: *Touretting* displaying the syndrome, *Tourettized* afflicted with the syndrome. (From Oliver Sacks, *The Man Who Mistook His Wife for a Hat*, 1985, and 'Being Moved by the Spirit', *Sunday Times*, 25 Sept. 1988.)

Paradigms and paraphrases. Although they often belong in clusters, complex words are usually formed one at a time in accordance with more or less established patterns. Such patterns or *paradigms* are built up analogically and differ for compounds and derivatives. Compound patterns involve a distinctive kind of stress on (the main syllable of) the first element, as in *TEApot*

and *eMERgency plan*, and paraphrase formulas gloss the relationships between the bases in a compound: a *flower pot* is a 'pot for flowers' and so a *slop bucket* is interpretable as a 'bucket for slops'; a *goatskin* is 'the skin of a goat' and so an *iguana skin* is interpretable as 'the skin of an iguana'. Derivational paradigms are often cumulative, as in the set *form/formal/formality*, the paraphrases expressing relationships between base and other elements: *formality* is the condition of being *formal*, and *formal* is the adjective that relates to *form*, and similar relations exist for the set *norm/normal/normality*, but not for *nature, natural, *naturality*.

The word-forming continuum. Although much of English word-formation is regular, few patterns are neat and tidy and many forms blend their categories and mix their patterns. It is useful therefore to introduce the concept *hybrid*: for example, compounds with derivational elements (*schoolboyish* and *mud-walled*) and abbreviations involved in attribution and compounding (*a NATO radar system*), in derivation (*ex-IBMer*, someone who no longer works for International Business Machines), or in both (*an ex-CFL player*, someone who no longer plays for the Canadian Football League). It is likely that word-formation can be most usefully discussed in terms of both a continuum in which categories shade into each other and self-contained classical containers, each more or less insulated from the others. The fluidity of word-formation arises both from complex processes of change over centuries and from casual usage untouched by theories of language and norms of 'good' formation. The American linguist Dwight Bolinger, reflecting on 'the high informality of word-making in English', puts the matter as follows:

Practically all words that are not imported bodily from some other language . . . are made up of old words and their parts. Sometimes those parts are pretty well standardized, like the suffix *-ness* and the prefix *un-*. Other times they are only broken pieces that some inventive speaker manages to re-fit . . . *Hamburger* yields *-burger*, which is reattached in *nutburger, Gainesburger*, and *cheeseburger*. *Cafeteria* yields *-teria*, which is reattached in *valeteria, groceteria*, and *washateria*. Trade names make easy use of almost any fragment, like the *-roni* of *macaroni* that is reattached in *Rice-a-Roni* and *Noodle-Roni*. The fabrication may re-use elements that have been re-used many times, or it may be a one-shot affair such as the punning reference to being a member of the *lowerarchy*, with *-archy* extracted from *hierarchy*. The principle is the same. Scientists and scholars may give themselves airs with high-bred affixes borrowed from classical languages, but they are linguistically no more sophisticated than the common speakers who are satisfied with leftovers from the vernacular (*Aspects of Language*, 1968).

Word-formation in English operates among hundreds of millions of people, drawing on centuries of complex hybridization and prompting idiosyncrasy in forms and uses. As a result, even the most well-defined categories and patterns identify tendencies rather than absolutes that are thoughtlessly 'flouted' by the ignorant and insensitive. Around such focal points as compounding and affixation, with their relative certainties, swarm innumerable and unpredictable fringe formations, of longer or shorter duration, such as *lowerarchy*, *Rice-a-Roni* and *Grandma Tourette*.

See ABBREVIATION, ACRONYM, AFFIX, ASSIMILATION, BACK-FORMATION, BASE, BIG WORD, BISOCIATION, BLEND, BORROWING, BOUND AND FREE, CLASSICAL COMPOUND, CLASSICAL ENDING, CLIPPING, COGNATE, COINAGE, COMBINING FORM, COMPOUND WORD, COMPUTERESE, COMPUTER USAGE, CONTRACTION, CONVERSION, DERIVATION, DERIVATIVE, DIMINUTIVE, DOUBLET, ELISION, -EME, ENCLITIC, ENDING, EPONYM, FORMATIVE, HARD WORD, HYBRID, INDO-EUROPEAN ROOTS, INITIAL, INITIALESE, INITIALISM, INTERFIX, INTERNATIONAL SCIENTIFIC VOCABULARY, -ISM, ITERATIVE, LEXEME, LOAN, LONG WORD, MCWORD, MORPHEME, MORPHOLOGY, NEOLOGISM, NONCE WORD, NONSENSE, ONOMATOPOEIA, PHON(A)ESTHESIA, PLURAL, PORTMANTEAU WORD, PREFIX, PRIVATIVE, ROOT, SHAKESPEARE, -SPEAK, STEM, STUNT WORD, SUFFIX, TELESCOPING, THEMATIC VOWEL, TMESIS, VAGUE WORD, VOCABULARY. [GRAMMAR, WORD]. T.MCA.

Adams, Valerie. 1973. *An Introduction to Modern English Word-Formation.* London & New York: Longman.

Bauer, Laurie. 1983. *English Word-Formation.* Cambridge: University Press.

Lipka, Leonhard. 1990. *An Outline of English Lexicology: Lexical Structure, Word Semantics, and Word-Formation.* Tübingen: Niemeyer.

Marchand, Hans. 1960/9. *The Categories and Types of Present-Day English Word-Formation.* Munich: Verlag C. H. Beck.

Matthews, Peter. 1974. *Morphology: An Introduction to the Theory of Word-Structure.* Cambridge: University Press.

Quirk, Randolph, Greenbaum, Sidney, Leech, Geoffrey, & Svartvik, Jan. 1985. *A Comprehensive Grammar of the English Language.* Appendix I: Word-formation. London & New York: Longman.

WORD FREQUENCY (COUNT). See FREQUENCY COUNT, VOCABULARY CONTROL.

WORD GAME.
Games can be played with the senses, sounds, construction, or order of words. Playing with the sense of words creates *puns* and such team games as the BBC's *Call My Bluff*. Playing with the sounds of words creates *tongue-twisters*, *spoonerisms*, and poetic games like *bout-rimés* and *echo verse*. Playing with the construction of words creates *anagrams*, *charades*, *lipograms*, *palindromes*, and *pangrams*. Playing with the order or positioning of words or their letters creates *concrete poetry* and *hidden words*, and cumulative games like *consequences*, in which a story develops, and *I Packed My Bag*, in which more and more things go into the bag and have to be remembered by each player in turn. Words can also be placed in patterns or grids, as in *acrostics*, *crosswords*, *Scrabble*, and *word squares*. There are also numerous guessing games involving words, such as the *conundrum*, the *rebus*, and the *riddle*. Currently, the popularity of word games is shown by the large numbers of publications and television shows involving words. Many newspapers contain at least one crossword, sometimes elevated to the status of a national institution, such as *The Times* crossword in Britain.

Literary devices such as *alliteration*, *assonance*, and *rhyme* can be regarded as forms of word-play, and many writers have been noted for playing with words. The riddles of Old English were games as well as literary exercises; poets like John Skelton and William Dunbar in the 15/16c intermingled English with Latin to make *macaronic verses*; and Sir Thomas Wyatt (16c) and Jonathan Swift and William Cowper (18c) wrote enigmatic poems. William Shakespeare, Jonathan Swift, Thomas Hood, and Lewis Carroll were all addicted to the pun. The 17c metaphysical poets John Donne and George Herbert revelled in the playful use of language; Herbert wrote shaped poetry and echo verses, and some of his other poems were based on anagrams and rebuses. Lewis Carroll was an incorrigible word-player, inventing several word games (including *doublets*) and writing riddles, acrostics, rebuses, charades, and, in the shape of 'The Mouse's Tale' (or tail) in *Alice in Wonderland*, an early specimen of *concrete poetry*. Twentieth-century writers noted for their playful ways with words include James Thurber, e. e. cummings, Ezra Pound, Ogden Nash, Flann O'Brien, and James Joyce. Joyce's *Ulysses* is full of word-play, and *Finnegans Wake* is an extended language game.

See ACROSTIC, ALLITERATION, ANAGRAM, ASSONANCE, BEHEADMENT AND CURTAILMENT, BOUT-RIMÉS, CALL MY BLUFF, CARROLL, CHARADE, CONCRETE POETRY, CONUNDRUM, CROSSWORD PUZZLE, DOUBLET, ETYMORPHS, HUMO(U)R, JOKE, JOYCE, LIPOGRAM, LONG WORD, MACARONIC, MALAPROPISM, NONSENSE, NONSENSE VERSE, ONOMATOPOEIA, PALINDROME, PANGRAM, PLAYING WITH WORDS, PUN, READER'S DIGEST, REBUS, REVERSAL, RIDDLE, SCRABBLE, SPOONERISM, TONGUE-TWISTER, VERSE, WIT, WITTICISM, WORD-FORMATION, WORD SQUARE. [WORD]. T.A.

Augarde, Tony. 1984. *The Oxford Guide to Word Games*. Oxford: University Press.

Borgmann, Dmitri, 1965. *Language on Vacation*. New York: Charles Scribner's Sons.

Brandreth, Giles. 1988. *The Word Book*. Part 2: Word Play. London: Robson.

D'Israeli, Isaac. 1824. *Curiosities of Literature*. London: Murray.

WORD LIST, WORD-LIST. See FREQUENCY COUNT, VOCABULARY CONTROL.

WORD-LORE, also **wordlore** [1860s]. A Saxonism for philology or knowledge of words. See PHILOLOGY, SAXONISM. [WORD].   T.MCA.

WORD-MONGER [16c]. An informal pejorative term for someone who uses words pretentiously, plays with them too much, or invents new words without sufficient cause. See VERBALISM. [STYLE, WORD].   T.MCA.

WORD ORDER. [Late 19c]. A term for the order in which words appear in phrases and sentences. In such highly inflected languages as Latin and Sanskrit, word order is relatively free, since the relations between words can be signalled by inflections, but it is relatively fixed in English: for example, an adjective generally precedes the noun it modifies (*tall woman*) and a preposition precedes its complement (*on my table*). The normal order of sentence elements in English is Subject–Verb–Object: *Tony wants an egg*. See INVERSION, SENTENCE, SHAKESPEARE. [GRAMMAR, WORD].   S.G.

WORD ORIGINS. An informal, non-technical phrase associated with general works on English etymology, such as Eric Partridge's *Origins: An Etymological Dictionary of English* (1958), Owen Barfield's *History in English Words* (1962), and John Ayto's *The Bloomsbury Dictionary of Word Origins* (1990). Whereas scholarly dictionaries of etymology describe the histories of many thousands of words in dense entries with often formidable arrays of abbreviations and parentheses, books and articles on word origins tend to discuss a more limited range of words whose unusual 'stories' are often described in an expansive and relaxed style, as in:

FAKE Until a hundred years ago this was one of the words frowned upon by the schoolmasters. It was slang. Not only that, but it was the slang used by thieves and gypsies, not by reputable speakers and writers. The true history is therefore unknown, but some suppose it to have been picked up long before by English soldiers during the Thirty Years War (1618–48) when they were in contact with German allies (Charles E. Funk, *Thereby Hangs a Tale: Stories of Curious Word Origins*, Harper & Row, 1950).

CAUCUS Where the word "caucus" comes from is a mystery. There is a Greek word, "kaukos," but this is a drinking cup. Our word "caucus" means a meeting where political candidates are chosen, usually in private. Some say it could have come from the Algonquin Indians of North America. They had what they called "cau-cau-su"—old, wise men who advised the tribes. "Cau-cau-su" was probably picked up by the early European settlers and changed to "caucus", which was often used by the settlers; the earliest recorded use of it came in 1763. It appeared in the private papers of John Adams, before he became the second President of the United States (Herbert Sutcliffe & Harold Berman, *Words and Their Stories*, Voice of America, 1978).

FLU. Even if they are not comforted, sufferers from flu may be interested in some stray facts about its etymology. The OED says that as well as the various senses of the word 'influence', the Italian *influenza* also has the sense—from the notion of 'astral' or 'occult influence'—of 'visitation' on many people at the same time and place of any disease (e.g. *influenza di catarro* or *influenza di febbre scarlatina*). In 1743 the word was 'applied specifically to "the epidemic" (called also *la grippe*) which then raged in Italy . . . for which the Italian word (anglicized in pronunciation) became the English specific name'. The first abbreviation was 'flue' (John Silverlight, *Words*, Macmillan, 1985, a collection of articles that first appeared in the *Observer* newspaper).

Similar light, often humorous comment can be found in works on words whose emphases are not historical, such as Philip Howard's *Weasel Words* (Hamish Hamilton, 1978), Paul Dickson's *A Connoisseur's Collection of Old and New, Weird and Wonderful, Useful and Outlandish Words* (Arena, 1983), and Gyles Brandreth's *The Word Book: or everything you ever wanted to know about the English language but had neither the verbal dexterity nor linguistic flexiloquence to ask!* (Robson Books, 1988). See ETYMOLOGY. [HISTORY, REFERENCE, STYLE].   T.MCA.

WORD PLAY. See PLAYING WITH WORDS.

WORD PROCESSOR, also **word-processor** [1970s]. In computing, a term for both the software and hardware that organizes text for display on a screen and/or for printing in various forms, and stores it for later use. Software for small computers includes the programs *Wordperfect, Microsoft Word, MacWrite, Nota Bene*; for large computers, *Troff, Tex, Scribe*. The services include: an *editor* to help enter and rearrange text; a *hyphenator and justifier* to help arrange words into paragraphs and produce the equivalent of a traditional galley proof; a *layout processor* to arrange paragraphs on pages, perhaps including automatic handling of footnotes, figures, and typographic details; *specialized processors* to handle mathematical equations, tables, bibliographies, diagrams, or other features; and *auxiliary processors*, for spelling checking, grammar checking, style checking, indexing, marking changes from version to version, searching text, and other activities. Most word processors require the user to type some kind of code to indicate typographic features such as paragraphing or changes of font. The user edits the document by means of the codes, and the program interprets the codes so that the printer can provide (more or less) the format, characters, and style required. Some programs display the document in one form on screen and another form in actual print. Others display it in the precise form in which it will appear on paper, a process known as *wysiwyg* (what you see is what you get). Such programs are essential to desktop publishing and require an extended form of the QWERTY keyboard, in which *function keys* augment the regular keys. Individually or in combination, such keys allow the user to shift text within a document or file, or from one document or file to another, to consult a *help* menu (for advice) when in doubt about something, and to print out the end-product. See COMPUTING, DESKTOP PUBLISHING, DIACRITIC, ELECTRONIC PUBLISHING, KEYBOARD, MENU, TYPEWRITER. [TECHNOLOGY, WRITING].

M.L.

WORD SALAD [1910s]. An informal term for incoherent speech and sometimes writing made up of real and concocted words, lacking overall sense, and often occurring in schizophrenia. Compare DOUBLE TALK. [WORD]. T.MCA.

WORDSMITH [1890s]. An informal, non-technical term for someone who is good with words, such as a competent and entertaining journalist or novelist. [WORD, WRITING]. T.MCA.

WORD SQUARE [1870s]. A square made from words of the same length. Word squares usually have the same words horizontally and vertically:

```
S A D        C U B E
A L E        U G L Y
D E N        B L U E
             E Y E S
```

but *double word squares* use different words in each direction:

```
A S          O R A L
T O          M A R E
             E V E N
             N E A T
```

Word squares using words of up to six letters are common; squares made of longer words are much harder to compose. Such squares were the precursors of crossword puzzles. See WORD GAME. [WORD]. T.A.

WORD STRESS. See STRESS, SUFFIX.

WORDS WITHIN WORDS, also **Words, Word-Builder, Word-Hunt, In-Words, Keyword, Multiwords, Target**. A game that involves making as many words as possible from the constituent letters of a word. For example, *Chambers's Journal* (20 Apr. 1872) listed 61 words of four or more letters that can be found within the single word *Cambridge*: bridge, image, ream, ridge, badger, crag, bride, acre, admire, game, dear, brig, crib, care, braid, ride, card, dream, dame, mare, gird, raid, bard, bream, abide, bare, garb, mire, drab, amber, bier, bear, bird, grab, grace, gear, dare, rice, race, mead, crab, brace, bead, cram, grade, read, brim, cigar, dire, dram, cadi, rage, grim, cider, maid, cream, badge, crime, cage, drag, mirage. A variation, usually called *Hidden Words*, looks for words concealed in sentences: for example, *Do come soon* (doc, docs, does, dose, dome, doom, noose, nose, etc.). In a further variant, known as *Hidden Words* and *Buried Words*, a single word is concealed in a sentence: thus, in *Zealots are not always brave*, the word *zebra* is hidden. In this version, players are invited to look for the name of an animal. See WORD GAME. [WORD]. T.MCA.

WORD WORD [1982: coined by the US writer Paul Dickson]. A non-technical, tongue-in-cheek term for a word repeated in contrastive statements and questions: 'Are you talking about an American Indian or an *Indian Indian*?'; 'It happens in Irish English as well as *English English*.' [WORD]. T.MCA.

WORDSWORTH, William [1770–1850]. English poet. Born in Cockermouth, Cumberland. Educated at Hawkshead Grammar School and St John's College, Cambridge. He went to France (1791-2) and admired the Revolution until disillusioned by the subsequent Terror. A small legacy in 1795 gave him leisure to continue writing poetry. He became friendly with Coleridge, with whom he published the influential *Lyrical Ballads* (1798). In the same year, they visited Germany and then settled near each other in the Lake District (hence the sobriquet *Lake Poets* by which they and Robert Southey came to be known). When Wordsworth married in 1802, his sister and constant companion Dorothy lived with the family. *Poems in Two Volumes* (1807), which included the 'Ode to Duty', 'Miscellaneous Sonnets', and 'Ode: Intimations of Immortality from Recollections of Early Childhood', increased his reputation. His long, unfinished philosophical poem *The Excursion* was printed in 1814. His personal and literary development was the subject of *The Prelude*, written between 1799 and 1805 but extensively revised, and published posthumously in 1850. Wordsworth received a government sinecure in 1813 and was made Poet Laureate on Southey's death in 1843.

In his long life, Wordsworth wrote a great deal of poetry; however, it is generally agreed that his later work shows a decline. He was a pioneer of English Romanticism. His love of the natural world, discovered (as he relates in *The Prelude*) during a lonely boyhood, grew into a sense of the mystic bond between humanity and nature. He loved to hear and tell stories of simple people and sought a style suitable to their condition. He regarded the *poetic diction* of his predecessors as mannered and artificial, challenging it in the 'Advertisement' to *Lyrical Ballads* and giving his views more fully in the Preface to the 1800 edition (with further expansion in 1802):

The language too of these men has been adopted (purified indeed from what appear to be its real defects, from all lasting and rational causes of dislike or disgust) because such men hourly communicate with the best objects from which the best part of language is originally derived . . . Accordingly such a language, arising out of repeated experience and regular feelings, is a more permanent, and far more philosophical language, than that which is frequently substituted for it by Poets, who think that they are conferring honour upon themselves and their art, in proportion as they separate themselves from the sympathies of men (Preface, *Lyrical Ballads*, 1800).

Wordsworth claimed that there should be no essential difference between the languages of poetry and prose, and accused the 18c neoclassicists of creating a false poetic style with excessive personifications and abstractions, instead of 'a selection of the language really used by men'. He did not always follow his own principles, however, and sometimes the attempted simplicity was bathetic, distorted by constraints of metre and rhyme as in the lines from 'Simon Lee' (1798):

> Few months of life has he in store
> As he to you will tell,
> For still the more he works, the more
> Do his weak ankles swell.

Yet he was more often grandly eloquent without resorting to stilted diction, as in 'Ode: Intimations of Immortality from Recollections of Early Childhood' (1807):

> Moving about in worlds not realized,
> High instincts before which our mortal Nature
> Did tremble like a guilty thing surprised.

Despite his reputation, Wordsworth had little direct influence on the language of later 19c poetry. It was not until the new departures of Modernism that 'the language really used by men' became the poetic norm. [BIOGRAPHY, EUROPE, LITERATURE].   R.C.

WORK OF REFERENCE. See REFERENCE.

WORLD BOOK DICTIONARY, short form *WBD*. A two-volume American dictionary edited by Clarence L. Barnhart and his son Robert K. Barnhart, available primarily with the *World Book Encyclopedia*. It contains *c.*225,000 entries, and is based on the Thorndike–Barnhart school dictionaries (1935, 1941), William Dwight Whitney's *Century Dictionary* (1889–91), *The New Century Dictionary* (1927), and the Barnhart citation file. A number of its features, such as the use in the pronunciations of schwa [ə] for unstressed vowels, were pioneered in the US by Clarence Barnhart. See BARNHART, CENTURY DICTIONARY, DICTIONARY, THORNDIKE, WHITNEY. [AMERICAS, REFERENCE].   J.A.

WORLD ENGLISH [1960s: with or without a capital *w*]. An increasingly common term for English as a world language: 'World English' (title, article by Tom McArthur, *Opinion*, Bombay, 28 Feb. 1967); 'We may definitely recognize Australian English and New Zealand English as [forms] making their own special contribution to world English' (Robert D. Eagleson, in Bailey & Görlach (eds.), *English as a World Language*, 1982); 'The traditional spelling system generally ignores both the changes in pronunciation over time and the variations in pronunciation through space; despite its notorious vagaries, it is a unifying force in world English' (Quirk *et al.*, *A Comprehensive Grammar of the English Language*, 1985). Some scholars use the term cautiously or avoid it, because for them it suggests global dominance by English and English-speaking countries, with an attendant downgrading of other languages. See ENGLISH, IMAGE, INTERNATIONAL ENGLISH, WORLD ENGLISHES, WORLD LANGUAGE. [GEOGRAPHY, VARIETY].   T.MCA.

WORLD ENGLISHES, full title *World Englishes: Journal of English as an International and Intranational Language*. Short form *WE*. A journal published by Pergamon Press, Oxford, a renaming and restructuring in 1985 of *World Language English*, an international journal about the teaching and learning of English as a foreign or second language that was founded in 1981 and edited till 1984 in the UK by William R. Lee. The new publication is edited in the US by Braj B. Kachru at the U. of Illinois and Larry E. Smith at the East–West Center, Honolulu, Hawaii, and documents and discusses varieties of English, native and non-native, such as *American English*, *British English*, *Indian English*, and *Japanese English*. The editorial stance of *WE* is that the language belongs to all who use it. It provides an international outlook on language, literature, and the methodology of English teaching, publishing articles, notes, book reviews, and notices with an emphasis on theory, research, and English in multilingual settings. See ENGLISHES, WORLD ENGLISH. [MEDIA, VARIETY]. L.E.S.

WORLD LANGUAGE [*c.*1860s, as *world-language*]. A language used throughout the entire world, such as late 20c English (as described for example in Richard W. Bailey & Manfred Görlach (eds.), *English as a World Language*, 1982). The term also refers to a language used in many parts of the world (such as Spanish and Portuguese), in specific large regions (such as the Latin of the Roman Empire, Arabic, Hindi, and Russian), and widely because of a special role (such as French for diplomatic purposes, especially in the 18–19c, and Sanskrit as the language of Hindu learning). Many such languages have risen and declined over the centuries, having achieved their status through empire-building, the spread of a religion, cultural significance, shifting populations, or a mixture of such factors. See CLASSICAL LANGUAGE, DIASPORA, IMPERIALISM, INTERNATIONAL LANGUAGE, KOINE, LINGUA FRANCA, WORLD ENGLISH, WORLD LITERATURE. [GEOGRAPHY, HISTORY, LANGUAGE]. T.MCA.

WORLD LANGUAGE ENGLISH. See WORLD ENGLISHES.

WORLD LITERATURE [1830s: compare German *Weltliteratur*]. A term used especially by literary critics for all literature worldwide: 'Instead of isolated, mutually repulsive National Literatures, a World Literature may one day be looked for?' (Thomas Carlyle, *Edinburgh Review*, 1831). It is used especially for that portion of the world's literary texts taken to have universal relevance and merit, as outlined in Tore Zetterholm & Peter Quennell's *An Illustrated Companion to World Literature: The Lives and Works of over 500 Great Novelists, Playwrights, Poets, Philosophers and Essayists* (London: Orbis, 1986: from an earlier version by Zetterholm alone, published in Swedish in 1981). This work classifies world literature in terms of historical and regional groups such as *Greek Antiquity* and *French classicism*. See ENGLISH LITERATURE, WORLD LANGUAGE, WORLD LITERATURE WRITTEN IN ENGLISH. [LITERATURE]. T.MCA.

WORLD LITERATURE WRITTEN IN ENGLISH, short form *WLWE*. The oldest of the journals devoted to critical discussion of post-colonial literatures in English. It began in 1962 as the newsletter of the *Conference on British Commonwealth Literature* (*CBCL*), a division of the Modern Language Association of America, and in due course it became a fully-fledged literary journal, taking its current name from MLA Group 12 in 1968. Its principal concern has been the spread of English and its literature beyond the British Isles (16–20c). It asserts the importance and uniqueness of the various literatures in English and seeks to discern relationships among them. Its editors have been: Joseph Jones, U. of Texas at Austin (1962–8), Robert MacDowell, U. of Texas at Arlington (1968–78), G. Douglas Killam, U. of Guelph, Ontario (1978–89), and Diana Brydon, U. of Guelph (1989–). See COMMONWEALTH LITERATURE, ENGLISH LITERATURE, WORLD LITERATURE. [LITERATURE, MEDIA]. G.D.K.

WRENN, C(harles) L(eslie) [1895–1969]. English philologist, born at Westcliff-on-Sea, Essex, and educated privately and at Oxford. After lecturing in English at the U. of Durham (1917–20), he went to India and became Professor of English at Madras (1920–1) and Dacca (1921–8). He was a lecturer in English at Leeds (1928–30) and in Anglo-Saxon at Oxford (1930–9), then Professor of English at King's College, London (1939–46) and Professor of Anglo-Saxon at Oxford (1946–63). His publications include: *The English Language* (1949), an edition of *Beowulf* (1953), *An Old English Grammar* (with Randolph Quirk, 1955), and *A Study of Old English Literature* (1967). Wrenn helped found the International Association of University Professors of English by convening the constituent conference in Oxford (1950) and was its chairman (1950–3). See index. [BIOGRAPHY, EDUCATION, EUROPE, LANGUAGE]. P.C.

WRIGHT, Joseph [1855–1930]. English philologist and dialectologist, born in the village of Thackley, in the township of Idle, Yorkshire; he liked to say 'I have been an idle man all my life, and shall remain an idle man till I die' (Elizabeth Mary Wright, *The Life of Joseph Wright*, Oxford University Press, 1932). His father worked for a time in the ironstone mines. His mother was widowed early and kept her children by taking in washing. Wright was unable to read and write until he was 15, and already supported his mother and brothers by working as a wool sorter at Salt's Mill in Saltaire, Yorkshire. In 1870, he started attending night schools, learned German and French, and, when the mill closed for a time in 1876, decided to further his education. He went to Heidelberg in Germany and had enough money to support him for eleven weeks. In 1877, he attended evening classes in Leeds and matriculated in 1878. In 1882, he passed the intermediate examination for the BA at the U. of London, but never took the full degree there. He went to Germany in 1882 where he stayed for six years, mainly in Heidelberg and Leipzig. He studied under Hermann Osthoff, Professor of Comparative Philology, and gained his doctorate in Heidelberg in 1885. His first work was a translation of K. Brugmann's *Comparative Grammar of the Indogermanic Languages* (1887). Wright became Assistant Professor of Comparative Philology at Oxford (1891). His *Windmill Dialect Grammar* (1893) broke new ground in language studies in being written by a native speaker of a living dialect and in treating dialect as a subject of serious research. He was secretary of the short-lived *English Dialect Society* from 1893 until it was wound up in 1896, by which time he was well on the way to publishing his great *English Dialect Dictionary* (1898-1905), which included, as Volume 6, his *English Dialect Grammar*. The *EDD* included 'so far as it is possible the complete vocabulary of all English dialect words which are still in use or are known to have been in use at any time during the last two hundred years in England, Ireland, Scotland, and Wales' (preface). The six volumes continue to be of immense value to scholars of local varieties of English. Nothing of comparable breadth or depth of dialect scholarship has been published in Britain since. See index. [BIOGRAPHY, EUROPE, LANGUAGE, VARIETY].   S.E., L.T.

WRITER [From Old English *wrītere*]. Someone who can write or engages in writing, especially for professional and/or artistic purposes: 'Writers are people who sit alone in rooms' (Salman Rushdie, *Newsweek*, 19 Nov. 1990). The term is often synonymous with *author* (especially of works of fiction: *a thriller writer*), and is sometimes employed in formal texts so as to avoid using the first person: *In the present writer's view, this matter has become a cause for concern*, rather than *I think (that) this matter has become a cause for concern.*

Writers and patrons. The craft of writing has long been basic to many occupations (such as scribe, priest, clerk, public letter-writer, bureaucrat, surveyor, merchant, lawyer, physician, teacher, scholar, mathematician, and scientist), but writing as a creative activity (of, for example, 'the man of letters', 'the lady novelist', or 'the literary hack') has been a regular paid form of employment only in recent centuries. Since at least the Middle Ages, creative writers have generally had other or additional means of livelihood; Chaucer was an official of the Crown, Shakespeare a partner in a theatre company, and Milton a Latin secretary in government service. Other means by which society has maintained creative writers have included sinecures (granted in consideration of literary merit) and various

scholarships, subsidies, and prizes (with sums of money attached). Until the 19c, those who needed financial support would send dedications and complimentary copies of their work to prominent people, in the hope of attracting gifts of money. In Britain, the system of direct and indirect patronage only slowly came to an end as the profession of letters developed in the 18c, with the spread of literacy, the growth of the novel and the periodical, and in the 19c a consequent capacity of publishers to support full-time paid writers. In 1755, Samuel Johnson completed his dictionary without the promised financial support of Lord Chesterfield. His letter to the Earl in the same year, after Chesterfield had sought to revive his claim to be Johnson's patron, includes a sardonic definition of patrons:

Is not a Patron, my Lord, one who looks with unconcern on a man struggling for life in the water, and, when he has reached ground, encumbers him with help? The notice which you are pleased to take of my labours, had it been early, had been kind; but it has been delayed till I am indifferent, and cannot enjoy it; till I am solitary, and cannot impart it; till I am known, and do not want it.

Writers, publishers, critics, and agents. In the early 19c, Walter Scott made a good living and paid substantial debts by writing novels. Direct payment for a manuscript sold to a printer, often meagre and useful only as a supplement to other income, was slowly replaced by the *royalty*, a percentage of the profits on sales agreed by contract before the publication or even the writing of the book in question. Many 19c novelists lived well from their writing and were respected as professionals in need of no other career. Financial rewards have been increased in the 20c by the sale of *rights* (translation rights, distribution rights in certain areas, paperback rights, and film and television rights), while a writer may be paid an *advance* on royalties to encourage the writing of a particular book or to keep other publishers at bay.

The production and distribution of books developed from the copying of single manuscripts to the mass production made possible by the printing press in the 15c and its further developments in the 19-20c. Private and public libraries increased the demand for books, a virtually guaranteed sale for popular authors that offset the many non-contributing readers of one library copy. The 20c increase in outlets (individual bookshops and chains of stores) has favoured writers, as has the growth of periodicals from the early 19c, providing openings for short stories, serialized novels, and poetry. The success of such publishing encouraged two subsidiary professions: the *literary critic*, commenting on and analysing the works of others, often while holding a post in a university department of English or another language, and the *literary agent*, a professional finder of publishers who receives a percentage of receipts in return for being a successful go-between.

Writers and the media. Currently, new works by well-established writers can be auctioned to publishers by agents. Even being short-listed for a significant literary prize, such as the *Booker Prize* in the UK, can greatly affect sales of hardbacks and paperbacks. Relatively few people, however, live solely by creative writing and even fewer make their fortunes from it. The principal financial rewards, apart from a rare 'best-seller' or 'blockbuster', are in films, television, lecturing, adjudicating, and winning a significant prize. Poets, novelists, and literary critics are, however, only a small minority of those for whom writing is a major part of their everyday work. Professional writers in this wider sense include journalists, scriptwriters for radio, television, and the motion-picture industry, advertising copywriters, and publicists, and writing is a key element in teaching, preaching, publishing, government, science, medicine, and commerce. See Victor Bonham-Carter, *Authors by Profession* (vol. 1, 1978, *From the Introduction of Printing until the Copyright Act 1911*; vol. 2, 1984, *From the Copyright Act 1911 until the End of 1981*, London, Society of Authors).

Compare AUTHOR, HACK, LETTERS, POET, SCRIBBLER, SCRIBE. See AMERICAN PUBLISHING, BRITISH PUBLISHING, CREATIVE WRITING, EDITING, EFFECTIVE WRITING, LITERACY. [LITERATURE, MEDIA, WRITING]. T.MCA., R.C.

WRITING [From Old English *wrītan* to write, engrave, draw: compare Old Frisian *wrīta* and Old Norse *rita* to write, score; Saxon *wrītan* to write, cut; Old High German *rīzan* to tear, draw; German *reissen*, to tear, pull, sketch]. The term *writing* encompasses four pairs of linked senses. It may refer to: (1) An activity (*reading and writing*) or the product of that activity (*What illegible writing!*). (2) A concrete process (a *writing exercise*) or the concept behind that process (*Writing was invented over 5,000 years ago*). (3) Handwriting alone (*specimens of their writing*) or both handwriting and print (*Writing systems were extended by the invention of movable type*). (4) A general skill regarded as a social necessity (*Writing is part of everybody's education*) or a minority art form, occupation, hobby, and/or obsession (*This novel is the best example of her writing to date*).

Although written signs need not be permanent (as in writing on a blackboard or sky-writing from an aircraft), they are generally taken to be more or less durable. In the Germanic languages, as the etymology above indicates, the concept of writing related to cutting signs on wood or inscribing them on stone (see RUNE), but in principle the making of graphic signs is not restricted in either materials or methods: they may be cut with knife, chisel, drill, and other tools on stone, wood, plastic, and similar surfaces, or applied by pen, brush, type, and other instruments to surfaces such as paper, parchment, or cloth. The electromagnetic charges of the computer are also understood to be writing, whether temporary on screens or more permanently on disks and other devices for information storage and retrieval.

A medium of language. Each medium that carries language (such as speech, writing, or signing among the deaf) has its special features. All language is linear, but each medium has its distinctive units and marshals them differently: for example, an alphabetic letter, a dash, or the indenting of a paragraph has no equivalent in speech. Forms of writing and print have cultural resonances distinct from those of speech and song, as for example the contrast between capital and small letters, or between the use of roman or italic script. Although each medium of language can 'say' things about another, there is no way in which one medium can *be* another. In addition, many scholars consider that social systems such as religions and governments for which writing is a normal activity are quite different from those that depend on the more fluid and ephemeral processes of speech and memory: issues of morality become more abstract, reasoning more rigorous, and language more open to objective and logical analysis. With the help of writing, draft plans can be formulated and administrative routines can develop, and in the process the speech of such communities is also changed, becoming imbued with the styles and patterns of written language.

Speech versus writing. Since classical times, there have been two contradictory approaches to speech and writing: (1) The view that writing is the primary and speech the secondary medium, because writing is more culturally significant and lastingly valuable than speech. The term *grammar*, for example, derives from the Greek verb *gráphein* to write. The systematization of classical Greek grammar by such theorists and teachers as Dionysius Thrax, *c*.100 BC, was the first attempt at language description in the Western world, and unlike the early studies of language in India, which were sound-based, it rested entirely on writing: see GRAMMAR. This tradition was extended to the study and teaching of many languages throughout the world with little change until the early 20c. (2) The view that speech is primary and writing secondary, because speech is prior to writing both historically and in terms of a child's acquisition of language. In the 4c BC, Aristotle said: 'Spoken sounds are symbols of affections of the soul, and written marks are symbols of spoken sounds' (*On Interpretation*, 16a 3-4). Comparably, but long afterwards, the Swiss philologist Ferdinand de Saussure observed: 'Speech and writing are two separate systems of signs; the sole purpose of the second is to represent the first' (1916: translated from *Cours de linguistique générale*, ed. Tullio de Mauro, Payot, Paris, 1978, Introduction, ch. 6). When Saussure made this comment, he was reacting against centuries of scholarship and education in which the text had been regarded as fundamental.

Writing systems. A major feature of writing is that it can operate over distance and time. Memorized and stylized speech that passes from person to person has some of this capacity, but has no existence apart from the performance of one speaker at one time. There is also no guarantee that an oral message will be the same after several stages of transmission, whereas a written document can be read at different times by different people and remain stable, unless overwritten. Although people may interpret such a document differently, they agree that it is an invariant object, and may accept it as incontrovertible evidence in a court of law. The signs on a well-kept 4,000-year-old clay tablet are virtually as legible and perhaps as intelligible today as at the time of writing, save that some shades of meaning and implications of context are likely to have been lost. There was nothing comparably durable for spoken language until the invention of the phonograph in the late 19c, but even so audio-recording remains distinct from text in its effect, its usefulness, and its technologies.

The first known system of writing was not a re-expression of spoken language. It was pictorial in origin, creating two-dimensional analogues of three-dimensional things in the world; only much later did writing systems acquire the capacity to 'reflect' or run parallel to the words and sounds of speech. The first writing was invented in West Asia 5,000-6,000 years ago, in Sumer in southern Mesopotamia. Since that time, writing systems have used a variety of symbolic forms, sometimes as relatively 'pure' systems of one kind of sign, but more commonly in combinations of the following two broad categories of signs:

Picture-based signs. The longer-established variety of sign is representational and analogous, as with early Sumerian. Scholars generally identify three types that are not always easy to set off one from another: (1) *Pictograms*, that directly represent things in the world, such as animals, people, houses, and geographical features, often in stylized and simplified outline forms such as a wavy line for water. (2) *Ideograms* (in effect 'idea grams'), that represent concepts, such as the numerals *I, II, III* or *1, 2, 3*, usually arising from the further stylizing and simplifying of pictograms. (3) *Logograms*, that represent words proper, such as the icons used in international airports: a drawing of a telephone directly standing for *telephone*, a man and a woman side by side indirectly standing for *toilets* (or their equivalents in different languages). The early writing systems of Sumer and Egypt and the writing of China belong almost wholly in the picture-based group, which deals directly in meanings and not in sounds.

Sound-based signs. The somewhat younger variety of sign is *phonographic*, relating sound to symbol. Two types can usually be kept distinct (but see ALPHABET): (1) *Syllabograms*, representing individual syllables, as in the *kana* systems of Japanese (see JAPAN). (2) *Phonograms*, or as they are more commonly known, *letters*, signs that represent individual sounds. Such signs have over the centuries often become detached from the specific language in which they were first used, as demonstrated by the many variants of the Roman alphabet (for English, French, German, Polish, etc.), and may therefore represent different sounds in different systems, as for example the letter *c* as used in English and Italian. Phonographic writing systems deal in sounds, not meanings.

Writing technologies. The development of technologies of writing is contingent on time, place, and environment. The Sumerian system, for example, developed in marshy terrain, where its inventors used a cut reed to impose wedge-like (*cuneiform*) marks on a soft clay tablet (the reed held in one hand, the tablet in the other). The inscribed clay was then left to dry in the hot sun, or for greater permanence was baked in an oven. Their system was an integrated technology of stylus, clay, and cuneiform that was at first pictographic and became in due course ideographic and syllabographic. The Egyptians, also a riverine people, did not develop clay but concentrated on plants, using a reed brush to paint their signs on papyrus stems that were pressed together to form sheets held in place by their own gum. Theirs was a technology of brush, papyrus, and hieroglyph that later developed phonographic elements. Both Sumerian and Egyptian writing methods were also applied successfully to large vertical surfaces, such as walls and pillars. In medieval Europe, scribes used trimmed feathers from the wings of large birds and various inks to mark a set of alphabetic letters on parchment skins. Theirs was a technology that combined pen, parchment, and alphabet. At the end of the 20c, as a sum of all the operations of the past throughout the world, a vast array of calligraphic and typographic options is available, for example word-processing, for the preparation of texts of many kinds on surfaces of many kinds.

Writing implements. The *pen* (a 13c term from Latin *penna* feather) is the oldest writing implement in general use. It has its origins in both the Sumerian reed and the medieval feather. Vast flocks of geese were once kept in Europe to provide quill pens that were sold in bunches. The writing ends of the goose quill feathers were cut and split with a *pen knife*, after which they could be dipped in *ink-wells* or *ink-horns* and put to use, the ink flowing down the split while one wrote until it was used up. Pens with metal nibs are an industrial-age adaptation of both the cut reed and quill. Letters made by reed or quill have thick and thin strokes, a feature that influenced the shapes given to letters in printing. The *fountain pen*, equipped with a reusable cartridge for holding a large supply of ink to be steadily fed to the nib, was a late 19c advance on the basic metal-nibbed pen. After the Second World War, however, all such pens were generally replaced by the cheap, easily disposable *ballpoint* (*pen*) or *biro* (named after László Biró, its Hungarian inventor). The present-day *pencil* (a 14c term from Latin *penicillum* a painter's brush, ultimately from *penis* a tail) is more recent than the pen. It consists of a stick of graphite (often erroneously called 'lead', as in *lead pencil*), protected by a machined sheath of wood. It developed as a variation of the markers that medieval scribes used to draw lines in manuscripts. The late 20c *felt-tip pen* (BrE) or *marker* (AmE) is a variation on the ancient reed brush, its ink supply stored in its stem like a biro.

Pen and print. Generally, documents written in ink have had both a higher social cachet and greater physical permanence than documents written in pencil, while texts in print have had still higher prestige and greater permanence (depending on the quality of paper used). Because documents written in pencil and pen are no longer widely circulated, there is less pressure on students to cultivate clear handwriting. Writing by hand continues to be basic to education while at the same time its value has declined in occupational terms. It is useful in note-taking, note-writing, and personal letters, but there are fewer and fewer clerical careers that require no more than the making of handwritten entries in books and ledgers. Handwriting and handwritten documents have become as a result increasingly demotic and spelling and grammar in personal letters appear to be increasingly seen as personal matters.

Type and word-processing. In 20c public life, writing by hand has long been displaced by typing. In recent years, the word-processing *personal computer* (the *PC*: whether desktop, laptop, or palmtop) has adopted and adapted many features from the typewriter, particularly the format of the keyboard, while advanced or 'smart' typewriters have come more and more to resemble PCs. With its battery of word-processing software, spelling and style checkers, dictionaries, thesauruses, and other built-in aids, the PC is, however, as different from the typewriter as the typewriter from the traditional printing press, and the press from the pen. Transmission systems known as *modems* (short for 'modulator demodulators') can send and receive texts electronically over distance, and scanners capable of *optical character recognition* (*OCR*) can read printed documents and transcribe them directly on to disk with ever greater accuracy. In addition, large computers routinely direct typesetting machinery in the production of books and periodicals. As a consequence, computers used for language work are changing many aspects of, and attitudes towards, traditional written and printed language: see COMPUTING, KEYBOARD.

Learning to write. All writing systems demand long periods of apprenticeship in which the student memorizes and learns to use the inventory of signs and the tools associated with them. Over the last two centuries, more and more societies have grown to expect more and more of their members to be able to write. Universal literacy became an aim in most industrialized nation-states over a century ago, but the concept of an adequately literate society remains unclear, and changes over time: see LITERACY. There is also ongoing controversy over the teaching and acquisition of styles and skills in handwriting, and in learning how to spell and read adequately in languages with complex orthographies, such as English and French: see READING, SPELLING, SPELLING REFORM.

Handwriting. Basically, methods of teaching children to write have not changed greatly over the centuries. The principal procedure remains an introduction to the elements of the writing system. Models are then provided for copying and developing in various ways: usually the teacher's own handwriting and specimens in copybooks. For English, as with other languages originating in Europe, a cardinal feature in learning to write is learning to join letters as opposed to leaving them in an unjoined form known as *print script*. The ability to link separate letters by means of connecting lines is highly valued as proof of a child's success in learning to write. A significant subsidiary feature is the ability to move from large early letters formed with great care to smaller letters in a maturer 'hand' that stays within an acceptable size range. Once this is achieved, individuals are free to develop their own handwriting, descriptions of which include such evaluative terms as *generous* or *cramped*, *neat* or *untidy*, *rounded* or *spiky*, *legible* or *illegible*. In educational terms, such matters as a steady reduction in the size of letters relate to stages in children's neuromuscular development and physical coordination.

Aids to learning. Analogies and mnemonic devices continue to be common in helping young children write individual letter forms. Such devices are often reminiscent of past or different kinds of writing, as with the pictorial analogy: 'Letter *S* is a swan who holds her head up high' (Ruth Fagg, *Everyday Writing*, University of London Press, 1963). The visual system developed by Lyn Wendon uses animal and other shapes as templates for the child to work with (*Pictograms*, Barton, Cambridge, 1973/84). One of her pictographic examples is the character Dippy Duck, used to teach the direction and flow necessary when forming small *d*: '*Stroke* Dippy's back. Go *round* his tum. Go *up* his neck. Then *down* you come!'

Factors in learning. Teaching people to write includes such factors as: (1) Eliminating tension, especially in very young learners, through preliminary relaxing exercises. (2) Checking writing postures and hand grips. (3) Ensuring good writing conditions, such as a suitable seat, desk surface, and lighting. (4) Determining hand dominance and ensuring that left-handers in a society dominated by right-handers are not directly or indirectly penalized or neglected. (5) Providing adequate graded pattern exercises, such as the angular diagonal patterns that underlie the writing of capital *M* and the rounded equivalents for *m*. (6) Helping learners to achieve rhythm, fluency, and reasonable speed. (7) Constructively working on faults (such as wrong pencil grips, ill-formed letters, and inefficient directionality in the shaping of letters). (8) In due course allowing the learner to develop a confident individual hand.

See ALPHABET, COMMUNICATIVE SHIFT, CREATIVE WRITING, EFFECTIVE WRITING, ILLITERACY, LITERACY, ORTHOGRAPHY, PRINTING, READING, SCRIPT, SPELLING, WORD PROCESSOR, WRITER. [HISTORY, WRITING]. T.MCA., W.W.B.

History and writing systems

Coulmas, F. 1989. *The Writing Systems of the World.* Oxford: Basil Blackwell.

Diringer, D. 1948/68. *The Alphabet: A Key to the History of Mankind.* London: Hutchinson.

Gelb, Ignace J. 1963. *A Study of Writing.* Chicago: University Press.

Harris, Roy. 1986. *The Origin of Writing.* London: Duckworth.

Hooker, J. T., *et al.* 1990. *Reading the Past: Ancient Writing from Cuneiform to the Alphabet.* London: British Museum Publications.

Sampson, G. 1985. *Writing Systems.* London: Hutchinson.

Senner, Wayne M. (ed.). 1989. *The Origins of Writing.* Lincoln: University of Nebraska Press.

Ullman, B. L. 1963. *Ancient Writing and Its Influence.* New York: Longman.

Vachek, J. 1973. *Written Language.* The Hague: Mouton.

The craft of writing and writing as part of education

Couture, Barbara (ed.). 1986. *Functional Approaches to Writing: Research Perspectives.* London: Frances Pinter.

Czerniewska, Pam, *et al.* 1989. *Becoming a Writer* (part of a series stemming from the National Writing Project, 1985-9, set up by the School Curriculum Development Committee, and centred on experience with children learning to write in England and Wales). London: Nelson.

Heim, Michael. 1987. *Electric Language: A Philosophical Study of Word Processing.* New Haven & London: Yale University Press.

Nystrand, M. (ed.). 1982. *What Writers Know: The Language, Process, and Structure of Written Discourse.* New York: Academic Press.

Smith, P. E. 1977. *Developing Handwriting.* London: Macmillan.

—— & Inglis, A. 1989. *New Nelson Handwriting: Teacher's Manual,* 2nd edition. Walton-on-Thames & Edinburgh: Nelson.

Tannen, Deborah (ed.). 1982. *Spoken and Written Language.* Norwood, NJ: Ablex.

The writing theme

A–L. ABBREVIATION, ABRIDG(E)MENT, ACCENT, ACUTE ACCENT, AELFRIC, ALPHABET, AMPERSAND, ANACHRONY, ANACOLUTHON, ANGLE, ANGLIC, APOSIOPESIS, ARTICLE[2], ASCENDER AND DESCENDER, ASH, AUREATE DICTION, AUTHOR, BIBLIOGRAPHY, BOILERPLATE, BRAILLE, BREVE, CEDILLA, CHAPTER, CHARACTER, CIRCUMFLEX, COHERENCE, COHESION, COLON, COMMA, COMMUNICATIVE SHIFT, COMPOSITION, COMPUTERATE, COMPUTER LITERACY, CONSONANT, CONSONANT CLUSTER, CONTRACTION, CONTROLLED COMPOSITION, COPY, COPYBOOK, COPYIST, COPYRIGHT, CREATIVE WRITING, CULTURAL LITERACY, DAGGER, DASH, DATE, DESKTOP PUBLISHING, DIACRITIC, DIA(E)RESIS, DIAGONAL, DIALOG(UE), DICTATION, DIGEST, DIGRAPH, DIRECT AND INDIRECT SPEECH, DISYLLABLE, DOCUMENT, DOCUMENTARY, DYSGRAPHIA, DYSLEXIA, EDITING, ELLIPSIS, EMENDATION, EMPHASIS, ENDNOTE, ENG, EPITOME, EPSILON, ESH, ESSAY, ETH, EUPHUISM, EXCLAMATION MARK/POINT, EYE DIALECT, FOOTNOTE, FORM, FORMAT, FULL STOP, FUNCTIONAL LITERACY, FUNK, GRAMMATOLOGY, GRAPHEME, GRAPHIC MEDIUM, GRAPHOLOGY, GRAVE ACCENT, GREENGROCER'S APOSTROPHE, HACK, HAND, HANDWRITING, HARD AND SOFT, HART'S RULES, HEADERS AND FOOTERS, HEADING, HEMPL, HOMEOTELEUTON, HOUSE STYLE, ILLITERACY, INDENTION, INITIAL, INITIAL TEACHING ALPHABET,

INKHORN TERM, INTERNATIONAL PHONETIC ALPHABET, INTERTEXTUALITY, INVERSION, IOTA, ITA, ITALIC, JOURNALISM, LAYOUT, LEMMA, LETTER[1], LETTER[2], LIGATURE, LINE, LITERACY, LITERATURE, LOGOGRAM, LONGHAND, LONG S.

M–Z. MACAULAY, MACRON, MAGIC E, MANUSCRIPT, MARGIN, MARK, MONOGRAPH, NARRATION, NOM DE PLUME, NOTATION, NOTE, NOTES AND REFERENCES, NOVEL, OBELISK, OBLIQUE, ORTHOGRAPHY, ORWELL, PARAGRAPH, PARAPHRASE, PARATAXIS, PARENTHESIS, PEN NAME, PERIOD, PERIODIC SENTENCE, PHATIC COMMUNION, PHONOGRAPHY, PHONOTYPE, PITMAN (I.), PITMAN (J.), PLAGIARISM, PLAIN ENGLISH, PLOT, POETIC PROSE, POSTSCRIPT, PRÉCIS, PREFACE, PROLOG(UE), PROOF-READING, PRINTING, PROSE, PUBLISHING, PUNCTUATION, PUNCTUATION MARK, PURPLE PATCH, QUESTION MARK, QUOTATION, QUOTATION MARKS, QUOTE UNQUOTE, READER, READING, REBUS, REFERENCE MARK, RESPELLING, REVISE, ROMAN, ROMAN NUMERAL, SCRIBBLER, SCRIBE, SCRIPT, SCRIPTURE, SCROLL, SEMI-LITERATE, SERIF, SHORTHAND, SIC, SIMPLIFIED SPELLING SOCIETY, SLANT, SLASH, SOLIDUS, SPACE, SPEEDHAND, SPELLER, SPELLING, SPELLING BEE, SPELLING CHECKER, SPELLING REFORM, STET, STYLE, SUB-EDITING, SUBHEAD(ING), SUBSCRIPT, SUMMARY, SUPERSCRIPT, SWUNG DASH, SYLLAB(IF)ICATION, SYNOPSIS, TEXT, THEME, THORN, TILDE, TOPIC, TRANSCRIPTION, TRANSLITERATION, TRIPHTHONG, UMLAUT, UNCIAL, UNIVOCALIC, VERBATIM, VIRGULE, VOLUME, WEBSTER, WHITE SPACE, WORD PROCESSOR, WORDSMITH, WRITER, WRITING, WYNN, WYSIWYG, YOGH.

WYCLIFFE, John, also **Wyclif, Wiclif,** and others [*c.*1320-1384]. English reformer and Bible translator, born at Wycliffe in Yorkshire, and Master of Balliol College, Oxford (*c.*1356-*c.*1382). His role in the Lollard movement and the politics of the Reformation have tended to overshadow his significant contribution to the language. His translations (with collaborators) of the Vulgate Bible were the first complete Bible in English and existed in two forms, the Early Version (*c.*1380-2) and the Late Version (*c.*1382-8), the second being more idiomatic, less archaic, and freer from Latinisms and generally more highly regarded. Wycliffe was a friend of Geoffrey Chaucer, who may have used him as the model for the Poor Parson in *The Canterbury Tales.* He did for Middle English prose what Chaucer did for poetry, making English a competitor with French and Latin; his sermons were written when London usage was coming together with the East Midlands dialect, to form a standard language accessible to all, and he included scientific references, such as to chemistry and optics. His style influenced Reformation and later nonconformist writing, and John Milton was among his admirers. More than 300 of his discourses survive, with some 170 manuscript copies of his Bible, circulated from Lutterworth, where he was rector (1374-84). Its opening words are: 'In the firste made God of nought heuene and erthe. The erthe forsothe was veyn withynne and void, and derknessis weren upon the face of the see.' Wycliffe's own share in the translations bearing his name is uncertain, but was probably considerable. See BIBLE and index. [BIOGRAPHY, EUROPE, HISTORY, LITERATURE].   M.LA.

WYLD, Henry Cecil Kennedy [1870-1945]. English philologist and lexicographer. Born in London of Scottish descent, he was educated at Charterhouse and in Switzerland, then at the universities of Bonn and Heidelberg in Germany, and at Oxford, where he was taught by Henry Sweet. In 1899, he was appointed lecturer in English Language at U. College, Liverpool, and in 1904 became the first Professor of English Language at the U. of Liverpool. In 1920, he was elected Merton Professor of English at Oxford. His publications include: *A Short History of English* (1914, revised 1927), *A History of Modern Colloquial English* (1920, enlarged edition 1936), and the monumental, one-volume *Universal Dictionary of the English Language* (1932). Wyld worked on the history of English sounds and used the terms *Public School English* and *Received Standard* for the accent currently known as *Received Pronunciation* (*RP*). His dictionary has phonetic transcriptions, detailed etymologies, and illustrations of modern idiomatic usage, and set a pattern followed by A. S. Hornby in the *Advanced Learner's Dictionary of Current English* and in other learner's dictionaries. See index. [BIOGRAPHY, EUROPE, REFERENCE, SPEECH].   P.C.

WYNN, also **wyn, wen** [Before 12c: from the Old English mnemonic name *wyn(n)* joy]. The name of a runic letter and its manuscript and printed form *p*, used in Old and early Middle English for *w*, as in *snap* snow, *hpit* white. See LETTER[1], RUNE. [WRITING].   E.W.

WYSIWYG. See WORD PROCESSOR.

X

X, x [Called 'eks']. The 24th letter of the Roman alphabet as used for English. It was adapted from the Greek letter *chi/khi* (X) by the Romans, with the value /ks/.

Sound value. Phonetically, *x* as used in English is redundant, its standard value /ks/ being equally represented by *cc* in *vaccine*, *ks* in *treks*, *cs* in *tocsin*, and *cks* in *socks*, allowing such homophones as *lax/lacks* and *cox/cocks*. However, *x* is not always pronounced as *ks*, different environments inducing the alternatives /gz/ in *example* and /z/ in *xenophobia*.

Initial *X* and *EX*-. (1) No vernacular English word begins with the sound /ks/, and the pronunciation is /z/ for initial *x* in such Greek-derived bases as *xantho-* yellow, *xeno-* foreign, *xero-* dry, *xylo-* wood, and such names as *Xanthippe* and *Xerxes*. (2) Older Spanish *x* as in *Mexico*, *Texas* is kept, with English pronunciation as *ks*, although in Spain these are today written *Méjico*, *Tejas*, and pronounced with a velar fricative /x/, as in ScoE *loch*. (3) When initial *x* stands for the letter *x* (*Xmas*, *X-ray*), it is pronounced 'eks'. (4) *X* in the Latin prefix *ex-* may be pronounced voiceless as /ks/ (typically when stressed, as in *export*, *extra*) or voiced as /gz/ (typically before a stressed vowel, as in *exact*, *exist*). In practice, however, voicing is often inconsistent, both realizations being heard in *exit*. The *c* in initial *exc-* (*excel*, *excite*) is assimilated into the voiceless value of *x*, while following *h* is usually assimilated into the voiced realization (*exhaust*, *exhibit*, but voicelessly in *exhibition*). A following root beginning with *s* loses the *s* (*ex + sert* becomes *exert*) and the *x* is voiced.

Medial *X*. (1) In medial position, *x* is typically voiceless (*maxim*, *vexatious*, *elixir*, *toxin*, *approximate*, *buxom*, *axle*, *sexton*), but when an *i*-glide

follows (whether represented by *i* with a following vowel, or by *u* with the value in *music*), the glide may be assimilated and *x* sounded as *ksh* (*noxious*, *luxury*, *sexual*), a palatalizing effect paralleled in other spelling patterns such as *fractious*, *actual*. (2) Voicing of this sound may occur medially before a stressed syllable, 'gzh' rather than 'ksh' being often heard in *luxurious*. (3) *Anxious* parallels *noxious* (though with the preceding *n* velarized as 'ng'), but in the noun *anxiety* the *i* is not assimilated, the *n* remains velarized, and *x* is voiced but loses its /k/, being pronounced /z/. (4) English usually retains *x* as derived from Latin, as in *exit* from *exitus* and *crucifixion* from *crucifixio/crucifixionis*, but, since the 17c, *connexion*, *inflexion* (the etymologically appropriate spellings) have increasingly been written *connection* and *inflection*, probably by analogy with *direction*. *Complexion* and *fluxion* do not have alternative forms.

Final and silent *X*. (1) Final *x* is common and except in recent loans has the value /ks/, usually after a short vowel (BrE *axe*, AmE *ax*, *flax*, *relax*, *climax*, *wax*, *index*, *flex*, *complex*, *sex*, *vex*, *fix*, *mix*, *six*, *executrix*, *phalanx*, *jinx*, *ox*, *box*, *fox*, *pox*, *flux*, *crux*), but in *coax*, *hoax* after a long vowel. Final /ks/ is normally spelt *x* in English, except when the /s/ is an inflection: contrast *tax/tacks*. (2) In French loans, final *x* is typically silent (*choux*, *prix*, *Montreux*) or pronounced /z/ if a plural inflection (*tableaux*). *Sioux* is modelled on French with silent *x*, although Amerindian in origin. (3) Latin morphology sometimes affects final *x*. When the plural of *appendix*, *index*, *matrix*, *vortex* follows Latin, *x* becomes *c* in *appendices*, *indices*, *matrices*, *vortices*. However, regular English pluralizing with *-es* (*appendixes*, *indexes*, *matrixes*) is common, though sometimes implying a distinct sense of the word concerned: for example,

THE CAPITAL LETTER						THE SMALL LETTER				
EARLY FORMS				CURRENT FORMS		EARLY FORMS			CURRENT FORMS	
Phoenician	Greek	Etruscan	Roman (Latin)	roman	italic	Roman cursive	Roman uncial	Carolingian minuscule	roman	italic
‡	‡ X Ξ		X	X	*X*	*X*	X	X	x	*x*

appendices in books, *appendixes* in the body. (4) Similarly, the Latin feminine suffix *-trix* is occasionally used as a counterpart to masculine *-tor* rather than the commoner French-derived *-tress*, as in *dominatrix, executrix, victrix*, as against *actress, benefactress*.

Miscellaneous. (1) *X* sometimes alternates with *sk* by metathesis: *Manx* for earlier *Mansk*; *piskey* as a variant of *pixie*; *ax* as a dialect form of *ask*. (2) *Buxom* was formerly *bucksome* and *pox* derives from the plural of *pock*. Comparably, a recent tendency in commercial spelling reduces the morphologically distinct *cs, cks* to *x*: *fax* for *facts* and *facsimile, pix* for *pictures, sox* for *socks, trux* for *trucks*. (3) Disyllables ending in *x* include technical terms from Latin (*helix, vortex*) and, apparently as a consequence, many commercial and trade names (*Kleenex, Tampax, Xerox*). See ALPHABET, C, K, LETTER[1], SPELLING. [WRITING]. C.U.

XEROGRAPHY. See PHOTOCOPYING.

X-HEIGHT. See ASCENDER AND DESCENDER.

XHOSA. See AFRICAN ENGLISH, BANTU, SOUTH AFRICA, SOUTH AFRICAN LANGUAGES.

Y

Y, y [Called 'wy', rhyming with *high*]. The 25th letter of the Roman alphabet as used for English. It originated as one of two letters derived by the Greeks from the Phoenician consonant symbol *waw*. The Greek letter *upsilon* (*Y*, lower case *υ*) had a value like *u*, which Latin wrote as *V*. Only later did the Romans adopt the form *Y* as a separate letter specifically to transliterate Greek *upsilon*, adding it to the end of the alphabet (*z* being a later addition still). Many European languages indicate the Greek origin in their name for *y*: French *i-grec*, Spanish *i-griega* (Greek *i*), German *Ypsilon*. The French and Spanish names imply that the letter is an alternative for *i*.

Origins and early uses. The name *wy* may derive (with changes in pronunciation) from the sound the letter represented in Old English: a fronted *u* as in French *tu* and the value of *y* in German and the International Phonetic Alphabet: see OLD ENGLISH[1]. In Middle English, this sound typically merged with that of short *i*. In medieval times, *y* was commonly written with a superimposed dot to distinguish it from the similar forms of the Old English letters *thorn* and *wynn*. After the Norman Conquest in 1066, fronted *u* was increasingly spelt in the French fashion as *u*, making *y* available as the alternative to *i*, which may have been useful for breaking up a series of vertical strokes, so that *min* (*mine*) might be more legibly written *myn*. There was, however, little consistency in the use of either *i* or *y*.

In addition, in Middle English, *y* often served to represent the Old English letter *yogh* (*ʒ*), especially word-initially. As this sound lost its velar quality, there emerged the semi-vowel value heard in *year*. This use was reinforced by its availability, unlike yogh, in printers' typefaces. A few words with initial yogh in Old English dropped it entirely, *enough*, *if*, *itch* now having an initial vowel. On the other hand, *you* has replaced an initial glide vowel with *y* (Old English *eow*). The similarity of the handwritten forms of *y* and thorn (*þ*) led to its occasional use as an alternative to *th*, the usual Roman equivalent of thorn, especially in *the*, *that*, etc., so producing shorthand forms for these words as *yᵉ*, *yᵗ* which persisted in private use well into the Early Modern English period. The form *yᵉ* is currently used on pseudo-antique shop-signs such as *Ye Olde Englishe Tea Shoppe* (jocularly pronounced 'ye oldy Englishy tea shoppy'), in which the *ye* is generally not recognized as an alternative spelling for *the*.

Sound values. (1) In English, *y* is widely used as an alternative letter for the sounds represented by *i*, sometimes interchangeably, but often with a different positional distribution: word-initially as a semi-vowel (*year*, *yes*, *you*); word-finally in vernacular words (*caddy*, *hilly*, *sorry*). (2) Like *i*, *y* commonly softens a preceding *c* or *g* (*cypress*, *gypsum*, *fancy*, *bulgy*), but there are exceptions and options in the pronunciation of words derived from Greek: in *Cythera* usually hard, in *gynecology* generally hard but sometimes soft, and in *demagogy*, *hegemony* both hard and soft. (3) The letter *y* alternates with *a* in *scallywag/scalawag*, and in the spellings BrE *pyjamas*, AmE *pajamas*.

Greek short Y. Short *y* has the value of short *i* in many words derived from Greek (transliterating upsilon), often borrowed through Latin and French: *analysis*, *anonymous*, *chrysanthemum*, *crypt*, *cylinder*, *cynic*, *cyst*, *dynasty*, *dyslexia*, *Egypt*, *etymology*, *gymnasium*, *hymn*, *hypnosis*, *hypocrite*, *idyllic*, *lyric*, *martyr*, *methylated*, *myriad*, *myrrh*, *myrtle*, *mystery*, *myth*, *oxygen*, *physic*, *polygon*, *polyp*, *pterodactyl*, *pyramid*, *rhythm*, *syllable*, *sympathy*, *synagogue*, *system*, *zephyr*. Some words in short *i* may look Greek, but are not, and often have variants in *i*:

THE CAPITAL LETTER						THE SMALL LETTER				
EARLY FORMS				CURRENT FORMS		EARLY FORMS			CURRENT FORMS	
Phoenician	Greek	Etruscan	Roman (Latin)	roman	italic	Roman cursive	Roman uncial	Carolingian minuscule	roman	italic
Υ	ꟼΥ	Υ	V	Y	*Y*	ꟼ	ʏ	ʒ	y	*y*

for example, *syllabub/sillabub*, *sylvan/silvan*, *syrup/sirup*. However, *gypsy/gipsy* and *pygmy/pigmy* are Greek in origin.

Word-final short Y. The short *i*-sound in which many native English words end in most accents is always spelt *y*: contrast traditional words with loans, as in *jetty/spaghetti, windy/Hindi, juicy/sushi*. In some accents, however, this vowel has the same value /ɪ/ as medial short *y*; in others, it is lengthened to /i/: for example, older RP has the value of medial short *y*, while more recent RP has a quality similar to that in *see*. These endings commonly change *y* to *ie* in inflected forms (*pity/pities/pitied*), and in Elizabethan times the base words were often spelt *-ie* (*citie, pitie*). Word-final *y* occurs in several common patterns: (1) Disyllabic concrete nouns: *baby, jetty, city, ivy, body, study*. (2) Disyllabic nouns (mainly concrete) in *-ey*: *abbey, alley, chimney, donkey, hockey, honey, jersey, journey, medley, money, monkey, parsley, spinney, turkey, valley*. (3) Adjectives: *happy, holy, merry, pretty, silly, tidy*. This *-y* is often a suffix added to another word: *crazy, catty, easy, fiery*. (4) Abstract nouns, such as those based on an adjective ending in *-ous* (*curiosity, pomposity, notoriety*), on a word ending in *t* (*difficulty, pregnancy, prophecy*), or otherwise (*facility, necessity, opportunity*). They include many Greek-derived words: *biology, economy, hierarchy, liturgy*. (5) Adverbs in which the suffix *-ly* has been added to an adjective: *grandly, hurriedly, slowly, stupidly*; sometimes some assimilation takes place with the root: *wholly, happily, ably, incredibly, nobly, volubly, simply*. A few adjectives are formed by the addition of *-ly* to a base: *brotherly, friendly, kindly*. (6) Verbs, as *carry, marry, vary, pity, worry, hurry*. In some words, such as *bogey, bogy, caddy, pixy, stymy*, final *-(e)y* is alternatively spelt *-ie*.

Long Y. The letter *y* often represents the sound of long stressed *i*: *by, lyre*. Some related words alternate long and short values: *lyre/lyric, paralyse/paralysis*. Long *y* occurs: (1) In monosyllables, typically of Old English origin, in final position: *buy, by, cry, fry, guy, my, ply, sty, thy, why, wry*. A silent *e* is added to avoid spelling a non-grammatical word with just two letters: *bye, dye, eye, rye*. (2) In verbs, in final position, such as *ally, defy, deny, modify, multiply, occupy, prophesy, qualify, satisfy, specify, supply*. Y in *multiply, supply* is short when these words are adverbs derived from *multiple, supple*. (3) As the dominant pronunciation of Greek-derived bases and prefixes such as *cycl-, dyn-, gyr-, hydro-, hyper-, hypo-* (but not *hypocrite*), *pyro-* and such words as *hyacinth, hyena, hygiene, hymen, hyphen, lyre, papyrus, type, tyrant*. In some words of non-Greek origin, medial long *y* is

interchangeable with *i*: *cyder, cypher, dyke, gybe, tyro*. (4) In such words as *rhyme* (see entry), *style* (see entry), *typhoon*, and BrE *tyre* (AmE *tire*).

Semi-vowel Y. (1) In medial positions, there is no clear phonetic distinction between the semi-vowel *y* and an *i*-glide. In the alternative spellings *lanyard/laniard* they are identical in pronunciation. (2) Semi-vowel *y* occurs in initial position in words mostly of Old English origin, formerly often spelt with yogh: *yard, yarn, year, yeast, yellow, yeoman, yes, yesterday, yew, yield, yoke, you, young, your, youth*. (3) Most other words beginning with *y* are more recent, and often loanwords: *yacht, yak, yam, yank, yodel, yoga*. (4) Medial *y* with a semi-vowel value as in *lawyer* is uncommon. (5) The semi-vowel value is also represented in the letter *u* (*cure, pure*) and the digraphs *eu, ew* (*eureka, spew*). The semi-vowel is normally so spelt after a consonant: *fuse, few, feud*. (6) Word-initially, *u* commonly has the sound of *you* (*union, use*), as do *eu, ew*; *ewe* and *yew* are homophones.

Digraphs. Like *i*, *y* serves as the second letter in digraphs after other vowel letters, *y* usually word-finally, with *i* medially. (1) The digraph *ay* occurs in common monosyllables. This *ay* has the value of long *a* like *ai* as in *rain*: *bray, clay, day, flay, fray, gay, may, pay, play, pray, ray, say, slay, spray, stay, tray, way*. When *-r* (syllabic or with preceding schwa) is added, the value of *ay* may be modified: *layer, prayer, mayor, Ayr*. Exceptionally, the two forms *ay, aye* have the value of long *i*, while *ay* in *quay* has the value of long *e*. (2) The digraph *ey*, as opposed to the *-ey* ending of *abbey*, occurs in a few monosyllables and disyllables with the value of *ei* in *vein* and *ay* in *day*: *prey, they, whey, convey, obey, survey*, with modification before *r* in the name *Eyre*. Exceptionally, *ey* has the value of long *e* as in *me* in *key, geyser, Seymour*, and of short *e* as in *men* in *Reynolds*. (3) The word-final digraph *oy* parallels medial *oi* (*boy/boil*), and represents a diphthong typically deriving from French (*employ*: compare Modern French *emploi*). It occurs in the monosyllables *boy, buoy, cloy, coy, joy, ploy, toy* and the disyllables *alloy, annoy, convoy, decoy, deploy, destroy, employ, enjoy, viceroy*, between vowels in *loyal, royal, voyage*, and medially before a consonant in *oyster*. See ALPHABET, I, LETTER[1], SPELLING, THORN, U, WYNN, YOGH. [WRITING]. C.U.

Y-. A prefix for the past participle in Middle English, as in Chaucer's *were yfounde* were found. The past participle in most Old English verbs began with *ge-*, as in *gefunden* found. By the 14c, this had dwindled to *y-* or vanished: Chaucer also has *hath founde* has found. Later writers used *y-* as a conscious archaism. Shakespeare, Milton, and Charlotte Bronte, among others, used *yclept* called, named; Spenser used many such forms. In the 19c, William Barnes reports *a-zet*, the equivalent of *y-set*, as the Dorset form of the past participle *set*; *a-* plus past participle remains a marker of dialect in southwestern England. See SPENSER, WEST COUNTRY, YOLA (AS EE-). [HISTORY, GRAMMAR].   W.F.B.

YANKEE [18c: origin uncertain. The currently favoured origin is *Jan Kees*, a variant of Dutch *Jan Kaas* (Johnny Cheese), a nickname mistakenly taken to be plural and used for an ordinary person. Other proposed origins include the Dutch *Janke*, diminutive of *Jan* John, used as a derisive nickname in New England, and versions of *English* and *Anglais* in Amerindian languages. *Yankee* and *Yank* may or may not have an initial capital]. An informal term associated with the US, with three distinct senses according to place of reference, emotional connotation, and user: (1) In the oldest and narrowest sense, a person from New England, as in the Revolutionary war song *Yankee Doodle*, which satirized the naïve and incompetent New England colonials opposing the redcoats. When the song was adopted as a marching tune by those it satirized, the term was popularized as an expression of pride, particularly after the defeat of the British. (2) A person from the northern states, especially as used (often pejoratively) by people in the southern states. Although it had originated earlier, this sense was particularly associated with the Civil War, when *confederate, rebel, reb,* or *Johnny Reb* was used for Southerners and *yankee* or *damn yankee* for Northerners. This wider reference is the most common in the US, although the precise limits of yankee territory are unclear. For almost all Americans, *yankee* applies to someone from the Northeast: New England, New York State, New Jersey, and Pennsylvania, the area north of the old *Mason Dixon Line*, the boundary between Pennsylvania and Maryland named for the surveyors who laid it out and later taken as the dividing line between free-soil and slave states. For many, yankee territory extends westward through the tier of northern states that formed the Union during the Civil War; there is, however, uncertainty about how far westward the term applies. Some think it appropriate for anyone outside the old Confederacy (the southeastern states) and thus to the newer western parts of the US as well. (3) Also *Yank*. The widest sense, an American, invented by the British shortly after the Revolutionary War and now used almost exclusively by non-Americans. The sense became popular during World War I: for example, in George M. Cohan's 1917 marching song *Over There*, with its line 'The Yanks are coming'. The term is often pejorative, as in *Yankees go home!* It is not used by Americans as a national term. British, European, and other applications of the term to any American are likely to conflict with its other meanings. To call a Georgian or a South Carolinian a *yankee* is equivalent to calling a Scot *English*. It is best not to do so. See ETHNIC NAME, NEW ENGLAND. [AMERICAS, NAME].   J.A.

YAT. See NEW ORLEANS.

YEAR'S WORK IN ENGLISH STUDIES, The, short form *YWES*. A critical bibliography published annually since 1921 by the English Association. Each volume has a general editor (of whom the first was Sir Sidney Lee); in it, books and articles of the year in question are listed and discussed in period chapters by a number of reviewers. Successive volumes reveal changes in the extent of 'English' studies: American literature was included for the first time in 1954 and Commonwealth literature in 1982. The growth of the literary-critical industry is also indicated: the volume for 1957 has 274 pages, that for 1987 933 pages. The volume for 1987, entitled *YWES 68* and published in 1990, was edited by Laurel Blake and published for the Association by Basil Blackwell (Oxford, 1990). It has the following sections: *I* Reference, Literary History, and Bibliography; *II* Literary Theory; *III* English Language; *IV* Old English Literature; *V* Middle English—Excluding Chaucer; *VI* Middle English—Chaucer; *VII* The Sixteenth Century: Excluding Drama After 1550; *VIII* Shakespeare; *IX* Renaissance Drama—Excluding Shakespeare; *X* The Earlier Seventeenth Century; *XI* Milton; *XII* The Later Seventeenth Century; *XIII* The Eighteenth Century; *XIV* The Nineteenth Century—Romantic Period; *XV* The Nineteenth Century—Victorian Period; *XVI* The Twentieth Century; *XVII* American Literature to 1900; *XVIII* American Literature—Twentieth Century; *XIX* New Literatures in English. These are followed by the appendices *Books Received, Best Books and Articles* (as selected by the *YWES* critics, and listed in the same order as the preceding sections), and *Indexes* (Critics; Authors and Subjects Treated). The headquarters of the Association are in London. Compare REFERENCE GUIDE FOR ENGLISH STUDIES. See BIBLIOGRAPHY, ENGLISH ASSOCIATION, ENGLISH STUDIES. [EUROPE, MEDIA].   R.C.

YELLOW PRESS, The [1890s: from the comic-strip character 'The Yellow Kid', who first appeared in *The Sunday World* (1895), a New York newspaper owned by Joseph Pulitzer]. A disparaging colloquial term for low-grade, sensational journalism. In the course of the circulation war between Joseph Pulitzer (1847-1911) and W. Randolph Hearst (1863-1951), 'The Yellow Kid' changed sides several times, and the term was born as each party strove to outdo the other. The equivalent British terms, *the gutter press* and *gutter journalism*, emerged in the same period. See AMERICAN PRESS, GUTTER, TABLOID. [MEDIA]. G.H.

YEMEN. See ARABIC.

YES-NO QUESTION. See QUESTION.

YIDDISH [1880s: called by its speakers *Yidish* Jewish, and *mame-loshn* mother tongue]. The language used by Jews of Eastern and Central Europe and their descendants, spoken for nearly a thousand years and until World War II the most widely used Jewish language of modern times, with over 11m speakers. Currently, there are about 4m speakers worldwide, mostly in North and South America, Israel, and the Soviet Union. Yiddish is a Germanic language akin to English, but with a distinctive lexical component of about 18% Hebrew-Aramaic and 16% Slavic (Czech, Polish, Russian, Ukrainian) as well as Romance elements from Old French and Old Italian. It is the only Germanic language to be written in a non-Roman alphabet: like other Jewish languages, Yiddish is written in the Hebrew alphabet, and words of Hebrew or Aramaic origin retain their original spellings, while those of Germanic or other origin are spelled according to phonetic rules. Scholars divide Yiddish historically into four phases: *Earliest Yiddish* from c.1000, *Old Yiddish* from 1250, *Middle Yiddish* from 1500, and *Modern Yiddish* from 1700. Of the two major dialect groups, *Western* and *Eastern*, only the latter survives; Western Yiddish (Germany, Switzerland, The Netherlands, Alsace-Lorraine) went into decline after 1700. The chief dialects of Eastern Yiddish are *North-Eastern* (Lithuania, Latvia, Byelorussia), *South-Eastern* (Ukraine, Romania, eastern Galicia), and *Central* (Poland, western Galicia). *Standard Yiddish* is closest to the North-Eastern dialect in pronunciation, and generally closest in grammar to Central Yiddish. In the US, colloquial Yiddish became heavily influenced by AmE. Many words were replaced by Americanisms, some embodying distinctly US concepts, others reflecting the everyday dominance of English. A number of American Yiddish innovations, such as *allrightnik* and *boychik*, have found their way into colloquial AmE. See AMERICAN LITERATURE, BORROWING, COCKNEY, DIALECT IN AMERICA, EUROPEAN COMMUNITY, HEBREW, JEWISH ENGLISH, YIDDISHISM. [AMERICAS, EUROPE, LANGUAGE]. S.S.

YIDDISHISM [1920s: from *Yiddish* and *-ism* as in *Scotticism*]. An expression or construction typical of the Yiddish language, especially when found in another language. Yiddishisms occur in such languages as Dutch, English, French, German, Hebrew, and Spanish. The earliest recorded Yiddishisms in English either refer to items of the Jewish religion (such as *kosher* ritually fit, and its antonym *treyf*, both first recorded in 1851) or were part of the argot of criminals (such as *ganef* a thief, *goy* a non-Jew, both first recorded in the 1830s). With the immigration of Eastern European Jews into the UK and US during the 1880s Yiddishisms began entering English in great numbers. The centrality of London and New York City, where most of the immigrants settled, played a major role in disseminating such usages as *Yid, Yiddish, shnorrer, shlemiel, gefilte fish, shul, bar mitzva*. Throughout the 20c, Yiddishisms have continued to make their way into English, increasingly as slang. The chief medium of transfer remains the Yiddish-influenced variety of English used by Jews of Eastern European origin or descent. See ETHNIC NAME, JEWISH ENGLISH. [VARIETY, WORD]. S.S.

YINGLISH [1951: a blend of *Yiddish* and *English*, perhaps the earliest of the *-(g)lish* terms]. An informal and often facetious term for: (1) English that contains many Yiddish words and expressions. It is an informal synonym of *Jewish English* (of the Ashkenazic or Eastern European variety). (2) Yiddish words and expressions that have become part of colloquial English, an informal collective term for *Yiddishisms*. (3) Words and expressions that blend Yiddish and English, such as *borscht circuit, fancy-shmancy, a whole megillah, a hearty mazel tov*. The term is viewed by scholars of Yiddish as slangy and disparaging. See -GLISH AND -LISH. [VARIETY]. S.S.

YOGH [Before 12c: a Middle English name, often associated with *yoke* and its Latin equivalent *iugum*]. The letter ʒ, a loosely written form of the letter *g* in Old English script. In Middle English, it became a distinct letter, having the values /j/ initially and medially, as in *ʒok* yoke, *beʒonde* beyond, /ɣ/ medially, as in *oʒen* own, *eʒe* eye, and /x/ medially and finally, as in *riʒt* right, *plouʒ* plough. In later Middle English, yogh was replaced by *y* and *gh*. See ALPHABET, LETTER[1], Y, Z. [WRITING]. E.W.

YOLA [From Old English, especially West Saxon, *yald* old]. A name for the first English spoken in Ireland, dating from the 12c and regarded as archaic by settlers in the 16-17c. It was slowly displaced by 17c norms, but survived into the 19c in Fort and Bargy in County Wexford and Fingal in County Dublin. In 'A Glossary of the old dialect of the Baronies of Forth and Bargy' (edited by William Barnes, 1867), Jacob Poole provided a piece of verse called 'A Yola Song':

Joud and moud vrem earchee ete was ee Lough.
Zitch vapereen, an shimereen, fan ee-daff ee aar scoth!
Zitch blakeen, an blayeen, fan ee ball was ee-drowe!
Chote well aar aim was t'yie ouz n'eer a blowe.
[Throngs and crowds from each quarter were at the Lough.
Such vapouring and glittering when stript in their shirts!
Such bawling and shouting, when the ball was thrown!
I saw their intent was to give us ne'er a stroke.]

See IRISH ENGLISH, OLD ENGLISH². [EUROPE, VARIETY]. L.T.

YORKSHIRE. Historically, the largest county of England, administered from the city of York. The city's name derives from Danish *Jorvik*, from Old English *Eoforwic*, from the Latinized Celtic *Eboracum* in Roman times. Although York was taken by the Angles in the early 5c, Celtic resistance continued in nearby *Leodis*, the present-day Leeds; it is sometimes suggested that the longer survival of Celtic control and language in that area may be responsible for some of the differences in pronunciation in West Yorkshire. The Old English term *scīr* (shire) for an administrative area was taken over by both Danes and Normans, the Danes adding the term *þriðjungr* ('thirding' or 'third part'). This survives in the subdivisions known as the *Yorkshire ridings* (East Riding, West Riding, and North Riding), the *t* or *th* of Middle English *t(h)riding* being absorbed by the *t* or *th* of *East, West, North*. These names were abandoned in the reorganization of counties in 1974, when the ridings became the counties of East, West, and North Yorkshire, with some territory contributed to the new county of Humberside. The name *Yorkshire* continues in informal use, however, for the area of the former county. Used attributively, the term refers to anything in or from the old county: *Yorkshire dialect, roast beef and Yorkshire pudding, Yorkshire terrier*. Used elliptically, it refers to the Yorkshire dialect: "'Tis as ridiculous . . . as it would be to talk broad Yorkshire or Somersetshire in the drawing room' (M. W. Montagu, *Letters*, 1 Apr. 1717).

Yorkshire dialect. The dialects of the region derive from the northern dialect of Old English known as *Anglian* or *Anglic*; an early text is the song of Caedmon, a lay brother at the monastery of Whitby (*c*.670). Scandinavian influence, from invasions and occupations from the 9c to 1066, had its most immediate influence on the non-literate in the area. However, a Danish element from the north entered the standard southern language in such words as *sky* and *outlaw*. Some Middle English writers can be identified as writing a northern English representing Yorkshire speech: for example, Richard Rolle, author of *The Ayenbite of Inwit* (Modern: *The Prick of Conscience*, written *c*.1340), a hermit who lived near Doncaster, and the authors of the Miracles or Mystery Plays from York and Wakefield. A feature of northern Middle English orthography was *quh* rather than *wh*, as in *quhilk* for the more southern *hwich* (which): compare SCOTS; see Q. Although English as used in Yorkshire is often taken to be a single homogeneous dialect, it is not in fact so. There are many kinds of Yorkshire usage, some of which are mutually unintelligible. The two main varieties are derived from the two groups of speakers in the county, and are divided by the boundary between the Midland and Northern groups of dialects.

Pronunciation. (1) Yorkshire accents are non-rhotic, with the exception of East Yorkshire, where a postvocalic alveolar *r* is occasionally heard in stressed syllables and final unstressed syllables, the word *farmer* having two such *r*-sounds. (2) The *a*-sound before *s*, *f*, and voiceless *th* is regularly short, as in *fast, staff*, and *path*. Yorkshire-speakers use a short /a/ vowel in *my aunt can't dance*. In southern England, the vowel is nasalized and long. (3) Some, mainly rural, speakers in the North and East Ridings have preserved something of the northern vowels of Middle English in the unrounded vowel of such words as /naː/ and /saː/ for *know* and *saw*, in /swan/ for *swan* and /kwari/ for *quarry*, and in an unchanged long vowel giving /huːs/ for *house* and /duːn/ for *down*. (4) The pronunciation or non-pronunciation of *the* is a well-known Yorkshire shibboleth. It varies from complete absence in the East, through a kind of suspended *t* in the central areas (often represented as *t' book, t' man*), to *d'* in the North before voiced consonants and *t'* before voiceless consonants (*d' book, t' packet*), and in the extreme West a *th'* before vowels and *t'* before consonants (*th' old man, t' book*). (5) Traditional short *u* in Yorkshire and throughout the north has the same sound in such words as *up, come* as in standard *wool, put*, but *-ook* words have remained long: /buːk/ and /kuːk/ for *book* and *cook*. (6) Regional variations often contrast greatly, especially between West on the one hand and North and East on the other: for example, *soon, road, stone* in the West sound like 'sooin', 'rooad', 'stooan', and in the North and East like 'see-en', 'reead', 'steean' (with 'sioon' for *soon* in the North-West).

Grammar. (1) The second-person singular *thou* survives in various forms, with /ðuː/ for *thou* in the East and North, and /ðaː/ in the West. In the West, *thou* can appear as /tə/, as in /wat duz tə want/ (What do you want?). The accusative form *thee* also survives, as in *Ah'll gi it thee* I'll give it to you. (2) *Happen* is widely used rather than *perhaps*, as in *Happen he'll come* Perhaps he'll come. (3) The form *summat* (somewhat), as in *There's summat up* and *I've summat to tell thee*, corresponds in use to *something*. (4) There is a common intransitive progressive use of the verb *like* in the question *Are you liking?* (Do you like it here?). (5) *Aye* and *nay* (yes and no) are widely used, especially in rural areas. (6) *While* is often used instead of *until*, as in *I'll stay here while eight*, a usage that occasionally causes confusion, as in the ambiguous *Wait while the light is green*. (7) The use of an echoic tag is common, usually *is that*, as in *It's a good buy, is that!* and *That's right nice, is that*.

Vocabulary. (1) The Scandinavian element is strong in rural and especially in agricultural usage that is obsolescent along with the objects it refers to: *flaycrow* scarecrow, *stoops* gateposts, *stower* rung (of a *stee* ladder), *lea* scythe, *flake* hurdle, *pike* small stack of hay. Most of such words were common to much of the north of England. (2) Many items in common use descend from Old Norse, and include: *addle* to earn, *beck* stream, *brook*, *cleg* horse-fly (shared with ScoE), *lake* or *laik* to play, *spaining* or *speaning* weaning (animals), and *ted* to spread hay. (3) The West Yorkshire form of the northern and Scots verb *thole* (permit, endure, tolerate) is *thoil*, which carries the Old English sense of *suffer*. It is applied mostly to spending money on something desirable but too expensive, as in *Nay, I couldn't thoil ten pound for that*. (4) The northern and ScoE term *bairn* (child) is common, as is the distinctive northern *childer*, plural of *child*, which descends from Middle English *childre* and *childer*, from late Old English *cildru* and *cildra*. The southern and standard *children* was assimilated to a now obsolete *-en* plural, as in *house/housen*. The cognate Scots *chiel(d)* (child, lad) has the regular plural *chiel(d)s*. Typical also, as part of northern English generally, are such usages as *lad* and *lass* (as in *We have a little lass*: a small daughter) and *love*, pronounced /lʊv/, as a form of address (as in *It's time to go, love*).

Processes of change. Although there has been considerable immigration from Ireland and Eastern Europe (late 19c, early 20c) and from the Caribbean and South Asia (since the 1950s, mainly to Leeds, Bradford, and Huddersfield), such influxes do not appear to have modified local speech. The usage of the children of these mainly working-class incomers is more often a variety of Yorkshire (with lexical influences from the parents' mother tongues) than of the standard language. Despite a continuing claim that increasing mobility and the standardization of education are causing dialectal differences to die out, observation of the working-class areas of Yorkshire cities shows that varieties distinct from the standard usage of England, especially in terms of traditional accents, continue to be used by schoolchildren.

Literary Yorkshire. Yorkshire dialect began to be written for literary purposes in the 17c with the publication of an anonymous poem, possibly from the Northallerton area, entitled *A Yorkshire Dialogue between an Awd Wife, a Lass and a Butcher* (printed at York, 1673). It opens:

AWD WIFE Pretha now lass, gang into t'hurn
            An' fetch me heame a skeel o' burn.
            Na pretha, barn, mak heeaste an' gang,
            I's mar my deagh, thou stays sae lang.
LASS   Why, Gom, I's gea, bud for my pains
            You's gie me a frundel o' your grains.
AWD WIFE My grains, my barn! Marry! not I,
            My draugh's for t'gilts an' galts i' t'sty.
            Than, pretha, look i' t'garth an' see
            What owsen I' the stand-hecks be.

[Prithee now, girl, go into the corner of the field / And fetch me home a bucket of water. / Now prithee, child, make haste and go, / I'll spoil my dough, you stay so long. / Why, grandmother, I will go, but for my trouble, give me a handful of your malt-grain. / My malt-grain, my child! Mary! Not I, / My grain-refuse is for the sows and boars in the sty. / Then, prithee, look in the yard and see what oxen there are in the stalls.]

This language would not at the time, nor would it now, be accepted over the whole area as Yorkshire dialect, but would be well understood, especially in parts of the North. Perhaps the most famous representation of Yorkshire dialect in literature is that by Emily Bronte in *Wuthering Heights* (1847), as in the following excerpt from Chapter 9, when the old servant Joseph says:

Yon lad gets wur an' wur! . . . He's left th' yate ut t'full swing and miss's pony has trodden dahn two rigs uh corn, un plottered through, raight o'r intuh t'meadow! Hahsomdiver, t'maister ull play t'divil to-morn, and he'll do weel. He's patience itsseln wi' sich careless, offald craters—patience itsseln he is! Bud he'll not be soa allus—yah's see, all on ye! Yah mumn't drive him out of his heead for nowt!

[That boy gets worse and worse. . . . He's left the gate wide open and the young lady's pony has pressed down two ridges of corn and floundered through right over into the meadow! However, the master will play the devil tomorrow, and he will be right. He's patience itself with such careless, awful creatures—patience itself he is! But he'll not be so always—you'll see, all of you! You mustn't drive him off his head for nothing!]

Many 19c working men tried to represent their vernacular in writing. Their works were often published in *Almanacks*, annual notes of supposed local events, calendar entries interspersed with passages of dialect, usually humorous and knockabout in character. This kind of prose continues in many Yorkshire newspapers. There was also a strain of poetry writing. One 19c poet was Sir Ben Turner, Mayor of Batley and Minister of Mines for the first Labour government. The poetry tradition continues and two 20c poets are Stanley Umpleby (North Yorkshire) and Fred Brown (West Yorkshire). Umpleby's writing is more rural, as in this stanza on the temptations for a country widow to remarry:

> There's yowes an' lambs bleeatin'
> A brawne i' t'ga'th reeatin'
> A wye cawf at's freeatin'
> What mud yan want mair?
> (from *T'Widda Weddin'*)

> [There are ewes and lambs bleating
> A pig rooting in the paddock,
> A heifer calf that is pasturing,
> What more could anyone want?]

Yorkshire Dialect Society. The first group concerned with the dialect came together in 1894 as a Yorkshire Committee of the *English Dialect Society*, to assist in the preparation of Joseph Wright's *English Dialect Dictionary*. After the disbandment of the EDS in 1896, the committee re-formed in 1897 as the Yorkshire Dialect Society, which publishes *The Transactions of the Yorkshire Dialect Society*. The society combines the scholarly study of local speech with the publication of prose and poetry in various forms of local dialect. It meets at colleges and university premises throughout the three Yorkshires as well as at industrial and folk museums, and promotes joint meetings with other groups. Papers on place-names and studies of local vocabularies are given as well as readings and recitations by dialect speakers.

See BRONTË (SISTERS), DIALECT IN ENGLAND, ENGLISH DIALECT SOCIETY, ENGLISH IN ENGLAND, ENGLISH PLACE-NAMES, GEORDIE, LANCASHIRE, MIDLANDS, NORSE, NORTHERN ENGLISH, NORTHUMBRIA, SURVEY OF ENGLISH DIALECTS. [EUROPE, NAME, VARIETY].   S.E.

YORUBA. See AFRICAN ENGLISH, AFRICAN LANGUAGES, NIGERIA.

Z

Z, z [In BrE called 'zed', in AmE 'zee']. The 26th and last letter of the Roman alphabet as used for English. It originated as the 7th letter of the Phoenician alphabet and became the 7th letter of the Hebrew and Greek alphabets. The Greeks called it *zeta* (Z, ζ), probably first pronouncing it /dz/, then /z/. The Romans adopted *Z* later than the rest of the alphabet, since /z/ was not a native Latin sound, adding it at the end of their list of letters and using it rarely. They did not always use it to transliterate *zeta*. Old English did not normally use *z*, the name *Elizabeth* being an exception. The use of *zed* as a term of abuse in Shakespeare's *King Lear* ('Thou whoreson zed! Thou unnecessary letter!', 2. 2) suggests that although it was then being increasingly written it was held in low esteem. The modification of BrE *zed* (from Old French *zede*, through Latin, from Greek *zeta*) to *zee* in AmE appears to have been by analogy with *bee, dee, vee*, etc.

Sound values and double Z. (1) In vernacular English, *z* represents a voiced alveolar fricative, pairing with *s* as its voiceless equivalent. It occurs initially, medially, and finally, sometimes doubled: *zebra, horizon, dazzle, daze, buzz.* (2) Before the ending *-ure*, the initial *i*-glide of the *u* is commonly assimilated to the *z*, producing the sound 'zh': *azure, seizure* (compare *measure*). (3) The sound /z/ is more frequently represented by *s* than *z*. (4) Some possibly echoic monosyllables have *zz* (*buzz, fizz, fuzz, jazz, whiz(z)*), as have disyllables with the iterative suffix *-le* (*dazzle, razzle, fizzle, sizzle, guzzle*). (5) Monosyllables ending in single *z* after a short vowel (*fez, quiz*) inflect with *zz*: *fez/fezzes, quiz/quizzing.* (6) Final *y* requires preceding *zz* if the preceding vowel is short (*dizzy, muzzy*), but only *z* if long (*lazy, crazy, dozy*).

Voiced and voiceless Z. The voiced/voiceless distinction of /s, z/ in Old English was predictable and did not need to be shown in spelling; medial *s* was voiced, as is still largely the case (*busy, weasel*), but French influence after the Norman Conquest in 1066 led to the writing of medial voiced *s* as *z* or *zz* in some words of Old English or Old Norse derivation: *adz(e), amaze, blaze, craze, daze, dazzle, dizzy, doze, drizzle, freeze, furze, gaze, hazel, ooze, sneeze, squeeze, wheeze, wizen.* Some related nouns have voiceless *s* (*brazen/brass, frozen/frost, glaze/glass, graze/grass*), others voiced *s* (*nuzzle/nose, wizard/wise*). Words of Old English origin were not spelt with final *z*: *sneeze, booze,* not **sneez,* **booz.*

English Z, French S. Many French-derived words contain *z* or *zz*, sometimes where French has or had *s*: English *breeze* (French *brise*), *buzzard, citizen, embezzle, frenzy* (French *frénésie*), *frieze* (French *frise*), *gizzard, grizzle* (French *grisailler*), *hazard* (French *hasard*), *lozenge* (French *losange*), *mizzen, muzzle* (French *museau*), *razor* (French *rasoir*), *seize* (French *saisir*). *Prize* corresponds to French *prix* and *size*, a clipping of *assize*, is derived from French *assise*. *Baize* appears to have been a misinterpretation of the French plural *baies*. Elsewhere, English *z* matches French *z*: *bizarre, bronze, dozen, gauze, lizard.*

Exotic Z. (1) Initial *z* was used from the 14c in new words derived from French or Latin, often originating in other languages such as Arabic, Spanish, and Greek: *zeal, zebra, zenith, zero, zest, zeugma, zirconium, zither, zodiac, zone, zoology.* German was the source of *zigzag, zinc*, while *zombie* originated in Africa. (2) Medial *z* occurs in more recent loans: Persian *bazaar*, Spanish *bonanza, maize*, Kongo *chimpanzee*, Greek *horizon*, German (from Italian) *marzipan*, Polish *mazurka*, Arabic *muezzin*, Italian *stanza*, French (through Latin from Greek) *trapeze*. (3) In recent loans, *z* usually retains the value given

THE CAPITAL LETTER						THE SMALL LETTER				
EARLY FORMS				CURRENT FORMS		EARLY FORMS			CURRENT FORMS	
Phoenician	Greek	Etruscan	Roman (Latin)	roman	italic	Roman cursive	Roman uncial	Carolingian minuscule	roman	italic
I	IZ	L	Z	Z	Z	Z	Z	Z	z	z

to it in the source language: /ts/ in German *Alzheimer's disease, Nazi, Zeitgeist* and Italian *pizzicato* (*mezzo-soprano* has /dz/ in Italian). Older German loans may have a preceding *t*: *quartz, waltz* (compare modern German *Quarz, Walzer*). (4) In the *tz* combination, the *t* induces devoicing of a following *z*, as in *blitz, chintz*. *Quartz* and *quarts* are homophones. (5) Silent *z* occurs in recent French loans: *laissez-faire, rendezvous, répondez s'il vous plaît*. (6) Because of German influence, in the Greek combining form *schizo-* (as in *schizophrenia*), *z* is pronounced as a voiceless affricate, /ts/. (7) In the word *Czech*, the digraph *cz* has the value of English *ch*, but in *czar* the initial *c* is silent and *z* has its normal value, as also in the alternative (and etymologically more accurate) spelling *tsar*. (8) Of unknown but recent origin are *bamboozle, blizzard, puzzle*.

Archaic Scots Z. In ScoE, some words, including names, have a silent *z* (*capercailzie* pronounced 'capercailie', *Dalrulzion* 'Dalrullion', *Dalziel* 'Deyell', *gaberlunzie* 'gabberloonie') or a digraph *nz* pronounced /ŋ/, as in the name *Menzies*, traditionally pronounced 'Mingis' (*ng* as in *singer*). Here *z* is an adaptation of the Old English letter yogh (*ȝ*) rather than etymological *z*.

British and American differences. Some alternative *s/z* spellings are found, the most widespread the Greek-derived suffix *-ise/ize* (*regularise/regularize*), where *z* is universal in AmE, and *s* is widely used in BrE and preferred in AusE. This variation also occurs in AmE *cozy, cognizant*, BrE *cosy, cognisant*. See ALPHABET, LETTER[1], S, SPELLING, X, YOGH. [WRITING]. C.U.

ZAMBIA. Official title: *Republic of Zambia*. A country of southern Africa and member of the Commonwealth. Capital: Lusaka. Currency: the kwacha (100 ngwee). Population: 7.5m (1988), 11.1m (projection for 2000). Ethnicity: 34% Bemba, 16% Tonga, 14% Chewa, 9% Lozi, various others, and 1% European. Religions: 46% Protestant, 29% traditional, 25% Roman Catholic. Languages: English (official); seven vernaculars are recognized, including Bemba, Nyanja, and Tonga. Education: primary 86%, secondary 19%, tertiary 2%, literacy 76%. The British colony of *Northern Rhodesia* gained its independence as *Zambia* in 1964. It is one of the most urbanized of East African countries, and the mix of languages in urban areas emphasizes the need for a link language. English is used exclusively in education from the first year and is important in the media. National English-language newspapers include *The Times of Zambia* (set up in 1943), the *Zambia Daily Mail*, and the *Sunday Times*. Zambian English is one of the most divergent forms of AfrE, with a good deal of borrowing from local languages, even to the extent of adding Bantu affixes to English roots: *maolanges* oranges (where *ma-* is a plural prefix and *l* replaces *r*); *cipoto* a pot (where *ci-* is a Bemba nominal prefix); *awashes* he or she washes, *adriver* he or she drives (where *a-* is a subject prefix). Examples of local innovations in the use of adverbial particles are illustrated by the omission of *up* in *I'll come to pick you at half eight*, its addition in *cope up with*, and a reassignment in its use in *I'm fed up* (I'm full). Lexical innovation includes *movious* always on the move. Discourse may be marked by elements that maintain age, sex, and status relationships: a younger man may address an elder as *uncle/ father* and be addressed in turn as *son/nephew*. Cultural influences are evidenced in the questions: *How have you stayed the day?* How have things gone since this morning?; *How are you suffering?* as a greeting to one who has suffered a misfortune. See EAST AFRICAN ENGLISH, ENGLISH, RHODESIA. [AFRICA, NAME, VARIETY]. C.L.N.

ZETLAND, ZETLANDIC. See SHETLAND, SHETLANDIC.

ZEUGMA [16c: through Latin from Greek *zeûgma* yoking]. (1) Also *syllepsis*. In rhetoric, a phrase in which a word, usually a verb, is followed by two or more other words that commonly collocate with it, but not together: 'The morning brought misty sunshine and the nurse' (Mary Stewart, *Wildfire at Midnight*, 1956). A figurative use usually precedes a literal use; in Pope's *Rape of the Lock* (1714), the heroine might 'stain her Honour, or her new Brocade' and 'lose her Heart, or Neck-lace, at a Ball'. (2) A form of ellipsis regarded as poor style: *I was on the plane and my bags on the ground*. Here, the singular *was* serves both *I* and *my bags*, but the sentence **My bags was on the ground* is ungrammatical in standard English. Zeugma is common in such constructions as *X is as big if not bigger than Y*, from which the **X is as big than Y* can be extracted. The balanced form is *X is as big as, if not bigger than, Y*. [GRAMMAR, STYLE, USAGE]. T.McA.

ZIMBABWE. Official title: *Republic of Zimbabwe*. A country of southern Africa and member of the Commonwealth. Capital: Harare. Currency: the dollar (100 cents). Population: 9.3m (1988), 13.2m (projection for 2000). Ethnicity: 71% Shona, 16% Ndebele, 11% other indigenous peoples, 2% European. Religions: 50% Protestant, 25% Roman Catholic, 25% mainly traditional. Languages; English (official); the indigenous languages Shona and Ndebele, which may be used in the Senate. Education: primary

92%, secondary 43%, tertiary 3%, literacy 74%. Zimbabwe, formerly the British colony of *Southern Rhodesia*, took its present form in 1980. English was introduced into the region toward the end of the 19c in colonial commerce (the ventures of Cecil Rhodes) and in missionary education. English-language newspapers include the *Sunday News* (set up in 1930), *The Chronicle* (1894), the *Herald* (1891), and the *Sunday Mail* (1935). The English of Zimbabwe is non-rhotic. There is some blending of vowels into a five-vowel system and simplification of consonant structures, features shared with other varieties of East and South African English: 'men' the pronunciation of both *man* and *men*, 'fit' of both *fit* and *feet*. Syntactic structures are often attributable to transfer from local languages: *He (has) grown up in my eyes* I saw him grow up; *when the rain is in the nose* when the rainy season approaches. There are loans from local languages in the vocabulary, such as *shimiyaan*

home-made liquor made from treacle, and *muti* medicine, as well as words of various origins common in southern Africa, such as *kraal* village, *veld* high open grassland, *commando* military unit, *trek* a journey (originally by ox-wagon). Local usages include *head-ring* a marker of elder or high status, *impi-line* a Zulu army unit, *love-muti* a love charm, *now-now girl* a modern young woman. Education in the area since the 19c has involved studying classical English literature, which has left this variety, like many others, with a 'bookish' style. See EAST AFRICAN ENGLISH, ENGLISH, RHODESIA. [AFRICA, NAME, VARIETY]. C.L.N.

ZULU. See AFRICAN ENGLISH, BANTU, FANAKALO, SOUTH AFRICA, SOUTH AFRICAN ENGLISH, SOUTH AFRICAN LANGUAGES, SOUTH AFRICAN PLACE-NAMES.

ZUMMERZET. See MUMMERSET, SOMERSET.

Index of Persons

Index of Persons

An asterisk (*) preceding an entry name indicates that the person concerned appears in the bibliography following that entry and not in the entry itself. Names mentioned in the *Chronology of English* are not listed.

Branford, J.
  South African dictionaries, *South
  African English
Branford, W.
  South African dictionaries
Brathwaite, D.
  Brathwaite
Brathwaite, E.
  Brathwaite, Caribbean literature in
  English, Nation Language, novel
Braun, E.
  *theatre
Bréal, M.
  semantics
Brecht, B.
  drama, theatre
Brereton, J.
  Anglo-Welsh literature, wit
Brewer, E.
  *Brewer's Dictionary of Phrase and
  Fable*
Bridges, R.
  BBC English[1], Bridges, metre,
  Society for Pure English
Bridgman, R.
  *American literature
Bridie, J.
  Bible
Bright, J.
  *TESL
Bright, T.
  shorthand
Bright, W.
  *linguistics
Brik, O.
  genre
Brink, A.
  South African English
Brink, B. ten
  English literature
Brink, D. T.
  *English Language Amendment
Brinsley, J.
  education
Britton, J.
  Bullock Report
Britz, M.
  South African dictionaries
Broca, P.
  aphasia
Brockett, O.
  *theatre
Brontë, C.
  biography, Brontë, English
  literature, Gothic, onomastics,
  Scott, Yorkshire
Brontë, E.
  Brontë, dialogue, English literature,
  Gothic, Scott, Yorkshire
Brook, G.
  Lancashire, *Old English[1],
  *Shakespeare
Brooke, C.
  Anglo-Irish literature
Brooke, F.
  Canadian literature
Brooke, R.
  couplet
Brooke-Rose, C.
  intertextuality, *metaphor

Brooks, C.
  *TESD
Brophy, J.
  Partridge
Broughton, G.
  glossary
Broughton, R.
  Anglo-Welsh literature
Brown, C.
  Gothic, novel
Brown, E. K.
  *linguistics
Brown, Gillian
  *discourse analysis
Brown, Goold
  grammar, usage guidance and
  criticism
Brown, H.
  language teaching
Brown, I.
  *Dickens, usage guidance and
  criticism, word buff
Brown, L.
  *African literature in English
Browne, (Sir) T.
  Biblical English, Cambridge
  University Press, literary standard,
  Stevenson, style
Browning, E. B.
  narrative poetry
Browning, R.
  blank verse, Caliban, English
  literature, figurative language,
  narrative poetry, Tennyson
Bruce, F.
  *Bible
Brudenell, J.
  toponymy
Brugmann, K.
  philology, Wright
Brumfit, C.
  *language teaching, *TESL
Brunell, A.
  regional dictionaries of English
Brunner, K.
  *Middle English
Bruno, G.
  censorship
Bryan, W.
  American publishing
Bryce, C.
  Facts on File
Bryson, Bill
  *English, nonsense
Bublitz, W.
  *Survey of English Usage
Buchan, J.
  English literature, Scottish literature
Buchanan, J.
  Scottish dictionaries
Buckley, S.
  newspaper
Bullokar, J.
  dictionary, Latin[1], usage guidance
  and criticism
Bulwer, J.
  rhetoric
Bulwer-Lytton, E.
  quotation, stilted
Bunyan, J.
  allegory, Bible, Bunyan,

Bunyan, J.—*cont.*
  English literature, fantasy,
  literature, novel, onomastics
Burchfield, R. W.
  BBC English[1], Burchfield, *English,
  Fowler, General American, *history
  of English, *lexicography, New
  Zealand dictionaries, *New Zealand
  English, *Oxford Dictionary of
  English Etymology*, Oxford English,
  Oxford English Dictionary, usage
  guidance and criticism
Burgess, A.
  Burgess, demotic, *English
  literature, essay, Fowler,
  Heinemann, *Hobson-Jobson*, novel,
  usage guidance and criticism
Burgess, F. G.
  blurb, Burgessism
Burgis, N.
  *Dickens
Burke, E.
  Anglo-Irish literature, letter[2], prose,
  Wollstonecraft
Burke, W.
  *slang
Burling, R.
  *Black American Vernacular
Burnell, A.
  Hobson-Jobson, regional
  dictionaries of English
Burness, E.
  *Shakespeare
Burney, F.
  diary, letter[2]
Burnley, D.
  *history of English
Burnley, J.
  *Chaucer
Burns, R.
  Broad Scots, Burns, Caledonia,
  Chambers, dialect, English
  literature, macaronic, MacDiarmid,
  Scotia, Scots, Scots literature,
  Scottish dictionaries, sexuality and
  language, Southron
Burroughs, E. R.
  Africa, anachorism, fantasy,
  root-creation, science fiction
Burton, E.
  *theatre
Burton L.
  Canadian style guides
Burton R.
  allusion
Burton, R. F.
  lallation, prose
Bush, G.
  American language, catchphrase,
  -ism, personal name
Bush, V.
  hypertext, information
Butcher, J.
  *proof-reading
Butler, C.
  spelling reform
Butler, F.
  home
Butler, R. A.
  abbreviation

Chaucer, G.—*cont.*
Chaucer, Cockney, couplet,
Dickens, dictionary, English,
English literature, fable, Great
Vowel Shift, history of English,
humour, imagination, leaf, literary
criticism, literature, London,
Middle English, Norman French,
plain English, prose, proverb,
Puttenham, Rickert, satire, short
story, slang, specialization, Spenser,
standard English, style, writer,
Wycliffe, y-
Chaudhuri, N. C.
Indian English[1], Indian English
literature
Chauvin, N.
chauvinism
Chavez, L.
English Language Amendment
Cheke, J.
Latin[1], Saxonism
Chekhov, A.
drama, short story
Chen, M. F.
conversion, italic
Chernikoff, S.
computer usage
Cherryh, C. H.
science fiction
Cheshire, J.
*dialect, *English
Chesterfield, Lord
chiasmus, illiteracy, style, wit, writer
Chida, A. R.
Indo-Anglian
Child, F. J.
American Dialect Society, ballad,
English literature, rhetoric
Chinweizu, O. J.
*African literature in English
Chomsky, N.
acceptability, axiom, child language
acquisition, Chomsky,
communicative competence,
competence and performance,
*Comprehensive Grammar of the
English Language*, description,
generative, history of English,
language acquisition device,
language universals, linguistics,
linguistic typology, logic, mistake,
model, passivization, poetics,
psycholinguistics, Sapir–Whorf
hypothesis, structural linguistics,
structure dependence,
transformational-generative
grammar
Christie, A.
detective story, ethnic name,
personal name, popular fiction
Christie, S.
*South African literature in English
Christophersen, P.
*language teaching
Chubbe, J.
lingo
Church, A.
knowledge representation
Churchill, Sir W. S.
alliteration, anadiplosis, Basic

Churchill, Sir W. S.—*cont.*
English[1], Britain, British
broadcasting, Churchill, education,
English-Speaking Union, personal
name, preposition, proper name,
quotation, repartee
Cicero, Marcus Tullius
Attic and Doric, Atticism,
chiasmus, Early Modern English,
language teaching, Latin analogy,
Latin literature, letter[2], prose,
rhetoric, shorthand
Cipolla, C. M.
*literacy
Claiborne, R.
*history of English
Clanchy, M. T.
*literacy
Clarendon, Lord
Oxford University Press
Clark, D. L.
*rhetoric
Clark, H. H.
*psycholinguistics
Clark, J.
*phonetics
Clark, J. O. E.
*idiom, usage guidance and
criticism
Clark, S. W.
American publishing
Clarke, A. C.
science fiction
Clarke, M.
novel
Clarke, S.
Newfoundland English
Clark Hall, J. R.
*Old English[1]
Clas, A.
Canadian dictionaries
Claudius
Britannia
Cleary, J.
proper
Cleather, B.
BBC English[2]
Cleland, J.
memoir
Clerc, L.
sign language
Clifford, G. J.
*literacy
Clifton, J.
Queen's English Society
Clough, A. H.
hymn, slipshod
Cluett, R.
Canadian literature in English
Clyne, M.
German
Coard, B.
TESD
Coates, J.
*sexism, *Survey of English Usage
Coats, J.
*modal verb
Cobbett, W.
Cobbett, journalism
Cochran, A. S.
English-Speaking Union

Cockeram, H.
dictionary, philology
Coelho, E.
*TESD
Coetzee, J. H.
South African literature in English
Cohan, G. M.
Yankee
Cole, S.
Facts on File
Coleridge, H.
Coleridge (H.), Furnivall, Murray,
Oxford English Dictionary, Trench
Coleridge, S. T.
alliterative verse, archaism, ballad,
Biblical English, blank verse,
Coleridge (H.), Coleridge (S.),
English literature, internal rhyme,
journalism, literary criticism,
Longman, metre, quality press,
Romanticism, slovenly,
Wordsworth
Coles, E.
dictionary
College, A.
BBC English[1]
Collins, F. H.
house style, Oxford University Press
Collins, J. C.
English literature
Collins, Jan
Collins, Urdang
Collins, Joan
soap opera
Collins, P.
*Australian English
Collins, Philip
*Dickens
Collins, Wilkie
detective story, novel
Collins, William (*poet*)
English literature, literature
Collins, William (*publisher*)
Collins
Collison, R. L.
bilingual dictionary
Collymore, F. A.
*Caribbean English
Columbus, C.
Indian, multiculturalism, Spanish
Compton-Burnett, I.
personal name
Comrie, B.
*language, *linguistic typology
Conan Doyle, (Sir) A.
characternym, detective story,
dialogue, novel, onomastics,
pastiche, personal name, science
fiction
Congreve, W.
Anglo-Irish literature, English
literature, lingo
Conklin, N. F.
American languages
Connolly, Billy
Glasgow
Connolly, C.
pen name
Conrad, A.
*English

Svartvik, J.
Comprehensive Grammar of the English Language, corpus, grammar, Longman, Quirk, Survey of English Usage
Swain, M.
*bilingualism
Swan, M.
*contrastive linguistics, ELT publishing
Swart, C.
South African dictionaries
Sweet, H.
American Dialect Society, Anglo-Frisian, applied linguistics, language teaching, Onions, Passy, Pygmalion, Shaw, Skeat, spelling reform, Sweet, Viëtor, Wyld
Swift, J.
Anglo-Irish literature, anticlimax, Augustan, autobiography, banter, bathos, Bible, clipping, Dublin, Early Modern English, English in England, history of English, letter², literary criticism, Newspeak, pamphlet, prose, satire, style, Swift, usage, usage guidance and criticism, voice, wit, word games
Swift, K.
sexism
Swift, S.
*effective writing
Swinburne, A.
aesthetics, Caribbean literature in English, English literature, internal rhyme
Swrdwal, I.
Anglo-Welsh literature
Sykes, J. B.
Concise Oxford Dictionary, generic pronoun, house style
Symon, M.
Scots literature
Synge, J. M.
drama, tragedy

Tacitus
Caledonia, Ingvaeonic
Taglicht, J.
*Survey of English Usage
Talbot, G.
Queen's English Society
Talbot, T.
*linguistics
Tallack, D.
*American literature
Tambling, J.
*literature
Tannen, D.
*writing
Tanton, J.
English Language Amendment
Tasso, T.
literary criticism
Tate, A.
literary criticism, ode
Taverner, R.
Bible
Taylor, G.
*Shakespeare

Taylor, J.
doggerel
Taylor, T.
Punch
Tebbel, J.
*American publishing
Tebbit, V.
Chambers
Telford, T.
English place-names
Temple, S.
personal names
Temple, (Archbishop) W.
Simplified Spelling Society
Tenniel, (Sir) J.
Carroll, *Punch*
Tennyson, Alfred (Lord)
Anglicize, blank verse, Caribbean literature in English, Coleridge (S.), dactyl, elegy, English literature, epanalepsis, hymn, Macmillan, metre, play on words, poet laureate, poetic diction, poetry, quatrain, spelling reform, spondee, Tennyson
Terence
drama
Thackeray, W. M.
capital, charade, dog-/dog, English literature, fantasy, *King's English* (*The*), mulatto, novel, onomastics, Oxbridge, prose, *Punch*, satire
Thales
logic
Thatcher, M.
Britannia, Bullock Report, Eng Lit, Euro-, metaphor, onomastics, personal name
Thavenius, C.
*Survey of English Usage
Theocritus
pastoral
Thody, P.
faux ami
Thomas, A.
linguistic atlas, *Welsh English
Thomas, B.
farce
Thomas, C.
Curme
Thomas, David
Punch
Thomas, Dylan
Anglo-Welsh literature, Bible, Celtic languages, figurative language, half rhyme, literature, sonnet, Thomas
Thomas, G.
Anglo-Welsh literature
Thompson, D.
American broadcasting
Thompson, T.
Anglicize
Thomson, D.
Scottish Gaelic
Thomson, G.
Burns
Thomson, James (*18c*)
Britannia
Thomson, James (*19c*)
blank verse, Scottish literature
Thomson, M.
*dyslexia

Thoreau, H. D.
American literature, New England, Romanticism
Thorndike, E. L.
Barnhart, defining vocabulary, frequency count, reading, Thorndike, vocabulary control
Thornley, G. C.
*English literature
Thorpe, B.
Romanticism
Thorpe, D.
*reading
Thrale, H.
synonymy, Piozzi
Thrax, Dionysius
analogy and anomaly, grammar, part of speech, sentence, word-formation, writing
Throne, B.
*sexism
Thucydides
Greek literature, Latin literature
Thurber, J.
fable, humour, *New Yorker*, word games
Tickoo, M.
learner's dictionary
Tiempo, Edilberto
Filipino literature in English
Tiempo, Edith
Filipino literature in English
Tilak, B. G.
Indian English literature
Tilling, P. M.
Survey of English Dialects
Tilly, G.
*Canadian literature
Tinio, R. S.
*Philippine English
Tiro, Marcus Tullius
shorthand
Tobin, Y.
*semiotics
Todd, L.
*African English, *Irish English, international language, *pidgin, *usage, Varieties of English around the World
Todd, M. J.
Longman
Todman, Bill
Call My Bluff
Todorov, T.
literary criticism, literature, poetics
Tolkien, J. R. R.
fantasy, onomastics, root-creation
Tollefson, J.
language planning, language rights
Toller, T. N.
*Old English¹, period dictionaries of English
Tolstoy, L.
Heinemann, Russian
Tomalin, N.
journalese
Tongue, R. K.
Indian Recommended Pronunciation, *Singapore English
Tooke, J. H.
etymology